McGraw-Hill's
HOMEWORK MANAGER PLUS™

THE COMPLETE SOLUTION

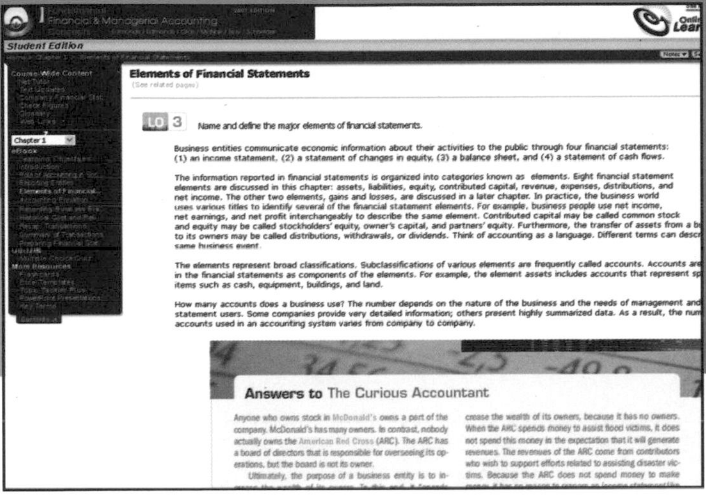

Interactive Online Version of the Textbook

Online LearningCenter with PowerWeb

In addition to the textbook, students can rely on this online version of the text for a convenient way to study. The interactive content is fully integrated with Homework Manager to give students quick access to relevant content as they work through

Features:

- Online version of the text integrated with Homework Manager
- Students referred to appropriate sections of the online book as they complete an assignment or take a practice quiz
- Direct link to related material that corresponds with the learning objective within the text

McGraw-Hill's Homework Manager Plus combines the power of Homework Manager with the latest interactive learning technology to create a comprehensive, fully integrated online study package. Students working on assignments in Homework Manager can click a simple hotlink and instantly review the appropriate material in the Interactive Online Textbook. NetTutor rounds out the package by offering live tutoring with a qualified expert in the course material.

By including Homework Manager Plus with your textbook adoption, you're giving your students a vital edge as they progress through the course and ensuring that the help they need is never more than a mouse click away. Contact your McGraw-Hill representative or visit the book's website to learn how to add Homework Manager Plus to your adoption.

McGraw-Hill's HM PLUS™

HOMEWORK **MANAGER**
HELPS YOU EFFICIENTLY

McGraw-Hill's
HOMEWORK
MANAGER™

Assign coursework online.

Problems and exercises from the book, as well as questions from the test bank, have been integrated into Homework Manager to give you a variety of options as you deliver assignments and quizzes to students via the web. You can choose from static or algorithmic questions and have the graded results automatically stored in your grade book online.

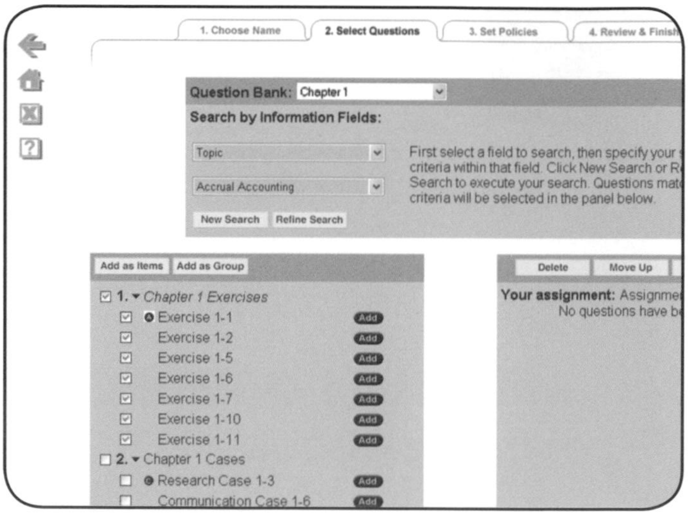

Have you ever wished that you could assign a different set of problems to each of your students, individualizing their educational experience? The algorithmic question capabilities of Homework Manager give you the opportunity to do so. The problem-making function inserts new numbers and data from an endless supply into the set question structure. Each student will have a different answer while learning the same principles from the text. This also enables the students to master concepts by revisiting the same questions with different data.

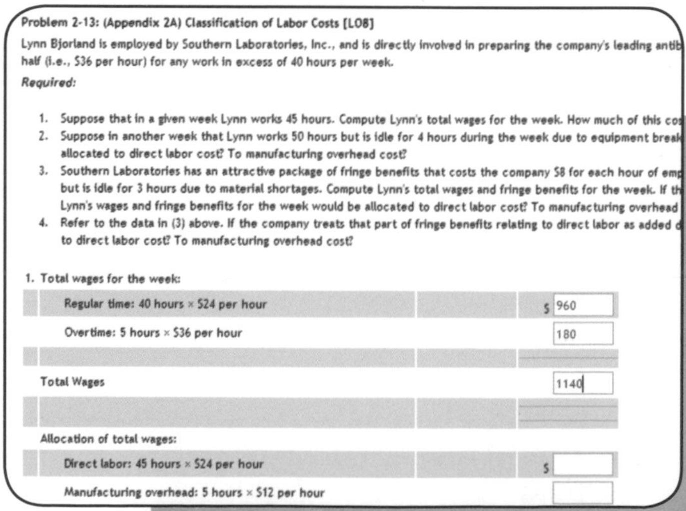

MANAGE YOUR CLASS.

Control how content is presented.

Homework Manager gives you a flexible and easy way to present course work to students. You determine which questions to ask and how much help students will receive as they work through assignments. You can determine the number of attempts a student can make with each problem or provide hints and feedback with each question. The questions can also be linked to an online version of the text for quick and simple reference while students complete an assignment.

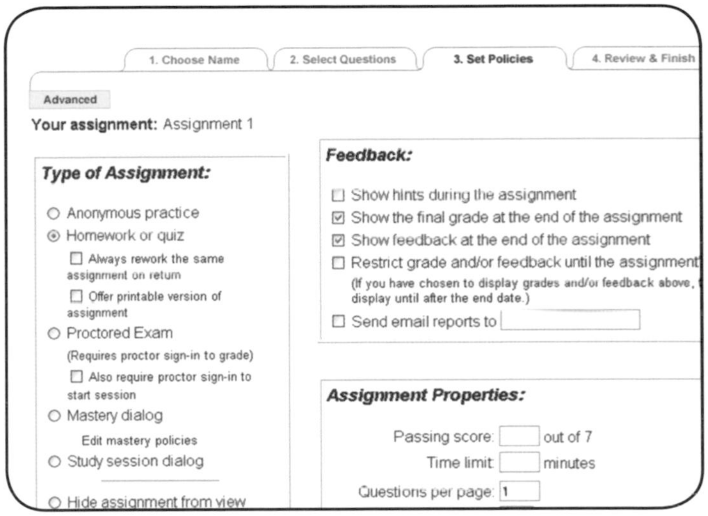

Track student progress.

Assignments are graded automatically, with the results stored in your private grade book. Detailed results let you see at a glance how each student does on an assignment or an individual problem. You can even see how many attempts it took them to solve it. You can monitor how the whole class does on each problem and even determine where individual students might need extra help.

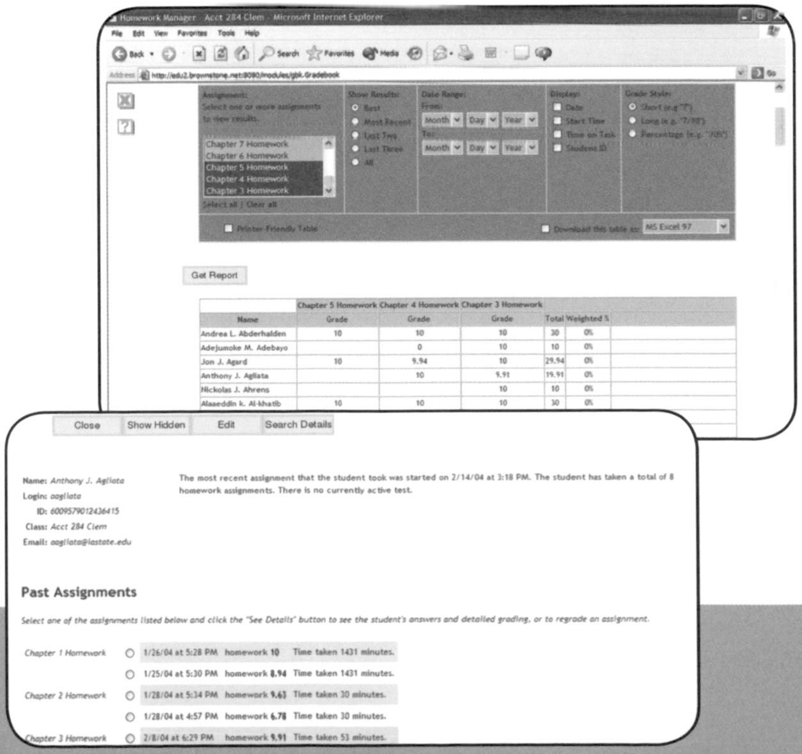

PROFESSORS CAN ALLOW HOMEWORK **MANAGER** TO GIVE STUDENTS HELPFUL FEEDBACK

Auto-grading and feedback.

Question 1: *Score 6.5/8*

Your response

Exercise 2-1: Using Cost Terms [LO2, LO5, LO7]

Following are a number of cost terms introduced in the chapter:

Period cost	Fixed cost
Variable cost	Prime cost
Opportunity cost	Conversion cost
Product cost	Sunk cost

Choose the cost term or terms above that most appropriately describe the costs identified in each of the following situations. A cost term can be used more than once.

1. Crestline Books, Inc., prints a small book titled *The Pocket Speller* . The paper going into the manufacture of the book would be called direct materials and classified as a Product cost (6%). In terms of cost behavior, the paper could also be described as a Product cost (0%) with respect to the number of books printed.
2. Instead of compiling the words in the book, the author hired by the company could have earned considerable fees consulting with business organizations. The consulting fees forgone by the author would be called Opportunity cost (6%).
3. The paper and other materials used in the manufacture of the book, combined with the direct labor cost involved, would be called Prime cost (6%).
4. The salary of Crestline Books' president would be classified as a Product cost (0%), and the salary will appear on the income statement as an expense in the time period in which it is incurred.
5. Depreciation on the equipment used to print the book would be classified by Crestline Books as a Product cost (6%). However, depreciation on any equipment used by the company in selling and administrative activities would be classified as a Period cost (6%). In terms of cost behavior, depreciation would probably be classified as a Fixed cost (6%) with respect to the number of books printed.
6. A Product cost (6%) is also known as an inventoriable cost,

Correct response

Exercise 2-1: Using Cost Terms [LO2, LO5, LO7]

Following are a number of cost terms introduced in the chapter:

Period cost	Fixed cost
Variable cost	Prime cost
Opportunity cost	Conversion cost
Product cost	Sunk cost

Choose the cost term or terms above that most appropriately describe the costs identified in each of the following situations. A cost term can be used more than once.

1. Crestline Books, Inc., prints a small book titled *The Pocket Speller* . The paper going into the manufacture of the book would be called direct materials and classified as a Product cost. In terms of cost behavior, the paper could also be described as a variable cost with respect to the number of books printed.
2. Instead of compiling the words in the book, the author hired by the company could have earned considerable fees consulting with business organizations. The consulting fees forgone by the author would be called Opportunity cost.
3. The paper and other materials used in the manufacture of the book, combined with the direct labor cost involved, would be called Prime cost.
4. The salary of Crestline Books' president would be classified as a Period cost, and the salary will appear on the income statement as an expense in the time period in which it is incurred.
5. Depreciation on the equipment used to print the book would be classified by Crestline Books as a Product cost. However, depreciation on any equipment used by the company in selling and administrative activities would be classified as a Period cost. In terms of cost behavior, depreciation would probably be classified as a Fixed cost with respect to the number of books printed.
6. A Product cost is also known as an inventoriable cost, since

Immediately after finishing an assignment, students can compare their answers side-by-side with the detailed solutions. Students can try again with new numbers to see if they have mastered the concept.

Fundamental Financial and Managerial Accounting Concepts

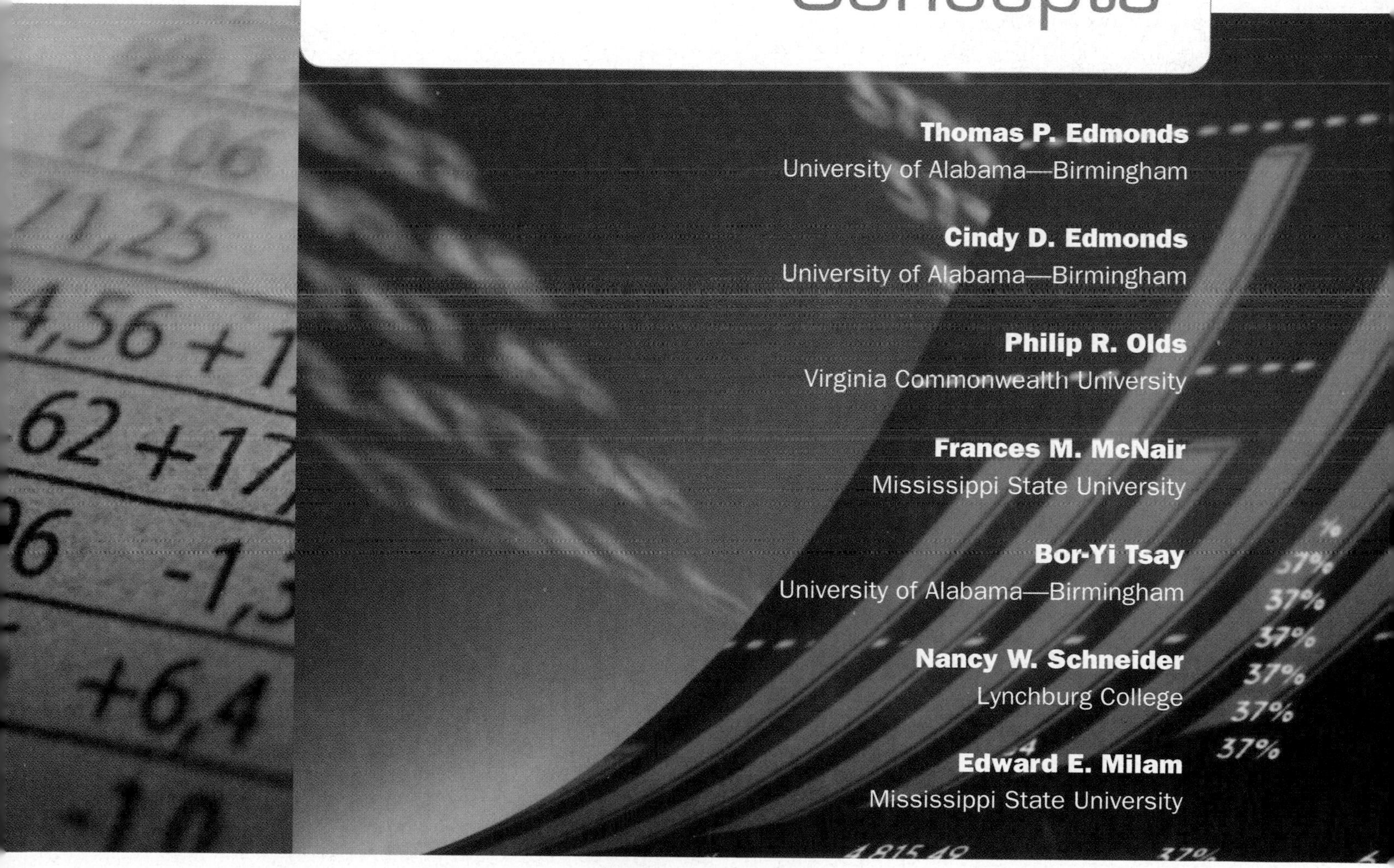

Thomas P. Edmonds
University of Alabama—Birmingham

Cindy D. Edmonds
University of Alabama—Birmingham

Philip R. Olds
Virginia Commonwealth University

Frances M. McNair
Mississippi State University

Bor-Yi Tsay
University of Alabama—Birmingham

Nancy W. Schneider
Lynchburg College

Edward E. Milam
Mississippi State University

McGraw-Hill Irwin

Boston Burr Ridge, IL Dubuque, IA Madison, WI New York
San Francisco St. Louis Bangkok Bogotá Caracas Kuala Lumpur
Lisbon London Madrid Mexico City Milan Montreal New Delhi
Santiago Seoul Singapore Sydney Taipei Toronto

McGraw-Hill Irwin

FUNDAMENTAL FINANCIAL AND MANAGERIAL ACCOUNTING CONCEPTS
Published by McGraw-Hill/Irwin, a business unit of The McGraw-Hill Companies, Inc., 1221 Avenue of the Americas, New York, NY, 10020.

This book is printed on acid-free paper.

1 2 3 4 5 6 7 8 9 0 WCK/WCK 0 9 8 7 6 5

ISBN-13: 978-0-07-284600-3
ISBN-10: 0-07-284600-3

Editorial director: *Stewart Mattson*
Senior sponsoring editor: *Steve Schuetz*
Managing developmental editor: *Gail Korosa*
Marketing manager: *Melissa Larmon*
Media producer: *Elizabeth Mavetz*
Lead project manager: *Pat Frederickson*
Production supervisor: *Debra R. Sylvester*
Senior designer: *Mary E. Kazak*
Senior photo research coordinator: *Jeremy Cheshareck*
Photo researcher: *Julie Tesser*
Media project manager: *Matthew Perry*
Senior supplement producer: *Carol Loreth*
Cover design: *Chris Bowyer*
Cover image: *Scott T. Smith/Corbis*
Interior design: *Amanda Kavanagh*
Typeface: *10/12 Times*
Compositor: *Cenveo*
Printer: *Quebecor World Versailles Inc.*

Library of Congress Cataloging-in-Publication Data

Fundamental financial and managerial accounting concepts / Thomas P. Edmonds . . . [et al.].
p. cm.
Includes index.
ISBN-13: 978-0-07-284600-3 (alk. paper)
ISBN-10: 0-07-284600-3 (alk. paper)
1. Accounting. 2. Managerial accounting. I. Edmonds, Thomas P.
HF5636.F955 2007
658.15'11—dc22

2005044579

www. mhhe. corn

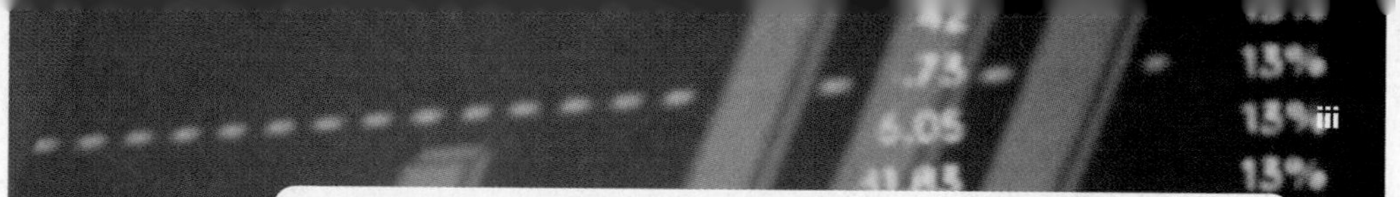

BRIEF CONTENTS

Contents

Coca-Cola
McDonald's

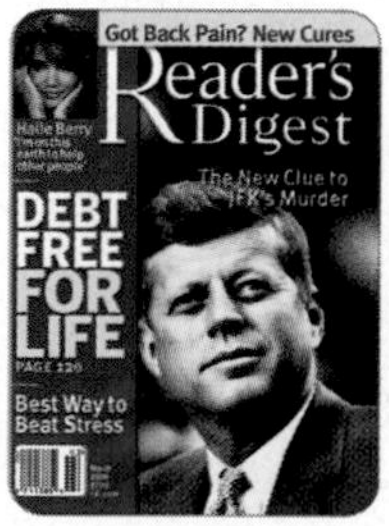
Got Back Pain? New Cures
Reader's Digest
DEBT FREE FOR LIFE
Best Way to Beat Stress

GAP

Chapter 4 Accounting for Merchandising Businesses 180

Chapter 5 Accounting for Inventories 236

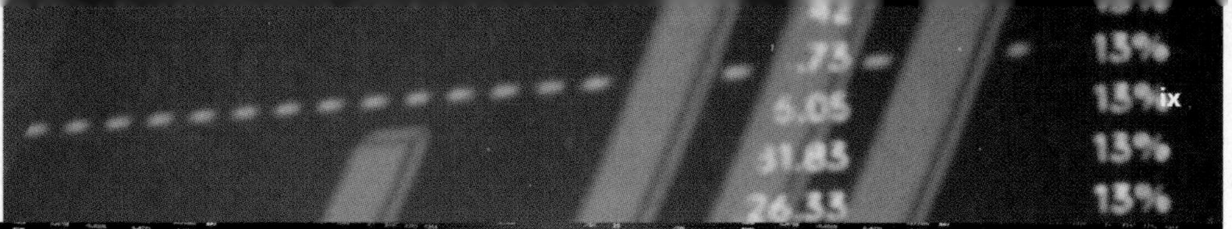

Chapter 7 Accounting for Receivables 330

Chapter 8 Accounting for Long-Term Operational Assets 384

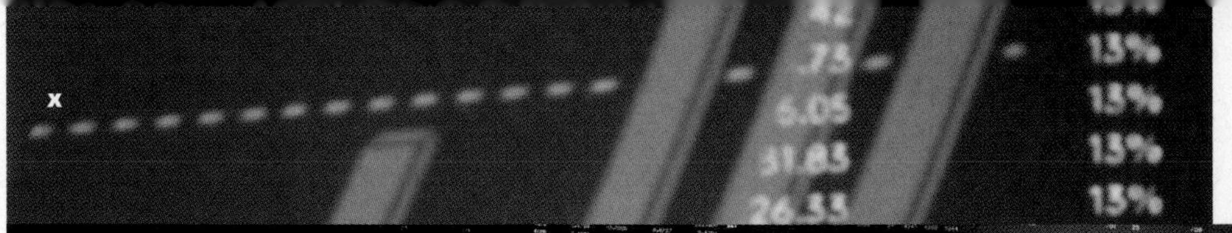
.75
6.05
31.85
26.33
13%
13%
13%
13%

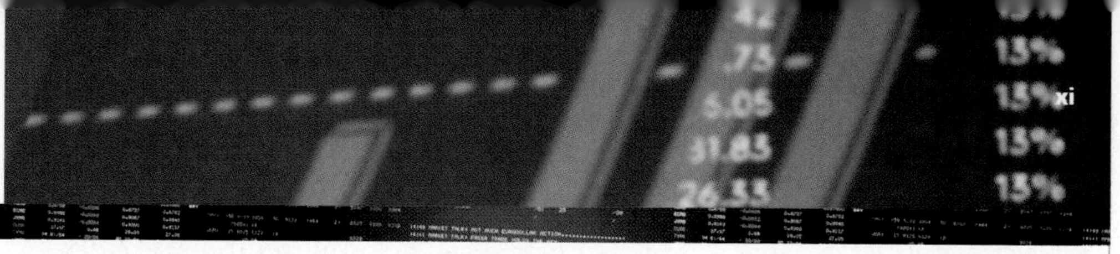

Chapter 10 Accounting For Long-Term Notes Payable and Bond Liabilities 496

Chapter 11 Proprietorships, Partnerships, and Corporations 554

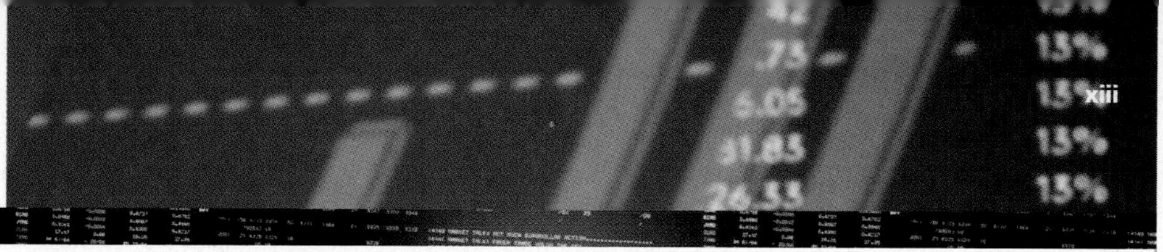

cingular

SOUTHWEST.COM
N445WN

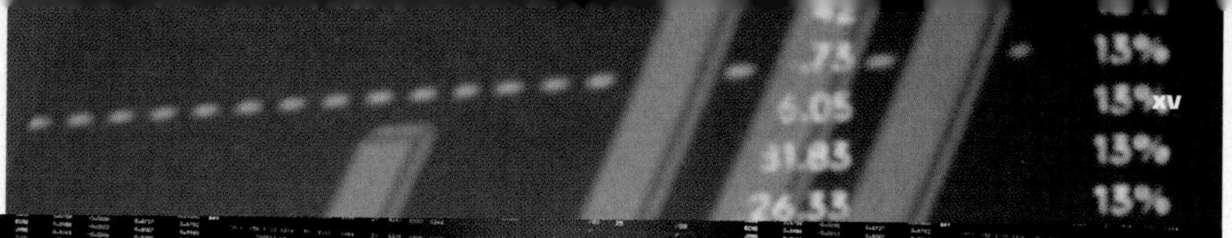

Chapter 16 Cost Accumulation, Tracing, and Allocation 792

Chapter 17 Product Costing in Service and Manufacturing Companies 832

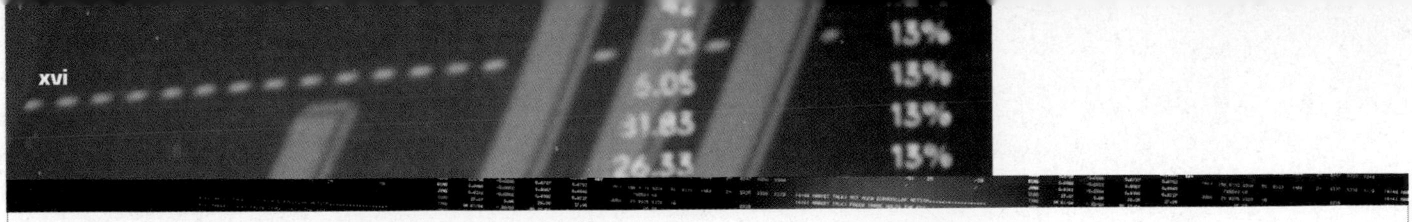

Chapter 21 Planning for Profit and Cost Control 1018

Chapter 22 Performance Evaluation 1060

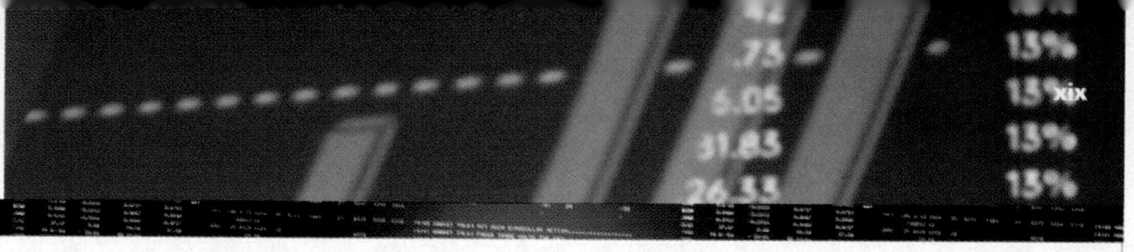

Chapter 23 Responsibility Accounting 1108

Chapter 24 Planning for Capital Investments 1148

ABOUT THE AUTHORS

Thomas P. Edmonds

Thomas P. Edmonds, Ph.D., is the Friends and Alumni Professor of Accounting at the University of Alabama at Birmingham (UAB). Dr. Edmonds has taught in the introductory area throughout his career. He has coordinated the accounting principles courses at the University of Houston and UAB. He currently teaches introductory accounting in mass sections and in UAB's distance learning program. He is actively involved in the accounting education change movement. He has conducted more that 50 workshops related to teaching introductory accounting during the last decade. Dr. Edmonds has received numerous prestigious teaching awards including the 2005 Alabama Society of CPAs Outstanding Educator Award and the UAB President's Excellence in Teaching Award. Dr. Edmonds' current research is education based. He has written articles that appeared in many publications including among others the *Accounting Review, Issues in Accounting, Journal of Accounting Education,* and *Advances in Accounting Education.* Dr. Edmonds has been a successful entrepreneur. He has worked as a management accountant for a transportation company and as a commercial lending officer for the Federal Home Loan Bank. Dr. Edmonds began his academic training at Young Harris Community College. His Ph.D. degree was awarded by Georgia State University. Dr. Edmonds' work experience and academic training has enabled him to bring a unique perspective to the classroom.

Cindy D. Edmonds

Cindy D. Edmonds, Ph.D., is an Associate Professor of Accounting at the University of Alabama at Birmingham. She serves as the coordinator of the introductory accounting courses at UAB. Dr. Edmonds has received five prestigious teaching awards. Dr. Edmonds' articles appear in numerous publications including *Advances in Accounting Education, Journal of Education for Business, Journal of Accounting Regulation, Advances in Accounting, Management Accounting, CMA Journal, Disclosures,* and *Business & Professional Ethics Journal.* Dr. Edmonds is heavily involved in service activities. She is a past president of the Birmingham Chapter of the American Society of Women Accountants. Dr. Edmonds has worked in the insurance industry, in a manufacturing company, and in a governmental agency. This work experience has enabled her to bring a real-world flavor to her writing. Dr. Edmonds holds a B.S. degree from Auburn University, an M.B.A degree from the University of Houston, and a Ph.D. degree from the University of Alabama.

Philip R. Olds

Philip R. Olds is Associate Professor of Accounting at Virginia Commonwealth University (VCU). He serves as the coordinator of the introduction to accounting courses at VCU. Professor Olds received his A.S. degree from Brunswick Junior College in Brunswick, Georgia (now Costal Georgia Community College). He received a B.B.A. in Accounting from Georgia Southern College (now Georgia Southern University) and his M.P.A. and Ph.D. degrees from Georgia State University. After graduating from Georgia Southern, he worked as an auditor with the U.S. Department of Labor in Atlanta, Georgia. A CPA in Virginia, Professor Olds has published articles in various professional journals and presented papers at national and regional conferences. He also served as the faculty adviser to the VCU chapter of Beta Alpha Psi for five years. In 1989, he was recognized with an Outstanding Faculty Vice-President Award by the national Beta Alpha Psi organization.

Frances M. McNair

Frances M. McNair holds the KPMG Peat Marwick Professorship in Accounting at Mississippi State University (MSU). She has been involved in teaching principles of accounting for the past 12 years and currently serves as the coordinator for the principles of accounting courses at MSU. She joined the MSU faculty in 1987 after receiving her Ph.D. from the University of Mississippi. The author of various articles that have appeared in the *Journal of Accountancy, Management Accounting, Business and Professional Ethics Journal, The Practical Accountant, Taxes,* and other publications, she also coauthored the book *The Tax Practitioner* with Dr. Denzil Causey. Dr. McNair is currently serving on committees of the American Taxation Association, the American Accounting Association, and the Institute of Management Accountants as well as numerous School of Accountancy and MSU committees.

Bor-Yi Tsay

Bor-Yi Tsay, Ph.D., CPA, is Professor of Accounting at the University of Alabama at Birmingham (UAB) where he has taught since 1986. He has taught principles of accounting courses at the University of Houston and UAB. Dr. Tsay received the 1996 Loudell Ellis Robinson Excellence in Teaching Award. He has also received numerous awards for his writing and publications including John L. Rhoads Manuscripts Award, John Pugsley Manuscripts Award, Van Pelt Manuscripts Award, and three certificates of merit from the Institute of Management Accountants. His articles appeared in *Journal of Accounting Education, Management Accounting, Journal of Managerial Issues, CPA Journal, CMA Magazine, Journal of Systems Management, and Journal of Medical Systems.* He currently serves as the treasurer of the Birmingham Chapter, Institute of Management Accountants. Dr. Tsay received a B.S. in Agricultural Economics from National Taiwan University, an MBA from Eastern Washington University, and a Ph.D. in Accounting from the University of Houston.

Nancy Schneider

Nancy Schneider, lead instructor for the accounting principles courses, is Professor of Accounting at Lynchburg College (LC) where she has received the Sydnor Award for Teaching Excellence in Business and the LC Rosser Excellence in Teaching Award. Professor Schneider has participated in the writing of college-level textbooks, textbook supplements, and related teaching materials; has made numerous conference presentations related to teaching strategies; and initiated a highly popular annual symposium in which professors across all disciplines at LC exchange good teaching ideas. She has been an auditor with an international public accounting firm and an internal auditor for a large oil and gas company. Professor Schneider has an active CPA license and also serves on the board of the local Institute of Management Accountants chapter where she regularly involves students in professional meetings. She received a B.S. in Mathematics Education from the University of Florida and an M.P.A. degree from Georgia State University.

Edward E. Milam

Edward E. Milam, Ph.D., CPA, is a Professor of Accounting at Mississippi State University (MSU). Dr. Milam has been the recipient of several prestigious teaching awards including the Federation of Schools of Accountancy Outstanding Educator Award, and the Mississippi Society of CPA's Educator of the Year Award. Dr. Milam is a past President of the Federation of Schools of Accountancy, and has served on various committees of the ATA, FSA, AICPA, American Accounting Association, and the Mississippi Society of Certified Public Accountants. He has authored numerous articles that appeared in publications including *Journal of Accountancy, Taxes, Management Accounting, Financial Executive, Estate Planning, Trusts and Estates,* the *CPA Journal,* and others. He has also coauthored seven books.

• NOTE FROM AUTHORS •

Over the past 15 years, major changes in accounting education have impacted the way most college and university professors teach introductory accounting. We are gratified that our concepts approach has been so effective that it has become a market leader in the change movement. The concepts approach takes traditional accounting to the next level, by not only covering debits and credits, but also explaining how those debits and credits impact financial statements.

"I heartily applaud the authors' goal of providing students with a concepts-based approach rather than a strictly procedure-based approach to be an important contribution to improving accounting education, one that appeals to both users and preparers and that enables students to "read between the lines."

MICHAEL R. DODGE, COASTAL CAROLINA COMMUNITY COLLEGE

HOW HAVE WE BECOME MARKET LEADERS IN THE INTRODUCTORY ACCOUNTING COURSE?

We look at ourselves as innovative traditionalists. We don't aim to radically transform accounting education, but to make it more effective. With the concepts approach, students follow a different path toward the accomplishment of a conventional set of learning objectives. However, the path is easier to walk and students complete the journey with a far greater understanding of accounting.

In contrast to traditional textbooks, this is a **concepts-based approach** that **focuses on the big picture**. Recording procedures and other details are presented after a conceptual foundation has been established. This approach enables students to understand rather than memorize. What do we mean by a concepts-based textbook? We mean the text stresses the relationships between business events and financial statements. The primary objective is to develop students who can explain how business events affect the income statement, balance sheet, and statement of cash flows. Do assets increase, decrease or remain unchanged? What effect does each event have on liabilities, equity, revenue, expense, gains, losses, net income, and dividends? Furthermore, how does the event affect cash flows? **The focus is on learning how business events affect financial statements.**

BALANCE BETWEEN THEORY AND PRACTICE.

This text addresses the issues raised by advocates for change in accounting education. Not only are students who understand concepts better able to communicate ideas and more effective at solving unstructured problems, but they are also better prepared to learn technical content. While seeing the big picture, students will learn the basics of double-entry bookkeeping including debits and credits, journal entries, T-accounts, and trial balances, allowing this text to maintain an appropriate balance between skill development and technical competence.

The concepts approach serves both users and preparers. By teaching concepts, you no longer have to choose between the interests of accounting majors and those of other business students. The concepts approach serves both groups.

"Very clear, concise, yet sophisticated treatment of topics."

NICHOLAS P. MARUDAS, AUBURN UNIVERSITY AT MONTGOMERY

IMPLEMENTING THE CONCEPTS APPROACH IS SURPRISINGLY SIMPLE.

Instead of teaching students to record transactions in journals or T-accounts, teach them to record transactions directly into financial statements. While this shift is easy for instructors, it represents a dramatic improvement in how students have traditionally studied accounting. Making a direct connection between business events and financial statements encourages students to analyze conceptual relationships rather than memorize procedures.

This text helps teachers move from the traditional educational paradigm more easily than you might imagine. The content focuses on essential concepts, reducing the amount of material you must cover, and giving you more time to work on skill development. The Instructor's Resource Manual provides step-by-step instructions for implementing innovative teaching methods such as active learning and group dynamics. It offers enticing short discovery learning cases which provide class-opening experiences that effectively stimulate student interest and help develop critical thinking skills.

"I would say it is a positive, new approach to teaching an old subject."

FRANK BAGAN, COUNTY COLLEGE OF MORRIS

"I couldn't recommend this text too highly to any of my colleagues. It literally puts the "sizzle" back into the teaching process!"

MICHAEL R. DODGE, COASTAL CAROLINA COMMUNITY COLLEGE

BUT DON'T TAKE OUR WORD FOR IT.

With over 200 colleges and universities successfully making the change to the concepts approach, we feel confident you will experience the same success as many of your colleagues. We would like to thank all of those who have been supportive of our teaching philosophy, and we highly encourage you to contact the author team or your local McGraw-Hill/Irwin representative to learn more about our texts.

Tom Edmonds+Cindy Edmonds+Frances McNair+Phil Olds +Bor-Yi Tsay+Nancy Schneider

HOW DOES THIS BOOK HELP STUDENTS SEE THE BIG PICTURE?

HORIZONTAL FINANCIAL STATEMENTS MODEL

"[The Horizontal Financial Statements Model is] well organized and a straightforward way to show the effects of transactions."

ANDY WILLIAMS, EDMONDS COMMUNITY COLLEGE

A horizontal financial statements model replaces the accounting equation as the predominant teaching platform in this text. The model arranges the balance sheet, income statement, and statement of cash flows horizontally across a single line of text as shown below.

Assets	=	Liabilities	+	Stockholders' Equity	Revenue	−	Expense	=	Net Income	Cash Flow

The statements model approach enables students to see how accounting relates to real-world decision making. The traditional approach teaches students to journalize a series of events and to present summarized information in financial statements. They never see how individual transactions affect financial statements. In contrast, when students record transactions into a statements model, they see a direct connection between business events and financial statements. Most business people think "if I take this particular action, how will it affect my financials," not "if I do these fifteen things, how will they be journalized." Accordingly, the statements model approach provides a learning experience that is more intuitive and relevant than the one provided by traditional teaching methodology.

ESTABLISHING THE CONCEPTUAL FRAMEWORK

"I see tremendous benefit in this horizontal analysis concept because, like I've said many times in this review, the idea is a new, very effective, and revolutionary technique that would do everything the preface describes."

FRANK BAGAN, COUNTY COLLEGE OF MORRIS

Chapter 1 introduces the key components of the conceptual framework for financial accounting. We expect students to master not only the definitions of financial statement elements but also the relationships between those elements. For example, the term "asset" is defined and then the term "revenue" is defined as an increase in assets. The definitions are expanded in a logical step-wise fashion. Once students have learned the elements, the text explains how to organize those elements into a set of financial statements. The financial statements model is introduced toward the end of the first chapter.

Accruals and deferrals are introduced in **Chapter 2** and it not only introduces new concepts but reinforces the core concepts introduced in Chapter 1. The basic conceptual components of the income statement are reinforced through repetition. By the time students have completed the first two chapters, they have a strong conceptual foundation.

Chapter 3 introduces recording procedures, including debits and credits. By the end of the first three chapters, students will have been exposed to the same accounting content as those who use traditional books. Instead of emerging from the learning experience with a memorized set of seemingly unrelated details, students using this text will emerge with a firmly established conceptual foundation.

After Chapter 3, the text demonstrates both the conceptual structure and the recording procedures in tandem. Each time a new type of business event is introduced, the text illustrates the effects of that event on the financial statements using the horizontal statements model. The statements model is then followed with an illustration of the relevant journal entry or T-account entries.

THE EFFECTS OF CASH FLOWS ARE SHOWN THROUGH THE ENTIRE TEXT.

The statement of cash flows is introduced in the first chapter and included throughout the text. Students learn to prepare a statement of cash flows in the first chapter by learning to analyze each increase and decrease in the cash account. They can prepare a statement of cash flows by classifying each entry in the cash account as an operating, investing, or financing activity. This logical approach helps students understand the essential differences between cash flows and accrual-based income.

EFFECTS OF FINANCIAL STATEMENTS OVER MULTIPLE ACCOUNTING CYCLES

The text also uses a vertical statements model that shows financial statements from top to bottom on a single page. This model displays financial results for consecutive accounting cycles in adjacent columns, thereby enabling the instructor to show how related events are reported over multiple accounting cycles.

Exhibit 2
Elden Enterprises
Financial Statements Under Double-declining-balance

Income Statements	2003	2004	2005	2006	2007
Rent Revenue	$15,000	$ 9,000	$ 5,000	$ 3,000	$ -0-
Depreciation Expense	12,000	6,000	2,000	-0-	-0-
Operating Income	3,000	3,000	3,000	3,000	-0-
Gain on sale of Van	-0-	-0-	-0-	-0-	500
Net Income	$ 3,000	$ 3,000	$ 3,000	$ 3,000	$ 500
Balance Sheets					
Assets:					
Cash	$16,000	$25,000	$30,000	$33,000	$37,500
Van	24,000	24,000	24,000	24,000	-0-
Accumulated Depreciation	(12,000)	(18,000)	(20,000)	(20,000)	-0-
Total Assets	$28,000	$31,000	$34,000	$37,000	$37,500
Stockholders' Equity					
Common Stock	$25,000	$25,000	$25,000	$25,000	$25,000
Retained Earnings	3,000	6,000	9,000	12,000	12,500
Total Stockholders' Equity	$28,000	$31,000	$34,000	$37,000	$37,500
Statements of Cash Flows					
Operating Activities					
Inflow from Customers	15,000	9,000	5,000	3,000	-0-
Investing Activities					
Outflow to Purchase Van	(24,000)				
Inflow from Sale of Van					4,500
Financing Activities					
Inflow from Stock Issue	25,000				
Net Change in Cash	16,000	9,000	5,000	3,000	4,500
Beginning Cash Balance	0	16,000	25,000	30,000	33,000
Ending Cash Balance	$16,000	$25,000	$30,000	$33,000	$37,500

"I really like this approach of bringing the conceptual framework up front, helping students see the big picture before they find themselves bogged down in details. I find that students who have the clearest appreciation of the conceptual framework early have the greatest chance of mastering the details later on."

**MICHAEL R. DODGE,
COASTAL CAROLINA
COMMUNITY COLLEGE**

"I wish I had learned it (cash flows) this way. This helps our accounting students tremendously as they have a smoother transition into immediate accounting. You make a difficult topic much easier to understand!"

**SONDRA SMITH,
UNIVERSITY OF WEST GEORGIA**

"I think the integration of the financial statements in the chapters is excellent. It reinforces the concepts."

RACHEL PERNIA, ESSEX COUNTY COLLEGE

MANAGERIAL ACCOUNTING CONCEPTS

Traditional texts have emphasized accounting practices for manufacturing companies, while the business environment has shifted toward service companies. This text recognizes this critical shift by emphasizing decision-making concepts applicable to both service and manufacturing companies. Topics such as cost behavior, operating leverage, and cost allocation are introduced early. Traditional topics such as manufacturing cost flow, job-order costing, and process costing are covered toward the end of the text. This placement reflects the decision-making concepts emphasis found throughout the text.

A CONSISTENT POINT OF REFERENCE

"The chapter on cost-volume-profit analysis is most likely the best I have read on the subject."

MICHAEL J. FARINA, CERRITOS COLLEGE

Why do good students sometimes have so much trouble grasping the simplest concepts? A recent introductory accounting workshop participant supplied the answer. Most accounting events are described from the perspective of the business entity. For example, we say the business borrowed money, purchased assets, earned revenue, or incurred expenses. However, we usually shift the point of reference when describing equity transactions. We say the owners contributed capital, provided cash, or invested assets in the business. This reference shift confuses an entry-level accounting student. Your students will appreciate the fact that this text uses the business entity as a consistent point of reference in describing all accounting events. Accounting is a new language for most business students, so this text makes a conscious effort to minimize the road blocks that are frequently raised by the inconsistent use of technical terminology.

FOCUS ON CORPORATE FORM OF ORGANIZATION

We want students to learn that businesses acquire assets from three primary sources: from creditors, from investors, and from earnings. The corporate organization structure highlights these three asset sources by using separate account categories for liabilities, contributed capital, and retained earnings. We have found the corporate form to be pedagogically superior to the proprietorship form in the educational setting. While we cover accounting for proprietorships and partnerships in a separate chapter of the text, we use the corporate form as the primary teaching platform.

LESS IS MORE

Many educators recognize the detrimental effect of information overload. Research suggests that students resort to memorization when faced with too much content, and are unable to comprehend basic concepts. We make a conscious choice to reduce the breadth of content coverage in order to enhance student comprehension of concepts. For example, you don't need to teach both the net and gross methods to explain how cash discounts affect financial statements. Demonstrating just one method is sufficient to demonstrate the critical interrelationships.

We have eliminated many of the alternative accounting practices typically found in traditional textbooks. Omitted topics include: alternative recording procedures for adjusting entries, reversing entries, accounting for discounting notes receivable, sum-of-the-years' digits depreciation, accounting for the exchange of like-kind assets, issuing bonds between interest dates, stock subscriptions, and differences in accounting for large versus small stock dividends. While this is not an exhaustive list of omitted topics, it illustrates the serious commitment to reduce the information overload problem. With only twenty-four chapters, this text eliminates less critical details and is able to focus on developing a conceptual framework. This framework enables students to understand, rather than memorize, and less detail results in greater comprehension.

"Very readable and understandable on the student level. Should be an easier approach for students to understand. Not too much material in any one chapter – smaller bites will be easier for students to digest."

LYNN A. SUBERLY, VALDOSTA STATE UNIVERSITY

"Excellent overall introduction to the whole subject, especially the role of accounting in society. The first text I have seen that distinguishes in a meaningful way between profit and nonprofit entities."

NICHOLAS P. MARUDAS, AUBURN UNIVERSITY AT MONTGOMERY

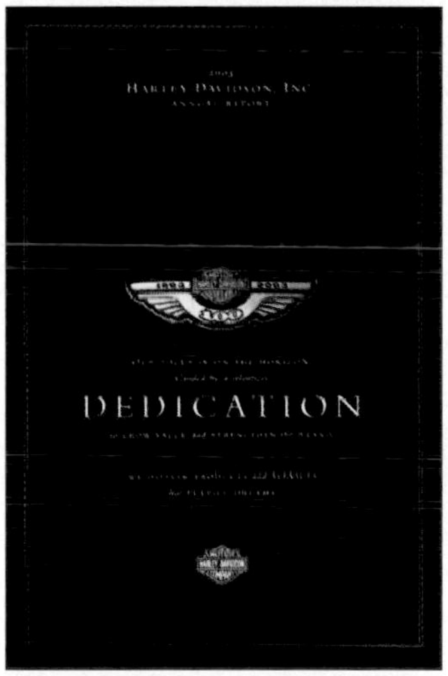

ANNUAL REPORTS

Two annual reports accompany the text.

- The 2003 annual report for Harley-Davidson, Inc., is packaged separately with the text.
- The 2003 annual report for The Topps Company, Inc., is printed in Appendix B.

Business application problems related to the annual reports from Harley-Davidson, Inc., and Topps Company are included at the end of each chapter.

In the Annual Report and Financial Statement Analysis Projects, located on the text website and the Instructor's Manual, projects for each of these companies are included as well as a general purpose annual report project instructors can assign for any company's annual report.

"Good conceptual order, elimination of superfluous material."

ANDY WILLIAMS, EDMONDS COMMUNITY COLLEGE

"I think this text did a great job of ferreting out the important topics to cover in a managerial text, and streamlined some of the coverage to a quick explanation that can introduce students to concepts, while leaving the actual materials and computations to the cost accounting class."

JAN RICHARD HEIER, AUBURN UNIVERSITY – MONTGOMERY

COMPREHENSIVE PROBLEM TO INTEGRATE CONCEPTS ACROSS CHAPTERS

Chapters include a comprehensive problem designed to integrate concepts across chapters. These problems help students understand interrelationships between various accounting concepts. The problem builds in each successive chapter, with the ending account balances in one chapter becoming the beginning account balances in the next chapter.

COMPREHENSIVE PROBLEM

The trial balance of Pacilio Security Services, Inc. as of January 1, 2003 had the following normal balances:

Cash	$8,900
Accounts Receivable	1,500
Supplies	65
Prepaid Rent	800
Land	4,000
Accounts Payable	1,050
Unearned Revenue	200
Salaries Payable	1,200
Notes Payable	2,000
Common Stock	8,000
Retained Earnings	2,815

During 2003, Pacilio Security Services experienced the following transactions:

1. Paid the salaries payable from 2002.
2. Paid the balance of $2,000 on the debt owed to the Small Business Government Agency. The loan is interest free.
3. Performed $32,000 of security services for numerous local events during the year; $21,000 was on account and $11,000 was for cash.
4. On May 1, paid $3,000 for 12 months' rent in advance.
5. Purchased supplies on account for $700.
6. Paid salaries expense for the year of $9,000.

EXCEL SPREADSHEETS

Spreadsheet applications are essential to contemporary accounting practice. Students must recognize the power of spreadsheets and know how accounting data are presented in spreadsheets. We discuss Excel applications where appropriate throughout the text. In most instances, the text illustrates actual spreadsheets. End-of-chapter materials include problems students can complete using spreadsheet software.

Understanding the Accounting Cycle 97

Problem 2-34A *Missing information in financial statements*

L.O. 5, 6

eXcel

mhhe.com/edmonds2007

Required

Fill in the blanks (as indicated by the alphabetic letters in parentheses) in the following financial statements. Assume the company started operations January 1, 2006, and that all transactions involve cash.

CHECK FIGURES

a. ($500)

o. $600

	For the Years		
	2006	2007	2008
Income Statements			
Revenue	$ 700	$ 1,300	$ 2,000
Expense	(a)	(700)	(1,300)
Net Income	$200	$ (m)	$ 700
Statements of Changes in Stockholders' Equity			
Beginning Common Stock	$ 0	$ (n)	$ 6,000
Plus: Common Stock Issued	5,000	1,000	2,000
Ending Common Stock	5,000	6,000	(t)
Beginning Retained Earnings	0	100	200
Plus: Net Income	(b)	(o)	700
Less: Dividends	(c)	(500)	(300)
Ending Retained Earnings	100	(p)	600
	$ (d)	$ 6,200	$ 8,600

USER-FRIENDLY WRITING STYLE

Every chapter of the text has been designed to encourage students to read the book. Students will find the content easy to read and comprehend.

"The writing style is excellent. It is clear and concise."

MICHAEL J. FARINA,
CERRITOS COLLEGE

FOCUS COMPANIES

A logo representing the focus company of each chapter in the managerial portions of the book has been included to add realism to these fictitious companies.

Name and Type of Company Used as Main Chapter Example

Chapter Title	Company Used as Main Chapter Example	Company Logo	Type of Company
14. Management Accounting: A Value-Added Discipline	Patillo Manufacturing Company	PATILLO	Manufactures wooden tables
15. Cost Behavior, Operating Leverage, and Profitability Analysis	Star Productions Inc. (SPI)		Promotes rock concerts
16. Cost Accumulation,Tracing, and Allocation	In Style Inc. (ISI)	STYLE	Retail clothing store
17. Product Costing in Service and Manufacturing Entities	Ventra Manufacturing Company	VENTRA	Constructs mahogany jewelry boxes
18. Job-Order, Process, and Hybrid Cost Systems	Benchmore Boat Company		Manufactures boats
	Janis Juice Company	JANIS	Makes fruit juice
19. Analysis of Cost, Volume, and Pricing to Increase Profitability	Bright Day Distributors		Sells nonprescription health food supplements
20. Relevant Information for Special Decisions	Premier Office Products	PREMIER	Manufactures printers
21. Planning for Profit and Cost Control	Hampton Hams (HH)		Sells cured hams nationwide through retail outlets
22. Performance Evaluation	Melrose Manufacturing Company		Makes small, high-quality trophies used in award ceremonies
23. Responsibility Accounting	Panther Holding Company	PANTHER	Furniture Manufacturing Division
24. Planning for Capital Investments	EZ Rentals		Rents computers, monitors, and projection equipment

"Very well-written."

KAREN WISNIEWSKI,
COUNTY COLLEGE OF MORRIS

HOW DOES THE BOOK MOTIVATE STUDENTS?

The text provides a variety of thought-provoking, real-world examples of financial and managerial accounting as an essential part of the management process. There are descriptions of accounting practices from Coca-Cola, Enron, General Motors, JCPenney, and Amazon.com. These companies are highlighted in blue in the text.

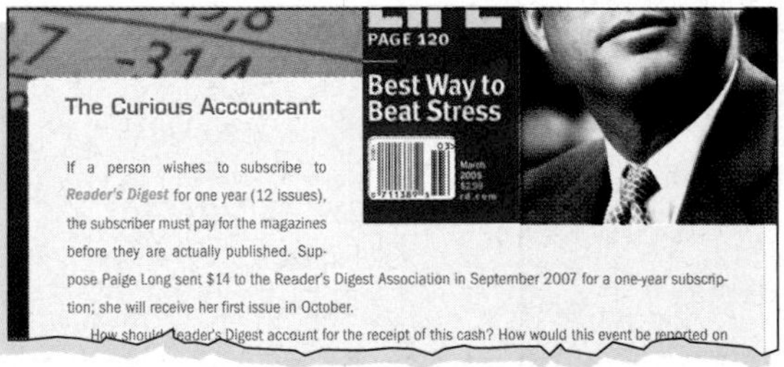

The Curious Accountant

If a person wishes to subscribe to *Reader's Digest* for one year (12 issues), the subscriber must pay for the magazines before they are actually published. Suppose Paige Long sent $14 to the Reader's Digest Association in September 2007 for a one-year subscription; she will receive her first issue in October.

How should Reader's Digest account for the receipt of this cash? How would this event be reported on

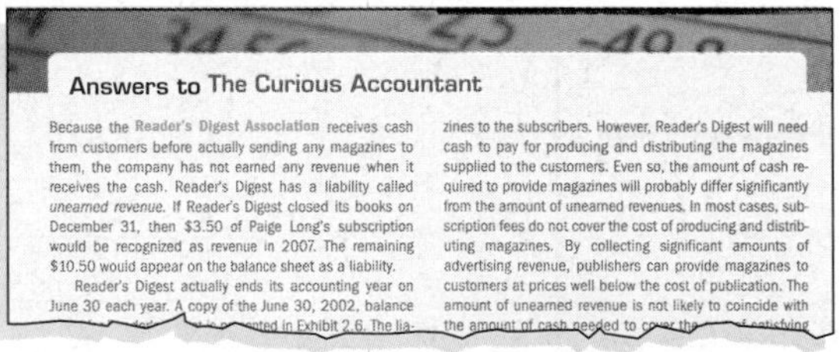

Answers to The Curious Accountant

Because the Reader's Digest Association receives cash from customers before actually sending any magazines to them, the company has not earned any revenue when it receives the cash. Reader's Digest has a liability called *unearned revenue*. If Reader's Digest closed its books on December 31, then $3.50 of Paige Long's subscription would be recognized as revenue in 2007. The remaining $10.50 would appear on the balance sheet as a liability.

Reader's Digest actually ends its accounting year on June 30 each year. A copy of the June 30, 2002, balance ... presented in Exhibit 2.6. The lia- ... zines to the subscribers. However, Reader's Digest will need cash to pay for producing and distributing the magazines supplied to the customers. Even so, the amount of cash required to provide magazines will probably differ significantly from the amount of unearned revenues. In most cases, subscription fees do not cover the cost of producing and distributing magazines. By collecting significant amounts of advertising revenue, publishers can provide magazines to customers at prices well below the cost of publication. The amount of unearned revenue is not likely to coincide with the amount of cash needed to cover the ... satisfying

THE CURIOUS ACCOUNTANT

Each chapter opens with a short vignette that sets the stage and helps pique student interest. These pose a question about a real-world accounting issue related to the topic of the chapter. The answer to the question appears in a separate sidebar a few pages further into the chapter.

FOCUS ON INTERNATIONAL ISSUES

IS THERE GLOBAL GAAP?

As explained in this chapter, financial reporting is a measurement and communication discipline based on generally accepted accounting principles (GAAP). The accounting rules described in this text represent the GAAP used in the United States. All economies in the world do not use the same accounting rules. Although there are similarities among the accounting principles used in different countries, there are also major differences. An independent body, the International Accounting Standards Board (IASB), has made an effort in recent years to create uniform international accounting standards. Individual countries, however, have retained the authority to establish their own accounting principles, so there is no single "global GAAP," though the work of the IASB has reduced the extent of variation in accounting principles that exists among countries.

Accounting rules differ among countries for such reasons as the economic and legal environments in each country and the way in which a country establishes its accounting principles. In the United States, the Financial Accounting Standards Board (FASB), a nongovernmental rule-making body that the accounting profession established, has primary responsibility for establishing accounting rules. In some countries accounting principles are established by governmental bodies ... laws and regulations are established in the United States.

FOCUS ON INTERNATIONAL ISSUES

These boxed inserts expose students to international issues in accounting.

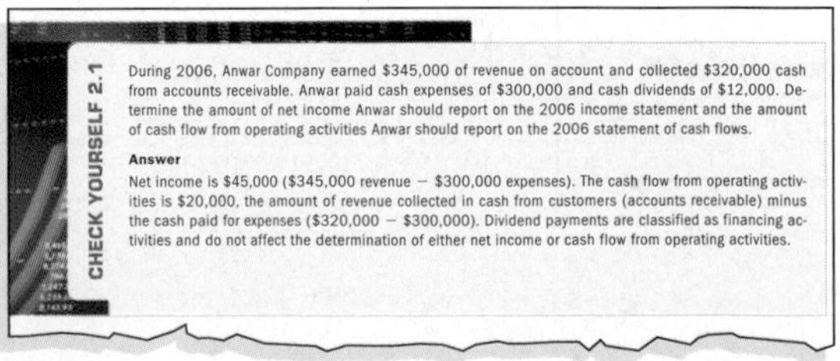

CHECK YOURSELF 2.1

During 2006, Anwar Company earned $345,000 of revenue on account and collected $320,000 cash from accounts receivable. Anwar paid cash expenses of $300,000 and cash dividends of $12,000. Determine the amount of net income Anwar should report on the 2006 income statement and the amount of cash flow from operating activities Anwar should report on the 2006 statement of cash flows.

Answer

Net income is $45,000 ($345,000 revenue − $300,000 expenses). The cash flow from operating activities is $20,000, the amount of revenue collected in cash from customers (accounts receivable) minus the cash paid for expenses ($320,000 − $300,000). Dividend payments are classified as financing activities and do not affect the determination of either net income or cash flow from operating activities.

CHECK YOURSELF

These short question/answer features occur at the end of each main topic and ask students to stop and think about the material just covered. The answer follows to provide immediate feedback before students go on to a new topic.

REALITY BYTES

This feature provides examples or expansions of the topics presented by highlighting companies and showing how they use the accounting concepts discussed in the chapter to make business decisions.

REALITY BYTES

Independent auditors are primarily responsible to the investing public, not to the company that hires and pays them. In 2002 numerous accounting scandals involving some very large public companies caused investors to question whether or not the external auditors really were independent. The public learned that external audit firms were often also serving as consultants to the companies they audited. The fees earned for consulting services were sometimes significantly higher than the fees earned for auditing the same company. These arrangements caused many people, including members of Congress, to doubt that auditors would take a tough stance with a company's management over financial reporting issues if doing so might threaten future consulting fees.

No situation demonstrated this concern more than that of Enron. The well-publicized accounting problems that led to Enron's downfall were equally devastating for its auditor, Arthur Andersen. Within six months after Enron's troubles became public knowledge, Arthur Andersen lost over half its public company audit clients and almost two-thirds of its employees. Further, Andersen was convicted of obstruction of justice by a Houston jury and was told by the SEC that it could no longer audit public companies. The partner in charge of the Enron audit was fired and pled guilty to obstruction of justice charges; the previous year, his compensation exceeded $1 million.

THE FINANCIAL ANALYST

Financial statement analysis is highlighted in each chapter under this heading.

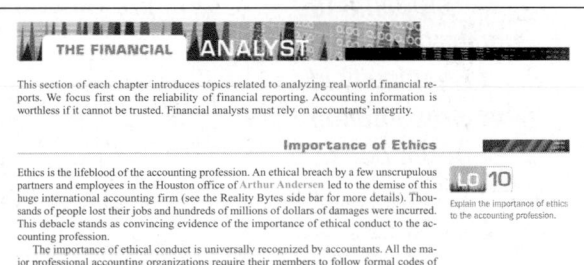

THE FINANCIAL ANALYST

This section of each chapter introduces topics related to analyzing real world financial reports. We focus first on the reliability of financial reporting. Accounting information is worthless if it cannot be trusted. Financial analysts must rely on accountants' integrity.

Importance of Ethics

Ethics is the lifeblood of the accounting profession. An ethical breach by a few unscrupulous partners and employees in the Houston office of Arthur Andersen led to the demise of this huge international accounting firm (see the Reality Bytes side bar for more details). Thousands of people lost their jobs and hundreds of millions of dollars of damages were incurred. This debacle stands as convincing evidence of the importance of ethical conduct to the accounting profession.

The importance of ethical conduct is universally recognized by accountants. All the major professional accounting organizations require their members to follow formal codes of ethical conduct. The underlying principles of the **Code of Professional Conduct**[6] adopted by the American Institute of Certified Public Accountants are summarized in Exhibit 1.7. Other codes follow similar principles.

LO 10

Explain the importance of ethics to the accounting profession.

TOPIC TACKLER PLUS

A logo indicates a topic explained on the Topic Tackler Plus DVD. The DVD includes two hard-to-learn topics for each chapter explained with video, PowerPoint, practice quizzes, self-tests, and a demonstration problem walkthrough.

Recording Business Events Under the Accounting Equation

An **accounting event** is an economic occurrence that changes an enterprise's assets, liabilities, or stockholders' equity. A **transaction** is a particular kind of event that involves transferring something of value between two entities. Examples of transactions include acquiring assets from owners, borrowing money from creditors, and purchasing or selling goods and services. The following section of the text explains how several different types of accounting events affect a company's accounting equation.

LO 5

Record business events in general ledger accounts organized under an accounting equation.

Topic Tackler PLUS

1-2

Asset Source Transactions

As previously mentioned, businesses obtain assets (resources) from three sources. They acquire assets from owners (stockholders); they borrow assets from creditors; and they earn assets through profitable operations. Asset source transactions increase total assets and total claims. A more detailed discussion of the effects of asset source transactions is provided below:

Event 1 **Rustic Camp Sites (RCS) was formed on January 1, 2004, when it acquired $120,000 cash from issuing common stock.**

When RCS issued stock, it received cash and gave each investor (owner) a stock certificate as a receipt. Since this transaction provided $120,000 of assets (cash) to the business, it is an **asset source transaction.** It increases the business's assets (cash) and its stockholders' equity (common stock).

A LOOK BACK / A LOOK FORWARD

Students need a roadmap to make sense of where the chapter topics fit into the whole picture. A Look Back reviews the chapter material and a Look Forward introduces new material to come in the next chapter.

<< A Look Back

This chapter introduced the role of accounting in society and business: to provide information helpful to operating and evaluating the performance of organizations. Accounting is a measurement discipline. To communicate effectively, users of accounting must agree on the rules of measurement. *Generally accepted accounting principles (GAAP)* constitute the rules used by the accounting profession in the United States to govern financial reporting. GAAP is a work in progress that continues to evolve.

This chapter has discussed eight elements of financial statements: *assets, liabilities, equity, common stock (contributed capital), revenue, expenses, dividends (distributions),* and *net income.* The elements represent broad classifications reported on financial statements. Four basic financial statements appear in the reports of public companies: the *balance sheet,* the *income statement,* the *statement of changes in stockholders' equity,* and the *statement of cash flows.* The chapter discussed the form and content of each statement as well as the interrelationships among the statements.

This chapter introduced a *horizontal financial statements model* as a tool to help you understand how business events affect a set of financial statements. This model is used throughout the text. You should carefully study this model before proceeding to Chapter 2.

>> A Look Forward

To keep matters as simple as possible and to focus on the interrelationships among financial statements, this chapter considered only cash events. Obviously, many real-world events do not involve an immediate exchange of cash. For example, customers use telephone service throughout the month without paying for it until the next month.

HOW ARE CHAPTER CONCEPTS REINFORCED?

"I like the way you complete a review of each chapter with 'A Look Back' but I especially like 'A Look Forward' section for the students to understand there is continuity in the presentation of the book."

Jan Richard Heier,
Auburn University - Montgomery

Regardless of the instructional approach, there is no shortcut to learning accounting. Students must practice to master basic accounting concepts. The text includes a prodigious supply of practice materials and exercises and problems.

SELF-STUDY REVIEW PROBLEM

These sections offer problems and solutions of major chapter concepts.

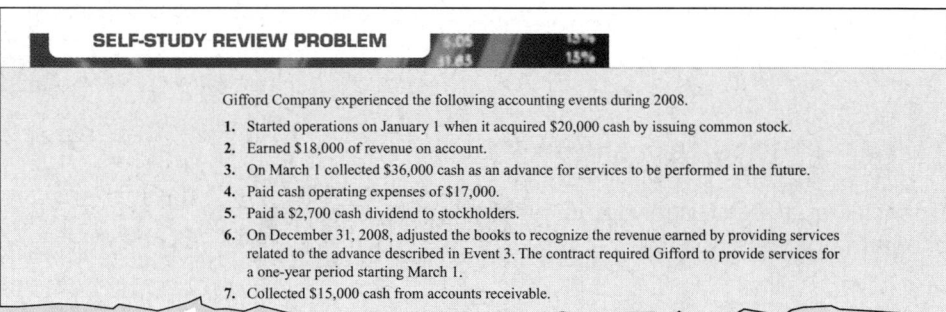

SELF-STUDY REVIEW PROBLEM

Gifford Company experienced the following accounting events during 2008.

1. Started operations on January 1 when it acquired $20,000 cash by issuing common stock.
2. Earned $18,000 of revenue on account.
3. On March 1 collected $36,000 cash as an advance for services to be performed in the future.
4. Paid cash operating expenses of $17,000.
5. Paid a $2,700 cash dividend to stockholders.
6. On December 31, 2008, adjusted the books to recognize the revenue earned by providing services related to the advance described in Event 3. The contract required Gifford to provide services for a one-year period starting March 1.
7. Collected $15,000 cash from accounts receivable.

EXERCISE SERIES A & B AND PROBLEM SERIES A & B

There are two sets of problems and exercises, Series A and B. Instructors can assign one set for homework and another set for classwork.

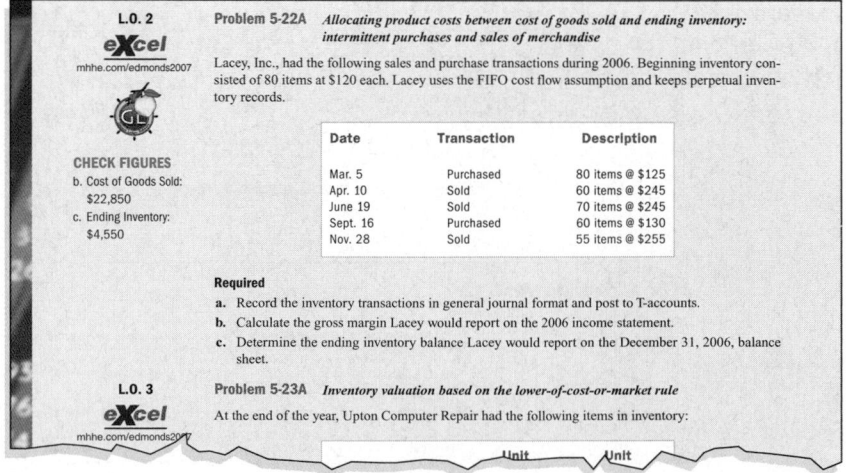

L.O. 2

excel
mhhe.com/edmonds2007

Problem 5-22A ***Allocating product costs between cost of goods sold and ending inventory: intermittent purchases and sales of merchandise***

Lacey, Inc., had the following sales and purchase transactions during 2006. Beginning inventory consisted of 80 items at $120 each. Lacey uses the FIFO cost flow assumption and keeps perpetual inventory records.

CHECK FIGURES
b. Cost of Goods Sold: $22,850
c. Ending Inventory: $4,550

Date	Transaction	Description
Mar. 5	Purchased	80 items @ $125
Apr. 10	Sold	60 items @ $245
June 19	Sold	70 items @ $245
Sept. 16	Purchased	60 items @ $130
Nov. 28	Sold	55 items @ $255

Required

a. Record the inventory transactions in general journal format and post to T-accounts.
b. Calculate the gross margin Lacey would report on the 2006 income statement.
c. Determine the ending inventory balance Lacey would report on the December 31, 2006, balance sheet.

L.O. 3

excel
mhhe.com/edmonds2007

Problem 5-23A ***Inventory valuation based on the lower-of-cost-or-market rule***

At the end of the year, Upton Computer Repair had the following items in inventory:

Unit Unit

• Check figures

The figures provide a quick reference for students to check on their progress in solving the problem. These are included for all problems in Series A.

• Excel

Many exercises and problems can be solved using the Excel™ spreadsheet templates contained on the text's Online Learning Center. A logo appears in the margins next to these exercises and problems for easy identification.

• General Ledger and Peachtree Software

If a problem can be solved using our General Ledger or Peachtree software, a logo is shown.

ANALYZE, THINK, COMMUNICATE (ATC)

Each chapter includes an innovative section entitled Analyze, Think, Communicate (ATC). This section contains:

- Business application cases related to the annual reports from Harley-Davidson and Topps Company

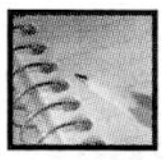

- **Writing assignments**

- **Group exercises**

- **Ethics cases**

- **Internet assignments**

eXcel
mhhe.com/edmonds2007

- **Excel spreadsheet applications**

- **Real company examples**

Harley-Davidson, Inc.

The Topps Company, Inc.

- **Research assignment**

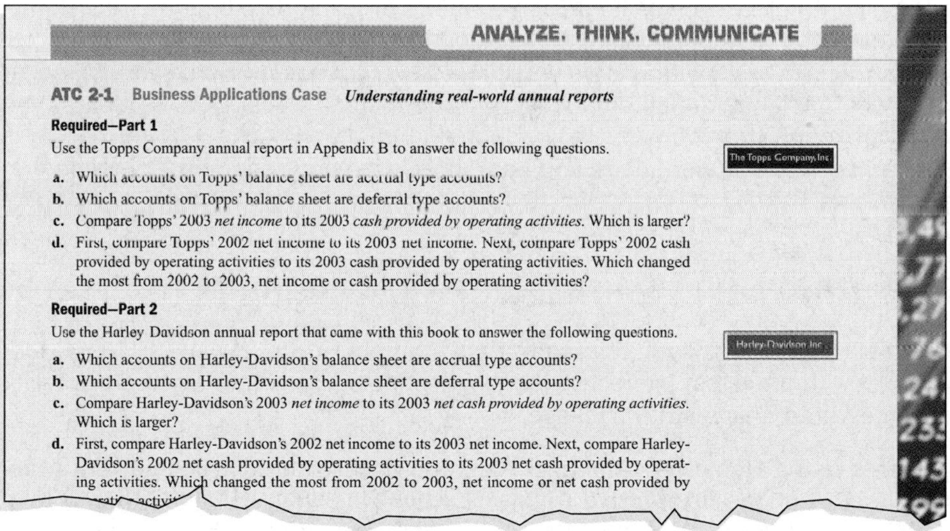

ANALYZE, THINK, COMMUNICATE

ATC 2-1 Business Applications Case *Understanding real-world annual reports*

Required—Part 1

Use the Topps Company annual report in Appendix B to answer the following questions.

a. Which accounts on Topps' balance sheet are accrual type accounts?
b. Which accounts on Topps' balance sheet are deferral type accounts?
c. Compare Topps' 2003 *net income* to its 2003 *cash provided by operating activities*. Which is larger?
d. First, compare Topps' 2002 net income to its 2003 net income. Next, compare Topps' 2002 cash provided by operating activities to its 2003 cash provided by operating activities. Which changed the most from 2002 to 2003, net income or cash provided by operating activities?

Required—Part 2

Use the Harley Davidson annual report that came with this book to answer the following questions.

a. Which accounts on Harley-Davidson's balance sheet are accrual type accounts?
b. Which accounts on Harley-Davidson's balance sheet are deferral type accounts?
c. Compare Harley-Davidson's 2003 *net income* to its 2003 *net cash provided by operating activities*. Which is larger?
d. First, compare Harley-Davidson's 2002 net income to its 2003 net income. Next, compare Harley-Davidson's 2002 net cash provided by operating activities to its 2003 net cash provided by operating activities. Which changed the most from 2002 to 2003, net income or net cash provided by

HOW CAN TECHNOLOGY SUPPORT STUDENT SUCCESS?

Our technology resources help students and instructors focus on learning success. By using the Internet and multimedia students get book-specific help at their convenience. Compare our technology to that of any other book and we're confident you'll agree that *Fundamental Financial and Managerial Accounting Concepts* has the best in the market. Teaching aids make in-class presentations easy and stimulating. These aids give you more power than ever to teach your class the way you want.

McGRAW-HILL'S HOMEWORK MANAGER™

McGraw-Hill's Homework Manager is a web-based homework management system that gives you unparalleled power and flexibility in creating homework assignments, tests, and quizzes. Homework Manager duplicates problem structures directly from the end-of-chapter material in your McGraw-Hill textbook, using algorithms to provide limitless variations of textbook problems. Use Homework Manager to supply online self-graded practice for students, or create assignments and tests with unique versions of every problem: Homework Manager can grade assignments automatically, provide instant feedback to students, and store all results in your private gradebook. Detailed results let you see at a glance how each student does and easily track the progress of every student in your course.

McGRAW-HILL'S HOMEWORK MANAGER PLUS™

McGraw-Hill's Homework Manager Plus combines the power of Homework Manager with the latest interactive learning technology to create a comprehensive, fully integrated online study package.

Students using Homework Manager Plus can access not only **Homework Manager** itself, but the **Interactive Online Textbook** as well. Far more than a textbook on a screen, this resource is completely integrated into Homework Manager, allowing students working on assignments to click a hotlink and instantly review the appropriate material in the textbook. **NetTutor** rounds out the package by offering live tutoring with a qualified expert in the course material, using our innovative virtual whiteboard to allow student and tutor to communicate in real time.

By including Homework Manager Plus with your textbook adoption, you're giving your students a vital edge as they progress through the course and ensuring that the help they need is never more than a mouse click away.

NETTUTOR

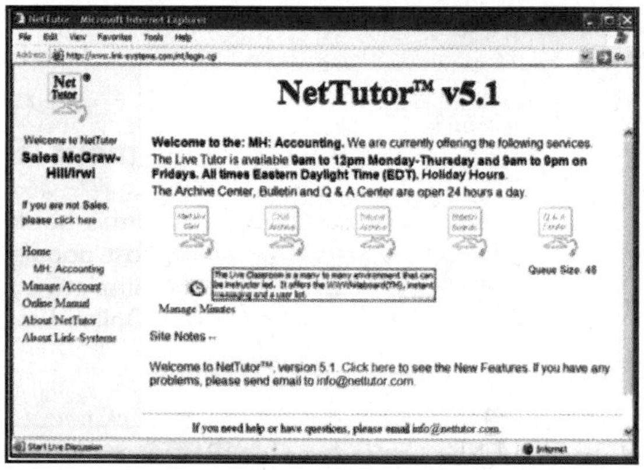

Many students work or have other commitments outside of class, making it difficult for them to get help with their questions during regular school hours. NetTutor connects students with qualified tutors online. Students can work with an online tutor in real time, or post a question to be answered within 24 hours. Only available through Homework Manager Plus, adopters receive unlimited tutoring time on NetTutor.

INTERACTIVE ONLINE VERSION OF THE TEXTBOOK

In addition to the textbook, students can rely on this online version of the text for a convenient way to study. While other publishers offer a simple PDF, this interactive Web-based textbook contains hotlinks to key definitions and is integrated with Homework Manager to give students quick access to relevant content as they work through problems, exercises, and practice quizzes.

TOPIC TACKLER PLUS DVD

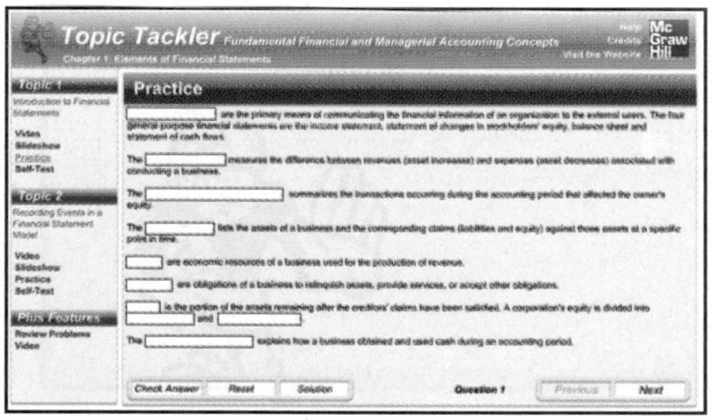

This software is a complete tutorial focusing on areas in the course that give students the most trouble. It provides help on two key topics for each chapter by use of

- Video clips
- PowerPoint slide shows
- Interactive exercises
- Self-grading quizzes

The DVD also includes the Self-Study Review Problems in the book presented in an audio-narrated slide presentation. A logo in the text marks the topic given further coverage in Topic Tackler Plus.

ONLINE LEARNING CENTER (OLC)

www.mhhe.com/edmonds/concepts

More and more students are studying online. That's why we offer an Online Learning Center (OLC) that follows *Fundamental Financial and Managerial Accounting Concepts* chapter by chapter.

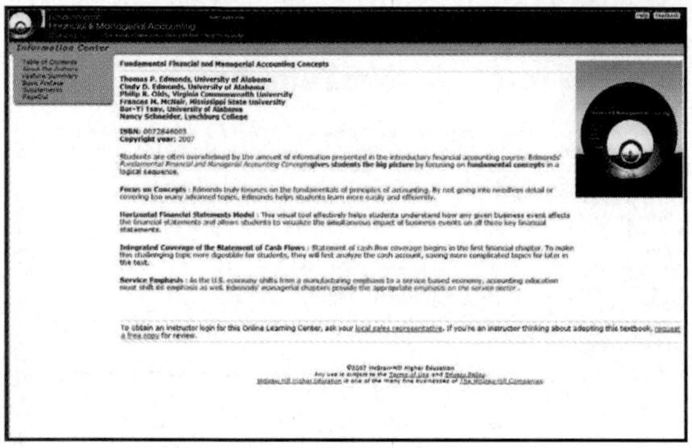

The OLC now includes the following:

- Excel Spreadsheets
- Spreadsheet Tips
- Text Updates
- Glossary
- Key Term Flashcards
- Chapter Learning Objectives
- Interactive Quizzes
- E Lectures (audio-narrated slide presentations)
- Additional Check Figures
- Mobile Resources
- Topic Tackler Plus

For instructors, the book's secured OLC contains essential course materials. You can pull all of this material into your PageOut course syllabus or use it as part of another online course management system. It doesn't require any building or maintenance on your part. It's ready to go the moment you type in the URL.

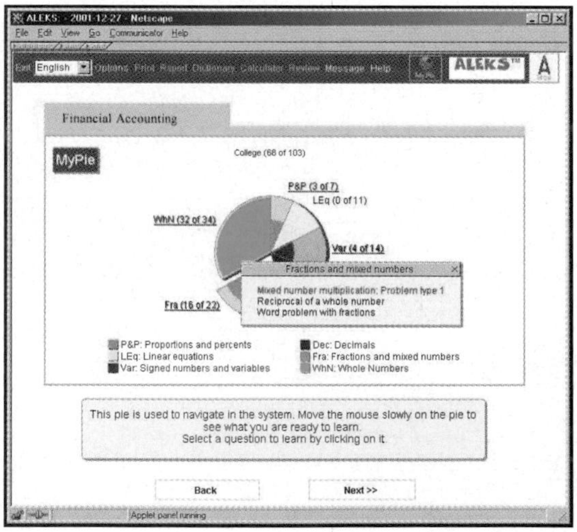

ALEKS

ALEKS for the Accounting Cycle and ALEKS for Financial Accounting provide precise assessment and individualized instruction in the fundamental skills your students need to succeed in accounting. ALEKS motivates your students because it can tell what a student knows, doesn't know, and is most ready to learn next. ALEKS uses an artificial intelligence engine to exactly identify a student's knowledge of accounting. To learn more about adding ALEKS to your accounting course, visit **www.business.aleks.com.**

CAROL YACHT'S GENERAL LEDGER & PEACHTREE COMPLETE 2005 CD

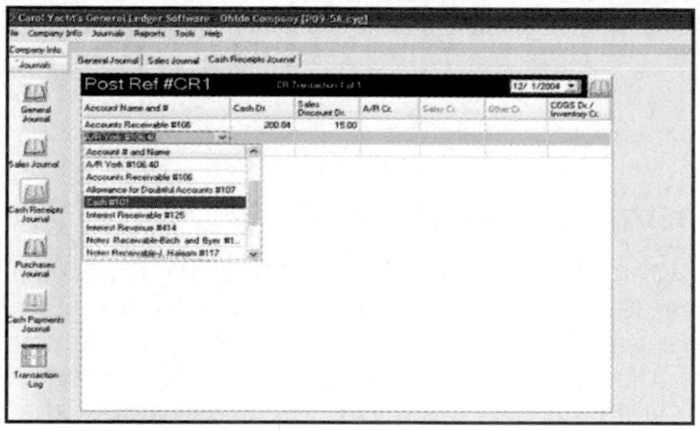

The CD-ROM includes fully functioning versions of McGraw-Hill's General Ledger Application software as well as Peachtree Complete 2005. Problem templates are included that allow you to assign text problems for working in either Yacht's General Ledger or Peachtree Complete 2005. These problems are indicated by the GL logo.

CPS CLASSROOM PERFORMANCE SYSTEM

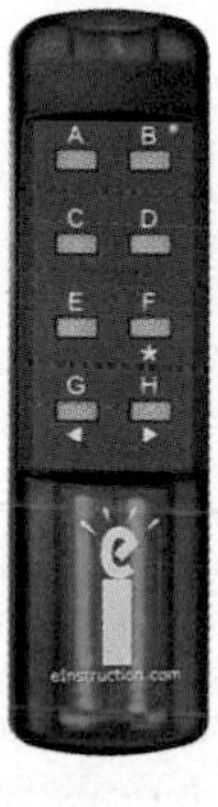

This is a revolutionary system that brings ultimate interactivity to the classroom. CPS is a wireless response system that gives you immediate feedback from every student in the class. CPS units include easy-to-use software for creating and delivering questions and assessments to your class. With CPS you can ask subjective and objective questions. Then every student simply responds with their individual, wireless response pad, providing instant results. CPS is the perfect tool for engaging students while gathering important assessment data.

PAGE OUT

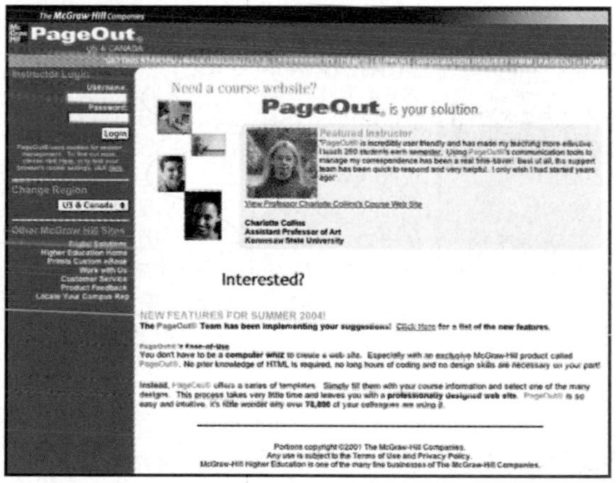

McGraw-Hill's Course Management System PageOut is the easiest way to create a website for your accounting course. Just fill in a series of boxes with plain English and click on one of our professional designs. In no time your course is online with a website that contains your syllabus. If you need help, our team of specialists is ready to take your course materials and build a custom website to your specifications. To learn more visit **www.pageout.net.**

ONLINE COURSE MANAGEMENT WEBCT, ECOLLEGE, AND BLACKBOARD

We offer *Fundamental Financial and Managerial Accounting Concepts* content for complete online courses. You can customize the Online Learning Center content and author your own course materials. No matter which online course solution you choose, you can count on the highest level of support. Our specialists offer free training and answer any question you have through the life of your adoption.

SUPPLEMENTS FOR INSTRUCTORS

Instructor's Resource CD

ISBN-13: 978-0-07-307962-2 (ISBN-10: 0-07-307962-6)
This CD includes electronic versions of the Instructor's Manual, Solutions Manual, Test Bank, and computerized Test Bank, as well as PowerPoint slides, video clips, all exhibits in the text in PowerPoint, and spreadsheet templates with solutions. This CD-ROM makes it easy for instructors to create multimedia presentations.

Instructor's Manual

ISBN-13: 978-0-07-307957-8
(ISBN-10: 0-07-307957-X)
(Also available on the password-protected Instructor Online Learning Center (OLC) and Instructor's Resource CD.) This comprehensive manual includes step-by-step, explicit instructions on how the text can be used to implement alternative teaching methods. It also provides guidance for instructors who use the traditional lecture method. The guide includes lesson plans and demonstration problems with student work papers, as well as solutions. It was prepared by Tom Edmonds and Jill Smith.

Solutions Manual

Volume 1 ISBN-13: 978-0-07-307955-4
(ISBN-10: 0-07-307955-3)
Volume 2 ISBN-13: 978-0-07-307956-1
(ISBN-10: 0-07-307956-1)
(Also available on the password-protected Instructor Online Learning Center (OLC) and Instructor Resource CD) Prepared by the authors, the manual contains complete solutions to all the text's end-of-chapter exercises, problems, and cases.

Solutions Transparencies

Volume 1 ISBN-13: 978-0-07-307958-5
(ISBN-10: 0-07-307958-8)
Volume 2 ISBN-13: 978-0-07-307959-2
(ISBN-10: 0-07-307959-6)
Transparencies are prepared in easy-to-read 14-point bold type. They are exact images of the answers provided in the solutions manual and are consistent with the forms contained in the working papers. This ensures congruence between your class presentations and the follow-up exposure that students attain when they view the solutions manual or use the working papers.

Test Bank

Volume 1 ISBN-13: 978-0-07-307960-8
(ISBN-10: 0-07-307960-X)
Volume 2 ISBN-13: 978-0-07-307961-5
(ISBN-10: 0-07-307961-8)
(Also available on the Instructor's Resource CD) This test bank in Word format contains multiple-choice questions, essay questions, and short problems. Each test item is coded for level of difficulty and learning objective. In addition to an expansive array of traditional test questions, the test bank includes new types of questions that focus exclusively on how business events affect financial statements.

Computerized Test Bank with Algorithmic Problem Generator

(Available on the Instructor's Resource CD) This computerized test bank is an algorithmic problem generator enabling instructors to create similarly structured problems with different values, allowing every student to be assigned a unique quiz or test. The user-friendly interface allows faculty to easily create different versions of the same test, change the answer order, edit or add questions, and even conduct online testing.

PowerPoint Presentation

(Available on the Online Learning Center and Instructor's Resource CD) These slides can serve as interactive class discussions.

SUPPLEMENTS FOR STUDENTS

McGraw-Hill's Homework Manager Plus™

Homework Manager Plus integrates all of the text's multimedia resources. With just one access code, students can obtain state-of-the-art study aids, including Homework Manager, NetTutor and an online version of the text.

McGraw-Hill's Homework Manager™

This web-based software duplicates problem structures directly from the end-of-chapter material in the textbook. It uses algorithms to provide a limitless supply of self-graded practice for students. It shows students where they made errors. All Exercises and Problems in Series A are available with Homework Manager.

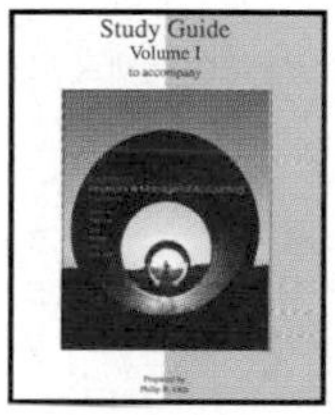

Study Guide

Volume 1 ISBN-13: 978-0-07-307968-4
(ISBN-10: 0-07-307968-5)
Volume 2 ISBN-13: 978-0-07-307969-1
(ISBN-10: 0-07-307969-3)

Each chapter contains a review and explanation of the chapter's learning objectives, as well as multiple-choice problems and short exercises. Unique to this Study Guide is a series of problems that require students to indicate how accounting events affect the elements of financial statements. The guide includes appropriate working papers and a complete set of solutions.

Working Papers

Volume 1 ISBN-13: 978-0-07-307970-7
(ISBN-10: 0-07-307970-7)
Volume 2 ISBN-13: 978-0-07-307971-4
(ISBN-10: 0-07-307971-5)

Working papers are available to direct students in solving text assignments.

Computerized Practice Sets

Wheels Exquisite, Level 1
Student ISBN 0072428457
Instructor ISBN 0072427531

Gold Run Snowmobile
Student ISBN 0072957883
Instructor ISBN 0072947683

Granite Bay Jet Ski, Level 2
Student ISBN 0072426950
Instructor ISBN 0072426209

Topic Tackler Plus DVD

This tutorial offers a virtual helping hand in understanding the most challenging topics in the introductory accounting course. Through a step-by-step sequence of video clips, PowerPoint slides, interactive practice exercises, and self tests, Topic Tackler Plus offers help on two key topics for each chapter. These topics are indicated by a logo in the text. Another component on the DVD takes the Self-Study Review Problem in the book and demonstrates how to solve it in an animated audio presentation.

Carol Yacht's General Ledger & Peachtree Complete 2005 CD

ISBN-13: 978-0-07-307967-7
(ISBN-10: 0-07-307967-7)

This software package includes both an easy-to-use general ledger software tool and a real-world accounting package on one CD-ROM. It will help students learn how to record transactions and create financial statements. Logos in the text highlight selected end-of-chapter problems where both the general ledger software and Peachtree Complete 2005 software are available to help students work through the problem.

Excel Templates

Available on the Online Learning Center (OLC) these templates allow students to develop spreadsheet skills to solve selected assignments identified by an icon in the end-of-chapter material.

E lectures

Available on the Online Learning Center (OLC) these slides cover key chapter topics in an **audio-narrated** presentation sure to help students learn.

ALEKS for Financial Accounting

ISBN 0072841966

ALEKS for the Accounting Cycle

ISBN 0072975326

Online Learning Center (OLC)

www.mhhe.com/edmonds/concepts

ACKNOWLEDGEMENTS

We would like to express our appreciation to the people who have provided assistance in the development of this textbook.

FOCUS GROUP PARTICIPANTS

Brenda Bindschatel	Green River Community College
Kelly Cranford	Georgia Perimeter College
Susan Davis	Green River Community College
Patti Davis	Keystone College
Daniel Gibbons	Waubonsee Community College
Hisel Gobble	Chattanooga Technical College
Cathy Larson	Middlesex Community College
Douglas Larson	Salem State College
Paris Lester	Southwest Virginia Community College
Bruce Lindsey	Genesee Community College
Mabel Machin	Edmonds Community College
Brenda Mattison	Tri-County Technical College
Ann Rowell	Central Piedmont Community College
Gina Shea	Community College of Baltimore
Ellen Sweatt	Georgia Perimeter College
Laverne Thomas-Vertrees	St. Louis Community College at Meramec
Gene Trenary	San Juan College

MANUSCRIPT REVIEWERS

Frank Bagan	County College of Morris
Eric Blazer	Millersville University
Julio Borges	Miami Dade College
Patrick Bouker	North Seattle Community College
Phil Brown	Harding University
Barry Buchoff	Towson University
Rita Buttermilch	SUNY College at Old Westbury
Harlow Callander	University of St. Thomas
Joseph Carthey	Northeast Iowa Community College
James Chimenti	Jamestown Community College
Margaret Costello Lambert	Oakland Community College
Helen Davis	Johnson & Wales University
Suryakant Desai	Cedar Valley College
Michael Dodge	Coastal Carolina Community College

Eileen Eichler	Farmingdale State University
Michael Farina	Cerritos College
Robert Fleming	Northern Michigan University
Jim Formosa	Nashville Community College
Philip Gilmore	Liberty University
Amy Haas	Kingsborough Community College City University of New York
Linda Hall	SUNY at Fredonia
Ward Harder	Motlow State Community College
Jan Heier	Auburn University at Montgomery
Paul Holt	Texas A&M University at Kingsville
Kathy Horton	College of DuPage
Janice Ivansek	Lakeland Community College
Charles Kee	Kingsborough Community College City University of New York
Cindy Killian	Wilkes Community College
Susan Koch	Austin Peay State University
Linda Kropp	Modesto Junior College
Tara Laken	Joliet Junior College
Dorinda Lynn	Pensacola Junior College
Linda Mallory	Central Virginia Community College
Nicholas Marudas	Auburn University at Montgomery
David Mautz	North Carolina A&T State University
Al McKinnie	Northeast State Technical Community College
Brian Nash	St. Petersburg College
Elizabeth Ott	Casper College
Debra Schmidt	Cerritos College
Jerry Scott	Ivy Tech State College
Lloyd Seaton	University of Nebraska at Kearney
G. Phillip Smilanick	Truckee Meadows Community College
Sondra Smith	University of West Georgia
Kimberly Smith	County College of Morris
Lynn Suberly	Valdosta State University
David Swarts	Clinton Community College
Carl Swoboda	Southwest Tennessee Community College
LaVerne Thomas-Vertrees	St. Louis Community College at Meramec
Leonard Weld	Valdosta College
Kathleen Wilcox	Kennesaw State University
Andrew Williams	Edmonds Community College
Karen Wisniewski	County College of Morris
Audrey Yancey	St. Petersburg College

Special thanks to the talented people who prepared the supplements. These take a great deal of time and effort to write and we appreciate their efforts. Sue Cullers of Tarleton State University wrote the Test Bank questions. Steve Muller of Valencia Community College prepared the Self-Review Problem Audio-narrated Slides. Tom Edmonds of the University of Alabama prepared the Instructor's Manual. Kimberly Temme of Maryville University wrote the Online Quizzes. Kathleen Wilcox prepared the Electronic Slide presentations. Linda Schain of Hofstra University developed Topic Tackler Plus. Peggy Hussey of Northern Kentucky University prepared the Excel templates. Carol Yacht prepared the Peachtree templates and General Ledger Accounting Software. We also thank our accuracy checkers. They include Barbara Schnathorst of The Write Solution, Inc. Beth Woods, Lynn Suberly of Valdosta State University, Steve Muller, and Kimberly Smith of County College of Morris. A special thanks to Linda Bell of William Jewell College for her contribution to the Financial Statement Analysis material that appears in the Instructor's Manual and text website.

We are deeply indebted to our sponsoring editor, Steve Schuetz. His direction and guidance have added clarity and quality to the text. We especially appreciate the efforts of our developmental editor, Gail Korosa. Gail has coordinated the exchange of ideas among our class testers, reviewers, copy editor, and error checkers; she has done far more than simply pass along ideas. She has contributed numerous original suggestions that have enhanced the quality of the text. Our editors have certainly facilitated our efforts to prepare a book that will facilitate a meaningful understanding of accounting. Even so, their contributions are to no avail unless the text reaches its intended audience. We are most grateful to Melissa Larmon and Jackie Powers and the sales staff for providing the informative advertising that has so accurately communicated the unique features of the concepts approach to accounting educators. Many others at McGraw-Hill/Irwin at a moment's notice redirected their attention to focus their efforts on the development of this text. We extend our sincere appreciation to Pat Frederickson, Elizabeth Mavetz, Debra Sylvester, Mary Kazak, Jeremy Cheshareck, Carol Loreth, and Matt Perry. We deeply appreciate the long hours that you committed to the formation of a high-quality text.

Thomas P. Edmonds
Cindy D. Edmonds
Frances M. McNair
Philip R. Olds
Bor-Yi Tsay
Nancy W. Schneider

CHAPTER 1

Elements of Financial Statements

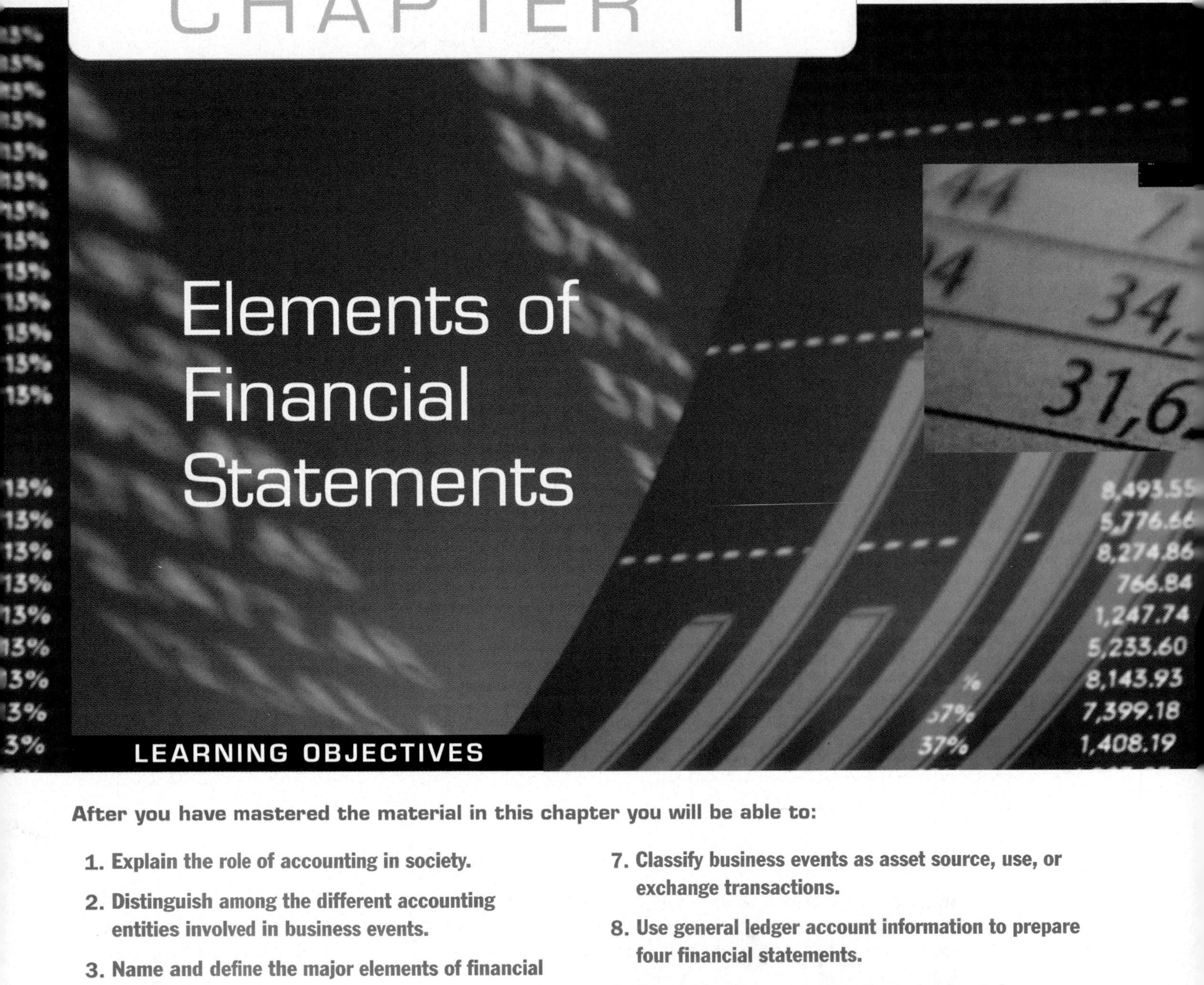

LEARNING OBJECTIVES

After you have mastered the material in this chapter you will be able to:

1. Explain the role of accounting in society.
2. Distinguish among the different accounting entities involved in business events.
3. Name and define the major elements of financial statements.
4. Describe the relationships expressed in the accounting equation.
5. Record business events in general ledger accounts organized under an accounting equation.
6. Explain how the historical cost and reliability concepts affect amounts reported in financial statements.
7. Classify business events as asset source, use, or exchange transactions.
8. Use general ledger account information to prepare four financial statements.
9. Record business events using a horizontal financial statements model.
10. Explain the importance of ethics to the accounting profession.
11. Identify three types of business organizations and some of the technical terms they use in their real world financial reports.

Chapter 1

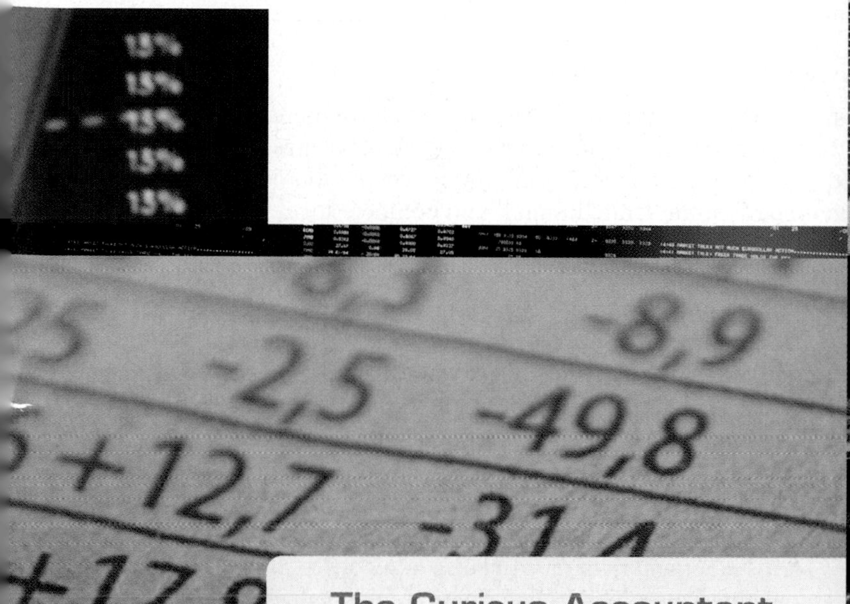

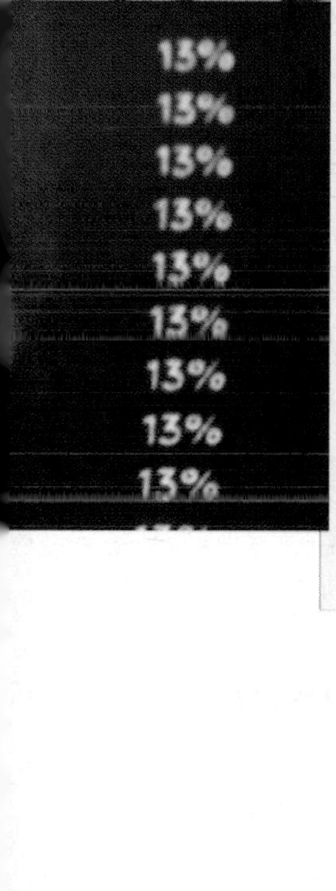

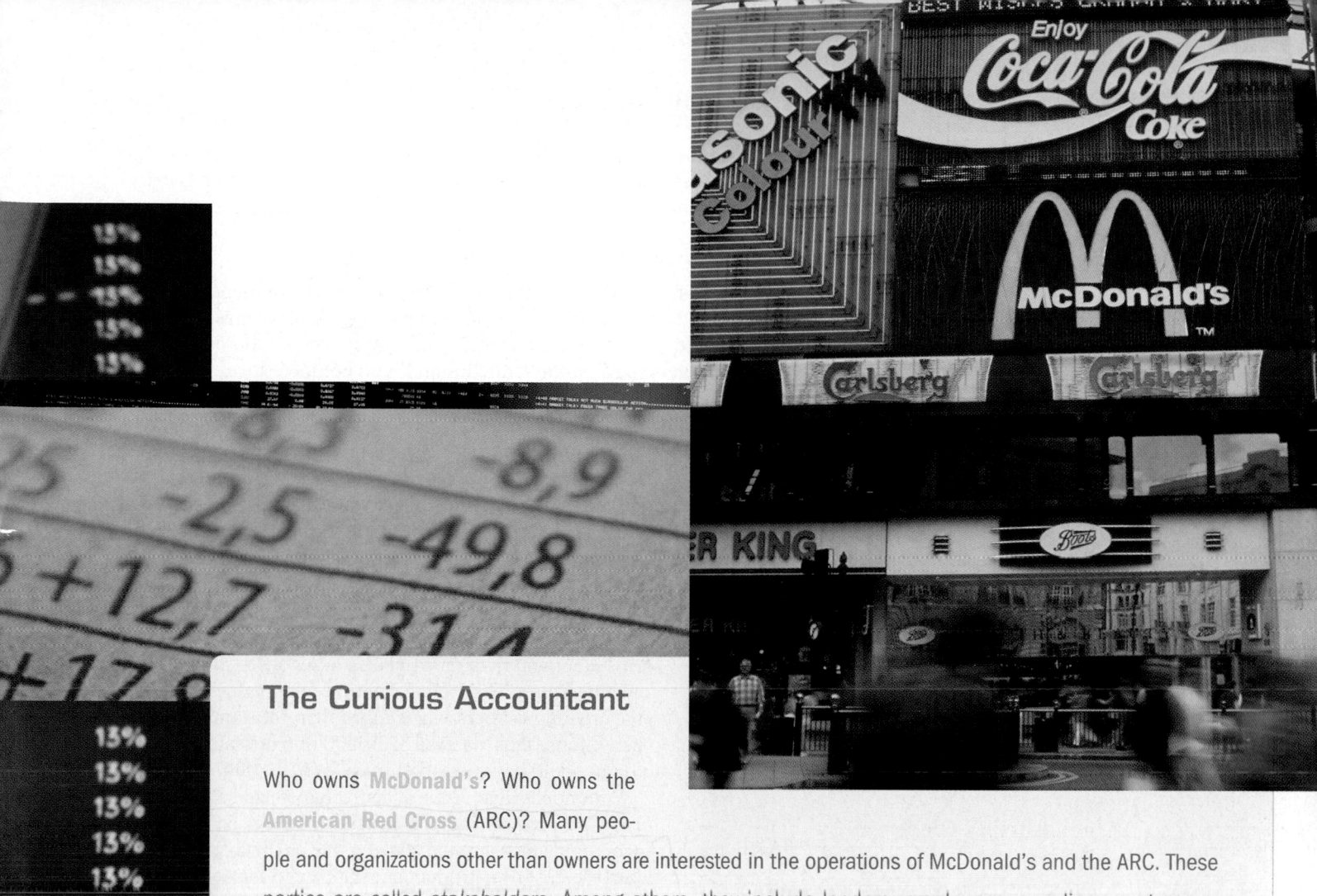

The Curious Accountant

Who owns McDonald's? Who owns the American Red Cross (ARC)? Many people and organizations other than owners are interested in the operations of McDonald's and the ARC. These parties are called *stakeholders.* Among others, they include lenders, employees, suppliers, customers, benefactors, research institutions, local governments, flood victims, lawyers, bankers, financial analysts, and government agencies such as the Internal Revenue Service and the Securities and Exchange Commission. Organizations communicate information to stakeholders through *financial reports.*

How do you think the financial reports of McDonald's differ from those of the ARC? (Answer on page 9.)

CHAPTER OPENING

Why should you study accounting? You should study accounting because it can help you succeed in business. Businesses use accounting to keep score. Imagine trying to play football without knowing how many points a touchdown is worth. Like sports, business is competitive. If you do not know how to keep score, you are not likely to succeed.

Accounting *is an information system that reports on the economic activities and financial condition of a business or other organization. Do not underestimate the importance of accounting information. If you had information that enabled you to predict business success, you could become a very wealthy Wall Street investor. Communicating economic information is so important that accounting is frequently called the* language of business.

Role of Accounting in Society

LO 1

Explain the role of accounting in society.

How should society allocate its resources? Should we spend more to harvest food or cure disease? Should we build computers or cars? Should we invest money in IBM or General Motors? Accounting provides information that helps answer such questions.

Using Free Markets to Set Resource Priorities

Suppose you want to start a business. You may have heard "you have to have money to make money." In fact, you will need more than just money to start and operate a business. You will likely need such resources as equipment, land, materials, and employees. If you do not have these resources, how can you get them? In the United States, you compete for resources in open markets.

A **market** is a group of people or entities organized to exchange items of value. The market for business resources involves three distinct participants: consumers, conversion agents, and resource owners. *Consumers* use resources. Resources are frequently not in a form consumers want. For example, nature provides trees but consumers want furniture. *Conversion agents* (businesses) transform resources such as trees into desirable products such as furniture. *Resource owners* control the distribution of resources to conversion agents. Thus resource owners provide resources (inputs) to conversion agents who provide goods and services (outputs) to consumers.

For example, a home builder (conversion agent) transforms labor and materials (inputs) into houses (output) that consumers use. The transformation adds value to the inputs, creating outputs worth more than the sum of the inputs. A house that required $220,000 of materials and labor to build could have a market value of $250,000.

Common terms for the added value created in the transformation process include **profit, income, or earnings.** Accountants measure the added value as the difference between the cost of a product or service and the selling price of that product or service. The profit on the house described above is $30,000, the difference between its $220,000 cost and $250,000 market value.

Conversion agents who successfully and efficiently (at low cost) satisfy consumer preferences are rewarded with high earnings. These earnings are shared with resource owners, so conversion agents who exhibit high earnings potential are more likely to compete successfully for resources.

Return to the original question. How can you get the resources you need to start a business? You must go to open markets and convince resource owners that you can produce profits. Exhibit 1.1 illustrates the market trilogy involved in resource allocation.

The specific resources businesses commonly use to satisfy consumer demand are financial resources, physical resources, and labor resources.

Financial Resources

Businesses (conversion agents) need **financial resources** (money) to get started and to operate. *Investors* and *creditors* provide financial resources.

- **Investors** provide financial resources in exchange for ownership interests in businesses. Owners expect businesses to return to them a share of the business income earned.
- **Creditors** lend financial resources to businesses. Instead of a share of business income, creditors expect businesses to repay borrowed resources at a future date.

The resources controlled by a business are called **assets.** If a business ceases to operate, its remaining assets are sold and the sale proceeds are returned to the investors and creditors through a process called business **liquidation.** Creditors have a priority claim on assets in business liquidations. After creditor claims are satisfied, any remaining assets are distributed to investors (owners).

EXHIBIT 1.1

Market Trilogy in Resource Allocation

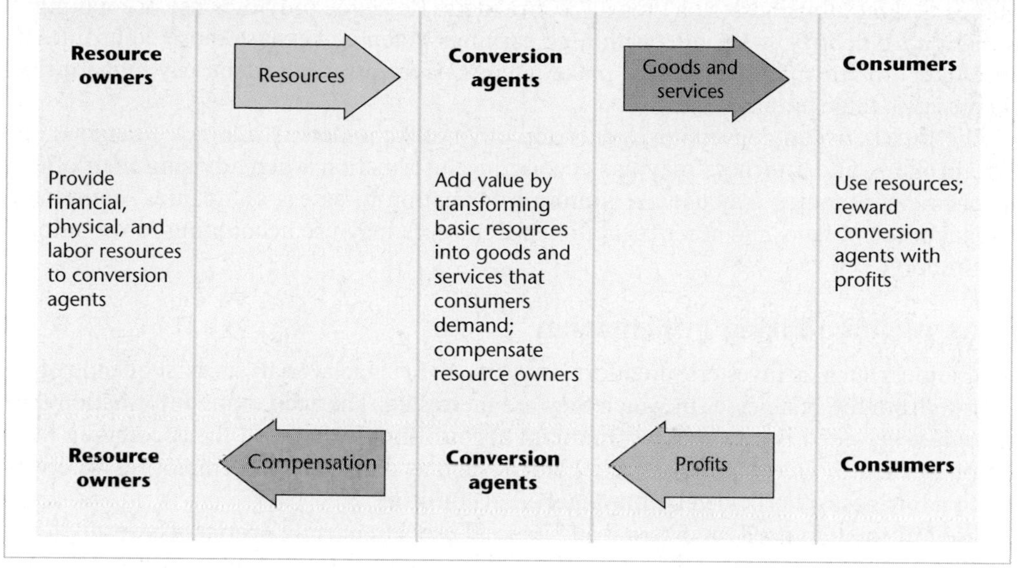

To illustrate, suppose a business acquired $100 cash from investors and $200 cash from creditors. Assume the business lost $75 and returned the remaining $225 ($300 − $75) to the resource providers. The creditors would receive $200; the owners would receive only $25. If the business lost $120, the creditors would receive only $180 ($300 − $120); the investors would receive nothing.

As this illustration suggests, both creditors and investors can lose resources when businesses fail. Creditors, however, are in a more secure position because of their priority claim on resources. In exchange for their more secure position, creditors normally do not share business profits. Instead, they receive a fixed amount of money called **interest.**

Investors and creditors prefer to provide financial resources to businesses with high earnings potential because such companies are better able to share profits and make interest payments. Profitable businesses are also less likely to experience bankruptcy and liquidation.

Physical Resources

In their most primitive form, **physical resources** are natural resources. Physical resources often move through numerous stages of transformation. For example, standing timber may be successively transformed into harvested logs, raw lumber, and finished furniture. Owners of physical resources seek to sell those resources to businesses with high earnings potential because profitable businesses are able to pay higher prices and make repeat purchases.

Labor Resources

Labor resources include both intellectual and physical labor. Like other resource providers, workers prefer businesses that have high income potential because these businesses are able to pay higher wages and offer continued employment.

Accounting Provides Information

How do providers of financial, physical, and labor resources identify conversion agents (businesses) with high profit potential? Investors, creditors, and workers rely heavily on accounting information to evaluate which businesses are worthy of receiving resources. In addition, other people and organizations have an interest in accounting information about businesses. The many **users** of accounting information are commonly called **stakeholders.** Stakeholders include resource providers, financial analysts, brokers, attorneys, government regulators, and news reporters.

The link between conversion agents (businesses) and those stakeholders who provide resources is direct: businesses pay resource providers. Resource providers use accounting information to identify companies with high earnings potential because those companies are more likely to return higher profits, make interest payments, repay debt, pay higher prices, and provide stable employment.

The link between conversion agents and other stakeholders is indirect. Financial analysts, brokers, and attorneys may use accounting information when advising their clients. Government agencies may use accounting information to assess companies' compliance with income tax laws and other regulations. Reporters may use accounting information in news reports.

Types of Accounting Information

Stakeholders such as investors, creditors, lawyers, and financial analysts exist outside of and separate from the businesses in which they are interested. The accounting information these *external users* need is provided by **financial accounting.** In contrast, the accounting information needed by *internal users,* stakeholders such as managers and employees who work within a business, is provided by **managerial accounting.**

The information needs of external and internal users frequently overlap. For example, external and internal users are both interested in the amount of income a business earns. Managerial accounting information, however, is usually more detailed than financial accounting reports. Investors are concerned about the overall profitability of Wendy's versus Burger King; a Wendy's regional manager is interested in the profits of individual Wendy's restaurants. In fact, a regional manager is also interested in nonfinancial measures, such as the number of employees needed to operate a restaurant, the times at which customer demand is high versus low, and measures of cleanliness and customer satisfaction.

Nonbusiness Resource Usage

The U.S. economy is not *purely* market based. Factors other than profitability often influence resource allocation priorities. For example, governments allocate resources to national defense, to redistribute wealth, or to protect the environment. Foundations, religious groups, the Peace Corps, and various benevolent organizations prioritize resource usage based on humanitarian concerns.

Like profit-oriented businesses, civic or humanitarian organizations add value through resource transformation. For example, a soup kitchen adds value to uncooked meats and vegetables by converting them into prepared meals. The individuals who consume the meals, however, are unable to pay for the kitchen's operating costs, much less for the added value. The soup kitchen's motivation is to meet humanitarian needs, not to earn profits. Organizations that are not motivated by profit are called **not-for-profit entities** (also called *nonprofit* or *nonbusiness organizations*).

Stakeholders interested in nonprofit organizations also need accounting information. Accounting systems measure the cost of the goods and services not-for-profit organizations provide, the efficiency and effectiveness of the organizations' operations, and the ability of the organizations to continue to provide goods and services. This information serves a host of stakeholders, including taxpayers, contributors, lenders, suppliers, employees, managers, financial analysts, attorneys, and beneficiaries.

The focus of accounting, therefore, is to provide information useful to making decisions for a variety of business and nonbusiness user groups. The different types of accounting information and the stakeholders that commonly use the information are summarized in Exhibit 1.2.

Measurement Rules

Suppose a store sells a compact disk player in December to a customer who agrees to pay for it in January. Should the business *recognize* (report) the sale as a December transaction or as

EXHIBIT 1.2

Accounting as Information Provider

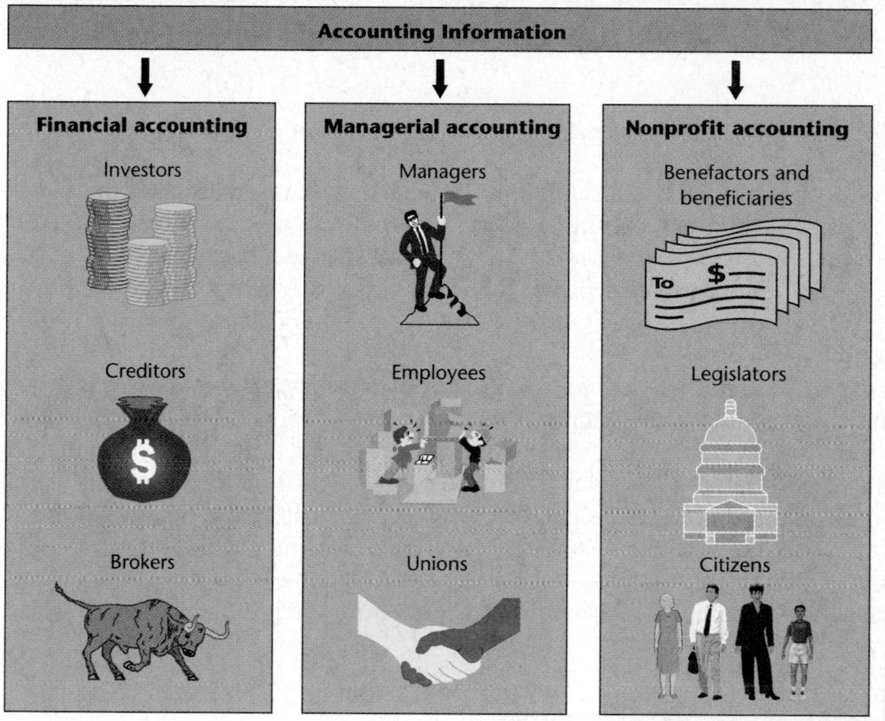

a January transaction? It really does not matter as long as the storeowner discloses the rule the decision is based on and applies it consistently to other transactions. Because businesses may use different reporting rules, however, clear communication also requires full and fair disclosure of the accounting rules chosen.

Communicating business results would be simpler if each type of business activity were reported using only one measurement method. World economies and financial reporting practices, however, have not evolved uniformly. Even in highly sophisticated countries such as the United States, companies exhibit significant diversity in reporting methods. Providers of accounting reports assume that users are educated about accounting practices.

The **Financial Accounting Standards Board (FASB)**[1] is a privately funded organization with the primary authority for establishing accounting standards in the United States. The measurement rules established by the FASB are called **generally accepted accounting principles (GAAP).** Financial reports issued to the public must follow GAAP. This textbook introduces these principles so you will be able to understand business activity reported by companies in the USA.

[1] The FASB consists of seven full-time members appointed by the supporting organization, the Financial Accounting Foundation (FAF). The FAF membership is intended to represent the broad spectrum of individuals and institutions that have an interest in accounting and financial reporting. FAF members include representatives of the accounting profession, industry, financial institutions, the government, and the investing public.

It is worth mentioning that, for convenience and efficiency, many internal business reports use accounting data that conform to GAAP. Companies are not required, however, to follow GAAP when preparing *management accounting* reports. Although there is considerable overlap between financial and managerial accounting, managers are free to construct internal reports in whatever fashion best suits the effective operation of their companies.

Reporting Entities

LO 2

Distinguish among the different accounting entities involved in business events.

Financial accounting reports disclose the financial activities of particular individuals or organizations described as **reporting entities.** Each entity is a separate reporting unit. For example, a business, the person who owns the business, and a bank that loans money to the business are viewed as three separate reporting entities. Accountants would prepare three separate sets of financial reports to describe the economic activities of each of the three entities.

This text describes accounting from the perspective of a business entity. This point of view may require that you mentally adjust the way you look at business transactions. You likely think from a customer perspective. For example, as a customer you consider a sales discount a great bargain. The view is different, however, from the perspective of the business granting the discount. A sales discount means an item did not sell at the expected price. To move the item, the business had to accept less money than it originally planned to accept. From this perspective, a sales discount is not a good thing. To understand accounting, train yourself to interpret transactions from the perspective of a business rather than a consumer.

CHECK YOURSELF 1.1

In a recent business transaction, land was exchanged for cash. Did the amount of cash increase or decrease?

Answer

The answer depends on the reporting entity to which the question pertains. One entity sold land. The other entity bought land. For the entity that sold land, cash increased. For the entity that bought land, cash decreased.

Elements of Financial Statements

LO 3

Name and define the major elements of financial statements.

Topic Tackler PLUS

1-1

Business entities communicate economic information about their activities to the public through four **financial statements:**[2] (1) an income statement, (2) a statement of changes in equity, (3) a balance sheet, and (4) a statement of cash flows.

The information reported in financial statements is organized into categories known as **elements.** Eight financial statement elements are discussed in this chapter: assets, liabili-

[2] In practice these statements have alternate names. For example, the income statement may be called *results of operations* or *statement of earnings.* The balance sheet is sometimes called the *statement of financial position.* The statement of changes in equity might be called *statement of capital* or *statement of stockholders' equity.* Since the Financial Accounting Standards Board (FASB) called for the title *statement of cash flows,* companies do not use alternate names for that statement.

Answers to The Curious Accountant

Anyone who owns stock in **McDonald's** owns a part of the company. McDonald's has many owners. In contrast, nobody actually owns the **American Red Cross** (ARC). The ARC has a board of directors that is responsible for overseeing its operations, but the board is not its owner.

Ultimately, the purpose of a business entity is to increase the wealth of its owners. To this end, it "spends money to make money." The expense that McDonald's incurs for advertising is a cost incurred in the hope that it will generate revenues when it sells hamburgers. The financial statements of a business show, among other things, whether and how the company made a profit during the current year.

The ARC is a not-for-profit entity. It operates to provide services to society at large, not to make a profit. It cannot increase the wealth of its owners, because it has no owners. When the ARC spends money to assist flood victims, it does not spend this money in the expectation that it will generate revenues. The revenues of the ARC come from contributors who wish to support efforts related to assisting disaster victims. Because the ARC does not spend money to make money, it has no reason to prepare an *income statement* like that of McDonald's.

Not-for-profit entities do prepare financial statements that are similar in appearance to those of commercial enterprises. The financial statements of not-for-profit entities are called the *statement of financial position*, the *statement of activities*, and the *cash flow statement*.

tics, equity, contributed capital, revenue, expenses, distributions, and net income. The other two elements, gains and losses, are discussed in a later chapter. In practice, the business world uses various titles to identify several of the financial statement elements. For example, business people use net income, net earnings, and net profit interchangeably to describe the same element. Contributed capital may be called *common stock* and equity may be called *stockholders' equity, owner's capital,* and *partners' equity.* Furthermore, the transfer of assets from a business to its owners may be called *distributions, withdrawals,* or *dividends.* Think of accounting as a language. Different terms can describe the same business event.

The elements represent broad classifications. Subclassifications of various elements are frequently called **accounts.** Accounts are reported in the financial statements as components of the elements. For example, the element assets includes accounts that represent specific items such as cash, equipment, buildings, and land.

How many accounts does a business use? The number depends on the nature of the business and the needs of management and financial statement users. Some companies provide very detailed information; others present highly summarized data. As a result, the number of accounts used in an accounting system varies from company to company.

Accounting Equation

LO 4

Describe the relationships expressed in the accounting equation.

The resources that a business uses to produce earnings are called *assets.* Examples of assets include land, buildings, equipment, materials, and supplies. Assets result from historical events. For example, if a business owns a truck that it purchased in a past transaction, the truck is an asset of the business. A truck that a business *plans* to purchase in the future, however, is not an asset of that business, no matter how certain the future purchase might be.

The assets of a business belong to the resource providers (creditors and investors). These resource providers have **claims** on the assets. The relationship between the assets and the providers' claims is described by the **accounting equation:**

$$\text{Assets} = \text{Claims}$$

Creditor claims are called **liabilities** and investor claims are called **equity.** Substituting these terms into the accounting equation produces the following expanded form:

$$\text{Assets} = \overbrace{\text{Liabilities} + \text{Equity}}^{\text{Claims}}$$

Liabilities can also be viewed as future *obligations of the enterprise.* To settle the obligations, the business will probably either relinquish some of its assets (e.g., pay off its debts with cash), provide services to its creditors (e.g., work off its debts), or accept other obligations (e.g., trade short-term debt for long-term debt).

As indicated by the accounting equation, the amount of total assets is equal to the total of the liabilities plus the equity. To illustrate, assume that Hagan Company has assets of \$500, liabilities of \$200, and equity of \$300. These amounts appear in the accounting equation as follows:

$$\begin{aligned} \text{Assets} &= \overbrace{\text{Liabilities} + \text{Equity}}^{\text{Claims}} \\ \$500 &= \quad \$200 \quad + \; \$300 \end{aligned}$$

The claims side of the accounting equation (liabilities plus equity) may also be viewed as listing the sources of the assets. For example, when a bank loans assets (money) to a business, it establishes a claim to have those assets returned at some future date. Liabilities can therefore be viewed as sources of assets.

Equity can also be viewed as a source of assets. In fact, equity represents two distinct sources of assets. First, businesses typically acquire assets from their owners (investors). Many businesses issue **common stock**[3] certificates as receipts to acknowledge assets received from owners. The owners of such businesses are often called **stockholders,** and the ownership interest in the business is called **stockholders' equity.**

Second, businesses usually obtain assets through their earnings activities (the business acquires assets by working for them). Assets a business has earned can either be distributed to the owners or kept in the business. The portion of assets that has been provided by earnings activities and not returned as dividends is called **retained earnings.** Since stockholders own the business, they are entitled to assets acquired through its earnings activities. Retained earnings is therefore a component of stockholders' equity. Further expansion of the accounting equation can show the three sources of assets (liabilities, common stock, and retained earnings):

$$\text{Assets} = \text{Liabilities} + \overbrace{\text{Common stock} + \text{Retained earnings}}^{\text{Stockholders' equity}}$$

[3] This presentation assumes the business is organized as a corporation. Other forms of business organization include proprietorships and partnerships. The treatment of equity for these types of businesses is slightly different from that of corporations. A detailed discussion of the differences is included in a later chapter of the text.

CHECK YOURSELF 1.2

Gupta Company has $250,000 of assets, $60,000 of liabilities, and $90,000 of common stock. What percentage of the assets was provided by retained earnings?

Answer

First, using algebra, determine the dollar amount of retained earnings:
Assets = Liabilities + Common stock + Retained earnings
Retained earnings = Assets − Liabilities − Common stock
Retained earnings = $250,000 − $60,000 − $90,000
Retained earnings = $100,000

Second, determine the percentage:
Percentage of assets provided by retained earnings = Retained earnings/Total assets
Percentage of assets provided by retained earnings = $100,000/$250,000 = 40%

Recording Business Events under the Accounting Equation

LO 5 Record business events in general ledger accounts organized under an accounting equation.

Topic Tackler PLUS 1-2

An **accounting event** is an economic occurrence that changes an enterprise's assets, liabilities, or stockholders' equity. A **transaction** is a particular kind of event that involves transferring something of value between two entities. Examples of transactions include acquiring assets from owners, borrowing money from creditors, and purchasing or selling goods and services. The following section of the text explains how several different types of accounting events affect a company's accounting equation.

Asset Source Transactions

As previously mentioned, businesses obtain assets (resources) from three sources. They acquire assets from owners (stockholders); they borrow assets from creditors; and they earn assets through profitable operations. Asset source transactions increase total assets and total claims. A more detailed discussion of the effects of asset source transactions is provided below:

Event 1 **Rustic Camp Sites (RCS) was formed on January 1, 2004, when it acquired $120,000 cash from issuing common stock.**

When RCS issued stock, it received cash and gave each investor (owner) a stock certificate as a receipt. Since this transaction provided $120,000 of assets (cash) to the business, it is an **asset source transaction.** It increases the business's assets (cash) and its stockholders' equity (common stock).

	Assets			=	Liab.	+	Stockholders' Equity		
	Cash	+	Land	=	N. Pay.	+	Com. Stk.	+	Ret. Earn.
Acquired cash through stock issue	120,000	+	NA	=	NA	+	120,000	+	NA

Notice the elements have been divided into accounts. For example, the element *assets* is divided into a Cash account and a Land account. Do not be concerned if some of these account titles are unfamiliar. They will be explained as new transactions are presented. Recall that the number of accounts a company uses depends on the nature of its business and the level of detail management needs to operate the business. For example, **Sears** would have an account called Cost of Goods Sold although **GEICO Insurance** would not. Why? Because Sears sells goods (merchandise) but GEICO does not.

Also, notice that a stock issue transaction affects the accounting equation in two places, both under an asset (cash) and also under the source of that asset (common stock). All transactions affect the accounting equation in at least two places. It is from this practice that the **double-entry bookkeeping** system derives its name.

Event 2 **RCS acquired an additional $400,000 of cash by borrowing from a creditor.**

This transaction is also an asset source transaction. It increases assets (cash) and liability claims (notes payable). The account title Notes Payable is used because the borrower (RCS) is required to issue a promissory note to the creditor (a bank). A promissory note describes, among other things, the amount of interest RCS will pay and for how long it will borrow the money.[4] The effect of the borrowing transaction on the accounting equation is indicated below.

	Assets			=	Liab.	+	Stockholders' Equity		
	Cash	+	Land	=	N. Pay.	+	Com. Stk.	+	Ret. Earn.
Beginning balances	120,000	+	NA	=	NA	+	120,000	+	NA
Acquired cash by issuing note	400,000	+	NA	=	400,000	+	NA	+	NA
Ending balances	520,000	+	NA	=	400,000	+	120,000	+	NA

The beginning balances above came from the ending balances produced by the prior transaction. This practice is followed throughout the illustration.

Asset Exchange Transactions

Businesses frequently trade one asset for another asset. In such cases, the amount of one asset decreases and the amount of the other asset increases. Total assets are unaffected by asset exchange transactions. Event 3 is an asset exchange transaction.

Event 3 **RCS paid $500,000 cash to purchase land.**

This asset exchange transaction reduces the asset account Cash and increases the asset account Land. The amount of total assets is not affected. An asset exchange transaction simply reflects changes in the composition of assets. In this case, the company traded cash for land. The amount of cash decreased by $500,000 and the amount of land increased by the same amount.

	Assets			=	Liab.	+	Stockholders' Equity		
	Cash	+	Land	=	N. Pay.	+	Com. Stk.	+	Ret. Earn.
Beginning balances	520,000	+	NA	=	400,000	+	120,000	+	NA
Paid cash to buy land	(500,000)	+	500,000	=	NA	+	NA	+	NA
Ending balances	20,000	+	500,000	=	400,000	+	120,000	+	NA

Another Asset Source Transaction

Event 4 **RCS obtained $85,000 cash by leasing camp sites to customers.**

Revenue represents an economic benefit a company obtains by providing customers with goods and services. In this example the economic benefit is an increase in the asset

[4]For simplicity, the effects of interest are ignored in this chapter. We discuss accounting for interest in future chapters.

cash. Revenue transactions can therefore be viewed as *asset source transactions*. The asset increase is balanced by an increase in the retained earnings section of stockholders' equity because producing revenue increases the amount of earnings retained in the business.

	Assets			=	Liab.	+	Stockholders' Equity		
	Cash	+	Land	=	N. Pay.	+	Com. Stk.	+	Ret. Earn.
Beginning balances	20,000	+	500,000	=	400,000	+	120,000	+	NA
Acquired cash by earning revenue	85,000	+	NA	=	NA	+	NA	+	85,000
Ending balances	105,000	+	500,000	=	400,000	+	120,000	+	85,000

Asset Use Transactions

Businesses use assets for a variety of purposes. For example, assets may be used to pay off liabilities or they may be transferred to owners. Assets may also be used in the process of generating earnings. All asset use transactions decrease the total amount of assets and the total amount of claims on assets (liabilities or stockholders' equity).

Event 5 **RCS paid $50,000 cash for operating expenses such as salaries, rent, and interest. (RCS could establish a separate account for each type of expense. However, the management team does not currently desire this level of detail. Remember, the number of accounts a business uses depends on the level of information managers need to make decisions.)**

In the normal course of generating revenue, a business consumes various assets and services. The assets and services consumed to generate revenue are called **expenses.** Revenue results from providing goods and services to customers. In exchange, the business acquires assets from its customers. Since the owners bear the ultimate risk and reap the rewards of operating the business, revenues increase stockholders' equity (retained earnings), and expenses decrease retained earnings. In this case, the asset account, Cash, decreased. This decrease is balanced by a decrease in the retained earnings section of stockholders' equity because expenses decrease the amount of earnings retained in the business.

	Assets			=	Liab.	+	Stockholders' Equity		
	Cash	+	Land	=	N. Pay.	+	Com. Stk.	+	Ret. Earn.
Beginning balances	105,000	+	500,000	=	400,000	+	120,000	+	85,000
Used cash to pay expenses	(50,000)	+	NA	=	NA	+	NA	+	(50,000)
Ending balances	55,000	+	500,000	=	400,000	+	120,000	+	35,000

Event 6 **RCS paid $4,000 in cash dividends to its owners.**

To this point the enterprise's total assets and equity have increased by $35,000 ($85,000 of revenue − $50,000 of expense) as a result of its earnings activities. RCS can keep the additional assets in the business or transfer them to the owners. If a business transfers some or all of its earned assets to owners, the transfer is frequently called a **dividend.** Since assets distributed to stockholders are not used for the purpose of generating revenue, *dividends are wealth transfers, not expenses.* Furthermore, dividends are a transfer of *earnings,* not a return of assets acquired in exchange for common stock.

	Assets			=	Liab.	+	Stockholders' Equity		
	Cash	+	Land	=	N. Pay.	+	Com. Stk.	+	Ret. Earn.
Beginning balances	55,000	+	500,000	=	400,000	+	120,000	+	35,000
Used cash to pay dividends	(4,000)	+	NA	=	NA	+	NA	+	(4,000)
Ending balances	51,000	+	500,000	=	400,000	+	120,000	+	31,000

Historical Cost and Reliability Concepts

LO 6

Explain how the historical cost and reliability concepts affect amounts reported in financial statements.

Event 7 **The land that RCS paid $500,000 to purchase had an appraised market value of $525,000 on December 31, 2004.**

Although the appraised value of the land is higher than the original cost, RCS will not increase the amount recorded in its accounting records above the land's $500,000 historical cost. In general, accountants do not recognize changes in market value. The **historical cost concept** requires that most assets be reported at the amount paid for them (their historical cost) regardless of increases in market value.

Surely investors would rather know what an asset is worth instead of how much it originally cost. So why do accountants maintain records and report financial information based on historical cost? Accountants rely heavily on the **reliability concept.** Information is reliable if it can be independently verified. For example, two people looking at the legal documents associated with RCS's land purchase will both conclude that RCS paid $500,000 for the land. That historical cost is a verifiable fact. The appraised value, in contrast, is an opinion. Even two persons who are experienced appraisers are not likely to come up with the same amount for the land's market value. Accountants do not report market values in financial statements because such values are not reliable.

Recap: Types of Transactions

LO 7

Classify business events as asset source, use, or exchange transactions.

The transactions described above have each been classified into one of three categories: (1) asset source transactions; (2) asset exchange transactions; and (3) asset use transactions. A fourth category, claims exchange transactions, is introduced in a later chapter. In summary

- ***Asset source transactions*** increase the total amount of assets and increase the total amount of claims. In its first year of operation, RCS acquired assets from three sources: first, from owners (Event 1); next, by borrowing (Event 2); and finally, through earnings activities (Event 4).
- ***Asset exchange transactions*** decrease one asset and increase another asset. The total amount of assets is unchanged by asset exchange transactions. RCS experienced one asset exchange transaction; it used cash to purchase land (Event 3).
- ***Asset use transactions*** decrease the total amount of assets and the total amount of claims. RCS used assets to pay expenses (Event 5) and to pay dividends (Event 6).

As you proceed through this text, practice classifying transactions into one of the four categories. Businesses engage in thousands of transactions every day. It is far more effective to learn how to classify the transactions into meaningful categories than to attempt to memorize the effects of thousands of transactions.

Summary of Transactions

The complete collection of a company's accounts is called the **general ledger.** The general ledger account information for RCS's 2004 accounting period is shown in Exhibit 1.3. The

EXHIBIT 1.3

General Ledger Accounts Organized Under the Accounting Equation

	Assets			=	Liabilities	+	Stockholders' Equity			
Event No.	Cash	+	Land	=	Notes Payable	+	Common Stock	+	Retained Earnings	Other Account Titles
Beg. bal.	0		0		0		0		0	
1.	120,000						120,000			
2.	400,000				400,000					
3.	(500,000)		500,000							
4.	85,000								85,000	Revenue
5.	(50,000)								(50,000)	Expense
6.	(4,000)								(4,000)	Dividend
7.	NA		NA		NA		NA		NA	
	51,000	+	500,000	=	400,000	+	120,000	+	31,000	

revenue, expense, and dividend account data appear in the retained earnings column. These account titles are shown immediately to the right of the dollar amounts listed in the retained earnings column. To help you review RCS's general ledger, the business events that the company experienced during 2004 are summarized below.

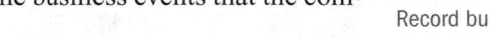

LO 5 Record business events in general ledger accounts organized under an accounting equation.

1. RCS issued common stock, acquiring $120,000 cash from its owners.
2. RCS borrowed $400,000 cash.
3. RCS paid $500,000 cash to purchase land.
4. RCS received $85,000 cash from earning revenue.
5. RCS paid $50,000 cash for expenses.
6. RCS paid dividends of $4,000 cash to the owners.
7. The land that RCS paid $500,000 to purchase had an appraised market value of $525,000 on December 31, 2004.

As indicated earlier, accounting information is normally presented to external users in four general-purpose financial statements. The information in the ledger accounts is used to prepare these financial statements. The data in the above ledger accounts are color coded to help you understand the source of information in the financial statements. The numbers in *green* are used in the *statement of cash flows.* The numbers in *red* are used to prepare the *balance sheet.* Finally, the numbers in *blue* are used to prepare the *income statement.* The numbers reported in the statement of changes in stockholders' equity have not been color coded because they appear in more than one statement. The next section explains how the information in the accounts is presented in financial statements.

Preparing Financial Statements

LO 8 Use general ledger account information to prepare four financial statements.

The financial statements for RCS are shown in Exhibit 1.4. The information used to prepare these statements was drawn from the ledger accounts. Information in one statement may relate to information in another statement. For example, the amount of net income reported on the income statement also appears on the statement of changes in stockholders' equity. Accountants use the term **articulation** to describe the interrelationships among the various elements of the financial statements. The key articulated relationships in RCS's financial statements are highlighted with arrows (Exhibit 1.4). A description of each statement follows.

EXHIBIT 1.4 Financial Statements

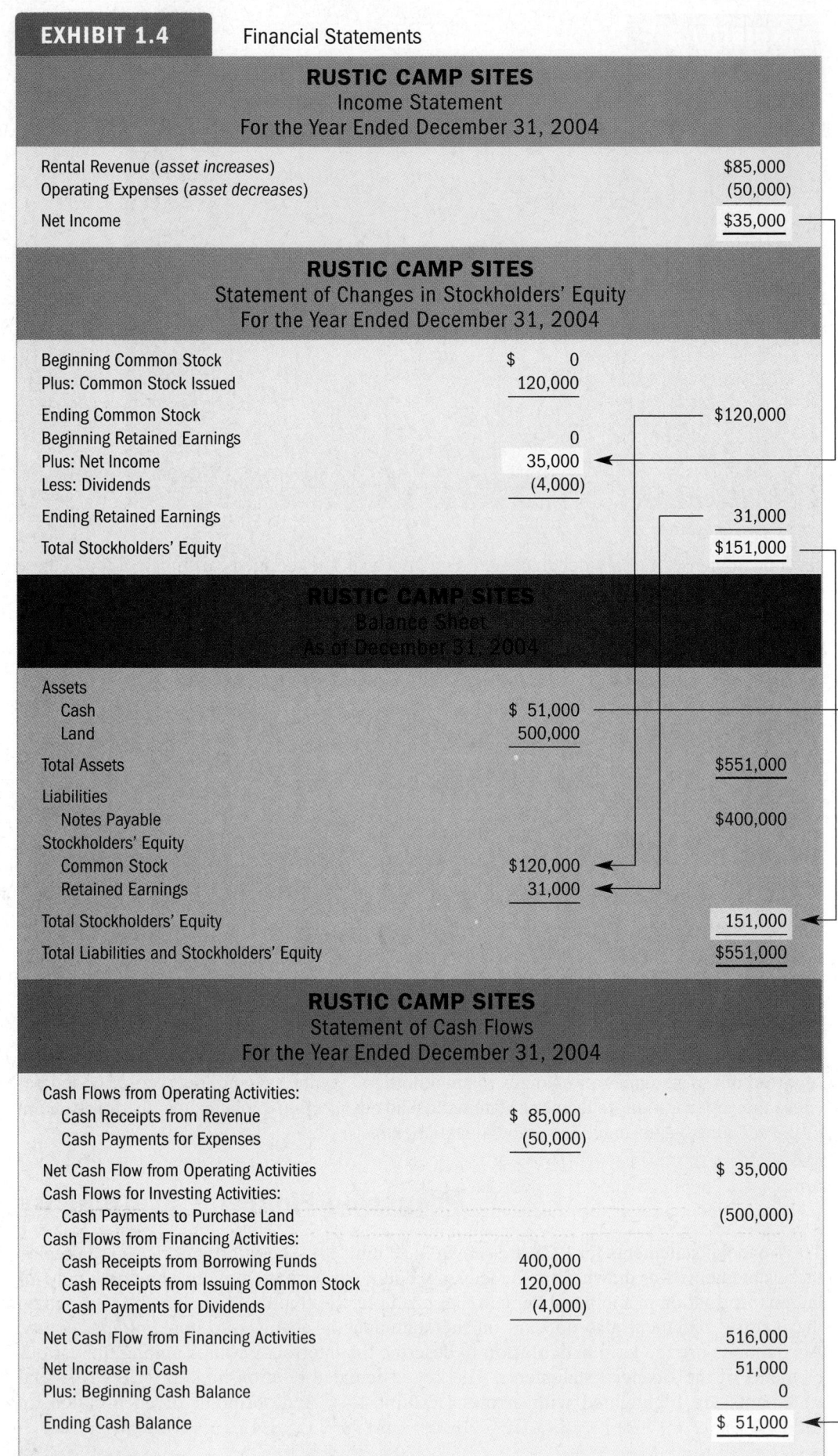

RUSTIC CAMP SITES
Income Statement
For the Year Ended December 31, 2004

Rental Revenue (*asset increases*)	$85,000
Operating Expenses (*asset decreases*)	(50,000)
Net Income	$35,000

RUSTIC CAMP SITES
Statement of Changes in Stockholders' Equity
For the Year Ended December 31, 2004

Beginning Common Stock	$ 0	
Plus: Common Stock Issued	120,000	
Ending Common Stock		$120,000
Beginning Retained Earnings	0	
Plus: Net Income	35,000	
Less: Dividends	(4,000)	
Ending Retained Earnings		31,000
Total Stockholders' Equity		$151,000

RUSTIC CAMP SITES
Balance Sheet
As of December 31, 2004

Assets		
Cash	$ 51,000	
Land	500,000	
Total Assets		$551,000
Liabilities		
Notes Payable		$400,000
Stockholders' Equity		
Common Stock	$120,000	
Retained Earnings	31,000	
Total Stockholders' Equity		151,000
Total Liabilities and Stockholders' Equity		$551,000

RUSTIC CAMP SITES
Statement of Cash Flows
For the Year Ended December 31, 2004

Cash Flows from Operating Activities:		
Cash Receipts from Revenue	$ 85,000	
Cash Payments for Expenses	(50,000)	
Net Cash Flow from Operating Activities		$ 35,000
Cash Flows for Investing Activities:		
Cash Payments to Purchase Land		(500,000)
Cash Flows from Financing Activities:		
Cash Receipts from Borrowing Funds	400,000	
Cash Receipts from Issuing Common Stock	120,000	
Cash Payments for Dividends	(4,000)	
Net Cash Flow from Financing Activities		516,000
Net Increase in Cash		51,000
Plus: Beginning Cash Balance		0
Ending Cash Balance		$ 51,000

Income Statement and the Matching Concept

Businesses consume assets and services in order to generate revenues, thereby creating greater quantities of other assets. For example, RCS may pay cash (asset use) to an employee who maintains the camp sites. Maintaining the sites is necessary in order to collect cash (obtain assets) from customers. The **income statement** *matches* asset increases from operating a business with asset decreases from operating the business.[5] Asset increases resulting from providing goods and services to customers in the course of normal operations are called *revenues.* Asset decreases resulting from consuming assets and services for the purpose of generating revenues are called *expenses.* If revenues are greater than expenses, the difference is called **net income.** If expenses exceed revenues, the difference is a **net loss.**

The income statement in Exhibit 1.4 indicates that RCS has earned more assets than it has used. The statement shows that RCS has increased its assets by $35,000 (net income) as a result of operating its business. Observe the phrase *For the Year Ended December 31, 2004,* in the heading of the income statement. Income is measured for a span of time called the **accounting period.** While accounting periods of one year are normal for external financial reporting, income can be measured weekly, monthly, quarterly, semiannually, or over any other desired time period. Notice that the cash RCS paid to its stockholders (dividends) is not reported as expense. The decrease in assets for dividend payments is not incurred for the purpose of generating revenue. Instead, dividends are transfers of wealth to the owners of the business. Dividend payments are not reported on the income statement.

CHECK YOURSELF 1.3

Mahoney, Inc. was started when it issued common stock to its owners for $300,000. During its first year of operation Mahoney received $523,000 cash for services provided to customers. Mahoney paid employees $233,000 cash. Advertising costs paid in cash amounted to $102,000. Other cash operating expenses amounted to $124,000. Finally, Mahoney paid a $25,000 cash dividend to its stockholders. What amount of net income would Mahoney's report on its earnings statement?

Answer

The amount of net income is $64,000 ($523,000 Revenue − $233,000 Salary Expense − $102,000 Advertising Expense − $124,000 Other Operating Expenses). The cash received from issuing stock is not revenue because it was not acquired from earnings activities. In other words, Mahoney did not work (perform services) for this money; it was contributed by owners of the business. The dividends are not expenses because the decrease in cash was not incurred for the purpose of generating revenue. Instead, the dividends represent a transfer of wealth to the owners.

Statement of Changes in Stockholders' Equity

The **statement of changes in stockholders' equity** explains the effects of transactions on stockholders' equity during the accounting period. It starts with the beginning balance in the common stock account. In the case of RCS, the beginning balance in the common stock account is zero because the company did not exist before the 2004 accounting period. The amount of stock issued during the accounting period is added to the beginning balance to determine the ending balance in the common stock account.

In addition to reporting the changes in common stock, the statement describes the changes in retained earnings for the accounting period. RCS had no beginning balance in retained earnings. During the period, the company earned $35,000 and paid $4,000 in dividends to the stockholders, producing an ending retained earning balance of $31,000 ($0 + $35,000 − $4,000). Since equity consists of common stock and retained earnings, the ending total equity balance is $151,000 ($120,000 + $31,000). This statement is also dated with

[5] This description of the income statement is expanded in subsequent chapters as additional relationships among the elements of financial statements are introduced.

the phrase *For the Year Ended December 31, 2004,* because it describes what happened to stockholders' equity during 2004.

Balance Sheet

The **balance sheet** draws its name from the accounting equation. Total assets balances with (equals) claims (liabilities and stockholders' equity) on those assets. The balance sheet for RCS is shown in Exhibit 1.4. Note that total claims (liabilities plus stockholders' equity) are equal to total assets ($551,000 = $551,000).

Note the order of the assets in the balance sheet. Cash appears first, followed by land. Assets are displayed in the balance sheet based on their level of **liquidity.** This means that assets are listed in order of how rapidly they will be converted to cash. Finally, note that the balance sheet is dated with the phrase *As of December 31, 2004,* indicating that it describes the company's financial condition on the last day of the accounting period.

CHECK YOURSELF 1.4

To gain a clear understanding of the balance sheet, try to create one that describes your personal financial condition. First list your assets, then your liabilities. Determine the amount of your equity by subtracting your liabilities from your assets.

Answer

Answers for this exercise will vary depending on the particular assets and liabilities each student identifies. Common student assets include automobiles, computers, stereos, TVs, phones, CD players, clothes, and textbooks. Common student liabilities include car loans, mortgages, student loans, and credit card debt. The difference between the assets and the liabilities is the equity.

Statement of Cash Flows

The **statement of cash flows** explains how a company obtained and used *cash* during the accounting period. Receipts of cash are called *cash inflows,* and payments are *cash outflows.* The statement classifies cash receipts (inflows) and payments (outflows) into three categories: financing activities, investing activities, and operating activities.

Businesses normally start with an idea. Implementing the idea usually requires cash. For example, suppose you decide to start an apartment rental business. First, you would need cash to finance acquiring the apartments. Acquiring cash to start a business is a financing activity. **Financing activities** include obtaining cash (inflow) from owners or paying cash (outflow) to owners (dividends). Financing activities also include borrowing cash (inflow) from creditors and repaying the principal (outflow) to creditors. Because interest on borrowed money is an expense, however, cash paid to creditors for interest is reported in the operating activities section of the statement of cash flows.

After obtaining cash from financing activities, you would invest the money by building or buying apartments. **Investing activities** involve paying cash (outflow) to purchase productive assets or receiving cash (inflow) from selling productive assets. **Productive assets** are sometimes called long-term assets because businesses normally use them for more than one year. Cash outflows to purchase land or cash inflows from selling a building are examples of investing activities.

After investing in the productive assets (apartments), you would engage in operating activities. **Operating activities** involve receiving cash (inflow) from revenue and paying cash (outflow) for expenses. Note that cash spent to purchase short-term assets such as office supplies is reported in the operating activities section because the office supplies would likely be used (expensed) within a single accounting period.

The primary cash inflows and outflows related to the types of business activity introduced in this chapter are summarized in Exhibit 1.5. The exhibit will be expanded as additional types of events are introduced in subsequent chapters.

The statement of cash flows for Rustic Camp Sites in Exhibit 1.4 shows that the amount of cash increased by $51,000 during the year. The beginning balance in the Cash account was zero; adding the $51,000 increase to the beginning balance results in a $51,000 ending balance. Notice that the $51,000 ending cash balance on the statement of cash flows is the same as the amount of cash reported in the asset section on the December 31 year-end balance sheet. Also, note that the statement of cash flows is dated with the phrase *For the Year Ended December 31, 2004,* because it describes what happened to cash over the span of the year.

EXHIBIT 1.5

Classification Scheme for Statement of Cash Flows

Cash Flows from Operating Activities:
- Cash Receipts (Inflows) from Revenue (Including Interest)
- Cash Payments (Outflows) for Expenses (Including Interest)

Cash Flows from Investing Activities:
- Cash Receipts (Inflows) from the Sale of Long-Term Assets
- Cash Payments (Outflows) for the Purchase of Long-Term Assets

Cash Flows from Financing Activities:
- Cash Receipts (Inflows) from Borrowing Funds
- Cash Receipts (Inflows) from Issuing Common Stock
- Cash Payments (Outflows) to Repay Borrowed Funds
- Cash Payments (Outflows) for Dividends

CHECK YOURSELF 1.5

Classify each of the following cash flows as an operating activity, investing activity, or financing activity.

1. Acquired cash from owners.
2. Borrowed cash from creditors.
3. Paid cash to purchase land.
4. Earned cash revenue.
5. Paid cash for salary expenses.
6. Paid cash dividend.
7. Paid cash for interest.

Answer

(1) financing activity; (2) financing activity; (3) investing activity; (4) operating activity; (5) operating activity; (6) financing activity; (7) operating activity.

The Horizontal Financial Statements Model

LO 9

Record business events using a horizontal financial statements model.

Financial statements are the scorecard for business activity. If you want to succeed in business, you must know how your business decisions affect your company's financial statements. This text uses a **horizontal statements model** to help you understand how business events affect financial statements. This model shows a set of financial statements horizontally across a single page of paper. The balance sheet is displayed first, adjacent to the income statement, and then the statement of cash flows. Because the effects of equity transactions can be analyzed by referring to certain balance sheet columns, and because of limited space, the statement of changes in stockholders' equity is not shown in the horizontal statements model.

The model frequently uses abbreviations. For example, activity classifications in the statement of cash flows are identified using OA for operating activities, IA for investing activities, and FA for financing activities. NC designates the net change in cash. The statements model uses "NA" when an account is not affected by an event. The background of the *balance sheet* is red, the *income statement* is blue, and the *statement of cash flows* is green. To demonstrate the usefulness of the horizontal statements model, we use it to display the seven accounting events that RCS experienced during its first year of operation (2004).

1. RCS acquired $120,000 cash from the owners.
2. RCS borrowed $400,000 cash.

3. RCS paid $500,000 cash to purchase land.
4. RCS received $85,000 cash from earning revenue.
5. RCS paid $50,000 cash for expenses.
6. RCS paid $4,000 of cash dividends to the owners.
7. The market value of the land owned by RCS was appraised at $525,000 on December 31, 2004.

Event No.	Balance Sheet									Income Statement					Statement of Cash Flows
	Assets			=	Liab.	+	Stockholders' Equity								
	Cash	+	Land	=	N. Pay.	+	Com. Stk.	+	Ret. Earn.	Rev.	−	Exp.	=	Net Inc.	
Beg. bal.	0	+	0	=	0	+	0	+	0	0	−	0	=	0	NA
1.	120,000	+	NA	=	NA	+	120,000	+	NA	NA	−	NA	=	NA	120,000 FA
2.	400,000	+	NA	=	400,000	+	NA	+	NA	NA	−	NA	=	NA	400,000 FA
3.	(500,000)	+	500,000	=	NA	+	NA	+	NA	NA	−	NA	=	NA	(500,000) IA
4.	85,000	+	NA	=	NA	+	NA	+	85,000	85,000	−	NA	=	85,000	85,000 OA
5.	(50,000)	+	NA	=	NA	+	NA	+	(50,000)	NA	−	50,000	=	(50,000)	(50,000) OA
6.	(4,000)	+	NA	=	NA	+	NA	+	(4,000)	NA	−	NA	=	NA	(4,000) FA
7.	NA	+	NA	=	NA	+	NA	+	NA	NA	−	NA	=	NA	NA
Totals	51,000	+	500,000	=	400,000	+	120,000	+	31,000	85,000	−	50,000	=	35,000	51,000 NC

Recognize that statements models are learning tools. Because they are helpful in understanding how accounting events affect financial statements, they are used extensively in this book. However, the models omit many of the details used in published financial statements. For example, the horizontal model shows only a partial set of statements. Also, since the statements are presented in aggregate, the description of dates (i.e., "as of" versus "for the period ended") does not distinguish periodic from cumulative data.

Careers in Accounting

LO 1

Explain the role of accounting in society.

An accounting career can take you to the top of the business world. *BusinessWeek* studied the backgrounds of the chief executive officers (CEOs) of the 1,000 largest public corporations. More CEOs had backgrounds in accounting than any other field. Exhibit 1.6 provides additional detail regarding the career paths followed by these executives.

What do accountants do? Accountants identify, record, analyze, and communicate information about the economic events that affect organizations. They may work in either public accounting or private accounting.

Public Accounting

You are probably familiar with the acronym CPA. CPA stands for certified *public* accountant. Public accountants provide services to various clients. They are usually paid a fee that varies depending on the service provided. Services typically offered by public accountants include (1) audit services, (2) tax services, and (3) consulting services.

- *Audit services* involve examining a company's accounting records in order to issue an opinion about whether the company's financial statements conform to generally accepted accounting principles. The auditor's opinion adds credibility to the statements, which are prepared by the company's management.

- *Tax services* include both determining the amount of tax due and tax planning to help companies minimize tax expense.
- *Consulting services* cover a wide range of activities that includes everything from installing sophisticated computerized accounting systems to providing personal financial advice.

All public accountants are not certified. Each state government establishes certification requirements applicable in that state. Although the requirements vary from state to state, CPA candidates normally must have a college education, pass a demanding technical examination, and obtain work experience relevant to practicing public accounting.

EXHIBIT 1.6

Career Paths of Chief Executive Officers

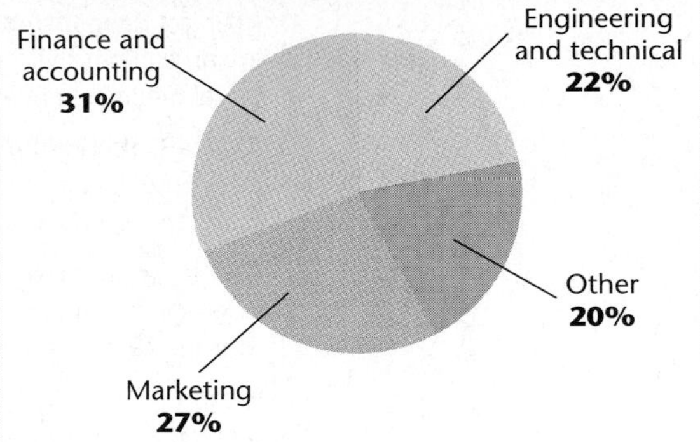

Private Accounting

Accountants employed in the private sector usually work for a specific company or nonprofit organization. Private sector accountants perform a wide variety of functions for their employers. Their duties include classifying and recording transactions, billing customers and collecting amounts due, ordering merchandise, paying suppliers, preparing and analyzing financial statements, developing budgets, measuring costs, assessing performance, and making decisions.

Private accountants may earn any of several professional certifications. For example, the Institute of Certified Management Accountants issues the *Certified Management Accounting (CMA)* designation. The Institute of Internal Auditors issues the *Certified Internal Auditor (CIA)* designation. These designations are widely recognized indicators of technical competence and integrity on the part of individuals who hold them. All professional accounting certifications call for meeting education requirements, passing a technical examination, and obtaining relevant work experience.

THE FINANCIAL ANALYST

This section of each chapter introduces topics related to analyzing real world financial reports. We focus first on the reliability of financial reporting. Accounting information is worthless if it cannot be trusted. Financial analysts must rely on accountants' integrity.

Importance of Ethics

LO 10

Explain the importance of ethics to the accounting profession.

Ethics is the lifeblood of the accounting profession. An ethical breach by a few unscrupulous partners and employees in the Houston office of **Arthur Andersen** led to the demise of this huge international accounting firm (see the Reality Bytes side bar for more details). Thousands of people lost their jobs and hundreds of millions of dollars of damages were incurred. This debacle stands as convincing evidence of the importance of ethical conduct to the accounting profession.

The importance of ethical conduct is universally recognized by accountants. All the major professional accounting organizations require their members to follow formal codes of ethical conduct. The underlying principles of the **Code of Professional Conduct**[6] adopted by the American Institute of Certified Public Accountants are summarized in Exhibit 1.7. Other codes follow similar principles.

[6]American Institute of Certified Public Accountants, Inc. (AICPA), *Code of Professional Conduct* (New York: AICPA, 1992).

EXHIBIT 1.7

Principles of AICPA Code of Professional Conduct

Article I Responsibilities
In carrying out their responsibilities as professionals, members should exercise sensitive professional and moral judgments in all their activities.

Article II The Public Interest
Members should accept the obligation to act in a way that will serve the public interest, honor the public trust, and demonstrate commitment to professionalism.

Article III Integrity
To maintain and broaden public confidence, members should perform all professional responsibilities with the highest sense of integrity.

Article IV Objectivity and Independence
A member should maintain objectivity and be free of conflicts of interest in discharging professional responsibilities. A member in public practice should be independent in fact and appearance when providing auditing and other attestation services.

Article V Due Care
A member should observe the profession's technical and ethical standards, strive continually to improve competence and the quality of services, and discharge professional responsibility to the best of the member's ability.

Article VI Scope and Nature of Services
A member in public practice should observe the principles of the Code of Professional Conduct in determining the scope and nature of services to be provided.

Sarbanes-Oxley Act of 2002

Codes of ethics cannot deter all unethical behavior. The massive surprise bankruptcies of Enron in late 2001 and WorldCom several months later suggested major audit failures on the part of the independent auditors. An audit failure means a company's auditor does not detect, or fails to report, that the company's financial reports are not in compliance with GAAP. The audit failures at Enron, WorldCom, and others prompted Congress to pass the Sarbanes-Oxley Act, which became effective on July 30, 2002. The provisions of this legislation are complex, and their full effects will not be known for some time. However, it is clear that the act has tightened the rules governing auditors' independence.

Prior to Sarbanes-Oxley, independent auditors often provided nonaudit services, such as installing computer systems, for their audit clients. The fees they earned for these services sometimes greatly exceeded the fees charged for the audit itself. This practice had been questioned prior to the audit failures at Enron and WorldCom. Critics felt the independent audit firm was subject to pressure from the company to conduct a less rigorous audit, or risk losing lucrative nonaudit work. The Sarbanes-Oxley Act prohibits auditors from providing most types of nonaudit services to companies they audit.

Another provision of Sarbanes-Oxley clarifies the legal responsibility that company management has for a company's financial reports. The company's chief executive officer (CEO) and chief financial officer (CFO) must certify in writing that they have reviewed the financial reports being issued, and that the reports present fairly the company's financial status. An executive who falsely certifies the company's financial reports is subject to significant fines and imprisonment.

Additional details of the Sarbanes-Oxley Act are presented in Chapters 11 and 14. Further discussion of the problems at WorldCom and Enron are presented in Chapters 6 and 10, respectively.

Common Features of Ethical Misconduct

People who become involved in unethical or criminal behavior usually do so unexpectedly. They start with small indiscretions that evolve gradually into more serious violations of trust. To reduce the incidence of unethical or illegal conduct, business persons must be aware of conditions that lead to trust violations. To increase awareness, Donald Cressey studied hun-

REALITY BYTES

Independent auditors are primarily responsible to the investing public, not to the company that hires and pays them. In 2002 numerous accounting scandals involving some very large public companies caused investors to question whether or not the external auditors really were independent. The public learned that external audit firms were often also serving as consultants to the companies they audited. The fees earned for consulting services were sometimes significantly higher than the fees earned for auditing the same company. These arrangements caused many people, including members of Congress, to doubt that auditors would take a tough stance with a company's management over financial reporting issues if doing so might threaten future consulting fees.

No situation demonstrated this concern more than that of **Enron**. The well-publicized accounting problems that led to Enron's downfall were equally devastating for its auditor, **Arthur Andersen**. Within six months after Enron's troubles became public knowledge, Arthur Andersen lost over half its public company audit clients and almost two-thirds of its employees. Further, Andersen was convicted of obstruction of justice by a Houston jury and was told by the **SEC** that it could no longer audit public companies. The partner in charge of the Enron audit was fired and pled guilty to obstruction of justice charges; the previous year, his compensation exceeded $1 million.

In addition to the consequences mentioned above, civil lawsuits were filed against Arthur Andersen, and legal experts believe its partners, even those not involved in the Enron audit, will likely be held personally liable for any damages resulting from inadequate audits. Congress has given CPAs a legal monopoly to provide independent audits for public companies. However, their protected status does not shelter them from the consequences of their actions. As the Enron case demonstrates, when CPAs fail, they are held to a high and costly standard.

dreds of criminal cases to identify the primary factors behind ethical misconduct. Cressey found three factors common to all cases: (1) the existence of a nonsharable problem, (2) the presence of an opportunity, and (3) the capacity for rationalization.[7]

As the term implies, a *nonsharable problem* is one that must be kept secret. Individuals differ about what they keep to themselves. Consider two responses to the problem of an imminent business failure. One person may feel so ashamed that he or she cannot discuss the problem with anyone. Another person in the same situation may want to talk to anyone, even a stranger, in the hope of getting help. Other nonsharable problems include personal vices such as drug addiction, gambling, and promiscuity. Cressey's findings suggest that the person who is inclined toward secrecy is more likely to accept an unethical or illegal solution. In other words, the perceived need for secrecy increases vulnerability.

Accountants establish policies and procedures designed to reduce *opportunities* for fraud. These policies and procedures are commonly called **internal controls.** Specific internal control procedures are tailored to meet the individual needs of particular businesses. For example, banks use vaults to protect cash, but universities have little use for this type of equipment. Chapter 6 discusses internal control procedures in more detail. At this point, simply

[7]D. R. Cressey, *Other People's Money* (Montclair, NJ: Paterson Smith, 1973).

recognize that accountants are aware of the need to reduce opportunities for unethical and criminal activities.

Few individuals think of themselves as dishonest, so they develop *rationalizations* to justify their misconduct. Cressey found a significant number of embezzlers who contended they were only "borrowing the money," even after being convicted and sentenced to jail. Common rationalizations include peer pressure, loyalty to unscrupulous superiors, family needs, revenge, and a sense of entitlement. To avoid involvement in ethical misconduct, accountants must develop a strong sense of personal responsibility. They cannot allow themselves to blame other people or unfair circumstances for their problems. They must learn to hold themselves personally accountable for their actions.

Ethical misconduct is a serious offense in the accounting profession. A single mistake can destroy an accounting career. If you commit a white-collar crime, you normally lose the opportunity to hold a white-collar job. Second chances are rarely granted; it is extremely important that you learn how to recognize and avoid the common features of ethical misconduct. To help you prepare for the real-world situations you are likely to encounter, we include ethical dilemmas in the end-of-chapter materials. When working with these dilemmas, try to identify the (1) secret, (2) opportunity, and (3) rationalization associated with the particular ethical situation described. If you are not an ethical person, accounting is not the career for you.

Real-World Financial Reports

LO 11

Identify three types of business organizations and some of the technical terms they use in their real world financial reports.

As previously indicated, organizations exist in many different forms, including *business* entities and *not-for-profit* entities. Business entities are typically service, merchandising, or manufacturing companies. **Service businesses,** which include doctors, attorneys, accountants, dry cleaners, and maids, provide services to their customers. **Merchandising businesses,** sometimes called *retail* or *wholesale companies,* sell goods to customers that other entities make. **Manufacturing businesses** make the goods that they sell to their customers.

Some business operations include combinations of these three categories. For example, an automotive repair shop might change oil (service function), sell parts such as oil filters (retail function), and rebuild engines (manufacturing function). The nature of the reporting entity affects the form and content of the information reported in an entity's financial statements. For example, not-for-profit entities provide statements of revenues, expenditures, and changes in fund equity while business entities provide income statements. Similarly, income statements of retail companies show an expense item called *cost of goods sold,* but service

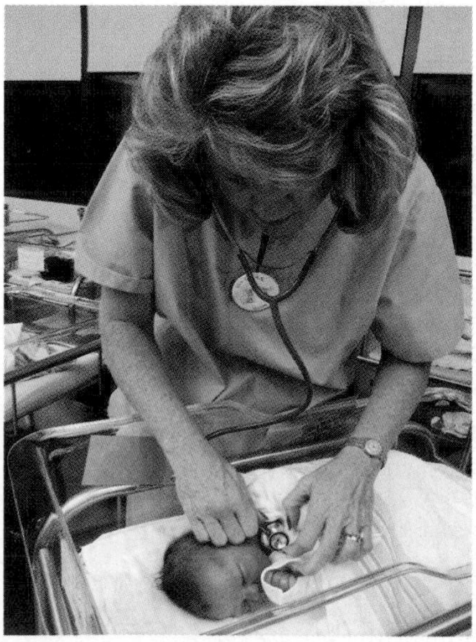

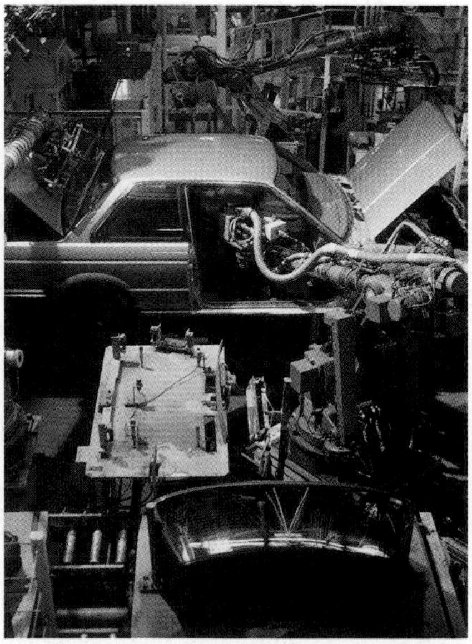

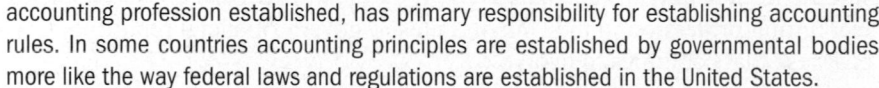

FOCUS ON INTERNATIONAL ISSUES

IS THERE GLOBAL GAAP?

As explained in this chapter, financial reporting is a measurement and communication discipline based on generally accepted accounting principles (GAAP). The accounting rules described in this text represent the GAAP used in the United States. All economies in the world do not use the same accounting rules. Although there are similarities among the accounting principles used in different countries, there are also major differences. An independent body, the International Accounting Standards Board (IASB), has made an effort in recent years to create uniform international accounting standards. Individual countries, however, have retained the authority to establish their own accounting principles, so there is no single "global GAAP," though the work of the IASB has reduced the extent of variation in accounting principles that exists among countries.

Accounting rules differ among countries for such reasons as the economic and legal environments in each country and the way in which a country establishes its accounting principles. In the United States, the Financial Accounting Standards Board (FASB), a nongovernmental rule-making body that the accounting profession established, has primary responsibility for establishing accounting rules. In some countries accounting principles are established by governmental bodies more like the way federal laws and regulations are established in the United States.

Finally, in the United States there is no direct connection between GAAP established by the FASB and the tax accounting rules established by Congress and the Internal Revenue Service (IRS). In some countries, government authorities require that companies use the same accounting rules for both financial and income tax reporting.

companies that do not sell goods have no such item in their income statements. You should expect some diversity when reviewing real-world financial statements.

Annual Report for The Topps Company, Inc.

Organizations normally provide information, including financial statements, to *stakeholders* yearly in a document known as an **annual report.** The annual report for **Topps** is reproduced in Appendix B of this text. This report includes the company's financial statements (see pages 12–15 of the report). Immediately following the statements are footnotes that provide additional details about the items described in the statements (see pages 16–30). The annual report contains the *auditors' report,* which is discussed in Chapter 6. Annual reports also include written commentary describing management's assessment of significant events that affected the company during the reporting period. This commentary is called *management's discussion and analysis* (MD&A).

The U.S. Securities and Exchange Commission (SEC) requires public companies to file an annual report on a document known as a 10-K. The SEC is discussed in more detail later. Even though the annual report is usually flashier (contains more color and pictures) than the 10-K, the 10-K is normally more comprehensive with respect to content. As a result, the 10-K report can substitute for the annual report, but the annual report cannot substitute for the 10-K. In an effort to reduce costs, some companies use the 10-K report as their annual report.

Special Terms in Real-World Reports

The financial statements of real-world companies include numerous items relating to advanced topics that are not covered in introductory accounting textbooks, especially the first chapter of an introductory accounting textbook. Do not, however, be discouraged from browsing through real-world annual reports. You will significantly enhance your learning if you look at many annual reports and attempt to identify as many items as you can. As your accounting knowledge grows, you will likely experience increased interest in real-world financial reports and the businesses they describe.

We encourage you to look for annual reports in the library or ask your employer for a copy of your company's report. The Internet is another excellent source for obtaining annual reports. Most companies provide links to their annual reports on their home pages. Look for links labeled "about the company" or "investor relations" or other phrases that logically lead to the company's financial reports. The best way to learn accounting is to use it. Accounting is the language of business. Learning the language will serve you well in almost any area of business that you pursue.

<< A Look Back

This chapter introduced the role of accounting in society and business: to provide information helpful to operating and evaluating the performance of organizations. Accounting is a measurement discipline. To communicate effectively, users of accounting must agree on the rules of measurement. *Generally accepted accounting principles (GAAP)* constitute the rules used by the accounting profession in the United States to govern financial reporting. GAAP is a work in progress that continues to evolve.

This chapter has discussed eight elements of financial statements: *assets, liabilities, equity, common stock (contributed capital), revenue, expenses, dividends (distributions),* and *net income.* The elements represent broad classifications reported on financial statements. Four basic financial statements appear in the reports of public companies: the *balance sheet,* the *income statement,* the *statement of changes in stockholders' equity,* and the *statement of cash flows.* The chapter discussed the form and content of each statement as well as the interrelationships among the statements.

This chapter introduced a *horizontal financial statements model* as a tool to help you understand how business events affect a set of financial statements. This model is used throughout the text. You should carefully study this model before proceeding to Chapter 2.

>> A Look Forward

To keep matters as simple as possible and to focus on the interrelationships among financial statements, this chapter considered only cash events. Obviously, many real-world events do not involve an immediate exchange of cash. For example, customers use telephone service throughout the month without paying for it until the next month. Such phone usage represents an expense in one month with a cash exchange in the following month. Events such as this are called *accruals.* Understanding the effects that accrual events have on the financial statements is included in Chapter 2.

SELF-STUDY REVIEW PROBLEM

During 2005 Rustic Camp Sites experienced the following transactions.

1. RCS acquired $32,000 cash by issuing common stock.

2. RCS received $116,000 cash for providing services to customers (leasing camp sites).
3. RCS paid $13,000 cash for salaries expense.
4. RCS paid a $9,000 cash dividend to the owners.
5. RCS sold land that had cost $100,000 for $100,000 cash.
6. RCS paid $47,000 cash for other operating expenses.

Required

a. Record the transaction data in a horizontal financial statements model like the following one. In the Cash Flow column, classify the cash flows as operating activities (OA), investing activities (IA), or financing activities (FA). The beginning balances have been recorded as an example. They are the ending balances shown on RCS's December 31, 2004, financial statements illustrated in the chapter. Note that the revenue and expense accounts have a zero beginning balance. Amounts in these accounts apply only to a single accounting period. Revenue and expense account balances are not carried forward from one accounting period to the next.

Event No.	Balance Sheet									Income Statement					Statement of Cash Flows
	Assets			=	Liab.	+	Stockholders' Equity								
	Cash	+	Land	=	N. Pay.	+	Com. Stk.	+	Ret. Earn.	Rev.	−	Exp.	=	Net Inc.	
Beg. bal.	51,000	+	500,000	=	400,000	+	120,000	+	31,000	NA	−	NA	=	NA	NA

b. Explain why there are no beginning balances in the Income Statement columns.

c. What amount of net income will RCS report on the 2005 income statement?

d. What amount of total assets will RCS report on the December 31, 2005, balance sheet?

e. What amount of retained earnings will RCS report on the December 31, 2005, balance sheet?

f. What amount of net cash flow from operating activities will RCS report on the 2005 statement of cash flows?

Solution

a.

Event No.	Balance Sheet									Income Statement					Statement of Cash Flows
	Assets			=	Liab.	+	Stockholders' Equity								
	Cash	+	Land	=	N. Pay.	+	Com. Stk.	+	Ret. Earn.	Rev.	−	Exp.	=	Net Inc.	
Beg. bal.	51,000	+	500,000	=	400,000	+	120,000	+	31,000	NA	−	NA	=	NA	NA
1.	32,000	+	NA	=	NA	+	32,000	+	NA	NA	−	NA	=	NA	32,000 FA
2.	116,000	+	NA	=	NA	+	NA	+	116,000	116,000	−	NA	=	116,000	116,000 OA
3.	(13,000)	+	NA	=	NA	+	NA	+	(13,000)	NA	−	13,000	=	(13,000)	(13,000) OA
4.	(9,000)	+	NA	=	NA	+	NA	+	(9,000)	NA	−	NA	=	NA	(9,000) FA
5.	100,000	+	(100,000)	=	NA	+	NA	+	NA	NA	−	NA	=	NA	100,000 IA
6.	(47,000)	+	NA	=	NA	+	NA	+	(47,000)	NA	−	47,000	=	(47,000)	(47,000) OA
Totals	230,000	+	400,000	=	400,000	+	152,000	+	78,000	116,000	−	60,000	=	56,000	179,000 NC*

*The letters NC on the last line of the column designate the net change in cash.

b. The revenue and expense accounts are temporary accounts used to capture data for a single accounting period. They are closed (amounts removed from the accounts) to retained earnings at the end of the accounting period and therefore always have zero balances at the beginning of the accounting cycle.

c. RCS will report net income of $56,000 on the 2005 income statement. Compute this amount by subtracting the expenses from the revenue ($116,000 Revenue − $13,000 Salaries expense − $47,000 Other operating expense).

d. RCS will report total assets of $630,000 on the December 31, 2005, balance sheet. Compute total assets by adding the cash amount to the land amount ($230,000 Cash + $400,000 Land).

e. RCS will report retained earnings of $78,000 on the December 31, 2005 balance sheet. Compute this amount using the following formula: Beginning retained earnings + Net income − Dividends = Ending retained earnings. In this case, $31,000 + $56,000 − $9,000 = $78,000.

f. Net cash flow from operating activities is the difference between the amount of cash collected from revenue and the amount of cash spent for expenses. In this case, $116,000 cash inflow from revenue − $13,000 cash outflow for salaries expense − $47,000 cash outflow for other operating expenses = $56,000 net cash inflow from operating activities.

KEY TERMS

accounts 9
accounting 3
accounting equation 9
accounting event 11
accounting period 17
annual report 25
articulation 15
assets 4
asset source transaction 11
balance sheet 18
claims 9
Code of Professional Conduct 21
common stock 10
creditors 4
dividend 13
double-entry bookkeeping 12
earnings 4
elements 8
equity 10
expenses 13
financial accounting 6
Financial Accounting Standards Board (FASB) 7
financial resources 4
financial statements 8
financing activities 18
general ledger 14
generally accepted accounting principles (GAAP) 7
historical cost concept 14
horizontal statements model 19
income 4
income statement 17
interest 5
internal controls 23
investing activities 18
investors 4
labor resources 5
liabilities 10
liquidation 4
liquidity 18
managerial accounting 6
manufacturing businesses 24
market 4
merchandising businesses 24
net income 17
net loss 17
not-for-profit entities 6
operating activities 18
physical resources 5
productive assets 18
profit 4
reliability concept 14
reporting entities 8
retained earnings 10
revenue 12
service businesses 24
stakeholders 6
statement of cash flows 18
statement of changes in stockholders' equity 17
stockholders 10
stockholders' equity 10
transaction 11
users 6

QUESTIONS

1. Explain the term *stakeholder.*
2. Why is accounting called the *language of business?*
3. What is the primary mechanism used to allocate resources in the United States?
4. In a business context, what does the term *market* mean?
5. What market trilogy component is involved in the process of transforming resources into finished products?
6. Give an example of a financial resource, a physical resource, and a labor resource.
7. What type of compensation does an investor expect to receive in exchange for providing financial resources to a business? What type of compensation does a creditor expect from providing financial resources to an organization or business?
8. How do financial and managerial accounting differ?
9. Describe a not-for-profit or nonprofit enterprise. What is the motivation for this type of entity?
10. What are the U.S. rules of accounting measurement called?
11. Is there a global GAAP (generally accepted accounting principles)? Explain your answer.
12. What body has the primary responsibility for establishing GAAP in the United States?
13. Distinguish between elements of financial statements and accounts.
14. What is the most basic form of the accounting equation?
15. What role do assets play in business profitability?
16. To whom do the assets of a business belong?
17. Explain the order of priority for asset distributions in a business liquidation.

18. Name the element used to describe the ownership interest in a business.
19. Name the element used to describe creditors' claims on the assets of a business.
20. What is the accounting equation? Describe each of its three components.
21. Who ultimately bears the risk and collects the rewards associated with operating a business?
22. What does *double-entry bookkeeping* mean?
23. Identify the three types of accounting transactions discussed in this chapter. Provide an example of each type of transaction, and explain how it affects the accounting equation.
24. How does acquiring resources from owners affect the accounting equation?
25. Name the two primary components of stockholders' equity.
26. How does earning revenue affect the accounting equation?
27. What are the three primary sources of assets?
28. What is included in retained earnings?
29. How does distributing assets (paying dividends) to owners affect the accounting equation?
30. What are the similarities and differences between dividends and expenses?
31. What four general-purpose financial statements do business enterprises use to communicate information to stakeholders?
32. Which of the general-purpose financial statements provides information about the enterprise at a specific designated date?
33. What causes a net loss?
34. What three categories of cash receipts and cash payments do businesses report on the statement of cash flows? Explain the types of cash flows reported in each category.
35. How are asset accounts usually arranged in the balance sheet?
36. What type of information does a business typically include in its annual report?
37. Name three types of service provided by certified public accountants.
38. Name three professional designations that accountants can earn.
39. What are the six principles of ethical conduct set out under section I of the AICPA's Code of Professional Conduct?

EXERCISES—SERIES A

All Exercises in Series A are available with McGraw-Hill's Homework Manager

Exercise 1-1A *Understanding markets* L.O. 1

Free economies use open markets to allocate resources.

Required

Identify the three participants in a free business market. Write a brief memo explaining how these participants interact to ensure that goods and services are distributed in a manner that satisfies consumers.

Exercise 1-2A *Distributions in a business liquidation* L.O. 2

Assume that Mallory Company acquires $700 cash from creditors and $900 cash from investors (stockholders). The company then has an operating loss of $1,000 cash and goes out of business.

Required

a. Define the term *business liquidation.*
b. What amount of cash will Mallory's creditors receive?
c. What amount of cash will Mallory's investors (stockholders) receive?

Exercise 1-3A *Identifying the reporting entities* L.O. 2

Reza Pierno recently started a business. During the first few days of operation, Mr. Pierno transferred $15,000 from his personal account into a business account for a company he named Pierno Enterprises. Pierno Enterprises borrowed $20,000 from the State Bank of Renu. Mr. Pierno's father-in-law, Edward Goebel, invested $32,000 into the business for which he received a 25 percent ownership interest. Pierno Enterprises purchased a building from Stokes Realty Company. The building cost $60,000 cash. Pierno Enterprises earned $28,000 in revenue from the company's customers and paid its employees $17,000 for salaries expense.

Required

Identify the entities that were mentioned in the scenario and explain what happened to the cash accounts of each entity that you identify.

L.O. 3

Exercise 1-4A ***Financial statement elements and accounts***

Required

Write a brief memo that distinguishes between the *elements* of financial statements and the *accounts* that appear on financial statements.

L.O. 3

Exercise 1-5A ***Titles and accounts appearing on financial statements***

Annual reports normally include an income statement, a statement of changes in stockholders' equity, a balance sheet, and a statement of cash flows.

Required

Identify the financial statements on which each of the following titles or accounts would appear. If a title or an account appears on more than one statement, list all statements that would include it.

a. Common Stock
b. Land
c. Ending Cash Balance
d. Beginning Cash Balance
e. Notes Payable
f. Retained Earnings
g. Revenue
h. Dividends
i. Financing Activities
j. Salary Expense

L.O. 4

Exercise 1-6A ***Components of the accounting equation***

Required

The following three requirements are independent of each other.

a. James Auto Parts has assets of $9,100 and equity of $6,500. What is the amount of liabilities? What is the amount of claims?
b. Best Candy Inc. has liabilities of $2,400 and equity of $5,400. What is the amount of assets?
c. Sam's Dive Shop has assets of $49,200 and liabilities of $21,600. What is the amount of its equity? What is the amount of the investors' claims on assets?

L.O. 4

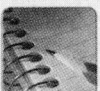

Exercise 1-7A ***Effect of events on the accounting equation***

Sun Co. experienced the following events during 2006.

1. Acquired cash from the issue of common stock.
2. Provided services to clients for cash.
3. Borrowed cash.
4. Paid operating expenses with cash.
5. Paid a cash dividend to the stockholders.
6. Purchased land with cash.

Required

Explain how each of these events affects the accounting equation by writing the letter I for increase, the letter D for decrease, and NA for no effect under each of the components of the accounting equation. The first event is shown as an example.

Event Number	Assets	=	Liabilities	+	Stockholders' Equity: Common Stock	+	Stockholders' Equity: Retained Earnings
1	I		NA		I		NA

Exercise 1-8A *Effects of issuing stock*

L.O. 4, 5

Jeter Company was started in 2009 when it acquired $18,000 cash by issuing common stock. The cash acquisition was the only event that affected the business in 2009.

Required

a. Write an accounting equation, and record the effects of the stock issue under the appropriate general ledger account headings.

b. What is the amount of net income appearing on the income statement?

c. Where would the stock issue be reported on the statement of cash flows?

Exercise 1-9A *Effects of borrowing*

L.O. 4, 5

South Pacific Company was started in 2007 when it issued a note to borrow $8,400 cash. Assume this is the only accounting event that occurred during 2007.

Required

a. Write an accounting equation, and record the effects of the borrowing transaction under the appropriate general ledger account headings.

b. What is the amount of net income reported on the income statement? (Ignore any effects of interest.)

c. Where would the note issue appear on the statement of cash flows?

Exercise 1-10A *Effects of revenue, expense, and dividend events*

L.O. 3, 4, 5, 8

Epps Company was started on January 1, 2005. During 2005, the company experienced the following three accounting events: (1) earned cash revenues of $13,500, (2) paid cash expenses of $8,600, and (3) paid a $1,000 cash dividend to stockholders. These were the only events that affected the company during 2005.

Required

a. Write an accounting equation, and record the effects of each accounting event under the appropriate general ledger account headings.

b. Prepare an income statement for the 2005 accounting period and a balance sheet at the end of 2005 for Epps Company.

Exercise 1-11A *Classifying items for the statement of cash flows*

L.O. 3

Required

Indicate whether each of the following would be classified on the statement of cash flows as operating activities (OA), investing activities (IA), financing activities (FA), or not applicable (NA).

a. Paid $4,000 cash for salary expense.

b. Borrowed $8,000 cash from First State Bank.

c. Received $30,000 cash from the issue of common stock.

d. Purchased land for $8,000 cash.

e. Performed services for $14,000 cash.

f. Paid $4,200 cash for utilities expense.

g. Sold land for $7,000 cash.

h. Paid a cash dividend of $1,000 to the stockholders.

i. Hired an accountant to keep the books.

j. Paid $3,000 cash on the loan from First State Bank.

L.O. 3, 4, 5, 6

Exercise 1-12A ***Effect of transactions on general ledger accounts***

At the beginning of 2004, Quick Service Company's accounting records had the following general ledger accounts and balances.

QUICK SERVICE COMPANY Accounting Equation								
Event	**Assets**		**=**	**Liabilities**	**+**	**Stockholders' Equity**		**Acct. Titles for Ret. Earn.**
	Cash	**Land**		**Notes Payable**		**Common Stock**	**Retained Earnings**	
Balance 1/1/2004	25,000	50,000		35,000		30,000	10,000	

Quick completed the following transactions during 2004:

1. Purchased additional land for $12,000 cash.
2. Acquired $20,000 cash from the issue of common stock.
3. Received $65,000 cash for providing services to customers.
4. Paid cash operating expenses of $42,000.
5. Paid $20,000 cash on notes payable.
6. Paid a $3,000 cash dividend to the stockholders.
7. Determined the market value of the land to be $72,000 at the end of the year.

Required

a. Record the transactions in the appropriate general ledger accounts. Record the amounts of revenue, expense, and dividends in the Retained Earnings column. Provide the appropriate titles for these accounts in the last column of the table.

b. Determine the amount of net income for the 2004 period.

c. What is the amount of total assets at the end of 2004? What is the amount of stockholders' equity at the end of 2004?

L.O. 3, 4, 5, 6, 8

Exercise 1-13A ***Preparing financial statements***

Dale Company experienced the following events during 2004.

1. Acquired $30,000 cash from the issue of common stock.
2. Paid $12,000 cash to purchase land.
3. Borrowed $8,000 cash.
4. Provided services for $20,000 cash.
5. Paid $1,000 cash for rent expense.
6. Paid $12,000 cash for other operating expenses.
7. Paid a $2,000 cash dividend to the stockholders.
8. Determined that the market value of the land purchased in Event 2 is now $12,700.

Required

a. The January 1, 2004, general ledger account balances are shown in the following accounting equation. Record the eight events in the appropriate general ledger accounts. Record the amounts of revenue, expense, and dividends in the Retained Earnings column. Provide the appropriate titles for these accounts in the last column of the table. The first event is shown as an example.

b. Prepare an income statement, statement of changes in stockholders' equity, year-end balance sheet, and statement of cash flows for the 2004 accounting period.

c. Determine the percentage of assets that was provided by retained earnings. How much cash is in the retained earnings account?

DALE COMPANY
Accounting Equation

Event	Assets		=	Liabilities	+	Stockholders' Equity		Acct. Titles for Ret. Earn.
	Cash	Land		Notes Payable		Common Stock	Retained Earnings	
Balance 1/1/2004	2,000	16,000		0		10,000	8,000	
1.	30,000					30,000		

Exercise 1-14A *Classifying events as asset source, use, or exchange*

L.O. 7

Foster Company experienced the following events during its first year of operations.

1. Acquired $10,000 cash from the issue of common stock.
2. Borrowed $8,000 cash from First Bank.
3. Paid $4,000 cash to purchase land.
4. Received $5,000 cash for providing boarding services.
5. Acquired an additional $2,000 cash from the issue of common stock.
6. Purchased additional land for $3,500 cash.
7. Paid $2,500 cash for salary expense.
8. Signed a contract to provide additional services in the future.
9. Paid $1,000 cash for rent expense.
10. Paid a $1,000 cash dividend to the stockholders.
11. Determined the market value of the land to be $8,000 at the end of the accounting period.

Required

Classify each event as an asset source, use, or exchange transaction or as not applicable (NA).

Exercise 1-15A *Relationship between assets and retained earnings*

L.O. 4

Eastern Company was organized when it acquired $1,000 cash from the issue of common stock. During its first accounting period the company earned $800 of cash revenue and incurred $500 of cash expenses. Also, during the accounting period the company paid its owners a $100 cash dividend.

Required

a. Determine the ending amount of the retained earnings account.

b. As of the end of the accounting period, determine what percentage of total assets was provided by earnings.

Exercise 1-16A *Historical cost versus market value*

L.O. 6

Feloma Company purchased land in April 2001 at a cost of $520,000. The estimated market value of the land is $600,000 as of December 31, 2004. Feloma purchased marketable equity securities (bought the common stock of a company that is independent of Feloma) in May 2001 at a cost of $320,000. These securities have a market value of $360,000 as of December 31, 2004. Generally accepted accounting principles require that the land be shown on the December 31, 2004, balance sheet at $520,000, while the marketable equity securities are required to be reported at $360,000.

Required

Write a brief memo that explains the contradiction regarding why GAAP requires Feloma to report historical cost with respect to the land versus market value with respect to the marketable securities. This answer may require speculation on your part. Use your knowledge about the historical cost and reliability concepts to formulate a logical response.

L.O. 2, 7

Exercise 1-17A *Relating accounting events to entities*

Hanson Company was started in 2004 when it acquired $50,000 cash by issuing common stock to Michael Hanson.

Required

a. Was this event an asset source, use, or exchange transaction for Hanson Company?

b. Was this event an asset source, use, or exchange transaction for Michael Hanson?

c. Was the cash flow an operating, investing, or financing activity on Hanson Company's 2004 statement of cash flows?

d. Was the cash flow an operating, investing, or financing activity on Michael Hanson's 2004 statement of cash flows?

L.O. 4

Exercise 1-18A *Missing information in the accounting equation*

Required

Calculate the missing amounts in the following table:

					Stockholders' Equity		
Company	Assets	=	Liabilities	+	Common Stock	+	Retained Earnings
A	$?		$48,000		$52,000		$36,000
B	90,000		?		25,000		40,000
C	87,000		15,000		?		37,000
D	102,000		29,000		42,000		?

L.O. 3, 9

Exercise 1-19A *Missing information in the accounting equation*

As of December 31, 2006, Thomas Company had total assets of $156,000, total liabilities of $85,600, and common stock of $48,400. During 2007 Thomas earned $36,000 of cash revenue, paid $22,000 for cash expenses, and paid a $1,000 cash dividend to the stockholders.

Required

a. Determine the amount of retained earnings as of December 31, 2006.

b. Determine the amount of net income earned in 2007.

c. Determine the amount of retained earnings as of December 31, 2007.

d. Determine the amount of cash that is in the retained earnings account as of December 31, 2007.

L.O. 6, 9

Exercise 1-20A *Missing information for determining net income*

The December 31, 2006, balance sheet for Kerr Company showed total stockholders' equity of $62,500. Total stockholders' equity increased by $53,400 between December 31, 2006, and December 31, 2007. During 2007 Kerr Company acquired $11,000 cash from the issue of common stock. Kerr Company paid an $8,000 cash dividend to the stockholders during 2007.

Required

Determine the amount of net income or loss Kerr reported on its 2007 income statement. (*Hint:* Remember that stock issues, net income, and dividends all change total stockholders' equity.)

L.O. 6, 7, 9

Exercise 1-21A *Effect of events on a horizontal financial statements model*

Hayes Consulting Services experienced the following events during 2006.

1. Acquired cash by issuing common stock.
2. Collected cash for providing tutoring services to clients.
3. Borrowed cash from a local government small business foundation.
4. Purchased land for cash.
5. Paid cash for operating expenses.
6. Paid a cash dividend to the stockholders.
7. Determined the year-end market value of the land to be higher than its historical cost.

Required

Use a horizontal statements model to show how each event affects the balance sheet, income statement, and statement of cash flows. Indicate whether the event increases (I), decreases (D), or does not affect (NA) each element of the financial statements. Also, in the Cash Flows column, classify the cash flows as operating activities (OA), investing activities (IA), or financing activities (FA). The first transaction is shown as an example.

Event No.	Balance Sheet									Income Statement					Statement of Cash Flows	
	Cash	+	Land	=	N. Pay.	+	Com. Stk.	+	Ret. Earn.	Rev.	−	Exp.	=	Net Inc.		
1.	I	+	NA	=	NA	+	I	+	NA	NA	−	NA	=	NA	I	FA

Exercise 1-22A *Record events in the horizontal statements model*

L.O. 3, 9

Marshall Co. was started in 2006. During 2006, the company (1) acquired $9,000 cash from the issue of common stock, (2) earned cash revenue of $18,000, (3) paid cash expenses of $12,500, and (4) paid a $1,000 cash dividend to the stockholders.

Required

a. Record these four events in a horizontal statements model. Also, in the Cash Flows column, classify the cash flows as operating activities (OA), investing activities (IA), or financing activities (FA). The first event is shown as an example.

Event No.	Balance Sheet							Income Statement					Statement of Cash Flows	
	Cash	=	N. Pay.	+	Com. Stk.	+	Ret. Earn.	Rev.	−	Exp.	=	Net Inc.		
1.	9,000	=	NA	+	9,000	+	NA	NA	−	NA	=	NA	9,000	FA

b. What does the income statement tell you about the assets of this business?

Exercise 1-23A *Effect of events on a horizontal statements model*

L.O. 6, 9

Tax Help Inc. was started on January 1, 2006. The company experienced the following events during its first year of operation.

1. Acquired $30,000 cash from the issue of common stock.
2. Paid $12,000 cash to purchase land.
3. Received $30,000 cash for providing tax services to customers.
4. Paid $9,500 cash for salary expense.
5. Acquired $5,000 cash from the issue of additional common stock.
6. Borrowed $10,000 cash from the bank.
7. Purchased additional land for $5,000 cash.
8. Paid $6,000 cash for other operating expenses.
9. Paid a $2,800 cash dividend to the stockholders.
10. Determined the market value of the land to be $18,000.

Required

a. Record these events in a horizontal statements model. Also, in the Cash Flows column, classify the cash flows as operating activities (OA), investing activities (IA), or financing activities (FA). The first event is shown as an example.

Event No.	Balance Sheet									Income Statement					Statement of Cash Flows	
	Cash	+	Land	=	N. Pay.	+	Com. Stk.	+	Ret. Earn.	Rev.	−	Exp.	=	Net Inc.		
1.	30,000	+	NA	=	NA	+	30,000	+	NA	NA	−	NA	=	NA	30,000	FA

b. What is the net income earned in 2006?

c. What is the amount of total assets at the end of 2006?

d. What is the net cash flow from operating activities for 2006?

e. What is the net cash flow from investing activities for 2006?

f. What is the net cash flow from financing activities for 2006?

g. What is the cash balance at the end of 2006?

h. As of the end of the year 2006, what percentage of total assets was provided by creditors, investors, and earnings?

L.O. 6, 7, 9

Exercise 1-24A *Types of transactions and the horizontal statements model*

The Shoe Shop experienced the following events during its first year of operations, 2008.

1. Acquired cash by issuing common stock.
2. Provided services and collected cash.
3. Borrowed cash from a bank.
4. Paid cash for operating expenses.
5. Purchased land with cash.
6. Paid a cash dividend to the stockholders.
7. Determined the market value of the land to be higher than the historical cost.

Required

a. Indicate whether each event is an asset source, use, or exchange transaction.

b. Use a horizontal statements model to show how each event affects the balance sheet, income statement, and statement of cash flows. Indicate whether the event increases (I), decreases (D), or does not affect (NA) each element of the financial statements. Also, in the Cash Flows column, classify the cash flows as operating activities (OA), investing activities (IA), or financing activities (FA). The first transaction is shown as an example.

	Balance Sheet									Income Statement					
Event No.	Cash	+	Land	=	N. Pay.	+	Com. Stk.	+	Ret. Earn.	Rev.	−	Exp.	=	Net Inc.	Statement of Cash Flows
1.	I	+	NA	=	NA	+	I	+	NA	NA	−	NA	=	NA	I FA

L.O. 1

Exercise 1-25A *Public accounting career*

Sam Shelton is a public accountant with a professional designation.

Required

a. What professional designation does Sam most likely hold?

b. Identify three services that Sam may perform for his clients.

L.O. 10

Exercise 1-26A *Code of Professional Conduct*

Jane Wong is a certified public accountant (CPA). She follows a code of professional conduct in the performance of her duties.

Required

a. Name the organization that established the code of conduct that Jane follows.

b. Name the six principles in the code of conduct that Jane follows.

PROBLEMS—SERIES A

All Problems in Series A are available with McGraw-Hill's Homework Manager

L.O. 1

Problem 1-27A *Accounting's role in not-for-profit organizations*

Charles Robertson is struggling to pass his introductory accounting course. Charles is intelligent but he likes to party. Studying is a low priority for Charles. When one of his friends tells him he is going to have trouble in business if he doesn't learn accounting, Charles responds that he doesn't plan to go into business. He says that he is arts oriented and plans someday to be a director of a museum. He is in the school of business to develop his social skills, not his quantitative skills. Charles says he won't have to worry about accounting since museums are not intended to make a profit.

Required

a. Write a brief memo explaining whether you agree or disagree with Charles's position regarding accounting and not-for-profit organizations.

b. Distinguish between financial accounting and managerial accounting.

c. Identify some of the stakeholders of not-for-profit institutions that would expect to receive financial accounting reports.

d. Identify some of the stakeholders of not-for-profit institutions that would expect to receive managerial accounting reports.

Problem 1-28A *Accounting entities*

L.O. 2

CHECK FIGURE

Entities mentioned:
Tilly Jensen
Jensen Business

The following business scenarios are independent of one another.

1. Tilly Jensen starts a business by transferring $5,000 from her personal checking account into a checking account for the business.
2. A business that Bart Angle owns earns $2,300 of cash revenue.
3. Phil Culver borrows $20,000 from the National Bank and uses the money to purchase a car from Henderson Ford.
4. Lipka Company pays its five employees $2,000 each to cover their salaries.
5. Kevin Dow loans his son Brian $5,000 cash.
6. Asthana Inc. paid $150,000 cash to purchase land from Waterbury Inc.
7. Moshe Liu and Chao Porat form a partnership by contributing $30,000 each from their personal bank accounts to a partnership bank account.
8. Ken Stanga pays cash to purchase $2,000 of common stock that is issued by Krishnan Inc.
9. Omni Company pays a $42,000 cash dividend to each of its seven shareholders.
10. McCann Inc. borrowed $5,000,000 from the National Bank.

Required

a. For each scenario create a list of all of the entities that are mentioned in the description.

b. Describe what happens to the cash account of each entity that you identified in Requirement *a*.

Problem 1-29A *Relating titles and accounts to financial statements*

L.O. 3

Required

Identify the financial statements on which each of the following items (titles, date descriptions, and accounts) appears by placing a check mark in the appropriate column. If an item appears on more than one statement, place a check mark in every applicable column.

Item	Income Statement	Statement of Changes in Stockholders' Equity	Balance Sheet	Statement of Cash Flows
Notes payable				
Beginning common stock				
Service revenue				
Utility expense				
Cash from stock issue				
Operating activities				
For the period ended (date)				

continued

Item	Income Statement	Statement of Changes in Stockholders' Equity	[redacted]	Statement of Cash Flows
Net income				
Investing activities				
Net loss				
Ending cash balance				
Salary expense				
Consulting revenue				
Dividends				
Financing activities				
Ending common stock				
Rent expense				
As of (date)				
Land				
Beginning cash balance				

L.O. 3, 4, 5, 6, 8

eXcel

mhhe.com/edmonds2007

CHECK FIGURES

a. Net Income 2006: $23,000

b. Retained Earnings 2007: $40,500

Problem 1-30A *Preparing financial statements for two complete accounting cycles*

Keller Consulting experienced the following transactions for 2006, its first year of operations, and 2007. *Assume that all transactions involve the receipt or payment of cash.*

Transactions for 2006

1. Acquired $20,000 by issuing common stock.
2. Received $65,000 cash for providing services to customers.
3. Borrowed $25,000 cash from creditors.
4. Paid expenses amounting to $42,000.
5. Purchased land for $30,000 cash.

Transactions for 2007

Beginning account balances for 2007 are:

Cash	$38,000
Land	30,000
Notes Payable	25,000
Common Stock	20,000
Retained Earnings	23,000

1. Acquired an additional $24,000 from the issue of common stock.
2. Received $95,000 for providing services.
3. Paid $10,000 to creditors to reduce loan.
4. Paid expenses amounting to $71,500.
5. Paid a $6,000 dividend to the stockholders.
6. Determined the market value of the land to be $47,000.

Required

a. Write an accounting equation, and record the effects of each accounting event under the appropriate headings for each year. Record the amounts of revenue, expense, and dividends in the Retained Earnings column. Provide appropriate titles for these accounts in the last column of the table.

b. Prepare an income statement, statement of changes in stockholders' equity, year-end balance sheet, and statement of cash flows for each year.

c. Determine the amount of cash that is in the retained earnings account at the end of 2006 and 2007.

d. Compare the information provided by the income statement with the information provided by the statement of cash flows. Point out similarities and differences.

Problem 1-31A *Interrelationships among financial statements*

L.O. 3, 5, 8

CHECK FIGURES
a. Net Income: $16,000
b. Total Assets: $48,000

O'Shea Enterprises started the 2006 accounting period with $30,000 of assets (all cash), $18,000 of liabilities, and $4,000 of common stock. During the year, O'Shea earned cash revenues of $48,000, paid cash expenses of $32,000, and paid a cash dividend to stockholders of $2,000. O'Shea also acquired $10,000 of additional cash from the sale of common stock and paid $6,000 cash to reduce the liability owed to a bank.

Required

a. Prepare an income statement, statement of changes in stockholders' equity, period-end balance sheet, and statement of cash flows for the 2006 accounting period. (*Hint:* Determine the amount of beginning retained earnings before considering the effects of the current period events. Record all events under an accounting equation before preparing the statements.)

b. Determine the percentage of total assets that was provided by creditors, investors, and earnings.

Problem 1-32A *Classifying events as asset source, use, or exchange*

L.O. 4, 7

CHECK FIGURE
Event 2 Asset Exchange

The following unrelated events are typical of those experienced by business entities.

1. Acquire cash by issuing common stock.
2. Purchase land with cash.
3. Purchase equipment with cash.
4. Pay monthly rent on an office building.
5. Hire a new office manager.
6. Borrow cash from a bank.
7. Pay a cash dividend to stockholders.
8. Pay cash for operating expenses.
9. Pay an office manager's salary with cash.
10. Receive cash for services that have been performed.
11. Provide services for cash.
12. Acquire land by accepting a liability (financing the purchase).
13. Pay cash to purchase a new office building.
14. Discuss plans for a new office building with an architect.
15. Repay part of a bank loan.

Required

Identify each of the events as an asset source, use, or exchange transaction. If an event would not be recorded under generally accepted accounting principles, identify it as *not applicable* (NA). Also indicate for each event whether total assets would increase, decrease, or remain unchanged. Organize your answer according to the following table. The first event is shown in the table as an example.

Event No.	Type of Event	Effect on Total Assets
1	Asset source	Increase

Problem 1-33A *Recording the effect of events in a horizontal statements model*

L.O. 6, 9

Lighthouse Services experienced the following transactions during 2006.

1. Acquired cash by issuing common stock.
2. Received cash for performing services.
3. Paid cash expenses.
4. Borrowed cash from the local bank.
5. Purchased land for cash.
6. Paid cash to reduce the principal balance of the bank loan.

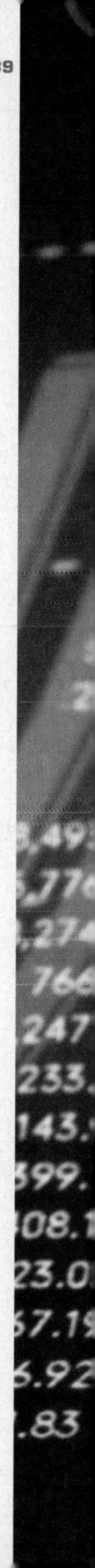

7. Paid a cash dividend to the stockholders.
8. Determined the market value of the land to be higher than its historical cost.

Required

Use a horizontal statements model to show how each event affects the balance sheet, income statement, and statement of cash flows. Indicate whether the event increases (I), decreases (D), or does not affect (NA) each element of the financial statements. Also, in the Cash Flows column, classify the cash flows as operating activities (OA), investing activities (IA), or financing activities (FA). The first transaction is shown as an example.

Event No.	Balance Sheet					Income Statement			Statement of Cash Flows	
	Cash +	Land =	N. Pay. +	Com. Stk. +	Ret. Earn.	Rev. −	Exp. =	Net Inc.		
1.	I +	NA =	NA +	I +	NA	NA −	NA =	NA	I	FA

L.O. 4, 6, 9

Problem 1-34A *Recording events in a horizontal statements model*

CHECK FIGURES
a. Net Income: $13,000
e. Net Cash Flow from Operating Activities: $13,000

Flick Company was started on January 1, 2007, and experienced the following events during its first year of operation.

1. Acquired $30,000 cash from the issue of common stock.
2. Borrowed $20,000 cash from State Bank.
3. Earned cash revenues of $48,000 for performing services.
4. Paid cash expenses of $35,000.
5. Paid a $4,000 cash dividend to the stockholders.
6. Acquired an additional $20,000 cash from the issue of common stock.
7. Paid $5,000 cash to reduce the principal balance of the bank note.
8. Paid $53,000 cash to purchase land.
9. Determined the market value of the land to be $60,000.

Required

a. Record the preceding transactions in the horizontal statements model. Also, in the Cash Flows column, classify the cash flows as operating activities (OA), investing activities (IA), or financing activities (FA). The first event is shown as an example.

Event No.	Balance Sheet					Income Statement			Statement of Cash Flows	
	Cash +	Land =	N. Pay. +	Com. Stk. +	Ret. Earn.	Rev. −	Exp. =	Net Inc.		
1.	30,000 +	NA =	NA +	30,000 +	NA	NA −	NA =	NA	30,000	FA

b. Determine the amount of total assets that Flick would report on the December 31, 2007, balance sheet.
c. Identify the sources of the assets that Flick would report on the December 31, 2007, balance sheet. Determine the amount of each of these sources.
d. Determine the net income that Flick would report on the 2007 income statement. Explain why dividends do not appear on the income statement.
e. Determine the net cash flows from operating activities, financing activities, and investing activities that Flick would report on the 2007 statement of cash flows.
f. Determine the percentage of assets that was provided by investors, creditors, and earnings.

L.O. 10

Problem 1-35A *Factors associated with white collar crime*

Clair Cubelic, a private accountant employed by a large corporation, holds the CMA professional designation. She is a trusted employee who is eager to help others whenever necessary. For example, Clair frequently orders merchandise when purchasing department personnel are overburdened. Clair's only problem is that she feels she is underpaid. Several men in her office make more money than she does and they are not even professionally certified accountants. Clair has significant debt that she acquired while she was a student and has trouble paying her monthly bills. A close friend of Clair's sells supplies to the company. When Clair complained to him about her pay situation, he joked that he could help her get even by sending the company less merchandise than was shown on the purchase orders. He laughed and suggested they could split the rewards of the rip-off between them. To his surprise she responded with a serious plan that would enable them to embezzle several thousand dollars per month from her company. She assured him that she could gain control of all phases of the purchasing system from ordering to payment. Unfortunately for Clair, what started as a joke ultimately ended with a jail sentence.

Required

Name the three factors that Donald Cressey found to be associated with white collar criminals. Identify these factors as they apply to Clair Cubelic's case.

EXERCISES—SERIES B

Exercise 1-1B *Identifying resources* L.O. 1

Resource owners provide three types of resources to conversion agents that transform the resources into products or services that satisfy consumer demands.

Required

Identify the three types of resources. Write a brief memo explaining how resource owners select the particular conversion agents to which they will provide resources.

Exercise 1-2B *Distributions in a business liquidation* L.O. 2

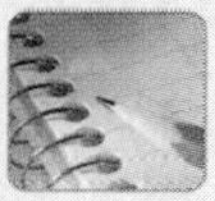

Assume that Clark Company acquires $800 cash from creditors and $900 cash from investors. The company then has operating losses of $600 cash and goes out of business.

Required

a. Explain the primary differences between investors and creditors.
b. What amount of cash will Clark's creditors receive?
c. What amount of cash will Clark's investors (stockholders) receive?

Exercise 1-3B *Identifying the reporting entities* L.O. 2

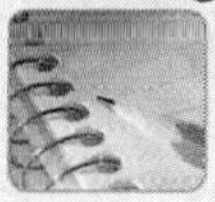

Wonda DeLeo helped organize a charity fund to help cover the medical expenses of a friend of hers who was seriously injured in a bicycle accident. The fund was named Gloria Novin Recovery Fund (GNRF). Wonda contributed $500 of her own money to the fund. The $500 was paid to WRCK, a local radio station that designed and played an advertising campaign to educate the public to the need for help. The campaign resulted in the collection of $12,000 cash. GNRF paid $10,000 to the Hillsboro Hospital to cover Gloria's outstanding hospital cost. The remaining $2,000 was contributed to the National Cyclist Fund.

Required

Identify the entities that were mentioned in the scenario and explain what happened to the cash accounts of each entity that you identify.

Exercise 1-4B *Financial statement names* L.O. 3

Accounting reports that are issued to the public normally contain four financial statements. The same statement may have more than one name.

Required

Provide two names that are commonly used for each statement. If a statement has only one name, indicate that this is the case.

Exercise 1-5B *Titles and accounts appearing on financial statements* L.O. 3

Annual reports normally include an income statement, statement of changes in stockholders' equity, balance sheet, and statement of cash flows.

Required

Identify the financial statements on which each of the following titles or accounts would appear. If a title or an account appears on more than one statement, list all statements that would include it.

a. Retained Earnings
b. Revenue
c. Common Stock
d. Financing Activities
e. Salaries Expense
f. Land
g. Ending Cash Balance
h. Beginning Cash Balance
i. Notes Payable
j. Dividends

L.O. 4

Exercise 1-6B *Components of the accounting equation*

Required

The following three requirements are independent of each other.

a. Jackson Camping Supplies has assets of $8,500 and equity of $3,200. What is the amount of liabilities? What is the amount of claims?
b. Betty's Snow Cones has liabilities of $2,400 and equity of $4,400. What is the amount of its assets?
c. Petrello Company has assets of $98,300 and liabilities of $56,200. What is the amount of its equity? What is the amount of creditor claims on assets?

L.O. 4

Exercise 1-7B *Effect of events on the accounting equation*

Olive Enterprises experienced the following events during 2007.

1. Acquired cash from the issue of common stock.
2. Paid cash to reduce the principal on a bank note.
3. Sold land for cash at an amount equal to its cost.
4. Provided services to clients for cash.
5. Paid utilities expense with cash.
6. Paid a cash dividend to the stockholders.

Required

Explain how each of the events would affect the accounting equation by writing the letter I for increase, the letter D for decrease, and NA for no effect under each of the components of the accounting equation. The first event is shown as an example.

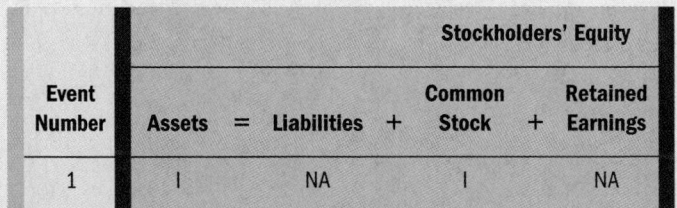

					Stockholders' Equity		
Event Number	Assets	=	Liabilities	+	Common Stock	+	Retained Earnings
1	I		NA		I		NA

L.O. 3

Exercise 1-8B *Effects of issuing stock*

Lambena Company was started in 2006 when it acquired $24,000 cash by issuing common stock. The cash acquisition was the only event that affected the business in 2006.

Required

Which financial statements would be affected by this event?

L.O. 3

Exercise 1-9B *Effects of borrowing*

Southern Pacific Company was started in 2007 when it borrowed $19,500 from National Bank.

Required

Which financial statements would be affected by this event?

Exercise 1-10B *Effects of revenue, expense, and dividend events* L.O. 3, 4, 5, 8

Kim Company was started on January 1, 2007. During 2007, the company completed three accounting events: (1) earned cash revenues of $12,500, (2) paid cash expenses of $8,600, and (3) paid a $1,000 cash dividend to the owner. These were the only events that affected the company during 2007.

Required

a. Write an accounting equation, and record the effects of each accounting event under the appropriate general ledger account headings.

b. Prepare an income statement for the 2007 accounting period and a balance sheet at the end of 2007 for Kim Company.

Exercise 1-11B *Classifying items for the statement of cash flows* L.O. 3

Required

Indicate whether each of the following would be classified on the statement of cash flows as operating activities (OA), investing activities (IA), financing activities (FA), or not applicable (NA).

a. Borrowed $8,000 cash from First State Bank.
b. Paid $5,000 cash for salary expense.
c. Signed a contract to provide services in the future.
d. Performed services for $25,000 cash.
e. Paid $9,000 cash to purchase land.
f. Paid $1,500 cash for utilities expense.
g. Sold land for $5,000 cash.
h. Paid $4,000 cash on the principal of a bank loan.
i. Paid a $2,000 cash dividend to the stockholders.
j. Received $30,000 cash from the issue of common stock.

Exercise 1-12B *Effect of transactions on general ledger accounts* L.O. 3, 4, 5, 6

At the beginning of 2008, Pete's Pest Control's accounting records had the following general ledger accounts and balances.

PETE'S PEST CONTROL
Accounting Equation

Event	Assets		=	Liabilities	+	Stockholders' Equity		Acct. Titles for Ret. Earn.
	Cash	Land		Notes Payable		Common Stock	Retained Earnings	
Balance 1/1/2008	15,000	20,000		15,000		7,000	13,000	

Pete's completed the following transactions during 2008.

1. Purchased additional land for $5,000 cash.
2. Acquired $25,000 cash from the issue of common stock.
3. Received $65,000 cash for providing services to customers.
4. Paid cash operating expenses of $42,000.
5. Borrowed $10,000 cash from the bank.
6. Paid a $2,500 cash dividend to the stockholders.
7. Determined the market value of the land to be $30,000 at the end of the year.

Required

a. Record the transactions in the appropriate general ledger accounts. Record the amounts of revenue, expense, and dividends in the Retained Earnings column. Provide the appropriate titles for these accounts in the last column of the table.

b. Determine the net cash flow from financing activities.
c. What is the balance in the Retained Earnings account as of January 1, 2009?

L.O. 3, 4, 5, 6, 8

Exercise 1-13B *Preparing financial statements*

J & A Inc. experienced the following events during 2007.

1. Acquired $55,000 cash from the issue of common stock.
2. Paid $15,000 cash to purchase land.
3. Borrowed $5,000 cash from First Bank.
4. Provided services for $21,000 cash.
5. Paid $1,500 cash for utilities expense.
6. Paid $11,000 cash for other operating expenses.
7. Paid a $2,000 cash dividend to the stockholders.
8. Determined the market value of the land purchased in Event 2 to be $20,000.

Required

a. The January 1, 2007, general ledger account balances are shown in the following accounting equation. Record the eight events in the appropriate general ledger accounts. Record the amounts of revenue, expense, and dividends in the Retained Earnings column. Provide the appropriate titles for these accounts in the last column of the table. The first event is shown as an example.

J & A INC.
Accounting Equation

Event	Assets		=	Liabilities	+	Stockholders' Equity		Acct. Titles for Ret. Earn.
	Cash	Land		Notes Payable		Common Stock	Retained Earnings	
Balance 1/1/2007	12,000	20,000		0		15,000	17,000	
1.	55,000					55,000		

b. Prepare an income statement, statement of changes in stockholders' equity, year-end balance sheet, and statement of cash flows for the 2007 accounting period.
c. Determine the percentage of assets that was provided by retained earnings. How much cash is in the Retained Earnings account?

L.O. 7

Exercise 1-14B *Classifying events as asset source, use, or exchange*

Hill Company experienced the following events during its first year of operations.

1. Acquired $8,000 cash from the issue of common stock.
2. Paid $3,500 cash for salary expense.
3. Borrowed $10,000 cash from New South Bank.
4. Paid $6,000 cash to purchase land.
5. Provided boarding services for $6,500 cash.
6. Acquired an additional $1,000 cash from the issue of common stock.
7. Paid $1,200 cash for utilities expense.
8. Paid a $1,500 cash dividend to the stockholders.
9. Provided additional services for $3,000 cash.
10. Purchased additional land for $2,500 cash.
11. Determined the market value of the land to be $12,000 at the end of the accounting period.

Required

Classify each event as an asset source, use, or exchange transaction.

Exercise 1-15B *Financial statement elements* L.O. 3

Western Company was organized by issuing $550 of common stock and by borrowing $250. During the accounting period, the company earned and retained $200. Also during the accounting period, the company purchased land for $950.

Required

a. What asset accounts would appear on the company's balance sheet? What are the balance sheet amounts in these accounts?

b. Determine the percentage of total assets that was provided by investors, creditors, and earnings.

c. How much cash is in the Retained Earnings account?

Exercise 1-16B *Historical cost versus market value* L.O. 6

ACCO Inc. purchased land in January 2004 at a cost of $230,000. The estimated market value of the land is $270,000 as of December 31, 2006.

Required

a. Name the December 31, 2006, financial statement(s) on which the land will be reported.

b. At what dollar amount will the land be reported in the financial statement(s)?

c. Name the key concept that will be used in determining the dollar amount that will be reported for land that is shown in the financial statement(s).

Exercise 1-17B *Relating accounting events to entities* L.O. 2, 7

Jackling Company sold land for $50,000 cash to Power Company in 2007.

Required

a. Was this event an asset source, use, or exchange transaction for Jackling Company?

b. Was this event an asset source, use, or exchange transaction for Power Company?

c. Was the cash flow an operating, investing, or financing activity on Jackling Company's 2007 statement of cash flows?

d. Was the cash flow an operating, investing, or financing activity on Power Company's 2007 statement of cash flows?

Exercise 1-18B *Missing information in the accounting equation* L.O. 4

Required

Calculate the missing amounts in the following table.

					Stockholders' Equity		
Company	**Assets**	=	**Liabilities**	+	**Common Stock**	+	**Retained Earnings**
A	$?		$25,000		$48,000		$25,000
B	50,000		?		15,000		30,000
C	75,000		20,000		?		42,000
D	125,000		45,000		75,000		?

Exercise 1-19B *Missing information in the accounting equation* L.O. 4

As of December 31, 2004, Stone Company had total assets of $132,000, retained earnings of $74,300, and common stock of $45,000. During 2005 Stone earned $42,000 of cash revenue, paid $21,500 for cash expenses, and paid a $600 cash dividend to the stockholders. Stone also paid $5,000 to reduce its debt during 2005.

Required

a. Determine the amount of liabilities at December 31, 2004.

b. Determine the amount of net income earned in 2005.

c. Determine the amount of total assets as of December 31, 2005.

d. Determine the amount of total liabilities as of December 31, 2005.

L.O. 3, 4

Exercise 1-20B ***Missing information for determining revenue***

Total stockholders' equity of Zullo Company increased by $46,500 between December 31, 2005, and December 31, 2006. During 2006 Zullo acquired $15,000 cash from the issue of common stock. The company paid a $5,000 cash dividend to the stockholders during 2006. Total expenses during 2006 amounted to $22,000.

Required

Determine the amount of revenue that Zullo reported on its 2006 income statement. (*Hint:* Remember that stock issues, net income, and dividends all change total stockholders' equity.)

L.O. 6, 9

Exercise 1-21B ***Effect of events on a horizontal financial statements model***

Lourens Auto Repair Inc. experienced the following events during 2007.

1. Purchased land for cash.
2. Issued common stock for cash.
3. Collected cash for providing auto repair services to customers.
4. Paid a cash dividend to the stockholders.
5. Paid cash for operating expenses.
6. Paid cash to reduce the principal balance on a liability.
7. Determined the year-end market value of the land to be higher than its historical cost.

Required

Use a horizontal statements model to show how each event affects the balance sheet, income statement, and statement of cash flows. Indicate whether the event increases (I), decreases (D), or does not affect (NA) each element of the financial statements. Also, in the Cash Flows column, classify the cash flows as operating activities (OA), investing activities (IA), or financing activities (FA). The first transaction is shown as an example.

Event No.	Balance Sheet									Income Statement					Statement of Cash Flows	
	Cash	+	Land	=	N. Pay.	+	Com. Stk.	+	Ret. Earn.	Rev.	−	Exp.	=	Net Inc.		
1.	D	+	I	=	NA	+	NA	+	NA	NA	−	NA	=	NA	D	IA

L.O. 3, 9

Exercise 1-22B ***Record events in the horizontal statements model***

Eaton Boat Repairs was started in 2006. During 2006, the company (1) acquired $9,000 cash from the issue of common stock, (2) earned cash revenue of $22,000, (3) paid cash expenses of $12,800, and (4) paid an $800 cash dividend to the stockholders.

Required

a. Record these four events in a horizontal statements model. Also, in the Cash Flows column, classify the cash flows as operating activities (OA), investing activities (IA), or financing activities (FA). The first event is shown as an example.

Event No.	Balance Sheet							Income Statement					Statement of Cash Flows	
	Cash	=	N. Pay.	+	Com. Stk.	+	Ret. Earn.	Rev.	−	Exp.	=	Net Inc.		
1.	9,000	=	NA	+	9,000	+	NA	NA	−	NA	=	NA	9,000	FA

b. Why is the net income different from the net increase in cash for this business?

L.O. 6, 9

Exercise 1-23B ***Effect of events on a horizontal statements model***

Joyce Higgins started Computer Software Services on January 1, 2006. The company experienced the following events during its first year of operation.

1. Acquired $20,000 cash by issuing common stock.

2. Paid $5,000 cash to purchase land.
3. Received $32,000 cash for providing computer consulting services to customers.
4. Paid $12,500 cash for salary expense.
5. Acquired $4,000 cash from the issue of additional common stock.
6. Borrowed $15,000 cash from the bank.
7. Purchased additional land for $15,000 cash.
8. Paid $14,000 cash for other operating expenses.
9. Paid a $2,500 cash dividend to the stockholders.
10. Determined the year-end market value of the land to be $18,000.

Required

a. Record these events in a horizontal statements model. Also, in the Cash Flows column, classify the cash flows as operating activities (OA), investing activities (IA), or financing activities (FA). The first event is shown as an example.

Event No.	Balance Sheet									Income Statement					Statement of Cash Flows
	Cash	+	Land	=	N. Pay.	+	Com. Stk.	+	Ret. Earn.	Rev.	−	Exp.	=	Net Inc.	
1.	20,000	+	NA	=	NA	+	20,000	+	NA	NA	−	NA	=	NA	20,000 FA

b. What is the net income earned in 2006?

c. What is the amount of total assets at the end of 2006?

d. What is the net cash flow from operating activities for 2006?

e. What is the net cash flow from investing activities for 2006?

f. What is the net cash flow from financing activities for 2006?

g. What is the cash balance at the end of 2006?

h. As of the end of the year 2006, what percentage of total assets was provided by creditors, investors, and earnings?

Exercise 1-24B *Types of transactions and the horizontal statements model*

L.O. 6, 7, 9

Computer Parts experienced the following events during its first year of operations, 2007.

1. Acquired cash by issuing common stock.
2. Purchased land with cash.
3. Borrowed cash from a bank.
4. Signed a contract to provide services in the future.
5. Paid a cash dividend to the stockholders.
6. Paid cash for operating expenses.
7. Determined that the market value of the land is higher than the historical cost.

Required

a. Indicate whether each event is an asset source, use, or exchange transaction.

b. Use a horizontal statements model to show how each event affects the balance sheet, income statement, and statement of cash flows. Indicate whether the event increases (I), decreases (D), or does not affect (NA) each element of the financial statements. Also, in the Cash Flows column, classify the cash flows as operating activities (OA), investing activities (IA), or financing activities (FA). The first transaction is shown as an example.

Event No.	Balance Sheet									Income Statement					Statement of Cash Flows
	Cash	+	Land	=	N. Pay.	+	Com. Stk.	+	Ret. Earn.	Rev.	−	Exp.	=	Net Inc.	
1.	I	+	NA	=	NA	+	I	+	NA	NA	−	NA	=	NA	I FA

L.O. 1

Exercise 1-25B *Private accounting career*

Gail Gilmore is a private accountant with a professional designation.

Required

a. Name two professional designations that Gail may hold.
b. Describe some duties that Gail may perform in her job.

L.O. 10

Exercise Exercise 1-26B *Factors associated with white collar crime*

Donald Cressey's research found three factors that were common among white collar criminals.

Required

Name the three factors identified by Cressey.

PROBLEMS—SERIES B

L.O. 1

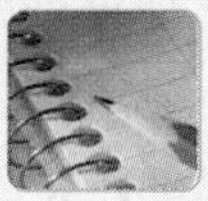

Problem 1-27B *Applying GAAP to financial reporting*

Kim Verhaeghe is a business consultant. She analyzed the business processes of one of her clients, Rector Companies, in November 2005. She prepared a report containing her recommendation for changes in some of the company's business practices. She presented Rector with the report in December 2005. Kim guarantees that her clients will save money by following her advice. She does not collect for the services she provides until the client is satisfied with the results of her work. In this case she received cash payment from Rector in February 2006.

Required

a. Define the acronym GAAP.
b. Assume that Kim's accountant tells her that GAAP permits Kim to recognize the revenue from Rector in either 2005 or 2006. What GAAP rule would justify reporting the same event in two different ways? Write a brief memo explaining the logic behind this rule.
c. If Kim were keeping records for managerial reporting purposes, would she be bound by GAAP rules? Write a brief memo to explain how GAAP applies to financial versus managerial reporting.

L.O. 2

Problem 1-28B *Accounting entities*

The following business scenarios are independent of one another.

1. Mary Poort purchased an automobile from Hayney Bros. Auto Sales for $9,000.
2. John Rodman loaned $15,000 to the business in which he is a stockholder.
3. First State Bank paid interest to Caleb Co. for a savings account that Caleb Co. has at First State Bank.
4. Parkside Restaurant paid the current utility bill of $128 to Gulf Utilities.
5. Gatemore Inc. borrowed $50,000 from City National Bank and used the funds to purchase land from Morgan Realty.
6. Steven Wong purchased $10,000 of common stock of International Sales Corporation from the corporation.
7. Dan Dow loaned $4,000 cash to his daughter.
8. Mega Service Co. earned $5,000 in cash revenue.
9. McCloud Co. paid $1,500 for salaries to each of its four employees.
10. Shim Inc. paid a cash dividend of $3,000 to its sole shareholder, Marcus Shim.

Required

a. For each scenario, create a list of all of the entities that are mentioned in the description.
b. Describe what happens to the cash account of each entity that you identified in Requirement *a.*

L.O. 3

Problem 1-29B *Relating titles and accounts to financial statements*

A random list of various financial statements components follows: (1) Retained Earnings account ending balance, (2) revenues, (3) Common Stock account beginning balance, (4) Common Stock account ending balance, (5) assets, (6) expenses, (7) operating activities, (8) dividends, (9) Retained Earnings beginning balance, (10) investing activities, (11) common stock issued during the period for cash, (12) liabilities, and (13) financing activities.

Required

Set up a table with the following headings. Identify the financial statements on which each of the preceding components appears by placing a check mark for the component in the appropriate column. If an item appears on more than one statement, place the check mark in every applicable column. The first component is shown as an example.

Component Number	Income Statement	Statement of Changes in Stockholders' Equity	[redacted]	Statement of Cash Flows
1		✓	✓	

Problem 1-30B *Preparing financial statements for two complete accounting cycles*

L.O. 3, 4, 5, 6, 8

Jim's Janitorial Services experienced the following transactions for 2007, the first year of operations, and 2008. *Assume that all transactions involve the receipt or payment of cash.*

Transactions for 2007

1. Acquired $60,000 by issuing common stock.
2. Received $100,000 for providing services to customers.
3. Borrowed $25,000 cash from creditors.
4. Paid expenses amounting to $70,000.
5. Purchased land for $40,000 cash.

Transactions for 2008

Beginning account balances for 2008 are:

Cash	$75,000
Land	40,000
Notes Payable	25,000
Common Stock	60,000
Retained Earnings	30,000

1. Acquired an additional $20,000 from the issue of common stock.
2. Received $120,000 for providing services in 2008.
3. Paid $10,000 to reduce notes payable.
4. Paid expenses amounting to $80,000.
5. Paid a $15,000 dividend to the stockholders.
6. Determined the market value of the land to be $45,000.

Required

a. Write an accounting equation, and record the effects of each accounting event under the appropriate headings for each year. Record the amounts of revenue, expense, and dividends in the Retained Earnings column. Provide appropriate titles for these accounts in the last column of the table.

b. Prepare an income statement, statement of changes in stockholders' equity, year-end balance sheet, and statement of cash flows for each year.

c. Determine the amount of cash that is in the Retained Earnings account at the end of 2007 and 2008.

d. Compare the information provided by the income statement with the information provided by the statement of cash flows. Point out similarities and differences.

Problem 1-31B *Interrelationships among financial statements*

L.O. 3, 5, 8

Best Electronics started the accounting period with $10,000 of assets, $2,200 of liabilities, and $4,550 of retained earnings. During the period, the Retained Earnings account increased by $3,565. The bookkeeper reported that Best paid cash expenses of $5,010 and paid a $625 cash dividend to stockholders,

but she could not find a record of the amount of cash that Best received for performing services. Best also paid $1,000 cash to reduce the liability owed to a bank, and the business acquired $2,000 of additional cash from the issue of common stock.

Required

a. Prepare an income statement, statement of changes in stockholders' equity, year-end balance sheet, and statement of cash flows for the accounting period. (*Hint:* Determine the beginning balance in the Common Stock account before considering the effects of the current period events. Record all events under an accounting equation before preparing the statements.)
b. Determine the percentage of total assets that was provided by creditors, investors, and earnings.

L.O. 4, 7

Problem 1-32B *Classifying events as asset source, use, or exchange*

The following unrelated events are typical of those experienced by business entities:

1. Acquire cash by issuing common stock.
2. Borrow cash from the local bank.
3. Pay office supplies expense.
4. Make plans to purchase office equipment.
5. Trade a used car for a computer with the same value.
6. Pay other operating expenses.
7. Agree to represent a client in an IRS audit and to receive payment when the audit is complete.
8. Receive cash from customers for services rendered.
9. Pay employee salaries with cash.
10. Pay back a bank loan with cash.
11. Pay rent to a bank with cash.
12. Transfer cash from a checking account to a money market account.
13. Sell land for cash at its original cost.
14. Pay a cash dividend to stockholders.

Required

Identify each of the events as an asset source, asset use, or asset exchange transaction. If an event would not be recorded under generally accepted accounting principles, identify it as *not applicable* (NA). Also indicate for each event whether total assets would increase, decrease, or remain unchanged. Organize your answer according to the following table. The first event is shown in the table as an example.

Event No.	Type of Event	Effect on Total Assets
1	Asset source	Increase

L.O. 6, 9

Problem 1-33B *Recording the effect of events in a horizontal statements model*

Belzio Company experienced the following transactions during 2006.

1. Paid a cash dividend to the stockholders.
2. Acquired cash by issuing additional common stock.
3. Signed a contract to perform services in the future.
4. Performed services for cash.
5. Paid cash expenses.
6. Sold land for cash at an amount equal to its cost.
7. Borrowed cash from a bank.
8. Determined the year-end market value of the land to be higher than its historical cost.

Required

Use a horizontal statements model to show how each event affects the balance sheet, income statement, and statement of cash flows. Indicate whether the event increases (I), decreases (D), or does not affect (NA) each element of the financial statements. Also, in the Cash Flows column, classify the cash flows as operating activities (OA), investing activities (IA), or financing activities (FA). The first transaction is shown as an example.

Event No.	Balance Sheet									Income Statement					Statement of Cash Flows
	Cash	+	Land	=	N. Pay.	+	Com. Stk.	+	Ret. Earn.	Rev.	−	Exp.	=	Net Inc.	
1.	D	+	NA	=	NA	+	NA	+	D	NA	−	NA	=	NA	D FA

Problem 1-34B *Recording events in a horizontal statements model*

L.O. 4, 6, 9

Foreman Company was started January 1, 2007, and experienced the following events during its first year of operation.

1. Acquired $32,000 cash from the issue of common stock.
2. Borrowed $20,000 cash from National Bank.
3. Earned cash revenues of $42,000 for performing services.
4. Paid cash expenses of $28,000.
5. Paid a $6,000 cash dividend to the stockholders.
6. Acquired $10,000 cash from the issue of additional common stock.
7. Paid $15,000 cash to reduce the principal balance of the bank note.
8. Paid $45,000 cash to purchase land.
9. Determined that the year-end market value of the land is $50,000.

Required

a. Record the preceding transactions in the horizontal statements model. Also, in the Cash Flows column, classify the cash flows as operating activities (OA), investing activities (IA), or financing activities (FA). The first event is shown as an example.

Event No.	Balance Sheet									Income Statement					Statement of Cash Flows
	Cash	+	Land	=	N. Pay.	+	Com. Stk.	+	Ret. Earn.	Rev.	−	Exp.	=	Net Inc.	
1.	32,000	+	NA	=	NA	+	32,000	+	D	NA	−	NA	=	NA	32,000 FA

b. Determine the amount of total assets that Foreman would report on the December 31, 2007, balance sheet.

c. Identify the asset source transactions and related amounts for 2007.

d. Determine the net income that Foreman would report on the 2007 income statement. Explain why dividends do not appear on the income statement.

e. Determine the net cash flows from operating activities, investing activities, and financing activities that Foreman would report on the 2007 statement of cash flows.

f. Determine the percentage of assets that was provided by investors, creditors, and earnings.

Problem 1-35B *Code of Professional Conduct*

L.O. 10

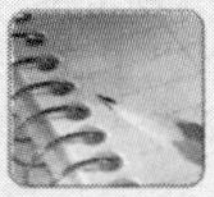

Pablo Gonzalez is a CPA. His sister, Maria, started a business two years ago. She has been successful enough that she wants to expand operations. She has contacted a local bank to inquire about obtaining a loan to finance the expansion. The bank loan officer was encouraging but insisted that she provide the bank with a set of financial statements that have been audited by a CPA. Maria has asked Pablo if he would agree to audit her financial statements in order to save her the expense of having to hire another accountant.

Required

Write a brief memo explaining how Pablo should respond to Maria's request. Your memo should contain relevant references to the AICPA's Code of Professional Conduct.

ANALYZE, THINK, COMMUNICATE

ATC 1-1 Business Applications Case *Understanding real world annual reports*

Required—Part 1

The Topps Company, Inc.

Use the **Topps Company's** annual report in Appendix B to answer the following questions.

a. What was Topps' net income for 2003?

b. Did Topps' net income increase or decrease from 2002 to 2003, and by how much?

c. What was Topps' accounting equation for 2003?

d. Which of the following had the largest percentage increase from 2002 to 2003: net sales, cost of sales, or selling, general, and administrative expenses? Show all computations.

Required—Part 2

Harley-Davidson, Inc.

Use the **Harley-Davidson's** annual report that came with this book to answer the following questions.

a. What was Harley-Davidson's net income for 2003?

b. Did Harley-Davidson's net income increase or decrease from 2002 to 2003, and by how much?

c. What was Harley-Davidson's accounting equation for 2003?

d. Which of the following had the largest percentage increase from 2002 to 2003: net revenue, cost of goods sold, or selling, general, and engineering expenses? Show all computations.

ATC 1-2 Group Assignment *Missing information*

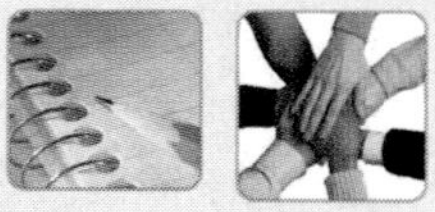

The following selected financial information is available for J&G Inc. Amounts are in millions of dollars.

Income Statements	2004	2003	2002	2001
Revenue	$ 661	$1,307	$ (a)	$ 894
Cost and Expenses	(a)	(a)	(1,859)	(769)
Income from Continuing Operations	(b)	174	71	(a)
Unusual Items	0	218	(b)	(b)
Net Income	$ 7	$ (b)	$ 47	$ 177

Balance Sheets	2004	2003	2002	2001
Assets				
Cash and Marketable Securities	$ 249	$1,247	$ (c)	$ 419
Other Assets	1,661	(c)	1,226	(c)
Total Assets	1,910	$2,904	$ (d)	$1,418
Liabilities	$ (c)	$ (d)	$ 907	$ (d)
Stockholders' Equity				
Common Stock	422	356	(e)	313
Retained Earnings	(d)	(e)	684	(e)
Total Stockholders' Equity	1,062	1,342	(f)	1,040
Total Liabilities and Stockholders' Equity	$1,910	$ (f)	$1,906	$1,418

Required

a. Divide the class into groups of four or five students each. Organize the groups into four sections. Assign Task 1 to the first section of groups, Task 2 to the second section, Task 3 to the third section, and Task 4 to the fourth section.

Group Tasks

(1) Fill in the missing information for 2001.

(2) Fill in the missing information for 2002.

(3) Fill in the missing information for 2003.

(4) Fill in the missing information for 2004.

b. Each section should select two representatives. One representative is to put the financial statements assigned to that section on the board, underlining the missing amounts. The second representative is to explain to the class how the missing amounts were determined.

c. Each section should list events that could have caused the unusual item category on the income statement.

ATC 1-3 Real-World Case *Classifying cash flow activities at five companies*

The following cash transactions occurred in five real world companies during 2004:

1. **FedEx Corp.**, which is the holding company of **Federal Express**, purchased **Kinko's, Inc.**, on February 12, 2004, for $2.4 billion.
2. **Google Inc.** issued 14.1 million shares of its stock on August 18, 2004, for $85 per share. On that same day, a few major shareholders of Google, including its founders, sold 5.5 million shares of its stock at the same price.
3. **Payless ShoeSource, Inc.**, had cash sales of $2.8 billion during its fiscal year ending on January 31, 2004.
4. **Red Hat, Inc.**, the leading provider of the open-source operating system Linux, issued $600 million of "convertible debentures" in January 2004. Convertible debentures are a form of long-term debt that is explained in more detail in Chapter 10.
5. **Sears, Roebuck and Company** completed the sale of its domestic Credit and Financial Products business to **Citicorp** on November 3, 2004, for $32 billion, $22 billion of which was received in cash.

Required

Determine if each of the above transactions should be classified as an *operating, investing,* or *financing* activity. Also, identify the amount of each cash flow and whether it was an *inflow* or an *outflow.*

ATC 1-4 Business Applications Case *Use of real-world numbers for forecasting*

The following information was drawn from the annual report of **Machine Import Company (MIC)**:

	For the Years	
	2001	**2002**
Income Statements		
Revenue	$600,000	$690,000
Operating Expenses	480,000	552,000
Income from Continuing Operations	120,000	138,000
Extraordinary Item—Lottery Win		62,000
Net Income	$120,000	$200,000
Balance Sheets		
Assets	$880,000	$880,000
Liabilities	$200,000	$ 0
Stockholders' Equity		
Common Stock	380,000	380,000
Retained Earnings	300,000	500,000
Total Liabilities and Stockholders' Equity	$880,000	$880,000

Required

a. Compute the percentage of growth in net income from 2001 to 2002. Can stockholders expect a similar increase between 2002 and 2003?

b. Assuming that MIC collected $200,000 cash from earnings (net income), explain how this money was spent in 2002.

c. Assuming that MIC experiences the same percentage of growth from 2002 to 2003 as it did from 2001 to 2002, determine the amount of income from continuing operations that the owners can expect to see on the 2003 income statement.

d. During 2003, MIC experienced a $40,000 loss due to storm damage (note that this would be shown as an extraordinary loss on the income statement). Liabilities and common stock were unchanged from 2002 to 2003. Use the information that you computed in Part *c* plus the additional information provided in the previous two sentences to prepare an income statement for 2003 and balance sheet as of December 31, 2003.

ATC 1-5 Writing Assignment *Elements of financial statements defined*

Bob and his sister Marsha both attend the state university. As a reward for their successful completion of the past year (Bob had a 3.2 GPA in business, and Marsha had a 3.7 GPA in art), their father gave each of them 100 shares of **The Walt Disney Company** stock. They have just received their first annual report. Marsha does not understand what the information means and has asked Bob to explain it to her. Bob is currently taking an accounting course, and she knows he will understand the financial statements.

Required

Assume that you are Bob. Write Marsha a memo explaining the following financial statement items to her. In your explanation, describe each of the two financial statements and explain the financial information each contains. Also define each of the elements listed for each financial statement and explain what it means.

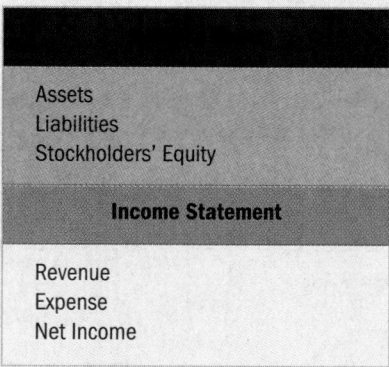

[redacted]
Assets Liabilities Stockholders' Equity
Income Statement
Revenue Expense Net Income

ATC 1-6 Ethical Dilemma *Loyalty versus the bottom line*

Assume that Jones has been working for you for five years. He has had an excellent work history and has received generous pay raises in response. The raises have been so generous that Jones is quite overpaid for the job he is required to perform. Unfortunately, he is not qualified to take on other, more responsible jobs available within the company. A recent job applicant is willing to accept a salary $5,000 per year less than the amount currently being paid to Jones. The applicant is well qualified to take over Jones's duties and has a very positive attitude. The following financial statements were reported by your company at the close of its most recent accounting period.

Financial Statements	
Income Statement	
Revenue	$ 57,000
Expense	(45,000)
Net Income	$12,000

continued

Statement of Changes in Stockholders' Equity		
Beginning Common Stock	$20,000	
Plus: Stock Issued	5,000	
Ending Common Stock		$25,000
Beginning Retained Earnings	50,000	
Net Income	12,000	
Dividends	(2,000)	
Ending Retained Earnings		60,000
Total Stockholders' Equity		$85,000

[redacted]	
Assets	
Cash	$85,000
Stockholders' Equity	
Common Stock	$25,000
Retained Earnings	60,000
Total Stockholders' Equity	$85,000

Statement of Cash Flows		
Operating Activities		
Inflow from Customers	$57,000	
Outflow for Expenses	(45,000)	
Net Inflow from Operating Activities		$12,000
Investing Activities		0
Financing Activities		
Inflow from Stock Issue	5,000	
Outflow for Dividends	(2,000)	
Net Inflow from Financing Activities		3,000
Net Change in Cash		15,000
Plus: Beginning Cash Balance		70,000
Ending Cash Balance		$85,000

Required

a. Reconstruct the financial statements, assuming that Jones was replaced at the beginning of the most recent accounting period. Both Jones and his replacement are paid in cash. No other changes are to be considered.

b. Assume that you are a CPA. Would any of the principles of the AICPA Code of Professional Conduct prevent you from replacing Jones? Explain your answer.

ATC 1-7 Research Assignment *Finding real-world accounting information*

The Curious Accountant story at the beginning of this chapter referred to **McDonald's Corporation** and discussed who its stakeholders are. This chapter introduced the basic four financial statements companies use annually to keep their stakeholders informed of their accomplishments and financial situation. Complete the requirements below using the 2003 financial statements available on the McDonald's website. Obtain the statements on the Internet by following the steps below. (The formatting of the company's website may have changed since these instructions were written.)

1. Go to www.mcdonalds.com.
2. Click on the "Corporate" link at the bottom of the page. (Most companies have a link titled "investor relations" that leads to their financial statements; McDonald's uses "corporate" instead.)
3. Click on the "INVESTORS" link at the top of the page.

4. Click on *"Publications"* and then on *"Annual Report Archives."*
5. Click on *"McDonald's 2003 Annual Report"* and then on *"2003 Financial Report."*
6. Go to the company's financial statements on pages 17 through 20 of the annual report.

Required

a. What was the company's net income in 2003, 2002, and 2001?
b. What amount of total assets did the company have at the end of 2003?
c. How much retained earnings did the company have at the end of 2003?
d. For 2003, what was the company's cash flow from operating activities, cash flow from investing activities, and cash flow from financing activities?

COMPREHENSIVE PROBLEM

The following information is available for Pacilio Security Services Inc. for 2001, its first year of operations. Pacilio provides security services for local sporting events.

The following summary transactions occurred during 2001.

1. Acquired $6,000 from the issue of common stock.
2. Borrowed $5,000 from the Small Business Government Agency. The loan is interest free.
3. Performed security services at local sporting events during the year for $9,000 cash.
4. Paid salaries expense of $3,000 for the year.
5. Purchased land for $4,000.
6. Paid other operating expenses of $2,000 for the year.
7. Paid a cash dividend to the shareholders of $2,500.
8. The market value of the land was determined to be $4,500 at December 31, 2001.

Required

a. Record the above transactions in an accounting equation. Provide the appropriate account titles for the amounts shown in the Retained Earnings column.
b. Prepare an income statement, statement of changes in stockholders' equity, balance sheet, and statement of cash flows for 2001.

CHAPTER 2

Understanding the Accounting Cycle

LEARNING OBJECTIVES

After you have mastered the material in this chapter, you will be able to:

1. **Record basic accrual and deferral events in a horizontal financial statements model.**
2. **Organize general ledger accounts under an accounting equation.**
3. **Prepare financial statements based on accrual accounting.**
4. **Describe the closing process, the accounting cycle, and the matching concept.**
5. **Prepare a vertical financial statements model.**
6. **Explain how business events affect financial statements over multiple accounting cycles.**
7. **Explain how to use the price-earnings ratio and growth percentage analysis to assess the market value of common stock.**
8. **Classify accounting events into one of four categories:**
   a. **asset source transactions.**
   b. **asset use transactions.**
   c. **asset exchange transactions.**
   d. **claims exchange transactions.**

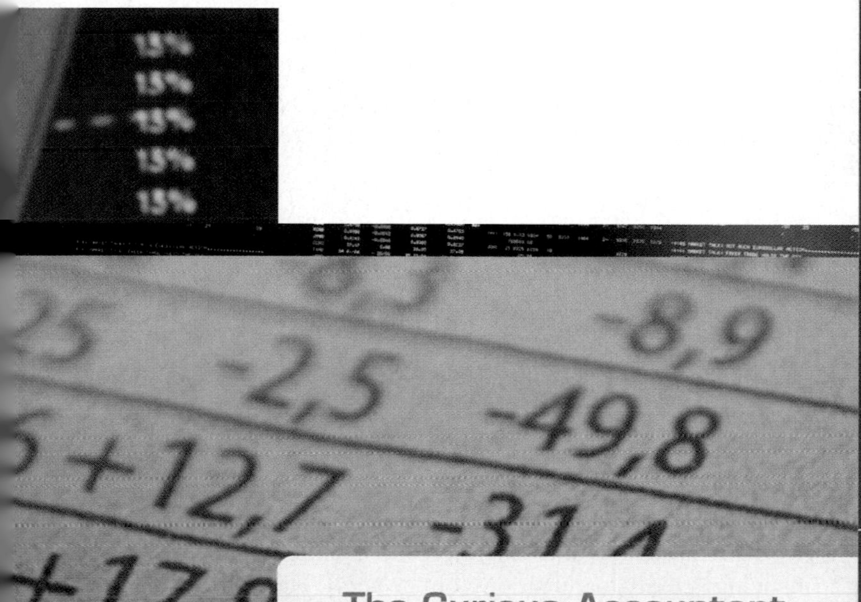

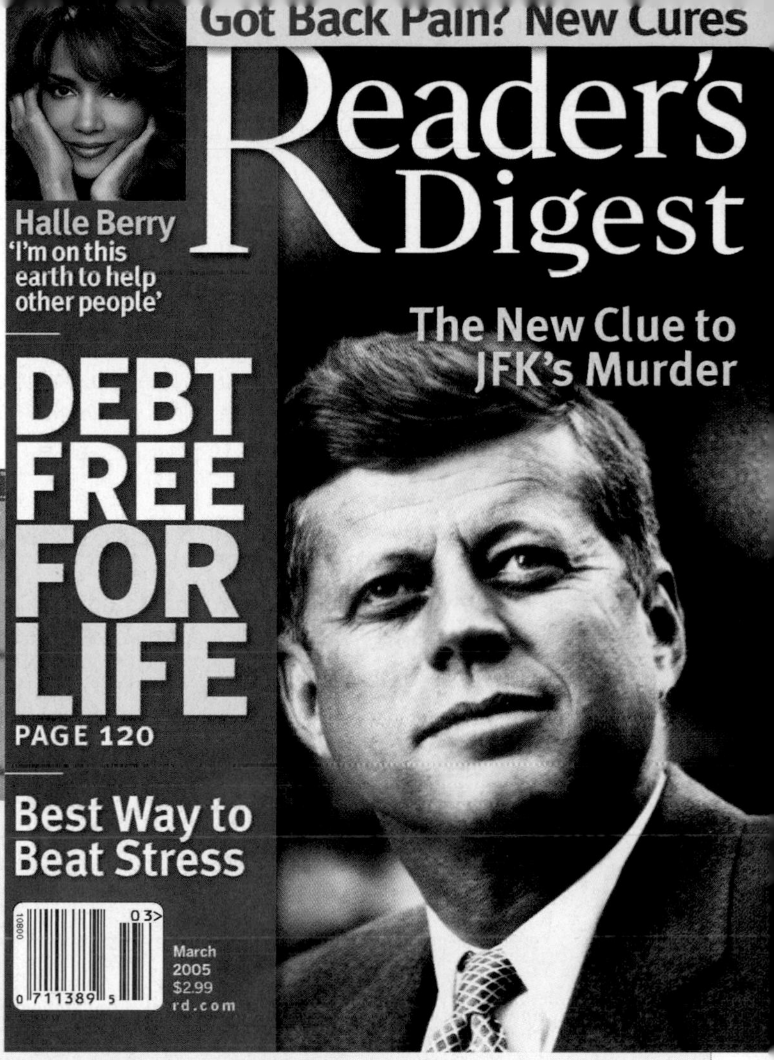

The Curious Accountant

If a person wishes to subscribe to *Reader's Digest* for one year (12 issues), the subscriber must pay for the magazines before they are actually published. Suppose Paige Long sent $14 to the Reader's Digest Association in September 2007 for a one-year subscription; she will receive her first issue in October.

How should Reader's Digest account for the receipt of this cash? How would this event be reported on Reader's Digest's December 31, 2007, financial statements? (Answers on page 74.)

CHAPTER OPENING

Users of financial statements must distinguish between the terms recognition *and* realization. **Recognition** *means formally* reporting *an economic item or event in the financial statements.* **Realization** *refers to collecting money, generally from the sale of products or services. Companies may recognize (report) revenue in the income statement in a different accounting period from the period in which they collect the cash related to the revenue. Furthermore, companies frequently make cash payments for expenses in accounting periods other than the periods in which the expenses are recognized in the income statement.*

To illustrate, assume Johnson Company provides services to customers in 2005 but collects cash for those services in 2006. In this case, realization occurs in 2006. When should Johnson recognize the services revenue?

Users of cash basis *accounting recognize (report) revenues and expenses in the period in which cash is collected or paid. Under cash basis accounting Johnson would recognize the revenue in 2006 when it collects the cash. In contrast, users of* **accrual accounting** *recognize revenues and expenses in the period in which they occur, regardless of when cash is collected or paid. Under accrual accounting Johnson would recognize the revenue in 2005 (the period in which it performed the services) even though it does not collect (realize) the cash until 2006.*

Accrual accounting is required by generally accepted accounting principles. Virtually all major companies operating in the United States use it. Its two distinguishing features are called accruals *and* deferrals.

- *The term* **accrual** *describes an earnings event that is recognized* **before** *cash is exchanged. Johnson's recognition of revenue in 2005 related to cash realized in 2006 is an example of an accrual.*
- *The term* **deferral** *describes an earnings event that is recognized* **after** *cash has been exchanged. Suppose Johnson pays cash in 2005 to purchase office supplies it uses in 2006. In this case the cash payment occurs in 2005 although supplies expense is recognized in 2006. This example is a deferral.* ■

Accrual Accounting

LO 1

Record basic accrual and deferral events in a horizontal financial statements model.

Topic Tackler PLUS

2-1

The next section of the text describes seven events experienced by Cato Consultants, a training services company that uses accrual accounting.

Event 1 **Cato Consultants was started on January 1, 2008, when it acquired $5,000 cash by issuing common stock.**

The issue of stock for cash is an **asset source transaction.** It increases the company's assets (cash) and its equity (common stock). The transaction does not affect the income statement. The cash inflow is classified as a financing activity (acquisition from owners). These effects are shown in the following financial statements model:

Assets	=	Liab.	+	Stockholders' Equity								
Cash	=			Com. Stk.	+	Ret. Earn.	Rev.	−	Exp.	=	Net Inc.	Cash Flow
5,000	=	NA	+	5,000	+	NA	NA	−	NA	=	NA	5,000 FA

Accounting for Accounts Receivable

Event 2 **During 2008 Cato Consultants provided $84,000 of consulting services to its clients. The business has completed the work and sent bills to the clients, but not yet collected any cash. This type of transaction is frequently described as providing services *on account.***

Accrual accounting requires companies to recognize revenue in the period in which the work is done regardless of when cash is collected. In this case, revenue is recognized in 2008 even though cash has not been realized (collected). Recall that revenue represents the economic benefit that results in an increase in assets from providing goods and services to customers. The specific asset that increases is called **Accounts Receivable.** The balance in Accounts Receivable represents the amount of cash the company expects to collect in the future. Since the revenue recognition causes assets (accounts receivable) to increase, it is classified as an asset source transaction. Its effect on the financial statements follows:

Assets			=	Liab.	+	Stockholders' Equity								
Cash	+	Accts. Rec.	=			Com. Stk.	+	Ret. Earn.	Rev.	−	Exp.	=	Net Inc.	Cash Flow
NA	+	84,000	=	NA	+	NA	+	84,000	84,000	−	NA	=	84,000	NA

Notice that the event affects the income statement but not the statement of cash flows. The statement of cash flows will be affected in the future when cash is collected.

Event 3 **Cato collected $60,000 cash from customers in partial settlement of its accounts receivable.**

The collection of an account receivable is an **asset exchange transaction.** One asset account (Cash) increases and another asset account (Accounts Receivable) decreases. The amount of total assets is unchanged. The effect of the $60,000 collection of receivables on the financial statements is as follows:

Assets			=	Liab.	+	Stockholders' Equity								
Cash	+	Accts. Rec.	=			Com. Stk.	+	Ret. Earn.	Rev.	−	Exp.	=	Net Inc.	Cash Flow
60,000	+	(60,000)	=	NA	+	NA	+	NA	NA	−	NA	=	NA	60,000 OA

Notice that collecting the cash did not affect the income statement. The revenue was recognized when the work was done (see Event 2). Revenue would be double counted if it were recognized again when the cash is collected. The statement of cash flows reflects a cash inflow from operating activities.

Other Events

Event 4 **Cato paid the instructor $10,000 for teaching training courses (salary expense).**

Cash payment for salary expense is an **asset use transaction.** Both the asset account Cash and the equity account Retained Earnings decrease by $10,000. Recognizing the expense decreases net income on the income statement. Since Cato paid cash for the expense, the statement of cash flows reflects a cash outflow from operating activities. These effects on the financial statements follow:

Assets			=	Liab.	+	Stockholders' Equity								
Cash	+	Accts. Rec.	=			Com. Stk.	+	Ret. Earn.	Rev.	−	Exp.	=	Net Inc.	Cash Flow
(10,000)	+	NA	=	NA	+	NA	+	(10,000)	NA	−	10,000	=	(10,000)	(10,000) OA

Event 5 **Cato paid $2,000 cash for advertising costs. The advertisements appeared in 2008.**

Cash payments for advertising expenses are asset use transactions. Both the asset account Cash and the equity account Retained Earnings decrease by $2,000. Recognizing the expense decreases net income on the income statement. Since the expense was paid with cash, the statement of cash flows reflects a cash outflow from operating activities. These effects on the financial statements follow:

Assets			=	Liab.	+	Stockholders' Equity								
Cash	+	Accts. Rec.	=			Com. Stk.	+	Ret. Earn.	Rev.	−	Exp.	=	Net Inc.	Cash Flow
(2,000)	+	NA	=	NA	+	NA	+	(2,000)	NA	−	2,000	=	(2,000)	(2,000) OA

Event 6 **Cato signed contracts for $42,000 of consulting services to be performed in 2009.**

The $42,000 for consulting services to be performed in 2009 is not recognized in the 2008 financial statements. Revenue is recognized for work actually completed, *not* work expected to be completed. This event does not affect any of the financial statements.

Assets			=	Liab.	+	Stockholders' Equity								
Cash	+	Accts. Rec.	=			Com. Stk.	+	Ret. Earn.	Rev.	−	Exp.	=	Net Inc.	Cash Flow
NA	+	NA	=	NA	+	NA	+	NA	NA	−	NA	=	NA	NA

Accounting for Accrued Salary Expense (Adjusting Entry)

It is impractical to record many business events as they occur. For example, Cato incurs salary expense continually as the instructor teaches courses. Imagine the impossibility of trying to record salary expense second by second! Companies normally record transactions when it is most convenient. The most convenient time to record many expenses is when they are paid. Often, however, a single business transaction pertains to more than one accounting period. To provide accurate financial reports in such cases, companies may need to recognize some expenses before paying cash for them. Expenses that are recognized before cash is paid are called **accrued expenses.** The accounting for Event 7 illustrates the effect of recognizing accrued salary expense.

Event 7 **At the end of 2008 Cato recorded accrued salary expense of $6,000 (the salary expense is for courses the instructor taught in 2008 that Cato will pay him for in 2009).**

Accrual accounting requires that companies recognize expenses in the period in which they are incurred regardless of when cash is paid. Cato must recognize all salary expense in the period in which the instructor worked (2008) even though Cato will not pay the instructor again until 2009. Cato must also recognize the obligation (liability) it has to pay the instructor. To accurately report all 2008 salary expense and year-end obligations, Cato must record the unpaid salary expense and salary liability before preparing its financial statements. The entry to recognize the accrued salary expense is called an **adjusting entry.** Like all adjusting entries, it is only to update the accounting records; it does not affect cash.

This adjusting entry decreases stockholders' equity (retained earnings) and increases a liability account called **Salaries Payable.** The balance in the Salaries Payable account represents the amount of cash the company is obligated to pay the instructor in the future. The effect of the expense recognition on the financial statements follows:

Assets			=	Liab.	+	Stockholders' Equity								
Cash	+	Accts. Rec.	=	Sal. Pay.	+	Com. Stk.	+	Ret. Earn.	Rev.	−	Exp.	=	Net Inc.	Cash Flow
NA	+	NA	=	6,000	+	NA	+	(6,000)	NA	−	6,000	=	(6,000)	NA

This event is a **claims exchange transaction.** The claims of creditors (liabilities) increase and the claims of stockholders (retained earnings) decrease. Total claims remain unchanged. The salary expense is reported on the income statement. The statement of cash flows is not affected.

Be careful not to confuse liabilities with expenses. Although liabilities may increase when a company recognizes expenses, liabilities are not expenses. Liabilities are obligations. They can arise from acquiring assets as well as recognizing expenses. For example, when a business borrows money from a bank, it recognizes an increase in assets (cash) and liabilities (notes payable). The borrowing transaction does not affect expenses.

CHECK YOURSELF 2.1

During 2006, Anwar Company earned $345,000 of revenue on account and collected $320,000 cash from accounts receivable. Anwar paid cash expenses of $300,000 and cash dividends of $12,000. Determine the amount of net income Anwar should report on the 2006 income statement and the amount of cash flow from operating activities Anwar should report on the 2006 statement of cash flows.

Answer

Net income is $45,000 ($345,000 revenue − $300,000 expenses). The cash flow from operating activities is $20,000, the amount of revenue collected in cash from customers (accounts receivable) minus the cash paid for expenses ($320,000 − $300,000). Dividend payments are classified as financing activities and do not affect the determination of either net income or cash flow from operating activities.

Summary of Events

The previous section of this chapter described seven events Cato Consultants experienced during the 2008 accounting period. These events are summarized below for your convenience.

Event 1 Cato Consultants acquired $5,000 cash by issuing common stock.
Event 2 Cato provided $84,000 of consulting services on account.
Event 3 Cato collected $60,000 cash from customers in partial settlement of its accounts receivable.
Event 4 Cato paid $10,000 cash for salary expense.
Event 5 Cato paid $2,000 cash for 2008 advertising costs.
Event 6 Cato signed contracts for $42,000 of consulting services to be performed in 2009.
Event 7 Cato recognized $6,000 of accrued salary expense.

The General Ledger

LO 2

Organize general ledger accounts under an accounting equation.

Exhibit 2.1 shows the 2008 transaction data recorded in general ledger accounts. The information in these accounts is used to prepare the financial statements. The revenue and expense items appear in the Retained Earnings column with their account titles immediately to the right of the dollar amounts. The amounts are color coded to help you trace the data to the financial statements. Data in red appear on the balance sheet, data in blue on the income statement, and data in green on the statement of cash flows. Before reading further, trace each transaction in the summary of events into Exhibit 2.1.

Vertical Statements Model

LO 3

Prepare financial statements based on accrual accounting.

The financial statements for Cato Consultants' 2008 accounting period are represented in a vertical statements model in Exhibit 2.2. A vertical statements model arranges a set of financial statement information vertically on a single page. Like horizontal statements models, vertical statements models are learning tools. They illustrate interrelationships among financial statements. The models do not, however, portray the full, formal presentation formats companies use in published financial statements. For example, statements models may use summarized formats with abbreviated titles and dates. As you read the following explanations of each financial statement, trace the color coded financial data from Exhibit 2.1 to Exhibit 2.2.

Income Statement

The income statement reflects accrual accounting. Consulting revenue represents the price Cato charged for all the services it performed in 2008, even though Cato had not by the end

EXHIBIT 2.1 Transaction Data for 2008 Recorded in General Ledger Accounts

	Assets			=	Liabilities	+	Stockholders' Equity			
Event No.	**Cash**	**+**	**Accounts Receivable**	**=**	**Salaries Payable**	**+**	**Common Stock**	**+**	**Retained Earnings**	**Other Account Titles**
Beg. bal.	0		0		0		0		0	
1	5,000						5,000			
2			84,000						84,000	Consulting Revenue
3	60,000		(60,000)							
4	(10,000)								(10,000)	Salary Expense
5	(2,000)								(2,000)	Advertising Expense
6										
7					6,000				(6,000)	Salary Expense
End bal.	53,000	+	24,000	=	6,000	+	5,000	+	66,000	

EXHIBIT 2.2 Vertical Statements Model

CATO CONSULTANTS
Financial Statements*
Income Statement
For the Year Ended December 31, 2008

Consulting Revenue		$84,000
Salary Expense		(16,000)
Advertising Expense		(2,000)
Net Income		$66,000

Statement of Changes in Stockholders' Equity
For the Year Ended December 31, 2008

Beginning Common Stock	$ 0	
Plus: Common Stock Issued	5,000	
Ending Common Stock		$ 5,000
Beginning Retained Earnings	0	
Plus: Net Income	66,000	
Less: Dividends	0	
Ending Retained Earnings		66,000
Total Stockholders' Equity		$71,000

Balance Sheet
As of December 31, 2008

Assets		
Cash	$53,000	
Accounts Receivable	24,000	
Total Assets		$77,000
Liabilities		
Salaries Payable		$ 6,000
Stockholders' Equity		
Common Stock	$ 5,000	
Retained Earnings	66,000	
Total Stockholders' Equity		71,000
Total Liabilities and Stockholders' Equity		$77,000

Statement of Cash Flows
For the Year Ended December 31, 2008

Cash Flows from Operating Activities		
Cash Receipts from Customers	$60,000	
Cash Payments for Salary Expense	(10,000)	
Cash Payments for Advertising Expenses	(2,000)	
Net Cash Flow from Operating Activities		$48,000
Cash Flow from Investing Activities		0
Cash Flows from Financing Activities		
Cash Receipt from Issuing Common Stock	5,000	
Net Cash Flow from Financing Activities		5,000
Net Change in Cash		53,000
Plus: Beginning Cash Balance		0
Ending Cash Balance		$53,000

*In real-world annual reports, financial statements are normally presented separately with appropriate descriptions of the date to indicate whether the statement applies to the entire accounting period or a specific point in time.

of the year received cash for some of the services performed. Expenses include all costs incurred to produce revenue, whether paid for by year-end or not. We can now expand the definition of expenses introduced in Chapter 1. Expenses were previously defined as assets consumed in the process of generating revenue. Cato's adjusting entry to recognize accrued salaries expense did not reflect consuming assets. Instead of a decrease in assets, Cato recorded an increase in liabilities (salaries payable). An **expense** can therefore be more precisely defined as *a decrease in assets or an increase in liabilities resulting from operating activities undertaken to generate revenue.*

Statement of Changes in Stockholders' Equity

The statement of changes in stockholders' equity reports the effects on equity of issuing common stock, earning net income, and paying dividends to stockholders. It identifies how an entity's equity increased and decreased during the period as a result of transactions with stockholders and operating the business. In the Cato case, the statement shows that equity increased when the business acquired $5,000 cash by issuing common stock. The statement also reports that equity increased by $66,000 from earning income and that none of the $66,000 of net earnings was distributed to owners (no dividends were paid). Equity at the end of the year is $71,000 ($5,000 + $66,000).

Balance Sheet

The balance sheet discloses an entity's assets, liabilities, and stockholders' equity at a particular point in time. Cato Consultants had two assets at the end of the 2008 accounting period: cash of $53,000 and accounts receivable of $24,000. These assets are listed on the balance sheet in order of liquidity. Of the $77,000 in total assets, creditors have a $6,000 claim, leaving stockholders with a $71,000 claim.

Statement of Cash Flows

The statement of cash flows explains the change in cash from the beginning to the end of the accounting period. It can be prepared by analyzing the Cash account. Since Cato Consultants was established in 2008, its beginning cash balance was zero. By the end of the year, the cash balance was $53,000. The statement of cash flows explains this increase. The Cash account increased because Cato collected $60,000 from customers and decreased because Cato paid $12,000 for expenses. As a result, Cato's net cash inflow from operating activities was $48,000. Also, the business acquired $5,000 cash through the financing activity of issuing common stock, for a cumulative cash increase of $53,000 ($48,000 + $5,000) during 2008.

Comparing Cash Flow from Operating Activities with Net Income

The amount of net income measured using accrual accounting differs from the amount of cash flow from operating activities. For Cato Consulting in 2008, the differences are summarized below:

	Accrual Accounting	Cash Flow
Consulting revenue	$84,000	$60,000
Salary expense	(16,000)	(10,000)
Advertising expense	(2,000)	(2,000)
Net income	$66,000	$48,000

Many students begin their first accounting class with the misconception that revenue and expense items are cash equivalents. The Cato illustration demonstrates that a company may recognize a revenue or expense without a corresponding cash collection or payment in the same accounting period.

The Closing Process

LO 4

Describe the closing process, the accounting cycle, and the matching concept.

Much of the information disclosed in a company's financial statements summarizes business activity for a specified time period. The end of one time period marks the beginning of the next time period. Each time period, which typically lasts one year, represents an **accounting cycle.** Accounting cycles follow one after the other from the time a business is formed until it is dissolved.

The amounts in balance sheet accounts (assets, liabilities, common stock, and retained earnings) at the end of an accounting cycle carry forward to the beginning of the next accounting cycle. For example, a company will begin 2009 with the same amount of cash it had at the end of 2008. Because their balances carry forward, balance sheet accounts are sometimes called **permanent accounts.**

In contrast, revenue, expense, and dividend accounts are **temporary accounts,** used to capture accounting information for a single accounting cycle. After the financial statements have been prepared at the end of the accounting cycle, the amounts in the temporary accounts are moved to Retained Earnings, a permanent account. Accountants call the process of moving the revenue, expense, and dividend account balances to retained earnings **closing the books,** or simply **closing.** After closing, every temporary account has a zero balance and the retained earnings account is updated to reflect the earning activities and dividend distributions that took place during the accounting period.

Exhibit 2.3 shows the general ledger accounts for Cato Consultants after the revenue and expense accounts have been closed to retained earnings. The closing entry labeled Cl.1 transfers the balance in the Consulting Revenue account to the Retained Earnings account.

EXHIBIT 2.3

General Ledger Accounts for Cato Consultants

Assets = Liabilities + Stockholders' Equity

Assets

Cash	
(1)	5,000
(3)	60,000
(4)	(10,000)
(5)	(2,000)
Bal.	53,000

Accounts Receivable	
(2)	84,000
(3)	(60,000)
Bal.	24,000

Liabilities

Salaries Payable	
(7)	6,000
Bal.	6,000

Stockholders' Equity

Common Stock	
(1)	5,000

Retained Earnings	
Cl.1	84,000
Cl.2	(16,000)
Cl.3	(2,000)
Bal.	66,000

Consulting Revenue	
(2)	84,000
Cl.1	(84,000)
Bal.	0

Salary Expense	
(4)	(10,000)
(7)	(6,000)
Cl.2	16,000
Bal.	0

Advertising Expense	
(5)	(2,000)
Cl.3	2,000
Bal.	0

Closing entries Cl.2 and Cl.3 transfer the balances in the expense accounts to retained earnings.

Steps in an Accounting Cycle

A complete accounting cycle, which is represented graphically in Exhibit 2.4, involves several steps. The four steps identified to this point are (1) recording transactions; (2) adjusting the accounts; (3) preparing financial statements; and (4) closing the temporary accounts. The first step occurs continually throughout the accounting period. Steps 2, 3, and 4 normally occur at the end of the accounting period. Additional steps are described in coming chapters of the text.

EXHIBIT 2.4

The Accounting Cycle

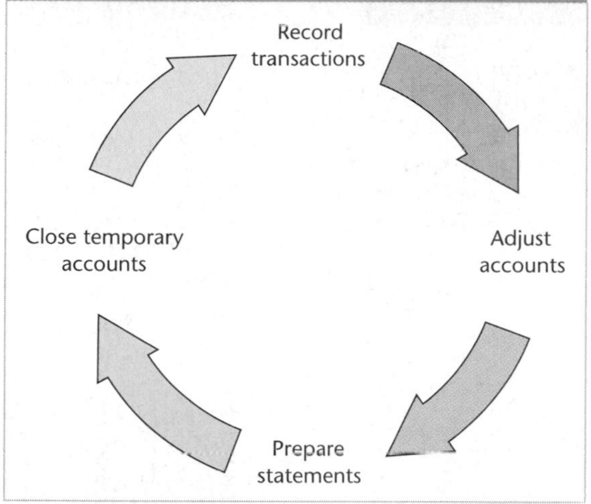

The Matching Concept

Cash basis accounting can distort reported net income because it sometimes fails to match expenses with the revenues they produce. To illustrate, consider the $6,000 of accrued salary expense that Cato Consultants recognized at the end of 2008. The instructor's teaching produced revenue in 2008. If Cato waited until 2009 (when it paid the instructor) to recognize $6,000 of the total $16,000 salary expense, then $6,000 of the expense would not be matched with the revenue it generated. By using accrual accounting, Cato recognized all the salary expense in the same accounting period in which the consulting revenue was recognized. A primary goal of accrual accounting is to appropriately match expenses with revenues, the **matching concept.**

Appropriately matching expenses with revenues can be difficult even when using accrual accounting. For example, consider Cato's advertising expense. Money spent on advertising may generate revenue in future accounting periods as well as in the current period. A prospective customer could save an advertising brochure for several years before calling Cato for training services. It is difficult to know when and to what extent advertising produces revenue. When the connection between an expense and the corresponding revenue is vague, accountants commonly match the expense with the period in which it is incurred. Cato matched (recognized) the entire $2,000 of advertising cost with the 2008 accounting period even though some of that cost might generate revenue in future accounting periods. Expenses that are matched with the period in which they are incurred are frequently called **period costs.**

Matching is not perfect. Although it would be more accurate to match expenses with revenues than with periods, there is sometimes no obvious direct connection between expenses and revenue. Accountants must exercise judgment to select the accounting period in which to recognize revenues and expenses. The concept of conservatism influences such judgment calls.

The Conservatism Principle

When faced with a recognition dilemma, **conservatism** guides accountants to select the alternative that produces the lowest amount of net income. In uncertain circumstances, accountants tend to delay revenue recognition and accelerate expense recognition. The conservatism principle holds that it is better to understate net income than to overstate it. If subsequent developments suggest that net income should have been higher, investors will respond more favorably than if they learn it was really lower. This practice explains why Cato recognized all of the advertising cost as expense in 2008 even though some of that cost may generate revenue in future accounting periods.

Second Accounting Cycle

LO 1

Record basic accrual and deferral events in a horizontal financial statements model.

Topic Tackler PLUS

2-2

The text next describes the effects of Cato Consultants' 2009 events.

Event 1 **Cato paid $6,000 to the instructor to settle the salaries payable obligation.**

Cash payments to creditors are ***asset use transactions.*** When Cato pays the instructor, both the asset account Cash and the liability account Salaries Payable decrease. The cash payment does not affect the income statement. The salary expense was recognized in 2008 when the instructor taught the classes. The statement of cash flows reflects a cash outflow from operating activities. The effects of this transaction on the financial statements are shown here:

Assets	=	Liab.	+	Stk. Equity						
Cash	=	Sal. Pay.			Rev.	−	Exp.	=	Net Inc.	Cash Flow
(6,000)	=	(6,000)	+	NA	NA	−	NA	=	NA	(6,000) OA

Prepaid Items (Cost versus Expense)

Event 2 **On March 1, Cato signed a one-year lease agreement and paid $12,000 cash in advance to rent office space. The one-year lease term began on March 1.**

Accrual accounting draws a distinction between the terms *cost* and *expense. A* **cost** *might be either an asset or an expense.* If a company has already consumed a purchased resource in the process of earning revenue, the cost of the resource is an *expense.* For example, companies normally pay for electricity the month after using it. The cost of electric utilities is therefore usually recorded as an expense. In contrast, if a company purchases a resource it will use in the future to generate revenue, the cost of the resource represents an *asset.* Accountants record such a cost in an asset account and ***defer*** recognizing an expense until the resource is used to produce revenue. Deferring the expense recognition provides more accurate ***matching*** of revenues and expenses.

The cost of the office space Cato leased in Event 2 is an asset. It is recorded in the asset account *Prepaid Rent.* Cato expects to benefit from incurring this cost for the next twelve months. Expense recognition is deferred until Cato uses the office space to help generate revenue. Other common deferred expenses include *prepaid insurance* and *prepaid taxes.* As these titles imply, deferred expenses are frequently called **prepaid items.** Exhibit 2.5 illustrates the relationship between costs, assets, and expenses.

EXHIBIT 2.5

Relationship between Cost and Expense

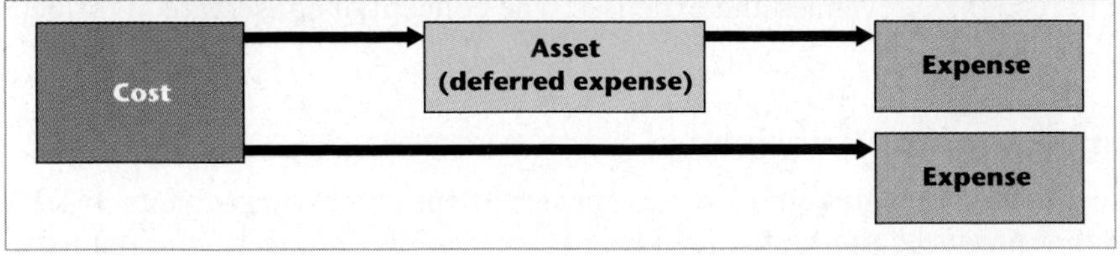

Purchasing prepaid rent is an asset exchange transaction. The asset account Cash decreases and the asset account Prepaid Rent increases. The amount of total assets is unaffected. The income statement is unaffected. Expense recognition is deferred until the office space is used. The statement of cash flows reflects a cash outflow from operating activities. The effects of this transaction on the financial statements are shown here:

Assets		= Liab.	+ Stk. Equity							
Cash	+ Prep. Rent			Rev.	−	Exp.	=	Net Inc.	Cash Flow	
(12,000) +	12,000	= NA	+ NA	NA	−	NA	=	NA	(12,000)	OA

Accounting for Receipt of Unearned Revenue

Event 3 **Cato received $18,000 cash in advance from Westberry Company for consulting services Cato agreed to perform over a one-year period beginning June 1.**

Cato must defer (delay) recognizing any revenue until it performs (does the work) the consulting services for Westberry. From Cato's point of view, the deferred revenue is a liability because Cato is obligated to perform services in the future. The liability is called **unearned revenue.** The cash receipt is an ***asset source transaction.*** The asset account Cash and the liability account Unearned Revenue both increase. Collecting the cash has no effect on the income statement. The revenue will be reported on the income statement after Cato performs the services. The statement of cash flows reflects a cash inflow from operating activities. The effects of this transaction on the financial statements are shown here:

Assets	= Liab.	+ Stk. Equity							
Cash	= Unearn. Rev.		Rev.	−	Exp.	=	Net Inc.	Cash Flow	
18,000	= 18,000	+ NA	NA	−	NA	=	NA	18,000	OA

Accounting for Supplies Purchase

Event 4 **Cato purchased $800 of supplies on account.**

The purchase of supplies on account is an ***asset source transaction.*** The asset account Supplies and the liability account Accounts Payable increase. The income statement is unaffected. Expense recognition is deferred until the supplies are used. The statement of cash flows is not affected. The effects of this transaction on the financial statements are shown here:

Assets	= Liab.	+ Stk. Equity						
Supplies	= Accts. Pay.		Rev.	−	Exp.	=	Net Inc.	Cash Flow
800	= 800	+ NA	NA	−	NA	=	NA	NA

Other 2009 Events

Event 5 **Cato provided $96,400 of consulting services on account.**

Providing services on account is an ***asset source transaction.*** The asset account Accounts Receivable and the stockholders' equity account Retained Earnings increase. Revenue and net income increase. The statement of cash flows is not affected. The effects of this transaction on the financial statements are shown here:

Assets	= Liab.	+ Stk. Equity						
Accts. Rec.	=	Ret. Earn.	Rev.	−	Exp.	=	Net Inc.	Cash Flow
96,400	= NA	+ 96,400	96,400	−	NA	=	96,400	NA

Event 6 Cato collected $105,000 cash from customers as partial settlement of accounts receivable.

Collecting money from customers who are paying accounts receivable are ***asset exchange transactions.*** One asset account (Cash) increases and another asset account (Accounts Receivable) decreases. The amount of total assets is unchanged. The income statement is not affected. The statement of cash flows reports a cash inflow from operating activities. The effects of this transaction on the financial statements are shown here:

Assets			=	Liab.	+	Stk. Equity						Cash Flow
Cash	+	Accts. Rec.					Rev.	−	Exp.	=	Net Inc.	
105,000	+	(105,000)	=	NA	+	NA	NA	−	NA	=	NA	105,000 OA

Event 7 Cato paid $32,000 cash for salary expense.

Cash payments for salary expense are ***asset use transactions.*** Both the asset account Cash and the equity account Retained Earnings decrease by $32,000. Recognizing the expense decreases net income on the income statement. The statement of cash flows reflects a cash outflow from operating activities. The effects of this transaction on the financial statements are shown here:

Assets	=	Liab.	+	Stk. Equity						Cash Flow
Cash	=			Ret. Earn.	Rev.	−	Exp.	=	Net Inc.	
(32,000)	=	NA	+	(32,000)	NA	−	32,000	=	(32,000)	(32,000) OA

Event 8 Cato incurred $21,000 of other operating expenses on account.

Recognizing expenses incurred on account are ***claims exchange transactions.*** One claims account (Accounts Payable) increases and another claims account (Retained Earnings) decreases. The amount of total claims is not affected. Recognizing the expenses decreases net income. The statement of cash flows is not affected. The effects of this transaction on the financial statements are shown here:

Assets	=	Liab.	+	Stk. Equity						Cash Flow
		Accts. Pay.	+	Ret. Earn.	Rev.	−	Exp.	=	Net Inc.	
NA	=	21,000	+	(21,000)	NA	−	21,000	=	(21,000)	NA

Event 9 Cato paid $18,200 in partial settlement of accounts payable.

Paying accounts payable is an ***asset use transaction.*** The asset account Cash and the liability account Accounts Payable decrease. The statement of cash flows reports a cash outflow for operating activities. The income statement is not affected. The effects of this transaction on the financial statements are shown here:

Assets	=	Liab.	+	Stk. Equity						Cash Flow
Cash	=	Accts. Pay.			Rev.	−	Exp.	=	Net Inc.	
(18,200)	=	(18,200)	+	NA	NA	−	NA	=	NA	(18,200) OA

Event 10 Cato paid $79,500 to purchase land it planned to use in the future as a building site for its home office.

Purchasing land with cash is an ***asset exchange transaction.*** One asset account, Cash, decreases and another asset account, Land, increases. The amount of total assets is unchanged. The income statement is not affected. The statement of cash flows reports a cash outflow for investing activities. The effects of this transaction on the financial statements are shown here:

Assets			=	Liab.	+	Stk. Equity						Cash Flow
Cash	+	Land					Rev.	−	Exp.	=	Net Inc.	Cash Flow
(79,500)	+	79,500	=	NA	+	NA	NA	−	NA	=	NA	(79,500) IA

Event 11 **Cato paid $21,000 in cash dividends to its stockholders.**

Cash payments for dividends are ***asset use transactions.*** Both the asset account Cash and the equity account Retained Earnings decrease. Recall that dividends are wealth transfers from the business to the stockholders, not expenses. They are not incurred in the process of generating revenue. They do not affect the income statement. The statement of cash flows reflects a cash outflow from financing activities. The effects of this transaction on the financial statements are shown here:

Assets	=	Liab.	+	Stk. Equity						
Cash	=			Ret. Earn.	Rev.	−	Exp.	=	Net Inc.	Cash Flow
(21,000)	=	NA	+	(21,000)	NA	−	NA	=	NA	(21,000) FA

Event 12 **Cato acquired $2,000 cash from issuing additional shares of common stock.**

Issuing common stock is an ***asset source transaction.*** The asset account Cash and the stockholders' equity account Common Stock increase. The income statement is unaffected. The statement of cash flows reports a cash inflow from financing activities. The effects of this transaction on the financial statements are shown here:

Assets	=	Liab.	+	Stk. Equity						
Cash	=			Com. Stk.	Rev.	−	Exp.	=	Net Inc.	Cash Flow
2,000	=	NA	+	2,000	NA	−	NA	=	NA	2,000 FA

Adjusting Entries

Recall that companies make adjusting entries at the end of an accounting period to update the account balances before preparing the financial statements. Adjusting entries ensure that companies report revenues and expenses in the appropriate accounting period; adjusting entries never affect the Cash account.

Accounting for Supplies (Adjusting Entry)

Event 13 **After determining through a physical count that it had $150 of unused supplies on hand as of December 31, Cato recognized supplies expense.**

Companies would find the cost of recording supplies expense each time a pencil, piece of paper, envelope, or other supply item is used to far outweigh the benefit derived from such tedious recordkeeping. Instead, accountants transfer to expense the total cost of all supplies used during the entire accounting period in a single year-end adjusting entry. The cost of supplies used is determined as follows:

$$\text{Beginning supplies balance} + \text{Supplies purchased} = \text{Supplies available for use} - \text{Ending supplies balance} = \text{Supplies used}$$

Companies determine the ending supplies balance by physically counting the supplies onhand at the end of the period. Cato used $650 of supplies during the year (zero beginning balance + $800 supplies purchase = $800 available for use − $150 ending balance).

Recognizing Cato's supplies expense is an ***asset use transaction.*** The asset account Supplies and the stockholders' equity account Retained Earnings decrease. Recognizing supplies expense reduces net income. The statement of cash flows is not affected. The effects of this transaction on the financial statements are shown here:

Assets	=	Liab.	+	Stk. Equity						
Supplies	**=**			**Ret. Earn.**	**Rev.**	**−**	**Exp.**	**=**	**Net Inc.**	**Cash Flow**
(650)	=	NA	+	(650)	NA	−	650	=	(650)	NA

Accounting for Prepaid Rent (Adjusting Entry)

Event 14 **Cato recognized rent expense for the office space used during the accounting period.**

Recall that Cato paid $12,000 on March 1 to rent office space for one year (see Event 2). The portion of the lease cost that represents using office space from March 1 through December 31 is computed as follows:

Cost of annual lease ÷ 12 = Cost per month × Months used = Rent expense

$12,000 cost of policy ÷ 12 = $1,000 per month × 10 months = $10,000 Rent expense

Recognizing the rent expense decreases the asset account Prepaid Rent and the stockholders' equity account Retained Earnings. Recognizing rent expense reduces net income. The statement of cash flows is not affected. The cash flow effect was recorded in the March 1 event. These effects on the financial statements follow:

Assets	=	Liab.	+	Stk. Equity						
Prep. Rent	**=**			**Ret. Earn.**	**Rev.**	**−**	**Exp.**	**=**	**Net Inc.**	**Cash Flow**
(10,000)	=	NA	+	(10,000)	NA	−	10,000	=	(10,000)	NA

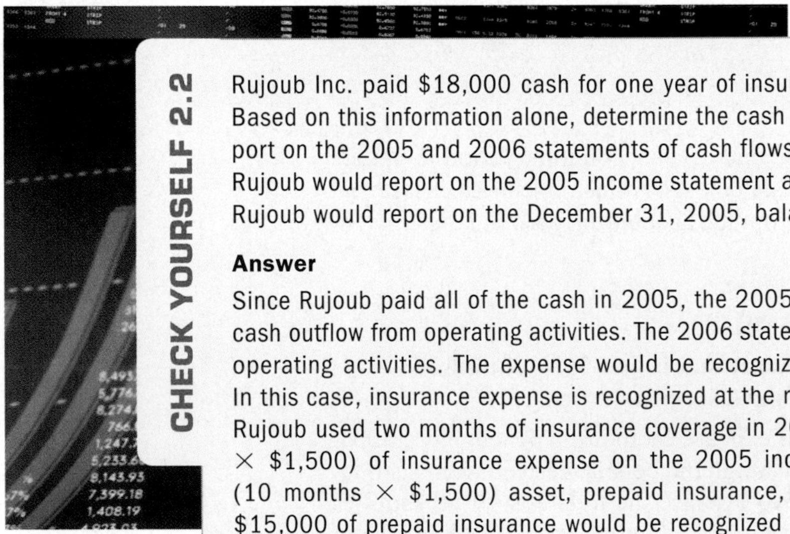

CHECK YOURSELF 2.2

Rujoub Inc. paid $18,000 cash for one year of insurance coverage that began on November 1, 2005. Based on this information alone, determine the cash flow from operating activities that Rujoub would report on the 2005 and 2006 statements of cash flows. Also, determine the amount of insurance expense Rujoub would report on the 2005 income statement and the amount of prepaid insurance (an asset) that Rujoub would report on the December 31, 2005, balance sheet.

Answer

Since Rujoub paid all of the cash in 2005, the 2005 statement of cash flows would report an $18,000 cash outflow from operating activities. The 2006 statement of cash flows would report zero cash flow from operating activities. The expense would be recognized in the periods in which the insurance is used. In this case, insurance expense is recognized at the rate of $1,500 per month ($18,000 ÷ 12 months). Rujoub used two months of insurance coverage in 2005 and therefore would report $3,000 (2 months × $1,500) of insurance expense on the 2005 income statement. Rujoub would report a $15,000 (10 months × $1,500) asset, prepaid insurance, on the December 31, 2005, balance sheet. The $15,000 of prepaid insurance would be recognized as insurance expense in 2006 when the insurance coverage is used.

Accounting for Unearned Revenue (Adjusting Entry)

Event 15 **Cato recognized the portion of the unearned revenue it earned during the accounting period.**

Recall that Cato received an $18,000 cash advance from Westberry Company to provide consulting services from June 1, 2009, to May 31, 2010 (see Event 3). By December 31,

Cato had earned 7 months (June 1 through December 31) of the revenue related to this contract. Rather than recording the revenue continuously as it performed the consulting services, Cato can simply recognize the amount earned in a single adjustment to the accounting records at the end of the accounting period. The amount of the adjustment is computed as follows:

$18,000 ÷ 12 months = $1,500 revenue earned per month

$1,500 × 7 months = $10,500 revenue to be recognized in 2009

The adjusting entry moves $10,500 from the Unearned Revenue account to the Consulting Revenue account. This entry is a ***claims exchange transaction.*** The liability account Unearned Revenue decreases and the equity account Retained Earnings increases. The effects of this transaction on the financial statements are shown here:

Assets	=	Liab.	+	Stk. Equity						
		Unearn. Rev.	+	Ret. Earn.	Rev.	−	Exp.	=	Net Inc.	Cash Flow
NA	=	(10,500)	+	10,500	10,500	−	NA	=	10,500	NA

Recall that revenue was previously defined as an economic benefit a company obtains by providing customers with goods and services. In this case the economic benefit is a decrease in the liability account Unearned Revenue. **Revenue** can therefore be more precisely defined as *an increase in assets or a decrease in liabilities that a company obtains by providing customers with goods or services.*

CHECK YOURSELF 2.3

Sanderson & Associates received a $24,000 cash advance as a retainer to provide legal services to a client. The contract called for Sanderson to render services during a one-year period beginning October 1, 2006. Based on this information alone, determine the cash flow from operating activities Sanderson would report on the 2006 and 2007 statements of cash flows. Also determine the amount of revenue Sanderson would report on the 2006 and 2007 income statements.

Answer

Since Sanderson collected all of the cash in 2006, the 2006 statement of cash flows would report a $24,000 cash inflow from operating activities. The 2007 statement of cash flows would report zero cash flow from operating activities. Revenue is recognized in the period in which it is earned. In this case revenue is earned at the rate of $2,000 per month ($24,000 ÷ 12 months = $2,000 per month). Sanderson rendered services for three months in 2006 and nine months in 2007. Sanderson would report $6,000 (3 months × $2,000) of revenue on the 2006 income statement and $18,000 (9 months × $2,000) of revenue on the 2007 income statement.

Accounting for Accrued Salary Expense (Adjusting Entry)

Event 16 **Cato recognized $4,000 of accrued salary expense.**

The adjusting entry to recognize the accrued salary expense is a ***claims exchange transaction.*** One claims account, Retained Earnings, decreases and another claims account, Salaries Payable, increases. The expense recognition reduces net income. The statement of cash flows is not affected. The effects of this transaction on the financial statements are shown here:

Assets	=	Liab.	+	Stk. Equity						
		Sal. Pay.	+	Ret. Earn.	Rev.	−	Exp.	=	Net Inc.	Cash Flow
NA	=	4,000	+	(4,000)	NA	−	4,000	=	(4,000)	NA

Answers to The Curious Accountant

Because the **Reader's Digest Association** receives cash from customers before actually sending any magazines to them, the company has not earned any revenue when it receives the cash. Reader's Digest has a liability called *unearned revenue.* If Reader's Digest closed its books on December 31, then $3.50 of Paige Long's subscription would be recognized as revenue in 2007. The remaining $10.50 would appear on the balance sheet as a liability.

Reader's Digest actually ends its accounting year on June 30 each year. A copy of the June 30, 2002, balance sheet for Reader's Digest is presented in Exhibit 2.6. The liability for unearned revenue was $561.7 ($426.9 + $134.8) million—which represented about 25 percent of Reader's Digest's total liabilities!

Will Reader's Digest need cash to pay these subscription liabilities? Not exactly. The liabilities will not be paid directly with cash. Instead, they will be satisfied by providing magazines to the subscribers. However, Reader's Digest will need cash to pay for producing and distributing the magazines supplied to the customers. Even so, the amount of cash required to provide magazines will probably differ significantly from the amount of unearned revenues. In most cases, subscription fees do not cover the cost of producing and distributing magazines. By collecting significant amounts of advertising revenue, publishers can provide magazines to customers at prices well below the cost of publication. The amount of unearned revenue is not likely to coincide with the amount of cash needed to cover the cost of satisfying the company's obligation to produce and distribute magazines. Even though the association between unearned revenues and the cost of providing magazines to customers is not direct, a knowledgeable financial analyst can use the information to make estimates of future cash flows and revenue recognition.

Summary of Events

The previous section of this chapter described sixteen events Cato Consultants experienced the during the 2009 accounting period. These events are summarized below for your convenience.

Event 1 Cato paid $6,000 to the instructor to settle the salaries payable obligation.

Event 2 On March 1, Cato paid $12,000 cash to lease office space for one year.

Event 3 Cato received $18,000 cash in advance from Westberry Company for consulting services to be performed for one year beginning June 1.

Event 4 Cato purchased $800 of supplies on account.

Event 5 Cato provided $96,400 of consulting services on account.

Event 6 Cato collected $105,000 cash from customers as partial settlement of accounts receivable.

Event 7 Cato paid $32,000 cash for salary expense.

Event 8 Cato incurred $21,000 of other operating expenses on account.

Event 9 Cato paid $18,200 in partial settlement of accounts payable.

Event 10 Cato paid $79,500 to purchase land it planned to use in the future as a building site for its home office.

Event 11 Cato paid $21,000 in cash dividends to its stockholders.

Event 12 Cato acquired $2,000 cash from issuing additional shares of common stock.

The year-end adjustments are:

Event 13 After determining through a physical count that it had $150 of unused supplies on hand as of December 31, Cato recognized supplies expense.

Event 14 Cato recognized rent expense for the office space used during the accounting period.

Event 15 Cato recognized the portion of the unearned revenue it earned during the accounting period.

Event 16 Cato recognized $4,000 of accrued salary expense.

EXHIBIT 2.6 2002 Balance Sheet for Reader's Digest

	At June 30,	
	2002	2001 Restated
Assets		
Current Assets		
Cash and Cash Equivalents	$ 107.6	$ 35.4
Accounts Receivable, Net	306.0	274.8
Inventories	156.0	167.4
Prepaid and Deferred Promotion Costs	140.9	106.7
Prepaid Expenses and Other Current Assets	153.2	192.1
Total Current Assets	863.7	776.4
Property, Plant, and Equipment, Net	168.1	160.2
Goodwill and Other Intangible Assets, Net	1,244.6	409.8
Other Noncurrent Assets	426.3	334.5
Total Assets	$2,702.7	$1,680.9
Liabilities and Stockholders' Equity		
Current Liabilities		
Loans and Notes Payable	$ 132.7	$ 160.3
Accounts Payable	102.8	86.4
Accrued Expenses	283.2	251.1
Income Taxes Payable	28.4	41.2
Unearned Revenues	426.9	291.6
Other Current Liabilities	6.8	28.9
Total Current Liabilities	980.8	859.5
Postretirement and Postemployment Benefits Other than Pensions	128.1	138.7
Unearned Revenues	134.8	54.1
Long-Term Debt	818.0	9.8
Other Noncurrent Liabilities	169.1	159.0
Total Liabilities	2,230.8	1,221.1
Commitments and Contingencies (Notes 11 and 13)		
Stockholders' Equity		
Capital Stock	25.5	29.6
Paid-In Capital	224.6	226.1
Retained Earnings	1,261.2	1,191.3
Accumulated Other Comprehensive (Loss) Income	(89.7)	(84.6)
Treasury Stock, at Cost	(949.7)	(902.6)
Total Stockholders' Equity	471.9	459.8
Total Liabilities and Stockholders' Equity	$2,702.7	$1,680.9

The General Ledger

LO 2

Organize general ledger accounts under an accounting equation.

Exhibit 2.7 shows Cato Consultants' 2009 transaction data recorded in general ledger form. The account balances at the end of 2008, shown in Exhibit 2.3, become the beginning balances for the 2009 accounting period. The 2009 transaction data are referenced to the accounting events with numbers in parentheses. The information in the ledger accounts is the basis for the financial statements in Exhibit 2.8. Before reading further, trace each transaction in the summary of events into Exhibit 2.7.

Vertical Statements Model

Financial statement users obtain helpful insights by analyzing company trends over multiple accounting cycles. Exhibit 2.8 presents for Cato Consultants a multicycle **vertical statements**

EXHIBIT 2.7

Ledger Accounts with 2009 Transaction Data

Assets = Liabilities + Stockholders' Equity

Assets

Cash

Bal.	53,000
(1)	(6,000)
(2)	(12,000)
(3)	18,000
(6)	105,000
(7)	(32,000)
(9)	(18,200)
(10)	(79,500)
(11)	(21,000)
(12)	2,000
Bal.	9,300

Accounts Receivable

Bal.	24,000
(5)	96,400
(6)	(105,000)
Bal.	15,400

Supplies

Bal.	0
(4)	800
(13)	(650)
Bal.	150

Prepaid Rent

Bal.	0
(2)	12,000
(14)	(10,000)
Bal.	2,000

Land

Bal.	0
(10)	79,500
Bal.	79,500

Liabilities

Accounts Payable

Bal.	0
(4)	800
(8)	21,000
(9)	(18,200)
Bal.	3,600

Unearned Revenue

Bal.	0
(3)	18,000
(15)	(10,500)
Bal.	7,500

Salaries Payable

Bal.	6,000
(1)	(6,000)
(16)	4,000
Bal.	4,000

Stockholders' Equity

Common Stock

Bal.	5,000
(12)	2,000
Bal.	7,000

Retained Earnings

Bal.	66,000

Dividends

Bal.	0
(11)	(21,000)
Bal.	(21,000)

Consulting Revenue

Bal.	0
(5)	96,400
(15)	10,500
Bal.	106,900

Other Operating Expenses

Bal.	0
(8)	(21,000)
Bal.	(21,000)

Salary Expense

Bal.	0
(7)	(32,000)
(16)	(4,000)
Bal.	(36,000)

Rent Expense

Bal.	0
(14)	(10,000)
Bal.	(10,000)

Supplies Expense

Bal.	0
(13)	(650)
Bal.	(650)

LO 6

Explain how business events affect financial statements over multiple accounting cycles.

model of 2008 and 2009 accounting data. To conserve space, we have combined all the expenses for each year into single amounts labeled "Operating Expenses," determined as follows:

	2008	2009
Other Operating Expenses	$ 0	$21,000
Salary Expense	16,000	36,000
Rent Expense	0	10,000
Advertising Expense	2,000	0
Supplies Expense	0	650
Total Operating Expenses	$18,000	$67,650

Similarly, we combined the cash payments for operating expenses on the statement of cash flows as follows:

	2008	2009
Supplies and Other Operating Expenses	$ 0	$18,200*
Salary Expense	10,000	38,000
Rent Expense	0	12,000
Advertising Expense	2,000	0
Total Cash Payments for Operating Expenses	$12,000	$68,200

*Amount paid in partial settlement of accounts payable

Recall that the level of detail reported in financial statements depends on user information needs. Most real-world companies combine many account balances together to report highly summarized totals under each financial statement caption. Before reading further, trace the remaining financial statement items from the ledger accounts in Exhibit 2.7 to where they are reported in Exhibit 2.8.

The vertical statements model in Exhibit 2.8 shows significant interrelationships among the financial statements. For each year, trace the amount of net income from the income statement to the statement of changes in stockholders' equity. Next, trace the ending balances of common stock and retained earnings reported on the statement of changes in stockholders' equity to the stockholders' equity section of the balance sheet. Also, confirm that the amount of cash reported on the balance sheet equals the ending cash balance on the statement of cash flows.

Other relationships connect the two accounting periods. For example, trace the ending retained earnings balance from the 2008 statement of stockholders' equity to the beginning retained earnings balance on the 2009 statement of stockholders' equity. Also, trace the ending cash balance on the 2008 statement of cash flows to the beginning cash balance on the 2009 statement of cash flows. Finally, confirm that the change in cash between the 2008 and 2009 balance sheets ($53,000 – $9,300 – $43,700 decrease) agrees with the net change in cash reported on the 2009 statement of cash flows.

THE FINANCIAL ANALYST

When you buy a share of stock, what do you really get? The stock certificate you receive is evidence of your right to share in the earnings of the company that issued the stock. The more the company earns, the more your wealth increases. Investors are willing to pay higher prices for companies with higher earnings potential.

LO 7

Explain how to use the price-earnings ratio and growth percentage analysis to assess the market value of common stock.

Price-earnings Ratio

The **price-earnings ratio,** frequently called the *P/E ratio,* is the most commonly reported measure of a company's value. The P/E ratio is a company's market price per share of stock divided by the company's annual earnings per share (EPS).[1]

Assume Western Company recently reported annual earnings per share of $3. Western's stock is currently selling for $54 per share. Western's stock is therefore selling at a P/E ratio

[1] The amount of earnings per share is provided in a company's annual report. In its simplest form, it is computed by dividing the company's net income (net earnings) by the number of shares of common stock outstanding.

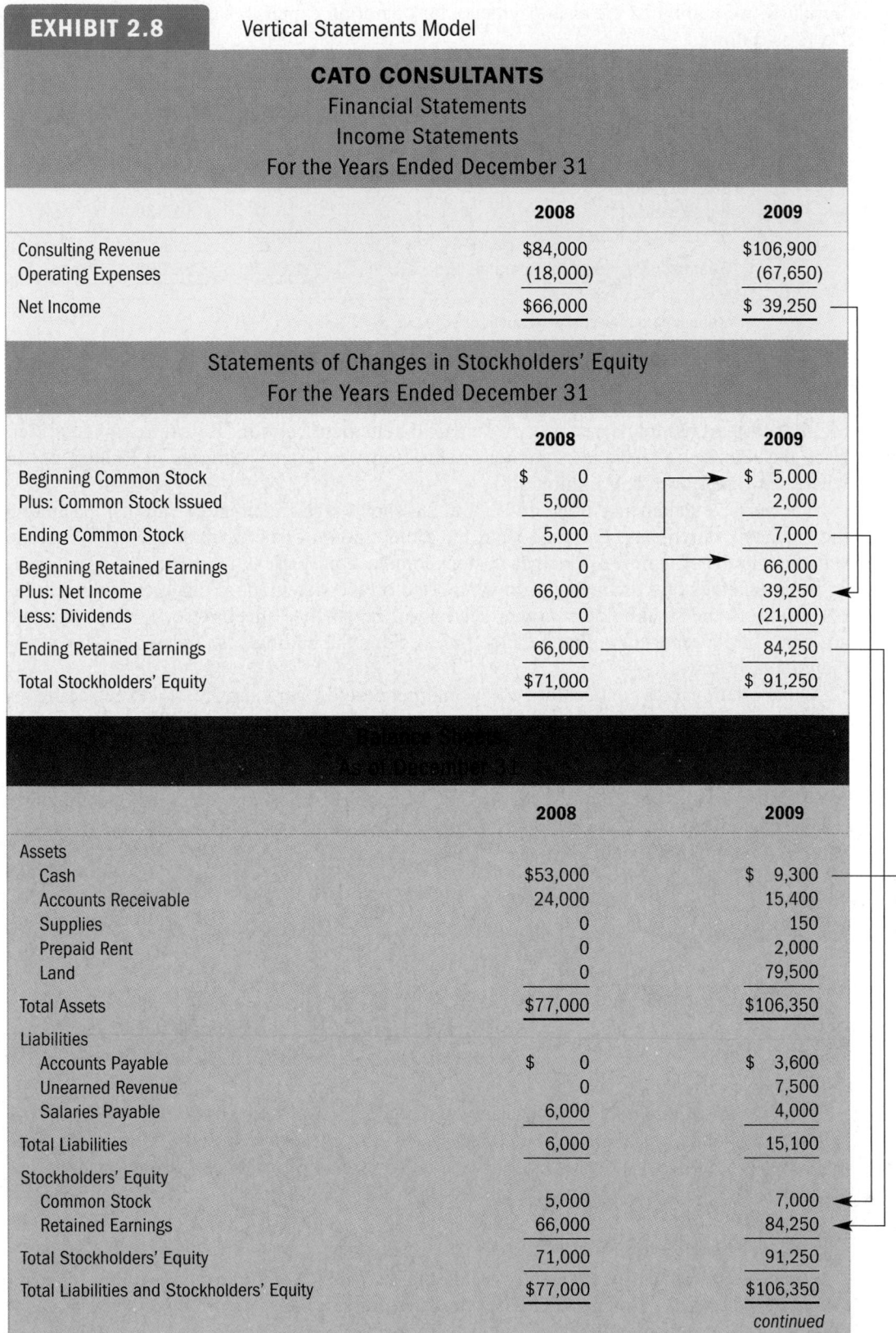

EXHIBIT 2.8 Vertical Statements Model

CATO CONSULTANTS
Financial Statements
Income Statements
For the Years Ended December 31

	2008	2009
Consulting Revenue	$84,000	$106,900
Operating Expenses	(18,000)	(67,650)
Net Income	$66,000	$ 39,250

Statements of Changes in Stockholders' Equity
For the Years Ended December 31

	2008	2009
Beginning Common Stock	$ 0	$ 5,000
Plus: Common Stock Issued	5,000	2,000
Ending Common Stock	5,000	7,000
Beginning Retained Earnings	0	66,000
Plus: Net Income	66,000	39,250
Less: Dividends	0	(21,000)
Ending Retained Earnings	66,000	84,250
Total Stockholders' Equity	$71,000	$ 91,250

Balance Sheets
As of December 31

	2008	2009
Assets		
Cash	$53,000	$ 9,300
Accounts Receivable	24,000	15,400
Supplies	0	150
Prepaid Rent	0	2,000
Land	0	79,500
Total Assets	$77,000	$106,350
Liabilities		
Accounts Payable	$ 0	$ 3,600
Unearned Revenue	0	7,500
Salaries Payable	6,000	4,000
Total Liabilities	6,000	15,100
Stockholders' Equity		
Common Stock	5,000	7,000
Retained Earnings	66,000	84,250
Total Stockholders' Equity	71,000	91,250
Total Liabilities and Stockholders' Equity	$77,000	$106,350

continued

of 18 ($54 market price ÷ $3 EPS). What does a P/E ratio of 18 mean? If Western continued earning $3 per share of stock each year and paid all its earnings out to stockholders in the form of cash dividends, it would take 18 years for an investor to recover the price paid for the stock.

EXHIBIT 2.8 *Concluded*

Statements of Cash Flows
For the Years Ended December 31

	2008	2009
Cash Flows from Operating Activities		
Cash Receipts from Customers	$60,000	$123,000
Cash Payments for Operating Expenses	(12,000)	(68,200)
Net Cash Flow from Operating Activities	48,000	54,800
Cash Flows from Investing Activities		
Cash Payment to Purchase Land	0	(79,500)
Cash Flows from Financing Activities		
Cash Receipts from Issuing Common Stock	5,000	2,000
Cash Payments for Dividends	0	(21,000)
Net Cash Flow from Financing Activities	5,000	(19,000)
Net Change in Cash	53,000	(43,700)
Plus: Beginning Cash Balance	0	53,000
Ending Cash Balance	$53,000	$ 9,300

In contrast, assume the stock of Eastern Company, which reported EPS of $4, is currently selling for $48 per share. Eastern's P/E ratio is 12 ($48 market price ÷ $4 EPS). Investors who buy Eastern Company stock would get their money back six years faster (18 − 12) than investors who buy Western Company stock.

Why would investors buy a stock with a P/E ratio of 18 when they could buy one with a P/E ratio of 12? If investors expect Western Company's earnings to grow faster than Eastern Company's earnings, the higher P/E ratio makes sense. For example, suppose Western Company's earnings were to double to $6 per share while Eastern's remained at $4 per share. Western's P/E ratio would drop to 9 ($54 market price ÷ $6 EPS) while Eastern's remains at 12. This explains why high-growth companies sell for higher P/E multiples than do low-growth companies.

Measuring Growth through Percentage Analysis

The income statements for Cammeron Inc. show that earnings increased by $4.2 million from 2005 to 2006. Comparable data for Diller Enterprises indicate earnings growth of $2.9 million. Is Cammeron a better-managed company than Diller? Not necessarily; perhaps Cammeron is simply a larger company than Diller. Investors frequently use percentage analysis to level the playing field when comparing companies of differing sizes. Consider the following actual earnings data for the two companies:

	2005*	2006*	Growth†
Cammeron	$42.4	$46.6	$4.2
Diller	9.9	12.8	2.9

*Earnings data shown in millions.

†Growth calculated by subtracting 2005 earnings from 2006 earnings.

EXHIBIT 2.9

Real-World Price-earnings Ratios and Growth Rates

Company	P/E Ratio	Average Annual Earnings Growth 1999–2001
High growth companies:		
Cisco Systems	90	35.3%
Microsoft	46	13.2
Medium growth companies:		
General Electric	20	6.2
General Mills	24	6.4
Low growth companies:		
DuPont	10	(4.2)
Sara Lee	10	1.4

Analysts can measure the percentage growth in earnings between 2005 and 2006 for each of the companies with the following formula:

$$\frac{\text{Alternative year earnings} - \text{Base year earnings}}{\text{Base year earnings}} = \text{Percentage growth rate}$$

Cammeron Inc.:

$$\frac{\$46.6 - \$42.4}{\$42.4} = 9.9\%$$

Diller Enterprises:

$$\frac{\$12.8 - \$9.9}{\$9.9} = 29.3\%$$

This analysis shows that Cammeron is the larger company, but Diller is growing much more rapidly. If this trend continues, Diller will eventually become the larger company and have higher earnings than Cammeron. This higher earnings potential is why investors value fast-growing companies. The P/E ratios of real-world companies are highly correlated with their growth rates, as demonstrated in the data reported in Exhibit 2.9. The data in this exhibit are based on the closing stock prices on June 25, 2002.

CHECK YOURSELF 2.4

Treadmore Company started the 2007 accounting period with $580 of supplies on hand. During 2007 the company purchased $2,200 of supplies. A physical count of supplies indicated that there was $420 of supplies on hand at the end of 2007. Treadmore pays cash for supplies at the time they are purchased. Based on this information alone, determine the amount of supplies expense to be recognized on the income statement and the amount of cash flow to be shown in the operating activities section of the statement of cash flows.

Answer

The amount of supplies expense recognized on the income statement is the amount of supplies that were used during the accounting period. This amount is computed below.

Beginning balance	+	Supplies purchased	=	Supplies available	−	Ending balance	=	Supplies used
$580	+	$2,200	=	$2,780	−	$420	=	$2,360

The cash flow from operating activities is the amount of cash paid for supplies during the accounting period. In this case, Treadmore paid $2,200 cash to purchase supplies. This amount would be shown as a cash outflow.

REALITY BYTES

Under accrual accounting, revenue is recognized only after a company completes work. In contrast, investors focus on anticipated income when purchasing stock. This helps explain why the stock of some companies sells for more than the stock of other companies. For example, since the silicon-chip industry has a higher growth potential than the grocery-store industry, **Intel's** stock will likely sell for a higher earnings multiple than **Kroger's** stock. Indeed, on August 19, 2003, Intel's stock sold for 50 times earnings, while Kroger's sold for only 11 times earnings.

Significant differences in P/E ratios occur because investors base their stock purchases on a company's potential to earn future profits rather than its past earnings. Does this mean historically based financial statements are not useful in making investment decisions? No! Past earnings provide insight into future earnings. A company with a history of 20 percent per year earnings growth is more likely to experience rapid growth in the future than a company with a 5 percent historical growth rate. Financial statements based on accrual accounting can provide insight into the future even though they are historically based.

A Look Back <<

LO 8

Classify accounting events into one of four categories:

a. asset source transactions.
b. asset use transactions.
c. asset exchange transactions.
d. claims exchange transactions.

Chapters 1 and 2 introduced four types of transactions. Although businesses engage in an infinite number of different transactions, all transactions fall into one of four types. By learning to identify transactions by type, you can understand how unfamiliar events affect financial statements. The four types of transactions are:

1. *Asset source transactions:* An asset account increases, and a corresponding claims account increases.
2. *Asset use transactions:* An asset account decreases, and a corresponding claims account decreases.
3. *Asset exchange transactions:* One asset account increases, and another asset account decreases.
4. *Claims exchange transactions:* One claims account increases, and another claims account decreases.

Also, the definitions of revenue and expense have been expanded. The complete definitions of these two elements are as follows:

1. **Revenue:** Revenue is the *economic benefit* derived from operating the business. Its recognition is accompanied by an increase in assets or a decrease in liabilities resulting from providing products or services to customers.
2. **Expense:** An expense is an *economic sacrifice* incurred in the process of generating revenue. Its recognition is accompanied by a decrease in assets or an increase in liabilities resulting from consuming assets and services in an effort to produce revenue.

This chapter introduced accrual accounting. Accrual accounting distinguishes between *recognition* and *realization.* Recognition means reporting an economic item or event in the financial statements. In contrast, realization refers to collecting cash from the sale of assets or services. Recognition and realization can occur in different accounting periods. In addition, cash payments for expenses often occur in different accounting periods from when a company recognizes the expenses. Accrual accounting uses both *accruals* and *deferrals.*

- The term *accrual* applies to earnings events that are recognized before cash is exchanged. Recognizing revenue on account or accrued salaries expense are examples of accruals.
- The term *deferral* applies to earnings events that are recognized after cash has been exchanged. Supplies, prepaid items, and unearned revenue are examples of deferrals.

Virtually all major companies operating in the United States use accrual accounting.

>> A Look Forward

To this point, we have used plus and minus signs to illustrate the effects of business events on financial statements. In real businesses, so many transactions occur that recording them with simple mathematical notations is impractical. In practice, accountants usually maintain records using a system of rules known as *double-entry bookkeeping.* Chapter 3 introduces the basic components of this bookkeeping system. You will learn how to record business events using a debit/credit format. You will be introduced to ledgers, journals, and trial balances. When you finish Chapter 3, you will have a clear understanding of how accountants maintain records of business activity.

SELF-STUDY REVIEW PROBLEM

Gifford Company experienced the following accounting events during 2008.

1. Started operations on January 1 when it acquired $20,000 cash by issuing common stock.
2. Earned $18,000 of revenue on account.
3. On March 1 collected $36,000 cash as an advance for services to be performed in the future.
4. Paid cash operating expenses of $17,000.
5. Paid a $2,700 cash dividend to stockholders.
6. On December 31, 2008, adjusted the books to recognize the revenue earned by providing services related to the advance described in Event 3. The contract required Gifford to provide services for a one-year period starting March 1.
7. Collected $15,000 cash from accounts receivable.

Gifford Company experienced the following accounting events during 2009.

1. Recognized $38,000 of cash revenue.
2. On April 1 paid $12,000 cash for an insurance policy that provides coverage for one year beginning immediately.
3. Collected $2,000 cash from accounts receivable.
4. Paid cash operating expenses of $21,000.
5. Paid a $5,000 cash dividend to stockholders.
6. On December 31, 2009, adjusted the books to recognize the remaining revenue earned by providing services related to the advance described in Event 3 of 2008.
7. On December 31, 2009, Gifford adjusted the books to recognize the amount of the insurance policy used during 2009.

Required

a. Record the events in a financial statements model like the following one. The first event is recorded as an example.

Event No.	Assets			=	Liab.	+	Stockholders' Equity				
	Cash +	Accts. Rec. +	Prep. Ins.	=	Unearn. Rev.	+	Com. Stk. +	Ret. Earn.	Rev. − Exp. = Net Inc.		Cash Flow
1	20,000 +	NA +	NA	=	NA	+	20,000 +	NA	NA − NA = NA		20,000 FA

b. What amount of revenue would Gifford report on the 2008 income statement?

c. What amount of cash flow from customers would Gifford report on the 2008 statement of cash flows?

d. What amount of unearned revenue would Gifford report on the 2008 and 2009 year-end balance sheets?

e. What are the 2009 opening balances for the revenue and expense accounts?

f. What amount of total assets would Gifford report on the December 31, 2008 balance sheet?

g. What claims on assets would Gifford report on the December 31, 2009 balance sheet?

Solution to Requirement a

The financial statements model follows.

	Assets			= Liab.	+ Stockholders' Equity						
Event No.	Cash	+ Accts. Rec.	+ Prep. Ins.	= Unearn. Rev.	+ Com. Stk.	+ Ret. Earn.	Rev.	− Exp.	= Net Inc.	Cash Flow	
2008											
1	20,000	NA	NA	NA	20,000	NA	NA	NA	NA	20,000	FA
2	NA	18,000	NA	NA	NA	18,000	18,000	NA	18,000	NA	
3	36,000	NA	NA	36,000	NA	NA	NA	NA	NA	36,000	OA
4	(17,000)	NA	NA	NA	NA	(17,000)	NA	17,000	(17,000)	(17,000)	OA
5	(2,700)	NA	NA	NA	NA	(2,700)	NA	NA	NA	(2,700)	FA
6*	NA	NA	NA	(30,000)	NA	30,000	30,000	NA	30,000	NA	
7	15,000	(15,000)	NA	NA	NA	NA	NA	NA	NA	15,000	OA
Bal.	51,300	3,000	NA	6,000	20,000	28,300	48,000	17,000	31,000	51,300	NC
	Asset, liability, and equity account balances carry forward						Rev. & exp. accts. are closed				
2009											
Bal.	51,300	3,000	NA	6,000	20,000	28,300	NA	NA	NA	NA	
1	38,000	NA	NA	NA	NA	38,000	38,000	NA	38,000	38,000	OA
2	(12,000)	NA	12,000	NA	NA	NA	NA	NA	NA	(12,000)	OA
3	2,000	(2,000)	NA	NA	NA	NA	NA	NA	NA	2,000	OA
4	(21,000)	NA	NA	NA	NA	(21,000)	NA	21,000	(21,000)	(21,000)	OA
5	(5,000)	NA	NA	NA	NA	(5,000)	NA	NA	NA	(5,000)	FA
6*	NA	NA	NA	(6,000)	NA	6,000	6,000	NA	6,000	NA	
7†	NA	NA	(9,000)	NA	NA	(9,000)	NA	9,000	(9,000)	NA	
Bal.	53,300	1,000	3,000	0	20,000	37,300	44,000	30,000	14,000	2,000	NC

*Revenue is earned at the rate of \$3,000 (\$36,000 ÷ 12 months) per month. Revenue recognized in 2008 is \$30,000 (\$3,000 × 10 months). Revenue recognized in 2009 is \$6,000 (\$3,000 × 2 months).

†Rent expense is incurred at the rate of \$1,000 (\$12,000 ÷ 12 months) per month. Rent expense recognized in 2009 is \$9,000 (\$1,000 × 9 months).

Solutions to Requirements b–g

b. Gifford would report \$48,000 of revenue in 2008 (\$18,000 revenue on account plus \$30,000 of the \$36,000 of unearned revenue).

c. The cash inflow from customers is \$51,000 (\$36,000 when the unearned revenue was received plus \$15,000 collection of accounts receivable).

d. The December 31, 2008, balance sheet will report \$6,000 of unearned revenue, which is the amount of the cash advance less the amount of revenue recognized in 2008 (\$36,000 − \$30,000). The December 31, 2009, unearned revenue balance is zero.

e. Since revenue and expense accounts are closed at the end of each accounting period, the beginning balances in these accounts are always zero.

f. Assets on the December 31, 2008, balance sheet are \$54,300 [Gifford's cash at year end plus the balance in accounts receivable (\$51,300 + \$3,000)].

g. Since all unearned revenue would be recognized before the financial statements were prepared at the end of 2009, there would be no liabilities on the 2009 balance sheet. Common stock and retained earnings would be the only claims as of December 31, 2009, for a claims total of \$57,300 (\$20,000 + \$37,300).

KEY TERMS

QUESTIONS

1. What does accrual accounting attempt to accomplish?
2. Define *recognition.* How is it independent of collecting or paying cash?
3. What does the term *deferral* mean?
4. If cash is collected in advance of performing services, when is the associated revenue recognized?
5. What does the term *asset source transaction* mean?
6. What effect does the issue of common stock have on the accounting equation?
7. How does the recognition of revenue on account (accounts receivable) affect the income statement compared to its effect on the statement of cash flows?
8. Give an example of an asset source transaction. What is the effect of this transaction on the accounting equation?
9. When is revenue recognized under accrual accounting?
10. Give an example of an asset exchange transaction. What is the effect of this transaction on the accounting equation?
11. What is the effect on the claims side of the accounting equation when cash is collected in advance of performing services?
12. What does the term *unearned revenue* mean?
13. What effect does expense recognition have on the accounting equation?
14. What does the term *claims exchange transaction* mean?
15. What type of transaction is a cash payment to creditors? How does this type of transaction affect the accounting equation?
16. When are expenses recognized under accrual accounting?
17. Why may net cash flow from operating activities on the cash flow statement be different from the amount of net income reported on the income statement?
18. What is the relationship between the income statement and changes in assets and liabilities?
19. How does net income affect the stockholders' claims on the business's assets?
20. What is the difference between a cost and an expense?
21. When does a cost become an expense? Do all costs become expenses?
22. How and when is the cost of the *supplies used* recognized in an accounting period?
23. What does the term *expense* mean?
24. What does the term *revenue* mean?
25. What is the purpose of the statement of changes in stockholders' equity?
26. What is the main purpose of the balance sheet?
27. Why is the balance sheet dated *as of* a specific date when the income statement, statement of changes in stockholders' equity, and statement of cash flows are dated with the phrase *for the period ended?*
28. In what order are assets listed on the balance sheet?
29. What does the statement of cash flows explain?
30. What does the term *adjusting entry* mean? Give an example.

31. What types of accounts are closed at the end of the accounting period? Why is it necessary to close these accounts?
32. Give several examples of period costs.
33. Give an example of a cost that can be directly matched with the revenue produced by an accounting firm from preparing a tax return.
34. List and describe the four stages of the accounting cycle discussed in Chapter 2.
35. What does the P/E ratio measure?
36. Why might a high-growth company sell for a higher P/E multiple than a low-growth company?

EXERCISES—SERIES A

All Exercises in Series A are available with McGraw-Hill's Homework Manager

Where applicable in all exercises, round computations to the nearest dollar.

Exercise 2-1A *Effect of accruals on the financial statements*

L.O. 2, 3

Hamby Inc. experienced the following events in 2006, in its first year of operation.

1. Received $15,000 cash from the issue of common stock.
2. Performed services on account for $48,000.
3. Paid the utility expense of $1,250.
4. Collected $36,000 of the accounts receivable.
5. Recorded $8,000 of accrued salaries at the end of the year.
6. Paid a $1,000 cash dividend to the shareholders.

Required

a. Record the events in general ledger accounts under an accounting equation. In the last column of the table, provide appropriate account titles for the Retained Earnings amounts. The first transaction has been recorded as an example.

HAMBY INC.
General Ledger Accounts

Event	Assets		=	Liabilities	+	Stockholders' Equity		Acct. Titles for Ret. Earn.
	Cash	Accounts Receivable		Salaries Payable		Common Stock	Retained Earnings	
1.	15,000					15,000		

b. Prepare the income statement, statement of changes in stockholders' equity, balance sheet, and statement of cash flows for the 2006 accounting period.
c. Why is the amount of net income different from the amount of net cash flow from operating activities?

Exercise 2-2A *Effect of collecting accounts receivable on the accounting equation and financial statements*

L.O. 2, 3

Pilgram Company earned $6,000 of service revenue on account during 2008. The company collected $5,200 cash from accounts receivable during 2008.

Required

Based on this information alone, determine the following. (*Hint:* Record the events in general ledger accounts under an accounting equation before satisfying the requirements.)

a. The balance of the accounts receivable that Pilgram would report on the December 31, 2008, balance sheet.

b. The amount of net income that Pilgram would report on the 2008 income statement.

c. The amount of net cash flow from operating activities that Pilgram would report on the 2008 statement of cash flows.

d. The amount of retained earnings that Pilgram would report on the 2008 balance sheet.

e. Why are the answers to Requirements *b* and *c* different?

L.O. 2, 3

Exercise 2-3A *Effect of prepaid rent on the accounting equation and financial statements*

The following events apply to 2005, the first year of operations of ITS Consulting Services:

1. Acquired $20,000 cash from the issue of common stock.
2. Paid $12,000 cash in advance for a one-year rental contract for office space.
3. Provided services for $25,000 cash.
4. Adjusted the records to recognize the use of the office space. The one-year contract started on March 1, 2005. The adjustment was made as of December 31, 2005.

Required

a. Write an accounting equation and record the effects of each accounting event under the appropriate general ledger account headings.

b. Prepare an income statement and statement of cash flows for the 2005 accounting period.

c. Explain the difference between the amount of net income and amount of net cash flow from operating activities.

L.O. 1, 3

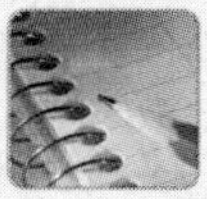

Exercise 2-4A *Effect of supplies on the financial statements*

The Copy Center Inc. started the 2005 accounting period with $8,000 cash, $6,000 of common stock, and $2,000 of retained earnings. The Copy Center was affected by the following accounting events during 2005:

1. Purchased $11,500 of paper and other supplies on account.
2. Earned and collected $27,000 of cash revenue.
3. Paid $10,000 cash on accounts payable.
4. Adjusted the records to reflect the use of supplies. A physical count indicated that $2,500 of supplies was still on hand on December 31, 2005.

Required

a. Show the effects of the events on the financial statements using a horizontal statements model like the following one. In the Cash Flows column, use OA to designate operating activity, IA for investing activity, FA for financing activity, and NC for net change in cash. Use NA to indicate accounts not affected by the event. The beginning balances are entered in the following example.

	Assets			=	Liab.	+	Stockholders' Equity								
Event No.	Cash	+	Supplies	=	Accts. Pay.	+	Com. Stk.	+	Ret. Earn.	Rev.	−	Exp.	=	Net Inc.	Cash Flows
Beg. bal.	8,000	+	0	=	0	+	6,000	+	2,000	0	−	0	=	0	0

b. Explain the difference between the amount of net income and amount of net cash flow from operating activities.

L.O. 1

Exercise 2-5A *Effect of unearned revenue on financial statements*

Meg Sanderfert started a personal financial planning business when she accepted $60,000 cash as advance payment for managing the financial assets of a large estate. Sanderfert agreed to manage the estate for a one-year period beginning April 1, 2007.

Required

a. Show the effects of the advance payment and revenue recognition on the 2007 financial statements using a horizontal statements model like the following one. In the Cash Flows column, use OA to designate operating activity, IA for investing activity, FA for financing activity, and NC for net change in cash. Use NA if the account is not affected.

Event	Assets	=	Liab.	+	Stockholders' Equity	Rev. − Exp. = Net Inc.	Cash Flows
	Cash	=	Unearn. Rev.	+	Ret. Earn.		

b. How much revenue would Meg recognize on the 2008 income statement?

c. What is the amount of cash flow from operating activities in 2008?

Exercise 2-6A *Unearned revenue defined as a liability*

L.O. 3

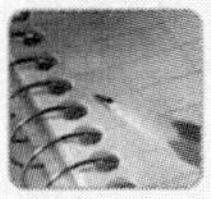

Steve Chang received $500 in advance for tutoring fees when he agreed to help Jon Seng with his introductory accounting course. Upon receiving the cash, Steve mentioned that he would have to record the transaction as a liability on his books. Seng asked, "Why a liability? You don't owe me any money, do you?"

Required

Respond to Seng's question regarding Chang's liability.

Exercise 2-7A *Distinguishing between an expense and a cost*

L.O. 3

Clair Seaton tells you that the accountants where she works are real hair splitters. For example, they make a big issue over the difference between a cost and an expense. She says the two terms mean the same thing to her.

Required

a. Explain to Clair the difference between a cost and an expense from an accountant's perspective.

b. Explain whether each of the following events produces an asset or an expense.

(1) Purchased a building for cash.
(2) Paid cash to purchase supplies.
(3) Used supplies on hand to produce revenue.
(4) Paid cash in advance for insurance.
(5) Recognized accrued salaries.

Exercise 2-8A *Revenue and expense recognition*

L.O. 1

Required

a. Describe an expense recognition event that results in an increase in liabilities.

b. Describe an expense recognition event that results in a decrease in assets.

c. Describe a revenue recognition event that results in a decrease in liabilities.

d. Describe a revenue recognition event that results in an increase in assets.

Exercise 2-9A *Transactions that affect the elements of financial statements*

L.O. 1

Required

Give an example of a transaction that will do the following:

a. Increase an asset and increase equity (asset source event).

b. Decrease an asset and decrease equity (asset use event).

c. Increase an asset and decrease another asset (asset exchange event).

d. Decrease a liability and increase equity (claims exchange event).

e. Increase a liability and decrease equity (claims exchange event).

f. Increase an asset and increase a liability (asset source event).

g. Decrease an asset and decrease a liability (asset use event).

Exercise 2-10A *Identifying deferral and accrual events*

L.O. 3

Required

Identify each of the following events as an accrual, a deferral, or neither.

a. Paid cash in advance for a one-year insurance policy.

b. Paid cash to settle an account payable.

c. Collected accounts receivable.
d. Paid cash for current salaries expense.
e. Paid cash to purchase supplies.
f. Provided services on account.
g. Provided services and collected cash.
h. Paid cash to purchase land.
i. Recognized accrued salaries at the end of the accounting period.
j. Paid a cash dividend to the stockholders.

L.O. 2

Exercise 2-11A ***Prepaid and unearned rent***

On September 1, 2007, Ameriship paid West Coast Rentals $36,000 for a 12-month lease on warehouse space.

Required

a. Record the deferral and the related December 31, 2007, adjustment for Ameriship in the accounting equation.
b. Record the deferral and the related December 31, 2007, adjustment for West Coast Rentals in the accounting equation.

L.O. 3

Exercise 2-12A ***Classifying events on the statement of cash flows***

The following transactions pertain to the operations of Stone Company for 2008:

1. Acquired $24,000 cash from the issue of common stock.
2. Provided $40,000 of services on account.
3. Incurred $25,000 of other operating expenses on account.
4. Collected $32,000 cash from accounts receivable.
5. Paid a $2,000 cash dividend to the stockholders.
6. Paid $18,000 cash on accounts payable.
7. Performed services for $8,000 cash.
8. Paid a $6,000 cash advance for a one year contract to rent equipment.
9. Recognized $9,000 of accrued salary expense.
10. Accepted an $18,000 cash advance for services to be performed in the future.

Required

a. Classify the cash flows from these transactions as operating activities (OA), investing activities (IA), or financing activities (FA). Use NA for transactions that do not affect the statement of cash flows.
b. Prepare a statement of cash flows. (There is no beginning cash balance.)

L.O. 3

Exercise 2-13A ***Effect of accounting events on the income statement and statement of cash flows***

Required

Explain how each of the following events or series of events and the related adjusting entry will affect the amount of *net income* and the amount of *cash flow from operating activities* reported on the year-end financial statements. Identify the direction of change (increase, decrease, or NA) and the amount of the change. Organize your answers according to the following table. The first event is recorded as an example. If an event does not have a related adjusting entry, record only the effects of the event.

	Net Income		Cash Flows from Operating Activities	
Event No.	**Direction of Change**	**Amount of Change**	**Direction of Change**	**Amount of Change**
a	NA	NA	NA	NA

a. Acquired $50,000 cash from the issue of common stock.
b. Earned $12,000 of revenue on account. Collected $10,000 cash from accounts receivable.
c. Paid $2,400 cash on October 1 to purchase a one-year insurance policy.

d. Collected $9,600 in advance for services to be performed in the future. The contract called for services to start on August 1 and to continue for one year.

e. Accrued salaries amounting to $4,000.

f. Sold land that cost $15,000 for $15,000 cash.

g. Provided services for $7,500 cash.

h. Purchased $1,200 of supplies on account. Paid $1,000 cash on accounts payable. The ending balance in the Supplies account, after adjustment, was $300.

i. Paid cash for other operating expenses of $1,500.

Exercise 2-14A *Identifying transaction type and effect on the financial statements* L.O. 1, 8

Required

Identify whether each of the following transactions is an asset source (AS), asset use (AU), asset exchange (AE), or claims exchange (CE). Also show the effects of the events on the financial statements using the horizontal statements model. Indicate whether the event increases (I), decreases (D), or does not affect (NA) each element of the financial statements. In the Cash Flows column, designate the cash flows as operating activities (OA), investing activities (IA), or financing activities (FA). The first two transactions have been recorded as examples.

						Stockholders' Equity								
Event No.	Type of Event	Assets	=	Liabilities	+	Common Stock	+	Retained Earnings	Rev.	−	Exp.	=	Net Inc.	Cash Flows
a	AS	I		NA		NA		I	I		NA		I	I OA
b	AS	I		I		NA		NA	NA		NA		NA	NA

a. Provided services and collected cash.

b. Purchased supplies on account to be used in the future.

c. Paid cash in advance for one year's rent.

d. Paid cash to purchase land.

e. Paid a cash dividend to the stockholders.

f. Received cash from the issue of common stock.

g. Paid cash on accounts payable.

h. Collected cash from accounts receivable.

i. Received cash advance for services to be provided in the future.

j. Incurred other operating expenses on account.

k. Performed services on account.

l. Adjusted books to reflect the amount of prepaid rent expired during the period.

m. Paid cash for operating expenses.

n. Adjusted the books to record the supplies used during the period.

o. Recorded accrued salaries.

p. Paid cash for salaries accrued at the end of a prior period.

Exercise 2-15A *Effect of accruals and deferrals on financial statements: the horizontal statements model* L.O. 1

D. Downs, Attorney at Law, experienced the following transactions in 2007, the first year of operations:

1. Purchased $1,200 of office supplies on account.
2. Accepted $18,000 on February 1, 2007, as a retainer for services to be performed evenly over the next 12 months.
3. Performed legal services for cash of $66,000.
4. Paid cash for salaries expense of $20,500.
5. Paid a cash dividend to the stockholders of $5,000.
6. Paid $900 of the amount due on accounts payable.
7. Determined that at the end of the accounting period, $125 of office supplies remained on hand.

8. On December 31, 2007, recognized the revenue that had been earned for services performed in accordance with Transaction 2.

Required

Show the effects of the events on the financial statements using a horizontal statements model like the following one. In the Cash Flow column, use the initials OA to designate operating activity, IA for investing activity, FA for financing activity, and NC for net change in cash. Use NA to indicate accounts not affected by the event. The first event has been recorded as an example.

Event No.	Assets		=	Liabilities		+ Stk. Equity				
	Cash +	Supplies	=	Accts. Pay. +	Unearn. Rev.	+ Ret. Earn.	Rev. −	Exp. =	Net Inc.	Cash Flow
1	NA +	1,200	=	1,200 +	NA	+ NA	NA −	NA =	NA	NA

L.O. 2, 3

Exercise 2-16A *Effect of an error on financial statements*

On May 1, 2007, Dobler Corporation paid $9,600 to purchase a 24-month insurance policy. Assume that Dobler records the purchase as an asset and that the books are closed on December 31.

Required

a. Show the purchase of the insurance policy and the related adjusting entry to recognize insurance expense in the accounting equation.

b. Assume that Dobler Corporation failed to record the adjusting entry to reflect the expiration of insurance. How would the error affect the company's 2007 income statement and balance sheet?

L.O. 2, 3

Exercise 2-17A *Net income versus changes in cash*

In 2008, Lott Inc. billed its customers $56,000 for services performed. The company collected $42,000 of the amount billed. Lott incurred $38,000 of other operating expenses on account. Lott paid $25,000 of the accounts payable. Lott acquired $30,000 cash from the issue of common stock. The company invested $12,000 cash in the purchase of land.

Required

Use the preceding information to answer the following questions. (*Hint:* Identify the six events described in the paragraph and record them in general ledger accounts under an accounting equation before attempting to answer the questions.)

a. What amount of revenue will Lott report on the 2008 income statement?

b. What amount of cash flow from revenue will Lott report on the statement of cash flows?

c. What is the net income for the period?

d. What is the net cash flow from operating activities for the period?

e. Why is the amount of net income different from the net cash flow from operating activities for the period?

f. What is the amount of net cash flow from investing activities?

g. What is the amount of net cash flow from financing activities?

h. What amounts of total assets, liabilities, and equity will Lott report on the year-end balance sheet?

L.O. 3

Exercise 2-18A *Adjusting the accounts*

Morgan Associates experienced the following accounting events during its 2006 accounting period.

1. Recognized revenue on account.
2. Issued common stock.
3. Paid cash to purchase supplies.
4. Collected a cash advance for services that will be provided during the coming year.
5. Paid a cash dividend to the stockholders.
6. Paid cash for an insurance policy that provides coverage during the next year.
7. Collected cash from accounts receivable.
8. Paid cash for operating expenses.

9. Paid cash to settle an account payable.
10. Paid cash to purchase land.

Required

a. Identify the events that would require a year-end adjusting entry.
b. Explain why adjusting entries are made at the end of the accounting period.

Exercise 2-19A *Closing the accounts*

L.O. 4

The following information was drawn from the accounting records of Pearson Company as of December 31, 2007, before the temporary accounts had been closed. The Cash balance was $3,000, and Notes Payable amounted to $2,500. The company had revenues of $4,000 and expenses of $2,500. The company's Land account had a $5,000 balance. Dividends amounted to $500. There was $1,000 of common stock issued.

Required

a. Identify which accounts would be classified as permanent and which accounts would be classified as temporary.
b. Assuming that Pearson's beginning balance (as of January 1, 2007) in the Retained Earnings account was $3,500, determine its balance after the temporary accounts were closed at the end of 2007.
c. What amount of net income would Pearson Company report on its 2007 income statement?
d. Explain why the amount of net income differs from the amount of the ending Retained Earnings balance.
e. What are the balances in the revenue, expense, and dividend accounts on January 1, 2008?

Exercise 2-20A *Closing accounts and the accounting cycle*

L.O. 4

Required

a. Identify which of the following accounts are temporary (will be closed to Retained Earnings at the end of the year) and which are permanent.
   (1) Cash
   (2) Salaries Expense
   (3) Prepaid Rent
   (4) Utilities Expense
   (5) Service Revenue
   (6) Dividends
   (7) Common Stock
   (8) Land
   (9) Salaries Payable
   (10) Retained Earnings
b. List and explain the four stages of the accounting cycle. Which stage must be first? Which stage is last?

Exercise 2-21A *Closing entries*

L.O. 4

Required

Which of the following accounts are closed at the end of the accounting period?

a. Accounts Payable
b. Unearned Revenue
c. Cash
d. Accounts Receivable
e. Service Revenue
f. Advertising Expense
g. Dividends
h. Retained Earnings
i. Utilities Expense
j. Salaries Payable
k. Land
l. Operating Expenses

L.O. 4

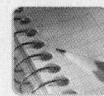

Exercise 2-22A ***Matching concept***

Companies make sacrifices known as *expenses* to obtain benefits called *revenues.* The accurate measurement of net income requires that expenses be matched with revenues. In some circumstances matching a particular expense directly with revenue is difficult or impossible. In these circumstances, the expense is matched with the period in which it is incurred.

Required

a. Identify an expense that could be matched directly with revenue.
b. Identify a period expense that would be difficult to match with revenue. Explain why.

L.O. 8

Exercise 2-23A ***Identifying source, use, and exchange transactions***

Required

Indicate whether each of the following transactions is an asset source (AS), asset use (AU), asset exchange (AE), or claims exchange (CE) transaction.

a. Acquired cash from the issue of stock.
b. Paid a cash dividend to the stockholders.
c. Paid cash on accounts payable.
d. Incurred other operating expenses on account.
e. Paid cash for rent expense.
f. Performed services for cash.
g. Performed services for clients on account.
h. Collected cash from accounts receivable.
i. Received cash for services to be performed in the future.
j. Purchased land with cash.

L.O. 8

Exercise 2-24A ***Identifying asset source, use, and exchange transactions***

Required

a. Name an asset use transaction that will *not* affect the income statement.
b. Name an asset exchange transaction that will affect the statement of cash flows.
c. Name an asset source transaction that will *not* affect the income statement.
d. Name an asset source transaction that will *not* affect the statement of cash flows.
e. Name an asset source transaction that will affect the income statement.

L.O. 5

Exercise 2-25A ***Relation of elements to financial statements***

Required

Identify whether each of the following items would appear on the income statement (IS), statement of changes in stockholders' equity (SE), balance sheet (BS), or statement of cash flows (CF). Some items may appear on more than one statement; if so, identify all applicable statements. If an item would not appear on any financial statement, label it NA.

a. Land
b. Consulting Revenue
c. Dividends
d. Salaries Expense
e. Net Income
f. Supplies
g. Ending Cash Balance
h. Cash Flow from Investing Activities
i. Prepaid Rent
j. Salaries Payable
k. Accounts Receivable
l. Retained Earnings
m. Accounts Payable
n. Utilities Payable
o. Unearned Revenue

Exercise 2-26A *Price-earnings ratio* **L.O. 7**

The following information is available for two companies.

	Henry Company	Pager Company
Earnings per share	$ 1.05	$ 4.50
Market price per share	38.50	108.00

Required

a. Compute the price-earnings ratio for each company.

b. Explain why one company would have a higher price-earnings ratio than the other.

PROBLEMS—SERIES A

All Problems in Series A are available with McGraw-Hill's Homework Manager

Problem 2-27A *Recording events in a horizontal statements model* **L.O. 1**

CHECK FIGURES
Net Income: $10,000
Ending Cash Balance: $19,100

The following events pertain to The Plains Company:

1. Acquired $12,000 cash from the issue of common stock.
2. Provided services for $4,000 cash.
3. Provided $12,000 of services on account.
4. Collected $9,000 cash from the account receivable created in Event 3.
5. Paid $900 cash to purchase supplies.
6. Had $100 of supplies on hand at the end of the accounting period.
7. Received $1,800 cash in advance for services to be performed in the future.
8. Performed one-half of the services agreed to in Event 7.
9. Paid $4,600 for salaries expense.
10. Incurred $1,500 of other operating expenses on account.
11. Paid $1,200 cash on the account payable created in Event 10.
12. Paid a $1,000 cash dividend to the stockholders.

Required

Show the effects of the events on the financial statements using a horizontal statements model like the following one. In the Cash Flows column, use the letters OA to designate operating activity, IA for investing activity, FA for financing activity, and NC for net change in cash. Use NA to indicate accounts not affected by the event. The first event is recorded as an example.

	Assets					=	Liabilities			+	Stockholders' Equity									
Event No.	Cash	+	Accts. Rec.	+	Supp.	=	Accts. Pay.	+	Unearn. Rev.	+	Com. Stk.	+	Ret. Earn.	Rev.	−	Exp.	=	Net Inc.	Cash Flows	
1	12,000	+	NA	+	NA	=	NA	+	NA	+	12,000	+	NA	NA	−	NA	=	NA	12,000	FA

Problem 2-28A *Effect of deferrals on financial statements: three separate single-cycle examples* **L.O. 1, 2, 3**

excel
mhhe.com/edmonds2007

CHECK FIGURES
a. Net Income: $56,000
b. Net Income: $10,000

Required

a. On February 1, 2005, Business Help Inc. was formed when it received $60,000 cash from the issue of common stock. On May 1, 2005, the company paid $36,000 cash in advance to rent office space for the coming year. The office space was used as a place to consult with clients. The consulting activity generated $80,000 of cash revenue during 2005. Based on this information alone, record the events and related adjusting entry in the general ledger accounts under the accounting equation. Determine the amount of net income and cash flows from operating activities for 2005.

b. On January 1, 2006, the accounting firm of Woo & Associates was formed. On August 1, 2006, the company received a retainer fee (was paid in advance) of $24,000 for services to be performed monthly during the coming year. Assuming that this was the only transaction completed in 2006, prepare an income statement, statement of changes in stockholders' equity, balance sheet, and statement of cash flows for 2006.

c. Sing Company had $350 of supplies on hand on January 1, 2007. Sing purchased $1,200 of supplies on account during 2007. A physical count of supplies revealed that $200 of supplies were on hand as of December 31, 2007. Determine the amount of supplies expense that should be recognized in the December 31, 2007, adjusting entry. Use a financial statements model to show how the adjusting entry would affect the balance sheet, income statement, and statement of cash flows.

L.O. 2

CHECK FIGURE
b. adjustment amount: $1,500

Problem 2-29A *Effect of adjusting entries on the accounting equation*

Required

Each of the following independent events requires a year-end adjusting entry. Show how each event and its related adjusting entry affect the accounting equation. Assume a December 31 closing date. The first event is recorded as an example.

	Total Assets						Stockholders' Equity		
Event/ Adjustment	Cash	+	Other Assets	=	Liabilities	+	Common Stock	+	Retained Earnings
a	−3,000		+3,000		NA		NA		NA
Adj.	NA		−2,250		NA		NA		−2,250

a. Paid $3,000 cash in advance on April 1 for a one-year insurance policy.
b. Purchased $1,600 of supplies on account. At year's end, $100 of supplies remained on hand.
c. Paid $6,000 cash in advance on March 1 for a one-year lease on office space.
d. Received a $15,000 cash advance for a contract to provide services in the future. The contract required a one-year commitment starting September 1.
e. Paid $12,000 cash in advance on October 1 for a one-year lease on office space.

L.O. 2, 5, 6, 8

eXcel

mhhe.com/edmonds2007

CHECK FIGURES
a. Net Income, 2008: $21,200
b. Net Income, 2009: $21,500

Problem 2-30A *Events for two complete accounting cycles*

Texas Drilling Company was formed on January 1, 2008.

Events Affecting the 2008 Accounting Period

1. Acquired cash of $50,000 from the issue of common stock.
2. Purchased $800 of supplies on account.
3. Purchased land that cost $12,000 cash.
4. Paid $800 cash to settle accounts payable created in Event 2.
5. Recognized revenue on account of $38,000.
6. Paid $15,000 cash for other operating expenses.
7. Collected $22,000 cash from accounts receivable.

Information for 2008 Adjusting Entries

8. Recognized accrued salaries of $1,200 on December 31, 2008.
9. Had $200 of supplies on hand at the end of the accounting period.

Events Affecting the 2009 Accounting Period

1. Acquired an additional $10,000 cash from the issue of common stock.
2. Paid $1,200 cash to settle the salaries payable obligation.
3. Paid $3,600 cash in advance for a lease on office facilities.
4. Sold land that had cost $12,000 for $12,000 cash.
5. Received $5,400 cash in advance for services to be performed in the future.
6. Purchased $1,000 of supplies on account during the year.
7. Provided services on account of $26,000.
8. Collected $28,000 cash from accounts receivable.
9. Paid a cash dividend of $5,000 to the stockholders.

Information for 2009 Adjusting Entries

10. The advance payment for rental of the office facilities (see Event 3) was made on March 1 for a one-year lease term.
11. The cash advance for services to be provided in the future was collected on October 1 (see Event 5). The one-year contract started October 1.
12. Had $150 of supplies on hand at the end of the period.
13. Recognized accrued salaries of $1,800 at the end of the accounting period.

Required

a. Identify each event affecting the 2008 and 2009 accounting periods as asset source (AS), asset use (AU), asset exchange (AE), or claims exchange (CE). Record the effects of each event under the appropriate general ledger account headings of the accounting equation.

b. Prepare an income statement, statement of changes in stockholders' equity, balance sheet, and statement of cash flows for 2008 and 2009, using the vertical statements model.

Problem 2-31A ***Effect of events on financial statements*** **L.O. 2, 3**

CHECK FIGURES
b. $25,000
h. $(3,000)

Rios Company had the following balances in its accounting records as of December 31, 2006:

Assets		Claims	
Cash	$ 50,000	Accounts Payable	$ 25,000
Accounts Receivable	45,000	Common Stock	80,000
Land	25,000	Retained Earnings	15,000
Totals	$120,000		$120,000

The following accounting events apply to Rios's 2007 fiscal year:

Jan.	1	Acquired an additional $40,000 cash from the issue of common stock.
April	1	Paid $5,400 cash in advance for a one-year lease for office space.
June	1	Paid a $2,000 cash dividend to the stockholders.
July	1	Purchased additional land that cost $25,000 cash.
Aug.	1	Made a cash payment on accounts payable of $10,000.
Sept.	1	Received $7,200 cash in advance as a retainer for services to be performed monthly during the next eight months.
Sept.	30	Sold land for $22,000 cash that had originally cost $22,000.
Oct.	1	Purchased $900 of supplies on account.
Dec.	31	Earned $60,000 of service revenue on account during the year.
	31	Received $56,000 cash collections from accounts receivable.
	31	Incurred $12,000 other operating expenses on account during the year.
	31	Recognized accrued salaries expense of $5,000.
	31	Had $150 of supplies on hand at the end of the period.
	31	The land purchased on July 1 had a market value of $28,000.

Required

Based on the preceding information, answer the following questions. All questions pertain to the 2007 financial statements. (*Hint:* Record the events in general ledger accounts under an accounting equation before answering the questions.)

a. What two additional adjusting entries need to be made at the end of the year?
b. What amount would be reported for land on the balance sheet?
c. What amount of net cash flow from operating activities would Rios report on the statement of cash flows?
d. What amount of rent expense would Rios report in the income statement?
e. What amount of total liabilities would Rios report on the balance sheet?
f. What amount of supplies expense would Rios report on the income statement?
g. What amount of unearned revenue would Rios report on the balance sheet?
h. What amount of net cash flow from investing activities would Rios report on the statement of cash flows?

i. What amount of total expenses would Rios report on the income statement?
j. What total amount of service revenues would Rios report on the income statement?
k. What amount of cash flows from financing activities would Rios report on the statement of cash flows?
l. What amount of net income would Rios report on the income statement?
m. What amount of retained earnings would Rios report on the balance sheet?

L.O. 5

CHECK FIGURES
a. Total Assets $70,650
b. Net Income $34,150

Problem 2-32A *Identifying and arranging elements on financial statements*

The following accounts and balances were drawn from the records of Warren Company at December 31, 2005:

Cash	$11,400	Accounts Receivable	$19,000
Land	37,000	Cash Flow from Operating Act.	7,500
Insurance Expense	1,100	Beginning Retained Earnings	7,500
Dividends	5,000	Beginning Common Stock	1,000
Prepaid Insurance	2,500	Service Revenue	80,000
Accounts Payable	29,000	Cash Flow from Financing Act.	5,500
Supplies	750	Ending Common Stock	5,000
Supplies Expense	250	Cash Flow from Investing Act.	(7,000)
Rent Expense	2,500	Other Operating Expenses	42,000

Required

Use the accounts and balances from Warren Company to construct an income statement, statement of changes in stockholders' equity, balance sheet, and statement of cash flows (show only totals for each activity on the statement of cash flows).

L.O. 3

CHECK FIGURES
a. IS
z. BS/SE

Problem 2-33A *Relationship of accounts to financial statements*

Required

Identify whether each of the following items would appear on the income statement (IS), statement of changes in stockholders' equity (SE), balance sheet (BS), or statement of cash flows (CF). Some items may appear on more than one statement; if so, identify all applicable statements. If an item would not appear on any financial statement, label it NA.

a. Rent Expense
b. Salary Expense
c. Total Stockholders' Equity
d. Unearned Revenue
e. Cash Flow from Investing Activities
f. Insurance Expense
g. Ending Retained Earnings
h. Price-earnings Ratio
i. Supplies
j. Beginning Retained Earnings
k. Utilities Payable
l. Cash Flow from Financing Activities
m. Accounts Receivable
n. Prepaid Insurance
o. Ending Cash Balance
p. Utilities Expense
q. Accounts Payable
r. Beginning Common Stock
s. Dividends
t. Total Assets
u. Consulting Revenue
v. Market Value of Land
w. Supplies Expense
x. Salaries Payable
y. Notes Payable
z. Ending Common Stock
aa. Beginning Cash Balance
bb. Prepaid Rent
cc. Net Change in Cash
dd. Land
ee. Operating Expenses
ff. Total Liabilities
gg. "As of" Date Notation
hh. Salaries Expense
ii. Net Income
jj. Service Revenue
kk. Cash Flow from Operating Activities
ll. Operating Income

Problem 2-34A ***Missing information in financial statements***

L.O. 5, 6

excel

mhhe.com/edmonds2007

CHECK FIGURES

a. ($500)

o. $600

Required

Fill in the blanks (as indicated by the alphabetic letters in parentheses) in the following financial statements. Assume the company started operations January 1, 2006, and that all transactions involve cash.

	For the Years		
	2006	**2007**	**2008**
Income Statements			
Revenue	$ 700	$ 1,300	$ 2,000
Expense	(a)	(700)	(1,300)
Net Income	$200	$ (m)	$ 700
Statements of Changes in Stockholders' Equity			
Beginning Common Stock	$ 0	$ (n)	$ 6,000
Plus: Common Stock Issued	5,000	1,000	2,000
Ending Common Stock	5,000	6,000	(t)
Beginning Retained Earnings	0	100	200
Plus: Net Income	(b)	(o)	700
Less: Dividends	(c)	(500)	(300)
Ending Retained Earnings	100	(p)	600
Total Stockholders' Equity	$ (d)	$ 6,200	$ 8,600
Balance Sheets			
Assets			
Cash	$ (e)	$ (q)	$ (u)
Land	0	(r)	8,000
Total Assets	$ (f)	$11,200	$10,600
Liabilities	$ (g)	$ 5,000	$ 2,000
Stockholders' Equity			
Common Stock	(h)	(s)	8,000
Retained Earnings	(i)	200	600
Total Stockholders' Equity	(j)	6,200	8,600
Total Liabilities and Stockholders' Equity	$8,100	$11,200	$10,600
Statements of Cash Flows			
Cash Flows from Operating Activities			
Cash Receipts from Revenue	$ (k)	$ 1,300	$ (v)
Cash Payments for Expenses	(l)	(700)	(w)
Net Cash Flows from Operating Activities	200	600	700
Cash Flows from Investing Activities			
Cash Payments for Land	0	(8,000)	0
Cash Flows from Financing Activities			
Cash Receipts from Loan	3,000	3,000	0
Cash Payments to Reduce Debt	0	(1,000)	(x)
Cash Receipts from Stock Issue	5,000	1,000	(y)
Cash Payments for Dividends	(100)	(500)	(z)
Net Cash Flows from Financing Activities	7,900	2,500	(1,300)
Net Change in Cash	8,100	(4,900)	(600)
Plus: Beginning Cash Balance	0	8,100	3,200
Ending Cash Balance	$8,100	$ 3,200	$ 2,600

L.O. 7

Problem 2-35A *Price-earnings relationships*

Beta One Inc. is a pharmaceutical company heavily involved in research leading to the development of genealogy-based medicines. Although the company has several promising research studies in progress, it has brought only two viable products to market during the last decade. Earnings per share and market price per share data for the latest three years of operation follow.

Beta One Inc.	2006	2007	2008
Earnings per share	$1.22	$1.19	$1.20
Market price per share	85.40	84.49	87.60

Required

a. Calculate the company's annual growth rate in earnings per share from 2006 to 2007 and from 2007 to 2008.

b. Based on the data shown in Exhibit 2.9, identify the company as a high-, medium-, or low-growth company.

EXERCISES—SERIES B

Where applicable in all exercises, round computations to the nearest dollar.

L.O. 2, 3

Exercise 2-1B *Effect of accruals on the financial statements*

Cook Inc. experienced the following events in 2005, its first year of operations.

1. Received $15,000 cash from the issue of common stock.
2. Performed services on account for $42,000.
3. Paid the utility expense of $800.
4. Collected $32,000 of the accounts receivable.
5. Recorded $5,000 of accrued salaries at the end of the year.
6. Paid a $1,000 cash dividend to the stockholders.

Required

a. Record these events in general ledger accounts under an accounting equation. In the last column of the table, provide appropriate account titles for the Retained Earnings amounts. The first transaction has been recorded as an example.

COOK INC.
General Ledger Accounts

Event	Assets		=	Liabilities	+	Stockholders' Equity		Acct. Titles for Ret. Earn.
	Cash	Accounts Receivable		Salaries Payable		Common Stock	Retained Earnings	
1.	15,000					15,000		

b. Prepare the income statement, statement of changes in stockholders' equity, balance sheet, and statement of cash flows for the 2005 accounting period.

c. Why is the ending cash balance the same as the net change in cash on the statement of cash flows?

L.O. 2, 3

Exercise 2-2B *Effect of collecting accounts receivable on the accounting equation and financial statements*

Solimon Company earned $13,000 of revenue on account during 2008. The company collected $7,000 cash from accounts receivable during 2008.

Required

Based on this information alone, determine the following. (*Hint:* Record the events in general ledger accounts under an accounting equation before satisfying the requirements.)

a. The balance of accounts receivable that Solimon would report on the December 31, 2008, balance sheet.

b. The amount of net income that Solimon would report on the 2008 income statement.

c. The amount of net cash flow from operating activities that Solimon would report on the 2008 statement of cash flows.

d. The amount of retained earnings that Solimon would report on the December 31, 2008, balance sheet.

e. Why are the answers to Requirements *b* and *c* different?

Exercise 2-3B *Effect of prepaid rent on the accounting equation and financial statements*

L.O. 2, 3

The following events apply to 2007, the first year of operations of Shay Services:

1. Acquired $25,000 cash from the issue of common stock.
2. Paid $18,000 cash in advance for a one-year rental contract for office space.
3. Provided services for $28,000 cash.
4. Adjusted the records to recognize the use of the office space. The one-year contract started on April 1, 2007. The adjustment was made as of December 31, 2007.

Required

a. Write an accounting equation and record the effects of each accounting event under the appropriate general ledger account headings.

b. Prepare a balance sheet at the end of the 2007 accounting period.

c. What amount of rent expense will Shay report on the 2007 income statement?

d. What amount of net cash flow from operating activities will Shay report on the 2007 statement of cash flows?

Exercise 2-4B *Effect of supplies on the financial statements*

L.O. 1, 3

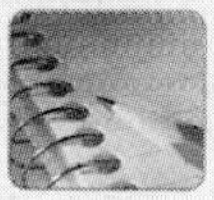

Package Express started the 2006 accounting period with $2,000 cash, $1,200 of common stock, and $800 of retained earnings. Package was affected by the following accounting events during 2006:

1. Purchased $2,400 of copier toner and other supplies on account.
2. Earned and collected $10,800 of cash revenue.
3. Paid $1,800 cash on accounts payable.
4. Adjusted the records to reflect the use of supplies. A physical count indicated that $200 of supplies was still on hand on December 31, 2006.

Required

a. Show the effects of the events on the financial statements using a horizontal statements model like the following one. In the Cash Flows column, use OA to designate operating activity, IA for investing activity, FA for financing activity, and NC for net change in cash. Use NA to indicate accounts not affected by the event. The beginning balances are entered in the following example.

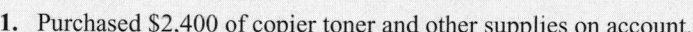

Event No.	Assets			=	Liab.	+	Stockholders' Equity									
	Cash	+	Supplies	=	Accts. Pay.	+	Com. Stk.	+	Ret. Earn.	Rev.	−	Exp.	=	Net Inc.		Cash Flows
Beg. bal.	2,000	+	0	=	0	+	1,200	+	800	0	−	0	=	0		0

b. Explain the difference between the amount of net income and amount of net cash flow from operating activities.

Exercise 2-5B *Effect of unearned revenue on financial statements*

L.O. 1

Donald Jones started a personal financial planning business when he accepted $30,000 cash as advance payment for managing the financial assets of a large estate. Donald agreed to manage the estate for a 12-month period, beginning April 1, 2008.

Required

a. Show the effects of the advance payment and revenue recognition on the 2008 financial statements using a horizontal statements model like the following one. In the Cash Flows column, use OA to designate operating activity, IA for investing activity, FA for financing activity, and NC for net change in cash. Use NA if the account is not affected.

Event	Assets	=	Liab.	+	Stockholders' Equity	Rev.	−	Exp.	=	Net Inc.	Cash Flows
	Cash	=	Unearn. Rev.	+	Ret. Earn.						

b. How much revenue would Jones recognize on the 2009 income statement?

c. What is the amount of cash flow from operating activities in 2009?

L.O. 3

Exercise 2-6B *Unearned revenue defined as a liability*

Lei, an accounting major, and Jim, a marketing major, are watching a *Matlock* rerun on late-night TV. Of course, there is a murder and the suspect wants to hire Matlock as the defense attorney. Matlock will take the case but requires an advance payment of $100,000. Jim remarks that Matlock has earned a cool $100,000 without lifting a finger. Lei tells Jim that Matlock has not earned anything but has a $100,000 liability. Jim asks "How can that be?"

Required

Assume you are Lei. Explain to Jim why Matlock has a liability and when Matlock would actually earn the $100,000.

L.O. 3

Exercise 2-7B *Asset versus expense*

A cost can be either an asset or an expense.

Required

a. Distinguish between a cost that is an asset and a cost that is an expense.

b. List three costs that are assets.

c. List three costs that are expenses.

L.O. 1

Exercise 2-8B *Revenue and expense recognition*

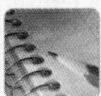

Required

a. Describe a revenue recognition event that results in an increase in assets.

b. Describe a revenue recognition event that results in a decrease in liabilities.

c. Describe an expense recognition event that results in an increase in liabilities.

d. Describe an expense recognition event that results in a decrease in assets.

L.O. 1

Exercise 2-9B *Transactions that affect the elements of financial statements*

Required

Give an example of a transaction that will

a. Increase an asset and decrease another asset (asset exchange event).

b. Increase an asset and increase a liability (asset source event).

c. Decrease an asset and decrease a liability (asset use event).

d. Decrease an asset and decrease equity (asset use event).

e. Increase a liability and decrease equity (claims exchange event).

f. Increase an asset and increase equity (asset source event).

g. Decrease a liability and increase equity (claims exchange event).

L.O. 3

Exercise 2-10B *Identifying deferral and accrual events*

Required

Identify each of the following events as an accrual, deferral, or neither.

a. Incurred other operating expenses on account.

b. Recorded expense for salaries owed to employees at the end of the accounting period.

c. Paid a cash dividend to the stockholders.
d. Paid cash to purchase supplies to be used over the next several months.
e. Paid cash to purchase land.
f. Provided services on account.
g. Collected accounts receivable.
h. Paid one year's rent in advance.
i. Paid cash for utilities expense.
j. Collected $2,400 in advance for services to be performed over the next 12 months.

Exercise 2-11B *Unearned and prepaid services* **L.O. 2**

On September 1, 2007, Anthony Park, attorney, accepted an $18,000 cash advance from his client, Slab Company, for services to be performed over the next six months.

Required

a. Record the deferral and the related December 31, 2007, adjustment for Anthony Park in an accounting equation.
b. Record the deferral and the related December 31, 2007, adjustment for Slab Company in an accounting equation.

Exercise 2-12B *Classifying events on the statement of cash flows* **L.O. 3**

The following transactions pertain to the operations of Colton Company for 2006:

1. Acquired $20,000 cash from the issue of common stock.
2. Provided $80,000 of services on account.
3. Paid $20,000 cash on accounts payable.
4. Performed services for $5,000 cash.
5. Collected $65,000 cash from accounts receivable.
6. Incurred $42,000 of operating expenses on account.
7. Paid $4,800 cash for one year's rent in advance.
8. Paid a $5,000 cash dividend to the stockholders.
9. Paid $900 cash for supplies to be used in the future.
10. Recognized $2,500 of accrued salaries expense.

Required

a. Classify the cash flows from each of these transactions as operating activities (OA), investing activities (IA), or financing activities (FA). Use NA for transactions that do not affect the statement of cash flows.
b. Prepare a statement of cash flows. (This is the first year of operations.)

Exercise 2-13B *Effect of accounting events on the income statement and statement of cash flows* **L.O. 3**

Required

Explain how each of the following events or series of events and any related adjusting entry will affect the amount of *net income* and the amount of *cash flow from operating activities* reported on the year-end financial statements. Identify the direction of change (increase, decrease, or NA) and the amount of the change. Organize your answers according to the following table. The first event is recorded as an example. If an event does not have a related adjusting entry, record only the effects of the event.

	Net Income		Cash Flows from Operating Activities	
Event No.	**Direction of Change**	**Amount of Change**	**Direction of Change**	**Amount of Change**
a	NA	NA	Decrease	$6,000
Adj	Decrease	$1,000	NA	NA

a. Paid $6,000 cash on November 1 to purchase a one-year insurance policy.
b. Purchased $1,000 of supplies on account. Paid $700 cash on accounts payable. The ending balance in the Supplies account, after adjustment, was $100.

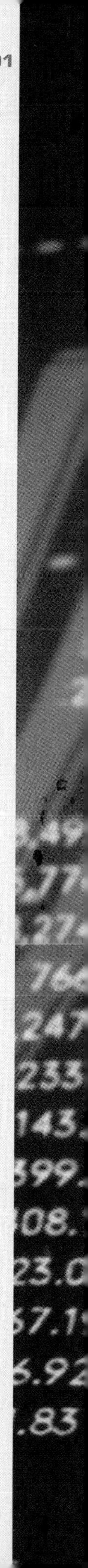

c. Provided services for $8,000 cash.
d. Collected $1,800 in advance for services to be performed in the future. The contract called for services to start on May 1 and to continue for one year.
e. Accrued salaries amounting to $3,200.
f. Sold land that cost $2,000 for $2,000 cash.
g. Acquired $20,000 cash from the issue of common stock.
h. Earned $8,000 of revenue on account. Collected $5,000 cash from accounts receivable.
i. Paid cash operating expenses of $3,000.

L.O. 1, 8

Exercise 2-14B *Identifying transaction type and effect on the financial statements*

Required

Identify whether each of the following transactions is an asset source (AS), asset use (AU), asset exchange (AE), or claims exchange (CE). Also show the effects of the events on the financial statements using the horizontal statements model. Indicate whether the event increases (I), decreases (D), or does not affect (NA) each element of the financial statements. In the Cash Flows column, designate the cash flows as operating activities (OA), investing activities (IA), or financing activities (FA). The first two transactions have been recorded as examples.

					Stockholders' Equity					
Event No.	Type of Event	Assets	=	Liabilities	+ Common Stock	+ Retained Earnings	Rev.	− Exp.	= Net Inc.	Cash Flows
a	AE	I D		NA	NA	NA	NA	NA	NA	D IA
b	AS	I		NA	I	NA	NA	NA	NA	I FA

a. Purchased land for cash.
b. Acquired cash from the issue of common stock.
c. Collected cash from accounts receivable.
d. Paid cash for operating expenses.
e. Recorded accrued salaries.
f. Purchased supplies on account.
g. Performed services on account.
h. Paid cash in advance for rent on office space.
i. Adjusted the books to record supplies used during the period.
j. Performed services for cash.
k. Paid cash for salaries accrued at the end of a prior period.
l. Paid a cash dividend to the stockholders.
m. Adjusted books to reflect the amount of prepaid rent expired during the period.
n. Incurred operating expenses on account.
o. Paid cash on accounts payable.
p. Received cash advance for services to be provided in the future.

L.O. 1

Exercise 2-15B *Effect of accruals and deferrals on financial statements: horizontal statements model*

Grange, Attorney at Law, experienced the following transactions in 2007, the first year of operations:

1. Accepted $24,000 on April 1, 2007, as a retainer for services to be performed evenly over the next 12 months.
2. Performed legal services for cash of $29,000.
3. Purchased $1,400 of office supplies on account.
4. Paid $1,000 of the amount due on accounts payable.
5. Paid a cash dividend to the stockholders of $5,000.
6. Paid cash for operating expenses of $16,200.
7. Determined that at the end of the accounting period $150 of office supplies remained on hand.
8. On December 31, 2007, recognized the revenue that had been earned for services performed in accordance with Transaction 1.

Required

Show the effects of the events on the financial statements using a horizontal statements model like the following one. In the Cash Flows column, use the initials OA to designate operating activity, IA for investing activity, FA for financing activity, and NC for net change in cash. Use NA to indicate accounts not affected by the event. The first event has been recorded as an example.

Event No.	Assets			=	Liabilities			+	Stk. Equity						Cash Flow
	Cash	+	Supplies	=	Accts. Pay.	+	Unearn. Rev.	+	Ret. Earn.	Rev.	−	Exp.	=	Net Inc.	
1	24,000	+	NA	=	NA	+	24,000	+	NA	NA	−	NA	=	NA	24,000 NA

Exercise 2-16B *Effect of an error on financial statements*

L.O. 2, 3

On May 1, 2007, Southern Corporation paid $9,000 cash in advance for a one-year lease on an office building. Assume that Southern records the prepaid rent as an asset and that the books are closed on December 31.

Required

a. Show the payment for the one-year lease and the related adjusting entry to recognize rent expense in the accounting equation.

b. Assume that Southern Corporation failed to record the adjusting entry to reflect using the office building. How would the error affect the company's 2007 income statement and balance sheet?

Exercise 2-17B *Net income versus changes in cash*

L.O. 2, 3

In 2008, Ace Company billed its customers $100,000 for services performed. The company subsequently collected $73,000 of the amount billed. Ace incurred $69,000 of operating expenses on account. Ace paid $62,000 of that amount. Ace acquired $30,000 cash from the issue of common stock. The company invested $40,000 cash in the purchase of land.

Required

Use the preceding information to answer the following questions. (*Hint:* Identify the six events described in the paragraph and record them in general ledger accounts under an accounting equation before answering the questions.)

a. What amount of revenue will Ace report on the 2008 income statement?

b. What is the net income for the period?

c. What amount of cash flow from revenue will Ace report on the statement of cash flows?

d. What is the net cash flow from operating activities for the period?

e. Why is the amount of net income different from the net cash flow from operating activities for the period?

f. What is the amount of net cash flow from investing activities?

g. What is the amount of net cash flow from financing activities?

h. What amount of total equity will Ace report on the year-end balance sheet?

Exercise 2-18B *Adjusting the accounts*

L.O. 3

Mendez Inc. experienced the following accounting events during its 2006 accounting period.

1. Paid cash to settle an account payable.
2. Collected a cash advance for services that will be provided during the coming year.
3. Paid a cash dividend to the stockholders.
4. Paid cash for a one-year lease to rent office space.
5. Collected cash from accounts receivable.
6. Recognized cash revenue.
7. Issued common stock.
8. Paid cash to purchase land.
9. Paid cash to purchase supplies.
10. Recognized operating expenses on account.

Required

a. Identify the events that would require a year-end adjusting entry.

b. Are adjusting or closing entries recorded first? Why?

L.O. 4

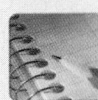

Exercise 2-19B *Closing the accounts*

The following information was drawn from the accounting records of Fulmer Company as of December 31, 2005, before the temporary accounts had been closed. The company's cash balance was $2,500, and its land account had a $6,500 balance. Notes payable amounted to $3,000. The balance in the Common Stock account was $1,500. The company had revenues of $5,500 and expenses of $2,000, and dividends amounted to $900.

Required

a. Identify the accounts that would be closed to Retained Earnings at the end of the accounting period.

b. Assuming that Fulmer's beginning balance (as of January 1, 2005) in the Retained Earnings account was $1,900, determine its balance after the temporary accounts were closed at the end of 2005.

c. What amount of net income would Fulmer Company report on its 2005 income statement?

d. Explain why the amount of net income differs from the amount of the ending Retained Earnings balance.

e. What are the balances in the revenue, expense, and dividend accounts on January 1, 2006?

L.O. 4

Exercise 2-20B *Closing accounts and the accounting cycle*

Required

a. Identify which of the following accounts are temporary (will be closed to Retained Earnings at the end of the year) and which are permanent.

(1) Common Stock
(2) Salaries Payable
(3) Cash
(4) Service Revenue
(5) Dividends
(6) Land
(7) Salaries Expense
(8) Retained Earnings
(9) Utilities Expense
(10) Other Operating Expenses

b. Bill bragged that he had five years of accounting experience. Jane disagreed, responding, "No. You have had one year of accounting experience five times." Explain what Jane meant. (*Hint:* Refer to the accounting cycle.)

L.O. 4

Exercise 2-21B *Closing entries*

Required

Which of the following accounts are closed at the end of the accounting period?

a. Land
b. Supplies Expense
c. Prepaid Rent
d. Rent Expense
e. Salaries Payable
f. Service Revenue
g. Retained Earnings
h. Cash
i. Dividends
j. Accounts Receivable
k. Common Stock
l. Advertising Expense

Exercise 2-22B *Matching concept* L.O. 4

Companies make sacrifices known as *expenses* to obtain benefits called *revenues.* The accurate measurement of net income requires that expenses be matched with revenues. In some circumstances, matching a particular expense directly with revenue is difficult or impossible. In these circumstances, the expense is matched with the period in which it is incurred.

Required

Distinguish the following items that could be matched directly with revenues from the items that would be classified as period expenses.

a. Sales commissions paid to employees.
b. Advertising expense.
c. Supplies.
d. The cost of land that has been sold.

Exercise 2-23B *Identifying source, use, and exchange transactions* L.O. 8

Required

Indicate whether each of the following transactions is an asset source (AS), asset use (AU), asset exchange (AE), or claims exchange (CE) transaction.

a. Performed services for clients on account.
b. Paid cash for salary expense.
c. Acquired cash from the issue of common stock.
d. Incurred other operating expenses on account.
e. Performed services for cash.
f. Paid cash on accounts payable.
g. Collected cash from accounts receivable.
h. Paid a cash dividend to the stockholders.
i. Received cash for services to be performed in the future.
j. Purchased land with cash.

Exercise 2-24B *Identifying asset source, use, and exchange transactions* L.O. 8

Required

a. Name an asset use transaction that will affect the income statement.
b. Name an asset use transaction that will *not* affect the income statement.
c. Name an asset exchange transaction that will *not* affect the statement of cash flows.
d. Name an asset exchange transaction that will affect the statement of cash flows.
e. Name an asset source transaction that will *not* affect the income statement.

Exercise 2-25B *Relation of elements to financial statements* L.O. 5

Required

Identify whether each of the following items would appear on the income statement (IS), statement of changes in stockholders' equity (SE), balance sheet (BS), or statement of cash flows (CF). Some items may appear on more than one statement; if so, identify all applicable statements. If an item would not appear on any financial statement, label it NA.

a. Accounts Receivable
b. Accounts Payable
c. Salaries Payable
d. Dividends
e. Beginning Cash Balance
f. Ending Retained Earnings
g. Rent Expense
h. Ending Cash Balance
i. Salaries Expense
j. Net Income
k. Utilities Expense

l. Price-earnings Ratio
m. Cash Flow from Operating Activities
n. Service Revenue
o. Unearned Revenue

L.O. 7

Exercise 2-26B ***Price-earnings ratio***

The following information is available for two companies:

	ARC Company	Pager Company
Earnings per share	$ 0.85	$ 2.25
Market price per share	46.50	75.40

Required

a. Compute the price-earnings ratio for each company.
b. Which company would you expect to have the higher earnings growth potential?

PROBLEMS—SERIES B

L.O. 1

Problem 2-27B ***Recording events in a horizontal statements model***

The following events pertain to Union Inc.:

1. Acquired $8,000 cash from the issue of common stock.
2. Provided $9,000 of services on account.
3. Provided services for $3,000 cash.
4. Received $2,500 cash in advance for services to be performed in the future.
5. Collected $5,600 cash from the account receivable created in Event 2.
6. Paid $1,100 for cash expenses.
7. Performed $1,400 of the services agreed to in Event 4.
8. Incurred $2,800 of expenses on account.
9. Paid $2,400 cash in advance for one-year contract to rent office space.
10. Paid $2,200 cash on the account payable created in Event 8.
11. Paid a $1,500 cash dividend to the stockholders.
12. Recognized rent expense for nine months' use of office space acquired in Event 9.

Required

Show the effects of the events on the financial statements using a horizontal statements model like the following one. In the Cash Flows column, use the letters OA to designate operating activity, IA for investing activity, FA for financing activity, and NC for net change in cash. Use NA to indicate accounts not affected by the event. The first event is recorded as an example.

	Assets					=	Liabilities			+	Stockholders' Equity								
Event No.	Cash	+	Accts. Rec.	+	Prep. Rent	=	Accts. Pay.	+	Unearn. Rev.	+	Common Stock	+	Ret. Earn.	Rev.	−	Exp.	=	Net Inc.	Cash Flows
1	8,000	+	NA	+	NA	=	NA	+	NA	+	8,000	+	NA	NA	−	NA	=	NA	8,000 FA

L.O. 1, 2, 3

Problem 2-28B ***Effect of deferrals on financial statements: three separate single-cycle examples***

Required

a. On February 1, 2006, Elder Company was formed when it acquired $10,000 cash from the issue of common stock. On June 1, 2006, the company paid $2,400 cash in advance to rent office space for the coming year. The office space was used as a place to consult with clients. The consulting activity generated $5,200 of cash revenue during 2006. Based on this information alone, record the events in general ledger accounts under the accounting equation. Determine the amount of net income and cash flows from operating activities for 2006.

b. On August 1, 2005, the consulting firm of Craig & Associates was formed. On September 1, 2005, the company received a $12,000 retainer (was paid in advance) for monthly services to be performed over a one-year period. Assuming that this was the only transaction completed in 2005, prepare an income statement, statement of changes in stockholders' equity, balance sheet, and statement of cash flows for 2005.

c. Snell Company had $650 of supplies on hand on January 1, 2008. During 2008 Snell Company purchased $1,500 of supplies on account. A physical count of supplies revealed that $350 of supplies were on hand as of December 31, 2008. Determine the amount of supplies expense that should be recognized in the December 31, 2008, adjusting entry. Use a financial statements model to show how the adjusting entry would affect the balance sheet, income statement, and statement of cash flows.

Problem 2-29B *Effect of adjusting entries on the accounting equation*

L.O. 2

Required

Each of the following independent events requires a year-end adjusting entry. Show how each event and its related adjusting entry affects the accounting equation. Assume a December 31 closing date. The first event is recorded as an example.

	Total Assets						Stockholders' Equity		
Event/ Adjustment	Cash	+	Other Assets	=	Liabilities	+	Common Stock	+	Retained Earnings
a	−3,600		+3,600		NA		NA		NA
Adj.	NA		−900		NA		NA		−900

a. Paid $3,600 cash in advance on October 1 for a one-year insurance policy.

b. Received an $1,800 cash advance for a contract to provide services in the future. The contract required a one-year commitment, starting April 1.

c. Purchased $800 of supplies on account. At year's end, $140 of supplies remained on hand.

d. Paid $7,200 cash in advance on August 1 for a one-year lease on office space.

Problem 2-30B *Events for two complete accounting cycles*

L.O. 2, 5, 6, 8

Southwest Plains Company was formed on January 1, 2005.

Events Affecting the 2005 Accounting Period

1. Acquired $25,000 cash from the issue of common stock.
2. Purchased $500 of supplies on account.
3. Purchased land that cost $12,000 cash.
4. Paid $500 cash to settle accounts payable created in Event 2.
5. Recognized revenue on account of $9,000.
6. Paid $2,400 cash for other operating expenses.
7. Collected $7,000 cash from accounts receivable.

Information for 2005 Adjusting Entries

8. Recognized accrued salaries of $3,200 on December 31, 2005.
9. Had $100 of supplies on hand at the end of the accounting period.

Events Affecting the 2006 Accounting Period

1. Acquired $12,000 cash from the issue of common stock.
2. Paid $3,200 cash to settle the salaries payable obligation.
3. Paid $6,000 cash in advance to lease office space.
4. Sold the land that cost $12,000 for $12,000 cash.
5. Received $8,400 cash in advance for services to be performed in the future.
6. Purchased $2,000 of supplies on account during the year.

7. Provided services on account of $11,000.
8. Collected $9,000 cash from accounts receivable.
9. Paid a cash dividend of $2,000 to the stockholders.

Information for 2006 Adjusting Entries

10. The advance payment for rental of the office space (see Event 3) was made on February 1 for a one-year term.
11. The cash advance for services to be provided in the future was collected on October 1 (see Event 5). The one-year contract started on October 1.
12. Had $200 of supplies remaining on hand at the end of the period.
13. Recognized accrued salaries of $6,000 at the end of the accounting period.

Required

a. Identify each event affecting the 2005 and 2006 accounting periods as an asset source (AS), asset use (AU), asset exchange (AE), or claims exchange (CE). Record the effects of each event under the appropriate general ledger account headings of the accounting equation.

b. Prepare an income statement, statement of changes in stockholders' equity, balance sheet, and statement of cash flows for 2005 and 2006, using the vertical statements model.

L.O. 2, 3

Problem 2-31B ***Effect of events on financial statements***

Caban Company had the following balances in its accounting records as of December 31, 2006:

Assets		Claims	
Cash	$23,000	Accounts Payable	$ 5,000
Accounts Receivable	7,000	Common Stock	24,000
Land	42,000	Retained Earnings	43,000
Total	$72,000	Total	$72,000

The following accounting events apply to Caban Company's 2007 fiscal year:

Jan.	1	Acquired $12,000 cash from the issue of common stock.
Feb.	1	Paid $3,000 cash in advance for a one-year lease for office space.
Mar.	1	Paid a $1,000 cash dividend to the stockholders.
April	1	Purchased additional land that cost $28,000 cash.
May	1	Made a cash payment on accounts payable of $2,000.
July	1	Received $5,400 cash in advance as a retainer for services to be performed monthly over the coming year.
Sept.	1	Sold land for $42,000 cash that had originally cost $42,000.
Oct.	1	Purchased $3,000 of supplies on account.
Dec.	31	Earned $35,000 of service revenue on account during the year.
	31	Received cash collections from accounts receivable amounting to $40,000.
	31	Incurred other operating expenses on account during the year that amounted to $6,000.
	31	Recognized accrued salaries expense of $4,800.
	31	Had $50 of supplies on hand at the end of the period.
	31	The land purchased on April 1 had a market value of $30,000.

Required

Based on the preceding information, answer the following questions. All questions pertain to the 2007 financial statements. (*Hint:* Enter items in general ledger accounts under the accounting equation before answering the questions.)

a. Based on the preceding transactions, identify two additional adjustments and describe them.
b. What amount would Caban report for land on the balance sheet?
c. What amount of net cash flow from operating activities would Caban report on the statement of cash flows?
d. What amount of rent expense would Caban report in the income statement?
e. What amount of total liabilities would Caban report on the balance sheet?
f. What amount of supplies expense would Caban report on the income statement?

g. What amount of unearned revenue would Caban report on the balance sheet?
h. What amount of net cash flow from investing activities would Caban report on the statement of cash flows?
i. What amount of total expenses would Caban report on the income statement?
j. What amount of service revenue would Caban report on the income statement?
k. What amount of cash flows from financing activities would Caban report on the statement of cash flows?
l. What amount of net income would Caban report on the income statement?
m. What amount of retained earnings would Caban report on the balance sheet?

Problem 2-32B *Preparing financial statements*

L.O. 5

The following accounts and balances were drawn from the records of Miller Company:

Required

The following accounts and balances were drawn from the 2006 accounting records of Miller Company. Use the information to construct an income statement, statement of changes in stockholders' equity, balance sheet, and statement of cash flows. (Show only totals for each activity on the statement of cash flows.)

Supplies	$ 300	Beginning Retained Earnings	$14,500
Cash Flow from Investing Act.	(7,800)	Cash Flow from Financing Act.	0
Prepaid Insurance	600	Rent Expense	1,500
Service Revenue	45,450	Dividends	6,000
Other Operating Expenses	35,000	Cash	19,000
Supplies Expense	750	Accounts Receivable	7,000
Insurance Expense	1,800	Prepaid Rent	6,000
Beginning Common Stock	24,000	Unearned Revenue	8,000
Cash Flow from Operating Act.	10,450	Land	36,000
Common Stock Issued	6,000	Accounts Payable	16,000

Problem 2-33B *Relationship of accounts to financial statements*

L.O. 3

Required

Identify whether each of the following items would appear on the income statement (IS), statement of changes in stockholders' equity (SE), balance sheet (BS), or statement of cash flows (CF). If some items appear on more than one statement, identify all applicable statements. If an item will not appear on any financial statement, label it NA.

a. Rent Expense
b. Price/earnings Ratio
c. Taxes Payable
d. Unearned Revenue
e. Service Revenue
f. Cash Flow from Investing Activities
g. Consulting Revenue
h. Utilities Expense
i. Ending Common Stock
j. Total Liabilities
k. Operating Cycle
l. Cash Flow from Operating Activities
m. Operating Expenses
n. Supplies Expense
o. Beginning Retained Earnings
p. Beginning Common Stock
q. Prepaid Insurance
r. Salary Expense
s. Beginning Cash Balance
t. Ending Cash Balance
u. Supplies
v. Cash Flow from Financing Activities
w. "As of" Date Notation
x. Ending Retained Earnings
y. Net Income
z. Dividends
aa. Net Change in Cash
bb. "For the Period Ended"
cc. Land
dd. Ending Common Stock
ee. Salaries Expense
ff. Prepaid Rent
gg. Accounts Payable
hh. Total Assets
ii. Salaries Payable
jj. Insurance Expense
kk. Notes Payable
ll. Accounts Receivable

L.O. 5, 6

Problem 2-34B ***Missing information in financial statements***

Required

Fill in the blanks (indicated by the alphabetic letters in parentheses) in the following financial statements. Assume the company started operations January 1, 2005, and all transactions involve cash.

	For the Years		
	2005	**2006**	**2007**
Income Statements			
Revenue	$ 400	$ 500	$ 800
Expense	(250)	(l)	(425)
Net Income	$ (a)	$ 100	$ 375
Statements of Changes in Stockholders' Equity			
Beginning Common Stock	$ 0	$ (m)	$ 9,100
Plus: Common Stock Issued	(b)	1,100	310
Ending Common Stock	8,000	9,100	(s)
Beginning Retained Earnings	0	25	75
Plus: Net Income	(c)	100	375
Less: Dividends	(d)	(50)	(150)
Ending Retained Earnings	25	(n)	300
Total Stockholders' Equity	$ (e)	$ 9,175	$ (t)
Balance Sheets			
Assets			
Cash	$ (f)	$ (o)	$ (u)
Land	0	(p)	2,500
Total Assets	$11,000	$11,650	$10,550
Liabilities	$ (g)	$ (q)	$ 840
Stockholders' Equity			
Common Stock	(h)	(r)	9,410
Retained Earnings	(i)	75	300
Total Stockholders' Equity	8,025	9,175	9,710
Total Liabilities and Stockholders' Equity	$11,000	$11,650	$10,550
Statements of Cash Flows			
Cash Flows from Operating Activities			
Cash Receipts from Revenue	$ (j)	$ 500	$ (v)
Cash Payments for Expenses	(k)	(400)	(w)
Net Cash Flows from Operating Activities	150	100	375
Cash Flows from Investing Activities			
Cash Payments for Land	0	(5,000)	0
Cash Receipt from Sale of Land	0	0	2,500
Net Cash Flows from Investing Activities	0	(5,000)	2,500
Cash Flows from Financing Activities			
Cash Receipts from Borrowed Funds	2,975	0	0
Cash Payments to Reduce Debt	0	(500)	(x)
Cash Receipts from Stock Issue	8,000	1,100	(y)
Cash Payments for Dividends	(125)	(50)	(z)
Net Cash Flows from Financing Activities	10,850	550	(1,475)
Net Change in Cash	11,000	(4,350)	1,400
Plus: Beginning Cash Balance	0	11,000	6,650
Ending Cash Balance	$11,000	$ 6,650	$ 8,050

Problem 2-35B *Price-earnings relationships*

L.O. 7

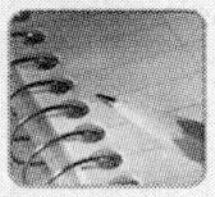

Earnings per share and market price per share data for Advantage Inc. and Hi-Lite Inc. follow.

Advantage Inc.	**2005**	**2006**	**2007**
Earnings per share	$ 4.22	$ 4.13	$ 4.18
Market price per share	50.64	45.43	45.98
Hi-Lite Inc.	**2005**	**2006**	**2007**
Earnings per share	$ 3.27	$ 4.19	$ 5.81
Market price per share	98.10	129.89	220.78

Required

a. Calculate the annual percentage growth rate in the earnings per share of each company from 2005 to 2006 and from 2006 to 2007.

b. Calculate the price-earnings ratio for each company for all three years.

c. Explain what the price-earnings ratio means.

d. Why would the price-earnings ratios of the two companies be different?

ANALYZE, THINK, COMMUNICATE

ATC 2-1 Business Applications Case *Understanding real-world annual reports*

Required—Part 1

Use the **Topps Company** annual report in Appendix B to answer the following questions.

The Topps Company, Inc.

a. Which accounts on Topps' balance sheet are accrual type accounts?

b. Which accounts on Topps' balance sheet are deferral type accounts?

c. Compare Topps' 2003 *net income* to its 2003 *cash provided by operating activities.* Which is larger?

d. First, compare Topps' 2002 net income to its 2003 net income. Next, compare Topps' 2002 cash provided by operating activities to its 2003 cash provided by operating activities. Which changed the most from 2002 to 2003, net income or cash provided by operating activities?

Required—Part 2

Use the **Harley-Davidson** annual report that came with this book to answer the following questions.

Harley-Davidson, Inc.

a. Which accounts on Harley-Davidson's balance sheet are accrual type accounts?

b. Which accounts on Harley-Davidson's balance sheet are deferral type accounts?

c. Compare Harley-Davidson's 2003 *net income* to its 2003 *net cash provided by operating activities.* Which is larger?

d. First, compare Harley-Davidson's 2002 net income to its 2003 net income. Next, compare Harley-Davidson's 2002 net cash provided by operating activities to its 2003 net cash provided by operating activities. Which changed the most from 2002 to 2003, net income or net cash provided by operating activities?

ATC 2-2 Group Assignment *Missing information*

Verizon Communications, Inc., is one of the world's largest providers of communication services. The following information, taken from the company's annual reports, is available for the years 2003, 2002, and 2001.

	2003	**2002**	**2001**
Revenue	$67,752	$67,304	$66,713
Operating Expenses	60,258	52,300	55,240
All dollar amounts are shown in millions.			
Net Income for 2000 was $16,758			

Required

a. Divide the class into groups of four or five students. Organize the groups into three sections. Assign each section of groups the financial data for one of the preceding accounting periods.

Group Tasks

(1) Determine the amount of net income for the year assigned.

(2) How does the result in item 1 above affect the retained earnings of the company?

(3) Compute the percentage growth rate for each year.

(4) Have representatives from each section put the income statement for their respective year on the board.

Class Discussion

b. Have the class discuss the trend in revenue and net income.

ATC 2-3 Real-World Case *Classifying which company is the best investment*

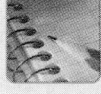

Following are the net earnings of four large companies for the fiscal years from 1999 to 2002. These amounts are in thousands of dollars.

		Net Earnings in $000			
Company	**Industry**	**2002**	**2001**	**2000**	**1999**
Autozone	Automobile parts retailer	$428,148	$175,526	$267,590	$244,783
Kohl's	Department store chain	643,381	495,676	372,148	258,142
Oshkosh B'Gosh	Children's clothing	32,045	32,808	32,217	32,448
Peoplesoft	Software development	182,589	191,554	145,691	(177,765)

Required

Based on this information alone, decide which of the companies you think would present the best investment opportunity for the future and which would be the worst. Write a brief memorandum supporting your choices, and show any computations that you used to reach your conclusions. As part of your analysis, compute the annual growth rates for each company's earnings. To do this, compute by what percentage each company's earnings increased or decreased from the year before. You will not be able to compute a growth rate for 1999 since the earnings for 1998 are not given. Perform whatever additional analysis you think is useful.

ATC 2-4 Business Applications Case *Calculating percentage growth rates at two companies*

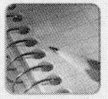

The following information relates to two companies in the same industry.

	Net Earnings by Year			
Company	**2007**	**2006**	**2005**	**2004**
Seven Grain	$2,000	$1,850	$1,660	$1,450
Whole Wheat	5,000	4,750	4,500	4,150

Required

a. Calculate the percentage growth rate of each company's net earnings from 2004 to 2007.

b. Based on this information alone, which company would you expect to have the higher price-earnings ratio? Explain your answer.

ATC 2-5 Business Applications Case *Calculating EPS and P/E ratios*

The following information was drawn from the financial statements of Last Minute Inc. and the Just-in-Time Co.

Statement Data	Last Minute Inc.	Just-in-Time Co.
Revenue	$15,000,000	$20,000,000
Net income	$ 1,150,000	$ 900,000
Number of shares of common stock outstanding	1,200,000	500,000
Market price per share	$ 17.25	$ 21.50

Required

a. Calculate the earnings per share (EPS) for each company.

b. Calculate the price-earnings (P/E) ratio for each company.

c. Which company does the market seem to be the most optimistic about?

ATC 2-6 Writing Assignment *Effect of stock options on real-world companies' P/E ratios*

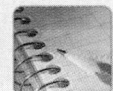

Many companies grant certain members of management stock options that allow them to purchase designated amounts of stock for less than its market price. These arrangements are referred to as *stock compensation plans* and are intended to help the company retain high-quality management and to encourage management to increase the market value of the company's stock.

Deciding on the appropriate way to account for these plans is complex and controversial. Therefore, companies are allowed to *exclude* the estimated costs of the options they grant their management from net earnings provided that they disclose the estimated costs in the footnotes to the financial statements.

Listed here are data from four different companies that grant stock options to members of their management. The data are based on information provided in the companies' 10-K reports.

Costco Wholesale Corporation	
Basic EPS as reported on the fiscal year 2002 income statement	$ 1.48
Basic EPS if stock compensation is deducted	1.32
Selling price of the company's stock on July 1, 2003	36.51
Target Corporation	
Basic EPS as reported on the fiscal year 2003 income statement	$ 1.82
Basic EPS if stock compensation is deducted	1.79
Selling price of the company's stock on July 1, 2003	37.62
Cisco Systems, Inc.	
Basic EPS as reported on the fiscal year 2002 income statement	$ 0.26
Basic EPS if stock compensation is deducted	0.05
Selling price of the company's stock on July 1, 2003	17.24
Oracle Corporation	
Basic EPS as reported on the fiscal year 2003 income statement	$ 0.44
Basic EPS if stock compensation is deducted	0.37
Selling price of the company's stock on July 1, 2003	12.33

Required

a. Compute each company's P/E ratio on July 1, 2003, based on (1) EPS as reported and (2) EPS with stock compensation deducted. You will have eight P/E ratios.

b. Assuming these companies are representative of their respective industries (department stores and software companies), what conclusions can you draw from the data provided and from your P/E computations? Write a brief report presenting your conclusions and the reasons for them.

ATC 2-7 Ethical Dilemma *What is a little deceit among friends?*

Glenn's Cleaning Services Company is experiencing cash flow problems and needs a loan. Glenn has a friend who is willing to lend him the money he needs provided she can be convinced that he will be able to repay the debt. Glenn has assured his friend that his business is viable, but his friend has asked to see the company's financial statements. Glenn's accountant produced the following financial statements:

Income Statement	
Service Revenue	$ 38,000
Operating Expenses	(70,000)
Net Loss	$(32,000)

[redacted]	
Assets	$85,000
Liabilities	$35,000
Stockholders' Equity	
Common Stock	82,000
Retained Earnings	(32,000)
Total Liabilities and Stockholders' Equity	$85,000

Glenn made the following adjustments to these statements before showing them to his friend. He recorded $82,000 of revenue on account from Barrymore Manufacturing Company for a contract to clean its headquarters office building that was still being negotiated for the next month. Barrymore had scheduled a meeting to sign a contract the following week, so Glenn was sure that he would get the job. Barrymore was a reputable company, and Glenn was confident that he could ultimately collect the $82,000. Also, he subtracted $30,000 of accrued salaries expense and the corresponding liability. He reasoned that since he had not paid the employees, he had not incurred any expense.

Required

a. Reconstruct the income statement and balance sheet as they would appear after Glenn's adjustments. Comment on the accuracy of the adjusted financial statements.

b. Suppose you are Glenn and the $30,000 you owe your employees is due next week. If you are unable to pay them, they will quit and the business will go bankrupt. You are sure you will be able to repay your friend when your employees perform the $82,000 of services for Barrymore and you collect the cash. However, your friend is risk averse and is not likely to make the loan based on the financial statements your accountant prepared. Would you make the changes that Glenn made to get the loan and thereby save your company? Defend your position with a rational explanation.

c. Discuss Donald Cressey's features of ethical misconduct (described in Chapter 1) as they apply to Glenn's decision to change the financial statements to reflect more favorable results.

ATC 2-8 Research Assignment *Investigating nonfinancial information in Nike's annual report*

Although most of this course is concerned with the financial statements themselves, all sections of a company's annual report are important. A company must file various reports with the SEC, and one of these, Form 10-K, is essentially the company's annual report. The requirements below ask you to investigate sections of **Nike's** annual report that explain various nonfinancial aspects of its business operations.

To obtain the Form 10-K you can use either the EDGAR system following the instructions in Appendix A or the company's website.

Required

a. In what year did Nike begin operations?

b. Other than athletic shoes, what products does Nike sell?

c. Does Nike operate businesses under names other than Nike? If so, what are they?

d. How many employees does Nike have?

e. In how many countries other than the United States does Nike sell its products?

COMPREHENSIVE PROBLEM

The trial balance of Pacilio Security Services Inc. as of January 1, 2002, was as follows:

Cash	$8,500
Land	4,000
Notes Payable	5,000
Common Stock	6,000
Retained Earnings	1,500

During 2002, Pacilio Security Services experienced the following transactions:

1. Acquired an additional $2,000 from the issue of common stock.
2. Paid $3,000 on the debt owed to the Small Business Government Agency. The loan is interest free.
3. Performed $21,000 of security services for numerous local events during the year; $15,000 was on account and $6,000 was cash.
4. On May 1, rented a small office building. Paid $2,400 for 12 months' rent in advance.
5. Purchased supplies on account for $650.
6. Paid salaries expense for the year of $8,000.
7. Incurred other operating expenses on account, $6,200.
8. On September 1, 2002, a customer paid $600 for services to be provided over the next six months.
9. Collected $13,500 of accounts receivable during the year.
10. Paid $5,800 on accounts payable.
11. Paid $1,500 of advertising expenses for the year.
12. Paid a cash dividend to the shareholders of $1,000.
13. The market value of the land was determined to be $5,000 at December 31, 2002.

Information for Adjustments

14. There was $65 of supplies on hand at the end of the year.
15. Recognized the expired rent.
16. Recognized the revenue earned from Transaction 8.
17. Accrued salaries were $1,200 at December 31, 2002.

Required

a. Record the above transactions in an accounting equation. Provide the appropriate account titles for the amounts shown in the Retained Earnings column.

b. Prepare an income statement, statement of changes in stockholders' equity, balance sheet, and statement of cash flows for 2002.

CHAPTER 3

The Double-Entry Accounting System

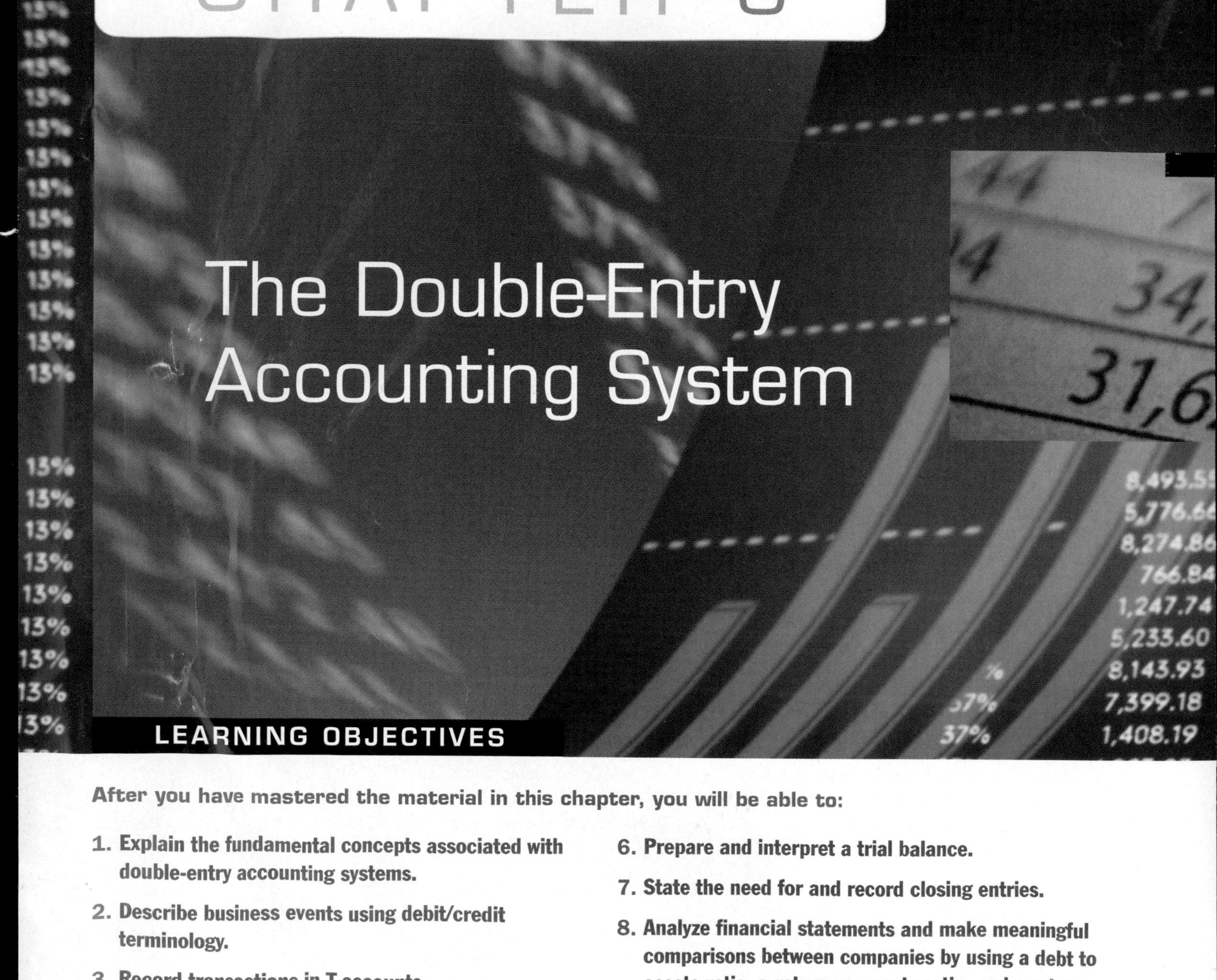

LEARNING OBJECTIVES

After you have mastered the material in this chapter, you will be able to:

1. **Explain the fundamental concepts associated with double-entry accounting systems.**
2. **Describe business events using debit/credit terminology.**
3. **Record transactions in T-accounts.**
4. **Identify the events that need adjusting entries and record them.**
5. **Record transactions using the general journal format.**
6. **Prepare and interpret a trial balance.**
7. **State the need for and record closing entries.**
8. **Analyze financial statements and make meaningful comparisons between companies by using a debt to assets ratio, a return on assets ratio, and a return on equity ratio.**

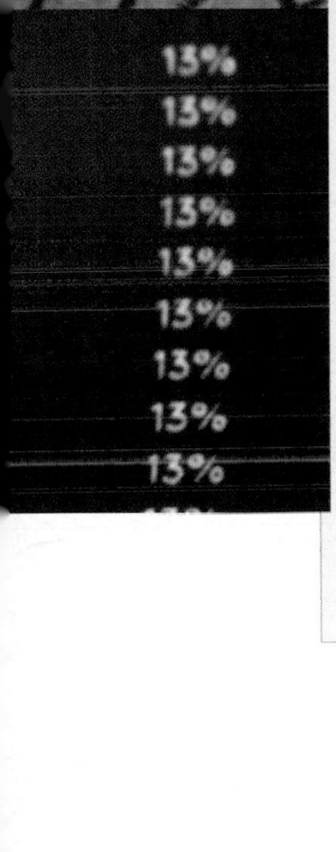

Chapter 3

The Curious Accountant

Most companies prepare financial statements at least once each year. The year about which financial statements report is called a **fiscal year.** Illustrations in this textbook usually assume the fiscal year coincides with the calendar year; that is, it ends on December 31. In practice, the fiscal years of many companies do not end on December 31. For example, **Levi Strauss**, a company that produces clothing, ends its fiscal year on the last Sunday in November. **Gap, Inc.**, a company that sells clothing, ends its fiscal year on the last Saturday in January or the first Saturday in February.

Why would these companies choose these dates to end their fiscal years? (Answers on pages 135 and 136)

CHAPTER OPENING

To prepare financial statements, a company must have a system for accurately capturing the vast numbers of business transactions in which it engages each year. The most widely used such system, double-entry accounting, is so effective it has been in use for hundreds of years! This chapter explains the rules for recording transactions using double-entry accounting.

Double-entry accounting rules are analogous to other rules people adopt to achieve various goals, such as rules governing traffic signals. A red signal means "stop," but it could just as easily mean "go." What matters is that all drivers agree on what red means. Similarly, double-entry accounting rules could have developed differently. In fact, the rules sometimes seem backwards at first. You likely use accounting terms like "debit" or "credit" from a consumer's point of view. To learn the accounting rules, however, you must view them from a business perspective. With practice, they will become second nature and you will know them as well as you know traffic signals. ■

Debit/Credit Terminology

LO 1

Explain the fundamental concepts associated with double-entry accounting systems.

LO 2

Describe business events using debit/credit terminology.

Topic Tackler PLUS

3-1

An account form known as a **T-account** is a good starting point for learning double-entry recording procedures. A T-account looks like the letter "T" drawn on a piece of paper. The account title is written across the top of the horizontal bar of the T. The left side of the vertical bar is the **debit** side, and the right side is the **credit** side. An account has been *debited* when an amount is written on the left side and *credited* when an amount is written on the right side. Accountants often abbreviate the term *debit* as "dr." and *credit* as "cr." For any given account, the difference between the total debit and credit amounts is the **account balance.**

The rules for using debits and credits to record transactions in T-accounts are as follows:

			Claims				
Assets		=	Liabilities		+	Equity	
Debit	Credit		Debit	Credit		Debit	Credit
+	−		−	+		−	+

Notice that a debit can represent an increase or a decrease. Likewise, a credit can represent an increase or a decrease. Whether a debit or credit is an increase or a decrease depends on the type of account (asset, liability, or stockholders' equity) in question. The rules of debits and credits are summarized as follows:

1. Debits increase asset accounts; credits decrease asset accounts.
2. Debits decrease liability and stockholders' equity accounts; credits increase liability and stockholders' equity accounts.

Collins Consultants Case

LO 3

Record transactions in T-accounts.

We will record the accounting events for a small business, Collins Consultants, to show how the rules for debits and credits work. Each event falls into one of the four transaction types:

1. Asset source transactions
2. Asset exchange transactions
3. Asset use transactions
4. Claims exchange transactions

Asset Source Transactions

A business may obtain assets from three primary sources: (1) from stockholders, (2) from creditors, or (3) through operating activities (earning revenue). An asset source transaction increases an asset account and a corresponding liability or stockholders' equity account. The increase in the asset account is recorded with a debit entry. The increase in a liability or stockholders' equity account is recorded with a credit entry. The following section demonstrates recording procedures for common asset source transactions.

Event 1 **Assets Acquired from Owners**

Collins Consultants was established on January 1, 2007, when it acquired $25,000 cash from Collins.

This accounting event increases both assets and stockholders' equity. The increase in assets (Cash) is recorded with a debit, and the increase in stockholders' equity (Common Stock) with a credit, shown in T-account form as follows:

Assets		=	Liabilities	+	Equity	
Cash					Common Stock	
Debit	Credit				Debit	Credit
+						+
(1) 25,000						25,000 (1)

Notice the entry included both debiting an account and crediting an account. This system is called **double-entry accounting.** Recording any transaction requires at least one debit and at least one credit. The total of the debit amounts must equal the total of the credit amounts. These requirements provide accountants with a built-in error detection tool.

This entry has the following effects on the financial statements:

Assets	=	Liab.	+	Equity	Rev.	−	Exp.	=	Net Inc.	Cash Flow
Cash	=			Com. Stk.						
25,000	=	NA	+	25,000	NA	−	NA	=	NA	25,000 FA

Event 2 **Assets Acquired from Creditors**

On February 17, Collins Consultants purchased $850 of office supplies on account (agreed to pay for the supplies at a later date) from Morris Supply Company.

Purchasing supplies on account increases both assets and liabilities. The increase in assets (Supplies) is recorded with a debit, and the increase in liabilities (Accounts Payable) is recorded with a credit, as shown in the following T-accounts:

Assets		=	Liabilities		+	Equity
Supplies			Accounts Payable			
Debit	Credit		Debit	Credit		
+				+		
(2) 850				850 (2)		

This entry has the following effects on the financial statements:

Assets	=	Liab.	+	Equity	Rev.	−	Exp.	=	Net Inc.	Cash Flow
Supplies	=	Accts. Pay.								
850	=	850	+	NA	NA	−	NA	=	NA	NA

Event 3 **Assets Acquired from Creditors**

On February 28, Collins Consultants signed a contract to evaluate the internal control system used by Kendall Food Stores. Kendall paid Collins $5,000 in advance for these future services.

Accepting the $5,000 in advance creates an obligation for Collins Consultants. The obligation is to provide future services to Kendall Food Stores. Collins will recognize a liability called *unearned revenue.* Recording the event increases both assets and liabilities. The increase in assets (Cash) is recorded with a debit, and the increase in liabilities (Unearned Revenue) is recorded with a credit, as shown in the following T-accounts:

Assets	=	Liabilities	+	Equity
Cash		**Unearned Revenue**		
Debit + (3) 5,000 / Credit		Debit / Credit + 5,000 (3)		

This entry has the following effects on the financial statements:

Assets	=	Liab.	+	Equity	Rev.	−	Exp.	=	Net Inc.	Cash Flow
Cash	=	Unearned Revenue								
5,000	=	5,000	+	NA	NA	−	NA	=	NA	5,000 OA

Event 4 Assets Acquired from Creditors

On March 1, Collins Consultants received $18,000 from signing a contract to provide professional advice to Harwood Corporation over a one-year period.

The event increases both assets and liabilities. The increase in assets (Cash) is recorded with a debit, and the increase in liabilities (Unearned Revenue) is recorded with a credit, as shown in the following T-accounts:

Assets	=	Liabilities	+	Equity
Cash		**Unearned Revenue**		
Debit + (4) 18,000 / Credit		Debit / Credit + 18,000 (4)		

This entry has the following effects on the financial statements:

Assets	=	Liab.	+	Equity	Rev.	−	Exp.	=	Net Inc.	Cash Flow
Cash	=	Unearned Revenue								
18,000	=	18,000	+	NA	NA	−	NA	=	NA	18,000 OA

Event 5 Assets Acquired through Operating Activities

On April 10, Collins Consultants provided $2,360 of services to Rex Company on account (agreed to let the customer pay at a future date).

Recognizing revenue earned on account increases both assets and stockholders' equity. The increase in assets (Accounts Receivable) is recorded with a debit, and the increase in stockholders' equity (Consulting Revenue) is recorded with a credit, as shown in the following T-accounts:

Assets	=	Liabilities	+	Equity
Accounts Receivable				**Consulting Revenue**
Debit + (5) 2,360 / Credit				Debit / Credit + 2,360 (5)

This entry has the following effects on the financial statements:

Assets	=	Liab.	+	Equity	Rev.	−	Exp.	=	Net Inc.	Cash Flow
Accts. Rec.	=			Ret. Earn.						
2,360	=	NA	+	2,360	2,360	−	NA	=	2,360	NA

Event 6 Assets Acquired through Operating Activities
On April 29, Collins performed services and received $8,400 cash.

Recognizing the revenue increases both assets and stockholders' equity. The increase in assets (Cash) is recorded with a debit, and the increase in stockholders' equity (Consulting Revenue) is recorded with a credit, as shown in the following T-accounts:

Assets		=	Liabilities	+	Equity	
Cash					Consulting Revenue	
Debit	Credit				Debit	Credit
+						+
(6) 8,400						8,400 (6)

This entry has the following effects on the financial statements:

Assets	=	Liab.	+	Equity	Rev.	−	Exp.	=	Net Inc.	Cash Flow
Cash	=			Ret. Earn.						
8,400	=	NA	+	8,400	8,400	−	NA	=	8,400	8,400 OA

Summary of the Previous Asset Source Transactions

Events 1 through 6 are asset source transactions. In each case, an asset account and a corresponding claims account increased. The increase in the asset account was recorded with a debit and the increase in the liability or stockholders' equity account was recorded with a credit. Any transaction that provides assets to a business is recorded similarly.

CHECK YOURSELF 3.1

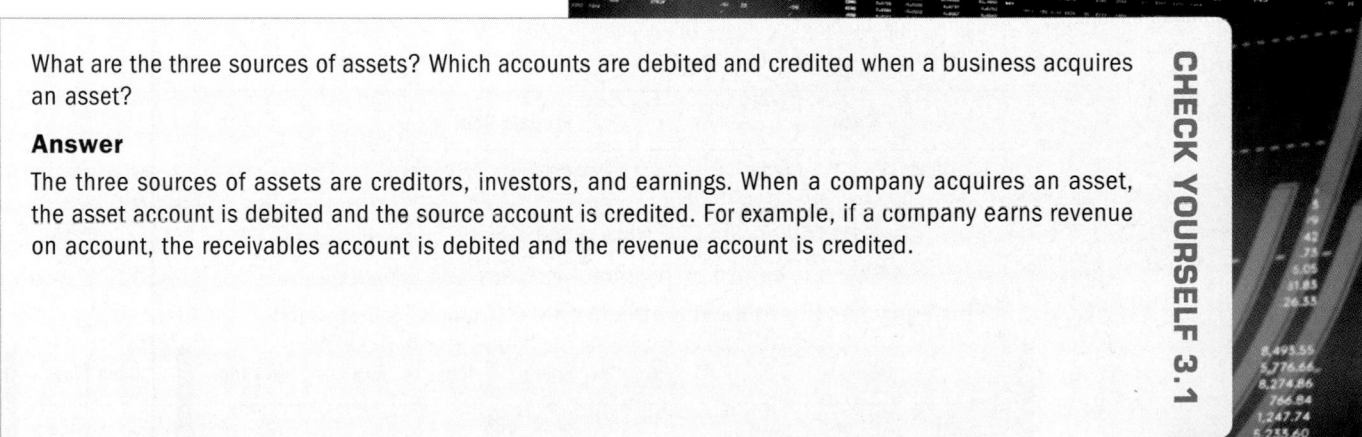

What are the three sources of assets? Which accounts are debited and credited when a business acquires an asset?

Answer

The three sources of assets are creditors, investors, and earnings. When a company acquires an asset, the asset account is debited and the source account is credited. For example, if a company earns revenue on account, the receivables account is debited and the revenue account is credited.

Asset Exchange Transactions

Asset exchange transactions involve trading one asset for another asset. One asset account increases; the other decreases. The total amount of assets remains unchanged. Asset exchange transactions are recorded by debiting the asset account that is increasing and crediting the asset account that is decreasing. In T-account form, asset exchange transactions have the following effects on the accounting equation:

Assets				=	Claims
Asset 1		Asset 2			
Debit	Credit	Debit	Credit		
+			−		

Event 7 **Cash Exchanged for Land**

On June 30, Collins purchased land for $42,000 cash.

The increase in assets (Land) is recorded with a debit, and the decrease in assets (Cash) is recorded with a credit, as shown in the following T-accounts:

Assets				=	Claims
Cash		Land			
Debit	Credit	Debit	Credit		
	−	+			
	42,000 (7)	(7) 42,000			

This entry has the following effects on the financial statements:

Assets			=	Liab.	+	Equity	Rev.	−	Exp.	=	Net Inc.	Cash Flow
Cash	+	Land										
(42,000)	+	42,000	=	NA	+	NA	NA	−	NA	=	NA	(42,000) IA

Event 8 **Cash Exchanged for Prepaid Rent**

On July 31, Collins paid $3,600 cash in advance for a one-year lease to rent office space beginning August 1.

The increase in assets (Prepaid Rent) is recorded with a debit, and the decrease in assets (Cash) is recorded with a credit, as shown in the following T-accounts:

Assets				=	Claims
Cash		Prepaid Rent			
Debit	Credit	Debit	Credit		
	−	+			
	3,600 (8)	(8) 3,600			

This entry has the following effects on the financial statements:

Assets			=	Liab.	+	Equity	Rev.	−	Exp.	=	Net Inc.	Cash Flow
Cash	+	Prep. Rent										
(3,600)	+	3,600	=	NA	+	NA	NA	−	NA	=	NA	(3,600) OA

Event 9 **Accounts Receivable Exchanged for Cash**

On August 8, Collins Consultants collected $1,200 from Rex Company as partial payment of the account receivable (see Event 5).

The increase in assets (Cash) is recorded with a debit, and the decrease in assets (Accounts Receivable) is recorded with a credit, as shown in the following T-accounts:

Assets				=	Claims
Cash		Accounts Receivable			
Debit	Credit	Debit	Credit		
+			−		
(9) 1,200			1,200 (9)		

This entry has the following effects on the financial statements:

Assets		=	Liab.	+	Equity	Rev.	−	Exp.	=	Net Inc.	Cash Flow
Cash +	Accts. Rec.										
1,200 +	(1,200)	=	NA	+	NA	NA	−	NA	=	NA	1,200 OA

Summary of the Previous Asset Exchange Transactions

Events 7 through 9 are all asset exchange transactions. In each case, one asset account increased and another decreased. The asset account that increased was debited, and the asset account that decreased was credited. These asset exchange transactions did not affect the total amounts of either assets or claims.

Asset Use Transactions

There are three primary asset use transactions: (1) expenses may use assets, (2) settling liabilities may use assets, or (3) paying dividends may use assets. An asset use transaction decreases an asset account and also decreases a claims account. The decrease in the asset account is recorded with a credit and the decrease in the claims account is recorded with a debit.

Event 10 **Used Assets to Produce Revenue**
On September 4, Collins Consultants paid employees who worked for the company $7,500 in salaries.

The decrease in assets (Cash) is recorded with a credit, and the decrease in stockholders' equity (Salaries Expense) is recorded with a debit, as shown in the following T-accounts:

Assets		=	Liabilities	+	Equity	
Cash					Salaries Expense	
Debit	Credit				Debit	Credit
	−				+ Expense	
	7,500 (10)				− Equity	
					(10) 7,500	

The debit to Salaries Expense represents an *increase* in the salaries expense account which is actually a *decrease* in stockholders' equity (Retained Earnings). Debit entries increase expense accounts. Expenses, however, decrease stockholders' equity (Retained Earnings). Debiting an expense account, therefore, reduces stockholders' equity.

This entry has the following effects on the financial statements:

Assets	=	Liab.	+	Equity	Rev.	−	Exp.	=	Net Inc.	Cash Flow
Cash	=			Ret. Earn.						
(7,500)	=	NA	+	(7,500)	NA	−	7,500	=	(7,500)	(7,500) OA

Event 11 Assets Transferred to Owners

On September 20, Collins Consultants paid a $1,500 cash dividend to its owner.

The decrease in assets (Cash) is recorded with a credit, and the decrease in stockholders' equity (Dividends) is recorded with a debit, as shown in the following T-accounts:

Assets		=	Liabilities	+	Equity	
Cash					**Dividends**	
Debit	Credit				Debit	Credit
	−				+ Div	
	1,500 (11)				− Equity	
					(11) 1,500	

The debit to Dividends represents both an increase in the dividends account and a decrease in stockholders' equity (Retained Earnings). Since dividends decrease stockholders' equity, an increase in the dividends account reduces stockholders' equity. Recall that dividends are wealth transfers, not expenses.

This entry has the following effects on the financial statements:

Assets	=	Liab.	+	Equity	Rev.	−	Exp.	=	Net Inc.	Cash Flow
Cash	=			Ret. Earn.						
(1,500)	=	NA	+	(1,500)	NA	−	NA	=	NA	(1,500) FA

Event 12 Used Assets to Pay Liabilities

On October 10, Collins Consultants paid Morris Supply Company the $850 owed from purchasing office supplies on account (see Event 2).

The decrease in assets (Cash) is recorded with a credit, and the decrease in liabilities (Accounts Payable) is recorded with a debit, as shown in the following T-accounts:

Assets		=	Liabilities		+	Equity
Cash			**Accounts Payable**			
Debit	Credit		Debit	Credit		
	−		−			
	850 (12)		(12) 850			

This entry has the following effects on the financial statements:

Assets	=	Liab.	+	Equity	Rev.	−	Exp.	=	Net Inc.	Cash Flow
Cash	=	Accts. Pay.								
(850)	=	(850)	+	NA	NA	−	NA	=	NA	(850) OA

Summary of Asset Use Transactions

Events 10 through 12 each reduced both an asset account and either a liability or stockholders' equity account. Even though debit entries to expense and dividends accounts represent increases in those accounts, the balances in expense and dividends accounts reduce stockholders' equity. Any asset use transaction is recorded with a debit to a liability or a stockholders' equity account and a credit to an asset account.

Claims Exchange Transactions

Certain transactions involve exchanging one claims account for another claims account. The total amount of claims remains unchanged. Such transactions are recorded by debiting the claims account which is decreasing and crediting the claims account which is increasing.

Event 13 **Revenue Recognized (Unearned to Earned)**
On November 15, Collins completed its consulting evaluation of the internal control system used by Kendall Food Stores (see Event 3).

Kendall expressed satisfaction with Collins's report. Recall Kendall had paid $5,000 in advance for the consulting services. Upon completing the project, Collins will recognize the revenue earned. Kendall's advance payment had created a liability; recognizing the revenue decreases liabilities and increases stockholders' equity. The decrease in liabilities (Unearned Revenue) is recorded with a debit, and the increase in stockholders' equity (Consulting Revenue) is recorded with a credit, as shown in the following T-accounts:

Assets	=	Liabilities		+	Equity	
		Unearned Revenue			Consulting Revenue	
		Debit	Credit		Debit	Credit
		−				+
		(13) 5,000				5,000 (13)

This entry has the following effects on the financial statements:

Assets	=	Liab.	+	Equity	Rev.	−	Exp.	=	Net Inc.	Cash Flow
		Unearned Revenue	+	Ret. Earn.						
NA	=	(5,000)	+	5,000	5,000	−	NA	=	5,000	NA

Event 14 **Expense Recognized**
On December 18, Collins Consultants received a $900 bill from Creative Ads for advertisements which had appeared in regional magazines. Collins plans to pay the bill later since it is not due until early the next year.

The event increases liabilities and decreases stockholders' equity. The increase in liabilities (Accounts Payable) is recorded with a credit, and the decrease in stockholders' equity (Advertising Expense) is recorded with a debit, as shown in the following T-accounts:

Assets	=	Liabilities		+	Equity	
		Accounts Payable			Advertising Expense	
		Debit	Credit		Debit	Credit
			+		+ Expense	
			900 (14)		− Equity	
					(14) 900	

This entry has the following effects on the financial statements:

Assets	=	Liab.	+	Equity	Rev.	−	Exp.	=	Net Inc.	Cash Flow
		Accts. Pay.	+	Ret. Earn.						
NA	=	900	+	(900)	NA	−	900	=	(900)	NA

Summary of Claims Exchange Transactions

Events 13 and 14 reflect exchanges on the claims side of the accounting equation. In each case, one claims account was debited, and another claims account was credited. Claims exchange transactions do not affect the total amounts of either assets or claims.

Adjusting the Accounts

LO 4

Identify the events that need adjusting entries and record them.

Assume that Collins Consultants' fiscal year ends on December 31, 2007. In order to prepare the financial statements, Collins must first adjust its accounting records to recognize any unrecorded accruals or deferrals. The appropriate adjustments are discussed in the next section of this chapter. Notice that adjusting entries do not affect the Cash account.

Adjustment 1 **Salary Expense Accrued**

Collins recognized accrued but unpaid salaries.

Collins Consultants last paid salaries to employees on September 4 (see Event 10). Assume that Collins owes $800 more to employees for work done in 2007 since September 4. Collins will pay these salaries in 2008. The required adjusting entry increases liabilities and decreases stockholders' equity. The increase in liabilities (Salaries Payable) is recorded with a credit, and the decrease in stockholders' equity (Salaries Expense) is recorded with a debit, as shown in the following T-accounts:

Assets	=	Liabilities		+	Equity	
		Salaries Payable			Salaries Expense	
		Debit	Credit		Debit	Credit
			+		+ Expense	
			800 (A1)		− Equity	
					(A1) 800	

This adjustment has the following effects on the financial statements:

Assets	=	Liab.	+	Equity	Rev.	−	Exp.	=	Net Inc.	Cash Flow
		Sal. Pay.	+	Ret. Earn.						
NA	=	800	+	(800)	NA	−	800	=	(800)	NA

Adjustment 2 **Rent Expense Recognized**

Collins recognized rent expense for the portion of prepaid rent used up since entering the lease agreement on July 31 (see Event 8).

Recall that Collins paid $3,600 in advance to lease office space for one year. The monthly rental cost is therefore $300 ($3,600 ÷ 12 months). By December 31, Collins had *used* the office for five months in 2007. Rent expense for those 5 months is therefore $1,500 ($300 × 5). Recognizing the rent expense decreases both assets and stockholders' equity. The decrease in assets (Prepaid Rent) is recorded with a credit, and the decrease in stockholders' equity (Rent Expense) is recorded with a debit, as shown in the following T-accounts:

Assets		=	Liabilities	+	Equity	
Prepaid Rent					Rent Expense	
Debit	Credit				Debit	Credit
	−				+ Expense	
	1,500 (A2)				− Equity	
					(A2) 1,500	

This adjustment has the following effects on the financial statements:

Assets	=	Liab.	+	Equity	Rev.	−	Exp.	=	Net Inc.	Cash Flow
Prep. Rent	=			Ret. Earn.						
(1,500)	=	NA	+	(1,500)	NA	−	1,500	=	(1,500)	NA

Adjustment 3 **Recognized Supplies Expense**

A physical count at the end of the year indicates that $125 worth of the supplies purchased on February 17 is still on hand (see Event 2).

Collins used $725 ($850 − $125) of supplies during the period. Recognizing the supplies expense decreases both assets and stockholders' equity. The decrease in assets (Supplies) is recorded with a credit and the decrease in stockholders' equity (Supplies Expense) is recorded with a debit, as shown in the following T-accounts:

Assets		=	Liabilities		+	Equity	
Supplies						Supplies Expense	
Debit	Credit					Debit	Credit
	−					+ Expense	
	725 (A3)					− Equity	
						(A3) 725	

This adjustment has the following effects on the financial statements:

Assets	=	Liab.	+	Equity	Rev.	−	Exp.	=	Net Inc.	Cash Flow
Supplies	=			Ret. Earn.						
(725)	=	NA	+	(725)	NA	−	725	=	(725)	NA

Adjustment 4 **Consulting Revenue Recognized**

Collins Consultants adjusted its accounting records to reflect revenue earned to date on the contract to provide services to Harwood Corporation for a one-year period beginning March 1 (see Event 4).

Recall that Collins collected $18,000 in advance for this contract. By December 31, 2007, Collins would have provided Harwood professional services for 10 months, earning $15,000 ($18,000 ÷ 12 = $1,500 × 10 = $15,000) of the contract revenue during 2007. This amount must be transferred from the liability account (Unearned Revenue) to an equity account (Consulting Revenue). Recognizing the revenue decreases liabilities and increases stockholders' equity. The decrease in liabilities (Unearned Revenue) is recorded with a debit, and the increase in stockholders' equity (Consulting Revenue) is recorded with a credit, as shown in the following T-accounts:

Assets	=	Liabilities		+	Equity	
		Unearned Revenue			Consulting Revenue	
		Debit	Credit		Debit	Credit
		−				+
		(A4) 15,000				15,000 (A4)

This adjustment has the following effects on the financial statements:

Assets	=	Liab.	+	Equity	Rev.	−	Exp.	=	Net Inc.	Cash Flow
		Unearned Revenue	+	Ret. Earn.						
NA	=	(15,000)	+	15,000	15,000	−	NA	=	15,000	NA

CHECK YOURSELF 3.2

Can an asset exchange transaction be an adjusting entry?

Answer

No. Adjusting entries always involve revenue or expense accounts. Since an asset exchange transaction involves only asset accounts, it cannot be an adjusting entry.

Overview of Debit/Credit Relationships

LO 2

Describe business events using debit/credit terminology.

Panel A of Exhibit 3.1 summarizes the rules for debits and credits. Panel B illustrates these rules in T-account form.

The balance in each account, which is the difference between all the debit entries and all the credit entries, is written on the plus (increase) side of that account. Asset, expense, and dividend accounts normally have *debit balances;* liability, stockholders' equity, and revenue accounts normally have *credit balances.*

The General Ledger

LO 1

Explain the fundamental concepts associated with double-entry accounting systems.

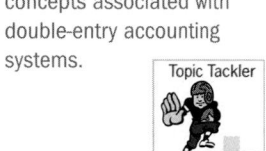

Topic Tackler PLUS 3-2

LO 5

Record transactions using the general journal format.

The collection of all the accounts used by a particular business is called the **general ledger.** The general ledger for Collins Consultants is displayed in Exhibit 3.2. In a manual system, the ledger could be a book with pages for each account where entries are recorded by hand. In more sophisticated systems, the general ledger is maintained in electronic form. Data is entered into electronic ledgers using computer keyboards or scanners. Companies typically assign each ledger account a name and a number. A list of all ledger accounts and their account numbers is called the **chart of accounts.**

The General Journal

Businesses find it impractical to record every individual transaction directly into general ledger accounts. Imagine the number of cash transactions a grocery store has each day. To simplify recordkeeping, businesses rely on **source documents** such as cash register tapes as the basis for entering transaction data into the accounting system. Other source documents include invoices, time cards, check stubs, and deposit tickets.

Accountants further simplify recordkeeping by initially recording data from source documents into **journals.** Journals provide a chronological record of business transactions. *Transactions are recorded in journals before they are entered into ledger accounts.* Journals

EXHIBIT 3.1

Debit/Credit Relationships

Panel A

Account	Debits	Credits
Assets	Increase	Decrease
Liabilities	Decrease	Increase
Equity	Decrease	Increase
Common Stock	Decrease	Increase
Revenue	Decrease	Increase
Expenses	Increase	Decrease
Dividends	Increase	Decrease

Panel B

Assets = Liabilities + Equity

Assets		=	Liabilities		+	Equity	
Debit +	Credit −		Debit −	Credit +		Debit −	Credit +

Common Stock

Debit	Credit
−	+

Dividends

Debit	Credit
− Equity	+ Equity
+ Div.	− Div.

Revenue

Debit	Credit
−	+

Expense

Debit	Credit
− Equity	+ Equity
+ Exp.	− Exp.

are therefore **books of original entry.** Companies may use different **special journals** to record specific types of recurring transactions. For example, a company may use one special journal to record sales on account, another to record purchases on account, a third to record cash receipts, and a fourth to record cash payments. Transactions that do not fall into any of these categories are recorded in the **general journal.** Although special journals can be useful, companies can keep records without them by recording all transactions in the general journal. For simplicity, this text illustrates a general journal only.

At a minimum, the general journal shows the dates, the account titles, and the amounts of each transaction. The date is recorded in the first column, followed by the title of the account to be debited. The title of the account to be credited is indented and written on the line directly below the account to be debited. The dollar amount of the transaction is recorded in the Debit and Credit columns. For example, providing services for $1,000 cash on August 1 would be recorded in general journal format as follows:

Date	Account Title	Debit	Credit
Aug. 1	Cash	1,000	
	Service Revenue		1,000

EXHIBIT 3.2

General Ledger Accounts

Assets = Liabilities + Equity

Assets

Cash

(1)	25,000	42,000	(7)
(3)	5,000	3,600	(8)
(4)	18,000	7,500	(10)
(6)	8,400	1,500	(11)
(9)	1,200	850	(12)
Bal.	2,150		

Accounts Receivable

(5)	2,360	1,200	(9)
Bal.	1,160		

Supplies

(2)	850	725	(A3)
Bal.	125		

Prepaid Rent

(8)	3,600	1,500	(A2)
Bal.	2,100		

Land

(7)	42,000		
Bal.	42,000		

Liabilities

Accounts Payable

(12)	850	850	(2)
		900	(14)
		900	Bal.

Unearned Revenue

(13)	5,000	5,000	(3)
(A4)	15,000	18,000	(4)
		3,000	Bal.

Salaries Payable

		800	(A1)
		800	Bal.

Equity

Common Stock

		25,000	(1)
		25,000	Bal.

Dividends

(11)	1,500		
Bal.	1,500		

Retained Earnings

Consulting Revenue

		2,360	(5)
		8,400	(6)
		5,000	(13)
		15,000	(A4)
		30,760	Bal.

Salaries Expense

(10)	7,500		
(A1)	800		
Bal.	8,300		

Advertising Expense

(14)	900		
Bal.	900		

Rent Expense

(A2)	1,500		
Bal.	1,500		

Supplies Expense

(A3)	725		
Bal.	725		

Total Assets	=	**Total Liabilities**	+	**Total Equity**
		4,700		42,835
47,535			**Total Claims** 47,535	

Exhibit 3.3 shows in general journal form all the Collins Consultants' transactions discussed thus far. After transactions are initially recorded in a journal, the dollar amounts of each debit and credit are copied into the ledger accounts, a process called **posting.**

Most companies today use computer technology to record transactions and prepare financial statements. Computers can record and post data pertaining to vast numbers of transactions with incredible speed and unparalleled accuracy. Both manual and computerized

REALITY BYTES

Do all accounting systems require using debits and credits? The answer is a definite no. Many small businesses use a single-entry system. A checkbook constitutes a sufficient accounting system for many business owners. Deposits represent revenues, and payments constitute expenses. Many excellent automated accounting systems do not require data entry through a debit/credit recording scheme. **QuickBooks** is a good example of this type of system. Data are entered into the QuickBooks software program through a user-friendly computer interface that does not require knowledge of debit/credit terminology. Even so, the QuickBooks program produces traditional financial reports such as an income statement, balance sheet, and statement of cash flows. How is this possible? Before you become too ingrained in the debit/credit system, recall that throughout the first two chapters of this text, we illustrated accounting records without using debits and credits. Financial reports can be produced in many ways without using a double-entry system. Having recognized this point, we also note that the vast majority of medium- to large-size companies use the double-entry system. Indeed, debit/credit terminology is a part of common culture. Most people have an understanding of what is happening when a business tells them that their account is being debited or credited. It is important for you to embrace the double-entry system as well as other financial reporting systems.

accounting systems, however, use the same underlying design. Analyzing a manual accounting system is a useful way to gain insight into how computer-based systems work.

Trial Balance

LO 6

Prepare and interpret a trial balance.

To test whether debits equal credits in the general ledger, accountants regularly prepare an internal accounting schedule called a **trial balance**. A trial balance lists every ledger account and its balance. Debit balances are listed in one column and credit balances are listed in an adjacent column. The columns are totaled and the totals are compared. Exhibit 3.4 displays the trial balance for Collins Consultants after the adjusting entries have been posted to the ledger.

If the debit total does not equal the credit total, the accountant knows to search for an error. Even if the totals are equal, however, there may be errors in the accounting records. For example, equal trial balance totals would not disclose errors like the following: failure to record transactions; misclassifications, such as debiting the wrong account; or incorrectly recording the amount of a transaction, such as recording a $200 transaction as $2,000. Equal debits and credits in a trial balance provide evidence rather than proof of accuracy.

Financial Statements

Supplemented with details from the Cash and Common Stock ledger accounts, the adjusted trial balance (Exhibit 3.4) provides the information to prepare the financial statements for Collins Consultants. The income statement, statement of changes in stockholders' equity, balance sheet, and statement of cash flows are shown in Exhibits 3.5, 3.6, 3.7, and 3.8.

EXHIBIT 3.3

General Journal

Date	Account Titles	Debit	Credit
Jan. 1	Cash	25,000	
	Common Stock		25,000
Feb. 17	Supplies	850	
	Accounts Payable		850
28	Cash	5,000	
	Unearned Revenue		5,000
Mar. 1	Cash	18,000	
	Unearned Revenue		18,000
April 10	Accounts Receivable	2,360	
	Consulting Revenue		2,360
29	Cash	8,400	
	Consulting Revenue		8,400
June 30	Land	42,000	
	Cash		42,000
July 31	Prepaid Rent	3,600	
	Cash		3,600
Aug. 8	Cash	1,200	
	Accounts Receivable		1,200
Sept. 4	Salaries Expense	7,500	
	Cash		7,500
20	Dividends	1,500	
	Cash		1,500
Oct. 10	Accounts Payable	850	
	Cash		850
Nov. 15	Unearned Revenue	5,000	
	Consulting Revenue		5,000
Dec. 18	Advertising Expense	900	
	Accounts Payable		900
	Adjusting Entries		
Dec. 31	Salaries Expense	800	
	Salaries Payable		800
31	Rent Expense	1,500	
	Prepaid Rent		1,500
31	Supplies Expense	725	
	Supplies		725
31	Unearned Revenue	15,000	
	Consulting Revenue		15,000

Closing Entries

LO 7

State the need for and record closing entries.

Exhibit 3.9 shows **closing entries** for Collins Consultants. These entries move all 2007 data from the temporary accounts (revenues, expenses, and dividends) into the Retained Earnings account. For example, the first closing entry in Exhibit 3.9 moves the balance in the Consulting Revenue account to the Retained Earnings account. As shown in the ad-

EXHIBIT 3.4

COLLINS CONSULTANTS
Adjusted Trial Balance
December 31, 2007

Account Titles	Debit	Credit
Cash	2,150	
Accounts Receivable	1,160	
Supplies	125	
Prepaid Rent	2,100	
Land	42,000	
Accounts Payable		900
Unearned Revenue		3,000
Salaries Payable		800
Common Stock		25,000
Retained Earnings		0
Dividends	1,500	
Consulting Revenue		30,760
Salaries Expense	8,300	
Advertising Expense	900	
Rent Expense	1,500	
Supplies Expense	725	
Totals	60,460	60,460

EXHIBIT 3.5

COLLINS CONSULTANTS
Income Statement
For the Year Ended December 31, 2007

Revenue		
Consulting Revenue		$30,760
Less: Expenses		
Salaries Expense	$8,300	
Advertising Expense	900	
Rent Expense	1,500	
Supplies Expense	725	
Total Expenses		(11,425)
Net Income		$19,335

EXHIBIT 3.6

COLLINS CONSULTANTS
Statement of Changes in Stockholders' Equity
For the Year Ended December 31, 2007

Beginning Common Stock	$ 0	
Plus: Stock Issued	25,000	
Ending Common Stock		$25,000
Beginning Retained Earnings	0	
Plus: Net Income	19,335	
Less: Dividends	(1,500)	
Ending Retained Earnings		17,835
Total Stockholders' Equity		$42,835

EXHIBIT 3.7

COLLINS CONSULTANTS
Balance Sheet
As of December 31, 2007

Assets		
Cash	$ 2,150	
Accounts Receivable	1,160	
Supplies	125	
Prepaid Rent	2,100	
Land	42,000	
Total Assets		$47,535
Liabilities		
Accounts Payable	$ 900	
Unearned Revenue	3,000	
Salaries Payable	800	
Total Liabilities		$ 4,700
Stockholders' Equity		
Common Stock	25,000	
Retained Earnings	17,835	
Total Stockholders' Equity		42,835
Total Liabilities and Stockholders' Equity		$47,535

EXHIBIT 3.8

COLLINS CONSULTANTS
Statement of Cash Flows
For the Year Ended December 31, 2007

Cash Flow from Operating Activities		
Inflow from Customers*	$32,600	
Outflow for Rent	(3,600)	
Outflow for Salaries	(7,500)	
Outflow for Supplies	(850)	
Net Cash Inflow from Operating Activities		$20,650
Cash Flow from Investing Activities		
Outflow to Purchase Land	(42,000)	
Net Cash Outflow for Investing Activities		(42,000)
Cash Flow from Financing Activities		
Inflow from Issue of Stock	25,000	
Outflow for Dividends	(1,500)	
Net Cash Inflow from Financing Activities		23,500
Net Change in Cash		2,150
Plus: Beginning Cash Balance		0
Ending Cash Balance		$ 2,150

*The sum of cash inflows from Events 3, 4, 6, and 9.

EXHIBIT 3.9

Closing Entries

Date	Account Title	Debit	Credit
Dec. 31	Consulting Revenue	30,760	
	Retained Earnings		30,760
31	Retained Earnings	8,300	
	Salaries Expense		8,300
31	Retained Earnings	900	
	Advertising Expense		900
31	Retained Earnings	1,500	
	Rent Expense		1,500
31	Retained Earnings	725	
	Supplies Expense		725
31	Retained Earnings	1,500	
	Dividends		1,500

justed trial balance (Exhibit 3.4), the Consulting Revenue account has a $30,760 credit balance before it is closed. Debiting the account for $30,760 brings its after-closing balance to zero. The corresponding $30,760 credit to Retained Earnings increases the balance in that account.

The second closing entry moves the balance in the Salaries Expense account to the Retained Earnings account. Before closing, the Salaries Expense account has an $8,300 debit balance; crediting the account for $8,300 leaves it with an after-closing balance of zero. The corresponding $8,300 debit to the Retained Earnings account reduces the balance in that

Answers to The Curious Accountant

Part 1

The process of closing the books and going through a year-end audit is time consuming for a business. Also, it is time spent that does not produce revenue. Thus, companies whose business is highly seasonal often choose "slow" periods to end their fiscal year. **Gap, Inc.** does heavy business during the Christmas season, so it might find December 31 an inconvenient time to close its books. Toward the end of January, business activity is slow, and inventory levels are at their low points. This is a good time to count the inventory and to assess the financial condition of the company. For these reasons, Gap, Inc. has chosen to close its books to end its fiscal year around the end of January.

Now that you know why a business like Gap, Inc. might choose to end its fiscal year at the end of January, can you think of a reason why **Levi Strauss** closes its books at the end of November? (See page 136.)

account. The remaining entries close the other expenses and the dividends accounts by crediting them and debiting the Retained Earnings account.

Closing entries can be recorded more efficiently than in Exhibit 3.9. For example, all of the expense accounts could be closed with one compound journal entry, like the one below.

Date	Account Title	Debit	Credit
Dec. 31	Retained earnings	11,425	
	Salaries Expense		8,300
	Advertising Expense		900
	Rent Expense		1,500
	Supplies Expense		725

Furthermore, revenue, expense, and dividend accounts could all be closed in a single compound journal entry. The form of the closing entries is not important. What matters is that all revenue, expense, and dividend amounts be moved to the Retained Earnings account. After the closing entries are posted to the ledger accounts, all revenue, expense, and dividends accounts have zero balances. The temporary accounts are then ready to capture revenue, expense, and dividend data for the next fiscal year.

If all companies closed their books on December 31 each year, accountants, printers, lawyers, government agencies, and others would be overburdened by the effort to produce the accounting reports of all companies at the same time. In an effort to balance the workload, many companies close their books at the end of the natural business year. A natural business year ends when operating activities are at their lowest point. For many companies the lowest point in the operating cycle occurs on a date other than December 31. A recent survey found that almost one-half of the companies sampled closed their books in months other than December (see Exhibit 3.10).

EXHIBIT 3.10

Distribution of Fiscal Closing Dates

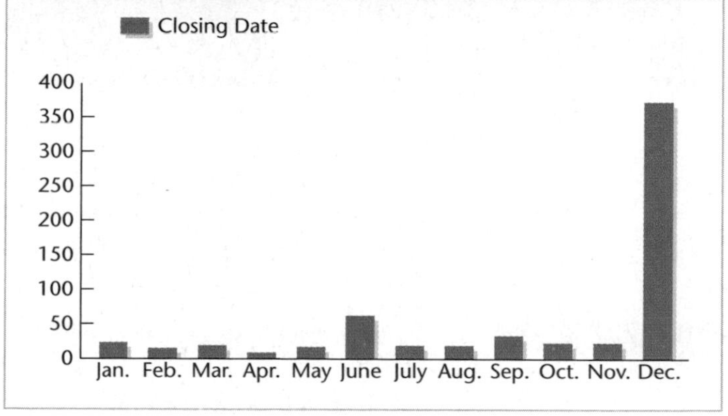

Data Source: AICPA Accounting Trends and Techniques

Answers to The Curious Accountant

Part 2

Levi Strauss does not sell its clothes directly to consumers; rather, it sells most of its clothes through retailers. Levi Strauss must deliver its jeans to retailers before Thanksgiving if the stores are going to have goods available to sell during the Christmas season. So, Levi's "Christmas season" is probably over by early November, making the end of November a good time to end its fiscal year. Some clothing manufacturers, such as **Tommy Hilfiger** and **Polo Ralph Lauren**, close their books around the end of March. By then, goods for both the Christmas and spring seasons have been shipped to retailers.

Trial Balance

LO 6

Prepare and interpret a trial balance.

How often should companies prepare a trial balance? Some companies prepare a trial balance daily; others may prepare one monthly, quarterly, or annually, depending on the needs of management. The heading of a trial balance describes the status of the account balances in it. For example, the trial balance in Exhibit 3.11 is described as a *Post-Closing Trial Balance* because it reflects the account balances immediately after the closing entries were posted. In contrast, the trial balance in Exhibit 3.4 is described as an *Adjusted Trial Balance* because it shows the account balances immediately after the adjusting entries were posted. A trial balance prepared at the end of each day may be described as a *Daily Trial Balance.*

CHECK YOURSELF 3.3

Describe an error that would not cause a trial balance to be out of balance.

Answer

Many potential errors would not cause a trial balance to be out of balance, such as debiting or crediting the wrong account. For example, if revenue earned on account were recorded with a debit to Cash instead of Accounts Receivable, total assets would be correct and the totals in the trial balance would equal each other even though the balances in the Cash and Accounts Receivable accounts would be incorrect. Recording the same incorrect amount in both the debit and credit part of an entry also would not cause a trial balance to be out of balance. For example, if $20 of revenue earned on account were recorded as a $200 debit to Accounts Receivable and a $200 credit to Consulting Revenue, the totals in the trial balance would equal each other although Accounts Receivable and Consulting Revenue amounts would be incorrect.

THE FINANCIAL ANALYST

Suppose a company earned net income of $1,000,000. Is the company's performance good or poor? If the company is **General Motors**, the performance is poor. If it is a small shoe store, the performance is outstanding. So, how do financial analysts compare the performance of differing size companies? Financial ratios are helpful in this regard.

Assessing the Effective Use of Assets

Evaluating performance requires considering the size of the investment base used to produce the income. In other words, you expect someone who has a $10 million investment

EXHIBIT 3.11

COLLINS CONSULTANTS
Post-Closing Trial Balance
December 31, 2007

Account Titles	Debit	Credit
Cash	2,150	
Accounts Receivable	1,160	
Supplies	125	
Prepaid Rent	2,100	
Land	42,000	
Accounts Payable		900
Unearned Revenue		3,000
Salaries Payable		800
Common Stock		25,000
Retained Earnings		17,835
Totals	47,535	47,535

base to earn more than someone who has a $10 thousand base. The relationship between the level of income and the size of the investment can be expressed as the **return on assets ratio,** as follows:

LO 8

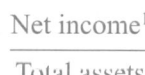

Analyze financial statements and make meaningful comparisons between companies by using a debt to assets ratio, a return on assets ratio, and a return on equity ratio.

$$\frac{\text{Net income}^1}{\text{Total assets}}$$

This ratio permits meaningful comparisons between different-size companies. Compare **The Nautilus Group, Inc.**, the company that makes exercise equipment, with **General Motors** (GM). In 2002, Nautilus's net income was $98 million and GM's was $1.7 billion, more than 17 times the earnings of Nautilus. However, the return on asset ratios for the two companies reveal that Nautilus produced higher earnings relative to the assets invested. GM's ratio was 0.5 percent while Nautilus' was 35.4 percent. Even though Nautilus earned fewer dollars of net income, the company did a better job than GM of managing its assets.

The preceding example demonstrates the usefulness of the relationship between income and assets. Two more ratios that enhance financial statement analysis are discussed in the following paragraphs.

Assessing Debt Risk

Borrowing money can be a risky business. To illustrate, assume two companies have the following financial structures:

	Assets	=	Liabilities	+	Stockholders' Equity
Eastern Company	100	=	20	+	80
Western Company	100	=	80	+	20

[1] The use of net income in this ratio ignores the effects of debt financing and income taxation. The effect of these variables on the return on assets ratio is explained in a later chapter.

Which company has the greater financial risk? If each company incurred a $30 loss, the financial structures would change as follows:

	Assets	=	Liabilities	+	Stockholders' Equity
Eastern Company	70	=	20	+	50
Western Company	70	=	80	+	(10)

Clearly, Western Company is at greater risk. Eastern Company could survive a $30 loss that reduced assets and stockholders' equity. It would still have a $50 balance in stockholders' equity and more than enough assets ($70) to satisfy the creditors' $20 claim. In contrast, a $30 loss would throw Western Company into bankruptcy. The company would have a $10 deficit (negative) balance in stockholders' equity and the remaining assets ($70) would be less than the creditors' $80 claim on assets.

The level of debt risk can be measured in part by using a **debt to assets ratio,** as follows:

$$\frac{\text{Total debt}}{\text{Total assets}}$$

For example, Eastern Company's debt to assets ratio is 20 percent ($20 ÷ $100) while Western Company's is 80 percent ($80 ÷ $100). Why would the owners of Western Company be willing to accept greater debt risk? Assume that both companies produce $12 of revenue and each must pay 10 percent interest on money owed to creditors. Income statements for the two companies appear as follows:[2]

	Eastern Company	Western Company
Revenue	$12	$12
Interest Expense	2	8
Net Income	$10	$ 4

At first glance, the owners of Eastern Company appear better off because Eastern produced higher net income. In fact, however, the owners of *Western* Company are better off. The owners of Eastern Company get $10 of income for investing $80 of their own money into the business, a return on their invested funds of 12.5 percent ($10 ÷ $80). In contrast, the owners of Western Company obtain $4 of net income for their $20 investment, a return on invested funds of 20 percent ($4 ÷ $20).

The relationship between net income and stockholders' equity used above is the **return on equity ratio,** computed as:

$$\frac{\text{Net income}}{\text{Stockholders' equity}}$$

Using borrowed money to increase the return on stockholders' investment is called **financial leverage.** Financial leverage explains why companies are willing to accept the risk of debt. Companies borrow money to make money. If a company can borrow money at 10 percent and invest it at 12 percent, the owners will be better off by 2 percent of the amount borrowed. A business that does not borrow may be missing an opportunity to increase its return on equity.

Real-World Data

Exhibit 3.12 shows the debt to assets, return on assets, and return on equity ratios for six real-world companies in two different industries. The data are drawn from the companies'

[2] This illustration ignores the effect of income taxes on debt financing. This subject is discussed in a later chapter.

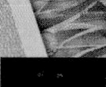

FOCUS ON INTERNATIONAL ISSUES

Although accounting rules vary from country to country, geographic, political, and social forces foster similar rules within selected sets of countries. For example, the accounting principles used in the United Kingdom more closely match those of New Zealand than those of Brazil.

An accounting research study concluded that accounting systems could be divided into four groups: (1) the British Commonwealth Model, (2) the Latin American Model, (3) the Continental European Model, and (4) the United States Model.* This study concluded that countries with accounting rules similar to (but not exactly the same as) U.S. GAAP include Canada, Japan, Mexico, Panama, and the Philippines.

If similarities exist among the accounting principles used in different countries, why not have only one set of rules for all countries? In fact, there is a serious attempt under way to achieve this objective. In 2001 the International Accounting Standards Committee Foundation Board (the foundation) was founded with these objectives:

(a) to develop, in the public interest, a single set of high quality, understandable and enforceable global accounting standards that require high quality, transparent and comparable information in financial statements and other financial reporting to help participants in the world's capital markets and other users make economic decisions; (b) to promote the use and rigorous application of those standards; and (c) to bring about convergence of national accounting standards and International Accounting Standards and International Financial Reporting Standards to high quality solutions.

The foundation's accounting standard-setting agency is the International Accounting Standards Board (IASB). Over 100 member countries participate in the foundation's activities and by 2005 over 90 of these countries either required or allowed their public companies to follow IASB standards. Most notably, all member countries of the European Union made IASB standards mandatory in 2005. U.S. GAAP does not follow IASB rules, but there is a formal relationship between the FASB and the IASB to achieve as much convergence as possible between the standards set by the two bodies. In addition to the United States, two large democratic economies that do not follow IASB rules are Japan and Canada.

The information about the IASB was taken from its website, which can be found at www.iasb.org.

*Nair, R. D. and Frank, W. G., "The Impact of Disclosure and Measurement Practices on International Accounting Classifications," *The Accounting Review*, July, 1980.

2002 financial reports. Notice **Hartford's** return on assets ratio was 0.4 percent and **Aflac's** was 1.8 percent. Neither ratio seems good; banks often pay more than 1.8 percent interest on deposits in savings accounts. The *return on equity* ratios, however, show a different picture; Hartford's was 9.8 percent and Aflac's was 12.8 percent—much better than banks pay depositors.

Exhibit 3.12 also shows that although Hartford's return on assets ratio was lower than **Chevron Texaco** (0.4 percent versus 1.5 percent), its return on equity ratio was higher than Chevron Texaco's (9.8 percent versus 3.6 percent). How can this happen? Compare the debt to assets ratios. Hartford financed 96 percent of its assets with debt compared to Chevron Texaco's 59 percent. Financial leverage is a contributing factor to Hartford's higher return on equity. While financial leverage can boost the return on equity, it is not the only factor that affects this ratio. For example, notice that compared to all of the companies in Exhibit 3.12, **ExxonMobil** has the highest return on equity but the lowest debt to assets ratio. Certainly, many factors other than debt management affect profitability. More financial leverage may have enabled ExxonMobil to increase its return on equity even further.

EXHIBIT 3.12

Three Ratios (in Percentages) for Six Real-World Companies

Industry	Company	Debt to Assets	Return on Assets	Return on Equity
Insurance	Aflac	86	1.8	12.8
	Hartford	96	0.4	9.8
	John Hancock	94	0.5	8.0
Oil	Chevron Texaco	59	1.5	3.6
	Conoco Phillips	60	0.9	2.4
	ExxonMobil	49	7.2	14.8

Since financial leverage offers the opportunity to increase return on equity, why doesn't every company leverage itself to the maximum? There is a down side. When the economy turns down, companies may not be able to produce investment returns that exceed interest rates. A company that has borrowed money at a fixed rate of 8 percent that can only earn 6 percent on its investments will suffer from financial leverage. In other words, financial leverage is a double-edged sword. It can have a negative as well as a positive impact on a company's return on equity ratio.

Finally, compare the ratios in Exhibit 3.12 for companies in the oil industry to the same ratios for companies in the insurance industry. There are significant differences *between* industries, but there are considerable similarities *within* each industry. The debt to assets ratio is much higher for the insurance industry than for the oil industry. However, within each industry, the ratios are clustered fairly close together. With ExxonMobil being the exception, distinct differences between industries and similarities within industries are common business features. When you compare accounting information for different companies, you must consider the industries in which those companies operate.

Scope of Coverage

Throughout this text, we introduce ratios directly related to chapter topics. Only a few of the many ratios available to users of financial statements are introduced. Introductory finance courses typically include a more extensive study of ratios and other topics related to financial statement analysis. Many business programs offer an entire course on financial statement analysis. These courses help students learn to judge whether the ratio results signal good or poor performance. Developing such judgment requires understanding how accounting policies and procedures can affect financial ratios. The ratios introduced in this text will enhance your understanding of accounting as a basis for studying more advanced topics in subsequent courses.

<< A Look Back

This chapter introduced the *double-entry accounting system.* This system was first documented in the 1400s, and is used by most companies today. Key components of the double-entry system are summarized below.

1. Business events can be classified concisely using debit/credit terminology. *Debits* are used to record increases in asset accounts and decreases in liability and stockholders' equity accounts. *Credits* are used to record decreases in asset accounts and increases in liability and stockholders' equity accounts.
2. *T-accounts* are frequently used to analyze and communicate account activity. The account title is placed at the top of the horizontal bar of the T, and increases and decreases are placed on either side of the vertical bar. In a T-account, debits are recorded on the left side and credits are recorded on the right side.
3. Accountants initially record transaction data in journals. The *general journal* is used not only for data entry but also as a shorthand communication tool. Each journal entry includes at least one debit and one credit. An entry is recorded using at least two lines, with the debit recorded on the top line and the credit on the bottom line. The credit is indented to distinguish it from the debit. The general journal format is illustrated here:

Debit	XXX	
Credit		XXX

4. Information is posted (copied) from the journals to *ledger* accounts. The ledger accounts provide the information used to prepare the financial statements.
5. *Trial balances* are used to check the mathematical accuracy of the recording process. Ledger accounts with their associated debit and credit balances are listed in the trial balance. The debit and credit amounts are totaled and compared. An equal amount of debits and credits provides evidence that transactions have been recorded correctly, although errors may still exist. If the debits and credits are *not* equal, it is proof that errors exist.

The double-entry system is just a way to organize accounting data. No matter how we organize the data, the objective is to summarize and report it in a way that is useful for making decisions.

A Look Forward >>

Chapters 1 through 3 focused on businesses that generate revenue by providing services to their customers. Examples of these types of businesses include consulting, real estate sales, medical services, and legal services. The next chapter introduces accounting practices for businesses that generate revenue by selling goods. Examples of these companies include **Wal-Mart**, **Circuit City**, **Office Depot**, and **Lowe's**.

SELF-STUDY REVIEW PROBLEM

The following events apply to the first year of operations for Mestro Financial Services Company:

1. Acquired $28,000 cash by issuing common stock on January 1, 2007.
2. Purchased $1,100 of supplies on account.

3. Paid $12,000 cash in advance for a one-year lease on office space.
4. Earned $23,000 of consulting revenue on account.
5. Incurred $16,000 of general operating expenses on account.
6. Collected $20,000 cash from receivables.
7. Paid $13,000 cash on accounts payable.
8. Paid a $1,000 cash dividend to stockholders.

Information for Adjusting Entries

9. There was $200 of supplies on hand at the end of the accounting period.
10. The one-year lease on the office space was effective beginning on October 1, 2007.
11. There was $1,200 of accrued salaries at the end of 2007.

Required

a. Record the preceding events in general journal format.

b. Post the transaction data from the general journal into general ledger T-accounts.

c. Prepare an adjusted trial balance.

d. Prepare an income statement, statement of changes in stockholders' equity, balance sheet, and statement of cash flows.

e. Prepare the appropriate closing entries in general journal format.

Solution to Requirement a

Event No.	Account Title	Debit	Credit
1	Cash	28,000	
	Common Stock		28,000
2	Supplies	1,100	
	Accounts Payable		1,100
3	Prepaid Rent	12,000	
	Cash		12,000
4	Accounts Receivable	23,000	
	Consulting Revenue		23,000
5	General Operating Expenses	16,000	
	Accounts Payable		16,000
6	Cash	20,000	
	Accounts Receivable		20,000
7	Accounts Payable	13,000	
	Cash		13,000
8	Dividends	1,000	
	Cash		1,000
9	Supplies Expense	900	
	Supplies		900
10	Rent Expense	3,000	
	Prepaid Rent		3,000
11	Salaries Expense	1,200	
	Salaries Payable		1,200

Solution to Requirement b

MESTRO FINANCIAL SERVICES COMPANY
T-Accounts, 2007

Assets = Liabilities + Equity

Assets

Cash

1.	28,000	3.	12,000
6.	20,000	7.	13,000
		8.	1,000
Bal.	22,000		

Accounts Receivable

4.	23,000	6.	20,000
Bal.	3,000		

Supplies

2.	1,100	9.	900
Bal.	200		

Prepaid Rent

3.	12,000	10.	3,000
Bal.	9,000		

Liabilities

Accounts Payable

7.	13,000	2.	1,100
		5.	16,000
		Bal.	4,100

Salaries Payable

		11.	1,200
		Bal.	1,200

Equity

Common Stock

		1.	28,000
		Bal.	28,000

Dividends

8.	1,000		

Consulting Revenue

		4.	23,000

General Operating Expenses

5.	16,000		

Salaries Expense

11.	1,200		

Supplies Expense

9.	900		

Rent Expense

10.	3,000		

Solution to Requirement c

MESTRO FINANCIAL SERVICES COMPANY
Trial Balance
December 31, 2007

Account Titles	Debit	Credit
Cash	$22,000	
Accounts Receivable	3,000	
Supplies	200	
Prepaid Rent	9,000	
Accounts Payable		$ 4,100
Salaries Payable		1,200
Common Stock		28,000
Dividends	1,000	
Consulting Revenue		23,000
General Operating Expenses	16,000	
Salaries Expense	1,200	
Supplies Expense	900	
Rent Expense	3,000	
Totals	$56,300	$56,300

Solution to Requirement d

MESTRO FINANCIAL SERVICES COMPANY
Financial Statements
For 2007

Income Statement
For the Year Ended December 31, 2007

Consulting Revenue		$23,000
Expenses		
General Operating Expenses	$16,000	
Salaries Expense	1,200	
Supplies Expense	900	
Rent Expense	3,000	
Total Expenses		(21,100)
Net Income		$ 1,900

Statement of Changes in Stockholders' Equity
For the Year Ended December 31, 2007

Beginning Common Stock	$ 0	
Plus: Common Stock Issued	28,000	
Ending Common Stock		$28,000
Beginning Retained Earnings	0	
Plus: Net Income	1,900	
Less: Dividends	(1,000)	
Ending Retained Earnings		900
Total Stockholders' Equity		$28,900

Balance Sheet
As of December 31, 2007

Assets		
Cash	$22,000	
Accounts Receivable	3,000	
Supplies	200	
Prepaid Rent	9,000	
Total Assets		$34,200
Liabilities		
Accounts Payable	$ 4,100	
Salaries Payable	1,200	
Total Liabilities		$ 5,300
Stockholders' Equity		
Common Stock	28,000	
Retained Earnings	900	
Total Stockholders' Equity		28,900
Total Liabilities and Stockholders' Equity		$34,200

continued

Statement of Cash Flows
For the Year Ended December 31, 2007

Cash Flows from Operating Activities		
Inflow from Customers	$20,000	
Outflow for Expenses	(25,000)	
Net Cash Flow for Operating Activities		$(5,000)
Cash Flows from Investing Activities		0
Cash Flows from Financing Activities		
Inflow from Issue of Common Stock	28,000	
Outflow for Dividends	(1,000)	
Net Cash Flow from Financing Activities		27,000
Net Change in Cash		22,000
Plus: Beginning Cash Balance		0
Ending Cash Balance		$22,000

Solution to Requirement e

Date	Account Title	Debit	Credit
	Closing Entries		
Dec. 31	Consulting Revenue	23,000	
	Retained Earnings		23,000
Dec. 31	Retained Earnings	21,100	
	General Operating Expenses		16,000
	Salaries Expense		1,200
	Supplies Expense		900
	Rent Expense		3,000
Dec. 31	Retained Earnings	1,000	
	Dividends		1,000

KEY TERMS

account balance 118
books of original entry 129
chart of accounts 128
closing entries 132
credit 118
debit 118
debt to assets ratio 138
double-entry accounting 119
financial leverage 138
fiscal year 117
general journal 129
general ledger 128
journals 128
posting 130
return on assets ratio 137
return on equity ratio 138
source documents 128
special journals 129
T-account 118
trial balance 131

QUESTIONS

1. What are the two fundamental equality requirements of the double-entry accounting system?
2. Define *debit* and *credit.* How are assets, liabilities, common stock, retained earnings, revenues, expenses, and dividends affected (increased or decreased) by debits and by credits?
3. How is the balance of an account determined?
4. What are the three primary sources of business assets?
5. What are the three primary ways a business may use assets?
6. Give an example of an asset exchange transaction.

7. How does a debit to an expense account ultimately affect retained earnings? Stockholders' equity?
8. What accounts normally have debit balances? What accounts normally have credit balances?
9. What is the primary source of information for preparing the financial statements?
10. What is the purpose of a journal?
11. What is the difference between the *general journal* and special journals?
12. What is a ledger? What is its function in the accounting system?
13. What is the purpose of closing entries?
14. Do all companies close their books on December 31? Why or why not?
15. At a minimum, what information is recorded in the general journal?
16. What is the purpose of a trial balance?
17. When should a trial balance be prepared?
18. What does the term *posting* mean?
19. What information does the return on assets ratio provide about a company?
20. What information does the debt to assets ratio provide about a company?
21. What is financial leverage?
22. Explain how financial leverage impacts the return on equity ratio.

EXERCISES—SERIES A

All Exercises in Series A are available with McGraw-Hill's Homework Manager

L.O. 2

Exercise 3-1A *Matching debit and credit terminology with accounts*

Required

Complete the following table by indicating whether a debit or credit is used to increase or decrease the balance of the following accounts. The appropriate debit/credit terminology has been identified for the first account as an example.

Account Titles	Used to Increase This Account	Used to Decrease This Account
Accounts Receivable	Debit	Credit
Accounts Payable		
Common Stock		
Land		
Unearned Revenue		
Service Revenue		
Retained Earnings		
Insurance Expense		
Rent Expense		
Prepaid Rent		

L.O. 1, 2

Exercise 3-2A *Debit/credit rules*

Matt, Allison, and Sarah, three accounting students, were discussing the rules of debits and credits. Matt says that debits increase account balances and credits decrease account balances. Allison says that Matt is wrong, that credits increase account balances and debits decrease account balances. Sarah interrupts and declares that they are both correct.

Required

Explain what Sarah meant and give examples of transactions where debits increase account balances, credits decrease account balances, credits increase account balances, and debits decrease account balances.

Exercise 3-3A *Matching debit and credit terminology with account titles* — L.O. 2

Required

Indicate whether each of the following accounts normally has a debit balance or a credit balance.

a. Unearned Revenue
b. Service Revenue
c. Dividends
d. Land
e. Accounts Receivable
f. Cash
g. Common Stock
h. Prepaid Rent
i. Supplies
j. Accounts Payable

Exercise 3-4A *Identifying increases and decreases in T-accounts* — L.O. 1, 2

Required

For each of the following T-accounts, indicate the side of the account that should be used to record an increase or decrease in the financial statement element.

Assets		=	Liabilities		+	Stockholders' Equity	
Debit	Credit		Debit	Credit		Debit	Credit
						Revenue	
						Debit	Credit
						Expense	
						Debit	Credit

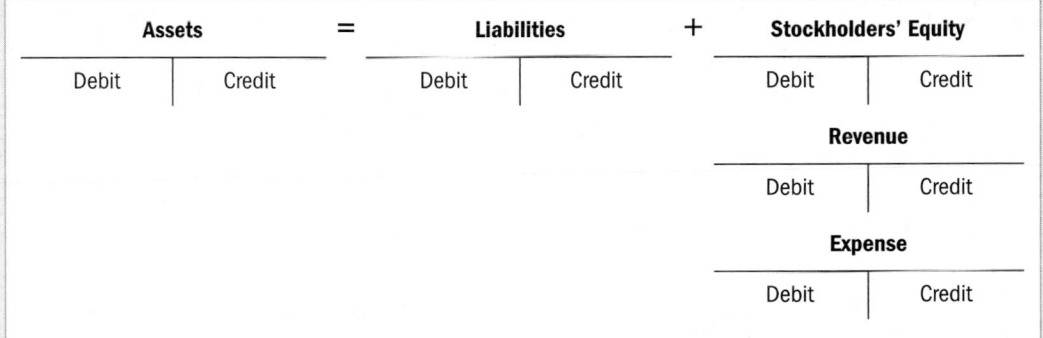

Exercise 3-5A *Applying debit/credit terminology to accounting events* — L.O. 1, 2

Required

a. In parallel columns, list the accounts that would be debited and credited for each of the following unrelated transactions:

(1) Provided services for cash.
(2) Paid cash for salaries expense.
(3) Paid in advance for two-year lease on office space.
(4) Acquired cash from the issue of common stock.
(5) Provided services on account.
(6) Purchased supplies for cash.
(7) Recognized expense for prepaid rent that had been used up by the end of the accounting period.
(8) Recorded accrued salaries at the end of the accounting period.

b. Show how each transaction affects the financial statements by placing a + for increase, − for decrease, and NA for not affected under each component in a horizontal statements model like the one shown below. Also, in the Cash Flow column, use the letters OA to designate operating activity, IA for investing activity, and FA for financing activity. The first event is recorded as an example.

Assets	=	Liab.	+	Equity	Rev.	−	Exp.	=	Net Inc.	Cash Flow
+		NA		+	+		NA		+	+ OA

Exercise 3-6A *T-accounts and the accounting equation* — L.O. 2, 3

Required

Record each of the following Cummings Co. events in T-accounts and then explain how the event affects the accounting equation.

a. Received $20,000 cash by issuing common stock.

b. Purchased supplies for $900 cash.
c. Performed services on account for $7,000.
d. Paid cash for $4,000 of salaries expense.

L.O. 3

Exercise 3-7A ***Recording transactions in general journal and T-accounts***

The following events apply to Pearson Service Co. for 2006, its first year of operation.

1. Received cash of $50,000 from the issue of common stock.
2. Performed $90,000 worth of services on account.
3. Paid $64,000 cash for salaries expense.
4. Purchased supplies for $12,000 on account.
5. Collected $78,000 of accounts receivable.
6. Paid $8,500 of the accounts payable.
7. Paid a $5,000 dividend to the stockholders.
8. Had $1,500 of supplies on hand at the end of the period.

Required

a. Record these events in general journal form.
b. Post the entries to T-accounts and determine the ending balance in each account.
c. Determine the amount of total assets at the end of 2006.
d. Determine the amount of net income for 2006.

L.O. 2

Exercise 3-8A ***Debit/credit terminology***

Required

For each of the following independent events, identify the account that would be debited and the account that would be credited. The accounts for the first event are identified as an example.

Event	Account Debited	Account Credited
a	Cash	Common Stock

a. Received cash by issuing common stock.
b. Received cash for services to be performed in the future.
c. Provided services on account.
d. Paid accounts payable.
e. Paid cash in advance for one year's rent.
f. Paid cash for operating expenses.
g. Paid salaries payable.
h. Purchased supplies on account.
i. Paid cash dividends to the stockholders.
j. Recognized revenue for services completed; previously collected the cash in Event *b*.
k. Received cash in payment of accounts receivable.
l. Paid salaries expense.
m. Recognized expense for prepaid rent that had been used up by the end of the accounting period.

L.O. 1, 2

Exercise 3-9A ***Identifying transaction type, its effect on the accounting equation, and whether the effect is recorded with a debit or credit***

Required

Identify whether each of the following transactions is an asset source (AS), asset use (AU), asset exchange (AE), or claims exchange (CE). Also explain how each event affects the accounting equation by placing a + for *increase,* − for *decrease,* and NA for *not affected* under each of the components of the accounting equation. Finally, indicate whether the effect requires a debit or credit entry. The first event is recorded as an example.

						Stockholders' Equity		
Event	Type of Event	Assets	=	Liabilities	+	Common Stock	+	Retained Earnings
a	AS	+ Debit		NA		NA		+ Credit

a. Provided services on account.
b. Received cash in payment of accounts receivable.
c. Purchased land by paying cash.
d. Recognized revenue for services completed; cash collected previously.
e. Paid a cash dividend to the stockholders.
f. Paid cash in advance for one year's rent.
g. Received cash for services to be performed in the future.
h. Incurred other operating expense on account.
i. Paid salaries payable.
j. Recognized expense for prepaid rent that had been used up by the end of the accounting period.
k. Provided services for cash.
l. Purchased supplies on account.
m. Recognized expense for supplies used during the period.

Exercise 3-10A *Recording events in the general journal and the effect on financial statements*

L.O. 5

Required

Record each of the following transactions in general journal form and then show the effect of the transaction in the horizontal statements model. The first transaction is shown as an example.

Account Title	Debit	Credit
Cash	8,000	
Unearned Revenue		8,000

Assets	=	Liab.	+	Equity	Rev.	−	Exp.	=	Net Inc.	Cash Flow
8,000		8,000		NA	NA		NA		NA	8,000 OA

a. Received $8,000 cash for services to be performed at a later date.
b. Purchased supplies for $1,200 cash.
c. Performed $25,000 worth of services on account.
d. Charged $1,500 on account for operating expense.
e. Collected $19,000 cash on accounts receivable.
f. Paid $900 on accounts payable.
g. Paid $4,800 cash in advance for an insurance policy.
h. Recorded the adjusting entry to recognize $3,600 of insurance expense.

Exercise 3-11A *Preparing a trial balance*

L.O. 6

Required

On December 31, 2008, Chang Company had the following normal account balances in its general ledger. Use this information to prepare a trial balance.

Common Stock	$25,000
Salaries Expense	16,000
Office Supplies	1,800
Advertising Expense	2,500
Retained Earnings, 1/1/2008	14,200
Unearned Revenue	18,000
Accounts Receivable	6,500
Cash	60,000
Service Revenue	76,000
Dividends	5,000
Prepaid Insurance	6,400
Land	22,000
Rent Expense	15,000
Accounts Payable	2,000

L.O. 5, 7

Exercise 3-12A ***Preparing closing entries***

The following financial information was taken from the books of Ritz Salon.

Account Balances as of December 31, 2008	
Accounts Receivable	$28,000
Accounts Payable	7,500
Advertising Expense	2,500
Cash	40,300
Common Stock	20,000
Dividends	5,000
Land	13,500
Prepaid Rent	3,200
Rent Expense	7,800
Retained Earnings 1/1/2008	19,400
Salaries Expense	32,000
Salaries Payable	11,800
Service Revenue	76,500
Supplies	400
Supplies Expense	2,500

Required

a. Prepare the necessary closing entries at December 31, 2008, for Ritz Salon.

b. What is the balance in the Retained Earnings account after the closing entries are posted?

L.O. 3, 6

Exercise 3-13A ***Recording events in the general journal, posting to T-accounts, and preparing a trial balance***

The following events apply to Complete Business Service in 2007, its first year of operations.

1. Received $30,000 cash from the issue of common stock.
2. Earned $25,000 of service revenue on account.
3. Incurred $10,000 of operating expenses on account.
4. Received $20,000 cash for performing services.
5. Paid $8,000 cash to purchase land.
6. Collected $22,000 of cash from accounts receivable.
7. Received a $6,000 cash advance for services to be provided in the future.
8. Purchased $900 of supplies on account.
9. Made a $7,500 payment on accounts payable.
10. Paid a $5,000 cash dividend to the stockholders.
11. Recognized $500 of supplies expense.
12. Recognized $5,000 of revenue for services provided to the customer in Event 7.

Required

a. Record the events in the general journal.

b. Post the events to T-accounts and determine the ending account balances.

c. Test the equality of the debit and credit balances of the T-accounts by preparing a trial balance.

Exercise 3-14A *Determining the effect of errors on the trial balance* L.O. 6

Required

Explain how each of the following posting errors affects a trial balance. State whether the trial balance will be out of balance because of the posting error, and indicate which side of the trial balance will have a higher amount after each independent entry is posted. If the posting error does not affect the equality of debits and credits in the trial balance, state that the error will not cause an inequality and explain why.

a. A $1,000 credit to Salaries Payable was not posted.

b. A $2,400 debit to Cash was posted as a $4,200 debit.

c. A $2,000 debit to Prepaid Rent was debited to Rent Expense.

d. The collection of $500 of accounts receivable was posted to Accounts Receivable twice.

e. A $2,000 credit to Accounts Payable was posted as a credit to Cash.

Exercise 3-15A *Recording events in the general journal, posting to T-accounts, and preparing closing entries* L.O. 3, 5, 7

At the beginning of 2005, Mitchell Cleaning Service had the following normal balances in its accounts:

Account	Balance
Cash	$30,000
Accounts Receivable	19,000
Accounts Payable	12,400
Common Stock	24,000
Retained Earnings	12,600

The following events apply to Mitchell for 2005.

1. Provided $65,000 of services on account.
2. Incurred $3,100 of operating expenses on account.
3. Collected $56,000 of accounts receivable.
4. Paid $36,000 cash for salaries expense.
5. Paid $15,000 cash as a partial payment on accounts payable.
6. Paid an $8,000 cash dividend to the stockholders.

Required

a. Record these events in a general journal.

b. Open T-accounts and post the beginning balances and the preceding transactions to the appropriate accounts. Determine the balance of each account.

c. Record the beginning balances and the events in a horizontal statements model such as the following one:

Assets			=	Liab.	+	Equity			Rev. − Exp. = Net Inc.	Cash Flow
Cash	+	Accts. Rec.	=	Accts. Pay.	+	Common Stock	+	Ret. Earn.		

d. Record the closing entries in the general journal and post them to the T-accounts. What is the amount of net income for the year?

e. What is the amount of *change* in retained earnings for the year? Is the change in retained earnings different from the amount of net income? If so, why?

L.O. 3, 7

Exercise 3-16A *Recording receivables and identifying their effect on financial statements*

Wong Company performed services on account for $60,000 in 2006, its first year of operations. Wong collected $48,000 cash from accounts receivable during 2006 and the remaining $12,000 in cash during 2007.

Required

a. Record the 2006 transactions in T-accounts.

b. Record the 2006 transactions in a horizontal statements model like the following one:

Assets			=	Liab.	+	Equity	Rev.	−	Exp.	=	Net Inc.	Cash Flow
Cash	+	Accts. Rec.	=			Ret. Earn.						

c. Determine the amount of revenue Wong would report on the 2006 income statement.

d. Determine the amount of cash flow from operating activities Wong would report on the 2006 statement of cash flows.

e. Open a T-account for Retained Earnings, and close the 2006 Service Revenue account to the Retained Earnings account.

f. Record the 2007 cash collection in the appropriate T-accounts.

g. Record the 2007 transaction in a horizontal statements model like the one shown in Requirement *b.*

h. Assuming no other transactions occur in 2007, determine the amount of net income and the net cash flow from operating activities for 2007.

L.O. 3, 4, 6, 7

Exercise 3-17A *Recording supplies and identifying their effect on financial statements*

Kim Perz started and operated a small family consulting firm in 2005. The firm was affected by two events: (1) Perz provided $18,000 of services on account, and (2) she purchased $5,000 of supplies on account. There were $900 of supplies on hand as of December 31, 2005.

Required

a. Open T-accounts and record the two transactions in the accounts.

b. Record the required year-end adjusting entry to reflect the use of supplies.

c. Record the above transactions in a horizontal statements model like the following one.

Assets			=	Liab.	+	Equity	Rev.	−	Exp.	=	Net Inc.	Cash Flow
Accts. Rec.	+	Supplies	=	Accts. Pay.	+	Ret. Earn.						

d. Explain why the amounts of net income and net cash flow from operating activities differ.

e. Record and post the required closing entries, and prepare an after-closing trial balance.

L.O. 4, 5

Exercise 3-18A *Recording prepaid items and identifying their effect on financial statements*

California Mining began operations by issuing common stock for $100,000. The company paid $90,000 cash in advance for a one-year contract to lease machinery for the business. The lease agreement was signed on March 1, 2005, and was effective immediately. California Mining earned $115,000 of cash revenue in 2005.

Required

a. Record the March 1 cash payment in general journal format.

b. Record in general journal format the adjustment required as of December 31, 2005.

c. Record all 2005 events in a horizontal statements model like the following one:

Assets			=	Liab.	+	Equity	Rev.	−	Exp.	=	Net Inc.	Cash Flow
Cash	+	Prep. Rent	=			Ret. Earn.						

d. What amount of net income would California Mining report on the 2005 income statement? What is the amount of net cash flow from operating activities for 2005?

e. Determine the amount of prepaid rent California Mining would report on the December 31, 2005, balance sheet.

Exercise 3-19A *Recording accrued salaries and identifying their effect on financial statements*

L.O. 4, 5

On December 31, 2008, Red River Company had accrued salaries of $9,500.

Required

a. Record in general journal format the adjustment required as of December 31, 2008.

b. Record the above adjustment in a horizontal statements model like the following one:

Assets	=	Liab.	+	Equity	Rev.	−	Exp.	=	Net Inc.	Cash Flow
		Sal. Pay.	+	Ret. Earn.						

c. Determine the amount of net income Red River would report on the 2008 income statement, assuming that Red River earns $25,000 of cash revenue. What is the amount of net cash flow from operating activities for 2008?

d. What amount of salaries payable would Red River report on the December 31, 2008, balance sheet?

Exercise 3-20A *Recording unearned revenue and identifying its effect on financial statements*

L.O. 3, 4

Zhen received a $60,000 cash advance on March 1, 2005, for legal services to be performed in the future. Services were to be provided for a one-year term beginning March 1, 2005.

Required

a. Record the March 1 cash receipt in T-accounts.

b. Record in T-accounts the adjustment required as of December 31, 2005.

c. Record the preceding transaction and related adjustment in a horizontal statements model like the following one:

Assets	=	Liab.	+	Equity	Rev.	−	Exp.	=	Net Inc.	Cash Flow

d. Determine the amount of net income on the 2005 income statement. What is the amount of net cash flow from operating activities for 2005?

e. What amount of unearned revenue would Zhen report on the December 31, 2005, balance sheet?

Exercise 3-21A *Using a T-account to determine cash flow from operating activities*

L.O. 3

Koch Inc. began the accounting period with a $75,000 debit balance in its Accounts Receivable account. During the accounting period, Koch earned revenue on account of $320,000. The ending Accounts Receivable balance was $62,000.

Required

Based on this information alone, determine the amount of cash inflow from operating activities during the accounting period. (*Hint:* Use a T-account for Accounts Receivable. Enter the debits and credits for the given events, and solve for the missing amount.)

Exercise 3-22A *Using a T-account to determine cash flow from operating activities*

L.O. 3

Cole Company began the accounting period with an $18,000 credit balance in its Accounts Payable account. During the accounting period, Cole incurred expenses on account of $54,000. The ending Accounts Payable balance was $24,000.

Required

Based on this information, determine the amount of cash outflow for expenses during the accounting period. (*Hint:* Use a T-account for Accounts Payable. Enter the debits and credits for the given events, and solve for the missing amount.)

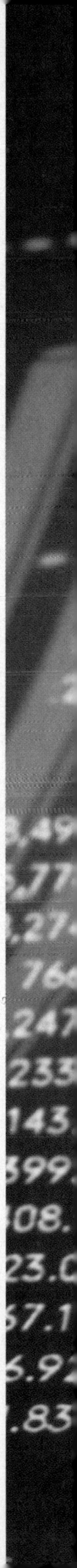

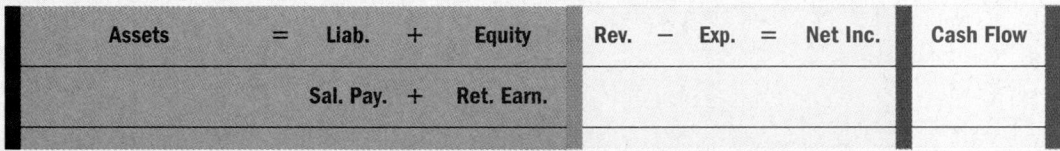

PROBLEMS—SERIES A

All Problems in Series A are available with McGraw-Hill's Homework Manager

L.O. 2

Problem 3-23A *Identifying debit and credit balances*

CHECK FIGURES
a. Land: Debit
o. Accounts Payable: Credit

Required

Indicate whether each of the following accounts normally has a debit or credit balance.

a. Land
b. Salaries Expense
c. Rent Expense
d. Common Stock
e. Cash
f. Salaries Payable
g. Accounts Receivable
h. Insurance Expense
i. Prepaid Insurance
j. Retained Earnings
k. Supplies Expense
l. Prepaid Rent
m. Service Revenue
n. Supplies
o. Accounts Payable
p. Unearned Revenue
q. Operating Expense
r. Dividends

L.O. 1, 2

Problem 3-24A *Transaction type and debit/credit terminology*

The following events apply to Box Enterprises.

1. Acquired $30,000 cash from the issue of common stock.
2. Paid salaries to employees, $8,000 cash.
3. Collected $9,000 cash for services to be performed in the future.
4. Paid cash for utilities expense, $1,200.
5. Recognized $28,000 of service revenue on account.
6. Paid a $5,000 cash dividend to the stockholders.
7. Purchased $2,000 of supplies on account.
8. Received $18,000 cash for services rendered.
9. Paid cash to rent office space for the next 12 months, $7,800.
10. Paid cash of $9,200 for operating expenses.
11. Paid on accounts payable, $1,200.
12. Recognized $3,250 of rent expense related to cash paid in a prior transaction (see Event 9).
13. Recognized $6,000 of revenue for services performed for which cash had been previously collected (see Event 3).
14. Recognized $4,800 of accrued salaries expense.

Required

Identify each event as asset source (AS), asset use (AU), asset exchange (AE), or claims exchange (CE). Also identify the account to be debited and the account to be credited when the transaction is recorded. The first event is recorded as an example.

Event No.	Type of Event	Account Debited	Account Credited
1	AS	Cash	Common Stock

L.O. 4, 5

Problem 3-25A *Recording adjusting entries in general journal format*

Required

Each of the following independent events requires a year-end adjusting entry. Record each event and the related adjusting entry in general journal format. The first event is recorded as an example. Assume a December 31 closing date.

Date	Account Title	Debit	Credit
Oct. 1	Prepaid Rent Cash	9,600	 9,600
Dec. 31	Rent Expense (9,600 × 3/12) Prepaid Rent	2,400	 2,400

CHECK FIGURES
d. Adjustment amount: $2,400

a. Paid $9,600 cash in advance on October 1 for a one-year lease on office space.
b. Purchased $3,200 of supplies on account on June 15. At year end, $300 of supplies remained on hand.
c. Received a $9,600 cash advance on September 1 for a contract to provide services for one year.
d. Paid $3,600 cash in advance on May 1 for a one-year insurance policy.

Problem 3-26A *One complete accounting cycle*

L.O. 3, 4, 6, 7

The following events apply to Paradise Vacations' first year of operations:

1. Acquired $20,000 cash from the issue of common stock on January 1, 2005.
2. Purchased $800 of supplies on account.
3. Paid $4,200 cash in advance for a one-year lease on office space.
4. Earned $28,000 of revenue on account.
5. Incurred $12,500 of other operating expenses on account.
6. Collected $24,000 cash from accounts receivable.
7. Paid $9,000 cash on accounts payable.
8. Paid a $3,000 cash dividend to the stockholders.

CHECK FIGURES
c. Ending Cash Balance: $27,800
Total debits of trial balance: $55,900

Information for Adjusting Entries

9. There was $150 of supplies on hand at the end of the accounting period.
10. The lease on the office space covered a one-year period beginning November 1.
11. There was $3,600 of accrued salaries at the end of the period.

Required

a. Record these transactions in general journal form.
b. Post the transaction data from the journal to ledger T-accounts.
c. Prepare a trial balance.
d. Prepare an income statement, statement of changes in stockholders' equity, a balance sheet, and a statement of cash flows.
e. Record the entries to close the temporary accounts (Revenue, Expense, and Dividends) to Retained Earnings in general journal form.
f. Post the closing entries to the T-accounts, and prepare an after-closing trial balance.

Problem 3-27A *Two complete accounting cycles*

L.O. 3–7

excel
mhhe.com/edmonds2007

Pacific Machining experienced the following events during 2007.

1. Started operations by acquiring $50,000 of cash from the issue of common stock.
2. Paid $6,000 cash in advance for rent during the period from February 1, 2007, to February 1, 2008.
3. Received $4,800 cash in advance for services to be performed evenly over the period from September 1, 2007, to September 1, 2008.
4. Performed services for customers on account for $65,200.
5. Incurred operating expenses on account of $31,500.
6. Collected $56,900 cash from accounts receivable.
7. Paid $22,000 cash for salaries expense.
8. Paid $28,000 cash as a partial payment on accounts payable.

CHECK FIGURES
b. Ending Cash Balance, 2007: $55,700
g. Net Income, 2008: $26,650

Adjusting Entries

9. Made the adjusting entry for the expired rent. (See Event 2.)

10. Recognized revenue for services performed in accordance with Event 3.
11. Recorded $2,100 of accrued salaries at the end of 2007.

Events for 2008

1. Paid $2,100 cash for the salaries accrued at the end of the previous year.
2. Performed services for cash, $40,500.
3. Paid $25,000 cash to purchase land.
4. Paid $5,400 cash in advance for rent during the period from February 1, 2008, to February 1, 2009.
5. Performed services for customers on account for $82,000.
6. Incurred operating expenses on account of $49,100.
7. Collected $76,300 cash from accounts receivable.
8. Paid $48,000 cash as a partial payment on accounts payable.
9. Paid $41,000 cash for salaries expense.
10. Paid a $5,000 cash dividend to the stockholders.

Adjusting Entries

11. Recognized revenue for services performed in accordance with Event 3 in 2007.
12. Made the adjusting entry for the expired rent. (*Hint:* Part of the rent was paid in 2007.)
13. Recorded $3,500 of accrued salaries at the end of 2008.

Required

a. Record the events and adjusting entries for 2007 in general journal form.
b. Post the events for 2007 to T-accounts.
c. Prepare a trial balance for 2007.
d. Prepare an income statement, statement of changes in stockholders' equity, balance sheet, and statement of cash flows for 2007.
e. Record the entries to close the 2007 temporary accounts to Retained Earnings in the general journal and post to the T-accounts.
f. Prepare an after-closing trial balance for December 31, 2007.
g. Repeat Requirements *a* through *f* for 2008.

L.O. 2, 5

Problem 3-28A *Identifying accounting events from journal entries*

Required

The following information is from the records of Swan Design. Write a brief description of the accounting event represented in each of the general journal entries.

Date	Account Titles	Debit	Credit
Jan. 1	Cash	12,500	
	Common Stock		12,500
Feb. 10	Supplies	1,550	
	Accounts Payable		1,550
Mar. 1	Cash	13,000	
	Unearned Revenue		13,000
Apr. 1	Prepaid Rent	10,200	
	Cash		10,200
20	Accounts Receivable	18,400	
	Service Revenue		18,400
June 15	Salaries Expense	6,100	
	Cash		6,100
30	Property Tax Expense	3,000	
	Cash		3,000
July 28	Cash	9,300	
	Service Revenue		9,300

continued

Date	Account Titles	Debit	Credit
Aug. 30	Dividends	3,000	
	Cash		3,000
Sept. 19	Cash	16,000	
	Accounts Receivable		16,000
Dec. 31	Supplies Expense	2,025	
	Supplies		2,025
31	Rent Expense	6,400	
	Prepaid Rent		6,400
31	Unearned Revenue	8,500	
	Service Revenue		8,500

Problem 3-29A ***Recording events in a statements model and T-accounts and preparing a trial balance***

L.O. 3, 4, 6

CHECK FIGURE

c. Total debits: $38,675

The following accounting events apply to Parks Co. for the year 2008:

Asset Source Transactions

1. Began operations when the business acquired $20,000 cash from the issue of common stock.
2. Performed services and collected cash of $1,000.
3. Collected $4,500 of cash in advance for services to be provided over the next 12 months.
4. Provided $12,000 of services on account.
5. Purchased supplies of $420 on account.

Asset Exchange Transactions

6. Purchased $4,000 of land for cash.
7. Collected $8,500 of cash from accounts receivable.
8. Purchased $500 of supplies with cash.
9. Paid $3,600 in advance for one year's rent.

Asset Use Transactions

10. Paid $3,000 cash for salaries of employees.
11. Paid a cash dividend of $2,000 to the stockholders.
12. Paid $420 for supplies that had been purchased on account.

Claims Exchange Transactions

13. Placed an advertisement in the local newspaper for $150 and agreed to pay for the ad later.
14. Incurred utilities expense of $125 on account.

Adjusting Entries

15. Recognized $3,000 of revenue for performing services. The collection of cash for these services occurred in a prior transaction. (See Event 3.)
16. Recorded $900 of accrued salary expense at the end of 2008.
17. Recorded supplies expense. Had $120 of supplies on hand at the end of the accounting period.
18. Recognized that three months of prepaid rent had been used up during the accounting period.

Required

a. Use a horizontal statements model to show how each event affects the balance sheet, income statement, and statement of cash flows. Indicate whether the event increases (+), decreases (−), or does not affect (NA) each element of the financial statements. Also, in the Cash Flow column, use the letters OA to designate operating activity, IA for investing activity, and FA for financing activity. The first event is recorded as an example.

Assets	=	Liab.	+	Equity	Rev.	−	Exp.	=	Net Inc.	Cash Flow
+		NA		+	NA		NA		NA	+ FA

b. Record each of the preceding transactions in T-accounts and determine the balance of each account.
c. Prepare a before-closing trial balance.

L.O. 1, 5

Problem 3-30A ***Effect of journal entries on financial statements***

Event No.	Account Title	Debit	Credit
1	Cash Common Stock	xxx	 xxx
2	Cash Unearned Revenue	xxx	 xxx
3	Supplies Accounts Payable	xxx	 xxx
4	Accounts Receivable Service Revenue	xxx	 xxx
5	Cash Accounts Receivable	xxx	 xxx
6	Cash Service Revenue	xxx	 xxx
7	Salaries Expense Cash	xxx	 xxx
8	Dividends Cash	xxx	 xxx
9	Prepaid Rent Cash	xxx	 xxx
10	Property Tax Expense Cash	xxx	 xxx
11	Supplies Expense Supplies	xxx	 xxx
12	Rent Expense Prepaid Rent	xxx	 xxx
13	Unearned Revenue Service Revenue	xxx	 xxx

Required

The preceding 13 different accounting events are presented in general journal format. Use a horizontal statements model to show how each event affects the balance sheet, income statement, and statement of cash flows. Indicate whether the event increases (+), decreases (−), or does not affect (NA) each element of the financial statements. Also, in the Cash Flow column, use the letters OA to designate operating activity, IA for investing activity, and FA for financing activity. The first event is recorded as an example.

Assets	=	Liab.	+	Equity	Rev.	−	Exp.	=	Net Inc.	Cash Flow
+		NA		+	NA		NA		NA	+ FA

L.O. 6

CHECK FIGURE
Error (e): Out of balance by $3,000

Problem 3-31A ***Effect of errors on the trial balance***

Required

Consider each of the following errors independently (assume that each is the only error that has occurred). Complete the following table. The first error is recorded as an example.

Error	Is the Trial Balance Out of Balance?	By What Amount?	Which Is Larger, Total Debits or Credits?
a	yes	90	credit

a. A credit of $780 to Accounts Payable was recorded as $870.
b. A credit of $500 to Accounts Receivable was not recorded.
c. A debit of $900 to Rent Expense was recorded as a debit of $700 to Salaries Expense.
d. An entry requiring a debit of $450 to Cash and a credit of $450 to Accounts Receivable was not posted to the ledger accounts.
e. A credit of $1,500 to Prepaid Insurance was recorded as a debit of $1,500 to Prepaid Insurance.
f. A debit of $500 to Cash was recorded as a credit of $500 to Cash.

Problem 3-32A ***Effect of errors on the trial balance***

L.O. 6

CHECK FIGURE
Corrected cash balance: $8,200

The following trial balance was prepared from the ledger accounts of Cook Inc.:

COOK INC.
Trial Balance
May 31, 2006

Account Title	Debit	Credit
Cash	$ 7,200	
Accounts Receivable	1,770	
Supplies	420	
Prepaid Insurance	2,400	
Land	5,000	
Accounts Payable		$ 1,500
Common Stock		1,800
Retained Earnings		7,390
Dividends	400	
Service Revenue		19,600
Rent Expense	3,600	
Salaries Expense	9,000	
Operating Expenses	2,500	
Totals	$32,290	$30,290

The accountant for Cook, Inc., made the following errors during May 2006.

1. The cash purchase of land for $3,000 was recorded as a $5,000 debit to Land and a $3,000 credit to Cash.
2. An $800 purchase of supplies on account was properly recorded as a debit to the Supplies account but was incorrectly recorded as a credit to the Cash account.
3. The company provided services valued at $8,600 to a customer on account. The accountant recorded the transaction in the proper accounts but in the incorrect amount of $6,800.
4. A $600 cash receipt for a payment on an account receivable was not recorded.
5. A $400 cash payment of an account payable was not recorded.
6. The May utility bill, which amounted to $550 on account, was not recorded.

Required

a. Identify the errors that would cause a difference in the total amounts of debits and credits that would appear in a trial balance. Indicate whether the Debit or Credit column would be larger as a result of the error.
b. Indicate whether each of the preceding errors would overstate, understate, or have no effect on the amount of total assets, liabilities, and equity. Your answer should take the following form:

Event No.	Assets	=	Liabilities	+	Stockholders' Equity
1	Overstate		No effect		No effect

c. Prepare a corrected trial balance.

L.O. 3-7

eXcel

mhhe.com/edmonds2007

CHECK FIGURES

d. Net Income: $12,900

Total Assets: $76,300

Problem 3-33A *Comprehensive problem: single cycle*

The following transactions pertain to Abbott Corporation for 2005.

Jan.	1	Began operations when the business acquired $50,000 cash from the issue of common stock.
Mar.	1	Paid rent for office space for two years, $16,800 cash.
Apr.	14	Purchased $800 of supplies on account.
June	30	Received $24,000 cash in advance for services to be provided over the next year.
July	5	Paid $600 of the accounts payable from April 14.
Aug.	1	Billed a customer $9,600 for services provided during July.
	8	Completed a job and received $3,200 cash for services rendered.
Sept.	1	Paid employee salaries of $36,000 cash.
	9	Received $8,500 cash from accounts receivable.
Oct.	5	Billed customers $34,000 for services rendered on account.
Nov.	2	Paid a $1,000 cash dividend to the stockholders.
Dec.	31	Adjusted records to recognize the services provided on the contract of June 30.
	31	Recorded $2,200 of accrued salaries as of December 31.
	31	Recorded the rent expense for the year. (See March 1.)
	31	Physically counted supplies; $100 was on hand at the end of the period.

Required

a. Record the preceding transactions in the general journal.
b. Post the transactions to T-accounts and calculate the account balances.
c. Prepare a trial balance.
d. Prepare the income statement, statement of changes in stockholders' equity, balance sheet, and statement of cash flows.
e. Prepare the closing entries at December 31.
f. Prepare a trial balance after the closing entries are posted.

L.O. 3-7

eXcel

mhhe.com/edmonds2007

CHECK FIGURES

Cash, April 30, 2007: $36,970

Net Income: $1,967

Problem 3-34A *Comprehensive problem: two cycles*

This is a two-cycle problem. The second cycle is in Problem 3-34B. The first cycle *can* be completed without referring to the second cycle.

John and Larry organized a cleaning business that began operations on April 1, 2007. Turner Cleaning consummated the following transactions during the first month of operation.

April	1	Acquired $40,000 from the issue of common stock.
	1	Paid $3,600 in advance rent for a one-year lease on office space.
	6	Purchased supplies for $220 cash.
	9	Received from Don Orr a $500 cash advance for services to be performed in May.
	10	Recorded services provided to customers. Cash receipts were $850, and invoices for services on account were $1,200.
	15	Paid $960 cash for employee salaries.
	16	Collected $450 from accounts receivable.
	23	Received monthly utility bills amounting to $233. The bills will be paid during May.
	25	Paid advertising expense for advertisements run during April, $240.
	30	Recorded services to customers. Cash sales were $1,150 and invoices for services on account were $1,600.
	30	Paid $960 cash for employee salaries.

Information for April 30 Adjusting Entries

1. Counted the supplies inventory. Had $80 of supplies on hand.
2. Made an adjustment for expired rent.

Required

a. Record the transactions for April in general journal format.
b. Open a general ledger, using T-accounts, and post the general journal entries to the ledger.
c. Prepare a trial balance.
d. Record and post the appropriate adjusting entries.
e. Prepare a before-closing trial balance.
f. Prepare an income statement, statement of changes in stockholders' equity, balance sheet, and statement of cash flows.
g. Record and post the closing entries.
h. Prepare an after-closing trial balance.

EXERCISES—SERIES B

Exercise 3-1B *Matching debit and credit terminology with accounting elements* L.O. 2

Required

Complete the following table by indicating whether a debit or credit is used to increase or decrease the balance of accounts belonging to each category of financial statement elements. The appropriate debit/credit terminology has been identified for the first category (assets) as an example.

Category of Elements	Used to Increase This Element	Used to Decrease This Element
Assets	Debit	Credit
Liabilities		
Common Stock		
Retained Earnings		
Revenue		
Expense		
Dividends		

Exercise 3-2B *Debit/credit terminology* L.O. 1, 2

Two introductory accounting students were arguing about how to record a transaction involving an exchange of cash for land. Trisha stated that the transaction should have a debit to Land and a credit to Cash; Tony argued that the reverse (debit to Cash and credit to Land) represented the appropriate treatment.

Required

Which student was correct? Defend your position.

Exercise 3-3B *Matching debit and credit terminology with account titles* L.O. 1, 2

Required

Indicate whether each of the following accounts normally has a debit balance or a credit balance.

a. Land
b. Dividends
c. Accounts Payable
d. Unearned Revenue
e. Consulting Revenue
f. Salaries Expense
g. Salaries Payable
h. Cash
i. Prepaid Insurance
j. Common Stock

Exercise 3-4B *Identifying increases and decreases in T-accounts* L.O. 1, 2

Required

For each of the following T-accounts, indicate the side of the account that should be used to record an increase or decrease in the account balance.

Cash	
Debit	Credit

Accounts Payable	
Debit	Credit

Common Stock	
Debit	Credit

Accounts Receivable	
Debit	Credit

Salaries Payable	
Debit	Credit

Dividends	
Debit	Credit

Supplies	
Debit	Credit

Service Revenue	
Debit	Credit

Other Operating Expense	
Debit	Credit

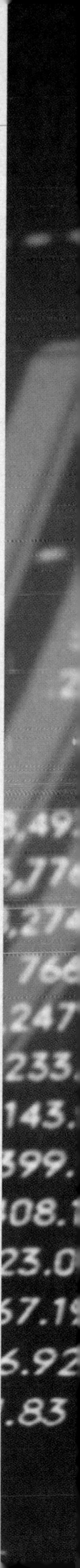

L.O. 2

Exercise 3-5B *Applying debit/credit terminology to accounting events*

Required

a. In parallel columns, list the accounts that would be debited and credited for each of the following unrelated transactions:

(1) Provided services on account.
(2) Paid cash for operating expenses.
(3) Acquired cash from the issue of common stock.
(4) Purchased supplies on account.
(5) Purchased land for cash.
(6) Paid a cash dividend to the stockholders.
(7) Provided services for cash.
(8) Recognized accrued salaries at the end of the period.

b. Show how each transaction affects the financial statements by placing a + for increase, − for decrease, and NA for not affected under each component in a horizontal statements model like the one shown below. Also, in the Cash Flow column, use the letters OA to designate operating activity, IA for investing activity, and FA for financing activity. The first event is recorded as an example.

Assets	=	Liab.	+	Equity	Rev.	−	Exp.	=	Net Inc.	Cash Flow
+		NA		+	+		NA		+	NA

L.O. 2, 3

Exercise 3-6B *T-accounts and the accounting equation*

Required

Record each of the following Lang Co. events in T-accounts, and then explain how the event affects the accounting equation.

a. Received $5,000 cash by issuing common stock.
b. Purchased supplies for $250 cash.
c. Purchased land for $10,000 cash.
d. Performed services for $800 cash.

L.O. 3

Exercise 3-7B *Recording transactions in the general journal and T-accounts*

The following events apply to Godwin Company for 2005, its first year of operation.

1. Received cash of $48,000 from the issue of common stock.
2. Performed $85,000 of services on account.
3. Incurred $8,000 of other operating expenses on account.
4. Paid $34,000 cash for salaries expense.
5. Collected $65,000 of accounts receivable.
6. Paid a $5,000 dividend to the stockholders.
7. Performed $9,200 of services for cash.
8. Paid $4,400 of the accounts payable.

Required

a. Record the preceding transactions in general journal form.
b. Post the entries to T-accounts and determine the ending balance in each account.
c. Determine the amount of total assets at the end of 2005.
d. Determine the amount of net income for 2005.

L.O. 2

Exercise 3-8B *Debit/credit terminology*

Required

For each of the following independent events, identify the account that would be debited and the account that would be credited. The accounts for the first event are identified as an example.

Event	Account Debited	Account Credited
a	Cash	Common Stock

a. Received cash by issuing common stock.
b. Received cash for services to be performed in the future.
c. Paid salaries payable.
d. Provided services on account.
e. Paid cash for operating expenses.
f. Purchased supplies on account.
g. Recognized revenue for services completed. Cash had been collected in Event *b*.
h. Paid accounts payable.
i. Received cash in payment of accounts receivable.
j. Paid a cash dividend to the stockholders.
k. Recognized accrued salaries expense.
l. Recognized expense for supplies used during the period.
m. Performed services for cash.

Exercise 3-9B ***Identifying transaction type, its effect on the accounting equation, and whether the effect is recorded with a debit or credit*** **L.O. 1, 2**

Required

Identify whether each of the following transactions is an asset source (AS), asset use (AU), asset exchange (AE), or claims exchange (CE). Also explain how each event affects the accounting equation by placing a + for *increase,* − for *decrease,* and NA for *not affected* under each of the components of the accounting equation. Finally, indicate whether the effect requires a debit or credit entry. The first event is recorded as an example.

						Stockholders' Equity		
Event	Type of Event	Assets	=	Liabilities	+	Common Stock	+	Retained Earnings
a	AE	+ Debit − Credit		NA		NA		NA

a. Purchased land with cash.
b. Provided services for cash.
c. Purchased supplies on account.
d. Paid accounts payable.
e. Acquired cash from the issue of common stock.
f. Received cash in payment of accounts receivable.
g. Paid cash in advance for one year of rent.
h. Paid salaries payable.
i. Received cash for services to be performed in the future.
j. Paid a cash dividend to the stockholders.
k. Recognized revenue for services completed for which cash had been collected previously.
l. Recognized expense for supplies used during the period.
m. Incurred other operating expenses on account.

Exercise 3-10B ***Recording events in the general journal and effect on financial statements*** **L.O. 5**

Required

Record each of the following transactions in general journal form and then show the effect of the transaction in a horizontal statements model. The first transaction is shown as an example.

Account Title	Debit	Credit
Accounts Receivable	19,000	
Service Revenue		19,000

Assets	=	Liab.	+	Equity	Rev.	−	Exp.	=	Net Inc.	Cash Flow
19,000				19,000	19,000		NA		19,000	NA

a. Performed $19,000 of services on account.
b. Purchased land for $24,000 cash.
c. Purchased supplies for $530 cash.
d. Received $3,000 cash for services to be performed at a later date.
e. Collected $8,400 cash on accounts receivable.
f. Paid $2,300 cash in advance for an insurance policy.
g. Paid $1,200 on accounts payable.
h. Recorded the adjusting entry to recognize $800 of insurance expense.

L.O. 6

Exercise 3-11B *Preparing a trial balance*

Required

On December 31, 2006, Grey Company had the following normal account balances in its general ledger. Use this information to prepare a trial balance.

Land	$80,000
Unearned Revenue	52,000
Dividends	20,000
Prepaid Rent	19,200
Cash	58,000
Salaries Expense	50,000
Accounts Payable	12,000
Common Stock	80,000
Operating Expense	50,000
Office Supplies	10,000
Advertising Expense	4,000
Retained Earnings, 1/1/2006	18,000
Service Revenue	184,000
Accounts Receivable	54,800

L.O. 5, 7

Exercise 3-12B *Preparing closing entries*

The following financial information was taken from the books of Better Shape Health Club, a small spa and health club.

Account Balances as of December 31, 2008	
Accounts Receivable	$16,150
Accounts Payable	5,500
Salaries Payable	2,150
Cash	20,725
Dividends	1,750
Operating Expense	31,550
Prepaid Rent	600
Rent Expense	4,200
Retained Earnings 1/1/2008	32,650
Salaries Expense	11,200

continued

Service Revenue	48,400
Supplies	450
Supplies Expense	4,240
Common Stock	6,515
Unearned Revenue	8,050
Land	12,400

Required

a. Prepare the necessary closing entries at December 31, 2008, for Better Shape Health Club.

b. What is the balance in the Retained Earnings account after the closing entries are posted?

Exercise 3-13B ***Recording events in the general journal, posting to T-accounts, and preparing a trial balance*** **L.O. 3, 6**

The following events apply to Electronics Services Inc. in its first year of operation.

1. Acquired $80,000 cash from the issue of common stock.
2. Earned $56,000 of service revenue on account.
3. Incurred $30,400 of operating expenses on account.
4. Collected $52,800 cash from accounts receivable.
5. Made a $27,200 payment on accounts payable.
6. Paid a $4,000 cash dividend to the stockholders.
7. Received a $14,200 cash advance for services to be provided in the future.
8. Purchased $3,200 of supplies on account.
9. Recognized $4,800 of revenue for services provided to the customer in Event 7.
10. Recognized $2,400 of supplies expense.
11. Recorded $3,200 of accrued salaries expense.

Required

a. Record the events in T-accounts and determine the ending account balances.

b. Test the equality of the debit and credit balances of the T-accounts by preparing a trial balance.

Exercise 3-14B ***Determining the effect of errors on the trial balance*** **L.O. 6**

Required

Explain how each of the following posting errors affects a trial balance. State whether the trial balance will be out of balance because of the posting error, and indicate which side of the trial balance will have a higher amount after each independent entry is posted. If the posting error does not affect the equality of debits and credits in the trial balance, state that the error will not cause an inequality and explain why.

a. A $400 debit to Rent Expense was posted twice.

b. A $1,200 credit to Accounts Payable was not posted.

c. A $400 credit to Unearned Revenue was credited to Service Revenue.

d. A $200 debit to Cash was posted as a $2,000 debit.

e. A $520 debit to Office Supplies was debited to Office Supplies Expense.

Exercise 3-15B ***Recording events in the general journal, posting to T-accounts, and preparing closing entries*** **L.O. 3, 5, 7**

At the beginning of 2006, Tim's Consulting had the following normal balances in its accounts:

Account	Balance
Cash	$13,000
Accounts Receivable	9,500
Accounts Payable	3,600
Common Stock	9,900
Retained Earnings	9,000

The following events apply to Tim's Consulting for 2006.

1. Provided $118,000 of services on account.
2. Incurred $11,980 of operating expenses on account.
3. Collected $124,000 of accounts receivable.
4. Paid $71,000 cash for salaries expense.
5. Paid $13,600 cash as a partial payment on accounts payable.
6. Paid an $11,000 cash dividend to the stockholders.

Required

a. Record these transactions in a general journal.
b. Open T-accounts, and post the beginning balances and the preceding transactions to the appropriate accounts.
c. Record the beginning balances and the transactions in a horizontal statements model such as the following one:

Assets			=	Liab.	+	Equity			Rev. − Exp. = Net Inc.	Cash Flow
Cash	+	Accts. Rec.	=	Accts. Pay.	+	Common Stock	+	Ret. Earn.		

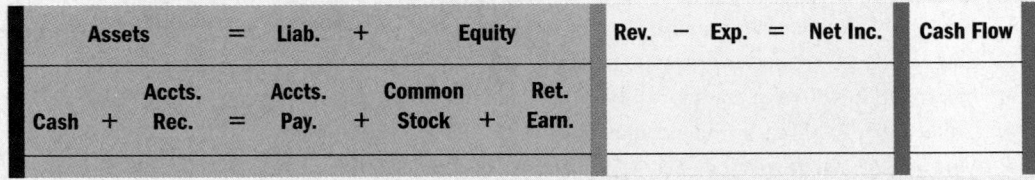

d. Record the closing entries in the general journal and post them to the T-accounts. What is the amount of net income for the year?
e. What is the amount of *change* in retained earnings for the year? Is the change in retained earnings different from the amount of net income? If so, why?

L.O. 3, 5

Exercise 3-16B *Recording receivables and identifying their effect on financial statements*

Boone Company performed services on account for $40,000 in 2006. Boone collected $25,000 cash from accounts receivable during 2006, and the remaining $15,000 was collected in cash during 2007.

Required

a. Record the 2006 transactions in T-accounts.
b. Record the 2006 transactions in a horizontal statements model like the following one:

Assets			=	Liab. + Equity	Rev. − Exp. = Net Inc.	Cash Flow
Cash	+	Accts. Rec.	=	Ret. Earn.		

c. Determine the amount of revenue Boone would report on the 2006 income statement.
d. Determine the amount of cash flow from operating activities Boone would report on the 2006 statement of cash flows.
e. Open a T-account for Retained Earnings, and close the 2006 Service Revenue account to the Retained Earnings account.
f. Record the 2007 cash collection in the appropriate T-accounts.
g. Record the 2007 transaction in a horizontal statements model like the one shown in Requirement *b.*
h. Assuming no other transactions occur in 2007, determine the amount of net income and the net cash flow from operating activities for 2007.

L.O. 3, 4, 6, 7

Exercise 3-17B *Recording supplies and identifying their effect on financial statements*

Wayne Dunn started and operated a small family architectural firm in 2007. The firm was affected by two events: (1) Dunn provided $25,000 of services on account, and (2) he purchased $6,000 of supplies on account. There were $500 of supplies on hand as of December 31, 2007.

Required

a. Open T-accounts and record the two transactions in the accounts.
b. Record the required year-end adjusting entry to reflect the use of supplies.

c. Record the preceding transactions in a horizontal statements model like the following one:

Assets			=	Liab.	+	Equity	Rev.	−	Exp.	=	Net Inc.	Cash Flow
Accts. Rec.	+	Supplies	=	Accts. Pay.	+	Ret. Earn.						

d. Explain why the amounts of net income and net cash flow from operating activities differ.

e. Record and post the required closing entries, and prepare an after-closing trial balance.

Exercise 3-18B *Recording prepaid items and identifying their effect on financial statements* L.O. 4, 5

The Far East Company began operations when it issued common stock for $50,000 cash. It paid $48,000 cash in advance for a one-year contract to lease delivery equipment for the business. It signed the lease agreement on March 1, 2007, which was effective immediately. Far East earned $60,000 of cash revenue in 2007.

Required

a. Record the March 1 cash payment in general journal format.

b. Record in general journal format the adjustment required as of December 31, 2007.

c. Record all events in a horizontal statements model like the following one:

Assets			=	Liab.	+	Equity	Rev.	−	Exp.	=	Net Inc.	Cash Flow
Cash	+	Prep. Rent				Ret. Earn.						

d. What amount of net income will Far East report on the 2007 income statement? What is the amount of net cash flow from operating activities for 2007?

e. Determine the amount of prepaid rent Far East would report on the December 31, 2007, balance sheet.

Exercise 3-19B *Recording accrued salaries and identifying their effect on financial statements* L.O. 4, 5

On December 31, 2008, IBC Company had accrued salaries of $9,600.

Required

a. Record in general journal format the adjustment required as of December 31, 2008.

b. Record the above adjustment in a horizontal statements model like the following one.

Assets	=	Liab.	+	Equity	Rev.	−	Exp.	=	Net Inc.	Cash Flow
		Sal. Pay.	+	Ret. Earn.						

c. Determine the amount of net income IBC would report on the 2008 income statement, assuming that IBC earns $12,000 of cash revenue. What is the amount of net cash flow from operating activities for 2008?

d. What amount of salaries payable would IBC report on the December 31, 2008, balance sheet?

Exercise 3-20B *Recording unearned revenue and identifying its effect on financial statements* L.O. 3, 4

Margarete received a $60,000 cash advance payment on June 1, 2005, for consulting services to be performed in the future. Services were to be provided for a one-year term beginning June 1, 2005.

Required

a. Record the June 1 cash receipt in T-accounts.

b. Record in T-accounts the adjustment required as of December 31, 2005.

c. Record the preceding transaction and related adjustment in a horizontal statements model like the following one:

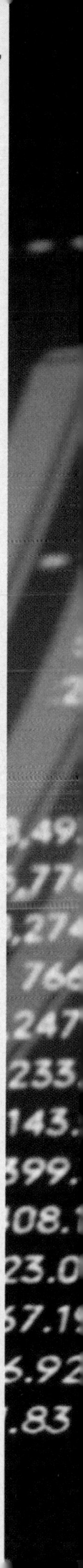

Assets	=	Liab.	+	Equity	Rev.	−	Exp.	=	Net Inc.	Cash Flow

d. Determine the amount of net income on the 2005 income statement. What is the amount of net cash flow from operating activities for 2005?

e. What amount of liabilities would Margarete report on the 2005 balance sheet?

L.O. 3

Exercise 3-21B *Using a T-account to determine cash flow from operating activities*

ABC began the accounting period with a $58,000 debit balance in its Accounts Receivable account. During the accounting period, ABC earned revenue on account of $126,000. The ending Accounts Receivable balance was $54,000.

Required

Based on this information alone, determine the amount of cash inflow from operating activities during the accounting period. (*Hint:* Use a T-account for Accounts Receivable. Enter the debits and credits for the given events, and solve for the missing amount.)

L.O. 3

Exercise 3-22B *Using a T-account to determine cash flow from operating activities*

The Dive Company began the accounting period with a $40,000 credit balance in its Accounts Payable account. During the accounting period, Dive incurred expenses on account of $95,000. The ending Accounts Payable balance was $28,000.

Required

Based on this information, determine the amount of cash outflow for expenses during the accounting period. (*Hint:* Use a T-account for Accounts Payable. Enter the debits and credits for the given events, and solve for the missing amount.)

PROBLEMS—SERIES B

L.O. 2

Problem 3-23B *Identifying debit and credit balances*

Required

Indicate whether each of the following accounts normally has a debit or credit balance.

a. Common Stock
b. Retained Earnings
c. Land
d. Accounts Receivable
e. Insurance Expense
f. Cash
g. Dividends
h. Unearned Revenue
i. Operating Expense
j. Accounts Payable
k. Service Revenue
l. Supplies
m. Utilities Payable
n. Consulting Revenue
o. Supplies Expense
p. Salaries Expense
q. Salaries Payable
r. Land
s. Prepaid Insurance

L.O. 1, 2

Problem 3-24B *Transaction type and debit/credit terminology*

The following events apply to Mask Enterprises.

1. Acquired $25,000 cash from the issue of common stock.
2. Paid salaries to employees, $1,750 cash.
3. Collected $8,100 cash for services to be performed in the future.
4. Paid cash for utilities expense, $402.
5. Recognized $22,500 of service revenue on account.
6. Paid a $1,250 cash dividend to the stockholders.
7. Purchased $1,600 of supplies on account.

8. Received $6,250 cash for services rendered.
9. Paid cash to rent office space for the next 12 months, $6,000.
10. Paid cash of $8,750 for other operating expenses.
11. Paid on account payable, $876.
12. Recognized $1,500 of rent expense. Cash had been paid in a prior transaction (see Event 9).
13. Recognized $2,500 of revenue for services performed. Cash had been previously collected (see Event 3).
14. Recognized $2,600 of accrued salaries expense.

Required

Identify each event as asset source (AS), asset use (AU), asset exchange (AE), or claims exchange (CE). Also identify the account that is to be debited and the account that is to be credited when the transaction is recorded. The first event is recorded as an example.

Event No.	Type of Event	Account Debited	Account Credited
1	AS	Cash	Common Stock

Problem 3-25B ***Recording adjusting entries in general journal format*** **L.O. 4, 5**

Required

Each of the following independent events requires a year-end adjusting entry. Record each event and the related adjusting entry in general journal format. The first event is recorded as an example. Assume a December 31 closing date.

Event No.	Date	Account Titles	Debit	Credit
a	Sept. 1	Prepaid Rent	15,000	
		Cash		15,000
a	Dec. 31	Rent Expense (15,000 × 4/12)	5,000	
		Prepaid Rent		5,000

a. Paid $15,000 cash in advance on September 1 for a one-year lease on office space.
b. Purchased $2,000 of supplies on account on April 15. At year-end, $300 of supplies remained on hand.
c. Received a $3,600 cash advance on July 1 for a contract to provide services for one year.
d. Paid $5,100 cash in advance on February 1 for a one-year insurance policy.

Problem 3-26B ***One complete accounting cycle*** **L.O. 3–7**

The following events apply to Jeater Company's first year of operations:

1. Acquired $20,000 cash from issuing common stock on January 1, 2006.
2. Purchased $600 of supplies on account.
3. Paid $12,000 cash in advance for a one-year lease on office space.
4. Earned $11,500 of revenue on account.
5. Incurred $8,970 of operating expenses on account.
6. Collected $5,900 cash from accounts receivable.
7. Paid $6,500 cash on accounts payable.

Information for Adjusting Entries

8. There was $100 of supplies on hand at the end of the accounting period.
9. The lease on the office space covered a one-year period beginning September 1, 2006.
10. There was $2,200 of accrued salaries at the end of the period.

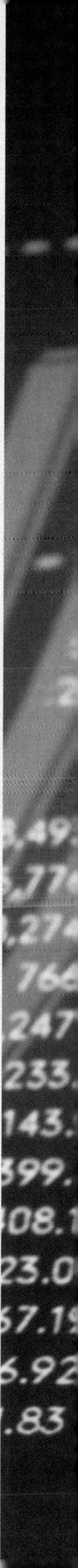

Required

a. Record these transactions in general journal form.
b. Post the transaction data from the journal to ledger T-accounts.
c. Prepare a trial balance.
d. Prepare an income statement, statement of changes in stockholders' equity, a balance sheet, and a statement of cash flows.
e. Close the temporary accounts (Revenue, Expense, and Dividends) to Retained Earnings.
f. Post the closing entries to the T-accounts, and prepare an after-closing trial balance.

L.O. 3-7

Problem 3-27B *Two complete accounting cycles*

Cummings Enterprises experienced the following events for 2006, the first year of operation.

1. Acquired $13,000 cash from the issue of common stock.
2. Paid $4,000 cash in advance for rent. The payment was for the period April 1, 2006, to March 31, 2007.
3. Performed services for customers on account for $27,000.
4. Incurred operating expenses on account of $13,500.
5. Collected $25,150 cash from accounts receivable.
6. Paid $8,500 cash for salary expense.
7. Paid $11,500 cash as a partial payment on accounts payable.

Adjusting Entries

8. Made the adjusting entry for the expired rent. (See Event 2.)
9. Recorded $900 of accrued salaries at the end of 2006.

Events for 2007

1. Paid $900 cash for the salaries accrued at the end of the prior accounting period.
2. Performed services for cash of $8,500.
3. Purchased $1,200 of supplies on account.
4. Paid $4,500 cash in advance for rent. The payment was for one year beginning April 1, 2007.
5. Performed services for customers on account for $42,000.
6. Incurred operating expense on account of $19,250.
7. Collected $40,500 cash from accounts receivable.
8. Paid $20,000 cash as a partial payment on accounts payable.
9. Paid $14,000 cash for salary expense.
10. Paid a $6,000 cash dividend to stockholders.

Adjusting Entries

11. Made the adjusting entry for the expired rent. (*Hint:* Part of the rent was paid in 2006.)
12. Recorded supplies expense. A physical count showed that $300 of supplies were still on hand.

Required

a. Record the events and adjusting entries for 2006 in general journal form.
b. Post the 2006 events to T-accounts.
c. Prepare a trial balance for 2006.
d. Prepare an income statement, statement of changes in stockholders' equity, balance sheet, and statement of cash flows for 2006.
e. Record the entries to close the 2006 temporary accounts to Retained Earnings in the general journal and post to the T-accounts.
f. Prepare an after-closing trial balance for December 31, 2006.
g. Repeat Requirements *a* through *f* for 2007.

L.O. 2, 5

Problem 3-28B *Identifying accounting events from journal entries*

Required

The following information is from the records of attorney Steve Ray. Write a brief description of the accounting event represented in each of the general journal entries.

Date	Account Titles	Debit	Credit
Jan. 1	Cash Common Stock	20,000	 20,000
Feb. 10	Cash Unearned Revenue	4,000	 4,000
Mar. 5	Supplies Cash	2,000	 2,000
Apr. 30	Prepaid Rent Cash	800	 800
May 1	Accounts Receivable Service Revenue	24,000	 24,000
June 1	Salaries Expense Cash	2,000	 2,000
Aug. 5	Accounts Receivable Service Revenue	12,000	 12,000
10	Dividends Cash	1,000	 1,000
Sept. 10	Cash Accounts Receivable	4,400	 4,400
Oct. 1	Property Tax Expense Cash	3,000	 3,000
Dec. 31	Supplies Expense Supplies	800	 800
31	Rent Expense Prepaid Rent	4,400	 4,400
31	Unearned Revenue Service Revenue	6,240	 6,240

Problem 3-29B ***Recording events in a statements model and T-accounts and preparing a trial balance*** **L.O. 3, 4, 6**

The following accounting events apply to Ginger's Designs for the year 2007.

Asset Source Transactions

1. Began operations by acquiring $40,000 of cash from the issue of common stock.
2. Performed services and collected cash of $2,000.
3. Collected $12,000 of cash in advance for services to be provided over the next 12 months.
4. Provided $24,000 of services on account.
5. Purchased supplies of $3,000 on account.

Asset Exchange Transactions

6. Purchased $8,000 of land for cash.
7. Collected $14,000 of cash from accounts receivable.
8. Purchased $1,260 of supplies with cash.
9. Paid $4,800 for one year's rent in advance.

Asset Use Transactions

10. Paid $8,000 cash for salaries of employees.
11. Paid a cash dividend of $4,000 to the stockholders.
12. Paid off $1,260 of the accounts payable with cash.

Claims Exchange Transactions

13. Placed an advertisement in the local newspaper for $1,600 on account.
14. Incurred utility expense of $1,200 on account.

Adjusting Entries

15. Recognized $8,800 of revenue for performing services. The collection of cash for these services occurred in a prior transaction. (See Event 3.)
16. Recorded $3,000 of accrued salary expense at the end of 2007.

17. Recorded supplies expense. Had $1,200 of supplies on hand at the end of the accounting period.
18. Recognized four months' of expense for prepaid rent that had been used up during the accounting period.

Required

a. Use a horizontal statements model to show how each event affects the balance sheet, income statement, and statement of cash flows. Indicate whether the event increases (+), decreases (−), or does not affect (NA) each element of the financial statements. Also, in the Cash Flow column, use the letters OA to designate operating activity, IA for investing activity, and FA for financing activity. The first event is recorded as an example.

Assets	=	Liab.	+	Equity	Rev.	−	Exp.	=	Net Inc.	Cash Flow
+		NA		+	NA		NA		NA	+ FA

b. Record each of the preceding events in T-accounts.
c. Prepare a before-closing trial balance.

L.O. 1, 5

Problem 3-30B *Effect of journal entries on financial statements*

Event No.	Account Title	Debit	Credit
1	Cash Common Stock	XXX	 XXX
2	Prepaid Rent Cash	XXX	 XXX
3	Dividends Cash	XXX	 XXX
4	Utility Expense Cash	XXX	 XXX
5	Accounts Receivable Service Revenue	XXX	 XXX
6	Salaries Expense Cash	XXX	 XXX
7	Cash Service Revenue	XXX	 XXX
8	Cash Unearned Revenue	XXX	 XXX
9	Supplies Accounts Payable	XXX	 XXX
10	Cash Accounts Receivable	XXX	 XXX
11	Rent Expense Prepaid Rent	XXX	 XXX
12	Supplies Expense Supplies	XXX	 XXX
13	Unearned Revenue Service Revenue	XXX	 XXX

Required

The preceding 13 different accounting events are presented in general journal format. Use a horizontal statements model to show how each event affects the balance sheet, income statement, and statement of cash flows. Indicate whether the event increases (+), decreases (−), or does not affect (NA) each element of the financial statements. Also, in the Cash Flow column, use the letters OA to designate operating activity, IA for investing activity, and FA for financing activity. The first event is recorded as an example.

Assets	=	Liab.	+	Equity	Rev.	−	Exp.	=	Net Inc.	Cash Flow
+		NA		+	NA		NA		NA	+ FA

Problem 3-31B *Effect of errors on the trial balance* **L.O. 6**

Required

Consider each of the following errors independently (assume that each is the only error that has occurred). Complete the following table. The first error is recorded as an example.

Error	Is the Trial Balance Out of Balance?	By What Amount?	Which Is Larger, Total Debits or Credits?
a	no	NA	NA

a. A debit of $800 to Supplies Expense was recorded as a debit of $800 to Rent Expense.
b. A credit of $500 to Consulting Revenue was not recorded.
c. A credit of $360 to Accounts Payable was recorded as $680.
d. A debit of $3,000 to Cash was recorded as a credit of $3,000 to Cash.
e. An entry requiring a debit to Cash of $850 and a credit to Accounts Receivable of $850 was not posted to the ledger accounts.
f. A debit of $4,200 to Prepaid Rent was recorded as a credit of $4,200 to Prepaid Rent.

Problem 3-32B *Effect of errors on the trial balance* **L.O. 6**

The following trial balance was prepared from the ledger accounts of Kona Company.

KONA COMPANY
Trial Balance
April 30, 2006

Account Title	Debit	Credit
Cash	$ 41,500	
Accounts Receivable	40,000	
Supplies	2,400	
Prepaid Insurance	3,200	
Land		$ 10,000
Accounts Payable		8,500
Common Stock		96,000
Retained Earnings		56,720
Dividends	6,000	
Service Revenue		40,000
Rent Expense	7,200	
Salaries Expense	26,400	
Operating Expense	65,240	
Totals	$191,940	$211,220

When the trial balance failed to balance, the accountant reviewed the records and discovered the following errors:

1. The company received $470 as payment for services rendered. The credit to Service Revenue was recorded correctly, but the debit to Cash was recorded as $740.
2. A $430 receipt of cash that was received as a payment on accounts receivable was not recorded.
3. A $450 purchase of supplies on account was properly recorded as a debit to the Supplies account. However, the credit to Accounts Payable was not recorded.
4. Land valued at $10,000 was contributed to the business in exchange for common stock. The entry to record the transaction was recorded as a $10,000 credit to both the Land account and the Common Stock account.
5. A $200 rent payment was properly recorded as a credit to Cash. However, the Salaries Expense account was incorrectly debited for $200.

Required

Based on this information, prepare a corrected trial balance for Kona Company.

L.O. 3-7

Problem 3-33B *Comprehensive problem: single cycle*

The following transactions pertain to Sky Training Company for 2008.

Jan.	30	Established the business when it acquired $75,000 cash from the issue of common stock.
Feb.	1	Paid rent for office space for two years, $24,000 cash.
Apr.	10	Purchased $5,300 of supplies on account.
July	1	Received $50,000 cash in advance for services to be provided over the next year.
	20	Paid $1,800 of the accounts payable from April 10.
Aug.	15	Billed a customer $32,000 for services provided during August.
Sept.	15	Completed a job and received $19,000 cash for services rendered.
Oct.	1	Paid employee salaries of $20,000 cash.
	15	Received $25,000 cash from accounts receivable.
Nov.	16	Billed customers $37,000 for services rendered on account.
Dec.	1	Paid a dividend of $6,000 cash to the stockholders.
	31	Adjusted records to recognize the services provided on the contract of July 1.
	31	Recorded $4,500 of accrued salaries as of December 31.
	31	Recorded the rent expense for the year. (See February 1.)
	31	Physically counted supplies; $480 was on hand at the end of the period.

Required

a. Record the preceding transactions in the general journal.

b. Post the transactions to T-accounts and calculate the account balances.

c. Prepare a trial balance.

d. Prepare the income statement, statement of changes in stockholders' equity, balance sheet, and statement of cash flows.

e. Prepare the closing entries at December 31.

f. Prepare a trial balance after the closing entries are posted.

L.O. 3-7

Problem 3-34B *Comprehensive problem: two cycles*

This problem extends Problem 3-34A involving Turner Cleaning and *should not* be attempted until that problem has been completed. The transactions consummated by Turner Cleaning during May 2007 (the company's second month of operation) consisted of the following:

May	1	Recorded services provided to customers. Cash receipts were $420, and invoices for services on account were $1,200.
	2	Purchased supplies on account that cost $300.
	7	Collected $2,500 cash from customer accounts receivable.
	8	Provided services to Don Orr that had been paid for in advance (see April 9 in Problem 3-34A).
	10	Paid the utility company for the monthly utility bills that had been received in the previous month, $233.
	15	Paid $2,100 cash for employee salaries.
	15	Purchased a one-year insurance policy that cost $1,200 with coverage beginning immediately.
	16	Paid $300 on the account payable that was established when supplies were purchased on May 2.
	20	Paid a $300 cash dividend to the stockholders.
	27	Received monthly utility bills amounting to $310. The bills will be paid during June.
	31	Recorded services provided to customers. Cash sales were $625, and invoices for services on account were $4,100.
	31	Paid $2,100 cash for employee salaries.
	31	Counted the supplies inventory. Had $40 of supplies on hand.

Required

a. Open a general ledger with T-accounts, using the ending account balances computed in Problem 3-34A.

b. Record the preceding transactions directly into the T-accounts.

c. Record the adjusting entries in the general journal, and post to the T-accounts. (*Note:* Refer to Problem 3-34A to obtain all the information needed to prepare the adjusting entries.)

d. Prepare an income statement, statement of changes in stockholders' equity, balance sheet, and statement of cash flows.

e. Record the closing entries in the general journal and post to the T-accounts.
f. Answer the following questions.
   (1) Why is the amount in the May 31, 2007, Retained Earnings account not equal to the amount of net income or loss for the month of May?
   (2) Why is the amount of supplies expense not $300?

ANALYZE, THINK, COMMUNICATE

ATC 3-1 Business Applications Case *Understanding real-world annual reports*

Required

The Topps Company, Inc.

a. Use the **Topps Company's** annual report in Appendix B to answer the following questions.
   (1) On March 1, 2003, Topps had a balance of $262,877,000 in Retained Earnings. On March 2, 2002, the balance in Retained Earnings was $245,941,000. Why did Retained Earnings change during 2003?
   (2) Why did Topps' Net Sales and Net Income decrease so much in 2003 compared to 2002?
   (3) Could Requirement 2 be answered by examining only Topps' income statement, balance sheet, and cash statement? If not, where did you find the information?
   (4) Who are the independent auditors for Topps?

Harley-Davidson, Inc.

b. Use the **Harley-Davidson's** annual report that came with this book to answer the following questions.
   (1) On December 31, 2003, Harley-Davidson had a balance of $3,074 million in Retained Earnings. On December 31, 2002, the balance in Retained Earnings was $2,372 million. Why did Retained Earnings change during 2003?
   (2) Harley-Davidson's Net Revenue increased during 2003 compared to 2002. The MD&A section of its annual report explains the reasons this occurred. What are these reasons?
   (3) Who are the independent auditors for Harley-Davidson?

ATC 3-2 Group Assignment *Financial statement analysis*

The beginning account balances for Mabry Company were as follows for 2005, 2006, and 2007:

	January 1		
	2005	**2006**	**2007**
Cash	$12,000	$19,000	$42,600
Accounts Receivable	6,000	10,000	6,000
Land	9,000	9,000	9,000
Prepaid Rent	0	1,000	1,400
Accounts Payable	12,300	11,300	15,300
Salaries Payable	0	0	2,100
Common Stock	10,000	10,000	10,000
Retained Earnings	4,700	17,700	31,600

Mabry Company experienced the following events for the accounting periods 2005, 2006, and 2007.

2005

1. Performed services for $36,000 on account.
2. Paid rent of $6,000 for the period March 1, 2005, to March 1, 2006.
3. Incurred operating expense of $18,000 on account.
4. Collected $32,000 of accounts receivable.
5. Paid $19,000 of accounts payable.
6. Recorded expired rent.

2006

1. Performed services on account of $48,000.
2. Paid rent of $8,400 for the period March 1, 2006, to March 1, 2007, and recorded the expired rent for the period January 1, 2006, to March 1, 2006.
3. Incurred operating expenses of $24,000 on account.

4. Collected $52,000 of accounts receivable.
5. Paid $20,000 of accounts payable.
6. Recorded expired rent.
7. Recorded accrued salaries of $2,100.

2007

1. Paid accrued salaries.
2. Performed services on account of $56,000.
3. Paid rent of $9,000 for the period March 1, 2007, to March 1, 2008, and recorded the expired rent for the period January 1, 2007, to March 1, 2007.
4. Incurred operating expenses of $32,000 on account.
5. Collected $55,000 of accounts receivable.
6. Paid $33,000 of accounts payable.
7. Sold land for $5,000; the land had a cost of $5,000.
8. Recorded expired rent.

Required

Divide the class into groups of four or five students. Organize the groups into three sections. Assign each section of groups the financial data for one of the preceding accounting periods.

Group Task

a. Prepare an income statement, balance sheet, and statement of cash flows. It may be helpful to open T-accounts and post transactions to these accounts before attempting to prepare the statements.

Class Discussion

b. Review the cash flows associated with the collection of receivables and the payment of payables. Comment on the company's collection and payment strategy.
c. Did net income increase or decrease between 2005 and 2006? What were the primary causes?
d. Did net income increase or decrease between 2006 and 2007? What were the primary causes?

ATC 3-3 Real-World Case *Choice of fiscal year*

Consider the following brief descriptions of four companies from different industries. **Toll Brothers, Inc.**, is one of the largest homebuilders in the nation, with operations in 22 states. **Toys R Us, Inc.**, is the well-known, international retailer of toys. **Six Flags, Inc.**, claims to be the world's largest operator of regional theme parks. It operates 39 parks worldwide, including 15 of the largest 50 parks in the United States. **Vail Resorts, Inc.**, operates several ski resorts in Colorado, including Vail Mountain, the largest in the United States, and Breckenridge Mountain Resort.

The chapter explained that companies often choose to close their books when business is slow. Each of these companies ends its fiscal year on a different date. The closing dates, listed chronologically, are:

January 31
July 31
October 31
December 31

Required

a. Try to determine which fiscal year-end matches which company. Write a brief explanation of the reason for your decisions.
b. Because many companies deliberately choose to prepare their financial statements at a slow time of year, try to identify problems this may present for someone trying to analyze the balance sheet for Toys R Us. Write a brief explanation of the issues you identify.

ATC 3-4 Business Applications Case *Using ratio analysis to assess financial risk*

The following information was drawn from the balance sheets of two companies:

Company	Assets	=	Liabilities	+	Stockholders' Equity
Frozen Treats	416,000		178,500		237,500
Perfect Pastries	164,000		57,500		106,500

Required

a. Compute the debt to assets ratio to measure the level of financial risk of both companies.

b. Compare the two ratios computed in Part *a* to determine which company has the higher level of financial risk.

ATC 3-5 Business Applications Case *Using ratio analysis to make comparisons between companies*

At the end of 2007, the following information is available for Fran's Flower Shop and Betty's Bouquets.

Statement Data	Fran's Flowers	Betty's Bouquets
Total Assets	$945,000	$273,000
Total Liabilities	585,000	191,000
Stockholders' Equity	360,000	82,000
Net Income	61,000	17,000

Required

a. For each company, compute the debt to assets ratio and the return on equity ratio.
b. Determine what percentage of each company's assets was financed by the owners.
c. Which company had a higher level of financial risk?
d. Based on profitability alone, which company performed better?
e. Do the preceding ratios support the concept of financial leverage? Explain.

ATC 3-6 Writing Assignment *Effect of land sale on return on assets*

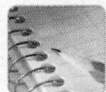

Toyo Company is holding land that cost $900,000 for future use. However, plans have changed and the company may not need the land in the foreseeable future. The president is concerned about the return on assets. Current net income is $425,000 and total assets are $3,500,000.

Required

a. Write a memo to the company president explaining the effect of disposing of the land, assuming that it has a current value of $1,500,000.
b. Write a memo to the company president explaining the effect of disposing of the land, assuming that it has a current value of $600,000.

ATC 3-7 Ethical Dilemma *Choice of brothers: ethics, risk, and accounting numbers in a medieval setting*

In the late 1400s, a wealthy land owner named Caster was trying to decide which of his twin sons, Rogan or Argon, to designate as the first heir to the family fortune. He decided to set up each son with a small farm consisting of 300 sheep and 20 acres of land. Each twin would be allowed to manage his property as he deemed appropriate. After a designated period, Caster would call his sons before him to account for their actions. The heir to the family fortune would be chosen on the basis of which son had produced a larger increase in wealth during the test period.

On the appointed day of reckoning, Argon boasted that he had 714 sheep under his control while Rogan had only 330. Furthermore, Argon stated that he had increased his land holdings to 27 acres. The seven-acre increase resulted from two transactions: first, on the day the contest started, Argon used 20 sheep to buy 10 additional acres; and second, he sold three of these acres for a total of 9 sheep on the day of reckoning. Also, Argon's flock had produced 75 newborn sheep during the period of accounting. He had been able to give his friends 50 sheep in return for the help that they had given him in building a fence, thereby increasing not only his own wealth but the wealth of his neighbors as well. Argon boasted that the fence was strong and would keep his herd safe from predatory creatures for five years (assume the fence had been used for one year during the contest period). Rogan countered that Argon was holding 400 sheep that belonged to another herder. Argon had borrowed these sheep on the day that the contest had started. Furthermore, Argon had agreed to return 424 sheep to the herder. The 24 additional sheep represented consideration for the use of the herder's flock. Argon had agreed to return the sheep immediately after the day of reckoning.

During the test period, Rogan's flock had produced 37 newborn sheep, but 2 sheep had gotten sick and died during the accounting period. Rogan had also lost 5 sheep to predatory creatures. He had no fence, and some of his sheep strayed from the herd, thereby exposing themselves to danger. Knowing that he was falling behind, Rogan had taken a wife in order to boost his productivity. His wife owned 170 sheep on the day they were married; her sheep had produced 16 newborn sheep since the date of her marriage to Rogan. Argon had not included the wife's sheep in his count of Rogan's herd. If his wife's sheep had been counted, Rogan's herd would contain 516 instead of 330 sheep suggested by Argon's count.

Argon charged that seven of Rogan's sheep were sick with symptoms similar to those exhibited by the two sheep that were now dead. Rogan interjected that he should not be held accountable for acts of nature such as illness. Furthermore, he contended that by isolating the sick sheep from the remainder of the herd, he had demonstrated prudent management practices that supported his case to be designated first heir.

Required

a. Prepare an income statement, balance sheet, statement of sheep flow (cash flow) for each twin, using contemporary (2007) accounting standards. Note that you have to decide whether to include the sheep owned by Rogan's wife when making his financial statements (what is the accounting entity?). (*Hint:* Use the number of sheep rather than the number of dollars as the common unit of measure.)

b. Refer to the statements you prepared in Requirement *a* to answer the following questions:

(1) Which twin has more owner's equity at the end of the accounting period?

(2) Which twin produced the higher net income during the accounting period?

(3) Which son should be designated heir based on conventional accounting and reporting standards?

c. What is the difference in the value of the land of the twins if the land is valued at market value (that is, three sheep per acre) rather than historical cost (that is, two sheep per acre)?

d. Did Argon's decision to borrow sheep increase his profitability? Support your answer with appropriate financial data.

e. Was Argon's decision to build a fence financially prudent? Support your answer with appropriate financial data.

f. Assuming that the loan resulted in a financial benefit to Argon, identify some reasons that the shepherd who owned the sheep may have been willing to loan them to Argon.

g. Which twin is likely to take risks to improve profitability? What would be the financial condition of each twin if one-half of the sheep in both flocks died as a result of illness? How should such risk factors be reported in financial statements?

h. Should Rogan's decision to "marry for sheep" be considered from an ethical perspective, or should the decision be made solely on the basis of the bottom-line net income figure?

i. Prepare a report that recommends which twin should be designated heir to the family business. Include a set of financial statements that supports your recommendation. Since this is a managerial report that will not be distributed to the public, you are not bound by generally accepted accounting principles.

ATC 3-8 Research Assignment *Assessing the financial situation of two airlines*

For several years many companies in the passenger airline industry have had financial difficulties. This chapter introduces three financial ratios that can be used to help users analyze a company's performance and its exposure to financial risk. Complete the requirements below using the most recent financial statements of **Delta Air Lines** and **Southwest Airlines**, which are available on the companies' websites. Obtain the statements on the Internet by following the steps below. (Be aware that the formatting of the companies' websites may have changed since these instructions were written.)

For Delta Air Lines

1. Go to www.delta.com.
2. Click on the "About Delta" link at the bottom of the page.
3. Click on the "*Investor Relations*" link on the left side of the page.
4. Click on "200X Summary *Annual Report.*" In addition to the complete, and often very complex, annual report that most large companies are required to publish, many also issue *Summary Reports.* These reports provide the major elements of the company's complete annual report, but omit some of the details that many nonprofessional users do not need.

For Southwest Airlines

1. Go to www.southwest.com.
2. Click on the "About SWA" link at the top of the page.
3. Click on the "INVESTOR RELATIONS" link on the left side of the page.
4. Click on the "ANNUAL REPORTS" link on the left side of the page.
5. Click on "*200X.*"

Required

a. Compute Delta's debt to assets ratio and return on assets ratio. Delta's balance sheet does not show total liabilities, so you will need to add current liabilities and noncurrent liabilities together in order to obtain total liabilities.

b. Compute Southwest's debt to assets ratio and return on assets ratio. Southwest's balance sheet does not show total liabilities, so you will need to subtract total stockholders' equity from total assets to obtain total liabilities.

c. Write a brief commentary about your perception of each company's financial situation. Your comments should include consideration of the ratios you calculated for Requirements *a* and *b,* but you may also wish to consider other information included in the company's financial statements.

COMPREHENSIVE PROBLEM

The trial balance of Pacilio Security Services Inc. as of January 1, 2003 had the following normal balances:

Cash	$8,900
Accounts Receivable	1,500
Supplies	65
Prepaid Rent	800
Land	4,000
Accounts Payable	1,050
Unearned Revenue	200
Salaries Payable	1,200
Notes Payable	2,000
Common Stock	8,000
Retained Earnings	2,815

During 2003, Pacilio Security Services experienced the following transactions:

1. Paid the salaries payable from 2002.
2. Paid the balance of $2,000 on the debt owed to the Small Business Government Agency. The loan is interest free.
3. Performed $32,000 of security services for numerous local events during the year; $21,000 was on account and $11,000 was for cash.
4. On May 1, paid $3,000 for 12 months' rent in advance.
5. Purchased supplies on account for $700.
6. Paid salaries expense for the year of $9,000.
7. Incurred other operating expenses on account, $4,200.
8. On October 1, 2003, a customer paid $1,200 for services to be provided over the next 12 months.
9. Collected $19,000 of accounts receivable during the year.
10. Paid $5,950 on accounts payable.
11. Paid $1,800 of advertising expenses for the year.
12. Paid a cash dividend to the shareholders of $4,650.
13. The market value of the land was determined to be $5,500 at December 31, 2003.

Adjustments

14. There was $120 of supplies on hand at the end of the year.
15. Recognized the expired rent.
16. Recognized the earned revenue from 2002 and transaction no. 8.
17. Accrued salaries were $1,000 at December 31, 2003.

Required

a. Record the above transactions in general journal form.
b. Post the transactions to T-accounts and determine the account balances.
c. Prepare a trial balance.
d. Prepare an income statement, statement of changes in stockholders' equity, balance sheet, and statement of cash flows for 2003.
e. Prepare the closing entries and post to the T-accounts.
f. Prepare an after-closing trial balance.

CHAPTER 4

Accounting for Merchandising Businesses

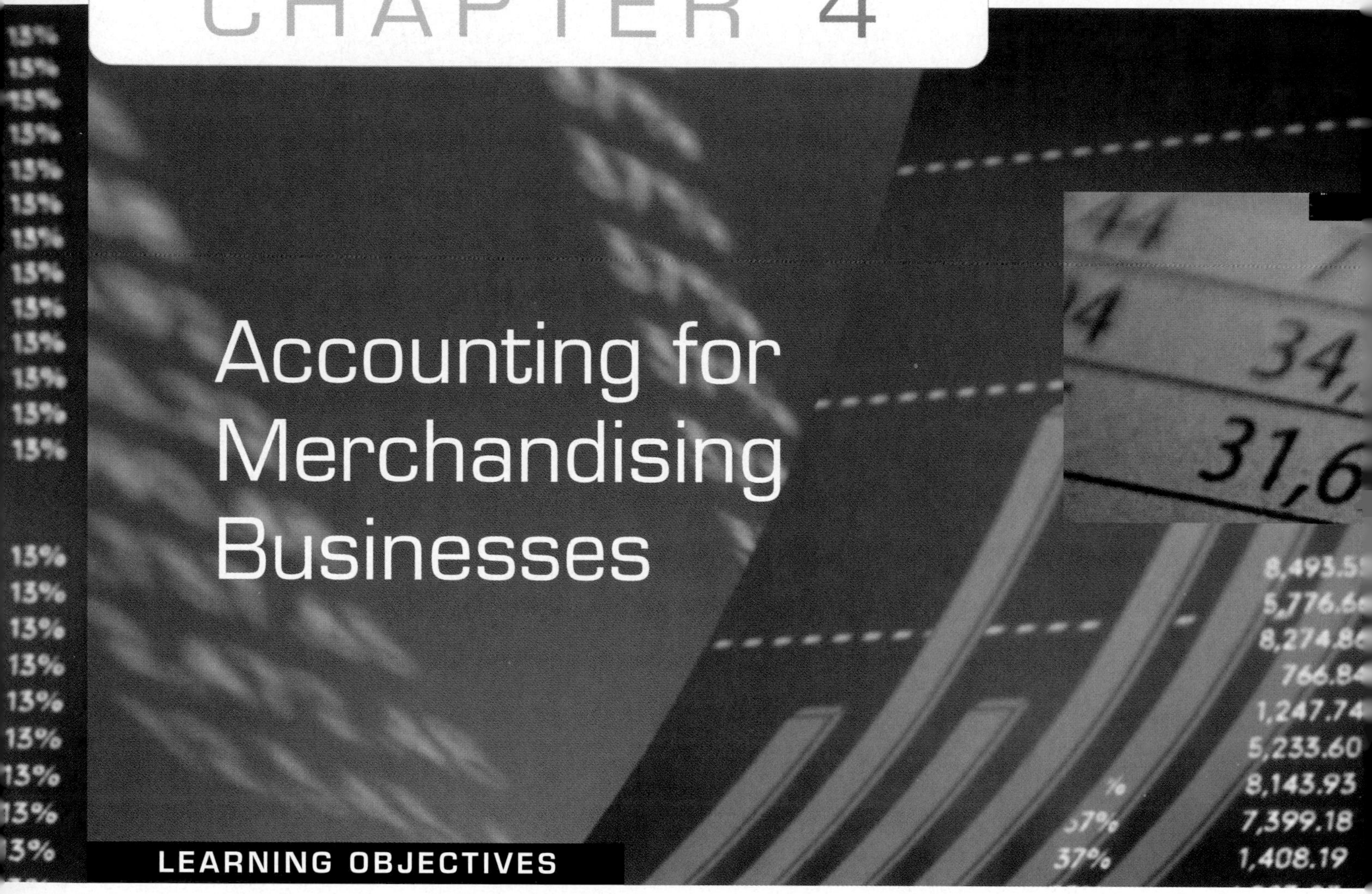

LEARNING OBJECTIVES

After you have mastered the material in this chapter you will be able to:

1. **Identify and explain the primary features of the perpetual inventory system.**
2. **Record and report inventory transactions in the double-entry accounting system.**
3. **Explain the meaning of terms used to describe transportation costs, cash discounts, returns or allowances, and financing costs.**
4. **Compare and contrast single and multistep income statements.**
5. **Show the effect of lost, damaged, or stolen inventory on financial statements.**
6. **Use common size financial statements to evaluate managerial performance.**
7. **Use ratio analysis to evaluate managerial performance.**
8. **Identify the primary features of the periodic inventory system. (Appendix)**

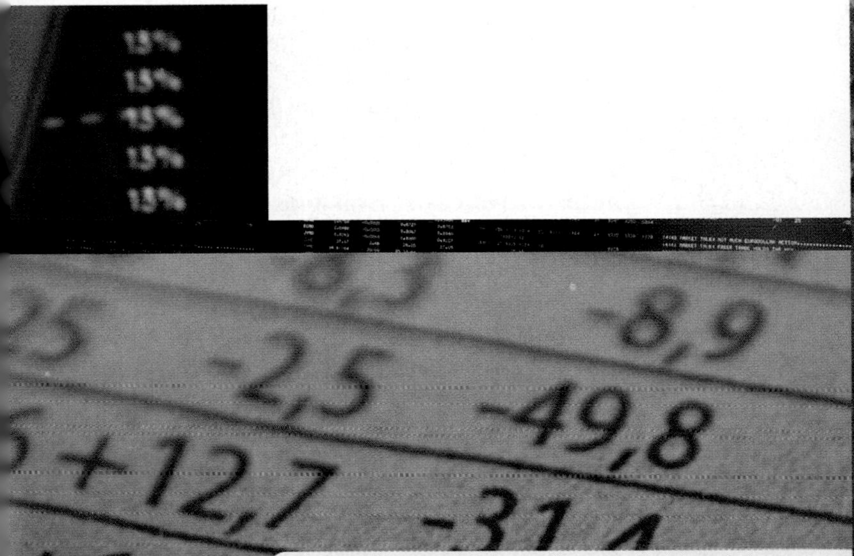

Chapter 4

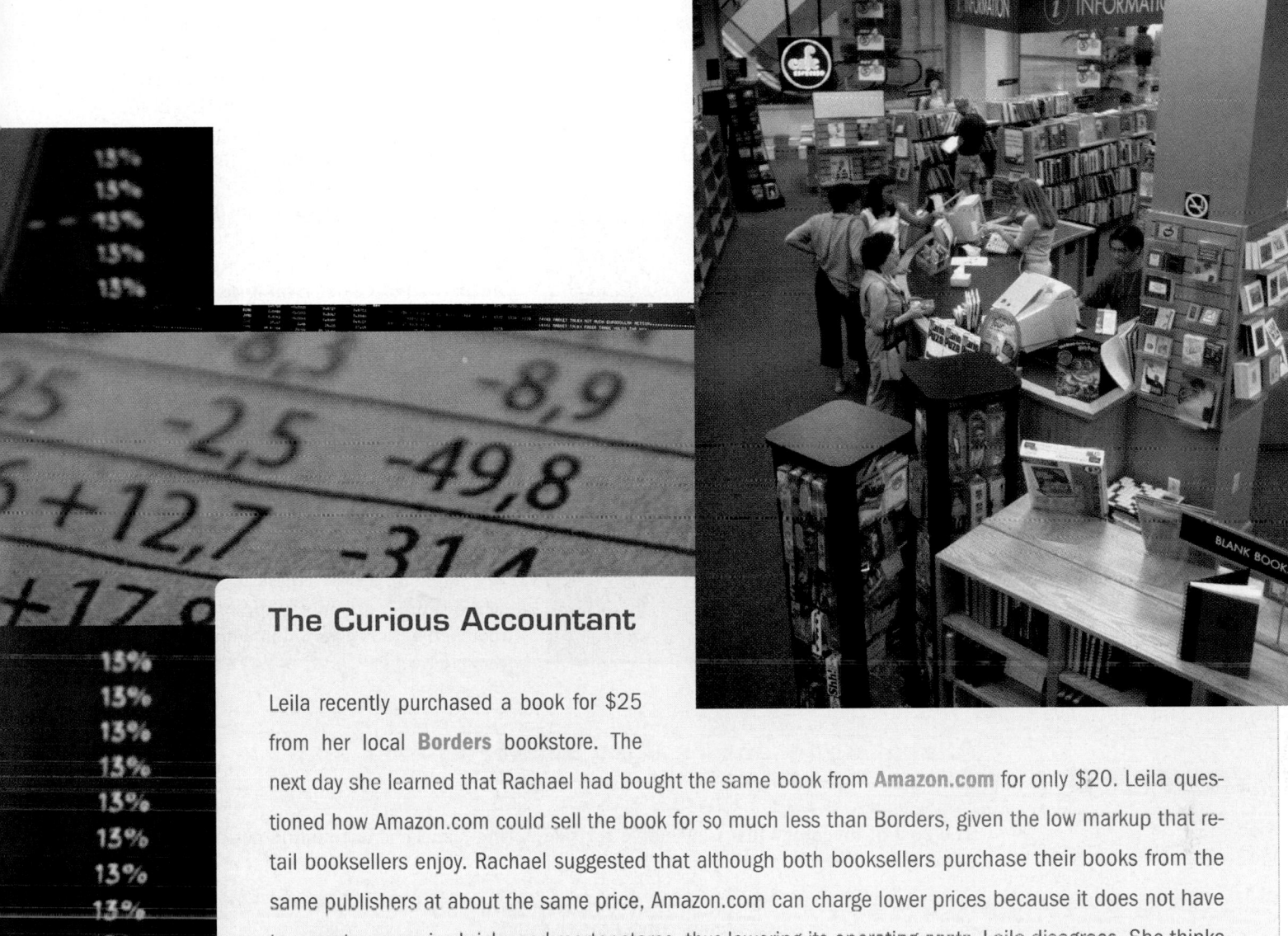

The Curious Accountant

Leila recently purchased a book for $25 from her local **Borders** bookstore. The next day she learned that Rachael had bought the same book from **Amazon.com** for only $20. Leila questioned how Amazon.com could sell the book for so much less than Borders, given the low markup that retail booksellers enjoy. Rachael suggested that although both booksellers purchase their books from the same publishers at about the same price, Amazon.com can charge lower prices because it does not have to operate expensive bricks-and-mortar stores, thus lowering its operating costs. Leila disagrees. She thinks the cost of operating huge distribution centers and Internet server centers would offset any cost savings Amazon.com enjoys from not owning retail bookstores.

Exhibit 4.1 presents the income statements for Amazon.com and Borders. Based on these income statements, do you think Leila or Rachael is correct? (Answer on page 184.)

CHAPTER OPENING

Previous chapters have discussed accounting for service businesses. These businesses obtain revenue by providing some kind of service such as medical or legal advice to their customers. Other examples of service companies include dry cleaning companies, maid service companies, and car washes. This chapter introduces accounting practices for merchandising businesses. **Merchandising businesses** *generate revenue by selling goods. They buy the merchandise they sell from companies called suppliers. The goods purchased for resale are called* **merchandise inventory.** *Merchandising businesses include* **retail companies** *(companies that sell goods to the final consumer) and* **wholesale companies** *(companies that sell to other businesses).* ***Sears, JCPenney, Target,*** *and* ***SAM'S CLUB*** *are real-world merchandising businesses.* ■

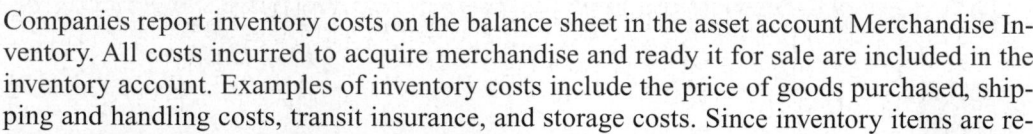

Product Costs Versus Selling and Administrative Costs

LO 1

Identify and explain the primary features of the perpetual inventory system.

Companies report inventory costs on the balance sheet in the asset account Merchandise Inventory. All costs incurred to acquire merchandise and ready it for sale are included in the inventory account. Examples of inventory costs include the price of goods purchased, shipping and handling costs, transit insurance, and storage costs. Since inventory items are referred to as products, inventory costs are frequently called **product costs.**

Costs that are not included in inventory are usually called **selling and administrative costs.** Examples of selling and administrative costs include advertising, administrative salaries, sales commissions, insurance, and interest. Since selling and administrative costs are usually recognized as expenses *in the period* in which they are incurred, they are sometimes called **period costs.** In contrast, product costs are expensed when inventory is sold regardless of when it was purchased. In other words, product costs are matched directly with sales revenue, while selling and administrative costs are matched with the period in which they are incurred.

Allocating Inventory Cost Between Asset and Expense Accounts

The cost of inventory that is available for sale during a specific accounting period is determined as follows:

$$\text{Beginning inventory balance} + \text{Inventory purchased during the period} = \text{Cost of goods available for sale}$$

The **cost of goods available for sale** is allocated between the asset account Merchandise Inventory and an expense account called **Cost of Goods Sold.** The cost of inventory items that have not been sold (Merchandise Inventory) is reported as an asset on the balance sheet, and the cost of the items sold (Cost of Goods Sold) is expensed on the income statement. This allocation is depicted graphically as follows.

Cost of goods available for sale → Merchandise Inventory (Balance Sheet)

Cost of goods available for sale → Cost of Goods Sold (Income Statement)

The difference between the sales revenue and the cost of goods sold is called **gross margin** or **gross profit.** The selling and administrative expenses (period costs) are subtracted from gross margin to obtain the net income.

Exhibit 4.1 displays income statements from the annual reports of **Amazon.com, Inc.**, and **Borders Group, Inc.** For each company, review the most current income statement and determine the amount of gross margin. You should find a gross profit of $992,618 (in thousands) for Amazon.com and a gross margin of $960.9 (in millions) for Borders.

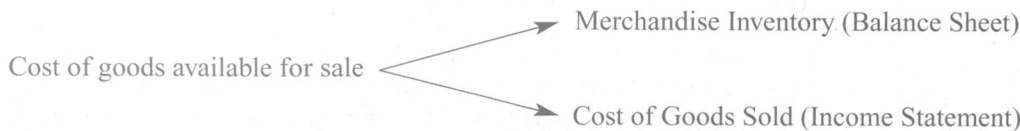

EXHIBIT 4.1 Comparative Income Statements

AMAZON.COM, INC.
Consolidated Statements of Operations
(dollars in thousands)

	Years Ended December 31,		
	2002	**2001**	**2000**
Net Sales	$3,932,936	$3,122,433	$2,761,983
Cost of Sales	2,940,318	2,323,875	2,106,206
Gross Profit	992,618	798,558	655,777
Operating Expenses:			
Fulfillment	392,467	374,250	414,509
Marketing	125,383	138,283	179,980
Technology and Content	215,617	241,165	269,326
General and Administrative	79,049	89,862	108,962
Stock-Based Compensation	68,927	4,637	24,797
Amortization of Goodwill and Other Intangibles	5,478	181,033	321,772
Restructuring-Related and Other	41,573	181,585	200,311
Total Operating Expenses	928,494	1,210,815	1,519,657
Income (Loss) from Operations	64,124	(412,257)	(863,880)
Interest Income	23,687	29,103	40,821
Interest Expense	(142,925)	(139,232)	(130,921)
Other Income (Expense), Net	5,623	(1,900)	(10,058)
Other Gains (Losses), Net	(96,273)	(2,141)	(142,639)
Total Nonoperating Expenses, Net	(209,888)	(114,170)	(242,797)
Loss before Equity in Losses of Equity-Method Investees	(145,764)	(526,427)	(1,106,677)
Equity in Losses of Equity-Method Investees	(4,169)	(30,327)	(304,596)
Net Loss before Change in Accounting Principle	(149,933)	(556,754)	(1,411,273)
Cumulative Effect of Change in Accounting Principle	801	(10,523)	–
Net Loss	$ (149,132)	$ (567,277)	$(1,411,273)

BORDERS GROUP, INC.
Consolidated Statements of Operations
(dollars in millions)

	Fiscal Year Ended		
	January 26, 2003	**January 27, 2002**	**January 28, 2001**
Sales	$ 3,486.1	$ 3,387.9	$ 3,271.2
Other Revenue	26.9	25.3	25.9
Total Revenue	3,513.0	3,413.2	3,297.1
Cost of Merchandise Sold (Includes Occupancy)	2,550.3	2,464.5	2,380.4
Fulfillment Center and Other Inventory Writedowns	1.8	10.1	–
Gross Margin	960.9	938.6	916.7
Selling, General, and Administrative Expenses	745.2	744.8	736.2
Legal Settlement Expense	–	2.4	–
Preopening Expense	6.9	6.3	6.4
Asset Impairments and Other Writedowns	14.9	25.4	36.2
Goodwill Amortization	–	2.7	2.8
Operating Income	193.9	157.0	135.1
Interest Expense	12.6	14.4	13.1
Income from Continuing Operations before Income Tax	181.3	142.6	122.0
Income Tax Provision	69.6	55.2	48.2
Income from Continuing Operations	111.7	87.4	73.8
Discontinued Operations (Note 3)			
Loss from Operations of All Wound Up, Net of Income Tax Credits of $7.0 and $2.4	–	–	10.8
Loss on Disposition of All Wound Up, Net of Deferred Income Tax Credit of $8.9	–	–	19.4
Net Income	$ 111.7	$ 87.4	$ 43.6

Answers to The Curious Accountant

The income statement data show that **Amazon.com** had higher operating expenses than **Borders** although it does not operate traditional stores. As explained later in this chapter, the *gross margin percentage* indicates to some degree how much a company is charging in relation to what it pays to purchase the goods it is selling (its cost of goods sold). The *return on sales ratio* reveals how much profit, as a percentage of sales, a company is making after *all* of its expenses have been taken into account. For the calendar year 2002, the gross margin percentage for Borders was 27.4 percent and for Amazon.com was 25.2 percent, indicating that, on average, Amazon.com really does charge less for its books. The return on sales for Borders was 3.2 percent and for Amazon.com was −3.8 percent, suggesting that Borders is the one with the lower operating costs. In fact, Amazon.com's expenses were higher than those of Borders. Excluding cost of goods sold, the expenses at Borders were 24.4 percent of sales and at Amazon.com were 29.7 percent.

Perpetual Inventory System

LO 1

Identify and explain the primary features of the perpetual inventory system.

Topic Tackler PLUS

4-1

Most modern companies maintain their inventory records using the **perpetual inventory system,** so-called because the inventory account is adjusted perpetually (continually) throughout the accounting period. Each time merchandise is purchased, the inventory account is increased; each time it is sold, the inventory account is decreased. The following illustration demonstrates the basic features of the perpetual inventory system.

June Gardener loved plants and grew them with such remarkable success that she decided to open a small retail plant store. She started June's Plant Shop (JPS) on January 1, 2006. The following discussion explains and illustrates the effects of the four events the company experienced during its first year of operation.

Effects of 2006 Events on Financial Statements

Event 1 ***JPS acquired $15,000 cash by issuing common stock.***

This event is an asset source transaction. It increases both assets (cash) and stockholders' equity (common stock). The income statement is not affected. The statement of cash flows reflects an inflow from financing activities. These effects are shown here:

Assets		= Liab. +	Stockholders' Equity		Rev. −	Exp. =	Net Inc.	Cash Flow
Cash +	Inventory =		Com. Stk. +	Ret. Earn.				
15,000 +	NA	= NA +	15,000 +	NA	NA −	NA =	NA	15,000 FA

Event 2 ***JPS purchased merchandise inventory for $14,000 cash.***

This event is an asset exchange transaction. One asset, cash, decreases and another asset, merchandise inventory, increases; total assets remain unchanged. Because product costs are expensed when inventory is sold, not when it is purchased, the event does not affect the income statement. The cash outflow, however, is reported in the operating activities section of the statement of cash flows. These effects are illustrated below:

Assets		= Liab. +	Stockholders' Equity		Rev. −	Exp. =	Net Inc.	Cash Flow
Cash +	Inventory =		Com. Stk. +	Ret. Earn.				
(14,000) +	14,000	= NA +	NA +	NA	NA −	NA =	NA	(14,000) OA

Event 3a ***JPS recognized sales revenue from selling inventory for $12,000 cash.***

The revenue recognition is the first part of a two-part transaction. The *sales part* represents a source of assets (cash increases from earning sales revenue). Both assets (cash) and stockholders' equity (retained earnings) increase. Sales revenue on the income statement increases. The $12,000 cash inflow is reported in the operating activities section of the statement of cash flows. These effects are shown in the following financial statements model:

Assets		= Liab. +	Stockholders' Equity		Rev. − Exp. = Net Inc.	Cash Flow
Cash +	Inventory =		Com. Stk. +	Ret. Earn.		
12,000 +	NA	= NA +	NA +	12,000	12,000 − NA = 12,000	12,000 OA

Event 3b ***JPS recognized $8,000 of cost of goods sold.***

The expense recognition is the second part of the two-part transaction. The *expense part* represents a use of assets. Both assets (merchandise inventory) and stockholders' equity (retained earnings) decrease. An expense account, Cost of Goods Sold, is reported on the income statement. This part of the transaction does not affect the statement of cash flows. A cash outflow occurred when the goods were bought, not when they were sold. These effects are shown here:

Assets		= Liab. +	Stockholders' Equity		Rev. − Exp. = Net Inc.	Cash Flow
Cash +	Inventory =		Com. Stk. +	Ret. Earn.		
NA +	(8,000)	= NA +	NA +	(8,000)	NA − 8,000 = (8,000)	NA

Event 4 ***JPS paid $1,000 cash for selling and administrative expenses.***

This event is an asset use transaction. The payment decreases both assets (cash) and stockholders' equity (retained earnings). The increase in selling and administrative expenses decreases net income. The $1,000 cash payment is reported in the operating activities section of the statement of cash flows. These effects are illustrated below:

Assets		= Liab. +	Stockholders' Equity		Rev. − Exp. = Net Inc.	Cash Flow
Cash +	Inventory =		Com. Stk. +	Ret. Earn.		
(1,000) +	NA	= NA +	NA +	(1,000)	NA − 1,000 = (1,000)	(1,000) OA

Recording and Reporting Inventory Events in the Double-Entry System

LO 2 Record and report inventory transactions in the double-entry accounting system.

The 2006 transactions JPS experienced are summarized below.

Event 1 JPS acquired $15,000 cash by issuing common stock.

Event 2 JPS purchased merchandise inventory (plants) for $14,000 cash.

Event 3 JPS sold merchandise inventory for $12,000 cash. This inventory had cost $8,000.

Event 4 JPS paid $1,000 cash for selling and administrative expenses.

Panel A of Exhibit 4.2 shows these transactions recorded in general journal format. Panel B of Exhibit 4.2 shows the general ledger T-accounts after the journal entries have been posted to them. The ledger accounts provide the data for the financial statements in Exhibit 4.3.

EXHIBIT 4.2

Journal Entries and General Ledger Accounts for 2006

Panel A Journal Entries

Event No.	Account Title	Debit	Credit
1	Cash	15,000	
	Common Stock		15,000
2	Merchandise Inventory	14,000	
	Cash		14,000
3a	Cash	12,000	
	Sales Revenue		12,000
3b	Cost of Goods Sold	8,000	
	Merchandise Inventory		8,000
4	Selling and Administrative Expenses	1,000	
	Cash		1,000

Panel B General Ledger Accounts

Assets = Liabilities + Equity

Assets

Cash

	Debit	Credit	
(1)	15,000	14,000	(2)
(3a)	12,000	1,000	(4)
Bal.	12,000		

Merchandise Inventory

	Debit	Credit	
(2)	14,000	8,000	(3b)
Bal.	6,000		

Liabilities

Accounts Payable

	Debit	Credit	
		0	Bal.

Equity

Common Stock

	Debit	Credit	
		15,000	(1)
		15,000	Bal.

Retained Earnings

	Debit	Credit	

Sales Revenue

	Debit	Credit	
		12,000	(3a)

Cost of Goods Sold

	Debit	Credit	
(3b)	8,000		

Selling and Admin. Expenses

	Debit	Credit	
(4)	1,000		

Although Exhibit 4.2 does not illustrate the 2006 year-end closing entries, recall that the closing entries will transfer the amounts from the revenue and expense accounts to the Retained Earnings account. The balance in the Retained Earnings account after closing will be $3,000. Before reading further, trace the transaction data from each journal entry in Panel A to the ledger accounts in Panel B and then from the ledger accounts to the financial statements in Exhibit 4.3.

Financial Statements for 2006

JPS had no beginning inventory in its first year, so the cost of merchandise inventory available for sale was $14,000 (the amount of inventory purchased during the period). Recall that JPS must allocate the ***Cost of Goods (Inventory) Available for Sale*** between the ***Cost of Goods Sold*** ($8,000) and the ending balance ($6,000) in the ***Merchandise Inventory*** account. The cost of goods sold is reported as an expense on the income statement and the end-

EXHIBIT 4.3

Financial Statements

2006 Income Statement

Sales Revenue	$12,000
Cost of Goods Sold	(8,000)
Gross Margin	4,000
Less: Operating Exp.	
Selling and Admin. Exp.	(1,000)
Net Income	$ 3,000

12/31/06 Balance Sheet

Assets		
Cash	$12,000	
Merchandise Inventory	6,000	
Total Assets		$18,000
Liabilities		$ 0
Stockholders' Equity		
Common Stock	$15,000	
Retained Earnings	3,000	
Total Stockholders' Equity		18,000
Total Liab. and Stk. Equity		$18,000

2006 Statement of Cash Flows

Operating Activities		
Inflow from Customers	$12,000	
Outflow for Inventory	(14,000)	
Outflow for Selling & Admin. Exp.	(1,000)	
Net Cash Outflow for Operating Activities		$ (3,000)
Investing Activities		0
Financing Activities		
Inflow from Stock Issue		15,000
Net Change in Cash		12,000
Plus: Beginning Cash Balance		0
Ending Cash Balance		$12,000

ing balance of merchandise inventory is reported as an asset on the balance sheet. The difference between the sales revenue ($12,000) and the cost of goods sold ($8,000) is labeled ***gross margin*** ($4,000) on the income statement.

CHECK YOURSELF 4.1

Phambroom Company began 2006 with $35,600 in its Inventory account. During the year, it purchased inventory costing $356,800 and sold inventory that had cost $360,000 for $520,000. Based on this information alone, determine (1) the inventory balance as of December 31, 2006, and (2) the amount of gross margin Phambroom would report on its 2006 income statement.

Answer

1. Beginning inventory + Purchases = Goods available − Ending inventory = Cost of goods sold
   $35,600 + $356,800 = $392,400 − Ending inventory = $360,000
   Ending inventory = $32,400
2. Sales revenue − Cost of goods sold = Gross margin
   $520,000 − $360,000 = $160,000

Transportation Cost, Purchase Returns and Allowances, and Cash Discounts Related to Inventory Purchases

LO 3

Explain the meaning of terms used to describe transportation costs, cash discounts, returns or allowances, and financing costs.

Purchasing inventory often involves: (1) incurring transportation costs, (2) returning inventory or receiving purchase allowances (cost reductions), and (3) taking cash discounts (also cost reductions). During its second accounting cycle, JPS encountered these kinds of events. The final account balances at the end of the 2006 fiscal year become the beginning balances for 2007: Cash, $12,000; Merchandise Inventory, $6,000; Common Stock, $15,000; and Retained Earnings, $3,000.

Effects of 2007 Events on Financial Statements

JPS experienced the following events during its 2007 accounting period. The effects of each of these events are explained and illustrated in the following discussion.

Event 1 ***JPS purchased merchandise inventory on account with a list price of $8,000. The payment terms were 2/10, n/30.***

Topic Tackler PLUS 4-2

The expression **2/10, n/30** (two-ten net thirty) means the seller will allow a 2 percent **cash discount** if the purchaser pays cash for the merchandise within 10 days from the date of purchase. If the purchaser pays later than 10 days from the purchase date, the full amount is due within 30 days. Based on these terms, the net (cash) cost of the inventory is computed as follows:

List price	$8,000
Purchase discount ($8,000 × .02)	160
Net price (Cash price $8,000 × .98)	$7,840

Since JPS could purchase the inventory for $7,840 cash, that is the cost JPS will record in the Merchandise Inventory account. The **purchase discount** is an additional charge JPS will incur if it chooses to delay payment. The real cost of the inventory is the net price. Although accounting practice permits recording the inventory cost at either the list price or the net price, the net price is theoretically preferable. This text uses the **net method** of accounting for inventory cost.

The inventory purchase increases both assets (merchandise inventory) and liabilities (accounts payable) on the balance sheet. The income statement is not affected until later, when inventory is sold. Since the inventory was purchased on account, there was no cash outflow. These effects are shown here:

Assets					=	Liab.	+	Stockholders' Equity			Rev.	−	Exp.	=	Net Inc.	Cash Flow
Cash	+	Accts. Rec.	+	Inventory	=	Accts. Pay.	+	Com. Stk.	+	Retained Earnings						
NA	+	NA	+	7,840	=	7,840	+	NA	+	NA	NA	−	NA	=	NA	NA

Event 2 ***JPS returned some of the inventory purchased in Event 1. The list price of the returned merchandise was $1,000.***

To promote customer satisfaction, many businesses allow customers to return goods for reasons such as wrong size, wrong color, wrong design, or even simply because the purchaser changed his mind. The effect of a purchase return is the *opposite* of the original purchase. For JPS the purchase return decreases both assets (merchandise inventory) and liabilities (accounts payable). There is no effect on either the income statement or the statement of cash flows. Since the inventory purchase was originally recorded at the net price (list price less purchase discount), the return is also recorded at the net price, $980 ($1,000 × .98). These effects are shown below:

Assets					=	Liab.	+	Stockholders' Equity			Rev.	−	Exp.	=	Net Inc.	Cash Flow
Cash	+	Accts. Rec.	+	Inventory	=	Accts. Pay.	+	Com. Stk.	+	Retained Earnings						
NA	+	NA	+	(980)	=	(980)	+	NA	+	NA	NA	−	NA	=	NA	NA

Sometimes dissatisfied buyers will agree to keep goods instead of returning them if the seller offers to reduce the price. Such reductions are called **allowances.** Purchase allowances affect the financial statements the same way purchase returns do.

Event 3 ***JPS paid cash to settle the account payable due on the inventory purchased in Event 1. The payment was made after the end of the discount period.***

Recall that JPS purchased merchandise inventory with a list price of $8,000 and returned merchandise with a list price of $1,000. JPS therefore has a liability for merchandise with a list price of $7,000. The net price of this merchandise is computed as follows:

List price	$7,000
Purchase discount ($7,000 × .02)	140
Net price (Cash price $7,000 × .98)	$6,860

Since JPS records inventory purchases at the net price, its account payable for this merchandise is recorded at $6,860. JPS must pay the list price ($7,000), however, because it failed to pay within the discount period. Delaying payment is equivalent to borrowing money from the supplier. The purchase discount ($140) is classified as interest expense.

The $7,000 cash payment results in a compound entry that reduces the asset account, Cash, reduces the liability account, Accounts Payable, and recognizes interest expense. The interest expense reduces net income. Since paying the account payable and paying interest expense are both operating activities, the statement of cash flows reflects a single outflow of $7,000. These effects are illustrated in the following financial statements model:

Assets					=	Liab.	+	Stockholders' Equity			Rev.	−	Exp.	=	Net Inc.	Cash Flow
Cash	+	Accts. Rec.	+	Inventory	=	Accts. Pay.	+	Com. Stk.	+	Retained Earnings						
(7,000)	+	NA	+	NA	=	(6,860)	+	NA	+	(140)	NA	−	140	=	(140)	(7,000) OA

Event 4 ***The shipping terms for the inventory purchased in Event 1 were FOB shipping point. JPS paid the freight company $300 cash for delivering the merchandise.***

The terms **FOB shipping point** and **FOB destination** identify whether the buyer or the seller is responsible for transportation costs. If goods are delivered FOB shipping point, the buyer is responsible for the freight cost. If goods are delivered FOB destination, the seller is responsible. When the buyer is responsible, the freight cost is called **transportation-in.** When the seller is responsible, the cost is called **transportation-out.** The following table summarizes freight cost terms.

Responsible Party	Buyer	Seller
Freight terms	FOB shipping point	FOB destination
Cost title	Transportation-in	Transportation-out

REALITY BYTES

Many real-world companies have found it more effective to impose a penalty for late payment than to use a cash discount to encourage early payment. The invoice from Arley Water Works is an example of the penalty strategy. Notice that the amount due, if paid by the due date, is $18.14. A $1.88 late charge is imposed if the bill is paid after the due date. The $1.88 late charge is in fact interest. If Arley Water Works collects the payment after the due date, the utility will receive cash of $20.02. The collection will increase cash ($20.02), reduce accounts receivable ($18.14), and increase interest revenue ($1.88).

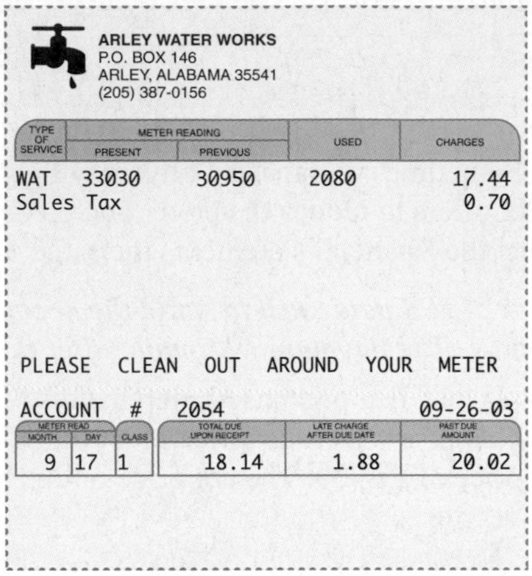
ARLEY WATER WORKS
P.O. BOX 146
ARLEY, ALABAMA 35541
(205) 387-0156

TYPE OF SERVICE	METER READING PRESENT	METER READING PREVIOUS	USED	CHARGES
WAT	33030	30950	2080	17.44
Sales Tax				0.70

PLEASE CLEAN OUT AROUND YOUR METER

ACCOUNT # 2054 09-26-03

METER READ MONTH	DAY	CLASS	TOTAL DUE UPON RECEIPT	LATE CHARGE AFTER DUE DATE	PAST DUE AMOUNT
9	17	1	18.14	1.88	20.02

Event 4 indicates the inventory was delivered FOB shipping point, so JPS (the buyer) is responsible for the $300 freight cost. Since incurring transportation-in costs is necessary to obtain inventory, these costs are added to the inventory account. The freight cost increases one asset account (Merchandise Inventory) and decreases another asset account (Cash). The income statement is not affected by this transaction because transportation-in costs are not expensed when they are incurred. Instead they are expensed as part of *cost of goods sold* when the inventory is sold. However, the cash paid for freight when inventory is delivered to customers is reported as an outflow in the operating activities section of the statement of cash flows. The effects of *transportation-in costs* are shown here:

Assets					=	Liab.	+	Stockholders' Equity			Rev.	−	Exp.	=	Net Inc.	Cash Flow
Cash	+	Accts. Rec.	+	Inventory	=	Accts. Pay.	+	Com. Stk.	+	Retained Earnings						
(300)	+	NA	+	300	=	NA	+	NA	+	NA	NA	−	NA	=	NA	(300) OA

Event 5a ***JPS recognized $24,750 of revenue on the cash sale of merchandise that cost $11,500.***

The sale increases assets (cash) and stockholders' equity (retained earnings). The revenue recognition increases net income. The $24,750 cash inflow from the sale is reported in the operating activities section of the statement of cash flows. These effects are shown below:

Assets					=	Liab.	+	Stockholders' Equity			Rev.	−	Exp.	=	Net Inc.	Cash Flow
Cash	+	Accts. Rec.	+	Inventory	=	Accts. Pay.	+	Com. Stk.	+	Retained Earnings						
24,750	+	NA	+	NA	=	NA	+	NA	+	24,750	24,750	−	NA	=	24,750	24,750 OA

Event 5b ***JPS recognized $11,500 of cost of goods sold.***

When goods are sold, the product cost—*including a proportionate share of transportation-in and adjustments for purchase returns and allowances*—is transferred from the Merchandise

Inventory account to the expense account, Cost of Goods Sold. Recognizing cost of goods sold decreases both assets (merchandise inventory) and stockholders' equity (retained earnings). The expense recognition for cost of goods sold decreases net income. Cash flow is not affected. These effects are shown here:

Assets					=	Liab.	+	Stockholders' Equity			Rev.	−	Exp.	=	Net Inc.	Cash Flow
Cash	+	Accts. Rec.	+	Inventory	=	Accts. Pay.	+	Com. Stk.	+	Retained Earnings						
NA	+	NA	+	(11,500)	=	NA	+	NA	+	(11,500)	NA	−	11,500	=	(11,500)	NA

Event 6 ***JPS incurred $450 of cash freight costs on inventory delivered to customers.***

Assume the merchandise sold in Event 5 was shipped FOB destination. Also assume JPS paid the freight cost in cash. FOB destination means the seller is responsible for the freight cost, which is called transportation-out. Transportation-out is reported on the income statement as an operating expense in the section below gross margin. The cost of freight on goods shipped to customers is incurred *after* the goods are sold. It is not part of the costs to obtain goods or ready them for sale. Recognizing the expense of transportation-out reduces assets (cash) and stockholders' equity (retained earnings). Operating expenses increase and net income decreases. The cash outflow is reported in the operating activities section of the statement of cash flows. These effects are shown below:

Assets					=	Liab.	+	Stockholders' Equity			Rev.	−	Exp.	=	Net Inc.	Cash Flow
Cash	+	Accts. Rec.	+	Inventory	=	Accts. Pay.	+	Com. Stk.	+	Retained Earnings						
(450)	+	NA	+	NA	=	NA	+	NA	+	(450)	NA	−	450	=	(450)	(450) OA

Event 7 ***JPS purchased $14,000 of merchandise inventory on account with credit terms of 1/10, n/30. The inventory was delivered FOB destination. The freight costs were $400.***

Merchandise inventory and accounts payable both increase by the net price of the merchandise, $13,860 ($14,000 × .99). Net income and cash flow are not affected. *The freight costs do not affect JPS since the freight terms are FOB destination and the seller is responsible for them.* These effects are shown here:

Assets					=	Liab.	+	Stockholders' Equity			Rev.	−	Exp.	=	Net Inc.	Cash Flow
Cash	+	Accts. Rec.	+	Inventory	=	Accts. Pay.	+	Com. Stk.	+	Retained Earnings						
NA	+	NA	+	13,860	=	13,860	+	NA	+	NA	NA	−	NA	=	NA	NA

Event 8a ***JPS recognized $16,800 of revenue from the sale on account of merchandise that cost $8,660. The freight terms were FOB shipping point. The party responsible paid freight costs of $275 in cash. JPS does not offer a cash discount to customers.***

The effect on the balance sheet of recognizing revenue is an increase in both assets (accounts receivable) and stockholders' equity (retained earnings). The event increases revenue and net income. Since JPS sold the inventory on account, cash flow is not currently affected. These effects are illustrated here:

Assets					=	Liab.	+	Stockholders' Equity			Rev.	−	Exp.	=	Net Inc.	Cash Flow
Cash	+	Accts. Rec.	+	Inventory	=	Accts. Pay.	+	Com. Stk.	+	Retained Earnings						
NA	+	16,800	+	NA	=	NA	+	NA	+	16,800	16,800	−	NA	=	16,800	NA

Event 8b ***JPS recognized $8,660 of cost of goods sold.***

As discussed previously, when inventory is sold, the product cost is transferred from the Merchandise Inventory account to the expense account, Cost of Goods Sold. Recognizing cost of goods sold decreases both assets (merchandise inventory) and stockholders' equity (retained earnings) by $8,660. The expense recognition for cost of goods sold decreases net income. Cash flow is not affected. *The freight costs do not affect JPS since the freight terms are FOB shipping point and the buyer is responsible for them.* These effects are shown here:

Assets					=	Liab.	+	Stockholders' Equity			Rev.	−	Exp.	=	Net Inc.	Cash Flow
Cash	+	Accts. Rec.	+	Inventory	=	Accts. Pay.	+	Com. Stk.	+	Retained Earnings						
NA	+	NA	+	(8,660)	=	NA	+	NA	+	(8,660)	NA	−	8,660	=	(8,660)	NA

Event 9 ***JPS paid $9,900 cash in partial settlement of the account payable that arose from purchasing inventory on account in Event 7. The partial payment was made within the discount period for merchandise with a list price of $10,000.***

Assume that JPS was not able to pay the entire account payable of $13,860 (recorded at the net amount) in time to receive the 1% purchase discount offered by the supplier, but JPS was able to pay part of the liability within the discount period. The effect of the event on the balance sheet is to decrease both assets (cash) and liabilities (accounts payable) by $9,900 ($10,000 × .99). The $9,900 cash outflow is included in the operating activities section of the statement of cash flows. These effects are shown below.

Assets					=	Liab.	+	Stockholders' Equity			Rev.	−	Exp.	=	Net Inc.	Cash Flow
Cash	+	Accts. Rec.	+	Inventory	=	Accts. Pay.	+	Com. Stk.	+	Retained Earnings						
(9,900)	+	NA	+	NA	=	(9,900)	+	NA	+	NA	NA	−	NA	=	NA	(9,900) OA

Event 10 ***JPS paid $8,000 cash for selling and administrative expenses.***

The effect on the balance sheet is to decrease both assets (cash) and stockholders' equity (retained earnings). Recognizing the selling and administrative expenses decreases net income. The $8,000 cash outflow is reported in the operating activities section of the statement of cash flows. These effects are shown below.

Assets					=	Liab.	+	Stockholders' Equity			Rev.	−	Exp.	=	Net Inc.	Cash Flow
Cash	+	Accts. Rec.	+	Inventory	=	Accts. Pay.	+	Com. Stk.	+	Retained Earnings						
(8,000)	+	NA	+	NA	=	NA	+	NA	+	(8,000)	NA	−	8,000	=	(8,000)	(8,000) OA

CHECK YOURSELF 4.2

Choi Company purchased $24,000 of inventory on account with payment terms of 2/10, n/30 and freight terms FOB shipping point. Freight costs were $1,200. Choi paid $18,000 of the accounts payable within the 10-day discount period and the remaining $6,000 after the discount period had expired. Choi sold all of the inventory for $32,000. Based on this information, determine the amount of gross margin and interest expense Choi would report on the income statement.

Answer

The cost of the inventory is determined as follows:

Net price ($24,000 × .98)	$23,520
Plus: Transportation-in	1,200
Total cost	$24,720

The gross margin is $7,280, the sales price less cost of goods sold ($32,000 − $24,720). The amount of interest expense is $120 ($6,000 × .02).

Recording and Reporting Inventory Events in the Double-Entry System

LO 2

Record and report inventory transactions in the double-entry accounting system.

Exhibit 4.4 illustrates the general journal entries and general ledger accounts for the 2007 transactions JPS experienced. A summary of these events follows here for your convenience. Before reading further, trace each event to the corresponding journal entry. Then trace each journal entry to its posting in the ledger accounts. Finally, trace the information in the ledger accounts to the 2007 financial statements displayed in Exhibit 4.5. Note that the ledger reflects the account balances prior to recording closing entries.

Event 1 JPS purchased on account merchandise inventory with a list price of $8,000, payment terms 2/10, n/30.

Event 2 JPS returned some of the inventory purchased in Event 1. The list price of the returned merchandise was $1,000.

Event 3 JPS paid cash to settle the account payable due on the inventory purchased in Event 1. The payment was made after the end of the discount period.

Event 4 The inventory purchased in Event 1 was delivered FOB shipping point. JPS paid the freight company $300 cash for delivering the merchandise.

Event 5a JPS recognized $24,750 of revenue on the cash sale of merchandise that cost $11,500.

Event 5b JPS recognized $11,500 of cost of goods sold.

Event 6 JPS incurred cash freight costs of $450 on inventory delivered to customers.

Event 7 JPS purchased $14,000 of merchandise inventory on account with credit terms of 1/10, n/30. The inventory was delivered FOB destination. The freight costs were $400.

Event 8a JPS recognized $16,800 of revenue from the sale on account of merchandise that cost $8,660. The freight terms were FOB shipping point. The party responsible paid freight costs of $275 in cash.

Event 8b JPS recognized $8,660 of cost of goods sold.

Event 9 JPS paid $9,900 cash in partial settlement of the account payable for inventory purchased on account in Event 7.

Event 10 JPS paid $8,000 cash for selling and administrative expenses.

EXHIBIT 4.4

Journal Entries and General Ledger Accounts for 2007

Panel A Journal Entries

Event No.	Account Title	Debit	Credit
1	Merchandise Inventory	7,840	
	Accounts Payable		7,840
2	Accounts Payable	980	
	Merchandise Inventory		980
3	Accounts Payable	6,860	
	Interest Expense	140	
	Cash		7,000
4	Merchandise Inventory	300	
	Cash		300
5a	Cash	24,750	
	Sales Revenue		24,750
5b	Cost of Goods Sold	11,500	
	Merchandise Inventory		11,500
6	Transportation-Out	450	
	Cash		450
7	Merchandise Inventory	13,860	
	Accounts Payable		13,860
8a	Accounts Receivable	16,800	
	Sales Revenue		16,800
8b	Cost of Goods Sold	8,660	
	Merchandise Inventory		8,660
9	Accounts Payable	9,900	
	Cash		9,900
10	Selling and Administrative Expenses	8,000	
	Cash		8,000

Panel B General Ledger Accounts

Assets = Liabilities + Equity

Assets

Cash

Bal.	12,000	7,000	(3)
(5a)	24,750	300	(4)
		450	(6)
		9,900	(9)
		8,000	(10)
Bal.	11,100		

Accounts Receivable

(8a)	16,800		
Bal.	16,800		

Merchandise Inventory

Bal.	6,000	980	(2)
(1)	7,840	11,500	(5b)
(4)	300	8,660	(8b)
(7)	13,860		
Bal.	6,860		

Liabilities

Accounts Payable

(2)	980	7,840	(1)
(3)	6,860	13,860	(7)
(9)	9,900		
		3,960	Bal.

Equity

Common Stock

		15,000	Bal.

Retained Earnings

		3,000	Bal.

Sales Revenue

		24,750	(5a)
		16,800	(8a)
		41,550	Bal.

Cost of Goods Sold

(5b)	11,500		
(8b)	8,660		
Bal.	20,160		

Transportation-out

(6)	450		

Selling and Admin. Expenses

(10)	8,000		

Interest Expense

(3)	140		

Total Assets = **Total Liabilities** + **Total Equity**

$34,760 = **$3,960** + **$30,800**

EXHIBIT 4.5

Financial Statements

2007 Income Statement

Sales Revenue	$41,550
Cost of Goods Sold	(20,160)
Gross Margin	21,390
Less: Operating Expenses	
Selling and Admin. Exp.	(8,000)
Transportation-out	(450)
Operating Income	12,940
Nonoperating Items	
Interest Expense	(140)
Net Income	$12,800

12/31/07 Balance Sheet

Assets		
Cash	$11,100	
Accounts Receivable	16,800	
Merchandise Inventory	6,860	
Total Assets		$34,760
Liabilities		
Accounts Payable		$ 3,960
Stockholders' Equity		
Common Stock	$15,000	
Retained Earnings	15,800	
Total Stockholders' Equity		30,800
Total Liab. and Stk. Equity		$34,760

2007 Statement of Cash Flows

Operating Activities		
Inflow from Customers	$24,750	
Outflow for Inventory	(17,060)	
Outflow for Transportation-out	(450)	
Outflow for Selling and Admin. Exp.	(8,000)	
Outflow for Interest	(140)	
Net Cash Outflow for Operating Activities		$ (900)
Investing Activities		-0-
Financing Activities		-0-
Net Change in Cash		(900)
Plus: Beginning Cash Balance		12,000
Ending Cash Balance		$11,100

Financial Statements

LO 4

Compare and contrast single and multistep income statements.

The income statement displayed in Exhibit 4.5 is more informative than one which simply subtracts expenses from revenues. By reporting gross margin, it shows the relationship between the cost of goods sold and the sales revenue earned from those particular goods. This income statement also separates routine operating results from nonoperating results, which enables analysts to distinguish between recurring revenues and expenses and those related to peripheral transactions, such as gains and losses, interest revenue, and interest expense. Income statements that show these additional relationships, including **operating income (or loss),** are called **multistep income statements.** Income statements that display a single comparison of total revenues and total expenses are called **single-step income statements.** Exhibit 4.6 shows the percentage of companies that use the multistep versus the single-step format.

On a multistep income statement, interest revenue and interest expense are classified as nonoperating items. In contrast, cash receipts of interest revenue and cash payments of interest expense are reported as operating activities on the statement of cash flows. When developing the statement of cash flows, the Financial Accounting Standards Board (FASB) faced two alternatives regarding how to classify interest, each of which had legitimate theoretical support. Even though interest is reported as a nonoperating item on the income statement, the FASB voted to require that interest be reported as an operating activity on the statement of cash flows. Awareness of this inconsistency is helpful in avoiding confusion when reading financial statements.

Whether using the single-step or multistep income statement format, companies are required to report revenues or expenses from discontinued operations or extraordinary items on separate lines just above net income.

EXHIBIT 4.6

Income Statement Format Used by U.S. Companies

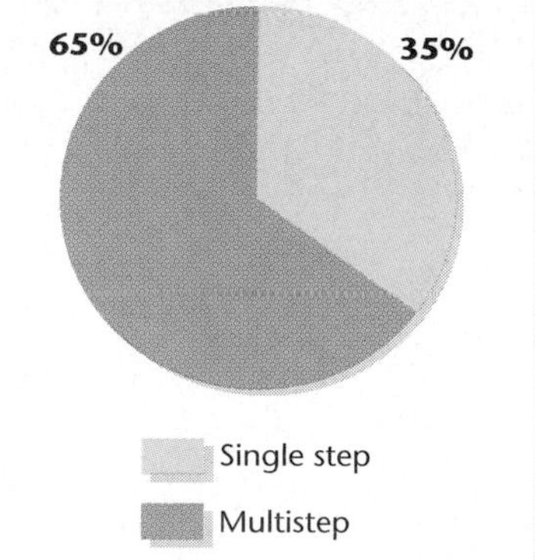

Data Source: AICPA, *Accounting Trends and Techniques,* 2002.

Events Affecting Sales

To this point we assumed JPS did not offer cash discounts to its customers. However, sales, as well as purchases, of inventory can be affected by returns, allowances, and discounts.

LO 1

Identify and explain the primary features of the perpetual inventory system.

Sales discounts are price reductions offered by sellers to encourage buyers to pay promptly. To illustrate, assume JPS engaged in the following selected events during January 2008.

Event 1a ***JPS sold on account merchandise with a list price of $8,500. Payment terms were 1/10, n/30. The merchandise had cost JPS $5,100.***

The sale is recorded at the net price of $8,415 ($8,500 × .99). It increases both assets (accounts receivable) and shareholders' equity (retained earnings). Recognizing revenue increases net income. The statement of cash flows is not affected. The journal entry for this event and its effects on the financial statements follow:

Event No.	Account Title	Debit	Credit
1a	Accounts Receivable Sales Revenue	8,415	 8,415

Assets					=	Liab.	+	Stockholders' Equity			Rev.	−	Exp.	=	Net Inc.	Cash Flow
Cash	+	Accts. Rec.	+	Inventory	=	Accts. Pay.	+	Com. Stk.	+	Retained Earnings						
NA	+	8,415	+	NA	=	NA	+	NA	+	8,415	8,415	−	NA	=	8,415	NA

Event 1b ***JPS recognized $5,100 of cost of goods sold.***

Recognizing the expense decreases assets (merchandise inventory) and stockholders' equity (retained earnings). Cost of goods sold increases and net income decreases. Cash flow is not affected. The journal entry for this event and its effects on the financial statements follow:

Event No.	Account Title	Debit	Credit
1b	Cost of Goods Sold Merchandise Inventory	5,100	 5,100

Assets					=	Liab.	+	Stockholders' Equity			Rev.	−	Exp.	=	Net Inc.	Cash Flow
Cash	+	Accts. Rec.	+	Inventory	=	Accts. Pay.	+	Com. Stk.	+	Retained Earnings						
NA	+	NA	+	(5,100)	=	NA	+	NA	+	(5,100)	NA	−	5,100	=	(5,100)	NA

Event 2a ***The customer from Event 1a returned inventory with a $1,000 list price that JPS had sold with 1/10, n/30 payment terms. The merchandise had cost JPS $600.***

Since JPS originally recorded the sales revenue at the net price, it must also record the sales return at the net price, $990 ($1,000 × .99). The return decreases both assets (accounts receivable) and stockholders' equity (retained earnings) on the balance sheet. Sales and net income decrease. Cash flow is not affected. The journal entry for this event and its effects on the financial statements follow:

Event No.	Account Title	Debit	Credit
2a	Sales Revenue Accounts Receivable	990	 990

Assets					=	Liab.	+	Stockholders' Equity			Rev.	−	Exp.	=	Net Inc.	Cash Flow
Cash	+	Accts. Rec.	+	Inventory	=	Accts. Pay.	+	Com. Stk.	+	Retained Earnings						
NA	+	(990)	+	NA	=	NA	+	NA	+	(990)	(990)	−	NA	=	(990)	NA

Event 2b ***The cost of the goods ($600) is returned to the inventory account.***

Since JPS got the inventory back, the sales return increases both assets (merchandise inventory) and stockholders' equity (retained earnings). The expense (cost of goods sold) decreases and net income increases. Cash flow is not affected. The journal entry for this event and its effects on the financial statements follow:

Event No.	Account Title	Debit	Credit
2b	Merchandise Inventory	600	
	Cost of Goods Sold		600

Assets					=	Liab.	+	Stockholders' Equity			Rev.	−	Exp.	=	Net Inc.	Cash Flow
Cash	+	Accts. Rec.	+	Inventory	=	Accts. Pay.	+	Com. Stk.	+	Retained Earnings						
NA	+	NA	+	600	=	NA	+	NA	+	600	NA	−	(600)	=	600	NA

Event 3 ***JPS collected the balance of the account receivable from the customer that purchased the goods in Event 1a.***

If the customer paid within the discount period, JPS would receive the net amount, which equals the balance in the Accounts Receivable account. The cash collection would represent an asset exchange, with cash increasing and accounts receivable decreasing for the net amount of $7,425 ($7,500 × .99). The statement of cash flows would report an inflow of $7,425 from operating activities. The journal entry for this event and its effects on the financial statements follow:

Event No.	Account Title	Debit	Credit
3	Cash	7,425	
	Accounts Receivable		7,425

Assets					=	Liab.	+	Stockholders' Equity			Rev.	−	Exp.	=	Net Inc.	Cash Flow
Cash	+	Accts. Rec.	+	Inventory	=	Accts. Pay.	+	Com. Stk.	+	Retained Earnings						
7,425	+	(7,425)	+	NA	=	NA	+	NA	+	NA	NA	−	NA	=	NA	7,425 OA

Alternatively, if the customer paid after the discount period expired, JPS would receive the list price of $7,500. The $75 ($7,500 − $7,425) difference between the list price and the net price is interest revenue. The asset cash would increase, the asset accounts receivable would decrease, and revenue would increase. The statement of cash flows would report an inflow of $7,500 from operating activities. The journal entry for this event and its effects on the financial statements follow:

Event No.	Account Title	Debit	Credit
3	Cash	7,500	
	Accounts Receivable		7,425
	Interest Revenue		75

Assets			=	Liab.	+	Stockholders' Equity		Rev.	−	Exp.	=	Net Inc.	Cash Flow
Cash +	Accts. Rec. +	Inventory	=	Accts. Pay.	+	Com. Stk. +	Retained Earnings						
7,500 +	(7,425) +	NA	=	NA	+	NA +	75	75	−	NA	=	75	7,500 OA

Lost, Damaged, or Stolen Inventory

LO 5

Show the effect of lost, damaged, or stolen inventory on financial statements.

Most merchandising companies experience some level of inventory **shrinkage,** a term that reflects decreases in inventory for reasons other than sales to customers. Inventory may be stolen by shoplifters, damaged by customers or employees, or even simply lost or misplaced. Since the *perpetual* inventory system is designed to record purchases and sales of inventory as they occur, the balance in the Merchandise Inventory account represents the amount of inventory that *should* be on hand at any given time. By taking a physical count of the merchandise inventory at the end of the accounting period and comparing that amount with the book balance in the Merchandise Inventory account, managers can determine the amount of any inventory shrinkage. If goods have been lost, damaged, or stolen, the book balance will be higher than the actual amount of inventory on hand and an adjusting entry is required to reduce assets and equity. The Merchandise Inventory account is reduced, and an expense for the amount of the lost, damaged, or stolen inventory is recognized.

Adjustment for Lost, Damaged, or Stolen Inventory

To illustrate, assume that Midwest Merchandising Company maintains perpetual inventory records. Midwest determined, through a physical count, that it had $23,500 of merchandise inventory on hand at the end of the accounting period. The balance in the Inventory account was $24,000. Midwest must make an adjusting entry to write down the Inventory account so the amount reported on the financial statements agrees with the amount actually on hand at the end of the period. The write-down decreases both assets (inventory) and stockholders' equity (retained earnings). The write-down increases expenses and decreases net income. Cash flow is not affected. The journal entry for this event and its effects on the financial statements follow:

Account Title	Debit	Credit
Inventory Loss (Cost of Goods Sold)	500	
Inventory		500

Assets		=	Liab.	+	Stockholders' Equity		Rev.	−	Exp.	=	Net Inc.	Cash Flow
Cash +	Inventory	=			Com. Stk. +	Ret. Earn.						
NA +	(500)	=	NA	+	NA +	(500)	NA	−	500	=	(500)	NA

Theoretically, inventory losses are operating expenses. Because such losses are normally immaterial in amount, however, they are usually added to cost of goods sold for external reporting purposes.

Recognizing Gains and Losses

When Pepper Place, a retail merchandising company, sells *merchandise inventory* for more than cost, Pepper includes the profit from the transaction in the amount of *gross margin* on its income statement. In contrast, if Pepper sells *land* for more than cost, Pepper labels the profit from the transaction as a *gain* on the income statement. In both cases, Pepper subtracts the cost of the asset sold (inventory or land) from its sales price. What is the difference between gross margin and a gain? By using these labels, Pepper discloses the different nature of the underlying transactions.

Pepper's primary business is selling inventory, not land. The term **gain** indicates profit resulting from an incidental transaction not likely to regularly recur. Pepper may sell land (store sites) occasionally as a side effect of its ongoing inventory sales business. If Pepper had sold the land for less than cost the expense would have been labeled a **loss,** which also indicates it did not result from normal, recurring operating activities.

Gains and losses are so labeled in financial statements to communicate the expectation that they are nonrecurring. To illustrate, assume Pepper Place started the accounting period with the following balance sheet:

Assets	
Cash	$ 2,000
Merchandise Inventory	16,000
Land (future building sites)	68,000
Total Assets	$86,000
Stockholders' Equity	
Common Stock	$24,000
Retained Earnings	62,000
Total Stockholders' Equity	$86,000

The three events Pepper experienced during the accounting period follow. Each event is also presented in general journal format.

Event 1 ***Sold inventory that cost $12,000 for $19,000 cash.***

Account Title	Debit	Credit
Cash	19,000	
Cost of Goods Sold	12,000	
Sales Revenue		19,000
Merchandise Inventory		12,000

Event 2 ***Sold land that cost $31,000 for $47,000 cash.***

Account Title	Debit	Credit
Cash	47,000	
Land		31,000
Gain on Sale of Land		16,000

Event 3 ***Paid $5,000 cash for operating expenses.***

Account Title	Debit	Credit
Operating Expenses	5,000	
Cash		5,000

Pepper's financial statements at the end of the period would appear as follows:

Pepper Place

Income Statement

Net Sales	$19,000
Cost of Goods Sold	(12,000)
Gross Margin	7,000
Less: Operating Exp.	(5,000)
Operating Income	2,000
Nonoperating Items	
Gain on Sale of Land	16,000
Net Income	$18,000

[redacted]

Assets	
Cash	$ 63,000
Merchandise Inventory	4,000
Land	37,000
Total Assets	$104,000
Stockholders' Equity	
Common Stock	$ 24,000
Retained Earnings	80,000
Total Stockholders' Equity	$104,000

Statement of Cash Flows

Operating Activities		
Inflow from Customers	$19,000	
Outflow for Operating Exp.	(5,000)	
Net Cash Inflow from Operating Activities		$14,000
Investing Activities		
Infow from Sale of Land		47,000
Financing Activities		0
Net Change in Cash		61,000
Plus: Beginning Cash Balance		2,000
Ending Cash Balance		$63,000

On the multistep income statement, the gain on the sale of land is reported as a nonoperating item. The gain does not appear in the operating activities section of the statement of cash flows. The entire amount received from the land sale is reported as an inflow from the sale of land in the investing activities section of the statement of cash flows.

THE FINANCIAL ANALYST

LO 6

Use common size financial statements to evaluate managerial performance.

Merchandising is a highly competitive business. In order to succeed, merchandisers develop different strategies to distinguish themselves in the marketplace. For example, companies like **Wal-Mart**, **Kmart**, and **Target** focus on price competition while others such as **Neiman Marcus** and **Saks Fifth Avenue** sell high price goods that offer superior quality, fashionable style, and strong guarantees. Financial analysts have developed specific tools that are useful in scrutinizing the success or failure of a company's sales strategy. The first step in the analysis is to develop common size statements so that comparisons can be made between companies.

Common Size Financial Statements

Raw accounting numbers can be difficult to interpret. Suppose that Smith Company earns a 10 percent return on its assets while Jones Company earns only 8 percent on its assets. If Smith Company's total assets are $1,000,000 and Jones Company's are $2,000,000, Smith Company would report less income ($1,000,000 × 0.10 = $100,000) than Jones Company ($2,000,000 × 0.08 = $160,000) even though Smith Company was doing a better job of investing its assets.

Similar difficulties arise when comparing a single company's current period financial statements to those of prior periods. How good is a $1,000,000 increase in net income?

The increase is certainly not as good if the company is IBM rather than a small computer store. To more easily compare between accounting periods or between companies, analysts prepare **common size financial statements** by converting absolute dollar amounts to percentages.

With respect to the income statement, we begin by defining net sales as the base figure, or 100%. **Net sales** is total sales minus sales returns, sales allowances, and sales discounts. The other amounts on the statement are then shown as a percentage of net sales. For example, the cost of goods sold percentage is the dollar amount of cost of goods sold divided by the dollar amount of net sales, and so on for the other items on the statement. Exhibit 4.7 displays a common size income statement derived from JPS's 2007 income statement shown in Exhibit 4.5.

EXHIBIT 4.7

JUNE'S PLANT SHOP
Common Size Income Statement*
For the Year Ended December 31, 2007

Net Sales	$41,550	100.00%
Cost of Goods Sold	(20,160)	(48.52)
Gross Margin	21,390	51.48
Less: Operating Expenses		
Selling and Administrative Expenses	(8,000)	(19.25)
Transportation-out	(450)	(1.08)
Operating Income	12,940	31.14
Nonoperating Items		
Interest Expense	(140)	(.34)
Net Income	$12,800	30.81%

*Percentages do not add exactly because they have been rounded.

Comparisons between Companies

Gross Margin Percentage

LO 7

Use ratio analysis to evaluate managerial performance.

Does Wal-Mart sell merchandise at a higher or lower price than Target? The gross margin percentage is useful in answering questions such as this. Specifically, the **gross margin percentage** is defined as:

$$\frac{\text{Gross margin}}{\text{Net sales}}$$

When comparing two retail companies, all other things being equal, the company with the higher gross margin percentage is pricing its products higher.

CHECK YOURSELF 4.3

The following sales data are from the records of two retail sales companies. All amounts are in thousands.

	Company A	Company B
Sales	$21,234	$43,465
Cost of goods sold	14,864	34,772
Gross margin	$ 6,370	$ 8,693

One company is an upscale department store, and the other is a discount store. Which company is the upscale department store?

Answer

The gross margin percentage for Company A is approximately 30 percent ($6,370 ÷ $21,234). The gross margin percentage for Company B is 20 percent ($8,693 ÷ $43,465). These percentages suggest that Company A is selling goods with a higher markup than Company B, which implies that Company A is the upscale department store.

EXHIBIT 4.8

JUNE'S PLANT SHOP
Common Size Income Statements*

	2007		2008	
Net Sales	$41,550	100%	$49,860	100%
Cost of Goods Sold	(20,160)	49	(19,944)	(40)
Gross Margin	21,390	51	29,916	60
Less: Operating Expenses				
Selling and Administrative Expenses	(8,000)	(19)	(12,465)	(25)
Transportation-out	(450)	(1)	(500)	(1)
Operating Income	12,940	31	16,951	34
Nonoperating Items				
Interest Expense	(140)	0	(400)	(1)
Net Income	$12,800	31%	$16,551	33%

Net Income Percentage

Another commonly used ratio is the net income percentage. The **net income percentage** (sometimes called **return on sales**) is determined as follows:

$$\frac{\text{Net income}}{\text{Net sales}}$$

Net income expressed as a percentage of sales provides insight as to how much of each sales dollar is left as net income after *all* expenses are paid. When comparing two companies, all other things being equal, the company with the higher return on sales ratio is doing a better job of controlling expenses.

Comparisons within a Particular Company

The previous discussion focused on using common size income data to make comparisons among different companies. Analysts also find it useful to compare a particular company's performance over different periods. To illustrate, assume that June's Plant Shop relocated its store to an upscale shopping mall with a wealthier customer base. June has to pay more for rent but believes she will more than offset the higher rent cost by selling her merchandise at higher prices. June changed locations on January 1, 2008. Exhibit 4.8 contains JPS's 2007 and 2008 income statements. Use the data in this exhibit to determine whether June's strategy was successful.

Analyzing the common size statements suggests that June's strategy did increase the profitability of her business. The increase in the gross margin percentage (51% to 60%) confirms the fact that JPS raised its prices. The increase in the return on sales ratio (31% to 33%) shows that the increase in sales revenue was larger than the increase in total expenses.

Real-World Data

Exhibit 4.9 shows the gross margin percentages and return on sales ratios for 10 companies. Three of the companies are manufacturers that produce pharmaceutical products, and the remaining seven companies sell various products at the retail level. These data are for the companies' fiscal years that ended in late 2002 or early 2003.

A review of the data confirms our earlier finding that ratios for companies in the same industry are often more similar than are ratios for companies from different industries. For example, note that the manufacturers have much higher margins, both for gross profit and for net earnings, than do the retailers. Manufacturers are often able to charge higher prices than are retailers because they obtain patents which give them a legal monopoly on the products they create. When a company such as Pfizer develops a new drug, no one else can produce that drug

EXHIBIT 4.9

Industry/Company	Gross Margin %	Return on Sales
Pharmaceutical manufacturers		
Bristol Myers-Squibb	64.7%	11.4%
Johnson & Johnson	71.2	18.2
Pfizer	87.5	28.2
Retail pharmacies		
CVS	25.1	3.0
Rite Aid	23.4	(0.7)
Walgreens	26.5	3.6
Department stores		
Neiman Marcus	32.2	3.4
Wal-Mart	21.5	3.3
Office supplies		
Office Depot	29.6	2.7
Staples	25.4	3.8

until the patent expires, giving it lots of control over its price at the wholesale level. Conversely, when Walgreens sells Pfizer's drug at the retail level, it faces price competition from CVS, a company that is trying to sell the same drug to the same consumers. One way CVS can try to get customers to shop at its store is to charge lower prices than its competitors, but this reduces its profit margins, since it must pay the same price to get Pfizer's drug as did Walgreens. As the data in Exhibit 4.9 show, in 2002 CVS had a lower gross margin percentage than did Walgreens, indicating it is charging slightly lower prices for similar goods.

In the examples presented in Exhibit 4.9, the companies with higher gross margin percentages usually had higher return on sales ratios than their competitors, but this was not always the case. In the office supplies business, Office Depot's gross margin percentage was significantly higher than that of its rival, Staples, but its return on sales ratio was considerably lower. Also, while Neiman Marcus had a gross margin percentage that was 50 percent greater than Wal-Mart's [(32.2 − 21.5) ÷ 21.5] their return on sales ratios were almost equal. This is not surprising when you consider how much more luxurious, and costly, the interior of a Neiman Marcus store is compared to a Wal-Mart.

Financing Merchandise Inventory

Suppose a store purchases inventory in October to sell during the holiday season. If the store sells the inventory on account, much of the cash from the sales won't be collected until January or February of the next year. With cash collections from customers lagging three or four months behind when the goods were purchased, how will the store pay for the inventory? One way is to borrow the money. The company could pay for the merchandise in October with money borrowed from a bank. When the cash from fall sales is collected in January and February, the company could repay the bank.

An obvious drawback to obtaining a loan to pay for inventory is the interest expense incurred on the borrowed funds. However, other alternatives for financing inventory purchases are also expensive. If the owner's money is used, it cannot be invested elsewhere, such as in an interest-earning savings account. This failure to earn interest revenue is called an **opportunity cost;** it is effectively a financing cost that is just as real as actual payment of interest expense. Net income falls regardless of whether a business incurs expenses or loses revenue.

A third alternative is to purchase the inventory on account. However, when purchases are made on account, the seller usually charges the buyer an interest fee. This charge may be hidden in the form of higher prices. So although interest costs are lower, the cost of goods sold is higher. As indicated earlier in this chapter, many companies recognize financing costs by offering buyers the opportunity to receive cash discounts by paying for purchases within a short time after the sale. From any perspective, merchandisers incur significant inventory-financing costs.

Accounting information can help companies minimize the cost of financing inventory. As much as possible, businesses should limit how long goods stay in inventory before they are sold. Ratios to help manage inventory turnover are explained in Chapter 5. Companies should also take steps to collect cash as quickly as possible from customers for the goods they purchase. Managing accounts receivable turnover is explained in Chapter 7. The preceding discussion explains the need for such management techniques.

<< A Look Back

Merchandising companies earn profits by selling inventory at prices that are higher than the cost paid for the goods. Merchandising companies include *retail companies* (companies that sell goods to the final consumer) and *wholesale companies* (companies that sell to other merchandising companies). The products sold by merchandising companies are called *inventory.* The costs to purchase inventory, to receive it, and to ready it for sale are *product costs,* which are first accumulated in an inventory account (balance sheet asset account) and then recognized as cost of goods sold (income statement expense account) in the period in which goods are sold. Purchases and sales of inventory can be recorded continually as goods are bought and sold (perpetual system) or at the end of the accounting period (periodic system, discussed in the chapter appendix).

Accounting for inventory includes the treatment of cash discounts, transportation costs, and returns and allowances. The cost of inventory is the list price less any *cash discount* offered by the seller. The cost of freight paid to acquire inventory (*transportation-in*) is considered a product cost. The cost of freight paid to deliver inventory to customers (*transportation-out*) is a selling expense. *Sales returns and allowances* and *sales discounts* are subtracted from sales revenue to determine the amount of *net sales* reported on the income statement. Purchase returns and allowances reduce product cost. Theoretically, the cost of lost, damaged, or stolen inventory is an operating expense. However, because these costs are usually immaterial in amount they are typically included as part of cost of goods sold on the income statement.

Some companies use a *multistep income statement* which reports product costs separately from selling and administrative costs. Cost of goods sold is subtracted from sales revenue to determine *gross margin.* Selling and administrative expenses are subtracted from gross margin to determine income from operations. Other companies report income using a *single-step format* in which the cost of goods sold is listed along with selling and administrative items in a single expense category that is subtracted in total from revenue to determine income from operations.

Managers of merchandising businesses operate in a highly competitive environment. They must manage company operations carefully to remain profitable. *Common size financial statements* (statements presented on a percentage basis) and ratio analysis are useful monitoring tools. Common size financial statements permit ready comparisons among different-size companies. Although a $1 million increase in sales may be good for a small company and bad for a large company, a 10 percent increase can apply to any size company. The two most common ratios used by merchandising companies are the *gross margin percentage* (gross margin ÷ net sales) and the *net income percentage* (net income ÷ net sales). Interpreting these ratios requires an understanding of industry characteristics. For example, a discount store such as **Wal-Mart** would be expected to have a much lower gross margin percentage than an upscale store such as **Neiman Marcus**.

Managers should be aware of the financing cost of carrying inventory. By investing funds in inventory, a firm loses the opportunity to invest them in interest-bearing assets. The cost of financing inventory is an *opportunity cost.* To minimize financing costs, a company should minimize the amount of inventory it carries, the length of time it holds the inventory, and the time it requires to collect accounts receivable after the inventory is sold.

A Look Forward >>

To this point, the text has explained the basic accounting cycle for service and merchandising businesses. Future chapters more closely address specific accounting issues. For example, in Chapter 5 you will learn how to deal with inventory items that are purchased at differing prices. Other chapters will discuss a variety of specific practices that are widely used by real-world companies.

APPENDIX

Periodic Inventory System

LO 8

Identify the primary features of the periodic inventory system.

Under certain conditions, it is impractical to record inventory sales transactions as they occur. Consider the operations of a fast-food restaurant. To maintain perpetual inventory records, the restaurant would have to transfer from the Inventory account to the Cost of Goods Sold account the *cost* of each hamburger, order of fries, soft drink, or other food items as they were sold. Obviously, recording the cost of each item at the point of sale would be impractical without using highly sophisticated computer equipment (recording the selling price the customer pays is captured by cash registers; the difficulty lies in capturing inventory cost).

The **periodic inventory system** offers a practical solution for recording inventory transactions in a low-technology, high-volume environment. Inventory costs are recorded in a Purchases account at the time of purchase. Purchase returns and allowances and transportation-in are recorded in separate accounts. No entries for the cost of merchandise purchases or sales are recorded in the Inventory account during the period. The cost of goods sold is determined at the end of the period as shown in Exhibit 4.11.

The perpetual and periodic inventory systems represent alternative procedures for recording the same information. The amounts of cost of goods sold and ending inventory reported in the financial statements will be the same regardless of the method used. Exhibit 4.10 presents the general journal entries JPS would make if it used the periodic inventory method for the 2007 transactions. Cost of goods sold is recorded in an adjusting entry at the end of the accounting period.

The **schedule of cost of goods sold** presented in Exhibit 4.11 is used for internal reporting purposes. It is normally not shown in published financial statements. The amount of cost of goods sold is reported as a single line item on the income statement. The financial statements in Exhibit 4.5 will be the same whether JPS maintains perpetual or periodic inventory records.

Advantages and Disadvantages of the Periodic System versus the Perpetual System

The chief advantage of the periodic method is recording efficiency. Recording inventory transactions occasionally (periodically) requires less effort than recording them continually (perpetually). Historically, practical limitations offered businesses like fast-food restaurants or grocery stores no alternative to using the periodic system. The sheer volume of transactions made recording individual decreases to the Inventory account balance as each item was sold impossible. Imagine the number of transactions a grocery store would have to record every business day to maintain perpetual records.

Although the periodic system provides a recordkeeping advantage over the perpetual system, perpetual inventory records provide significant control advantages over periodic records. With perpetual records, the book balance in the Inventory account should agree with the amount of inventory in stock at any given time. By comparing that book balance with the results of a

EXHIBIT 4.10

General Journal Entries for 2007

Event No.	Account Title	Debit	Credit
1	Purchases	7,840	
	Accounts Payable		7,840
2	Accounts Payable	980	
	Purchase Returns and Allowances		980
3	Accounts Payable	6,860	
	Interest Expense	140	
	Cash		7,000
4	Transportation-in	300	
	Cash		300
5	Cash	24,750	
	Sales Revenue		24,750
6	Transportation-out	450	
	Cash		450
7	Purchases	13,860	
	Accounts Payable		13,860
8	Accounts Receivable	16,800	
	Sales Revenue		16,800
9	Accounts Payable	9,900	
	Cash		9,900
10	Selling and Administrative Expenses	8,000	
	Cash		8,000
ADJ	Cost of Goods Sold	20,160	
	Inventory	860	
	Purchases Returns and Allowances	980	
	Purchases		21,700
	Transportation-in		300
CL	Sales Revenue	41,550	
	Cost of Goods Sold		20,160
	Transportation-out		450
	Selling and Administrative Expenses		8,000
	Interest Expense		140
	Retained Earnings		12,800

EXHIBIT 4.11

Schedule of Cost of Goods Sold for 2007

Beginning Inventory	$ 6,000
Purchases	21,700
Purchase Returns and Allowances	(980)
Transportation-in	300
Cost of Goods Available for Sale	27,020
Ending Inventory	(6,860)
Cost of Goods Sold	$20,160

physical inventory count, management can determine the amount of lost, damaged, destroyed, or stolen inventory. Perpetual records also permit more timely and accurate reorder decisions and profitability assessments.

When a company uses the *periodic* inventory system, lost, damaged, or stolen merchandise is automatically included in cost of goods sold. Because such goods are not included in the year-end physical count, they are treated as sold regardless of the reason for their absence. Since the periodic system does not separate the cost of lost, damaged, or stolen merchandise from the cost of goods sold, the amount of any inventory shrinkage is unknown. This feature is a major disadvantage of the periodic system. Without knowing the amount of inventory losses, management cannot weigh the costs of various security systems against the potential benefits.

Advances in such technology as electronic bar code scanning and increased computing power have eliminated most of the practical constraints that once prevented merchandisers with high-volume, low dollar-value inventories from recording inventory transactions on a continual basis. As a result, use of the perpetual inventory system has expanded rapidly in recent years and continued growth can be expected. This text, therefore, concentrates on the perpetual inventory system.

SELF-STUDY REVIEW PROBLEM

Academy Sales Company (ASC) started the 2007 accounting period with the balances given in the following financial statements model. During 2007 ASC experienced the following business events.

1. Purchased $16,000 of merchandise inventory on account, terms 2/10, n/30.
2. The goods that were purchased in Event 1 were delivered FOB shipping point. Freight costs of $600 were paid in cash by the responsible party.
3. Returned $500 of goods purchased in Event 1.
4. Paid the balance due on the account payable. The payment was made after the discount period had expired.

5a. Recognized $21,000 of cash revenue from the sale of merchandise.

5b. Recognized $15,000 of cost of goods sold.

6. The merchandise in Event 5a was sold to customers FOB destination. Freight costs of $950 were paid in cash by the responsible party.
7. Paid cash of $4,000 for selling and administrative expenses.

Required

a. Record these transactions in a financial statements model like the following one.

Event No.	Cash	+	Inv.	=	Accts. Pay.	+	Com. Stk.	+	Ret. Earn.	Rev.	−	Exp.	=	Net Inc.	Cash Flow
Bal.	25,000	+	3,000	=	0	+	18,000	+	10,000	NA		NA	=	NA	NA

b. Calculate the gross margin percentage. Based on ASC's gross margin percentage and the information shown in Exhibit 4.9, classify ASC as an upscale department store, a retail discount store, or an office supplies store.

Solution to Requirement a

Event No.	Cash	+	Inv.	=	Accts. Pay.	+	Com. Stk.	+	Ret. Earn.	Rev.	−	Exp.	=	Net Inc.	Cash Flow
Bal.	25,000	+	3,000	=	0	+	18,000	+	10,000	NA	−	NA	=	NA	NA
1		+	15,680	=	15,680	+		+			−		=		
2	(600)	+	600	=		+		+			−		=		(600) OA
3		+	(490)	=	(490)	+		+			−		=		
4	(15,500)	+		=	(15,190)	+		+	(310)		−	310	=	(310)	(15,500) OA
5a	21,000	+		=		+		+	21,000	21,000	−		=	21,000	21,000 OA
5b		+	(15,000)	=		+		+	(15,000)		−	15,000	=	(15,000)	
6	(950)	+		=		+		+	(950)		−	950	=	(950)	(950) OA
7	(4,000)	+		=		+		+	(4,000)		−	4,000	=	(4,000)	(4,000) OA
Bal.	24,950	+	3,790	=	0	+	18,000	+	10,740	21,000	−	20,260	=	740	(50) NC

Solution to Requirement b

Gross margin equals sales minus cost of goods sold. In this case, the gross margin is $6,000 ($21,000 − $15,000). The gross margin percentage is computed by dividing gross margin by sales. In this case, the gross margin percentage is 28.6 percent ($6,000 ÷ $21,000). Since this percentage is closest to the percentage shown for **Office Depot**, the data suggest ASC may be an office supplies store.

KEY TERMS

allowances 189
cash discount 188
common size financial statements 201
cost of goods available for sale 182
cost of goods sold 182
FOB (free on board) destination 189
FOB (free on board) shipping point 189
gain 199
gross margin 182
gross margin percentage 201
gross profit 182
loss 199
merchandise inventory 181
merchandising businesses 181
multistep income statement 195
net income percentage 202
net method 188
net sales 201
operating income (or loss) 195
opportunity cost 203
period costs 182
periodic inventory system 205
perpetual inventory system 184
product costs 182
purchase discount 188
retail companies 181
return on sales 202
sales discounts 196
schedule of cost of goods sold 205
selling and administrative costs 182
shrinkage 198
single-step income statement 195
transportation-in (freight-in) 189
transportation-out (freight-out) 189
2/10, n/30 188
wholesale companies 181

QUESTIONS

1. Define *merchandise inventory.* What types of costs are included in the Merchandise Inventory account?
2. What is the difference between a product cost and a selling and administrative cost?
3. How is the cost of goods available for sale determined?
4. What portion of cost of goods available for sale is shown on the balance sheet? What portion is shown on the income statement?
5. When are period costs expensed? When are product costs expensed?
6. If PetCo had net sales of $600,000, goods available for sale of $450,000, and cost of goods sold of $375,000, what is its gross margin? What amount of inventory will be shown on its balance sheet?
7. Describe how the perpetual inventory system works. What are some advantages of using the perpetual inventory system? Is it necessary to take a physical inventory when using the perpetual inventory system?
8. What are the effects of the following types of transactions on the accounting equation? Also identify the financial statements that are affected. (Assume that the perpetual inventory system is used.)
   a. Acquisition of cash from the issue of common stock.
   b. Contribution of inventory by an owner of a company.
   c. Purchase of inventory with cash by a company.
   d. Sale of inventory for cash.
9. Northern Merchandising Company sold inventory that cost $12,000 for $20,000 cash. How does this event affect the accounting equation? What financial statements and accounts are affected? (Assume that the perpetual inventory system is used.)
10. If goods are shipped FOB shipping point, which party (buyer or seller) is responsible for the shipping costs?
11. Define *transportation-in.* Is it a product or a period cost?
12. Quality Cellular Co. paid $80 for freight on merchandise that it had purchased for resale to customers (transportation-in) and paid $135 for freight on merchandise delivered to customers (transportation-out). What account is debited for the $80 payment? What account is debited for the $135 payment?
13. Why would a seller grant an allowance to a buyer of the seller's merchandise?
14. Dyer Department Store purchased goods with the terms 2/10, n/30. What do these terms mean?
15. Eastern Discount Stores incurred a $5,000 cash cost. How does the accounting for this cost differ if the cash were paid for inventory versus commissions to sales personnel?
16. What is the purpose of giving a cash discount to charge customers?
17. Define *transportation-out.* Is it a product cost or a period cost for the seller?
18. Ball Co. purchased inventory with a list price of $4,000 with the terms 2/10, n/30. What amount will be debited to the Merchandise Inventory account?

19. Explain the difference between purchase returns and sales returns. How do purchase returns affect the financial statements of both buyer and seller? How do sales returns affect the financial statements of both buyer and seller?
20. How is net sales determined?
21. What is the difference between a multistep income statement and a single-step income statement?
22. What is the advantage of using common size income statements to present financial information for several accounting periods?
23. What information is provided by the net income percentage (return on sales ratio)?
24. What is the purpose of preparing a schedule of cost of goods sold?
25. Explain how the periodic inventory system works. What are some advantages of using the periodic inventory system? What are some disadvantages of using the periodic inventory system? Is it necessary to take a physical inventory when using the periodic inventory system?
26. Why does the periodic inventory system impose a major disadvantage for management in accounting for lost, stolen, or damaged goods?

EXERCISES—SERIES A

All Exercises in Series A are available with McGraw-Hill's Homework Manager

When the instructions for *any* exercise or problem call for the preparation of an income statement, use the *multistep format* unless otherwise indicated.

Exercise 4-1A *Comparing a merchandising company with a service company* L.O. 1, 2

The following information is available for two different types of businesses for the 2007 accounting period. Markin Consulting is a service business that provides consulting services to small businesses. College Book Mart is a merchandising business that sells books to college students.

Data for Markin Consulting

1. Received $20,000 from issuing common stock to start the business.
2. Performed services for customers and collected $15,000 cash.
3. Paid salary expense of $9,600.

Data for College Book Mart

1. Received $20,000 from issuing common stock to start the business.
2. Purchased $9,500 of inventory for cash.
3. Inventory costing $8,400 was sold for $15,000 cash.
4. Paid $1,200 cash for operating expenses.

Required

a. Prepare an income statement, balance sheet, and statement of cash flows for each of the companies.
b. What is different about the income statements of the two businesses?
c. What is different about the balance sheets of the two businesses?
d. How are the statements of cash flow different for the two businesses?

Exercise 4-2A *Effect of inventory transactions on journals, ledgers, and financial statements: perpetual system* L.O. 2

Justin Harris started a small merchandising business in 2006. The business experienced the following events during its first year of operation. Assume that Harris uses the perpetual inventory system.

1. Acquired $30,000 cash from the issue of common stock.
2. Purchased inventory for $25,000 cash.
3. Sold inventory costing $18,000 for $28,000 cash.

Required

a. Record the events in general journal format.
b. Post the entries to T-accounts.
c. Record the events in a statements model like the one shown below.

Assets			=	Equity			Rev.	−	Exp.	=	Net Inc.	Cash Flow
Cash	+	Inv.	=	Com. Stk.	+	Ret. Earn.						

d. Prepare an income statement for 2006 (use the multistep format).

e. What is the amount of total assets at the end of the period?

L.O. 2

Exercise 4-3A *Effect of inventory transactions on the income statement and statement of cash flows: perpetual system*

During 2007, Etc. Merchandising Company purchased $40,000 of inventory on account. The company sold inventory on account that cost $30,000 for $45,000. Cash payments on accounts payable were $25,000. There was $40,000 cash collected from accounts receivable. Etc. also paid $8,000 cash for operating expenses. Assume that Etc. started the accounting period with $36,000 in both cash and common stock.

Required

a. Identify the events described in the preceding paragraph and record them in a horizontal statements model like the following one:

Assets					=	Liab.	+	Equity			Rev.	−	Exp.	=	Net Inc.	Cash Flow
Cash	+	Accts. Rec.	+	Inv.	=	Accts. Pay.	+	Com. Stk.	+	Ret. Earn.						
36,000	+	NA	+	NA	=	NA	+	36,000	+	NA	NA	−	NA	=	NA	NA

b. What is the balance of accounts receivable at the end of 2007?

c. What is the balance of accounts payable at the end of 2007?

d. What are the amounts of gross margin and net income for 2007?

e. Determine the amount of net cash flow from operating activities.

f. Explain any differences between net income and net cash flow from operating activities.

L.O. 2

Exercise 4-4A *Recording inventory transactions in the general journal and posting entries to T-accounts: perpetual system*

Tom's Paint Supply experienced the following events during 2006, its first year of operation:

1. Acquired $15,000 cash from the issue of common stock.
2. Purchased inventory for $12,000 cash.
3. Sold inventory costing $6,500 for $11,000 cash.
4. Paid $800 for advertising expense.

Required

a. Record the general journal entries for the preceding transactions.

b. Post each of the entries to T-accounts.

c. Prepare a trial balance to prove the equality of debits and credits.

d. Record the events in a statements model like the one shown below.

Assets			=	Equity			Rev.	−	Exp.	=	Net Inc.	Cash Flow
Cash	+	Inv.	=	Com. Stk.	+	Ret. Earn.						

L.O. 3

Exercise 4-5A *Determining which party is responsible for freight cost*

Required

Determine which party, buyer or seller, is responsible for freight charges in each of the following situations:

a. Sold merchandise, freight terms, FOB destination.

b. Sold merchandise, freight terms, FOB shipping point.
c. Purchased merchandise, freight terms, FOB destination.
d. Purchased merchandise, freight terms, FOB shipping point.

Exercise 4-6A ***Effect of purchase returns and allowances and freight costs on the journal, ledger, and financial statements: perpetual system*** **L.O. 2, 3**

The trial balance for The Copy Shop as of January 1, 2006, was as follows:

Account Titles	Debit	Credit
Cash	$12,000	
Inventory	6,000	
Common Stock		$15,000
Retained Earnings		3,000
Total	$18,000	$18,000

The following events affected the company during the 2006 accounting period:

1. Purchased merchandise on account that cost $8,200.
2. Purchased goods FOB shipping point with freight cost of $300 cash.
3. Returned $1,000 of damaged merchandise for credit on account.
4. Agreed to keep other damaged merchandise for which the company received a $500 allowance.
5. Sold merchandise that cost $5,500 for $9,500 cash.
6. Delivered merchandise to customers under terms FOB destination with freight costs amounting to $200 cash.
7. Paid $6,000 on the merchandise purchased in Event 1.

Required

a. Record the transactions in general journal format.
b. Open general ledger T-accounts with the appropriate beginning balances, and post the journal entries to the T-accounts.
c. Prepare an income statement and statement of cash flows for 2006.
d. Explain why a difference does or does not exist between net income and net cash flow from operating activities.

Exercise 4-7A ***Accounting for product costs: perpetual inventory system*** **L.O. 2, 3**

Which of the following would be debited to the Inventory account for a merchandising business using the perpetual inventory system?

Required

a. Transportation-out.
b. Purchase discount.
c. Transportation-in.
d. Purchase of supplies to be used by the business.
e. Purchase of inventory.
f. Allowance received for damaged inventory.

Exercise 4-8A ***Effect of product cost and period cost: horizontal statements model*** **L.O. 1, 2, 3**

Brislin Co. experienced the following events for the 2007 accounting period:

1. Acquired $5,000 cash from the issue of common stock.
2. Purchased $18,000 of inventory on account.
3. Received goods purchased in Event 2 FOB shipping point. Freight cost of $500 paid in cash.
4. Returned $2,000 of goods purchased in Event 2 because of poor quality.
5. Sold inventory on account that cost $14,300 for $22,000.

6. Freight cost on the goods sold in Event 5 was $200. The goods were shipped FOB destination. Cash was paid for the freight cost.
7. Collected $16,500 cash from accounts receivable.
8. Paid $12,000 cash on accounts payable.
9. Paid $1,100 for advertising expense.
10. Paid $2,200 cash for insurance expense.

Required

a. Which of these transactions result in period (selling and administrative) costs? Which result in product costs? If neither, label the transaction NA.

b. Record each event in a horizontal statements model like the following one. The first event is recorded as an example.

Assets					=	Liab.	+	Equity			Rev.	−	Exp.	=	Net Inc.	Cash Flow
Cash	+	Accts. Rec.	+	Inv.	=	Accts. Pay.	+	Com. Stk.	+	Ret. Earn.						
5,000	+	NA	+	NA	=	NA	+	5,000	+	NA	NA	−	NA	=	NA	5,000 FA

L.O. 3

Exercise 4-9A *Cash discounts and purchase returns (net method)*

On March 6, 2006, Lie's Imports purchased merchandise from The Glass Exchange with a list price of $15,500, terms 2/10, n/45. On March 10, Lie's returned merchandise to The Glass Exchange for credit. The list price of the returned merchandise was $3,200. Lie's paid cash to settle the accounts payable on March 15, 2006.

Required

a. What is the amount of the check that Lie's must write to The Glass Exchange on March 15?

b. Record the events in a horizontal statements model like the following one.

Assets			=	Liab.	+	Equity			Rev.	−	Exp.	=	Net Inc.	Cash Flow
Cash	+	Inv.	=	Accts. Pay.	+	Com. Stk.	+	Ret. Earn.						

c. How much would Lie's pay for the merchandise purchased if the payment is not made until March 20, 2006?

d. Record the payment of the merchandise in Event *c* in a horizontal statements model like the one shown above.

e. Why would The Glass Exchange sell merchandise with the terms 2/10, n/45?

L.O. 2, 3

Exercise 4-10A *Effect of sales returns and allowances and freight costs on the journal, ledger, and financial statements: perpetual system*

Cain Company began the 2006 accounting period with $18,000 cash, $50,000 inventory, $40,000 common stock, and $28,000 retained earnings. During the 2006 accounting period, Cain experienced the following events:

1. Sold merchandise costing $38,200 for $66,500 on account to Jones' General Store.
2. Delivered the goods to Jones under terms FOB destination. Freight costs were $600 cash.
3. Received returned damaged goods from Jones. The goods cost Cain $4,000 and were sold to Jones for $7,600.
4. Granted Jones a $2,000 allowance for other damaged goods that Jones agreed to keep.
5. Collected partial payment of $52,000 cash from accounts receivable.

Required

a. Record the transactions in general journal format.

b. Open general ledger T-accounts with the appropriate beginning balances and post the journal entries to the T-accounts.

c. Record the events in a statements model like the one shown below.

Assets					=	Equity			Rev. − Exp. = Net Inc.	Cash Flow
Cash	+	Accts. Rec.	+	Inv.	=	Com. Stk.	+	Ret. Earn.		

d. Prepare an income statement, balance sheet, and statement of cash flows.
e. Why would Cain grant the $2,000 allowance to Jones? Who benefits more?

Exercise 4-11A ***Effect of cash discounts on the journal, ledger, and financial statements: perpetual system (net method)*** **L.O. 2, 3**

Lane Sales was started in 2006. The company experienced the following accounting events during its first year of operation:

1. Started business when it acquired $40,000 cash from the issue of common stock.
2. Purchased merchandise with a list price of $42,000 on account, terms 2/10, n/30.
3. Paid off one-half of the accounts payable balance within the discount period.
4. Sold merchandise on account that had a list price of $25,000. Credit terms were 1/20, n/30. The merchandise had cost Lane $18,000.
5. Collected cash from the account receivable within the discount period.
6. Paid $2,600 cash for operating expenses.
7. Paid the balance due on accounts payable. The payment was not made within the discount period.

Required

a. Record the transactions in general journal format.
b. Open general ledger T-accounts, and post the journal entries to the T-accounts.
c. Record the events in a horizontal statements model like the following one.

Assets					=	Liab.	+	Equity			Rev. − Exp. = Net Inc.	Cash Flow
Cash	+	Accts. Rec.	+	Inv.	=	Accts. Pay.	+	Com. Stk.	+	Ret. Earn.		

d. What is the amount of gross margin for the period? What is the net income for the period?
e. Why would Lane sell merchandise with the terms 1/20, n/30?
f. What do the terms 2/10, n/30 in event 2 mean to Lane?

Exercise 4-12A ***Effect of inventory transactions on the financial statements: comprehensive exercise with sales and purchase returns and discounts*** **L.O. 2, 3**

Boone Sales Company had the following balances in its accounts on January 1, 2005:

Cash	$30,000
Merchandise Inventory	20,000
Common Stock	40,000
Retained Earnings	10,000

Boone experienced the following events during 2005:

1. Purchased merchandise inventory on account with a list price of $30,000, terms 1/10, n/30.
2. Paid freight of $600 on the merchandise purchased.
3. Sold merchandise inventory with a list price of $30,000 on account, terms 2/10, n/45. The inventory had cost Boone $19,000.
4. Returned damaged merchandise purchased in Event 1. The list price of the returned merchandise was $1,000.
5. Agreed to keep other merchandise that was slightly damaged and was granted an allowance of $200.
6. The customer in Event 3 returned for credit inventory with a list price of $5,000. The inventory had cost Boone $3,200.

7. Collected the balance of accounts receivable within the discount period.
8. Paid for one-half of the accounts payable within the discount period.
9. Paid $3,200 cash for selling and administrative expenses.
10. Paid the balance of accounts payable (not within the discount period).

Required

a. Record each of these events in general journal format.
b. Open general ledger T-accounts. Post the beginning balances and the events to the accounts.
c. Prepare a trial balance.
d. Prepare an income statement, balance sheet, and a statement of cash flows.

L.O. 2, 5

Exercise 4-13A *Effect of inventory losses: perpetual system*

Mia Sales experienced the following events during 2005, its first year of operation:

1. Started the business when it acquired $50,000 cash from the issue of common stock.
2. Paid $42,000 cash to purchase inventory.
3. Sold inventory costing $25,000 for $53,000 cash.
4. Physically counted inventory showing $15,800 inventory was on hand at the end of the accounting period.

Required

a. Open appropriate ledger T-accounts, and record the events in the accounts.
b. Prepare an income statement and balance sheet for 2005.
c. Explain how differences between the book balance and the physical count of inventory could arise. Why is being able to determine whether differences exist useful to management?

L.O. 2

Exercise 4-14A *Determining the effect of inventory transactions on the horizontal statements model: perpetual system*

Lopez Sales Company experienced the following events:

1. Purchased merchandise inventory for cash.
2. Purchased merchandise inventory on account.
3. Sold merchandise inventory for cash. Label the revenue recognition 3a and the expense recognition 3b.
4. Sold merchandise inventory on account. Label the revenue recognition 4a and the expense recognition 4b.
5. Returned merchandise purchased on account.
6. Paid cash for selling and administrative expenses.
7. Paid cash on accounts payable not within the discount period.
8. Paid cash for transportation-in.
9. Collected cash from accounts receivable.
10. Paid cash for transportation-out.

Required

Identify each event as asset source (AS), asset use (AU), asset exchange (AE), or claims exchange (CE). Also explain how each event affects the financial statements by placing a + for increase, − for decrease, or NA for not affected under each of the components in the following statements model. Assume the use of the perpetual inventory system. The first event is recorded as an example.

Event No.	Event Type	Assets	=	Liab.	+	Equity	Rev.	−	Exp.	=	Net Inc.	Cash Flow
1	AE	+ −	=	NA	+	NA	NA	−	NA	=	NA	− OA

L.O. 4

Exercise 4-15A *Single-step and multistep income statements*

The following information was taken from the accounts of Good Foods Store, a delicatessen. The accounts are listed in alphabetical order, and each has a normal balance.

Accounts Payable	$315
Accounts Receivable	200
Advertising Expense	100
Cash	205
Common Stock	100
Cost of Goods Sold	300
Merchandise Inventory	225
Prepaid Rent	20
Retained Earnings	255
Sales Revenue	500
Salaries Expense	65
Supplies Expense	55

Required

First, prepare an income statement using the single-step approach. Then prepare another income statement using the multistep approach.

Exercise 4-16A *Determining the cost of financing inventory*

L.O. 2

On January 1, 2008, Mel Stark started a small sailboat merchandising business that he named Mel's Sails. The company experienced the following events during the first year of operation:

1. Started the business by issuing common stock for $20,000 cash.
2. Paid $14,000 cash to purchase inventory.
3. Sold a sailboat that cost $9,000 for $16,000 on account.
4. Collected $10,000 cash from accounts receivable.
5. Paid $2,500 for operating expenses.

Required

a. Record the events in general journal format, using the perpetual system.
b. Open general ledger T-accounts, and post the journal entries to the T-accounts.
c. Prepare an income statement, balance sheet, and statement of cash flows.
d. Since Mel sold inventory for $16,000, he will be able to recover more than half of the $20,000 he invested in the stock. Do you agree with this statement? Why or why not?

Exercise 4-17A *Financing inventory and cash discounts*

L.O. 3

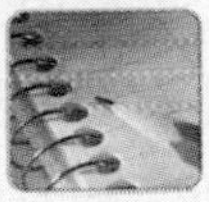

May Haynes came to you for advice. She has just purchased a large amount of inventory with the terms 2/10, n/60. The amount of the invoice is $260,000. She is currently short on cash but has good credit. She can borrow the money at the appropriate time to take advantage of the discount. The annual interest rate is 7% if she decides to borrow the money. Haynes is sure she will have the necessary cash by the due date of the invoice (but not by the discount date).

Required

a. For how long would Haynes need to borrow the money to take advantage of the discount?
b. How much money would Haynes need to borrow?
c. Write a memo to Haynes outlining the most cost-effective strategy for her to follow. Include in your memo the amount of savings from the alternative you suggest.

Exercise 4-18A *Effect of inventory transactions on the income statement and balance sheet: periodic system (Appendix)*

L.O. 8

Don Moon is the owner of The Clothes Shop. At the beginning of the year, Moon had $1,200 in inventory. During the year, Moon purchased inventory that cost $6,500. At the end of the year, inventory on hand amounted to $1,800.

Required

Calculate the following:

a. Cost of goods available for sale during the year.
b. Cost of goods sold for the year.
c. Inventory amount The Clothes Shop would report on its year-end balance sheet.

L.O. 8

Exercise 4-19A *Determining cost of goods sold: periodic system (Appendix)*

Sunset Retailers uses the periodic inventory system to account for its inventory transactions. The following account titles and balances were drawn from Sunset's records for the year 2007: beginning balance in inventory, $24,900; purchases, $306,400; purchase returns and allowances, $9,600; sales, $680,000; sales returns and allowances, $6,370; transportation-in, $2,160; and operating expenses, $51,400. A physical count indicated that $29,300 of merchandise was on hand at the end of the accounting period.

Required

a. Prepare a schedule of cost of goods sold.
b. Prepare a multistep income statement.

L.O. 8

Exercise 4-20A *Basic transactions: periodic system, single cycle (Appendix)*

The following events apply to Tops Gift Shop for 2007, its first year of operation:

1. Acquired $33,500 cash from the issue of common stock.
2. Issued common stock to Kayla Taylor, one of the owners, in exchange for gift merchandise worth $2,500 Taylor had acquired prior to opening the shop.
3. Purchased $43,500 of inventory on account.
4. Paid $2,750 for advertising expense.
5. Sold inventory for $77,500.
6. Paid $8,000 in salary to a part-time salesperson.
7. Paid $35,000 on accounts payable (see Event 3).
8. Physically counted inventory, which indicated that $7,000 of inventory was on hand at the end of the accounting period.

Required

a. Record each of these events in general journal form. Tops Gift Shop uses the periodic system.
b. Post each of the events to ledger T-accounts.
c. Prepare an income statement, statement of changes in stockholders' equity, balance sheet, and statement of cash flows for 2007.
d. Prepare the necessary closing entries at the end of 2007, and post them to the appropriate T-accounts.
e. Prepare an after-closing trial balance.
f. Discuss an advantage of using the periodic system instead of the perpetual system.
g. Why is the common stock issued amount on the statement of changes in stockholders' equity different from the common stock issued amount in the cash flow from financing activities section of the cash flow statement?

PROBLEMS—SERIES A

All Problems in Series A are available with McGraw-Hill's Homework Manager

L.O. 2

CHECK FIGURES
2007 Net Income: $5,300
2009 Total Assets: $45,300

Problem 4-21A *Basic transactions for three accounting cycles: perpetual system*

Ramsey Company was started in 2007 when it acquired $30,000 from the issue of common stock. The following data summarize the company's first three years' operating activities. Assume that all transactions were cash transactions.

	2007	2008	2009
Purchases of Inventory	$24,000	$12,000	$18,500
Sales	26,000	32,000	36,000
Cost of Goods Sold	15,200	18,500	20,000
Selling and Administrative Expenses	5,500	9,400	10,100

Required

Prepare an income statement (use the multistep format) and balance sheet for each fiscal year. (*Hint:* Record the transaction data for each accounting period in T-accounts before preparing the statements for that year.)

Problem 4-22A *Identifying product and period costs*

L.O. 1

Required

Indicate whether each of the following costs is a product cost or a period cost:

a. Insurance on vans used to deliver goods to customers.
b. Salaries of sales supervisors.
c. Monthly maintenance expense for a leased copier.
d. Goods purchased for resale.
e. Cleaning supplies for the office.
f. Freight on goods purchased for resale.
g. Salary of the marketing director.
h. Freight on goods sold to customer with terms FOB destination.
i. Utilities expense incurred for office building.

Problem 4-23A *Identifying freight cost*

L.O. 3

CHECK FIGURE
Event (b): Freight Costs Paid: $150

Required

For each of the following events, determine the amount of freight paid by Tom's Parts House. Also indicate whether the freight is classified as a product or period cost.

a. Purchased inventory with freight costs of $700, FOB destination.
b. Shipped merchandise to customers with freight costs of $150, FOB destination.
c. Purchased additional merchandise with costs of $250, FOB shipping point.
d. Sold merchandise to a customer. Freight costs were $400, FOB shipping point.

Problem 4-24A *Effect of purchase returns and allowances and purchase discounts on the financial statements; perpetual system (net method)*

L.O. 2, 3

CHECK FIGURES
a. Ending Cash: $16,062
d. Net Income: $2,338

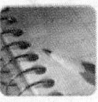

The following events were completed by Chris Toy Shop in September 2009:

Sept.	1	Acquired $30,000 cash from the issue of common stock.
	1	Purchased $22,000 of merchandise on account with terms 2/10, n/30.
	5	Paid $500 cash for freight to obtain merchandise purchased on September 1.
	8	Sold merchandise that cost $5,000 to customers for $9,500 on account, with terms 1/10, n/30.
	8	Returned $800 of defective merchandise from the September 1 purchase to the supplier.
	10	Paid cash for one-half of the balance due on the merchandise purchased on September 1.
	20	Received cash from customers of September 8 sale in settlement of the account balances, but not within the discount period.
	30	Paid the balance due on the merchandise purchased on September 1.
	30	Paid $1,950 cash for selling expenses.

Required

a. Record each event in a statements model like the following one. The first event is recorded as an example.

Assets					=	Liab.	+	Equity			Rev.	−	Exp.	=	Net Inc.	Cash Flow
Cash	+	Accts. Rec.	+	Inv.	=	Accts. Pay.	+	Com. Stk.	+	Ret. Earn.						
30,000	+	NA	+	NA	=	NA	+	30,000	+	NA	NA	−	NA	=	NA	30,000 FA

b. Record each of these transactions in general journal form.
c. Post each of the transactions to general ledger T-accounts.
d. Prepare an income statement for the month ending September 30.
e. Prepare a statement of cash flows for the month ending September 30.
f. Explain why there is a difference between net income and cash flow from operating activities.

L.O. 2, 3, 5

Problem 4-25A *Comprehensive cycle problem: perpetual system*

eXcel

mhhe.com/edmonds2007

CHECK FIGURES

d. Retained Earnings Ending Balance: $7,220

Net Income: $1,720

At the beginning of 2005, the C. Eaton Company had the following balances in its accounts:

Cash	$ 6,500
Inventory	9,000
Common Stock	10,000
Retained Earnings	5,500

During 2005, the company experienced the following events.

1. Purchased inventory with a list price of $3,000 on account from Blue Company under terms 1/10, n/30. The merchandise was delivered FOB shipping point. Freight costs of $150 were paid in cash.
2. Returned $300 of the inventory that it had purchased because the inventory was damaged in transit. The freight company agreed to pay the return freight cost.
3. Paid the amount due on its account payable to Blue Company but not within the cash discount period.
4. Sold inventory with a list price of $6,000 and a cost of $3,500 on account, under terms 2/10, n/45.
5. Received returned merchandise from a customer. The merchandise originally cost $400 and was sold to the customer for $650 cash. The customer was paid $650 cash for the returned merchandise.
6. Delivered goods in Event 4 FOB destination. Freight costs of $80 were paid in cash.
7. Collected the amount due on the account receivable but not within the discount period.
8. Took a physical count indicating that $8,300 of inventory was on hand at the end of the accounting period.

Required

a. Identify each of these events as asset source (AS), asset use (AU), asset exchange (AE), or claims exchange (CE). Also explain how each event would affect the financial statements by placing a + for increase, − for decrease, or NA for not affected under each of the components in the following statements model. Assume that the perpetual inventory method is used. When an event has more than one part, use letters to distinguish the effects of each part. The first event is recorded as an example.

Event No.	Event Type	Assets	=	Liab.	+	Equity	Rev.	−	Exp.	=	Net Inc.	Cash Flow
1a	AS	+	=	+	+	NA	NA	−	NA	=	NA	NA
1b	AE	+ −	=	NA	+	NA	NA	−	NA	=	NA	− OA

b. Record the events in general journal format.
c. Open ledger T-accounts, and post the beginning balances and the events to the accounts.
d. Prepare an income statement, a statement of changes in stockholders' equity, a balance sheet, and a statement of cash flows.
e. Record and post the closing entries, and prepare an after-closing trial balance.

L.O. 6

Problem 4-26A *Using common size income statements to make comparisons*

The following income statements were drawn from the annual reports of Hall Company:

	2005*	2006*
Net Sales	$302,900	$370,500
Cost of Goods Sold	(217,400)	(264,700)
Gross Margin	85,500	105,800
Less: Operating Expense		
Selling and Administrative Expenses	(40,800)	(58,210)
Net Income	$ 44,700	$ 47,590

*All dollar amounts are reported in thousands.

The president's message in the company's annual report stated that the company had implemented a strategy to increase market share by spending more on advertising. The president indicated that prices held steady and sales grew as expected. Write a memo indicating whether you agree with the president's statements. How has the strategy affected profitability? Support your answer by measuring growth in sales and selling expenses. Also prepare common size income statements and make appropriate references to the differences between 2005 and 2006.

Problem 4-27A ***Preparing a schedule of cost of goods sold and multistep and single-step income statements: periodic system (Appendix)***

L.O. 4, 8

excel

mhhe.com/edmonds2007

CHECK FIGURES

a. Cost of Goods Available for Sale: $150,800

b. Net Income: $49,050

The following account titles and balances were taken from the adjusted trial balance of Scoggins Sales Co. at December 31, 2004. The company uses the periodic inventory method.

Account Title	Balance
Advertising Expense	$ 12,800
Supplies Expense	10,700
Interest Expense	150
Merchandise Inventory, January 1	18,000
Merchandise Inventory, December 31	20,100
Miscellaneous Expense	800
Purchases	130,000
Purchase Returns and Allowances	2,700
Rent Expense	14,000
Salaries Expense	53,000
Sales	290,000
Sales Returns and Allowances	8,000
Transportation-in	5,500
Transportation-out	10,800

Required

a. Prepare a schedule to determine the amount of cost of goods sold.
b. Prepare a multistep income statement.
c. Prepare a single-step income statement.

Problem 4-28A ***Comprehensive cycle problem: periodic system (Appendix)***

L.O. 8

excel

mhhe.com/edmonds2007

CHECK FIGURES

b. Ending Cash: $100,640

c. Cost of Goods Sold: $50,810

The following trial balance pertains to Reeves Hardware as of January 1, 2005:

Account Title	Debit	Credit
Cash	$ 74,000	
Accounts Receivable	9,000	
Merchandise Inventory	60,000	
Accounts Payable		$ 5,000
Common Stock		70,000
Retained Earnings		68,000
Total	$143,000	$143,000

The following events occurred in 2005. Assume that Reeves Hardware uses the periodic inventory system.

1. Purchased land for $25,000 cash.
2. Purchased merchandise on account for $23,000, terms 2/10, n/30.
3. The merchandise purchased was shipped FOB shipping point for $230 cash.
4. Returned $2,000 of defective merchandise purchased in Event 2.
5. Sold merchandise for $27,000 cash.
6. Sold merchandise on account for $50,000, terms 1/20, n/30.
7. Paid cash within the discount period on accounts payable due on merchandise purchased in Event 2.
8. Paid $1,200 cash for selling expenses.

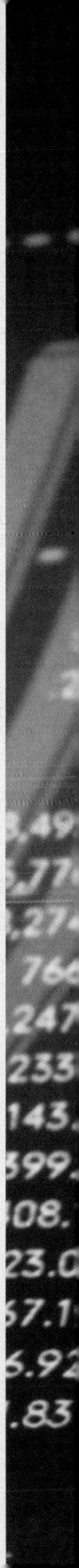

9. Collected part of the balance due from accounts receivable in Event 6. Collections were made after the discount period on $12,000 list amount of sales on account. Collections were made during the discount period on $35,000 list amount of sales on account.
10. Performed a physical count indicating that $30,000 of inventory was on hand at the end of the accounting period.

Required

a. Record these transactions in a general journal.
b. Post the transactions to ledger T-accounts.
c. Prepare a schedule of cost of goods sold, an income statement, a statement of changes in stockholders' equity, a balance sheet, and a statement of cash flows for 2005.

EXERCISES—SERIES B

When the instructions for *any* exercise or problem call for the preparation of an income statement, use the *multistep format* unless otherwise indicated.

L.O. 1, 2

Exercise 4-1B *Comparing a merchandising company with a service company*

The following information is available for two different types of businesses for the 2006 accounting period. Moore CPAs is a service business that provides accounting services to small businesses. Campus Sports Shop is a merchandising business that sells diving gear to college students.

Data for Moore CPAs

1. Received $20,000 cash from the issue of common stock to start the business.
2. Provided $15,000 of services to customers and collected $15,000 cash.
3. Paid salary expense of $10,000.

Data for Campus Sports Shop

1. Received $20,000 cash from the issue of common stock to start the business.
2. Purchased $12,500 inventory for cash.
3. Inventory costing $8,200 was sold for $15,000 cash.
4. Paid $1,800 cash for operating expenses.

Required

a. Prepare an income statement, balance sheet, and statement of cash flows for each of the companies.
b. Which of the two businesses would have product costs? Why?
c. Why does Moore CPAs not compute gross margin on its income statement?
d. Compare the assets of both companies. What assets do they have in common? What assets are different? Why?

L.O. 2

Exercise 4-2B *Effect of inventory transactions on journals, ledgers, and financial statements: perpetual system*

Troy Lane started a small merchandising business in 2005. The business experienced the following events during its first year of operation. Assume that Lane uses the perpetual inventory system.

1. Acquired $20,000 cash from the issue of common stock.
2. Purchased inventory for $15,000 cash.
3. Sold inventory costing $10,000 for $16,000 cash.

Required

a. Record the events in general journal format.
b. Post the entries to T-accounts.
c. Record the events in a statements model like the one shown below.

Assets			=	Equity			Rev.	−	Exp.	=	Net Inc.	Cash Flow
Cash	+	Inv.	=	Com. Stk.	+	Ret. Earn.						

d. Prepare an income statement for 2005 (use the multistep format).

e. What is the amount of net cash flow from operating activities for 2005?

Exercise 4-3B *Effect of inventory transactions on the income statement and statement of cash flows: perpetual system*

L.O. 2

During 2005, Bond Merchandising Company purchased $30,000 of inventory on account. Bond sold inventory on account that cost $25,000 for $35,000. Cash payments on accounts payable were $20,000. There was $22,000 cash collected from accounts receivable. Bond also paid $7,000 cash for operating expenses. Assume that Bond started the accounting period with $28,000 in both cash and common stock.

Required

a. Identify the events described in the preceding paragraph and record them in a horizontal statements model like the following one:

Assets					=	Liab.	+	Equity			Rev.	−	Exp.	=	Net Inc.	Cash Flow
Cash	+	Accts. Rec.	+	Inv.	=	Accts. Pay.	+	Com. Stk.	+	Ret. Earn.						
28,000	+	NA	+	NA	=	NA	+	28,000	+	NA	NA	−	NA	=	NA	NA

b. What is the balance of accounts receivable at the end of 2005?

c. What is the balance of accounts payable at the end of 2005?

d. What are the amounts of gross margin and net income for 2005?

e. Determine the amount of net cash flow from operating activities.

f. Explain why net income and retained earnings are the same for Bond. Normally would these amounts be the same? Why or why not?

Exercise 4-4B *Recording inventory transactions in the general journal and posting entries to T-accounts: perpetual system*

L.O. 2

Toro Clothing experienced the following events during 2006, its first year of operation:

1. Acquired $7,000 cash from the issue of common stock.
2. Purchased inventory for $4,000 cash.
3. Sold inventory costing $3,000 for $4,500 cash.
4. Paid $400 for advertising expense.

Required

a. Record the general journal entries for the preceding transactions.

b. Post each of the entries to T-accounts.

c. Prepare a trial balance to prove the equality of debits and credits.

d. Record the events in a statements model like the one shown below.

Assets			=	Equity			Rev.	−	Exp.	=	Net Inc.	Cash Flow
Cash	+	Inv.	=	Com. Stk.	+	Ret. Earn.						

Exercise 4-5B *Understanding the freight terms FOB shipping point and FOB destination*

L.O. 3

Required

For each of the following events, indicate whether the freight terms are FOB destination or FOB shipping point.

a. Sold merchandise and paid the freight costs.

b. Purchased merchandise and paid the freight costs.

c. Sold merchandise and the buyer paid the freight costs.

d. Purchased merchandise and the seller paid the freight costs.

L.O. 2, 3

Exercise 4-6B ***Effect of purchase returns and allowances and freight costs on the journal, ledger, and financial statements: perpetual system***

The trial balance for The Garden Shop as of January 1, 2005, follows:

Account Titles	Debit	Credit
Cash	$32,000	
Inventory	12,000	
Common Stock		$40,000
Retained Earnings		4,000
Total	$44,000	$44,000

The following events affected the company during the 2005 accounting period:

1. Purchased merchandise on account that cost $22,000.
2. Purchased goods in Event 1 FOB shipping point with freight cost of $1,000 cash.
3. Returned $3,200 of damaged merchandise for credit on account.
4. Agreed to keep other damaged merchandise for which the company received a $1,400 allowance.
5. Sold merchandise that cost $16,000 for $31,000 cash.
6. Delivered merchandise to customers in Event 5 under terms FOB destination with freight costs amounting to $800 cash.
7. Paid $15,000 on the merchandise purchased in Event 1.

Required

a. Record the events in general journal format.
b. Open general ledger T-accounts with the appropriate beginning balances, and post the journal entries to the T-accounts.
c. Prepare an income statement, balance sheet, and statement of cash flows.
d. Explain why a difference does or does not exist between net income and net cash flow from operating activities.

L.O. 2, 3

Exercise 4-7B ***Accounting for product costs: perpetual inventory system***

Which of the following would be debited to the Inventory account for a merchandising business using the perpetual inventory system?

Required

a. Purchase of inventory.
b. Allowance received for damaged inventory.
c. Transportation-in.
d. Cash discount given on goods sold.
e. Transportation-out.
f. Purchase of office supplies.

L.O. 1, 2, 3

Exercise 4-8B ***Effect of product cost and period cost: horizontal statements model***

The Health Food Store experienced the following events for the 2006 accounting period:

1. Acquired $10,000 cash from the issue of common stock.
2. Purchased $56,000 of inventory on account.
3. Received goods purchased in Event 2 FOB shipping point; freight cost of $600 paid in cash.
4. Sold inventory on account that cost $33,000 for $57,400.
5. Freight cost on the goods sold in Event 4 was $420. The goods were shipped FOB destination. Cash was paid for the freight cost.
6. Customer in Event 4 returned $2,000 worth of goods that had a cost of $1,400.
7. Collected $47,000 cash from accounts receivable.

8. Paid $40,000 cash on accounts payable.
9. Paid $1,100 for advertising expense.
10. Paid $2,000 cash for insurance expense.

Required

a. Which of these events result in period (selling and administrative) costs? Which result in product costs? If neither, label the transaction NA.

b. Record each event in a horizontal statements model like the following one. The first event is recorded as an example.

Assets					=	Liab.	+	Equity			Rev. − Exp. = Net Inc.	Cash Flow
Cash	+	Accts. Rec.	+	Inv.	=	Accts. Pay.	+	Com. Stk.	+	Ret. Earn.		
10,000	+	NA	+	NA	=	NA	+	10,000	+	NA	NA − NA = NA	10,000 FA

Exercise 4-9B *Cash discounts and purchase returns* L.O. 3

On April 6, 2007, Ming Furnishings purchased $6,200 of merchandise from Exchange Emporium, terms 2/10, n/45. On April 5, Ming returned $600 of the merchandise to the Exchange Emporium for credit. Ming paid cash for the merchandise on April 15, 2007.

Required

a. What is the amount that Ming must pay the Exchange Emporium on April 15?

b. Record the events in a horizontal statements model like the following one.

Assets			=	Liab.	+	Equity			Rev. − Exp. = Net Inc.	Cash Flow
Cash	+	Inv.	=	Accts. Pay.	+	Com. Stk.	+	Ret. Earn.		

c. How much must Ming pay for the merchandise purchased if the payment is not made until April 20, 2007?

d. Record the payment in Event *c* in a horizontal statements model like the one above.

e. Why would Ming want to pay for the merchandise by April 15?

Exercise 4-10B *Effect of sales returns and allowances and freight costs on the journal, ledger, and financial statements: perpetual system* L.O. 2, 3

Rainey Company began the 2006 accounting period with $7,000 cash, $38,000 inventory, $25,000 common stock, and $20,000 retained earnings. During 2006, Rainey experienced the following events:

1. Sold merchandise costing $32,000 for $50,000 on account to Mitchell's Furniture Store.
2. Delivered the goods to Mitchell under terms FOB destination. Freight costs were $500 cash.
3. Received returned damaged goods from Mitchell. The goods cost Rainey $3,000 and were sold to Mitchell for $4,000.
4. Granted Mitchell a $2,000 allowance for other damaged goods that Mitchell agreed to keep.
5. Collected partial payment of $30,000 cash from accounts receivable.

Required

a. Record the events in general journal format.

b. Open general ledger T-accounts with the appropriate beginning balances and post the journal entries to the T-accounts.

c. Record the events in a statements model like the one shown below.

Assets					=	Equity			Rev. − Exp. = Net Inc.	Cash Flow
Cash	+	Accts. Rec.	+	Inv.	=	Com. Stk.	+	Ret. Earn.		

d. Prepare an income statement, balance sheet, and statement of cash flows.

e. Why would Mitchell agree to keep the damaged goods? Who benefits more?

L.O. 2, 3

Exercise 4-11B *Effect of cash discounts on the journal, ledger, and financial statements: perpetual system*

Batte Supply Inc. was started in 2006 and experienced the following accounting events during its first year of operation:

1. Started business when it acquired $15,000 cash from the issue of common stock.
2. Purchased merchandise with a list price of $9,000 on account, terms 2/10, n/30.
3. Paid off the account payable but not within the discount period.
4. Sold inventory on account with a list price of $7,500 that had a cost of $5,000. Credit terms were 1/20, n/30.
5. Collected cash from the account receivable but not within the discount period.
6. Paid $1,900 cash for operating expenses.

Required

a. Record the transactions in general journal format.

b. Open general ledger T-accounts, and post the journal entries to the T-accounts.

c. Record the events in a horizontal statements model like the following one.

Assets					=	Liab.	+	Equity			Rev. − Exp. = Net Inc.	Cash Flow
Cash	+	Accts. Rec.	+	Inv.	=	Accts. Pay.	+	Com. Stk.	+	Ret. Earn.		

d. What is the amount of gross margin for the period? What is the net income for the period?

e. Why would Batte sell merchandise with the terms 1/20, n/30?

f. What do the terms 2/10, n/30 mean to Batte?

L.O. 2, 3

Exercise 4-12B *Effect of inventory transactions on the financial statements: comprehensive exercise with sales and purchase returns and discounts*

Fuller Merchandise Company had the following balances in its accounts on January 1, 2006:

Cash	$20,000
Merchandise Inventory	15,000
Common Stock	25,000
Retained Earnings	10,000

Fuller experienced the following events during 2006:

1. Purchased merchandise inventory on account for $45,000, terms 2/10, n/30.
2. Paid freight of $600 on the merchandise purchased.
3. Sold merchandise inventory that cost $23,000 for a list price of $42,000 on account, terms 1/10, n/45.
4. Returned $1,500 of damaged merchandise purchased in Event 1.
5. Agreed to keep other merchandise that was slightly damaged and was granted an allowance of $500.
6. The customer in Event 3 returned merchandise that had a list price of $6,000 and a cost of $3,400.
7. Collected the balance of accounts receivable within the discount period.
8. Paid for one-half of the accounts payable within the discount period.
9. Paid $4,300 cash for selling and administrative expenses.
10. Paid the balance of accounts payable (not within the discount period).

Required

a. Record each of these events in general journal format.

b. Open general ledger T-accounts. Post the beginning balances and the events to the accounts.

c. Prepare a trial balance.
d. Prepare an income statement, balance sheet, and a statement of cash flows.

Exercise 4-13B *Effect of inventory losses: perpetual system* L.O. 2, 5

Dodd Traders experienced the following events during 2005, its first year of operation:

1. Started the business when it acquired $20,000 cash from the issue of common stock.
2. Paid $14,000 cash to purchase inventory.
3. Sold inventory costing $10,750 for $17,100 cash.
4. Physically counted inventory; had inventory of $2,900 on hand at the end of the accounting period.

Required

a. Open appropriate ledger T-accounts, and record the events in the accounts.
b. Prepare an income statement and balance sheet.
c. If all purchases and sales of merchandise are reflected as increases or decreases to the merchandise inventory account, why is it necessary for management to even bother to take a physical count of goods on hand (ending inventory) at the end of the year?

Exercise 4-14B *Determining the effect of inventory transactions on the accounting equation: perpetual system* L.O. 2

Marshall Company experienced the following events:

1. Purchased merchandise inventory on account.
2. Purchased merchandise inventory for cash.
3. Sold merchandise inventory on account. Label the revenue recognition 3a and the expense recognition 3b.
4. Returned merchandise purchased on account.
5. Sold merchandise inventory for cash. Label the revenue recognition 5a and the expense recognition 5b.
6. Paid cash on accounts payable within the discount period.
7. Paid cash for selling and administrative expenses.
8. Collected cash from accounts receivable not within the discount period.
9. Paid cash for transportation-out.
10. Paid cash for transportation-in.

Required

Identify each event as asset source (AS), asset use (AU), asset exchange (AE), or claims exchange (CE). Also explain how each event affects the financial statements by placing a + for increase, − for decrease, or NA for not affected under each of the components in the following statements model. Assume the company uses the perpetual inventory system. The first event is recorded as an example.

Event No.	Event Type	Assets	=	Liab.	+	Equity	Rev.	−	Exp.	=	Net Inc.	Cash Flow
1	AS	+	=	+	+	NA	NA	−	NA	=	NA	NA

Exercise 4-15B *Single-step and multistep income statements* L.O. 4

The following information was taken from the accounts of North Street Market, a small grocery store. The accounts are listed in alphabetical order, and all have normal balances.

Accounts Payable	$600
Accounts Receivable	700
Advertising Expense	400
Cash	820
Common Stock	400
Cost of Goods Sold	900

continued

Merchandise Inventory	300
Prepaid Rent	80
Retained Earnings	910
Sales Revenue	1,600
Salaries Expense	260
Supplies Expense	50

Required

First, prepare an income statement using the single-step approach. Then prepare another income statement using the multistep approach.

L.O. 2

Exercise 4-16B *Determining the cost of financing inventory*

Jay Xie started J's Appliances, a home appliance merchandising business. J's uses the perpetual system. The company experienced the following events during the first year of operation:

1. On January 1, 2006, started the business when Xie issued common stock for $100,000 cash.
2. Paid $80,000 cash to purchase inventory.
3. Sold appliances that cost $36,000 for $68,000 on account.
4. Collected $28,000 cash from accounts receivable.
5. Paid $10,000 for operating expenses.

Required

a. Record the transactions in general journal format.
b. Open general ledger T-accounts, and post the journal entries to the T-accounts.
c. Prepare an income statement, balance sheet, and statement of cash flows.
d. Since J's earned $68,000 of sales revenue, Xie will recover a large part of his investment in the first year. Do you agree? Explain.

L.O. 3

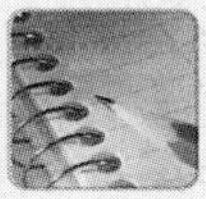

Exercise 4-17B *Financing inventory and cash discounts*

Tarius Henry came to you for advice. He has just purchased a large amount of inventory with the terms 1/10, n/45. The amount of the invoice is $65,000. He is currently short on cash but has good credit and so can borrow the money at the appropriate time to take advantage of the discount. The annual interest rate is 7 percent if he decides to borrow the money. Henry is sure he will have the necessary cash by the due date of the invoice (but not by the discount date).

Required

a. For how long would Henry need to borrow the money to take advantage of the discount?
b. How much money would Henry need to borrow?
c. What action would you recommend Henry take? Explain.

L.O. 8

Exercise 4-18B *Effect of inventory transactions on the income statement and balance sheet: periodic system (Appendix)*

Nat Briscoe owns Nat's Sporting Goods. At the beginning of the year, Nat's had $4,200 in inventory. During the year, Nat's purchased inventory that cost $21,000. At the end of the year, inventory on hand amounted to $8,800.

Required

Calculate the following:

a. Cost of goods available for sale during the year.
b. Cost of goods sold for the year.
c. Amount of inventory Nat's would report on the year-end balance sheet.

L.O. 8

Exercise 4-19B *Determining cost of goods sold: periodic system (Appendix)*

Hill Antiques uses the periodic inventory system to account for its inventory transactions. The following account titles and balances were drawn from Hill's records: beginning balance in inventory, $12,000; purchases, $150,000; purchase returns and allowances, $5,000; sales, $400,000; sales returns and allowances, $3,000; freight-in, $1,000; and operating expenses, $26,000. A physical count indicated that $15,000 of merchandise was on hand at the end of the accounting period.

Required

a. Prepare a schedule of cost of goods sold.
b. Prepare a multistep income statement.

Exercise 4-20B ***Basic transactions: periodic system, single cycle (Appendix)*** L.O. 8

The following transactions apply to Kay's Specialties Shop for 2005, its first year of operations:

1. Acquired $70,000 cash from the issue of common stock.
2. Acquired $8,000 of gift merchandise from Kay Pierce, the owner, who had acquired the merchandise prior to opening the shop. Issued common stock to Kay in exchange for the merchandise.
3. Purchased $90,000 of inventory on account.
4. Paid $6,000 for radio ads.
5. Sold inventory for $160,000 cash.
6. Paid $20,000 in salary to a part-time salesperson.
7. Paid $75,000 on accounts payable (see Event 3).
8. Physically counted inventory, which indicated that $20,000 of inventory was on hand at the end of the accounting period.

Required

a. Record each of these transactions in general journal form using the periodic method.
b. Post each of the transactions to ledger T-accounts.
c. Prepare an income statement, statement of changes in stockholders' equity, balance sheet, and statement of cash flows for 2005.
d. Prepare the necessary closing entries at the end of 2005, and post them to the appropriate T-accounts.
e. Prepare an after-closing trial balance.
f. Give an example of a business that may want to use the periodic system. Give an example of a business that may use the perpetual system.
g. Give some examples of assets other than cash that are commonly contributed to a business in exchange for stock.

PROBLEMS—SERIES B

Problem 4-21B ***Basic transactions for three accounting cycles: perpetual system*** L.O. 2

Carol's Flower Company was started in 2005 when it acquired $80,000 cash from the issue of common stock. The following data summarize the company's first three years' operating activities. Assume that all transactions were cash transactions.

	2005	2006	2007
Purchases of Inventory	$ 60,000	$ 90,000	$130,000
Sales	102,000	146,000	220,000
Cost of Goods Sold	54,000	78,000	140,000
Selling and Administrative Expenses	40,000	52,000	72,000

Required

Prepare an income statement (use multistep format) and balance sheet for each fiscal year. (*Hint:* Record the transaction data for each accounting period in T-accounts before preparing the statements for that year.)

Problem 4-22B ***Identifying product and period costs*** L.O. 1

Required

Indicate whether each of the following costs is a product cost or a period (selling and administrative) cost.

a. Transportation-in.
b. Insurance on the office building.
c. Office supplies.
d. Costs incurred to improve the quality of goods available for sale.
e. Goods purchased for resale.
f. Salaries of salespersons.
g. Advertising costs.
h. Transportation-out.
i. Salary of the company president.

L.O. 3

Problem 4-23B *Identifying freight costs*

Required

For each of the following events, determine the amount of freight paid by The Book Shop. Also indicate whether the freight cost would be classified as a product or period (selling and administrative) cost.

a. Purchased additional merchandise with freight costs of $300. The merchandise was shipped FOB shipping point.
b. Shipped merchandise to customers, freight terms FOB shipping point. The freight costs were $100.
c. Purchased inventory with freight costs of $1,000. The goods were shipped FOB destination.
d. Sold merchandise to a customer. Freight costs were $500. The goods were shipped FOB destination.

L.O. 2, 3

Problem 4-24B *Effect of purchase returns and allowances and purchase discounts on the financial statements: perpetual system*

The following transactions were completed by The Jewel Shop in May 2008.

May	1	Acquired $100,000 cash from the issue of common stock.
	1	Purchased $60,000 of merchandise on account with terms 2/10, n/30.
	2	Paid $1,200 cash for freight to obtain merchandise purchased on May 1.
	4	Sold merchandise that cost $44,000 for $74,000 to customers on account.
	4	Returned $5,000 of defective merchandise from the May 1 purchase for credit on account.
	10	Paid cash for one-half of the balance due on the merchandise purchased on May 1.
	13	Received cash from customers of May 4 sale in settlement of the account balance.
	31	Paid the balance due on the merchandise purchased on May 1.
	31	Paid selling expenses of $7,800.

Required

a. Record each event in a horizontal statements model like the following one. The first event is recorded as an example.

Assets							=	Liab.	+	Equity			Rev.	−	Exp.	=	Net Inc.	Cash Flow
Cash	+	Accts. Rec.	+	Inv.			=	Accts. Pay.	+	Com. Stk.	+	Ret. Earn.						
100,000	+	NA	+	NA			=	NA	+	100,000	+	NA	NA	−	NA	=	NA	100,000 FA

b. Record each of the transactions in general journal form.
c. Post each of the transactions to general ledger T-accounts.
d. Prepare an income statement for the month ending May 31.
e. Prepare a statement of cash flows for the month ending May 31.
f. Explain why there is a difference between net income and cash flow from operating activities.

L.O. 2, 3, 5

Problem 4-25B *Comprehensive cycle problem: perpetual system*

At the beginning of 2006, M & M Enterprises had the following balances in its accounts:

Cash	$8,400
Inventory	2,000
Common Stock	8,000
Retained Earnings	2,400

During 2006, M & M Enterprises experienced the following events:

1. Purchased inventory with a list price of $5,600 on account from Smoot Company under terms 2/10, n/30. The merchandise was delivered FOB shipping point. Freight costs of $500 were paid in cash.
2. Returned inventory with a list price of $400 because the inventory had been damaged in transit. The freight company agreed to pay the return freight cost.
3. Paid the amount due on its account payable to Smoot Company but not within the cash discount period.
4. Sold inventory that had cost $6,000 for a list price of $9,000. The sale was on account under terms 2/10, n/45.
5. Received returned merchandise from a customer. The merchandise had originally cost $520 and had been sold to the customer for $840 cash. The customer was paid $840 cash for the returned merchandise.
6. Delivered goods in Event 4 FOB destination. Freight costs of $600 were paid in cash.
7. Collected the amount due on accounts receivable but not within the discount period.
8. Took a physical count indicating that $1,800 of inventory was on hand at the end of the accounting period.

Required

a. Identify each of these events as asset source (AS), asset use (AU), asset exchange (AE), or claims exchange (CE). Also explain how each event affects the financial statements by placing a + for increase, − for decrease, or NA for not affected under each of the components in the following statements model. Assume that the perpetual inventory method is used. When an event has more than one part, use letters to distinguish the effects of each part. The first event is recorded as an example.

Event No.	Event Type	Assets	=	Liab.	+	Equity	Rev.	−	Exp.	=	Net Inc.	Cash Flow
1a	AS	+	=	+	+	NA	NA	−	NA	=	NA	NA
1b	AE	+ −	=	NA	+	NA	NA	−	NA	=	NA	− OA

b. Record the events in general journal format.

c. Open ledger T-accounts and post the beginning balances and the events to the accounts.

d. Prepare an income statement, statement of changes in stockholders' equity, balance sheet, and statement of cash flows.

e. Record and post the closing entries, and prepare an after-closing trial balance.

Problem 4-26B ***Using common size income statements to make comparisons*** L.O. 6

The following income statements were drawn from the annual reports of Madison Company:

	2006*	2007*
Net Sales	$74,507	$80,000
Cost of Goods Sold	(28,317)	(34,400)
Gross Margin	46,190	45,600
Less: Operating Expenses		
Selling and Administrative Expenses	(43,210)	(40,800)
Net Income	$ 2,980	$ 4,800

*All figures are reported in thousands of dollars.

Required

The president's message in the company's annual report stated that the company increased profitability by decreasing prices and controlling operating expenses. Write a memorandum indicating whether you agree with the president's statement. Support your answer by preparing common size income statements and making appropriate references to the differences between 2006 and 2007.

L.O. 4, 8

Problem 4-27B ***Preparing schedule of cost of goods sold and multistep and single-step income statements: periodic system (Appendix)***

The following account titles and balances were taken from the adjusted trial balance of Huggins Farm Co. for 2006. The company uses the periodic inventory system.

Account Title	Balance
Sales Returns and Allowances	$ 2,250
Supplies Expense	3,700
Miscellaneous Expense	400
Transportation-out	600
Sales	69,750
Advertising Expense	2,750
Salaries Expense	7,900
Transportation-in	1,725
Purchases	40,000
Interest Expense	360
Merchandise Inventory, January 1	5,075
Rent Expense	5,000
Merchandise Inventory, December 31	4,050
Purchase Returns and Allowances	1,450

Required

a. Prepare a schedule to determine the amount of cost of goods sold.

b. Prepare a multistep income statement.

c. Prepare a single-step income statement.

L.O. 8

Problem 4-28B ***Comprehensive cycle problem: periodic system (Appendix)***

The following trial balance pertains to John's Jungle as of January 1, 2008:

Account Title	Debit	Credit
Cash	$ 86,000	
Accounts Receivable	4,000	
Merchandise Inventory	50,000	
Accounts Payable		$ 4,000
Common Stock		43,000
Retained Earnings		93,000
Totals	$140,000	$140,000

The following events occurred in 2008. Assume that John's uses the periodic inventory method.

1. Purchased land for $50,000 cash.
2. Purchased merchandise on account for $126,000, terms 1/10, n/45.
3. Paid freight of $1,000 cash on merchandise purchased FOB shipping point.
4. Returned $3,600 of defective merchandise purchased in Event 2.
5. Sold merchandise for $86,000 cash.
6. Sold merchandise on account for $120,000, terms 2/10, n/30.
7. Paid cash within the discount period on accounts payable due on merchandise purchased in Event 2.
8. Paid $11,600 cash for selling expenses.
9. Collected part of the balance due from accounts receivable in Event 6. Collections were made after the discount period on $60,000 list amount of sales on account. Collections were made during the discount period on $50,000 list amount of sales on account.
10. A physical count indicated that $27,600 of inventory was on hand at the end of the accounting period.

Required

a. Record these transactions in a general journal.

b. Post the transactions to ledger T-accounts.

c. Prepare a schedule of costs of goods sold, an income statement, statement of changes in stockholders' equity, balance sheet, and statement of cash flows for 2008.

ANALYZE, THINK, COMMUNICATE

ATC 4-1 Business Applications Case *Understanding real world annual reports*

Required

a. Use the Topps Company's annual report in Appendix B to answer the following questions.

The Topps Company, Inc.

(1) What was Topps' gross margin percentage for 2003 and 2002?

(2) What was Topps' return on sales percentage for 2003 and 2002?

(3) Topps' Gross Profit on Sales was about $12 million lower in 2003 than in 2002 and this caused its Net Income to be lower as well. However, its gross margin percentage also decreased in 2003. Ignoring taxes, how much higher would its 2003 net income have been if the gross margin percentage in 2003 had been the same as for 2002?

b. Use the Harley-Davidson's annual report that came with this book to answer the following questions.

Harley-Davidson, Inc.

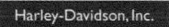

(1) What was Harley-Davidson's gross margin percentage for 2003 and 2002?

(2) What was Harley-Davidson's return on sales percentage for 2003 and 2002?

(3) Harley-Davidson's gross margin percentage increased during 2003 compared to 2002. The MD&A section of its annual report explains the reasons this occurred. What are these reasons?

ATC 4-2 Group Exercise *Multistep income statement*

The following quarterly information is given for Raybon for the year ended 2002 (amounts shown are in millions).

	First Quarter	Second Quarter	Third Quarter	Fourth Quarter
Net Sales	$736.0	$717.4	$815.2	$620.1
Gross Margin	461.9	440.3	525.3	252.3
Net Income	37.1	24.6	38.6	31.4

Required

a. Divide the class into groups and organize the groups into four sections. Assign each section financial information for one of the quarters.

(1) Each group should compute the cost of goods sold and operating expenses for the specific quarter assigned to its section and prepare a multistep income statement for the quarter.

(2) Each group should compute the gross margin percentage and cost of goods sold percentage for its specific quarter.

(3) Have a representative of each group put that quarter's sales, cost of goods sold percentage, and gross margin percentage on the board.

Class Discussion

b. Have the class discuss the change in each of these items from quarter to quarter and explain why the change might have occurred. Which was the best quarter and why?

ATC 4-3 Real-World Case *Identifying companies based on financial statement information*

Presented here is selected information from the 2002 fiscal-year reports of four companies. The four companies, in alphabetical order, are Caterpillar, Inc., a manufacturer of heavy machinery; Oracle

Corporation, a company that develops software; Peet's Coffee & Tea, a company that sells coffee products; and Tiffany & Company, a company that operates high-end jewelry and department stores. The data for the companies, presented in the order of the amount of their sales in millions of dollars, follow:

	A	B	C	D
Sales	$18,648	$ 9,673	$1,706.6	$104.1
Cost of goods sold	14,709	2,406	695.2	48.1
Net earnings	798	2,224	189.9	4.7
Inventory	2,763	0	732.1	11.0
Accounts receivable	2,838	2,036	113.1	2.2
Total assets	32,851	10,800	1,923.6	95.1

Required

Based on these financial data and your knowledge and assumptions about the nature of the businesses that the companies operate, determine which data relate to which companies. Write a memorandum explaining your decisions. Include a discussion of which ratios you used in your analysis, and show the computations of these ratios in your memorandum.

ATC 4-4 Business Applications Case *Using ratios to make comparisons*

The following income statements were drawn from the annual reports of Design Company and Royal Company.

	Design	Royal
Net Sales	$95,700	$52,300
Cost of Goods Sold	68,900	31,400
Gross Margin	26,800	20,900
Less: Selling and Admin. Expenses	22,000	18,800
Net Income	$ 4,800	$ 2,100

*All figures are reported in thousands of dollars

Required

a. One of the companies is a high-end retailer that operates in exclusive shopping malls. The other operates discount stores located in low-cost stand-alone buildings. Identify the high-end retailer and the discounter. Support your answer with appropriate ratios.

b. If Design and Royal have equity of $40,000 and $21,000, respectively, which company is the more profitable?

ATC 4-5 Business Applications Case *Using common size statements and ratios to make comparisons*

At the end of 2006, the following information is available for Kinlaw and Parker companies:

	Kinlaw	Parker
Sales	$2,000	$2,000,000
Cost of Goods Sold	1,400	1,200,000
Selling and Administrative Expenses	520	640,000
Total Assets	2,500	2,500,000
Stockholders' Equity	750	730,000

Required

a. Prepare common size income statements for each company.

b. Compute the return on assets and return on equity for each company.

c. Which company is more profitable from the stockholders' perspective?

d. One company is a high-end retailer, and the other operates a discount store. Which is the discounter? Support your selection by referring to appropriate ratios.

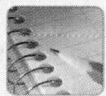

ATC 4-6 Written Assignment, Critical Thinking *Effect of sales returns on financial statements*

Bell Farm and Garden Equipment reported the following information for 2005:

Net sales of equipment	$2,450,567
Other income	6,786
Cost of goods sold	1,425,990
Selling, general, and administrative expense	325,965
Net operating income	$ 705,398

Selected information from the balance sheet as of December 31, 2005, follows:

Cash and Marketable Securities	$113,545
Inventory	248,600
Accounts Receivable	82,462
Property, Plant, and Equipment—net	335,890
Other Assets	5,410
Total Assets	$785,907

Assume that a major customer returned a large order to Bell on December 31, 2005. The amount of the sale had been $146,800 with a cost of sales of $94,623. The return was recorded in the books on January 1, 2006. The company president does not want to correct the books. He argues that it makes no difference as to whether the return is recorded in 2005 or 2006. Either way, the return has been duly recognized.

Required

a. Assume that you are the CFO for Bell Farm and Garden Equipment Co. Write a memo to the president explaining how omitting the entry on December 31, 2005, could cause the financial statements to be misleading to investors and creditors. Explain how omitting the return from the customer would affect net income and the balance sheet.

b. Why might the president want to record the return on January 1, 2006, instead of December 31, 2005?

c. Would the failure to record the customer return violate the AICPA Code of Professional Conduct? (See Exhibit 1–7 in Chapter 1.)

d. If the president of the company refuses to correct the financial statements, what action should you take?

ATC 4-7 Ethical Dilemma *Wait until I get mine*

Ada Fontanez is the president of a large company that owns a chain of athletic shoe stores. The company was in dire financial condition when she was hired three years ago. To motivate Fontanez, the board of directors included a bonus plan as part of her compensation package. According to her employment contract, on January 15 of each year, Fontanez is paid a cash bonus equal to 5 percent of the amount of net income reported on the preceding December 31 income statement. Fontanez was sufficiently motivated. Through her leadership, the company prospered. Her efforts were recognized throughout the industry, and she received numerous lucrative offers to leave the company. One offer was so enticing that she decided to change jobs. Her decision was made in late December 2005. However, she decided to resign effective February 1, 2006, to ensure the receipt of her January bonus. On December 31, 2005, the chief accountant, Walter Smith, advised Fontanez that the company had a sizable quantity of damaged inventory. A warehouse fire had resulted in smoke and water damage to approximately $600,000 of inventory. The warehouse was not insured, and the accountant recommended that the loss be recognized immediately. After examining the inventory, Fontanez argued that it could be sold as *damaged goods* to customers at reduced prices. She refused to allow the write-off the accountant recommended. She stated that so long as she is president, the inventory stays on the books at cost. She told the accountant that he could take up the matter with the new president in February.

Required

a. How would an immediate write-off of the damaged inventory affect the December 31, 2005, income statement, balance sheet, and statement of cash flows?

b. How would the write-off affect Fontanez's bonus?

c. If the new president is given the same bonus plan, how will Fontanez's refusal to recognize the loss affect his or her bonus?

d. Assuming that the damaged inventory is truly worthless, comment on the ethical implications of Fontanez's refusal to recognize the loss in the 2005 accounting period.

e. Assume that the damaged inventory is truly worthless and that you are Smith. How would you react to Fontanez's refusal to recognize the loss?

ATC 4-8 Research Assignment *Analyzing Alcoa's profit margins*

Using either Alcoa's most current Form 10-K or the company's annual report, answer the questions below. To obtain the Form 10-K you can use either the EDGAR system following the instructions in Appendix A, or the company's website. The company's annual report is available on its website.

Required

a. What was Alcoa's gross margin percentage for the most current year?

b. What was Alcoa's gross margin percentage for the previous year? Has it changed significantly?

c. What was Alcoa's return on sales percentage for the most current year?

d. What percentage of Alcoa's total sales for the most current year was from operations in the United States?

e. Comment on the appropriateness of comparing Alcoa's gross margin with that of Ford Motor Company. If Ford has a higher/lower margin, does that mean that Ford is a better managed company?

COMPREHENSIVE PROBLEM

The trial balance of Pacilio Security Services Inc. as of January 1, 2004, had the following normal balances:

Cash	$12,500
Accounts Receivable	3,500
Supplies	120
Prepaid Rent	1,000
Land	4,000
Unearned Revenue	900
Salaries Payable	1,000
Common Stock	8,000
Retained Earnings	11,220

In 2004, Pacilio Security Services decided to expand its business to sell security systems and offer 24-hour alarm monitoring services. It plans to phase out its current service of providing security personnel at various events. The following summary transactions occurred during 2004.

1. Paid the salaries payable from 2003.
2. Acquired an additional $42,000 cash from the issue of common stock.
3. Rented a larger building on May 1; paid $6,000 for 12 months' rent in advance.
4. Paid $800 cash for supplies to be used over the next several months by the business.
5. Purchased 50 alarm systems for resale at a list price of $12,245. The alarm systems were purchased on account with the terms 2/10, n/30.

6. Returned one of the alarm systems that had a list price of $245.
7. Installed 40 alarm systems during the year for a total sales amount of $20,000. The cost of these systems amounted to $9,600. $15,000 of the sales were on account and $5,000 were cash sales.
8. Paid the installers and other employees a total of $9,500 in salaries.
9. Sold $36,000 of monitoring services for the year. The services are billed to the customers each month.
10. Paid cash on accounts payable. The payment was made before the discount period expired. At the time of purchase, the inventory had a list price of $8,000 and a net price of $7,840.
11. Paid cash to settle additional accounts payable. The payment was made after the discount period expired. At the time of purchase, the inventory had a list price of $3,000 and a net price of $2,940.
12. Collected $43,000 of accounts receivable during the year.
13. Performed $12,000 of security services for area events; $9,000 was on account and $3,000 was for cash.
14. Paid advertising cost of $1,400 for the year.
15. Paid $1,100 for utilities expense for the year.
16. Paid a dividend of $12,000 to the shareholders.

Adjustment Information

17. Supplies of $150 were on hand at the end of the year.
18. Recognized the expired rent for the year.
19. Recognized the balance of the unearned revenue; cash was received in 2003.
20. Accrued salaries at December 31, 2004, were $1,500.

Required

a. Record the above transactions in general journal form. (Round amounts to the nearest dollar.)
b. Post the transactions to T-accounts.
c. Prepare a trial balance.
d. Prepare an income statement, statement of changes in stockholders' equity, balance sheet, and statement of cash flows.
e. Close the temporary accounts to retained earnings.
f. Post the closing entries to the T-accounts and prepare an after-closing trial balance.

CHAPTER 5

Accounting for Inventories

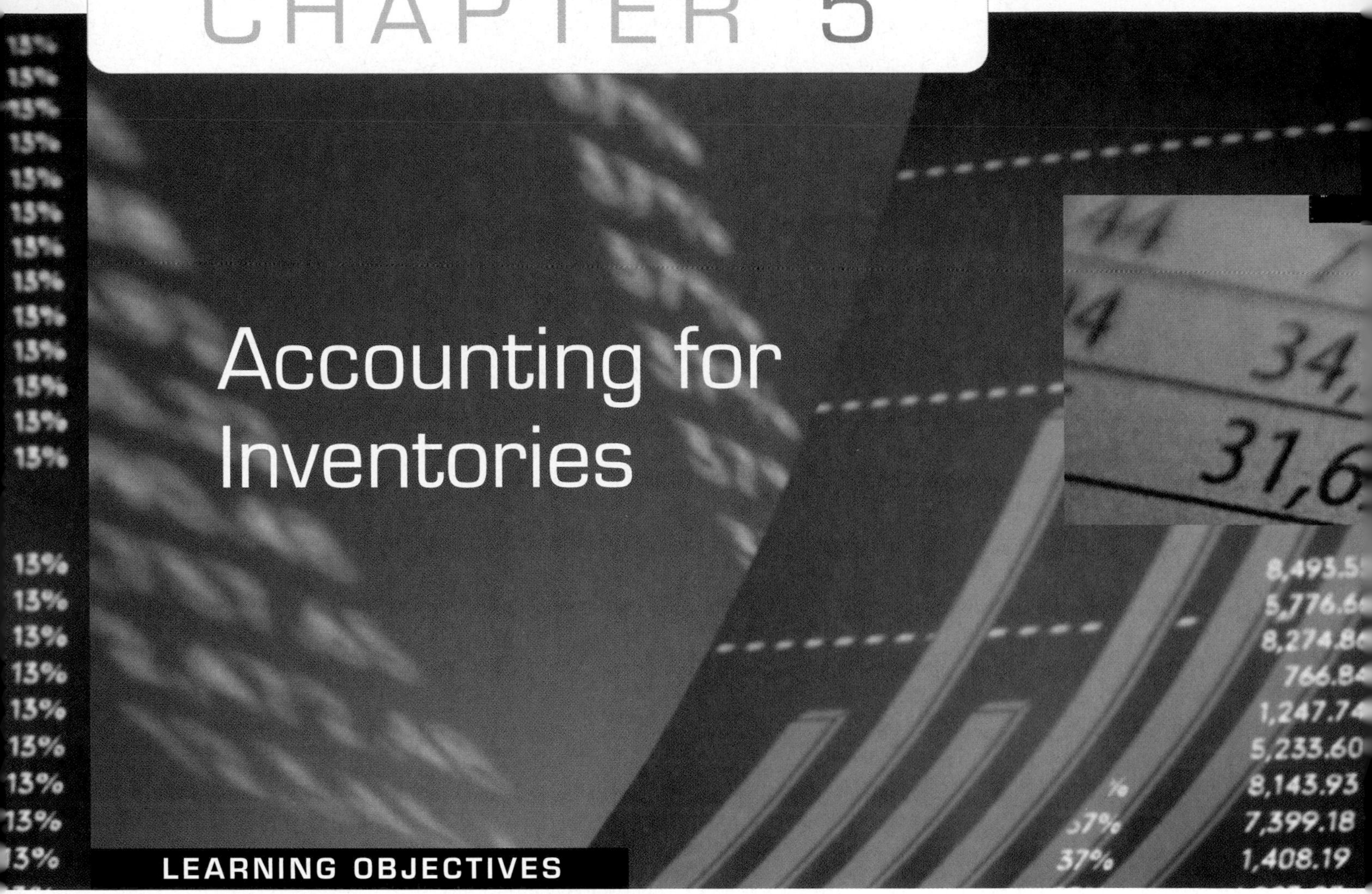

LEARNING OBJECTIVES

After you have mastered the material in this chapter, you will be able to:

1. **Explain how different inventory cost flow methods (specific identification, FIFO, LIFO, and weighted average) affect financial statements.**
2. **Demonstrate the computational procedures for FIFO, LIFO, and weighted average.**
3. **Apply the lower-of-cost-or-market rule to inventory valuation.**
4. **Explain how fraud can be avoided through inventory control.**
5. **Use the gross margin method to estimate ending inventory.**
6. **Explain the importance of inventory turnover to a company's profitability.**
7. **Explain how accounting for investment securities differs when the securities are classified as held to maturity, trading, or available for sale. (Appendix)**

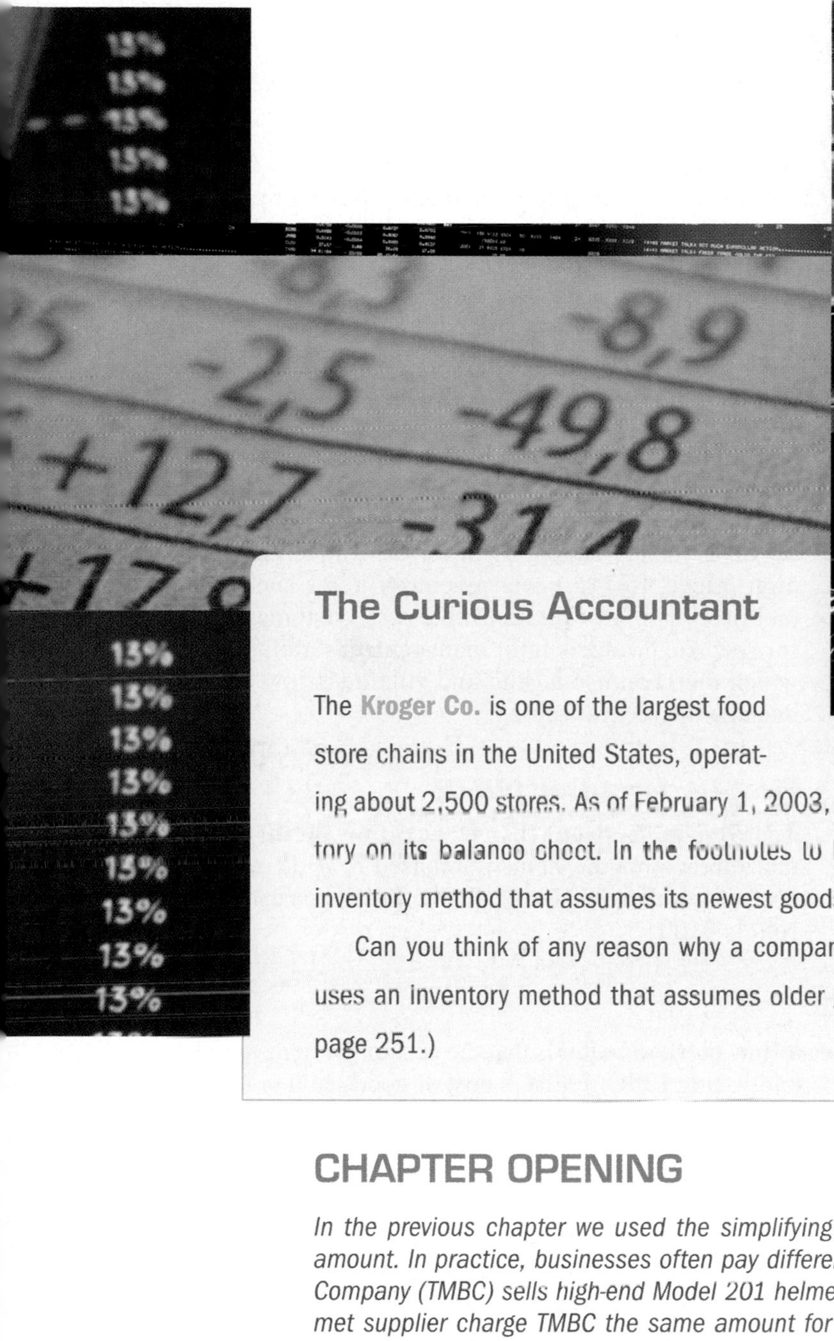

The Curious Accountant

The **Kroger Co.** is one of the largest food store chains in the United States, operating about 2,500 stores. As of February 1, 2003, the company reported approximately $4.2 billion of inventory on its balance sheet. In the footnotes to its financial statements, Kroger reported that it uses an inventory method that assumes its newest goods are sold first and its oldest goods are kept in inventory.

Can you think of any reason why a company selling perishable goods such as milk and vegetables uses an inventory method that assumes older goods are kept while newer goods are sold? (Answer on page 251.)

Chapter 5

CHAPTER OPENING

In the previous chapter we used the simplifying assumption that identical inventory items cost the same amount. In practice, businesses often pay different amounts for identical items. Suppose The Mountain Bike Company (TMBC) sells high-end Model 201 helmets. Since all Model 201 helmets are identical, does the helmet supplier charge TMBC the same amount for each helmet? Probably not. You have likely observed that prices change frequently.

Assume TMBC purchases one Model 201 helmet at a cost of $100. Two weeks later TMBC purchases a second Model 201 helmet. Because the supplier has raised prices, the second helmet costs $110. If TMBC sells one of its two helmets, should it record $100 or $110 as cost of goods sold? The following section of this chapter discusses several acceptable alternative methods for determining the amount of cost of goods sold from which companies may choose under generally accepted accounting principles. ■

Inventory Cost Flow Methods

LO 1

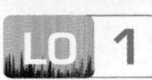

Explain how different inventory cost flow methods (specific identification, FIFO, LIFO, and weighted average) affect financial statements.

5-1

Recall that when goods are sold, product costs flow (are transferred) from the Inventory account to the Cost of Goods Sold account. Four acceptable methods for determining the amount of cost to transfer are (1) specific identification; (2) first-in, first-out (FIFO); (3) last-in, first-out (LIFO); and weighted average.

Specific Identification

Suppose TMBC tags inventory items so that it can identify which one is sold at the time of sale. TMBC could then charge the actual cost of the specific item sold to cost of goods sold. Recall that the first inventory item TMBC purchased cost $100 and the second item cost $110. Using **specific identification,** cost of goods sold would be $100 if the first item purchased were sold or $110 if the second item purchased were sold.

When a company's inventory consists of many low-priced, high-turnover goods the record keeping necessary to use specific identification isn't practical. Imagine the difficulty of recording the cost of each specific food item in a grocery store. Another disadvantage of the specific identification method is the opportunity for managers to manipulate the income statement. For example, TMBC can report a lower cost of goods sold by selling the first instead of the second item. Specific identification is, however, frequently used for high-priced, low-turnover inventory items such as automobiles. For big ticket items like cars, customer demands for specific products limit management's ability to select which merchandise is sold and volume is low enough to manage the recordkeeping.

First-In, First-Out (FIFO)

The **first-in, first-out (FIFO) cost flow method** requires that the cost of the items purchased *first* be assigned to cost of goods sold. Using FIFO, TMBC's cost of goods sold is $100.

Last-In, First-Out (LIFO)

The **last-in, first-out (LIFO) cost flow method** requires that the cost of the items purchased *last* be charged to cost of goods sold. Using LIFO, TMBC's cost of goods sold is $110.

Weighted Average

To use the **weighted-average cost flow method,** first calculate the average cost per unit by dividing the *total cost* of the inventory available by the *total number* of units available. In the case of TMBC, the average cost per unit of the inventory is $105 ([$100 + $110] ÷ 2). Cost of goods sold is then calculated by multiplying the average cost per unit by the number of units sold. Using weighted average, TMBC's cost of goods sold is $105 ($105 × 1).

Physical Flow

The preceding discussion pertains to the flow of *costs* through the accounting records, *not* the actual **physical flow of goods.** Goods usually move physically on a FIFO basis, which means that the first items of merchandise acquired by a company (first-in) are the first items sold to its customers (first-out). The inventory items on hand at the end of the accounting period are typically the last items in (the most recently acquired goods). If companies did not sell their oldest inventory items first, inventories would include dated, less marketable merchandise. *Cost flow,* however, can differ from *physical flow.* For example, a company may use LIFO or weighted average for financial reporting even if its goods flow physically on a FIFO basis.

Effect of Cost Flow on Financial Statements

Effect on Income Statement

The cost flow method a company uses can significantly affect the gross margin reported in the income statement. To demonstrate, assume that TMBC sold the inventory item discussed previously for $120. The amounts of gross margin using the FIFO, LIFO, and weighted-average cost flow assumptions are shown in the following table:

	FIFO	LIFO	Weighted Average
Sales	$120	$120	$120
Cost of Goods Sold	100	110	105
Gross Margin	$ 20	$ 10	$ 15

Even though the physical flow is assumed to be identical for each method, the gross margin reported under FIFO is double the amount reported under LIFO. Companies experiencing identical economic events (same units of inventory purchased and sold) can report significantly different results in their financial statements. Meaningful financial analysis requires an understanding of financial reporting practices.

Effect on Balance Sheet

Since total product costs are allocated between costs of goods sold and ending inventory, the cost flow method a company uses affects its balance sheet as well as its income statement. Since FIFO transfers the first cost to the income statement, it leaves the last cost on the balance sheet. Similarly, by transferring the last cost to the income statement, LIFO leaves the first cost in ending inventory. The weighted-average method bases both cost of goods sold and ending inventory on the average cost per unit. To illustrate, the ending inventory TMBC would report on the balance sheet using each of the three cost flow methods is shown in the following table:

	FIFO	LIFO	Weighted Average
Ending Inventory	$110	$100	$105

EXHIBIT 5.1

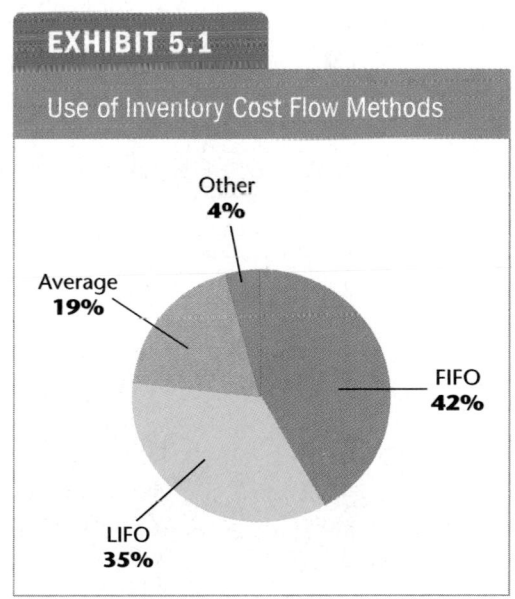

Use of Inventory Cost Flow Methods

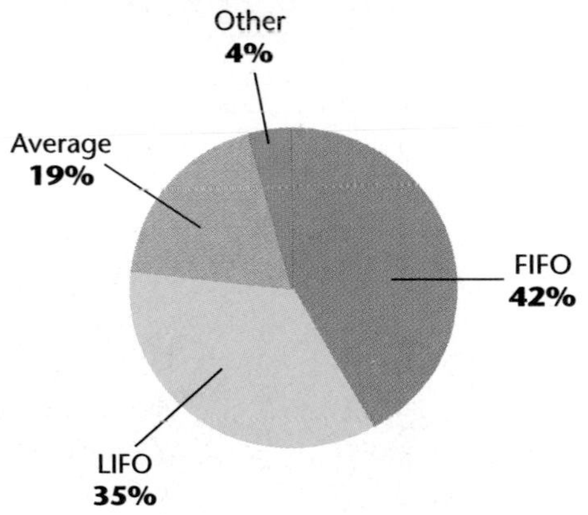

Data source: AICPA, *Accounting Trends and Techniques,* 2000.

The FIFO, LIFO, and weighted-average methods are all used extensively in business practice. The same company may even use one cost flow method for some of its products and different cost flow methods for other products. Exhibit 5.1 illustrates the relative use of the different cost flow methods among U.S. companies.

CHECK YOURSELF 5.1

Nash Office Supply (NOS) purchased two Model 303 copiers at different times. The first copier purchased cost $400 and the second copier purchased cost $450. NOS sold one of the copiers for $600. Determine the gross margin on the sale and the ending inventory balance assuming NOS accounts for inventory using (1) FIFO, (2) LIFO, and (3) weighted average.

Answer

	FIFO	LIFO	Weighted Average
Sales	$600	$600	$600
Cost of Goods Sold	(400)	(450)	(425)
Gross Margin	$200	$150	$175
Ending Inventory	$450	$400	$425

Inventory Cost Flow under a Perpetual System

Multiple Layers with Multiple Quantities

LO 2

Demonstrate the computational procedures for FIFO, LIFO, and weighted average.

The previous example illustrates different **inventory cost flow methods** using only two cost layers ($100 and $110) with only one unit of inventory in each layer. Actual business inventories are considerably more complex. Most real-world inventories are composed of multiple cost layers with different quantities of inventory in each layer. The underlying allocation concepts, however, remain unchanged.

For example, a different inventory item The Mountain Bike Company (TMBC) carries in its stores is a bike called the Eraser. TMBC's beginning inventory and two purchases of Eraser bikes are described below.

Jan. 1	Beginning inventory	10 units @ $200	=	$ 2,000
Mar. 18	First purchase	20 units @ $220	=	4,400
Aug. 21	Second purchase	25 units @ $250	=	6,250
Total cost of the 55 bikes available for sale				$12,650

The accounting records for the period show that TMBC paid cash for all Eraser bike purchases and that it sold 43 bikes at a cash price of $350 each.

Allocating Cost of Goods Available for Sale

The following discussion shows how to determine the cost of goods sold and ending inventory amounts under FIFO, LIFO, and weighted average. We show all three methods to demonstrate how they affect the financial statements differently; TMBC would actually use only one of the methods.

Regardless of the cost flow method chosen, TMBC must allocate the cost of goods available for sale ($12,650) between cost of goods sold and ending inventory. The amounts assigned to each category will differ depending on TMBC's cost flow method. Computations for each method are shown below.

FIFO Inventory Cost Flow

Recall that TMBC sold 43 Eraser bikes during the accounting period. The FIFO method transfers to the Cost of Goods Sold account the *cost of the first 43 bikes* TMBC had available to sell. The first 43 bikes acquired by TMBC were the 10 bikes in the beginning inventory (these were purchased in the prior period) plus the 20 bikes purchased in March and 13 of the bikes purchased in August. The expense recognized for the cost of these bikes ($9,650) is computed as follows:

Jan. 1	Beginning inventory	10 units @ $200	=	$2,000
Mar. 18	First purchase	20 units @ $220	=	4,400
Aug. 21	Second purchase	13 units @ $250	=	3,250
Total cost of the 43 bikes sold				$9,650

Since TMBC had 55 bikes available for sale it would have 12 bikes (55 available − 43 sold) in ending inventory. The cost assigned to these 12 bikes (the ending balance in the Inventory account) equals the cost of goods available for sale minus the cost of goods sold as shown below:

Cost of goods available for sale	$12,650
Cost of goods sold	9,650
Ending inventory balance	$ 3,000

We show the allocation of the cost of goods available for sale between cost of goods sold and ending inventory graphically below.

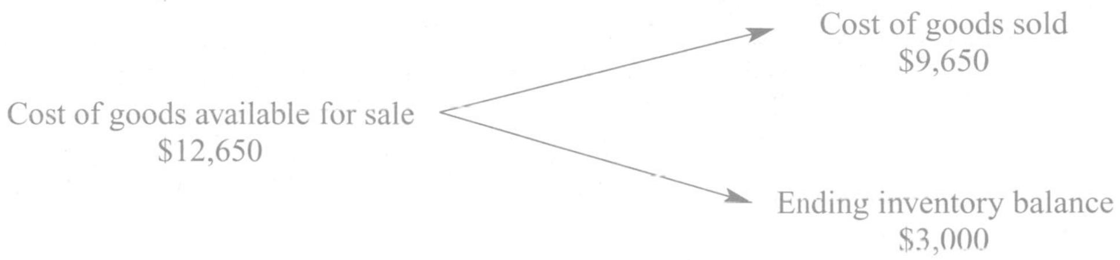

LIFO Inventory Cost Flow

Under LIFO, the cost of goods sold is the cost of the last 43 bikes acquired by TMBC, computed as follows:

Aug. 21	Second purchase	25 units @ $250	=	$ 6,250
Mar. 18	First purchase	18 units @ $220	=	3,960
Total cost of the 43 bikes sold				$10,210

The LIFO cost of the 12 bikes in ending inventory is computed as shown below:

Cost of goods available for sale	$12,650
Cost of goods sold	10,210
Ending inventory balance	$ 2,440

We show the allocation of the cost of goods available for sale between cost of goods sold and ending inventory graphically below.

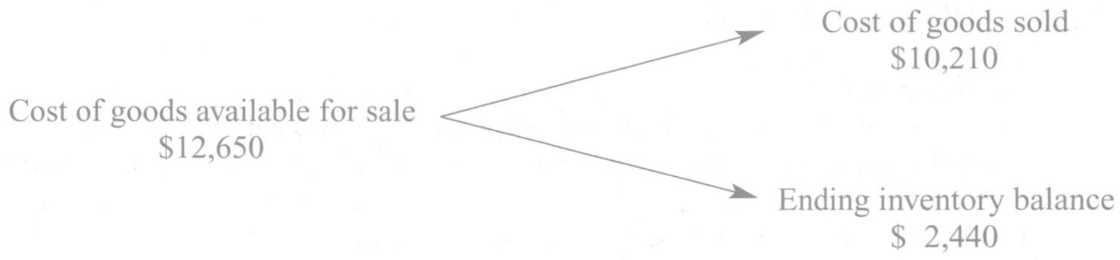

Weighted-Average Cost Flow

The weighted-average cost per unit is determined by dividing the *total cost of goods available for sale* by the *total number of units* available for sale. For TMBC, the weighted-average cost per unit is \$230 (\$12,650 ÷ 55). The weighted-average cost of goods sold is determined by multiplying the average cost per unit by the number of units sold (\$230 × 43 = \$9,890). The cost assigned to the 12 bikes in ending inventory is \$2,760 (12 × \$230).

We show the allocation of the cost of goods available for sale between cost of goods sold and ending inventory graphically below.

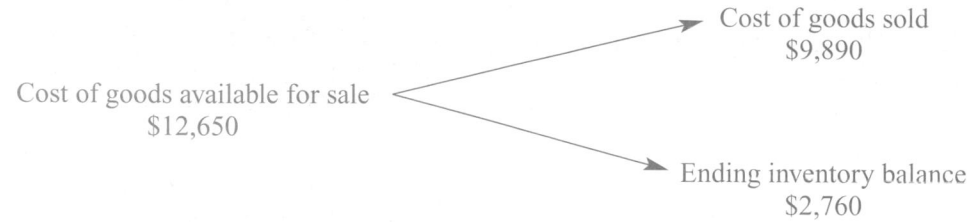

Cost of goods available for sale \$12,650 → Cost of goods sold \$9,890

Cost of goods available for sale \$12,650 → Ending inventory balance \$2,760

Effect of Cost Flow on Financial Statements

LO 1

Explain how different inventory cost flow methods (specific identification, FIFO, LIFO, and weighted average) affect financial statements.

Exhibit 5.2 displays partial financial statements for The Mountain Bike Company (TMBC). This exhibit includes only information pertaining to the Eraser bikes inventory item described above. Other financial statement data are omitted.

Recall that assets are reported on the balance sheet in order of liquidity (how quickly they are expected to be converted to cash). Since companies frequently sell inventory on account, inventory is less liquid than accounts receivable. As a result, companies commonly report inventory below accounts receivable on the balance sheet.

Exhibit 5.2 demonstrates that the amounts reported for gross margin on the income statement and inventory on the balance sheet differ significantly. The cash flow from operating activities on the statement of cash flows, however, is identical under all three methods. Regardless of cost flow reporting method, TMBC paid \$10,650 cash (\$4,400 first purchase + \$6,250 second purchase) to purchase inventory and received \$15,050 cash for inventory sold.

The Impact of Income Tax

Based on the financial statement information in Exhibit 5.2, which cost flow method should TMBC use? Most people initially suggest FIFO because FIFO reports the highest gross margin and the largest balance in ending inventory. However, other factors are relevant. FIFO produces the highest gross margin; it also produces the highest net income and the highest income tax expense. In contrast, LIFO results in recognizing the lowest gross margin, lowest net income, and the lowest income tax expense.

Will investors favor a company with more assets and higher net income or one with lower tax expense? Recognize that specific identification, FIFO, LIFO, and weighted average are ***different methods of reporting the same information.*** TMBC experienced only one set of events pertaining to Eraser bikes. Exhibit 5.2 reports those same events three different ways. However, if the FIFO reporting method causes TMBC to pay more taxes than the LIFO method, using FIFO will cause a real reduction in the value of the company. Paying more money in taxes leaves less money in the company. Knowledgeable investors would be more attracted to TMBC if it uses LIFO because the lower tax payments allow the company to keep more value in the business.

EXHIBIT 5.2

TMBC COMPANY
Comparative Financial Statements

Partial Income Statements			
	FIFO	**LIFO**	**Weighted Average**
Sales	$15,050	$15,050	$15,050
Cost of Goods Sold	(9,650)	(10,210)	(9,890)
Gross Margin	5,400	4,840	5,160
Partial Balance Sheets			
	FIFO	**LIFO**	**Weighted Average**
Assets			
Cash	$ xx	$ xx	$ xx
Accounts Receivable	xx	xx	xx
Inventory	3,000	2,440	2,760
Partial Statements of Cash Flows			
	FIFO	**LIFO**	**Weighted Average**
Operating Activities			
Cash Inflow from Customers	$15,050	$15,050	$15,050
Cash Outflow for Inventory	(10,650)	(10,650)	(10,650)

Research suggests that, as a group, investors are knowledgeable. They make investment decisions based on economic substance regardless of how information is reported in financial statements.

The Income Statement versus the Tax Return

In some instances companies may use one accounting method for financial reporting and a different method to compute income taxes (the tax return must explain any differences). With respect to LIFO, however, the Internal Revenue Service requires that companies using LIFO for income tax purposes must also use LIFO for financial reporting. A company could not, therefore, get both the lower tax benefit provided by LIFO and the financial reporting advantage offered under FIFO.

Inflation versus Deflation

Our illustration assumes an inflationary environment (rising inventory prices). In a deflationary environment, the impact of using LIFO versus FIFO is reversed. LIFO produces tax advantages in an inflationary environment, while FIFO produces tax advantages in a deflationary environment. Companies operating in the computer industry where prices are falling would obtain a tax advantage by using FIFO. In contrast, companies that sell medical supplies in an inflationary environment would obtain a tax advantage by using LIFO.

Full Disclosure and Consistency

Generally accepted accounting principles allow each company to choose the inventory cost flow method best suited to its reporting needs. Because results can vary considerably among methods, however, the GAAP principle of **full disclosure** requires that financial statements disclose the method chosen. In addition, so that a company's financial statements are comparable from year to year, the GAAP principle of **consistency** generally requires that companies use the same cost flow method each period. The limited exceptions to the consistency principle are described in more advanced accounting courses.

CHECK YOURSELF 5.2

The following information was drawn from the inventory records of Fields, Inc.

Beginning inventory	200 units @ $20
First purchase	400 units @ $22
Second purchase	600 units @ $24

Assume that Fields sold 900 units of inventory.

1. Determine the amount of cost of goods sold using FIFO.
2. Would using LIFO produce a higher or lower amount of cost of goods sold? Why?

Answer

1. Cost of goods sold using FIFO

Beginning inventory	200 units @ $20	=	$ 4,000
First purchase	400 units @ $22	=	8,800
Second purchase	300 units @ $24	=	7,200
Total cost of goods sold			$20,000

2. The inventory records reflect an inflationary environment of steadily rising prices. Since LIFO charges the latest costs (in this case the highest costs) to the income statement, using LIFO would produce a higher amount of cost of goods sold than would using FIFO.

Inventory Cost Flow When Sales and Purchases Occur Intermittently

LO 2

Demonstrate the computational procedures for FIFO, LIFO, and weighted average.

In the previous illustrations, all purchases were made before any goods were sold. This section addresses more realistic conditions, when sales transactions occur intermittently with purchases. Consider a third product The Mountain Bike Company (TMBC) carries in its inventory, an energy bar called NeverStop. NeverStop is sold at concession booths sponsored by TMBC at bike races. TMBC purchases and sells NeverStop in bulk boxes. It refers to each box as a unit of product. TMBC's beginning inventory, purchases, and sales of NeverStop for the period are described below.

Date	Transaction	Description
Jan. 1	Beginning inventory	100 units @ $20.00
Feb. 14	Purchased	200 units @ $21.50
Apr. 5	Sold	220 units @ $30.00
June 21	Purchased	160 units @ $22.50
Aug. 18	Sold	100 units @ $30.00
Sept. 2	Purchased	280 units @ $23.50
Nov. 10	Sold	330 units @ $30.00

FIFO Cost Flow

Exhibit 5.3 displays the computations for cost of goods sold and inventory if TMBC uses the FIFO cost flow method. The inventory records are maintained in layers. Each time a sales transaction occurs, the unit cost in the first layer of inventory is assigned to the items sold. If

EXHIBIT 5.3

Inventory Balance and Cost of Goods Sold using FIFO Cost Flow

		Inventory						Cost of Goods Sold
Date	**Description**	**Units**		**Cost**		**Total**		
Jan. 1	Beginning Balance	100	@	$20.00	=	$2,000		
Feb. 14	Purchase	200	@	21.50	=	4,300		
Apr. 5	Sale of 220 Units	(100)	@	20.00	=	(2,000)		
		(120)	@	21.50	=	(2,580)		$ 4,580
	Inventory Balance after Sale	80	@	21.50	=	1,720		
June 21	Purchase	160	@	22.50	=	3,600		
Aug. 18	Sale of 100 Units	(80)	@	21.50	=	(1,720)		
		(20)	@	22.50	=	(450)		2,170
	Inventory Balance after Sale	140	@	22.50	=	3,150		
Sept. 2	Purchase	280	@	23.50	=	6,580		
Nov. 10	Sale of 330 Units	(140)	@	22.50	=	(3,150)		
		(190)	@	23.50	=	(4,465)		7,615
	Ending Inventory Balance	90	@	23.50	=	$2,115		
	Total Cost of Goods Sold							$14,365

the number of items sold exceeds the number of items in the first layer, the unit cost of the next layer is assigned to the remaining number of units sold, and so on. For example, the cost assigned to the 220 units of inventory sold on April 5 is determined as follows:

100 units of inventory in the first layer × $20.00 per unit	=	$2,000
+ 120 units of inventory in the second layer × $21.50 per unit	=	2,580
220 units for total cost of goods sold for the April 5 sale	=	$4,580

The cost of goods sold for subsequent sales transactions is similarly computed.

Using FIFO, and assuming a selling price of $30 per unit, gross margin for the period is computed as follows:

Sales (650 units @ $30 each)	$19,500
Cost of Goods Sold	14,365
Gross Margin	$ 5,135

Weighted-Average and LIFO Cost Flows

When maintaining perpetual inventory records, using the weighted-average or LIFO cost flow methods leads to timing difficulties. For example, under LIFO, the cost of the *last* items purchased *during an accounting period* is the first amount transferred to cost of goods sold. When sales and purchases occur intermittently, the cost of the last items purchased isn't known at the time earlier sales occur. For example, when TMBC sold merchandise in April, it did not know what the replacement inventory purchased in September would cost.

Accountants can solve cost flow timing problems by keeping perpetual records of the quantities (number of units) of items purchased and sold separately from the related costs.

FOCUS ON INTERNATIONAL ISSUES

THE INFLUENCE OF TAX ACCOUNTING ON GAAP

As noted in this chapter, a U.S. company can use LIFO for income tax reporting *only* if it also uses LIFO for GAAP. This is unusual because tax accounting in the United States is separate and distinct from financial reporting under GAAP; the Internal Revenue Service has no formal power to establish GAAP. In the case of LIFO, however, the IRS has an indirect influence on the inventory method that a company chooses for financial reporting. The tax accounting rules of most other countries do not allow the use of the LIFO cost flow method, even if the country's GAAP does allow its use. If U.S. tax rules did not allow the use of LIFO under any circumstances, how many companies would use it for financial reporting? Very few!

The separation between tax accounting and GAAP accounting that exists in the United States does not exist in many other countries. In some countries, a company cannot deduct a cost for tax purposes unless the same cost is shown as an expense on the company's GAAP-based income statement. In other words, the unusual situation that exists in the United States only for the use of LIFO is the general rule in many countries. Countries whose tax laws greatly influence GAAP reporting include France, Germany, and Japan.

Keeping records of quantities moving in and out of inventory, even though cost information is unavailable, provides many of the benefits of a perpetual inventory system. For example, management can determine the quantity of lost, damaged, or stolen goods and the point at which to reorder merchandise. At the end of the accounting period, when the cost of all inventory purchases is available, costs are assigned to the quantity data that have been maintained perpetually. Although further discussion of the weighted-average and LIFO cost flow methods is beyond the scope of this text, recognize that timing problems associated with intermittent sales are manageable.

Lower-of-Cost-or-Market Rule

LO 3

Apply the lower-of-cost-or-market rule to inventory valuation.

Regardless of whether a company uses FIFO, LIFO, weighted average, or specific identification, once the cost of ending inventory has been determined, generally accepted accounting principles require that the cost be compared with the end of period market value and that the inventory be reported at *lower of cost or market. Market* is defined as the amount the company would have to pay to *replace* the merchandise. If the replacement cost is less than the actual cost, regardless of whether the decline in market value is due to physical damage, deterioration, obsolescence, or a general price-level decline, the loss must be recognized in the current period.

The **lower-of-cost-or-market rule** can be applied to (1) each individual inventory item, (2) major classes or categories of inventory, or (3) the entire stock of inventory in the aggregate. The most common practice is the individualized application. To illustrate applying the rule to individual inventory items, assume that The Mountain Bike Company (TMBC) has in ending inventory 100 T-shirts it purchased at a cost of $14 each. If the year-end replacement cost of the shirts is above $14, TMBC will report the ending inventory at cost (100 × $14 =

REALITY BYTES

To avoid spoilage or obsolescence, most companies use a first-in, first-out (FIFO) approach for the flow of physical goods. The older goods (first units purchased) are sold before the newer goods are sold. For example, **Kroger** and other food stores stack older merchandise at the front of the shelf where customers are more likely to pick it up first. As a result, merchandise is sold before it becomes dated. However, when timing is not an issue, convenience may dictate the use of the last-in, first-out (LIFO) method. Examples of products that frequently move on a LIFO basis include rock, gravel, dirt, or other nonwasting assets. Indeed, rock, gravel, and dirt are normally stored in piles that are unprotected from weather. New inventory is simply piled on top of the old. Inventory that is sold is taken from the top of the pile because it is convenient to do so. Accordingly, the last inventory purchased is the first inventory sold. Regardless of whether the flow of physical goods occurs on a LIFO or FIFO basis, costs can flow differently. The flow of inventory through the physical facility is a separate issue from the flow of costs through the accounting system.

$1,400). However, if outsourcing permits the manufacturer to reduce the unit price of the shirts to $11, then TMBC's replacement cost falls below the historical cost, and the inventory must be written down to $1,100 (100 × $11).

Exhibit 5.4 illustrates computing the ending inventory value on an item-by-item basis for a company that has four different inventory items. The company must write down the $30,020 historical cost of its ending inventory to $28,410. This $1,610 write-down reduces the company's gross margin for the period. If the company keeps perpetual inventory records, the effect of the write-down and the journal entry to record it are as follows:

Assets	=	Liab.	+	Equity	Rev.	−	Exp.	=	Net Inc.	Cash Flow
(1,610)	=	NA	+	(1,610)	NA	−	1,610	=	(1,610)	NA

EXHIBIT 5.4

Determination of Ending Inventory at Lower of Cost or Market

Item	Quantity (a)	Unit Cost (b)	Unit Market (c)	Total Cost (a × b)	Total Market (a × c)	Lower of Cost or Market
A	320	$21.50	$22.00	$ 6,880	$ 7,040	$ 6,880
B	460	18.00	16.00	8,280	7,360	7,360
C	690	15.00	14.00	10,350	9,660	9,660
D	220	20.50	23.00	4,510	5,060	4,510
				$30,020	$29,120	$28,410

Account Title	Debit	Credit
Cost of Goods Sold (Inventory Loss)	1,610	
Inventory		1,610

Conceptually, the loss should be reported as an operating expense on the income statement. However, if the amount is immaterial, it can be included in cost of goods sold.

Avoiding Fraud in Merchandising Businesses

LO 4

Explain how fraud can be avoided through inventory control.

Topic Tackler PLUS

5-2

For merchandising businesses, inventory is often the largest single asset reported on the balance sheet and cost of goods sold is normally the largest single expense reported on the income statement. For example, the 2002 income statement for **Publix** (a large grocery store chain) reported $16.0 billion of sales and approximately $11.6 billion of cost of goods sold, which means cost of goods sold for Publix was about 72% of revenue. In contrast, the next largest expense (operating and administrative expense) was approximately $3.4 billion, or 21% of revenue. While cost of goods sold represents only one expense account, the operating and administrative expense category actually combines many, perhaps hundreds, of individual expense accounts, such as depreciation, salaries, utilities, and so on. Because the inventory and cost of goods sold accounts are so significant, they are attractive targets for concealing fraud. For example, suppose a manager attempts to perpetrate a fraud by deliberately understating expenses. The understatement is less likely to be detected if it is hidden in the $11.6 billion Cost of Goods Sold account than if it is recorded in one of the smaller operating expense accounts.

Because the inventory and cost of goods sold accounts are susceptible to abuse, auditors and financial analysts carefully examine them for signs of fraud. Using tools to detect possible inventory misstatements requires understanding how overstatement or understatement of inventory affects the financial statements. To illustrate, assume that a company overstates its year-end inventory balance by $1,000. This inventory overstatement results in a $1,000 understatement of cost of goods sold, as shown in the following schedule:

	Ending Inventory Is Accurate	Ending Inventory Is Overstated	Effect
Beginning inventory	$ 4,000	$ 4,000	
Purchases	6,000	6,000	
Cost of goods available for sale	10,000	10,000	
Ending inventory	(3,000)	(4,000)	$1,000 Overstated
Cost of goods sold	$ 7,000	$ 6,000	$1,000 Understated

The understatement of cost of goods sold results in the overstatement of gross margin, which leads to an overstatement of net earnings, as indicated in the following income statement:

	Ending Inventory Is Accurate	Ending Inventory Is Overstated	Effect
Sales	$11,000	$11,000	
Cost of Goods Sold	(7,000)	(6,000)	$1,000 Understated
Gross Margin	$ 4,000	$ 5,000	$1,000 Overstated

On the balance sheet, assets (inventory) and stockholders' equity (retained earnings) are overstated as follows:

	Ending Inventory Is Accurate	Ending Inventory Is Overstated	Effect
Assets			
Cash	$1,000	$ 1,000	
Inventory	3,000	4,000	$1,000 Overstated
Other Assets	5,000	5,000	
Total Assets	$9,000	$10,000	
Stockholders' Equity			
Common Stock	$5,000	$5,000	
Retained Earnings	4,000	5,000	$1,000 Overstated
Total Stockholders' Equity	$9,000	$10,000	

Managers may be tempted to overstate the physical count of the ending inventory in order to report higher amounts of gross margin on the income statement and larger amounts of assets on the balance sheet. How can companies discourage managers from deliberately overstating the physical count of the ending inventory? The first line of defense is to assign the task of recording inventory transactions to different employees from those responsible for counting inventory.

Recall that under the perpetual system, increases and decreases in inventory are recorded at the time inventory is purchased and sold. If the records are maintained accurately, the balance in the inventory account should agree with the amount of physical inventory on hand. If a manager were to attempt to manipulate the financial statements by overstating the physical count of inventory, there would be a discrepancy between the accounting records and the physical count. In other words, a successful fraud requires controlling both the physical count and the recording process. If the counting and recording duties are performed by different individuals, fraud requires collusion, which reduces the likelihood of its occurrence. The separation of duties is an internal control procedure discussed further in the next chapter.

Because motives for fraud persist, even the most carefully managed companies cannot guarantee that no fraud will ever occur. As a result, auditors and financial analysts have developed tools to test for financial statement manipulation. The gross margin method of estimating the ending inventory balance is such a tool.

Estimating the Ending Inventory Balance

LO 5

Use the gross margin method to estimate ending inventory.

The **gross margin method** assumes that the percentage of gross margin to sales remains relatively stable over time. To the extent that this assumption is accurate, the gross margin ratio from prior periods can be used to accurately estimate the current period's ending inventory. To illustrate, first review the information in Exhibit 5.5 which pertains to the T-Shirt Company.

EXHIBIT 5.5

THE T-SHIRT COMPANY
Schedule for Estimating the Ending Inventory Balance
For the Six Months Ending June 30, 2006

Beginning inventory	$ 5,100	
Purchases	18,500	
Cost of goods available for sale		$23,600
Sales through June 30, 2006	22,000	
Less: Estimated gross margin*	?	
Estimated cost of goods sold		?
Estimated ending inventory		$?

*Historically, gross margin has amounted to approximately 25 percent of sales.

The estimated cost of ending inventory can be computed as follows:

1. Calculate the expected gross margin ratio using financial statement data from prior periods. Accuracy may be improved by averaging gross margin and sales data over several accounting periods. For the T-Shirt Company, assume the average gross margin for the prior five years ÷ the average sales for the same five-year period = 25% expected gross margin ratio.
2. Multiply the expected gross margin ratio by the current period's sales ($22,000 × 0.25 = $5,500) to estimate the amount of gross margin.
3. Subtract the estimated gross margin from sales ($22,000 − $5,500 = $16,500) to estimate the amount of cost of goods sold.
4. Subtract the estimated cost of goods sold from the amount of goods available for sale ($23,600 − $16,500 = $7,100) to estimate the amount of ending inventory.

The estimated amount of ending inventory ($7,100) can be compared to the book balance and the physical count of inventory. If the book balance or the physical count is significantly higher than the estimated inventory balance, the analysis suggests the possibility of financial statement manipulation.

Other analytical comparisons are also useful. For example, the current year's gross margin ratio can be compared to last year's ratio. If cost of goods sold has been understated (ending inventory overstated), the gross margin ratio will be inflated. If this year's ratio is significantly higher than last year's, further analysis is required.

Although it may seem common because of the intense publicity generated when it occurs, fraud is the exception rather than the norm. In fact, growth in the inventory account balance usually results from natural business conditions. For example, a company that is adding new stores is expected to report growth in its inventory balance. Nevertheless, significant growth in inventory that is not explained by accompanying sales growth signals the need to analyze further for evidence of manipulation.

Since one year's ending inventory balance becomes the next year's beginning inventory balance, inaccuracies carry forward from one accounting period to the next. Persistent inventory overstatements result in an inventory account balance that spirals higher and higher. A fraudulently increasing inventory balance is likely to be discovered eventually.

To avoid detection, a manager who has previously overstated inventory will need to write the inventory back down in a subsequent accounting period. Therefore significant decreases, as well as increases, in the inventory balance or the gross margin ratio should be investigated. A manager may try to justify inventory write-downs by claiming that the inventory was lost, damaged, stolen, or had declined in value below historical cost. While there are valid reasons for writing down inventory, the possibility of fraud should be investigated.

Answers to The Curious Accountant

Even though **The Kroger Co.** uses the last-in, first-out *cost flow assumption* for financial reporting purposes, it, like most other companies, actually sells its oldest inventory first. As explained in the text material, GAAP allows a company to report its costs of goods sold in an order that is different from the actual physical flow of its goods. The primary reason some companies use the LIFO assumption is to reduce income taxes. Over the years, Kroger has saved approximately $100 million in taxes by using the LIFO versus the FIFO cost flow assumption when computing its taxable income.

CHECK YOURSELF 5.3

A physical count of Cantrell Inc.'s inventory revealed an ending balance of $6,020. The company's auditor decided to use the gross margin method to test the accuracy of the physical count. The accounting records indicate that the beginning inventory balance had been $20,000. During the period Cantrell had purchased $70,000 of inventory and had recognized $140,000 of sales revenue. Cantrell's gross margin percentage is normally 40 percent of sales. Develop an estimate of the amount of ending inventory and comment on the accuracy of the physical count.

Answer

Goods available for sale is $90,000 ($20,000 beginning inventory + $70,000 purchases). Estimated cost of goods sold is $84,000 ($140,000 sales − [$140,000 × 0.40] gross margin). Estimated ending inventory is $6,000 ($90,000 goods available for sale − $84,000 cost of goods sold). The difference between the physical count and the estimated balance ($6,020 − $6,000 = $20) is immaterial. Therefore the gross margin estimate is consistent with the physical count.

THE FINANCIAL ANALYST

LO 6

Explain the importance of inventory turnover to a company's profitability.

Assume a grocery store sells two brands of kitchen cleansers, Zjax and Cosmos. Zjax costs $1 and sells for $1.25, resulting in a gross margin of $0.25 ($1.25 − $1.00). Cosmos costs $1.20 and sells for $1.60, resulting in a gross margin of $0.40 ($1.60 − $1.20). Is it more profitable to stock Cosmos than Zjax? Not if the store can sell significantly more cans of Zjax.

Suppose the lower price results in higher customer demand for Zjax. If the store can sell 7,000 units of Zjax but only 3,000 units of Cosmos, Zjax will provide a total gross profit of $1,750 (7,000 units × $0.25 per unit), while Cosmos will provide only $1,200 (3,000 units × $0.40 per unit). How fast inventory sells is as important as the spread between cost and selling price. To determine how fast inventory is selling, financial analysts calculate a ratio that measures the *average number of days it takes to sell inventory.*

Average Number of Days to Sell Inventory

The first step in calculating the average number of days it takes to sell inventory is to compute the **inventory turnover,** as follows:

$$\frac{\text{Cost of goods sold}}{\text{Inventory}}$$

The result of this computation is the number of times the balance in the Inventory account is turned over (sold) each year. To more easily interpret the inventory turnover ratio, analysts often take a further step and determine the **average number of days to sell inventory** (also called the **average days in inventory**), computed as

$$\frac{365}{\text{Inventory turnover}}$$

Is It a Marketing or an Accounting Decision?

As suggested, overall profitability depends upon two elements: gross margin and inventory turnover. The most profitable combination would be to carry high margin inventory that turns over rapidly. To be competitive, however, companies must often concentrate on one or the other of the elements. For example, *discount merchandisers* such as Wal-Mart offer lower prices to stimulate greater sales. In contrast, fashionable stores such as Saks Fifth Avenue charge higher prices to compensate for their slower inventory turnover. These upscale stores justify their higher prices by offering superior style, quality, convenience, service, etc. While decisions about pricing, advertising, service, and so on are often viewed as marketing decisions, effective choices require understanding the interaction between the gross margin percentage and inventory turnover.

Real-World Data

LO 6

Explain the importance of inventory turnover to a company's profitability.

Exhibit 5.6 shows the *average number of days to sell inventory* for eight real-world companies in three different industries. The numbers pertain to fiscal years that ended in late 2002 or early 2003. The data raise several questions.

EXHIBIT 5.6

Industry	Company	Average Number of Days to Sell Inventory
Fast Food	Domino's	9
	McDonald's	10
	Starbucks	65
Office Supplies	Office Depot	58
	OfficeMax	92
	Staples	64
Wine	Chalone	642
	Mondavi	548

First, why do Chalone and Mondavi take so long to sell their inventories compared to the other companies? Both of these companies produce and sell wine. Quality wine is aged before it is sold; time spent in inventory is actually a part of the production process. In the wine world, wines produced by Chalone are, on average, considered to be of higher quality than those produced by Mondavi. This higher quality results, in part, from the longer time Chalone's wines spend aging prior to sale.

Why does Starbucks hold its inventory so much longer than the other two fast-food businesses? Starbucks' inventory is mostly coffee. It is more difficult for Starbucks to obtain coffee than it is for McDonald's to obtain beef or Domino's to obtain flour, cheese, and fresh vegetables. Very little coffee is grown in the United States (Hawaii is the only state that produces coffee). Since purchasing coffee requires substantial delivery time, Starbucks cannot order its inventory at the last minute. This problem is further complicated by the fact that coffee harvests are seasonal. Cattle, on the other hand, can be processed into hamburgers year-round. As a result, Starbucks must hold inventory longer than McDonald's or Domino's.

Finally, why do companies in the office supply business take longer to sell inventory than those in the fast-food business? Part of the answer is that food is perishable and stationery is not. But there is also the fact that office supply stores carry many more inventory items than do fast-food restaurants. It is much easier to anticipate customer demand if a company sells only 20 different items than if the company sells 20,000 different items. The problem of anticipating customer demand is solved by holding larger quantities of inventory.

Effects of Cost Flow on Ratio Analysis

Since the amounts of ending inventory and cost of goods sold are affected by the cost flow method (FIFO, LIFO, etc.) a company uses, the gross margin and inventory turnover ratios are also affected by the cost flow method used. Further, since cost of goods sold affects the amount of net income and retained earnings, many other ratios are also affected by the inventory cost flow method that a company uses. Financial analysts must consider that the ratios they use can be significantly influenced by which accounting methods a company chooses.

A Look Back <<

This chapter discussed the inventory cost flow methods of first-in, first-out (FIFO), last-in, first-out (LIFO), weighted average, and specific identification. Under *FIFO,* the cost of the items purchased first is reported on the income statement, and the cost of the items purchased last is reported on the balance sheet. Under *LIFO,* the cost of the items purchased last is reported on the income statement, and the cost of the items purchased first is reported on the balance sheet. Under the *weighted-average method,* the average cost of inventory is reported on both the income statement and the balance sheet. Finally, under specific identification the actual cost of the goods is reported on the income statement and the balance sheet.

Generally accepted accounting principles often allow companies to account for the same types of events in different ways. The different cost flow methods presented in this chapter—FIFO, LIFO, weighted average, and specific identification—are examples of alternative accounting procedures allowed by GAAP. Financial analysts must be aware that financial statement amounts are affected by the accounting methods that a company uses as well as the economic activity it experiences.

This chapter also explained how to calculate the time it takes a company to sell its inventory. The measure of how fast inventory sells is called *inventory turnover;* it is computed by dividing cost of goods sold by inventory. The result of this computation is the number of times the balance in the inventory account is turned over each year. The *average number of days to sell inventory* can be determined by dividing the number of days in a year (365) by the inventory turnover ratio.

Accounting for investment securities is discussed in the appendix to this chapter.

A Look Forward >>

Chapter 6 examines accounting for cash and the system of internal controls. Internal controls are the accounting practices and procedures that companies use to protect assets and to ensure that transactions are recorded accurately. You will learn that companies account for small disbursements of cash, called *petty cash disbursements,* differently than they do for large disbursements. You will also learn how to prepare a formal bank reconciliation.

APPENDIX

Types of Investment Securities

LO 7

Explain how accounting for investment securities differs when the securities are classified as held to maturity, trading, or available for sale. (Appendix)

A financial investment occurs when one entity provides assets or services to another entity in exchange for a certificate known as a *security.* The entity that provides the assets and receives the security certificate is called the **investor.** The entity that receives the assets or services and gives the security certificate is called the **investee.** This appendix discusses accounting practices that apply to securities held by investors.

There are two primary types of investment securities: debt securities and equity securities. An investor receives a **debt security** when assets *are loaned* to the investee. In general, a debt security describes the investee's obligation to return the assets and to pay interest for the use of the assets. Common types of debt securities include bonds, notes, certificates of deposit, and commercial paper.

An **equity security** is obtained when an investor acquires an *ownership interest* in the investee. An equity security usually describes the rights of ownership, including the right to influence the operations of the investee and to share in profits or losses that accrue from those operations. The most common types of equity securities are common stock and preferred stock. In summary, **investment securities** are certificates that describe the rights and privileges that investors receive when they loan or give assets or services to investees.

Transactions between the investor and the investee constitute the **primary securities market.** There is a **secondary securities market** in which investors exchange (buy and sell) investment securities with other investors. Securities that regularly trade in established secondary markets are called **marketable securities.** Investee companies are affected by secondary-market transactions only to the extent that their obligations are transferred to a different party. For example, assume that Tom Williams (investor) loans assets to American Can Company (investee). Williams receives a bond (investment security) from American Can that describes American Can's obligation to return assets and pay interest to Williams. This exchange represents a primary securities market transaction. Now assume that in a secondary-market transaction Williams sells his investment security (bond) to Tina Tucker. American Can Company is affected by this transaction only to the extent that the company's obligation transfers from Williams to Tucker. In other words, American Can's obligation to repay principal and interest does not change. The only thing that changes is the party to whom American Can makes payments. *An investee's financial statements are not affected when the securities it has issued to an investor are traded in the secondary market.*

The **fair value,** also called **market value,** of an investor's securities is established by the prices at which they sell in the secondary markets. For financial reporting purposes, fair value is established as the closing (last) price paid for an identical security on the investor's fiscal closing date. Whether securities are reported at fair value or historical cost depends on whether the investor intends to sell or hold the securities. Generally accepted accounting principles require companies to classify their investment securities into one of three categories: (1) held-to-maturity securities, (2) trading securities, and (3) available-for-sale securities.

Held-to-Maturity Securities

Since equity securities representing ownership interests have no maturity date, the held-to-maturity classification applies only to debt securities. Debt securities should be classified as held-to-maturity securities if the investor has a *positive intent* and the *ability* to hold the securities until the maturity date. **Held-to-maturity securities** are reported on the balance sheet at *amortized historical cost.*[1]

Trading Securities

Both debt and equity securities can be classified as *trading securities.* **Trading securities** are bought and sold for the purpose of generating profits on the short-term appreciation of stock or bond prices. They are usually traded within three months of when they are acquired. Trading securities are reported on the investor's balance sheet at their fair value on the investor's fiscal closing date.

Available-for-Sale Securities

All marketable securities that are not classified as held-to-maturity or trading securities must be classified as **available-for-sale securities.** These securities are also reported on the investor's balance sheet at fair value as of the investor's fiscal closing date.

Two of the three classifications, therefore, must be reported at fair value, which is a clear exception to the historical cost concept. Other exceptions to the use of historical cost measures for asset valuation are discussed in later sections of this appendix.

---

[1]Debt securities are frequently purchased for amounts that are more or less than their face value (the amount of principal due at the maturity date). If the purchase price is above the face value, the difference between the face value and the purchase price is called a *premium.* If the purchase price is below the face value, the difference is called a *discount.* Premiums and discounts increase or decrease the amount of interest revenue earned and affect the carrying value of the bond investment reported on the balance sheet. The presentation in this section of the text makes the simplifying assumption that the bonds are purchased at a price equal to their face value. Accounting for discounts and premiums is discussed in Chapter 10.

Reporting Events that Affect Investment Securities

The effects on the investor's financial statements of four distinct accounting events involving marketable investment securities are illustrated in the following section. The illustration assumes that the investor, Arapaho Company, started the accounting period with cash of $10,000 and common stock of $10,000.

Event 1 Investment Purchase

Arapaho paid $9,000 cash to purchase marketable investment securities.

This event is an asset exchange. One asset (cash) decreases, and another asset (investment securities) increases. The income statement is not affected. The $9,000 cash outflow is reported as either an operating activity or an investing activity, depending on how the securities are classified. Since *trading securities* are short-term assets that are regularly traded for the purpose of producing income, cash flows from the purchase or sale of trading securities are reported in the operating activities section of the statement of cash flows. In contrast, cash flows involving the purchase or sale of securities classified as *held to maturity* or *available for sale* are reported in the investing activities section of the statement of cash flows. The only difference among the three alternatives lies in the classification of the cash outflow reported on the statement of cash flows, as shown in the following statements model:

Event No.	Type	Assets			=	Liab.	+	Equity	Rev.	−	Exp.	=	Net Inc.	Cash Flow	
		Cash	+	Inv. Sec.											
1	Held	(9,000)	+	9,000	=	NA	+	NA	NA	−	NA	=	NA	(9,000)	IA
1	Trading	(9,000)	+	9,000	=	NA	+	NA	NA	−	NA	=	NA	(9,000)	OA
1	Available	(9,000)	+	9,000	=	NA	+	NA	NA	−	NA	=	NA	(9,000)	IA

Event 2 Recognition of Investment Revenue

Arapaho earned $1,600 of cash investment revenue.

Investment revenue is reported the same way regardless of whether the investment securities are classified as held to maturity, trading, or available for sale. Investment revenue comes in two forms. Earnings from equity investments are called **dividends.** Revenue from debt securities is called **interest.** Both forms have the same impact on the financial statements. Recognizing the investment revenue increases both assets and stockholders' equity. Revenue and net income increase. The cash inflow from investment revenue is reported in the operating activities section of the statement of cash flows regardless of how the investment securities are classified.

Event No.	Assets	=	Liab.	+	Equity	Rev.	−	Exp.	=	Net Inc.	Cash Flow	
	Cash	=			Ret. Earn.							
2	1,600	=	NA	+	1,600	1,600	−	NA	=	1,600	1,600	OA

Event 3 Sale of Investment Securities

Arapaho sold securities that cost $2,000 for $2,600 cash.

This event results in recognizing a $600 realized (actual) gain that increases both total assets and stockholders' equity. The asset cash increases by $2,600 and the asset investment securities decreases by $2,000, resulting in a $600 increase in total assets. The $600 realized gain is reported on the income statement, increasing net income and retained earnings. The $600 gain does not appear on the statement of cash flows. Instead, the entire $2,600 cash inflow is reported in one section of the statement of cash flows. Cash inflows from the sale of held-to-maturity and available-for-sale securities are reported as investing activities. Cash flows involving trading securities are reported as operating activities. These effects are shown below.

Event No.	Type	Assets			=	Liab.	+	Equity	Rev. or Gain	−	Exp. or Loss	=	Net Inc.	Cash Flow	
		Cash	+	Inv. Sec.											
3	Held	2,600	+	(2,000)	=	NA	+	600	600	−	NA	=	600	2,600	IA
3	Trading	2,600	+	(2,000)	=	NA	+	600	600	−	NA	=	600	2,600	OA
3	Available	2,600	+	(2,000)	=	NA	+	600	600	−	NA	=	600	2,600	IA

Event 4 Market Value Adjustment
Arapaho recognized a $700 unrealized gain.

After Event 3, the historical cost of Arapaho's portfolio of remaining investment securities is $7,000 ($9,000 purchased less $2,000 sold). Assume that at Arapaho's fiscal closing date, these securities have a fair value of $7,700, giving Arapaho a $700 unrealized gain on its investment. This type of gain (sometimes called a *paper profit*) is classified as *unrealized* because the securities have not been sold. The treatment of **unrealized gains or losses** in the financial statements depends on whether the securities are classified as held to maturity, trading, or available for sale. Unrealized gains or losses on securities classified as *held to maturity* are not recognized in the financial statements; they have no effect on the balance sheet, income statement, and statement of cash flows. Even so, many companies choose to disclose the market value of the securities as part of the narrative description or in the footnotes that accompany the statements. Whether or not the market value is disclosed, held-to-maturity securities are reported on the balance sheet at amortized cost.

Investments classified as trading securities are reported in the financial statements at fair value. Unrealized gains or losses on *trading securities* are recognized in net income even though the securities have not been sold. In Arapaho's case, the $700 gain increases the carrying value of the investment securities. The gain increases net income, which in turn increases retained earnings. Unrealized gains and losses have no effect on cash flows.

Investments classified as available-for-sale securities are also reported in the financial statements at fair value. However, an important distinction exists with respect to how the unrealized gains and losses affect the financial statements. Even though unrealized gains or losses on available-for-sale securities are included in the assets on the balance sheet, they *are not* recognized in determining net income.[2] On Arapaho's balance sheet, the $700 gain increases the carrying value of the investment securities. A corresponding increase is reported in a separate equity account called Unrealized Gain or Loss on Available-for-Sale Securities. The statement of cash flows is not affected by recognizing unrealized gains and losses on available-for-sale securities.

The effects of these alternative treatments of unrealized gains and losses on Arapaho's financial statements are shown here:

Event No.	Type	Assets	=	Liab.	+	Equity			Rev. or Gain	−	Exp. or Loss	=	Net Inc.	Cash Flow
		Inv. Sec.	=			Ret. Earn.	+	Unreal. Gain						
4	Held	NA	=	NA	+	NA	+	NA	NA	−	NA	=	NA	NA
4	Trading	700	=	NA	+	700	+	NA	700	−	NA	=	700	NA
4	Available	700	=	NA	+	NA	+	700	NA	−	NA	=	NA	NA

Financial Statements

As the preceding discussion implies, the financial statements of Arapaho Company are affected by not only the business events relating to its security transactions but also the accounting treatment used to

[2] *Statement of Financial Accounting Standards No. 130* permits companies to report unrealized gains and losses on available-for-sale securities as additions to or subtractions from net income with the result being titled *comprehensive income.* Alternatively, the unrealized gains and losses can be reported on a separate statement or as part of the statement of changes in stockholders' equity.

EXHIBIT 5.7

ARAPAHO COMPANY
Comparative Financial Statements

Income Statements

Investment Securities Classified as	**Held**	**Trading**	**Available**
Investment Revenue	$ 1,600	$ 1,600	$ 1,600
Realized Gain	600	600	600
Unrealized Gain		700	
Net Income	$ 2,200	$ 2,900	$ 2,200

Balance Sheets

	Held	**Trading**	**Available**
Assets			
Cash	$ 5,200	$ 5,200	$ 5,200
Investment Securities, at Cost (Market Value $7,700)	7,000		
Investment Securities, at Market (Cost $7,000)		7,700	7,700
Total Assets	$12,200	$12,900	$12,900
Stockholders' Equity			
Common Stock	$10,000	$10,000	$10,000
Retained Earnings	2,200	2,900	2,200
Unrealized Gain on Investment Securities			700
Total Stockholders' Equity	$12,200	$12,900	$12,900

Statements of Cash Flows

	Held	**Trading**	**Available**
Operating Activities			
Cash Inflow from Investment Revenue	$ 1,600	$ 1,600	$ 1,600
Outflow to Purchase Securities		(9,000)	
Inflow from Sale of Securities		2,600	
Investing Activities			
Outflow to Purchase Securities	(9,000)		(9,000)
Inflow from Sale of Securities	2,600		2,600
Financing Activities*	0	0	0
Net Decrease in Cash	(4,800)	(4,800)	(4,800)
Beginning Cash Balance	10,000	10,000	10,000
Ending Cash Balance	$ 5,200	$ 5,200	$ 5,200

*The $10,000 capital acquisition is assumed to have occurred prior to the start of the accounting period.

report those events. In other words, the same economic events are reflected differently in the financial statements depending on whether the securities are classified as held to maturity, trading, or available for sale. Exhibit 5.7 displays the financial statements for Arapaho under each investment classification alternative.

The net income reported under the trading securities alternative is $700 higher than that reported under the held-to-maturity and available-for-sale alternatives because unrealized gains and losses on trading securities are recognized on the income statement. Similarly, total assets and total stockholders' equity are $700 higher under the trading and available-for-sale alternatives than they are under the held-to-maturity category because the $700 unrealized gain is recognized on the balance sheet for those two classifications. The gain is not reported on the income statement for available-for-sale

EXHIBIT 5.8

Investment Category	Types of Securities	Types of Revenue Recognized	Reported on Balance Sheet at	Recognition of Unrealized Gains and Losses on the Income Statement	Cash Flow from Purchase or Sale of Securities Classified As
Held to maturity	Debt	Interest	Amortized cost	No	Investing activity
Trading	Debt and equity	Interest and dividends	Market value	Yes	Operating activity
Available for sale	Debt and equity	Interest and dividends	Market value	No	Investing activity

securities; it is reported on the balance sheet in a special equity account called Unrealized Gain on Investment Securities. The statements of cash flows report purchases and sales of trading securities as operating activities while purchases and sales of available-for-sale and held-to-maturity securities are investing activities. Exhibit 5.8 summarizes the reporting differences among the three classifications of investment securities.

Alternative Reporting Practices for Equity Securities

If an investor owns 20 percent or more of an investee's equity securities, the investor is presumed able, unless there is evidence to the contrary, to exercise *significant influence* over the investee company. Investors owning more than 50 percent of the stock of an investee company are assumed to have control over the investee. The previous discussion of accounting rules for equity securities assumed the investor did not significantly influence or control the investee. Alternative accounting rules apply to securities owned by investors who exercise significant influence or control over an investee company. Accounting for equity investment securities differs depending on the level of the investor's ability to influence or control the operating, investing, and financing activities of the investee.

As previously demonstrated, investors who do not have significant influence (they own less than 20 percent of the stock of the investee) account for their investments in equity securities at fair value. Investors exercising significant influence (they own 20 to 50 percent of the investee's stock) must account for their investments using the **equity method.** A detailed discussion of the equity method is beyond the scope of this text. However, *be aware that investments reported using the equity method represent a measure of the book value of the investee rather than the cost or fair value of the equity securities owned.*

Investors who have a controlling interest (they own more than 50 percent of the investee's stock) in an investee company are required to issue **consolidated financial statements.** The company that holds the controlling interest is referred to as the **parent company,** and the company that is controlled is called the **subsidiary company.** Usually, the parent and subsidiary companies maintain separate accounting records. However, a parent company is also required to report to the public its accounting data along with that of its subsidiaries in a single set of combined financial statements. These consolidated statements represent a separate accounting entity composed of the parent and its subsidiaries. A parent company that owns one subsidiary will produce three sets of financial statements: statements for the parent company, statements for the subsidiary company, and statements for the consolidated entity.

SELF-STUDY REVIEW PROBLEM

Erie Jewelers sells gold earrings. Its beginning inventory of Model 407 gold earrings consisted of 100 pairs of earrings at $50 per pair. Erie purchased two batches of Model 407 earrings during the year. The first batch purchased consisted of 150 pairs at $53 per pair; the second batch consisted of 200 pairs at $56 per pair. During the year, Erie sold 375 pairs of Model 407 earrings.

Required

Determine the amount of product cost Erie would allocate to cost of goods sold and ending inventory assuming that Erie uses (a) FIFO, (b) LIFO, and (c) weighted average.

Solution to Requirements a–c

Goods Available for Sale					
Beginning inventory	100	@	$50	=	$ 5,000
First purchase	150	@	53	=	7,950
Second purchase	200	@	56	=	11,200
Goods available for sale	450				$24,150

a. FIFO

Cost of Goods Sold	Pairs		Cost per Pair		Cost of Goods Sold
From beginning inventory	100	@	$50	=	$ 5,000
From first purchase	150	@	53	=	7,950
From second purchase	125	@	56	=	7,000
Total pairs sold	375				$19,950

Ending inventory = Goods available for sale − Cost of goods sold

Ending inventory = $24,150 − $19,950 = $4,200

b. LIFO

Cost of Goods Sold	Pairs		Cost per Pair		Cost of Goods Sold
From second purchase	200	@	$56	=	$11,200
From first purchase	150	@	53	=	7,950
From beginning inventory	25	@	50	=	1,250
Total pairs sold	375				$20,400

Ending inventory = Goods available for sale − Cost of goods sold

Ending inventory = $24,150 − $20,400 = $3,750

c. Weighted average

Goods available for sale ÷ Total pairs = Cost per pair

$24,150 ÷ 450 = $53.6667

Cost of goods sold 375 units @ $53.6667 = $20,125

Ending inventory 75 units @ $53.6667 = $4,025

KEY TERMS

available-for-sale securities 254
average number of days to sell inventory (also called the average days in inventory) 252
consistency 243
consolidated financial statements 258
debt security 253
dividends 255
equity method 258
equity security 254
fair value 254
first-in, first-out (FIFO) cost flow method 238
full disclosure 243
gross margin method 249
held-to-maturity securities 254
interest 255
inventory cost flow methods 240
inventory turnover 251

QUESTIONS

1. Name and describe the four cost flow methods discussed in this chapter.
2. What are some advantages and disadvantages of the specific identification method of accounting for inventory?
3. What are some advantages and disadvantages of using the FIFO method of inventory valuation?
4. What are some advantages and disadvantages of using the LIFO method of inventory valuation?
5. In an inflationary period, which inventory cost flow method will produce the highest net income? Explain.
6. In an inflationary period, which inventory cost flow method will produce the largest amount of total assets on the balance sheet? Explain.
7. What is the difference between the flow of costs and the physical flow of goods?
8. Does the choice of cost flow method (FIFO, LIFO, or weighted average) affect the statement of cash flows? Explain.
9. Assume that Key Co. purchased 1,000 units of merchandise in its first year of operations for $25 per unit. The company sold 850 units for $40. What is the amount of cost of goods sold using FIFO? LIFO? Weighted average?
10. Assume that Key Co. purchased 1,500 units of merchandise in its second year of operation for $27 per unit. Its beginning inventory was determined in Question 9. Assuming that 1,500 units are sold, what is the amount of cost of goods sold using FIFO? LIFO? Weighted average?
11. Refer to Questions 9 and 10. Which method might be preferable for financial statements? For income tax reporting? Explain.
12. In an inflationary period, which cost flow method, FIFO or LIFO, produces the larger cash flow? Explain.
13. Which inventory cost flow method produces the highest net income in a deflationary period?
14. How does the phrase *lower-of-cost-or-market* apply to inventory valuation?
15. If some merchandise declined in value because of damage or obsolescence, what effect will the lower-of-cost-or-market rule have on the income statement? Explain.
16. What is a situation in which estimates of the amount of inventory may be useful or even necessary?
17. How can management manipulate net income using inventory fraud?
18. If the amount of goods available for sale is $123,000, the amount of sales is $130,000, and the gross margin is 25 percent of sales, what is the amount of ending inventory?
19. Assume that inventory is overstated by $1,500 at the end of 2006 but is corrected in 2007. What effect will this have on the 2006 income statement? The 2006 balance sheet? The 2007 income statement? The 2007 balance sheet?
20. What information does inventory turnover provide?
21. What is an example of a business that would have a high inventory turnover? A low inventory turnover?
22. Why are historical costs generally used in financial statements?
23. What are some instances in which the Financial Accounting Standards Board requires using market values for financial reporting?
24. What is an example of an asset easily valued at fair market value? What is an example of an asset that is difficult to value at fair market value?
25. What are the two primary types of investment securities?
26. What is a debt security? Give an example.
27. What is an equity security? Give an example.

28. What is the difference between the primary securities market and the secondary securities market?
29. What are marketable securities?
30. Generally accepted accounting principles require companies to classify investment securities into three categories. Name and describe them.
31. When must the equity method of accounting for investments be used for financial statement reporting?

EXERCISES—SERIES A

All Exercises in Series A are available with McGraw-Hill's Homework Manager

Exercise 5-1A *Effect of inventory cost flow assumption on financial statements* — L.O. 1

Required

For each of the following situations, indicate whether FIFO, LIFO, or weighted average applies.

a. In a period of rising prices, net income would be highest.
b. In a period of rising prices, cost of goods sold would be highest.
c. In a period of rising prices, ending inventory would be highest.
d. In a period of falling prices, net income would be highest.
e. In a period of falling prices, the unit cost of goods would be the same for ending inventory and cost of goods sold.

Exercise 5-2A *Allocating product cost between cost of goods sold and ending inventory* — L.O. 1, 2

Mix Co. started the year with no inventory. During the year, it purchased two identical inventory items. The inventory was purchased at different times. The first purchase cost $1,200 and the other, $1,500. One of the items was sold during the year.

Required

Based on this information, how much product cost would be allocated to cost of goods sold and ending inventory on the year-end financial statements, assuming use of

a. FIFO?
b. LIFO?
c. Weighted average?

Exercise 5-3A *Allocating product cost between cost of goods sold and ending inventory: multiple purchases* — L.O. 1, 2

Laird Company sells coffee makers used in business offices. Its beginning inventory of coffee makers was 200 units at $45 per unit. During the year, Laird made two batch purchases of coffee makers. The first was a 300-unit purchase at $50 per unit; the second was a 350-unit purchase at $52 per unit. During the period, Laird sold 800 coffee makers.

Required

Determine the amount of product costs that would be allocated to cost of goods sold and ending inventory, assuming that Laird uses

a. FIFO.
b. LIFO.
c. Weighted average.

Exercise 5-4A *Effect of inventory cost flow (FIFO, LIFO, and weighted average) on gross margin* — L.O. 1, 2

The following information pertains to Porter Company for 2005.

Beginning inventory	70 units @ $13
Units purchased	280 units @ $18

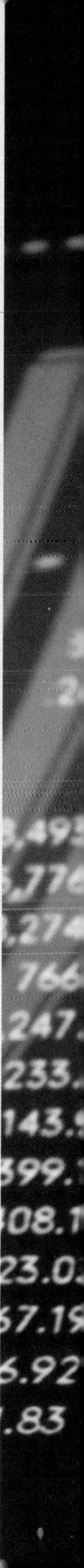

Ending inventory consisted of 30 units. Porter sold 320 units at $30 each. All purchases and sales were made with cash.

Required

a. Compute the gross margin for Porter Company using the following cost flow assumptions: (1) FIFO, (2) LIFO, and (3) weighted average.

b. What is the dollar amount of difference in net income between using FIFO versus LIFO? (Ignore income tax considerations.)

c. Determine the cash flow from operating activities, using each of the three cost flow assumptions listed in Requirement *a.* Ignore the effect of income taxes. Explain why these cash flows have no differences.

L.O. 1, 2

Exercise 5-5A *Effect of inventory cost flow on ending inventory balance and gross margin*

Bristol Sales had the following transactions for DVDs in 2004, its first year of operations.

Jan. 20	Purchased 75 units @ $17	=	$1,275
Apr. 21	Purchased 450 units @ $19	=	8,550
July 25	Purchased 200 units @ $23	=	4,600
Sept. 19	Purchased 100 units @ $29	=	2,900

During the year, Bristol Sales sold 775 DVDs for $60 each.

Required

a. Compute the amount of ending inventory Bristol would report on the balance sheet, assuming the following cost flow assumptions: (1) FIFO, (2) LIFO, and (3) weighted average.

b. Record the above transactions in general journal form and post to T-accounts using (1) FIFO, (2) LIFO, and (3) weighted average. Use a separate set of journal entries and T-accounts for each method. Assume all transactions are cash transactions.

c. Compute the difference in gross margin between the FIFO and LIFO cost flow assumptions.

L.O. 1, 2

Exercise 5-6A *Income tax effect of shifting from FIFO to LIFO*

The following information pertains to the inventory of the La Bonne Company:

Jan. 1	Beginning Inventory	500 units @ $20
Apr. 1	Purchased	2,500 units @ $25
Oct. 1	Purchased	800 units @ $26

During the year, La Bonne sold 3,400 units of inventory at $40 per unit and incurred $17,000 of operating expenses. La Bonne currently uses the FIFO method but is considering a change to LIFO. All transactions are cash transactions. Assume a 30 percent income tax rate. La Bonne started the period with cash of $42,000, inventory of $10,000, common stock of $20,000 and retained earnings of $32,000.

Required

a. Record the above transactions in general journal form and post to T-accounts using (1) FIFO and (2) LIFO. Use a separate set of journal entries and T-accounts for each method.

b. Prepare income statements using FIFO and LIFO.

c. Determine the amount of income taxes La Bonne would save if it changed cost flow methods.

d. Determine the cash flow from operating activities under FIFO and LIFO.

e. Explain why cash flow from operating activities is lower under FIFO when that cost flow method produced the higher gross margin.

L.O. 1, 2

Exercise 5-7A *Effect of FIFO versus LIFO on income tax expense*

Holly Hocks Inc. had sales of $225,000 for 2006, its first year of operation. On April 2, the company purchased 200 units of inventory at $190 per unit. On September 1, an additional 150 units were purchased for $210 per unit. The company had 50 units on hand at the end of the year. The company's income tax rate is 40 percent. All transactions are cash transactions.

Required

a. The preceding paragraph describes five accounting events: (1) a sales transaction, (2) the first purchase of inventory, (3) a second purchase of inventory, (4) the recognition of cost of goods sold expense, and (5) the payment of income tax expense. Record the amounts of each event in horizontal statements models like the following ones, assuming first a FIFO and then a LIFO cost flow.

Effect of Events on Financial Statements

Panel 1: FIFO Cost Flow

Event No.	Balance Sheet							Income Statement					Statement of Cash Flows
	Cash	+	Inventory	=	Com. Stk.	+	Ret. Earn.	Rev.	−	Exp.	=	Net Inc.	

Panel 2: LIFO Cost Flow

Event No.	Balance Sheet							Income Statement					Statement of Cash Flows
	Cash	+	Inventory	=	Com. Stk.	+	Ret. Earn.	Rev.	−	Exp.	=	Net Inc.	

b. Compute net income using FIFO.

c. Compute net income using LIFO.

d. Explain the difference, if any, in the amount of income tax expense incurred using the two cost flow assumptions.

e. How does the use of the FIFO versus the LIFO cost flow assumptions affect the statement of cash flows?

Exercise 5-8A *Recording inventory transactions using the perpetual system: intermittent sales and purchases* L.O. 2

The following inventory transactions apply to TNT Company for 2004.

Jan. 1	Purchased	250 units @ $10
Apr. 1	Sold	125 units @ $18
Aug. 1	Purchased	400 units @ $11
Dec. 1	Sold	500 units @ $19

The beginning inventory consisted of 175 units at $11 per unit. All transactions are cash transactions.

Required

a. Record these transactions in general journal format assuming TNT uses the FIFO cost flow assumption and keeps perpetual records.

b. Compute the ending balance in the Inventory account.

Exercise 5-9A *Effect of cost flow on ending inventory: intermittent sales and purchases* L.O. 2

Solar Heating, Inc., had the following transactions for 2007:

Date	Transaction	Description
Jan. 1	Beginning inventory	50 units @ $20
Mar. 15	Purchased	200 units @ $24
May 30	Sold	170 units @ $40
Aug. 10	Purchased	275 units @ $25
Nov. 20	Sold	340 units @ $40

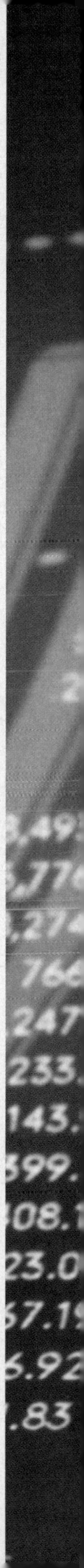

Required

a. Determine the quantity and dollar amount of inventory at the end of the year, assuming Solar Heating Inc. uses the FIFO cost flow assumption and keeps perpetual records.

b. Write a memo explaining why Solar Heating, Inc., would have difficulty applying the LIFO method on a perpetual basis. Include a discussion of how to overcome these difficulties.

L.O. 3

Exercise 5-10A *Lower-of-cost-or-market rule: perpetual system*

The following information pertains to Royal Auto Parts's ending inventory for the current year.

Item	Quantity	Unit Cost	Unit Market Value
P	100	$6	$7
D	50	8	6
S	20	7	8
J	15	9	7

Required

a. Determine the value of the ending inventory using the lower-of-cost-or-market rule applied to (1) each individual inventory item and (2) the inventory in aggregate.

b. Prepare any necessary journal entries, assuming the decline in value is immaterial, using the (1) individual method and (2) aggregate method. Royal Auto Parts uses the perpetual inventory system.

L.O. 3

Exercise 5-11A *Lower-of-cost-or-market rule*

Guzman Company carries three inventory items. The following information pertains to the ending inventory:

Item	Quantity	Unit Cost	Unit Market Value
O	200	$10	$ 9
J	250	15	14
R	175	5	8

Required

a. Determine the ending inventory that will be reported on the balance sheet, assuming that Guzman applies the lower-of-cost-or-market rule to individual inventory items.

b. Prepare the necessary journal entry, assuming the decline in value is immaterial.

L.O. 4, 5

Exercise 5-12A *Estimating ending inventory using the gross margin method*

Rich French, the owner of Rich's Fishing Supplies, is surprised at the amount of actual inventory at the end of the year. He thought there should be more inventory on hand based on the amount of sales for the year. The following information is taken from the books of Rich's Fishing Supplies:

Beginning Inventory	$200,000
Purchases for the year	400,000
Sales for the year	600,000
Inventory at the end of the year (based on actual count)	100,000

Historically, Rich has made a 20 percent gross margin on his sales. Rich thinks there may be some problem with the inventory. Evaluate the situation based on the historical gross profit percentage.

Required

Estimate the following:

a. Gross margin in dollars.
b. Cost of goods sold in dollars.
c. Estimated ending inventory.
d. Inventory shortage.
e. Give an explanation for the shortage.

Exercise 5-13A *Estimating ending inventory: perpetual system* — L.O. 4, 5

Carol Lapaz owned a small company that sold boating equipment. The equipment was expensive, and a perpetual system was maintained for control purposes. Even so, lost, damaged, and stolen merchandise normally amounted to 5 percent of the inventory balance. On June 14, Carol's warehouse was destroyed by fire. Just prior to the fire, the accounting records contained a $150,000 balance in the Inventory account. However, inventory costing $15,000 had been sold and delivered to customers the day of the fire but had not been recorded in the books at the time of the fire. The fire did not affect the showroom, which contained inventory that cost $40,000.

Required

Estimate the amount of inventory destroyed by fire.

Exercise 5-14A *Effect of inventory error on financial statements: perpetual system* — L.O. 4, 5

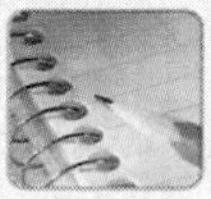

Marshall Company failed to count $12,000 of inventory in its 2007 year-end physical count.

Required

Explain how this error will affect Marshall's 2007 financial statements, assuming that Marshall uses the perpetual inventory system.

Exercise 5-15A *Effect of inventory misstatement on elements of financial statements* — L.O. 4, 5

The ending inventory for Tokro Co. was erroneously written down causing an understatement of $5,200 at the end of 2005.

Required

Was each of the following amounts overstated, understated, or not affected by the error?

Item No.	Year	Amount
1	2005	Beginning inventory
2	2005	Purchases
3	2005	Goods available for sale
4	2005	Cost of goods sold
5	2005	Gross margin
6	2005	Net income
7	2006	Beginning inventory
8	2006	Purchases
9	2006	Goods available for sale
10	2006	Cost of goods sold
11	2006	Gross margin
12	2006	Net income

Exercise 5-16A *Identifying asset values for financial statements (Appendix)* — L.O. 7

Required

Indicate whether each of the following assets should be valued at fair market value (FMV), lower of cost or market (LCM), or historical cost (HC) on the balance sheet. For certain assets, historical cost may be called amortized cost (AC).

Asset	FMV	LCM	HC/AC
Supplies			
Land			
Trading Securities			
Cash			
Held-to-Maturity Securities			
Buildings			
Available-for-Sale Securities			
Office Equipment			
Inventory			

L.O. 7

Exercise 5-17A *Accounting for investment securities (Appendix)*

Brooks Bros. purchased $18,000 of marketable securities on March 1, 2004. On the company's fiscal year closing date, December 31, 2004, the securities had a market value of $13,500. During 2004, Brooks recognized $5,000 of revenue and $1,000 of expenses.

Required

a. Record a +, −, or NA in a horizontal statements model to show how the purchase of the securities affects the financial statements, assuming that the securities are classified as (1) held to maturity, (2) trading, or (3) available for sale. In the Cash Flow column, indicate whether the event is an operating activity (OA), investing activity (IA), or financing activity (FA). Record only the effects of the purchase event.

Event No.	Type	Cash	+	Inv. Sec.	=	Liab.	+	Equity	Rev.	−	Exp.	=	Net Inc.	Cash Flow
1	Held													
2	Trading													
3	Available													

b. Determine the amount of net income that would be reported on the 2004 income statement, assuming that the marketable securities are classified as (1) held to maturity, (2) trading, or (3) available for sale.

L.O. 7

Exercise 5-18A *Effect of investment securities transactions on financial statements (Appendix)*

The following information pertains to Regan Supply Co. for 2006.

1. Purchased $100,000 of marketable investment securities.
2. Earned $5,000 of cash investment revenue.
3. Sold for $30,000 securities that cost $28,000.
4. The fair value of the remaining securities at December 31, 2006, was $92,000.

Required

a. Record the four events in a statements model like the following one. Use a separate model for each classification: (1) held to maturity, (2) trading, and (3) available for sale. The first event for the first classification is shown as an example.

Held to Maturity

Event No.	Cash	+	Inv. Sec.	=	Liab.	+	Ret. Earn.	+	Unreal. Gain.	Rev. or Gains	−	Exp. or Loss	=	Net Inc.	Cash Flow
1	(100,000)	+	100,000	=	NA	+	NA	+	NA	NA	−	NA	=	NA	(100,000) IA

b. What is the amount of net income under each of the three classifications?

c. What is the change in cash from operating activities under each of the three classifications?

d. Are the answers to Requirements *b* and *c* different for each of the classifications? Why or why not?

Exercise 5-19A *Preparing financial statements for investment securities (Appendix)* L.O. 7

Barnett, Inc., began 2007 with $50,000 in both cash and common stock. The company engaged in the following investment transactions during 2007:

1. Purchased $20,000 of marketable investment securities.
2. Earned $800 cash from investment revenue.
3. Sold investment securities for $14,000 that cost $12,000.
4. Purchased $9,000 of additional marketable investment securities.
5. Determined that the investment securities had a fair value of $22,000 at the end of 2007.

Required

a. Record the above transaction in general journal form and post to T-accounts assuming the securities were (1) held to maturity, (2) trading, and (3) available for sale. (Use a separate set of journal entries and T-accounts for each type of security.)

b. Use a vertical statements model to prepare income statements, balance sheets, and statements of cash flow for Barnett, Inc., assuming the securities were (1) held to maturity, (2) trading, and (3) available for sale.

Exercise 5-20A *Differences among marketable investment securities classifications (Appendix)* L.O. 7

Complete the following table for the three categories of marketable investment securities:

Investment Category	Types of Securities	Types of Revenue Recognized	Value Reported on Balance Sheet	Recognition of Unrealized Gains and Losses on the Income Statement	Cash Flow from Purchase or Sale of Securities Is Classified as
Held-to-maturity	Debt	Interest	Amortized Cost	No	Investing Activity
Trading					
Available-for-sale					

PROBLEMS—SERIES A

All Problems in Series A are available with McGraw-Hill's Homework Manager

HM™

Problem 5-21A *Effect of different inventory cost flow methods on financial statements* L.O. 1, 2

excel

mhhe.com/edmonds2007

CHECK FIGURES

a. Cost of Goods Sold–FIFO: $27,540

c. Net Income–LIFO: $6,780

The accounting records of Clear Photography, Inc., reflected the following balances as of January 1, 2007:

Cash	$18,000
Beginning Inventory	13,500 (150 units @ $90)
Common Stock	15,000
Retained Earnings	16,500

The following five transactions occurred in 2007:

1. First purchase (cash) 120 units @ $92
2. Second purchase (cash) 200 units @ $100
3. Sales (all cash) 300 units @ $185
4. Paid $15,000 cash for operating expenses.

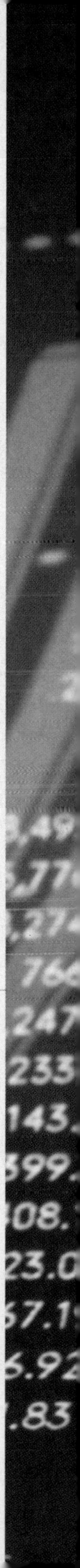

5. Paid cash for income tax at the rate of 40 percent of income before taxes.

Required

a. Compute the cost of goods sold and ending inventory, assuming (1) FIFO cost flow, (2) LIFO cost flow, and (3) weighted-average cost flow. Compute income tax expense for each method.

b. Record the above transactions in general journal form and post to T-accounts assuming (1) FIFO cost flow, (2) LIFO cost flow, and (3) weighted-average cost flow.

c. Use a vertical model to show the 2007 income statement, balance sheet, and statement of cash flows under FIFO, LIFO, and weighted average.

L.O. 2

excel

mhhe.com/edmonds2007

CHECK FIGURES

b. Cost of Goods Sold: $22,850

c. Ending Inventory: $4,550

Problem 5-22A *Allocating product costs between cost of goods sold and ending inventory: intermittent purchases and sales of merchandise*

Lacey, Inc., had the following sales and purchase transactions during 2006. Beginning inventory consisted of 80 items at $120 each. Lacey uses the FIFO cost flow assumption and keeps perpetual inventory records.

Date	Transaction	Description
Mar. 5	Purchased	80 items @ $125
Apr. 10	Sold	60 items @ $245
June 19	Sold	70 items @ $245
Sept. 16	Purchased	60 items @ $130
Nov. 28	Sold	55 items @ $255

Required

a. Record the inventory transactions in general journal format.

b. Calculate the gross margin Lacey would report on the 2006 income statement.

c. Determine the ending inventory balance Lacey would report on the December 31, 2006, balance sheet.

L.O. 3

excel

mhhe.com/edmonds2007

CHECK FIGURES

a. $5,980

c. $6,640

Problem 5-23A *Inventory valuation based on the lower-of-cost-or-market rule*

At the end of the year, Upton Computer Repair had the following items in inventory:

Item	Quantity	Unit Cost	Unit Market Value
D1	60	$20	$26
D2	30	50	48
D3	44	35	42
D4	40	60	45

Required

a. Determine the amount of ending inventory using the lower-of-cost-or-market rule applied to each individual inventory item.

b. Provide the general journal entry necessary to write down the inventory based on Requirement *a.* Assume that Upton Computer Repair uses the perpetual inventory system.

c. Determine the amount of ending inventory, assuming that the lower-of-cost-or-market rule is applied to the inventory in aggregate.

d. Provide the general journal entry necessary to write down the inventory based on Requirement *c.* Assume that Upton Computer Repair uses the perpetual inventory system.

L.O. 5

Problem 5-24A *Estimating ending inventory: gross margin method*

Metal Supplies had its inventory destroyed by a hurricane on September 21 of the current year. Although some of the accounting information was destroyed, the following information was discovered for the period of January 1 through September 21:

Beginning inventory, January 1	$ 70,000
Purchases through September 21	360,000
Sales through September 21	500,000

The gross margin for Metal Supplies has traditionally been 25 percent of sales.

CHECK FIGURES
a. Gross Margin: $125,000
b. Total Inventory Loss: $45,000

Required

a. For the period ending September 21, compute the following:
   (1) Estimated gross margin.
   (2) Estimated cost of goods sold.
   (3) Estimated inventory at September 21.

b. Assume that $10,000 of the inventory was not damaged. What is the amount of the loss from the hurricane?

c. Metal Supplies uses the perpetual inventory system. If some of the accounting records had not been destroyed, how would Metal determine the amount of the inventory loss?

Problem 5-25A ***Estimating ending inventory: gross margin method*** **L.O. 5**

CHECK FIGURE
b. Estimated Ending Inventory: $114,400

Don Green, owner of Plains Company, is reviewing the quarterly financial statements and thinks the cost of goods sold is out of line with past years. The following historical data is available for 2004 and 2005:

	2004	2005
Net sales	$160,000	$200,000
Cost of goods sold	70,000	90,000

At the end of the first quarter of 2006, Plains Company's ledger had the following account balances:

Sales	$240,000
Purchases	160,000
Beginning Inventory, January 1, 2006	60,000

Required

Using the information provided, estimate the following for the first quarter of 2006:

a. Cost of goods sold. (Use average cost of goods sold percentage.)
b. Ending inventory at March 31 based on the historical cost of goods sold percentage.
c. Inventory shortage if the inventory balance as of March 31 is $100,000.

Problem 5-26A ***Effect of inventory errors on financial statements*** **L.O. 4**

The following income statement was prepared for Bell Company for the year 2006:

BELL COMPANY Income Statement For the Year Ended December 31, 2006	
Sales	$69,000
Cost of Goods Sold	(38,640)
Gross Margin	30,360
Operating Expenses	(9,100)
Net Income	$21,260

During the year-end audit, the following errors were discovered.

1. A $1,400 payment for repairs was erroneously charged to the Cost of Goods Sold account. (Assume that the perpetual inventory system is used.)

2. Sales to customers for $2,400 at December 31, 2006, were not recorded in the books for 2006. Also, the $1,344 cost of goods sold was not recorded. The error was not discovered in the physical count because the goods had not been delivered to the customer.
3. A mathematical error was made in determining ending inventory. Ending inventory was understated by $1,200. (The Inventory account was written down in error to the Cost of Goods Sold account.)

Required

Determine the effect, if any, of each of the errors on the following items. Give the dollar amount of the effect and whether it would overstate (+), understate (−), or not affect (NA) the account. The effect on sales is recorded as an example.

Error No. 1	Amount of Error	Effect
Sales, 2006	NA	NA
Ending inventory, December 31, 2006		
Gross margin, 2006		
Beginning inventory, January 1, 2007		
Cost of goods sold, 2006		
Net income, 2006		
Retained earnings, December 31, 2006		
Total assets, December 31, 2006		

Error No. 2	Amount of Error	Effect
Sales, 2006	$2,400	−
Ending inventory, December 31, 2006		
Gross margin, 2006		
Beginning inventory, January 1, 2007		
Cost of goods sold, 2006		
Net income, 2006		
Retained earnings, December 31, 2006		
Total assets, December 31, 2006		

Error No. 3	Amount of Error	Effect
Sales, 2006	NA	NA
Ending inventory, December 31, 2006		
Gross margin, 2006		
Beginning inventory, January 1, 2007		
Cost of goods sold, 2006		
Net income, 2006		
Retained earnings, December 31, 2006		
Total assets, December 31, 2006		

L.O. 7

CHECK FIGURES

Net Income–Held to Maturity: $50,500
Net Income–Trading: $47,500

Problem 5-27A *Effect of marketable investment securities transactions on financial statements (Appendix)*

The following transactions pertain to Quality Answering Service for 2007:

1. Started business by acquiring $30,000 cash from the issue of common stock.
2. Provided $70,000 of services for cash.
3. Invested $35,000 in marketable investment securities.
4. Paid $24,000 of operating expense.
5. Received $500 of investment income from the securities.
6. Invested an additional $12,000 in marketable investment securities.
7. Paid a $2,000 cash dividend to the stockholders.
8. Sold investment securities that cost $8,000 for $11,000.

9. Received another $1,000 in investment income.
10. Determined the market value of the investment securities at the end of the year was $36,000.

Required

Use a vertical model to show a 2007 income statement, balance sheet, and statement of cash flows, assuming that the marketable investment securities were classified as (a) held to maturity, (b) trading, and (c) available for sale. (*Hint:* Record the events in T-accounts prior to preparing the financial statements.)

Problem 5-28A *Comprehensive horizontal statements model (Appendix)*

L.O. 1, 3, 7

Woody's Catering experienced the following independent events.

1. Acquired cash from issuing common stock.
2. Purchased inventory on account.
3. Paid cash to purchase marketable securities classified as trading securities.
4. There was an unrealized loss on marketable securities that were classified as trading securities.
5. There was an unrealized loss on marketable securities that were classified as available-for-sale securities.
6. There was an unrealized loss on marketable securities that were classified as held-to-maturity securities.
7. Wrote down inventory to comply with lower-of-cost-or-market rule. (Assume the company uses the perpetual inventory system.)
8. Recognized cost of goods sold under FIFO.
9. Recognized cost of goods sold under the weighted-average method.

Required

a. Show the effect of each event on the elements of the financial statements using a horizontal statements model like the following one. Use + for increase, − for decrease, and NA for not affected. In the Cash Flow column, indicate whether the item is an operating activity (OA), investing activity (IA), or financing activity (FA). The first transaction is entered as an example.

Event No.	Assets	=	Liab.	+	Equity	Rev. or Gain	−	Exp. or Loss	=	Net Inc.	Cash Flow
1	+		NA		+	NA		NA		NA	+ FA

b. Explain why there is or is not a difference in the way Events 8 and 9 affect the financial statements model.

EXERCISES—SERIES B

Exercise 5-1B *Effect of inventory cost flow assumption on financial statements*

L.O. 1

Required

For each of the following situations, fill in the blank with *FIFO, LIFO,* or *weighted average.*

a. ______ would produce the highest amount of net income in an inflationary environment.
b. ______ would produce the highest amount of assets in an inflationary environment.
c. ______ would produce the lowest amount of net income in a deflationary environment.
d. ______ would produce the same unit cost for assets and cost of goods sold in an inflationary environment.
e. ______ would produce the lowest amount of net income in an inflationary environment.
f. ______ would produce an asset value that was the same regardless of whether the environment was inflationary or deflationary.
g. ______ would produce the lowest amount of assets in an inflationary environment.
h. ______ would produce the highest amount of assets in a deflationary environment.

L.O. 1, 2

Exercise 5-2B *Allocating product cost between cost of goods sold and ending inventory*

Berryhill Co. started the year with no inventory. During the year, it purchased two identical inventory items at different times. The first purchase cost $750 and the other, $1,000. Berryhill sold one of the items during the year.

Required

Based on this information, how much product cost would be allocated to cost of goods sold and ending inventory on the year-end financial statements, assuming use of

a. FIFO?

b. LIFO?

c. Weighted average?

L.O. 1, 2

Exercise 5-3B *Allocating product cost between cost of goods sold and ending inventory: multiple purchases*

Alfonza Company sells chairs that are used at computer stations. Its beginning inventory of chairs was 100 units at $40 per unit. During the year, Alfonza made two batch purchases of this chair. The first was a 150-unit purchase at $50 per unit; the second was a 200-unit purchase at $60 per unit. During the period, it sold 260 chairs.

Required

Determine the amount of product costs that would be allocated to cost of goods sold and ending inventory, assuming that Alfonza uses

a. FIFO.

b. LIFO.

c. Weighted average.

L.O. 1, 2

Exercise 5-4B *Effect of inventory cost flow (FIFO, LIFO, and weighted average) on gross margin*

The following information pertains to Ping Company for 2006.

Beginning inventory	40 units @ $20
Units purchased	200 units @ $25

Ending inventory consisted of 30 units. Ping sold 210 units at $50 each. All purchases and sales were made with cash.

Required

a. Compute the gross margin for Ping Company using the following cost flow assumptions: (1) FIFO, (2) LIFO, and (3) weighted average.

b. What is the amount of net income using FIFO, LIFO, and weighted average? (Ignore income tax considerations.)

c. Compute the amount of ending inventory using (1) FIFO, (2) LIFO, and (3) weighted average.

L.O. 1, 2

Exercise 5-5B *Effect of inventory cost flow on ending inventory balance and gross margin*

University Sales had the following transactions for T-shirts for 2006, its first year of operations.

Jan. 20	Purchased 450 units @ $ 5	=	$2,250
Apr. 21	Purchased 200 units @ $ 6	=	1,200
July 25	Purchased 100 units @ $10	=	1,000
Sept. 19	Purchased 75 units @ $ 8	=	600

During the year, University Sales sold 725 T-shirts for $20 each.

Required

a. Compute the amount of ending inventory University would report on the balance sheet, assuming the following cost flow assumptions: (1) FIFO, (2) LIFO, and (3) weighted average.

b. Record the above transactions in general journal form and post to T-accounts assuming (1) FIFO, (2) LIFO, and (3) weighted average methods. Use a separate set of journal entries and T-accounts for each method. Assume all transactions are cash transactions.

c. Compute the difference in gross margin between the FIFO and LIFO cost flow assumptions.

Exercise 5-6B *Income tax effect of shifting from FIFO to LIFO*

L.O. 1, 2

The following information pertains to the inventory of Starr Company:

Jan. 1	Beginning Inventory	500 units @ $20
Apr. 1	Purchased	2,500 units @ $22
Oct. 1	Purchased	800 units @ $28

During 2007, Starr sold 3,400 units of inventory at $40 per unit and incurred $34,000 of operating expenses. Starr currently uses the FIFO method but is considering a change to LIFO. All transactions are cash transactions. Assume a 30 percent income tax rate. Starr Co. started the period with cash of $60,000, inventory of $10,000, common stock of $40,000, and retained earnings of $30,000.

Required

a. Record the above transactions in general journal form and post to T-accounts using (1) FIFO and (2) LIFO. Use a separate set of journal entries and T-accounts for each method.

b. Prepare income statements using FIFO and LIFO.

c. Determine the amount of income taxes that Starr would pay using each cost flow method.

d. Determine the cash flow from operating activities under FIFO and LIFO.

e. Why is the cash flow from operating activities different under FIFO and LIFO?

Exercise 5-7B *Effect of FIFO versus LIFO on income tax expense*

L.O. 1, 2

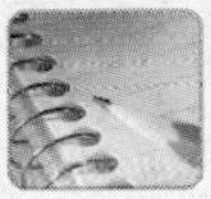

The Keys Company had sales of $250,000 for 2005, its first year of operation. On April 2, the company purchased 200 units of inventory at $350 per unit. On September 1, an additional 150 units were purchased for $375 per unit. The company had 100 units on hand at the end of the year. The company's income tax rate is 40 percent. All transactions are cash transactions.

Required

a. The preceding paragraph describes five accounting events: (1) a sales transaction, (2) the first purchase of inventory, (3) a second purchase of inventory, (4) the recognition of cost of goods sold expense, and (5) the payment of income tax expense. Record the amounts of each event in horizontal statements models like the following ones, assuming first a FIFO and then a LIFO cost flow.

Effect of Events on Financial Statements

Panel 1: FIFO Cost Flow

Event No.	Balance Sheet					Income Statement					Statement of Cash Flows
	Cash	+	Inventory	=	Ret. Earn.	Rev.	−	Exp.	=	Net Inc.	

Panel 2: LIFO Cost Flow

Event No.	Balance Sheet					Income Statement					Statement of Cash Flows
	Cash	+	Inventory	=	Ret. Earn.	Rev.	−	Exp.	=	Net Inc.	

b. Compute net income using FIFO.

c. Compute net income using LIFO.

d. Explain the difference, if any, in the amount of income tax expense incurred using the two cost flow assumptions.

e. Which method, FIFO or LIFO, produced the larger amount of assets on the balance sheet?

L.O. 2

Exercise 5-8B ***Recording inventory transactions using the perpetual method: intermittent sales and purchases***

The following inventory transactions apply to Willow Company for 2006.

Jan. 1	Purchased	250 units @ $40
Apr. 1	Sold	125 units @ $70
Aug. 1	Purchased	400 units @ $44
Dec. 1	Sold	500 units @ $76

The beginning inventory consisted of 175 units at $34 per unit. All transactions are cash transactions.

Required

a. Record these transactions in general journal format assuming Willow uses the FIFO cost flow assumption and keeps perpetual records.

b. Compute cost of goods sold for 2006.

L.O. 2

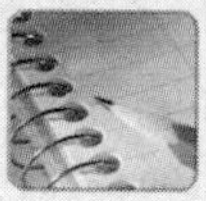

Exercise 5-9B ***Effect of cost flow on ending inventory: intermittent sales and purchases***

Sand Hill, Inc., had the following series of transactions for 2008:

Date	Transaction	Description
Jan. 1	Beginning inventory	50 units @ $30
Mar. 15	Purchased	200 units @ $35
May 30	Sold	170 units @ $70
Aug. 10	Purchased	275 units @ $40
Nov. 20	Sold	340 units @ $75

Required

a. Determine the quantity and dollar amount of inventory at the end of the year, assuming Sand Hill uses the FIFO cost flow assumption and keeps perpetual records.

b. Write a memo explaining why Sand Hill, Inc., would have difficulty applying the weighted-average method on a perpetual basis.

L.O. 3

Exercise 5-10B ***Lower-of-cost-or-market rule: perpetual system***

The following information pertains to Superior Woodwork Co.'s ending inventory for the current year.

Item	Quantity	Unit Cost	Unit Market Value
P	100	$16	$12
D	50	18	16
S	20	24	26
J	15	20	22

Required

a. Determine the value of the ending inventory using the lower-of-cost-or-market rule applied to (1) each individual inventory item and (2) the inventory in aggregate.

b. Prepare any necessary journal entries, assuming the decline in value is immaterial. Superior Woodwork Co. uses the perpetual inventory system. (Make entries for both methods.)

L.O. 3

Exercise 5-11B ***Lower-of-cost-or-market rule***

Wygal Company carries three inventory items. The following information pertains to the ending inventory:

Item	Quantity	Unit Cost	Unit Market Value
B	100	$40	$36
C	150	60	56
D	90	20	30

Required

a. Determine the ending inventory that Wygal will report on the balance sheet, assuming that it applies the lower-of-cost-or-market rule to individual inventory items.

b. Prepare the necessary journal entry, assuming the decline in value was immaterial.

Exercise 5-12B ***Estimating ending inventory*** L.O. 4, 5

A substantial portion of inventory owned by Prairie Hunting Goods was recently destroyed when the roof collapsed during a rainstorm. Prairie also lost some of its accounting records. Prairie must estimate the loss from the storm for insurance reporting and financial statement purposes. Prairie uses the periodic inventory system. The following accounting information was recovered from the damaged records.

Beginning inventory	$ 25,000
Purchases to date of storm	100,000
Sales to date of storm	137,500

The value of undamaged inventory counted was $2,000. Historically Prairie's gross margin percentage has been approximately 25 percent of sales.

Required

Estimate the following:

a. Gross margin in dollars.

b. Cost of goods sold.

c. Ending inventory.

d. Amount of lost inventory.

Exercise 5-13B ***Estimating ending inventory: perpetual system*** L.O. 4, 5

Ralph Kaye owned a small company that sold garden equipment. The equipment was expensive, and a perpetual system was maintained for control purposes. Even so, lost, damaged, and stolen merchandise normally amounted to 5 percent of the inventory balance. On June 14, Kaye's warehouse was destroyed by fire. Just prior to the fire, the accounting records contained a $338,000 balance in the Inventory account. However, inventory costing $42,000 had been sold and delivered to customers but had not been recorded in the books at the time of the fire. The fire did not affect the showroom, which contained inventory that cost $75,000.

Required

Estimate the amount of inventory destroyed by fire.

Exercise 5-14B ***Effect of inventory error on financial statements: perpetual system*** L.O. 4, 5

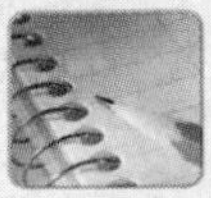

Sharp Company failed to count $50,000 of inventory in its 2005 year-end physical count.

Required

Write a memo explaining how Sharp Company's balance sheet will be affected in 2005. Assume Sharp uses the perpetual inventory system.

Exercise 5-15B ***Effect of inventory error on elements of financial statements*** L.O. 4, 5

The ending inventory for Elm Co. was incorrectly adjusted, which caused it to be understated by $12,500 for 2006.

Required

Was each of the following amounts overstated, understated, or not affected by the error?

Item No.	Year	Amount
1	2006	Beginning inventory
2	2006	Purchases
3	2006	Goods available for sale
4	2006	Cost of goods sold
5	2006	Gross margin
6	2006	Net income
7	2007	Beginning inventory
8	2007	Purchases
9	2007	Goods available for sale
10	2007	Cost of goods sold
11	2007	Gross margin
12	2007	Net income

L.O. 7

Exercise 5-16B *Identifying asset values for financial statements (Appendix)*

Required

Indicate whether each of the following assets should be valued at fair market value (FMV), lower-of-cost-or-market (LCM), or historical cost (HC) on the balance sheet. For certain assets, historical cost may be called amortized cost (AC).

Asset	FMV	LCM	HC/AC
Inventory			
Prepaid Rent			
Cash			
Held-to-Maturity Securities			
Machinery			
Available-for-Sale Securities			
Supplies			
Trading Securities			

L.O. 7

Exercise 5-17B *Accounting for investment securities (Appendix)*

Jones Bros. purchased $20,000 of marketable securities on March 1, 2005. On the company's fiscal closing date, December 31, 2005, the securities had a market value of $27,000. During 2005, Jones recognized $10,000 of revenue and $4,000 of expenses.

Required

a. Record a +, −, or NA in a horizontal statements model to show how the purchase of the securities affects the financial statements, assuming that the securities are classified as (1) held to maturity, (2) trading, or (3) available for sale. In the Cash Flow column, indicate whether the event is an operating activity (OA), investing activity (IA), or financing activity (FA). Record only the effects of the purchase event.

Event No.	Type	Cash	+	Inv. Sec.	=	Liab.	+	Equity	Rev.	−	Exp.	=	Net Inc.	Cash Flow
1	Held													
2	Trading													
3	Available													

b. Determine the amount of net income that would be reported on the 2005 income statement, assuming that the marketable securities are classified as (1) held to maturity, (2) trading, or (3) available for sale.

Exercise 5-18B *Effect of investment securities transactions on financial statements (Appendix)* L.O. 7

The following information pertains to City Electronics for 2003.

1. Purchased $75,000 of marketable investment securities.
2. Earned $4,500 of cash investment revenue.
3. Sold for $15,000 securities that cost $12,500.
4. The fair market value of the remaining securities at December 31, 2003, was $50,000.

Required

a. Record the four events in a statements model like the following one. Use a separate model for each classification: (1) held to maturity, (2) trading, and (3) available for sale. The first event for the first classification is shown as an example.

Held to Maturity

Event No.	Cash	+	Inv. Sec.	=	Liab.	+	Ret. Earn.	+	Unreal. Gain.	Rev. or Gains	−	Exp. or Loss	=	Net Inc.	Cash Flow
1	(75,000)	+	75,000	=	NA	+	NA	+	NA	NA	−	NA	=	NA	(75,000) IA

b. What is the amount of net income under each of the three classifications?

c. What is the change in cash from operating activities under each of the three assumptions?

d. What is the ending amount of Investment Securities under each of the three assumptions?

Exercise 5-19B *Preparing financial statements for investment securities (Appendix)* L.O. 7

Coopers, Inc., began 2006 with $60,000 in both cash and common stock. The company engaged in the following investment transactions during 2006:

1. Purchased $30,000 of marketable investment securities.
2. Earned $800 cash from investment revenue.
3. Sold investment securities for $10,000 that cost $7,000.
4. Purchased $10,000 of additional marketable investment securities.
5. Determined that the investment securities had a fair value of $34,000 at the end of 2006.

Required

a. Record the above transactions in general journal form and post to T-accounts assuming the securities were (1) held to maturity, (2) trading, and (3) available for sale. (Use a separate set of journal entries and T-accounts for each type of security.)

b. Use a vertical statements model to prepare income statements, balance sheets, and statements of cash flow for Coopers, Inc., assuming the securities were (1) held to maturity, (2) trading, and (3) available for sale.

Exercise 5-20B *Differences among classifications of marketable investment securities (Appendix)* L.O. 7

Required

List the three classifications of investment securities and give an example of each.

PROBLEMS—SERIES B

Problem 5-21B *Effect of different inventory cost flow methods on financial statements* L.O. 1, 2

The accounting records of Helen's Clock Shop reflected the following balances as of January 1, 2007.

Cash	$50,800
Beginning Inventory	56,000 (200 units @ $280)
Common Stock	43,000
Retained Earnings	63,800

The following five transactions occurred in 2007:

1. First purchase (cash) 120 units @ $300
2. Second purchase (cash) 140 units @ $330
3. Sales (all cash) 400 units @ $450
4. Paid $30,000 cash for salaries expense.
5. Paid cash for income tax at the rate of 25 percent of income before taxes.

Required

a. Compute the cost of goods sold and ending inventory, assuming (1) FIFO cost flow, (2) LIFO cost flow, and (3) weighted-average cost flow. Compute the income tax expense for each method.

b. Record the five transactions in general journal form and post to T-accounts assuming (1) FIFO cost flow, (2) LIFO cost flow, and (3) weighted-average cost flow.

c. Use a vertical model to show the 2007 income statement, balance sheet, and statement of cash flows under FIFO, LIFO, and weighted average. (*Hint:* Record the events under an accounting equation before preparing the statements.)

L.O. 2

Problem 5-22B ***Allocating product costs between cost of goods sold and ending inventory: intermittent purchases and sales of merchandise***

The Fireplace Shop had the following sales and purchase transactions during 2008. Beginning inventory consisted of 60 items at $350 each. The company uses the FIFO cost flow assumption and keeps perpetual inventory records.

Date	Transaction	Description
Mar. 5	Purchased	50 items @ $370
Apr. 10	Sold	40 items @ $450
June 19	Sold	50 items @ $450
Sept. 16	Purchased	50 items @ $390
Nov. 28	Sold	35 items @ $470

Required

a. Record the inventory transactions in general journal format.

b. Calculate the gross margin The Fireplace Shop would report on the 2008 income statement.

c. Determine the ending inventory balance The Fireplace Shop would report on the December 31, 2008, balance sheet.

L.O. 3

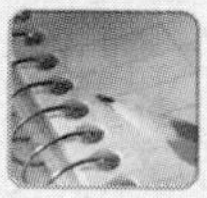

Problem 5-23B ***Inventory valuation based on the lower-of-cost-or-market rule***

At the end of the year, Ralph's Repair Service had the following items in inventory:

Item	Quantity	Unit Cost	Unit Market Value
P1	80	$ 80	$ 90
P2	60	60	66
P3	100	140	130
P4	50	130	140

Required

a. Determine the amount of ending inventory using the lower-of-cost-or-market rule applied to each individual inventory item.

b. Provide the general journal entry necessary to write down the inventory based on Requirement *a.* Assume that Ralph's Repair Service uses the perpetual inventory system.

c. Determine the amount of ending inventory, assuming that the lower-of-cost-or-market rule is applied to the total inventory in aggregate.

d. Provide the general journal entry necessary to write down the inventory based on Requirement *c.* Assume that Ralph's Repair Service uses the perpetual inventory system.

e. Explain how the inventory loss would be reported when the periodic inventory system is used.

Problem 5-24B ***Estimating ending inventory: gross margin method*** **L.O. 5**

Second Chance Grocery had its inventory destroyed by a tornado on October 6 of the current year. Fortunately, some of the accounting records were at the home of one of the owners and were not damaged. The following information was available for the period of January 1 through October 6:

Beginning inventory, January 1	$ 162,000
Purchases through October 6	680,000
Sales through October 6	1,140,000

Gross margin for Second Chance has traditionally been 30 percent of sales.

Required

a. For the period ending October 6, compute the following:
   (1) Estimated gross margin.
   (2) Estimated cost of goods sold.
   (3) Estimated inventory at October 6.

b. Assume that $20,000 of the inventory was not damaged. What is the amount of the loss from the tornado?

c. If Second Chance Grocery had used the perpetual inventory system, how would it have determined the amount of the inventory loss?

Problem 5-25B ***Estimating ending inventory: gross margin method*** **L.O. 5**

Mae's Market Place wishes to produce quarterly financial statements, but it takes a physical count of inventory only at year end. The following historical data were taken from the 2006 and 2007 accounting records:

	2006	2007
Net sales	$60,000	$70,000
Cost of goods sold	31,000	36,500

At the end of the first quarter of 2008, Mae's ledger had the following account balances:

Sales	$56,500
Purchases	41,000
Beginning Inventory 1/1/2008	12,500
Ending Inventory 3/31/2008	15,000

Based on purchases and sales, Mae thinks her inventory is low.

Required

Using the information provided, estimate the following for the first quarter of 2008:

a. Cost of goods sold. (Use the average cost of goods sold percentage.)

b. Ending inventory at March 31.

c. What could explain the difference between actual and estimated inventory?

L.O. 4

Problem 5-26B ***Effect of inventory errors on financial statements***

The following income statement was prepared for Hot Fireworks for the year 2006:

HOT FIREWORKS Income Statement For the Year Ended December 31, 2006	
Sales	$140,000
Cost of Goods Sold	(77,200)
Gross Margin	62,800
Operating Expenses	(40,900)
Net Income	$21,900

During the year-end audit, the following errors were discovered:

1. A $2,000 payment for repairs was erroneously charged to the Cost of Goods Sold account. (Assume that the perpetual inventory system is used.)
2. Sales to customers for $500 at December 31, 2006, were not recorded in the books for 2006. Also, the $300 cost of goods sold was not recorded. The error was not discovered in the physical count because the goods had not been delivered to the customers.
3. A mathematical error was made in determining ending inventory. Ending inventory was understated by $1,800. (The Inventory account was written down in error to the Cost of Goods Sold account.)

Required

Determine the effect, if any, of each of the errors on the following items. Give the dollar amount of the effect and whether it would overstate (+), understate (−), or not affect (NA) the account. The first item for each error is recorded as an example.

Error No. 1	Amount of Error	Effect
Sales, 2006	NA	NA
Ending inventory, December 31, 2006		
Gross margin, 2006		
Beginning inventory, January 1, 2007		
Cost of goods sold, 2006		
Net income, 2006		
Retained earnings, December 31, 2006		
Total assets, December 31, 2006		
Error No. 2	**Amount of Error**	**Effect**
Sales, 2006	$500	−
Ending inventory, December 31, 2006		
Gross margin, 2006		
Beginning inventory, January 1, 2007		
Cost of goods sold, 2006		
Net income, 2006		
Retained earnings, December 31, 2006		
Total assets, December 31, 2006		
Error No. 3	**Amount of Error**	**Effect**
Sales, 2006	NA	NA
Ending inventory, December 31, 2006		
Gross margin, 2006		
Beginning inventory, January 1, 2007		
Cost of goods sold, 2006		
Net income, 2006		
Retained earnings, December 31, 2006		
Total assets, December 31, 2006		

Problem 5-27B *Effect of marketable investment securities on financial statements (Appendix)*

L.O. 7

The following transactions pertain to Five State Trucking Co. for 2007.

1. Heather Brogan started the business when it acquired $15,000 cash from a stock issue.
2. Provided $50,000 of services for cash.
3. Invested $12,000 in marketable investment securities.
4. Paid $17,000 of operating expense.
5. Received $400 investment income from the securities.
6. Invested an additional $16,000 in marketable investment securities.
7. Paid a $1,000 cash dividend to the owner.
8. Sold investment securities that cost $6,000 for $6,400.
9. Received $900 in investment income.
10. Determined the fair value of the investment securities at the end of the year to be $20,000.

Required

Use a vertical model to show an income statement, balance sheet, and statement of cash flows, assuming that the marketable investment securities were classified as (a) held to maturity, (b) trading, and (c) available for sale. (*Hint:* Record the events in T-accounts prior to preparing the financial statements.)

Problem 5-28B *Comprehensive horizontal statements model (Appendix)*

L.O. 1, 3, 7

Beach Front Sales Co. experienced the following independent events.

1. Acquired cash from the issue of common stock.
2. Paid cash to purchase marketable securities classified as available for sale.
3. Paid cash to purchase inventory.
4. There was an unrealized gain on marketable securities that were classified as trading securities.
5. There was an unrealized gain on marketable securities that were classified as available-for-sale securities.
6. There was an unrealized gain on marketable securities that were classified as held-to-maturity securities.
7. Wrote down inventory to comply with the lower-of-cost-or-market rule. (Assume that the company uses the perpetual inventory system.)
8. Recognized cost of goods sold under FIFO.
9. Recognized cost of goods sold under LIFO.

Required

a. Show the effect of each event on the elements of the financial statements using a horizontal statements model like the following one. Use + for increase, − for decrease, and NA for not affected. In the Cash Flow column, indicate whether the item is an operating activity (OA), investing activity (IA) or financing activity (FA). The first transaction is entered as an example.

Event No.	Assets	=	Liab.	+	Equity	Rev. or Gain	−	Exp. or Loss	=	Net Inc.	Cash Flow
1	+		NA		+	NA		NA		NA	+ FA

b. Explain why there is or is not a difference in the way Events 8 and 9 affect the financial statements model.

ANALYZE, THINK, COMMUNICATE

ATC 5-1 Business Applications Case *Understanding real world annual reports*

Required—Part 1

Use the Topps Company's annual report in Appendix B to answer the following questions.

The Topps Company, Inc.

a. What was Topps' inventory turnover ratio and average days to sell inventory for the years ended March 1, 2003, and March 2, 2002?
b. Is the company's management of inventory getting better or worse?
c. What cost flow method(s) did Topps use to account for inventory?

Required—Part 2

Harley-Davidson, Inc.

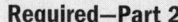

Use the Harley-Davidson's annual report that came with this book to answer the following questions.

a. What was Harley-Davidson's inventory turnover ratio and average days to sell inventory for the year ended December 31, 2003?
b. What cost flow method(s) did Harley-Davidson use to account for inventory?
c. How much different, lower or higher, would Harley-Davidson's ending inventory have been if it had used the FIFO cost flow method for all of its inventory (see Note 2)?

Required—Part 3

Speculate as to why Harley-Davidson sells its inventory more quickly than Topps.

ATC 5-2 Group Assignment *Inventory cost flow*

The accounting records of Blue Bird Co. showed the following balances at January 1, 2008:

Cash	$30,000
Beginning inventory (100 units @ $50, 70 units @ $55)	8,850
Common stock	20,000
Retained earnings	18,850

Transactions for 2008 were as follows:

Purchased 100 units @ $54 per unit.
Sold 220 units @ $80 per unit.
Purchased 250 units @ $58 per unit.
Sold 200 units @ $90 per unit.
Paid operating expenses of $3,200.
Paid income tax expense. The income tax rate is 30%.

Required

a. Organize the class into three sections, and divide each section into groups of three to five students. Assign each section one of the cost flow methods, FIFO, LIFO, or weighted average. The company uses the perpetual inventory system.

Group Tasks

Determine the amount of ending inventory, cost of goods sold, gross margin, and net income after income tax for the cost flow method assigned to your section. Also prepare an income statement using that cost flow assumption.

Class Discussion

b. Have a representative of each section put its income statement on the board. Discuss the effect that each cost flow method has on assets (ending inventory), net income, and cash flows. Which method is preferred for tax reporting? For financial reporting? What restrictions are placed on the use of LIFO for tax reporting?

ATC 5-3 Real-World Case *Analyzing inventory management issues at Campbell's Soup*

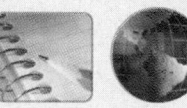

After more than a decade of generally positive economic news, the United States economy began to slow in 2000. At that time, the Campbell Soup Company (Campbell's), like many other companies, saw its earnings decline. Campbell's net earnings fell from $714 million in its 2000 fiscal year to $525 million in 2002, but then profits began to improve. By 2004 its earnings were back up to $647 million.

The data below, for Campbell's fiscal years ending on August 3, 2003, and August 1, 2004, pertain to analyzing the company's management of inventory. All dollar amounts are in millions.

	2004	2003
Sales	$7,109	$6,678
Cost of goods sold	4,187	3,805
Ending inventory	795	709
Income before taxes	947	924
Net earnings	647	595*
Income tax rate	32%	32%

*Includes a special charge for a change in accounting principle of ($31). This expense does not affect the requirements below.

Required

a. Compute Campbell's gross margin percentage for 2004 and 2003.
b. Compute Campbell's average days to sell inventory for 2004 and 2003.
c. Did Campbell's earnings improve from 2003 to 2004 due to either better gross margins or better inventory management (turnover)? Explain.
d. How much higher or lower would Campbell's *earnings before taxes* have been in 2004 if its gross margin percentage had been the same as it was in 2003? Show all supporting computations.
e. How much higher or lower would Campbell's *net earnings* have been in 2004 if its gross margin percentage had been the same as it was in 2003? Show all supporting computations.

ATC 5-4 Business Applications Case *Using the average days to sell inventory ratio to make a lending decision*

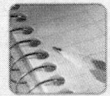

Edna Valley Fruits has applied for a loan and has agreed to use its inventory to collateralize the loan. The company currently has an inventory balance of $206,000. The cost of goods sold for the past year was $5,781,000. The average shelf life for the fruit that Edna Valley sells is 10 days, after which time it begins to spoil and must be sold at drastically reduced prices to dispose of it rapidly. The company maintained steady sales over the past three years and expects to continue at current levels for the foreseeable future.

Required

Based on your knowledge of inventory turnover, write a memo that describes the quality of the inventory as collateral for the loan.

ATC 5-5 Business Applications Case *Using ratios to make comparisons*

The following accounting information pertains to Java Joint and Coffee Corner at the end of 2008. The only difference between the two companies is that Java uses FIFO while Coffee uses LIFO.

	Java Joint	Coffee Corner
Cash	$ 60,000	$ 60,000
Accounts Receivable	240,000	240,000
Merchandise Inventory	180,000	140,000
Accounts Payable	160,000	160,000
Cost of Goods Sold	900,000	940,000
Building	300,000	300,000
Sales	1,500,000	1,500,000

Required

a. Compute the gross margin percentage for each company, and identify the company that *appears* to be charging the higher prices in relation to its costs.
b. For each company, compute the inventory turnover ratio and the average number of days to sell inventory. Identify the company that *appears* to be incurring the higher inventory financing cost.
c. Explain why the company with the lower gross margin percentage has the higher inventory turnover ratio.

ATC 5-6 Writing Assignment *Marketable securities in financial statements*

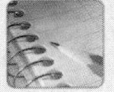

The following information for investment securities is taken from the annual report of The Maximum Companies at December 31, 2005 (amounts in millions):

	Amortized Cost	Gross Unrealized Gains	Gross Unrealized Losses	Estimated Fair Value
Investments				
Available for sale	$19,107.1	$951.3	$79.9	$19,978.5
Held to maturity	143.0	21.7	.4	164.3
Trading securities	16,521.9	13.8	0.0	16,535.7

Required

a. Using the preceding information, what amounts would Maximum report on the balance sheet at December 31, 2005?

b. Write a memo to the shareholders explaining why some investments are reported at cost and others are reported at market value. Explain how the values of these investments are reported at market value. Also explain how gains and losses on the various types of securities are reported in the financial statements.

ATC 5-7 Ethical Dilemma *Show them only what you want them to see*

Clair Coolage is the chief accountant for a sales company called Far Eastern Imports. The company has been highly successful and is trying to increase its capital base by attracting new investors. The company operates in an inflationary environment and has been using the LIFO inventory cost flow method to minimize its net earnings and thereby reduce its income taxes. Katie Bailey, the vice president of finance, asked Coolage to estimate the change in net earnings that would occur if the company switched to FIFO. After reviewing the company's books, Coolage estimated that pretax income would increase by $1,200,000 if the company adopted the FIFO cost flow method. However, the switch would result in approximately $400,000 of additional taxes. The overall effect would result in an increase of $800,000 in net earnings. Bailey told Coolage to avoid the additional taxes by preparing the tax return on a LIFO basis but to prepare a set of statements on a FIFO basis to be distributed to potential investors.

Required

a. Comment on the legal and ethical implications of Bailey's decision.

b. How will the switch to FIFO affect Far Eastern's balance sheet?

c. If Bailey reconsiders and makes a decision to switch to FIFO for tax purposes as well as financial reporting purposes, net income will increase by $800,000. Comment on the wisdom of paying $400,000 in income taxes to obtain an additional $800,000 of net income.

ATC 5-8 Research Assignment *Analyzing inventory at Gap Company*

Using either **Gap's** most current Form 10-K or the company's annual report, answer the questions below. To obtain the Form 10-K use either the EDGAR system following the instructions in Appendix A, or the company's website. The company's annual report is available on its website.

Required

a. What was the average amount of inventory per store? Use *all* stores operated by The Gap, Inc., not just those called *The Gap.* (*Hint:* The answer to this question must be computed. The number of stores in operation at the end of the most recent year can be found in the MD&A of the 10-K.)

b. How many *new* stores did Gap open during the year?

c. Using the quarterly financial information in the 10-K, complete the following chart.

Quarter	Sales During Each Quarter
1	$
2	
3	
4	

d. Referring to the chart in Requirement *c*, explain why Gap's sales vary so widely throughout its fiscal year. Do you believe that Gap's inventory level varies throughout the year in relation to sales?

COMPREHENSIVE PROBLEM

The trial balance of Pacilio Security Services Inc. as of January 1, 2005, had the following normal balances:

Cash	$62,860
Accounts Receivable	20,500
Supplies	150
Prepaid Rent	2,000
Merchandise Inventory (9 @ $240)	2,160
Land	4,000
Accounts Payable	980
Salaries Payable	1,500
Common Stock	50,000
Retained Earnings	39,190

During 2005, Pacilio Security Services experienced the following transactions:

1. Paid the salaries payable from 2004.
2. On January 15, purchased 20 standard alarm systems for cash at a cost of $250 each.
3. On February 1, paid the accounts payable of $980, but not within the discount period. Total cash paid was $1,000.
4. On March 1, leased a business van. Paid $4,800 for one year's lease in advance.
5. Paid $7,200 on May 1 for one year's rent on the office in advance.
6. Purchased with cash $500 of supplies to be used over the next several months by the business.
7. Purchased with cash another 25 alarm systems on August 1 for resale at a cost of $260 each.
8. On September 5, purchased on account 30 standard alarm systems at a cost of $265.
9. Installed 60 standard alarm systems for $33,000. $22,000 of the sales were on account and $11,000 were cash sales. (*Note:* Be sure to record cost of goods sold using the perpetual FIFO method.)
10. Made a full refund to a dissatisfied customer who returned her alarm system. The sale had been a cash sale for $550 with a cost of $260.
11. Paid installers and other employees a total of $21,000 cash for salaries.
12. Sold $45,000 of monitoring services during the year. The services are billed to the customers each month.
13. Sold an additional monitoring service for $1,200 for one year's service. The customer paid the full amount of $1,200 on October 1.
14. Collected $74,000 of accounts receivable during the year.
15. Paid an additional $6,000 to settle some of the accounts payable.
16. Paid $3,500 of advertising expense during the year.
17. Paid $2,300 of utilities expense for the year.
18. Paid a dividend of $15,000 to the shareholders.

Adjustments

19. There was $200 of supplies on hand at the end of the year.
20. Recognized the expired rent for both the van and the office building for the year.
21. Recognized the revenue earned from transaction 13.
22. Accrued salaries at December 31, 2005, were $1,000.

Required

a. Record the above transactions in general journal form.
b. Post the transactions to T-accounts.
c. Prepare a trial balance.
d. Prepare an income statement, statement of changes in stockholders' equity, balance sheet, and statement of cash flows.
e. Close the temporary accounts to retained earnings.
f. Post the closing entries to the T-accounts and prepare an after-closing trial balance.

CHAPTER 6

Internal Control and Accounting for Cash

LEARNING OBJECTIVES

After you have mastered the material in this chapter, you will be able to:

1. **Identify the key elements of a strong system of internal control.**
2. **Identify special internal controls for cash.**
3. **Prepare a bank reconciliation.**
4. **Explain the use of a petty cash fund.**
5. **Describe the auditor's role in financial reporting.**

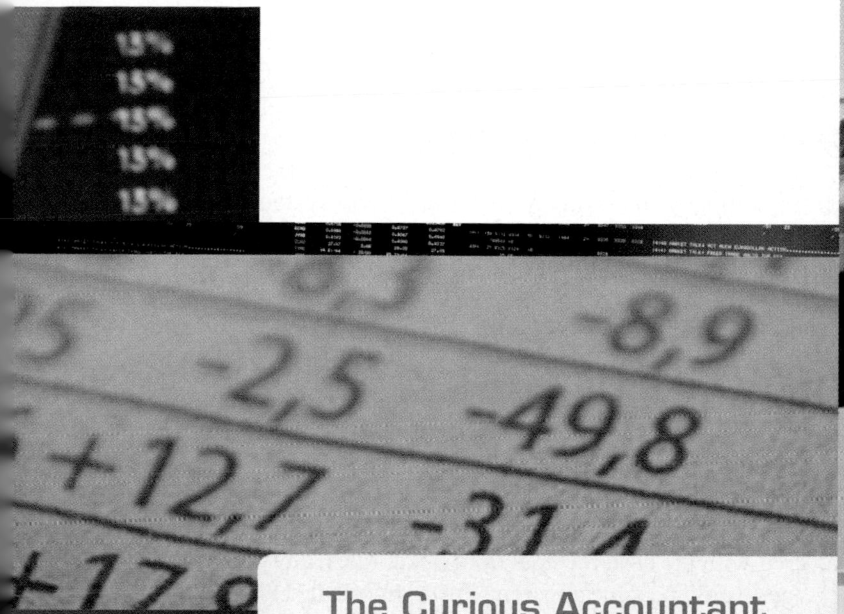

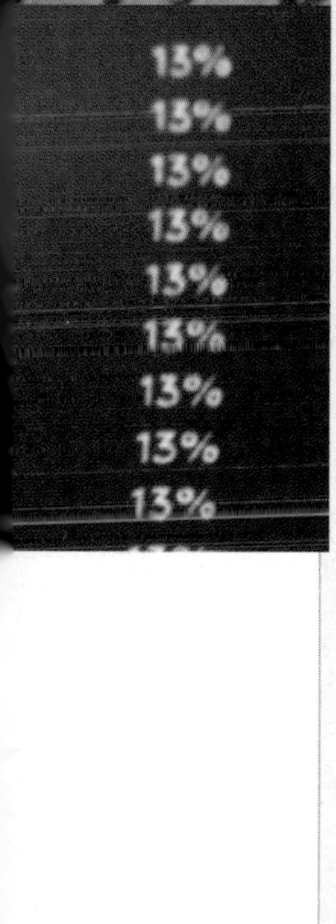

Chapter 6

The Curious Accountant

On June 25, 2002, **WorldCom**, the second largest long-distance telecommunications company in the United States, announced that its expenses had been incorrectly understated by approximately $3.6 billion. This understatement occurred because certain costs that should have been recorded as expenses were, instead, recorded as assets. On June 26, the company, which was experiencing difficulties before the revelation of its accounting problems, announced it would lay off 17,000 of its 80,000 employees, and the NASDAQ stopped trading of its stock. The company predicted its accounting misstatements would total over $11 billion by August 2003.

The restatement of WorldCom's earnings resulting from this discovery was the largest in corporate history, replacing the previous record set by **Waste Management** in 1998. Obviously, this is not a record a company wants to hold. As a result of these accounting irregularities, some members of management were fired or asked to resign.

How do you think such a large understatement of expenses goes undetected? Try to *speculate as to how it was ultimately discovered.* (Answer on page 291.)

CHAPTER OPENING

To operate successfully, businesses must establish systems of control. How can ***Wal-Mart's*** *upper-level managers ensure that every store will open on time? How can the president of* ***General Motors*** *be confident that the company's financial reports fairly reflect the company's operations? How can the owner of a restaurant prevent a waiter from serving food to his friends and relatives without charging them for it? The answer: by exercising* *effective control over company activities. The policies and procedures used to provide reasonable assurance that the objectives of an enterprise will be accomplished are called* **internal controls.**[1]

Internal controls can be divided into two categories: (1) **accounting controls** *are designed to safeguard company assets and ensure reliable accounting records; and (2)* **administrative controls** *are concerned with evaluating performance and assessing the degree of compliance with company policies and public laws.* ■

Key Features of Internal Control Systems

LO 1

Identify the key elements of a strong system of internal control.

Topic Tackler PLUS 6-1

Internal control systems vary from company to company. However, most systems include certain basic policies and procedures that have proven effective over time. A discussion of the more common features of a strong system of internal control follows.

Separation of Duties

The likelihood of fraud or theft is reduced if collusion is required to accomplish it. Clear **separation of duties** is frequently used as a deterrent to corruption. When duties are separated, the work of one employee can act as a check on the work of another employee. For example, a person selling seats to a movie may be tempted to steal money received from customers who enter the theater. This temptation is reduced if the person staffing the box office is required to issue tickets that a second employee collects as people enter the theater. If ticket stubs collected by the second employee are compared with the cash receipts from ticket sales, any cash shortages would become apparent. Furthermore, friends and relatives of the ticket agent could not easily enter the theater without paying. Theft or unauthorized entry would require collusion between the ticket agent and the usher who collects the tickets. Both individuals would have to be dishonest enough to steal, yet trustworthy enough to convince each other they would keep the embezzlement secret. Whenever possible, the functions of *authorization, recording,* and *custody of assets* should be performed by separate individuals.

Quality of Employees

A business is only as good as the people it employs. Cheap labor is not a bargain if the employees are incompetent. Employees should be properly trained. In fact, they should be trained to perform a variety of tasks. The ability of employees to substitute for one another prevents disruptions when co-workers are absent because of illnesses, vacations, or other commitments. The capacity to rotate jobs also relieves boredom and increases respect for the contributions of other employees. Every business should strive to maximize the productivity of every employee. Ongoing training programs are essential to a strong system of internal control.

Bonded Employees

The best way to ensure employee honesty is to hire individuals with *high levels of personal integrity.* Employers should screen job applicants using interviews, background checks, and recommendations from prior employers or educators. Even so, screening programs may fail to identify character weaknesses. Further, unusual circumstances may cause honest employees to go astray. Therefore, employees in positions of trust should be bonded. A **fidelity bond** provides insurance that protects a company from losses caused by employee dishonesty.

Required Absences

Employees should be required to take regular vacations and their duties should be rotated periodically. Employees may be able to cover up fraudulent activities if they are always present

[1]*AICPA Professional Standards,* vol. 1, sec. 320, par. 6 (June 1, 1989).

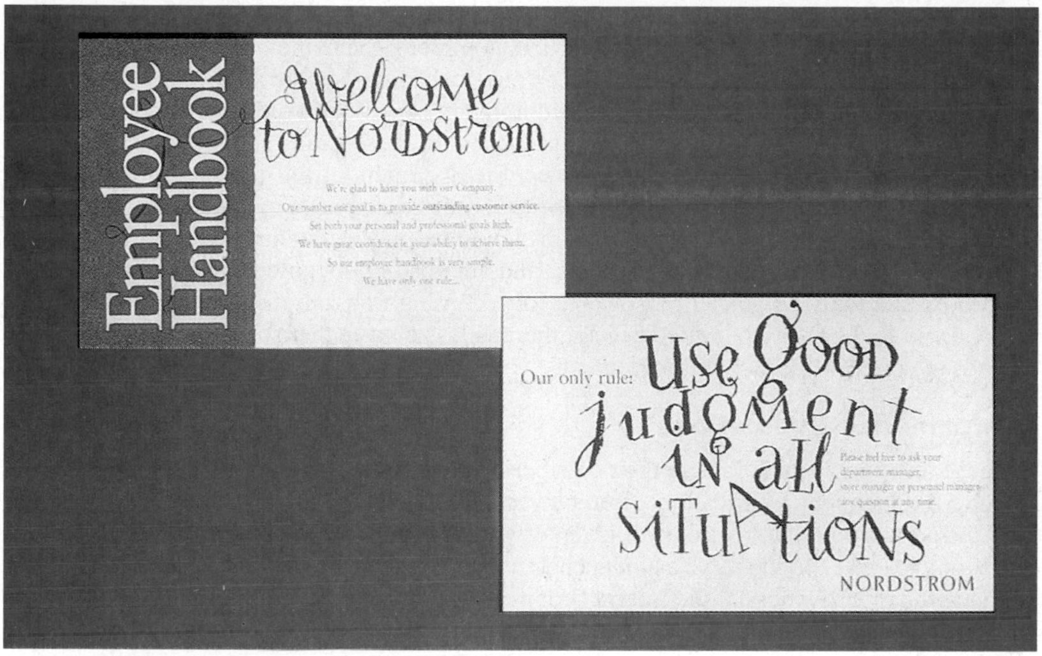

at work. Consider the case of a parking meter collection agent who covered the same route for several years with no vacation. When the agent became sick, a substitute collected more money each day than the regular reader usually reported. Management checked past records and found that the ill meter reader had been understating the cash receipts and pocketing the difference. If management had required vacations or rotated the routes, the embezzlement would have been discovered much earlier.

Procedures Manual

Appropriate accounting procedures should be documented in a **procedures manual**. The manual should be routinely updated. Periodic reviews should be conducted to ensure that employees are following the procedures outlined in the manual.

Authority and Responsibility

Employees are motivated by clear lines of authority and responsibility. They work harder when they have the authority to use their own judgment and they exercise reasonable caution when they are held responsible for their actions. Businesses should prepare an **authority manual** that establishes a definitive *chain of command.* The authority manual should guide both specific and general authorizations. **Specific authorizations** apply to specific positions within the organization. For example, investment decisions are authorized at the division level while hiring decisions are authorized at the departmental level. In contrast, **general authority** applies across different levels of management. For example, employees at all levels may be required to fly coach or to make purchases from specific vendors.

Prenumbered Documents

How would you know if a check were stolen from your check book? If you keep a record of your check numbers, the missing number would tip you off immediately. Businesses also use prenumbered checks to avoid the unauthorized use of their bank accounts. In fact, prenumbered forms are used for all important documents such as purchase orders, receiving reports, invoices, and checks. To reduce errors, prenumbered forms should be as simple and easy to use as possible. Also, the documents should allow for authorized signatures. For example, credit sales slips should be signed by the customer to clearly establish who made the purchase, reducing the likelihood of unauthorized transactions.

Physical Control

Employees walk away with billions of dollars of business assets each year. To limit losses, companies should establish adequate physical control over valuable assets. For example, inventory should be kept in a storeroom and not released without proper authorization. Serial numbers on equipment should be recorded along with the name of the individual who is responsible for the equipment. Unannounced physical counts should be conducted randomly to verify the presence of company-owned equipment. Certificates of deposit and marketable securities should be kept in fireproof vaults. Access to these vaults should be limited to authorized personnel. These procedures protect the documents from fire and limit access to only those individuals who have the appropriate security clearance to handle the documents.

In addition to safeguarding assets, there should be physical control over the accounting records. The accounting journals, ledgers, and supporting documents should be kept in a fireproof safe. Only personnel responsible for recording transactions in the journals should have access to them. With limited access, there is less chance that someone will change the records to conceal fraud or embezzlement.

Performance Evaluations

Because few people can evaluate their own performance objectively, internal controls should include independent verification of employee performance. For example, someone other than the person who has control over inventory should take a physical count of inventory. Internal and external audits serve as independent verification of performance. Auditors should evaluate the effectiveness of the internal control system as well as verify the accuracy of the accounting records. In addition, the external auditors attest to the company's use of generally accepted accounting principles in the financial statements.

Limitations

A system of internal controls is designed to prevent or detect errors and fraud. However, no control system is foolproof. Internal controls can be circumvented by collusion among employees. Two or more employees working together can hide embezzlement by covering for each other. For example, if an embezzler goes on vacation, fraud will not be reported by a replacement who is in collusion with the embezzler. No system can prevent all fraud. However, a good system of internal controls minimizes illegal or unethical activities by reducing temptation and increasing the likelihood of early detection.

CHECK YOURSELF 6.1

What are nine features of an internal control system?

Answer

The nine features follow.

1. Separating duties so that fraud or theft requires collusion.
2. Hiring and training competent employees.
3. Bonding employees to recover losses through insurance.
4. Requiring employees to be absent from their jobs so that their replacements can discover errors or fraudulent activity that might have occurred.
5. Establishing proper procedures for processing transactions.
6. Establishing clear lines of authority and responsibility.
7. Using prenumbered documents.
8. Implementing physical controls such as locking cash in a safe.
9. Conducting performance evaluations through independent internal and external audits.

Accounting for Cash

LO 2

Identify special internal controls for cash.

For financial reporting purposes, **cash** generally includes currency and other items that are payable *on demand,* such as checks, money orders, bank drafts, and certain savings accounts. Savings accounts that impose substantial penalties for early withdrawal should be classified as *investments* rather than cash. Postdated checks or IOUs represent *receivables* and should not be included in cash. As illustrated in Exhibit 6.1, most companies combine currency and other payable on demand items in a single balance sheet account with varying titles.

Answers to The Curious Accountant

Bernie Ebbers, founder of **WorldCom**, is quoted as once having ordered Cynthia Cooper, WorldCom's vice president of internal audit, never to use the phrase *internal control.* Ebbers said he didn't understand it. Apparently, he was right. It was Mrs. Cooper and her team of internal auditors who ultimately uncovered the vast fraud. Perhaps a different attitude at the top about internal control could have avoided this fiasco.

As noted earlier, WorldCom had been experiencing difficulties prior to June 2002. In April 2002 its longtime CEO was ousted, and its board of directors launched an internal investigation of the company's operations. Mrs. Cooper found the questionable accounting procedures and reported them to the company's audit committee. The chief financial officer at WorldCom was fired upon discovery of the accounting fraud. He and a few other key executives were ultimately indicted on criminal charges. After others had pled guilty to the fraud charges, the chief financial officer reportedly continued to claim the company was within the rules to record the costs in question as assets and depreciate them in future periods, rather than recognize them immediately as expenses. The company's external auditor and board of directors did not agree with him.

Another question to consider is why no one asked to see the $3.6 billion of assets the company was supposed to be purchasing. The answer to this is not as obvious as one might expect. In the telecommunications business, many legitimate assets do not have any physical existence; they are said to be intangible assets, so it is not surprising that no one noticed they did not exist. Intangible assets are discussed in Chapter 8. WorldCom has since changed its name to **MCI**, but all of the legal issues surrounding the accounting fraud at the company have not yet been settled.

Companies must maintain a sufficient amount of cash to pay employees, suppliers, and other creditors. When a company fails to pay its legal obligations, its creditors can force the company into bankruptcy. Even so, management should avoid accumulating more cash than is needed. The failure to invest excess cash in earning assets reduces profitability. Cash inflows and outflows must be managed to prevent a shortage or surplus of cash.

EXHIBIT 6.1

Balance Sheet Classifications that Include the Word Cash

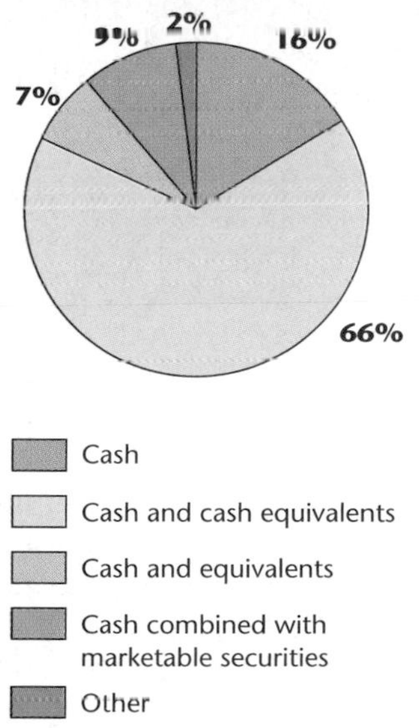

Data Source: AICPA, *Accounting Trends and Techniques,* 2002.

Controlling Cash

Controlling cash, more than any other asset, requires strict adherence to internal control procedures. Cash has universal appeal. A relatively small suitcase filled with high-denomination currency can represent significant value. Furthermore, the rightful owner of currency is difficult to prove. In most cases, possession constitutes ownership. As a result, cash is highly susceptible to theft and must be carefully protected. Cash is most susceptible to embezzlement when it is received or disbursed. The following controls should be employed to reduce the likelihood of theft.

Cash Receipts

A record of all cash collections should be prepared immediately upon receipt. The amount of cash on hand should be counted regularly. Missing amounts of money can be detected by comparing the actual cash on hand with the book balance. Employees who receive cash should give customers a copy of a written receipt. Customers usually review their receipts to ensure they have gotten credit for the amount paid and call any errors to the receipts clerk's attention. This not only reduces errors but also provides a control on the clerk's honesty. Cash receipts should be deposited in a bank on a timely basis. Cash collected late in the day should be deposited in a night depository. Every effort should be made to minimize the amount of cash on hand. Keeping large amounts of cash on hand not only increases the risk of loss from theft but also places employees in danger of being harmed by criminals who may be tempted to rob the company.

Cash Payments

To effectively control cash, a company should make all disbursements using checks, thereby providing a record of cash payments. All checks should be prenumbered, and unused checks should be locked up. Using prenumbered checks allows companies to easily identify lost or

REALITY BYTES

THE COST OF PROTECTING CASH

Could you afford to buy a safe like the one shown here? The vault is only one of many expensive security devices used by banks to safeguard cash. By using checking accounts, companies are able to avoid many of the costs associated with keeping cash safe. In addition to providing physical control, checking accounts enable companies to maintain a written audit trail of cash receipts and payments. Checking accounts represent the most widely used internal control device in modern society. It is difficult to imagine a business operating without the use of checking accounts.

stolen checks by comparing the numbers on unused and canceled checks with the numbers used for legitimate disbursements.

The duties of approving disbursements, signing checks, and recording transactions should be separated. If one person is authorized to approve, sign, and record checks, he or she could falsify supporting documents, write an unauthorized check, and record a cover-up transaction in the accounting records. By separating these duties, the check signer reviews the documentation provided by the approving individual before signing the check. Likewise, the recording clerk reviews the work of both the approving person and the check signer when the disbursement is recorded in the accounting records. Thus writing unauthorized checks requires trilevel collusion.

Supporting documents with authorized approval signatures should be required when checks are presented to the check signer. For example, a warehouse receiving order should be matched with a purchase order before a check is approved to pay a bill from a supplier. Before payments are approved, invoice amounts should be checked and payees verified as valid vendors. Matching supporting documents with proper authorization discourages employees from creating phony documents for a disbursement to a friend or fictitious business. Also, the approval process serves as a check on the accuracy of the work of all employees involved.

Supporting documents should be marked *Paid* when the check is signed. If the documents are not indelibly marked, they could be retrieved from the files and resubmitted for a duplicate, unauthorized payment. A payables clerk could collude with the payee to split extra cash paid out by submitting the same supporting documents for a second payment.

All spoiled and voided checks should be defaced and retained. If defaced checks are not retained, an employee could steal a check and then claim that it was written incorrectly and thrown away. The clerk could then use the stolen check to make an unauthorized payment.

Checking Account Documents

The previous section explained the need for businesses to use checking accounts. A description of four main types of forms associated with a bank checking account follows:

Signature Card

A bank **signature card** shows the bank account number and the signatures of the people authorized to sign checks. The card is retained in the bank's files. If a bank employee is unfamiliar with the signature on a check, he or she can refer to the signature card to verify the signature before cashing the check.

Deposit Ticket

Each deposit of cash or checks is accompanied by a **deposit ticket,** which normally identifies the account number and the name of the account. The depositor lists the individual amounts of currency, coins, and checks, as well as the total deposited, on the deposit ticket.

Bank Check

A written check affects three parties: (1) the person or business writing the check (the *payer*); (2) the bank on which the check is drawn; and (3) the person or business to whom the check is payable (the *payee*). Companies often write **checks** using multicopy, prenumbered forms, with the name of the issuing business preprinted on the face of each check. A remittance notice is usually attached to the check forms. This portion of the form provides the issuer space to record what the check is for (e.g., what invoices are being paid), the amount being disbursed, and the date of payment. When signed by the person whose signature is on the signature card, the check authorizes the bank to transfer the face amount of the check from the payer's account to the payee.

Bank Statement

Periodically, the bank sends the depositor a **bank statement.** The bank statement is presented from the bank's point of view. Checking accounts are liabilities to a bank because the bank is obligated to pay back the money that customers have deposited in their accounts. Therefore, in the bank's accounting records a customer's checking account has a *credit* balance. As a result, **bank statement debit memos** describe transactions that reduce the customer's account balance (the bank's liability). **Bank statement credit memos** describe activities that increase the customer's account balance (the bank's liability). Since a checking account is an asset (cash) to the depositor, a *bank statement debit memo* requires a *credit entry* to the cash account on the depositor's books. Likewise, when a bank tells you that it has credited your account, you will debit your cash account in response.

Bank statements normally report (a) the balance of the account at the beginning of the period; (b) additions for customer deposits made during the period; (c) other additions described in credit memos (e.g., for interest earned); (d) subtractions for the payment of checks drawn on the account during the period; (e) other subtractions described in debit memos (e.g., for service charges); (f) a running balance of the account; and (g) the balance of the account at the end of the period. The sample bank statement in Exhibit 6.2 illustrates these items with references to the preceding letters in parentheses. Normally, the canceled checks or copies of them are enclosed with the bank statement.

Reconciling the Bank Account

LO 3

Prepare a bank reconciliation.

Topic Tackler PLUS

6-2

Usually the ending balance reported on the bank statement differs from the balance in the depositor's cash account as of the same date. The discrepancy is normally attributable to timing differences. For example, a depositor deducts the amount of a check from its cash account when it writes the check. However, the bank does not deduct the amount of the check from the depositor's account until the payee presents it for payment, which may be days, weeks, or even months after the check is written. As a result, the balance on the depositor's books is lower than the balance on the bank's books. Companies prepare a **bank reconciliation** to explain the differences between the cash balance reported on the bank statement and the cash balance recorded in the depositor's accounting records.

Determining True Cash Balance

A bank reconciliation normally begins with the cash balance reported by the bank which is called the **unadjusted bank balance.** The adjustments necessary to determine the amount of cash that the depositor actually owns as of the date of the bank statement are then added to and subtracted from the unadjusted bank balance. The final total is the **true cash balance.** The true cash balance is independently reached a second time by making adjustments to the **unadjusted book balance.** The bank account is reconciled when the true cash balance determined from the perspective of the unadjusted *bank* balance agrees with the true cash balance determined from the perspective of the unadjusted *book* balance. The procedures a company uses to determine the *true cash balance* from the two different perspectives are outlined here.

EXHIBIT 6.2

FIRST STATE BANK
of Frisco County

2121 Westbury Drive • Harrison, Nevada • 54269 - 0001

Green Shades Resorts, Inc
1439 Lazy Lane
Harrison, Nevada 54275 - 0023

Account Number
53-9872-3

Checking Account Summary	On This Date	Your Balance Was	Deposits Added	No. Deposits	Checks Paid	No. Checks
	8/31/2003	(a) 4,779.86	3,571.72	5	4,537.22	22
	Other Debits	Resulting in a Balance of		On This Date		Enclosures
	297.91	(g) 3,516.45		9/30/2003		29

Checks and Debits		Deposits and Credits	Date	Balance
(d) 15.82	24.85	(b) 600.25	9/3	(f) 5,339.44
249.08	497.00		9/5	4,593.36
42.53	124.61		9/7	4,426.22
79.87	859.38		9/8	3,486.97
685.00	742.59	711.43	9/9	2,770.81
25.75	38.98		9/12	2,706.08
36.45	59.91		9/14	2,609.72
	(e) 8.40 DM	(c) 940.00 CM	9/15	3,541.32
61.40		689.47	9/18	4,169.39
289.51 NS			9/19	3,879.88
71.59	82.00		9/21	3,726.29
312.87			9/24	3,413.42
25.00		630.57	9/27	4,018.99
227.00			9/28	3,791.99
95.06	180.48		9/30	3,516.45

LEGEND – NS Nonsufficient Funds • DM Debit Memo • CM Credit Memo

FIRST STATE BANK OF FRISCO COUNTY

Adjustments to the Bank Balance

A typical format for determining the true cash balance beginning with the unadjusted bank balance is

	Unadjusted bank balance
+	Deposits in transit
−	Outstanding checks
=	True cash balance

Deposits in transit. Companies frequently leave deposits in the bank's night depository or make them on the day following the receipt of cash. Such deposits are called **deposits in transit.** Since these deposits have been recorded in the depositor's accounting records but have not yet been added to the depositor's account by the bank, they must be added to the unadjusted bank balance.

Outstanding checks. These are disbursements that have been properly recorded as cash deductions on the depositor's books. However, the bank has not deducted the amounts from the depositor's bank account because the checks have not yet been presented by the payee to the bank for payment; that is, the checks have not cleared the bank. **Outstanding checks** must be subtracted from the unadjusted bank balance to determine the true cash balance.

Adjustments to the Book Balance

A typical format for determining the true cash balance beginning with the unadjusted book balance is as follows:

	Unadjusted book balance
+	Accounts receivable collections
+	Interest earned
−	Bank service charges
−	Non-sufficient-funds (NSF) checks
=	True cash balance

Accounts receivable collections. To collect cash as quickly as possible, many companies have their customers send payments directly to the bank. The bank adds the collection directly to the depositor's account and notifies the depositor about the collection through a credit memo that is included on the bank statement. The depositor adds the amount of the cash collections to the unadjusted book balance in the process of determining the true cash balance.

Interest earned. Banks pay interest on certain checking accounts. The amount of the interest is added directly to the depositor's bank account. The bank notifies the depositor about the interest through a credit memo that is included on the bank statement. The depositor adds the amount of the interest revenue to the unadjusted book balance in the process of determining the true cash balance.

Service charges. Banks frequently charge depositors fees for services performed. They may also charge a penalty if the depositor fails to maintain a specified minimum cash balance throughout the period. Banks deduct such fees and penalties directly from the depositor's account and advise the depositor of the deduction through a debit memo that is included on the bank statement. The depositor deducts such **service charges** from the unadjusted book balance to determine the true cash balance.

Non-sufficient-funds (NSF) checks. **NSF checks** are checks that a company obtains from its customers and deposits in its checking account. However, when the checks are submitted to the customers' banks for payment, the banks refuse payment because there is insufficient money in the customers' accounts. When such checks are returned, the amounts of the checks are deducted from the company's bank account balance. The company is advised of NSF checks through debit memos that appear on the bank statement. The depositor deducts the amounts of the NSF checks from the unadjusted book balance in the process of determining the true cash balance.

Correction of Errors

In the course of reconciling the bank statement with the cash account, the depositor may discover errors in the bank's records, the depositor's records, or both. If an error is found on the bank statement, an adjustment for it is made to the unadjusted bank balance to determine the true cash balance, and the bank should be notified immediately to correct its records. Errors made by the depositor require adjustments to the book balance to arrive at the true cash balance.

Certified Checks

A **certified check** is guaranteed for payment by a bank. Whereas a regular check is deducted from the customer's account when it is presented for payment, a certified check is deducted from the customer's account when the bank certifies that the check is good. Certified checks, therefore, *have* been deducted by the bank in determining the unadjusted bank balance, whether they have cleared the bank or remain outstanding as of the date of the bank statement. Since certified checks are deducted both from bank and depositor records immediately, they do not cause differences between the depositor and bank balances. As a result, certified checks are not included in a bank reconciliation.

EXHIBIT 6.3

GREEN SHADES RESORTS, INC.
Bank Reconciliation
September 30, 2003

Unadjusted bank balance, September 30, 2003	$3,516.45
Add: Deposits in transit	724.11
Bank error: Check drawn on Green Valley Resorts charged to GSRI	25.00
Less: Outstanding checks	

Check No.	Date	Amount
639	Sept. 18	$ 13.75
646	Sept. 20	29.00
672	Sept. 27	192.50

Total	(235.25)
True cash balance, September 30, 2003	$4,030.31
Unadjusted book balance, September 30, 2003	$3,361.22
Add: Receivable collected by bank	940.00
Error made by accountant (Check no. 633 recorded as $63.45 instead of $36.45)	27.00
Less: Bank service charges	(8.40)
NSF check	(289.51)
True cash balance, September 30, 2003	$4,030.31

Illustrating a Bank Reconciliation

The following example illustrates preparing the bank reconciliation for Green Shades Resorts, Inc. (GSRI). The bank statement for GSRI is displayed in Exhibit 6.2. Exhibit 6.3 illustrates the completed bank reconciliation. The items on the reconciliation are described below.

Adjustments to the Bank Balance

As of September 30, 2003, the bank statement showed an unadjusted balance of $3,516.45. A review of the bank statement disclosed three adjustments that had to be made to the unadjusted bank balance to determine GSRI's true cash balance.

1. Comparing the deposits on the bank statement with deposits recorded in GSRI's accounting records indicated there was $724.11 of deposits in transit.
2. An examination of the returned checks disclosed that the bank had erroneously deducted a $25 check written by Green Valley Resorts from GSRI's bank account. This amount must be added back to the unadjusted bank balance to determine the true cash balance.
3. The checks returned with the bank statement were sorted and compared to the cash records. Three checks with amounts totaling $235.25 were outstanding.

   After these adjustment are made GSRI's true cash balance is determined to be $4,030.31.

Adjustments to the Book Balance

As indicated in Exhibit 6.3, GSRI's unadjusted book balance as of September 30, 2003, was $3,361.22. This balance differs from GSRI's true cash balance because of four unrecorded accounting events:

1. The bank collected a $940 account receivable for GSRI.
2. GSRI's accountant made a $27 recording error.

3. The bank charged GSRI an $8.40 service fee.
4. GSRI had deposited a $289.51 check from a customer who did not have sufficient funds to cover the check.

Two of these four adjustments increase the unadjusted cash balance. The other two decrease the unadjusted cash balance. After the adjustments have been recorded, the cash account reflects the true cash balance of $4,030.31 ($3,361.22 unadjusted cash balance + $940.00 receivable collection + $27.00 recording error − $8.40 service charge − $289.51 NSF check). Since the true balance determined from the perspective of the bank statement agrees with the true balance determined from the perspective of GSRI's books, the bank statement has been successfully reconciled with the accounting records.

Updating GSRI's Accounting Records

Each of the adjustments to the book balance must be recorded in GSRI's financial records. The effects of each adjustment on the financial statements are as follows.

Adjustment 1 ***Recording the $940 receivable collection increases cash and reduces accounts receivable.***

The event is an asset exchange transaction. The effect of the collection on GSRI's financial statements is:

Assets			=	Liab.	+	Equity	Rev.	−	Exp.	=	Net Inc.	Cash Flow
Cash	+	Accts. Rec.										
940	+	(940)	=	NA	+	NA	NA	−	NA	=	NA	940 OA

Adjustment 2 ***Assume the $27 recording error occurred because GSRI's accountant accidentally transposed two numbers when recording check no. 633 for utilities expense.***

The check was written to pay utilities expense of $36.45 but was recorded as a $63.45 disbursement. Since cash payments are overstated by $27.00 ($63.45 − $36.45), this amount must be added back to GSRI's cash balance and deducted from the utilities expense account, which increases net income. The effects on the financial statements are:

Assets	=	Liab.	+	Equity	Rev.	−	Exp.	=	Net Inc.	Cash Flow
Cash	=			Ret. Earn.						
27	=	NA	+	27	NA	−	(27)	=	27	27 OA

Adjustment 3 ***The $8.40 service charge is an expense that reduces assets, stockholders' equity, net income, and cash.***

The effects are:

Assets	=	Liab.	+	Equity	Rev.	−	Exp.	=	Net Inc.	Cash Flow
Cash	=			Ret. Earn.						
(8.40)	=	NA	+	(8.40)	NA	−	8.40	=	(8.40)	(8.40)

Adjustment 4 ***The $289.51 NSF check reduces GSRI's cash balance.***

When it originally accepted the customer's check, GSRI increased its cash account. Since there is not enough money in the customer's bank account to pay the check, GSRI didn't actually receive cash so GSRI must reduce its cash account. GSRI will still try to collect the money from the customer. In the meantime, it will show the amount of the NSF check as an account receivable. The adjusting entry to record the NSF check is an asset exchange transaction. Cash decreases and accounts receivable increases. The effect on GSRI's financial statements is:

Assets			=	Liab.	+	Equity	Rev.	−	Exp.	=	Net Inc.	Cash Flow
Cash	+	Accts. Rec.										
(289.51)	+	289.51	=	NA	+	NA	NA	−	NA	=	NA	(289.51) OA

Journal Entries

The journal entries for the four adjustments described above are as follows:

Account Title	Debit	Credit
Cash	940.00	
Accounts Receivable		940.00
To record the account receivable collected by the bank		
Cash	27.00	
Utilities Expense		27.00
To correct error on recording check no. 633		
Bank Service Charge Expense	8.40	
Cash		8.40
To record service charge expense		
Accounts Receivable	289.51	
Cash		289.51
To establish receivable from customer who wrote a bad check		

Cash Short and Over

Sometimes employees make mistakes when collecting cash from or making change for customers. When such errors occur, the amount of money in the cash register will not agree with the amount of cash receipts recorded on the cash register tape. For example, suppose that when a customer paid for $17.95 of merchandise with a $20 bill, the sales clerk returned $3.05 in change instead of $2.05. If, at the end of the day, the cash register tape shows total receipts of $487.50, the cash drawer would contain only $486.50. The actual cash balance is less than the expected cash balance by $1. Any shortage of cash or excess of cash is recorded in a special account called **Cash Short and Over.** In this example, the shortage is recorded with the following journal entry:

Account Title	Debit	Credit
Cash	486.50	
Cash Short and Over	1.00	
Sales		487.50

A cash shortage is an expense. It is recorded by debiting the Cash Short and Over account. An overage of cash represents revenue and is recorded by crediting the Cash Short and Over account. As with other expense and revenue items, the balance of the Cash Short and Over account is closed to the Retained Earnings account at the end of the accounting period.

CHECK YOURSELF 6.2

The following information was drawn from Reliance Company's October bank statement. The unadjusted bank balance on October 31 was $2,300. The statement showed that the bank had collected a $200 account receivable for Reliance. The statement also included $20 of bank service charges for October and a $100 check payable to Reliance that was returned NSF. A comparison of the bank statement with company accounting records indicates that there was a $500 deposit in transit and $1,800 of checks outstanding at the end of the month. Based on this information, determine the true cash balance on October 31.

Answer

Since the unadjusted book balance is not given, start with the unadjusted bank balance to determine the true cash balance. The collection of the receivable, the bank service charges, and the NSF check are already recognized in the unadjusted bank balance, so these items are not used to determine the true cash balance. Determine the true cash balance by adding the deposit in transit to and subtracting the outstanding checks from the unadjusted bank balance. The true cash balance is $1,000 ($2,300 unadjusted

Using Petty Cash Funds

LO 4

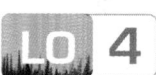

Explain the use of a petty cash fund.

Although businesses use checks for most disbursements, they often pay for small items such as postage, delivery charges, taxi fares, employees' supper money, and so on with currency. They frequently establish a **petty cash fund** to maintain effective control over these small cash disbursements. The fund is established for a specified dollar amount, such as $300, and is controlled by one employee, called the *petty cash custodian.*

Petty cash funds are usually maintained on an **imprest basis,** which means that the money disbursed is periodically replenished. The fund is created by drawing a check on the regular checking account, cashing it, and giving the currency to the petty cash custodian. The custodian normally keeps the currency under lock and key. The amount of the petty cash fund depends on what it is used for, how often it is used, and how often it is replenished. It should be large enough to handle disbursements for a reasonable time period, such as several weeks or a month.

Establishing a petty cash fund merely transfers money from a bank to a safety box inside the company offices. The establishment is an asset exchange event. The Cash account decreases, and an account called Petty Cash increases. The effects on the financial statements of establishing a $300 petty cash fund and the related journal entry are shown here:

Assets			=	Liab.	+	Equity	Rev.	−	Exp.	=	Net Inc.	Cash Flow
Cash	+	Petty Cash										
(300)	+	300	=	NA	+	NA	NA	−	NA	=	NA	NA

Account Title	Debit	Credit
Petty Cash	300.00	
Cash		300.00

When money is disbursed from the petty cash fund, the custodian should complete a **petty cash voucher,** such as the one in Exhibit 6.4. Any supporting documents, such as an invoice, restaurant bill, or parking fee receipt, should be attached to the petty cash voucher. The person who receives the currency should sign the voucher as evidence of receiving the money. The total of the amounts recorded on the petty cash vouchers plus the remaining coins and currency should equal the balance of the petty cash ledger account. *No journal entry is made in the accounting records when petty cash funds are disbursed.* The effects on the

EXHIBIT 6.4

Petty cash voucher no. ________

To: ______________________________ Date ________, 20____

Explanation: Account No. ____________ Amount ________

Approved by ______________ Received by ______________

financial statements are recorded when the petty cash fund is replenished (when additional currency is put into the petty cash safety box).

When the amount of currency in the petty cash fund is relatively low, the fund is replenished. The petty cash vouchers are totaled, the amount of any cash short or over is determined, and a check is issued to the bank to obtain the currency needed to return the fund to its imprest balance. For example, suppose the $300 petty cash fund is replenished when the total of the petty cash vouchers is $216. The vouchers can be classified according to different types of expenses or listed in total as miscellaneous expense. Assuming the company classifies petty cash expenditures as miscellaneous expense, the journal entries to record replenishing the fund are as follows:

Account Title	Debit	Credit
Miscellaneous Expense	216.00	
Petty Cash		216.00
To record expenses paid from the petty cash fund		
Petty Cash	216.00	
Cash		216.00
To replenish the petty cash fund		

If desired, the effect of the entries could be recorded more efficiently. Since the credit to the Petty Cash account is offset by a debit to the same account, a single entry debiting miscellaneous expense and crediting cash would have the same effect on the accounts. The entry more frequently used in practice to record replenishing petty cash is:

Account Title	Debit	Credit
Miscellaneous Expense	216.00	
Cash		216.00

The replenishment affects the financial statements in the same manner as any other cash expense. It reduces assets, stockholders' equity, net income, and cash flow, as follows:

Assets	=	Liab.	+	Equity	Rev.	−	Exp.	=	Net Inc.	Cash Flow
Cash	=			Ret. Earn.						
(216)	=	NA	+	(216)	NA	−	216	=	(216)	(216) OA

If management desires more detailed information about petty cash expenditures, the vouchers can be sorted into postage, $66; delivery charges, $78.40; taxi fares, $28; and supper money, $43.60, in which case the journal entry to replenish the fund could be recorded as follows:

Account Title	Debit	Credit
Postage Expense	66.00	
Delivery Expense	78.40	
Taxi Fares Expense	28.00	
Employee Meal Expense	43.60	
Cash		216.00

Once the vouchers are checked, the fund replenished, and the journal entry recorded, the vouchers should be indelibly marked *Paid* so they cannot be reused.

Sometimes, cash shortages and overages are discovered when the money in the petty cash fund is physically counted. Suppose that a physical count discloses $212.30 in petty cash vouchers and only $87 in currency and coins. Assuming an imprest petty cash balance of $300, the journal entry necessary to replenish the fund is as follows:

Account Title	Debit	Credit
Miscellaneous Expense	212.30	
Cash Short and Over	.70	
Cash		213.00
To replenish the petty cash fund		

If cash shortages or overages do not occur frequently and are of insignificant amounts, companies are likely to include them in miscellaneous expense or miscellaneous revenue.

CHECK YOURSELF 6.3

Cornerstone Corporation established a $400 petty cash fund that was replenished when it contained $30 of currency and coins and $378 of receipts for miscellaneous expenses. Based on this information, determine the amount of cash short or over to be recognized. Explain how the shortage or overage would be reported in the financial statements. Also determine the amount of petty cash expenses that were recognized when the fund was replenished.

Answer

The fund contained $408 of currency and receipts ($30 currency + $378 of receipts), resulting in a cash overage of $8 ($408 − $400). The overage would be reported as miscellaneous revenue on the income statement. The amount of petty cash expenses recognized would equal the amount of the expense receipts, which is $378.

THE FINANCIAL ANALYST

LO 5

Describe the auditor's role in financial reporting.

As previously explained, financial statements are prepared in accordance with certain rules called *generally accepted accounting principles (GAAP)*. Thus, when **General Electric** publishes its financial statements, it is saying, "here are our financial statements prepared according to GAAP." How can a financial analyst know that a company really did follow GAAP? Analysts and other statement users rely on **audits** conducted by **certified public accountants (CPAs).**

The primary roles of an independent auditor (CPA) are summarized below:

1. Conducts a financial audit (a detailed examination of a company's financial statements and underlying accounting records).
2. Assumes both legal and professional responsibilities to the public as well as to the company paying the auditor.
3. Determines if financial statements are *materially* correct rather than *absolutely* correct.
4. Presents conclusions in an audit report that includes an opinion as to whether the statements are prepared in conformity with GAAP. In rare cases, the auditor issues a disclaimer.
5. Maintains professional confidentiality of client records. The auditor is not, however, exempt from legal obligations such as testifying in court.

The Financial Audit

What is an audit? There are several different types of audits. The type most relevant to this course is a **financial audit.** The financial audit is a detailed examination of a company's financial statements and the documents that support those statements. It also tests the reliability of the accounting system used to produce the financial reports. A financial audit is conducted by an **independent auditor** who must be a CPA.

The term *independent auditor* typically refers to a *firm* of certified public accountants. CPAs are licensed by state governments to provide services to the public. They are to be as independent of the companies they audit as is reasonably possible. To help assure independence, CPAs and members of their immediate families may not be employees of the companies they audit. Further, they cannot have investments in the companies they audit. Although CPAs are paid by the companies they audit, the audit fee may not be based on the outcome of the audit.

Although the independent auditors are chosen by, paid by, and can be fired by their client companies, the auditors are primarily responsible to *the public.* In fact, auditors have a legal responsibility to those members of the public who have a financial interest in the company being audited. If investors in a company lose money, they sometimes sue the independent auditors in an attempt to recover their losses, especially if the losses were related to financial failure. A lawsuit against auditors will succeed only if the auditors failed in their professional responsibilities when conducting the audit. Auditors are not responsible for the success or failure of a company. Instead, they are responsible for the appropriate reporting of that success or failure. While recent debacles such as Enron produce spectacular headlines, auditors are actually not sued very often, considering the number of audits they perform.

Materiality and Financial Audits

Auditors do not guarantee that financial statements are absolutely correct—only that they are *materially* correct. This is where things get a little fuzzy. What is a *material error?* The concept of materiality is very subjective. If Wal-Mart inadvertently overstated its sales by $1 million, would this be material? In 2002, Wal-Mart had approximately $245 billion of sales! A $1 million error in computing sales at Wal-Mart is like a $1 error in computing the pay of a person who makes $245,000 per year—not material at all! An error, or other reporting problem, is **material** if knowing about it would influence the decisions of an *average prudent investor.*

Financial audits are not directed toward the discovery of fraud. Auditors are, however, responsible for providing *reasonable assurance* that statements are free from material misstatements, whether caused by errors or fraud. Also, auditors are responsible for evaluating whether internal control procedures are in place to help prevent fraud. If fraud is widespread in a company, normal audit procedures should detect it.

Accounting majors take at least one and often two or more courses in auditing to understand how to conduct an audit. An explanation of auditing techniques is beyond the scope of this course, but at least be aware that auditors do not review how the company accounted for every transaction. Along with other methods, auditors use statistics to choose representative samples of transactions to examine.

REALITY BYTES

This chapter explains the role independent auditors play in the financial reporting process. Although the auditor performs a key function, the primary responsibility for the integrity of a company's financial statements rests with the company's management.

If an auditor fails to detect fraudulent financial reporting by a company, the auditor may be required to pay for financial damages suffered by investors, and may lose the privilege of performing audits. Company executives convicted of fraudulent financial reporting can be held criminally liable. They cannot simply blame the auditor for not correcting their mistakes.

In 2000, **Rite Aid Corp.** restated its earnings downward by $1.6 billion to correct the overstatement of earnings that had occurred in previous years. By mid-2004 six former executives of Rite Aid had been convicted for their roles in the accounting fraud, and four of them received prison time. The company's former CEO, Martin Grass, who pled guilty to two felony charges, received the harshest sentence. He was fined $500,000, sentenced to eight years in prison, and given three years of probation. Even with the benefits of good behavior, Mr. Grass, who is 50, is expected to serve almost seven years in jail. Additionally, the SEC barred him from ever serving again as an officer or director of a public company.

For more details on this story, see "Rite Aid's Ex-CEO Sentenced to 8 Years for Accounting Fraud," by Mark Maremont, *The Wall Street Journal*, May 28, 2004, pp. A-3 and A-5.

Types of Audit Opinions

Once an audit is complete, the auditors present their conclusions in a report that includes an *audit opinion.* There are three basic types of audit opinions.

An **unqualified opinion,** despite its negative-sounding name, is the most favorable opinion auditors can express. It means the auditor believes the financial statements are in compliance with GAAP without qualification, reservation, or exception. Most audits result in unqualified opinions because companies correct any reporting deficiencies the auditors find before the financial statements are released.

The most negative report an auditor can issue is an **adverse opinion.** An adverse opinion means that one or more departures from GAAP are so material the financial statements do not present a fair picture of the company's status. The auditor's report explains the unacceptable accounting practice(s) that resulted in the adverse opinion being issued. Adverse opinions are very rare because public companies are required by law to follow GAAP.

A **qualified opinion** falls between an unqualified and an adverse opinion. A qualified opinion means that for the most part, the company's financial statements are in compliance with GAAP, but the auditors have reservations about something in the statements. The auditors' report explains why the opinion is qualified. A qualified opinion usually does not imply a serious accounting problem, but users should read the auditors' report and draw their own conclusions.

If an auditor is unable to perform the audit procedures necessary to determine whether the statements are prepared in accordance with GAAP, the auditor cannot issue an opinion on the financial statements. Instead, the auditor issues a **disclaimer of opinion.** A disclaimer is neither negative nor positive. It simply means that the auditor is unable to obtain enough information to confirm compliance with GAAP.

Regardless of the type of report they issue, auditors are only expressing their judgment about whether the financial statements present a fair picture of a company. They do not provide opinions regarding the investment quality of a company.

The ultimate responsibility for financial statements rests with the executives of the reporting company. Just like auditors, managers can be sued by investors who believe they lost money due to improper financial reporting. This is one reason all business persons should understand accounting fundamentals.

Confidentiality

The **confidentiality** rules in the code of ethics for CPAs prohibits auditors from *voluntarily disclosing* information they have acquired as a result of their accountant-client relationships. However, accountants may be required to testify in a court of law. In general, federal law does not recognize an accountant-client privilege as it does with attorneys and clergy. Some federal courts have taken exception to this position, especially as it applies to tax cases. State law varies with respect to accountant-client privilege. Furthermore, if auditors terminate a client relationship because of ethical or legal disagreements and they are subsequently contacted by a successor auditor, they may be required to inform the successor of the reasons for the termination. In addition, auditors must consider the particular circumstances of a case when assessing the appropriateness of disclosing confidential information. Given the diverse legal positions governing accountant-client confidentiality, auditors should seek legal counsel prior to disclosing any information obtained in an accountant-client relationship.

To illustrate, assume that Joe Smith, CPA, discovers that his client Jane Doe is misrepresenting information reported in her financial statements. Smith tries to convince Doe to correct the misrepresentations, but she refuses to do so. Smith is required by the code of ethics to terminate his relationship with Doe. However, Smith is not permitted to disclose Doe's dishonest reporting practices unless he is called on to testify in a legal hearing or to respond to an inquiry by Doe's successor accountant.

With respect to the discovery of significant fraud, the auditor is required to inform management at least one level above the position of the employee who is engaged in the fraud and to notify the board of directors of the company. Suppose that Joe Smith, CPA, discovers that Jane Doe, employee of Western Company, is embezzling money from Western. Smith is required to inform Doe's supervisor and to notify Western's board of directors. However, Smith is prohibited from publicly disclosing the fraud.

<< A Look Back

The policies and procedures used to provide reasonable assurance that the objectives of an enterprise will be accomplished are called *internal controls,* which can be subdivided into two categories: accounting controls and administrative controls. *Accounting controls* are composed of procedures designed to safeguard the assets and ensure that the accounting records contain reliable information. *Administrative controls* are designed to evaluate performance and the degree of compliance with company policies and public laws. While the mechanics of internal control systems vary from company to company, the more prevalent features include the following:

1. *Separation of duties.* Whenever possible, the functions of authorization, recording, and custody should be exercised by different individuals.
2. *Quality of employees.* Employees should be qualified to competently perform the duties that are assigned to them. Companies must establish hiring practices to screen out

unqualified candidates. Furthermore, procedures should be established to ensure that employees receive appropriate training to maintain their competence.

3. *Bonded employees.* Employees in sensitive positions should be covered by a fidelity bond that provides insurance to reimburse losses due to illegal actions committed by employees.
4. *Required absences.* Employees should be required to take extended absences from their jobs so that they are not always present to hide unscrupulous or illegal activities.
5. *Procedures manual.* To promote compliance, the procedures for processing transactions should be clearly described in a manual.
6. *Authority and responsibility.* To motivate employees and promote effective control, clear lines of authority and responsibility should be established.
7. *Prenumbered documents.* Prenumbered documents minimize the likelihood of missing or duplicate documents. Prenumbered forms should be used for all important documents such as purchase orders, receiving reports, invoices, and checks.
8. *Physical control.* Locks, fences, security personnel, and other physical devices should be employed to safeguard assets.
9. *Performance evaluations.* Because few people can evaluate their own performance objectively, independent performance evaluations should be performed. Substandard performance will likely persist unless employees are encouraged to take corrective action.

Because cash is such an important business asset and because it is tempting to steal, much of the discussion of internal controls in this chapter focused on cash controls. Special procedures should be employed to control the receipts and payments of cash. One of the most common control policies is to use *checking accounts* for all except petty cash disbursements.

A *bank reconciliation* should be prepared each month to explain differences between the bank statement and a company's internal accounting records. A common reconciliation format determines the true cash balance based on both bank and book records. Items that typically appear on a bank reconciliation include the following:

Unadjusted Bank Balance	xxx	Unadjusted Book Balance	xxx
Add		Add	
Deposits in Transit	xxx	Interest Revenue	xxx
		Collection of Receivables	xxx
Subtract		Subtract	
Outstanding Checks	xxx	Bank Service Charges	xxx
		NSF Checks	xxx
True Cash Balance	xxx	True Cash Balance	xxx

Agreement of the two true cash balances provides evidence that accounting for cash transactions has been accurate.

Another common internal control policy for protecting cash is using a *petty cash fund.* Normally, an employee who is designated as the petty cash custodian is entrusted with a small amount of cash. The custodian reimburses employees for small expenditures made on behalf of the company in exchange for authorized receipts from the employees at the time they are reimbursed. The total of these receipts plus the remaining currency in the fund should always equal the amount of funds entrusted to the custodian. Journal entries to recognize the expenses incurred are made at the time the fund is replenished.

Finally, the chapter discussed the auditor's role in financial reporting, including the materiality concept and the types of audit opinions that may be issued.

A Look Forward >>

Accounting for receivables and payables was introduced in Chapter 2 using relatively simple illustrations. For example, we assumed that customers who purchased services on account always paid their bills. In real business practice, some customers do not pay their bills. Among other topics, Chapter 7 examines how companies account for uncollectible accounts receivable.

SELF-STUDY REVIEW PROBLEM

The following information pertains to Terry's Pest Control Company (TPCC) for July:

1. The unadjusted bank balance at July 31 was $870.
2. The bank statement included the following items:
   (a) A $60 credit memo for interest earned by TPCC.
   (b) A $200 NSF check made payable to TPCC.
   (c) A $110 debit memo for bank service charges.
3. The unadjusted book balance at July 31 was $1,400.
4. A comparison of the bank statement with company accounting records disclosed the following:
   (a) A $400 deposit in transit at July 31.
   (b) Outstanding checks totaling $120 at the end of the month.

Required

a. Prepare a bank reconciliation.
b. Prepare in general journal format the entries necessary to adjust TPCC's cash account to its true balance.

Solution to Requirement *a*

TERRY'S PEST CONTROL COMPANY Bank Reconciliation July 31	
Unadjusted bank balance	$ 870
Add: Deposits in transit	400
Less: Outstanding checks	(120)
True cash balance	$1,150
Unadjusted book balance	$1,400
Add: Interest revenue	60
Less: NSF check	(200)
Less: Bank service charges	(110)
True cash balance	$1,150

Solution to Requirement *b*

Ref.	Account Title	Debit	Credit
1.	Cash	60	
	Interest Revenue		60
2.	Accounts Receivable	200	
	Cash		200
3.	Service Charge Expense	110	
	Cash		110

KEY TERMS

accounting controls 288
administrative controls 288
adverse opinion 303
audits 301
authority manual 289
bank reconciliation 293
bank statement 293
bank statement credit memo 293
bank statement debit memo 293
cash 290
cash short and over 298
certified check 295
certified public accountants (CPAs) 301
checks 293
confidentiality 304
deposit ticket 293
deposits in transit 294
disclaimer of opinion 303
fidelity bond 288
financial audit 302
general authority 289
imprest basis 299
independent auditor 302
internal controls 288
material 302
non-sufficient-funds (NSF) checks 295
outstanding checks 294
petty cash fund 299
petty cash voucher 299
procedures manual 289
qualified opinion 303
separation of duties 288
service charges 295
signature card 292
specific authorizations 289
true cash balance 293
unadjusted bank balance 293
unadjusted book balance 293
unqualified opinion 303

QUESTIONS

1. What are the policies and procedures called that are used to provide reasonable assurance that the objectives of an enterprise will be accomplished?
2. What is the difference between accounting controls and administrative controls?
3. What are several features of an effective internal control system?
4. What is meant by *separation of duties*? Give an illustration.
5. What are the attributes of a high-quality employee?
6. What is a fidelity bond? Explain its purpose.
7. Why is it important that every employee periodically take a leave of absence or vacation?
8. What are the purpose and importance of a procedures manual?
9. What is the difference between specific and general authorizations?
10. Why should documents (checks, invoices, receipts) be prenumbered?
11. What procedures are important in the physical control of assets and accounting records?
12. What is the purpose of independent verification of performance?
13. What items are considered cash?
14. Why is cash more susceptible to theft or embezzlement than other assets?
15. Giving written copies of receipts to customers can help prevent what type of illegal acts?
16. What procedures can help to protect cash receipts?
17. What procedures can help protect cash disbursements?
18. What effect does a debit memo in a bank statement have on the Cash account? What effect does a credit memo in a bank statement have on the Cash account?
19. What information is normally included in a bank statement?
20. Why might a bank statement reflect a balance that is larger than the balance recorded in the depositor's books? What could cause the bank balance to be smaller than the book balance?
21. What is the purpose of a bank reconciliation?
22. What is an outstanding check?
23. What is a deposit in transit?
24. What is a certified check?
25. How is an NSF check accounted for in the accounting records?
26. What is the purpose of the Cash Short and Over account?
27. What is the purpose of a petty cash fund?
28. What types of expenditures are usually made from a petty cash fund?
29. What is a financial audit? Who is qualified to perform it?
30. What is an independent auditor? Why must auditors be independent?
31. What makes an error in the financial statements material?

32. What three basic types of auditors' opinions can be issued on audited financial statements? Describe each.
33. What are the implications of an unqualified audit opinion?
34. When might an auditor issue a disclaimer on financial statements?
35. In what circumstances can an auditor disclose confidential information about a client without the client's permission?
36. What is the purpose of internal controls in an organization?

EXERCISES—SERIES A

All Exercises in Series A are available with McGraw-Hill's Homework Manager

L.O. 1

Exercise 6-1A *Features of a strong internal control system*

Required

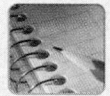

List and describe nine features of a strong internal control system discussed in this chapter.

L.O. 1, 2

Exercise 6-2A *Internal controls for small businesses*

Required

Assume you are the owner of a small business that has only two employees.

a. Which of the internal control procedures are most important to you?
b. How can you overcome the limited opportunity to use the separation-of-duties control procedure?

L.O. 2

Exercise 6-3A *Internal control for cash*

Required

a. Why are special controls needed for cash?
b. What is included in the definition of *cash*?

L.O. 1

Exercise 6-4A *Internal control procedures to prevent embezzlement*

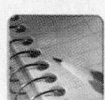

Bell Gates was in charge of the returns department at The Software Company. She was responsible for evaluating returned merchandise. She sent merchandise that was reusable back to the warehouse, where it was restocked in inventory. Gates was also responsible for taking the merchandise that she determined to be defective to the city dump for disposal. She had agreed to buy a friend a tax planning program at a discount through her contacts at work. That is when the idea came to her. She could simply classify one of the reusable returns as defective and bring it home instead of taking it to the dump. She did so and made a quick $150. She was happy, and her friend was ecstatic; he was able to buy a $400 software package for only $150. He told his friends about the deal, and soon Gates had a regular set of customers. She was caught when a retail store owner complained to the marketing manager that his pricing strategy was being undercut by The Software Company's direct sales to the public. The marketing manager was suspicious because The Software Company had no direct marketing program. When the outside sales were ultimately traced back to Gates, the company discovered that it had lost over $10,000 in sales revenue because of her criminal activity.

Required

Identify an internal control procedure that could have prevented the company's losses. Explain how the procedure would have stopped the embezzlement.

L.O. 1

Exercise 6-5A *Internal control procedures to prevent deception*

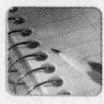

Emergency Care Medical Centers (ECMC) hired a new physician, Ken Major, who was an immediate success. Everyone loved his bedside manner; he could charm the most cantankerous patient. Indeed, he was a master salesman as well as an expert physician. Unfortunately, Major misdiagnosed a case that resulted in serious consequences to the patient. The patient filed suit against ECMC. In preparation for the defense, ECMC's attorneys discovered that Major was indeed an exceptional salesman. He had worked for several years as district marketing manager for a pharmaceutical company. In fact, he was not a physician at all! He had changed professions without going to medical school. He had lied on his application form. His knowledge of medical terminology had enabled him to fool everyone. ECMC was found negligent and lost a $3 million lawsuit.

Required

Identify the relevant internal control procedures that could have prevented the company's losses. Explain how these procedures would have prevented Major's deception.

Exercise 6-6A *Treatment of NSF check* L.O. 3

The bank statement of Zone Supplies included a $200 NSF check that one of Zone's customers had written to pay for services that were provided by Zone.

Required

a. Show the effects of recognizing the NSF check on the financial statements by recording the appropriate amounts in a horizontal statements model like the following one.

Assets	= Liab. + Equity	Rev. − Exp. = Net Inc.	Cash Flow
Cash + Accts. Rec.			

b. Is the recognition of the NSF check on Zone's books an asset source, use, or exchange transaction?

c. Suppose the customer redeems the check by giving Zone $225 cash in exchange for the bad check. The additional $25 paid a service fee charged by Zone. Show the effects on the financial statements in the horizontal statements model in Requirement *a.*

d. Is the receipt of cash referred to in Requirement *c* an asset source, use, or exchange transaction?

e. Record in general journal form the adjusting entry for the NSF check and the subsequent entry for redemption of the check by the customer.

Exercise 6-7A *Adjustments to the balance per books* L.O. 3

Required

Identify which of the following items are added to or subtracted from the unadjusted *book balance* to arrive at the true cash balance. Distinguish the additions from the subtractions by placing a + beside the items that are added to the unadjusted book balance and a − beside those that are subtracted from it. The first item is recorded as an example.

Reconciling Items	Book Balance Adjusted?	Added or Subtracted?
Outstanding checks	No	N/A
Interest revenue earned on the account		
Deposits in transit		
Service charge		
Automatic debit for utility bill		
Charge for checks		
NSF check from customer		
ATM fee		

Exercise 6-8A *Adjustments to the balance per bank* L.O. 3

Required

Identify which of the following items are added to or subtracted from the unadjusted *bank balance* to arrive at the true cash balance. Distinguish the additions from the subtractions by placing a + beside the items that are added to the unadjusted bank balance and a − beside those that are subtracted from it. The first item is recorded as an example.

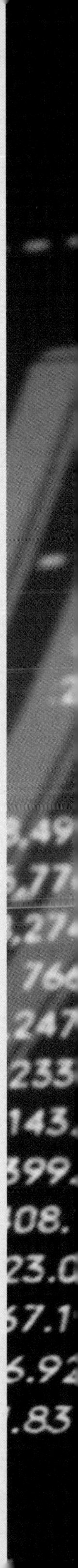

Reconciling Items	Bank Balance Adjusted?	Added or Subtracted?
Bank service charge	No	N/A
Outstanding checks		
Deposits in transit		
Debit memo		
Credit memo		
ATM fee		
Petty cash voucher		
NSF check from customer		
Interest revenue		

L.O. 3

Exercise 6-9A ***Adjusting the cash account***

As of May 31, 2004, the bank statement showed an ending balance of $17,250. The unadjusted Cash account balance was $16,450. The following information is available:

1. Deposit in transit, $2,630.
2. Credit memo in bank statement for interest earned in May, $12.
3. Outstanding check, $3,428.
4. Debit memo for service charge, $10.

Required

a. Determine the true cash balance by preparing a bank reconciliation as of May 31, 2004, using the preceding information.
b. Record in general journal format the adjusting entries necessary to correct the unadjusted book balance.

L.O. 3

Exercise 6-10A ***Determining the true cash balance, starting with the unadjusted bank balance***

The following information is available for Stone Company for the month of August:

1. The unadjusted balance per the bank statement on August 31 was $56,300.
2. Deposits in transit on August 31 were $2,600.
3. A debit memo was included with the bank statement for a service charge of $20.
4. A $4,925 check written in August had not been paid by the bank.
5. The bank statement included a $1,000 credit memo for the collection of a note. The principal of the note was $950, and the interest collected was $50.

Required

Determine the true cash balance as of August 31. (*Hint:* It is not necessary to use all of the preceding items to determine the true balance.)

L.O. 3

Exercise 6-11A ***Determining the true cash balance, starting with the unadjusted book balance***

Lee Company had an unadjusted cash balance of $7,850 as of April 30. The company's bank statement, also dated April 30, included a $75 NSF check written by one of Lee's customers. There were $920 in outstanding checks and $250 in deposits in transit as of April 30. According to the bank statement, service charges were $50, and the bank collected a $900 note receivable for Lee. The bank statement also showed $12 of interest revenue earned by Lee.

Required

Determine the true cash balance as of April 30. (*Hint:* It is not necessary to use all of the preceding items to determine the true balance.)

Exercise 6-12A ***Effect of establishing a petty cash fund*** **L.O. 4**

Macon Timber Company established a $150 petty cash fund on January 1, 2003.

Required

a. Is the establishment of the petty cash fund an asset source, use, or exchange transaction?

b. Record the establishment of the petty cash fund in a horizontal statements model like the following one:

Assets		=	Liab.	+	Equity	Rev.	−	Exp.	=	Net Inc.	Cash Flow
Cash +	Petty Cash										

c. Record the establishment of the fund in general journal format.

Exercise 6-13A ***Effect of petty cash events on the financial statements*** **L.O. 4**

Toro Inc. established a petty cash fund of $200 on January 2. On January 31, the fund contained cash of $15.30 and vouchers for the following cash payments:

Postage	$25.00
Office supplies	48.50
Printing expense	30.00
Entertainment expense	79.20

The three distinct accounting events affecting the petty cash fund for the period were (1) establishment of the fund, (2) reimbursements made to employees, and (3) recognition of expenses and replenishment of the fund.

Required

a. Record each of the three events in a horizontal statements model like the following one. In the Cash Flow column, indicate whether the item is an operating activity (OA), investing activity (IA), or a financing activity (FA). Use NA to indicate that an account was not affected by the event.

Assets		=	Liab.	+	Equity	Rev.	−	Exp.	=	Net Inc.	Cash Flow
Cash +	Petty Cash										

b. Record the events in general journal format.

Exercise 6-14A ***Determining the amount of petty cash expense*** **L.O. 4**

Consider the following events:

1. A petty cash fund of $100 was established on April 1, 2006.
2. Employees were reimbursed when they presented petty cash vouchers to the petty cash custodian.
3. On April 30, 2006, the petty cash fund contained vouchers totaling $87.30 plus $13.50 of currency.

Required

Answer the following questions:

a. How did the establishment of the petty cash fund affect (increase, decrease, or have no effect on) total assets?

b. What is the amount of total petty cash expenses to be recognized during April?

c. When are petty cash expenses recognized (at the time of establishment, reimbursement, or replenishment)?

Exercise 6-15A ***Confidentiality and the auditor*** **L.O. 5**

West Aston discovered a significant fraud in the accounting records of a high profile client. The story has been broadcast on national airways. Aston was unable to resolve his remaining concerns with the

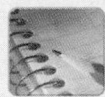

company's management team and ultimately resigned from the audit engagement. Aston knows that he will be asked by several interested parties, including his friends and relatives, the successor auditor, and prosecuting attorneys in a court of law, to tell what he knows. He has asked you for advice.

Required

Write a memo that explains Aston's disclosure responsibilities to each of the interested parties.

PROBLEMS—SERIES A

All Problems in Series A are available with McGraw-Hill's Homework Manager

L.O. 1, 2

Problem 6-16A *Using internal control to restrict illegal or unethical behavior*

Required

For each of the following fraudulent acts, describe one or more internal control procedures that could have prevented (or helped prevent) the problems.

a. Everyone in the office has noticed what a dedicated employee Jennifer Reidel is. She never misses work, not even for a vacation. Reidel is in charge of the petty cash fund. She transfers funds from the company's bank account to the petty cash account on an as-needed basis. During a surprise audit, the petty cash fund was found to contain fictitious receipts. Over a three-year period, Reidel had used more than $4,000 of petty cash to pay for personal expenses.

b. Bill Bruton was hired as the vice president of the manufacturing division of a corporation. His impressive resume listed a master's degree in business administration from a large state university and numerous collegiate awards and activities, when in fact Bruton had only a high school diploma. In a short time, the company was in poor financial condition because of his inadequate knowledge and bad decisions.

c. Havolene Manufacturing has good internal control over its manufacturing materials inventory. However, office supplies are kept on open shelves in the employee break room. The office supervisor has noticed that he is having to order paper, tape, staplers, and pens with increasing frequency.

L.O. 3

CHECK FIGURE
a. True Cash Balance, October 31, 2006: $9,350

Problem 6-17A *Preparing a bank reconciliation*

Jim Guidry owns a construction business, Guidry Supply Co. The following cash information is available for the month of October 2006.

As of October 31, the bank statement shows a balance of $12,300. The October 31 unadjusted balance in the Cash account of Guidry Supply Co. is $11,200. A review of the bank statement revealed the following information:

1. A deposit of $1,500 on October 31, 2006, does not appear on the October 31 bank statement.
2. A debit memo for $50 was included in the bank statement for the purchase of a new supply of checks.
3. When checks written during the month were compared with those paid by the bank, three checks amounting to $4,450 were found to be outstanding.
4. It was discovered that a check to pay for repairs was correctly written and paid by the bank for $3,100 but was recorded on the books as $1,300.

Required

a. Prepare a bank reconciliation at the end of October showing the true cash balance.

b. Prepare any necessary journal entries to adjust the books to the true cash balance.

L.O. 3

eXcel
mhhe.com/edmonds2007

Problem 6-18A *Missing information in a bank reconciliation*

The following data apply to Smoot Sports Inc. for April 2007:

1. Balance per the bank on April 30, $12,250.
2. Deposits in transit not recorded by the bank, $2,100.
3. Bank error; check written by Smoot on his personal checking account was drawn on Smoot Sports Inc.'s account, $800.
4. The following checks written and recorded by Smoot Sports Inc. were not included in the bank statement:

1901	$ 220
1920	580
1921	1,500

CHECK FIGURE
True Cash Balance, April 30, 2007: $12,850

5. Credit memo for note collected by the bank, $700.
6. Service charge for collection of note, $10.
7. The bookkeeper recorded a check written for $560 to pay for April's office supplies as $650 in the cash disbursements journal.
8. Bank service charge in addition to the note collection fee, $30.
9. NSF checks returned by the bank, $150.

Required

Determine the amount of the unadjusted cash balance per Smoot Sports Inc.'s books.

Problem 6-19A *Adjustments to the cash account based on the bank reconciliation*

L.O. 3

eXcel
mhhe.com/edmonds2007

CHECK FIGURE
h. Theft Loss: $800

Determine whether the following items in National Imports' bank reconciliation require adjusting or correcting entries on National Imports' books. When an entry is required, record it in general journal format.

a. The bank collected $5,000 of National Imports' accounts receivable. National Imports had instructed its customers to send their payments directly to the bank.
b. The bank mistakenly gave Imports Inc. credit for a $500 deposit made by National Imports.
c. Deposits in transit were $5,600.
d. National Imports' bank statement contained a $525 NSF check. National Imports had received the check from a customer and had included it in one of its bank deposits.
e. The bank statement indicated that National Imports earned $80 of interest revenue.
f. National Imports' accountant mistakenly recorded a $230 check that was written to purchase supplies as $320.
g. Bank service charges for the month were $50.
h. The bank reconciliation disclosed that $800 had been stolen from National Imports' business.
i. Outstanding checks amounted to $1,700.

Problem 6-20A *Bank reconciliation and adjustments to the cash account*

L.O. 3

CHECK FIGURE
a. True Cash Balance, July 31, 2005: $16,234

The following information is available for Mountain Top Hotel for July 2005:

Bank Statement
STATE BANK
Bolta Vista, NV 10001

Mountain Top Hotel
10 Main Street
Bolta Vista, NV 10001

Account number
12-4567
July 31, 2005

Beginning balance 6/30/2005	$ 9,031
Total deposits and other credits	29,800
Total checks and other debits	23,902
Ending balance 7/31/2005	14,929

Checks and Debits		Deposits and Credits		
Check No.	Amount	Date		Amount
2350	$3,761	July	1	$1,102
2351	1,643	July	10	6,498
2352	8,000	July	15	4,929
2354	2,894	July	21	6,174
2355	1,401	July	26	5,963
2357	6,187	July	30	2,084
DM	16	CM		3,050

The following is a list of checks and deposits recorded on the books of the Mountain Top Hotel for July 2005:

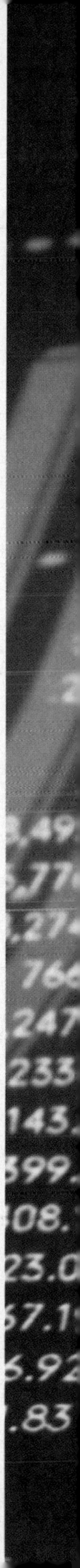

Date		Check No.	Amount of Check	Date		Amount of Deposit
July	2	2351	$1,643	July	8	$6,498
July	4	2352	8,000	July	14	4,929
July	10	2353	1,500	July	21	6,174
July	10	2354	2,894	July	26	5,963
July	15	2355	1,401	July	29	2,084
July	20	2356	745	July	30	3,550
July	22	2357	6,187			

Other Information

1. Check no. 2350 was outstanding from June.
2. The credit memo was for collection of notes receivable.
3. All checks were paid at the correct amount.
4. The debit memo was for printed checks.
5. The June 30 bank reconciliation showed a deposit in transit of $1,102.
6. The unadjusted Cash account balance at July 31 was $13,200.

Required

a. Prepare the bank reconciliation for Mountain Top Hotel at the end of July.

b. Record in general journal form any necessary entries to the Cash account to adjust it to the true cash balance.

L.O. 3

Problem 6-21A *Effect of adjustments to cash on the accounting equation*

After reconciling its bank account, Hull Equipment Company made the following adjusting entries:

Entry No.	Account Titles	Debit	Credit
1	Cash	40	
	Interest Revenue		40
	To record interest revenue		
2	Accounts Receivable	250	
	Cash		250
	To record NSF check from Wilson		
3	Rent Expense	35	
	Cash		35
	To correct understatement of expense		
4	Service Charge Expense	15	
	Cash		15
	To record bank service charge		
5	Cash	175	
	Accounts Receivable		175
	To record bank collection		

Required

Identify the event depicted in each journal entry as asset source (AS), asset use (AU), asset exchange (AE), or claims exchange (CE). Also explain how each entry affects the accounting equation by placing a + for increase, − for decrease, or NA for not affected under the following components of the accounting equation. The first event is recorded as an example.

						Stockholders' Equity		
Event No.	Type of Event	Assets	=	Liabilities	+	Common Stock	+	Retained Earnings
1	AS	+		NA		NA		+

Problem 6-22A *Bank reconciliation and internal control*

L.O. 1, 2, 3

CHECK FIGURE
a. True Cash Balance, May 31, 2006: $22,550

Following is a bank reconciliation for Holt's Sandwich Shop for May 31, 2006:

	Cash Account	Bank Statement
Balance as of 5/31/06	$25,000	$22,000
Deposit in transit		4,250
Outstanding checks		(465)
Note collected by bank	1,815	
Bank service charge	(30)	
Automatic payment on loan	(1,000)	
Adjusted cash balance as of 5/31/06	$25,785	$25,785

Because of limited funds, Holt's employed only one accountant who was responsible for receiving cash, recording receipts and disbursements, preparing deposits, and preparing the bank reconciliation. The accountant left the company on June 8, 2006, after preparing the preceding statement. His replacement compared the checks returned with the bank statement to the cash disbursements journal and found the total of outstanding checks to be $3,700.

Required

a. Prepare a corrected bank reconciliation.

b. What is the total amount of cash missing, and how was the difference between the "true cash" per the bank and the "true cash" per the books hidden on the reconciliation prepared by the former employee?

c. What could Holt's do to avoid cash theft in the future?

Problem 6-23A *Petty cash fund*

L.O. 4

CHECK FIGURE
a. Cash Short: $3

The following data pertain to the petty cash fund of Zelda Company:

1. The petty cash fund was established on an imprest basis at $150 on March 1.
2. On March 31, a physical count of the fund disclosed $18 in currency and coins, vouchers authorizing meal allowances totaling $75, vouchers authorizing purchase of postage stamps of $19, and vouchers for payment of delivery charges of $35.

Required

a. Prepare all general journal entries necessary to (1) establish the fund, (2) reimburse employees, and (3) recognize the expenses and replenish the fund as of March 31. (*Hint:* Journal entries may not be required for all three events.)

b. Explain how the Cash Short and Over account required in this case affects the income statement.

c. Identify the event depicted in each journal entry recorded in Requirement *a* as asset source (AS), asset use (AU), asset exchange (AE), or claims exchange (CE).

d. Record the effects on the financial statements of the events in Requirement *a* using a horizontal statements model like the following one. In the Cash Flow column, indicate whether the item is an operating activity (OA), investing activity (IA), or financing activity (FA). Use NA to indicate that an account was not affected by the event.

Assets			=	Liab.	+	Equity	Rev.	−	Exp.	=	Net Inc.	Cash Flow
Cash	+	Petty Cash										

Problem 6-24A *Auditor responsibilities*

L.O. 5

You have probably heard it is unwise to bite the hand that feeds you. Independent auditors are chosen by, paid by, and can be fired by the companies they audit. What keeps the auditor independent? In other words, what stops an auditor from blindly following the orders of a client?

Required

Write a memo that explains the reporting responsibilities of an independent auditor.

EXERCISES—SERIES B

L.O. 1

Exercise 6-1B *Internal control procedures*

Required

a. Name and describe the two categories of internal controls.

b. What is the purpose of internal controls?

L.O. 1

Exercise 6-2B *Internal controls for equipment*

Required

List the internal control procedures that pertain to the protection of business equipment.

L.O. 2

Exercise 6-3B *Features of internal control procedures for cash*

Required

List and discuss effective internal control procedures that apply to cash.

L.O. 1

Exercise 6-4B *Internal control procedures*

Dick Haney is opening a new business that will sell sporting goods. It will initially be a small operation, and he is concerned about the security of his assets. He will not be able to be at the business all of the time and will have to rely on his employees and internal control procedures to ensure that transactions are properly accounted for and assets are safeguarded. He will have a store manager and two other employees who will be sales personnel and stock personnel and who will also perform any other duties necessary. Dick will be in the business on a regular basis. He has come to you for advice.

Required

Write a memo to Dick outlining the procedures that he should implement to ensure that his store assets are protected and that the financial transactions are properly recorded.

L.O. 1

Exercise 6-5B *Internal controls to prevent theft*

Rhonda Cox worked as the parts manager for State Line Automobiles, a local automobile dealership. Rhonda was very dedicated and never missed a day of work. Since State Line was a small operation, she was the only employee in the parts department. Her duties consisted of ordering parts for stock and as needed for repairs, receiving the parts and checking them in, distributing them as needed to the shop or to customers for purchase, and keeping track of and taking the year-end inventory of parts. State Line decided to expand and needed to secure additional financing. The local bank agreed to a loan contingent on an audit of the dealership. One requirement of the audit was to oversee the inventory count of both automobiles and parts on hand. Rhonda was clearly nervous, explaining that she had just inventoried all parts in the parts department. She supplied the auditors with a detailed list. The inventory showed parts on hand worth $225,000. The auditors decided they needed to verify a substantial part of the inventory. When the auditors began their counts, a pattern began to develop. Each type of part seemed to be one or two items short when the actual count was taken. This raised more concern. Although Rhonda assured the auditors the parts were just misplaced, the auditors continued the count. After completing the count of parts on hand, the auditors could document only $155,000 of actual parts. Suddenly, Rhonda quit her job and moved to another state.

Required

a. What do you suppose caused the discrepancy between the actual count and the count that Rhonda had supplied?

b. What procedures could be put into place to prevent this type of problem?

L.O. 3

Exercise 6-6B *Treatment of NSF check*

Rankin Stationery's bank statement contained a $250 NSF check that one of its customers had written to pay for supplies purchased.

Required

a. Show the effects of recognizing the NSF check on the financial statements by recording the appropriate amounts in a horizontal statements model like the following one:

Assets		= Liab.	+ Equity	Rev.	− Exp.	= Net Inc.	Cash Flow
Cash	+ Accts. Rec.						

b. Is the recognition of the NSF check on Rankin's books an asset source, use, or exchange transaction?

c. Suppose the customer redeems the check by giving Rankin $270 cash in exchange for the bad check. The additional $20 paid a service fee charged by Rankin. Show the effects on the financial statements in the horizontal statements model in Requirement *a.*

d. Is the receipt of cash referenced in Requirement *c* an asset source, use, or exchange transaction?

e. Record in general journal form the adjusting entry for the NSF check and the entry for redemption of the check by the customer.

Exercise 6-7B *Adjustments to the balance per books*

L.O. 3

Required

Identify which of the following items are added to or subtracted from the unadjusted *book balance* to arrive at the true cash balance. Distinguish the additions from the subtractions by placing a + beside the items that are added to the unadjusted book balance and a − beside those that are subtracted from it. The first item is recorded as an example.

Reconciling Items	Book Balance Adjusted?	Added or Subtracted?
Interest revenue	Yes	+
Deposits in transit		
Debit memo		
Service charge		
Charge for checks		
NSF check from customer		
Note receivable collected by the bank		
Outstanding checks		
Credit memo		

Exercise 6-8B *Adjustments to the balance per bank*

L.O. 3

Required

Identify which of the following items are added to or subtracted from the unadjusted *bank balance* to arrive at the true cash balance. Distinguish the additions from the subtractions by placing a + beside the items that are added to the unadjusted bank balance and a − beside those that are subtracted from it. The first item is recorded as an example.

Reconciling Items	Bank Balance Adjusted?	Added or Subtracted?
Deposits in transit	Yes	+
Debit memo		
Credit memo		
Certified checks		
Petty cash voucher		
NSF check from customer		
Interest revenue		
Bank service charge		
Outstanding checks		

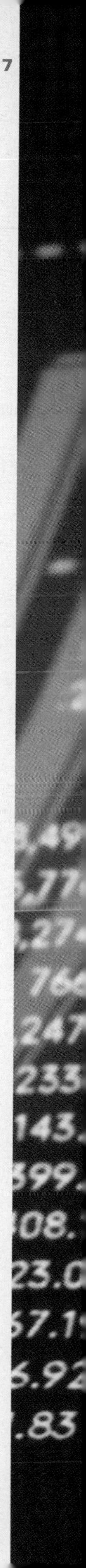

L.O. 3

Exercise 6-9B *Adjusting the cash account*

As of June 30, 2006, the bank statement showed an ending balance of $13,879.85. The unadjusted Cash account balance was $13,483.75. The following information is available:

1. Deposit in transit, $1,476.30.
2. Credit memo in bank statement for interest earned in June, $35.
3. Outstanding check, $1,843.74.
4. Debit memo for service charge, $6.34.

Required

a. Determine the true cash balance by preparing a bank reconciliation as of June 30, 2006, using the preceding information.

b. Record in general journal format the adjusting entries necessary to correct the unadjusted book balance.

L.O. 3

Exercise 6-10B *Determining the true cash balance, starting with the unadjusted bank balance*

The following information is available for Hamby Company for the month of June:

1. The unadjusted balance per the bank statement on June 30 was $68,714.35.
2. Deposits in transit on June 30 were $1,464.95.
3. A debit memo was included with the bank statement for a service charge of $25.38.
4. A $4,745.66 check written in June had not been paid by the bank.
5. The bank statement included a $944 credit memo for the collection of a note. The principal of the note was $859, and the interest collected amounted to $85.

Required

Determine the true cash balance as of June 30. (*Hint:* It is not necessary to use all of the preceding items to determine the true balance.)

L.O. 3

Exercise 6-11B *Determining the true cash balance, starting with the unadjusted book balance*

Crumbley Company had an unadjusted cash balance of $6,450 as of May 31. The company's bank statement, also dated May 31, included a $38 NSF check written by one of Crumbley's customers. There were $548.60 in outstanding checks and $143.74 in deposits in transit as of May 31. According to the bank statement, service charges were $30, and the bank collected a $450 note receivable for Crumbley. The bank statement also showed $18 of interest revenue earned by Crumbley.

Required

Determine the true cash balance as of May 31. (*Hint:* It is not necessary to use all of the preceding items to determine the true balance.)

L.O. 4

Exercise 6-12B *Effect of establishing a petty cash fund*

Manu Company established a $300 petty cash fund on January 1, 2003.

Required

a. Is the establishment of the petty cash fund an asset source, use, or exchange transaction?

b. Record the establishment of the petty cash fund in a horizontal statements model like the following one:

Assets		=	Liab.	+	Equity	Rev.	−	Exp.	=	Net Inc.	Cash Flow
Cash +	Petty Cash										

c. Record the establishment of the fund in general journal format.

L.O. 4

Exercise 6-13B *Effect of petty cash events on the financial statements*

Family Medical Center established a petty cash fund of $100 on January 2. On January 31, the fund contained cash of $16.75 and vouchers for the following cash payments:

Postage	$34.68
Office supplies	18.43
Printing expense	7.40
Transportation expense	23.92

The three distinct accounting events affecting the petty cash fund for the period were (1) establishment of the fund, (2) reimbursements made to employees, and (3) recognition of expenses and replenishment of the fund.

Required

a. Record each of the three events in a horizontal statements model like the following one. In the Cash Flow column, indicate whether the item is an operating activity (OA), investing activity (IA), or a financing activity (FA). Use NA to indicate that an account was not affected by the event.

Assets			=	Liab.	+	Equity	Rev.	−	Exp.	=	Net Inc.	Cash Flow
Cash	+	Petty Cash										

b. Record the events in general journal format.

Exercise 6-14B *Determining the amount of petty cash expense*

L.O. 4

Consider the following events:

1. A petty cash fund of $220 was established on April 1, 2008.
2. Employees were reimbursed when they presented petty cash vouchers to the petty cash custodian.
3. On April 30, 2008, the petty cash fund contained vouchers totaling $184.93 plus $28.84 of currency.

Required

Answer the following questions:

a. How did the establishment of the petty cash fund affect (increase, decrease, or have no effect on) total assets?

b. What is the amount of total petty cash expenses to be recognized during April?

c. When are petty cash expenses recognized (at the time of establishment, reimbursement, or replenishment)?

Exercise 6-15B *Materiality and the auditor*

L.O. 5

Sharon Waters is an auditor. Her work at two companies disclosed inappropriate recognition of revenue. Both cases involved dollar amounts in the $100,000 range. In one case, Waters considered the item material and required her client to restate earnings. In the other case, Waters dismissed the misstatement as being immaterial.

Required

Write a memo that explains how a $100,000 misstatement of revenue is acceptable for one company but unacceptable for a different company.

PROBLEMS—SERIES B

Problem 6-16B *Using internal control to restrict illegal or unethical behavior*

L.O. 1, 2

Required

For each of the following fraudulent acts, describe one or more internal control procedures that could have prevented (or helped prevent) the problems.

a. Paula Wissel, the administrative assistant in charge of payroll, created a fictitious employee, wrote weekly checks to the fictitious employee, and then personally cashed the checks for her own benefit.

b. Larry Kent, the receiving manager of Southern Lumber, created a fictitious supplier named F&M Building Supply. F&M regularly billed Southern Lumber for supplies purchased. Kent had printed shipping slips and billing invoices with the name of the fictitious company and opened a post office box as the mailing address. Kent simply prepared a receiving report and submitted it for payment to the accounts payable department. The accounts payable clerk then paid the invoice when it was received because Kent acknowledged receipt of the supplies.

c. Holly Baker works at a local hobby shop and usually operates the cash register. She has developed a way to give discounts to her friends. When they come by, she rings a lower price or does not charge the friend for some of the material purchased. At first, Baker thought she would get caught, but no one seemed to notice. Indeed, she has become so sure that there is no way for the owner to find out that she has started taking home some supplies for her own personal use.

L.O. 3

Problem 6-17B *Preparing a bank reconciliation*

Bob Carson owns a card shop, Card Talk. The following cash information is available for the month of August, 2006.

As of August 31, the bank statement shows a balance of $17,000. The August 31 unadjusted balance in the Cash account of Card Talk is $16,000. A review of the bank statement revealed the following information:

1. A deposit of $2,260 on August 31, 2006, does not appear on the August bank statement.
2. It was discovered that a check to pay for baseball cards was correctly written and paid by the bank for $4,040 but was recorded on the books as $4,400.
3. When checks written during the month were compared with those paid by the bank, three checks amounting to $3,000 were found to be outstanding.
4. A debit memo for $100 was included in the bank statement for the purchase of a new supply of checks.

Required

a. Prepare a bank reconciliation at the end of August showing the true cash balance.

b. Prepare any necessary journal entries to adjust the books to the true cash balance.

L.O. 3

Problem 6-18B *Missing information in a bank reconciliation*

The following data apply to Superior Auto Supply Inc. for May 2007.

1. Balance per the bank on May 31, $8,000.
2. Deposits in transit not recorded by the bank, $975.
3. Bank error; check written by Allen Auto Supply was charged to Superior Auto Supply's account, $650.
4. The following checks written and recorded by Superior Auto Supply were not included in the bank statement:

3013	$ 385
3054	735
3056	1,900

5. Note collected by the bank, $500.
6. Service charge for collection of note, $10.
7. The bookkeeper recorded a check written for $188 to pay for the May utilities expense as $888 in the cash disbursements journal.
8. Bank service charge in addition to the note collection fee, $25.
9. Customer checks returned by the bank as NSF, $125.

Required

Determine the amount of the unadjusted cash balance per Superior Auto Supply's books.

L.O. 3

Problem 6-19B *Adjustments to the cash account based on the bank reconciliation*

Required

Determine whether the following items included in Yang Company's bank reconciliation will require adjusting or correcting entries on Yang's books. When an entry is required, record it in general journal format.

a. An $877 deposit was recorded by the bank as $778.

b. Four checks totaling $450 written during the month of January were not included with the January bank statement.

c. A $54 check written to Office Max for office supplies was recorded in the general journal as $45.

d. The bank statement indicated that the bank had collected a $330 note for Yang.

e. Yang recorded $500 of receipts on January 31, 2006, which was deposited in the night depository of the bank. These deposits were not included in the bank statement.

f. Service charges of $22 for the month of January were listed on the bank statement.

g. The bank charged a $297 check drawn on Cave Restaurant to Yang's account. The check was included in Yang's bank statement.

h. A check of $31 was returned to the bank because of insufficient funds and was noted on the bank statement. Yang received the check from a customer and thought that it was good when it was deposited into the account.

Problem 6-20B ***Bank reconciliation and adjustments to the cash account*** L.O. 3

The following information is available for Cooters Garage for March 2007:

BANK STATEMENT
HAZARD STATE BANK
215 MAIN STREET
HAZARD, GA 30321

Cooters Garage
629 Main Street
Hazard, GA 30321

Account number
62-00062
March 31, 2007

Beginning balance 3/1/2007	$15,000.00
Total deposits and other credits	7,000.00
Total checks and other debits	6,000.00
Ending balance 3/31/2007	16,000.00

Checks and Debits		Deposits and Credits	
Check No.	Amount	Date	Amount
1462	$1,163.00	March 1	$1,000.00
1463	62.00	March 2	1,340.00
1464	1,235.00	March 6	210.00
1465	750.00	March 12	1,940.00
1466	1,111.00	March 17	855.00
1467	964.00	March 22	1,480.00
DM	15.00	CM	175.00
1468	700.00		

The following is a list of checks and deposits recorded on the books of Cooters Garage for March 2007:

Date	Check No.	Amount of Check	Date	Amount of Deposit
March 1	1463	$ 62.00	March 1	$1,340.00
March 5	1464	1,235.00	March 5	210.00
March 6	1465	750.00		
March 9	1466	1,111.00	March 10	1,940.00
March 10	1467	964.00		
March 14	1468	70.00	March 16	855.00
March 19	1469	1,500.00	March 19	1,480.00
March 28	1470	102.00	March 29	2,000.00

Other Information

1. Check no. 1462 was outstanding from February.
2. A credit memo for collection of accounts receivable was included in the bank statement.
3. All checks were paid at the correct amount.

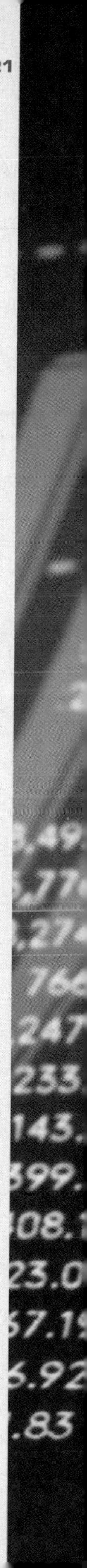

4. The bank statement included a debit memo for service charges.
5. The February 28 bank reconciliation showed a deposit in transit of $1,000.
6. Check no. 1468 was for the purchase of equipment.
7. The unadjusted Cash account balance at March 31 was $16,868.

Required

a. Prepare the bank reconciliation for Cooters Garage at the end of March.
b. Record in general journal form any necessary entries to the Cash account to adjust it to the true cash balance.

L.O. 3

Problem 6-21B ***Effect of adjustments to cash on the accounting equation***

After reconciling its bank account, Obian Company made the following adjusting entries:

Entry No.	Account Titles	Debit	Credit
1	Cash	845	
	Accounts Receivable		845
	To record bank collection		
2	Cash	44	
	Interest Revenue		44
	To record interest revenue		
3	Service Charge Expense	35	
	Cash		35
	To record bank service charge		
4	Accounts Receivable	174	
	Cash		174
	To record NSF check from Beat		
5	Cash	20	
	Supplies Expense		20
	To correct overstatement of expense		

Required

Identify the event depicted in each journal entry as asset source (AS), asset use (AU), asset exchange (AE), or claims exchange (CE). Also explain how each entry affects the accounting equation by placing a + for increase, − for decrease, or NA for not affected under the following components of the accounting equation. The first event is recorded as an example.

						Stockholders' Equity		
Event No.	Type of Event	Assets	=	Liabilities	+	Common Stock	+	Retained Earnings
1	AE	+ −		NA		NA		NA

L.O. 1, 2, 3

Problem 6-22B ***Bank reconciliation and internal control***

Following is a bank reconciliation for Surf Shop for June 30, 2005:

	Cash Account	Bank Statement
Balance as of 6/30/05	$1,618	$3,000
Deposit in transit		600
Outstanding checks		(1,507)
Note collected by bank	2,000	
Bank service charge	(25)	
NSF check	(1,500)	
Adjusted cash balance as of 6/30/05	$2,093	$2,093

When reviewing the bank reconciliation, Surf's auditor was unable to locate any reference to the NSF check on the bank statement. Furthermore, the clerk who reconciles the bank account and records the adjusting entries could not find the actual NSF check that should have been included in the bank statement. Finally, there was no specific reference in the accounts receivable supporting records identifying a party who had written a bad check.

Required

a. Prepare the adjusting entry that the clerk would have made to record the NSF check.

b. Assume that the clerk who prepares the bank reconciliation and records the adjusting entries also makes bank deposits. Explain how the clerk could use a fictitious NSF check to hide the theft of cash.

c. How could Surf avoid the theft of cash that is concealed by the use of fictitious NSF checks?

Problem 6-23B *Petty cash fund*

L.O. 4

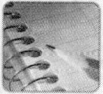

Martinez Co. established a petty cash fund by issuing a check for $250 and appointing Bob Potts as petty cash custodian. Potts had vouchers for the following petty cash payments during the month:

Stamps	$14.00
Miscellaneous items	25.00
Employee supper money	75.00
Taxi fare	80.00
Window-washing service	22.00

There was $32 of currency in the petty cash box at the time it was replenished.

Required

a. Prepare all general journal entries necessary to (1) establish the fund, (2) reimburse employees, (3) recognize expenses, and (4) replenish the fund. (*Hint:* Journal entries may not be required for all the events.)

b. Explain how the Cash Short and Over account required in this case will affect the income statement.

c. Identify the event depicted in each journal entry recorded in Requirement *a* as asset source (AS), asset use (AU), asset exchange (AE), or claims exchange (CE).

d. Record the effects of the events in Requirement *a* on the financial statements using a horizontal statements model like the following one. In the Cash Flow column, indicate whether the item is an operating activity (OA), investing activity (IA), or financing activity (FA). Use NA to indicate that an account was not affected by the event.

Assets			=	Liab.	+	Equity	Rev.	−	Exp.	=	Net Inc.	Cash Flow
Cash	+	Petty Cash										

Problem 6-24B *Types of audit reports*

L.O. 5

Shay Ding is a partner of a regional accounting firm. Ms. Ding was hired by a client to audit the company's books. After extensive work, Ms. Ding determined that she was unable to perform the appropriate audit procedures.

Required

a. Name the type of audit report that Ms. Ding should issue with respect to the work that she did accomplish.

b. If Ms. Ding had been able to perform the necessary audit procedures, there are three types of audit reports that she could have issued depending on the outcome of the audit. Name and describe these three types of audit reports.

ANALYZE, THINK, COMMUNICATE

ATC 6-1 Business Applications Case *Understanding real-world annual reports*

Required—Part 1

The Topps Company, Inc.

Use the **Topps Company**'s annual report in Appendix B to answer the following questions.

a. Who are the independent auditors for Topps?

b. What type of opinion did the independent auditors issue on Topps' financial statements?

c. On what date does it appear the independent auditors completed their work related to Topps' 2003 financial statements?

d. Does the auditors' report give any information about how the audit was conducted? If so, what does it suggest was done?

e. Does the auditors' report tell the reader that the audit was concerned with materiality rather than absolute accuracy in the financial statements?

Required—Part 2

Harley-Davidson, Inc.

Use the **Harley-Davidson**'s annual report that came with this book to answer the following questions.

a. Who are the independent auditors for Harley-Davidson?

b. What type of opinion did the independent auditors issue on Harley-Davidson's financial statements?

c. On what date does it appear the independent auditors completed their work related to Harley-Davidson's 2003 financial statements?

d. Does the auditors' report tell the reader that the audit was concerned with materiality rather than absolute accuracy in the financial statements?

e. Read the *Report of Management,* on page 92, and the *Report of the Audit Committee,* on page 93, of Harley's annual report. Based on these reports, and the auditors' report, which you read to answer items a, b, c, and d above, who is primarily responsible for the company's financial statements?

Required—Part 3

Why did the auditors for Topps finish their audit work so much later in the year than did the auditors for Harley-Davidson?

ATC 6-2 Group Assignment *Bank reconciliations*

The following cash and bank information is available for three companies at June 30, 2007.

Cash and Adjustment Information	Peach Co.	Apple Co.	Pear Co.
Unadjusted cash balance per books, 6/30	$45,620	$32,450	$23,467
Outstanding checks	1,345	2,478	2,540
Service charge	50	75	35
Balance per bank statement, 6/30	48,632	37,176	24,894
Credit memo for collection of notes receivable	4,500	5,600	3,800
NSF check	325	145	90
Deposits in transit	2,500	3,200	4,800
Credit memo for interest earned	42	68	12

Required

a. Organize the class into three sections and divide each section into groups of three to five students. Assign Peach Co. to section 1, Apple Co. to section 2, and Pear Co. to section 3.

Group Tasks

(1) Prepare a bank reconciliation for the company assigned to your group.

(2) Prepare any necessary journal entries for the company assigned to your group.

(3) Select a representative from a group in each section to put the bank reconciliation and required journal entries on the board.

Class Discussion:

b. Discuss the cause of the difference between the unadjusted cash balance and the ending balance for the bank statement. Also, discuss types of adjustment that are commonly made to the bank balance and types of adjustment that are commonly made to the unadjusted book balance.

ATC 6-3 Real-World Case *Whose numbers are they anyway?*

The following excerpt, sometimes referred to as *management's statement of responsibility,* was taken from **JCPenney's** 10-K report for its 2003 fiscal year. The authors have italicized and numbered selected portions of the excerpt.

Company Statement on Financial Information (partial)

[1] *The Company is responsible for the information presented in this Annual Report.* The consolidated financial statements have been prepared in accordance with accounting principles generally accepted in the United States of America and present fairly, in all material respects, the Company's results of operations, financial position, and cash flows. The Company's CEO and CFO have signed certification statements as required by Sections 302 and 906 of the Sarbanes-Oxley Act of 2002. These signed certifications have been filed with the Securities and Exchange Commission as part of the Company's 2002 Form 10-K. Certain amounts included in the consolidated financial statements are estimated based on currently available information and judgment as to the outcome of future conditions and circumstances. . . .

The Company's system of internal controls is supported by written policies and procedures and supplemented by a staff of internal auditors. **[2]** *This system is designed to provide reasonable assurance, at suitable costs,* that assets are safeguarded and that transactions are executed in accordance with appropriate authorization and are recorded and reported properly. The system is continually reviewed, evaluated and where appropriate, modified to accommodate current conditions. Emphasis is placed on the careful **[3]** *selection,* **[4]** *training, and development of professional finance and internal audit managers.*

An organizational alignment that is premised upon appropriate **[5]** *delegation of authority* and **[6]** *division of responsibility* is fundamental to this system. **[7]** *Communication programs are aimed at assuring that established policies and procedures are disseminated and understood throughout the Company.*

The consolidated financial statements have been audited by independent auditors whose report appears below. Their audit was conducted in accordance with auditing standards generally accepted in the United States of America, which include the consideration of the Company's internal controls to the extent necessary to form an independent opinion on the consolidated financial statements prepared by management.

The Audit Committee of the Board of Directors is composed solely of directors who are not officers or employees of the Company . . .

Required

Assume that a colleague, who has never taken an accounting course, asks you to explain JCPenney's "company statement on financial information." Write a memorandum that explains each of the numbered portions of the material. When appropriate, include examples to explain these concepts of internal control to your colleague.

ATC 6-4 Business Applications Case *Decisions about materiality*

The accounting firm of Espey & Davis, CPAs, recently completed the audits of three separate companies. During these audits, the following events were discovered, and Espey & Davis is trying to decide if each event is material. If an item is material, the CPA firm will insist that the company modify the financial statements.

1. In 2003, Foxx Company reported service revenues of $1,000,000 and earnings before tax of $80,000. Because of an accounting error, the company recorded $6,000 as revenue in 2003 for services that will not be performed until early 2004.
2. Guzza Company plans to report a cash balance of $70,000. Because of an accounting error, this amount is $5,000 too high. Guzza also plans to report total assets of $4,000,000 and net earnings of $415,000.
3. Jeter Company's 2003 balance sheet shows a cash balance of $200,000 and total assets of $9,000,000. For 2003, the company had a net income of $750,000. These balances are all

correct, but they would have been $5,000 higher if the president of the company had not claimed business travel expenses that were, in fact, the cost of personal vacations for him and his family. He charged the costs of these trips on the company's credit card. The president of Jeter Company owns 25 percent of the business.

Required

Write a memorandum to the partners of Espey & Davis, explaining whether each of these events is material.

ATC 6-5 Business Applications Case *Limitations of audit opinion*

The statement of financial position (balance sheet) of Trident Company reports assets of $4,500,000. Jan Lewis advises you that a major accounting firm has audited the statements and attested that they were prepared in accordance with generally accepted accounting principles. She tells you that she can buy the total owner's interest in the business for only $2,750,000 and is seriously considering the opportunity. She says that the auditor's unqualified opinion validates the $4,500,000 value of the assets. Lewis believes she would be foolish to pass up the opportunity to purchase the assets at a price of only $2,750,000.

Required

a. What part of the accounting equation is Lewis failing to consider?

b. Comment on Lewis's misconceptions regarding the auditor's role in providing information that is useful in making investment decisions.

ATC 6-6 Writing Assignment *Internal control procedures*

Alison Marsh was a trusted employee of Small City State Bank. She was involved in everything. She worked as a teller, she accounted for the cash at the other teller windows, and she recorded many of the transactions in the accounting records. She was so loyal that she never would take a day off, even when she was really too sick to work. She routinely worked late to see that all the day's work was posted into the accounting records. She would never take even a day's vacation because they might need her at the bank. Tick and Tack, CPAs, were hired to perform an audit, the first complete audit that had been done in several years. Marsh seemed somewhat upset by the upcoming audit. She said that everything had been properly accounted for and that the audit was a needless expense. When Tick and Tack examined some of the bank's internal control procedures, it discovered problems. In fact, as the audit progressed, it became apparent that a large amount of cash was missing. Numerous adjustments had been made to customer accounts with credit memorandums, and many of the transactions had been posted several days late. In addition, there were numerous cash payments for "office expenses." When the audit was complete, it was determined that more than $200,000 of funds was missing or improperly accounted for. All fingers pointed to Marsh. The bank's president, who was a close friend of Marsh, was bewildered. How could this type of thing happen at this bank?

Required

Prepare a written memo to the bank president, outlining the procedures that should be followed to prevent this type of problem in the future.

ATC 6-7 Ethical Dilemma *I need just a little extra money*

Terry Bailey, an accountant, has worked for the past eight years as a payroll clerk for Fairwell Furniture, a small furniture manufacturing firm in the northeast. Terry recently experienced unfortunate circumstances. Her teenage son required minor surgery and the medical bills not covered by Terry's insurance have financially strained Terry's family.

Terry works hard and is a model employee. Although she received regular performance raises during her first few years with Fairwell, Terry's wages have not increased in three years. Terry asked her supervisor, Bill Jameson, for a raise. Bill agreed that Terry deserved a raise, but told her he could not currently approve one because of sluggish sales.

A disappointed Terry returned to her duties while the financial pressures in her life continued. Two weeks later, Larry Tyler, an assembly worker at Fairwell, quit over a dispute with management. Terry conceived an idea. Terry's duties included not only processing employee terminations but also approving time cards before paychecks were issued and then distributing the paychecks to firm personnel. Terry decided to delay processing Mr. Tyler's termination, to forge timecards for Larry Tyler for the next few weeks, and to cash the checks herself. Since she distributed paychecks, no one would find out, and Terry reasoned that she was really entitled to the extra money anyway. In fact, no one did discover her maneuver and Terry stopped the practice after three weeks.

Required

a. Does Terry's scheme affect Fairwell's balance sheet? Explain your answer.

b. Review the AICPA's Articles of Professional Conduct (see Chapter 1) and comment on any of the standards that have been violated.

c. Donald Cressey (see Chapter 1) identified three common features of unethical and criminal conduct. Name these features and explain how they pertain to this case.

ATC 6-8 Research Assignment *Accounting fraud at Nortel Networks Corporation*

Read the article "**Nortel Networks** Fires 7 More Finance Officials" that appears on page A-3 of the August 20, 2004, issue of *The Wall Street Journal* and answer the following questions.

Required

a. What was the general nature of the fraud the finance officials are accused of committing?

b. How high in the company's management ranks were the employees who were accused of committing the accounting fraud?

c. Describe the magnitude of the fraud. How much money was involved, and what percentage of the company's net earnings did it comprise?

d. What incentive did the people accused of committing the accounting fraud have that may have motivated them to behave unethically? Be specific.

e. What penalties, other than being fired, are those accused of the fraud expected to suffer?

COMPREHENSIVE PROBLEM

The trial balance of Pacilio Security Services Inc. as of January 1, 2006, had the following normal balances:

Cash	$74,210
Accounts Receivable	13,500
Supplies	200
Prepaid Rent	3,200
Merchandise Inventory (24 @ $265; 1 @ $260)	6,620
Land	4,000
Accounts Payable	1,950
Unearned Revenue	900
Salaries Payable	1,000
Common Stock	50,000
Retained Earnings	47,880

During 2006 Pacilio Security Services experienced the following transactions:

1. Paid the salaries payable from 2005.
2. On March 1, 2006, Pacilio established a $100 petty cash fund to handle small expenditures.
3. Paid $4,800 on March 1, 2006, for one year's lease on the company van in advance.
4. Paid $7,200 on May 2, 2006, for one year's rent in advance.
5. Purchased $400 of supplies on account.
6. Purchased 100 alarm systems for $28,000 cash during the year.
7. Sold 102 alarm systems for $57,120. All sales were on account. (Compute cost of goods sold using the FIFO cost flow method.)
8. Paid $2,100 on accounts payable during the year.

9. Replenished the petty cash fund on August 1. At this time, the petty cash fund had only $7 of currency left. It contained the following receipts: office supplies expense $23, cutting grass $55, and miscellaneous expense $14.
10. Billed $52,000 of monitoring services for the year.
11. Paid installers and other employees a total of $25,000 cash for salaries.
12. Collected $89,300 of accounts receivable during the year.
13. Paid $3,600 of advertising expense during the year.
14. Paid $2,500 of utilities expense for the year.
15. Paid a dividend of $10,000 to the shareholders.

Adjustments

16. There was $160 of supplies on hand at the end of the year.
17. Recognized the expired rent for both the van and the office building for the year.
18. Recognized the balance of the revenue earned in 2006 where cash had been collected in 2005.
19. Accrued salaries at December 31, 2006, were $1,400.

Required

a. Record the above transactions in general journal form.
b. Post the transactions to the T-accounts.
c. Prepare a bank reconciliation at the end of the year. The following information is available for the bank reconciliation:
   (1) Checks written but not paid by the bank, $8,350.
   (2) A deposit of $6,500 made on December 31, 2006, had been recorded but was not shown on the bank statement.
   (3) A debit memo for $55 for a new supply of checks. (Hint: Use Office Supplies Expense account.)
   (4) A credit memo for $30 for interest earned on the checking account.
   (5) An NSF check for $120.
   (6) The balance shown on the bank statement was $80,822.
d. Record and post any adjustments necessary from the bank reconciliation.
e. Prepare a trial balance.
f. Prepare an income statement, statement of changes in stockholders' equity, balance sheet, and statement of cash flows.
g. Close the temporary accounts to retained earnings.
h. Post the closing entries to the T-accounts and prepare an after-closing trial balance.

CHAPTER 7

Accounting for Receivables

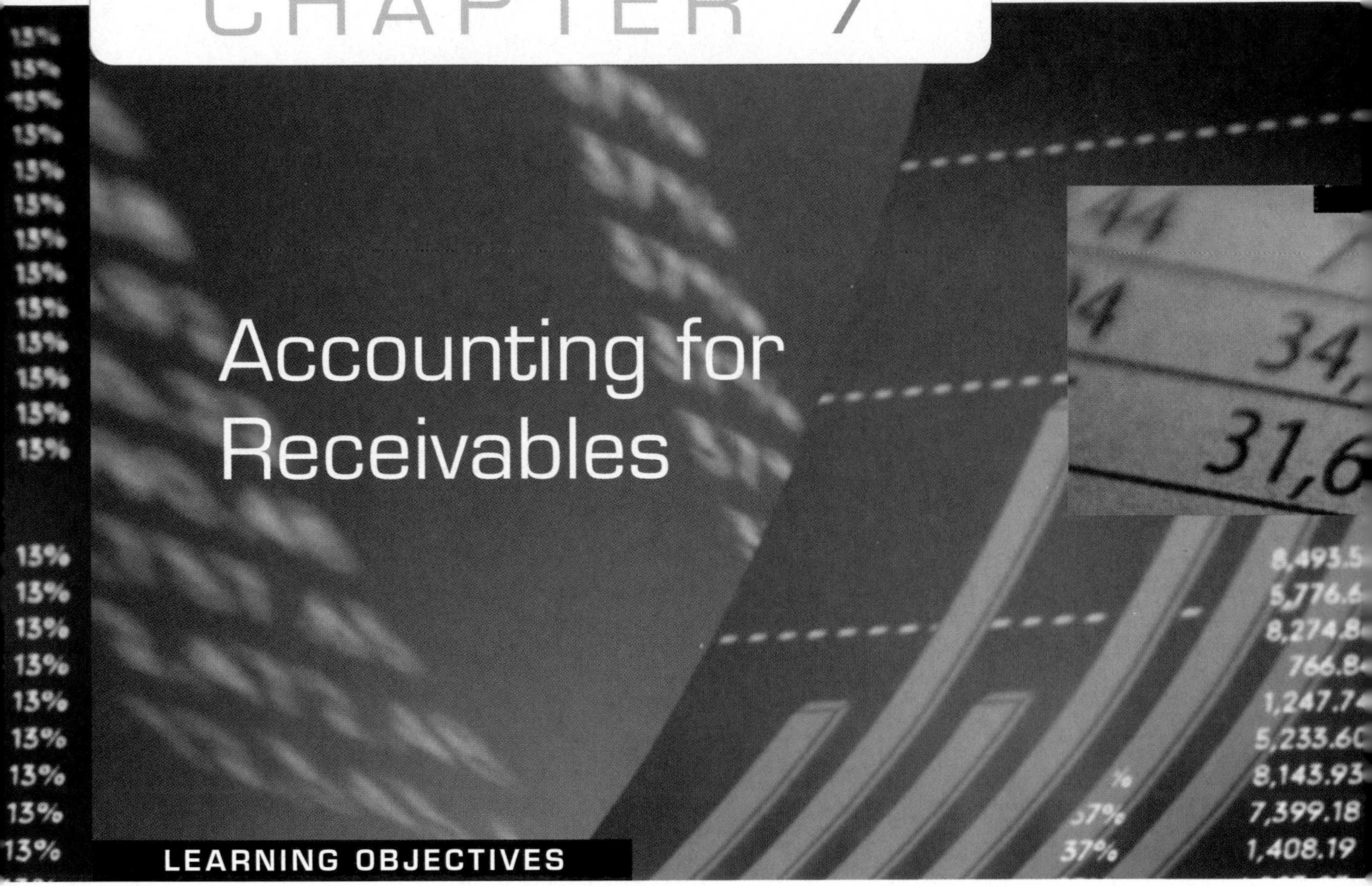

LEARNING OBJECTIVES

After you have mastered the material in this chapter, you will be able to:

1. **Explain the importance of offering credit terms to customers.**
2. **Explain how the allowance method of accounting for uncollectible accounts affects financial statements.**
3. **Show how the direct write-off method of accounting for uncollectible accounts affects financial statements.**
4. **Explain how accounting for notes receivable and accrued interest affects financial statements.**
5. **Explain how accounting for credit card sales affects financial statements.**
6. **Explain the effects of the cost of financing credit sales.**

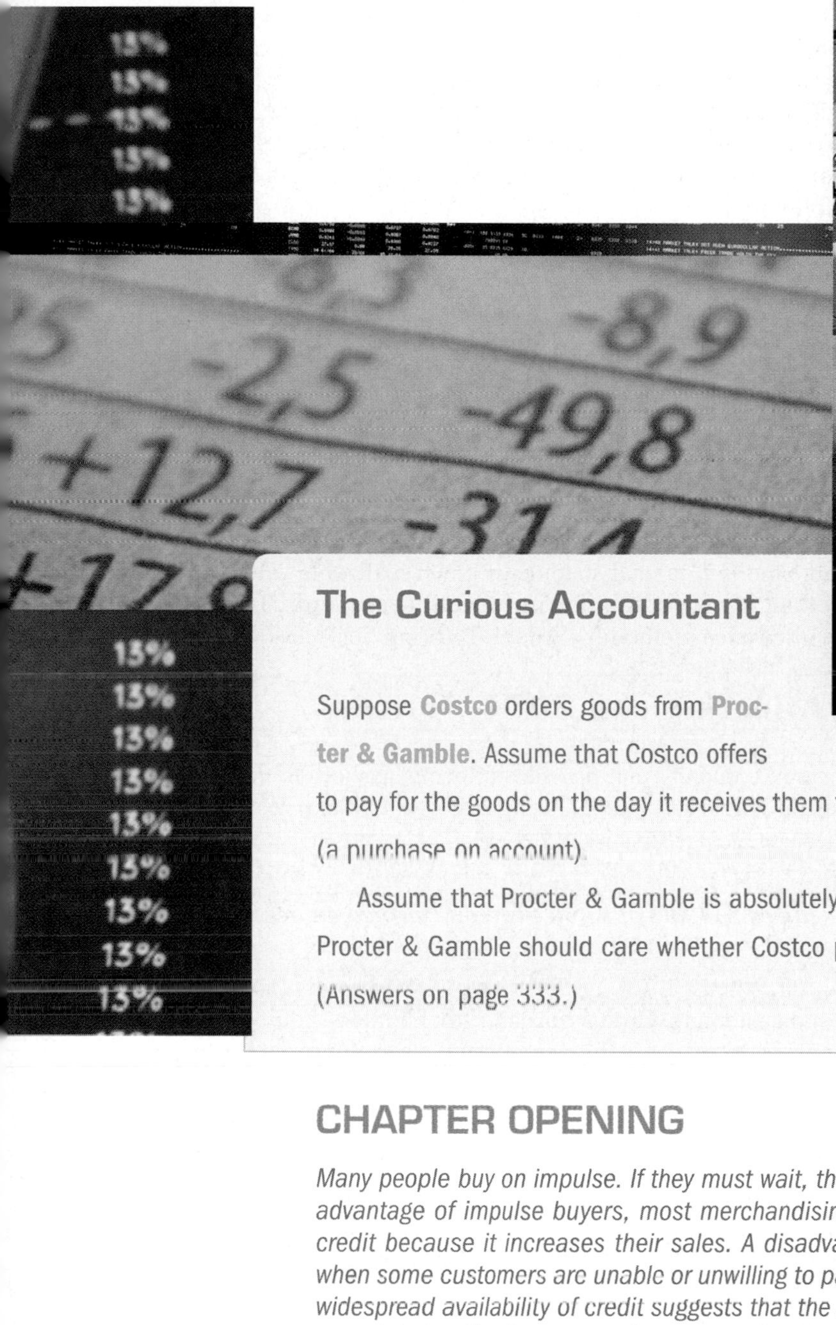

Chapter 7

The Curious Accountant

Suppose **Costco** orders goods from **Procter & Gamble**. Assume that Costco offers to pay for the goods on the day it receives them from Procter & Gamble (a cash purchase) or 30 days later (a purchase on account).

Assume that Procter & Gamble is absolutely sure Costco will pay its account when due. Do you think Procter & Gamble should care whether Costco pays for the goods upon delivery or 30 days later? Why? (Answers on page 333.)

CHAPTER OPENING

LO 1

Explain the importance of offering credit terms to customers.

Many people buy on impulse. If they must wait, the desire to buy wanes. To take advantage of impulse buyers, most merchandising companies offer customers credit because it increases their sales. A disadvantage of this strategy occurs when some customers are unable or unwilling to pay their bills. Nevertheless, the widespread availability of credit suggests that the advantages of increased sales outweigh the disadvantages of some uncollectible accounts.

When a company allows a customer to "buy now and pay later," the company's right to collect cash in the future is called an **account receivable.** *Typically, amounts due from individual accounts receivable are relatively small and the collection period is short. Most accounts receivable are collected within 30 days. When a longer credit term is needed or when a receivable is large, the seller usually requires the buyer to issue a note reflecting a credit agreement between the parties. The note specifies the maturity date, interest rate, and other credit terms. Receivables evidenced by such notes are called* **notes receivable.** *Accounts and notes receivable are reported as assets on the balance sheet.*

Allowance Method of Accounting for Uncollectible Accounts

LO 2

Explain how the allowance method of accounting for uncollectible accounts affects financial statements.

Most companies do not expect to collect the full amount (face value) of their accounts receivable. Even carefully screened credit customers sometimes don't pay their bills. The **net realizable value** of accounts receivable represents the amount of receivables a company estimates it will actually collect. The net realizable value is the *face value* less an *allowance for doubtful accounts.*

The **allowance for doubtful accounts** represents a company's estimate of the amount of uncollectible receivables. To illustrate, assume a company with total accounts receivable of $50,000 estimates that $2,000 of its receivables will not be collected. The net realizable value of receivables is computed as follows:

Accounts receivable	$50,000
Less: Allowance for doubtful accounts	(2,000)
Net realizable value of receivables	$48,000

A company cannot know today, of course, the exact amount of the receivables it will not be able to collect in the future. The *allowance for doubtful accounts* and the *net realizable value* are necessarily *estimated amounts.* The net realizable value, however, more closely measures the cash that will ultimately be collected than does the face value. To avoid overstating assets, companies usually report receivables on their balance sheets at the net realizable value.

Reporting accounts receivable in the financial statements at net realizable value is commonly called the **allowance method of accounting for uncollectible accounts.** The following section illustrates using the allowance method for Allen's Tutoring Services (ATS).

Accounting Events Affecting the 2006 Period

LO 2

Explain how the allowance method of accounting for uncollectible accounts affects financial statements.

Topic Tackler PLUS 7-1

Allen's Tutoring Services is a small company that provides tutoring services to college students. Allen's started operations on January 1, 2006. During 2006, Allen's experienced three types of accounting events. These events are discussed below.

Event 1 **Revenue Recognition**

Allen's Tutoring Services recognized $14,000 of service revenue earned on account during 2006.

This is an asset source transaction. Allen's Tutoring Services obtained assets (accounts receivable) by providing services to customers. Both assets and stockholders' equity (retained earnings) increase. The event increases revenue and net income. Cash flow is not affected. These effects follow:

Event No.	Assets	=	Liab.	+	Equity	Rev.	−	Exp.	=	Net Inc.	Cash Flow
	Accts. Rec.	=			Ret. Earn.						
1	14,000	=	NA	+	14,000	14,000	−	NA	=	14,000	NA

Event 2 **Collection of Receivables**

Allen's Tutoring Services collected $12,500 cash from accounts receivable in 2006.

This event is an asset exchange transaction. The asset cash increases; the asset accounts receivable decreases. Total assets remains unchanged. Net income is not affected because the revenue was recognized in the previous transaction. The cash inflow is reported in the operating activities section of the statement of cash flows.

Event No.	Assets			=	Liab.	+	Equity	Rev.	−	Exp.	=	Net Inc.	Cash Flow
	Cash	+	Accts. Rec.										
2	12,500	+	(12,500)	=	NA	+	NA	NA	−	NA	=	NA	12,500 OA

Answers to The Curious Accountant

Procter & Gamble would definitely prefer to make the sale to Costco in cash rather than on account. Even though it may be certain to collect its accounts receivable from Costco, the sooner Procter & Gamble gets its cash, the sooner the cash can be reinvested.

The interest cost related to a small account receivable of $50 that takes 30 days to collect may seem immaterial; at 4 percent, the lost interest amounts to less than $.20. However, when one considers that Procter & Gamble had approximately $3.4 billion of accounts receivable on June 30, 2002, the cost of financing receivables for a real-world company becomes apparent. At 4 percent, the cost of waiting 30 days to collect $3.4 billion of cash is $11.2 million ($3.4 billion × 0.04 × [30 ÷ 365]). For one full year, the cost to Procter & Gamble would be more than $136 million ($3.4 billion × 0.04). In 2002 it took Procter & Gamble approximately 31 days to collect its accounts receivable, and the weighted-average interest rate on its debt was approximately 3.7 percent.

Event 3 Recognizing Uncollectible Accounts Expense

Allen's Tutoring Services recognized uncollectible accounts expense for accounts expected to be uncollectible in the future.

The year-end balance in the accounts receivable account is $1,500 ($14,000 of revenue on account − $12,500 of collections). Although Allen's Tutoring Services has the legal right to receive this $1,500 in 2007, the company is not likely to collect the entire amount because some of its customers may not pay the amounts due. Allen's will not know the actual amount of uncollectible accounts until some future time when the customers default (fail to pay). However, the company can *estimate* the amount of receivables that will be uncollectible.

Suppose Allen's Tutoring Services estimates that $75 of the receivables is uncollectible. To improve financial reporting, the company can recognize the estimated expense in 2006. In this way, uncollectible accounts expense and the related revenue will be recognized in the same accounting period (2006). Recognizing an estimated expense is more useful than recognizing no expense. The *matching* of revenues and expenses is improved and the statements are, therefore, more accurate.

The estimated amount of **uncollectible accounts expense** is recognized in a year-end adjusting entry. The adjusting entry reduces the book value of total assets, reduces stockholders' equity (retained earnings), and reduces the amount of reported net income. The statement of cash flows is not affected. The effects of recognizing uncollectible accounts expense are shown here:

Event No.	Assets			=	Liab.	+	Equity	Rev.	−	Exp.	=	Net Inc.	Cash Flow
	Accts. Rec.	−	Allow.	=			Ret. Earn.						
3	NA	−	75	=	NA	+	(75)	NA	−	75	=	(75)	NA

Instead of decreasing the receivables account directly, the asset reduction is recorded in the **contra asset account,** Allowance for Doubtful Accounts. Recall that the contra account is subtracted from the accounts receivable balance to determine the net realizable value of receivables, as follows for ATS:

Accounts receivable	$1,500
Less: Allowance for doubtful accounts	(75)
Net realizable value of receivables	$1,425

Generally accepted accounting principles require disclosure of both the net realizable value and the amount of the allowance account. Many companies disclose these amounts directly in the balance sheet in a manner similar to that shown in the text box above. Other companies disclose this information in the footnotes to the financial statements.

Recording and Reporting Uncollectible Accounts Events in the Double-Entry System

The transactions experienced by Allen's Tutoring Services during 2006 are summarized below.

Event 1 ATS earned $14,000 of revenue on account.

Event 2 ATS collected $12,500 cash from accounts receivable.

Event 3 ATS adjusted its accounts to reflect management's estimate that uncollectible accounts expense would be $75.

Exhibit 7.1, Panel A, shows these transactions in general journal format. Panel B shows the general ledger T-accounts after the journal entries have been posted to them. The amounts in the ledger accounts provide the information for the financial statements in Exhibit 7.2. Although Exhibit 7.1 does not illustrate the 2006 year-end closing entries, recall that the closing entries will transfer the amounts from the revenue and expense accounts to the Retained Earnings account. The balance in the Retained Earnings account after closing will be $13,925, as reported on the year-end balance sheet. Before reading further, trace the transaction data from each journal entry in Panel A to the ledger accounts in Panel B and then from the ledger accounts to the financial statements in Exhibit 7.2.

EXHIBIT 7.1

Journal Entries and General Ledger Accounts

Panel A Journal Entries

Event No.	Account Title	Debit	Credit
1	Accounts Receivable	14,000	
	Service Revenue		14,000
2	Cash	12,500	
	Accounts Receivable		12,500
3	Uncollectible Accounts Expense	75	
	Allowance for Doubtful Accounts		75

Panel B General Ledger Accounts

Assets = Liabilities + Equity

Cash

	Debit	Credit	
(2)	12,500		
Bal.	12,500		

Accounts Receivable

	Debit	Credit	
(1)	14,000	12,500	(2)
Bal.	1,500		

Allowance for Doubtful Accounts

	Debit	Credit	
		75	(3)
		75	Bal.

Retained Earnings

	Debit	Credit	

Service Revenue

	Debit	Credit	
		14,000	(1)

Uncollectible Accts. Expense

	Debit	Credit	
(3)	75		

EXHIBIT 7.2

Financial Statements for 2006

Income Statement

Service Revenue	$14,000
Uncollectible Accts. Exp.	(75)
Net Income	$13,925

Assets		
Cash		$12,500
Accounts Receivable	$1,500	
Less: Allowance	(75)	
Net Realizable Value		1,425
Total Assets		$13,925
Stockholders' Equity		
Retained Earnings		$13,925

Statement of Cash Flows

Operating Activities	
Inflow from Customers	$12,500
Investing Activities	0
Financing Activities	0
Net Change in Cash	12,500
Plus: Beginning Cash Balance	0
Ending Cash Balance	$12,500

Financial Statements

As previously indicated, estimating uncollectible accounts improves the usefulness of the 2006 financial statements in two ways. First, the balance sheet reports the amount of cash ($1,500 − $75 = $1,425) the company actually expects to collect (net realizable value of accounts receivable). Second, the income statement provides a clearer picture of managerial performance because it better *matches* the uncollectible accounts expense with the revenue it helped produce. The statements in Exhibit 7.2 show that the cash flow from operating activities ($12,500) differs from net income ($13,925). The statement of cash flows reports only cash collections, whereas the income statement reports revenues earned on account less the estimated amount of uncollectible accounts expense.

CHECK YOURSELF 7.1

Pamlico Inc. began operations on January 1, 2008. During 2008, it earned $400,000 of revenue on account. The company collected $370,000 of accounts receivable. At the end of the year, Pamlico estimates uncollectible accounts expense will be 1 percent of sales. Based on this information alone, what is the net realizable value of accounts receivable as of December 31, 2008?

Answer

Accounts receivable at year end are $30,000 ($400,000 sales on account − $370,000 collection of receivables). The amount in the allowance for doubtful accounts would be $4,000 ($400,000 credit sales × 0.01). The net realizable value of accounts receivable is therefore $26,000 ($30,000 − $4,000).

Accounting Events Affecting the 2007 Period

To further illustrate accounting for uncollectible accounts, we discuss six accounting events affecting Allen's Tutoring Services during 2007.

LO 2

Explain how the allowance method of accounting for uncollectible accounts affects financial statements.

Event 1 **Write-Off of Uncollectible Accounts Receivable**
Allen's Tutoring Services wrote off $70 of uncollectible accounts receivable.

This is an asset exchange transaction. The amount of the uncollectible accounts is removed from the Accounts Receivable account and from the Allowance for Doubtful Accounts account. Since the balances in both the Accounts Receivable and the Allowance accounts decrease, the net realizable value of receivables—and therefore total assets—remains unchanged. The write-off does not affect the income statement. Since the uncollectible accounts expense was recognized in the previous year, the expense would be double counted if it were recognized again at the time an uncollectible account is written off. Finally, the statement of cash flows is not affected by the write-off. These effects are shown in the following statements model:

Event No.	Assets			=	Liab.	+	Equity	Rev.	−	Exp.	=	Net Inc.	Cash Flow
	Accts. Rec.	−	Allow.										
1	(70)	−	(70)	=	NA	+	NA	NA	−	NA	=	NA	NA

The computation of the *net realizable value,* before and after the write-off, is shown below.

	Before Write-Off	After Write-Off
Accounts receivable	$1,500	$1,430
Less: Allowance for doubtful accounts	(75)	(5)
Net realizable value	$1,425	$1,425

Event 2 Revenue Recognition

Allen's Tutoring Services provided $10,000 of tutoring services on account during 2007.

Assets (accounts receivable) and stockholders' equity (retained earnings) increase. Recognizing revenue increases net income. Cash flow is not affected. These effects are illustrated below:

Event No.	Assets	=	Liab.	+	Equity	Rev.	−	Exp.	=	Net Inc.	Cash Flow
	Accts. Rec.	=			Ret. Earn.						
2	10,000	=	NA	+	10,000	10,000	−	NA	=	10,000	NA

Event 3 Collection of Accounts Receivable

Allen's Tutoring Services collected $8,430 cash from accounts receivable.

The balance in the Cash account increases, and the balance in the Accounts Receivable account decreases. Total assets are unaffected. Net income is not affected because revenue was recognized previously. The cash inflow is reported in the operating activities section of the statement of cash flows.

Event No.	Assets			=	Liab.	+	Equity	Rev.	−	Exp.	=	Net Inc.	Cash Flow
	Cash	+	Accts. Rec.										
3	8,430	+	(8,430)	=	NA	+	NA	NA	−	NA	=	NA	8,430 OA

Event 4 Recovery of an Uncollectible Account: Reinstate Receivable

Allen's Tutoring Services recovered a receivable that it had previously written off.

Occasionally, a company receives payment from a customer whose account was previously written off. In such cases, the customer's account should be reinstated and the cash received should be recorded the same way as any other collection on account. The account receivable is reinstated because a complete record of the customer's payment history may be useful if the customer requests credit again at some future date. To illustrate, assume that Allen's Tutoring Services received a $10 cash payment from a customer whose account had previously been written off. The first step is to **reinstate** the account receivable by reversing the previous write-off. The balances in the Accounts Receivable and the Allowance accounts increase. Since the Allowance is a contra asset account, the increase in it offsets the increase in the Accounts Receivable account, and total assets are unchanged. Net income and cash flow are unaffected. These effects are shown here:

Event No.	Assets			=	Liab.	+	Equity	Rev.	−	Exp.	=	Net Inc.	Cash Flow
	Accts. Rec.	−	Allow.										
4	10	−	10	=	NA	+	NA	NA	−	NA	=	NA	NA

Event 5 **Recovery of an Uncollectible Account: Collection of Receivable**
Allen's Tutoring Services recorded collection of the reinstated receivable.

The collection of $10 is recorded like any other collection of a receivable account. Cash increases, and accounts receivable decreases.

Event No.	Assets			=	Liab.	+	Equity	Rev.	−	Exp.	=	Net Inc.	Cash Flow
	Cash	+	Accts. Rec.										
5	10	+	(10)	=	NA	+	NA	NA	−	NA	=	NA	10 OA

Estimating Uncollectible Accounts Expense Using the Percent of Revenue (Sales) Method

Companies recognize the estimated amount of uncollectible accounts expense in a period-end adjusting entry. Since Allen's Tutoring Service began operations in 2006, it had no previous credit history upon which to base its estimate. After consulting trade publications and experienced people in the same industry, ATS made an educated guess as to the amount of expense it should recognize for its first year. In its second year of operation, however, ATS can use its first-year experience as a starting point for estimating the second year (2007) uncollectible accounts expense.

At the end of 2006 ATS estimated uncollectible accounts expense to be $75 on service revenue of $14,000. In 2007 ATS actually wrote off $70 of which $10 was later recovered. ATS therefore experienced actual uncollectible accounts of $60 on service revenue of $14,000 for an uncollectible accounts rate of approximately .43 percent of service revenue. ATS could apply this percentage to the 2007 service revenue to estimate the 2007 uncollectible accounts expense. In practice, many companies determine the percentage estimate of uncollectible accounts on a three- or five-year moving average.

Companies adjust the historical percentage for anticipated future circumstances. For example, they reduce it if they adopt more rigorous approval standards for new credit applicants. Alternatively, they may increase the percentage if economic forecasts signal an economic downturn that would make future defaults more likely. A company will also increase the percentage if it has specific knowledge one or more of its customers is financially distressed. Multiplying the service revenue by the percentage estimate of uncollectible accounts is commonly called the **percent of revenue method** of estimating uncollectible accounts expense.

Event 6 **Adjustment for Recognition of Uncollectible Accounts Expense**
Using the percent of revenue method, Allen's Tutoring Services recognized uncollectible accounts expense for 2007.

ATS must record this adjustment as of December 31, 2007, to update its accounting records before preparing the 2007 financial statements. After reviewing its credit history, economic forecasts, and correspondence with customers, management estimates uncollectible accounts expense to be 1.35 percent of service revenue, or $135 ($10,000 service revenue × .0135). Recognizing the $135 uncollectible accounts expense decreases both assets (net realizable of receivables) and stockholders' equity (retained earnings). The expense recognition decreases net income. The statement of cash flows is not affected. The financial statements are affected as shown here:

Event No.	Assets			=	Liab.	+	Equity	Rev.	−	Exp.	=	Net Inc.	Cash Flow
	Accts. Rec.	−	Allow.	=			Ret. Earn.						
6	NA	−	135	=	NA	+	(135)	NA	−	135	=	(135)	NA

Recording and Reporting Uncollectible Accounts Events in the Double-Entry System

The 2007 transactions experienced by Allen's Tutoring Services are summarized below.

Event 1 ATS wrote off $70 of uncollectible accounts receivable.
Event 2 ATS earned $10,000 of revenue on account.
Event 3 ATS collected $8,430 cash from accounts receivable.
Event 4 ATS reinstated a $10 account receivable it had previously written off.
Event 5 ATS recorded collecting $10 from the reinstated receivable referenced in Event 5.
Event 6 ATS adjusted its accounts to recognize $135 of uncollectible accounts expense.

Panel A of Exhibit 7.3 shows these transactions recorded in general journal format. Panel B of the exhibit shows the general ledger T-accounts after the journal entries have been posted into them. The amounts in the ledger accounts are used to prepare the financial statements that appear in Exhibit 7.4. Exhibit 7.3 does not include the closing entries. Closing the accounts will transfer the amounts from the revenue and expense accounts to the Retained Earnings account, resulting in a $23,790 ending balance in this account as shown on the 2007 balance sheet. We recommend that you trace the transaction data from each journal entry to the ledger accounts and the amounts in the ledger accounts to the financial statements.

Analysis of Financial Statements

Exhibit 7.4 displays the 2007 financial statements. The amount of uncollectible accounts expense ($135) differs from the ending balance of the Allowance account ($150). The balance in the Allowance account was $15 before the 2007 adjusting entry for uncollectible accounts expense was recorded. At the end of 2006, Allen's Tutoring Services estimated there would be $75 of uncollectible accounts as a result of 2006 credit sales. Actual write-offs, however, amounted to $70 and $10 of that amount was recovered, indicating the actual uncollectible accounts expense for 2006 was only $60. Hindsight shows the expense for 2006 was overstated by $15. However, if no estimate had been made, the amount of uncollectible accounts expense would have been understated by $60. In some accounting periods estimated uncollectible accounts expense will likely be overstated; in others it may be understated. The

EXHIBIT 7.3

Journal Entries and General Ledger Accounts

Panel A Journal Entries

Event No.	Account Title	Debit	Credit
1	Allowance for Doubtful Accounts	70	
	Accounts Receivable		70
2	Accounts Receivable	10,000	
	Service Revenue		10,000
3	Cash	8,430	
	Accounts Receivable		8,430
4	Accounts Receivable	10	
	Allowance for Doubtful Accounts		10
5	Cash	10	
	Accounts Receivable		10
6	Uncollectible Accounts Expense	135	
	Allowance for Doubtful Accounts		135

Panel B General Ledger Accounts

Assets = **Liabilities** + **Equity**

Cash

	Debit	Credit	
Bal.	12,500		
(3)	8,430		
(5)	10		
Bal.	20,940		

Accounts Receivable

	Debit	Credit	
Bal.	1,500	70	(1)
(2)	10,000	8,430	(3)
(4)	10	10	(5)
Bal.	3,000		

Allowance for Doubtful Accounts

	Debit	Credit	
(1)	70	75	Bal.
		10	(4)
		135	(6)
		150	Bal.

Retained Earnings

	Debit	Credit	
		13,925	Bal.

Service Revenue

	Debit	Credit	
		10,000	(2)

Uncollectible Accts. Expense

	Debit	Credit	
(6)	135		

allowance method cannot produce perfect results, but it does improve the accuracy of the financial statements.

Since no dividends were paid, retained earnings at the end of 2007 equals the December 31, 2006, retained earnings plus 2007 net income (that is, \$13,925 + \$9,865 = \$23,790). Again, the cash flow from operating activities (\$8,440) differs from net income (\$9,865) because the statement of cash flows does not include the effects of revenues earned on account or the recognition of uncollectible accounts expense.

EXHIBIT 7.4

Financial Statements for 2007

Income Statement

Service Revenue	$10,000
Uncollectible Accts. Exp.	(135)
Net Income	$ 9,865

Balance Sheet

Assets		
Cash		$20,940
Accounts Receivable	$3,000	
Less: Allowance	(150)	
Net Realizable Value		2,850
Total Assets		$23,790
Stockholders' Equity		
Retained Earnings		$23,790

Statement of Cash Flows

Operating Activities	
Inflow from Customers	$ 8,440
Investing Activities	0
Financing Activities	0
Net Change in Cash	8,440
Plus: Beginning Cash Balance	12,500
Ending Cash Balance	$20,940

CHECK YOURSELF 7.2

Maher Company had beginning balances in Accounts Receivable and Allowance for Doubtful Accounts of $24,200 and $2,000, respectively. During the accounting period Maher earned $230,000 of revenue on account and collected $232,500 of cash from receivables. The company also wrote off $1,950 of uncollectible accounts during the period. Maher estimates uncollectible accounts expense will be 1 percent of credit sales. Based on this information, what is the net realizable value of receivables at the end of the period?

Answer

The balance in the Accounts Receivable account is $19,750 ($24,200 + $230,000 − $232,500 − $1,950). The amount of uncollectible accounts expense for the period is $2,300 ($230,000 × 0.01). The balance in the Allowance for Doubtful Accounts is $2,350 ($2,000 − $1,950 + $2,300). The net realizable value of receivables is therefore $17,400 ($19,750 − $2,350).

Estimating Uncollectible Accounts Expense Using the Percent of Receivables Method

As an alternative to the percent of revenue method, which focuses on estimating the *expense* of uncollectible accounts, companies may estimate the amount of the adjusting entry to record uncollectible accounts expense using the **percent of receivables method.** The percent of receivables method focuses on estimating the most accurate amount for the balance sheet *Allowance for Doubtful Accounts* account.

The longer an account receivable remains outstanding, the less likely it is to be collected. Companies using the percent of receivables method typically determine the age of their individual accounts receivable accounts as part of estimating the allowance for doubtful accounts. An **aging of accounts receivable** schedule classifies all receivables by their due date. Exhibit 7.5 shows an aging schedule for Pyramid Corporation as of December 31, 2007.

A company estimates the required Allowance for Doubtful Accounts balance by applying different percentages to each category in the aging schedule. The percentage for each category is based on a company's previous collection experience for each of the categories. The percentages become progressively higher as the accounts become older. Exhibit 7.6 illustrates computing the allowance balance Pyramid Corporation requires.

The computations in Exhibit 7.6 mean the *ending balance* in the Allowance for Doubtful Accounts account should be $3,760. This balance represents the amount Pyramid will subtract from total accounts receivable to determine the net realizable value of receivables. To determine the amount of the adjusting entry to recognize uncollectible accounts expense,

EXHIBIT 7.5

PYRAMID CORPORATION
Accounts Receivable Aging Schedule
December 31, 2007

Customer Name	Total Balance	Current	Number of Days Past Due 0–30	31–60	61–90	Over 90
J. Davis	$ 6,700	$ 6,700				
B. Diamond	4,800	2,100	$ 2,700			
K. Eppy	9,400	9,400				
B. Gilman	2,200				$1,000	$1,200
A. Kelly	7,300	7,300				
L. Niel	8,600	1,000	6,000	$ 1,600		
L. Platt	4,600			4,600		
J. Turner	5,500			3,000	2,000	500
H. Zachry	6,900		3,000	3,900		
Total	$56,000	$26,500	$11,700	$13,100	$3,000	$1,700

EXHIBIT 7.6

Balance Required in the Allowance for Doubtful Accounts at December 31, 2007

Number of Days Past Due	Receivables Amount	Percentage Likely to Be Uncollectible	Required Allowance Account Balance
Current	$26,500	.01	$ 265
0–30	11,700	.05	585
31–60	13,100	.10	1,310
61–90	3,000	.25	750
Over 90	1,700	.50	850
Total	$56,000		$3,760

Pyramid must take into account any existing balance in the allowance account *before* recording the adjustment. For example, if Pyramid Corporation had a $500 credit balance in the Allowance account before the year-end adjustment, the adjusting entry would need to add $3,260 ($3,760 − $500) to the account. The journal entry to record the uncollectible accounts expense and its effects on the financial statements are shown below:

Account Title	Debit	Credit
Uncollectible Accounts Expense	3,260	
Allowance for Doubtful Accounts		3,260

Assets			=	Liab.	+	Equity	Rev.	−	Exp.	=	Net Inc.	Cash Flow
Accts. Rec.	−	Allow.	=			Ret. Earn.						
NA	−	3,260	=	NA	+	(3,260)	NA	−	3,260	=	3,260	NA

Matching Revenues and Expenses versus Asset Measurement

The *percent of revenue* method, with its focus on determining the uncollectible accounts expense, is often called the income statement approach. The *percent of receivables* method, focused on determining the best estimate of the allowance balance, is frequently called the balance sheet approach. Which estimating method is better? In any given year, the results will vary slightly between approaches. In the long run, however, the percentages used in either approach are based on a company's actual history of uncollectible accounts. Accountants routinely revise their estimates as more data become available, using hindsight to determine if the percentages should be increased or decreased. Either approach provides acceptable results.

Recognizing Uncollectible Accounts Expense Using the Direct Write-Off Method

LO 3

Show how the direct write-off method of accounting for uncollectible accounts affects financial statements.

If uncollectible accounts are not material, generally accepted accounting principles allow companies to account for them using the **direct write-off method.** Under the direct write-off method, a company simply recognizes uncollectible accounts expense *in the period in which it identifies and writes off uncollectible accounts.* No estimates, allowance account, or adjusting entries are needed.

The direct write-off method fails to match revenues with expenses. Revenues are recognized in one period and any related uncollectible accounts expense is recognized in a later period. Also, the direct write-off method overstates assets because receivables are reported at *face value* rather than *net realizable value.* If the amount of uncollectible accounts is immaterial, however, companies accept the minor reporting inaccuracies as a reasonable trade-off for recording convenience.

To illustrate the direct write-off method, return to the first year (2006) that Allen's Tutoring Service (ATS) operated. Assume ATS decided the direct write-off method was appropriate to account for its receivables. Recall that during 2006 ATS recognized $14,000 of revenue on account. The journal entry and its effects on the financial statements are shown below:

Account Title	Debit	Credit
Accounts Receivable	14,000	
Service Revenue		14,000

Assets	=	Liab.	+	Equity	Rev.	−	Exp.	=	Net Inc.	Cash Flow
Accts. Rec.	=			Ret. Earn.						
14,000	=	NA	+	14,000	14,000	−	NA	=	14,000	NA

ATS believed only an immaterial amount of the $14,000 of accounts receivable would prove uncollectible. It therefore made no year-end adjusting entry for estimated uncollectible accounts. Instead, ATS recognizes uncollectible accounts expense when it determines an account is uncollectible.

In its second accounting period (2007), ATS determined that $70 of accounts receivable were uncollectible. ATS recognized the uncollectible accounts expense in the entry to write off the uncollectible receivables. With the direct write-off method, the write-off reduces the asset account Accounts Receivable and decreases the stockholders' equity account Retained Earnings. On the income statement, expenses increase and net income decreases. The statement of cash flows is not affected by the write-off. The journal entry and its effects on the financial statements are shown below:

Account Title	Debit	Credit
Uncollectible Accounts Expense	70	
Accounts Receivable		70

Assets	=	Liab.	+	Equity	Rev.	−	Exp.	=	Net Inc.	Cash Flow
Accts. Rec.	=			Ret. Earn.						
(70)	=	NA	+	(70)	NA	−	70	=	(70)	NA

Also in 2007 ATS recovered a $10 account receivable it had previously written off. Recording the recovery of a previously written-off account requires two entries. First, ATS must *reinstate* the receivable (merely reverse the write-off entry above) because it has proved to be collectible after all. Second, ATS must record collecting the reinstated account. With the direct write-off method, reinstating the receivable increases the asset account Accounts Receivable and increases the stockholders' equity account Retained Earnings. On the income statement, expenses decrease and net income increases. The statement of cash flows is not affected. The journal entry and its effects on the financial statements are shown below:

Account Title	Debit	Credit
Accounts Receivable	10	
Uncollectible Accounts Expense		10

Assets	=	Liab.	+	Equity	Rev.	−	Exp.	=	Net Inc.	Cash Flow
Accts. Rec.	=			Ret. Earn.						
10	=	NA	+	10	NA	−	(10)	=	10	NA

Like the collection of any other receivable, collection of the reinstated account receivable increases the asset account Cash and decreases the asset account Accounts Receivable. The income statement is not affected. The cash inflow is reported in the operating activities section of the statement of cash flows. The journal entry and its effects on the financial statements are shown below:

Account Title	Debit	Credit
Cash	10	
Accounts Receivable		10

Assets			=	Liab.	+	Equity	Rev.	−	Exp.	=	Net Inc.	Cash Flow
Cash	−	Accts. Rec.										
10		(10)	=	NA	+	NA	NA	−	NA	=	NA	10 OA

Characteristics of Notes Receivable (Promissory Notes)

Companies typically do not charge their customers interest on accounts receivable that are not past due. When a company extends credit for a long time or when the amount of credit it extends is large, however, the cost of granting free credit and the potential for disputes about

EXHIBIT 7.7

Promissory Note

Promissory Note

$15,000 (3) — November 1, 2008

Amount — **Date**

For consideration received, Stanford Cummings **hereby promises to pay to the order of:**

Allen's Tutoring Services (2)

Fifteen thousand and no/100 **Dollars**

payable on October 31, 2009 (5)

plus interest thereon at the rate of 6 **percent per year.** (4)

Collateral Description Automobile title (6)

Signature *Stanford Cummings* (1)

Topic Tackler PLUS

7-1

payment terms both increase. To address these concerns, the parties frequently enter into a credit agreement, the terms of which are legally documented in a **promissory note.**

To illustrate, assume Allen's Tutoring Services (ATS) loans some of its idle cash to an individual, Stanford Cummings, so Cummings can buy a car. ATS and Cummings agree that Cummings will repay the money borrowed plus interest at the end of one year. They also agree that ATS will hold the title to the car to secure the debt. Exhibit 7.7 illustrates a promissory note that outlines this credit agreement. For ATS, the credit arrangement represents a *note receivable.*

Features of this note are discussed below. Each feature is cross referenced with a number that corresponds to an item on the promissory note in Exhibit 7.7. Locate each feature in Exhibit 7.7 and read the corresponding description of the feature below.

1. Maker—The person responsible for making payment on the due date is the **maker** of the note. The maker may also be called the *borrower* or *debtor.*
2. Payee—The person to whom the note is made payable is the **payee.** The payee may also be called the *creditor* or *lender.* The payee loans money to the maker and expects the return of the principal and the interest due.
3. Principal—The amount of money loaned by the payee to the maker of the note is the **principal.**
4. Interest—The economic benefit earned by the payee for loaning the principal to the maker is **interest,** which is normally expressed as an annual percentage of the principal amount. For example, a note with a 6 percent interest rate requires interest payments equal to 6 percent of the principal amount every year the loan is outstanding.
5. Maturity Date—The date on which the maker must repay the principal and make the final interest payment to the payee is the **maturity date.**
6. Collateral—Assets belonging to the maker that are assigned as security to ensure that the principal and interest will be paid when due are called **collateral.** In this example, if Cummings fails to pay ATS the amount due, ownership of the car Cummings purchased will be transferred to ATS.

Accounting for Notes Receivable

We illustrate accounting for notes receivable using the credit agreement evidenced by the promissory note in Exhibit 7.7. Allen's Tutoring Services engaged in many transactions during 2008; we discuss here only transactions directly related to the note receivable.

LO 4

Explain how accounting for notes receivable and accrued interest affects financial statements.

Event 1 Loan of Money

The note shows that ATS loaned $15,000 to Stanford Cummings on November 1, 2008. This event is an asset exchange. The asset account Cash decreases and the asset account Notes Receivable increases. The income statement is not affected. The statement of cash flows shows a cash outflow for investing activities. The journal entry and its effects on the financial statements are shown below:

Account Title	Debit	Credit
Notes Receivable	15,000	
Cash		15,000

Date	Assets					=	Liab.	+	Equity	Rev.	−	Exp.	=	Net Inc.	Cash Flow
	Cash	+	Notes Rec.	+	Int. Rec.	=			Ret. Earn.						
11/01/08	(15,000)	+	15,000	+	NA	=	NA	+	NA	NA	−	NA	=	NA	(15,000) IA

Event 2 Accrual of Interest

For ATS, loaning money to the maker of the note, Stanford Cummings, represents investing in the note receivable. Cummings will repay the principal ($15,000) plus interest of 6 percent of the principal amount ($0.06 \times \$15,000 = \$900$), or a total of $15,900, on October 31, 2009, one year from the date he borrowed the money from ATS.

Conceptually, lenders *earn* interest continually even though they do not *collect* cash payment for it every day. Each day, the amount of interest due, called **accrued interest,** is greater than the day before. Companies would find it highly impractical to attempt to record (recognize) accrued interest continually as the amount due increased.

Businesses typically solve the recordkeeping problem by only recording accrued interest when it is time to prepare financial statements or when it is due. At such times, the accounts are *adjusted* to reflect the amount of interest currently due. For example, ATS recorded the asset exchange immediately upon investing in the Note Receivable on November 1, 2008. ATS did not, however, recognize any interest earned on the note until the balance sheet date, December 31, 2008. At year-end ATS made an entry to recognize the interest it had earned during the previous two months (November 1 through December 31). This entry is an **adjusting entry** because it adjusts (updates) the account balances prior to preparing financial statements.

ATS computed the amount of accrued interest by multiplying the principal amount of the note by the annual interest rate and by the length of time for which the note has been outstanding.

$$\text{Principal} \times \text{Annual interest rate} \times \text{Time outstanding} = \text{Interest revenue}$$

$$\$15{,}000 \times 0.06 \times (2/12) = \$150$$

ATS recognized the $150 of interest revenue in 2008 although ATS will not collect the cash until 2009. This practice illustrates the **matching concept.** Interest revenue is recognized in (matched with) the period in which it is earned regardless of when the related cash is collected. The adjusting entry is an asset source transaction. The asset account Interest Receivable increases, and the stockholders' equity account Retained Earnings increases. The income statement reflects an increase in revenue and net income. The statement of cash flows is not affected because ATS will not collect cash until the maturity date (October 31, 2009). The adjusting entry and its effects on the financial statements are shown below:

Account Title	Debit	Credit
Interest Receivable	150	
Interest Revenue		150

Date	Assets					=	Liab.	+	Equity	Rev.	−	Exp.	=	Net Inc.	Cash Flow
	Cash	+	Notes Rec.	+	Int. Rec.	=			Ret. Earn.						
12/31/08	NA	+	NA	+	150	=	NA	+	150	150	−	NA	=	150	NA

Event 3 Collection of Principal and Interest on the Maturity Date

ATS collected $15,900 cash on the maturity date. The collection included $15,000 for the principal plus $900 for the interest. Recall that ATS previously accrued interest in the December 31, 2008, adjusting entry for the two months in 2008 that the note was outstanding. Since year-end, ATS has earned an additional 10 months of interest revenue. ATS must recognize this interest revenue before recording the cash collection. The amount of interest earned in 2009 is computed as follows:

$$\text{Principal} \times \text{Annual interest rate} \times \text{Time outstanding} = \text{Interest revenue}$$

$$\$15{,}000 \times 0.06 \times (10/12) = \$750$$

The journal entry and effects on the financial statements are shown below.

Account Title	Debit	Credit
Interest Receivable	750	
Interest Revenue		750

Date	Assets					=	Liab.	+	Equity	Rev.	−	Exp.	=	Net Inc.	Cash Flow
	Cash	+	Notes Rec.	+	Int. Rec.	=			Ret. Earn.						
10/31/09	NA	+	NA	+	750	=	NA	+	750	750	−	NA	=	750	NA

The total amount of accrued interest is now $900 ($150 accrued in 2008 plus $750 accrued in 2009). The $15,900 cash collection is an asset exchange transaction. The asset account Cash increases and two asset accounts, Notes Receivable and Interest Receivable, decrease. The income statement is not affected. The statement of cash flows shows a $15,000 inflow from investing activities (recovery of principal) and a $900 inflow from operating activities (interest collection). The journal entry and effects on the financial statements are shown below.

Account Title	Debit	Credit
Cash	15,900	
Notes Receivable		15,000
Interest Receivable		900

Date	Assets					=	Liab.	+	Equity	Rev.	−	Exp.	=	Net Inc.	Cash Flow
	Cash	+	Notes Rec.	+	Int. Rec.	=			Ret. Earn.						
10/31/09	15,900	+	(15,000)	+	(900)	=	NA	+	NA	NA	−	NA	=	NA	15,000 IA 900 OA

To clarify the illustration, we showed the interest accrual and the cash collection as two separate entries. Experienced accountants often record the two events in a single journal entry as follows:

Account Title	Debit	Credit
Cash	15,900	
Notes Receivable		15,000
Interest Receivable		150
Interest Revenue		750

Financial Statements

The financial statements reveal key differences between the timing of revenue recognition and the exchange of cash. These differences are highlighted below:

	2008	2009	Total
Interest revenue recognized	$150	$750	$900
Cash inflow from operating activities	0	900	900

Accrual accounting calls for recognizing revenue in the period in which it is earned regardless of when cash is collected.

Income statement

Although generally accepted accounting principles require reporting receipts of or payments for interest on the statement of cash flows as operating activities, they do not specify how to classify interest on the income statement. In fact, companies traditionally report interest on the income statement as a nonoperating item. Interest is therefore frequently reported in two different categories within the same set of financial statements.

Balance Sheet

As with other assets, companies report interest receivable and notes receivable on the balance sheet in order of their liquidity. **Liquidity** refers to how quickly assets are expected to be converted to cash during normal operations. In the preceding example, ATS expects to convert its accounts receivable to cash before it collects the interest receivable and note receivable. Companies commonly report interest and notes receivable after accounts receivable. Exhibit 7.8 shows a partial balance sheet for Southern Company to illustrate the presentation of receivables.

EXHIBIT 7.8

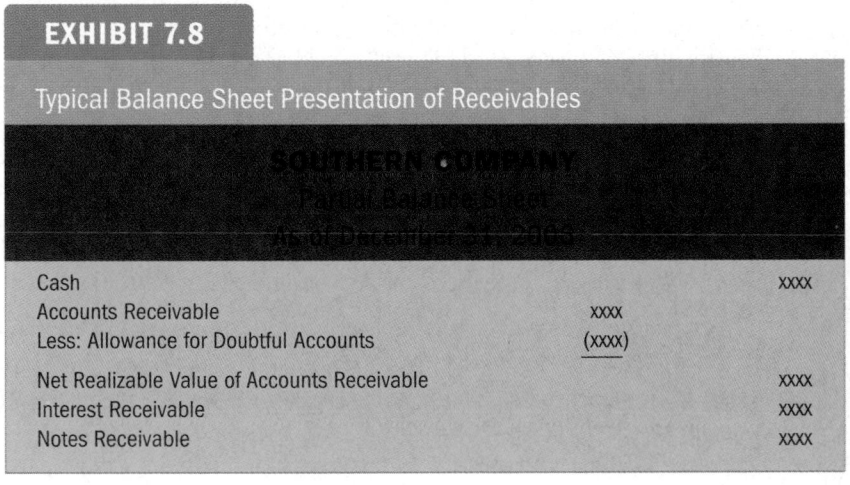

Typical Balance Sheet Presentation of Receivables

SOUTHERN COMPANY
Partial Balance Sheet
As of December 31, 2008

Cash		xxxx
Accounts Receivable	xxxx	
Less: Allowance for Doubtful Accounts	(xxxx)	
Net Realizable Value of Accounts Receivable		xxxx
Interest Receivable		xxxx
Notes Receivable		xxxx

CHECK YOURSELF 7.3

On October 1, 2006, Mei Company accepted a promissory note for a loan it made to the Asia Pacific Company. The note had a $24,000 principal amount, a four-month term, and an annual interest rate of 4 percent. Determine the amount of interest revenue and the cash inflow from operating activities Mei will report in its 2006 and 2007 financial statements. Also provide in general journal form the year-end adjusting entry needed to recognize 2006 interest revenue.

Answer

The computation of accrued interest revenue is shown below. The interest rate is stated in annual terms even though the term of the note is only four months. Interest rates are commonly expressed as an annual percentage regardless of the term of the note. The *time outstanding* in the following formulas is therefore expressed as a fraction of a year. Mei charged annual interest of 4 percent, but the note was outstanding for only 3/12 of a year in 2006 and 1/12 of a year in 2007.

2006

Principal	×	Annual interest rate	×	Time outstanding	=	Interest revenue
$24,000	×	0.04	×	(3/12)	=	$240

2007

Principal	×	Annual interest rate	×	Time outstanding	=	Interest revenue
$24,000	×	0.04	×	(1/12)	=	$80

In 2006, Mei's cash inflow from interest will be zero.

In 2007, Mei will report a $320 ($240 + $80) cash inflow from operating activities for interest. The adjusting entry to recognize 2006 accrued interest is as follows:

Interest Receivable	240	
Interest Revenue		240

Accounting for Credit Card Sales

LO 5

Explain how accounting for credit card sales affects financial statements.

Maintaining accounts and notes receivable is expensive. In addition to uncollectible accounts expense, companies extending credit to their customers incur considerable costs for such clerical tasks as running background checks and maintaining customer records. Many businesses find it more efficient to accept third-party credit cards instead of offering credit directly to their customers. Credit card companies service the merchant's credit sales for a fee that typically ranges between 2 and 8 percent of gross sales.

The credit card company provides customers with plastic cards that permit cardholders to charge purchases at various retail outlets. When a sale takes place, the seller records the transaction on a receipt the customer signs. The receipt is forwarded to the credit card company, which immediately pays the merchant.

The credit card company deducts its service fee from the gross amount of the sale and pays the merchant the net balance (gross amount of sale less credit card fee) in cash. The credit card company collects the gross sale amount directly from the customer. The merchant avoids the risk of uncollectible accounts as well as the cost of maintaining customer credit records. To illustrate, assume that Allen's Tutoring Service experiences the following events.

Event 1 Recognition of Revenue and Expense on Credit Card Sales
ATS accepts a credit card payment for $1,000 of services rendered.

Assume the credit card company charges a 5 percent fee for handling the transaction ($1,000 × 0.05 = $50). ATS's income increases by the amount of revenue ($1,000) and decreases by the amount of the credit card expense ($50). Net income increases by $950. The event increases an asset, accounts receivable, due from the credit card company, and stockholders' equity (retained earnings) by $950 ($1,000 revenue − $50 credit card expense). Cash flow is not affected. These effects are shown here:

Event No.	Assets	=	Liab.	+	Equity	Rev.	−	Exp.	=	Net Inc.	Cash Flow
	Accts. Rec.	=			Ret. Earn.						
1	950	=	NA	+	950	1,000	−	50	=	950	NA

In general journal form, the entry to record the transaction is as follows:

Account Title	Debit	Credit
Accounts Receivable–Credit Card Company	950	
Credit Card Expense	50	
Service Revenue		1,000

Event 2 **Collection of Credit Card Receivable**

The collection of the receivable due from the credit card company is recorded like any other receivable collection.

When ATS collects the net amount of $950 ($1,000 − $50) from the credit card company, one asset account (Cash) increases and another asset account (Accounts Receivable) decreases. Total assets are not affected. The income statement is not affected. A $950 cash inflow is reported in the operating activities section of the statement of cash flows. These effects are illustrated below:

Event No.	Assets			=	Liab.	+	Equity	Rev.	−	Exp.	=	Net Inc.	Cash Flow
	Cash	+	Accts. Rec.										
2	950	+	(950)	=	NA	+	NA	NA	−	NA	=	NA	950 OA

The following entry records the transaction in the general journal.

Account Title	Debit	Credit
Cash	950	
Accounts Receivable–Credit Card Company		950

THE FINANCIAL ANALYST

Costs of Credit Sales

LO 6 Explain the effects of the cost of financing credit sales.

As mentioned earlier, two costs of extending credit to customers are uncollectible accounts expense and recordkeeping costs. These costs can be significant. Large companies spend literally millions of dollars to buy the equipment and pay the staff necessary to operate entire departments devoted to managing accounts receivable. Further, there is an implicit interest cost associated with extending credit. When a customer is permitted to delay payment, the creditor foregoes the opportunity to invest the amount the customer owes.

Topic Tackler PLUS

7-2

Exhibit 7.9 presents part of a footnote from the 2002 annual report of PepsiCo, Inc. This excerpt provides insight into the credit costs real companies incur. First, observe that PepsiCo was owed \$2.65 billion of accounts receivable. These receivables represent money that could be in the bank earning interest if all sales had been made in cash. If PepsiCo could have earned interest at 5 percent on that money, the opportunity cost of this lost interest is approximately \$132.5 million (\$2.65 billion × .05) a year. Next, observe that PepsiCo expects to have uncollectible accounts amounting to \$116 million (balance in the allowance account). These are significant costs.

EXHIBIT 7.9

PepsiCo Dec. 28, 2002
PARTIAL FOOTNOTE regarding Receivables
(amounts are shown in millions)

Note 14 Supplemental Financial Information

	2002	**2001**
Accounts receivable:		
Trade receivables	$1,924	$1,663
Other receivables	723	600
	2,647	2,263
Allowance, beginning of year	121	126
Charged to expense	38	41
Other additions (a)	3	2
Deductions (b)	(46)	(48)
Allowance, end of year	116	121
Net receivables	$2,531	$2,142

Average Number of Days to Collect Accounts Receivable

The longer it takes to collect accounts receivable, the greater the opportunity cost of lost income. Also, business experience indicates that the older an account receivable becomes, the less likely it is to be collected. Finally, taking longer to collect an account typically costs more for salaries, equipment, and supplies used in the process of trying to collect it. Businesses are therefore concerned about how long it takes to collect their receivables.

Two ratios help management, or other users, measure a company's collection period. One is the **accounts receivable turnover ratio,** computed as:[1]

$$\frac{\text{Sales}}{\text{Accounts receivable}}$$

Dividing a company's sales by its accounts receivable tells how many times the accounts receivable balance is "turned over" (converted into cash) each year. The higher the turnover, the shorter the collection period. To simplify its interpretation, the accounts receivable turnover ratio is often taken one step further to determine the **average number of days to collect accounts receivable,** sometimes called the *average collection period.* This is computed as:

$$\frac{365}{\text{Accounts receivable turnover ratio}}$$

This ratio measures how many days, on average, it takes a company to collect its accounts receivable. Since longer collection periods increase costs, shorter periods are obviously more desirable. To illustrate computing the *average number of days to collect accounts receivable* for Allen's Tutoring Services, refer to the 2007 financial statements in Exhibit 7.4. On average, the company takes 104 days to collect its receivables, computed in two steps:

1. The accounts receivable turnover is 3.509 (\$10,000 ÷ \$2,850) times.
2. The average number of days to collect receivables is 104 (365 ÷ 3.509) days.

In the preceding computations, the net realizable value of accounts receivable was used because that is the amount typically reported in published financial statements. The results would not have been materially different had total accounts receivable been used.

[1] To be more precise, the ratio could be computed using only credit sales and average accounts receivable. Usually, however, companies do not report credit sales separately from cash sales in published financial statements. Average accounts receivable, if desired, is computed as [(beginning receivables + ending receivables) ÷ 2]. For this course, use the simpler computation shown here (sales ÷ accounts receivable).

EXHIBIT 7.10

Industry	Company	Average Days to Sell Inventory	Average Days to Collect Receivables	Length of Operating Cycle
Fast Food	Domino's	9	16	25
	McDonald's	10	21	31
	Starbucks	65	10	75
Office Supplies	Office Depot	58	25	83
	OfficeMax	92	7	99
	Staples	64	11	75
Wine	Chalone	642	74	716
	Mondavi	548	82	630

Real-World Data

What is the collection period for real companies? The time required to collect receivables varies among industries and among companies within industries. Column 4 in Exhibit 7.10 displays the average number of days to collect receivables for eight companies in three different industries. These numbers are for the 2002 calendar year.

Since fast-food restaurants require customers to pay cash when they purchase hamburgers or coffee, why do these companies have accounts receivable? The accounts receivable for Domino's, McDonald's, and Starbucks arise because these companies sell goods to restaurants that are independent franchisees. So, for example, Domino's accounts receivable represents future collections from restaurant owners, not customers who purchase pepperoni pizzas.

Are the collection periods for Mondavi and Chalone Wine Group too long? The answer depends on their credit policies. If they are selling goods to customers on net 30-day terms, there may be reason for concern, but if they allow customers 90 days to pay and the cost of this policy has been built into their pricing structure, the collection periods may not be unreasonable.

Some companies allow their customers extended time to pay their bills because the customers would otherwise have difficulty coming up with the money. For example, Mondavi may sell to a wine retailer that does not have the cash available to pay immediately. If Mondavi allows the retailer sufficient time, the retailer can sell the wine to customers and obtain the cash it needs to pay Mondavi. Many small companies do not have cash available to pay up front. Buying on credit is the only way they can obtain the inventory they need. If a manufacturer or wholesaler wants to sell to such companies, credit sales represent the only option available.

The length of the **operating cycle** is the average time it takes a business to convert inventory to accounts receivable plus the time it takes to convert accounts receivable into cash. The average number of days to collect receivables is one component of the operating cycle for a particular company. The other component is the average number of days to sell inventory that was explained in Chapter 5. The length of the operating cycles for the real-world companies discussed herein is shown in the last column of Exhibit 7.10.

What is the significance of the different operating cycle lengths in Exhibit 7.10? As previously explained, the longer the operating cycle takes, the more it costs the company. Exhibit 7.10 shows it takes OfficeMax an average of 24 days longer than Staples to complete an operating cycle. All other things being equal, approximately how much did this longer time reduce OfficeMax's earnings? Assume OfficeMax could invest excess cash at 8 percent (or alternatively, assume it pays 8 percent to finance its inventory and accounts receivable). Using the accounting information reported in OfficeMax's January 25, 2003, financial statements, we can answer the question as follows:

REALITY BYTES

This chapter explains that, in general, companies want to collect their receivables as quickly as possible. There is a notable exception to this generalization. If a company charges its customers interest on unpaid receivables, the company makes money on the unpaid balance. Many sellers of "big-ticket" goods like furniture, large appliances, and automobiles offer to finance their customers' purchases, allowing customers extended time to pay off their receivables in exchange for the customers' paying additional charges for interest.

For example, most people probably think General Motors (GM) makes its profits primarily by selling cars and trucks, but GM often earns more from *financing* vehicle sales than from the sales themselves. In 2003 GM's income from operations, after taxes, was $2,862 million, of which almost all—$2,648—was actually earned from its financing businesses. Only $35 million came from profits directly related to vehicle sales. Even the company's insurance activities produced more profit ($179 million) than selling vehicles.

Should GM therefore stop selling cars and trucks? No. If it did not sell vehicles, GM would have far fewer opportunities to finance the sale of automobiles. For the record, almost half of GM's financing income comes from mortgage activities, not automotive financing. The familiar ditech.com of the "lost another loan to ditech" commercial is a wholly owned subsidiary of GM.

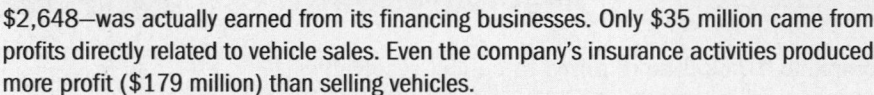

$$\text{OfficeMax's investment in inventory} \times \text{Interest rate} \times \text{Time} = \text{Cost}$$

$$\$906{,}253{,}000 \times 8\% \times 24/365 = \$4{,}767{,}139$$

With 3.69 operating cycles per year (365 ÷ 99), the extended operating cycle costs OfficeMax $17.6 million annually. Based on the assumptions used here, OfficeMax would increase its after-tax net earnings by approximately 15 percent if it could reduce its operating cycle by 24 days. Although this illustration is a rough estimate, it demonstrates that it is important for businesses to minimize the length of their operating cycles.

CHECK YOURSELF 7.4

Randolph Corporation had sales for the year of $535,333 and an accounts receivable balance at year end of $22,000. Determine Randolph's average number of days to collect accounts receivable.

Answer

The accounts receivable turnover is 24.33 ($535,333 ÷ $22,000) times per year. The average number of days to collect accounts receivable is 15 (365 ÷ 24.33).

FOCUS ON INTERNATIONAL ISSUES

A ROSE BY ANY OTHER NAME . . .

If a person who studied U.S. GAAP wanted to look at the financial statements of a non-U.S. company, choosing statements of a company from another English-speaking country might seem logical. Presumably, this would eliminate language differences, and only the differences in GAAP would remain. However, this is not true.

When an accountant in the United States uses the term *turnover,* she or he is usually thinking of a financial ratio, such as the accounts receivable turnover ratio. However, in the United Kingdom, the term *turnover* refers to what U.S. accountants call *sales.* U.K. balance sheets do not usually show an account named *Inventory;* rather, they use the term *Stocks.* In the United States, accountants typically use the term *stocks* to refer to certificates representing ownership in a corporation. Finally, if an accountant or banker from the United Kingdom should ever ask you about your *gearing ratio,* he or she probably is not interested in your bicycle but in your debt to assets ratio.

A Look Back <<

We first introduced accounting for receivables in Chapter 2. This chapter presented additional complexities related to accounts receivable, such as the *allowance method of accounting for uncollectible accounts.* The allowance method improves matching of expenses with revenues. It also provides a more accurate measure of the value of accounts receivable on the balance sheet.

Under the allowance method, estimated uncollectible accounts expense is recorded in an adjusting entry at the end of the period in which a company has made credit sales. There are two methods commonly used to estimate the amount of uncollectible accounts expense: the percent of revenue method and the percent of receivables method. With the percent of revenue method, uncollectible accounts expense is measured as a percent of the period's sales. With the percent of receivables method, a company analyzes its accounts receivable at the end of the period, usually classifying them by age, to estimate the amount of the accounts receivable balance that is likely to be uncollectible. The balance in the Allowance for Doubtful Accounts account is then adjusted to equal the estimated amount of uncollectible accounts. Uncollectible accounts expense decreases the net realizable value of receivables (accounts receivable − allowance for doubtful accounts), stockholders' equity, and net income.

The allowance method of accounting for uncollectible accounts is conceptually superior to the *direct write-off method,* in which uncollectible accounts expense is recognized when an account is determined to be uncollectible. The direct write-off method fails to match revenues with expenses and overstates accounts receivable on the balance sheet. It is easier to use, however, and is permitted by generally accepted accounting principles if the amount of uncollectible accounts expense is immaterial.

The chapter also introduced notes receivable and accounting for *accrued interest.* When the term of a promissory note extends over more than one accounting period, companies must record adjusting entries to recognize interest in the appropriate accounting period, even if the cash exchange of interest occurs in a different accounting period.

We also discussed accounting for credit card sales, a vehicle that shifts uncollectible accounts expense to the credit card issuer. Many companies find the benefits of accepting major credit cards to be worth the credit card expense consequently incurred.

Finally, we addressed the costs of making credit sales. In addition to uncollectible accounts expense, interest is a major cost of financing receivables. The length of the collection period provides a measure of the quality of receivables. Short collection periods usually indicate lower amounts of uncollectible accounts and interest cost. Long collection periods imply higher costs. The collection period can be measured in two steps. First, divide sales by the accounts receivable balance to determine the accounts receivable turnover ratio. Then divide the number of days in the year (365) by the accounts receivable turnover ratio.

>> A Look Forward

Chapter 8 discusses accounting for long-term assets such as buildings and equipment. As with inventory cost flow, discussed in Chapter 5, GAAP allows companies to use different accounting methods to report on similar types of business events. Life would be easier for accounting students if all companies used the same accounting methods. However, the business world is complex. For the foreseeable future, people are likely to continue to have diverse views as to the best way to account for a variety of business transactions. To function effectively in today's business environment, it is important for you to be able to recognize differences in reporting practices.

SELF-STUDY REVIEW PROBLEM

During 2007 Calico Company experienced the following accounting events:

1. Provided $120,000 of services on account.
2. Collected $85,000 cash from accounts receivable.
3. Wrote off $1,800 of accounts receivable that were uncollectible.
4. Loaned $3,000 to an individual, Emma Gardner, in exchange for a note receivable.
5. Paid $90,500 cash for operating expenses.
6. Estimated that uncollectible accounts expense would be 2 percent of credit sales. Recorded the year-end adjusting entry.
7. Recorded the year-end adjusting entry for accrued interest on the note receivable (see Event 4). Calico made the loan on August 1. It had a six-month term and a 6 percent rate of interest.

Calico's ledger balances on January 1, 2007 were as follows:

Event No.	Assets									=	Liab.	+	Equity		
	Cash	+	Accts. Rec.	−	Allow.	+	Notes Rec.	+	Int. Rec.	=			Com. Stk.	+	Ret. Earn.
Bal.	12,000		18,000		2,200	+	NA	+	NA	=	NA	+	20,000	+	7,800

Required

a. Record the 2007 events in ledger accounts using the horizontal format shown above.
b. Determine net income for 2007.
c. Determine net cash flow from operating activities for 2007.
d. Determine the net realizable value of accounts receivable at December 31, 2007.
e. What amount of interest revenue will Calico recognize on its note receivable in 2008?

Solution to Requirement *a*.

Event No.	Assets									=	Liab.	+	Equity		
	Cash	+	Accts. Rec.	−	Allow.	+	Notes Rec.	+	Int. Rec.	=			Com. Stk.	+	Ret. Earn.
Bal.	12,000	+	18,000	−	2,200	+	NA	+	NA	=	NA	+	20,000	+	7,800
1	NA	+	120,000	−	NA	+	NA	+	NA	=	NA	+	NA	+	120,000
2	85,000	+	(85,000)	−	NA	+	NA	+	NA	=	NA	+	NA	+	NA
3	NA	+	(1,800)	−	(1,800)	+	NA	+	NA	=	NA	+	NA	+	NA
4	(3,000)	+	NA	−	NA	+	3,000	+	NA	=	NA	+	NA	+	NA
5	(90,500)	+	NA	−	NA	+	NA	+	NA	=	NA	+	NA	+	(90,500)
6	NA	+	NA	−	2,400	+	NA	+	NA	=	NA	+	NA	+	(2,400)
7	NA	+	NA	−	NA	+	NA	+	75*	=	NA	+	NA	+	75
Totals	3,500	+	51,200	−	2,800	+	3,000	+	75	=	NA	+	20,000	+	34,975

*$3,000 × .06 × 5/12 = $75.

Solution to Requirements *b–e*.

b. Net income is $27,175 ($120,000 − $90,500 − $2,400 + $75).

c. Net cash flow from operating activities is an outflow of $5,500 ($85,000 − $90,500).

d. The net realizable value of accounts receivable is $48,400 ($51,200 − $2,800).

e. In 2008, Calico will recognize interest revenue for one month: $3,000 × .06 × 1/12 = $15.

KEY TERMS

account receivable 331
accounts receivable turnover ratio 350
accrued interest 345
adjusting entry 345
aging of accounts receivable 340
allowance for doubtful accounts 332
allowance method of accounting for uncollectible accounts 332
average number of days to collect accounts receivable 350
collateral 344
contra asset account 333
direct write-off method 342
interest 344
liquidity 347
maker 347
matching concept 345
maturity date 344
net realizable value 332
notes receivable 331
operating cycle 351
payee 344
percent of receivables method 340
percent of revenue method 338
principal 344
promissory note 344
reinstate 337
uncollectible accounts expense 333

QUESTIONS

1. What is the difference between accounts receivable and notes receivable?
2. What is the *net realizable value* of receivables?
3. What type of account is the Allowance for Doubtful Accounts?
4. What are two ways in which estimating uncollectible accounts improves the accuracy of the financial statements?
5. When using the allowance method, why is uncollectible accounts expense an estimated amount?
6. What is the most common format for reporting accounts receivable on the balance sheet? What information does this method provide beyond showing only the net amount?
7. Why is it necessary to make an entry to reinstate a previously written off account receivable before the collection is recorded?

8. What are some factors considered in estimating the amount of uncollectible accounts receivable?
9. What is the effect on the accounting equation of recognizing uncollectible accounts expense?
10. What is the effect on the accounting equation of writing off an uncollectible account receivable when the allowance method is used? When the direct write-off method is used?
11. How does the recovery of a previously written-off account affect the income statement when the allowance method is used? How does the recovery of a previously written-off account affect the statement of cash flows when the allowance method is used?
12. What is the advantage of using the allowance method of accounting for uncollectible accounts? What is the advantage of using the direct write-off method?
13. How do companies determine the percentage estimate of uncollectible accounts when using the percent of revenue method?
14. What is an advantage of using the percent of receivables method of estimating uncollectible accounts expense?
15. What is "aging of accounts receivable"?
16. What is the difference between the allowance method and the direct write-off method of accounting for uncollectible accounts?
17. When is it acceptable to use the direct write-off method of accounting for uncollectible accounts?
18. What is a promissory note?
19. Define the following terms:
    a. Maker
    b. Payee
    c. Principal
    d. Interest
    e. Maturity date
    f. Collateral
20. What is the formula for computing interest revenue?
21. What is accrued interest?
22. When is an adjusting entry for accrued interest generally recorded?
23. Assume that on July 1, 2006, Big Corp. loaned Little Corp. $12,000 for a period of one year at 6 percent interest. What amount of interest revenue will Big report for 2006? What amount of cash will Big receive upon maturity of the note?
24. In which section of the statement of cash flows will Big report the cash collected in question 23?
25. Why is it generally beneficial for a business to accept major credit cards as payment for goods and services even when the fee charged by the credit card company is substantial?
26. What types of costs do businesses avoid when they accept major credit cards as compared with handling credit sales themselves?
27. How is the accounts receivable turnover ratio computed? What information does the ratio provide?
28. How is the average number of days to collect accounts receivable computed? What information does the ratio provide?
29. Is accounting terminology standard in all countries? What term is used in the United Kingdom to refer to *sales?* What term is used to refer to *inventory?* What is a *gearing ratio?* Is it important to know about these differences?
30. What is the operating cycle of a business?

EXERCISES—SERIES A

All Exercises in Series A are available with McGraw-Hill's Homework Manager

L.O. 2

Exercise 7-1A *Analysis of financial statement effects of accounting for uncollectible accounts under the allowance method*

Businesses using the allowance method for the recognition of uncollectible accounts expense commonly experience four accounting events:

1. Recognition of revenue on account.
2. Collection of cash from accounts receivable.
3. Recognition of uncollectible accounts expense through a year-end adjusting entry.
4. Write-off of uncollectible accounts.

Required

Show the effect of each event on the elements of the financial statements, using a horizontal statements model like the one shown here. Use the following coding scheme to record your answers: increase is +, decrease is −, not affected is NA. In the cash flow column, indicate whether the item is an operating activity (OA), investing activity (IA), or financing activity (FA). The first transaction is entered as an example.

Event No.	Assets	=	Liab.	+	Equity	Rev.	−	Exp.	=	Net Inc.	Cash Flow
1	+		NA		+	+		NA		+	NA

Exercise 7-2A *Accounting for bad debts: allowance method*

L.O. 2

Nina's Accounting Service began operation on January 1, 2007. The company experienced the following events for its first year of operations.

Events Affecting 2007:

1. Provided $120,000 of accounting services on account.
2. Collected $90,000 cash from accounts receivable.
3. Paid salaries of $24,000 for the year.
4. Adjusted the accounts to reflect management's expectations that uncollectible accounts expense would be $1,200.

Required

a. Prepare general journal entries for the above events.
b. Post the general journal entries to T-accounts.
c. Prepare an income statement, balance sheet, and statement of cash flows for 2007.

Exercise 7-3A *Effect of recognizing uncollectible accounts expense on financial statements: percent of revenue allowance method*

L.O. 2

Big A's Auto Service was started on January 1, 2006. The company experienced the following events during its first two years of operation

Events Affecting 2006

1. Provided $30,000 of repair services on account.
2. Collected $25,000 cash from accounts receivable.
3. Adjusted the accounting records to reflect the estimate that uncollectible accounts expense would be 1 percent of the service revenue on account.

Events Affecting 2007

1. Wrote off a $280 account receivable that was determined to be uncollectible.
2. Provided $35,000 of repair services on account.
3. Collected $31,000 cash from accounts receivable.
4. Adjusted the accounting records to reflect the estimate that uncollectible accounts expense would be 1 percent of the service revenue on account.

Required

a. Record the events for 2006 in general journal form and post them to T-accounts.
b. Determine the following amounts:
   (1) Net income for 2006.
   (2) Net cash flow from operating activities for 2006.
   (3) Balance of accounts receivable at the end of 2006.
   (4) Net realizable value of accounts receivable at the end of 2006.
c. Repeat Requirements *a* and *b* for the 2007 accounting period.

L.O. 2

Exercise 7-4A ***Analyzing financial statement effects of accounting for uncollectible accounts using the percent of revenue allowance method***

Gray Bros. uses the allowance method to account for uncollectible accounts expense. Gray experienced the following four events in 2005:

1. Recognized $48,000 of revenue on account.
2. Collected $42,000 cash from accounts receivable.
3. Determined that $300 of accounts receivable were not collectible and wrote them off.
4. Recognized uncollectible accounts expense for the year. Gray estimates that uncollectible accounts expense will be 2 percent of its sales.

Required

a. Show the effect of each of these events on the elements of the financial statements, using a horizontal statements model like the following one. Use + for increase, − for decrease, and NA for not affected. In the cash flow column, indicate whether the item is an operating activity (OA), investing activity (IA), or financing activity (FA).

Event No.	Assets			= Liab.	+ Equity	Rev.	− Exp.	= Net Inc.	Cash Flow
	Cash +	Accts. Rec. −	Allow. =		Ret. Earn.				

b. Record the above transactions in general journal form.

L.O. 2

Exercise 7-5A ***Analyzing account balances for a company using the allowance method of accounting for uncollectible accounts***

The following account balances come from the records of Teton Company.

	Beginning Balance	Ending Balance
Accounts Receivable	$3,000	$3,500
Allowance for Doubtful Accounts	120	200

During the accounting period, Teton recorded $12,000 of service revenue on account. The company also wrote off a $150 account receivable.

Required

a. Determine the amount of cash collected from receivables.

b. Determine the amount of uncollectible accounts expense recognized during the period.

L.O. 2

Exercise 7-6A ***Effect of recovering a receivable previously written off***

The accounts receivable balance for City Shoe Repair at December 31, 2006, was $84,000. Also on that date, the balance in the Allowance for Doubtful Accounts was $2,400. During 2007, $2,100 of accounts receivable were written off as uncollectible. In addition, City Shoe Repair unexpectedly collected $150 of receivables that had been written off in a previous accounting period. Sales on account during 2007 were $218,000, and cash collections from receivables were $220,000. Uncollectible accounts expense was estimated to be 1 percent of the sales on account for the period.

Required

a. Record the transactions in general journal form and post them to T-accounts.

b. Based on the preceding information, compute (after year-end adjustment):

(1) Balance of Allowance for Doubtful Accounts at December 31, 2007.

(2) Balance of Accounts Receivable at December 31, 2007.

(3) Net realizable value of Accounts Receivable at December 31, 2007.

c. What amount of uncollectible accounts expense will City Shoe Repair report for 2007?

d. Explain how the $150 recovery of receivables affected the accounting equation.

Exercise 7-7A ***Accounting for uncollectible accounts: percent of receivables allowance method*** L.O. 2

King Service Co. experienced the following transactions for 2009, its first year of operations:

1. Provided $66,000 of services on account.
2. Collected $42,000 cash from accounts receivable.
3. Paid $26,000 of salaries expense for the year.
4. King adjusted the accounts using the following information from an accounts receivable aging schedule:

Number of Days Past Due	Amount	Percent Likely to Be Uncollectible	Allowance Balance
Current	$16,000	.01	
0–30	3,000	.05	
31–60	2,000	.10	
61–90	1,000	.30	
Over 90 days	2,000	.50	

Required

a. Record the above transactions in general journal form and post them to T-accounts.
b. Prepare the income statement for King Service Co. for 2009.
c. What is the net realizable value of the accounts receivable at December 31, 2009?

Exercise 7-8A ***Effect of recognizing uncollectible accounts on the financial statements: percent of receivables allowance method*** L.O. 2

Bourret Inc. experienced the following events for the first two years of its operations.

2009:

1. Provided $60,000 of services on account.
2. Provided $25,000 of services and received cash.
3. Collected $35,000 cash from accounts receivable.
4. Paid $12,000 of salaries expense for the year.
5. Adjusted the accounting records to reflect uncollectible accounts expense for the year. Bourret estimates that 5 percent of the ending accounts receivable balance will be uncollectible.

2010:

1. Wrote off an uncollectible account of $650.
2. Provided $80,000 of services on account.
3. Provided $15,000 of services and collected cash.
4. Collected $62,000 cash from accounts receivable.
5. Paid $20,000 of salaries expense for the year.
6. Adjusted the accounts to reflect uncollectible accounts expense for the year. Bourret estimates that 5 percent of the ending accounts receivable balance will be uncollectible.

Required

a. Record the 2009 events in general journal form and post them to T-accounts.
b. Prepare the income statement, statement of changes in stockholders' equity, balance sheet, and statement of cash flows for 2009.
c. What is the net realizable value of the accounts receivable at December 31, 2009?
d. Repeat Requirements *a, b,* and *c* for 2010.

Exercise 7-9A ***Accounting for uncollectible accounts: percent of revenue allowance versus direct write-off method*** L.O. 2, 3

Classic Auto Parts sells new and used auto parts. Although a majority of its sales are cash sales, it makes a significant amount of credit sales. During 2008, its first year of operations, Classic Auto Parts experienced the following:

Sales on account	$280,000
Cash sales	650,000
Collections of accounts receivable	265,000
Uncollectible accounts charged off during the year	1,200

Required

a. Assume that Classic Auto Parts uses the allowance method of accounting for uncollectible accounts and estimates that 1 percent of its sales on account will not be collected. Answer the following questions:

(1) What is the Accounts Receivable balance at December 31, 2008?
(2) What is the ending balance of the Allowance for Doubtful Accounts at December 31, 2008, after all entries and adjusting entries are posted?
(3) What is the amount of uncollectible accounts expense for 2008?
(4) What is the net realizable value of accounts receivable at December 31, 2008?

b. Assume that Classic Auto Parts uses the direct write-off method of accounting for uncollectible accounts. Answer the following questions:

(1) What is the Accounts Receivable balance at December 31, 2008?
(2) What is the amount of uncollectible accounts expense for 2008?
(3) What is the net realizable value of accounts receivable at December 31, 2008?

L.O. 3

Exercise 7-10A *Accounting for uncollectible accounts: direct write-off method*

Hogan Business Systems has a small number of sales on account but is mostly a cash business. Consequently, it uses the direct write-off method to account for uncollectible accounts. During 2006 Hogan Business Systems earned $32,000 of cash revenue and $8,000 of revenue on account. Cash operating expenses were $26,500. After numerous attempts to collect a $250 account receivable from Sam Smart, the account was determined to be uncollectible in 2007.

Required

a. Record the effects of (1) cash revenue, (2) revenue on account, (3) cash expenses, and (4) write-off of the uncollectible account on the financial statements using a horizontal statements model like the one shown here. In the Cash Flow column, indicate whether the item is an operating activity (OA), investing activity (IA), or financing activity (FA). Use NA to indicate that an element is not affected by the event.

Assets			=	Liab.	+	Equity	Rev.	−	Exp.	=	Net Inc.	Cash Flow
Cash	+	Accts. Rec.										

b. What amount of net income did Hogan Business Systems report on the 2006 income statement?

c. Prepare the general journal entries for the four accounting events listed in Requirement *a.*

L.O. 5

Exercise 7-11A *Effect of credit card sales on financial statements*

Royal Carpet Cleaning provided $90,000 of services during 2006, its first year of operations. All customers paid for the services with major credit cards. Royal submitted the credit card receipts to the credit card company immediately. The credit card company paid Royal cash in the amount of face value less a 3 percent service charge.

Required

a. Record the credit card sales and the subsequent collection of accounts receivable in a horizontal statements model like the one shown here. In the Cash Flow column, indicate whether the item is an operating activity (OA), investing activity (IA), or financing activity (FA). Use NA to indicate that an element is not affected by the event.

Assets			=	Liab.	+	Equity	Rev.	−	Exp.	=	Net Inc.	Cash Flow
Cash	+	Accts. Rec.										

b. Answer the following questions:

(1) What is the amount of total assets at the end of the accounting period?

(2) What is the amount of revenue reported on the income statement?

(3) What is the amount of cash flow from operating activities reported on the statement of cash flows?

(4) Why would Royal Carpet Cleaning accept credit cards instead of providing credit directly to its customers? In other words, why would Royal be willing to pay 3 percent of sales to have the credit card company handle its sales on account?

Exercise 7-12A *Recording credit card sales* L.O. 5

Baucom Company accepted credit cards in payment for $6,850 of services performed during March 2006. The credit card company charged Baucom a 4 percent service fee. The credit card company paid Baucom as soon as it received the invoices.

Required

a. Prepare the general journal entry to record the service revenue.

b. Prepare the general journal entry for the collection of the receivable from the credit card company.

c. Based on this information alone, what is the amount of net income earned during the month of March?

Exercise 7-13A *Accounting for notes receivable* L.O. 4

Babb Enterprises loaned $25,000 to Sneathen Co. on September 1, 2008, for one year at 6 percent interest.

Required

a. Record these general journal entries for Babb Enterprises:

(1) The loan to Sneathen Co.

(2) The adjusting entry at December 31, 2008.

(3) The adjusting entry and collection of the note on September 1, 2009.

b. Show the effects of the three above transactions in a horizontal statements model like the one shown below.

	Assets					=	Liab.	+	Equity	Rev.	−	Exp.	=	Net Inc.	Cash Flows
Date	Cash	+	Notes Rec.	+	Int. Rec.	=			Ret. Earn.						

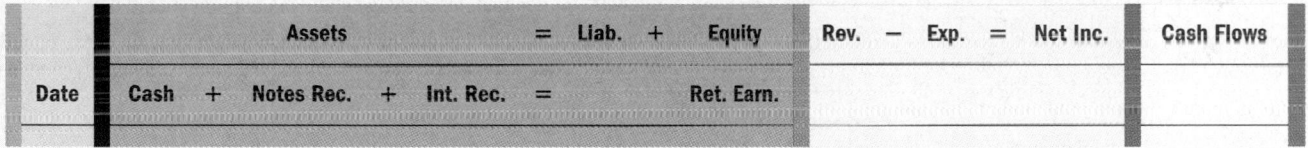

Exercise 7-14A *Notes receivable—accrued interest* L.O. 4

On March 1, 2007, Jason's Deli loaned $12,000 to Mark Johnson for one year at 5 percent interest.

Required

Answer the following questions.

a. What is Jason's interest income for 2007?

b. What is Jason's total amount of receivables at December 31, 2007?

c. What amounts will be reported on Jason's 2007 statement of cash flows?

d. What is Jason's interest income for 2008?

e. What is the total amount of cash that Jason's will collect in 2008 from Mark Johnson?

f. What amounts will be reported on Jason's 2008 statement of cash flows?

g. What is the total amount of interest Jason's Deli earned from the loan to Mark Johnson?

Exercise 7-15A *Comprehensive single-cycle problem* L.O. 2, 4

The following after-closing trial balance was drawn from the accounts of Spruce Timber Co. as of December 31, 2006.

	Debit	Credit
Cash	$ 6,000	
Accounts Receivable	18,000	
Allowance for Doubtful Accounts		$ 2,000
Inventory	24,000	
Accounts Payable		9,200
Common Stock		20,000
Retained Earnings		16,800
Totals	$48,000	$48,000

Transactions for 2007

1. Acquired an additional $10,000 cash from the issue of common stock.
2. Purchased $60,000 of inventory on account.
3. Sold inventory that cost $62,000 for $95,000. Sales were made on account.
4. Wrote off $1,100 of uncollectible accounts.
5. On September 1, Spruce loaned $9,000 to Pine Co. The note had a 7 percent interest rate and a one-year term.
6. Paid $15,800 cash for salaries expense.
7. Collected $80,000 cash from accounts receivable.
8. Paid $52,000 cash on accounts payable.
9. Paid a $5,000 cash dividend to the stockholders.
10. Estimated uncollectible accounts expense to be 1 percent of sales on account.
11. Recorded the accrued interest at December 31, 2007.

Required

a. Record the above transactions in general journal form.
b. Open T-accounts and record the beginning balances and the 2007 transactions.
c. Prepare an income statement, statement of changes in stockholders' equity, balance sheet, and statement of cash flows for 2007.

L.O. 6

Exercise 7-16A ***Accounts receivable turnover and average days to collect accounts receivable***

The following information is available for Market Inc. and Supply Inc. at December 31, 2008:

Accounts	Market, Inc.	Supply, Inc.
Accounts Receivable	$ 56,200	$ 75,400
Allowance for Doubtful Accounts	2,248	2,256
Sales Revenue	606,960	867,100

Required

a. What is the accounts receivable turnover for each of the companies for 2008?
b. What is the average days to collect the receivables for 2008?
c. Assuming both companies use the percent of receivables allowance method, what is the estimated percentage of uncollectible accounts for each company?

PROBLEMS—SERIES A

All Problems in Series A are available with McGraw-Hill's Homework Manager

L.O. 2

Problem 7-17A ***Accounting for uncollectible accounts—two cycles using the percent of revenue allowance method***

The following transactions apply to Sharp Consulting for 2006, the first year of operation:

1. Recognized $65,000 of service revenue earned on account.
2. Collected $58,000 from accounts receivable.
3. Adjusted accounts to recognize uncollectible accounts expense. Sharp uses the allowance method of accounting for uncollectible accounts and estimates that uncollectible accounts expense will be 2 percent of sales on account.

CHECK FIGURES
c. Ending Accounts Receivable, 2006: $7,000
d. Net Income, 2007: $23,275

The following transactions apply to Sharp Consulting for 2007:

1. Recognized $72,500 of service revenue on account.
2. Collected $66,000 from accounts receivable.
3. Determined that $900 of the accounts receivable were uncollectible and wrote them off.
4. Collected $100 of an account that had been previously written off.
5. Paid $48,500 cash for operating expenses.
6. Adjusted accounts to recognize uncollectible accounts expense for 2007. Sharp estimates that uncollectible accounts expense will be 1 percent of sales on account.

Required

Complete all the following requirements for 2006 and 2007. Complete all requirements for 2006 prior to beginning the requirements for 2007.

a. Identify the type of each transaction (asset source, asset use, asset exchange, or claims exchange).
b. Show the effect of each transaction on the elements of the financial statements, using a horizontal statements model like the one shown here. Use + for increase, − for decrease, and NA for not affected. Also, in the Cash Flow column, indicate whether the item is an operating activity (OA), investing activity (IA), or financing activity (FA). The first transaction is entered as an example. (*Hint:* Closing entries do not affect the statements model.)

Event No.	Assets	=	Liab.	+	Equity	Rev.	−	Exp.	=	Net Inc.	Cash Flow
1	+		NA		+	+		NA		+	NA

c. Record the transactions in general journal form, and post them to T-accounts (begin 2007 with the ending T-account balances from 2006).
d. Prepare the income statement, statement of changes in stockholders' equity, balance sheet, and statement of cash flows.
e. Prepare closing entries and post these closing entries to the T-accounts. Prepare an after-closing trial balance.

Problem 7-18A ***Determination of account balances and preparation of journal entries—percent of receivables allowance method of accounting for uncollectible accounts***

L.O. 2

CHECK FIGURE
d. Net Realizable Value $55,104

During the first year of operation, 2006, Martin's Appliance recognized $292,000 of service revenue on account. At the end of 2006, the accounts receivable balance was $57,400. Even though this is his first year in business, the owner believes he will collect all but about 4 percent of the ending balance.

Required

a. What amount of cash was collected by Martin's during 2006?
b. Assuming the use of an allowance system to account for uncollectible accounts, what amount should Martin record as uncollectible accounts expense in 2006?
c. Prepare the journal entries to
   (1) Record service revenue on account.
   (2) Record collection of accounts receivable.
   (3) Record the entry to recognize uncollectible accounts expense.
d. What is the net realizable value of receivables at the end of 2006?
e. Show the effect of the transactions listed in Requirement *c* on the financial statements by recording the appropriate amounts in a horizontal statements model like the one shown here. When you record amounts in the Cash Flow column, indicate whether the item is an operating activity (OA), investing activity (IA), or financing activity (FA). The letters NA indicate that an element is not affected by the event.

Assets			=	Liab.	+	Equity	Rev.	−	Exp.	=	Net Inc.	Cash Flow
Cash	+ Accts. Rec.	− Allow.										

L.O. 2

CHECK FIGURES

b. Net Income: $62,520
Total Assets: $157,520

Problem 7-19A ***Accounting for uncollectible accounts: percent of receivables allowance method***

Hammond Inc. experienced the following transactions for 2007, its first year of operations:

1. Issued common stock for $80,000 cash.
2. Purchased $225,000 of merchandise on account.
3. Sold merchandise that cost $148,000 for $294,000 on account.
4. Collected $242,000 cash from accounts receivable.
5. Paid $210,000 on accounts payable.
6. Paid $46,000 of salaries expense for the year.
7. Paid other operating expenses of $35,000.
8. Hammond adjusted the accounts using the following information from an accounts receivable aging schedule.

Number of Days Past Due	Amount	Percent Likely to Be Uncollectible	Allowance Balance
Current	$33,000	.01	
0–30	12,000	.05	
31–60	3,000	.10	
61–90	2,500	.20	
Over 90 days	1,500	.50	

Required

a. Record the above transactions in general journal form and post them to T-accounts.
b. Prepare the income statement, statement of changes in stockholders' equity, balance sheet, and statement of cash flows for Hammond Inc. for 2007.
c. What is the net realizable value of the accounts receivable at December 31, 2007?

L.O. 2

CHECK FIGURE

b. Net Realizable Value: $82,775

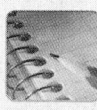

Problem 7-20A ***Determining account balances and preparing journal entries: percent of revenue allowance method of accounting for uncollectible accounts***

The following information pertains to Bay Cabinet Company's sales on account and accounts receivable:

Accounts Receivable Balance, January 1, 2007	$125,400
Allowance for Doubtful Accounts, January 1, 2007	3,250
Sales on Account, 2007	875,000
Cost of Goods Sold, 2007	620,000
Collections of Accounts Receivable, 2007	910,000

After several collection attempts, Bay Cabinet Company wrote off $2,800 of accounts that could not be collected. Bay estimates that uncollectible accounts expense will be 0.5 percent of sales on account.

Required

a. Prepare the general journal entries to:
   (1) Record sales on account for 2007.
   (2) Record cash collections from accounts receivable for 2007.
   (3) Write off the accounts that are not collectible.
   (4) Record the estimated uncollectible accounts expense for 2007.

b. Compute the following amounts:

(1) Using the allowance method, the amount of uncollectible accounts expense for 2007.

(2) Net realizable value of receivables at the end of 2007.

c. Explain why the uncollectible accounts expense amount is different from the amount that was written off as uncollectible.

Problem 7-21A ***Accounting for credit card sales and uncollectible accounts: percent of receivables allowance method***

L.O. 2, 5

eXcel

mhhe.com/edmonds2007

Bishop Supply Company had the following transactions in 2006:

1. Acquired $60,000 cash from the issue of common stock.
2. Purchased $180,000 of merchandise for cash in 2006.
3. Sold merchandise that cost $110,000 for $200,000 during the year under the following terms:

$ 50,000	Cash Sales
140,000	Credit Card Sales (The credit card company charges a 3 percent service fee.)
10,000	Sales on Account

4. Collected all the amount receivable from the credit card company.
5. Collected $9,200 of accounts receivable.
6. Paid selling and administrative expenses of $46,000.
7. Determined that 5 percent of the ending accounts receivable balance would be uncollectible.

CHECK FIGURES

c. Net Income: $39,760

Total Assets: $99,760

Required

a. Show the effects of each of the transactions on the elements of the financial statements, using a horizontal statements model like the one shown here. Use + for increase, − for decrease, and NA for not affected. The first transaction is entered as an example. (*Hint:* Closing entries do not affect the statements model.)

Event No.	Assets	=	Liab.	+	Equity	Rev.	−	Exp.	=	Net Inc.	Cash Flow
1	+		NA		+	NA		NA		NA	+ FA

b. Prepare general journal entries for each of the transactions, and post them to T-accounts.

c. Prepare an income statement, statement of changes in stockholders' equity, balance sheet, and statement of cash flows for 2006.

Problem 7-22A ***Accounting for notes receivable and uncollectible accounts using the direct write-off method***

L.O. 3, 4

The following transactions apply to Bialis Co. for 2006, its first year of operations.

1. Issued $100,000 of common stock for cash.
2. Provided $86,000 of services on account.
3. Collected $75,000 cash from accounts receivable.
4. Loaned $10,000 to Horne Co. on October 1, 2006. The note had a one-year term to maturity and an 8 percent interest rate.
5. Paid $32,000 of salaries expense for the year.
6. Paid a $2,000 dividend to the stockholders.
7. Recorded the accrued interest on December 31, 2006 (see item 4).
8. Determined that $560 of accounts receivable were uncollectible.

Required

a. Record the above transactions in general journal form.

b. Post the entries to T-accounts.

c. Prepare the income statement, balance sheet, and statement of cash flows for 2006.

d. Show the effects of the above transactions in a horizontal statements model like the one shown below.

	Assets				= Liab. +	Equity	Rev. − Exp. = Net Inc.	Cash Flows
Event	Cash +	Accts. Rec. +	Notes Rec. +	Int. Rec.	=	Com. Stk. + Ret. Earn.		

L.O. 2, 4, 5

Problem 7-23A *Effect of transactions on the elements of financial statements*

Required

Identify each of the following independent transactions as asset source (AS), asset use (AU), asset exchange (AE), or claims exchange (CE). Also explain how each event affects assets, liabilities, stockholders' equity, net income, and cash flow by placing a + for increase, − for decrease, or NA for not affected under each of the categories. The first event is recorded as an example.

Event	Type of Event	Assets	Liabilities	Common Stock	Retained Earnings	Net Income	Cash Flow
a	AE	+/−	NA	NA	NA	NA	+

a. Collected cash from customers paying their accounts.
b. Recovered an uncollectible account that was previously written off (assume direct write-off method was used).
c. Paid cash for land.
d. Paid cash for other operating expenses.
e. Sold merchandise at a price above cost. Accepted payment by credit card. The credit card company charges a service fee. The receipts have not yet been forwarded to the credit card company.
f. Sold land for cash at its cost.
g. Paid cash to satisfy salaries payable.
h. Submitted receipts to the credit card company (see *e* above) and collected cash.
i. Loaned Carl Maddox cash. The loan had a 5 percent interest rate and a one-year term to maturity.
j. Paid cash to creditors on accounts payable.
k. Accrued three months' interest on the note receivable (see *i* above).
l. Provided services for cash.
m. Paid cash for salaries expense.
n. Provided services on account.
o. Wrote off an uncollectible account (use direct write-off method).

L.O. 2, 4

excel

mhhe.com/edmonds2007

CHECK FIGURES

Total Current Assets: $338,800

Total Current Liabilities: $130,000

Problem 7-24A *Multistep income statement and balance sheet*

Required

Use the following information to prepare a multistep income statement and a balance sheet for Daniels Company for 2006. (*Hint:* Some of the items will *not* appear on either statement, and ending retained earnings must be calculated.)

Operating Expenses	$ 90,000	Allowance for Doubtful Accounts	7,000
Accounts Payable	60,000	Sales Revenue	400,000
Land	77,000	Uncollectible Accounts Expense	14,000
Dividends	12,000	Accounts Receivable	113,000
Beginning Retained Earnings	171,070	Salaries Payable	12,000
Interest Revenue	16,000	Supplies	3,000
Inventory	125,000	Prepaid Rent	14,000
Notes Receivable (short term)	17,000	Common Stock	52,000
Cash	73,000	Cost of Goods Sold	179,000
Interest Receivable (short term)	800	Salaries Expense	58,270
Cash Flow from Investing Activities	102,000	Unearned Revenue	58,000

Problem 7-25A ***Missing information***

L.O. 2, 4

CHECK FIGURES
a. Net Realizable Value: $33,600
b. Interest Revenue: $4,000

The following information comes from the accounts of Kemper Company:

Account Title	Beginning Balance	Ending Balance
Accounts Receivable	$30,000	$36,000
Allowance for Doubtful Accounts	1,800	2,400
Notes Receivable	50,000	50,000
Interest Receivable	1,000	5,000

Required

a. There were $180,000 in sales on account during the accounting period. Write-offs of uncollectible accounts were $2,100. What was the amount of cash collected from accounts receivable? What amount of uncollectible accounts expense was reported on the income statement? What was the net realizable value of receivables at the end of the accounting period?

b. The note has an 8 percent interest rate and 24 months to maturity. What amount of interest revenue was recognized during the period? How much cash was collected for interest?

Problem 7-26A ***Comprehensive accounting cycle problem (uses percent of revenue allowance method)***

L.O. 2, 4, 5

CHECK FIGURES
Net Income: $113,150
Total Assets: $308,650

The following trial balance was prepared for Lakeview Sales and Service on December 31, 2006, after the closing entries were posted.

Account Title	Debit	Credit
Cash	$ 87,100	
Accounts Receivable	18,760	
Allowance for Doubtful Accounts		$ 960
Inventory	94,600	
Accounts Payable		44,000
Common Stock		90,000
Retained Earnings		65,500
Totals	$200,460	$200,460

Lakeview had the following transactions in 2007:

1. Purchased merchandise on account for $270,000.
2. Sold merchandise that cost $215,000 on account for $350,000.
3. Performed $80,000 of services for cash.
4. Sold merchandise for $76,000 to credit card customers. The merchandise cost $47,500. The credit card company charges a 5 percent fee.
5. Collected $360,000 cash from accounts receivable.
6. Paid $274,000 cash on accounts payable.
7. Paid $126,000 cash for selling and administrative expenses.
8. Collected cash for the full amount due from the credit card company (see item 4).
9. Loaned $60,000 to R. Shell. The note had an 8 percent interest rate and a one-year term to maturity.
10. Wrote off $650 of accounts as uncollectible.
11. Made the following adjusting entries:
    (a) Recorded three months' interest on the note at December 31, 2007 (see item 9).
    (b) Estimated uncollectible accounts expense to be .5 percent of sales on account.

Required

Prepare general journal entries for these transactions; post the entries to T-accounts; and prepare an income statement, a statement of changes in stockholders' equity, a balance sheet, and a statement of cash flows for 2007.

EXERCISES—SERIES B

L.O. 2

Exercise 7-1B ***Analysis of financial statement effects of accounting for uncollectible accounts under the direct write-off method***

Burgess Services Co. experienced the following events in 2008:

1. Provided services on account.
2. Collected cash for accounts receivable.
3. Attempted to collect an account and, when unsuccessful, wrote the amount off to uncollectible accounts expense.

Required

Show the effect of each event on the elements of the financial statements, using a horizontal statements model like the one shown here. Use the following coding scheme to record your answers: increase is +, decrease is −, not affected is NA. In the cash flow column, indicate whether the item is an operating activity (OA), investing activity (IA), or financing activity (FA).

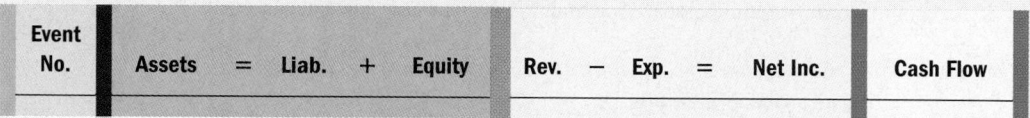

Event No.	Assets	=	Liab.	+	Equity	Rev.	−	Exp.	=	Net Inc.	Cash Flow

L.O. 2

Exercise 7-2B ***Accounting for uncollectible accounts: allowance method***

Justin's Cleaning Service began operation on January 1, 2007. The company experienced the following events for its first year of operations.

Events Affecting 2007:

1. Provided $80,000 of cleaning services on account.
2. Collected $65,000 cash from accounts receivable.
3. Paid salaries of $12,000 for the year.
4. Adjusted the accounts to reflect management's expectations that uncollectible accounts expense would be $900.

Required

a. Prepare general journal entries for the above events.
b. Post the general journal entries to T-accounts.
c. Prepare an income statement, balance sheet, and statement of cash flows for 2007.

L.O. 2

Exercise 7-3B ***Effect of recognizing uncollectible accounts expense on financial statements: percent of revenue allowance method***

Hughes Dry Cleaning was started on January 1, 2006. It experienced the following events during its first two years of operation.

Events Affecting 2006

1. Provided $10,000 of cleaning services on account.
2. Collected $8,000 cash from accounts receivable.
3. Adjusted the accounting records to reflect the estimate that uncollectible accounts expense would be 1 percent of the cleaning revenue on account.

Events Affecting 2007

1. Wrote off an $80 account receivable that was determined to be uncollectible.
2. Provided $12,000 of cleaning services on account.
3. Collected $10,000 cash from accounts receivable.
4. Adjusted the accounting records to reflect the estimate that uncollectible accounts expense would be 1 percent of the cleaning revenue on account.

Required

a. Record the events for 2006 in T-accounts.

b. Determine the following amounts:
  (1) Net income for 2006.
  (2) Net cash flow from operating activities for 2006.
  (3) Balance of accounts receivable at the end of 2006.
  (4) Net realizable value of accounts receivable at the end of 2006.

c. Repeat Requirements *a* and *b* for the 2007 accounting period.

Exercise 7-4B *Analyzing financial statement effects of accounting for uncollectible accounts using the percent of revenue allowance method*

L.O. 2

Smith Inc. uses the allowance method to account for uncollectible accounts expense. Smith experienced the following four accounting events in 2008:

1. Recognized $72,000 of revenue on account.
2. Collected $60,000 cash from accounts receivable.
3. Wrote off uncollectible accounts of $520.
4. Recognized uncollectible accounts expense. Smith estimated that uncollectible accounts expense will be 1 percent of sales on account.

Required

a. Show the effect of each event on the elements of the financial statements, using a horizontal statements model like the one shown here. Use + for increase, − for decrease, and NA for not affected. In the cash flow column, indicate whether the item is an operating activity (OA), investing activity (IA), or financing activity (FA). The first transaction is entered as an example.

Event No.	Assets	=	Liab.	+	Equity	Rev.	−	Exp.	=	Net Inc.	Cash Flow
1	+		NA		+	+		NA		+	NA

b. Record the above transactions in general journal form.

Exercise 7-5B *Analyzing account balances for a company using the allowance method of accounting for uncollectible accounts*

L.O. 2

The following account balances come from the records of Fiesta Company.

	Beginning Balance	Ending Balance
Accounts Receivable	$1,500	$2,000
Allowance for Doubtful Accounts	150	175

During the accounting period, Fiesta recorded $7,000 of sales revenue on account. The company also wrote off an $80 account receivable.

Required

a. Determine the amount of cash collected from receivables.

b. Determine the amount of uncollectible accounts expense recognized during the period.

Exercise 7-6B *Effect of recovering a receivable previously written off*

L.O. 2

The accounts receivable balance for Get-N-Shape Spa at December 31, 2007, was $80,000. Also on that date, the balance in the Allowance for Doubtful Accounts was $3,000. During 2008, $3,500 of accounts receivable were written off as uncollectible. In addition, Get-N-Shape unexpectedly collected $900 of receivables that had been written off in a previous accounting period. Sales on account during 2008 were $200,000, and cash collections from receivables were $190,000. Uncollectible accounts expense was estimated to be 2 percent of the sales on account for the period.

Required

a. Record the transactions in general journal form and post to T-accounts.

b. Based on the preceding information, compute (after year-end adjustment):
  (1) Balance of Allowance for Doubtful Accounts at December 31, 2008.
  (2) Balance of Accounts Receivable at December 31, 2008.
  (3) Net realizable value of Accounts Receivable at December 31, 2008.

c. What amount of uncollectible accounts expense will Get-N-Shape report for 2008?

d. Explain how the $900 recovery of receivables affects the income statement.

L.O. 2

Exercise 7-7B ***Accounting for uncollectible accounts: percent of receivables allowance method***

Harper Service Co. experienced the following transactions for 2009, its first year of operations:

1. Provided $98,000 of services on account.
2. Collected $76,000 cash from accounts receivable.
3. Paid $32,000 of salaries expense for the year.
4. Adjusted the accounts using the following information from an accounts receivable aging schedule:

Number of Days Past Due	Amount	Percent Likely to Be Uncollectible	Allowance Balance
Current	$13,000	.01	
0–30	4,000	.05	
31–60	2,000	.10	
61–90	1,500	.20	
Over 90 days	1,500	.50	

Required

a. Record the above transactions in general journal form and post to T-accounts.

b. Prepare the income statement for Harper Service Co. for 2009.

c. What is the net realizable value of the accounts receivable at December 31, 2009?

L.O. 2

Exercise 7-8B ***Effect of recognizing uncollectible accounts on the financial statements: percent of receivables allowance method***

Swanson Inc. experienced the following events for the first two years of its operations.

2009:

1. Provided $75,000 of services on account.
2. Provided $30,000 of services and received cash.
3. Collected $60,000 cash from accounts receivable.
4. Paid $22,000 of salaries expense for the year.
5. Adjusted the accounting records to reflect uncollectible accounts expense for the year. Swanson estimates that 5 percent of the ending accounts receivable balance will be uncollectible.

2010:

1. Wrote off an uncollectible account for $850.
2. Provided $80,000 of services on account.
3. Provided $15,000 of services and collected cash.
4. Collected $62,000 cash from accounts receivable.
5. Paid $20,000 of salaries expense for the year.
6. Adjusted the accounts to reflect uncollectible accounts expense for the year. Swanson estimates that 5 percent of the ending accounts receivable balance will be uncollectible.

Required

a. Record the 2009 events in general journal form and post them to T-accounts.

b. Prepare the income statement, statement of changes in stockholders' equity, balance sheet, and statement of cash flows for 2009.

c. What is the net realizable value of the accounts receivable at December 31, 2009?

d. Repeat Requirements *a, b,* and *c* for 2010.

Exercise 7-9B ***Accounting for uncollectible accounts: percent of revenue allowance versus direct write-off method*** **L.O. 2, 3**

Ted's Bike Shop sells new and used bicycle parts. Although a majority of its sales are cash sales, it makes a significant amount of credit sales. During 2004, its first year of operations, Ted's Bike Shop experienced the following:

Sales on account	$300,000
Cash sales	555,000
Collections of Accounts Receivable	260,000
Uncollectible accounts charged off during the year	250

Required

a. Assume that Ted's Bike Shop uses the allowance method of accounting for uncollectible accounts and estimates that 1 percent of its sales on account will not be collected. Answer the following questions:

(1) What is the Accounts Receivable balance at December 31, 2004?

(2) What is the ending balance of the Allowance for Doubtful Accounts at December 31, 2004, after all entries and adjusting entries are posted?

(3) What is the amount of uncollectible accounts expense for 2004?

(4) What is the net realizable value of accounts receivable at December 31, 2004?

b. Assume that Ted's Bike Shop uses the direct write-off method of accounting for uncollectible accounts. Answer the following questions:

(1) What is the Accounts Receivable balance at December 31, 2004?

(2) What is the amount of uncollectible accounts expense for 2004?

(3) What is the net realizable value of accounts receivable at December 31, 2004?

Exercise 7-10B ***Accounting for uncollectible accounts: direct write-off method*** **L.O. 3**

Hunan Service Co. does make a few sales on account but is mostly a cash business. Consequently, it uses the direct write-off method to account for uncollectible accounts. During 2005 Hunan Service Co. earned $10,000 of cash revenue and $2,000 of revenue on account. Cash operating expenses were $8,000. After numerous attempts to collect a $70 account receivable from Bill Smith, the account was determined to be uncollectible in 2005.

Required

a. Record the effects of (1) cash revenue, (2) revenue on account, (3) cash expenses, and (4) write-off of the uncollectible account on the financial statements using a horizontal statements model like the one shown here. In the Cash Flow column, indicate whether the item is an operating activity (OA), investing activity (IA), or financing activity (FA). Use NA to indicate that an element is not affected by the event.

Assets			=	Liab.	+	Equity	Rev.	−	Exp.	=	Net Inc.	Cash Flow
Cash	+	Accts. Rec.										

b. What amount of net income did Hunan Service Co. report on the 2005 income statement?

c. Prepare the general journal entries for the four accounting events listed in Requirement *a*.

Exercise 7-11B ***Effect of credit card sales on financial statements*** **L.O. 5**

Super Day Spa provided $120,000 of services during 2004. All customers paid for the services with credit cards. Super submitted the credit card receipts to the credit card company immediately. The credit card company paid Super cash in the amount of face value less a 5 percent service charge.

Required

a. Record the credit card sales and the subsequent collection of accounts receivable in a horizontal statements model like the one shown here. In the Cash Flow column, indicate whether the item is an operating activity (OA), investing activity (IA), or financing activity (FA). Use NA to indicate that an element is not affected by the event.

Assets			=	Liab.	+	Equity	Rev.	−	Exp.	=	Net Inc.	Cash Flow
Cash	+	Accts. Rec.										

b. Based on this information alone, answer the following questions:

(1) What is the amount of total assets at the end of the accounting period?
(2) What is the amount of revenue reported on the income statement?
(3) What is the amount of cash flow from operating activities reported on the statement of cash flows?
(4) What costs would a business incur if it maintained its own accounts receivable? What cost does a business incur by accepting credit cards?

L.O. 5

Exercise 7-12B *Recording credit card sales*

Elk Company accepted credit cards in payment for $3,000 of services performed during July 2004. The credit card company charged Elk a 4 percent service fee; it paid Elk as soon as it received the invoices.

Required

a. Prepare the general journal entry to record the service revenue.
b. Prepare the general journal entry for the collection of the receivable from the credit card company.
c. Based on this information alone, what is the amount of net income earned during the month of July?

L.O. 4

Exercise 7-13B *Accounting for notes receivable*

Mann Enterprises loaned $12,000 to Snell Co. on June 1, 2008, for one year at 5 percent interest.

Required

a. Record these general journal entries for Mann Enterprises:
(1) The loan to Snell Co.
(2) The adjusting entry at December 31, 2008.
(3) The adjusting entry and collection of the note on June 1, 2009.
b. Show the effects of the three above transactions in a horizontal statements model like the one shown below.

Date	Assets					=	Liab.	+	Equity	Rev.	−	Exp.	=	Net Inc.	Cash Flows
	Cash	+	Notes Rec.	+	Int. Rec.	=			Ret. Earn.						

L.O. 4

Exercise 7-14B *Notes receivable—accrued interest*

On May 1, 2007, Lenny's Sandwich Shop loaned $20,000 to Joe Lopez for one year at 6 percent interest.

Required

Answer the following questions:

a. What is Lenny's interest income for 2007?
b. What is Lenny's total amount of receivables at December 31, 2007?
c. What amounts will be reported on Lenny's 2007 statement of cash flows?
d. What is Lenny's interest income for 2008?
e. What is the total amount of cash that Lenny's will collect in 2008 from Joe Lopez?
f. What amounts will be reported on Lenny's 2008 statement of cash flows?
g. What is the total amount of interest that Lenny's earned on the loan to Joe Lopez?

Exercise 7-15B ***Comprehensive single-cycle problem*** L.O. 2, 4

The following after-closing trial balance was drawn from the accounts of Millers Metal Co. (MMC) as of December 31, 2004.

	Debit	Credit
Cash	$ 4,000	
Accounts Receivable	20,000	
Allowance for Doubtful Accounts		$ 1,000
Inventory	40,000	
Accounts Payable		10,000
Common Stock		20,000
Retained Earnings		33,000
Totals	$64,000	$64,000

Transactions for 2005

1. MMC acquired an additional $4,000 cash from the issue of common stock.
2. MMC purchased $80,000 of inventory on account.
3. MMC sold inventory that cost $76,000 for $128,000. Sales were made on account.
4. The company wrote off $800 of uncollectible accounts.
5. On September 1, MMC loaned $10,000 to King Co. The note had a 9 percent interest rate and a one-year term.
6. MMC paid $16,000 cash for operating expenses.
7. The company collected $133,200 cash from accounts receivable.
8. A cash payment of $68,000 was paid on accounts payable.
9. The company paid a $2,000 cash dividend to the stockholders.
10. Uncollectible accounts are estimated to be 1 percent of sales on account.
11. Recorded the accrued interest at December 31, 2005 (see item 5).

Required

a. Record the above transactions in general journal form.
b. Open T-accounts and record the beginning balances and the 2005 transactions.
c. Prepare an income statement, statement of changes in stockholders' equity, balance sheet, and statement of cash flows for 2005.

Exercise 7-16B ***Accounts receivable turnover and average days to collect accounts receivable*** L.O. 6

The following information is available for Spring Inc. and Winter Inc. at December 31, 2008:

Accounts	Spring, Inc.	Winter, Inc.
Accounts Receivable	$ 88,200	$ 103,400
Allowance for Doubtful Accounts	3,528	3,102
Sales Revenue	977,500	1,230,500

Required

a. What is the accounts receivable turnover for each of the companies for 2008?
b. What is the average days to collect the receivables for 2008?
c. Assuming both companies use the percent of receivables allowance method, what is the estimated percentage of uncollectible accounts for each company?

PROBLEMS—SERIES B

L.O. 2

Problem 7-17B ***Accounting for uncollectible accounts: two cycles using the percent of revenue allowance method***

The following transactions apply to KC Company for 2005, the first year of operation:

1. Recognized $255,000 of service revenue earned on account.
2. Collected $159,000 from accounts receivable.
3. Paid $150,000 cash for operating expenses.
4. Adjusted the accounts to recognize uncollectible accounts expense. KC uses the allowance method of accounting for uncollectible accounts and estimates that uncollectible accounts expense will be 1 percent of sales on account.

The following transactions apply to KC for 2006:

1. Recognized $408,000 of service revenue on account.
2. Collected $411,000 from accounts receivable.
3. Determined that $1,800 of the accounts receivable were uncollectible and wrote them off.
4. Collected $600 of an account that had previously been written off.
5. Paid $126,000 cash for operating expenses.
6. Adjusted the accounts to recognize uncollectible accounts expense for 2006. KC estimates uncollectible accounts expense will be 0.5 percent of sales on account.

Required

Complete the following requirements for 2005 and 2006. Complete all requirements for 2005 prior to beginning the requirements for 2006.

a. Identify the type of each transaction (asset source, asset use, asset exchange, or claims exchange).
b. Show the effect of each transaction on the elements of the financial statements, using a horizontal statements model like the one shown here. Use + for increase, − for decrease, and NA for not affected. Also, in the Cash Flow column, indicate whether the item is an operating activity (OA), investing activity (IA), or financing activity (FA). The first transaction is entered as an example. (*Hint:* Closing entries do not affect the statements model.)

Event No.	Assets	=	Liab.	+	Equity	Rev.	−	Exp.	=	Net Inc.	Cash Flow
1	+		NA		+	+		NA		+	NA

c. Record the transactions in general journal form, and post them to T-accounts (begin 2006 with the ending T-account balances from 2005).
d. Prepare the income statement, statement of changes in stockholders' equity, balance sheet, and statement of cash flows.
e. Prepare closing entries and post these closing entries to the T-accounts. Prepare the after-closing trial balance.

L.O. 2

Problem 7-18B ***Determination of account balances and preparation of journal entries—percent of receivables allowance method of accounting for uncollectible accounts***

The following information is available for Book Barn Company's sales on account and accounts receivable:

Accounts Receivable Balance, January 1, 2007	$ 172,800
Allowance for Doubtful Accounts, January 1, 2007	5,184
Sales on Account, 2007	1,269,800
Collection on Accounts Receivable, 2007	1,284,860

After several collection attempts, Book Barn wrote off $4,500 of accounts that could not be collected. Book Barn estimates that 4 percent of the ending accounts receivable balance will be uncollectible.

Required

a. Compute the following amounts:

(1) Using the allowance method, the amount of uncollectible accounts expense for 2007.
(2) Net realizable value of receivables at the end of 2007.

b. Record the general journal entries to:

(1) Record sales on account for 2007.
(2) Record cash collections from accounts receivable for 2007.
(3) Write off the accounts that are not collectible.
(4) Record the estimated uncollectible accounts expense for 2007.

c. Explain why the uncollectible accounts expense amount is different from the amount that was written off as uncollectible.

Problem 7-19B *Accounting for uncollectible accounts: percent of receivables allowance method*

L.O. 2

Ming Inc. experienced the following transactions for 2007, its first year of operations:

1. Issued common stock for $50,000 cash.
2. Purchased $145,000 of merchandise on account.
3. Sold merchandise that cost $85,000 for $136,000 on account.
4. Collected $115,000 cash from accounts receivable.
5. Paid $85,000 on accounts payable.
6. Paid $25,000 of salaries expense for the year.
7. Paid other operating expenses of $15,000.
8. Ming adjusted the accounts using the following information from an accounts receivable aging schedule:

Number of Days Past Due	Amount	Percent Likely to Be Uncollectible	Allowance Balance
Current	$12,000	.01	
0–30	4,000	.05	
31–60	2,000	.10	
61–90	2,000	.20	
Over 90 days	1,000	.50	

Required

a. Record the above transactions in general journal form and post to T-accounts.

b. Prepare the income statement, statement of changes in stockholders' equity, balance sheet, and statement of cash flows for Ming Inc. for 2007.

c. What is the net realizable value of the accounts receivable at December 31, 2007?

Problem 7-20B *Determining account balances and preparing journal entries: percent of revenue allowance method of accounting for uncollectible accounts*

L.O. 2

During the first year of operation, 2006, Wells Appliance Co. recognized $300,000 of service revenue on account. At the end of 2006, the accounts receivable balance was $58,000. For this first year in business, the owner believes uncollectible accounts expense will be about 1 percent of sales on account.

Required

a. What amount of cash did Wells collect from accounts receivable during 2006?

b. Assuming Wells uses the allowance method to account for uncollectible accounts, what amount should Wells record as uncollectible accounts expense for 2006?

c. Prepare the general journal entries to:

(1) Record service revenue on account.
(2) Record collections from accounts receivable.
(3) Record the entry to recognize uncollectible accounts expense.

d. What is the net realizable value of receivables at the end of 2006?

e. Show the effects of the transactions in Requirement *c* on the financial statements by recording the appropriate amounts in a horizontal statements model like the one shown here. In the Cash Flow column, indicate whether the item is an operating activity (OA), investing activity (IA), or financing activity (FA). Use NA for not affected.

Assets					=	Liab.	+	Equity	Rev.	−	Exp.	=	Net Inc.	Cash Flow
Cash	+	Accts. Rec.	−	Allow.										

L.O. 2, 5

Problem 7-21B *Accounting for credit card sales and uncollectible accounts: percent of receivables allowance method*

Northeast Sales had the following transactions in 2005:

1. The business was started when it acquired $500,000 cash from the issue of common stock.
2. Northeast purchased $1,200,000 of merchandise for cash in 2005.
3. During the year, the company sold merchandise for $1,600,000. The merchandise cost $900,000. Sales were made under the following terms:

a.	$600,000	Cash sales
b.	500,000	Credit card sales (The credit card company charges a 4 percent service fee.)
c.	500,000	Sales on account

4. The company collected all the amount receivable from the credit card company.
5. The company collected $400,000 of accounts receivable.
6. The company paid $100,000 cash for selling and administrative expenses.
7. Determined that 5 percent of the ending accounts receivable balance would be uncollectible.

Required

a. Show the effects of each of the transactions on the elements of the financial statements, using a horizontal statements model like the one shown here. Use + for increase, − for decrease, and NA for not affected. The first transaction is entered as an example. (*Hint:* Closing entries do not affect the statements model.)

Event No.	Assets	=	Liab.	+	Equity	Rev.	−	Exp.	=	Net Inc.	Cash Flow
1	+		NA		+	NA		NA		NA	+ FA

b. Prepare general journal entries for each of the transactions, and post them to T-accounts.

c. Prepare an income statement, statement of changes in stockholders' equity, balance sheet, and statement of cash flows for 2005.

L.O. 3, 4

Problem 7-22B *Accounting for notes receivable and uncollectible accounts using the direct write-off method*

The following transactions apply to Kenyon Co. for 2006, its first year of operations.

1. Issued $80,000 of common stock for cash.
2. Provided $110,000 of services on account.
3. Collected $92,000 cash from accounts receivable.
4. Loaned $20,000 to Harpst Co. on November 30, 2006. The note had a one-year term to maturity and a 6 percent interest rate.
5. Paid $24,000 of salaries expense for the year.
6. Paid a $1,000 dividend to the stockholders.
7. Recorded the accrued interest on December 31, 2006 (see item 4).
8. Determined that $840 of accounts receivable were uncollectible.

Required

a. Record the above transactions in general journal form.

b. Post the entries to T-accounts.

c. Prepare the income statement, balance sheet, and statement of cash flows for 2006.

d. Show the effects of the above transactions in a horizontal statements model like the one shown below.

	Assets				= Liab. +	Equity	Rev. − Exp. = Net Inc.	Cash Flows
Event	Cash +	Accts. Rec. +	Notes Rec. +	Int. Rec.	=	Com. Stk. + Ret. Earn.		

Problem 7-23B *Effect of transactions on the elements of financial statements*

L.O. 2, 4, 5

Required

Identify each of the following independent transactions as asset source (AS), asset use (AU), asset exchange (AE), or claims exchange (CE). Also explain how each event affects assets, liabilities, stockholders' equity, net income, and cash flow by placing a + for increase, − for decrease, or NA for not affected under each of the categories. The first event is recorded as an example.

Event	Type of Event	Assets	Liabilities	Common Stock	Retained Earnings	Net Income	Cash Flow
a	AE	+/−	NA	NA	NA	NA	−

a. Paid cash for land.

b. Sold merchandise at a price above cost. Accepted payment by credit card. The credit card company charges a service fee. The receipts have not yet been forwarded to the credit card company.

c. Submitted receipts to the credit card company (see *b* above) and collected cash.

d. Sold land at its cost.

e. Provided services for cash.

f. Paid cash for operating expenses.

g. Paid cash for salaries expense.

h. Recovered an uncollectible account that had been previously written off (assume the direct write off method is used to account for uncollectible accounts).

i. Paid cash to creditors on accounts payable.

j. Loaned cash to H. Phillips for one year at 6 percent interest.

k. Provided services on account.

l. Wrote off an uncollectible account (use the direct write-off method).

m. Recorded three months of accrued interest on the note receivable (see *j* above).

n. Collected cash from customers paying their accounts.

Problem 7-24B *Multistep income statement and balance sheet*

L.O. 2, 4

Required

Use the following information to prepare a multistep income statement and a balance sheet for Belmont Equipment Co. for 2007. (*Hint:* Some of the items will *not* appear on either statement, and ending retained earnings must be calculated.)

Salaries Expense	$ 96,000	Interest Revenue	10,600
Common Stock	140,000	Sales Revenue	396,000
Notes Receivable (short term)	12,000	Dividends	8,000
Allowance for Doubtful Accounts	4,000	Interest Receivable (short term)	500
Uncollectible Accounts Expense	10,800	Beginning Retained Earnings	10,400
Supplies	1,600		*continued*

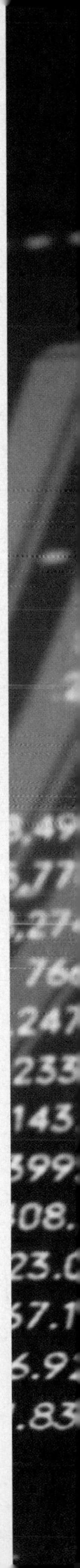

Operating Expenses	70,000	Inventory	122,800
Cash Flow from Investing Activities	80,000	Accounts Payable	46,000
Prepaid Rent	9,600	Salaries Payable	9,200
Land	36,000	Cost of Goods Sold	143,000
Cash	17,800	Accounts Receivable	88,100

L.O. 2, 4

Problem 7-25B ***Missing information***

The following information comes from the accounts of Jersey Company:

Account Title	Beginning Balance	Ending Balance
Accounts Receivable	$30,000	$34,000
Allowance for Doubtful Accounts	1,800	1,700
Notes Receivable	40,000	40,000
Interest Receivable	1,200	3,600

Required

a. There were $170,000 of sales on account during the accounting period. Write-offs of uncollectible accounts were $1,400. What was the amount of cash collected from accounts receivable? What amount of uncollectible accounts expense was reported on the income statement? What was the net realizable value of receivables at the end of the accounting period?

b. The note receivable has a two-year term with a 6 percent interest rate. What amount of interest revenue was recognized during the period? How much cash was collected from interest?

L.O. 2, 3, 4, 5

Problem 7-26B ***Comprehensive accounting cycle problem (uses percent of sales allowance method)***

The following trial balance was prepared for Candles, Etc., Inc., on December 31, 2006, after the closing entries were posted.

Account Title	Debit	Credit
Cash	$118,000	
Accounts Receivable	172,000	
Allowance for Doubtful Accounts		$ 10,000
Inventory	690,000	
Accounts Payable		142,000
Common Stock		720,000
Retained Earnings		108,000
Totals	$980,000	$980,000

Candles, Etc. had the following transactions in 2007:

1. Purchased merchandise on account for $420,000.
2. Sold merchandise that cost $288,000 for $480,000 on account.
3. Sold for $240,000 cash merchandise that had cost $144,000.
4. Sold merchandise for $180,000 to credit card customers. The merchandise had cost $108,000. The credit card company charges a 4 percent fee.
5. Collected $526,000 cash from accounts receivable.
6. Paid $540,000 cash on accounts payable.
7. Paid $134,000 cash for selling and administrative expenses.
8. Collected cash for the full amount due from the credit card company (see item 4).
9. Loaned $48,000 to D. Carnes. The note had a 10 percent interest rate and a one-year term to maturity.

10. Wrote off $7,200 of accounts as uncollectible.
11. Made the following adjusting entries:
    (a) Recorded uncollectible accounts expense estimated at 1 percent of sales on account.
    (b) Recorded seven months of accrued interest on the note at December 31, 2007 (see item 9).

Required

a. Prepare general journal entries for these transactions; post the entries to T-accounts; and prepare an income statement, a statement of changes in stockholders' equity, a balance sheet, and a statement of cash flows for 2007.
b. Compute the net realizable value of accounts receivable at December 31, 2007.
c. If Candles, Etc. used the direct write-off method, what amount of uncollectible accounts expense would it report on the income statement?

ANALYZE, THINK, COMMUNICATE

ATC 7-1 Business Applications Case *Understanding real-world annual reports*

Required—Part 1

Use the Topps Company's annual report in Appendix B to answer the following questions.

The Topps Company, Inc.

a. How long did it take Topps to collect accounts receivable during the year ended March 1, 2003?
b. Approximately what percentage of accounts receivable, as of March 1, 2003, does the company think will not be collected (see Note 3)? Caution, "Reserve for returns," also shown in Note 3, is not related to uncollectible accounts receivable.
c. What do you think the balance in the Reserve for Returns account represents?

Required—Part 2

Use the Harley-Davidson's annual report that came with this book to answer the following questions.

Harley-Davidson, Inc.

a. How long did it take Harley-Davidson to collect receivables during the year ended December 31, 2003? Note: For the purposes of this computation, use all three receivables accounts shown on Harley-Davidson's balance sheet.
b. Why does Harley-Davidson take so long to collect its receivables? Does this indicate the company has a problem with its receivables?
c. Approximately what percentage of accounts receivable, as of December 31, 2003, does the company think will not be collected (see Note 2)?

ATC 7-2 Group Assignment *Missing information*

The following selected financial information is available for three companies:

	Bell	Card	Zore
Total sales	$125,000	$210,000	?
Cash sales	?	26,000	$120,000
Sales on account	40,000	?	75,000
Accounts receivable, January 1, 2008	6,200	42,000	?
Accounts receivable, December 31, 2008	5,600	48,000	7,500
Allowance for doubtful accounts, January 1, 2008	?	?	405
Allowance for doubtful accounts, December 31, 2008	224	1,680	?
Uncollectible accounts expense, 2008	242	1,200	395
Uncollectible accounts written off	204	1,360	365
Collections of accounts receivable, 2008	?	?	75,235

Required

a. Divide the class into three sections and divide each section into groups of three to five students. Assign one of the companies to each of the sections.

Group Tasks

(1) Determine the missing amounts for your company.

(2) Determine the percentage of accounts receivable estimated to be uncollectible at the end of 2007 and 2008 for your company.

(3) Determine the percentage of total sales that are sales on account for your company.

(4) Determine the accounts receivable turnover for your company.

Class Discussion

b. Have a representative of each section put the missing information on the board and explain how it was determined.

c. Which company has the highest percentage of sales that are on account?

d. Which company is doing the best job of collecting its accounts receivable? What procedures and policies can a company use to better collect its accounts receivable?

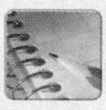

ATC 7-3 Real-World Case *Time needed to collect accounts receivable*

Presented here are the average days to collect accounts receivable for four companies in different industries. The data are for 2002.

Company	Average Days to Collect Accounts Receivable
Boeing (aircraft manufacturer)	34
Ford (automobile manufacturer)	6
Haverty's (furniture retailer)	81
Colgate Palmolive (consumer products manufacturer)	45

Required

Write a brief memorandum that provides possible answers to each of the following questions:

a. Why would a company that manufactures cars (Ford) collect its accounts receivable faster than a company that sells furniture (Haverty's)? (*Hint:* Ford sells cars to dealerships, not to individual customers.)

b. Why would a company that manufactures and sells large airplanes (Boeing) collect its accounts receivable faster than a company that sells toothpaste and soap (Colgate Palmolive)?

ATC 7-4 Business Applications Case *Using average number of days to collect accounts receivable to make comparisons*

The following information was drawn from the accounting records of Oakville and Monteray.

Account Title	Oakville	Monteray
Accounts Receivable (year end)	$ 60,000	$ 90,000
Sales on Account	610,000	1,200,000

Required

a. Determine the average number of days to collect accounts receivable for each company.

b. Which company is likely to incur more costs associated with extending credit?

c. Identify and discuss some of the costs associated with extending credit.

d. Explain why a company would be willing to accept the costs of extending credit to its customers.

ATC 7-5 Business Applications Case *Using ratios to make comparisons*

The following accounting information exists for Blackjack and Roulette companies at the end of 2007.

	Blackjack	Roulette
Cash	$ 50,000	$ 60,000
Accounts receivable	190,000	200,000
Allowance for doubtful accounts	5,000	10,000
Merchandise inventory	175,000	165,000
Accounts payable	185,000	175,000
Cost of goods sold	1,125,000	700,000
Sales	1,500,000	1,000,000

Required

a. For each company, compute the gross margin percentage and the average number of days to collect accounts receivable (use the net realizable value of receivables to compute the average days to collect accounts receivable).

b. In relation to cost, which company is charging more for its merchandise?

c. Which company is likely to incur higher financial costs associated with the granting of credit to customers? Explain.

d. Which company appears to have more restrictive credit standards when authorizing credit to its customers? (*Hint:* There is no specific answer to this question. Use your judgment and general knowledge of ratios to answer.)

ATC 7-6 Writing Assignment *Cost of charge sales*

Paul Smith is opening a plumbing supply store in University City. He plans to sell plumbing parts and materials to both wholesale and retail customers. Since contractors (wholesale customers) prefer to charge parts and materials and pay at the end of the month, Paul expects he will have to offer charge accounts. He plans to offer charge sales to the wholesale customers only and to require retail customers to pay with either cash or credit cards. Paul wondered what expenses his business would incur relative to the charge sales and the credit cards.

Required

a. What issues will Paul need to consider if he allows wholesale customers to buy plumbing supplies on account?

b. Write a memo to Paul Smith outlining the potential cost of accepting charge customers. Discuss the difference between the allowance method for uncollectible accounts and the direct write-off method. Also discuss the cost of accepting credit cards.

ATC 7-7 Ethical Dilemma *How bad can it be?*

Alonzo Saunders owns a small training services company that is experiencing growing pains. The company has grown rapidly by offering liberal credit terms to its customers. Although his competitors require payment for services within 30 days, Saunders permits his customers to delay payment for up to 90 days. Saunders' customers thereby have time to fully evaluate the training that employees receive before they must pay for that training. Saunders guarantees satisfaction. If a customer is unhappy, the customer does not have to pay. Saunders works with reputable companies, provides top-quality training, and rarely encounters dissatisfied customers.

The long collection period, however, has created a cash flow problem. Saunders has a $100,000 accounts receivable balance, but needs cash to pay current bills. He has recently negotiated a loan agreement with National Bank of Brighton County that should solve his cash flow problems. The loan agreement requires that Saunders pledge the accounts receivable as collateral for the loan. The bank agreed to loan Saunders 70 percent of the receivables balance, thereby giving him access to $70,000 cash. Saunders is satisfied with this arrangement because he estimates he needs approximately $60,000.

On the day Saunders was to execute the loan agreement, he heard a rumor that his biggest customer was experiencing financial problems and might declare bankruptcy. The customer owed Saunders $45,000. Saunders promptly called the customer's chief accountant and learned "off the record" that the rumor was true. The accountant told Saunders that the company's net worth was negative and most of its assets were pledged as collateral for bank loans. In his opinion, Saunders was unlikely to collect the balance due. Saunders' immediate concern was the impact the circumstances would have on his loan agreement with the bank.

Saunders uses the direct write-off method to recognize uncollectible accounts expense. Removing the $45,000 receivable from the collateral pool would leave only $55,000 of receivables, reducing the available credit to $38,500 ($55,000 × 0.70). Even worse, recognizing the uncollectible accounts expense would so adversely affect his income statement that the bank might further reduce the available credit by reducing the percentage of receivables allowed under the loan agreement. Saunders will have to attest to the quality of the receivables at the date of the loan but reasons that since the information he obtained about the possible bankruptcy was "off the record" he is under no obligation to recognize the uncollectible accounts expense until the receivable is officially uncollectible.

Required

a. How are income and assets affected by the decision not to act on the bankruptcy information?

b. Review the AICPA's Articles of Professional Conduct (see Chapter 1) and comment on any of the standards that would be violated by the actions Saunders is contemplating.

c. Donald Cressey identified three common features of unethical and criminal conduct (see Chapter 1). Identify these features and explain how they apply to this case.

ATC 7-8 Research Assignment *Comparing Maytag's and Papa John's time to collect accounts receivable*

Using the most current annual reports or the Forms 10-K, for **Maytag Company** and for **Papa John's International, Inc.**, complete the requirements below. To obtain the Forms 10-K, use either the EDGAR system following the instructions in Appendix A or the companies' websites. The annual reports can be found on the companies' websites.

Required

a. What was Maytag's average days to collect accounts receivable? Show your computations.

b. What percentage of accounts receivable did Maytag estimate would not be collected?

c. What was Papa John's average days to collect accounts receivable? Show your computations.

d. What percentage of accounts receivable did Papa John's estimate would not be collected?

e. Briefly explain why Maytag would take longer than Papa John's to collect its accounts receivable.

COMPREHENSIVE PROBLEM

The trial balance of Pacilio Security Services Inc. as of January 1, 2007, had the following normal balances:

Cash	$ 78,972
Petty Cash	100
Accounts Receivable	33,440
Supplies	160
Prepaid Rent	3,200
Merchandise Inventory (23 @ $280)	6,440
Land	4,000
Accounts Payable	250
Salaries Payable	1,400
Common Stock	50,000
Retained Earnings	74,662

During 2007 Pacilio Security Services experienced the following transactions:

1. Paid the salaries payable from 2006.
2. Paid $4,800 on March 1, 2007, for one year's lease on the company van in advance.

3. Paid $8,400 on May 2, 2007, for one year's rent in advance.
4. Purchased $550 of supplies on account.
5. Paid cash to purchase 105 alarm systems at a cost of $285 each.
6. Pacilio has noticed its accounts receivable balance is growing more than desired and some collection problems exist. It appears that uncollectible accounts expense is approximately 3 percent of total credit sales. Pacilio has decided it will, starting this year, adopt the allowance method of accounting for uncollectible accounts. It will record an adjusting entry to recognize the estimate at the end of the year.
7. In trying to collect several of its delinquent accounts, Pacilio has learned that these customers have either declared bankruptcy or moved and left no forwarding address. These uncollectible accounts amount to $1,900.
8. Sold 110 alarm systems for $63,800. All sales were on account. (Compute cost of goods sold using the FIFO cost flow method.)
9. Paid the balance of the accounts payable.
10. Pacilio began accepting credit cards for some of its monitoring service sales. The credit card company charges a fee of 4 percent. Total monitoring services for the year were $68,000. Pacilio accepted credit cards for $24,000 of this amount. The other $44,000 was sales on account.
11. On July 1, 2007, Pacilio replenished the petty cash fund. The fund contained $21 of currency and receipts of $50 for yard mowing, $22 for office supplies expense, and $9 for miscellaneous expenses.
12. Collected the amount due from the credit card company.
13. Paid installers and other employees a total of $45,000 cash for salaries.
14. Collected $116,800 of accounts receivable during the year.
15. Paid $9,500 of advertising expense during the year.
16. Paid $5,200 of utilities expense for the year.
17. Paid a dividend of $20,000 to the shareholders.

Adjustments

18. There was $250 of supplies on hand at the end of the year.
19. Recognized the expired rent for both the van and the office building for the year.
20. Recognized the uncollectible accounts expense for the year using the allowance method.
21. Accrued salaries at December 31, 2007, were $2,100.

Required

a. Record the above transactions in general journal form.
b. Post the transactions to the T-accounts.
c. Prepare a trial balance.
d. Prepare an income statement, statement of changes in stockholders' equity, balance sheet, and statement of cash flows.
e. Close the temporary accounts to retained earnings.
f. Post the closing entries to the T-accounts and prepare an after-closing trial balance.

CHAPTER 8

Accounting for Long-Term Operational Assets

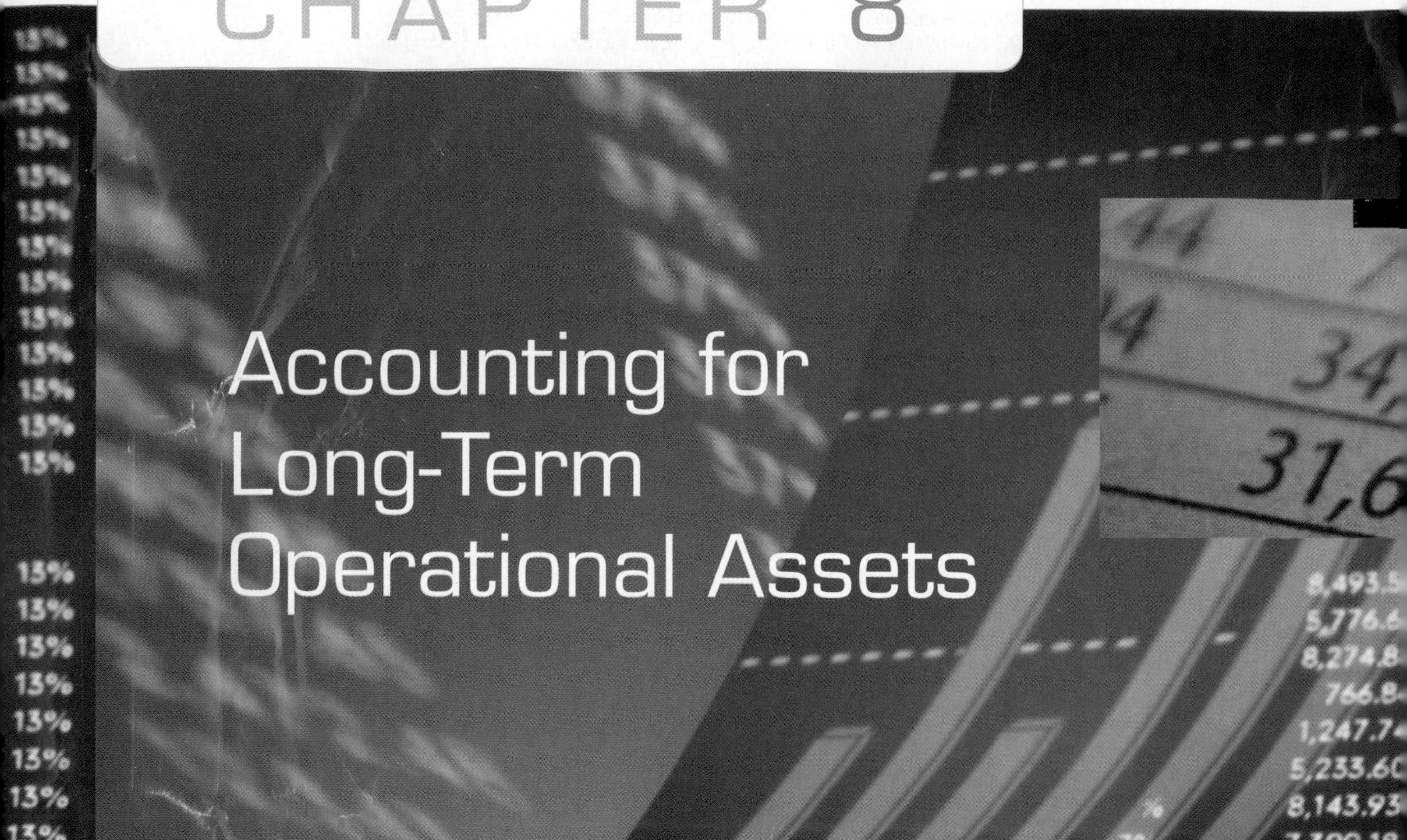

LEARNING OBJECTIVES

After you have mastered the material in this chapter, you will be able to:

1. **Identify different types of long-term operational assets.**
2. **Determine the cost of long-term operational assets.**
3. **Explain how different depreciation methods affect financial statements.**
4. **Determine how gains and losses on disposals of long-term operational assets affect financial statements.**
5. **Identify some of the tax issues that affect long-term operational assets.**
6. **Show how revising estimates affects financial statements.**
7. **Explain how continuing expenditures for operational assets affect financial statements.**
8. **Explain how expense recognition for natural resources (depletion) affects financial statements.**
9. **Explain how expense recognition for intangible assets (amortization) affects financial statements.**
10. **Understand how expense recognition choices and industry characteristics affect financial performance measures.**

Chapter 8

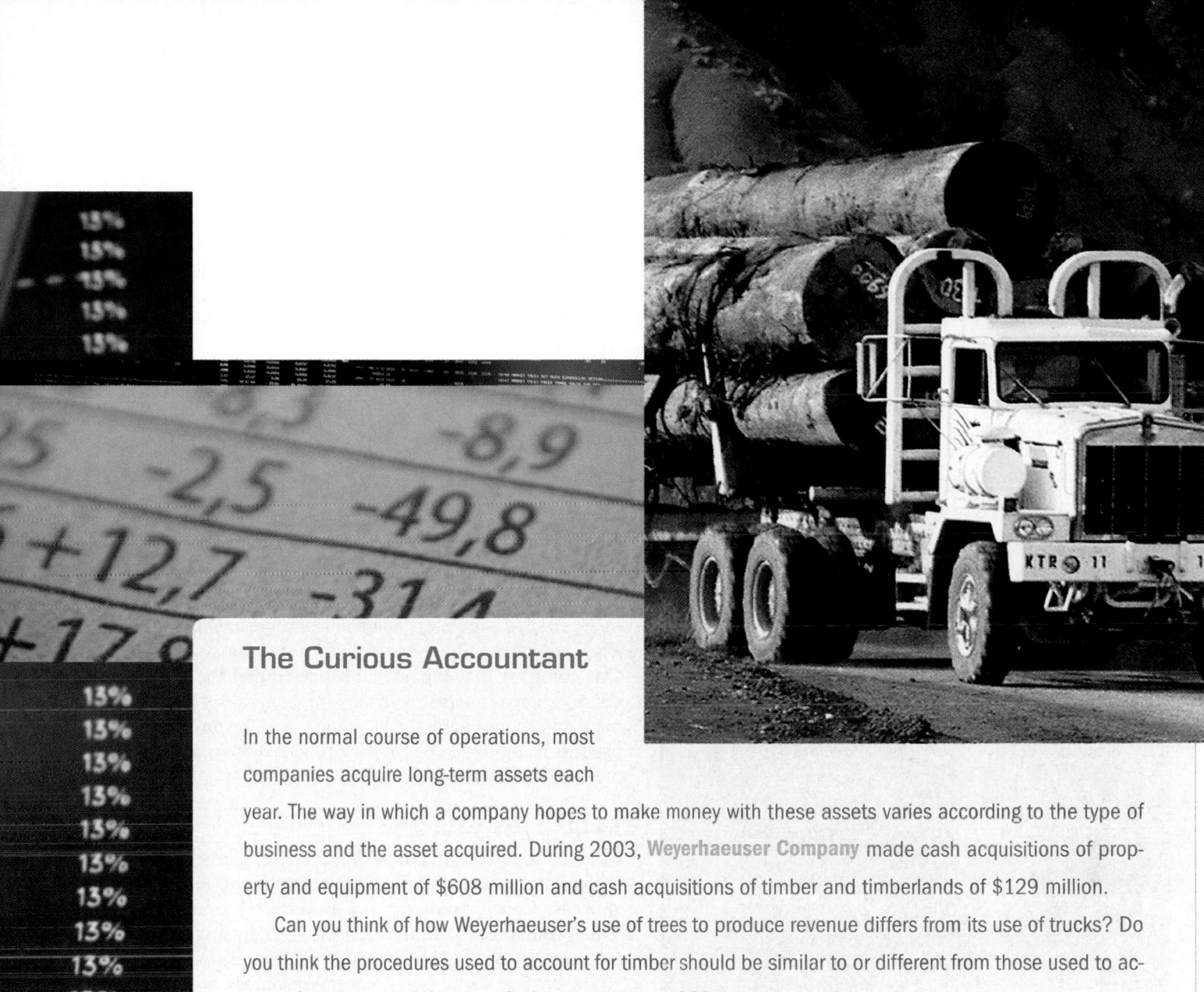

The Curious Accountant

In the normal course of operations, most companies acquire long-term assets each year. The way in which a company hopes to make money with these assets varies according to the type of business and the asset acquired. During 2003, **Weyerhaeuser Company** made cash acquisitions of property and equipment of $608 million and cash acquisitions of timber and timberlands of $129 million.

Can you think of how Weyerhaeuser's use of trees to produce revenue differs from its use of trucks? Do you think the procedures used to account for timber should be similar to or different from those used to account for trucks, and if so, how? (Answers on page 380.)

CHAPTER OPENING

Companies use assets to produce revenue. Some assets, like inventory or office supplies, are called **current assets** *because they are used relatively quickly (within a single accounting period). Other assets, like equipment or buildings, are used for extended periods of time (two or more accounting periods). These assets are called* **long-term operational assets.**[1] *Accounting for long-term assets raises several questions. For example, what is the cost of the asset? Is it the list price only or should the cost of transportation, transit insurance, setup, and so on be added to the list price? Should the cost of a long-term asset be recognized as expense in the period the asset is purchased or should the cost be expensed over the useful life of the asset? What happens in the accounting records when a long-term asset is retired from use? This chapter answers these questions. It explains accounting for long-term operational assets from the date of purchase through the date of disposal.* ■

[1] Classifying assets as current versus long term is explained in more detail in Chapter 9.

Tangible Versus Intangible Assets

LO 1

Identify different types of long-term operational assets.

Topic Tackler PLUS

8-1

Long-term assets may be tangible or intangible. **Tangible assets** have a physical presence; they can be seen and touched. Tangible assets include equipment, machinery, natural resources, and land. In contrast, intangible assets have no physical form. Although they may be represented by physical documents, **intangible assets** are, in fact, rights or privileges. They cannot be seen or touched. For example, a patent represents an exclusive legal *privilege* to produce and sell a particular product. It protects inventors by making it illegal for others to profit by copying their inventions. Although a patent may be represented by legal documents, the privilege is the actual asset. Since the privilege cannot be seen or touched, the patent is an intangible asset.

Tangible Long-Term Assets

Tangible long-term assets are classified as (1) property, plant, and equipment; (2) natural resources, or (3) land.

Property, Plant, and Equipment

Property, plant, and equipment is sometimes called *plant assets* or *fixed assets.* Examples of property, plant, and equipment include furniture, cash registers, machinery, delivery trucks, computers, mechanical robots, and buildings. The level of detail used to account for these assets varies. One company may include all office equipment in one account, whereas another company might divide office equipment into computers, desks, chairs, and so on. The term used to recognize expense for property, plant, and equipment is **depreciation.**

Natural Resources

Mineral deposits, oil and gas reserves, timber stands, coal mines, and stone quarries are examples of **natural resources.** Conceptually, natural resources are inventories. When sold, the cost of these assets is frequently expensed as *cost of goods sold.* Although inventories are usually classified as short-term assets, natural resources are normally classified as long term because the resource deposits generally have long lives. For example, it may take decades to extract all of the diamonds from a diamond mine. The term used to recognize expense for natural resources is **depletion.**

Land

Land is classified separately from other property because land is not subject to depreciation or depletion. Land has an infinite life. It is not worn out or consumed as it is used. When buildings or natural resources are purchased simultaneously with land, the amount paid must be divided between the land and the other assets because of the nondepreciable nature of the land.

Intangible Assets

Intangible assets fall into two categories, those with *identifiable useful lives* and those with *indefinite useful lives.*

Intangible Assets with Identifiable Useful Lives

Intangible assets with identifiable useful lives include patents and copyrights. These assets may become obsolete (a patent may become worthless if new technology provides a superior product) or may reach the end of their legal lives. The term used when recognizing expense for intangible assets with identifiable useful lives is called **amortization.**

Intangible Assets with Indefinite Useful Lives

The benefits of some intangible assets may extend so far into the future that their useful lives cannot be estimated. For how many years will the Coca-Cola trademark attract customers? When will the value of a McDonald's franchise end? There are no answers to these questions. Intangible assets such as renewable franchises, trademarks, and goodwill have indefinite useful lives. The costs of such assets are not expensed unless the value of the assets becomes impaired.

Determining the Cost of Long-Term Assets

LO 2

Determine the cost of long-term operational assets.

The **historical cost concept** requires that an asset be recorded at the amount paid for it. This amount includes the purchase price plus any costs necessary to get the asset in the location and condition for its intended use. Common cost components are:

- ***Buildings:*** (1) purchase price, (2) sales taxes, (3) title search and transfer document costs, (4) realtor's and attorney's fees, and (5) remodeling costs.
- ***Land:*** (1) purchase price, (2) sales taxes, (3) title search and transfer document costs, (4) realtor's and attorney's fees, (5) costs for removal of old buildings, and (6) grading costs.
- ***Equipment:*** (1) purchase price (less discounts), (2) sales taxes, (3) delivery costs, (4) installation costs, and (5) costs to adapt for intended use.

The cost of an asset does not include payments for fines, damages, and so on that could have been avoided.

CHECK YOURSELF 8.1

Sheridan Construction Company purchased a new bulldozer that had a $260,000 list price. The seller agreed to allow a 4 percent cash discount in exchange for immediate payment. The bulldozer was delivered FOB shipping point at a cost of $1,200. Sheridan hired a new employee to operate the dozer for an annual salary of $36,000. The employee was trained to operate the dozer for a onetime training fee of $800. The cost of the company's theft insurance policy increased by $300 per year as a result of adding the dozer to the policy. The dozer had a five-year useful life and an expected salvage value of $26,000. Determine the asset's cost.

Answer

List price	$260,000
Less: Cash discount ($260,000 × 0.04)	(10,400)
Shipping cost	1,200
Training cost	800
Total asset cost (amount capitalized)	$251,600

Basket Purchase Allocation

Acquiring a group of assets in a single transaction is known as a **basket purchase.** The total price of a basket purchase must be allocated among the assets acquired. Accountants commonly allocate the purchase price using the **relative fair market value method.** To illustrate, assume that Beatty Company purchased land and a building for $240,000 cash. A real estate appraiser determined the fair market value of each asset to be:

Building	$270,000
Land	90,000
Total	$360,000

The appraisal indicates that the land is worth 25 percent ($90,000 ÷ $360,000) of the total value and the building is worth 75 percent ($270,000 ÷ $360,000). Using these percentages, the actual purchase price is allocated as follows:

Topic Tackler PLUS

8-2

Building	0.75 × $240,000 =	$180,000
Land	0.25 × $240,000 =	60,000
Total		$240,000

Methods of Recognizing Depreciation Expense

LO 3

Explain how different depreciation methods affect financial statements.

The life cycle of an operational asset involves (1) acquiring the funds to buy the asset, (2) purchasing the asset, (3) using the asset, and (4) retiring (disposing of) the asset. These stages are illustrated in Exhibit 8.1. The stages involving (1) acquiring funds and (2) purchasing assets have been discussed previously. This section of the chapter describes how accountants recognize the *use* of assets (Stage 3). As they are used, assets suffer from wear and tear called *depreciation.* Ultimately, assets depreciate to the point that they are no longer useful in the process of earning revenue. This process usually takes several years. The amount of an asset's cost that is allocated to expense during an accounting period is called **depreciation expense.**

EXHIBIT 8.1

Life Cycle of an Operational Asset

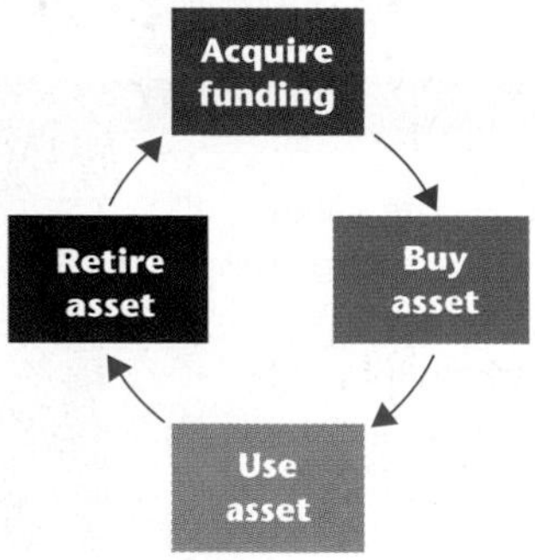

An asset that is fully depreciated by one company may still be useful to another company. For example, a rental car that is no longer useful to Hertz may still be useful to a local delivery company. As a result, companies are frequently able to sell their fully depreciated assets to other companies or individuals. The expected market value of a fully depreciated asset is called its **salvage value.** The total amount of depreciation a company recognizes for an asset, its **depreciable cost,** is the difference between its original cost and its salvage value.

For example, assume a company purchases an asset for $5,000. The company expects to use the asset for 5 years (the **estimated useful life**) and then to sell it for $1,000 (salvage value). The depreciable cost of the asset is $4,000 ($5,000 − $1,000). The portion of the depreciable cost ($4,000) that represents its annual usage is recognized as depreciation expense.

Accountants must exercise judgment to estimate the amount of depreciation expense to recognize each period. For example, suppose you own a personal computer. You know how much the computer cost, and you know you will eventually need to replace it. How would you determine the amount the computer depreciates each year you use it? Businesses may use any of several acceptable methods to estimate the amount of depreciation expense to recognize each year.

EXHIBIT 8.2

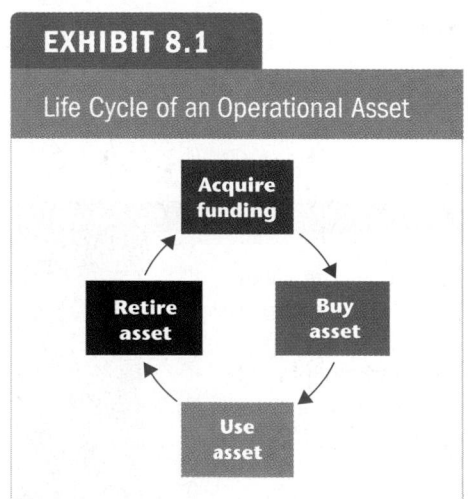

Depreciation Methods Used by U.S. Companies

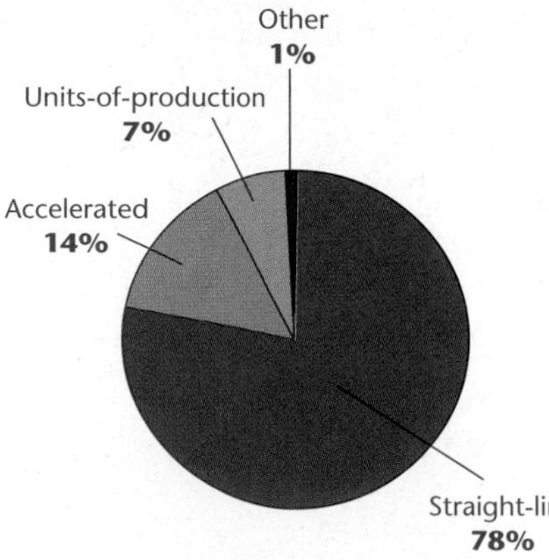

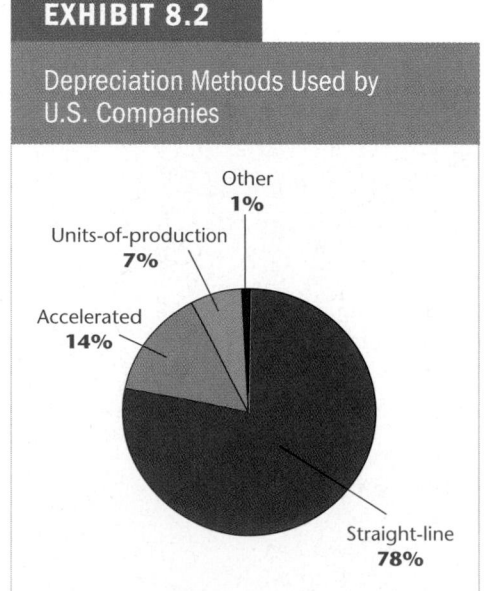

Data source: AICPA Accounting Trends and Techniques, 2002.

The method used to recognize depreciation expense should match the asset's usage pattern. More expense should be recognized in periods when the asset is used more and less in periods when the asset is used less. Since assets are used to produce revenue, matching expense recognition with asset usage also matches expense recognition with revenue recognition. Three alternative methods for recognizing depreciation expense are (1) straight-line, (2) double-declining-balance, and (3) units-of-production.

The *straight-line* method produces the same amount of depreciation expense each accounting period. *Double-declining-balance,* an accelerated method, produces more depreciation expense in the early years of an asset's life, with a declining amount of expense in later years. *Units-of-production* produces varying amounts of depreciation expense in different accounting periods (more in some accounting periods and less in others). Exhibit 8.2 contrasts the different depreciation methods that U.S. companies use.

Answers to The Curious Accountant

Equipment is a long-term asset used for the purpose of producing revenue. A portion of the equipment's cost is recognized as depreciation expense each accounting period. The expense recognition for the cost of equipment is therefore spread over the useful life of the asset. Timber, however, is not used until the trees are grown. Conceptually, the costs of the trees should be treated as inventories and expensed as cost of goods sold at the time the products made from trees are sold. Even so, some timber companies recognize a periodic charge called *depletion* in a manner similar to that used for depreciation.

Accounting for unusual long-term assets such as timber requires an understanding of specialized "industry practice" accounting rules that are beyond the scope of this course. Many industries have unique accounting problems, and business managers in such industries must understand specialized accounting rules that relate to their companies.

Dryden Enterprises Illustration

To illustrate the different depreciation methods, consider a van purchased by Dryden Enterprises. Dryden plans to use the van as rental property. The van had a list price of $23,500. Dryden obtained a 10 percent cash discount from the dealer. The van was delivered FOB shipping point, and Dryden paid an additional $250 for transportation costs. Dryden also paid $2,600 for a custom accessory package to increase the van's appeal as a rental vehicle. The cost of the van is computed as follows:

List price	$23,500	
Less: Cash discount	(2,350)	$23,500 × 0.10
Plus: Transportation costs	250	
Plus: Cost of customization	2,600	
Total	$24,000	

The van has an estimated *salvage value* of $4,000 and an *estimated useful life* of four years. The following section examines three different patterns of expense recognition for this van.

Straight-Line Depreciation

The first scenario assumes the van is used evenly over its four-year life. The revenue from renting the van is assumed to be $8,000 per year. The matching concept calls for the expense recognition pattern to match the revenue stream. Since the same amount of revenue is recognized in each accounting period, Dryden should use **straight-line depreciation** because it produces equal amounts of depreciation expense each year.

Life Cycle Phase 1

The first phase of the asset life cycle is to acquire funds to purchase the asset. Assume Dryden acquired $25,000 cash on January 1, 2005, by issuing common stock. The journal entry and its effects on the financial statements follow:

Account Title	Debit	Credit
Cash	25,000	
Common Stock		25,000

Assets					=	Equity			Rev.	−	Exp.	=	Net Inc.	Cash Flow
Cash	+	Van	−	Acc. Dep.	=	Com. Stk.	+	Ret. Earn.						
25,000	+	NA	−	NA	=	25,000	+	NA	NA	−	NA	=	NA	25,000 FA

Life Cycle Phase 2

The second phase of the life cycle is to purchase the van. Assume Dryden bought the van on January 1, 2005, using funds from the stock issue. The cost of the van, previously computed, was $24,000 cash. The journal entry and its effects on the financial statements are:

Account Title	Debit	Credit
Van	24,000	
Cash		24,000

Assets							=	Equity			Rev.	−	Exp.	=	Net Inc.	Cash Flow
Cash	+	Van	−	Acc. Dep.	=	Com. Stk.	+	Ret. Earn.								
(24,000)	+	24,000	−	NA	=	NA	+	NA			NA	−	NA	=	NA	(24,000) IA

Life Cycle Phase 3

Dryden used the van by renting it to customers. The rent revenue each year is $8,000 cash. The annual journal entry and its effects on the financial statements are shown next:

Account Title	Debit	Credit
Cash	8,000	
Rent Revenue		8,000

Assets							=	Equity	Rev.	−	Exp.	=	Net Inc.	Cash Flow
Cash	+	Van	−	Acc. Dep.	=	Com. Stk.	+	Ret. Earn.						
8,000	+	NA	−	NA	=	NA	+	8,000	8,000	−	NA	=	8,000	8,000 OA

Although illustrated only once, these effects occur four times—once for each year Dryden earns revenue by renting the van.

At the end of each year, Dryden adjusts its accounts to recognize depreciation expense. The amount of depreciation recognized using the straight-line method is calculated as follows:

$$\text{(Asset cost} - \text{Salvage value)} \div \text{Useful life} = \text{Depreciation expense}$$

$$(\$24{,}000 - \$4{,}000) \div 4 \text{ years} = \$5{,}000 \text{ per year.}$$

Recognizing depreciation expense is an asset use transaction that reduces assets and equity. The asset reduction is reported using a **contra asset account** called **Accumulated Depreciation.** Recognizing depreciation expense *does not affect cash flow.* The entire cash outflow for this asset occurred in January 2005 when Dryden purchased the van. Depreciation reflects *using* tangible assets, not spending cash to purchase them. The journal entry and its effects on the financial statements are as follows:

Account Title	Debit	Credit
Depreciation Expense	5,000	
Accumulated Depreciation		5,000

Assets							=	Equity			Rev.	−	Exp.	=	Net Inc.	Cash Flow
Cash	+	Van	−	Acc. Dep.	=	Com. Stk.	+	Ret. Earn.								
NA	+	NA	−	5,000	=	NA	+	(5,000)			NA	−	5,000	=	(5,000)	NA

Although illustrated only once, these effects occur four times—once for each year Dryden uses the asset.

The Depreciation *Expense* account, like other expense accounts, is closed to the Retained Earnings account at the end of each year. The *Accumulated* Depreciation account, in contrast, increases each year, *accumulating* the total amount of depreciation recognized on the asset to date.

Life Cycle Phase 4

LO 4

Determine how gains and losses on disposals of long-term operational assets affect financial statements.

The final stage in the life cycle of a tangible asset is its disposal and removal from the company's records. Dryden retired the van from service on January 1, 2009, selling it for $4,500 cash. The van's **book value** (cost − accumulated depreciation) when it was sold was $4,000 ($24,000 cost − $20,000 accumulated depreciation), so Dryden recognized a $500 gain ($4,500 − $4,000) on the sale.

Gains are *like* revenues in that they increase assets or decrease liabilities. Gains are *unlike* revenues in that gains result from peripheral (incidental) transactions rather than routine operating activities. Dryden is not in the business of selling vans. Dryden's normal business activity is renting vans. Since selling vans is incidental to Dryden's normal operations, gains are reported separately, after operating income, on the income statement.

If Dryden had sold the asset for less than book value, the company would have recognized a loss on the asset disposal. Losses are similar to expenses in that they decrease assets or increase liabilities. However, like gains, losses result from peripheral transactions. Losses are also reported as nonoperating items on the income statement.

The journal entry to record the asset disposal and its effects on the financial statements are shown next:

Account Title	Debit	Credit
Cash	4,500	
Accumulated Depreciation	20,000	
Van		24,000
Gain on Sale of Van		500

Assets					=	Equity			Rev. or Gain	−	Exp. or Loss	=	Net Inc.	Cash Flow
Cash	+	Van	−	Acc. Dep.	=	Com. Stk.	+	Ret. Earn.						
4,500	+	(24,000)	−	(20,000)	=	NA	+	500	500	−	NA	=	500	4,500 IA

Although the gain reported on the 2009 income statement is $500, the cash inflow from selling the van is $4,500. Gains and losses are not reported on the statement of cash flows. Instead they are included in the total amount of cash collected from the sale of the asset. In this case, the entire $4,500 is shown in the cash flow from investing activities section of the 2009 statement of cash flows.

Financial Statements

Exhibit 8.3 displays a vertical statements model that shows the financial results for the Dryden illustration from 2005 through 2009. Study the exhibit until you understand how all the

EXHIBIT 8.3 Financial Statements under Straight-Line Depreciation

DRYDEN ENTERPRISES
Financial Statements

	2005	2006	2007	2008	2009
Income Statements					
Rent Revenue	$ 8,000	$ 8,000	$ 8,000	$ 8,000	$ 0
Depreciation Expense	(5,000)	(5,000)	(5,000)	(5,000)	0
Operating Income	3,000	3,000	3,000	3,000	0
Gain on Sale of Van	0	0	0	0	500
Net Income	$ 3,000	$ 3,000	$ 3,000	$ 3,000	$ 500
Balance Sheets					
Assets					
Cash	$ 9,000	$17,000	$25,000	$33,000	$37,500
Van	24,000	24,000	24,000	24,000	0
Accumulated Depreciation	(5,000)	(10,000)	(15,000)	(20,000)	0
Total Assets	$28,000	$31,000	$34,000	$37,000	$37,500
Stockholders' Equity					
Common Stock	$25,000	$25,000	$25,000	$25,000	$25,000
Retained Earnings	3,000	6,000	9,000	12,000	12,500
Total Stockholders' Equity	$28,000	$31,000	$34,000	$37,000	$37,500
Statements of Cash Flows					
Operating Activities					
Inflow from Customers	$ 8,000	$ 8,000	$ 8,000	$ 8,000	$ 0
Investing Activities					
Outflow to Purchase Van	(24,000)				
Inflow from Sale of Van					4,500
Financing Activities					
Inflow from Stock Issue	25,000				
Net Change in Cash	9,000	8,000	8,000	8,000	4,500
Beginning Cash Balance	0	9,000	17,000	25,000	33,000
Ending Cash Balance	$9,000	$17,000	$25,000	$33,000	$37,500

figures were derived. The amount of depreciation expense ($5,000) reported on the income statement is constant each year from 2005 through 2008. The amount of accumulated depreciation reported on the balance sheet grows from $5,000 to $10,000, to $15,000, and finally to $20,000. The Accumulated Depreciation account is a *contra asset account* that is subtracted from the Van account in determining total assets.

Study the timing differences between cash flow and net income. Dryden spent $24,000 cash to acquire the van. Over the van's life cycle, Dryden collected $36,500 [($8,000 revenue × 4 years = $32,000) plus ($4,500 from the asset disposal) = $36,500]. The $12,500 difference between the cash collected and the cash paid ($36,500 − $24,000) equals the total net income earned during the van's life cycle.

Although the amounts are the same, the timing of the cash flows and the income recognition are different. For example, in 2005 there was a $24,000 cash outflow to purchase the van and an $8,000 cash inflow from customers. In contrast, the income statement reports net income of $3,000. In 2009, Dryden reported a $500 gain on the asset disposal, but the amount of operating income and the cash flow from operating activities is zero for that year. The gain is only indirectly related to cash flows. The $4,500 of cash received on disposal is reported as a cash inflow from investing activities. Since gains and losses result from peripheral transactions, they do not affect operating income or cash flow from operating activities.

Double-Declining-Balance Depreciation

LO 3

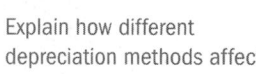

Explain how different depreciation methods affect financial statements.

For the second scenario, assume demand for the van is strong when it is new, but fewer people rent the van as it ages. As a result, the van produces smaller amounts of revenue as time goes by. To match expenses with revenues, it is reasonable to recognize more depreciation expense in the van's early years and less as it ages.

Double-declining-balance depreciation produces a large amount of depreciation in the first year of an asset's life and progressively smaller levels of expense in each succeeding year. Since the double-declining-balance method recognizes depreciation expense more rapidly than the straight-line method does, it is called an **accelerated depreciation method.** Depreciation expense recognized using double-declining-balance is computed in three steps.

1. *Determine the straight-line rate.* Divide one by the asset's useful life. Since the estimated useful life of Dryden's van is four years, the straight-line rate is 25 percent (1 ÷ 4) per year.
2. *Determine the double-declining-balance rate.* Multiply the straight-line rate by 2 (*double* the rate). The double-declining-balance rate for the van is 50 percent (25 percent × 2).
3. *Determine the depreciation expense.* Multiply the double-declining-balance rate by the book value of the asset *at the beginning of the period* (recall that book value is historical cost minus *accumulated depreciation*). The following table shows the amount of depreciation expense Dryden will recognize over the van's useful life (2005–2008).

Year	Book Value at Beginning of Period	×	Double the Straight-Line Rate	=	Annual Depreciation Expense	
2005	($24,000 − $ 0)	×	0.50	=	$12,000	
2006	(24,000 − 12,000)	×	0.50	=	6,000	
2007	(24,000 − 18,000)	×	0.50	=	~~3,000~~	2,000
2008	(24,000 − 20,000)	×	0.50	=	~~2,000~~	0

Regardless of the depreciation method used, *an asset cannot be depreciated below its salvage value.* This restriction affects depreciation computations for the third and fourth years. Because the van had a cost of $24,000 and a salvage value of $4,000, the total amount of depreciable cost (historical cost − salvage value) is $20,000 ($24,000 − $4,000). Since $18,000 ($12,000 + $6,000) of the depreciable cost is recognized in the first two years, only $2,000 ($20,000 − $18,000) remains to be recognized after the second year. Depreciation expense recognized in the third year is therefore $2,000 even though double-declining-balance computations suggest that $3,000 should be recognized. Similarly, zero depreciation expense is recognized in the fourth year even though the computations indicate a $2,000 charge.

EXHIBIT 8.4 Financial Statements under Double-Declining-Balance Depreciation

DRYDEN ENTERPRISES Financial Statements					
	2005	**2006**	**2007**	**2008**	**2009**
Income Statements					
Rent Revenue	$15,000	$ 9,000	$ 5,000	$ 3,000	$ 0
Depreciation Expense	(12,000)	(6,000)	(2,000)	0	0
Operating Income	3,000	3,000	3,000	3,000	0
Gain on Sale of Van	0	0	0	0	500
Net Income	$ 3,000	$ 3,000	$ 3,000	$ 3,000	$ 500
[redacted]					
Assets					
Cash	$16,000	$25,000	$30,000	$33,000	$37,500
Van	24,000	24,000	24,000	24,000	0
Accumulated Depreciation	(12,000)	(18,000)	(20,000)	(20,000)	0
Total Assets	$28,000	$31,000	$34,000	$37,000	$37,500
Stockholders' Equity					
Common Stock	$25,000	$25,000	$25,000	$25,000	$25,000
Retained Earnings	3,000	6,000	9,000	12,000	12,500
Total Stockholders' Equity	$28,000	$31,000	$34,000	$37,000	$37,500
Statements of Cash Flows					
Operating Activities					
Inflow from Customers	$15,000	$ 9,000	$ 5,000	$ 3,000	$ 0
Investing Activities					
Outflow to Purchase Van	(24,000)				
Inflow from Sale of Van					4,500
Financing Activities					
Inflow from Stock Issue	25,000				
Net Change in Cash	16,000	9,000	5,000	3,000	4,500
Beginning Cash Balance	0	16,000	25,000	30,000	33,000
Ending Cash Balance	$16,000	$25,000	$30,000	$33,000	$37,500

Effects on the Financial Statements

Exhibit 8.4 displays financial statements for the life of the asset assuming Dryden uses double-declining-balance depreciation. The illustration assumes a cash revenue stream of $15,000, $9,000, $5,000, and $3,000 for the years 2005, 2006, 2007, and 2008, respectively. Trace the depreciation expense from the table above to the income statements. Reported depreciation expense is greater in the earlier years and smaller in the later years of the asset's life.

The double-declining-balance method smoothes the amount of net income reported over the asset's useful life. In the early years, when heavy asset use produces higher revenue, depreciation expense is also higher. Similarly, in the later years, lower levels of revenue are matched with lower levels of depreciation expense. Net income is constant at $3,000 per year.

CHECK YOURSELF 8.2

Olds Company purchased an asset that cost $36,000 on January 1, 2005. The asset had an expected useful life of five years and an estimated salvage value of $5,000. Assuming Olds uses the double-declining-balance method, determine the amount of depreciation expense and the amount of accumulated depreciation Olds would report on the 2007 financial statements.

Answer

Year	Book Value at Beginning of Period	×	Double the Straight-Line Rate*	=	Annual Depreciation Expense
2005	($36,000 − $ 0)	×	0.40	=	$14,400
2006	(36,000 − 14,400)	×	0.40	=	8,640
2007	(36,000 − 23,040)	×	0.40	=	5,184
Total accumulated depreciation at December 31, 2007					$28,224

*Double-declining-balance rate = 2 × Straight-line rate = 2 × (1 ÷ 5 years) = 0.40

The depreciation method a company uses *does not* affect how it acquires the financing, invests the funds, and retires the asset. For Dryden's van, the accounting effects of these life cycle phases are the same as under the straight-line approach. Similarly, the *recording procedures* are not affected by the depreciation method. Different depreciation methods affect only the amounts of depreciation expense recorded each year, not which accounts are used. The general journal entries are therefore not illustrated for the double-declining-balance or the units-of-production depreciation methods.

Units-of-Production Depreciation

LO 3

Explain how different depreciation methods affect financial statements.

Suppose rental demand for Dryden's van depends on general economic conditions. In a robust economy, travel increases, and demand for renting vans is high. In a stagnant economy, demand for van rentals declines. In such circumstances, revenues fluctuate from year to year. To accomplish the matching objective, depreciation should also fluctuate from year to year. A method of depreciation known as **units-of-production depreciation** accomplishes this goal by basing depreciation expense on actual asset usage.

Computing depreciation expense using units-of-production begins with identifying a measure of the asset's productive capacity. For example, the number of miles Dryden expects its van to be driven may be a reasonable measure of its productive capacity. If the depreciable asset were a saw, an appropriate measure of productive capacity could be the number of board feet the saw was expected to cut during its useful life. In other words, the basis for measuring production depends on the nature of the depreciable asset.

To illustrate computing depreciation using the units-of-production depreciation method, assume that Dryden measures productive capacity based on the total number of miles the van will be driven over its useful life. Assume Dryden estimates this productive capacity to be 100,000 miles. The first step in determining depreciation expense is to compute the cost per unit of production. For Dryden's van, this amount is total depreciable cost (historical cost − salvage value) divided by total units of expected productive capacity (100,000 miles). The depreciation cost per mile is therefore $0.20 ([$24,000 cost − $4,000 salvage] ÷ 100,000 miles). Annual depreciation expense is computed by multiplying the cost per mile by the number of miles driven. Odometer readings indicate the van was driven 40,000 miles, 20,000 miles, 30,000 miles, and 15,000 miles in 2005, 2006, 2007, and 2008, respectively. Dryden developed the following schedule of depreciation charges.

Year	Cost per Mile (a)	Miles Driven (b)	Depreciation Expense (a × b)
2005	$.20	40,000	$8,000
2006	.20	20,000	4,000
2007	.20	30,000	6,000
2008	.20	15,000	~~3,000~~ 2,000

As pointed out in the discussion of the double-declining-balance method, an asset cannot be depreciated below its salvage value. Since $18,000 of the $20,000 ($24,000 cost − $4,000 salvage) depreciable cost is recognized in the first three years of using the van, only $2,000 ($20,000 − $18,000) remains to be charged to depreciation in the fourth year, even though the depreciation computations suggest the charge should be $3,000. As the preceding table indicates, the general formula for computing units-of-production depreciation is:

$$\frac{\text{Cost} - \text{Salvage value}}{\text{Total estimated units of production}} \times \begin{array}{c}\text{Units of production}\\ \text{in current}\\ \text{year}\end{array} = \begin{array}{c}\text{Annual}\\ \text{depreciation}\\ \text{expense}\end{array}$$

Exhibit 8.5 displays financial statements that assume Dryden uses units-of-production depreciation. The exhibit assumes a cash revenue stream of $11,000, $7,000, $9,000, and $5,000 for 2005, 2006, 2007, and 2008, respectively. Trace the depreciation expense from the schedule above to the income statements. Depreciation expense is greater in years the van is driven more and smaller in years the van is driven less, providing a reasonable matching of depreciation expense with revenue produced. Net income is again constant at $3,000 per year.

Comparing the Depreciation Methods

LO 3

Explain how different depreciation methods affect financial statements.

The total amount of depreciation expense Dryden recognized using each of the three methods was $20,000 ($24,000 cost − $4,000 salvage value). The different methods affect the *timing,* but not the *total amount,* of expense recognized. The different methods simply assign the $20,000 to different accounting periods. Exhibit 8.6 presents graphically the differences among the three depreciation methods discussed above. A company should use the method that most closely matches expenses with revenues.

EXHIBIT 8.6

Depreciation Expense under Different Depreciation Methods

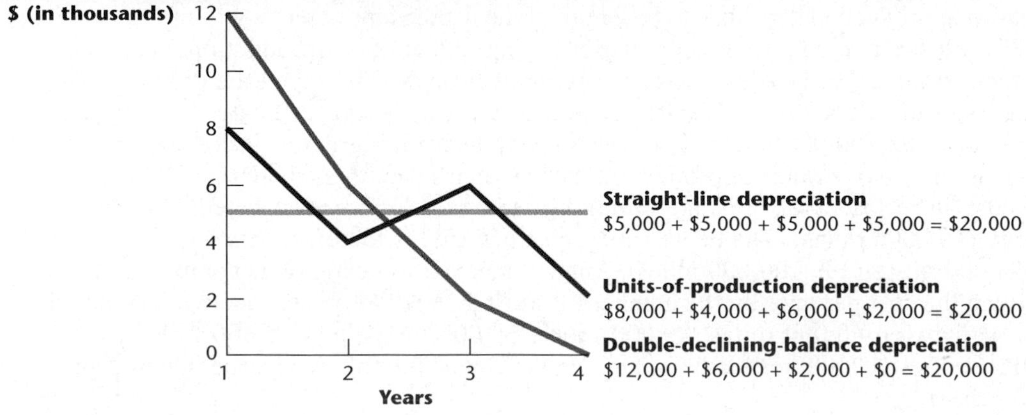

EXHIBIT 8.5 Financial Statements under Units-of-Production Depreciation

DRYDEN ENTERPRISES
Financial Statements

	2005	2006	2007	2008	2009
Income Statements					
Rent Revenue	$11,000	$ 7,000	$ 9,000	$ 5,000	$ 0
Depreciation Expense	(8,000)	(4,000)	(6,000)	(2,000)	0
Operating Income	3,000	3,000	3,000	3,000	0
Gain on Sale of Van	0	0	0	0	500
Net Income	$ 3,000	$ 3,000	$ 3,000	$ 3,000	$ 500
Balance Sheets					
Assets					
Cash	$12,000	$19,000	$28,000	$33,000	$37,500
Van	24,000	24,000	24,000	24,000	0
Accumulated Depreciation	(8,000)	(12,000)	(18,000)	(20,000)	0
Total Assets	$28,000	$31,000	$34,000	$37,000	$37,500
Stockholders' Equity					
Common Stock	$25,000	$25,000	$25,000	$25,000	$25,000
Retained Earnings	3,000	6,000	9,000	12,000	12,500
Total Stockholders' Equity	$28,000	$31,000	$34,000	$37,000	$37,500
Statements of Cash Flows					
Operating Activities					
Inflow from Customers	$11,000	$ 7,000	$ 9,000	$ 5,000	$ 0
Investing Activities					
Outflow to Purchase Van	(24,000)				
Inflow from Sale of Van					4,500
Financing Activities					
Inflow from Stock Issue	25,000				
Net Change in Cash	12,000	7,000	9,000	5,000	4,500
Beginning Cash Balance	0	12,000	19,000	28,000	33,000
Ending Cash Balance	$12,000	$19,000	$28,000	$33,000	$37,500

Income Tax Considerations

LO 5

Identify some of the tax issues that affect long-term operational assets.

The matching principle is not relevant to income tax reporting. The objective of tax reporting is to minimize tax expense. For tax purposes the most desirable depreciation method is the one that produces the highest amount of depreciation expense. Higher expenses mean lower taxes.

The maximum depreciation currently allowed by tax law is computed using an accelerated depreciation method known as the **modified accelerated cost recovery system (MACRS).** MACRS specifies the useful life for designated categories of assets. For example, under the law, companies must base depreciation computations for automobiles, light trucks, technological equipment, and other similar asset types on a 5-year useful life. In contrast, a 7-year life must be used for office furniture, fixtures, and many types of conventional machinery. The law classifies depreciable property, excluding real estate, into one of six categories: 3-year property, 5-year property, 7-year property, 10-year property, 15-year property, and 20-year property. Tables have been established for each category that specify the percentage of cost that can be expensed (deducted) in determining the amount of taxable income. A tax table for 5- and 7-year property is shown here as an example.

Year	5-Year Property, %	7-Year Property, %
1	20.00	14.29
2	32.00	24.49
3	19.20	17.49
4	11.52	12.49
5	11.52	8.93
6	5.76	8.92
7		8.93
8		4.46

The amount of depreciation a company can deduct each year for tax purposes is determined by multiplying the cost of a depreciable asset by the percentage shown in the table. For example, the depreciation expense for year 1 of a 7-year property asset is the cost of the asset multiplied by 14.29 percent. Depreciation for year 2 is the cost multiplied by 24.49 percent.

The tables present some apparent inconsistencies. For example, if MACRS is an accelerated depreciation method, why is less depreciation permitted in year 1 than in years 2 and 3? Also, why is depreciation computed in year 6 for property with a 5-year life and in year 8 for property with a 7-year life? These conditions are the consequence of using the **half-year convention.**

The half-year convention is designed to simplify computing taxable income. Instead of requiring taxpayers to calculate depreciation from the exact date of purchase to the exact date of disposal, the tax code requires one-half year's depreciation to be charged in the year in which an asset is acquired and one-half year's depreciation in the year of disposal. As a result, the percentages shown in the table for the first and last years represent depreciation for one-half year instead of the actual time of usage.

To illustrate computing depreciation using MACRS, assume that Wilson Company purchased furniture (7-year property) for $10,000 cash on July 21. Tax depreciation charges over the useful life of the asset are computed as shown:

Year	Table Factor, %	×	Cost	=	Depreciation Amount
1	14.29		$10,000		$ 1,429
2	24.49		10,000		2,449
3	17.49		10,000		1,749
4	12.49		10,000		1,249
5	8.93		10,000		893
6	8.92		10,000		892
7	8.93		10,000		893
8	4.46		10,000		446
Total over useful life					$10,000

As an alternative to MACRS, the tax code permits using straight-line depreciation. For certain types of assets such as real property (buildings), the tax code requires using straight-line depreciation.

There is no requirement that depreciation methods used for financial reporting be consistent with those used in preparing the income tax return. For example, a company may use straight-line depreciation in its financial statements and MACRS for the tax return. A company making this choice would reduce taxes in the early years of an asset's life because it would report higher depreciation charges on the tax return than in the financial statements. In later years, however, taxes will be higher because under MACRS, the amount of depreciation declines as the asset becomes older. Taxes are delayed but not avoided. The amount of taxes delayed for future payment represent a **deferred tax liability.** Delaying tax payments is advantageous. During the delay period, the money that would have been used to pay taxes can be used instead to make revenue-generating investments.

Revision of Estimates

LO 6

Show how revising estimates affects financial statements.

In order to report useful financial information on a timely basis, accountants must make many estimates of future results, such as the salvage value and useful life of depreciable assets and uncollectible accounts expense. Estimates are frequently revised when new information surfaces. Because revisions of estimates are common, generally accepted accounting principles call for incorporating the revised information into present and future calculations. Prior reports are not corrected.

To illustrate, assume that McGraw Company purchased a machine on January 1, 2003, for $50,000. McGraw estimated the machine would have a useful life of eight years and a salvage value of $3,000. Using the straight-line method, McGraw determined the annual depreciation charge as follows:

$$(\$50{,}000 - \$3{,}000) \div 8 \text{ years} = \$5{,}875 \text{ per year}$$

At the beginning of the fifth year, accumulated depreciation on the machine is $23,500 ($5,875 × 4). The machine's book value is $26,500 ($50,000 − $23,500). At this point, what happens if McGraw changes its estimates of useful life or the salvage value? Consider the following revision examples independently of each other.

Revision of Life

Assume McGraw revises the expected life to 14, rather than 8, years. The machine's *remaining* life would then be 10 more years instead of 4 more years. Assume salvage value remains $3,000. Depreciation for each remaining year is:

$$(\$26{,}500 \text{ book value} - \$3{,}000 \text{ salvage}) \div 10\text{-year remaining life} = \$2{,}350$$

Revision of Salvage

Alternatively, assume the original expected life remained eight years, but McGraw revised its estimate of salvage value to $6,000. Depreciation for each of the remaining four years would be

$$(\$26{,}500 \text{ book value} - \$6{,}000 \text{ salvage}) \div 4\text{-year remaining life} = \$5{,}125$$

The revised amounts are determined for the full year, regardless of when McGraw revised its estimates. For example, if McGraw decides to change the estimated useful life on October 1, 2008, the change would be effective as of January 1, 2008. The year-end adjusting entry for depreciation would include a full year's depreciation calculated on the basis of the revised estimated useful life.

Continuing Expenditures for Plant Assets

LO 7

Explain how continuing expenditures for operational assets affect financial statements.

Most plant assets require additional expenditures for maintenance or improvement during their useful lives. Accountants must determine if these expenditures should be expensed or capitalized (recorded as assets).

Costs that Are Expensed

The costs of routine maintenance and minor repairs that are incurred to *keep* an asset in good working order are expensed in the period in which they are incurred. Because they reduce net income when incurred, accountants often call repair and maintenance costs **revenue expenditures** (companies subtract them from revenue).

With respect to the previous example, assume McGraw spent $500 for routine lubrication and to replace minor parts. The effect of the expenditure on the financial statements and the journal entry necessary to record it follow:

Assets	=	Equity			Rev. − Exp. = Net Inc.					Cash Flow
Cash	=	Com. Stk.	+	Ret. Earn.						
(500)	=	NA	+	(500)	NA	−	500	=	(500)	(500) OA

Account Title	Debit	Credit
Repairs Expense	500	
Cash		500

Costs that Are Capitalized

Substantial amounts spent to improve the quality or extend the life of an asset are described as **capital expenditures.** Capital expenditures are accounted for in one of two ways, depending on whether the cost incurred *improves the quality* or *extends the life* of the asset.

Improving Quality

Expenditures such as adding air conditioning to an existing building or installing a trailer hitch on a vehicle improve the quality of service these assets provide. If a capital expenditure improves an asset's quality, the amount is added to the historical cost of the asset. The additional cost is expensed through higher depreciation charges over the asset's remaining useful life.

To demonstrate, return to the McGraw Company example. Recall that the machine originally cost $50,000, had an estimated salvage of $3,000, and had a predicted life of eight years. Recall further that accumulated depreciation at the beginning of the fifth year is $23,500 ($5,875 × 4) so the book value is $26,500 ($50,000 − $23,500). Assume McGraw makes a major expenditure of $4,000 in the machine's fifth year to improve its productive capacity. The effect of the $4,000 expenditure on the financial statements and the journal entry necessary to record it follow:

Assets					=	Equity			Rev. − Exp. = Net Inc.					Cash Flow
Cash	+	Mach.	−	Acc. Dep.	=	Com. Stk.	+	Ret. Earn.						
(4,000)	+	4,000	−	NA	=	NA	+	NA	NA	−	NA	=	NA	(4,000) IA

Account Title	Debit	Credit
Machine	4,000	
Cash		4,000

After recording the expenditure, the machine account balance is $54,000 and the asset's book value is $30,500 ($54,000 − $23,500). The depreciation charges for each of the remaining four years are:

($30,500 book value − $3,000 salvage) ÷ 4-year remaining life = $6,875

Extending Life

Expenditures such as replacing the roof of an existing building or putting a new engine in an older vehicle extend the useful life of these assets. If a capital expenditure extends the life of an asset rather than improving the asset's quality of service, accountants view the expenditure as canceling some of the depreciation previously charged to expense. The event is still an asset exchange; cash decreases, and the book value of the machine increases. However, the increase in the book value of the machine results from reducing the balance in the contra asset account, Accumulated Depreciation.

To illustrate, assume that instead of increasing productive capacity, McGraw's $4,000 expenditure had extended the useful life of the machine by two years. The effect of the expenditure on the financial statements and the journal entry necessary to record it follow:

Assets					=	Equity			Rev.	−	Exp.	=	Net Inc.	Cash Flow
Cash	+	Mach.	−	Acc. Dep.	=	Com. Stk.	+	Ret. Earn.						
(4,000)	+	NA	−	(4,000)	=	NA	+	NA	NA	−	NA	=	NA	(4,000) IA

Account Title	Debit	Credit
Accumulated Depreciation—Machine	4,000	
Cash		4,000

After the expenditure is recorded, the book value is the same as if the $4,000 had been added to the Machine account ($50,000 cost − $19,500 adjusted balance in Accumulated Depreciation = $30,500). Depreciation expense for each of the remaining six years follows:

($30,500 book value − $3,000 salvage) ÷ 6-year remaining life = $4,583

CHECK YOURSELF 8.3

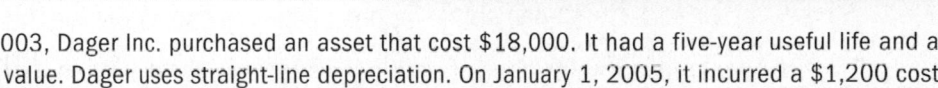

On January 1, 2003, Dager Inc. purchased an asset that cost $18,000. It had a five-year useful life and a $3,000 salvage value. Dager uses straight-line depreciation. On January 1, 2005, it incurred a $1,200 cost related to the asset. With respect to this asset, determine the amount of expense and accumulated depreciation Dager would report in the 2005 financial statements under each of the following assumptions.

1. The $1,200 cost was incurred to repair damage resulting from an accident.
2. The $1,200 cost improved the operating capacity of the asset. The total useful life and salvage value remained unchanged.
3. The $1,200 cost extended the useful life of the asset by one year. The salvage value remained unchanged.

Answer

1. Dager would report the $1,200 repair cost as an expense. Dager would also report depreciation expense of $3,000 ([$18,000 − $3,000] ÷ 5). Total expenses related to this asset in 2005 would be $4,200 ($1,200 repair expense + $3,000 depreciation expense). Accumulated depreciation at the end of 2005 would be $9,000 ($3,000 depreciation expense × 3 years).
2. The $1,200 cost would be capitalized in the asset account, increasing both the book value of the asset and the annual depreciation expense.

	After Effects of Capital Improvement
Amount in asset account ($18,000 + $1,200)	$19,200
Less: Salvage value	(3,000)
Accumulated depreciation on January 1, 2005	(6,000)
Remaining depreciable cost before recording 2005 depreciation	$10,200
Depreciation for 2005 ($10,200 ÷ 3 years)	$ 3,400
Accumulated depreciation at December 31, 2005 ($6,000 + $3,400)	$ 9,400

continued

CHECK YOURSELF 8.3

3. The $1,200 cost would be subtracted from the Accumulated Depreciation account, increasing the book value of the asset. The remaining useful life would increase to four years, which would decrease the depreciation expense.

	After Effects of Capital Improvement
Amount in asset account	$18,000
Less: Salvage value	(3,000)
Accumulated depreciation on January 1, 2005 ($6,000 − $1,200)	(4,800)
Remaining depreciable cost before recording 2005 depreciation	$10,200
Depreciation for 2005 ($10,200 ÷ 4 years)	$ 2,550
Accumulated depreciation at December 31, 2005 ($4,800 + $2,550)	$ 7,350

Natural Resources

LO 8

Explain how expense recognition for natural resources (depletion) affects financial statements.

The cost of natural resources includes not only the purchase price but also related items such as the cost of exploration, geographic surveys, and estimates. The process of expensing natural resources is commonly called depletion.[2] The most common method used to calculate depletion is units-of-production.

To illustrate, assume Apex Coal Mining paid $4,000,000 cash to purchase a mine with an estimated 16,000,000 tons of coal. The unit depletion charge is:

$$\$4{,}000{,}000 \div 16{,}000{,}000 \text{ tons} = \$0.25 \text{ per ton}$$

If Apex mines 360,000 tons of coal in the first year, the depletion charge is:

$$360{,}000 \text{ tons} \times \$0.25 \text{ per ton} = \$90{,}000$$

The depletion of a natural resource has the same effect on the accounting equation as other expense recognition events. Assets (in this case, a *coal mine*) and stockholders' equity decrease. The depletion expense reduces net income. The effect on the financial statements and the journal entries necessary to record the acquisition and depletion of the coal mine follow:

Assets			=	Equity			Rev.	−	Exp.	=	Net Inc.	Cash Flow
Cash	+	Coal Mine	=	Com. Stk.	+	Ret. Earn.						
(4,000,000)	+	4,000,000	=	NA	+	NA	NA	−	NA	=	NA	(4,000,000) IA
NA	+	(90,000)	=	NA	+	(90,000)	NA	−	90,000	=	(90,000)	NA

Account Title	Debit	Credit
Coal Mine	4,000,000	
Cash		4,000,000
Depletion Expense	90,000	
Coal Mine		90,000

[2]In practice, the depletion charge is considered a product cost and allocated between inventory and cost of goods sold. This text uses the simplifying assumption that all resources are sold in the same accounting period in which they are extracted. The full depletion charge is therefore expensed in the period in which the resources are extracted.

Intangible Assets

LO 9

Explain how expense recognition for intangible assets (amortization) affects financial statements.

Intangible assets provide rights, privileges, and special opportunities to businesses. Common intangible assets include trademarks, patents, copyrights, franchises, and goodwill. Some of the unique characteristics of these intangible assets are described in the following sections.

Trademarks

A **trademark** is a name or symbol that identifies a company or a product. Familiar trademarks include the Polo emblem, the name *Coca-Cola*, and the Nike slogan, "Just do it." Trademarks are registered with the federal government and have an indefinite legal lifetime.

The costs incurred to design, purchase, or defend a trademark are capitalized in an asset account called Trademarks. Companies want their trademarks to become familiar but also face the risk of a trademark being used as the generic name for a product. To protect a trademark, companies in this predicament spend large sums on legal fees and extensive advertising programs to educate consumers. Well-known trademarks that have been subject to this problem include Coke, Xerox, Kleenex, and Vaseline.

Patents

A **patent** grants its owner an exclusive legal right to produce and sell a product that has one or more unique features. Patents issued by the U.S. Patent Office have a legal life of 17 years. Companies may obtain patents through purchase, lease, or internal development. The costs capitalized in the Patent account are usually limited to the purchase price and legal fees to obtain and defend the patent. The research and development costs that are incurred to develop patentable products are usually expensed in the period in which they are incurred.

Copyrights

A **copyright** protects writings, musical compositions, works of art, and other intellectual property for the exclusive benefit of the creator or persons assigned the right by the creator. The cost of a copyright includes the purchase price and any legal costs associated with obtaining and defending the copyright. Copyrights granted by the federal government extend for the life of the creator plus 70 years. A radio commercial could legally use a Bach composition as background music; it could not, however, use the theme song from the movie, *The Matrix,* without obtaining permission from the copyright owner. The cost of a copyright is often expensed early because future royalties may be uncertain.

Franchises

Franchises grant exclusive rights to sell products or perform services in certain geographic areas. Franchises may be granted by governments or private businesses. Franchises granted by governments include federal broadcasting licenses. Private business franchises include fast-food restaurant chains and brand labels such as Healthy Choice. The legal and useful lives of a franchise are frequently difficult to determine. Judgment is often crucial to establishing the estimated useful life for franchises.

Goodwill

Goodwill is the value attributable to favorable factors such as reputation, location, and superior products. Consider the most popular restaurant in your town. If the owner sold the restaurant, do you think the purchase price would be simply the total value of the chairs, tables, kitchen equipment, and building? Certainly not, because much of the restaurant's value

FOCUS ON INTERNATIONAL ISSUES

U.S. GAAP: A COMPETITIVE DISADVANTAGE?

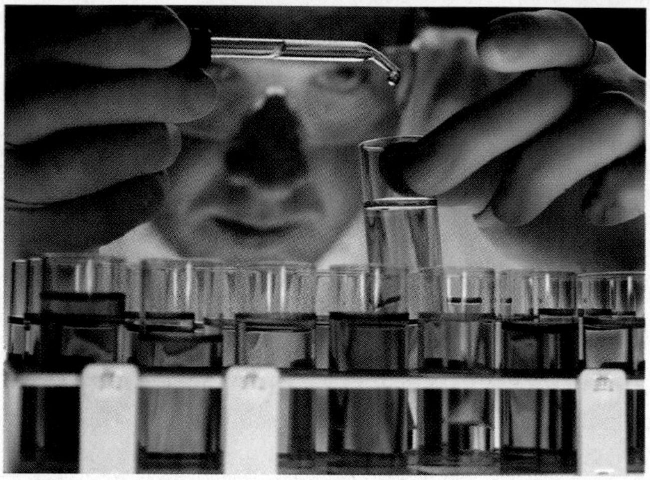

The accounting rules of various countries have many differences, but, over the years, perhaps none caused as much concern to companies involved in global competition as the rules related to accounting for goodwill and research and development (R&D).

Suppose that Company A paid $300,000 to purchase Company B's assets. Furthermore, suppose Company B's assets have a market value of only $200,000. In the United States, the $100,000 difference is classified as *goodwill.* Before July 2001, this goodwill would have been amortized (expensed) over its useful life. In the United Kingdom, the accounting is very different. A U.K. company is allowed to charge the entire $100,000 *directly against equity* in the year of the purchase. Normally, a cost is first recorded in an asset account and then expensed. When the expense is recognized, net income decreases and retained earnings decreases. Under the U.K. approach, you simply skip the income statement by making a charge directly to Retained Earnings.

In July 2001, the FASB voted to change radically the U.S. GAAP related to accounting for business combinations, which includes accounting for goodwill. Now goodwill is reported on the balance sheet as an asset, but it never has to be written off as an expense, so long as the value of the goodwill does not decrease. The rules governing accounting for business combinations in the United States are now more like those of other industrialized nations.

Suppose Company X is a pharmaceutical company that spends $10 million on the R&D of a new drug. Under U.S. GAAP, the company is required to expense the $10 million immediately. In Japan, the company is allowed to capitalize the cost in an asset account and then to expense it gradually over the useful life of the asset. Therefore, in the year in which R&D costs are incurred, a U.S. company reports more expense and less income than its Japanese counterpart.

Some businesspeople believe that U.S. GAAP can put U.S. companies at a competitive disadvantage in the search for capital. Certainly, the rules pertaining to goodwill and R&D demonstrate how U.S. companies may be forced to report lower earnings. Foreign companies that report higher earnings may be able to attract international investors who would otherwise invest in U.S. companies. Keep in mind that well-informed business professionals know how different accounting rules affect a company's financial statements. If they believe that U.S. GAAP cause a company's earnings to be understated, they take this into consideration when making investment decisions.

lies in its popularity; in other words, its ability to generate a high return is based on the goodwill (reputation) of the business.

Calculating goodwill can be complex; here we present a simple example to illustrate how it is determined. Suppose the accounting records of a restaurant named Bendigo's show:

Assets	=	Liabilities	+	Stockholders' Equity
$200,000	=	$50,000	+	$150,000

Assume a buyer agrees to purchase the restaurant by paying the owner $300,000 cash and assuming the existing liabilities. In other words, the restaurant is purchased at a price of $350,000 ($300,000 cash + $50,000 assumed liabilities). Now assume that the assets of the business (tables, chairs, kitchen equipment, etc.) have a fair market value of only $280,000.

REALITY BYTES

In September 2001, **Hewlett-Packard Company (HP)** agreed to pay approximately $24 billion to acquire **Compaq Computer Corporation**. At the time, Compaq's balance sheet showed net assets (assets minus liabilitics) of approximately $11.7 billion. Why would HP pay the owners of Compaq twice the value of the assets reported on the company's balance sheet?

HP was likely willing to pay twice the book value of the assets for three reasons. First, the value of the assets on Compaq's balance sheet represented the historical cost of the assets. The current market value of these assets was probably higher than their historical cost, especially for assets such as the Compaq trademark. Second, HP believed that the two companies combined could operate at a lower cost than the two could as separate companies, thus increasing the total income they could generate. Finally, HP probably believed that Compaq had *goodwill,* which enables a company to generate above average earnings from using its assets. In other words, HP was paying for a hidden asset not reported on Compaq's balance sheet.

Just because a company is willing to pay for goodwill does not mean it exists. In February 2005 HP's board of directors fired the company's CEO, Carly Fiorina, (pictured here) due in large part to the disappointing performance of HP since its acquisition of Compaq.

Why would the buyer pay $350,000 to purchase assets with a market value of $280,000? Obviously, the buyer is purchasing more than just the assets. The buyer is purchasing the business's goodwill. The amount of the goodwill is the difference between the purchase price and the fair market value of the assets. In this case, the goodwill is $70,000 ($350,000 − $280,000). The effects of the purchase on the financial statements of the buyer follow:

Assets					=	Liab.	+	Equity	Rev.	−	Exp.	=	Net Inc.	Cash Flow
Cash	+	Rest. Assets	+	Goodwill										
(300,000)	+	280,000	+	70,000	=	50,000	+	NA	NA	−	NA	=	NA	(300,000) IA

The journal entry to record the purchase of the restaurant is:

Account Title	Debit	Credit
Restaurant Assets	280,000	
Goodwill	70,000	
Cash		300,000
Liabilities		50,000

The fair market value of the restaurant assets represents the historical cost to the new owner. It becomes the basis for future depreciation charges.

Expense Recognition for Intangible Assets

As mentioned earlier, intangible assets fall into two categories, those with *identifiable useful lives* and those with *indefinite useful lives.* Expense recognition for intangible assets depends on which classification applies.

Expensing Intangible Assets with Identifiable Useful Lives

The costs of intangible assets with identifiable useful lives are normally expensed on a straight-line basis using a process called *amortization.* An intangible asset should be amortized over the shorter of two possible time periods: (1) its legal life or (2) its useful life.

To illustrate, assume that Flowers Industries purchased a newly granted patent for \$44,000 cash. Although the patent has a legal life of 17 years, Flowers estimates that it will be useful for only 11 years. The annual amortization charge is therefore \$4,000 (\$44,000 ÷ 11 years). The effect on the financial statements of the patent purchase and first year amortization and the journal entries to record these events follow:

Assets			=	Equity			Rev.	−	Exp.	=	Net Inc.	Cash Flow
Cash	+	Patent	=	Com. Stk.	+	Ret. Earn.						
(44,000)	+	44,000	=	NA	+	NA	NA	−	NA	=	NA	(44,000) IA
NA	+	(4,000)	=	NA	+	(4,000)	NA	−	4,000	=	(4,000)	NA

Account Title	Debit	Credit
Patent	44,000	
Cash		44,000
Amortization Expense, Patent	4,000	
Patent		4,000

Impairment Losses for Intangible Assets with Indefinite Useful Lives

Intangible assets with indefinite useful lives must be tested for impairment annually. The impairment test consists of comparing the fair value of the intangible asset to its carrying value (book value). If the fair value is less than the book value, an impairment loss must be recognized.

To illustrate, return to the example of the Bendigo's restaurant purchase. Recall that the buyer of Bendigo's paid \$70,000 for goodwill. Assume the restaurant experiences a significant decline in revenue because many of its former regular customers are dissatisfied with the food prepared by the new chef. Suppose the decline in revenue is so substantial that the new owner believes the Bendigo's name is permanently impaired. The owner decides to hire a different chef and change the name of the restaurant. In this case, the business has suffered a permanent decline in value of goodwill. The company must recognize an impairment loss.

The restaurant's name has lost its value, but the owner believes the location continues to provide the opportunity to produce above-average earnings. Some, but not all, of the goodwill has been lost. Assume the fair value of the remaining goodwill is determined to be \$40,000. The impairment loss to recognize is \$30,000 (\$70,000 − \$40,000). The loss reduces the intangible asset (goodwill), stockholder's equity (retained earnings), and net income. The statement of cash flows would not be affected. These effects on the financial statements follow:

Assets	=	Liab.	+	Equity	Rev.	−	Exp./Loss	=	Net Inc.	Cash Flow
Goodwill	=			Ret. Earn.						
(30,000)	=	NA	+	(30,000)	NA	−	30,000	=	(30,000)	NA

The journal entry to recognize the impairment loss is:

Account Title	Debit	Credit
Impairment Loss	30,000	
Goodwill		30,000

Balance Sheet Presentation

This chapter explained accounting for the acquisition, expense recognition, and disposal of a wide range of long-term assets. Exhibit 8.7 illustrates typical balance sheet presentation of many of the assets discussed.

EXHIBIT 8.7

Balance Sheet Presentation of Operational Assets

Partial Balance Sheet			
Long-Term Assets			
Plant and Equipment			
Buildings	$4,000,000		
Less: Accumulated Depreciation	(2,500,000)	$1,500,000	
Equipment	1,750,000		
Less: Accumulated Depreciation	(1,200,000)	550,000	
Total Plant and Equipment			$2,050,000
Land			850,000
Natural Resources			
Mineral Deposits (Less: Depletion)		2,100,000	
Oil Reserves (Less: Depletion)		890,000	
Total Natural Resources			2,990,000
Intangibles			
Patents (Less: Amortization)		38,000	
Goodwill		175,000	
Total Intangible Assets			213,000
Total Long-Term Assets			$6,103,000

THE FINANCIAL ANALYST

Managers may have differing opinions about which allocation method (straight-line, accelerated, or units-of-production) best matches expenses with revenues. As a result, one company may use straight-line depreciation while another company in similar circumstances uses double-declining-balance. Since the allocation method a company uses affects the amount of expense it recognizes, analysts reviewing financial statements must consider the accounting procedures companies use in preparing the statements.

LO 10

Understand how expense recognition choices and industry characteristics affect financial performance measures.

Effect of Judgment and Estimation

Assume that two companies, Alpha and Zeta, experience identical economic events in 2005 and 2006. Both generate revenue of $50,000 and incur cost of goods sold of $30,000 during each year. In 2005, each company pays $20,000 for an asset with an expected useful life of five years and no salvage value. How will the companies' financial statements differ if one uses straight-line depreciation and the other uses the double-declining-balance method? To answer this question, first compute the depreciation expense for both companies for 2005 and 2006.

If Alpha Company uses the straight-line method, depreciation for 2005 and 2006 is:

(Cost − Salvage) ÷ Useful life = Depreciation expense per year

($20,000 − $0) ÷ 5 years = $4,000

In contrast, if Zeta Company uses the double-declining-balance method, Zeta recognizes the following amounts of depreciation expense for 2005 and 2006:

	(Cost − Accumulated Depreciation)	×	2 × (Straight-Line Rate)	=	Depreciation Expense
2005	($20,000 − $ 0)	×	[2 × (1 ÷ 5)]	=	$8,000
2006	($20,000 − $8,000)	×	[2 × (1 ÷ 5)]	=	$4,800

Based on these computations, the income statements for the two companies are:

Income Statements				
	2005		2006	
	Alpha Co.	Zeta Co.	Alpha Co.	Zeta Co.
Sales	$50,000	$50,000	$50,000	$50,000
Cost of Goods Sold	(30,000)	(30,000)	(30,000)	(30,000)
Gross Margin	20,000	20,000	20,000	20,000
Depreciation Expense	(4,000)	(8,000)	(4,000)	(4,800)
Net Income	$16,000	$12,000	$16,000	$15,200

The relevant sections of the balance sheets are:

[illegible]				
	2005		2006	
	Alpha Co.	Zeta Co.	Alpha Co.	Zeta Co.
Asset	$20,000	$20,000	$20,000	$20,000
Accumulated Depreciation	(4,000)	(8,000)	(8,000)	(12,800)
Book Value	$16,000	$12,000	$12,000	$ 7,200

The depreciation method is not the only aspect of expense recognition that can vary between companies. Companies may also make different assumptions about the useful lives and salvage values of long-term operational assets. Thus, even if the same depreciation method is used, depreciation expense may still differ.

Since the depreciation method and the underlying assumptions regarding useful life and salvage value affect the determination of depreciation expense, they also affect the amounts of net income, retained earnings, and total assets. Financial statement analysis is affected if it is based on ratios that include these items. Previously defined ratios that are affected include the (1) debt to assets ratio, (2) return on assets ratio, (3) return on equity ratio, and (4) return on sales ratio.

To promote meaningful analysis, public companies are required to disclose all significant accounting policies used to prepare their financial statements. This disclosure is usually provided in the footnotes that accompany the financial statements.

Effect of Industry Characteristics

As indicated in previous chapters, industry characteristics affect financial performance measures. For example, companies in manufacturing industries invest heavily in machinery while insurance companies rely more on human capital. Manufacturing companies therefore

have relatively higher depreciation charges than insurance companies. To illustrate how the type of industry affects financial reporting, examine Exhibit 8.8. This exhibit compares the ratio of sales to property, plant, and equipment for two companies in each of three different industries. These data are for 2002.

The table indicates that for every $1.00 invested in property, plant, and equipment, **Manpower, Inc.** produced $56.20 of sales. In contrast, **Comcast Corp.** and **Delta Airlines** produced only $0.66 and $.80, respectively for each $1.00 they invested in operational assets. Does this mean the management of Manpower, Inc. is doing a better job than the management of Comcast or Delta? Not necessarily. It means that these companies operate in different economic environments. In other words, it takes significantly more equipment to operate a cable company or an airline than it takes to operate an employment agency.

Effective financial analysis requires careful consideration of industry characteristics, accounting policies, and the reasonableness of assumptions such as useful life and salvage value.

EXHIBIT 8.8

Industry Data Reflecting the Use of Long-Term Tangible Assets

Industry	Company	Sales ÷ Property, Plant, and Equipment
Cable Companies	Comcast Corp.	0.66
	Cox Communication	0.65
Airlines	Dolta	0.00
	United	0.85
Employment Agencies	Kelly Services	21.37
	Manpower, Inc.	56.20

A Look Back <<

This chapter explains that the primary objective of recognizing depreciation is to match the cost of a long-term tangible asset with the revenues the asset is expected to generate. The matching concept also applies to natural resources (depletion) and intangible assets (amortization). The chapter explains how alternative methods can be used to account for the same event (e.g., straight-line versus double-declining-balance depreciation). Companies experiencing exactly the same business events could produce different financial statements. The alternative accounting methods for depreciating, depleting, or amortizing assets include the (1) straight-line, (2) double-declining-balance, and (3) units-of-production methods.

The *straight-line method* produces equal amounts of expense in each accounting period. The amount of the expense recognized is determined using the formula [(cost − salvage) ÷ number of years of useful life]. The *double-declining-balance method* produces proportionately larger amounts of expense in the early years of an asset's useful life and increasingly smaller amounts of expense in the later years of the asset's useful life. The formula for calculating double-declining-balance depreciation is [book value at beginning of period × (2 × the straight-line rate)]. The *units-of-production method* produces expense in direct proportion to the number of units produced during an accounting period. The formula for the amount of expense recognized each period is [(cost − salvage) ÷ total estimated units of production = allocation rate × units of production in current accounting period].

The chapter also discussed *MACRS depreciation,* an accelerated tax reporting method. MACRS is not acceptable under GAAP for public reporting. A company may use MACRS depreciation for tax purposes and straight-line or one of the other methods for public reporting. As a result, differences may exist between the amount of tax expense and the amount of tax liability. Such differences are reported as *deferred income taxes.*

This chapter showed how to account for *changes in estimates* such as the useful life or the salvage value of a depreciable asset. Changes in estimates do not affect the amount of depreciation recognized previously. Instead, the remaining book value of the asset is expensed over its remaining useful life.

After an asset has been placed into service, companies typically incur further costs for maintenance, quality improvement, and extensions of useful life. *Maintenance costs* are expensed in the period in which they are incurred. *Costs that improve the quality* of an asset are added to the cost of the asset, increasing the book value and the amount of future depreciation charges. *Costs that extend the useful life* of an asset are subtracted from the asset's Accumulated Depreciation account, increasing the book value and the amount of future depreciation charges.

>> A Look Forward

In Chapter 9 we move from the assets section of the balance sheet to issues in accounting for short-term liabilities. You will also study the basic components of a payroll accounting system.

SELF-STUDY REVIEW PROBLEM

The following information pertains to a machine purchased by Bakersfield Company on January 1, 2005.

Purchase price	$ 63,000
Delivery cost	$ 2,000
Installation charge	$ 3,000
Estimated useful life	8 years
Estimated units the machine will produce	130,000
Estimated salvage value	$ 3,000

The machine produced 14,400 units during 2005 and 17,000 units during 2006.

Required

Determine the depreciation expense Bakersfield would report for 2005 and 2006 using each of the following methods.

a. Straight-line.

b. Double-declining-balance.

c. Units-of-production.

d. MACRS assuming that the machine is classified as seven-year property.

Solution to Requirements a–d.

a. Straight-line

Purchase price	$63,000
Delivery cost	2,000
Installation charge	3,000
Total cost of machine	68,000
Less: Salvage value	(3,000)
	$65,000 ÷ 8 = $8,125 Depreciation per year
2005	$ 8,125
2006	$ 8,125

b. Double-declining-balance

Year	Cost	−	Accumulated Depreciation at Beginning of Year	×	2 × S-L Rate	=	Annual Depreciation
2005	$68,000	−	$ 0	×	(2 × 0.125)	=	$17,000
2006	68,000	−	17,000	×	(2 × 0.125)	=	12,750

c. Units-of-production

(1) (Cost − Salvage value) ÷ Estimated units of production = Depreciation cost per unit produced

$$\frac{\$68{,}000 - \$3{,}000}{130{,}000} = \$0.50 \text{ per unit}$$

(2) Cost per unit × Annual units produced = Annual depreciation expense

2005 $0.50 × 14,400 = $7,200

2006 0.50 × 17,000 = 8,500

d. MACRS

Cost × MACRS percentage = Annual depreciation

2005 $68,000 × 0.1429 = $ 9,717

2006 68,000 × 0.2449 = 16,653

KEY TERMS

accelerated depreciation method 393
accumulated depreciation 390
amortization 386
basket purchase 387
book value 391
capital expenditures 400
contra asset account 390
copyright 403
current assets 385
deferred tax liability 399
depletion 386
depreciable cost 388
depreciation 386
depreciation expense 388
double-declining-balance depreciation 393
estimated useful life 388
franchise 403
goodwill 403
half-year convention 398
historical cost concept 387
intangible assets 386
long-term operational assets 385
modified accelerated cost recovery system (MACRS) 397
natural resources 386
patent 403
property, plant, and equipment 386
relative fair market value method 387
revenue expenditures 400
salvage value 388
straight line depreciation 389
tangible assets 386
trademark 403
units-of-production depreciation 395

QUESTIONS

1. What is the difference between the functions of long-term operational assets and investments?
2. What is the difference between tangible and intangible assets? Give an example of each.
3. What is the difference between goodwill and specifically identifiable intangible assets?
4. Define *depreciation*. What kind of asset depreciates?
5. Why are natural resources called *wasting assets?*
6. Is land a depreciable asset? Why or why not?
7. Define *amortization*. What kind of assets are amortized?
8. Explain the historical cost concept as it applies to long-term operational assets. Why is the book value of an asset likely to be different from the current market value of the asset?
9. What different kinds of expenditures might be included in the recorded cost of a building?

10. What is a basket purchase of assets? When a basket purchase is made, how is cost assigned to individual assets?
11. What are the stages in the life cycle of a long-term operational asset?
12. Explain straight-line, units-of-production, and double-declining-balance depreciation. When is it appropriate to use each of these depreciation methods?
13. What effect does the recognition of depreciation expense have on total assets? On total equity?
14. Does the recognition of depreciation expense affect cash flows? Why or why not?
15. MalMax purchased a depreciable asset. What would be the difference in total assets at the end of the first year if MalMax chooses straight-line depreciation versus double-declining-balance depreciation?
16. John Smith mistakenly expensed the cost of a long-term tangible fixed asset. Specifically, he charged the cost of a truck to a delivery expense account. How will this error affect the income statement and the balance sheet in the year in which the mistake is made?
17. What is *salvage value?*
18. What type of account (classification) is Accumulated Depreciation?
19. How is the book value of an asset determined?
20. Why is depreciation that has been recognized over the life of an asset shown in a contra account? Why not just reduce the asset account?
21. Assume that a piece of equipment cost $5,000 and had accumulated depreciation recorded of $3,000. What is the book value of the equipment? Is the book value equal to the fair market value of the equipment? Explain.
22. Why would a company choose to depreciate one piece of equipment using the double-declining-balance method and another piece of equipment using straight-line depreciation?
23. Explain MACRS depreciation. When is its use appropriate?
24. Does the method of depreciation required to be used for tax purposes reflect the use of a piece of equipment? Can you use double-declining-balance depreciation for tax purposes?
25. Define *deferred taxes.* Where does the account *Deferred Taxes* appear in the financial statements?
26. Why may it be necessary to revise the estimated life of a plant asset? When the estimated life is revised, does it affect the amount of depreciation per year? Why or why not?
27. How are capital expenditures made to improve the quality of a capital asset accounted for? Would the answer change if the expenditure extended the life of the asset but did not improve quality? Explain.
28. When a long-term operational asset is sold at a gain, how is the balance sheet affected? Is the statement of cash flows affected? If so, how?
29. Define *depletion.* What is the most commonly used method of computing depletion?
30. List several common intangible assets. How is the life determined that is to be used to compute amortization?
31. List some differences between U.S. GAAP and GAAP of other countries.
32. How do differences in expense recognition and industry characteristics affect financial performance measures?

EXERCISES—SERIES A

All Exercises in Series A are available with McGraw-Hill's Homework Manager

Unless specifically included, ignore income tax considerations in all exercises and problems.

L.O. 1

Exercise 8-1A *Long-term operational assets used in a business*

Required

Give some examples of long-term operational assets that each of the following companies is likely to own: *(a)* AT&T, *(b)* Caterpillar, *(c)* Amtrak, and *(d)* The Walt Disney Co.

Exercise 8-2A *Identifying long-term operational assets*

L.O. 1

Required

Which of the following items should be classified as long-term operational assets?

a. Cash
b. Buildings
c. Production machinery
d. Accounts receivable
e. Prepaid rent
f. Franchise
g. Inventory
h. Patent
i. Tract of timber
j. Land
k. Computer
l. Goodwill

Exercise 8-3A *Classifying tangible and intangible assets*

L.O. 1

Required

Identify each of the following long-term operational assets as either tangible (T) or intangible (I).

a. Retail store building
b. Shelving for inventory
c. Trademark
d. Gas well
e. Drilling rig
f. FCC license for TV station
g. 18-wheel truck
h. Timber
i. Log loader
j. Dental chair
k. Goodwill
l. Business Web page

Exercise 8-4A *Determining the cost of an asset*

L.O. 2

Northeast Logging Co. purchased an electronic saw to cut various types and sizes of logs. The saw had a list price of $120,000. The seller agreed to allow a 5 percent discount because Northeast paid cash. Delivery terms were FOB shipping point. Freight cost amounted to $2,500. Northeast had to hire an individual to operate the saw. Northeast had to build a special platform to mount the saw. The cost of the platform was $1,000. The saw operator was paid an annual salary of $40,000. The cost of the company's theft insurance policy increased by $2,000 per year as a result of acquiring of the saw. The saw had a four-year useful life and an expected salvage value of $10,000.

Required

a. Determine the amount to be capitalized in an asset account for the purchase of the saw.
b. Record the purchase in general journal format.

Exercise 8-5A *Allocating costs on the basis of relative market values*

L.O. 2

Midwest Company purchased a building and the land on which the building is situated for a total cost of $900,000 cash. The land was appraised at $200,000 and the building at $800,000.

Required

a. What is the accounting term for this type of acquisition?
b. Determine the amount of the purchase cost to allocate to the land and the amount to allocate to the building.
c. Would the company recognize a gain on the purchase? Why or why not?
d. Record the purchase in a statements model like the following one.

Assets			=	Liab.	+	Equity	Rev.	−	Exp.	=	Net Inc.	Cash Flow
Cash +	Land +	Building										

e. Record the purchases in general journal format.

Exercise 8-6A *Allocating costs for a basket purchase*

L.O. 2

Jourdan Company purchased a restaurant building, land, and equipment for $700,000 cash. The appraised value of the assets was as follows:

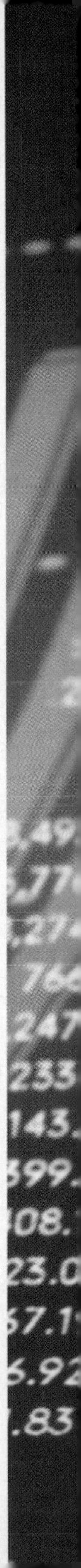

Land	$160,000
Building	400,000
Equipment	240,000
Total	$800,000

Required

a. Compute the amount to be recorded on the books for each of the assets.

b. Record the purchase in a horizontal statements model like the following one.

Assets	= Liab. + Equity	Rev. − Exp. = Net Inc.	Cash Flow
Cash + Land + Building + Equip.			

c. Prepare the general journal entry to record the purchase.

L.O. 3

Exercise 8-7A ***Effect of depreciation on the accounting equation and financial statements***

The following events apply to The Pizza Factory for the 2008 fiscal year:

1. The company started when it acquired $18,000 cash from the issue of common stock.
2. Purchased a new pizza oven that cost $15,000 cash.
3. Earned $26,000 in cash revenue.
4. Paid $13,000 cash for salaries expense.
5. Paid $6,000 cash for operating expenses.
6. Adjusted the records to reflect the use of the pizza oven. The oven, purchased on January 1, 2008, has an expected useful life of five years and an estimated salvage value of $3,000. Use straight-line depreciation. The adjusting entry was made as of December 31, 2008.

Required

a. Record the events in general journal format and post to T-accounts.

b. What amount of depreciation expense would The Pizza Factory report on the 2009 income statement?

c. What amount of accumulated depreciation would The Pizza Factory report on the December 31, 2009, balance sheet?

d. Would the cash flow from operating activities be affected by depreciation in 2009?

L.O. 3

Exercise 8-8A ***Effect of double-declining-balance depreciation on financial statements***

Smith Company started operations by acquiring $100,000 cash from the issue of common stock. On January 1, 2005, the company purchased equipment that cost $100,000 cash. The equipment had an expected useful life of five years and an estimated salvage value of $20,000. Smith Company earned $92,000 and $65,000 of cash revenue during 2005 and 2006, respectively. Smith Company uses double-declining-balance depreciation.

Required

Prepare income statements, balance sheets, and statements of cash flows for 2005 and 2006. Use a vertical statements format. (*Hint:* Record the events in T-accounts prior to preparing the statements.)

L.O. 3, 4

Exercise 8-9A ***Events related to the acquisition, use, and disposal of a tangible plant asset: straight-line depreciation***

CJ's Pizza purchased a delivery van on January 1, 2005, for $25,000. In addition, CJ's paid sales tax and title fees of $1,000 for the van. The van is expected to have a four-year life and a salvage value of $6,000.

Required

a. Using the straight-line method, compute the depreciation expense for 2005 and 2006.

b. Prepare the general journal entry to record the 2005 depreciation.

c. Assume the van was sold on January 1, 2008, for $12,000. Prepare the journal entry for the sale of the van in 2008.

Exercise 8-10A ***Computing and recording straight-line versus double-declining-balance depreciation*** **L.O. 3**

At the beginning of 2006, Precision Manufacturing purchased a new computerized drill press for $50,000. It is expected to have a five-year life and a $5,000 salvage value.

Required

a. Compute the depreciation for each of the five years, assuming that the company uses
   (1) Straight-line depreciation.
   (2) Double-declining-balance depreciation.

b. Record the purchase of the drill press and the depreciation expense for the first year under the straight-line and double-declining-balance methods in a financial statements model like the following one:

Assets							=	Equity	Rev.	−	Exp.	=	Net Inc.	Cash Flow
Cash	+	Drill Press	−	Acc. Dep.			=	Ret. Earn						

c. Prepare the journal entries to recognize depreciation for each of the five years, assuming that the company uses
   (1) Straight-line depreciation.
   (2) Double-declining-balance depreciation.

Exercise 8-11A ***Effect of the disposal of plant assets on the financial statements*** **L.O. 4**

A plant asset with a cost of $40,000 and accumulated depreciation of $36,000 is sold for $6,000.

Required

a. What is the book value of the asset at the time of sale?

b. What is the amount of gain or loss on the disposal?

c. How would the sale affect net income (increase, decrease, no effect) and by how much?

d. How would the sale affect the amount of total assets shown on the balance sheet (increase, decrease, no effect) and by how much?

e. How would the event affect the statement of cash flows (inflow, outflow, no effect) and in what section?

Exercise 8-12A ***Effect of gains and losses on the accounting equation and financial statements*** **L.O. 8**

On January 1, 2008, Gert Enterprises purchased a parcel of land for $12,000 cash. At the time of purchase, the company planned to use the land for future expansion. In 2009, Gert Enterprises changed its plans and sold the land.

Required

a. Assume that the land was sold for $11,200 in 2009.
   (1) Show the effect of the sale on the accounting equation.
   (2) What amount would Gert report on the income statement related to the sale of the land?
   (3) What amount would Gert report on the statement of cash flows related to the sale of the land?

b. Assume that the land was sold for $13,500 in 2009.
   (1) Show the effect of the sale on the accounting equation.
   (2) What amount would Gert report on the income statement related to the sale of the land?
   (3) What amount would Gert report on the statement of cash flows related to the sale of the land?

Exercise 8-13A ***Double-declining-balance and units-of-production depreciation: gain or loss on disposal*** **L.O. 3, 4**

Print Service Co. purchased a new color copier at the beginning of 2005 for $35,000. The copier is expected to have a five-year useful life and a $5,000 salvage value. The expected copy production was estimated at 2,000,000 copies. Actual copy production for the five years was as follows:

2005	550,000
2006	480,000
2007	380,000
2008	390,000
2009	240,000
Total	2,040,000

The copier was sold at the end of 2009 for $5,200.

Required

a. Compute the depreciation expense for each of the five years, using double-declining-balance depreciation.

b. Compute the depreciation expense for each of the five years, using units-of-production depreciation. (Round cost per unit to three decimal places.)

c. Calculate the amount of gain or loss from the sale of the asset under each of the depreciation methods.

L.O. 5

Exercise 8-14A ***Computing depreciation for tax purposes***

Quality Lumber Company purchased $120,000 of equipment on September 1, 2006.

Required

a. Compute the amount of depreciation expense that is deductible under MACRS for 2006 and 2007, assuming that the equipment is classified as seven-year property.

b. Compute the amount of depreciation expense that is deductible under MACRS for 2006 and 2007, assuming that the equipment is classified as five-year property.

L.O. 6

Exercise 8-15A ***Revision of estimated useful life***

On January 1, 2006, Harris Machining Co. purchased a compressor and related installation equipment for $64,000. The equipment had a three-year estimated life with a $4,000 salvage value. Straight-line depreciation was used. At the beginning of 2008, Harris revised the expected life of the asset to four years rather than three years. The salvage value was revised to $3,000.

Required

Compute the depreciation expense for each of the four years.

L.O. 7

Exercise 8-16A ***Distinguishing between revenue expenditures and capital expenditures***

Zell's Shredding Service has just completed a minor repair on a shredding machine. The repair cost was $900, and the book value prior to the repair was $5,000. In addition, the company spent $8,000 to replace the roof on a building. The new roof extended the life of the building by five years. Prior to the roof replacement, the general ledger reflected the Building account at $90,000 and related Accumulated Depreciation account at $40,000.

Required

After the work was completed, what book value should Zell's report on the balance sheet for the shredding machine and the building?

L.O. 7

Exercise 8-17A ***Effect of revenue expenditures versus capital expenditures on financial statements***

Sequoia Construction Company purchased a forklift for $110,000 cash. It had an estimated useful life of four years and a $10,000 salvage value. At the beginning of the third year of use, the company spent an additional $8,000 that was related to the forklift. The company's financial condition just prior to this expenditure is shown in the following statements model.

Assets					=	Equity			Rev.	−	Exp.	=	Net Inc.	Cash Flow
Cash	+	Forklift	−	Acc. Dep.	=	Com. Stk.	+	Ret. Earn.						
12,000	+	110,000	−	50,000	=	24,000	+	48,000	NA	−	NA	=	NA	NA

Required

Record the $8,000 expenditure in the statements model under each of the following *independent* assumptions:

a. The expenditure was for routine maintenance.
b. The expenditure extended the forklift's life.
c. The expenditure improved the forklift's operating capacity.

Exercise 8-18A *Effect of revenue expenditures versus capital expenditures on financial statements* L.O. 7

On January 1, 2005, Valley Power Company overhauled four turbine engines that generate power for customers. The overhaul resulted in a slight increase in the capacity of the engines to produce power. Such overhauls occur regularly at two-year intervals and have been treated as maintenance expense in the past. Management is considering whether to capitalize this year's $25,000 cash cost in the engine asset account or to expense it as a maintenance expense. Assume that the engines have a remaining useful life of two years and no expected salvage value. Assume straight-line depreciation.

Required

a. Determine the amount of additional depreciation expense Valley would recognize in 2005 and 2006 if the cost were capitalized in the Engine account.
b. Determine the amount of expense Valley would recognize in 2005 and 2006 if the cost were recognized as maintenance expense.
c. Determine the effect of the overhaul on cash flow from operating activities for 2005 and 2006 if the cost were capitalized and expensed through depreciation charges.
d. Determine the effect of the overhaul on cash flow from operating activities for 2005 and 2006 if the cost were recognized as maintenance expense.

Exercise 8-19A *Computing and recording depletion expense* L.O. 8

Ecru Sand and Gravel paid $600,000 to acquire 800,000 cubic yards of sand reserves. The following statements model reflects Ecru's financial condition just prior to purchasing the sand reserves. The company extracted 420,000 cubic yards of sand in year 1 and 360,000 cubic yards in year 2.

Assets			=	Equity			Rev.	−	Exp.	=	Net Inc.	Cash Flow
Cash	+	Sand Res.	=	Com. Stk.	+	Ret. Earn.						
700,000	+	NA	=	700,000	+	NA	NA	−	NA	=	NA	NA

Required

a. Compute the depletion charge per unit.
b. Record the acquisition of the sand reserves and the depletion expense for years 1 and 2 in a financial statements model like the preceding one.
c. Prepare the general journal entries to record the depletion expense for years 1 and 2.

Exercise 8-20A *Computing and recording the amortization of intangibles* L.O. 9

Texas Manufacturing paid cash to purchase the assets of an existing company. Among the assets purchased were the following items:

Patent with 5 remaining years of legal life	$36,000
Goodwill	40,000

Texas's financial condition just prior to the purchase of these assets is shown in the following statements model:

Assets					=	Liab.	+	Equity	Rev.	−	Exp.	=	Net Inc.	Cash Flow
Cash	+	Patent	+	Goodwill										
94,000	+	NA	+	NA	=	NA	+	94,000	NA	−	NA	+	NA	NA

Required

a. Compute the annual amortization expense for these items if applicable.

b. Record the purchase of the intangible assets and the related amortization expense for year 1 in a horizontal statements model like the preceding one.

c. Prepare the journal entries to record the purchase of the intangible assets and the related amortization for year 1.

L.O. 9

Exercise 8-21A *Computing and recording goodwill*

Mike Wallace purchased the business Magnum Supply Co. for $275,000 cash and assumed all liabilities at the date of purchase. Magnum's books showed tangible assets of $280,000, liabilities of $40,000, and equity of $240,000. An appraiser assessed the fair market value of the tangible assets at $270,000 at the date of purchase. Wallace's financial condition just prior to the purchase is shown in the following statements model:

Assets					=	Liab.	+	Equity	Rev.	−	Exp.	=	Net Inc.	Cash Flow
Cash	+	Tang. Assets	+	Goodwill										
325,000	+	NA	+	NA	=	NA	+	325,000	NA	−	NA	=	NA	NA

Required

a. Compute the amount of goodwill purchased.

b. Record the purchase in a financial statements model like the preceding one.

c. Record the purchase in general journal format.

PROBLEMS—SERIES A

HM™

All Problems in Series A are available with McGraw-Hill's Homework Manager

L.O. 2

Problem 8-22A *Accounting for acquisition of assets including a basket purchase*

CHECK FIGURES
Total cost of equipment: $40,900
Cost allocated to copier: $7,500

Khan Company made several purchases of long-term assets in 2009. The details of each purchase are presented here.

New Office Equipment

1. List price: $40,000; terms: 1/10 n/30; paid within the discount period.
2. Transportation-in: $800.
3. Installation: $500.
4. Cost to repair damage during unloading: $500.
5. Routine maintenance cost after eight months: $120.

Basket Purchase of Office Furniture, Copier, Computers, and Laser Printers for $50,000 with Fair Market Values

1. Office furniture, $24,000.
2. Copier, $9,000.
3. Computers and printers, $27,000.

Land for New Headquarters with Old Barn Torn Down

1. Purchase price, $80,000.
2. Demolition of barn, $5,000.
3. Lumber sold from old barn, $2,000.
4. Grading in preparation for new building, $8,000.
5. Construction of new building, $250,000.

Required

In each of these cases, determine the amount of cost to be capitalized in the asset accounts.

Problem 8-23A ***Accounting for depreciation over multiple accounting cycles: straight-line depreciation***

L.O. 3, 4

eXcel

mhhe.com/edmonds2007

KC Company began operations when it acquired $30,000 cash from the issue of common stock on January 1, 2005. The cash acquired was immediately used to purchase equipment for $30,000 that had a $5,000 salvage value and an expected useful life of four years. The equipment was used to produce the following revenue stream (assume all revenue transactions are for cash). At the beginning of the fifth year, the equipment was sold for $4,500 cash. KC uses straight-line depreciation.

CHECK FIGURES
Net Income, 2005: $1,250
Total Assets, 2009: $35,200

	2005	2006	2007	2008	2009
Revenue	$7,500	$8,000	$8,200	$7,000	$0

Required

Prepare income statements, statements of changes in stockholders' equity, balance sheets, and statements of cash flows for each of the five years.

Problem 8-24A ***Purchase and use of tangible asset: three accounting cycles, double-declining-balance depreciation***

L.O. 2, 3, 6, 7

CHECK FIGURES
c. Net Income, 2007: $23,200
Total Assets, 2009: $139,770

The following transactions pertain to Optimal Solutions Inc. Assume the transactions for the purchase of the computer and any capital improvements occur on January 1 each year.

2007

1. Acquired $60,000 cash from the issue of common stock.
2. Purchased a computer system for $25,000. It has an estimated useful life of five years and a $3,000 salvage value.
3. Paid $1,500 sales tax on the computer system.
4. Collected $35,000 in data entry fees from clients.
5. Paid $1,200 in fees to service the computers.
6. Recorded double-declining-balance depreciation on the computer system for 2007.
7. Closed the revenue and expense accounts to Retained Earnings at the end of 2007.

2008

1. Paid $800 for repairs to the computer system.
2. Bought a case of toner cartridges for the printers that are part of the computer system, $1,200.
3. Collected $38,000 in data entry fees from clients.
4. Paid $900 in fees to service the computers.
5. Recorded double-declining-balance depreciation for 2008.
6. Closed the revenue and expense accounts to Retained Earnings at the end of 2008.

2009

1. Paid $3,000 to upgrade the computer system, which extended the total life of the system to six years.
2. Paid $900 in fees to service the computers.
3. Collected $35,000 in data entry fees from clients.
4. Recorded double-declining-balance depreciation for 2009.
5. Closed the revenue and expense accounts at the end of 2009.

Required

a. Use a horizontal statements model like the following one to show the effect of these transactions on the elements of financial statements. Use + for increase, − for decrease, and NA for not affected. The first event is recorded as an example.

2007 Event No.	Assets	=	Liabilities	+	Equity	Net Inc.	Cash Flow
1	+		NA		+	NA	+ FA

b. For each year, record the transactions in general journal form and post them to T-accounts.
c. Use a vertical model to present financial statements for 2007, 2008, and 2009.

L.O. 3, 5

excel

mhhe.com/edmonds2007

CHECK FIGURES
b. Depreciation Expense, 2008: $4,600
c. Depreciation Expense, 2009: $4,300

Problem 8-25A *Calculating depreciation expense using four different methods*

O'Brian Service Company purchased a copier on January 1, 2008, for $17,000 and paid an additional $200 for delivery charges. The copier was estimated to have a life of four years or 800,000 copies. Salvage was estimated at $1,200. The copier produced 230,000 copies in 2008 and 250,000 copies in 2009.

Required

Compute the amount of depreciation expense for the copier for calendar years 2008 and 2009, using these methods:

a. Straight-line.
b. Units-of-production.
c. Double-declining-balance.
d. MACRS, assuming that the copier is classified as five-year property.

L.O. 3, 4

excel

mhhe.com/edmonds2007

CHECK FIGURES
a. Depreciation Expense, Year 2: $6,400
b. Depreciation Expense, Year 2: $8,400

Problem 8-26A *Effect of straight-line versus double-declining-balance depreciation on the recognition of expense and gains or losses*

Same Day Laundry Services purchased a new steam press on January 1, for $35,000. It is expected to have a five-year useful life and a $3,000 salvage value. Same Day expects to use the steam press more extensively in the early years of its life.

Required

a. Calculate the depreciation expense for each of the five years, assuming the use of straight-line depreciation.
b. Calculate the depreciation expense for each of the five years, assuming the use of double-declining-balance depreciation.
c. Would the choice of one depreciation method over another produce a different amount of cash flow for any year? Why or why not?
d. Assume that Same Day Laundry Services sold the steam press at the end of the third year for $20,000. Compute the amount of gain or loss using each depreciation method.

L.O. 3, 4

Problem 8-27A *Computing and recording units-of-production depreciation*

McNabb Corporation purchased a delivery van for $25,500 in 2007. The firm's financial condition immediately prior to the purchase is shown in the following horizontal statements model:

Assets					=	Equity			Rev.	−	Exp.	=	Net Inc.	Cash Flow
Cash	+	Van	−	Acc. Dep.	=	Com. Stk.	+	Ret. Earn.						
50,000	+	NA	−	NA	=	50,000	+	NA	NA	−	NA	=	NA	NA

CHECK FIGURES
a. Depreciation Expense, 2007: $7,500
c. Gain on Sale: $1,000

The van was expected to have a useful life of 150,000 miles and a salvage value of $3,000. Actual mileage was as follows:

2007	50,000
2008	70,000
2009	58,000

Required

a. Compute the depreciation for each of the three years, assuming the use of units-of-production depreciation.
b. Assume that McNabb earns $21,000 of cash revenue during 2007. Record the purchase of the van and the recognition of the revenue and the depreciation expense for the first year in a financial statements model like the preceding one.
c. Assume that McNabb sold the van at the end of the third year for $4,000. Record the general journal entry for the sale.

Problem 8-28A ***Determining the effect of depreciation expense on financial statements*** **L.O. 3**

CHECK FIGURES
a. Company A, Net Income: $20,000
c. Company C, Book Value: $17,750

Three different companies each purchased a machine on January 1, 2005, for $54,000. Each machine was expected to last five years or 200,000 hours. Salvage value was estimated to be $4,000. All three machines were operated for 50,000 hours in 2005, 55,000 hours in 2006, 40,000 hours in 2007, 44,000 hours in 2008, and 31,000 hours in 2009. Each of the three companies earned $30,000 of cash revenue during each of the five years. Company A uses straight-line depreciation, company B uses double-declining-balance depreciation, and company C uses units-of-production depreciation.

Required

Answer each of the following questions. Ignore the effects of income taxes.

a. Which company will report the highest amount of net income for 2005?
b. Which company will report the lowest amount of net income for 2007?
c. Which company will report the highest book value on the December 31, 2007, balance sheet?
d. Which company will report the highest amount of retained earnings on the December 31, 2008, balance sheet?
e. Which company will report the lowest amount of cash flow from operating activities on the 2007 statement of cash flows?

Problem 8-29A ***Accounting for depletion*** **L.O. 6, 8**

CHECK FIGURES
a. Coal Mine Depletion, 2007: $280,000
b. Total Natural Resources: $1,757,000

Favre Exploration Corporation engages in the exploration and development of many types of natural resources. In the last two years, the company has engaged in the following activities:

Jan. 1, 2007	Purchased a coal mine estimated to contain 200,000 tons of coal for $800,000.
July 1, 2007	Purchased for $1,950,000 a tract of timber estimated to yield 3,000,000 board feet of lumber and to have a residual land value of $150,000.
Feb. 1, 2008	Purchased a silver mine estimated to contain 30,000 tons of silver for $750,000.
Aug. 1, 2008	Purchased for $736,000 oil reserves estimated to contain 250,000 barrels of oil, of which 20,000 would be unprofitable to pump.

Required

a. Prepare the journal entries to account for the following:
  (1) The 2007 purchases.
  (2) Depletion on the 2007 purchases, assuming that 70,000 tons of coal were mined and 1,000,000 board feet of lumber were cut.
  (3) The 2008 purchases.
  (4) Depletion on the four reserves, assuming that 62,000 tons of coal, 1,200,000 board feet of lumber, 9,000 tons of silver, and 80,000 barrels of oil were extracted.
b. Prepare the portion of the December 31, 2008, balance sheet that reports natural resources.
c. Assume that in 2009 the estimates changed to reflect only 50,000 tons of coal remaining. Prepare the depletion journal entry for 2009 to account for the extraction of 35,000 tons of coal.

Problem 8-30A ***Recording continuing expenditures for plant assets*** **L.O. 3, 4, 6, 7**

CHECK FIGURES
b. 2007 Depreciation Expense: $7,000
d. Loss on Sale: $3,250

Big Sky Inc. recorded the following transactions over the life of a piece of equipment purchased in 2005:

Jan. 1, 2005	Purchased the equipment for $36,000 cash. The equipment is estimated to have a five-year life and $6,000 salvage value and was to be depreciated using the straight-line method.
Dec. 31, 2005	Recorded depreciation expense for 2005.
May 5, 2006	Undertook routine repairs costing $750.
Dec. 31, 2006	Recorded depreciation expense for 2006.
Jan. 1, 2007	Made an adjustment costing $3,000 to the equipment. It improved the quality of the output but did not affect the life estimate.
Dec. 31, 2007	Recorded depreciation expense for 2007.
Mar. 1, 2008	Incurred $320 cost to oil and clean the equipment.
Dec. 31, 2008	Recorded depreciation expense for 2008.
Jan. 1, 2009	Had the equipment completely overhauled at a cost of $7,500. The overhaul was estimated to extend the total life to seven years and revised the salvage value to $4,000.

Dec. 31, 2009 Recorded depreciation expense for 2009.
July 1, 2010 Sold the equipment for $9,000 cash.

Required

a. Use a horizontal statements model like the following one to show the effects of these transactions on the elements of the financial statements. Use + for increase, − for decrease, and NA for not affected. The first event is recorded as an example.

Date	Assets	=	Liabilities	+	Equity	Net Inc.	Cash Flow
Jan. 1, 2005	+ −		NA		NA	NA	− IA

b. Determine amount of depreciation expense Big Sky will report on the income statements for the years 2005 through 2009.

c. Determine the book value (cost − accumulated depreciation) Big Sky will report on the balance sheets at the end of the years 2005 through 2009.

d. Determine the amount of the gain or loss Big Sky will report on the disposal of the equipment on July 1, 2010.

e. Prepare the journal entry for the disposal of the equipment on July 1, 2010.

L.O. 6, 7

Problem 8-31A *Accounting for continuing expenditures*

Vernon Manufacturing paid $58,000 to purchase a computerized assembly machine on January 1, 2002. The machine had an estimated life of eight years and a $2,000 salvage value. Vernon's financial condition as of January 1, 2005, is shown in the following financial statements model. Vernon uses the straight-line method for depreciation.

Assets					=	Equity			Rev.	−	Exp.	=	Net Inc.	Cash Flow
Cash	+	Mach.	−	Acc. Dep.	=	Com. Stk.	+	Ret. Earn.						
15,000	+	58,000	−	21,000	=	8,000	+	44,000	NA	−	NA	=	NA	NA

CHECK FIGURE
b. Depreciation Expense: $8,000

Vernon Manufacturing made the following expenditures on the computerized assembly machine in 2005.

Jan. 2 Added an overdrive mechanism for $6,000 that would improve the overall quality of the performance of the machine but would not extend its life. The salvage value was revised to $3,000.
Aug. 1 Performed routine maintenance, $1,150.
Oct. 2 Replaced some computer chips (considered routine), $950.
Dec. 31 Recognized 2005 depreciation expense.

Required

a. Record the 2005 transactions in a statements model like the preceding one.

b. Prepare journal entries for the 2005 transactions.

L.O. 9

Problem 8-32A *Accounting for intangible assets*

CHECK FIGURE
a. Goodwill Purchased: $130,000

Mia-Tora Company purchased a fast-food restaurant for $1,400,000. The fair market values of the assets purchased were as follows. No liabilities were assumed.

Equipment	$320,000
Land	200,000
Building	650,000
Franchise (5-year life)	100,000

Required

a. Calculate the amount of goodwill purchased.

b. Prepare the journal entry to record the amortization of the franchise fee at the end of year 1.

Problem 8-33A ***Accounting for goodwill*** **L.O. 9**

Springhill Co. purchased the assets of Canyon Co. for $1,000,000 in 2005. The estimated fair market value of the assets at the purchase date was $920,000. Goodwill of $80,000 was recorded at purchase. In 2007, because of negative publicity, one-half of the goodwill purchased from Canyon Co. was judged to be permanently impaired.

CHECK FIGURE
b. Impairment Loss: $40,000

Required

a. How will Springhill account for the impairment of the goodwill?

b. Prepare the journal entry to record the permanent impairment of goodwill.

EXERCISES—SERIES B

Unless specifically included, ignore income tax considerations in all exercises and problems.

Exercise 8-1B ***Long-term operational assets used in a business*** **L.O. 1**

Required

Give some examples of long-term operational assets that each of the following companies is likely to own: *(a)* Lansing Farms, *(b)* American Airlines, *(c)* IBM, and *(d)* Northwest Mutual Insurance Co.

Exercise 8-2B ***Identifying long-term operational assets*** **L.O. 1**

Required

Which of the following items should be classified as long-term operational assets?

a. Prepaid insurance
b. Coal mine
c. Office equipment
d. Accounts receivable
e. Supplies
f. Copyright
g. Delivery van
h. Land used in the business
i. Goodwill
j. Cash
k. Filing cabinet
l. Tax library of accounting firm

Exercise 8-3B ***Classifying tangible and intangible assets*** **L.O. 1**

Required

Identify each of the following long-term operational assets as either tangible (T) or intangible (I).

a. Pizza oven
b. Land
c. Franchise
d. Filing cabinet
e. Copyright
f. Silver mine
g. Office building
h. Drill press
i. Patent
j. Oil well
k. Desk
l. Goodwill

Exercise 8-4B ***Determining the cost of an asset*** **L.O. 2**

Xpert Milling Co. purchased a front-end loader to move stacks of lumber. The loader had a list price of $100,000. The seller agreed to allow a 4 percent discount because Xpert Milling paid cash. Delivery terms were FOB shipping point. Freight cost amounted to $500. Xpert Milling had to hire a consultant to train an employee to operate the loader. The training fee was $1,000. The loader operator is paid an annual salary of $30,000. The cost of the company's theft insurance policy increased by $800 per year as a result of acquiring the loader. The loader had a four-year useful life and an expected salvage value of $6,500.

Required

a. Determine the amount to be capitalized in an asset account for the purchase of the loader.

b. Record the purchase in general journal format.

L.O. 2

Exercise 8-5B *Allocating costs on the basis of relative market values*

Diaz Inc. purchased a building and the land on which the building is situated for a total cost of $800,000 cash. The land was appraised at $270,000 and the building at $630,000.

Required

a. Determine the amount of the purchase cost to allocate to the land and the amount to allocate to the building.

b. Would the company recognize a gain on the purchase? Why or why not?

c. Record the purchase in a statements model like the following one.

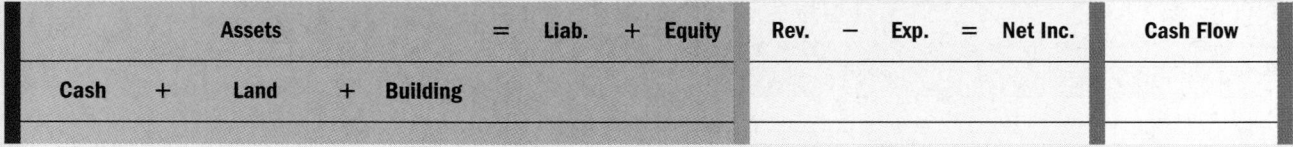

Assets			= Liab.	+ Equity	Rev. − Exp. = Net Inc.	Cash Flow
Cash +	Land +	Building				

d. Record the purchase in general journal format.

L.O. 2

Exercise 8-6B *Allocating costs for a basket purchase*

Marker Co. purchased an office building, land, and furniture for $300,000 cash. The appraised value of the assets was as follows:

Land	$105,000
Building	210,000
Furniture	35,000
Total	$350,000

Required

a. Compute the amount to be recorded on the books for each asset.

b. Record the purchase in a horizontal statements model like the following one.

Assets				= Liab.	+ Equity	Rev. − Exp. = Net Inc.	Cash Flow
Cash +	Land +	Building +	Furn.				

c. Prepare the general journal entry to record the purchase.

L.O. 3

Exercise 8-7B *Effect of depreciation on the accounting equation and financial statements*

The following events apply to Jim's Deli for the 2006 fiscal year:

1. The company started when it acquired $30,000 cash by issuing common stock.
2. Purchased a new stove that cost $22,000 cash.
3. Earned $21,000 in cash revenue.
4. Paid $4,000 cash for salaries expense.
5. Adjusted the records to reflect the use of the stove. Purchased on January 1, 2006, the stove has an expected useful life of four years and an estimated salvage value of $1,000. Use straight line depreciation. The adjusting entry was made as of December 31, 2006.

Required

a. Record the events in general journal format and post to T-accounts.

b. Prepare a balance sheet and a statement of cash flows for the 2006 accounting period.

c. What is the net income for 2006?

d. What amount of depreciation expense would Jim's report on the 2007 income statement?

e. What amount of accumulated depreciation would Jim's report on the December 31, 2007, balance sheet?

f. Would the cash flow from operating activities be affected by depreciation in 2007?

Exercise 8-8B *Effect of double-declining-balance depreciation on financial statements* L.O. 3

Ram Manufacturing Company started operations by acquiring $120,000 cash from the issue of common stock. On January 1, 2006, the company purchased equipment that cost $120,000 cash, had an expected useful life of six years, and had an estimated salvage value of $6,000. Ram Manufacturing earned $76,000 and $85,200 of cash revenue during 2006 and 2007, respectively. Ram Manufacturing uses double-declining-balance depreciation.

Required

Prepare income statements, balance sheets, and statements of cash flows for 2006 and 2007. Use a vertical statements format. (*Hint:* Record the events in T-accounts prior to preparing the statements.)

Exercise 8-9B *Events related to the acquisition, use, and disposal of a tangible plant asset: straight-line depreciation* L.O. 3, 4

Fast Taxi Service purchased a new auto to use as a taxi on January 1, 2008, for $27,000. In addition, Fast paid sales tax and title fees of $500 for the vehicle. The taxi is expected to have a five-year life and a salvage value of $2,500.

Required

a. Using the straight-line method, compute the depreciation expense for 2008 and 2009.

b. Prepare the general journal entry to record the 2008 depreciation.

c. Assume that the taxi was sold on January 1, 2010, for $15,000. Prepare the journal entry for the sale of the taxi in 2010.

Exercise 8-10B *Computing and recording straight-line versus double-declining-balance depreciation* L.O. 3

At the beginning of 2006, Macon Drugstore purchased a new computer system for $48,000. It is expected to have a five-year life and a $3,000 salvage value.

Required

a. Compute the depreciation for each of the five years, assuming that the company uses

(1) Straight-line depreciation.

(2) Double-declining-balance depreciation.

b. Record the purchase of the computer system and the depreciation expense for the first year under straight-line and double-declining-balance methods in a financial statements model like the following one:

Assets						=	Equity	Rev.	−	Exp.	=	Net Inc.	Cash Flow
Cash	+	Comp. Sys.	−	Acc. Dep.		=	Ret. Earn.						

c. Prepare the journal entries to recognize depreciation for each of the five years, assuming that the company uses

(1) Straight-line depreciation.

(2) Double-declining-balance depreciation.

Exercise 8-11B *Effect of the disposal of plant assets on the financial statements* L.O. 4

Mertz Company sold office equipment with a cost of $27,000 and accumulated depreciation of $13,000 for $14,000.

Required

a. What is the book value of the asset at the time of sale?

b. What is the amount of gain or loss on the disposal?

c. How would the sale affect net income (increase, decrease, no effect) and by how much?

d. How would the sale affect the amount of total assets shown on the balance sheet (increase, decrease, no effect) and by how much?

e. How would the event affect the statement of cash flows (inflow, outflow, no effect) and in what section?

L.O. 8

Exercise 8-12B ***Effect of gains and losses on the accounting equation and financial statements***

On January 1, 2005, Arizona Enterprises purchased a parcel of land for $16,000 cash. At the time of purchase, the company planned to use the land for a warehouse site. In 2007, Arizona Enterprises changed its plans and sold the land.

Required

a. Assume that the land was sold for $15,000 in 2007.
  (1) Show the effect of the sale on the accounting equation.
  (2) What amount would Arizona report on the 2007 income statement related to the sale of the land?
  (3) What amount would Arizona report on the 2007 statement of cash flows related to the sale of the land?

b. Assume that the land was sold for $18,000 in 2007.
  (1) Show the effect of the sale on the accounting equation.
  (2) What amount would Arizona report on the 2007 income statement related to the sale of the land?
  (3) What amount would Arizona report on the 2007 statement of cash flows related to the sale of the land?

L.O. 3, 4

Exercise 8-13B ***Double-declining-balance and units-of-production depreciation: gain or loss on disposal***

Kate's Photo Service purchased a new color printer at the beginning of 2006 for $28,000. The printer is expected to have a four-year useful life and a $2,000 salvage value. The expected print production is estimated at 1,300,000 pages. Actual print production for the four years was as follows:

2006	350,000
2007	370,000
2008	280,000
2009	320,000
Total	1,320,000

The printer was sold at the end of 2009 for $1,500.

Required

a. Compute the depreciation expense for each of the four years, using double-declining-balance depreciation.

b. Compute the depreciation expense for each of the four years, using units-of-production depreciation. (Round cost per unit to three decimal places.)

c. Calculate the amount of gain or loss from the sale of the asset under each of the depreciation methods.

L.O. 5

Exercise 8-14B ***Computing depreciation for tax purposes***

Vision Eye Care Company purchased $40,000 of equipment on March 1, 2008.

Required

a. Compute the amount of depreciation expense that is deductible under MACRS for 2008 and 2009, assuming that the equipment is classified as seven-year property.

b. Compute the amount of depreciation expense that is deductible under MACRS for 2008 and 2009, assuming that the equipment is classified as five-year property.

L.O. 6

Exercise 8-15B ***Revision of estimated useful life***

On January 1, 2007, Maxie Storage Company purchased a freezer and related installation equipment for $36,000. The equipment had a three-year estimated life with a $6,000 salvage value. Straight-line depreciation was used. At the beginning of 2009, Maxie revised the expected life of the asset to four years rather than three years. The salvage value was revised to $4,000.

Required

Compute the depreciation expense for each of the four years.

Exercise 8-16B ***Distinguishing between revenue expenditures and capital expenditures*** **L.O. 7**

Reliable Wrecker Service has just completed a minor repair on a tow truck. The repair cost was $620, and the book value prior to the repair was $5,600. In addition, the company spent $4,000 to replace the roof on a building. The new roof extended the life of the building by five years. Prior to the roof replacement, the general ledger reflected the Building account at $90,000 and related Accumulated Depreciation account at $26,500.

Required

After the work was completed, what book value should appear on the balance sheet for the tow truck and the building?

Exercise 8-17B ***Effect of revenue expenditures versus capital expenditures on financial statements*** **L.O. 7**

Kauai Construction Company purchased a compressor for $42,000 cash. It had an estimated useful life of four years and a $4,000 salvage value. At the beginning of the third year of use, the company spent an additional $3,000 related to the equipment. The company's financial condition just prior to this expenditure is shown in the following statements model.

Assets					=	Equity			Rev.	−	Exp.	=	Net Inc.	Cash Flow
Cash	+	Compressor	−	Acc. Dep.	=	Com. Stk.	+	Ret. Earn.						
37,000	+	42,000	−	19,000	=	40,000	+	20,000	NA	−	NA	=	NA	NA

Required

Record the $3,000 expenditure in the statements model under each of the following *independent* assumptions:

a. The expenditure was for routine maintenance.
b. The expenditure extended the compressor's life.
c. The expenditure improved the compressor's operating capacity.

Exercise 8-18B ***Effect of revenue expenditures versus capital expenditures on financial statements*** **L.O. 7**

On January 1, 2006, Grayson Construction Company overhauled four cranes resulting in a slight increase in the life of the cranes. Such overhauls occur regularly at two-year intervals and have been treated as maintenance expense in the past. Management is considering whether to capitalize this year's $26,000 cash cost in the Cranes asset account or to expense it as a maintenance expense. Assume that the cranes have a remaining useful life of two years and no expected salvage value. Assume straight-line depreciation.

Required

a. Determine the amount of additional depreciation expense Grayson would recognize in 2006 and 2007 if the cost were capitalized in the Cranes account.
b. Determine the amount of expense Grayson would recognize in 2006 and 2007 if the cost were recognized as maintenance expense.
c. Determine the effect of the overhaul on cash flow from operating activities for 2006 and 2007 if the cost were capitalized and expensed through depreciation charges.
d. Determine the effect of the overhaul on cash flow from operating activities for 2006 and 2007 if the cost were recognized as maintenance expense.

Exercise 8-19B ***Computing and recording depletion expense*** **L.O. 8**

Mountain Coal paid $450,000 to acquire a mine with 22,500 tons of coal reserves. The following statements model reflects Mountain's financial condition just prior to purchasing the coal reserves. The company extracted 10,000 tons of coal in year 1 and 8,000 tons in year 2.

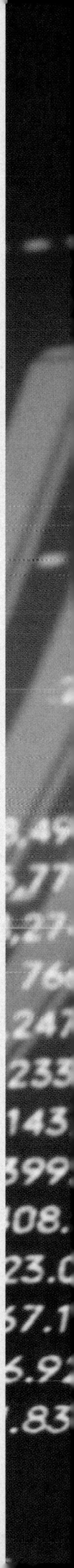

Assets			=	Equity			Rev.	−	Exp.	=	Net Inc.	Cash Flow
Cash	+	Coal Res.	=	Com. Stk.	+	Ret. Earn.						
600,000	+	NA	=	600,000	+	NA	NA	−	NA	=	NA	NA

Required

a. Compute the depletion charge per unit.

b. Record the acquisition of the coal reserves and the depletion expense for years 1 and 2 in a financial statements model like the preceding one.

c. Prepare the general journal entries to record the depletion expense for years 1 and 2.

L.O. 9

Exercise 8-20B *Computing and recording the amortization of intangibles*

Hi-Tech Manufacturing paid cash to purchase the assets of an existing company. Among the assets purchased were the following items:

Patent with 2 remaining years of legal life	$24,000
Goodwill	20,000

Hi-Tech's financial condition just prior to the purchase of these assets is shown in the following statements model:

Assets					=	Liab.	+	Equity	Rev.	−	Exp.	=	Net Inc.	Cash Flow
Cash	+	Patent	+	Goodwill										
90,000	+	NA	+	NA	=	NA	+	90,000	NA	−	NA	=	NA	NA

Required

a. Compute the annual amortization expense for these items.

b. Record the purchase of the intangible assets and the related amortization expense for year 1 in a horizontal statements model like the preceding one.

c. Prepare the journal entries to record the purchase of the intangible assets and the related amortization for year 1.

L.O. 9

Exercise 8-21B *Computing and recording goodwill*

Sea Corp purchased the business Beta Resources for $200,000 cash and assumed all liabilities at the date of purchase. Beta's books showed tangible assets of $150,000, liabilities of $40,000, and stockholders' equity of $110,000. An appraiser assessed the fair market value of the tangible assets at $185,000 at the date of purchase. Sea Corp's financial condition just prior to the purchase is shown in the following statements model:

Assets					=	Liab.	+	Equity	Rev.	−	Exp.	=	Net Inc.	Cash Flow
Cash	+	Tang. Assets	+	Goodwill										
300,000	+	NA	+	NA	=	NA	+	300,000	NA	−	NA	=	NA	NA

Required

a. Compute the amount of goodwill purchased.

b. Record the purchase in a financial statements model like the preceding one.

c. When will the goodwill be written off under the impairment rules?

d. Record the purchase in general journal format.

PROBLEMS—SERIES B

Problem 8-22B ***Accounting for acquisition of assets including a basket purchase*** **L.O. 2**

Moon Co., Inc., made several purchases of long-term assets in 2009. The details of each purchase are presented here.

New Office Equipment

1. List price: $60,000; terms: 2/10 n/30; paid within discount period.
2. Transportation-in: $1,600.
3. Installation: $2,200.
4. Cost to repair damage during unloading: $1,000.
5. Routine maintenance cost after six months: $300.

Basket Purchase of Copier, Computer, and Scanner for $15,000 with Fair Market Values

1. Copier, $10,000.
2. Computer, $6,000.
3. Scanner, $4,000.

Land for New Warehouse with an Old Building Torn Down

1. Purchase price, $200,000.
2. Demolition of building, $10,000.
3. Lumber sold from old building, $7,000.
4. Grading in preparation for new building, $14,000.
5. Construction of new building, $500,000.

Required

In each of these cases, determine the amount of cost to be capitalized in the asset accounts.

Problem 8-23B ***Accounting for depreciation over multiple accounting cycles: straight-line depreciation*** **L.O. 3, 4**

Altoids Company started business by acquiring $60,000 cash from the issue of common stock on January 1, 2006. The cash acquired was immediately used to purchase equipment for $60,000 that had a $12,000 salvage value and an expected useful life of four years. The equipment was used to produce the following revenue stream (assume that all revenue transactions are for cash). At the beginning of the fifth year, the equipment was sold for $6,800 cash. Altoids uses straight-line depreciation.

	2006	2007	2008	2009	2010
Revenue	$15,200	$14,400	$13,000	$12,000	$0

Required

Prepare income statements, statements of changes in stockholders' equity, balance sheets, and statements of cash flows for each of the five years. Present the statements in the form of a vertical statements model.

Problem 8-24B ***Purchase and use of tangible asset: three accounting cycles, straight-line depreciation*** **L.O. 3, 6, 7**

The following transactions relate to Jim's Towing Service. Assume the transactions for the purchase of the wrecker and any capital improvements occur on January 1 of each year.

2007

1. Acquired $40,000 cash from the issue of common stock.
2. Purchased a used wrecker for $26,000. It has an estimated useful life of three years and a $2,000 salvage value.

3. Paid sales tax on the wrecker of $1,800.
4. Collected $17,600 in towing fees.
5. Paid $3,000 for gasoline and oil.
6. Recorded straight-line depreciation on the wrecker for 2007.
7. Closed the revenue and expense accounts to Retained Earnings at the end of 2007.

2008

1. Paid for a tune-up for the wrecker's engine, $400.
2. Bought four new tires, $600.
3. Collected $18,000 in towing fees.
4. Paid $4,200 for gasoline and oil.
5. Recorded straight-line depreciation for 2008.
6. Closed the revenue and expense accounts to Retained Earnings at the end of 2008.

2009

1. Paid to overhaul the wrecker's engine, $1,400, which extended the life of the wrecker to a total of four years.
2. Paid for gasoline and oil, $3,600.
3. Collected $30,000 in towing fees.
4. Recorded straight-line depreciation for 2009.
5. Closed the revenue and expense accounts at the end of 2009.

Required

a. Use a horizontal statements model like the following one to show the effect of these transactions on the elements of financial statements. Use + for increase, − for decrease, and NA for not affected. The first event is recorded as an example.

2007 Event No.	Assets	=	Liabilities	+	Equity	Net Inc.	Cash Flow
1	+		NA		+	NA	+ FA

b. For each year, record the transactions in general journal form and post them to T-accounts.
c. Use a vertical model to present financial statements for 2007, 2008, and 2009.

L.O. 3

Problem 8-25B *Calculating depreciation expense using four different methods*

Action Inc. manufactures sporting goods. The following information applies to a machine purchased on January 1, 2007:

Purchase price	$ 70,000
Delivery cost	$ 2,000
Installation charge	$ 1,000
Estimated life	5 years
Estimated units	140,000
Salvage estimate	$ 3,000

During 2007, the machine produced 26,000 units and during 2008, it produced 21,000 units.

Required

Determine the amount of depreciation expense for 2007 and 2008 using each of the following methods:

a. Straight line.
b. Double-declining-balance.
c. Units of production.
d. MACRS, assuming that the machine is classified as seven-year property.

Problem 8-26B ***Effect of straight-line versus double-declining-balance depreciation on the recognition of expense and gains or losses*** **L.O. 3, 4**

Graves Office Service purchased a new computer system in 2008 for $60,000. It is expected to have a five-year useful life and a $5,000 salvage value. The company expects to use the system more extensively in the early years of its life.

Required

a. Calculate the depreciation expense for each of the five years, assuming the use of straight-line depreciation.

b. Calculate the depreciation expense for each of the five years, assuming the use of double-declining-balance depreciation.

c. Would the choice of one depreciation method over another produce a different amount of cash flow for any year? Why or why not?

d. Assume that Graves Office Service sold the computer system at the end of the fourth year for $15,000. Compute the amount of gain or loss using each depreciation method.

e. Explain any differences in gain or loss due to using the different methods.

Problem 8-27B ***Computing and recording units-of-production depreciation*** **L.O. 3, 4**

Marvel purchased assembly equipment for $700,000 on January 1, 2007. Marvel's financial condition immediately prior to the purchase is shown in the following horizontal statements model:

Assets					=	Equity			Rev.	−	Exp.	=	Net Inc.	Cash Flow
Cash	+	Equip.	−	Acc. Dep.	=	Com. Stk.	+	Ret. Earn.						
800,000	+	NA	−	NA	=	800,000	+	NA	NA	−	NA	=	NA	NA

The equipment is expected to have a useful life of 100,000 machine hours and a salvage value of $20,000. Actual machine-hour use was as follows:

2007	32,000
2008	33,000
2009	35,000
2010	28,000
2011	12,000

Required

a. Compute the depreciation for each of the five years, assuming the use of units-of-production depreciation.

b. Assume that Marvel earns $320,000 of cash revenue during 2007. Record the purchase of the equipment and the recognition of the revenue and the depreciation expense for the first year in a financial statements model like the preceding one.

c. Assume that Marvel sold the equipment at the end of the fifth year for $18,000. Record the general journal entry for the sale.

Problem 8-28B ***Determining the effect of depreciation expense on financial statements*** **L.O. 3**

Three different companies each purchased trucks on January 1, 2007, for $40,000. Each truck was expected to last four years or 200,000 miles. Salvage value was estimated to be $5,000. All three trucks were driven 66,000 miles in 2007, 42,000 miles in 2008, 40,000 miles in 2009, and 60,000 miles in 2010. Each of the three companies earned $30,000 of cash revenue during each of the four years. Company A uses straight-line depreciation, company B uses double-declining-balance depreciation, and company C uses units-of-production depreciation.

Required

Answer each of the following questions. Ignore the effects of income taxes.

a. Which company will report the highest amount of net income for 2007?

b. Which company will report the lowest amount of net income for 2010?

c. Which company will report the highest book value on the December 31, 2009, balance sheet?

d. Which company will report the highest amount of retained earnings on the December 31, 2010, balance sheet?

e. Which company will report the lowest amount of cash flow from operating activities on the 2009 statement of cash flows?

L.O. 6, 8

Problem 8-29B ***Accounting for depletion***

Sanchez Company engages in the exploration and development of many types of natural resources. In the last two years, the company has engaged in the following activities:

Jan. 1, 2006	Purchased for $1,600,000 a silver mine estimated to contain 100,000 tons of silver ore.
July 1, 2006	Purchased for $1,500,000 a tract of timber estimated to yield 1,000,000 board feet of lumber and the residual value of the land was estimated at $100,000.
Feb. 1, 2007	Purchased for $1,800,000 a gold mine estimated to yield 30,000 tons of gold-veined ore.
Sept. 1, 2007	Purchased oil reserves for $1,360,000. The reserves were estimated to contain 282,000 barrels of oil, of which 10,000 would be unprofitable to pump.

Required

a. Prepare the journal entries to account for the following:

(1) The 2006 purchases.

(2) Depletion on the 2006 purchases, assuming that 12,000 tons of silver were mined and 500,000 board feet of lumber were cut.

(3) The 2007 purchases.

(4) Depletion on the four natural resource assets, assuming that 20,000 tons of silver ore, 300,000 board feet of lumber, 4,000 tons of gold ore, and 50,000 barrels of oil were extracted.

b. Prepare the portion of the December 31, 2007, balance sheet that reports natural resources.

c. Assume that in 2008 the estimates changed to reflect only 20,000 tons of gold ore remaining. Prepare the depletion journal entry in 2008 to account for the extraction of 6,000 tons of gold ore.

L.O. 3, 4, 6, 7

Problem 8-30B ***Recording continuing expenditures for plant assets***

Harris Inc. recorded the following transactions over the life of a piece of equipment purchased in 2007:

Jan. 1, 2007	Purchased equipment for $80,000 cash. The equipment was estimated to have a five-year life and $5,000 salvage value and was to be depreciated using the straight-line method.
Dec. 31, 2007	Recorded depreciation expense for 2007.
Sept. 30, 2008	Undertook routine repairs costing $750.
Dec. 31, 2008	Recorded depreciation expense for 2008.
Jan. 1, 2009	Made an adjustment costing $3,000 to the equipment. It improved the quality of the output but did not affect the life estimate.
Dec. 31, 2009	Recorded depreciation expense for 2009.
June 1, 2010	Incurred $620 cost to oil and clean the equipment.
Dec. 31, 2010	Recorded depreciation expense for 2010.
Jan. 1, 2011	Had the equipment completely overhauled at a cost of $8,000. The overhaul was estimated to extend the total life to seven years.
Dec. 31, 2011	Recorded depreciation expense for 2011.
Oct. 1, 2012	Received and accepted an offer of $18,000 for the equipment.

Required

a. Use a horizontal statements model like the following one to show the effects of these transactions on the elements of the financial statements. Use + for increase, − for decrease, and NA for not affected. The first event is recorded as an example.

Date	Assets	=	Liabilities	+	Equity	Net Inc.	Cash Flow
Jan. 1, 2007	+ −		NA		NA	NA	− IA

b. Determine the amount of depreciation expense to be reported on the income statements for the years 2007 through 2012.

c. Determine the book value (cost − accumulated depreciation) Harris will report on the balance sheets at the end of the years 2007 through 2012.

d. Determine the amount of the gain or loss Harris will report on the disposal of the equipment on October 1, 2012.

e. Prepare the general entry for the disposal of the equipment on October 1, 2012.

Problem 8-31B *Continuing expenditures with statements model*

L.O. 6, 7

Venus Company owned a service truck that was purchased at the beginning of 2007 for $20,000. It had an estimated life of three years and an estimated salvage value of $2,000. Venus uses straight-line depreciation. Its financial condition as of January 1, 2009, is shown in the following financial statements model:

Assets					=	Equity			Rev.	−	Exp.	=	Net Inc.	Cash Flow
Cash	+	Truck	−	Acc. Dep.	=	Com. Stk.	+	Ret. Earn.						
14,000	+	20,000	−	12,000	=	4,000	+	18,000	NA	−	NA	=	NA	NA

In 2009, Venus spent the following amounts on the truck:

Jan.	4	Overhauled the engine for $4,000. The estimated life was extended one additional year, and the salvage value was revised to $3,000.
July	6	Obtained oil change and transmission service, $160.
Aug.	7	Replaced the fan belt and battery, $360.
Dec.	31	Purchased gasoline for the year, $5,000.
	31	Recognized 2009 depreciation expense.

Required

a. Record the 2009 transactions in a statements model like the preceding one.

b. Prepare journal entries for the 2009 transactions.

Problem 8-32B *Accounting for intangible assets*

L.O. 9

Xie Company purchased Atlantic Transportation Co. for $1,200,000. The fair market values of the assets purchased were as follows. No liabilities were assumed.

Equipment	$400,000
Land	100,000
Building	400,000
Franchise (10-year life)	20,000

Required

a. Calculate the amount of goodwill purchased.

b. Prepare the journal entry to record the amortization of the franchise fee at the end of year 1.

Problem 8-33B *Accounting for goodwill*

L.O. 9

Sulley Equipment Manufacturing Co. purchased the assets of Malcom Inc., a competitor, in 2007. It recorded goodwill of $50,000 at purchase. Because of defective machinery Malcom had produced prior to the purchase, it has been determined that all of the purchased goodwill has been permanently impaired.

Required

Prepare the journal entry to record the permanent impairment of the goodwill.

ANALYZE, THINK, COMMUNICATE

ATC 8-1 Business Applications Case *Understanding real-world annual reports*

Required—Part 1

The Topps Company, Inc.

Use the **Topps Company**'s annual report in Appendix B to answer the following questions.

a. What method of depreciation does Topps use?

b. What types of intangible assets does Topps have?

c. What are the estimated lives that Topps uses for the various types of long-term assets?

d. As of March 1, 2003, what is the original cost of Topps': Land; Buildings and improvements; and Machinery, equipment and software (see the footnotes)?

e. What was Topps' depreciation expense and amortization expense for 2003 (see the footnotes)?

Required—Part 2

Harley-Davidson, Inc.

Use the **Harley-Davidson**'s annual report that came with this book to answer the following questions.

a. What method of depreciation does Harley-Davidson use?

b. What types of intangible assets, if any, does Harley-Davidson have?

c. What are the estimated lives that Harley-Davidson uses for the various types of long-term assets?

d. What dollar amount of Harley-Davidson's "identifiable assets" is associated with its Motorcycles Segment and what amount is associated with its Financial Services segment (see Note 11)?

e. What dollar amount of Harley-Davidson's "long-lived assets" is located in the United States and what amount is located in other countries (see Note 11)?

ATC 8-2 Group Assignment *Different depreciation methods*

Sweet's Bakery makes cakes, pies, and other pastries that it sells to local grocery stores. The company experienced the following transactions during 2008.

1. Started business by acquiring $60,000 cash from the issue of common stock.
2. Purchased bakery equipment for $46,000.
3. Had sales in 2008 amounting to $42,000.
4. Paid $8,200 of cash for supplies which were all used during the year to make baked goods.
5. Incurred other operating expenses of $12,000 for 2008.
6. Recorded depreciation assuming the equipment had a four-year life and a $6,000 salvage value. The MACRS recovery period is five years.
7. Paid income tax. The rate is 30 percent.

Required

a. Organize the class into three sections and divide each section into groups of three to five students. Assign each section a depreciation method: straight-line, double-declining-balance, or MACRS.

Group Task

Prepare an income statement and balance sheet using the preceding information and the depreciation method assigned to your group.

Class Discussion

b. Have a representative of each section put its income statement on the board. Are there differences in net income? In the amount of income tax paid? How will these differences in the amount of depreciation expense change over the life of the equipment?

ATC 8-3 Real-World Case *Different numbers for different industries*

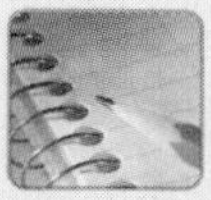

The following ratios are for four companies in different industries. Some of these ratios have been discussed in the textbook; others have not, but their names explain how the ratio was computed. The four sets of ratios, presented randomly are:

Ratio	Company 1	Company 2	Company 3	Company 4
Operating cycle	39 days	11 days	27 days	234 days
Return on assets	24%	11%	14%	2%
Gross margin	54%	39%	40%	27%
Sales ÷ Property, plant and equipment	64.8 times	2.6 times	1.6 times	2.9 times
Sales ÷ Number of full-time employees	$21,000	$40,000	$585,000	$284,000

The four companies to which these ratios relate, listed in alphabetical order, are:

1. **Anheuser Busch Companies, Inc.**, a company that produces beer and related products. Its fiscal year-end was December 31, 2002.
2. **Caterpillar, Inc.**, a company that manufactures heavy construction equipment. Its fiscal year-end was December 31, 2002.
3. **Outback Steakhouse, Inc.**, which operates over 800 restaurants worldwide, most of them under the name Outback Steakhouse. Its fiscal year-end was December 31, 2002.
4. **Weight Watchers International, Inc.**, a company that provides weight loss services and products. During its fiscal year ending December 28, 2002, 64 percent of its revenues came from meeting fees, and 29 percent came from product sales.

Required

Determine which company should be matched with each set of ratios. Write a memorandum explaining the rationale for your decisions.

ATC 8-4 Business Applications Case *Effect of depreciation on the return on assets ratio*

Organic Bagel Bakery (OBB) was started on January 1, 2005, when it acquired $100,000 cash from the issue of common stock. The company immediately purchased an oven that cost $100,000 cash. The oven had an estimated salvage value of $10,000 and an expected useful life of eight years. OBB used the oven during 2005 to produce $30,000 of cash revenue. Assume that these were the only events affecting OBB during 2005.

Required

(*Hint:* Prepare an income statement and a balance sheet prior to completing the following requirements.)

a. Compute the return on assets ratio as of December 31, 2005, assuming OBB uses the straight-line depreciation method.
b. Recompute the ratio assuming OBB uses the double-declining-balance method.
c. Which depreciation method makes it *appear* that OBB is utilizing its assets more effectively?

ATC 8-5 Business Applications Case *Effect of depreciation on financial statement analysis: straight-line versus double-declining-balance*

Qin Company and Roche Company experienced the exact same set of economic events during 2006. Both companies purchased machines on January 1, 2006. Except for the effects of this purchase, the accounting records of both companies had the following accounts and balances.

As of January 1, 2006	
Total Assets	$200,000
Total Liabilities	80,000
Total Stockholders' Equity	120,000
During 2006	
Total Sales Revenue	100,000
Total Expenses (not including depreciation)	60,000
Liabilities were not affected by transactions in 2006.	

The machines purchased by the companies each cost $40,000 cash. The machines had expected useful lives of five years and estimated salvage values of $4,000. Qin uses straight-line depreciation. Roche uses double-declining-balance depreciation.

Required

a. For both companies, calculate the balances in the preceding accounts on December 31, 2006, after the effects of the purchase and depreciation of the machines have been applied. [*Hint:* The purchases of the machines are asset exchange transactions that do not affect total assets. However, the effect of depreciating the machines changes the amounts in total assets, expense, and equity (retained earnings)].

b. Based on the revised account balances determined in Requirement *a,* calculate the following ratios for both companies:

(1) Debt to assets ratio.

(2) Return on assets ratio.

(3) Return on equity ratio.

c. Disregarding the effects of income taxes, which company produced the higher increase in real economic wealth during 2006?

ATC 8-6 Writing Assignment *Impact of historical cost on asset presentation on the balance sheet*

Assume that you are examining the balance sheets of two companies and note the following information:

	Company A	Company B
Equipment	$1,130,000	$900,000
Accumulated Depreciation	(730,000)	(500,000)
Book Value	$ 400,000	$400,000

Maxie Smith, a student who has had no accounting courses, remarks that Company A and Company B have the same amount of equipment.

Required

In a short paragraph, explain to Maxie that the two companies do not have equal amounts of equipment. You may want to include in your discussion comments regarding the possible age of each company's equipment, the impact of the historical cost concept on balance sheet information, and the impact of different depreciation methods on book value.

ATC 8-7 Ethical Dilemma *What's an expense?*

Several years ago, Wilson Blowhard founded a communications company. The company became successful and grew by expanding its customer base and acquiring some of its competitors. In fact, most of its growth resulted from acquiring other companies. Mr. Blowhard is adamant about continuing the company's growth and increasing its net worth. To achieve these goals, the business's net income must continue to increase at a rapid pace.

If the company's net worth continues to rise, Mr. Blowhard plans to sell the company and retire. He is, therefore, focused on improving the company's profit any way he can.

In the communications business, companies often use the lines of other communications companies. This line usage is a significant operating expense for Mr. Blowhard's company. Generally accepted accounting principles require operating costs like line use to be expensed as they are incurred each year. Each dollar of line cost reduces net income by a dollar.

After reviewing the company's operations, Mr. Blowhard concluded that the company did not currently need all of the line use it was paying for. It was really paying the owner of the lines now so that the line use would be available in the future for all of Mr. Blowhard's expected new customers. Mr. Blowhard instructed his accountant to capitalize all of the line cost charges and depreciate them over 10 years. The accountant reluctantly followed Mr. Blowhard's instructions and the company's net income for the current year showed a significant increase over the prior year's net income. Mr. Blowhard had found a way to report continued growth in the company's net income and increase the value of the company.

Required

a. How does Mr. Blowhard's scheme affect the amount of income that the company would otherwise report in its financial statements and how does the scheme affect the company's balance sheet? Explain your answer.

b. Review the AICPA's Articles of Professional Conduct (see Chapter 1) and comment on any of the standards that were violated.

c. Review Donald Cressey's identified features of unethical and criminal conduct (see Chapter 1) and comment on which of these features are evident in this case.

ATC 8-8 Research Assignment *Comparing Microsoft's and Intel's operational assets*

This chapter discussed how companies in different industries often use different proportions of current versus long-term assets to accomplish their business objective. The technology revolution resulting from the silicon microchip has often been led by two well-known companies: **Microsoft** and **Intel**. Although often thought of together, these companies are really very different. Using either the most current Forms 10-K or annual reports for Microsoft Corporation and Intel Corporation, complete the requirements below. To obtain the Forms 10-K, use either the EDGAR system following the instructions in Appendix A or the company's website. Microsoft's annual report is available on its website; Intel's annual report is its Form 10-K.

Required

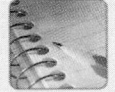

a. Fill in the missing data in the following table. The percentages must be computed; they are not included in the companies' 10-Ks. (*Note:* The percentages for current assets and property, plant, and equipment will not sum to 100.)

	Current Assets	Property, Plant, and Equipment	Total Assets
Microsoft			
Dollar Amount	$ ______	$ ______	$ ______
% of Total Assets	______ %	______ %	100%
Intel			
Dollar Amount	$ ______	$ ______	$ ______
% of Total Assets	______ %	______ %	100%

b. Briefly explain why these two companies have different percentages of their assets in current assets versus property, plant, and equipment.

COMPREHENSIVE PROBLEM

The trial balance of Pacilio Security Services Inc. as of January 1, 2008, had the following normal balances:

Cash	$93,708
Petty Cash	100
Accounts Receivable	22,540
Allowance for Doubtful Accounts	1,334
Supplies	250
Prepaid Rent	3,600
Merchandise Inventory (18 @ $285)	5,130
Land	4,000
Salaries Payable	2,100
Common Stock	50,000
Retained Earnings	75,894

During 2008 Pacillo Security Services experienced the following transactions:

1. Paid the salaries payable from 2007.
2. Purchased equipment and a van for a lump sum of $36,000 cash on January 2, 2008. The equipment was appraised for $10,000 and the van was appraised for $30,000.
3. Paid $9,000 on May 2, 2008, for one year's office rent in advance.
4. Purchased $300 of supplies on account.
5. Purchased 120 alarm systems at a cost of $280 each. Paid cash for the purchase.
6. After numerous attempts to collect from customers, wrote off $2,350 of uncollectible accounts receivable.
7. Sold 115 alarm systems for $580 each. All sales were on account. (Be sure to compute cost of goods sold using the FIFO cost flow method.)
8. Billed $86,000 of monitoring services for the year. Credit card sales amounted to $36,000, and the credit card company charged a 4 percent fee. The remaining $50,000 were sales on account.
9. Replenished the petty cash fund on June 30. The fund had $12 cash and receipts of $45 for yard mowing, $28 for office supplies expense, and $11 for miscellaneous expenses.
10. Collected the amount due from the credit card company.
11. Paid installers and other employees a total of $52,000 cash for salaries.
12. Collected $115,500 of accounts receivable during the year.
13. Paid $12,500 of advertising expense during the year.
14. Paid $6,800 of utilities expense for the year.
15. Sold the land, which was purchased in 2001, for $12,000.
16. Paid the accounts payable.
17. Paid a dividend of $10,000 to the shareholders.

Adjustments

18. Determined that $180 of supplies were on hand at the end of the year.
19. Recognized the expired rent for both the van and the office building for the year. The lease on the van was not renewed.
20. Recognized uncollectible accounts expense for the year using the allowance method. Pacilio estimates that 3 percent of sales on account will not be collected.
21. Recognized depreciation expense on the equipment and the van. The equipment has a five-year life and a $2,000 salvage value. The van has a four-year life and a $6,000 salvage value. The company uses double-declining-balance for the van and straight-line for the equipment.
22. Accrued salaries at December 31, 2008, were $1,500.

Required

a. Record the above transactions in general journal form.
b. Post the transactions to T-accounts.
c. Prepare a trial balance.
d. Prepare an income statement, statement of changes in stockholders' equity, balance sheet, and statement of cash flows.
e. Close the temporary accounts to retained earnings.
f. Post the closing entries to the T-accounts and prepare an after-closing trial balance.

CHAPTER 9

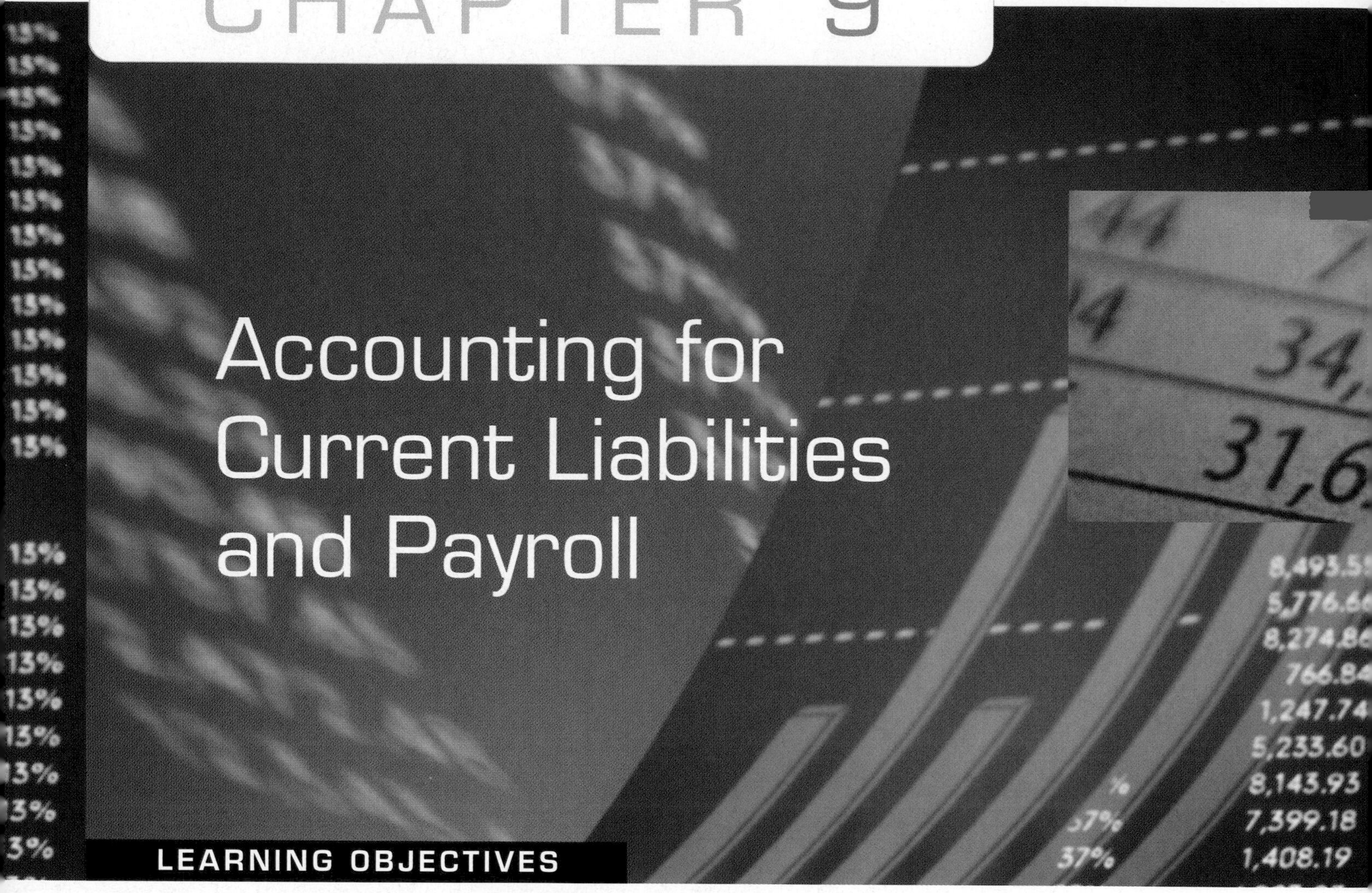

Accounting for Current Liabilities and Payroll

LEARNING OBJECTIVES

After you have mastered the material in this chapter, you will be able to:

1. Show how notes payable and related interest expense affect financial statements.
2. Show how sales tax liabilities affect financial statements.
3. Define contingent liabilities and explain how they are reported in financial statements.
4. Explain how warranty obligations affect financial statements.
5. Define basic terms and identify common documents associated with payroll accounting.
6. Explain how payroll accounting affects financial statements.
7. Compute FICA and unemployment payroll taxes.
8. Distinguish between current and noncurrent assets and liabilities.
9. Prepare a classified balance sheet.
10. Use the current ratio to assess the level of liquidity.
11. Show how discount notes and related interest charges affect financial statements. (Appendix)

Chapter 9

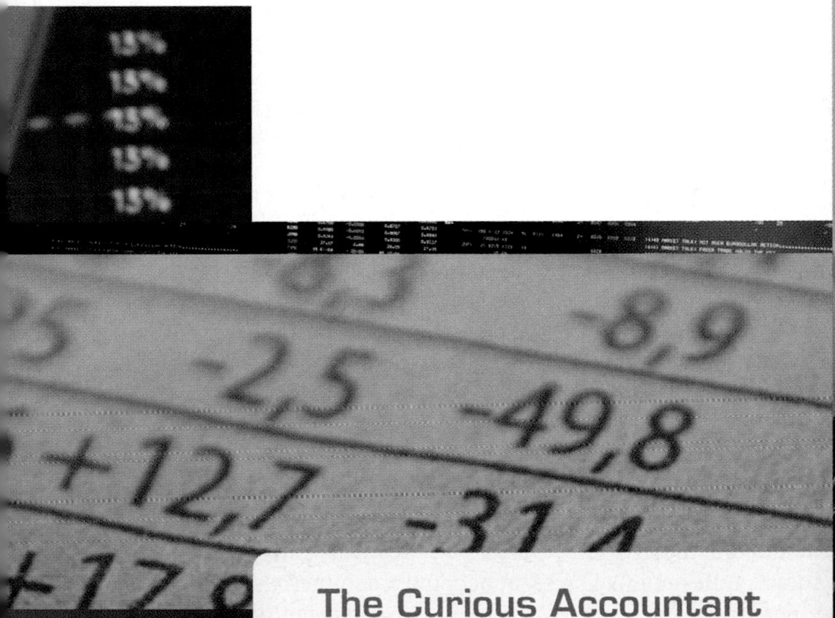

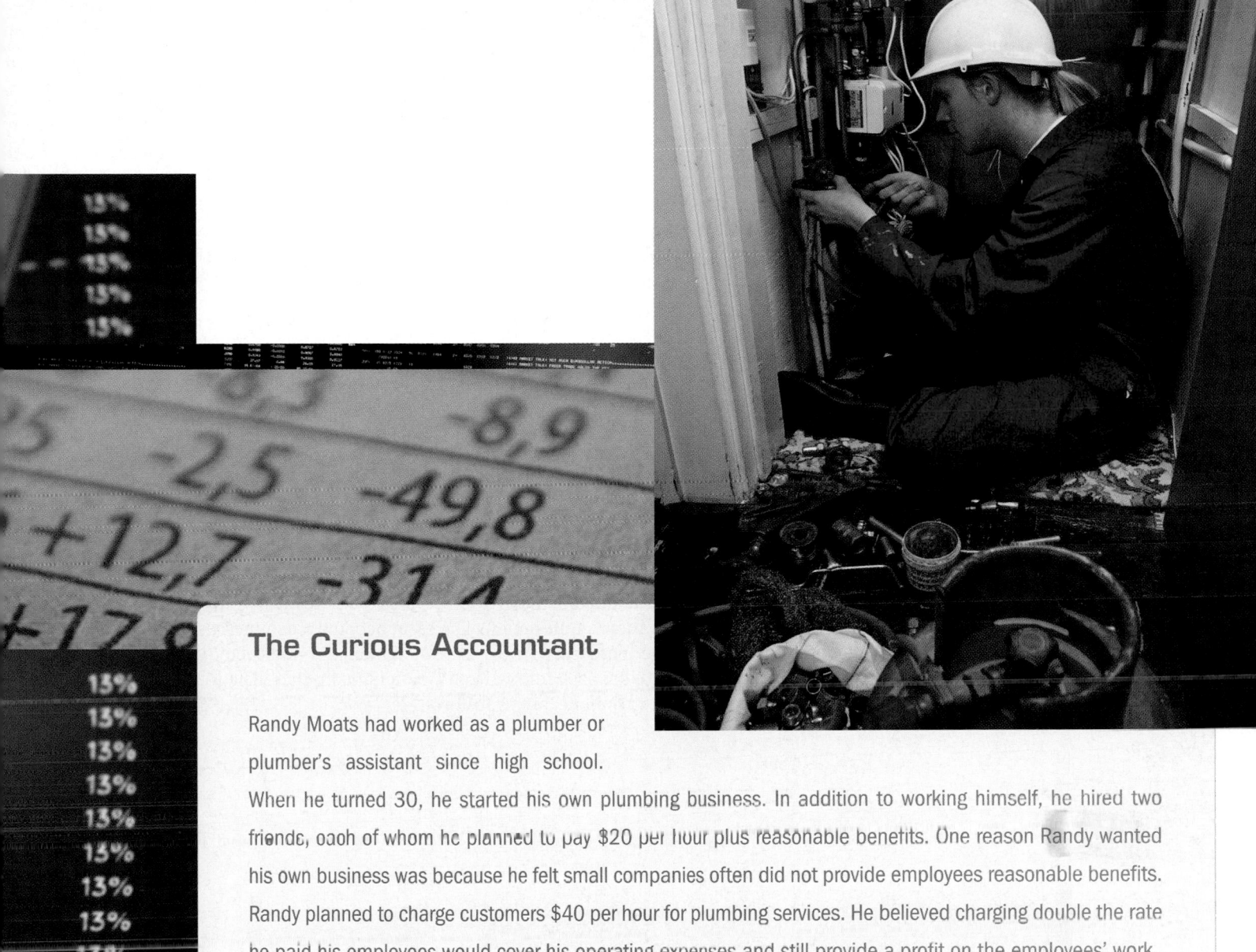

The Curious Accountant

Randy Moats had worked as a plumber or plumber's assistant since high school. When he turned 30, he started his own plumbing business. In addition to working himself, he hired two friends, each of whom he planned to pay $20 per hour plus reasonable benefits. One reason Randy wanted his own business was because he felt small companies often did not provide employees reasonable benefits. Randy planned to charge customers $40 per hour for plumbing services. He believed charging double the rate he paid his employees would cover his operating expenses and still provide a profit on the employees' work.

Randy hired a local accounting firm for his accounting needs, including handling his company's payroll records. After getting the business established, he and his employees kept busy, but the business was not as profitable as Randy had expected. His accountant explained that the total compensation cost of his employees was averaging around $25 per hour. Randy knew the employees would cost more than their $20 per hour wage rate because of their fringe benefits, but he had not expected the benefits cost to be one-fourth of their base pay.

What could cause Randy's compensation expenses to be so unexpectedly high? (Answers on page 457.)

CHAPTER OPENING

Chapter 7 explained the need to estimate the net realizable value of receivables (the amount of receivables a company expects to actually collect). Do companies also estimate the net realizable value of payables (the amount they expect to actually pay)? The answer is no. Unless there is evidence to the contrary, companies are assumed to be going concerns that will continue to operate. Under this **going concern assumption,** *companies expect to pay their obligations in full. Accounts and notes payable are therefore reported at face value. In* *addition to reporting liabilities for which the amounts due are known, companies report liabilities for which the amounts due are uncertain. Liabilities that are uncertain as to amount are contingent liabilities.*

Chapter 2 discussed several types of liabilities with known amounts due, including accounts payable, salaries payable, and unearned revenue. This chapter introduces other liabilities with known amounts due: notes payable, sales taxes payable, and payroll liabilities; and contingent liabilities including warranties payable and vacation pay. We limit the discussion in this chapter to current liabilities, *those that are payable within one year or the operating cycle, whichever is longer.* ■

Accounting for Current Liabilities

Accounting for Notes Payable

LO 1

Show how notes payable and related interest expense affect financial statements.

Topic Tackler PLUS 9-1

Our discussion of promissory notes in Chapter 7 focused on the payee, the company with a note receivable on its books. In this chapter we focus on the maker of the note, the company with a note payable on its books. Since the maker of the note issues (gives) the note to the payee, the maker is sometimes called the **issuer.**

To illustrate, assume that on September 1, 2006, Herrera Supply Company (HSC) borrowed $90,000 from the National Bank. As evidence of the debt, Herrera issued a **note payable** that had a one-year term and an annual interest rate of 9 percent.

Issuing the note is an asset source transaction. The asset account Cash increases and the liability account Notes Payable increases. The income statement is not affected. The statement of cash flows shows a $90,000 cash inflow from financing activities. The journal entry and its effects on the financial statements are as follows:

Account Title	Debit	Credit
Cash	90,000	
Notes Payable		90,000

	Assets	=	Liabilities			+	Stockholders' Equity			Rev.	−	Exp.	=	Net Inc.	Cash Flow
Date	Cash	=	Notes Pay.	+	Int. Pay.	+	Com. Stk.	+	Ret. Earn.						
09/01/06	90,000	=	90,000	+	NA	+	NA	+	NA	NA	−	NA	=	NA	90,000 FA

On December 31, 2006, HSC would record an adjusting entry to recognize four months (September 1 through December 31) of accrued interest expense. The accrued interest is $2,700 [$90,000 × 0.09 × (4 ÷ 12)]. The adjusting entry is a claims exchange. The liability account Interest Payable increases, and the equity account Retained Earnings decreases. The income statement would report interest expense although HSC had not paid any cash for interest in 2006. The journal entry and its effects on the financial statements are as follows:

Account Title	Debit	Credit
Interest Expense	2,700	
Interest Payable		2,700

	Assets	=	Liabilities			+	Stockholders' Equity			Rev.	−	Exp.	=	Net Inc.	Cash Flow
Date	Cash	=	Notes Pay.	+	Int. Pay.	+	Com. Stk.	+	Ret. Earn.						
12/31/06	NA	=	NA	+	2,700	+	NA	+	(2,700)	NA	−	2,700	=	(2,700)	NA

HSC would record three journal entries on August 31, 2007 (the maturity date). The first entry recognizes $5,400 of interest expense that accrued in 2007 from January 1 through August 31 [$90,000 × 0.09 × (8 ÷ 12)]. The entry and its effects on the financial statements are as follows:

Account Title	Debit	Credit
Interest Expense	5,400	
Interest Payable		5,400

	Assets =	Liabilities	+	Stockholders' Equity		Rev. − Exp. = Net Inc.	Cash Flow
Date	Cash =	Notes Pay. +	Int. Pay. +	Com. Stk. +	Ret. Earn.		
08/31/07	NA =	NA +	5,400 +	NA +	(5,400)	NA − 5,400 = (5,400)	NA

The second entry records HSC's cash payment for interest on August 31, 2007. This entry is an asset use transaction that reduces both the Cash and Interest Payable accounts for the total amount of interest due, $8,100 [$90,000 × 0.09 × (12 ÷ 12)]. The interest payment includes the four months' interest accrued in 2006 and the eight months accrued in 2007 ($2,700 + $5,400 = $8,100). There is no effect on the income statement because HSC recognized the interest expense in two previous journal entries. The statement of cash flows would report an $8,100 cash outflow from operating activities. The journal entry and its effects on the financial statements follow:

Account Title	Debit	Credit
Interest Payable	8,100	
Cash		8,100

	Assets =	Liabilities	+	Stockholders' Equity		Rev. − Exp. = Net Inc.	Cash Flow
Date	Cash =	Notes Pay. +	Int. Pay. +	Com. Stk. +	Ret. Earn.		
08/31/07	(8,100) =	NA +	(8,100) +	NA +	NA	NA − NA = NA	(8,100) OA

The third entry on August 31, 2007, reflects repaying the principal. This entry is an asset use transaction. The Cash account and the Notes Payable account each decrease by $90,000. There is no effect on the income statement. The statement of cash flows would show a $90,000 cash outflow from financing activities. Recall that paying interest is classified as an operating activity even though repaying the principal is a financing activity. The journal entry and its effects on the financial statements are as follows:

Account Title	Debit	Credit
Notes Payable	90,000	
Cash		90,000

	Assets =	Liabilities	+	Stockholders' Equity		Rev. − Exp. = Net Inc.	Cash Flow
Date	Cash =	Notes Pay. +	Int. Pay. +	Com. Stk. +	Ret. Earn.		
08/31/07	(90,000) =	(90,000) +	NA +	NA +	NA	NA − NA = NA	(90,000) FA

Alternatively, HSC could combine the three separate journal entries recorded on the maturity date (August 31, 2007) into a single compound journal entry as shown below:

Account Title	Debit	Credit
Interest Expense	5,400	
Interest Payable	2,700	
Notes Payable	90,000	
Cash		98,100

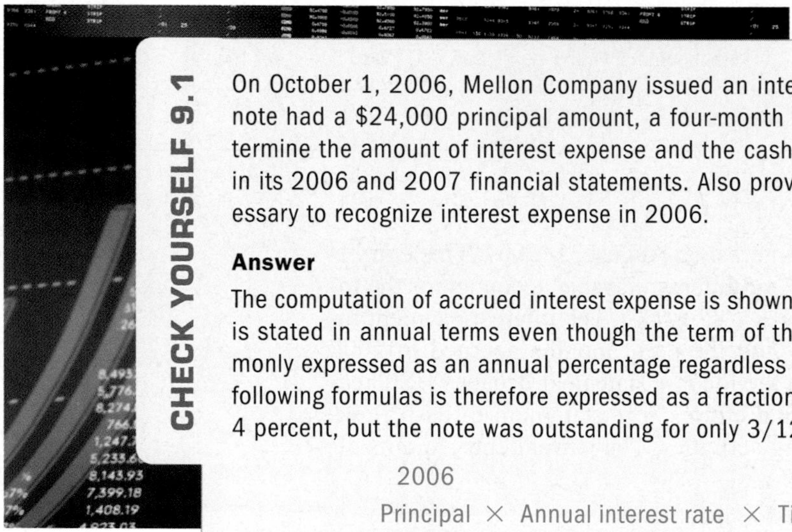

CHECK YOURSELF 9.1

On October 1, 2006, Mellon Company issued an interest-bearing note payable to Better Banks Inc. The note had a $24,000 principal amount, a four-month term, and an annual interest rate of 4 percent. Determine the amount of interest expense and the cash outflow from operating activities Mellon will report in its 2006 and 2007 financial statements. Also provide in general journal form the adjusting entry necessary to recognize interest expense in 2006.

Answer

The computation of accrued interest expense is shown below. Unless otherwise specified, the interest rate is stated in annual terms even though the term of the note is only four months. Interest rates are commonly expressed as an annual percentage regardless of the term of the note. The *time outstanding* in the following formulas is therefore expressed as a fraction of a year. Mellon paid interest at an annual rate of 4 percent, but the note was outstanding for only 3/12 of a year in 2006 and 1/12 of a year in 2007.

2006

Principal × Annual interest rate × Time outstanding = Interest expense

$24,000 × 0.04 × (3/12) = $240

2007

Principal × Annual interest rate × Time outstanding = Interest expense

$24,000 × 0.04 × (1/12) = $80

Mellon will report a $320 ($240 + $80) cash outflow from operating activities for interest in 2007. The adjusting entry required to recognize accrued interest at the end of 2006 is as follows:

Interest Expense	240	
Interest Payable		240

Accounting for Sales Tax

LO 2

Show how sales tax liabilities affect financial statements.

Most states require retail companies to collect a sales tax on items sold to their customers. The retailer collects the tax from its customers and remits the tax to the state at regular intervals. The retailer has a current liability for the amount of sales tax collected but not yet paid to the state.

To illustrate, assume Herrera Supply Company (HSC) sells merchandise to a customer for $2,000 cash in a state where the sales tax rate is 6 percent. The journal entry to record the sale and its effects on the financial statements are shown below.

Account Title	Debit	Credit
Cash	2,120	
Sales Tax Payable		120
Sales Revenue[1]		2,000

[1]The entry to record cost of goods sold for this sale is intentionally omitted.

Assets	=	Liab.	+	Equity			Rev. − Exp. = Net Inc.	Cash Flow
Cash	=	Sales Tax Pay.	+	Com. Stk.	+	Ret. Earn.		
2,120	=	120	+	NA	+	2,000	2,000 − NA = 2,000	2,120 OA

Remitting the tax (paying cash to the tax authority) is an asset use transaction. Both the Cash account and the Sales Tax Payable account decrease. The journal entry and its effects on the financial statements are as follows:

Account Title	Debit	Credit
Sales Tax Payable	120	
Cash		120

Assets	=	Liab.	+	Equity			Rev. − Exp. = Net Inc.	Cash Flow
Cash	=	Sales Tax Pay.	+	Com. Stk.	+	Ret. Earn.		
(120)	=	(120)	+	NA	+	NA	NA − NA = NA	(120) OA

Contingent Liabilities

A **contingent liability** is a potential obligation arising from a past event. The amount or existence of the obligation depends on some future event. A pending lawsuit, for example, is a contingent liability. Depending on the outcome, a defendant company could be required to pay a large monetary settlement or could be relieved of any obligation. Generally accepted accounting principles require that companies classify contingent liabilities into three different categories depending on the likelihood of their becoming actual liabilities. The categories and the accounting for each are described below:

LO 3

Define contingent liabilities and explain how they are reported in financial statements.

1. If the likelihood of a future obligation arising is *probable* (likely) and its amount can be *reasonably estimated,* a liability is recognized in the financial statements. Contingent liabilities in this category include warranties, vacation pay, and sick leave.
2. If the likelihood of a future obligation arising is *reasonably possible* but not likely or if it is probable but *cannot be reasonably estimated,* no liability is reported on the balance sheet. The potential liability is, however, disclosed in the footnotes to the financial statements. Contingent liabilities in this category include legal challenges, environmental damages, and government investigations.
3. If the likelihood of a future obligation arising is *remote,* no liability need be recognized in the financial statements or disclosed in the footnotes to the statements.[2]

Determining whether a contingent liability is probable, reasonably possible, or remote requires professional judgment. Even seasoned accountants seek the advice of attorneys, engineers, insurance agents, and government regulators before classifying significant contingent liabilities. Professional judgment is also required to distinguish between contingent liabilities and **general uncertainties.** All businesses face

[2] Companies may, if desired, voluntarily disclose contingent liabilities classified as remote.

EXHIBIT 9.1

Reporting Contingent Liabilities

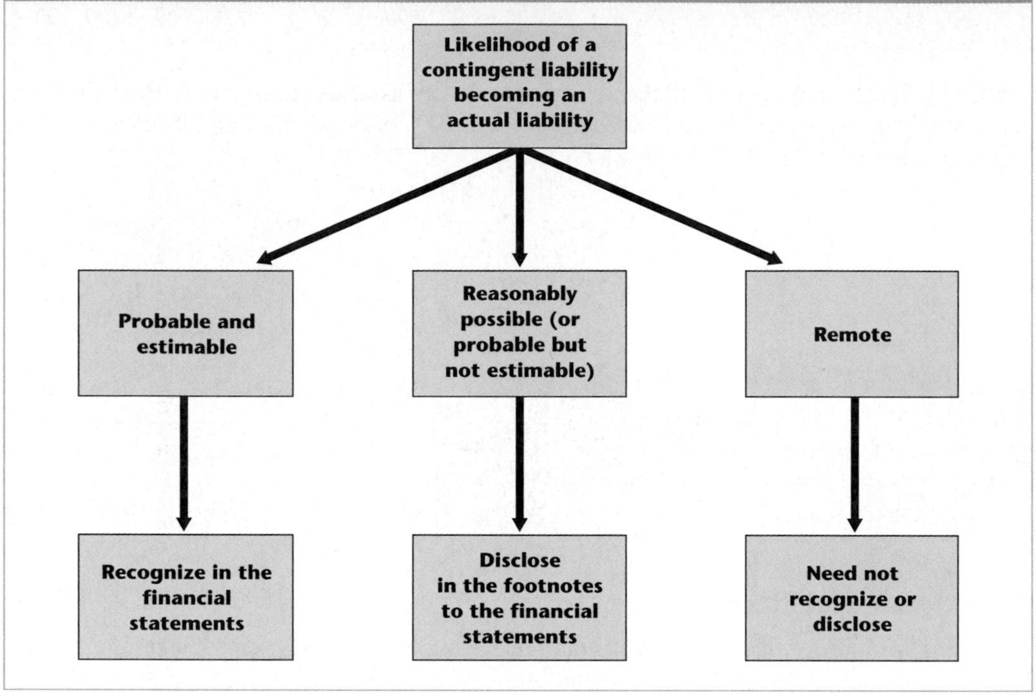

uncertainties such as competition and damage from floods or storms. Such uncertainties are not contingent liabilities, however, because they do not arise from past events.

Exhibit 9.1 summarizes the three categories of contingent liabilities and the accounting for each category.

Warranty Obligations

LO 4

Explain how warranty obligations affect financial statements.

To attract customers, many companies guarantee their products or services. Such guarantees are called **warranties.** Warranties take many forms. Usually, they extend for a specified period of time. Within this period, the seller promises to replace or repair defective products without charge. Although the amount and timing of warranty obligations are uncertain, warranties usually represent liabilities that must be reported in the financial statements.

To illustrate accounting for warranty obligations, assume Herrera Supply Company (HSC) had cash of $2,000, inventory of $6,000, common stock of $5,000, and retained earnings of $3,000 on January 1, 2005. The 2005 accounting period is affected by three accounting events: (1) sale of merchandise under warranty; (2) recognition of warranty obligations to customers who purchased the merchandise; and (3) settlement of a customer's warranty claim.

Event 1 **Sale of Merchandise**

HSC sold for $7,000 cash merchandise that had cost $4,000.

In the following statements model, revenue from the sale is referenced as 1a and the cost of the sale as 1b. The journal entries for the sales transaction and their effects on the financial statements are shown below:

Account Title	Debit	Credit
Cash	7,000	
Sales Revenue		7,000
Cost of Goods Sold	4,000	
Inventory		4,000

Event No.	Assets			=	Liab.	+	Equity	Rev.	−	Exp.	=	Net Inc.	Cash Flow
	Cash	+	Inventory	=			Ret. Earn.						
1a	7,000	+	NA	=	NA	+	7,000	7,000	−	NA	=	7,000	7,000 OA
1b	NA	+	(4,000)	=	NA	+	(4,000)	NA	−	4,000	=	(4,000)	NA

Event 2 **Recognition of Warranty Expense**

HSC guaranteed the merchandise sold in Event 1 to be free from defects for one year following the date of sale.

Although the exact amount of future warranty claims is unknown, HSC must inform financial statement users of the company's obligation. HSC must estimate the amount of the warranty liability and report the estimate in the 2005 financial statements. Assume the warranty obligation is estimated to be $100. Recognizing this obligation increases liabilities (warranties payable) and reduces stockholders' equity (retained earnings). Recognizing the warranty expense reduces net income. The statement of cash flows is not affected when the obligation and the corresponding expense are recognized. The journal entry and its effects on the financial statements follow:

Account Title	Debit	Credit
Warranty Expense	100	
Warranties Payable		100

Event No.	Assets	=	Liab.	+	Equity	Rev.	−	Exp.	=	Net Inc.	Cash Flow
			Warr. Pay.	+	Ret. Earn.						
2	NA	=	100	+	(100)	NA	−	100	=	(100)	NA

Event 3 **Settlement of Warranty Obligation**

HSC paid $40 cash to repair defective merchandise returned by a customer.

The cash payment for the repair is not an expense. Warranty expense was recognized in the period in which the sale was made (when the Warranties Payable account was credited). The payment reduces an asset (cash) and a liability (warranties payable). The income statement is not affected by the repairs payment. However, there is a $40 cash outflow reported in the operating activities section of the statement of cash flows. The journal entry and its effects on the financial statements follow:

Account Title	Debit	Credit
Warranties Payable	40	
Cash		40

Event No.	Assets	=	Liab.	+	Equity	Rev.	−	Exp.	=	Net Inc.	Cash Flow
	Cash	=	Warr. Pay.	+	Ret. Earn.						
3	(40)	=	(40)	+	NA	NA	−	NA	=	NA	(40) OA

General Ledger T-Accounts and Financial Statements

Exhibit 9.2 presents in T-account form the ledger accounts for the business events experienced by HSC. The entry to close the revenue and expense accounts at the end of the 2005

EXHIBIT 9.2

General Ledger

Assets = **Liabilities** + **Equity**

Cash

Bal.	2,000	40	(3)
(1a)	7,000		
Bal.	8,960		

Inventory

Bal.	6,000	4,000	(1b)
Bal.	2,000		

Warranties Payable

(3)	40	100	(2)
		60	Bal.

Common Stock

		5,000	Bal.

Retained Earnings

		3,000	Bal.
		2,900	(cl.)
		5,900	Bal.

Sales Revenue

(cl.)	7,000	7,000	(1a)
0	Bal.		

Cost of Goods Sold

(1b)	4,000	4,000	(cl.)
		Bal.	0

Warranty Expense

(2)	100	100	(cl.)
Bal.	0		

EXHIBIT 9.3

Financial Statements for 2005

Income Statement

Sales Revenue	$7,000
Cost of Goods Sold	(4,000)
Gross Margin	3,000
Warranty Expense	(100)
Net Income	$2,900

Balance Sheet

Assets	
Cash	$ 8,960
Inventory	2,000
Total Assets	$10,960
Liabilities	
Warranties Payable	$ 60
Stockholders' Equity	
Common Stock	5,000
Retained Earnings	5,900
Total Liab. and Stockholders' Equity	$10,960

Statement of Cash Flows

Operating Activities	
Inflow from Customers	$7,000
Outflow for Warranty	(40)
Net Inflow from Operating Activities	6,960
Investing Activities	0
Financing Activities	0
Net Change in Cash	6,960
Plus: Beginning Cash Balance	2,000
Ending Cash Balance	$8,960

accounting period is included. The ledger accounts provide the information to prepare the financial statements in Exhibit 9.3. The accounting events are summarized here:

Transactions for 2005

1. Sold merchandise that cost $4,000 for $7,000 cash.
2. Recognized a $100 warranty obligation and the corresponding expense.
3. Paid $40 to satisfy a warranty claim.
4. Closed the revenue and expense accounts (referenced *cl.*).

The transaction data in the T-accounts for events 1 through 3 are referenced by event number shown in parentheses. Event 4 is referenced with the letters *cl* indicating that journal entry is for closing the accounts.

CHECK YOURSELF 9.2

Flotation Systems Inc. (FSI) began operations in 2006. Its sales were $360,000 in 2006 and $410,000 in 2007. FSI estimates the cost of its one-year product warranty will be 2 percent of sales. Actual cash payments for warranty claims amounted to $5,400 during 2006 and $8,500 during 2007. Prepare the journal entries required to record warranty expense and cash paid to settle warranty claims for 2006 and 2007. Determine the amount of warranties payable FSI would report on its 2006 and 2007 year-end balance sheets.

Answer

Journal Entries for 2006

Account Title	Debit	Credit
Warranty Expense ($360,000 × .02)	7,200	
Warranties Payable		7,200
Warranties Payable	5,400	
Cash		5,400

Journal Entries for 2007

Account Title	Debit	Credit
Warranty Expense ($410,000 × .02)	8,200	
Warranties Payable		8,200
Warranties Payable	8,500	
Cash*		8,500

*The 2007 cash payment exceeds the 2007 accrued expense because some of the warranty expense accrued in 2006 was actually paid in 2007.

FSI would report Warranties Payable on the December 31, 2006, balance sheet of $1,800 ($7,200 − $5,400). Warranties Payable on the December 31, 2007, balance sheet is $1,500 ($1,800 + $8,200 − $8,500).

Accounting for Payroll

LO 5

Define basic terms and identify common documents associated with payroll accounting.

Topic Tackler PLUS 9-2

If you've had a job, you know the amount of your paycheck is less than the amount of your salary. Employers are required to withhold part of each employee's earnings. The money withheld is used to pay such items as income taxes, union dues, and medical insurance premiums for which the *employee* is responsible. The *employer* is also required to make matching payments for certain items such as social security and to pay additional amounts for unemployment taxes. This section of the chapter explains how employers account for *employee withholdings* as well as *employer payroll expenses.*

Identifying Employees

Businesses use the services of independent contractors as well as employees. They must distinguish between the two because payroll taxes apply only to employees. When a business supervises, directs, and controls an individual's work, the individual is an **employee** of the business. When a business pays an individual for specific services, but the individual supervises and controls the work, then that individual is an **independent contractor.**

REALITY BYTES

Most electrical appliances come with a manufacturer's warranty that obligates the manufacturer to pay for defects that occur during some designated period of time after the point of sale. Why would **Best Buy** issue warranties that obligate it to pay for defects that occur after the manufacturer's warranty has expired? Warranties are in fact insurance policies that generate profits. Best Buy reported that the gross dollar sales from extended warranty programs were 3.6 percent of its total sales in fiscal year 2003. Even more important, Best Buy notes that gross profit margins on products sold with extended warranties are higher than the gross profit margins on products sold without extended warranties. Warranties produce revenues for manufacturers as well as retailers. The only difference is that the revenues generated from manufacturer's warranties are embedded in the sales price. Products with longer, more comprehensive warranties usually sell at higher prices than products with shorter, less extensive warranties.

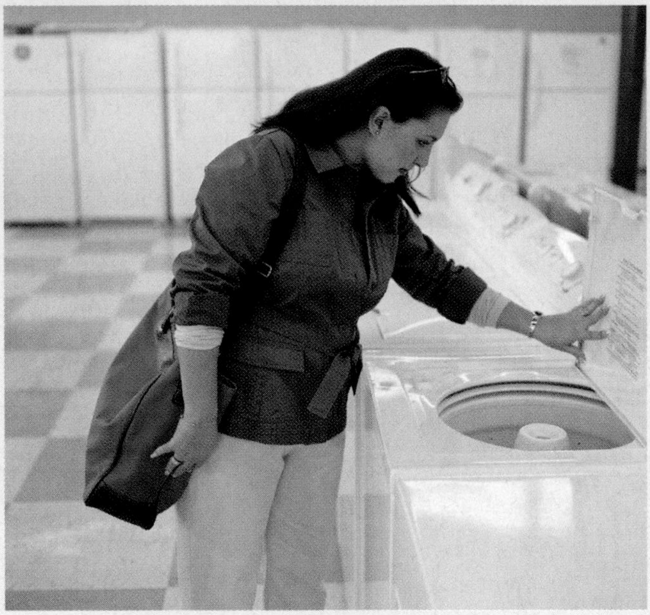

The distinction between independent contractor and employee depends upon control and supervision rather than the type of work performed. A company's chief financial officer (CFO) is a company *employee;* the company's outside auditor is an *independent contractor.* Although both individuals provide accounting services, the company controls the CFO's work while the auditor is independent. If a business hired Randy Moats' company (see The Curious Accountant at the start of the chapter) for plumbing services, Randy would be an independent contractor with respect to his customer. Randy's workers, however, are employees of Randy's plumbing company.

Employees' Gross Earnings

The compensation earned by employees who are paid based on the number of hours they work is normally called **wages.** The compensation earned by employees who are paid a set amount per week, month, or other earnings period regardless of the number of hours worked is normally called **salaries.** The total amount of wages or salaries earned, before any deductions for withholding, represents employees' **gross earnings.** Gross earnings is the sum of regular pay plus any bonuses, overtime, or other additions.

Deductions from Employees' Gross Earnings

Employers withhold money from employees' gross earnings. Employers are obligated (have liabilities) to pay the funds withheld on behalf of the employees. Employers determine each employee's net pay (cash paid to the employee) by *deducting* the withholdings from the gross earnings. This section of the chapter introduces common withholdings.

Federal Income Taxes

LO 6 Explain how payroll accounting affects financial statements.

To help the federal government collect income taxes due on a timely basis, the tax laws adopted by Congress require employers to withhold income taxes from employee earnings. The employers then pay the withheld taxes directly to the government.

For example, assume an employee earns \$2,000. Assume further the employee owes \$300 of income tax on these earnings. On payday, the employer withholds \$300 of the earnings and pays the employee \$1,700 cash. The employer then has a \$300 liability (obligation) to the federal government for the income tax withheld. The employer will use the money withheld to pay the employee's federal income tax liability. The journal entry to record paying the employee and its effects on the financial statements is shown below.

Account Title	Debit	Credit
Salary Expense	2,000	
Employee Income Tax Payable		300
Cash		1,700

Assets	=	Liab.	+	Equity			Rev. − Exp. = Net Inc.	Cash Flow
Cash	=	EIT Pay.	+	Com. Stk.	+	Ret. Earn.		
(1,700)	=	300	+	NA	+	(2,000)	NA − 2,000 = (2,000)	(1,700) OA

When the employer pays the liability, both cash and liabilities will decrease. The income statement will not be affected. The statement of cash flows will show a cash outflow from operating activities. The journal entry and its effects on the financial statements are shown below:

Account Title	Debit	Credit
Employee Income Tax Payable	300	
Cash		300

Assets	=	Liab.	+	Equity			Rev. − Exp. = Net Inc.	Cash Flow
Cash	=	EIT Pay.	+	Com. Stk.	+	Ret. Earn.		
(300)	=	(300)	+	NA	+	NA	NA − NA = NA	(300) OA

The federal tax laws require employers to withhold funds for employee Social Security (FICA) taxes and Medicare taxes as well as income taxes. Employers may also be required to withhold amounts to pay state, county, and municipal government taxes from employees' paychecks. These withholdings have the same effects on the financial statements as those described above for federal income taxes.

Federal Income Tax Documents

The amount withheld from an employee's salary depends on the employee's *gross pay* and the number of *withholding allowances* the employee claims. Each allowance reduces the amount the employer must withhold. Employees are generally allowed to claim one allowance for themselves and one for each legal dependent. For example, a married person with two dependent children could claim four allowances (the employee, the dependent spouse, and the two dependent children). Exhibit 9.4 shows an **Employee's Withholding Allowance Certificate, Form W-4,** the form used to document the number of allowances claimed by an employee.

The federal government provides tax withholding tables that indicate the amount to withhold for any amount of earnings and any number of allowances. At the end of the calendar year, the employer must notify each employee of the amount of his or her gross earnings for the year and of the amounts the employer withheld. Employers provide this information to employees on a **Wage and Tax Statement, Form W-2,** illustrated in Exhibit 9.5. The employer sends one copy of form W-2 to the Internal Revenue Service and other copies to the employee.

EXHIBIT 9.4

Employee's Withholding Allowance Certificate, Form W-4

------------------Cut here and give Form W-4 to your employer. Keep the top part for your records.------------------

Form **W-4**
Department of the Treasury
Internal Revenue Service

Employee's Withholding Allowance Certificate

▶ Your employer must send a copy of this form to the IRS if: (a) you claim more than 10 allowances or (b) you claim "Exempt" and your wages are normally more than $200 per week.

OMB No. 1545-0010

2004

1 Type or print your first name and middle initial	Last name	2 Your social security number
Home address (number and street or rural route)	3 ☐ Single ☐ Married ☐ Married, but withhold at higher Single rate. **Note:** *If married, but legally separated, or spouse is a nonresident alien, check the "Single" box.*	
City or town, state, and ZIP code	**4 If your last name differs from that shown on your social security card, check here. You must call 1-800-772-1213 for a new card . . . ▶** ☐	

5 Total number of allowances you are claiming (from line **H** above **or** from the applicable worksheet on page 2) **5**

6 Additional amount, if any, you want withheld from each paycheck . . . . **6** $

7 I claim exemption from withholding for 2004, and I certify that I meet **both** of the following conditions for exemption:

- Last year I had a right to a refund of **all** Federal income tax withheld because I had **no** tax liability **and**
- This year I expect a refund of **all** Federal income tax withheld because I expect to have **no** tax liability.

If you meet both conditions, write "Exempt" here . . . . ▶ **7**

Under penalties of perjury, I certify that I am entitled to the number of withholding allowances claimed on this certificate, or I am entitled to claim exempt status.

Employee's signature
(Form is not valid
unless you sign it.) ▶ **Date ▶**

8 Employer's name and address (Employer: Complete lines 8 and 10 only if sending to the IRS.)	9 Office code (optional)	10 Employer identification number (EIN)

For Privacy Act and Paperwork Reduction Act Notice, see page 2. Form **W-4** (2004)

JSA
3W9041 1.000

Employers are required to file the **Employer's Quarterly Federal Tax Return, Form 941** no later than one month after each quarter ends. This form reports the amounts due and paid to the government for federal withholdings. Failure to pay withheld taxes in a timely manner is serious. The government has the right to impose significant penalties and can even close a business, seize its assets, and take legal action against those who fail to pay taxes due.

LO 7

Compute FICA and unemployment payroll taxes.

Social Security and Medicare Taxes (FICA)

Congress adopted the Federal Insurance Contributions Act (FICA) to provide funding for the Social Security and Medicare programs. **Social Security** provides qualified individuals with old age, survivor's, and disability insurance (OASDI); **Medicare** provides health insurance. During their working years, employees pay a percentage of their earnings (up to a specified limit) to the federal government for Social Security. At retirement, a qualified person is entitled to receive monthly Social Security payments. Workers who become disabled before retirement are eligible to receive disability benefits. If a worker or retired person dies, any legal dependents are eligible to receive survivor benefits.

In order to meet the required benefit payments, Congress has frequently increased the FICA tax rates and the amount of earnings to which the rates apply. Future changes in FICA tax rates and earnings maximums are likely. These changes will affect only the amount of FICA taxes, however, not how to account for them. *To simplify computations this text assumes a Social Security rate of 6 percent on the first $90,000 of income and a Medicare rate of 1.5 percent on all earnings.* For example, an em-

EXHIBIT 9.5

Wage and Tax Statement, Form W-2

a Control number	22222 Void	For Official Use Only ▶ OMB No. 1545-0008	
b Employer identification		1 Wages, tips, other compensation	2 Federal income tax withheld
c Employer's name, address, and ZIP code		3 Social security wages	4 Social security tax withheld
		5 Medicare wages and tips	6 Medicare tax withheld
		7 Social security tips	8 Allocated tips
d Employee's social security number		9 Advance EIC payment	10 Dependent care benefits
e Employee's first name and initial	Last name	11 Nonqualified plans	12a See instructions for box 12
		13 Statutory employee / Retirement plan / Third-party sick pay	12b
		14 Other	12c
			12d
f Employee's address and ZIP code			

15 State / Employer's state ID number	16 State wages, tips, etc.	17 State income tax	18 Local wages, tips, etc	19 Local income tax	20 Locality name

Form **W-2** Wage and Tax Statement **2004** Department of the Treasury—Internal Revenue Service

Copy A for Social Security Administration - Send this entire page with Form W-3 to the Social Security Administration; photocopies are not acceptable.

4W9846 2.000 0000/1062

For Privacy Act and Paperwork Reduction Act Notice, see back of Copy D.

ployee earning $100,000 per year will have the following FICA taxes withheld from his or her salary:

Social Security	$ 90,000	×	6.0%	=	$5,400
Medicare	100,000	×	1.5%	=	1,500
Total withheld					$6,900

Not only employees are required to pay FICA taxes; the FICA legislation requires employers to pay a matching amount. The total FICA tax paid to the federal government for an employee earning $100,000 per year is $13,800 ($6,900 × 2), half paid by the employee and half paid by the employer. We discuss accounting for employer taxes later in the chapter.

Voluntary Withholdings (Deductions)

One reason governments require employers to withhold taxes from employee earnings is that many people have difficulty managing their spending. If employees received their gross earnings amount, they might not be able to pay their taxes because they would spend the money on other things first. Many people have this tendency with regard to other spending responsibilities as well. To ensure they make important payments, they voluntarily allow their employer to withhold money from their salaries. The employer then uses the money withheld to make payment in the employees' names for such items as medical insurance premiums, union dues, charitable contributions, and contributions to private retirement funds or savings accounts. Even employees who manage their personal finances without difficulty find it convenient to allow their employers to withhold funds and make payments on their behalf.

Withholding voluntary deductions from an employee's gross earnings represents a service on the employer's part. The employer must deduct the amounts authorized by each employee and remit the withheld money to the proper recipients. The employer must maintain additional records and undertake additional transactions to ensure the proper amounts are withheld and paid as specified on a timely basis. Employers normally itemize all deductions from gross pay on the pay stub to explain how an employee's net pay was determined.

Computing Employee Net Pay

LO 6

Explain how payroll accounting affects financial statements.

Net pay is the employee's gross earnings less all deductions (withholdings). Net pay, often called take-home pay, is the amount of cash the employee receives from the employer.

To illustrate assume that Herrera Supply Company (HSC) has an employee named Sarah Jennings. Ms. Jennings earns a monthly salary of $6,000. Based on Ms. Jennings's Form W-4, the tax tables require withholding $450 per month for income taxes. Since Ms. Jennings earns less than $90,000 per year, her full monthly salary is subject to FICA withholdings. Ms. Jennings has authorized HSC to deduct $320 per month for medical insurance and $25 per month for a charitable contribution to the American Cancer Society. Ms. Jennings' net pay is computed as follows:

Gross monthly salary		$6,000
Deductions		
Federal income taxes	$450	
FICA Tax–Social Security ($6,000 × 6%)	360	
FICA Tax–Medicare ($6,000 × 1.5%)	90	
Medical insurance premiums	320	
American Cancer Society	25	
Total deductions		1,245
Net pay		$4,755

The journal entry to recognize salary expense for Ms. Jennings and its effects on HSC's financial statements are as follows.

Account Title	Debit	Credit
Salary Expense	6,000	
Employee Income Tax Payable		450
FICA Tax–Social Security Payable		360
FICA Tax–Medicare Payable		90
Medical Insurance Premiums Payable		320
American Cancer Society Payable		25
Cash		4,755

Assets	=	Liab.	+	Equity			Rev.	−	Exp.	=	Net Inc.	Cash Flow
Cash	=	Various Payables	+	Com. Stk.	+	Ret. Earn.						
(4,755)	=	1,245	+	NA	+	(6,000)	NA	−	6,000	=	(6,000)	(4,755) OA

Employer Payroll Taxes

LO 7

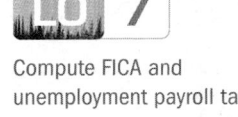

Compute FICA and unemployment payroll taxes.

As mentioned above, employers are required to match employees' FICA taxes, and FICA tax rates are subject to change. This text uses the same assumed tax rates for employers as it uses for employees. *Assume a Social Security rate of 6% on the first $90,000 of each employee's earnings and a Medicare rate of 1.5% on all earnings.* The employers' portion of FICA taxes is a payroll tax expense to the employer.

Employers also incur a payroll tax expense for *unemployment* taxes. Congress adopted the **Federal Unemployment Tax Act (FUTA)** to finance temporary relief to qualified *unemployed* persons. The tax is determined by multiplying the wages of employees (up to a specified maximum limit) by a specified rate. The FUTA tax provides money to both state and federal government workforce agencies. States may enact supplemental unemployment tax laws based on higher maximum earnings or tax rates and could assess employees, rather than employers, for all or part of the supplemental coverage.

As of January 2005, the unemployment tax rate was 6.2 percent of the first $7,000 of wages earned by each employee during a calendar year. FUTA allows employers a credit of up to 5.4 percent for amounts paid to a state unemployment program, leaving a rate of .8 percent to be paid to the federal government. For example, on a tax of $434 (6.2% × $7,000), an employer would pay $56 (.8% × $7,000) to the federal government and $378 (5.4% × $7,000) to the state government. State governments receive a larger percentage because they are responsible for administering the unemployment programs. The rates may be reduced to reward employers with few or no unemployment claims.

Recording and Reporting Payroll Taxes

LO 6

Explain how payroll accounting affects financial statements.

To illustrate computing employer payroll tax expense, return to HSC's employee, Ms. Jennings, who earns $6,000 per month. HSC's February payroll tax expense for Ms. Jennings is computed as follows:

FICA tax expense—Social Security ($6,000 × 6%)	$360
FICA tax expense—Medicare ($6,000 × 1.5%)	90
Federal unemployment tax expense ($1,000 × .8%)	8
State unemployment tax expense ($1,000 × 5.4%)	54
Total payroll tax expense	$512

The unemployment taxes apply only to the first $7,000 of income earned each year by each employee. Since Ms. Jennings earned $6,000 in January, unemployment tax only applies to $1,000 of her February salary. The journal entry to record the payroll tax expense and its effects on the financial statements is as follows.

Account Title	Debit	Credit
Payroll Tax Expense	512	
FICA Tax—Social Security Payable		360
FICA Tax—Medicare Payable		90
Federal Unemployment Tax Payable		8
State Unemployment Tax Payable		54

Assets	=	Liab.	+	Equity			Rev. − Exp. = Net Inc.	Cash Flow
Cash	=	Various Payables	+	Com. Stk.	+	Ret. Earn.		
NA	=	512	+	NA	+	(512)	NA − 512 = (512)	NA

CHECK YOURSELF 9.3

Bill Chavez, an employee of Bombay Company, earns a salary of $110,000 per year. Based on the tax rates assumed in this chapter, determine the annual payroll tax expense Bombay Company would incur with respect to Mr. Chavez. How much payroll tax would Mr. Chavez be required to pay?

Answer

Payroll tax expense for Bombay Company	
FICA tax expense–Social Security ($90,000 × 6%)	$5,400
FICA tax expense–Medicare ($110,000 × 1.5%)	1,650
Federal unemployment tax expense ($7,000 × .8%)	56
State unemployment tax expense ($7,000 × 5.4%)	378
Total payroll tax expense	$7,484

Mr. Chavez would not pay any payroll taxes. Payroll taxes apply to employers, not employees.

Employee Fringe Benefits

LO 6

Explain how payroll accounting affects financial statements.

In addition to salaries and wages, many employers provide their employees with a variety of fringe benefits such as paid vacations, sick leave, maternity leave, and medical, dental, life, and disability insurance. These benefits plus payroll taxes frequently amount to as much as 25% of the employees' gross salaries and wages. Fringe benefits are reported as expenses on the income statement.

To illustrate, assume HSC provides the following fringe benefits to an employee, Alice Worthington, who earns approximately $200 per day. Ms. Worthington earns one day of vacation for each month she works. HSC pays $250 per month for Ms. Worthington's medical insurance and contributes $150 per month to a pension (retirement) program for Ms. Worthington. The monthly entry to record the accrued fringe benefits expenses and its effects on the financial statements are shown below:

Account Title	Debit	Credit
Vacation Pay Expense	200	
Employee Medical Insurance Expense	250	
Employee Pension Expense	150	
Vacation Pay Payable		200
Employee Medical Insurance Payable		250
Employee Pension Liability		150

Assets	=	Liab.	+	Equity			Rev. − Exp. = Net Inc.	Cash Flow
Cash	=	Various Payables	+	Com. Stk.	+	Rct. Earn.		
NA	=	600	+	NA	+	(600)	NA − 600 = (600)	NA

THE FINANCIAL ANALYST

Current Versus Noncurrent

Because meeting obligations on time is critical to business survival, financial analysts and creditors are interested in whether companies will have enough money available to pay bills

Answers to The Curious Accountant

As the chapter has explained, employers must match the FICA taxes employees are required to pay. Using an assumed rate of 7.5%, the employer's share of these FICA taxes is $1.50 per hour for an employee earning $20 per hour. Employers must also pay federal and state unemployment insurance (FUTA) taxes. Although the FUTA tax amount varies from company to company even within a given state, we assume for illustration a rate of 6.2%, which comes to $1.24 per hour. Randy may also be contributing to his employees' 401(k) retirement funds. According to the United States Department of Labor and Chamber of Commerce, about half of all companies match employees' 401(k) retirement contributions, and the average amount provided is 4.1% of employees' salaries. Such a contribution would cost Randy $.82 per hour. Health care insurance paid by one of the authors' employers costs his university $300 per month. At this rate, Randy would pay $1.80 per hour for the health insurance benefits of an employee working 40 hours per week. A small employer would probably have to pay more. The costs listed here would increase Randy's per hour cost by $5.36, or 27% of employee base wages, and we have not even considered the costs of vacation time, sick leave, and workers' compensation insurance.

when they are due. Most businesses provide information about their bill-paying ability by classifying their assets and liabilities according to liquidity. The more quickly an asset is converted to cash or consumed, the more *liquid* it is. Assets are usually divided into two major classifications: *current* and *noncurrent*. Current items are also referred to as *short term* and noncurrent items as *long term*.

LO 8

Distinguish between current and noncurrent assets and liabilities.

A **current (short-term) asset** is expected to be converted to cash or consumed within one year or an operating cycle, whichever is longer. An **operating cycle** is defined as the average time it takes a business to convert cash to inventory, inventory to accounts receivable, and accounts receivable back to cash. The financial tools used to measure the length of an operating cycle for particular businesses are discussed in Chapter 7. For most businesses, the operating cycle is less than one year. As a result, the one-year rule normally prevails with respect to classifying assets as current. The current assets section of a balance sheet typically includes the following items:

Current Assets
Cash
Marketable Securities
Accounts Receivable
Short-Term Notes Receivable
Interest Receivable
Inventory
Supplies
Prepaid Items

Given the definition of current assets, it seems reasonable to assume that **current (short-term) liabilities** would be those due within one year or an operating cycle, whichever is longer. This assumption is usually correct. However, an exception is made for long-term renewable debt. For example, consider a liability that was issued with a 20-year term to maturity. After 19 years, the liability becomes due within one year and is, therefore, a current liability. Even so, the liability will be classified as long term if the company plans to issue new long-term debt and to use the proceeds from that debt to repay the maturing liability. This situation is described as *refinancing short-term debt on a long-term basis.* In general, if a business does not plan to use any of its current assets to repay a debt, that debt is listed as long term even if it is due within one year. The current liabilities section of a balance sheet typically includes the following items:

Current Liabilities
- Accounts Payable
- Short-Term Notes Payable
- Wages Payable
- Taxes Payable
- Interest Payable

LO 9

Prepare a classified balance sheet.

Balance sheets that distinguish between current and noncurrent items are called **classified balance sheets.** To enhance the usefulness of accounting information, most real-world balance sheets are classified. Exhibit 9.6 displays an example of a classified balance sheet.

EXHIBIT 9.6

LIMBAUGH COMPANY
Classified Balance Sheet
As of December 31, 2006

Current Assets			
Cash		$ 20,000	
Accounts Receivable		35,000	
Inventory		230,000	
Prepaid Rent		3,600	
Total Current Assets			$288,600
Property, Plant, and Equipment			
Office Equipment	$ 80,000		
Less: Accumulated Depreciation	(25,000)	55,000	
Building	340,000		
Less: Accumulated Depreciation	(40,000)	300,000	
Land		120,000	
Total Property, Plant, and Equipment			475,000
Total Assets			$763,600
Current Liabilities			
Accounts Payable		$ 32,000	
Notes Payable		120,000	
Salaries Payable		32,000	
Unearned Revenue		9,800	
Total Current Liabilities			$193,800
Long-Term Liabilities			
Note Payable			100,000
Total Liabilities			293,800
Stockholders' Equity			
Common Stock		200,000	
Retained Earnings		269,800	469,800
Total Liabilities and Stockholders' Equity			$763,600

Liquidity Versus Solvency

Liquidity describes the ability to generate sufficient short-term cash flows to pay obligations as they come due. **Solvency** is the ability to repay liabilities in the long run. Liquidity and solvency are both important to the survival of a business. Financial analysts rely on several

FOCUS ON INTERNATIONAL ISSUES

WHY ARE THESE BALANCE SHEETS BACKWARD?

Many of the differences in accounting rules used around the world would be difficult to detect by merely comparing financial statements of companies in different countries. For example, if a balance sheet for a U.S. company and one for a U.K. company both report an asset called *land,* it might not be clear whether the reported amounts were computed by using the same measurement rules or different measurement rules. Did both companies use historical cost as a basis for measurement? Perhaps not, but this would be difficult to determine by comparing their balance sheets.

However, one difference between financial reporting in the United Kingdom and the United States that is obvious is the arrangement of assets on the balance sheet. In this chapter, we explain that U.S. GAAP requires current assets to be shown first and noncurrent assets second; the same is true of liabilities. In the United Kingdom, noncurrent assets appear first, followed by current assets; however, liabilities are shown in the same order as in the United States. In other countries (e.g., France), both assets and liabilities are shown with noncurrent items first. The accounting rules of some countries require that equity be shown before liabilities; this is the opposite of U.S. GAAP. Therefore, to someone who learned accounting in the United States, the balance sheets of companies from some countries may appear backward or upside down.

No matter in what order the assets, liabilities, and equity accounts are arranged on a company's balance sheet, one accounting concept is true throughout the free world:

$$\text{Assets} = \text{Liabilities} + \text{Equity}$$

For a real-world example of the items discussed here, look up the financial statements of ITV, the largest commercial television network in the United Kingdom. Go to www.itvplc.com. Click on "Company Reports" under "FINANCIAL INFORMATION." Next click on "Financial review 2003" or whatever is the most current fiscal year.

ratios to help them evaluate a company's liquidity and solvency. The *debt to assets* ratio introduced in Chapter 3 is one tool used to measure solvency. The primary ratio used to evaluate liquidity is the current ratio.

Current Ratio

LO 10

Use the current ratio to assess the level of liquidity.

The **current ratio** is defined as:

$$\frac{\text{Current assets}}{\text{Current liabilities}}$$

Since current assets normally exceed current liabilities, this ratio is usually greater than 100 percent. For example, if a company has \$250 in current assets and \$100 in current liabilities, current assets are 250 percent of current liabilities. The current ratio is traditionally expressed as a decimal rather than as a percentage, however; most analysts would describe this example as a current ratio of 2.5 to 1 (\$250 ÷ \$100 = \$2.50 in current assets for every \$1 in current liabilities). This book uses the traditional format when referring to the current ratio.

The current ratio is among the most widely used ratios in analyzing financial statements. Current ratios can be too high as well as too low. A low ratio suggests that the company may have difficulty paying its short-term obligations. A high ratio suggests that a company is not maximizing its earnings potential because investments in liquid assets usually do not earn as much money as investments in other assets. Companies must try to maintain an effective balance between liquid assets (so they can pay bills on time) and nonliquid assets (so they can earn a good return).

Real-World Data

Exhibit 9.7 presents the 2002 current ratios and debt to assets ratios for six companies in three different industries.

EXHIBIT 9.7

Industry	Company	Current Ratio	Debt to Assets Ratio
Electric utilities	**Duke Energy**	0.99	0.72
	Dominion Resources	0.81	0.72
Grocery stores	**Albertsons**	1.24	0.66
	Safeway	1.08	0.77
Building supplies	**Home Depot**	1.48	0.34
	Lowe's	1.56	0.48

Which of these companies has the highest level of financial risk? Perhaps **Safeway** because it has the highest debt to assets ratio. The electric utilities have higher debt to assets ratios and lower current ratios than those of the companies in the building supplies business. Does this mean that electric utilities are riskier investments? Not necessarily; since the companies are in different industries, the ratios may not be comparable. Utility companies have a more stable revenue base than building companies. If the economy turns downward, people are likely to continue to use electricity. However, they are less likely to buy a new home or to add on to their existing home. Because utility companies have a stable source of revenue, creditors are likely to feel comfortable with higher levels of debt for them than they would for building companies. As previously stated, the industry must be considered when interpreting ratios.

Finally, note that the debt to assets ratios, with the exception of the grocery stores, tend to be grouped by industry. Current ratios do vary somewhat among different industries, but they probably do not vary as much as the debt to assets ratios. Why? Because all companies, regardless of how they finance their total assets, must keep sufficient current assets on hand to repay current liabilities.

>> A Look Back

Chapter 9 discussed accounting for current liabilities and payroll. Current liabilities are obligations due within one year or the company's operating cycle, whichever is longer. The chapter expanded the discussion of promissory notes begun in Chapter 7. Chapter 7 introduced accounting for the note payee, the lender; Chapter 9 discussed accounting for the note maker (issuer), the borrower. Notes payable and related interest payable are reported as liabilities on the balance sheet. Chapter 9 also discussed accounting for sales tax liabilities, warranty obligations, and contingent liabilities.

Payroll costs and payroll taxes constitute a major expense for most businesses. An employer is responsible for withholding money from an employee's salary. The most common withholdings are for federal income taxes, FICA taxes, insurance premiums, savings or retirement contributions, union dues, and charitable donations. The employer uses the withholdings to pay the employees' obligations. The difference between the *gross pay* and the money withheld is called net pay. The *net pay* is the amount of cash the employer pays to the employee.

In addition to making payments for its employees, the employer is responsible for certain taxes on its employees' salaries and wages. These taxes are called payroll taxes. They include matching FICA Social Security and Medicare taxes, and federal and state unemployment taxes. Governments periodically change the rates of these taxes. The accounting for them, however, is not affected by rate changes. The rates used in this text are as follows: FICA Social Security—6 percent of the first $90,000 of each employee's wages with a matching payment for the employer; FICA Medicare—1.5 percent of the total wages of each employee with a matching payment for the employer; federal unemployment taxes—.8 percent (6.2 percent less a 5.4 percent credit for state unemployment taxes) of the first $7,000 of each employee's wages; and state unemployment—5.4 percent of the first $7,000 of each employee's wages.

Finally, Chapter 9 discussed assessing companies' liquidity. The current ratio is current assets divided by current liabilities. The higher the current ratio, the more liquid the business.

A Look Forward >>

Chapter 10 investigates issues related to accounting for long-term liabilities. As you will learn, income tax consequences enter into decisions to borrow money.

APPENDIX

Accounting for Discount Notes

LO 11

Show how discount notes and related interest charges affect financial statements.

All notes payable discussed previously have been "add-on" **interest-bearing notes.** The amount due at maturity for add-on notes is the *face value* of the note *plus accrued interest.* In contrast, the interest on a **discount note** is included in the face value of the note. A $5,000 face value discount note is repaid with $5,000 cash at maturity. This payment includes both principal and accrued interest.

To illustrate, assume Beacon Management Services experienced the following events.

Event 1 **Borrowed Money by Issuing a Discount Note**
Beacon Management Services was started when it issued a $10,000 face value discount note to State Bank on March 1, 2006.

The note had a 9 percent *discount rate* and a one-year term to maturity. As with interest-bearing notes, the *issuer* of a discount note exchanges the promissory note for cash. Accounting for the discount note requires dividing the face amount between the **discount** and the **principal,** or **proceeds** (amount of cash borrowed). The discount is computed by multiplying the face value of the note by the interest rate by the time period. Subtracting the discount from the face value of the note determines the principal (proceeds). The computations follow:

Face value of note	$10,000
Less discount ($10,000 × 0.09 × 1) =	900
Proceeds (amount borrowed)	$ 9,100

On the issue date, both assets and liabilities increase by the amount borrowed (the $9,100 principal). The borrowing transaction on the issue date has no effect on the income statement. The $9,100 cash inflow is reported in the financing activities section of the statement of cash flows. The journal entry to record issuing the discount note and its effects on the financial statements are shown here:

Account Title	Debit	Credit
Cash	9,100	
Discount on Notes Payable	900	
Notes Payable		10,000

Event No.	Assets	=	Liabilities			+	Equity			Rev. − Exp. = Net Inc.	Cash Flow
	Cash	=	Notes Pay.	−	Disc. on N/P	+	Com. Stk.	+	Ret. Earn.		
1	9,100	=	10,000	−	900	+	NA	+	NA	NA − NA = NA	9,100 FA

The discount is recorded in a **contra liability account** called **Discount on Notes Payable.** The *carrying value* of the liability is the difference between the Notes Payable and Discount accounts. Carrying value, also called *book value,* is the amount at which the liability is carried on the books. In this case, the Notes Payable account in Beacon's ledger has a $10,000 credit balance and the Discount on Notes Payable account has a $900 debit balance. The carrying value on the issue date is as follows:

Notes Payable	$10,000
Discount on Notes Payable	(900)
Carrying value of liability	$ 9,100

Event 2 **Recognized Operating Expenses**

Beacon incurred $8,000 of cash operating expenses.

Paying these expenses reduces both assets and stockholders' equity. The effect on the income statement is to increase expenses and decrease net income. The cash outflow is reported in the operating activities section of the statement of cash flows. The journal entry and its effects are shown below:

Account Title	Debit	Credit
Operating Expenses	8,000	
Cash		8,000

Event No.	Assets	=	Liabilities			+	Equity			Rev. − Exp. = Net Inc.	Cash Flow
	Cash	=	Notes Pay.	−	Disc. on N/P	+	Com. Stk.	+	Ret. Earn.		
2	(8,000)	=	NA	−	NA	+	NA	+	(8,000)	NA − 8,000 = (8,000)	(8,000) OA

Event 3 **Recognized Revenue**

Beacon recognized $12,000 of cash service revenue.

Recognizing revenue increases both assets and stockholders' equity. Net income increases. The cash inflow is reported in the operating activities section of the statement of cash flows. The journal entry and its effects follow:

Account Title	Debit	Credit
Cash	12,000	
Service Revenue		12,000

Event No.	Assets	=	Liabilities			+	Equity			Rev.	− Exp.	= Net Inc.	Cash Flow
	Cash	=	Notes Pay.	−	Disc. on N/P	+	Com. Stk.	+	Ret. Earn.				
3	12,000	=	NA	−	NA	+	NA	+	12,000	12,000	− NA	= 12,000	12,000 OA

Event 4 **Recognized Accrued Interest**

Beacon recorded an adjusting entry to recognize interest accrued since March 1.

On December 31, 2006, Beacon must adjust its accounting records to recognize the 10 months of interest expense it incurred in 2006. For this note, interest expense accrues at $75 per month ($900 discount ÷ 12). As of December 31, $750 ($75 × 10) of interest expense has accrued. Since no cash payment is due until the note matures in 2007, the reduction in equity from recognizing the interest expense is accompanied by an increase in liabilities.

The increase in liabilities is recorded by *reducing the contra liability account,* Discount on Notes Payable. Recall that the carrying value of the liability was $9,100 on the day the note was issued. The adjusting entry to record the accrued interest expense removes $750 from the Discount account, leaving a discount balance of $150 ($900 − $750) after the adjusting entry is posted.

The bookkeeping technique of converting the discount to interest expense over the term of the loan is described as **amortizing** the discount. After amortizing 10 months' interest expense, the carrying value of the liability reported on the December 31, 2006, balance sheet (see Exhibit 9.9) is $9,850 ($10,000 face value − $150 discount). The effect of the interest recognition on the income statement is to increase expenses and decrease net income by $750. The statement of cash flows is not affected by the accrual. Beacon recognizes the cash effects of the interest on the maturity date when it pays the maturity (face) value of the note to State Bank.

The journal entry to amortize the discount and its effects on the financial statements are shown here:

Account Title	Debit	Credit
Interest Expense	750	
Discount on Notes Payable		750

Event No.	Assets	=	Liabilities			+	Equity			Rev.	− Exp.	= Net Inc.	Cash Flow
	Cash	=	Notes Pay.	−	Disc. on N/P	+	Com. Stk.	+	Ret. Earn.				
4	NA	=	NA	−	(750)	+	NA	+	(750)	NA	− 750	= (750)	NA

General Ledger T-Accounts and Financial Statements

Exhibit 9.8 displays in T-account form the ledger accounts for Beacon's 2006 business events. The entry to close the revenue and expense accounts at the end of 2006 is included. The ledger accounts provide the information to prepare the financial statements in Exhibit 9.9. The accounting events are summarized here:

1. Beacon issued a $10,000 face value, one-year, discount note with a 9 percent discount rate.
2. Beacon paid $8,000 cash for operating expenses.
3. Beacon earned cash service revenue of $12,000.
4. Beacon recognized $750 of accrued interest expense.
5. Beacon closed the revenue and expense accounts. The letters *cl* are the posting reference for the closing entry.

Accounting Events Affecting 2007

LO 11

Show how discount notes and related interest charges affect financial statements.

This section illustrates four accounting events that apply to Beacon's 2007 accounting cycle.

Event 1 **Recognized Accrued Interest for 2007**

Beacon recorded an adjusting entry to recognize interest accrued since December 31.

EXHIBIT 9.8

General Ledger

Assets = **Liabilities** + **Equity**

Cash

(1)	9,100	8,000	(2)
(3)	12,000		
Bal.	13,100		

Notes Payable

		10,000	(1)
		10,000	Bal.

Discount on Notes Payable

(1)	900	750	(4)
Bal.	150		

Retained Earnings

		3,250	(cl.)
		3,250	Bal.

Service Revenue

(cl.)	12,000	12,000	(3)
		0	Bal.

Operating Expenses

(2)	8,000	8,000	(cl.)
Bal.	0		

Interest Expense

(4)	750	750	(cl.)
Bal.	0		

EXHIBIT 9.9

Financial Statements for 2006

Income Statement

Service Revenue	$12,000
Operating Expenses	(8,000)
Operating Income	4,000
Interest Expense	(750)
Net Income	$ 3,250

Balance Sheet

Assets		
Cash		$13,100
Liabilities		
Notes Payable	$10,000	
Less: Disc. on Notes Pay.	(150)	
Total Liabilities		$ 9,850
Stockholders' Equity		
Retained Earnings		3,250
Total Liab. and Stockholders' Equity		$13,100

Statement of Cash Flows

Operating Activities	
Inflow from Customers	$12,000
Outflow for Expenses	(8,000)
Net Inflow from Operating Activities	4,000
Investing Activities	0
Financing Activities	
Inflow from Creditors	9,100
Net Change in Cash	13,100
Plus: Beginning Cash Balance	0
Ending Cash Balance	$13,100

Since the note had a one-year term, interest for two months remains to be accrued at the maturity date on March 1, 2007. Interest on this note accrues at $75 per month ($900 discount ÷ 12), so there is $150 ($75 × 2) of interest expense to recognize in 2007. Recognizing the interest increases liabilities (the Discount account is reduced to zero) and decreases stockholders' equity. The effect on the income statement of recognizing interest is to increase expenses and decrease net income by $150. The statement of cash flows is not affected by the interest recognition. The journal entry and financial statement effects follow:

Account Title	Debit	Credit
Interest Expense	150	
Discount on Notes Payable		150

Event No.	Assets	=	Liabilities			+	Equity			Rev. − Exp. = Net Inc.	Cash Flow
	Cash	=	Notes Pay.	−	Disc. on N/P	+	Com. Stk.	+	Ret. Earn.		
1	NA	=	NA	−	(150)	+	NA	+	(150)	NA − 150 = (150)	NA

Event 2 **Payment of Face Value**
Beacon paid the face value of the note.

The face value ($10,000) of the note is due on the maturity date. Paying the maturity value is an asset use transaction that decreases both assets and liabilities. The income statement is not affected by the payment. The $10,000 cash payment includes $900 for interest and $9,100 for principal. On the statement of cash flows a $900 outflow for interest is reported in the operating activities section and a $9,100 outflow for repaying the loan is reported in the financing activities section. The journal entry and financial statement effects are shown below:

Account Title	Debit	Credit
Notes Payable	10,000	
Cash		10,000

Event No.	Assets	=	Liabilities			+	Equity			Rev. − Exp. = Net Inc.	Cash Flow
	Cash	=	Notes Pay.	−	Disc. on N/P	+	Com. Stk.	+	Ret. Earn.		
2	(10,000)	=	(10,000)	−	NA	+	NA	+	NA	NA − NA = NA	(900) OA (9,100) FA

Event 3 **Recognized Revenue**
Beacon recognized $13,000 of cash service revenue.

Recognizing the revenue increases both assets and stockholders' equity. Net income also increases. The cash inflow is reported in the operating activities section of the statement of cash flows. These effects follow:

Account Title	Debit	Credit
Cash	13,000	
Service Revenue		13,000

Event No.	Assets	=	Liabilities			+	Equity			Rev. − Exp. = Net Inc.	Cash Flow
	Cash	=	Notes Pay.	−	Disc. on N/P	+	Com. Stk.	+	Ret. Earn.		
3	13,000	=	NA	−	NA	+	NA	+	13,000	13,000 − NA = 13,000	13,000 OA

Event 4 **Recognized Operating Expenses**
Beacon incurred $8,500 of cash operating expenses.

This event decreases both assets and stockholders' equity. Net income also decreases. The cash outflow is reported in the operating activities section of the statement of cash flows. The journal entry and its effects are shown below:

Account Title	Debit	Credit
Operating Expenses	8,500	
Cash		8,500

Event No.	Assets =		Liabilities	+	Equity				Rev. − Exp. = Net Inc.	Cash Flow
	Cash	=	Notes Pay.	− Disc. on N/P	+	Com. Stk.	+	Ret. Earn.		
4	(8,500)	=	NA	− NA	+	NA	+	(8,500)	NA − 8,500 = (8,500)	(8,500) OA

General Ledger T-Accounts and Financial Statements

Exhibits 9.10 and 9.11 present the relevant ledger T-accounts and financial statements, respectively. No liabilities are reported in Exhibit 9.11 because Beacon has repaid both principal and interest on the discount note. Since Beacon did not pay any dividends in 2006 or 2007, retained earnings represents the sum of net income for the two years.

EXHIBIT 9.10

General Ledger

Assets = Liabilities + Equity

Cash

	Debit	Credit	
Bal.	13,100	10,000	(2)
(3)	13,000	8,500	(4)
Bal.	7,600		

Notes Payable

	Debit	Credit	
(2)	10,000	10,000	Bal.
		0	Bal.

Discount on Notes Payable

	Debit	Credit	
Bal.	150	150	(1)
Bal.	0		

Retained Earnings

	Debit	Credit	
		3,250	Bal.
		4,350	(cl.)
		7,600	Bal.

Service Revenue

	Debit	Credit	
(cl.)	13,000	13,000	(3)
		0	Bal.

Operating Expenses

	Debit	Credit	
(4)	8,500	8,500	(cl.)
Bal.	0		

Interest Expense

	Debit	Credit	
(1)	150	150	(cl.)
Bal.	0		

EXHIBIT 9.11

Financial Statements for 2007

Income Statement

Service Revenue	$13,000
Operating Expenses	(8,500)
Operating Income	4,500
Interest Expense	(150)
Net Income	$ 4,350

Balance Sheet

Assets	
Cash	$7,600
Liabilities	$ 0
Stockholders' Equity	
Retained Earnings	7,600
Total Liab. and Stockholders' Equity	$7,600

Statement of Cash Flows

Operating Activities	
Inflow from Customers	$13,000
Outflow for Expenses	(8,500)
Outflow for Interest	(900)
Net Inflow from Operating Activities	3,600
Investing Activities	0
Financing Activities	
Outflow to Creditors	(9,100)
Net Change in Cash	(5,500)
Plus: Beginning Cash Balance	13,100
Ending Cash Balance	$ 7,600

SELF-STUDY REVIEW PROBLEM

Perfect Picture Inc. (PPI) experienced the following transactions during 2007. The transactions are summarized (transaction data pertain to the full year) and limited to those that affect the company's current liabilities.

1. PPI had cash sales of $820,000. The state requires that PPI charge customers an 8 percent sales tax (ignore cost of goods sold).
2. PPI paid the state sales tax authority $63,000.
3. On March 1, PPI issued a note payable to the County Bank. PPI received $50,000 cash (principal balance). The note had a one-year term and a 6 percent annual interest rate.
4. On December 31, PPI recognized accrued interest on the note issued in Event 3.
5. On December 31, PPI recognized warranty expense at the rate of 3 percent of sales.
6. PPI paid $22,000 cash to settle warranty claims.
7. PPI has five employees. Four of the employees each earn $40,000 per year. The fifth employee, the store manager, earns $110,000 per year. The annual amount withheld for income tax for all employees is $54,000. Each of the five employees has volunteered to have $50 per month withheld as a charitable contribution to the United Way. Record the net pay as a liability.
8. Based on the salary data described in Event 7, PPI recognized payroll tax expense for FICA and unemployment taxes.
9. During the year PPI remitted the following amounts of cash in partial settlement of the indicated liabilities.

Employee income tax payable	$ 52,000
FICA tax–Social Security payable	27,000
FICA tax–Medicare payable	7,000
United Way payable	2,500
Salaries payable	190,250
Federal unemployment tax payable	200
State unemployment tax payable	1,500

10. PPI pays $320 per month for medical insurance premiums for each employee. The company also contributes an amount equal to 4 percent of salaries to a pension fund for each employee. Each employee accrues vacation pay at a rate of $300 per month.
11. During the year PPI remitted the following amount of cash in partial settlement of the indicated liabilities.

Medical insurance payable	$18,000
Employee pension fund payable	8,200
Vacation pay payable	16,400

Required

a. Prepare in general journal form the entries to record the transactions described above.

b. Prepare the current liabilities section of the December 31, 2007, balance sheet.

Solution to Requirement *a*

Event No.	Account Title	Debit	Credit
1	Cash	885,600	
	Sales Revenue		820,000
	Sales Tax Payable		65,600
2	Sales Tax Payable	63,000	
	Cash		63,000
3	Cash	50,000	
	Notes Payable		50,000

continued

Event No.	Account Title	Debit	Credit
4	Interest Expense ($50,000 × .06 × 10/12)	2,500	
	Interest Payable		2,500
5	Warranty Expense ($820,000 × 0.03)	24,600	
	Warranties Payable		24,600
6	Warranties Payable	22,000	
	Cash		22,000
7	Salary Expense [(4 × $40,000) + $110,000)]	270,000	
	Employee income Tax Payable		54,000
	FICA Tax–Social Security Payable*		15,000
	FICA Tax–Medicare Payable ($270,000 × 0.015)		4,050
	United Way Payable ($50 × 5 × 12)		3,000
	Salaries Payable		193,950
8	Payroll Tax Expense	21,220	
	FICA Tax–Social Security Payable*		15,000
	FICA Tax–Medicare Payable ($270,000 × .015)		4,050
	Federal Unemployment Tax Payable ($7,000 × 5 × .008)		280
	State Unemployment Tax Payable ($7,000 × 5 × .054)		1,890
9	Employee income Tax Payable	52,000	
	FICA Tax–Social Security Payable	27,000	
	FICA Tax–Medicare Payable	7,000	
	United Way Payable	2,500	
	Salaries Payable	190,250	
	Federal Unemployment Tax Payable	200	
	State Unemployment Tax Payable	1,500	
	Cash		280,450
10	Fringe Benefits Expense	48,000	
	Medical Insurance Payable ($320 × 12 × 5)		19,200
	Employee Pension Fund Payable ($270,000 × .04)		10,800
	Vacation Pay Payable ($300 × 12 × 5)		18,000
11	Medical Insurance Payable	18,000	
	Employee Pension Fund Payable	8,200	
	Vacation Pay Payable	16,400	
	Cash		42,600

*[($40,000 × .06 = $2,400 × 4 = $9,600) + ($90,000 × .06 = $5,400)] = $15,000

Solution to Requirement *b*

[redacted]

Current Liabilities	
Sales Tax Payable ($65,600 − $63,000)	$ 2,600
Notes Payable	50,000
Interest Payable	2,500
Warranties Payable ($24,600 − $22,000)	2,600
Employee income Tax Payable ($54,000 − $52,000)	2,000
FICA - Social Security Payable ($15,000 + $15,000 − $27,000)	3,000
FICA - Medicare Payable ($4,050 + $4,050 − $7,000)	1,100
United Way Payable ($3,000 − $2,500)	500
Salaries Payable ($193,950 − $190,250)	3,700
Federal Unemployment Tax Payable ($280 − $200)	80
State Unemployment Tax Payable ($1,890 − 1,500)	390
Medical Insurance Payable ($19,200 − $18,000)	1,200
Employee Pension Fund Payable ($10,800 − $8,200)	2,600
Vacation Pay Payable ($18,000 − $16,400)	1,600
Total Current Liabilities	$73,870

KEY TERMS

QUESTIONS

1. What type of transaction is a cash payment to creditors? How does this type of transaction affect the accounting equation?
2. What is a current liability? Distinguish between a current liability and a long-term debt.
3. What type of entry is the entry to record accrued interest expense? How does it affect the accounting equation?
4. Who is the maker of a note payable?
5. What is the going concern assumption? Does it affect the way liabilities are reported in the financial statements?
6. Why is it necessary to make an adjusting entry at the end of the accounting period for unpaid interest on a note payable?
7. Assume that on October 1, 2007, Big Company borrowed $10,000 from the local bank at 6 percent interest. The note is due on October 1, 2008. How much interest does Big pay in 2007? How much interest does Big pay in 2008? What amount of cash does Big pay back in 2008?
8. When a business collects sales tax from customers, is it revenue? Why or why not?
9. What is a contingent liability?
10. List the three categories of contingent liabilities.
11. Are contingent liabilities recorded on a company's books? Explain.
12. What is the difference in accounting procedures for a liability that is probable and estimable and one that is reasonably possible but not estimable?
13. What type of liabilities are not recorded on a company's books?
14. What does the term *warranty* mean?
15. What effect does recognizing future warranty obligations have on the balance sheet? On the income statement?
16. When is warranty cost reported on the statement of cash flows?
17. What is the difference between an employee and an independent contractor?
18. What is the difference between wages and salaries?
19. What is the purpose of the W-2 form? What is the purpose of the W-4 form?
20. What two taxes are components of the FICA tax? What programs do they fund?
21. Who pays the FICA tax? Is there a ceiling on the amount of tax that is paid?
22. What is the difference between gross pay and net pay for an employee?
23. Why are amounts withheld from employees' pay considered liabilities of the employer?
24. What is the purpose of the Federal Unemployment Tax? What are the maximum amount of wages subject to the tax?
25. What items are included in compensation cost for a company in addition to the gross salaries of the employees?
26. Give two examples of fringe benefits.

27. What is a classified balance sheet?
28. What is the difference between the liquidity and the solvency of a business?
29. The higher the company's current ratio, the better the company's financial condition. Do you agree with this statement? Explain.
30. What is the difference between an interest-bearing note and a discount note?
31. How is the carrying value of a discount note computed?
32. Will the effective rate of interest be the same on a $10,000 face value, 6 percent interest-bearing note and a $10,000 face value, 6 percent discount note? Is the amount of cash received upon making these two loans the same? Why or why not?
33. How does the *amortization* of a discount affect the income statement, balance sheet, and statement of cash flows?
34. How does issuing an $8,000 discount note with an 8 percent discount rate and a one-year term to maturity affect the accounting equation?
35. What type of account is Discount on Notes Payable?

EXERCISES—SERIES A

All Exercises in Series A are available with McGraw-Hill's Homework Manager

L.O. 1

Exercise 9-1A *Recognizing accrued interest expense*

Classic Corporation borrowed $90,000 from the bank on November 1, 2007. The note had an 8 percent annual rate of interest and matured on April 30, 2008. Interest and principal were paid in cash on the maturity date.

Required

a. What amount of cash did Classic pay for interest in 2007?
b. What amount of interest expense was reported on the 2007 income statement?
c. What amount of total liabilities was reported on the December 31, 2007, balance sheet?
d. What total amount of cash was paid to the bank on April 30, 2008 for principal and interest?
e. What amount of interest expense was reported on the 2008 income statement?

L.O. 1

Exercise 9-2A *Effects of recognizing accrued interest on financial statements*

Scott Perkins started Perkins Company on January 1, 2005. The company experienced the following events during its first year of operation.

1. Earned $1,500 of cash revenue for performing services.
2. Borrowed $2,400 cash from the bank.
3. Adjusted the accounting records to recognize accrued interest expense on the bank note. The note, issued on August 1, 2005, had a one-year term and a 7 percent annual interest rate.

Required

a. What is the amount of interest expense in 2005?
b. What amount of cash was paid for interest in 2005?
c. Use a horizontal statements model to show how each event affects the balance sheet, income statement, and statement of cash flows. Indicate whether the event increases (I), decreases (D), or does not affect (NA) each element of the financial statements. In the Cash Flows column, designate the cash flows as operating activities (OA), investing activities (IA), or financing activities (FA). The first transaction has been recorded as an example.

Event No.	Balance Sheet									Income Statement					Statement of Cash Flows
	Cash	=	Notes Pay.	+	Int. Pay.	+	Com. Stk.	+	Ret. Earn.	Rev.	−	Exp.	=	Net Inc.	
1	I	=	NA	+	NA	+	NA	+	I	I	−	NA	=	I	I OA

Exercise 9-3A *Recording sales tax expense* L.O. 2

The University Book Store sells books and other supplies to students in a state where the sales tax rate is 7 percent. The University Book Store engaged in the following transactions for 2008. Sales tax of 7 percent is collected on all sales.

1. Book sales, not including sales tax, for 2008 amounted to $275,000 cash.
2. Cash sales of miscellaneous items in 2008 were $150,000, not including tax.
3. Cost of goods sold amounted to $210,000 for the year.
4. Paid $130,000 in operating expenses for the year.
5. Paid the sales tax collected to the state agency.

Required

a. What is the total amount of sales tax the University Book Store collected and paid for the year?
b. Prepare the journal entries for the above transactions.
c. What is the University Book Store's net income for the year?

Exercise 9-4A *Recognizing sales tax payable* L.O. 2

The following selected transactions apply to Big Stop for November and December 2008. November was the first month of operations. Sales tax is collected at the time of sale but is not paid to the state sales tax agency until the following month.

1. Cash sales for November 2008 were $65,000 plus sales tax of 8 percent.
2. Big Stop paid the November sales tax to the state agency on December 10, 2008.
3. Cash sales for December 2008 were $80,000 plus sales tax of 8 percent.

Required

a. Record the above transactions in general journal form.
b. Show the effect of the above transactions on a statements model like the one shown below.

Assets =	Liabilities +		Equity	Income Statement			
Cash =	Sales Tax Pay. +	Com. Stk. +	Ret. Earn.	Rev. −	Exp. =	Net Inc.	Cash Flow

c. What was the total amount of sales tax paid in 2008?
d. What was the total amount of sales tax collected in 2008?
e. What is the amount of the sales tax liability as of December 31, 2008?
f. On what financial statement will the sales tax liability appear?

Exercise 9-5A *Contingent liabilities* L.O. 3

The following legal situations apply to Stringer Corp. for 2009:

1. A customer slipped and fell on a slick floor while shopping in the retail store. The customer has filed a $5 million lawsuit against the company. Stringer's attorney knows that the company will have to pay some damages but is reasonably certain that the suit can be settled for $500,000.
2. The EPA has assessed a fine against Stringer of $250,000 for hazardous emissions from one of its manufacturing plants. The EPA had previously issued a warning to Stringer and required Stringer to make repairs within six months. Stringer began to make the repairs, but was not able to complete them within the six-month period. Since Stringer has started the repairs, Stringer's attorney thinks the fine will be reduced to $100,000. He is approximately 80 percent certain that he can negotiate the fine reduction because of the repair work that has been completed.
3. One of Stringer's largest manufacturing facilities is located in "tornado alley." Property is routinely damaged by storms. Stringer estimates it may have property damage of as much as $300,000 this coming year.

Required

For each item above, determine the correct accounting treatment. Prepare any required journal entries.

L.O. 4

Exercise 9-6A *Effect of warranties on income and cash flow*

To support herself while attending school, Ellen Abba sold computers to other students. During her first year of operation, she sold computers that had cost her $120,000 cash for $260,000 cash. She provided her customers with a one-year warranty against defects in parts and labor. Based on industry standards, she estimated that warranty claims would amount to 5 percent of sales. During the year she paid $920 cash to replace a defective hard drive.

Required

a. Prepare the journal entries to record the:
   (1) Purchase of inventory.
   (2) Sale of computers.
   (3) Warranty expense.
   (4) Payment for repairs.

b. Post the above transactions to T-accounts.

c. Prepare an income statement and statement of cash flows for Abba's first year of operation.

d. Explain the difference between net income and the amount of cash flow from operating activities.

L.O. 4

Exercise 9-7A *Effect of warranty obligations and payments on financial statements*

The Ja-San Appliance Co. provides a 120-day parts-and-labor warranty on all merchandise it sells. Ja-San estimates the warranty expense for the current period to be $1,250. During the period a customer returned a product that cost $920 to repair.

Required

a. Show the effects of these transactions on the financial statements using a horizontal statements model like the example shown here. Use a + to indicate increase, a − for decrease, and NA for not affected. In the Cash Flow column, indicate whether the item is an operating activity (OA), investing activity (IA), or financing activity (FA).

Assets	=	Liab.	+	Equity	Rev.	−	Exp.	=	Net Inc.	Cash Flow

b. Prepare the journal entry to record the warranty expense for the period.

c. Prepare the journal entry to record payment for the actual repair costs.

d. Discuss the advantage of estimating the amount of warranty expense.

L.O. 2, 4, 8

Exercise 9-8A *Current liabilities*

The following transactions apply to Mabry Equipment Sales Corp. for 2007:

1. The business was started when Mabry Corp. received $50,000 from the issue of common stock.
2. Purchased $175,000 of merchandise on account.
3. Sold merchandise for $200,000 cash (not including sales tax). Sales tax of 8 percent is collected when the merchandise is sold. The merchandise had a cost of $125,000.
4. Provided a six-month warranty on the merchandise sold. Based on industry estimates, the warranty claims would amount to 4 percent of merchandise sales.
5. Paid the sales tax to the state agency on $150,000 of the sales.
6. On September 1, 2007, borrowed $20,000 from the local bank. The note had a 6 percent interest rate and matures on March 1, 2008.
7. Paid $5,600 for warranty repairs during the year.
8. Paid operating expenses of $54,000 for the year.
9. Paid $125,000 of accounts payable.
10. Recorded accrued interest at the end of the year.

Required

a. Show the effect of these transactions on the financial statements using a horizontal statements model like the one shown here. Use a + to indicate increase, a − for decrease, and NA for not affected. In the Cash Flow column, indicate whether the item is an operating activity (OA), investing activity (IA), or financing activity (FA). The first transaction is recorded as an example.

Assets	=	Liabilities	+	Equity	Rev.	−	Exp.	=	Net Inc.	Cash Flow
+		NA		+	NA		NA		NA	+ FA

b. Prepare the journal entries for the above transactions and post them to the appropriate T-accounts.
c. Prepare the income statement, balance sheet, and statement of cash flows for 2007.
d. What is the total amount of current liabilities at December 31, 2007?

Exercise 9-9A *Calculating payroll* L.O. 6, 7

Karim Enterprises has two hourly employees, Kala and Carl. Both employees earn overtime at the rate of 1½ times the hourly rate for hours worked in excess of 40 per week. Assume the Social Security tax rate is 6 percent on the first $90,000 of wages and the Medicare tax rate is 1.5 percent on all earnings. Federal income tax withheld for Kala and Carl was $250 and $220 respectively. The following information is for the first week in January 2007:

Employee	Hours Worked	Wage Rate per Hour
Kala	52	$20
Carl	47	$25

Required

a. Calculate the gross pay for each employee for the week.
b. Calculate the net pay for each employee for the week.
c. Prepare the general journal entry to record payment of the wages.

Exercise 9-10A *Calculating payroll* L.O. 6, 7

Mega Mart has two employees in 2007. Marsha earns $4,200 per month and Tom, the manager, earns $8,500 per month. Neither is paid extra if they work overtime. Assume the Social Security tax rate is 6 percent on the first $90,000 of earnings and the Medicare tax rate is 1.5 percent on all earnings. The federal income tax withholding is 15 percent of gross earnings for Marsha and 20 percent for Tom. Both Marsha and Tom have been employed all year.

Required

a. Calculate the net pay for both Marsha and Tom for March.
b. Calculate the net pay for both Marsha and Tom for December.
c. Is the net pay the same in March as December for both employees? Why or why not?
d. What amounts will Mega Mart report on the 2007 W-2s for each employee?

Exercise 9-11A *Calculating employee and employer payroll taxes* L.O. 6, 7

Marion Co. employed Juan Lopez in 2007. Juan earned $5,000 per month and worked the entire year. Assume the Social Security tax rate is 6 percent and the Medicare tax rate is 1.5 percent. Juan's federal income tax withholding amount is $900 per month. Use 6.2 percent for the unemployment tax rate.

Required

a. Answer the following questions:
   (1) What is Juan's net pay per month?
   (2) What amount does Juan pay monthly in FICA payroll taxes?
   (3) What is the total payroll tax expense for Marion Co. for January 2007? February 2007? March 2007? December 2007?
b. Assume that instead of $5,000 per month Juan earned $8,000 per month. Answer the questions in Requirement *a*.

Exercise 9-12A *Fringe benefits and payroll expense* L.O. 6, 7

Lynch Co. provides various fringe benefits for its three employees. It provides vacation and personal leave at the rate of one day for each month worked. Its employees earn a combined total of approximately $600 per day. In addition, Lynch Co. pays $750 per month in medical insurance premiums for its employees. Lynch also contributes $300 per month into a retirement plan for the employees. Assume the Social Security tax rate is 6% of the first $90,000 of salaries and the Medicare tax rate is 1.5%. The unemployment tax rate is 5.2%.

Required

a. Prepare the monthly journal entry for the accrued fringe benefits.

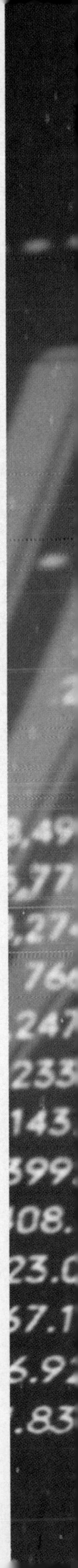

b. Show the effect of the above transaction on a statements model like the one shown below.

Assets	=	Liabilities	+	Equity		Income Statement			Cash Flow
Cash	=	Various Payables	+	Com. Stk.	+ Ret. Earn.	Rev.	− Exp.	= Net Inc.	

c. If the three employees each worked 250 days, what is Lynch Co.'s total payroll cost (salary, payroll taxes, and fringe benefits) for the year? (Assume that each employee earns $200 per day.)

L.O. 3

Exercise 9-13A *Comprehensive single cycle problem*

The following transactions apply to Design Co. for 2009:

1. Received $30,000 cash from the issue of common stock.
2. Purchased inventory on account for $142,000.
3. Sold inventory for $175,000 cash that had cost $108,000. Sales tax was collected at the rate of 5 percent on the inventory sold.
4. Borrowed $20,000 from the First State Bank on October 1, 2009. The note had a 6 percent interest rate and a one-year term to maturity.
5. Paid the accounts payable (see transaction 2).
6. Paid the sales tax due on $150,000 of sales. Sales tax on the other $25,000 is not due until after the end of the year.
7. Salaries for the year for the one employee amounted $30,000. Assume the Social Security tax rate is 6 percent and the Medicare tax rate is 1.5 percent. Federal income tax withheld was $5,200.
8. Paid $2,600 for warranty repairs during the year.
9. Paid $12,000 of other operating expenses during the year.
10. Paid a dividend of $5,000 to the shareholders.

Adjustments:

11. The products sold in transaction 3 were warranted. Design estimated that the warranty cost would be 4 percent of sales.
12. Record the accrued interest at December 31, 2009.
13. Record the accrued payroll tax at December 31, 2009. Assume no payroll taxes have been paid for the year and that the unemployment tax rate is 6.2 percent (federal unemployment tax rate is .8 percent and the state unemployment tax rate is 5.4 percent).

Required

a. Record the above transactions in general journal form.

b. Post the transactions to T-accounts.

c. Prepare an income statement, statement of changes in stockholders' equity, balance sheet, and statement of cash flows for 2009.

L.O. 9

Exercise 9-14A *Preparing a classified balance sheet*

Required

Use the following information to prepare a classified balance sheet for Steller Co. at the end of 2008.

Accounts Receivable	$42,500
Accounts Payable	8,000
Cash	15,260
Common Stock	42,000
Long-Term Notes Payable	23,000
Merchandise Inventory	29,000
Office Equipment	28,500
Retained Earnings	45,460
Prepaid Insurance	3,200

Exercise 9-15A *Current ratio*

L.O. 10

The following information is available for two companies:

	Pacer Co.	Sprinter Co.
Cash	$ 20,000	$ 15,000
Accounts Receivable	35,000	45,000
Merchandise Inventory	120,000	70,000
Building and Equipment	220,000	120,000
Accounts Payable	80,000	60,000
Salaries Payable	20,000	30,000
Taxes Payable	12,000	25,000
Long-Term Notes Payable	150,000	100,000

Required

a. Compute the current ratios for the above companies.

b. Which company would more likely be able to pay its short-term debts? Explain.

Exercise 9-16A *Effect of a discount note on financial statements (Appendix)*

L.O. 11

Pat Waverly started a moving company on January 1, 2006. On March 1, 2006, Waverly borrowed cash from a local bank by issuing a one-year $50,000 face value note with annual interest based on a 12 percent discount. During 2006, Waverly provided services for $36,800 cash.

Required

Answer the following questions. Record the events in T-accounts prior to answering the questions.

a. What is the amount of total liabilities on the December 31, 2006, balance sheet?

b. What is the amount of net income on the 2006 income statement?

c. What is the amount of cash flow from operating activities on the 2006 statement of cash flows?

d. Provide the general journal entries necessary to record issuing the note on March 1, 2006; recognizing accrued interest on December 31, 2006; and repaying the loan on February 28, 2007.

Exercise 9-17A *Comparing effective interest rates on discount versus interest-bearing notes (Appendix)*

L.O. 11

Glen Pounds borrowed money by issuing two notes on January 1, 2006. The financing transactions are described here.

1. Borrowed funds by issuing a $30,000 face value discount note to State Bank. The note had an 8 percent discount rate, a one-year term to maturity, and was paid off on December 31, 2006.
2. Borrowed funds by issuing a $30,000 face value, interest-bearing note to Community Bank. The note had an 8 percent stated rate of interest, a one-year term to maturity, and was paid off on December 31, 2006.

Required

a. Show the effects of issuing the two notes on the financial statements using separate horizontal financial statement models like the ones here. Record the transaction amounts under the appropriate categories. In the Cash Flow column, indicate whether the item is an operating activity (OA), investing activity (IA), or financing activity (FA). Record only the events occurring on the date of issue. Do not record accrued interest or the repayment at maturity.

Discount Note

Assets =	Liabilities		+ Equity	Rev. − Exp. = Net Inc.	Cash Flow
Cash =	Notes Pay. −	Disc. on Notes Pay.	+ Ret. Earn.		

Interest-Bearing Note

Assets	=	Liabilities	+	Equity	Rev. − Exp. = Net Inc.	Cash Flow
Cash	=	Notes Pay.	+	Ret. Earn.		

b. What is the total amount of interest to be paid on each note?
c. What amount of cash was received from each note when it was issued?
d. Which note has the higher effective interest rate? Support your answer with appropriate computations.

L.O. 11

Exercise 9-18A *Recording accounting events for a discount note (Appendix)*

Cross Co. issued a $50,000 face value discount note to First Bank on June 1, 2006. The note had a 6 percent discount rate and a one-year term to maturity.

Required

Prepare general journal entries for the following transactions:

a. The issuance of the note on June 1, 2006.
b. The adjustment for accrued interest at the end of the year, December 31, 2006.
c. Recording interest expense for 2007 and repaying the principal on May 31, 2007.

PROBLEMS—SERIES A

All Problems in Series A are available with McGraw-Hill's Homework Manager

L.O. 1. 2, 3, 4

Problem 9-19A *Accounting for short-term debt and sales tax—two accounting cycles*

The following transactions apply to Artesia Co. for 2009, its first year of operations.

1. Received $40,000 cash from the issue of a short-term note with a 5 percent interest rate and a one-year maturity. The note was made on April 1, 2009.
2. Received $120,000 cash plus applicable sales tax from performing services. The services are subject to a sales tax rate of 6 percent.
3. Paid $72,000 cash for other operating expenses during the year.
4. Paid the sales tax due on $100,000 of the service revenue for the year. Sales tax on the balance of the revenue is not due until 2010.
5. Recognized the accrued interest at December 31, 2009.

The following transactions apply to Artesia Co. for 2010.

1. Paid the balance of the sales tax due for 2009.
2. Received $145,000 cash plus applicable sales tax from performing services. The services are subject to a sales tax rate of 6 percent.
3. Repaid the principal of the note and applicable interest on April 1, 2010.
4. Paid $85,000 of other operating expense during the year.
5. Paid the sales tax due on $120,000 of the service revenue. The sales tax on the balance of the revenue is not due until 2011.

Required

a. Record the 2009 transactions in general journal form.
b. Post the transactions to T-accounts.
c. Prepare a balance sheet, statement of changes in stockholders' equity, income statement, and statement of cash flows for 2009.
d. Prepare the closing entries and post them to the T-accounts.
e. Prepare an after-closing trial balance.
f. Repeat Requirements *a* through *e* for 2010.

Problem 9-20A *Effect of accrued interest on financial statements*

L.O. 1

CHECK FIGURES
a. $12,000
h. $38,800

Norman Co. borrowed $15,000 from the local bank on April 1, 2008, when the company was started. The note had an 8 percent annual interest rate and a one-year term to maturity. Norman Co. recognized $42,000 of revenue on account in 2008 and $56,000 of revenue on account in 2009. Cash collections from accounts receivable were $38,000 in 2008 and $58,000 in 2009. Norman Co. paid $26,000 of salaries expense in 2008 and $32,000 of salaries expense in 2009. Repaid loan and interest at maturity date.

Required

Based on the preceding information, answer the following questions. (*Hint:* Record the events in T-accounts before answering the questions.)

a. What amount of net cash flow from operating activities would Norman report on the 2008 cash flow statement?

b. What amount of interest expense would Norman report on the 2008 income statement?

c. What amount of total liabilities would Norman report on the December 31, 2008, balance sheet?

d. What amount of retained earnings would Norman report on the December 31, 2008, balance sheet?

e. What amount of cash flow from financing activities would Norman report on the 2008 statement of cash flows?

f. What amount of interest expense would Norman report on the 2009 income statement?

g. What amount of cash flows from operating activities would Norman report on the 2009 cash flow statement?

h. What amount of total assets would Norman report on the December 31, 2009, balance sheet?

Problem 9-21A *Current liabilities*

L.O. 1, 2, 4

The following selected transactions were taken from the books of Caledonia Company for 2008.

1. On March 1, 2008, borrowed $50,000 cash from the local bank. The note had a 6 percent interest rate and was due on September 1, 2008.
2. Cash sales for the year amounted to $225,000 plus sales tax at the rate of 7 percent.
3. Caledonia provides a 90-day warranty on the merchandise sold. The warranty expense is estimated to be 2 percent of sales.
4. Paid the sales tax to the state sales tax agency on $190,000 of the sales.
5. Paid the note due on September 1 and the related interest.
6. On October 1, 2008, borrowed $40,000 cash from the local bank. The note had a 7 percent interest rate and a one-year term to maturity.
7. Paid $3,600 in warranty repairs.
8. A customer has filed a lawsuit against Caledonia for $100,000 for breach of contract. The company attorney does not believe the suit has merit.

Required

a. Answer the following questions:

(1) What amount of cash did Caledonia pay for interest during the year?

(2) What amount of interest expense is reported on Caledonia's income statement for the year?

(3) What is the amount of warranty expense for the year?

b. Prepare the current liabilities section of the balance sheet at December 31, 2008. (*Hint:* first post the liabilities transactions to T-accounts.)

c. Show the effect of these transactions on the financial statements using a horizontal statements model like the one shown here. Use a + to indicate increase, a − for decrease, and NA for not affected. In the Cash Flow column, indicate whether the item is an operating activity (OA), investing activity (IA), or financing activity (FA). The first transaction is recorded as an example.

Assets	=	Liabilities	+	Equity	Rev.	−	Exp.	=	Net Inc.	Cash Flow
+		+		NA	NA		NA		NA	+ FA

L.O. 3

Problem 9-22A *Contingent liabilities*

Required

a. Give an example of a contingent liability that is probable and reasonably estimable. How would this type of liability be shown in the accounting records?

b. Give an example of a contingent liability that is reasonably possible or probable but not reasonably estimable. How would this type of liability be shown in the accounting records?

c. Give an example of a contingent liability that is remote. How is this type of liability shown in the accounting records?

L.O. 6, 7

Problem 9-23A *Accounting for payroll and payroll taxes*

Sturgis Co. pays salaries monthly on the last day of the month. The following information is available from Sturgis Co. for the month ended December 31, 2008.

Administrative salaries	$76,000
Sales salaries	58,000
Office salaries	42,000

Assume the Social Security tax rate is 6 percent on the first $90,000 of salaries and the Medicare tax rate is 1.5 percent on all salaries. Ralph reached the $90,000 amount in October. His salary in December amounted to $10,000 and is included in the $76,000. No one else will reach the $90,000 amount for the year. None of the employee salaries are subject to unemployment tax in December.

Other amounts withheld from salaries in December were as follows:

Federal income tax	$18,000
State income tax	5,600
U.S. Savings Bonds	2,000

Required

1. Prepare the journal entry to record the payment of payroll on December 31, 2008.
2. Prepare the journal entry to record the payroll tax expense for Sturgis Co. for December 2008.

L.O. 6, 7

Problem 9-24A *Computation of net pay and payroll expense*

The following information is available for the employees of Rockwell Company for the first week of January 2009:

1. John earns $26 per hour and 1½ times his regular rate for hours over 40 per week. John worked 46 hours the first week in January. John's federal income tax withholding is equal to 10 percent of his gross pay. Rockwell pays medical insurance of $75 per week for John and contributes $50 per week to a retirement plan for him.
2. Ken earns a weekly salary of $1,200. Ken's federal income tax withholding is 15 percent of his gross pay. Rockwell pays medical insurance of $120 per week for Ken and contributes $100 per week to a retirement plan for him.
3. Vacation pay is accrued at the rate of 1/4 of the regular pay rate per hour for John and $75 per week for Ken.

Assume the Social Security tax rate is 6 percent on the first $90,000 of salaries and the Medicare tax rate is 1.5 percent of total salaries. The state unemployment tax rate is 4.2 percent and the federal unemployment tax rate is .8 percent of the first $7,000 of salary for each employee.

Required

a. Compute the gross pay for John for the first week in January.

b. Compute the net pay for both John and Ken for the first week in January.

c. Prepare the journal entry to record the payment of the payroll for the week.

d. Prepare the journal entry to record the payroll tax expense and fringe benefit expense for Rockwell for the week.

e. What is the total cost of compensation expense for the first week of January 2009 for Rockwell Company?

Problem 9-25A *Multistep income statement and classified balance sheet*

L.O. 9

excel
mhhe.com/edmonds2007

Required

Use the following information to prepare a multistep income statement and a classified balance sheet for Douglas Company for 2004. (*Hint:* Some of the items will *not* appear on either statement, and ending retained earnings must be calculated.)

Operating Expenses	$ 90,000	Cash	$ 23,000
Land	50,000	Interest Receivable (short term)	800
Accumulated Depreciation	38,000	Cash Flow from Investing Activities	102,000
Accounts Payable	60,000	Allowance for Doubtful Accounts	7,000
Unearned Revenue	58,000	Interest Payable (short term)	3,000
Warranties Payable (short term)	2,000	Sales Revenue	500,000
Equipment	77,000	Uncollectible Accounts Expense	14,000
Notes Payable (long term)	129,000	Interest Expense	32,000
Salvage Value of Equipment	7,000	Accounts Receivable	113,000
Dividends	12,000	Salaries Payable	12,000
Warranty Expense	5,000	Supplies	3,000
Beginning Retained Earnings	28,800	Prepaid Rent	14,000
Interest Revenue	6,000	Common Stock	52,000
Gain on Sale of Equipment	10,000	Cost of Goods Sold	179,000
Inventory	154,000	Salaries Expense	122,000
Notes Receivable (short term)	17,000		

CHECK FIGURES
Total Current Assets: $317,800
Total Current Liabilities: $135,000

Problem 9-26A *Accounting for a discount note—two accounting cycles (Appendix)*

L.O. 11

excel
mhhe.com/edmonds2007

Una Corp. was started in 2006. The following summarizes transactions that occurred during 2006:

1. Issued a $20,000 face value discount note to Golden Savings Bank on April 1, 2006. The note had a 6 percent discount rate and a one-year term to maturity.
2. Recognized revenue from services performed for cash, $125,000.
3. Incurred and paid $95,000 cash for selling and administrative expenses.
4. Amortized the discount on the note at the end of the year, December 31, 2006.
5. Prepared the necessary closing entries at December 31, 2006.

The following summarizes transactions that occurred in 2007:

1. Recognized $195,000 of service revenue in cash.
2. Incurred and paid $146,000 for selling and administrative expenses.
3. Amortized the remainder of the discount for 2007 and paid the face value of the note.
4. Prepared the necessary closing entries at December 31, 2007.

CHECK FIGURES
c. Net Income: $109,250
Total Assets: $368,550

Required

a. Show the effects of each of the transactions on the elements of the financial statements, using a horizontal statements model like the one shown here. Use + for increase, − for decrease, and NA for not affected. The first transaction is entered as an example. (*Hint:* Closing entries do not affect the statements model.)

Event No.	Assets	=	Liab.	+	Equity	Rev.	−	Exp.	=	Net Inc.	Cash Flow
1	+		+		NA	NA		NA		NA	+ FA

b. Prepare entries in general journal form for the transactions for 2006 and 2007, and post them to T-accounts.

c. Prepare an income statement, statement of changes in stockholders' equity, balance sheet, and statement of cash flows for 2006 and 2007.

EXERCISES—SERIES B

L.O. 1

Exercise 9-1B *Recognizing accrued interest expense*

Whitewater Corporation borrowed $40,000 from the bank on October 1, 2007. The note had a 9 percent annual rate of interest and matured on March 31, 2008. Interest and principal were paid in cash on the maturity date.

Required

a. What amount of cash did Whitewater pay for interest in 2007?
b. What amount of interest expense was recognized on the 2007 income statement?
c. What amount of total liabilities was reported on the December 31, 2007, balance sheet?
d. What total amount of cash was paid to the bank on March 31, 2008, for principal and interest?
e. What amount of interest expense was reported on the 2008 income statement?

L.O. 1

Exercise 9-2B *Effects of recognizing accrued interest on financial statements*

Bill Parker started Parker Company on January 1, 2007. The company experienced the following events during its first year of operation.

1. Earned $6,200 of cash revenue.
2. Borrowed $4,000 cash from the bank.
3. Adjusted the accounting records to recognize accrued interest expense on the bank note. The note, issued on September 1, 2007, had a one-year term and a 10 percent annual interest rate.

Required

a. What is the amount of interest payable at December 31, 2007?
b. What is the amount of interest expense in 2007?
c. What is the amount of interest paid 2007?
d. Use a horizontal statements model to show how each event affects the balance sheet, income statement, and statement of cash flows. Indicate whether the event increases (I), decreases (D), or does not affect (NA) each element of the financial statements. In the Cash Flows column, designate the cash flows as operating activities (OA), investing activities (IA), or financing activities (FA). The first transaction has been recorded as an example.

	Balance Sheet									Income Statement					
Event No.	Cash	=	Notes Pay.	+	Int. Pay.	+	Com. Stk.	+	Ret. Earn.	Rev.	−	Exp.	=	Net Inc.	Statement of Cash Flows
1	I	=	NA	+	NA	+	NA	+	I	I	−	NA	=	I	I OA

L.O. 2

Exercise 9-3B *Recording sales tax expense*

The College Book Mart sells books and other supplies to students in a state where the sales tax rate is 8 percent. The College Book Mart engaged in the following transactions for 2008. Sales tax of 8 percent is collected on all sales.

1. Book sales, not including sales tax, for 2008 amounted to $320,000 cash.
2. Cash sales of miscellaneous items in 2008 were $80,000, not including tax.
3. Cost of goods sold was $190,000 for the year.
4. Paid $150,000 in operating expenses for the year.
5. Paid the sales tax collected to the state agency.

Required

a. What is the total amount of sales tax the College Book Mart collected and paid for the year?
b. Prepare the journal entries for the above transactions.
c. What is the College Book Mart's net income for the year?

L.O. 2

Exercise 9-4B *Recognizing sales tax payable*

The following selected transactions apply to Mountain Supply for November and December 2008. November was the first month of operations. Sales tax is collected at the time of sale but is not paid to the state sales tax agency until the following month.

1. Cash sales for November 2008 were $135,000 plus sales tax of 7 percent.
2. Mountain Supply paid the November sales tax to the state agency on December 10, 2008.
3. Cash sales for December 2008 were $160,000 plus sales tax of 7 percent.

Required

a. Record the above transactions in general journal form.

b. Show the effect of the above transactions on a statements model like the one shown below.

Assets:	=	Liabilities	+	Equity			Income Statement					Cash Flow
Cash	=	Sales Tax Pay.	+	Com. Stk.	+	Ret. Earn.	Rev.	−	Exp.	=	Net Inc.	

c. What was the total amount of sales tax paid in 2008?

d. What was the total amount of sales tax collected in 2008?

e. What amount of sales tax expense will be reported on the 2008 income statement?

Exercise 9-5B *Contingent liabilities*

L.O. 3

The following three independent sets of facts relate to contingent liabilities:

1. In November of the current year an automobile manufacturing company recalled all minivans manufactured during the past two years. A flaw in the seat belt fastener was discovered and the recall provides for replacement of the defective fasteners. The estimated cost of this recall is $1 million.
2. The EPA has notified a company of violations of environmental laws relating to hazardous waste. These actions seek cleanup costs, penalties, and damages to property. The company is reasonably certain that the cleanup cost will be approximately $5 million. In addition, potential reimbursements for property damage could be as much as $2 million or as little as $100,000. There is no way to more accurately estimate the property damage at this time.
3. Big Company does not carry property damage insurance because of the cost. The company suffered substantial losses each year of the past three years. However, it has had no losses for the current year. Management thinks this is too good to be true and is sure there will be significant losses in the coming year. However, the exact amount cannot be determined.

Required

a. Discuss the various categories of contingent liabilities.

b. For each item above determine the correct accounting treatment. Prepare any required journal entries.

Exercise 9-6B *Effect of warranties on income and cash flow*

L.O. 4

To support herself while attending school, Kim Lee sold stereo systems to other students. During her first year of operation, she sold systems that had cost her $95,000 cash for $140,000 cash. She provided her customers with a one-year warranty against defects in parts and labor. Based on industry standards, she estimated that warranty claims would amount to 6 percent of sales. During the year she paid $200 cash to replace a defective tuner.

Required

Prepare an income statement and statement of cash flows for Lee's first year of operation. Based on the information given, what is Lee's total warranties liability at the end of the accounting period?

Exercise 9-7B *Effect of warranty obligations and payments on financial statements*

L.O. 4

The Cycle Company provides a 120-day parts-and-labor warranty on all merchandise it sells. Cycle estimates the warranty expense for the current period to be $1,400. During the period a customer returned a product that cost $596 to repair.

Required

a. Show the effects of these transactions on the financial statements using a horizontal statements model like the example shown here. Use a + to indicate increase, a − for decrease, and NA for not affected. In the Cash Flow column, indicate whether the item is an operating activity (OA), investing activity (IA), or financing activity (FA).

Assets	=	Liab.	+	Equity	Rev.	−	Exp.	=	Net Inc.	Cash Flow

b. Prepare the journal entry to record the warranty expense for the period.

c. Prepare the journal entry to record payment for the actual repair costs.

d. Why do companies estimate warranty expense and record the expense before the repairs are actually made?

L.O. 2, 4, 8

Exercise 9-8B *Current liabilities*

The following transactions apply to Comfort Mattress Sales for 2007:

1. The business was started when the company received $30,000 from the issue of common stock.
2. Purchased mattress inventory of $200,000 on account.
3. Sold mattresses for $300,000 cash (not including sales tax). Sales tax of 8 percent is collected when the merchandise is sold. The merchandise had a cost of $150,000.
4. Provided a six-month warranty on the mattresses sold. Based on industry estimates, the warranty claims would amount to 2 percent of mattress sales.
5. Paid the sales tax to the state agency on $250,000 of the sales.
6. On September 1, 2007, borrowed $30,000 from the local bank. The note had a 6 percent interest rate and matured on March 1, 2008.
7. Paid $4,600 for warranty repairs during the year.
8. Paid operating expenses of $96,000 for the year.
9. Paid $175,000 of accounts payable.
10. Record accrued interest on the note issued in transaction no. 6.

Required

a. Show the effect of these transactions on the financial statements using a horizontal statements model like the one shown here. Use a + to indicate increase, a − for decrease, and NA for not affected. In the Cash Flow column, indicate whether the item is an operating activity (OA), investing activity (IA), or financing activity (FA). The first transaction is recorded as an example.

Assets	=	Liabilities	+	Equity	Rev.	−	Exp.	=	Net Inc.	Cash Flow
+		NA		+	NA		NA		NA	+ FA

b. Prepare the journal entries for the above transactions and post them to the appropriate T-accounts.

c. Prepare the income statement, balance sheet, and statement of cash flows for 2007.

d. What is the total amount of current liabilities at December 31, 2007?

L.O. 6, 7

Exercise 9-9B *Calculating payroll*

Khonkar Enterprises has two hourly employees, Matt and Sam. Both employees earn overtime at the rate of 1½ times the hourly rate for hours worked in excess of 40 per week. Assume the Social Security tax rate is 6 percent on the first $90,000 of wages and the Medicare tax rate is 1.5 percent on all earnings. Federal income tax withheld for Matt and Sam was $290 and $240 respectively for the first week of January. The following information is for the first week in January 2007:

Employee	Hours Worked	Wage Rate per Hour
Matt	56	$26
Sam	48	$22

Required

a. Calculate the gross pay for each employee for the week.

b. Calculate the net pay for each employee for the week.

c. Prepare the general journal entry to record payment of the wages.

Exercise 9-10B *Calculating payroll* — L.O. 6, 7

Holiday Hall has two employees in 2007. Seon earns $4,600 per month and Hun, the manager, earns $8,800 per month. Neither is paid extra for working overtime. Assume the Social Security tax rate is 6 percent on the first $90,000 of earnings and the Medicare tax rate is 1.5 percent on all earnings. The federal income tax withholding is 15 percent of gross earnings for Seon and 20 percent for Hun. Both Seon and Hun have been employed all year.

Required

a. Calculate the net pay for both Seon and Hun for March.
b. Calculate the net pay for both Seon and Hun for December.
c. Is the net pay the same in March as December for both employees? Why or why not?
d. What amounts will Holiday Hall report on the 2007 W-2s for each employee?

Exercise 9-11B *Calculating employee and employer payroll taxes* — L.O. 6, 7

Carter Co. employed Sam Goldman in 2007. Sam earned $5,200 per month and worked the entire year. Assume the Social Security tax rate is 6 percent and the Medicare tax rate is 1.5 percent. Sam's federal income tax withholding amount is $900 per month. Use 5.4 percent for the state unemployment tax rate and .8 percent for the federal unemployment tax rate.

Required

a. Answer the following questions.
  (1) What is Sam's net pay per month?
  (2) What amount does Sam pay monthly in FICA payroll taxes?
  (3) What is the total payroll tax expense for Carter Co. for January 2007? February 2007? March 2007? December 2007?

b. Assume that instead of $5,200 per month Sam earned $9,000 per month. Answer the questions in Requirement *a*.

Exercise 9-12B *Fringe benefits and payroll expense* — L.O. 6, 7

Faello Co. provides various fringe benefits for its three employees. It provides vacation and personal leave at the rate of one day for each month worked. Its employees earn a combined total of approximately $450 per day. In addition, Faello Co. pays $600 per month in medical insurance premiums for its employees. Faello also contributes $350 per month into a retirement plan for the employees. The federal unemployment tax rate is .8 percent and the state unemployment tax rate is 4.0 percent.

Required

a. Prepare the monthly journal entry for the accrued fringe benefits.
b. Show the effect of the above transaction on a statements model like the one shown below.

Assets	=	Liabilities	+	Equity			Income Statement	Cash Flow
Cash	=	Various Payables	+	Com. Stk.	+	Ret. Earn.	Rev. − Exp. = Net Inc.	

c. If the three employees each worked 250 days, what is Faello Co.'s total payroll cost (salary, payroll taxes, and fringe benefits) for the year? (Assume that each employee earns $150 per day.)

Exercise 9-13B *Comprehensive single cycle problem* — L.O. 3

The following transactions apply to Toro Co. for 2009:

1. Received $50,000 cash from the issue of common stock.
2. Purchased inventory on account for $230,000.
3. Sold inventory for $245,000 cash that had cost $130,000. Sales tax was collected at the rate of 5 percent on the inventory sold.
4. Borrowed $30,000 from the First State Bank on March 1, 2009. The note had a 7 percent interest rate and a one-year term to maturity.
5. Paid the accounts payable (see transaction 2).

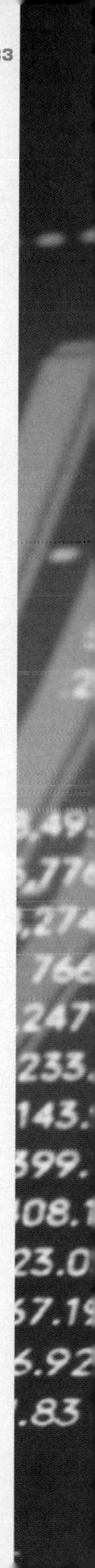

6. Paid the sales tax due on $180,000 of sales. Sales tax on the other $65,000 is not due until after the end of the year.
7. Salaries for the year for the one employee amounted to $40,000. Assume the Social Security tax rate is 6 percent and the Medicare tax rate is 1.5 percent. Federal income tax withheld was $6,500.
8. Paid $5,600 for warranty repairs during the year.
9. Paid $35,000 of other operating expenses during the year.
10. Paid a dividend of $6,000 to the shareholders.

Adjustments:

11. The products sold in transaction 3 were warranted. Toro estimated that the warranty cost would be 3 percent of sales.
12. Record the accrued interest at December 31, 2009.
13. Record the accrued payroll tax at December 31, 2009. Assume no payroll taxes have been paid for the year and that the unemployment tax rate is 6.2 percent (federal unemployment tax rate is .8 percent and the state unemployment tax rate is 5.4 percent).

Required

a. Record the above transactions in general journal form.

b. Post the transactions to T-accounts.

c. Prepare an income statement, statement of changes in stockholders' equity, balance sheet, and statement of cash flows for 2009.

L.O. 9

Exercise 9-14B ***Preparing a classified balance sheet***

Required

Use the following information to prepare a classified balance sheet for Chapley Co. at the end of 2007.

Accounts Receivable	$12,150
Accounts Payable	5,500
Cash	10,992
Common Stock	12,000
Land	12,500
Long-Term Notes Payable	11,500
Merchandise Inventory	16,000
Retained Earnings	22,642

L.O. 10

Exercise 9-15B ***Current ratio***

The following information is available for two companies:

	Snapper Co.	Clapper Co.
Cash	$ 90,000	$ 35,000
Accounts Receivable	85,000	65,000
Merchandise Inventory	70,000	150,000
Building and Equipment	439,000	220,000
Accounts Payable	70,000	90,000
Salaries Payable	40,000	60,000
Taxes Payable	20,000	40,000
Long-term Notes Payable	150,000	100,000

Required

a. Compute the current ratios for the above companies.

b. Which company would more likely be able to pay its short-term debts? Explain.

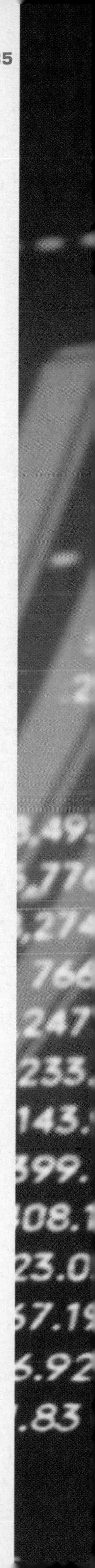

Exercise 9-16B *Effect of a discount note on financial statements (Appendix)* L.O. 11

Ken Kersey started a design company on January 1, 2004. On April 1, 2004, Kersey borrowed cash from a local bank by issuing a one-year $200,000 face value note with annual interest based on a 10 percent discount. During 2004, Kersey provided services for $55,000 cash.

Required

Answer the following questions. (*Hint:* Record the events in T-accounts prior to answering the questions.)

a. What is the amount of total liabilities on the December 31, 2004, balance sheet?

b. What is the amount of net income on the 2004 income statement?

c. What is the amount of cash flow from operating activities on the 2004 statement of cash flows?

d. Provide the general journal entries necessary to record issuing the note on April 1, 2004; recognizing accrued interest on December 31, 2004; and repaying the loan on March 31, 2005.

Exercise 9-17B *Comparing effective interest rates on discount versus interest-bearing notes (Appendix)* L.O. 11

Cheyenne Ross borrowed money by issuing two notes on March 1, 2005. The financing transactions are described here.

1. Borrowed funds by issuing a $30,000 face value discount note to Farmers Bank. The note had a 10 percent discount rate, a one-year term to maturity, and was paid off on March 1, 2006.
2. Borrowed funds by issuing a $30,000 face value, interest-bearing note to Valley Bank. The note had a 10 percent stated rate of interest, a one-year term to maturity, and was paid off on March 1, 2006.

Required

a. Show the effects of issuing the two notes on the financial statements using separate horizontal financial statement models like the ones here. Record the transaction amounts under the appropriate categories. In the Cash Flow column, indicate whether the item is an operating activity (OA), investing activity (IA), or financing activity (FA). Record only the events occurring on the date of issue. Do not record accrued interest or the repayment at maturity.

Discount Note

Assets =	Liabilities		+ Equity	Rev. − Exp. = Net Inc.	Cash Flow
Cash =	Notes Pay. −	Disc. on Notes Pay.	+ Ret. Earn.		

Interest-Bearing Note

Assets =	Liabilities	+ Equity	Rev. − Exp. = Net Inc.	Cash Flow
Cash =	Notes Pay.	+ Ret. Earn.		

b. What is the total amount of interest to be paid on each note?

c. What amount of cash was received from each note when it was issued?

d. Which note has the higher effective interest rate? Support your answer with appropriate computations.

Exercise 9-18B *Recording accounting events for a discount note (Appendix)* L.O. 11

Hopkins Co. issued a $40,000 face value discount note to National Bank on July 1, 2005. The note had a 12 percent discount rate and a one-year term to maturity.

Required

Prepare general journal entries for the following:

a. The issuance of the note on July 1, 2005.

b. The adjustment for accrued interest at the end of the year, December 31, 2005.

c. Recording interest expense for 2006 and repaying the principal on June 30, 2006.

PROBLEMS—SERIES B

L.O. 1, 2, 3, 4

Problem 9-19B *Account for short-term debt and sales tax—two accounting cycles*

The following transactions apply to Allied Enterprises for 2009, its first year of operations.

1. Received $50,000 cash from the issue of a short-term note with a 6 percent interest rate and a one-year maturity. The note was made on April 1, 2009.
2. Received $180,000 cash plus applicable sales tax from performing services. The services are subject to a sales tax rate of 6 percent.
3. Paid $90,000 cash for other operating expenses during the year.
4. Paid the sales tax due on $140,000 of the service revenue for the year. Sales tax on the balance of the revenue is not due until 2010.
5. Recognized the accrued interest at December 31, 2009.

The following transactions apply to Allied Enterprises for 2010.

1. Paid the balance of the sales tax due for 2009.
2. Received $215,000 cash plus applicable sales tax from performing services. The services are subject to a sales tax rate of 6 percent.
3. Repaid the principal of the note and applicable interest on April 1, 2010.
4. Paid $125,000 of other operating expenses during the year.
5. Paid the sales tax due on $180,000 of the service revenue. The sales tax on the balance of the revenue is not due until 2011.

Required

a. Record the 2009 transactions in general journal form.
b. Post the transactions to T-accounts.
c. Prepare a balance sheet, statement of changes in stockholders' equity, income statement, and statement of cash flows for 2009.
d. Prepare the closing entries and post them to the T-accounts.
e. Prepare an after-closing trial balance.
f. Repeat Requirements *a* through *d* for 2010.

L.O. 1

Problem 9-20B *Effect of accrued interest on financial statements*

Magic Enterprises borrowed $18,000 from a local bank on July 1, 2006, when the company was started. The note had a 10 percent annual interest rate and a one-year term to maturity. Magic Enterprises recognized $42,500 of revenue on account in 2006 and $45,000 of revenue on account in 2007. Cash collections of accounts receivable were $36,000 in 2006 and $35,000 in 2007. Magic paid $24,000 of other operating expenses in 2006 and $28,000 of other operating expenses in 2007. Repaid the loan and interest at the maturity date.

Required

Based on this information, answer the following questions. (*Hint:* Record the events in T-accounts before answering the questions.)

a. What amount of interest expense would Magic report on the 2006 income statement?
b. What amount of net cash flow from operating activities would Magic report on the 2006 statement of cash flows?
c. What amount of total liabilities would Magic report on the December 31, 2006, balance sheet?
d. What amount of retained earnings would Magic report on the December 31, 2006, balance sheet?
e. What amount of net cash flow from financing activities would Magic report on the 2006 statement of cash flows?
f. What amount of interest expense would Magic report on the 2007 income statement?
g. What amount of net cash flow from operating activities would Magic report on the 2007 statement of cash flows?
h. What amount of total assets would Magic report on the December 31, 2007, balance sheet?
i. What amount of net cash flow from investing activities would Magic report on the 2007 statement of cash flows?

j. If Magic Enterprises paid a $1,500 dividend during 2007, what retained earnings balance would it report on the December 31, 2007, balance sheet?

Problem 9-21B *Current liabilities*

L.O. 1, 2, 4

The following selected transactions were taken from the books of Chandra Company for 2008.

1. On February 1, 2008, borrowed $60,000 cash from the local bank. The note had a 6 percent interest rate and was due on June 1, 2008.
2. Cash sales for the year amounted to $310,000 plus sales tax at the rate of 7 percent.
3. Chandra provides a 90-day warranty on the merchandise sold. The warranty expense is estimated to be 1 percent of sales.
4. Paid the sales tax to the state sales tax agency on $280,000 of the sales.
5. Paid the note due on June 1 and the related interest.
6. On November 1, 2008, borrowed $50,000 cash from the local bank. The note had a 6 percent interest rate and a one-year term to maturity.
7. Paid $2,400 in warranty repairs.
8. A customer has filed a lawsuit against Chandra for $500,000 for breach of contract. The company attorney does not believe the suit has merit.

Required

a. Answer the following questions.

  (1) What amount of cash did Chandra pay for interest during the year?

  (2) What amount of interest expense is reported on Chandra's income statement for the year?

  (3) What is the amount of warranty expense for the year?

b. Prepare the current liabilities section of the balance sheet at December 31, 2008. (*Hint:* First post the liabilities transactions to T-accounts.)

c. Show the effect of these transactions on the financial statements using a horizontal statements model like the one shown here. Use a + to indicate increase, a − for decrease, and NA for not affected. In the Cash Flow column, indicate whether the item is an operating activity (OA), investing activity (IA), or financing activity (FA). The first transaction has been recorded as an example.

Assets	=	Liabilities	+	Equity	Rev.	−	Exp.	=	Net Inc.	Cash Flow
+		+		NA	NA		NA		NA	+ FA

Problem 9-22B *Contingent liabilities*

L.O. 3

Required

How should each of the following situations be reported in the financial statements?

a. It has been determined that one of the company's products has caused a safety hazard. It is considered probable that liabilities have been incurred and a reasonable estimate of the amount can be made.

b. A company warehouse is located in a section of the city that has routinely flooded in the past. Consequently the company can no longer find a source of insurance for the warehouse. No flood has yet occurred this year.

c. Because of newly passed legislation, a company will have to upgrade its facilities over the next two years. Significant expenditures will occur, but at this time the amount has not been determined.

Problem 9-23B *Accounting for payroll and payroll taxes*

L.O. 6, 7

Seaside Service Co. pays salaries monthly on the last day of the month. The following information is available from Seaside for the month ended December 31, 2008.

Administrative salaries	$92,000
Sales salaries	66,000
Office salaries	45,000

Assume the Social Security tax rate is 6 percent on the first $90,000 of salaries. Kirk reached the $90,000 amount in September. His salary in December amounted to $12,000 and is included in the

$92,000. No one else will reach the $90,000 amount for the year. None of the employee salaries are subject to unemployment tax in December.

Other amounts withheld from salaries in December were as follows:

Federal income tax	$16,000
State income tax	7,200
U.S. Savings Bonds	3,000

Required

a. Prepare the journal entry to record the payment of payroll on December 31, 2008.

b. Prepare the journal entry to record the payroll tax expense for Seaside Service Co. for December 2008.

L.O. 6, 7

Problem 9-24B *Computation of net pay and payroll expense*

The following information is available for the employees of Lighthouse Packing Company for the first week of January 2009:

1. Sarah earns $25 per hour and 1½ times her regular rate for hours over 40 per week. Sarah worked 52 hours the first week in January. Sarah's federal income tax withholding is equal to 15 percent of her gross pay. Lighthouse pays medical insurance of $60 per week for Sarah and contributes $40 per week to a retirement plan for her.
2. Karen earns a weekly salary of $1,500. Karen's federal income tax withholding is 18 percent of her gross pay. Lighthouse pays medical insurance of $80 per week for Karen and contributes $120 per week to a retirement plan for her.
3. Vacation pay is accrued at the rate of 2 hours per week (based on the regular pay rate) for Sarah and $80 per week for Karen.

Assume the Social Security tax rate is 6 percent on the first $90,000 of salaries and the Medicare tax rate is 1.5 percent of total salaries. The state unemployment tax rate is 4.2 percent and the federal unemployment tax rate is .8 percent of the first $7,000 of salary for each employee.

Required

a. Compute the gross pay for Sarah for the first week in January.

b. Compute the net pay for both Sarah and Karen for the first week in January.

c. Prepare the journal entry to record the payment of the payroll for the week.

d. Prepare the journal entry to record the payroll tax expense and fringe benefit expense for Lighthouse Packing Company for the week.

e. What is the total cost of compensation expense for the first week of January 2009 for Lighthouse Packing Company?

L.O. 9

Problem 9-25B *Multistep income statement and classified balance sheet*

Required

Use the following information to prepare a multistep income statement and a classified balance sheet for Beamer Equipment Co. for 2007. (*Hint:* Some of the items will *not* appear on either statement, and ending retained earnings must be calculated.)

Salaries Expense	$ 96,000	Interest Receivable (short term)	$ 500
Common Stock	40,000	Beginning Retained Earnings	10,400
Notes Receivable (short term)	12,000	Warranties Payable (short term)	1,300
Allowance for Doubtful Accounts	4,000	Gain on Sale of Equipment	6,400
Accumulated Depreciation	30,000	Operating Expenses	70,000
Notes Payable (long term)	103,600	Cash Flow from Investing Activities	80,000
Salvage Value of Building	4,000	Prepaid Rent	9,600
Interest Payable (short term)	1,800	Land	36,000
Uncollectible Accounts Expense	10,800	Cash	17,800
Supplies	1,600	Inventory	122,800
Equipment	60,000	Accounts Payable	46,000
Interest Revenue	4,200	Interest Expense	24,000
Sales Revenue	396,000	Salaries Payable	9,200
Dividends	8,000	Unearned Revenue	52,600
Warranty Expense	3,400	Cost of Goods Sold	143,000
		Accounts Receivable	90,000

Problem 9-26B ***Accounting for a discount note across two accounting cycles (Appendix)*** **L.O. 11**

Laura White opened White & Company, an accounting practice, in 2006. The following summarizes transactions that occurred during 2006:

1. Issued a $200,000 face value discount note to First National Bank on July 1, 2006. The note had a 10 percent discount rate and a one-year term to maturity.
2. Recognized cash revenue of $336,000.
3. Incurred and paid $132,000 of operating expenses.
4. Adjusted the books to recognize interest expense at December 31, 2006.
5. Prepared the necessary closing entries at December 31, 2006.

The following summarizes transactions that occurred in 2007:

1. Recognized $984,000 of cash revenue.
2. Incurred and paid $416,000 of operating expenses.
3. Recognized the interest expense for 2007 and paid the face value of the note.
4. Prepared the necessary closing entries at December 31, 2007.

Required

a. Show the effects of each of the transactions on the elements of the financial statements, using a horizontal statements model like the one shown here. Use + for increase, − for decrease, and NA for not affected. The first transaction is entered as an example. (*Hint:* Closing entries do not affect the statements model.)

Event No.	Assets	=	Liab.	+	Equity	Rev.	−	Exp.	=	Net Inc.	Cash Flow
1	+		+		NA	NA		NA		NA	+ FA

b. Prepare entries in general journal form for the transactions for 2006 and 2007, and post them to T-accounts.

c. Prepare an income statement, statement of changes in stockholders' equity, balance sheet, and statement of cash flows for 2006 and 2007.

ANALYZE, THINK, COMMUNICATE

ATC 9-1 **Business Applications Case** ***Understanding real-world annual reports***

Required – Part 1

Use the **Topps Company**'s annual report in Appendix B to answer the following questions.

The Topps Company, Inc.

a. What was Topps' current ratio as of March 1, 2003, and March 2, 2002?
b. Did the current ratio get stronger or weaker from 2002 to 2003? Explain briefly why this happened.
c. Topps' balance sheet reports "Accrued expenses and other liabilities." What is included in this category? (See the footnotes.)

Required – Part 2

Use the **Harley-Davidson**'s annual report that came with this book to answer the following questions.

Harley-Davidson, Inc.

a. What was Harley-Davidson's current ratio as of December 31, 2003, and December 31, 2002?
b. Did the current ratio get stronger or weaker from 2002 to 2003?
c. Harley-Davidson's balance sheet reports "Accrued expenses and other liabilities." What is included in this category? (See the footnotes.)
d. How much warranty liability did Harley-Davidson have as of December 31, 2003 (see Note 1)?

ATC 9-2 **Group Assignment** ***Accounting for payroll***

The following payroll information is available for three companies for 2007. Each company has two employees. Assume that the Social Security tax rate is 6 percent on the first $90,000 of earnings and the Medicare tax rate is 1.5 percent on all earnings.

Company No. 1				
Brooks Company	**Hourly Rate**	**Regular Hours**	**Overtime Rate**	**Overtime Hours**
Employee No. 1	$40	2,000	$60	300
Employee No. 2	$20	2,000	$30	100

Other benefits provided for the employees:	
Medical insurance	$250 per month for each employee
Pension benefits	$100 per month for one employee

Federal income tax withheld is 15 percent of gross earnings for each employee. The state unemployment tax rate is 3.5 percent and the federal unemployment tax rate is .8 percent.

Company No. 2				
Hill Company	**Weekly Rate/Hourly Rate**	**Weeks/Hours Worked**	**Overtime Rate**	**Overtime Hours**
Employee No. 1	$2,000	52	NA	NA
Employee No. 2	$18	2,000	$27	60

Other benefits provided for the employees:	
Medical and dental insurance	$325 per month for each employee.
Pension benefits	$150 per month for one employee and $100 per month for the other employee.

Federal income tax withheld is 15 percent of gross earnings for each employee. The state unemployment tax rate is 3.5 percent and the federal unemployment tax rate is .8 percent.

Company No. 3				
Valley Company	**Monthly Rate/Hourly Rate**	**Months/Hours Worked**	**Overtime Rate**	**Overtime Hours**
Employee No. 1	$10,500	12	NA	NA
Employee No. 2 (part time)	$20	860	NA	NA

Other benefits provided for the employees:	
Medical and dental insurance	$375 per month for only one employee.
Pension benefits	10% of Gross salary for the full time employee.

Federal income tax withheld is 15 percent of gross earnings for each employee. The state unemployment tax rate is 3.0 percent and the federal unemployment tax rate is .8 percent.

Required

a. Divide the class into groups of four or five students. Organize the groups into three sections. Assign each section of groups the payroll data for one of the above companies.

Group tasks

(1) Determine the gross and net payroll for your company for the year.

(2) Determine the total compensation cost for your company for the year.

(3) Have a representative from each section put the compensation on the board broken down by salaries cost, payroll tax, and fringe benefit cost.

Class Discussion

b. Have the class discuss how the categories of compensation cost are similar and why some are more or less than those of the other companies.

ATC 9-3 Real-World Case *Unusual types of liabilities*

In the liabilities section of its 2002 balance sheet, **Wachovia Corporation** reported "noninterest-bearing deposits" of over $44 billion. Wachovia is a very large banking company. In the liabilities section of its 2002 balance sheet, **Newmont Mining Corporation** reported "reclamation and remediation liabilities" of more than $302 million. Newmont Mining is involved in gold mining and refining activities. In the accrued liabilities reported on its 2002 balance sheet, **Conoco Phillips** included $1.7 billion for "accrued dismantlement, removal, and environmental costs."

Required

a. For each of the preceding liabilities, write a brief explanation of what you believe the nature of the liability to be and how the company will pay it off. To develop your answers, think about the nature of the industry in which each of the companies operates.

b. Of the three liabilities described, which do you think poses the most risk for the company? In other words, for which liability are actual costs most likely to exceed the liability reported on the balance sheet? Uncertainty creates risk.

ATC 9-4 Business Applications Case *Using the current ratio*

	Hamburger House	Hot Dog Heaven
Current assets	$90,000	$60,000
Current liabilities	65,000	33,000

Required

a. Compute the current ratio for each company.

b. Which company has the greater likelihood of being able to pay its bills?

c. Assuming that both companies have the same amount of total assets, which company would produce the higher return on assets ratio?

ATC 9-5 Business Applications Case *Using current ratios to make comparisons*

The following accounting information pertains to Eckert and Ragland companies at the end of 2006:

Account Title	Eckert	Ragland
Cash	$ 22,000	$ 30,000
Wages Payable	30,000	30,000
Merchandise Inventory	45,000	66,000
Building	120,000	95,000
Accounts Receivable	53,000	37,000
Long-term Notes Payable	115,000	145,000
Land	68,000	60,000
Accounts Payable	60,000	54,000
Sales Revenue	330,000	325,000
Expenses	285,000	295,000

Required

a. Identify the current assets and current liabilities, and compute the current ratio for each company.

b. Assuming that all assets and liabilities are listed here, compute the debt to assets ratio for each company.

c. Determine which company has the greater financial risk in both the short term and the long term.

ATC 9-6 Writing Assignment *Definition of elements of financial statements*

Putting "yum" on people's faces around the world is the mission of **YUM Bands. Inc.** Yum was spun off from **PepsiCo** in 1997. A spin-off occurs when a company separates its operations into two or more distinct companies The company was originally composed of KFC, Pizza Hut, and Taco Bell and was operated as a part of PepsiCo prior to the spin-off. In 2002 YUM acquired A & W All American Foods and Long John Silver's units. The acquisition pushed YUM's debt to $4.8 billion. YUM's net income before interest and taxes in 2002 was $1.03 million.

Required

a. If YUM's debt remains constant at $4.8 billion for 2003, how much interest will YUM incur in 2003, assuming the average interest rate is 7 percent?

b. Does the debt seem excessive compared with the amount of 2002 net income before interest and taxes? Explain.

c. Assuming YUM pays tax at the rate of 30 percent, what amount of tax will YUM pay in 2002?

d. Assume you are the president of the company. Write a memo to the shareholders explaining how YUM is able to meet its obligations and increase stockholders' equity.

ATC 9-7 ETHICAL DILEMMA *Who pays FICA taxes?*

Scott Putman owns and operates a lawn care company. Like most companies in the lawn care business, his company experiences a high level of employee turnover. However, he finds it relatively easy to replace employees because he pays above market wages. He attributes his ability to pay high wages to a little accounting trick he discovered several years ago. Instead of paying his half of each employee's FICA taxes to the government, he decided to pay that money to the employees in the form of higher wages. He then doubles their FICA tax payroll deduction and uses half of the deduction to pay his share of the Social Security tax. For example, suppose he plans to pay an employee $2,000 per month. Technically, the employee would have to pay 7.5 percent FICA and Medicare tax ($2,000 × .075 = $150) and Mr. Putman's company would have to make a $150 matching payment. Instead of doing it this way, he devised the following plan. He pays the employee $2,150 and then deducts $300 for FICA and Medicare tax from the employee's salary. The end result is the same. Either way the employee ends up with net pay of $1,850 ($2,000 − $150 = $1,850 or $2,150 − $300 = $1,850). Also, the government gets $300 FICA tax, regardless of how it gets divided between the employee and the employer. Mr. Putman is convinced that he is right in what he is doing. Certainly, it benefits his company by allowing him to offer higher starting salaries. Further, he believes it is a more honest way of showing the real cost of Social Security and Medicare.

Required

a. Is Mr. Putnam right in his assumption that the total tax paid is the same under his approach as it would be if proper accounting procedures were applied? Explain.

b. Assuming that Mr. Putman is a CPA, do his actions violate any of the articles of the AICPA Code of Professional Conduct shown in Chapter 1 (Exhibit 1-7)? If so, discuss some of the articles that are violated.

c. Discuss Mr. Putman's actions within the context of Donald Cressey's common features of ethical misconduct that were outlined in Chapter 1.

ATC 9-8 Research Assignment *Analyzing Pep Boys' liquidity*

Using either the most current Form 10-K for The Pep Boys—Manny, Moe & Jack, or the company's annual report, answer the questions below. To obtain the Form 10-K either use the EDGAR system following the instructions in Appendix A, or the company's website. The company's annual report is available on its website.

Required

a. What is Pep Boys' current ratio?

b. Which of Pep Boys' current assets had the largest balance?

c. What percentage of Pep Boys' total assets consisted of current assets?

d. Did Pep Boys have any "currently maturing" long-term debt included in current liabilities on its balance sheet (see note 2)?

e. If Pep Boys were a company that manufactured auto parts rather than a retailer of auto parts, how do you think its balance sheet would be different?

COMPREHENSIVE PROBLEM

The trial balance of Pacilio Security Services Inc. as of January 1, 2009, had the following normal balances:

Cash	$93,380
Petty Cash	100
Accounts Receivable	21,390
Allowance for Doubtful Accounts	2,485
Supplies	180
Prepaid Rent	3,000
Merchandise Inventory (23 @ $280)	6,440
Equipment	9,000
Van	27,000
Accumulated Depreciation	14,900
Salaries Payable	1,500
Common Stock	50,000
Retained Earnings	91,605

During 2009 Pacilio Security Services experienced the following transactions:

1. Paid the salaries payable from 2008.
2. Paid $9,000 on May 2, 2009, for one year's office rent in advance.
3. Purchased $425 of supplies on account.
4. Purchased 145 alarm systems at a cost of $290 each. Paid cash for the purchase.
5. After numerous attempts to collect from customers, wrote off $2,060 of uncollectible accounts receivable.
6. Sold 130 alarm systems for $580 each plus sales tax of 5 percent. All sales were on account. (Be sure to compute cost of goods sold using the FIFO cost flow method.)
7. Billed $107,000 of monitoring services for the year. Credit card sales amounted to $42,000, and the credit card company charged a 4 percent fee. The remaining $65,000 were sales on account. Sales tax is not charged on this service.
8. Replenished the petty cash fund on June 30. The fund had $5 cash and receipts of $60 for yard mowing, $15 for office supplies expense, and $17 for miscellaneous expenses.
9. Collected the amount due from the credit card company.
10. Paid the sales tax collected on $69,600 of the alarm sales.
11. Paid installers and other employees a total of $65,000 for salaries for the year. Assume the Social Security tax rate is 6 percent and the Medicare tax rate is 1.5 percent. Federal income taxes withheld amounted to $7,500. Cash was paid for the net amount of salaries due.
12. Pacilio now offers a one-year warranty on its alarm systems. Paid $1,950 in warranty repairs during the year.
13. On September 1, borrowed $12,000 from State Bank. The note had an 8 percent interest rate and a one-year term to maturity.
14. Collected $136,100 of accounts receivable during the year.
15. Paid $15,000 of advertising expense during the year.
16. Paid $7,200 of utilities expense for the year.
17. Paid the payroll taxes, both the amounts withheld from the salaries plus the employer share of Social Security tax and Medicare tax, on $60,000 of the salaries plus $7,000 of the federal income tax that was withheld. (Unemployment taxes were not paid at this time.)
18. Paid the accounts payable.
19. Paid a dividend of $10,000 to the shareholders.

Adjustments

20. There was $165 of supplies on hand at the end of the year.

21. Recognized the expired rent for the office building for the year.
22. Recognized uncollectible accounts expense for the year using the allowance method. The company revised its estimate of uncollectible accounts based on prior years' experience. This year Pacilio estimates that 2.75 percent of sales on account will not be collected.
23. Recognized depreciation expense on the equipment and the van. The equipment has a 5-year life and a $2,000 salvage value. The van has a 4-year life and a $6,000 salvage value. The company uses double-declining-balance for the van and straight-line for the equipment. (A full year's depreciation was taken in 2008, the year of acquisition.)
24. The alarm systems sold in transaction 6 were covered with a one-year warranty. Pacilio estimated that the warranty cost would be 3 percent of alarm sales.
25. Recognized the accrued interest on the note payable at December 31, 2009.
26. The unemployment tax on salaries has not been paid. Record the accrued unemployment tax on the salaries for the year. The unemployment tax rate is 4.5 percent. ($14,000 of salaries is subject to this tax.)
27. Recognized the employer Social Security and Medicare payroll tax that has not been paid on $5,000 of salaries expense.

Required

a. Record the above transactions in general journal form. Round all amounts to nearest whole dollar.
b. Post the transactions to the T-accounts.
c. Prepare a trial balance.
d. Prepare an income statement, statement of changes in stockholders' equity, a classified balance sheet, and statement of cash flows.
e. Close the temporary accounts to retained earnings.
f. Post the closing entries to the T-accounts and prepare an after-closing trial balance.

CHAPTER 10

Accounting For Long-Term Notes Payable and Bond Liabilities

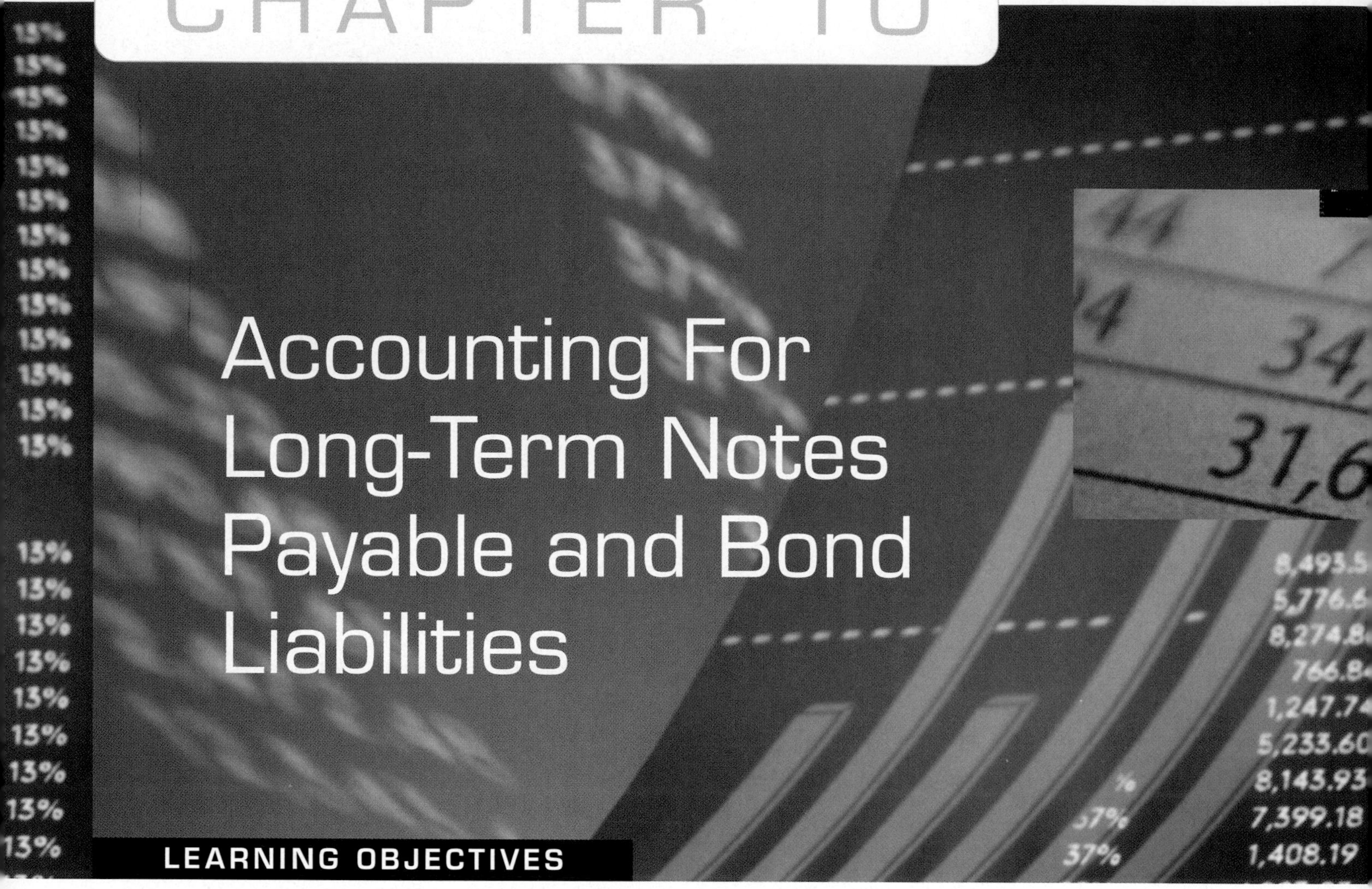

LEARNING OBJECTIVES

After you have mastered the material in this chapter, you will be able to:

1. **Show how the amortization of long-term notes affects financial statements.**
2. **Show how a line of credit affects financial statements.**
3. **Describe the different types of bonds that companies issue.**
4. **Show how bond liabilities and their related interest costs affect financial statements.**
5. **Explain how to account for bonds and their related interest costs.**
6. **Explain why bonds are issued at face value, a discount, or a premium.**
7. **Explain the advantages and disadvantages of debt financing.**
8. **Explain the time value of money. (Appendix)**

Chapter 10

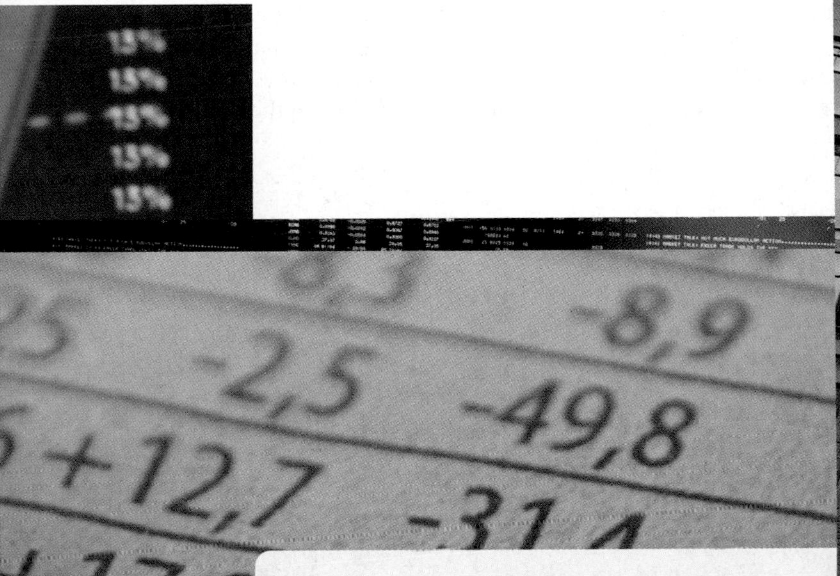

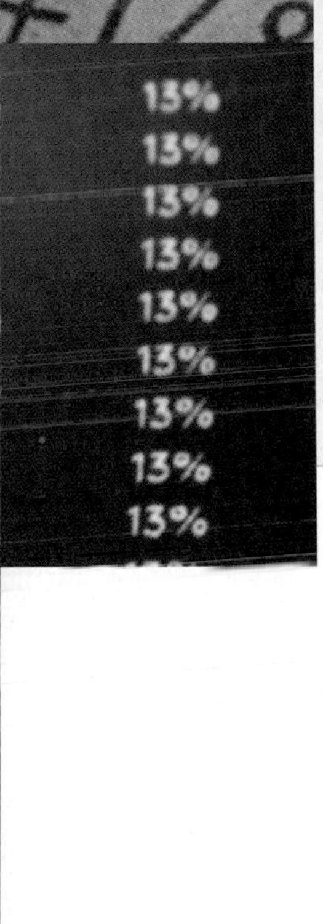

The Curious Accountant

For its 2002 fiscal year, **AOL Time Warner** (now called Time Warner) reported a net loss of $98.7 billion. That same year, the company had $1.8 billion of interest expense.

With such a huge loss on its income statement, do you think Time Warner was able to make the interest payments on its debt? If so, how? (Answers on page 499.)

CHAPTER OPENING

Most businesses finance their investing activities with long-term debt. Recall that current liabilities mature within one year or a company's operating cycle, whichever is longer. Other liabilities are **long-term liabilities.** *Long-term debt agreements vary with respect to requirements for paying interest charges and repaying principal (the amount borrowed). Interest payments may be due monthly, annually, at some other interval, or at the maturity date. Interest charges may be based on a* **fixed interest rate** *that remains constant during the term of the loan or may be based on a* **variable interest rate** *that fluctuates up or down during the loan period.*

Principal repayment is generally required either in one lump sum at the maturity date or in installments that are spread over the life of the loan. For example, each monthly payment on your car loan probably includes both paying interest and repaying some of the principal. Repaying a portion of the principal with regular payments that also include interest is often called loan **amortization.**[1] *This chapter explains accounting for interest and principal with respect to the major forms of long-term debt financing.* ■

[1] In Chapter 8 the term *amortization* described the expense recognized when the *cost of an intangible asset* is systematically allocated to expense over the useful life of the asset. This chapter shows that the term amortization refers more broadly to a variety of allocation processes. Here it means the systematic process of allocating the *principal repayment* over the life of a loan.

Installment Notes Payable

LO 1

Show how the amortization of long-term notes affects financial statements.

Topic Tackler PLUS 10-1

Loans that require payments of principal and interest at regular intervals (amortizing loans) are typically represented by **installment notes.** The terms of installment notes usually range from two to five years. To illustrate accounting for installment notes, assume Blair Company was started on January 1, 2005, when it borrowed $100,000 cash from the National Bank. In exchange for the money, Blair issued the bank a five-year installment note with a 9 percent fixed interest rate. The journal entry to record issuing the note and its effects on the financial statements are as follows:

Date	Account Title	Debit	Credit
2005 Jan. 1	Cash	100,000	
	Installment Note Payable		100,000

	Assets	=	Liab.	+	Equity			Rev.	−	Exp.	=	Net Inc.	Cash Flow
Date	Cash	=	Note Pay.	+	Com. Stk.	+	Ret. Earn.						
2005 Jan. 1	100,000	=	100,000	+	NA	+	NA	NA	−	NA	=	NA	100,000 FA

The loan agreement required Blair to pay five equal installments of $25,709[2] on December 31 of each year from 2005 through 2009. Exhibit 10.1 shows the allocation of each payment between principal and interest. When Blair pays the final installment, both the principal and interest will be paid in full. The amounts shown in Exhibit 10.1 are computed as follows:

1. The Interest Expense (Column D) is computed by multiplying the Principal Balance on Jan. 1 (Column B) by the interest rate. For example, interest expense for 2005 is $100,000 × .09 = $9,000; for 2006 it is $83,291 × .09 = $7,496; and so on.
2. The Principal Repayment (Column E) is computed by subtracting the Interest Expense (Column D) from the Cash Payment on Dec. 31 (Column C). For example, the Principal

EXHIBIT 10.1

Amortization Schedule for Installment Note Payable

Accounting Period Column A	Principal Balance on Jan. 1 Column B	Cash Payment on Dec. 31 Column C	Interest Expense Column D	Principal Repayment Column E	Principal Balance on Dec. 31 Column F
2005	$100,000	$25,709	$9,000	$16,709	$83,291
2006	83,291	25,709	7,496	18,213	65,078
2007	65,078	25,709	5,857	19,852	45,226
2008	45,226	25,709	4,070	21,639	23,587
2009	23,587	25,710*	2,123	23,587	0

*All computations are rounded to the nearest dollar. To fully liquidate the liability, the final payment is one dollar more than the others because of rounding differences.

[2] The amount of the annual payment is determined using the present value concepts presented in the appendix to this chapter. Usually the lender (bank or other financial institution) calculates the amount of the payment for the customer.

Answers To The Curious Accountant

Time Warner, Inc., was able to make its interest payments in 2002 for two reasons. (1) Interest is paid with cash, not accrual earnings. Many of the expenses on the company's income statement did not require the use of cash. The company's statement of cash flows shows that net cash flow from operating activities, *after making interest payments,* was a positive \$7.0 billion during 2002. (2) The net loss the company incurred was *after* interest expense had been deducted. The capacity of operations to support interest payments is measured by the amount of earnings before interest deductions. For example, look at the 2005 income statement for Blair Company in Exhibit 10.2. This statement shows only \$3,000 of net income, but \$12,000 of cash revenue was available for the payment of interest. Similarly, Time Warner's 2002 net loss is not an indication of the company's ability to pay interest in the short run.

Repayment for 2005 is \$25,709 − \$9,000 = \$16,709; for 2006 it is \$25,709 − \$7,496 = \$18,213; and so on.

3. The Principal Balance on Dec. 31 (Column F) is computed by subtracting the Principal Repayment (Column E) from the Principal Balance on Jan. 1 (Column B). For example, the Principal Balance on Dec. 31 for 2005 is \$100,000 − \$16,709 = \$83,291; on December 31, 2006, the principal balance is \$83,291 − \$18,213 = \$65,078; and so on. The Principal Balance on Dec. 31 (ending balance) for 2005 (\$83,291) is also the Principal Balance on Jan. 1 (beginning balance) for 2006; the principal balance on December 31, 2006 is the principal balance on January 1, 2007; and so on.

Although the amounts for interest expense and principal repayment differ each year, the effects of the annual payment on the financial statements are the same. On the balance sheet, assets (cash) decrease by the total amount of the payment; liabilities (note payable) decrease by the amount of the principal repayment; and stockholders' equity (retained earnings) decreases by the amount of interest expense. Net income decreases from recognizing interest expense. On the statement of cash flows, the portion of the cash payment applied to interest is reported in the operating activities section and the portion applied to principal is reported in the financing activities section. The journal entry to record the December 31, 2005, cash payment and its effects on the financial statements is as follows:

Date	Account Title	Debit	Credit
2005			
Dec. 31	Interest Expense	9,000	
	Installment Note Payable	16,709	
	Cash		25,709

	Assets	=	Liab.	+	Equity			Rev. − Exp. = Net Inc.	Cash Flow
Date	Cash	=	Note Pay.	+	Com. Stk.	+	Ret. Earn.		
2005 Dec. 31	(25,709)	=	(16,709)	+	NA	+	(9,000)	NA − 9,000 = (9,000)	(9,000) OA (16,709) FA

Exhibit 10.2 displays income statements, balance sheets, and statements of cash flows for Blair Company for the accounting periods 2005 through 2009. The illustration assumes that Blair earned \$12,000 of rent revenue each year. Since some of the principal is repaid each

EXHIBIT 10.2

BLAIR COMPANY Financial Statements	2005	2006	2007	2008	2009
Income Statements					
Rent Revenue	$12,000	$12,000	$12,000	$12,000	$12,000
Interest Expense	(9,000)	(7,496)	(5,857)	(4,070)	(2,123)
Net Income	$ 3,000	$ 4,504	$ 6,143	$ 7,930	$ 9,877
Balance Sheets					
Assets					
Cash	$86,291	$72,582	$58,873	$45,164	$31,454
Liabilities					
Note Payable	$83,291	$65,078	$45,226	$23,587	$ 0
Stockholders' Equity					
Retained Earnings	3,000	7,504	13,647	21,577	31,454
Total Liabilities and Stk. Equity	$86,291	$72,582	$58,873	$45,164	$31,454
Statements of Cash Flows					
Operating Activities					
Inflow from Customers	$ 12,000	$12,000	$12,000	$12,000	$12,000
Outflow for Interest	(9,000)	(7,496)	(5,857)	(4,070)	(2,123)
Investing Activities	0	0	0	0	0
Financing Activities					
Inflow from Note Issue	100,000	0	0	0	0
Outflow to Repay Note	(16,709)	(18,213)	(19,852)	(21,639)	(23,587)
Net Change in Cash	86,291	(13,709)	(13,709)	(13,709)	(13,710)
Plus: Beginning Cash Balance	0	86,291	72,582	58,873	45,164
Ending Cash Balance	$ 86,291	$72,582	$58,873	$45,164	$31,454

year, the note payable amount reported on the balance sheet and the amount of the interest expense on the income statement both decline each year.

CHECK YOURSELF 10.1

On January 1, 2004, Krueger Company issued a $50,000 installment note to State Bank. The note had a 10-year term and an 8 percent interest rate. Krueger agreed to repay the principal and interest in 10 annual payments of $7,451.47 at the end of each year. Determine the amount of principal and interest Krueger paid during the first and second year that the note was outstanding.

Answer

Accounting Period	Principal Balance January 1 A	Cash Payment December 31 B	Applied to Interest C = A × 0.08	Applied to Principal B − C
2004	$50,000.00	$7,451.47	$4,000.00	$3,451.47
2005	46,548.53	7,451.47	3,723.88	3,727.59

Line of Credit

LO 2

Show how a line of credit affects financial statements.

A **line of credit** enables a company to borrow or repay funds as needed. For example, a business may borrow $50,000 one month and make a partial repayment of $10,000 the next month. Credit agreements usually specify a limit on the amount that can be borrowed. Exhibit 10.3 shows that credit agreements are widely used.

Interest rates on lines of credit normally vary with fluctuations in some designated interest rate benchmark such as the rate paid on U.S. Treasury bills. For example, a company may pay 4 percent interest one month and 4.5 percent the next month, even if the principal balance remains constant.

Lines of credit typically have one-year terms. Although they are classified on the balance sheet as short-term liabilities, lines of credit are frequently extended indefinitely by simply renewing the credit agreement.

To illustrate accounting for a line of credit, assume Lagoon Company owns a wholesale jet-ski distributorship. In the spring, Lagoon borrows money using a line of credit to finance building up its inventory. Lagoon repays the loan over the summer months using cash generated from jet-ski sales. Borrowing or repaying events occur on the first of the month. Interest payments occur at the end of each month. Exhibit 10.4 presents all 2006 line of credit events.

Each borrowing event (March 1, April 1, and May 1) is an asset source transaction. Both cash and the line of credit liability increase. Each repayment (June 1, July 1, and August 1) is an asset use transaction. Both cash and the line of credit liability decrease. Each month's interest expense recognition and payment is an asset use transaction. Assets (cash) and stockholders' equity (retained earnings) decrease, as does net income. The journal entries to record the events are shown in Panel A of Exhibit 10.5. The effects of the events on the financial statements are shown in Panel B.

EXHIBIT 10.3

Percentage of U.S. Companies Disclosing Credit Agreements

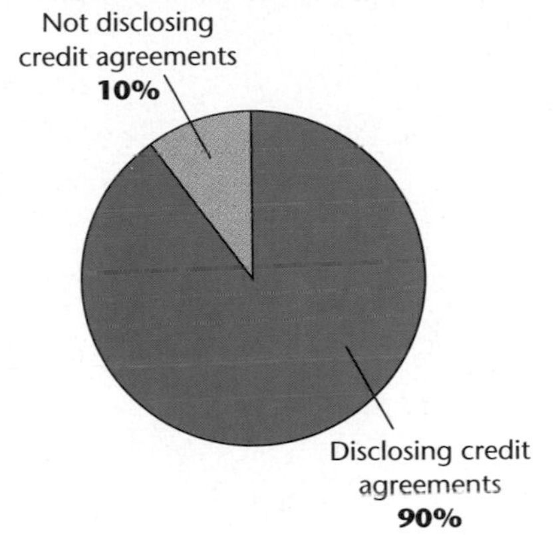

Data source: AICPA, *Accounting Trends and Techniques,* 2002.

EXHIBIT 10.4

Summary of Line of Credit Events

Date	Amount Borrowed (Repaid)	Loan Balance at End of Month	Effective Interest Rate per Month (%)	Interest Expense (rounded to nearest $1)
Mar. 1	$20,000	$ 20,000	0.09 ÷ 12	$150
Apr. 1	30,000	50,000	0.09 ÷ 12	375
May 1	50,000	100,000	0.105 ÷ 12	875
June 1	(10,000)	90,000	0.10 ÷ 12	750
July 1	(40,000)	50,000	0.09 ÷ 12	375
Aug. 1	(50,000)	0	0.09 ÷ 12	0

Bond Liabilities

LO 3

Describe the different types of bonds that companies issue.

Many companies borrow money directly from the public by selling **bond certificates,** otherwise called *issuing* bonds. Bond certificates describe a company's obligation to pay interest and to repay the principal. The seller, or **issuer,** of a bond is the borrower; the buyer of a bond, or **bondholder,** is the lender.

From the issuer's point of view, a bond represents an obligation to pay a sum of money to the bondholder on the bond's maturity date. The amount due at maturity is the **face value** of the bond. Most bonds also require the issuer to make cash interest payments based on a

EXHIBIT 10.5

Panel A Journal Entries

Date	Account Title	Debit	Credit
Mar. 1	Cash	20,000	
	Note Payable		20,000
Mar. 31	Interest Expense	150	
	Cash		150
Apr. 1	Cash	30,000	
	Note Payable		30,000
Apr. 30	Interest Expense	375	
	Cash		375
May 1	Cash	50,000	
	Note Payable		50,000
May 31	Interest Expense	875	
	Cash		875
June 1	Note Payable	10,000	
	Cash		10,000
June 30	Interest Expense	750	
	Cash		750
July 1	Note Payable	40,000	
	Cash		40,000
July 31	Interest Expense	375	
	Cash		375
Aug. 1	Note Payable	50,000	
	Cash		50,000

Panel B Effects on Financial Statements

Date	Assets	=	Liabilities	+	Equity	Rev.	−	Exp.	=	Net Inc.	Cash Flow	
Mar. 1	20,000	=	20,000	+	NA	NA	−	NA	=	NA	20,000	FA
31	(150)	=	NA	+	(150)	NA	−	150	=	(150)	(150)	OA
Apr. 1	30,000	=	30,000	+	NA	NA	−	NA	=	NA	30,000	FA
30	(375)	=	NA	+	(375)	NA	−	375	=	(375)	(375)	OA
May 1	50,000	=	50,000	+	NA	NA	−	NA	=	NA	50,000	FA
31	(875)	=	NA	+	(875)	NA	−	875	=	(875)	(875)	OA
June 1	(10,000)	=	(10,000)	+	NA	NA	−	NA	=	NA	(10,000)	FA
30	(750)	=	NA	+	(750)	NA	−	750	=	(750)	(750)	OA
July 1	(40,000)	=	(40,000)	+	NA	NA	−	NA	=	NA	(40,000)	FA
31	(375)	=	NA	+	(375)	NA	−	375	=	(375)	(375)	OA
Aug. 1	(50,000)	=	(50,000)	+	NA	NA	−	NA	=	NA	(50,000)	FA
31	NA	=	NA	+	NA	NA	−	NA	=	NA	NA	

Topic Tackler PLUS

10-2

stated interest rate at regular intervals over the life of the bond. Exhibit 10.6 shows a typical bond certificate.

Advantages of Issuing Bonds

Bond financing offers companies the following advantages.

1. Bonds usually have longer terms than notes issued to banks. While typical bank loan terms range from 2 to 5 years, bonds normally have 20-year terms to maturity. Longer terms to maturity allow companies to implement long-term strategic plans without having to worry about frequent refinancing arrangements.
2. Bond interest rates may be lower than bank interest rates. Banks earn profits by borrowing money from the public (depositors) at low interest rates, then loaning that money to companies at higher rates. By issuing bonds directly to the public, companies can pay lower interest costs by eliminating the middle man (banks).

EXHIBIT 10.6

Bond Certificate

Security of Bonds

Bonds may be either secured or unsecured.

1. **Secured bonds** grant their holders a priority legal claim on specified identifiable assets should the issuer default. A common type of secured bond is a **mortgage bond,** which conditionally transfers the title of designated property to the bondholder until the bond is paid.
2. **Unsecured bonds,** also called **debentures,** are issued based on the general strength of the borrower's credit. Bond certificates often specify the priority of debenture holders' claims relative to other creditors. Holders of **subordinated debentures** have lower priority claims than other creditors, whereas holders of **unsubordinated debentures** have equal claims.

Timing of Maturity

The maturity dates of bonds can be specified in various ways. Even bonds sold as separate components of a single issue may have different maturity dates.

1. **Term bonds** mature on a specified date in the future.
2. **Serial bonds** mature at specified intervals throughout the life of the total issue. For example, bonds with a total face value of $1,000,000 may mature in increments of $100,000 every year for 10 years.

To ensure there is enough cash available at maturity to pay off the debt, a bond agreement may require the issuer to make regular payments into a **sinking fund.** Money deposited in the sinking fund is usually managed by an independent trustee who invests the funds until the bonds mature. At maturity, the funds and the proceeds from the investments are used to repay the bond debt.

Special Features

Some bonds feature one or both of the following characteristics.

1. **Convertible bonds** are liabilities that can be exchanged at the option of the bondholder for common stock or some other specified ownership interest. The issuing company benefits because bondholders (investors) are willing to accept a lower interest rate in exchange for the conversion feature. Bondholders benefit because they obtain the option to share in potential rewards of ownership. If the market value of the company's stock increases, bondholders can convert their bonds to stock. If the stock price does not increase bondholders are still guaranteed interest payments and priority claims in bankruptcy settlements.
2. **Callable bonds** allow the issuing company to redeem (pay off) the bond debt before the maturity date. If interest rates decline, this feature benefits the issuing company because it could borrow additional money at a lower rate and use the proceeds to pay off its higher rate bonds. Since an early redemption would eliminate their higher interest bond investments,

REALITY BYTES

On November 8, 2001, **Enron Corporation** announced that it would have to reduce its stockholders' equity by approximately $1.2 billion. On December 2, 2001, the company filed for Chapter 11 bankruptcy protection.

When covering this story, most of the media's attention focused on the overstatement of earnings that resulted from Enron's improper use of a form of partnerships called "special purpose entities." However, these entities were also used to improperly keep as much as $1 billion of debt off of Enron's balance sheet. Why did this matter to Enron? Enron was a very rapidly growing company and it used lots of debt to finance this growth. From 1999 to 2000 its assets grew from $33.4 billion to $65.5 billion, but its debt grew from $23.8 billion to $54.0 billion. This caused its debt to assets ratio to rise from 71.3 percent to 82.4 percent. The higher debt burden put Enron at risk of having to pay higher interest rates, an unattractive option for a company with this much debt.

bondholders consider call features undesirable. To encourage investors to buy callable bonds, the **call price** normally exceeds the *face value* of the bonds. For example, the issuing company may agree to pay the holder of a $1,000 face value bond a call price of $1,050 if the bond is redeemed before its maturity date. The difference between the call price and the face value ($50 [$1,050 − $1,000] in this case) is commonly called a **call premium.**

Bond Ratings

Various financial services, such as Moody's, analyze the risk of default for corporate bond issues and publish ratings of the risk as guides to bond investors. The highest rating (lowest risk) a company can achieve is AAA, the next highest AA, and so forth. Bond issuers try to maintain high credit ratings because lower ratings require them to pay higher interest rates.

Bonds Issued at Face Value

Fixed-Rate, Fixed-Term, Annual Interest Bonds

LO 4

Show how bond liabilities and their related interest costs affect financial statements.

Assume Marsha Mason needs cash in order to seize a business opportunity. Mason knows of a company seeking a plot of land on which to store its inventory of crushed stone. Mason also knows of a suitable tract of land she could purchase for $100,000. The company has agreed to lease the land it needs from Mason for $12,000 per year. Mason lacks the funds to buy the land.

Some of Mason's friends recently complained about the low interest rates banks were paying on certificates of deposit. Mason suggested that her friends invest in bonds instead of CDs. She offered to sell them bonds with a 9 percent stated interest rate. The terms specified in the bond agreement Mason drafted included making interest payments in cash on December 31 of each year, a five-year term to maturity, and pledging the land as collateral for the bonds.[3] Her friends were favorably impressed, and Mason issued the bonds to them in exchange for cash on January 1, 2001.

[3] In practice, bonds are usually issued for much larger sums of money, often hundreds of millions of dollars. Also, terms to maturity are normally long, with 20 years being common. Using such large amounts for such long terms is unnecessarily cumbersome for instructional purposes. The effects of bond issues can be illustrated efficiently by using smaller amounts of debt with shorter maturities, as assumed in the case of Marsha Mason.

Mason used the bond proceeds to purchase the land and immediately contracted to lease it for five years. On December 31, 2005, the maturity date of the bonds, Mason sold the land for its $100,000 book value and used the proceeds from the sale to repay the bond liability.

Mason's business venture involved six distinct accounting events:

1. Received $100,000 cash from issuing five-year bonds at face value.
2. Invested proceeds from the bond issue to purchase land for $100,000 cash.
3. Earned $12,000 cash revenue annually from leasing the land.
4. Paid $9,000 annual interest on December 31 of each year.
5. Sold the land for $100,000 cash.
6. Repaid the bond principal to bondholders.

Recording Procedures

LO 5

Explain how to account for bonds and their related interest costs.

Exhibit 10.7 presents the general journal entries to record the six events that Mason Company experienced.

EXHIBIT 10.7

Event No.	Account Title	Debit	Credit
1	Cash Bonds Payable *Entry on January 1, 2001, to record bond issue*	100,000	 100,000
2	Land Cash *Entry on January 1, 2001, to record investment in land*	100,000	 100,000
3	Cash Rent Revenue *Revenue recognition entries on December 31, 2001–2005*	12,000	 12,000
4	Interest Expense Cash *Expense recognition entries on December 31, 2001–2005*	9,000	 9,000
5	Cash Land *Entry on December 31, 2005, to record sale of land*	100,000	 100,000
6	Bonds Payable Cash *Entry on December 31, 2005, to record bond payment*	100,000	 100,000

Effect of Events on Financial Statements

LO 4

Show how bond liabilities and their related interest costs affect financial statements.

Event 1 **Issue Bonds for Cash**

Issuing bonds is an asset source transaction.

Assets (cash) and liabilities (bonds payable) increase. Net income is not affected. The $100,000 cash inflow is reported in the financing activities section of the statement of cash flows. These effects are shown here:

Assets	=	Liab.	+	Equity	Rev.	−	Exp.	=	Net Inc.	Cash Flow
Cash	=	Bonds Pay.								
100,000	=	100,000	+	NA	NA	−	NA	=	NA	100,000 FA

Event 2 **Investment in Land**

Paying $100,000 cash to purchase land is an asset exchange transaction.

The asset cash decreases and the asset land increases. The income statement is not affected. The cash outflow is reported in the investing activities section of the statement of cash flows. These effects are illustrated below:

Assets			=	Liab.	+	Equity	Rev.	−	Exp.	=	Net Inc.	Cash Flow
Cash	+	Land										
(100,000)	+	100,000	=	NA	+	NA	NA	−	NA	=	NA	(100,000) IA

Event 3 Revenue Recognition

Recognizing $12,000 cash revenue from renting the property is an asset source transaction.

This event is repeated each year from 2001 through 2005. The event increases assets and stockholders' equity. Recognizing revenue increases net income. The cash inflow is reported in the operating activities section of the statement of cash flows. These effects follow:

Assets	=	Liab.	+	Equity	Rev.	−	Exp.	=	Net Inc.	Cash Flow
Cash	=			Ret. Earn.						
12,000	=	NA	+	12,000	12,000	−	NA	=	12,000	12,000 OA

Event 4 Expense Recognition

Mason's $9,000 ($100,000 × 0.09) cash payment represents interest expense.

This event is also repeated each year from 2001 through 2005. The interest payment is an asset use transaction. Cash and stockholders' equity (retained earnings) decrease. The expense recognition decreases net income. The cash outflow is reported in the operating activities section of the statement of cash flows. These effects follow:

Assets	=	Liab.	+	Equity	Rev.	−	Exp.	=	Net Inc.	Cash Flow
Cash	=			Ret. Earn.						
(9,000)	=	NA	+	(9,000)	NA	−	9,000	=	(9,000)	(9,000) OA

Event 5 Sale of Investment in Land

Selling the land for cash equal to its $100,000 book value is an asset exchange transaction.

Cash increases and land decreases. Since there was no gain or loss on the sale, the income statement is not affected. The cash inflow is reported in the investing activities section of the statement of cash flows. These effects follow:

Assets			=	Liab.	+	Equity	Rev.	−	Exp.	=	Net Inc.	Cash Flow
Cash	+	Land										
100,000	+	(100,000)	=	NA	+	NA	NA	−	NA	=	NA	100,000 IA

Event 6 Payoff of Bond Liability

Repaying the face value of the bond liability is an asset use transaction.

Cash and bonds payable decrease. The income statement is not affected. The cash outflow is reported in the financing activities section of the statement of cash flows:

Assets	=	Liab.	+	Equity	Rev.	−	Exp.	=	Net Inc.	Cash Flow
Cash	=	Bonds Pay.								
(100,000)	=	(100,000)	+	NA	NA	−	NA	=	NA	(100,000) FA

Financial Statements

LO 4

Show how bond liabilities and their related interest costs affect financial statements.

Exhibit 10.8 displays Mason Company's financial statements. For simplicity, the income statement does not distinguish between operating and nonoperating items. Rent revenue and interest expense are constant across all accounting periods, so Mason recognizes $3,000 of net income in each accounting period. On the balance sheet, cash increases by $3,000 each year because cash revenue exceeds cash paid for interest. Land remains constant each year at its $100,000 historical cost until it is sold in 2005. Similarly, the bonds payable liability is reported at $100,000 from the date the bonds were issued in 2001 until they are paid off on December 31, 2005.

Compare Blair Company's income statements in Exhibit 10.2 with Mason Company's income statements in Exhibit 10.8. Both Blair and Mason borrowed $100,000 cash at a 9 percent stated interest rate for five-year terms. Blair, however, repaid its liability under the

EXHIBIT 10.8

Mason Company Financial Statements

Bonds Issued at Face Value					
	2001	**2002**	**2003**	**2004**	**2005**
Income Statements					
Rent Revenue	$ 12,000	$ 12,000	$ 12,000	$ 12,000	$ 12,000
Interest Expense	(9,000)	(9,000)	(9,000)	(9,000)	(9,000)
Net Income	$ 3,000	$ 3,000	$ 3,000	$ 3,000	$ 3,000
Balance Sheets					
Assets					
Cash	$ 3,000	$ 6,000	$ 9,000	$ 12,000	$ 15,000
Land	100,000	100,000	100,000	100,000	0
Total Assets	$103,000	$106,000	$109,000	$112,000	$ 15,000
Liabilities					
Bonds Payable	$100,000	$100,000	$100,000	$100,000	$ 0
Stockholders' Equity					
Retained Earnings	3,000	6,000	9,000	12,000	15,000
Total Liabilities and Stockholders' Equity	$103,000	$106,000	$109,000	$112,000	$ 15,000
Statements of Cash Flows					
Operating Activities					
Inflow from Customers	$ 12,000	$ 12,000	$ 12,000	$ 12,000	$ 12,000
Outflow for Interest	(9,000)	(9,000)	(9,000)	(9,000)	(9,000)
Investing Activities					
Outflow to Purchase Land	(100,000)				
Inflow from Sale of Land					100,000
Financing Activities					
Inflow from Bond Issue	100,000				
Outflow to Repay Bond Liab.					(100,000)
Net Change in Cash	3,000	3,000	3,000	3,000	3,000
Plus: Beginning Cash Balance	0	3,000	6,000	9,000	12,000
Ending Cash Balance	$ 3,000	$ 6,000	$ 9,000	$ 12,000	$ 15,000

terms of an installment note while Mason did not repay any principal until the end of the five-year bond term. Because Blair repaid part of the principal balance on the installment loan each year, Blair's interest expense declined each year. The interest expense on Mason's bond liability, however, remained constant because the full principal amount was outstanding for the entire five-year bond term.

Bonds Issued at a Discount

LO 6

Explain why bonds are issued at face value, a discount, or a premium.

Return to the Mason Company illustration with one change. Assume Mason's bond certificates have a 9 percent stated rate of interest printed on them. Suppose Mason's friends find they can buy bonds from another entrepreneur willing to pay a higher rate of interest. They explain to Mason that business decisions cannot be made on the basis of friendship. Mason provides a counteroffer. There is no time to change the bond certificates, so Mason offers to accept $95,000 for the bonds today and still repay the full face value of $100,000 at the maturity date. The $5,000 difference is called a **bond discount.** Mason's friends agree to buy the bonds for $95,000.

Effective Interest Rate

The bond discount increases the interest Mason must pay. First, Mason must still make the annual cash payments described in the bond agreement. In other words, Mason must pay cash of $9,000 (.09 × $100,000) annually even though she actually borrowed only $95,000. Second, Mason will have to pay back $5,000 more than she received ($100,000 − $95,000). The extra $5,000 (bond discount) is additional interest. Although the $5,000 of additional interest is not paid until maturity, when spread over the life of the bond it amounts to $1,000 of additional interest expense per year.

The actual rate of interest that Mason must pay is called the **effective interest rate.** A rough estimate of the effective interest rate for the discounted Mason bonds is 10.5 percent [($9,000 annual stated interest + $1,000 annual amortization of the discount) ÷ $95,000 amount borrowed]. Selling the bonds at a $5,000 discount permits Mason to raise the 9 percent stated rate of interest to an effective rate of roughly 10.5 percent. Deeper discounts would raise the effective rate even higher. More shallow discounts would reduce the effective rate of interest. Mason can set the effective rate of interest to any level desired by adjusting the amount of the discount.

Bond Prices

It is common business practice to use discounts to raise the effective rate of interest above the stated rate. Bonds frequently sell for less than face value. Bond prices are normally expressed *as a percentage of the face value.* For example, Mason's discounted bonds sold for 95, meaning the bonds sold at 95 percent of face value ($100,000 × .95 = $95,000). Amounts of less than 1 percentage point are usually expressed as a fraction. Therefore, a bond priced at 98 3/4 sells for 98.75 percent of face value.

Mason Company Revisited

LO 5

Explain how to account for bonds and their related interest costs.

To illustrate accounting for bonds issued at a discount, return to the Mason Company example using the assumption the bonds are issued for 95 instead of face value. We examine the same six events using this revised assumption. This revision changes some amounts reported on the financial statements. For example, Event 1 in year 2001 reflects receiving only $95,000 cash from the bond issue. Since Mason had only $95,000 available to invest in land, the illustration assumes that Mason acquired a less desirable piece of property which generated only $11,400 of rent revenue per year.

Event 1 **Issue Bonds for Cash**
Bonds with a face value of $100,000 are issued at 95.

Because Mason must pay the face value at maturity, the $100,000 face value of the bonds is recorded in the Bonds Payable account. The $5,000 discount is recorded in a separate contra account called **Discount on Bonds Payable.** As shown below, the contra account is subtracted from the face value to determine the **carrying value** (book value) of the bond liability on January 1, 2001.

Bonds Payable	$100,000
Less: Discount on Bonds Payable	(5,000)
Carrying Value	$ 95,000

The bond issue is an asset source transaction. Both assets and total liabilities increase by $95,000. Net income is not affected. The cash inflow is reported in the financing activities section of the statement of cash flows. The effect of the bond issue on the financial statements and the journal entry to record it follow:

Assets	=	Liabilities			+	Equity	Rev. − Exp. = Net Inc.	Cash Flow
Cash	=	Bonds Pay.	−	Discount	+	Equity		
95,000	=	100,000	−	5,000	+	NA	NA − NA = NA	95,000 FA

Account Title	Debit	Credit
Cash	95,000	
Discount on Bonds Payable	5,000	
Bonds Payable		100,000

Event 2 Investment in Land

Paying $95,000 cash to purchase land is an asset exchange transaction.

The asset cash decreases and the asset land increases. The income statement is not affected. The cash outflow is reported in the investing activities section of the statement of cash flows. These effects follow:

Assets			=	Liab.	+	Equity	Rev. − Exp. = Net Inc.	Cash Flow
Cash	+	Land						
(95,000)	+	95,000	=	NA	+	NA	NA − NA = NA	(95,000) IA

Event 3 Revenue Recognition

Recognizing $11,400 cash revenue from renting the property is an asset source transaction.

This event is repeated each year from 2001 through 2005. The event is an asset source transaction that increases assets and stockholders' equity. Recognizing revenue increases net income. The cash inflow is reported in the operating activities section of the statement of cash flows. These effects follow:

Assets	=	Liab.	+	Equity	Rev. − Exp. = Net Inc.	Cash Flow
Cash	=			Ret. Earn.		
11,400	=	NA	+	11,400	11,400 − NA = 11,400	11,400 OA

Event 4 Expense Recognition

The interest cost of borrowing has two components: the $9,000 paid in cash each year and the $5,000 discount paid at maturity.

Using **straight-line amortization,** the amount of the discount recognized as expense in each accounting period is $1,000 ($5,000 discount ÷ 5 years). Mason will therefore recognize $10,000 of interest expense each year ($9,000 at the stated interest rate plus $1,000 amortization of the bond discount). On the balance sheet, the asset cash decreases by $9,000, the carrying value of the bond liability increases by $1,000 (through a decrease in the bond discount), and retained earnings (interest expense) decreases by $10,000. The effect on the financial statements of recognizing the interest expense and the journal entry to record it for each accounting period are shown here:

Assets	=	Liabilities			+	Equity	Rev. − Exp. = Net Inc.	Cash Flow
Cash	=	Bonds Pay.	−	Discount	+	Ret. Earn.		
(9,000)	=	NA	−	(1,000)	+	(10,000)	NA − 10,000 = (10,000)	(9,000) OA

Account Title	Debit	Credit
Interest Expense	10,000	
Cash		9,000
Discount on Bonds Payable		1,000

Event 5 Sale of Investment in Land

Selling the land for cash equal to its $95,000 book value is an asset exchange transaction.

Cash increases and land decreases. Since there was no gain or loss on the sale, the income statement is not affected. The cash inflow is reported in the investing activities section of the statement of cash flows. These effects follow:

Assets			=	Liab.	+	Equity	Rev. − Exp. = Net Inc.	Cash Flow
Cash	+	Land						
95,000	+	(95,000)	=	NA	+	NA	NA − NA = NA	95,000 IA

Event 6 Payoff of Bond Liability

Repaying the face value of the bond liability is an asset use transaction.

Cash and bonds payable decrease. The income statement is not affected. For reporting purposes, the cash outflow is separated into two parts on the statement of cash flows: $95,000 of the cash outflow is reported in the financing activities section because it represents repaying the principal amount borrowed; the remaining $5,000 cash outflow is reported in the operating activities section because it represents the interest arising from issuing the bonds at a discount. In practice, the amount of the discount is frequently immaterial and is combined in the financing activities section with the principal repayment.

Assets	=	Liab.	+	Equity	Rev. − Exp. = Net Inc.	Cash Flow
Cash	=	Bonds Pay.				
(100,000)	=	(100,000)	+	NA	NA − NA = NA	(95,000) FA (5,000) OA

LO 4

Show how bond liabilities and their related interest costs affect financial statements.

Effect on Financial Statements

Exhibit 10.9 displays Mason Company's financial statements assuming the bonds were issued at a discount. Contrast the net income reported in Exhibit 10.9 (bonds issued at a discount) with the net income reported in Exhibit 10.8 (bonds sold at face value). Two factors

EXHIBIT 10.9

Mason Company Financial Statements

Bonds Issued at a Discount	2001	2002	2003	2004	2005
Income Statements					
Rent Revenue	$ 11,400	$ 11,400	$ 11,400	$ 11,400	$11,400
Interest Expense	(10,000)	(10,000)	(10,000)	(10,000)	(10,000)
Net Income	$ 1,400	$ 1,400	$ 1,400	$ 1,400	$ 1,400
Balance Sheets					
Assets					
Cash	$ 2,400	$ 4,800	$ 7,200	$ 9,600	$ 7,000
Land	95,000	95,000	95,000	95,000	0
Total Assets	$ 97,400	$ 99,800	$102,200	$104,600	$ 7,000
Liabilities					
Bonds Payable	$100,000	$100,000	$100,000	$100,000	$ 0
Discount on Bonds Payable	(4,000)	(3,000)	(2,000)	(1,000)	0
Carrying Value of Bond Liab.	96,000	97,000	98,000	99,000	0
Stockholders' Equity					
Retained Earnings	1,400	2,800	4,200	5,600	7,000
Total Liabilities and Stockholders' Equity	$ 97,400	$ 99,800	$102,200	$104,600	$ 7,000
Statements of Cash Flows					
Operating Activities					
Inflow from Customers	$ 11,400	$ 11,400	$ 11,400	$ 11,400	$11,400
Outflow for Interest	(9,000)	(9,000)	(9,000)	(9,000)	(14,000)
Investing Activities					
Outflow to Purchase Land	(95,000)				
Inflow from Sale of Land					95,000
Financing Activities					
Inflow from Bond Issue	95,000				
Outflow to Repay Bond Liab.					(95,000)
Net Change in Cash	2,400	2,400	2,400	2,400	(2,600)
Plus: Beginning Cash Balance	0	2,400	4,800	7,200	9,600
Ending Cash Balance	$ 2,400	$ 4,800	$ 7,200	$ 9,600	$ 7,000

cause the net income in Exhibit 10.9 to be lower. First, since the bonds were sold at a discount, Mason Company had less money to spend on its land investment. It bought less desirable land which generated less revenue. Second, the effective interest rate was higher than the stated rate, resulting in higher interest expense. Lower revenues coupled with higher expenses result in less profitability.

On the balance sheet, the carrying value of the bond liability increases each year until the maturity date, December 31, 2005, when it is equal to the $100,000 face value of the bonds (the amount Mason is obligated to pay). Because Mason did not pay any dividends, retained earnings ($7,000) on December 31, 2005, is equal to the total amount of net income reported over the five-year period ($1,400 × 5). All earnings were retained in the business.

Several factors account for the differences between net income and cash flow. First, although \$10,000 of interest expense is reported on each income statement, only \$9,000 of cash was paid for interest each year until 2005, when \$14,000 was paid for interest (\$9,000 based on the stated rate + \$5,000 for discount). The \$1,000 difference between interest expense and cash paid for interest in 2001, 2002, 2003, and 2004 results from amortizing the bond discount. The cash outflow for the interest related to the discount is included in the \$100,000 payment made at maturity on December 31, 2005. Even though \$14,000 of cash is paid for interest in 2005, only \$10,000 is recognized as interest expense on the income statement that year. Although the total increase in cash over the five-year life of the business (\$7,000) is equal to the total net income reported for the same period, there are significant timing differences between when the interest expense is recognized and when the cash outflows occur to pay for it.

CHECK YOURSELF 10.2

On January 1, 2004, Moffett Company issued bonds with a \$600,000 face value at 98. The bonds had a 9 percent annual interest rate and a 10-year term. Interest is payable in cash on December 31 of each year. What amount of interest expense will Moffett report on the 2006 income statement? What carrying value for bonds payable will Moffett report on the December 31, 2006, balance sheet?

Answer

The bonds were issued at a \$12,000 (\$600,000 × 0.02) discount. The discount will be amortized over the 10-year life at the rate of \$1,200 (\$12,000 ÷ 10 years) per year. The amount of interest expense for 2006 is \$55,200 (\$600,000 × .09 = \$54,000 annual cash interest + \$1,200 discount amortization).

The carrying value of the bond liability is equal to the face value less the unamortized discount. By the end of 2006, \$3,600 of the discount will have been amortized (\$1,200 × 3 years = \$3,600). The unamortized discount as of December 31, 2006, will be \$8,400 (\$12,000 − \$3,600). The carrying value of the bond liability as of December 31, 2006, will be \$591,600 (\$600,000 − \$8,400).

Effect of Semiannual Interest Payments

LO 5

Explain how to account for bonds and their related interest costs.

The previous examples assumed that interest payments were made annually. In practice, most bond agreements call for interest to be paid semiannually, which means that interest is paid in cash twice each year. If Marsha Mason's bond certificate had stipulated semiannual interest payments, her company would have paid \$4,500 (\$100,000 × 0.09 = \$9,000 ÷ 2 = \$4,500) cash to bondholders for interest on June 30 and December 31 of each year. The journal entries to record semiannual interest payments each year (for the bonds issued at a discount) are as follows:

Date	Account Title	Debit	Credit
June 30	Interest Expense	5,000	
	Discount on Bonds Payable		500
	Cash		4,500
Dec. 31	Interest Expense	5,000	
	Discount on Bonds Payable		500
	Cash		4,500

Bonds Issued at a Premium

When bonds are sold for more than their face value, the difference between the amount received and the face value is called a **bond premium.** Bond premiums reduce the effective interest rate. For example, assume Mason Company issued its 9 percent bonds at 105, receiving $105,000 cash on the issue date. The company is still only required to repay the $100,000 face value of the bonds at the maturity date. The $5,000 difference between the amount received and the amount repaid at maturity reduces the total amount of interest expense. The premium is recorded in a separate liability account called Premium on Bonds Payable. This account is reported on the balance sheet as an addition to Bonds Payable, increasing the carrying value of the bond liability. On the issue date, the bond liability would be reported on the balance sheet as follows:

LO 6

Explain why bonds are issued at face value, a discount, or a premium.

Bonds Payable	$100,000
Plus: Premium on Bonds Payable	5,000
Carrying Value	$105,000

The effect on the financial statements of issuing the bonds at a premium follows:

Assets	=	Liabilities	+	Equity	Rev. − Exp. = Net Inc.	Cash Flow
Cash	=	Bonds Pay. + Premium				
105,000	=	100,000 + 5,000	+	NA	NA − NA = NA	105,000 FA

The entire $105,000 cash inflow is reported in the financing activities section of the statement of cash flows even though the $5,000 premium is conceptually an operating activities cash flow because it pertains to interest. In practice, premiums are usually so small they are immaterial and the entire cash inflow is normally classified as a financing activity.

The journal entries to record issuing the bonds at a premium and the first interest payment are as follows (assume annual interest payments):

Date	Account Title	Debit	Credit
Jan. 1	Cash	105,000	
	Bonds Payable		100,000
	Premium on Bonds Payable		5,000
Dec. 31	Interest Expense	8,000	
	Premium on Bonds Payable	1,000	
	Cash		9,000

The Market Rate of Interest

When a bond is issued, the effective interest rate is determined by current market conditions. Market conditions are influenced by many factors such as the state of the economy, government policy, and the law of supply and demand. These conditions are collectively reflected in the **market interest rate.** The *effective rate of interest* investors are willing to accept *for a particular bond* equals the *market rate of interest* for other investments with similar levels of risk at the time the bond is issued. When the market rate of interest is higher than the stated rate of interest, bonds will sell at a discount so as to increase the effective rate of interest to the market rate. When the market rate is lower than the stated rate, bonds will sell at a premium so as to reduce the effective rate to the market rate.

LO 6

Explain why bonds are issued at face value, a discount, or a premium.

Bond Redemptions

In the previous illustration, Mason Company's five-year, 9 percent bonds were redeemed (paid off) on the maturity date. After Mason Company paid the bondholders the face value of the bonds, the balance in the bonds payable account was zero. The balance in the fully amortized discount account was also zero.

LO 5

Explain how to account for bonds and their related interest costs.

Companies may redeem bonds with a *call provision* prior to the maturity date. If a company calls bonds prior to maturity, it must pay the bondholders the call price. As explained previously, the call price is normally above face value. For example, suppose Mason Company's bond certificate allows it to call the bonds at 103. Assume Marsha Mason's client breaks the land rental contract two years early, at the end of 2003. Mason is forced to sell the land and pay off the bonds. Assuming the bonds were originally issued at a $5,000 discount, Exhibit 10.9 shows there is a $2,000 balance in the Discount on Bonds Payable account at the end of 2003.

To redeem the bonds on January 1, 2004, Mason must pay the bondholders $103,000 ($100,000 face value × 1.03 call price). Since the book value of the bond liability is $98,000 ($100,000 face value − $2,000 remaining discount), Mason recognizes a $5,000 loss ($103,000 redemption price − $98,000 book value) when the bonds are called. The early redemption decreases cash, the carrying value of the bond liability, and stockholders' equity. The effect of the redemption on the financial statements follows:

Assets	=	Liabilities			+	Equity	Rev.	−	Exp.	=	Net Inc.	Cash Flow
Cash	=	Bond Pay.	−	Discount	+	Ret. Earn.						
(103,000)	=	(100,000)	−	(2,000)	+	(5,000)	NA	−	5,000	=	(5,000)	(103,000) FA

The entire $103,000 cash outflow is reported in the financing activities section of the statement of cash flows. Conceptually, some of this outflow is attributable to activities other than financing. In practice, the amounts paid in an early redemption which are not attributable to financing activities are usually immaterial and the entire cash outflow is therefore classified as a financing activity.

The general journal entry to record the bond redemption follows:

Account Title	Debit	Credit
Loss on Bond Redemption	5,000	
Bonds Payable	100,000	
Discount on Bonds Payable		2,000
Cash		103,000

Security for Loan Agreements

In general, large loans with long terms to maturity pose more risk to lenders (creditors) than small loans with short terms. To reduce the risk that they won't get paid, lenders frequently require borrowers (debtors) to pledge designated assets as **collateral** for loans. For example, when a bank makes a car loan, it usually retains legal title to the car until the loan is fully repaid. If the borrower fails to make the monthly payments, the bank repossesses the car, sells it to someone else, and uses the proceeds to pay the original owner's debt. Similarly, assets like accounts receivable, inventory, equipment, buildings, and land may be pledged as collateral for business loans.

In addition to requiring collateral, creditors often obtain additional protection by including **restrictive covenants** in loan agreements. Such covenants may restrict additional borrowing, limit dividend payments, or restrict salary increases. If the loan restrictions are violated, the borrower is in default and the loan balance is due immediately.

Finally, creditors often ask key personnel to provide copies of their personal tax returns and financial statements. The financial condition of key executives is important because they may be asked to pledge personal property as collateral for business loans, particularly for small businesses.

THE FINANCIAL ANALYST

Bond financing has advantages and disadvantages for the stockholders of a business. Assessing a company's investment potential requires understanding both the potential rewards and the potential risks of debt financing.

LO 7

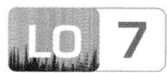

Explain the advantages and disadvantages of debt financing.

Financial Leverage and Tax Advantage of Debt Financing

As with other forms of credit, bonds may provide companies increased earnings through **financial leverage.** If a company can borrow money at 7 percent through a bond issue and invest the proceeds at 12 percent, the company's earnings benefit from the 5 percent (12 percent − 7 percent) **spread.**

Also, bond interest expense, like other forms of interest expense, is tax deductible, making the effective cost of borrowing less than the interest expense because the interest expense reduces the tax expense. Because dividend payments are not tax deductible, equity financing (e.g., issuing common stock) does not offer this advantage.

To illustrate, assume its organizers obtain $100,000 to start Maduro Company. During its first year of operation, Maduro earns $60,000 of revenue and incurs $40,000 of expenses other than interest expense. Consider two different forms of financing. First, assume the initial $100,000 is obtained by issuing common stock (equity financing) and Maduro pays an 8 percent dividend ($100,000 × .08 = $8,000 dividend). Second, assume Maduro issues $100,000 of bonds that pay 8 percent annual interest ($100,000 × .08 = $8,000). Assuming a 30 percent tax rate, which form of financing produces the larger increase in retained earnings? Refer to the following computations:

Computation of Addition to Retained Earnings

	Equity Financing	Debt Financing
Revenue	$60,000	$60,000
Expense (excluding interest)	(40,000)	(40,000)
Earnings before Interest and Taxes	20,000	20,000
Interest ($100,000 × 8%)	0	(8,000)
Pretax Income	20,000	12,000
Income Tax (30%)	(6,000)	(3,600)
Net Income	14,000	8,400
Dividend	(8,000)	0
Addition to Retained Earnings	$ 6,000	$ 8,400

Debt financing produces $2,400 more retained earnings than equity financing. If equity financing is obtained, the company pays $6,000 in income taxes; debt financing requires only $3,600 of income taxes. Maduro's cost of financing, whether paid in dividends to investors or interest to creditors, is $8,000. With debt financing, however, the Internal Revenue Service receives $2,400 less.

The after-tax interest cost of debt can be computed as:

$$\text{Total interest expense} \times (1.0 - \text{Tax rate})$$

$$\$8{,}000 \times (1.0 - 0.30) = \$5{,}600$$

The after-tax interest rate that Maduro is paying can be computed using the same logic:

$$\text{Debt interest rate} \times (1.0 - \text{Tax rate})$$

$$8\% \times (1.0 - 0.30) = 5.6\%$$

Unlike interest expense, there is no difference in the before-tax and after-tax effects of a dividend. For Maduro, $1 of dividends costs the company a full $1 of retained earnings, while $1 of interest has an after-tax cost of only $0.70 (assuming a 30 percent tax rate). This tax benefit only applies to profitable businesses. There are no tax savings if a company has no income because businesses that produce losses pay no taxes.

EBIT and Ratio Analysis

The tax consequences of debt financing can influence ratio analysis. For example, consider the *return on assets* (ROA) ratio discussed in Chapter 3. In that chapter ROA was defined as:

$$\text{Net income} \div \text{Total assets}$$

Recall that the ROA ratio is used to measure the effectiveness of asset management. In general, higher ROAs suggest better performance. However, the Maduro example demonstrates that a higher ROA can be obtained by using equity financing rather than debt financing without regard to how assets are managed. Recall that Maduro obtained $100,000 of assets whether through equity or debt financing. The assets were used exactly the same way regardless of the financing method used. With equity financing, Maduro's ROA is 14 percent ($14,000 ÷ $100,000) and with debt financing it is 8.4 percent ($8,400 ÷ $100,000). The difference in the ROA results from the financing approach rather than asset management.

The effects of the financing strategy can be avoided in ROA calculations by using *earnings before interest and taxes* (EBIT) rather than net income when computing the ratio. For example, if Maduro uses EBIT to compute ROA, the result is 20 percent ($20,000 ÷ $100,000) regardless of whether debt or equity financing is used. Using EBIT to compute ROA provides a less biased measure of asset utilization. For simplicity, however, this text uses net income to determine ROA unless otherwise indicated.

Times Interest Earned Ratio

Financing with bonds also has disadvantages. The issuer is legally obligated to make interest payments on time and to repay the principal at maturity. If a company fails to make scheduled payments, the creditors (bondholders) can force the company into bankruptcy. The claims on a company's assets held by bondholders and other creditors have priority over the claims of the owners. If a company in bankruptcy is forced to liquidate its assets, creditor claims must be fully paid before any owner claims can be paid. Bond issues therefore increase the owners' risk.

Financial analysts use several ratios to help assess the risk of bankruptcy. One is the *debt to assets ratio,* explained in Chapter 3. Another is the **times interest earned** ratio, defined as:

$$\text{EBIT} \div \text{Interest expense}$$

This ratio measures *how many times* a company would be able to pay its interest using its earnings. The *times interest earned ratio* is based on EBIT rather than net income because it is the amount of earnings before interest and taxes that is available to pay interest. The higher the ratio, the less likely a company will be unable to make its interest payments. Higher times interest earned ratios suggest lower levels of risk. Examples of times interest earned ratios and debt to assets ratios for six real-world companies follow. These numbers are based on financial data for the year 2002.

Industry	Company	Times Interest Earned	Debt to Assets
Breakfast Cereal	Kellogg's	3.93 times	0.91
	General Mills	2.60	0.77
Tools	Black & Decker	6.32	0.85
	Stanley Works	10.56	0.59
Hotel	Hilton Hotels	1.82	0.75
	Marriott	6.48	0.57

Since bills are paid with cash, not income, a company may be able to make interest payments even if it has a negative times interest earned ratio. A company with no EBIT may yet have cash. Meaningful financial statement analysis cannot rely on any single ratio or any set of ratios. Making sound business decisions requires considering other information in addition to the insights provided from analyzing ratios. A company with inferior ratios and a patent on a newly discovered drug that cures cancer may be a far better investment than a company with great ratios and a patent on a chemotherapy product that will soon be out of date. Ratio computations are based on historical data. They are useful only to the extent that history is likely to repeat itself.

CHECK YOURSELF 10.3

Selected financial data pertaining to Shaver and Goode Companies follow (amounts are in thousands):

	Shaver Company	Goode Company
Earnings before interest and taxes	$750,720	$2,970,680
Interest expense	234,600	645,800

Based on this information, which company is more likely to be able to make its interest payments?

Answer

The times interest earned ratio for Shaver Company is 3.2 ($750,720 ÷ $234,600) times. The times interest earned ratio for Goode Company is 4.6 ($2,970,680 ÷ $645,800) times. Based on this data, Goode Company is more likely to be able to make its interest payments.

A Look Back <<

This chapter explained basic accounting for long-term debt. *Long-term notes payable* mature in two to five years and usually require payments that include a return of principal plus interest. *Lines of credit* enable companies to borrow limited amounts on an as-needed basis. Although lines of credit normally have one-year terms, companies frequently renew them, extending the effective maturity date to the intermediate range of five or more years. Interest on a line of credit is normally paid monthly.

Long-term debt financing for more than 10 years usually requires issuing *bonds.* Bond agreements normally commit a company to pay *semiannual interest* at a fixed percentage of the bond face value. The amount of interest required by the bond agreement is based on the *stated interest rate.* If bonds are issued when the *market interest rate* is different from the stated interest rate, companies will receive more or less than the face value in order for the effective rate of interest to be consistent with market conditions. Selling bonds at a *discount* (below face value) increases the effective interest rate above the stated rate. Selling bonds at a *premium* decreases the effective rate of interest.

This chapter explained the tax advantages of using debt versus equity financing. Interest is a *tax-deductible expense* subtracted prior to determining taxable income. In contrast, dividends paid to owners are not deductible in determining taxable income.

>> A Look Forward

A company seeking long-term financing might choose to use debt, such as the types of bonds or term loans that were discussed in this chapter. Owners' equity is another source of long-term financing. Several equity alternatives are available, depending on the type of business organization the owners choose to establish. For example, a company could be organized as a sole proprietorship, partnership, or corporation. Chapter 11 presents accounting issues related to equity transactions for each of these types of business structures.

APPENDIX

Time Value of Money

Future Value

LO 8

Explain the time value of money.

Suppose you recently won $10,000 cash in a local lottery. You save the money to have funds available to obtain a masters of business administration (MBA) degree. You plan to enter the program three years from today. Assuming you invest the money in an account that earns 8 percent annual interest, how much money will you have available in three years? The answer depends on whether your investment will earn *simple* or *compound* interest.

To determine the amount of funds available assuming you earn 8 percent **simple interest,** multiply the principal balance by the interest rate to determine the amount of interest earned per year ($10,000 × 0.08 = $800). Next, multiply the amount of annual interest by the number of years the funds will be invested ($800 × 3 = $2,400). Finally, add the interest earned to the principal balance to determine the total amount of funds available at the end of the three-year term ($10,000 principal + $2,400 interest = $12,400 cash available at the end of three years).

Investors can increase their returns by reinvesting the income earned from their investments. For example, at the beginning of the second year, you will have available for investment not only the original $10,000 principal balance but also $800 of interest earned during the first year. In other words, you will be able to earn interest on the interest that you previously earned. Earning interest on interest is called **compounding.** Assuming you earn 8 percent compound interest, the amount of funds available to you at the end of three years can be computed as shown in Exhibit 10.10.

EXHIBIT 10.10

Year	Amount Invested	×	Interest Rate	=	Interest Earned	+	Amount Invested	=	New Balance
1	$10,000.00	×	0.08	=	$ 800.00	+	$10,000.00	=	$10,800.00
2	10,800.00	×	0.08	=	864.00	+	10,800.00	=	11,664.00
3	11,664.00	×	0.08	=	933.12	+	11,664.00	=	12,597.12
Total interest earned				=	$2,597.12				

Obviously, you earn more with compound interest ($2,597.12 compound versus $2,400 simple). The computations required for **compound interest** can become cumbersome when the investment term is long. Fortunately, there are mathematical formulas, interest tables, and computer programs that reduce the computational burden. For example, a compound interest factor can be developed from the formula

$$(1 + i)^n$$

where i = interest

n = number of periods

The value of the investment is determined by multiplying the compound interest factor by the principal balance. The compound interest factor for a three-year term and an 8 percent interest rate is 1.259712 (1.08 × 1.08 × 1.08 = 1.259712). Assuming a $10,000 original investment, the value of the investment at the end of three years is $12,597.12 ($10,000 × 1.259712). This is, of course, the same amount that was computed in the previous illustration (see final figure in the New Balance column of Exhibit 10.10).

The mathematical formulas have been used to develop tables of interest factors that can be used to determine the **future value** of an investment for a variety of interest rates and time periods. For example, Table I on page 523 contains the interest factor for an investment with a three-year term earning 8 percent compound interest. To confirm this point, move down the column marked n to the third period. Next move across to the column marked 8%, where you will find the value 1.259712. This is identical to the amount computed using the mathematical formula in the preceding paragraph. Here also, the value of the investment at the end of three years can be determined by multiplying the principal balance by the compound interest factor ($10,000 × 1.259712 = $12,597.12). These same factors and amounts can be determined using computer programs in calculators and spreadsheet software.

Clearly, a variety of ways can be used to determine the future value of an investment, given a principal balance, interest rate, and term to maturity. In our case, we showed that your original investment of $10,000 would be worth $12,597 in three years, assuming an 8 percent compound interest rate. Suppose you determine this amount is insufficient to get you through the MBA program you want to complete. Assume you believe you will need $18,000 three years from today to sustain yourself while you finish the degree. Suppose your parents agree to cover the shortfall. They ask how much money you need today in order to have $18,000 three years from now.

Present Value

The mathematical formula required to convert the future value of a dollar to its **present value** equivalent is

$$\frac{1}{(1 + i)^n}$$

where i = interest

n = number of periods

For easy conversion, the formula has been used to develop Table II, Present Value of $1. At an 8 percent annual compound interest rate, the present value equivalent of $18,000 to be received three years from today is computed as follows: Move down the far left column to where $n = 3$. Next, move right to the column marked 8%. At this point, you should see the interest factor 0.793832. Multiplying this factor by the desired future value of $18,000 yields the present value of $14,288.98 ($18,000 × 0.793832). This means if you invest $14,288.98 (present value) today at an annual compound interest rate of 8 percent, you will have the $18,000 (future value) you need to enter the MBA program three years from now.

If you currently have $10,000, you will need an additional $4,288.98 from your parents to make the required $14,288.98 investment that will yield the future value of $18,000 you need. Having $14,288.98 today is the same as having $18,000 three years from today, assuming you can earn 8 percent compound interest. To validate this conclusion, use Table I to determine the future value of $14,288.98, given a three-year term and 8 percent annual compound interest. As previously indicated, the future-value conversion factor under these conditions is 1.259712. Multiplying this factor by the $14,288.98 present value produces the expected future value of $18,000 ($14,288.98 × 1.259712 = $18,000). The factors in Table I can be used to convert present values to future values, and the corresponding factors in Table II are used to convert future values to present values.

Future Value Annuities

The previous examples described present and future values of a single lump-sum payment. Many financial transactions involve a series of payments. To illustrate, we return to the example in which you want to have $18,000 available three years from today. We continue the assumption that you can earn 8 percent compound interest. However, now we assume that you do not have $14,288.98 to invest today. Instead, you decide to save part of the money during each of the next three years. How much money must you save each year to have $18,000 at the end of three years? *The series of equal payments made over a number of periods in order to acquire a future value is called an* **annuity.** The factors in Table III, Future Value of an Annuity of $1, can be used to determine the amount of the annuity needed to produce the desired $18,000 future value. The table is constructed so that future values can be determined by multiplying the conversion factor by the amount of the annuity. These relationships can be expressed algebraically as follows:

Amount of annuity payment × Table conversion factor = Future value

To determine the amount of the required annuity payment in our example, first locate the future value conversion factor. In Table III, move down the first column on the left-hand side until you locate period 3. Next move to the right until you locate the 8% column. At this location you will see a conversion factor of 3.2464. This factor can be used to determine the amount of the annuity payment as indicated here:

Amount of annuity payment × Table conversion factor = Future value

Amount of annuity payment = Future value ÷ Table conversion factor

Amount of annuity payment = $18,000.00 ÷ 3.2464

Amount of annuity payment = $5,544.60

If you deposit $5,544.60 in an investment account at the end of each of the next three years,[4] the investment account balance will be $18,000, assuming your investment earns 8 percent interest compounded annually. This conclusion is confirmed by the following schedule.

End of Year	Beg. Acct. Bal.	+	Interest Computation	+	Payment	=	End. Acct. Bal.
1	NA	+	NA	+	$5,544.60	=	$ 5,544.60
2	$ 5,544.60	+	$ 5,544.60 × 0.08 = $443.57	+	5,544.60	=	11,532.77
3	11,532.77	+	11,532.77 × 0.08 = 922.62	+	5,544.60	=	18,000.00*

*Total does not add exactly due to rounding.

Present Value Annuities

We previously demonstrated that a future value of $18,000 is equivalent to a present value of $14,288.98, given annual compound interest of 8 percent for a three-year period. If the future value of a $5,544.60 annuity for three years is equivalent to $18,000, that same annuity should have a present value of $14,288.98. We can test this conclusion by using the conversion factors in Table IV, Present Value of an Annuity of $1. The present value annuity table is constructed so that present values can be determined by multiplying the conversion factor by the amount of the annuity. These relationships can be expressed algebraically as follows:

Amount of annuity payment × Table conversion factor = Present value

To determine the present value of the annuity payment in our example, first locate the present value conversion factor. In Table IV, move down the first column on the left-hand side until you locate period 3. Next move to the right until you locate the column for the 8 percent interest rate. At this location you will see a conversion factor of 2.577097. This factor can be used to determine the amount of the present value of the annuity payment, as indicated:

Amount of annuity payment	×	Table conversion factor	=	Present value
$5,544.60	×	2.577097	=	$14,288.97*

*The 1 cent difference between this value and the expected value of $14,288.98 is due to rounding.

In summary, Tables III and IV can be used to convert annuities to future or present values for a variety of different assumptions regarding interest rates and time periods.

[4] A payment made at the end of a period is known as an *ordinary annuity.* A payment made at the beginning of a period is called an *annuity due.* Tables are generally set up to assume ordinary annuities. Minor adjustments must be made when dealing with an annuity due. For the purposes of this text, we consider all annuities to be ordinary.

Business Applications

Long-Term Notes Payable

In the early part of this chapter, we considered a case in which Blair Company borrowed $100,000 from National Bank. We indicated that Blair agreed to repay the bank through a series of annual payments (an *annuity*) of $25,709 each. How was this amount determined? Recall that Blair agreed to pay the bank 9 percent interest over a five-year term. Under these circumstances, we are trying to find the annuity equivalent to the $100,000 present value that the bank is loaning Blair. The first step in determining the annuity (annual payment) is to locate the appropriate present value conversion factor from Table IV. At the fifth row under the 9% column, you will find the value 3.889651. This factor can be used to determine the amount of the annuity payment as indicated here:

Amount of annuity payment × Table conversion factor = Present value

Amount of annuity payment = Present value ÷ Table conversion factor

Amount of annuity payment = $100,000 ÷ 3.889651

Amount of annuity payment = $25,709

There are many applications in which debt repayment occurs through annuities. Common examples with which you are probably familiar include auto loans and home mortgages. Payment schedules for such loans may be determined from the interest tables, as demonstrated here. However, most real-world businesses have further refined the computational process through the use of sophisticated computer programs. The software program prompts the user to provide the relevant information regarding the present value of the amount borrowed, number of payments, and interest rate. Given this information and a few keystrokes, the computer program produces the amount of the amortization payment along with an amortization schedule showing the amounts of principal and interest payments over the life of the loan. Similar results can be obtained with spreadsheet software applications such as Excel and Lotus. Even many handheld calculators have present and future value functions that enable users to quickly compute annuity payments for an infinite number of interest rate and time period assumptions.

Bond Liabilities: Determine Price

We discussed the use of discounts and premiums as means of producing an effective rate of interest that is higher or lower than the stated rate of interest. For example, if the stated rate of interest is lower than the market rate of interest at the time the bonds are issued, the issuer can increase the effective interest rate by selling the bonds for a price lower than their face value. At maturity, the issuer will settle the obligation by paying the face value of the bond. The difference between the discounted bond price and the face value of the bond is additional interest. To illustrate, assume that Tower Company issues $100,000 face value bonds with a 20-year term and a 9 percent stated rate of annual interest. At the time the bonds are issued, the market rate of interest for bonds of comparable risk is 10 percent annual interest. For what amount would Tower Company be required to sell the bonds in order to move its 9 percent stated rate of interest to an effective rate of 10 percent?

Information from present value Tables II and IV is required to determine the amount of the discount required to produce a 10 percent effective rate of interest. First, we identify the future cash flows that will be generated by the bonds. Based on the stated interest rate, the bonds will pay $9,000 ($100,000 face value × 0.09 interest) interest per year. This constitutes a 20-year annuity that should be discounted back to its present value equivalent. Also, at the end of 20 years, the bonds will require a single $100,000 lump-sum payment to settle the principal obligation. This amount must also be discounted back to its present value in order to determine the bond price. The computations required to determine the discounted bond price are shown here:

Present value of principal	$100,000 × 0.148644 (Table II, n = 20, i = 10%)	=	$14,864.40
Present value of interest	$9,000 × 8.513564 (Table IV, n = 20, i = 10%)	=	76,622.08
Bond price (proceeds received)			$91,486.48

Tower Company bonds sell at an $8,513.52 discount ($100,000 − $91,486.48) to produce a 10 percent effective interest rate. Note that in these computations, the stated rate of interest was used to determine the amount of cash flow, and the effective rate of interest was used to determine the table conversion factors.

Bond Liabilities: Effective Interest Rate Method of Amortization

To this point, the straight-line method has been used to amortize bond discounts or premiums. This method is commonly used in practice because it is simple to apply and easy to understand. However, the method is theoretically deficient because it results in the recognition of a constant amount of interest expense while the carrying value of the bond liability fluctuates. Consider the discount on Tower Company bonds just discussed as an example. In this case, the amount of interest expense recognized each period is computed as follows:

Stated rate of interest	$100,000.00 × 0.09	=	$9,000.00
Amortization of discount	8,513.52 ÷ 20	=	425.68
Interest expense recognized each accounting period		=	$9,425.68

As previously demonstrated, the amortization of the bond discount increases the carrying value of the bond liability. Under the straight-line method, the bond liability increases while the amount of interest expense recognized remains constant. Logically, the amount of interest expense should increase as the amount of liability increases. This rational relationship can be achieved by applying the **effective interest rate method** to the amortization of bond discounts and premiums. The effective interest rate method is required when the result of its application will have a material effect on the financial statements.

Under the effective interest rate method, the amount of interest expense recognized in the financial statements is determined by multiplying the effective rate of interest by the carrying value of the bond liability. The amount of the discount to be amortized is determined by the difference between the interest expense and the cash outflow, as defined by the stated rate of interest. The following schedule demonstrates the application of the effective interest rate method for the recognition of interest expense during the first three years that Tower Company bonds were outstanding.

End of Year	Cash Payment	Interest Expense	Discount Amortization	Carrying Value
Issue Date				$91,486.48
1	$9,000*	$9,148.65†	$148.65‡	91,635.13§
2	9,000	9,163.51	163.51	91,798.64
3	9,000	9,179.86	179.86	91,978.50

*Cash outflow based on the stated rate of interest ($100,000 × 0.09).

†Effective interest rate times the carrying value (.10 × $91,486.48).

‡Interest expense minus cash outflow ($9,148.65 − $9,000.00).

§Previous carrying value plus portion of discount amortized ($91,486.48 + $148.65).

The effective interest rate method results in increasingly larger amounts of expense recognition as the carrying value of the bond liability increases. The effect of the expense recognition on the financial statements and the journal entry necessary to record it for the first accounting period are as follows:

Assets	=	Liabilities	+	Equity	Rev.	−	Exp.	=	Net Inc.	Cash Flow
Cash	=	Bond Liab.	+	Ret. Earn.						
(9,000)	=	148.65*	+	(9,148.65)	NA	−	9,148.65	=	(9,148.65)	(9,000) OA

*The decrease in the amount of the discount increases the bond liability.

Account Title	Debit	Credit
Interest Expense	9,148.65	
Cash		9,000.00
Discount on Bonds Payable		148.65

TABLE I Future Value of $1

n	4%	5%	6%	7%	8%	9%	10%	12%	14%	16%	20%
1	1.040000	1.050000	1.060000	1.070000	1.080000	1.090000	1.100000	1.120000	1.140000	1.160000	1.200000
2	1.081600	1.102500	1.123600	1.144900	1.166400	1.188100	1.210000	1.254400	1.299600	1.345600	1.440000
3	1.124864	1.157625	1.191016	1.225043	1.259712	1.295029	1.331000	1.404928	1.481544	1.560896	1.728000
4	1.169859	1.215506	1.262477	1.310796	1.360489	1.411582	1.464100	1.573519	1.688960	1.810639	2.073600
5	1.216653	1.276282	1.338226	1.402552	1.469328	1.538624	1.610510	1.762342	1.925415	2.100342	2.488320
6	1.265319	1.340096	1.418519	1.500730	1.586874	1.677100	1.771561	1.973823	2.194973	2.436396	2.985984
7	1.315932	1.407100	1.503630	1.605781	1.713824	1.828039	1.948717	2.210681	2.502269	2.826220	3.583181
8	1.368569	1.477455	1.593848	1.718186	1.850930	1.992563	2.143589	2.475963	2.852586	3.278415	4.299817
9	1.423312	1.551328	1.689479	1.838459	1.999005	2.171893	2.357948	2.773079	3.251949	3.802961	5.159780
10	1.480244	1.628895	1.790848	1.967151	2.158925	2.367364	2.593742	3.105848	3.707221	4.411435	6.191736
11	1.539454	1.710339	1.898299	2.104852	2.331639	2.580426	2.853117	3.478550	4.226232	5.117265	7.430084
12	1.601032	1.795856	2.012196	2.252192	2.518170	2.812665	3.138428	3.895976	4.817905	5.936027	8.916100
13	1.665074	1.885649	2.132928	2.409845	2.719624	3.065805	3.452271	4.363493	5.492411	6.885791	10.699321
14	1.731676	1.979932	2.260904	2.578534	2.937194	3.341727	3.797498	4.887112	6.261349	7.987518	12.839185
15	1.800944	2.078928	2.396558	2.759032	3.172169	3.642482	4.177248	5.473566	7.137938	9.265521	15.407022
16	1.872981	2.182875	2.540352	2.952164	3.425943	3.970306	4.594973	6.130394	8.137249	10.748004	18.488426
17	1.947900	2.292018	2.692773	3.158815	3.700018	4.327633	5.054470	6.866041	9.276464	12.467685	22.186111
18	2.025817	2.406619	2.854339	3.379932	3.996019	4.717120	5.559917	7.689966	10.575169	14.462514	26.623333
19	2.106849	2.526950	3.025600	3.616528	4.315701	5.141661	6.115909	8.612762	12.055693	16.776517	31.948000
20	2.191123	2.653298	3.207135	3.869684	4.660957	5.604411	6.727500	9.646293	13.743490	19.460759	38.337600

TABLE II Present Value of $1

n	4%	5%	6%	7%	8%	9%	10%	12%	14%	16%	20%
1	0.961538	0.952381	0.943396	0.934579	0.925926	0.917431	0.909091	0.892857	0.877193	0.862069	0.833333
2	0.924556	0.907029	0.889996	0.873439	0.857339	0.841680	0.826446	0.797194	0.769468	0.743163	0.694444
3	0.888996	0.863838	0.839619	0.816298	0.793832	0.772183	0.751315	0.711780	0.674972	0.640658	0.578704
4	0.854804	0.822702	0.792094	0.762895	0.735030	0.708425	0.683013	0.635518	0.592080	0.552291	0.482253
5	0.821927	0.783526	0.747258	0.712986	0.680583	0.649931	0.620921	0.567427	0.519369	0.476113	0.401878
6	0.790315	0.746215	0.704961	0.666342	0.630170	0.596267	0.564474	0.506631	0.455587	0.410442	0.334898
7	0.759918	0.710681	0.665057	0.622750	0.583490	0.547034	0.513158	0.452349	0.399637	0.353830	0.279082
8	0.730690	0.676839	0.627412	0.582009	0.540269	0.501866	0.466507	0.403883	0.350559	0.305025	0.232568
9	0.702587	0.644609	0.591898	0.543934	0.500249	0.460428	0.424098	0.360610	0.307508	0.262953	0.193807
10	0.675564	0.613913	0.558395	0.508349	0.463193	0.422411	0.385543	0.321973	0.269744	0.226684	0.161506
11	0.649581	0.584679	0.526788	0.475093	0.428883	0.387533	0.350494	0.287476	0.236617	0.195417	0.134588
12	0.624597	0.556837	0.496969	0.444012	0.397114	0.355535	0.318631	0.256675	0.207559	0.168463	0.112157
13	0.600574	0.530321	0.468839	0.414964	0.367698	0.326179	0.289664	0.229174	0.182069	0.145227	0.093464
14	0.577475	0.505068	0.442301	0.387817	0.340461	0.299246	0.263331	0.204620	0.159710	0.125195	0.077887
15	0.555265	0.481017	0.417265	0.362446	0.315242	0.274538	0.239392	0.182696	0.140096	0.107927	0.064905
16	0.533908	0.458112	0.393646	0.338735	0.291890	0.251870	0.217629	0.163122	0.122892	0.093041	0.054088
17	0.513373	0.436297	0.371364	0.316574	0.270269	0.231073	0.197845	0.145644	0.107800	0.080207	0.045073
18	0.493628	0.415521	0.350344	0.295864	0.250249	0.211994	0.179859	0.130040	0.094561	0.069144	0.037561
19	0.474642	0.395734	0.330513	0.276508	0.231712	0.194490	0.163508	0.116107	0.082948	0.059607	0.031301
20	0.456387	0.376889	0.311805	0.258419	0.214548	0.178431	0.148644	0.103667	0.072762	0.051385	0.026084

TABLE III Future Value of an Annuity of $1

n	4%	5%	6%	7%	8%	9%	10%	12%	14%	16%	20%
1	1.000000	1.000000	1.000000	1.000000	1.000000	1.000000	1.000000	1.000000	1.000000	1.000000	1.000000
2	2.040000	2.050000	2.060000	2.070000	2.080000	2.090000	2.100000	2.120000	2.140000	2.160000	2.200000
3	3.121600	3.152500	3.183600	3.214900	3.246400	3.278100	3.310000	3.374400	3.439600	3.505600	3.640000
4	4.246464	4.310125	4.374616	4.439943	4.506112	4.573129	4.641000	4.779328	4.921144	5.066496	5.368000
5	5.416323	5.525631	5.637093	5.750739	5.866601	5.984711	6.105100	6.352847	6.610104	6.877135	7.441600
6	6.632975	6.801913	6.975319	7.153291	7.335929	7.523335	7.715610	8.115189	8.535519	8.977477	9.929920
7	7.898294	8.142008	8.393838	8.654021	8.922803	9.200435	9.487171	10.089012	10.730491	11.413873	12.915904
8	9.214226	9.549109	9.897468	10.259803	10.636628	11.028474	11.435888	12.299693	13.232760	14.240093	16.499085
9	10.582795	11.026564	11.491316	11.977989	12.487558	13.021036	13.579477	14.775656	16.085347	17.518508	20.798902
10	12.006107	12.577893	13.180795	13.816448	14.486562	15.192930	15.937425	17.548735	19.337295	21.321469	25.958682
11	13.486351	14.206787	14.971643	15.783599	16.645487	17.560293	18.531167	20.654583	23.044516	25.732904	32.150419
12	15.025805	15.917127	16.869941	17.888451	18.977126	20.140720	21.384284	24.133133	27.270749	30.850169	39.580502
13	16.626838	17.712983	18.882138	20.140643	21.495297	22.953385	24.522712	28.029109	32.088654	36.786196	48.496603
14	18.291911	19.598632	21.015066	22.550488	24.214920	26.019189	27.974983	32.392602	37.581065	43.671987	59.195923
15	20.023588	21.578564	23.275970	25.129022	27.152114	29.360916	31.772482	37.279715	43.842414	51.659505	72.035108
16	21.824531	23.657492	25.672528	27.888054	30.324283	33.003399	35.949730	42.753280	50.980352	60.925026	87.442129
17	23.697512	25.840366	28.212880	30.840217	33.750226	36.973705	40.544703	48.883674	59.117601	71.673030	105.930555
18	25.645413	28.132385	30.905653	33.999033	37.450244	41.301338	45.599173	55.749715	68.394066	84.140715	128.116666
19	27.671229	30.539004	33.759992	37.378965	41.446263	46.018458	51.159090	63.439681	78.969235	98.603230	154.740000
20	29.778079	33.065954	36.785591	40.995492	45.761964	51.160120	57.274999	72.052442	91.024928	115.379747	186.688000

TABLE IV Present Value of an Annuity of $1

n	4%	5%	6%	7%	8%	9%	10%	12%	14%	16%	20%
1	0.961538	0.952381	0.943396	0.934579	0.925926	0.917431	0.909091	0.892857	0.877193	0.862069	0.833333
2	1.886095	1.859410	1.833393	1.808018	1.783265	1.759111	1.735537	1.690051	1.646661	1.605232	1.527778
3	2.775091	2.723248	2.673012	2.624316	2.577097	2.531295	2.486852	2.401831	2.321632	2.245890	2.106481
4	3.629895	3.545951	3.465106	3.387211	3.312127	3.239720	3.169865	3.037349	2.913712	2.798181	2.588735
5	4.451822	4.329477	4.212364	4.100197	3.992710	3.889651	3.790787	3.604776	3.433081	3.274294	2.990612
6	5.242137	5.075692	4.917324	4.766540	4.622880	4.485919	4.355261	4.111407	3.888668	3.684736	3.325510
7	6.002055	5.786373	5.582381	5.389289	5.206370	5.032953	4.868419	4.563757	4.288305	4.038565	3.604592
8	6.732745	6.463213	6.209794	5.971299	5.746639	5.534819	5.334926	4.967640	4.638864	4.343591	3.837160
9	7.435332	7.107822	6.801692	6.515232	6.246888	5.995247	5.759024	5.328250	4.946372	4.606544	4.030967
10	8.110896	7.721735	7.360087	7.023582	6.710081	6.417658	6.144567	5.650223	5.216116	4.833227	4.192472
11	8.760477	8.306414	7.886875	7.498674	7.138964	6.805191	6.495061	5.937699	5.452733	5.028644	4.327060
12	9.385074	8.863252	8.383844	7.942686	7.536078	7.160725	6.813692	6.194374	5.660292	5.197107	4.439217
13	9.985648	9.393573	8.852683	8.357651	7.903776	7.486904	7.103356	6.423548	5.842362	5.342334	4.532681
14	10.563123	9.898641	9.294984	8.745468	8.244237	7.786150	7.366687	6.628168	6.002072	5.467529	4.610567
15	11.118387	10.379658	9.712249	9.107914	8.559479	8.060688	7.606080	6.810864	6.142168	5.575456	4.675473
16	11.652296	10.837770	10.105895	9.446649	8.851369	8.312558	7.823709	6.973986	6.265060	5.668497	4.729561
17	12.165669	11.274066	10.477260	9.763223	9.121638	8.543631	8.021553	7.119630	6.372859	5.748704	4.774634
18	12.659297	11.689587	10.827603	10.059087	9.371887	8.755625	8.201412	7.249670	6.467420	5.817848	4.812195
19	13.133939	12.085321	11.158116	10.335595	9.603599	8.905115	8.364920	7.365777	6.550369	5.877455	4.843496
20	13.590326	12.462210	11.469921	10.594014	9.818147	9.128546	8.513564	7.469444	6.623131	5.928841	4.869580

SELF-STUDY REVIEW PROBLEM

During 2004 and 2005, Herring Corp. completed the following selected transactions relating to its bond issue. The corporation's fiscal year ends on December 31.

2004

Jan. 1 Sold $400,000 of 10-year, 9 percent bonds at 97. Interest is payable in cash on December 31 each year.

Dec. 31 Paid the bond interest and recorded the amortization of the discount using the straight-line method.

2005

Dec. 31 Paid the bond interest and recorded the amortization of the discount using the straight-line method.

Required

a. Show how these events would affect Herring's financial statements by recording them in a financial statements model like the following one.

	Assets	=	Liab.			+	Equity	Rev.	−	Exp.	=	Net Inc.	Cash Flow
Date	Cash	=	Bond Pay.	−	Discount	+	Ret. Earn.						
1/1/04													
12/31/04													
12/31/05													

b. Determine the carrying value of the bond liability as of December 31, 2005.

c. Assuming Herring had earnings before interest and taxes of $198,360 in 2005, calculate the times interest earned ratio.

Solution

a.

	Assets	=	Liab.			+	Equity	Rev.	−	Exp.	=	Net Inc.	Cash Flow
Date	Cash	=	Bond Pay.	−	Discount	+	Ret. Earn.						
1/1/04	388,000	=	400,000	−	12,000	+	NA	NA	−	NA	=	NA	388,000 FA
12/31/04	(36,000)	=	NA	−	(1,200)	+	(37,200)	NA	−	37,200	=	(37,200)	(36,000) OA
12/31/05	(36,000)	=	NA	−	(1,200)	+	(37,200)	NA	−	37,200	=	(37,200)	(36,000) OA

b. The unamortized discount as of December 31, 2005, is $9,600 ($12,000 − $1,200 − $1,200). The carrying value of the bond liability is $390,400 ($400,000 − $9,600).

c. The times interest earned ratio is 5.3 times ($198,360 ÷ $37,200).

KEY TERMS

QUESTIONS

1. What is the difference between classification of a note as short term or long term?
2. At the beginning of year 1, B Co. has a note payable of $72,000 that calls for an annual payment of $16,246, which includes both principal and interest. If the interest rate is 8 percent, what is the amount of interest expense in year 1 and in year 2? What is the balance of the note at the end of year 2?
3. What is the purpose of a line of credit for a business? Why would a company choose to obtain a line of credit instead of issuing bonds?
4. What are the primary sources of debt financing for most large companies?
5. What are some advantages of issuing bonds versus borrowing from a bank?
6. What are some disadvantages of issuing bonds?
7. Why can a company usually issue bonds at a lower interest rate than the company would pay if the funds were borrowed from a bank?
8. What effect does income tax have on the cost of borrowing funds for a business?
9. What is the concept of financial leverage?
10. Which type of bond, secured or unsecured, is likely to have a lower interest rate? Explain.
11. What is the function of restrictive covenants attached to bond issues?
12. What is the difference between term bonds and serial bonds?
13. What is the purpose of establishing a sinking fund?
14. What is the call price of a bond? Is it usually higher or lower than the face amount of the bond? Explain.
15. If Roc Co. issued $100,000 of 5 percent, 10-year bonds at the face amount, what is the effect of the issuance of the bonds on the financial statements? What amount of interest expense will Roc Co. recognize each year?
16. What mechanism is used to adjust the stated interest rate to the market rate of interest?
17. When the effective interest rate is higher than the stated interest rate on a bond issue, will the bond sell at a discount or premium? Why?
18. What type of transaction is the issuance of bonds by a company?
19. What factors may cause the effective interest rate and the stated interest rate to be different?
20. If a bond is selling at 97½, how much cash will the company receive from the sale of a $1,000 bond?
21. How is the carrying value of a bond computed?
22. Gay Co. has a balance in the Bonds Payable account of $25,000 and a balance in the Discount on Bonds Payable account of $5,200. What is the carrying value of the bonds? What is the total amount of the liability?
23. When the effective interest rate is higher than the stated interest rate, will interest expense be higher or lower than the amount of interest paid?
24. Assuming that the selling price of the bond and the face value are the same, would the issuer of a bond rather make annual or semiannual interest payments? Why?
25. Which method of financing, debt or equity, is generally more advantageous from a tax standpoint? Why?
26. If a company has a tax rate of 30 percent and interest expense was $10,000, what is the after-tax cost of the debt?
27. Which type of financing, debt or equity, increases the risk factor of a business? Why?

28. What information does the times interest earned ratio provide?
29. What is the difference between simple and compound interest?
30. What is meant by the future value of an investment? How is it determined?
31. If you have $10,000 to invest at the beginning of year 1 at an interest rate of 8 percent, what is the future value of the investment at the end of year 4?
32. What is meant by the present value of an investment? How is it determined?
33. Assume that your favorite aunt gave you $25,000, but you will not receive the gift until you are 25 years old. You are presently 22 years old. What is the current value of the gift, assuming an interest rate of 8 percent?
34. What is the present value of four payments of $4,000 each to be received at the end of each of the next four years, assuming an interest rate of 8 percent?
35. How does the effective interest rate method of amortization differ from the straight-line method of amortization? Which method is conceptually more correct?

EXERCISES—SERIES A

All Exercises in Series A are available with McGraw-Hill's Homework Manager

Unless stated otherwise, use straight-line amortization for all exercises and problems when appropriate.

Exercise 10-1A *How credit terms affect financial statements*

L.O. 1

Marshall Co. is planning to finance an expansion of its operations by borrowing $50,000. City Bank has agreed to loan Marshall the funds. Marshall has two repayment options: (1) to issue a note with the principal due in 10 years and with interest payable annually or (2) to issue a note to repay $5,000 of the principal each year along with the annual interest based on the unpaid principal balance. Assume the interest rate is 9 percent for each option.

Required

a. What amount of interest will Marshall pay in year 1
 (1) Under option 1?
 (2) Under option 2?
b. What amount of interest will Marshall pay in year 2
 (1) Under option 1?
 (2) Under option 2?
c. Explain the advantage of each option.

Exercise 10-2A *Accounting for an installment note payable with annual payments that include interest and principal*

L.O. 1

On January 1, 2007, Mooney Co. borrowed $60,000 cash from First Bank by issuing a four-year, 6 percent note. The principal and interest are to be paid by making annual payments in the amount of $17,315. Payments are to be made December 31 of each year, beginning December 31, 2007.

Required

Prepare an amortization schedule for the interest and principal payments for the four-year period.

Exercise 10-3A *Long-term installment note payable*

L.O. 1

Jim Felix started a business by issuing an $80,000 face value note to State National Bank on January 1, 2008. The note had a 7 percent annual rate of interest and a 10-year term. Payments of $11,390 are to be made each December 31 for 10 years.

Required

a. What portion of the December 31, 2008, payment is applied to
 (1) Interest expense?
 (2) Principal?
b. What is the principal balance on January 1, 2009?

c. What portion of the December 31, 2009, payment is applied to
(1) Interest expense?
(2) Principal?

L.O. 1

Exercise 10-4A *Amortization of a long-term loan*

A partial amortization schedule for a five-year note payable that Chacon Co. issued on January 1, 2008, is shown here:

Accounting Period	Principal Balance January 1	Cash Payment	Applied to Interest	Applied to Principal
2008	$120,000	$30,851	$10,800	$20,051
2009	99,949	30,851	8,995	21,856

Required

a. What rate of interest is Chacon Co. paying on the note?

b. Using a financial statements model like the one shown below, record the appropriate amounts for the following two events:
(1) January 1, 2008, issue of the note payable.
(2) December 31, 2009, payment on the note payable.

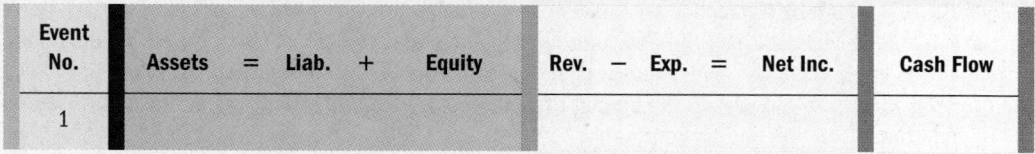

Event No.	Assets	=	Liab.	+	Equity	Rev.	−	Exp.	=	Net Inc.	Cash Flow
1											

c. If the company earned $90,000 cash revenue and paid $50,000 in cash expenses in addition to the interest in 2008, what is the amount of each of the following? (Disregard income taxes.)
(1) Net income for 2008.
(2) Cash flow from operating activities for 2008.
(3) Cash flow from financing activities for 2008.

d. What is the amount of interest expense on this loan for 2010?

L.O. 2

Exercise 10-5A *Accounting for a line of credit*

Casper Company has a line of credit with Federal Bank. Casper can borrow up to $400,000 at any time over the course of the 2007 calendar year. The following table shows the prime rate expressed as an annual percentage along with the amounts borrowed and repaid during the first four months of 2007. Casper agreed to pay interest at an annual rate equal to 2 percent above the bank's prime rate. Funds are borrowed or repaid on the first day of each month. Interest is payable in cash on the last day of the month. The interest rate is applied to the outstanding monthly balance. For example, Casper pays 6 percent (4 percent + 2 percent) annual interest on $80,000 for the month of January.

Month	Amount Borrowed or (Repaid)	Prime Rate for the Month, %
January	$80,000	4
February	40,000	3
March	(20,000)	3.5
April	30,000	4

Required

Provide all journal entries pertaining to Casper's line of credit for the first four months of 2007.

Exercise 10-6A *Accounting for a line of credit*

L.O. 2

King Co. uses an approved line of credit not to exceed $200,000 with the local bank to provide short-term financing for its business operations. King either borrows or repays funds on the first day of a month. Interest is payable monthly at the bank's prime interest rate plus .5 percent. The following table shows the amounts borrowed and repaid for 2006 along with the bank's prime interest rate.

Month	Amount Borrowed or (Repaid)	Prime rate for the month, %
January	0	4
February	$40,000	4
March	20,000	4.5
April	(10,000)	5
May	(30,000)	4
June	10,000	5
July–October	0	5
November	50,000	5.5
December	(30,000)	5.25

Required

a. Prepare all of the journal entries pertaining to the line of credit for 2006. (Round to the nearest dollar.)

b. Show the effects of these transactions on the financial statements using a horizontal statements model like the one shown here. Use a + to indicate increase, a − for decrease, and NA for not affected. In the Cash Flow column, indicate whether the item is an operating activity (OA), investing activity (IA), or financing activity (FA).

Assets	=	Liabilities.	+	Equity	Rev.	−	Exp.	=	Net Inc.	Cash Flow

c. What is the total amount of interest expense paid for 2006?

Exercise 10-7A *Annual versus semiannual interest payments*

L.O. 5

Gardner Co. issued bonds with a face value of $100,000 on January 1, 2007. The bonds had a 6 percent stated rate of interest and a five-year term. The bonds were issued at face value.

Required

a. What total amount of interest will Gardner pay in 2007 if bond interest is paid annually each December 31?

b. What total amount of interest will Gardner pay in 2007 if bond interest is paid semiannually each June 30 and December 31?

c. Write a memo explaining which option Gardner would prefer.

Exercise 10-8A *Determining cash receipts from bond issues*

L.O. 5, 6

Required

Compute the cash proceeds from bond issues under the following terms. For each case, indicate whether the bonds sold at a premium or discount.

a. May Inc. issued $200,000 of 8-year, 7 percent bonds at 101.

b. Tom Co. issued $100,000 of 4-year, 6 percent bonds at 98.

c. Hill Co. issued $150,000 of 10-year, 7 percent bonds at 102¼.

d. Day Inc. issued $50,000 of 5-year, 6 percent bonds at 97½.

L.O. 6

Exercise 10-9A *Identifying the relationship between the stated rate of interest and the market rate of interest*

Required

Indicate whether a bond will sell at a premium (P), discount (D), or face value (F) for each of the following conditions:

a. ______ The market rate of interest is less than the stated rate.
b. ______ The market rate of interest is equal to the stated rate.
c. ______ The stated rate of interest is higher than the market rate.
d. ______ The market rate of interest is higher than the stated rate.
e. ______ The stated rate of interest is less than the market rate.

L.O. 6

Exercise 10-10A *Identifying bond premiums and discounts*

Required

In each of the following situations, state whether the bonds will sell at a premium or discount.

a. Jaco issued $100,000 of bonds with a stated interest rate of 6.5 percent. At the time of issue, the market rate of interest for similar investments was 6 percent.

b. Webnet issued $150,000 of bonds with a stated interest rate of 5.5 percent. At the time of issue, the market rate of interest for similar investments was 6 percent.

c. Pearl Inc. issued callable bonds with a stated interest rate of 6 percent. The bonds were callable at 102. At the date of issue, the market rate of interest was 6.5 percent for similar investments.

L.O. 6

Exercise 10-11A *Determining the amount of bond premiums and discounts*

Required

For each of the following situations, calculate the amount of bond discount or premium, if any.

a. Lind Co. issued $60,000 of 7 percent bonds at 101¼.
b. Schwarz Inc. issued $90,000 of 10-year, 6 percent bonds at 95½.
c. Zoe Inc. issued $200,000 of 20-year, 6 percent bonds at 102.
d. Uddin Co. issued $150,000 of 15-year, 7 percent bonds at 98.

L.O. 4, 5

Exercise 10-12A *Effect of a bond discount on financial statements: annual interest*

Keeley Company issued $100,000 face value of bonds on January 1, 2008. The bonds had a 7 percent stated rate of interest and a 10-year term. Interest is paid in cash annually, beginning December 31, 2008.The bonds were issued at 98.

Required

a. Use a financial statements model like the one shown below to demonstrate how (1) the January 1, 2008 bond issue and (2) the December 31, 2008 recognition of interest expense, including the amortization of the discount and the cash payment, affects the company's financial statements. Use + for increase, − for decrease, and NA for not affected.

Event No.	Assets	=	Liab.	+	Equity	Rev.	−	Exp.	=	Net Inc.	Cash Flow
1											

b. Determine the amount of interest expense reported on the 2008 income statement.

c. Determine the carrying value (face value less discount) of the bond liability as of December 31, 2008.

d. Determine the amount of interest expense reported on the 2009 income statement.

e. Determine the carrying value (face value less discount) of the bond liability as of December 31, 2009.

Exercise 10-13A *Effect of a bond premium on financial statements: annual interest*

L.O. 4, 5

Ball Company issued $200,000 face value of bonds on January 1, 2007. The bonds had a 6 percent stated rate of interest and a 10-year term. Interest is paid in cash annually, beginning December 31, 2007. The bonds were issued at 102.

Required

a. Use a financial statements model like the one shown below to demonstrate how (1) the January 1, 2007, bond issue and (2) the December 31, 2007, recognition of interest expense, including the amortization of the premium and the cash payment, affects the company's financial statements. Use + for increase, − for decrease, and NA for not affected.

Event No.	Assets	=	Liab.	+	Equity	Rev.	−	Exp.	=	Net Inc.	Cash Flow
1											

b. Determine the carrying value (face value plus premium) of the bond liability as of December 31, 2007.

c. Determine the amount of interest expense reported on the 2007 income statement.

d. Determine the carrying value of the bond liability as of December 31, 2008.

e. Determine the amount of interest expense reported on the 2008 income statement.

Exercise 10-14A *Effect of bonds issued at a discount on financial statements: semiannual interest*

L.O. 4, 5

Farm Supplies Inc. issued $150,000 of 10-year, 6 percent bonds on July 1, 2008, at 95. Interest is payable in cash semiannually on June 30 and December 31.

Required

a. Prepare the journal entries to record issuing the bonds and any necessary journal entries for 2008 and 2009. Post the journal entries to T-accounts.

b. Prepare the liabilities section of the balance sheet at the end of 2008 and 2009.

c. What amount of interest expense will Farm Supplies report on the financial statements for 2008 and 2009?

d. What amount of cash will Farm Supplies pay for interest in 2008 and 2009?

Exercise 10-15A *Recording bonds issued at face value and associated interest for two accounting cycles: annual interest*

L.O. 5

On January 1, 2008, Demski Corp. issued $300,000 of 10-year, 5 percent bonds at their face amount. Interest is payable on December 31 of each year with the first payment due December 31, 2008.

Required

Prepare all the general journal entries related to these bonds for 2008 and 2009.

Exercise 10-16A *Recording bonds issued at a discount: annual interest*

L.O. 5

On January 1, 2008, Marva Co. issued $200,000 of five-year, 6 percent bonds at 96. Interest is payable annually on December 31. The discount is amortized using the straight-line method.

Required

Prepare the journal entries to record the bond transactions for 2008 and 2009.

Exercise 10-17A *Recording bonds issued at a premium: annual interest*

L.O. 5

On January 1, 2006, Stone Company issued $200,000 of five-year, 6 percent bonds at 102. Interest is payable annually on December 31. The premium is amortized using the straight-line method.

Required

Prepare the journal entries to record the bond transactions for 2006 and 2007.

L.O. 4, 5

Exercise 10-18A *Two complete accounting cycles: bonds issued at face value with annual interest*

Wyatt Company issued $400,000 of 20-year, 6 percent bonds on January 1, 2007. The bonds were issued at face value. Interest is payable in cash on December 31 of each year. Wyatt immediately invested the proceeds from the bond issue in land. The land was leased for an annual $60,000 of cash revenue, which was collected on December 31 of each year, beginning December 31, 2007.

Required

a. Prepare the journal entries for these events, and post them to T-accounts for 2007 and 2008.

b. Prepare the income statement, balance sheet, and statement of cash flows for 2007 and 2008.

L.O. 5

Exercise 10-19A *Recording callable bonds*

Ball Co. issued $200,000 of 6 percent, 10-year, callable bonds on January 1, 2006, for their face value. The call premium was 2 percent (bonds are callable at 102). Interest was payable annually on December 31. The bonds were called on December 31, 2009.

Required

Prepare the journal entries to record the bond issue on January 1, 2006, and the bond redemption on December 31, 2009. Assume that all entries to accrue and pay interest were recorded correctly.

L.O. 7

Exercise 10-20A *Determining the after-tax cost of debt*

The following 2006 information is available for three companies:

	Crow Co.	Dahl Co.	Snow Co.
Face value of bonds payable	$300,000	$600,000	$500,000
Interest rate	8%	7%	6%
Income tax rate	35%	20%	25%

Required

a. Determine the annual before-tax interest cost for each company *in dollars.*

b. Determine the annual after-tax interest cost for each company *in dollars.*

c. Determine the annual after-tax interest cost for each company *as a percentage* of the face value of the bonds.

L.O. 8

Exercise 10-21A *Future value and present value (Appendix)*

Required

Using Tables I, II, III, or IV in the appendix, calculate the following:

a. The future value of $20,000 invested at 6 percent for 10 years.

b. The future value of eight annual payments of $1,200 at 7 percent interest.

c. The amount that must be deposited today (present value) at 6 percent to accumulate $50,000 in five years.

d. The annual payment on a 10-year, 6 percent, $40,000 note payable.

L.O. 8

Exercise 10-22A *Computing the payment amount (Appendix)*

Nancy Swift is a business major at State U. She will be graduating this year and is planning to start a consulting business. She will need to purchase computer equipment that costs $22,000. She can borrow the money from the local bank but will have to make annual payments of principal and interest.

Required

a. Compute the annual payment Nancy will be required to make on a $22,000, four-year, 7 percent loan.

b. If Nancy can afford to make annual payments of $8,000, how much can she borrow?

Exercise 10-23A ***Saving for a future value (Appendix)*** **L.O. 8**

Billy Joe and Betty Ann were recently married and want to start saving for their dream home. They expect the house they want will cost approximately $250,000. They hope to be able to purchase the house for cash in 10 years.

Required

a. How much will Billy Joe and Betty Ann have to invest each year to purchase their dream home at the end of 10 years? Assume an interest rate of 8 percent.
b. Billy Joe's parents want to give the couple a substantial wedding gift for the purchase of their future home. How much must Billy Joe's parents give them now if they are to have the desired amount of $250,000 in 12 years? Assume an interest rate of 8 percent.

Exercise 10-24A ***Sale of bonds at a discount using present value (Appendix)*** **L.O. 6, 8**

Jones Corporation issued $60,000 of 6 percent, 10-year bonds on January 1, 2007, for a price that reflected a 7 percent market rate of interest. Interest is payable annually on December 31.

Required

a. What was the selling price of the bonds?
b. Prepare the journal entry to record issuing the bonds.
c. Prepare the journal entry for the first interest payment on December 31, 2007, using the effective interest rate method.

Exercise 10-25A ***Comparing the effective interest rate method with the straight-line method (Appendix)*** **L.O. 6, 8**

Required

Write a short memo explaining why the effective interest rate method produces a different amount of interest expense from the straight-line method in any given year.

PROBLEMS—SERIES A

All Problems in Series A are available with McGraw-Hill's Homework Manager

Problem 10-26A ***Effect of an installment loan on financial statements*** **L.O. 1**

On January 1, 2006, Miller Co. borrowed cash from First City Bank by issuing a $60,000 face value, three-year installment note that had a 7 percent annual interest rate. The note is to be repaid by making annual payments of $22,863 that include both interest and principal on December 31 each year. Jones invested the proceeds from the loan in land that generated lease revenues of $30,000 cash per year.

CHECK FIGURES
a. 2006 Ending Principal Balance: $41,337
b. 2008 Net Income: $28,505

Required

a. Prepare an amortization schedule for the three-year period.
b. Prepare an income statement, balance sheet, and statement of cash flows for each of the three years. (*Hint:* Record the transactions for each year in T-accounts before preparing the financial statements.)
c. Does cash outflow from operating activities remain constant or change each year? Explain.

Problem 10-27A ***Accounting for an installment note payable*** **L.O. 1**

The following transactions apply to Marque Co. for 2008, its first year of operations.

1. Received $30,000 cash in exchange for issuance of common stock.
2. Secured a $100,000, 10-year installment loan from First Bank. The interest rate was 6 percent and annual payments are $13,587.
3. Purchased land for $20,000.
4. Provided services for $85,000 cash.

5. Paid other operating expenses of $34,000.
6. Paid the annual payment on the loan.

Required

a. Prepare the journal entries for 2008 and post to T-accounts.
b. Prepare an income statement and balance sheet for 2008.
c. What is the interest expense for 2009? 2010?

L.O. 2

Problem 10-28A *Accounting for a line of credit*

Quality Sports Equipment uses a line of credit to help finance its inventory purchases. Quality sells ski equipment and uses the line of credit to build inventory for its peak sales months, which tend to be clustered in the winter months. Account balances at the beginning of 2009 were as follows:

Cash	$50,000
Inventory	75,000
Common Stock	60,000
Retained Earnings	65,000

Quality experienced the following transactions for January, February, and March, 2009.

1. January 1, 2009, obtained approval for a line of credit of up to $200,000. Funds are to be obtained or repaid on the first day of each month. The interest rate is the bank prime rate plus 1 percent.
2. January 1, 2009, borrowed $30,000 on the line of credit. The bank's prime interest rate is 5 percent for January.
3. January 15, purchased inventory on account, $68,000.
4. January 31, paid other operating expenses of $8,000.
5. In January, sold inventory for $65,000 on account. The inventory had cost $42,000.
6. January 31, paid the interest due on the line of credit.
7. February 1, borrowed $60,000 on the line of credit. The bank's prime rate is 6 percent for February.
8. February 1, paid the accounts payable from transaction 3.
9. February 10, collected $62,000 of the sales on account.
10. February 20, purchased inventory on account, $72,000.
11. February sales on account were $110,000. The inventory had cost $75,000.
12. February 28, paid the interest due on the line of credit.
13. March 1, repaid $20,000 on the line of credit. The bank's prime rate is 5 percent for March.
14. March 5, paid $50,000 of the accounts payable.
15. March 10, collected $105,000 from accounts receivable.
16. March 20, purchased inventory on account, $72,000.
17. March sales on account were $135,000. The inventory had cost $87,000.
18. March 31, paid the interest due on the line of credit.

Required

a. Prepare the journal entries for the above transactions and post them to T-accounts.
b. What is the amount of interest expense for January? February? March?
c. What amount of cash was paid for interest in January? February? March?

L.O. 2

Problem 10-29A *Effect of a line of credit on financial statements*

Shim Company has a line of credit with Bay Bank. Shim can borrow up to $200,000 at any time over the course of the 2006 calendar year. The following table shows the prime rate expressed as an annual percentage along with the amounts borrowed and repaid during 2006. Shim agreed to pay interest at an annual rate equal to 1 percent above the bank's prime rate. Funds are borrowed or repaid on the first day of each month. Interest is payable in cash on the last day of the month. The interest rate is applied to the outstanding monthly balance. For example, Shim pays 5 percent (4 percent + 1 percent) annual interest on $70,000 for the month of January.

Month	Amount Borrowed or (Repaid)	Prime Rate for the Month, %
January	$70,000	4
February	40,000	4
March	(20,000)	5
April through October	No change	No change
November	(30,000)	5
December	(20,000)	4

CHECK FIGURES
a. Interest Expense: $4,817
Total Assets: $53,183

Shim earned $18,000 of cash revenue during 2006.

Required

a. Prepare an income statement, balance sheet, and statement of cash flows for 2006.

b. Write a memo discussing the advantages to a business of arranging a line of credit.

Problem 10-30A ***Accounting for a bond premium over multiple accounting cycles***

L.O. 4, 5

eXcel

mhhe.com/edmonds2007

Tyrone Company was started when it issued bonds with $200,000 face value on January 1, 2006. The bonds were issued for cash at 105. They had a 15-year term to maturity and an 8 percent annual interest rate. Interest was payable annually. Tyrone immediately purchased land with the proceeds (cash received) from the bond issue. Tyrone leased the land for $20,000 cash per year. On January 1, 2009, the company sold the land for $211,000 cash. Immediately after the sale, Tyrone repurchased its bonds (repaid the bond liability) at 106. Assume that no other accounting events occurred in 2009.

CHECK FIGURES
2008 Operating Income: $4,667
2009 Total Assets: $11,000

Required

Prepare an income statement, statement of changes in equity, balance sheet, and statement of cash flows for each of the 2006, 2007, 2008, and 2009 accounting periods. Assume that the company closes its books on December 31 of each year. Prepare the statements using a vertical statements format. (*Hint:* Record each year's transactions in T-accounts prior to preparing the financial statements.)

Problem 10-31A ***Recording and reporting a bond discount over two cycles: semiannual interest***

L.O. 4-6

During 2007 and 2008, Martin Co. completed the following transactions relating to its bond issue. The company's fiscal year ends on December 31.

2007

Mar.	1	Issued $60,000 of eight-year, 7 percent bonds for $57,000. The semiannual cash payment for interest is due on March 1 and September 1, beginning September 2007.
Sept.	1	Recognized interest expense including the amortization of the discount and made the semiannual cash payment for interest.
Dec.	31	Recognized accrued interest expense including the amortization of the discount.
Dec.	31	Closed the interest expense account.

2008

Mar.	1	Recognized interest expense including the amortization of the discount and made the semiannual cash payment for interest.
Sept.	1	Recognized interest expense including the amortization of the discount and made the semiannual cash payment for interest.
Dec.	31	Recognized accrued interest expense including the amortization of the discount.
Dec.	31	Closed the interest expense account.

CHECK FIGURES
d. 2007 Interest Expense: $3,812.50
e. 2007 Interest Paid: $2,100.00

Required

a. When the bonds were issued, was the market rate of interest more or less than the stated rate of interest? If the bonds had sold at face value, what amount of cash would Martin Co. have received?

b. Prepare the general journal entries for these transactions.

c. Prepare the liabilities section of the balance sheet at December 31, 2007 and 2008.

d. Determine the amount of interest expense Martin would report on the income statements for 2007 and 2008.

e. Determine the amount of interest Martin would pay to the bondholders in 2007 and 2008.

L.O. 4, 5

Problem 10-32A *Effect of a bond premium on the elements of financial statements*

Valley Land Co. was formed when it acquired cash from the issue of common stock. The company then issued bonds at a premium on January 1, 2006. Interest is payable annually on December 31 of each year, beginning December 31, 2006. On January 2, 2006, Valley Land Co. purchased a piece of land and leased it for an annual rental fee. The rent is received annually on December 31, beginning December 31, 2006. At the end of the eight-year period (December 31, 2013), the land was sold at a gain, and the bonds were paid off. A summary of the transactions for each year follows:

2006

1. Acquired cash from the issue of common stock.
2. Issued eight-year bonds.
3. Purchased land.
4. Received land-lease income.
5. Recognized interest expense including the amortization of the premium and made the cash payment for interest on December 31.
6. Prepared the December 31 entry to close Rent Revenue.
7. Prepared the December 31 entry to close Interest Expense.

2007–2012

8. Received land-lease income.
9. Recognized interest expense including the amortization of the premium and made the cash payment for interest on December 31.
10. Prepared the December 31 entry to close Rent Revenue.
11. Prepared the December 31 entry to close Interest Expense.

2013

12. Sold land at a gain.
13. Retired bonds at face value.

Required

Identify each of these 13 transactions as asset source (AS), asset use (AU), asset exchange (AE), or claims exchange (CE). Explain how each event affects assets, liabilities, equity, net income, and cash flow by placing a + for increase, − for decrease, or NA for not affected under each category. In the Cash Flow column, indicate whether the item is an operating activity (OA), investing activity (IA), or financing activity (FA). The first event is recorded as an example.

Event No.	Type of Event	Assets	=	Liab.	+	Common Stock	+	Retained Earnings	Net Income	Cash Flow
1	AS	+		NA		+		NA	NA	+ FA

L.O. 4, 5

CHECK FIGURES

b. Interest Expense: $9,600

b. Loss on Bond Redemption $1,800

Problem 10-33A *Recording transactions for callable bonds*

Franklin Co. issued $120,000 of 10-year, 8 percent, callable bonds on January 1, 2006, with interest payable annually on December 31. The bonds were issued at their face amount. The bonds are callable at 101½. The fiscal year of the corporation is the calendar year.

Required

a. Show the effect of the following events on the financial statements by recording the appropriate amounts in a horizontal statements model like the following one. In the Cash Flow column, indicate whether the item is an operating activity (OA), investing activity (IA), or financing activity (FA). Use NA if an element was not affected by the event.

(1) Issued the bonds on January 1, 2006.

(2) Paid interest due to bondholders on December 31, 2006.

(3) On January 1, 2010, Franklin Co. called the bonds. Assume that all interim entries were correctly recorded.

Event No.	Assets	=	Liab.	+	Equity	Rev.	−	Exp.	=	Net Inc.	Cash Flow
1											

b. Prepare journal entries for the three events listed in Requirement *a.*

Problem 10-34A *Effect of debt transactions on financial statements*

L.O. 1, 2, 4

Required

Show the effect of each of the following independent accounting events on the financial statements using a horizontal statements model like the following one. Use + for increase, − for decrease, and NA for not affected. The first event is recorded as an example.

Event No.	Assets	=	Liab.	+	Equity	Rev.	−	Exp.	=	Net Inc.	Cash Flow
a	+		+		NA	NA		NA		NA	+ FA

a. Issued a bond at a premium.

b. Made an interest payment on a bond that had been issued at a premium and amortized the premium.

c. Borrowed funds using a line of credit.

d. Made an interest payment for funds that had been borrowed against a line of credit.

e. Made a cash payment on a note payable for both interest and principal.

f. Issued a bond at face value.

g. Made an interest payment on a bond that had been issued at face value.

h. Issued a bond at a discount.

i. Made an interest payment on a bond that had been issued at a discount and amortized the discount.

Problem 10-35A *Sale of bonds at a premium and amortization using the effective interest rate method (Appendix)*

L.O. 5, 8

CHECK FIGURES

a. Selling price of bond: $321,071

c. 2007 Interest Expense: $22,475

On January 1, 2007, Keel Corp. sold $300,000 of its own 8 percent, 10-year bonds. Interest is payable annually on December 31. The bonds were sold to yield an effective interest rate of 7 percent. Keel Corp. uses the effective interest rate method.

Required

a. Using the information in the appendix, calculate the selling price of the bonds.

b. Prepare the journal entry for the issuance of the bonds.

c. Prepare the journal entry for the amortization of the bond premium and the payment of the interest on December 31, 2009.

d. Calculate the amount of interest expense for 2010.

EXERCISES—SERIES B

Exercise 10-1B *How credit terms affect financial statements*

L.O. 1

Marco Co. borrowed $40,000 from the National Bank by issuing a note with a five-year term. Marco has two options with respect to the payment of interest and principal. Option 1 requires the payment of interest only on an annual basis with the full amount of the principal due at maturity. Option 2 calls for an annual payment that includes interest due plus a partial repayment of the principal balance. The effective annual interest rate on both notes is identical.

Required

Write a memo explaining how the two alternatives will affect (*a*) the carrying value of liabilities, (*b*) the amount of annual interest expense, (*c*) the total amount of interest that will be paid over the life of the note, and (*d*) the cash flow consequences.

L.O. 1

Exercise 10-2B *Accounting for an installment note payable with annual payments that include interest and principal*

On January 1, 2006, Baco Co. borrowed $120,000 cash from Central Bank by issuing a five-year, 8 percent note. The principal and interest are to be paid by making annual payments in the amount of $30,055. Payments are to be made December 31 of each year, beginning December 31, 2006.

Required

Prepare an amortization schedule for the interest and principal payments for the five-year period.

L.O. 1

Exercise 10-3B *Long-term installment note payable*

Terek Amer started a business by issuing an $80,000 face value note to First State Bank on January 1, 2006. The note had a 10 percent annual rate of interest and a five-year term. Payments of $21,104 are to be made each December 31 for five years.

Required

a. What portion of the December 31, 2006, payment is applied to
  (1) Interest expense?
  (2) Principal?

b. What is the principal balance on January 1, 2007?

c. What portion of the December 31, 2007, payment is applied to
  (1) Interest expense?
  (2) Principal?

L.O. 1

Exercise 10-4B *Amortization of a long-term loan*

A partial amortization schedule for a 10-year note payable issued on January 1, 2006, is shown below:

Accounting Period	Principal Balance January 1	Cash Payment	Applied to Interest	Applied to Principal
2006	$200,000	$32,549	$20,000	$12,549
2007	187,451	32,549	18,745	13,804
2008	173,647	32,549	17,365	15,184

Required

a. Using a financial statements model like the one shown here, record the appropriate amounts for the following two events:
  (1) January 1, 2006, issue of the note payable.
  (2) December 31, 2006, payment on the note payable.

Event No.	Assets	=	Liab.	+	Equity	Rev.	−	Exp.	=	Net Inc.	Cash Flow
1											

b. If the company earned $100,000 cash revenue and paid $50,000 in cash expenses in addition to the interest in 2006, what is the amount of each of the following?
  (1) Net income for 2006.
  (2) Cash flow from operating activities for 2006.
  (3) Cash flow from financing activities for 2006.

c. What is the amount of interest expense on this loan for 2009?

L.O. 2

Exercise 10-5B *Accounting for a line of credit*

Vanheis Company has a line of credit with United Bank. Vanheis can borrow up to $200,000 at any time over the course of the 2007 calendar year. The following table shows the prime rate expressed as an annual percentage along with the amounts borrowed and repaid during the first three months of 2007. Vanheis agreed to pay interest at an annual rate equal to 2 percent above the bank's prime rate. Funds are borrowed or repaid on the first day of each month. Interest is payable in cash on the last day of the month. The interest rate is applied to the outstanding monthly balance. For example, Vanheis pays 6 percent (4 percent + 2 percent) annual interest on $80,000 for the month of February.

Month	Amount Borrowed or (Repaid)	Prime Rate for the Month, %
January	$50,000	3.0
February	30,000	4.0
March	(40,000)	4.5

Required

Provide all journal entries pertaining to Vanheis's line of credit for the first three months of 2007.

Exercise 10-6B *Effect of a line of credit on financial statements*

L.O. 2

Babb Co. uses an approved line of credit not to exceed $100,000 with the local bank to provide short-term financing for its business operations. Babb either borrows or repays funds on the first day of a month. Interest is payable monthly at the bank's prime interest rate plus 1.5 percent. The following table shows the amounts borrowed and repaid for 2007 along with the bank's prime interest rate.

Month	Amount Borrowed or (Repaid)	Prime rate for the month, %
January	0	4
February	$20,000	4
March	30,000	4.5
April	(10,000)	5
May	(25,000)	4
June	20,000	5
July–October	0	5
November	40,000	5.5
December	(50,000)	5.25

Required

a. Prepare all of the journal entries pertaining to the line of credit for 2007.

b. Show the effects of these transactions on the financial statements using a horizontal statements model like the one shown here. Use a + to indicate increase, a − for decrease, and NA for not affected. In the Cash Flow column, indicate whether the item is an operating activity (OA), investing activity (IA), or financing activity (FA).

Assets	=	Liabilities	+	Equity	Rev.	−	Exp.	=	Net Inc.	Cash Flow

c. What is the total amount of interest expense paid for 2007?

Exercise 10-7B *Annual versus semiannual interest payments*

L.O. 5

Colgan Company issued bonds with a face value of $10,000 on January 1, 2006. The bonds had an 8 percent stated rate of interest and a six-year term. The bonds were issued at face value. Interest is payable on an annual basis.

Required

Write a memo explaining whether the total cash outflow for interest would be more, less, or the same if the bonds pay semiannual versus annual interest.

L.O. 5, 6

Exercise 10-8B *Determining cash receipts from bond issues*

Required

Compute the cash proceeds from bond issues under the following terms. For each case, indicate whether the bonds sold at a premium or discount.

a. Petal Inc. issued $200,000 of 10-year, 8 percent bonds at 103.
b. Stem Inc. issued $80,000 of five-year, 12 percent bonds at 95½.
c. Rose Co. issued $100,000 of five-year, 6 percent bonds at 101¾.
d. Tulip Inc. issued $50,000 of four-year, 8 percent bonds at 98.

L.O. 6

Exercise 10-9B *Identifying the relationship between the stated rate of interest and the market rate of interest*

Required

Indicate whether a bond will sell at a premium (P), discount (D), or face value (F) for each of the following conditions:

a. ______ The market rate of interest is equal to the stated rate.
b. ______ The market rate of interest is less than the stated rate.
c. ______ The market rate of interest is higher than the stated rate.
d. ______ The stated rate of interest is higher than the market rate.
e. ______ The stated rate of interest is less than the market rate.

L.O. 6

Exercise 10-10B *Identifying bond premiums and discounts*

Required

In each of the following situations, state whether the bonds will sell at a premium or discount.

a. Stokes issued $200,000 of bonds with a stated interest rate of 8 percent. At the time of issue, the market rate of interest for similar investments was 7 percent.
b. Shaw issued $100,000 of bonds with a stated interest rate of 8 percent. At the time of issue, the market rate of interest for similar investments was 9 percent.
c. Link Inc. issued callable bonds with a stated interest rate of 8 percent. The bonds were callable at 104. At the date of issue, the market rate of interest was 9 percent for similar investments.

L.O. 6

Exercise 10-11B *Determining the amount of bond premiums and discounts*

Required

For each of the following situations, calculate the amount of bond discount or premium, if any.

a. Ball Co. issued $80,000 of 6 percent bonds at 102.
b. Link Inc. issued $50,000 of 10-year, 8 percent bonds at 98.
c. Hall Inc. issued $100,000 of 15-year, 9 percent bonds at 102¼.
d. Mink Co. issued $500,000 of 20-year, 8 percent bonds at 98¾.

L.O. 4, 5

Exercise 10-12B *Effect of a bond discount on financial statements: annual interest*

Landry Company issued $100,000 face value of bonds on January 1, 2007. The bonds had an 8 percent stated rate of interest and a five-year term. Interest is paid in cash annually, beginning December 31, 2007. The bonds were issued at 96.

Required

a. Use a financial statements model like the one shown below to demonstrate how (1) the January 1, 2007, bond issue and (2) the December 31, 2007, recognition of interest expense, including the amortization of the discount and the cash payment, affects the company's financial statements. Use + for increase, − for decrease, and NA for not affected.

Event No.	Assets	=	Liab.	+	Equity	Rev.	−	Exp.	=	Net Inc.	Cash Flow
1											

b. Determine the carrying value (face value less discount) of the bond liability as of December 31, 2007.

c. Determine the amount of interest expense reported on the 2007 income statement.

d. Determine the carrying value (face value less discount) of the bond liability as of December 31, 2008.

e. Determine the amount of interest expense reported on the 2008 income statement.

Exercise 10-13B *Effect of a bond premium on financial statements: annual interest*

L.O. 4, 5

Switzer Company issued $100,000 face value of bonds on January 1, 2007. The bonds had an 8 percent stated rate of interest and a five-year term. Interest is paid in cash annually, beginning December 31, 2007. The bonds were issued at 102.

Required

a. Use a financial statements model like the one shown below to demonstrate how (1) the January 1, 2007, bond issue and (2) the December 31, 2007, recognition of interest expense, including the amortization of the premium and the cash payment, affects the company's financial statements. Use + for increase, − for decrease, and NA for not affected.

Event No.	Assets	=	Liab.	+	Equity	Rev.	−	Exp.	=	Net Inc.	Cash Flow
1											

b. Determine the carrying value (face value plus premium) of the bond liability as of December 31, 2007.

c. Determine the amount of interest expense reported on the 2007 income statement.

d. Determine the carrying value of the bond liability as of December 31, 2008.

e. Determine the amount of interest expense reported on the 2008 income statement.

Exercise 10-14B *Effect of bonds issued at a premium on financial statements: semiannual interest*

L.O. 4, 5

Garden Supplies Inc. issued $200,000 of 10-year, 6 percent bonds on July 1, 2006, at 104. Interest is payable in cash semiannually on June 30 and December 31.

Required

a. Prepare the journal entries to record issuing the bonds and any necessary journal entries for 2006 and 2007. Post the journal entries to T-accounts.

b. Prepare the liabilities section of the balance sheet at the end of 2006 and 2007.

c. What amount of interest expense will Garden report on the financial statements for 2006 and 2007?

d. What amount of cash will Garden pay for interest in 2006 and 2007?

Exercise 10-15B *Recording bonds issued at face value and associated interest for two accounting cycles: annual interest*

L.O. 5

On January 1, 2006, Miller Corp. issued $100,000 of 10-year, 9 percent bonds at their face amount. Interest is payable on December 31 of each year with the first payment due December 31, 2006.

Required

Prepare all the general journal entries related to these bonds for 2006 and 2007.

Exercise 10-16B *Recording bonds issued at a discount: annual interest*

L.O. 5

On January 1, 2007, Creason Co. issued $100,000 of five-year, 8 percent bonds at 97½. Interest is payable annually on December 31. The discount is amortized using the straight-line method.

Required

Prepare the journal entries to record the bond transactions for 2007 and 2008.

L.O. 5

Exercise 10-17B *Recording bonds issued at a premium: semiannual interest*

On January 1, 2006, Vickers Company issued $200,000 of five-year, 12 percent bonds at 103. Interest is payable semiannually on June 30 and December 31. The premium is amortized using the straight-line method.

Required

Prepare the journal entries to record the bond transactions for 2006 and 2007.

L.O. 4, 5

Exercise 10-18B *Two complete accounting cycles: bonds issued at face value with annual interest*

Upton Company issued $1,000,000 of 10-year, 10 percent bonds on January 1, 2007. The bonds were issued at face value. Interest is payable in cash on December 31 of each year. Upton immediately invested the proceeds from the bond issue in land. The land was leased for an annual $140,000 of cash revenue, which was collected on December 31 of each year, beginning December 31, 2007.

Required

a. Prepare the journal entries for these events, and post them to T-accounts for 2007 and 2008.

b. Prepare the income statement, balance sheet, and statement of cash flows for 2007 and 2008.

L.O. 5

Exercise 10-19B *Recording callable bonds*

Han Co. issued $500,000 of 8 percent, 10-year, callable bonds on January 1, 2006, for their face value. The call premium was 4 percent (bonds are callable at 104). Interest was payable annually on December 31. The bonds were called on December 31, 2010.

Required

Prepare the journal entries to record the bond issue on January 1, 2006, and the bond redemption on December 31, 2010. Assume that all entries for accrual and payment of interest were recorded correctly.

L.O. 7

Exercise 10-20B *Determining the after-tax cost of debt*

The following 2006 information is available for three companies:

	Pace Co.	Pile Co.	Park Co.
Face value of bonds payable	$300,000	$600,000	$500,000
Interest rate	10%	9%	8%
Income tax rate	40%	30%	35%

Required

a. Determine the annual before-tax interest cost for each company *in dollars.*

b. Determine the annual after-tax interest cost for each company *in dollars.*

c. Determine the annual after-tax interest cost for each company *as a percentage* of the face value of the bonds.

L.O. 8

Exercise 10-21B *Future value and present value (Appendix)*

Required

Using Tables I, II, III, or IV in the appendix, calculate the following:

a. The future value of $10,000 invested at 6 percent for four years.

b. The future value of five annual payments of $2,000 at 10 percent interest.

c. The amount that must be deposited today (present value) at 9 percent to accumulate $200,000 in 10 years.

d. The annual payment on a five-year, 8 percent, $100,000 note payable.

Exercise 10-22B ***Computing the amount of payment (Appendix)*** **L.O. 8**

Required

a. Donna Kirk has just graduated from Ivory Tower University with a degree in theater. She wants to buy a new car but does not know if she can afford the payments. Since Kirk knows that you have had an accounting course, she asks you to compute the annual payment on a $30,000, 10 percent, five-year note. What would Kirk's annual payment be?

b. If Kirk can afford an annual payment of only $4,000, what price vehicle should she look for, assuming an interest rate of 10 percent and a five-year term?

Exercise 10-23B ***Saving for a future value (Appendix)*** **L.O. 8**

Mary and Mark Yuppy are celebrating the birth of their son, Marcus Andrew Yuppy IV. They want to send Little Andy to the best university and know they must begin saving for his education right away. They project that Little Andy's education will cost $500,000.

Required

a. How much must the Yuppys set aside annually to accumulate the necessary $500,000 in 18 years? Assume an 8 percent interest rate.

b. If the Yuppys wish to make a one-time investment currently for Little Andy's education, how much must they deposit today, assuming an 8 percent interest rate?

Exercise 10-24B ***Sale of bonds at a discount using present value (Appendix)*** **L.O. 6, 8**

Thompson Corporation issued $100,000 of 10 percent, 10-year bonds on January 1, 2006, for a price that reflected a 9 percent market rate of interest. Interest is payable annually on December 31.

Required

a. What was the selling price of the bonds?

b. Prepare the journal entry to record issuing the bonds.

c. Prepare the journal entry for the first interest payment on December 31, 2006, using the effective interest rate method.

Exercise 10-25B ***Effect of semiannual interest on investment returns (Appendix)*** **L.O. 6, 8**

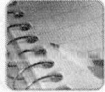

Required

Write a short memo explaining why an investor would find a bond that pays semiannual interest more attractive than one that pays annual interest.

PROBLEMS—SERIES B

Problem 10-26B ***Effect of an installment note payable on financial statements*** **L.O. 1**

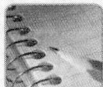

On January 1, 2007, Mixon Co. borrowed cash from Best Bank by issuing a $100,000 face value, four-year installment note that had a 10 percent annual interest rate. The note is to be repaid by making annual cash payments of $31,547 that include both interest and principal on December 31 of each year. Mixon used the proceeds from the loan to purchase land that generated rental revenues of $40,000 cash per year.

Required

a. Prepare an amortization schedule for the four-year period.

b. Prepare an income statement, balance sheet, and statement of cash flows for each of the four years. (*Hint:* Record the transactions for each year in T-accounts before preparing the financial statements.)

c. Given that revenue is the same for each period, explain why net income increases each year.

Problem 10-27B ***Accounting for an installment note payable*** **L.O. 1**

The following transactions apply to Luther Co. for 2008, its first year of operations.

1. Received $50,000 cash in exchange for issuance of common stock.
2. Secured a $150,000, eight-year installment loan from First Bank. The interest rate was 5 percent and annual payments are $22,569.
3. Purchased land for $40,000.
4. Provided services for $120,000 cash.
5. Paid other operating expenses of $84,000.
6. Paid the annual payment on the loan.

Required

a. Prepare the journal entries for 2008 and post to T-accounts.
b. Prepare an income statement and balance sheet for 2008.
c. What is the interest expense for 2009? 2010?

L.O. 2

Problem 10-28B *Accounting for a line of credit*

Beach Sports Equipment uses a line of credit to help finance its inventory purchases. Beach sells water sports equipment and uses the line of credit to build inventory for its peak sales months. Account balances at the beginning of 2009 were as follows:

Cash	$ 60,000
Inventory	80,000
Common Stock	40,000
Retained Earnings	100,000

Beach experienced the following transactions for January, February, and March, 2009.

1. January 1, 2009, obtained approval for a line of credit of up to $100,000. Funds are to be obtained or repaid on the first day of each month. The interest rate is the bank prime rate plus 1 percent.
2. January 1, 2009, borrowed $20,000 on the line of credit. The bank's prime interest rate is 5 percent for January.
3. January 15, purchased inventory on account, $80,000.
4. January 31, paid other operating expenses of $18,000.
5. In January, sold inventory for $95,000 on account. The inventory had cost $58,000.
6. January 31, paid the interest due on the line of credit.
7. February 1, borrowed $50,000 on the line of credit. The bank's prime rate is 6 percent for February.
8. February 1, paid the accounts payable from transaction 3.
9. February 10, collected $90,000 of the sales on account.
10. February 20, purchased inventory on account, $102,000.
11. February sales on account were $140,000. The inventory had cost $100,000.
12. February 28, paid the interest due on the line of credit.
13. March 1, repaid $20,000 on the line of credit. The bank's prime rate is 5.5 percent for March.
14. March 5, paid $80,000 of the accounts payable.
15. March 10, collected $130,000 from accounts receivable.
16. March 20, purchased inventory on account, $110,000.
17. March sales on account were $165,000. The inventory had cost $105,000.
18. March 31, paid the interest due on the line of credit.

Required

a. Prepare the journal entries for the above transactions and post them to T-accounts.
b. What is the amount of interest expense for January? February? March?
c. What amount of cash was paid for interest in January? February? March?

L.O. 2

Problem 10-29B *Effect of a line of credit on financial statements*

Libby Company has a line of credit with State Bank. Libby can borrow up to $200,000 at any time over the course of the 2006 calendar year. The following table shows the prime rate expressed as an annual percentage along with the amounts borrowed and repaid during 2006. Libby agreed to pay interest at an annual rate equal to 2 percent above the bank's prime rate. Funds are borrowed or repaid on the first day of each month. Interest is payable in cash on the last day of the month. The interest rate is applied to the outstanding monthly balance. For example, Libby pays 7 percent (5 percent + 2 percent) annual interest on $100,000 for the month of January.

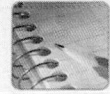

Month	Amount Borrowed or (Repaid)	Prime Rate for the Month, %
January	$100,000	5
February	50,000	6
March	(40,000)	7
April through October	No change	No change
November	(80,000)	6
December	(20,000)	5

Libby earned $30,000 of cash revenue during 2006.

Required

a. Prepare an income statement, balance sheet, and statement of cash flows for 2006. (*Note:* Round computations to the nearest dollar.)

b. Write a memo to explain how the business was able to generate retained earnings when the owner contributed no assets to the business.

Problem 10-30B *Accounting for a bond discount over multiple accounting cycles*

L.O. 4, 5

Box Company was started when it issued bonds with a $400,000 face value on January 1, 2005. The bonds were issued for cash at 96. They had a 20-year term to maturity and an 8 percent annual interest rate. Interest was payable on December 31 of each year. Box Company immediately purchased land with the proceeds (cash received) from the bond issue. Box leased the land for $50,000 cash per year. On January 1, 2008, the company sold the land for $400,000 cash. Immediately after the sale of the land, Box redeemed the bonds at 98. Assume that no other accounting events occurred during 2008.

Required

Prepare an income statement, statement of changes in equity, balance sheet, and statement of cash flows for the 2005, 2006, 2007, and 2008 accounting periods. Assume that the company closes its books on December 31 of each year. Prepare the statements using a vertical statements format. (*Hint:* Record each year's transactions in T-accounts prior to preparing the financial statements.)

Problem 10-31B *Recording and reporting bond discount over two cycles*

L.O. 4, 5, 6

During 2006 and 2007, Joy Corp. completed the following transactions relating to its bond issue. The corporation's fiscal year is the calendar year.

2006

Jan. 1 Issued $100,000 of 10-year, 10 percent bonds for $96,000. The annual cash payment for interest is due on December 31.

Dec. 31 Recognized interest expense, including the amortization of the discount, and made the cash payment for interest.

Dec. 31 Closed the interest expense account.

2007

Dec. 31 Recognized interest expense, including the amortization of the discount, and made the cash payment for interest.

Dec. 31 Closed the interest expense account.

Required

a. When the bonds were issued, was the market rate of interest more or less than the stated rate of interest? If Joy had sold the bonds at their face amount, what amount of cash would Joy have received?

b. Prepare the general journal entries for these transactions.

c. Prepare the liabilities section of the balance sheet at December 31, 2006 and 2007.

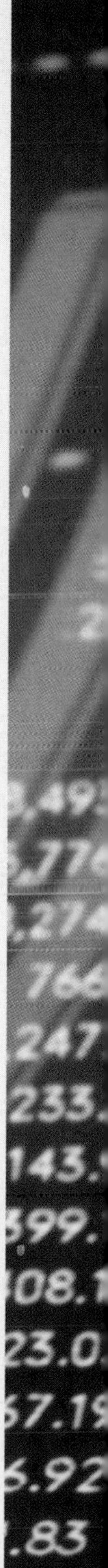

d. Determine the amount of interest expense that will be reported on the income statements for 2006 and 2007.

e. Determine the amount of interest that will be paid in cash to the bondholders in 2006 and 2007.

L.O. 4, 5

Problem 10-32B *Effect of a bond discount on the elements of financial statements*

Stafford Co. was formed when it acquired cash from the issue of common stock. The company then issued bonds at a discount on January 1, 2007. Interest is payable on December 31 with the first payment made December 31, 2007. On January 2, 2007, Stafford Co. purchased a piece of land that produced rent revenue annually. The rent is collected on December 31 of each year, beginning December 31, 2007. At the end of the six-year period (January 1, 2013), the land was sold at a gain, and the bonds were paid off at face value. A summary of the transactions for each year follows:

2007

1. Acquired cash from the issue of common stock.
2. Issued six-year bonds.
3. Purchased land.
4. Received land-lease income.
5. Recognized interest expense, including the amortization of the discount, and made the cash payment for interest on December 31.
6. Prepared December 31 entry to close Rent Revenue.
7. Prepared December 31 entry to close Interest Expense.

2008–2012

8. Received land-lease income.
9. Recognized interest expense, including the amortization of the discount, and made the cash payment for interest December 31.
10. Prepared December 31 entry to close Rent Revenue.
11. Prepared December 31 entry to close Interest Expense.

2013

12. Sold the land at a gain.
13. Retired the bonds at face value.

Required

Identify each of these 13 transactions as asset source (AS), asset use (AU), asset exchange (AE), or claims exchange (CE). Explain how each event affects assets, liabilities, equity, net income, and cash flow by placing a + for increase, − for decrease, or NA for not affected under each of the categories. In the Cash Flow column, indicate whether the item is an operating activity (OA), investing activity (IA), or financing activity (FA). The first event is recorded as an example.

Event No.	Type of Event	Assets	=	Liab.	+	Common Stock	+	Retained Earnings	Net Income	Cash Flow
1	AS	+		NA		+		NA	NA	+ FA

L.O. 4, 5

Problem 10-33B *Recording transactions for callable bonds*

IHL Corp. issued $300,000 of 20-year, 10 percent, callable bonds on January 1, 2008, with interest payable annually on December 31. The bonds were issued at their face amount. The bonds are callable at 105. The fiscal year of the corporation ends December 31.

Required

a. Show the effect of the following events on the financial statements by recording the appropriate amounts in a horizontal statements model like the following one. In the Cash Flow column, indicate whether the item is an operating activity (OA), investing activity (IA), or financing activity (FA). Use NA if an element was not affected by the event.

(1) Issued the bonds on January 1, 2008.

(2) Paid interest due to bondholders on December 31, 2008.

(3) On January 1, 2013, IHL Corp. called the bonds. Assume that all interim entries were correctly recorded.

Event No.	Assets	=	Liab.	+	Equity	Rev.	−	Exp.	=	Net Inc.	Cash Flow
1											

b. Prepare journal entries for the three events listed in Requirement *a*.

Problem 10-34B *Effect of debt transactions on financial statements*

L.O. 4, 5

The three typical accounting events associated with borrowing money through a bond issue are:

1. Exchanging the bonds for cash on the day of issue.
2. Making cash payments for interest expense and recording amortization when applicable.
3. Repaying the principal at maturity.

Required

a. Assuming the bonds are issued at face value, show the effect of each of the three events on the financial statements, using a horizontal statements model like the following one. Use + for increase, − for decrease, and NA for not affected.

Event No.	Assets	=	Liab.	+	Equity	Rev.	−	Exp.	=	Net Inc.	Cash Flow
1											

b. Repeat the requirements in Requirement *a,* but assume instead that the bonds are issued at a discount.

c. Repeat the requirements in Requirement *a,* but assume instead that the bonds are issued at a premium.

Problem 10-35B *Sale of bonds at a discount and amortization using the effective interest method (Appendix)*

L.O. 5, 8

On January 1, 2008, Pond Corp. sold $500,000 of its own 8 percent, 10-year bonds. Interest is payable annually on December 31. The bonds were sold to yield an effective interest rate of 9 percent. Pond uses the effective interest rate method.

Required

a. Using the information in the appendix, calculate the selling price of the bonds.

b. Prepare the journal entry for the issuance of the bonds.

c. Prepare the journal entry for the amortization of the bond discount and the payment of the interest at December 31, 2008.

d. Calculate the amount of interest expense for 2009.

ANALYZE, THINK, COMMUNICATE

ATC 10-1 Business Applications Case *Understanding real-world annual reports*

Required–Part 1

Use the **Topps Company**'s annual report in Appendix B to answer the following questions.

The Topps Company, Inc.

a. On its balance sheet Topps shows "Other liabilities" of $22,601,000. Does the company explain what these are? If so, what are they?

b. In the footnotes, Topps reveals that it entered into a credit agreement with two banks in 2000. What amount of credit is available to Topps under this agreement, and when does it expire?

c. What restrictions does the credit agreement place on Topps? Be specific.

Required—Part 2

Harley-Davidson, Inc.

Use the **Harley-Davidson**'s annual report that came with this book to answer the following questions.

a. As of December 31, 2003, Harley-Davidson has $994,305,000 of "finance debt." How much of this is current debt and how much is long-term debt (see the footnotes)?

b. Specifically, what types of borrowings are included in this $994,305,000 of finance debt?

c. What is the range of interest rates that Harley-Davidson has to pay on its finance debt?

ATC 10-2 Group Assignment *Missing information*

The following three companies issued the following bonds:

1. Lot Inc. issued $100,000 of 8 percent, five-year bonds at 102¼ on January 1, 2006. Interest is payable annually on December 31.

2. Max Inc. issued $100,000 of 8 percent, five-year bonds at 98 on January 1, 2006. Interest is payable annually on December 31.

3. Par Inc. issued $100,000 of 8 percent, five-year bonds at 104 on January 1, 2006. Interest is payable annually on December 31.

Required

a. Organize the class into three sections and divide each section into groups of three to five students. Assign each of the sections one of the companies.

Group Tasks

(1) Compute the following amounts for your company:

(a) Cash proceeds from the bond issue.

(b) Interest paid in 2006.

(c) Interest expense for 2006.

(2) Prepare the liabilities section of the balance sheet as of December 31, 2006.

Class Discussion

b. Have a representative of each section put the liabilities section for its company on the board.

c. Is the amount of interest expense different for the three companies? Why or why not?

d. Is the amount of interest paid different for each of the companies? Why or why not?

e. Is the amount of total liabilities different for each of the companies? Why or why not?

ATC 10-3 Real-World Case *Using accounting numbers to assess creditworthiness*

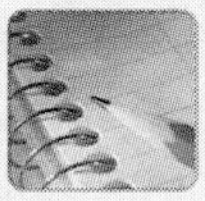

Standard & Poor's (S&P) and **Moody's** are two credit-rating services that evaluate the creditworthiness of various companies. Their grading systems are similar, but not exactly the same. S&P's grading scheme works as follows: AAA is the highest rating, followed by AA, then A, then BBB, and so on. For each grade, a "+" or "−" may also be used.

The following are selected financial data for four companies whose overall, long-term creditworthiness was rated by S&P. The companies, listed alphabetically, are:

Alliance Imaging, Inc., provides mobile imaging services to hospitals and other healthcare providers.

American Airlines, Inc., is one of the largest scheduled airlines in the United States.

3M Company develops, manufactures, and markets a wide variety of products for uses ranging from healthcare, to communications, to consumer products.

7-Eleven, Inc., operates, franchises or licenses over 24,000 convenience stores worldwide.

Dollar amounts are in thousands.

	Net Income	Cash Flow from Oper. Act.	Current Ratio	Debt to Assets Ratio	Times Interest Earned	Return on Assets Ratio
Alliance Imaging						
2002	$ 35,939	$ 138,960	1.78	1.06	2.3	5%
2001	10,530	96,364	1.42	1.12	1.3	2%

continued

	Net Income	Cash Flow from Oper. Act.	Current Ratio	Debt to Assets Ratio	Times Interest Earned	Return on Assets Ratio
American Airlines						
2002	(3,495,000)	(1,379,000)	0.68	.97	(7.3)	(13%)
2001	(1,562,000)	380,000	0.90	.82	(9.0)	(5%)
3M						
2002	1,974,000	2,992,000	1.36	.61	38.6	13%
2001	1,430,000	3,078,000	1.40	.58	18.6	10%
7-Eleven						
2002	12,777	496,747	0.81	.95	2.4	0%
2001	83,720	278,235	0.80	.95	3.6	3%

Each company received a different credit rating by S&P. The grades awarded, as of June 9, 2003, in descending order, were AA, BBB, B+, and CCC.

Required

Determine which grade was assigned to each company. Write a memorandum explaining the rationale for your decisions.

ATC 10-4 Business Applications Case *Using ratios to make comparisons*

The following accounting information pertains to On-Time Cleaners and Drive-Thru Laundry Inc. at the end of 2007.

	On-Time Cleaners	Drive-Thru Laundry
Current assets	$ 30,000	$ 30,000
Total assets	530,000	530,000
Current liabilities	38,000	52,000
Total liabilities	330,000	450,000
Stockholders' equity	200,000	80,000
Interest expense	30,000	41,000
Income tax expense	50,500	46,000
Net income	76,500	70,000

Required

a. Compute the following ratios for each company: debt to assets, current, and times interest earned (EBIT must be computed). Identify the company with the greater financial risk.

b. For each company, compute the return on equity and return on assets ratios. Use EBIT instead of net income to compute the return on assets ratio. Identify the company that is managing its assets more effectively. Identify the company that is producing the higher return from the stockholders' perspective. Explain how one company was able to produce a higher return on equity than the other.

ATC 10-5 Business Applications Case *Determining the effects of financing alternatives on ratios*

Fenn Research Associates has the following account balances:

Current Assets	$200,000	Current Liabilities	$125,000
Noncurrent Assets	500,000	Noncurrent Liabilities	300,000
		Stockholders' Equity	275,000

The company wishes to raise $100,000 in cash and is considering two financing options. Either it can sell $100,000 of bonds payable, or it can issue additional common stock for $100,000. To help in the decision process, Fenn's management wants to determine the effects of each alternative on its current ratio and debt to assets ratio.

Required

a. Help the company's management by completing the following chart:

Ratio	Currently	If Bonds Are Issued	If Stock Is Issued
Current ratio			
Debt to assets ratio			

b. Assume that after the funds are invested, EBIT amounts to $50,000. Also assume that the company pays $10,000 in dividends or $10,000 in interest, depending on which source of financing is used. Based on a 30 percent tax rate, determine the amount of the increase in retained earnings under each financing option.

ATC 10-6 Writing Assignment *Debt versus equity financing*

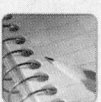

Mack Company plans to invest $50,000 in land that will produce annual rent revenue equal to 15 percent of the investment starting on January 1, 2007. The revenue will be collected in cash at the end of each year, starting December 31, 2007. Mack can obtain the cash necessary to purchase the land from two sources. Funds can be obtained by issuing $50,000 of 10 percent, five-year bonds at their face amount. Interest due on the bonds is payable on December 31 of each year with the first payment due on December 31, 2007. Alternatively, the $50,000 needed to invest in land can be obtained from equity financing. In this case, the stockholders (holders of the equity) will be paid a $5,000 annual distribution. Mack Company is in a 30 percent income tax bracket.

Required

a. Prepare an income statement and statement of cash flows for 2007 under the two alternative financing proposals.

b. Write a short memorandum explaining why one financing alternative provides more net income but less cash flow than the other.

ATC 10-7 Ethical Dilemma *Sometimes debt is not debt*

David Sheridan was a well-respected CPA in his mid-fifties. After spending 10 years at a national accounting firm, he was hired by Global, Inc., a multinational corporation headquartered in the United States. He patiently worked his way up to the top of Global's accounting department and in the early 1990's, took over as chief financial officer for the company. As the Internet began to explode, management at Global, Inc. decided to radically change the nature of its business to one of e-commerce. Two years after the transition, Internet commerce began to slow down, and Global was in dire need of cash in order to continue operations. Management turned to the accounting department.

Global, Inc. needed to borrow a substantial amount of money but couldn't afford to increase the amount of liabilities on the balance sheet for fear of the stock price dropping and banks becoming nervous and demanding repayment of existing loans. David discovered a way that would allow the company to raise the needed cash to continue operations without having to report the long-term notes payable on the balance sheet. Under an obscure rule, companies can set up separate legal organizations that do not have to be reported on the parent company's financial statements, if a third party contributes just 3 percent of the start-up capital. David called a friend, Brian Johnson, and asked him to participate in a business venture with Global. Brian agreed, and created a special purpose entity with Global named BrianCo. For his participation, Brian was awarded a substantial amount of valuable Global stock. Brian then went to a bank and used the stock as collateral to borrow a large sum of money for BrianCo. Then, Global sold some of its poor or underperforming assets to BrianCo for the cash that Brian borrowed. In the end, Global got rid of bad assets, received the proceeds of the long-term note payable, and did not have to show the liability on the balance sheet. Only the top executives and the accountants that worked closely with David knew of the scheme, and they planned to use this method only until the e-commerce portion of Global became profitable again.

Required

a. How did David's scheme affect the overall appearance of Global's financial statements? Why was this important to investors and creditors?

b. Review the AICPA's Articles of Professional conduct (see Chapter 1) and comment on any of the standards that have been violated.

c. Donald Cressey identified three common features of unethical and criminal conduct (see Chapter 1). Name these features and explain how they materialize in this case.

ATC 10-8 Research Assignment *Analyzing long-term debt at Union Pacific Railroad*

Many companies have a form of debt called *capital leases.* A capital lease is created when a company agrees to rent an asset, such as equipment or a building, for such a long time that GAAP treats the lease as if the asset were purchased using borrowed funds. A capital lease creates a liability for the company that acquired the leased asset because it has promised to make payments to another company for several years in the future. If a company has any capital leases, it must disclose them in the footnotes to the financial statements, and will sometimes disclose them in a separate account in the liabilities section of the balance sheet.

Using the most current Forms 10-K for Union Pacific Corporation, complete the requirements below. To obtain the 10-Ks use either the EDGAR system following the instructions in Appendix A, or the company's website.

Required

a. What was Union Pacific's debt to assets ratio? (You will need to compute total liabilities by subtracting "Common shareholders' equity" from total assets.)

b. How much interest expense did Union Pacific incur?

c. What amount of liabilities did Union Pacific have as a result of capital leases? Footnote 5 presents information about Union Pacific's leases.

d. What percentage of Union Pacific's long-term liabilities was the result of capital leases?

e. Many companies try to structure (design) leasing agreements so their leases will *not* be classified as capital leases. Explain why a company such as Union Pacific might want to avoid reporting capital leases.

COMPREHENSIVE PROBLEM

The trial balance of Pacilio Security Services Inc, as of January 1, 2010, had the following normal balances:

Cash	$122,475
Petty Cash	100
Accounts Receivable	27,400
Allowance for Doubtful Accounts	4,390
Supplies	165
Prepaid Rent	3,000
Merchandise Inventory (38 @ $290)	11,020
Equipment	9,000
Van	27,000
Accumulated Depreciation	23,050
Sales Tax Payable	290
Employee Income Tax Payable	500
FICA–Social Security Tax Payable	600
FICA–Medicare Tax Payable	150
Warranty Payable	312
Unemployment Tax Payable	630
Interest Payable	320
Notes Payable	12,000
Common Stock	50,000
Retained Earnings	107,918

During 2010 Pacilio Security Services experienced the following transactions:

1. Paid the sales tax payable from 2009.
2. Paid the balance of the payroll liabilities due for 2009 (federal income tax, FICA taxes, and unemployment taxes).
3. On January 1, 2010, purchased land and a building for $150,000. The building was appraised at $125,000 and the land at $25,000. Pacilio paid $50,000 cash and financed the balance. The balance was financed with a 10-year installment note. The note had an interest rate of 7 percent and annual payments of $14,238 due on the last day of the year.
4. On January 1, 2010, issued $50,000 of 6 percent, five year bonds. The bonds were issued at 98.
5. Purchase $660 of supplies on account.
6. Purchased 170 alarm systems at a cost of $300. Cash was paid for the purchase.
7. After numerous attempts to collect from customers, wrote off $2,450 of uncollectible accounts receivable.
8. Sold 160 alarm systems for $580 each plus sales tax of 5 percent. All sales were on account. (Be sure to compute cost of goods sold using the FIFO cost flow method.)
9. Billed $120,000 of monitoring services for the year. Credit card sales amounted to $36,000, and the credit card company charged a 4 percent fee. The remaining $84,000 were sales on account. Sales tax is not charged on this service.
10. Replenished the petty cash fund on June 30. The fund had $11 cash and receipts of $65 for yard mowing and $24 for office supplies expense.
11. Collected the amount due from the credit card company.
12. Paid the sales tax collected on $85,000 of the alarm sales.
13. Collected $167,000 of accounts receivable during the year.
14. Paid installers and other employees a total of $82,000 for salaries for the year. Assume the Social Security tax rate is 6 percent and the Medicare tax rate is 1.5 percent. Federal income taxes withheld amounted to $9,600. The net amount of salaries was paid in cash.
15. Paid $1,250 in warranty repairs during the year.
16. On September 1, paid the note and interest owed to State Bank.
17. Paid $18,000 of advertising expense during the year.
18. Paid $5,600 of utilities expense for the year.
19. Paid the payroll liabilities, both the amounts withheld from the salaries plus the employer share of Social Security tax and Medicare tax, on $75,000 of the salaries plus $8,600 of the federal income tax that was withheld. (Disregard unemployment taxes in this entry.)
20. Paid the accounts payable.
21. Paid bond interest and amortized the discount.
22. Paid the annual installment on the amortized note.
23. Paid a dividend of $10,000 to the shareholders.

Adjustments

24. There was $210 of supplies on hand at the end of the year.

25. Recognized the expired rent for the office building for the year.

26. Recognized the uncollectible accounts expense for the year using the allowance method. Pacilio now estimates that 1.5 percent of sales on account will not be collected.

27. Recognized depreciation expense on the equipment, van, and building. The equipment has a five-year life and a $2,000 salvage value. The van has a four-year life and a $6,000 salvage value. The building has a 40-year life and a $10,000 salvage value. The company uses double-declining-balance for the van and straight-line for the equipment and the building. The equipment and van were purchased in 2008 and a full year of depreciation was taken for both in 2008.

28. The alarms systems sold in transaction 8 were covered with a one-year warranty. Pacilio estimated that the warranty cost would be 2 percent of alarm sales.

29. The unemployment tax on the three employees has not been paid. Record the accrued unemployment tax on the salaries for the year. The unemployment tax rate is 4.5 percent and gross wages for all employees exceeded $7,000.

30. Recognized the employer Social Security and Medicare payroll tax that has not been paid on $7,000 of salaries expense.

Required

a. Record the above transactions in general journal form. Round all amounts to nearest whole dollar.

b. Post the transactions to the T-accounts.

c. Prepare a trial balance.

d. Prepare an income statement, statement of changes in stockholders' equity, a classified balance sheet, and statement of cash flows.

e. Close the temporary accounts to retained earnings.

f. Post the closing entries to the T-accounts and prepare an after-closing trial balance.

CHAPTER 11

Proprietorships, Partnerships, and Corporations

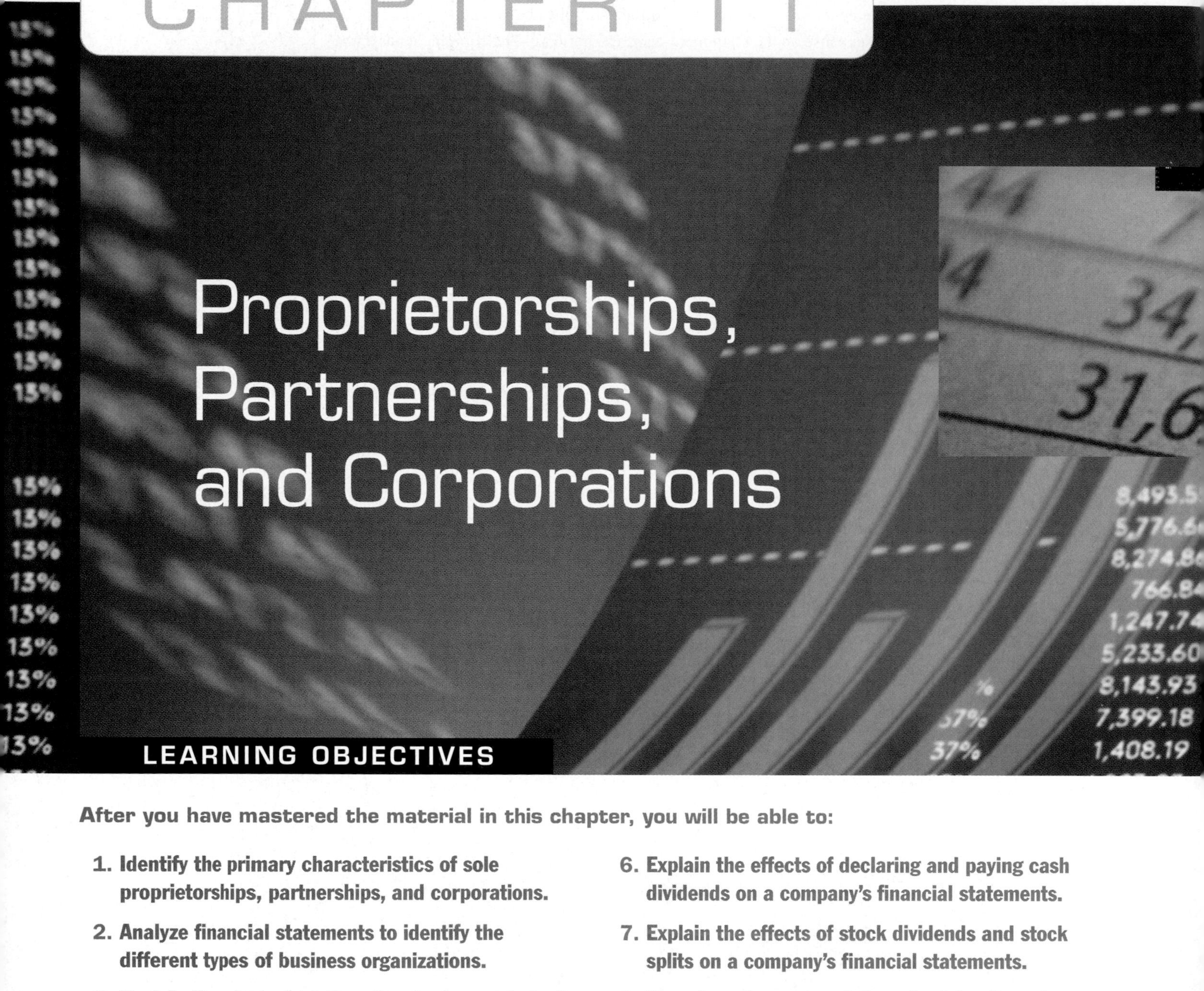

LEARNING OBJECTIVES

After you have mastered the material in this chapter, you will be able to:

1. **Identify the primary characteristics of sole proprietorships, partnerships, and corporations.**
2. **Analyze financial statements to identify the different types of business organizations.**
3. **Explain the characteristics of major types of stock issued by corporations.**
4. **Explain how to account for different types of stock issued by corporations.**
5. **Show how treasury stock transactions affect a company's financial statements.**
6. **Explain the effects of declaring and paying cash dividends on a company's financial statements.**
7. **Explain the effects of stock dividends and stock splits on a company's financial statements.**
8. **Show how the appropriation of retained earnings affects financial statements.**
9. **Explain some uses of accounting information in making stock investment decisions.**
10. **Explain accounting for not-for-profit entities and governmental organizations. (Appendix)**

Chapter 11

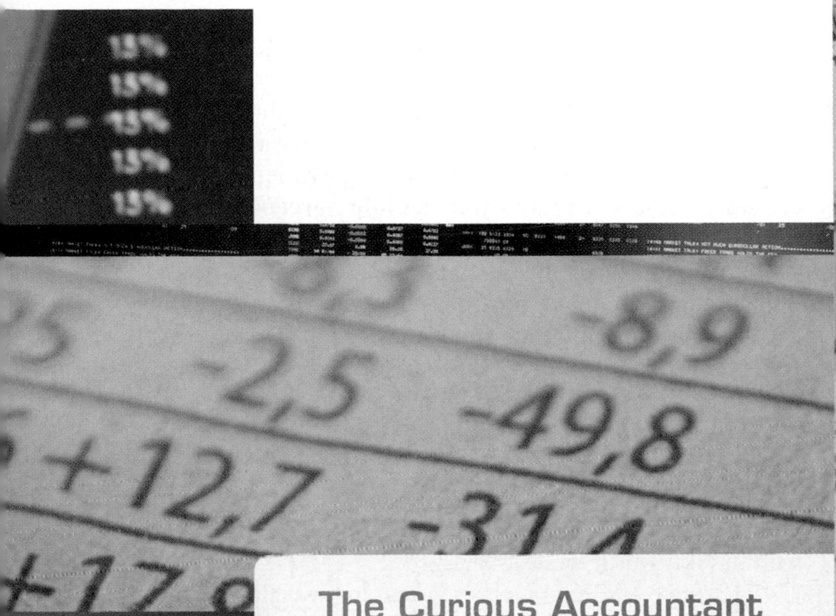

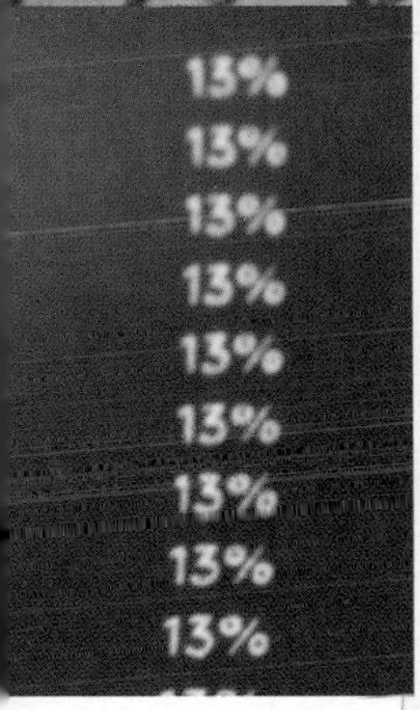

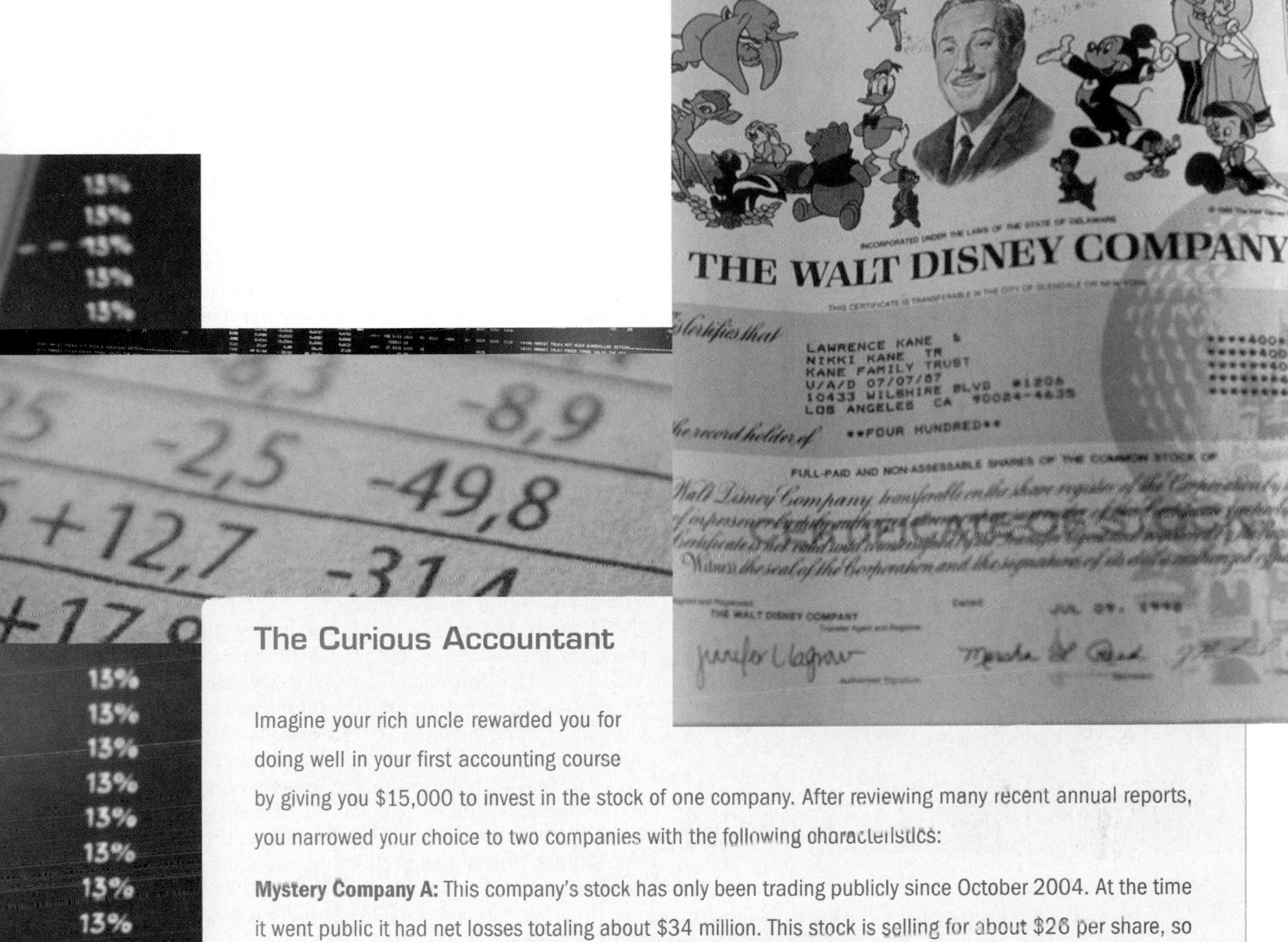

The Curious Accountant

Imagine your rich uncle rewarded you for doing well in your first accounting course by giving you $15,000 to invest in the stock of one company. After reviewing many recent annual reports, you narrowed your choice to two companies with the following characteristics:

Mystery Company A: This company's stock has only been trading publicly since October 2004. At the time it went public it had net losses totaling about $34 million. This stock is selling for about $26 per share, so you can buy about 577 shares. A friend told you it was a "sure winner," especially at its current price, since it is just starting out and has a lot of growth potential.

Mystery Company B: This company has been in existence since 1923 and has made a profit most years. In the most recent five years, its net earnings totaled over $6 *billion,* and it paid dividends of over $2.1 *billion.* This stock is selling for about $28 per share, so you can buy 535 shares of it. Your friend said "you would have to be goofy to buy this stock."

The names of the real-world companies described above are disclosed later. Based on the information provided, which company's stock would you buy? (Answer on page 558.)

CHAPTER OPENING

You want to start a business. How should you structure it? Should it be a sole proprietorship, partnership, or corporation? Each form of business structure presents advantages and disadvantages. For example, a sole proprietorship allows maximum independence and control while partnerships and corporations allow individuals to pool resources and talents with other people. This chapter discusses these and other features of the three primary forms of business structure. ■

Forms of Business Organizations

LO 1

Identify the primary characteristics of sole proprietorships, partnerships, and corporations.

Topic Tackler PLUS

11-1

Sole proprietorships are owned by a single individual who is responsible for making business and profit distribution decisions. If you want to be the absolute master of your destiny, you should organize your business as a proprietorship. Establishing a sole proprietorship is usually as simple as obtaining a business license from local government authorities. Usually no legal ownership agreement is required.

Partnerships allow persons to share their talents, capital, and the risks and rewards of business ownership. Since two or more individuals share ownership, partnerships require clear agreements about how authority, risks, and profits will be shared. Prudent partners minimize misunderstandings by hiring attorneys to prepare a **partnership agreement** which defines the responsibilities of each partner and describes how income or losses will be divided. Since the measurement of income affects the distribution of profits, partnerships frequently hire accountants to ensure that records are maintained in accordance with generally accepted accounting principles (GAAP). Partnerships (and sole proprietorships) also may need professional advice to deal with tax issues.

A **corporation** is a separate legal entity created by the authority of a state government. The paperwork to start a corporation is complex. For most laypersons, engaging professional attorneys and accountants to assist with the paperwork is well worth the fees charged.

Each state has separate laws governing establishing corporations. Many states follow the standard provisions of the Model Business Corporation Act. All states require the initial application to provide **articles of incorporation** which normally include the following information: (1) the corporation's name and proposed date of incorporation; (2) the purpose of the corporation; (3) the location of the business and its expected life (which can be *perpetuity,* meaning *endless*); (4) provisions for capital stock; and (5) the names and addresses of the members of the first board of directors, the individuals with the ultimate authority for operating the business. If the articles are in order, the state establishes the legal existence of the corporation by issuing a charter of incorporation. The charter and the articles are public documents.

Advantages and Disadvantages of Different Forms of Business Organization

LO 1

Identify the primary characteristics of sole proprietorships, partnerships, and corporations.

Each form of business organization presents a different combination of advantages and disadvantages. Persons wanting to start a business or invest in one should consider the characteristics of each type of business structure.

Regulation

Few laws specifically affect the operations of proprietorships and partnerships. Corporations, however, are usually heavily regulated. The extent of government regulation depends on the size and distribution of a company's ownership interests. Ownership interests in corporations are normally evidenced by **stock certificates.**

Ownership of corporations can be transferred from one individual to another through exchanging stock certificates. As long as the exchanges (buying and selling of shares of stock, often called *trading*) are limited to transactions between individuals, a company is defined as a **closely held corporation.** However, once a corporation reaches a certain size, it may list its stock on a stock exchange such as the New York Stock Exchange or the American Stock Exchange. Trading on a stock exchange is limited to the stockbrokers who are members of the exchange. These brokers represent buyers and sellers who are willing to pay the brokers commissions for exchanging stock certificates on their behalf. Although closely held corpo-

REALITY BYTES

Edward Nusbaum, CEO of **Grant Thornton**, a Chicago accounting firm, believes that "Sarbanes-Oxley is most likely creating the desired effect of making businesses realize that very strong responsibilities come with being a public company." However, a recent study conducted by Grant Thornton indicates that the cost of regulatory compliance is so significant that many smaller companies are taking their firms' stock off the exchanges. The study found that the number of public companies making the switch to private ownership is up 30 percent since the Sarbanes-Oxley Act went into effect July 30, 2002. A different study by Thomson Financial found similar results. The Thomson study found 60 public companies went private in the first nine months of 2003, up from 49 during the same period in 2002 and nearly double the 32 firms that went private in 2001. Clearly, the expense of regulatory compliance is a distinct disadvantage of the corporate form of business. In contrast, ease of formation and limited regulation are clear advantages of proprietorships and, to a lesser extent, partnerships.

rations are relatively free from government regulation, companies whose stock is publicly traded on the exchanges by brokers are subject to extensive regulation.

The extensive regulation of trading on stock exchanges began in the 1930s. The stock market crash of 1929 and the subsequent Great Depression led Congress to pass the **Securities Act of 1933** and the **Securities Exchange Act of 1934** to regulate issuing stock and to govern the exchanges. The 1934 act also created the Securities and Exchange Commission (SEC) to enforce the securities laws. Congress gave the SEC legal authority to establish accounting principles for corporations that are registered on the exchanges. However, the SEC has generally deferred its rule-making authority to private sector accounting bodies such as the Financial Accounting Standards Board (FASB), effectively allowing the accounting profession to regulate itself.

A number of high-profile business failures around the turn of the century raised questions about the effectiveness of self-regulation and the usefulness of audits to protect the public. The **Sarbanes-Oxley Act of 2002** was adopted to address these concerns. The act creates a five-member Public Company Accounting Oversight Board (PCAOB) with the authority to set and enforce auditing, attestation, quality control, and ethics standards for auditors of public companies. The PCAOB is empowered to impose disciplinary and remedial sanctions for violations of its rules, securities laws, and professional auditing and accounting standards. Public corporations operate in a complex regulatory environment that requires the services of attorneys and professional accountants.

Double Taxation

Corporations pay income taxes on their earnings and then owners pay income taxes on distributions (dividends) received from corporations. As a result, distributed corporate profits are taxed twice—first when income is reported on the corporation's income tax return and a second time when distributions are reported on individual owners' tax returns. This phenomenon is commonly called **double taxation** and is a significant disadvantage of the corporate form of business organization.

To illustrate, assume Glide Corporation earns pretax income of \$100,000. Glide is in a 30 percent tax bracket. The corporation itself will pay income tax of \$30,000 (\$100,000 × 0.30). If the corporation distributes the after-tax income of \$70,000 (\$100,000 − \$30,000) to individual

Answers to The Curious Accountant

Mystery Company A is **Shopping.com, Ltd.** (as of December 16, 2004), a company that offers a free, online, comparison shopping service. The origins of the company can be traced back to 1998. On October 25, 2004, Shopping.com's stock was sold to the public in an *initial public offering* (IPO) at $18. The first day its stock traded on NASDAQ it closed at $28.80. During its first month of trading its price ranged from a low of $22.92 per share to a high of $35.62 per share. Obviously, the people trading Shopping.com's stock were not paying much attention to its past profits. Instead, they were focusing on the company's potential.

Mystery Company B is **Walt Disney Company, Inc.** (as of December 16, 2004). Of course, only the future will tell which company is the better investment.

stockholders in 15 percent tax brackets,[1] the $70,000 dividend will be reported on the individual tax returns, requiring tax payments of $10,500 ($70,000 × .15). Total income tax of $40,500 ($30,000 + $10,500) is due on $100,000 of earned income. In contrast, consider a proprietorship that is owned by an individual in a 30 percent tax bracket. If the proprietorship earns and distributes $100,000 profit, the total tax would be only $30,000 ($100,000 × .30).

Double taxation can be a burden for small companies. To reduce that burden, tax laws permit small closely held corporations to elect "S Corporation" status. S Corporations are taxed as proprietorships or partnerships. Also, many states have recently enacted laws permitting the formation of **limited liability companies (LLCs)** which offer many of the benefits of corporate ownership yet are in general taxed as partnerships. Since proprietorships and partnerships are not separate legal entities, company earnings are taxable to the owners rather than the company itself.

Limited Liability

Given the disadvantages of increased regulation and double taxation, why would anyone choose the corporate form of business structure over a partnership or proprietorship? A major reason is that the corporate form limits an investor's potential liability as an owner of a business venture. Because a corporation is legally separate from its owners, creditors cannot claim owners' personal assets as payment for the company's debts. Also, plaintiffs must sue the corporation, not its owners. The most that owners of a corporation can lose is the amount they have invested in the company (the value of the company's stock).

Unlike corporate stockholders, the owners of proprietorships and partnerships are *personally liable* for actions they take in the name of their companies. In fact, partners are responsible not only for their own actions but also for those taken by any other partner on behalf of the partnership. The benefit of **limited liability** is one of the most significant reasons the corporate form of business organization is so popular.

Continuity

Unlike partnerships or proprietorships, which terminate with the departure of their owners, a corporation's life continues when a shareholder dies or sells his or her stock. Because of **continuity** of existence, many corporations formed in the 1800s still thrive today.

Transferability of Ownership

The **transferability** of corporate ownership is easy. An investor simply buys or sells stock to acquire or give up an ownership interest in a corporation. Hundreds of millions of shares of stock are bought and sold on the major stock exchanges each day.

[1] As a result of the Jobs and Growth Tax Relief Reconciliation Act (JGTRRA) of 2003, dividends received in tax years after 2002 are taxed at a maximum rate of 15 percent for most taxpayers. Lower income individuals pay a 5 percent tax on dividends received on December 31, 2007, or earlier. This rate falls to zero in 2008. The provisions of JGTRRA are set to expire on December 31, 2008.

Transferring the ownership of proprietorships is much more difficult. To sell an ownership interest in a proprietorship, the proprietor must find someone willing to purchase the entire business. Since most proprietors also run their businesses, transferring ownership also requires transferring management responsibilities. Consider the difference in selling $1 million of **Exxon** stock versus selling a locally owned gas station. The stock could be sold on the New York Stock Exchange within minutes. In contrast, it could take years to find a buyer who is financially capable of and interested in owning and operating a gas station.

Transferring ownership in partnerships can also be difficult. As with proprietorships, ownership transfers may require a new partner to make a significant investment and accept management responsibilities in the business. Further, a new partner must accept and be accepted by the other partners. Personality conflicts and differences in management style can cause problems in transferring ownership interests in partnerships.

Management Structure

Partnerships and proprietorships are usually managed by their owners. Corporations, in contrast, have three tiers of management authority. The *owners* (**stockholders**) represent the highest level of organizational authority. The stockholders *elect* a **board of directors** to oversee company operations. The directors then *hire* professional executives to manage the company on a daily basis. Since large corporations can offer high salaries and challenging career opportunities, they can often attract superior managerial talent.

While the management structure used by corporations is generally effective, it sometimes complicates dismissing incompetent managers. The chief executive officer (CEO) is usually a member of the board of directors and is frequently influential in choosing other board members. The CEO is also in a position to reward loyal board members. As a result, board members may be reluctant to fire the CEO or other top executives even if the individuals are performing poorly. Corporations operating under such conditions are said to be experiencing **entrenched management.**

Ability to Raise Capital

Because corporations can have millions of owners (shareholders), they have the opportunity to raise huge amounts of capital. Few individuals have the financial means to build and operate a telecommunications network such as **AT&T** or a marketing distribution system such as **Wal-Mart**. However, by pooling the resources of millions of owners through public stock and bond offerings, corporations generate the billions of dollars of capital needed for such massive investments. In contrast, the capital resources of proprietorships and partnerships are limited to a relatively small number of private owners. Although proprietorships and partnerships can also obtain resources by borrowing, the amount creditors are willing to lend them is usually limited by the size of the owners' net worth.

Appearance of Capital Structure in Financial Statements

LO 2

Analyze financial statements to identify the different types of business organizations.

The ownership interest (equity) in a business is composed of two elements: (1) owner/investor contributions and (2) retained earnings. The way these two elements are reported in the financial statements differs for each type of business structure (proprietorship, partnership, or corporation).

Presentation of Equity in Proprietorships

Owner contributions and retained earnings are combined in a single Capital account on the balance sheets of proprietorships. To illustrate, assume that Worthington Sole Proprietorship was started on January 1, 2005, when it acquired a $5,000 capital contribution from its owner, Phil Worthington. During the first year of operation, the company generated $4,000 of cash revenues, incurred $2,500 of cash expenses, and distributed $1,000 cash to the owner. Exhibit 11.1 displays 2005 financial statements for Worthington's company. Note on the *capital statement* that distributions are called **withdrawals.** Verify that the $5,500 balance in the Capital account on the balance sheet includes the $5,000 owner contribution and the retained earnings of $500 ($1,500 net income − $1,000 withdrawal).

EXHIBIT 11.1

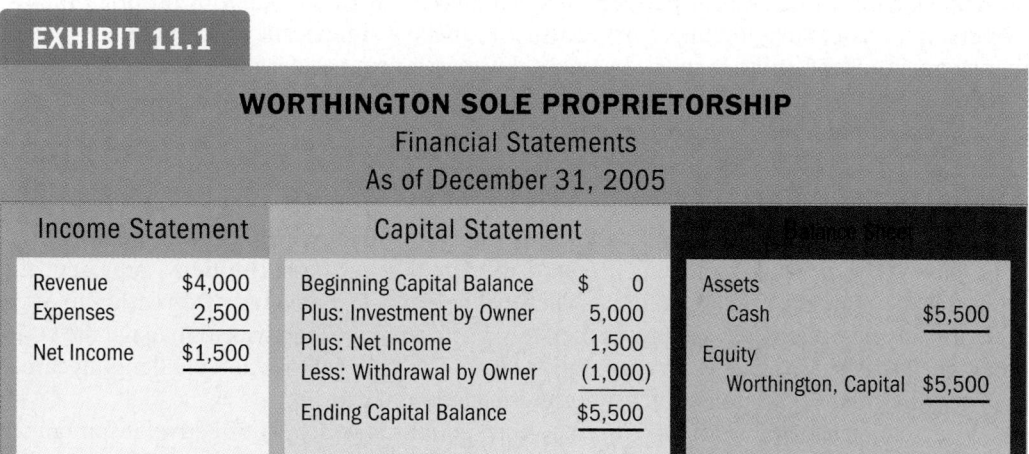

WORTHINGTON SOLE PROPRIETORSHIP
Financial Statements
As of December 31, 2005

Income Statement	
Revenue	$4,000
Expenses	2,500
Net Income	$1,500

Capital Statement	
Beginning Capital Balance	$ 0
Plus: Investment by Owner	5,000
Plus: Net Income	1,500
Less: Withdrawal by Owner	(1,000)
Ending Capital Balance	$5,500

Balance Sheet	
Assets	
Cash	$5,500
Equity	
Worthington, Capital	$5,500

CHECK YOURSELF 11.1

Weiss Company was started on January 1, 2004, when it acquired $50,000 cash from its owner(s). During 2004 the company earned $72,000 of net income. Explain how the equity section of Weiss's December 31, 2004, balance sheet would differ if the company were a proprietorship versus a corporation.

Answer

Proprietorship records combine capital acquisitions from the owner and earnings from operating the business in a single capital account. In contrast, *corporation* records separate capital acquisitions from the owners and earnings from operating the business. If Weiss were a proprietorship, the equity section of the year-end balance sheet would report a single capital component of $122,000. If Weiss were a corporation, the equity section would report two separate equity components, most likely common stock of $50,000 and retained earnings of $72,000.

Presentation of Equity in Partnerships

The financial statement format for reporting partnership equity is similar to that used for proprietorships. Contributed capital and retained earnings are combined. However, a separate capital account is maintained for each partner in the business to reflect each partner's ownership interest.

To illustrate, assume that Sara Slater and Jill Johnson formed a partnership on January 1, 2006. The partnership acquired $2,000 of capital from Slater and $4,000 from Johnson. The partnership agreement called for each partner to receive an annual distribution equal to 10 percent of her capital contribution. Any further earnings were to be retained in the business and divided equally between the partners. During 2006, the company earned $5,000 of cash revenue and incurred $3,000 of cash expenses, for net income of $2,000 ($5,000 − $3,000). As specified by the partnership agreement, Slater received a $200 ($2,000 × 0.10) cash withdrawal and Johnson received $400 ($4,000 × 0.10). The remaining $1,400 ($2,000 − $200 − $400) of income was retained in the business and divided equally, adding $700 to each partner's capital account.

Exhibit 11.2 displays financial statements for the Slater and Johnson partnership. Again, note that distributions are called *withdrawals*. Also find on the balance sheet a *separate cap-*

EXHIBIT 11.2

SLATER AND JOHNSON PARTNERSHIP
Financial Statements
As of December 31, 2006

Income Statement

Revenue	$5,000
Expenses	3,000
Net Income	$2,000

Capital Statement

Beginning Capital Balance	$ 0
Plus: Investment by Owners	6,000
Plus: Net Income	2,000
Less: Withdrawal by Owners	(600)
Ending Capital Balance	$7,400

Balance Sheet

Assets	
Cash	$7,400
Equity	
Slater, Capital	$2,700
Johnson, Capital	4,700
Total Capital	$7,400

ital account for each partner. Each capital account includes the amount of the partner's contributed capital plus her proportionate share of the retained earnings.

Topic Tackler PLUS 11-2

Presentation of Equity in Corporations

Corporations have more complex capital structures than proprietorships and partnerships. Explanations of some of the more common features of corporate capital structures and transactions follow.

Characteristics of Capital Stock

LO 3 Explain the characteristics of major types of stock issued by corporations

Stock issued by corporations may have a variety of different characteristics. For example, a company may issue different classes of stock that grant owners different rights and privileges. Also, the number of shares a corporation can legally issue may differ from the number it actually has issued. Further, a corporation can even buy back its own stock. Finally, a corporation may assign different values to the stock it issues. Accounting for corporate equity transactions is discussed in the next section of the text.

Par Value

Many states require assigning a **par value** to stock. Historically, par value represented the maximum liability of the investors. Par value multiplied by the number of shares of stock issued represents the minimum amount of assets that must be retained in the company as protection for creditors. This amount is known as **legal capital.** To ensure that the amount of legal capital is maintained in a corporation, many states require that purchasers pay at least the par value for a share of stock initially purchased from a corporation. To minimize the amount of assets that owners must maintain in the business, many corporations issue stock with very low par values, often $1 or less. Therefore, *legal capital* as defined by par value has come to have very little relevance to investors or creditors. As a result, many states allow corporations to issue no-par stock.

Stated Value

No-par stock may have a stated value. Like par value, **stated value** is an arbitrary amount assigned by the board of directors to the stock. It also has little relevance to investors and creditors. Stock with a par value and stock with a stated value are accounted for exactly the same way. When stock has no par or stated value, accounting for it is slightly different. These accounting differences are illustrated later in this chapter.

Other Valuation Terminology

The price an investor must pay to purchase a share of stock is the **market value.** The sales price of a share of stock may be more or less than the par value. Another term analysts frequently associate with stock is *book value.* **Book value per share** is calculated by dividing total stockholders' equity (assets − liabilities) by the number of shares of stock owned by investors. Book value per share differs from market value per share because equity is measured in historical dollars and market value reflects investors' estimates of a company's current value.

Stock: Authorized, Issued, and Outstanding

As part of the regulatory function, states approve the maximum number of shares of stock corporations are legally permitted to issue. This maximum number is called **authorized stock.** Authorized stock that has been sold to the public is called **issued stock.** When a corporation buys back some of its issued stock from the public, the repurchased stock is called **treasury stock.** Treasury stock is still considered to be issued stock, but it is no longer outstanding. **Outstanding stock** (total issued stock minus treasury stock) is stock owned by investors outside the corporation. For example, assume a company that is authorized to issue 150 shares of stock issues 100 shares to investors, and then buys back 20 shares of treasury stock. There are 150 shares authorized, 100 shares issued, and 80 shares outstanding.

Classes of Stock

The corporate charter defines the number of shares of stock authorized, the par value or stated value (if any), and the classes of stock that a corporation can issue. Most stock issued is either *common* or *preferred.*

FOCUS ON INTERNATIONAL ISSUES

WHO PROVIDES THE FINANCING?

The accounting rules in a country are affected by who provides financing to businesses in that country. Equity (versus debt) financing is a major source of financing for most businesses in the United States. The stock (equity ownership) of most large U.S. companies is said to be *widely held.* This means that many different institutional investors (e.g., pension funds) and individuals own stock. At the other extreme is a country in which the government owns most industries. In between might be a country in which large banks provide a major portion of business financing, such as Japan or Germany.

It is well beyond the scope of this course to explain specifically how a country's accounting principles are affected by who provides the financing for the country's major industries. Nevertheless, a businessperson should be aware that the source of a company's financing affects its financial reporting. Do not assume that business practices or accounting rules in other countries are like those in the United States.

Common Stock

All corporations issue **common stock.** Common stockholders bear the highest risk of losing their investment if a company is forced to liquidate. On the other hand, they reap the greatest rewards when a corporation prospers. Common stockholders generally enjoy several rights, including: (1) the right to buy and sell stock, (2) the right to share in the distribution of profits, (3) the right to share in the distribution of corporate assets in the case of liquidation, (4) the right to vote on significant matters that affect the corporate charter, and (5) the right to participate in the election of directors.

Preferred Stock

Many corporations issue **preferred stock** in addition to common stock. Holders of preferred stock receive certain privileges relative to holders of common stock. In exchange for special privileges in some areas, preferred stockholders give up rights in other areas. Preferred stockholders usually have no voting rights and the amount of their dividends is usually limited. Preferences granted to preferred stockholders include the following:

1. *Preference as to assets.* Preferred stock often has a liquidation value. In case of bankruptcy, preferred stockholders must be paid the liquidation value before any assets are distributed to common stockholders. However, preferred stockholder claims still fall behind creditor claims.
2. *Preference as to dividends.* Preferred shareholders are frequently guaranteed the right to receive dividends before common stockholders. The amount of the preferred dividend is normally stated on the stock certificate. It may be stated as a dollar value (say, $5) per share or as a percentage of the par value. Most preferred stock has **cumulative dividends,** meaning that if a corporation is unable to pay the preferred dividend in any year, the dividend is not lost but begins to accumulate. Cumulative dividends that have not been paid are called **dividends in arrears.** When a company pays dividends, any preferred stock arrearages must be paid before any other dividends are paid. Noncumulative preferred stock is not often issued because preferred stock is much less attractive if missed dividends do not accumulate.

To illustrate the effects of preferred dividends, consider Dillion, Incorporated, which has the following shares of stock outstanding:

Preferred stock, 4%, $10 par, 10,000 shares
Common stock, $10 par, 20,000 shares

Assume the preferred stock dividend has not been paid for two years. If Dillion pays $22,000 in dividends, how much will each class of stock receive? It depends on whether the preferred stock is cumulative.

Allocation of Distribution for Cumulative Preferred Stock		
	To Preferred	**To Common**
Dividends in arrears	$ 8,000	$ 0
Current year's dividends	4,000	10,000
Total distribution	$12,000	$10,000

Allocation of Distribution for Noncumulative Preferred Stock		
	To Preferred	**To Common**
Dividends in arrears	$ 0	$ 0
Current year's dividends	4,000	18,000
Total distribution	$ 4,000	$18,000

EXHIBIT 11.3

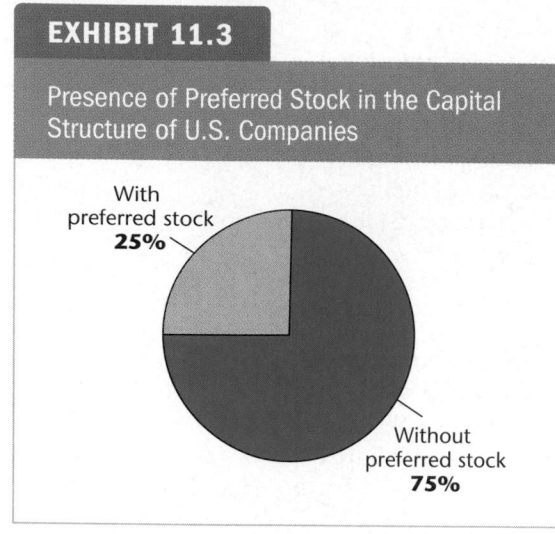

Presence of Preferred Stock in the Capital Structure of U.S. Companies

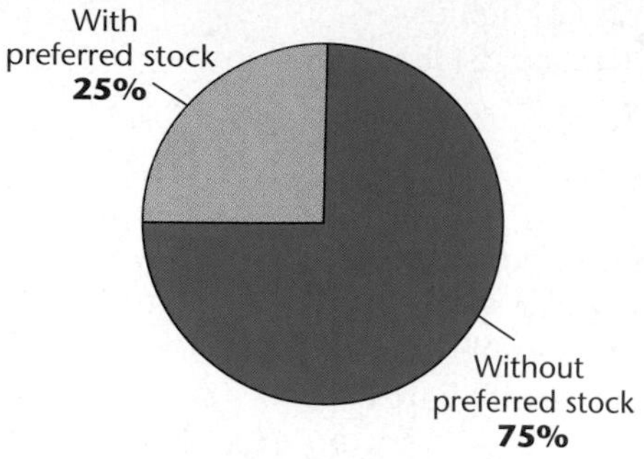

Data source: AICPA, *Accounting Trends and Techniques,* 2002.

The total annual dividend on the preferred stock is $4,000 (0.04 × $10 par × 10,000 shares). If the preferred stock is cumulative, the $8,000 in arrears must be paid first. Then $4,000 for the current year's dividend is paid next. The remaining $10,000 goes to common stockholders. If the preferred stock is noncumulative, the $8,000 of dividends from past periods is ignored. This year's $4,000 preferred dividend is paid first, with the remaining $18,000 going to common.

Other features of preferred stock may include the right to participate in distributions beyond the established amount of the preferred dividend, the right to convert preferred stock to common stock or to bonds, and the potential for having the preferred stock called (repurchased) by the corporation. Detailed discussion of these topics is left to more advanced courses. Exhibit 11.3 indicates that roughly 25 percent of U.S. companies have preferred shares outstanding.

Accounting for Stock Transactions on the Day of Issue

LO 4

Explain how to account for different types of stock issued by corporations.

Issuing stock with a par or stated value is accounted for differently from issuing no-par stock. For stock with either a par or stated value, the total amount acquired from the owners is divided between two separate equity accounts. The amount of the par or stated value is recorded in the stock account. Any amount received above the par or stated value is recorded in an account called **Paid-in Capital in Excess of Par** (or **Stated**) **Value.**

Issuing Par Value Stock

To illustrate the issue of common stock with a par value, assume that Nelson Incorporated is authorized to issue 250 shares of common stock. During 2005, Nelson issued 100 shares of $10 par common stock for $22 per share. The event increases assets and stockholders' equity by $2,200 ($22 × 100 shares). The increase in stockholders' equity is divided into two parts, $1,000 of par value ($10 per share × 100 shares) and $1,200 ($2,200 − $1,000) received in excess of par value. The income statement is not affected. The $2,200 cash inflow is reported in the financing activities section of the statement of cash flows. The effects on the financial statements and the journal entry to record the event follow:

Assets	=	Liab.	+	Equity			Rev.	−	Exp.	=	Net Inc.	Cash Flow
Cash	=			Com. Stk.	+	PIC in Excess						
2,200	=	NA	+	1,000	+	1,200	NA	−	NA	=	NA	2,200 FA

Account Title	Debit	Credit
Cash	2,200	
Common Stock, $10 Par Value		1,000
Paid-in Capital in Excess of Par Value—Common		1,200

The *legal capital* of the corporation is $1,000, the total par value of the issued common stock. The number of shares issued can be easily verified by dividing the total amount in the common stock account by the par value ($1,000 ÷ $10 = 100 shares).

Stock Classification

Assume Nelson Incorporated obtains authorization to issue 400 shares of Class B, $20 par value common stock. The company issues 150 shares of this stock at $25 per share. The event increases assets and stockholders' equity by $3,750 ($25 × 150 shares). The increase in stockholders' equity is divided into two parts, $3,000 of par value ($20 per share × 150 shares) and $750 ($3,750 − $3,000) received in excess of par value. The income statement is not affected. The $3,750 cash inflow is reported in the financing activities section of the statement of cash flows. The effects on the financial statements and the journal entry to record the event follow:

Assets	=	Liab.	+	Equity			Rev.	−	Exp.	=	Net Inc.	Cash Flow
Cash	=			Com. Stk.	+	PIC in Excess						
3,750	=	NA	+	3,000	+	750	NA	−	NA	=	NA	3,750 FA

Account Title	Debit	Credit
Cash	3,750	
Common Stock, Class B, $20 Par Value		3,000
Paid-In Capital in Excess of Par Value—Class B Common		750

As the preceding event suggests, companies can issue numerous classes of common stock. The specific rights and privileges for each class are described in the individual stock certificates.

Stock Issued at Stated Value

Assume Nelson is authorized to issue 300 shares of a third class of stock, 7 percent cumulative preferred stock with a stated value of $10 per share. Nelson issued 100 shares of the preferred stock at a price of $22 per share. The effect on the financial statements is identical to that described for the issue of the $10 par value common stock. The journal entry differs only to reflect the name of the different class of stock.

Assets	=	Liab.	+	Equity			Rev.	−	Exp.	=	Net Inc.	Cash Flow
Cash	=			Pfd. Stk.	+	PIC in Excess						
2,200	=	NA	+	1,000	+	1,200	NA	−	NA	=	NA	2,200 FA

Account Title	Debit	Credit
Cash	2,200	
Preferred Stock, $10 Stated Value, 7% cumulative		1,000
Paid-in Capital in Excess of Stated Value—Preferred		1,200

Stock Issued with No Par Value

Assume that Nelson Incorporated is authorized to issue 150 shares of a fourth class of stock. This stock is no-par common stock. Nelson issues 100 shares of this no-par stock at $22 per share. The entire amount received ($22 × 100 = $2,200) is recorded in the stock account. The effects on the financial statements and the journal entry to record the event follow:

Assets	=	Liab.	+	Equity			Rev.	−	Exp.	=	Net Inc.	Cash Flow
Cash	=			Com. Stk.	+	PIC in Excess						
2,200	=	NA	+	2,200	+	NA	NA	−	NA	=	NA	2,200 FA

Account Title	Debit	Credit
Cash	2,200	
Common Stock, No Par		2,200

Financial Statement Presentation

Exhibit 11.4 displays Nelson Incorporated's balance sheet after the four stock issuances described above. The exhibit assumes that Nelson earned and retained $5,000 of cash income during 2005. The stock accounts are presented first, followed by the paid-in capital in excess of par (or stated) value accounts. A wide variety of reporting formats is used in practice. For example, another popular format is to group accounts by stock class, with the paid-in capital in excess accounts listed with their associated stock accounts. Alternatively, many companies combine the different classes of stock into a single amount and provide the detailed information in footnotes to the financial statements.

EXHIBIT 11.4

NELSON, INCORPORATED
Balance Sheet
As of December 31, 2005

Assets	
Cash	$15,350
Stockholders' Equity	
Preferred Stock, $10 Stated Value, 7% cumulative, 300 shares authorized, 100 issued and outstanding	$ 1,000
Common Stock, $10 Par Value, 250 shares authorized, 100 issued and outstanding	1,000
Common Stock, Class B, $20 Par Value, 400 shares authorized, 150 issued and outstanding	3,000
Common Stock, No Par, 150 shares authorized, 100 issued and outstanding	2,200
Paid-in Capital in Excess of Stated Value—Preferred	1,200
Paid-in Capital in Excess of Par Value—Common	1,200
Paid-in Capital in Excess of Par Value—Class B Common	750
Total Paid-in Capital	10,350
Retained Earnings	5,000
Total Stockholders' Equity	$15,350

Stockholders' Equity Transactions after the Day of Issue

Treasury Stock

When a company buys its own stock, the stock purchased is called *treasury stock.* Why would a company buy its own stock? Common reasons include (1) to have stock available to give employees pursuant to stock option plans, (2) to accumulate stock in preparation for a merger or business combination, (3) to reduce the number of shares outstanding in order to increase earnings per share, (4) to keep the price of the stock high when it appears to be falling, and (5) to avoid a hostile takeover (removing shares from the open market reduces the opportunity for outsiders to obtain enough voting shares to gain control of the company).

LO 5

Show how treasury stock transactions affect a company's financial statements.

Conceptually, purchasing treasury stock is the reverse of issuing stock. When a business issues stock, the assets and equity of the business increase. When a business buys treasury stock, the assets and equity of the business decrease. To illustrate, return to the Nelson Incorporated example. Assume that in 2006 Nelson paid $20 per share to buy back 50 shares of the $10 par value common stock that it originally issued at $22 per share. The purchase of treasury stock is an asset use transaction. Assets and stockholders' equity decrease by the cost of the purchase ($20 × 50 shares = $1,000). The income statement is not affected. The cash outflow is reported in the financing activities section of the statement of cash flows. The effects on the financial statements and the journal entry to record the event follow:

Assets	=	Liab.	+	Equity			Rev.	−	Exp.	=	Net Inc.	Cash Flow
Cash	=			Other Equity Accts.	−	Treasury Stk.						
(1,000)	=	NA	+	NA	−	1,000	NA	−	NA	=	NA	(1,000) FA

Account Title	Debit	Credit
Treasury Stock	1,000	
Cash		1,000

The Treasury Stock account is a contra equity account. It is deducted from the other equity accounts in determining total stockholders' equity. In this example, the Treasury Stock account is debited for the full amount paid ($1,000). The original issue price and the par value of the stock have no effect on the entry. Recording the full amount paid in the treasury stock account is called the **cost method of accounting for treasury stock** transactions. Although other methods could be used, the cost method is the most common.

Assume Nelson reissues 30 shares of treasury stock at a price of $25 per share. As with any other stock issue, the sale of treasury stock is an asset source transaction. In this case, assets and stockholders' equity increase by $750 ($25 × 30 shares). The income statement is not affected. The cash inflow is reported in the financing activities section of the statement of cash flows. The effect of this event on the financial statements and the journal entry to record it follow:

Assets	=	Liab.	+	Equity					Rev.	−	Exp.	=	Net Inc.	Cash Flow
Cash	=			Other Equity Accounts	−	Treasury Stock	+	PIC from Treasury Stk.						
750	=	NA	+	NA	−	(600)	+	150	NA	−	NA	=	NA	750 FA

Account Title	Debit	Credit
Cash	750	
Treasury Stock		600
Paid-in Capital in Excess of Cost of Treasury Stock		150

The decrease in the Treasury Stock account increases stockholders' equity. The $150 difference between the cost of the treasury stock ($20 per share × 30 shares = $600) and the sales price ($750) is *not* reported as a gain. The sale of treasury stock is a capital acquisition, not a revenue transaction. The $150 is additional paid-in capital. *Corporations do not recognize gains or losses on the sale of treasury stock.*

After selling 30 shares of treasury stock, 20 shares remain in Nelson's possession. These shares cost $20 each, so the balance in the Treasury Stock account is now $400 ($20 × 20 shares). Treasury stock is reported on the balance sheet directly below retained earnings. Although this placement suggests that treasury stock reduces retained earnings, the reduction actually applies to the entire stockholders' equity section. Exhibit 11.5 shows the presentation of treasury stock in the balance sheet.

CHECK YOURSELF 11.2

On January 1, 2006, Janell Company's Common Stock account balance was $20,000. On April 1, 2006, Janell paid $12,000 cash to purchase some of its own stock. Janell resold this stock on October 1, 2006, for $14,500. What is the effect on the company's cash and stockholders' equity from both the April 1 purchase and the October 1 resale of the stock?

Answer

The April 1 purchase would reduce both cash and stockholders' equity by $12,000. The treasury stock transaction represents a return of invested capital to those owners who sold stock back to the company.

The sale of the treasury stock on October 1 would increase both cash and stockholders' equity by $14,500. The difference between the sales price of the treasury stock and its cost ($14,500 − $12,000) represents additional paid-in capital from treasury stock transactions. The stockholders' equity section of the balance sheet would include Common Stock, $20,000, and Additional Paid-in Capital from Treasury Stock Transactions, $2,500.

Cash Dividend

LO 6

Explain the effects of declaring and paying cash dividends on a company's financial statements.

Cash dividends are affected by three significant dates: *the declaration date, the date of record,* and *the payment date.* Assume that on October 15, 2006, the board of Nelson Incorporated declared the cash dividend on the 100 outstanding shares of its $10 stated value preferred stock. The dividend will be paid to stockholders of record as of November 15, 2006. The cash payment will be made on December 15, 2006.

Declaration Date

Although corporations are not required to declare dividends, they are legally obligated to pay dividends once they have been declared. They must recognize a liability on the **declaration date** (in this case, October 15, 2006). The increase in liabilities is accompanied by a decrease in retained earnings. The income statement and statement of cash flows are not affected. The effect on the financial statements of *declaring* the $70 (0.07 × $10 × 100 shares) dividend and the journal entry to record the declaration follow:

Assets	=	Liab.	+	Equity			Rev.	−	Exp.	=	Net Inc.	Cash Flow
Cash	=	Div. Pay.	+	Com. Stk.	+	Ret. Earn.						
NA	=	70	+	NA	+	(70)	NA	−	NA	=	NA	NA

Account Title	Debit	Credit
Dividends	70	
Dividends Payable		70

Date of Record

Cash dividends are paid to investors who owned the preferred stock on the **date of record** (in this case November 15, 2006). Any stock sold after the date of record but before the payment date (in this case December 15, 2006) is traded **ex-dividend,** meaning the buyer will not receive the upcoming dividend. The date of record is merely a cutoff date. It does not affect the financial statements.

Payment Date

Nelson actually paid the cash dividend on the **payment date.** This event has the same effect as paying any other liability. Assets (cash) and liabilities (dividends payable) both decrease. The income statement is not affected. The cash outflow is reported in the financing activities section of the statement of cash flows. The effect of the cash payment on the financial statements and the journal entry to record it follow:

Assets	=	Liab.	+	Equity			Rev.	−	Exp.	=	Net Inc.	Cash Flow
Cash	=	Div. Pay.	+	Com. Stk.	+	Ret. Earn.						
(70)	=	(70)	+	NA	+	NA	NA	−	NA	=	NA	(70) FA

Account Title	Debit	Credit
Dividends Payable	70	
Cash		70

Stock Dividend

LO 7

Explain the effects of stock dividends and stock splits on a company's financial statements.

Dividends are not always paid in cash. Companies sometimes choose to issue **stock dividends,** wherein they distribute additional shares of stock to the stockholders. To illustrate, assume that Nelson Incorporated decided to issue a 10 percent stock dividend on its class B, \$20 par value common stock. Since dividends apply to outstanding shares only, Nelson will issue 15 (150 outstanding shares × 0.10) additional shares of class B stock.

Assume the new shares are distributed when the market value of the stock is \$30 per share. As a result of the stock dividend, Nelson will transfer \$450 (\$30 × 15 new shares) from retained earnings to paid-in capital.[2] The stock dividend is an equity exchange transaction. The income statement and statement of cash flows are not affected. The effect of the stock dividend on the financial statements and the journal entry to record it follow:

Assets	=	Liab.	+	Equity					Rev.	−	Exp.	=	Net Inc.	Cash Flow
				Com. Stk.	+	PIC in Excess	+	Ret. Earn.						
NA	=	NA	+	300	+	150	+	(450)	NA	−	NA	=	NA	NA

Account Title	Debit	Credit
Retained Earnings	450	
Common Stock, Class B, \$20 Par Value		300
Paid-in Capital in Excess of Par Value—Class B Common		150

Stock dividends have no effect on assets. They merely increase the number of shares of stock outstanding. Since a greater number of shares represents the same ownership interest

[2] The accounting here applies to small stock dividends. Accounting for large stock dividends is explained in a more advanced course.

in the same amount of assets, the market value per share of a company's stock normally declines when a stock dividend is distributed. A lower market price makes the stock more affordable and may increase demand for the stock, which benefits both the company and its stockholders.

Stock Split

A corporation may also reduce the market price of its stock through a **stock split.** A stock split replaces existing shares with a greater number of new shares. Any par or stated value of the stock is proportionately reduced to reflect the new number of shares outstanding. For example, assume Nelson Incorporated declared a 2-for-1 stock split on the 165 outstanding shares (150 originally issued + 15 shares distributed in a stock dividend) of its $20 par value, class B common stock. Nelson notes in the accounting records that the 165 old $20 par shares are replaced with 330 new $10 par shares. Investors who owned the 165 shares of old common stock would now own 330 shares of the new common stock.

Stock splits have no effect on the dollar amounts of assets, liabilities, and stockholders' equity. They only affect the number of shares of stock outstanding. In Nelson's case, the ownership interest that was previously represented by 165 shares of stock is now represented by 330 shares. Since twice as many shares now represent the same ownership interest, the market value per share should be one-half as much as it was prior to the split. However, as with a stock dividend, the lower market price will probably stimulate demand for the stock. As a result, doubling the number of shares will likely reduce the market price to slightly more than one-half of the pre-split value. For example, if the stock were selling for $30 per share before the 2-for-1 split, it might sell for $15.50 after the split.

Appropriation of Retained Earnings

LO 8

Show how the appropriation of retained earnings affects financial statements.

The board of directors may restrict the amount of retained earnings available to distribute as dividends. The restriction may be required by credit agreements, or it may be discretionary. A retained earnings restriction, often called an *appropriation,* is an equity exchange event. It transfers a portion of existing retained earnings to **Appropriated Retained Earnings.** Total retained earnings remains unchanged. To illustrate, assume that Nelson appropriates $1,000 of retained earnings for future expansion. The income statement and the statement of cash flows are not affected. The effect on the financial statements of appropriating $1,000 of retained earnings and the journal entry to record it follow:

Assets	=	Liab.	+	Equity					Rev.	−	Exp.	=	Net Inc.	Cash Flow
				Com. Stk.	+	Ret. Earn.	+	App. Ret. Earn.						
NA	=	NA	+	NA	+	(1,000)	+	1,000	NA	−	NA	=	NA	NA

Account Title	Debit	Credit
Retained Earnings	1,000	
Appropriated Retained Earnings		1,000

Financial Statement Presentation

The 2005 and 2006 events for Nelson Incorporated are summarized below. Events 1 through 8 are cash transactions. The results of the 2005 transactions (nos. 1–5) are reflected in Exhibit 11.4. The results of the 2006 transactions (nos. 6–9) are shown in Exhibit 11.5.

1. Issued 100 shares of $10 par value common stock at a market price of $22 per share.

EXHIBIT 11.5

NELSON INCORPORATED
Balance Sheet
As of December 31, 2006

Assets		
Cash		$21,030
Stockholders' Equity		
Preferred Stock, $10 Stated Value, 7% cumulative, 300 shares authorized, 100 issued and outstanding	$1,000	
Common Stock, $10 Par Value, 250 shares authorized, 100 issued, and 80 outstanding	1,000	
Common Stock, Class B, $10 Par, 800 shares authorized, 330 issued and outstanding	3,300	
Common Stock, No Par, 150 shares authorized, 100 issued and outstanding	2,200	
Paid-in Capital in Excess of Stated Value—Preferred	1,200	
Paid-in Capital in Excess of Par Value—Common	1,200	
Paid-in Capital in Excess of Par Value—Class B Common	900	
Paid-in Capital in Excess of Cost of Treasury Stock	150	
Total Paid-in Capital		$10,950
Retained Earnings		
Appropriated	1,000	
Unappropriated	9,480	
Total Retained Earnings		10,480
Less: Treasury Stock, 20 shares @ $20 per share		(400)
Total Stockholders' Equity		$21,030

2. Issued 150 shares of class B, $20 par value common stock at a market price of $25 per share.
3. Issued 100 shares of $10 stated value, 7 percent cumulative preferred stock at a market price of $22 per share.
4. Issued 100 shares of no-par common stock at a market price of $22 per share.
5. Earned and retained $5,000 cash from operations.
6. Purchased 50 shares of $10 par value common stock as treasury stock at a market price of $20 per share.
7. Sold 30 shares of treasury stock at a market price of $25 per share.
8. Declared and paid a $70 cash dividend on the preferred stock.
9. Issued a 10 percent stock dividend on the 150 shares of outstanding class B, $20 par value common stock (15 additional shares). The additional shares were issued when the market price of the stock was $30 per share. There are 165 (150 + 15) class B common shares outstanding after the stock dividend.
10. Issued a 2-for-1 stock split on the 165 shares of class B, $20 par value common stock. After this transaction, there are 330 shares outstanding of the class B common stock with a $10 par value.
11. Appropriated $1,000 of retained earnings.

The illustration assumes that Nelson earned net income of $6,000 in 2006. The ending retained earnings balance is determined as follows: Beginning Balance $5,000 − $70 Cash Dividend − $450 Stock Dividend + $6,000 Net Income = $10,480.

THE FINANCIAL ANALYST

LO 9

Explain some uses of accounting information in making stock investment decisions.

Stockholders may benefit in two ways when a company generates earnings. The company may distribute the earnings directly to the stockholders in the form of dividends. Alternatively, the company may retain some or all of the earnings to finance growth and increase its potential for future earnings. If the company retains earnings, the market value of its stock should increase to reflect its greater earnings prospects. How can analysts use financial reporting to help assess the potential for dividend payments or growth in market value?

Receiving Dividends

Is a company likely to pay dividends in the future? The financial statements can help answer this question. They show if dividends were paid in the past. Companies with a history of paying dividends usually continue to pay dividends. Also, to pay dividends in the future, a company must have sufficient cash and retained earnings. These amounts are reported on the balance sheet and the statement of cash flows.

Increasing the Price of Stock

Is the market value (price) of a company's stock likely to increase? Increases in a company's stock price occur when investors believe the company's earnings will grow. Financial statements provide information that is useful in predicting the prospects for earnings growth. Here also, a company's earnings history is an indicator of its growth potential. However, because published financial statements report historical information, investors must recognize their limitations. Investors want to know about the future. Stock prices are therefore influenced more by forecasts than by history.

For example:

- On May 6, 2003, Cisco Systems, Inc., announced that its profits for the third quarter of the 2003 fiscal year were 35 percent higher than profits in the same quarter of 2002. In reaction to this news, the price of Cisco's stock *fell* 2.6 percent. Why? Because on the same day, Cisco announced that it believed revenue for the fourth quarter of 2003 would be flat compared to the third quarter, and analysts who follow the company were expecting revenues to grow slightly.
- On May 8, 2003, Comcast Corporation announced a first quarter *loss* of $297 million. This loss was over three times greater than its loss had been for the first quarter of the 2002 fiscal year. Yet the stock market's reaction to the news was to *increase* the price of Comcast's stock by 3 percent. In that same announcement the company reported strong revenue growth, which made investors more optimistic about Comcast's future.

In each case, investors reacted to the potential for earnings growth rather than the historical earnings reports. Because investors find forecasted statements more relevant to decision making than historical financial statements, most companies provide forecasts in addition to historical financial statements.

The value of a company's stock is also influenced by nonfinancial information that financial statements cannot provide. For example, suppose ExxonMobil announced in the middle of its fiscal year that it had just discovered substantial oil reserves on property to which it held drilling rights. Consider the following questions:

- What would happen to the price of ExxonMobil's stock on the day of the announcement?
- What would happen to ExxonMobil's financial statements on that day?

The price of ExxonMobil's stock would almost certainly increase as soon as the discovery was made public. However, nothing would happen to its financial statements on that day. There would probably be very little effect on its financial statements for that year. Only after the company began to develop the oil field and sell the oil would its financial statements reflect the discovery. Changes in financial statements tend to lag behind the announcements companies make regarding their earnings potential.

Stock prices are also affected by general economic conditions and consumer confidence as well as the performance measures reported in financial statements. For example, the stock prices of virtually all companies declined sharply immediately after the September 11, 2001, terrorist attacks on the World Trade Center and the Pentagon. Historically-based financial statements are of little benefit in predicting general economic conditions or changes in consumer confidence.

Price-earnings Ratio

The most commonly reported measure of a company's value is the price-earnings ratio, frequently called the P/E ratio. The P/E ratio is a company's market price per share of stock divided by the company's annual earnings per share (EPS). In general, high P/E ratios indicate that investors are optimistic about a company's earnings growth potential. For a more a detailed discussion of this important ratio refer back to the coverage in Chapter 2.

Exercising Control through Stock Ownership

The more influence an investor has over the operations of a company, the more the investor can benefit from owning stock in the company. For example, consider a power company that needs coal to produce electricity. The power company may purchase some common stock in a coal mining company to ensure a stable supply of coal. What percentage of the mining company's stock must the power company acquire to exercise significant influence over the mining company? The answer depends on how many investors own stock in the mining company and how the number of shares is distributed among the stockholders.

The greater its number of stockholders, the more *widely held* a company is. If stock ownership is concentrated in the hands of a few persons, a company is *closely held.* Widely held companies can generally be controlled with smaller percentages of ownership than closely held companies. Consider a company in which no existing investor owns more than 1 percent of the voting stock. A new investor who acquires a 5 percent interest would immediately become, by far, the largest shareholder and would likely be able to significantly influence board decisions. In contrast, consider a closely held company in which one current shareholder owns 51 percent of the company's stock. Even if another investor acquired the remaining 49 percent of the company, that investor could not control the company.

Financial statements contain some, but not all, of the information needed to help an investor determine ownership levels necessary to permit control. For example, the financial statements disclose the total number of shares of stock outstanding, but they normally contain little information about the number of shareholders and even less information about any relationships between shareholders. Relationships between shareholders are critically important because related shareholders, whether bound by family or business interests, might exercise control by voting as a block. For publicly traded companies, information about the number of shareholders and the identity of some large shareholders is disclosed in reports filed with the Securities and Exchange Commission.

<< A Look Back

Starting a business requires obtaining financing; it takes money to make money. Although some money may be borrowed, lenders are unlikely to make loans to businesses that lack some degree of owner financing. Equity financing is therefore critical to virtually all profit-oriented businesses. This chapter has examined some of the issues related to accounting for equity transactions.

The idea that a business must obtain financing from its owners was one of the first events presented in this textbook. This chapter discussed the advantages and disadvantages of organizing a business as a sole proprietorship versus a partnership versus a corporation. These advantages and disadvantages include the following:

1. *Double taxation*—Income of corporations is subject to double taxation, but that of proprietorships and partnerships is not.
2. *Regulation*—Corporations are subject to more regulation than are proprietorships and partnerships.
3. *Limited liability*—An investor's personal assets are not at risk as a result of owning corporate securities. The investor's liability is limited to the amount of the investment. In general proprietorships and partnerships do not offer limited liability. However, laws in some states permit the formation of limited liability companies which operate like proprietorships and partnerships yet place some limits on the personal liability of their owners.
4. *Continuity*—Proprietorships and partnerships dissolve when one of the owners leaves the business. Corporations are separate legal entities that continue to exist regardless of changes in ownership.
5. *Transferability*—Ownership interests in corporations are easier to transfer than those of proprietorships or partnerships.
6. *Management structure*—Corporations are more likely to have independent professional managers than are proprietorships or partnerships.
7. *Ability to raise capital*—Because they can be owned by millions of investors, corporations have the opportunity to raise more capital than proprietorships or partnerships.

Corporations issue different classes of common stock and preferred stock as evidence of ownership interests. In general, *common stock* provides the widest range of privileges including the right to vote and participate in earnings. *Preferred stockholders* usually give up the right to vote in exchange for preferences such as the right to receive dividends or assets upon liquidation before common stockholders. Stock may have a *par value* or *stated value,* which relates to legal requirements governing the amount of capital that must be maintained in the corporation. Corporations may also issue *no-par stock,* avoiding some of the legal requirements that pertain to par or stated value stock.

Stock that a company issues and then repurchases is called *treasury stock.* Purchasing treasury stock reduces total assets and stockholders' equity. Reselling treasury stock represents a capital acquisition. The difference between the reissue price and the cost of the treasury stock is recorded directly in the equity accounts. Treasury stock transactions do not result in gains or losses on the income statement.

Companies may issue *stock splits* or *stock dividends.* These transactions increase the number of shares of stock without changing the net assets of a company. The per share market value usually drops when a company issues stock splits or dividends.

>> A Look Forward

Chapter 12 examines the statement of cash flows in more detail than past chapters have. It introduces a more practical way to prepare the statement than analyzing every single entry in the cash account, and presents the more formal format for the statement of cash flows used by most real-world companies.

APPENDIX

Accounting for Not-for-Profit (NFP) Organizations

LO 10

Explain accounting for not-for-profit entities and governmental organizations.

To this point, our primary focus has been on profit-oriented business organizations. We turn now to a group of organizations classified as *not-for-profit (NFP) entities.* These NFP organizations are distinguished from profit-oriented businesses by three characteristics: (1) the receipt of significant resources from contributors not expecting repayment or economic returns, (2) the operation for purposes other than profit, and (3) the absence of defined ownership interests. Types of organizations that clearly fall within the scope of the NFP classification include museums, churches, clubs, professional associations, and foundations. Organizations that clearly fall outside the scope of the NFP classification include investor-owned enterprises and mutual organizations that provide dividends, lower costs, or other economic benefits directly and proportionately to their owners, members, or participants. The line of demarcation between business and NFP organizations can be vague. Consider a nonprofit school that finances the majority of its capital needs from the proceeds of debt and operating activities. Should this organization be classified as a business or an NFP organization? The ultimate decision is left to the judgment of the interested parties.

Fortunately, much of the information about accounting for business organizations that you have learned is applicable to NFP organizations as well. For example, the financial statements of both profit and NFP organizations contain assets, liabilities, revenues, expenses, gains, and losses. However, investments by owners and distributions to them are not appropriate for NFP entities. Also, the composition of net assets for business and NFP organizations differs. Business organizations subdivide net assets into owner contributions and retained earnings. In contrast, NFP entities subdivide net assets into three classes based on the degree of donor-imposed restrictions: (1) permanently restricted, (2) temporarily restricted, or (3) unrestricted. The double-entry recording system, including debits and credits, journal entries, ledgers, T-accounts, trial balances, and so on, applies to organizations operating in an NFP context. Also, like business organizations, NFP entities are governed by a set of generally accepted accounting principles (GAAP) established by the Financial Accounting Standards Board (FASB).

The NFP organizations issue three general-purpose external financial statements designed to help external users assess (1) the services an NFP organization provides, (2) the organization's ability to continue providing those services, and (3) the performance of the organization's management. The complete set of financial statements and accompanying notes includes a:

1. Statement of financial position as of the end of the period.
2. Statement of activities for the period.
3. Statement of cash flows for the period.

The **statement of financial position** reports on the organization's assets, liabilities, and net assets. This statement contains many common account titles, including Cash, Cash Equivalents, Accounts and Notes Receivable and Payable, Inventories, Marketable Securities, Long-Term Assets and Liabilities, Buildings, and Land. However, as indicated, the equity section of the statement of financial position is subdivided into three categories: *permanently restricted net assets, temporarily restricted net assets,* and *unrestricted net assets.*

The **statement of activities** reports on revenues, expenses, gains, and losses that increase or decrease net assets. Revenues and gains are increases in assets or decreases in liabilities generated by the organization's operating activities. Donor contributions are classified as revenues. Expenses and losses are decreases in assets or increases in liabilities incurred through operating activities. The statement is arranged in three sections: (1) changes in unrestricted net assets, (2) changes in temporarily restricted net assets, and (3) changes in permanently restricted net assets. The bottom-line figure is computed by adding the net change in net assets to the beginning balance in net assets to arrive at the ending net asset balance.

The **statement of cash flows** reports the cash consequences of the organization's operating, investing, and financing activities. Unrestricted and temporarily restricted donor contributions are included in the operating activities section of the statement of cash flows. Permanently restricted donor contributions are considered financing activities. Other items are treated in a manner similar to the treatment used by profit-oriented businesses.

To illustrate financial reporting for NFP entities, assume that a private nonprofit school, Palmer Primary School of Excellence, is established when it receives a $10 million cash contribution from

Dana Palmer, a wealthy benefactor who wants to promote excellence in early childhood education for minority students. A total of $1 million was designated as unrestricted funds; $2 million was temporarily restricted for the purchase of land and construction of buildings. The remaining $7 million was permanently restricted for an endowed investment fund that will produce investment income to be used to supplement school operations. Parents are required to pay the school for educational services on a scale based on their level of income. During 2001, the first year of operation, $1,200,000 cash was spent to acquire land and buildings. The $7 million of cash was invested in the endowed fund. The endowment generated investment income amounting to $700,000 cash. Operating revenues amounted to $100,000 cash. Cash operating expenses amounted to $950,000, not including $50,000 of depreciation expense. The results of these events are reported in the set of financial statements in Exhibit 11.6. Study these statements, noting the following differentiating features:

1. That which is classified as equity in business statements is called *net assets* in the NFP statement. The net assets are subdivided into three components, depending on the nature of the donor restrictions originally placed on the use of the resources.
2. The statement of activities is divided into three categories, including activities that affect unrestricted, temporarily restricted, and permanently restricted assets. Notice that unrestricted contributions are treated in a manner similar to the way revenue is treated in profit-oriented businesses. Finally, observe the reconciliation between the beginning and ending balances in net assets shown at the bottom of the statement.
3. With respect to the statement of cash flows, unrestricted and temporarily restricted donor contributions are classified as operating activities. Only permanently restricted donor contributions are classified as financing activities. In contrast, all contributed capital of profit-oriented businesses is classified as a financing activity.

Governmental Accounting

LO 10

Explain accounting for not-for-profit entities and governmental organizations.

Governmental entities have characteristics that require a unique accounting system in order to satisfy the needs of information users. These characteristics include (1) involuntary contributors of resources known as *taxpayers;* (2) monopoly supplier of goods and services; (3) resources heavily invested in nonrevenue-producing assets such as buildings, bridges, highways, schools, and military and police forces; and (4) management by elected representation. The primary users of governmental financial reports include citizens, researchers, media agents, special-interest groups, legislative and oversight bodies, and investors and creditors. The information contained in the financial reports is used to (1) compare actual results with budgeted estimates, (2) assess the entities' financial condition and operating results, (3) determine compliance with the laws and regulations, and (4) evaluate the effectiveness and efficiency of management.

The GAAP for governmental accounting is set forth by the Governmental Accounting Standards Board (GASB), a sister organization of the FASB. The presence of two separate standards-setting authorities can lead to confusion regarding which authoritative body has jurisdiction over certain types of organizations. For example, a hospital can be operated as a profit-oriented business enterprise, a private nonprofit entity, or a branch of a governmental entity. Often a single hospital possesses some mixture of the characteristics of the two or three forms of organization. Accordingly, the lines of distinction can be vague, and judgment may be required as to which GAAP applies.

The GASB has concluded that *the diversity of governmental activities and the need for legal compliance preclude the use of a single accounting entity approach* for governmental bodies. Instead, financial reporting is structured using distinct fiscal entities called *funds* or *account groups.* Governmental accounting is frequently called **fund accounting.** A **fund** is an independent accounting entity with a self-balancing set of accounts segregated for the purpose of carrying on specific activities. For example, a local governmental municipality may maintain separate funds for schools, police, and parks and recreation.

Because governmental entities are not subject to the constraints imposed by competition in the free markets, the GASB has taken a budgetary approach to accounting. Governmental entities frequently are required by law to establish budgets. When a governmental entity adopts a budget, GASB principles require that the budget be incorporated into the accounts, including the adoption of a report form that provides comparisons between budget and actual data in the financial statements. A formal budget is a critical component of accounting for government entities because it (1) provides an expression of public policy, (2) represents a statement of financial intent with

EXHIBIT 11.6

PALMER PRIMARY SCHOOL OF EXCELLENCE

Financial Statements

As of December 31, 2001

Statement of Activities

Changes in Unrestricted Net Assets	
Donor Contributions	$1,000,000
Released from Temp. Building Restriction	1,200,000
Investment Revenue	700,000
Tuition	100,000
Expenses for Educational Programs	(950,000)
Depreciation Expense	(50,000)
Net Change in Unrestricted Net Assets	2,000,000
Changes in Temporarily Restricted Net Assets	
Temp. Restricted Contributions for Buildings	2,000,000
Released from Temp. Building Restriction	(1,200,000)
Changes in Permanently Restricted Net Assets	
Donor Contributions	7,000,000
Increase in Net Assets	9,800,000
Net Assets at Beginning of Year	0
Net Assets at End of Year	$9,800,000

Statement of Financial Position

Assets	
Cash	$1,650,000
Endowed Investment Fund	7,000,000
Buildings and Land	1,200,000
Less: Accumulated Depreciation	(50,000)
Total Assets	$9,800,000
Net Assets	
Permanently Restricted	$7,000,000
Temporarily Restricted	800,000
Unrestricted	2,000,000
Total Net Assets	$9,800,000

Statement of Cash Flows

Operating Activities	
Temp. Restricted Donor Contributions	$2,000,000
Unrestricted Donor Contributions	1,000,000
Investment Revenue	700,000
Tuition	100,000
Operating Expenses	(950,000)
Net Inflow from Operating Activities	2,850,000
Investing Activities	
Endowed Investment Fund	(7,000,000)
Purchase Building and Land	(1,200,000)
Financing Activities	
Perm. Restricted Donor Contributions	7,000,000
Net Change in Cash	$1,650,000

regard to how funds raised through taxation will be spent, (3) acts as a legally enforceable instrument that limits spending by requiring financial managers to attain formally approved budgetary amendments prior to making expenditures that exceed the budgetary limits, (4) provides a standard to which actual results can be compared, thereby enabling the evaluation of performance, and (5) facilitates the planning process for the future needs of the governmental entity.

Governmental entities are required to issue a **comprehensive annual financial report (CAFR)** that covers all funds and account groups under their jurisdictions. The CAFR includes (1) the report of the independent auditor, (2) general-purpose financial statements, (3) combined statements organized by fund type when the primary entity has more than one fund of a given type, (4) individual fund statements when the primary governmental entity has only one fund of a given type, (5) schedules that provide detail sufficient to demonstrate compliance with specific regulations, and (6) appropriate statistical tables. Governmental reports are characterized by multiple columns that provide information on individual funds and account groups. No single summation is provided for the entity as a whole. Clearly, the appearance of financial statements prepared by governmental entities will differ significantly from that of those prepared by profit-oriented businesses.

The details of accounting for governmental entities are beyond the scope of this book, but the preceding discussion should improve your understanding of the need for flexibility in financial reporting. Always remember that accounting should provide information that is useful to current and potential resource providers, consumers, and monitors of a variety of organizational entities. To preserve its relevance, accounting must maintain an appropriate level of versatility in reporting practices so as to meet the needs of its users.

SELF-STUDY REVIEW PROBLEM

Edwards Inc. experienced the following events:

1. Issued common stock for cash.
2. Declared a cash dividend.
3. Issued noncumulative preferred stock for cash.
4. Appropriated retained earnings.
5. Distributed a stock dividend.
6. Paid cash to purchase treasury stock.
7. Distributed a 2-for-1 stock split.
8. Issued cumulative preferred stock for cash.
9. Paid a cash dividend that had previously been declared.
10. Sold treasury stock for cash at a higher amount than the cost of the treasury stock.

Required

Show the effect of each event on the elements of the financial statements using a horizontal statements model like the one shown here. Use + for increase, − for decrease, and NA for not affected. In the Cash Flow column, indicate whether the item is an operating activity (OA), investing activity (IA), or a financing activity (FA). The first transaction is entered as an example.

Event	Assets	=	Liab.	+	Equity	Rev.	−	Exp.	=	Net Inc.	Cash Flow
1	+		NA		+	NA		NA		NA	+ FA

Solution to Self-Study Review Problem

Event	Assets	=	Liab.	+	Equity	Rev.	−	Exp.	=	Net Inc.	Cash Flow
1	+		NA		+	NA		NA		NA	+ FA
2	NA		+		−	NA		NA		NA	NA
3	+		NA		+	NA		NA		NA	+ FA
4	NA		NA		−+	NA		NA		NA	NA
5	NA		NA		−+	NA		NA		NA	NA
6	−		NA		−	NA		NA		NA	− FA
7	NA		NA		NA	NA		NA		NA	NA
8	+		NA		+	NA		NA		NA	+ FA
9	−		−		NA	NA		NA		NA	− FA
10	+		NA		+	NA		NA		NA	+ FA

KEY TERMS

appropriated retained earnings 570
articles of incorporation 556
authorized stock 562
board of directors 559
book value per share 562
closely held corporation 556
common stock 563
comprehensive annual financial report (CAFR) 578
continuity 558
corporation 556
cost method of accounting for treasury stock 567
cumulative dividends 563
date of record 568
declaration date 568
dividends in arrears 563
double taxation 557
entrenched management 559
ex-dividend 569
fund 576
fund accounting 576
issued stock 562
legal capital 561
limited liability 558
limited liability companies (LLCs) 558
market value 562
outstanding stock 562
Paid-in Capital in Excess of Par Value 564
par value 561
partnerships 556
partnership agreement 556
payment date 569
preferred stock 563
Sarbanes-Oxley Act of 2002 557
Securities Act of 1933 and Securities Exchange Act of 1934 557
sole proprietorships 556
stated value 561
statement of activities 575
statement of cash flows 575
statement of financial position 575
stock certificates 556
stock dividends 569
stockholders 559
stock split 570
transferability 558
treasury stock 562
withdrawals 560

QUESTIONS

1. What are the three major forms of business organizations? Describe each.
2. How are sole proprietorships formed?
3. Discuss the purpose of a partnership agreement. Is such an agreement necessary for partnership formation?
4. What is meant by the phrase *separate legal entity?* To which type of business organization does it apply?
5. What is the purpose of the articles of incorporation? What information do they provide?
6. What is the function of the stock certificate?
7. What prompted Congress to pass the Securities Act of 1933 and the Securities Exchange Act of 1934? What is the purpose of these laws?
8. What are the advantages and disadvantages of the corporate form of business organization?
9. What is a limited liability company? Discuss its advantages and disadvantages.
10. How does the term *double taxation* apply to corporations? Give an example of double taxation.

11. What is the difference between contributed capital and retained earnings for a corporation?
12. What are the similarities and differences in the equity structure of a sole proprietorship, a partnership, and a corporation?
13. Why is it easier for a corporation to raise large amounts of capital than it is for a partnership?
14. What is the meaning of each of the following terms with respect to the corporate form of organization?
    (a) Legal capital
    (b) Par value of stock
    (c) Stated value of stock
    (d) Market value of stock
    (e) Book value of stock
    (f) Authorized shares of stock
    (g) Issued stock
    (h) Outstanding stock
    (i) Treasury stock
    (j) Common stock
    (k) Preferred stock
    (l) Dividends
15. What is the difference between cumulative preferred stock and noncumulative preferred stock?
16. What is no-par stock? How is it recorded in the accounting records?
17. Assume that Best Co. has issued and outstanding 1,000 shares of $100 par value, 10 percent, cumulative preferred stock. What is the dividend per share? If the preferred dividend is two years in arrears, what total amount of dividends must be paid before the common shareholders can receive any dividends?
18. If Best Co. issued 10,000 shares of $20 par value common stock for $30 per share, what amount is credited to the Common Stock account? What amount of cash is received?
19. What is the difference between par value stock and stated value stock?
20. Why might a company repurchase its own stock?
21. What effect does the purchase of treasury stock have on the equity of a company?
22. Assume that Day Company repurchased 1,000 of its own shares for $30 per share and sold the shares two weeks later for $35 per share. What is the amount of gain on the sale? How is it reported on the balance sheet? What type of account is treasury stock?
23. What is the importance of the declaration date, record date, and payment date in conjunction with corporate dividends?
24. What is the difference between a stock dividend and a stock split?
25. Why would a company choose to distribute a stock dividend instead of a cash dividend?
26. What is the primary reason that a company would declare a stock split?
27. If Best Co. had 10,000 shares of $20 par value common stock outstanding and declared a 5-for-1 stock split, how many shares would then be outstanding and what would be their par value after the split?
28. When a company appropriates retained earnings, does the company set aside cash for a specific use? Explain.
29. What is the largest source of financing for most U.S. businesses?
30. What is meant by *equity financing?* What is meant by *debt financing?*
31. What is a widely held corporation? What is a closely held corporation?
32. What are some reasons that a corporation might not pay dividends?

EXERCISES—SERIES A

All Exercises in Series A are available with McGraw-Hill's Homework Manager

L.O. 1, 2

Exercise 11-1A ***Effect of accounting events on the financial statements of a sole proprietorship***

A sole proprietorship was started on January 1, 2005, when it received $60,000 cash from Mark Pruitt, the owner. During 2005, the company earned $40,000 in cash revenues and paid $19,300 in cash expenses. Pruitt withdrew $5,000 cash from the business during 2005.

Required

Prepare an income statement, capital statement (statement of changes in equity), balance sheet, and statement of cash flows for Pruitt's 2005 fiscal year.

Exercise 11-2A *Effect of accounting events on the financial statements of a partnership* L.O. 1, 2

Justin Harris and Paul Berryhill started the HB partnership on January 1, 2006. The business acquired $56,000 cash from Harris and $84,000 from Berryhill. During 2006, the partnership earned $65,000 in cash revenues and paid $32,000 for cash expenses. Harris withdrew $2,000 cash from the business, and Berryhill withdrew $3,000 cash. The net income was allocated to the capital accounts of the two partners in proportion to the amounts of their original investments in the business.

Required

Prepare an income statement, capital statement, balance sheet, and statement of cash flows for the HB partnership for the 2006 fiscal year.

Exercise 11-3A *Effect of accounting events on the financial statements of a corporation* L.O. 1, 2

Morris Corporation was started with the issue of 5,000 shares of $10 par common stock for cash on January 1, 2007. The stock was issued at a market price of $18 per share. During 2007, the company earned $63,000 in cash revenues and paid $41,000 for cash expenses. Also a $4,000 cash dividend was paid to the stockholders.

Required

Prepare an income statement, statement of changes in stockholders' equity, balance sheet, and statement of cash flows for Morris Corporation's 2007 fiscal year.

Exercise 11-4A *Effect of issuing common stock on the balance sheet* L.O. 4

Newly formed Home Medical Corporation has 100,000 shares of $5 par common stock authorized. On March 1, 2006, Home Medical issued 10,000 shares of the stock for $12 per share. On May 2 the company issued an additional 20,000 shares for $20 per share. Home Medical was not affected by other events during 2006.

Required

a. Record the transactions in a horizontal statements model like the following one. In the Cash Flow column, indicate whether the item is an operating activity (OA), investing activity (IA), or financing activity (FA). Use NA to indicate that an element was not affected by the event.

Assets	=	Liab.	+	Equity			Rev. − Exp. = Net Inc.	Cash Flow
Cash	=			Com. Stk.	+	PIC in Excess		

b. Determine the amount Home Medical would report for common stock on the December 31, 2006, balance sheet.

c. Determine the amount Home Medical would report for paid-in capital in excess of par.

d. What is the total amount of capital contributed by the owners?

e. What amount of total assets would Home Medical report on the December 31, 2006, balance sheet?

f. Prepare journal entries to record the March 1 and May 2 transactions.

Exercise 11-5A *Recording and reporting common and preferred stock transactions* L.O. 4

Rainey Inc. was organized on June 5, 2007. It was authorized to issue 400,000 shares of $10 par common stock and 50,000 shares of 4 percent cumulative class A preferred stock. The class A stock had a stated value of $25 per share. The following stock transactions pertain to Rainey Inc.:

1. Issued 20,000 shares of common stock for $15 per share.
2. Issued 10,000 shares of the class A preferred stock for $30 per share.
3. Issued 50,000 shares of common stock for $18 per share.

Required

a. Prepare general journal entries for these transactions.

b. Prepare the stockholders' equity section of the balance sheet immediately after these transactions.

L.O. 4

Exercise 11-6A *Effect of no-par common and par preferred stock on the horizontal statements model*

Eaton Corporation issued 5,000 shares of no-par common stock for $20 per share. Eaton also issued 2,000 shares of $50 par, 6 percent noncumulative preferred stock at $60 per share.

Required

a. Record these events in a horizontal statements model like the following one. In the cash flow column, indicate whether the item is an operating activity (OA), investing activity (IA), or financing activity (FA). Use NA to indicate that an element was not affected by the event.

Assets	=	Equity					Rev. − Exp. = Net Inc.	Cash Flow
Cash	=	Pfd. Stk.	+	Com. Stk.	+	PIC in Excess		

b. Prepare journal entries to record these transactions.

L.O. 4

Exercise 11-7A *Issuing stock for assets other than cash*

Kaylee Corporation was formed when it issued shares of common stock to two of its shareholders. Kaylee issued 5,000 shares of $10 par common stock to K. Breslin in exchange for $60,000 cash (the issue price was $12 per share). Kaylee also issued 2,500 shares of stock to T. Lindsay in exchange for a one-year-old delivery van on the same day. Lindsay had originally paid $35,000 for the van.

Required

a. What was the market value of the delivery van on the date of the stock issue?

b. Show the effect of the two stock issues on Kaylee's books in a horizontal statements model like the following one. In the Cash Flow column, indicate whether the item is an operating activity (OA), investing activity (IA), or financing activity (FA). Use NA to indicate that an element was not affected by the event.

Assets			=	Equity			Rev. − Exp. = Net Inc.	Cash Flow
Cash	+	Van	=	Com. Stk.	+	PIC in Excess		

c. Prepare the journal entries to record these transactions.

L.O. 5

Exercise 11-8A *Treasury stock transactions*

Graves Corporation repurchased 2,000 shares of its own stock for $40 per share. The stock has a par of $10 per share. A month later Graves resold 1,200 shares of the treasury stock for $48 per share.

Required

a. Record the two events in general journal format.

b. What is the balance of the treasury stock account after these transactions?

L.O. 5

Exercise 11-9A *Recording and reporting treasury stock transactions*

The following information pertains to Smoot Corp. at January 1, 2006.

Common stock, $10 par, 10,000 shares authorized, 2,000 shares issued and outstanding	$20,000
Paid-in capital in excess of par, common stock	15,000
Retained earnings	65,000

Smoot Corp. completed the following transactions during 2006:

1. Issued 1,000 shares of $10 par common stock for $28 per share.
2. Repurchased 200 shares of its own common stock for $25 per share.
3. Resold 50 shares of treasury stock for $26 per share.

Required

a. How many shares of common stock were outstanding at the end of the period?
b. How many shares of common stock had been issued at the end of the period?
c. Prepare journal entries for these transactions and post them to T-accounts.
d. Prepare the stockholders' equity section of the balance sheet reflecting these transactions. Include the number of shares authorized, issued, and outstanding in the description of the common stock.

Exercise 11-10A ***Effect of cash dividends on financial statements*** L.O. 6

On October 1, 2005, Smart Corporation declared a $60,000 cash dividend to be paid on December 30 to shareholders of record on November 20.

Required

a. Record the events occurring on October 1, November 20, and December 30 in a horizontal statements model like the following one. In the Cash Flow column, indicate whether the item is an operating activity (OA), investing activity (IA), or financing activity (FA).

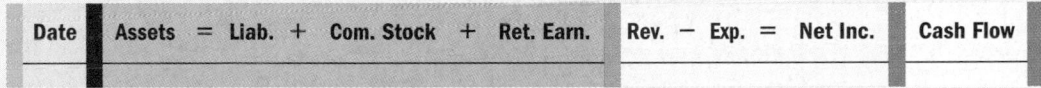

Date	Assets	=	Liab.	+	Com. Stock	+	Ret. Earn.	Rev.	−	Exp.	=	Net Inc.	Cash Flow

b. Prepare journal entries for all events associated with the dividend.

Exercise 11-11A ***Accounting for cumulative preferred dividends*** L.O. 6

When Polledo Corporation was organized in January 2007, it immediately issued 5,000 shares of $50 par, 5 percent, cumulative preferred stock and 10,000 shares of $10 par common stock. The company's earnings history is as follows: 2007, net loss of $15,000; 2008, net income of $60,000; 2009, net income of $95,000. The corporation did not pay a dividend in 2007.

Required

a. How much is the dividend arrearage as of January 1, 2008?
b. Assume that the board of directors declares a $40,000 cash dividend at the end of 2008 (remember that the 2007 and 2008 preferred dividends are due). How will the dividend be divided between the preferred and common stockholders?

Exercise 11-12A ***Cash dividends for preferred and common shareholders*** L.O. 6

B&S Corporation had the following stock issued and outstanding at January 1, 2007:

1. 100,000 shares of $5 par common stock.
2. 5,000 shares of $100 par, 5 percent, noncumulative preferred stock.

On May 10, B&S Corporation declared the annual cash dividend on its 5,000 shares of preferred stock and a $1 per share dividend for the common shareholders. The dividends will be paid on June 15 to the shareholders of record on May 30.

Required

a. Determine the total amount of dividends to be paid to the preferred shareholders and common shareholders.
b. Prepare general journal entries to record the declaration and payment of the cash dividends (be sure to date your entries).

Exercise 11-13A ***Cash dividends: common and preferred stock*** L.O. 6

Wu Corp. had the following stock issued and outstanding at January 1, 2006:

1. 50,000 shares of no-par common stock.
2. 10,000 shares of $100 par, 4 percent, cumulative preferred stock. (Dividends are in arrears for one year, 2005.)

On February 1, 2006, Wu declared a $100,000 cash dividend to be paid March 31 to shareholders of record on March 10.

Required

a. What amount of dividends will be paid to the preferred shareholders versus the common shareholders?

b. Prepare the journal entries required for these transactions. (Be sure to include the dates of the entries.)

L.O. 7

Exercise 11-14A *Accounting for stock dividends*

Merino Corporation issued a 4 percent stock dividend on 30,000 shares of its $10 par common stock. At the time of the dividend, the market value of the stock was $25 per share.

Required

a. Compute the amount of the stock dividend.

b. Show the effects of the stock dividend on the financial statements using a horizontal statements model like the following one.

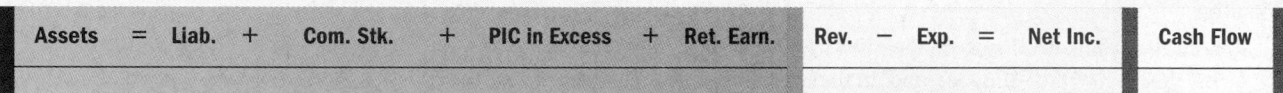

Assets	=	Liab.	+	Com. Stk.	+	PIC in Excess	+	Ret. Earn.	Rev.	−	Exp.	=	Net Inc.	Cash Flow

c. Prepare the journal entry to record the stock dividend.

L.O. 7

Exercise 11-15A *Determining the effects of stock splits on the accounting records*

The market value of Coe Corporation's common stock had become excessively high. The stock was currently selling for $180 per share. To reduce the market price of the common stock, Coe declared a 2-for-1 stock split for the 300,000 outstanding shares of its $10 par common stock.

Required

a. How will Coe Corporation's books be affected by the stock split?

b. Determine the number of common shares outstanding and the par value after the split.

c. Explain how the market value of the stock will be affected by the stock split.

L.O. 9

Exercise 11-16A *Corporate announcements*

Mighty Drugs (one of the three largest drug makers) just reported that its 2004 third quarter profits are essentially the same as the 2003 third quarter profits. In addition to this announcement, the same day, Mighty Drugs also announced that the Food and Drug Administration has just approved a new drug used to treat high blood pressure that Mighty Drugs developed. This new drug has been shown to be extremely effective and has few or no side effects. It will also be less expensive than the other drugs currently on the market.

Required

Using the above information, answer the following questions:

a. What do you think will happen to the stock price of Mighty Drugs on the day these two announcements are made? Explain your answer.

b. How will the balance sheet be affected on that day by the above announcements?

c. How will the income statement be affected on that day by the above announcements?

d. How will the statement of cash flows be affected on that day by the above announcements?

L.O. 10

Exercise 11-17A *Not for profit (Appendix)*

Kelly Curtis, an enterprising accounting student, agreed to prepare financial statements for Salem City Arts Theater. She prepared the financial statements using the format for profit institutions (income statement, balance sheet, and statement of cash flows). She has asked you to review the statements.

Required

Write a memo that describes the financial statements that are required for not-for-profit entities. In the memo explain the differences in the financial statements required for profit businesses and those required for not-for-profit entities.

PROBLEMS—SERIES A

All Problems in Series A are available with McGraw-Hill's Homework Manager

Problem 11-18A *Effect of business structure on financial statements*

L.O. 1, 2

eXcel mhhe.com/edmonds2007

Ja-San Company was started on January 1, 2007, when the owners invested $160,000 cash in the business. During 2007, the company earned cash revenues of $90,000 and incurred cash expenses of $65,000. The company also paid cash distributions of $10,000.

CHECK FIGURES
a. Net Income: $25,000
b. James Capital: $103,000

Required

Prepare a 2007 income statement, capital statement (statement of changes in equity), balance sheet, and statement of cash flows using each of the following assumptions. (Consider each assumption separately.)

a. Ja-San is a sole proprietorship owned by J. Sanford.

b. Ja-San is a partnership with two partners, Kim James and Mary Sanders. James invested $100,000 and Sanders invested $60,000 of the $160,000 cash that was used to start the business. Sanders was expected to assume the vast majority of the responsibility for operating the business. The partnership agreement called for Sanders to receive 60 percent of the profits and James the remaining 40 percent. With regard to the $10,000 distribution, Sanders withdrew $3,000 from the business and James withdrew $7,000.

c. Ja-San is a corporation. The owners were issued 10,000 shares of $10 par common stock when they invested the $160,000 cash in the business.

Problem 11-19A *Recording and reporting stock transactions and cash dividends across two accounting cycles*

L.O. 4–6

eXcel mhhe.com/edmonds2007

Lane Corporation was authorized to issue 100,000 shares of $5 par common stock and 20,000 shares of $100 par, 6 percent, cumulative preferred stock. Lane Corporation completed the following transactions during its first two years of operation:

CHECK FIGURES
b. Preferred Stock, 2006: $200,000
c. Common Shares Outstanding, 2007: 34,500

2006

Jan. 2	Issued 15,000 shares of $5 par common stock for $7 per share.
15	Issued 2,000 shares of $100 par preferred stock for $110 per share.
Feb. 14	Issued 20,000 shares of $5 par common stock for $9 per share.
Dec. 31	During the year, earned $310,000 of cash revenues and paid $240,000 of cash operating expenses.
31	Declared the cash dividend on outstanding shares of preferred stock for 2006. The dividend will be paid on January 31 to stockholders of record on January 15, 2007.
31	Closed revenue, expense, and dividend accounts to the retained earnings account.

2007

Jan. 31	Paid the cash dividend declared on December 31, 2006.
Mar. 1	Issued 3,000 shares of $100 par preferred stock for $120 per share.
June 1	Purchased 500 shares of common stock as treasury stock at $10 per share.
Dec. 31	During the year, earned $250,000 of cash revenues and paid $175,000 of cash operating expenses.
31	Declared the dividend on the preferred stock and a $0.50 per share dividend on the common stock.
31	Closed revenue, expense, and dividend accounts to the retained earnings account.

Required

a. Prepare journal entries for these transactions for 2006 and 2007 and post them to T-accounts.

b. Prepare the stockholders' equity section of the balance sheet at December 31, 2006.

c. Prepare the balance sheet at December 31, 2007.

Problem 11-20A *Recording and reporting treasury stock transactions*

L.O. 5, 6, 8

eXcel mhhe.com/edmonds2007

Midwest Corp. completed the following transactions in 2007, the first year of operation:

1. Issued 20,000 shares of $10 par common stock at par.

CHECK FIGURE
b. Total Paid-In Capital: $264,900

2. Issued 2,000 shares of $30 stated value preferred stock at $32 per share.
3. Purchased 500 shares of common stock as treasury stock for $15 per share.
4. Declared a 5 percent cash dividend on preferred stock.
5. Sold 300 shares of treasury stock for $18 per share.
6. Paid the cash dividend on preferred stock that was declared in Event 4.
7. Earned revenue of $75,000 and incurred operating expenses of $42,000.
8. Closed revenue, expense, and dividend accounts to the retained earnings account.
9. Appropriated $6,000 of retained earnings.

Required

a. Prepare journal entries to record these transactions and post them to T-accounts.
b. Prepare the stockholders' equity section of the balance sheet as of December 31, 2007.

L.O. 5

CHECK FIGURES
b. Total Paid-In Capital: $451,200
b. Total Stockholders' Equity: $570,000

Problem 11-21A *Recording and reporting treasury stock transactions*

Boley Corporation reports the following information in its January 1, 2006, balance sheet:

Stockholders' Equity	
Common Stock, $10 Par Value, 50,000 shares authorized, 30,000 shares issued and outstanding	$300,000
Paid-in Capital in Excess of Par Value	150,000
Retained Earnings	100,000
Total Stockholders' Equity	$550,000

During 2006, Boley was affected by the following accounting events:

1. Purchased 1,000 shares of treasury stock at $18 per share.
2. Reissued 600 shares of treasury stock at $20 per share.
3. Earned $64,000 of cash revenues.
4. Paid $38,000 of cash operating expenses.

Required

a. Provide journal entries to record these transactions.
b. Prepare the stockholders' equity section of the year-end balance sheet.

L.O. 4, 6, 7

CHECK FIGURES
c. Total Paid-In Capital: $895,000
c. Retained Earnings: $17,500

Problem 11-22A *Recording and reporting stock dividends*

Chen Corp. completed the following transactions in 2007, the first year of operation:

1. Issued 20,000 shares of $20 par common stock for $30 per share.
2. Issued 5,000 shares of $50 par, 5 percent, preferred stock at $51 per share.
3. Paid the annual cash dividend to preferred shareholders.
4. Issued a 5 percent stock dividend on the common stock. The market value at the dividend declaration date was $40 per share.
5. Later that year, issued a 2-for-1 split on the 21,000 shares of outstanding common stock.
6. Earned $210,000 of cash revenues and paid $140,000 of cash operating expenses.
7. Closed the revenue, expense, and dividend accounts to retained earnings.

Required

a. Record each of these events in a horizontal statements model like the following one. In the Cash Flow column, indicate whether the item is an operating activity (OA), investing activity (IA), or financing activity (FA). Use NA to indicate that an element is not affected by the event.

Assets = Liab. +	Equity	Rev. − Exp. = Net Inc.	Cash Flow
	Pfd. Stk. + Com. Stk. + PIC in Excess PS + PIC in Excess CS + Ret. Earn.		

b. Record the 2007 transactions in general journal form and post them to T-accounts.

c. Prepare the stockholders' equity section of the balance sheet at the end of 2007.

Problem 11-23A *Analyzing the stockholders' equity section of the balance sheet*

L.O. 4, 7

The stockholders' equity section of the balance sheet for Atkins Company at December 31, 2007, is as follows:

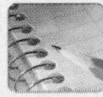

Stockholders' Equity		
Paid-in Capital		
Preferred Stock, ? Par Value, 6% cumulative, 50,000 shares authorized, 30,000 shares issued and outstanding	$300,000	
Common Stock, $10 Stated Value, 150,000 shares authorized, 50,000 shares issued and ? outstanding	500,000	
Paid-in Capital in Excess of Par—Preferred	30,000	
Paid-in Capital in Excess of Stated Value—Common	200,000	
Total Paid-in Capital		$1,030,000
Retained Earnings		250,000
Treasury Stock, 1,000 shares		(100,000)
Total Stockholders' Equity		$1,180,000

Note: The market value per share of the common stock is $25, and the market value per share of the preferred stock is $12.

CHECK FIGURES

a. Par value per share: $10

b. Dividend per share: $.60

Required

a. What is the par value per share of the preferred stock?

b. What is the dividend per share on the preferred stock?

c. What is the number of common stock shares outstanding?

d. What was the average issue price per share (price for which the stock was issued) of the common stock?

e. Explain the difference between the average issue price and the market price of the common stock.

f. If Atkins declared a 2-for-1 stock split on the common stock, how many shares would be outstanding after the split? What amount would be transferred from the retained earnings account because of the stock split? Theoretically, what would be the market price of the common stock immediately after the stock split?

Problem 11-24A *Different forms of business organization*

L.O. 1

Shawn Bates was working to establish a business enterprise with four of his wealthy friends. Each of the five individuals would receive a 20 percent ownership interest in the company. A primary goal of establishing the enterprise was to minimize the amount of income taxes paid. Assume that the five investors are in a 35 percent personal tax bracket and that the corporate tax rate is 25 percent. Also assume that the new company is expected to earn $200,000 of cash income before taxes during its first year of operation. All earnings are expected to be immediately distributed to the owners.

Required

Calculate the amount of after-tax cash flow available to each investor if the business is established as a partnership versus a corporation. Write a memo explaining the advantages and disadvantages of these two forms of business organization. Explain why a limited liability company may be a better choice than either a partnership or a corporation.

Problem 11-25A *Effects of equity transactions on financial statements*

L.O. 4-8

The following events were experienced by Abbot Inc.:

1. Issued cumulative preferred stock for cash.

2. Issued common stock for cash.
3. Distributed a 2-for-1 stock split on the common stock.
4. Issued noncumulative preferred stock for cash.
5. Appropriated retained earnings.
6. Sold treasury stock for an amount of cash that was more than the cost of the treasury stock.
7. Distributed a stock dividend.
8. Paid cash to purchase treasury stock.
9. Declared a cash dividend.
10. Paid the cash dividend declared in Event 9.

Required

Show the effect of each event on the elements of the financial statements using a horizontal statements model like the following one. Use + for increase, − for decrease, and NA for not affected. In the Cash Flow column, indicate whether the item is an operating activity (OA), investing activity (IA), or financing activity (FA). The first transaction is entered as an example.

Event No.	Assets	=	Liab.	+	Equity	Rev.	−	Exp.	=	Net Inc.	Cash Flow
1	+		NA		+	NA		NA		NA	+ FA

L.O. 10

Problem 11-26A *Not for profit (Appendix)*

CHECK FIGURES
Total Unrestricted Assets: $549,750
Net Cash Flow from Operating Assets: $570,000

The City Theater is an NFP organization established to encourage the performing arts in Monroe, Louisiana. The City Theater experienced the following accounting events during 2006. Assume that all transactions are cash transactions unless otherwise stated.

1. Acquired cash contributions from donors, including $500,000 of permanently restricted, $300,000 of temporarily restricted, and $200,000 of unrestricted contributions.
2. The $500,000 of permanently restricted funds was invested in an endowed fund designed to provide investment income that will be made available for operating expenses.
3. The endowed investment fund produced $40,000 of cash revenue.
4. The $300,000 of temporarily restricted funds was used in accordance with donor restrictions to purchase a theater in which plays will be presented. The theater had an expected useful life of 40 years and an anticipated salvage value of $50,000.
5. Of the unrestricted assets, $70,000 was spent to purchase theatrical equipment. The equipment was expected to have a five-year useful life and zero salvage value.
6. Tickets sales produced $140,000 of revenue during the accounting period.
7. The company incurred and paid $110,000 of operating expenses.
8. Recognized depreciation on the theater and theatrical equipment.

Required

Prepare a statement of activities, statement of financial position, and statement of cash flows.

EXERCISES—SERIES B

L.O. 1, 2

Exercise 11-1B *Effect of accounting events on the financial statements of a sole proprietorship*

A sole proprietorship was started on January 1, 2009, when it received $20,000 cash from Dan Jones, the owner. During 2009, the company earned $14,500 in cash revenues and paid $9,300 in cash expenses. Jones withdrew $500 cash from the business during 2009.

Required

Prepare an income statement, capital statement (statement of changes in equity), balance sheet, and statement of cash flows for Jones's 2009 fiscal year.

Exercise 11-2B *Effect of accounting events on the financial statements of a partnership* L.O. 1, 2

Claire Mills and Polly Price started the M&P partnership on January 1, 2009. The business acquired $24,500 cash from Mills and $45,500 from Price. During 2009, the partnership earned $15,000 in cash revenues and paid $6,300 for cash expenses. Mills withdrew $600 cash from the business, and Price withdrew $1,400 cash. The net income was allocated to the capital accounts of the two partners in proportion to the amounts of their original investments in the business.

Required

Prepare an income statement, capital statement, balance sheet, and statement of cash flows for M&P's 2009 fiscal year.

Exercise 11-3B *Effect of accounting events on the financial statements of a corporation* L.O. 1, 2

Stone Corporation was started with the issue of 1,000 shares of $5 par stock for cash on January 1, 2009. The stock was issued at a market price of $18 per share. During 2009, the company earned $23,000 in cash revenues and paid $17,000 for cash expenses. Also a $1,200 cash dividend was paid to the stockholders.

Required

Prepare an income statement, statement of changes in stockholders' equity, balance sheet, and statement of cash flows for Stone Corporation's 2009 fiscal year.

Exercise 11-4B *Effect of issuing common stock on the balance sheet* L.O. 4

Newly formed Super Max Corporation has 30,000 shares of $10 par common stock authorized. On March 1, 2009, Super Max issued 5,000 shares of the stock for $20 per share. On May 2 the company issued an additional 6,000 shares for $24 per share. Super Max was not affected by other events during 2009.

Required

a. Record the transactions in a horizontal statements model like the following one. In the Cash Flow column, indicate whether the item is an operating activity (OA), investing activity (IA), or financing activity (FA). Use NA to indicate that an element was not affected by the event.

Assets	=	Liab.	+	Equity			Rev. − Exp. = Net Inc.	Cash Flow
Cash	=			Com. Stk.	+	PIC in Excess		

b. Determine the amount Super Max would report for common stock on the December 31, 2009, balance sheet.

c. Determine the amount Super Max would report for paid-in capital in excess of par.

d. What is the total amount of capital contributed by the owners?

e. What amount of total assets would Super Max report on the December 31, 2009, balance sheet?

f. Prepare journal entries to record the March 1 and May 2 transactions.

Exercise 11-5B *Recording and reporting common and preferred stock transactions* L.O. 4

E.Com Inc. was organized on June 5, 2009. It was authorized to issue 200,000 shares of $5 par common stock and 20,000 shares of 5 percent cumulative class A preferred stock. The class A stock had a stated value of $50 per share. The following stock transactions pertain to E.Com Inc.:

1. Issued 10,000 shares of common stock for $8 per share.
2. Issued 3,000 shares of the class A preferred stock for $80 per share.
3. Issued 80,000 shares of common stock for $10 per share.

Required

a. Prepare general journal entries for these transactions.

b. Prepare the stockholders' equity section of the balance sheet immediately after these transactions.

L.O. 4

Exercise 11-6B *Effect of no-par common and par preferred stock on the horizontal statements model*

Master Corporation issued 4,000 shares of no-par common stock for $30 per share. Master also issued 1,000 shares of $50 par, 6 percent noncumulative preferred stock at $80 per share.

Required

a. Record these events in a horizontal statements model like the following one. In the Cash Flow column, indicate whether the item is an operating activity (OA), investing activity (IA), or financing activity (FA). Use NA to indicate that an element was not affected by the event.

Assets	=	Equity					Rev. − Exp. = Net Inc.	Cash Flow
Cash	=	Pfd. Stk.	+	Com. Stk.	+	PIC in Excess		

b. Prepare journal entries to record these transactions.

L.O. 4

Exercise 11-7B *Issuing stock for assets other than cash*

James Lee, a wealthy investor, exchanged a plot of land that originally cost him $30,000 for 1,000 shares of $10 par common stock issued to him by Bay Corp. On the same date, Bay Corp. issued an additional 400 shares of stock to Lee for $31 per share.

Required

a. What was the value of the land at the date of the stock issue?

b. Show the effect of the two stock issues on Bay's books in a horizontal statements model like the following one. In the Cash Flow column, indicate whether the item is an operating activity (OA), investing activity (IA), or financing activity (FA). Use NA to indicate that an element was not affected by the event.

Assets			=	Equity			Rev. − Exp. = Net Inc.	Cash Flow
Cash	+	Land	=	Com. Stk.	+	PIC in Excess		

c. Prepare the journal entries to record these transactions.

L.O. 5

Exercise 11-8B *Treasury stock transactions*

Hawk Corporation repurchased 1,000 shares of its own stock for $38 per share. The stock has a par of $10 per share. A month later Hawk resold 500 shares of the treasury stock for $55 per share.

Required

a. Record the two events in general journal format.

b. What is the balance of the treasury stock account after these transactions?

L.O. 5

Exercise 11-9B *Recording and reporting treasury stock transactions*

The following information pertains to Sneed Corp. at January 1, 2006.

Common stock, $10 par, 10,000 shares authorized, 800 shares issued and outstanding	$ 8,000
Paid-in capital in excess of par, common stock	12,000
Retained earnings	75,000

Sneed Corp. completed the following transactions during 2006:

1. Issued 2,000 shares of $10 par common stock for $43 per share.
2. Repurchased 300 shares of its own common stock for $38 per share.
3. Resold 100 shares of treasury stock for $40 per share.

Required

a. How many shares of common stock were outstanding at the end of the period?

b. How many shares of common stock had been issued at the end of the period?

c. Prepare journal entries for these transactions and post them to T-accounts.

d. Prepare the stockholders' equity section of the balance sheet reflecting these transactions. Include the number of shares authorized, issued, and outstanding in the description of the common stock.

Exercise 11-10B *Effect of cash dividends on financial statements* L.O. 6

On May 1, 2005, Lott Corporation declared a $120,000 cash dividend to be paid on May 31 to shareholders of record on May 15.

Required

a. Record the events occurring on May 1, May 15, and May 31 in a horizontal statements model like the following one. In the Cash Flow column, indicate whether the item is an operating activity (OA), investing activity (IA), or financing activity (FA).

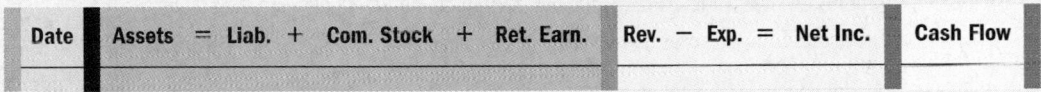

Date	Assets	=	Liab.	+	Com. Stock	+	Ret. Earn.	Rev.	−	Exp.	=	Net Inc.	Cash Flow

b. Prepare journal entries for all events associated with the dividend.

Exercise 11-11B *Accounting for cumulative preferred dividends* L.O. 6

When Express Corporation was organized in January 2007, it immediately issued 2,000 shares of $50 par, 7 percent, cumulative preferred stock and 30,000 shares of $20 par common stock. Its earnings history is as follows: 2007, net loss of $25,000; 2008, net income of $120,000; 2009, net income of $250,000. The corporation did not pay a dividend in 2007.

Required

a. How much is the dividend arrearage as of January 1, 2008?

b. Assume that the board of directors declares a $30,000 cash dividend at the end of 2008 (remember that the 2007 and 2008 preferred dividends are due). How will the dividend be divided between the preferred and common stockholders?

Exercise 11-12B *Cash dividends for preferred and common shareholders* L.O. 6

Iuka Corporation had the following stock issued and outstanding at January 1, 2005:

1. 100,000 shares of $1 par common stock.
2. 10,000 shares of $100 par, 8 percent, noncumulative preferred stock.

On June 10, Iuka Corporation declared the annual cash dividend on its 10,000 shares of preferred stock and a $1 per share dividend for the common shareholders. The dividends will be paid on July 1 to the shareholders of record on June 20.

Required

a. Determine the total amount of dividends to be paid to the preferred shareholders and common shareholders.

b. Prepare general journal entries to record the declaration and payment of the cash dividends (be sure to date your entries).

Exercise 11-13B *Cash dividends: common and preferred stock* L.O. 6

Varsity Inc. had the following stock issued and outstanding at January 1, 2006:

1. 200,000 shares of no-par common stock.
2. 10,000 shares of $100 par, 8 percent, cumulative preferred stock. (Dividends are in arrears for one year, 2005.)

On March 8, 2006, Varsity declared a $200,000 cash dividend to be paid March 31 to shareholders of record on March 20.

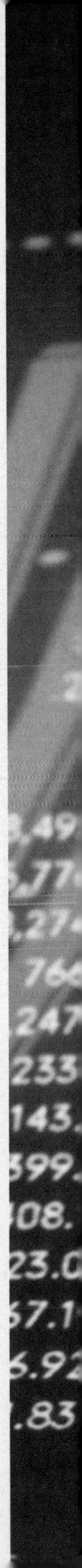

Required

a. What amount of dividends will be paid to the preferred shareholders versus the common shareholders?

b. Prepare the journal entries required for these transactions. (Be sure to include the dates of the entries.)

L.O. 7

Exercise 11-14B *Accounting for stock dividends*

Rollins Corporation issued a 5 percent stock dividend on 10,000 shares of its $10 par common stock. At the time of the dividend, the market value of the stock was $14 per share.

Required

a. Compute the amount of the stock dividend.

b. Show the effects of the stock dividend on the financial statements using a horizontal statements model like the following one.

Assets	=	Liab.	+	Com. Stock	+	PIC in Excess	+	Ret. Earn.	Rev.	−	Exp.	=	Net Inc.	Cash Flow

c. Prepare the journal entry to record the stock dividend.

L.O. 7

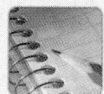

Exercise 11-15B *Determining the effects of stock splits on the accounting records*

The market value of West Corporation's common stock had become excessively high. The stock was currently selling for $240 per share. To reduce the market price of the common stock, West declared a 4-for-1 stock split for the 100,000 outstanding shares of its $20 par value common stock.

Required

a. What entry will be made on the books of West Corporation for the stock split?

b. Determine the number of common shares outstanding and the par value after the split.

c. Explain how the market value of the stock will be affected by the stock split.

L.O. 9

Exercise 11-16B *Accounting information*

The Cutting Edge (TCE) is one of the world's largest lawn mower distributors. TCE is concerned about maintaining an adequate supply of the economy-line mowers that it sells in its stores. TCE currently obtains its economy-line mowers from two suppliers. To ensure a steady supply of mowers, the management of TCE is considering the purchase of an ownership interest in one of the companies that supply its mowers. More specifically, TCE wants to own enough stock of one of the suppliers to enable it to exercise significant influence over the management of the company. The following is a description of the two suppliers.

The first supplier, Dobbs Incorporated, is a closely held company. Large blocks of the Dobbs stock are held by individual members of the Dobbs family. TCE's investment advisor has discovered that one of the members of the Dobbs family is interested in selling her 5 percent share of the company's stock.

The second supplier, National Mowers Inc., has widely disbursed ownership with no one single stockholder owning more than 1 percent of the stock. TCE's investment advisor believes that 5 percent of this company's stock could be acquired gradually over an extended period of time without having a significant effect on the company's stock price.

Required

Provide a recommendation to TCE's management as to whether it should pursue the purchase of 5 percent of Dobbs Incorporated, or 5 percent of National Mowers Inc. Your answer should be supported by an explanation of your recommendation.

L.O. 10

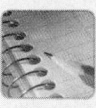

Exercise 11-17B *Not for profit (Appendix)*

Mark Hayes was arguing with his friend Sewon Ow regarding contributions of financial resources that are acquired by an organization. Ow contends that such events constitute revenue that should be reported on the income statement and in the operating activities section of the statement of cash flows. Hayes disagrees. He believes that acquisitions of capital should not be shown on the income statement and should be shown as a financing activity in the statement of cash flows.

Required

Write a brief memo explaining how both of the apparently contradictory arguments could be correct.

PROBLEMS—SERIES B

Problem 11-18B *Effect of business structure on financial statements*

L.O. 1, 2

Calloway Company was started on January 1, 2009, when it acquired $40,000 cash from the owners. During 2009, the company earned cash revenues of $18,000 and incurred cash expenses of $12,500. The company also paid cash distributions of $3,000.

Required

Prepare a 2009 income statement, capital statement (statement of changes in equity), balance sheet, and statement of cash flows under each of the following assumptions. (Consider each assumption separately.)

a. Calloway is a sole proprietorship owned by Macy Calloway.

b. Calloway is a partnership with two partners, Macy Calloway and Artie Calloway. Macy Calloway invested $25,000 and Artie Calloway invested $15,000 of the $40,000 cash that was used to start the business. A. Calloway was expected to assume the vast majority of the responsibility for operating the business. The partnership agreement called for A. Calloway to receive 60 percent of the profits and M. Calloway to get the remaining 40 percent. With regard to the $3,000 distribution, A. Calloway withdrew $1,200 from the business and M. Calloway withdrew $1,800.

c. Calloway is a corporation. It issued 5,000 shares of $5 par common stock for $40,000 cash to start the business.

Problem 11-19B *Recording and reporting stock transactions and cash dividends across two accounting cycles*

L.O. 4-6

Hamby Corporation received a charter that authorized the issuance of 100,000 shares of $10 par common stock and 50,000 shares of $50 par, 6 percent cumulative preferred stock. Hamby Corporation completed the following transactions during its first two years of operation.

2008

Jan.	5	Sold 10,000 shares of the $10 par common stock for $28 per share.
	12	Sold 1,000 shares of the 6 percent preferred stock for $70 per share.
Apr.	5	Sold 40,000 shares of the $10 par common stock for $40 per share.
Dec.	31	During the year, earned $170,000 in cash revenue and paid $110,000 for cash operating expenses.
	31	Declared the cash dividend on the outstanding shares of preferred stock for 2008. The dividend will be paid on February 15 to stockholders of record on January 10, 2009.
	31	Closed the revenue, expense, and dividend accounts to the retained earnings account.

2009

Feb.	15	Paid the cash dividend declared on December 31, 2008.
Mar.	3	Sold 10,000 shares of the $50 par preferred stock for $78 per share.
May	5	Purchased 500 shares of the common stock as treasury stock at $43 per share.
Dec.	31	During the year, earned $210,000 in cash revenues and paid $140,000 for cash operating expenses.
	31	Declared the annual dividend on the preferred stock and a $0.60 per share dividend on the common stock.
	31	Closed revenue, expense, and dividend accounts to the retained earnings account.

Required

a. Prepare journal entries for these transactions for 2008 and 2009 and post them to T-accounts.

b. Prepare the balance sheets at December 31, 2008 and 2009.

c. What is the number of common shares *outstanding* at the end of 2008? At the end of 2009? How many common shares had been *issued* at the end of 2008? At the end of 2009? Explain any differences between issued and outstanding common shares for 2008 and for 2009.

Problem 11-20B *Recording and reporting treasury stock transactions*

L.O. 4, 5, 8

One Co. completed the following transactions in 2009, the first year of operation:

1. Issued 20,000 shares of $5 par common stock for $5 per share.
2. Issued 1,000 shares of $20 stated value preferred stock for $20 per share.

3. Purchased 1,000 shares of common stock as treasury stock for $7 per share.
4. Declared a $1,500 cash dividend on preferred stock.
5. Sold 500 shares of treasury stock for $10 per share.
6. Paid $1,500 cash for the preferred dividend declared in Event 4.
7. Earned cash revenues of $54,000 and incurred cash expenses of $32,000.
8. Closed revenue, expense, and dividend accounts to the retained earnings account.
9. Appropriated $5,000 of retained earnings.

Required

a. Prepare journal entries to record these transactions and post them to T-accounts.
b. Prepare a balance sheet as of December 31, 2009.

L.O. 4, 5

Problem 11-21B *Analyzing journal entries for treasury stock transactions*

The following correctly prepared entries without explanations pertain to Triangle Corporation.

	Account Title	Debit	Credit
1.	Cash	2,100,000	
	Common Stock		1,000,000
	Paid-in Capital in Excess of Par Value		1,100,000
2.	Treasury Stock	22,500	
	Cash		22,500
3.	Cash	13,600	
	Treasury Stock		12,000
	Paid-in Capital in Excess of Cost of Treasury Stock		1,600

The original sale (Entry 1) was for 200,000 shares, and the treasury stock was acquired for $15 per share (Entry 2).

Required

a. What was the sales price per share of the original stock issue?
b. How many shares of stock did the corporation acquire in Event 2?
c. How many shares were reissued in Event 3?
d. How many shares are outstanding immediately following Events 2 and 3, respectively?

L.O. 4, 6, 7

Problem 11-22B *Recording and reporting stock dividends*

Deaton Co. completed the following transactions in 2006, the first year of operation:

1. Issued 20,000 shares of no-par common stock for $10 per share.
2. Issued 5,000 shares of $20 par, 6 percent, preferred stock for $20 per share.
3. Paid a cash dividend of $6,000 to preferred shareholders.
4. Issued a 10 percent stock dividend on no-par common stock. The market value at the dividend declaration date was $15 per share.
5. Later that year, issued a 2-for-1 split on the shares of outstanding common stock. The market price of the stock at that time was $35 per share.
6. Produced $145,000 of cash revenues and incurred $97,000 of cash operating expenses.
7. Closed the revenue, expense, and dividend accounts to retained earnings.

Required

a. Record each of these events in a horizontal statements model like the following one. In the Cash Flow column, indicate whether the item is an operating activity (OA), investing activity (IA), or financing activity (FA). Use NA to indicate that an element is not affected by the event.

Assets	=	Equity	Rev. − Exp. = Net Inc.	Cash Flow
		P. Stk. + C. Stk. + Ret. Earn.		

b. Record the 2006 transactions in general journal form and post them to T-accounts.
c. Prepare the stockholders' equity section of the balance sheet at the end of 2006. (Include all necessary information.)
d. Theoretically, what is the market value of the common stock after the stock split?

Problem 11-23B ***Analyzing the stockholders' equity section of the balance sheet*** **L.O. 4, 7**

The stockholders' equity section of the balance sheet for Cross Electric Co. at December 31, 2007, is as follows:

Stockholders' Equity		
Paid-in Capital		
Preferred Stock, ? Par Value, 8% cumulative, 100,000 shares authorized, 5,000 shares issued and outstanding	$ 250,000	
Common Stock, $20 Stated Value, 200,000 shares authorized, 100,000 shares issued and outstanding	2,000,000	
Paid-in Capital in Excess of Par—Preferred	100,000	
Paid-in Capital in Excess of Stated Value—Common	500,000	
Total Paid-in Capital		$2,850,000
Retained Earnings		500,000
Total Stockholders' Equity		$3,350,000

Note: The market value per share of the common stock is $36, and the market value per share of the preferred stock is $75.

Required

a. What is the par value per share of the preferred stock?
b. What is the dividend per share on the preferred stock?
c. What was the average issue price per share (price for which the stock was issued) of the common stock?
d. Explain the difference between the par value and the market price of the preferred stock.
e. If Cross declares a 3-for-1 stock split on the common stock, how many shares will be outstanding after the split? What amount will be transferred from the retained earnings account because of the stock split? Theoretically, what will be the market price of the common stock immediately after the stock split?

Problem 11-24B ***Different forms of business organization*** **L.O. 1**

Paul Salvy established a partnership with Lisa Witlow. The new company, S&W Fuels, purchased coal directly from mining companies and contracted to ship the coal via waterways to a seaport where it was delivered to ships that were owned and operated by international utilities companies. Salvy was primarily responsible for running the day-to-day operations of the business. Witlow negotiated the buy-and-sell agreements. She recently signed a deal to purchase and deliver $2,000,000 of coal to Solar Utilities. S&W Fuels purchased the coal on account from Miller Mining Company. After accepting title to the coal, S&W Fuels agreed to deliver the coal under terms FOB destination, Port of Long Beach. Unfortunately, Witlow failed to inform Salvy of the deal in time for Salvy to insure the shipment. While in transit, the vessel carrying the coal suffered storm damage that rendered the coal virtually worthless by the time it reached its destination. S&W Fuels immediately declared bankruptcy. The company not only was responsible for the $2,000,000 due to Miller Mining Company but also was sued by Solar for breach of contract. Witlow had a personal net worth of virtually zero, but Salvy was a wealthy individual with a net worth approaching $2,500,000. Accordingly, Miller Mining and Solar filed suit against Salvy's personal assets. Salvy claimed that he was not responsible for the problem because Witlow had failed to inform him of the contracts in time to obtain insurance coverage. Witlow admitted that she was personally responsible for the disaster.

Required

Write a memo describing Salvy's risk associated with his participation in the partnership. Comment on how other forms of ownership would have affected his level of risk.

L.O. 4–8

Problem 11-25B *Effects of equity transactions on financial statements*

The following events were experienced by Baskin, Inc.

1. Issued common stock for cash.
2. Paid cash to purchase treasury stock.
3. Declared a cash dividend.
4. Issued cumulative preferred stock.
5. Issued noncumulative preferred stock.
6. Appropriated retained earnings.
7. Sold treasury stock for an amount of cash that was more than the cost of the treasury stock.
8. Distributed a stock dividend.
9. Declared a 2-for-1 stock split on the common stock.
10. Paid a cash dividend that was previously declared.

Required

Show the effect of each event on the elements of the financial statements using a horizontal statements model like the following one. Use + for increase, − for decrease, and NA for not affected. In the Cash Flow column indicate whether the item is an operating activity (OA), investing activity (IA), or financing activity (FA). The first transaction is entered as an example.

Event No.	Assets	=	Liab.	+	Equity	Rev.	−	Exp.	=	Net Inc.	Cash Flow
1	+		NA		+	NA		NA		NA	+ FA

L.O. 10

Problem 11-26B *Not for profit (Appendix)*

Marshall County Public Library (MCPL) experienced the following accounting events during 2009. Assume that all transactions are cash transactions unless otherwise stated.

1. Acquired $500,000 in contributions.
2. Paid $450,000 for facilities and equipment.
3. Earned $120,000 of revenue.
4. Incurred $80,000 in operating expenses.
5. Recognized $25,000 of depreciation expense.

Required

a. Assume that MCPL is a profit-oriented corporation and that the first event results from the issue of no-par common stock. Prepare an income statement, balance sheet, and statement of cash flows.

b. Assume that MCPL is a not-for-profit organization and that the first event represents an unrestricted donor contribution. Prepare a statement of activities, statement of financial position, and statement of cash flows.

ANALYZE, THINK, COMMUNICATE

ATC 11-1 Business Applications Case *Understanding real world annual reports*

Required—Part 1

The Topps Company, Inc.

Use the **Topps Company**'s annual report in Appendix B to answer the following questions.

a. Does Topps' common stock have a par value, and if so how much is it?

b. How many shares of Topps' common stock were *outstanding* as of March 1, 2003? Do not forget to consider treasury stock.

c. The dollar-value balance in Topps' Treasury Stock account is larger than the balance in its Common Stock and Additional Paid-In-Capital accounts. How can this be?

d. How many members of Topps' Board of Directors are also officers (employees) of the company as of March 1, 2003?

e. What was the highest and lowest price per share that Topps' common stock sold for during the fiscal year ending on March 1, 2003?

Required—Part 2

Use the **Harley-Davidson**'s annual report that came with this book to answer the following questions.

Harley-Davidson, Inc.

a. Does Harley-Davidson's common stock have a par value, and if so how much is it?

b. How many shares of Harley-Davidson's common stock were outstanding as of December 31, 2003?

c. Did Harley-Davidson pay cash dividends in 2003, and if so, how much?

d. What was the highest and lowest price per share that Harley-Davidson's common stock sold for during the fiscal year ending on December 31, 2003?

ATC 11-2 Group Assignment *Missing information*

Listed here are the stockholders' equity sections of three public companies for years ending in 2003 and 2002:

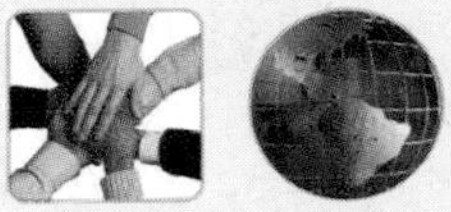

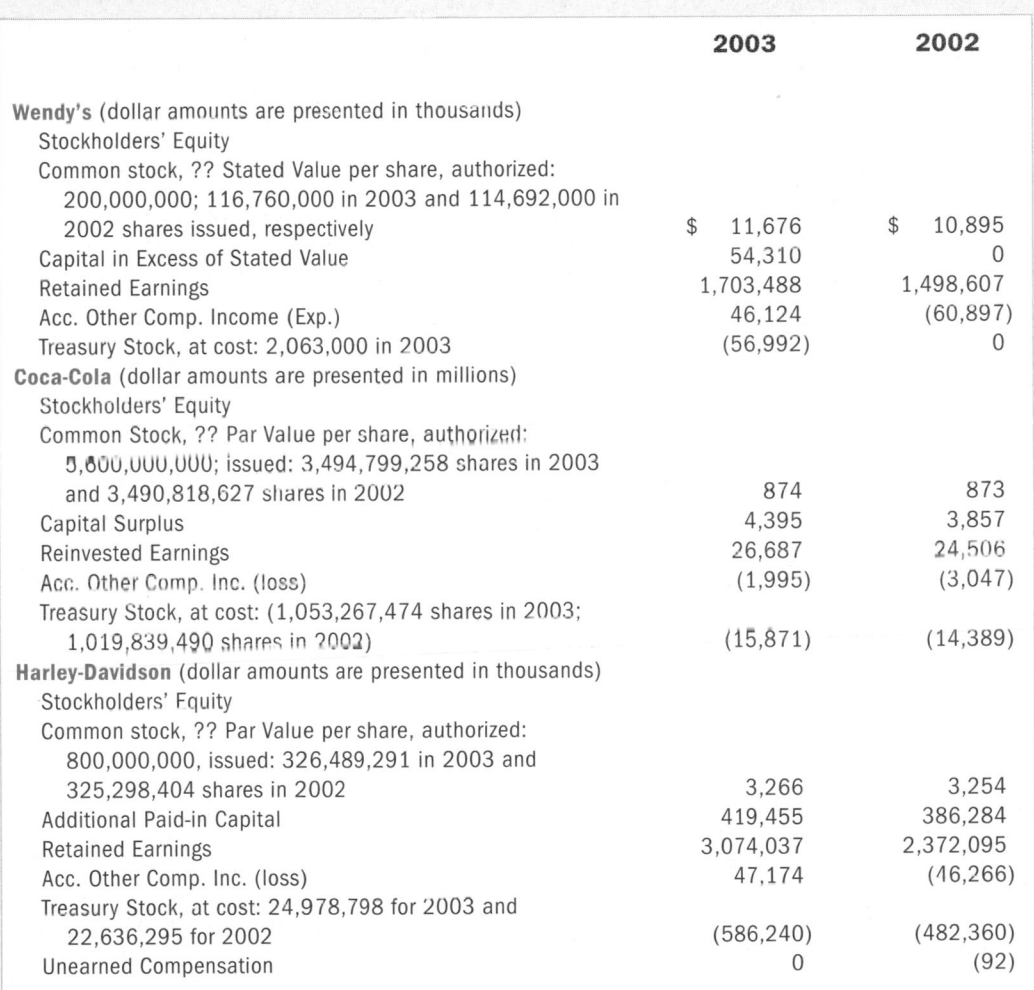

	2003	2002
Wendy's (dollar amounts are presented in thousands)		
Stockholders' Equity		
Common stock, ?? Stated Value per share, authorized: 200,000,000; 116,760,000 in 2003 and 114,692,000 in 2002 shares issued, respectively	$ 11,676	$ 10,895
Capital in Excess of Stated Value	54,310	0
Retained Earnings	1,703,488	1,498,607
Acc. Other Comp. Income (Exp.)	46,124	(60,897)
Treasury Stock, at cost: 2,063,000 in 2003	(56,992)	0
Coca-Cola (dollar amounts are presented in millions)		
Stockholders' Equity		
Common Stock, ?? Par Value per share, authorized: 5,600,000,000; issued: 3,494,799,258 shares in 2003 and 3,490,818,627 shares in 2002	874	873
Capital Surplus	4,395	3,857
Reinvested Earnings	26,687	24,506
Acc. Other Comp. Inc. (loss)	(1,995)	(3,047)
Treasury Stock, at cost: (1,053,267,474 shares in 2003; 1,019,839,490 shares in 2002)	(15,871)	(14,389)
Harley-Davidson (dollar amounts are presented in thousands)		
Stockholders' Equity		
Common stock, ?? Par Value per share, authorized: 800,000,000, issued: 326,489,291 in 2003 and 325,298,404 shares in 2002	3,266	3,254
Additional Paid-in Capital	419,455	386,284
Retained Earnings	3,074,037	2,372,095
Acc. Other Comp. Inc. (loss)	47,174	(46,266)
Treasury Stock, at cost: 24,978,798 for 2003 and 22,636,295 for 2002	(586,240)	(482,360)
Unearned Compensation	0	(92)

Required

a. Divide the class in three sections and divide each section into groups of three to five students. Assign each section one of the companies.

Group Tasks

Based on the company assigned to your group, answer the following questions.

b. What is the per share par or stated value of the common stock in 2003?

c. What was the average issue price of the common stock for each year?

d. How many shares of stock are outstanding at the end of each year?
e. What is the average cost per share of the treasury stock for 2003?
f. Do the data suggest that your company was profitable in 2003?
g. Can you determine the amount of net income from the information given? What is missing?
h. What is the total stockholders' equity of your company for each year?

Class Discussion

i. Have each group select a representative to present the information about its company. Compare the share issue price and the par or stated value of the companies.
j. Compare the average issue price to the current market price for each of the companies. Speculate about what might cause the difference.

ATC 11-3 Real-World Case *Which stock is most valuable?*

Listed here are data for five companies. These data are from companies' annual reports for the fiscal year indicated in the parentheses. The market price per share is the closing price of the companies' stock as of November 17, 2004. Except for market price per share, all amounts are in thousands. The shares outstanding number is the weighted-average number of shares the company used to compute its basic earnings per share.

Company (Fiscal Year-End)	Net Earnings	Shares Outstanding	Stockholders' Equity	Market Price per Share
Amazon.com (12/31/2003)	$ 35,282	395,479	$ (1,036,107)	$39.90
ExxonMobil (12/31/2003)	21,510,000	6,634,000	89,915,000	50.05
Genetech (12/31/2003)	562,527	517,240	6,520,298	49.88
Krispy Kreme (2/01/2004)	57,087	59,188	452,207	12.43
Temple-Inland (1/03/2004)	96,000,000	54,200,000	1,968,000	62.31

Required:

a. Compute the earnings per share (EPS) for each company.
b. Compute the P/E ratio for each company.
c. Using the P/E ratios, rank the companies' stock in the order that the stock market appears to value the companies, from most valuable to least valuable. Identify reasons the ranking based on P/E ratios may not represent the market's optimism about one or two companies.
d. Compute the book value per share for each company.
e. Compare each company's book value per share to its market price per share. Based on the data, rank the companies from most valuable to least valuable. (The higher the ratio of market value to book value, the greater the value the stock market appears to be assigning to a company's stock.)

ATC 11-4 Business Applications Case *Finding stock market information*

This problem requires stock price quotations for the New York Stock Exchange, the American Stock Exchange, and NASDAQ. These are available in *The Wall Street Journal* and in the business sections of many daily newspapers as well as on various websites. Stock prices are also available on electronic data services such as CompuServe.

Required

For each company listed here, provide the requested information as of Thursday of last week. (*Hint:* Information about Thursday's stock market is in Friday's newspaper.)

Name of Company	Stock Exchange Where Listed	Closing Price	P/E Ratio
Berkshire Hathaway A			
Devron Energy Corp.			
Intel			
Yahoo			
Xerox			

ATC 11-5 Business Applications Case *Using the P/E ratio*

During 2007, Musicland Corporation and Jazztown Corporation reported net incomes of $62,000 and $54,000, respectively. Each company had 10,000 shares of common stock issued and outstanding. The market price per share of Musicland's stock was $80, while Jazztown's stock sold for $88 per share.

Required

a. Determine the P/E ratio for each company.

b. Based on the P/E ratios computed in Requirement *a*, which company do investors believe has more potential for growth in income?

ATC 11-6 Writing Assignment *Comparison of organizational forms*

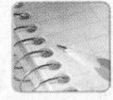

Jim Baku and Scott Hanson are thinking about opening a new restaurant. Baku has extensive marketing experience but does not know that much about food preparation. However, Hanson is an excellent chef. Both will work in the business, but Baku will provide most of the funds necessary to start the business. At this time, they cannot decide whether to operate the business as a partnership or a corporation.

Required

Prepare a written memo to Baku and Hanson describing the advantages and disadvantages of each organizational form. Also, from the limited information provided, recommend the organizational form you think they should use.

ATC 11-7 Ethical Dilemma *Bad news versus very bad news*

Louise Stinson, the chief financial officer of Bostonian Corporation, was on her way to the president's office. She was carrying the latest round of bad news. There would be no executive bonuses this year. Corporate profits were down. Indeed, if the latest projections held true, the company would report a small loss on the year-end income statement. Executive bonuses were tied to corporate profits. The executive compensation plan provided for 10 percent of net earnings to be set aside for bonuses. No profits meant no bonuses. While things looked bleak, Stinson had a plan that might help soften the blow.

After informing the company president of the earnings forecast, Stinson made the following suggestion: Since the company was going to report a loss anyway, why not report a big loss? She reasoned that the directors and stockholders would not be much more angry if the company reported a large loss than if it reported a small one. There were several questionable assets that could be written down in the current year. This would increase the current year's loss but would reduce expenses in subsequent accounting periods. For example, the company was carrying damaged inventory that was estimated to have a value of $2,500,000. If this estimate were revised to $500,000, the company would have to recognize a $2,000,000 loss in the current year. However, next year when the goods were sold, the expense for cost of goods sold would be $2,000,000 less and profits would be higher by that amount. Although the directors would be angry this year, they would certainly be happy next year. The strategy would also have the benefit of adding $200,000 to next year's executive bonus pool ($2,000,000 × 0.10). Furthermore, it could not hurt this year's bonus pool because there would be no pool this year since the company is going to report a loss.

Some of the other items that Stinson is considering include (1) converting from straight-line to accelerated depreciation, (2) increasing the percentage of receivables estimated to be uncollectible in the current year and lowering the percentage in the following year, and (3) raising the percentage of estimated warranty claims in the current period and lowering it in the following period. Finally, Stinson notes that two of the company's department stores have been experiencing losses. The company could sell these stores this year and thereby improve earnings next year. Stinson admits that the sale would result in significant losses this year, but she smiles as she thinks of next year's bonus check.

Required

a. Explain how each of the three numbered strategies for increasing the amount of the current year's loss would affect the stockholders' equity section of the balance sheet in the current year. How would the other elements of the balance sheet be affected?

b. If Stinson's strategy were effectively implemented, how would it affect the stockholders' equity in subsequent accounting periods?

c. Comment on the ethical implications of running the company for the sake of management (maximization of bonuses) versus the maximization of return to stockholders.

d. Formulate a bonus plan that will motivate managers to maximize the value of the firm instead of motivating them to manipulate the reporting process.

e. How would Stinson's strategy of overstating the amount of the reported loss in the current year affect the company's current P/E ratio?

ATC 11-8 Research Assignment *Analyzing PepsiCo's equity structure*

Using either **PepsiCo**'s most current Form 10-K or the company's annual report, answer the questions below. To obtain the Form 10-K use either the EDGAR system following the instructions in Appendix A or the company's website. The company's annual report is available on its website.

Required

a. What is the *book value* of PepsiCo's stockholders' equity that is shown on the company's balance sheet?

b. What is the par value of PepsiCo's common stock?

c. Does PepsiCo have any treasury stock? If so, how many shares of treasury stock does the company hold?

d. Why does the stock of a company such as a PepsiCo have a market value that is higher than its book value?

COMPREHENSIVE PROBLEM

The trial balance of Pacilio Security Services Inc. as of January 1, 2011, had the following normal balances:

Cash	$113,718
Petty Cash	100
Accounts Receivable	39,390
Allowance for Doubtful Accounts	4,662
Supplies	210
Merchandise Inventory (48 @ $300)	14,400
Equipment	9,000
Van	27,000
Building	125,000
Accumulated Depreciation	28,075
Land	25,000
Sales Tax Payable	390
Employee Income Tax Payable	1,000
FICA—Social Security Tax Payable	840
FICA—Medicare Tax Payable	210
Warranty Payable	918
Unemployment Tax Payable	945
Notes Payable—Building	92,762
Bonds Payable	50,000
Discount on Bonds Payable	800
Common Stock	50,000
Retained Earnings	124,816

During 2011, Pacilio Security Services experienced the following transactions:

1. Paid the sales tax payable from 2010.
2. Paid the balance of the payroll liabilities due for 2010 (federal income tax, FICA taxes, and unemployment taxes).
3. Issued 5,000 additional shares of the $5 par value common stock for $8 per share and 1,000 shares of $50 stated value, 5 percent cumulative preferred stock for $52 per share.
4. Purchased $500 of supplies on account.
5. Purchased 190 alarm systems at a cost of $310. Cash was paid for the purchase.

6. After numerous attempts to collect from customers, wrote off $3,670 of uncollectible accounts receivable.
7. Sold 210 alarm systems for $600 each plus sales tax of 5 percent. All sales were on account. (Be sure to compute cost of goods sold using the FIFO cost flow method.)
8. Billed $125,000 of monitoring services for the year. Credit card sales amounted to $58,000, and the credit card company charged a 4 percent fee. The remaining $67,000 were sales on account. Sales tax is not charged on this service.
9. Replenished the petty cash fund on June 30. The fund had $10 cash and receipts of $75 for yard mowing and $15 for office supplies expense.
10. Collected the amount due from the credit card company.
11. Paid the sales tax collected on $105,000 of the alarm sales.
12. Collected $198,000 of accounts receivable during the year.
13. Paid installers and other employees a total of $96,000 for salaries for the year. Assume the Social Security tax rate is 6 percent and the Medicare tax rate is 1.5 percent. Federal income taxes withheld amounted to $10,600. No employee exceeded $90,000 in total wages. The net salaries were paid in cash.
14. On October 1, declared a dividend on the preferred stock and a $1 per share dividend on the common stock to be paid to shareholders of record on October 15, payable on November 1, 2011.
15. Paid $1,625 in warranty repairs during the year.
16. On November 1, 2011, paid the dividends that had been previously declared.
17. Paid $18,500 of advertising expense during the year.
18. Paid $6,100 of utilities expense for the year.
19. Paid the payroll liabilities, both the amounts withheld from the salaries plus the employer share of Social Security tax and Medicare tax, on $88,000 of the salaries plus $9,200 of the federal income tax that was withheld.
20. Paid the accounts payable.
21. Paid bond interest and amortized the discount.
22. Paid the annual installment of $14,238 on the amortized note.

Adjustments

23. There was $190 of supplies on hand at the end of the year.
24. Recognized the uncollectible accounts expense for the year using the allowance method. Pacilio now estimates that 1 percent of sales on account will not be collected.
25. Recognized depreciation expense on the equipment, van, and building. The equipment has a five-year life and a $2,000 salvage value. The van has a four-year life and a $6,000 salvage value. The building has a 40-year life and a $10,000 salvage value. The company uses double declining balance for the van and straight-line for the equipment and the building.
26. The alarms systems sold in transaction 7 were covered with a one-year warranty. Pacilio estimated that the warranty cost would be 2 percent of alarm sales.
27. The unemployment tax on the three employees has not been paid. Record the accrued unemployment tax on the salaries for the year. The unemployment tax rate is 4.5 percent and gross wages for all three employees exceeded $7,000.
28. Recognized the employer Social Security and Medicard payroll tax that has not been paid on $8,000 of salaries expense.

Required

a. Record the above transactions in general journal form. Round all amounts to the nearest whole dollar.
b. Post the transactions to the T-accounts.
c. Prepare a trial balance.
d. Prepare an income statement, a balance sheet, and a statement of cash flows.
e. Close the temporary accounts to retained earnings.
f. Post the closing entries to the T-accounts and prepare an after-closing trial balance.

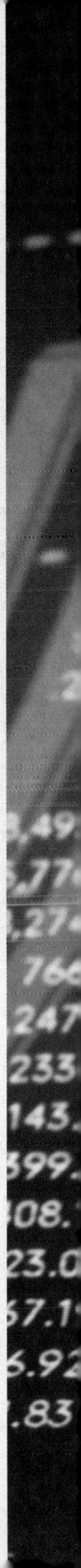

CHAPTER 12

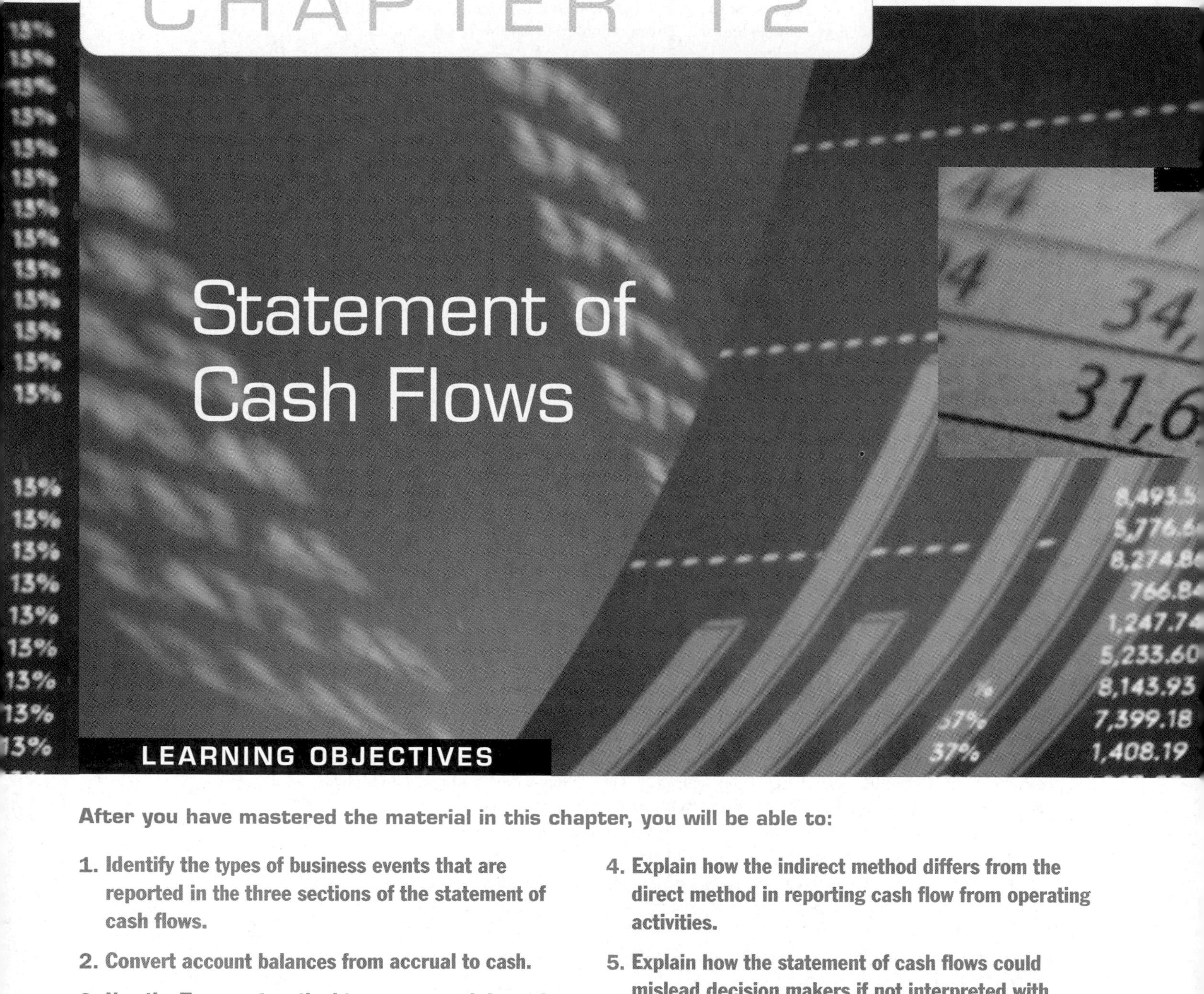

Statement of Cash Flows

LEARNING OBJECTIVES

After you have mastered the material in this chapter, you will be able to:

1. **Identify the types of business events that are reported in the three sections of the statement of cash flows.**
2. **Convert account balances from accrual to cash.**
3. **Use the T-account method to prepare a statement of cash flows.**
4. **Explain how the indirect method differs from the direct method in reporting cash flow from operating activities.**
5. **Explain how the statement of cash flows could mislead decision makers if not interpreted with care.**

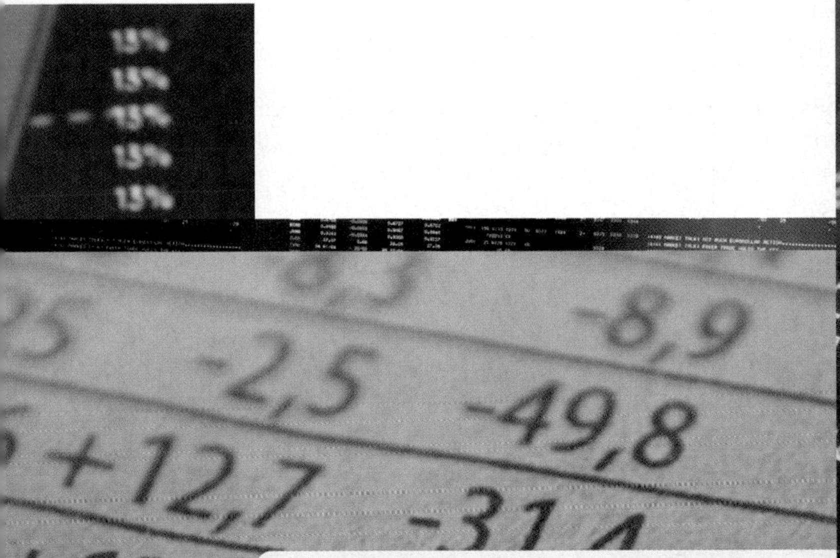

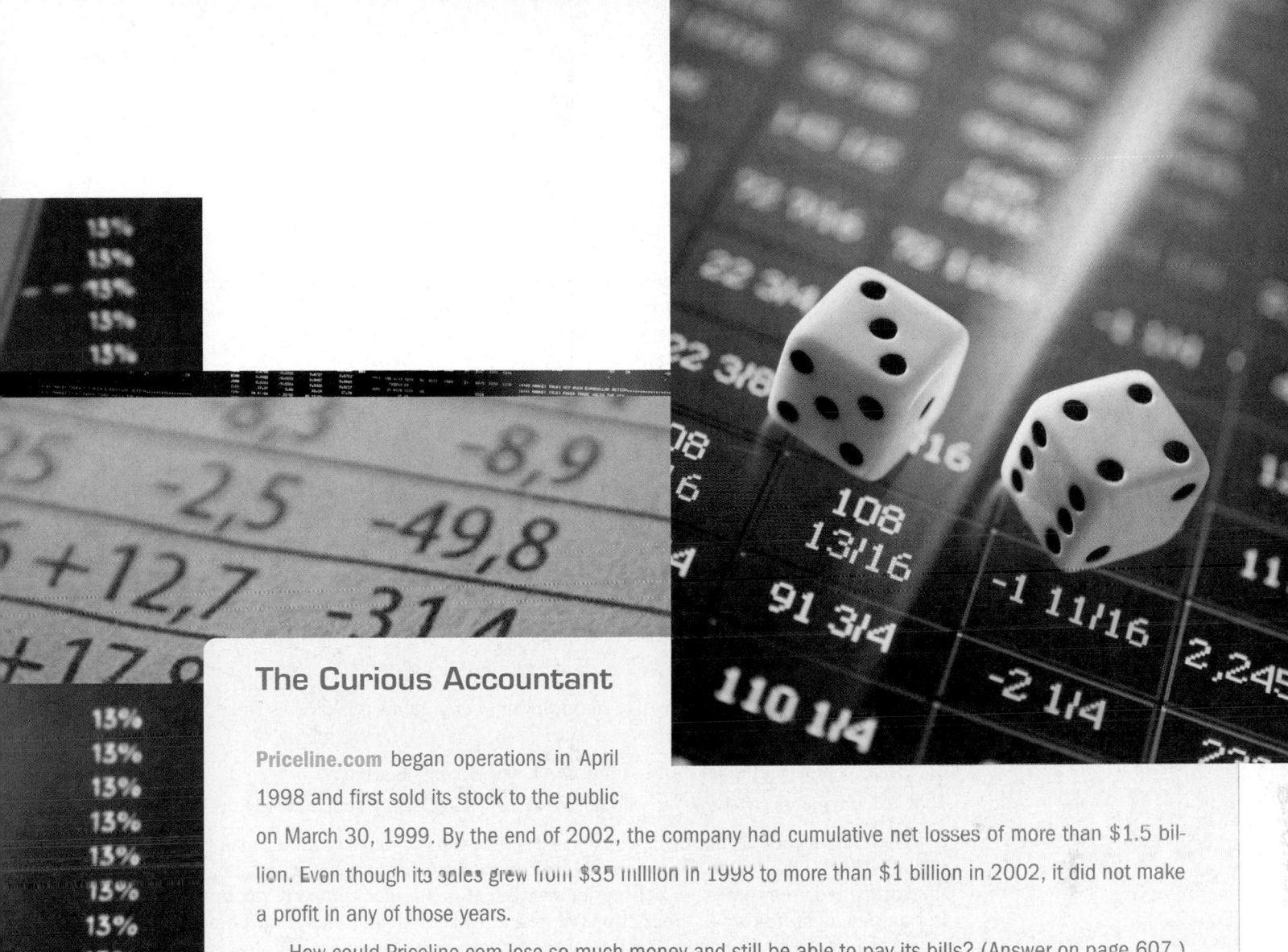

The Curious Accountant

Priceline.com began operations in April 1998 and first sold its stock to the public on March 30, 1999. By the end of 2002, the company had cumulative net losses of more than $1.5 billion. Even though its sales grew from $35 million in 1998 to more than $1 billion in 2002, it did not make a profit in any of those years.

How could Priceline.com lose so much money and still be able to pay its bills? (Answer on page 607.)

Chapter 12

CHAPTER OPENING

To make informed investment and credit decisions, financial statement users need information to help them assess the amounts, timing, and uncertainty of a company's prospective cash flows. This chapter explains more about the items reported on the statement of cash flows and describes a more practical way to prepare the statement than analyzing every entry in the cash account. As previously shown, the statement of cash flows reports how a company obtained and spent cash during an accounting period. Sources of cash are ***cash inflows,*** *and uses are* ***cash outflows.*** *Cash receipts (inflows) and payments (outflows) are reported as either operating activities, investing activities, or financing activities.* ■

Topic Tackler PLUS 12-1

LO 1

Identify the types of business events that are reported in the three sections of the statement of cash flows.

Operating Activities

Routine cash inflows and outflows resulting from running (operating) a business are classified as **operating activities.** Items reported as operating activities include:

1. Cash receipts from sales, commissions, fees, and receipts from interest and dividends.
2. Cash payments for inventories, salaries, operating expenses, interest, and taxes.

Gains and *losses* from disposals of long-term operational assets are not reported on the statement of cash flows. The total amount of cash collected from selling long-term assets (including cash associated with gains and losses) is reported in the investing activities section of the statement of cash flows.

Investing Activities

Investing activities always involve *assets.* Items reported as investing activities include:

1. Cash receipts (inflows) from selling property, plant, equipment, or marketable securities as well as collecting loans.
2. Cash payments (outflows) for purchasing property, plant, equipment, or marketable securities as well as lending to others.

Financing Activities

Financing activities always involve *liabilities* or *equity.* Items reported as financing activities include:

1. Cash receipts (inflows) from issuing stock and borrowing money.
2. Cash payments (outflows) to purchase treasury stock, repay debt, and pay dividends.

The classification of cash flows is based on the type of activity rather than the type of account. For example, cash flows involving common stock represent investing activities if the company is purchasing or selling its investment in another company's common stock. In contrast, common stock transactions represent financing activities if the company is issuing or buying back its own stock (treasury stock). Similarly, receiving dividends is an operating activity, but paying dividends is a financing activity. Furthermore, lending cash is an investing activity while borrowing cash is a financing activity.

Noncash Investing and Financing Activities

Occasionally, companies engage in significant **noncash investing and financing activities.** For example, a company could issue common stock in exchange for land or acquire a building by accepting a mortgage obligation. Since these types of transactions do not involve exchanging cash, they cannot be reported in the main body of the statement of cash flows. However, the Financial Accounting Standards Board (FASB) has concluded that full and fair reporting requires disclosing all material investing and financing activities whether or not they involve exchanging cash. Companies must therefore include with the statement of cash flows a separate schedule that reports noncash investing and financing activities.

Reporting Format for the Statement of Cash Flows

Cash flows are shown on the statement of cash flows in the following order: (1) operating activities, (2) investing activities, and (3) financing activities. At the end of each category, the difference between the inflows and outflows is presented as a *net* cash inflow or outflow for the category. These net amounts are combined to determine the net change (increase or

EXHIBIT 12.1

WESTERN COMPANY
Statement of Cash Flows
For the Year Ended December 31, 2001

Cash Flows from Operating Activities		
Plus: List of Individual Inflows	$XXX	
Less: List of Individual Outflows	(XXX)	
Net Increase (Decrease) from Operating Activities		$XXX
Cash Flows from Investing Activities		
Plus: List of Individual Inflows	XXX	
Less: List of Individual Outflows	(XXX)	
Net Increase (Decrease) from Investing Activities		XXX
Cash Flows from Financing Activities		
Plus: List of Individual Inflows	XXX	
Less: List of Individual Outflows	(XXX)	
Net Increase (Decrease) from Financing Activities		XXX
Net Increase (Decrease) in Cash		XXX
Plus: Beginning Cash Balance		XXX
Ending Cash Balance		$XXX
Schedule of Noncash Investing and Financing Activities		
List of Noncash Transactions		$XXX

EXHIBIT 12.2

Placement of Statement of Cash Flows Relative to Other Financial Statements

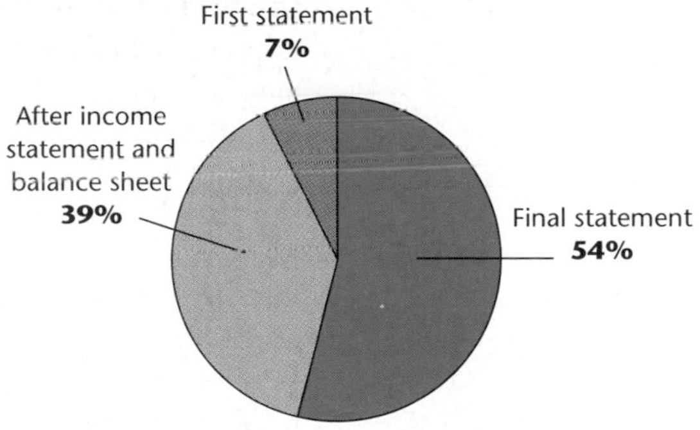

Data source: AICPA, *Accounting Trends and Techniques*, 2002.

decrease) in the company's cash for the period. The net change in cash is combined with the beginning cash balance to determine the ending cash balance. The ending cash balance on the statement of cash flows is the same as the cash balance shown on the balance sheet. The schedule of noncash investing and financing activities is typically presented at the bottom of the statement of cash flows. Exhibit 12.1 outlines this format.

As indicated in Exhibit 12.2, most companies present the statement of cash flows as the last of the four primary financial statements. However, a sizable number of companies present it after the income statement and balance sheet but before the statement of changes in stockholders' equity. Some companies place the statement of cash flows first, before the other three statements.

Converting from Accrual to Cash-Basis Accounting

LO 2
Convert account balances from accrual to cash.

The operating activities section of the statement of cash flows is essentially a cash-basis income statement. Since accounting records are normally maintained on an accrual basis, determining the cash flow from operating activities requires converting the accrual based records to cash equivalents.

Operating Activities

Converting Accruals to Cash

The adjustments to convert **accrual transactions** to cash are explained in the following sections.

Revenue Transactions. The amount of revenue a company recognizes in a given accounting period normally differs from the amount of cash the company collects from customers. The amount of revenue recognized on the income statement can be converted to the amount of cash collected from customers by analyzing the change in the Accounts Receivable balance. For example, assume a company reported on its income statement $500 of sales revenue for the period. Also assume the company's Accounts Receivable balance at the beginning of the period was $100 and at the end of the period was $160 for an increase in receivables of $60 ($160 − $100). These circumstances indicate that $60 of the $500 in sales has not yet been collected from customers. Therefore, the amount of cash collected must have been $440 ($500 revenue − $60 increase in accounts receivable).

LO 3

Use the T-account method to prepare a statement of cash flows.

The conclusion that $440 of cash was collected from the revenue transactions can be confirmed using the **T-account method.** This method uses a T-account to analyze the changes in Accounts Receivable for the period. The beginning and ending Accounts Receivable balances are entered in the T-account, in this case, the beginning balance of $100, and the ending balance of $160. Next a $500 debit is posted to the account to reflect the sales on account recognized during the period. The T-account then appears as follows:

	Accounts Receivable	
Beginning balance	100	
Debit to record sales	500	?
Ending balance	160	

Since adding $500 to the beginning balance of $100 does not produce the ending balance of $160, we know that Accounts Receivable must have been credited for some amount. We can use algebra to determine the amount of the credit in the receivables account ($\$100 + \$500 - x = \$160; x = \$440$). Since credits to Accounts Receivable are normally the result of cash collections from customers, the Cash account would have been debited when the receivables account was credited. T-account analysis, therefore, suggests that $440 of cash was collected from revenue generating activities.

Expense Transactions. Accrual accounting requires recognizing expenses when they are incurred, which is frequently before the accounting period when cash is paid for the expenses. Expenses on the income statement that include accrued amounts must be analyzed in conjunction with related balance sheet liabilities in order to determine the amount of cash paid for the expenses during the period. For example, assume a company reports $200 of utilities expense on its income statement. Furthermore, assume the beginning and ending balances of Utilities Payable are $70 and $40, respectively. The company therefore paid not only for the current period's utilities but also paid an additional $30 ($70 − $40) to reduce utility obligations from prior periods. The cash outflow for utility use must have been $230 ($200 expense incurred + $30 reduction in liability).

The T-account method confirms that $230 cash was paid. Enter the beginning and ending balances of Utilities Payable into a T-account. Post a credit of $200 to the account to reflect recognizing the current period's utility expense. The T-account then appears as follows:

Utilities Payable		
	70	Beginning balance
?	200	Credit to record expense
	40	Ending balance

Algebra dictates that the account must have been debited $230 to produce the $40 ending balance ($\$70 + \$200 - x = \$40; x = \$230$). Since debits to payable accounts are normally the result of cash payments, the Cash account would have been credited when Utilities Payable was debited, indicating that cash outflows for utility expenses were $230.

Answers to The Curious Accountant

First, remember GAAP requires that earnings and losses be computed on an accrual basis. A company can have negative earnings and still have positive cash flows from operating activities. This was not the case at **Priceline.com**, however. From 1998 through 2001, the company's cash flows from operating activities totaled a negative $94.8 million. Although this is much less than the $1.5 billion cumulative losses the company incurred during the same period, it still does not pay the bills.

Priceline.com, like many new companies, was able to stay in business because of the cash it raised through financing activities. These cash flows were a positive $376.9 million for 1998 through 2001. The company also had some significant noncash transactions. Exhibit 12.3 presents Priceline.com's statement of cash flows from the first four years (1998–2001) of its life.

EXHIBIT 12.3

PRICELINE.COM INCORPORATED
Statements of Cash Flows
(dollars in thousands)

	Year Ended December 31			
	2001	**2000**	**1999**	**1998**
Operating Activities				
Net loss	$ (7,303)	$(315,145)	$(1,055,090)	$(112,243)
Adjustments to reconcile net loss to net cash used in operating activities:				
Depreciation and amortization	16,578	17,385	5,348	1,860
Provision for uncollectible accounts	18,548	7,354	3,127	581
Warrant costs	–	8,595	1,189,111	67,866
Webhouse warrant	–	189,000	(189,000)	–
Net loss on disposal of fixed assets	17	12,398	–	–
Net loss on sale of equity investments	946	2,558	–	–
Impairment of Myprice loan	–	4,886	–	–
Equity in net income of priceline mortgage	(551)	–	–	–
Noncash severance	3,076	–	–	–
Enhanced withholding on restricted shares	3,136	–	–	–
Compensation expense arising from deferred stock awards	13,395	1,711	–	–
Changes in assets and liabilities:				
Accounts receivable	(19,768)	7,401	(29,617)	(4,757)
Prepaid expenses and other current assets	699	1,194	(12,043)	(1,922)
Related party receivables	–	(3,484)	–	–
Accounts payable and accrued expenses	(1,501)	45,155	28,470	8,300
Other	824	1,276	(3,331)	112
Net cash used in operating activities	28,096	(19,716)	(63,025)	(40,203)
Investing Activities				
Additions to property and equipment	(9,415)	(37,320)	(27,416)	(6,607)
Proceeds from sales of fixed assets	170	–	–	–
Purchase of convertible notes and warrants of licensees	–	(25,676)	(2,000)	–
Proceeds from sales/maturities of investments	770	31,101	–	–
Funding of restricted cash and bank certificate of deposits	2,646	(4,779)	(8,789)	(680)
Investment in priceline.com europe Ltd.	(14,248)	–	–	–
Cash acquired from acquisition of priceline europe Ltd.	2,779	–	–	–
Investment in marketable securities	(38,878)	(5,000)	(38,771)	–
Net cash used in investing activities	(56,176)	(41,674)	(76,976)	(7,287)
Financing Activities				
Related party payable	–	–	–	(1,072)
Issuance of long-term debt	–	–	–	1,000
Payment of long-term debt	–	–	(1,000)	–
Principal payments under capital lease obligations	–	–	(25)	(22)
Shares reacquired for withholding taxes	(8,716)	–	–	–
Proceeds from sale of common stock, net	49,459	–	208,417	26,495
Proceeds from exercise of stock options and warrants	10,256	14,031	3,399	–
Payment received on stockholder note	–	–	–	250
Issuance of Series A convertible preferred stock	–	–	–	20,000
Issuance of Series B convertible preferred stock	–	–	–	54,415
Net cash provided by financing activities	50,999	14,031	210,791	101,066
Net increase (decrease) in cash and cash equivalents	22,919	(47,359)	70,790	53,576
Cash and cash equivalents, beginning of period	77,024	124,383	53,593	17
Cash and cash equivalents, end of period	$99,943	$ 77,024	$ 124,383	$ 53,593
Supplemental Cash Flow Information				
Cash paid during the period for interest	$ –	$ 4	$ 37	$ 61
Acquisition of priceline.com europe Ltd. —net liabilities assumed	$ 7,896	$ –	$ –	$ –

CHECK YOURSELF 12.1

Hammer Inc. had a beginning balance of $22,400 in its Accounts Receivable account. During the accounting period, Hammer earned $234,700 of revenue on account. The ending balance in the Accounts Receivable account was $18,200. Based on this information alone, determine the amount of cash received from revenue transactions. In what section of the statement of cash flows would this cash flow appear?

Answer

Beginning accounts receivable balance	$ 22,400
Plus: Revenue earned on account during the period	234,700
Receivables available for collection	257,100
Less: Ending accounts receivable balance	(18,200)
Cash collected from receivables (revenue)	$238,900

A $238,900 credit to accounts receivable is required to balance the account. This credit would be offset by a corresponding debit to cash. Cash received from revenue transactions appears in the operating activities section of the statement of cash flows.

Converting Deferrals to Cash

With **deferral transactions,** cash receipts or payments occur before the related revenue or expense is recognized. The following section explains how to convert deferred income and expense items to their cash equivalents.

Revenue Transactions. When a company collects cash from customers before it delivers goods or services, it incurs an obligation (liability) to provide the goods or services at some future date. If the goods or services are provided in a different accounting period from the cash collection, the amount of revenue reported on the income statement will differ from the amount of cash collected. Converting deferred revenue to its cash equivalent requires analyzing the revenue reported on the income statement in conjunction with the liability unearned revenue.

To illustrate, assume revenue of $400 was recognized and Unearned Revenue increased from a beginning balance of $80 to an ending balance of $110. The increase in the liability means that the company received more cash than the amount of revenue it recognized. Not only did the company earn the $400 of revenue reported on the income statement but also it received $30 ($110 − $80) for goods and services to be provided in a future period. Cash receipts from customers was $430 ($400 earned revenue + $30 unearned revenue).

Analyzing the T-account for Unearned Revenue confirms that $430 cash was received. Enter the beginning and ending balances into the Unearned Revenue account. Post a debit of $400 to reflect the revenue earned. The account then appears as follows:

	Unearned Revenue		
		80	Beginning balance
Debit to recognize revenue	400	?	
		110	Ending balance

Use algebra to determine that $430 must have been credited to the account ($\$80 + x - \$400 = \$110; x = \$430$). Since credit entries to the Unearned Revenue account are normally the result of cash collections, the T-account analysis indicates that $430 of cash receipts was generated by revenue activities.

Expense Transactions. Companies often pay cash for goods or services before using them. The costs of such goods or services are normally recorded first in asset accounts. The assets are then recognized as expenses in later periods when the goods or services are used. The amount of cash paid for expenses therefore normally differs from the amount of expense recognized in a given period.

Expenses recognized on the income statement can be converted to cash flows by analyzing the changes in relevant asset accounts in conjunction with their corresponding expenses. For example, assume the beginning and ending balances of Prepaid Rent are $60 and $80, respectively, and reported rent expense is $800. These circumstances indicate the company not only paid enough cash for the $800 of recognized expense but also paid an additional $20 ($80 − $60) to increase the Prepaid Rent account. Therefore, the cash outflow for rent was $820 ($800 recognized expense + $20 prepaid rent).

Analyzing the T-account for Prepaid Rent confirms that $820 was paid for rent. Enter the beginning and ending balances, then post an $800 credit to reflect the rent expense. The account then appears as follows:

	Prepaid Rent		
Beginning balance	60		
	?	800	Credit to recognize expense
Ending balance	80		

Use algebra to determine that the account must have been debited for $820 ($60 + x − $800 = $80; x = $820). Since debit entries to the Prepaid Rent account are normally the result of cash payments, the analysis confirms that the cash outflow for rent was $820.

Investing Activities

Determining cash flow from investing activities also requires analyzing changes in various account balances along with related income statement amounts. For example, assume the beginning and ending balances in the Land account were $900 and $300, respectively. Furthermore, assume the income statement recognized a $200 gain on the sale of land. The $600 ($900 − $300) decrease in book value means land was sold. The gain on the income statement means the land was sold for $200 more than its book value. This suggests that land was sold for $800 cash ($600 decrease in Land account + $200 Gain). The cash flow amount is different from the gain amount reported on the income statement. The full $800 cash inflow is reported in the investing activities section of the statement of cash flows. The gain has no effect on the operating activities section of the statement of cash flows.

The $800 cash inflow from selling land can be confirmed using the T-account method. Analyzing the beginning and ending Land account balances indicates that land costing $600 ($900 beginning balance − $300 ending balance) was sold. Because of the $200 gain (which is closed to Retained Earnings), $800 cash must have been collected from the sale. The relevant T-accounts appear as follows:

Cash		Land		Retained Earnings	
?		900	600		200
		300			

Financing Activities

Cash flow from financing activities can frequently be determined by simply analyzing the changes in liability and stockholders' equity accounts. For example, an increase in bond liabilities from $500 to $800 implies that a company issued new bonds for $300 cash. The T-account method supports this conclusion. Enter the beginning and ending balances in Bonds Payable as shown:

Bonds Payable		
	500	Beginning balance
	?	
	800	Ending balance

To have an ending balance of $800, the T-account must have been credited for $300. Since increases in bond liabilities are normally the result of borrowing cash, the analysis suggests $300 of cash inflow must have been derived from issuing bonds.

Other explanations are possible. Some of the company's stockholders may have exchanged their equity securities for debt securities or the company may have incurred the obligation in exchange for some asset (property, plant, or equipment) other than cash. Such transactions would be reported in the schedule of noncash investing and financing activities.

Comprehensive Example Using the T-Account Approach

LO 3

Use the T-account method to prepare a statement of cash flows.

The preceding discussion suggests that a statement of cash flows can be prepared by analyzing other financial statements. Beginning and ending asset, liability, and equity account balances can be obtained from two successive balance sheets. Revenues, expenses, gains, and losses can be found on the intervening income statement. Notes to the financial statements may contain information about noncash transactions. Exhibits 12.4 and 12.5 display the balance sheets, income statement, and additional information needed to prepare a statement of cash flows.

EXHIBIT 12.4

THE NEW SOUTH CORPORATION
Comparative Balance Sheets
As of December 31

	2004	2005
Current Assets		
Cash	$ 400	$ 900
Accounts Receivable	1,200	1,000
Interest Receivable	300	400
Inventory	8,200	8,900
Prepaid Insurance	1,400	1,100
Total Current Assets	11,500	12,300
Long-Term Assets		
Marketable Securities	3,500	5,100
Equipment	4,600	5,400
Less: Accumulated Depreciation	(1,200)	(900)
Land	6,000	8,500
Total Long-Term Assets	12,900	18,100
Total Assets	$24,400	$30,400
Current Liabilities		
Accounts Payable—Inventory Purchases	$ 1,100	$ 800
Salaries Payable	900	1,000
Other Operating Expenses Payable	1,300	1,500
Interest Payable	500	300
Unearned Rent Revenue	1,600	600
Total Current Liabilities	5,400	4,200
Long-Term Liabilities		
Mortgage Payable	0	2,500
Bonds Payable	4,000	1,000
Total Long-Term Liabilities	4,000	3,500
Stockholders' Equity		
Common Stock	8,000	10,000
Retained Earnings	7,000	12,700
Total Stockholders' Equity	15,000	22,700
Total Liabilities and Stockholders' Equity	$24,400	$30,400

EXHIBIT 12.5

THE NEW SOUTH CORPORATION Income Statement For the Year Ended December 31, 2005		
Sales		$20,600
Cost of Goods Sold		(10,500)
Gross Margin		10,100
Operating Expenses		
Depreciation Expense	$ 800	
Salaries Expense	2,700	
Insurance Expense	600	
Other Operating Expenses	1,400	
Total Operating Expenses		(5,500)
		4,600
Other Income—Rent Revenue		2,400
Operating Income		7,000
Nonoperating Revenue and Expenses		
Interest Revenue	700	
Interest Expense	(400)	
Loss on Sale of Equipment	(100)	
Total Nonoperating Items		200
Net Income		$ 7,200

Additional information

1. The corporation sold equipment for $300 cash. This equipment had an original cost of $1,500 and accumulated depreciation of $1,100 at the time of the sale.
2. The corporation issued a $2,500 mortgage note in exchange for land.
3. There was a $1,500 cash dividend paid during the accounting period.

Preparing a Statement of Cash Flows

Analyzing the financial statements begins by setting up T-accounts for each balance sheet item, entering beginning balances from the 2004 balance sheet (see Exhibit 12.4) and ending balances from the 2005 balance sheet. Enough room is left in the Cash account to separately record cash flows as operating, investing, and financing activities. For convenience, the T-account analysis uses only balance sheet accounts; any entries to revenue, expense, or dividend accounts is posted directly to retained earnings. Exhibit 12.6 displays the full set of T-accounts after all transactions have been analyzed. Each transaction is labeled with a lowercase letter and a number to clarify the details of the analysis. The following section explains each transaction. Trace every transaction from its explanation to Exhibit 12.6.

Cash Flows from Operating Activities

Determining cash flows from operating activities essentially requires converting the accrual-based revenues and expenses reported on the income statement to their cash equivalents. Each income statement amount should be analyzed separately to assess its cash flow consequences.

Cash Receipts from Sales

The first item reported on the income statement is $20,600 of sales revenue. Assuming all sales were on account, the entry to record sales would have debited Accounts Receivable and credited Sales Revenue. Since sales revenue increases retained earnings, the entry posted to the T-accounts is a debit to Accounts Receivable and a credit to Retained Earnings. This entry is labeled (a1) in Exhibit 12.6.

After recording the sales revenue transaction, the cash inflow from sales can be determined by analyzing the Accounts Receivable T-account. Use algebra to determine that $20,800 ($1,200 + $20,600 − x = $1,000; x = $20,800) of receivables must have been

EXHIBIT 12.6

Balance Sheet T-Accounts

Assets = Liabilities + Equity

Assets

Cash

	Debit	Credit	
Bal.	400		

Operating Activities

	Debit	Credit	
(a2)	20,800	11,500	(b3)
(g2)	1,400	2,600	(d2)
(h2)	600	300	(e2)
		1,200	(f2)
		600	(i2)

Investing Activities

	Debit	Credit	
(k1)	300	1,600	(j1)
		2,300	(l1)

Financing Activities

	Debit	Credit	
(o1)	2,000	3,000	(n1)
		1,500	(p1)
Bal.	900		

Accounts Receivable

	Debit	Credit	
Bal.	1,200	20,800	(a2)
(a1)	20,600		
Bal.	1,000		

Interest Receivable

	Debit	Credit	
Bal.	300	600	(h2)
(h1)	700		
Bal.	400		

Inventory

	Debit	Credit	
Bal.	8,200	10,500	(b1)
(b2)	11,200		
Bal.	8,900		

Prepaid Insurance

	Debit	Credit	
Bal.	1,400	600	(e1)
(e2)	300		
Bal.	1,100		

Marketable Securities

	Debit	Credit	
Bal.	3,500		
(j1)	1,600		
Bal.	5,100		

Equipment

	Debit	Credit	
Bal.	4,600	1,500	(k1)
(l1)	2,300		
Bal.	5,400		

Accumulated Depreciation

	Debit	Credit	
(k1)	1,100	1,200	Bal.
		800	(c1)
		900	Bal.

Land

	Debit	Credit	
Bal.	6,000		
(m1)	2,500		
Bal.	8,500		

Liabilities

Accounts Payable—Inventory

	Debit	Credit	
(b3)	11,500	1,100	Bal.
		11,200	(b2)
		800	Bal.

Salaries Payable

	Debit	Credit	
(d2)	2,600	900	Bal.
		2,700	(d1)
		1,000	Bal.

Other Operating Exp. Payable

	Debit	Credit	
(f2)	1,200	1,300	Bal.
		1,400	(f1)
		1,500	Bal.

Interest Payable

	Debit	Credit	
(i2)	600	500	Bal.
		400	(i1)
		300	Bal.

Unearned Rent Revenue

	Debit	Credit	
(g1)	2,400	1,600	Bal.
		1,400	(g2)
		600	Bal.

Mortgage Payable

	Debit	Credit	
		0	Bal.
		2,500	(m1)
		2,500	Bal.

Bonds Payable

	Debit	Credit	
(n1)	3,000	4,000	Bal.
		1,000	Bal.

Equity

Common Stock

	Debit	Credit	
		8,000	Bal.
		2,000	(o1)
		10,000	Bal.

Retained Earnings

	Debit	Credit	
(b1)	10,500	7,000	Bal.
(c1)	800	20,600	(a1)
(d1)	2,700	2,400	(g1)
(e1)	600	700	(h1)
(f1)	1,400		
(i1)	400		
(k1)	100		
(p1)	1,500		
		12,700	Bal.

collected. The cash inflow is recorded with a debit to the Cash account in the operating activities section and a credit to the Accounts Receivable account. This entry is labeled (a2) in Exhibit 12.6.

The analysis is complete when the difference between the beginning and ending balances in an account has been fully explained. In this case, the analysis of Accounts Receivable is complete. However, the analysis of retained earning will not be complete until all revenue, expense, and dividend events have been recorded.

Cash Payments Associated with Cost of Goods Sold (Inventory Purchases)

The next item on the income statement is cost of goods sold.

When analyzing the inventory account, it is helpful to make two simplifying assumptions. First, assume the company maintains perpetual inventory records; second, assume all inventory purchases are made on account. The following analysis uses these two assumptions.

Recording the \$10,500 cost of goods sold (reported on the income statement in Exhibit 12.5) would have required crediting Inventory and debiting Cost of Goods Sold. Since cost of goods sold reduces retained earnings, the entry is posted as a debit to Retained Earnings and a credit to Inventory. This entry is labeled (b1) in Exhibit 12.6. Further review of the Inventory account indicates that some inventory must have been purchased. Use algebra to determine that \$11,200 (\$8,200 + x − \$10,500 = \$8,900; x = \$11,200) of inventory must have been purchased. The entry to record the inventory purchase, labeled (b2), involves a debit to Inventory and a credit to Accounts Payable. This entry completes the analysis of the Inventory account.

The Accounts Payable analysis is still incomplete. Use algebra and entry (b2) to determine that Accounts Payable decreased by \$11,500 (\$1,100 + \$11,200 − x = \$800; x = \$11,500), reflecting cash payments that must have been made to reduce the liability. The entry to record this cash outflow, labeled (b3), involves a debit to Accounts Payable and a credit in the operating activities section of the Cash account. The analysis of the Accounts Payable account is now complete.

Noncash Effects of Depreciation

The next item on the income statement is depreciation expense, a noncash charge against revenues. No cash is paid when depreciation expense is recorded. The entry to record depreciation expense (c1) involves a debit to Retained Earnings (depreciation expense) and a credit to Accumulated Depreciation. This entry only partly explains the change in accumulated depreciation. Since cash flow consequences related to long-term assets and their respective contra accounts affect the investing activities section of the statement of cash flows, the analysis of Accumulated Depreciation will be completed in the discussion of investing activities after the analysis of cash flows from operating activities is completed.

Cash Payments for Salaries

The entry to record \$2,700 of salaries expense (d1) involves a debit to Retained Earnings (salaries expense) and a credit to Salaries Payable. This entry partly explains the change in the Salaries Payable account. Use algebra to determine that Salaries Payable decreased \$2,600 (\$900 + \$2,700 − x – \$1,000; x = \$2,600), reflecting cash paid for salaries. The entry to record the cash outflows for salaries (d2) involves a debit to the Salaries Payable account and a credit to the operating activities section of the Cash account.

Cash Payments for Insurance

The entry to record \$600 of insurance expense (e1) requires a debit to Retained Earnings (insurance expense) and a credit to Prepaid Insurance. This entry partly explains the change in the Prepaid Insurance account. Use algebra to determine that Prepaid Insurance increased \$300 (\$1,400 + x − \$600 = \$1,100; x = \$300), reflecting cash payments to purchase Prepaid Insurance during the accounting period. The entry to record the cash outflow for the purchase of insurance (e2) involves a debit to the Prepaid Insurance account and a credit to the operating activities section of the Cash account.

Cash Payments for Other Operating Expenses

The \$1,400 of other operating expenses reported on the income statement is recorded in the T-accounts with a debit to Retained Earnings and a credit to the Other Operating Expenses Payable account. This entry (f1) partly explains the change in the Other Operating Expenses Payable account. Use algebra to determine that the liability decreased by \$1,200 (\$1,300 + \$1,400 − x = \$1,500; x = \$1,200), reflecting cash payments for other operating expenses. The entry to record the cash outflow (f2) involves a debit to the Other Operating Expenses Payable account and a credit to the operating activities section of the Cash account.

Cash Receipts for Rent

The entry to record \$2,400 of rent revenue (g1) involves a debit to the Unearned Rent Revenue account and a credit to the Retained Earnings account. This entry partly explains the change in the Unearned Rent Revenue account. Use algebra to determine that the account must have been credited for \$1,400 (\$1,600 + x − \$2,400 = \$600; x = \$1,400), reflecting cash received in advance for rent revenue. The entry to record the cash inflow involves a credit to the Unearned Rent Revenue account and a debit to the operating activities section of the Cash account, (g2) in Exhibit 12.6.

Cash Receipts of Interest Revenue

The entry to record \$700 of interest revenue (h1) involves a debit to the Interest Receivable account and a credit to Retained Earnings (interest revenue). This entry partly explains the change in the Interest Receivable account. Use algebra to determine that interest receivable must have decreased by \$600 (\$300 + \$700 − x = \$400; x = \$600), reflecting cash collection of interest revenue. The entry to record this cash inflow (h2) involves a credit to Interest Receivable and a debit to the operating activities section of the Cash account.

Cash Payments for Interest Expense

The entry to record \$400 of interest expense (i1) involves a debit to Retained Earnings (interest expense) and a credit to Interest Payable. The entry partly explains the change in the Interest Payable account. Use algebra to determine that interest payable decreased by \$600 (\$500 + \$400 − x = \$300; x = \$600), reflecting cash payments of interest obligations. The entry to recognize the cash outflow for interest payments (i2) involves a debit to the Interest Payable account and a credit to the operating activities section of the Cash account.

Noncash Effects of Loss

The loss on sale of equipment does not represent a cash flow. The cash flow represented by the proceeds of the sale is explained shortly in the investing activities discussion. Cash flow from operating activities is not affected by gains or losses on the disposal of long-term assets.

Completion of Analysis of Operating Activities

Since all income statement items have now been analyzed, the conversion of revenues and expenses from accrual to cash for operating activities is complete. The example now moves to cash flows from investing activities.

CHECK YOURSELF 12.2

Q Magazine Inc. reported \$234,800 of revenue for the month. At the beginning of the month, its Unearned Revenue account had a balance of \$78,000. At the end of the month, the account had a balance of \$67,000. Based on this information alone, determine the amount of cash received from revenue.

Answer

The Unearned Revenue account decreased by \$11,000 (\$78,000 − \$67,000). This decrease in unearned revenue would have coincided with an increase in revenue that did not involve receiving cash. As a result, \$11,000 of the revenue earned had no effect on cash flow during this month. To determine the cash received from revenue, subtract the noncash increase from reported revenue. Cash received from revenue is \$223,800 (\$234,800 − \$11,000).

Cash Flows from Investing Activities

Since investing activities generally involve the acquisition (purchase) or disposal (sale) of long-term assets, determining cash flows from investing activities centers on analyzing balance sheet changes in these asset accounts.

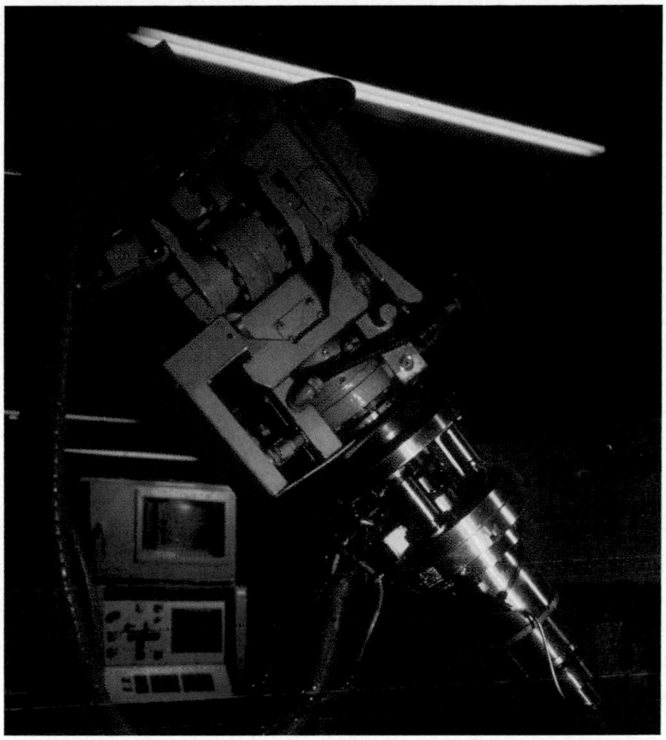

Cash Payments to Purchase Marketable Securities

The first long-term asset reported on the balance sheets, Marketable Securities, increased from \$3,500 at the beginning of the year to \$5,100 at the end of the year. The increase most likely resulted from purchasing additional securities for \$1,600 (\$5,100 − \$3,500). In the absence of evidence to the contrary, it is assumed securities were purchased with cash. The entry to record the purchase (j1) involves a debit to the Marketable Securities account and a credit to the investing activities section of the Cash account. Trace this entry into Exhibit 12.6.

Cash Receipts from Sale of Equipment

The next asset on the balance sheets is Equipment. Previous review of the income statement disclosed a loss on sale of equipment, indicating some equipment was sold during the period. The additional information below the income statement discloses that equipment costing \$1,500 with accumulated depreciation of \$1,100 was sold for \$300. The difference between the \$400 (\$1,500 − \$1,100) book value and the \$300 sales price explains the \$100 loss on the income statement. The cash inflow from the sale, \$300, is unaffected by the original cost, accumulated depreciation, or the amount of the loss. The entry to recognize the cash receipt (k1) involves a debit to the investing activities section of the Cash account, a debit to Retained Earnings (loss), a debit to the Accumulated Depreciation account, and a credit to the Equipment account. Trace this entry into Exhibit 12.6.

Cash Payments to Purchase Equipment

The sale of equipment partly explains the change in the Equipment account. However, further analysis indicates some equipment must have been purchased. Use algebra and entry (k1) to determine that the Equipment account must have increased by \$2,300 (\$4,600 + x − \$1,500 = \$5,400; x = \$2,300), reflecting the purchase of additional equipment. The entry to record the equipment purchase (l1) involves a debit to the Equipment account and a credit to the investing activities section of the Cash account.

Noncash Transaction for Land Acquisition

Land increased from \$6,000 to \$8,500, indicating that land costing \$2,500 (\$8,500 − \$6,000) was acquired during the accounting period. The additional information below the income statement discloses that the corporation issued a mortgage to acquire this land. The entry to record the transaction (m1), a noncash exchange, involves a debit to Land and a credit to Mortgage Payable in Exhibit 12.6. Since the transaction does not affect cash, it is reported in the separate schedule for noncash investing and financing activities included with the statement of cash flows.

Since the changes in all long-term asset accounts have now been explained, the analysis of cash flows from investing activities is complete. The example continues with determining cash flows from financing activities.

Cash Flows from Financing Activities

Since financing activities involve borrowing and repayment transactions and transactions with owners, determining cash flows from financing activities requires analyzing the long-term liability and stockholders' equity sections of the balance sheets. The first long-term liability on the balance sheet is Mortgage Payable. The change in this account was explained previously in conjunction with analyzing the Land account. The financing activity of issuing the mortgage payable is reported along with the investing activity of acquiring land in the separate schedule for noncash transactions.

REALITY BYTES

How did **Florida Power and Light (FPL)** acquire $501 million of property and equipment without spending any cash? Oddly enough, the answer can be found in the company's statement of cash flows. The supplemental schedule of noncash investing and financing activities section of FPL's cash statement shows that it acquired $81 million of equipment by accepting lease obligations and that it acquired $420 million of property by assuming debt. In other words, FPL acquired $501 million ($81 million + $420 million) in property and equipment by agreeing to pay for it later.

Cash Repayment for Bond Principal

The Bonds Payable balance decreased from $4,000 to $1,000. In the absence of evidence to the contrary, it is likely that $3,000 ($4,000 − $1,000) cash was paid to reduce bond liabilities. The entry to record the cash outflow (n1) involves a debit to the Bonds Payable account and a credit to the financing activities section of the Cash account.

Cash Receipt from Stock Issue

The Common Stock balance increased from $8,000 to $10,000. It is reasonable to assume the company issued common stock for $2,000 ($10,000 − $8,000) cash. The entry to record this cash inflow (o1) involves a credit to Common Stock and a debit to the financing activities section of the Cash account.

Cash Payments for Dividends

Finally, additional information below the income statement discloses a cash dividend of $1,500. The transaction to record this cash outflow (p1) involves a debit to the Retained Earnings account and a credit to the financing activities section of the Cash account.

Now all income statement items have been accounted for, all changes in balance sheet accounts have been analyzed, and all additional information has been considered. Review the analysis by tracing each entry into the T-accounts in Exhibit 12.6.

Presenting Information in the Statement of Cash Flows

To prepare the formal statement of cash flows, the inflows and outflows summarized in the Cash T-account must be appropriately organized and labeled. Cash flows from operating activities are presented first, followed by cash flows from investing activities, and finally, cash flows from financing activities. Noncash investing and financing activities are reported in a separate schedule or in the footnotes. Exhibit 12.7 displays the statement of cash flows and a separate schedule for noncash activities.

EXHIBIT 12.7

THE NEW SOUTH CORPORATION Statement of Cash Flows For the Year Ended December 31, 2005			
Cash Flows from Operating Activities			
Cash Receipts from			
Sales	$20,800		
Rent	1,400		
Interest	600		
Total Cash Inflows		$22,800	
Cash Payments for			
Inventory Purchases	11,500		
Salaries	2,600		
Insurance	300		
Other Operating Expenses	1,200		
Interest	600		
Total Cash Outflows		(16,200)	
Net Cash Flow from Operating Activities			$6,600
Cash Flows from Investing Activities			
Inflow from Sale of Equipment		300	
Outflow to Purchase Marketable Securities		(1,600)	
Outflow to Purchase Equipment		(2,300)	
Net Cash Flow for Investing Activities			(3,600)
Cash Flows from Financing Activities			
Inflow from Stock Issue		2,000	
Outflow to Repay Debt		(3,000)	
Outflow for Dividends		(1,500)	
Net Cash Flow for Financing Activities			(2,500)
Net Increase in Cash			500
Plus: Beginning Cash Balance			400
Ending Cash Balance			$ 900
Schedule of Noncash Investing and Financing Activities			
Issue of Mortgage for Land			$2,500

Statement of Cash Flows Presented under the Indirect Method

LO 4

Explain how the indirect method differs from the direct method in reporting cash flow from operating activities.

Topic Tackler PLUS

12-2

In all previous examples this textbook has illustrated the operating activities section of the statement of cash flows using the **direct method.** Although the direct method is easier to understand and is preferred by the Financial Accounting Standards Board, most companies use an alternative format called the **indirect method.** The amount of net cash flow from operating activities is the same using either method, but the presentation of the operating activities section differs. The indirect method starts with net income as reported on the income statement followed by the adjustments necessary to convert the accrual-based net income figure to a cash-basis equivalent. The conversion process uses three basic rules.

Rule 1: Increases in current assets are deducted from net income, and decreases in current assets are added to net income. For example, an increase in accounts receivable suggests that not all sales were collected in cash. The amount of sales revenue reported on the income statement exceeds the amount of cash collections. The increase in receivables must therefore be subtracted from the amount of net income to convert the net income figure to its cash equivalent. Similarly, a decrease in receivables must be added to the net income figure. Comparable logic holds for all current assets.

Rule 2: Increases in current liabilities are added to net income, and decreases in current liabilities are deducted from net income. The rule for current liabilities is the opposite of the rule for current assets. For example, an increase in accounts payable suggests that not all expenses were paid in cash. A greater amount of expenses was subtracted in determining net income than the amount of cash payments for those expenses. The increase in payables must be added to the amount of net income to convert the net income figure to its cash equivalent. Conversely, decreases in payable accounts are deducted from net income. This logic applies to all current liabilities that are affected by operating activities.

CHECK YOURSELF 12.3

The following account balances were drawn from the accounting records of Loeb Inc.

Account Title	Beginning Balance	Ending Balance
Prepaid Rent	$4,200	$3,000
Interest Payable	2,900	2,650

Loeb reported $7,400 of net income during the accounting period. Based on this information alone, determine the amount of cash flow from operating activities.

Answer

Based on Rule 1, the $1,200 decrease ($3,000 − $4,200) in Prepaid Rent (current asset) must be added to net income to determine the amount of cash flow from operating activities. Rule 2 requires that the $250 decrease ($2,650 − $2,900) in Interest Payable (current liability) must be deducted from net income. Accordingly, the cash flow from operating activities is $8,350 ($7,400 + $1,200 − $250). Note that paying interest is defined as an operating activity and should not be confused with dividend payments, which are classified as financing activities.

Rule 3: All noncash expenses and losses are added to net income, and all noncash revenue and gains are subtracted from net income. Some expense and revenue transactions do not have cash consequences. For example, although depreciation is an expense subtracted in determining net income, it does not require a cash payment. The amount of depreciation expense must therefore be added to net income to convert net income to its cash equivalent. Similarly, losses and gains reported on the income statement do not have cash consequences. Net income must be adjusted to remove the effects of losses and gains to convert it to cash flow.

CHECK YOURSELF 12.4

Arley Company's income statement reported net income (in millions) of $326 for the year. The income statement included depreciation expense of $45 and a net loss on the sale of disposable assets of $22. Based on this information alone, determine the net cash flow from operating activities.

Answer

Based on Rule 3, both the depreciation expense and the loss would have to be added to net income to determine cash flow from operating activities. Net cash flow from operating activities would be $393 ($326 + $45 + $22).

Exhibit 12.8 displays the statement of cash flows with operating activities presented using the indirect method. The statement was constructed by applying the three basic conversion rules to The New South Corporation data from Exhibits 12.4 and 12.5. The only

EXHIBIT 12.8

THE NEW SOUTH CORPORATION
Statement of Cash Flows (Indirect Method)
For the Year Ended December 31, 2005

Cash Flows from Operating Activities		
Net Income	$7,200	
Plus: Decreases in Current Assets and Increases in Current Liabilities		
Decrease in Accounts Receivable	200	
Decrease in Prepaid Insurance	300	
Increase in Salaries Payable	100	
Increase in Other Operating Expenses Payable	200	
Less: Increases in Current Assets and Decreases in Current Liabilities		
Increase in Interest Receivable	(100)	
Increase in Inventory	(700)	
Decrease in Accounts Payable	(300)	
Decrease in Interest Payable	(200)	
Decrease in Unearned Rent Revenue	(1,000)	
Plus: Noncash Charges		
Depreciation Expense	800	
Loss on Sale of Equipment	100	
Net Cash Flow from Operating Activities		$6,600
Cash Flows from Investing Activities		
Inflow from Sale of Equipment	300	
Outflow to Purchase Marketable Securities	(1,600)	
Outflow to Purchase Equipment	(2,300)	
Net Cash Flow for Investing Activities		(3,600)
Cash Flows from Financing Activities		
Inflow from Stock Issue	2,000	
Outflow to Repay Debt	(3,000)	
Outflow for Dividends	(1,500)	
Net Cash Flow for Financing Activities		(2,500)
Net Increase in Cash		500
Plus: Beginning Cash Balance		400
Ending Cash Balance		$ 900
Schedule of Noncash Investing and Financing Activities		
Issue of Mortgage for Land		$2,500

difference between the indirect method (Exhibit 12.8) and the direct method (Exhibit 12.7) is in the presentation of the cash flows from operating activities section. Cash flows from investing and financing activities and the schedule of noncash investing and financing activities are the same for both reporting formats.

THE FINANCIAL ANALYST

Why are financial analysts interested in the statement of cash flows? Understanding the cash flows of a business is essential because cash is used to pay the bills. A company, especially one experiencing rapid growth, can be short of cash in spite of earning substantial net income. To illustrate, assume you start a computer sales business. You borrow $2,000 and spend the money to purchase two computers for $1,000 each. You sell one of the computers on account for $1,500. If your loan required a payment at this time, you could not make it. Even though you have net income of $500 ($1,500 sales − $1,000 cost of goods sold), you

LO 5

Explain how the statement of cash flows could mislead decision makers if not interpreted with care.

have no cash until you collect the $1,500 account receivable. A business cannot survive without managing cash flow carefully. It is little wonder that financial analysts are keenly interested in cash flow.

Real-World Data

The statement of cash flows frequently provides a picture of business activity that would otherwise be lost in the complexities of accrual accounting. For example, IBM Corporation's combined operating losses (before taxes) for 1991, 1992, and 1993 were more than $17.9 *billion.* During this same period, IBM reported "restructuring charges" of more than $24 billion. Restructuring costs relate to reorganizing a company. They may include the costs of closing facilities and losses on asset disposals. Without the restructuring charges, IBM would have reported operating *profits* of about $6 billion (before taxes). Do restructuring charges signal positive or negative changes? Different financial analysts have different opinions about this issue. However, one aspect of IBM's performance during these years is easily understood. The company produced over $21 billion in positive cash flow from operating activities. It had no trouble paying its bills.

Investors consider cash flow information so important that they are willing to pay for it, even when the FASB discourages its use. The FASB *prohibits* companies from disclosing *cash flow per share* in audited financial statements. However, one prominent stock analysis service, *Value Line Investment Survey,* sells this information to a significant customer base. Clearly, Value Line's customers value information about cash flows.

Exhibit 12.9 compares income from operations and cash flow from operating activities for six real-world companies from five different industries for the 2000, 2001, and 2002 fiscal years.

Several things are apparent from Exhibit 12.9. The cash flow from operating activities exceeds income from operations for all of the companies except Toll Brothers. Many real-world companies report such a result because depreciation, a noncash expense, is usually significant. The most dramatic example is for Sprint in 2001. Even though Sprint reported a *net loss* from operations of approximately $2.3 billion, it generated *positive* cash flow from

EXHIBIT 12.9

Operating Income versus Cash Flow From Operating Activities (Amounts in $000)

Company		2002	2001	2000
Alaska Airlines	Operating Income	$ (57,000)	$ (11,800)	$ (14,800)
	Cash Flow Operating Activities	119,600	202,000	282,900
Southwest Airlines	Operating Income	240,969	511,147	625,224
	Cash Flow Operating Activities	520,209	1,484,608	1,298,286
Boeing	Operating Income	2,319,000	2,826,000	2,128,000
	Cash Flow Operating Activities	4,375,000	3,894,000	6,226,000
Mattel	Operating Income	455,042	310,920	170,177
	Cash Flow Operating Activities	1,156,084	756,793	555,090
Sprint	Operating Income	468,000	(2,274,000)	(963,000)
	Cash Flow Operating Activities	6,206,000	4,563,000	4,096,000
Toll Brothers	Operating Income	219,887	213,673	145,943
	Cash Flow Operating Activities	(94,105)	(148,379)	(16,863)

operating activities of more than $4.5 *billion.* This difference between cash flow from operating activities and operating income helps explain how some companies can have significant losses over a few years and continue to stay in business and pay their bills.

The exhibit shows that cash flow from operating activities can be more stable than operating income. Results for Sprint also demonstrate this clearly. Although the company's earnings were negative in 2000, more negative in 2001, and positive in 2002, its cash flows from operating activities were always positive. Stability is one of the reasons many financial analysts prefer cash flow over earnings as a predictor of future performance.

Finally, what could explain why Toll Brothers has *less* cash flow from operating activities than operating income? Does the company have a problem? Not necessarily. Toll Brothers is experiencing the kind of growth described earlier for your computer sales business. Its cash is supporting growth in inventory levels. Toll Brothers is one of the nation's largest new-home construction companies. Its growth rates, based on revenue from sales of new homes, for the 2002, 2001, and 2000 fiscal years were 5 percent, 24 percent, and 23 percent, respectively. When Toll Brothers begins to build new homes, it needs more inventory. Increases in inventory *do* affect cash flow from operating activities. Remember, increases in current assets decrease cash flow from operating activities. This condition alone might explain why the company has less cash flow from operating activities than operating income. Is this situation unfavorable? Chapter 5 made the point that, *other things being equal,* it is better to have less inventory. At Toll Brothers, however, other things are not equal. The company has been growing rapidly.

The Toll Brothers situation highlights a potential weakness in the format of the statement of cash flows. Some accountants consider it misleading to classify all increases in long-term assets as *investing activities* and all changes in inventory as affecting cash flow from operating activities. They argue that the increase in inventory at Toll Brothers that results from building more houses should be classified as an investing activity, just as the cost of a new building is. Although inventory is classified as a current asset and buildings are classified as long-term assets, in reality there is a certain level of inventory a company must permanently maintain to stay in business. The GAAP format of the statement of cash flows penalizes cash flow from operating activities for increases in inventory that are really a permanent investment in assets.

Conversely, the same critics might argue that some purchases of long-term assets are not actually *investments* but merely replacements of old, existing property, plant, and equipment. In other words, the *investing activities* section of the statement of cash flows makes no distinction between expenditures that expand the business and those that simply replace old equipment (sometimes called *capital maintenance* expenditures).

Users of the statement of cash flows must exercise the same care interpreting it as when they use the balance sheet or the income statement. Numbers alone are insufficient. Users must evaluate numbers based on knowledge of the particular business and industry they are analyzing.

Accounting information alone cannot guide a businessperson to a sound decision. Making good business decisions requires an understanding of the business in question, the environmental and economic factors affecting the operation of that business, and the accounting concepts on which the financial statements of that business are based.

A Look Back <<

Thus far in this text, you have considered many different accounting events that businesses experience. You have been asked to consider the effects these events have on a company's balance sheet, income statement, and statement of cash flows. By now, you should recognize that each financial statement shows a different, but equally important, view of a company's financial situation.

This chapter examined in detail only one financial statement, the statement of cash flows. The chapter provided a more comprehensive discussion of how accrual accounting relates to cash-based accounting. Effective use of financial statements requires understanding not only accrual and cash-based accounting systems but also how they relate to each other. That relationship is why a statement of cash flows can begin with a reconciliation of net income, an accrual measurement, to net cash flow from operating activities, a cash measurement. Finally, this chapter explained how the conventions for classifying cash flows as operating, investing, or financing activities require analysis and understanding to make informed decisions with the financial information.

>> A Look Forward

Chapter 13 focuses on financial statement analysis. It explains and illustrates a number of tools analysts can use to evaluate a company's profitability, financial soundness, and levels of risk based on reported financial statement information.

SELF-STUDY REVIEW PROBLEM

The following financial statements pertain to Schlemmer Company.

Balance Sheets
As of December 31

	2003	2004
Cash	$ 2,800	$48,400
Accounts Receivable	1,200	2,200
Inventory	6,000	5,600
Equipment	22,000	18,000
Accumulated Depreciation–Equip.	(17,400)	(13,650)
Land	10,400	17,200
Total Assets	$25,000	$77,750
Accounts Payable	$ 4,200	$ 5,200
Long-Term Debt	6,400	5,600
Common Stock	10,000	19,400
Retained Earnings	4,400	47,550
Total Liabilities and Equity	$25,000	$77,750

Income Statement
For the Year Ended December 31, 2004

Sales Revenue	$67,300
Cost of Goods Sold	(24,100)
Gross Margin	43,200
Depreciation Expense	(1,250)
Operating Income	41,950
Gain on Sale of Equipment	2,900
Loss on Disposal of Land	(100)
Net Income	$44,750

Additional Data

1. During 2004 the company sold equipment for $8,900 that had originally cost $11,000. Accumulated depreciation on this equipment was $5,000 at the time of sale. Also, the company purchased equipment for $7,000.
2. The company sold for $2,500 land that had cost $2,600, resulting in the recognition of a $100 loss. Also, common stock was issued in exchange for land valued at $9,400 at the time of the exchange.
3. The company declared and paid dividends of $1,600.

Required

a. Use T-accounts to analyze the preceding data.

b. Using the direct method, prepare in good form a statement of cash flows for the year ended December 31, 2004.

Solution to Requirement *a*

Transactions Legend

a1. Revenue, $67,300.
a2. Collection of accounts receivable, $66,300 ($1,200 + $67,300 − $2,200).
b1. Cost of goods sold, $24,100.
b2. Inventory purchases, $23,700 ($5,600 + $24,100 − $6,000).
b3. Payments for inventory purchases, $22,700 ($4,200 + $23,700 − $5,200).
c1. Depreciation expense, $1,250 (noncash).
d1. Sale of equipment, $8,900; cost of equipment sold, $11,000; accumulated depreciation on equipment sold, $5,000.
d2. Purchase of equipment, $7,000.
e1. Sale of land, $2,500; cost of land sold, $2,600.
f1. Issue of stock in exchange for land, $9,400.
g1. Paid dividends, $1,600.
h1. Paid off portion of long-term debt, $800.

SCHLEMMER COMPANY

T-Accounts

Assets = Liabilities + Equity

Assets

Cash

Bal.	2,800		
(a2)	66,300	(b3)	22,700
(d1)	8,900	(d2)	7,000
(e1)	2,500	(g1)	1,600
		(h1)	800
Bal.	48,400		

Accounts Receivable

Bal.	1,200		
(a1)	67,300	(a2)	66,300
Bal.	2,200		

Inventory

Bal.	6,000		
(b2)	23,700	(b1)	24,100
Bal.	5,600		

Equipment

Bal.	22,000		
(d2)	7,000	(d1)	11,000
Bal.	18,000		

Accumulated Depreciation

		Bal.	17,400
(d1)	5,000	(c1)	1,250
		Bal.	13,650

Land

Bal.	10,400		
(f1)	9,400	(e1)	2,600
Bal.	17,200		

Liabilities

Accounts Payable

		Bal.	4,200
(b3)	22,700	(b2)	23,700
		Bal.	5,200

Long-Term Debt

		Bal.	6,400
(h1)	800		
		Bal.	5,600

Equity

Common Stock

		Bal.	10,000
		(f1)	9,400
		Bal.	19,400

Retained Earnings

		Bal.	4,400
(b1)	24,100	(a1)	67,300
(c1)	1,250	(d1)	2,900
(e1)	100		
(g1)	1,600		
		Bal.	47,550

Solution to Requirement b

SCHLEMMER COMPANY Statement of Cash Flows For the Year Ended December 31, 2004		
Cash Flows from Operating Activities		
Cash Receipts from Customers	$66,300	
Cash Payments for Inventory Purchases	(22,700)	
Net Cash Flow Provided by Operating Activities		$43,600
Cash Flows from Investing Activities		
Inflow from Sale of Equipment	8,900	
Inflow from Sale of Land	2,500	
Outflow to Purchase Equipment	(7,000)	
Net Cash Flow Provided by Investing Activities		4,400
Cash Flows from Financing Activities		
Outflow for Dividends	(1,600)	
Outflow for Repayment of Debt	(800)	
Net Cash Flow Used by Financing Activities		(2,400)
Net Increase in Cash		45,600
Plus: Beginning Cash Balance		2,800
Ending Cash Balance		$48,400
Schedule of Noncash Investing and Financing Activities		
Issued Common Stock for Land		$ 9,400

KEY TERMS

accrual transactions 605
cash inflows 603
cash outflows 603
deferral transactions 608
direct method 617
expense transactions 606
financing activities 604
indirect method 617
investing activities 604
noncash investing and financing activities 604
operating activities 604
revenue transactions 606
T-account method 606

QUESTIONS

1. What is the purpose of the statement of cash flows?
2. What are the three categories of cash flows reported on the cash flow statement? Discuss each and give an example of an inflow and an outflow for each category.
3. What are noncash investing and financing activities? Provide an example. How are such transactions shown on the statement of cash flows?
4. Best Company had beginning accounts receivable of $12,000 and ending accounts receivable of $14,000. If total sales were $110,000, what amount of cash was collected?
5. Best Company's Utilities Payable account had a beginning balance of $3,300 and an ending balance of $5,200. Utilities expense reported on the income statement was $87,000. What was the amount of cash paid for utilities for the period?
6. Best Company had a balance in the Unearned Revenue account of $4,300 at the beginning of the period and an ending balance of $5,700. If the portion of unearned revenue Best recognized as earned during the period was $15,600, what amount of cash did Best collect?
7. Which of the following activities are financing activities?
   (a) Payment of accounts payable.
   (b) Payment of interest on bonds payable.

(c) Sale of common stock.
(d) Sale of preferred stock at a premium.
(e) Payment of a cash dividend.

8. Does depreciation expense affect net cash flow? Explain.
9. If Best Company sold land that cost $4,200 at a $500 gain, how much cash did it collect from the sale of land?
10. If Best Company sold office equipment that originally cost $7,500 and had $7,200 of accumulated depreciation at a $100 loss, what was the selling price for the office equipment?
11. In which section of the statement of cash flows would the following transactions be reported?
    (a) Cash receipt of interest income.
    (b) Cash purchase of marketable securities.
    (c) Cash purchase of equipment.
    (d) Cash sale of merchandise.
    (e) Cash sale of common stock.
    (f) Payment of interest expense.
    (g) Cash proceeds from loan.
    (h) Cash payment on bonds payable.
    (i) Cash receipt from sale of old equipment.
    (j) Cash payment for operating expenses.
12. What is the difference between preparing the statement of cash flows using the direct method and using the indirect method?
13. Which method (direct or indirect) of presenting the statement of cash flows is more intuitively logical? Why?
14. What is the major advantage of using the indirect method to present the statement of cash flows?
15. What is the advantage of using the direct method to present the statement of cash flows?
16. How would Best Company report the following transactions on the statement of cash flows?
    (a) Purchased new equipment for $46,000 cash.
    (b) Sold old equipment for $8,700 cash. The equipment had a book value of $4,900.
17. Can a company report negative net cash flows from operating activities for the year on the statement of cash flows but still have positive net income on the income statement? Explain.
18. Why does the FASB prohibit disclosing cash flow per share in audited financial statements?

EXERCISES—SERIES A

All Exercises in Series A are available with McGraw-Hill's Homework Manager

Exercise 12-1A *Classifying cash flows into categories—direct method* L.O. 1

Required

Classify each of the following as operating activities, investing activities, financing activities, or non-cash transactions. (Assume the use of the direct method.)

a. Paid cash to settle note payable.
b. Sold land for cash.
c. Paid cash to purchase a computer.
d. Paid cash for employee compensation.
e. Received cash interest from a bond investment.
f. Recognized depreciation expense.
g. Acquired cash from issue of common stock.
h. Provided services for cash.
i. Acquired cash by issuing a note payable.
j. Paid cash for interest.
k. Paid cash dividends.

L.O. 1

Exercise 12-2A ***Cash outflows from operating activities—direct method***

Required

Which of the following transactions produce cash outflows from operating activities (assume the use of the direct method)?

a. Cash receipt from collecting accounts receivable.
b. Cash receipt from sale of land.
c. Cash payment for dividends.
d. Cash payment to settle an account payable.
e. Cash payment to purchase inventory.
f. Cash payment for equipment.

L.O. 2

Exercise 12-3A ***Using account balances to determine cash flows from operating activities—direct method***

The following account balances are available for Max Company for 2007.

Account Title	Beginning of Year	End of Year
Accounts Receivable	$42,000	$46,000
Interest Receivable	6,000	5,000
Accounts Payable	22,000	26,000
Salaries Payable	12,000	15,000

Other Information for 2007

Sales on account	$680,000
Interest revenue	24,000
Operating expenses	270,000
Salaries expense for the year	172,000

Required

(*Hint:* It may be helpful to assume that all revenues and expenses are on account.)

a. Compute the amount of cash *inflow* from operating activities.
b. Compute the amount of cash *outflow* from operating activities.

L.O. 2

Exercise 12-4A ***Using account balances to determine cash flow from operating activities—direct method***

The following account balances were available for Theri Enterprises for 2007.

Account Title	Beginning of Year	End of Year
Unearned Revenue	$5,000	$6,500
Prepaid Rent	2,400	1,800

During the year, $68,000 of unearned revenue was recognized as having been earned. Rent expense for the period was $15,000. Theri Enterprises maintains its books on the accrual basis.

Required

Using T-accounts and the preceding information, determine the amount of cash inflow from revenue and cash outflow for rent.

Exercise 12-5A *Using account balances to determine cash flow from investing activities* L.O. 2, 3

The following account information pertains to Guidry Company for 2005.

Land		Marketable Securities	
Bal. 46,000	56,000	Bal. 82,000	46,000
128,000		120,000	
Bal. 118,000		Bal. 156,000	

The income statement reported a $3,000 loss on the sale of land and a $2,500 gain on the sale of marketable securities.

Required

Prepare the investing activities section of the 2005 statement of cash flows.

Exercise 12-6A *Using account balances to determine cash flow from financing activities* L.O. 2, 3

The following account balances pertain to Olack Inc. for 2006.

Bonds Payable		Common Stock		Paid-in Capital in Excess of Par Value	
	Bal. 220,000		Bal. 280,000		Bal. 90,000
90,000			180,000		50,000
	Bal. 130,000		Bal. 460,000		Bal. 140,000

Required

Prepare the financing activities section of the 2006 statement of cash flows.

Exercise 12-7A *Using account balances to determine cash outflow for inventory purchases* L.O. 2

The following account information pertains to Maze Company, which uses the perpetual inventory method and purchases all inventory on account.

Inventory		Accounts Payable	
Bal. 52,000			Bal. 44,000
?	352,000	?	?
Bal. 61,000			Bal. 41,000

Required

Compute the amount of cash paid for the purchase of inventory.

Exercise 12-8A *Using account balances to determine cash flow from operating activities—indirect method* L.O. 2, 4

Kwon Company presents its statement of cash flows using the indirect method. The following accounts and corresponding balances were drawn from Kwon's accounting records for the period.

Account Titles	Beginning Balances	Ending Balances
Accounts Receivable	$32,000	$28,000
Prepaid Rent	1,500	1,800
Interest Receivable	500	700
Accounts Payable	9,800	8,500
Salaries Payable	3,200	3,600
Unearned Revenue	6,000	4,000

Net income for the period was $52,000.

Required

Using the preceding information, compute the net cash flow from operating activities using the indirect method.

L.O. 2, 3, 4

Exercise 12-9A ***Using account balances to determine cash flow from operating activities—direct and indirect methods***

The following account balances are from Marlin Company's accounting records. Assume Marlin had no investing or financing transactions during 2007.

December 31	2006	2007
Cash	$65,000	$107,000
Accounts Receivable	75,000	78,000
Prepaid Rent	900	800
Accounts Payable	33,000	34,000
Utilities Payable	1,200	1,500
Sales Revenue		$272,000
Operating Expenses		(168,000)
Utilities Expense		(36,400)
Rent Expense		(24,000)
Net Income		$ 43,600

Required

a. Prepare the operating activities section of the 2007 statement of cash flows using the direct method.

b. Prepare the operating activities section of the 2007 statement of cash flows using the indirect method.

L.O. 3, 5

Exercise 12-10A ***Interpreting statement of cash flows information***

The following selected transactions pertain to Johnston Corporation for 2007.

1. Paid $35,200 cash to purchase delivery equipment.
2. Sold delivery equipment for $3,500. The equipment had originally cost $18,000 and had accumulated depreciation of $12,000.
3. Borrowed $50,000 cash by issuing bonds at face value.
4. Purchased a building that cost $220,000. Paid $50,000 cash and issued a mortgage for the remaining $170,000.
5. Exchanged no-par common stock for machinery valued at $38,700.

Required

a. Prepare the appropriate sections of the 2007 statement of cash flows.

b. Explain how a company could spend more cash on investing activities than it collected from financing activities during the same accounting period.

PROBLEMS—SERIES A

All Problems in Series A are available with McGraw-Hill's Homework Manager

L.O. 1

Problem 12-11A ***Classifying cash flows***

Required

Classify each of the following as an operating activity (OA), an investing activity (IA), or a financing activity (FA) cash flow, or a noncash transaction (NT).

a. Provided services for cash.
b. Purchased marketable securities with cash.
c. Paid cash for rent.
d. Received interest on note receivable.
e. Paid cash for salaries.
f. Received advance payment for services.
g. Paid a cash dividend.
h. Provided services on account.
i. Purchased office supplies on account.
j. Bought land with cash.
k. Collected cash from accounts receivable.
l. Issued common stock for cash.
m. Repaid principal and interest on a note payable.
n. Declared a stock split.
o. Purchased inventory with cash.
p. Recorded amortization of intangibles.
q. Paid insurance with cash.
r. Issued a note payable in exchange for equipment.
s. Recorded depreciation expense.

Problem 12-12A *Using transaction data to prepare a statement of cash flows*

L.O. 2, 3

CHECK FIGURE
Net Cash Flow from Operating Activities: $(110,775)

Store Company engaged in the following transactions during the 2007 accounting period. The beginning cash balance was $28,600.

1. Sales on account were $250,000. The beginning receivables balance was $87,000 and the ending balance was $83,000.
2. Salaries expense for the period was $56,000. The beginning salaries payable balance was $3,500 and the ending balance was $2,000.
3. Other operating expenses for the period were $125,000. The beginning operating expense payable balance was $4,500 and the ending balance was $8,500.
4. Recorded $19,500 of depreciation expense. The beginning and ending balances in the Accumulated Depreciation account were $14,000 and $33,500, respectively.
5. The Equipment account had beginning and ending balances of $210,000 and $240,000, respectively. The increase was caused by the cash purchase of equipment.
6. The beginning and ending balances in the Notes Payable account were $50,000 and $150,000, respectively. The increase was caused by additional cash borrowing.
7. There was $6,000 of interest expense reported on the income statement. The beginning and ending balances in the Interest Payable account were $1,500 and $1,000, respectively.
8. The beginning and ending Merchandise Inventory account balances were $90,000 and $108,000, respectively. The company sold merchandise with a cost of $156,000 (cost of goods sold for the period was $156,000). The beginning and ending balances of Accounts Payable were $9,500 and $11,500, respectively.
9. The beginning and ending balances of Notes Receivable were $5,000 and $10,000, respectively. The increase resulted from a cash loan to one of the company's employees.
10. The beginning and ending balances of the Common Stock account were $100,000 and $120,000, respectively. The increase was caused by the issue of common stock for cash.
11. Land had beginning and ending balances of $50,000 and $41,000, respectively. Land that cost $9,000 was sold for $12,200, resulting in a gain of $3,200.
12. The tax expense for the period was $7,700. The Taxes Payable account had a $950 beginning balance and an $875 ending balance.
13. The Investments account had beginning and ending balances of $25,000 and $29,000, respectively. The company purchased investments for $18,000 cash during the period, and investments that cost $14,000 were sold for $9,000, resulting in a $5,000 loss.

Required

Convert the preceding information to cash-equivalent data and prepare a statement of cash flows.

L.O. 2, 3

excel

mhhe.com/edmonds2007

CHECK FIGURE

a. Net Cash Flow from Operating Activities: $(7,600)

Problem 12-13A *Using financial statement data to determine cash flow from operating activities*

The following account information is available for Park Company for 2004:

Account Title	Beginning of Year	End of Year
Accounts Receivable	$26,000	$24,000
Merchandise Inventory	52,000	56,000
Prepaid Insurance	24,000	20,000
Accounts Payable (Inventory)	20,000	23,000
Salaries Payable	4,200	4,600

Other Information

1. Sales for the period were $180,000.
2. Purchases of merchandise for the period were $90,000.
3. Insurance expense for the period was $42,000.
4. Other operating expenses (all cash) were $30,000.
5. Salary expense was $35,000.

Required

a. Compute the net cash flow from operating activities.
b. Prepare the cash flow from operating activities section of the statement of cash flows.

L.O. 2, 3

excel

mhhe.com/edmonds2007

CHECK FIGURE

a. Net Cash Flow from Investing Activities: $(152,000)

Problem 12-14A *Using financial statement data to determine cash flow from investing activities*

The following information pertaining to investing activities is available for Leach Company for 2005:

Account Title	Beginning of Year	End of Year
Machinery and Equipment	$425,000	$520,000
Marketable Securities	112,000	102,000
Land	90,000	140,000

Other Information for 2005

1. Marketable securities were sold at book value. No gain or loss was recognized.
2. Machinery was purchased for $120,000. Old machinery with a book value of $5,000 (cost of $25,000, accumulated depreciation of $20,000) was sold for $8,000.
3. No land was sold during the year.

Required

a. Compute the net cash flow from investing activities.
b. Prepare the cash flow from investing activities section of the statement of cash flows.

L.O. 2, 3

CHECK FIGURE

a. Net Cash Flow from Financing Activities: $(25,000)

Problem 12-15A *Using financial statement data to determine cash flow from financing activities*

The following information pertaining to financing activities is available for Rebel Company for 2007:

Account Title	Beginning of Year	End of Year
Bonds Payable	$300,000	$210,000
Common Stock	200,000	260,000
Paid-in Capital in Excess of Par	75,000	110,000

Other Information

1. Dividends paid during the period amounted to $30,000.
2. No new funds were borrowed during the period.

Required

a. Compute the net cash flow from financing activities for 2007.
b. Prepare the cash flow from financing activities section of the statement of cash flows.

Problem 12-16A ***Using financial statements to prepare a statement of cash flows—direct method***

L.O. 2, 3

CHECK FIGURES
Net Cash Flow from Operating Activities: $18,750
Net Increase in Cash: $21,400

The following financial statements were drawn from the records of Pacific Company.

Balance Sheets
As of December 31

	2006	2007
Assets		
Cash	$ 2,800	$24,200
Accounts Receivable	1,200	2,000
Inventory	6,000	6,400
Equipment	42,000	19,000
Accumulated Depreciation—Equipment	(17,400)	(9,000)
Land	10,400	18,400
Total Assets	$45,000	$61,000
Liabilities and Equity		
Accounts Payable	$ 4,200	$ 2,600
Long-Term Debt	6,400	2,800
Common Stock	10,000	22,000
Retained Earnings	24,400	33,600
Total Liabilities and Equity	$45,000	$61,000

Income Statement
For the Year Ended December 31, 2007

Sales Revenue	$35,700
Cost of Goods Sold	(14,150)
Gross Margin	21,550
Depreciation Expense	(3,600)
Operating Income	17,950
Gain on Sale of Equipment	500
Loss on Disposal of Land	(50)
Net Income	$18,400

Additional Data

1. During 2007, the company sold equipment for $18,500; it had originally cost $30,000. Accumulated depreciation on this equipment was $12,000 at the time of the sale. Also, the company purchased equipment for $7,000 cash.
2. The company sold land that had cost $4,000. This land was sold for $3,950, resulting in the recognition of a $50 loss. Also, common stock was issued in exchange for title to land that was valued at $12,000 at the time of exchange.
3. Paid dividends of $9,200.

Required

Use the T-account method to analyze the data and prepare a statement of cash flows using the direct method.

L.O. 2, 3

CHECK FIGURES

Net Cash Flow from Operating Activities: $86,800

Net Increase in Cash: $95,400

Problem 12-17A ***Using financial statements to prepare a statement of cash flows—direct method***

The following financial statements were drawn from the records of Raceway Sports:

Balance Sheets As of December 31	2006	2007
Assets		
Cash	$ 28,200	$123,600
Accounts Receivable	66,000	57,000
Inventory	114,000	126,000
Notes Receivable	30,000	0
Equipment	255,000	147,000
Accumulated Depreciation–Equipment	(141,000)	(74,740)
Land	52,500	82,500
Total Assets	$404,700	$461,360
Liabilities and Equity		
Accounts Payable	$ 48,600	$ 42,000
Salaries Payable	24,000	30,000
Utilities Payable	1,200	600
Interest Payable	1,800	0
Note Payable	60,000	0
Common Stock	240,000	300,000
Retained Earnings	29,100	88,760
Total Liabilities and Equity	$404,700	$461,360

Income Statement For the Year Ended December 31, 2007	
Sales Revenue	$580,000
Cost of Goods Sold	(288,000)
Gross Margin	292,000
Operating Expenses	
Salary Expense	(184,000)
Depreciation Expense	(17,740)
Utilities Expense	(12,200)
Operating Income	78,060
Nonoperating Items	
Interest Expense	(3,000)
Loss on Sale of Equipment	(1,800)
Net Income	$ 73,260

Additional Information

1. Sold equipment costing $108,000 with accumulated depreciation of $84,000 for $22,200 cash.
2. Paid a $13,600 cash dividend to owners.

Required

Use the T-account method to analyze the data and prepare a statement of cash flows using the direct method.

Problem 12-18A ***Using financial statements to prepare a statement of cash flows—indirect method***

L.O. 2, 4

eXcel

mhhe.com/edmonds2007

The comparative balance sheets for Redwood Corporation for 2006 and 2007 follow:

CHECK FIGURES

Net Cash Flow from Operating Activities: $170,200

Net Increase in Cash: $28,200

Balance Sheets As of December 31	2006	2007
Assets		
Cash	$ 40,600	$ 68,800
Accounts Receivable	22,000	30,000
Merchandise Inventory	176,000	160,000
Prepaid Rent	4,800	2,400
Equipment	288,000	256,000
Accumulated Depreciation	(236,000)	(146,800)
Land	80,000	192,000
Total Assets	$375,400	$562,400
Liabilities		
Accounts Payable (Inventory)	$ 76,000	$ 67,000
Salaries Payable	24,000	28,000
Stockholders' Equity		
Common Stock, $25 Par Value	200,000	250,000
Retained Earnings	75,400	217,400
Total Liabilities and Equity	$375,400	$562,400

Income Statement For the Year Ended December 31, 2007	
Sales	$1,500,000
Cost of Goods Sold	(797,200)
Gross Profit	702,800
Operating Expenses	
Depreciation Expense	(22,800)
Rent Expense	(24,000)
Salaries Expense	(256,000)
Other Operating Expenses	(258,000)
Net Income	$ 142,000

Other Information

1. Purchased land for $112,000.
2. Purchased new equipment for $100,000.
3. Sold old equipment that cost $132,000 with accumulated depreciation of $112,000 for $20,000 cash.
4. Issued common stock for $50,000.

Required

Prepare the statement of cash flows for 2007 using the indirect method.

EXERCISES—SERIES B

Exercise 12-1B ***Classifying cash flows into categories—direct method***

L.O. 1

Required

Identify whether the cash flows in the following list should be classified as operating activities, investing activities, or financing activities on the statement of cash flows (assume the use of the direct method).

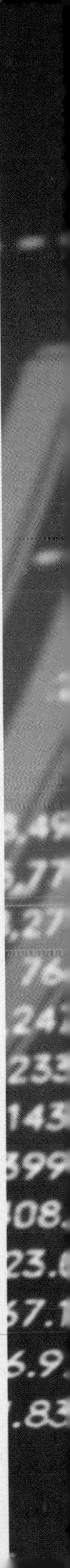

a. Sold merchandise on account.
b. Paid employee salary.
c. Received cash proceeds from bank loan.
d. Paid dividends.
e. Sold used equipment for cash.
f. Received interest income on a certificate of deposit.
g. Issued stock for cash.
h. Repaid bank loan.
i. Purchased equipment for cash.
j. Paid interest on loan.

L.O. 1

Exercise 12-2B ***Cash inflows from operating activities—direct method***

Required

Which of the following transactions produce cash inflows from operating activities (assume the use of the direct method)?

a. Cash payment for utilities expense.
b. Cash payment for equipment.
c. Cash receipt from interest.
d. Cash payment for dividends.
e. Collection of cash from accounts receivable.
f. Provide services for cash.

L.O. 2

Exercise 12-3B ***Using account balances to determine cash flow from operating activities—direct method***

The following account balances are available for Norstom Company for 2006.

Account Title	Beginning of Year	End of Year
Accounts Receivable	$40,000	$46,000
Interest Receivable	5,000	3,000
Accounts Payable	30,000	33,000
Salaries Payable	12,000	10,500

Other Information for 2006

Sales on account	$275,000
Interest revenue	25,000
Operating expenses	196,000
Salaries expense for the year	75,000

Required

(*Hint:* It may be helpful to assume that all revenues and expenses are on account.)

a. Compute the amount of cash *inflow* from operating activities.
b. Compute the amount of cash *outflow* from operating activities.

L.O. 2

Exercise 12-4B ***Using account balances to determine cash flow from operating activities—direct method***

The following account balances were available for Earles Candy Company for 2007:

Account Title	Beginning of Year	End of Year
Unearned Revenue	$18,000	$8,000
Prepaid Rent	2,000	900

During the year, $41,000 of unearned revenue was recognized as having been earned. Rent expense for the period was $8,000. Earles Candy Company maintains its books on the accrual basis.

Required

Using T-accounts and the preceding information, determine the amount of cash inflow from revenue and cash outflow for rent.

Exercise 12-5B ***Using account balances to determine cash flow from investing activities*** **L.O. 2, 3**

The following account information is available for McClung Inc. for 2005:

Land			Marketable Securities		
Bal.	20,000	50,000	Bal.	75,000	30,000
	100,000			40,000	
Bal.	70,000		Bal.	85,000	

The income statement reported a $9,000 gain on the sale of land and a $1,200 loss on the sale of marketable securities.

Required

Prepare the investing activities section of the statement of cash flows for 2005.

Exercise 12-6B ***Using account balances to determine cash flow from financing activities*** **L.O. 2, 3**

The following account balances were available for Golden Company for 2007:

Mortgage Payable			Common Stock			Paid-in Capital In Excess of Par		
	148,000	Bal.		200,000	Bal.		65,000	Bal.
62,000				50,000			30,000	
	86,000	Bal.		250,000	Bal.		95,000	Bal.

Required

Prepare the financing activities section of the statement of cash flows for 2007.

Exercise 12-7B ***Using account balances to determine cash outflow for inventory purchases*** **L.O. 2**

The following account information is available for Sherman Company. The company uses the perpetual inventory method and makes all inventory purchases on account.

Inventory			Accounts Payable		
Bal.	41,000			42,000	Bal.
	?	120,000	?	?	
Bal.	65,000			52,000	Bal.

Required

Compute the amount of cash paid for the purchase of inventory.

Exercise 12-8B ***Using account balances to determine cash flow from operating activities—indirect method*** **L.O. 2, 4**

Maple Company presents its statement of cash flows using the indirect method. The following accounts and corresponding balances were drawn from Maple's accounting records.

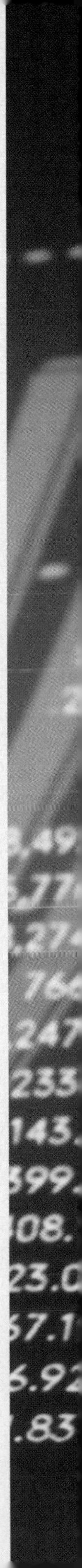

Account Titles	Beginning Balances	Ending Balances
Accounts Receivable	$30,000	$35,000
Prepaid Rent	2,000	1,200
Interest Receivable	800	400
Accounts Payable	9,000	9,500
Salaries Payable	2,500	2,100
Unearned Revenue	1,200	2,200

Net income for the period was $45,000.

Required

Using the preceding information, compute the net cash flow from operating activities using the indirect method.

L.O. 2-4

Exercise 12-9B ***Using account balances to determine cash flow from operating activities—direct and indirect methods***

The following information is from the accounting records of Mong Company:

	2008	2009
Cash	$ 42,000	$ 88,800
Accounts Receivable	158,000	159,800
Prepaid Rent	3,000	5,600
Accounts Payable	120,000	125,000
Utilities Payable	12,000	8,400
Sales Revenue		$212,000
Operating Expenses		(135,000)
Utilities Expense		(17,200)
Rent Expense		(10,000)
Net Income		$ 49,800

Required

a. Prepare the operating activities section of the 2009 statement of cash flows using the direct method.

b. Prepare the operating activities section of the 2009 statement of cash flows using the indirect method.

L.O. 3, 5

Exercise 12-10B ***Interpreting statement of cash flows information***

The following selected transactions pertain to Johnston Company for 2008.

1. Purchased new office equipment for $9,800 cash.
2. Sold old office equipment for $2,000 that originally cost $12,000 and had accumulated depreciation of $11,000.
3. Borrowed $20,000 cash from the bank for six months.
4. Purchased land for $125,000 by paying $50,000 in cash and issuing a note for the balance.
5. Exchanged no-par common stock for an automobile valued at $26,500.

Required

a. Prepare the appropriate sections of the statement of cash flows for 2008.

b. What information does the noncash investing and financing activities section of the statement provide? If this information were omitted, could it affect a decision to invest in a company?

PROBLEMS—SERIES B

Problem 12-11B *Classifying cash flows*

L.O. 1

Required

Classify each of the following as an operating activity (OA), an investing activity (IA), or a financing activity (FA) cash flow, or a noncash transaction (NT).

a. Paid cash for operating expenses.
b. Wrote off an uncollectible account receivable using the allowance method.
c. Wrote off an uncollectible account receivable using the direct write-off method.
d. Issued common stock for cash.
e. Declared a stock split.
f. Issued a mortgage to purchase a building.
g. Purchased equipment with cash.
h. Repaid the principal balance on a note payable.
i. Made a cash payment for the balance due in the Dividends Payable account.
j. Received a cash dividend from an investment in marketable securities.
k. Purchased supplies on account.
l. Collected cash from accounts receivable.
m. Accrued warranty expense.
n. Borrowed cash by issuing a bond.
o. Loaned cash to a business associate.
p. Paid cash for interest expense.
q. Incurred a loss on the sale of equipment.
r. Wrote down inventory because the year-end physical count was less than the balance in the Inventory account.
s. Paid cash to purchase inventory.

Problem 12-12B *Using transaction data to prepare a statement of cash flows*

L.O. 2, 3

Greenstein Company engaged in the following transactions during 2008. The beginning cash balance was $86,000.

1. Sales on account were $548,000. The beginning receivables balance was $128,000 and the ending balance was $90,000.
2. Salaries expense was $232,000. The beginning Salaries Payable balance was $16,000 and the ending balance was $8,000.
3. Other operating expenses were $236,000. The beginning Operating Expense Payable balance was $16,000 and the ending balance was $10,000.
4. Recorded $30,000 of depreciation expense. The beginning and ending balances in the Accumulated Depreciation account were $12,000 and $42,000, respectively.
5. The Equipment account had beginning and ending balances of $44,000 and $56,000, respectively. The increase was caused by the cash purchase of equipment.
6. The beginning and ending balances in the Notes Payable account were $44,000 and $36,000, respectively. The decrease was caused by the cash repayment of debt.
7. There was $4,600 of interest expense reported on the income statement. The beginning and ending balances in the Interest Payable account were $8,400 and $7,500, respectively.
8. The beginning and ending Merchandise Inventory account balances were $22,000 and $29,400, respectively. The company sold merchandise with a cost of $83,600. The beginning and ending balances of Accounts Payable were $8,000 and $6,400, respectively.
9. The beginning and ending balances of Notes Receivable were $100,000 and $60,000, respectively. The decline resulted from the cash collection of a portion of the receivable.
10. The beginning and ending balances of the Common Stock account were $120,000 and $160,000, respectively. The increase was caused by the issue of common stock for cash.

11. Land had beginning and ending balances of $24,000 and $14,000, respectively. Land that cost $10,000 was sold for $6,000, resulting in a loss of $4,000.
12. The tax expense for 2008 was $6,600. The Tax Payable account had a $2,400 beginning balance and a $2,200 ending balance.
13. The Investments account had beginning and ending balances of $20,000 and $60,000, respectively. The company purchased investments for $50,000 cash during 2008, and investments that cost $10,000 were sold for $22,000, resulting in a $12,000 gain.

Required

Convert the preceding information to cash-equivalent data and prepare a statement of cash flows.

L.O. 2, 3

Problem 12-13B *Using financial statement data to determine cash flow from operating activities*

The following account information is available for Gables Auto Supplies for 2008:

Account Title	Beginning of Year	End of Year
Accounts Receivable	$ 17,800	$ 21,000
Merchandise Inventory	136,000	142,800
Prepaid Insurance	1,600	1,200
Accounts Payable (Inventory)	18,800	19,600
Salaries Payable	6,400	5,800

Other Information

1. Sales for the period were $248,000.
2. Purchases of merchandise for the period were $186,000.
3. Insurance expense for the period was $8,000.
4. Other operating expenses (all cash) were $27,400.
5. Salary expense was $42,600.

Required

a. Compute the net cash flow from operating activities.
b. Prepare the cash flow from operating activities section of the statement of cash flows.

L.O. 2, 3

Problem 12-14B *Using financial statement data to determine cash flow from investing activities*

The following information pertaining to investing activities is available for Tony's Flea Markets Inc. for 2007.

Account Title	Beginning of Year	End of Year
Trucks and Equipment	$162,000	$170,000
Marketable Securities	66,000	51,200
Land	42,000	34,000

Other Information for 2007

1. Tony's sold marketable securities at book value. No gain or loss was recognized.
2. Trucks were purchased for $40,000. Old trucks with a cost of $32,000 and accumulated depreciation of $24,000 were sold for $11,000.
3. Land that cost $8,000 was sold for $10,000.

Required

a. Compute the net cash flow from investing activities.
b. Prepare the cash flow from investing activities section of the statement of cash flows.

Problem 12-15B ***Using financial statement data to determine cash flow from financing activities*** **L.O. 2, 3**

The following information pertaining to financing activities is available for Engineered Components Company for 2007.

Account Title	Beginning of Year	End of Year
Bonds Payable	$170,000	$180,000
Common Stock	210,000	280,000
Paid-in Capital in Excess of Par	84,000	116,000

Other Information

1. Dividends paid during the period amounted to $28,000.
2. Additional funds of $40,000 were borrowed during the period by issuing bonds.

Required

a. Compute the net cash flow from financing activities for 2007.

b. Prepare the cash flow from financing activities section of the statement of cash flows.

Problem 12-16B ***Using financial statements to prepare a statement of cash flows—direct method*** **L.O. 2, 3**

The following financial statements were drawn from the records of Healthy Products Co.

Balance Sheets
As of December 31

	2006	2007
Assets		
Cash	$ 1,940	$16,120
Accounts Receivable	2,000	2,400
Inventory	2,600	2,000
Equipment	17,100	13,700
Accumulated Depreciation–Equipment	(12,950)	(11,300)
Land	8,000	13,000
Total Assets	$18,690	$35,920
Liabilities and Equity		
Accounts Payable	$ 2,400	$ 3,600
Long-Term Debt	4,000	3,200
Common Stock	10,000	17,000
Retained Earnings	2,290	12,120
Total Liabilities and Stockholders' Equity	$18,690	$35,920

Income Statement
For the Year Ended December 31, 2007

Sales Revenue	$17,480
Cost of Goods Sold	(6,200)
Gross Margin	11,280
Depreciation Expense	(1,750)
Operating Income	9,530
Gain on Sale of Equipment	1,800
Loss on Disposal of Land	(600)
Net Income	$10,730

Additional Data

1. During 2007, the company sold equipment for $6,800; it had originally cost $8,400. Accumulated depreciation on this equipment was $3,400 at the time of the sale. Also, the company purchased equipment for $5,000 cash.
2. The company sold land that had cost $2,000. This land was sold for $1,400, resulting in the recognition of a $600 loss. Also, common stock was issued in exchange for title to land that was valued at $7,000 at the time of exchange.
3. Paid dividends of $900.

Required

Use the T-account method to analyze the data and prepare a statement of cash flows using the direct method.

L.O. 2, 3

Problem 12-17B ***Using financial statements to prepare a statement of cash flows—direct method***

The following financial statements were drawn from the records of Norton Materials Inc.

Balance Sheets As of December 31	2006	2007
Assets		
Cash	$ 14,100	$ 94,300
Accounts Receivable	40,000	36,000
Inventory	64,000	72,000
Notes Receivable	16,000	0
Equipment	170,000	98,000
Accumulated Depreciation–Equipment	(94,000)	(47,800)
Land	30,000	46,000
Total Assets	$240,100	$298,500
Liabilities and Equity		
Accounts Payable	$ 26,400	$ 24,000
Salaries Payable	10,000	15,000
Utilities Payable	1,400	800
Interest Payable	1,000	0
Note Payable	24,000	0
Common Stock	110,000	150,000
Retained Earnings	67,300	108,700
Total Liabilities and Equity	$240,100	$298,500

Income Statement For the Year Ended December 31, 2007	
Sales Revenue	$300,000
Cost of Goods Sold	(144,000)
Gross Margin	156,000
Operating Expenses	
Salary Expense	(88,000)
Depreciation Expense	(9,800)
Utilities Expense	(6,400)
Operating Income	51,800
Nonoperating Items	
Interest Expense	(2,400)
Loss on Sale of Equipment	(800)
Net Income	$ 48,600

Additional Information

1. Sold equipment costing $72,000 with accumulated depreciation of $56,000 for $15,200 cash.
2. Paid a $7,200 cash dividend to owners.

Required

Use the T-account method to analyze the data and prepare a statement of cash flows using the direct method.

Problem 12-18B ***Using financial statements to prepare a statement of cash flows—indirect method*** **L.O. 2, 4**

The comparative balance sheets for Lind Beauty Products Inc. for 2006 and 2007 follow:

Balance Sheets As of December 31	2006	2007
Assets		
Cash	$ 48,400	$ 6,300
Accounts Receivable	7,260	10,200
Merchandise Inventory	56,000	45,200
Prepaid Rent	2,140	700
Equipment	144,000	140,000
Accumulated Depreciation	(118,000)	(73,400)
Land	50,000	116,000
Total Assets	$189,800	$245,000
Liabilities and Equity		
Accounts Payable (Inventory)	$ 40,000	$ 37,200
Salaries Payable	10,600	12,200
Stockholders' Equity		
Common Stock, $50 Par Value	120,000	150,000
Retained Earnings	19,200	45,600
Total Liabilities and Equity	$189,800	$245,000

Income Statement For the Year Ended December 31, 2007	
Sales	$480,000
Cost of Goods Sold	(264,000)
Gross Profit	216,000
Operating Expenses	
Depreciation Expense	(11,400)
Rent Expense	(7,000)
Salaries Expense	(95,200)
Other Operating Expenses	(76,000)
Net Income	$ 26,400

Other Information

1. Purchased land for $66,000.
2. Purchased new equipment for $62,000.
3. Sold old equipment that cost $66,000 with accumulated depreciation of $56,000 for $10,000 cash.
4. Issued common stock for $30,000.

Required

Prepare the statement of cash flows for 2007 using the indirect method.

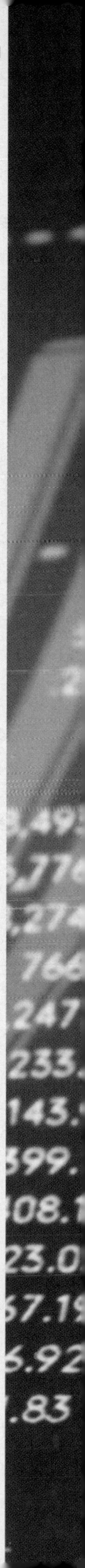

ANALYZE, THINK, COMMUNICATE

ATC 12-1 Business Applications Case *Understanding real-world annual reports*

Required—Part 1

The Topps Company, Inc.

Use the Topps Company's annual report in Appendix B to answer the following questions.

a. For the 2003 fiscal year, which was larger, Topps' *net income* or its *cash flow from operating activities*? By what amount did they differ?

b. What two items are most responsible for the difference between Topps' *net income* and its *cash flow from operating activities* in 2003?

c. In 2003 Topps generated approximately $6.2 million of cash from operating activities, and its cash balance decreased by about $6.8 million. How did the company use this $13 million of cash?

Required—Part 2

Harley-Davidson, Inc.

Use the Harley-Davidson's annual report that came with this book to answer the following questions.

a. For the 2003 fiscal year, which was larger, Harley-Davidson's *net income* or its *cash flow from operating activities*? By what amount did they differ?

b. What item is most responsible for the difference between Harley-Davidson's *net income* and its *cash flow from operating activities* in 2003?

c. In 2003 Harley-Davidson generated approximately $936 million of cash from operating activities. What did the company do with this cash?

ATC 12-2 Real-World Case *Following the cash*

Panera Bread Company (Panera) is the name of the company formally known as Au Bon Pain Company (ABP). Panera operates retail bakery-cafes under the names Panera Bread and Saint Louis Bread Company. The company has experienced rapid growth in recent years. In 1996, only 62 stores were in operation. By the end of 2003, this number had grown to 602. The following table shows the number of these cafes in operation for each year from 2000 through 2003.

Year	Company Owned	Franchise Owned	Total
2003	173	429	602
2002	132	346	478
2001	110	259	369
2000	90	172	262

Panera's statements of cash flows for 2001, 2002, and 2003 appear as follows:

PANERA BREAD COMPANY
Consolidated Statements of Cash Flows
($ in thousands)

	For the fiscal years ended		
	December 27, 2003	December 28, 2002	December 29, 2001
Cash flows from operating activities:			
Net income	$30,409	$21,765	$13,152
Adjustments to reconcile net income to net cash provided by operating activities:			
Cumulative effect of accounting change, net of tax	239	–	–
Depreciation and amortization	19,487	13,965	10,839

continued

	For the fiscal years ended		
	December 27, 2003	December 28, 2002	December 29, 2001
Tax benefit from exercise of stock options	6,847	8,064	8,023
Deferred income taxes	8,798	4,193	252
Minority interest	365	180	8
Other	148	113	27
Changes in operating assets and liabilities:			
Trade and other accounts receivable	(2,808)	(4,454)	(2,078)
Inventories	(2,417)	(1,675)	(998)
Prepaid expenses	538	(172)	(622)
Accounts payable	2,085	716	(125)
Accrued expenses	5,162	3,786	2,383
Deferred revenue	(497)	(137)	(636)
Other	172	(21)	335
Net cash provided by operating activities	68,528	46,323	30,560
Cash flows from investing activities:			
Purchase of investments	(4,000)	(9,200)	–
Investment maturities	4,000	–	–
Additions to property and equipment	(41,187)	(27,119)	(27,528)
Acquisitions	(20,969)	(3,267)	–
Increase in deposits and other	(126)	(529)	(271)
Other	–	–	(749)
Net cash used in investing activities	(62,282)	(40,115)	(28,548)
Cash flows from financing activities:			
Exercise of employee stock options	4,211	3,032	6,714
Proceeds from note receivable	–	248	–
Proceeds from issuance of common stock	814	923	395
Principal payments on long-term debt and computer equipment financing	–	–	(374)
Increase in deferred financing costs	(2)	–	(6)
Investments by minority interest owner	1,209	1,461	300
Net cash provided by financing activities	6,232	5,664	7,029
Net increase in cash and cash equivalents	12,478	11,872	9,041
Cash and cash equivalents at beginning of period	29,924	18,052	9,011
Cash and cash equivalents at end of period	$42,402	$29,924	$18,052
Supplemental cash flow information:			
Cash paid during the year for:			
Interest	$ 22	$ 17	$ 32
Income taxes	$ 783	$ 424	$ 73

Required

Using the information provided, including an analysis of Panera's statements of cash flows, answer the following questions. Explain the rationale for your answers, and present any computations necessary to support them.

a. What is the dollar amount of difference between Panera's net income and its cash flow from operating activities in 2003? What adjustment is most responsible for this difference?

b. As shown in the table above, Panera has expanded its operations for each of the past four years. Approximately how much cash did Panera spend in 2001, 2002, and 2003 to increase the number of stores it operates?

c. What were the sources of cash that Panera used to expand its operations in those three years?

ATC 12-3 Group Assignment *Preparing a statement of cash flows*

The following financial statements and information are available for Blythe Industries Inc.

Balance Sheets
As of December 31

	2004	2005
Assets		
Cash	$120,600	$ 160,200
Accounts Receivable	85,000	103,200
Inventory	171,800	186,400
Marketable Securities (Available for Sale)	220,000	284,000
Equipment	490,000	650,000
Accumulated Depreciation	(240,000)	(310,000)
Land	120,000	80,000
Total Assets	$967,400	$1,153,800
Liabilities and Equity		
Liabilities		
Accounts Payable (Inventory)	$ 66,200	$ 36,400
Notes Payable–Long-Term	250,000	230,000
Bonds Payable	100,000	200,000
Total Liabilities	416,200	466,400
Stockholders' Equity		
Common Stock, No Par	200,000	240,000
Preferred Stock, $50 Par	100,000	110,000
Paid-in Capital in Excess of Par–Preferred Stock	26,800	34,400
Total Paid-In Capital	326,800	384,400
Retained Earnings	264,400	333,000
Less: Treasury Stock	(40,000)	(30,000)
Total Stockholders' Equity	551,200	687,400
Total Liabilities and Stockholders' Equity	$967,400	$1,153,800

Income Statement
For the Year Ended December 31, 2005

Sales Revenue		$1,050,000
Cost of Goods Sold		(766,500)
Gross Profit		283,500
Operating Expenses		
Supplies Expense	$20,400	
Salaries Expense	92,000	
Depreciation Expense	90,000	
Total Operating Expenses		(202,400)
Operating Income		81,100
Nonoperating Items		
Interest Expense		(16,000)
Gain from the Sale of Marketable Securities		30,000
Gain from the Sale of Land and Equipment		12,000
Net Income		$ 107,100

Additional Information

1. Sold land that cost $40,000 for $44,000.
2. Sold equipment that cost $30,000 and had accumulated depreciation of $20,000 for $18,000.
3. Purchased new equipment for $190,000.
4. Sold marketable securities, classified as available-for-sale, that cost $40,000 for $70,000.

5. Purchased new marketable securities, classified as available-for-sale, for $104,000.
6. Paid $20,000 on the principal of the long-term note.
7. Paid off a $100,000 bond issue and issued new bonds for $200,000.
8. Sold 100 shares of treasury stock at its cost.
9. Issued some new common stock.
10. Issued some new $50 par preferred stock.
11. Paid dividends. (*Note:* The only transactions to affect retained earnings were net income and dividends.)

Required

Organize the class into three sections, and divide each section into groups of three to five students. Assign each section of groups an activity section of the statement of cash flows (operating activities, investing activities, or financing activities).

Group Task

Prepare your assigned portion of the statement of cash flows. Have a representative of your section put your activity section of the statement of cash flows on the board. As each section adds its information on the board, the full statement of cash flows will be presented.

Class Discussion

Have the class finish the statement of cash flows by computing the net change in cash. Also have the class answer the following questions:

a. What is the cost per share of the treasury stock?
b. What was the issue price per share of the preferred stock?
c. What was the book value of the equipment sold?

ATC 12-4 Business Applications Case *Identifying different presentation formats*

In *Statement of Financial Accounting Standards No. 95,* the Financial Accounting Standards Board (FASB) recommended but did not require that companies use the direct method. In Appendix B, Paragraphs 106–121, the FASB discussed its reasons for this recommendation.

Required

Obtain a copy of *Standard No. 95* and read Appendix B Paragraphs 106–121. Write a brief response summarizing the issues that the FASB considered and its specific reaction to those issues. Your response should draw heavily on paragraphs 119–121.

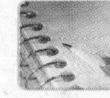

ATC 12-5 Writing Assignment *Explaining discrepancies between cash flow and operating income*

The following selected information was drawn from the records of Fleming Company:

Assets	2005	2006
Accounts Receivable	$ 400,000	$ 840,200
Merchandise Inventory	720,000	1,480,000
Equipment	1,484,000	1,861,200
Accumulated Depreciation	(312,000)	(402,400)

Fleming is experiencing cash flow problems. Despite the fact that it reported significant increases in operating income, operating activities produced a net cash outflow. Recent financial forecasts predict that Fleming will have insufficient cash to pay its current liabilities within three months.

Required

Write an explanation of Fleming's cash shortage. Include a recommendation to remedy the problem.

ATC 12-6 Ethical Dilemma *Would I lie to you, baby?*

Andy and Jean Crocket are involved in divorce proceedings. When discussing a property settlement, Andy told Jean that he should take over their investment in an apartment complex because she would be unable to absorb the loss that the apartments are generating. Jean was somewhat distrustful and asked Andy to support his contention. He produced the following income statement, which was supported by a CPA's unqualified opinion that the statement was prepared in accordance with generally accepted accounting principles.

CROCKET APARTMENTS Income Statement For the Year Ended December 31, 2003		
Rent Revenue		$580,000
Less: Expenses		
Depreciation Expense	$280,000	
Interest Expense	184,000	
Operating Expense	88,000	
Management Fees	56,000	
Total Expenses		(608,000)
Net Loss		$ (28,000)

All revenue is earned on account. Interest and operating expenses are incurred on account. Management fees are paid in cash. The following accounts and balances were drawn from the 2002 and 2003 year-end balance sheets.

Account Title	2002	2003
Rent Receivable	$40,000	$44,000
Interest Payable	12,000	18,000
Accounts Payable (Oper. Exp.)	6,000	4,000

Jean is reluctant to give up the apartments but feels that she must because her present salary is only $40,000 per year. She says that if she takes the apartments, the $28,000 loss would absorb a significant portion of her salary, leaving her only $12,000 with which to support herself. She tells you that while the figures seem to support her husband's arguments, she believes that she is failing to see something. She knows that she and her husband collected a $20,000 distribution from the business on December 1, 2003. Also, $150,000 cash was paid in 2003 to reduce the principal balance on a mortgage that was taken out to finance the purchase of the apartments two years ago. Finally, $24,000 cash was paid during 2003 to purchase a computer system used in the business. She wonders, "If the apartments are losing money, where is my husband getting all the cash to make these payments?"

Required

a. Prepare a statement of cash flows for the 2003 accounting period.

b. Compare the cash flow statement prepared in Requirement *a* with the income statement and provide Jean Crocket with recommendations.

c. Comment on the value of an unqualified audit opinion when using financial statements for decision-making purposes.

ATC 12-7 Research Assignment *Analyzing cash flow information*

On March 19, 2003, the United States military began operations in Iraq. Soon afterwards it was announced that the **Halliburton Company** and its subsidiaries had been awarded contracts to provide services, such as meals, to service men and women serving there. Complete the requirements below using the 2003 financial statements available on the company's website. Obtain these by following these steps:

- Go to www.halliburton.com.
- Click on the "INVESTOR RELATIONS" link, shown under "CORPORATE."
- On this screen, click on the "Annual Report and Proxy" link.
- Next, click on "2003 Annual Report—PDF Version."
- The financial statements are on pages 69 through 72 of the annual report.

Required

a. What were Halliburton's revenues in 2001, 2002, and 2003?

b. What was the company's net income (loss) in 2001, 2002, and 2003?

c. What was Halliburton's cash flow from operating activities in 2003?

d. What was the increase or decrease in the company's cash balance from 2002 to 2003?

e. Using the company's statement of cash flows, explain why this increase or decrease occurred.

f. Do you consider the change in Halliburton's cash position from 2002 to 2003 to be good or bad? Explain your answer.

g. Does it appear that Halliburton's acceptance of the government contracts in 2003 required it to make significant new cash investments?

CHAPTER 13

Financial Statement Analysis

LEARNING OBJECTIVES

After you have mastered the material in this chapter you will be able to:

1. **Describe factors associated with communicating useful information.**
2. **Differentiate between horizontal and vertical analysis.**
3. **Explain ratio analysis.**
4. **Calculate ratios for assessing a company's liquidity.**
5. **Calculate ratios for assessing a company's solvency.**
6. **Calculate ratios for assessing company management's effectiveness.**
7. **Calculate ratios for assessing a company's position in the stock market.**
8. **Identify different forms for presenting analytical data.**
9. **Explain the limitations of financial statement analysis.**

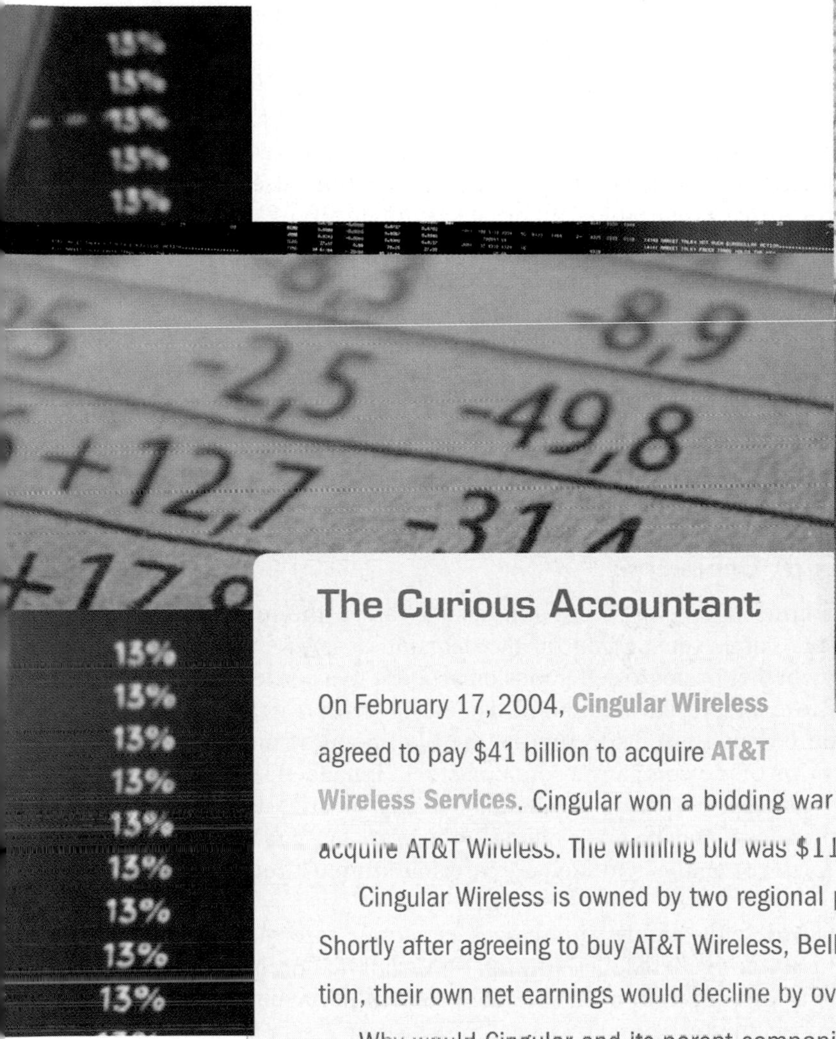

Chapter 13

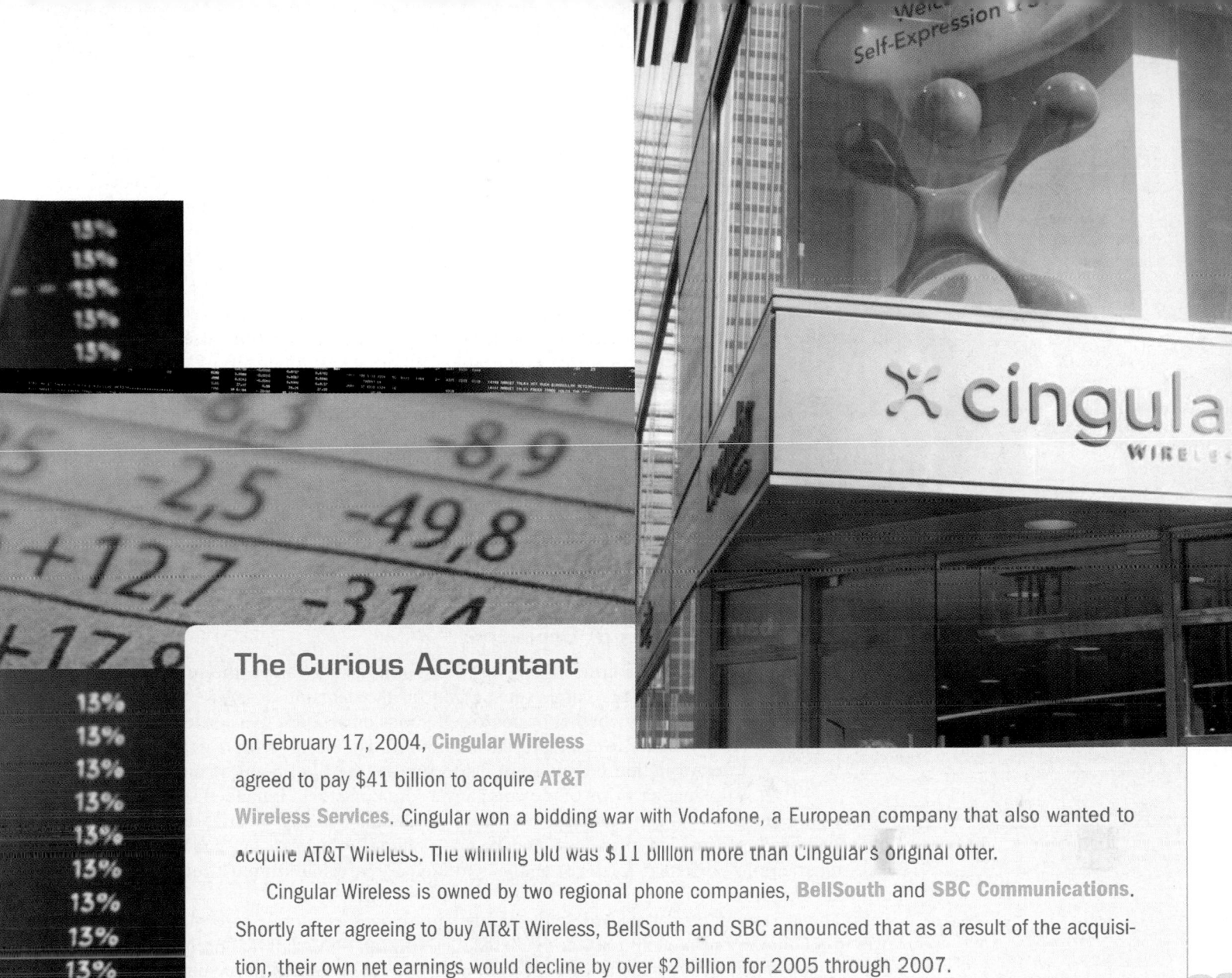

The Curious Accountant

On February 17, 2004, **Cingular Wireless** agreed to pay $41 billion to acquire **AT&T Wireless Services**. Cingular won a bidding war with Vodafone, a European company that also wanted to acquire AT&T Wireless. The winning bid was $11 billion more than Cingular's original offer.

Cingular Wireless is owned by two regional phone companies, **BellSouth** and **SBC Communications**. Shortly after agreeing to buy AT&T Wireless, BellSouth and SBC announced that as a result of the acquisition, their own net earnings would decline by over $2 billion for 2005 through 2007.

Why would Cingular and its parent companies agree to a deal that would reduce their earnings by so much over the next three years? What type of analysis would these companies use to make this decision? (Answers on page 653.)

CHAPTER OPENING

Expressing financial statement information in the form of ratios enhances its usefulness. Ratios permit comparisons over time and among companies, highlighting similarities, differences, and trends. Proficiency with common financial statement analysis techniques benefits both internal and external users. Before beginning detailed explanations of numerous ratios and percentages, however, we consider factors relevant to communicating useful information. ■

Factors in Communicating Useful Information

LO 1

Describe factors associated with communicating useful information.

The primary objective of accounting is to provide information useful for decision making. To provide information that supports this objective, accountants must consider the intended users, the types of decisions users make with financial statement information, and available means of analyzing the information.

The Users

Users of financial statement information include managers, creditors, stockholders, potential investors, and regulatory agencies. These individuals and organizations use financial statements for different purposes and bring varying levels of sophistication to understanding business activities. For example, investors range from private individuals who know little about financial statements to large investment brokers and institutional investors capable of using complex statistical analysis techniques. At what level of user knowledge should financial statements be aimed? Condensing and reporting complex business transactions at a level easily understood by nonprofessional investors is increasingly difficult. Current reporting standards target users that have a reasonably informed knowledge of business, though that level of sophistication is difficult to define.

The Types of Decisions

Just as the knowledge level of potential users varies, the information needs of users varies, depending on the decision at hand. A supplier considering whether or not to sell goods on account to a particular company wants to evaluate the likelihood of getting paid; a potential investor in that company wants to predict the likelihood of increases in the market value of the company's common stock. Financial statements, however, are designed for general purposes; they are not aimed at any specific user group. Some disclosed information, therefore, may be irrelevant to some users but vital to others. Users must employ different forms of analysis to identify information most relevant to a particular decision.

Financial statements can provide only highly summarized economic information. The costs to a company of providing excessively detailed information would be prohibitive. In addition, too much detail leads to **information overload,** the problem of having so much data that important information becomes obscured by trivial information. Users faced with reams of data may become so frustrated attempting to use it that they lose the value of *key* information that is provided.

Information Analysis

Topic Tackler PLUS

13-1

Because of the diversity of users, their different levels of knowledge, the varying information needs for particular decisions, and the general nature of financial statements, a variety of analysis techniques has been developed. In the following sections, we explain several common methods of analysis. The choice of method depends on which technique appears to provide the most relevant information in a given situation.

Methods of Analysis

LO 2

Differentiate between horizontal and vertical analysis.

Financial statement analysis should focus primarily on isolating information useful for making a particular decision. The information required can take many forms but usually involves comparisons, such as comparing changes in the same item for the same company over a number of years, comparing key relationships within the same year, or comparing the operations of several different companies in the same industry. This chapter discusses three categories of analysis methods: horizontal, vertical, and ratio. Exhibits 13.1 and 13.2 present comparative financial statements for Milavec Company. We refer to these statements in the examples of analysis techniques.

EXHIBIT 13.1

MILAVEC COMPANY
Income Statements and Statements of Retained Earnings
For the Years Ending December 31

	2008	2007
Sales	$900,000	$800,000
Cost of Goods Sold		
Beginning Inventory	43,000	40,000
Purchases	637,000	483,000
Goods Available for Sale	680,000	523,000
Ending Inventory	70,000	43,000
Cost of Goods Sold	610,000	480,000
Gross Margin	290,000	320,000
Operating Expenses	248,000	280,000
Income before Taxes	42,000	40,000
Income Taxes	17,000	18,000
Net Income	25,000	22,000
Plus: Retained Earnings, Beginning Balance	137,000	130,000
Less: Dividends	0	15,000
Retained Earnings, Ending Balance	$162,000	$137,000

EXHIBIT 13.2

MILAVEC COMPANY
Balance Sheets
As of December 31

	2008	2007
Assets		
Cash	$ 20,000	$ 17,000
Marketable Securities	20,000	22,000
Notes Receivable	4,000	3,000
Accounts Receivable	50,000	56,000
Merchandise Inventory	70,000	43,000
Prepaid Items	4,000	4,000
Property, Plant, and Equipment (net)	340,000	310,000
Total Assets	$508,000	$455,000
Liabilities and Stockholders' Equity		
Accounts Payable	$ 40,000	$ 38,000
Salaries Payable	2,000	3,000
Taxes Payable	4,000	2,000
Bonds Payable, 8%	100,000	100,000
Preferred Stock, 6%, $100 par, cumulative	50,000	50,000
Common Stock, $10 par	150,000	125,000
Retained Earnings	162,000	137,000
Total Liabilities and Stockholders' Equity	$508,000	$455,000

Horizontal Analysis

Horizontal analysis, also called **trend analysis,** refers to studying the behavior of individual financial statement items over several accounting periods. These periods may be several quarters within the same fiscal year or they may be several different years. The analysis of a given item may focus on trends in the absolute dollar amount of the item or trends in percentages. For example, a user may observe that revenue increased from one period to the next by $42 million (an absolute dollar amount) or that it increased by a percentage such as 15 percent.

Absolute Amounts

The **absolute amounts** of particular financial statement items have many uses. Various national economic statistics, such as gross domestic product and the amount spent to replace productive capacity, are derived by combining absolute amounts reported by businesses. Financial statement users with expertise in particular industries might evaluate amounts reported for research and development costs to judge whether a company is spending excessively or conservatively. Users are particularly concerned with how amounts change over time. For example, a user might compare a pharmaceutical company's revenue before and after the patent expired on one of its drugs.

Comparing only absolute amounts has drawbacks, however, because *materiality* levels differ from company to company or even from year to year for a given company. The **materiality** of information refers to its relative importance. An item is considered material if knowledge of it would influence the decision of a reasonably informed user. Generally accepted accounting principles permit companies to account for *immaterial* items in the most convenient way, regardless of technical accounting rules. For example, companies may expense, rather than capitalize and depreciate, relatively inexpensive long-term assets like pencil sharpeners or waste baskets even if the assets have useful lives of many years. The concept of materiality, which has both quantitative and qualitative aspects, underlies all accounting principles.

It is difficult to judge the materiality of an absolute financial statement amount without considering the size of the company reporting it. For reporting purposes, Exxon Corporation's financial statements are rounded to the nearest million dollars. For Exxon, a $400,000 increase in sales is not material. For a small company, however, $400,000 could represent total sales, a highly material amount. Meaningful comparisons between the two companies' operating performance are impossible using only absolute amounts. Users can surmount these difficulties with percentage analysis.

Percentage Analysis

Percentage analysis involves computing the percentage relationship between two amounts. In horizontal percentage analysis, a financial statement item is expressed as a percentage of the previous balance for the same item. Percentage analysis sidesteps the materiality problems of comparing different size companies by measuring changes in percentages rather than absolute amounts. Each change is converted to a percentage of the base year. Exhibit 13.3 presents a condensed version of Milavec's income statement with horizontal percentages for each item.

EXHIBIT 13.3

MILAVEC COMPANY
Comparative Income Statements
For the Years Ending December 31

	2008	2007	Percentage Difference
Sales	$900,000	$800,000	+12.5%*
Cost of Goods Sold	610,000	480,000	+27.1
Gross Margin	290,000	320,000	−9.4
Operating Expenses	248,000	280,000	−11.4
Income before Taxes	42,000	40,000	+5.0
Income Taxes	17,000	18,000	−5.6
Net Income	$ 25,000	$ 22,000	+13.6

*($900,000 − $800,000) ÷ $800,000; all changes expressed as percentages of previous totals.

The percentage changes disclose that, even though Milavec's net income increased slightly more than total sales, products may be underpriced. Cost of goods sold increased much more than sales, resulting in a lower gross margin. Users would also want to investigate why operating expenses decreased substantially despite the increase in sales volume.

Whether basing their analyses on absolute amounts, percentages, or ratios, users must avoid drawing overly simplistic conclusions about the reasons for the results. Numerical relationships flag conditions requiring further study. A change which appears favorable on the surface may not necessarily be a good sign. Users must evaluate the underlying reasons for the change.

CHECK YOURSELF 13.1

The following information was drawn from the annual reports of two retail companies (amounts are shown in millions). One company is an upscale department store; the other is a discount store. Based on this limited information, identify which company is the upscale department store.

	Jenkins Co.	Horn's Inc.
Sales	$325	$680
Cost of Goods Sold	130	408
Gross Margin	$195	$272

Answer

Jenkins' gross margin represents 60 percent ($195 ÷ $325) of sales. Horn's gross margin represents 40 percent ($272 ÷ $680) of sales. Since an upscale department store would have higher margins than a discount store, the data suggest that Jenkins is the upscale department store.

Answers to The Curious Accountant

Although BellSouth and SBC expect the acquisition of AT&T Wireless to depress earnings from 2005 through 2007, they believe the acquisition will significantly increase earnings after 2007. They expect to achieve this benefit by reducing capital expenditures and operating costs; one combined company will need less equipment than two separate companies and will not need to spend as much as two companies for such items as marketing and personnel. They estimate these cost savings will range from $1.4 to $2.1 billion annually.

Not all analysts agree with the two companies' forecasts. After studying the same basic information some analysts think competition from rivals such as Verizon may force Cingular to spend more on advertising than it expects in order to keep customers from switching providers. These analysts believe the year or so it takes to implement the merger will give rivals the opportunity to steal existing customers from AT&T Wireless. Additionally, some think Verizon currently has a technically superior network, which may cause Cingular to spend more on equipment than it estimated when bidding for AT&T Wireless. These analysts' think Cingular paid too much for AT&T Wireless.

Financial analysis techniques can help managers make decisions, but cannot guarantee success. When using such tools as ratios and trend analysis, decision makers must understand the businesses being evaluated, and they must make assumptions about future events. Only the future will tell whether Cingular paid too much for AT&T Wireless, but we can be sure that many ratio and capital budgeting computations were made before Cingular decided how much its winning bid would be.

Source: Companies' filings with the SEC and Roger O. Crockett, "How the Cingular Deal Helps Verizon," *BusinessWeek*, March 1, 2004, pp. 36–37.

When comparing more than two periods, analysts use either of two basic approaches: (1) choosing one base year from which to calculate all increases or decreases or (2) calculating each period's percentage change from the preceding figure. For example, assume Milavec's sales for 2005 and 2006 were $600,000 and $750,000, respectively.

	2008	2007	2006	2005
Sales	$900,000	$800,000	$750,000	$600,000
Increase over 2005 sales	50.0%	33.3%	25.0%	–
Increase over preceding year	12.5%	6.7%	25.0%	–

Analysis discloses that Milavec's 2008 sales represented a 50 percent increase over 2005 sales, and a large increase (25 percent) occurred in 2006. From 2006 to 2007, sales increased only 6.7 percent but in the following year increased much more (12.5 percent).

Vertical Analysis

Vertical analysis uses percentages to compare individual components of financial statements to a key statement figure. Horizontal analysis compares items over many time periods; vertical analysis compares many items within the same time period.

Vertical Analysis of the Income Statement

Vertical analysis of an income statement (also called a *common size* income statement) involves converting each income statement component to a percentage of sales. Although vertical analysis suggests examining only one period, it is useful to compare common size income statements for several years. Exhibit 13.4 presents Milavec's income statements, along with vertical percentages, for 2008 and 2007. This analysis discloses that cost of goods sold increased significantly as a percentage of sales. Operating expenses and income taxes, however, decreased in relation to sales. Each of these observations indicates a need for more analysis regarding possible trends for future profits.

Vertical Analysis of the Balance Sheet

Vertical analysis of the balance sheet involves converting each balance sheet component to a percentage of total assets. The vertical analysis of Milavec's balance sheets in Exhibit 13.5

EXHIBIT 13.4

MILAVEC COMPANY
Vertical Analysis of Comparative Income Statements

	2008		2007	
	Amount	Percentage of Sales	Amount	Percentage of Sales
Sales	$900,000	100.0%	$800,000	100.0%
Cost of Goods Sold	610,000	67.8	480,000	60.0
Gross Margin	290,000	32.2	320,000	40.0
Operating Expenses	248,000	27.6	280,000	35.0
Income before Taxes	42,000	4.7	40,000	5.0
Income Taxes	17,000	1.9	18,000	2.3
Net Income	$ 25,000	2.8%	$ 22,000	2.8%

EXHIBIT 13.5

[redacted]

	2008	Percentage of Total	2007	Percentage of Total
Assets				
Cash	$ 20,000	3.9%	$ 17,000	3.7%
Marketable Securities	20,000	3.9	22,000	4.8
Notes Receivable	4,000	0.8	3,000	0.7
Accounts Receivable	50,000	9.8	56,000	12.3
Merchandise Inventory	70,000	13.8	43,000	9.5
Prepaid Items	4,000	0.8	4,000	0.9
Total Current Assets	168,000	33.1	145,000	31.9
Property, Plant, and Equipment	340,000	67.0	310,000	68.1
Total Assets	$508,000	100.0%	$455,000	100.0%
Liabilities and Stockholders' Equity				
Accounts Payable	$ 40,000	7.9%	$ 38,000	8.4%
Salaries Payable	2,000	0.4	3,000	0.7
Taxes Payable	4,000	0.8	2,000	0.4
Total Current Liabilities	46,000	9.1	43,000	9.5
Bonds Payable, 8%	100,000	19.7	100,000	22.0
Total Liabilities	146,000	28.7	143,000	31.4
Preferred Stock 6%, $100 par	50,000	9.8	50,000	11.0
Common Stock, $10 par	150,000	29.5	125,000	27.5
Retained Earnings	162,000	31.9	137,000	30.1
Total Stockholders' Equity	362,000	71.3	312,000	68.6
Total Liabilities and Stockholders' Equity	$508,000	100.0%	$455,000	100.0%

discloses few large percentage changes from the preceding year. Even small individual percentage changes, however, may represent substantial dollar increases. Inventory, one of the less liquid current assets, has increased 62.8 percent ([$70,000 − $43,000] ÷ $43,000) from 2007 to 2008, which may have unfavorable consequences. Careful analysis requires considering changes in both percentages *and* absolute amounts.

Ratio Analysis

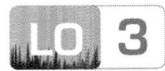

LO 3 Explain ratio analysis.

Ratio analysis involves studying various relationships between different items reported in a set of financial statements. For example, net earnings (net income) reported on the income statement may be compared to total assets reported on the balance sheet. Analysts calculate many different ratios for a wide variety of purposes. The remainder of this chapter is devoted to discussing some of the more commonly used ratios.

Objectives of Ratio Analysis

As suggested earlier, various users approach financial statement analysis with many different objectives. Creditors are interested in whether a company will be able to pay its debts on time. Both creditors and stockholders are concerned with how the company is financed, whether through debt, equity, or earnings. Stockholders and potential investors analyze past earnings performance and dividend policy for clues to the future value of their investments. In addition to using internally generated data to analyze operations, company managers find much information prepared for external purposes useful for examining past operations and planning future policies. Although many of these objectives are interrelated, it is convenient to group ratios into categories such as measures of debt-paying ability and measures of profitability.

Measures of Debt-Paying Ability

Liquidity Ratios

LO 4 Calculate ratios for assessing a company's liquidity.

Liquidity ratios indicate a company's ability to pay short-term debts. They focus on current assets and current liabilities. The examples in the following section use the financial statement information reported by Milavec Company.

Working Capital

Working capital is current assets minus current liabilities. Current assets include assets most likely to be converted into cash or consumed in the current operating period. Current liabilities represent debts that must be satisfied in the current period. Working capital therefore measures the excess funds the company will have available for operations, excluding any new funds it generates during the year. Think of working capital as the cushion against short-term debt-paying problems. Working capital at the end of 2008 and 2007 for Milavec Company was as follows.

	2008	2007
Current assets	$168,000	$145,000
− Current liabilities	46,000	43,000
Working capital	$122,000	$102,000

Milavec's working capital increased dramatically from 2007 to 2008, but the numbers themselves say little. Whether $122,000 is sufficient or not depends on such factors as the industry in which Milavec operates, its size, and the maturity dates of its current obligations. We can see, however, that the increase in working capital is primarily due to the increase in inventories.

Current Ratio

Working capital is an absolute amount. Its usefulness is limited by the materiality difficulties discussed earlier. It is hard to draw meaningful conclusions from comparing Milavec's working capital of $122,000 with another company that also has working capital of $122,000. By expressing the relationship between current assets and current liabilities as a ratio, however, we have a more useful measure of the company's debt-paying ability relative to other companies. The **current ratio,** also called the **working capital ratio,** is calculated as follows.

$$\text{Current ratio} = \frac{\text{Current assets}}{\text{Current liabilities}}$$

To illustrate using the current ratio for comparisons, consider Milavec's current position relative to Laroque's, a larger firm with current assets of $500,000 and current liabilities of $378,000.

	Milavec	Laroque
Current assets (a)	$168,000	$500,000
− Current liabilities (b)	46,000	378,000
Working capital	$122,000	$122,000
Current ratio (a ÷ b)	3.65:1	1.32:1

The current ratio is expressed as the number of dollars of current assets for each dollar of current liabilities. In the above example, both companies have the same amount of working capital. Milavec, however, appears to have a much stronger working capital position. Any conclusions from this analysis must take into account the circumstances of the particular companies; there is no single ideal current ratio that suits all companies. In recent years the average current ratio of the 30 companies that constitute the Dow Jones Industrial Average was around 1.35:1; the individual company ratios, however, ranged from .37:1 to 4.22:1. A current ratio can be too high. Money invested in factories and developing new products is usually more profitable than money held as large cash balances or invested in inventory.

Quick Ratio

The **quick ratio,** also known as the **acid-test ratio,** is a conservative variation of the current ratio. The quick ratio measures a company's *immediate* debt-paying ability. Only cash, receivables, and current marketable securities *(quick assets)* are included in the numerator. Less liquid current assets, such as inventories and prepaid items, are omitted. Inventories may take several months to sell; prepaid items reduce otherwise necessary expenditures but do not lead eventually to cash receipts. The quick ratio is computed as follows.

$$\text{Quick ratio} = \frac{\text{Quick assets}}{\text{Current liabilities}}$$

Milavec Company's current ratios and quick ratios for 2008 and 2007 follow.

	2008	2007
Current ratio	$168,000 ÷ $46,000 3.65:1	$145,000 ÷ $43,000 3.37:1
Quick ratio	$94,000 ÷ $46,000 2.04:1	$98,000 ÷ $43,000 2.28:1

The decrease in the quick ratio from 2007 to 2008 reflects both a decrease in quick assets and an increase in current liabilities. The result indicates that the company is less liquid (has less ability to pay its short-term debt) in 2008 than it was in 2007.

Accounts Receivable Ratios

Offering customers credit plays an enormous role in generating revenue, but it also increases expenses and delays cash receipts. To minimize uncollectible accounts expense and collect cash for use in current operations, companies want to collect receivables as quickly as possible without losing customers. Two relationships are often examined to assess a company's collection record: *accounts receivable turnover* and *average number of days to collect receivables (average collection period).*

Accounts receivable turnover is calculated as follows.

$$\text{Accounts receivable turnover} = \frac{\text{Net credit sales}}{\text{Average accounts receivable}}$$

Net credit sales refers to total sales on account less sales discounts, allowances, and returns. When most sales are credit sales or when a breakdown of total sales between cash sales and credit sales is not available, the analyst must use total sales in the numerator. The denominator is based on *net accounts receivable* (receivables after subtracting the allowance for doubtful accounts). Since the numerator represents a whole period, it is preferable to use average receivables in the denominator if possible. When comparative statements are available, the average can be based on the beginning and ending balances. Milavec Company's accounts receivable turnover is computed as follows:

	2008	2007
Net sales (assume all on account) (a)	$900,000	$800,000
Beginning receivables (b)	$ 56,000	$ 55,000*
Ending receivables (c)	50,000	56,000
Average receivables (d) = (a + c) ÷ 2	$ 53,000	$ 55,500
Accounts receivable turnover (a ÷ d)	16.98	14.41

*The beginning receivables balance was drawn from the 2006 financial statements, which are not included in the illustration.

The 2008 accounts receivable turnover of 16.98 indicates Milavec collected its average receivables almost 17 times that year. The higher the turnover, the faster the collections. A company can have cash flow problems and lose substantial purchasing power if resources are tied up in receivables for long periods.

Average number of days to collect receivables is calculated as follows.

$$\text{Average number of days to collect receivables} = \frac{\text{365 days}}{\text{Accounts receivable turnover}}$$

This ratio offers another way to look at turnover by showing the number of days, on average, it takes to collect a receivable. If receivables were collected 16.98 times in 2008, the average collection period was 21 days, 365 ÷ 16.98 (the number of days in the year divided by accounts receivable turnover). For 2007, it took an average of 25 days (365 ÷ 14.41) to collect a receivable.

Although the collection period improved, no other conclusions can be reached without considering the industry, Milavec's past performance, and the general economic environment. In recent years the average time to collect accounts receivable for the 25 nonfinancial companies that make up the Dow Jones Industrial Average was around 60 days. (Financial firms are excluded because, by the nature of their business, they have very long collection periods.)

Inventory Ratios

A fine line exists between having too much and too little inventory in stock. Too little inventory can result in lost sales and costly production delays. Too much inventory can use needed space, increase financing and insurance costs, and become obsolete. To help analyze how

efficiently a company manages inventory, we use two ratios similar to those used in analyzing accounts receivable.

Inventory turnover indicates the number of times, on average, that inventory is totally replaced during the year. The relationship is computed as follows.

$$\text{Inventory turnover} = \frac{\text{Cost of goods sold}}{\text{Average inventory}}$$

The average inventory is usually based on the beginning and ending balances that are shown in the financial statements. Inventory turnover for Milavec was as follows.

	2008	2007
Cost of goods sold (a)	$610,000	$480,000
Beginning inventory (b)	43,000	40,000*
Ending inventory (c)	70,000	43,000
Average inventory (d) = (b + c) ÷ 2	$ 56,500	$ 41,500
Inventory turnover (a ÷ d)	10.80	11.57

*The beginning inventory balance was drawn from the company's 2006 financial statements, which are not included in the illustration.

Generally, a higher turnover indicates that merchandise is being handled more efficiently. Trying to compare firms in different industries, however, can be misleading. Inventory turnover for grocery stores and many retail outlets is high. Because of the nature of the goods being sold, inventory turnover is much lower for appliance and jewelry stores. We look at this issue in more detail when we discuss return on investment.

Average number of days to sell inventory is determined by dividing the number of days in the year by the inventory turnover as follows.

$$\text{Average number of days to sell inventory} = \frac{\text{365 days}}{\text{Inventory turnover}}$$

The result approximates the number of days the firm could sell inventory without purchasing more. For Milavec, this figure was 34 days in 2008 (365 ÷ 10.80) and 32 days in 2007 (365 ÷ 11.57). In recent years it took around 30 days, on average, for the companies in the Dow Jones Industrial Average that have inventory to sell their inventory. The time it took individual companies to sell their inventory varied by industry, ranging from 3 days to 55 days.

Solvency Ratios

LO 5

Calculate ratios for assessing a company's solvency.

Solvency ratios are used to analyze a company's long-term debt-paying ability and its financing structure. Creditors are concerned with a company's ability to satisfy outstanding obligations. The larger a company's liability percentage, the greater the risk that the company could fall behind or default on debt payments. Stockholders, too, are concerned about a company's solvency. If a company is unable to pay its debts, the owners could lose their investment. Each user group desires that company financing choices minimize its investment risk, whether their investment is in debt or stockholders' equity.

Debt Ratios

The following ratios represent two different ways to express the same relationship. Both are frequently used.

Debt to assets ratio. This ratio measures the percentage of a company's assets that are financed by debt.

Debt to equity ratio. As used in this ratio, *equity* means stockholders' equity. The debt to equity ratio compares creditor financing to owner financing. It is expressed as the dollar amount of liabilities for each dollar of stockholder's equity.

These ratios are calculated as follows.

$$\text{Debt to assets} = \frac{\text{Total liabilities}}{\text{Total assets}}$$

$$\text{Debt to equity} = \frac{\text{Total liabilities}}{\text{Total stockholders' equity}}$$

Applying these formulas to Milavec Company's results produces the following.

	2008	2007
Total liabilities (a)	$146,000	$143,000
Total stockholders' equity (b)	362,000	312,000
Total assets (liabilities + stockholders' equity) (c)	$508,000	$455,000
Debt to assets (a ÷ c)	29%	31%
Debt to equity ratio (a ÷ b)	0.40:1	0.46:1

Each year less than one-third of the company's assets were financed with debt. The amount of liabilities per dollar of stockholders' equity declined by 0.06. It is difficult to judge whether the reduced percentage of liabilities is favorable. In general, a lower level of liabilities provides greater security because the likelihood of bankruptcy is reduced. Perhaps, however, the company is financially strong enough to incur more liabilities and benefit from financial leverage. The 30 companies that make up the Dow Jones Industrial Average report around 64 percent of their assets, on average, are financed through borrowing.

Number of Times Interest Is Earned

The **times interest earned** ratio measures the burden a company's interest payments represent. Users often consider times interest is earned along with the debt ratios when evaluating financial risk. The numerator of this ratio uses *earnings before interest and taxes (EBIT),* rather than net earnings, because the amount of earnings *before* interest and income taxes is available for paying interest.

$$\text{Times interest earned} = \frac{\text{Earnings before interest expense and taxes}}{\text{Interest expense}}$$

Dividing EBIT by interest expense indicates how many times the company could have made its interest payments. Obviously, interest is paid only once, but the more times it *could* be paid, the bigger the company's safety net. Although interest is paid from cash, not accrual earnings, it is standard practice to base this ratio on accrual-based EBIT, not a cash-based amount. For Milavec, this calculation is as follows.

	2008	2007
Income before taxes	$42,000	$40,000
Interest expense (b)	8,000	8,000*
Earnings before interest and taxes (a)	$50,000	$48,000
Times interest earned (a ÷ b)	6.25 times	6 times

*Interest on bonds: $100,000 × .08 = $8,000.

Any expense or dividend payment can be analyzed this way. Another frequently used calculation is the number of times the preferred dividend is earned. In that case, the numerator is net income (after taxes) and the denominator is the amount of the annual preferred dividend.

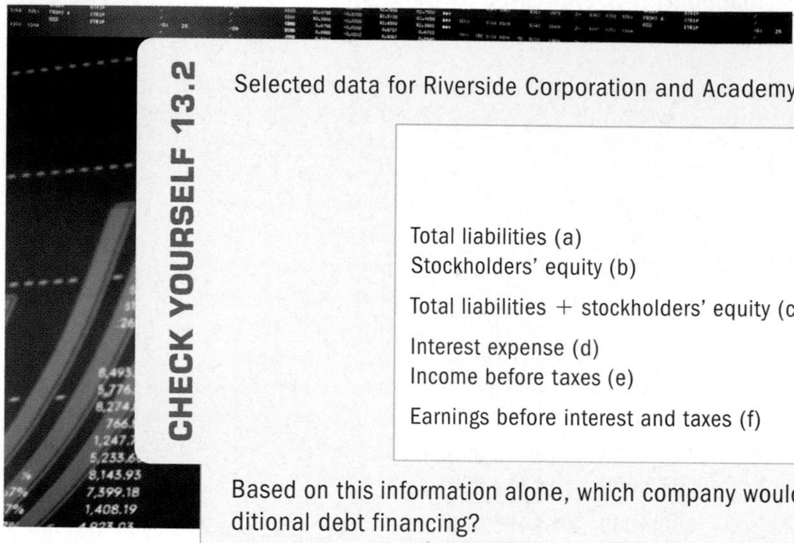

CHECK YOURSELF 13.2

Selected data for Riverside Corporation and Academy Company follow (amounts are shown in millions).

	Riverside Corporation	Academy Company
Total liabilities (a)	$650	$450
Stockholders' equity (b)	300	400
Total liabilities + stockholders' equity (c)	$950	$850
Interest expense (d)	$ 65	$ 45
Income before taxes (e)	140	130
Earnings before interest and taxes (f)	$205	$175

Based on this information alone, which company would likely obtain the less favorable interest rate on additional debt financing?

Answer

Interest rates vary with risk levels. Companies with less solvency (long-term debt-paying ability) generally must pay higher interest rates to obtain financing. Two solvency measures for the two companies follow. Recall:

Total assets = Liabilities + Stockholders' equity

	Riverside Corporation	Academy Company
Debt to assets ratio (a ÷ c)	68.4%	52.9%
Times interest earned (f ÷ d)	3.15 times	3.89 times

Since Riverside has a higher percentage of debt and a lower times interest earned ratio, the data suggest that Riverside is less solvent than Academy. Riverside would therefore likely have to pay a higher interest rate to obtain additional financing.

Plant Assets to Long-Term Liabilities

Companies often pledge plant assets as collateral for long-term liabilities. Financial statement users may analyze a firm's ability to obtain long-term financing on the strength of its asset base. Effective financial management principles dictate that asset purchases should be financed over a time span about equal to the expected lives of the assets. Short-term assets should be financed with short-term liabilities; the current ratio, introduced earlier, indicates how well a company manages current debt. Long-lived assets should be financed with long-term liabilities, and the **plant assets to long-term liabilities** ratio suggests how well long-term debt is managed. It is calculated as follows.

$$\text{Plant assets to long-term liabilities} = \frac{\text{Net plant assets}}{\text{Long-term liabilities}}$$

For Milavec Company, these ratios follow.

	2008	2007
Net plant assets (a)	$340,000	$310,000
Bonds payable (b)	100,000	100,000
Plant assets to long-term liabilities (a ÷ b)	3.4:1	3.1:1

Measures of Profitability

Profitability refers to a company's ability to generate earnings. Both management and external users desire information about a company's success in generating profits and how these profits are used to reward investors. Some of the many ratios available to measure different aspects of profitability are discussed in the following two sections.

Measures of Managerial Effectiveness

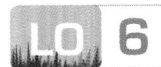

LO 6

Calculate ratios for assessing company management's effectiveness.

The most common ratios used to evaluate managerial effectiveness measure what percentage of sales results in earnings and how productive assets are in generating those sales. As mentioned earlier, the *absolute amount* of sales or earnings means little without also considering company size.

Net Margin (or Return on Sales)

Gross margin and *gross profit* are alternate terms for the amount remaining after subtracting the expense cost of goods sold from sales. **Net margin,** sometimes called *operating margin, profit margin,* or the *return on sales ratio,* describes the percent remaining of each sales dollar after subtracting other expenses as well as cost of goods sold. Net margin can be calculated in several ways; some of the more common methods only subtract normal operating expenses or all expenses other than income tax expense. For simplicity, our calculation uses net income (we subtract all expenses). Net income divided by net sales expresses net income (earnings) as a percentage of sales, as follows.

$$\text{Net margin} = \frac{\text{Net income}}{\text{Net sales}}$$

For Milavec Company, the net margins for 2008 and 2007 were as follows.

	2008	2007
Net income (a)	$ 25,000	$ 22,000
Net sales (b)	900,000	800,000
Net margin (a ÷ b)	2.78%	2.75%

Milavec has maintained approximately the same net margin. Obviously, the larger the percentage, the better; a meaningful interpretation, however, requires analyzing the company's history and comparing the net margin to other companies in the same industry. The average net margin for the 30 companies that make up the Dow Jones Industrial Average has been around 10 percent in recent years; some companies, such as Microsoft with 31 percent, have been much higher than the average. Of course, if a company has a net loss, its net margin for that year will be negative.

Asset Turnover Ratio

The **asset turnover ratio** (sometimes called *turnover of assets ratio*) measures how many sales dollars were generated for each dollar of assets invested. As with many ratios used in financial statement analysis, users may define the numerator and denominator of this ratio in different ways. For example, they may use total assets or only include operating assets. Since the numerator represents a whole period, it is preferable to use average assets in the denominator if possible, especially if the amount of assets changed significantly during the year. We use average total assets in our illustration.

$$\text{Asset turnover} = \frac{\text{Net sales}}{\text{Average total assets}}$$

For Milavec, the asset turnover ratios were as follows.

	2008	2007
Net sales (a)	$900,000	$800,000
Beginning assets (b)	$455,000	$420,000*
Ending assets (c)	508,000	455,000
Average assets (d) = (b + c) ÷ 2	$481,500	$437,500
Asset turnover (a ÷ d)	1.87	1.83

*The beginning asset balance was drawn from the 2006 financial statements, which are not included in the illustration.

As with most ratios, the implications of a given asset turnover ratio are affected by other considerations. Asset turnover will be high in an industry that requires only minimal investment to operate, such as real estate sales companies. On the other hand, industries that require large investments in plant and machinery, like the auto industry, are likely to have lower asset turnover ratios. The asset turnover ratios of the companies that make up the Dow Jones Industrial Average have averaged around 0.75 in recent years. This means that annual sales have averaged 75 percent of their assets.

Return on Investment

Return on investment (ROI), also called *return on assets* or *earning power,* is the ratio of wealth generated (net income) to the amount invested (average total assets) to generate the wealth. ROI can be calculated as follows.[1]

$$\text{ROI} = \frac{\text{Net income}}{\text{Average total assets}}$$

For Milavec, ROI was as follows.

2008

$25,000 ÷ $481,500* = 5.19%

2007

$22,000 ÷ $437,500* = 5.03%

*The computation of average assets is shown above.

In general, higher ROIs suggest better performance. The ROI of the large companies that make up the Dow Jones Industrial Average has averaged around 7 percent in recent years. These data suggest that Milavec is performing below average, and therefore signals a need for further evaluation that would lead to improved performance.

Return on Equity

Return on equity (ROE) is often used to measure the profitability of the stockholders' investment. ROE is usually higher than ROI because of financial leverage. Financial leverage refers to using debt financing to increase the assets available to a business beyond the amount of assets financed by owners. As long as a company's ROI exceeds its cost of bor-

[1] Detailed coverage of the return on investment ratio is provided in Chapter 23. As discussed in that chapter, companies frequently manipulate the formula to improve managerial motivation and performance. For example, instead of using net income, companies frequently use operating income because net income may be affected by items that are not controllable by management such as loss on a plant closing, storm damage, and so on.

rowing (interest expense), the owners will earn a higher return on their investment in the company by using borrowed money. For example, if a company borrows money at 8 percent and invests it at 10 percent, the owners will enjoy a return that is higher than 10 percent. ROE is computed as follows.

$$\text{ROE} = \frac{\text{Net income}}{\text{Average total stockholders' equity}}$$

If the amount of stockholders' equity changes significantly during the year, it is desirable to use average equity rather than year-end equity in the denominator. The ROE figures for Milavec Company were as follows.

	2008	2007
Net income (a)	$ 25,000	$ 22,000
Preferred stock, 6%, $100 par, cumulative	50,000	50,000
Common stock, $10 par	150,000	125,000
Retained earnings	162,000	137,000
Total stockholders' equity (b)	$362,000	$312,000
ROE (a ÷ b)	6.9%	7.1%

The slight decrease in ROE is due primarily to the increase in common stock. The effect of the increase in total stockholders' equity offsets the effect of the increase in earnings. This information does not disclose whether Milavec had the use of the additional stockholder investment for all or part of the year. If the data are available, calculating a weighted average amount of stockholders' equity provides more meaningful results.

We mentioned earlier the companies that make up the Dow Jones Industrial Average had an average ROI of 7 percent. The average ROE for the companies in the Dow was 19 percent, indicating effective use of financial leverage.

Stock Market Ratios

LO 7

Calculate ratios for assessing a company's position in the stock market.

Existing and potential investors in a company's stock use many common ratios to analyze and compare the earnings and dividends of different size companies in different industries. Purchasers of stock can profit in two ways: through receiving dividends and through increases in stock value. Investors consider both dividends and overall earnings performance as indicators of the value of the stock they own.

Earnings per Share

Perhaps the most frequently quoted measure of earnings performance is **earnings per share (EPS).** EPS represents an attempt to express a company's annual earnings in one easily understood figure. Investors may appreciate knowing that a large company's net income increased from $437 million in 2006 to $493 million in 2007. But, if they also learn that the company's EPS increased from $2.19 to $2.47, the increase is easier to understand. When financial analysts cite companies' earnings, they usually speak of EPS, not total net earnings.

EPS differs from *dividends per share.* Rarely would a company distribute all the year's earnings to stockholders. EPS calculations are among the most complex in accounting, and more advanced textbooks devote entire chapters to the subject. At this level, we use the following basic formula.

$$\text{Earnings per share} = \frac{\text{Net earnings available for common stock}}{\text{Average number of outstanding common shares}}$$

EPS pertains to shares of *common stock.* Limiting the numerator to earnings available for common stock eliminates the annual preferred dividend ($0.06 \times \$50{,}000 = \$3{,}000$) from the calculation. Exhibit 13.1 shows that Milavec did not pay the preferred dividends in 2008. Since the preferred stock is cumulative, however, the preferred dividend is in arrears and not available to the common stockholders. The number of common shares outstanding is determined by dividing the book value of the common stock by its par value per share ($150,000 ÷ $10 = 15,000 for 2008 and $125,000 ÷ $10 = 12,500 for 2007). Using these data, Milavec's 2008 EPS is calculated as follows.

$$\frac{\$25{,}000 \text{ (net income)} - \$3{,}000 \text{ (preferred dividend)}}{(15{,}000 + 12{,}500)/2 \text{ (average outstanding common shares)}} = \$1.60 \text{ per share}$$

Investors attribute a great deal of importance to EPS figures. The amounts used in calculating EPS, however, have limitations. Many accounting choices, assumptions, and estimates underlie net income computations, including alternative depreciation methods, different inventory cost flow assumptions, and estimates of future uncollectible accounts or warranty expenses, to name only a few. The denominator is also inexact because various factors (discussed in advanced accounting courses) affect the number of shares to include. Numerous opportunities therefore exist to manipulate EPS figures. Prudent investors consider these variables in deciding how much weight to attach to earnings per share.

Book Value

Book value per share is another frequently quoted measure of a share of stock. It is calculated as follows.

$$\text{Book value per share} = \frac{\text{Stockholders' equity} - \text{Preferred rights}}{\text{Outstanding common shares}}$$

Instead of describing the numerator as stockholders' equity, we could have used assets minus liabilities, the algebraic computation of a company's "net worth." Net worth is a misnomer. A company's accounting records reflect book values, not worth. Because assets are recorded at historical costs and different methods are used to transfer asset costs to expense, the book value of assets after deducting liabilities means little if anything. Nevertheless, investors use the term *book value per share* frequently.

Preferred rights represents the amount of money required to satisfy the claims of preferred stockholders. If the preferred stock has a call premium, the call premium amount is subtracted. In our example, we assume the preferred stock can be retired at par. Book value per share for 2008 was therefore as follows.

$$\frac{\$362{,}000 - \$50{,}000}{15{,}000} = \$20.80 \text{ per share}$$

Price-Earnings Ratio

The **price-earnings ratio,** or *P/E ratio,* compares the earnings per share of a company to the market price for a share of the company's stock. Assume Avalanche Company and Brushfire Company each report earnings per share of $3.60. For the same year, Cyclone Company reports EPS of $4.10. Based on these data alone, Cyclone stock may seem to be the best investment. Suppose, however, that the price for one share of stock in each company is $43.20, $36.00, and $51.25, respectively. Which stock would you buy? Cyclone's stock price is the highest, but so is its EPS. The P/E ratio provides a common base of comparison:

$$\text{Price-earnings ratio} = \frac{\text{Market price per share}}{\text{Earnings per share}}$$

The P/E ratios for the three companies are:

Avalanche	Brushfire	Cyclone
12.0	10.0	12.5

Brushfire might initially seem to be the best buy for your money. Yet there must be some reason that Cyclone's stock is selling at 12½ times earnings. In general, a higher P/E ratio indicates the market is more optimistic about a company's growth potential than it is about a company with a lower P/E ratio. The market price of a company's stock reflects judgments about both the company's current results and expectations about future results. Investors cannot make informed use of these ratios for investment decisions without examining the reasons behind the ratios. In May 2004, the average P/E ratio for the companies in the Dow Jones Industrial Average was around 20.

Dividend Yield

There are two ways to profit from a stock investment. One, investors can sell the stock for more than they paid to purchase it (if the stock price rises). Two, the company that issued the stock can pay cash dividends to the shareholders. Most investors view rising stock prices as the primary reward for investing in stock. The importance of receiving dividends, however, should not be overlooked. Evaluating dividend payments is more complex than simply comparing the dividends per share paid by one company to the dividends per share paid by another company. Receiving a \$1 dividend on a share purchased for \$10 is a much better return than receiving a \$1.50 dividend on stock bought for \$100. Computing the **dividend yield** simplifies comparing dividend payments. Dividend yield measures dividends received as a percentage of a stock's market price.

$$\text{Dividend yield} = \frac{\text{Dividends per share}}{\text{Market price per share}}$$

To illustrate, consider Dragonfly Inc. and Elk Company. The information for calculating dividend yield follows:

	Dragonfly	Elk
Dividends per share (a)	\$ 1.80	\$ 3.00
Market price per share (b)	40.00	75.00
Dividend yield (a ÷ b)	4.5%	4.0%

Even though the dividend per share paid by Elk Company is higher, the yield is lower (4.5 percent versus 4.0 percent) because Elk's stock price is so high. The dividend yields for the companies included in the Dow Jones Industrial Average were averaging around 2 percent in May of 2004.

Other Ratios

Investors can also use a wide array of other ratios to analyze profitability. Most **profitability ratios** use the same reasoning. For example, you can calculate the *yield* of a variety of financial investments. Yield represents the percentage the amount received is of the amount invested. The dividend yield explained above could be calculated for either common or preferred stock. Investors could measure the earnings yield by calculating earnings per share as a percentage of market price. Yield on a bond can be calculated the same way: interest received divided by the price of the bond.

The specific ratios presented in this chapter are summarized in Exhibit 13.6.

Presentation of Analytical Relationships

LO 8

Identify different forms for presenting analytical data.

To communicate with users, companies present analytical information in endless different ways in annual reports. Although providing diagrams and illustrations in annual reports is not usually required, companies often include various forms of graphs and charts along with the underlying numbers to help users interpret financial statement data more easily. Common types presented include bar charts, pie charts, and line graphs. Exhibits 13.7, 13.8, and 13.9 show examples of these forms.

EXHIBIT 13.6

Summary of Key Relationships

Liquidity Ratios	1. Working capital	Current assets − Current liabilities
	2. Current ratio	Current assets ÷ Current liabilities
	3. Quick (acid-test) ratio	(Current assets − Inventory − Prepaid Items) ÷ Current liabilities
	4. Accounts receivable turnover	Net credit sales ÷ Average net receivables
	5. Average number of days to collect receivables	365 ÷ Accounts receivable turnover
	6. Inventory turnover	Cost of goods sold ÷ Average inventory
	7. Average number of days to sell inventory	365 ÷ Inventory turnover
Solvency Ratios	8. Debt to assets ratio	Total liabilities ÷ Total assets
	9. Debt to equity ratio	Total liabilities ÷ Total stockholders' equity
	10. Times interest earned	Earnings before interest expense and taxes ÷ interest expense
	11. Plant assets to long-term liabilities	Net plant assets ÷ Long-term liabilities
Profitability Ratios	12. Net margin	Net income ÷ Net sales
	13. Asset turnover	Net sales ÷ Average total assets
	14. Return on investment (also: return on assets)	Net income ÷ Average total assets
	15. Return on equity	Net income ÷ Average total stockholders' equity
Stock Market Ratios	16. Earnings per share	Net earnings available for common stock ÷ Average outstanding common shares
	17. Book value per share	(Stockholders' equity − Preferred rights) ÷ Outstanding common shares
	18. Price-earnings ratio	Market price per share ÷ Earnings per share
	19. Dividend yield	Dividends per share ÷ Market price per share

EXHIBIT 13.7

Earnings and Dividends on Common Stock

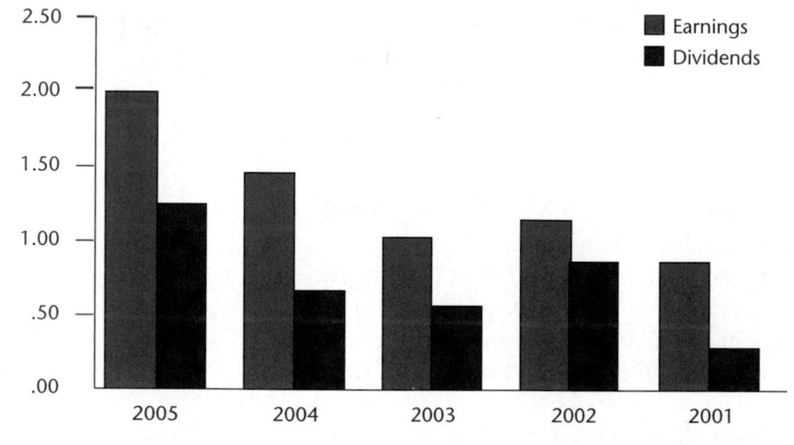

EXHIBIT 13.8

Percentage of Sales Dollar

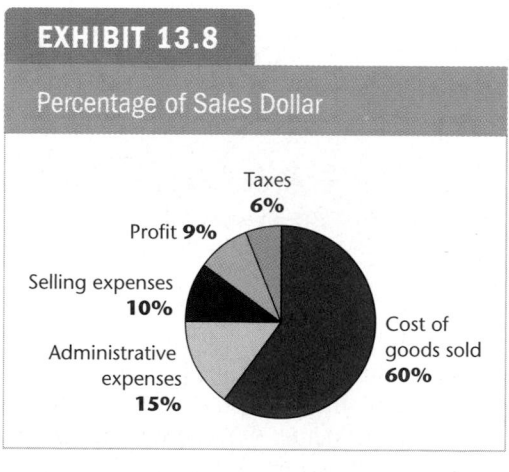

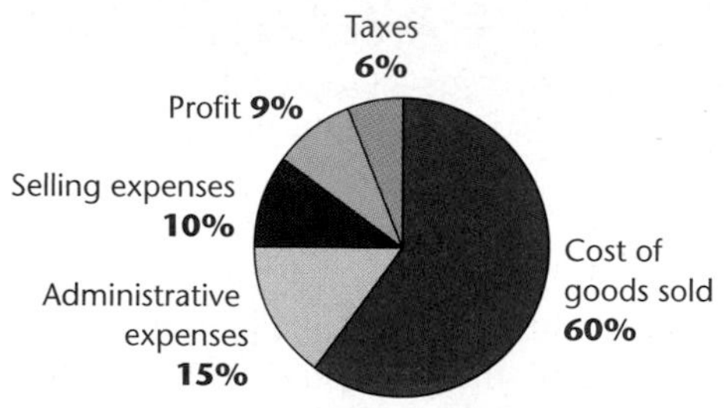

Limitations of Financial Statement Analysis

LO 9

Explain the limitations of financial statement analysis.

Analyzing financial statements is analogous to choosing a new car. Each car is different, and prospective buyers must evaluate and weigh a myriad of features: gas mileage, engine size, manufacturer's reputation, color, accessories, and price, to name a few. Just as it is difficult to compare a Toyota minivan to a Ferrari sports car, so it is difficult to compare a small

REALITY BYTES

The most important source of financial information comes from companies' reports, but decision makers should also consult other sources. Interested persons can access quarterly and annual reports through the SEC's EDGAR database and often from company web sites. Many companies will provide printed versions of these reports upon request. Companies also post information on their web sites that is not included in their annual reports. For example, some automobile companies provide detailed production data on their web sites.

Users can frequently obtain information useful in analyzing a particular company from independent sources as well as from the company itself. For example, the web sites of popular news services, such as CNN (*money.cnn.com*) and CNBC (*moneycentral.msn.com*) provide archived news stories and independent financial information about many companies. The web sites of brokerage houses like *www.schwab.com* offer free financial information about companies. Finally, libraries often subscribe to independent services that evaluate companies as potential investments. One example worth reviewing is *Value Line Investment Survey*.

textile firm to a giant oil company. To make a meaningful assessment, the potential car buyer must focus on key data that can be comparably expressed for each car, such as gas mileage. The superior gas mileage of the minivan may pale in comparison to the thrill of driving the sports car, but the price of buying and operating the sports car may be the characteristic that determines the ultimate choice.

EXHIBIT 13.9

Profits by Major Industry Segment

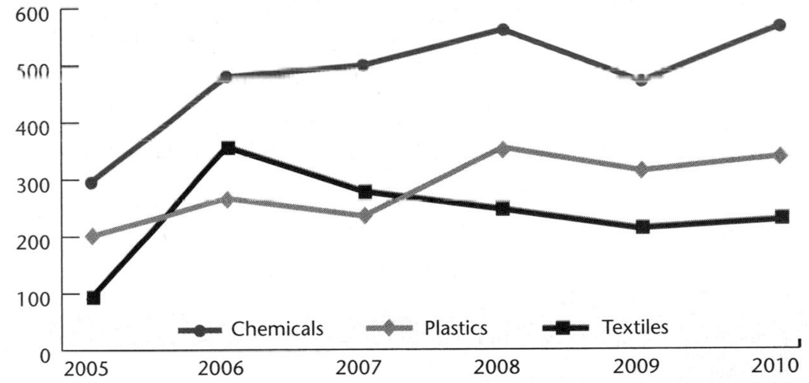

External users can rely on financial statement analysis only as a general guide to the potential of a business. They should resist placing too much weight on any particular figure or trend. Many factors must be considered simultaneously before making any judgments. Furthermore, the analysis techniques discussed in this chapter are all based on historical information. Future events and unanticipated changes in conditions will also influence a company's operating results.

Different Industries

Different industries may be affected by unique social policies, special accounting procedures, or other individual industry attributes. Ratios of companies in different industries are not comparable without considering industry characteristics. A high debt to assets ratio is more acceptable in some industries than others. Even within an industry, a particular business may require more or less working capital than the industry average. If so, the working capital and quick ratios would mean little compared to those of other firms, but may still be useful for trend analysis.

Because of industry-specific factors, most professional analysts specialize in one, or only a few, industries. Financial institutions such as brokerage houses, banks, and insurance companies typically employ financial analysts who specialize in areas such as mineral or oil extraction, chemicals, banking, retail, insurance, bond markets, or automobile manufacturing.

Changing Economic Environment

When comparing firms, analysts must be alert to changes in general economic trends from year to year. Significant changes in fuel costs and interest rates in recent years make old rule-of-thumb guidelines for evaluating these factors obsolete. In addition, the presence or absence of inflation affects business prospects.

Accounting Principles

Financial statement analysis is only as reliable as the data on which it is based. Although most companies follow generally accepted accounting principles, a wide variety of acceptable accounting methods is available from which to choose, including different inventory and depreciation methods, different schedules for recognizing revenue, and different ways to account for oil and gas exploration costs. Analyzing statements of companies that seem identical may produce noncomparable ratios if the companies used different accounting methods. Analysts may seek to improve comparability by trying to recast different companies' financial statements as if the same accounting methods had been applied.

Accrual accounting requires the use of many estimates; uncollectible accounts expense, warranty expense, asset lives, and salvage value are just a few. The reliability of the resulting financial reports depends on the expertise and integrity of the persons who make the estimates.

The quality and usefulness of accounting information are influenced by underlying accounting concepts. Two particular concepts, *conservatism* and *historical cost,* have a tremendous impact on financial reporting. Conservatism dictates recognizing estimated losses as soon as they occur, but gain recognition is almost always deferred until the gains are actually realized. Conservatism produces a negative bias in financial statements. There are persuasive arguments for the conservatism principle, but users should be alert to distortions it may cause in accounting information.

The pervasive use of the historical cost concept is probably the greatest single cause of distorted financial statement analysis results. The historical cost of an asset does not represent its current value. The asset purchased in 1980 for $10,000 is not comparable in value to the asset purchased in 1995 for $10,000 because of changes in the value of the dollar. Using historical cost produces financial statements that report dollars with differing purchasing power in the same statement. Combining these differing dollar values is akin to adding miles to kilometers. To get the most from analyzing financial statements, users should be cognizant of these limitations.

CHECK YOURSELF 13.3

The return on equity for Gup Company is 23.4 percent and for Hunn Company is 17 percent. Does this mean Gup Company is better managed than Hunn Company?

Answer

No single ratio can adequately measure management performance. Even analyzing a wide range of ratios provides only limited insight. Any useful interpretation requires the analyst to recognize the limitations of ratio analysis. For example, ratio norms typically differ between industries and may be affected by changing economic factors. In addition, companies' use of different accounting practices and procedures produces different ratio results even when underlying circumstances are comparable.

A Look Back <<

Financial statement analysis involves many factors, among them user characteristics, information needs for particular types of decisions, and how financial information is analyzed. Analytical techniques include *horizontal, vertical,* and *ratio analysis.* Users commonly calculate ratios to measure a company's liquidity, solvency, and profitability. The specific ratios presented in this chapter are summarized in Exhibit 13.6. Although ratios are easy to calculate and provide useful insights into business operations, when interpreting analytical results, users should consider limitations resulting from differing industry characteristics, differing economic conditions, and the fundamental accounting principles used to produce reported financial information.

A Look Forward >>

This chapter concludes the *financial* accounting portion of the text. Beginning with chapter 14, we introduce various tools from a branch of the field called *managerial* accounting. Managerial accounting focuses on meeting the accounting information needs of decision makers inside, rather than outside, a company. In addition to financial statement data, inside users require detailed, forward looking information that includes nonfinancial as well as financial components. We begin with a chapter that discusses the value management accounting adds to the decision making process.

SELF-STUDY REVIEW PROBLEM

Financial statements for Stallings Company follow.

INCOME STATEMENTS
for the Years Ended December 31

	2009	2008
Revenues		
Net Sales	$315,000	$259,000
Expenses		
Cost of Goods Sold	(189,000)	(154,000)
General, Selling, and Administrative Expenses	(54,000)	(46,000)
Interest Expense	(4,000)	(4,500)
Income Before Taxes	68,000	54,500
Income Tax Expense (40%)	(27,200)	(21,800)
Net Earnings	$ 40,800	$ 32,700

[redacted]

	2009	2008
Assets		
Current Assets		
Cash	$ 6,500	$ 11,500
Accounts Receivable	51,000	49,000
Inventories	155,000	147,500
Total Current Assets	212,500	208,000
Plant and Equipment (net)	187,500	177,000
Total Assets	$400,000	$385,000

continued

	2009	2008
Liabilities and Stockholders' Equity		
Liabilities		
Current Liabilities		
Accounts Payable	$ 60,000	$ 81,500
Other	25,000	22,500
Total Current Liabilities	85,000	104,000
Bonds Payable	100,000	100,000
Total Liabilities	185,000	204,000
Stockholders' Equity		
Common Stock (50,000 shares, $3 par)	150,000	150,000
Paid-In Capital in Excess of Par Value	20,000	20,000
Retained Earnings	45,000	11,000
Total Stockholders' Equity	215,000	181,000
Total Liabilities and Stockholders' Equity	$400,000	$385,000

Required

a. Use horizontal analysis to determine which expense item increased by the highest percentage from 2008 to 2009.

b. Use vertical analysis to determine whether the inventory balance is a higher percentage of total assets at the end of 2008 or 2009.

c. Calculate the following ratios for 2008 and 2009. When data limitations prohibit computing averages, use year-end balances in your calculations.

(1) Net margin
(2) Return on investment
(3) Return on equity
(4) Earnings per share
(5) Price-earnings ratio (market price per share at the end of 2009 and 2008 was $12.04 and $8.86, respectively)
(6) Book value per share of common stock
(7) Times interest earned
(8) Working capital
(9) Current ratio
(10) Acid-test ratio
(11) Accounts receivable turnover
(12) Inventory turnover
(13) Debt to equity

Solution to Requirement *a*

Income tax expense increased by the greatest percentage. Computations follow.

Cost of goods sold ($189,000 − $154,000) ÷ $154,000 = 22.73%

General, selling, and administrative ($54,000 − $46,000) ÷ $46,000 = 17.39%

Interest expense decreased.

Income tax expense ($27,200 − $21,800) ÷ $21,800 = 24.77%

Solution to Requirement *b*

2008: $147,500 ÷ $385,000 = 38.31%

2009: $155,000 ÷ $400,000 = 38.75%

Inventory is slightly larger relative to total assets at the end of 2009.

Solution to Requirement c

		2009	2008
1.	$\frac{\text{Net income}}{\text{Net sales}}$	$\frac{\$40{,}800}{\$315{,}000} = 12.95\%$	$\frac{\$32{,}700}{\$259{,}000} = 12.63\%$
2.	$\frac{\text{Net income}}{\text{Average total assets}}$	$\frac{\$40{,}800}{\$392{,}500} = 10.39\%$	$\frac{\$32{,}700}{\$385{,}000} = 8.49\%$
3.	$\frac{\text{Net income}}{\text{Average total stockholders' equity}}$	$\frac{\$40{,}800}{\$198{,}000} = 20.61\%$	$\frac{\$32{,}700}{\$181{,}000} = 18.07\%$
4.	$\frac{\text{Net income}}{\text{Average common shares outstanding}}$	$\frac{\$40{,}800}{50{,}000} = \$0.816$	$\frac{\$32{,}700}{50{,}000} = \$0.654$
5.	$\frac{\text{Market price per share}}{\text{Earnings per share}}$	$\frac{\$12.04}{\$0.816} = 14.75\text{ times}$	$\frac{\$8.86}{\$0.654} = 13.55\text{ times}$
6.	$\frac{\text{Stockholders' equity} - \text{Preferred rights}}{\text{Outstanding common shares}}$	$\frac{\$215{,}000}{50{,}000} = \$4.30$	$\frac{\$181{,}000}{50{,}000} = \$3.62$
7.	$\frac{\text{Net income} + \text{Taxes} + \text{Interest expense}}{\text{Interest expense}}$	$\frac{\$40{,}800 + \$27{,}200 + \$4{,}000}{\$4{,}000} = 18\text{ times}$	$\frac{\$32{,}700 + \$21{,}800 + \$4{,}500}{\$4{,}500} = 13.1\text{ times}$
8.	Current assets − Current liabilities	$\$212{,}500 - \$85{,}000 = \$127{,}500$	$\$208{,}000 - \$104{,}000 = \$104{,}000$
9.	$\frac{\text{Current assets}}{\text{Current liabilities}}$	$\frac{\$212{,}500}{\$85{,}000} = 2.5{:}1$	$\frac{\$208{,}000}{\$104{,}000} = 2{:}1$
10.	$\frac{\text{Quick assets}}{\text{Current liabilities}}$	$\frac{\$57{,}500}{\$85{,}000} = 0.68{:}1$	$\frac{\$60{,}500}{\$104{,}000} = 0.58{:}1$
11.	$\frac{\text{Net credit sales}}{\text{Average net accounts receivable}}$	$\frac{\$315{,}000}{\$50{,}000} = 6.3\text{ times}$	$\frac{\$259{,}000}{\$49{,}000} = 5.29\text{ times}$
12.	$\frac{\text{Cost of goods sold}}{\text{Average inventory}}$	$\frac{\$189{,}000}{\$151{,}250} = 1.25\text{ times}$	$\frac{\$154{,}000}{\$147{,}500} = 1.04\text{ times}$
13.	$\frac{\text{Total liabilities}}{\text{Total stockholders' equity}}$	$\frac{\$185{,}000}{\$215{,}000} = 86.05\%$	$\frac{\$204{,}000}{\$181{,}000} = 112.71\%$

KEY TERMS

absolute amounts 651
accounts receivable turnover 657
acid-test ratio 656
asset turnover ratio 661
average number of days to collect receivables 657
average number of days to sell inventory 658
book value per share 664
current ratio 656
debt to assets ratio 659
debt to equity ratio 659
dividend yield 665
earnings per share 663
horizontal analysis 651
information overload 650
inventory turnover 658
liquidity ratios 655
materiality 651
net margin 661
percentage analysis 652
plant assets to long-term liabilities 660
price-earnings ratio 664
profitability ratios 665
quick ratio 656
ratio analysis 655
return on equity 662
return on investment 662
solvency ratios 658
times interest earned 659
trend analysis 651
vertical analysis 653
working capital 655
working capital ratio 656

QUESTIONS

1. Why are ratios and trends used in financial analysis?
2. What do the terms *liquidity* and *solvency* mean?
3. What is apparent from a horizontal presentation of financial statement information? A vertical presentation?
4. What is the significance of inventory turnover, and how is it calculated?
5. What is the difference between the current ratio and the quick ratio? What does each measure?
6. Why are absolute amounts of limited use when comparing companies?
7. What is the difference between return on investment and return on equity?
8. Which ratios are used to measure long-term debt-paying ability? How is each calculated?

9. What are some limitations of the earnings per share figure?
10. What is the formula for calculating return on investment (ROI)?
11. What is information overload?
12. What is the price-earnings ratio? Explain the difference between it and the dividend yield.
13. What environmental factors must be considered in analyzing companies?
14. How do accounting principles affect financial statement analysis?

EXERCISES—SERIES A

All Exercises in Series A are available with McGraw-Hill's Homework Manager.

L.O. 4

Exericse 13-1A *Inventory turnover*

Selected financial information for Wingo Company for 2007 follows.

Sales	$120,000
Cost of Goods Sold	88,000
Merchandise Inventory	
Beginning of Year	10,000
End of Year	24,000

Required

Assuming that the merchandise inventory buildup was relatively constant, how many times did the merchandise inventory turn over during 2007?

L.O. 5

Exericse 13-2A *Times interest earned*

The following data come from the financial records of Cowser Corporation for 2005.

Sales	$135,000
Interest Expense	4,500
Income Tax Expense	22,500
Net Income	30,000

Required

How many times was interest earned in 2005?

L.O. 4

Exericse 13-3A *Current ratio*

Moran Corporation wrote off a $1,000 uncollectible account receivable against the $8,500 balance in its allowance account.

Required

Explain the effect of the write-off on Moran's current ratio.

L.O. 4

Exericse 13-4A *Working capital and current ratio*

On June 30, 2006, Victor Company's total current assets were $160,000 and its total current liabilities were $100,000. On July 1, 2006, Victor issued a short-term note to a bank for $25,000 cash.

Required

a. Compute Victor's working capital before and after issuing the note.
b. Compute Victor's current ratio before and after issuing the note.

L.O. 4

Exericse 13-5A *Working capital and current ratio*

On June 30, 2006, Victor Company's total current assets were $160,000 and its total current liabilities were $100,000. On July 1, 2006, Victor issued a long-term note to a bank for $25,000 cash.

Required

a. Compute Victor's working capital before and after issuing the note.
b. Compute Victor's current ratio before and after issuing the note.

Exericse 13-6A *Horizontal analysis*

L.O. 2

Fredrick Corporation reported the following operating results for two consecutive years.

	2005	2004	Percentage Change
Sales	$1,250,000	$1,000,000	
Cost of Goods Sold	750,000	600,000	
Gross Margin	500,000	400,000	
Operating Expenses	300,000	200,000	
Income before Taxes	200,000	200,000	
Income Taxes	61,000	53,000	
Net Income	$ 139,000	$ 147,000	

Required

a. Compute the percentage changes in Fredrick Corporation's income statement components between the two years.
b. Comment on apparent trends disclosed by the percentage changes computed in Requirement *a*.

Exericse 13-7A *Vertical analysis*

L.O. 2

Sanchez Company reported the following operating results for two consecutive years.

2004	Amount	Percent of Sales
Sales	$500,000	
Cost of Goods Sold	320,000	
Gross Margin	180,000	
Operating Expenses	100,000	
Income before Taxes	80,000	
Income Taxes	24,000	
Net Income	$ 56,000	
2005	**Amount**	**Percent of Sales**
Sales	$480,000	
Cost of Goods Sold	307,000	
Gross Margin	173,000	
Operating Expenses	120,000	
Income before Taxes	53,000	
Income Taxes	16,000	
Net Income	$ 37,000	

Required

Express each income statement component for each of the two years as a percent of sales.

Exericse 13-8A *Ratio analysis*

L.O. 2

Balance sheet data for Embry Corporation follow.

Current Assets	$ 750,000
Long-Term Assets (net)	4,250,000
Total Assets	$5,000,000
Current Liabilities	$ 420,000
Long-Term Liabilities	2,460,000
Total Liabilities	2,880,000
Common Stock and Retained Earnings	2,120,000
Total Liabilities and Stockholders' Equity	$5,000,000

Required

Compute the following:

Working capital	________
Current ratio	________
Debt to assets ratio	________
Debt to equity ratio	________

L.O. 7

Exericse 13-9A *Ratio analysis*

For 2006, Ethridge Corporation reported after-tax net income of $3,600,000. During the year, the number of shares of stock outstanding remained constant at 10,000 of $100 par, 9 percent preferred stock and 400,000 shares of common stock. The company's total stockholders' equity was $20,000,000 at December 31, 2006. Ethridge Corporation's common stock was selling at $52 per share at the end of its fiscal year. All dividends for the year had been paid, including $4.80 per share to common stockholders.

Required

Compute the following:

a. Earnings per share
b. Book value per share of common stock
c. Price-earnings ratio
d. Dividend yield

L.O. 2, 3, 4, 5, 6, 7

Exericse 13-10A *Ratio analysis*

Required

Match each of the following ratios with the formula used to compute it.

______	**1.** Working capital	**a.** Net income ÷ Average total stockholders' equity
______	**2.** Current ratio	**b.** Cost of goods sold ÷ Average inventory
______	**3.** Quick ratio	**c.** Current assets − Current liabilities
______	**4.** Accounts receivable turnover	**d.** 365 ÷ Inventory turnover
______	**5.** Average number of days to collect receivables	**e.** Net income ÷ Average total assets
______	**6.** Inventory turnover	**f.** (Net income − Preferred dividends) ÷ Average outstanding common shares
______	**7.** Average number of days to sell inventory	**g.** (Current assets − Inventory − Prepaid items) ÷ Current liabilities
______	**8.** Debt to assets ratio	**h.** Total liabilities ÷ Total assets
______	**9.** Debt to equity ratio	**i.** 365 ÷ Accounts receivable turnover
______	**10.** Return on investment	**j.** Total liabilities ÷ Total stockholders' equity
______	**11.** Return on equity	**k.** Net credit sales ÷ Average net receivables
______	**12.** Earnings per share	**l.** Current assets ÷ Current liabilities

L.O. 2

Exericse 13-11A *Horizontal and vertical analysis*

Income statements for Shirley Company for 2005 and 2006 follow.

	2006	2005
Sales	$240,000	$200,000
Cost of Goods Sold	147,900	108,000
Selling Expenses	40,100	22,000
Administrative Expenses	24,000	28,000
Interest Expense	6,000	12,000
Total Expenses	218,000	170,000
Income before Taxes	22,000	30,000
Income Taxes Expense	6,000	8,000
Net Income	$ 16,000	$ 22,000

Required

a. Perform a horizontal analysis, showing the percentage change in each income statement component between 2005 and 2006.

b. Perform a vertical analysis, showing each income statement component as a percent of sales for each year.

Exericse 13-12A ***Ratio analysis*** **L.O. 2, 3, 4, 5, 6, 7**

Compute the specified ratios using Kale Company's balance sheet at December 31, 2004.

Assets	
Cash	$ 15,000
Marketable Securities	8,000
Accounts Receivable	13,000
Inventory	11,000
Property and Equipment	170,000
Accumulated Depreciation	(12,500)
Total Assets	$204,500
Equities	
Accounts Payable	$ 8,500
Current Notes Payable	3,500
Mortgage Payable	4,500
Bonds Payable	21,500
Common Stock, $50 Par	110,000
Paid-In Capital in Excess of Par Value	4,000
Retained Earnings	52,500
Total Liabilities and Stockholders' Equity	$204,500

The average number of common stock shares outstanding during 2004 was 880 shares. Net income for the year was $15,000.

Required

Compute each of the following:

a. Current ratio

b. Earnings per share

c. Quick (acid-test) ratio

d. Return on investment

e. Return on equity

f. Debt to equity ratio

L.O. 4, 5, 6, 7

Exericse 13-13A *Comprehensive analysis*

Required

Indicate the effect of each of the following transactions on (1) the current ratio, (2) working capital, (3) stockholders' equity, (4) book value per share of common stock, (5) retained earnings. Assume that the current ratio is greater than 1.0.

a. Collected account receivable.
b. Wrote off account receivable.
c. Purchased treasury stock.
d. Purchased inventory on account.
e. Declared cash dividend.
f. Sold merchandise on account at a profit.
g. Issued stock dividend.
h. Paid account payable.
i. Sold building at a loss.

L.O. 4, 7

Exericse 13-14A *Accounts receivable turnover, inventory turnover, and net margin*

Selected data from Walker Company follow.

Balance Sheet Data As of December 31		
	2004	**2003**
Accounts Receivable	$400,000	$376,000
Allowance for Doubtful Accounts	(20,000)	(16,000)
Net Accounts Receivable	$380,000	$360,000
Inventories, Lower of Cost or Market	$480,000	$440,000

Income Statement Data For the Year Ended December 31		
	2004	**2003**
Net Credit Sales	$2,000,000	$1,760,000
Net Cash Sales	400,000	320,000
Net Sales	2,400,000	2,080,000
Cost of Goods Sold	1,600,000	1,440,000
Selling, General, & Administrative Expenses	240,000	216,000
Other Expenses	40,000	24,000
Total Operating Expenses	$1,880,000	$1,680,000

Required

Compute the following:

a. The accounts receivable turnover for 2004.
b. The inventory turnover for 2004.
c. The net margin for 2003.

L.O. 4, 5

Exericse 13-15A *Comprehensive analysis*

The December 31, 2005, balance sheet for Ivey Inc. is presented here. These are the only accounts on Ivey's balance sheet. Amounts indicated by question marks (?) can be calculated using the additional information following the balance sheet.

Assets	
Cash	$ 25,000
Accounts Receivable (net)	?
Inventory	?
Property, Plant, and Equipment (net)	294,000
	$432,000
Liabilities and Stockholders' Equity	
Accounts Payable (trade)	$?
Income Taxes Payable (current)	25,000
Long-Term Debt	?
Common Stock	300,000
Retained Earnings	?
	$?
Additional Information	
Current ratio (at year end)	1.5 to 1.0
Total liabilities ÷ Total stockholders' equity	0.8
Gross margin percent	30%
Inventory turnover (Cost of goods sold ÷ Ending inventory)	10.5 times
Gross margin for 2005	$315,000

Required

Determine the following:

a. The balance in trade accounts payable as of December 31, 2005.

b. The balance in retained earnings as of December 31, 2005.

c. The balance in the inventory account as of December 31, 2005.

PROBLEMS—SERIES A

All Problems in Series A are available with McGraw-Hill's Homework Manager.

Problem 13-16A ***Vertical analysis***

L.O. 2

CHECK FIGURES
NI of 2006: $36,000
Total Expenses of 2005: $135,000

The following percentages apply to Walden Company for 2005 and 2006.

	2006	**2005**
Sales	100.0%	100.0%
Cost of Goods Sold	61.0	64.0
Gross Margin	39.0	36.0
Selling and Administrative Expenses	26.5	20.5
Interest Expense	2.5	2.0
Total Expenses	29.0	22.5
Income before Taxes	10.0	13.5
Income Tax Expense	5.5	7.0
Net Income	4.5%	6.5%

Required

Assuming that sales were $600,000 in 2005 and $800,000 in 2006, prepare income statements for the two years.

L.O. 5, 6, 7

excel

mhhe.com/edmonds2007

CHECK FIGURES

a. 2004: 12.22 times
c. 2003: 8.5 times

Problem 13-17A *Ratio analysis*

Oxmoore Company's income statement information follows.

	2004	2003
Net Sales	$420,000	$260,000
Income before Interest and Taxes	110,000	85,000
Net Income after Taxes	55,500	63,000
Interest Expense	9,000	8,000
Stockholders' Equity, December 31 (2002: $200,000)	305,000	235,000
Common Stock, par $50, December 31	260,000	230,000

The average number of shares outstanding was 7,800 for 2004 and 6,900 for 2003.

Required

Compute the following ratios for Oxmoore for 2004 and 2003.

a. Times interest earned.
b. Earnings per share based on the average number of shares outstanding.
c. Price-earnings ratio (market prices: 2004, $64 per share; 2003, $78 per share).
d. Return on average equity.
e. Net margin.

L.O. 4

Problem 13-18A *Effect of transactions on current ratio and working capital*

Bellaire Manufacturing has a current ratio of 3:1 on December 31, 2003. Indicate whether each of the following transactions would increase (+), decrease (−), or not affect (NA) Bellaire's current ratio and its working capital.

Required

a. Paid cash for a trademark.
b. Wrote off an uncollectible account receivable.
c. Sold equipment for cash.
d. Sold merchandise at a profit (cash).
e. Declared a cash dividend.
f. Purchased inventory on account.
g. Scrapped a fully depreciated machine (no gain or loss).
h. Issued a stock dividend.
i. Purchased a machine with a long-term note.
j. Paid a previously declared cash dividend.
k. Collected accounts receivable.
l. Invested in current marketable securities.

L.O. 7

CHECK FIGURE

a. Earnings per share: $4.38

Problem 13-19A *Ratio analysis*

Selected data for Faulkner Company for 2005 and additional information on industry averages follow.

Earnings (net income)		$ 174,000
Preferred Stock (13,200 shares at $50 par, 4%)		$ 660,000
Common Stock (30,000 shares at $1 par, market value $56)		30,000
Paid-in Capital in Excess of Par Value—Common		480,000
Retained Earnings		562,500
		1,732,500
Less: Treasury Stock		
Preferred (1,200 shares)	$54,000	
Common (1,200 shares)	24,000	78,000
Total Stockholders' Equity		$1,654,500

Note: Dividends in arrears on preferred stock: $24,000. The preferred stock can be called for $51 per share.

Industry averages	
Earnings per share	$ 5.20
Price-earnings ratio	9.50
Return on equity	11.20%

Required

a. Calculate and compare Faulkner Company's ratios with the industry averages.
b. Discuss factors you would consider in deciding whether to invest in the company.

Problem 13-20A ***Supply missing balance sheet numbers*** **L.O. 2**

The bookkeeper for Clifford's Country Music Bar went insane and left this incomplete balance sheet. Clifford's working capital is $90,000 and its debt to assets ratio is 40 percent.

CHECK FIGURES
d. $337,500
f. $97,500

Assets	
Current Assets	
Cash	$ 21,000
Accounts Receivable	42,000
Inventory	(A)
Prepaid Items	9,000
Total Current Assets	(B)
Long-Term Assets	
Building	(C)
Less: Accumulated Depreciation	(39,000)
Total Long-Term Assets	210,000
Total Assets	$ (D)
Equities	
Liabilities	
Current Liabilities	
Accounts Payable	$ (E)
Notes Payable	12,000
Income Tax Payable	10,500
Total Current Liabilities	37,500
Long-Term Liabilities	
Mortgage Payable	(F)
Total Liabilities	(G)
Stockholders' Equity	
Common Stock	105,000
Retained Earnings	(H)
Total Stockholders' Equity	(I)
Total Liabilities and Stockholders' Equity	$ (J)

Required

Complete the balance sheet by supplying the missing amounts.

Problem 13-21A ***Ratio analysis*** **L.O. 2, 3, 4, 5, 6, 7**

excel
mhhe.com/edmonds2007

CHECK FIGURES
d. 2005: $0.72
k. 2004: 5.47 times

The following financial statements apply to Maronge Company.

	2005	2004
Revenues		
Net Sales	$210,000	$175,000
Other Revenues	4,000	5,000
Total Revenues	214,000	180,000

continued

	2005	2004
Expenses		
Cost of Goods Sold	126,000	103,000
Selling Expenses	21,000	19,000
General and Administrative Expenses	11,000	10,000
Interest Expense	3,000	3,000
Income Tax Expense (40%)	21,000	18,000
Total Expenses	182,000	153,000
Earnings from Continuing Operations before Extraordinary Items	32,000	27,000
Extraordinary Gain (net of $3,000 tax)	4,000	0
Net Earnings	$ 36,000	$ 27,000
Assets		
Current Assets		
Cash	$ 4,000	$ 8,000
Marketable Securities	1,000	1,000
Accounts Receivable	35,000	32,000
Inventories	100,000	96,000
Prepaid Items	3,000	2,000
Total Current Assets	143,000	139,000
Plant and Equipment (net)	105,000	105,000
Intangibles	20,000	0
Total Assets	$268,000	$244,000
Equities		
Liabilities		
Current Liabilities		
Accounts Payable	$ 40,000	$ 54,000
Other	17,000	15,000
Total Current Liabilities	57,000	69,000
Bonds Payable	66,000	67,000
Total Liabilities	123,000	136,000
Stockholders' Equity		
Common Stock ($2 par)	100,000	100,000
Paid-In Capital in Excess of Par Value	15,000	15,000
Retained Earnings	30,000	(7,000)
Total Stockholders' Equity	145,000	108,000
Total Liabilities and Stockholders' Equity	$268,000	$244,000

Required

Calculate the following ratios for 2004 and 2005. When data limitations prohibit computing averages, use year-end balances in your calculations.

a. Net margin
b. Return on investment
c. Return on equity
d. Earnings per share
e. Price-earnings ratio (market prices at the end of 2004 and 2005 were $5.94 and $4.77, respectively)
f. Book value per share of common stock
g. Times interest earned
h. Working capital
i. Current ratio
j. Quick (acid-test) ratio
k. Accounts receivable turnover
l. Inventory turnover
m. Debt to equity ratio
n. Debt to assets ratio

Problem 13-22A ***Horizontal analysis***

L.O. 2

Financial statements for Pocca Company follow.

CHECK FIGURES

Total Assets: +11.6%

Total Liabilities: +14.4%

POCCA COMPANY
Balance Sheets
As of December 31

	2006	2005
Assets		
Current Assets		
Cash	$ 16,000	$ 12,000
Marketable Securities	20,000	6,000
Accounts Receivable (net)	54,000	46,000
Inventories	135,000	143,000
Prepaid Items	25,000	10,000
Total Current Assets	250,000	217,000
Investments	27,000	20,000
Plant (net)	270,000	255,000
Land	29,000	24,000
Total Assets	$576,000	$516,000
Equities		
Liabilities		
Current Liabilities		
Notes Payable	$ 17,000	$ 6,000
Accounts Payable	113,800	100,000
Salaries Payable	21,000	15,000
Total Current Liabilities	151,800	121,000
Noncurrent Liabilities		
Bonds Payable	100,000	100,000
Other	32,000	27,000
Total Noncurrent Liabilities	132,000	127,000
Total Liabilities	283,800	248,000
Stockholders' Equity		
Preferred Stock, par value $10, 4% cumulative, non-participating; 7,000 shares authorized and issued; no dividends in arrears	70,000	70,000
Common Stock, $5 par value; 50,000 shares authorized; 10,000 shares issued	50,000	50,000
Paid-In Capital in excess of par value—Preferred	10,000	10,000
Paid-In Capital in excess of par value—Common	30,000	30,000
Retained Earnings	132,200	108,000
Total Stockholders' Equity	292,200	268,000
Total Liabilities and Stockholders' Equity	$576,000	$516,000

POCCA COMPANY
Statements of Income and Retained Earnings
For the Years Ended December 31

	2006	2005
Revenues		
Sales (net)	$230,000	$210,000
Other Revenues	8,000	5,000
Total Revenues	238,000	215,000

continued

	2006	2005
Expenses		
Cost of Goods Sold	120,000	103,000
Selling, General, and Administrative Expenses	55,000	50,000
Interest Expense	8,000	7,200
Income Tax Expense	23,000	22,000
Total Expenses	206,000	182,200
Net Earnings (Net Income)	32,000	32,800
Retained Earnings, January 1	108,000	83,000
Less: Preferred Stock Dividends	2,800	2,800
Common Stock Dividends	5,000	5,000
Retained Earnings, December 31	$132,200	$108,000

Required

Prepare a horizontal analysis of both the balance sheet and income statement.

L.O. 2, 3, 4, 5, 6, 7

excel

mhhe.com/edmonds2007

CHECK FIGURES

k. 2006: 2.05:1

p. 2005: $3.00

Problem 13-23A *Ratio analysis*

Required

Use the financial statements for Pocca Company from Problem 13–22A to calculate the following ratios for 2006 and 2005.

a. Working capital
b. Current ratio
c. Quick ratio
d. Accounts receivable turnover (beginning receivables at January 1, 2005, were $47,000.)
e. Average number of days to collect accounts receivable
f. Inventory turnover (beginning inventory at January 1, 2005, was $140,000.)
g. Average number of days to sell inventory
h. Debt to assets ratio
i. Debt to equity ratio
j. Times interest earned
k. Plant assets to long-term debt
l. Net margin
m. Asset turnover
n. Return on investment
o. Return on equity
p. Earnings per share
q. Book value per share of common stock
r. Price-earnings ratio (market price per share: 2005, $11.75; 2006, $12.50)
s. Dividend yield on common stock

L.O. 2

excel

mhhe.com/edmonds2007

CHECK FIGURE

2006 Retained Earnings: 23%

Problem 13-24A *Vertical analysis*

Required

Use the financial statements for Pocca Company from Problem 13–22A to perform a vertical analysis of both the balance sheets and income statements for 2006 and 2005.

EXERCISES—SERIES B

L.O. 4

Exericse 13-1B *Inventory turnover*

Selected financial information for Hyman Company for 2006 follows.

Sales	$1,100,000
Cost of Goods Sold	960,000
Merchandise Inventory	
Beginning of Year	136,000
End of Year	248,000

Required

Assuming that the merchandise inventory buildup was relatively constant, how many times did the merchandise inventory turn over during 2006?

Exericse 13-2B *Times interest earned*

L.O. 5

The following data come from the financial records of the Hickel Corporation for 2005.

Sales	$2,000,000
Interest Expense	100,000
Income Tax	280,000
Net Income	520,000

Required

How many times was interest earned in 2005?

Exericse 13-3B *Current ratio*

L.O. 4

Jeter Corporation purchased $200 of merchandise on account.

Required

Explain the effect of the purchase on Jeter's current ratio.

Exericse 13-4B *Working capital and current ratio*

L.O. 4

On October 31, 2006, Morey Company's total current assets were $50,000 and its total current liabilities were $20,000. On November 1, 2006, Morey purchased current marketable securities for $10,000 cash.

Required

a. Compute Morey's working capital before and after the securities purchase.
b. Compute Morey's current ratio before and after the securities purchase.

Exericse 13-5B *Working capital and current ratio*

L.O. 4

On October 31, 2006, Morey Company's total current assets were $50,000 and its total current liabilities were $20,000. On November 1, 2006, Morey bought manufacturing equipment for $10,000 cash.

Required

a. Compute Morey's working capital before and after the equipment purchase.
b. Compute Morey's current ratio before and after the equipment purchase.

Exericse 13-6B *Horizontal analysis*

L.O. 2

Kawai Corporation reported the following operating results for two consecutive years.

	2006	2005	Percentage Change
Sales	$440,000	$400,000	
Cost of Goods Sold	264,000	254,000	
Gross Margin	176,000	146,000	
Operating Expenses	75,000	65,000	
Income before Taxes	101,000	81,000	
Income Taxes	45,000	31,600	
Net Income	$ 56,000	$ 49,400	

Required

a. Compute the percentage changes in Kawai Corporation's income statement components for the two years.

b. Comment on apparent trends disclosed by the percentage changes computed in Requirement *a*.

L.O. 2

Exericse 13-7B ***Vertical analysis***

Julius Company reported the following operating results for two consecutive years.

2003	**Amount**	**Percentage of Sales**
Sales	$100,000	
Cost of Goods Sold	64,000	
Gross Margin	36,000	
Operating Expenses	19,000	
Income before Taxes	17,000	
Income Taxes	5,400	
Net Income	$ 11,600	
2004	**Amount**	**Percentage of Sales**
Sales	$128,000	
Cost of Goods Sold	81,600	
Gross Margin	46,400	
Operating Expenses	23,000	
Income before Taxes	23,400	
Income Taxes	6,200	
Net Income	$ 17,200	

Required

Express each income statement component for each of the two years as a percentage of sales.

L.O. 2

Exericse 13-8B ***Ratio analysis***

Balance sheet data for the Mathis Corporation follow.

Current Assets	$ 20,000
Long-Term Assets (Net)	140,000
Total Assets	$160,000
Current Liabilities	$ 15,000
Long-Term Liabilities	45,000
Total Liabilities	60,000
Common Stock and Retained Earnings	100,000
Total Liabilities and Stockholders' Equity	$160,000

Required

Compute the following:

a. Working capital

b. Current ratio

c. Debt to assets ratio

d. Debt to equity ratio

Exericse 13-9B *Ratio analysis*

L.O. 7

During 2004, Santini Corporation reported net income after taxes of $192,000. During the year, the number of shares of stock outstanding remained constant at 20,000 shares of $20 par 8 percent preferred stock and 200,000 shares of common stock. The company's total equities at December 31, 2004, were $700,000, which included $128,000 of liabilities. The common stock was selling for $8 per share at the end of the year. All dividends for the year were declared and paid, including $0.72 per share to common stockholders.

Required

Compute the following:

a. Earnings per share
b. Book value per share
c. Price-earnings ratio
d. Dividend yield

Exericse 13-10B *Ratio analysis*

L.O. 2, 3, 4, 5, 6, 7

Match each of the following ratios with its formula.

______ 1. Price-earnings ratio
______ 2. Dividend yield
______ 3. Book value per share
______ 4. Plant assets to long-term liabilities
______ 5. Times interest earned
______ 6. Earnings per share
______ 7. Net margin
______ 8. Debt to equity ratio
______ 9. Current ratio
______ 10. Asset turnover
______ 11. Average number of days to collect A/R
______ 12. Average number of days to sell inventory

a. Total liabilities ÷ Total stockholders' equity
b. Current assets ÷ Current liabilities
c. 365 ÷ Accounts receivable turnover
d. (Net income − Preferred dividends) ÷ Average outstanding common shares
e. (Stockholders' equity − Preferred rights) ÷ Outstanding common shares
f. 365 ÷ Inventory turnover
g. Dividends per share ÷ Market price per share
h. Net plant assets ÷ Long-term liabilities
i. Market price per share ÷ Earnings per share
j. Net income ÷ Net sales
k. Net sales ÷ Average total assets
l. Income before interest expense and taxes ÷ Interest expense

Exericse 13-11B *Horizontal and vertical analysis*

L.O. 2

Tewalt Company reported the following operating results for 2005 and 2006.

	2006	2005
Sales	$480,000	$432,000
Cost of Goods Sold	252,000	228,000
Selling Expenses	30,000	24,000
Administrative Expenses	54,000	50,000
Interest Expense	8,000	10,000
Total Expenses	344,000	312,000
Income before Taxes	136,000	120,000
Income Taxes Expense	28,000	24,000
Net Income	$108,000	$ 96,000

Required

a. Perform a horizontal analysis, showing the percentage change in each income statement component between 2005 and 2006.
b. Perform a vertical analysis, showing each income statement component as a percent of sales for each year.

L.O. 2, 3, 4, 5, 6, 7

Exericse 13-12B *Ratio analysis*

Compute the specified ratios using the following December 31, 2006, statement of financial position for Clay Company.

Assets	
Cash	$ 32,000
Marketable Securities	9,000
Accounts Receivable	72,800
Inventory	112,200
Property and Equipment	150,000
Accumulated Depreciation	(24,000)
Total Assets	$352,000
Equities	
Accounts Payable	$ 39,200
Current Notes Payable	6,800
Mortgage Payable	62,000
Bonds Payable	42,000
Common Stock	128,000
Retained Earnings	74,000
Total Liabilities and Stockholders' Equity	$352,000

The average number of common shares outstanding during 2006 was 1,500. Net earnings for the year were $48,000.

Required

Compute each of the following:

a. Current ratio
b. Earnings per share
c. Acid-test ratio
d. Return on investment
e. Return on equity
f. Debt to equity ratio

L.O. 4, 5, 6, 7

Exericse 13-13B *Comprehensive analysis*

The following is a list of transactions.

a. Paid cash for short-term marketable securities.
b. Purchased a computer, issuing a short-term note for the purchase price.
c. Purchased factory equipment, issuing a long-term note for the purchase price.
d. Sold merchandise on account at a profit.
e. Paid cash on accounts payable.
f. Received cash from issuing common stock.
g. Sold a factory for cash at a profit.
h. Purchased inventory on account.
i. Paid cash for property taxes on buildings.

Required

Indicate the effect of each of the preceding independent transactions on (a) the quick ratio, (b) working capital, (c) stockholders' equity, (d) the debt to equity ratio, (e) retained earnings. Assume that the current ratio is greater than 1.0.

Exericse 13-14B ***Accounts receivable turnover, inventory turnover, and net margin*** **L.O. 4, 7**

Selected data from Gilman Company follow.

Balance Sheet Data As of December 31	2004	2003
Accounts Receivable	$640,000	$600,000
Allowance for Doubtful Accounts	(32,000)	(28,000)
Net Accounts Receivable	$608,000	$572,000
Inventories, Lower of Cost or Market	$400,000	$420,000

Income Statement Data Year Ended December 31	2004	2003
Net Credit Sales	$4,000,000	$3,000,000
Net Cash Sales	800,000	600,000
Net Sales	$4,800,000	$3,600,000
Cost of Goods Sold	$2,800,000	$2,200,000
Selling, General, and Administrative Expenses	400,000	280,000
Other Expenses	200,000	160,000
Total Operating Expenses	$3,400,000	$2,640,000

Required

Compute the following:

a. The accounts receivable turnover for 2004.
b. The inventory turnover for 2004.
c. The net margin for 2003.

Exericse 13-15B ***Comprehensive analysis*** **L.O. 4, 5**

December 31, 2005, balance sheet data for Zabel Company follow. All accounts are represented. Amounts indicated by question marks (?) can be calculated using the additional information following the balance sheet.

Assets	
Cash	$ 30,000
Accounts Receivable (net)	?
Inventory	?
Property, Plant, and Equipment (net)	556,000
	$?
Liabilities and Stockholders' Equity	
Accounts Payable (trade)	$ 52,000
Income Taxes Payable (current)	28,000
Long-Term Debt	?
Common Stock	320,000
Retained Earnings	?
	$?
	continued

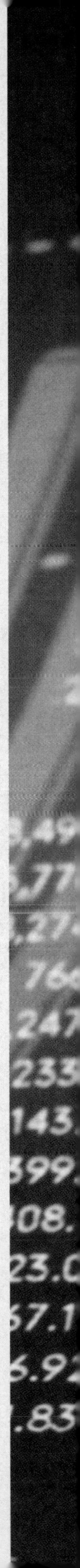

Additional Information	
Quick ratio (at year end)	1.3 to 1
Working capital	$84,000
Inventory turnover (Cost of goods sold ÷ Ending inventory)	12 times
Debt to equity ratio	0.8
Gross margin for 2005	$252,000

Required

Determine the following:

a. The balance in accounts receivable as of December 31, 2005.

b. The asset turnover for 2005.

c. The balance of long-term debt as of December 31, 2005.

d. The balance in retained earnings as of December 2005.

PROBLEMS—SERIES B

L.O. 2

Problem 13-16B *Vertical analysis*

Posey Corporation's controller has prepared the following vertical analysis for the president.

	2006	2005
Sales	100.0%	100.0%
Cost of Goods Sold	57.0	54.0
Gross Margin	43.0	46.0
Selling and Administrative Expenses	18.0	20.0
Interest Expense	2.8	4.0
Total Expenses	20.8	24.0
Income before Taxes	22.2	22.0
Income Tax Expense	10.0	8.0
Net Income	12.2%	14.0%

Required

Sales were $400,000 in 2005 and $800,000 in 2006. Convert the analysis to income statements for the two years.

L.O. 5, 6, 7

Problem 13-17B *Ratio analysis*

Information from Gaut Company's financial statements follows.

	2004	2003
Net sales	$1,440,000	$1,000,000
Income before interest and taxes	320,000	260,000
Net income after taxes	148,000	96,000
Interest expense	36,000	24,000
Stockholders' equity, December 31 (2002: $480,000)	720,000	600,000
Common stock, par $24, December 31	420,000	360,000

Average number of shares outstanding was 16,000 for 2004 and 15,000 for 2003.

Required

Compute the following ratios for Gaut Company for 2004 and 2003.

a. Times interest earned
b. Earnings per share based on the average number of shares outstanding
c. Price-earnings ratio (market prices: 2004, $60 per share; 2003, $48 per share)
d. Return on average equity
e. Net margin

Problem 13-18B ***Effect of transactions on current ratio and working capital*** L.O. 4

Moreno Company has a current ratio of 2:1 on June 30, 2006. Indicate whether each of the following transactions would increase (+), decrease (−), or not affect (NA) Moreno's current ratio and its working capital.

Required

a. Issued 10-year bonds for $100,000 cash.
b. Paid cash to settle an account payable.
c. Sold merchandise for more than cost.
d. Recognized depreciation on plant equipment.
e. Purchased a machine by issuing a long-term note payable.
f. Purchased merchandise inventory on account.
g. Received customer payment on accounts receivable.
h. Paid cash for federal income tax expense (assume that the expense has not been previously accrued).
i. Declared cash dividend payable in one month.
j. Received cash for interest on a long-term note receivable (assume that interest has not been previously accrued).
k. Received cash from issuing a short-term note payable.
l. Traded a truck for a sedan.

Problem 13-19B ***Ratio analysis*** L.O. 7

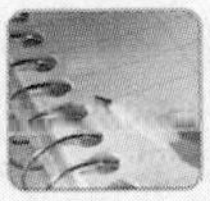

Selected data for Taft Company for 2003 and additional information on industry averages follow.

Earnings (net income)		$ 168,000
Preferred Stock (20,000 shares at $28 par, 6%)		$560,000
Common Stock (40,500 shares at $8 par, market value $30.40)		324,000
Paid-in Capital in Excess of par value—common		360,000
Retained Earnings		480,000
		1,724,000
Less: Treasury Stock		
Preferred (1,000 shares)	$28,800	
Common (500 shares)	12,800	41,600
Total Stockholders' Equity		$1,682,400

Note: Dividends in arrears on preferred stock: $31,920. The preferred stock can be called for $36.80 per share.

Industry averages	
Earnings per share	$2.00
Price-earnings ratio	8.00
Return on equity	7.30%

Required

a. Calculate and compare Taft Company's ratios with the industry averages.
b. Discuss factors you would consider in deciding whether to invest in the company.

L.O. 2

Problem 13-20B *Supply missing balance sheet numbers*

Agnes Hale discovered a piece of wet and partially burned balance sheet after her office was destroyed by fire. She could recall a current ratio of 1.75 and a debt to assets ratio of 45 percent.

Assets	
Current Assets	
Cash	$ 37,500
Accounts Receivable	(A)
Inventory	63,000
Prepaid Items	13,500
Total Current Assets	(B)
Long-Term Assets	
Building	(C)
Less: Accumulated Depreciation	(45,000)
Total Long-Term Assets	270,000
Total Assets	$ (D)
Liabilities and Stockholders' Equity	
Liabilities	
Current Liabilities	
Accounts Payable	$ 63,000
Notes Payable	(E)
Income Tax Payable	27,000
Total Current Liabilities	120,000
Long-Term Liabilities	
Bonds Payable	67,500
Mortgage Payable	(F)
Total Liabilities	(G)
Stockholders' Equity	
Common Stock	135,000
Retained Earnings	(H)
Total Stockholders' Equity	(I)
Total Liabilities and Stockholders' Equity	$ (J)

Required

Complete the balance sheet by supplying the missing amounts.

L.O. 2, 3, 4, 5, 6, 7

Problem 13-21B *Ratio analysis*

The following financial statements apply to Wells Appliances, Inc.

WELLS APPLIANCES, INC.
Balance Sheets
As of December 31

	2006	2005
Assets		
Current Assets		
Cash	$118,000	$ 91,000
Marketable Securities	24,000	18,000
Accounts Receivable (net)	112,000	108,000
Inventories	180,000	192,000
Prepaid Items	27,000	14,000
Total Current Assets	461,000	423,000

continued

	2006	2005
Investments	120,000	120,000
Plant (net)	260,000	254,000
Other	80,000	74,000
Total Assets	$921,000	$871,000
Equities		
Liabilities		
Current Liabilities		
Notes Payable	$ 20,000	$ 15,000
Accounts Payable	80,000	38,000
Other	66,000	9,000
Total Current Liabilities	166,000	62,000
Noncurrent Liabilities		
Bonds Payable	110,000	210,000
Other	26,000	12,000
Total Noncurrent Liabilities	136,000	222,000
Total Liabilities	302,000	284,000
Stockholders' Equity		
Preferred Stock ($100 par, 4% cumulative, nonparticipating; $100 liquidating value; 1,000 shares authorized and issued; no dividends in arrears)	100,000	100,000
Common Stock ($10 par; 50,000 shares authorized; 12,000 shares issued)	120,000	120,000
Paid-In Capital in excess of par value—Preferred	36,000	36,000
Paid-In Capital in excess of par value—Common	120,000	120,000
Retained Earnings	243,000	211,000
Total Stockholders' Equity	619,000	587,000
Total Liabilities and Stockholders' Equity	$921,000	$871,000

WELLS APPLIANCES, INC.
Statements of Income and Retained Earnings
For the Years Ended December 31

	2006	2005
Revenues		
Sales (net)	$240,000	$230,000
Other Revenues	7,000	4,000
Total Revenues	247,000	234,000
Expenses		
Cost of Goods Sold	143,000	130,000
Selling, General, and Administrative	46,000	57,000
Interest Expense	7,000	10,000
Income Tax Expense	8,000	14,000
Total Expenses	204,000	211,000
Net Earnings (net income)	43,000	23,000
Retained Earnings, January 1	210,000	198,000
Less: Preferred Stock Dividends	4,000	4,000
Common Stock Dividends	6,000	6,000
Retained Earnings, December 31	$243,000	$211,000

Required

Calculate the following ratios for 2006:

a. Working capital
b. Current ratio
c. Quick ratio
d. Accounts receivable turnover
e. Average number of days to collect accounts receivable
f. Inventory turnover
g. Average number of days to sell inventory
h. Debt to assets ratio
i. Debt to equity ratio
j. Times interest earned
k. Plant assets to long-term debt
l. Net margin
m. Asset turnover
n. Return on investment
o. Return on equity
p. Earnings per share
q. Book value
r. Price-earnings ratio (market price: $13.26)
s. Dividend yield on common stock

L.O. 2, 3, 4, 5, 6, 7

excel

mhhe.com/edmonds2007

Problem 13-22B *Ratio analysis*

Galin Company's stock is quoted at $16 per share at December 31, 2006 and 2005. Galin's financial statements follow.

GALIN COMPANY
Balance Sheets
As of December 31
(In thousands)

	2006	2005
Assets		
Current Assets		
Cash	$ 3,000	$ 2,000
Marketable Securities, at cost which approximates market	5,000	4,000
Accounts Receivable, net of allowance for doubtful accounts	47,000	44,000
Inventories, lower of cost or market	50,000	60,000
Prepaid Items	2,000	1,000
Total Current Assets	107,000	111,000
Property, Plant, and Equipment, net of accumulated depreciation	100,000	105,000
Investments	1,000	1,000
Long-Term Receivables	3,000	2,000
Goodwill and Patents, net of accumulated amortization	2,000	4,000
Other Assets	2,000	3,000
Total Assets	$215,000	$226,000
Liabilities and Stockholders' Equity		
Current Liabilities		
Notes Payable	$ 3,000	$ 5,000
Accounts Payable	12,000	16,000
Accrued Expenses	9,000	11,000
Income Taxes Payable	1,000	1,000
Payments Due within one year	3,000	2,000
Total Current Liabilities	28,000	35,000
Long-Term Debt	50,000	60,000
Deferred Income Taxes	30,000	27,000
Other Liabilities	5,000	4,000
Total Liabilities	113,000	126,000

continued

Stockholders' Equity		
5% Cumulative Preferred Stock, par value $100 per share; $100 liquidating value; authorized 250,000 shares; issued and outstanding 200,000 shares	20,000	20,000
Common Stock, $1 par value; 10,000,000 shares authorized and 5,000,000 shares issued and outstanding	5,000	5,000
Additional Paid-In Capital, common	35,000	35,000
Retained Earnings	42,000	40,000
Total Stockholders' Equity	102,000	100,000
Total Liabilities and Stockholders' Equity	$215,000	$226,000

GALIN COMPANY
Statements of Income and Retained Earnings
For the Years Ended December 31
(in thousands)

	2006	2005
Net Sales	$180,000	$150,000
Expenses		
Cost of Goods Sold	147,000	120,000
Selling, General, and Administrative Expenses	20,000	18,000
Other	2,000	2,000
Total Expenses	169,000	140,000
Income Before Income Taxes	11,000	10,000
Income Taxes	5,000	4,000
Net Income	6,000	6,000
Retained Earnings at Beginning of Period	40,000	38,000
Less: Dividends on Common Stock	3,000	3,000
Dividends on Preferred Stock	1,000	1,000
Retained Earnings at End of Period	$ 42,000	$ 40,000

Required

Based on the preceding information, compute the following for 2006 only.

a. Current ratio
b. Quick (acid-test) ratio
c. Average number of days to collect accounts receivable, assuming all sales on account
d. Inventory turnover
e. Book value per share of common stock
f. Earnings per share on common stock
g. Price-earnings ratio on common stock
h. Debt to assets ratio
i. Return on investment
j. Return on equity

Problem 13-23B ***Horizontal analysis*** L.O. 2

Required

Use the financial statements for Galin Company from Problem 13-22B to perform a horizontal analysis of both the balance sheet and income statement for 2006 and 2005.

Problem 13-24B ***Vertical analysis*** L.O. 2

Required

Use the financial statements for Galin Company from Problem 13-22B to perform a vertical analysis (based on total assets, total equities, and sales) of both the balance sheets and income statements for 2006 and 2005.

ANALYZE, THINK, COMMUNICATE

ATC 13-1 Business Applications Case ***Analyzing Best Buy Company and Circuit City Stores***

The following information relates to Best Buy and Circuit City Stores, Inc., for their 2003 and 2002 fiscal years.

BEST BUY CO., INC.
Selected Financial Information
(Amounts in millions, except per share amounts)

	March 1, 2003	March 2, 2002
Total current assets	$ 4,867	$ 4,600
Merchandise inventories	2,046	1,875
Property and equipment, net of depreciation	2,062	1,661
Total assets	7,663	7,367
Total current liabilities	3,793	3,705
Total long-term liabilities	1,140	1,141
Total liabilities	4,933	4,846
Total shareholders' equity	2,730	2,521
Total liabilities and shareholders' equity	7,663	7,367
Revenue	20,946	17,711
Cost of goods sold	15,710	13,941
Gross profit	5,236	3,770
Operating income	1,010	908
Interest expense	30	21
Earnings from continuing operations before income tax expense	1,014	926
Income tax expense	392	356
Earnings from continuing operations	622	570
Net earnings	99	570
Basic earnings per share	$ 0.31	$ 1.80

CIRCUIT CITY STORES, INC.
Selected Financial Information
(Amounts in millions except per share data)

	February 28, 2003	February 28, 2002
Total current assets	$3,103	$3,653
Merchandise inventory	1,410	1,234
Property and equipment, net of depreciation	650	733
Total assets	3,799	4,542
Total current liabilities	1,280	1,641
Total long-term liabilities	178	167
Total liabilities	1,458	1,808
Total stockholders' equity	2,342	2,734
Revenues	9,954	9,518
Cost of sales, buying and warehousing	7,603	7,180
Gross profit	2,350	2,328
Interest expense	1	1
Earnings from continuing operations before income taxes	67	206
Provision for income taxes	25	78
Earnings from continuing operations	42	128
Net earnings	106	219
Basic earnings per share:		
Continuing operations	$ 0.20	$ 0.62

Required

a. Compute the following ratios for the companies' 2003 fiscal years:

(1) Current ratio.

(2) Average number of days to sell inventory. (Use average inventory)

(3) Debt to assets ratio.

(4) Return on investment. (Use average assets and use "earnings from continuing operations" rather than "net earnings.")

(5) Gross margin percentage.

(6) Asset turnover. (Use average assets.)

(7) Return on sales. (Use "earnings from continuing operations" rather than "net earnings.")

(8) Plant assets to long-term debt ratio.

b. Which company appears to be more profitable? Explain your answer and identify which of the ratio(s) from Requirement *a* you used to reach your conclusion.

c. Which company appears to have the higher level of financial risk? Explain your answer and identify which of the ratio(s) from Requirement *a* you used to reach your conclusion.

d. Which company appears to be charging higher prices for its goods? Explain your answer and identify which of the ratio(s) from Requirement *a* you used to reach your conclusion.

e. Which company appears to be the more efficient at using its assets? Explain your answer and identify which of the ratio(s) from Requirement *a* you used to reach your conclusion.

ATC 13-2 Group Assignment *Ratio analysis and logic*

Presented here are selected data from the 10-K reports of four companies for the 1997 fiscal year. The four companies, in alphabetical order, are

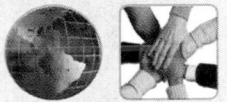

1. BellSouth Corporation, a telephone company that operates in the southeastern United States.
2. Caterpillar, Inc., a manufacturer of heavy machinery.
3. Dollar General Corporation, a company that owns Dollar General Stores discount stores.
4. Tiffany & Company, a company that operates high-end jewelry stores

The data, presented in the order of the amount of sales, are as follows. Dollar amounts are in millions.

	A	B	C	D
Sales	$20,561	$18,110	$2,627.3	$1,017.6
Cost of goods sold	6,254	13,374	1,885.2	453.4
Net earnings	3,261	1,665	144.6	72.8
Inventory or NA	2,603	632.0	386.4	
Materials and supplies	398	NA	NA	NA
Accounts receivable	4,750	3,331	0	99.5
Total assets	36,301	20,756	914.8	827.1

Required

a. Divide the class into groups of four or five students per group and then organize the groups into four sections. Assign Task 1 to the first section of groups, Task 2 to the second section, Task 3 to the third section, and Task 4 to the fourth section.

Group Tasks

(1) Assume that you represent BellSouth Corporation. Identify the set of financial data (Column A, B, C, or D) that relates to your company.

(2) Assume that you represent Caterpillar, Inc. Identify the set of financial data (Column A, B, C, or D) that relates to your company.

(3) Assume that you represent Dollar General Corporation. Identify the set of financial data (Column A, B, C, or D) that relates to your company.

(4) Assume that you represent Tiffany & Company. Identify the set of financial data (Column A, B, C, or D) that relates to your company.

Hint: Use a gross margin ratio (gross margin ÷ sales), a net margin ratio (net income ÷ sales), and return on assets (net income ÷ total assets) to facilitate identifying the financial data related to your particular company.

b. Select a representative from each section. Have the representatives explain the rationale for the group's selection. The explanation should include a set of ratios that support the group's conclusion.

ATC 13-3 Research Assignment *Financial analysis information in Dell's annual report*

Dell, Inc., uses its SEC Form 10-K as its official annual report. The company also produces a "Year in Review" summary, which it refers to as an annual report, but that document does not provide sufficient detail to answer the following questions. Using the most current Forms 10-K for Dell, Inc., complete the requirements below. To find the Forms 10-K use either the SEC EDGAR system following the instructions in Appendix A, or the company's website.

Required

a. Find the Management's Discussion and Analysis section (MD&A) of Dell's 10-K. In the first subsection of the MD&A, "Overview," a table summarizes Dell's results of operations for the past three years. Does this table present information in a horizontal or a vertical format?

b. Using the table identified in Requirement *a*, explain how Dell's net income changed over the past three years in absolute amounts and in percentages.

c. Which reflected the greater percentage change, revenue, or net income?

d. Near the middle of the MD&A section there is a subsection called "Liquidity, Capital Commitments, and Contractual Cash Obligations." The second table in this subsection presents data for three items related to Dell's "Cash conversion cycle." Identify these three items and explain what the data related to them tell the reader.

Note: The directions for finding Dell's 10-K were accurate for 2004 and several prior fiscal years. The company may have moved this information in later reports.

ATC 13-4 Writing Assignment *Interpreting ratios*

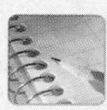

Following are the debt to assets, return on assets, and return on equity ratios for four companies from two different industries. The range of interest rates each company was paying on its long-term debt is provided. Each of these public companies is a leader in its particular industry, and the data are for the fiscal years ending in 1997. All numbers are percentages.

	Debt to Assets*	Return on Assets	Return on Equity	Interest Rates
Banking Industry				
Wachovia Corporation	92	1.0	11.5	5.7–7.0
Wells Fargo & Co.	87	1.2	9.0	6.1–11.0
Home Construction Industry				
Pulte Corporation	62	2.5	6.5	7.0–10.1
Toll Brothers, Inc.	66	5.8	16.9	7.8–10.5

*Debt to assets ratio is defined as total liabilities divided by total assets.

Required

a. Based only on the debt to assets ratios, the banking companies appear to have the most financial risk. Generally, companies that have more financial risk are charged higher interest rates. Write a brief explanation of why the banking companies can borrow money at lower interest rates than the construction companies.

b. Explain why the return on equity ratio for Wachovia is more than 10 times higher than its return on assets ratio, and Pulte's return on equity ratio is less than 3 times higher than its return on assets ratio.

ATC 13-5 Ethical Dilemma *Making the ratios look good*

J. Talbot is the accounting manager for Kolla Waste Disposal Corporation. Kolla is having its worst financial year since its inception. The company is expected to report a net loss. In the midst of such bad news, Ms. Talbot surprised the company president, Mr. Winston, by suggesting that the company write off approximately 25 percent of its garbage trucks. Mr. Winston responded by noting that the trucks could still be operated for another two or three years. Ms. Talbot replied, "We may use them for two or three more years, but you couldn't sell them on the street if you had to. Who wants to buy a bunch of old garbage trucks and besides, it will make next year's financials so sweet. No one will care about the additional write-off this year. We are already showing a loss. Who will care if we lose a little bit more?"

Required

a. How will the write-off affect the following year's return on assets ratio?

b. How will the write-off affect the asset and income growth percentages?

c. Would writing off the garbage trucks for the reasons stated present any ethical concerns for Kolla? Explain.

Comprehensive financial statements analysis projects are available at www.mhhe.com/edmonds/concepts.

CHAPTER 14

Management Accounting: A Value-Added Discipline

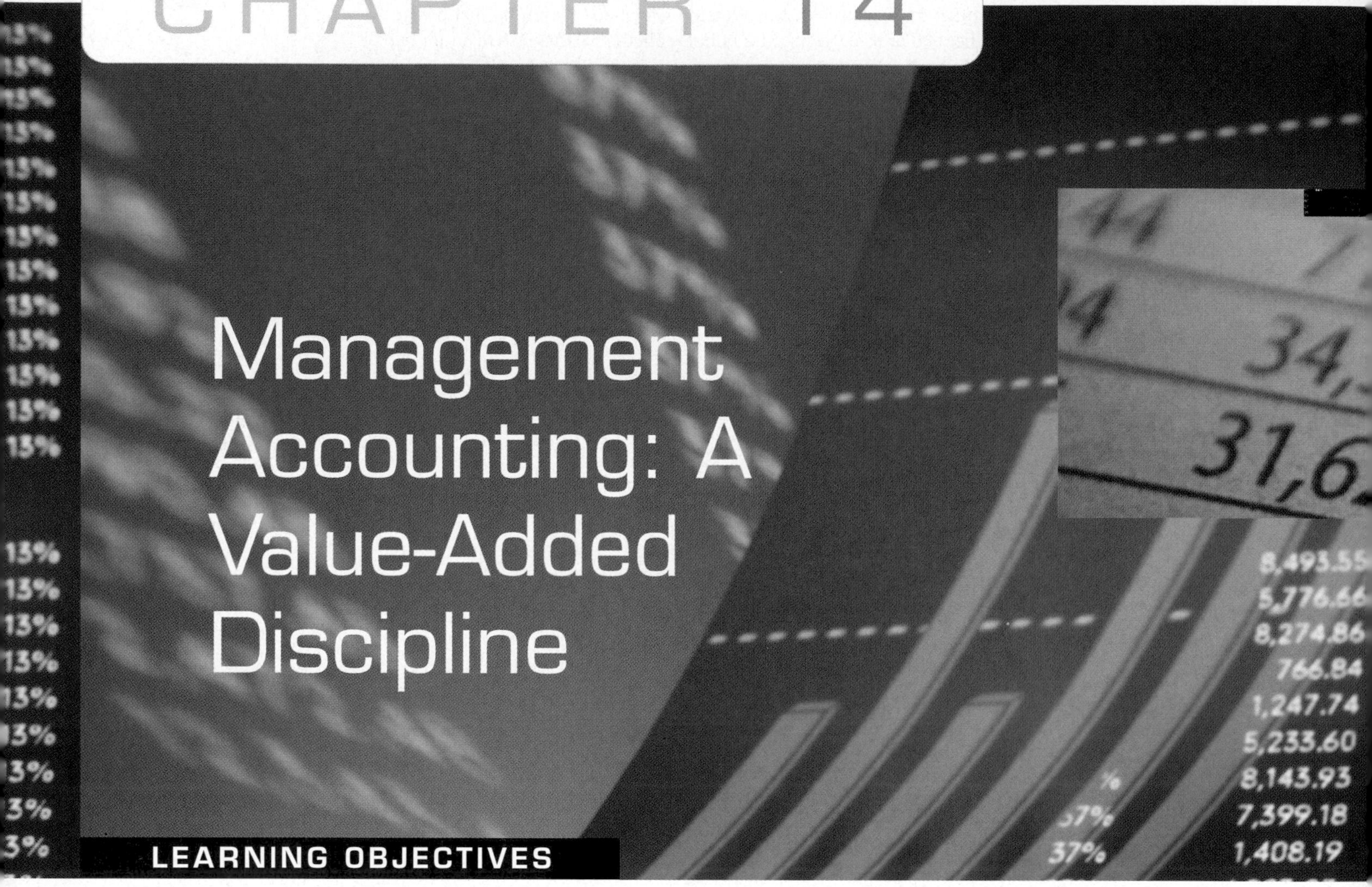

LEARNING OBJECTIVES

After you have mastered the material in this chapter, you will be able to:

1. Distinguish between managerial and financial accounting.
2. Identify the cost components of a product made by a manufacturing company: the cost of materials, labor, and overhead.
3. Explain the need for determining the average cost per unit of a product.
4. Distinguish between a cost and an expense.
5. Explain the effects on financial statements of product costs versus general, selling, and administrative costs.
6. Explain how cost classification affects financial statements and managerial decisions.
7. Identify the standards of ethical conduct and the features that motivate misconduct.
8. Distinguish product costs from upstream and downstream costs.
9. Explain how products provided by service companies differ from products made by manufacturing companies.
10. Explain how emerging trends such as activity-based management, value-added assessment, and just-in-time inventory are affecting the managerial accounting discipline.

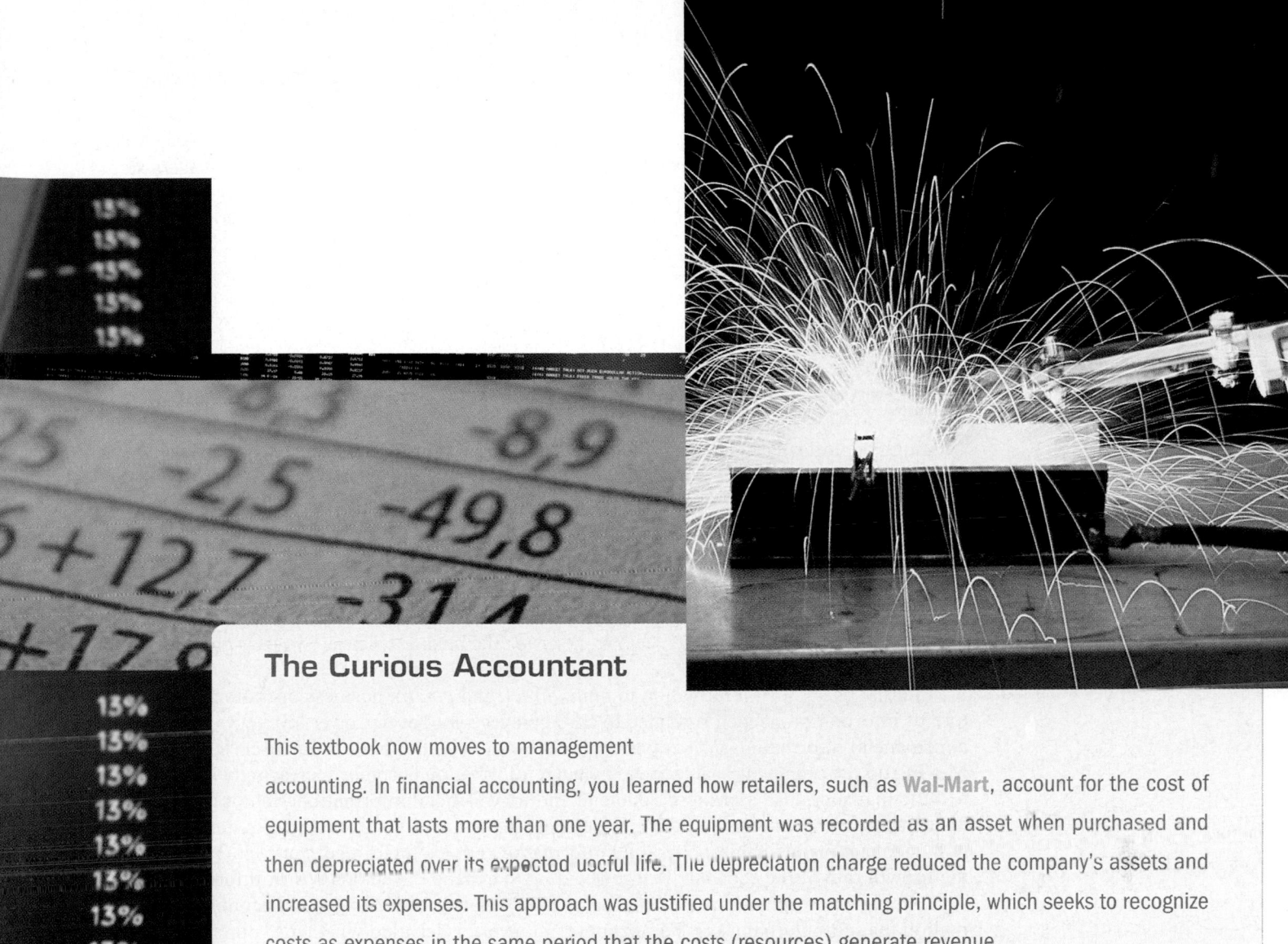

The Curious Accountant

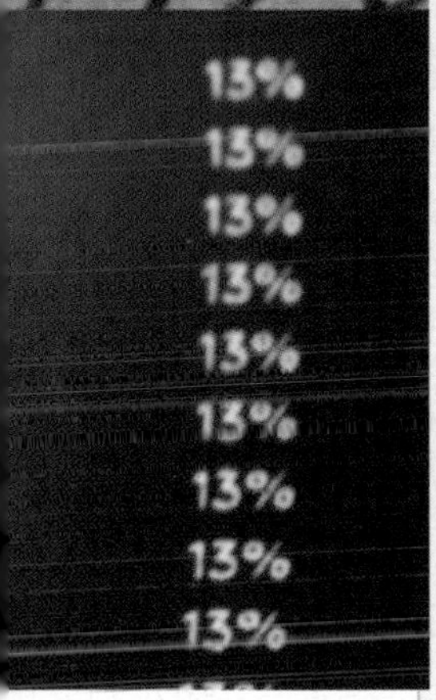

This textbook now moves to management accounting. In financial accounting, you learned how retailers, such as **Wal-Mart**, account for the cost of equipment that lasts more than one year. The equipment was recorded as an asset when purchased and then depreciated over its expected useful life. The depreciation charge reduced the company's assets and increased its expenses. This approach was justified under the matching principle, which seeks to recognize costs as expenses in the same period that the costs (resources) generate revenue.

In management accounting, the focus will often be on manufacturing entities. Consider the following scenario. **Black & Decker** manufactures cordless hedge trimmers that it sells to Wal-Mart. In order to produce the hedge trimmers, Black & Decker purchased a robotic machine that it expects can be used to produce 1 million hedge trimmers.

Should Black & Decker account for depreciation of its manufacturing equipment the same way Wal-Mart accounts for depreciation of its registers at the checkout counters? If not, how should Black & Decker account for its depreciation? Consider the matching principle when thinking of your answer. (Answer on page 714.)

Chapter 14

CHAPTER OPENING

*Andy Grove, president and CEO of **Intel Corporation**, is credited with the motto "Only the paranoid survive." Mr. Grove describes a wide variety of concerns that make him paranoid. He declares:*

> *I worry about products getting screwed up, and I worry about products getting introduced prematurely. I worry about factories not performing well, and I worry about having too many factories. I worry about hiring the right people, and I worry about morale slacking off. And, of course, I worry about competitors. I worry*

about other people figuring out how to do what we do better or cheaper, and displacing us with our customers.

Do Intel's historically-based financial statements contain the information Mr. Grove needs? No. **Financial accounting** *is not designed to satisfy all the information needs of business managers. Its scope is limited to the needs of external users such as investors and creditors. The field of accounting designed to meet the needs of internal users is called* **managerial accounting.** ■

Differences Between Managerial and Financial Accounting

LO 1

Distinguish between managerial and financial accounting.

Although the information needs of internal and external users overlap, the needs of managers differ from those of investors or creditors. Some distinguishing characteristics are discussed in the following section.

Users and Types of Information

Financial accounting provides information used primarily by investors, creditors, and others *outside* a business. In contrast, managerial accounting focuses on information used by executives, managers, and employees who work *inside* the business. These two user groups need different types of information.

Internal users need information to *plan*, *direct*, and *control* business operations. The nature of information needed is related to an employee's job level. Lower level employees use nonfinancial information such as work schedules, store hours, and customer service policies. Moving up the organizational ladder, financial information becomes increasingly important. Middle managers use a blend of financial and nonfinancial information. Senior executives concentrate on financial data. To a lesser degree, senior executives also use general economic data and nonfinancial operating information. For example, an executive may consider the growth rate of the economy before deciding to expand the company's workforce.

External users (investors and creditors) have greater needs for general economic information than do internal users. For example, an investor debating whether to purchase stock versus bond securities might be more interested in government tax policy than financial statement data. Exhibit 14.1 summarizes the information needs of different user groups.

Level of Aggregation

External users desire *global information* that reflects the performance of a company as a whole. For example, an investor is not so much interested in the performance of a particular Sears store as she is in the performance of Sears Roebuck Company versus that of JCPenney Company. In contrast, internal users focus on detailed information about specific subunits of the company. To meet the needs of the different user groups financial accounting data are more aggregated than managerial accounting data.

Regulation

Financial accounting is designed to generate information for the general public. In an effort to protect the public interest, Congress established the **Securities and Exchange Commission (SEC)** and gave it authority to regulate public financial reporting practices. The SEC has delegated much of its authority for developing accounting rules to the

EXHIBIT 14.1

Relationship Between Type of User and Type of Information

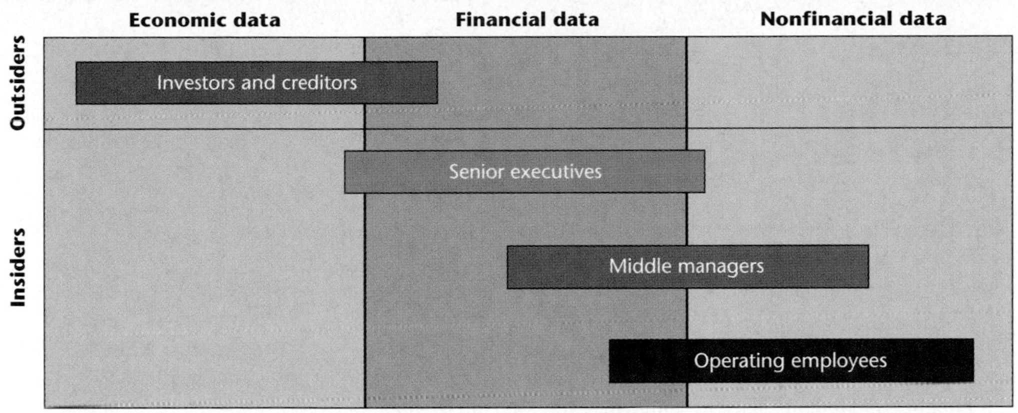

private sector **Financial Accounting Standards Board (FASB),** thereby allowing the accounting profession considerable influence over financial accounting reports. The FASB supports the broad base of pronouncements and practices known as **generally accepted accounting principles (GAAP).** GAAP severely restricts the accounting procedures and practices permitted in published financial statements.

Around the turn of the century, a number of high-profile business failures raised questions about the effectiveness of self-regulation and the usefulness of audits to protect the public. The **Sarbanes-Oxley Act of 2002** was adopted to address these concerns. The act creates a five-member Public Company Accounting Oversight Board (PCAOB) with the authority to set and enforce auditing, attestation, quality control, and ethics standards for auditors of public companies. The PCAOB is empowered to impose disciplinary and remedial sanctions for violations of its rules, securities laws, and professional auditing and accounting standards.

Beyond financial statement data, much of the information generated by management accounting systems is proprietary information not available to the public. Since this information is not distributed to the public, it need not be regulated to protect the public interest. Management accounting is restricted only by the **value-added principle**. Management accountants are free to engage in any information gathering and reporting activity so long as the activity adds value in excess of its cost. For example, management accountants are free to provide forecasted information to internal users. In contrast, financial accounting as prescribed by GAAP does not permit forecasting.

Information Characteristics

While financial accounting is characterized by its objectivity, reliability, consistency, and historical nature, managerial accounting is concerned with relevance and timeliness. Managerial accounting uses more estimates and fewer facts than financial accounting. Financial accounting reports what happened yesterday; managerial accounting reports what is expected to happen tomorrow.

Time Horizon and Reporting Frequency

Financial accounting information is reported periodically, normally at the end of a year. Management cannot wait until the end of the year to discover problems. Planning, controlling, and directing require immediate attention. Managerial accounting information is delivered on a continual basis.

EXHIBIT 14.2

Comparative Features of Managerial Versus Financial Accounting Information

Features	Managerial Accounting	Financial Accounting
Users	Insiders including executives, managers, and operators	Outsiders including investors, creditors, government agencies, analysts, and reporters
Information type	Economic and physical data as well as financial data	Financial data
Level of aggregation	Local information on subunits of the organization	Global information on the company as a whole
Regulation	No regulation, limited only by the value-added principle	Regulation by SEC, FASB, and other determinors of GAAP
Information characteristics	Estimates that promote relevance and enable timeliness	Factual information that is characterized by objectivity, reliability, consistency, and accuracy
Time horizon	Past, present, and future	Past only, historically based
Reporting frequency	Continuous reporting	Delayed with emphasis on annual reports

Exhibit 14.2 summarizes significant differences between financial and managerial accounting.

Product Costing

LO 2

Identify the cost components of a product made by a manufacturing company: the cost of materials, labor, and overhead.

A major focus for managerial accountants is determining **product cost.**[1] Managers need to know the cost of their products for a variety of reasons. For example, **cost-plus pricing** is a common business practice.[2] **Product costing** is also used to control business operations. It is useful in answering questions such as: Are costs higher or lower than expected? Who is responsible for the variances between expected and actual costs? What action can be taken to control the variances?

Product Costs in Manufacturing Companies

Topic Tackler PLUS

14-1

The cost of making products includes the cost of materials, labor, and other resources (usually called **overhead**). To understand how these costs affect financial statements, consider the example of Tabor Manufacturing Company.

Tabor Manufacturing Company

Tabor Manufacturing Company makes wooden tables. The company spent $1,000 cash to build four tables: $390 for materials, $470 for a carpenter's labor, and $140 for tools used in making the tables. How much is Tabor's expense? The answer is zero. The $1,000 cash has been converted into products (four tables). The cash payments for materials, labor, and tools were *asset exchange* transactions. One asset (cash) decreased while another asset (tables) increased. Tabor will not recognize any expense until the tables are sold; in the meantime, the cost of the tables is held in an asset account called **Finished Goods Inventory.** Exhibit 14.3 illustrates how cash is transformed into inventory.

[1] This text uses the term *product* in a generic sense to mean both goods and services.

[2] Other pricing strategies will be introduced in subsequent chapters.

EXHIBIT 14.3

Transforming the Asset Cash Into the Asset Finished Goods Inventory

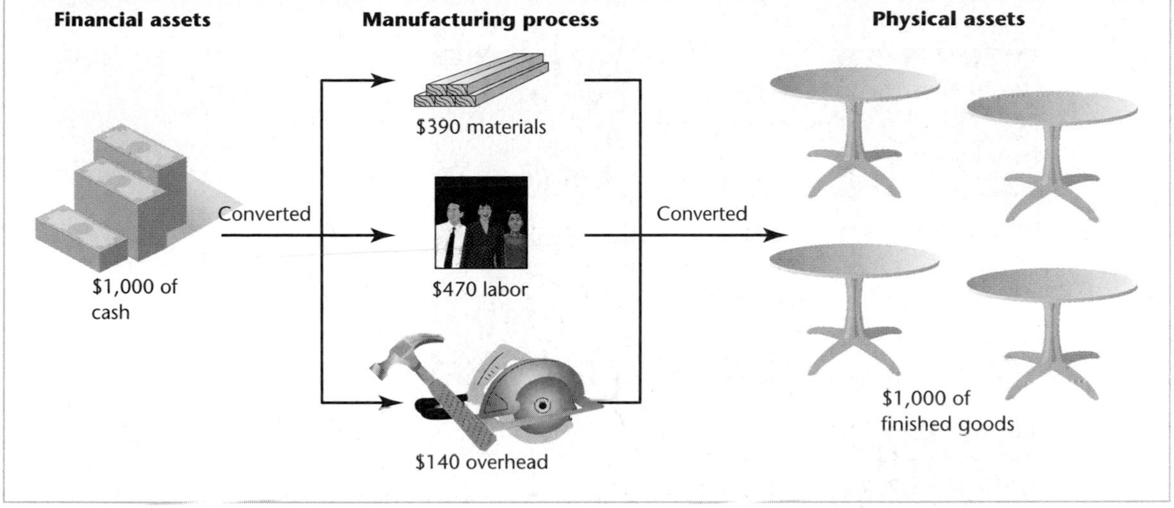

Average Cost per Unit

LO 3

Explain the need for determining the average cost per unit of a product.

How much did each table made by Tabor cost? The actual cost of each of the four tables likely differs. The carpenter probably spent a little more time on some of the tables than others. Material and tool usage probably varied from table to table. Determining the exact cost of each table is virtually impossible. Minute details such as a second of labor time cannot be effectively measured. Even if Tabor could determine the exact cost of each table, the information would be of little use. Minor differences in the cost per table would make no difference in pricing or other decisions management needs to make. Accountants therefore normally calculate cost per unit as an *average*. In the case of Tabor Manufacturing, the **average cost** per table is $250 ($1,000 ÷ 4 units). Unless otherwise stated, assume *cost per unit* means *average cost per unit.*

CHECK YOURSELF 14.1

All boxes of General Mills' Total Raisin Bran cereal are priced at exactly the same amount in your local grocery store. Does this mean that the actual cost of making each box of cereal was exactly the same?

Answer

No, making each box would not cost exactly the same amount. For example, some boxes contain slightly more or less cereal than other boxes. Accordingly, some boxes cost slightly more or less to make than others do. General Mills uses average cost rather than actual cost to develop its pricing strategy.

Costs Can Be Assets or Expenses

LO 4

Distinguish between a cost and an expense.

It might seem odd that wages earned by production workers are recorded as inventory instead of being expensed. Remember, however, that expenses are assets used in the process of *earning revenue*. The cash paid to production workers is not used to produce revenue. Instead, the cash is used to produce inventory. Revenue will be earned when the inventory is used (sold). So long as the inventory remains on hand, all product costs (materials, labor, and overhead) remain in an inventory account.

EXHIBIT 14.4

Cost Classification for Tabor Manufacturing Company

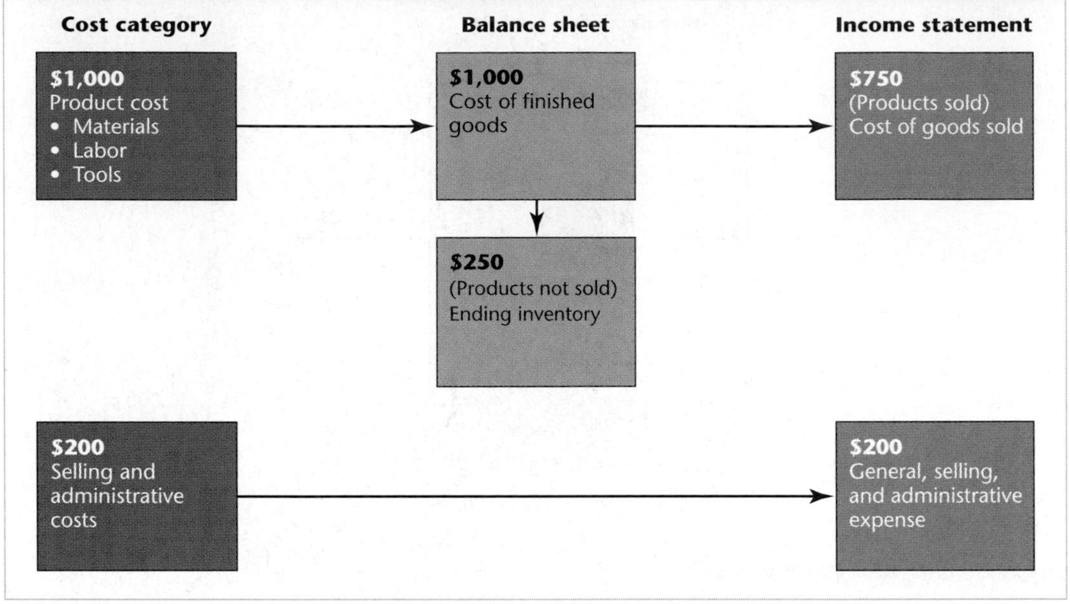

When a table is sold, the average cost of the table is transferred from the Inventory account to the Cost of Goods Sold (expense) account. If some tables remain unsold at the end of the accounting period, part of the *product cost* is reported as an asset (inventory) on the balance sheet while the other part is reported as an expense (cost of goods sold) on the income statement.

Costs that are not classified as product costs are normally expensed in the period in which they are incurred. These costs include *general operating costs, selling and administrative costs, interest costs*, and the *cost of income taxes*.

To illustrate, return to the Tabor Manufacturing example. Recall that Tabor made four tables at an average cost per unit of $250. Assume Tabor pays an employee who sells three of the tables a $200 sales commission. The sales commission is expensed immediately. The total product cost for the three tables (3 tables × $250 each = $750) is expensed on the income statement as cost of goods sold. The portion of the total product cost remaining in inventory is $250 (one table × $250). Exhibit 14.4 shows the relationship between the costs incurred and the expenses recognized for Tabor Manufacturing Company.

Effect of Product Costs on Financial Statements

LO 5

Explain the effects on financial statements of product costs versus general, selling, and administrative costs.

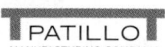

We illustrate accounting for product costs in manufacturing companies with Patillo Manufacturing Company, a producer of ceramic pottery. Patillo, started on January 1, 2004, experienced the following accounting events during its first year of operations.[3] *Assume that all transactions except 6, 8, and 10 are cash transactions.*

1. Acquired $15,000 cash by issuing common stock.
2. Paid $2,000 for materials that were used to make products. All products started were completed during the period.

[3] This illustration assumes that all inventory started during the period was completed during the period. Patillo therefore uses only one inventory account, Finished Goods Inventory. Many manufacturing companies normally have three categories of inventory on hand at the end of an accounting period: Raw Materials Inventory, Work in Process Inventory (inventory of partially completed units), and Finished Goods Inventory. Chapter 17 discusses these inventories in greater detail.

EXHIBIT 14.5

Effect of Product Versus Selling and administrative Costs on Financial Statements

Event No.	Assets								Equity								
	Cash	+	Inventory	+	Office Furn.*	+	Manuf. Equip.*	=	Com. Stk.	+	Ret. Earn.	Rev.	−	Exp.	=	Net Inc.	Cash Flow
1	15,000							=	15,000								15,000 FA
2	(2,000)	+	2,000														(2,000) OA
3	(1,200)							=			(1,200)		−	1,200	=	(1,200)	(1,200) OA
4	(3,000)	+	3,000														(3,000) OA
5	(2,800)	+			2,800												(2,800) IA
6					(600)			=			(600)		−	600	=	(600)	
7	(4,500)	+					4,500										(4,500) IA
8			1,000	+			(1,000)										
9	7,500							=			7,500	7,500			=	7,500	7,500 OA
10			(4,000)					=			(4,000)		−	4,000	=	(4,000)	
Totals	9,000	+	2,000	+	2,200	+	3,500	=	15,000	+	1,700	7,500	−	5,800	=	1,700	9,000 NC

*Negative amounts in these columns represent accumulated depreciation.

3. Paid $1,200 for salaries of selling and administrative employees.
4. Paid $3,000 for wages of production workers.
5. Paid $2,800 for furniture used in selling and administrative offices.
6. Recognized depreciation on the office furniture purchased in Event 5. The furniture was acquired on January 1, had a $400 estimated salvage value, and a four-year useful life. The annual depreciation charge is $600 [($2,800 − $400) ÷ 4].
7. Paid $4,500 for manufacturing equipment.
8. Recognized depreciation on the equipment purchased in Event 7. The equipment was acquired on January 1, had a $1,500 estimated salvage value, and a three-year useful life. The annual depreciation charge is $1,000 [($4,500 − $1,500) ÷ 3].
9. Sold inventory to customers for $7,500 cash.
10. The inventory sold in Event 9 cost $4,000 to make.

The effects of these transactions on the balance sheet, income statement, and statement of cash flows are shown in Exhibit 14.5. Study each row in this exhibit, paying particular attention to how similar costs such as salaries for selling and administrative personnel and wages for production workers have radically different effects on the financial statements. The example illustrates the three elements of product costs, materials (Event 2), labor (Event 4), and overhead (Event 8). These events are discussed in more detail below.

Materials Costs (Event 2)

Materials used to make products are usually called **raw materials**. The cost of raw materials is first recorded in an asset account (Inventory). The cost is then transferred from the Inventory account to the Cost of Goods Sold account at the time the goods are sold. Remember that materials cost is only one component of total manufacturing costs. When inventory is sold, the combined cost of materials, labor, and overhead is expensed as *cost of goods sold*. The costs of materials that can be easily and conveniently traced to products are called **direct raw materials** costs.

Labor Costs (Event 4)

The salaries paid to selling and administrative employees (Event 3) and the wages paid to production workers (Event 4) are accounted for differently. Salaries paid to selling and administrative employees are expensed immediately, but the cost of production wages is added to inventory. Production wages are expensed as part of cost of goods sold at the time the inventory is sold. Labor costs that can be easily and conveniently traced to products are called **direct labor** costs. The cost flow of wages for production employees versus salaries for selling and administrative personnel is shown in Exhibit 14.6.

EXHIBIT 14.6

Flow of Labor Costs

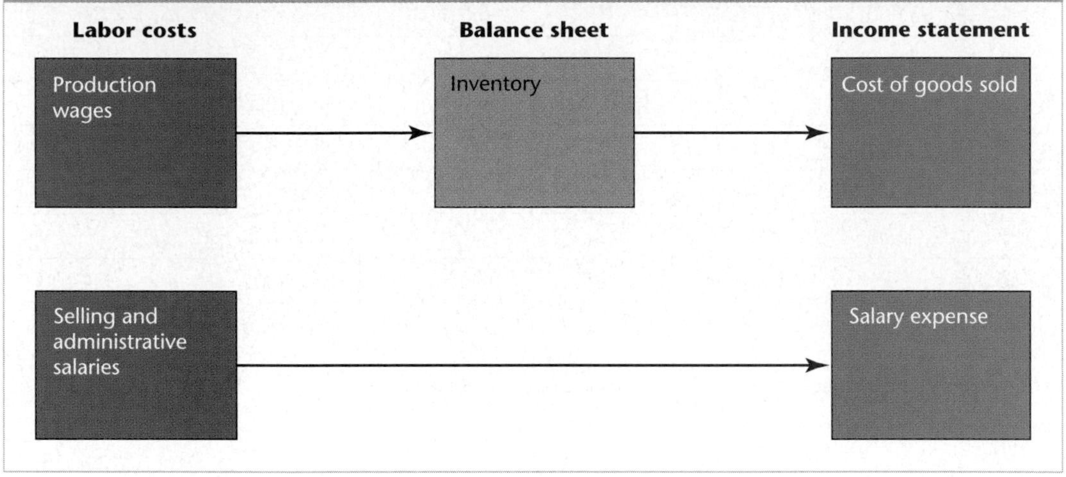

Overhead Costs (Event 8)

Although depreciation cost totaled $1,600 ($600 on office furniture and $1,000 on manufacturing equipment), only the $600 of depreciation on the office furniture is expensed directly on the income statement. The depreciation on the manufacturing equipment is split between the income statement (cost of goods sold) and the balance sheet (inventory). The depreciation cost flow for the manufacturing equipment versus the office furniture is shown in Exhibit 14.7.

EXHIBIT 14.7

Flow of Depreciation Costs

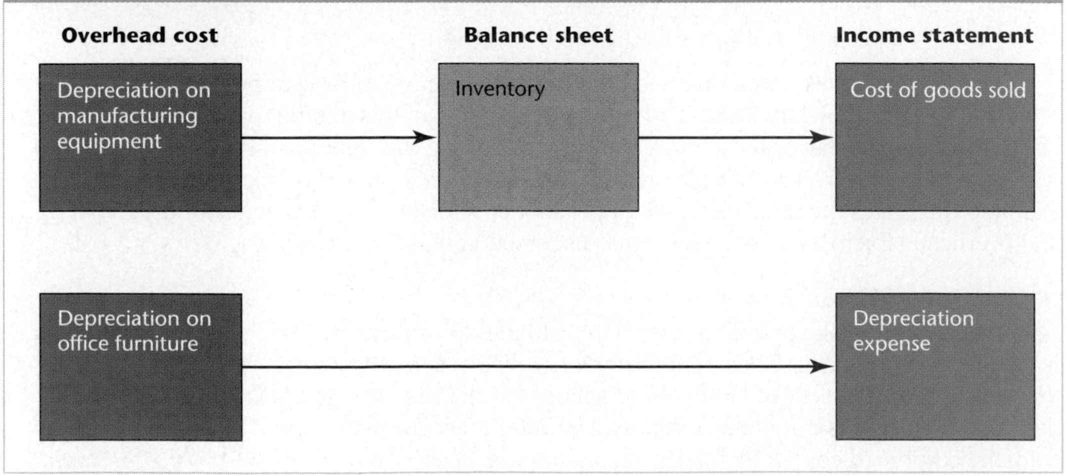

Total Product Cost. A summary of Patillo Manufacturing's total product cost is shown in Exhibit 14.8.

EXHIBIT 14.8

Schedule of Inventory Costs

Materials	$2,000
Labor	3,000
Manufacturing overhead*	1,000
Total product costs	6,000
Less: Cost of goods sold	(4,000)
Ending inventory balance	$2,000

*Depreciation ([$4,500 − $1,500] ÷ 3)

EXHIBIT 14.9

PATILLO MANUFACTURING COMPANY

Financial Statements

Income Statement for 2004

Sales Revenue		$7,500
Cost of Goods Sold		(4,000)
Gross Margin		3,500
G, S, & A Expenses		
Salaries Expense		(1,200)
Depreciation Expense—Office Furniture		(600)
Net Income		$1,700

Balance Sheet as of December 31, 2004

Cash		$ 9,000
Finished Goods Inventory		2,000
Office Furniture	$2,800	
Accumulated Depreciation	(600)	
Book Value		2,200
Manufacturing Equipment	4,500	
Accumulated Depreciation	(1,000)	
Book Value		3,500
Total Assets		$16,700
Stockholders' Equity		
Common Stock		$15,000
Retained Earnings		1,700
Total Stockholders' Equity		$16,700

Statement of Cash Flows for 2004

Operating Activities	
Inflow from Revenue	$ 7,500
Outflow for Inventory	(5,000)
Outflow for S&A Salaries	(1,200)
Net Inflow from Operating Activities	1,300
Investing Activities	
Outflow for Equipment and Furniture	(7,300)
Financing Activities	
Inflow from Stock Issue	15,000
Net Change in Cash	9,000
Beginning Cash Balance	-0-
Ending Cash Balance	$ 9,000

General, Selling, and Administrative Costs

General, selling, and administrative costs (G,S,&A) are normally expensed *in the period* in which they are incurred. Because of this recognition pattern, nonproduct expenses are sometimes called **period costs.** In Patillo's case, the salary expense for selling and administrative employees and the depreciation on office furniture are period costs reported directly on the income statement.

The income statement, balance sheet, and statement of cash flows for Patillo Manufacturing are displayed in Exhibit 14.9.

The $4,000 cost of goods sold reported on the income statement includes a portion of the materials, labor, and overhead costs incurred by Patillo during the year. Similarly, the $2,000 of finished goods inventory on the balance sheet includes materials, labor, and overhead costs. These product costs will be recognized as expense in the next accounting period when the goods are sold. Initially classifying a cost as a product cost delays, but does not eliminate, its recognition as an expense. All product costs are ultimately recognized as expense (cost of goods sold). Cost classification does not affect cash flow. Cash inflows and outflows are recognized in the period that cash is collected or paid regardless of whether the cost is recorded as an asset or expensed on the income statement.

Overhead Costs: A Closer Look

Costs such as depreciation on manufacturing equipment cannot be easily traced to products. Suppose that Patillo Manufacturing makes both tables and chairs. What part of the depreciation is caused by manufacturing tables versus manufacturing chairs? Similarly, suppose a production supervisor oversees employees who work on both tables and chairs. How much of the supervisor's salary relates to tables and how much to chairs? Likewise, the cost of glue used in the production department would be difficult to trace to tables versus chairs. You could count the drops of glue used on each product, but the information would not be useful enough to merit the time and money spent collecting the data.

Costs that cannot be traced to products and services in a *cost-effective* manner are called **indirect costs.** The indirect costs incurred to make products are called **manufacturing overhead**. Some of the items commonly included in manufacturing overhead are indirect materials, indirect labor, factory utilities, rent of manufacturing facilities, and depreciation on manufacturing assets.

CHECK YOURSELF 14.2

Lawson Manufacturing Company paid production workers wages of $100,000. It incurred materials costs of $120,000 and manufacturing overhead costs of $160,000. Selling and administrative salaries were $80,000. Lawson started and completed 1,000 units of product and sold 800 of these units. The company sets sales prices at $220 above the average per unit production cost. Based on this information alone, determine the amount of gross margin and net income. What is Lawson's pricing strategy called?

Answer

Total product cost is $380,000 ($100,000 labor + $120,000 materials + $160,000 overhead). Cost per unit is $380 ($380,000 ÷ 1,000 units). The sales price per unit is $600 ($380 + $220). Cost of goods sold is $304,000 ($380 × 800 units). Sales revenue is $480,000 ($600 × 800 units). Gross margin is $176,000 ($480,000 revenue − $304,000 cost of goods sold). Net income is $96,000 ($176,000 gross margin − $80,000 selling and administrative salaries). Lawson's pricing strategy is called *cost-plus* pricing.

Since indirect costs cannot be effectively traced to products, they are normally assigned to products using **cost allocation**, a process of dividing a total cost into parts and assigning the parts to relevant cost objects. To illustrate, suppose that production workers spend an eight-hour day making a chair and a table. The chair requires two hours to complete and the table requires six hours. Now suppose that $120 of utilities cost is consumed during the day. How much of the $120 should be assigned to each piece of furniture? The utility cost cannot be directly traced to each specific piece of furniture, but the piece of furniture that required more labor also likely consumed more of the utility cost. Using this line of reasoning, it is rational to allocate the utility cost to the two pieces of furniture based on *direct labor hours* at a rate of $15 per hour ($120 ÷ 8 hours). The chair would be assigned $30 ($15 per hour × 2 hours) of the utility cost and the table would be assigned the remaining $90 ($15 × 6 hours) of utility cost. The allocation of the utility cost is shown in Exhibit 14.10.

We discuss the details of cost allocation in a later chapter. For now, recognize that overhead costs are normally allocated to products rather than traced directly to them.

EXHIBIT 14.10

Cost Allocation

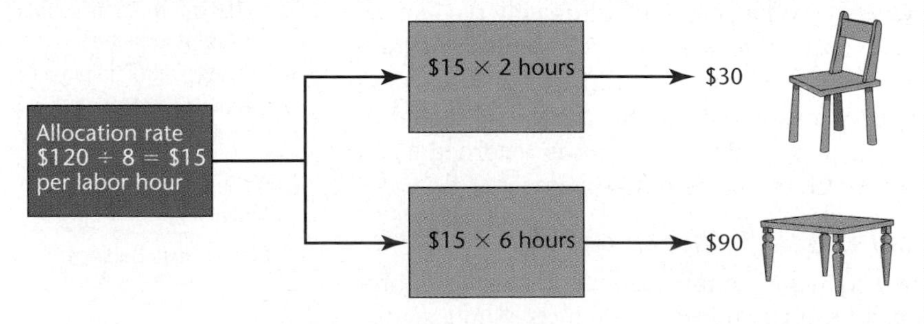

Manufacturing Product Cost Summary

As explained, the cost of a product made by a manufacturing company normally consists of three categories: direct materials, direct labor, and manufacturing overhead. Relevant information about these three cost components is summarized in Exhibit 14.11.

Importance of Cost Classification

What if an expense is misclassified as an asset? Financial statements appear more favorable than the actual condition of the company. Specifically, total assets and net income are overstated. This distortion may have significant consequences for management, investors, and the

EXHIBIT 14.11

Components of Manufacturing Product Costs

Component 1–Direct Materials
Sometimes called *raw materials.* In addition to basic resources such as wood or metals, direct materials can include manufactured parts. For example, engines, glass, and car tires are raw materials for an automotive manufacturer. If the amount of a material in a product is known, it can usually be classified as a direct material. The cost of direct materials can be easily traced to specific products.

Component 2–Direct Labor
The cost of wages paid to factory workers involved in hands-on contact with the products being manufactured. If the amount of time employees worked on a product can be measured, this cost can usually be classified as direct labor. Like direct materials, labor costs must be easily traced to a specific product in order to be classified as direct costs.

Component 3–Manufacturing Overhead
Costs that cannot be easily traced to specific products. These costs are called *indirect costs.* They can include but are not limited to the following:

1. Indirect materials such as glue, nails, paper, and oil. Indirect materials used in the production process may not be part of the finished product. An example is a chemical solvent used to clean products during the production process but not a component material found in the final product.
2. Indirect labor such as the cost of salaries paid to production supervisors, inspectors, and maintenance personnel.
3. Rental cost for manufacturing facilities and equipment.
4. Utility costs.
5. Depreciation on manufacturing facilities and equipment.
6. Security.
7. The cost of preparing equipment for the manufacturing process (setup costs).
8. Maintenance cost for the manufacturing facility and equipment.

government. For example, managers who earn bonuses based on net income will benefit. Similarly, the inflated financial reports may encourage investors to buy stock or lenders to make loans. On the negative side, the inflated earnings will result in the overpayment of income taxes.

LO 6

Explain how cost classification affects financial statements and managerial decisions.

Marion Manufacturing Company

To illustrate practical implications of cost classification, consider the events experienced by Marion Manufacturing Company (MMC) during its first year of operations. All transactions are cash transactions.

1. MMC was started when it acquired $12,000 from issuing common stock.
2. MMC incurred $4,000 of costs to design its product and plan the manufacturing process.
3. MMC incurred specifically identifiable product costs (materials, labor, and overhead) of $8,000.
4. MMC made 1,000 units of product and sold 700 of the units for $18 each.

Exhibit 14.12 displays a set of financial statements prepared under the following two scenarios.

Scenario 1: The $4,000 of design and planning costs are classified as selling and administrative expenses.

Scenario 2: The $4,000 of design and planning costs are classified as product costs, meaning they are first accumulated in the Inventory account and then expensed when the goods are sold. Given that MMC made 1,000 units and sold 700 units of inventory, 70 percent (700 ÷ 1,000) of the design cost has passed through the Inventory account into the Cost of Goods Sold account, leaving 30 percent (300 ÷ 1,000) remaining in the Inventory account.

EXHIBIT 14.12

Financial Statements Under Alternative Cost Classification Scenarios

Income Statements	**Scenario 1**	**Scenario 2**
Sales Revenue (700 × $18)	$12,600	$12,600
Cost of Goods Sold	(5,600)	(8,400)
Gross Margin	7,000	4,200
Selling and Administrative Expense	(4,000)	0
Net Income	$ 3,000	$ 4,200
Balance Sheets		
Assets		
Cash	$12,600	$12,600
Inventory	2,400	3,600
Total Assets	$15,000	$16,200
Stockholders' Equity		
Common Stock	$12,000	$12,000
Retained Earnings	3,000	4,200
Total Stockholders' Equity	$15,000	$16,200
Statements of Cash Flows		
Operating Activities		
Inflow from Customers	$12,600	$12,600
Outflow for Inventory	(8,000)	(12,000)
Outflow for S&A	(4,000)	0
Net Inflow from Operating Activities	600	600
Investing Activities	0	0
Financing Activities		
Inflow from Stock Issue	12,000	12,000
Net Change in Cash	12,600	12,600
Beginning Cash Balance	0	0
Ending Cash Balance	$12,600	$12,600

Statement Differences

Comparing the financial statements prepared under Scenario 1 with those prepared under Scenario 2 reveals the following.

1. There are no selling and administrative expenses under Scenario 2. The design cost was treated as a product cost and placed into the Inventory account rather than being expensed.
2. Cost of goods sold is $2,800 ($4,000 design cost × .70) higher under Scenario 2.
3. Net income is $1,200 higher under Scenario 2 ($4,000 understated expense − $2,800 overstated cost of goods sold).
4. Ending inventory is $1,200 ($4,000 design cost × .30) higher under Scenario 2.

While the Scenario 2 income statement and balance sheet are overstated, cash flow is not affected by the alternative cost classifications. Regardless of how the design cost is classified, the same amount of cash was collected and paid. This explains why financial analysts consider the statement of cash flows to be a critical source of information.

Practical Implications

The financial statement differences shown in Exhibit 14.12 are *timing differences.* When MMC sells the remaining 300 units of inventory, the $1,200 of design and planning costs included in inventory under Scenario 2 will be expensed through cost of goods sold. In other words, once the entire inventory is sold, total expenses and retained earnings will be the same under both scenarios. Initially recording cost in an inventory account only delays eventual expense recognition. However, the temporary effects on the financial statements can influence the (1) availability of financing, (2) motivations of management, and (3) timing of income tax payments.

Availability of Financing

The willingness of creditors and investors to provide capital to a business is influenced by their expectations of the business's future financial performance. In general, more favorable financial statements enhance a company's ability to obtain financing from creditors or investors.

Management Motivation

Financial statement results might affect executive compensation. For example, assume that Marion Manufacturing adopted a management incentive plan that provides a bonus pool equal to 10 percent of net income. In Scenario 1, managers would receive \$300 (\$3,000 × 0.10). In Scenario 2, however, managers would receive \$420 (\$4,200 × 0.10). Do not be deceived by the small numbers used for convenience in the example. We could illustrate with millions of dollars just as well as with hundreds of dollars. Managers would clearly favor Scenario 2. In fact, managers might be tempted to misclassify costs to manipulate the content of financial statements.

Income Tax Considerations

Since income tax expense is calculated as a designated percentage of taxable income, managers seek to minimize taxes by reporting the minimum amount of taxable income. Scenario 1 in Exhibit 14.12 depicts the most favorable tax condition. In other words, with respect to taxes, managers prefer to classify costs as expenses rather than assets. The Internal Revenue Service is responsible for enforcing the proper classification of costs. Disagreements between the Internal Revenue Service and taxpayers are ultimately settled in federal courts.

Ethical Considerations

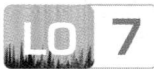

LO 7

Identify the standards of ethical conduct and the features that motivate misconduct.

Topic Tackler PLUS 14-2

The preceding discussion provides some insight into conflicts of interest management accountants might face. It is tempting to misclassify a cost if doing so will significantly increase a manager's bonus. Management accountants must be prepared not only to make difficult choices between legitimate alternatives but also to face conflicts of a more troubling nature, such as pressure to:

1. Undertake duties they have not been trained to perform competently.
2. Disclose confidential information.
3. Compromise their integrity through falsification, embezzlement, bribery, and so on.
4. Issue biased, misleading, or incomplete reports.

Yielding to such temptations can have disastrous consequences. The primary job of a management accountant is to provide information useful in making decisions. Information is worthless if its provider cannot be trusted. Accountants have an obligation to themselves, their organizations, and the public to maintain high standards of ethical conduct. In recognition of this obligation, the Institute of Management Accountants (IMA) has issued *Standards of Ethical Conduct for Management Accountants*, which are summarized in Exhibit 14.13. Management accountants are also frequently required to abide by organizational codes of ethics. Failure to adhere to professional and organizational ethical standards can lead to personal disgrace and loss of employment.

EXHIBIT 14.13

Standards of Ethical Conduct for Management Accountants

Competence Management accountants have a responsibility to

- Maintain an appropriate level of professional competence by ongoing development of their knowledge and skills.
- Perform their professional duties in accordance with relevant laws, regulations, and technical standards.
- Prepare complete and clear reports and recommendations after appropriate analysis of relevant and reliable information.

Confidentiality Management accountants have a responsibility to

- Refrain from disclosing confidential information acquired in the course of their work except when authorized, unless legally obligated to do so.
- Inform subordinates as appropriate regarding the confidentiality of information acquired in the course of their work and monitor their activities to ensure the maintenance of the confidentiality.
- Refrain from using or appearing to use confidential information acquired in the course of their work for unethical or illegal advantage either personally or through third parties.

Integrity Management accountants have a responsibility to

- Avoid actual or apparent conflicts of interest and advise all appropriate parties of any potential conflict.
- Refrain from engaging in any activity that would prejudice their ability to carry out their duties ethically.
- Refuse any gift, favor, or hospitality that would influence or would appear to influence their actions.
- Refrain from either actively or passively subverting the attainment of the organization's legitimate and ethical objectives.
- Recognize and communicate professional limitations or other constraints that would preclude responsible judgment or successful performance of an activity.
- Communicate unfavorable as well as favorable information and professional judgments or opinions.
- Refrain from engaging in or supporting any activity that would discredit the profession.

Objectivity Management accountants have a responsibility to

- Communicate information fairly and objectively.
- Disclose fully all relevant information that could reasonably be expected to influence an intended user's understanding of the reports, comments, and recommendations presented.

Upstream and Downstream Costs

LO 8

Distinguish product costs from upstream and downstream costs.

Most companies incur product-related costs before and after, as well as during, the manufacturing process. For example, Ford Motor Company incurs significant research and development costs prior to mass producing a new car model. These **upstream costs** occur before the manufacturing process begins. Similarly, companies normally incur significant costs after the manufacturing process is complete. Examples of **downstream costs** include transportation, advertising, sales commissions, and uncollectible accounts receivable. While upstream and downstream costs are not considered product costs for financial reporting purposes, profitability analysis requires that they be considered in cost-plus pricing decisions. To be profitable, a company must recover the total cost of developing, producing, and delivering its products to customers.

Product Costs in Service Companies

Service businesses, such as doctors' offices, chimney sweeps, and real estate agencies, differ from manufacturing companies in that they provide assistance rather than goods to their customers. *Nevertheless, service companies, like manufacturing companies, incur materials,*

REALITY BYTES

In March 2002, Gene Morse, an accountant employed by **WorldCom**, discovered accounting fraud at the company. He relayed his findings to his boss, Cynthia Cooper, the company's vice president of internal audit. After further investigation, Ms. Cooper reported her findings to WorldCom's board of directors in June 2002, and the chief financial officer, Scott Sullivan, was fired.

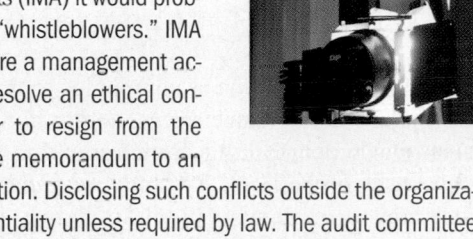

If company management had refused to let Ms. Cooper address the board, would it have been appropriate for her and Mr. Morse to tell the press about the fraud? If they were members of the Institute of Management Accountants (IMA) it would probably have been unethical for them to be "whistleblowers." IMA standards (*SMA Number 1C*, 1983) require a management accountant who is unable to satisfactorily resolve an ethical conflict between himself and his employer to resign from the organization and to submit an informative memorandum to an appropriate representative of the organization. Disclosing such conflicts outside the organization is an inappropriate breach of confidentiality unless required by law. The audit committee of the company's board of directors is an "appropriate representative." In a matter as significant as the WorldCom fraud, the employee would be well advised to seek legal counsel.

For more details on this story, see: "How Three Unlikely Sleuths Discovered Fraud at WorldCom," by Susan Pullman and Deborah Solomon, *The Wall Street Journal*, October 30, 2002, pp. 1 and 16.

labor, and overhead costs in the process of providing services. For example, a hospital providing medical service to a patient incurs costs for medical supplies (materials), salaries of doctors and nurses (labor), and depreciation, utilities, insurance, and so on (overhead).

LO 9 Explain how products provided by service companies differ from products made by manufacturing companies.

The primary difference between manufacturing entities and service companies is that the products provided by service companies are consumed immediately. In contrast, products made by manufacturing companies can be held in the form of inventory until they are sold to customers. Managers of service companies are expected to control costs, improve quality, and increase productivity. Product costing information is useful in achieving these goals regardless of whether a company's product is consumed immediately or later. Although service companies might not report product costs as inventory in their financial statements, they certainly segregate and analyze product costs for internal decision making.

CHECK YOURSELF 14.3

The cost of making a **Burger King** hamburger includes the cost of materials, labor, and overhead. Does this mean that Burger King is a manufacturing company?

Answer

No, Burger King is not a manufacturing company. It is a service company because its products are consumed immediately. In contrast, there may be a considerable delay between the time the product of a manufacturing company is made and the time it is consumed. For example, it could be several months between the time **Ford Motor Company** makes an Explorer and the time the Explorer is ultimately sold to a customer. The primary difference between service and manufacturing companies is that manufacturing companies have inventories of products and service companies do not.

Answers to The Curious Accountant

As you have seen, accounting for depreciation related to manufacturing assets is different from accounting for depreciation for nonmanufacturing assets. Depreciation on the checkout equipment at Wal-Mart is recorded as depreciation expense. Depreciation on manufacturing equipment at Black & Decker is considered a product cost. It is included first as a part of the cost of inventory and eventually as a part of the expense, cost of goods sold. Recording depreciation on manufacturing equipment as an inventory cost is simply another example of the matching principle, because the cost does not become an expense until revenue from the product sale is recognized.

Emerging Trends in Managerial Accounting

LO 10

Explain how emerging trends such as activity-based management, value-added assessment, and just-in-time inventory are affecting the managerial accounting discipline.

Global competition has forced many companies to reengineer their production and delivery systems to eliminate waste, reduce errors, and minimize costs. A key ingredient of successful **reengineering** is benchmarking. **Benchmarking** involves identifying the **best practices** used by world-class competitors. By studying and mimicking these practices, a company uses benchmarking to implement highly effective and efficient operating methods. Best practices employed by world-class companies include total quality management (TQM), activity-based management (ABM), value-added assessment, and just-in-time inventory (JIT).

Total Quality Management

To promote effective and efficient operations, many companies practice **total quality management (TQM)**. TQM is a two-dimensional management philosophy using (1) a systematic problem-solving philosophy that encourages front-line workers to achieve *zero defects* and (2) an organizational commitment to achieving *customer satisfaction.* A key component of TQM is **continuous improvement**, an ongoing process through which employees strive to eliminate waste, reduce response time, minimize defects, and simplify the design and delivery of products and services to customers.

Activity-Based Management

Simple changes in perspective can have dramatic results. For example, imagine how realizing the world is round instead of flat changed the nature of travel. A recent change in perspective developing in management accounting is the realization that an organization cannot manage *costs.* Instead, it manages the *activities* that cause costs to be incurred. **Activities** represent the measures an organization takes to accomplish its goals.

The primary goal of all organizations is to provide products (goods and services) their customers *value.* The sequence of activities used to provide products is called a **value chain. Activity-based management** assesses the value chain to create new or refine existing **value-added activities** and to eliminate or reduce *nonvalue-added activities*. A value-added activity is any unit of work that contributes to a product's ability to satisfy customer needs. For example, cooking is an activity that adds value to food served to a hungry customer. **Nonvalue-added activities** are tasks undertaken that do not contribute to a product's ability to satisfy customer needs. Waiting for the oven to preheat so that food can be cooked does not add value. Most customers value cooked food, but they do not value waiting for it.

To illustrate, consider the value-added activities undertaken by a pizza restaurant. Begin with a customer who is hungry for pizza; certain activities must occur to satisfy that hunger. These activities are pictured in Exhibit 14.14. At a minimum, the restaurant must conduct research and development (devise a recipe), obtain raw materials (acquire the ingredients), manufacture the product (combine and bake the ingredients), market the product (advertise its availability), and deliver the product (transfer the pizza to the customer).

FOCUS ON INTERNATIOAL SALES

WHERE IN THE WORLD DO NEW MANAGERIAL ACCOUNTING PRACTICES COME FROM?

Many of the emerging practices in managerial accounting have their foundations in Asian companies. These companies established employee relationships that achieve continuous improvement by encouraging employees to participate in the design as well as the execution of their work. Employee empowerment through the practice known as *kaizen management* recognizes gradual, continuous improvement as the ultimate key to cost reduction and quality control. Employees are encouraged to identify and eliminate nonvalue-added activities, idle time, and waste. The response is overwhelming when employee suggestions are taken seriously. For example, the **Toyota Motor Corporation** reported the receipt of approximately two million employee suggestions in one year alone.

Source: Takao Tanaka, "Kaizen Budgeting: Toyota's Cost Control System Under TQC," *Journal of Cost Management*, Winter 1996, p. 62.

EXHIBIT 14.14

Value Chain

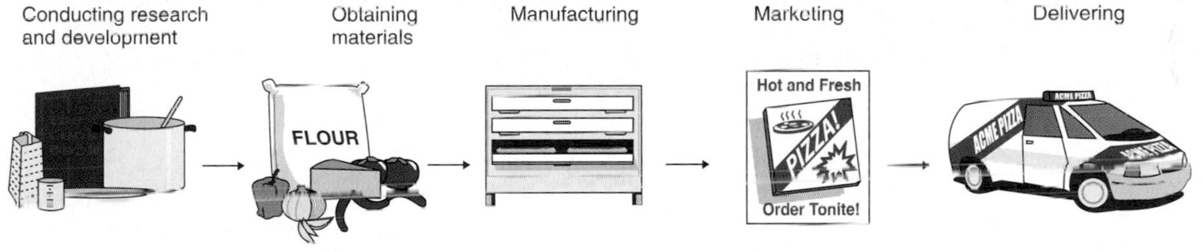

Businesses gain competitive advantages by adding activities that satisfy customer needs. For example, **Domino's Pizza** grew briskly by recognizing the value customers placed on the convenience of home pizza delivery. Alternatively, **Little Caesar's** has been highly successful by satisfying customers who value low prices. Other restaurants capitalize on customer values pertaining to taste, ambiance, or location. Businesses can also gain competitive advantages by identifying and eliminating nonvalue-added activities, providing products of comparable quality at lower cost than competitors. Some of the more common nonvalue-added activities and approaches taken to eliminate them are discussed next.

Just-in-Time Inventory

A common nonvalue-added activity found in many business organizations is maintaining excess amounts of inventory. Consumers want products to be available when requested, but they do not benefit when businesses maintain more inventory than necessary to meet demand. In fact, customers could suffer if businesses hold excessive inventory because inventory holding costs must be passed on in the form of higher prices.

Many **inventory holding costs** are obvious: financing, warehouse space, supervision, theft, damage, and obsolescence. Other costs are hidden: diminished motivation, sloppy

■ At Ford Motor Company's plant in Valencia, Spain, suppliers feed parts such as these bumpers just in time and in the right order directly to the assembly line.

work, inattentive attitudes, and increased production time. Many managers work closely with their suppliers to minimize the amount of inventory they carry. They may guarantee the supplier a steady stream of purchases and prompt payment. In exchange, the supplier grants **most-favored customer status** that ensures priority treatment over other customers when shortages exist. Assured priority delivery from a reliable supplier enables a company to minimize the amount of inventory it carries and thereby reduces inventory holding cost.

Many businesses have been able to simultaneously reduce their inventory holding costs and increase customer satisfaction by making products available **just in time (JIT)** for customer consumption. For example, hamburgers that are cooked to order are fresher and more individualized than those that are prepared in advance and stored until a customer orders one. Many fast-food restaurants have discovered that JIT systems lead not only to greater customer satisfaction but also to lower costs through reduced waste.

CHECK YOURSELF 14.4

A strike at a General Motors brake plant caused an almost immediate shutdown of many of the company's assembly plants. What could have caused such a rapid and widespread shutdown?

Answer

A rapid and widespread shutdown could have occurred because General Motors uses a just-in-time inventory system. With a just-in-time inventory system, there is no stockpile of inventory to draw on when strikes or other forces disrupt inventory deliveries. This illustrates a potential negative effect of using a just-in-time inventory system.

Just-in-Time Illustration

To illustrate the benefits of a JIT system, consider Paula Elliot, a student at a large urban university. She helps support herself by selling flowers. Three days each week, Paula drives to a florist, purchases 25 single stem roses, returns to the school, and sells the flowers to individuals from a street corner. She pays $2 per rose and sells each one for $3. Some days she does not have enough flowers to meet customer demand. Other days, she must discard one or two unsold flowers; she believes quality is important and refuses to sell flowers that are not fresh. During May, she purchased 300 roses and sold 280. She calculated her driving cost to be $45. Exhibit 14.15 displays Paula's May income statement.

EXHIBIT 14.15

Income Statement

Sales Revenue (280 units × $3 per unit)	$840
Cost of Goods Sold (300 units × $2 per unit)	(600)
Gross Margin	240
Driving Expense	(45)
Net Income	$195

After studying just-in-time inventory systems in her managerial accounting class, Paula decided to apply the concepts to her small business. She *reengineered* her distribution system by purchasing her flowers from a florist within walking distance of her sales location. She had considered purchasing from this florist earlier but had rejected the idea because the florist's regular selling price of $2.25 per rose was too high. After learning about *most-favored customer status,* she developed a strategy to get a price reduction. By guaranteeing that she would buy at least 30 roses per week, she was able to convince the local florist to match her current cost of $2.00 per rose. The local florist agreed that she could make purchases in batches of any size so long as the total amounted to at least 30 per week. Under this arrangement, Paula was able to buy roses *just in time* to meet customer demand. Each day she purchased a small number of flowers. When she ran out, she simply returned to the florist for additional ones.

The JIT system also enabled Paula to eliminate the cost of the *nonvalue-added activity* of driving to her former florist. Customer satisfaction actually improved because no one was ever turned away because of the lack of inventory. In June, Paula was able to buy and sell 310 roses with no waste and no driving expense. The June income statement is shown in Exhibit 14.16.

EXHIBIT 14.16

Income Statement

Sales Revenue (310 units × $3 per unit)	$930
Cost of Goods Sold (310 units × $2 per unit)	(620)
Gross Margin	310
Driving Expense	0
Net Income	$310

Paula was ecstatic about her $115 increase in profitability ($310 in June − $195 in May = $115 increase), but she was puzzled about the exact reasons for the change. She had saved $40 (20 flowers × $2 each) by avoiding waste and eliminated $45 of driving expenses. These two factors explained only $85 ($40 waste + $45 driving expense) of the $115 increase. What had caused the remaining $30 ($115 − $85) increase in profitability? Paula asked her accounting professor to help her identify the remaining $30 difference.

The professor explained that May sales had suffered from *lost opportunities.* Recall that under the earlier inventory system, Paula had to turn away some prospective customers because she sold out of flowers before all customers were served. Sales increased from 280 roses in May to 310 roses in June. A likely explanation for the 30 unit difference (310 − 280) is that customers who would have purchased flowers in May were unable to do so because of a lack of availability. May's sales suffered from the lost opportunity to earn a gross margin of $1 per flower on 30 roses, a $30 **opportunity cost.** This opportunity cost is the missing link in explaining the profitability difference between May and June. The total $115 difference consists of (1) $40 savings from waste elimination, (2) $45 savings from eliminating driving expense, and (3) opportunity cost of $30. The subject of opportunity cost has widespread application and is discussed in more depth in subsequent chapters of the text.

Value Chain Analysis Across Companies

Comprehensive value chain analysis extends from obtaining raw materials to the ultimate disposition of finished products. It encompasses the activities performed not only by a particular organization but also by that organization's suppliers and those who service its finished products. For example, **PepsiCo** must be concerned with the activities of the company that supplies the containers for its soft drinks as well as the retail companies that sell its products. If cans of Pepsi fail to open properly, the customer is more likely to blame PepsiCo than the supplier of the cans. Comprehensive value chain analysis can lead to identifying and eliminating nonvalue-added activities that occur between companies. For example, container producers could be encouraged to build manufacturing facilities near Pepsi's bottling factories, eliminating the nonvalue-added activity of transporting empty containers from the manufacturer to the bottling facility. The resulting cost savings benefits customers by reducing costs without affecting quality.

A Look Back >>

Managerial accounting focuses on the information needs of *internal users,* while *financial accounting* focuses on the information needs of *external* users. Managerial accounting uses economic, operating, and nonfinancial, as well as financial, data. Managerial accounting information is local (pertains to the company's subunits), is limited by cost/benefit considerations, is more concerned with relevance and timeliness, and is future oriented. Financial accounting information, on the other hand, is more global than managerial accounting information. It supplies information that applies to the whole company. Financial accounting is regulated by numerous authorities, is characterized by objectivity, is focused on reliability and accuracy, and is historical in nature.

Both managerial and financial accounting are concerned with product costing. Financial accountants need product cost information to determine the amount of inventory reported on the balance sheet and the amount of cost of goods sold reported on the income statement. Managerial accountants need to know the cost of products for pricing decisions and for control and evaluation purposes. When determining unit product costs, managers use the average cost per unit. The actual cost of each product requires an unreasonable amount of time and record keeping and makes no difference in product pricing and product cost control decisions.

Product costs are the costs incurred to make products: the costs of direct materials, direct labor, and overhead. *Overhead costs* are product costs that cannot be cost effectively traced to a product; therefore, they are assigned to products using *cost allocation*. Overhead costs include indirect materials, indirect labor, depreciation, rent, and utilities for manufacturing facilities. Product costs are first accumulated in an asset account (Inventory). They are expensed as cost of goods sold in the period the inventory is sold. The difference between sales revenue and cost of goods sold is called *gross margin*.

General, selling, and administrative costs are classified separately from product costs. They are subtracted from gross margin to determine net income. General, selling, and administrative costs can be divided into two categories. Costs incurred before the manufacturing process begins (research and development costs) are *upstream costs*. Costs incurred after manufacturing is complete (transportation) are *downstream costs*. Service companies, like manufacturing companies, incur materials, labor, and overhead costs, but the products provided by service companies are consumed immediately. Therefore, service company product costs are not accumulated in an Inventory account. A *code of ethical conduct* is needed in the accounting profession because accountants hold positions of trust and face conflicts of interest. In recognition of the temptations that accountants face, the IMA has issued *Standards of Ethical Conduct for Management Accountants*, which provides accountants guidance in resisting temptations and in making difficult decisions.

Emerging trends such as *just-in-time inventory* and *activity-based management* are methods that many companies have used to reengineer their production and delivery systems to eliminate waste, reduce errors, and minimize costs. Activity-based management seeks to eliminate or reduce *nonvalue-added activities* and to create new *value-added activities*. Just-in-time inventory seeks to reduce inventory holding costs and to lower prices for customers by making inventory available just in time for customer consumption.

>> A Look Forward

In addition to distinguishing costs by product versus G, S, & A classification, other classifications can be used to facilitate managerial decision making. In the next chapter, costs are classified according to the *behavior* they exhibit when the number of units of product increases or decreases (volume of activity changes). You will learn to distinguish between costs that vary with activity volume changes versus costs that remain fixed with activity volume changes. You will learn not only to recognize *cost behavior* but also how to use such recognition to evaluate business risk and opportunity.

SELF-STUDY REVIEW PROBLEM

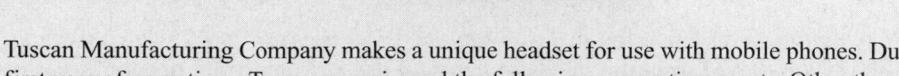

Tuscan Manufacturing Company makes a unique headset for use with mobile phones. During 2006, its first year of operations, Tuscan experienced the following accounting events. Other than the adjusting entries for depreciation, assume that all transactions are cash transactions.

1. Acquired $850,000 cash from the issue of common stock.
2. Paid $50,000 of research and development costs to develop the headset.
3. Paid $140,000 for the materials used to make headsets, all of which were started and completed during the year.
4. Paid salaries of $82,200 to selling and administrative employees.

5. Paid wages of $224,000 to production workers.
6. Paid $48,000 to purchase furniture used in selling and administrative offices.
7. Recognized depreciation on the office furniture. The furniture, acquired January 1, had an $8,000 estimated salvage value and a four-year useful life. The amount of depreciation is computed as ([cost − salvage] ÷ useful life). Specifically, ([$48,000 − $8,000] ÷ 4 = $10,000).
8. Paid $65,000 to purchase manufacturing equipment.
9. Recognized depreciation on the manufacturing equipment. The equipment, acquired January 1, had a $5,000 estimated salvage value and a three-year useful life. The amount of depreciation is computed as ([cost − salvage] ÷ useful life). Specifically, ([$65,000 − $5,000] ÷ 3 = $20,000).
10. Paid $136,000 for rent and utility costs on the manufacturing facility.
11. Paid $41,000 for inventory holding expenses for completed headsets (rental of warehouse space, salaries of warehouse personnel, and other general storage costs).
12. Tuscan started and completed 20,000 headset units during 2006. The company sold 18,400 headsets at a price of $38 per unit.
13. Compute the average product cost per unit and recognize the appropriate amount of cost of goods sold.

Required

a. Show how these events affect the balance sheet, income statement, and statement of cash flows by recording them in a horizontal financial statements model.
b. Explain why Tuscan's recognition of cost of goods sold expense had no impact on cash flow.
c. Prepare a formal income statement for the year.
d. Distinguish between the product costs and the upstream and downstream costs that Tuscan incurred.
e. The company president believes that Tuscan could save money by buying the inventory that it currently makes. The warehouse supervisor said that would not be possible because the purchase price of $27 per unit was above the $26 average cost per unit of making the product. Assuming the purchased inventory would be available on demand, explain how the company president could be correct and why the warehouse supervisor could be biased in his assessment of the option to buy the inventory.

Solution to Requirement *a*

	Assets				=	Equity						
Event No.	Cash +	Inventory +	Office Furn.* +	Manuf. Equip.*	=	Com. Stk. +	Ret. Earn.	Rev. −	Exp. =	Net Inc.	Cash Flow	
1	850,000				=	850,000					850,000	FA
2	(50,000)				=		(50,000)		− 50,000	= (50,000)	(50,000)	OA
3	(140,000) +	140,000									(140,000)	OA
4	(82,200)				=		(82,200)		− 82,200	= (82,200)	(82,200)	OA
5	(224,000) +	224,000									(224,000)	OA
6	(48,000) +		48,000								(48,000)	IA
7			(10,000)		=		(10,000)		10,000	= (10,000)		
8	(65,000) +			65,000							(65,000)	IA
9		20,000 +		(20,000)								
10	(136,000) +	136,000									(136,000)	OA
11	(41,000)				=		(41,000)		− 41,000	= (41,000)	(41,000)	OA
12	699,200				=		699,200	699,200		= 699,200	699,200	OA
13		(478,400)			=		(478,400)		− 478,400	= (478,400)		
Totals	763,000 +	41,600 +	38,000 +	45,000	=	850,000 +	37,600	699,200 −	661,600 =	37,600	763,000	NC

*Negative amounts in these columns represent accumulated depreciation.

The average cost per unit of product is determined by dividing the total product cost by the number of headsets produced. Specifically, ($140,000 + $224,000 + $20,000 + $136,000) ÷ 20,000 = $26. Cost of goods sold is $478,400 ($26 × 18,400).

Solution to Requirement *b*

The impact on cash flow occurs when Tuscan pays for various product costs. In this case, cash outflows occurred when Tuscan paid for materials, labor, and overhead. The cash flow consequences of these transactions were recognized before the cost of goods sold expense was recognized.

Solution to Requirement *c*

TUSCAN MANUFACTURING COMPANY Income Statement For the Year Ended December 31, 2006	
Sales Revenue (18,400 units × $38)	$699,200
Cost of Goods Sold (18,400 × $26)	(478,400)
Gross Margin	220,800
R & D Expenses	(50,000)
Selling and Admin. Salary Expense	(82,200)
Admin. Depreciation Expense	(10,000)
Inventory Holding Expense	(41,000)
Net Income	$ 37,600

Solution to Requirement *d*

Inventory product costs for manufacturing companies focus on the costs necessary to make the product. The cost of research and development (Event 2) occurs before the inventory is made and is therefore an upstream cost, not an inventory (product) cost. The inventory holding costs (Event 11) are incurred after the inventory has been made and are therefore downstream costs, not product costs. Selling costs (included in Events 4 and 7) are normally incurred after products have been made and are therefore usually classified as downstream costs. Administrative costs (also included in Events 4 and 7) are not related to making products and are therefore not classified as product costs. Administrative costs may be incurred before, during, or after products are made, so they may be classified as either upstream or downstream costs. Only the costs of materials, labor, and overhead that are actually incurred for the purpose of making goods (Events 3, 5, 9, and 10) are classified as product costs.

Solution to Requirement *e*

Since the merchandise would be available on demand, Tuscan could operate a just-in-time inventory system thereby eliminating the inventory holding expense. Since the additional cost to purchase is $1 per unit ($27 − $26), it would cost Tuscan an additional $20,000 ($1 × 20,000 units) to purchase its product. However, the company would save $41,000 of inventory holding expense. The warehouse supervisor could be biased by the fact that his job would be lost if the company purchased its products and thereby could eliminate the need for warehousing inventory. If Tuscan does not maintain inventory, it would not need a warehouse supervisor.

KEY TERMS

Securities and Exchange Commission (SEC) 700
total quality management (TQM) 714
upstream costs 712
value-added activity 714
value-added principle 701
value chain 714

QUESTIONS

1. What are some differences between financial and managerial accounting?
2. What does the value-added principle mean as it applies to managerial accounting information? Give an example of value-added information that may be included in managerial accounting reports but is not shown in publicly reported financial statements.
3. What are the two dimensions of a total quality management (TQM) program? Why is TQM being used in business practice?
4. How does product costing used in financial accounting differ from product costing used in managerial accounting?
5. What does the statement "costs can be assets or expenses" mean?
6. Why are the salaries of production workers accumulated in an inventory account instead of being directly expensed on the income statement?
7. How do product costs affect the financial statements? How does the classification of product cost (as an asset vs. an expense) affect net income?
8. What is an indirect cost? Provide examples of product costs that would be classified as indirect.
9. How does a product cost differ from a general, selling, and administrative cost? Give examples of each.
10. Why is cost classification important to managers?
11. What does the term *reengineering* mean? Name some reengineering practices.
12. What is cost allocation? Give an example of a cost that needs to be allocated.
13. How has the Institute of Management Accountants responded to the need for high standards of ethical conduct in the accounting profession?
14. What are some of the common ethical conflicts that accountants encounter?
15. What costs should be considered in determining the sales price of a product?
16. What does the term *activity-based management* mean?
17. What is a value chain?
18. What do the terms *value-added activity* and *nonvalue-added activity* mean? Provide an example of each type of activity.
19. What is a just-in-time (JIT) inventory system? Name some inventory costs that can be eliminated or reduced by its use.

EXERCISES—SERIES A

All Exercises in Series A are available with McGraw-Hill's Homework Manager

Exercise 14-1A *Identifying financial versus managerial accounting characteristics*

L.O. 1

Required

Indicate whether each of the following is representative of managerial or of financial accounting.

a. Information is historically based and usually reported annually.
b. Information is local and pertains to subunits of the organization.
c. Information includes economic and nonfinancial data as well as financial data.
d. Information is global and pertains to the company as a whole.
e. Information is provided to insiders including executives, managers, and operators.
f. Information is factual and is characterized by objectivity, reliability, consistency, and accuracy.
g. Information is reported continuously and has a current or future orientation.

h. Information is provided to outsiders including investors, creditors, government agencies, analysts, and reporters.
i. Information is regulated by the SEC, FASB, and other sources of GAAP.
j. Information is based on estimates that are bounded by relevance and timeliness.

L.O. 5

Exercise 14-2A *Identifying product versus general, selling, and administrative costs*

Required

Indicate whether each of the following costs should be classified as a product cost or as a general, selling, and administrative cost.

a. Indirect labor used to manufacture inventory.
b. Attorney's fees paid to protect the company from frivolous lawsuits.
c. Research and development costs incurred to create new drugs for a pharmaceutical company.
d. The cost of secretarial supplies used in a doctor's office.
e. Depreciation on the office furniture of the company president.
f. Direct materials used in a manufacturing company.
g. Indirect materials used in a manufacturing company.
h. Salaries of employees working in the accounting department.
i. Commissions paid to sales staff.
j. Interest on the mortgage for the company's corporate headquarters.

L.O.. 5

Exercise 14-3A *Classifying costs: product or G,S,&A/asset or expense*

Required

Use the following format to classify each cost as a product cost or a general, selling, and administrative (G, S, & A) cost. Also indicate whether the cost would be recorded as an asset or an expense. The first item is shown as an example.

Cost Category	Product/ G, S, & A	Asset/ Expense
Wages of production workers	Product	Asset
Advertising costs		
Promotion costs		
Production supplies		
Depreciation on administration building		
Depreciation on manufacturing equipment		
Research and development costs		
Cost to set up manufacturing equipment		
Utilities used in factory		
Cars for sales staff		
Distributions to stockholders		
General office supplies		
Raw materials used in the manufacturing process		
Cost to rent office equipment		

L.O. 5

Exercise 14-4A *Identifying effect of product versus general, selling, and administrative costs on financial statements*

Required

Cadeshia Industries recognized accrued compensation cost. Use the following model to show how this event would affect the company's financial statement under the following two assumptions: (1) the compensation is for office personnel and (2) the compensation is for production workers. Use pluses or minuses to show the effect on each element. If an element is not affected, indicate so by placing the letters NA under the appropriate heading.

	Assets	=	Liab.	+	Equity	Rev.	−	Exp.	=	Net Inc.	Cash Flow
1											
2											

Exercise 14-5A *Identify effect of product versus general, selling, and administrative costs on financial statements*

L.O. 5

Required

Chappell Industries recognized the annual cost of depreciation on December 31, 2007. Using the following horizontal financial statements model, indicate how this event affected the company's financial statements under the following two assumptions: (1) the depreciation was on office furniture and (2) the depreciation was on manufacturing equipment. Indicate whether the event increases (I), decreases (D), or has no affect (NA) on each element of the financial statements. Also, in the Cash column, indicate whether the cash flow is for operating activities (OA), investing activities (IA), or financing activities (FA). (Note: Show accumulated depreciation as a decrease in the book value of the appropriate asset account.)

	Assets									Equity								
Event No.	Cash	+	Inventory	+	Manuf. Equip.	+	Office Furn.	=	Com. Stk.	+	Ret. Earn.	Rev.	−	Exp.	=	Net Inc.	Cash Flow	
1																		
2																		

Exercise 14-6A *Identifying product costs in a manufacturing company*

L.O. 2

Andrea Pomare was talking to another accounting student, Don Cantrell. Upon discovering that the accounting department offered an upper-level course in cost measurement, Andrea remarked to Don, "How difficult can it be? My parents own a toy store. All you have to do to figure out how much something costs is look at the invoice. Surely you don't need an entire course to teach you how to read an invoice."

Required

a. Identify the three main components of product cost for a manufacturing entity.

b. Explain why measuring product cost for a manufacturing entity is more complex than measuring product cost for a retail toy store.

c. Assume that Andrea's parents rent a store for $8,000 per month. Different types of toys use different amounts of store space. For example, displaying a bicycle requires more store space than displaying a deck of cards. Also, some toys remain on the shelf longer than others. Fad toys sell quickly, but traditional toys sell more slowly. Under these circumstances, how would you determine the amount of rental cost required to display each type of toy? Identify two other costs incurred by a toy store that may be difficult to allocate to individual toys.

✓ Exercise 14-7A *Identifying product versus general, selling, and administrative costs*

L.O. 5

A review of the accounting records of Zammon Manufacturing indicated that the company incurred the following payroll costs during the month of August.

1. Salary of the company president—$75,000.
2. Salary of the vice president of manufacturing—$50,000. b * watch for on test
3. Salary of the chief financial officer—$40,000.
4. Salary of the vice president of marketing—$35,000.
5. Salaries of middle managers (department heads, production supervisors) in manufacturing plant—$75,000. b

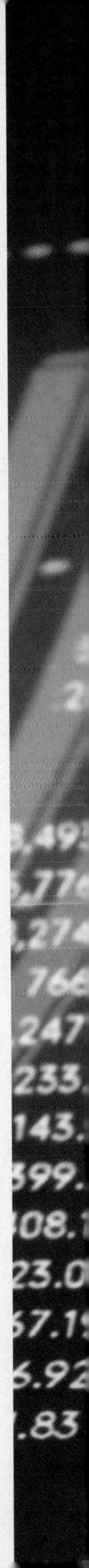

6. Wages of production workers—$540,000.
7. Salaries of administrative secretaries—$78,000.
8. Salaries of engineers and other personnel responsible for maintaining production equipment—$135,000.
9. Commissions paid to sales staff—$128,000.

Required

a. What amount of payroll cost would be classified as general, selling, and administrative expense?
b. Assuming that Zammon made 4,000 units of product and sold 3,600 of them during the month of August, determine the amount of payroll cost that would be included in cost of goods sold.

L.O. 2, 4, 5

Exercise 14-8A *Recording product versus general, selling, and administrative costs in a financial statements model*

Trammell Manufacturing experienced the following events during its first accounting period.

1. Recognized depreciation on manufacturing equipment.
2. Recognized depreciation on office furniture.
3. Recognized revenue from cash sale of products.
4. Recognized cost of goods sold from sale referenced in Event 3.
5. Acquired cash by issuing common stock.
6. Paid cash to purchase raw materials that were used to make products.
7. Paid wages to production workers.
8. Paid salaries to administrative staff.

Required

Use the following horizontal financial statements model to show how each event affects the balance sheet, income statement, and statement of cash flows. Indicate whether the event increases (I), decreases (D), or has no effect (NA) on each element of the financial statements. In the Cash Flow column, indicate whether the cash flow is for operating activities (OA), investing activities (IA), or financing activities (FA). The first transaction has been recorded as an example. (*Note:* Show accumulated depreciation as decrease in the book value of the appropriate asset account.)

	Assets								Equity								
Event No.	Cash	+	Inventory	+	Manuf. Equip.	+	Office Furn.	=	Com. Stk.	+	Ret. Earn.	Rev.	−	Exp.	=	Net Inc.	Cash Flow
1	NA		I		D		NA		NA		NA	NA		NA		NA	NA

L.O. 2, 3, 4

Exercise 14-9A *Allocating product costs between ending inventory and cost of goods sold*

Kasey Manufacturing Company began operations on January 1. During the year, it started and completed 4,000 units of product. The company incurred the following costs.

1. Raw materials purchased and used—$6,000.
2. Wages of production workers—$9,000.
3. Salaries of administrative and sales personnel—$3,600.
4. Depreciation on manufacturing equipment—$10,800.
5. Depreciation on administrative equipment—$4,000.

Kasey sold 3,000 units of product.

Required

a. Determine the total product cost for the year.
b. Determine the total cost of the ending inventory.
c. Determine the total of cost of goods sold.

L.O. 4, 5

Exercise 14-10A *Financial statement effects for manufacturing versus service organizations*

The following financial statements model shows the effects of recognizing depreciation in two different circumstances. One circumstance represents recognizing depreciation on a machine used in a factory. The other circumstance recognizes depreciation on computers used in a consulting firm. The effects of each event have been recorded using the letter (I) to represent increase, (D) for decrease, and (NA) for no effect.

	Assets				Equity							
Event No.	Cash	+ Inventory	+ Equip.	=	Com. Stk.	+ Ret. Earn.	Rev.	−	Exp.	=	Net Inc.	Cash Flow
1	NA	NA	D		NA	D	NA		I		D	NA
2	NA	I	D		NA	NA	NA		NA		NA	NA

Required

a. Identify the event that represents depreciation on the computers.

b. Explain why recognizing depreciation on equipment used in a manufacturing company affects financial statements differently from recognizing depreciation on equipment used in a service organization.

Exercise 14-11A *Identifying the effect of product versus general, selling, and administrative cost on the income statement and statement of cash flows*

L.O. 5

Required

Each of the following events describes acquiring an asset that requires a year-end adjusting entry. Explain how acquiring the asset and making the adjusting entry affect the amount of net income and the cash flow reported on the year-end financial statements. Also, in the Cash Flow column, indicate whether the cash flow is for operating activities (OA), investing activities (IA), or financing activities (FA). Use (NA) for no effect. Assume a December 31 annual closing date. The first event has been recorded as an example. Assume that any products that have been made have not been sold.

	Net Income	Cash Flow
Event No.	Amount of Change	Amount of Change
1. Purchase of printers	NA	(4,000) IA
1. Make adjusting entry	(1,000)	NA

1. Paid $4,000 cash on January 1 to purchase printers to be used for administrative purposes. The printers had an estimated useful life of three years and a $1,000 salvage value.
2. Paid $4,000 cash on January 1 to purchase manufacturing equipment. The equipment had an estimated useful life of three years and a $1,000 salvage value.
3. Paid $5,400 cash in advance on May 1 for a one-year rental contract on administrative offices.
4. Paid $5,400 cash in advance on May 1 for a one-year rental contract on manufacturing facilities.
5. Paid $1,000 cash to purchase supplies to be used by the marketing department. At the end of the year, $50 of supplies was still on hand.
6. Paid $1,000 cash to purchase supplies to be used in the manufacturing process. At the end of the year, $50 of supplies was still on hand.

Exercise 14-12A *Upstream and downstream costs*

L.O. 8

During 2008, Wake Manufacturing Company incurred $9,000,000 of research and development (R&D) costs to create a long-life battery to use in computers. In accordance with FASB standards, the entire R&D cost was recognized as an expense in 2008. Manufacturing costs (direct materials, direct labor, and overhead) were expected to be $26 per unit. Packaging, shipping, and sales commissions were expected to be $5 per unit. Wake expected to sell 200,000 batteries before new research renders the battery design technologically obsolete. During 2008, Wake made 22,000 batteries and sold 20,000 of them.

Required

a. Identify the upstream and downstream costs.

b. Determine the 2008 amount of cost of goods sold and the ending inventory balance.

c. Determine the sales price assuming that Wake desired to earn a profit margin equal to 25 percent of the *total cost* of developing, making, and distributing the batteries.

d. Prepare an income statement for 2008. Use the sales price developed in Requirement *c*.

e. Why would Wake price the batteries at a level that would generate a loss for the 2008 accounting period?

L.O. 10

Exercise 14-13A *Value chain analysis*

Autosound Company manufactures and sells high-quality audio speakers. The speakers are encased in solid walnut cabinets supplied by Garrison Cabinet Inc. Garrison packages the speakers in durable moisture-proof boxes and ships them by truck to Autosound's manufacturing facility, which is located 50 miles from the cabinet factory.

Required

Identify the nonvalue-added activities that occur between the companies described in the preceding scenario. Explain how these nonvalue-added activities could be eliminated.

L.O. 10

Exercise 14-14A *Identify the effect of a just-in-time inventory system on financial statements*

After reviewing the financial statements of Baird Company, Tim Hanson concluded that Baird was a service company because its financial statements displayed no inventory accounts.

Required

Explain how Baird's implementation of a 100 percent effective just-in-time inventory system could have led Mr. Hanson to a false conclusion regarding the nature of Baird's business.

L.O. 10

Exercise 14-15A *Using JIT to minimize waste and lost opportunity*

Lucy Quinn, a teacher at Grove Middle School, is in charge of ordering the T-shirts to be sold for the school's annual fund-raising project. The T-shirts are printed with a special Grove School logo. In some years, the supply of T-shirts has been insufficient to satisfy the number of sales orders. In other years, T-shirts have been left over. Excess T-shirts are normally donated to some charitable organization. T-shirts cost the school $4 each and are normally sold for $6 each. Ms. Quinn has decided to order 800 shirts.

Required

a. If the school receives actual sales orders for 750 shirts, what amount of profit will the school earn? What is the cost of waste due to excess inventory?

b. If the school receives actual sales orders for 850 shirts, what amount of profit will the school earn? What amount of opportunity cost will the school incur?

c. Explain how a JIT inventory system could maximize profitability by eliminating waste and opportunity cost.

L.O. 10

Exercise 14-16A *Using JIT to minimize holding costs*

Jay's Pet Supplies purchases its inventory from a variety of suppliers, some of which require a six-week lead time before delivery. To ensure that she has a sufficient supply of goods on hand, Ms. Lane, the owner, must maintain a large supply of inventory. The cost of this inventory averages $40,000. She usually finances the purchase of inventory and pays a 10 percent annual finance charge. Ms. Lane's accountant has suggested that she establish a relationship with a single large distributor who can satisfy all of her orders within a two-week time period. Given this quick turnaround time, she will be able to reduce her average inventory balance to $10,000. Ms. Lane also believes that she could save $6,000 per year by reducing phone bills, insurance, and warehouse rental space costs associated with ordering and maintaining the larger level of inventory.

Required

a. Is the new inventory system available to Ms. Lane a pure or approximate just-in-time system?

b. Based on the information provided, how much of Ms. Lane's inventory holding cost could be eliminated by taking the accountant's advice?

PROBLEMS—SERIES A

All Problems in Series A are available with McGraw-Hill's Homework Manager

Problem 14-17A *Product versus general, selling, and administrative costs*

L.O. 2, 3, 4, 5, 6

CHECK FIGURES
a. Average Cost per Unit: $8.40
f. $90,400

Reavis Manufacturing Company was started on January 1, 2006, when it acquired $90,000 cash by issuing common stock. Reavis immediately purchased office furniture and manufacturing equipment costing $10,000 and $28,000, respectively. The office furniture had a five-year useful life and a zero salvage value. The manufacturing equipment had a $4,000 salvage value and an expected useful life of three years. The company paid $12,000 for salaries of administrative personnel and $16,000 for wages to production personnel. Finally, the company paid $18,000 for raw materials that were used to make inventory. All inventory was started and completed during the year. Reavis completed production on 5,000 units of product and sold 4,000 units at a price of $12 each in 2006. (Assume all transactions are cash transactions.)

Required

a. Determine the total product cost and the average cost per unit of the inventory produced in 2006.

b. Determine the amount of cost of goods sold that would appear on the 2006 income statement. 4,000×12 = 36,000

c. Determine the amount of the ending inventory balance that would appear on the December 31, 2006, balance sheet. 1000 X 8.40

d. Determine the amount of net income that would appear on the 2006 income statement.

e. Determine the amount of retained earnings that would appear on the December 31, 2006, balance sheet.

f. Determine the amount of total assets that would appear on the December 31, 2006, balance sheet.

g. Determine the amount of net cash flow from operating activities that would appear on the 2006 statement of cash flows.

h. Determine the amount of net cash flow from investing activities that would appear on the 2006 statement of cash flows.

Problem 14-18A *Effect of product versus period costs on financial statements*

L.O. 2, 4, 5

excel
mhhe.com/edmonds2007

CHECK FIGURES
Cash balance: $47,400
Net income: $10,700

Chateau Manufacturing Company experienced the following accounting events during its first year of operation. With the exception of the adjusting entries for depreciation, all transactions are cash transactions.

1. Acquired $67,000 cash by issuing common stock.
2. Paid $9,500 for the materials used to make products, all of which were started and completed during the year.
3. Paid salaries of $5,300 to selling and administrative employees.
4. Paid wages of $6,200 to production workers.
5. Paid $9,600 for furniture used in selling and administrative offices. The furniture was acquired on January 1. It had a $1,600 estimated salvage value and a four-year useful life.
6. Paid $27,000 for manufacturing equipment. The equipment was acquired on January 1. It had a $3,000 estimated salvage value and a three-year useful life.
7. Sold inventory to customers for $38,000 that had cost $20,000 to make.

Required

Explain how these events would affect the balance sheet, income statement, and statement of cash flows by recording them in a horizontal financial statements model as indicated here. The first event is recorded as an example. In the Cash Flow column, indicate whether the amounts represent financing activities (FA), investing activities (IA), or operating activities (OA).

Event No.	Assets					Equity					
	Cash +	Inventory +	Manuf. Equip.* +	Office Furn.*	=	Com. Stk. +	Ret. Earn.	Rev. −	Exp. =	Net Inc.	Cash Flow
1	67,000					67,000					67,000 FA

*Record accumulated depreciation as negative amounts in these columns.

L.O. 2, 3, 4, 5

CHECK FIGURES
Net income: $540
Total assets: $3,540

√ Problem 14-19A *Product versus general, selling, and administrative costs*

The following transactions pertain to 2007, the first year operations of Lakeview Company. All inventory was started and completed during 2007. Assume that all transactions are cash transactions.

1. Acquired $3,000 cash by issuing common stock.
2. Paid $600 for materials used to produce inventory.
3. Paid $900 to production workers.
4. Paid $300 rental fee for production equipment.
5. Paid $240 to administrative employees.
6. Paid $120 rental fee for administrative office equipment.
7. Produced 300 units of inventory of which 200 units were sold at a price of $10.50 each.

Required

Prepare an income statement, balance sheet, and statement of cash flows.

L.O. 2, 3, 4, 5

eXcel
mhhe.com/edmonds2007

CHECK FIGURES
a. Net loss: $24,000
b. Total assets: $66,000
c. Net income: $13,200

Problem 14-20A *Service versus manufacturing companies*

Savoy Company began operations on January 1, 2006, by issuing common stock for $36,000 cash. During 2006, Savoy received $48,000 cash from revenue and incurred costs that required $72,000 of cash payments.

Required

Prepare an income statement, balance sheet, and statement of cash flows for Savoy Company for 2006, under each of the following independent scenarios.

a. Savoy is a promoter of rock concerts. The $72,000 was paid to provide a rock concert that produced the revenue.

b. Savoy is in the car rental business. The $72,000 was paid to purchase automobiles. The automobiles were purchased on January 1, 2006, had four-year useful lives and no expected salvage value. Savoy uses straight-line depreciation. The revenue was generated by leasing the automobiles.

c. Savoy is a manufacturing company. The $72,000 was paid to purchase the following items:
   (1) Paid $9,600 cash to purchase materials that were used to make products during the year.
   (2) Paid $24,000 cash for wages of factory workers who made products during the year.
   (3) Paid $2,400 cash for salaries of sales and administrative employees.
   (4) Paid $36,000 cash to purchase manufacturing equipment. The equipment was used solely to make products. It had a three-year life and a $7,200 salvage value. The company uses straight-line depreciation.
   (5) During 2005, Savoy started and completed 2,000 units of product. The revenue was earned when Savoy sold 1,500 units of product to its customers.

d. Refer to Requirement *c*. Could Savoy determine the actual cost of making the 500th unit of product? How likely is it that the actual cost of the 500th product was exactly the same as the cost of producing the 501st unit of product? Explain why management may be more interested in average cost than in actual cost.

L.O. 2, 3, 4, 5, 6

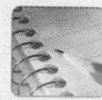

Problem 14-21A *Importance of cost classification*

Dextron Manufacturing Company (DMC) was started when it acquired $60,000 by issuing common stock. During the first year of operations, the company incurred specifically identifiable product costs (materials, labor, and overhead) amounting to $30,000. DMC also incurred $20,000 of engineering design and planning costs. There was a debate regarding how the design and planning costs should be classified. Advocates of Option 1 believe that the costs should be classified as general, selling, and administrative costs. Advocates of Option 2 believe it is more appropriate to classify the design and planning costs as product costs. During the year, DMC made 4,000 units of product and sold 3,000 units at a price of $18 each. All transactions were cash transactions.

CHECK FIGURES
a. Option 1: NI = $11,500
Option 2: Total Assets = $76,500

Required

a. Prepare an income statement, balance sheet, and statement of cash flows under each of the two options.
b. Identify the option that results in financial statements more likely to leave a favorable impression on investors and creditors.
c. Assume that DMC provides an incentive bonus to the company president equal to 10 percent of net income. Compute the amount of the bonus under each of the two options. Identify the option that provides the president with the higher bonus.
d. Assume a 35 percent income tax rate. Determine the amount of income tax expense under each of the two options. Identify the option that minimizes the amount of the company's income tax expense.
e. Comment on the conflict of interest between the company president as determined in Requirement *c* and the owners of the company as indicated in Requirement *d*. Describe an incentive compensation plan that would avoid a conflict of interest between the president and the owners.

Problem 14-22A *Value chain analysis*

L.O. 10

Hacienda Company invented a new process for manufacturing ice cream. The ingredients are mixed in high-tech machinery that forms the product into small round beads. Like a bag of balls, the ice cream beads are surrounded by air pockets in packages. This design has numerous advantages. First, each bite of ice cream melts quickly in a person's mouth, creating a more flavorful sensation when compared to ordinary ice cream. Also, the air pockets mean that a typical serving includes a smaller amount of ice cream. This not only reduces materials cost but also provides the consumer with a low-calorie snack. A cup appears full of ice cream, but it is really half full of air. The consumer eats only half the ingredients that are contained in a typical cup of blended ice cream. Finally, the texture of the ice cream makes scooping it out of a large container easy. The frustration of trying to get a spoon into a rock-solid package of blended ice cream has been eliminated. Hacienda Company named the new product Sonic Cream.

Like many other ice cream producers, Hacienda Company purchases its raw materials from a food wholesaler. The ingredients are mixed in Hacienda's manufacturing plant. The packages of finished product are distributed to privately owned franchise ice cream shops that sell Sonic Cream directly to the public.

Hacienda provides national advertising and is responsible for all research and development costs associated with making new flavors of Sonic Cream.

Required

a. Based on the information provided, draw a comprehensive value chain for Hacienda Company that includes its suppliers and customers.
b. Identify the place in the chain where Hacienda Company is exercising its opportunity to create added value beyond that currently being provided by its competitors.

Problem 14-23A *Using JIT to reduce inventory holding costs*

L.O. 10

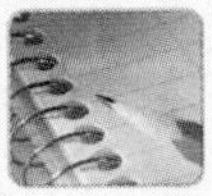

CHECK FIGURE
a. $360,000

Levis Manufacturing Company obtains its raw materials from a variety of suppliers. Levis's strategy is to obtain the best price by letting the suppliers know that it buys from the lowest bidder. Approximately four years ago, unexpected increased demand resulted in materials shortages. Levis was unable to find the materials it needed even though it was willing to pay premium prices. Because of the lack of raw materials, Levis was forced to close its manufacturing facility for two weeks. Its president vowed that her company would never again be at the mercy of its suppliers. She immediately ordered her purchasing agent to perpetually maintain a one-month supply of raw materials. Compliance with the president's orders resulted in a raw materials inventory amounting to approximately $2,000,000. Warehouse rental and personnel costs to maintain the inventory amounted to $10,000 per month. Levis has a line of credit with a local bank that calls for a 12 percent annual rate of interest. Assume that Levis finances the raw materials inventory with the line of credit.

Required

a. Based on the information provided, determine the annual holding cost of the raw materials inventory.

b. Explain how a JIT system could reduce Levis's inventory holding cost.
c. Explain how most-favored customer status could enable Levis to establish a JIT inventory system without risking the raw materials shortages experienced in the past.

L.O. 10

excel

mhhe.com/edmonds2007

CHECK FIGURES
a. $900
b. $3,700

Problem 14-24A *Using JIT to minimize waste and lost opportunity*

Pass CPA Inc. provides review courses for students studying to take the CPA exam. The cost of textbooks is included in the registration fee. Text material requires constant updating and is useful for only one course. To minimize printing costs and ensure availability of books on the first day of class, Pass CPA has books printed and delivered to its offices two weeks in advance of the first class. To ensure that enough books are available, Pass CPA normally orders 10 percent more than expected enrollment. Usually there is an oversupply of books that is thrown away. However, demand occasionally exceeds expectations by more than 10 percent and there are too few books available for student use. Pass CPA had been forced to turn away students because of a lack of textbooks. Pass CPA expects to enroll approximately 100 students per course. The tuition fee is $800 per student. The cost of teachers is $25,000 per course, textbooks cost $60 each, and other operating expenses are estimated to be $35,000 per course.

Required

a. Prepare an income statement, assuming that 95 students enroll in a course. Determine the cost of waste associated with unused books.
b. Prepare an income statement, assuming that 115 students attempt to enroll in the course. Note that five students are turned away because of too few textbooks. Determine the amount of lost profit resulting from the inability to serve the five additional students.
c. Suppose that textbooks can be produced through a high-speed copying process that permits delivery *just in time* for class to start. The cost of books made using this process, however, is $65 each. Assume that all books must be made using the same production process. In other words, Pass CPA cannot order some of the books using the regular copy process and the rest using the high-speed process. Prepare an income statement under the JIT system assuming that 95 students enroll in a course. Compare the income statement under JIT with the income statement prepared in Requirement *a*. Comment on how the JIT system would affect profitability.
d. Assume the same facts as in Requirement *c* with respect to a JIT system that enables immediate delivery of books at a cost of $65 each. Prepare an income statement under the JIT system, assuming that 115 students enroll in a course. Compare the income statement under JIT with the income statement prepared in Requirement *b*. Comment on how the JIT system would affect profitability.
e. Discuss the possible effect of the JIT system on the level of customer satisfaction.

EXERCISES—SERIES B

L.O. 1

Exercise 14-1B *Financial versus managerial accounting items*

Required

Indicate whether each of the following is representative of financial or managerial accounting.

a. Monthly sales reports used by the vice president of marketing to help allocate funds.
b. Divisional profit reports used by the company president to determine bonuses for divisional vice presidents.
c. Financial results used by stockbrokers to evaluate a company's profitability.
d. Quarterly budgets used by management to determine future borrowing needs.
e. Financial statements prepared in accordance with generally accepted accounting principles.
f. Annual financial reports submitted to the SEC in compliance with federal securities laws.
g. Projected budget information used to make logistical decisions.
h. Condensed financial information sent to current investors at the end of each quarter.
i. Audited financial statements submitted to bankers when applying for a line of credit.
j. A weekly cash budget used by the treasurer to determine whether cash on hand is excessive.

Exercise 14-2B *Identifying product versus general, selling, and administrative costs*

L.O. 5

Required

Indicate whether each of the following costs should be classified as a product cost or as a general, selling, and administrative cost.

a. The fabric used in building a customized sofa for a customer.
b. The salary of an engineer who maintains all manufacturing plant equipment.
c. Wages paid to workers in a manufacturing plant.
d. The salary of the receptionist working in the sales department.
e. Supplies used in the sales department.
f. Wages of janitors who clean the factory floor.
g. The salary of the company president.
h. The salary of the cell phone manufacturing plant manager.
i. The depreciation on administrative buildings.
j. The depreciation on the company treasurer's computer.

Exercise 14-3B *Classifying costs: product or period/asset or expense*

L.O. 5

Required

Use the following format to classify each cost as a product cost or a general, selling, and administrative (G,S,&A) cost. Also indicate whether the cost would be recorded as an asset or an expense. The first cost item is shown as an example.

Cost Category	Product/ G, S, & A	Asset/ Expense
Raw material used to make products	Product	Asset
Lubricant used to maintain factory equipment		
Cost of a delivery truck		
Cash dividend to stockholders		
Cost of merchandise shipped to customers		
Depreciation on vehicles used by salespeople		
Wages of administrative building security guards		
Supplies used in the plant manager's office		
Computers for the accounting department		
Depreciation on computers used in factory		
Natural gas used in the factory		
Cost of television commercials		
Wages of factory workers		
Paper and ink cartridges used in the cashier's office		

Exercise 14-4B *Effect of product versus general, selling, and administrative costs on financial statements*

L.O. 5

Required

Ashton Plastics Company accrued a tax liability for $2,500. Use the following horizontal financial statements model to show the effect of this accrual under the following two assumptions: (1) the tax is on administrative buildings or (2) the tax is on production equipment. Use plus signs or minus signs to show the effect on each element. If an element is not affected, indicate so by placing the letters NA under the appropriate heading.

	Assets = Liab. + Equity	Rev. − Exp. = Net Inc.	Cash Flow
1			
2			

L.O. 5

Exercise 14-5B *Effect of product versus general, selling, and administrative cost on financial statements*

Required

Seffner Corporation recognized the annual expiration of insurance on December 31, 2008. Using the following horizontal financial statements model, indicate how this event affected the company's financial statements under the following two assumptions: (1) the insurance was for office equipment or (2) the insurance was for manufacturing equipment. Indicate whether the event increases (I), decreases (D), or does not affect (NA) each element of the financial statements. In the Cash Flow column, indicate whether the cash flow is for operating activities (OA), investing activities (IA), or financing activities (FA).

	Assets					=	Equity								
Event No.	Cash	+	Prepaid Insurance	+	Inventory	=	Com. Stk.	+	Ret. Earn.	Rev.	−	Exp.	=	Net Inc.	Cash Flow
1															
2															

L.O. 2

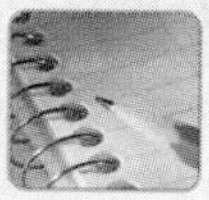

Exercise 14-6B *Product costs in a manufacturing company*

Because friends and neighbors frequently praise her baking skills, Susan Spann plans to start a new business baking cakes for customers. She wonders how to determine the cost of her cakes.

Required

a. Identify and give examples of the three components of product cost incurred in producing cakes.

b. Explain why measuring product cost for a bakery is more complex than measuring product cost for a retail store.

c. Assume that Susan decides to bake cakes for her customers at her home. Consequently, she will avoid the cost of renting a bakery. However, her home utility bills will increase. She also plans to offer different types of cakes for which baking time will vary. Cakes mixed with ice cream will require freezing, and other cakes will need refrigeration. Some can cool at room temperature. Under these circumstances, how can Susan estimate the amount of utility cost required to produce a given cake? Identify two costs other than utility cost that she will incur that could be difficult to measure.

L.O. 5

Exercise 14-7B *Product versus general, selling, and administrative costs*

In reviewing Desoto Company's September accounting records, Don Albani, the chief accountant, noted the following depreciation costs.

1. Factory buildings—$30,000.
2. Computers used in manufacturing—$4,800.
3. A building used to display finished products—$9,600.
4. Trucks used to deliver merchandise to customers—$16,800.
5. Forklifts used in the factory—$26,400.
6. Furniture used in the president's office—$10,800.
7. Elevators in administrative buildings—$7,200.
8. Factory machinery—$10,800.

Required

a. What amount of depreciation cost would be classified as general, selling, and administrative expense?

b. Assume that Desoto manufactured 4,500 units of product and sold 3,000 units of product during the month of September. Determine the amount of depreciation cost that would be included in cost of goods sold.

L.O. 2, 4, 5

Exercise 14-8B *Recording product versus general, selling, and administrative costs in a financial statements model*

Upton Electronics Company experienced the following events during its first accounting period.

1. Received $200,000 cash by issuing common stock.
2. Paid $30,000 cash for wages to production workers.
3. Paid $20,000 for salaries to administrative staff.
4. Purchased for cash and used $18,000 of raw materials.
5. Recognized $2,000 of depreciation on administrative offices.
6. Recognized $3,000 of depreciation on manufacturing equipment.
7. Recognized $96,000 of sales revenue from cash sales of products.
8. Recognized $60,000 of cost of goods sold from the sale referenced in Event 7.

Required

Use a horizontal financial statements model to show how each event affects the balance sheet, income statement, and statement of cash flows. Indicate whether the event increases (I), decreases (D), or does not affect (NA) each element of the financial statements. In the Cash Flow column, indicate whether the cash flow is for operating activities (OA), investing activities (IA), or financing activities (FA). The first transaction is shown as an example. (*Note:* Show accumulated depreciation as a decrease in the book value of the appropriate asset account.)

	Assets				Equity					
Event No.	**Cash +**	**Inventory +**	**Manuf. Equip. +**	**Adm. Offices =**	**Com. Stk. +**	**Ret. Earn.**	**Rev. −**	**Exp. =**	**Net Inc.**	**Cash Flow**
1	I	NA	NA	NA	I	NA	NA	NA	NA	I FA

Exercise 14-9B *Allocating product costs between ending inventory and cost of goods sold*

L.O. 2, 3, 4

Tanaka Manufacturing Company began operations on January 1. During January, it started and completed 2,000 units of product. The company incurred the following costs:

1. Raw materials purchased and used—$2,000.
2. Wages of production workers—$1,600.
3. Salaries of administrative and sales personnel—$800.
4. Depreciation on manufacturing equipment—$1,200.
5. Depreciation on administrative equipment—$960.

Tanaka sold 1,600 units of product.

Required

a. Determine the total product cost.

b. Determine the total cost of the ending inventory.

c. Determine the total of cost of goods sold.

Exercise 14-10B *Financial statement effects for manufacturing versus service organizations*

L.O. 4 & 5

The following horizontal financial statements model shows the effects of recording the expiration of insurance in two different circumstances. One circumstance represents the expiration of insurance on a factory building. The other circumstance represents the expiration of insurance on an administrative building. The cash flow effects are shown using (I) for increase, (D) for decrease, and (NA) for no effect.

	Assets			Equity					
Event No.	**Cash +**	**Prepaid Insurance +**	**Inventory =**	**Com. Stk. +**	**Ret. Earn.**	**Rev. −**	**Exp. =**	**Net Inc.**	**Cash Flow**
1	NA	D	I	NA	NA	NA	NA	NA	NA
2	NA	D	NA	NA	D	NA	I	D	NA

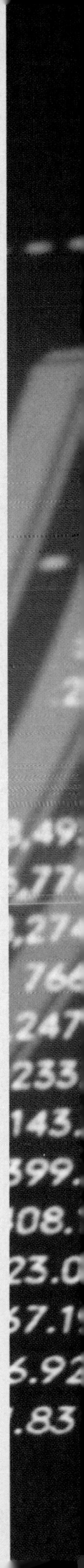

Required

a. Identify the event that represents the expiration of insurance on the factory building.

b. Explain why recognizing the expiration of insurance on a factory building affects financial statements differently from recognizing the expiration of insurance on an administrative building.

L.O. 5

Exercise 14-11B *Effect of product versus general, selling, and administrative cost on the income statement and statement of cash flows*

Each of the following asset acquisitions requires a year-end adjusting entry.

	Net Income	Cash Flow
Event No.	Amount of Change	Amount of Change
1. Purchased franchise	NA	(75,000) IA
1. Adjusting Entry	(7,500)	NA

1. Paid $75,000 cash on January 1 to purchase a hamburger franchise that had an estimated expected useful life of 10 years and no salvage value.
2. Paid $75,000 cash on January 1 to purchase a patent to manufacture a special product. The patent had an estimated expected useful life of 10 years.
3. Paid $4,800 cash on April 1 for a one-year insurance policy on the administrative building.
4. Paid $4,800 cash on April 1 for a one-year insurance policy on the manufacturing building.
5. Paid $2,500 cash to purchase office supplies for the accounting department. At the end of the year, $600 of office supplies was still on hand.
6. Paid $2,500 cash to purchase factory supplies. At the end of the year, $600 of factory supplies was still on hand.

Required

Explain how both acquiring the asset and recording the adjusting entry affect the amount of net income and the cash flow reported in the annual financial statements. In the Cash Flow Column, indicate whether the cash flow is for operating activities (OA), investing activities (IA), or financing activities (FA). Assume a December 31 annual closing date. The first event is shown as an example. Assume that any products that have been made have not been sold.

L.O. 8

Exercise 14-12B *Upstream and downstream costs*

During 2007 Troy Pharmaceutical Company incurred $10,000,000 of research and development (R&D) costs to develop a new hay fever drug called Allergone. In accordance with FASB standards, the entire R&D cost was recognized as expense in 2007. Manufacturing costs (direct materials, direct labor, and overhead) to produce Allergone are expected to be $40 per unit. Packaging, shipping, and sales commissions are expected to be $5 per unit. Troy expects to sell 1,000,000 units of Allergone before developing a new drug to replace it in the market. During 2007, Troy produced 160,000 units of Allergone and sold 100,000 of them.

Required

a. Identify the upstream and downstream costs.

b. Determine the 2007 amount of cost of goods sold and the December 31, 2007, ending inventory balance.

c. Determine the unit sales price Troy should establish assuming it desires to earn a profit margin equal to 40 percent of the *total cost* of developing, manufacturing, and distributing Allergone.

d. Prepare an income statement for 2007 using the sales price from Requirement *c*.

e. Why would Troy price Allergone at a level that would generate a loss for 2007?

L.O. 10

Exercise 14-13B *Value chain analysis*

Fastidious Vincent washed his hair at home and then went to a barbershop for a haircut. The barber explained that shop policy is to shampoo each customer's hair before cutting, regardless of how recently it had been washed. Somewhat annoyed, Vincent submitted to the shampoo, after which the barber skillfully cut his hair. After the haircut, the barber dried his hair and complimented Vincent on his appearance. He added, "That will be $18, $3 for the shampoo and $15 for the cut and dry." Vincent did not tip the barber.

Required

Identify the nonvalue-added activity described. How could the barber modify this nonvalue-added activity?

Exercise 14-14B *Effect of a just-in-time inventory system on financial statements* — L.O. 10

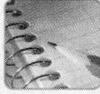

In reviewing Kelowna Company's financial statements for the past two years, Sylvia Peters, a bank loan officer, noticed that the company's inventory level had increased significantly while sales revenue had remained constant. Such a trend typically indicates increasing inventory carrying costs and slowing cash inflows. Ms. Peters concluded that the bank should deny Kelowna's credit line application.

Required

Explain how implementing an effective just-in-time inventory system would affect Kelowna's financial statements and possibly reverse Ms. Peters's decision about its credit line application.

Exercise 14-15B *Using JIT to minimize waste and lost opportunity* — L.O. 10

Dawn Choi is the editor-in-chief of her school's yearbook. The school has 800 students and 60 faculty and staff members. The firm engaged to print copies of the yearbook charges the school $15 per book and requires a 10-day lead time for delivery. Dawn and her editors plan to order 700 copies to sell at the school fair for $24 each.

Required

a. If the school sells 600 yearbooks, what amount of profit will it earn? What is the cost of waste due to excess inventory?

b. If 100 buyers are turned away after all yearbooks have been sold, what amount of profit will the school earn? What amount of opportunity cost will the school incur?

c. How could Dawn use a JIT inventory system to maximize profits by eliminating waste and opportunity cost?

Exercise 14-16B *Using JIT to minimize holding costs* — L.O. 10

Angie's Beauty Salon purchases inventory supplies from a variety of vendors, some of which require a four-week lead time before delivering inventory purchases. To ensure that she will not run out of supplies, Angie Hammond, the owner, maintains a large inventory. The average cost of inventory on hand is $9,000. Ms. Hammond usually finances inventory purchases with a line of credit that has a 12 percent annual interest charge. Her accountant has suggested that she purchase all inventory from a single large distributor that can satisfy all of her orders within a three-day period. With such prompt delivery, Ms. Hammond would be able to reduce her average inventory balance to $2,000. She also believes that she could save $1,000 per year through reduced phone bills, insurance costs, and warehouse rental costs associated with ordering and maintaining the higher level of inventory.

Required

a. Is the inventory system the accountant suggested to Ms. Hammond a pure or approximate just-in-time system?

b. Based on the information provided, how much inventory holding cost could Ms. Hammond eliminate by taking the accountant's advice?

PROBLEMS—SERIES B

Problem 14-17B *Product versus general, selling, and administrative costs* — L.O. 2, 3, 4, 5, 6

Looney Manufacturing Company was started on January 1, 2007, when it acquired $167,500 cash by issuing common stock. Looney immediately purchased office furniture and manufacturing equipment costing $25,000 and $47,500, respectively. The office furniture had a four-year useful life and a zero salvage value. The manufacturing equipment had a $5,500 salvage value and an expected useful life of six years. The company paid $17,500 for salaries of administrative personnel and $22,500 for wages of production personnel. Finally, the company paid $30,500 for raw materials that were used to make inventory. All inventory was started and completed during the year. Looney completed production on 6,000 units of product and sold 5,600 units at a price of $17.50 each in 2007. (Assume all transactions are cash transactions.)

Required

a. Determine the total product cost and the average cost per unit of the inventory produced in 2007.

b. Determine the amount of cost of goods sold that would appear on the 2007 income statement.

c. Determine the amount of the ending inventory balance that would appear on the December 31, 2007, balance sheet.

d. Determine the amount of net income that would appear on the 2007 income statement.

e. Determine the amount of retained earnings that would appear on the December 31, 2007, balance sheet.

f. Determine the amount of total assets that would appear on the December 31, 2007, balance sheet.

g. Determine the amount of net cash flow from operating activities that would appear on the 2007 statement of cash flows.

h. Determine the amount of net cash flow from investing activities that would appear on the 2007 statement of cash flows.

L.O. 2, 4, 5

Problem 14-18B ***Effect of product versus general, selling, and administrative costs on financial statements***

Watson Company experienced the following accounting events during its first year of operation. With the exception of the adjusting entries for depreciation, all transactions were cash transactions.

1. Acquired $99,000 cash by issuing common stock.
2. Paid $18,750 for the materials used to make products. All products started were completed during the period.
3. Paid salaries of $7,500 to selling and administrative employees.
4. Paid wages of $11,250 to production workers.
5. Paid $15,000 for furniture used in selling and administrative offices. The furniture was acquired on January 1. It had a $1,875 estimated salvage value and a seven-year useful life.
6. Paid $27,500 for manufacturing equipment. The equipment was acquired on January 1. It had a $2,500 estimated salvage value and a five-year useful life.
7. Sold inventory to customers for $53,750 that had cost $31,250 to make.

Required

Explain how these events would affect the balance sheet, income statement, and statement of cash flows by recording them in a horizontal financial statements model as indicated here. The first event is recorded as an example. In the Cash Flow column, indicate whether the amounts represent financing activities (FA), investing activities (IA), or operating activities (OA).

	Assets								Equity								
Event No.	Cash	+	Inventory	+	Manuf. Equip.*	+	Office Furn.*	=	Com. Stk.	+	Ret. Earn.	Rev.	−	Exp.	=	Net Inc.	Cash Flow
1	99,000								99,000								99,000 FA

*Record accumulated depreciation as negative amounts in these columns.

L.O. 2, 3, 4, 5

Problem 14-19B ***Product versus general, selling, and administrative costs***

The following transactions pertain to 2008, the first year of operations of Womack Company. All inventory was started and completed during the accounting period. All transactions were cash transactions.

1. Acquired $44,800 cash by issuing common stock.
2. Paid $7,680 for materials used to produce inventory.

3. Paid $3,520 to production workers.
4. Paid $4,000 rental fee for production equipment.
5. Paid $1,200 to administrative employees.
6. Paid $2,560 rental fee for administrative office equipment.
7. Produced 1,900 units of inventory of which 1,500 units were sold at a price of $13.92 each.

Required

Prepare an income statement, balance sheet, and statement of cash flows.

Problem 14-20B ***Service versus manufacturing companies*** **L.O. 2, 3, 4, 5**

Hague Company began operations on January 1, 2006, by issuing common stock for $75,200 cash. During 2006, Hague received $61,600 cash from revenue and incurred costs that required $72,000 of cash payments.

Required

Prepare an income statement, balance sheet, and statement of cash flows for Hague Company for 2006, under each of the following independent scenarios.

a. Hague is an employment agency. The $72,000 was paid for employee salaries and advertising.

b. Hague is a trucking company. The $72,000 was paid to purchase two trucks. The trucks were purchased on January 1, 2006, had five-year useful lives, and had no expected salvage value. Hague uses straight-line depreciation.

c. Hague is a manufacturing company. The $72,000 was paid to purchase the following items:

(1) Paid $14,400 cash to purchase materials used to make products during the year.

(2) Paid $22,400 cash for wages to production workers who made products during the year.

(3) Paid $3,200 cash for salaries of sales and administrative employees.

(4) Paid $32,000 cash to purchase manufacturing equipment. The equipment was used solely for the purpose of making products. It had a six-year life and a $3,200 salvage value. The company uses straight-line depreciation.

(5) During 2006, Hague started and completed 2,600 units of product. The revenue was earned when Hague sold 2,200 units of product to its customers.

d. Refer to Requirement *c*. Could Hague determine the actual cost of making the 500th unit of product? How likely is it that the actual cost of the 500th unit of product was exactly the same as the cost of producing the 501st unit of product? Explain why management may be more interested in average cost than in actual cost.

Problem 14-21B ***Importance of cost classification*** **L.O. 2, 3, 4, 5, 6**

Addison Company was started when it acquired $84,000 by issuing common stock. During the first year of operations, the company incurred specifically identifiable product costs (materials, labor, and overhead) amounting to $48,000. Addison also incurred $24,000 of product development costs. There was a debate regarding how the product development costs should be classified. Advocates of Option 1 believed that the costs should be included in the general, selling, and administrative cost category. Advocates of Option 2 believed it would be more appropriate to classify the product development costs as product costs. During the first year, Addison made 10,000 units of product and sold 8,000 units at a price of $16.80 each. All transactions were cash transactions.

Required

a. Prepare an income statement, balance sheet, and statement of cash flows under each of the two options.

b. Identify the option that results in financial statements more likely to leave a favorable impression on investors and creditors.

c. Assume that Addison provides an incentive bonus to the company president that is equal to 8 percent of net income. Compute the amount of the bonus under each of the two options. Identify the option that provides the president with the higher bonus.

d. Assume a 35 percent income tax rate. Determine the amount of income tax expense under each of the two options. Identify the option that minimizes the amount of the company's income tax expense.

e. Comment on the conflict of interest between the company president as determined in Requirement *c* and the stockholders of the company as indicated in Requirement *d*. Describe an incentive compensation plan that would avoid conflicts between the interests of the president and the owners.

L.O. 10

Problem 14-22B *Value chain analysis*

Kelly Doss visited her personal physician for treatment of flu symptoms. She was greeted by the receptionist, who gave her personal history and insurance forms to complete. She needed no instructions; she completed these same forms every time she visited the doctor. After completing the forms, Ms. Doss waited for 30 minutes before being ushered into the examining room. After an additional 15 minutes, Dr. Brannon entered the room. The doctor ushered Ms. Doss into the hallway where he weighed her and called her weight out to the nurse for recording. Ms. Doss had gained 10 pounds since her last visit, and the doctor suggested that she consider going on a diet. Dr. Brannon then took her temperature and asked her to return to the examining room. Ten minutes later, he returned to take a throat culture and draw blood. She waited another 15 minutes for the test results. Finally, the doctor returned and told Ms. Doss that she had strep throat and bronchitis. Dr. Brannon prescribed an antibiotic and told her to get at least two days of bed rest. Ms. Doss was then ushered to the accounting department to settle her bill. The accounting clerk asked her several questions; the answers to most of them were on the forms she had completed when she first arrived at the office. Finally, Ms. Doss paid her required copayment and left the office. Three weeks later, she received a bill indicating that she had not paid the copayment. She called the accounting department, and, after a search of the records, the clerk verified that the bill had, in fact, been paid. The clerk apologized for the inconvenience and inquired as to whether Ms. Doss's health had improved.

Required

a. Identify at least three value-added and three nonvalue-added activities suggested in this scenario.
b. Provide suggestions for how to eliminate the nonvalue-added activities.

L.O. 10

Problem 14-23B *Using JIT to reduce inventory holding costs*

McCoy Automobile Dealership Inc. (MAD) buys and sells a variety of cars made by Saig Motor Corporation. MAD maintains about 30 new cars in its parking lot for customers' selection; the cost of this inventory is approximately $320,000. Additionally, MAD hires security guards to protect the inventory from theft and a maintenance crew to keep the facilities attractive. The total payroll cost for the guards and maintenance crew amounts to $80,000 per year. MAD has a line of credit with a local bank that calls for a 15 percent annual rate of interest. Recently, David Mazur, the president of MAD, learned that a competitor in town, Wade Dealership, has been attracting some of MAD's usual customers because Wade could offer them lower prices. Mr. Mazur also discovered that Wade carries no inventory at all but shows customers a catalog of cars as well as pertinent information from on-line computer databases. Wade promises to deliver any car that a customer identifies within three working days.

Required

a. Based on the information provided, determine MAD's annual inventory holding cost.
b. Name the inventory system that Wade uses and explain how the system enables Wade to sell at reduced prices.

L.O. 10

Problem 14-24B *Using JIT to minimize waste and lost opportunity*

Donna's Hamburger is a small fast-food shop in a busy shopping center that operates only during lunch hours. Donna Hudson, the owner and manager of the shop, is confused. On some days, she does not have enough hamburgers to satisfy customer demand. On other days, she has more hamburgers than she can sell. When she has excess hamburgers, she has no choice but to dump them. Usually, Ms. Hudson prepares about 160 hamburgers before the busy lunch hour. The product cost per hamburger is approximately $0.75; the sales price is $2.50 each. Ms. Hudson pays general, selling, and administrative expenses that include daily rent of $50 and daily wages of $40.

Required

a. Prepare an income statement based on sales of 100 hamburgers per day. Determine the cost of wasted hamburgers if 160 hamburgers were prepared in advance.
b. Prepare an income statement assuming that 200 customers attempt to buy hamburgers. Since Ms. Hudson has prepared only 160 hamburgers, she must reject 40 customer orders because of insufficient supply. Determine the amount of lost profit.

c. Suppose that hamburgers can be prepared quickly after each customer orders. However, Ms. Hudson must hire an additional part-time employee at a cost of approximately $20 per day. The per unit cost of each hamburger remains at $0.75. Prepare an income statement under the JIT system assuming that 100 hamburgers are sold. Compare the income statement under JIT with the income statement prepared in Requirement *a*. Comment on how the JIT system would affect profitability.

d. Assume the same facts as in Requirement *c* with respect to a JIT system that requires additional labor costing $20 per day. Prepare an income statement under the JIT system, assuming that 200 hamburgers are sold. Compare the income statement under JIT with the income statement prepared in Requirement *b*. Comment on how the JIT system would affect profitability.

e. Explain how the JIT system might be able to improve customer satisfaction as well as profitability.

ANALYZE, THINK, COMMUNICATE

ATC 14-1 Business Applications Case *Financial versus managerial accounting*

An article in the April 12, 2004, edition of *BusinessWeek,* "The Costco Way—Higher Wages Mean Higher Profits" compared **Costco Wholesale Corporation** data with **Wal-Mart's Sam's Club** data. The tables below present some of the data used to support this claim.

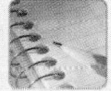

How Costco Spends More on Employees

	Costco	Sam's Club
Average hourly wage rate	$15.97	$11.53
Employees covered by a health-care plan	82%	47%
Average annual health-care costs per employee	$5,735	$3,500
Employees covered by a retirement plan	91%	64%
Average annual retirement costs per employee	$1,330	$747

Benefits to Costco from Spending More on Emplyees

	Costco	Sam's Club
Annual employee trunover	6%	21%
Labor and overhead cost as a percent of sales	9.8%	17%
Annual sales per square foot	$795	$516
Annual profit per employee	$13,647	$11,039

Required

a. Is the information in the tables above best described as primarily financial accounting data or managerial accounting data in nature? Explain.

b. Provide additional examples of managerial and financial accounting information that could apply to Costco.

c. Explain why a manager of an individual Costco store needs different kinds of information than someone who is considering lending the company money or investing in its common stock.

ATC 14-2 Group Assignment *Product versus upstream and downstream costs*

Victor Holt, the accounting manager of Sexton Inc., gathered the following information for 2006. Some of it can be used to construct an income statement for 2006. Ignore items that do not appear on an income statement. Some computations may be required. For example, the cost of manufacturing equipment would not appear on the income statement. However, the cost of manufacturing equipment is needed to compute the amount of depreciation. All units of product were started and completed in 2006.

1. Issued $864,000 of common stock.
2. Paid engineers in the product design department $10,000 for salaries that were accrued at the end of the previous year.
3. Incurred advertising expenses of $70,000.
4. Paid $720,000 for materials used to manufacture the company's product.
5. Incurred utility costs of $160,000. These costs were allocated to different departments on the basis of square footage of floor space. Mr. Holt identified three departments and determined the square footage of floor space for each department to be as shown in the table below:

Department	Square Footage
Research and development	10,000
Manufacturing	60,000
Selling and administrative	30,000
Total	100,000

6. Paid $880,000 for wages of production workers.
7. Paid cash of $658,000 for salaries of administrative personnel. There was $16,000 of accrued salaries owed to administrative personnel at the end of 2006. There was no beginning balance in the Salaries Payable account for administrative personnel.
8. Purchased manufacturing equipment two years ago at a cost of $10,000,000. The equipment had an eight-year useful life and a $2,000,000 salvage value.
9. Paid $390,000 cash to engineers in the product design department.
10. Paid a $258,000 cash dividend to owners.
11. Paid $80,000 to set up manufacturing equipment for production.
12. Paid a one-time $186,000 restructuring cost to redesign the production process to implement a just-in-time inventory system.
13. Prepaid the premium on a new insurance policy covering nonmanufacturing employees. The policy cost $72,000 and had a one-year term with an effective starting date of May 1. Four employees work in the research and development department and eight employees in the selling and administrative department. Assume a December 31 closing date.
14. Made 69,400 units of product and sold 60,000 units at a price of $70 each.

Required

a. Divide the class into groups of four or five students per group, and then organize the groups into three sections. Assign Task 1 to the first section of groups, Task 2 to the second section of groups, and Task 3 to the third section of groups.

Group Tasks

(1) Identify the items that are classified as product costs and determine the amount of cost of goods sold reported on the 2006 income statement.

(2) Identify the items that are classified as upstream costs and determine the amount of upstream cost expensed on the 2006 income statement.

(3) Identify the items that are classified as downstream costs and determine the amount of downstream cost expensed on the 2006 income statement.

b. Have the class construct an income statement in the following manner. Select a member of one of the groups assigned the first group task identifying the product costs. Have that person go to the board and list the costs included in the determination of cost of goods sold. Anyone in the other groups who disagrees with one of the classifications provided by the person at the board should voice an objection and explain why the item should be classified differently. The instructor should lead the class to a consensus on the disputed items. After the amount of cost of goods sold is determined, the student at the board constructs the part of the income statement showing the determination of gross margin. The exercise continues in a similar fashion with representatives from the other sections explaining the composition of the upstream and downstream costs. These items are added to the income statement started by the first group representative. The final result is a completed income statement.

ATC 14-3 Research Assignment *Skills needed by managerial accountants*

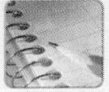

The September 1999 issue of *Strategic Finance* contains the article "Counting More, Counting Less: Transformations in the Management Accounting Profession," written by Keith Russell, Gary Siegel, and C. S. Kuleszo. It appears on pages 38 to 44. This article reviews findings from a survey of managerial accountants conducted by the Institute of Management Accountants (IMA). Read this article and complete the following requirements.

Required

a. What skills did the management accountants identify as being most important for their success?

b. Did the respondents see their work as being more closely associated with the accounting or finance function?

c. Like all business professionals, management accountants must continuously update their skills. What were the five most important skills the respondents said they had acquired in the five years prior to the survey?

d. Non-accountants often view accountants as persons who work alone sitting at a desk. What percentage of the respondents to the IMA survey said they work on cross-functional teams?

ATC 14-4 Writing Assignment *Emerging practices in managerial accounting*

The 1998 annual report of the **Maytag Corporation** contained the following excerpt:

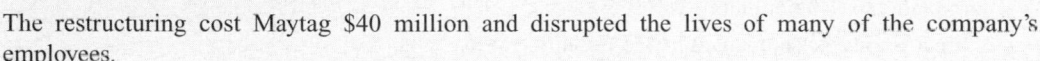

> *During the first quarter of 1996, the Company announced the restructuring of its major appliance operations in an effort to strengthen its position in the industry and to deliver improved performance to both customers and shareowners. This included the consolidation of two separate organizational units into a single operation responsible for all activities associated with the manufacture and distribution of the Company's brands of major appliances and the closing of a cooking products plant in Indianapolis, Indiana, with transfer of that production to an existing plant in Cleveland, Tennessee.*

The restructuring cost Maytag $40 million and disrupted the lives of many of the company's employees.

Required

Assume that you are Maytag's vice president of human relations. Write a letter to the employees who are affected by the restructuring. The letter should explain why it was necessary for the company to undertake the restructuring. Your explanation should refer to the ideas discussed in the section "Emerging Trends in Managerial Accounting" of this chapter.

ATC 14-5 Ethical Dilemma *Product cost versus selling and administrative expense*

Eddie Emerson is a proud woman with a problem. Her daughter has been accepted into a prestigious law school. While Ms. Emerson beams with pride, she is worried sick about how to pay for the school; she is a single parent who has to support herself and her three children. She had to go heavily into debt to finance her own education. Even though she now has a good job, family needs have continued to outpace her income and her debt burden is staggering. She knows she will be unable to borrow the money needed for her daughter's law school.

Ms. Emerson is the controller of a small manufacturing company. She has just accepted a new job offer. She has not yet told her employer that she will be leaving in a month. She is concerned that her year-end incentive bonus may be affected if her boss learns of her plans to leave. She plans to inform the company immediately after receiving the bonus. She knows her behavior is less than honorable, but she believes that she has been underpaid for a long time. Her boss, a relative of the company's owner, makes twice what she makes and does half the work. Why should she care about leaving with a little extra cash? Indeed, she is considering an opportunity to boost the bonus.

Ms. Emerson's bonus is based on a percentage of net income. Her company recently introduced a new product line that required substantial production start-up costs. Ms. Emerson is fully aware that GAAP requires these costs to be expensed in the current accounting period, but no one else in the company has the technical expertise to know exactly how the costs should be treated. She is considering misclassifying the start-up costs as product costs. If the costs are misclassified, net income will be significantly higher, resulting in a nice boost in her incentive bonus. By the time the auditors discover the misclassification, Ms. Emerson will have moved on to her new job. If the matter is brought to the attention of her new employer, she will simply plead ignorance. Considering her daughter's needs, Ms. Emerson decides to classify the start-up costs as product costs.

Required

a. Based on this information, indicate whether Ms. Emerson believes the number of units of product sold will be equal to, less than, or greater than, the number of units made. Write a brief paragraph explaining the logic that supports your answer.

b. Explain how the misclassification could mislead an investor or creditor regarding the company's financial condition.

c. Explain how the misclassification could affect income taxes.

d. Identify the factors that contributed to the breach of ethical conduct. When constructing your answer, you may want to refer to the section "Common Features of Ethical Misconduct" in Chapter 1 of this text.

e. Review the standards of ethical conduct shown in Exhibit 14.13 and identify at least two standards that Ms. Emerson's misclassification of the start-up costs violated.

COMPREHENSIVE PROBLEM

Magnificent Modems Inc. makes modem cards that are used in notebook computers. The company completed the following transactions during 2006. All purchases and sales were made with cash.

1. Acquired $750,000 of cash by issuing common stock.
2. Purchased $270,000 of manufacturing equipment. The equipment has a $30,000 salvage value and a four-year useful life. Label the purchase of the equipment as **Event 2a** and the recognition of depreciation as **Event 2b.**
3. The company started and completed 5,000 modems. Direct materials purchased and used amounted to $40 per unit.
4. Direct labor costs amounted to $25 per unit.
5. The cost of manufacturing supplies used amounted to $4 per unit.
6. The company paid $50,000 to rent the manufacturing facility.
7. Magnificent sold all 5,000 units at a cash price of $120 per unit. Label the recognition of the sales revenue as **Event 7a** and the cost of goods sold as **Event 7b.** (Hint: It will be necessary to determine the manufacturing costs in order to record the cost of goods sold.)
8. The sales staff was paid a $6 per unit sales commission.
9. Paid $39,000 to purchase equipment for administrative offices. The equipment was expected to have a $3,000 salvage value and a three-year useful life. Label the purchase of the equipment as **Event 9a** and the recognition of depreciation as **Event 9b.**
10. Administrative expenses consisting of office rental and salaries amounted to $71,950.

Required

Record the transaction data for Magnificent Modems Inc. in a financial statements model like the one shown below. In the Cash Flow column, use parentheses to indicate cash outflows. Indicate whether each cash flow item is a financing activity (FA), investing activity (IA), or operating activity (OA). The first transaction is recorded as an example.

	Assets				=	Equity					
Event No.	**Cash +**	**Inventory +**	**Manuf. Equip.* +**	**Office Equip.***	**=**	**Com. Stock +**	**Ret. Earn.**	**Rev. –**	**Exp.**	**= Net Inc.**	**Cash Flow**
1	750,000					750,000					750,000 FA
Ck. Fig.	544,050 +	0	+ 210,000 +	27,000	=	750,000 +		31,050	600,000 –	568,950	=

*Negative amounts in these columns represent accumulated depreciation.

CHAPTER 15

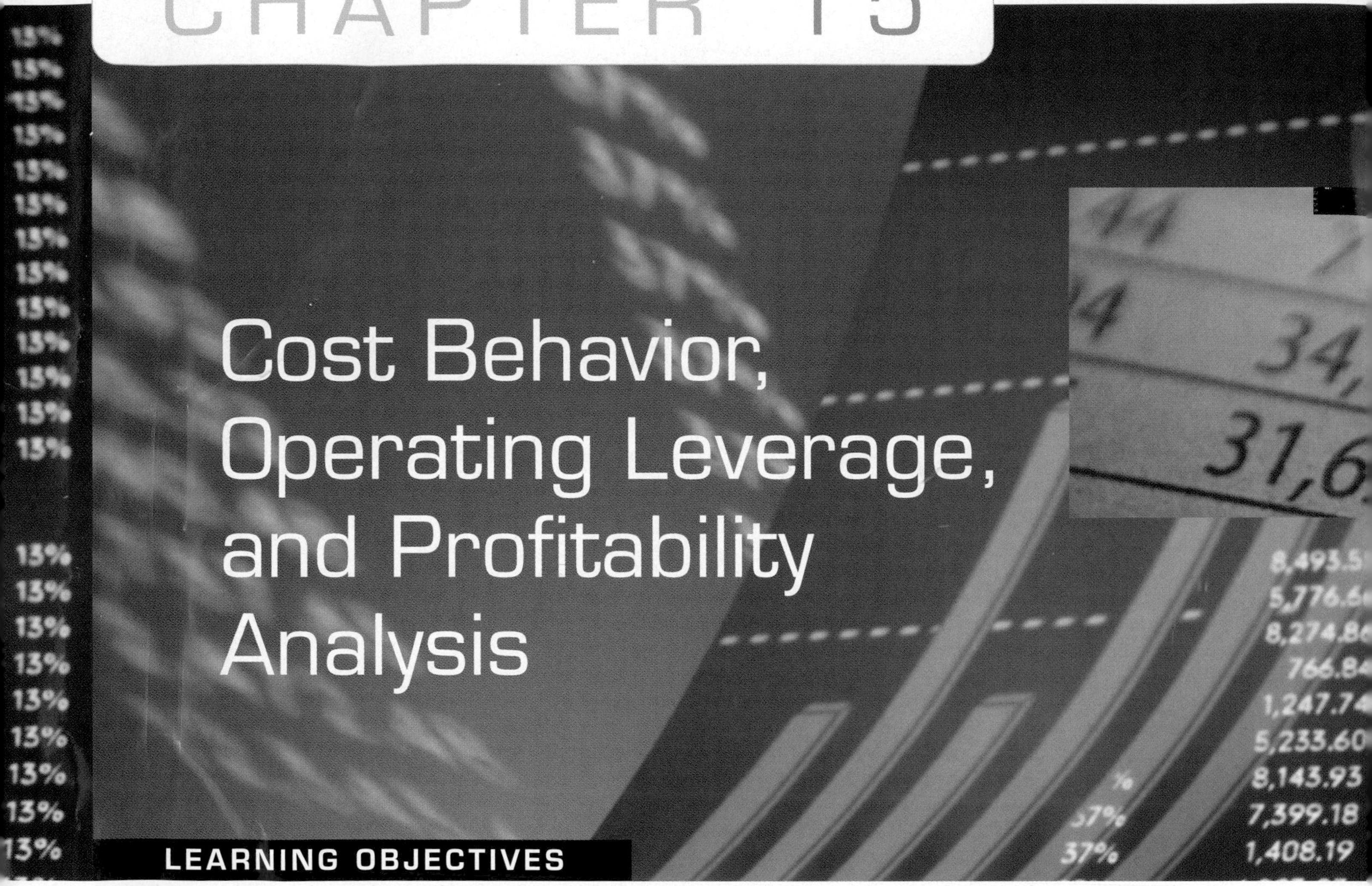

Cost Behavior, Operating Leverage, and Profitability Analysis

LEARNING OBJECTIVES

After you have mastered the material in this chapter, you will be able to:

1. **Distinguish between fixed and variable cost behavior.**
2. **Demonstrate the effects of operating leverage on profitability.**
3. **Show how cost behavior affects profitability.**
4. **Prepare an income statement using the contribution margin approach.**
5. **Calculate the magnitude of operating leverage.**
6. **Use cost behavior to create a competitive operating advantage.**
7. **Demonstrate how the relevant range and the decision-making context affect cost behavior.**
8. **Select an appropriate time period for calculating the average cost per unit.**
9. **Define the term *mixed costs.***
10. **Use the high-low method and scattergraphs to estimate fixed and variable costs.**

Chapter 15

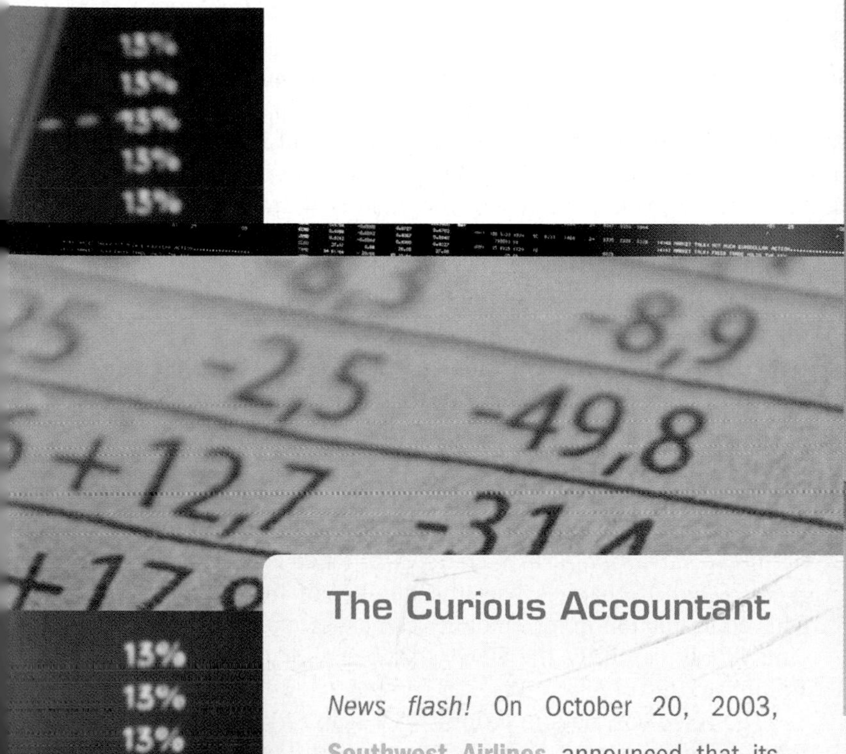

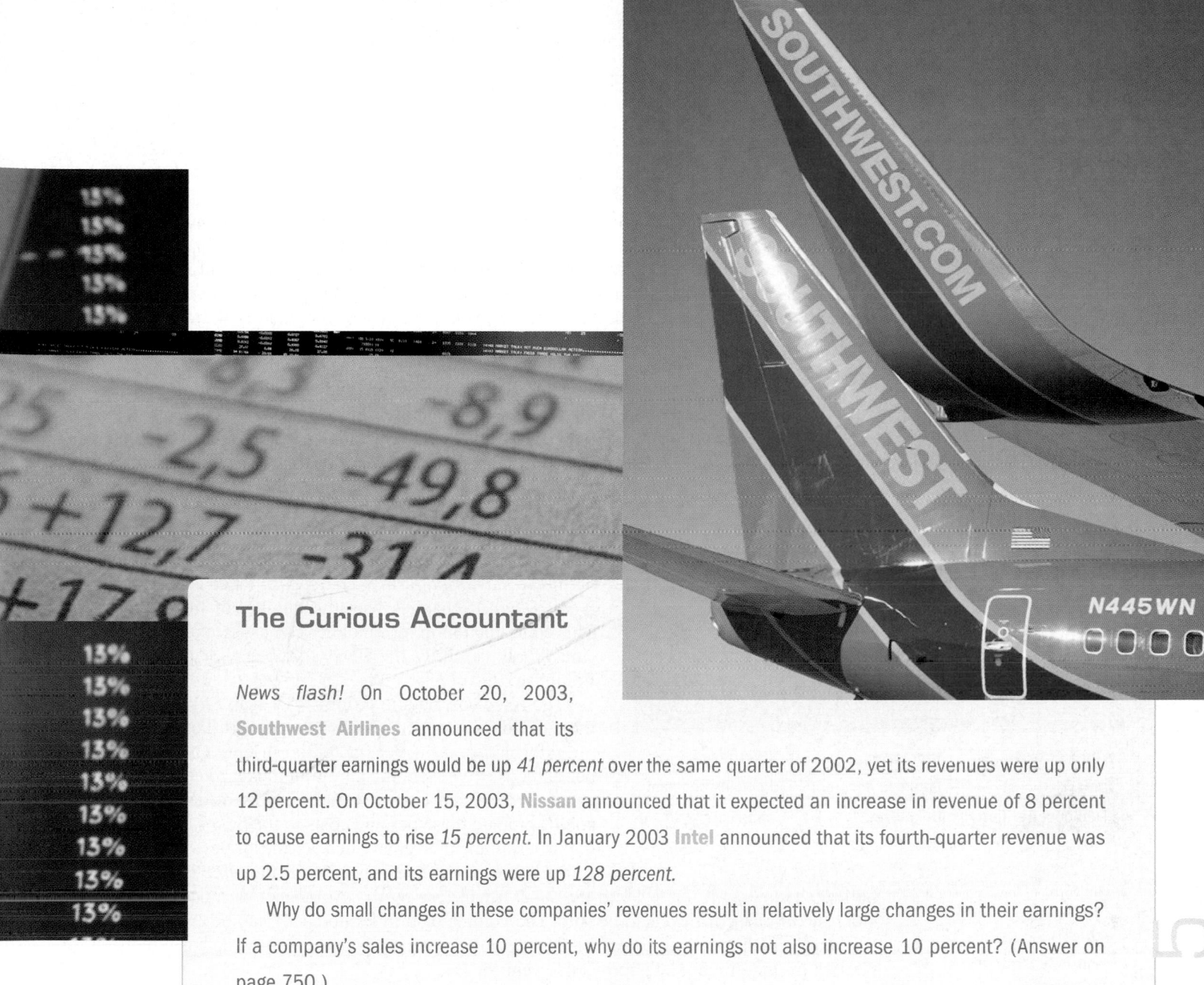

The Curious Accountant

News flash! On October 20, 2003, **Southwest Airlines** announced that its third-quarter earnings would be up *41 percent* over the same quarter of 2002, yet its revenues were up only 12 percent. On October 15, 2003, **Nissan** announced that it expected an increase in revenue of 8 percent to cause earnings to rise *15 percent.* In January 2003 **Intel** announced that its fourth-quarter revenue was up 2.5 percent, and its earnings were up *128 percent.*

Why do small changes in these companies' revenues result in relatively large changes in their earnings? If a company's sales increase 10 percent, why do its earnings not also increase 10 percent? (Answer on page 750.)

CHAPTER OPENING

Three college students are planning a vacation. One of them suggests inviting a fourth person along, remarking that four can travel for the same cost as three. Certainly, some costs will be the same whether three or four people go on the trip. For example, the hotel room costs $800 per week, regardless of whether three or four people stay in the room. In accounting terms, the cost of the hotel room is a **fixed cost.** *The total amount of a fixed cost does not change when volume changes. The total hotel room cost is $800 whether 1, 2, 3, or 4 people use the room. In contrast, some costs vary in direct proportion with changes in volume. When volume increases, total variable cost increases; when volume decreases, total variable cost decreases. For example, the cost of tickets to a theme park is a* **variable cost.** *The total cost of tickets increases proportionately with each vacationer who goes to the theme park.* **Cost behavior** *(fixed versus variable) can significantly impact profitability. This chapter explains cost behavior and ways it can be used to increase profitability.* ■

Fixed Cost Behavior

LO 1

Distinguish between fixed and variable cost behavior.

Topic Tackler PLUS

15-1

How much more will it cost to send one additional employee to a sales meeting? If more people buy our products, can we charge less? If sales increase by 10 percent, how will profits be affected? Managers seeking answers to such questions must understand cost behavior. Knowing how costs behave relative to the level of business activity enables managers to more effectively plan and control costs. To illustrate, consider the entertainment company Star Productions Inc. (SPI).

SPI specializes in promoting rock concerts. It is considering paying a band $48,000 to play a concert. Obviously, SPI must sell enough tickets to cover this cost. In this example, the relevant activity base is the number of tickets sold. The cost of the band is a *fixed cost* because it does not change regardless of the number of tickets sold. Exhibit 15.1 illustrates the fixed cost behavior pattern, showing the *total cost* and the *cost per unit* at three different levels of activity.

EXHIBIT 15.1

Fixed Cost Behavior

Number of tickets sold (a)	2,700	3,000	3,300
Total cost of band (b)	$48,000	$48,000	$48,000
Cost per ticket sold (b ÷ a)	$17.78	$16.00	$14.55

Total versus *per unit* fixed costs behave differently. The total cost for the band remains constant (fixed) at $48,000. In contrast, fixed cost per unit decreases as volume (number of tickets sold) increases. The term *fixed cost* is consistent with the behavior of *total cost.* Total fixed cost remains constant (fixed) when activity changes. However, there is a contradiction between the term *fixed cost per unit* and the *per unit behavior pattern of a fixed cost.* Fixed cost per unit is *not* fixed. It changes with the number of tickets sold. This contradiction in terminology can cause untold confusion. Study carefully the fixed cost behavior patterns in Exhibit 15.2.

EXHIBIT 15.2

Fixed Cost Behavior

When Activity	Increases	Decreases
Total fixed cost	Remains constant	Remains constant
Fixed cost **per unit**	Decreases	Increases

The fixed cost data in Exhibit 15.1 help SPI's management decide whether to sponsor the concert. For example, the information influences potential pricing choices. The per unit costs represent the minimum ticket prices required to cover the fixed cost at various levels of activity. SPI could compare these per unit costs to the prices of competing entertainment events (such as the prices of movies, sporting events, or theater tickets). If the price is not competitive, tickets will not sell and the concert will lose money. Management must also consider the number of tickets to be sold. The volume data in Exhibit 15.1 can be compared to the band's track record of ticket sales at previous concerts. Analyzing these data can reduce the risk of undertaking an unprofitable venture.

LO 2

Demonstrate the effects of operating leverage on profitability.

Operating Leverage

EXHIBIT 15.3

Operating Leverage

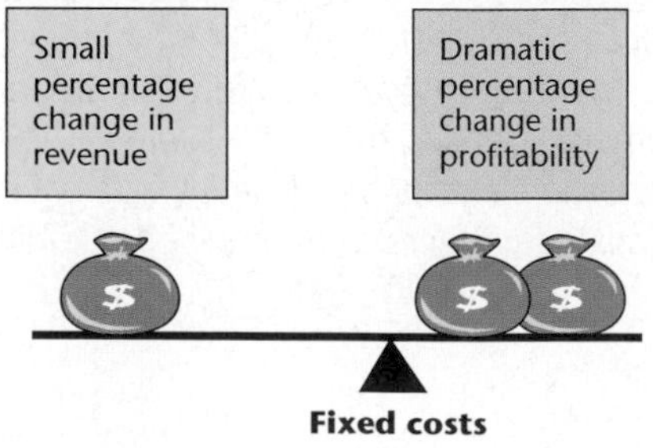

Heavy objects can be moved with little effort using *physical* leverage. Business managers apply **operating leverage** to magnify small changes in revenue into dramatic changes in profitability. The *lever* managers use to achieve disproportionate changes between revenue and profitability is fixed costs. The leverage relationships between revenue, fixed costs, and profitability are displayed in Exhibit 15.3.

When all costs are fixed, every sales dollar contributes one dollar toward the potential profitability of a project. Once sales dollars cover fixed costs, each additional sales dollar represents pure profit. As a result, a small change in sales volume can significantly affect profitability. To illustrate, assume SPI estimates it will sell 3,000 tickets for $18 each. A 10 percent difference in actual sales volume will produce a 90 percent difference in profitability. Examine the data in Exhibit 15.4 to verify this result.

FOCUS ON INTERNATIONAL ISSUES

FIXED COSTS BRING INTERNATIONAL INTRIGUE INTO THE AUTOMOBILE INDUSTRY

In 2000, amidst great fanfare, **General Motors (GM)** and **Fiat S.p.A.** of Italy announced that GM had purchased a 20 percent equity stake in Fiat for $2.4 billion. The two automakers planned to combine some operations that had been separate, reducing the operating costs for both companies. In some cases these savings were achieved. A special clause in the contract, however, became problematic for GM in 2005.

As part of the financial agreement, Fiat insisted on the right to require GM to purchase all of Fiat between 2005 and 2010. This arrangement is called a *put option.* When the deal was struck neither company thought Fiat would ever exercise the option, but if it did, the two companies would have to negotiate a purchase price. By late 2004, circumstances had changed.

Fiat's CEO suggested he might force GM to purchase Fiat unless GM paid a significant price to void the put option. GM did not want to make such a payment, and the two sides entered difficult negotiations with legal action looking likely. What caused this drastic change in conditions? As *The Wall Street Journal* put it, "Fiat Auto ... is caught in a trap of high fixed costs and shrinking market share." The same could be said of GM and the automobile manufacturing business in general. Manufacturing vehicles requires high fixed costs. By 2005 automakers' worldwide excess capacity was 24 million units. In 2004, GM, the largest company in the auto industry, produced only 9.1 million vehicles worldwide. GM was already at risk of experiencing a downgrade in its debt rating and did not need the added burden of Fiat's unprofitable operations and high debt. Facing high fixed costs and the inability to raise prices due to the glut of cars on the market, Fiat was at risk of bankruptcy without a new source of cash.

Both companies faced difficult choices. The heavily fixed-cost structure of the auto industry, coupled with excess capacity, is a major source of their problems. If a company had only variable costs, it would have no excess capacity, but it would have no economies of scale either. When times are good and sales are expanding, fixed costs can cause profits to soar. In recent years, however, the auto industry has not experienced great sales growth, so its high fixed costs have created problems for many manufacturers.

In March of 2005, GM agreed to pay Fiat $2 billion to cancel the deal described above.

Source: Company data and "Separation Anxiety: For GM and Fiat, a Messy Breakup Could Be in the Works," *The Wall Street Journal,* January 24, 2005, pp. A-1 and A-13.

EXHIBIT 15.4

Effect of Operating Leverage on Profitability

Number of tickets sold	2,700	⇐−10% ⇐	3,000	⇒+10% ⇒	3,300
Sales revenue ($18 per ticket)	$48,600		$54,000		$59,400
Cost of band (fixed cost)	(48,000)		(48,000)		(48,000)
Gross margin	$ 600	⇐−90% ⇐	$ 6,000	⇒+90% ⇒	$11,400

Calculating Percentage Change

The percentages in Exhibit 15.4 are computed as follows:

$$[(\text{Alternative measure} - \text{Base measure}) \div \text{Base measure}] \times 100 = \%\ \text{change}$$

The *base measure is the starting point.* To illustrate, compute the percentage change in gross margin when moving from 3,000 units (base measure) to 3,300 units (the alternative measure).

$$[(\text{Alternative measure} - \text{Base measure}) \div \text{Base measure}] \times 100 = \%\ \text{change}$$

$$[(\$11{,}400 - \$6{,}000) \div \$6{,}000] \times 100 = 90\%$$

The percentage *decline* in profitability is similarly computed:

$$[(\text{Alternative measure} - \text{Base measure}) \div \text{Base measure}] \times 100 = \%\ \text{change}$$

$$[(\$600 - \$6{,}000) \div \$6{,}000] \times 100 = (90\%)$$

Risk and Reward Assessment

Risk refers to the possibility that sacrifices may exceed benefits. A fixed cost represents a commitment to an economic sacrifice. It represents the ultimate risk of undertaking a particular business project. If SPI pays the band but nobody buys a ticket, the company will lose $48,000. SPI can avoid this risk by substituting *variable costs* for the *fixed cost.*

Variable Cost Behavior

LO 2

Demonstrate the effects of operating leverage on profitability.

To illustrate variable cost behavior, assume SPI arranges to pay the band $16 per ticket sold instead of a fixed $48,000. Exhibit 15.5 shows the total cost of the band and the cost per ticket sold at three different levels of activity.

Since SPI will pay the band $16 for each ticket sold, the *total* variable cost increases in direct proportion to the number of tickets sold. If SPI sells one ticket, total band cost will be $16 (1 × $16); if SPI sells two tickets, total band cost will be $32 (2 × $16); and so on. The total cost of the band increases proportionately as ticket sales move from 2,700 to 3,000 to 3,300. The variable cost *per ticket* remains $16, however, regardless of whether the number of tickets sold is 1, 2, 3, or 3,000. The behavior of variable cost *per unit* is contradictory to the word *variable.* Variable cost per unit remains *constant* regardless of how many tickets are sold. Study carefully the variable cost behavior patterns in Exhibit 15.6.

EXHIBIT 15.5

Variable Cost Behavior

Number of tickets sold (a)	2,700	3,000	3,300
Total cost of band (b)	$43,200	$48,000	$52,800
Cost per ticket sold (b ÷ a)	$16	$16	$16

EXHIBIT 15.6

Variable Cost Behavior

When Activity	**Increases**	**Decreases**
Total variable cost	Increases proportionately	Decreases proportionately
Variable cost **per unit**	Remains constant	Remains constant

Shifting the cost structure from fixed to variable enables SPI to avoid the fixed cost risk. If no one buys a ticket, SPI loses nothing because it incurs no cost. If only one person buys a ticket at an $18 ticket price, SPI earns a $2 profit ($18 sales revenue − $16 cost of band). Should managers therefore avoid fixed costs whenever possible? Not necessarily.

Shifting the cost structure from fixed to variable reduces not only the level of risk but also the potential for profits. Managers cannot avoid the risk of fixed costs without also sacrificing the benefits. Variable costs do not offer operating leverage. Exhibit 15.7 shows that

EXHIBIT 15.7

Variable Cost Eliminates Operating Leverage

Number of tickets sold	2,700	⇐ −10% ⇐	3,000	⇒ +10% ⇒	3,300
Sales revenue ($18 per ticket)	$48,600		$54,000		$59,400
Cost of band (variable cost)	(43,200)		(48,000)		(52,800)
Gross margin	$ 5,400	⇐ −10% ⇐	$ 6,000	⇒ +10% ⇒	$ 6,600

a variable cost structure produces a proportional relationship between sales and profitability. A 10 percent increase or decrease in sales results in a corresponding 10 percent increase or decrease in profitability.

CHECK YOURSELF 15.1

Suppose you are sponsoring a political rally at which Ralph Nader will speak. You estimate that approximately 2,000 people will buy tickets to hear Mr. Nader's speech. The tickets are expected to be priced at $12 each. Would you prefer a contract that agrees to pay Mr. Nader $10,000 or one that agrees to pay him $5 per ticket purchased?

Answer

Your answer would depend on how certain you are that 2,000 people will purchase tickets. If it were likely that many more than 2,000 tickets would be sold, you would be better off with a fixed cost structure, agreeing to pay Mr. Nader a flat fee of $10,000. If attendance numbers are highly uncertain, you would be better off with a variable cost structure thereby guaranteeing a lower cost if fewer people buy tickets.

Relationship Between Cost Behavior and Revenue

LO 1 Distinguish between fixed and variable cost behavior.

Exhibit 15.8 compares the relationship between revenue and total fixed cost with the relationship between revenue and total variable cost. A pure fixed cost structure offers greater risk and higher potential rewards. A company will incur losses unless it generates enough revenue to cover its fixed cost. Thereafter, every dollar of revenue represents pure profit. As volume increases, the percentage change in net income is disproportionately larger than the percentage change in revenue. In contrast, a pure variable cost structure offers the security of earning a profit at any level of sales. But since costs increase proportionately with increases in revenue, the percentage change in net income is always equal to the percentage change in revenue. A pure variable cost structure offers no operating leverage.

EXHIBIT 15.8

Cost Behavior and Revenue Relationships

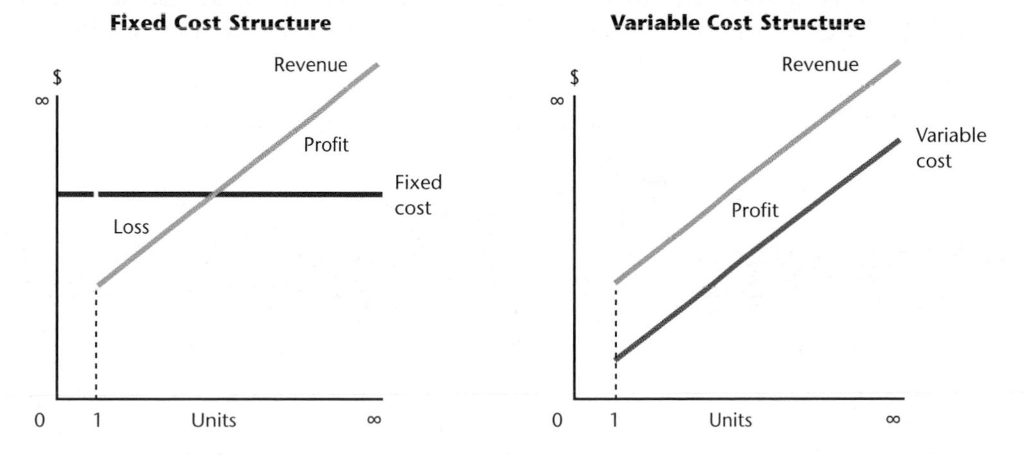

Effect of Cost Structure on Profit Stability

LO 3 Show how cost behavior affects profitability.

The preceding discussion suggests that companies with higher levels of fixed costs are more likely to experience earnings volatility. To illustrate, suppose three companies produce and sell the same product. Each company sells 10 units for $10 each. Furthermore, each company incurs costs of $60 in the process of making and selling its products. However, the companies

Answers to The Curious Accountant

The explanation for how a company's earnings can rise faster, as a percentage, than its revenue rises is operating leverage, and operating leverage is due entirely to fixed costs. When a company's output increases, its fixed cost per unit decreases. As long as it can keep prices about the same, this lower unit cost will result in higher profit per unit sold. In real world companies, the relationship between changing sales levels and changing earnings levels can be very complex, but the existence of fixed costs helps to explain why an 8 percent rise in revenue can cause a 15 percent rise in net earnings. Chapter 19 further investigates the relationships among an entity's cost structure, output level, pricing strategy, and profits earned.

operate under radically different **cost structures.** The entire $60 of cost incurred by Company A is fixed. Company B incurs $30 of fixed cost and $30 of variable cost ($3 per unit). All $60 of cost incurred by Company C is variable ($6 per unit). Exhibit 15.9 displays income statements for the three companies.

When sales change, the amount of the corresponding change in net income is directly influenced by the company's cost structure. The more fixed cost, the greater the fluctuation in net income. To illustrate, assume sales increase by one unit; the resulting income statements are displayed in Exhibit 15.10.

Company A, with the highest level of fixed costs, experienced a $10 ($50 − $40) increase in profitability; Company C, with the lowest level of fixed cost (zero), had only a $4 ($44 − $40) increase in profitability. Company B, with a 50/50 mix of fixed and variable cost, had a mid-range $7 ($47 − $40) increase in net income. The effect of fixed cost on volatility applies to decreases as well as increases in sales volume. To illustrate, assume sales decrease by one unit (from 10 to 9 units). The resulting income statements are displayed in Exhibit 15.11.

Company A again experiences the largest variance in earnings ($10 decrease). Company B had a moderate decline of $7, and Company C had the least volatility with only a $4 decline.

What cost structure is best? Should a manager use fixed or variable costs? The answer depends on sales volume

EXHIBIT 15.9

Income Statements

	Company		
	A	B	C
Variable Cost per Unit (a)	$ 0	$ 3	$ 6
Sales Revenue (10 units × $10)	$100	$100	$100
Variable Cost (10 units × a)	0	(30)	(60)
Fixed Cost	(60)	(30)	0
Net Income	$ 40	$ 40	$ 40

EXHIBIT 15.10

Income Statements

	Company		
	A	B	C
Variable Cost per Unit (a)	$ 0	$ 3	$ 6
Sales Revenue (11 units × $10)	$110	$110	$110
Variable Cost (11 units × a)	0	(33)	(66)
Fixed Cost	(60)	(30)	0
Net Income	$ 50	$ 47	$ 44

EXHIBIT 15.11

Income Statements

	Company		
	A	B	C
Variable Cost per Unit (a)	$ 0	$ 3	$ 6
Sales Revenue (9 units × $10)	$90	$90	$90
Variable Cost (9 units × a)	0	(27)	(54)
Fixed Cost	(60)	(30)	0
Net Income	$30	$33	$36

expectations. A manager who expects revenues to increase should use a fixed cost structure. On the other hand, if future sales growth is uncertain or if the manager believes revenue is likely to decline, a variable cost structure makes more sense.

CHECK YOURSELF 15.2

If both **Kroger Food Stores** and **Delta Airlines** were to experience a 5 percent increase in revenues, which company would be more likely to experience a higher percentage increase in net income?

Answer

Delta would be more likely to experience a higher percentage increase in net income because a large portion of its cost (e.g., employee salaries and depreciation) is fixed cost, while a large portion of Kroger's cost is variable (e.g., cost of goods sold).

An Income Statement under the Contribution Margin Approach

LO 4

Prepare an income statement using the contribution margin approach.

The impact of cost structure on profitability is so significant that managerial accountants frequently construct income statements that classify costs according to their behavior patterns. Such income statements first subtract variable costs from revenue; the resulting subtotal is called the **contribution margin.** The contribution margin represents the amount available to cover fixed expenses and thereafter to provide company profits. Net income is computed by subtracting the fixed costs from the contribution margin. A contribution margin style income statement cannot be used for public reporting (GAAP prohibits its use in external financial reports), but it is widely used for internal reporting purposes. Exhibit 15.12 illustrates income statements prepared using the contribution margin approach.

EXHIBIT 15.12

Income Statements

	Company	
	Bragg Co.	**Biltmore Co.**
Variable Cost per Unit (a)	$ 6	$ 12
Sales Revenue (10 units × $20)	$200	$200
Variable Cost (10 units × a)	(60)	(120)
Contribution Margin	140	80
Fixed Cost	(120)	(60)
Net Income	$ 20	$ 20

Measuring Operating Leverage Using Contribution Margin

A contribution margin income statement allows managers to easily measure operating leverage. The magnitude of operating leverage can be determined as follows:

LO 5

Calculate the magnitude of operating leverage.

$$\text{Magnitude of operating leverage} = \frac{\text{Contribution margin}}{\text{Net income}}$$

Applying this formula to the income statement data reported for Bragg Company and Biltmore Company in Exhibit 15.12 produces the following measures.

Bragg Company:

$$\text{Magnitude of operating leverage} = \frac{\$140}{\$20} = 7$$

Biltmore Company:

$$\text{Magnitude of operating leverage} = \frac{\$80}{\$20} = 4$$

The computations show that Bragg is more highly leveraged than Biltmore. Bragg's change in profitability will be seven times greater than a given percentage change in revenue. In contrast, Biltmore's profits change by only four times the percentage change in revenue. For example, a 10 percent increase in revenue produces a 70 percent increase (10 percent × 7) in profitability for Bragg Company and a 40 percent increase (10 percent × 4) in profitability for Biltmore Company. The income statements in Exhibits 15.13 and 15.14 confirm these expectations.

Operating leverage itself is neither good nor bad; it represents a strategy that can work to a company's advantage or disadvantage, depending on how it is used. The next section explains how managers can use operating leverage to create a competitive business advantage.

EXHIBIT 15.13

Comparative Income Statements for Bragg Company

Units (a)	10		11
Sales Revenue ($20 × a)	$200	⇒+10% ⇒	$220
Variable Cost ($6 × a)	(60)		(66)
Contribution Margin	140		154
Fixed Cost	(120)		(120)
Net Income	$ 20	⇒+70% ⇒	$ 34

EXHIBIT 15.14

Comparative Income Statements for Biltmore Company

Units (a)	10		11
Sales Revenue ($20 × a)	$200	⇒+10% ⇒	$220
Variable Cost ($12 × a)	(120)		(132)
Contribution Margin	80		88
Fixed Cost	(60)		(60)
Net Income	$ 20	⇒+40% ⇒	$ 28

CHECK YOURSELF 15.3

Boeing Company's 2001 10K annual report filed with the Securities and Exchange Commission refers to "higher commercial airlines segment margins." Is Boeing referring to gross margins or contribution margins?

Answer

Since the data come from the company's external annual report, the reference must be to gross margins (revenue − cost of goods sold), a product cost measure. The contribution margin (revenue − variable cost) is a measure used in internal reporting.

Using Fixed Cost to Provide a Competitive Operating Advantage

LO 6

Use cost behavior to create a competitive operating advantage.

Mary MaHall and John Strike have established tutoring companies to support themselves while they attend college. Both Ms. MaHall and Mr. Strike function as owner/managers; they each hire other students to actually provide the tutoring services. Ms. MaHall pays her tutors salaries; her labor costs are fixed at $16,000 per year regardless of the number of hours of tutoring performed. Mr. Strike pays his employees $8 per hour; his labor is therefore a variable cost. Both businesses currently provide 2,000 hours of tutoring services at a price of $11 per hour. As shown in Exhibit 15.15, both companies currently produce the same profit.

EXHIBIT 15.15

Comparative Profitability at 2,000 Hours of Tutoring

		MaHall		Strike
Number of hours of tutoring provided		2,000		2,000
Service revenue ($11 per hour)		$22,000		$22,000
Cost of tutors	Fixed	(16,000)	Variable ($8 × 2,000)	(16,000)
Net income		$ 6,000		$ 6,000

Suppose Ms. MaHall adopts a strategy to win over Mr. Strike's customers by reducing the price of tutoring services from $11 per hour to $7 per hour. If Ms. MaHall succeeds, her company's income will double as shown in Exhibit 15.16. Mr. Strike is in a vulnerable position because if he matches MaHall's price cut he will lose $1 ($7 new per hour price − $8 cost per hour for tutor) for each hour of tutoring service that his company provides.

EXHIBIT 15.16

MaHall's Profitability at 4,000 Hours of Tutoring

		MaHall
Number of hours of tutoring provided		4,000
Service revenue ($7 per hour)		$28,000
Cost of tutors	Fixed	(16,000)
Net income		$12,000

Is Mr. Strike's business doomed? Not necessarily; Ms. MaHall's operating leverage strategy only works if volume increases. If Mr. Strike matches Ms. MaHall's price, thereby maintaining the existing sales volume levels between the two companies, both companies incur losses. Exhibit 15.17 verifies this conclusion. Under these circumstances, Ms. MaHall would be forced to raise her price or to face the same negative consequences that she is attempting to force on Mr. Strike.

EXHIBIT 15.17

Comparative Profitability at 2,000 Hours of Tutoring

		MaHall		Strike
Number of hours of tutoring provided		2,000		2,000
Service revenue ($7 per hour)		$14,000		$14,000
Cost of tutors	Fixed	(16,000)	Variable ($8 × 2,000)	(16,000)
Net income (loss)		$ (2,000)		$ (2,000)

Cost Behavior Summarized

LO 1

Distinguish between fixed and variable cost behavior.

The term *fixed* refers to the behavior of *total* fixed cost. The cost *per unit* of a fixed cost *varies inversely* with changes in the level of activity. As activity increases, fixed cost per unit decreases. As activity decreases, fixed cost per unit increases. These relationships are graphed in Exhibit 15.18.

EXHIBIT 15.18

Graphical Presentation of Fixed Cost Behavior

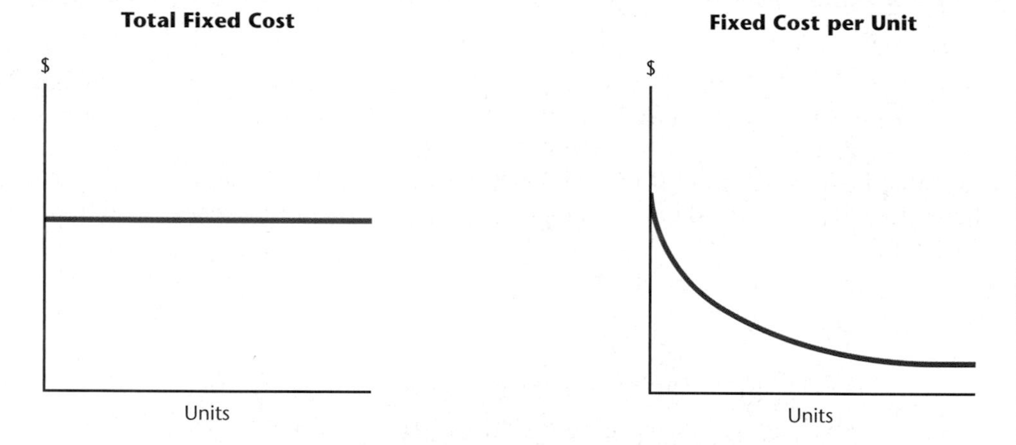

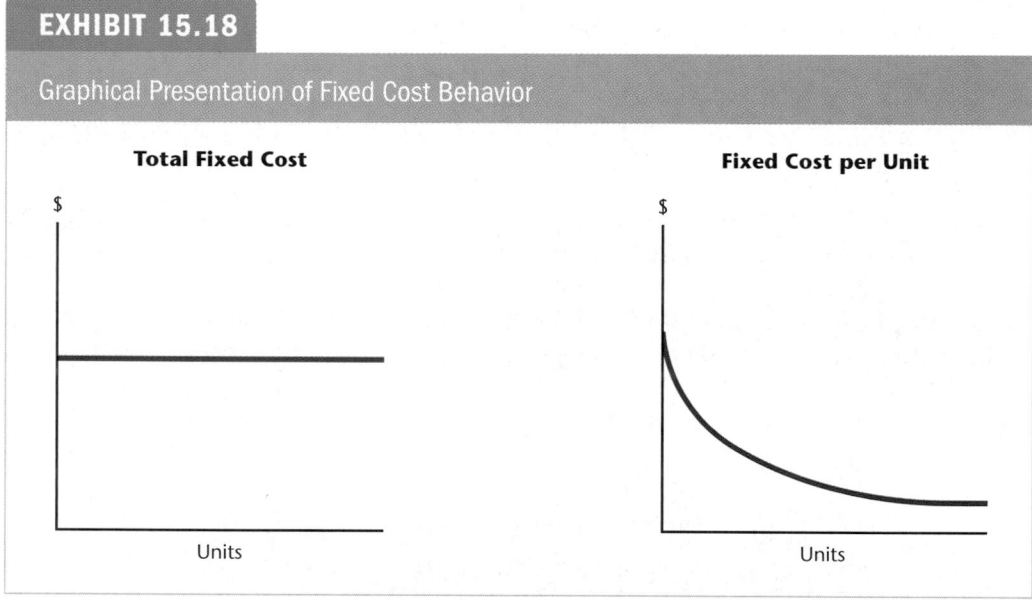

The term *variable* refers to the behavior of *total* variable cost. Total variable cost increases or decreases proportionately with changes in the volume of activity. In contrast, variable cost *per unit* remains *fixed* at all levels of activity. These relationships are graphed in Exhibit 15.19.

The relationships between fixed and variable costs are summarized in the chart in Exhibit 15.20. Study these relationships thoroughly.

The Relevant Range

LO 7

Demonstrate how the relevant range and the decision-making context affect cost behavior.

Suppose SPI, the rock concert promoter mentioned earlier, must pay $5,000 to rent a concert hall with a seating capacity of 4,000 people. Is the cost of the concert hall fixed or variable? Since total cost remains unchanged regardless of whether one ticket, 4,000 tickets, or any number in between is sold, the cost is fixed relative to ticket sales. However, what if demand for tickets is significantly more than 4,000? In that case, SPI might rent a larger concert hall at a higher cost. In other words, *the cost is fixed only for a designated range of activity (1 to 4,000).*

EXHIBIT 15.19

Graphical Presentation of Variable Cost Behavior

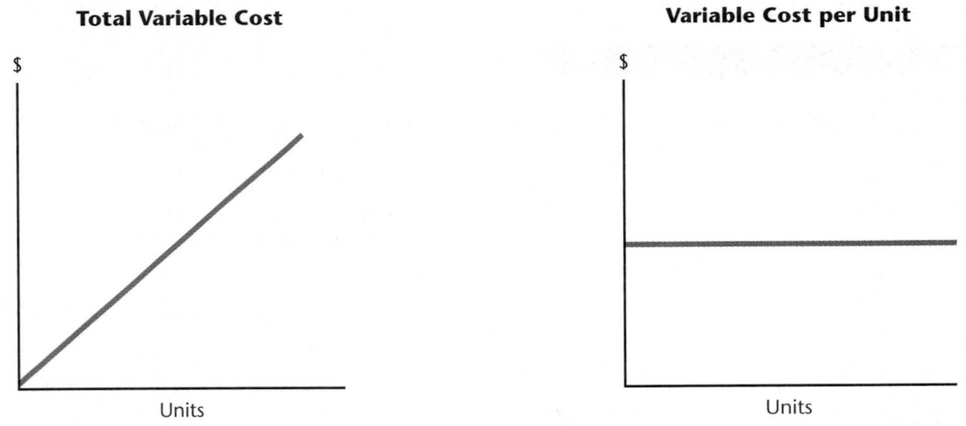

EXHIBIT 15.20

Fixed and Variable Cost Behavior

When Activity Level Changes	Total Cost	Cost per Unit
Fixed cost	Remains constant	Changes *inversely*
Variable cost	Changes in direct proportion	Remains constant

A similar circumstance affects many variable costs. For example, a supplier may offer a volume discount to buyers who purchase more than a specified number of products. Descriptions of cost behavior pertain to a specified range of activity. The range of activity over which the definitions of fixed and variable costs are valid is commonly called the **relevant range.**

Context-Sensitive Definitions of Fixed and Variable

The behavior pattern of a particular cost may be either fixed or variable, depending on the context. For example, the cost of the band was fixed at $48,000 when SPI was considering hiring it to play a single concert. Regardless of how many tickets SPI sold, the total band cost was $48,000. However, the band cost becomes variable if SPI decides to hire it to perform at a series of concerts. The total cost and the cost per concert for one, two, three, four, or five concerts are shown in Exhibit 15.21.

EXHIBIT 15.21

Cost Behavior Relative to Number of Concerts

Number of concerts (a)	1	2	3	4	5
Cost per concert (b)	$48,000	$48,000	$ 48,000	$ 48,000	$ 48,000
Total cost (a × b)	$48,000	$96,000	$144,000	$192,000	$240,000

In this context, the total cost of hiring the band increases proportionately with the number of concerts while cost per concert remains constant. The band cost is therefore variable.

The same cost can behave as either a fixed cost or a variable cost, depending on the **activity base.** When identifying a cost as fixed or variable, first ask, fixed or variable *relative to what activity base?* The cost of the band is fixed relative to *the number of tickets sold for a specific concert;* it is variable relative to *the number of concerts produced.*

CHECK YOURSELF 15.4

Is the compensation cost for managers of **Pizza Hut Restaurants** a fixed cost or a variable cost?

Answer

The answer depends on the context. For example, since a store manager's salary remains unchanged regardless of how many customers enter a particular restaurant, it can be classified as a fixed cost relative to the number of customers at a particular restaurant. However, the more restaurants Pizza Hut operates, the higher the total managers' compensation cost will be. Managers' salary cost would be classified as variable relative to the number of restaurants opened.

Cost Averaging

LO 8

Select an appropriate time period for calculating the average cost per unit.

Lake Resorts Inc. (LRI) offers water skiing lessons for guests. Since the demand for lessons is seasonal (guests buy more lessons in July than in December), LRI has chosen to rent (rather than own) the necessary equipment (boat, skis, ropes, life jackets) only when it is needed. LRI's accountant has collected the following data pertaining to providing ski lessons:

1. The daily fee to rent equipment is $80.
2. Instructors are paid $15 per lesson hour.
3. Fuel costs are $2 per lesson hour.
4. Lessons take one hour each.
5. LRI can provide up to ten lessons in one day.

Management wants to know the cost per lesson if 2, 5, or 10 lessons are provided per day. The cost is computed in Exhibit 15.22.

EXHIBIT 15.22

Analysis of Total and Unit Cost

Number of Lessons (a)	2	5	10
Cost of equipment rental	$ 80	$ 80	$ 80
Cost of instruction (a × $15)	30	75	150
Cost of fuel (a × $2)	4	10	20
Total cost (b)	$114	$165	$250
Cost per lesson (b ÷ a)	$ 57	$ 33	$ 25

The cost per lesson in Exhibit 15.22 is an example of **cost averaging.** Accountants focus on average costs because they are relatively easy to compute and are frequently more relevant to decision making than are actual costs. Imagine the difficulty of measuring the actual cost of each individual lesson. Because the equipment rental cost covers any number of lessons within the relevant range, it cannot be identified as an actual cost of any particular lesson. Towing heavier skiers behind the boat uses more gas than towing lighter ones. Wind conditions, water currents, the number of times a skier falls, and the presence of other boats affect cost factors such as fuel consumption and the actual time required to conduct a lesson. Determining the exact cost for each lesson is impossible.

Even if LRI could compute the actual cost per lesson, the information would be of little value. Of what use is knowing that on a given day the fifth lesson cost a little more or less to provide than the sixth? Customers expect standardized pricing. They do not want pricing that depends on which way the wind is blowing, even if the wind affects the actual cost of a ski les-

REALITY BYTES

Stella, a business student, works part time at **Costco Wholesale, Inc.,** to help pay her college expenses. She is currently taking a managerial accounting course, and has heard her instructor refer to depreciation as a fixed cost. However, as a requirement for her first accounting course, Stella reviewed Costco's financial statements for 2000, 2001, and 2002. The depreciation expense increased about 34 percent over these three years. She is not sure why depreciation expense would be considered a fixed cost.

Stella's accounting instructor reminded her that when an accountant says a cost is fixed, he or she means the cost is fixed in relation to one particular factor. A cost that is fixed in relation to one factor can be variable when compared to some other factor. For example, the depreciation for a retailer may be fixed relative to the number of customers who visit a particular store, but variable relative to the number of stores the company opens. In fact, Costco's depreciation increased from 2000 to 2002 mainly because the company built and opened additional stores.

Stella's instructor suggested Costco's depreciation expense would be more stable if analyzed on a per store basis, rather than in total. Being curious, Stella prepared the following table, where costs are in thousands. Over the three years, she noted that total depreciation expense increased 34.3 percent, while depreciation per store increased only 12.4 percent. Although the costs on a per store basis were more stable than the total depreciation costs, they still were not fixed, so she asked her instructor for further explanation.

Fiscal year	Total Depreciation Expense	Average Depreciation Expense per Store
2000	$254,397	$812.8
2001	301,297	873.3
2002	341,781	913.9

The instructor suggested Costco's average per store depreciation costs were increasing because the equipment and buildings purchased for the new stores (opened from 2000 to 2002) probably cost more than those purchased for the older stores. This would raise the average depreciation expense per store. The instructor also reminded her that in the real world very few costs are perfectly fixed or perfectly variable.

son. Also, customers prefer price data in advance to help them decide whether to take a lesson. They do not want to wait until after the lesson for someone to determine the exact cost. Average cost data may be more useful than actual cost information for pricing decisions.

Average cost data can help managers evaluate employee performance and control costs. Knowing an instructor spent a few minutes more or less on a particular lesson is of little use. Knowing, however, that an instructor averages 10 extra minutes per lesson signals the need for correction. Knowing what happens *on average* is more useful than knowing what happened in a particular instance.

Computing the average cost per unit requires choosing the time span over which to average costs. Suppose the following: on a single day in 2007 an instructor conducted 10 lessons for a total cost of $250. During the 2006 season, LRI provided a total of 589 lessons for a cost of $19,437. During the last five seasons, LRI provided 2,500 lessons for a total cost of

$55,000. Exhibit 15.23 shows the average cost per lesson for the day, the year, and the five-year period.

EXHIBIT 15.23

Cost per Lesson

	Span of Time		
	One Day	**One Year**	**Five Years**
Total cost of lessons (a)	$250	$19,437	$55,000
Number of lessons (b)	10	589	2,500
Cost per lesson (a ÷ b)	$ 25	$ 33	$ 22

If management decides to price individual ski lessons at average cost plus $5, should the price be $30 ($25 + $5), $38 ($33 + $5) or $27 ($22 + $5)?[1] The shortest time interval (one day) represents the most current information, but it may also be the least relevant. Suppose the one-day average reflects costs on a Sunday when demand for ski lessons was extremely high. The fixed cost of equipment rental is spread over a large number of lessons, resulting in a low cost per lesson. However, the Sunday average has little relevance to setting Monday's prices when customer demand drops sharply as many weekend vacationers return to work.

Distortions can also result from using time spans that are too long. For example, averaging costs over the previous five seasons may not reflect current costs or recent changes in customer demand. Equipment rental cost was probably less five years ago than it is today.

In this case a one-year average is probably most appropriate. If last year's season is a good predictor of this year's demand, pricing lessons at $38 provides a return that approximates management's $5 per lesson target profit. On days when demand is high, cost per unit will be low, and LRI will earn more than $5 per lesson. On days when demand is low, it will earn less than $5. However, on average, it will earn the desired return. Selecting the most appropriate time span requires using accounting judgment. *A professional management accountant provides much more than number crunching.*

Use of Estimates in Real-World Problems

LO 9

Define the term *mixed costs.*

Imagine trying to classify as fixed or variable all the different costs incurred by a large company such as Delta Airlines. Recordkeeping would be horrendous. Further complications would arise because some costs have both fixed and variable components. Consider the cost Delta incurs to use airport facilities. An airport may charge Delta a flat annual rental fee for terminal space plus a charge each time a plane takes off or lands. The flat rental fee is a fixed cost while the charge per flight is variable. The total facilities cost is mixed. Such costs are called **mixed costs** or **semivariable costs.**

To minimize the recordkeeping difficulties involved in identifying actual fixed and variable costs, many companies make decisions using estimated rather than actual costs. Several techniques exist to divide total cost into estimated fixed and variable components.

High-Low Method of Estimating Fixed and Variable Costs

LO 10

Use the high-low method and scattergraphs to estimate fixed and variable costs.

The management of Rainy Day Books (RDB) wants to expand operations. To help evaluate risks involved in opening an additional store, the company president wants to know the amount of fixed cost a new store will likely incur. Suppose RDB's accountant decides to

[1] The cost plus method is only one of several possible pricing strategies. Other pricing practices are discussed in subsequent chapters.

use the **high-low method** to supply the president with the requested information. The estimated amount of fixed cost for the new store would be developed in the following four steps.

Step 1 ***Assemble sales volume and cost history for an existing store.*** Assuming the new store would operate with roughly the same cost structure, the accountant can use the historical data to estimate the fixed cost likely to be incurred by the new store. To illustrate, the accounting data set for the existing store is displayed in Exhibit 15.24.

EXHIBIT 15.24

Cost Data

Month	Units Sold	Total Cost
January	30,000	$450,000
February	14,000	300,000
March	12,000	150,000
April	25,000	440,000
May	10,000	180,000
June	11,000	240,000
July	20,000	350,000
August	18,000	400,000
September	17,000	360,000
October	16,000	320,000
November	27,000	490,000
December	34,000	540,000

Step 2 ***Select the high and low points in the data set.*** In this example, the month with the lowest number of units sold does not correspond to the month with the lowest total cost. The lowest point in units sold occurred in May; the lowest total cost occurred in March. Because the total cost depends on the *number of units sold,* May should be classified as the low point. The high point in sales volume occurred in December. The units sold and cost data for the December and May high and low points follow:

	Units Sold	Total Cost
High (December)	34,000	$540,000
Low (May)	10,000	$180,000

Step 3 ***Determine the estimated variable cost per unit.*** The variable cost per unit is determined by dividing the difference in the total cost by the difference in the number of units sold. In this case, the variable cost per unit is as follows:

$$\text{Variable cost per unit} = \frac{\text{Difference in total cost}}{\text{Difference in volume}} = \frac{(\$540{,}000 - \$180{,}000)}{(34{,}000 - 10{,}000)} = \frac{\$360{,}000}{24{,}000} = \$15$$

Step 4 ***Determine the estimated total fixed costs.*** The total fixed cost can now be determined by subtracting the variable cost from the total cost using either the high point or the low point. Either point yields the same result. Computations using the high point follow:

$$\text{Fixed cost} + \text{Variable cost} = \text{Total cost}$$
$$\text{Fixed cost} = \text{Total cost} - \text{Variable cost}$$
$$\text{Fixed cost} = \$540{,}000 - (\$15 \times 34{,}000 \text{ units})$$
$$\text{Fixed cost} = \$30{,}000$$

Although 12 data points are available, the high-low method uses only 2 of them to estimate the amounts of fixed and variable costs. If either or both of these points is not representative of the true relationship between fixed and variable costs, the estimates produced by the high-low method will be inaccurate. *The chief advantage of the high-low method is its simplicity; the chief disadvantage is its vulnerability to inaccuracy.* RDB's accountant decides to test the accuracy of the high-low method results.

Scattergraph Method of Estimating Fixed and Variable Costs

LO 10

Use the high-low method and scattergraphs to estimate fixed and variable costs.

Scattergraphs are sometimes used as an estimation technique for dividing total cost into fixed and variable cost components. To assess the accuracy of the high-low estimate of fixed cost, RDB's accountant constructs a **scattergraph.** The horizontal axis is labeled with the number of books sold and the vertical axis with total costs. The 12 data points are plotted on the graph, and a line is drawn through the high and low points in the data set. The result is shown in Exhibit 15.25.

After studying the scattergraph in Exhibit 15.25, the accountant is certain that the high and low points are not representative of the data set. Most of the data points are above the high-low line. As shown in the second scattergraph in Exhibit 15.26, the line should be shifted upward to reflect the influence of the other data points.

The graph in Exhibit 15.26 is identical to the graph in Exhibit 15.25 except the straight line is plotted through the center of the entire data set rather than just the high and low points. The new line, a **visual fit line,** is drawn to visually minimize the total distance between the data points and the line. Usually, half of the data points are above and half below a visual fit line. The estimated variable cost per unit is measured by the slope (steepness) of the visual fit line. The fixed cost is the point (the *intercept*) where the visual fit line intersects the vertical axis (the total cost line).

The intercept in Exhibit 15.26 provides a fixed cost estimate of $100,000. Although RDB's president had only asked for the amount of fixed cost, the variable cost can be easily determined by subtracting the fixed cost from the total cost at any point along the visual fit line. For example, at 15,000 units, total cost is $300,000. Variable cost is determined as follows:

Fixed cost + Variable cost = Total cost

Variable cost = Total cost − Fixed cost

Variable cost = $300,000 − $100,000

Variable cost = $200,000

Variable cost per unit is $13.33, calculated by dividing the total variable cost by the number of units ($200,000 ÷ 15,000 units = $13.33 per unit).

EXHIBIT 15.25

Scattergraph Depicting High-Low Estimate

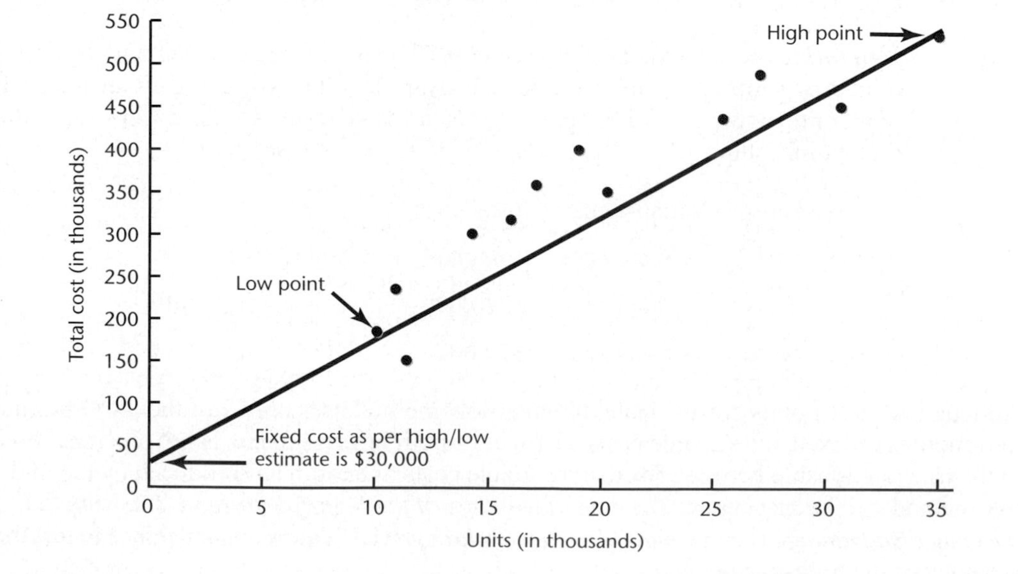

EXHIBIT 15.26

Scattergraph Depicting Line Drawn by Visual Inspection

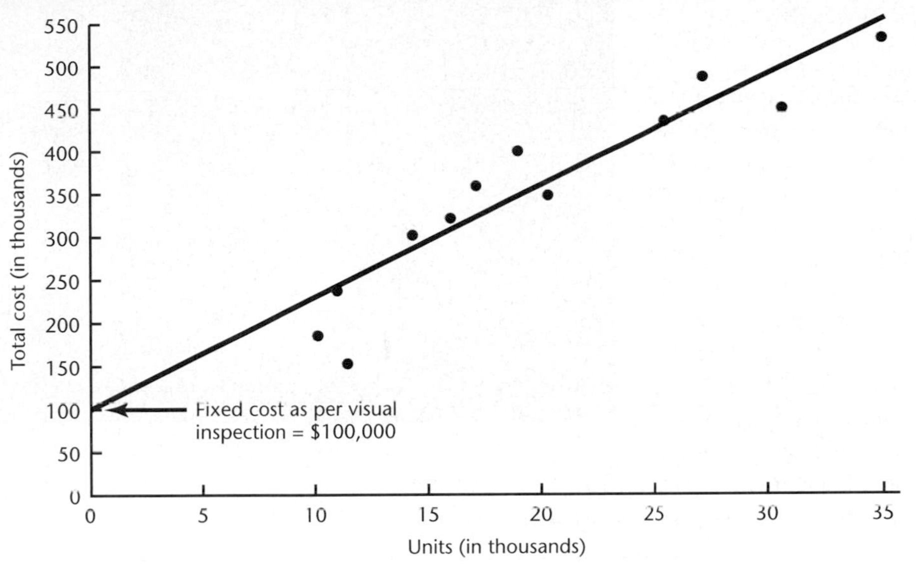

Statistical tools like least-squares regression can improve the accuracy of fitting a line through the data points. While such tools are beyond the scope of this text, you may have the opportunity to study them in other courses.

A Look Back <<

To plan and control business operations effectively, managers need to understand how different costs behave in relation to changes in the volume of activity. Total *fixed cost* remains constant when activity changes. Fixed cost per unit decreases with increases in activity and increases with decreases in activity. In contrast, total *variable cost* increases proportionately with increases in activity and decreases proportionately with decreases in activity. Variable cost per unit remains constant regardless of activity levels. The definitions of fixed and variable costs have meaning only within the context of a specified range of activity (the relevant range) for a defined period of time. In addition, cost behavior depends on the relevant volume measure (a store manager's salary is fixed relative to the number of customers visiting a particular store but is variable relative to the number of stores operated). A mixed cost has both fixed and variable cost components.

Fixed costs allow companies to take advantage of *operating leverage.* With operating leverage, each additional sale decreases the cost per unit. This principle allows a small percentage change in volume of revenue to cause a significantly larger percentage change in profits. The *magnitude of operating leverage* can be determined by dividing the contribution margin by net income. When all costs are fixed and revenues have covered fixed costs, each additional dollar of revenue represents pure profit. Having a fixed cost structure (employing operating leverage) offers a company both risks and rewards. If sales volume increases, costs do not increase, allowing profits to soar. Alternatively, if sales volume decreases, costs do not decrease and profits decline significantly more than revenues. Companies with high variable costs in relation to fixed costs do not experience as great a level of operating leverage. Their costs increase or decrease in proportion to changes in revenue. These companies face less risk but fail to reap disproportionately higher profits when volume soars.

Under the contribution margin approach, variable costs are subtracted from revenue to determine the *contribution margin.* Fixed costs are then subtracted from the contribution

FOCUS ON INTERNATIONAL ISSUES

ANOTHER REASON FIXED COSTS AREN'T ALWAYS FIXED

Suppose that a company is renting a facility at an annual rental rate that does not change for the next five years *no matter what.* Is this a fixed cost? By now, you are aware that the proper response is to ask fixed in relation to what? Is the rental cost of this facility fixed in relation to the activity at this facility? The answer seems to be yes, but it might be "not necessarily."

Consider the **Exxon Mobil Corporation**. If Exxon Mobil rents facilities in a country in the eastern hemisphere, Malaysia for example, the annual rental fee may be stated and paid in the local currency. In Malaysia, this is the ringgit. Even though Exxon Mobil may be paying the same number of ringgit in rent each year, Exxon Mobil's rental cost in U.S. dollars could vary greatly over time. Such potential foreign currency exchange fluctuations cause companies to enter very complex hedging arrangements to add stability to transactions that must be paid in foreign currencies.

Exxon Mobil was founded and has its headquarters in the United States. It does much business in the United States. Furthermore, it is listed on the New York Stock Exchange and presents its financial statements in U.S. dollars. However, it does much more business and has many more assets in countries outside the United States. Consider the following table from Exxon Mobil's 2002 financial statements. Before a multinational company can determine whether a cost is fixed, it must determine the applicable currency.

Geographical Area	Earnings*	Percentage of Total	Long-Term Assets*	Percentage of Total
United States	$2,131	28%	$34,138	36%
Non-United States	5,444	72	60,802	64
Totals	$7,575	100%	$94,940	100%

*Amounts in millions.

margin to determine net income. The contribution margin represents the amount available to pay fixed costs and provide a profit. Although not permitted by GAAP for external reporting, many companies use the contribution margin format for internal reporting purposes.

Cost per unit is an average cost that is easier to compute than the actual cost of each unit and is more relevant to decision making than actual cost. Accountants must use judgment when choosing the time span from which to draw data for computing the average cost per unit. Distortions can result from using either too long or too short a time span.

Fixed and variable costs can be estimated using such tools as the *high-low method* and *scattergraphs.* Both are easy to use and can be reasonably accurate.

>> A Look Forward

The next chapter begins investigating cost measurement. Accountants seek to determine the cost of certain objects. A cost object may be a product, a service, a department, a customer, or any other thing for which the cost is being determined. Some costs can be directly traced to a cost object, while others are difficult to trace. Costs that are difficult to trace to cost objects are called *indirect costs,* or *overhead.* Indirect costs are assigned to cost objects through *cost allocation.* The next chapter introduces the basic concepts and procedures of cost allocation.

SELF-STUDY REVIEW PROBLEM

Mensa Mountaineering Company (MMC) provides guided mountain climbing expeditions in the Rocky Mountains. Its only major expense is guide salaries; it pays each guide $4,800 per climbing expedition. MMC charges its customers $1,500 per expedition and expects to take five climbers on each expedition.

Part 1

Base your answers on the preceding information.

Required

a. Determine the total cost of guide salaries and the cost of guide salaries per climber assuming that four, five, or six climbers are included in a trip. Relative to the number of climbers in a single expedition, is the cost of guides a fixed or a variable cost?

b. Relative to the number of expeditions, is the cost of guides a fixed or a variable cost?

c. Determine the profit of an expedition assuming that five climbers are included in the trip.

d. Determine the profit assuming a 20 percent increase (six climbers total) in expedition revenue. What is the percentage change in profitability?

e. Determine the profit assuming a 20 percent decrease (four climbers total) in expedition revenue. What is the percentage change in profitability?

f. Explain why a 20 percent shift in revenue produces more than a 20 percent shift in profitability. What term describes this phenomenon?

Part 2

Assume that the guides offer to make the climbs for a percentage of expedition fees. Specifically, MMC will pay guides $960 per climber on the expedition. Assume also that the expedition fee charged to climbers remains at $1,500 per climber.

Required

g. Determine the total cost of guide salaries and the cost of guide salaries per climber assuming that four, five, or six climbers are included in a trip. Relative to the number of climbers in a single expedition, is the cost of guides a fixed or a variable cost?

h. Relative to the number of expeditions, is the cost of guides a fixed or a variable cost?

i. Determine the profit of an expedition assuming that five climbers are included in the trip.

j. Determine the profit assuming a 20 percent increase (six climbers total) in expedition revenue. What is the percentage change in profitability?

k. Determine the profit assuming a 20 percent decrease (four climbers total) in expedition revenue. What is the percentage change in profitability?

l. Explain why a 20 percent shift in revenue does not produce more than a 20 percent shift in profitability.

Solution to Part 1, Requirement *a*

Number of climbers (a)	4	5	6
Total cost of guide salaries (b)	$4,800	$4,800	$4,800
Cost per climber (b ÷ a)	1,200	960	800

Since the total cost remains constant (fixed) regardless of the number of climbers on a particular expedition, the cost is classified as fixed. Note that the cost per climber decreases as the number of climbers increases. This is the *per unit* behavior pattern of a fixed cost.

Solution to Part 1, Requirement *b*

Since the total cost of guide salaries changes proportionately each time the number of expeditions increases or decreases, the cost of salaries is variable relative to the number of expeditions.

Solution to Part 1, Requirements *c, d,* and *e*

Number of Climbers	4	Percentage Change	5	Percentage Change	6
Revenue ($1,500 per climber)	$6,000	⇐(20%) ⇐	$7,500	⇒+20% ⇒	$9,000
Cost of guide salaries (fixed)	4,800		4,800		4,800
Profit	$1,200	⇐(55.6%) ⇐	$2,700	⇒+55.6% ⇒	$4,200

Percentage change in revenue: ±$1,500 ÷ $7,500 = ±20%
Percentage change in profit: ±$1,500 ÷ $2,700 = ±55.6%

Solution to Part 1, Requirement *f*

Since the cost of guide salaries remains fixed while volume (number of climbers) changes, the change in net income, measured in absolute dollars, exactly matches the change in revenue. More specifically, each time MMC increases the number of climbers by one, revenue and net income increase by $1,500. Since the base figure for net income ($2,700) is lower than the base figure for revenue ($7,500), the percentage change in net income ($1,500 ÷ $2,700 = 55.6%) is higher than percentage change in revenue ($1,500 ÷ $7,500). This phenomenon is called *operating leverage.*

Solution for Part 2, Requirement *g*

Number of climbers (a)	4	5	6
Per climber cost of guide salaries (b)	$ 960	$ 960	$ 960
Cost per climber (b × a)	3,840	4,800	5,760

Since the total cost changes in proportion to changes in the number of climbers, the cost is classified as variable. Note that the cost per climber remains constant (stays the same) as the number of climbers increases or decreases. This is the *per unit* behavior pattern of a variable cost.

Solution for Part 2, Requirement *h*

Since the total cost of guide salaries changes proportionately with changes in the number of expeditions, the cost of salaries is also variable relative to the number of expeditions.

Solution for Part 2, Requirements *i, j,* and *k*

Number of Climbers	4	Percentage Change	5	Percentage Change	6
Revenue ($1,500 per climber)	$6,000	⇐(20%) ⇐	$7,500	⇒+20% ⇒	$9,000
Cost of guide salaries (variable)	3,840		4,800		5,760
Profit	$2,160	⇐(20%) ⇐	$2,700	⇒+20% ⇒	$3,240

Percentage change in revenue: ±$1,500 ÷ $7,500 = ±20%
Percentage change in profit: ±$540 ÷ $2,700 = ±20%

Solution for Part 2, Requirement *l*

Since the cost of guide salaries changes when volume (number of climbers) changes, the change in net income is proportionate to the change in revenue. More specifically, each time the number of climbers increases by one, revenue increases by $1,500 and net income increases by $540 ($1,500 − $960). Accordingly, the percentage change in net income will always equal the percentage change in revenue. This means that there is no operating leverage when all costs are variable.

KEY TERMS

activity base 756
contribution margin 751
cost averaging 756
cost behavior 745
cost structure 749
fixed cost 745
high-low method 759
mixed costs (semivariable costs) 758
operating leverage 746
relevant range 755
scattergraph method 760
variable cost 745
visual fit line 760

QUESTIONS

1. Define *fixed cost* and *variable cost* and give an example of each.
2. How can knowing cost behavior relative to volume fluctuations affect decision making?
3. Define the term *operating leverage* and explain how it affects profits.
4. How is operating leverage calculated?
5. Explain the limitations of using operating leverage to predict profitability.
6. If volume is increasing, would a company benefit more from a pure variable or a pure fixed cost structure? Which cost structure would be advantageous if volume is decreasing?
7. When are economies of scale possible? In what types of businesses would you most likely find economies of scale?
8. Explain the risk and rewards to a company that result from having fixed costs.
9. Are companies with predominately fixed cost structures likely to be most profitable?
10. How is the relevant range of activity related to fixed and variable cost? Give an example of how the definitions of these costs become invalid when volume is outside the relevant range.
11. Sam's Garage is trying to determine the cost of providing an oil change. Why would the average cost of this service be more relevant information than the actual cost for each customer?
12. When would the high-low method be appropriate for estimating variable and fixed costs? When would least-squares regression be the most desirable?
13. Which cost structure has the greater risk? Explain.
14. The president of Bright Corporation tells you that he sees a dim future for his company. He feels that his hands are tied because fixed costs are too high. He says that fixed costs do not change and therefore the situation is hopeless. Do you agree? Explain.
15. All costs are variable because if a business ceases operations, its costs fall to zero. Do you agree with the statement? Explain.
16. Because of seasonal fluctuations, Norel Corporation has a problem determining the unit cost of the products it produces. For example, high heating costs during the winter months cause per unit cost to be higher than per unit cost in the summer months even when the same number of units of product is produced. Suggest several ways that Norel can improve the computation of per unit costs.
17. Verna Salsbury tells you that she thinks the terms fixed cost and variable cost are confusing. She notes that fixed cost per unit changes when the number of units changes. Furthermore, variable cost per unit remains fixed regardless of how many units are produced. She concludes that the terminology seems to be backward. Explain why the terminology appears to be contradictory.

EXERCISES—SERIES A

All Exercises in Series A are available with McGraw-Hill's Homework Manager

Exercise 15-1A *Identifying cost behavior* — L.O. 1

Hoover's Kitchen, a fast-food restaurant company, operates a chain of restaurants across the nation. Each restaurant employs eight people; one is a manager paid a salary plus a bonus equal to 3 percent of sales. Other employees, two cooks, one dishwasher, and four waitresses, are paid salaries. Each manager is budgeted $3,000 per month for advertising cost.

Required

Classify each of the following costs incurred by Hoover's Kitchen as fixed, variable, or mixed.

a. Manager's compensation relative to the number of customers.
b. Waitresses' salaries relative to the number of restaurants.
c. Advertising costs relative to the number of customers for a particular restaurant.
d. Rental costs relative to the number of restaurants.
e. Cooks' salaries at a particular location relative to the number of customers.
f. Cost of supplies (cups, plates, spoons, etc.) relative to the number of customers.

L.O. 1

Exercise 15-2A *Identifying cost behavior*

At the various activity levels shown, Taylor Company incurred the following costs.

	Units sold	20	40	60	80	100
a.	Total salary cost	$1,200.00	$1,600.00	$2,000.00	$2,400.00	$2,800.00
b.	Total cost of goods sold	1,800.00	3,600.00	5,400.00	7,200.00	9,000.00
c.	Depreciation cost per unit	240.00	120.00	80.00	60.00	48.00
d.	Total rent cost	3,200.00	3,200.00	3,200.00	3,200.00	3,200.00
e.	Total cost of shopping bags	2.00	4.00	6.00	8.00	10.00
f.	Cost per unit of merchandise sold	90.00	90.00	90.00	90.00	90.00
g.	Rental cost per unit of merchandise sold	36.00	18.00	12.00	9.00	7.20
h.	Total phone expense	80.00	100.00	120.00	140.00	160.00
i.	Cost per unit of supplies	1.00	1.00	1.00	1.00	1.00
j.	Total insurance cost	480.00	480.00	480.00	480.00	480.00

Required

Identify each of these costs as fixed, variable, or mixed.

L.O. 1

Exercise 15-3A *Determining fixed cost per unit*

Simon Corporation incurs the following annual fixed costs:

Item	Cost
Depreciation	$ 30,000
Officers' salaries	100,000
Long-term lease	40,000
Property taxes	10,000

Required

Determine the total fixed cost per unit of production, assuming that Simon produces 4,000, 4,500, or 5,000 units.

L.O. 1

Exercise 15-4A *Determining total variable cost*

The following variable production costs apply to goods made by Keller Manufacturing Corporation.

Item	Cost per Unit
Materials	$5.00
Labor	2.80
Variable overhead	0.40
Total	$8.20

Required

Determine the total variable production cost, assuming that Keller makes 10,000, 15,000, or 20,000 units.

Exercise 15-5A *Fixed versus variable cost behavior*

L.O. 1

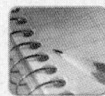

Whaley Company's cost and production data for two recent months included the following:

	January	February
Production (units)	100	200
Rent	$2,000	$2,000
Utilities	$ 500	$1,000

Required

a. Separately calculate the rental cost per unit and the utilities cost per unit for both January and February.

b. Based on both total and per unit amounts, identify which cost is variable and which is fixed. Explain your answer.

Exercise 15-6A *Fixed Versus variable cost behavior*

L.O. 1

Hernadez Trophies makes and sells trophies it distributes to little league ballplayers. The company normally produces and sells between 10,000 and 13,000 trophies per year. The following cost data apply to various activity levels.

Number of trophies	10,000	11,000	12,000	13,000
Total costs incurred				
Fixed	$ 60,000			
Variable	50,000			
Total costs	$110,000			
Cost per unit				
Fixed	$ 6.00			
Variable	5.00			
Total cost per trophy	$11.00			

Required

a. Complete the preceding table by filling in the missing amounts for the levels of activity shown in the first row of the table. Round all cost per unit figures to the nearest whole penny.

b. Explain why the total cost per trophy decreases as the number of trophies increases.

Exercise 15-7A *Fixed versus variable cost behavior*

L.O. 1

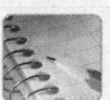

Barlow Entertainment sponsors rock concerts. The company is considering a contract to hire a band at a cost of $50,000 per concert.

Required

a. What are the total band cost and the cost per person if concert attendance is 2,000, 2,500, 3,000, 3,500, or 4,000?

b. Is the cost of hiring the band a fixed or a variable cost?

c. Draw a graph and plot total cost and cost per unit if attendance is 2,000, 2,500, 3,000, 3,500, or 4,000.

d. Identify Barlow's major business risks and explain how they can be minimized.

L.O. 1

Exercise 15-8A *Fixed versus variable cost behavior*

Barlow Entertainment sells souvenir T-shirts at each rock concert that it sponsors. The shirts cost $8 each. Any excess shirts can be returned to the manufacturer for a full refund of the purchase price. The sales price is $12 per shirt.

Required

a. What are the total cost of shirts and cost per shirt if sales amount to 2,000, 2,500, 3,000, 3,500, or 4,000?

b. Is the cost of T-shirts a fixed or a variable cost?

c. Draw a graph and plot total cost and cost per shirt if sales amount to 2,000, 2,500, 3,000, 3,500, or 4,000.

d. Comment on Barlow's likelihood of incurring a loss due to its operating activities.

L.O. 1

Exercise 15-9A *Graphing fixed cost behavior*

The following graphs depict the dollar amount of fixed cost on the vertical axes and the level of activity on the horizontal axes.

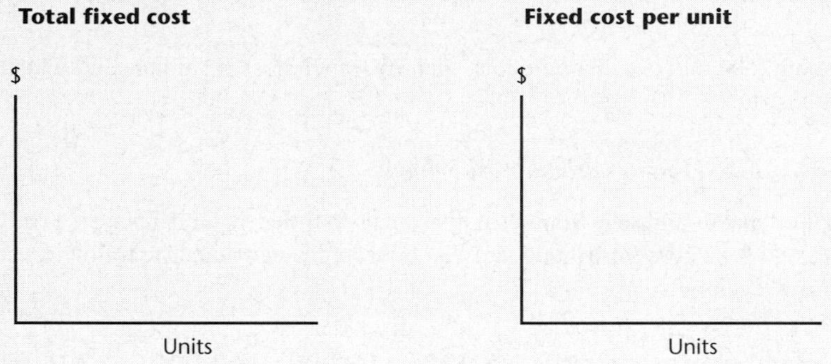

Required

a. Draw a line that depicts the relationship between total fixed cost and the level of activity.

b. Draw a line that depicts the relationship between fixed cost per unit and the level of activity.

L.O. 1

Exercise 15-10A *Graphing variable cost behavior*

The following graphs depict the dollar amount of variable cost on the vertical axes and the level of activity on the horizontal axes.

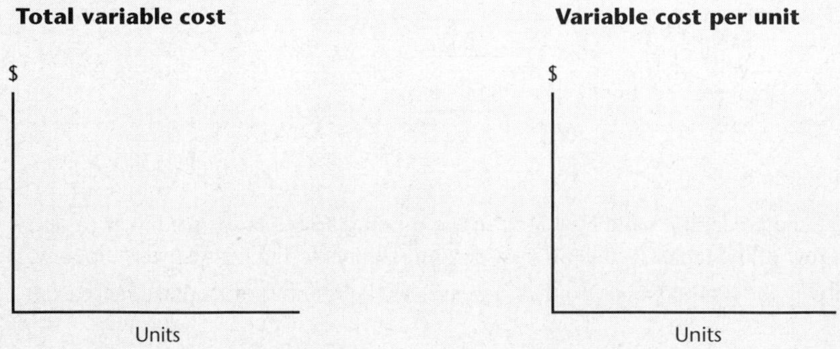

Required

a. Draw a line that depicts the relationship between total variable cost and the level of activity.

b. Draw a line that depicts the relationship between variable cost per unit and the level of activity.

L.O. 1

Exercise 15-11A *Mixed cost at different levels of activity*

Damon Corporation paid one of its sales representatives $5,000 during the month of March. The rep is paid a base salary plus $15 per unit of product sold. During March, the rep sold 200 units.

Required

Calculate the total monthly cost of the sales representative's salary for each of the following months.

Month	April	May	June	July
Number of units sold	240	160	250	160
Total variable cost				
Total fixed cost				
Total salary cost				

Exercise 15-12A ***Using fixed cost as a competitive business strategy*** **L.O. 1, 2, 3, 6**

The following income statements illustrate different cost structures for two competing companies.

Income Statements		
	Company Name	
	Keef	**Reef**
Number of Customers (a)	80	80
Sales Revenue (a × $250)	$20,000	$20,000
Variable Cost (a × $200)	N/A	(16,000)
Variable Cost (a × $0)	0	N/A
Contribution Margin	20,000	4,000
Fixed Cost	(16,000)	0
Net Income	$ 4,000	$ 4,000

Required

a. Reconstruct Keef's income statement, assuming that it serves 160 customers when it lures 80 customers away from Reef by lowering the sales price to $150 per customer.

b. Reconstruct Reef's income statement, assuming that it serves 160 customers when it lures 80 customers away from Keef by lowering the sales price to $150 per customer.

c. Explain why the price-cutting strategy increased Keef Company's profits but caused a net loss for Reef Company.

Exercise 15-13A ***Using contribution margin format income statement to measure the magnitude of operating leverage*** **L.O. 4, 5**

The following income statement was drawn from the records of Mantooth Company, a merchandising firm.

MANTOOTH COMPANY Income Statement For the Year Ended December 31, 2006	
Sales Revenue (3,500 units × $120)	$420,000
Cost of Goods Sold (3,500 units × $64)	(224,000)
Gross Margin	196,000
Sales Commissions (10% of sales)	(42,000)
Administrative Salaries Expense	(60,000)
Advertising Expense	(20,000)
Depreciation Expense	(25,000)
Shipping and Handling Expenses (3,500 units × $4.00)	(14,000)
Net Income	$ 35,000

Required

a. Reconstruct the income statement using the contribution margin format.

b. Calculate the magnitude of operating leverage.

c. Use the measure of operating leverage to determine the amount of net income Mantooth will earn if sales increase by 10 percent.

L.O. 5

Exercise 15-14A *Assessing the magnitude of operating leverage*

The following income statement applies to Lyons Company for the current year:

Income Statement	
Sales Revenue (400 units × $25)	$10,000
Variable Cost (400 units × $10)	(4,000)
Contribution Margin	6,000
Fixed Costs	(3,500)
Net Income	$ 2,500

Required

a. Use the contribution margin approach to calculate the magnitude of operating leverage.

b. Use the operating leverage measure computed in Requirement *a* to determine the amount of net income that Lyons Company will earn if it experiences a 20 percent increase in revenue. The sales price per unit is not affected.

c. Verify your answer to Requirement *b* by constructing an income statement based on a 20 percent increase in sales revenue. The sales price is not affected. Calculate the percentage change in net income for the two income statements.

L.O. 8

Exercise 15-15A *Averaging costs*

Mallory Camps Inc. leases the land on which it builds camp sites. Mallory is considering opening a new site on land that requires $2,500 of rental payment per month. The variable cost of providing service is expected to be $4 per camper. The following chart shows the number of campers Mallory expects for the first year of operation of the new site.

Jan.	Feb.	Mar.	Apr.	May	June	July	Aug.	Sept.	Oct.	Nov.	Dec.	Total
150	100	250	250	350	500	700	700	400	250	100	250	4,000

Required

Assuming that Mallory wants to earn $8 per camper, determine the price it should charge for a camp site in February and August.

L.O. 10

Exercise 15-16A *Estimating fixed and variable costs using the high-low method*

Petrosky Boat Company makes inexpensive aluminum fishing boats. Production is seasonal, with considerable activity occurring in the spring and summer. Sales and production tend to decline in the fall and winter months. During 2007, the high point in activity occurred in June when it produced 300 boats at a total cost of $175,000. The low point in production occurred in January when it produced 140 boats at a total cost of $111,000.

Required

Use the high-low method to estimate the amount of fixed cost incurred each month by Petrosky Boat Company.

PROBLEMS—SERIES A

All Problems in Series A are available with McGraw-Hill's Homework Manager

Problem 15-17A *Identifying cost behavior*

L.O. 1

Required

Identify the following costs as fixed or variable.

Costs related to plane trips between San Diego, California, and Orlando, Florida, follow. Pilots are paid on a per trip basis.

a. Pilots' salaries relative to the number of trips flown.
b. Depreciation relative to the number of planes in service.
c. Cost of refreshments relative to the number of passengers.
d. Pilots' salaries relative to the number of passengers on a particular trip.
e. Cost of a maintenance check relative to the number of passengers on a particular trip.
f. Fuel costs relative to the number of trips.

National Union Bank operates several branch offices in grocery stores. Each branch employs a supervisor and two tellers.

g. Tellers' salaries relative to the number of tellers in a particular district.
h. Supplies cost relative to the number of transactions processed in a particular branch.
i. Tellers' salaries relative to the number of customers served at a particular branch.
j. Supervisors' salaries relative to the number of branches operated.
k. Supervisors' salaries relative to the number of customers served in a particular branch.
l. Facility rental costs relative to the size of customer deposits.

Costs related to operating a fast-food restaurant follow.

m. Depreciation of equipment relative to the number of restaurants.
n. Building rental cost relative to the number of customers served in a particular restaurant.
o. Manager's salary of a particular restaurant relative to the number of employees.
p. Food cost relative to the number of customers.
q. Utility cost relative to the number of restaurants in operation.
r. Company president's salary relative to the number of restaurants in operation.
s. Land costs relative to the number of hamburgers sold at a particular restaurant.
t. Depreciation of equipment relative to the number of customers served at a particular restaurant.

Problem 15-18A *Cost behavior and averaging*

L.O. 1

eXcel

mhhe.com/edmonds2007

Jenny Tang has decided to start Tang Cleaning, a residential housecleaning service company. She is able to rent cleaning equipment at a cost of $600 per month. Labor costs are expected to be $50 per house cleaned and supplies are expected to cost $5 per house.

CHECK FIGURES

c. Total supplies cost for cleaning 30 houses: $150

d. Total cost for 20 houses: $1,700

Required

a. Determine the total expected cost of equipment rental and the average expected cost of equipment rental per house cleaned, assuming that Tang Cleaning cleans 10, 20, or 30 houses during one month. Is the cost of equipment a fixed or a variable cost?
b. Determine the total expected cost of labor and the average expected cost of labor per house cleaned, assuming that Tang Cleaning cleans 10, 20, or 30 houses during one month. Is the cost of labor a fixed or a variable cost?
c. Determine the total expected cost of supplies and the average expected cost of supplies per house cleaned, assuming that Tang Cleaning cleans 10, 20, or 30 houses during one month. Is the cost of supplies a fixed or a variable cost?
d. Determine the total expected cost of cleaning houses, assuming that Tang Cleaning cleans 10, 20, or 30 houses during one month.

e. Determine the average expected cost per house, assuming that Tang Cleaning cleans 10, 20, or 30 houses during one month. Why does the cost per unit decrease as the number of houses increases?

f. If Ms. Tang tells you that she prices her services at 25 percent above cost, would you assume that she means average or actual cost? Why?

L.O. 1

CHECK FIGURE
b. Average teller cost for 60,000 transactions: $1.33

Problem 15-19A *Context-sensitive nature of cost behavior classifications*

Citizens Bank's start-up division establishes new branch banks. Each branch opens with three tellers. Total teller cost per branch is $80,000 per year. The three tellers combined can process up to 80,000 customer transactions per year. If a branch does not attain a volume of at least 50,000 transactions during its first year of operations, it is closed. If the demand for services exceeds 80,000 transactions, an additional teller is hired, and the branch is transferred from the start-up division to regular operations.

Required

a. What is the relevant range of activity for new branch banks?

b. Determine the amount of teller cost in total and the average teller cost per transaction for a branch that processes 50,000, 60,000, 70,000, or 80,000 transactions. In this case (the activity base is the number of transactions for a specific branch), is the teller cost a fixed or a variable cost?

c. Determine the amount of teller cost in total and the average teller cost per branch for Citizens Bank, assuming that the start-up division operates 10, 15, 20, or 25 branches. In this case (the activity base is the number of branches), is the teller cost a fixed or a variable cost?

L.O. 1

eXcel

mhhe.com/edmonds2007

CHECK FIGURES
a. Average cost at 300 units: $225
b. Average price at 150 units: $310

Problem 15-20A *Context-sensitive nature of cost behavior classifications*

Adriane Dawkins operates a sales booth in computer software trade shows, selling an accounting software package, *Accountech.* She purchases the package from a software manufacturer for $200 each. Booth space at the convention hall costs $7,500 per show.

Required

a. Sales at past trade shows have ranged between 100 and 300 software packages per show. Determine the average cost of sales per unit if Ms. Dawkins sells 100, 150, 200, 250, or 300 units of *Accountech* at a trade show. Use the following chart to organize your answer. Is the cost of booth space fixed or variable?

	Sales Volume in Units (a)				
	100	150	200	250	300
Total cost of software (a × $200)	$20,000				
Total cost of booth rental	7,500				
Total cost of sales (b)	$27,500				
Average cost per unit (b ÷ a)	$275.00				

b. If Ms. Dawkins wants to earn a $60 profit on each package of software she sells at a trade show, what price must she charge at sales volumes of 100, 150, 200, 250, or 300 units?

c. Record the total cost of booth space if Ms. Dawkins attends one, two, three, four, or five trade shows. Record your answers in the following chart. Is the cost of booth space fixed or variable relative to the number of shows attended?

	Number of Trade Shows Attended				
	1	2	3	4	5
Total cost of booth rental	$7,500				

d. Ms. Dawkins provides decorative shopping bags to customers who purchase software packages. Some customers take the bags; others do not. Some customers stuff more than one software package into a single bag. The number of bags varies in relation to the number of units sold, but the relationship is not proportional. Assume that Ms. Dawkins uses $40 of bags for every 50 software packages sold. What is the additional cost per unit sold? Is the cost fixed or variable?

Problem 15-21A *Effects of operating leverage on profitability*

L.O. 2

excel

mhhe.com/edmonds2007

Smartt Training Services (STS) provides instruction on the use of computer software for the employees of its corporate clients. It offers courses in the clients' offices on the clients' equipment. The only major expense STS incurs is instructor salaries; it pays instructors $4,000 per course taught. STS recently agreed to offer a course of instruction to the employees of Cartee Incorporated at a price of $360 per student. Cartee estimated that 20 students would attend the course.

Base your answer on the preceding information.

CHECK FIGURES
Part 1, b: $3,200
Part 2, c: 10%
Part 3, a: cost per student for 22 students: $20

Part 1:

Required

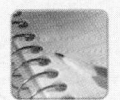

a. Relative to the number of students in a single course, is the cost of instruction a fixed or a variable cost?
b. Determine the profit, assuming that 20 students attend the course.
c. Determine the profit, assuming a 10 percent increase in enrollment (i.e., enrollment increases to 22 students). What is the percentage change in profitability?
d. Determine the profit, assuming a 10 percent decrease in enrollment (i.e., enrollment decreases to 18 students). What is the percentage change in profitability?
e. Explain why a 10 percent shift in enrollment produces more than a 10 percent shift in profitability. Use the term that identifies this phenomenon.

Part 2:

The instructor has offered to teach the course for a percentage of tuition fees. Specifically, she wants $200 per person attending the class. Assume that the tuition fee remains at $360 per student.

Required

f. Is the cost of instruction a fixed or a variable cost?
g. Determine the profit, assuming that 20 students take the course.
h. Determine the profit, assuming a 10 percent increase in enrollment (i.e., enrollment increases to 22 students). What is the percentage change in profitability?
i. Determine the profit, assuming a 10 percent decrease in enrollment (i.e., enrollment decreases to 18 students). What is the percentage change in profitability?
j. Explain why a 10 percent shift in enrollment produces a proportional 10 percent shift in profitability.

Part 3:

STS sells a workbook with printed material unique to each course to each student who attends the course. Any workbooks that are not sold must be destroyed. Prior to the first class, STS printed 20 copies of the books based on the client's estimate of the number of people who would attend the course. Each workbook costs $20 and is sold to course participants for $32. This cost includes a royalty fee paid to the author and the cost of duplication.

Required

k. Calculate the workbook cost in total and per student, assuming that 18, 20, or 22 students attempt to attend the course.
l. Classify the cost of workbooks as fixed or variable relative to the number of students attending the course.
m. Discuss the risk of holding inventory as it applies to the workbooks.
n. Explain how a just-in-time inventory system can reduce the cost and risk of holding inventory.

Problem 15-22A *Effects of fixed and variable cost behavior on the risk and rewards of business opportunities*

L.O. 2, 3, 6

Autumn and Zogby Universities offer executive training courses to corporate clients. Autumn pays its instructors $6,000 per course taught. Zogby pays its instructors $300 per student enrolled in the class. Both universities charge executives a $360 tuition fee per course attended.

CHECK FIGURES
a. Zogby NI: $1,200
b. NI: $2,000

Required

a. Prepare income statements for Autumn and Zogby, assuming that 20 students attend a course.

b. Autumn University embarks on a strategy to entice students from Zogby University by lowering its tuition to $200 per course. Prepare an income statement for Autumn, assuming that the university is successful and enrolls 40 students in its course.

c. Zogby University embarks on a strategy to entice students from Autumn University by lowering its tuition to $200 per course. Prepare an income statement for Zogby, assuming that the university is successful and enrolls 40 students in its course.

d. Explain why the strategy described in Requirement *b* produced a profit but the same strategy described in Requirement *c* produced a loss.

e. Prepare income statements for Autumn and Zogby Universities, assuming that 15 students attend a course, assuming that both universities charge executives a $360 tuition fee per course attended.

f. It is always better to have fixed than variable cost. Explain why this statement is false.

g. It is always better to have variable than fixed cost. Explain why this statement is false.

L.O. 5

excel

mhhe.com/edmonds2007

CHECK FIGURES
b. % of change for Bailey: 50
c. % of change for Morton: (20)

Problem 15-23A *Analyzing operating leverage*

Norm Champion is a venture capitalist facing two alternative investment opportunities. He intends to invest $500,000 in a start-up firm. He is nervous, however, about future economic volatility. He asks you to analyze the following financial data for the past year's operations of the two firms he is considering and give him some business advice.

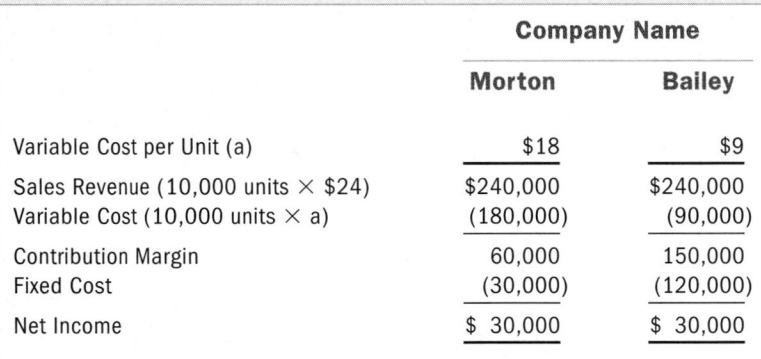

	Company Name	
	Morton	**Bailey**
Variable Cost per Unit (a)	$18	$9
Sales Revenue (10,000 units × $24)	$240,000	$240,000
Variable Cost (10,000 units × a)	(180,000)	(90,000)
Contribution Margin	60,000	150,000
Fixed Cost	(30,000)	(120,000)
Net Income	$ 30,000	$ 30,000

Required

a. Use the contribution margin approach to compute the operating leverage for each firm.

b. If the economy expands in coming years, Morton and Bailey will both enjoy a 10 percent per year increase in sales, assuming that the selling price remains unchanged. Compute the change in net income for each firm in dollar amount and in percentage. (*Note:* Since the number of units increases, both revenue and variable cost will increase.)

c. If the economy contracts in coming years, Morton and Bailey will both suffer a 10 percent decrease in sales volume, assuming that the selling price remains unchanged. Compute the change in net income for each firm in dollar amount and in percentage. (*Note:* Since the number of units decreases, both total revenue and total variable cost will decrease.)

d. Write a memo to Norm Champion with your analyses and advice.

L.O. 8

CHECK FIGURES
a. Monday: $3.20
b. Friday: $4.78

Problem 15-24A *Selecting the appropriate time period for cost averaging*

Fernandez Cinemas is considering a contract to rent a movie for $1,600 per day. The contract requires a minimum one-week rental period. Estimated attendance is as follows:

Monday	Tuesday	Wednesday	Thursday	Friday	Saturday	Sunday
500	400	100	500	900	1,000	600

Required

a. Determine the average cost per person of the movie rental contract separately for each day.

b. Suppose that Fernandez chooses to price movie tickets at cost as computed in Requirement *a* plus $3.00. What price would it charge per ticket on each day of the week?

c. Use weekly averaging to determine a reasonable price to charge for movie tickets.

d. Comment on why weekly averaging may be more useful to business managers than daily averaging.

Problem 15-25A *Identifying relevant issues for cost averaging*

L.O. 8

Mountaintop Inc. offers mountain-climbing expeditions for its customers, providing food, equipment, and guides. Climbs normally require one week to complete. The company's accountant is reviewing historical cost data to establish a pricing strategy for the coming year. The accountant has prepared the following table showing cost data for the most recent climb, the company's average cost per year, and the five-year average cost.

	Span of Time		
	Recent Climb	**One Year**	**Five Years**
Total cost of climbs (a)	$9,000	$524,800	$1,550,000
Number of climbers (b)	12	640	2,500
Cost per climber (a ÷ b)	$750	$820	$620

Required

Write a memo that explains the potential advantages and disadvantages of using each of the per unit cost figures as a basis for establishing a price to charge climbers during the coming year. What other factors must be considered in developing a pricing strategy?

Problem 15-26A *Estimating fixed and variable cost*

L.O. 10

CHECK FIGURE
b. FC = $1,540

Dorough Computer Services, Inc., has been in business for six months. The following are basic operating data for that period.

	Month					
	July	**Aug.**	**Sept.**	**Oct.**	**Nov.**	**Dec.**
Service hours	120	136	260	420	320	330
Revenue	$6,000	$6,800	$13,000	$21,000	$16,000	$16,500
Operating costs	$4,300	$5,300	$ 7,100	$11,200	$ 9,100	$10,600

Required

a. What is the average service revenue per hour for the six-month time period?

b. Use the high-low method to estimate the total monthly fixed cost and the variable cost per hour.

c. Determine the average contribution margin per hour.

d. Use the scattergraph method to estimate the total monthly fixed cost and the variable cost per hour.

e. Compare the results of the two methods and comment on the difference.

Problem 15-27A *Estimating fixed and variable cost*

L.O. 10

CHECK FIGURE
c. VC/unit: $5

Zassoda Handcrafts Inc. manufactures "antique" wooden cabinets to house modern radio and CD players. ZHI began operations in January of last year. Marie Lamb, the owner, asks for your assistance. She believes that she needs to better understand the cost of the cabinets for pricing purposes. You have collected the following data concerning actual production over the past year:

Month	Number of Cabinets Produced	Total Cost
January	800	$22,000
February	3,600	33,500
March	1,960	30,500
April	600	19,600
May	1,600	30,000
June	1,300	28,000
July	1,100	26,600
August	1,800	32,000
September	2,280	33,000
October	2,940	32,500
November	3,280	33,000
December	400	17,500

Required

a. To understand the department's cost behavior, you decide to plot the points on graph paper and sketch a total cost line.
 (1) Enter the number of units and their costs in increasing order.
 (2) Plot the points on the graph.
 (3) Sketch a line so the line "splits" all of the points (half of the points appear above and half below the line).

b. Using the line you just sketched, visually estimate the total cost to produce 2,000 units.

c. Using the high-low method, compute the total cost equation for the preceding data.
 (1) Compute the variable cost per unit.
 (2) Compute total fixed costs.
 (3) Assemble the total cost equation.
 (4) Sketch a line between the high and low points on your graph.

d. Using the high-low method, estimate the total cost to produce 2,000 units.

e. After discussing the results with your classmates, decide which method you believe is better.

EXERCISES—SERIES B

L.O. 1

Exercise 15-1B *Identifying cost behavior*

Zulu Copies Inc. provides professional copying services to customers through the 15 copy stores it operates in the southwestern United States. Each store employs a manager and four assistants. The manager earns $4,000 per month plus a bonus of 3 percent of sales. The assistants earn hourly wages. Each copy store costs $3,000 per month to lease. The company spends $5,000 per month on corporate-level advertising and promotion.

Required

Classify each of the following costs incurred by Zulu Copies as fixed, variable, or mixed.

a. Store manager's salary relative to the number of copies made for customers.

b. Cost of paper relative to the number of copies made for customers.

c. Lease cost relative to the number of stores.

d. Advertising and promotion costs relative to the number of copies a particular store makes.

e. Lease cost relative to the number of copies made for customers.

f. Assistants' wages relative to the number of copies made for customers.

Exercise 15-2B ***Identifying cost behavior*** **L.O. 1**

At the various sales levels shown, Attala Company incurred the following costs.

	Units sold	50	100	150	200	250
a.	Total shipping cost	$ 40.00	$ 80.00	$ 120.00	$ 160.00	$ 200.00
b.	Rent cost per unit of merchandise sold	12.00	6.00	4.00	3.00	2.40
c.	Total utility cost	200.00	300.00	400.00	500.00	600.00
d.	Supplies cost per unit	4.00	4.00	4.00	4.00	4.00
e.	Total insurance cost	500.00	500.00	500.00	500.00	500.00
f.	Total salary cost	1,500.00	2,000.00	2,500.00	3,000.00	3,500.00
g.	Cost per unit of merchandise sold	8.00	8.00	8.00	8.00	8.00
h.	Total cost of goods sold	4,000.00	8,000.00	12,000.00	16,000.00	20,000.00
i.	Depreciation cost per unit	30.00	15.00	10.00	7.50	6.00
j.	Total rent cost	600.00	600.00	600.00	600.00	600.00

Required

Identify each of these costs as fixed, variable, or mixed.

Exercise 15-3B ***Determining fixed cost per unit*** **L.O. 1**

Bali Corporation incurs the following annual fixed production costs:

Item	Cost
Insurance cost	$ 80,000
Patent amortization cost	1,500,000
Depreciation cost	750,000
Property tax cost	100,000

Required

Determine the total fixed production cost per unit if Bali produces 10,000, 20,000, or 50,000 units.

Exercise 15-4B ***Determining total variable cost*** **L.O. 1**

The following variable manufacturing costs apply to goods produced by Orlando Manufacturing Corporation.

Item	Cost per Unit
Materials	$3.00
Labor	2.00
Variable overhead	1.00
Total	$6.00

Required

Determine the total variable manufacturing cost if Orlando produces 4,000, 6,000, or 8,000 units.

L.O. 1

Exercise 15-5B *Fixed versus variable cost behavior*

Larose Company's production and total cost data for two recent months follow.

	January	February
Units produced	400	800
Total depreciation cost	$4,000	$4,000
Total factory supplies cost	$2,000	$4,000

Required

a. Separately calculate the depreciation cost per unit and the factory supplies cost per unit for both January and February.

b. Based on total and per unit amounts, identify which cost is variable and which is fixed. Explain your answer.

L.O. 1

Exercise 15-6B *Fixed versus variable cost behavior*

Professional Chairs Corporation produces ergonomically designed chairs favored by architects. The company normally produces and sells from 5,000 to 8,000 chairs per year. The following cost data apply to various production activity levels.

Number of Chairs	5,000	6,000	7,000	8,000
Total costs incurred				
Fixed	$ 84,000			
Variable	60,000			
Total costs	$144,000			
Per unit chair cost				
Fixed	$ 16.80			
Variable	12.00			
Total cost per chair	$ 28.80			

Required

a. Complete the preceding table by filling in the missing amounts for the levels of activity shown in the first row of the table.

b. Explain why the total cost per chair decreases as the number of chairs increases.

L.O. 1

Exercise 15-7B *Fixed versus variable cost behavior*

Bo Shuttler needs extra money quickly because his mother's sudden hospitalization has resulted in unexpected medical bills. Mr. Shuttler has learned fortune-telling skills through his long friendship with Frank Lopez, who tells fortunes during the day at the city market. Mr. Lopez has agreed to let Mr. Shuttler use his booth to tell fortunes during the evening for a rent of $50 per night.

Required

a. What is the booth rental cost both in total and per customer if the number of customers is 5, 10, 15, 20, or 25?

b. Is the cost of renting the fortune-telling booth fixed or variable relative to the number of customers?

c. Draw two graphs. On one, plot total booth rental cost for 5, 10, 15, 20, and 25 customers; on the other, plot booth rental cost per customer for 5, 10, 15, 20, or 25 customers.

d. Mr. Shuttler has little money. What major business risks would he take by renting the fortune-telling booth? How could he minimize those risks?

Exercise 15-8B *Fixed versus variable cost behavior* — L.O. 1

In the evenings, Bo Shuttler works telling fortunes using his friend Frank Lopez's booth at the city market. Mr. Lopez pays the booth rental, so Mr. Shuttler has no rental cost. As a courtesy, Mr. Shuttler provides each customer a soft drink. The drinks cost him $0.50 per customer.

Required

a. What is the soft drink cost both in total and per customer if the number of customers is 5, 10, 15, 20, or 25?

b. Is the soft drink cost fixed or variable?

c. Draw two graphs. On one, plot total soft drink cost for 5, 10, 15, 20, and 25 customers; on the other, plot soft drink cost per customer for 5, 10, 15, 20, and 25 customers.

d. Comment on the likelihood that Mr. Shuttler will incur a loss on this business venture.

Exercise 15-9B *Graphing fixed cost behavior* — L.O. 1

Rudolf Computers leases space in a mall at a monthly rental cost of $3,000. The following graphs depict rental cost on the vertical axes and activity level on the horizontal axes.

Total monthly rental cost

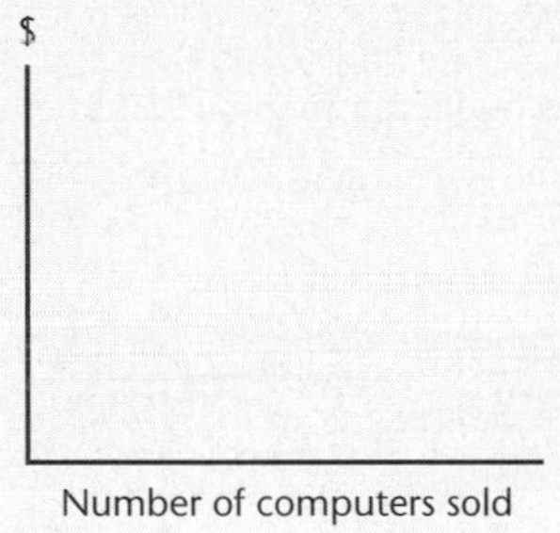

Rental cost per computer

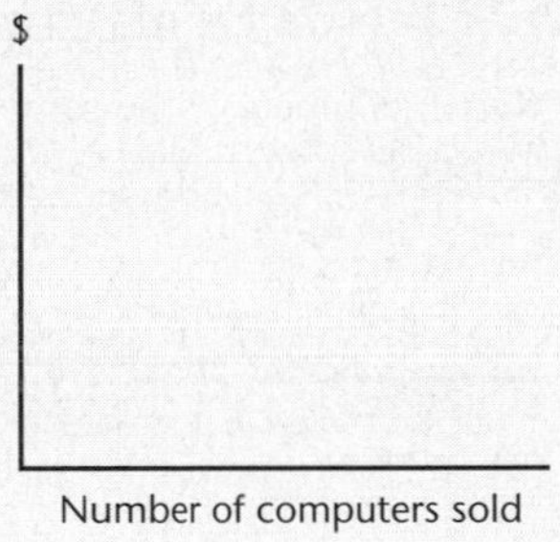

Required

a. Draw a line that depicts the relationship between the total monthly rental cost and the number of computers sold.

b. Draw a line that depicts the relationship between rental cost per computer and the number of computers sold.

Exercise 15-10B *Graphing variable cost behavior* — L.O. 1

Larsen Computers purchases computers from a manufacturer for $500 per computer. The following graphs depict product cost on the vertical axes and activity level on the horizontal axes.

Total product cost

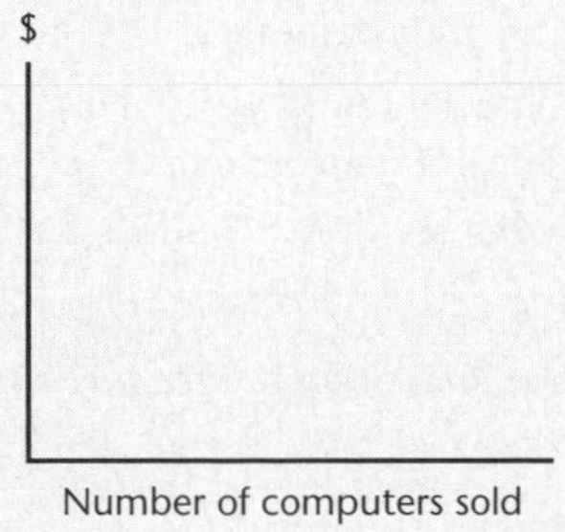

Product cost per computer

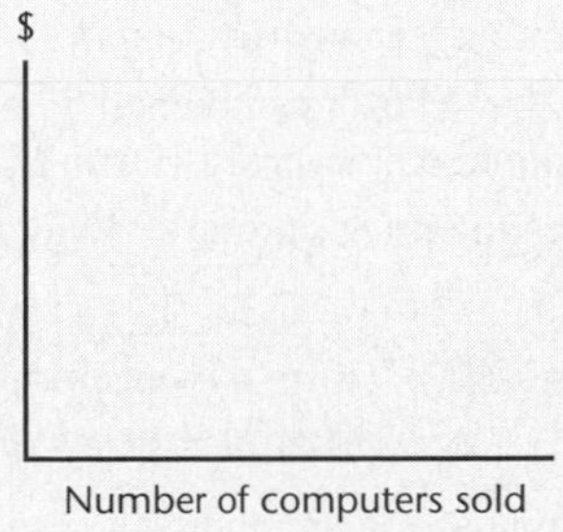

Required

a. Draw a line that depicts the relationship between total product cost and the number of computers sold.

b. Draw a line that depicts the relationship between cost per computer and the number of computers sold.

L.O. 1

Exercise 15-11B *Mixed cost at different levels of activity*

Lebron Hats Corporation uses workers in the Philippines to manually weave straw hats. The company pays the workers a daily base wage plus $0.20 per completed hat. On Monday, workers produced 100 hats for which the company paid wages of $30.

Required

Calculate the total cost of the workers' wages for each of the following days.

Day	Monday	Tuesday	Wednesday	Thursday
Number of hats woven	100	120	160	80
Total variable cost				
Total fixed cost				
Total wages cost				

L.O. 1, 2, 3, 6

Exercise 15-12B *Effect of cost structure on projected profits*

Logan and Martin compete in the same market. The following budgeted income statements illustrate their cost structures.

Income Statements		
	Company	
	Logan	Martin
Number of Customers (a)	80	80
Sales Revenue (a × $125)	$10,000	$10,000
Variable Cost (a × $80)	NA	(6,400)
Contribution Margin	10,000	3,600
Fixed Costs	(6,400)	0
Net Income	$ 3,600	$ 3,600

Required

a. Assume that Logan can lure all 80 customers away from Martin by lowering its sales price to $75 per customer. Reconstruct Logan's income statement based on 160 customers.

b. Assume that Martin can lure all 80 customers away from Logan by lowering its sales price to $75 per customer. Reconstruct Martin's income statement based on 160 customers.

c. Why does the price-cutting strategy increase Logan's profits but result in a net loss for Martin?

L.O. 3

Exercise 15-13B *Using a contribution margin format income statement to measure the magnitude of operating leverage*

Dothan Company, a merchandising firm, reported the following operating results.

Income Statement	
Sales Revenue (7,500 units × $80)	$600,000
Cost of Goods Sold (7,500 units × $48)	(360,000)
Gross Margin	240,000
Sales Commissions (10% of sales revenue)	(60,000)
Administrative Salaries Expense	(67,000)
Advertising Expense	(20,000)
Depreciation Expense	(41,000)
Shipping and Handling Expense (7,500 units × $1.60)	(12,000)
Net Income	$ 40,000

Required

a. Reconstruct the income statement using the contribution margin format.

b. Calculate the magnitude of operating leverage.

c. Use the measure of operating leverage to determine the amount of net income that Dothan will earn if sales revenue increases by 10 percent.

Exercise 15-14B *Assessing the magnitude of operating leverage* L.O. 5

The following budgeted income statement applies to Hope Company:

Income Statement	
Sales Revenue (600 units × $90)	$54,000
Variable Cost (600 units × $50)	(30,000)
Contribution Margin	24,000
Fixed Costs	(16,000)
Net Income	$ 8,000

Required

a. Use the contribution margin approach to calculate the magnitude of operating leverage.

b. Use the operating leverage measure computed in Requirement *a* to determine the amount of net income that Hope Company will earn if sales volume increases by 10 percent. Assume the sales price per unit remains unchanged at $90.

c. Verify your answer to Requirement *b* by constructing an alternative income statement based on a 10 percent increase in sales volume. The sales price per unit remains unchanged at $90. Calculate the percentage change in net income for the two income statements.

Exercise 15-15B *Averaging costs* L.O. 8

Nassar Entertainment Inc. operates a movie theater that has monthly fixed expenses of $9,000. In addition, the company pays film distributors $1.50 per ticket sold. The following chart shows the number of tickets Nassar expects to sell in the coming year:

Jan.	Feb.	Mar.	Apr.	May	June	July	Aug.	Sept.	Oct.	Nov.	Dec.	Total
2,600	1,400	3,000	3,600	4,000	4,800	6,000	5,400	4,200	3,000	3,800	3,200	45,000

Required

Assume that Nassar wants to earn $2.50 per movie patron. What price should it charge for a ticket in January and in September?

L.O. 10

Exercise 15-16B *Estimating fixed and variable costs using the high-low method*

Carmichael Ice Cream Company produces various ice cream products for which demand is highly seasonal. The company sells more ice cream in warmer months and less in colder ones. Last year, the high point in production activity occurred in August when Carmichael produced 45,000 gallons of ice cream at a total cost of $36,000. The low point in production activity occurred in February when the company produced 21,000 gallons of ice cream at a total cost of $30,000.

Required

Use the high-low method to estimate the amount of fixed cost per month incurred by Carmichael Ice Cream Company.

PROBLEMS—SERIES B

L.O. 1

Problem 15-17B *Identifying cost behavior*

Required

Identify the following costs as fixed or variable.

Costs related to operating a retail gasoline company.

a. The company's cost of national TV commercials relative to the number of stations in operation.
b. Depreciation of equipment relative to the number of customers served at a station.
c. Property and real estate taxes relative to the amount of gasoline sold at a particular station.
d. Depreciation of equipment relative to the number of stations.
e. Cashiers' wages relative to the number of customers served in a station.
f. Salary of a manager of a particular station relative to the number of employees.
g. Gasoline cost relative to the number of customers.
h. Utility cost relative to the number of stations in operation.

Costs related to shuttle bus trips between Chicago's O'Hare Intercontinental Airport and downtown Chicago. Each bus driver receives a specific salary per month. A manager schedules bus trips and supervises drivers, and a secretary receives phone calls.

i. Fuel costs relative to the number of passengers on a particular trip.
j. Drivers' salaries relative to the number of trips driven.
k. Office staff salaries relative to the number of passengers on a particular trip.
l. Depreciation relative to the number of buses in service.
m. A driver's salary relative to the number of passengers on a particular trip.
n. Fuel costs relative to the number of trips.

Janet's Barbershop operates several stores in shopping centers. Each store employs a supervisor and three barbers. Each barber receives a specific salary per month plus a 10 percent commission based on the service revenues he or she has generated.

o. Store rental costs relative to the number of customers.
p. Barbers' commissions relative to the number of customers.
q. Supervisory salaries relative to the number of customers served in a particular store.
r. Barbers' salaries relative to the number of barbers in a particular district.
s. Supplies cost relative to the number of hair services provided in a particular store.
t. Barbers' salaries relative to the number of customers served at a particular store.

L.O. 1

Problem 15-18B *Cost behavior and averaging*

Gene Solarz asks you to analyze the operating cost of his lawn services business. He has bought the needed equipment with a cash payment of $27,000. Upon your recommendation, he agrees to adopt straight-line depreciation. The equipment has an expected life of three years and no salvage value. Mr. Solarz pays his workers $30 per lawn service. Material costs, including fertilizer, pesticide, and supplies, are expected to be $6 per lawn service.

Required

a. Determine the total cost of equipment depreciation and the average cost of equipment depreciation per lawn service, assuming that Mr. Solarz provides 20, 25, or 30 lawn services during one month. Is the cost of equipment a fixed or a variable cost?

b. Determine the total expected cost of labor and the average expected cost of labor per lawn service, assuming that Mr. Solarz provides 20, 25, or 30 lawn services during one month. Is the cost of labor a fixed or a variable cost?

c. Determine the total expected cost of materials and the average expected cost of materials per lawn service, assuming that Mr. Solarz provides 20, 25, or 30 lawn services during one month. Is the cost of fertilizer, pesticide, and supplies a fixed or a variable cost?

d. Determine the total expected cost per lawn service, assuming that Mr. Solarz provides 20, 25, or 30 lawn services during one month.

e. Determine the average expected cost per lawn service, assuming that Mr. Solarz provides 20, 25, or 30 lawn services during one month. Why does the cost per unit decrease as the number of lawn services increases?

f. If Mr. Solarz tells you that he prices his services at 30 percent above cost, would you assume that he means average or actual cost? Why?

Problem 15-19B *Context-sensitive nature of cost behavior classifications*

L.O. 1

Sanchez and Adams Tax Services' Development Department is responsible for establishing new community branches. Each branch opens with two tax accountants. Total cost of payroll per branch is $75,000 per year. Together the two accountants can process up to 2,500 simple tax returns per year. The firm's policy requires closing branches that do not reach the quota of 1,500 tax returns per year. On the other hand, the firm hires an additional accountant for a branch and elevates it to the status of a regular operation if the customer demand for services exceeds 2,500 tax returns.

Required

a. What is the relevant range of activity for a new branch established by the Development Department?

b. Determine the amount of payroll cost in total and the average payroll cost per transaction for a branch that processes 1,500, 2,000, or 2,500 tax returns. In this case (the activity base is the number of tax returns for a specific branch), is the payroll cost a fixed or a variable cost?

c. Determine the amount of payroll cost in total and the average payroll cost per branch for Sanchez and Adams Tax Services, assuming that the Development Department operates 20, 30, or 40 branches. In this case (the activity base is the number of branches), is the payroll cost a fixed or a variable cost?

Problem 15-20B *Context-sensitive nature of cost behavior classifications*

L.O. 1

Bill Lankey sells a newly developed camera, Superb Image. He purchases the cameras from the manufacturer for $150 each and rents a store in a shopping mall for $5,000 per month.

Required

a. Determine the average cost of sales per unit if Mr. Lankey sells 100, 200, 300, 400, or 500 units of Superb Image per month. Use the following chart to organize your answer.

	Sales Volume in Units (a)				
	100	200	300	400	500
Total cost of cameras (a × $150)	$15,000				
Total cost of store rental	5,000				
Total cost of sales (b)	$20,000				
Average cost per unit (b ÷ a)	$200.00				

b. If Mr. Lankey wants to make a gross profit of $20 on each camera he sells, what price should he charge at sales volumes of 100, 200, 300, 400, or 500 units?

c. Record the total cost of store rental if Mr. Lankey opens a camera store at one, two, three, four, or five shopping malls. Record your answers in the following chart. Is the cost of store rental fixed or variable relative to the number of stores opened?

	Malls				
	1	2	3	4	5
Total cost of store rental	$5,000				

d. Mr. Lankey provides decorative ornaments to customers who purchase cameras. Some customers take the ornaments, others do not, and some take more than one. The number of ornaments varies in relation to the number of cameras sold, but the relationship is not proportional. Assume that, on average, Mr. Lankey gives away $150 worth of ornaments for every 100 cameras sold. What is the additional cost per camera sold? Is the cost fixed or variable?

L.O. 2

Problem 15-21B *Effects of operating leverage on profitability*

CMAs R Us conducts CMA review courses. Public universities that permit free use of a classroom support the classes. The only major expense incurred by CMAs R Us is the salary of instructors, which is $10,000 per course taught. The company recently planned to offer a review course in Boston for $500 per candidate; it estimated that 60 candidates would attend the course. Complete these requirements based on the preceding information.

Part 1:

Required

a. Relative to the number of CMA candidates in a single course, is the cost of instruction a fixed or a variable cost?

b. Determine the profit, assuming that 60 candidates attend the course.

c. Determine the profit, assuming a 10 percent increase in enrollment (i.e., enrollment increases to 66 students). What is the percentage change in profitability?

d. Determine the profit, assuming a 10 percent decrease in enrollment (i.e., enrollment decreases to 54 students). What is the percentage change in profitability?

e. Explain why a 10 percent shift in enrollment produces more than a 10 percent shift in profitability. Use the term that identifies this phenomenon.

Part 2:

The instructor has offered to teach the course for a percentage of tuition fees. Specifically, he wants $250 per candidate attending the class. Assume that the tuition fee remains at $500 per candidate.

Required

f. Is the cost of instruction a fixed or a variable cost?

g. Determine the profit, assuming that 60 candidates take the course.

h. Determine the profit, assuming a 10 percent increase in enrollment (i.e., enrollment increases to 66 students). What is the percentage change in profitability?

i. Determine the profit, assuming a 10 percent decrease in enrollment (i.e., enrollment decreases to 54 students). What is the percentage change in profitability?

j. Explain why a 10 percent shift in enrollment produces a proportional 10 percent shift in profitability.

Part 3:

CMAs R Us sells a workbook to each student who attends the course. The workbook contains printed material unique to each course. Workbooks that are not sold must be destroyed. Prior to the first class, CMAs R Us printed 60 copies of the books based on the estimated number of people who would attend the course. Each workbook costs $40 and is sold for $50. This cost includes a royalty fee paid to the author and the cost of duplication.

Required

k. Calculate the total cost and the cost per candidate of the workbooks, assuming that 54, 60, or 66 candidates attempt to attend the course.

l. Classify the cost of workbooks as fixed or variable relative to the number of candidates attending the course.

m. Discuss the risk of holding inventory as it applies to the workbooks.

n. Explain how a just-in-time inventory system can reduce the cost and risk of holding inventory.

Problem 15-22B ***Effects of fixed and variable cost behavior on the risk and rewards of business opportunities***

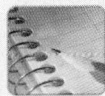

L.O. 2, 3, 6

Hoover Club and Beaver Club are competing health and recreation clubs in Seattle. They both offer tennis training clinics to adults. Hoover pays its coaches $6,000 per season. Beaver pays its coaches $200 per student enrolled in the clinic per season. Both clubs charge a tuition fee of $300 per season.

Required

a. Prepare income statements for Hoover and Beaver, assuming that 30 students per season attend each clinic.

b. The ambitious new director of Hoover Club tries to increase his market share by reducing the club's tuition per student to $180 per clinic. Prepare an income statement for Hoover, assuming that the club attracts all of Beaver's customers and therefore is able to enroll 60 students in its clinics.

c. Independent of Requirement *b,* Beaver Club tries to lure Hoover's students by lowering its price to $180 per student. Prepare an income statement for Beaver, assuming that the club succeeds in enrolling 60 students in its clinics.

d. Explain why the strategy described in Requirement *b* produced a profit while the same strategy described in Requirement *c* produced a loss.

e. Prepare an income statement for Hoover Club and Beaver Club, assuming that 18 students attend a clinic at the original $300 tuition price.

f. It is always better to have fixed rather than variable cost. Explain why this statement is false.

g. It is always better to have variable rather than fixed cost. Explain why this statement is false.

Problem 15-23B ***Analysis of operating leverage***

L.O. 7, 8

Wendy Ludman has invested in two start-up companies. At the end of the first year, she asks you to evaluate their operating performance. The following operating data apply to the first year.

	Company Name	
	Nanya	**Tatung**
Variable cost per unit (a)	$30	$15
Sales revenue (20,000 units × $45)	$900,000	$900,000
Variable cost (20,000 units × a)	(600,000)	(300,000)
Contribution margin	300,000	600,000
Fixed cost	(150,000)	(450,000)
Net income	$150,000	$150,000

Required

a. Use the contribution margin approach to compute the operating leverage for each firm.

b. If the economy expands in the coming year, Nanya and Tatung will both enjoy a 10 percent per year increase in sales volume, assuming that the selling price remains unchanged. (*Note:* Since the number of units increases, both revenue and variable cost will increase.) Compute the change in net income for each firm in dollar amount and in percentage.

c. If the economy contracts in the following year, Nanya and Tatung will both suffer a 10 percent decrease in sales volume, assuming that the selling price remains unchanged. (*Note:* Since the number of units decreases, both revenue and variable cost decrease.) Compute the change in net income for each firm in both dollar amount and percentage.

d. Write a memo to Wendy Ludman with your evaluation and recommendations.

L.O. 8

Problem 15-24B ***Selecting the appropriate time period for cost averaging***

The Greenland Amusement Park is considering signing a contract to hire a circus at a cost of $2,700 per day. The contract requires a minimum performance period of one week. Estimated circus attendance is as follows:

Monday	Tuesday	Wednesday	Thursday	Friday	Saturday	Sunday
600	500	450	700	960	1,450	1,340

Required

a. For each day, determine the average cost of the circus contract per person attending.

b. Suppose that the park prices circus tickets at cost as computed in Requirement *a* plus $1.80. What would be the price per ticket charged on each day of the week?

c. Use weekly averaging to determine a reasonable price to charge for the circus tickets.

d. Comment on why weekly averaging may be more useful to business managers than daily averaging.

L.O. 7

Problem 15-25B ***Identifying relevant issues for cost averaging***

Arizona Tours Inc. organizes adventure tours for people interested in visiting a desert environment. A desert tour generally lasts three days. Arizona provides food, equipment, and guides. Victor Vladmyer, the president of Arizona Tours, needs to set prices for the coming year. He has available the company's past cost data in the following table.

	Span of Time		
	Recent Tour	**One Year**	**Ten Years**
Total cost of tours (a)	$8,100	$456,000	$3,150,000
Number of tourists (b)	30	1,600	14,000
Cost per tourist (a ÷ b)	$270	$285	$225

Required

Write a memo to Mr. Vladmyer explaining the potential advantages and disadvantages of using each of the different per tourist cost figures as a basis for establishing a price to charge tourists during the coming year. What other factors must Mr. Vladmyer consider in developing a pricing strategy?

L.O. 10

Problem 15-26B ***Estimating fixed and variable costs***

Chapman Legal Services provides legal advice to clients. The following data apply to the first six months of operation.

	Month					
	Jan.	**Feb.**	**Mar.**	**Apr.**	**May**	**June**
Service hours	50	80	125	140	170	195
Revenue	$4,000	$6,400	$10,000	$11,200	$13,600	$15,600
Operating costs	6,200	7,100	8,380	8,500	8,761	9,680

Required

a. What is the average service revenue per hour for the six-month time period?

b. Use the high-low method to estimate the total monthly fixed cost and the variable cost per hour.

c. Determine the average contribution margin per hour.

d. Use the scattergraph method to estimate the total monthly fixed cost and the variable cost per hour.

e. Compare the results of the two methods and comment on any differences.

Problem 15-27B *Estimating fixed and variable cost*

L.O. 10

Pretty Frames Inc. (PFI) which manufactures ornate frames for original art work, began operations in January 2005. Justin Jamail, the owner, asks for your assistance. He believes that he needs to better understand the cost of the frames for pricing purposes. You have collected the following data concerning actual production over the past year:

Month	Number of Frames Produced	Total Cost
January	1,600	$42,000
February	7,200	65,000
March	3,920	59,000
April	1,200	37,200
May	3,200	58,000
June	2,600	54,000
July	2,200	51,200
August	3,600	62,000
September	4,560	64,000
October	5,880	63,000
November	6,560	64,000
December	800	33,000

Required

a. To understand the department's cost behavior, you decide to plot the points on graph paper and sketch a total cost line.

(1) Enter the number of units and their costs in increasing order.

(2) Plot the points on the graph.

(3) Sketch a line so the line "splits" all of the points (half of the points appear above and half appear below the line).

b. Using the line you just sketched, visually estimate the total cost to produce 4,000 units.

c. Using the high-low method, compute the total cost equation for the preceding data.

(1) Compute the variable cost per unit.

(2) Compute total fixed costs.

(3) Assemble the total cost equation.

(4) Sketch a line between the high and low points on your graph.

d. Using the high-low method, estimate the total cost to produce 4,000 units.

e. After discussing the results with your classmates, decide which method you believe is better.

ANALYZE, THINK, COMMUNICATE

ATC 15-1 Business Applications *Operating leverage*

The following information was taken from the Form 10-K SEC filings for **CSX Corporation** and **Starbucks Corporation**. It is from the 2002 fiscal year reports, and all dollar amounts are in millions.

Description of Business for CSX Corporation

CSX Corporation (CSX or the Company), operates one of the largest rail networks in the United States and also provides intermodal transportation services across the United States and key markets in Canada and Mexico. Its marine operations include an international terminal services company and a domestic container-shipping company.

CSX Corporation	2002	2001
Operating revenues	$8,172	$8,110
Operating earnings	424	293

Description of Business for Starbucks Corporation

Starbucks Corporation (together with its subsidiaries, Starbucks or the Company) purchases and roasts high-quality whole bean coffees and sells them, along with fresh, rich-brewed coffees, Italian-style espresso beverages, cold blended beverages, a variety of pastries and confections, coffee-related accessories and equipment, a selection of premium teas, and a line of compact discs primarily through Company-operated retail stores.

At fiscal year-end, Starbucks had 3,496 Company-operated stores in 43 states, the District of Columbia, and five Canadian provinces (which comprise the Company's North American Retail operating segment), as well as 322 stores in the United Kingdom, 33 stores in Australia, and 29 stores in Thailand.

Starbucks	2002	2001
Operating revenues	$3,289	$2,649
Operating earnings	319	281

Required

a. Determine which company appears to have the higher operating leverage.

b. Write a paragraph or two explaining why the company you identified in Requirement *a* might be expected to have the higher operating leverage.

c. If revenues for both companies declined, which company do you think would likely experience the greatest decline in operating earnings? Explain your answer.

ATC 15-2 Group Assignment *Operating leverage*

The Parent Teacher Association (PTA) of Meadow High School is planning a fund-raising campaign. The PTA is considering the possibility of hiring Eric Logan, a world-renowned investment counselor, to address the public. Tickets would sell for $28 each. The school has agreed to let the PTA use Harville Auditorium at no cost. Mr. Logan is willing to accept one of two compensation arrangements. He will sign an agreement to receive a fixed fee of $10,000 regardless of the number of tickets sold. Alternatively, he will accept payment of $20 per ticket sold. In communities similar to that in which Meadow is located, Mr. Logan has drawn an audience of approximately 500 people.

Required

a. In front of the class, present a statement showing the expected net income assuming 500 people buy tickets.

b. Divide the class into groups and then organize the groups into four sections. Assign one of the following tasks to each section of groups.

Group Tasks

(1) Assume the PTA pays Mr. Logan a fixed fee of $10,000. Determine the amount of net income that the PTA will earn if ticket sales are 10 percent higher than expected. Calculate the percentage change in net income.

(2) Assume that the PTA pays Mr. Logan a fixed fee of $10,000. Determine the amount of net income that the PTA will earn if ticket sales are 10 percent lower than expected. Calculate the percentage change in net income.

(3) Assume that the PTA pays Mr. Logan $20 per ticket sold. Determine the amount of net income that the PTA will earn if ticket sales are 10 percent higher than expected. Calculate the percentage change in net income.

(4) Assume that the PTA pays Mr. Logan $20 per ticket sold. Determine the amount of net income that the PTA will earn if ticket sales are 10 percent lower than expected. Calculate the percentage change in net income.

c. Have each group select a spokesperson. Have one of the spokespersons in each section of groups go to the board and present the results of the analysis conducted in Requirement *b.* Resolve any discrepancies in the computations presented at the board and those developed by the other groups.

d. Draw conclusions regarding the risks and rewards associated with operating leverage. At a minimum, answer the following questions.

(1) Which type of cost structure (fixed or variable) produces the higher growth potential in profitability for a company?

(2) Which type of cost structure (fixed or variable) produces the higher risk of declining profitability for a company?

(3) Under what circumstances should a company seek to establish a fixed cost structure?

(4) Under what circumstances should a company seek to establish a variable cost structure?

ATC 15-3 Research Assignment *Fixed versus variable cost*

The March 8, 2004, edition of *BusinessWeek* contained an article titled "Courting the Mass Affluent" (see page 68). The article discusses the efforts of **Charles Schwab Corp.** to attract a bigger share of investors who have $100,000 to $1 million to invest. Read this article and complete the following requirements.

Required

a. Schwab increased its marketing budget during the first quarter of 2004. What was the amount of the increase? Is this cost fixed or variable relative to the number of new customers that the company attracts?

b. Assume that Schwab acquires a significant number of new customers. Name several costs that are likely to remain fixed as revenue increases.

c. Assume that Schwab acquires a significant number of new customers. Name several costs that are likely to vary with increasing revenue.

d. Consider the cost of establishing a new customer account. Describe a set of circumstances under which this would be a fixed cost and a different set of circumstances under which this would be a variable cost.

ATC 15-4 Writing Assignment *Cost averaging*

Candice Sterling, a veterinarian, has always been concerned for the pets of low-income families. These families love their pets but frequently do not have the means to provide them proper veterinary care. Dr. Sterling decided to open a part-time veterinary practice in a low-income neighborhood. She plans to volunteer her services free of charge two days per week. Clients will be charged only for the actual costs of materials and overhead. Dr. Sterling leased a small space for $300 per month. Utilities and other miscellaneous costs are expected to be approximately $180 per month. She estimates the variable cost of materials to be approximately $10 per pet served. A friend of Dr. Sterling who runs a similar type of clinic in another area of town indicates that she should expect to treat the following number of pets during her first year of operation.

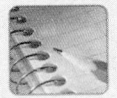

Jan.	Feb.	Mar.	Apr.	May	June	July	Aug.	Sept.	Oct.	Nov.	Dec.
18	26	28	36	42	54	63	82	42	24	20	15

Dr. Sterling's friend has noticed that visits increase significantly in the summer because children who are out of school tend to bring their pets to the vet more often. Business tapers off during the winter and reaches a low point in December when people spend what little money they have on holiday presents for their children. After looking at the data, Dr. Sterling became concerned that the people in the neighborhood would not be able to afford pet care during some months of operation even if it is offered at cost. For example, the cost of providing services in December would be approximately $42 per pet treated ($480 overhead ÷ 15 pets = $32 per pet, plus $10 materials cost). She is willing to provide her services free of charge, but she cannot afford to subsidize the practice further by personally paying for the costs of materials and overhead in the months of low activity. She decides to discuss the matter with her accountant to find a way to cut costs even more. Her accountant tells her that her problem is cost *measurement* rather than cost *cutting.*

Required

Assume that you are Dr. Sterling's accountant. Write a memo describing a pricing strategy that resolves the apparent problem of high costs during months of low volume. Recommend in your memo the price to charge per pet treated during the month of December.

ATC 15-5 Ethical Dilemma *Profitability versus social conscience (effects of cost behavior)*

Advances in biological technology have enabled two research companies, Bio Labs Inc. and Scientific Associates, to develop an insect-resistant corn seed. Neither company is financially strong enough to develop the distribution channels necessary to bring the product to world markets. World Agra Distributors Inc. has negotiated contracts with both companies for the exclusive right to market their seed. Bio Labs signed an agreement to receive an annual royalty of $1,000,000. In contrast, Scientific Associates chose an agreement that provides for a royalty of $0.50 per pound of seed sold. Both agreements have a 10-year term. During 2004, World Agra sold approximately 1,600,000 pounds of the Bio Labs Inc. seed and 2,400,000 pounds of the Scientific Associates seed. Both types of seed were sold for $1.25 per pound. By the end of 2004, it was apparent that the seed developed by Scientific Associates was superior. Although insect infestation was virtually nonexistent for both types of seed, the seed developed by Scientific Associates produced corn that was sweeter and had consistently higher yields.

World Agra Distributors' chief financial officer, Roger Weatherstone, recently retired. To the astonishment of the annual planning committee, Mr. Weatherstone's replacement, Ray Borrough, adamantly recommended that the marketing department develop a major advertising campaign to promote the seed developed by Bio Labs Inc. The planning committee reluctantly approved the recommendation. A $100,000 ad campaign was launched; the ads emphasized the ability of the Bio Labs seed to avoid insect infestation. The campaign was silent with respect to taste or crop yield. It did not mention the seed developed by Scientific Associates. World Agra's sales staff was instructed to push the Bio Labs seed and to sell the Scientific Associates seed only on customer demand. Although total sales remained relatively constant during 2005, sales of the Scientific Associates seed fell to approximately 1,300,000 pounds while sales of the Bio Labs Inc. seed rose to 2,700,000 pounds.

Required

a. Determine the amount of increase or decrease in profitability experienced by World Agra in 2005 as a result of promoting Bio Labs seed. Support your answer with appropriate commentary.

b. Did World Agra's customers in particular and society in general benefit or suffer from the decision to promote the Bio Labs seed?

c. Review the standards of ethical conduct in Exhibit 14.13 of Chapter 14 and comment on whether Mr. Borrough's recommendation violated any of the standards in the code of ethical conduct.

d. Comment on your belief regarding the adequacy of the Standards of Ethical Conduct for Managerial Accountants to direct the conduct of management accountants.

COMPREHENSIVE PROBLEM

Use the same transaction data for Magnificent Modems Inc. as was used in Chapter 14 (see page 742).

Required

a. Based on these data, identify each cost incurred by the company as (1) fixed versus variable relative to the number of units produced and sold; and (2) product versus general, selling, and administrative (G, S, & A). The solution for the first item is shown as an example.

Cost Item	Fixed	Variable	Product	G,S,&A
Depreciation on manufacturing equipment	X		X	
Direct materials				
Direct labor				
Production supplies				
Rent on manufacturing facility				
Sales commissions				
Depreciation on administrative equipment				
Administrative costs (rent and salaries)				

b. Replace the question marks in the following table to indicate the product cost per unit assuming levels of production of 5,000, 6,000, 7,000, and 8,000 units.

Cost of goods sold	$455,000	?	?	?
Divided by number of units	5,000	6,000	7,000	8,000
Cost per unit	$91	?	?	?

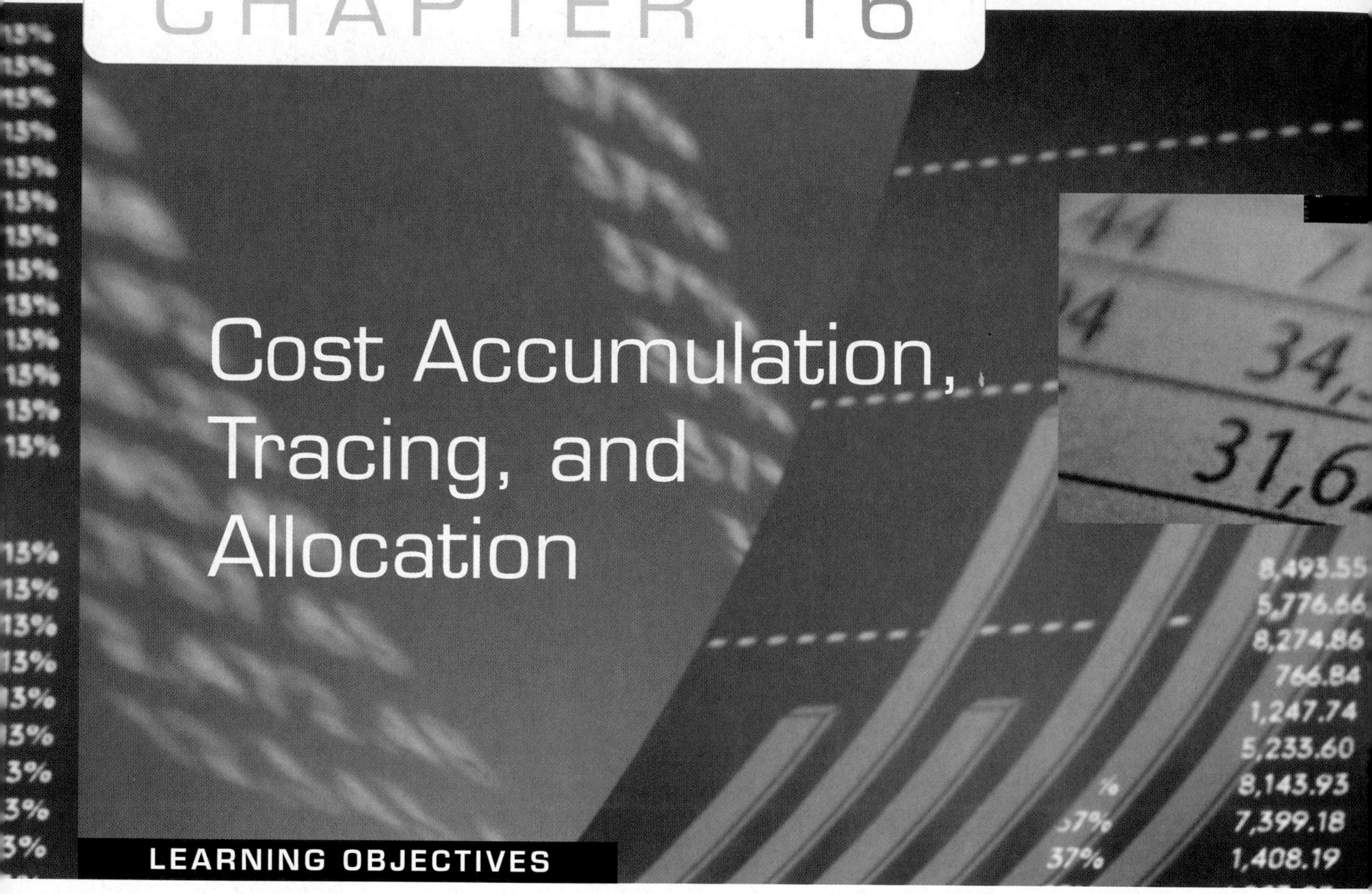

CHAPTER 16

Cost Accumulation, Tracing, and Allocation

LEARNING OBJECTIVES

After you have mastered the material in this chapter, you will be able to:

1. **Describe the relationships among cost objects, cost drivers, and cost accumulation.**
2. **Distinguish direct costs from indirect costs.**
3. **Use basic mathematics to compute indirect cost allocations.**
4. **Select appropriate cost drivers for allocating indirect costs in a variety of different circumstances.**
5. **Use allocation to solve problems that emerge in the process of making cost-plus pricing decisions.**
6. **Explain why companies establish indirect cost pools.**
7. **Explain the nature and allocation of joint product and by-product common costs.**
8. **Recognize human motivation as a key variable in the allocation process.**

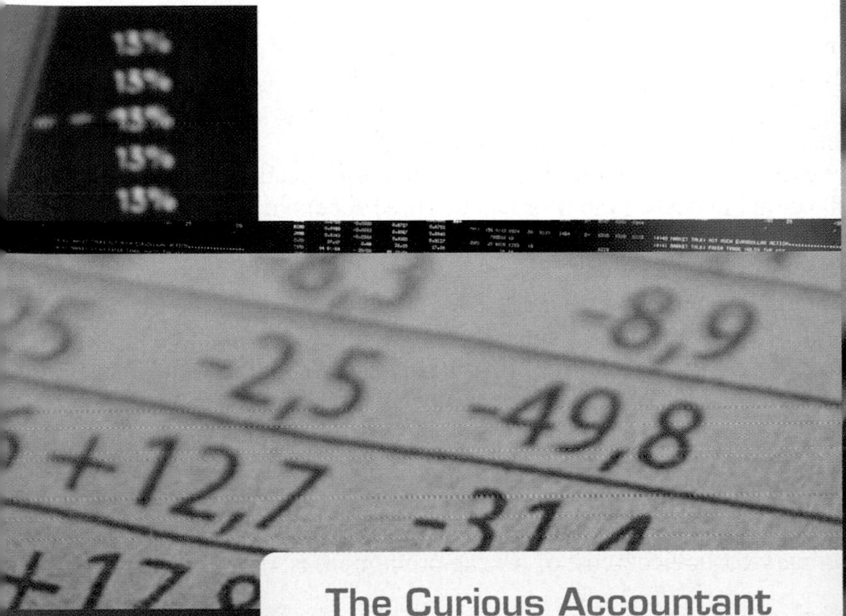

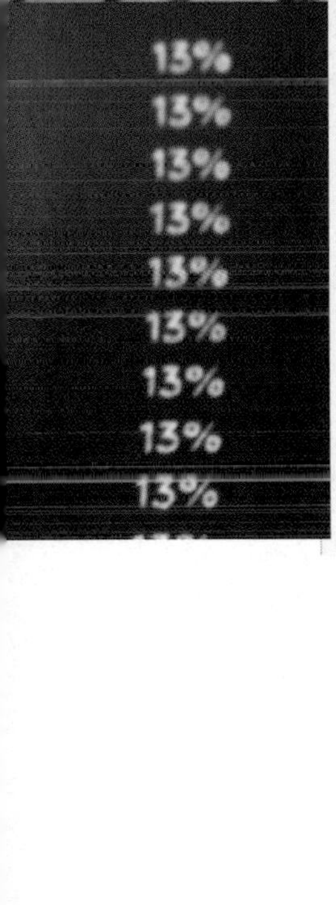

Chapter 16

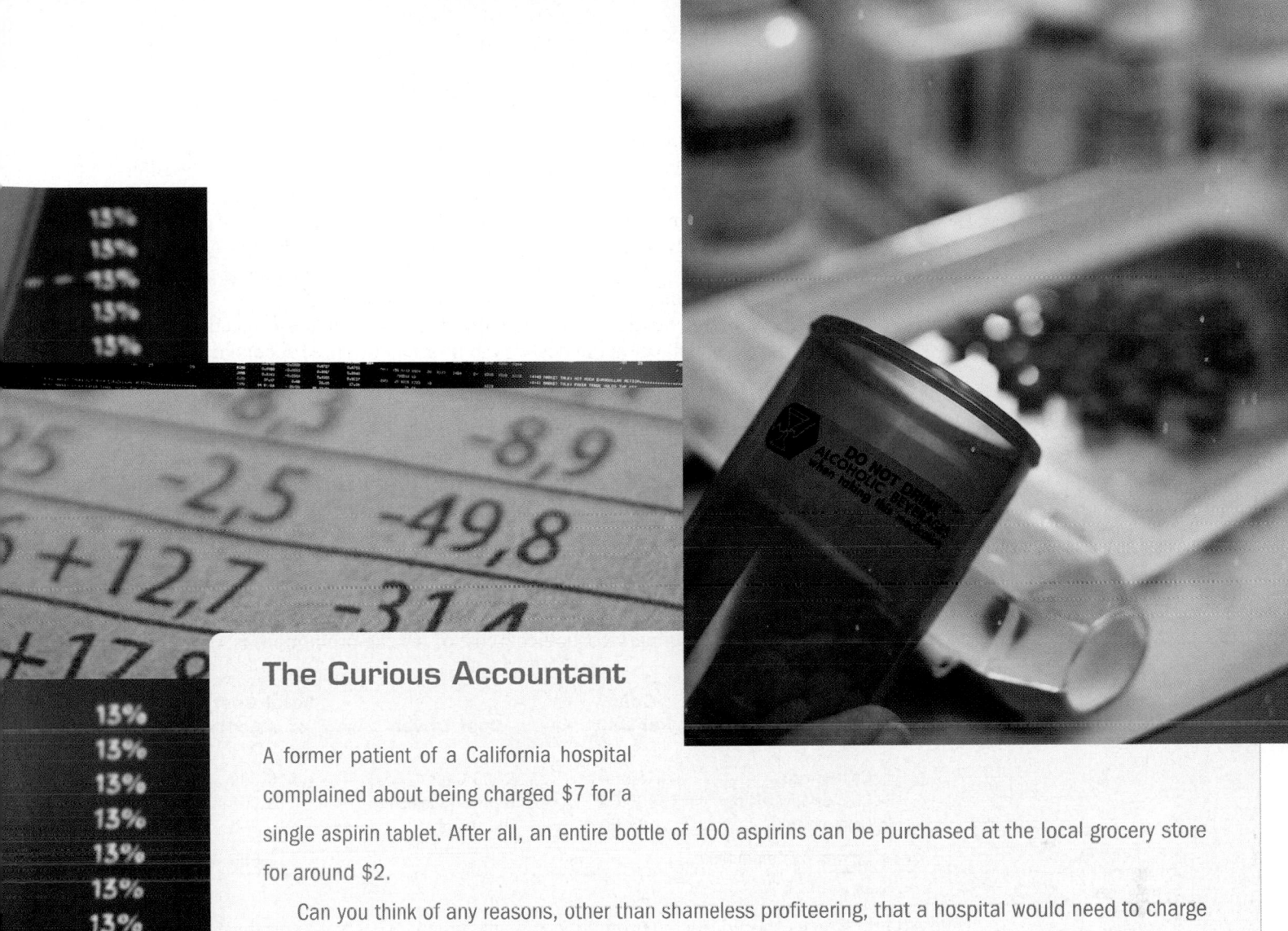

The Curious Accountant

A former patient of a California hospital complained about being charged $7 for a single aspirin tablet. After all, an entire bottle of 100 aspirins can be purchased at the local grocery store for around $2.

Can you think of any reasons, other than shameless profiteering, that a hospital would need to charge $7 for an aspirin? Remember that the hospital is not just selling the aspirin; it is also delivering it to the patient. (Answer on page 801.)

CHAPTER OPENING

What does it cost? This is one of the questions most frequently asked by business managers. Managers must have reliable cost estimates to price products, evaluate performance, control operations, and prepare financial statements. As this discussion implies, managers need to know the cost of many different things. The things we are trying to determine the cost of are commonly called **cost objects.** *For example, if we are trying to determine the cost of operating a department, that department is the cost object. Cost objects may be products, processes, departments, services, activities, and so on. This chapter explains techniques managerial accountants use to determine the cost of a variety of cost objects.* ■

Use of Cost Drivers to Accumulate Costs

LO 1

Describe the relationships among cost objects, cost drivers, and cost accumulation.

Accountants use **cost accumulation** to determine the cost of a particular object. Suppose the Atlanta Braves advertising manager wants to promote a Tuesday night ball game by offering free baseball caps to all children who attend. What would the promotion cost? The team's accountant must *accumulate* many individual costs and add them together. For simplicity consider only three cost components: (1) the cost of the caps, (2) the cost of advertising the promotion, and (3) the cost of an employee to work on the promotion.

Cost accumulation begins with identifying the cost objects. The primary cost object is the cost of the promotion. Three secondary cost objects are (1) the cost of caps, (2) the cost of advertising, and (3) the cost of labor. The costs of the secondary cost objects are combined to determine the cost of the primary cost object.

Determining the costs of the secondary cost objects requires identifying what *drives* those costs. A **cost driver** has a *cause-and-effect* relationship with a cost object. For example, the *number of caps* (cost driver) has an effect on the *cost of caps* (cost object). The *number of advertisements* is a cost driver for the *advertising cost* (cost object); the *number of labor* hours worked is a cost driver for the *labor cost* (cost object). Using the following assumptions about unit costs and cost drivers, the accumulated cost of the primary cost object (cost of the cap promotion) is:

Cost Object	Cost Per Unit	×	Cost Driver	=	Total Cost of Object
Cost of caps	$2.50	×	4,000 Caps	=	$10,000
Cost of advertising	$100.00	×	50 Advertisements	=	5,000
Cost of labor	$8.00	×	100 Hours	=	800
Cost of cap promotion					$15,800

The Atlanta Braves should run the promotion if management expects it to produce additional revenues exceeding $15,800.

Estimated Versus Actual Cost

The accumulated cost of the promotion—$15,800—is an *estimate.* Management cannot know *actual* costs and revenues until after running the promotion. While actual information is more accurate, it is not relevant for deciding whether to run the promotion because the decision must be made before the actual cost is known. Managers must accept a degree of inaccuracy in exchange for the relevance of timely information. Many business decisions are based on estimated rather than actual costs.

Managers use cost estimates to set prices, bid on contracts, evaluate proposals, distribute resources, plan production, and set goals. Certain circumstances, however, require actual cost data. For example, published financial reports and managerial performance evaluations use actual cost data. Managers frequently accumulate both estimated and actual cost data for the same cost object. For example, companies use cost estimates to establish goals and use actual costs to evaluate management performance in meeting those goals. The following discussion provides a number of business examples that use estimated data, actual data, or a combination of both.

Assignment of Cost to Objects in a Retail Business

Exhibit 16.1 displays the January income statement for In Style, Inc. (ISI), a retail clothing store. ISI subdivides its operations into women's, men's, and children's departments. To encourage the departmental managers to maximize sales, ISI began paying the manager of each department a bonus based on a percentage of departmental sales revenue.

Although the bonus incentive increased sales revenue, it also provoked negative consequences. The departmental managers began to argue over floor space; each manager wanted more space to display merchandise. The managers reduced prices; they increased sales commissions. In the drive to maximize sales, the managers ignored the need to control costs. To improve the situation, the store manager decided to base future bonuses on each department's contribution to profitability rather than its sales revenue.

EXHIBIT 16.1

Income Statement

IN STYLE, INC. Income Statement For the Month Ended January 31	
Sales	$360,000
Cost of Goods Sold	(216,000)
Gross Margin	144,000
Sales Commissions	(18,000)
Dept. Managers' Salaries	(12,000)
Store Manager's Salary	(9,360)
Depreciation	(16,000)
Rental Fee for Store	(18,400)
Utilities	(2,300)
Advertising	(7,200)
Supplies	(900)
Net income	$ 59,840

Identifying Direct Versus Indirect Costs

The new bonus strategy requires determining the cost of operating each department. Each department is a separate *cost object*. Assigning costs to the departments (cost objects) requires **cost tracing** and cost allocation. **Direct costs** can be easily traced to a cost object. **Indirect costs** cannot be easily traced to a cost object. Whether or not a cost is easily traceable requires *cost/benefit analysis.*

Some of ISI's costs can be easily traced to the cost objects (specific departments). The cost of goods sold is an example of an easily traced cost. Price tags on merchandise can be coded so cash register scanners capture the departmental code for each sale. The cost of goods sold is not only easily traceable but also useful information. Companies need cost of goods sold information for financial reporting (income statement) and for management decisions (determining inventory reorder points, pricing strategies, and cost control). Because the cost of tracing *cost of goods sold* is small relative to the benefits obtained, cost of goods sold is a *direct cost.*

LO 2

Distinguish direct costs from indirect costs.

In contrast, the cost of supplies (shopping bags, sales slips, pens, staples, price tags) used by each department is much more difficult to trace. How could the number of staples used to seal shopping bags be traced to any particular department? The sales staff could count the number of staples used, but doing so would be silly for the benefits obtained. Although tracing the cost of supplies to each department may be possible, it is not worth the effort of doing so. The cost of supplies is therefore an *indirect cost*. Indirect costs are also called **overhead costs.**

Direct and indirect costs can be described as follows.

Direct costs can be traced to cost objects in a *cost-effective* manner.
Indirect costs cannot be traced to objects in a *cost-effective* manner.

By analyzing the accounting records, ISI's accountant classified the costs from the income statement in Exhibit 16.1 as direct or indirect, as shown in Exhibit 16.2. The next paragraph explains the classifications.

All figures represent January costs. Items 1 though 4 are direct costs, traceable to the cost objects in a cost-effective manner. Cost of goods sold is traced to departments at the point of sale using cash register scanners. Sales commissions are based on a percentage of departmental sales and are therefore easy to trace to the departments. Departmental managers' salaries are also easily traceable to the departments. Equipment, furniture, and fixtures are tagged with department codes that permit tracing depreciation charges directly to specific departments. Items 5 through 8 are incurred on behalf of the company as a whole and are therefore not directly traceable to a specific department. Although Item 9 could be traced to specific departments, the cost of doing so would exceed the benefits. The cost of supplies is therefore also classified as indirect.

Cost Classifications—Independent and Context Sensitive

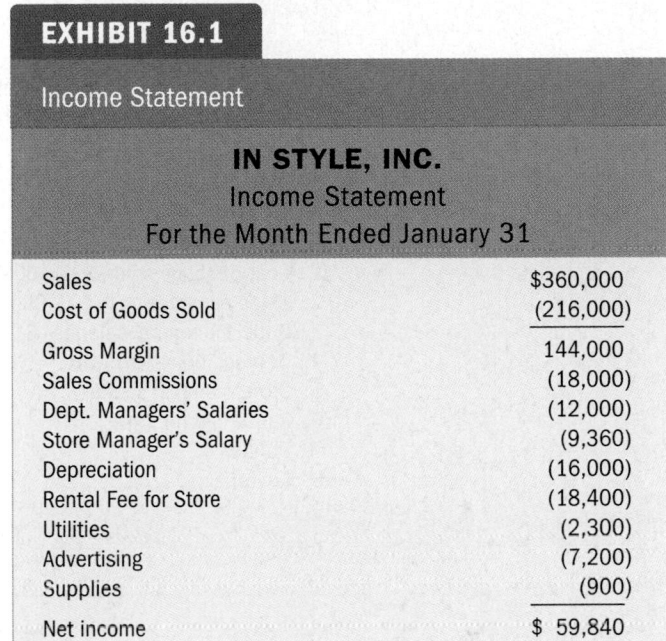

Whether a cost is direct or indirect is independent of whether it is fixed or variable. In the ISI example, both cost of goods sold and the cost of supplies vary relative to sales volume (both

EXHIBIT 16.2

Classification of Income Statement Costs

Cost Item	Direct Costs Women's	Men's	Children's	Indirect Costs
1. Cost of goods sold–$216,000	$120,000	$58,000	$38,000	
2. Sales commissions–$18,000	9,500	5,500	3,000	
3. Dept. managers' salaries–$12,000	5,000	4,200	2,800	
4. Depreciation–$16,000	7,000	5,000	4,000	
5. Store manager's salary				$ 9,360
6. Rental fee for store				18,400
7. Utilities				2,300
8. Advertising				7,200
9. Supplies				900
Totals	$141,500	$72,700	$47,800	$38,160

are variable costs), but cost of goods sold is direct and the cost of supplies is indirect. Furthermore, the cost of rent and the cost of depreciation are both fixed relative to sales volume, but the cost of rent is indirect and the cost of depreciation is direct. In fact, the very same cost can be classified as direct or indirect, depending on the cost object. The store manager's salary is not directly traceable to a specific department, but it is traceable to a particular store.

Similarly, identifying costs as direct or indirect is independent of whether the costs are relevant to a given decision. ISI could avoid both cost of goods sold and the cost of supplies for a particular department if that department were eliminated. Both costs are relevant to a segment elimination decision, yet one is direct, and the other is indirect. You cannot memorize costs as direct or indirect, fixed or variable, relevant or not relevant. When trying to identify costs as to type or behavior, you must consider the context in which the costs occur.

Allocating Indirect Costs to Objects

LO 3

Use basic mathematics to compute indirect cost allocations.

Topic Tackler PLUS

16-1

Cost **allocation** involves dividing a total cost into parts and assigning the parts to designated cost objects. How should ISI allocate the $38,160 of indirect costs to each of the three departments? First, identify a cost driver for each cost to be allocated. For example, there is a cause and effect relationship between store size and rent cost; the larger the building, the higher the rent cost. This relationship suggests that the more floor space a department occupies, the more rent cost that department should bear. To illustrate, assume ISI's store capacity is 23,000 square feet and the women's, men's, and children's departments occupy 12,000, 7,000, and 4,000 square feet, respectively. ISI can achieve a rational allocation of the rent cost using the following two-step process.[1]

Step 1. Compute the *allocation rate* by dividing the *total cost to be allocated* ($18,400 rental fee) by the *cost driver* (23,000 square feet of store space). The *cost driver is also called the* **allocation base.** This computation produces the **allocation rate,** as follows:

Total cost to be allocated	÷	Cost driver (allocation base)	=	Allocation rate
$18,400 rental fee	÷	23,000 square feet	=	$0.80 per square foot

[1] Other mathematical approaches achieve the same result. This text consistently uses the two-step method described here. Specifically, the text determines allocations by (1) computing a *rate* and (2) multiplying the *rate* by the *weight of the base* (cost driver).

REALITY BYTES

How does **Southwest Airlines** know the cost of flying a passenger from Houston, Texas, to Los Angeles, California? The fact is that Southwest does not know the actual cost of flying particular passengers anywhere. There are many indirect costs associated with flying passengers. Some of these include the cost of planes, fuel, pilots, office buildings, and ground personnel. Indeed, besides insignificant food and beverage costs, there are few costs that could be traced directly to customers. Southwest and other airlines must use allocation and averaging to determine the estimated cost of providing transportation services to customers. Estimated rather than actual cost is used for decision-making purposes.

Step 2. Multiply the *allocation rate* by the *weight of the cost driver* (weight of the base) to determine the allocation per *cost object,* as follows:

Cost Object	Allocation Rate	×	Number of Square Feet	=	Allocation per Cost Object
Women's department	$0.80	×	12,000	=	$ 9,600
Men's department	0.80	×	7,000	=	5,600
Children's department	0.80	×	4,000	=	3,200
Total			23,000		$18,400

It is also plausible to presume utilities cost is related to the amount of floor space a department occupies. Larger departments will consume more heating, lighting, air conditioning, and so on than smaller departments. Floor space is a reasonable cost driver for utility cost. Based on square footage, ISI can allocate utility cost to each department as follows:

Step 1. Compute the allocation rate by dividing the total cost to be allocated ($2,300 utility cost) by the cost driver (23,000 square feet of store space):

Total cost to be allocated	÷	Cost driver	=	Allocation rate
$2,300 utility cost	÷	23,000 square feet	=	$0.10 per square foot

Step 2. Multiply the *allocation rate* by the weight of the *cost driver* to determine the allocation per *cost object*:

Cost Object	Allocation Rate	×	Number of Square Feet	=	Allocation per Cost Object
Women's department	$0.10	×	12,000	=	$1,200
Men's department	0.10	×	7,000	=	700
Children's department	0.10	×	4,000	=	400
Total			23,000		$2,300

CHECK YOURSELF 16.1

HealthCare Inc. wants to estimate the cost of operating the three departments (Dermatology, Gynecology, and Pediatrics) that serve patients in its Health Center. Each department performed the following number of patient treatments during the most recent year of operation: Dermatology, 2,600; Gynecology, 3,500; and Pediatrics, 6,200. The annual salary of the Health Center's program administrator is $172,200. How much of the salary cost should HealthCare allocate to the Pediatrics Department?

Answer

Step 1 Compute the *allocation rate.*

Total cost to be allocated	÷	Cost driver (patient treatments)	=	Allocation rate
$172,200 salary cost	÷	(2,600 + 3,500 + 6,200)	=	$14 per patient treatment

Step 2 Multiply the *allocation rate* by the *weight of the cost driver* (weight of the base) to determine the allocation per *cost object.*

Cost Object	Allocation Rate	×	No. of Treatments	=	Allocation per Cost Object
Pediatrics department	$14	×	6,200	=	$86,800

Selecting a Cost Driver

LO 4

Select appropriate cost drivers for allocating indirect costs in a variety of different circumstances.

Topic Tackler PLUS 16-2

Companies can frequently identify more than one cost driver for a particular indirect cost. For example, ISI's shopping bag cost is related to both the *number of sales transactions* and the *volume of sales dollars.* As either of these potential cost drivers increases, shopping bag usage also increases. The most useful cost driver is the one with the strongest cause and effect relationship.

Consider shopping bag usage for T-shirts sold in the children's department versus T-shirts sold in the men's department. Assume ISI studied T-shirt sales during the first week of June and found the following:

Department	Children's	Men's
Number of sales transactions	120	92
Volume of sales dollars	$1,440	$1,612

Given that every sales transaction uses a shopping bag, the children's department uses far more shopping bags than the men's department even though it has a lower volume of sales dollars. A reasonable explanation for this circumstance is that children's T-shirts sell for less than men's T-shirts. The number of sales transactions is the better cost driver because it has a stronger cause and effect relationship with shopping bag usage than does the volume of sales dollars. Should ISI therefore use the number of sales transactions to allocate supply cost to the departments? Not necessarily.

The *availability of information* also influences cost driver selection. Although the number of sales transactions is the more accurate cost driver, ISI could not use this allocation base unless it maintains records of the number of sales transactions per department. If the store tracks the volume of sales dollars but not the number of transactions, it must use dollar volume even if the number of transactions is the better cost driver. For ISI, sales volume in dollars appears to be the best *available* cost driver for allocating supply cost.

Assuming that sales volume for the women's, men's, and children's departments was $190,000, $110,000, and $60,000, respectively, ISI can allocate the supplies cost as follows:

Step 1. Compute the allocation rate by dividing the total cost to be allocated ($900 supplies cost) by the cost driver ($360,000 total sales volume):

Total cost to be allocated	÷	Cost driver	=	Allocation rate
$900 supplies cost	÷	$360,000 sales volume	=	$0.0025 per sales dollar

Step 2. Multiply the allocation rate by the weight of the cost driver to determine the allocation per cost object:

Cost Object	Allocation Rate	×	Sales Volume	=	Allocation per Cost Object
Women's department	$0.0025	×	$190,000	=	$475
Men's department	0.0025	×	110,000	=	275
Children's department	0.0025	×	60,000	=	150
Total			$360,000		$900

ISI believes sales volume is also the appropriate allocation base for advertising cost. The sales generated in each department were likely influenced by the general advertising campaign. ISI can allocate advertising cost as follows:

Step 1. Compute the allocation rate by dividing the total cost to be allocated ($7,200 advertising cost) by the cost driver ($360,000 total sales volume):

Total cost to be allocated	÷	Cost driver	=	Allocation rate
$7,200 advertising cost	÷	$360,000 sales volume	=	$0.02 per sales dollar

Step 2. Multiply the allocation rate by the weight of the cost driver to determine the allocation per cost object:

Cost Object	Allocation Rate	×	Sales Volume	=	Allocation per Cost Object
Women's department	$0.02	×	$190,000	=	$3,800
Men's department	0.02	×	110,000	=	2,200
Children's department	0.02	×	60,000	=	1,200
Total			$360,000		$7,200

There is no strong cause and effect relationship between the store manager's salary and the departments. ISI pays the store manager the same salary regardless of sales level, square footage of store space, number of labor hours, or any other identifiable variable. Because no plausible cost driver exists, ISI must allocate the store manager's salary arbitrarily. Here the manager's salary is simply divided equally among the departments as follows:

Step 1. Compute the allocation rate by dividing the total cost to be allocated ($9,360 manager's monthly salary) by the allocation base (number of departments):

Total cost to be allocated	÷	Cost driver	=	Allocation rate
$9,360 store manager's salary	÷	3 departments	=	$3,120 per department

Step 2. Multiply the allocation rate by the weight of the cost driver to determine the allocation per cost object:

Cost Object	Allocation Rate	×	Number of Departments	=	Allocation per Cost Object
Women's department	$3,120	×	1	=	$3,120
Men's department	3,120	×	1	=	3,120
Children's department	3,120	×	1	=	3,120
Total			3		$9,360

As the allocation of the store manager's salary demonstrates, many allocations are arbitrary or based on a weak relationship between the allocated cost and the allocation base (cost driver). Managers must use care when making decisions using allocated costs.

Behavioral Implications

Using the indirect cost allocations just discussed, Exhibit 16.3 shows the profit each department generated in January. ISI paid the three departmental managers bonuses based on each department's contribution to profitability. The store manager noticed an immediate change in the behavior of the departmental managers. For example, the manager of the women's department offered to give up 1,000 square feet of floor space because she believed reducing the selection of available products would not reduce sales significantly. Customers would simply buy different brands. Although sales would not decline dramatically, rent and utility cost allocations to the women's department would decline, increasing the profitability of the department.

In contrast, the manager of the children's department wanted the extra space. He believed the children's department was losing sales because it did not have enough floor space to display a competitive variety of merchandise. Customers came to the store to shop at the women's department, but they did not come specifically for children's wear. With additional space, the children's department could carry items that would draw customers to the store specifically to buy children's clothing. He believed the extra space would increase sales enough to cover the additional rent and utility cost allocations.

The store manager was pleased with the emphasis on profitability that resulted from tracing and assigning costs to specific departments.

EXHIBIT 16.3

Profit Analysis by Department

	Department			
	Women's	Men's	Children's	Total
Sales	$190,000	$110,000	$60,000	$360,000
Cost of goods sold	(120,000)	(58,000)	(38,000)	(216,000)
Sales commissions	(9,500)	(5,500)	(3,000)	(18,000)
Dept. managers' salary	(5,000)	(4,200)	(2,800)	(12,000)
Depreciation	(7,000)	(5,000)	(4,000)	(16,000)
Store manager's salary	(3,120)	(3,120)	(3,120)	(9,360)
Rental fee for store	(9,600)	(5,600)	(3,200)	(18,400)
Utilities	(1,200)	(700)	(400)	(2,300)
Advertising	(3,800)	(2,200)	(1,200)	(7,200)
Supplies	(475)	(275)	(150)	(900)
Departmental profit	$ 30,305	$ 25,405	$ 4,130	$ 59,840

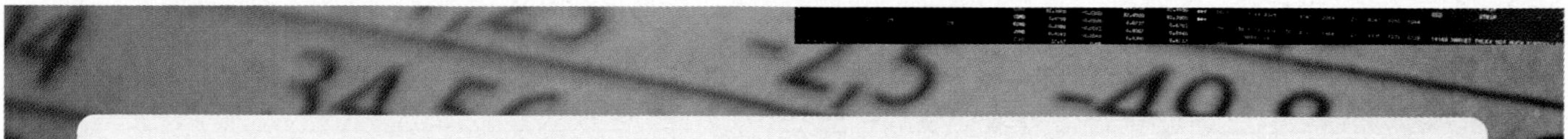

Answers to The Curious Accountant

When we compare the cost that a hospital charges for an aspirin to the price we pay for an aspirin, we are probably not considering the full cost that we incur to purchase aspirin. If someone asks you what you pay for an aspirin, you would probably take the price of a bottle, say $2, and divide it by the number of pills in the bottle, say 100. This would suggest their cost is $.02 each. What does it cost to buy the aspirins when all costs are considered? First, there is your time to drive to the store; what do you get paid per hour? Then, there is the cost of operating your automobile. You get the idea; in reality, the cost of an aspirin, from a business perspective, is much more than just the cost of the pills themselves.

Exhibit 16.4 shows the income statement of Tenent Healthcare Corporation for three recent years. Tenent Healthcare claims to be " . . . the second largest investor-owned health care services company in the United States." In 2002 it operated 114 hospitals with 27,870 beds in 16 states. As you can see, while it generated almost $14 billion in revenue, it also incurred a lot of expenses. Look at its first two expense categories. Although it incurred $2 billion in supplies expenses, it incurred almost three times this amount in compensation expense. In other words, it cost a lot more to have someone deliver the aspirin to your bed than the aspirin itself costs.

In 2002 Tenent earned $785 million from its $13.9 billion in sales. This is a return on sales percentage of 5.6 percent ($785 ÷ $13,913). Therefore, on a $7 aspirin, Tenent would earn 39 cents of profit, which is still not a bad profit for selling one aspirin. As a comparison, in 2002, Kroger's return on sales was 2.3 percent.

EXHIBIT 16.4

TENENT HEALTHCARE CORPORATION
Consolidated Statements of Income
(Dollars in Millions)

	Years ended May 31		
	2000	**2001**	**2002**
Net operating revenues	$11,414	$12,053	$13,913
Operating expenses:			
Salaries and benefits	4,508	4,680	5,346
Supplies	1,595	1,677	1,960
Provision for doubtful accounts	851	849	986
Other operating expenses	2,525	2,603	2,824
Depreciation	411	428	472
Goodwill amortization	94	00	101
Other amortization	28	27	31
Impairment of goodwill and long-lived assets and restructuring charges	355	143	99
Loss from early extinguishment of debt	–	56	383
Operating income	1,047	1,491	1,711
Interest expense	(479)	(456)	(327)
Investment earnings	22	37	32
Minority interests	(21)	(14)	(38)
Net gains on sales of facilities and long-term investments	49	28	–
Income before income taxes	618	1,086	1,378
Income taxes	(278)	(443)	(593)
Income from continuing operations, before discontinued operations and cumulative effect of accounting change	340	643	785
Discontinued operations, net of taxes	(19)	–	–
Cumulative effect of accounting change, net of taxes	(19)	–	–
Net income	$ 302	$ 643	$ 785

Effects of Cost Behavior on Selecting the Most Appropriate Cost Driver

LO 4

Select appropriate cost drivers for allocating indirect costs in a variety of different circumstances.

As previously mentioned, indirect costs may exhibit variable or fixed cost behavior patterns. Failing to consider the effects of cost behavior when allocating indirect costs can lead to significant distortions in product cost measurement. We examine the critical relationships between cost behavior and cost allocation in the next section of the text.

Using Volume Measures to Allocate Variable Overhead Costs

A *causal relationship* exists between variable overhead product costs (indirect materials, indirect labor, inspection costs, utilities, etc.) and the volume of production. For example, the cost of indirect materials such as glue, staples, screws, nails, and varnish will increase or decrease in proportion to the number of desks a furniture manufacturing company makes. *Volume measures are good cost drivers* for allocating variable overhead costs.

Volume can be expressed by such measures as the number of units produced, the number of labor hours worked, or the amount of *direct* materials used in production. Given the variety of possible volume measures, how does management identify the most appropriate cost driver (allocation base) for assigning particular overhead costs? Consider the case of Filmier Furniture Company.

Using Units as the Cost Driver

During the most recent year, Filmier Furniture Company produced 4,000 chairs and 1,000 desks. It incurred $60,000 of *indirect materials* cost during the period. How much of this cost should Filmier allocate to chairs versus desks? Using number of units as the cost driver produces the following allocation.

Step 1. Compute the allocation rate.

Total cost to be allocated	÷ Cost driver	=	Allocation rate
$60,000 indirect materials cost	÷ 5,000 units	=	$12 per unit

Step 2. Multiply the allocation rate by the weight of the cost driver to determine the allocation per cost object.

Product	Allocation Rate	×	Number of Units Produced	=	Allocated Cost
Desks	$12	×	1,000	=	$12,000
Chairs	12	×	4,000	=	48,000
Total			5,000	=	$60,000

Using Direct Labor Hours as the Cost Driver

Using the number of units as the cost driver assigns an *equal amount* ($12) of indirect materials cost to each piece of furniture. However, if Filmier uses more indirect materials to make a desk than to make a chair, assigning the same amount of indirect materials cost to each is inaccurate. Assume Filmier incurs the following direct costs to make chairs and desks:

	Desks	Chairs	Total
Direct labor hours	3,500 hrs.	2,500 hrs.	6,000 hrs.
Direct materials cost	$1,000,000	$500,000	$1,500,000

Both direct labor hours and direct materials cost are volume measures that indicate Filmier uses more indirect materials to make a desk than a chair. It makes sense that the amount of direct labor used is related to the amount of indirect materials used. Because production workers use materials to make furniture, it is plausible to assume that the more hours they work, the more materials they use. Using this reasoning, Filmier could assign the indirect materials cost to the chairs and desks as follows:

Step 1. Compute the allocation rate.

Total cost to be allocated	÷	Cost driver	=	Allocation rate
$60,000 indirect materials cost	÷	6,000 hours	=	$10 per hour

Step 2. Multiply the allocation rate by the weight of the cost driver.

Product	Allocation Rate	×	Number of Labor Hours	=	Allocated Cost
Desks	$10.00	×	3,500	=	$35,000
Chairs	10.00	×	2,500	=	25,000
Total			6,000	=	$60,000

Basing the allocation on labor hours rather than number of units assigns a significantly larger portion of the indirect materials cost to desks ($35,000 versus $12,000). Is this allocation more accurate? Suppose the desks, but not the chairs, require elaborate, labor-intensive carvings. A significant portion of the labor is then not related to consuming indirect materials (glue, staples, screws, nails, and varnish). It would therefore be inappropriate to allocate the indirect materials cost based on direct labor hours.

Using Direct Material Dollars as the Cost Driver

If labor hours is an inappropriate allocation base, Filmier can consider direct material usage, measured in material dollars, as the allocation base. It is likely that the more lumber (direct material) Filmier uses, the more glue, nails, and so forth (indirect materials) it uses. It is reasonable to presume direct materials usage drives indirect materials usage. Using direct materials dollars as the cost driver for indirect materials produces the following allocation:

Step 1. Compute the allocation rate.

Total cost to be allocated	÷	Cost driver	=	Allocation rate
$60,000 indirect materials cost	÷	$1,500,000 direct material dollars	=	$0.04 per direct material dollar

Step 2. Multiply the allocation rate by the weight of the cost driver.

Product	Allocation Rate	×	Number of Direct Material Dollars	=	Allocated Cost
Desks	$0.04	×	$1,000,000	=	$40,000
Chairs	0.04	×	500,000	=	20,000
Total			$1,500,000	=	$60,000

Selecting the Best Cost Driver

Which of the three volume-based cost drivers (units, labor hours, or direct material dollars) results in the most accurate allocation of the overhead cost? Management must use judgment to decide. In this case, direct material dollars appears to have the most convincing relationship to indirect materials usage. If the cost Filmier was allocating were fringe benefits, however, direct labor hours would be a more appropriate cost driver. If the cost Filmier was allocating were machine maintenance cost, a different volume-based cost driver, machine hours, would be an appropriate base. The most accurate allocations of indirect costs may actually require using multiple cost drivers.

CHECK YOURSELF 16.2

Boston Boat Company builds custom sailboats for customers. During the current accounting period, the company built five different size boats that ranged in cost from $35,000 to $185,000. The company's manufacturing overhead cost for the period was $118,000. Would you recommend using the number of units (boats) or direct labor hours as the base for allocating the overhead cost to the five boats? Why?

Answer

Using the number of units as the allocation base would assign the same amount of overhead cost to each boat. Since larger boats require more overhead cost (supplies, utilities, equipment, etc.) than smaller boats, there is no logical link between the number of boats and the amount of overhead cost required to build a particular boat. In contrast, there is a logical link between direct labor hours used and overhead cost incurred. The more labor used, the more supplies, utilities, equipment, and so on used. Since larger boats require more direct labor than smaller boats, using direct labor hours as the allocation base would allocate more overhead cost to larger boats and less overhead cost to smaller boats, producing a logical overhead allocation. Therefore, Boston should use direct labor hours as the allocation base.

Allocating Fixed Overhead Costs

Fixed costs present a different cost allocation problem. By definition, the volume of production does not drive fixed costs. Suppose Lednicky Bottling Company rents its manufacturing facility for $28,000 per year. The rental cost is fixed regardless of how much product Lednicky bottles. However, Lednicky may still use a volume-based cost driver as the allocation base. The purpose of allocating fixed costs to products is to distribute a *rational share* of the overhead cost to each product. Selecting an allocation base that spreads total overhead cost equally over total production often produces a rational distribution. For example, assume Lednicky produced 2,000,000 bottles of apple juice during 2006. If it sold 1,800,000 bottles of the juice during 2006, how much of the $28,000 of rental cost should Lednicky allocate to ending inventory and how much to cost of goods sold? A rational allocation follows:

Step 1. Compute the allocation rate.

Total cost to be allocated	÷	Allocation base (cost driver)	=	Allocation rate
$28,000 rental cost	÷	2,000,000 bottles	=	$0.014 per bottle of juice

Because the base (number of units) used to allocate the cost does not drive the cost, it is sometimes called an *allocation base* instead of a *cost driver*. However, many managers use the term cost driver in conjunction with fixed cost even though that usage is technically inaccurate. The terms allocation base and cost driver are frequently used interchangeably.

Step 2. Multiply the allocation rate by the weight of the cost driver.

Financial Statement Item	Allocation Rate	×	Number of Bottles	=	Allocated Cost
Inventory	$0.014	×	200,000	=	$ 2,800
Cost of goods sold	0.014	×	1,800,000	=	25,200

Using number of units as the allocation base assigns equal amounts of the rental cost to each unit of product. Equal allocation is appropriate so long as the units are homogeneous. If the units are not identical, however, Lednicky may need to choose a different allocation base to rationally distribute the rental cost. For example, if some of the bottles are significantly larger than others, Lednicky may find using some physical measure, like liters of direct material used, to be a more appropriate allocation base. Whether an indirect cost is fixed or variable, selecting the most appropriate allocation base requires sound reasoning and judgment.

Allocating Costs to Solve Timing Problems

LO 5

Use allocation to solve problems that emerge in the process of making cost-plus pricing decisions.

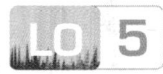

Monthly fluctuations in production volume complicate fixed cost allocations. To illustrate, assume Grave Manufacturing pays its production supervisor a monthly salary of $3,000. Furthermore, assume Grave makes 800 units of product in January and 1,875 in February. How much salary cost should Grave assign to the products made in January and February, respectively? The allocation seems simple. Just divide the $3,000 monthly salary cost by the number of units of product made each month as follows:

January	$3,000	÷	800 units	=	$3.75 cost per unit
February	$3,000	÷	1,875 units	=	$1.60 cost per unit

If Grave Manufacturing based a cost-plus pricing decision on these results, it would price products made in January significantly higher than products made in February. It is likely such price fluctuations would puzzle and drive away customers. Grave needs an allocation base that will spread the annual salary cost evenly over annual production. A timing problem exists, however, because Grave must allocate the salary cost before the end of the year. In order to price its products, Grave needs to know the allocated amount before the actual cost information is available. Grave can manage the timing problem by using estimated rather than actual costs.

Grave Manufacturing can *estimate* the annual cost of the supervisor's salary (indirect labor) as $36,000 ($3,000 × 12 months). The *actual* cost of indirect labor may differ because the supervisor might receive a pay raise or be replaced with a person who earns less. Based on current information, however, $36,000 is a reasonable estimate of the annual indirect labor cost. Grave must also estimate total annual production volume. Suppose Grave produced 18,000 units last year and expects no significant change in the current year. It can allocate indirect labor cost for January and February as follows:

Step 1. Compute the allocation rate.

Total cost to be allocated	÷	Allocation base (cost driver)	=	Allocation rate
$36,000	÷	18,000 units	=	$2.00 per unit

Step 2. Multiply the rate by the weight of the base (number of units per month) to determine how much of the salary cost to allocate to each month's production.

Month	Allocation Rate	×	Number of Units Produced	=	Allocation per Month
January	$2.00	×	800	=	$1,600
February	2.00	×	1,875	=	3,750

Grave Manufacturing will add these indirect cost allocations to other product costs to determine the total estimated product cost to use in cost-plus pricing or other managerial decisions.

Because the overhead allocation rate is determined *before* actual cost and volume data are available, it is called the **predetermined overhead rate.** Companies use predetermined overhead rates for product costing estimates and pricing decisions during a year, but they must use actual costs in published year-end financial statements. If necessary, companies adjust their accounting records at year-end when they have used estimated data on an interim basis. The procedures for making such adjustments are discussed in a later chapter.

Establishing Cost Pools

LO 6

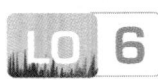

Explain why companies establish indirect cost pools.

Allocating *individually* every single indirect cost a company incurs would be tedious and not particularly useful relative to the benefit obtained. Instead, companies frequently accumulate many individual costs into a single **cost pool.** The *total* of the pooled costs is then allocated to the cost objects. For example, a company may accumulate costs for gas, water, electricity, and telephone service into a single *utilities* cost pool. It would then allocate the total cost in the utilities cost pool to the cost objects rather than individually allocating each of the four types of utility cost.

How far should pooling costs go? Why not pool utility costs with fringe benefit costs? The most accurate cost information comes from pooling costs with common cost drivers. To obtain rational allocations of various indirect costs to cost objects, companies must use different allocation bases (cost drivers). They should therefore limit pooling to costs with common cost drivers.

Allocating Joint Costs

LO 7

Explain the nature and allocation of joint product and by-product common costs.

Joint costs are common costs incurred in the process of making two or more **joint products.** The cost of raw milk is a joint cost of producing the joint products cream, whole milk, 2 percent milk, and skim milk. Joint costs include not only materials costs but also the labor and overhead costs of converting the materials into separate products. The point in the production process at which products become separate and identifiable is the **split-off point.** For financial reporting of inventory and cost of goods sold, companies must allocate the joint costs to the separate joint products. Some joint products require additional processing after the split-off point. Any additional materials, labor, or overhead costs incurred after the split-off point are assigned to the specific products to which they relate.

To illustrate, assume Westar Chemical Company produces from common raw materials the joint products Compound AK and Compound AL. Compound AL requires further processing before Westar can sell it. The diagram in Exhibit 16.5 illustrates the joint product costs.

EXHIBIT 16.5

Allocation of Joint Cost

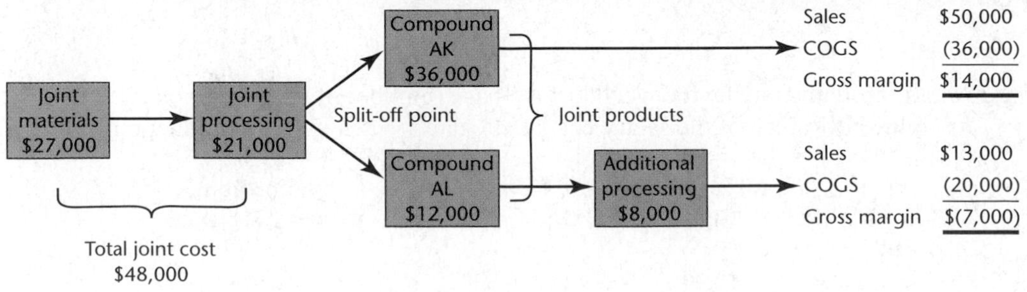

The joint cost of producing a batch of the two compounds is $48,000, representing $27,000 of materials cost and $21,000 of processing cost. A batch results in 3,000 gallons of Compound AK and 1,000 gallons of Compound AL. Westar allocates joint costs to the products based on the number of gallons produced, as follows:

Step 1. Compute the allocation rate.

Total cost to be allocated	÷	Allocation base	=	Allocation rate
$48,000 joint cost	÷	4,000 gallons	=	$12 per gallon

Step 2. Multiply the allocation rate by the weight of the base.

Joint Product	Allocation Rate	×	Number of Gallons Produced	=	Allocated Cost
Compound AK	$12	×	3,000	=	$36,000
Compound AL	12	×	1,000	=	12,000

Westar sells 3,000 gallons of Compound AK for $50,000, and 1,000 gallons of Compound AL for $13,000. Exhibit 16.5 shows the gross margins for each product using the joint cost allocations computed above.

Relative Sales Value as the Allocation Base

Because Compound AL shows a $7,000 loss, a manager might mistakenly conclude that Westar should stop making and selling this product. If Westar stops making Compound AL, the total joint cost ($48,000) would be assigned to Compound AK and total gross margin would decline as shown below.

	With Compound AL		Without Compound AL
Sales	$63,000	($50,000 + $13,000)	$50,000
Cost of goods sold	(56,000)	($36,000 + $20,000)	(48,000)
Gross Margin	$ 7,000		$ 2,000

To avoid the appearance that a product such as Compound AL is producing losses, many companies allocate joint cost to products based on the relative sales value of each product at the split-off point. Westar Chemical would allocate all of the joint cost to Compound AK because Compound AL has no market value at the split-off point. The resulting gross margins follow.

	Compound AK	Compound AL
Sales	$50,000	$13,000
Cost of goods sold	(48,000)	(8,000)
Gross margin	$ 2,000	$ 5,000

Westar's total profit on the joint products is $7,000 whether it allocates the joint costs using gallons or relative market value. However, using market value as the allocation base produces a positive gross margin for both products, reducing the likelihood that a manager will mistakenly eliminate a product that is contributing to profitability.

CHECK YOURSELF 16.3

What are some logical split-off points for a meat processing company engaged in butchering beef?

Answer

The first logical split-off point occurs when processing separates the hide (used to produce leather) from the carcass. Other split-off points occur as further processing produces different cuts of meat (T-bone and New York strip steaks, various roasts, chops, ground chuck, etc.).

By-Product Costs

Like joint products, **by-products** share common materials, labor, and overhead costs. Unlike joint products, by-products have a relatively insignificant market value. For example, sawdust is a by-product of producing lumber. Although accounting for by-products is not discussed in this text, be aware that the common costs of producing them are not relevant to further processing decisions.

Cost Allocation: The Human Factor

LO 8

Recognize human motivation as a key variable in the allocation process.

Cost allocations significantly affect individuals. They may influence managers' performance evaluations and compensation. They may dictate the amount of resources various departments, divisions, and other organizational subunits receive. Control over resources usually offers managers prestige and influence over organization operations. The following scenario illustrates the emotional impact and perceptions of fairness of cost allocation decisions.

Using Cost Allocations in a Budgeting Decision

Sharon Southport, dean of the School of Business at a major state university, is in dire need of a budgeting plan. Because of cuts in state funding, the money available to the School of Business for copying costs next year will be reduced substantially. Dean Southport supervises four departments: management, marketing, finance, and accounting. The Dean knows the individual department chairpersons will be unhappy and frustrated with the deep cuts they face.

Using Cost Drivers to Make Allocations

To address the allocation of copying resources, Dean Southport decided to meet with the department chairs. She explained that the total budgeted for copying costs will be \$36,000. Based on past usage, department allocations would be as follows: \$12,000 for management, \$10,000 for accounting, \$8,000 for finance, and \$6,000 for marketing.

Dr. Bill Thompson, the management department chair, immediately protested that his department could not operate on a \$12,000 budget for copy costs. Management has more faculty members than any other department. Dr. Thompson argued that copy costs are directly related to the number of faculty members, so copy funds should be allocated based on the number of faculty members. Dr. Thompson suggested that number of faculty members rather than past usage should be the allocation base.

Since the School of Business has 72 faculty members (29 in management, 16 in accounting, 12 in finance, and 15 in marketing), the allocation should be as follows:

Step 1. Compute the allocation rate.

Total cost to be allocated	÷	Cost driver	=	Allocation rate
\$36,000	÷	72	=	\$500 per faculty member

Step 2. Multiply the rate by the weight of the driver (the number of faculty per department) to determine the allocation per cost object (department).

Department	Allocation Rate	×	Number of Faculty	=	Allocation per Department	Allocation Based on Past Usage
Management	\$500	×	29		\$14,500	\$12,000
Accounting	500	×	16		8,000	10,000
Finance	500	×	12		6,000	8,000
Marketing	500	×	15		7,500	6,000
Total					\$36,000	\$36,000

Seeing these figures, Dr. Bob Smethers, chair of the accounting department, questioned the accuracy of using the number of faculty members as the cost driver. Dr. Smethers suggested the number of *students* rather than the number of *faculty* members drives the cost of copying. He argued that most copying results from duplicating syllabi, exams, and handouts. The accounting department teaches mass sections of introductory accounting that have extremely high student/teacher ratios. Because his department teaches more students, it spends more on copying costs even though it has fewer faculty members. Dr. Smethers recomputed the copy cost allocation as follows.

Step 1. Compute the allocation rate based on number of students. University records indicate that the School of Business taught 1,200 students during the most recent academic year. The allocation rate (copy cost per student) follows.

Total cost to be allocated	÷	Cost driver	=	Allocation rate
\$36,000	÷	1,200	=	\$30 per student

Step 2. Multiply the rate by the weight of the driver (number of students taught by each department) to determine the allocation per cost object (department).

Department	Allocation Rate	×	Number of Students	=	Allocation per Department	Allocation Based on Past Usage
Management	\$30	×	330		\$ 9,900	\$12,000
Accounting	30	×	360		10,800	10,000
Finance	30	×	290		8,700	8,000
Marketing	30	×	220		6,600	6,000
Total					\$36,000	\$36,000

Choosing the Best Cost Driver

Dr. Thompson objected vigorously to using the number of students as the cost driver. He continued to argue that the size of the faculty is a more appropriate allocation base. The chair of the finance department sided with Dr. Smethers, the chair of the marketing department kept quiet, and the dean had to settle the dispute.

Dean Southport recognized that the views of the chairpersons were influenced by self-interest. The allocation base affects the amount of resources available to each department. Furthermore, the dean recognized that the size of the faculty does drive some of the copying costs. For example, the cost of copying manuscripts that faculty submit for publication relates to faculty size. The more articles faculty submit, the higher the copying cost. Nevertheless, the dean decided the number of students has the most significant impact on copying costs. She also wanted to encourage faculty members to minimize the impact of funding cuts on student services. Dean Southport therefore decided to allocate copying costs based on the number of students taught by each department. Dr. Thompson stormed angrily out of the meeting. The dean developed a budget by assigning the available funds to each department using the number of students as the allocation base.

Controlling Emotions

Dr. Thompson's behavior may relieve his frustration but it doesn't indicate clear thinking. Dean Southport recognized that Dr. Thompson's contention that copy costs were related to faculty size had some merit. Had Dr. Thompson offered a compromise rather than an emotional outburst, he might have increased his department's share of the funds. Perhaps a portion of the allocation could have been based on the number of faculty members with the balance allocated based on the number of students. Had Dr. Thompson controlled his anger, the others might have agreed to compromise. Technical expertise in computing numbers is of little use without the interpersonal skills to persuade others. Accountants may provide numerical measurements, but they should never forget the impact of their reports on the people in the organization.

<< A Look Back

Managers need to know the costs of products, processes, departments, activities, and so on. The target for which accountants attempt to determine cost is a *cost object*. Knowing the cost of specific objects enables management to control costs, evaluate performance, and price products. *Direct costs* can be cost-effectively traced to a cost object. *Indirect costs* cannot be easily traced to designated cost objects.

The same cost can be direct or indirect, depending on the cost object to which it relates. For example, the salary of a Burger King restaurant manager can be directly traced to a particular store but cannot be traced to particular food items made and sold in the store. Classifying a cost as direct or indirect is independent of whether the cost behaves as fixed or variable; it is also independent of whether the cost is relevant to a given decision. A direct cost could be either fixed or variable or either relevant or irrelevant, depending on the context and the designated cost object.

Indirect costs are assigned to cost objects using *cost allocation*. Allocation divides an indirect cost into parts and distributes the parts among the relevant cost objects. Companies frequently allocate costs to cost objects in proportion to the *cost drivers* that cause the costs to be incurred. The first step in allocating an indirect cost is to determine the allocation rate by dividing the total cost to be allocated by the chosen cost driver. The next step is to multiply the allocation rate by the amount of the cost driver for a particular object. The result is the amount of indirect cost to assign to the cost object.

A particular indirect cost may be related to more than one driver. The best cost driver is the one that most accurately reflects the amount of the resource used by the cost object. Objects that consume the most resources should be allocated a proportionately greater share of the costs. If no suitable cost driver exists, companies may use arbitrary allocations such as dividing a total cost equally among cost objects.

Cost allocations have behavioral implications. Using inappropriate cost drivers can distort allocations and lead managers to make choices that are detrimental to the company's profitability.

To avoid the inefficiency of allocating every individual indirect cost, managers accumulate many indirect costs into *cost pools*. The costs combined in a pool should have a common cost driver. A single allocation can then be made of the cost pool total.

The joint costs incurred in the process of making two or more products are allocated among the products at the *split-off point*, the point at which products become separate and identifiable. The allocation base can be the products' relative sales values or some quantity measure of the amount of each product made. If one of the joint products requires additional processing costs to bring it to market, only these additional processing costs are relevant to a decision about whether to undertake further processing. The allocated joint costs are not relevant because they will be incurred whether or not the joint product is processed after the split-off point. By-products share common costs with other products but have an insignificant market value relative to their joint products.

A Look Forward >>

The next chapter moves into unexplored territory. It explains the concept of inventory cost flow, showing how inventory costs move through the inventory accounts Raw Materials, Work in Process, and Finished Goods. It presents techniques for assigning overhead cost to inventory as the inventory is produced. It identifies differences in product costing for service and manufacturing companies. Finally, it contrasts two approaches to valuing inventory, variable costing versus full-absorption costing.

SELF-STUDY REVIEW PROBLEM

New budget constraints have pressured Body Perfect Gym to control costs. The owner of the gym, Mr. Ripple, has notified division managers that their job performance evaluations will be highly influenced by their ability to minimize costs. The gym has three divisions, weight lifting, aerobics, and spinning.

The owner has formulated a report showing how much it cost to operate each of the three divisions last year. In preparing the report, Mr. Ripple identified several indirect costs that must be allocated among the divisions. These indirect costs are $4,200 of laundry expense, $48,000 of gym supplies, $350,000 of office rent, $50,000 of janitorial services, and $120,000 for administrative salaries. To provide a reasonably accurate cost allocation, Mr. Ripple has identified several potential cost drivers. These drivers and their association with each division follow.

Cost Driver	Weight Lifting	Aerobics	Spinning	Total
Number of participants	26	16	14	56
Number of instructors	10	8	6	24
Square feet of gym space	12,000	6,000	7,000	25,000
Number of staff	2	2	1	5

Required

a. Identify the appropriate cost objects.

b. Identify the most appropriate cost driver for each indirect cost, and compute the allocation rate for assigning each indirect cost to the cost objects.

c. Determine the amount of supplies expense that should be allocated to each of the three divisions.

d. The spinning manager wants to use the number of staff rather than the number of instructors as the allocation base for the supplies expense. Explain why the spinning manager would take this position.

e. Identify two cost drivers other than your choice for Requirement *b* that could be used to allocate the cost of the administrative salaries to the three divisions.

Solution to Requirement *a*

The objective is to determine the cost of operating each division. Therefore, the cost objects are the three divisions (weight lifting, aerobics, and spinning).

Solution to Requirement *b*

The costs, appropriate cost drivers, and allocation rates for assigning the costs to the departments follow:

Cost	Base	Computation	Allocation Rate
Laundry expense	Number of participants	$ 4,200 ÷ 56	$75 per participant
Supplies expense	Number of instructors	48,000 ÷ 24	$2,000 per instructor
Office rent	Square feet	350,000 ÷ 25,000	$14 per square foot
Janitorial service	Square feet	50,000 ÷ 25,000	$2 per square foot
Administrative salaries	Number of divisions	120,000 ÷ 3	$40,000 per division

There are other logical cost drivers. For example, supplies expense could be allocated based on the number of staff. It is also logical to use a combination of cost drivers. For example, the allocation of supplies expense could be based on the combined number of instructors and staff. For this problem, we assumed that Mr. Ripple chose the number of instructors as the base for allocating supplies expense.

Solution to Requirement *c*

Department	Cost to Be Allocated	Allocation Rate	×	Weight of Base	=	Amount Allocated
Weight lifting	Supplies expense	$2,000	×	10	=	$20,000
Aerobics	Supplies expense	2,000	×	8	=	16,000
Spinning	Supplies expense	2,000	×	6	=	12,000
Total						$48,000

Solution to Requirement *d*

If the number of staff were used as the allocation base, the allocation rate for supplies expense would be as follows:

$48,000 ÷ 5 staff = $9,600 per staff member

Using this rate, the total supplies expense would be allocated among the three divisions as follows:

Department	Cost to Be Allocated	Allocation Rate	×	Weight of Base	=	Amount Allocated
Weight lifting	Supplies expense	$9,600	×	2	=	$19,200
Aerobics	Supplies expense	9,600	×	2	=	19,200
Spinning	Supplies expense	9,600	×	1	=	9,600
Total						$48,000

By using the number of staff as the allocation base instead of the number of instructors, the amount of overhead cost allocated to the spinning division falls from $12,000 to $9,600. Since managers are evaluated based on minimizing costs, it is clearly in the spinning manager's self-interest to use the number of staff as the allocation base.

Solution to Requirement *e*

Among other possibilities, bases for allocating the administrative salaries include the number of participants, the number of lessons, or the number of instructors.

KEY TERMS

allocation 796
allocation base 796
allocation rate 796
by-products 808
cost accumulation 808
cost allocation 794
cost driver 794
cost objects 793
cost pool 806
cost tracing 795
direct cost 795
indirect cost 795
joint costs 806
joint products 806
overhead costs 795
predetermined overhead rate 806
split-off point 806

QUESTIONS

1. What is a cost object? Identify four different cost objects in which an accountant would be interested.
2. Why is cost accumulation imprecise?
3. If the cost object is a manufactured product, what are the three major cost categories to accumulate?
4. What is a direct cost? What criteria are used to determine whether a cost is a direct cost?
5. Why are the terms *direct cost* and *indirect cost* independent of the terms *fixed cost* and *variable cost*? Give an example to illustrate.
6. Give an example of why the statement, "All direct costs are avoidable," is incorrect.
7. What are the important factors in determining the appropriate cost driver to use in allocating a cost?
8. How is an allocation rate determined? How is an allocation made?
9. In a manufacturing environment, which costs are direct and which are indirect in product costing?
10. Why are some manufacturing costs not directly traceable to products?
11. What is the objective of allocating indirect manufacturing overhead costs to the product?
12. On January 31, the managers of Integra Inc. seek to determine the cost of producing their product during January for product pricing and control purposes. The company can easily determine the costs of direct materials and direct labor used in January production, but many fixed indirect costs are not affected by the level of production activity and have not yet been incurred. The managers can reasonably estimate the overhead costs for the year based on the fixed indirect costs incurred

in past periods. Assume the managers decide to allocate an equal amount of these estimated costs to the products produced each month. Explain why this practice may not provide a reasonable estimate of product costs in January.

13. Respond to the following statement: "The allocation base chosen is unimportant. What is important in product costing is that overhead costs be assigned to production in a specific period by an allocation process."
14. Larry Kwang insists that the costs of his school's fund-raising project should be determined after the project is complete. He argues that only after the project is complete can its costs be determined accurately and that it is a waste of time to try to estimate future costs. Georgia Sundum counters that waiting until the project is complete will not provide timely information for planning expenditures. How would you arbitrate this discussion? Explain the trade-offs between accuracy and timeliness.
15. Define the term *cost pool*. How are cost pools important in allocating costs?
16. What is the difference between a joint product and a by-product?

EXERCISES—SERIES A

All Exercises in Series A are available with McGraw-Hill's Homework Manager

L.O. 1, 3

Exercise 16-1A *Allocating costs between divisions*

Loftis Services Company (LSC) has 50 employees, 36 of whom are assigned to Division A and 14 to Division B. LSC incurred $360,000 of fringe benefits cost during 2006.

Required

Determine the amount of the fringe benefits cost to be allocated to Division A and to Division B.

L.O. 2

Exercise 16-2A *Direct versus indirect costs*

Burr Ridge Construction Company is composed of two divisions: (1) Home Construction and (2) Commercial Construction. The Home Construction Division is in the process of building 12 houses and the Commercial Construction Division is working on 3 projects. Cost items of the company follow:

Labor on a particular house
Salary of the supervisor of commercial construction projects
Supplies, such as glue and nails, used by the Home Construction Division
Cost of building permits
Materials used in commercial construction projects
Depreciation on home building equipment (small tools such as hammers or saws)
Company president's salary
Depreciation on crane used in commercial construction
Depreciation on home office building
Salary of corporate office manager
Wages of workers assigned to a specific construction project
Supplies used by the Commercial Construction Division

Required

a. Identify each cost as being a direct or indirect cost assuming the cost objects are the individual products (houses or projects).
b. Identify each cost as being a direct or indirect cost, assuming the cost objects are the two divisions.
c. Identify each cost as being a direct or indirect cost assuming the cost object is Burr Ridge Construction Company as a whole.

L.O. 3, 4

Exercise 16-3A *Allocating overhead cost among products*

Donna Hats Inc. manufactures three different styles of hats: Vogue, Beauty, and Deluxe. Donna expects to incur $600,000 of overhead cost during the next fiscal year. Other budget information follows.

	Vogue	Beauty	Deluxe	Total
Direct labor hours	3,000	5,000	4,500	12,500
Machine hours	1,000	1,000	1,000	3,000

Required

a. Use direct labor hours as the cost driver to compute the allocation rate and the budgeted overhead cost for each product.

b. Use machine hours as the cost driver to compute the allocation rate and the budgeted overhead cost for each product.

c. Describe a set of circumstances where it would be more appropriate to use direct labor hours as the allocation base.

d. Describe a set of circumstances where it would be more appropriate to use machine hours as the allocation base.

Exercise 16-4A *Allocating overhead costs among products* L.O. 3, 4

Ritchey Company makes three products in its factory: plastic cups, plastic tablecloths, and plastic bottles. The expected overhead costs for the next fiscal year include the following.

Factory manager's salary	$150,000
Factory utility cost	70,000
Factory supplies	30,000
Total overhead costs	$250,000

Ritchey uses machine hours as the cost driver to allocate overhead costs. Budgeted machine hours for the products are as follows.

Cups	500 Hours
Tablecloths	800
Bottles	1,200
Total machine hours	2,500

Required

a. Allocate the budgeted overhead costs to the products.

b. Provide a possible explanation as to why Ritchey chose machine hours, instead of labor hours, as the allocation base.

Exercise 16-5A *Allocating costs among products* L.O. 3, 4

Sudderth Construction Company expects to build three new homes during a specific accounting period. The estimated direct materials and labor costs are as follows.

Expected Costs	Home 1	Home 2	Home 3
Direct labor	$120,000	$180,000	$340,000
Direct materials	180,000	260,000	360,000

Assume Sudderth needs to allocate two major overhead costs ($80,000 of employee fringe benefits and $40,000 of indirect materials costs) among the three jobs.

Required

Choose an appropriate cost driver for each of the overhead costs and determine the total cost of each house.

L.O. 3, 5

Exercise 16-6A *Allocating to smooth cost over varying levels of production*

Production workers for Bakari Manufacturing Company provided 320 hours of labor in January and 480 hours in February. Bakari expects to use 4,000 hours of labor during the year. The rental fee for the manufacturing facility is $7,200 per month.

Required

Explain why allocation is needed. Based on this information, how much of the rental cost should be allocated to the products made in January and to those made in February?

L.O. 3, 5

Exercise 16-7A *Allocating to solve a timing problem*

Production workers for Poole Manufacturing Company provided 2,700 hours of labor in January and 1,800 hours in February. The company, whose operation is labor intensive, expects to use 36,000 hours of labor during the year. Poole paid a $45,000 annual premium on July 1 of the prior year for an insurance policy that covers the manufacturing facility for the following 12 months.

Required

Explain why allocation is needed. Based on this information, how much of the insurance cost should be allocated to the products made in January and to those made in February?

L.O. 3, 5

Exercise 16-8A *Allocating a fixed cost*

Coastal Air is a large airline company that pays a customer relations representative $4,000 per month. The representative, who processed 1,000 customer complaints in January and 1,300 complaints in February, is expected to process 16,000 customer complaints during 2007.

Required

a. Determine the total cost of processing customer complaints in January and in February.

b. Explain why allocating the cost of the customer relations representative would or would not be relevant to decision making.

L.O. 3, 5

Exercise 16-9A *Allocating overhead cost to accomplish smoothing*

Mimosa Corporation expects to incur indirect overhead costs of $72,000 per month and direct manufacturing costs of $11 per unit. The expected production activity for the first four months of 2007 is as follows.

	January	February	March	April
Estimated production in units	4,000	7,000	3,000	6,000

Required

a. Calculate a predetermined overhead rate based on the number of units of product expected to be made during the first four months of the year.

b. Allocate overhead costs to each month using the overhead rate computed in Requirement *a*.

c. Calculate the total cost per unit for each month using the overhead allocated in Requirement *b*.

L.O. 3, 5

Exercise 16-10A *Allocating overhead for product costing*

Seiko Manufacturing Company produced 1,200 units of inventory in January 2007. It expects to produce an additional 8,400 units during the remaining 11 months of the year. In other words, total production for 2007 is estimated to be 9,600 units. Direct materials and direct labor costs are $64 and $52 per unit, respectively. Seiko Company expects to incur the following manufacturing overhead costs during 2007:

Production supplies	$ 4,800
Supervisor salary	192,000
Depreciation on equipment	144,000
Utilities	36,000
Rental fee on manufacturing facilities	96,000
Total	$472,800

Required

a. Determine the cost of the 1,200 units of product made in January.

b. Is the cost computed in Requirement *a* actual or estimated? Could Seiko improve accuracy by waiting until December to determine the cost of products?

Exercise 16-11A *How fixed cost allocation affects a pricing decision*

L.O. 3, 5

Barnhart Manufacturing Co. expects to make 48,000 chairs during 2006. The company made 8,000 chairs in January. Materials and labor costs for January were $32,000 and $48,000, respectively. Barnhart produced 3,000 chairs in February. Materials and labor costs for February were $12,000 and $18,000, respectively. The company paid the $240,000 annual rental fee on its manufacturing facility on January 1, 2006. Ignore other manufacturing overhead costs.

Required

Assuming that Barnhart desires to sell its chairs for cost plus 30 percent of cost, what price should be charged for the chairs produced in January and February?

Exercise 16-12A *Cost pools*

L.O. 6

McLaurin Department Stores, Inc. has three departments: women's, men's, and children's. The following are the indirect costs related to its operations:

Payroll taxes
Paper rolls for cash registers
Medical insurance
Salaries of secretaries
Water bill
Vacation pay
Sewer bill
Staples
Natural gas bill
Pens
Ink cartridges

Required

a. Organize the costs in the following three pools: indirect materials, indirect labor, and indirect utilities, assuming that each department is a cost object.

b. Identify an appropriate cost driver for each pool.

c. Explain why accountants use cost pools.

Exercise 16-13A *Allocating joint product cost*

L.O. 3, 7

Mistrot Chemical Company makes three products, B217, K360, and X639, which are joint products from the same materials. In a standard batch of 150,000 pounds of raw materials, the company generates 35,000 pounds of B217, 75,000 pounds of K360, and 40,000 pounds of X639. A standard batch costs $1,800,000 to produce. The sales prices per pound are $8.00, $19.20, and $32.00 for B217, K360, and X639, respectively.

Required

a. Allocate the joint product cost among the three final products using weight as the allocation base.

b. Allocate the joint product cost among the three final products using market value as the allocation base.

Exercise 16-14A *Human factor*

L.O. 8

Brentwood Clinics provides medical care in three departments: internal medicine (IM), pediatrics (PD), and obstetrics gynecology (OB). The estimated costs to run each department follow:

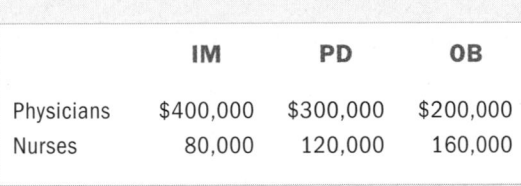

	IM	PD	OB
Physicians	$400,000	$300,000	$200,000
Nurses	80,000	120,000	160,000

Brentwood expects to incur $360,000 of indirect (overhead) costs in the next fiscal year.

Required

a. Based on the information provided, name four allocation bases that could be used to assign the overhead cost to each department.

b. Assume the manager of each department is permitted to recommend how the overhead cost should be allocated to the departments. Which of the allocation bases named in Requirement *a* is the manager of OB most likely to recommend? Explain why. What argument may the manager of OB use to justify his choice of the allocation base?

c. Which of the allocation bases would result in the fairest allocation of the overhead cost from the perspective of the company president?

d. Explain how classifying overhead costs into separate pools could improve the fairness of the allocation of the overhead costs.

PROBLEMS—SERIES A

All Problems in Series A are available with McGraw-Hill's Homework Manager

L.O. 1, 2, 3, 4, 5

eXcel

mhhe.com/edmonds2007

CHECK FIGURE

a. (2) $590,000

Problem 16-15A *Cost accumulation and allocation*

Belcher Manufacturing Company makes two different products, M and N. The company's two departments are named after the products; for example, Product M is made in Department M. Belcher's accountant has identified the following annual costs associated with these two products.

Financial data	
Salary of vice president of production division	$ 90,000
Salary of supervisor Department M	38,000
Salary of supervisor Department N	28,000
Direct materials cost Department M	150,000
Direct materials cost Department N	210,000
Direct labor cost Department M	120,000
Direct labor cost Department N	340,000
Direct utilities cost Department M	60,000
Direct utilities cost Department N	12,000
General factorywide utilities	18,000
Production supplies	18,000
Fringe benefits	69,000
Depreciation	360,000
Nonfinancial data	
Machine hours Department M	5,000
Machine hours Department N	1,000

Required

a. Identify the costs that are (1) direct costs of Department M, (2) direct costs of Department N, and (3) indirect costs.

b. Select the appropriate cost drivers for the indirect costs and allocate these costs to Departments M and N.

c. Determine the total estimated cost of the products made in Departments M and N. Assume that Belcher produced 2,000 units of Product M and 4,000 units of Product N during the year. If Belcher prices its products at cost plus 30 percent of cost, what price per unit must it charge for Product M and for Product N?

L.O. 1, 3, 4

Problem 16-16A *Selecting an appropriate cost driver (What is the base?)*

The Newman School of Vocational Technology has organized the school training programs into three departments. Each department provides training in a different area as follows: nursing assistant, dental hygiene, and office technology. The school's owner, Lucy Newman, wants to know how much it costs to operate each of the three departments. To accumulate the total cost for each department, the accountant has identified several indirect costs that must be allocated to each. These costs are $15,750 of phone expense, $3,360 of office supplies, $864,000 of office rent, $96,000 of janitorial services, and $72,000 of salary paid to the dean of students. To provide a reasonably accurate allocation of costs, the accountant has identified several possible cost drivers. These drivers and their association with each department follow.

Cost Driver	Department 1	Department 2	Department 3
Number of telephones	28	16	19
Number of faculty members	20	16	12
Square footage of office space	24,000	14,000	10,000
Number of secretaries	2	2	2

Required

a. Identify the appropriate cost objects.

b. Identify the appropriate cost driver for each indirect cost and compute the allocation rate for assigning each indirect cost to the cost objects.

c. Determine the amount of telephone expense that should be allocated to each of the three departments.

d. Determine the amount of supplies expense that should be allocated to Department 3.

e. Determine the amount of office rent that should be allocated to Department 2.

f. Determine the amount of janitorial services cost that should be allocated to Department 1.

g. Identify two cost drivers not listed here that could be used to allocate the cost of the dean's salary to the three departments.

Problem 16-17A *Cost allocation in a service industry*

L.O. 1, 2

CHECK FIGURES
b. To SF: $1,114;
To Chi: $546

Eagle Airlines is a small airline that occasionally carries overload shipments for the overnight delivery company Never-Fail Inc. Never-Fail is a multimillion-dollar company started by Peter Never immediately after he failed to finish his first accounting course. The company's motto is "We Never-Fail to Deliver Your Package on Time." When Never-Fail has more freight than it can deliver, it pays Eagle to carry the excess. Eagle contracts with independent pilots to fly its planes on a per trip basis. Eagle recently purchased an airplane that cost the company $6,000,000. The plane has an estimated useful life of 100,000,000 miles and a zero salvage value. During the first week in January, Eagle flew two trips. The first trip was a round trip flight from Chicago to San Francisco, for which Eagle paid $500 for the pilot and $350 for fuel. The second flight was a round trip from Chicago to New York. For this trip, it paid $300 for the pilot and $150 for fuel. The round trip between Chicago and San Francisco is approximately 4,400 miles and the round trip between Chicago and New York is 1,600 miles.

Required

a. Identify the direct and indirect costs that Eagle incurs for each trip.

b. Determine the total cost of each trip.

c. In addition to depreciation, identify three other indirect costs that may need to be allocated to determine the cost of each trip.

Problem 16-18A *Cost allocation in a manufacturing company*

L.O. 1, 3, 4

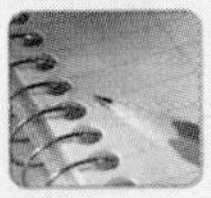

CHECK FIGURES
d. Jan.: $8,000
Feb.: $6,000

McCord Manufacturing Company makes tents that it sells directly to camping enthusiasts through a mail-order marketing program. The company pays a quality control expert $75,000 per year to inspect completed tents before they are shipped to customers. Assume that the company completed 1,600 tents in January and 1,200 tents in February. For the entire year, the company expects to produce 15,000 tents.

Required

a. Explain how changes in the cost driver (number of tents inspected) affect the total amount of fixed inspection cost.

b. Explain how changes in the cost driver (number of tents inspected) affect the amount of fixed inspection cost per unit.

c. If the cost objective is to determine the cost per tent, is the expert's salary a direct or an indirect cost?

d. How much of the expert's salary should be allocated to tents produced in January and February?

L.O. 1, 4, 8

excel

mhhe.com/edmonds2007

Problem 16-19A *Fairness in the allocation process*

Foreman Manufacturing Company uses two departments to make its products. Department I is a cutting department that is machine intensive and uses very few employees. Machines cut and form parts and then place the finished parts on a conveyor belt that carries them to Department II where they are assembled into finished goods. The assembly department is labor intensive and requires many workers to assemble parts into finished goods. The company's manufacturing facility incurs two significant overhead costs, employee fringe benefits and utility costs. The annual costs of fringe benefits are $504,000 and utility costs are $360,000. The typical consumption patterns for the two departments are as follows.

	Department I	Department II	Total
Machine hours used	16,000	4,000	20,000
Direct labor hours used	5,000	13,000	18,000

The supervisor of each department receives a bonus based on how well the department controls costs. The company's current policy requires using a single activity base (machine hours or labor hours) to allocate the total overhead cost of $864,000.

Required

a. Assume that you are the supervisor of Department I. Choose the allocation base that would minimize your department's share of the total overhead cost. Calculate the amount of overhead that would be allocated to both departments using the base that you selected.

b. Assume that you are the supervisor of Department II. Choose the allocation base that would minimize your department's share of the total overhead cost. Calculate the amount of overhead that would be allocated to both departments using the base that you selected.

c. Assume that you are the plant manager and have the authority to change the company's overhead allocation policy. Formulate an overhead allocation policy that would be fair to the supervisors of both Department I and Department II. Compute the overhead allocations for each department using your policy.

L.O. 1, 3, 5

CHECK FIGURES

a. $5.60

c. March: $59.20

Problem 16-20A *Allocation to accomplish smoothing*

Roddick Corporation estimated its overhead costs would be $36,000 per month except for January when it pays the $72,000 annual insurance premium on the manufacturing facility. Accordingly, the January overhead costs were expected to be $108,000 ($72,000 + $36,000). The company expected to use 7,000 direct labor hours per month except during July, August, and September when the company expected 9,000 hours of direct labor each month to build inventories for high demand that normally occurs during the holiday season. The company's actual direct labor hours were the same as the estimated hours. The company made 3,500 units of product in each month except July, August, and September in which it produced 4,500 units each month. Direct labor costs were $29 per unit, and direct materials costs were $19 per unit.

Required

a. Calculate a predetermined overhead rate based on direct labor hours.

b. Determine the total allocated overhead cost for January, March, and August.

c. Determine the cost per unit of product for January, March, and August.

d. Determine the selling price for the product, assuming that the company desires to earn a gross margin of $20 per unit.

L.O. 1, 3, 5

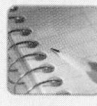

Problem 16-21A *Allocating indirect costs between products*

Dana Helton is considering expanding her business. She plans to hire a salesperson to cover trade shows. Because of compensation, travel expenses, and booth rental, fixed costs for a trade show are expected to be $15,000. The booth will be open 30 hours during the trade show. Ms. Helton also plans to add a new product line, ProOffice, which will cost $180 per package. She will continue to sell the existing product, EZRecords, which costs $100 per package. Ms. Helton believes that the salesperson will spend approximately 20 hours selling EZRecords and 10 hours marketing ProOffice.

CHECK FIGURES
a. Cost/unit for EZRecords: $225
b. Cost/unit for ProOffice: $230

Required

a. Determine the estimated total cost and cost per unit of each product, assuming that the salesperson is able to sell 80 units of EZRecords and 50 units of ProOffice.

b. Determine the estimated total cost and cost per unit of each product, assuming that the salesperson is able to sell 200 units of EZRecords and 100 units of ProOffice.

c. Explain why the cost per unit figures calculated in Requirement *a* are different from the amounts calculated in Requirement *b*. Also explain how the differences in estimated cost per unit will affect pricing decisions.

Problem 16-22A *Allocating joint product cost*

L.O. 3, 7

CHECK FIGURES
a. GM for drumsticks: $(980)
b. Total cost of breasts: $7,087.50

Merkle Chicken Inc. processes and packages chicken for grocery stores. It purchases chickens from farmers and processes them into two different products: chicken drumsticks and chicken steak. From a standard batch of 12,000 pounds of raw chicken that costs $7,000, the company produces two parts: 2,800 pounds of drumsticks and 4,200 pounds of breast for a processing cost of $2,450. The chicken breast is further processed into 3,200 pounds of steak for a processing cost of $2,000. The market price of drumsticks per pound is $1.00 and the market price per pound of chicken steak is $3.40. If Merkle decided to sell chicken breast instead of steak, the price per pound would be $2.00.

Required

a. Allocate the joint cost to the joint products, drumsticks and breasts, using weight as the allocation base. Calculate the net income for each product. Since the drumsticks are producing a net loss, should that product line be eliminated?

b. Reallocate the joint cost to the joint products, drumsticks and breasts, using relative market values as the allocation base. Calculate the net income for each product. Compare the total net income (drumsticks + breasts) computed in Requirement *b* with that computed in Requirement *a* above. Explain why the total amount is the same. Comment on which allocation base (weight or market value) is more appropriate.

c. Should Merkle further process chicken breasts into chicken steak?

EXERCISES—SERIES B

Exercise 16-1B *Allocating costs between divisions*

L.O. 1, 3

Thornton and Hart, LLP, has three departments: auditing, tax, and information systems. The departments occupy 2,500 square feet, 1,500 square feet, and 1,000 square feet of office space, respectively. The firm pays $9,000 per month to rent its offices.

Required

How much monthly rent cost should Thornton and Hart allocate to each department?

Exercise 16-2B *Direct versus indirect costs*

L.O. 2

Kackle and Associates, LLP, is an accounting firm that provides two major types of professional services: (1) tax services provided by the tax department and (2) auditing services provided by the audit department. Each department has numerous clients. Each engagement with each individual client is a separate service (i.e., product) and each department has several engagements in each period. Cost items of the firm follow.

Salary of the partner in charge of the audit department
Salary of the managing partner of the firm
Cost of office supplies such as paper, pencils, erasers, etc.
Depreciation of computers used in the tax department
License fees of the firm
Professional labor for a tax engagement
Secretarial labor supporting both departments

Professional labor for an audit engagement
Depreciation of computers used in the audit department
Salary of the partner in charge of the tax department
Travel expenditures of an audit engagement

Required

a. Identify each cost as a direct or an indirect cost assuming the cost objects are the individual engagements (audit engagements or tax engagements).

b. Identify each cost as a direct or an indirect cost assuming the cost objects are the two departments.

c. Identify each cost as a direct or an indirect cost assuming the cost object is Kackle and Associates, LLP, as a whole.

L.O. 3, 5

Exercise 16-3B ***Allocating overhead costs among products***

Ager Inc. manufactures three different sizes of automobile sunscreens—large, medium, and small. Ager expects to incur $720,000 of overhead costs during the next fiscal year. Other budget information for the coming year follows:

	Large	Medium	Small	Total
Direct labor hours	2,500	5,000	4,500	12,000
Machine hours	700	1,300	1,000	3,000

Required

a. Use direct labor hours as the cost driver to compute the allocation rate and the budgeted overhead cost for each product.

b. Use machine hours as the cost driver to compute the allocation rate and the budgeted overhead cost for each product.

c. Describe a set of circumstances where it would be more appropriate to use direct labor hours as the allocation base.

d. Describe a set of circumstances where it would be more appropriate to use machine hours as the allocation base.

L.O. 3, 4

Exercise 16-4B ***Allocating overhead costs among products***

Fraser Company makes three models of computer disks in its factory: Zip100, Zip250, and Zip40. The expected overhead costs for the next fiscal year are as follows:

Payroll for factory managers	$270,000
Factory maintenance costs	110,000
Factory insurance	40,000
Total overhead costs	$420,000

Fraser uses labor hours as the cost driver to allocate overhead cost. Budgeted labor hours for the products are as follows:

Zip100	2,000 hours
Zip250	1,300
Zip40	900
Total labor hours	4,200

Required

a. Allocate the budgeted overhead costs to the products.

b. Provide a possible explanation as to why Fraser chose labor hours, instead of machine hours, as the allocation base.

Exercise 16-5B *Allocating costs among products* L.O. 3, 4

Pillson Company makes household plastic bags in three different sizes: Snack, Sandwich, and Storage. The estimated direct materials and direct labor costs are as follows.

Expected Costs	Snack	Sandwich	Storage
Direct materials	$140,000	$235,000	$375,000
Direct labor	60,000	120,000	240,000

Pillson allocates two major overhead costs among the three products: $72,000 of indirect labor cost for workers who move various materials and products to different stations in the factory and $126,000 of employee pension costs.

Required

Determine the total cost of each product.

Exercise 16-6B *Allocating indirect cost over varying levels of production* L.O. 3, 5

Malone Company's annual factory depreciation is $18,000. Malone estimated it would operate the factory a total of 2,400 hours this year. The factory operated 200 hours in November and 150 hours in December.

Required

Why would Malone need to allocate factory depreciation cost? How much depreciation cost should Malone allocate to products made in November and those made in December?

Exercise 16-7B *Allocating to solve a timing problem* L.O. 3, 5

On January 1, Kinzey Corporation paid the annual royalty of $810,000 for rights to use patented technology to make batteries for laptop computers. Kinzey plans to use the patented technology to produce five different models of batteries. Kinzey uses machine hours as a common cost driver and plans to operate its machines 54,000 hours in the coming year. The company used 3,000 machine hours in June and 3,600 hours in July.

Required

Why would Kinzey need to allocate the annual royalty payment rather than simply assign it in total to January production? How much of the royalty cost should Kinzey allocate to products made in June and those made in July?

Exercise 16-8B *Allocating a fixed cost* L.O. 3, 5

Last year, Hermit Nassar bought an automobile for $29,000 to use in his taxi business. He expected to drive the vehicle for 150,000 miles before disposing of it for $2,000. Hermit drove 3,200 miles this week and 2,800 miles last week.

Required

a. Determine the total cost of vehicle depreciation this week and last week.

b. Explain why allocating the vehicle cost would or would not be relevant to decision making.

Exercise 16-9B *Allocating overhead cost to accomplish smoothing* L.O. 3, 5

In 2007, Harris Corporation incurred direct manufacturing costs of $30 per unit and manufacturing overhead costs of $270,000. The production activity for the four quarters of 2007 follows:

	1st Quarter	2nd Quarter	3rd Quarter	4th Quarter
Number of units produced	3,300	2,700	4,500	2,000

Required

a. Calculate a predetermined overhead rate based on the number of units produced during the year.

b. Allocate overhead costs to each quarter using the overhead rate computed in Requirement *a*.
c. Using the overhead allocation determined in Requirement *b*, calculate the total cost per unit for each quarter.

L.O. 3, 5

Exercise 16-10B *Allocating overhead for product costing*

Tricon Manufacturing Company produced 500 units of inventory in January 2006. The company expects to produce an additional 5,900 units of inventory during the remaining 11 months of the year, for total estimated production of 6,400 units in 2006. Direct materials and direct labor costs are $74 and $84 per unit, respectively. Tricon expects to incur the following manufacturing overhead costs during 2006:

Indirect materials	$ 6,800
Depreciation on equipment	104,000
Utilities cost	29,200
Salaries of plant manager and staff	304,000
Rental fee on manufacturing facilities	84,000
Total	$528,000

Required

a. Determine the cost of the 500 units of product made in January.
b. Is the cost computed in Requirement *a* actual or estimated? Could Tricon improve accuracy by waiting until December to determine the cost of products?

L.O. 3, 5

Exercise 16-11B *How fixed cost allocation affects a pricing decision*

Sonola Manufacturing Company expects to make 45,000 travel sewing kits during 2005. In January, the company made 1,800 kits. Materials and labor costs for January were $7,200 and $9,000, respectively. In February, Sonola produced 2,200 kits. Material and labor costs for February were $8,800 and $11,000, respectively. The company paid $54,000 for annual factory insurance on January 10, 2005. Ignore other manufacturing overhead costs.

Required

Assuming that Sonola desires to sell its sewing kits for cost plus 25 percent of cost, what price should it charge for the kits produced in January and February?

L.O. 6

Exercise 16-12B *Cost pools*

Wilson Furniture Company incurred the following costs in the process of making tables and chairs.

Glue	Paint
Supervisor salaries	Water bill
Gas bill	Vacation pay
Payroll taxes	Sewer bill
Cost of nails	Staples
Medical insurance	Electric bill

Required

a. Organize the costs in the following three pools: indirect materials, indirect labor, and indirect utilities.
b. Identify an appropriate cost driver for each pool.
c. Explain why accountants use cost pools.

L.O. 3, 7

Exercise 16-13B *Allocating joint product cost*

Bailey Food Corporation makes two products from soybeans, cooking oil and cattle feed. From a standard batch of 100,000 pounds of soybeans, Bailey produces 20,000 pounds of cooking oil and 80,000 pounds of cattle feed. Producing a standard batch costs $12,000. The sales prices per pound are $1.20 for cooking oil and $0.90 for cattle feed.

Required

a. Allocate the joint product cost to the two products using weight as the allocation base.
b. Allocate the joint product cost to the two products using market value as the allocation base.

Exercise 16-14B ***Human factor*** **L.O. 8**

Kramer Company builds custom sailboats. Kramer currently has three boats under construction. The estimated costs to complete each boat are shown below.

	Boat 1	Boat 2	Boat 3
Direct materials	$25,000	$32,000	$12,000
Direct labor	22,000	20,000	14,000

Kramer expects to incur $36,000 of indirect (overhead) costs in the process of making the boats.

Required

a. Based on the information provided, name four allocation bases that could be used to assign the overhead costs to each boat.

b. Assume that the production manager of each boat is permitted to recommend how the overhead costs should be allocated to the boats. Which of the allocation bases named in Requirement *a* is the manager of Boat 2 most likely to recommend? Explain why. What argument may the manager of Boat 2 use to justify his choice of the allocation base?

c. Which of the allocation bases would result in the fairest allocation of the overhead costs from the perspective of the company president?

d. Explain how classifying overhead costs into separate pools could improve the fairness of the allocation of the overhead costs.

PROBLEMS—SERIES B

Problem 16-15B ***Cost accumulation and allocation*** **L.O. 1, 2, 3, 4, 5**

Ridgewood Tools Company has two production departments in its manufacturing facilities. Home tools specializes in hand tools for individual home users, and professional tools makes sophisticated tools for professional maintenance workers. Ridgewood's accountant has identified the following annual costs associated with these two products:

Financial data	
Salary of vice president of production	$180,000
Salary of manager, home tools	54,000
Salary of manager, professional tools	43,500
Direct materials cost, home tools	300,000
Direct materials cost, professional tools	375,000
Direct labor cost, home tools	336,000
Direct labor cost, professional tools	414,000
Direct utilities cost, home tools	75,000
Direct utilities cost, professional tools	30,000
General factorywide utilities	31,500
Production supplies	40,500
Fringe benefits	112,500
Depreciation	360,000
Nonfinancial data	
Machine hours, home tools	4,000
Machine hours, professional tools	2,000

Required

a. Identify the costs that are the (1) direct costs of home tools, (2) direct costs of professional tools, and (3) indirect costs.

b. Select the appropriate cost drivers and allocate the indirect costs to home tools and to professional tools.

c. Assume that each department makes only a single product. Home tools produces its Deluxe Drill for home use, and professional tools produces the Professional Drill. The company made 30,000 Deluxe Drills and 20,000 Professional Drills during the year. Determine the total estimated cost of the products made in each department. If Ridgewood prices its products at cost plus 30 percent of cost, what price per unit must it charge for the Deluxe Drill and the Professional Drill?

L.O. 1, 3, 4

Problem 16-16B *Selecting an appropriate cost driver (What is the base?)*

Perrion Research Institute has three departments: biology, chemistry, and physics. The institute's controller wants to estimate the cost of operating each department. He has identified several indirect costs that must be allocated to each department including $22,400 of phone expense, $4,800 of office supplies, $2,240,000 of office rent, $280,000 of janitorial services, and $300,000 of salary paid to the director. To provide a reasonably accurate allocation of costs, the controller identified several possible cost drivers. These drivers and their association with each department follow.

Cost Driver	Biology	Chemistry	Physics
Number of telephones	20	28	32
Number of researchers	16	20	24
Square footage of office space	8,000	8,000	12,000
Number of secretaries	1	1	1

Required

a. Identify the appropriate cost objects.

b. Identify the appropriate cost driver for each indirect cost, and compute the allocation rate for assigning each indirect cost to the cost objects.

c. Determine the amount of telephone expense that should be allocated to each of the three departments.

d. Determine the amount of supplies expense that should be allocated to the physics department.

e. Determine the amount of office rent cost that should be allocated to the chemistry department.

f. Determine the amount of janitorial services cost that should be allocated to the biology department.

g. Identify two cost drivers not listed here that could be used to allocate the cost of the director's salary to the three departments.

L.O. 1, 2

Problem 16-17B *Cost allocation in a service industry*

Solarz, Adams, and Associates provides legal services for its local community. In addition to its regular attorneys, the firm hires some part-time attorneys to handle small cases. Two secretaries assist all part-time attorneys exclusively. In 2009, the firm paid $48,000 for the two secretaries who worked a total of 3,200 hours. Moreover, the firm paid Sue Rivera $60 per hour and Tim Gasden $50 per hour for their part-time legal services.

In August 2009, Ms. Rivera completed a case that took her 60 hours. Mr. Gasden finished a case on which he worked 20 hours. The firm also paid a private investigator to uncover relevant facts. The investigation fees cost $1,000 for Ms. Rivera's case and $750 for Mr. Gasden's case. Ms. Rivera used 30 hours of secretarial assistance, and Mr. Gasden used 40 hours.

Required

a. Identify the direct and indirect costs incurred in each case completed in August 2009.

b. Determine the total cost of each case.

c. In addition to secretaries' salaries, identify three other indirect costs that may need to be allocated to determine the cost of the cases.

L.O. 1, 3, 4

Problem 16-18B *Cost allocation in a manufacturing company*

Calla's Doors Inc. makes a particular type of door. The labor cost is $120 per door and the material cost is $200 per door. Calla's rents a factory building for $84,000 a month. Calla's plans to produce 24,000 doors annually. In March and April, it made 2,000 and 3,000 doors, respectively.

Required

a. Explain how changes in the cost driver (number of doors made) affect the total amount of fixed rental cost.
b. Explain how changes in the cost driver (number of doors made) affect the fixed rental cost per unit.
c. If the cost objective is to determine the cost per door, is the factory rent a direct or an indirect cost?
d. How much of the factory rent should be allocated to doors produced in March and April?

Problem 16-19B *Fairness in the allocation process*

L.O. 1, 4, 8

Hillshire Furniture Company has two production departments. The parts department uses automated machinery to make parts; as a result, it uses very few employees. The assembly department is labor intensive because workers manually assemble parts into finished furniture. Employee fringe benefits and utility costs are the two major overhead costs of the company's production division. The fringe benefits and utility costs for the year are $600,000 and $288,000, respectively. The typical consumption patterns for the two departments follow.

	Parts	Assembly	Total
Machine hours used	52,000	8,000	60,000
Direct labor hours used	3,500	20,500	24,000

The supervisor of each department receives a bonus based on how well the department controls costs. The company's current policy requires using a single activity base (machine hours or labor hours) to allocate the total overhead cost of $888,000.

Required

a. Assume that you are the parts department supervisor. Choose the allocation base that would minimize your department's share of the total overhead cost. Calculate the amount of overhead to allocate to both departments using the base that you selected.
b. Assume that you are the assembly department supervisor. Choose the allocation base that would minimize your department's share of the total overhead cost. Calculate the amount of overhead to allocate to both departments using the base that you selected.
c. Assume that you are the plant manager and that you have the authority to change the company's overhead allocation policy. Formulate an overhead allocation policy that would be fair to the supervisors of both the parts and assembly departments. Compute the overhead allocation for each department using your policy.

Problem 16-20B *Allocation to accomplish smoothing*

L.O. 1, 3, 5

Zivago Corporation's overhead costs are usually $48,000 per month. However, the company pays $108,000 of real estate tax on the factory facility in March. Thus, the overhead costs for March increase to $156,000. The company normally uses 5,000 direct labor hours per month except for August, September, and October, in which the company requires 9,000 hours of direct labor per month to build inventories for high demand in the holiday season. Last year, the company's actual direct labor hours were the same as usual. The company made 5,000 units of product in each month except August, September, and October, in which it produced 9,000 units per month. Direct labor costs were $16 per unit; direct materials costs were $14 per unit.

Required

a. Calculate a predetermined overhead rate based on direct labor hours.
b. Determine the total allocated overhead cost for the months of March, August, and December.
c. Determine the cost per unit of product for the months of March, August, and December.
d. Determine the selling price for the product, assuming that the company desires to earn a gross margin of $10 per unit.

Problem 16-21B *Allocating indirect cost between products*

L.O. 1, 3, 5

Darcy Corporation has hired a marketing representative to sell the company's two products, Marvelous and Wonderful. The representative's total salary and fringe benefits are $8,000 monthly. The product cost is $90 per unit for Marvelous and $144 per unit for Wonderful. Darcy expects the representative to spend 48 hours per month marketing Marvelous and 112 hours promoting Wonderful.

Required

a. Determine the estimated total cost and cost per unit, assuming that the representative is able to sell 100 units of Marvelous and 70 units of Wonderful in a month. Allocate indirect cost on the basis of labor hours.

b. Determine the estimated total cost and cost per unit, assuming that the representative is able to sell 250 units of Marvelous and 140 units of Wonderful. Allocate indirect cost on the basis of labor hours.

c. Explain why the cost per unit figures calculated in Requirement *a* differ from the amounts calculated in Requirement *b*. Also explain how the differences in estimated cost per unit will affect pricing decisions.

L.O. 3, 9

Problem 16-22B *Allocating joint product cost*

Yu-San Tea Co. makes two products: a high-grade tea branded Wulong and a low-grade tea branded San Tea for the Asian market. Yu-San purchases tea leaves from tea producers in mountainous villages of Taiwan and processes the tea leaves into a high-quality product. The tea leaves are dried and baked in the manufacturing process. Yu-San pays farmers $600 for 900 kilograms of tea leaves. For 900 kilograms of green leaves, the company can produce 100 kilograms of Wulong and 200 kilograms of tea fragments including dried leaf stems and broken dried leaves. The cost of this process is $300 per batch. The tea fragments are packaged into San Tea. The market price for San Tea is $2.00 per kilogram. The market price is $20 per kilogram for Wulong. Yu-San has the option of undertaking an additional process to further refine the 100 kilograms of Wulong into 30 kilograms of Donding, a prestigious brand. The market price of Donding is $100 per kilogram. The cost of the additional processing is $250 per batch.

Required

a. Allocate the joint cost to the joint products, Wulong and San Tea, using weight as the allocation base. Calculate the net income for each product. Since the San Tea is sold at a loss, should that product line be eliminated?

b. Allocate the joint cost to the joint products, Wulong and San Tea, using relative market value as the allocation base. Calculate the net income for each product. Compare the total net income (Wulong + San Tea) computed in Requirement *b* with that computed in Requirement *a* above. Explain why the total amount is the same. Comment on which allocation base (weight or relative market value) is more appropriate.

c. Should Yu-San further process Wulong into Donding?

ANALYZE, THINK, COMMUNICATE

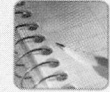

ATC 16-1 Business Applications Case *Allocating fixed costs at Porsche*

During its fiscal year ending on July 31, 2004, the Dr. Ing. h.c. F. Porsche AG, commonly known as "Porsche," manufactured 81,531 vehicles. During that same year Porsche recorded depreciation of €186,302,000. (Porsche's financial information is reported in euros. The symbol € represents the euro.) For this case, assume all depreciation relates to manufacturing activities.

Required

a. Indicate whether the depreciation charge is a:

(1) Product cost, or general, selling, and administrative cost.

(2) Fixed or variable cost relative to the volume of production.

(3) Direct or indirect cost if the cost object is the cost of vehicles made in the 2004 fiscal year.

b. Assume that Porsche incurred depreciation of €15,500,000 in each month of the 2004 fiscal year. It produced 6,000 vehicles during February and 7,000 during March. What was the average amount of depreciation cost per vehicle produced during each of these two months?

c. If Porsche had expected to produce 80,000 vehicles during 2004, what would its predetermined overhead charge per vehicle for depreciation have been? Explain the advantage of using this amount to determine the cost of manufacturing a car in February and March versus the amounts you computed in Requirement *b*.

d. If Porsche's management had estimated the profit per vehicle based on its budgeted production of 80,000 units, would you expect its actual profit per vehicle to be higher or lower than expected? Explain.

ATC 16-2 Group Assignment *Selection of the cost driver*

Vulcan College School of Business is divided into three departments, accounting, marketing, and management. Relevant information for each of the departments follows.

Cost Driver	Accounting	Marketing	Management
Number of students	1,400	800	400
Number of classes per semester	64	36	28
Number of professors	20	24	10

Vulcan is a private school that expects each department to generate a profit. It rewards departments for profitability by assigning 20 percent of each department's profits back to that department. Departments have free rein as to how to use these funds. Some departments have used them to supply professors with computer technology. Others have expanded their travel budgets. The practice has been highly successful in motivating the faculty to control costs. The revenues and direct costs for the year 2004 follow.

	Accounting	Marketing	Management
Revenue	$29,600,000	$16,600,000	$8,300,000
Direct costs	24,600,000	13,800,000	6,600,000

Vulcan allocates to the School of Business $4,492,800 of indirect overhead costs such as administrative salaries and costs of operating the registrar's office and the bookstore.

Required

a. Divide the class into groups and organize the groups into three sections. Assign each section a department. Assume that the dean of the school is planning to assign an equal amount of the college overhead to each department. Have the students in each group prepare a response to the dean's plan. Each group should select a spokesperson who is prepared to answer the following questions.

(1) Is your group in favor of or opposed to the allocation plan suggested by the dean?

(2) Does the plan suggested by the dean provide a fair allocation? Why?

The instructor should lead a discussion designed to assess the appropriateness of the dean's proposed allocation plan.

b. Have each group select the cost driver (allocation base) that best serves the self-interest of the department it represents.

c. Consensus on Requirement *c* should be achieved before completing Requirement *d.* Each group should determine the amount of the indirect cost to be allocated to each department using the cost driver that best serves the self-interest of the department it represents. Have a spokesperson from each section go to the board and show the income statement that would result for each department.

d. Discuss the development of a cost driver(s) that would promote fairness rather than self-interest in allocating the indirect costs.

ATC 16-3 Research Assignment *Cost accounting issues at real-world companies*

The July 2003 issue of *Strategic Finance* contains the article "Roles and Practices in Management Accounting Today: Results From the 2003 IMA-E&Y Survey" written by Ashish Garg, Debashis Ghosh, James Hudick, and Chwen Nowacki. This article reviews findings from a survey of managerial accountants conducted by the Institute of Management Accountants (IMA). Read this article and complete the following requirements.

Required

a. The article notes that cost management is an important element for strategic decision making. Why did respondents to the survey believe this was the case?

b. The authors noted that decision makers were most interested in "actionable" cost information. What are the attributes of actionable cost information?

c. Ninety-eight percent of respondents to the survey said that factors exist that cause distortions of cost information. What factors were identified that are responsible for these distortions?

d. Considering the proliferation of "off the shelf" software that is available, many people believe only a minority of companies develop their own cost management systems. According to the article, what percentage of companies actually do develop their systems "in house," and what do you think are the implications of the in-house development for managerial accountants?

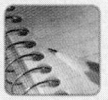

ATC 16-4 Writing Assignment *Selection of the appropriate cost driver*

Bullions Enterprises, Inc. (BEI), makes gold, silver, and bronze medals used to recognize outstanding athletic performance in regional and national sporting events. The per unit direct costs of producing the medals follows.

	Gold	Silver	Bronze
Direct materials	$300	$130	$ 35
Labor	120	120	120

During 2002, BEI made 1,200 units of each type of medal for a total of 3,600 (1,200 × 3) medals. All medals are created through the same production process, and they are packaged and shipped in identical containers. Indirect overhead costs amounted to $324,000. BEI currently uses the number of units as the cost driver for the allocation of overhead cost. As a result, BEI allocated $90 ($324,000 ÷ 3,600 units) of overhead cost to each medal produced.

Required

The president of the company has questioned the wisdom of assigning the same amount of overhead to each type of medal. He believes that overhead should be assigned on the basis of the cost to produce the medals. In other words, more overhead should be charged to expensive gold medals, less to silver, and even less to bronze. Assume that you are BEI's chief financial officer. Write a memo responding to the president's suggestion.

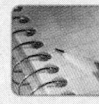

ATC 16-5 Ethical Dilemma *Allocation to achieve fairness*

The American Acupuncture Association offers continuing professional education courses for its members at its annual meeting. Instructors are paid a fee for each student attending their courses but are charged a fee for overhead costs that is deducted from their compensation. Overhead costs include fees paid to rent instructional equipment such as overhead projectors, provide supplies to participants, and offer refreshments during coffee breaks. The number of courses offered is used as the allocation base for determining the overhead charge. For example, if overhead costs amount to $5,000 and 25 courses are offered, each course is allocated an overhead charge of $200 ($5,000 ÷ 25 courses). Heidi McCarl, who taught one of the courses, received the following statement with her check in payment for her instructional services.

Instructional fees (20 students × $50 per student)	$1,000
Less: Overhead charge	(200)
Less: Charge for sign language assistant	(240)
Amount due instructor	$ 560

Although Ms. McCarl was well aware that one of her students was deaf and required a sign language assistant, she was surprised to find that she was required to absorb the cost of this service.

Required

a. Given that the Americans with Disabilities Act stipulates that the deaf student cannot be charged for the cost of providing sign language, who should be required to pay the cost of sign language services?

b. Explain how allocation can be used to promote fairness in distributing service costs to the disabled. Describe two ways to treat the $240 cost of providing sign language services that improve fairness.

COMPREHENSIVE PROBLEM

Magnificent Modems has excess production capacity and is considering the possibility of making and selling paging equipment. The following estimates are based on a production and sales volume of 1,000 pagers.

Unit-level manufacturing costs are expected to be $20. Sales commissions will be established at $1 per unit. The current facility-level costs, including depreciation on manufacturing equipment ($60,000), rent on the manufacturing facility ($50,000), depreciation on the administrative equipment ($12,000), and other fixed administrative expenses ($71,950), will not be affected by the production of the pagers. The chief accountant has decided to allocate the facility-level costs to the existing product (modems) and to the new product (pagers) on the basis of the number of units of product made (i.e., 5,000 modems and 1,000 pagers).

Required

a. Determine the per-unit cost of making and selling 1,000 pagers.

b. Assuming the pagers could be sold at a price of $34 each, should Magnificent make the pagers?

c. Comment on the validity of using the number of units as an allocation base.

CHAPTER 17

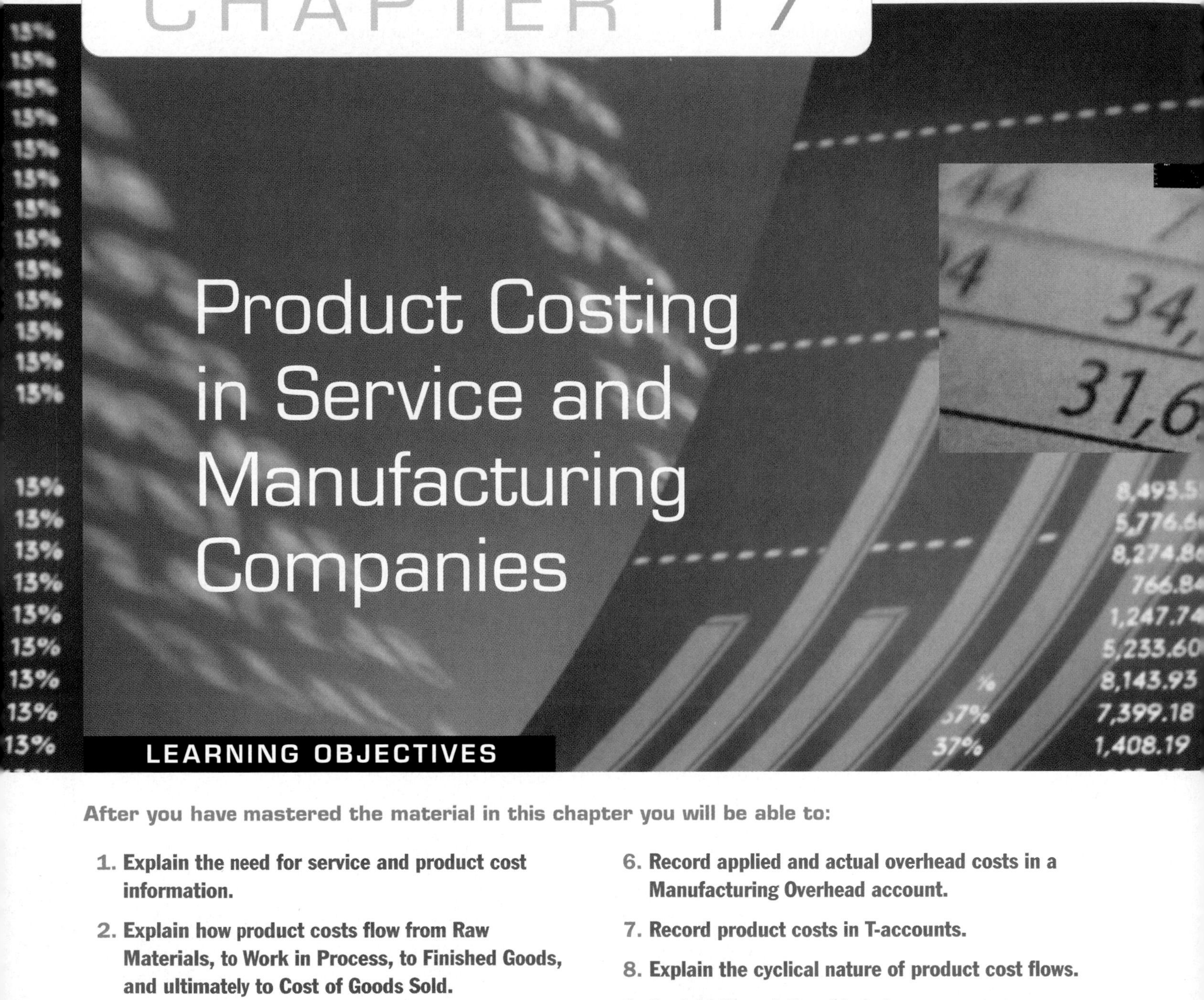

Product Costing in Service and Manufacturing Companies

LEARNING OBJECTIVES

After you have mastered the material in this chapter you will be able to:

1. **Explain the need for service and product cost information.**
2. **Explain how product costs flow from Raw Materials, to Work in Process, to Finished Goods, and ultimately to Cost of Goods Sold.**
3. **Distinguish between costing for service and manufacturing companies.**
4. **Demonstrate, using a horizontal financial statements model, how product cost flows affect financial statements.**
5. **Explain the need to assign estimated overhead costs to inventory and cost of goods sold during an accounting period.**
6. **Record applied and actual overhead costs in a Manufacturing Overhead account.**
7. **Record product costs in T-accounts.**
8. **Explain the cyclical nature of product cost flows.**
9. **Explain the relationship between over- or underapplied overhead and variance analysis.**
10. **Prepare a schedule of cost of goods manufactured and sold.**
11. **Prepare financial statements for a manufacturing company.**
12. **Distinguish between absorption and variable costing.**

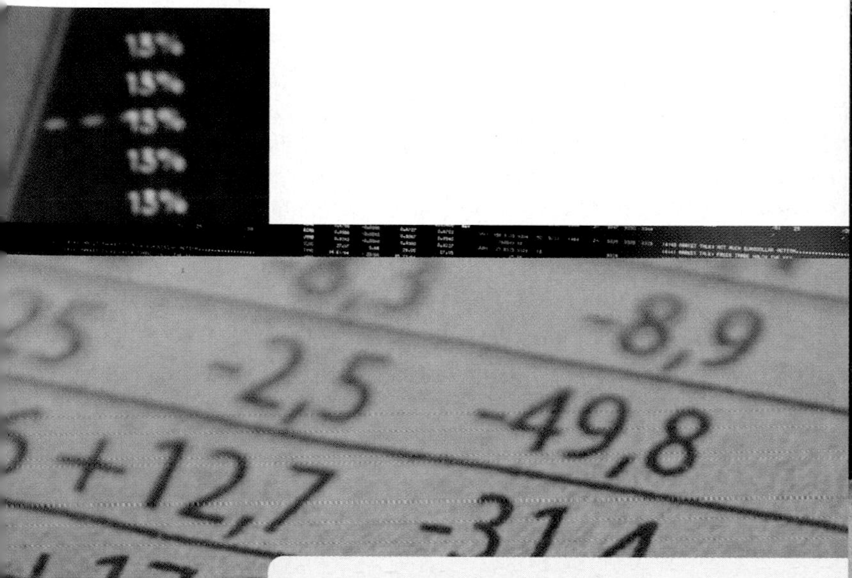

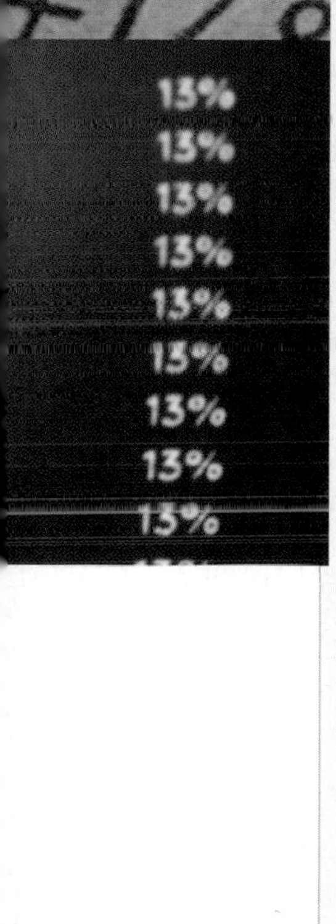

Chapter 17

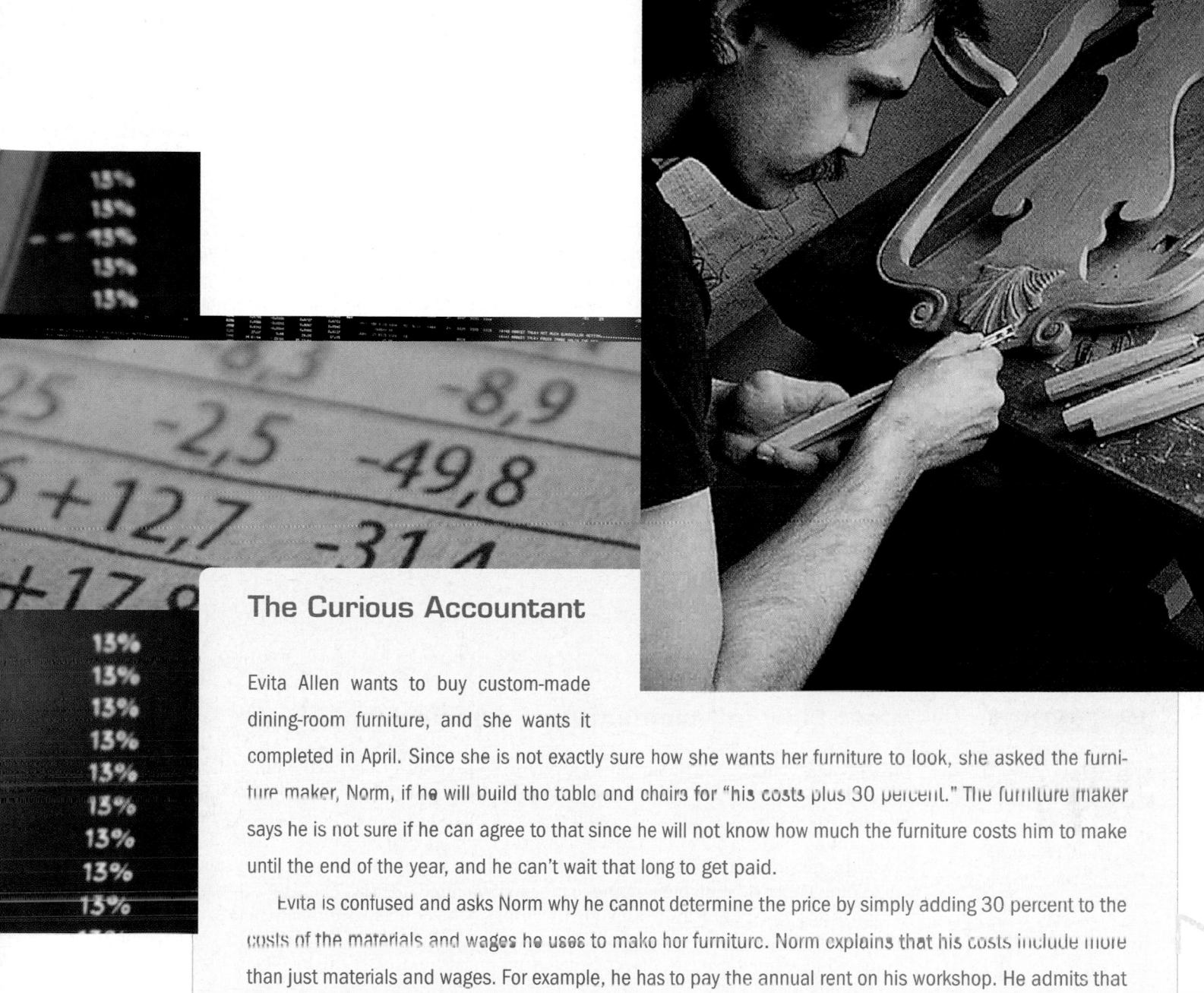

The Curious Accountant

Evita Allen wants to buy custom-made dining-room furniture, and she wants it completed in April. Since she is not exactly sure how she wants her furniture to look, she asked the furniture maker, Norm, if he will build the table and chairs for "his costs plus 30 percent." The furniture maker says he is not sure if he can agree to that since he will not know how much the furniture costs him to make until the end of the year, and he can't wait that long to get paid.

Evita is confused and asks Norm why he cannot determine the price by simply adding 30 percent to the costs of the materials and wages he uses to make her furniture. Norm explains that his costs include more than just materials and wages. For example, he has to pay the annual rent on his workshop. He admits that his rent is a fixed amount and he knows how much it will be, but he will not know how much of that rent is related to Evita's furniture until he knows how many other jobs he has throughout the year. In other words, if he completes 10 jobs during the year, the cost of Evita's furniture would include 10 percent of his rent, but if he has 20 jobs, then she would be responsible for only 5 percent of his rent.

How can a manufacturer, such as Norm's Furniture Shop, know what price to charge its customers when it does not know the real cost of any one job until the year ends? (Answer on page 843.)

CHAPTER OPENING

Service and product costing systems supply information about the cost of providing services or making products. Organizations need service and product cost information for financial reporting, managerial accounting, and contract negotiations.

For financial reporting, companies are required by generally accepted accounting principles (GAAP) to report service and product costs in their published financial statements. For example, product costs for manufacturing companies must be allocated between inventory (reported on the balance sheet) and cost of goods sold (reported on the income statement). Similarly, service companies must match on their income statements the costs of providing services with the revenues generated from the services provided.

For managerial accounting, managers need to know the cost of providing services or making products so they can plan company operations. For example, companies could not prepare budgets without knowing the cost of services or products. Service and product costing is also needed for cost control. Managers compare expected costs with actual costs to identify problems that need correcting. Service and product cost information may be used for pricing and other short-term decisions. For example, the cost of a service or product may be used in special order, outsourcing, or product elimination decisions.

Service and product costing information may be used by governmental agencies to regulate rates for public service entities such as utility companies or hospitals. Service and product costs are also used in determining the amount due on contracts that compensate companies for the costs they incur plus a reasonable profit (cost-plus contracts). For example, many governmental defense contracts are negotiated on a cost-plus basis. Cost-plus pricing may also be used by private companies. For example, many builders of custom homes charge customers based on cost-plus contracts. Cost information is therefore necessary for contract negotiations. This chapter shows how manufacturing companies determine the cost of the products they make. ■

Cost Flow in Manufacturing Companies

LO 1

Explain the need for service and product cost information.

In previous chapters, we assumed all inventory started during an accounting period was also completed during that accounting period. All product costs (materials, labor, and manufacturing overhead) were either in inventory or expensed as cost of goods sold. At the end of an accounting period, however, most real-world companies have raw materials on hand, and manufacturing companies are likely to have in inventory items that have been started but are not completed. Most manufacturing companies accumulate product costs in three distinct inventory accounts: (1) **Raw Materials Inventory,** which includes lumber, metals, paints, and chemicals that will be used to make the company's products; (2) **Work in Process Inventory,** which includes partially completed products; and (3) **Finished Goods Inventory,** which includes completed products that are ready for sale.

The cost of materials is first recorded in the Raw Materials Inventory account. The cost of materials placed in production is then transferred from the Raw Materials Inventory account to the Work in Process Inventory account. The costs of labor and overhead are added to the Work in Process Inventory account. The cost of the goods completed during the period is transferred from the Work in Process Inventory account to the Finished Goods Inventory account. The cost of the goods that are sold during the accounting period is transferred from the Finished Goods Inventory account to the Cost of Goods Sold account. The balances that remain in the Raw Materials, Work in Process, and Finished Goods Inventory accounts are reported on the balance sheet. The amount of product cost transferred to the Cost of Goods Sold account is expensed on the income statement. Exhibit 17.1 shows the flow of manufacturing costs through the accounting records.

Cost Flow in Service Companies

Like manufacturing companies, many service companies purchase raw materials and transform them through production stages such as work in process, finished goods, and

EXHIBIT 17.1

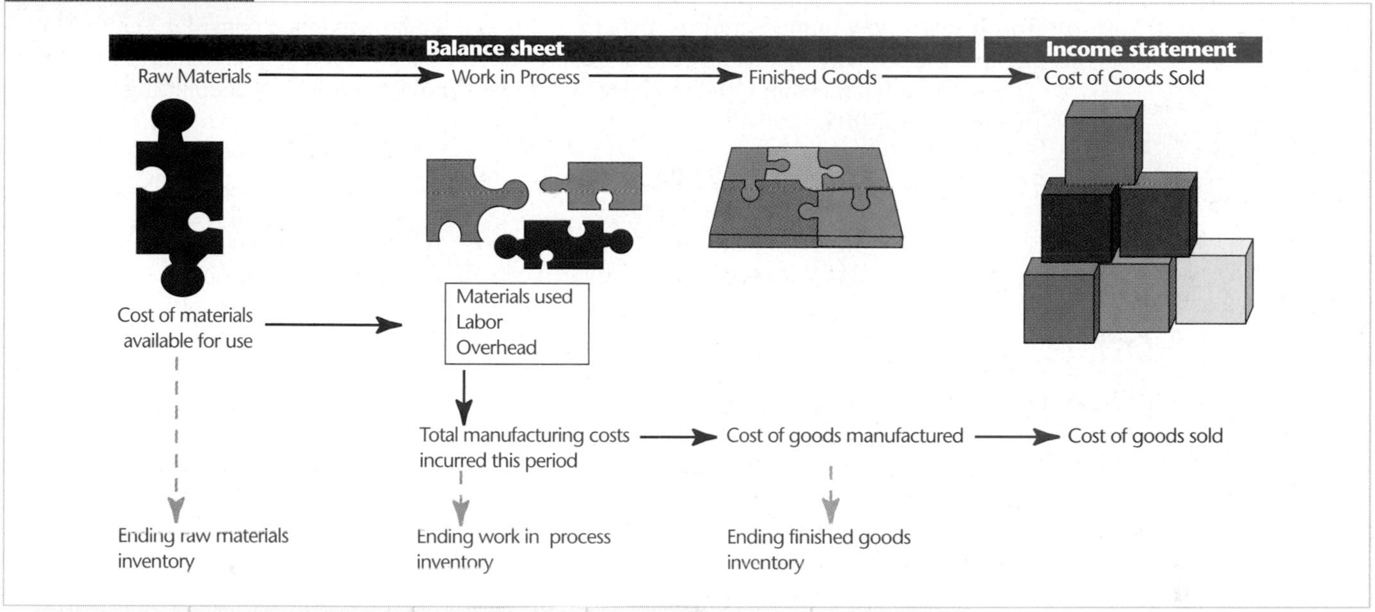

LO 2

Explain how product costs flow from Raw Materials, to Work in Process, to Finished Goods, and ultimately to Cost of Goods Sold.

LO 3

Distinguish between costing for service and manufacturing companies.

cost of goods sold. For example, a **McDonald's** hamburger starts with raw materials (meat, bun, and condiments), goes through work in process (is cooked, assembled, and wrapped), becomes a finished product, and is sold to a customer. Why then is McDonald's considered a *service* rather than a *manufacturing* company? The distinguishing feature is that products from McDonald's are consumed immediately. In general, services cannot be stored and sold later. Service companies do not have Work in Process and Finished Goods Inventory accounts for collecting costs before transferring them to a Cost of Goods Sold account. At the end of the day, McDonald's has no work in process or finished goods inventory.

Is a retail company such as **Toys "R" Us** a service company or a manufacturing company? Because wholesale and retail companies have large inventories, it may seem odd to think of them as service companies. Consider, however, what employees of a wholesale or retail company do. Their efforts cannot be stored and used later. The services of a salesperson are consumed as customers are assisted. Other service organizations include insurance companies, banks, cleaning establishments, airlines, law firms, hospitals, hotels, and governmental agencies.

Even though service companies do not collect costs in inventory accounts for financial reporting purposes, they do accumulate cost information for decision making. For example, a hotel manager needs to know the cost of providing a room to assess whether the pricing policy is appropriate. A private school may compare the expected and actual cost of offering a course to ensure that costs are controlled. Airline executives need to know the cost of serving a specific route to decide whether to maintain or eliminate the route. Measuring the cost of providing services is just as necessary as measuring the cost of making products whether the cost is collected in an inventory account or charged directly to the income statement.

Manufacturing Cost Flow Illustrated

LO 4

Demonstrate, using a horizontal financial statements model, how product cost flows affect financial statements.

VENTRA

Topic Tackler PLUS

17-1

To illustrate how manufacturing costs flow through ledger accounts, consider Ventra Manufacturing Company, which makes mahogany jewelry boxes that it sells to department stores. The account balances in Exhibit 17.2 were drawn from the company's accounting records as of January 1, 2005.

EXHIBIT 17.2

Trial Balance as of January 1, 2005

Cash	$ 64,500	
Raw Materials Inventory	500	
Work in Process Inventory	0	
Finished Goods Inventory	836	
Manufacturing Equipment	40,000	
Accumulated Depreciation		$ 10,000
Common Stock		76,000
Retained Earnings		19,836
Totals	$105,836	$105,836

Ventra Manufacturing's 2005 accounting events are explained here. The effects of the events are summarized in the T-accounts in Exhibit 17.4 on page 843. Study the entries in Exhibit 17.4 as you read the event descriptions in the following section of this chapter. The illustration assumes Ventra determines the cost of making its jewelry boxes on a monthly basis. Accounting events for January are described next.

Events Affecting Manufacturing Cost Flow in January

Event 1 **Ventra Manufacturing paid $26,500 cash to purchase raw materials.**

For simplicity, assume Ventra purchased all raw materials needed for the year at the beginning of the year. In practice, materials are usually purchased much more frequently. The effects of the materials purchase on the company's financial statements are shown in the following horizontal financial statements model.[1]

Assets			=	Liabilities	+	Equity	Revenue	−	Expenses	=	Net Income	Cash Flow
Cash	+	Raw Materials Inventory										
(26,500)	+	26,500	=	NA	+	NA	NA	−	NA	=	NA	(26,500) OA

This event is an asset exchange. One asset—cash—decreases, and another asset—raw materials inventory—increases. Neither total assets reported on the balance sheet nor any revenues or expenses on the income statement are affected. Raw materials costs are only one component of total manufacturing (product) costs. The raw materials costs will be included in the cost of goods sold (expense) recognized when completed jewelry boxes are sold to customers. Because Ventra spent cash for a current asset it will use in routine business operations, the cash outflow is classified as an operating activity (OA) on the statement of cash flows.

Event 2 **Ventra placed $1,100 of raw materials into production in the process of making jewelry boxes.**

[1] The horizontal model arranges the major financial statement elements horizontally across a single page. Reading from left to right, balance sheet elements are presented first, followed by income statement elements, and then the statement of cash flows. Cash flow classifications are identified by the letters OA for operating activities, IA for investing activities, and FA for financing activities.

This event is also an asset exchange. One asset—raw materials inventory—decreases, and another asset—work in process inventory—increases. Total assets reported on the balance sheet are not affected. Neither the income statement nor the statement of cash flows is affected. The effects on the company's financial statements of using the raw materials follow.

Assets			=	Liabilities	+	Equity	Revenue	−	Expenses	=	Net Income	Cash Flow
Raw Materials Inventory	+	Work in Process Inventory										
(1,100)	+	1,100	=	NA	+	NA	NA	−	NA	=	NA	NA

Ventra's raw materials are *direct* inputs to the production process. They are accounted for using the *perpetual inventory method.* Because the raw materials are traced directly to products, it is easy to match the cost flow with the physical flow. Every time direct raw materials are moved from storage to work in process, their cost is transferred in the accounting records as well.

Event 3 Ventra paid $2,000 cash to purchase production supplies (glue, nails, sandpaper).

This event is also an asset exchange. One asset—cash—decreases, and another asset—production supplies—increases. Total assets reported on the balance sheet are not affected. Net income is not affected. The cash paid for the supplies purchased is reported in the operating activities section of the statement of cash flows. The effects of this event on the company's financial statements follow.

Assets			=	Liabilities	+	Equity	Revenue	−	Expenses	=	Net Income	Cash Flow
Cash	+	Production Supplies										
(2,000)	+	2,000	=	NA	+	NA	NA	−	NA	=	NA	(2,000) OA

The production supplies are recorded in a separate asset account because Ventra finds it more practical to account for them using the *periodic inventory method.* Production supplies are *indirect* inputs. Such small quantities are used on each jewelry box that it is not worth the trouble to track the actual costs as the materials are used. Nobody wants to make a journal entry every time a few nails are used. *Instead of recognizing production supplies usage as it occurs (perpetually), Ventra determines at the end of the accounting period (periodically) the cost of supplies used.* The record-keeping procedures for including the cost of production supplies in the flow of manufacturing costs are described in the explanation of the Manufacturing Overhead account described shortly.

Event 4 Ventra paid production workers $1,400 cash.

These wages are *not* classified as salary expense. Because the labor was used to make jewelry boxes, the cost is added to the Work in Process Inventory account. This event is yet another asset exchange. Ventra exchanged cash for the value added by making the inventory. One asset—cash—decreases, and another asset—work in process inventory—increases. Total assets reported on the balance sheet are not affected. The income statement is not affected. The cash outflow is reported in the operating activities section of the statement of cash flows. The effects on the company's financial statements of incurring production labor costs follow.

Assets			=	Liabilities	+	Equity	Revenue	−	Expenses	=	Net Income	Cash Flow
Cash	+	Work in Process Inventory										
(1,400)	+	1,400	=	NA	+	NA	NA	−	NA	=	NA	(1,400) OA

Flow of Overhead Costs

LO 5

Explain the need to assign estimated overhead costs to inventory and cost of goods sold during an accounting period.

Topic Tackler PLUS

17-2

Assume Ventra made 500 jewelry boxes during January. What is the cost per jewelry box? Why does management need to know this cost? If Ventra uses a cost-plus pricing strategy, management must know the cost per jewelry box to determine what price to charge for each one. Product cost information is also used to control costs and evaluate managerial performance. By comparing current production costs with historical or standard costs, management can evaluate whether performance meets expectations and take appropriate action to ensure the company accomplishes its goals. Ventra has many reasons for needing to know in January the cost of products made in January.

The *direct costs* of making the 500 jewelry boxes in January are \$1,100 for materials and \$1,400 for labor. The *actual indirect overhead costs* are unknown. Ventra will not know the exact amount of some of these indirect costs until the end of the year. For example, Ventra uses the periodic inventory method to determine the cost of production supplies consumed. The actual cost of supplies consumed is unknown until the end of the year when Ventra counts any unused supplies. Similarly, the actual cost for 2005 of taxes, insurance, landscaping, supervisory bonuses, and other indirect costs may be unknown in January. Ventra cannot delay making managerial decisions until actual cost data become available. Ventra needs information on January 31 that will not be available until December 31. This dilemma is depicted in the following graphic.

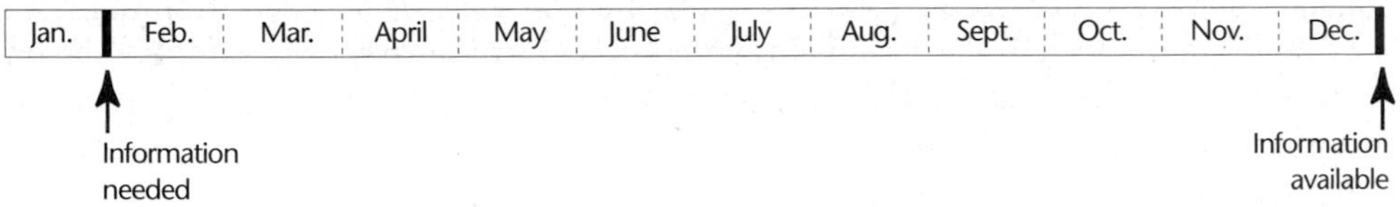

To solve the problem of needing cost information before it is available, Ventra *records estimated costs* in its accounting system *during the accounting period.* To illustrate, assume the accountant estimated Ventra will incur total indirect overhead costs of \$40,320 during 2005. This *estimate* of overhead cost includes \$1,600 for the cost of production supplies Ventra will use, \$10,000 of depreciation cost, and \$28,720 of other costs such as supervisory salaries, rent on the manufacturing facility, utilities, and maintenance. How much of the \$40,320 *estimated* overhead cost should Ventra allocate to the units produced in January? Ventra must first identify the most appropriate allocation base. Assuming the jewelry boxes are identical, it makes sense to use number of units as the allocation base, assigning an equal amount of overhead cost to each box.

Suppose Ventra's accountant expected Ventra to produce 12,000 jewelry boxes during the year. Based on this estimate, the allocation rate is \$3.36 per unit (\$40,320 expected cost ÷ 12,000 units). Because the overhead allocation rate is determined before the actual overhead costs are known, it is called a **predetermined overhead rate.** Using the \$3.36 predetermined overhead rate, Ventra allocated \$1,680 of overhead cost to the 500 jewelry boxes made in January (\$3.36 × 500 boxes).

Manufacturing Overhead Account

LO 6

Record applied and actual overhead costs in a Manufacturing Overhead account.

How are overhead costs recorded in the accounting records? Estimated overhead costs are *applied* (assigned) to work in process inventory *at the time goods are produced.* As shown in event 5 below, for January Ventra Manufacturing would apply (transfer) \$1,680 of overhead cost to the Work in Process Inventory account. Actual overhead costs may be incurred at different times from when goods are made. For example, Ventra may recognize depreciation or supplies use at year-end. Actual and estimated overhead costs are therefore recorded at different times during the accounting period.

At the time estimated overhead is added (a debit) to the Work in Process Inventory account, a corresponding entry is recorded on the credit side of a *temporary* account called *Manufacturing Overhead.* This credit entry in the Manufacturing Overhead account is **applied overhead.** Think of the **Manufacturing Overhead account** as a temporary asset account. Recognizing estimated overhead can be viewed as an asset exchange transaction. When estimated overhead is recognized, the temporary account, Manufacturing Overhead, decreases and the Work in Process Inventory account increases.

REALITY BYTES

Like manufacturing companies, service companies must use predetermined overhead rates to make timely decisions, such as determining what price to charge customers. Consider the Engineering and Evaluation (E&E) segment of **National Technical Systems, Inc.**, a large technical services company headquartered in Calabasas, California. In its 2003 fiscal year, the E&E segment generated over $54 million in revenues.

According to the company's 2003 annual report, its E&E segment "provides highly trained technical personnel for product certification, product safety testing, and product evaluation . . . " including " . . . performing structural testing and analysis . . . of large articles such as complete airframes." Fixed pricing is one method the company uses to price its goods.

Since the company has a lot of fixed overhead costs that include, among other things, depreciation of its testing facilities and equipment, it does not know the actual cost of completing a job until the end of the year. However, it cannot wait until then to give the customer a price for a test to be performed in March. How does it determine the price to charge? According to the company's annual report, "At the time the Company enters into a contract that includes multiple tasks, the Company *estimates* the amount of actual labor *and other costs* that will be required to complete each task based on historical experience." (Emphasis supplied.) These cost estimates are used to establish a price to be charged.

Actual overhead costs are recorded as increases (debits) in the Manufacturing Overhead account. For example, at the end of the year, Ventra will reduce the Production Supplies account and increase the Manufacturing Overhead account by the actual amount of supplies used. The balance in the Production Supplies account will be decreased and the balance in the Manufacturing Overhead account will be increased. When Ventra pays monthly rent cost for the manufacturing facilities, it will increase Manufacturing Overhead and decrease Cash. Other actual overhead costs are recorded the same way.

Since differences normally exist between estimated and actual overhead costs, the Manufacturing Overhead account is likely to have a balance at the end of the year. If more overhead has been applied than was actually incurred, the account balance represents the amount of **overapplied overhead.** If less overhead was applied than was incurred, the account balance is **underapplied overhead.** Overapplied overhead means the amount of estimated overhead cost recorded in the Work in Process Inventory account exceeded the actual overhead cost incurred. Underapplied overhead means the amount of estimated overhead cost recorded in the Work in Process Inventory account was less than the actual overhead cost incurred.

Because costs flow from Work in Process Inventory to Finished Goods Inventory and then to Cost of Goods Sold, these accounts will also be overstated or understated relative to actual costs. If the amount of overapplied or underapplied overhead is significant, it must be allocated proportionately at the end of the year to the Work in Process Inventory, Finished Goods Inventory, and Cost of Goods Sold accounts so these accounts will reflect actual, rather than estimated, amounts for financial reporting.

In most cases, over- or underapplied overhead is not significant and companies may allocate it in any convenient manner. In these circumstances, companies normally assign the total amount of the overhead correction directly to Cost of Goods Sold. We have adopted this simplifying practice throughout the text and in the end-of-chapter exercises and problems.

EXHIBIT 17.3

Flow of Product Costs

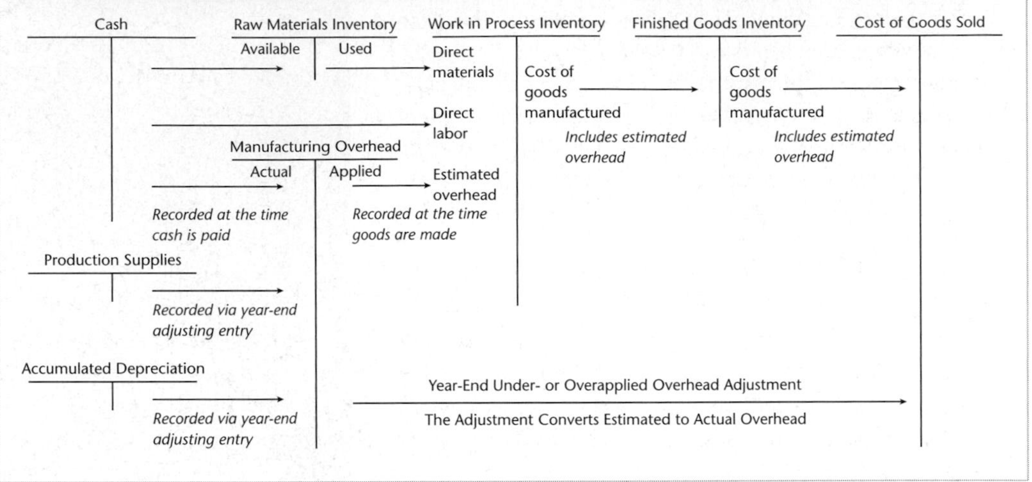

Exhibit 17.3 shows the flow of product costs, including actual and applied overhead. To illustrate using a Manufacturing Overhead account, return to Ventra Manufacturing Company.

Event 5 Ventra recognized \$1,680 of estimated manufacturing overhead costs at the end of January (see previous section entitled Flow of Overhead Costs to review computing this amount).

This event is another asset exchange. Total assets reported on the balance sheet, net income, and cash flow are not affected. The temporary asset account Manufacturing Overhead decreases, and the asset account Work in Process Inventory increases. The effects of this event on the company's financial statements follow.

Assets			=	Liabilities	+	Equity	Revenue	−	Expenses	=	Net Income	Cash Flow
Manufacturing Overhead	+	Work in Process Inventory										
(1,680)	+	1,680	=	NA	+	NA	NA	−	NA	=	NA	NA

Event 6 Ventra transferred the total cost of the 500 jewelry boxes made in January (\$1,100 materials + \$1,400 labor + \$1,680 estimated overhead = \$4,180 cost of goods manufactured) from work in process to finished goods.

This event is an asset exchange. Total assets reported on the balance sheet, net income, and cash flow are not affected. The asset account Work in Process Inventory decreases, and the asset account Finished Goods Inventory increases. The effects of this event on the company's financial statements follow.

Assets			=	Liabilities	+	Equity	Revenue	−	Expenses	=	Net Income	Cash Flow
Work in Process Inventory	+	Finished Goods Inventory										
(4,180)	+	4,180	=	NA	+	NA	NA	−	NA	=	NA	NA

Event 7 Ventra transferred the cost of 400 sold jewelry boxes from finished goods inventory to cost of goods sold.

Recall that Ventra made 500 jewelry boxes costing \$4,180 during January. Also, the beginning balance in the Finished Goods Inventory account was \$836. Assume this balance represented

100 jewelry boxes that had been made in 2004. Therefore, 600 units (100 + 500) of finished goods costing $5,016 ($836 + $4,180) were available for sale. If Ventra sold 400 units, it had 200 units in finished goods inventory at the end of January. The cost of the 600 boxes available ($5,016) must be allocated between the Finished Goods Inventory account and the Cost of Goods Sold account. The allocation is based on the cost per unit of jewelry boxes. Given that 600 boxes cost $5,016, the cost per unit is $8.36 ($5,016 ÷ 600). Based on this cost per unit, Ventra transferred $3,344 ($8.36 × 400 boxes) from finished goods inventory to cost of goods sold, leaving an ending balance of $1,672 ($8.36 × 200 boxes) in the Finished Goods Inventory account.

Transferring cost from finished goods inventory to cost of goods sold is an asset use event. Both total assets and stockholders' equity reported on the balance sheet decrease. The asset finished goods inventory decreases, and the expense cost of goods sold increases, decreasing stockholders' equity (retained earnings). Net income decreases. Recognizing the expense does not affect cash flow. The sales transaction encompasses two events. The following horizontal model shows the effects of the expense recognition. The effects of the corresponding revenue recognition are discussed separately as Event 8.

Assets	=	Liabilities	+	Equity	Revenue	−	Expenses	=	Net Income	Cash Flow
Finished Goods Inventory	=			Retained Earnings						
(3,344)	=	NA	+	(3,344)	NA	−	3,344	=	(3,344)	NA

Knowing the cost per jewelry box is useful for many purposes. For example, the amount of the allocation between the ending Finished Goods Inventory and the Cost of Goods Sold accounts is needed for the financial statements. Ventra must compute the cost per unit data if it wishes to prepare interim (monthly or quarterly) financial reports. The cost per unit for the month of January also could be compared to the cost per unit for the previous accounting period or to standard cost data to evaluate cost control and managerial performance. Finally, the cost per unit data are needed for setting the price under a cost-plus pricing strategy. Assume Ventra desires to earn a gross margin of $5.64 per jewelry box. It would therefore charge $14 ($8.36 cost + $5.64 gross margin) per unit for each jewelry box. When recording the effects of recognizing revenue for the 400 boxes sold, we assume that Ventra charges its customers $14 per unit.

Event 8 Ventra recognized $5,600 ($14 per unit × 400 units) of sales revenue for the cash sale of 400 jewelry boxes.

Recognizing revenue is an asset source transaction. The asset cash increases and stockholders' equity (retained earnings) increases. Net income increases. The cash inflow is reported in the operating activities section of the statement of cash flows. These effects are shown here.

Assets	=	Liabilities	+	Equity	Revenue	−	Expenses	=	Net Income	Cash Flow
Cash	=			Retained Earnings						
5,600	=	NA	+	5,600	5,600	−	NA	=	5,600	5,600 OA

Event 9 Ventra paid $1,200 cash for manufacturing overhead costs including indirect labor, utilities, and rent.

Paying for actual overhead costs is an asset exchange event. Ventra transfers cost from the asset account Cash to the temporary asset account Manufacturing Overhead. Total assets on the balance sheet and net income are unaffected. The cash outflow is reported as a reduction in the operating activities section of the statement of cash flows. These effects follow.

Assets			=	Liabilities	+	Equity	Revenue	−	Expenses	=	Net Income	Cash Flow
Cash	+	Manufacturing Overhead										
(1,200)	+	1,200	=	NA	+	NA	NA	−	NA	=	NA	(1,200) OA

Recall that $1,680 of overhead cost was applied to the January work in process inventory. This amount is significantly more than the $1,200 of actual overhead costs paid for above. These amounts differ because the estimated (applied) overhead includes several costs that have not yet been recognized. For example, the amount of supplies used and depreciation expense are not recognized until Ventra records adjusting entries on December 31. Although these costs are not recognized until December, a portion of them must be included in the cost of products made in January. Otherwise, all of the supplies cost and depreciation cost would be assigned to products made in December.

The manufacturing equipment and supplies are actually used throughout the year. Assigning the total cost of these resources to December alone would overstate the cost of December production and understate the cost of production during other months. Such distortions in measuring product cost could mislead managers making decisions based on the reported costs. By using *estimated* overhead costs during the accounting period, management reduces the distortions that using actual monthly costs would create. The difference between actual and estimated overhead is corrected in a *year-end adjusting entry.* Companies do not adjust for these differences on an interim basis.

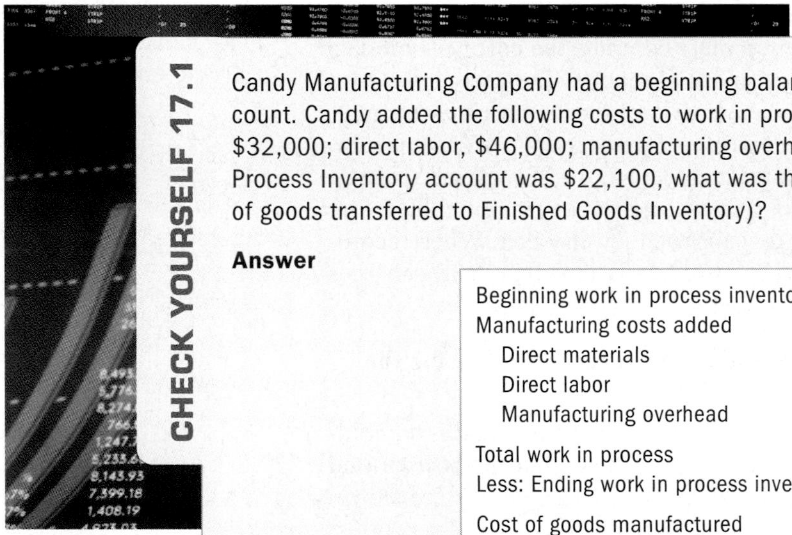

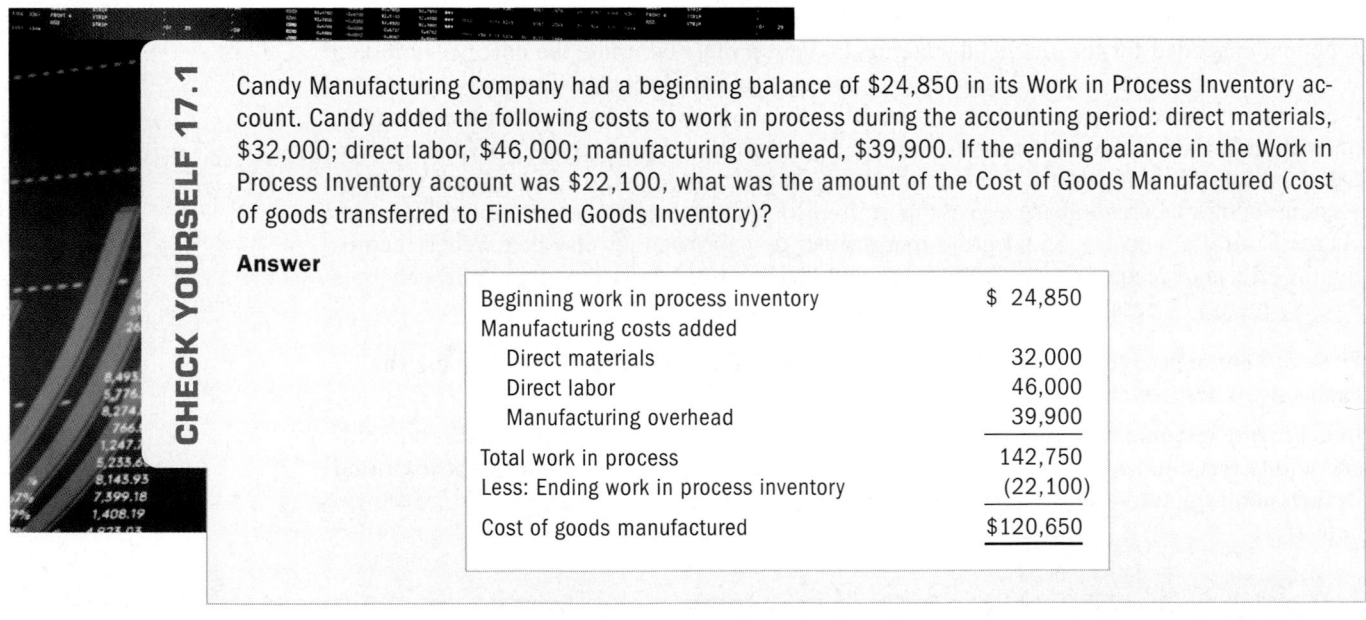

CHECK YOURSELF 17.1

Candy Manufacturing Company had a beginning balance of $24,850 in its Work in Process Inventory account. Candy added the following costs to work in process during the accounting period: direct materials, $32,000; direct labor, $46,000; manufacturing overhead, $39,900. If the ending balance in the Work in Process Inventory account was $22,100, what was the amount of the Cost of Goods Manufactured (cost of goods transferred to Finished Goods Inventory)?

Answer

Beginning work in process inventory	$ 24,850
Manufacturing costs added	
Direct materials	32,000
Direct labor	46,000
Manufacturing overhead	39,900
Total work in process	142,750
Less: Ending work in process inventory	(22,100)
Cost of goods manufactured	$120,650

Summary of January Events

LO 7

Record product costs in T-accounts.

Exhibit 17.4 summarizes the events that occurred during January. The upper section of the exhibit illustrates the *physical flow* of the resources used to make the jewelry boxes. The lower section shows the product *cost flow* through Ventra's ledger accounts. The exhibit illustrates Events 1 through 7. Event 8 recognizes the sales revenue, and Event 9 reflects the actual overhead cost incurred in January. The January balances in the Work in Process Inventory, Finished Goods Inventory, and Cost of Goods Sold accounts include the cost of materials, labor, and an *estimated* amount of overhead. Estimated overhead cost is applied to work in process inventory throughout the year. Actual overhead costs are accumulated in the Manufacturing Overhead account as they are incurred. The accounts are adjusted at year-end to reconcile the difference between the estimated and actual overhead costs.

Answers to The Curious Accountant

Obviously, Norm's Furniture Shop cannot stay in business if it cannot give customers a price for the goods it is selling. As the chapter has explained, manufacturers estimate the manufacturing overhead cost of a job using a predetermined overhead rate. These estimates allow companies to price their goods before they are manufactured. If a company does not do a reasonably good job of estimating the costs it will incur to complete a job, it will suffer by either pricing its goods too high, which will cause it to lose business to its competitors, or pricing its goods too low, which will cause it to not make a profit adequate to stay in business.

EXHIBIT 17.4

Flow of Product Costs for Ventra Manufacturing Company's January Production

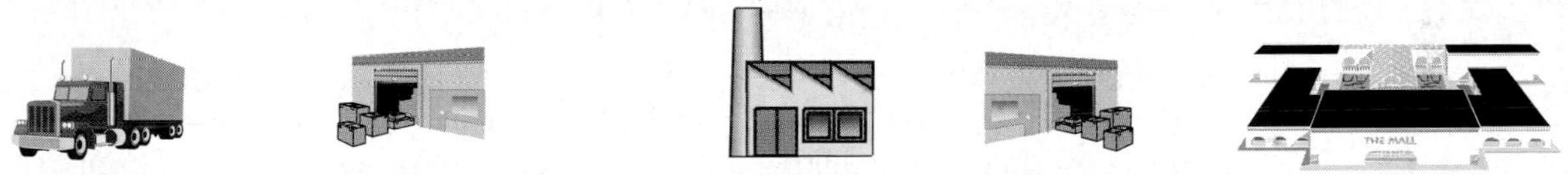

Supplier	Raw materials warehouse	Factory production	Finished goods warehouse	Retail store
Events 1 and 3	Event 2	Events 4 and 5	Event 6	Event 7
Purchase materials from suppliers and store them for future use	Transfer direct materials to factory production	Add direct labor and overhead to convert materials to finished goods	Store goods in finished goods warehouse	Sell goods to customers

Assets = Equity

Cash
Bal. 64,500
(8) 5,600
| (1) 26,500
| (3) 2,000
| (4) 1,400
| (9) 1,200

Production Supplies
(3) 2,000

Manufacturing Equipment
Bal. 40,000

Accumulated Depreciation
| Bal. 10,000

Raw Materials
Available | Used
Bal. 500 | (2) 1,100
(1) 26,500 |

Manufacturing Overhead
Actual | Estimated
(9) 1,200 | (5) 1,680

Work in Process
Materials
(2) 1,100 | (6) 4,180
Labor
(4) 1,400
Applied OH
(5) 1,680

Finished Goods
Bal. 836 | (7) 3,344
(6) 4,180 |

Common Stock
| Bal. 76,000

Retained Earnings
| Bal. 19,836

Sales Revenue
| (8) 5,600

Cost of Goods Sold
(7) 3,344

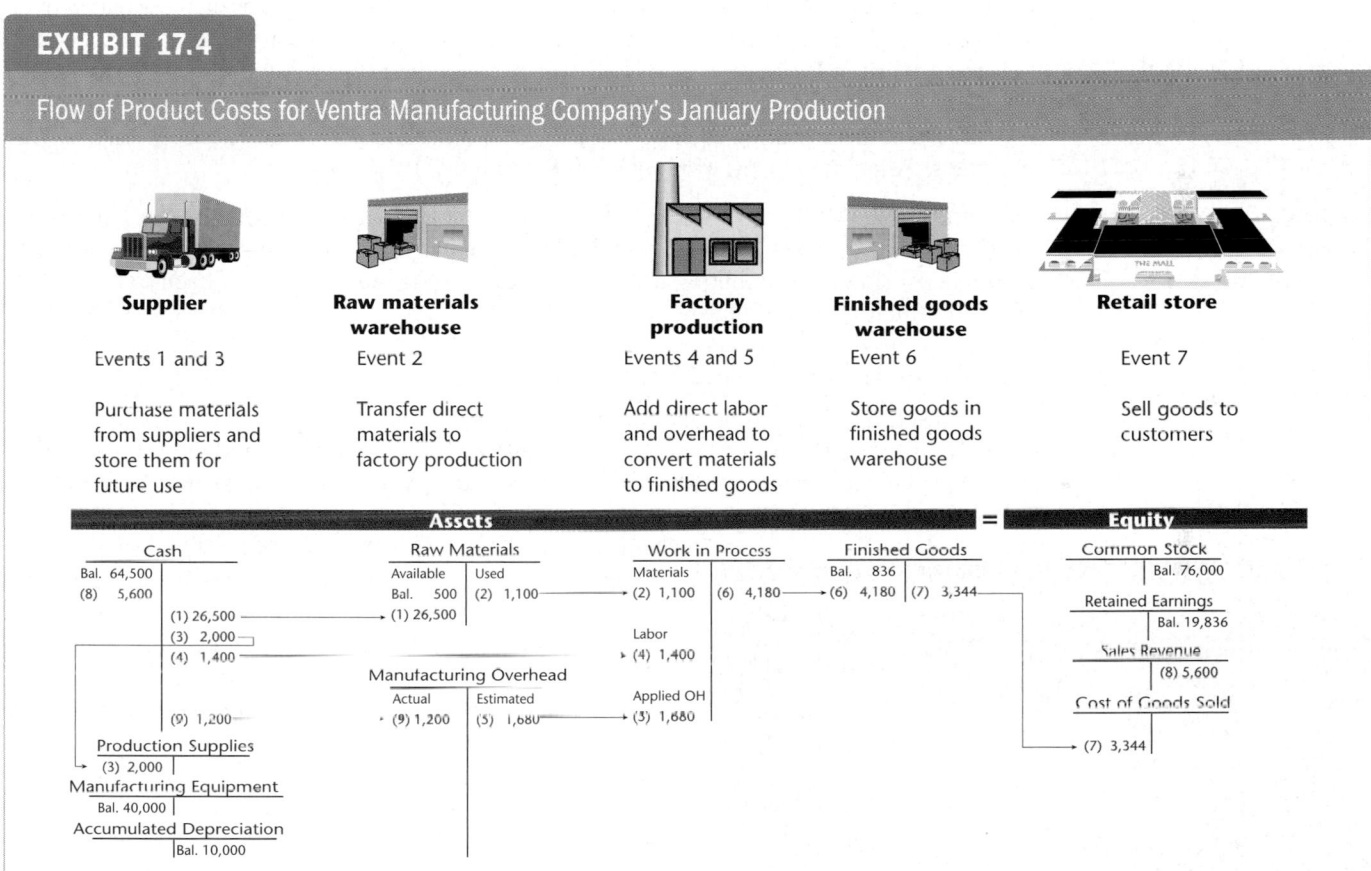

Manufacturing Cost Flow Events for February Through December

LO 8 Explain the cyclical nature of product cost flows.

Ventra Manufacturing Company's accounting events for February through December are summarized here. The sequence of events continues from the January activity. Since nine events occurred in January, the first February event is Event 10. The events for the remainder of 2005 follow.

10. Ventra used $24,860 of raw materials.
11. The company paid production workers $31,640 cash.
12. Ventra started production of an additional 11,300 jewelry boxes. Ventra applied overhead of $37,968 (11,300 units × the predetermined overhead rate of $3.36 per unit) to work in process inventory.
13. The company completed 10,300 units and transferred $86,108 of cost of goods manufactured from work in process inventory to finished goods inventory.

14. Ventra sold 9,600 units and recorded $80,256 of cost of goods sold.
15. The company recognized $134,400 of cash revenue for the products sold in Event 14.
16. The company paid $30,500 cash for overhead costs including indirect labor, rent, and utilities.
17. The year-end count of production supplies indicated $300 of supplies were on hand at December 31. Ventra recognized $1,700 ($2,000 supplies available − $300 ending balance) of indirect materials cost for supplies used during the year. This entry reflects year-end recognition of an actual overhead cost.
18. Ventra recognized $10,000 of actual overhead cost for depreciation of manufacturing equipment.
19. The company paid $31,400 cash for general, selling, and administrative expenses.
20. A year-end review of the Manufacturing Overhead account disclosed that overhead cost was underapplied by $3,752. Actual overhead ($43,400) was higher than estimated overhead ($39,648). Because estimated overhead cost passes through the ledger accounts from Work in Process Inventory, to Finished Goods Inventory, and ultimately to Cost of Goods Sold, the balance in the Cost of Goods Sold account is understated. Ventra recorded the adjusting entry to close the Manufacturing Overhead account and increase the balance in the Cost of Goods Sold account.

LO 7

Record product costs in T-accounts.

Exhibit 17.5 shows the flow of the 2005 costs through the ledger accounts. The January entries are shown in blue to distinguish them from the entries for the remainder of the year. The product cost flows are highlighted with black arrows. Trace the effects of each transaction to the exhibit before reading further.

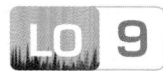

LO 9

Explain the relationship between over- or underapplied overhead and variance analysis.

Analyzing Underapplied Overhead

What caused overhead to be underapplied by $3,752? Recall that the predetermined overhead rate is based on two estimates, the estimated total overhead cost and the estimated total annual production volume. At the beginning of 2005, Ventra estimated total overhead cost would be $40,320, but actual overhead costs were $43,400, indicating Ventra spent $3,080 more than expected for overhead cost. This $3,080 is a *spending variance.* The remaining $672 of the underapplied overhead ($3,752 − $3,080) results from the difference between the actual and estimated volume of activity; it is called a *volume variance.* Recall that Ventra estimated production volume would be 12,000 units, but actual volume was only 11,800[2] units (500 units made in January + 11,300 units made from February through December). The predetermined overhead rate of $3.36 per unit was applied to 200 fewer units (12,000 units − 11,800 units) than expected, resulting in a volume variance of $672 ($3.36 predetermined overhead rate × 200 units). The combination of the spending and volume variances[3] explains the total underapplied overhead ($3,080 + $672 = $3,752).

Because the actual cost is higher than the expected cost, the spending variance is unfavorable. The volume variance

[2] There were 11,800 units placed into production. There were 10,800 units completed, leaving an ending work in process inventory balance of 1,000 units.

[3] The predetermined overhead rate in this chapter represents the standard cost and quantity of both variable and fixed inputs. As discussed in Chapter 22, companies may establish separate standards for variable costs and fixed costs. In this chapter, we assume the variable cost variances are insignificant and focus the discussion on the effects of fixed cost variances only.

EXHIBIT 17.5

Product Cost Flow for Ventra Manufacturing Company's 2005 Accounting Period

Cash

Bal.	64,500		
(8)	5,600		
(15)	134,400	(1)	26,500 →
		(3)	2,000 →
		(4)	1,400 →
		(11)	31,640 →
		(9)	1,200 →
		(16)	30,500 →
		(19)	31,400 →
Bal.	79,860		

Raw Materials Inventory

Available		Used	
Bal.	500	(2)	1,100 →
→ (1)	26,500	(10)	24,860 →
Bal.	1,040		

Work in Process Inventory

Materials			
→ (2)	1,100	(6)	4,180 →
→ (10)	24,860	(13)	86,108 →
Labor			
→ (4)	1,400		
→ (11)	31,640		
Applied OH			
→ (5)	1,680		
→ (12)	37,968		
Bal.	8,360		

Finished Goods Inventory

Bal.	836		
→ (6)	4,180	(7)	3,344 →
→ (13)	86,108	(14)	80,256 →
Bal.	7,524		

Common Stock

		Bal.	76,000

Retained Earnings

		Bal.	19,836

Manufacturing Overhead

Actual		Estimated	
→ (9)	1,200	(5)	1,680 →
→ (16)	30,500	(12)	37,968 →
→ (17)	1,700		
→ (18)	10,000	(20)	3,752 →
Bal.	0		

Sales Revenue

		(8)	5,600
		(15)	134,400
		Bal.	140,000

G, S&A Expense

→ (19)	31,400		

Production Supplies

→ (3)	2,000	(17)	1,700 →
Bal.	300		

Manufacturing Equip.

Bal.	40,000		

Accumulated Depreciation

		Bal.	10,000
		(18)	10,000 →
		Bal.	20,000

Cost of Goods Sold

→ (7)	3,344		
→ (14)	80,256		
→ (20)	3,752		
Bal.	87,352		

is also unfavorable because actual volume is less than expected, suggesting the manufacturing facilities were not utilized to the extent anticipated. In other words, fixed costs such as depreciation, rent, and supervisory salaries were spread over fewer units of product than expected, thereby increasing the cost per unit of product. If the variances are significant, estimated product costs could have been understated enough to have distorted decisions using the data. For example, products may have been underpriced, adversely affecting profitability. Making estimates as accurately as possible is critically important. Nevertheless, some degree of inaccuracy is inevitable. No one knows precisely what the future will bring. Managers seek to improve decision making. Although managers cannot make exact predictions, the more careful the estimates, the more useful will be the resulting information for timely decision making.

CHECK YOURSELF 17.2

At the beginning of the accounting period, Nutrient Manufacturing Company estimated its total manufacturing overhead cost for the coming year would be $124,000. Furthermore, the company expected to use 15,500 direct labor hours during the year. Nutrient actually incurred overhead costs of $128,500 for the year and actually used 15,800 direct labor hours. Nutrient allocates overhead costs to production based on direct labor hours. Would overhead costs be overapplied or underapplied? What effect will closing the overhead account have on cost of goods sold?

Answer

Predetermined overhead rate = Total expected overhead cost ÷ Allocation base

Predetermined overhead rate = $124,000 ÷ 15,500 hours = $8 per direct labor hour

Applied overhead = Predetermined overhead rate × Actual direct labor hours

Applied overhead = $8 × 15,800 = $126,400

Since the applied overhead ($126,400) is less than the actual overhead ($128,500), the overhead is underapplied. Closing the overhead account will increase Cost of Goods Sold by $2,100 ($128,500 − $126,400).

Preparing the Schedule of Cost of Goods Manufactured and Sold

LO 10

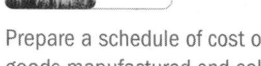

Prepare a schedule of cost of goods manufactured and sold.

In practice, a general ledger system like that shown in Exhibit 17.5 may capture millions of events. Analyzing operations with such vast numbers of transactions is exceedingly difficult. To help managers analyze manufacturing results, companies summarize the ledger data in a *schedule* that shows the overall cost of goods manufactured and sold. The schedule is an internal document which is not presented with a company's published financial statements. Only the final total on the schedule (cost of goods sold) is disclosed; it is reported on the income statement. Exhibit 17.6 illustrates Ventra's 2005 **schedule of cost of goods manufactured and sold.**

The schedule in Exhibit 17.6 reflects the transaction data in the ledger accounts. Confirm this relationship by comparing the information in the Raw Materials Inventory account in Exhibit 17.5 with the computation of the cost of direct raw materials used in the schedule in Exhibit 17.6. The beginning raw materials inventory, purchases, and ending raw materials inventory amounts in the ledger account agree with the schedule. The schedule, however, presents various amounts in summary form. For example, in the schedule the amount of direct raw materials used is $25,960. In Exhibit 17.5 this same amount is shown as two separate entries ($1,100 + $24,860) in the T-account. Similarly, the $33,040 shown as direct labor in the schedule represents the total of the two amounts ($1,400 + $31,640) of labor cost entered in the Work in Process Inventory account in Exhibit 17.5. In practice, one number in the schedule may represent thousands of individual events captured in the

EXHIBIT 17.6

VENTRA MANUFACTURING COMPANY
Schedule of Cost of Goods Manufactured and Sold
For the Year Ended December 31, 2005

Beginning raw materials inventory	$ 500
Plus: Purchases	26,500
Raw materials available for use	27,000
Less: Ending raw materials inventory	(1,040)
Direct raw materials used	25,960
Direct labor	33,040
Overhead (actual overhead cost)	43,400
Total manufacturing costs	102,400
Plus: Beginning work in process inventory	0
Total work in process inventory	102,400
Less: Ending work in process inventory	(8,360)
Cost of goods manufactured	94,040
Plus: Beginning finished goods inventory	836
Cost of goods available for sale	94,876
Less: Ending finished goods inventory	(7,524)
Cost of goods sold	$ 87,352

ledger accounts. The schedule simplifies analyzing manufacturing cost flow data for decision-making purposes.

The schedule of cost of goods manufactured and sold includes the *actual* amount of overhead cost. Data for financial statement reports are summarized at the end of the year when actual cost data are available. Although companies use estimated costs for internal records and decision making during the year, they use actual historical cost data in this schedule prepared at the end of the year.

Financial Statements

LO 11

Prepare financial statements for a manufacturing company.

The final total on the schedule of cost of goods manufactured and sold is reported as the single line item *cost of goods sold* on the company's income statement. Cost of goods sold is subtracted from sales revenue to determine gross margin. Selling and administrative expenses are subtracted from gross margin to reach net income. Exhibit 17.7 shows Ventra Manufacturing's 2005 income statement; Exhibit 17.8 shows the year-end balance sheet. In Exhibit 17.8 we show the three inventory accounts (Raw Materials, Work in Process, and Finished Goods) separately for teaching purposes. In practice, these accounts are frequently combined and reported as a single amount (Inventories) on the balance sheet. Exhibit 17.9 shows the statement of cash flows. Study each statement, tracing the information from the T-accounts in Exhibit 17.5 to the exhibits to see how companies gather the information they report to the public in their published financial statements.

EXHIBIT 17.7

VENTRA MANUFACTURING COMPANY
Income Statement
For the Year Ended December 31, 2005

Sales Revenue	$140,000
Cost of Goods Sold	(87,352)
Gross Margin	52,648
Selling and Administrative Expenses	(31,400)
Net Income	$ 21,248

EXHIBIT 17.8

[redacted]

Assets	
Cash	$ 79,860
Raw Materials Inventory	1,040
Work in Process Inventory	8,360
Finished Goods Inventory	7,524
Production Supplies	300
Manufacturing Equipment	40,000
Accumulated Depreciation–Manufac. Equip.	(20,000)
Total Assets	$117,084
Stockholders' Equity	
Common Stock	$ 76,000
Retained Earnings	41,084
Total Stockholders' Equity	$117,084

EXHIBIT 17.9

VENTRA MANUFACTURING COMPANY
Statement of Cash Flows
For the Year Ended December 31, 2005

Cash Flows from Operating Activities	
Inflow from Customers	$140,000
Outflow for Production of Inventory*	(93,240)
Outflow for Selling and Administrative Expenses	(31,400)
Net Inflow from Operating Activities	15,360
Cash Flow from Investing Activities	0
Cash Flow from Financing Activities	0
Net Change in Cash	15,360
Plus: Beginning Cash Balance	64,500
Ending Cash Balance	$ 79,860

*See Cash account in Exhibit 17.5: $26,500 + $2,000 + $1,400 + $31,640 + $1,200 + $30,500 = $93,240.

Motive to Overproduce

Absorption Costing Versus Variable Costing

LO 12

Distinguish between absorption and variable costing.

As discussed previously, managers frequently separate product manufacturing costs into variable and fixed categories based on how the costs behave. For example, the cost of materials, labor, and supplies usually increases and decreases in direct proportion to the number of units produced. Other product costs, such as rent, depreciation, and supervisory salaries are fixed; they remain constant regardless of the number of products made. Generally accepted accounting principles require that *all* product costs, both variable and fixed, be reported as inventory until the products are sold, when the product costs are expensed as cost of goods sold. This practice is called **absorption (full) costing.**[4] To illustrate, assume Hokai Manufacturing Company incurs the following costs to produce 2,000 units of inventory.

Inventory Costs	Cost per Unit	×	Units	=	Total
Variable manufacturing costs	$9	×	2,000	=	$18,000
Fixed overhead				=	12,000
Total (full absorption product cost)				=	$30,000

Suppose Hokai sells all 2,000 units of inventory for $20 per unit (sales = 2,000 × $20 = $40,000). Gross margin is therefore $10,000 ($40,000 sales − $30,000 cost of goods sold). What happens to reported profitability if Hokai increases production without also increasing sales? Profitability increases because cost of goods sold decreases. Overproducing spreads the fixed cost over more units, thereby reducing the cost per unit and the amount charged to cost of goods sold. Exhibit 17.10 illustrates this effect; it shows the cost per unit at production levels of 2,000, 3,000, and 4,000 units.

[4] Since all manufacturing costs are classified as product costs under absorption costing, absorption costing is also called *full costing.*

EXHIBIT 17.10

Cost per Unit

Inventory Costs			
Fixed overhead (a)	$12,000	$12,000	$12,000
Number of units (b)	2,000	3,000	4,000
Fixed overhead per unit (a ÷ b)	$ 6	$ 4	$ 3
Variable manufacturing costs	9	9	9
Full absorption product cost per unit	$ 15	$ 13	$ 12

Exhibit 17.11 illustrates for Hokai alternate income statements assuming sales of 2,000 units and production levels of 2,000, 3,000, and 4,000 units.

EXHIBIT 17.11

Absorption Costing Income Statements at Different Levels of Production With Sales Held Constant at 2,000 Units

Level of Production	2,000		3,000		4,000
Sales ($20 per unit × 2,000 units)	$40,000		$40,000		$40,000
Cost of goods sold ($15 × 2,000) =	30,000	($13 × 2,000) =	26,000	($12 × 2,000) =	24,000
Gross margin	$10,000		$14,000		$16,000

Suppose Hokai's management is under pressure to increase profitability but cannot control sales because customers make buying decisions. Management may be tempted to increase reported profitability by increasing production. What is wrong with increasing production without also increasing sales? The problem lies in inventory accumulation. Notice inventory increases by 1,000 units when 3,000 units are produced but only 2,000 are sold. Likewise, inventory rises to 2,000 units when 4,000 are produced but 2,000 are sold. Holding excess inventory entails considerable risks and costs. Inventory is subject to obsolescence, damage, theft, destruction by fire or weather, or other disasters. Furthermore, holding inventory requires expenditures for warehouse space, employee handling, financing, and insurance coverage. These risks and costs reduce a company's profitability. Overproducing inventory is a poor business practice. To motivate managers to increase profitability without tempting them to overproduce, many companies use *variable costing* for internal reporting.

Variable Costing

Under **variable costing,** inventory includes only *variable* product costs. The income statement is presented using the contribution margin approach, with variable product costs subtracted from sales revenue to determine the contribution margin. Fixed costs are then subtracted from the contribution margin to determine net income.

Fixed manufacturing costs are expensed in the period in which they are incurred (the period in which the resources are used) regardless of when inventory is sold. Using variable costing, increases in production have no effect on the amount of reported profit as shown in the income statements in Exhibit 17.12.

Although managers may still overproduce under variable costing, they are not tempted to do so by the lure of reporting higher profits. The variable costing reporting format encourages management to make business decisions that have a more favorable impact on long-term profitability. Variable costing can be used only for internal reporting because generally accepted accounting principles prohibit its use in external financial statements.

EXHIBIT 17.12

Variable Costing Income Statements at Different Levels of Production with Sales Held Constant at 2,000 Units

Level of Production	2,000		3,000		4,000
Sales ($20 per unit × 2,000 units)	$40,000		$40,000		$40,000
Variable cost of goods sold ($9 × 2,000) =	(18,000)	($9 × 2,000) =	(18,000)	($9 × 2,000) =	(18,000)
Contribution margin	22,000		22,000		22,000
Fixed manufacturing costs	(12,000)		(12,000)		(12,000)
Net income	$10,000		$10,000		$10,000

CHECK YOURSELF 17.3

If production exceeds sales, will absorption or variable costing produce the higher amount of net income? Which method (absorption or variable costing) is required for external financial reporting?

Answer

Absorption costing produces a higher amount of net income when production exceeds sales. With absorption costing, fixed manufacturing costs are treated as inventory and remain in inventory accounts until the inventory is sold. In contrast, all fixed manufacturing costs are expensed with variable costing. Therefore, with absorption costing, some fixed manufacturing costs will be in inventory rather than in expense accounts, so expenses will be lower and net income will be higher than with variable costing (when production exceeds sales). Generally accepted accounting principles require companies to use absorption costing for external financial reporting purposes.

<< A Look Back

Most manufacturing companies accumulate product costs in three inventory accounts. The *Raw Materials Inventory account* is used to accumulate the cost of direct *raw materials* purchased for use in production. The *Work in Process Inventory account* includes the cost of partially completed products. Finally, the *Finished Goods Inventory account* contains the costs of fully completed products that are ready for sale. When direct materials are purchased, their costs are first recorded in raw materials inventory. The costs of the materials used in production are transferred from raw materials inventory to work in process inventory. The cost of direct labor and overhead are added to work in process inventory. As goods are completed, their costs are transferred from work in process inventory to finished goods inventory. When goods are sold, their cost is transferred from finished goods inventory to cost of goods sold. The ending balances in the Raw Materials, Work in Process, and Finished Goods Inventory accounts are reported in the balance sheet. The product cost in the Cost of Goods Sold account is subtracted from sales revenue on the income statement to determine gross margin.

The actual amounts of many indirect overhead costs incurred to make products are unknown until the end of the accounting period. Examples of such costs include the cost of rent, supplies, utilities, indirect materials, and indirect labor. Because many managerial decisions require product cost information before year-end, companies frequently estimate the amount of overhead cost. The estimated overhead costs are assigned to products using a *predetermined overhead rate.*

Actual and applied overhead costs are accumulated in the temporary asset account *Manufacturing Overhead.* Differences between actual and applied overhead result in a balance in the Manufacturing Overhead account at the end of the accounting period. If actual overhead exceeds applied overhead, the account balance represents *underapplied overhead.* If actual overhead is less than applied overhead, the balance represents *overapplied overhead.* If the amount of over- or underapplied overhead is insignificant, it is closed directly to cost of goods sold through a year-end adjusting entry.

Manufacturing cost information is summarized in a report known as a *schedule of cost of goods manufactured and sold.* This schedule shows how the amount of cost of goods sold reported on the income statement was determined. Actual, rather than applied, overhead cost is used in the schedule.

Generally accepted accounting principles require all product costs (fixed and variable) to be included in inventory until the products are sold. This practice is called *absorption costing.* Results reported under absorption costing may tempt management to increase profitability by producing more units than the company can sell (overproducing). Overproducing spreads fixed costs over more units, reducing the cost per unit and the amount charged to cost of goods sold. Overproducing has the adverse effect of reducing profitability in the long-term by increasing the risks and costs of inventory accumulation. To eliminate the temptation to overproduce, for internal reporting many companies determine product cost using *variable costing.* Under variable costing, only the variable product costs are included in inventory. Fixed product costs are expensed in the period they are incurred, regardless of when products are sold. As a result, overproduction does not decrease the product cost per unit and managers are not tempted to overproduce to increase reported profitability.

A Look Forward >>

Would you use the same product cost system to determine the cost of a bottle of Pepsi as to determine the cost of a stealth bomber? We answer this question in the next chapter, which expands on the basic cost flow concepts introduced in this chapter. You will be introduced to job-order, process, and hybrid cost systems. You will learn to identify the types of services and products that are most appropriate for each type of cost system.

SELF-STUDY REVIEW PROBLEM

Tavia Manufacturing Company's first year of operation is summarized in the following list. All transactions are cash transactions unless otherwise indicated.

1. Acquired cash by issuing common stock.
2. Purchased administrative equipment.
3. Purchased manufacturing equipment.
4. Purchased direct raw materials.
5. Purchased indirect materials (production supplies).
6. Used direct raw materials in making products.
7. Paid direct labor wages to manufacturing workers.
8. Applied overhead costs to Work in Process Inventory.
9. Paid indirect labor salaries (production supervisors).
10. Paid administrative and sales staff salaries.
11. Paid rent and utilities on the manufacturing facilities.
12. Completed work on products.
13. Sold completed inventory for cash (revenue event only).
14. Recognized cost of goods sold.
15. Recognized depreciation on manufacturing equipment.
16. Recognized depreciation on administrative equipment.
17. Recognized the amount of production supplies that had been used during the year.
18. Closed the Manufacturing Overhead account. Overhead had been underapplied during the year.

Required

a. Use the horizontal statements model to show how each event affects the balance sheet, income statement, and statement of cash flows. Indicate whether the event increases (+), decreases (−), or does not affect (NA) each element of the financial statements. Also designate the classification of cash flows using the letters OA for operating activity, IA for investing activity, and FA for financing activity.

b. Identify the accounts affected by each event and indicate whether they increased or decreased as a result of the event.

Solution to Requirement *a*

Event No.	Assets	=	Liab.	+	Equity	Rev.	−	Exp.	=	Net Inc.	Cash Flow
1	+		NA		+	NA		NA		NA	+FA
2	−+		NA		NA	NA		NA		NA	−IA
3	−+		NA		NA	NA		NA		NA	−IA
4	−+		NA		NA	NA		NA		NA	−OA
5	−+		NA		NA	NA		NA		NA	−OA
6	−+		NA		NA	NA		NA		NA	NA
7	−+		NA		NA	NA		NA		NA	−OA
8	−+		NA		NA	NA		NA		NA	NA
9	−+		NA		NA	NA		NA		NA	−OA
10	−		NA		−	NA		+		−	−OA
11	−+		NA		NA	NA		NA		NA	−OA
12	−+		NA		NA	NA		NA		NA	NA
13	+		NA		+	+		NA		+	+OA
14	−		NA		−	NA		+		−	NA
15	−+		NA		NA	NA		NA		NA	NA
16	−		NA		−	NA		+		−	NA
17	−+		NA		NA	NA		NA		NA	NA
18	−		NA		−	NA		+		−	NA

Solution to Requirement *b*

Event No.	Account Title	Increase/ Decrease	Account Title	Increase/ Decrease
1	Cash	+	Common Stock	+
2	Administrative Equipment	+	Cash	−
3	Manufacturing Equipment	+	Cash	−
4	Raw Materials Inventory	+	Cash	−
5	Production Supplies	+	Cash	−
6	Work in Process Inventory	+	Raw Materials Inventory	−
7	Work in Process Inventory	+	Cash	−
8	Work in Process Inventory	+	Manufacturing Overhead	−
9	Manufacturing Overhead	+	Cash	−
10	Salary Expense	+	Cash	−
11	Manufacturing Overhead	+	Cash	−
12	Finished Goods Inventory	+	Work in Process Inventory	−
13	Cash	+	Sales Revenue	+
14	Cost of Goods Sold	+	Finished Goods Inventory	−
15	Manufacturing Overhead	+	Accumulated Depreciation	+
16	Depreciation Expense	+	Accumulated Depreciation	+
17	Manufacturing Overhead	+	Production Supplies	−
18	Cost of Goods Sold	+	Manufacturing Overhead	−

KEY TERMS

QUESTIONS

1. What is the difference between direct and indirect raw materials costs?
2. Direct raw materials were purchased on account, and the costs were subsequently transferred to Work in Process Inventory. How would the transfer affect assets, liabilities, equity, and cash flows? What is the effect on the income statement? Would your answers change if the materials had originally been purchased for cash?
3. How do manufacturing costs flow through inventory accounts?
4. Goods that cost $2,000 to make were sold for $3,000 on account. How does their sale affect assets, liabilities, and equity? What is the effect on the income statement? What is the effect on the cash flow statement?
5. At the end of the accounting period, an adjusting entry is made for the accrued wages of production workers. How would this entry affect assets, liabilities, and equity? What is the effect on the income statement? What is the effect on the cash flow statement?
6. X Company recorded the payment for utilities used by the manufacturing facility by crediting Cash and debiting Manufacturing Overhead. Why was the debit made to Manufacturing Overhead instead of Work in Process Inventory?
7. Why is the salary of a production worker capitalized while the salary of a marketing manager is expensed?
8. Al Carmon says that his company has a difficult time establishing a predetermined overhead rate because the number of units of product produced during a period is difficult to measure. What are two measures of production other than the number of units of product that Mr. Carmon could use to establish a predetermined overhead rate?
9. What do the terms *overapplied overhead* and *underapplied overhead* mean?
10. What are *product costs* and *selling, general, and administrative costs?* Give examples of product costs and of selling, general, and administrative costs.
11. How does the entry to close an insignificant amount of overapplied overhead to the Cost of Goods Sold account affect net income?
12. Why are actual overhead costs not used in determining periodic product cost?
13. Because of seasonal fluctuations, Buresch Corporation has a problem determining the unit cost of its products. For example, high heating costs during the winter months cause the cost per unit to be higher than the per unit cost in the summer months even when the same number of units of product is produced. Suggest how Buresch can improve the computation of per unit cost.
14. What is the purpose of the Manufacturing Overhead account?
15. For what purpose is the schedule of cost of goods manufactured and sold prepared? Do all companies use the statement?
16. How does the variable costing approach differ from the absorption costing approach? Explain the different income statement formats used with each approach.
17. How is profitability affected by increases in productivity under the variable and absorption costing approaches?
18. Under what circumstance is a variable costing statement format used? What potential problem could it eliminate?

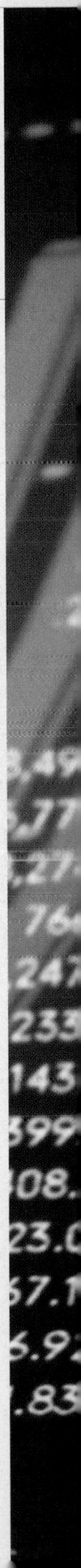

EXERCISES—SERIES A

All Exercises in Series A are available with McGraw-Hill's Homework Manager

L.O. 2, 4, 10, 11

Exercise 17-1A *Product cost flow and financial statements*

Weltin Manufacturing Company was started on January 1, 2006. The company was affected by the following events during its first year of operation.

1. Acquired $800 cash from the issue of common stock.
2. Paid $250 cash for direct raw materials.
3. Transferred $200 of direct raw materials to work in process.
4. Paid production employees $300 cash.
5. Paid $150 cash for manufacturing overhead costs.
6. Applied $123 of manufacturing overhead costs to work in process.
7. Completed work on products that cost $500.
8. Sold products that cost $400 for $700 cash.
9. Paid $200 cash for selling and administrative expenses.
10. Paid a $25 cash dividend to the owners.
11. Closed the Manufacturing Overhead account.

Required

a. Record these events in a horizontal statements model. Also designate the classification of cash flows using the letters OA for operating activities, IA for investing activities, and FA for financing activities. The first event is shown as an example.

Assets									=	Equity								
Cash	+	MOH	+	Raw M.	+	WIP	+	F. Goods	=	Com. Stk.	+	Ret. Earn.	Rev.	−	Exp.	=	Net Inc.	Cash Flow
800	+	NA	+	NA	+	NA	+	NA	=	800	+	NA	NA	−	NA	=	NA	800 FA

b. Prepare a schedule of cost of goods manufactured and sold.

L.O. 2, 7, 10, 11

Exercise 17-2A *Recording events in T-accounts and preparing financial statements*

Leimen Manufacturing Company was started on January 1, 2005, when it acquired $2,000 cash from the issue of common stock. During the first year of operation, $800 of direct raw materials was purchased with cash, and $600 of the materials was used to make products. Direct labor costs of $1,000 were paid in cash. Leimen applied $640 of overhead cost to the Work in Process account. Cash payments of $640 were made for actual overhead costs. The company completed products that cost $1,600 and sold goods that had cost $1,200 for $2,000 cash. Selling and administrative expenses of $480 were paid in cash.

Required

a. Open T-accounts and record the events affecting Leimen Manufacturing. Include closing entries.

b. Prepare a schedule of cost of goods manufactured and sold, an income statement, a balance sheet, and a statement of cash flows.

c. Explain the difference between net income and cash flow from operating activities.

L.O. 4

Exercise 17-3A *Effect of accounting events on financial statements*

Required

Use a horizontal statements model to indicate how each of the following independent accounting events affects the elements of the balance sheet, income statement, and statement of cash flows. Indicate whether the event increases (I), decreases (D), or does not affect (NA) each element of the financial statements. Also designate the classification of cash flows using the letters OA for operating activities, IA for investing activities, and FA for financing activities. The first two transactions are shown as examples.

a. Paid cash to purchase raw materials.
b. Recorded cash sales revenue.
c. Paid cash for actual manufacturing overhead cost.
d. Closed the Manufacturing Overhead account when overhead was overapplied.
e. Transferred cost of completed inventory to finished goods.
f. Paid cash for wages of production workers.
g. Paid cash for salaries of selling and administrative personnel.
h. Recorded adjusting entry to recognize amount of manufacturing supplies used (the company uses the periodic inventory method to account for manufacturing supplies).

Event No.	Balance Sheet								Income Statement					Statement of Cash Flows
	Assets	=	Liab.	+	Com. Stk.	+	Ret. Earn.		Rev.	−	Exp.	=	Net Inc.	
a.	I D		NA		NA		NA		NA		NA		NA	D OA
b.	I		NA		NA		I		I		NA		I	I OA

Exercise 17-4A *Preparing financial statements*

L.O. 2, 10, 11

Sahag Corporation began fiscal year 2005 with the following balances in its inventory accounts.

Raw Materials	$56,000
Work in Process	84,000
Finished Goods	28,000

During the accounting period, Sahag purchased $240,000 of raw materials and issued $248,000 of materials to the production department. Direct labor costs for the period amounted to $324,000, and factory overhead of $48,000 was applied to Work in Process Inventory. Assume that there was no over- or underapplied overhead. Goods costing $612,000 to produce were completed and transferred to Finished Goods Inventory. Goods costing $602,000 were sold for $800,000 during the period. Selling and administrative expenses amounted to $72,000.

Required

a. Determine the ending balance of each of the three inventory accounts that would appear on the year-end balance sheet.
b. Prepare a schedule of cost of goods manufactured and sold and an income statement.

Exercise 17-5A *Missing information in a schedule of cost of goods manufactured*

L.O. 10

Required

Supply the missing information on the following schedule of cost of goods manufactured.

PUMA CORPORATION
Schedule of Cost of Goods Manufactured
For the Year Ended December 31, 2005

Raw Materials		
Beginning Inventory	$?	
Plus: Purchases	120,000	
Raw Materials Available for Use	148,000	
Minus: Ending Raw Materials Inventory	?	
Cost of Direct Raw Materials Used		$124,000
Direct Labor		?
Manufacturing Overhead		24,000
Total Manufacturing Costs		310,000
Plus: Beginning Work in Process Inventory		?
Total Work in Process during the Period		?
Minus: Ending Work in Process Inventory		46,000
Cost of Goods Manufactured		$306,000

L.O. 10

Exercise 17-6A *Cost of goods manufactured and sold*

The following information pertains to Bluegrass Manufacturing Company for March 2005. Assume actual overhead equaled applied overhead.

March 1	
Inventory balances	
Raw materials	$ 95,000
Work in process	120,000
Finished goods	78,000
March 31	
Inventory balances	
Raw materials	$ 60,000
Work in process	145,000
Finished goods	80,000
During March	
Costs of raw materials purchased	$120,000
Costs of direct labor	100,000
Costs of manufacturing overhead	63,000
Sales revenues	310,000

Required

a. Prepare a schedule of cost of goods manufactured and sold.

b. Calculate the amount of gross margin on the income statement.

L.O. 6, 9

Exercise 17-7A *Calculating applied overhead*

Stenzil Inc. estimates manufacturing overhead costs for the 2005 accounting period as follows.

Equipment depreciation	$ 69,000
Supplies	18,000
Materials handling	20,000
Property taxes	16,000
Production setup	24,000
Rent	50,000
Maintenance	23,000
Supervisory salaries	135,000

The company uses a predetermined overhead rate based on machine hours. Estimated hours for labor in 2005 were 125,000 and for machines were 100,000.

Required

a. Calculate the predetermined overhead rate.

b. Determine the amount of manufacturing overhead applied to Work in Process Inventory during the 2005 period if actual machine hours were 120,000.

L.O. 5, 9

Exercise 17-8A *Treatment of over- or underapplied overhead*

Beeston Company estimates that its overhead costs for 2007 will be $450,000 and output in units of product will be 300,000 units.

Required

a. Calculate Beeston's predetermined overhead rate based on expected production.

b. If 24,000 units of product were made in March 2007, how much overhead cost would be allocated to the Work in Process Inventory account during the month?

c. If actual overhead costs in March were $35,000, would overhead be overapplied or underapplied and by how much?

Exercise 17-9A *Recording overhead costs in T-accounts*

L.O. 6, 9

Ard Company and Ciza Company both apply overhead to the Work in Process Inventory account using direct labor hours. The following information is available for both companies for the year.

	Ard Company	Ciza Company
Actual manufacturing overhead	$400,000	$800,000
Actual direct labor hours	10,000	12,000
Underapplied overhead		40,000
Overapplied overhead	80,000	

Required

a. Compute the predetermined overhead rate for each company.
b. Using T-accounts, record the entry to close the overapplied or underapplied overhead at the end of the accounting period for each company, assuming the amounts are immaterial.

Exercise 17-10A *Over- or underapplied overhead*

L.O. 6, 9

Korb Company and Mang Company assign manufacturing overhead to the Work in Process Inventory using direct labor cost. The following information is available for the companies for the year:

	Korb Company	Mang Company
Actual direct labor cost	$580,000	$480,000
Estimated direct labor cost	600,000	400,000
Actual manufacturing overhead cost	224,000	368,000
Estimated manufacturing overhead cost	240,000	320,000

Required

a. Compute the predetermined overhead rate for each company.
b. Determine the amount of overhead cost that would be applied to Work in Process Inventory for each company.
c. Compute the amount of overapplied or underapplied manufacturing overhead cost for each company.

Exercise 17-11A *Recording manufacturing overhead costs in T-accounts*

L.O. 6

Parrish Corporation manufactures model airplanes. The company purchased for $375,000 automated production equipment that can make the model parts. The equipment has a $15,000 salvage value and a 10-year useful life.

Required

a. Assuming that the equipment was purchased on March 1, record in T-accounts the adjusting entry that the company would make on December 31 to record depreciation on equipment.
b. In which month would the depreciation costs be assigned to units produced?

Exercise 17-12A *Missing information in T-accounts*

L.O. 2, 6, 9

Ostberg Manufacturing recorded the following amounts in its inventory accounts in 2007.

Raw Materials Inventory

Debit	Credit
60,000	(a)
16,000	

Work in Process Inventory

Debit	Credit
(a)	16,000
32,000	
24,000	
(c)	

Finished Goods Inventory

Debit	Credit
16,000	(d)
2,000	

Cost of Goods Sold

Debit	Credit
(d)	
(e)	

Manufacturing Overhead

Debit	Credit
(b)	24,000
2,000	

Required

Determine the dollar amounts for (a), (b), (c), (d), and (e). Assume that underapplied and overapplied overhead is closed to Cost of Goods Sold.

L.O. 12

Exercise 17-13A *Variable costing versus absorption costing*

Hume Company incurred manufacturing overhead cost for the year as follows.

Direct materials	$40/unit
Direct labor	$28/unit
Manufacturing overhead	
Variable	$12/unit
Fixed ($20/unit for 1,500 units)	$30,000
Variable selling & admin. expenses	$ 8,000
Fixed selling & admin. expenses	$16,000

The company produced 1,500 units and sold 1,000 of them at $180 per unit. Assume that the production manager is paid a 2 percent bonus based on the company's net income.

Required

a. Prepare an income statement using absorption costing.

b. Prepare an income statement using variable costing.

c. Determine the manager's bonus using each approach. Which approach would you recommend for internal reporting and why?

L.O. 5

Exercise 17-14A *Smoothed unit cost*

Canty Manufacturing estimated its product costs and volume of production for 2008 by quarter as follows.

	First Quarter	Second Quarter	Third Quarter	Fourth Quarter
Direct raw materials	$ 80,000	$ 40,000	$120,000	$ 60,000
Direct labor	48,000	24,000	72,000	36,000
Manufacturing overhead	80,000	124,000	160,000	92,000
Total production costs	$208,000	$188,000	$352,000	$188,000
Expected units produced	16,000	8,000	24,000	12,000

Canty Company sells a souvenir item at various resorts across the country. Its management uses the product's estimated quarterly cost to determine the selling price of its product. The company expects a large variance in demand for the product between quarters due to its seasonal nature. The company does not expect overhead costs, which are predominately fixed, to vary significantly as to production volume or with amounts for previous years. Prices are established by using a cost-plus pricing strategy. The company finds variations in short-term unit cost confusing to use. Unit cost variations complicate pricing decisions and many other decisions for which cost is a consideration.

Required

a. Based on estimated total production cost, determine the expected quarterly cost per unit for Canty's product.

b. How could overhead costs be estimated each quarter to solve the company's unit cost problem? Calculate the unit cost per quarter based on your recommendation.

PROBLEMS—SERIES A

HM™ **All Problems in Series A are available with McGraw-Hill's Homework Manager**

L.O. 2, 4, 8, 10, 11

Problem 17-15A *Manufacturing cost flow across three accounting cycles*

The following accounting events affected Estrada Manufacturing Company during its first three years of operation. Assume that all transactions are cash transactions.

CHECK FIGURE
b. Cost of goods sold: $578
NI: $152

Transactions for 2004

1. Started manufacturing company by issuing common stock for $3,000.
2. Purchased $1,200 of direct raw materials.
3. Used $800 of direct raw materials to produce inventory.
4. Paid $400 of direct labor wages to employees to make inventory.
5. Applied $250 of manufacturing overhead cost to Work in Process Inventory.
6. Finished work on inventory that cost $900.
7. Sold goods that cost $600 for $1,100.
8. Paid $370 for selling and administrative expenses.
9. Actual manufacturing overhead cost amounted to $228 for the year.

Transactions for 2005

1. Acquired additional $800 of cash from common stock.
2. Purchased $1,200 of direct raw materials.
3. Used $1,300 of direct raw materials to produce inventory.
4. Paid $600 of direct labor wages to employees to make inventory.
5. Applied $320 of manufacturing overhead cost to Work in Process Inventory.
6. Finished work on inventory that cost $1,800.
7. Sold goods that cost $1,600 for $2,800.
8. Paid $500 for selling and administrative expenses.
9. Actual manufacturing overhead cost amounted to $330 for the year.

Transactions for 2006

1. Paid a cash dividend of $700.
2. Purchased $1,400 of direct raw materials.
3. Used $1,200 of direct raw materials to produce inventory.
4. Paid $440 of direct labor wages to employees to make inventory.
5. Applied $290 of manufacturing overhead cost to work in process.
6. Finished work on inventory that cost $2,000.
7. Sold goods that cost $2,200 for $3,500.
8. Paid $710 for selling and administrative expenses.
9. Annual manufacturing overhead costs were $280 for the year.

Required

a. Record the 2004 events in a horizontal statements model. Close overapplied or underapplied overhead to Cost of Goods Sold. Also designate the classification of cash flows using the letters OA for operating activities, IA for investing activities, and FA for financing activities. The first event is shown as an example.

Assets									=	Equity								
Cash	+	**MOH**	+	**Raw M.**	+	**WIP**	+	**F. Goods**	=	**Com. Stk.**	+	**Ret. Earn.**	**Rev.**	−	**Exp.**	=	**Net Inc.**	**Cash Flow**
3,000	+	NA	+	NA	+	NA	+	NA	=	3,000	+	NA	NA	−	NA	=	NA	3,000 FA

b. Prepare a schedule of cost of goods manufactured and sold, an income statement, a balance sheet, and a statement of cash flows as of the close of business on December 31, 2004.

c. Close appropriate accounts.

d. Repeat Requirements *a* through *c* for years 2005 and 2006.

Problem 17-16A *Manufacturing cost flow for monthly and annual accounting periods*

L.O. 2, 6, 8, 9, 10, 11

Marcia Deavers started Eufala Manufacturing Company to make a universal television remote control device that she had invented. The company's labor force consisted of part-time employees. The following accounting events affected Eufala Manufacturing Company during its first year of operation. (Assume that all transactions are cash transactions unless otherwise stated.)

CHECK FIGURES
b. Cost of goods sold: $12,198
Total assets: $29,078

Transactions for January 2004, first month of operation

1. Issued common stock for $3,000.
2. Purchased $420 of direct raw materials and $60 of production supplies.
3. Used $240 of direct raw materials.
4. Used 80 direct labor hours; production workers were paid $9.60 per hour.
5. Expected total overhead costs for the year to be $3,300, and direct labor hours used during the year to be 1,000. Calculate an overhead rate and apply the appropriate amount of overhead costs to Work in Process Inventory.
6. Paid $144 for salaries to administrative and sales staff.
7. Paid $24 for indirect manufacturing labor.
8. Paid $210 for rent and utilities on the manufacturing facilities.
9. Started and completed 100 remote controls; all costs were transferred from the Work in Process Inventory account to the Finished Goods Inventory account.
10. Sold 75 remote controls at a price of $21.60 each.

Transactions for remainder of 2004

11. Acquired an additional $20,000 by issuing common stock.
12. Purchased $3,900 of direct raw materials and $900 of production supplies.
13. Used $3,000 of direct raw materials.
14. Paid production workers $9.60 per hour for 900 hours of work.
15. Applied the appropriate overhead cost to Work in Process Inventory.
16. Paid $1,560 for salaries of administrative and sales staff.
17. Paid $240 of indirect manufacturing labor cost.
18. Paid $2,400 for rental and utility costs on the manufacturing facilities.
19. Transferred 950 additional remote controls that cost $12.72 each from the Work in Process Inventory account to the Finished Goods Inventory account.
20. Determined that $168 of production supplies was on hand at the end of the accounting period.
21. Sold 850 remote controls for $21.60 each.
22. Determine whether the overhead is over- or underapplied. Close the Manufacturing Overhead account to the Cost of Goods Sold account.
23. Closed the revenue and expense accounts.

Required

a. Open T-accounts and post transactions to the accounts.
b. Prepare a schedule of cost of goods manufactured and sold, an income statement, a balance sheet, and a statement of cash flows for 2004.

L.O. 2, 4, 9, 10, 11

Problem 17-17A ***Manufacturing cost flow for one-year period***

CHECK FIGURE
b. NI: $430

Biro Manufacturing started 2005 with the following account balances.

Cash	$ 800
Raw Materials Inventory	960
Work in Process Inventory	640
Finished Goods Inventory (320 units @$5)	1,600
Common Stock	1,600
Retained Earnings	2,400

Transactions during 2005

1. Purchased $2,304 of raw materials with cash.
2. Transferred $3,000 of raw materials to the production department.
3. Incurred and paid cash for 180 hours of direct labor @ $12.80 per hour.
4. Applied overhead costs to the Work in Process Inventory account. The predetermined overhead rate is $13.20 per direct labor hour.
5. Incurred actual overhead costs of $2,400 cash.

6. Completed work on 1,200 units for $5.12 per unit.
7. Paid $1,120 in selling and administrative expenses in cash.
8. Sold 1,200 units for $7,680 cash revenue (assume FIFO cost flow).

Biro charges overapplied or underapplied overhead directly to Cost of Goods Sold.

Required

a. Record the preceding events in a horizontal statements model. Also designate the classification of cash flows using the letters OA for operating activities, IA for investing activities, and FA for financing activities. The beginning balances are shown as an example.

Assets					=	Equity						
Cash +	MOH +	Raw M. +	WIP +	F. Goods	=	Com. Stk. +	Ret. Earn.	Rev. −	Exp.	=	Net Inc.	Cash Flow
800 +	NA +	960 +	640 +	1,600	=	1,600 +	2,400	NA −	NA	=	NA	NA

b. Prepare a schedule of cost of goods manufactured and sold, an income statement, a balance sheet, and a statement of cash flows for 2005.

Problem 17-18A *Manufacturing cost flow for one accounting cycle*

L.O. 2, 6, 7, 10, 11

excel
mhhe.com/edmonds2007

CHECK FIGURE
NI: $3,974

The following trial balance was taken from the records of Maetz Manufacturing Company at the beginning of 2004.

Cash	$ 3,000	
Raw Materials Inventory	750	
Work in Process Inventory	1,200	
Finished Goods Inventory	2,100	
Property, Plant, and Equipment	7,500	
Accumulated Depreciation		$ 3,000
Common Stock		5,400
Retained Earnings		6,150
Total	$14,550	$14,550

Transactions for the accounting period

1. Maetz purchased $5,700 of direct raw materials and $300 of indirect raw materials on account. The indirect materials are capitalized in the Production Supplies account. Materials requisitions showed that $5,400 of direct raw materials had been used for production during the period. The use of indirect materials is determined at the end of the year by physically counting the supplies on hand.
2. By the end of the year, $5,250 of the accounts payable had been paid in cash.
3. During the year, direct labor amounted to 950 hours recorded in the Wages Payable account at $10.50 per hour.
4. By the end of the year, $9,000 of wages payable had been paid in cash.
5. At the beginning of the year, the company expected overhead cost for the period to be $6,300 and 1,000 direct labor hours to be worked. Overhead is allocated based on direct labor hours, which, as indicated in Event 3, amounted to 950 for the year.
6. Administrative and sales expenses for the year amounted to $900 paid in cash.
7. Utilities and rent for production facilities amounted to $4,650 paid in cash.
8. Depreciation on the plant and equipment used in production amounted to $1,500.
9. Assume that $12,000 of goods were completed during the year.
10. Assume that $12,750 of finished goods inventory was sold for $18,000 cash.
11. A count of the production supplies revealed a balance of $89 on hand at the end of the year.
12. Any over- or underapplied overhead is considered to be insignificant.

Required

a. Open T-accounts with the beginning balances shown in the preceding list and record all transactions for the year including closing entries in the T-accounts. (*Note:* Open new T-accounts as needed.)

b. Prepare a schedule of cost of goods manufactured and sold, an income statement, a balance sheet, and a statement of cash flows for the 2004 accounting period.

L.O. 2, 6, 7, 8, 9, 10, 11

CHECK FIGURES

b. NI for 2004: $22,860
NI for 2005: $33,040

Problem 17-19A ***Manufacturing cost flow for multiple accounting cycles***

The following events apply to Sapp Manufacturing Company. Assume that all transactions are cash transactions unless otherwise indicated.

Transactions for the 2004 accounting period

1. The company was started on January 1, 2004, when it acquired $162,000 cash by issuing common stock.
2. The company purchased $36,000 of direct raw materials with cash and used $2,430 of these materials to make its products in January.
3. Employees provided 900 hours of labor at $5.70 per hour during January. Wages are paid in cash.
4. The estimated manufacturing overhead costs for 2004 were $64,800. Overhead is applied on the basis of direct labor hours. The company expected to use 12,000 direct labor hours during 2004. Calculate an overhead rate and apply the overhead for January to work in process inventory.
5. The employees completed work on all inventory items started in January. The cost of this production was transferred to the Finished Goods Inventory account. Determine the cost per unit of product produced in January, assuming that a total of 1,800 units of product were started and completed during the month.
6. The company used an additional $31,050 of direct raw materials and 11,500 hours of direct labor at $5.70 per hour during the remainder of 2004. Overhead was allocated on the basis of direct labor hours.
7. The company completed work on inventory items started between February 1 and December 31, and the cost of the completed inventory was transferred to the Finished Goods Inventory account. Determine the cost per unit for goods produced between February 1 and December 31, assuming that 23,000 units of inventory were produced. If the company desires to earn a gross profit of $2.70 per unit, what price per unit must it charge for the merchandise sold?
8. The company sold 22,000 units of inventory for cash at $9.60 per unit. Determine the number of units in ending inventory and the cost per unit of this inventory.
9. Actual manufacturing overhead costs paid in cash were $65,700.
10. The company paid $37,800 cash for selling and administrative expenses.
11. Closed the Manufacturing Overhead account.
12. Closed the revenue and expense accounts.

Transactions for the 2005 accounting period

1. The company purchased $40,500 of direct raw materials with cash and used $2,280 of these materials to make products in January.
2. Employees provided 800 hours of labor at $5.70 per hour during January.
3. On January 1, 2005, Sapp hired a production supervisor at an expected cost of $1,080 cash per month. The company paid cash to purchase $4,500 of manufacturing supplies; it anticipated that $4,140 of these supplies would be used by year end. Other manufacturing overhead costs were expected to total $64,800. Overhead is applied on the basis of direct labor hours. Sapp expected to use 14,000 hours of direct labor during 2005. Based on this information, determine the total expected overhead cost for 2005. Calculate the predetermined overhead rate and apply the overhead cost to the January production.
4. The company recorded a $1,080 cash payment to the production supervisor.
5. The employees completed work on all inventory items started in January. The cost of this production was transferred to the Finished Goods Inventory account. Determine the cost per unit of product produced in January, assuming that 1,600 units of product were started and completed during the month.
6. During February 2005, the company used $2,850 of raw materials and 1,000 hours of labor at $5.70 per hour. Overhead was allocated on the basis of direct labor hours.
7. The company recorded a $1,080 cash payment to the production supervisor for February.
8. The employees completed work on all inventory items started in February; the cost of this production was transferred to the Finished Goods Inventory account. Determine the cost per unit of product produced in February, assuming that 2,000 units of product were started and completed during the month.
9. The company used an additional $34,200 of direct raw materials and 12,000 hours of direct labor at $5.70 per hour during the remainder of 2005. Overhead was allocated on the basis of direct labor hours.

10. The company recorded $10,800 of cash payments to the production supervisor for work performed between March 1 and December 31.
11. The company completed work on inventory items started between March 1 and December 31. The cost of the completed goods was transferred to the Finished Goods Inventory account. Compute the cost per unit of this inventory, assuming that there were 24,000 units of inventory produced.
12. The company sold 26,000 units of product for $9.90 cash per unit. Assume that the company uses the FIFO inventory cost flow method to determine the cost of goods sold.
13. The company paid $38,700 cash for selling and administrative expenses.
14. As of December 31, 2005, $450 of production supplies was on hand.
15. Actual cost of other manufacturing overhead was $63,020 cash.
16. Closed the manufacturing overhead account.
17. Closed the revenue and expense accounts.

Required

a. Open T-accounts and record the effects of the preceding events.

b. Prepare a schedule of cost of goods manufactured and sold, an income statement, a balance sheet, and a statement of cash flows for both years.

Problem 17-20A *Comprehensive review problem*

L.O. 10

CHECK FIGURE
c. Cost per computer with 2,000 units produced: $409.80

During their senior year at Preston College, two business students, John Pickett and Naomi Hayes, began a part-time business making personal computers. They bought the various components from a local supplier and assembled the machines in the basement of a friend's house. Their only cost was $360 for parts; they sold each computer for $630. They were able to make three machines per week and to sell them to fellow students. The activity was called Pickett Hayes Computers (PHC). The product quality was good, and as graduation approached, orders were coming in much faster than PHC could fill them.

A national CPA firm made Ms. Hayes an attractive offer of employment, and a large electronic company was ready to hire Mr. Pickett. Students and faculty at Preston College, however, encouraged the two to make PHC a full-time venture. The college administration had decided to require all students in the schools of business and engineering to buy their own computers beginning in the coming fall term. It was believed that the quality and price of the PHC machines would attract the college bookstore to sign a contract to buy a minimum of 1,000 units the first year for $540 each. The bookstore sales were likely to reach 2,000 units per year, but the manager would not make an initial commitment beyond 1,000.

The prospect of $540,000 in annual sales for PHC caused the two young entrepreneurs to wonder about the wisdom of accepting their job offers. Before making a decision, they decided to investigate the implications of making PHC a full-time operation. Their study provided the following information relating to the production of their computers.

Components from wholesaler	$360 per computer
Assembly labor	$15 per hour
Manufacturing space rent	$2,250 per month
Utilities	$450 per month
Janitorial services	$360 per month
Depreciation of equipment	$2,880 per year
Labor	2 hours per computer

The two owners expected to devote their time to the sales and administrative aspects of the business.

Required

a. Classify each cost item into the categories of direct materials, direct labor, and manufacturing overhead.

b. Classify each cost item as either variable or fixed.

c. What is the cost per computer if PHC produces 1,000 units per year? What is the cost per unit if PHC produces 2,000 units per year?

d. If the job offers for Mr. Pickett and Ms. Hayes totaled $96,000, would you recommend that they accept the offers or proceed with plans to make PHC a full-time venture?

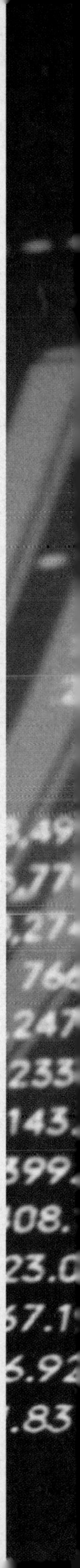

L.O. 12

eXcel

mhhe.com/edmonds2007

CHECK FIGURES
a. NI: $31,500
b. NI: $27,750

Problem 17-21A *Absorption versus variable costing*

Pace Manufacturing Company makes a product that sells for $27 per unit. Manufacturing costs for the product amount to $10.50 per unit variable, and $30,000 fixed. During the current accounting period, Pace made 4,000 units of the product and sold 3,500 units.

Required

a. Prepare an absorption costing income statement.
b. Prepare a variable costing income statement.
c. Explain why the amount of net income on the absorption costing income statement differs from the amount of net income on the variable costing income statement. Your answer should include the amount of the inventory balance that would exist under the two costing approaches.

L.O. 12

CHECK FIGURES
a. NI when 1,000 lamps are produced: $22,500
b. NI when 1,500 lamps are produced: $22,500

Problem 17-22A *Absorption versus variable costing*

Hardy Glass Company makes stained glass lamps. Each lamp sells for $315 and requires $18 of direct materials and $72 of direct labor. Fixed overhead costs are expected to be $202,500 per year. Hardy Glass expects to sell 1,000 lamps during the coming year.

Required

a. Prepare income statements using absorption costing, assuming that Hardy Glass makes 1,000, 1,250, and 1,500 lamps during the year.
b. Prepare income statements using variable costing, assuming that Hardy Glass makes 1,000, 1,250, and 1,500 lamps during the year.
c. Explain why Hardy Glass may produce income statements under both absorption and variable costing formats. Your answer should include an explanation of the advantages and disadvantages associated with using the two reporting formats.

L.O. 12

eXcel

mhhe.com/edmonds2007

CHECK FIGURES
a. NI for 2004: $24,000
d. $138,000

Problem 17-23A *Absorption and variable costing*

Kwan Manufacturing pays its production managers a bonus based on the company's profitability. During the two most recent years, the company maintained the same cost structure to manufacture its products.

Year	Units Produced	Units Sold
Production and Sales		
2004	4,000	4,000
2005	6,000	4,000
Cost Data		
Direct materials		$15 per unit
Direct labor		$24 per unit
Manufacturing overhead–variable		$12 per unit
Manufacturing overhead–fixed		$108,000
Variable selling and administrative expenses		$9 per unit sold
Fixed selling and administrative expenses		$60,000

(Assume that selling and administrative expenses are associated with goods sold.)

Kwan sells its products for $108 a unit.

Required

a. Prepare income statements based on absorption costing for 2004 and 2005.
b. Since Kwan sold the same number of units in 2004 and 2005, why did net income increase in 2005?
c. Discuss management's possible motivation for increasing production in 2005.
d. Determine the cost of ending inventory for 2005. Comment on the risks and costs associated with the accumulation of inventory.
e. Based on your answers to Requirements *b* and *c*, suggest a different income statement format. Prepare income statements for 2004 and 2005 using your suggested format.

EXERCISES—SERIES B

Exercise 17-1B *Product cost flow and financial statements* L.O. 2, 4

Wells Manufacturing began business on January 1, 2005. The following events pertain to its first year of operation.

1. Acquired $1,440 cash by issuing common stock.
2. Paid $480 cash for direct raw materials.
3. Transferred $400 of direct raw materials to Work in Process Inventory.
4. Paid production employees $560 cash.
5. Applied $260 of manufacturing overhead costs to Work in Process Inventory.
6. Completed work on products that cost $880.
7. Sold products for $1,280 cash.
8. Recognized cost of goods sold from Event 7 of $700.
9. Paid $360 cash for selling and administrative expenses.
10. Paid $280 cash for actual manufacturing overhead costs.
11. Paid an $80 cash dividend to owners.
12. Closed the Manufacturing Overhead account.

Required

a. Record the preceding events in a horizontal statements model. Also designate the classification of cash flows using the letters OA for operating activities, IA for investing activities, and FA for financing activities. The first event is shown as an example.

Assets									=	Equity									
Cash	+	MOH	+	Raw M.	+	WIP	+	F. Goods	=	Com. Stk.	+	Ret. Earn.	Rev.	−	Exp.	=	Net Inc.	Cash Flow	
1,440	+	NA	+	NA	+	NA	+	NA	=	1,440	+	NA	NA	−	NA	=	NA	1,440	FA

b. Prepare a schedule of cost of goods manufactured and sold.

Exercise 17-2B *Recording events in T-accounts and preparing financial statements* L.O. 2, 7, 10, 11

Zinn Manufacturing Company was started on January 1, 2005, when it acquired $1,600 cash by issuing common stock. During its first year of operation, it purchased $480 of direct raw materials with cash and used $360 of the materials to make products. Zinn paid $640 of direct labor costs in cash. The company applied $464 of overhead costs to Work in Process Inventory. It made cash payments of $464 for actual overhead costs. The company completed products that cost $1,040 to make. It sold goods that had cost $824 to make for $1,360 cash. It paid $320 of selling and administrative expenses in cash.

Required

a. Open the necessary T-accounts and record the 2005 events in the accounts. Include closing entries.
b. Prepare a schedule of cost of goods manufactured and sold, an income statement, a balance sheet, and a statement of cash flows.

Exercise 17-3B *Effect of accounting events on financial statements* L.O. 4

Required

Use a horizontal statements model to show how each of the following independent accounting events affects the elements of the balance sheet, income statement, and statement of cash flows. Indicate whether the event increases (I), decreases (D), or does not affect (NA) each element of the financial statements. Also designate the classification of cash flows using the letters OA for operating activities, IA for investing activities, and FA for financing activities. The first two transactions are shown as examples.

a. Paid cash to purchase raw materials.
b. Recorded cash sales revenue.
c. Applied overhead to Work in Process Inventory based on the predetermined overhead rate.

d. Closed the manufacturing overhead account when overhead was underapplied.
e. Recognized cost of goods sold.
f. Recognized depreciation expense on manufacturing equipment.
g. Purchased manufacturing supplies on account.
h. Sold fully depreciated manufacturing equipment for the exact amount of its salvage value.

Event No.	Balance Sheet: Assets	= Liab.	+ Com. Stk.	+ Ret. Earn.	Income Statement: Rev.	− Exp.	= Net Inc.	Statement of Cash Flows
a.	I D	NA	NA	NA	NA	NA	NA	D OA
b.	I	NA	NA	I	I	NA	I	I OA

L.O. 2, 10, 11

Exercise 17-4B *Preparing financial statements*

Kerr Manufacturing Company started 2005 with the following balances in its inventory accounts: Raw Materials, $5,400; Work in Process, $5,600; Finished Goods, $6,600. During 2005 Kerr purchased $34,000 of raw materials and issued $33,000 of materials to the production department. It incurred $38,000 of direct labor costs and applied manufacturing overhead of $37,400 to Work in Process Inventory. Assume there was no over- or underapplied overhead at the end of the year. Kerr completed goods costing $105,000 to produce and transferred them to finished goods inventory. During the year, Kerr sold goods costing $101,400 for $153,800. Selling and administrative expenses for 2005 were $36,000.

Required

a. Using T-accounts, determine the ending balance Kerr would report for each of the three inventory accounts that would appear on the December 31, 2005, balance sheet.
b. Prepare the 2005 schedule of cost of goods manufactured and sold and the 2005 income statement.

L.O. 10

Exercise 17-5B *Missing information in a schedule of cost of goods manufactured and sold*

Required

Supply the missing information on the following schedule of cost of goods manufactured and sold.

HILLIARD CORPORATION
Statement of Cost of Goods Manufactured and Sold
For the Year Ended December 31, 2006

Raw Materials	
Beginning Inventory	$ 8,000
Plus: Purchases	?
Raw Materials Available for Use	64,000
Minus: Ending Raw Materials Inventory	?
Cost of Direct Raw Materials Used	58,000
Direct Labor	48,000
Manufacturing Overhead	?
Total Manufacturing Costs	150,000
Plus: Beginning Work in Process Inventory	?
Total Work in Process during the Year	157,200
Minus: Ending Work in Process Inventory	(8,200)
Cost of Goods Manufactured	?
Plus: Beginning Finished Goods Inventory	?
Finished Goods Available for Sale	159,600
Minus: Ending Finished Goods Inventory	?
Cost of Goods Sold	$151,200

Exercise 17-6B *Cost of goods manufactured and sold*

L.O. 10

The following information was drawn from the accounting records of Dismuke Manufacturing Company.

	Beginning	Ending
Raw materials inventory	$4,000	$4,600
Work in process inventory	6,200	5,000
Finished goods inventory	6,800	5,800

During the accounting period, Dismuke paid $16,000 to purchase raw materials, $15,000 for direct labor, and $11,000 for overhead costs. Assume that actual overhead equaled applied overhead.

Required

a. Determine the amount of raw materials used.

b. Determine the amount of cost of goods manufactured (the amount transferred from Work in Process Inventory to Finished Goods Inventory).

c. Assuming sales revenue of $76,800, determine the amount of gross margin.

Exercise 17-7B *Calculating applied overhead*

L.O. 6, 9

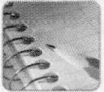

Gentry Enterprises' budget included the following estimated costs for the 2007 accounting period.

Depreciation on manufacturing equipment	$ 17,200
Cost of manufacturing supplies	3,000
Direct labor cost	86,400
Rent on manufacturing facility	7,600
Direct materials cost	74,000
Manufacturing utilities cost	6,000
Maintenance cost for manufacturing facility	5,200
Administrative salaries cost	30,500

The company uses a predetermined overhead rate based on machine hours. It estimated machine hour usage for 2007 would be 30,000 hours.

Required

a. Identify the manufacturing overhead costs Gentry would use to calculate the predetermined overhead rate.

b. Calculate the predetermined overhead rate.

c. Explain why the rate is called "predetermined."

d. Assuming Gentry actually used 29,200 machine hours during 2007, determine the amount of manufacturing overhead it would have applied to Work in Process Inventory during the period.

Exercise 17-8B *Treatment of over- or underapplied overhead*

L.O. 5, 9

On January 1, 2006, Bragg Company estimated that its total overhead costs for the coming year would be $139,400 and that it would make 34,000 units of product. Bragg actually produced 34,600 units of product and incurred actual overhead costs of $140,500 during 2006.

Required

a. Calculate Bragg's predetermined overhead rate based on expected costs and production.

b. Determine whether overhead was overapplied or underapplied during 2006.

c. Explain how the entry to close the Manufacturing Overhead account will affect the Cost of Goods Sold account.

Exercise 17-9B *Recording overhead costs in a T-account*

L.O. 6, 9

Zuber Manufacturing Company incurred actual overhead costs of $29,800 during 2006. It uses direct labor dollars as the allocation base for overhead costs. In 2006, actual direct labor costs were $42,000, and overhead costs were underapplied by $400.

Required

a. Calculate the predetermined overhead rate for 2006.

b. Open T-accounts for Manufacturing Overhead and Cost of Goods Sold. Record the overhead costs and the adjusting entry to close Manufacturing Overhead in these accounts.

c. Explain how the entry to close the Manufacturing Overhead account at the end of 2006 would affect the amount of net income reported on the 2006 income statement.

L.O. 6, 9

Exercise 17-10B *Over- or underapplied overhead*

Craig Company and Rowland Company base their predetermined overhead rates on machine hours. The following information pertains to the companies' most recent accounting periods.

	Craig	Rowland
Actual machine hours	12,300	19,500
Estimated machine hours	12,000	20,000
Actual manufacturing overhead costs	$17,000	$34,500
Estimated manufacturing overhead costs	$16,800	$34,800

Required

a. Compute the predetermined overhead rate for each company.

b. Determine the amount of overhead cost that would be applied to work in process for each company and compute the amount of overapplied or underapplied manufacturing overhead cost for each company.

c. Explain how closing the Manufacturing Overhead account would affect the Cost of Goods Sold account for each company.

L.O. 6, 9

Exercise 17-11B *Recording manufacturing overhead costs*

Patton Manufacturing Company incurred the following actual manufacturing overhead costs: (1) cash paid for plant supervisor's salary, $116,000; (2) depreciation on manufacturing equipment, $54,000; and (3) manufacturing supplies used, $4,600 (Patton uses the periodic inventory method for manufacturing supplies). Applied overhead amounted to $176,000.

Required

a. Open the appropriate T-accounts and record the manufacturing overhead costs described.

b. Record the entry Patton would make to close the Manufacturing Overhead account to Cost of Goods Sold.

L.O. 6, 9

Exercise 17-12B *Missing information in inventory T-accounts*

The following incomplete T-accounts were drawn from the records of Oser Manufacturing Company:

Raw Materials Inventory

25,000	(a)
1,200	

Work in Process Inventory

(a)	52,000
15,600	
(b)	

Finished Goods Inventory

(c)	
5,000	

Cost of Goods Sold

(d)	

Manufacturing Overhead

17,000	(e)
	800

Required

Determine the dollar amounts for (a), (b), (c), (d), and (e). Assume that underapplied and overapplied overhead is closed to Cost of Goods Sold.

Exercise 17-13B *Variable costing versus absorption costing*

L.O. 12

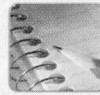

The following information was drawn from the records of Norwood Company:

Variable costs (per unit)		Fixed costs (in total)	
Direct materials	$16	Manufacturing overhead	$48,000
Direct labor	20	Selling and administrative	49,600
Manufacturing overhead	6		
Selling and administrative	14		

During the most recent month Norwood produced 4,000 units of product and sold 3,800 units of product at a sales price of $98 per unit.

Required

a. Prepare an income statement for the month using absorption costing.

b. Prepare an income statement for the month using variable costing.

c. Explain why a company might use one type of income statement for external reporting and a different type for internal reporting.

Exercise 17-14B *Smoothing unit cost*

L.O. 5

Unit-level (variable) manufacturing costs for Dixon Manufacturing Company amount to $4. Fixed manufacturing costs are $4,500 per month. Production workers provided 800 hours of direct labor in January and 1,400 hours in February. Dixon expects to use 12,000 hours of labor during the year. It actually produced 1,200 units of product in January and 2,100 units of product in February.

Required

a. For each month, determine the total product cost and the per unit product cost, assuming that actual fixed overhead costs are charged to monthly production.

b. Use a predetermined overhead rate based on direct labor hours to allocate the fixed overhead costs to each month's production. For each month, calculate the total product cost and the per unit product cost.

c. Dixon employs a cost-plus pricing strategy. Would you recommend charging production with actual or allocated fixed overhead costs? Explain.

PROBLEMS—SERIES B

Problem 17-15B *Manufacturing cost flow across three accounting cycles*

L.O. 2, 4, 6, 8, 10, 11

The following accounting events affected Ruff Manufacturing Company during its first three years of operation. Assume that all transactions are cash transactions.

Transactions for 2004

1. Started manufacturing company by issuing common stock for $1,440.
2. Purchased $576 of direct raw materials.
3. Used $432 of direct raw materials to produce inventory.
4. Paid $360 of direct labor wages to employees to make inventory.
5. Applied $360 of manufacturing overhead to Work in Process Inventory.
6. Actual manufacturing overhead costs amounted to $366.
7. Finished work on inventory that cost $648.
8. Sold goods that cost $432 for $576.
9. Paid $36 for selling and administrative expenses.

Transactions for 2005

1. Acquired additional $720 of cash from issuance of common stock.
2. Purchased $576 of direct raw materials.
3. Used $504 of direct raw materials to produce inventory.

4. Paid $432 of direct labor wages to employees to make inventory.
5. Applied $384 of manufacturing overhead to Work in Process Inventory.
6. Actual manufacturing overhead costs amounted to $378.
7. Finished work on inventory that cost $1,080.
8. Sold goods that cost $1,008 for $1,152.
9. Paid $72 for selling and administrative expenses.

Transactions for 2006

1. Purchased $360 of direct raw materials.
2. Used $576 of direct raw materials to produce inventory.
3. Paid $216 of direct labor wages to employees to make inventory.
4. Applied $300 of manufacturing overhead to Work in Process Inventory.
5. Actual manufacturing overhead costs amounted to $312.
6. Finished work on inventory that cost $1,188.
7. Sold goods that cost $1,296 for $1,584.
8. Paid $144 for selling and administrative expenses.
9. Paid a cash dividend of $288.

Required

a. Record the 2004 events in a horizontal statements model. Close overapplied or underapplied overhead to Cost of Goods Sold. Also designate the classification of cash flows using the letters OA for operating activities, IA for investing activities, and FA for financing activities. The first event is shown as an example.

Assets									=	Equity									
Cash	+	MOH	+	Raw M.	+	WIP	+	F. Goods	=	Com. Stk.	+	Ret. Earn.	Rev.	−	Exp.	=	Net Inc.	Cash Flow	
1,440	+	NA	+	NA	+	NA	+	NA	=	1,440	+	NA	NA	−	NA	=	NA	1,440	FA

b. Prepare a schedule of cost of goods manufactured and sold, an income statement, a balance sheet, and a statement of cash flows as of the close of business on December 31, 2004.
c. Close appropriate accounts to the Retained Earnings account.
d. Repeat Requirements *a* through *c* for years 2005 and 2006.

L.O. 2, 6, 7, 10, 11 **Problem 17-16B** ***Manufacturing cost for one accounting cycle***

The following trial balance was taken from the records of Aura Manufacturing Company at the beginning of 2004.

Cash	$ 2,800	
Raw Materials Inventory	200	
Work in Process Inventory	600	
Finished Goods Inventory	400	
Property, Plant, & Equipment	7,000	
Accumulated Depreciation		$ 2,000
Common Stock		4,200
Retained Earnings		4,800
Total	$11,000	$11,000

Transactions for the accounting period

1. Aura purchased $4,600 of direct raw materials and $500 of indirect raw materials on account. The indirect materials are capitalized in the Production Supplies account. Materials requisitions showed that $4,000 of direct raw materials had been used for production during the period. The use of indirect materials is determined at the end of the period by physically counting the supplies on hand at the end of the year.
2. By the end of the accounting period, $3,500 of the accounts payable had been paid in cash.

3. During the year, direct labor amounted to 1,200 hours recorded in the Wages Payable account at $6 per hour.
4. By the end of the accounting period, $6,500 of the Wages Payable account had been paid in cash.
5. At the beginning of the accounting period, the company expected overhead cost for the period to be $5,500 and 1,250 direct labor hours to be worked. Overhead is applied based on direct labor hours, which, as indicated in Event 3, amounted to 1,200 for the year.
6. Administrative and sales expenses for the period amounted to $1,400 paid in cash.
7. Utilities and rent for production facilities amounted to $3,000 paid in cash.
8. Depreciation on the plant and equipment used in production amounted to $2,000.
9. Assume that $15,000 of goods were completed during the period.
10. Assume that $10,000 of finished goods inventory was sold for $14,000 cash.
11. A count of the production supplies revealed a balance of $150 on hand at the end of the accounting period.
12. Any over- or underapplied overhead is considered to be insignificant.

Required

a. Open T-accounts with the beginning balances shown in the preceding list and record all transactions for the period including closing entries in the T-accounts. (*Note:* Open new T-accounts as needed.)

b. Prepare a schedule of cost of goods manufactured and sold, an income statement, a balance sheet, and a statement of cash flows.

Problem 17-17B *Manufacturing cost flow for one-year period*

L.O. 2, 4, 6, 10, 11

Clifton Manufacturing started 2005 with the following account balances.

Cash	$1,800
Raw Materials Inventory	80
Work in Process Inventory	176
Finished Goods Inventory (80 units @ $1.80/unit)	144
Common Stock	1,600
Retained Earnings	600

Transactions during 2005

1. Purchased $600 of raw materials with cash.
2. Transferred $400 of raw materials to the production department.
3. Incurred and paid cash for 80 hours of direct labor at $6.00 per hour.
4. Applied overhead costs to Work in Process Inventory. The predetermined overhead rate is $6.00 per direct labor hour.
5. Incurred actual overhead costs of $520 cash.
6. Completed work on 300 units for $2.88 per unit.
7. Paid $160 in selling and administrative expenses in cash.
8. Sold 200 units for $1,000 cash revenue (assume LIFO cost flow).

Clifton charges overapplied or underapplied overhead directly to Cost of Goods Sold.

Required

a. Record the preceding events in a horizontal statements model. Also designate the classification of cash flows using the letters OA for operating activities, IA for investing activities, and FA for financing activities. The beginning balances are shown as an example.

Assets									=	Equity									
Cash	+	MOH	+	Raw M.	+	WIP	+	F. Goods	=	Com. Stk.	+	Ret. Earn.	Rev.	−	Exp.	=	Net Inc.		Cash Flow
1,800	+	NA	+	80	+	176	+	144	=	1,600	+	600	NA	−	NA	=	NA		NA

b. Prepare a schedule of cost of goods manufactured and sold, an income statement, a balance sheet, and a statement of cash flows for 2005.

L.O. 2, 6, 7, 10, 11

Problem 17-18B ***Manufacturing cost flow for monthly and annual accounting periods***

Pratt Manufacturing Company manufactures puzzles that depict the works of famous artists. The company rents a small factory and uses local labor on a part-time basis. The following accounting events affected Pratt during its first year of operation. (Assume that all transactions are cash transactions unless otherwise stated.)

Transactions for first month of operation 2005

1. Issued common stock for $25,000.
2. Purchased $4,000 of direct raw materials and $300 of indirect raw materials. Indirect materials are recorded in a Production Supplies account.
3. Used $3,896 of direct raw materials.
4. Used 700 direct labor hours; production workers were paid $6 per hour.
5. Expected total overhead costs for the year to be $16,800 and direct labor hours used during the year to be 9,600. Calculate an overhead rate and apply the appropriate amount of overhead costs to Work in Process.
6. Paid $800 for salaries to administrative and sales staff.
7. Paid $700 for indirect manufacturing labor.
8. Paid $600 for rent and utilities on the manufacturing facilities.
9. Started and completed 956 puzzles; all costs were transferred from the Work in Process Inventory account to the Finished Goods Inventory account.
10. Sold 800 puzzles at a price of $12 each.

Transactions for remainder of 2005

11. Acquired an additional $200,000 by issuing common stock.
12. Purchased $46,000 of direct raw materials and $4,000 of indirect raw materials.
13. Used $41,050 of direct raw materials.
14. Paid production workers $6 per hour for 9,800 hours of work.
15. Applied the appropriate overhead cost to Work in Process Inventory.
16. Paid $8,800 for salaries of administrative and sales staff.
17. Paid $7,700 for the salary of the production supervisor.
18. Paid $6,600 for rental and utility costs on the manufacturing facilities.
19. Transferred 12,000 additional puzzles that cost $9.75 each from Work in Process Inventory to Finished Goods Inventory accounts.
20. Determined that $2,900 of production supplies was on hand at the end of the accounting period.
21. Sold 8,000 puzzles for $12 each.
22. Determined whether overhead is over- or underapplied. Closed the manufacturing overhead account to cost of goods sold.
23. Closed the revenue and expense accounts.

Required

a. Open T-accounts and post transactions to the accounts.

b. Prepare a schedule of cost of goods manufactured and sold, an income statement, a balance sheet, and a statement of cash flows for 2005.

L.O. 2, 6, 7, 8, 9, 10, 11

Problem 17-19B ***Manufacturing cost flow for multiple accounting cycles***

The following events apply to Gurganes Manufacturing Company. Assume that all transactions are cash transactions unless otherwise indicated.

Transactions for the 2006 accounting period

1. The company was started on January 1, 2006, when it acquired $700,000 cash by issuing common stock.
2. The company purchased $300,000 of direct raw materials with cash and used $26,000 of these materials to make its products in January.
3. Employees provided 1,500 hours of labor at $8 per hour during January. Wages are paid in cash.
4. The estimated manufacturing overhead costs for 2006 are $650,000. Overhead is applied on the basis of direct labor costs. The company expected $130,000 of direct labor costs during 2006. Record applied overhead for January.

5. By the end of January, the employees completed work on all inventory items started in January. The cost of this production was transferred to the Finished Goods Inventory account. Determine the cost per unit of product produced in January, assuming that a total of 10,000 units of product were started and completed during the month.
6. The company used an additional $234,000 of direct raw materials and 13,500 hours of direct labor at $8 per hour during the remainder of 2006. Overhead was allocated on the basis of direct labor cost.
7. The company completed work on inventory items started between February 1 and December 31, and the cost of the completed inventory was transferred to the Finished Goods Inventory account. Determine the cost per unit for goods produced between February 1 and December 31, assuming that 90,000 units of inventory were produced. If the company desires to earn a gross profit of $3 per unit, what price per unit must it charge for the merchandise sold?
8. The company sold 60,000 units of inventory for cash at $12.80 per unit. Determine the number of units in ending inventory and the cost per unit of this inventory.
9. Actual manufacturing overhead costs paid in cash were $610,000.
10. The company paid $150,000 cash for selling and administrative expenses.
11. Closed the Manufacturing Overhead account.
12. Closed the revenue and expense accounts.

Transactions for the 2007 accounting period

1. The company acquired $350,000 cash from the owners.
2. The company purchased $200,000 of direct raw materials with cash and used $20,800 of these materials to make products in January.
3. Employees provided 1,200 hours of labor at $8 per hour during January.
4. On January 1, 2007, Gurganes expected the production facilities to cost $1,500 cash per month. The company paid cash to purchase $7,000 of manufacturing supplies, and it anticipated that $7,000 of these supplies would be used by year end. Other manufacturing overhead costs were expected to total $455,000. Overhead is applied on the basis of direct labor costs. Gurganes expects direct labor costs of $80,000 during 2007. Based on this information, determine the total expected overhead cost for 2007. Calculate the predetermined overhead rate and apply the overhead cost for the January production. Also, record the purchase of manufacturing supplies.
5. The company recorded a $1,500 cash payment for production facilities in January.
6. In January, the employees completed work on all inventory items started in January. The cost of this production was transferred to the Finished Goods Inventory account. Determine the cost per unit of product produced in January assuming that a total of 8,000 units of product were started and completed during the month.
7. During February 2007, the company used $15,600 of raw materials and 900 hours of labor at $8 per hour. Overhead was allocated on the basis of direct labor cost.
8. The company recorded a $1,500 cash payment for production facilities in February.
9. In February, the employees completed work on all inventory items started in February; the cost of this production was transferred to the Finished Goods Inventory account. Determine the cost per unit of product produced in February, assuming that 6,000 units of product were started and completed during the month.
10. The company used an additional $143,000 of direct raw materials and 8,250 hours of direct labor at $8 per hour during the remainder of 2007. Overhead was allocated on the basis of direct labor cost.
11. The company recorded $15,000 of cash payments for production facilities for the period between March 1 and December 31.
12. The company completed work on inventory items started between March 1 and December 31. The cost of the completed goods was transferred to the Finished Goods Inventory account. Compute the cost per unit of this inventory, assuming that 55,000 units of inventory were produced.
13. The company sold 90,000 units of product for $14 per unit cash. Assume that the company uses the FIFO inventory cost flow method to determine the cost of goods sold.
14. The company paid $130,000 cash for selling and administrative expenses.
15. As of December 31, 2007, $1,200 of production supplies was on hand.
16. Actual cost of other manufacturing overhead was $461,000 cash.
17. Closed the manufacturing overhead account.
18. Closed the revenue and expense accounts.

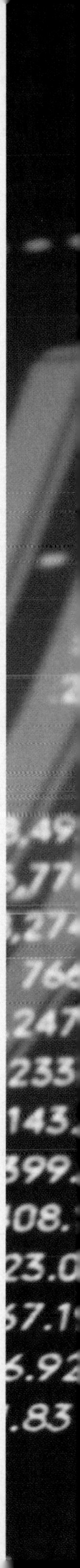

Required

a. Open T-accounts and record the effects of the preceding events.

b. Prepare a schedule of cost of goods manufactured and sold, an income statement, a balance sheet, and a statement of cash flows for both years.

L.O. 10

Problem 17-20B *Comprehensive review problem*

Lauren Cobb has worked as the plant manager of Sheppard Corporation, a large manufacturing company, for 10 years. The company produces stereo CD players for automotive vehicles and sells them to some of the largest car manufacturers in the country. Ms. Cobb has always toyed with the idea of starting her own car stereo manufacturing business. With her experience and knowledge, she is certain that she can produce a superior stereo at a low cost. Ms. Cobb's business strategy would be to market the product to smaller, more specialized car manufacturers. Her potential market is car manufacturers who sell at a lower volume to discriminating customers. She is confident that she could compete in this market that values low-cost quality production. She would not compete with Sheppard or the other large stereo producers that dominate the market made up of the largest automotive producers.

Ms. Cobb already has firm orders for 800 stereos from several automotive producers. Based on the contacts that she has made working for Sheppard, Ms. Cobb is confident that she can make and sell 2,000 stereos during the first year of operation. However, before making a final decision, she decides to investigate the profitability of starting her own business. Relevant information follows.

Components from wholesaler	$36.00 per stereo
Assembly labor	$8.40 per hour
Rent of manufacturing buildings	$9,600.00 per year
Utilities	$240.00 per month
Sales salaries	$480.00 per month
Depreciation of equipment	$1,600.00 per year
Labor	3 hours per stereo

During the first year, Ms. Cobb expects to be able to produce the stereos with only two production workers and a part-time salesperson to market the product. Ms. Cobb expects to devote her time to the administrative aspects of the business and to provide back-up support in the production work. She has decided not to pay herself a salary but to live off the profits of the business.

Required

a. Classify each cost item into the categories of direct materials, direct labor, and manufacturing overhead.

b. Classify each cost item as either variable or fixed.

c. What is the cost per stereo if Ms. Cobb's company produces 800 units per year? What is the unit cost if the company produces 2,000 units per year?

d. If Ms. Cobb's job presently pays her $12,000 a year, would you recommend that she proceed with the plans to start the new company if she could sell stereos for $96 each?

L.O. 12

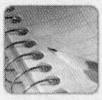

Problem 17-21B *Absorption versus variable costing*

Carney Manufacturing Company makes a product that sells for $25 per unit. Manufacturing costs for the product amount to $12 per unit variable, and $80,000 fixed. During the current accounting period, Carney made 8,000 units of the product and sold 7,600 units.

Required

a. Prepare an absorption costing income statement.

b. Prepare a variable costing income statement.

c. Explain why the amount of net income on the absorption costing income statement differs from the amount of net income on the variable costing income statement. Your answer should include the amount of the inventory balance that would exist under the two costing approaches.

Problem 17-22B *Absorption versus variable costing*

L.O. 12

King Company makes ladderback chairs that it sells for $200 per chair. Each chair requires $28 of direct materials and $72 of direct labor. Fixed overhead costs are expected to be $120,000 per year. King expects to sell 1,500 chairs during the coming year.

Required

a. Prepare income statements using absorption costing, assuming that King makes 1,500, 2,000, and 2,500 chairs during the year.

b. Prepare income statements using variable costing, assuming that King makes 1,500, 2,000, and 2,500 chairs during the year.

c. Explain why King may produce income statements under both absorption and variable costing formats. Your answer should include an explanation of the advantages or disadvantages associated with using the two reporting formats.

Problem 17-23B *Absorption and variable costing*

L.O. 12

Wofford Manufacturing pays its production managers a bonus based on the company's profitability. During the two most recent years, the company maintained the same cost structure to manufacture its products.

Year	Units Produced	Units Sold
Production and Sales		
2005	4,000	4,000
2006	6,000	4,000
Cost Data		
Direct materials		$8 per unit
Direct labor		$12 per unit
Manufacturing overhead–variable		$4 per unit
Manufacturing overhead–fixed		$72,000
Variable selling and administrative expenses		$4 per unit sold
Fixed selling and administrative expenses		$30,000

(Assume that selling and administrative expenses are associated with goods sold.)

Wofford's sales revenue for both years was $230,000.

Required

a. Prepare income statements based on absorption costing for the years 2005 and 2006.

b. Since Wofford sold the same amount in 2005 and 2006, why did net income increase in 2006?

c. Discuss management's possible motivation for increasing production in 2006.

d. Determine the cost of ending inventory for 2006. Comment on the risks and costs associated with the accumulation of inventory.

e. Based on your answers to Requirements *b* and *c*, suggest a different income statement format and prepare income statements for 2005 and 2006 using your suggested format.

ANALYZE, THINK, COMMUNICATE

ATC 17-1 Business Applications Case *Predetermined overhead rate*

Bytes Storage Company (BSC) makes memory storage chips that it sells to independent computer manufacturers. The average materials cost per set of chips is $3.15, and the average labor cost is $1.25. BSC incurs approximately $5,200,000 of fixed manufacturing overhead costs annually. The marketing department estimated that BSC would sell approximately 700,000 sets of chips during the coming year. BSC has experienced a steady decline in sales even though the computer industry has had a steady increase in the number of computers sold. The chief accountant, Stella Peng, was overheard saying that when she calculated the predetermined overhead rate, she deliberately lowered the estimated number of chips expected to be sold because she had lost faith in the marketing department's ability to deliver on its estimated sales numbers. Ms. Peng explained, "This way, our actual cost is always below the estimated cost. It is about the only way we continue to make a profit." Indeed, the company had a significant amount of overapplied overhead at the end of each year.

Required

a. Explain how the overapplied overhead affects the determination of year-end net income.

b. Assume that Ms. Peng used 600,000 sets of chips as the estimated sales to calculate the predetermined overhead rate. Determine the difference in expected cost per set of chips she calculated and the cost per set of chips that would result if the marketing department's estimate (700,000 units) had been used.

c. Assuming that BSC uses a cost-plus pricing policy, speculate how Ms. Pengs' behavior could be contributing to the decline in sales.

ATC 17-2 Group Assignment *Schedule of cost of goods manufactured and sold*

The following information is from the accounts of Depree Manufacturing Company for 2006.

Required

a. Divide the class into groups of four or five students per group and organize the groups into three sections. Assign Task 1 to the first section of groups, Task 2 to the second section, and Task 3 to the third section.

Group Tasks

(1) The ending balance in the Raw Materials Inventory account was $208,000. During the accounting period, Depree used $2,348,900 of raw materials inventory and purchased $2,200,000 of raw materials. Determine the beginning Raw Materials Inventory balance.

(2) During the accounting period, Depree used $2,348,900 of raw materials inventory and $2,780,200 of direct labor. Actual overhead costs were $3,300,000. Ending work in process inventory amounted to $450,000, and cost of goods manufactured amounted to $8,389,100. Determine the beginning balance in the Work in Process Inventory account.

(3) The cost of goods manufactured was $8,389,100, and the cost of goods sold was $8,419,100. Ending finished goods inventory amounted to $360,000. Determine the beginning balance in the Finished Goods Inventory account.

b. Select a spokesperson from each section. Use input from the three spokespersons to prepare a schedule of cost of goods manufactured and sold. The spokesperson from the first section should provide information for the computation of the cost of raw materials used. The spokesperson from the second section should provide information for the determination of the cost of goods manufactured. The spokesperson from the third section should provide information for the determination of the cost of goods sold.

ATC 17-3 Research Assignment *Distinction between service and manufacturing companies*

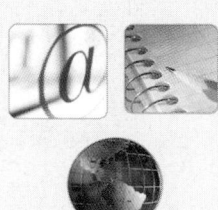

Electronic Arts, Inc., more commonly known as EA Sports, develops and markets games for Sony's Play Station 2 and Microsoft's X Box. Using either the company's March 31, 2004, Form 10-K or its annual report, answer the following questions. Access the company's website to obtain the Form 10-K or use the EDGAR system by following the instructions in Appendix A. An interactive version of the company's annual report is available on its website.

Required

a. Read the "Overview" and "Method of Delivery" subsections of the "Business" section of the company's 10-K or annual report. The business section is near the beginning of the documents. Based on this information, is EA Sports a service or a manufacturing business? Explain.

b. Based on your response to Requirement *a,* what types of inventory do you expect EA Sports to have? Review the information in Note (9) of the company's financial statements. Does the company have any inventory? If so, what is (are) the type(s) and dollar amounts of any inventory that EA Sports has? Does the information in Note (9) lead you to rethink your answer to Requirement *a?*

c. What are some cost drivers EA Sports might use to allocate common costs to the various games it markets?

ATC 17-4 Writing Assignment *Inventory cost flow in a manufacturing environment*

Barret Cameron, a student in Professor Wagner's managerial accounting course, asked the following question. "In the first accounting course, the teacher said inventory costs flow on a FIFO, LIFO, or weighted-average pattern. Now you are telling us inventory costs flow through raw materials, to work in process, and then to finished goods. Is this manufacturing stuff a new cost flow method or what?"

Required

Assume that you are Professor Wagner. Write a brief memo responding to Mr. Cameron's question.

ATC 17-5 Ethical Dilemma *Absorption costing*

Cliff Dennis may become a rich man. He is the creative force behind Amazing Drives, a new company. Amazing makes external drives that permit computer users to store large amounts of information on small floppy diskettes. Amazing has experienced tremendous growth since its inception three years ago. Investors have recognized the company's potential, and its stock is currently selling at 60 times projected earnings. More specifically, the company's 2004 earnings forecast shows estimated income to be \$0.30 per share and the current market price is \$18 per share (\$0.30 × 60). Mr. Dennis has stock options permitting him to buy 2,000,000 shares of stock for \$12 per share on January 1, 2005. This means that he could earn \$6 per share on the options. In other words, he would buy the stock at \$12 per share and sell it at \$18 per share. As a result, Mr. Dennis would earn \$12,000,000 (\$6 × 2,000,000 shares).

Weak economies in foreign countries have caused low demand for Amazing's products in international markets. Company insiders are painfully aware that Amazing Drives is going to be unable to meet its projected income numbers. If actual earnings fall short of the projected earnings, the market will manifest its disappointment by discounting the stock price. Mr. Dennis is concerned that the value of his stock options could plummet.

At its inception three years ago, Amazing invested heavily in manufacturing equipment. Expecting dramatic growth, the company purchased a significant amount of excess capacity. As a result, the company incurs approximately \$28,800,000 in fixed manufacturing costs annually. If Amazing continues to produce at its current level, it will make and sell approximately 800,000 drives during 2004. In the face of declining sales, Mr. Dennis has issued a puzzling order to his production manager. Specifically, he has told the production manager to increase production so that 1,200,000 drives will be completed during 2004. Mr. Dennis explained that he believes the economies in foreign countries will surge ahead in 2005 and that he wants Amazing to have the inventory necessary to satisfy the demand.

Required

a. Suppose that actual earnings for 2004 are \$0.18 per share. The market becomes disappointed, and the price-earnings ratio falls to 40 times earnings. What is the value of Mr. Dennis' stock options under these circumstances?

b. Determine the impact on income reported in 2004 if production is 800,000 units versus 1,200,000 units.

c. Why would Mr. Dennis order the increase in production?

d. Does Mr. Dennis' behavior violate any of the standards of ethical conduct in Exhibit 14-13 of Chapter 14?

e. Identify the features described in this case that could motivate criminal and ethical misconduct. (It may be helpful to reread the ethics material in Chapter 14 before attempting to satisfy this requirement.)

COMPREHENSIVE PROBLEM

Magnificent Modems Inc. acquired a subsidiary named Anywhere Inc. (AI). AI manufactures a wireless modem that enables users to access the Internet through cell phones. The following trial balance was drawn from the accounts of the subsidiary.

Cash	$200,000	
Raw Materials Inventory	4,000	
Work in Process Inventory	6,000	
Finished Goods Inventory	7,000	
Common Stock		$129,000
Retained Earnings		88,000
Totals	$217,000	$217,000

The subsidiary completed the following transactions during 2005.

1. Paid $60,000 cash for direct raw materials.
2. Transferred $50,000 of direct raw materials to work in process.
3. Paid production employees $80,000 cash.
4. Applied $53,000 of manufacturing overhead costs to work in process.
5. Completed work on products that cost $163,000.
6. Sold products that cost $143,000 for $182,000 cash. Record the recognition of revenue in a row labeled 6a and the cost of goods sold in a row labeled 6b.
7. Paid $20,000 cash for selling and administrative expenses.
8. Actual overhead costs paid in cash amounted to $55,000.
9. Closed the Manufacturing Overhead account. The amount of over- or underapplied overhead was insignificant (immaterial).
10. Paid a $5,000 cash dividend to the owners.

Required

a. For Anywhere Inc., record the events in a financial statements model like the one shown below. In the last column of the model indicate whether the cash inflows or outflows are financing activities (FA), investing activities (IA), or operating activities (OA).

Assets							=	Equity									
Cash	+	**MOH**	+	**Raw M.**	+	**WIP**	+	**F. Goods**	=	**Com. Stk.**	+	**Ret. Earn.**	**Rev.**	−	**Exp.**	=	**Net Inc.**	**Cash Flow**
200,000	+	0	+	4,000	+	6,000	+	7,000	=	129,000	+	88,000	NA	−	NA	=	NA	NA

b. Prepare a schedule of cost of goods manufactured and sold.

c. Prepare an income statement, balance sheet, and statement of cash flows.

CHAPTER 18

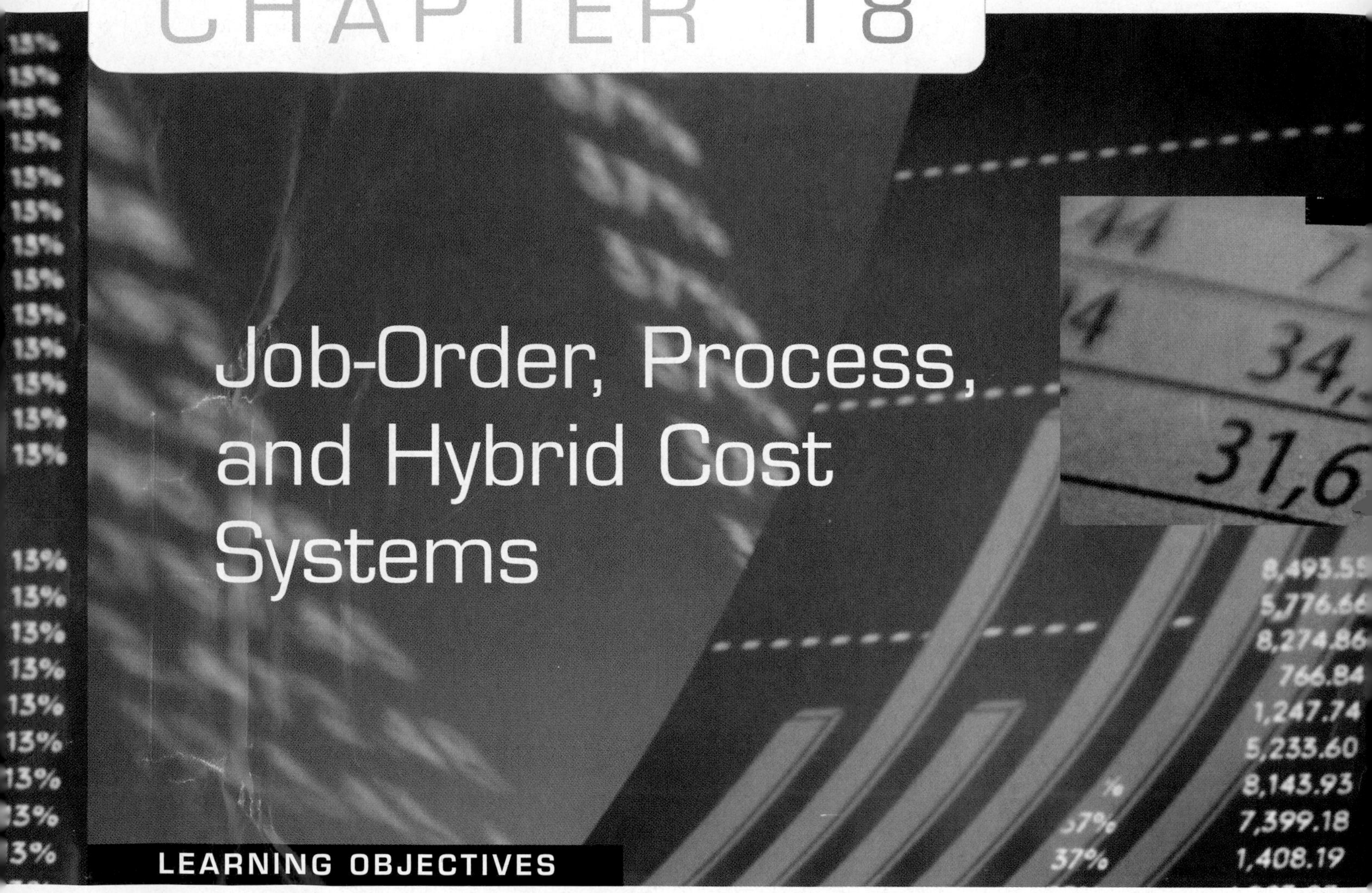

Job-Order, Process, and Hybrid Cost Systems

LEARNING OBJECTIVES

After you have mastered the material in this chapter you will be able to:

1. **Distinguish between job-order and process cost systems.**
2. **Identify how product costs flow through a job-order cost system.**
3. **Identify how product costs flow through a process cost system.**
4. **Distinguish between raw materials cost and transferred-in cost.**
5. **Explain how hybrid accounting systems combine components of job-order and process cost systems.**
6. **Identify the various forms of documentation used in a job-order cost system.**
7. **Explain how accounting events in a job-order cost system affect financial statements.**
8. **Explain how accounting events in a process cost system affect financial statements.**
9. **Convert partially completed units into equivalent whole units.**

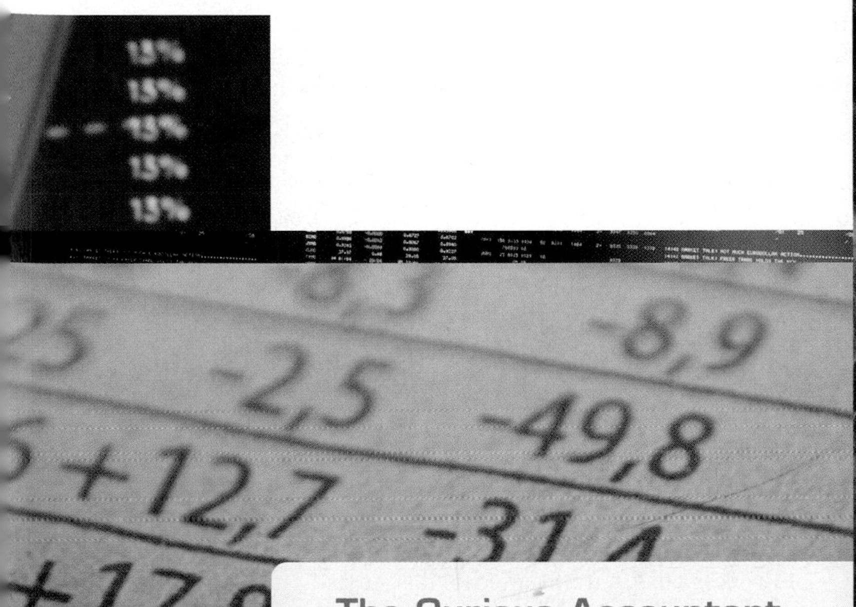

Chapter 18

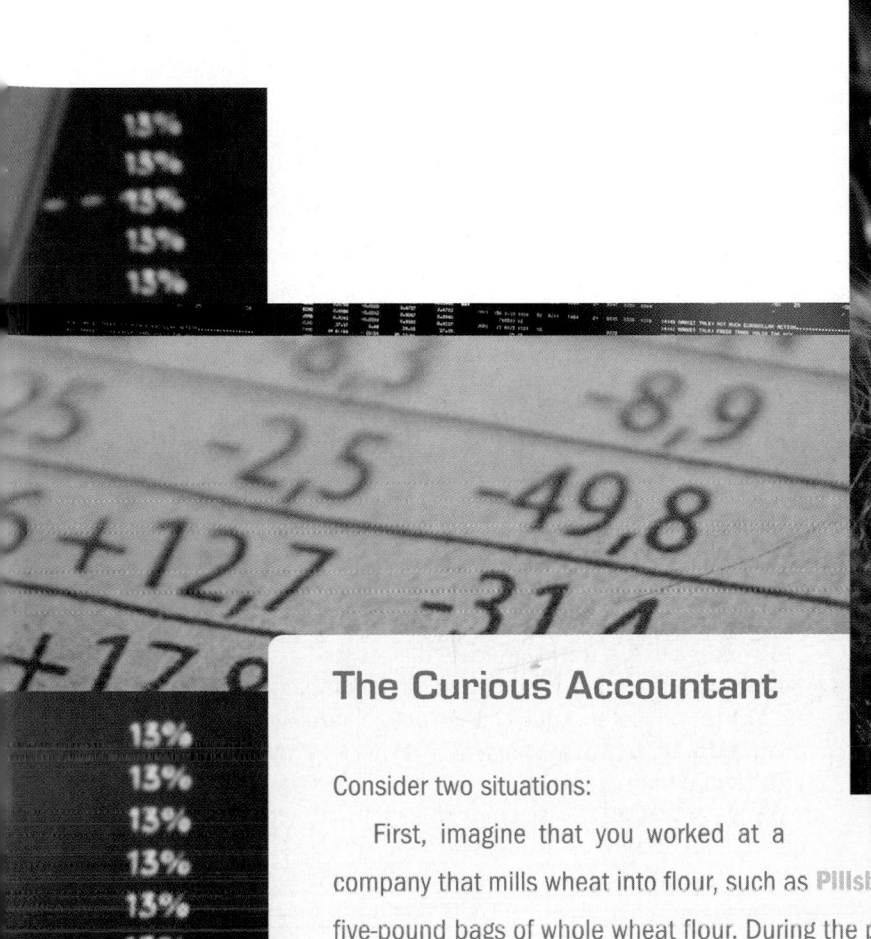

The Curious Accountant

Consider two situations:

First, imagine that you worked at a company that mills wheat into flour, such as **Pillsbury**, and that your company produced only one product, five-pound bags of whole wheat flour. During the past year, your company incurred manufacturing costs of $32.5 million to produce 50 million bags of flour.

Next, imagine you worked for a company that constructed houses. All activity for the past year has been in one particular neighborhood, Estate Homes. Your company incurred construction costs during the past year of $17.8 million to build 50 houses from start to finish; no two of these houses were the same.

How would you determine the cost of one bag of flour? How would you determine the cost incurred to construct the house on lot 131? Which of these questions is the more difficult for a real-world company to answer? (Answers on page 898.)

CHAPTER OPENING

Benchmore Boat Company built five boats during the current year. Each boat has unique characteristics that affect its cost. For example, an 80-foot yacht required more labor and materials than a 30-foot sailboat. Because different boats cost different amounts, Benchmore needs a cost system that traces product costs to individual inventory items (specific boats).

In contrast, Janis Juice Company produced 500,000 cans of apple juice during the same year. Each can of juice is identical to the others. Determining the cost of a boat built by Benchmore requires a different cost system than the system Janis needs to determine the cost of a can of juice. Benchmore needs a cost system that captures the unique cost of each individual inventory item. Janis needs a cost system that distributes costs evenly across total production (number of cans of juice produced during an accounting period). ■

Cost Systems

LO 1

Distinguish between job-order and process cost systems.

The type of product a company produces affects the type of accounting system needed to determine product cost. The two most common types of costing systems are job-order costing and process costing. Some companies use hybrid costing systems that combine features of both job-order and process systems. The following section of the text discusses the types of products most suited to each costing system and the accounting procedures used in each type of costing system.

Cost Systems and Type of Product

Job-order cost systems accumulate costs by individual products. The boats Benchmore builds are suited to job-order costing. Other products for which job-order costing is suitable include movies made by **Walt Disney Productions**, office buildings constructed by **Rust Engineering**, and airplanes made by **Boeing**. Job-order cost systems apply not only to individual inventory items but also to batches of inventory items. For example, **Hernandes Shirt Company** may account for producing a special order of 20,000 shirts sold to the United States Army as a single job. Companies use job-order cost systems when they need to know the costs of individual products or batches of products.

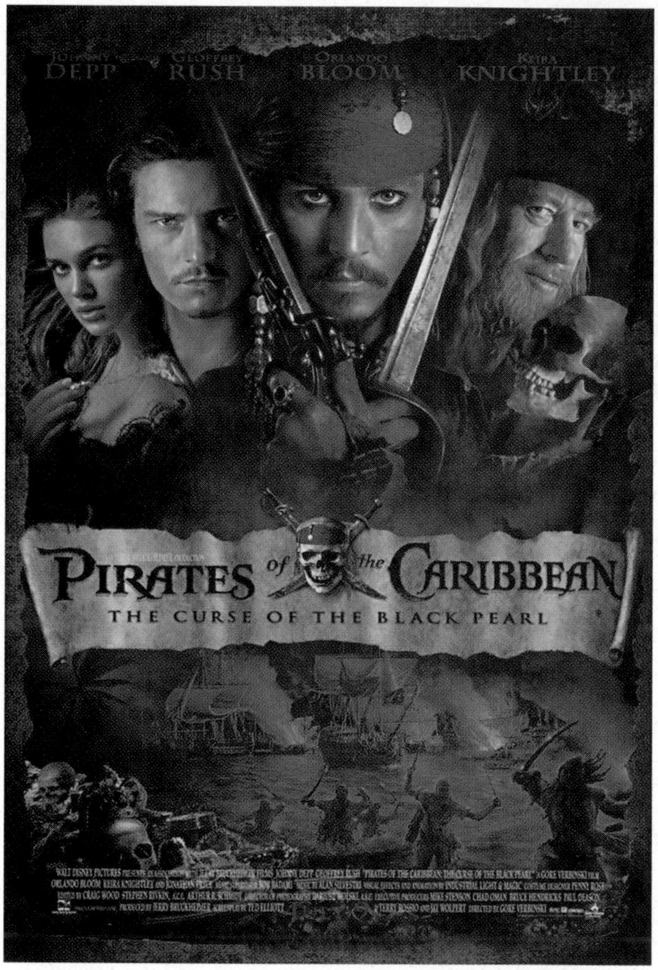

Process cost systems allocate costs evenly to homogeneous products. In addition to beverage companies such as Janis Juice, oil refiners such as **Texaco**, chemical producers such as **Dow Chemical**, food processors such as **General Mills**, and paint manufacturers such as **Sherwin-Williams** use process costing. These companies normally make products in mass quantities using continuous processes. The *per unit product cost* is determined by dividing the *total* product cost by the number of units produced during the accounting period. Process cost systems provide *average* product costs.

To a lesser extent, job-order costing systems also use average costs. It is either not possible or not cost effective to trace costs of indirect materials, indirect labor, utilities, rent, and depreciation directly to particular jobs. Companies normally combine these costs and allocate them to individual products using an average overhead rate based on a common measure of production such as labor hours, machine hours, or square footage. When jobs are produced in batches of a number of similar products, the cost per unit is determined by dividing the total cost of the job by the number of units in the batch. Although more costs are traced to specific products under a job-order system than a process system, *both* systems require *some* form of *cost averaging.*

Job-Order Cost Flow

LO 2

Identify how product costs flow through a job-order cost system.

Job-order and process costing systems are patterned after the physical flow of products moving through production. For example, consider how Benchmore Boat Company builds custom boats. Each boat is a separate project. Benchmore starts a project by requisitioning raw materials from materials storage. It assigns specific employees to work on specific boats. Finally, it assigns indirect (overhead) costs to each boat based on the number of direct labor hours required to build the boat.

Benchmore's *job-order cost system* accumulates cost in a manner parallel to physical boat construction. Benchmore assigns each boat a specific job identification number. It records transactions in inventory accounts on a perpetual basis. Product costs are accumulated separately for each job identification number. The costs of each boat move through the Work in Process Inventory account to the Finished Goods Inventory account and finally to

EXHIBIT 18.1

Cost Flow in a Job-Order Cost System

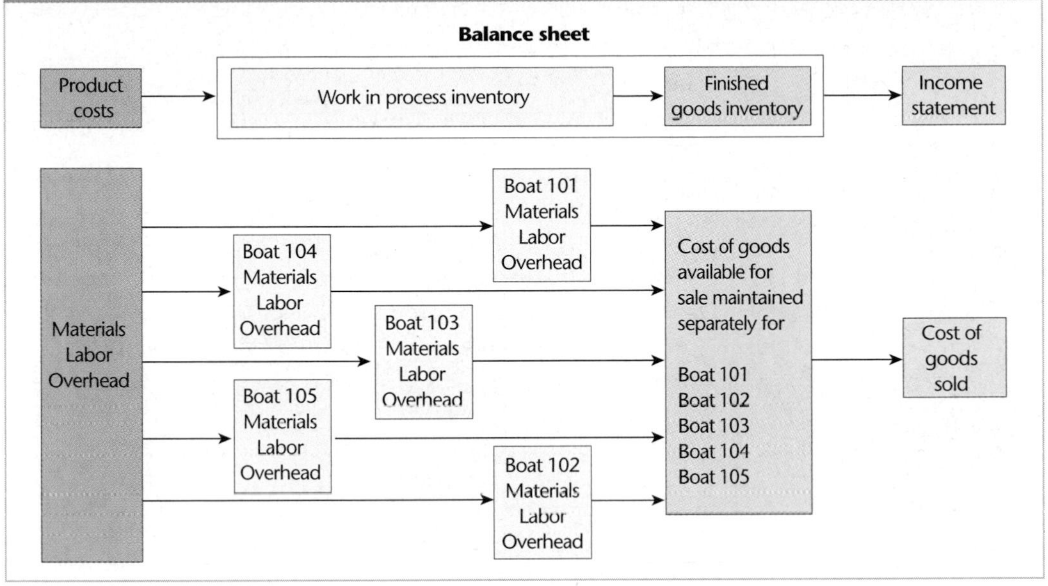

the Cost of Goods Sold account as the boat is produced and sold. Exhibit 18.1 shows the flow of product costs for the five boats Benchmore worked on in 2007 and 2008.

In a job-order system, the amount recorded in the Work in Process Inventory account is the total cost to date of distinct jobs. Each distinct job represents the costs of materials, labor, and overhead accumulated for that specific inventory project. The Work in Process Inventory account is a *control* account supported by numerous *subsidiary* accounts (the records for individual jobs). The Finished Goods Inventory account is also a control account. It is supported by subsidiary accounts in which are recorded the separate costs of each completed, but not yet sold, boat.

Process Cost Flow

LO 3

Identify how product costs flow through a process cost system.

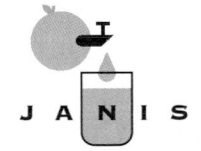

Process cost systems use the same general ledger accounts as job-order cost systems. Product costs flow from Raw Materials Inventory to Work in Process Inventory to Finished Goods Inventory to Cost of Goods Sold. The primary difference between the two systems centers on accounting for the work in process inventory. The physical products move continuously through a series of processing centers. Instead of accumulating product costs by jobs that add up to a single Work in Process Inventory control account, process cost systems accumulate product costs by processing centers, or *departments.*

Each department has its own separate Work in Process Inventory account. For example, Janis Juice Company uses three distinct processes to produce cans of apple juice. Raw apples enter the extraction department where juice concentrate is pressed from whole fruit. The concentrate moves to the mixing department where Janis adds water, sugar, food coloring, and preservatives. The resulting juice mixture moves to the packaging department where it is canned and boxed. The materials, labor, and overhead costs incurred as products move through a processing center (department) are charged to that center's Work in Process Inventory account.

Parallel to the physical flow of product through the manufacturing process, cost accumulations pass from one department to the next. The end products of one department become the raw materials of the next department. The costs transferred from one department to the next are **transferred-in costs**. Transferred-in costs are combined with the additional materials, labor, and overhead costs incurred by each succeeding department. When goods are complete, the total product cost transferred to the Finished Goods Inventory account represents the sum of product costs from all the departments. Exhibit 18.2 illustrates cost flow for the process costing system used by Janis Juice Company. Compare the cost flow patterns in Exhibits 18.1 and 18.2 to clarify the distinction between job-order and process cost systems.

EXHIBIT 18.2

Cost Flow in a Process Cost System

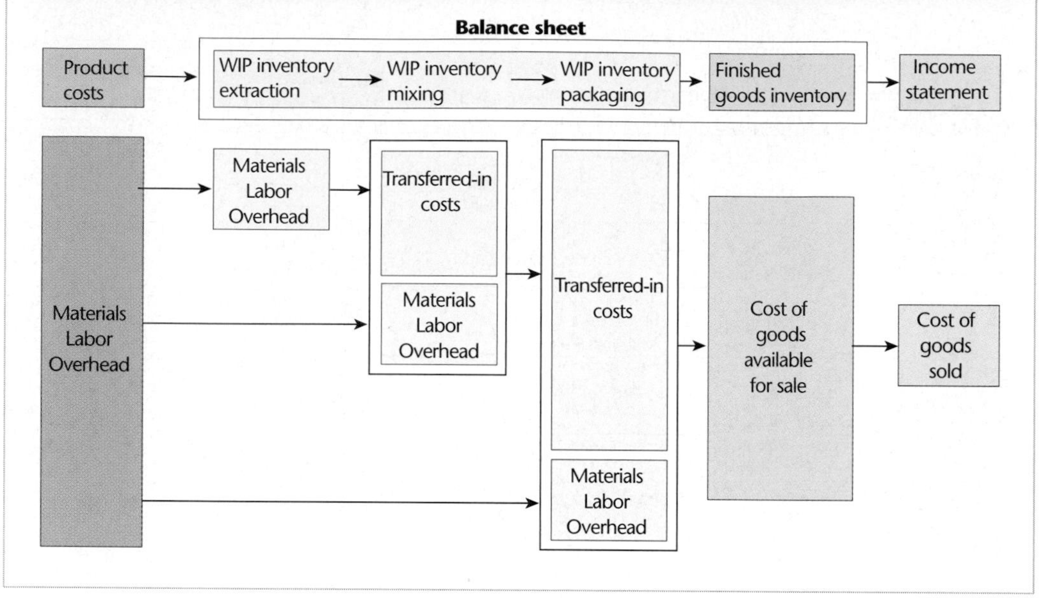

LO 4

Distinguish between raw materials cost and transferred-in cost.

LO 5

Explain how hybrid accounting systems combine components of job-order and process cost systems.

Hybrid Accounting Systems

Many companies use **hybrid cost systems**. Hybrid systems combine features of both process and job-order cost systems. For example, Gateway 2000 makes thousands of identical computers using a continuous assembly line that is compatible with process costing. Each unit requires the same amount of labor to assemble a standard set of parts into a finished computer ready for immediate sale. Gateway also builds custom computers with unique features. Customers can order larger monitors, more memory, or faster processors than Gateway's standard model has. Gateway meets these requests by customizing the computers as they move through production. The costs of customized features must be traced to products with a job-order type of system. Gateway charges customers a premium for the custom items.

LO 6

Identify the various forms of documentation used in a job-order cost system.

Topic Tackler PLUS

18-1

Documentation in a Job-Order Cost System

In a job-order cost system, product costs for each individual job are accumulated on a **job cost sheet**, also called a *job-order cost sheet* or a *job record*. As each job moves through production, detailed cost information for materials, labor, and overhead is recorded on the job cost sheet. When a job is finished, the job cost sheet summarizes all costs incurred to complete that job.

Two primary source documents, materials requisition forms and work tickets, provide the information recorded on the job cost sheet. Before starting a job, the job supervisor prepares a **materials requisition form** which lists the materials needed to begin work. The materials requisition represents the authorization for raw materials to be released from storage to production. Some companies deliver hard-copy forms to and from the different departments, but most modern businesses deliver requests electronically through a computer network. Whether recorded on paper documents or in electronic files, the information from material requisitions for each job is sent to the accounting department to be summarized on the job cost sheet.

The **work ticket**, sometimes called a *time card,* provides space for the job number, employee identification, and work description. Employees record on the work ticket the amount of time they spend on each job. This information is forwarded to the accounting department. Using wage rate records, the accounting department computes the amount of labor cost and records it on the job cost sheet. The data can be gathered manually or electronically.

Finally, each job cost sheet provides space for applied overhead. Companies maintain job cost sheet records perpetually, adding additional cost data as work on jobs progresses. Using

REALITY BYTES

Job-order, process, and hybrid costing systems apply to service businesses as well as manufacturing concerns. Consider a local franchisee of Lawn Doctor who is pricing lawn maintenance contracts for a variety of residential customers. A separate price will be quoted for each lawn, and this price will be based on what the company believes it will cost to maintain that particular lawn. Some customers have larger lawns than others, which cost more to service. Some customers want less lawn care service than others, which costs less. This type of service business will use a job-order system.

Now, consider a company in the clothes laundering business. The price the company charges to wash, press, and hang a man's shirt is the same for all shirts because the cost of servicing each shirt, whether large or small, is about the same. This business will use a process cost system to determine the cost of laundering one shirt.

EXHIBIT 18.3

Job-Order Cost Sheet and Source Documents

Job cost sheet

Job Order No. Boat 101 Customer Name: Arturo Martinez

Due Date: 03/15/2008 Date Started: 01/01/2007 Date Finished: 12/31/2007

Direct materials		Direct labor			Applied overhead		
Req. No.	Cost	Ticket	Hours	Cost	Rate	Hours	Cost
24585	7,100	367	1,400	9,100	3.90	1,400	5,460
24600	5,600	360	1,600	10,400	3.90	1,600	6,240
24609	6,100						
Total	18,800	Total		19,500	Total		11,700

Cost summary

Direct materials	$18,800
Direct labor	19,500
Overhead	11,700
Total	$50,000

Material requisitions

	Date	Quantity
Package K	1/1	Mixed
Package R	2/1	Mixed
Package T	3/1	Mixed

Information transferred electronically

Work tickets

	Date	Hours
Process 1	1/30	1,400
Process 2	2/28	1,600

Information transferred electronically

predetermined overhead rates, estimated overhead costs are regularly added to job cost sheets. Exhibit 18.3 illustrates a job cost sheet along with materials requisition forms and work tickets for Benchmore Boat Company's job-order number Boat 101.

EXHIBIT 18.4

BENCHMORE BOAT COMPANY
Trial Balance
As of January 1, 2008

	Debit	Credit
Cash	$ 73,000	
Raw Materials Inventory	7,000	
Work in Process Inventory	34,000	
Finished Goods Inventory	85,000	
Production Supplies	300	
Manufacturing Equipment	90,000	
Accumulated Depreciation		$ 32,000
Common Stock		200,000
Retained Earnings		57,300
Total	$289,300	$289,300

EXHIBIT 18.4 *continued*

Subsidiary Account Balances

Work in Process Inventory		Finished Goods Inventory	
Boat 103	$14,000	Boat 101	$50,000
Boat 104	8,000	Boat 102	35,000
Boat 105	12,000		
Total	$34,000	Total	$85,000

Job-Order Cost System Illustrated

LO 7

Explain how accounting events in a job-order cost system affect financial statements.

To illustrate how a job-order cost system works, we follow the operations of Benchmore Boat Company during 2008. Exhibit 18.4 shows the company's 2008 beginning account balances.

Entries for Benchmore's 2008 accounting events, described next, are shown in ledger T-accounts in Exhibit 18.5 on page 888. As you study each event, trace it to the T-accounts. The entries in Exhibit 18.5 are cross-referenced to sequential event numbers. The individual effect of each event on the financial statements is shown and discussed in the following section.

Event 1 **Benchmore paid $14,000 cash to purchase raw materials.**

The effects of this event on the company's financial statements follow.

Assets			=	Liabilities	+	Equity	Revenue	−	Expenses	=	Net Income	Cash Flow
Cash	+	Raw Materials Inventory										
(14,000)	+	14,000	=	NA	+	NA	NA	−	NA	=	NA	(14,000) OA

Event 1 is an asset exchange; it does not affect total assets reported on the balance sheet. The asset cash decreases and the asset raw materials inventory increases. The income statement is not affected. The cash outflow is reported in the operating activities section of the statement of cash flows.

Event 2 **Benchmore used $17,000 of direct raw materials in the process of making boats.**

The amounts used for Boat 103, Boat 104, and Boat 105 were $8,000, $3,400, and $5,600, respectively. The effects of this event on the financial statements follow.

Assets			=	Liabilities	+	Equity	Revenue	−	Expenses	=	Net Income	Cash Flow
Raw Materials Inventory	+	Work in Process Inventory										
(17,000)	+	17,000	=	NA	+	NA	NA	−	NA	=	NA	NA

This event is an asset exchange. It does not affect total assets reported on the balance sheet. The asset raw materials inventory decreases and the asset work in process inventory increases. The income statement and the statement of cash flows are not affected. In addition to recording the effects in the Work in Process Inventory control account, Benchmore adjusted the individual job cost sheets to reflect the raw material used on each job, as shown in Exhibit 18.5.

Event 3 Benchmore paid $1,200 cash to purchase production supplies.

The effects of this event on the company's financial statements are shown here.

Assets				=	Liabilities	+	Equity	Revenue	−	Expenses	=	Net Income	Cash Flow
Cash	+	Production Supplies											
(1,200)	+	1,200		=	NA	+	NA	NA	−	NA	=	NA	(1,200) OA

This event is also an asset exchange. It does not affect total assets reported on the balance sheet. One asset, cash, decreases and another asset, production supplies, increases. Purchasing production supplies does not affect the income statement. The cost of supplies is allocated to work in process inventory as part of overhead and is expensed as part of cost of goods sold. The cash outflow for the supplies purchase is reported in the operating activities section of the statement of cash flows.

Event 4 Benchmore paid $8,000 cash to production employees who worked on Boat 103.

The effects of this event on the company's financial statements follow.

Assets				=	Liabilities	+	Equity	Revenue	−	Expenses	=	Net Income	Cash Flow
Cash	+	Work in Process Inventory											
(8,000)	+	8,000		=	NA	+	NA	NA	−	NA	=	NA	(8,000) OA

These wages are *not* salary expense. Because the employees worked to make inventory, the cost of their labor is added to work in process inventory. This event is an asset exchange. The asset cash decreases, and the asset work in process inventory increases. Neither total assets reported on the balance sheet nor any revenues or expenses on the income statement are affected. The cash outflow is reported in the operating activities section of the statement of cash flows. In addition to recording the effects in the Work in Process Inventory control account, Benchmore adjusted the Boat 103 job cost sheet to reflect the labor used on the job. Refer to Exhibit 18.5; the $8,000 labor cost is entered in both the Work in Process Inventory control account and on the job cost sheet for Boat 103.

Event 5 Benchmore applied estimated manufacturing overhead costs of $6,240 to the Boat 103 job.

Production employees completed Boat 103. When the boat was finished, the actual amount of many costs to make it were not then known. During the year, Benchmore sells boats before knowing the exact costs of making them. Although a portion of the total production supplies, depreciation, supervisory salaries, rental cost, and utilities were used while Boat 103 was under construction, the actual cost of these resources is not known until the end of the year. To make timely decisions, such as setting the selling prices for boats, Benchmore must assign estimated overhead costs to boats as they are completed.

To estimate overhead as accurately as possible, Benchmore first reviewed the previous year's actual overhead costs. It then adjusted those amounts for expected changes. Assume Benchmore estimated total overhead costs for 2008 would be as follows: production supplies, $1,400; depreciation, $4,000; utilities and other indirect costs, $10,590, for a total of $15,990 ($1,400 + $4,000 + $10,590).

Benchmore has identified a cause and effect relationship between direct labor time and overhead cost. Boats that require more labor also require more overhead. For example, the more hours production employees work, the more supplies they use. Similarly, more labor

EXHIBIT 18.5

Ledger T-Accounts for Benchmore Boat Company

Cash

Bal.	73,000	(1)	14,000
(13)	91,000	(3)	1,200
		(4)	8,000
		(7)	24,500
		(8)	12,000
		(10)	10,100
Bal.	94,200		

Production Supplies

Bal.	300	(12)	1,100
(3)	1,200		
Bal.	400		

Manufacturing Equipment

Bal.	90,000		

Accumulated Dep.

		Bal.	32,000
		(11)	4,000
		Bal.	36,000

Raw Materials Inventory

Bal.	7,000	(2)	17,000
(1)	14,000		
Bal.	4,000		

Manufacturing Overhead

(10)	10,100	(5)	6,240
(11)	4,000	(9)	9,360
(12)	1,100		
(15)	400		
Bal.	0		

Work in Process Inventory

Bal.	34,000	(6)	36,240
(2)	17,000		
(4)	8,000		
(5)	6,240		
(8)	12,000		
(9)	9,360		
Bal.	50,360		

Job Cost Sheets (Subsidiary accounts)

Boat 103

Beginning Balance	14,000
Materials	8,000
Labor	8,000
Overhead	6,240
Product Cost	36,240
To Finished Goods	(36,240)
Ending Balance	0

Boat 104

Beginning Balance	8,000
Materials	3,400
Labor	5,000
Overhead	3,900
Ending Balance	20,300

Boat 105

Beginning Balance	12,000
Materials	5,600
Labor	7,000
Overhead	5,460
Ending Balance	30,060

Finished Goods Inventory

Bal.	85,000	(14)	50,000
(6)	36,240		
Bal.	71,240		

Boat 101

Balance	50,000
Sold	(50,000)
Balance	0

Boat 102

Balance	35,000
Cost Transferred	0
Balance	35,000

Boat 103

Balance	0
Cost Transferred	36,240
Balance	36,240

Common Stock

		Bal.	200,000

Retained Earnings

		Bal.	57,300

Sales Revenue

		(13)	91,000

Cost of Goods Sold

(14)	50,000	(15)	400
Bal.	49,600		

Selling and Admin. Exp.

(7)	24,500		

Boat 101

Cost Sheet Data Transferred to Permanent Storage

hours translates into more equipment use, causing more utilities and depreciation costs. Because of the relationship between labor and indirect costs, Benchmore uses *direct labor hours* as the allocation base for overhead costs. Benchmore estimated it would use a total of 4,100 labor hours during 2008. It established a *predetermined overhead rate* as follows:

$$\frac{\text{Predetermined}}{\text{overhead rate}} = \frac{\text{Total estimated}}{\text{overhead costs}} \div \frac{\text{Total estimated}}{\text{direct labor hours}}$$

$$\text{Predetermined overhead rate} = \$15{,}990 \div 4{,}100$$
$$= \$3.90 \text{ per direct labor hour}$$

Boat 103 required 1,600 actual direct labor hours. Benchmore applied $6,240 (1,600 hours × $3.90) of overhead to that job. The effects of the overhead application on the company's financial statements follow.

Assets			=	Liabilities	+	Equity	Revenue	−	Expenses	=	Net Income	Cash Flow
Manufacturing Overhead	+	Work in Process Inventory										
(6,240)	+	6,240	=	NA	+	NA	NA	−	NA	=	NA	NA

The event is an asset exchange. One asset, work in process inventory, increases and a temporary asset, manufacturing overhead, decreases. Applying overhead costs to work in process inventory does not affect the income statement. When finished goods are sold, overhead costs affect the income statement through cost of goods sold. Applying overhead does not affect cash flow either. Cash flow is affected when Benchmore *pays* indirect costs, not when it *applies* them to work in process inventory. The job cost sheet for Boat 103 reflects the applied (estimated) overhead cost. The T-accounts in Exhibit 18.5 also show the overhead application.

Event 6 **Benchmore transferred $36,240 of product costs for completed Boat 103 from work in process inventory to finished goods inventory.**

The effects of this transfer on the company's financial statements follow.

Assets			=	Liabilities	+	Equity	Revenue	−	Expenses	=	Net Income	Cash Flow
Work in Process Inventory	+	Finished Goods Inventory										
(36,240)	+	36,240	=	NA	+	NA	NA	−	NA	=	NA	NA

This event is an asset exchange. Benchmore transferred cost from the Work in Process Inventory control account to the Finished Goods Inventory control account. The transfer does not affect total assets reported on the balance sheet, nor does it affect the income statement or the statement of cash flows. The job cost sheet is moved to the finished goods file folder. Exhibit 18.5 illustrates these effects.

Event 7 **Benchmore paid $24,500 cash for selling and administrative expenses.**

The effects of this transaction on the financial statements follow.

Assets	=	Liabilities	+	Equity	Revenue	−	Expenses	=	Net Income	Cash Flow
Cash	=			Ret.Earn.						
(24,500)	=	NA	+	(24,500)	NA	−	24,500	=	(24,500)	(24,500) OA

This is an asset use transaction. Cash and stockholders' equity (retained earnings) decrease. Recognizing the expense decreases net income. The cash outflow reduces cash flow from operating activities.

Event 8 Benchmore paid $12,000 cash to production employees for work on Boats 104 and 105.

The cost of direct labor used was $5,000 for Boat 104 and $7,000 for Boat 105. These jobs were still incomplete at the end of 2008. The effects of this event on the financial statements follow.

Assets			=	Liabilities	+	Equity	Revenue	−	Expenses	=	Net Income	Cash Flow
Cash	+	Work in Process Inventory										
(12,000)	+	12,000	=	NA	+	NA	NA	−	NA	=	NA	(12,000) OA

This event is an asset exchange. It does not affect total assets reported on the balance sheet. It does not affect the income statement. The cash outflow is reported in the operating activities section of the statement of cash flows. In addition to the effects on the Work in Process Inventory control account, Benchmore adjusted the individual job cost sheets to reflect the labor used on each job. Exhibit 18.5 illustrates these effects.

Event 9 Benchmore applied estimated manufacturing overhead costs to the Boat 104 and Boat 105 jobs.

As previously explained, the predetermined overhead rate was $3.90 per direct labor hour (see Event 5). Assume the work described in Event 8 represented 1,000 direct labor hours for Boat 104 and 1,400 direct labor hours for Boat 105. The amount of estimated overhead cost Benchmore applied to the two jobs is calculated as follows:

Job Number	Predetermined Overhead Rate	×	Actual Labor Hours Used	=	Amount of Applied Overhead
Boat 104	$3.90	×	1,000	=	$3,900
Boat 105	3.90	×	1,400	=	5,460
Total					$9,360

The effects on the company's financial statements of applying the overhead follow.

Assets			=	Liabilities	+	Equity	Revenue	−	Expenses	=	Net Income	Cash Flow
Manufacturing Overhead	+	Work in Process Inventory										
(9,360)	+	9,360	=	NA	+	NA	NA	−	NA	=	NA	NA

Applying overhead is an asset exchange. Total assets, net income, and cash flow are not affected. Overhead costs of $3,900 for Boat 104 and $5,460 for Boat 105 are recorded on the job cost sheets. The total, $9,360, is recorded in the Work in Process Inventory control account. Trace these allocations to Exhibit 18.5.

Event 10 Benchmore paid $10,100 cash for utilities and other indirect product costs.

The effects of this event on the financial statements are shown here.

Assets			=	Liabilities	+	Equity	Revenue	−	Expenses	=	Net Income	Cash Flow
Cash	+	Manufacturing Overhead										
(10,100)	+	10,100	=	NA	+	NA	NA	−	NA	=	NA	(10,100) OA

Paying for *actual* overhead costs is an asset exchange. Total assets, net income, and job cost sheets are not affected. The cash outflow is reported in the operating activities section of the statement of cash flows. Recall that estimated overhead costs were previously recorded in work in process inventory and on the job cost sheets (Events 5 and 9).

Event 11 Benchmore recognized $4,000 of actual manufacturing equipment depreciation.

The effects of this event on the financial statements follow.

Assets			=	Liabilities	+	Equity	Revenue	−	Expenses	=	Net Income	Cash Flow
Book Value of Manufacturing Equipment	+	Manufacturing Overhead										
(4,000)	+	4,000	=	NA	+	NA	NA	−	NA	=	NA	NA

Depreciation of manufacturing equipment represents an *actual* indirect product cost (overhead), *not* an expense (even though the *amount* of depreciation is an estimate). Recognizing this depreciation is an asset exchange. The book value of the manufacturing equipment decreases and the Manufacturing Overhead account increases. Neither the total amount of assets reported on the balance sheet, nor the income statement or the statement of cash flows are affected. The job cost sheets are also not affected when *actual* overhead cost (depreciation) is recognized. The inventory accounts and job cost sheets reflect *estimated* overhead.

Event 12 Benchmore counted the production supplies on hand at year-end and recognized actual overhead cost for the supplies used.

During 2008, Benchmore had available for use $1,500 of production supplies ($300 beginning balance + $1,200 supplies purchased). A physical count disclosed there were $400 of supplies on hand at the end of 2008. Benchmore therefore must have used $1,100 of supplies ($1,500 $400). The effects on the company's financial statements of recognizing supplies used follow:

Assets			=	Liabilities	+	Equity	Revenue	−	Expenses	=	Net Income	Cash Flow
Production Supplies	+	Manufacturing Overhead										
(1,100)	+	1,100	=	NA	+	NA	NA	−	NA	=	NA	NA

The event is an asset exchange. Total assets, net income, and cash flow are not affected. The job cost sheets are not affected. Remember that estimated overhead costs were previously recorded on the job cost sheets.

Event 13 Benchmore sold Boat 101 for $91,000 cash.

The effects of this event on the financial statements follow.

Assets	=	Liabilities	+	Equity	Revenue	−	Expenses	=	Net Income	Cash Flow
Cash	=			Ret.Earn.						
91,000	=	NA	+	91,000	91,000	−	NA	=	91,000	91,000 OA

Recognizing revenue from selling inventory is an asset source event. Both assets (cash) and stockholders' equity (retained earnings) increase. Revenue recognition also increases the net income reported on the income statement. The cash inflow is reported in the operating activities section of the statement of cash flows.

Event 14 Benchmore recognized cost of goods sold for Boat 101.

The effects of this event on the financial statements follow.

Assets	=	Liabilities	+	Equity	Revenue	−	Expenses	=	Net Income	Cash Flow
Finished Goods Inventory	=			Ret.Earn.						
(50,000)	=	NA	+	(50,000)	NA	−	50,000	=	(50,000)	NA

Recognizing cost of goods sold is an asset use transaction. It decreases assets (finished goods inventory) and stockholders' equity (retained earnings). The expense recognition decreases net income, but does not affect cash flow. Benchmore recognized the cash flow impact when it spent cash in the process of building the boat. The job cost sheet for Boat 101 is transferred to the permanent files. The cost sheet is retained because information from it could be useful for estimating costs of future jobs.

Event 15 Benchmore closed the Manufacturing Overhead account, reducing cost of goods sold by $400.

During 2008, Benchmore applied $15,600 of estimated overhead cost to production. Actual overhead costs were $15,200. Overhead was therefore overapplied by $400 ($15,600 − $15,200), meaning too much overhead was transferred to the Work in Process Inventory, Finished Goods Inventory, and Cost of Goods Sold accounts. If the amount of overapplied overhead were significant, Benchmore would have to allocate it proportionately among the inventory and Cost of Goods Sold accounts. In this case, the amount is insignificant and Benchmore assigned it entirely to cost of goods sold. The effects of this event on the company's financial statements follow.

Assets	=	Liabilities	+	Equity	Revenue	−	Expenses	=	Net Income	Cash Flow
Manufacturing Overhead	=			Ret.Earn.						
400	=	NA	+	400	NA	−	(400)	=	400	NA

Overapplied overhead indicates the estimated cost transferred from the asset accounts to cost of goods sold was too high. The entry to close manufacturing overhead corrects the overstatement. Recording $400 in the overhead account increases total assets. The increase in assets is matched by a decrease in cost of goods sold, which reduces expenses, increases net income, and increases stockholders' equity (retained earnings). Cash flow is not affected. After this adjustment, the total increases in the overhead account (actual costs) equal the total decreases (estimated costs). Manufacturing Overhead is a temporary account. It is closed at year-end and does not appear in the financial statements. Exhibit 18.6 displays Benchmore Boat Company's preclosing trial balance at the end of 2008.

EXHIBIT 18.6

BENCHMORE BOAT COMPANY
Trial Balance
As of December 31, 2008

	Debit	Credit
Cash	$ 94,200	
Raw Materials Inventory	4,000	
Work in Process Inventory	50,360	
Finished Goods Inventory	71,240	
Production Supplies	400	
Manufacturing Equipment	90,000	
Accumulated Depreciation		$ 36,000
Common Stock		200,000
Retained Earnings		57,300
Sales Revenue		91,000
Cost of Goods Sold	49,600	
Selling and Administrative Expense	24,500	
Total	$384,300	$384,300

CHECK YOURSELF 18.1

Wilson Cabinets makes custom cabinets for home builders. It incurred the following costs during the most recent month.

Inventory	Materials	Labor
Job 1	$4,200	$2,700
Job 2	2,300	5,000
Job 3	1,700	800

Wilson's predetermined overhead rate is $0.80 per direct labor dollar. Actual overhead costs were $7,100. Wilson completed and sold Jobs 1 and 2 during the month, but Job 3 was not complete at month-end. The selling prices for Jobs 1 and 2 were $14,900 and $16,600, respectively. What amount of gross margin would Wilson report on the income statement for the month?

Answer

Cost accumulated in the Work in Process account:

Inventory	Materials	Labor	Overhead*	Total
Job 1	$4,200	$2,700	$2,160	$ 9,060
Job 2	2,300	5,000	4,000	11,300
Job 3	1,700	800	640	3,140

*80% of direct labor cost.

Total allocated overhead is $6,800 ($2,160 + $4,000 + $640). Since actual overhead is $7,100, overhead is underapplied by $300 ($7,100 − $6,800).

Sales Revenue ($14,900 + $16,600)	$31,500
Cost of Goods Sold (Job 1, $9,060 + Job 2, $11,300 + Underapplied overhead, $300)	(20,660)
Gross Margin	$10,840

Process Cost System Illustrated

LO 8

Explain how accounting events in a process cost system affect financial statements.

In process cost systems, product costs flow through the same general ledger accounts as in job-order cost systems: Raw Materials Inventory, Work in Process Inventory, Finished Goods Inventory, and ultimately Cost of Goods Sold. Accounting for work in process inventory, however, differs between the two systems. Instead of accumulating work in process costs by jobs, process cost systems accumulate product costs by departments. The costs of all goods that move through a processing department during a given accounting period are charged to that department. Work in process subsidiary documents (job cost sheets) are not needed. Process cost systems are easier to use than job-order systems. They do not, however, distinguish the cost of one product from another. Process systems are therefore not appropriate for manufacturers of distinctly different products; they are suited to account for continuous mass production of uniform products. Process cost systems produce the same cost per unit for all products.

To illustrate how a process cost system operates, we analyze the operations of Janis Juice Company during 2008. Recall that Janis uses three distinct processes to produce cans of

EXHIBIT 18.7

JANIS JUICE COMPANY
Trial Balance
As of January 1, 2008

	Debit	Credit
Cash	$320,000	
Raw Materials–Fruit	7,800	
Raw Materials–Additives	3,100	
Raw Materials–Containers	9,500	
Work in Process–Extraction	22,360	
Work in Process–Mixing	7,960	
Work in Process–Packaging	21,130	
Finished Goods Inventory	20,700	
Common Stock		$180,000
Retained Earnings		232,550
Total	$412,550	$412,550

apple juice. Raw materials (whole apples) enter the *extraction department* where juice concentrate is extracted from whole fruit. The juice extract passes to the *mixing department* where Janis adds water, sugar, food coloring, and preservatives. The juice mixture then moves to the *packaging department* where it is canned and boxed for shipment. Exhibit 18.7 shows the company's 2008 beginning account balances.

The entries for Janis Juice Company's 2008 accounting events, discussed individually in the following sections, are shown in ledger T-accounts in Exhibit 18.9 on page 902. The T-account entries are cross-referenced to sequential event numbers. As you study each event, trace it to the T-accounts.

Event 1 **Janis paid $84,000 cash to purchase raw materials.**

The effects of this event on the company's financial statements follow.

Assets			=	Liabilities	+	Equity	Revenue	−	Expenses	=	Net Income	Cash Flow
Cash	+	Raw Materials Inventory										
(84,000)	+	84,000	=	NA	+	NA	NA	−	NA	=	NA	(84,000) OA

This event is an asset exchange. Total assets and net income are not affected. The cash outflow is reported in the operating activities section of the statement of cash flows. The total purchase was for $25,000 of whole fruit, $30,000 of additives, and $29,000 of containers. Janis maintains separate inventory accounts for each category of raw material. Trace the entries for this event to the ledger accounts in Exhibit 18.9.

Event 2 **Janis processed $26,720 of whole fruit to produce juice extract.**

The effects of this event on the financial statements follow.

Assets			=	Liabilities	+	Equity	Revenue	−	Expenses	=	Net Income	Cash Flow
Raw Materials–Fruit	+	WIP–Extraction										
(26,720)	+	26,720	=	NA	+	NA	NA	−	NA	=	NA	NA

This event is an asset exchange. It does not affect total assets, net income, or cash flow. Janis assigns the cost of the materials used to the extraction *department* rather than to any particular product or batch of products. The extraction department adds the same amount of value to each can of juice.

Event 3 **Janis paid $38,000 cash to production employees who worked in the extraction department.**

The effects of this event on the financial statements follow.

Assets			=	Liabilities	+	Equity	Revenue	−	Expenses	=	Net Income	Cash Flow
Cash	+	WIP–Extraction										
(38,000)	+	38,000	=	NA	+	NA	NA	−	NA	=	NA	(38,000) OA

This event is also an asset exchange. Production labor cost is not salary expense. Total assets and net income are not affected. The cash outflow is reported in the operating activities section of the statement of cash flows. Like the raw materials, the labor cost is assigned to the department rather than to individual products.

Event 4 Janis applied estimated manufacturing overhead costs to the extraction department work in process inventory.

Janis has identified a relationship between labor dollars and indirect overhead costs. The more labor dollars paid, the more indirect resources consumed. Janis estimated total indirect costs in 2008 would be $96,000 and that it would pay $120,000 to production employees. Using these estimates, Janis established a *predetermined overhead rate* as follows.

$$\text{Predetermined overhead rate} = \text{Total estimated overhead costs} \div \text{Total estimated direct labor dollars}$$

$$\text{Predetermined overhead rate} = \$96{,}000 \div \$120{,}000$$

$$= \$0.80 \text{ per direct labor dollar}$$

Since the extraction department incurred $38,000 of labor cost (see Event 3), Janis applied $30,400 ($38,000 × $0.80) of overhead to that department. The effects of the overhead application on the financial statements follow.

Assets			=	Liabilities	+	Equity	Revenue	−	Expenses	=	Net Income	Cash Flow
Manufacturing Overhead	+	WIP–Extraction										
(30,400)	+	30,400	=	NA	+	NA	NA	−	NA	=	NA	NA

The event is an asset exchange. Total assets, net income, and cash flow are not affected.

18-2

LO 9

Convert partially completed units into equivalent whole units.

Event 5 Janis finished processing some of the whole fruit and transferred the related cost from the extraction department Work in Process Inventory account to the mixing department Work in Process Inventory account.

Total product costs in the extraction department Work in Process Inventory account amounted to $117,480 ($22,360 beginning balance + $26,720 materials + $38,000 labor + $30,400 applied overhead). The beginning inventory represented 100,000 units of product (cans) and the fruit Janis added started an additional 485,000 cans. The amount of fruit placed into production therefore represented 585,000 (100,000 + 485,000) units. Assume the extract transferred to the mixing department represented 500,000 cans of juice. The extraction department therefore had 85,000 (585,000 − 500,000) units in ending inventory that were *started but not completed.*

Janis had to allocate the total $117,480 product cost between the 85,000 partially completed units in ending inventory and the 500,000 completed units it transferred to the mixing department. A rational allocation requires converting the 85,000 partially completed units into equivalent whole units. The logic behind **equivalent whole units** relies on basic arithmetic. For example, 2 units that are 50 percent complete are equivalent to 1 whole (100 percent complete) unit (2 × 0.5 = 1). Similarly, 4 units that are 25 percent complete are equivalent to 1 whole unit (4 × 0.25 = 1). Further, 100 units that are 30 percent complete are equivalent to 30 whole units (100 units × 0.30 = 30).

An engineer estimated the 85,000 units in the extraction department's ending inventory were 40 percent complete. The equivalent whole units in ending inventory was therefore 34,000

(85,000 × 0.4). The *total* equivalent units processed by the extraction department during 2008 was 534,000 (500,000 units finished and transferred to the mixing department plus 34,000 equivalent whole units in ending inventory). Janis determined the average **cost per equivalent unit** as follows:

Cost per equivalent unit = Total cost ÷ Number of equivalent whole units

Cost per equivalent unit = $117,480 ÷ 534,000

= $0.22 per equivalent unit

Janis used the *cost per equivalent unit* to allocate the total cost incurred in the extraction department between the amount transferred to the mixing department and the amount in the extraction department's ending work in process inventory as follows.

	Equivalent Units	×	Cost per Unit	Cost to Be Allocated
Transferred-out costs	500,000	×	$0.22	$110,000
Ending inventory	34,000	×	0.22	7,480
Total				$117,480

The effects of transferring $110,000 from the extraction department's work in process inventory to the mixing department's work in process inventory follow.

Assets			=	Liabilities	+	Equity	Revenue	−	Expenses	=	Net Income	Cash Flow
WIP— Extraction	+	WIP— Mixing										
(110,000)	+	110,000	=	NA	+	NA	NA	−	NA	=	NA	NA

This event is an asset exchange. Total assets, net income, and the statement of cash flows are unaffected.

The allocation of costs between units transferred out and ending inventory is frequently summarized in a *cost of production report.* Cost of production reports usually provide details for three categories: the computation of equivalent units; the determination of cost per equivalent unit; and the allocation of total production cost between the units transferred out and the units in ending inventory. Exhibit 18.8 illustrates Janis's 2008 cost of production report for the extraction department.

The method used here to determine equivalent units is the **weighted average method.** The weighted average method does not account for the state of completion of units in *beginning* inventory. Equivalent units are computed for *ending* inventory only. Failing to account for equivalent units in beginning as well as ending inventories can distort the accuracy of the cost assigned to goods transferred out and goods in inventory accounts at the end of the period. Managers frequently tolerate some inaccuracy because the weighted average method is relatively easy to use. If accuracy is of paramount importance, however, a company might use the **first-in, first-out (FIFO) method.** The FIFO method accounts for the degree of completion of both beginning and ending inventories, but it is more complex to apply. Applying the FIFO method in process costing applications is explained in upper-level accounting courses. It is beyond the scope of this text.

Event 6 Janis mixed (used) $24,400 of additives with the extract transferred from the extraction department.

Conceptually, the juice extract transferred from the extraction department is a raw material to the mixing department. The mixing department adds other materials to the juice extract, such as sweetener, food coloring, and preservatives. Although both *transferred-in costs* and *additives* represent raw materials, they are traditionally classified separately. Review the

EXHIBIT 18.8

JANIS JUICE COMPANY
Cost of Production Report
Extraction Department
For the Year Ended December 31, 2008

	Actual		Equivalent
Determination of Equivalent Units			
Beginning inventory	100,000		
Units added to production	485,000		
Total	585,000		
Transferred to finished goods	500,000	100% Complete	500,000
Ending inventory	85,000	40% Complete	34,000
Total	585,000		534,000
Determination of Cost per Unit			
Cost accumulation			
Beginning inventory	$ 22,360		
Materials	26,720		
Labor	38,000		
Overhead	30,400		
Total	$117,480		
Divided by	÷		
Equivalent units	534,000		
Cost per equivalent unit (i.e., per can)	$ 0.22		
Cost Allocation			
To work in process inventory, mixing dept. (500,000 × $0.22)	$110,000		
To ending inventory (34,000 × $0.22)	7,480		
Total	$117,480		

mixing department's Work in Process account in Exhibit 18.9 to see these costs. The effects of using additional materials in the mixing department follow.

Assets			=	Liabilities	+	Equity	Revenue	−	Expenses	=	Net Income	Cash Flow
Raw Materials—Additives	+	WIP—Mixing										
(24,400)	+	24,400	=	NA	+	NA	NA	−	NA	=	NA	NA

This event is an asset exchange. Total assets, net income, and cash flow are not affected.

Event 7 **Janis paid $48,000 cash to production employees who worked in the mixing department.**

The effects of this event on the financial statements follow.

Assets			=	Liabilities	+	Equity	Revenue	−	Expenses	=	Net Income	Cash Flow
Cash	+	WIP—Mixing										
(48,000)	+	48,000	=	NA	+	NA	NA	−	NA	=	NA	(48,000) OA

Answers to The Curious Accountant

The company that produces flour should use a process costing system. This system is conceptually simple, especially when there is no beginning or ending work in process inventory. In the situation described in the Curious Accountant, the cost of one bag of whole wheat flour would be calculated by dividing $32.5 million by 50 million bags, yielding a cost per bag of $0.65.

The company that builds houses should use a job-order costing system. This system, as you have seen, requires extensive recordkeeping. The cost of each item of material that goes into a house and the wages of each worker who helps build a house must be tracked to the specific house in question. These costs, along with the appropriate amount of overhead, will constitute the cost of that particular house; it is unlikely that the cost of any two houses will be exactly the same.

This is an asset exchange. Total assets and net income are not affected. The cash outflow is reported in the operating activities section of the statement of cash flows.

Event 8 Janis applied estimated manufacturing overhead costs to the mixing department work in process inventory.

Using the *predetermined overhead rate* calculated in Event 4, Janis determined it should apply $38,400 ($48,000 labor × $0.80 overhead rate) of overhead costs to the mixing department's work in process inventory. The effects of the overhead application on the financial statements follow.

Assets			=	Liabilities	+	Equity	Revenue	−	Expenses	=	Net Income	Cash Flow
Manufacturing Overhead	+	WIP— Mixing										
(38,400)	+	38,400	=	NA	+	NA	NA	−	NA	=	NA	NA

The event is an asset exchange. Total assets, net income, and cash flow are not affected.

Event 9 Janis finished mixing some of the juice extract with additives and transferred the related cost from the mixing department Work in Process Inventory account to the packaging department Work in Process Inventory account.

Total product costs in the mixing department were $228,760 ($7,960 beginning balance + $110,000 transferred-in cost + $24,400 materials + $48,000 labor + $38,400 overhead). An engineer estimated that Janis transferred 510,000 units of mixed juice from the mixing department to the packaging department and that the 88,000 units of juice in the mixing department ending inventory were 25 percent complete.

The mixing department ending inventory therefore represented 22,000 (88,000 × 0.25) *equivalent whole units.* The total equivalent whole units produced by the mixing department was 532,000 (510,000 + 22,000). The average *cost per equivalent unit* was therefore $0.43 ($228,760 ÷ 532,000). Janis allocated the total product costs incurred in the mixing department between the amount transferred to the packaging department and the amount in the mixing department's *ending* work in process inventory as follows.

	Equivalent Units	×	Cost per Unit	Cost to Be Allocated
Transferred-out costs	510,000	×	$0.43	$219,300
Ending inventory	22,000	×	0.43	9,460
Total				$228,760

The effects of transferring $219,300 from the mixing department work in process inventory to the packaging department work in process inventory are as follows.

Assets			=	Liabilities	+	Equity	Revenue	−	Expenses	=	Net Income	Cash Flow
WIP—Mixing	+	WIP—Packaging										
(219,300)	+	219,300	=	NA	+	NA	NA	−	NA	=	NA	NA

This event is an asset exchange. Total assets, net income, and the statement of cash flows are unaffected. Find the ending balance in the mixing department's Work in Process Inventory account in Exhibit 18.9. Also find the entry that transfers $219,300 of product cost from the mixing department's Work in Process Inventory account to the packaging department's Work in Process Inventory account.

Event 10 **Janis added containers and other packaging materials costing $32,000 to work in process in the packaging department.**

The effects of this event on the financial statements follow:

Assets			=	Liabilities	+	Equity	Revenue	−	Expenses	=	Net Income	Cash Flow
Raw Materials—Containers	+	WIP—Packaging										
(32,000)	+	32,000	=	NA	+	NA	NA	−	NA	=	NA	NA

This event is an asset exchange. Total assets, net income, and cash flow are not affected.

Event 11 **Janis paid $43,000 cash to production employees who worked in the packaging department.**

The effects of this event on the financial statements follow.

Assets			=	Liabilities	+	Equity	Revenue	−	Expenses	=	Net Income	Cash Flow
Cash	+	WIP—Packaging										
(43,000)	+	43,000	=	NA	+	NA	NA	−	NA	=	NA	(43,000) OA

This is an asset exchange. Total assets and net income are not affected. The cash outflow is reported in the operating activities section of the statement of cash flows.

Event 12 **Janis applied estimated manufacturing overhead costs to the packaging department work in process inventory.**

Using the *predetermined overhead rate* calculated in Event 4, Janis determined it should apply $34,400 ($43,000 labor × $0.80 overhead rate) of overhead costs to the packaging department's work in process inventory. The effects of the overhead application on the financial statements follow.

Assets			=	Liabilities	+	Equity	Revenue	−	Expenses	=	Net Income	Cash Flow
Manufacturing Overhead	+	WIP—Packaging										
(34,400)	+	34,400	=	NA	+	NA	NA	−	NA	=	NA	NA

The event is an asset exchange. Total assets, net income, and cash flow are not affected.

Event 13 **Janis finished packaging some of the juice and transferred the related cost from the packaging department Work in Process Inventory account to the Finished Goods Inventory account.**

Total product costs in the packaging department were $349,830 ($21,130 beginning balance + $219,300 transferred-in cost + $32,000 materials + $43,000 labor + $34,400 overhead). An engineer estimated that Janis transferred 480,000 units of packaged juice from the packaging department to finished goods inventory and that the 90,000 units of juice in the packaging department ending inventory were 30 percent complete.

The packaging department ending inventory therefore represented 27,000 (90,000 × 0.30) *equivalent whole units.* The total equivalent whole units produced by the packaging department was 507,000 (480,000 + 27,000). The average *cost per equivalent unit* was therefore $0.69 ($349,830 ÷ 507,000). Janis allocated the total product costs incurred in the packaging department between the amount transferred to finished goods inventory and the amount in the packaging department's ending work in process inventory as follows.

	Equivalent Units	×	Cost per Unit	Cost to Be Allocated
Transferred-out costs	480,000	×	$0.69	$331,200
Ending inventory	27,000	×	0.69	18,630
Total				$349,830

The effects of transferring $331,200 from the packaging department work in process inventory to the finished goods inventory follow.

Assets			=	Liabilities	+	Equity	Revenue	−	Expenses	=	Net Income	Cash Flow
WIP—Packaging	+	Finished Goods Inventory										
(331,200)	+	331,200	=	NA	+	NA	NA	−	NA	=	NA	NA

This event is an asset exchange. Total assets, net income, and the statement of cash flows are unaffected. Find the ending balance in the packaging department's Work in Process Inventory account in Exhibit 18.9. Also find the entry that transfers $331,200 of product cost from the packaging department's Work in Process Inventory account to the Finished Goods Inventory account.

Event 14 Janis paid $106,330 cash for actual overhead costs.

The effects of this event on the financial statements follow.

Assets			=	Liabilities	+	Equity	Revenue	−	Expenses	=	Net Income	Cash Flow
Cash	+	Manufacturing Overhead										
(106,330)	+	106,330	=	NA	+	NA	NA	−	NA	=	NA	(106,330) OA

Incurring *actual overhead costs* is an asset exchange event. Total assets and net income are not affected. The cash outflow is reported in the operating activities section of the statement of cash flows.

Event 15 Janis sold 490,000 cans of juice for cash of $1 per can.

The effects of this event on the financial statements follow.

Assets	=	Liabilities	+	Equity	Revenue	−	Expenses	=	Net Income	Cash Flow
Cash	=			Ret.Earn.						
490,000	=	NA	+	490,000	490,000	−	NA	=	490,000	490,000 OA

Recognizing revenue from the sale of inventory is an asset source event. Assets (cash) and stockholders' equity (retained earnings) both increase, as do revenue and net income reported on the income statement. Since Janis received the revenue in cash, the operating activities section of the statement of cash flows reports the inflow.

Event 16 Janis recognized cost of goods sold for the 490,000 cans of juice sold in Event 15.

The average cost per finished can of juice was $0.69 (see Event 13). Cost of goods sold was therefore $338,100 (490,000 units × $0.69). The effects of this event on the financial statements follow.

Assets	=	Liabilities	+	Equity	Revenue	−	Expenses	=	Net Income	Cash Flow
Finished Goods Inventory	=			Ret.Earn.						
(338,100)	=	NA	+	(338,100)	NA	−	338,100	=	(338,100)	NA

Recognizing cost of goods sold is an asset use transaction. Both assets (finished goods inventory), and stockholders' equity (retained earnings), decrease. The increase in the expense, cost of goods sold, decreases net income. Cash flow is not affected.

Event 17 Janis paid $78,200 cash for selling and administrative expenses.

The effects of this event on the financial statements follow.

Assets	=	Liabilities	+	Equity	Revenue	−	Expenses	=	Net Income	Cash Flow
Cash	=			Ret.Earn.						
(78,200)	=	NA	+	(78,200)	NA	−	78,200	=	(78,200)	(78,200) OA

Recognizing selling and administrative expense is an asset use transaction. It decreases assets (cash) and stockholders' equity (retained earnings). Recognizing the expense decreases net income. The cash outflow is reported as a decrease in the operating activities section of the statement of cash flows.

Event 18 Janis closed the Manufacturing Overhead account and increased the Cost of Goods Sold account by $3,130.

During 2008, Janis applied $103,200 of overhead cost to production. Actual overhead costs were $106,330. Overhead was therefore underapplied by $3,130 ($106,330 − $103,200), indicating that too little overhead was transferred to work in process inventory, finished goods inventory, and cost of goods sold. Janis considered the underapplied amount insignificant and assigned it directly to cost of goods sold. The effects of this event on the financial statements follow.

Assets	=	Liabilities	+	Equity	Revenue	−	Expenses	=	Net Income	Cash Flow
Manufacturing Overhead	=			Ret.Earn.						
(3,130)	=	NA	+	(3,130)	NA	−	3,130	=	(3,130)	NA

Since underapplied overhead means too little estimated cost was transferred from the asset accounts to the Cost of Goods Sold account, closing the Manufacturing Overhead account to cost of goods sold corrects the understatement. The additional overhead costs of $3,130 increase cost of goods sold and decrease net income. Cash flow is unaffected. After this adjustment, the total increases in the overhead account (actual costs) equal the total decreases (estimated costs). The ending balance in the Manufacturing Overhead account is zero. Manufacturing overhead is not reported on any financial statement.

Exhibit 18.10 shows the year-end adjusted trial balance for Janis Juice Company.

EXHIBIT 18.9

Ledger T-Accounts for Janis Juice Company

Cash

Bal.	320,000	(1)	84,000
(15)	490,000	(3)	38,000
		(7)	48,000
		(11)	43,000
		(14)	106,330
		(17)	78,200
Bal.	412,470		

Raw Materials—Fruit

Bal.	7,800	(2)	26,720
(1)	25,000		
Bal.	6,080		

Raw Materials—Additives

Bal.	3,100	(6)	24,400
(1)	30,000		
Bal.	8,700		

Raw Materials—Containers

Bal.	9,500	(10)	32,000
(1)	29,000		
Bal.	6,500		

Manufacturing Overhead

(14)	106,330	(4)	30,400
		(8)	38,400
		(12)	34,400
		(18)	3,130
Bal.	0		

Work in Process—Extraction

Bal.	22,360	(5)	110,000
(2)	26,720		
(3)	38,000		
(4)	30,400		
Bal.	7,480		

Work in Process —Mixing

Bal.	7,960	(9)	219,300
(5)	110,000		
(6)	24,400		
(7)	48,000		
(8)	38,400		
Bal.	9,460		

Work in Process—Packaging

Bal.	21,130	(13)	331,200
(9)	219,300		
(10)	32,000		
(11)	43,000		
(12)	34,400		
Bal.	18,630		

Finished Goods Inventory

Bal.	20,700	(16)	338,100
(13)	331,200		
Bal.	13,800		

Common Stock

		Bal.	180,000

Retained Earnings

		Bal.	232,550

Sales Revenue

		(15)	490,000

Cost of Goods Sold

(16)	338,100		
(18)	3,130		
Bal.	341,230		

Selling and Admin. Exp.

(17)	78,200		

EXHIBIT 18.10

JANIS JUICE COMPANY Adjusted Trial Balance As of December 31, 2008		
	Debit	**Credit**
Cash	$412,470	
Raw Materials–Fruit	6,080	
Raw Materials–Additives	8,700	
Raw Materials–Containers	6,500	
Work in Process–Extraction	7,480	
Work in Process–Mixing	9,460	
Work in Process–Packaging	18,630	
Finished Goods Inventory	13,800	
Common Stock		$180,000
Retained Earnings		232,550
Sales Revenue		490,000
Cost of Goods Sold	341,230	
Selling and Administrative Expenses	78,200	
Total	$902,550	$902,550

CHECK YOURSELF 18.2

Western Manufacturing Company uses a process cost system. Its products pass through two departments. Beginning inventory in Department I's Work in Process (WIP) account was $5,000. During the month the department added $13,200 of product costs to the WIP account. There were 200 units of product in beginning inventory, and 500 units were started during the month. Ending inventory consisted of 300 units 40 percent complete. Prepare a cost of production report showing the cost of goods transferred from Department I to Department II and the cost of Department I's ending work in process inventory.

Answer

Cost of Production Report			
	Actual		**Equivalent Units**
Determination of Equivalent Units			
Beginning inventory	200		
Units added to production	500		
Total	700		
Transferred to finished goods	400	100% Complete	400
Ending inventory	300	40% Complete	120
Total	700		520
Determination of Cost per Unit			
Cost accumulation			
Beginning inventory	$ 5,000		
Product costs added	13,200		
Total product costs	$18,200		
Divide by	÷		
Equivalent units	520		
Cost per equivalent unit	$ 35		
Cost Allocation			
Transferred to Department II (400 × $35)	$14,000		
Ending WIP inventory (120 × $35)	4,200		
Total	$18,200		

FOCUS ON INTERNATIONAL ISSUES

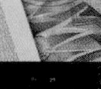

JOB-ORDER, PROCESS, AND HYBRID COST SYSTEMS CROSS INTERNATIONAL BORDERS

Companies throughout the world use job-order, process, and hybrid cost systems. **Nestlé Group**, a Swiss company, makes chocolate morsels, among many other products. A homogenous product like candy morsels requires the use of a process cost system. In contrast, **Airbus** is an aircraft manufacturing company headquartered in Toulouse, France. When it completes an order for five A320 airplanes for Air New Zealand, the cost of this order will be determined using a job-order cost system.

<< A Look Back

Job-order and *process cost systems* represent the two primary methods of accounting for product cost flows in manufacturing companies. In both systems, entries in the accounting records parallel the physical flow of products as they move through production. Job-order cost systems are used by manufacturers that produce distinct products or distinct batches of products. Products suited to job-order systems include buildings, ships, airplanes, and special-order batches. A job-order cost system accumulates costs for individual products or batches of products. Each product or batch has a job identification number. Costs are accumulated separately by job number. A job-order cost system requires detailed accounting information. The total cost of all jobs is accumulated in one Work in Process Inventory control account; details of the cost of materials, labor, and overhead for each job are kept in subsidiary records called job-order cost sheets. Process cost systems are used by manufacturers that make homogeneous products in a continuous production process. Products suited to a process cost system include paint, gasoline, and soft drinks. A process cost system accumulates product costs for each processing department (e.g., cutting, processing, assembling, packaging). Because the units are homogeneous, the cost per unit can be determined by dividing the total processing cost by the number of units (cost averaging). Any units that are partially complete at the end of an accounting period must be converted into equivalent whole units prior to determining the average cost per unit. The cost per equivalent whole unit is used to allocate the total processing cost among departments and ending inventories.

>> A Look Forward

The next chapter will show you how changes in cost, volume, and pricing affect profitability. You will learn to determine the number of units of product that must be produced and sold in order to break even (number of units that will produce an amount of revenue that is exactly equal to total cost). You will learn to establish the price of a product using a cost-plus pricing approach and to establish the cost of a product using a target-pricing approach. Finally, the chapter will show you how to use a break-even chart to examine potential profitability over a range of operating activity and how to use a technique known as *sensitivity analysis* to examine how simultaneous changes in sale price, volume, fixed cost, and variable cost affect profitability.

SELF-STUDY REVIEW PROBLEM 1

Hill Construction Company uses a job-order cost system. The company had three jobs in process at the beginning of the month. The beginning balance in the Work in Process control account was $145,400, made up of $42,400, $65,100, and $37,900 shown on the job cost sheets for Jobs 302, 303, and 304, respectively. During the month, Hill added the following materials and labor costs to each job:

Inventory	Materials	Labor
Job 302	$10,200	$32,000
Job 303	12,400	18,000
Job 304	16,500	10,000
Total	$39,100	$60,000

Overhead cost is applied at the predetermined rate of $0.60 per direct labor dollar. Actual overhead costs for the month were $36,800. Hill completed Job 303 and sold it for $129,000 cash during the month.

Required

a. Determine the balance in the Work in Process account at the end of the month.

b. Explain how the entry to close the Manufacturing Overhead account would affect the Cost of Goods Sold account.

c. Determine the amount of gross margin Hill would report on its income statement for the month.

Solution to Requirement *a*

Cost accumulated in the Work in Process account:

Inventory	Beg. Bal.	+	Materials	+	Labor	+	Overhead*	=	Total
Job 302	$42,400		$10,200		$32,000		$10,200		$103,800
Job 303	65,100		12,400		18,000		10,800		106,300
Job 304	37,900		16,500		10,000		6,000		70,400

*60% of direct labor cost.

Since Hill has sold Job 303, work in process at the end of the month is the sum of costs assigned to Jobs 302 and 304, $174,200 ($103,800 + $70,400).

Solution to Requirement *b*

Total applied overhead is $36,000 ($19,200 + $10,800 + $6,000). Since actual overhead is $36,800, overhead is underapplied by $800 ($36,800 − $36,000). Since the overhead is underapplied, cost of goods sold is understated. The entry to close the overhead account would increase the amount of cost of goods sold by $800.

Solution to Requirement *c*

Sales Revenue	$129,000
Cost of Goods Sold (Job 303, $106,300 + Underapplied Overhead, $800)	(107,100)
Gross Margin	$ 21,900

SELF-STUDY REVIEW PROBLEM 2

United Technology Manufacturing Company (UTMC) uses a process cost system. Products pass through two departments. The following information applies to the Assembly Department. Beginning inventory in the department's Work in Process (WIP) account was $18,400. During the month UTMC added $200,273 of product costs to the WIP account. There were 5,700 units of product in the beginning inventory and 45,300 units started during the month. The ending inventory consisted of 4,200 units, which were 30 percent complete.

Required

Prepare a cost of production report for the month.

Solution

Cost of Production Report

	Actual		Equivalent Units
Determination of Equivalent Units			
Beginning inventory	5,700		
Units added to production	45,300		
Total	51,000		
Transferred to finished goods	46,800	100% Complete	46,800
Ending inventory	4,200	30% Complete	1,260
Total	51,000		48,060
Determination of Cost per Unit			
Cost accumulation			
Beginning inventory	$ 18,400		
Product costs added	200,273		
Total product costs	$218,673		
Divide by	÷		
Equivalent units	48,060		
Cost per equivalent unit	$ 4.55		
Cost Allocation			
Transferred out (46,800 × $4.55)	$212,940		
Ending WIP inventory (1,260 × $4.55)	5,733		
Total	$218,673		

KEY TERMS

cost per equivalent unit 896
equivalent whole units 895
first-in, first-out (FIFO) method 896
hybrid cost system 884
job cost sheet 884
job-order cost system 882
materials requisition form 884
process cost system 882
transferred-in costs 883
weighted average method 896
work ticket 884

QUESTIONS

1. To what types of products is a job-order cost system best suited? Provide examples.
2. To what types of products is a process cost system best suited? Provide examples.
3. Why do both job-order and process costing require some form of cost averaging?
4. How is the unit cost of a product determined in a process cost system?
5. Ludwig Company, which normally operates a process cost system to account for the cost of the computers that it produces, has received a special order from a corporate client to produce and sell 5,000 computers. Can Ludwig use a job-order cost system to account for the costs associated with the special order even though it uses a process cost system for its normal operations?

6. Which system, a job-order or a process cost system, requires more documentation?
7. How do source documents help accountants operate a cost system?
8. In a job-order cost system, what are the Work in Process Inventory subsidiary records called? What information is included in these subsidiary records?
9. How is indirect labor recorded in ledger accounts? How is this labor eventually assigned to the items produced in a job-order cost system?
10. How is depreciation on manufacturing equipment recorded in ledger accounts? How is this depreciation assigned to the items produced in a job-order cost system and in a process cost system?
11. Why is a process cost system not appropriate for companies that produce items that are distinctly different from one another?
12. The president of Videl Corporation tells you that her company has a difficult time determining the cost per unit of product that it makes. It seems that some units are always partially complete. Counting these units as complete understates the cost per unit because all of the units but only part of the cost is included in the unit cost computation. Conversely, ignoring the number of partially completed products overstates the cost per unit because all of the costs are included but some of the number of units are omitted from the per unit computation. How can Videl obtain a more accurate cost per unit figure?
13. Bindon Furniture Manufacturing has completed its monthly inventory count for dining room chairs and recorded the following information for ending inventory: 600 units 100 percent complete, 300 units 60 percent complete, and 100 units 20 percent complete. The company uses a process cost system to determine unit cost. Why would unit cost be inaccurate if 1,000 units were used to determine unit cost?
14. What is the weighted average method of determining equivalent units? Why is it used? What are its weaknesses?
15. What is the purpose of each of the three primary steps in a process cost system? Describe each.
16. In a process cost system, what does the term *transferred-in costs* mean? How is the amount of transferred-in costs determined?
17. The finishing department is the last of four sequential production departments for Kowalski Graphics Inc. The company's other production departments are design, layout, and printing. The finishing department incurred the following costs in March 2006: direct materials, $40,000; direct labor, $80,000; applied overhead, $90,000; and transferred-in costs, $120,000. Which department incurred the transferred-in costs? In what month were the transferred-in costs incurred?

EXERCISES—SERIES A

All Exercises in Series A are available with McGraw-Hill's Homework Manager

Exercise 18-1A *Matching products with appropriate cost systems* L.O. 1

Required

Indicate which cost system (job-order, process, or hybrid) would be most appropriate for the type of product listed in the left-hand column. The first item is shown as an example.

Type of Product	Type of Cost System
a. Apartment building	Job order
b. Automobile	
c. Hollywood movie	
d. Concorde aircraft	
e. Personal computer with special features	
f. Coffee table	
g. Plastic storage containers	
h. TV set	

continued

Type of Product	Type of Cost System
i. Ship	
j. Boom box	
k. House	
l. Custom-made suit	
m. Van with custom features	
n. CPA review course	
o. Shirts	
p. Pots and pans	

L.O. 1

Exercise 18-2A *Identifying the appropriate cost system*

Extra Space Inc. makes small aluminum storage bins that it sells through a direct marketing mail-order business. The typical bin measures 6 × 8 feet. The bins are normally used to store garden tools or other small household items. Extra Space customizes bins for special-order customers by adding shelving; occasionally, it makes large bins following the unique specifications of commercial customers.

Required

Recommend the type of cost system (job-order, process, or hybrid) that Extra Space should use. Explain your recommendation.

L.O. 1, 2

Exercise 18-3A *Job-order or process cost system and a pricing decision*

Spence Chang, a tailor in his home country, recently immigrated to the United States. He is interested in starting a business making custom suits for men. Mr. Chang is trying to determine the cost of making a suit so he can set an appropriate selling price. He estimates that his materials cost will range from $50 to $80 per suit. Because he will make the suits himself, he assumes there will be no labor cost. Some suits will require more time than others, but Mr. Chang considers this fact to be irrelevant because he is personally supplying the labor, which costs him nothing. Finally, Mr. Chang knows that he will incur some overhead costs such as rent, utilities, advertising, packaging, delivery, and so on; however, he is uncertain as to the exact cost of these items.

Required

a. Should Mr. Chang use a job-order or a process cost system?

b. How can Mr. Chang determine the cost of suits he makes during the year when he does not know what the total overhead cost will be until the end of the year?

c. Is it appropriate for Mr. Chang to consider labor cost to be zero?

d. With respect to the overhead costs mentioned in the problem, distinguish the *manufacturing overhead* costs from the *selling and administrative* expenses. Comment on whether Mr. Chang should include the selling and administrative expenses in determining the product cost if he uses cost-plus pricing. Comment on whether the selling and administrative expenses should be included in determining the product cost for financial reporting purposes.

L.O. 2, 7

Exercise 18-4A *Job-order costing in a manufacturing company*

Seahawk Inc. builds sailboats. On January 1, 2004, the company had the following account balances: $40,000 for both cash and common stock. Boat 25 was started on February 10 and finished on May 31. To build the boat, Seahawk had incurred cash costs of $5,100 for labor and $4,350 for materials. During the same period, Seahawk paid $6,600 cash for actual manufacturing overhead costs. The company expects to incur $175,500 of indirect overhead cost during 2004. The overhead is allocated to jobs based on direct labor cost. The expected total labor cost for the year is $135,000.

Seahawk uses a just-in-time inventory management system. Consequently, it does not have raw materials inventory. Raw materials purchases are recorded directly in the Work in Process Inventory account.

Required

a. Use the horizontal financial statements model, as illustrated here, to record Seahawk's manufacturing events. In the Cash Flow column, designate the cash flows as operating activities (OA), investing activities (IA), or financing activities (FA). The first row shows beginning balances.

Assets								=	Equity								
Cash	+	Work in Process	+	Finished Goods	+	Manuf. Overhead		=	Com. Stk.	+	Ret. Earn.	Rev.	−	Exp.	=	Net Inc.	Cash Flow
40,000	+	NA	+	NA	+	NA		=	40,000	+	NA	NA	−	NA	=	NA	NA

b. If Seahawk desires to earn a profit equal to 20 percent of cost, for what price should it sell the boat?

c. If the boat is not sold by year end, what amount would appear in Work in Process Inventory and Finished Goods Inventory on the balance sheet for Boat 25?

d. Is the amount of inventory you calculated in Requirement *c* the actual or the estimated cost of the boat?

e. When is it appropriate to use estimated inventory cost on a year-end balance sheet?

Exercise 18-5A *Job-order costing in a manufacturing company*

L.O. 2, 7

Tanner Special Furniture Inc. makes custom-order furniture to meet the needs of disabled persons. On January 1, 2005, the company had the following account balances: $28,000 for both cash and common stock. In 2005, Tanner worked on three special orders. The relevant direct operating costs follow.

	Direct Labor	Direct Materials
Job 1	$1,200	$1,600
Job 2	720	560
Job 3	2,880	1,440
Total	$4,800	$3,600

Tanner's predetermined manufacturing overhead rate was $0.25 per direct labor dollar. Actual manufacturing overhead costs amounted to $1,286. Tanner paid cash for all costs. The company completed and delivered Jobs 1 and 2 to customers during the year. Job 3 was incomplete at the end of the year. The company sold Job 1 for $5,280 cash and Job 2 for $2,560 cash. Tanner also paid $1,200 cash for selling and administrative expenses for the year.

Tanner uses a just-in-time inventory management system. Consequently, it does not have raw materials inventory. Raw materials purchases are recorded directly in the Work in Process Inventory account.

Required

a. Record the preceding events in a horizontal statements model. In the Cash Flow column, designate the cash flow as operating activities (OA), investing activities (IA), or financing activities (FA). The first row shows beginning balances.

Assets								=	Equity								
Cash	+	Work in Process	+	Finished Goods	+	Manuf. Overhead		=	Com. Stk.	+	Ret. Earn.	Rev.	−	Exp.	=	Net Inc.	Cash Flow
28,000	+	NA	+	NA	+	NA		=	28,000	+	NA	NA	−	NA	=	NA	NA

b. Record the entry to close the amount of underapplied or overapplied overhead for the year to Cost of Goods Sold (in the expense category) in the horizontal financial statements model.

c. Determine the gross margin for the year.

Exercise 18-6A *Job-order costing in a service company*

L.O. 2, 7

Sertoma Condos Inc. a small company owned by Adam Garner, leases three condos of differing sizes to customers as vacation facilities. Labor costs for each condo consist of maid service and maintenance cost. Other direct operating costs consist of interest and depreciation. The direct operating costs for each condo follow.

	Direct labor	Other Direct Operating costs
Condo 1	$ 7,200	$18,000
Condo 2	9,300	21,000
Condo 3	11,250	28,500
Total	$27,750	$67,500

Indirect operating expenses, which amounted to $20,250, are allocated to the condos in proportion to the amount of other direct operating costs incurred for each.

Required

a. Assuming that the amount of rent revenue from Condo 2 is $48,000, what amount of income did it earn?

b. Based on the preceding information, will the company show finished goods inventory on its balance sheet? If so, what is the amount of this inventory? If not, explain why not.

L.O. 2

Exercise 18-7A *Job-order cost system*

The following information applies to Job 730 completed by Ritter Manufacturing Company during October 2005. The amount of labor cost for the job was $67,350. Applied overhead amounted to $96,000. The project was completed and delivered to Lancer Company at a contract price of $285,000. Ritter recognized a gross profit of $51,000 on the project.

Required

Determine the amount of raw materials used to complete Job 730.

L.O. 3

Exercise 18-8A *Process cost system—determine equivalent units*

Scott Furniture Company's cutting department had 200 units in its beginning work in process inventory. During the accounting period it began work on 800 units of product and had 400 partially complete units in its ending inventory.

Required

(Each requirement is independent of the others.)

a. Assuming the ending inventory units were 75 percent complete, determine the total number of equivalent units (number transferred out plus number in ending inventory) accounted for by the cutting department.

b. Assuming that the total number of equivalent units (number transferred out plus number in ending inventory) accounted for by the cutting department was 700, what was the ending inventory percentage of completion?

L.O. 3

Exercise 18-9A *Cost allocation in a process system*

Accurate Watches Inc. makes watches. Its assembly department started the accounting period with a beginning inventory balance of $43,000. During the accounting period, the department incurred $82,000 of transferred-in cost, $39,000 of materials cost, $120,000 of labor cost, and $130,800 of applied overhead cost. The department processed 3,050 total equivalent units of product during the accounting period.

Required

(Each requirement is independent of the others.)

a. Assuming that 600 equivalent units of product were in the ending work in process inventory, determine the amount of cost transferred out of the Work in Process Inventory account of the assembly department to the Finished Goods Inventory account. What was the assembly department's cost of ending work in process inventory?

b. Assuming that 2,800 units of product were transferred out of the assembly department's work in process inventory to finished goods inventory, determine the amount of the assembly department's cost of ending work in process inventory. What was the cost of the finished goods inventory transferred out of the assembly department?

Exercise 18-10A *Process cost system—determine equivalent units and allocate costs*

L.O. 3

Boulder Ski Company manufactures snow skis. During the most recent accounting period, the company's finishing department transferred 4,200 sets of skis to finished goods. At the end of the accounting period, 450 sets of skis were estimated to be 40 percent complete. Total product costs for the finishing department amounted to $657,000.

Required

a. Determine the cost per equivalent.
b. Determine the cost of the goods transferred out of the finishing department.
c. Determine the cost of the finishing department's ending work in process inventory.

Exercise 18-11A *Process cost system*

L.O. 3

Littrell Inc. is a cosmetics manufacturer. Its assembly department receives raw cosmetics from the molding department. The assembly department places the raw cosmetics into decorative containers and transfers them to the packaging department. The assembly department's Work in Process Inventory account had a $88,500 balance as of August 1. During August, the department incurred raw materials, labor, and overhead costs amounting to $108,000, $127,500, and $120,000, respectively. The department transferred products that cost $513,000 to the packaging department. The balance in the assembly department's Work in Process Inventory account as of August 31 was $61,500.

Required

Determine the cost of raw cosmetics transferred from the molding department to the assembly department during August.

Exercise 18-12A *Selecting the appropriate cost system*

L.O. 5

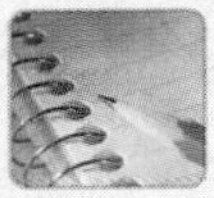

Tony's Car Wash (TCW) offers customers three cleaning options. Under Option 1, only the exterior is cleaned. With Option 2, the exterior and interior are cleaned. Option 3 provides exterior waxing as well as exterior and interior cleaning. TCW completed 4,000 Option 1 cleanings, 5,200 Option 2 cleanings, and 3,200 Option 3 cleanings during 2004. The average cost of completing each cleaning option and the price charged for it are shown here.

	Option 1	Option 2	Option 3
Price charged	$8	$12	$20
Costs of completing task	4	5	15

Required

a. Is TCW a manufacturing or a service company? Explain.
b. Which cost system, job-order or process, is most appropriate for TCW? Why?
c. What is the balance in TCW's Work in Process and Finished Goods Inventory accounts on the December 31 balance sheet?
d. Speculate as to the major costs that TCW incurs to complete a cleaning job.

PROBLEMS—SERIES A

All Problems in Series A are available with McGraw-Hill's Homework Manager.

HM™

Problem 18-13A *Job-order cost system*

L.O. 2, 7

eXcel

mhhe.com/edmonds2007

Holly Manufacturing Corporation was started with the issuance of common stock for $8,000. It purchased $5,000 of raw materials and worked on three job orders during 2004 for which data follow. (Assume that all transactions are for cash unless otherwise indicated.)

CHECK FIGURE
d. COGM: $6,750
NI: $1,550

	Direct Raw Materials Used	Direct Labor
Job 1	$ 500	$1,000
Job 2	1,000	2,000
Job 3	1,500	1,000
Total	$3,000	$4,000

Factory overhead is applied using a predetermined overhead rate of $0.50 per direct labor dollar. Jobs 2 and 3 were completed during the period and Job 3 was sold for $4,500. Holly paid $200 for selling and administrative expenses. Actual factory overhead was $1,750.

Required

a. Record the preceding events in a horizontal statements model. In the Cash Flow column, designate the cash flows as operating activities (OA), investing activities (IA), or financing activities (FA). The first event for 2004 has been recorded as an example.

Assets									=	Equity								
Cash	+	MOH	+	Raw M.	+	WIP	+	F. Goods	=	Com. Stk.	+	Ret. Earn.	Rev.	−	Exp.	=	Net Inc.	Cash Flow
8,000	+	NA	+	NA	+	NA	+	NA	=	8,000	+	NA	NA	−	NA	=	NA	8,000 FA

b. Reconcile all subsidiary accounts with their respective control accounts.

c. Record the closing entry for over- or underapplied manufacturing overhead, assuming that the amount is insignificant. Close revenue and expense accounts.

d. Prepare a schedule of cost of goods manufactured and sold, an income statement, a balance sheet, and a statement of cash flows for 2004.

L.O. 2, 7

CHECK FIGURES
d. COGM: $2,140
Total Assets: $6,135

Problem 18-14A *Job-order cost system*

Canto Construction Company began operations on January 1, 2005, when it acquired $6,000 cash from the issuance of common stock. During the year, Canto purchased $2,600 of direct raw materials and used $2,400 of the direct materials. There were 108 hours of direct labor worked at an average rate of $4 per hour paid in cash. The predetermined overhead rate was $2.50 per direct labor hour. The company started construction on three prefabricated buildings. The job cost sheets reflected the following allocations of costs to each building.

	Direct Materials	Direct Labor Hours
Job 1	$ 600	30
Job 2	1,000	50
Job 3	800	28

The company paid $80 cash for indirect labor costs. Actual overhead cost paid in cash other than indirect labor was $210. Canto completed Jobs 1 and 2 and sold Job 1 for $1,050 cash. The company incurred $100 of selling and administrative expenses that were paid in cash. Over- or underapplied overhead is closed to Cost of Goods Sold.

Required

a. Record the preceding events in a horizontal statements model. In the Cash Flow column, designate the cash flows as operating activities (OA), investing activities (IA), or financing activities (FA). The first event for 2005 has been recorded as an example.

Assets									=	Equity								
Cash	+	MOH	+	Raw M.	+	WIP	+	F. Goods	=	Com. Stk.	+	Ret. Earn.	Rev.	−	Exp.	=	Net Inc.	Cash Flow
6,000	+	NA	+	NA	+	NA	+	NA	=	6,000	+	NA	NA	−	NA	=	NA	6,000 FA

b. Reconcile all subsidiary accounts with their respective control accounts.

c. Record the closing entry for over- or underapplied manufacturing overhead, assuming that the amount is insignificant. Close revenue and expense accounts.

d. Prepare a schedule of cost of goods manufactured and sold, an income statement, a balance sheet, and a statement of cash flows for 2005.

Problem 18-15A *Process cost system*

L.O. 3, 8

CHECK FIGURES
d. COGS: $27,600
Cash: $40,500

Chairs Inc. makes rocking chairs. The chairs move through two departments during production. Lumber is cut into chair parts in the cutting department, which transfers the parts to the assembly department for completion. The company sells the unfinished chairs to hobby shops. The following transactions apply to Chairs' operations for its first year, 2006. (Assume that all transactions are for cash unless otherwise stated.)

1. The company was started when it acquired a $75,000 cash contribution from the owners.
2. The company purchased $22,500 of direct raw materials and $600 of indirect materials. Indirect materials are capitalized in the Production Supplies account.
3. Direct materials totaling $9,000 were issued to the cutting department.
4. Labor cost was $42,300. Direct labor for the cutting and assembly departments was $15,000 and $19,500, respectively. Indirect labor costs were $7,800.
5. The predetermined overhead rate was $0.50 per direct labor dollar.
6. Actual overhead costs other than indirect materials and indirect labor were $9,600 for the year.
7. The cutting department transferred $18,000 of inventory to the assembly department.
8. The assembly department transferred $30,000 of inventory to finished goods.
9. The company sold inventory costing $27,000 for $45,000.
10. Selling and administrative expenses were $4,500.
11. A physical count revealed $150 of production supplies on hand at the end of 2006.
12. Assume that over- or underapplied overhead is insignificant.

Required

a. Record the data in T-accounts.

b. Record the closing entry for over- or underapplied manufacturing overhead, assuming that the amount is insignificant.

c. Close the revenue and expense accounts.

d. Prepare a schedule of cost of goods manufactured and sold, an income statement, a balance sheet, and a statement of cash flows for 2006.

Problem 18-16A *Process cost system*

L.O. 3, 4, 8

CHECK FIGURES
d. NI: $16,350
Cash: $5,025

Use the ending balances from Problem 18-15A as the beginning balances for this problem. The transactions for the second year of operation (2007) are described here. (Assume that all transactions are cash transactions unless otherwise indicated.)

1. The company purchased $30,000 of direct raw materials and $975 of indirect materials.
2. Materials totaling $10,050 were issued to the cutting department.
3. Labor cost was $35,250. Direct labor for the cutting and assembly departments was $16,500 and $15,000, respectively. Indirect labor costs were $3,750. (*Note:* Assume that sufficient cash is available when periodic payments are made. These amounts represent summary data for the entire year and are not presented in exact order of collection and payment.)
4. The predetermined overhead rate was $0.50 per direct labor dollar.
5. Actual overhead costs other than indirect materials and indirect labor for the month were $10,950.
6. The cutting department transferred $22,500 of inventory to the assembly department.
7. The assembly department transferred $45,000 of inventory to finished goods.
8. The company sold inventory costing $25,500 for $48,000.
9. Selling and administrative expenses were $6,300.
10. At the end of 2007, $225 of production supplies was on hand.
11. Assume that over- or underapplied overhead is insignificant.

Required

a. Record the data in T-accounts.

b. Record the closing entry for over- or underapplied manufacturing overhead, assuming that the amount is insignificant.

c. Close the revenue and expense accounts.

d. Prepare a schedule of cost of goods manufactured and sold, an income statement, a balance sheet, and a statement of cash flows for 2007.

L.O. 3

excel

mhhe.com/edmonds2007

CHECK FIGURE
b. $15.60

Problem 18-17A *Process cost system cost of production report*

Hamby Company had 250 units of product in its work in process inventory at the beginning of the period and started 2,000 additional units during the period. At the end of the period, 750 units were in work in process inventory. The ending work in process inventory was estimated to be 60 percent complete. The cost of work in process inventory at the beginning of the period was $3,420, and $27,000 of product costs was added during the period.

Required

Prepare a cost of production report showing the following.

a. The number of equivalent units of production.

b. The product cost per equivalent unit.

c. The total cost allocated between the ending Work in Process Inventory and Finished Goods Inventory accounts.

L.O. 3

CHECK FIGURE
b. $29.50

Problem 18-18A *Determining inventory cost using a process cost system*

Mickel Company had 200 units of product in work in process inventory at the beginning of the period. It started 1,400 units during the period and transferred 1,200 units to finished goods inventory. The ending work in process inventory was estimated to be 80 percent complete. Cost data for the period follow.

	Product Costs
Beginning balance	$15,800
Added during period	29,040
Total	$44,840

Required

Prepare a cost of production report showing the following.

a. The number of equivalent units of production.

b. The product cost per equivalent unit.

c. The total cost allocated between ending work in process inventory and finished goods inventory.

L.O. 3

CHECK FIGURE
b. $11.00

Problem 18-19A *Process cost system*

Slaton Plastic Products Inc. makes a plastic toy using two departments, parts and assembly. The following data pertain to the parts department's transactions in 2006.

1. The beginning balance in the Work in Process Inventory account was $5,700. This inventory consisted of parts for 2,000 toys. The beginning balances in the Raw Materials Inventory, Production Supplies, and Cash accounts were $64,000, $1,000, and $200,000, respectively.
2. Direct materials costing $52,000 were issued to the parts department. The materials were sufficient to make 10,000 additional toys.
3. Direct labor cost was $47,000, and indirect labor costs are $4,600. All labor costs were paid in cash.
4. The predetermined overhead rate was $0.30 per direct labor dollar.
5. Actual overhead costs other than indirect materials and indirect labor for the year were $9,500, which was paid in cash.

6. The department completed parts work for 9,000 toys. The remaining toy parts were 60 percent complete. The completed parts were transferred to the assembly department.
7. All of the production supplies had been used by the end of 2006.
8. Over- or underapplied overhead was closed to the Cost of Goods Sold account.

Required

a. Determine the number of equivalent units of production.
b. Determine the product cost per equivalent unit.
c. Allocate the total cost between the ending work in process inventory and parts transferred to the assembly department.
d. Record the transactions in a partial set of T-accounts.

Problem 18-20A ***Process cost system***

L.O. 3

excel

mhhe.com/edmonds2007

CHECK FIGURE

b. $0.12

Royal Cola Corporation produces a new soft drink brand, Sweet Spring, using two production departments, mixing and bottling. Royal's beginning balances and data pertinent to the mixing department's activities for 2005 follow.

Account	Beginning Balances
Cash	$ 45,000
Raw Materials Inventory	14,800
Production Supplies	400
Work in Process Inventory (400,000 units)	40,000
Common Stock	100,200

1. Royal Cola issued additional common stock for $54,000 cash.
2. The company purchased raw materials and production supplies for $29,600 and $800, respectively, in cash.
3. The company issued $40,000 of raw materials to the mixing department for the production of 800,000 units of Sweet Spring that were started in 2005. A unit of soft drink is the amount needed to fill a bottle.
4. The mixing department used 2,700 hours of labor during 2005, consisting of 2,500 hours for direct labor and 200 hours for indirect labor. The average wage was $9.60 per hour. All wages were paid in 2005 in cash.
5. The predetermined overhead rate was $1.60 per direct labor hour.
6. Actual overhead costs other than indirect materials and indirect labor for the year amounted to $1,440, which was paid in cash.
7. The mixing department completed 600,000 units of Sweet Spring. The remaining inventory was 50 percent complete.
8. The completed soft drink was transferred to the bottling department.
9. The ending balance in the Production Supplies account was $560.

Required

a. Determine the number of equivalent units of production.
b. Determine the product cost per equivalent unit.
c. Allocate the total cost between the ending work in process inventory and units transferred to the bottling department.
d. Record the transactions in T-accounts.

Problem 18-21A ***Process cost system***

L.O. 3, 8

CHECK FIGURES

a. Cost/unit: $1.00
b. Cost/unit: $1.60

Greene Corporation makes a health beverage named Greene that is manufactured in a two-stage production process. The drink is first created in the Conversion Department where material ingredients (natural juices, supplements, preservatives, etc.) are combined. On July 1, 2005 the company had a sufficient quantity of partially completed beverage mix in the Conversion Department to make 40,000 containers of Greene. This beginning inventory had a cost of $30,000. During July, the company added

ingredients necessary to make 160,000 containers of Greene. The cost of these ingredients was $154,000. During July, liquid mix representing 180,000 containers of the beverage was transferred to the Finishing Department. The beverage mix is poured into containers and packaged for shipment in the Finishing Department. Beverage that remained in the Conversion Department at the end of July was 20 percent complete. At the beginning of July the Finishing Department had 10,000 containers of beverage mix. The cost of this mix was $24,000. The department added $44,000 of manufacturing costs (materials, labor, and overhead) during July. During July 120,000 containers of Greene were completed. The ending inventory for this department was 50 percent complete at the end of July.

Required

a. Prepare a cost of production report for the Conversion Department for July.

b. Prepare a cost of production report for the Finishing Department for July.

c. If 100,000 containers of Greene are sold in July for $240,000, determine the company's gross margin for July.

EXERCISES—SERIES B

L.O. 1

Exercise 18-1B *Matching products with appropriate cost systems*

Required

Indicate which cost system (job-order, process, or hybrid) would be most appropriate for the type of product listed in the left-hand column. The first item is shown as an example.

Type of Product	Type of Cost System
a. Audit engagement	Job order
b. Shoes	
c. Treadmill	
d. Textbook	
e. House	
f. Oil	
g. Luxury yacht	
h. Special-order personal computer	
i. Over-the-counter personal computer	
j. Mouse pad for a computer	
k. Aircraft carrier	
l. Makeup sponge	
m. Handheld video game player	
n. Generic coffee mug	
o. Personalized coffee mug	
p. Surgery	

L.O. 1

Exercise 18-2B *Identifying the appropriate cost system*

Cracco Corporation's Valley Plant in Little Rock, Arkansas, produces the company's weed-control chemical solution, Weed Terminator. Production begins with pure water from a controlled stream to which the plant adds different chemicals in the production process. Finally, the plant bottles the resulting chemical solution. The process is highly automated with different computer-controlled maneuvers and testing to ensure the quality of the end product. With only 15 employees, the plant can produce up to 6,000 bottles per day.

Required

Recommend the type of cost system (job-order, process, or hybrid) Valley Plant should use. Explain your recommendation.

L.O. 1, 2

Exercise 18-3B *Job-order or process costing*

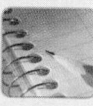

Jocey Smith, an artist, plans to make her living drawing customer portraits at a stand in Underground Atlanta. She will carry her drawing equipment and supplies to work each day in bags. By displaying two of her best hand-drawn portraits on either side of her stand, she expects to attract tourists' attention. Ms. Smith can usually draw a customer's portrait in 30 minutes. Her materials cost is minimal, about $1.60 for a portrait. Her most significant cost will be leasing the stand for $960 per month. She estimates she can replace supplies and worn out equipment for $40 per month. She plans to work 20 days each month from noon to 9:00 p.m. After surveying her planned work environment before beginning the business, she observed that six other artists were providing customer portraits in that section of Underground Atlanta. Their portrait prices ranged from $20 to $36 per portrait. They also offered to frame portraits for customers at $12 per frame. Ms. Smith found that she could obtain comparable frames for $4 each and that properly framing a portrait takes about 10 minutes. The biggest challenge, Ms. Smith observed, was attracting tourists' interest. If she could draw portraits continuously during her workdays, she could earn quite a respectable income. But she noticed several of the artists were reading magazines as she walked by.

Required

a. Should Ms. Smith use a job-order or process cost system for her art business?

b. List the individual types of costs Ms. Smith will likely incur in providing portraits.

c. How could Ms. Smith estimate her overhead rate per portrait when she does not know the number of portraits she will draw in a month?

d. Ms. Smith will not hire any employees. Will she have labor cost? Explain.

Exercise 18-4B *Job-Order costing in a manufacturing company*

L.O. 2, 7

Maher Drapery Inc. specializes in making custom draperies for both commercial and residential customers. It began business on August 1, 2004, by acquiring $40,000 cash through issuing common stock. In August 2004, Maher accepted drapery orders, Jobs 801 and 802, for two new commercial buildings. The company paid cash for the following costs related to the orders:

Job 801	
Raw materials	$ 7,360
Direct labor (512 hours at $20 per hour)	10,240
Job 802	
Raw materials	5,200
Direct labor (340 hours at $20 per hour)	6,800

During the same month, Maher paid $14,400 for various indirect costs such as utilities, equipment leases, and factory-related insurance. The company estimated its annual manufacturing overhead cost would be $240,000 and expected to use 20,000 direct labor hours in its first year of operation. It planned to allocate overhead based on direct labor hours. On August 31, 2004, Maher completed Job 801 and collected the contract price of $28,000. Job 802 was still in process.

Maher uses a just-in-time inventory management system. Consequently, it has no raw materials inventory. Raw materials purchases are recorded directly in the Work in Process Inventory account.

Required

a. Use a horizontal financial statements model as follows to record Maher's accounting events for August 2004. The first event is shown as an example.

Assets									=	Equity										
Cash	+	Manuf. Overhead	+	Work in Process	+	Finished Goods			=	Com. Stk.	+	Ret. Earn.		Rev.	−	Exp.	=	Net Inc.		Cash Flow
40,000	+	NA	+	NA	+	NA			=	40,000	+	NA		NA	−	NA	=	NA		40,000 FA

b. What was Maher's ending inventory on August 31, 2004? Is this amount the actual or the estimated inventory cost?

c. When is it appropriate to use estimated inventory cost on a year-end balance sheet?

Exercise 18-5B *Job-order costing in a manufacturing company*

L.O. 2, 7

McCoy Advertisements Inc. designs and produces television commercials for clients. On March 1, 2005, the company issued common stock for $48,000 cash. During March, McCoy worked on three jobs. Pertinent data follow.

Special Orders	Material	Labor
Job 301	$3,600	450 hours @ $32 per hour
Job 302	6,480	360 hours @ $60 per hour
Job 303	5,840	680 hours @ $28 per hour

Actual production overhead cost: $24,080
Predetermined overhead rate: $16 per direct labor hour

McCoy paid these costs in cash. Jobs 301 and 302 were completed and sold for cash to customers during March. Job 303 was incomplete at month end. Job 301 sold for $30,400, and Job 302 sold for $43,200. McCoy also paid $8,000 cash in March for selling and administrative expenses.

McCoy uses a just-in-time inventory management system. Consequently, it has no raw materials inventory. Raw materials purchases are recorded directly in the Work in Process Inventory account.

Required

a. Use a horizontal financial statements model, as follows, to record McCoy's accounting events for March 2005. The first event is shown as an example.

Assets								=	Equity										
Cash	+	Manuf. Overhead	+	Work in Process	+	Finished Goods		=	Com. Stk.	+	Ret. Earn.		Rev.	−	Exp.	=	Net Inc.		Cash Flow
48,000	+	NA	+	NA	+	NA		=	48,000	+	NA		NA	−	NA	=	NA		48,000 FA

b. Record the entry to close the amount of underapplied or overapplied manufacturing overhead to Cost of Goods Sold (in the expense category) in the horizontal financial statements model.

c. Determine the gross margin for March.

L.O. 2, 7

Exercise 18-6B *Job-order costing in a service company*

Jarman Consulting Inc. provides financial and estate planning services on a retainer basis for the executive officers of its corporate clients. It incurred the following labor costs on services for three corporate clients during March 2006:

	Direct Labor
Contract 1	$12,000
Contract 2	7,200
Contract 3	28,800
Total	$48,000

Jarman allocated March overhead costs of $21,600 to the contracts based on the amount of direct labor costs incurred on each contract.

Required

a. Assuming the revenue from Contract 3 was $65,600, what amount of income did Jarman earn from this contract?

b. Based on the preceding information, will Jarman report finished goods inventory on its balance sheet for Contract 1? If so, what is the amount of this inventory? If not, explain why not.

L.O. 2

Exercise 18-7B *Determine missing information for a job order*

The following information pertains to Job 712 that Dothan Manufacturing Company completed during January 2004. Materials and labor costs for the job were $62,000 and $38,000, respectively. Applied overhead costs were $44,000. Dothan completed and delivered the job to its customer and earned a $50,000 gross profit.

Required

Determine the contract price for the job.

Exercise 18-8B *Process costing: determining equivalent units*

L.O. 3

In March 2005, Finkel Corporation's battery plant had 1,500 units in its beginning work in process inventory. During March, the company added 18,000 units to production. At the end of the month, 6,000 units of product were in process.

Required

(Each requirement is independent of the other.)

a. Assuming the ending inventory units were 40 percent complete, determine the total number of equivalent units (number transferred out plus number in ending inventory) processed by the battery plant.

b. Assuming the total number of equivalent units (number transferred out plus number in ending inventory) processed by the battery plant was 15,000, what was the ending inventory percentage of completion?

Exercise 18-9B *Allocating costs in a process costing system*

L.O. 3

Osburn Corporation, a manufacturer of diabetic testing kits, started November production with $60,000 in beginning inventory. During the month, the company incurred $336,000 of materials cost and $192,000 of labor cost. It applied $132,000 of overhead cost to inventory. The company processed 18,000 total equivalent units of product.

Required

(Each requirement is independent of the other.)

a. Assuming 3,000 equivalent units of product were in ending work in process inventory, determine the amount of cost transferred from the Work in Process Inventory account to the Finished Goods Inventory account. What was the cost of the ending work in process inventory?

b. Assuming 14,000 equivalent units of product were transferred from work in process inventory to finished goods inventory, determine the cost of the ending work in process inventory. What was the cost of the finished goods inventory transferred from work in process?

Exercise 18-10B *Process costing: determining equivalent units and allocating costs*

L.O. 3

Burnside Corporation, which makes suitcases, completed 21,000 suitcases in August 2004. At the end of August, work in process inventory consisted of 3,000 suitcases estimated to be 40 percent complete. Total product costs for August amounted to $666,000.

Required

a. Determine the cost per equivalent unit.

b. Determine the cost of the goods transferred to finished goods.

c. Determine the cost of the ending work in process inventory.

Exercise 18-11B *Process costing: supply missing information*

L.O. 3

Gospel Publications Inc. produces Bibles in volume. It printed and sold 120,000 Bibles last year. Demand is sufficient to support producing a particular edition continuously throughout the year. For this operation, Gospel uses two departments, printing and binding. The printing department prints all pages and transfers them to the binding department, which binds the pages into books. The binding department's Work in Process Inventory account had a $60,000 balance on September 1. During September, the binding department incurred raw materials, labor, and overhead costs of $22,000, $76,000, and $142,000, respectively. During the month, the binding department transferred Bibles that cost $720,000 to finished goods. The balance in the binding department's Work in Process Inventory account as of September 30 was $106,000.

Required

Determine the cost of pages transferred from the printing department to the binding department during the month of September.

Exercise 18-12B *Selecting the appropriate costing system*

L.O. 5

Towns Automotive Specialties Inc. has a successful market niche. It customizes automobile interiors to fit the various needs of disabled customers. Some customers need special equipment to accommodate

disabled drivers. Others need modified entrance and seating arrangements for disabled passengers. Customer vehicles vary according to different brands and models of sedans, minivans, sport utility vehicles, and full-size vans. Towns' engineers interview customers directly to ascertain their special needs. The engineers then propose a design, explaining it and its cost for the customer's approval. Customers have the opportunity to request changes. Once the company and customer agree on an engineering design and its price, they sign a contract, and the customer's vehicle is delivered to Towns's factory. The factory manager directs mechanics to customize the vehicle according to the engineering design.

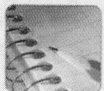

Required

a. Is Towns a manufacturing company or a service company? Explain.

b. Which cost system, job-order or process, would be most appropriate for Towns? Why?

c. Does Towns have work in process and finished goods inventories?

d. Should Towns classify engineering design costs as materials, labor, or overhead? Why?

PROBLEMS—SERIES B

L.O. 2, 7

Problem 18-13B *Job-order cost system*

Chief Corporation was created on January 1, 2006, when it received a stockholder's contribution of $32,000. It purchased $6,320 of raw materials and worked on three job orders during the year. Data about these jobs follow. (Assume all transactions are for cash unless otherwise indicated.)

	Direct Raw Materials Used	Direct Labor
Job 1	$1,680	$2,560
Job 2	1,360	3,840
Job 3	2,560	3,584
Total	$5,600	$9,984

The average wage rate is $12.80 per hour. Manufacturing overhead is applied using a predetermined overhead rate of $6 per direct labor hour. Jobs 1 and 3 were completed during the year, and Job 1 was sold for $7,840. Chief paid $1,120 for selling and administrative expenses. Actual factory overhead was $4,800.

Required

a. Record the preceding events in a horizontal statements model. In the Cash Flow column, designate the cash flows as operating activities (OA), investing activities (IA), or financing activities (FA). The first event for 2006 has been recorded as an example.

Assets									=	Equity									
Cash	+	MOH	+	Raw M.	+	WIP	+	F. Goods	=	Com. Stk.	+	Ret. Earn.	Rev.	−	Exp.	=	Net Inc.	Cash Flow	
32,000	+	NA	+	NA	+	NA	+	NA	=	32,000	+	NA	NA	−	NA	=	NA	32,000	FA

b. Reconcile all subsidiary accounts with their respective control accounts.

c. Record the closing entry for over- or underapplied manufacturing overhead, assuming that the amount is insignificant. Close revenue and expense accounts.

d. Prepare a schedule of cost of goods manufactured and sold, an income statement, a balance sheet, and a statement of cash flows for 2006.

L.O. 2, 7

Problem 18-14B *Job-order cost system*

Sayers Roofing Corporation was founded on January 1, 2005, when stockholders contributed $2,800 for common stock. During the year, Sayers purchased $2,400 of direct raw materials and used $2,160 of direct materials. There were 80 hours of direct labor worked at an average rate of $8 per hour paid in cash. The predetermined overhead rate was $6.50 per direct labor hour. The company started three custom roofing jobs. The job cost sheets reflected the following allocations of costs to each.

	Direct Materials	Direct Labor Hours
Roof 1	$800	20
Roof 2	400	12
Roof 3	960	48

The company paid $176 cash for indirect labor costs and $240 cash for production supplies, which were all used during 2005. Actual overhead cost paid in cash other than indirect materials and indirect labor was $144. Sayers completed Roofs 1 and 2 and collected the contract price for Roof 1 of $2,160 cash. The company incurred $496 of selling and administrative expenses that were paid with cash. Over- or underapplied overhead is closed to Cost of Goods Sold.

Required

a. Record the preceding events in a horizontal statements model. In the Cash Flow column, designate the cash flows as operating activities (OA), investing activities (IA), or financing activities (FA). The first event for 2005 has been recorded as an example.

Assets							=	Equity									
Cash	+	MOH	+	Raw M.	+	WIP	+	F. Goods	=	Com. Stk.	+	Ret. Earn.	Rev.	−	Exp.	=	Net Inc.	Cash Flow
2,800	+	NA	+	NA	+	NA	+	NA	=	2,800	+	NA	NA	−	NA	=	NA	2,800 FA

b. Reconcile all subsidiary accounts with their respective control accounts.

c. Record the closing entry for over- or underapplied manufacturing overhead, assuming that the amount is insignificant. Close revenue and expense accounts.

d. Prepare a schedule of cost of goods manufactured and sold, an income statement, a balance sheet, and a statement of cash flows for 2005.

Problem 18-15B *Process cost system*

L.O. 3, 8

Rivera Food Company makes frozen vegetables. Production involves two departments, processing and packaging. Raw materials are cleaned and cut in the processing department and then transferred to the packaging department where they are packaged and frozen. The following transactions apply to Rivera's first year (2004) of operations. (Assume that all transactions are for cash unless otherwise stated.)

1. The company was started when it acquired $64,000 cash from the issue of common stock.
2. Rivera purchased $33,600 of direct raw materials and $6,000 of indirect materials. Indirect materials are capitalized in the Production Supplies account.
3. Direct materials totaling $30,400 were issued to the processing department.
4. Labor cost was $61,600. Direct labor for the processing and packaging departments was $26,000 and $20,400, respectively. Indirect labor costs were $15,200.
5. The predetermined overhead rate was $0.80 per direct labor dollar.
6. Actual overhead costs other than indirect materials and indirect labor were $18,000 for the year.
7. The processing department transferred $48,400 of inventory to the packaging department.
8. The packaging department transferred $56,000 of inventory to finished goods.
9. The company sold inventory costing $50,400 for $94,000.
10. Selling and administrative expenses were $18,800.
11. A physical count revealed $2,400 of production supplies on hand at the end of 2004.
12. Assume that over- or underapplied overhead is insignificant.

Required

a. Record the data in T-accounts.

b. Record the closing entry for over- or underapplied manufacturing overhead, assuming that the amount is insignificant.

c. Close the revenue and expense accounts.

d. Prepare a schedule of cost of goods manufactured and sold, an income statement, a balance sheet, and a statement of cash flows for 2004.

L.O. 3, 4, 8

Problem 18-16B ***Process cost system***

Use the ending balances from Problem 18-15B as the beginning balances for this problem. The transactions for the second year of operation (2005) are described here. (Assume that all transactions are cash transactions unless otherwise indicated.)

1. The company purchased $40,800 of direct raw materials and $7,200 of indirect materials.
2. Materials costing $32,800 were issued to the processing department.
3. Labor cost was $71,600. Direct labor for the processing and packaging departments was $28,800 and $23,600, respectively. Indirect labor costs were $19,200. (*Note:* Assume that sufficient cash is available when periodic payments are made. These amounts represent summary data for the entire year and are not presented in exact order of collection and payment.)
4. The predetermined overhead rate was $0.80 per direct labor dollar.
5. Actual overhead costs other than indirect materials and indirect labor for the year were $20,000.
6. The processing department transferred $100,000 of inventory to the packaging department.
7. The packaging department transferred $140,000 of inventory to finished goods.
8. The company sold inventory costing $136,800 for $260,000.
9. Selling and administrative expenses amounted to $25,600.
10. At the end of the year, $1,600 of production supplies was on hand.
11. Assume that over- or underapplied overhead is insignificant.

Required

a. Record the data in T-accounts.

b. Record the closing entry for over- or underapplied manufacturing overhead, assuming that the amount is insignificant.

c. Close the revenue and expense accounts.

d. Prepare a schedule of cost of goods manufactured and sold, an income statement, a balance sheet, and a statement of cash flows for 2005.

L.O. 3

Problem 18-17B ***Process cost system cost of production report***

At the beginning of 2004, Dozier Company had 1,800 units of product in its work in process inventory, and it started 19,200 additional units of product during the year. At the end of the year, 6,000 units of product were in the work in process inventory. The ending work in process inventory was estimated to be 50 percent complete. The cost of work in process inventory at the beginning of the period was $9,000, and $108,000 of product costs was added during the period.

Required

Prepare a cost of production report showing the following.

a. The number of equivalent units of production.

b. The product cost per equivalent unit.

c. The total cost allocated between the ending Work in Process Inventory and Finished Goods Inventory accounts.

L.O. 3

Problem 18-18B ***Determining inventory cost using process costing***

Carri Company's beginning work in process inventory consisted of 4,500 units of product on January 1, 2006. During 2006, the company started 24,000 units of product and transferred 23,500 units to finished goods inventory. The ending work in process inventory was estimated to be 30 percent complete. Cost data for 2006 follow.

	Product Costs
Beginning balance	$ 19,000
Added during period	151,000
Total	$170,000

Required

Prepare a cost of production report showing the following.

a. The number of equivalent units of production.
b. The product cost per equivalent unit.
c. The total cost allocated between ending work in process inventory and finished goods inventory.

Problem 18-19B ***Process cost system*** L.O. 3, 8

Lloyd Corporation makes blue jeans. Its process involves two departments, cutting and sewing. The following data pertain to the cutting department's transactions in 2006.

1. The beginning balance in work in process inventory was $8,772. This inventory consisted of fabric for 6,000 pairs of jeans. The beginning balances in raw materials inventory, production supplies, and cash were $45,000, $2,100 and $135,600, respectively.
2. Direct materials costing $28,068 were issued to the cutting department; this amount of materials was sufficient to start work on 15,000 pairs of jeans.
3. Direct labor cost was $33,600, and indirect labor cost was $2,700. All labor costs were paid in cash.
4. The predetermined overhead rate was $0.25 per direct labor dollar.
5. Actual overhead costs other than indirect materials and indirect labor for the year amounted to $3,840, which was paid in cash.
6. The cutting department completed cutting 16,000 pairs of jeans. The remaining jeans were 40 percent complete.
7. The completed units of cut fabric were transferred to the sewing department.
8. All of the production supplies had been used by the end of the year.
9. Over- or underapplied overhead was closed to the Cost of Goods Sold account.

Required

a. Determine the number of equivalent units of production.
b. Determine the product cost per equivalent unit.
c. Allocate the total cost between ending work in process inventory and units transferred to the sewing department.
d. Record the transactions in a partial set of T-accounts.

Problem 18-20B ***Process cost system*** L.O. 3, 8

Vinson Paper Products Corporation produces paper cups using two production departments, printing and forming. Beginning balances and printing department data for 2006 follow.

Account	Beginning Balances
Cash	$50,000
Raw Materials	21,000
Production Supplies	1,500
Work in Process Inventory (300,000 units)	18,000
Common Stock	90,500

1. Vinson Paper Products issued additional common stock for $110,000 cash.
2. The company purchased raw materials and production supplies for $40,000 and $3,500, respectively, in cash.
3. The company issued $57,000 of raw materials and $3,600 of production supplies to the printing department for the production of 800,000 paper cups.
4. The printing department used 6,200 hours of labor during 2006, consisting of 5,600 hours for direct labor and 600 hours for indirect labor. The average wage was $5 per hour. All the wages were paid in 2006 in cash.
5. The predetermined overhead rate was $0.50 per direct labor dollar.
6. Actual overhead costs other than indirect materials and indirect labor for the year amounted to $7,400, which was paid in cash.

7. The printing department completed 700,000 paper cups. The remaining cups were 50 percent complete.
8. The completed paper cups were transferred to the forming department.
9. The ending balance in the Production Supplies account was $1,400.

Required

a. Determine the number of equivalent units of production.
b. Determine the product cost per equivalent unit.
c. Allocate the total cost between the ending work in process inventory and units transferred to the forming department.
d. Record the transactions in T-accounts.

L.O. 3, 8

Problem 18-21B ***Process cost system***

Gun Smoke Gifts makes unique western gifts that are sold at souvenir shops. One of the company's more popular products is a ceramic eagle that is produced in a mass production process that entails two manufacturing stages. In the first production stage ceramic glass is heated and molded into the shape of the eagle by the Compression Department. Finally, color and artistic detail is applied to the eagle by the Finishing Department. The company has just hired a new accountant who will be responsible for preparing the cost of production report for June 2006. The accountant is given the following information from which to prepare his report.

Departmental Cost Information for June

	Compression	Finishing
Costs in beginning inventory	$ 3,000	$14,400
Costs added during June:		
Materials	42,000	18,120
Labor	20,000	13,200
Overhead	90,000	62,000

Departmental Product Information for June

	Compression	Finishing
Units in beginning inventory	10,000	3,600
Units started	52,000	46,000
Units in ending inventory	16,000 (25% complete)	9,600 (80% complete)

Required

a. Prepare a cost of production report for the Conversion Department for June.
b. Prepare a cost of production report for the Finishing Department for June.
c. If 24,000 units are sold in June for $160,000, determine the company's gross margin for June.

ANALYZE, THINK, COMMUNICATE

ATC 18-1 **Business Application Case** ***Comprehensive job-order costing problem***

This problem uses concepts presented in Chapters 17 and 18 concerning job-order costing systems.

Custom Automobile Restoration Shop (CARS) is a small shop dedicated to high-quality restorations of vintage cars. Although it will restore a customer's automobile, usually the shop buys an old vehicle, restores it, and then sells it in a private party sale or at a classic-car auction. The shop has been in existence for 10 years, but for the sake of simplicity, assume it has no beginning inventories for

2007. CARS worked on five automobile restoration projects during 2007. By the end of the year, four of these projects were completed and three of these four were sold.

The following selected data are from CARS' 2007 *budget:*

Advertising	$ 5,000
Direct materials	150,000
Direct labor	130,000
Rent on office space	6,000
Rent on factory space	20,000
Indirect materials	11,000
Maintenance costs for factory equipment	3,000
Utilities costs for office space	1,000
Utilities costs for factory space	2,000
Depreciation on factory equipment	8,000
Machine hours expected to be used	4,000
Direct labor hours expected to be worked	6,500

The following information relates to production events during 2007.

1. Raw materials were purchased for $155,000.
2. Materials used in production totaled $150,800; $11,500 of these were considered indirect materials costs. The remaining $139,300 of direct materials costs related to individual restoration jobs as follows:

Job Number	Direct Materials Cost
701	$ 28,200
702	32,100
703	25,800
704	31,700
705	21,500

3. Labor costs incurred for production totaled $133,100. The workers are highly skilled craftsmen who require little supervision. Therefore all of these were considered direct labor costs and related to individual restoration jobs as follows:

Job Number	Direct Labor Cost
701	$30,900
702	29,300
703	22,100
704	36,600
705	14,200

4. Paid factory rent of $18,000.
5. Recorded depreciation on factory equipment of $8,500.
6. Made $2,500 of payments to outside vendors for maintenance of factory equipment.
7. Paid factory utilities costs of $2,400.
8. Applied manufacturing overhead using a predetermined rate of $11.00 per machine hour. The 3,750 machine hours that were used relate to each job as follows:

Job Number	Machine Hours Used
701	850
702	720
703	870
704	900
705	410

9. Completed all restoration jobs except 705 and transferred the projects to finished goods.
10. Sold three jobs for the following amounts:

Job Number	Sales Price
701	$88,900
702	93,000
703	74,800

11. Closed the Manufacturing Overhead account to transfer any overapplied or underapplied overhead to the Cost of Goods Sold account.

Required

a. Assume CARS had used direct labor hours (versus machine hours) as its cost driver. Compute its predetermined overhead rate.
b. Determine the ending balance in Raw Materials Inventory.
c. Determine the ending balance in Finished Goods Inventory.
d. Determine the ending balance in Work in Process Inventory.
e. Determine the costs of goods manufactured.
f. Determine the amount of cost of goods sold.
g. Determine the amount of gross margin that was earned on Jobs 701, 702, and 703.
h. Determine the amount of overapplied or underapplied overhead that existed at the end of the year.

Hint: You might find it helpful to organize the data using a horizontal financial statements model, although it will still be necessary to prepare a job cost sheet for each individual job.

ATC 18-2 Group Assignment *Job-order cost system*

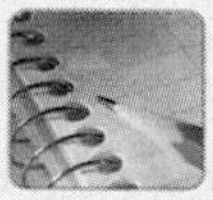

Bowen Bridge Company constructs bridges for the State of Kentucky. During 2006, Bowen started work on three bridges. The cost of materials and labor for each bridge follows.

Special Orders	Materials	Labor
Bridge 305	$407,200	$352,700
Bridge 306	362,300	375,000
Bridge 307	801,700	922,800

The predetermined overhead rate is $1.20 per direct labor dollar. Actual overhead costs were $2,170,800. Bridge 306 was completed for a contract price of $1,357,000 and was turned over to the state. Construction on Bridge 305 was also completed but the state had not yet finished its inspection process. General selling and administrative expenses amounted to $210,000. Over- or underapplied overhead is closed directly to the Cost of Goods Sold account. The company recognizes revenue when it turns over a completed bridge to a customer.

Required

a. Divide the class into groups of four or five students each and organize the groups into three sections. Assign Task 1 to the first section of groups, Task 2 to the second section, and Task 3 to the third section.

Group Tasks

(1) Determine the cost of construction for Bridge 305.
(2) Determine the cost of construction for Bridge 306.
(3) Determine the cost of construction for Bridge 307.

b. Select a spokesperson from each section. Use input from the three spokespersons to prepare an income statement and the asset section of the balance sheet.
c. Does the net income accurately reflect the profitability associated with Bridge 306? Explain.
d. Would converting to a process cost system improve the accuracy of the amount of reported net income? Explain.

ATC 18-3 Research Assignment *What type of cost system to use?*

In the *BusinessWeek* article " How Would You Like Your Ford?" Kathleen Kerwin reports on ways **Ford Motor Company** is changing procedures used to produce some of its car models. Read this article, which appears on page 34 of the August 9, 2004, issue, and complete the following requirements.

Required

a. Should Ford use a job-order, process, or hybrid cost system to account for vehicles produced in its new flexible-manufacturing system? Explain.

b. The article mentions that Ford's flexible-manufacturing system relies in part on 11 major component suppliers locating near its own plant. When Ford receives an item from one of these suppliers, should its cost be considered a *raw material cost* or a *transferred-in-cost*?

c. Ford expects its new production setup to reduce its manufacturing cost in several ways. Identify and briefly explain these cost reductions.

ATC 18-4 Writing Assignment *Determining the proper cost system*

Professor Julia Silverman received the following e-mail message.

"I don't know if you remember me. I am Tim Wallace. I was in your introductory accounting class a couple of years ago. I recently graduated and have just started my first real job. I remember your talking about job-order and process cost systems. I even looked the subject up in the textbook you wrote. In that book, you say that a process cost system is used when a company produces a single, homogeneous, high-volume, low-cost product. Well, the company I am working for makes T-shirts. All of the shirts are the same. They don't cost much, and we make nearly a million of them every year. The only difference in any of the shirts is the label we sew in them. We make the shirts for about 20 different companies. It seems to me that we should be using a process costing system. Even so, our accounting people are using a job order cost system. Unfortunately, you didn't tell us what to do when the company we work for is screwed up. I need some advice. Should I tell them they are using the wrong accounting system? I know I am new around here, and I don't want to offend anybody, but if your book is right, the company would be better off if it started using a process cost system. Some of these people around here didn't go to college, and I'm afraid they don't know what they are doing. I guess that's why they hired someone with a degree. Am I right about this or what?"

Required

Assume that you are Professor Silverman. Write a return e-mail responding to Mr. Wallace's inquiry.

ATC 18-5 Ethical Dilemma *Amount of equivalent units*

René Alverez knew she was in over her head soon after she took the job. Even so, the opportunity for promotion comes along rarely and she believed that she would grow into it. Ms. Alverez is the cost accounting specialist assigned to the finishing department of Standard Tool Company. Bill Sawyer, the manager of the finishing department, knows exactly what he is doing. In each of the three years he has managed the department, the cost per unit of product transferred out of his Work in Process Inventory account has declined. His ability to control cost is highly valued, and it is widely believed that he will be the successor to the plant manager, who is being promoted to manufacturing vice president. One more good year would surely seal the deal for Mr. Sawyer. It was little wonder that Ms. Alverez was uncomfortable in challenging Mr. Sawyer's estimate of the percentage of completion of the department's ending inventory. He contended that the inventory was 60 percent complete, but she believed that it was only about 40 percent complete.

After a brief altercation, Ms. Alverez agreed to sign off on Mr. Sawyer's estimate. The truth was that although she believed she was right, she did not know how to support her position. Besides, Mr. Sawyer was about to be named plant manager, and she felt it unwise to challenge such an important person.

The department had beginning inventory of 5,500 units of product and it started 94,500 units during the period. It transferred out 90,000 units during the period. Total transferred-in and production cost for the period was $902,400. This amount included the cost in beginning inventory plus additional costs incurred during the period. The target (standard) cost per unit is $9.45.

Required

a. Determine the equivalent cost per unit, assuming that the ending inventory is considered to be 40 percent complete.

b. Determine the equivalent cost per unit, assuming that the ending inventory is considered to be 60 percent complete.

c. Comment on Mr. Sawyer's motives for establishing the percentage of completion at 60 percent rather than 40 percent.

d. Assuming that Ms. Alverez is a certified management accountant, would informing the chief accountant of her dispute with Mr. Sawyer violate the confidentiality standards of ethical conduct in Exhibit 14.13 of Chapter 14?

e. Did Ms. Alverez violate any of the standards of ethical conduct in Exhibit 14.13 of Chapter 14? If so, which ones?

COMPREHENSIVE PROBLEM

This is a continuation of the comprehensive problem in Chapter 17. During 2006, Anywhere Inc. (AI) incurred the following product costs.

Raw materials	$62,000
Labor	89,422
Overhead	58,000

Recall that the 2005 ending balance in the Work in Process (WIP) account was $26,000. Accordingly, this is the beginning WIP balance for 2006. There were 110 units of product in beginning WIP inventory. AI started 1,840 units of product during 2006. Ending WIP inventory consisted of 90 units that were 60 percent complete.

Required

Prepare a cost of production report by filling in the cells that contain question marks.

Equivalent Unit Computations

	Units	% Complete	Equivalent Units
Beginning inventory	110		
Units started	1,840		
Total units available for completion	?		
Units in ending inventory	(90)	?	?
Units complete	1,860	100%	?
Total equivalent units			1,914

Cost per Equivalent Unit

	Cost	÷	Units	=	Cost Per Unit
Beginning inventory	$26,000				
Raw materials	?				
Labor	?				
Overhead	58,000				
Total product cost	?	÷	1,914	=	?

Allocation of Product Cost

Cost transferred to finished goods	?
Cost in ending inventory	?
Total product cost	$235,422

CHAPTER 19

Analysis of Cost, Volume, and Pricing to Increase Profitability

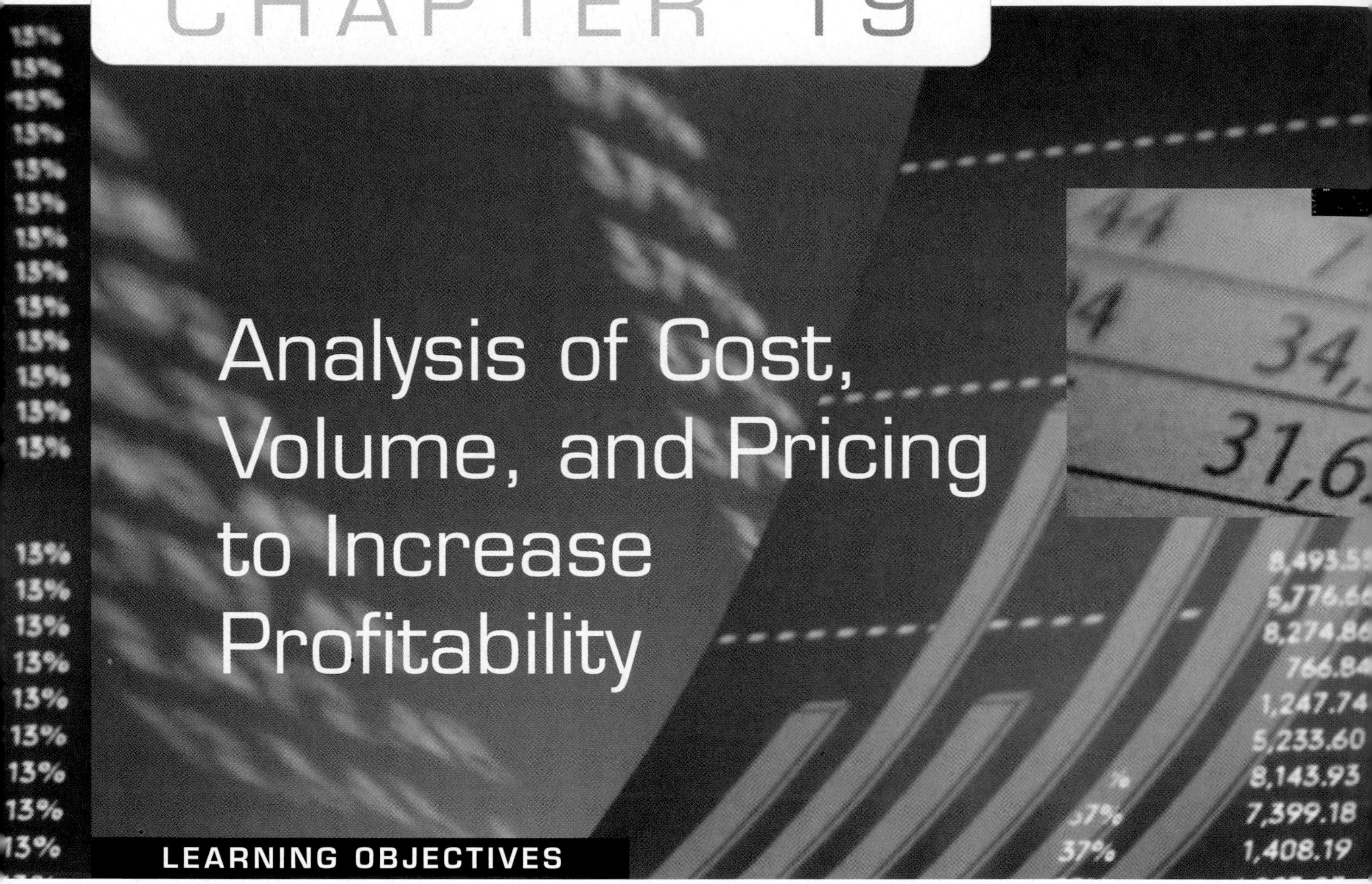

LEARNING OBJECTIVES

After you have mastered the material in this chapter, you will be able to:

1. **Determine the sales price of a product using a cost-plus pricing approach.**
2. **Use the contribution per unit approach to calculate the break-even point.**
3. **Use the contribution per unit approach to calculate the sales volume required to realize a target profit.**
4. **Use the contribution per unit approach to conduct cost-volume-profit analysis.**
5. **Use target pricing to reengineer a product.**
6. **Draw and interpret a cost-volume-profit graph.**
7. **Calculate the margin of safety in units, dollars, and percentage.**
8. **Explain how spreadsheet software can be used to conduct sensitivity analysis for cost-volume-profit relationships.**
9. **Use the contribution margin ratio and the equation method to conduct cost-volume-profit analysis.**
10. **Identify the limitations of cost-volume-profit analysis.**
11. **Perform multiple-product break-even analysis. (Appendix)**

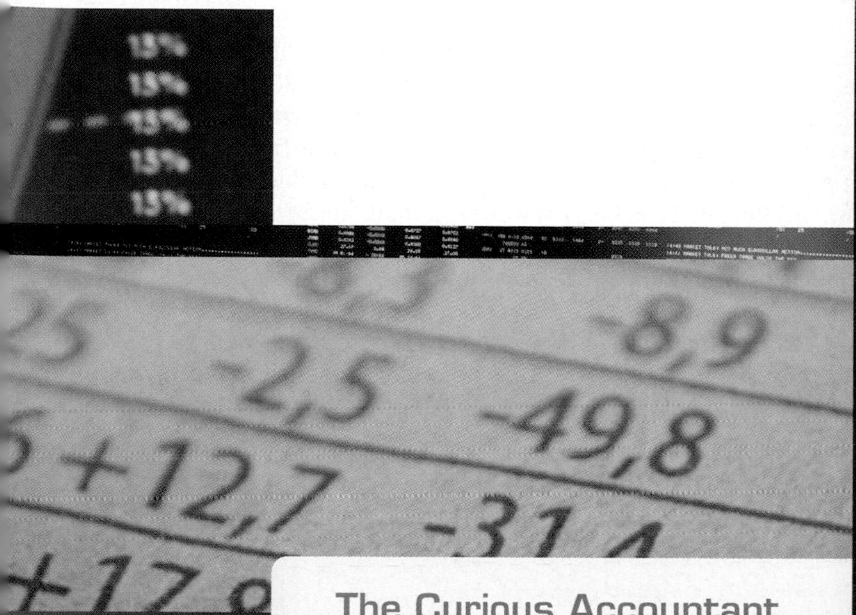

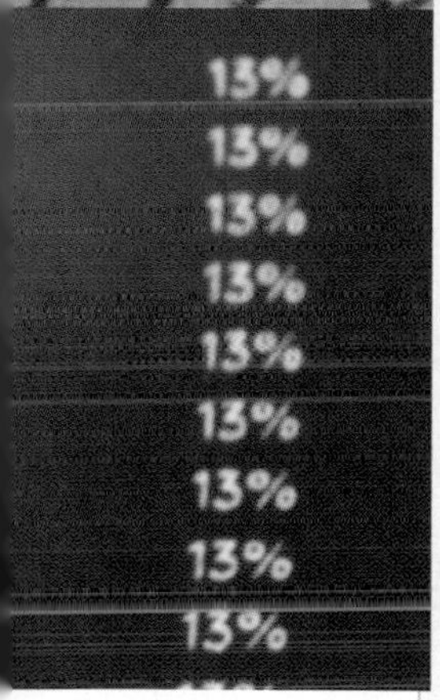

Chapter 19

The Curious Accountant

In August 2002, **American Airlines** announced several changes in its way of doing business. These changes included eliminating all of the first-class seats on some routes.

In February 2003, **Circuit City** laid off 3,900 sales personnel throughout its more than 600 stores in the United States. What makes this action unusual is that many of those fired were among the most productive salespeople in the company.

Why would American Airlines eliminate some of its highest priced seats at a time when airline traffic was already down around the globe? Why would Circuit City fire its best salespeople and replace them with less experienced, less proven employees? (Answers on page 936.)

CHAPTER OPENING

The president of Bright Day Distributors recently completed a managerial accounting course. He was particularly struck by the operating leverage concept. His instructor had demonstrated how a small percentage increase in sales volume could produce a significantly higher percentage increase in profitability. Unfortunately, the discussion had been limited to the effects of changes in sales volume. In practice, changes in sales volume are often related to changes in sales price. For example, reducing selling prices often leads to increases in sales volume. Sales volume may also change in response to cost changes such as increasing the advertising budget. Furthermore, significant changes in sales volume could redefine the relevant range, changing the fixed and variable costs. Bright Day's president realized that understanding operating leverage was only one piece of understanding how to manage a business. He also needed to understand how changes in prices, costs, and volume affect profitability. Bright Day's president is interested in ***cost-volume-profit (CVP) analysis.***

Determining the Contribution Margin per Unit

LO 1

Determine the sales price of a product using a cost-plus pricing approach.

Topic Tackler PLUS

19-1

Analyzing relationships among the CVP variables is simplified by using an income statement organized using the contribution margin format. Recall that the *contribution margin* is the difference between sales revenue and variable costs. It measures the amount available to cover fixed costs and thereafter to provide enterprise profits. Consider the following illustration.

Bright Day Distributors sells nonprescription health food supplements including vitamins, herbs, and natural hormones in the northwestern United States. Bright Day recently obtained the rights to distribute the new herb mixture Delatine. Recent scientific research found that Delatine delayed aging in laboratory animals. The researchers hypothesized that the substance would have a similar effect on humans. Their theory could not be confirmed because of the relatively long human life span. The news media reported the research findings; as stories turned up on television and radio news, talk shows, and in magazines, demand for Delatine increased.

Delatine costs \$24 per bottle. Bright Day uses a **cost-plus pricing** strategy; it sets prices at cost plus a markup equal to 50 percent of cost. A bottle of Delatine is priced at \$36 (\$24 + [0.50 × \$24]). The **contribution margin per unit** is:

Sales revenue per unit	\$36
Variable cost per unit	24
Contribution margin per unit	\$12

For every bottle of Delatine it sells, Bright Day earns a \$12 contribution margin. Bright Day's first concern is whether it can sell enough units for total contribution margin to cover fixed costs. The president made this position clear when he said, "We don't want to lose money on this product. We have to sell enough units to pay our fixed costs." Bright Day can use the per unit contribution margin to determine the quantity of sales required to break even.

Determining the Break-Even Point

LO 2

Use the contribution per unit approach to calculate the break-even point.

Bright Day's management team suspects that enthusiasm for Delatine will abate quickly as the news media shift to other subjects. To attract customers immediately, the product managers consider television advertising. The marketing manager suggests running a campaign of several hundred cable channel ads at an estimated cost of \$60,000. The company president asks, "How many bottles of Delatine would we have to sell to *break even?*"

The **break-even point** is the point where *total revenue equals total costs*. The cost of the advertising campaign is \$60,000 regardless of the number of bottles of Delatine sold. It is a *fixed cost*. Given Bright Day's expected contribution margin of \$12 per bottle, the break-even point measured in units is:

$$\text{Break-even volume in units} = \frac{\text{Fixed costs}}{\text{Contribution margin per unit}}$$

$$= \frac{\$60{,}000}{\$12} = 5{,}000 \text{ units}$$

The break-even point measured in *sales dollars* is the number of units that must be sold to break even multiplied by the sales price per unit. For Delatine, the break-even point in sales dollars is \$180,000 (5,000 units × \$36). The following income statement confirms these results.

Sales Revenue (5,000 units × \$36)	\$180,000
Total Variable Expenses (5,000 units × \$24)	(120,000)
Total Contribution Margin (5,000 units × \$12)	60,000
Fixed Expenses	(60,000)
Net Income	\$ 0

Once fixed costs have been covered (5,000 units have been sold), net income will increase by $12 (*per unit contribution margin*) for each additional bottle sold. Similarly, profitability will decrease by $12 for each per unit decrease in sales volume. Study the effect of the per unit contribution margin on profitability by comparing the following income statements.

	Number of Units Sold (a)				
	4,998	4,999	5,000	5,001	5,002
Sales Revenue					
($36 per unit × a)	$179,928	$179,964	$180,000	$180,036	$180,072
Total Variable Expenses					
($24 per unit × a)	(119,952)	(119,976)	(120,000)	(120,024)	(120,048)
Total Contribution Margin					
($12 per unit × a)	59,976	59,988	60,000	60,012	60,024
Fixed Expenses	(60,000)	(60,000)	(60,000)	(60,000)	(60,000)
Net Income (Loss)	$ (24)	$ (12)	$ 0	$ 12	$ 24

As sales increase from 5,000 to 5,001, net income increases from zero to $12. When sales increase by one additional unit, net income again rises by $12 (moves from $12 to $24). Income increases by the $12 per unit contribution margin with each additional unit sold. The effect of an increase or decrease in sales volume on net income can be computed by multiplying the amount of the change in sales volume by the contribution margin per unit. Suppose sales increase from 5,400 to 5,600 units. This increase will affect profitability by $2,400 ([5,600 − 5,400] × $12). The following comparative income statements confirm this result.

	Number of Units Sold		
	5,400	5,600	200 Unit Difference
Sales Revenue ($36 per unit)	$194,400	$201,600	$7,200
Total Variable Expenses ($24 per unit)	(129,600)	(134,400)	(4,800)
Total Contribution Margin ($12 per unit)	64,800	67,200	2,400
Fixed Expenses	(60,000)	(60,000)	0
Net Income	$ 4,800	$ 7,200	$2,400

Using the Contribution Approach to Estimate the Sales Volume Necessary to Reach a Target Profit

LO 3

Use the contribution per unit approach to calculate the sales volume required to realize a target profit.

Bright Day's president decides the ad campaign should produce a $40,000 profit. He asks the accountant to determine the sales volume that is required to achieve this level of profitability. For this result, the contribution margin must be sufficient to cover the fixed costs and to provide the desired profit. The required sales volume in units can be computed as shown here:

$$\text{Sales volume in units} = \frac{\text{Fixed costs} + \text{Desired profit}}{\text{Contribution margin per unit}}$$

$$= \frac{\$60{,}000 + \$40{,}000}{\$12} = 8{,}333.33 \text{ units}$$

The required volume in sales dollars is this number of units multiplied by the sales price per unit (8,333.33 units × $36 = $300,000). The following income statement confirms this result; all amounts are rounded to the nearest whole dollar.

Sales Revenue (8,333.33 units × $36)	$300,000
Total Variable Expenses (8,333.33 units × $24)	(200,000)
Total Contribution Margin (8,333.33 units × $12)	100,000
Fixed Expenses	(60,000)
Net Income	$ 40,000

In practice, the company will not sell partial bottles of Delatine. The accountant rounds 8,333.33 bottles to whole units. For planning and decision making, managers frequently make decisions using approximate data. Accuracy is desirable, but it is not as important as relevance. Do not be concerned when computations do not produce whole numbers. Rounding and approximation are common characteristics of managerial accounting data.

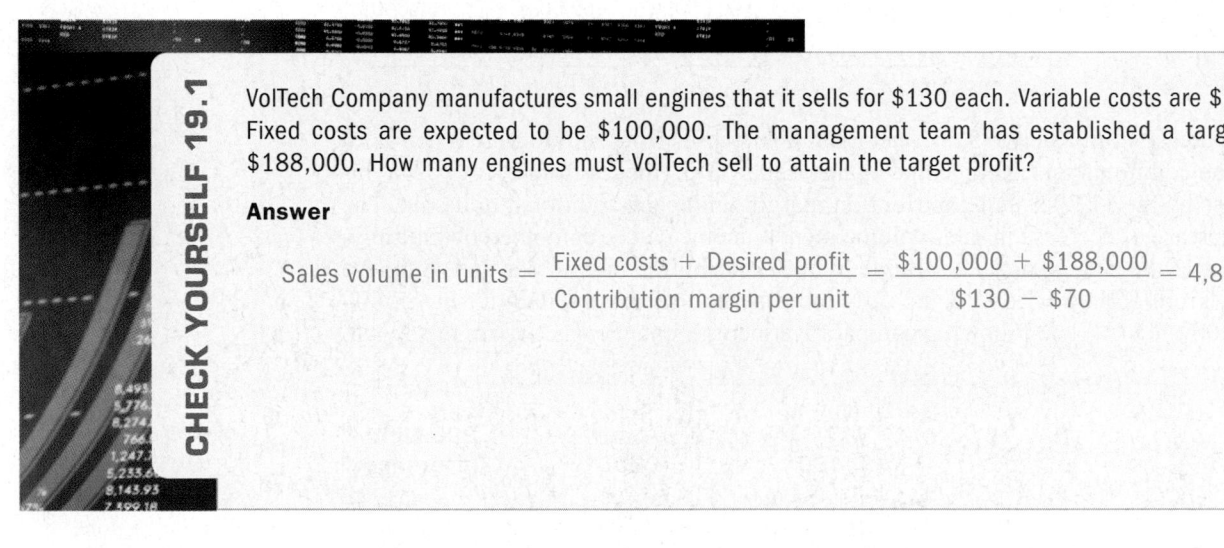

CHECK YOURSELF 19.1

VolTech Company manufactures small engines that it sells for $130 each. Variable costs are $70 per unit. Fixed costs are expected to be $100,000. The management team has established a target profit of $188,000. How many engines must VolTech sell to attain the target profit?

Answer

$$\text{Sales volume in units} = \frac{\text{Fixed costs} + \text{Desired profit}}{\text{Contribution margin per unit}} = \frac{\$100{,}000 + \$188{,}000}{\$130 - \$70} = 4{,}800 \text{ units}$$

Using the Contribution Approach to Estimate the Effects of Changes in Sales Price

LO 4

Use the contribution per unit approach to conduct cost-volume-profit analysis.

After reviewing the accountant's computations, the president asks the marketing manager, "What are our chances of reaching a sales volume of 8,334 units?" The manager replies, "Slim to none." She observes that no Bright Day product has ever sold more than 4,000 bottles when initially offered. Also, market research revealed that customers are resistant to paying $36. Based on prices for competing products, the marketing manager believes customers would pay $28 per bottle for Delatine. The company president asks how changing the projected sales price will affect the sales volume required to produce the $40,000 target profit.

Reducing the sales price from $36 to $28 will significantly decrease the contribution margin. If the sales price is $28 per bottle, the new contribution margin becomes a mere $4 ($28 − $24) per unit. As shown here, the significant drop in contribution margin per unit (from $12 to $4) will cause a dramatic increase in the sales volume necessary to attain the target profit:

$$\text{Sales volume in units} = \frac{\text{Fixed costs} + \text{Desired profit}}{\text{Contribution margin per unit}}$$

$$= \frac{\$60{,}000 + \$40{,}000}{\$4} = 25{,}000 \text{ units}$$

The required sales volume *in dollars* is $700,000 (25,000 units × $28 per bottle). The following income statement confirms these results.

Sales Revenue (25,000 units × $28)	$700,000
Total Variable Expenses (25,000 units × $24)	(600,000)
Total Contribution Margin (25,000 units × $4)	100,000
Fixed Expenses	(60,000)
Net Income	$ 40,000

Target Pricing

LO 5

Use target pricing to reengineer a product.

The marketing manager concludes it would be impossible to sell 25,000 bottles of Delatine at any price. She suggests that the company drop its cost-plus pricing strategy and replace it with *target pricing*. **Target pricing** begins by determining the *market price* at which a product will sell. This becomes the target price. The focus then shifts to developing the product at a *cost* that will enable the company to be profitable selling the product at the *target price*. Since the target price leads to a target cost, this market-based pricing strategy is also called *target costing*.

Target pricing focuses on the design stage of product development. With respect to Delatine the target price is $28 per bottle. Bright Day must design the product *at a cost* that will support this price and provide the desired profit of $40,000. Fortunately, the marketing manager had some suggestions.

Using the Contribution Approach to Estimate the Effects of Changes in Variable Costs

LO 4

Use the contribution per unit approach to conduct cost-volume-profit analysis.

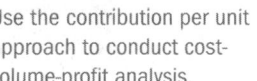

The previously discussed $24 cost is for a bottle of 100 capsules, each containing 90 milligrams (mg) of pure Delatine. The manufacturer is willing to provide Delatine to Bright Day in two alternative package sizes: (1) a bottle costing $12 that contains 100 capsules of 30 mg strength pure Delatine and (2) a bottle costing $3 that contains 100 capsules containing 5 mg of Delatine mixed with a vitamin C compound. The 5 mg dosage is the minimum required to permit a package label to indicate the product contains Delatine. The marketing manager observes that either option would enable Bright Day to sell Delatine at a price customers would be willing to pay.

The president vehemently rejected the second option, calling it a blatant attempt to deceive customers by suggesting they were buying Delatine when in fact they were getting vitamin C. *He considered the idea unethical and dangerous.* He vowed that he would not be seen on the six o'clock news trying to defend a fast buck scheme while his company's reputation went up in smoke. After calming down, he agreed that the first option had merit. The appropriate dosage for Delatine was uncertain; customers who wanted 90 mg per day could take three capsules instead of one. He asked the accountant, "What's the effect on the bottom line?"

The variable cost changes from $24 to $12 per bottle. The contribution margin per unit increases from $4 per bottle ($28 sales price − $24 variable cost per bottle) to $16 per bottle ($28 sales price − $12 variable cost per bottle). The significant increase in contribution margin per unit dramatically decreases the sales volume necessary to attain the target profit. The computations follow:

Answers to The Curious Accountant

American Airlines eliminated some first-class seats to increase its operating efficiency, even if it meant forgoing some revenue. To accomplish this, the company decided to reduce the number of flights it operated per day, and to reduce the number of different types of airplanes it uses. By reducing the number of flights, the occupancy level of each flight was increased. Since airlines have a significant amount of fixed costs for each flight operated, higher occupancy rates reduce the cost per passenger, and this should increase profits per flight. By reducing the number of different types of airplanes used, the company could reduce the costs of maintenance, since each type of plane requires its own inventory of replacement parts and special training for maintenance personnel.

Circuit City fired many of its most productive salespeople to reduce operating costs. These sales personnel were paid in part on a commission basis, so the more they sold, the greater Circuit City's selling expenses were. The company's main rival, **Best Buy**, was paying its sales personnel an hourly wage only rather than commissions. Although sales commissions motivate employees to be more aggressive in selling the company's goods, the sales commission is paid on *all* sales made, not just on the additional sales that result from motivation of the commission. Circuit City decided that the higher sales generated by the most successful members of the sales staff were not sufficient to justify their higher costs, so they were laid off.

Neither American Airlines nor Circuit City made their decisions by focusing only on revenues or only on costs. Rather, their decisions were based on an analysis of the interactions of costs, revenues, and the volume of sales that would be generated as cost and pricing strategies were altered.

$$\text{Sales volume in units} = \frac{\text{Fixed costs} + \text{Desired profit}}{\text{Contribution margin per unit}}$$

$$= \frac{\$60{,}000 + \$40{,}000}{\$16} = 6{,}250 \text{ units}$$

The required sales volume in sales dollars is $175,000 (6,250 units × $28 per bottle). The following income statement confirms these amounts.

Sales Revenue (6,250 units × $28)	$175,000
Total Variable Expenses (6,250 units × $12)	(75,000)
Total Contribution Margin (6,250 units × $16)	100,000
Fixed Expenses	(60,000)
Net Income	$ 40,000

Although the drop in required sales from 25,000 units to 6,250 was significant, the marketing manager was still uneasy about the company's ability to sell 6,250 bottles of Delatine. She observed again that no other Bright Day product had produced sales of that magnitude. The accountant suggested reducing projected fixed costs by advertising on radio rather than television. While gathering cost data for the potential television ad campaign, the accountant had consulted radio ad executives who had assured him radio ads could equal the TV audience exposure at about half the cost. Even though the TV ads would likely be more effective, he argued that since radio advertising costs would be half those of TV, the desired profit could be attained at a significantly lower volume of sales. The company president was impressed with the possibilities. He asked the accountant to determine the required sales volume if advertising costs were $30,000 instead of $60,000.

Using the Contribution Approach to Estimate the Effects of Changes in Fixed Costs

Since the contribution margin will cover a smaller amount of fixed costs, changing the fixed costs from $60,000 to $30,000 will dramatically reduce the sales level required to earn the target profit. The computations follow:

$$\text{Sales volume in units} = \frac{\text{Fixed costs} + \text{Desired profit}}{\text{Contribution margin per unit}}$$

$$= \frac{\$30{,}000 + \$40{,}000}{\$16} = 4{,}375 \text{ units}$$

LO 4

Use the contribution per unit approach to conduct cost-volume-profit analysis.

The required sales volume in sales dollars is $122,500 (4,375 units × $28). The following income statement confirms these amounts.

Sales Revenue (4,375 units × $28)	$122,500
Total Variable Expenses (4,375 units × $12)	(52,500)
Total Contribution Margin (4,375 units × $16)	70,000
Fixed Expenses	(30,000)
Net Income	$ 40,000

The marketing manager supported using radio instead of television ads. Obviously, she could not guarantee any specific sales volume, but she felt confident that sales projections within a range of 4,000 to 5,000 units were reasonable.

Using the Cost-Volume Profit Graph

LO 6

Draw and interpret a cost-volume-profit graph.

To visually analyze the revised projections, Bright Day's accountant prepared a cost-volume-profit (CVP) chart that pictured CVP relationships over a range of sales activity from zero to 6,000 units. The accountant followed the steps below to produce the CVP graph (sometimes called a *break-even chart*) shown in Exhibit 19.1. The graph uses the following assumptions:

- The contribution margin is $16 (sales price $28 − variable cost $12 per bottle).
- The fixed cost is $30,000.
- The desired profit is $40,000.

Procedures for Drawing the CVP Graph

1. *Draw and label the axes*: The horizontal axis represents activity (expressed in units) and the vertical axis represents dollars.
2. *Draw the fixed cost line*: Total fixed costs are constant for all levels of activity. Draw a horizontal line representing the amount of fixed costs across the graph at $30,000, the fixed-cost level.
3. *Draw the total cost line*: The total cost line representing the combination of fixed and variable costs is a diagonal line that rises as it moves from left to right. To draw the line, plot one point of the total cost line at the intersection of the fixed-cost line and the vertical axis. In this case, plot the first point at the zero level of activity and $30,000 (fixed cost). Next, select an arbitrary activity level. In this case we assume 6,000 units. At this volume, the total cost is $102,000 [(6,000 units × $12) + $30,000 fixed cost]. Plot a point at the coordinates of 6,000 units and $102,000. Draw a straight line through these two points.
4. *Draw the sales line*: Draw the revenue line using a procedure similar to that described for drawing the total cost line. Select some arbitrary level of activity and multiply that volume by the sales price per unit. Plot the result on the graph and draw a line from the origin (zero units, zero revenue) through this point. For example, at a volume of 6,000 units, the revenue is $168,000 (6,000 units × $28). Plot a point at the coordinates of 6,000 units and $168,000. Draw a line from the origin through the plotted point.

Trace these steps to the graph in Exhibit 19.1.

EXHIBIT 19.1

Cost-Volume-Profit Graph

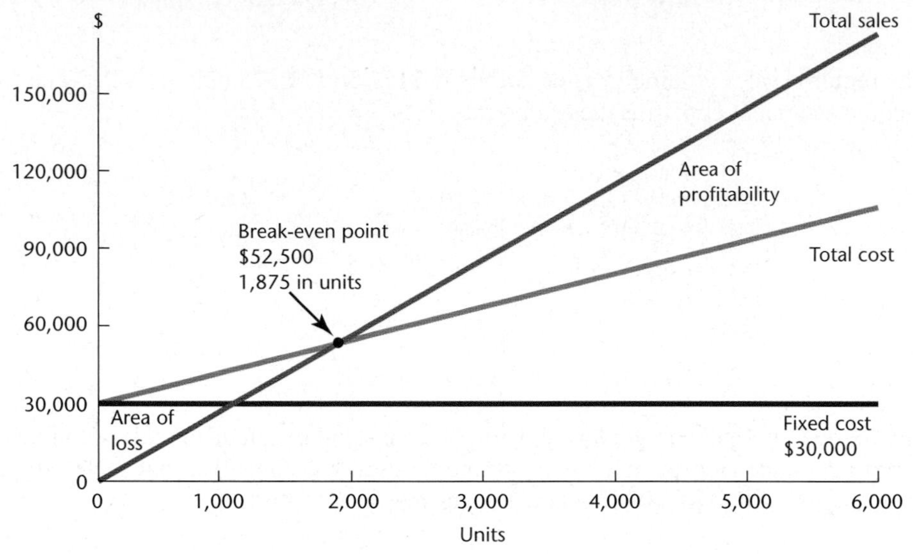

Calculating the Margin of Safety

LO 7

Calculate the margin of safety in units, dollars, and percentage.

The final meeting of Bright Day's management team focused on the reliability of the data used to construct the CVP chart. The accountant called attention to the sales volume figures in the area of profitability. Recall that Bright Day must sell 4,375 bottles of Delatine to earn the desired profit. In dollars, budgeted sales are $122,500 (4,375 bottles × $28 per bottle). The accountant highlighted the large gap between these budgeted sales and break-even sales. The amount of this gap, called the *margin of safety*, can be measured in units or in sales dollars as shown here:

	In Units	In Dollars
Budgeted sales	4,375	$122,500
Break-even sales	(1,875)	(52,500)
Margin of safety	2,500	$ 70,000

The **margin of safety** measures the cushion between budgeted sales and the break-even point. It quantifies the amount by which actual sales can fall short of expectations before the company will begin to incur losses.

To help compare diverse products or companies of different sizes, the margin of safety can be expressed as a percentage. Divide the margin of safety by the budgeted sales volume[1] as shown here:

$$\text{Margin of safety} = \frac{\text{Budgeted sales} - \text{Break-even sales}}{\text{Budgeted sales}}$$

$$\text{Margin of safety} = \frac{\$122{,}500 - \$52{,}500}{\$122{,}500} \times 100 = 57.14\%$$

[1] The margin of safety percentage can be based on actual as well as budgeted sales. For example, an analyst could compare the margins of safety of two companies under current operating conditions by substituting actual sales for budgeted sales in the computation, as follows: ([Actual sales − Break-even sales] ÷ Actual sales).

Recap of Delatine Decision Process

Management considers a new product named Delatine. Delatine has a projected sales price of $36 and variable cost of $24 per bottle. Fixed cost is projected to be $60,000. The break-even point is 5,000 units ($60,000 ÷ [$36 – $24] = 5,000).

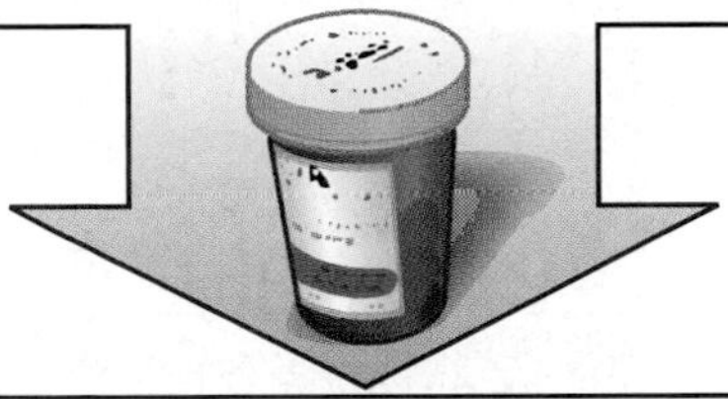

Management desires to earn a $40,000 profit on Delatine. The sales volume required to earn the desired profit is 8,334 units ([$60,000 + $40,000] ÷ [$36 – $24] = 8,334).

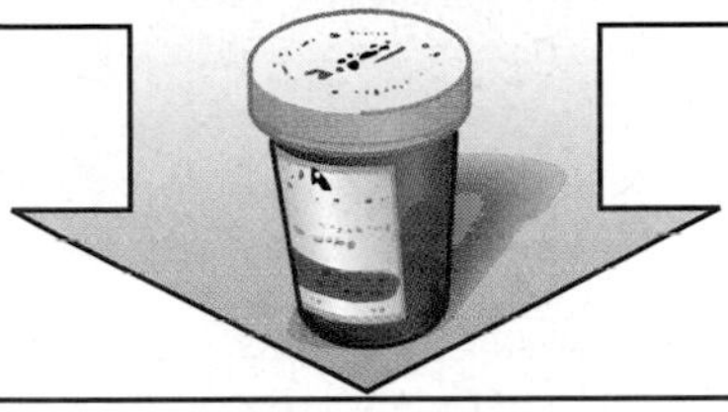

The marketing manager advocates a target pricing approach that lowers the proposed selling price to $28 per bottle. The sales volume required to earn a $40,000 profit increases to 25,000 units ([$60,000 + $40,000] ÷ [$28 – $24] = 25,000).

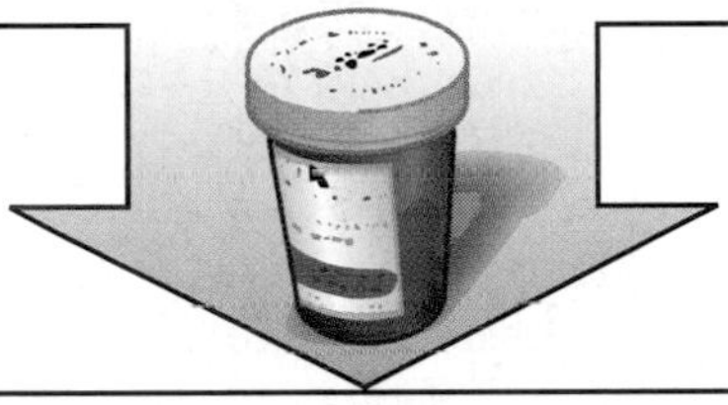

Target costing is employed to reengineer the product, thereby reducing variable cost to $12 per bottle. The sales volume required to earn a $40,000 profit decreases to 6,250 units ([$60,000 + $40,000] ÷ [$28 – $12] = 6,250).

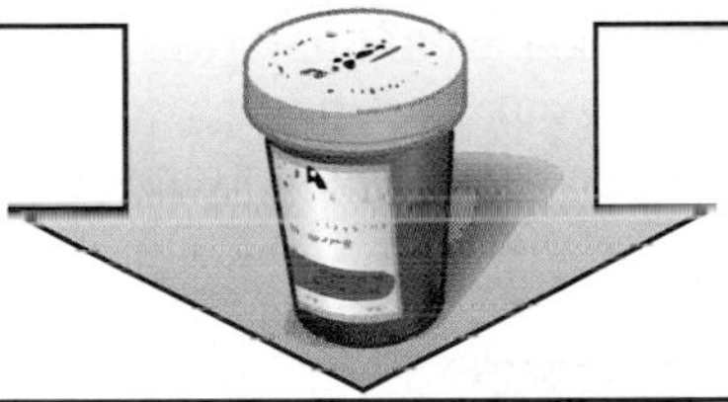

Target costing is applied further to reduce fixed cost to $30,000. The sales volume required to earn a $40,000 profit decreases to 4,375 units ([$30,000 + $40,000] ÷ [$28 – $12] = 4,375). The new break-even point is 1,875 units ($30,000 ÷ [$28 – $12] = 1,875).

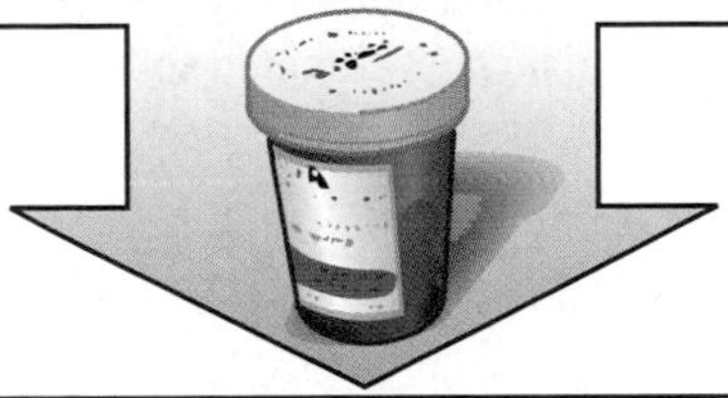

In view of a 57.14% margin of safety ([4,375 – 1,875] ÷ 4,375 = .5714), management decides to add Delatine to its product line.

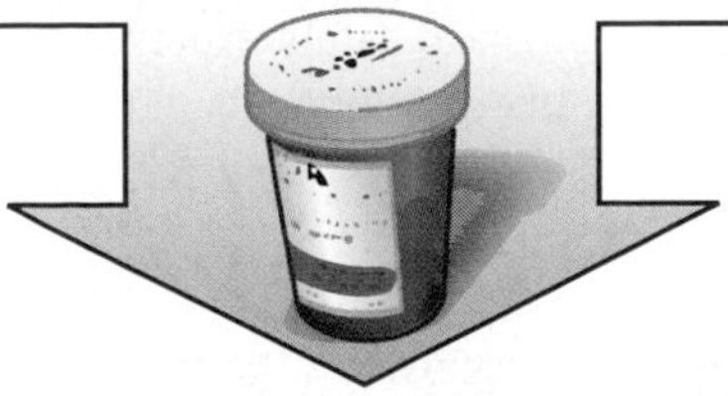

FOCUS ON INTERNATIONAL ISSUES

COST-VOLUME-PROFIT ANALYSIS AT A GERMAN SOFTWARE COMPANY

The higher the percentage of a company's total costs that are fixed, the more sensitive the company's earnings are to changes in revenue or volume. Operating leverage, the relationship between changes in revenue and changes in earnings introduced earlier, applies to companies throughout the world, large or small.

Software development companies have high fixed costs relative to total costs. It costs a lot to develop a new computer program, but it costs little to produce additional copies. **SAP**, a German company founded in 1972, is a leading provider of enterprise resource planning (ERP) software. From 2001 through 2003 SAP's earnings *increased* by 31.4 percent although its revenue *decreased* by 4.3 percent. No doubt the high fixed cost of developing software is one of the reasons that SAP's three major competitors, **J.D. Edwards**, **PeopleSoft**, and **Oracle**, went from being three separate firms in 2003 to only one firm, Oracle, by 2005.

Studying SAP offers insight into the global company. Though headquartered in Germany, in its 2003 fiscal year 57 percent of its revenues came from European customers, 25 percent from customers in the United States, and 14 percent from Asian customers. SAP's decline in revenues in 2003 was not caused by lower unit sales, but by the rise of the value of the euro against the dollar, a risk of international business. SAP's financial statements are presented in accordance with U.S. GAAP, but they are audited using German audit standards. The statements are mostly presented in euros, but some data are duplicated in U.S. dollars. You can review SAP's annual report at www.sap.com, under "Investor Relations."

This analysis suggests actual sales would have to fall short of expected sales by more than 57 percent before Bright Day would experience a loss on Delatine. The large margin of safety suggests the proposed radio advertising program to market bottles of 30mg Delatine capsules has minimal risk.

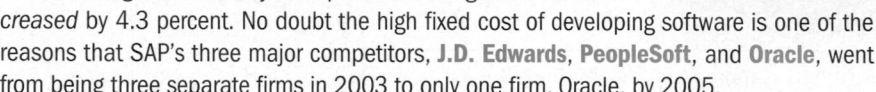

CHECK YOURSELF 19.2

Suppose that Bright Day is considering the possibility of selling a protein supplement that will cost Bright Day $5 per bottle. Bright Day believes that it can sell 4,000 bottles of the supplement for $25 per bottle. Fixed costs associated with selling the supplement are expected to be $42,000. Does the supplement have a wider margin of safety than Delatine?

Answer

Calculate the break-even point for the protein supplement.

$$\text{Break-even volume in units} = \frac{\text{Fixed costs}}{\text{Contribution margin per unit}} = \frac{\$42{,}000}{\$25 - \$5} = 2{,}100 \text{ units}$$

Calculate the margin of safety. Note that the margin of safety expressed as a percentage can be calculated using the number of units or sales dollars. Using either units or dollars yields the same percentage.

$$\text{Margin of safety} = \frac{\text{Budgeted sales} - \text{Break-even sales}}{\text{Budgeted sales}} = \frac{4{,}000 - 2{,}100}{4{,}000} = 47.5\%$$

The margin of safety for Delatine (57.14 percent) exceeds that for the protein supplement (47.5 percent). This suggests that Bright Day is less likely to incur losses selling Delatine than selling the supplement.

Performing Sensitivity Analysis Using Spreadsheet Software

LO 8

Explain how spreadsheet software can be used to conduct sensitivity analysis for cost-volume-profit relationships.

Although useful, the margin of safety offers only a one dimensional measure of risk—change in sales volume. Profitability is affected by multidimensional forces. Fixed or variable costs, as well as sales volume, could differ from expectations. Exhibit 19.2 uses data pertaining to Bright Day's proposed project for marketing Delatine to illustrate an Excel spreadsheet showing the sensitivity of profits to simultaneous changes in fixed cost, variable cost, and sales volume. Recall the accountant estimated the radio ad campaign would cost $30,000. The spreadsheet projects profitability if advertising costs are as low as $20,000 or as high as $40,000. The effects of potential simultaneous changes in variable cost and sales volume are similarly projected.

The range of scenarios illustrated in the spreadsheet represents only a few of the many alternatives management can analyze with a few quick keystrokes. The spreadsheet program recalculates profitability figures instantly when one of the variables changes. If the president asks what would happen if Bright Day sold 10,000 units, the accountant merely substitutes the new number for one of the existing sales volume figures, and revised profitability numbers are instantly available. By changing the variables, management can get a feel for the sensitivity of profits to changes in cost and volume. Investigating a multitude of what-if possibilities involving simultaneous changes in fixed cost, variable cost, and volume is called **sensitivity analysis.**

Assessing the Pricing Strategy

LO 2

Use the contribution per unit approach to calculate the break-even point.

After reviewing the spreadsheet analysis, Bright Day's management team is convinced it should undertake radio advertising for Delatine. Only under the most dire circumstances (if actual sales are significantly below expectations while costs are well above expectations) will the company incur a loss. In fact, the president feels uneasy because the projections seem too

EXHIBIT 19.2

Spreadsheet Report to Facilitate "What-If" Analysis

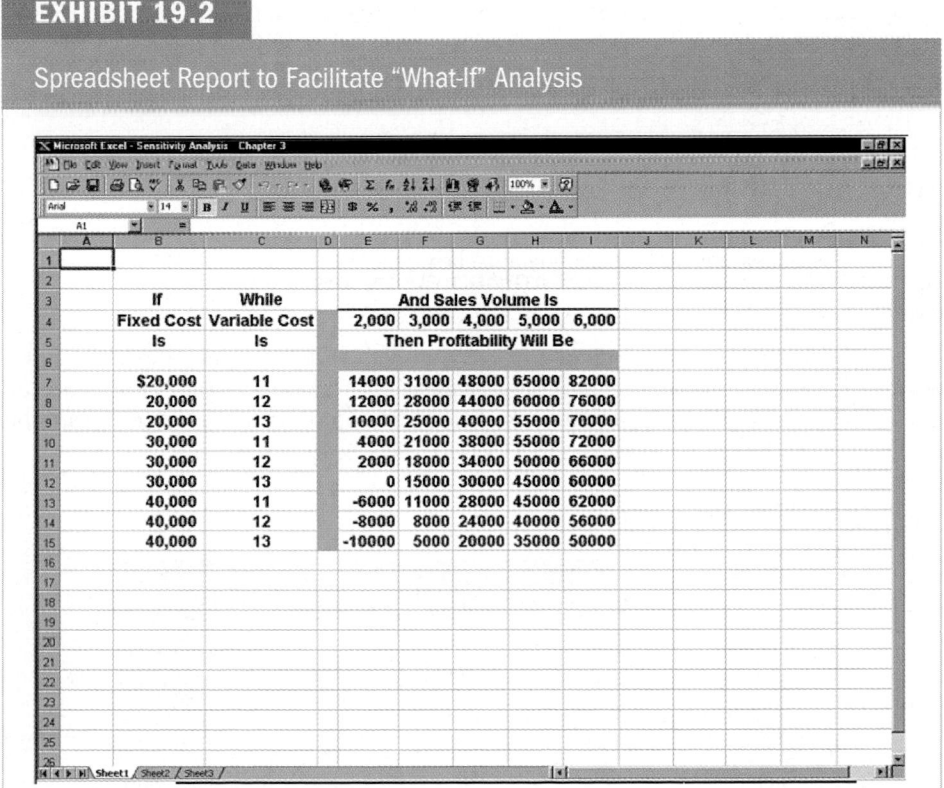

Microsoft Excel - Sensitivity Analysis Chapter 3

If	While	And Sales Volume Is				
Fixed Cost Is	Variable Cost Is	2,000	3,000	4,000	5,000	6,000
		Then Profitability Will Be				
$20,000	11	14000	31000	48000	65000	82000
20,000	12	12000	28000	44000	60000	76000
20,000	13	10000	25000	40000	55000	70000
30,000	11	4000	21000	38000	55000	72000
30,000	12	2000	18000	34000	50000	66000
30,000	13	0	15000	30000	45000	60000
40,000	11	-6000	11000	28000	45000	62000
40,000	12	-8000	8000	24000	40000	56000
40,000	13	-10000	5000	20000	35000	50000

Sheet1 / Sheet2 / Sheet3

good to be true. If Bright Day pays $12 per bottle for Delatine and sells it for $28 per bottle as projected, the effective markup on cost would be 133 percent [($28 - $12) ÷ $12]. Recall the company's normal markup is only 50 percent of cost. The president asks the marketing manager, "Are you sure people will buy this stuff at that price?"

The marketing manager explains she is advocating a pricing strategy known as **prestige pricing.** Many people will pay a premium to be the first to use a new product, especially when it receives widespread news media attention, as is the case with Delatine. Similarly, people will pay more for a product with a prestigious brand name. As news coverage of Delatine fades, competitors begin to offer alternatives, and customer interest wanes, the time will come to reduce prices. The marketing manager is confident the product will sell initially at the proposed price.

Using the Contribution Approach to Assess the Effect of Simultaneous Changes in CVP Variables

LO 4

Use the contribution per unit approach to conduct cost-volume-profit analysis.

The contribution approach previously illustrated to analyze one dimensional CVP relationships easily adapts to studying the effects of simultaneous changes in CVP variables. To illustrate several possible scenarios, assume Bright Day has developed the budgeted income statement in Exhibit 19.3.

A Decrease in Sales Price Accompanied by an Increase in Sales Volume

The marketing manager believes reducing the sales price per bottle to $25 will increase sales volume by 625 units. The per unit contribution margin would drop to $13 ($25 sales price − $12 cost per bottle). The expected sales volume would become 5,000 (4,375 + 625). Should Bright Day reduce the price? Compare the projected profit without these changes ($40,000) with the projected profit if the sales price is $25, computed as follows:

$$\text{Profit} = \text{Contribution margin} - \text{Fixed cost}$$

$$\text{Profit} = (5{,}000 \times \$13) - \$30{,}000 = \$35{,}000$$

Since budgeted income falls from $40,000 to $35,000, Bright Day should not reduce the sales price.

An Increase in Fixed Cost Accompanied by an Increase in Sales Volume

Return to the budgeted income statement in Exhibit 19.3. If the company buys an additional $12,000 of advertising, management believes sales can increase to 6,000 units. The contribution margin per unit will remain $16 ($28 − $12). Should Bright Day incur the additional advertising cost, increasing fixed costs to $42,000? The expected profit would be:

EXHIBIT 19.3

Budgeted Income Statement

Sales Revenue (4,375 units × $28 sale price)	$122,500
Total Variable Expenses (4,375 units × $12 cost per bottle)	(52,500)
Total Contribution Margin (4,375 units × $16)	70,000
Fixed Expenses	(30,000)
Net Income	$ 40,000

$$\text{Profit} = \text{Contribution margin} - \text{Fixed cost}$$

$$\text{Profit} = (6{,}000 \times \$16) - \$42{,}000 = \$54{,}000$$

Since budgeted income increases from $40,000 to $54,000, Bright Day should seek to increase sales through additional advertising.

A Simultaneous Reduction in Sales Price, Fixed Costs, Variable Costs, and Sales Volume

Return again to the budgeted income statement in Exhibit 19.3. Suppose Bright Day negotiates a $4 reduction in the cost of a bottle of Delatine. The management team considers passing some of the savings on to customers by reducing the sales price to $25 per bottle. Furthermore, the team believes it could reduce advertising costs by $8,000 and still achieve sales of 4,200 units. Should Bright Day adopt this plan to reduce prices and advertising costs?

The contribution margin would increase to $17 per bottle ($25 revised selling price − $8 revised variable cost per bottle) and fixed cost would fall to $22,000 ($30,000 − $8,000). Based on a sales volume of 4,200 units, the expected profit is:

$$\text{Profit} = \text{Contribution margin} - \text{Fixed cost}$$

$$\text{Profit} = (4{,}200 \times \$17) - \$22{,}000 = \$49{,}400$$

Because budgeted income increases from $40,000 to $49,400, Bright Day should proceed with the revised operating strategy.

Many other possible scenarios could be considered. The contribution approach can be used to analyze independent or simultaneous changes in the CVP variables.

Performing Cost-Volume-Profit (CVP) Analysis Using the Contribution Margin Ratio

LO 9

Use the contribution margin ratio and the equation method to conduct cost volume profit analysis.

The **contribution margin ratio** is the contribution margin divided by sales, computed using either total figures or per unit figures. The contribution margin *ratio* can be used in CVP analysis as an alternative to using the *per unit* contribution margin. To illustrate, assume Bright Day is considering selling a new product called Multi Minerals. The expected sales price, variable cost, and contribution margin per unit for Multi Minerals are:

Sales revenue per unit	$20
Variable cost per unit	12
Contribution margin per unit	$ 8

Based on these data, the *contribution margin ratio* for Multi Minerals is 40 percent ($8 ÷ $20). This ratio means every dollar of sales provides 40 cents ($1.00 × 0.40) to cover fixed costs. After fixed costs have been covered, each dollar of sales provides 40 cents of profit.

While the *per unit contribution margin* approach produces results measured in units, the *contribution margin ratio* approach produces results expressed in dollars. The two approaches represent different ways to reach the same conclusion. To illustrate, the two alternative approaches to calculate the break-even point are shown here, assuming Bright Day expects to incur $24,000 of fixed expenses to market Multi Minerals:

Per Unit Contribution Approach Break-even in Units	Contribution Ratio Approach Break-even in Dollars
$\dfrac{\text{Fixed costs}}{\text{Contribution margin per unit}} = \text{Units}$	$\dfrac{\text{Fixed costs}}{\text{Contribution margin ratio}} = \text{Dollars}$
$\dfrac{\$24{,}000}{\$8} = 3{,}000 \text{ units}$	$\dfrac{\$24{,}000}{40\%} = \$60{,}000$

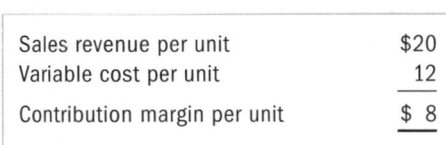

Recall the break-even point in units can be converted to sales dollars by multiplying the number of units to break even by the sales price per unit (3,000 units × $20 per unit = $60,000). Alternatively, the break-even point in sales dollars can be converted to units by dividing ($60,000 ÷ $20 = 3,000). The two approaches represent different views of the same data. The relationship between the two approaches holds when other CVP variables are added or changed. For example, either approach can provide the sales volume necessary to reach a target profit of $8,000, as follows:

Per Unit Contribution Approach Sales Volume in Units	**Contribution Ratio Approach Sales Volume in Dollars**
$\frac{\text{Fixed costs} + \text{Desired profit}}{\text{Contribution margin per unit}} = \text{Units}$	$\frac{\text{Fixed costs} + \text{Desired profit}}{\text{Contribution margin ratio}} = \text{Dollars}$
$\frac{\$24{,}000 + \$8{,}000}{\$8} = 4{,}000 \text{ units}$	$\frac{\$24{,}000 + \$8{,}000}{40\%} = \$80{,}000$

Once again, multiplying the $20 sales price by the sales volume expressed in units equals the sales volume in dollars ($20 × 4,000 = $80,000).

Performing Cost-Volume-Profit Analysis Using the Equation Method

LO 9

Use the contribution margin ratio and the equation method to conduct cost-volume-profit analysis.

Topic Tackler
PLUS

19-2

A third way to analyze CVP relationships uses the **equation method.** Begin with expressing the break-even point as an algebraic equation, as shown here.[2]

$$\text{Sales} = \text{Variable cost} + \text{Fixed cost}$$

Expanding the equation provides the basis for computing the break-even point in number of units, as shown here:

$$\begin{matrix}\text{Selling price per unit} \\ \times \\ \text{Number of units sold}\end{matrix} = \begin{matrix}\text{Variable cost per unit} \\ \times \\ \text{Number of units sold}\end{matrix} + \text{Fixed cost}$$

Using the Multi Minerals $20 sales price, $12 variable cost, and $24,000 fixed cost, the *break-even point in units* is:

$$\begin{aligned}\$20 \times \text{Units} &= \$12 \times \text{Units} + \$24{,}000 \\ \$8 \times \text{Units} &= \$24{,}000 \\ \text{Units} &= 3{,}000\end{aligned}$$

As before, the break-even sales volume in *units* can be converted into break-even sales volume in *dollars* by multiplying the sales price per unit by the number of units sold. The *break-even point* for Multi Minerals expressed in *dollars* is:

$$\begin{matrix}\text{Selling price per unit} & \times & \text{Number of units sold} & = & \text{Sales volume in dollars} \\ \$20 & \times & 3{,}000 & = & \$60{,}000\end{matrix}$$

[2] The equation method results in the same computation as the per unit contribution margin approach. Consider the following. Using the per unit contribution margin approach, the break-even point is determined as follows (X is the break-even point in units):

$$X = \text{Fixed cost} \div \text{Per unit contribution margin}$$

Using the equation method, the break-even point is determined as follows (X is the break-even point in units):

$$\begin{aligned}&\text{Unit sales price } (X) = \text{Variable cost per unit } (X) + \text{Fixed cost} \\ &(\text{Unit sales price} - \text{Variable cost per unit})\ (X) = \text{Fixed cost} \\ &\text{Per unit contribution margin } (X) = \text{Fixed cost} \\ &X = \text{Fixed cost} \div \text{Per unit contribution margin}\end{aligned}$$

The equation method can also be used to analyze additional CVP relationships. For example, the equation to determine the sales volume necessary to attain a target profit of \$8,000 is:

$$\begin{matrix}\text{Selling price per unit} \\ \times \\ \text{Number of units sold}\end{matrix} = \begin{matrix}\text{Variable cost per unit} \\ \times \\ \text{Number of units sold}\end{matrix} + \text{Fixed cost} + \text{Desired profit}$$

The computations are:

$$\$20 \times \text{Units} = \$12 \times \text{Units} + \$24{,}000 + \$8{,}000$$
$$\$8 \times \text{Units} = \$32{,}000$$
$$\text{Units} = 4{,}000$$

Comparing these results with those determined using the per unit contribution approach and the contribution margin ratio approach demonstrates that the equation method is another way to achieve the same result. The method to use depends on personal and management preferences.

CHECK YOURSELF 19.3

Recall the information presented in Check Yourself 19.1 on page 934. VolTech Company manufactures small engines that it sells for \$130 each, with variable costs of \$70 per unit, expected fixed costs of \$100,000, and a target profit of \$188,000. Use the equation method to calculate the number of engines VolTech must sell to attain the target profit.

Answer

$$\begin{matrix}\text{Selling price per unit} \\ \times \\ \text{Number of units sold}\end{matrix} = \begin{matrix}\text{Variable cost per unit} \\ \times \\ \text{Number of units sold}\end{matrix} + \text{Fixed cost} + \text{Desired profit}$$

$$\$130 \times \text{Units} = \$70 \times \text{Units} + \$100{,}000 + \$188{,}000$$
$$\$60 \times \text{Units} = \$288{,}000$$
$$\text{Units} = 4{,}800$$

This is the same result determined in the Check Yourself 19.1 exercise. The only difference is in the method used to make the computation.

Cost-Volume-Profit Limitations

LO 10

Identify the limitations of cost-volume-profit analysis.

Because cost-volume-profit analysis presumes strictly linear behavior among the variables, its accuracy is limited. Actual CVP variables rarely behave with true linearity. Suppose, for example, a business receives volume discounts on materials purchases: the more material purchased, the lower the cost per unit. The total cost varies but not in direct proportion to the amount of material purchased. Similarly, fixed costs can change. A supervisor's fixed salary may change if the supervisor receives a raise. Likewise, the cost of telephone service, rent, insurance, taxes, and so on may increase or decrease. In practice, fixed costs frequently fluctuate. Furthermore, sales prices may vary as a result of promotions or other factors. None of the CVP variables is likely to behave with strict linearity.

Finally, CVP analysis presumes inventory levels remain constant during the period. In other words, sales and production are assumed to be equal. CVP formulas provide the estimated number of units that must be *produced and sold* to break even or to achieve some designated target profit. Manufacturing or acquiring, but not selling, inventory generates costs without producing corresponding revenue. Changes in inventory levels undoubtedly affect CVP relationships. The assumptions underlying CVP analysis are rarely entirely valid in business practice. Within the relevant range of activity, however, deviations from the basic assumptions are normally insignificant. A prudent business manager who exercises good judgment will find the projections generated by cost-volume-profit analysis useful regardless of these limitations.

<< A Look Back

Profitability is affected by changes in sale price, costs, and the volume of activity. The relationship among these variables is examined using *cost-volume-profit (CVP) analysis*. The *contribution margin*, determined by subtracting variable costs from the sales price, is a useful variable in CVP analysis. The *contribution margin per unit* is the amount each unit sold provides to cover fixed costs. Once fixed costs have been covered, each additional unit sold increases net income by the amount of the per unit contribution margin.

The *break-even point* (the point where total revenue equals total cost) in units can be determined by dividing fixed costs by the contribution margin per unit. The break-even point in sales dollars can be determined by multiplying the number of break-even units by the sales price per unit. To determine sales in units to obtain a designated profit, the sum of fixed costs and desired profit is divided by the contribution margin per unit. The contribution margin per unit can also be used to assess the effects on the company's profitability of changes in sales price, variable costs, and fixed costs.

Many methods are available to determine the prices at which products should sell. In *cost-plus pricing*, the sales price per unit is determined by adding a percentage markup to the cost per unit. In contrast, *target pricing* (*target costing*) begins with an estimated market price customers would be willing to pay for the product and then develops the product at a cost that will enable the company to earn its desired profit.

A *break-even graph* can depict cost-volume-profit relationships for a product over a range of sales activity. The horizontal axis represents volume of activity and the vertical axis represents dollars. Lines for fixed costs, total costs, and sales are drawn based on the sales price per unit, variable cost per unit, and fixed costs. The graph can be used to determine the break-even point in units and sales dollars.

The *margin of safety* is the number of units or the amount of sales dollars by which actual sales can fall below expected sales before a loss is incurred. The margin of safety can also be expressed as a percentage to permit comparing different size companies. The margin of safety can be computed as a percentage by dividing the difference between budgeted sales and break-even sales by the amount of budgeted sales.

Spreadsheet software as well as the contribution margin approach can be used to conduct sensitivity analysis of cost-volume-profit relationships. *Sensitivity analysis* predicts the effect on profitability of different scenarios of fixed costs, variable costs, and sales volumes. The effects of simultaneous changes in all three variables can be assessed. A *contribution margin ratio* can be used to determine the break-even point in sales dollars. The ratio is a percentage determined by dividing the contribution margin per unit by the sales price per unit. Using the contribution margin ratio, the break-even volume in dollars can be determined by dividing the total fixed costs by the ratio. Cost-volume-profit relationships can also be examined using this algebraic equation:

$$\text{Sales} = \text{Variable cost} + \text{Fixed cost}$$

Cost-volume-profit analysis is built upon certain simplifying assumptions. The analysis assumes true linearity among the CVP variables and a constant level of inventory. Although these assumptions are not literally valid in actual practice, CVP analysis nevertheless provides managers with helpful insights for decision making.

>> A Look Forward

The next chapter introduces the concept of *relevance*. Applying the concepts you have learned to real-world business problems can be challenging. Frequently, so much data is available that it is difficult to distinguish important from useless information. The next chapter will help you learn to identify information that is relevant in a variety of short-term decision-making scenarios including special orders, outsourcing, segment elimination, and asset replacement.

APPENDIX

Multiple-Product Break-Even Analysis

LO 11

Perform multiple-product break-even analysis.

When a company analyzes CVP relationships for multiple products that sell simultaneously, the break-even point can be affected by the relative number (sales mix) of the products sold. For example, suppose Bright Day decides to run a special sale on its two leading antioxidants, vitamins C and E. The income statements at the break-even point are presented in Exhibit 19.4.

Recall that the break-even point is the point where total sales equal total costs. Net income is zero at that point. The data in Exhibit 19.4 indicate that the budgeted break-even sales volume for the antioxidant special is 2,700 bottles of vitamins with a sales mix of 2,000 bottles of vitamin C and 700 bottles of vitamin E. What happens if the relative sales mix changes? Exhibit 19.5 depicts the expected condition if total sales remain at 2,700 units but the sales mix changes to 2,100 bottles of vitamin C and 600 bottles of vitamin E.

Although the total number of bottles sold remains at 2,700 units, profitability shifts from breaking even to a $280 loss because of the change in the sales mix of the two products, that is, selling more vitamin C than expected and less vitamin E. Because vitamin C has a lower contribution margin ($1.20 per bottle) than vitamin E ($4.00 per bottle), selling more of C and less of E reduces profitability. The opposite impact occurs if Bright Day sells more E and less C. Exhibit 19.6 depicts the expected condition if total sales remain at 2,700 units but the sales mix changes to 1,350 bottles each of vitamin C and vitamin E.

EXHIBIT 19.4

Budgeted Data for Antioxidant Special

	Vitamin C			Vitamin E			Total	
	Budgeted Number	Per Unit	Budgeted Amount	Budgeted Number	Per Unit	Budgeted Amount	Budgeted Number	Budgeted Amount
Sales	2,000	@ $7.20 =	$14,400	700	@ $11.00 =	$7,700	2,700	$22,100
Variable Cost	2,000	@ 6.00 =	(12,000)	700	@ 7.00 =	(4,900)	2,700	(16,900)
Contribution Margin	2,000	@ 1.20 =	2,400	700	@ 4.00 =	2,800	2,700	5,200
Fixed Cost			(2,400)			(2,800)		(5,200)
Net income			$ 0			$ 0		$ 0

EXHIBIT 19.5

Budgeted Data for Antioxidant Special

	Vitamin C			Vitamin E			Total	
	Budgeted Number	Per Unit	Budgeted Amount	Budgeted Number	Per Unit	Budgeted Amount	Budgeted Number	Budgeted Amount
Sales	2,100	@ $7.20 =	$15,120	600	@ $11.00 =	$6,600	2,700	$21,720
Variable Cost	2,100	@ 6.00 =	(12,600)	600	@ 7.00 =	(4,200)	2,700	(16,800)
Contribution Margin	2,100	@ 1.20 =	2,520	600	@ 4.00 =	2,400	2,700	4,920
Fixed Cost			(2,400)			(2,800)		(5,200)
Net Income			$ 120			$ (400)		$ (280)

Companies must consider sales mix when conducting break-even analysis for multiproduct business ventures. The multiple product break-even point can be determined using the per unit contribution margin approach. However, it is necessary to use a weighted average to determine the per unit contribution margin. The contribution margin of each product must be weighted by its proportionate share of units sold. For example, in the preceding case, the relative sales mix between the two products is one half (1,350 units ÷ 2,700 units = 50 percent). What is the break-even point given a relative sales mix of one-half for each product? To answer this question, the companies must first determine the weighted average per unit contribution margin by multiplying the contribution margin of each product by 50 percent. The required computation is shown here.

Weighted Average Contribution Margin	
Vitamin C ($1.20 × 0.50)	$0.60
Vitamin E ($4.00 × 0.50)	2.00
Weighted average per unit contribution margin	$2.60

The break-even point in total units at a 50/50 sales mix is computed as follows.

Break-even point = Fixed costs ÷ Weighted average per unit contribution margin

Break-even point = $5,200 ÷ $2.60 = 2,000 total units

Next divide the total units to break even in proportion to the relative sales mix. In other words, the break-even point occurs at 1,000 bottles of Vitamin C (50 percent of 2,000) and 1,000 bottles of Vitamin E (50 percent of 2,000). The income statements presented in Exhibit 19.7 illustrate these results.

EXHIBIT 19.6

Budgeted Data for Antioxidant Special

	Vitamin C				Vitamin E				Total	
	Budgeted Number	Per Unit		Budgeted Amount	Budgeted Number	Per Unit		Budgeted Amount	Budgeted Number	Budgeted Amount
Sales	1,350	@ $7.20	=	$9,720	1,350	@ $11.00	=	$14,850	2,700	$24,570
Variable Cost	1,350	@ 6.00	=	(8,100)	1,350	@ 7.00	=	(9,450)	2,700	(17,550)
Contribution Margin	1,350	@ 1.20	=	1,620	1,350	@ 4.00	=	5,400	2,700	7,020
Fixed Cost				(2,400)				(2,800)		(5,200)
Net Income				$ (780)				$ 2,600		$ 1,820

EXHIBIT 19.7

Budgeted Data for Antioxidant Special

	Vitamin C				Vitamin E				Total	
	Budgeted Number	Per Unit		Budgeted Amount	Budgeted Number	Per Unit		Budgeted Amount	Budgeted Number	Budgeted Amount
Sales	1,000	@ $7.20	=	$ 7,200	1,000	@ $11.00	=	$11,000	2,000	$18,200
Variable Cost	1,000	@ 6.00	=	(6,000)	1,000	@ 7.00	=	(7,000)	2,000	(13,000)
Contribution Margin	1,000	@ 1.20	=	1,200	1,000	@ 4.00	=	4,000	2,000	5,200
Fixed Cost				(2,400)				(2,800)		(5,200)
Net Income				$(1,200)				$ 1,200		$ 0

SELF-STUDY REVIEW PROBLEM

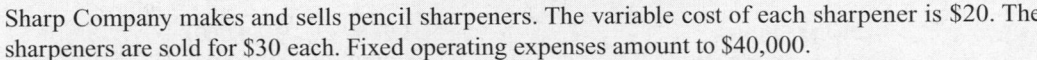

Sharp Company makes and sells pencil sharpeners. The variable cost of each sharpener is $20. The sharpeners are sold for $30 each. Fixed operating expenses amount to $40,000.

Required

a. Determine the break-even point in units and sales dollars.

b. Determine the sales volume in units and dollars that is required to attain a profit of $12,000. Verify your answer by preparing an income statement using the contribution margin format.

c. Determine the margin of safety between sales required to attain a profit of $12,000 and break-even sales.

d. Prepare a break-even graph using the cost and price assumptions outlined above.

Solution to Requirement *a*

Formula for Computing Break-even Point in Units

$$\frac{\text{Fixed cost} + \text{Target profit}}{\text{Contribution margin per unit}} = \frac{\$40{,}000 + \$0}{\$30 - \$20} = 4{,}000 \text{ Units}$$

Break-even Point in Sales Dollars	
Sales price	$ 30
Times number of units	4,000
Sales volume in dollars	$120,000

Solution to Requirement *b*

Formula for Computing Unit Sales Required to Attain Desired Profit

$$\frac{\text{Fixed cost} + \text{Target profit}}{\text{Contribution margin per unit}} = \frac{\$40{,}000 + \$12{,}000}{\$30 - \$20} = 5{,}200 \text{ units}$$

Sales Dollars Required to Attain Desired Profit	
Sales price	$ 30
Times number of units	5,200
Sales volume in dollars	$156,000

Income Statement	
Sales Volume in Units (a)	5,200
Sales Revenue (a × $30)	$156,000
Variable Costs (a × $20)	(104,000)
Contribution Margin	52,000
Fixed Costs	(40,000)
Net Income	$ 12,000

Solution to Requirement *c*

Margin of Safety Computations	Units	Dollars
Budgeted sales	5,200	$156,000
Break-even sales	(4,000)	(120,000)
Margin of safety	1,200	$ 36,000

Percentage Computation

$$\frac{\text{Margin of safety in \$}}{\text{Budgeted sales}} = \frac{\$36{,}000}{\$156{,}000} = 23.08\%$$

Solution to Requirement *d*

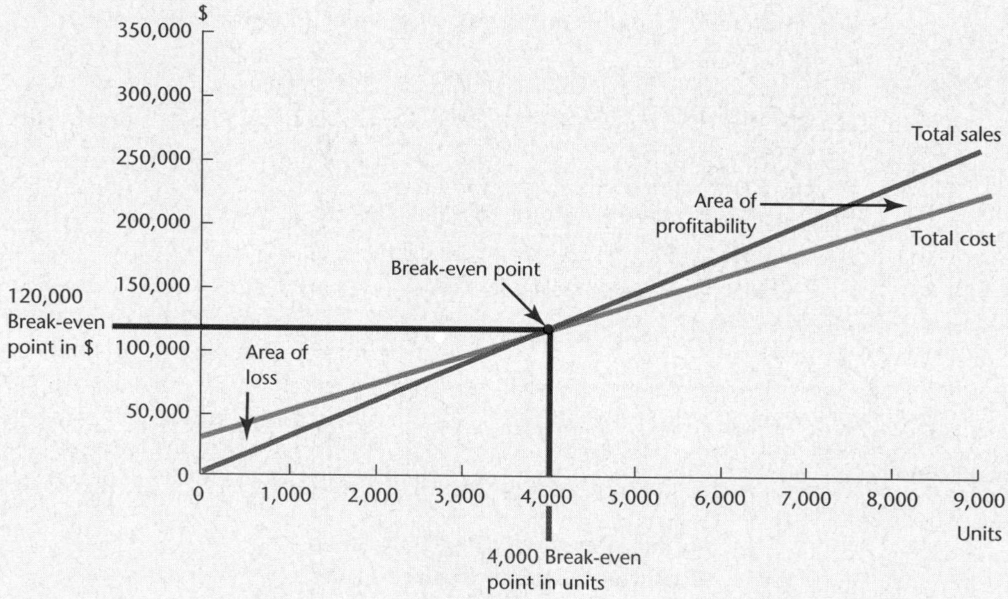

KEY TERMS

break-even point 932
contribution margin per unit 932
contribution margin ratio 943
cost-plus pricing 932
cost-volume-profit (CVP) analysis 931
equation method 944
margin of safety 938
prestige pricing 942
sensitivity analysis 941
target pricing (target costing) 935

QUESTIONS

1. What does the term *break-even point* mean? Name the two ways it can be measured.
2. How does a contribution margin income statement differ from the income statement used in financial reporting?
3. In what three ways can the contribution margin be useful in cost-volume-profit analysis?

4. If Company A has a projected margin of safety of 22 percent while Company B has a margin of safety of 52 percent, which company is at greater risk when actual sales are less than budgeted?
5. What variables affect profitability? Name two methods for determining profitability when simultaneous changes occur in these variables.
6. When would the customer be willing to pay a premium price for a product or service? What pricing strategy would be appropriate under these circumstances?
7. What are three alternative approaches to determine the break-even point? What do the results of these approaches show?
8. What is the equation method for determining the break-even point? Explain how the results of this method differ from those of the contribution margin approach.
9. If a company is trying to find the break-even point for multiple products that sell simultaneously, what consideration must be taken into account?
10. What assumptions are inherent in cost-volume-profit analysis? Since these assumptions are usually not wholly valid, why do managers still use the analysis in decision making?
11. Mary Hartwell and Jane Jamail, college roommates, are considering the joint purchase of a computer that they can share to prepare class assignments. Ms. Hartwell wants a particular model that costs $2,000; Ms. Jamail prefers a more economical model that costs $1,500. In fact, Ms. Jamail is adamant about her position, refusing to contribute more than $750 toward the purchase. If Ms. Hartwell is also adamant about her position, should she accept Ms. Jamail's $750 offer and apply that amount toward the purchase of the more expensive computer?
12. How would the algebraic formula used to compute the break-even point under the equation method be changed to solve for a desired target profit?
13. Setting the sales price is easy: Enter cost information and desired profit data into one of the cost-volume-profit formulas, and the appropriate sales price can be computed mathematically. Do you agree with this line of reasoning? Explain.
14. What is the relationship between cost-volume-profit analysis and the relevant range?

EXERCISES—SERIES A

All Exercises in Series A are available with McGraw-Hill's Homework Manager

Exercise 19-1A *Per unit contribution margin approach* — L.O. 2

Thorpe Corporation sells products for $15 each that have variable costs of $10 per unit. Thorpe's annual fixed cost is $300,000.

Required

Use the per unit contribution margin approach to determine the break-even point in units and dollars.

Exercise 19-2A *Equation method* — L.O. 2

Moreno Corporation produces products that it sells for $7 each. Variable costs per unit are $4, and annual fixed costs are $81,000.

Required

Use the equation method to determine the break-even point in units and dollars.

Exercise 19-3A *Contribution margin ratio* — L.O. 3

Jaffe Company incurs annual fixed costs of $60,000. Variable costs for Jaffe's product are $7.50 per unit, and the sales price is $12.50 per unit. Jaffe desires to earn an annual profit of $40,000.

Required

Use the contribution margin ratio approach to determine the sales volume in dollars and units required to earn the desired profit.

L.O. 3

Exercise 19-4A ***Equation method***

Crespo Company produces a product that sells for $21 per unit and has a variable cost of $15 per unit. Crespo incurs annual fixed costs of $230,000. It desires to earn a profit of $70,000.

Required

Use the equation method to determine the sales volume in units and dollars required to earn the desired profit.

L.O. 3

Exercise 19-5A ***Determining fixed and variable cost per unit***

Vidal Corporation produced and sold 24,000 units of product during October. It earned a contribution margin of $96,000 on sales of $336,000 and determined that cost per unit of product was $12.50.

Required

Based on this information, determine the variable and fixed cost per unit of product.

L.O. 3

Exercise 19-6A ***Determining variable cost from incomplete cost data***

Amaya Corporation produced 150,000 watches that it sold for $24 each during 2006. The company determined that fixed manufacturing cost per unit was $6 per watch. The company reported a $600,000 gross margin on its 2006 financial statements.

Required

Determine the total variable cost, the variable cost per unit, and the total contribution margin.

L.O. 2, 3

Exercise 19-7A ***Contribution margin per unit approach for break-even and desired profit***

Information concerning a product produced by Cheung Company appears here.

Sales price per unit	$160
Variable cost per unit	$35
Total annual fixed manufacturing and operating costs	$900,000

Required

Determine the following:

a. Contribution margin per unit.

b. Number of units that Cheung must sell to break even.

c. Sales level in units that Cheung must reach to earn a profit of $360,000.

L.O. 4

Exercise 19-8A ***Changing sales price***

Dansby Company produces a product that has a variable cost of $6 per unit; the product sells for $13 per unit. The company's annual fixed costs total $350,000; it had net income of $70,000 in the previous year. In an effort to increase the company's market share, management is considering lowering the selling price to $11.60 per unit.

Required

If Dansby desires to maintain net income of $70,000, how many additional units must it sell to justify the price decline?

L.O. 4

Exercise 19-9A ***Simultaneous change in sales price and desired profit***

Use the cost data presented in Exercise 19-8A but assume that in addition to increasing its market share by lowering its selling price to $11.60, Dansby desires to increase its net income by $14,000.

Required

Determine the number of units the company must sell to earn the desired income.

Exercise 19-10A *Components of break-even graph*

L.O. 2, 3, 6

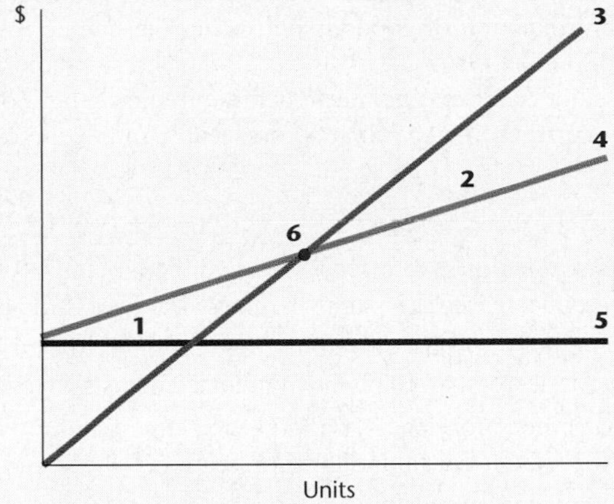

Required

Match the numbers shown in the graph with the following items.

a. Fixed cost line
b. Total cost line
c. Break-even point
d. Area of profit
e. Revenue line
f. Area of loss

Exercise 19-11A *Evaluating simultaneous changes in fixed and variable costs*

L.O. 4

Dennis Company currently produces and sells 7,500 units annually of a product that has a variable cost of $12 per unit and annual fixed costs of $200,000. The company currently earns a $70,000 annual profit. Assume that Dennis has the opportunity to invest in new labor-saving production equipment that will enable the company to reduce variable costs to $9 per unit. The investment would cause fixed costs to increase by $20,000 because of additional depreciation cost.

Required

a. Use the equation method to determine the sales price per unit under existing conditions (current equipment is used).
b. Prepare a contribution margin income statement, assuming that Dennis invests in the new production equipment. Recommend whether Dennis should invest in the new equipment.

Exercise 19-12A *Margin of safety*

L.O. 7

Bates Company makes a product that sells for $18 per unit. The company pays $8 per unit for the variable costs of the product and incurs annual fixed costs of $150,000. Bates expects to sell 24,000 units of product.

Required

Determine Bates' margin of safety expressed as a percentage.

Exercise 19-13A *Cost-volume-profit relationship*

L.O. 2, 3, 4

Clemmons, Inc., a manufacturing company, makes small electric motors it sells for $72 per unit. The variable costs of production are $48 per motor, and annual fixed costs of production are $144,000.

Required

a. How many units of product must Clemmons make and sell to break even?
b. How many units of product must Clemmons make and sell to earn a $36,000 profit?
c. The marketing manager believes that sales would increase dramatically if the price were reduced to $68 per unit. How many units of product must Clemmons make and sell to earn a $36,000 profit if the sales price is set at $68 per unit?

Exercise 19-14A *Understanding of the global economy through CVP relationships*

L.O. 4

An article published in the December 8, 1997, issue of *U.S. News & World Report* summarized several factors likely to support a continuing decline in the rate of inflation over the next decade. Specifically,

the article stated that "global competition has . . . fostered an environment of cheap labor, cost cutting, and increased efficiency." The article notes that these developments in the global economy have led to a condition in which "the production of goods is outpacing the number of consumers able to buy them." Even so, the level of production is not likely to decline because factories have been built in developing countries where labor is cheap. The recent decline in the strength of the Asian economies is likely to have a snowballing effect so that within the foreseeable future, there will "be too many goods chasing too few buyers."

Required

a. Identify the production cost factor(s) referred to that exhibit variable cost behavior. Has (have) the cost factor(s) increased or decreased? Explain why the variable costs have increased or decreased.

b. Identify the production cost factor(s) referred to that exhibit fixed cost behavior. Has (have) the cost factor(s) increased or decreased? Explain why the fixed costs have increased or decreased.

c. The article implies that production levels are likely to remain high even though demand is expected to be weak. Explain the logic behind this implication.

d. The article suggests that manufacturers will continue to produce goods even though they may have to sell goods at a price that is below the total cost of production. Considering what you know about fixed and variable costs, speculate on how low manufacturers would permit prices to drop before they would stop production.

L.O. 5

Exercise 19-15A ***Target costing***

The marketing manager of Cline Corporation has determined that a market exists for a telephone with a sales price of $43 per unit. The production manager estimates the annual fixed costs of producing between 20,000 and 40,000 telephones would be $450,000.

Required

Assume that Cline desires to earn a $150,000 profit from the phone sales. How much can Cline afford to spend on variable cost per unit if production and sales equal 30,000 phones?

Appendix

L.O. 4

Exercise 19-16A ***Multiple product break-even analysis***

Roberts Company manufactures two products. The budgeted per unit contribution margin for each product follows.

	Ascend	Advance
Sales price	$85	$98
Variable cost per unit	(45)	(38)
Contribution margin per unit	$40	$60

Roberts expects to incur annual fixed costs of $90,000. The relative sales mix of the products is 75 percent for Ascend and 25 percent for Advance.

Required

a. Determine the total number of products (units of Ascend and Advance combined) Roberts must sell to break even.

b. How many units each of Ascend and Advance must Roberts sell to break even?

PROBLEMS—SERIES A

All Problems in Series A are available with McGraw-Hill's Homework Manager

L.O. 2

excel

mhhe.com/edmonds2007

Problem 19-17A ***Determining the break-even point and preparing a contribution margin income statement***

Dester Manufacturing Company makes a product that it sells for $50 per unit. The company incurs variable manufacturing costs of $20 per unit. Variable selling expenses are $5 per unit, annual fixed manufacturing costs are $187,000, and fixed selling and administrative costs are $113,000 per year.

CHECK FIGURE
a. 12,000 units

Required

Determine the break-even point in units and dollars using each of the following approaches.

a. Contribution margin per unit.
b. Equation method.
c. Contribution margin ratio.
d. Confirm your results by preparing a contribution margin income statement for the break-even sales volume.

Problem 19-18A *Determining the break-even point and preparing a break-even graph*

L.O. 2, 6

Steinmetz Company is considering the production of a new product. The expected variable cost is $45 per unit. Annual fixed costs are expected to be $570,000. The anticipated sales price is $60 each.

CHECK FIGURE
a. $2,280,000

Required

Determine the break-even point in units and dollars using each of the following.

a. Contribution margin per unit approach.
b. Equation method.
c. Contribution margin ratio approach.
d. Prepare a break-even graph to illustrate the cost-volume-profit relationships.

Problem 19-19A *Effect of converting variable to fixed costs*

L.O. 2, 3, 4

Pinkerton Manufacturing Company reported the following data regarding a product it manufactures and sells. The sales price is $27.

CHECK FIGURE
b. 30,000 units

Variable costs	
Manufacturing	$10 per unit
Selling	6 per unit
Fixed costs:	
Manufacturing	$190,000 per year
Selling and administrative	85,000 per year

Required

a. Use the per unit contribution margin approach to determine the break-even point in units and dollars.
b. Use the per unit contribution margin approach to determine the level of sales in units and dollars required to obtain a profit of $55,000.
c. Suppose that variable selling costs could be eliminated by employing a salaried sales force. If the company could sell 45,000 units, how much could it pay in salaries for salespeople and still have a profit of $95,000? (*Hint:* Use the equation method.)

Problem 19-20A *Analyzing change in sales price using the contribution margin ratio*

L.O. 2, 3, 4

Aliant Company reported the following data regarding the product it sells.

CHECK FIGURE
c. 37,500 units

Sales price	$32
Contribution margin ratio	20%
Fixed costs	$540,000

Required

Use the contribution margin ratio approach and consider each requirement separately.

a. What is the break-even point in dollars? In units?
b. To obtain a profit of $80,000, what must the sales be in dollars? In units?
c. If the sales price increases to $40 and variable costs do not change, what is the new break-even point in dollars? In units?

L.O. 2

eXcel

mhhe.com/edmonds2007

CHECK FIGURE

a. 8,000 units

Problem 19-21A ***Analyzing sales price and fixed cost using the equation method***

Kruse Company is considering adding a new product. The cost accountant has provided the following data.

Expected variable cost of manufacturing	$41 per unit
Expected annual fixed manufacturing costs	$69,000

The administrative vice president has provided the following estimates.

Expected sales commission	$4 per unit
Expected annual fixed administrative costs	$31,000

The manager has decided that any new product must at least break even in the first year.

Required

Use the equation method and consider each requirement separately.

a. If the sales price is set at $57.50, how many units must Kruse sell to break even?

b. Kruse estimates that sales will probably be 10,000 units. What sales price per unit will allow the company to break even?

c. Kruse has decided to advertise the product heavily and has set the sales price at $60. If sales are 9,000 units, how much can the company spend on advertising and still break even?

L.O. 7

CHECK FIGURES

b. NI:

Skin Cream $102,000

Bath Oil $88,000

Color Gel $90,000

Problem 19-22A ***Margin of safety and operating leverage***

Musso Company is considering the addition of a new product to its cosmetics line. The company has three distinctly different options: a skin cream, a bath oil, or a hair coloring gel. Relevant information and budgeted annual income statements for each of the products follow.

	Relevant Information		
	Skin Cream	**Bath Oil**	**Color Gel**
Budgeted Sales in Units (a)	70,000	120,000	40,000
Expected Sales Price (b)	$8	$3	$12
Variable Costs Per Unit (c)	$5	$1	$ 7
Income Statements			
Sales Revenue (a × b)	$560,000	$360,000	$480,000
Variable Costs (a × c)	(350,000)	(120,000)	(280,000)
Contribution Margin	210,000	240,000	200,000
Fixed Costs	(150,000)	(200,000)	(150,000)
Net Income	$ 60,000	$ 40,000	$ 50,000

Required

a. Determine the margin of safety as a percentage for each product.

b. Prepare revised income statements for each product, assuming a 20 percent increase in the budgeted sales volume.

c. For each product, determine the percentage change in net income that results from the 20 percent increase in sales. Which product has the highest operating leverage?

d. Assuming that management is pessimistic and risk averse, which product should the company add to its cosmetic line? Explain your answer.

e. Assuming that management is optimistic and risk aggressive, which product should the company add to its cosmetics line? Explain your answer.

L.O. 2, 3, 4, 6, 7

Problem 19-23A ***Comprehensive CVP analysis***

Weissman Company makes and sells products with variable costs of $50 each. Weissman incurs annual fixed costs of $32,000. The current sales price is $70.

Required

The following requirements are interdependent. For example, the $8,000 desired profit introduced in Requirement *c* also applies to subsequent requirements. Likewise, the $60 sales price introduced in Requirement *d* applies to the subsequent requirements.

CHECK FIGURES
b. 1,600 units
c. 2,000 units
e. 3,200 units

a. Determine the contribution margin per unit.
b. Determine the break-even point in units and in dollars. Confirm your answer by preparing an income statement using the contribution margin format.
c. Suppose that Weissman desires to earn an $8,000 profit. Determine the sales volume in units and dollars required to earn the desired profit. Confirm your answer by preparing an income statement using the contribution margin format.
d. If the sales price drops to $60 per unit, what level of sales is required to earn the desired profit? Express your answer in units and dollars. Confirm your answer by preparing an income statement using the contribution margin format.
e. If fixed costs drop to $24,000, what level of sales is required to earn the desired profit? Express your answer in units and dollars. Confirm your answer by preparing an income statement using the contribution margin format.
f. If variable cost drops to $40 per unit, what level of sales is required to earn the desired profit? Express your answer in units and dollars. Confirm your answer by preparing an income statement using the contribution margin format.
g. Assume that Weissman concludes that it can sell 1,600 units of product for $60 each. Recall that variable costs are $40 each and fixed costs are $24,000. Compute the margin of safety in units and dollars and as a percentage.
h. Draw a break-even graph using the cost and price assumptions described in Requirement *g.*

Problem 19-24A ***Assessing simultaneous changes in CVP relationships***

L.O. 2, 3, 4, 6, 7

Green Shades Inc. (GSI) sells hammocks; variable costs are $75 each, and the hammocks are sold for $125 each. GSI incurs $250,000 of fixed operating expenses annually.

CHECK FIGURES
a. $750,000
c. 6,750 units

Required

a. Determine the sales volume in units and dollars required to attain a $50,000 profit. Verify your answer by preparing an income statement using the contribution margin format.
b. GSI is considering implementing a quality improvement program. The program will require a $10 increase in the variable cost per unit. To inform its customers of the quality improvements, the company plans to spend an additional $20,000 for advertising. Assuming that the improvement program will increase sales to a level that is 3,000 units above the amount computed in Requirement *a*, should GSI proceed with plans to improve product quality? Support your answer by preparing a budgeted income statement.
c. Determine the new break-even point in units and sales dollars as well as the margin of safety percentage, assuming that the quality improvement program is implemented.
d. Prepare a break-even graph using the cost and price assumptions outlined in Requirement *b.*

Appendix

Problem 19-25A ***Determining the break-even point and margin of safety for a company with multiple products***

L.O. 11

excel
mhhe.com/edmonds2007

Pinson Company produces two products. Budgeted annual income statements for the two products are provided here.

	Power					Lite					Total	
	Budgeted Number		Per Unit		Budgeted Amount	Budgeted Number		Per Unit		Budgeted Amount	Budgeted Number	Budgeted Amount
Sales	160	@	$500	=	$80,000	640	@	$450	=	$288,000	800	$368,000
Variable Cost	160	@	320	=	(51,200)	640	@	330	=	(211,200)	800	(262,400)
Contribution Margin	160	@	180	=	28,800	640	@	120	=	76,800	800	105,600
Fixed Cost					(12,000)					(54,000)		(66,000)
Net Income					$16,800					$ 22,800		$ 39,600

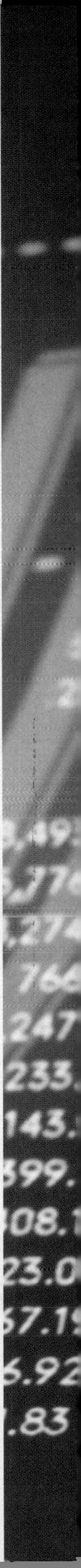

CHECK FIGURE
d. Power: 100 units
Lite: 400 units

Required

a. Based on budgeted sales, determine the relative sales mix between the two products.
b. Determine the weighted-average contribution margin per unit.
c. Calculate the break-even point in total number of units.
d. Determine the number of units of each product Pinson must sell to break even.
e. Verify the break-even point by preparing an income statement for each product as well as an income statement for the combined products.
f. Determine the margin of safety based on the combined sales of the two products.

EXERCISES—SERIES B

L.O. 2

Exercise 19-1B *Per unit contribution margin approach*

Sloan Corporation manufactures products that have variable costs of $10 per unit. Its fixed cost amounts to $81,000. It sells the products for $13 each.

Required
Use the per unit contribution margin approach to determine the break-even point in units and dollars.

L.O. 2

Exercise 19-2B *Equation method*

Rapaka Corporation manufactures products that it sells for $29 each. Variable costs are $20 per unit, and annual fixed costs are $450,000.

Required
Use the equation method to determine the break-even point in units and dollars.

L.O. 3

Exercise 19-3B *Contribution margin ratio*

Hooten Company incurs annual fixed costs of $310,000. Variable costs for Hooten's product are $18 per unit, and the sales price is $24 per unit. Hooten desires to earn a profit of $50,000.

Required
Use the contribution margin ratio approach to determine the sales volume in dollars and units required to earn the desired profit.

L.O. 3

Exercise 19-4B *Equation method*

Lundy Company manufactures a product that sells for $71 per unit. It incurs fixed costs of $390,000. Variable cost for its product is $50 per unit. Lundy desires to earn a target profit of $240,000.

Required
Use the equation method to determine the sales volume in units and dollars required to earn the desired profit.

L.O. 3

Exercise 19-5B *Fixed and variable cost per unit*

Nall Corporation broke even by producing and selling 37,000 units of product during 2005. It earned a contribution margin of $111,000 on sales of $740,000. The company determined that cost per unit of product was $20.

Required
Based on this information, determine the variable and fixed cost per unit of product.

L.O. 3

Exercise 19-6B *Determining variable cost from incomplete data*

Johnston Corporation produced 75,000 tires and sold them for $60 each during 2007. The company determined that fixed manufacturing cost per unit was $16 per tire. The company reported gross profit of $900,000 on its 2007 financial statements.

Required
Determine the total variable cost, the variable cost per unit, and the total contribution margin.

Exercise 19-7B *Contribution margin per unit approach for break-even and desired profit* — L.O. 2, 3

Information concerning a product produced by Odess Company appears here:

Sales price per unit	$786
Variable cost per unit	$426
Total fixed manufacturing and operating costs	$450,000

Required

Determine the following:

a. Contribution margin per unit.

b. Number of units Odess must sell to break even.

c. Sales level in units that Odess must reach in order to earn a profit of $90,000.

Exercise 19-8B *Change in sales price* — L.O. 4

Belcher Company manufactures a product that has a variable cost of $13 per unit. The company's fixed costs total $280,000. Belcher had net income of $80,000 in the previous year. Its product sells for $25 per unit. In an effort to increase the company's market share, management is considering lowering the product's selling price to $23 per unit.

Required

If Belcher desires to maintain net income of $80,000, how many additional units must it sell in order to justify the price decline?

Exercise 19-9B *Simultaneous change in sales price and desired profit* — L.O. 4

Use the cost data presented in Exercise 19-8B, but assume that in addition to increasing its market share by lowering its selling price to $23, Belcher desires to increase its net income by $40,000.

Required

Determine the number of units that Belcher must sell to earn the desired income.

Exercise 19-10B *Components of break-even graph* — L.O. 2, 3, 6

Austin, a 10-year-old boy, wants to sell lemonade on a hot summer day. He hopes to make enough money to buy a new Game Boy. Mark, his elder brother, tries to help him compute his prospect of doing so. The following is the relevant information:

Variable costs		
Lemonade		$0.30 per cup
Paper cup		$0.10 per cup
Fixed costs		
Table and chair	$36.00	
Price		$1.00 per cup

The adjacent graph depicts the dollar amount of cost or revenue on the vertical axis and the number of lemonade cups sold on the horizontal axis.

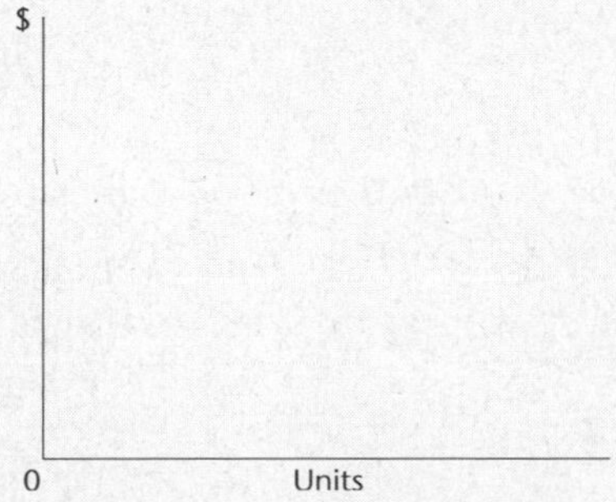

Required

a. Draw a line that depicts the total cost.

b. Draw a line that depicts the total revenue.

c. Identify the break-even point.

d. Identify the area representing profit.

e. Identify the area representing loss.

Exercise 19-11B *Evaluating simultaneous changes in fixed and variable costs* — L.O. 4

Crenshaw Company currently produces and sells 10,000 units of a telephone per year that has a variable cost of $10 per unit and a fixed cost of $275,000. The company currently earns a $125,000 annual

profit. Assume that Crenshaw has the opportunity to invest in a new machine that will enable the company to reduce variable costs to \$7 per unit. The investment would cause fixed costs to increase by \$18,000.

Required

a. Use the equation method to determine the sales price per unit under existing conditions (current machine is used).

b. Prepare a contribution margin income statement assuming Crenshaw invests in the new machine. Recommend whether Crenshaw should invest in the new machine.

L.O. 7

Exercise 19-12B *Margin of safety*

Suarez Company manufactures scanners that sell for \$135 each. The company pays \$55 per unit for the variable costs of the product and incurs fixed costs of \$1,600,000. Suarez expects to sell 36,000 scanners.

Required

Determine Suarez's margin of safety expressed as a percentage.

L.O. 2, 3, 4

Exercise 19-13B *Cost-volume-profit relationship*

Plutchak Corporation manufactures faucets. The variable costs of production are \$9 per faucet. Fixed costs of production are \$94,500. Plutchak sells the faucets for a price of \$30 per unit.

Required

a. How many faucets must Plutchak make and sell to break even?

b. How many faucets must Plutchak make and sell to earn a \$21,000 profit?

c. The marketing manager believes that sales would increase dramatically if the price were reduced to \$29 per unit. How many faucets must Plutchak make and sell to earn a \$21,000 profit, assuming the sales price is set at \$29 per unit?

L.O. 4

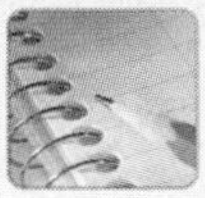

Exercise 19-14B *Understanding the global economy through CVP relationships*

An article published in the April 2, 2001, issue of *BusinessWeek* summarized several factors that had contributed to the economic slowdown that started in the fourth quarter of 2000. Specifically, the article stated, "When companies lowered their demand forecasts, they concluded that they didn't have just a little excess capacity—they had massive excessive capacity, . . ." The article continues to argue that companies with too much capacity have no desire to invest, no matter how low interest rates are.

Required

a. Identify the production cost factor(s) referred to that exhibit variable cost behavior. Has (have) the cost factor(s) increased or decreased? Explain why the variable costs have increased or decreased.

b. Identify the production cost factor(s) referred to that exhibit fixed cost behavior. Has (have) the cost factor(s) increased or decreased? Explain why the fixed costs have increased or decreased.

c. The article argues that new investments in production facilities will decrease. Explain the logic behind this argument.

d. In an economic downturn, manufacturers are pressured to sell their product at low prices. Comment on how low a manufacturer's prices can go before management decides to quit production.

L.O. 5

Exercise 19-15B *Target costing*

After substantial marketing research, Traynor Corporation management believes that it can make and sell a new battery with a prolonged life for laptop computers. Management expects the market demand for its new battery to be 10,000 units per year if the battery is priced at \$150 per unit. A team of engineers and accountants determines that the fixed costs of producing 8,000 units to 16,000 units is \$450,000.

Required

Assume that Traynor desires to earn a \$300,000 profit from the battery sales. How much can it afford to spend on variable cost per unit if production and sales equal 10,000 batteries?

Appendix

Exercise 19-16B ***Multiple product break-even analysis*** L.O. 11

Cain Company makes two products. The budgeted per unit contribution margin for each product follows:

	Product M	Product N
Sales price	$48	$75
Variable cost per unit	33	40
Contribution margin per unit	$15	$35

Cain expects to incur fixed costs of $115,000. The relative sales mix of the products is 60 percent for Product M and 40 percent for Product N.

Required

a. Determine the total number of products (units of M and N combined) Cain must sell to break even.
b. How many units each of Product M and Product N must Cain sell to break even?

PROBLEMS—SERIES B

Problem 19-17B ***Determining the break-even point and preparing a contribution margin income statement*** L.O. 2

Perkins Company manufactures radio and cassette players and sells them for $360 each. According to the company's records, the variable costs, including direct labor and direct materials, are $240. Factory depreciation and other fixed manufacturing costs are $292,000 per year. Perkins pays its salespeople a commission of $30 per unit. Annual fixed selling and administrative costs are $158,000.

Required

Determine the break-even point in units and dollars, using each of the following.

a. Contribution margin per unit approach.
b. Equation method.
c. Contribution margin ratio approach.
d. Confirm your results by preparing a contribution margin income statement for the break-even sales volume.

Problem 19-18B ***Determining the break-even point and preparing a break-even graph*** L.O. 2, 6

Executive officers of Rosenthal Company are assessing the profitability of a potential new product. They expect that the variable cost of making the product will be $36 per unit and fixed manufacturing cost will be $480,000. The executive officers plan to sell the product for $60 per unit.

Required

Determine the break-even point in units and dollars using each of the following approaches.

a. Contribution margin per unit.
b. Equation method.
c. Contribution margin ratio.
d. Prepare a break-even graph to illustrate the cost-volume-profit relationships.

Problem 19-19B ***Effect of converting variable to fixed costs*** L.O. 2, 3, 4

Hollis Company manufactures and sells its own brand of cameras. It sells each camera for $78. The company's accountant prepared the following data:

Manufacturing costs	
Variable	$18 per unit
Fixed	$150,000 per year
Selling and administrative expenses	
Variable	$6 per unit
Fixed	$66,000 per year

Required

a. Use the per unit contribution margin approach to determine the break-even point in units and dollars.

b. Use the per unit contribution margin approach to determine the level of sales in units and dollars required to obtain a $270,000 profit.

c. Suppose that variable selling and administrative costs could be eliminated by employing a salaried sales force. If the company could sell 9,500 units, how much could it pay in salaries for the salespeople and still have a profit of $270,000? (*Hint:* Use the equation method.)

L.O. 2, 3, 4

Problem 19-20B *Analyzing change in sales price using the contribution margin ratio*

Milby Company reported the following data regarding the one product it sells.

Sales price	$80
Contribution margin ratio	20%
Fixed costs	$160,000 per year

Required

Use the contribution margin ratio approach and consider each requirement separately.

a. What is the break-even point in dollars? In units?

b. To obtain an $80,000 profit, what must the sales be in dollars? In units?

c. If the sales price increases to $84 and variable costs do not change, what is the new break-even point in units? In dollars?

L.O. 2, 3, 4

Problem 19-21B *Analyzing sales price and fixed cost using the equation method*

Berger Company is analyzing whether its new product will be profitable. The following data are provided for analysis.

Expected variable cost of manufacturing	$39 per unit
Expected fixed manufacturing costs	$65,000 per year
Expected sales commission	$9 per unit
Expected fixed administrative costs	$16,000 per year

The company has decided that any new product must at least break even in the first year.

Required

Use the equation method and consider each requirement separately.

a. If the sales price is set at $75, how many units must Berger sell to break even?

b. Berger estimates that sales will probably be 4,000 units. What sales price per unit will allow the company to break even?

c. Berger has decided to advertise the product heavily and has set the sales price at $80. If sales are 3,500 units, how much can the company spend on advertising and still break even?

L.O. 7

Problem 19-22B *Margin of safety and operating leverage*

Fine Company has three distinctly different options available as it considers adding a new product to its automotive division: engine oil, coolant, or windshield washer. Relevant information and budgeted annual income statements for each product follow.

Relevant Information	Engine Oil	Coolant	Windshield Washer
Budgeted Sales in Units (a)	20,000	30,000	125,000
Expected Sales Price (b)	$2.40	$2.85	$1.15
Variable Costs Per Unit (c)	$1.00	$1.25	$0.35
Income Statements			
Sales Revenue (a × b)	$48,000	$85,500	$143,750
Variable Costs (a × c)	(20,000)	(37,500)	(43,750)
Contribution Margin	28,000	48,000	100,000
Fixed Costs	(21,000)	(32,000)	(50,000)
Net Income	$ 7,000	$16,000	$ 50,000

Required

a. Determine the margin of safety as a percentage for each product.

b. Prepare revised income statements for each product, assuming 20 percent growth in the budgeted sales volume.

c. For each product, determine the percentage change in net income that results from the 20 percent increase in sales. Which product has the highest operating leverage?

d. Assuming that management is pessimistic and risk averse, which product should the company add? Explain your answer.

e. Assuming that management is optimistic and risk aggressive, which product should the company add? Explain your answer.

Problem 19-23B ***Comprehensive CVP analysis*** **L.O. 2, 3, 4, 6, 7**

Mahdi Company makes a product that it sells for $75. Mahdi incurs annual fixed costs of $80,000 and variable costs of $50 per unit.

Required

The following requirements are interdependent. For example, the $20,000 desired profit introduced in Requirement *c* also applies to subsequent requirements. Likewise, the $70 sales price introduced in Requirement *d* applies to the subsequent requirements.

a. Determine the contribution margin per unit.

b. Determine the break-even point in units and in dollars. Confirm your answer by preparing an income statement using the contribution margin format.

c. Suppose that Mahdi desires to earn a $20,000 profit. Determine the sales volume in units and dollars required to earn the desired profit. Confirm your answer by preparing an income statement using the contribution margin format.

d. If the sales price drops to $70 per unit, what level of sales is required to earn the desired profit? Express your answer in units and dollars. Confirm your answer by preparing an income statement using the contribution margin format.

e. If fixed costs drop to $70,000, what level of sales is required to earn the desired profit? Express your answer in units and dollars. Confirm your answer by preparing an income statement using the contribution margin format.

f. If variable costs drop to $40 per unit, what level of sales is required to earn the desired profit? Express your answer in units and dollars. Confirm your answer by preparing an income statement using the contribution margin format.

g. Assume that Mahdi concludes that it can sell 4,800 units of product for $68 each. Recall that variable costs are $40 each and fixed costs are $70,000. Compute the margin of safety in units and dollars and as a percentage.

h. Draw a break-even graph using the cost and price assumptions described in Requirement *g*.

L.O. 2, 3, 4, 6, 7

Problem 19-24B ***Assessing simultaneous changes in CVP relationships***

Sarris Company sells tennis racquets; variable costs for each are \$75, and each is sold for \$105. Sarris incurs \$270,000 of fixed operating expenses annually.

Required

a. Determine the sales volume in units and dollars required to attain a \$120,000 profit. Verify your answer by preparing an income statement using the contribution margin format.

b. Sarris is considering establishing a quality improvement program that will require a \$10 increase in the variable cost per unit. To inform its customers of the quality improvements, the company plans to spend an additional \$60,000 for advertising. Assuming that the improvement program will increase sales to a level that is 5,000 units above the amount computed in Requirement *a,* should Sarris proceed with plans to improve product quality? Support your answer by preparing a budgeted income statement.

c. Determine the new break-even point and the margin of safety percentage, assuming Sarris adopts the quality improvement program.

d. Prepare a break-even graph using the cost and price assumptions outlined in Requirement *b.*

Appendix

L.O. 11

Problem 19-25B ***Determining the break-even point and margin of safety for a company with multiple products***

Executive officers of Witt Company have prepared the annual budgets for its two products, Washer and Dryer, as follows.

	Washer					Dryer					Total	
	Budgeted Number		Per Unit		Budgeted Amount	Budgeted Quantity		Per Unit		Budgeted Amount	Budgeted Quantity	Budgeted Amount
Sales	400	@	\$540	=	\$216,000	1,200	@	\$300	=	\$360,000	1,600	\$576,000
Variable Cost	400	@	300	=	(120,000)	1,200	@	180	=	(216,000)	1,600	(336,000)
Contribution Margin	400	@	240	=	96,000	1,200	@	120	=	144,000	1,600	240,000
Fixed Costs					(34,000)					(44,000)		(78,000)
Net Income					\$ 62,000					\$100,000		\$162,000

Required

a. Based on the number of units budgeted to be sold, determine the relative sales mix between the two products.

b. Determine the weighted-average contribution margin per unit.

c. Calculate the break-even point in total number of units.

d. Determine the number of units of each product Witt must sell to break even.

e. Verify the break-even point by preparing an income statement for each product as well as an income statement for the combined products.

f. Determine the margin of safety based on the combined sales of the two products.

ANALYZE, THINK, COMMUNICATE

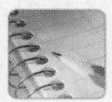

ATC 19-1 **Business Applications Case** ***Cost-volume-profit behavior at Apple Computer, Inc.***

On April 14, 2004, **Apple Computer** announced that revenues for the second quarter of its 2004 fiscal year rose 29 percent, causing earnings to increase by 300 percent compared with the second quarter of the previous year. This increase was largely due to significantly higher sales of its iPod MP3 music players. Sales for this quarter were \$1.91 billion.

On January 12, 2005, Apple announced that revenue for the first quarter of its 2005 fiscal year rose 74 percent causing earnings to increase by 468 percent compared with the second quarter of the previous year. Sales for this quarter were $3.49 billion. As in the previous year, sales of Apple's iPod continued to rise much faster than sales of its personal computers. By the end of 2004, revenue generated from iPod sales was considerably more than revenue from Apple's computer sales.

Required

a. What concept explains how Apple's net income could rise 300 percent when its revenue rose only 29 percent?

b. Does the concept identified in Requirement *a* result from fixed costs or variable costs?

c. Notice that in the second quarter of 2004 Apple's percentage increase in earnings was over 10 times more than the percentage increase in its revenue ($300 \div 29 = 10.3$). In the first quarter of 2005, however, Apple's percentage increase in earnings was only about six times that of revenue ($468 \div 74 = 6.3$). Explain why the ratio of increase in earnings to increase in revenue was lower in 2005 than in 2004. Assume Apple's general pricing policies and cost structure did not change.

ATC 19-2 Group Assignment *Effect of changes in fixed and variable cost on profitability*

In a month when it sold 200 units of product, Queen Manufacturing Company (QMC) produced the following internal income statement.

Revenue	$8,000
Variable Costs	(4,800)
Contribution Margin	3,200
Fixed Costs	(2,400)
Net Income	$ 800

QMC has the opportunity to alter its operations in one of the following ways:

1. Increasing fixed advertising costs by $1,600, thereby increasing sales by 120 units.
2. Lowering commissions paid to the sales staff by $8 per unit, thereby reducing sales by 10 units.
3. Decreasing fixed inventory holding cost by $800, thereby decreasing sales by 20 units.

Required

a. The instructor will divide the class into groups and then organize the groups into two sections. For a large class (12 or more groups), four sections may be necessary. At least three groups in each section are needed. Having more groups in one section than another section is acceptable because offsetting advantages and disadvantages exist. Having more groups is advantageous because more people will work on the task but is disadvantageous because having more people complicates communication.

Group Task

The sections are to compete with each other to see which section can identify the most profitable alternative in the shortest period of time. No instruction is provided regarding how the sections are to proceed with the task. In other words, each section is required to organize itself with respect to how to accomplish the task of selecting the best alternative. A total quality management (TQM) constraint is imposed that requires zero defects. A section that turns in a wrong answer is disqualified. Once an answer has been submitted to the instructor, it cannot be changed. Sections continue to turn in answers until all sections have submitted a response. The first section to submit the correct answer wins the competition.

b. If any section submits a wrong answer, the instructor or a spokesperson from the winning group should explain how the right answer was determined.

c. Discuss the dynamics of group interaction. How was the work organized? How was leadership established?

ATC 19-3 Research Assignment *Effect of costs changes*

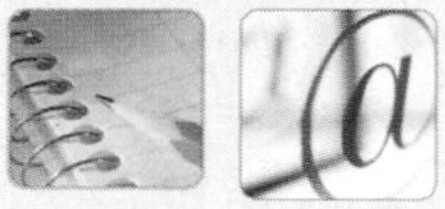

An article in the January 26, 2004, issue of *BusinessWeek* explains how automobile manufacturers in the United States are beginning to adopt a practice already prevalent among Japanese manufacturers.

Specifically, rather than build each model of vehicle on its own unique chassis, or platform, the same basic platform is being used as the foundation for several very different models. For example, **Honda** uses the platform designed for the Civic as the platform for the CR-V, Element, and Acura RSX.

Required

Read the article, "Detroit Tries It the Japanese Way," *BusinessWeek,* January 26, 2004, pp. 76–77. Based on the information in the article, prepare a memorandum that identifies as many reasons as you can think of to explain how using the same platform to produce several different models will reduce automobile manufacturers' costs. Be specific, and consider not only the concepts introduced in this chapter but also those from Chapters 14 and 15. For each reason you identify, provide a brief explanation about how this factor will help reduce the companies' costs. Also, explain which type of cost, fixed or variable, would be affected the most by the use of one platform to produce multiple models.

ATC 19-4 Writing Assignment *Operating leverage, margin of safety, and cost behavior*

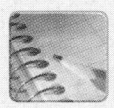

The article "Up Front: More Condensing at the Digest?" in the October 19, 1998, issue of *BusinessWeek* reported that Thomas Ryder, CEO of **Reader's Digest Association**, was considering a spin-off of Reader's Digest's direct-marketing operations into a joint venture with **Time Warner**. The article's author, Robert McNatt, noted that the direct marketing of books, music, and videos is a far larger part of the Reader's Digest business than is its namesake magazine. Furthermore, the article stated that 1998 direct-marketing sales of $1.6 billion were down 11 percent from 1997. The decline in revenue caused the division's operating profits to decline 58 percent. The article stated that the contemplated alliance with Time Warner could provide some fast help. Gerald Levin, Time Warner chairman, has said that his company's operations provide customer service and product fulfillment far better than other Web sellers do because of Time Warner's established 250 Web sites.

Required

a. Write a memo explaining how an 11 percent decrease in sales could result in a 58 percent decline in operating profits.

b. Explain briefly how the decline in revenue will affect the company's margin of safety.

c. Explain why a joint venture between Reader's Digest's direct-marketing division and Time Warner could work to the advantage of both companies. (*Hint:* Consider the effects of fixed cost behavior in formulating your response.)

ATC 19-5 Ethical Dilemma *Manipulating reported earnings*

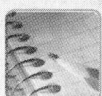

The article "Garbage In, Garbage Out" (*Fortune,* May 25, 1998, pp. 130–38) describes a litany of questionable accounting practices that ultimately led to the demise of **Waste Management, Inc.** Under pressure to retain its reputation on Wall Street as a growth company, Waste Management extended its estimates of the lives of its garbage trucks two to four years beyond the standard used in the industry. It also began to use a $25,000 expected salvage value on each truck when the industry standard was to recognize a zero salvage value. Because Waste Management owned approximately 20,000 trucks, these moves had a significant impact on the company's earnings. Extended lives and exaggerated salvage values were also applied to the company's 1.5 million steel dumpsters and its landfill facilities. These accounting practices boosted reported earnings by approximately $110 million per year. The long-term effect on real earnings was disastrous, however; maintenance costs began to soar and the company was forced to spend millions to keep broken-down trucks on the road. Overvalued assets failed to generate expected revenues. The failure to maintain earnings growth ultimately led to the replacement of management. When the new managers discovered the misstated accounting numbers, the company was forced to recognize a pretax charge of $3.54 billion in its 1997 income statement. The stock price plummeted, and the company was ultimately merged out of existence.

Required

a. Did Waste Management manipulate the recognition of fixed or variable costs?

b. Explain how extending the life estimate of an asset increases earnings and the book value of assets.

c. Explain how inflating the salvage value of an asset increases earnings and the book value of assets.

d. Speculate as to what motive would cause executives to manipulate earnings.

e. Review the standards of ethical conduct shown in Exhibit 14.13 of Chapter 14 and comment on whether Waste Management's accounting practices violated any standards.

COMPREHENSIVE PROBLEM

Use the same transaction data for Magnificent Modems Inc. as was used in Chapter 14. (See page 742).

Required

a. Use the following partially completed form to prepare an income statement using the contribution margin format.

Sales Revenue	$600,000
Variable Costs:	
Contribution Margin	225,000
Fixed costs	
Net income	$31,050

b. Determine the break-even point in units and in dollars.

c. Assume that next year's sales are budgeted to be the same as the current year's sales. Determine the margin of safety expressed as a percentage.

CHAPTER 20

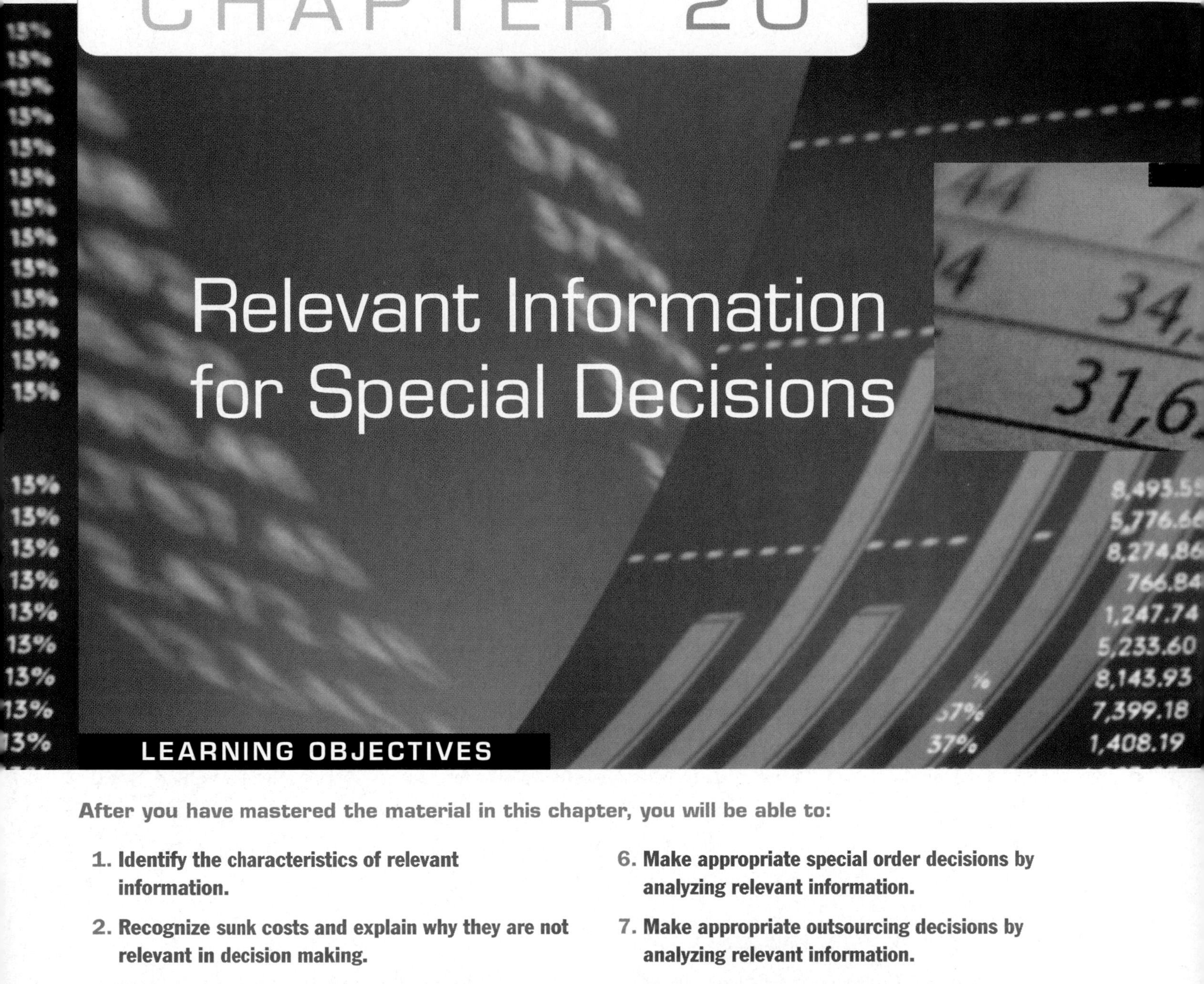

Relevant Information for Special Decisions

LEARNING OBJECTIVES

After you have mastered the material in this chapter, you will be able to:

1. **Identify the characteristics of relevant information.**
2. **Recognize sunk costs and explain why they are not relevant in decision making.**
3. **Distinguish between unit-level, batch-level, product-level, and facility-level costs and understand how these costs affect decision making.**
4. **Identify opportunity costs and explain why they are relevant in decision making.**
5. **Distinguish between quantitative and qualitative characteristics of decision making.**
6. **Make appropriate special order decisions by analyzing relevant information.**
7. **Make appropriate outsourcing decisions by analyzing relevant information.**
8. **Make appropriate segment elimination decisions by analyzing relevant information.**
9. **Make appropriate asset replacement decisions by analyzing relevant information.**
10. **Explain the conflict between short- and long-term profitability. (Appendix)**
11. **Make decisions about allocating scarce resources by analyzing relevant information. (Appendix)**

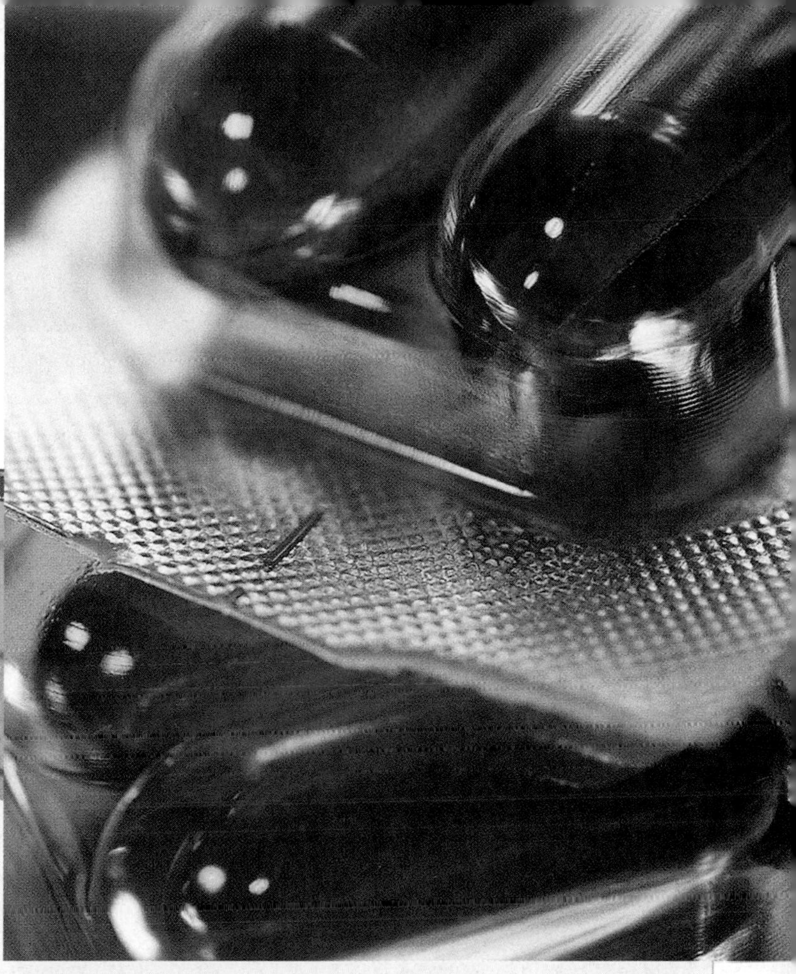

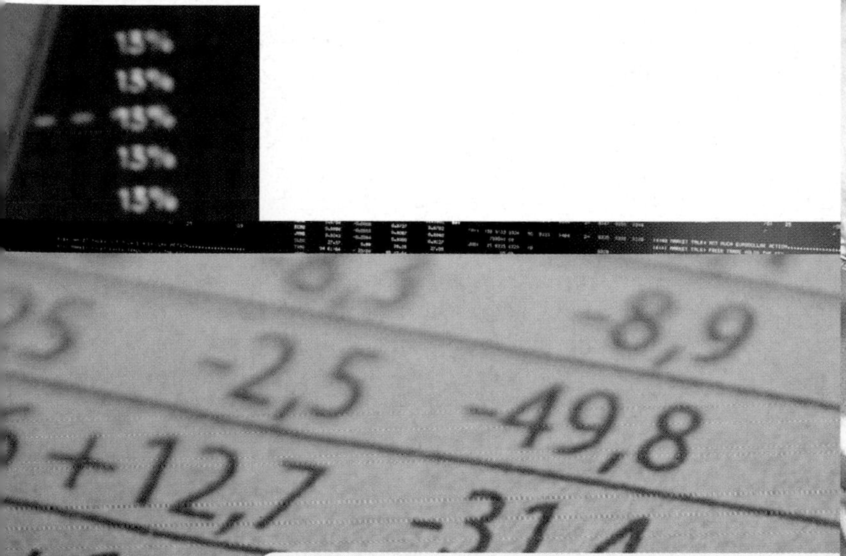

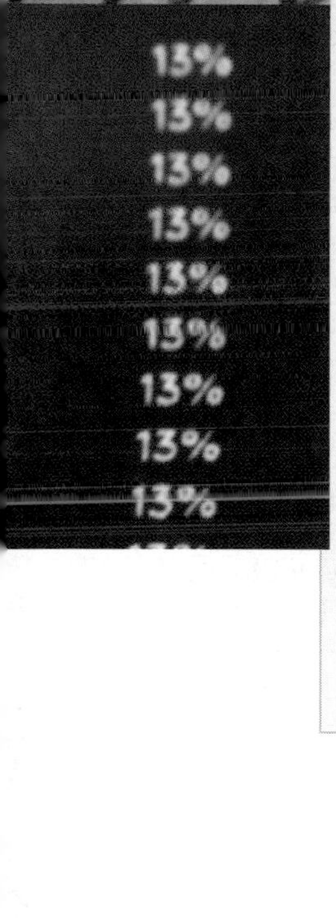

Chapter 20

The Curious Accountant

In February 2003 *The Wall Street Journal* ran an article about the difference between prescription drug prices in the United States and Canada. The article showed the Canadian prices for 10 popular prescription drugs, such as **Celebrex** and **Zocor**, were only 38 percent of prices charged in the United States.

Major pharmaceutical companies have *earnings before tax* that average around 25 percent of sales, indicating that their costs average around 75 percent of the prices they charge. In other words, it cost approximately 75 cents to generate one dollar of revenue. Given that drugs are sold in Canada for 38 percent of the U.S. sales price, a drug that is sold in the U.S. for a dollar would be sold in Canada for only 38 cents.

How can drugs be sold in Canada for less (38 cents) than cost (75 cents)? (Answer on page 976.)

CHAPTER OPENING

Mary Daniels is a partner in a small investment company. Her research indicates that Secor Inc. is a likely takeover target of a multinational corporation. Ms. Daniels wants to buy some Secor stock because she is certain its price will appreciate significantly in the immediate future. She is, however, short of cash. She wishes she had known about Secor last week when she bought 1,000 shares of Telstar Communications Inc. at $24 per share. Telstar had recently launched a series of satellites designed to make worldwide phone service feasible and convenient. With a small device not much larger than a thick credit card, customers could send and receive phone calls anywhere in the world. The day after Ms. Daniels bought the stock, Telstar announced technical difficulties with the satellites, and its stock price dropped to $20 per share. She told herself that Telstar stock is going nowhere, but if she sold it now, she'd take a $4,000 loss [($24 cost − $20 market) × 1,000 shares]. Ms. Daniels decided to hold the Telstar stock instead of selling it and buying Secor. The Secor stock seemed like a sure thing, but she didn't want to incur a loss. Did Ms. Daniels make the right decision? ■

The Decision Environment

Business decision makers cope with enormous challenges. They frequently must make decisions with incomplete information, yet are also faced with an overabundance of useless information. Highly successful executives may seem to have an uncanny knack for distinguishing between relevant and irrelevant data. Success, however, is not a matter of luck. The keys to effective decision making are discussed in the following pages.

Relevant Information

LO 1

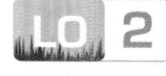

Identify the characteristics of relevant information.

Two primary characteristics distinguish relevant from useless information. First, **relevant information** *differs among the alternatives under consideration.* Suppose you are deciding between two job offers. Both jobs offer the same salary. Salary, therefore, is not *relevant* to the decision-making process. Although salary is important in choosing a job, it is not relevant in choosing between these two job offers. If you receive a third job offer that pays a different salary, salary then becomes relevant because you could differentiate the third offer from the other two.

A second characteristic of relevant information is that it is *future oriented.* "Don't cry over spilled milk." "It's water over the dam." These aphorisms remind people they cannot change the past. With regard to business decisions, the principle means *you cannot avoid a cost that has already been incurred.*

To illustrate, return to the opening of this chapter. Recall that Mary Daniels had purchased 1,000 shares of Telstar stock at $24 per share. She had an opportunity to sell the Telstar stock at $20 per share and invest the proceeds in Secor shares, which were expected to increase in value because Secor was rumored to be the target of a takeover attempt. Ms. Daniels decided to keep her investment in Telstar because she did not want to incur a loss. Did she make the right choice?

Whether Ms. Daniels will make more money by holding the Telstar stock instead of selling it and buying Secor is unknown. The stock price of either company could go up or down. However, she based the decision on *irrelevant* data. Ms. Daniels incurred a loss *when the price of Telstar dropped.* She cannot *avoid* a loss that already exists. Past mistakes should not affect current decisions. Owning the Telstar stock is equivalent to having $20,000 cash today. The relevant question is whether to invest the $20,000 in Telstar or Secor. If Secor is the better alternative, Ms. Daniels should sell the Telstar stock and buy Secor stock.

Sunk Cost

LO 2

Recognize sunk costs and explain why they are not relevant in decision making.

Ms. Daniels' Telstar stock investment is an example of a *sunk cost.* A **sunk cost** has been incurred in a past transaction. *Since* sunk costs *have been incurred in past transactions and cannot be changed, they are not relevant for making current decisions.*

Why even bother to collect historical information if it is not relevant? Historical information may be useful in predicting the future. A company that earned $5,000,000 last year is more likely to earn $5,000,000 this year than a company that earned $5,000 last year. The predictive capacity is relevant because it provides insight into the future.

Relevant (Differential) Revenues

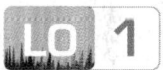

LO 1 Identify the characteristics of relevant information.

As indicated, relevant revenues must (1) be future oriented and (2) differ for the alternatives under consideration. Since relevant revenues differ between the alternatives, they are sometimes called **differential revenues.** For example, suppose that Pecks Department Stores sells men's, women's, and children's clothing and is considering eliminating the children's line. The revenue generated by the children's department is *differential (relevant) revenue* because Pecks' total revenue would be different if the department were eliminated.

Relevant (Avoidable) Costs

LO 1 Identify the characteristics of relevant information.

Businesses seek to minimize cost. Managers *avoid* costs whenever possible. In fact, **relevant costs** are frequently called **avoidable costs.** Avoidable (relevant) costs are the costs managers can eliminate by making specific choices. Return to the Pecks Department Stores example. Costs management could avoid by eliminating the children's department include: merchandise cost; the salaries of buyers and sales staff; interest on debt used to finance the inventory; packaging and transportation; insurance; lost, damaged, and stolen merchandise; uncollectible accounts; shopping bags; sales slips; price tags; and other supplies. Many other costs could *not* be avoided. For example, the company president's salary cannot be avoided by closing down the children's line. Pecks will pay the president her salary whether or not it closes the children's department. Other costs that cannot be avoided include depreciation on the buildings, rent, property taxes, general advertising, and storewide utilities. If a cost is the same (does not *differ*) for two alternatives, it cannot be avoided by selecting one of the alternatives. In other words, *avoidable costs differ between the alternatives.*

Topic Tackler PLUS 20-1

Relationship of Cost Avoidance to a Cost Hierarchy

LO 3 Distinguish between unit-level, batch-level, product-level, and facility-level costs and understand how these costs affect decision making.

Classifying costs into one of four hierarchical levels helps identify avoidable costs.[1]

1. *Unit-level costs.* Costs incurred each time a company generates one unit of product are **unit-level costs.**[2] Examples include the cost of direct materials, direct labor, inspections, packaging, shipping, and handling. Incremental (additional) unit-level costs increase *with each additional unit of product generated. Unit-level costs can be avoided by eliminating the production of a single unit of product.*

[1] R. Cooper and R. S. Kaplan, *The Design of Cost Management Systems* (Englewood Cliffs, NJ: Prentice-Hall, 1991). Our classifications are broader than those typically presented. They encompass service and merchandising companies as well as manufacturing businesses. The original cost hierarchy was developed as a platform for activity-based costing. These classifications are equally useful as a tool for identifying avoidable costs.

[2] Recall that we use the term *product* in a generic sense to represent producing goods or services.

2. *Batch-level costs.* Many products are generated in batches rather than individual units. For example, a heating and air conditioning technician may service a batch of air conditioners in an apartment complex. Some of the job costs apply only to individual units, and other costs relate to the entire batch. For instance, the labor to service each air conditioner is a unit-level cost, but the cost of driving to the site is a **batch-level cost.**

   Classifying costs as unit- versus batch-level frequently depends on the context rather than the type of cost. For example, shipping and handling costs to send 200 computers to a university are batch-level costs. In contrast, the shipping and handling cost to deliver a single computer to each of a number of individual customers is a unit-level cost. Eliminating a batch of work avoids both batch-level and unit-level costs. Similarly, adding a batch of work increases batch-level and unit-level costs. Increasing the number of units in a particular batch increases unit-level but not batch-level costs. Decreasing the number of units in a batch reduces unit-level costs but not batch-level costs.

3. *Product-level costs.* Costs incurred to support specific products or services are called **product-level costs.** Product-level costs include quality inspection costs, engineering design costs, the costs of obtaining and defending patents, the costs of regulatory compliance, and inventory holding costs such as interest, insurance, maintenance, and storage. *Product-level costs can be avoided by discontinuing a product line.* For example, suppose the Snapper Company makes the engines used in its lawn mowers. Buying engines from an outside supplier instead of making them would allow Snapper to avoid the product-level costs such as legal fees for patents, manufacturing supervisory costs of producing the engines, and the maintenance and inventory costs of holding engine parts.
4. *Facility-level costs.* **Facility-level costs** are incurred to support the entire company. They are not related to any specific product, batch, or unit of product. Because these costs maintain the facility as a whole, they are frequently called *facility-sustaining costs.* Facility-level costs include building rent or depreciation, personnel administration and training, property and real estate taxes, insurance, maintenance, administrative salaries, general selling costs, landscaping, utilities, and security. Total facility-level costs cannot be avoided unless the entire company is dissolved. However, eliminating a business segment (such as a division, department, or office) may enable a company to avoid some facility-level costs. For example, if a bank eliminates one of its branches, it can avoid the costs of renting, maintaining, and insuring that particular branch building. In general, *segment-level* facility costs can be avoided when a segment is eliminated. In contrast, *corporate-level* facility costs cannot be avoided unless the corporation is eliminated.

Precise distinctions between the various categories are often difficult to draw. One company may incur sales staff salaries as a facility-level cost while another company may pay sales commissions traceable to product lines or even specific units of a product line. Cost classifications cannot be memorized. Classifying specific cost items into the appropriate categories requires thoughtful judgment.

Relevance Is an Independent Concept

The concept of relevance is independent from the concept of cost behavior. In a given circumstance, relevant costs could be either fixed or variable. Consider the following illustration. Executives of Better Bakery Products are debating whether to add a new product, either cakes or pies, to the company's line. Projected costs for the two options follow.

Cost of Cakes		Cost of Pies	
Materials (per unit)	$ 1.50	Materials (per unit)	$ 2.00
Direct labor (per unit)	1.00	Direct labor (per unit)	1.00
Supervisor's salary*	25,000.00	Supervisor's salary*	25,000.00
Franchise fee†	50,000.00	Advertising‡	40,000.00

*It will be necessary to hire a new production supervisor at a cost of $25,000 per year.
†Cakes will be distributed under a nationally advertised label. Better Bakery pays an annual franchise fee for the right to use the product label. Because of the established brand name, Better Bakery will not be required to advertise the product.
‡Better Bakery will market the pies under its own name and will advertise the product in the local market in which the product sells.

Which costs are relevant? Fifty cents per unit of the materials can be avoided by choosing cakes instead of pies. A portion of the materials cost is therefore relevant. Labor costs will be one dollar per unit whether Better Bakery makes cakes or pies. Labor cost is therefore not relevant. Although both materials and direct labor are variable costs, one is relevant but the other is not.

Since Better Bakery must hire a supervisor under either alternative, the supervisor's salary is not relevant. The franchise fee can be avoided if Better Bakery makes pies and advertising costs can be avoided if it makes cakes. All three of these costs are fixed, but only two are relevant. Finally, all the costs (whether fixed or variable) could be avoided if Better Bakery rejects both products. Whether a cost is fixed or variable has no bearing on its relevance.

LO 1

Identify the characteristics of relevant information.

Relevance of Opportunity Costs

LO 4

Identify opportunity costs and explain why they are relevant in decision making.

Suppose you pay $50 for a highly sought-after ticket to an Olympic event. Just outside the stadium, someone offers to buy your ticket for $500. If you decline the offer, how much does attending the event cost you? From a decision-making perspective, the cost is $500. If you enter the stadium, you give up the *opportunity* to obtain $500 cash. The relevant cost is $500. The $50 original purchase price is an irrelevant *sunk cost.* The sacrifice represented by a lost opportunity is an **opportunity cost.** Opportunity costs that are (1) future oriented and (2) differ between the alternatives are relevant for decision-making purposes.

Suppose a few minutes after you turn down the offer to sell your ticket for $500, another person offers you $600 for the ticket. If you decline the second offer, has your opportunity cost risen to $1,100 (the first $500 offer plus the second $600 offer)? No; opportunity costs are not cumulative. If you had accepted the first offer, you could not have accepted the second. You may have many opportunities, but accepting one alternative eliminates the possibility of accepting any others. Accountants normally measure opportunity cost as the highest value of the available alternative courses of action. In this case, the opportunity cost of attending the Olympic event is $600.

Opportunity costs are not recorded in financial accounting records and are not reported in financial statements. You would not report the above described $600 opportunity cost as an expense on the income statement, but it will certainly affect your decision about whether to attend the Olympic event. *Opportunity costs are relevant costs.*

CHECK YOURSELF 20.1

Aqua Inc. makes statues for use in fountains. On January 1, 2003, the company paid $13,500 for a mold to make a particular type of statue. The mold had an expected useful life of four years and a salvage value of $1,500. On January 1, 2005, the mold had a market value of $3,000 and a salvage value of $1,200. The expected useful life did not change. What is the relevant cost of using the mold during 2005?

Answer

The relevant cost of using the mold in 2005 is the opportunity cost ([market value − salvage value] ÷ remaining useful life), in this case, ($3,000 − $1,200) ÷ 2 = $900. The book value of the asset and associated depreciation is based on a sunk cost that cannot be avoided because it has already been incurred and therefore is not relevant to current decisions. In contrast, Aqua could avoid the opportunity cost (market value) by selling the mold.

REALITY BYTES

Determining what price to charge for their company's goods or services is one of the most difficult decisions that business managers make. Charge too much and customers will go elsewhere. Charge less than customers are willing to pay and lose the opportunity to earn profits. This problem is especially difficult when managers are deciding if they should reduce (mark down) the price of aging inventory—for example, flowers that are beginning to wilt, fruit that is beginning to over-ripen, or clothing that is going out of season.

At first managers may be reluctant to mark down the inventory below its cost because this would cause the company to take a loss on the aging inventory. However, the concept of sunk cost applies here. Since the existing inventory has already been paid for, its cost is sunk. Since the cost is sunk it is not relevant to the decision. Does this mean the merchandise should be sold for any price? Not necessarily. The concept of opportunity cost must also be considered.

If the goods are marked down too far, too quickly, they may be sold for less than is possible. The lost potential revenue is an opportunity cost. To minimize the opportunity cost, the amount of a markdown must be the smallest amount necessary to sell the merchandise. The decision is further complicated by qualitative considerations. If a business develops a reputation for repeated markdowns, customers may hesitate to buy goods, thinking that the price will fall further if they only wait a while. The result is a dilemma as to when and how much to mark down aging inventories.

How do managers address this dilemma? Part of the answer has been the use of technology. For years airlines have used computerized mathematical models to help them decide how many seats on a particular flight should be sold at a discount. More recently, retailers have used this same type of modeling software. Such software allows retailers to take fewer markdowns at more appropriate times, thereby resulting in higher overall gross profit margins.

(For a more complete discussion of this topic, see *The Wall Street Journal,* August 7, 2001, pp. A-1, A-6.)

Relevance Is Context-Sensitive

LO 1

Identify the characteristics of relevant information.

A particular cost that is relevant in one context may be irrelevant in another. Consider a store that carries men's, women's, and children's clothing. The store manager's salary could not be avoided by eliminating the children's department, but it could be avoided if the entire store were closed. The salary is not relevant to deciding whether to eliminate the children's department but is relevant with respect to deciding to close a store. In one context, the salary is not relevant. In the other context, it is relevant.

Relationship Between Relevance and Accuracy

LO 1

Identify the characteristics of relevant information.

Information need not be exact to be relevant. You may decide to delay purchasing a laptop computer you want if you know its price is going to drop even if you don't know exactly how much the price decrease will be. You know part of the cost can be avoided by waiting; you are just not sure of the amount.

The most useful information is both relevant and precise. Totally inaccurate information is useless. Likewise, irrelevant information is useless regardless of its accuracy.

Quantitative Versus Qualitative Characteristics of Decision Making

LO 5

Distinguish between quantitative and qualitative characteristics of decision making.

Relevant information can have both **quantitative** and **qualitative characteristics.** The previous examples focused on quantitative data. Now consider qualitative issues. Suppose you are deciding which of two laptop computers to purchase. Computer A costs $300 more than Computer B. Both computers satisfy your technical requirements; however, Computer A has a more attractive appearance. From a quantitative standpoint, you would select Computer B because you could avoid $300 of cost. However, if the laptop will be used in circumstances when clients need to be impressed, appearance—a qualitative characteristic—may be more important than minimizing cost. You might purchase Computer A even though quantitative factors favor Computer B. Both qualitative and quantitative data are relevant to decision making.

As with quantitative data, qualitative features must *differ* between the alternatives to be relevant. If the two computers were identical in appearance, attractiveness would not be relevant to making the decision.

Topic Tackler PLUS

20-2

Relevant Information and Special Decisions

LO 6

Make appropriate special order decisions by analyzing relevant information.

Five types of special decisions are frequently encountered in business practice: (1) special order, (2) outsourcing, (3) segment elimination, (4) asset replacement, and (5) scarce resource allocation. The following sections discuss using relevant information in making the first four types of special decisions. The Appendix to this chapter discusses scarce resource decisions.

Special Order Decisions

Occasionally, a company receives an offer to sell its goods at a price significantly below its normal selling price. The company must make a **special order decision** to accept or reject the offer.

Quantitative Analysis

Assume Premier Office Products manufactures printers. Premier expects to make and sell 2,000 printers in 10 batches of 200 units per batch during the coming year. Expected production costs are summarized in Exhibit 20.1.

Adding its normal markup to the total cost per unit, Premier set the selling price at $360 per printer.

Suppose Premier receives a *special order* from a new customer for 200 printers. If Premier accepts the order, its expected sales would increase from 2,000 units to 2,200 units. But the special order customer is willing to pay only $250 per printer. This price is well below not only Premier's normal selling price of $360 but also the company's expected per unit cost of $329.25. Should Premier accept or reject the special order? At first glance, it seems Premier should reject the special order because the customer's offer is below the expected cost per unit. Analyzing relevant costs and revenue leads, however, to a different conclusion.

EXHIBIT 20.1

Budgeted Cost for Expected Production of 2,000 Printers

Unit-level costs		
Materials costs (2,000 units × $90)	$180,000	
Labor costs (2,000 units × $82.50)	165,000	
Overhead (2,000 units × $7.50)	15,000	
Total unit-level costs (2,000 × $180)		$360,000
Batch-level costs		
Assembly setup (10 batches × $1,700)	17,000	
Materials handling (10 batches × $500)	5,000	
Total batch-level costs (10 batches × $2,200)		22,000
Product-level costs		
Engineering design	14,000	
Production manager salary	63,300	
Total product-level costs		77,300
Facility-level costs		
Segment-level costs		
Division manager's salary	85,000	
Administrative costs	12,700	
Corporate-level costs		
Company president's salary	43,200	
Depreciation	27,300	
General expenses	31,000	
Total facility-level costs		199,200
Total expected cost		$658,500
Cost per unit: $658,500 ÷ 2,000 = $329.25		

Answers to The Curious Accountant

There are several factors that enable drug companies to reduce their prices to certain customers. One significant factor is the issue of relevant cost. Pharmaceutical manufacturers have a substantial amount of fixed cost, such as research and development. For example, in 2002 Pfizer, Inc., had research and development expenses that were 16 percent of sales, while its cost of goods sold expense was only 12.5 percent of sales. With respect to a special order decision, the research and development costs would not change and therefore would not be relevant. In contrast, the unit-level cost of goods sold would increase and therefore would be relevant. Clearly, relevant costs are significantly less than the total cost. If Canadian prices are based on relevant costs, that is, if drug companies view Canadian sales as a special order opportunity, the lower prices may provide a contribution to profitability even though they are significantly less than the prices charged in the United States.

The quantitative analysis follows in three steps.

Step 1 **Determine the amount of the relevant (differential) revenue Premier will earn by accepting the special order.** Premier's alternatives are (1) to accept or (2) to reject the special order. If Premier accepts the special order, additional revenue will be \$50,000 (\$250 × 200 units). If Premier rejects the special order, additional revenue will be zero. Since the amount of revenue differs between the alternatives, the \$50,000 is relevant.

Step 2 **Determine the amount of the relevant (differential) cost Premier will incur by accepting the special order.** Examine the costs in Exhibit 20.1. If Premier accepts the special order, it will incur additional unit-level costs (materials, labor, and overhead). It will also incur the cost of one additional 200-unit batch. The unit- and batch-level costs are relevant because Premier could avoid them by rejecting the special order. The other costs in Exhibit 20.1 are not relevant because Premier will incur them whether it accepts or rejects the special order.

Step 3 **Accept the special order if the relevant revenue exceeds the relevant (avoidable) cost. Reject the order if relevant cost exceeds relevant revenue.** Exhibit 20.2 summarizes the relevant figures. Since the relevant revenue exceeds the relevant cost, Premier should accept the special order because profitability will increase by \$11,800.

EXHIBIT 20.2

Relevant Information for Special Order of 200 Printers

Differential revenue (\$250 × 200 units)	\$50,000
Avoidable unit-level costs (\$180 × 200 units)	(36,000)
Avoidable batch-level costs (\$2,200 × 1 batch)	(2,200)
Contribution to income	\$11,800

Opportunity Costs

Premier can consider the special order because it has enough excess productive capacity to make the additional units. Suppose Premier has the opportunity to lease its excess capacity (currently unused building and equipment) for \$15,000. If Premier uses the excess capacity to make the additional printers, it must forgo the opportunity to lease the excess capacity to a third party. Sacrificing the potential leasing income represents an opportunity cost of accepting the special order. Adding this opportunity cost to the other relevant costs increases the cost of accepting the special order to \$53,200 (\$38,200 unit-level and batch-level costs + \$15,000 opportunity cost). The avoidable costs would then exceed the differential revenue, resulting in a projected loss of $3,200 ($50,000 differential revenue − $53,200 avoidable costs). Under these circumstances Premier would be better off rejecting the special order and leasing the excess capacity.

Relevance and the Decision Context

Assume Premier does not have the opportunity to lease its excess capacity. Recall the original analysis indicated the company could earn an $11,800 contribution to profit by accepting a special order to sell 200 printers at $250 per unit (see Exhibit 20.2). Because Premier can earn a contribution to profit by selling printers for $250 each, can the company reduce its normal selling price (price charged to existing customers) to $250? The answer is no, as illustrated in Exhibit 20.3.

EXHIBIT 20.3

Projections Based on 2,200 Printers at a Sales Price of $250 per Unit

Revenue ($250 × 2,200 units)		$ 550,000
Unit-level costs ($180 × 2,200 units)	$396,000	
Batch-level costs ($2,200 × 11 batches)	24,200	
Product-level costs	77,300	
Facility-level costs	199,200	
Total cost		(696,700)
Projected loss		$(146,700)

If a company is to be profitable, it must ultimately generate revenue in excess of total costs. Although the facility-level and product-level costs are not relevant to the special order decision, they are relevant to the operation of the business as a whole.

Qualitative Characteristics

LO 7

Make appropriate outsourcing decisions by analyzing relevant information.

Should a company ever reject a special order if the relevant revenues exceed the relevant costs? Qualitative characteristics may be even more important than quantitative ones. If Premier's regular customers learn the company sold printers to another buyer at $250 per unit, they may demand reduced prices on future purchases. Exhibit 20.3 shows Premier cannot reduce the price for all customers. Special order customers should therefore come from outside Premier's normal sales territory. In addition, special order customers should be advised that the special price does not apply to repeat business. Cutting off a special order customer who has been permitted to establish a continuing relationship is likely to lead to ill-feelings and harsh words. A business's reputation can depend on how management handles such relationships. Finally, at full capacity, Premier should reject any special orders at reduced prices because filling those orders reduces its ability to satisfy customers who pay full price.

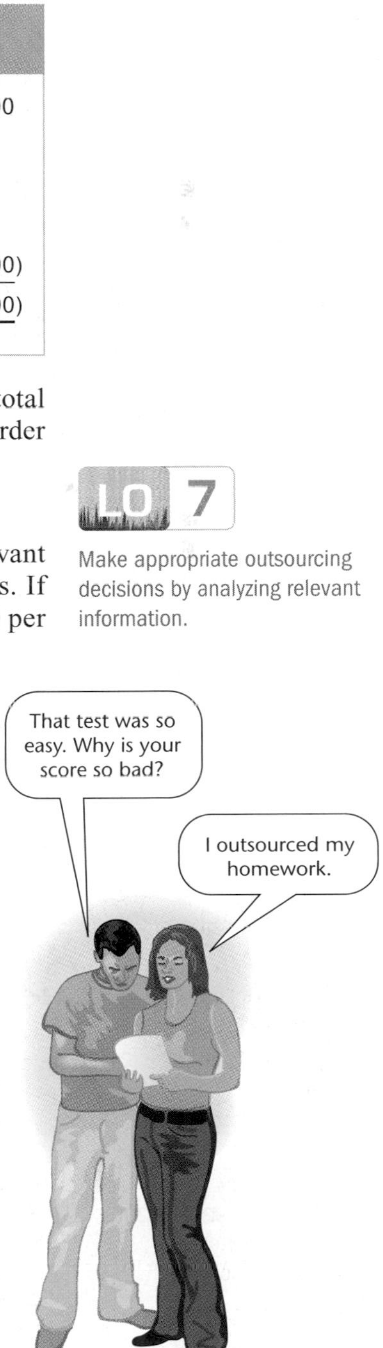

Outsourcing Decisions

Companies can sometimes purchase products they need for less than it would cost to make them. This circumstance explains why automobile manufacturers purchase rather than make many of the parts in their cars or why a caterer might buy gourmet desserts from a specialty company. Buying goods and services from other companies rather than producing them internally is commonly called **outsourcing.**

Quantitative Analysis

Assume Premier Office Products is considering whether to outsource production of the printers it currently makes. A supplier has offered to sell an unlimited supply of printers to Premier for $240 each. The estimated cost of making the printers is $329.25 per unit (see Exhibit 20.1). The data suggest that Premier could save money by outsourcing. Analyzing relevant costs proves this presumption wrong.

A two-step quantitative analysis for the outsourcing decision follows:

Step 1 **Determine the production costs Premier can avoid if it outsources printer production.** A review of Exhibit 20.1 discloses the costs Premier could avoid by outsourcing. If Premier purchases the printers, it can avoid the unit-level costs (materials, labor, overhead), assembly setup costs, and materials handling costs. It can also avoid the product-level costs (engineering design costs and production manager salary). Deciding to outsource will not, however, affect the facility-level costs. Because Premier will incur them whether or not it outsources printer production, the facility-level costs are not relevant to the outsourcing decision. Exhibit 20.4 shows the avoidable (relevant) costs of outsourcing.

EXHIBIT 20.4

Relevant Cost of Expected Production for Outsourcing 2,000 Printers

Unit-level costs ($180 × 2,000 units)	$360,000
Batch-level costs ($2,200 × 10 batches)	22,000
Product-level costs	77,300
Total relevant cost	$459,300
Cost per unit: $459,300 ÷ 2,000 = $229.65	

Step 2 **Compare the avoidable (relevant) production costs with the cost of buying the product and select the lower-cost option.** Because the relevant production cost is less than the purchase price of the printers ($229.65 per unit versus $240.00), the quantitative analysis suggests that Premier should continue to make the printers. Profitability would decline by $20,700 [$459,300 − ($240 × 2,000)] if printer production were outsourced.

Opportunity Costs

Suppose Premier's accountant determines that the space Premier currently uses to manufacture printers could be converted to warehouse space for storing finished goods. Using this space for warehouse storage would save Premier the $40,000 per year it currently spends to rent warehouse space. By using the space to manufacture printers, Premier is *forgoing the opportunity* to save $40,000 in warehouse costs. Because this *opportunity cost* can be avoided by purchasing the printers, it is relevant to the outsourcing decision. After adding the opportunity cost to the other relevant costs, the total relevant cost increases to $499,300 ($459,300 + $40,000) and the relevant cost per unit becomes $249.65 ($499,300 ÷ 2,000). Since Premier can purchase printers for $240, it should outsource printer production. It would be better off buying the printers and using the warehouse space to store finished goods than to continue producing the printers.

Evaluating the Effect of Growth on the Level of Production

The decision to outsource would change if expected production increased from 2,000 to 3,000 units. Because some of the avoidable costs are fixed relative to the level of production, cost per unit decreases as volume increases. For example, the product-level costs (engineering design, production manager's salary, and opportunity cost) are fixed relative to the level of production. Exhibit 20.5 shows the relevant cost per unit if Premier expects to produce 3,000 printers.

EXHIBIT 20.5

Relevant Cost of Expected Production for Outsourcing 3,000 Printers

Unit-level costs ($180 × 3,000 units)	$540,000
Batch-level costs ($2,200 × 15 batches)	33,000
Product-level costs	77,300
Opportunity cost	40,000
Total relevant cost	$690,300
Cost per unit: $690,300 ÷ 3,000 units = $230.10	

At 3,000 units of production, the relevant cost of making printers is less than the cost of outsourcing ($230.10 versus $240.00). If management believes

FOCUS ON INTERNATIONAL ISSUES

OUTSOURCING—HOW DO THEY DO IT IN JAPAN?

Many outsourcing opportunities suffer from a lack of long-term commitment. For example, a supplier may be able to attain economic efficiencies by redesigning its facilities to produce a product needed by a special order customer. Unfortunately, the redesign cost cannot be recovered on a small order quantity. The supplier needs assurances of a long-term relationship to justify a significant investment in the supply relationship. Japanese businesses have resolved this problem through what are sometimes called *obligational contract relationships*. While these contracts are renewable annually, most suppliers expect to form a supply relationship that will last more than five years. Indeed, Japanese custom establishes a commitment between the supplier and the buyer that includes the exchange of sensitive cost information. If deficiencies in price, delivery, or quality conformance occur, the buyer is likely to send production engineers to the offices of the supplier. The buyer's engineers will study the facilities of the supplier and give detailed advice as to how to achieve improved results. In the process of analyzing the supplier's operations, the buyer obtains detailed information regarding the supplier's costs. This information is used to negotiate prices that ensure reasonable rather than excessive profits for the supplier. Costs are controlled for not only the supplier but also the buyer.

Source: Miles B. Gietzmann, "Emerging Practices in Cost Accounting," *Management Accounting* (UK), January 1995, pp. 24–25.

the company is likely to experience growth in the near future, it should reject the outsourcing option. Managers must consider potential growth when making outsourcing decisions.

Qualitative Features

A company that uses **vertical integration** controls the full range of activities from acquiring raw materials to distributing goods and services. Outsourcing reduces the level of vertical integration, passing some of a company's control over its products to outside suppliers. The reliability of the supplier is critical to an outsourcing decision. An unscrupulous supplier may lure an unsuspecting manufacturer into an outsourcing decision using **low-ball pricing.** Once the manufacturer is dependent on the supplier, the supplier raises prices. If a price sounds too good to be true, it probably is too good to be true. Other potential problems include product quality and delivery commitments. If the printers do not work properly or are not delivered on time, Premier's customers will be dissatisfied with Premier, not the supplier. Outsourcing requires that Premier depend on the supplier to deliver quality products at designated prices according to a specified schedule. Any supplier failures will become Premier's failures.

To protect themselves from unscrupulous or incompetent suppliers, many companies establish a select list of reliable **certified suppliers.** These companies seek to become the preferred customers of the suppliers by offering incentives such as guaranteed volume purchases with prompt payments. These incentives motivate the suppliers to ship high-quality products on a timely basis. The purchasing companies recognize that prices ultimately depend on the suppliers' ability to control costs, so the buyers and suppliers work together to minimize costs. For example, buyers may share confidential information about their production plans with suppliers if such information would enable the suppliers to more effectively control costs.

Companies must approach outsourcing decisions cautiously even when relationships with reliable suppliers are ensured. Outsourcing has both internal and external effects. It usually displaces employees. If the supplier experiences difficulties, reestablishing internal production capacity is expensive once a trained workforce has been released. Loyalty and trust are difficult to build but easy to destroy. In fact, companies must consider not only the employees who will be discharged but also the morale of those who remain. Cost reductions achieved through outsourcing are of little benefit if they are acquired at the expense of low morale and reduced productivity.

In spite of potential pitfalls outsourcing entails, the vast majority of U.S. businesses engage in some form of it. Such widespread acceptance suggests that most companies believe the benefits achieved through outsourcing exceed the potential shortcomings.

CHECK YOURSELF 20.2

Addison Manufacturing Company pays a production supervisor a salary of $48,000 per year. The supervisor manages the production of sprinkler heads that are used in water irrigation systems. Should the production supervisor's salary be considered a relevant cost to a special order decision? Should the production supervisor's salary be considered a relevant cost to an outsourcing decision?

Answer

The production supervisor's salary is not a relevant cost to a special order decision because Addison would pay the salary regardless of whether it accepts or rejects a special order. Since the cost does not differ for the alternatives, it is not relevant. In contrast, the supervisor's salary would be relevant to an outsourcing decision. Addison could dismiss the supervisor if it purchased the sprinkler heads instead of making them. Since the salary could be avoided by purchasing heads instead of making them, the salary is relevant to an outsourcing decision.

Segment Elimination Decisions

LO 8

Make appropriate segment elimination decisions by analyzing relevant information.

Businesses frequently organize operating results into subcomponents called **segments.** Segment data are used to make comparisons among different products, departments, or divisions. For example, in addition to the companywide income statement provided for external users, JCPenney may prepare separate income statements for each retail store for internal users. Executives can then evaluate managerial performance by comparing profitability measures among stores. *Segment reports* can be prepared for products, services, departments, branches, centers, offices, or divisions. These reports normally show segment revenues and costs. The primary objective of segment analysis is to determine whether relevant revenues exceed relevant costs.

Quantitative Analysis

Assume Premier Office Products makes copy equipment and computers as well as printers. Each product line is made in a separate division of the company. Division (segment) operating results for the most recent year are shown in Exhibit 20.6. Initial review of the results suggests the copier division should be eliminated because it is operating at a loss. However, analyzing the relevant revenues and expenses leads to a different conclusion.

A three-step quantitative analysis for the segment elimination decision follows:

Step 1 **Determine the amount of relevant (differential) revenue that pertains to eliminating the copier division.** The alternatives are (1) to eliminate or (2) to continue to operate the copier division. If Premier eliminates the copier line it will lose the $550,000 of revenue the copier division currently produces. If the division continues to operate Premier will earn the revenue. Since the revenue differs between the alternatives, it is relevant.

Step 2 **Determine the amount of cost Premier can avoid if it eliminates the copier division.** If it eliminates copiers, Premier can avoid the unit-level, batch-level, product-level, and segment-level facility-sustaining costs. The relevant revenue and the avoidable costs are shown in Exhibit 20.7.

EXHIBIT 20.6

Projected Revenues and Costs by Segment

	Copiers	Computers	Printers	Total
Projected revenue	$550,000	$850,000	$780,000	$2,180,000
Projected costs				
Unit-level costs				
Materials costs	(120,000)	(178,000)	(180,000)	(478,000)
Labor costs	(160,000)	(202,000)	(165,000)	(527,000)
Overhead	(30,800)	(20,000)	(15,000)	(65,800)
Batch-level costs				
Assembly setup	(15,000)	(26,000)	(17,000)	(58,000)
Materials handling	(6,000)	(8,000)	(5,000)	(19,000)
Product-level costs				
Engineering design	(10,000)	(12,000)	(14,000)	(36,000)
Production manager salary	(52,000)	(55,800)	(63,300)	(171,100)
Facility-level costs				
Segment level				
Division manager salary	(82,000)	(92,000)	(85,000)	(259,000)
Administrative costs	(12,200)	(13,200)	(12,700)	(38,100)
Allocated—corporate level				
Company president salary	(34,000)	(46,000)	(43,200)	(123,200)
Building rental	(19,250)	(29,750)	(27,300)	(76,300)
General facility expenses	(31,000)	(31,000)	(31,000)	(93,000)
Projected profit (loss)	$ (22,250)	$136,250	$121,500	$ 235,500

Premier will incur the corporate-level facility-sustaining costs whether it eliminates the copier segment or continues to operate it. Since these costs do not differ between the alternatives, they are not relevant to the elimination decision. These indirect costs have been *allocated* to the three segments. In this case the total $93,000 of general corporate-level facility expenses has been allocated equally among the three segments, $31,000 to each. The other two corporate-level facility costs (president's salary and building rental) have not been allocated equally among the three segments. As shown in Chapter 16, a total cost can be allocated among segments in many ways. Regardless of the allocation, the total cost is unchanged before and after the segment elimination. These and other allocated costs are not relevant.

Step 3 **If the relevant revenue is less than the avoidable cost, eliminate the segment (division). If not, continue to operate it.** Because operating the segment is contributing $62,000 per year to company profitability (see Exhibit 20.7), Premier should not eliminate the copier division. Exhibit 20.8 shows Premier's estimated revenues and costs if the computer and printer divisions were operated without the copier division. Projected company profit declines by $62,000 ($235,500 − $173,500) without

EXHIBIT 20.7

Relevant Revenue and Cost Data for Copier Segment

Projected revenue	$550,000
Projected costs	
Unit-level costs	
Materials costs	(120,000)
Labor costs	(160,000)
Overhead	(30,800)
Batch-level costs	
Assembly setup	(15,000)
Materials handling	(6,000)
Product-level costs	
Engineering design	(10,000)
Production manager salary	(52,000)
Facility-level costs	
Segment level	
Division manager salary	(82,000)
Administrative costs	(12,200)
Projected profit (loss)	$ 62,000

EXHIBIT 20.8

Projected Revenues and Costs Without Copier Division

	Computers	Printers	Total
Projected revenue	$850,000	$780,000	$1,630,000
Projected costs			
Unit-level costs			
Materials costs	(178,000)	(180,000)	(358,000)
Labor costs	(202,000)	(165,000)	(367,000)
Overhead	(20,000)	(15,000)	(35,000)
Batch-level costs			
Assembly setup	(26,000)	(17,000)	(43,000)
Materials handling	(8,000)	(5,000)	(13,000)
Product-level costs			
Engineering design	(12,000)	(14,000)	(26,000)
Production manager salary	(55,800)	(63,300)	(119,100)
Facility-level costs			
Segment level			
Division manager salary	(92,000)	(85,000)	(177,000)
Administrative costs	(13,200)	(12,700)	(25,900)
Allocated—corporate level*			
Company president salary	(63,000)	(60,200)	(123,200)
Depreciation	(39,375)	(36,925)	(76,300)
General facility expenses	(46,500)	(46,500)	(93,000)
Projected profit (loss)	$ 94,125	$ 79,375	$ 173,500

*The general corporate-level facility costs that were previously *allocated* to the copier division have been reassigned on the basis of one-half to the computer division and one-half to the printer division.

the copier segment, confirming that eliminating it would be detrimental to Premier's profitability.

Qualitative Considerations in Decisions to Eliminate Segments

As with other special decisions, management should consider qualitative factors when determining whether to eliminate segments. Employee lives will be disrupted; some employees may be reassigned elsewhere in the company, but others will be discharged. As with outsourcing decisions, reestablishing internal production capacity is difficult once a trained workforce has been released. Furthermore, employees in other segments, suppliers, customers, and investors may believe that the elimination of a segment implies the company as a whole is experiencing financial difficulty. These individuals may lose confidence in the company and seek business contacts with other companies they perceive to be more stable.

Management must also consider the fact that sales of different product lines are frequently interdependent. Some customers prefer one-stop shopping; they want to buy all their office equipment from one supplier. If Premier no longer sells copiers, customers may stop buying its computers and printers. Eliminating one segment may reduce sales of other segments.

What will happen to the space Premier used to make the copiers? Suppose Premier decides to make telephone systems in the space it previously used for copiers. The contribution to profit of the telephone business would be an *opportunity cost* of operating the copier segment. As demonstrated in previous examples, adding the opportunity cost to the avoidable costs of operating the copier segment could change the decision.

As with outsourcing, volume changes can affect elimination decisions. Because many costs of operating a segment are fixed, the cost per unit decreases as production increases. Growth can transform a segment that is currently producing real losses into a segment that produces real profits. Managers must consider growth potential when making elimination decisions.

CHECK YOURSELF 20.3

Capital Corporation is considering eliminating one of its operating segments. Capital employed a real estate broker to determine the marketability of the building that houses the segment. The broker obtained three bids for the building: $250,000, $262,000, and $264,000. The book value of the building is $275,000. Based on this information alone, what is the relevant cost of the building?

Answer

The book value of the building is a sunk cost that is not relevant. There are three bids for the building, but only one is relevant because Capital could sell the building only once. The relevant cost of the building is the highest opportunity cost, which in this case is $264,000.

Summary of Relationships Between Avoidable Costs and the Hierarchy of Business Activity

LO 3 Distinguish between unit-level, batch-level, product-level, and facility-level costs and understand how these costs affect decision making.

A relationship exists between the cost hierarchy and the different types of special decisions just discussed. A special order involves making additional units of an existing product. Deciding to accept a special order affects unit-level and possibly batch-level costs. In contrast, outsourcing a product stops the production of that product. Outsourcing can avoid many product-level as well as unit- and batch-level costs. Finally, if a company eliminates an entire business segment, it can avoid some of the facility-level costs. The more complex the decision level, the more opportunities there are to avoid costs. Moving to a higher category does not mean, however, that all costs at the higher level of activity are avoidable. For example, all product-level costs may not be avoidable if a company chooses to outsource a product. The company may still incur inventory holding costs or advertising costs whether it makes or buys the product. Understanding the relationship between decision type and level of cost hierarchy helps when identifying avoidable costs. The relationships are summarized in Exhibit 20.9. For each type of decision, look for avoidable costs in the categories marked with an X. Remember also that sunk costs cannot be avoided.

EXHIBIT 20.9

Relationship Between Decision Type and Level of Cost Hierarchy

Decision Type	Unit level	Batch level	Product level	Facility level
Special order	X	X		
Outsourcing	X	X	X	
Segment elimination	X	X	X	X

Equipment Replacement Decisions

LO 9 Make appropriate asset replacement decisions by analyzing relevant information.

Equipment may become technologically obsolete long before it fails physically. Managers should base **equipment replacement decisions** on profitability analysis rather than physical deterioration. Assume Premier Office Products is considering replacing an existing machine with a new one. The following table summarizes pertinent information about the two machines:

Old Machine		New Machine	
Original cost	$ 90,000	Cost of the new machine	$29,000
Accumulated depreciation	(33,000)	Salvage value (in 5 years)	4,000
Book value	$ 57,000	Operating expenses ($4,500 × 5 years)	22,500
Market value (now)	$ 14,000		
Salvage value (in 5 years)	2,000		
Annual depreciation expense	11,000		
Operating expenses ($9,000 × 5 years)	45,000		

Quantitative Analysis

First determine what relevant costs Premier will incur if it keeps the *old machine.*

1. The *original cost* ($90,000), *current book value* ($57,000), *accumulated depreciation* ($33,000), and *annual depreciation expense* ($11,000) are different measures of a cost that was incurred in a prior period. They represent irrelevant sunk costs.
2. The $14,000 market value represents the current sacrifice Premier must make if it keeps using the existing machine. In other words, if Premier does not keep the machine, it can sell it for $14,000. In economic terms, *forgoing the opportunity* to sell the machine costs as much as buying it. The *opportunity cost* is therefore relevant to the replacement decision.
3. The salvage value of the old machine reduces the opportunity cost. Premier can sell the old machine now for $14,000 or use it for five more years and then sell it for $2,000. The opportunity cost of using the old machine for five more years is therefore $12,000 ($14,000 − $2,000).
4. Because the $45,000 ($9,000 × 5) of operating expenses will be incurred if the old machine is used but can be avoided if it is replaced, the operating expenses are relevant costs.

Next, determine what relevant costs will be incurred if Premier purchases and uses the *new machine.*

1. The cost of the new machine represents a future economic sacrifice Premier must incur if it buys the new machine. It is a relevant cost.
2. The salvage value reduces the cost of purchasing the new machine. Part ($4,000) of the $29,000 cost of the new machine will be recovered at the end of five years. The relevant cost of purchasing the new machine is $25,000 ($29,000 − $4,000).
3. The $22,500 ($4,500 × 5) of operating expenses will be incurred if the new machine is purchased; it can be avoided if the new machine is not purchased. The operating expenses are relevant costs.

The relevant costs for the two machines are summarized here:

Old Machine		New Machine	
Opportunity cost	$14,000	Cost of the new machine	$29,000
Salvage value	(2,000)	Salvage value	(4,000)
Operating expenses	45,000	Operating expenses	22,500
Total	$57,000	Total	$47,500

The analysis suggests that Premier should acquire the new machine because buying it produces the lower relevant cost. The $57,000 cost of using the old machine can be *avoided* by incurring the $47,500 cost of acquiring and using the new machine. Over the five-year period, Premier would save $9,500 ($57,000 − $47,500) by purchasing the new machine.

One caution: this analysis ignores income tax effects and the time value of money, which are explained in a later chapter. The discussion in this chapter focuses on identifying and using relevant costs in decision making.

A Look Back <<

Decision making requires managers to choose from alternative courses of action. Successful decision making depends on a manager's ability to identify *relevant information*. Information that is relevant for decision making differs among the alternatives and is future oriented. Relevant revenues are sometimes called *differential revenues* because they differ among the alternatives. Relevant costs are sometimes called *avoidable costs* because they can be eliminated or avoided by choosing a specific course of action.

Costs that do not differ among the alternatives are not avoidable and therefore not relevant. *Sunk costs* are not relevant in decision making because they have been incurred in past transactions and therefore cannot be avoided. *Opportunity costs* are relevant because they represent potential benefits that may or may not be realized, depending on the decision maker's choice. In other words, future benefits that differ among the alternatives are relevant. Opportunity costs are not recorded in the financial accounting records.

Classifying costs into one of four hierarchical levels facilitates identifying relevant costs. *Unit-level costs* such as materials and labor are incurred each time a single unit of product is made. These costs can be avoided by eliminating the production of a single unit of product. *Batch-level costs* are associated with producing a group of products. Examples include setup costs and inspection costs related to a batch (group) of work rather than a single unit. Eliminating a batch would avoid both batch-level costs and unit-level costs. *Product-level costs* are incurred to support specific products or services (design and regulatory compliance costs). Product-level costs can be avoided by discontinuing a product line. *Facility-level costs*, like the president's salary, are incurred on behalf of the whole company or a segment of the company. In segment elimination decisions, the facility-level costs related to a particular segment being considered for elimination are relevant and avoidable. Those applying to the company as a whole are not avoidable.

Cost behavior (fixed or variable) is independent from the concept of relevance. Furthermore, a cost that is relevant in one decision context may be irrelevant in another context. Decision making depends on qualitative as well as quantitative information. *Quantitative information refers to information that can be measured using numbers. Qualitative information* is nonquantitative information such as personal preferences or opportunities.

Four types of special decisions that are frequently encountered in business are (1) *special orders*, (2) *outsourcing*, (3) *elimination decisions*, and (4) *asset replacement*. The relevant costs in a special order decision are the unit-level and batch-level costs that will be incurred if the special order is accepted. If the differential revenues from the special order exceed the relevant costs, the order should be accepted. Outsourcing decisions determine whether goods and services should be purchased from other companies. The relevant costs are the unit-level, batch-level, and product-level costs that could be avoided if the company outsources the product or service. If these costs are more than the cost to buy and the qualitative characteristics are satisfactory, the company should outsource. Segment-related unit-level, batch-level, product-level, and facility-level costs that can be avoided when a segment is eliminated are relevant. If the segment's avoidable costs exceed its differential revenues, it should be eliminated, assuming favorable qualitative factors. Asset replacement decisions compare the relevant costs of existing equipment with the relevant costs of new equipment to determine whether replacing the old equipment would be profitable.

A Look Forward >>

The next chapter introduces the topics of planning and cost control. You will learn how to prepare budgets and projected (pro forma) financial statements. Finally, you will learn the importance of considering human factors as well as the quantitative aspects of the budgeting process.

APPENDIX

Short-Term Versus Long-Term Goals

LO 10

Explain the conflict between short- and long-term profitability.

To examine conflicts between short-term and long-term goals, return to the equipment replacement decision made by the management team of Premier Office Products (see page 983 for details). Suppose the final equipment replacement decision is made by a departmental supervisor under significant pressure to maximize profitability. If profitability declines, she will lose her job. Because the beneficial impact of the new machine is realized in the second through fifth years, the supervisor may choose to keep the old machine even though it is to the company's advantage to purchase the new one. Replacing the equipment will result in more expense/loss recognition in the first year. To illustrate, study the following information.

Year	First	Second	Third	Fourth	Fifth	Totals
Keep old machine						
Depreciation expense*	$11,000	$11,000	$11,000	$11,000	$11,000	$ 55,000
Operating expense	9,000	9,000	9,000	9,000	9,000	45,000
Total	$20,000	$20,000	$20,000	$20,000	$20,000	$100,000
Replace old machine						
Loss on disposal†	$43,000	$ 0	$ 0	$ 0	$ 0	$ 43,000
Depreciation expense‡	5,000	5,000	5,000	5,000	5,000	25,000
Operating expense	4,500	4,500	4,500	4,500	4,500	22,500
Total	$52,500	$ 9,500	$ 9,500	$ 9,500	$ 9,500	$ 90,500

*($57,000 book value − $2,000 salvage) ÷ 5 years = $11,000

†($57,000 book value − $14,000 market value) = $43,000

‡($29,000 cost − $4,000 salvage) ÷ 5 years = $5,000

This analysis verifies that total cost at the end of the five-year period is $9,500 less if the equipment is replaced ($100,000 − $90,500). Total costs, however, at the end of the first year are higher by $32,500 ($52,500 − $20,000) if the old machine is replaced. A decision maker under significant pressure to report higher profitability may be willing to sacrifice tomorrow's profits to look better today. By emphasizing short-term profitability, she may secure a promotion before the long-term effects of her decision become apparent. The department supervisor's intent is to survive the moment and let the future take care of itself. Misguided reward systems can be as detrimental as threats of punishment. For example, a manager may choose short-term profitability to obtain a bonus based on reported profitability. It is the responsibility of upper-level management to establish policies and procedures that motivate subordinates to perform in ways that maximize the company's long-term profitability.

Decisions Regarding the Allocation of Scarce Resources

LO 11

Make decisions about allocating scarce resources by analyzing relevant information.

Suppose that Premier Office Products makes two types of computers: a high-end network server and an inexpensive personal computer. The relevant sales and variable cost data for each unit follow.

Network Server		Personal Computer	
Sales price	$4,000	Sales price	$1,500
Less: Variable cost	(3,760)	Less: Variable cost	(1,370)
Contribution margin	$ 240	Contribution margin	$ 130

In many circumstances, variable costs act as proxies for *avoidable costs*. For example, by definition, unit-level costs increase and decrease in direct proportion to the number of units of product made and sold. As previously indicated, unit-level costs are avoidable with respect to many special decisions. To the extent that variable costs are proxies for avoidable costs, the contribution margin can be used as a measure of profitability. Other things being equal, higher contribution margins translate into more profitable products. If Premier could sell 1,000 computers, the company would certainly prefer that they be network servers. The contribution to profitability on those machines is almost double the contribution margin on the personal computer.

Even though the contribution margin is higher for network servers, selling personal computers may be more profitable. Why? If Premier can sell more of the personal computers, the volume of activity may make up for the lower margin. In other words, selling three personal computers produces more total margin (3 × $130 = $390) than selling one network server (1 × $240). Many factors could limit the sales of one or both of the products. Factors that limit a business's ability to satisfy the demand for its product are called **constraints.** Suppose that warehouse space is limited. Premier cannot warehouse all of the computers it needs to satisfy customer orders. If a network server requires more warehouse space than a personal computer, stocking and selling personal computers may be more profitable than stocking and selling network servers. To illustrate, assume it requires 5 square feet of warehouse space for a network server and 2 square feet for a personal computer. If only 2,100 square feet of warehouse space are available, which computer should Premier stock and sell?

In this case, the warehouse space is considered a scarce resource. The computer that produces the highest contribution margin per unit of scarce resource (per square foot) is the more profitable product. The per unit computations for each product are shown here.

	Network Server	Personal Computer
Contribution margin per unit (a)	$ 240	$ 130
Divide by warehouse space needed to store one unit (b)	5 sq. ft.	2 sq. ft.
Contribution margin per unit of scarce resource (a ÷ b)	$ 48	$ 65

The data suggest that Premier should focus on the personal computer. Even though the personal computer produces a lower contribution margin per product, its contribution margin per scarce resource is higher. The effect on total profitability follows.

	Network Server	Personal Computer
Amount of available warehouse space (a)	2,100	2,100
Divide by warehouse space needed to store one unit (b)	5 sq. ft.	2 sq. ft.
Warehouse capacity in number of units (a ÷ b) = (c)	420	1,050
Times contribution margin per unit (d)	$ 240	$ 130
Total profit potential (c × d)	$100,800	$136,500

Although the quantitative data suggest Premier will maximize profitability by limiting its inventory to personal computers, qualitative considerations may compel the company to maintain a reasonable sales mix between the two products. For example, a business that buys several personal computers may also need a network server. A customer who cannot obtain both products from Premier may choose to buy nothing. Instead, the customer will find a supplier who will satisfy all of his needs. Premier may still need to stock some servers to offer a competitive product line.

The chairman of the board of directors asked Premier's president why company sales had remained level while the company's chief competitor had experienced significant increases. The president replied, "You cannot sell what you do not have. Our warehouse is too small. We stop production when we fill up the warehouse. The products sell out rapidly, and then we have to wait around for the next batch of computers to be made. When we are out of stock, our customers turn to the competition. We are constrained by the size of the warehouse." In business terms, the warehouse is a **bottleneck.** Its size is limiting the company's ability to sell its products.

Many businesses use a management practice known as the **theory of constraints (TOC)** to increase profitability by managing bottlenecks or constrained resources. TOC's primary objective is to identify the bottlenecks restricting the operations of the business and then to open those bottlenecks through a practice known as **relaxing the constraints.** The effect of applying TOC to the Premier case is apparent via contribution margin analysis. According to the preceding computations, a new server and a new personal computer produce a contribution margin of $48 and $65 per square foot of storage space, respectively. So long as additional warehouse space can be purchased for less than these amounts, Premier can increase its profitability by acquiring the space.

SELF-STUDY REVIEW PROBLEM

Flying High Inc. (FHI) is a division of The Master Toy Company. FHI makes remote-controlled airplanes. During 2004, FHI incurred the following costs in the process of making 5,000 planes.

Unit-level materials costs (5,000 units @ $80)	$ 400,000
Unit-level labor costs (5,000 units @ $90)	450,000
Unit-level overhead costs (5,000 @ $70)	350,000
Depreciation cost on manufacturing equipment*	50,000
Other manufacturing overhead†	140,000
Inventory holding costs	240,000
Allocated portion of The Master Toy Company's facility-level costs	600,000
Total costs	$2,230,000

*The manufacturing equipment, which originally cost $250,000, has a book value of $200,000, a remaining useful life of four years, and a zero salvage value. If the equipment is not used in the production process, it can be leased for $30,000 per year.

†Includes supervisors' salaries and rent for the manufacturing building.

Required

a. FHI uses a cost-plus pricing strategy. FHI sets its price at product cost plus $100. Determine the price that FHI should charge for its remote-controlled airplanes.

b. Assume that a potential customer that operates a chain of high-end toy stores has approached FHI. A buyer for this chain has offered to purchase 1,000 planes from FHI at a price of $275 each. Ignoring qualitative considerations, should FHI accept or reject the order?

c. FHI has the opportunity to purchase the planes from Arland Manufacturing Company for $325 each. Arland maintains adequate inventories so that it can supply its customers with planes on demand. Should FHI accept the opportunity to outsource the making of its planes?

d. Use the contribution margin format to prepare an income statement based on historical cost data. Prepare a second income statement that reflects the relevant cost data that Master Toy should consider in a segment elimination decision. Based on a comparison of these two statements, indicate whether Master Toy should eliminate the FHI division.

e. FHI is considering replacing the equipment it currently uses to manufacture its planes. It could purchase replacement equipment for $480,000 that has an expected useful life of four years and a salvage value of $40,000. The new equipment would increase productivity substantially, reducing unit-level labor costs by 20 percent. Assume that FHI would maintain its production and sales at 5,000 planes per year. Prepare a schedule that shows the relevant costs of operating the old equipment versus the costs of operating the new equipment. Should FHI replace the equipment?

Solution to Requirement *a*

Product Cost for Remote-Controlled Airplanes

Unit-level materials costs (5,000 units × $80)	$ 400,000
Unit-level labor costs (5,000 units × $90)	450,000
Unit-level overhead costs (5,000 units × $70)	350,000
Depreciation cost on manufacturing equipment	50,000
Other manufacturing overhead	140,000
Total product cost	$1,390,000

The cost per unit is $278 ($1,390,000 ÷ 5,000 units). The sales price per unit is $378 ($278 + $100). Depreciation expense is included because cost-plus pricing is usually based on historical cost rather than relevant cost. To be profitable in the long run, a company must ultimately recover the amount it paid for the equipment (the historical cost of the equipment).

Solution to Requirement *b*

The incremental (relevant) cost of making 1,000 additional airplanes follows. The depreciation expense is not relevant because it represents a sunk cost. The other manufacturing overhead costs are not relevant because they will be incurred regardless of whether FHI makes the additional planes.

Per Unit Relevant Product Cost for Airplanes

Unit-level materials costs	$ 80
Unit-level labor costs	90
Unit-level overhead costs	70
Total relevant product cost	$240

Since the relevant (incremental) cost of making the planes is less than the incremental revenue, FHI should accept the special order. Accepting the order will increase profits by $35,000 [($275 incremental revenue − $240 incremental cost) × 1,000 units].

Solution to Requirement *c*

Distinguish this decision from the special order opportunity discussed in Requirement *b*. That special order (Requirement *b*) decision hinged on the cost of making additional units with the existing production process. In contrast, a make-or-buy decision compares current production with the possibility of making zero units (closing down the entire manufacturing process). If the manufacturing process were shut down, FHI could avoid the unit-level costs, the cost of the lost opportunity to lease the equipment, the other manufacturing overhead costs, and the inventory holding costs. Since the planes can be purchased on demand, there is no need to maintain any inventory. The allocated portion of the facility-level costs is not relevant because it would be incurred regardless of whether FHI manufactured the planes. The relevant cost of making the planes follows.

Relevant Manufacturing Cost for Airplanes

Unit-level materials costs (5,000 units × $80)	$ 400,000
Unit-level labor costs (5,000 units × $90)	450,000
Unit-level overhead costs (5,000 units × $70)	350,000
Opportunity cost of leasing the equipment	30,000
Other manufacturing overhead costs	140,000
Inventory holding cost	240,000
Total product cost	$1,610,000

The relevant cost per unit is $322 ($1,610,000 ÷ 5,000 units). Since the relevant cost of making the planes ($322) is less than the cost of purchasing them ($325), FHI should continue to make the planes.

Solution to Requirement *d*

Income Statements

	Historical Cost Data	Relevant Cost Data
Revenue (5,000 units × $378)	$1,890,000	$1,890,000
Less variable costs:		
Unit-level materials costs (5,000 units × $80)	(400,000)	(400,000)
Unit-level labor costs (5,000 units × $90)	(450,000)	(450,000)
Unit-level overhead costs (5,000 units × $70)	(350,000)	(350,000)
Contribution Margin	690,000	690,000
Depreciation cost on manufacturing equipment	(50,000)	

continued

	Historical Cost Data	Relevant Cost Data
Opportunity cost of leasing manufacturing equipment		(30,000)
Other manufacturing overhead costs	(140,000)	(140,000)
Inventory holding costs	(240,000)	(240,000)
Allocated facility-level administrative costs	(600,000)	
Net Loss	$ (340,000)	
Contribution to Master Toy's Profitability		$ 280,000

Master Toy should not eliminate the segment (FHI). Although it appears to be incurring a loss, the allocated facility-level administrative costs are not relevant because Master Toy would incur these costs regardless of whether it eliminated FHI. Also, the depreciation cost on the manufacturing equipment is not relevant because it is a sunk cost. However, since the company could lease the equipment if the segment were eliminated, the $30,000 potential rental fee represents a relevant opportunity cost. The relevant revenue and cost data show that FHI is contributing $280,000 to the profitability of The Master Toy Company.

Solution to Requirement *e*

The relevant costs of using the old equipment versus the new equipment are the costs that differ for the two alternatives. In this case relevant costs include the purchase price of the new equipment, the opportunity cost of the old equipment, and the labor costs. These items are summarized in the following table. The data show the total cost over the four-year useful life of the replacement equipment.

Relevant Cost Comparison

	Old Equipment	New Equipment
Opportunity to lease the old equipment ($30,000 × 4 years)	$ 120,000	
Cost of new equipment ($480,000 − $40,000)		$ 440,000
Unit-level labor costs (5,000 units × $90 × 4 years)	1,800,000	
Unit-level labor costs (5,000 units × $90 × 4 years × .80)		1,440,000
Total relevant costs	$1,920,000	$1,880,000

Since the relevant cost of operating the new equipment is less than the cost of operating the old equipment, FHI should replace the equipment.

KEY TERMS

avoidable costs 971
batch-level costs 972
bottleneck 987
certified suppliers 979
constraints 987
differential revenues 971
equipment replacement decisions 983
facility-level costs 972
low-ball pricing 979
opportunity costs 973
outsourcing 977
product-level costs 972
qualitative characteristics 975
quantitative characteristics 975
relaxing the constraints 987
relevant costs 971
relevant information 970
segment 980
special order decision 975
sunk costs 970
theory of constraints (TOC) 987
unit-level costs 971
vertical integration 979

QUESTIONS

1. Identify the primary qualities of revenues and costs that are relevant for decision making.
2. Are variable costs always relevant? Explain.
3. Identify the four hierarchical levels used to classify costs. When can each of these levels of costs be avoided?

4. Describe the relationship between relevance and accuracy.
5. "It all comes down to the bottom line. The numbers never lie." Do you agree with this conclusion? Explain your position.
6. Carmon Company invested $300,000 in the equity securities of Mann Corporation. The current market value of Carmon's investment in Mann is $250,000. Carmon currently needs funds for operating purposes. Although interest rates are high, Carmon's president has decided to borrow the needed funds instead of selling the investment in Mann. He explains that his company cannot afford to take a $50,000 loss on the Mann stock. Evaluate the president's decision based on this information.
7. What is an opportunity cost? How does it differ from a sunk cost?
8. A local bank advertises that it offers a free noninterest-bearing checking account if the depositor maintains a $500 minimum balance in the account. Is the checking account truly free?
9. A manager is faced with deciding whether to replace machine A or machine B. The original cost of machine A was $20,000 and that of machine B was $30,000. Because the two cost figures differ, they are relevant to the manager's decision. Do you agree? Explain your position.
10. Are all fixed costs unavoidable?
11. Identify two qualitative considerations that could be associated with special order decisions.
12. Which of the following would not be relevant to a make-or-buy decision?
    (a) Allocated portion of depreciation expense on existing facilities.
    (b) Variable cost of labor used to produce products currently purchased from suppliers.
    (c) Warehousing costs for inventory of completed products (inventory levels will be constant regardless of whether products are purchased or produced).
    (d) Cost of materials used to produce the items currently purchased from suppliers.
    (e) Property taxes on the factory building.
13. What two factors should be considered in deciding how to allocate shelf space in a retail establishment?
14. What level(s) of costs is(are) relevant in special order decisions?
15. Why would a company consider outsourcing products or services?
16. Chris Sutter, the production manager of Satellite Computers, insists that the floppy drives used in the company's upper-end computers be outsourced since they can be purchased from a supplier at a lower cost per unit than the company is presently incurring to produce the drives. Jane Meyers, his assistant, insists that if sales growth continues at the current levels, the company will be able to produce the drives in the near future at a lower cost because of the company's predominately fixed cost structure. Does Ms. Meyers have a legitimate argument? Explain.
17. Identify some qualitative factors that should be considered in addition to quantitative costs in deciding whether to outsource.
18. The managers of Wilcox Inc. are suggesting that the company president eliminate one of the company's segments that is operating at a loss. Why may this be a hasty decision?
19. Why would a supervisor choose to continue using a more costly old machine instead of replacing it with a less costly new machine?
20. Identify some of the constraints that limit a business's ability to satisfy the demand for its products or services.

EXERCISES—SERIES A

All Exercises in Series A are available with McGraw-Hill's Homework Manager

Exercise 20-1A *Distinction between relevance and cost behavior* L.O. 1

Lucy Taylor is trying to decide which of two different kinds of candy to sell in her retail candy store. One type is a name-brand candy that will practically sell itself. The other candy is cheaper to purchase but does not carry an identifiable brand name. Ms. Taylor believes that she will have to incur significant advertising costs to sell this candy. Several cost items for the two types of candy are as follows:

Brandless Candy		Name-Brand Candy	
Cost per box	$ 4.00	Cost per box	$ 6.00
Sales commissions per box	0.50	Sales commissions per box	1.00
Rent of display space	1,500.00	Rent of display space	1,500.00
Advertising	3,000.00	Advertising	2,000.00

Required

Identify each cost as being relevant or irrelevant to Ms. Taylor's decision and indicate whether it is fixed or variable relative to the number of boxes sold.

L.O. 1, 2

Exercise 20-2A ***Distinction between relevance and cost behavior***

Bron Company makes and sells a single product. Bron incurred the following costs in its most recent fiscal year.

Cost Items Appearing on the Income Statement	
Materials Cost ($7 per unit)	Sales Commissions (2% of sales)
Company President's Salary	Salaries of Administrative Personnel
Depreciation on Manufacturing Equipment	Shipping and Handling ($0.25 per unit)
Customer Billing Costs (1% of sales)	Depreciation on Office Furniture
Rental Cost of Manufacturing Facility	Manufacturing Supplies ($0.25 per unit)
Advertising Costs ($250,000 per year)	Production Supervisor's Salary
Labor Cost ($5 per unit)	

Bron could purchase the products that it currently makes. If it purchased the items, the company would continue to sell them using its own logo, advertising program, and sales staff.

Required

Identify each cost as relevant or irrelevant to the outsourcing decision and indicate whether the cost is fixed or variable relative to the number of products manufactured and sold.

L.O. 1

Exercise 20-3A ***Distinction between avoidable costs and cost behavior***

Elegance Company makes fine jewelry that it sells to department stores throughout the United States. Elegance is trying to decide which of two bracelets to manufacture. Elegance has a labor contract that prohibits the company from laying off workers freely. Cost data pertaining to the two choices follow.

	Bracelet A	Bracelet B
Cost of materials per unit	$ 30	$ 50
Cost of labor per unit	40	40
Advertising cost per year	8,000	6,000
Annual depreciation on existing equip.	5,000	4,000

Required

a. Identify the fixed costs and determine the amount of fixed cost for each product.
b. Identify the variable costs and determine the amount of variable cost per unit for each product.
c. Identify the avoidable costs and determine the amount of avoidable cost for each product.

L.O. 1, 2, 6

Exercise 20-4A ***Special order decision***

Solid Concrete Company pours concrete slabs for single-family dwellings. Russell Construction Company, which operates outside Solid's normal sales territory, asks Solid to pour 40 slabs for Russell's new development of homes. Solid has the capacity to build 300 slabs and is presently working on 250 of them. Russell is willing to pay only $3,000 per slab. Solid estimates the cost of a typical job to include unit-level materials, $1,500; unit-level labor, $1,000; and an allocated portion of facility-level overhead, $700.

Required

Should Solid accept or reject the special order to pour 40 slabs for $3,000 each? Support your answer with appropriate computations.

Exercise 20-5A ***Special order decision*** **L.O. 1, 2, 6**

Lance Company manufactures a personal computer designed for use in schools and markets it under its own label. Lance has the capacity to produce 20,000 units a year but is currently producing and selling only 15,000 units a year. The computer's normal selling price is $1,600 per unit with no volume discounts. The unit-level costs of the computer's production are $600 for direct materials, $200 for direct labor, and $250 for indirect unit-level manufacturing costs. The total product- and facility-level costs incurred by Lance during the year are expected to be $2,000,000 and $800,000, respectively. Assume that Lance receives a special order to produce and sell 4,000 computers at $1,200 each.

Required

Should Lance accept or reject the special order? Support your answer with appropriate computations.

Exercise 20-6A ***Identifying qualitative factors for a special order decision*** **L.O. 5**

Required

Describe the qualitative factors that Lance should consider before accepting the special order described in Exercise 20-5A.

Exercise 20-7A ***Using the contribution margin approach for a special order decision*** **L.O. 6**

Shane Company, which produces and sells a small digital clock, bases its pricing strategy on a 30 percent markup on total cost. Based on annual production costs for 15,000 units of product, computations for the sales price per clock follow.

Unit-level costs	$180,000
Fixed costs	60,000
Total cost (a)	240,000
Markup (a × 0.30)	72,000
Total sales (b)	$312,000
Sales price per unit (b ÷ 15,000)	$20.80

Required

a. Shane has excess capacity and receives a special order for 6,000 clocks for $15 each. Calculate the contribution margin per unit; based on it, should Shane accept the special order?

b. Support your answer by preparing a contribution margin income statement for the special order.

Exercise 20-8A ***Outsourcing decision*** **L.O. 7**

Rider Bicycle Manufacturing Company currently produces the handlebars used in manufacturing its bicycles, which are high-quality racing bikes with limited sales. Rider produces and sells only 5,000 bikes each year. Due to the low volume of activity, Rider is unable to obtain the economies of scale that larger producers achieve. For example, Rider could buy the handlebars for $30 each; they cost $34 each to make. The following is a detailed breakdown of current production costs.

Item	Unit Cost	Total
Unit-level costs		
Materials	$14	$ 70,000
Labor	11	55,000
Overhead	4	20,000
Allocated facility-level costs	5	25,000
Total	$34	$170,000

After seeing these figures, Rider's president remarked that it would be foolish for the company to continue to produce the handlebars at $34 each when it can buy them for $30 each.

Required

Do you agree with the president's conclusion? Support your answer with appropriate computations.

L.O. 7

Exercise 20-9A *Establishing price for an outsourcing decision*

Easy Cut Inc. makes and sells lawn mowers for which it currently makes the engines. It has an opportunity to purchase the engines from a reliable manufacturer. The annual costs of making the engines are shown here.

Cost of materials (20,000 Units × $20)	$ 400,000
Labor (20,000 Units × $25)	500,000
Depreciation on manufacturing equipment*	45,000
Salary of supervisor of engine production	180,000
Rental cost of equipment used to make engines	120,000
Allocated portion of corporate-level facility-sustaining costs	45,000
Total cost to make 20,000 engines	$1,290,000

*The equipment has a book value of $72,000 but its market value is zero.

Required

a. Determine the maximum price per unit that Easy Cut would be willing to pay for the engines.

b. Would the price computed in Requirement *a* change if production increased to 25,000 units? Support your answer with appropriate computations.

L.O. 5, 7

Exercise 20-10A *Outsourcing decision with qualitative factors*

Surround Sound Inc. (SSI), which makes and sells 80,000 radios annually, currently purchases the radio speakers it uses for $8 each. Each radio uses one speaker. The company has idle capacity and is considering the possibility of making the speakers that it needs. SSI estimates that the cost of materials and labor needed to make speakers would be a total of $7 for each speaker. In addition, the costs of supervisory salaries, rent, and other manufacturing costs would be $160,000. Allocated facility-level costs would be $96,000.

Required

a. Determine the change in net income SSI would experience if it decides to make the speakers.

b. Discuss the qualitative factors that SSI should consider.

L.O. 4, 7

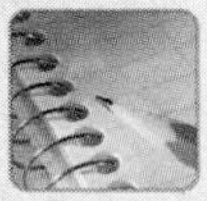

Exercise 20-11A *Outsourcing decision affected by opportunity costs*

Sertoma Electronics currently produces the shipping containers it uses to deliver the electronics products it sells. The monthly cost of producing 9,000 containers follows.

Unit-level materials	$ 4,500
Unit-level labor	6,000
Unit-level overhead	3,900
Product-level costs*	9,000
Allocated facility-level costs	22,500

*One-third of these costs can be avoided by purchasing the containers.

Loehman Container Company has offered to sell comparable containers to Sertoma for $2.25 each.

Required

a. Should Sertoma continue to make the containers? Support your answer with appropriate computations.

b. Sertoma could lease the space it currently uses in the manufacturing process. If leasing would produce $9,000 per month, would your answer to Requirement *a* be different? Explain.

L.O. 4

Exercise 20-12A *Opportunity cost*

Swift Truck Lines Inc. owns a truck that cost $80,000. Currently, the truck's book value is $48,000, and its expected remaining useful life is four years. Swift has the opportunity to purchase for $60,000 a replacement truck that is extremely fuel efficient. Fuel cost for the old truck is expected to be $8,000 per year more than fuel cost for the new truck. The old truck is paid for but, in spite of being in good condition, can be sold for only $32,000.

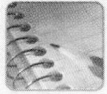

Required

Should Swift Truck Lines replace the old truck with the new fuel-efficient model, or should it continue to use the old truck until it wears out? Explain.

Exercise 20-13A ***Opportunity costs*** **L.O. 4, 5**

Tim Kozlowski owns his own taxi, for which he bought a $20,000 permit to operate two years ago. Mr. Kozlowski earns $37,000 a year operating as an independent but has the opportunity to sell the taxi and permit for $75,000 and take a position as dispatcher for Trenton Taxi Co. The dispatcher position pays $31,000 a year for a 40-hour week. Driving his own taxi, Mr. Kozlowski works approximately 55 hours per week. If he sells his business, he will invest the $75,000 and can earn a 10 percent return.

Required

a. Determine the opportunity cost of owning and operating the independent business.
b. Based solely on financial considerations, should Mr. Kozlowski sell the taxi and accept the position as dispatcher?
c. Discuss the qualitative as well as quantitative factors that Mr. Kozlowski should consider.

Exercise 20-14A ***Segment elimination decision*** **L.O. 8**

Quell Company operates three segments. Income statements for the segments imply that profitability could be improved if Segment A were eliminated.

QUELL COMPANY
Income Statements for the Year 2009

Segment	A	B	C
Sales	$196,000	$260,000	$345,000
Cost of Goods Sold	(143,000)	(98,000)	(190,000)
Sales Commissions	(20,000)	(38,000)	(22,000)
Contribution Margin	33,000	124,000	133,000
General Fixed Oper. Exp. (allocation of president's salary)	(44,000)	(52,000)	(44,000)
Advertising Expense (specific to individual divisions)	(3,000)	(10,000)	0
Net Income	$ (14,000)	$ 62,000	$ 89,000

Required

a. Explain the effect on profitability if Segment A is eliminated.
b. Prepare comparative income statements for the company as a whole under two alternatives: (1) the retention of Segment A and (2) the elimination of Segment A.

Exercise 20-15A ***Segment elimination decision*** **L.O. 8**

Moreno Transport Company divides its operations into four divisions. A recent income statement for Hess Division follows.

MORENO TRANSPORT COMPANY
Hess Division
Income Statement for the Year 2005

Revenue	$650,000
Salaries for Drivers	(420,000)
Fuel Expenses	(80,000)
Insurance	(110,000)
Division-Level Facility-Sustaining Costs	(60,000)
Companywide Facility-Sustaining Costs	(130,000)
Net Loss	$(150,000)

Required

a. Should Hess Division be eliminated? Support your answer by explaining how the division's elimination would affect the net income of the company as a whole. By how much would companywide income increase or decrease?

b. Assume that Hess Division is able to increase its revenue to $700,000 by raising its prices. Would this change the decision you made in Requirement *a*? Determine the amount of the increase or decrease that would occur in companywide net income if the segment were eliminated if revenue were $700,000.

c. What is the minimum amount of revenue required to justify continuing the operation of Hess Division?

L.O. 8

Exercise 20-16A *Identifying avoidable cost of a segment*

Howell Corporation is considering the elimination of one of its segments. The segment incurs the following fixed costs. If the segment is eliminated, the building it uses will be sold.

Advertising expense	$ 97,000
Supervisory salaries	159,000
Allocation of companywide facility-level costs	45,000
Original cost of building	100,000
Book value of building	60,000
Market value of building	70,000
Maintenance costs on equipment	50,000
Real estate taxes on building	7,000

Required

Based on this information, determine the amount of avoidable cost associated with the segment.

L.O. 9

Exercise 20-17A *Asset replacement decision*

A machine purchased three years ago for $200,000 has a current book value using straight-line depreciation of $120,000; its operating expenses are $30,000 per year. A replacement machine would cost $250,000, have a useful life of nine years, and would require $14,000 per year in operating expenses. It has an expected salvage value of $66,000 after nine years. The current disposal value of the old machine is $60,000; if it is kept nine more years, its residual value would be $10,000.

Required

Based on this information, should the old machine be replaced? Support your answer.

L.O. 9

Exercise 20-18A *Asset replacement decision*

McKee Company is considering replacement of some of its manufacturing equipment. Information regarding the existing equipment and the potential replacement equipment follows.

Existing Equipment		Replacement Equipment	
Cost	$ 90,000	Cost	$95,000
Operating expenses*	105,000	Operating expenses*	20,000
Salvage value	10,000	Salvage value	14,000
Market value	60,000	Useful life	8 years
Book value	32,000		
Remaining useful life	8 years		

*The amounts shown for operating expenses are the cumulative total of all such expected expenses to be incurred over the useful life of the equipment.

Required

Based on this information, recommend whether to replace the equipment. Support your recommendation with appropriate computations.

Exercise 20-19A *Asset replacement decision*

L.O. 9

Pendorric Company paid $72,000 to purchase a machine on January 1, 2006. During 2008, a technological breakthrough resulted in the development of a new machine that costs $125,000. The old machine costs $40,000 per year to operate, but the new machine could be operated for only $12,000 per year. The new machine, which will be available for delivery on January 1, 2009, has an expected useful life of four years. The old machine is more durable and is expected to have a remaining useful life of four years. The current market value of the old machine is $20,000. The expected salvage value of both machines is zero.

Required

Based on this information, recommend whether to replace the machine. Support your recommendation with appropriate computations.

Exercise 20-20A *Annual versus cumulative data for replacement decision*

L.O. 4, 9

Because of rapidly advancing technology, Sayre Publications Inc. is considering replacing its existing typesetting machine with leased equipment. The old machine, purchased two years ago, has an expected useful life of six years and is in good condition. Apparently, it will continue to perform as expected for the remaining four years of its expected useful life. A four-year lease for equipment with comparable productivity can be obtained for $15,000 per year. The following data apply to the old machine.

Original cost	$180,000
Accumulated depreciation	60,000
Current market value	77,500
Estimated salvage value	7,500

Required

a. Determine the annual opportunity cost of using the old machine. Based on your computations, recommend whether to replace it.

b. Determine the total cost of the lease over the four-year contract. Based on your computations, recommend whether to replace the old machine.

Appendix

Exercise 20-21A *Scarce resource decision*

L.O. 11

Ensor Funtime Novelties has the capacity to produce either 25,000 corncob pipes or 12,000 cornhusk dolls per year. The pipes cost $3 each to produce and sell for $6 each. The dolls sell for $10 each and cost $4 to produce.

Required

Assuming that Ensor Funtime Novelties can sell all it produces of either product, should it produce the corncob pipes or the cornhusk dolls? Show computations to support your answer.

PROBLEMS—SERIES A

All Problems in Series A are available with McGraw-Hill's Homework Manager

Problem 20-22A *Context-sensitive relevance*

L.O. 1

Required

Respond to each requirement independently.

a. Describe two decision-making contexts, one in which unit-level materials costs are avoidable, and the other in which they are unavoidable.

b. Describe two decision-making contexts, one in which batch-level setup costs are avoidable, and the other in which they are unavoidable.

c. Describe two decision-making contexts, one in which advertising costs are avoidable, and the other in which they are unavoidable.

d. Describe two decision-making contexts, one in which rent paid for a building is avoidable, and the other in which it is unavoidable.

e. Describe two decision-making contexts, one in which depreciation on manufacturing equipment is avoidable, and the other in which it is unavoidable.

L.O. 1

CHECK FIGURES

a. Contribution to profit for Job A: $168,000

b. Contribution to profit: $(1,000)

Problem 20-23A *Context-sensitive relevance*

Myl Construction Company is a building contractor specializing in small commercial buildings. The company has the opportunity to accept one of two jobs; it cannot accept both because they must be performed at the same time and Myl does not have the necessary labor force for both jobs. Indeed, it will be necessary to hire a new supervisor if either job is accepted. Furthermore, additional insurance will be required if either job is accepted. The revenue and costs associated with each job follow.

Cost Category	Job A	Job B
Contract price	$700,000	$600,000
Unit-level materials	250,000	220,000
Unit-level labor	240,000	243,000
Unit-level overhead	17,000	14,000
Supervisor's salary	80,000	80,000
Rental equipment costs	25,000	28,000
Depreciation on tools (zero market value)	20,000	20,000
Allocated portion of companywide facility-sustaining costs	9,000	8,000
Insurance cost for job	16,000	16,000

Required

a. Assume that Myl has decided to accept one of the two jobs. Identify the information relevant to selecting one job versus the other. Recommend which job to accept and support your answer with appropriate computations.

b. Assume that Job A is no longer available. Myl's choice is to accept or reject Job B alone. Identify the information relevant to this decision. Recommend whether to accept or reject Job B. Support your answer with appropriate computations.

L.O. 3, 5, 6

CHECK FIGURE

a. Relevant cost per unit: $56

Problem 20-24A *Effect of order quantity on special order decision*

Bogati Quilting Company makes blankets that it markets through a variety of department stores. It makes the blankets in batches of 1,000 units. Bogati made 20,000 blankets during the prior accounting period. The cost of producing the blankets is summarized here.

Materials cost ($20 per unit × 20,000)	$ 400,000
Labor cost ($25 per unit × 20,000)	500,000
Manufacturing supplies ($3 × 20,000)	60,000
Batch-level costs (20 batches at $4,000 per batch)	80,000
Product-level costs	140,000
Facility-level costs	300,000
Total costs	$1,480,000
Cost per unit = $1,480,000 ÷ 20,000 = $74	

Required

a. Quality Motels has offered to buy a batch of 500 blankets for $55 each. Bogati's normal selling price is $90 per unit. Based on the preceding quantitative data, should Bogati accept the special order? Support your answer with appropriate computations.

b. Would your answer to Requirement *a* change if Quality offered to buy a batch of 1,000 blankets for $55 per unit? Support your answer with appropriate computations.

c. Describe the qualitative factors that Bogati Quilting Company should consider before accepting a special order to sell blankets to Quality Motels.

Problem 20-25A *Effects of the level of production on an outsourcing decision*

L.O. 5, 6

Vaida Chemical Company makes a variety of cosmetic products, one of which is a skin cream designed to reduce the signs of aging. Vaida produces a relatively small amount (15,000 units) of the cream and is considering the purchase of the product from an outside supplier for $4.50 each. If Vaida purchases from the outside supplier, it would continue to sell and distribute the cream under its own brand name. Vaida's accountant constructed the following profitability analysis.

CHECK FIGURE
a. Total relevant cost: $75,000

Revenue (15,000 units × $10)	$150,000
Unit-level materials costs (15,000 units × $1.40)	(21,000)
Unit-level labor costs (15,000 units × $0.50)	(7,500)
Unit-level overhead costs (15,000 × $0.10)	(1,500)
Unit-level selling expenses (15,000 × $0.25)	(3,750)
Contribution margin	116,250
Skin cream production supervisor's salary	(45,000)
Allocated portion of facility-level costs	(11,250)
Product-level advertising cost	(36,000)
Contribution to companywide income	$ 24,000

Required

a. Identify the cost items relevant to the make-or-outsource decision.

b. Should Vaida continue to make the product or buy it from the supplier? Support your answer by determining the change in net income if Vaida buys the cream instead of making it.

c. Suppose that Vaida is able to increase sales by 10,000 units (sales will increase to 25,000 units). At this level of production, should Vaida make or buy the cream? Support your answer by explaining how the increase in production affects the cost per unit.

d. Discuss the qualitative factors that Vaida should consider before deciding to outsource the skin cream. How can Vaida minimize the risk of establishing a relationship with an unreliable supplier?

Problem 20-26A *Outsourcing decision affected by equipment replacement*

L.O. 5, 7, 9

Grant Bike Company (GBC) makes the frames used to build its bicycles. During 2006, GBC made 20,000 frames; the costs incurred follow.

CHECK FIGURES
a. Avoidable cost per unit: $119
b. Avoidable cost per unit with new equipment: $31

Unit-level materials costs (20,000 units × $40)	$ 800,000
Unit-level labor costs (20,000 units × $50)	1,000,000
Unit-level overhead costs (20,000 × $10)	200,000
Depreciation on manufacturing equipment	100,000
Bike frame production supervisor's salary	80,000
Inventory holding costs	300,000
Allocated portion of facility-level costs	500,000
Total costs	$2,980,000

GBC has an opportunity to purchase frames for $102 each.

Additional Information

1. The manufacturing equipment, which originally cost $500,000, has a book value of $400,000, a remaining useful life of four years, and a zero salvage value. If the equipment is not used to produce bicycle frames, it can be leased for $60,000 per year.
2. GBC has the opportunity to purchase for $960,000 new manufacturing equipment that will have an expected useful life of four years and a salvage value of $80,000. This equipment will increase productivity substantially, reducing unit-level labor costs by 60 percent. Assume that GBC will continue to produce and sell 20,000 frames per year in the future.
3. If GBC outsources the frames, the company can eliminate 80 percent of the inventory holding costs.

Required

a. Determine the avoidable cost per unit of making the bike frames, assuming that GBC is considering the alternatives between making the product using the existing equipment and outsourcing the product to the independent contractor. Based on the quantitative data, should GBC outsource the bike frames? Support your answer with appropriate computations.

b. Assuming that GBC is considering whether to replace the old equipment with the new equipment, determine the avoidable cost per unit to produce the bike frames using the new equipment and the avoidable cost per unit to produce the bike frames using the old equipment. Calculate the impact on profitability if the bike frames were made using the old equipment versus the new equipment.

c. Assuming that GBC is considering to either purchase the new equipment or outsource the bike frame, calculate the impact on profitability between the two alternatives.

d. Discuss the qualitative factors that GBC should consider before making a decision to outsource the bike frame. How can GBC minimize the risk of establishing a relationship with an unreliable supplier?

L.O. 8

eXcel

mhhe.com/edmonds2007

CHECK FIGURE

a. Contribution to profit: $12,000

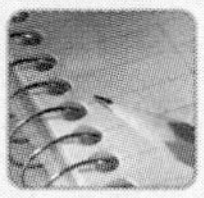

Problem 20-27A *Eliminating a segment*

Lackey Boot Co. sells men's, women's, and children's boots. For each type of boot sold, it operates a separate department that has its own manager. The manager of the men's department has a sales staff of nine employees, the manager of the women's department has six employees, and the manager of the children's department has three employees. All departments are housed in a single store. In recent years, the children's department has operated at a net loss and is expected to continue doing so. Last year's income statements follow.

	Men's Department	Women's Department	Children's Department
Sales	$580,000	$430,000	$165,000
Cost of Goods Sold	(260,000)	(180,000)	(103,000)
Gross Margin	320,000	250,000	62,000
Department Manager's Salary	(50,000)	(40,000)	(20,000)
Sales Commissions	(106,000)	(82,000)	(30,000)
Rent on Store Lease	(20,000)	(20,000)	(20,000)
Store Utilities	(5,000)	(5,000)	(5,000)
Net Income (loss)	$139,000	$103,000	$ (13,000)

Required

a. Determine whether to eliminate the children's department.

b. Confirm the conclusion you reached in Requirement *a* by preparing income statements for the company as a whole with and without the children's department.

c. Eliminating the children's department would increase space available to display men's and women's boots. Suppose management estimates that a wider selection of adult boots would increase the store's net earnings by $32,000. Would this information affect the decision that you made in Requirement *a*? Explain your answer.

L.O. 4, 8

CHECK FIGURE

a. Contribution to profit: $(40,000)

Problem 20-28A *Effect of activity level and opportunity cost on segment elimination decision*

Partlow Manufacturing Co. produces and sells specialized equipment used in the petroleum industry. The company is organized into three separate operating branches: Division A, which manufactures and sells heavy equipment; Division B, which manufactures and sells hand tools; and Division C, which makes and sells electric motors. Each division is housed in a separate manufacturing facility. Company headquarters is located in a separate building. In recent years, Division B has been operating at a net loss and is expected to continue doing so. Income statements for the three divisions for 2008 follow.

	Division A	Division B	Division C
Sales	$3,200,000	$ 750,000	$4,000,000
Less: Cost of Goods Sold			
Unit-Level Manufacturing Costs	(1,900,000)	(450,000)	(2,400,000)
Rent on Manufacturing Facility	(400,000)	(220,000)	(300,000)
Gross Margin	900,000	80,000	1,300,000
Less: Operating Expenses			
Unit-Level Selling and Admin. Expenses	(200,000)	(35,000)	(250,000)
Division-Level Fixed Selling and Admin. Expenses	(250,000)	(85,000)	(300,000)
Headquarters Facility-Level Costs	(150,000)	(150,000)	(150,000)
Net Income (loss)	$ 300,000	$(190,000)	$ 600,000

Required

a. Based on the preceding information, recommend whether to eliminate Division B. Support your answer by preparing companywide income statements before and after eliminating Division B.

b. During 2008, Division B produced and sold 20,000 units of hand tools. Would your recommendation in response to Requirement *a* change if sales and production increase to 30,000 units in 2009? Support your answer by comparing differential revenue and avoidable cost for Division B, assuming that it sells 30,000 units.

c. Suppose that Partlow could sublease Division B's manufacturing facility for $320,000. Would you operate the division at a production and sales volume of 30,000 units, or would you close it? Support your answer with appropriate computations.

Problem 20-29A ***Comprehensive problem including special order, outsourcing, and segment elimination decisions***

L.O. 6, 7, 8

excel

mhhe.com/edmonds2007

CHECK FIGURE

a. CM: $7,500

Weems Inc. makes and sells state-of-the-art electronics products. One of its segments produces The Math Machine, an inexpensive four-function calculator. The company's chief accountant recently prepared the following income statement showing annual revenues and expenses associated with the segment's operating activities. The relevant range for the production and sale of the calculators is between 30,000 and 60,000 units per year.

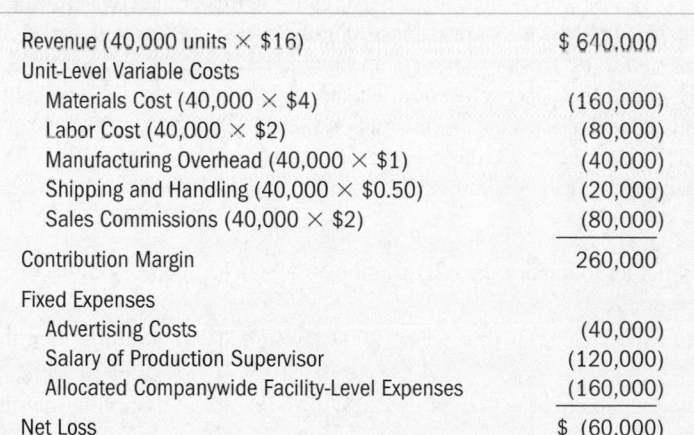

Revenue (40,000 units × $16)	$ 640,000
Unit-Level Variable Costs	
Materials Cost (40,000 × $4)	(160,000)
Labor Cost (40,000 × $2)	(80,000)
Manufacturing Overhead (40,000 × $1)	(40,000)
Shipping and Handling (40,000 × $0.50)	(20,000)
Sales Commissions (40,000 × $2)	(80,000)
Contribution Margin	260,000
Fixed Expenses	
Advertising Costs	(40,000)
Salary of Production Supervisor	(120,000)
Allocated Companywide Facility-Level Expenses	(160,000)
Net Loss	$ (60,000)

Required (Consider each of the requirements independently.)

a. A large discount store has approached the owner of Weems about buying 5,000 calculators. It would replace The Math Machine's label with its own logo to avoid affecting Weems' existing customers. Because the offer was made directly to the owner, no sales commissions on the transaction would be involved, but the discount store is willing to pay only $9.00 per calculator. Based on quantitative factors alone, should Weems accept the special order? Support your answer with appropriate computations. Specifically, by what amount would the special order increase or decrease profitability?

b. Weems has an opportunity to buy the 40,000 calculators it currently makes from a reliable competing manufacturer for $9.80 each. The product meets Weems' quality standards. Weems could continue to use its own logo, advertising program, and sales force to distribute the products. Should Weems buy the calculators or continue to make them? Support your answer with appropriate computations. Specifically, how much more or less would it cost to buy the calculators than to make them? Would your answer change if the volume of sales were increased to 60,000 units?

c. Because the calculator division is currently operating at a loss, should it be eliminated from the company's operations? Support your answer with appropriate computations. Specifically, by what amount would the segment's elimination increase or decrease profitability?

Appendix

L.O. 11

CHECK FIGURES

a. Contribution margin per hour: $2 for A and $1.50 for B

Problem 20-30A *Allocating scarce resources*

The following information applies to the products of Hardaway Company.

	Product A	Product B
Selling price per unit	$26	$24
Variable cost per unit	22	18

Required

Identify the product that should be produced or sold under each of the following constraints. Consider each constraint separately.

a. One unit of Product A requires 2 hours of labor to produce, and one unit of Product B requires 4 hours of labor to produce. Due to labor constraints, demand is higher than the company's capacity to make both products.

b. The products are sold to the public in retail stores. The company has limited floor space and cannot stock as many products as it would like. Display space is available for only one of the two products. Expected sales of Product A are 10,000 units and of Product B are 8,000 units.

c. The maximum number of machine hours available is 40,000. Product A uses 2 machine hours, and Product B uses 5 machine hours. The company can sell all the products it produces.

L.O. 10

eXcel

mhhe.com/edmonds2007

CHECK FIGURE

a. Relevant costs: $560,000 for keeping the old machine

Problem 20-31A *Conflict between short-term and long-term performance*

Bill Oakes manages the cutting department of Rancont Timber Company. He purchased a tree-cutting machine on January 1, 2006, for $400,000. The machine had an estimated useful life of five years and zero salvage value, and the cost to operate it is $90,000 per year. Technological developments resulted in the development of a more advanced machine available for purchase on January 1, 2007, that would allow a 25 percent reduction in operating costs. The new machine would cost $240,000 and have a four-year useful life and zero salvage value. The current market value of the old machine on January 1, 2007, is $200,000, and its book value is $320,000 on that date. Straight-line depreciation is used for both machines. The company expects to generate $224,000 of revenue per year from the use of either machine.

Required

a. Recommend whether to replace the old machine on January 1, 2007. Support your answer with appropriate computations.

b. Prepare income statements for four years (2007 through 2010) assuming that the old machine is retained.

c. Prepare income statements for four years (2007 through 2010) assuming that the old machine is replaced.

d. Discuss the potential ethical conflicts that could result from the timing of the loss and expense recognition reported in the two income statements.

EXERCISES—SERIES B

L.O. 1

Exercise 20-1B *Distinction between relevance and cost behavior*

Ken Griffith is planning to rent a small shop for a new business. He can sell either sandwiches or donuts. The following costs pertain to the two products.

Sandwiches		Donuts	
Cost per sandwich	$2.00	Cost per dozen donuts	$1.45
Sales commissions per sandwich	0.05	Sales commissions per dozen donuts	0.07
Monthly shop rental cost	1,000.00	Monthly shop rental cost	1,000.00
Monthly advertising cost	500.00	Monthly advertising cost	300.00

Required

Identify each cost as relevant or irrelevant to Mr. Griffith's product decision and indicate whether the cost is fixed or variable relative to the number of units sold.

Exercise 20-2B *Distinction between relevance and cost behavior* L.O. 1, 2

Rhodes Company makes and sells a toy plane. Rhodes incurred the following costs in its most recent fiscal year:

Cost Items Reported on Income Statement
Costs of TV Commercials
Labor Costs ($3 per unit)
Sales Commissions (1% of sales)
Sales Manager's Salary
Shipping and Handling Costs ($0.75 per unit)
Cost of Renting the Administrative Building
Utility Costs for the Manufacturing Plant ($0.25 per unit produced)
Manufacturing Plant Manager's Salary
Materials Costs ($4 per unit produced)
Real Estate Taxes on the Manufacturing Plant
Depreciation on Manufacturing Equipment
Packaging Cost ($1 per unit produced)
Wages of the Plant Security Guard

Rhodes could purchase the toy planes from a supplier. If it did, the company would continue to sell them using its own logo, advertising program, and sales staff.

Required

Identify each cost as relevant or irrelevant to the outsourcing decision and indicate whether the cost is fixed or variable relative to the number of toy planes manufactured and sold.

Exercise 20-3B *Distinction between avoidable costs and cost behavior* L.O. 1

Dublar Phones Inc. makes telephones that it sells to department stores throughout the United States. Dublar is trying to decide which of two telephone models to manufacture. The company could produce either telephone with its existing machinery. Cost data pertaining to the two choices follow:

	Model 90	Model 30
Materials cost per unit	$ 36	$ 36
Labor cost per unit	40	24
Product design cost	12,000	7,000
Depreciation on existing manufacturing machinery	3,000	3,000

Required

a. Identify the fixed costs and determine the amount of fixed cost for each model.

b. Identify the variable costs and determine the amount of variable cost for each model.

c. Identify the avoidable costs.

L.O. 1, 2, 6

Exercise 20-4B ***Special order decision***

Mai Textile Company manufactures high-quality bed sheets and sells them in sets to a well-known retail company for $40 a set. Mai has sufficient capacity to produce 100,000 sets of sheets annually; the retail company currently purchases 80,000 sets each year. Mai's unit-level cost is $25 per set and its fixed cost is $800,000 per year. A motel chain has offered to purchase 10,000 sheet sets from Mai for $32 per set. If Mai accepts the order, the contract will prohibit the motel chain from reselling the bed sheets.

Required

Should Mai accept or reject the special order? Support your answer with appropriate computations.

L.O. 1, 2, 6

Exercise 20-5B ***Special order decision***

Estrada Automotive Company manufactures an engine designed for motorcycles and markets the product using its own brand name. Although Estrada has the capacity to produce 28,000 engines annually, it currently produces and sells only 25,000 units per year. The engine normally sells for $650 per unit, with no quantity discounts. The unit-level costs to produce the engine are $200 for direct materials, $150 for direct labor, and $60 for indirect manufacturing costs. Estrada expects total annual product- and facility-level costs to be $500,000 and $750,000, respectively. Assume Estrada receives a special order from a new customer seeking to buy 1,000 engines for $460 each.

Required

Should Estrada accept or reject the special order? Support your answer with appropriate computations.

L.O. 5

Exercise 20-6B ***Identifying qualitative factors for a special order decision***

Required

Describe the qualitative factors that Estrada should consider before accepting the special order described in Exercise 20-5B.

L.O. 5

Exercise 20-7B ***Using the contribution margin approach for a special order decision***

Merkel Company produces and sells a food processor that it prices at a 25 percent markup on total cost. Based on data pertaining to producing and selling 30,000 food processors, Merkel computes the sales price per food processor as follows.

Unit-level costs	$ 600,000
Fixed costs	480,000
Total cost (a)	1,080,000
Markup (a × .25)	270,000
Total sales revenue (b)	$1,350,000
Sales price per unit (b ÷ 30,000)	$45.00

Required

a. Merkel receives a special order for 7,000 food processors for $19 each. Merkel has excess capacity. Calculate the contribution margin per unit for the special order. Based on the contribution margin per unit, should Merkel accept the special order?

b. Support your answer by preparing a contribution margin income statement for the special order.

L.O. 7

Exercise 20-8B ***Making an outsourcing decision***

Boutwell Boats Company currently produces a battery used in manufacturing its boats. The company annually manufactures and sells 2,000 units of a particular model of fishing boat. Because of the low volume of activity, Boutwell is unable to obtain the economies of scale that larger producers achieve. For example, the costs associated with producing the batteries it uses are almost 30 percent more than the cost of purchasing comparable batteries. Boutwell could buy batteries for $75 each; it costs $100 each to make them. A detailed breakdown of current production costs for the batteries follows:

Item	Unit Cost	Total
Unit-level costs:		
Materials	$ 30	$ 60,000
Labor	25	50,000
Overhead	5	10,000
Allocated facility-level costs	40	80,000
Total	$100	$200,000

Based on these figures, Boutwell's president asserted that it would be foolish for the company to continue to produce the batteries at $100 each when it can buy them for $75 each.

Required

Do you agree with the president's conclusion? Support your answer with appropriate computations.

Exercise 20-9B ***Establishing a price for an outsourcing decision*** **L.O. 7**

Smiles Inc. makes and sells skateboards. Smiles currently makes the 60,000 wheels used annually in its skateboards but has an opportunity to purchase the wheels from a reliable manufacturer. The costs of making the wheels follow.

Annual Costs Associated with Manufacturing Skateboard Wheels	
Materials (60,000 units × $4.50)	$270,000
Labor (60,000 units × $2.50)	150,000
Depreciation on manufacturing equipment*	30,000
Salary of wheel production supervisor	65,000
Rental cost of equipment used to make wheels	55,000
Allocated portion of corporate-level facility-sustaining costs	40,000
Total cost to make 60,000 wheels	$610,000

*The equipment has a book value of $74,000 but its market value is zero.

Required

a. Determine the maximum price per unit that Smiles would be willing to pay for the wheels.

b. Would the price computed in Requirement *a* change if production were increased to 80,000 units? Support your answer with appropriate computations.

Exercise 20-10B ***Making an outsourcing decision with qualitative factors considered*** **L.O. 5, 7**

Cox Computers currently purchases for $15 each keyboard it uses in the 50,000 computers it makes and sells annually. Each computer uses one keyboard. The company has idle capacity and is considering whether to make the keyboards that it needs. Cox estimates that materials and labor costs for making keyboards would be $9 each. In addition, supervisory salaries, rent, and other manufacturing costs would be $400,000. Allocated facility-level costs would amount to $70,000.

Required

a. Determine the change in net income that Cox would experience if it decides to make the keyboards.

b. Discuss the qualitative factors that Cox should consider.

Exercise 20-11B ***Outsourcing decision affected by opportunity costs*** **L.O. 4, 7**

Kwang Doors Company currently produces the doorknobs for the doors it makes and sells. The monthly cost of producing 3,000 doorknobs is as follows:

Unit-level materials	$2,700
Unit-level labor	2,400
Unit-level overhead	1,800
Product-level costs*	3,000
Allocated facility-level costs	9,600

*Twenty percent of these costs can be avoided if the doorknobs are purchased.

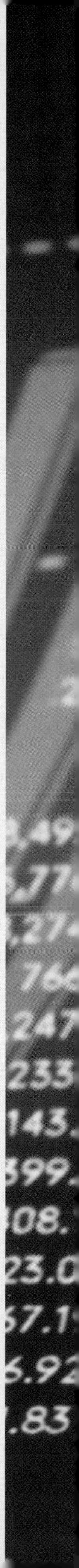

Nash Company has offered to sell comparable doorknobs to Kwang for $3 each.

Required

a. Should Kwang continue to make the doorknobs? Support your answer with appropriate computations.
b. For $3,000 per month, Kwang could lease the manufacturing space to another company. Would this potential cash inflow affect your response to Requirement *a*? Explain.

L.O. 4

Exercise 20-12B *Opportunity cost*

Bester Fishing Tours Inc. owns a boat that originally cost $98,000. Currently, the boat's net book value is $25,000, and its expected remaining useful life is four years. Bester has an opportunity to purchase for $72,000 a replacement boat that is extremely fuel efficient. Fuel costs for the old boat are expected to be $12,000 per year more than fuel costs would be for the replacement boat. Bester could sell the old boat, which is fully paid for and in good condition, for only $32,000.

Required

Should Bester replace the old boat with the new fuel-efficient model, or should it continue to use the old one until it wears out? Explain.

L.O. 4, 5

Exercise 20-13B *Opportunity costs*

Two years ago, Patrick Hale bought a truck for $28,000 to offer delivery service. Patrick earns $35,000 a year operating as an independent trucker. He has an opportunity to sell his truck for $15,000 and take a position as an instructor in a truck driving school. The instructor position pays $28,000 a year for working 40 hours per week. Driving his truck, Patrick works approximately 60 hours per week. If Patrick sells his truck, he will invest the proceeds of the sale in bonds that pay a 12 percent return.

Required

a. Determine the opportunity cost of owning and operating the independent delivery business.
b. Based solely on financial considerations, should Patrick sell his truck and accept the instructor position?
c. Discuss the qualitative as well as quantitative characteristics that Patrick should consider.

L.O. 8

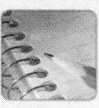

Exercise 20-14B *Segment elimination decision*

The Mosley Company operates three segments. Income statements for the segments imply that Mosley could improve profitability if Segment X were eliminated.

THE MOSLEY COMPANY
Income Statements
For the Year 2009

Segment	X	Y	Z
Sales	$ 58,000	$140,000	$132,000
Cost of Goods Sold	(44,000)	(55,000)	(56,000)
Sales Commissions	(4,000)	(14,000)	(13,000)
Contribution Margin	10,000	71,000	63,000
General Fixed Oper. Exp. (allocation of president's salary)	(10,000)	(10,000)	(10,000)
Advertising Expense (specific to individual segments)	(6,000)	(7,000)	0
Net Income	$ (6,000)	$ 54,000	$ 53,000

Required

a. Explain the effect on Mosley's profitability if segment X is eliminated.
b. Prepare comparative income statements for the company as a whole under the two alternatives: (1) Segment X is retained or (2) Segment X is eliminated.

L.O. 8

Exercise 20-15B *Segment elimination decision*

Hanson Company divides its operations into six divisions. A recent income statement for the Clairmont Division follows:

Income Statement	
Revenue	$ 800,000
Salaries for Employees	(550,000)
Operating Expenses	(145,000)
Insurance	(48,000)
Division-Level Facility-Sustaining Costs	(98,000)
Companywide Facility-Sustaining Costs	(60,000)
Net Loss	$(101,000)

Required

a. Should Hanson eliminate the Clairmont Division? Support your answer by explaining how the division's elimination would affect the net income of the company as a whole. By how much would companywide income increase or decrease?

b. Assume that the Clairmont Division could increase its revenue to $850,000 by raising prices. Would this change the decision you made in response to Requirement *a*? Assuming Hanson's revenue becomes $850,000, determine the amount of the increase or decrease that would occur in companywide net income if the segment were eliminated.

c. What is the minimum amount of revenue the Clairmont Division must generate to justify its continued operation?

Exercise 20-16B *Identifying avoidable cost of a segment* L.O. 8

The Ohldin Corporation is considering the elimination of one of its segments. The following fixed costs pertain to the segment. If the segment is eliminated, the building it uses will be sold.

Annual advertising expense	$169,000
Market value of the building	48,000
Annual depreciation on the building	18,000
Annual maintenance costs on equipment	26,000
Annual real estate taxes on the building	8,000
Annual supervisory salaries	72,000
Annual allocation of companywide facility-level costs	30,000
Original cost of the building	75,000
Current book value of the building	54,000

Required

Based on this information, determine the amount of avoidable cost associated with the segment.

Exercise 20-17B *Asset replacement decision* L.O. 9

Tench Electronics purchased a manufacturing plant four years ago for $8,000,000. The plant costs $2,000,000 per year to operate. Its current book value using straight-line depreciation is $6,000,000. Tench could purchase a replacement plant for $12,000,000 that would have a useful life of 10 years. Because of new technology, the replacement plant would require only $500,000 per year in operating expenses. It would have an expected salvage value of $1,000,000 after 10 years. The current disposal value of the old plant is $1,400,000, and if Tench keeps it 10 more years, its residual value would be $500,000.

Required

Based on this information, should Tench replace the old plant? Support your answer with appropriate computations.

Exercise 20-18B *Asset replacement decision* L.O. 9

Calder Company is considering whether to replace some of its manufacturing equipment. Information pertaining to the existing equipment and the potential replacement equipment follows:

Existing Equipment		Replacement Equipment	
Cost	$60,000	Cost	$45,000
Operating expenses*	50,000	Operating expenses*	10,000
Salvage value	12,000	Salvage value	10,000
Market value	20,000	Useful life	10 years
Book value	30,000		
Remaining useful life	10 years		

*The amounts shown for operating expenses are the cumulative total of all such expenses expected to be incurred over the useful life of the equipment.

Required

Based on this information, recommend whether to replace the equipment. Support your recommendation with appropriate computations.

L.O. 9

Exercise 20-19B *Asset replacement decision*

Kase Company, a Texas-based corporation, paid $65,000 to purchase an air conditioner on January 1, 1995. During 2005, surging energy costs prompted management to consider replacing the air conditioner with a more energy-efficient model. The new air conditioner would cost $90,000. Electricity for the existing air conditioner costs the company $35,000 per year; the new model would cost only $24,000 per year. The new model, which has an expected useful life of 10 years, would be installed on January 1, 2006. Because the old air conditioner is more durable, Kase estimates it still has a remaining useful life of 10 years even though it has been used. The current market value of the old air conditioner is $30,000. The expected salvage value of both air conditioners is zero.

Required

Based on this information, recommend whether to replace the equipment. Support your recommendation with appropriate computations.

L.O. 4, 9

Exercise 20-20B *Annual versus cumulative data for replacement decision*

Because their three adult children have all at last left home, Dan and Alberta Quaker recently moved to a smaller house. Dan owns a riding lawnmower he bought three years ago to take care of the former house's huge yard; it should last another five years. With the new house's smaller yard, Dan thinks he could hire someone to cut his grass for $350 per year. He wonders if this option is financially sound. Relevant information follows.

Riding Lawn Mower	Amount
Original cost	$1,800
Accumulated depreciation	720
Current market value	1,000
Estimated salvage value	0

Required

a. What is the annual opportunity cost of using the riding mower? Based on your computations, recommend whether Dan should sell it and hire a lawn service.

b. Determine the total cost of hiring a lawn service for the next five years. Based on your computations, recommend whether Dan should sell the mower and hire a lawn service.

Appendix

L.O. 11

Exercise 20-21B *Scarce resource decision*

Centech has the capacity to annually produce either 50,000 desktop computers or 28,000 laptop computers. Relevant data for each product follow:

	Desktop	Laptop
Sales price	$1,000	$1,800
Variable costs	400	650

Required

Assuming that Centech can sell all it produces of either product, should the company produce the desktop computers or the laptop computers? Provide computations to support your answer.

PROBLEMS–SERIES B

Problem 20-22B *Context-sensitive relevance* L.O. 1

Required

Respond to each requirement independently.

a. Describe two decision-making contexts, one in which unit-level labor costs are avoidable, and the other in which they are unavoidable.

b. Describe two decision-making contexts, one in which batch-level shipping costs are avoidable, and the other in which they are unavoidable.

c. Describe two decision-making contexts, one in which administrative costs are avoidable, and the other in which they are unavoidable.

d. Describe two decision-making contexts, one in which the insurance premium paid on a building is avoidable, and the other in which it is unavoidable.

e. Describe two decision-making contexts, one in which amortization of a product patent is avoidable, and the other in which it is unavoidable.

Problem 20-23B *Context-sensitive relevance* L.O. 1

Reeves Machines Company is evaluating two customer orders from which it can accept only one because of capacity limitations. The data associated with each order follow.

Cost Category	Order A	Order B
Contract price	$940,000	$860,000
Unit-level materials	350,000	306,000
Unit-level labor	330,000	304,800
Unit-level overhead	106,000	98,000
Supervisor's salary	80,000	80,000
Rental equipment costs	20,000	24,000
Depreciation on tools (zero market value)	28,000	28,000
Allocated portion of companywide facility-sustaining costs	8,000	7,200
Insurance coverage	54,000	54,000

Required

a. Assume that Reeves has decided to accept one of the two orders. Identify the information relevant to selecting one order versus the other. Recommend which job to accept, and support your answer with appropriate computations.

b. The customer presenting Order A has withdrawn it because of its financial hardship. Under this circumstance, Reeves' choice is to accept or reject Order B alone. Identify the information relevant to this decision. Recommend whether to accept or reject Order B. Support your answer with appropriate computations.

Problem 20-24B *Effect of order quantity on special order decision* L.O. 3, 5, 6

Wayland Company made 100,000 electric drills in batches of 1,000 units each during the prior accounting period. Normally, Wayland markets its products through a variety of hardware stores. The following is the summarized cost to produce electric drills.

Materials cost ($5.00 per unit × 100,000)	$ 500,000
Labor cost ($4.00 per unit × 100,000)	400,000
Manufacturing supplies ($0.50 × 100,000)	50,000
Batch-level costs (100 batches at $2,000 per batch)	200,000
Product-level costs	150,000
Facility-level costs	180,000
Total costs	$1,480,000
Cost per unit = $1,480,000 ÷ 100,000 = $14.80	

Required

a. Bypassing Wayland's regular distribution channel, Good Home Repair and Maintenance Inc. has offered to buy a batch of 500 electric drills for $12.50 each directly from Wayland. Wayland's normal selling price is $20 per unit. Based on the preceding quantitative data, should Wayland accept the special order? Support your answer with appropriate computations.

b. Would your answer to Requirement *a* change if Good Home Repair and Maintenance offered to buy a batch of 1,000 electric drills for $11.60 each? Support your answer with appropriate computations.

c. Describe the qualitative factors that Wayland Company should consider before accepting a special order to sell electric drills to Good Home Repair and Maintenance.

L.O. 5, 6

Problem 20-25B *Effects of the level of production on an outsourcing decision*

One of Aree Company's major products is a fuel additive designed to improve fuel efficiency and keep engines clean. Aree, a petrochemical firm, makes and sells 200,000 units of the fuel additive per year. Its management is evaluating the possibility of having an outside supplier manufacture the product for Aree for $1.28 each. Aree would continue to sell and distribute the fuel additive under its own brand name for either alternative. Aree's accountant constructed the following profitability analysis.

Revenue (200,000 units × $2.50)	$500,000
Unit-level materials costs (200,000 units × $0.50)	(100,000)
Unit-level labor costs (200,000 units × $0.10)	(20,000)
Unit-level overhead costs (200,000 × $0.25)	(50,000)
Unit-level selling expenses (200,000 × $0.15)	(30,000)
Contribution margin	300,000
Fuel additive production supervisor's salary	(100,000)
Allocated portion of facility-level costs	(40,000)
Product-level advertising cost	(60,000)
Contribution to companywide income	$100,000

Required

a. Identify the cost items relevant to the make-or-outsource decision.

b. Should Aree continue to make the fuel additive or buy it from the supplier? Support your answer by determining the change in net income if Aree buys the fuel additive instead of making it.

c. Suppose that Aree is able to increase sales by 200,000 units (sales will increase to 400,000 units). At this level of sales, should Aree make or buy the fuel additive? Support your answer by explaining how the increase in production affects the cost per unit.

d. Discuss the qualitative factors that Aree should consider before deciding to outsource the fuel additive. How can Aree minimize the risk of establishing a relationship with an unreliable supplier?

L.O. 5, 7, 9

Problem 20-26B *Outsourcing decision affected by equipment replacement*

During 2007, K-Bee Toy Company made 15,000 units of Model T, the costs of which follow.

Unit-level materials costs (15,000 units × $6)	$ 90,000
Unit-level labor costs (15,000 units × $20)	300,000
Unit-level overhead costs (15,000 × $8)	120,000
Depreciation on manufacturing equipment	48,000
Model T production supervisor's salary	42,000
Inventory holding costs	108,000
Allocated portion of facility-level costs	72,000
Total costs	$780,000

An independent contractor has offered to make the same product for K-Bee for $42 each.

Additional Information:

1. The manufacturing equipment originally cost $420,000 and has a book value of $240,000, a remaining useful life of four years, and a zero salvage value. If the equipment is not used to produce Model T in the production process, it can be leased for $36,000 per year.
2. K-Bee has the opportunity to purchase for $200,000 new manufacturing equipment that will have an expected useful life of four years and a salvage value of $80,000. This equipment will increase productivity substantially, thereby reducing unit-level labor costs by 20 percent.
3. If K-Bee discontinues the production of Model T, the company can eliminate 50 percent of its inventory holding cost.

Required

a. Determine the avoidable cost per unit to produce Model T assuming that K-Bee is considering the alternatives between making the product using the existing equipment and outsourcing the product to the independent contractor. Based on the quantitative data, should K-Bee outsource Model T? Support your answer with appropriate computations.

b. Assuming that K-Bee is considering whether to replace the old equipment with the new equipment, determine the avoidable cost per unit to produce Model T using the new equipment and the avoidable cost per unit to produce Model T using the old equipment. Calculate the impact on profitability if Model T were made using the old equipment versus the new equipment.

c. Assuming that K-Bee is considering to either purchase the new equipment or to outsource Model T, calculate the impact on profitability between the two alternatives.

d. Discuss the qualitative factors that K-Bee should consider before making a decision to outsource Model T. How can K-Bee minimize the risk of establishing a relationship with an unreliable supplier?

Problem 20-27B *Eliminating a segment* L.O. 8

Howell's Grocery Store has three departments, meat, canned food, and produce, each of which has its own manager. All departments are housed in a single store. Recently, the produce department has been suffering a net loss and is expected to continue doing so. Last year's income statements follow.

	Meat Department	Canned Food Department	Produce Department
Sales	$650,000	$580,000	$ 420,000
Cost of Goods Sold	(270,000)	(330,000)	(260,000)
Gross Margin	380,000	250,000	160,000
Departmental Manager's Salary	(42,000)	(30,000)	(35,000)
Rent on Store Lease	(80,000)	(80,000)	(80,000)
Store Utilities	(20,000)	(20,000)	(20,000)
Other General Expenses	(98,000)	(98,000)	(98,000)
Net Income (loss)	$140,000	$ 22,000	$ (73,000)

Required

a. Determine whether to eliminate the produce department.

b. Confirm the conclusion you reached in Requirement *a* by preparing a before and an after income statement, assuming that the produce department is eliminated.

c. Eliminating the produce department would allow the meat department to expand. It could add seafood to its products. Suppose that management estimates that offering seafood would increase the store's net earnings by $160,000. Would this information affect the decision that you made in Requirement *a*? Explain your answer.

L.O. 4, 8

Problem 20-28B ***Effect of activity level and opportunity cost on segment elimination decision***

Ozaydin Company has three separate operating branches: Division X, which manufactures utensils; Division Y, which makes plates; and Division Z, which makes cooking pots. Each division operates its own facility. The company's administrative offices are located in a separate building. In recent years, Division Z has experienced a net loss and is expected to continue to do so. Income statements for 2008 follow.

	Division X	Division Y	Division Z
Sales	$2,000,000	$1,600,000	$1,710,000
Less: Cost of Goods Sold			
Unit-Level Manufacturing Costs	(1,100,000)	(580,000)	(900,000)
Rent on Manufacturing Facility	(240,000)	(220,000)	(450,000)
Gross Margin	660,000	800,000	360,000
Less: Operating Expenses			
Unit-Level Selling and Admin. Expenses	(60,000)	(45,000)	(150,000)
Division-Level Fixed Selling and Admin. Expenses	(140,000)	(125,000)	(240,000)
Administrative Facility-Level Costs	(80,000)	(80,000)	(80,000)
Net Income (loss)	$ 380,000	$ 550,000	$ (110,000)

Required

a. Based on the preceding information, recommend whether to eliminate Division Z. Support your answer by preparing companywide income statements before and after eliminating Division Z.

b. During 2008, Division Z produced and sold 30,000 units of product. Would your recommendation in Requirement *a* change if sales and production increase to 45,000 units in 2009? Support your answer by comparing differential revenue and avoidable cost for Division Z, assuming that 45,000 units are sold.

c. Suppose that Ozaydin could sublease Division Z's manufacturing facility for $910,000. Would you operate the division at a production and sales volume of 45,000 units, or would you close it? Support your answer with appropriate computations.

L.O. 6, 7, 8

Problem 20-29B ***Comprehensive problem including special order, outsourcing, and segment elimination decisions***

Yelton Company's electronics division produces a radio/cassette player. The vice president in charge of the division is evaluating the income statement showing annual revenues and expenses associated with the division's operating activities. The relevant range for the production and sale of the radio/cassette player is between 40,000 and 120,000 units per year.

Income Statement	
Revenue (50,000 units × $40)	$2,000,000
Unit-Level Variable Costs	
Materials Cost (50,000 × $18)	(900,000)
Labor Cost (50,000 × $10)	(500,000)
Manufacturing Overhead (50,000 × $2)	(100,000)
Shipping and Handling (50,000 × $1)	(50,000)
Sales Commissions (50,000 × $3)	(150,000)
Contribution Margin	300,000
Fixed Expenses	
Advertising Costs Related to the Division	(40,000)
Salary of Production Supervisor	(150,000)
Allocated Companywide Facility-Level Expenses	(220,000)
Net Loss	$ (110,000)

Required (Consider each of the requirements independently.)

a. An international trading firm has approached top management about buying 30,000 radio/cassette players for $33 each. It would sell the product in a foreign country, so that Yelton's existing customers would not be affected. Because the offer was made directly to top management, no sales commissions on the transaction would be involved. Based on quantitative features alone, should Yelton accept the special order? Support your answer with appropriate computations. Specifically, by what amount would profitability increase or decrease if the special order is accepted?

b. Yelton has an opportunity to buy the 50,000 radio/cassette players it currently makes from a foreign manufacturer for $32 each. The manufacturer has a good reputation for reliability and quality, and Yelton could continue to use its own logo, advertising program, and sales force to distribute the products. Should Yelton buy the radio/cassette players or continue to make them? Support your answer with appropriate computations. Specifically, how much more or less would it cost to buy the radio/cassette players than to make them? Would your answer change if the volume of sales were increased to 120,000 units?

c. Because the electronics division is currently operating at a loss, should it be eliminated from the company's operations? Support your answer with appropriate computations. Specifically, by what amount would the segment's elimination increase or decrease profitability?

Appendix

Problem 20-30B *Allocating scarce resources* L.O. 11

Deen Company makes two products, M and N. Product information follows.

	Product M	Product N
Selling price per unit	$75	$90
Variable cost per unit	48	55

Required

Identify the product that should be produced or sold under each of the following constraints. Consider each constraint separately.

a. One unit of Product M requires 3 hours of labor to produce, and one unit of Product N requires 5 hours of labor to produce. Due to labor constraints, demand is higher than the company's capacity to make both products.

b. The products are sold to the public in retail stores. The company has limited floor space and cannot stock as many products as it would like. Display space is available for only one of the two products. Expected sales of Product M are 8,000 units, and expected sales of Product N are 7,000 units.

c. The maximum number of machine hours available is 36,000. Product M uses 6 machine hours, and Product N uses 10 machine hours. The company can sell all the products it produces.

Problem 20-31B *Conflict between short-term and long-term performance* L.O. 10

Curtis Construction Components Inc. purchased a machine on January 1, 2003, for $480,000. The chief engineer estimated the machine's useful life to be six years and its salvage value to be zero. The operating cost of this machine is $240,000 per year. By January 1, 2005, a new machine that requires 30 percent less operating cost than the existing machine has become available for $360,000; it would have a four-year useful life with zero salvage. The current market value of the old machine on January 1, 2005, is $200,000, and its book value is $320,000 on that date. Straight-line depreciation is used for both machines. The company expects to generate $640,000 of revenue per year from the use of either machine.

Required

a. Recommend whether to replace the old machine on January 1, 2005. Support your answer with appropriate computations.

b. Prepare income statements for four years (2005 through 2008) assuming that the old machine is retained.

c. Prepare income statements for four years (2005 through 2008) assuming that the old machine is replaced.

d. Discuss the potential ethical conflicts that could result from the timing of the loss and expense recognition reported in the two income statements.

ANALYZE, THINK, COMMUNICATE

ATC 20-1 Business Application Case *Elimination of a product line*

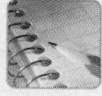

The following excerpts were drawn from the article entitled "The Scottish Shogun," published in *U.S. News & World Report,* May 19, 1997, on pages 44 and 45.

The Japanese car maker [**Mazda Motor Company**] has accumulated nearly a billion dollars in operating losses in three years. Its market share in Japan fell from nearly 8 percent to below 5 percent in the first half of the decade, and its overall car production dropped by a stunning 46 percent. In fact, Mazda has been fighting for its life. To salvage the company, **Ford Motor Co.**, Mazda's biggest shareholder, gambled $430 million [in 1996] and raised its equity stake in Mazda to 33.4 percent, which in practice gave it operating control. The U.S. car maker chose Henry Wallace, a Ford man for 25 years, to spearhead a turnaround. Mr. Wallace is the first foreigner to lead a big Japanese company. In this case, Mr. Wallace has been warmly embraced by the Japanese—both inside and outside Mazda. Wallace's first move was to retrench—cut product lines, consolidate sales channels, reduce inventory, and in the United States, halt unprofitable fleet and car-rental sales. Wallace also took action to instill a profit motive among the board of directors. Wallace observed, "I don't think previously there was a strong profit motive within the company." Instead, Mazda was a club of engineers who turned out wonderful niche cars—some with exotic styling, others with superb performance—that few consumers wanted to buy. When drivers developed a taste for sport utility vehicles, Mazda's beautiful sedans collected dust on the lots.

Required

a. The article indicated that one action Mr. Wallace took was to cut product lines. Explain which levels (unit, batch, product, and/or facility) of costs could be avoided by eliminating product lines. What sacrifices will Mazda likely have to make to obtain the cost savings associated with eliminating product lines?

b. Suppose that the cost data in the table below apply to three sales channels that were eliminated through the consolidation program.

Additional Information

(1) Sales are expected to drop by 10 percent because of the consolidation program. The remaining sales volume was absorbed by other sales channels.

(2) Half of the sales staff accepted transfers that placed them in positions in other sales channels. The other half left the company.

(3) The supervisor of Channel 1 accepted a job transfer. The other two supervisors left the company.

Annual Costs of Operating Each Sales Channel	Channel 1	Channel 2	Channel 3
Unit-level selling costs:			
Selling supplies	$ 32,000	$ 22,000	$ 40,000
Sales commissions	355,000	225,000	425,000
Shipping and handling	40,000	24,000	49,000
Miscellaneous	20,000	17,000	29,000
Facility-level selling costs:			
Rent	245,000	236,000	240,000
Utilities	40,000	48,000	50,000
Staff salaries	900,000	855,000	1,088,000
Supervisory salaries	150,000	100,000	170,000
Depreciation on equipment	300,000	307,000	303,000
Allocated companywide expenses	100,000	100,000	100,000

(4) The combined equipment, with an expected remaining useful life of four years and a $700,000 salvage value, had a market value of $625,000.

(5) The offices operated by the eliminated channels were closed.

Determine the amount of annual costs saved by consolidating the sales channels.

c. How will reducing inventory save costs?

d. Although the cost-cutting measures are impressive, Mr. Wallace was quoted as saying, "Obviously no one is going to succeed in our business just by reducing costs." Speculate as to some other measures that Mr. Wallace could take to improve Mazda's profitability.

ATC 20-2 Group Assignment *Relevance and cost behavior*

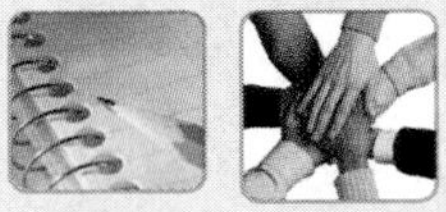

Maccoa Soft, a division of Zayer Software Company, produces and distributes an automated payroll software system. A contribution margin format income statement for Maccoa Soft for the past year follows.

Revenue (12,000 units × $1,200)	$14,400,000
Unit-Level Variable Costs	
Product Materials Cost (12,000 × $60)	(720,000)
Installation Labor Cost (12,000 × $200)	(2,400,000)
Manufacturing Overhead (12,000 × $2)	(24,000)
Shipping and Handling (12,000 × $25)	(300,000)
Sales Commissions (12,000 × $300)	(3,600,000)
Nonmanufacturing Miscellaneous Costs (12,000 × $5)	(60,000)
Contribution Margin (12,000 × $608)	7,296,000
Fixed Costs	
Research and Development	(2,700,000)
Legal Fees to Ensure Product Protection	(780,000)
Advertising Costs	(1,200,000)
Rental Cost of Manufacturing Facility	(600,000)
Depreciation on Production Equipment (zero market value)	(300,000)
Other Manufacturing Costs (salaries, utilities, etc.)	(744,000)
Division-Level Facility Sustaining Costs	(1,730,000)
Allocated Companywide Facility-Level Costs	(1,650,000)
Net Loss	$(2,408,000)

Required

a. Divide the class into groups and then organize the groups into three sections. Assign Task 1 to the first section, Task 2 to the second section, and Task 3 to the third section. Each task should be considered independently of the others.

Group Tasks

(1) Assume that Maccoa has excess capacity. The sales staff has identified a large franchise company with 200 outlets that is interested in Maccoa's software system but is willing to pay only $800 for each system. Ignoring qualitative considerations, should Maccoa accept the special order?

(2) Maccoa has the opportunity to purchase a comparable payroll system from a competing vendor for $600 per system. Ignoring qualitative considerations, should Maccoa outsource producing the software? Maccoa would continue to sell and install the software if the manufacturing activities were outsourced.

(3) Given that Maccoa is generating a loss, should Zayer eliminate it? Would your answer change if Maccoa could increase sales by 1,000 units?

b. Have a representative from each section explain its respective conclusions. Discuss the following:

(1) Representatives from Section 1 should respond to the following: The analysis related to the special order (Task 1) suggests that all variable costs are always relevant. Is this conclusion valid? Explain your answer.

(2) Representatives from Section 2 should respond to the following: With respect to the outsourcing decision, identify a relevant fixed cost and a nonrelevant fixed cost. Discuss the criteria for determining whether a cost is or is not relevant.

(3) Representatives from Section 3 should respond to the following: Why did the segment elimination decision change when the volume of production and sales increased?

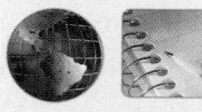

ATC 20-3 Research Assignment *Systems replacement decision*

The April 2003 issue of *Strategic Finance* contains an article "Why Automate Payables and Receivables? Electronic Are More Accurate and Less Costly," written by Suzanne Hurt. It appears on pages 33 to 35. This article notes that while financial resource management (FRM) software is available to automate processing transactions such as receivables and payables, 86 percent of these transactions are still paper based. In the article, the author explains some of the reasons companies should consider switching to an Internet-based FRM system and gives some examples of the cost savings that companies such as General Electric have realized by adopting such software. Read this article and complete the following requirements.

Required

a. Identify the relevant costs a company should consider when considering the switch from a manual system to an Internet-based FRM system of accounting for receivables and payables. Think carefully. The article does not specify all of these costs.

b. The article notes that one advantage of an Internet-based FRM system is that it allows companies to get money from receivables collected and deposited into the bank more quickly. What type of cost does this represent for a company that continues to use a manual system rather than adopt an automated system?

c. The author identifies what she thinks is the biggest challenge facing a company trying to switch to an Internet-based FRM system. What is this challenge?

ATC 20-4 Writing Assignment *Relevant versus full cost*

State law permits the State Department of Revenue to collect taxes for municipal governments that operate within the state's jurisdiction and allows private companies to collect taxes for municipalities. To promote fairness and to ensure the financial well-being of the state, the law dictates that the Department of Revenue must charge municipalities a fee for collection services that is above the cost of providing such services but does not define the term *cost.* Until recently, Department of Revenue officials have included a proportionate share of all departmental costs such as depreciation on buildings and equipment, supervisory salaries, and other facility-level overhead costs when determining the cost of providing collection services, a measurement approach known as full costing. The full costing approach has led to a pricing structure that places the Department of Revenue at a competitive disadvantage relative to private collection companies. Indeed, highly efficient private companies have been able to consistently underbid the Revenue Department for municipal customers. As a result, it has lost 30 percent of its municipal collection business over the last two years. The inability to be price competitive led the revenue commissioner to hire a consulting firm to evaluate the current practice of determining the cost to provide collection services.

The consulting firm concluded that the cost to provide collection services should be limited to the relevant costs associated with providing those services, defined as the difference between the costs that would be incurred if the services were provided and the costs that would be incurred if the services were not provided. According to this definition, the costs of depreciation, supervisory salaries, and other facility-level overhead costs are not included because they are the same regardless of whether the Department of Revenue provides collection services to municipalities. The Revenue Department adopted the relevant cost approach and immediately reduced the price it charges municipalities to collect their taxes and rapidly recovered the collection business it had lost. Indeed, several of the private collection companies were forced into bankruptcy. The private companies joined together and filed suit against the Revenue Department, charging that the new definition of cost violates the intent of the law.

Required

a. Assume that you are an accountant hired as a consultant for the private companies. Write a brief memo explaining why it is inappropriate to limit the definition of the costs of providing collection services to relevant costs.

b. Assume that you are an accountant hired as a consultant for the Department of Revenue. Write a brief memo explaining why it is appropriate to limit the definition of the costs of providing collection services to relevant costs.

c. Speculate on how the matter will be resolved.

ATC 20-5 Ethical Dilemma *Asset replacement clouded by self-interest*

John Dillworth is in charge of buying property used as building sites for branch offices of the National Bank of Commerce. Mr. Dillworth recently paid $110,000 for a site located in a growing section of the city. Shortly after purchasing this lot, Mr. Dillworth had the opportunity to purchase a more desirable lot at a significantly lower price. The traffic count at the new site is virtually twice that of the old site, but the price of the lot is only $80,000. It was immediately apparent that he had overpaid for the previous purchase. The current market value of the purchased property is only $75,000. Mr. Dillworth believes that it would be in the bank's best interest to buy the new lot, but he does not want to report a loss to his boss, Kelly Fullerton. He knows that Ms. Fullerton will severely reprimand him, even though she has made her share of mistakes. In fact, he is aware of a significant bad loan that Ms. Fullerton recently approved. When confronted with the bad debt by the senior vice president in charge of commercial lending, Ms. Fullerton blamed the decision on one of her former subordinates, Ira Sacks. Ms. Fullerton implied that Mr. Sacks had been dismissed for reckless lending decisions when, in fact, he had been an excellent loan officer with an uncanny ability to assess the creditworthiness of his customers. Indeed, Mr. Sacks had voluntarily resigned to accept a better position.

Required

a. Determine the amount of the loss that would be recognized on the sale of the existing branch site.

b. Identify the type of cost represented by the $110,000 original purchase price of the land. Also identify the type of cost represented by its current market value of $75,000. Indicate which cost is relevant to a decision as to whether the original site should be replaced with the new site.

c. Is Mr. Dillworth's conclusion that the old site should be replaced supported by quantitative analysis? If not, what facts do justify his conclusion?

d. Assuming that Mr. Dillworth is a certified management accountant (CMA), do you believe the failure to replace the land violates any of the standards of ethical conduct in Exhibit 14.13 in Chapter 14? If so, which standards would be violated?

e. Discuss the ethical dilemma that Mr. Dillworth faces within the context of Donald Cressey's common features of ethical misconduct that were outlined in Chapter 1.

COMPREHENSIVE PROBLEM

Use the same transaction data for Magnificent Modems Inc. as was used in Chapter 14. (See page 742.)

Required

a. One of Magnificent Modems' sales representatives receives a special order to sell 1,000 modems at a price of $72 each. Should the order be accepted?

b. Magnificent Modems has the opportunity to purchase the modems that it currently makes. The modems can be purchased at a price of $76 each. Assuming the manufacturing equipment has a zero market value, should Magnificent buy the modems?

c. Assume that Magnificent Modems expects production and sales to grow to 10,000. At this volume of production, should Magnificent buy the modems?

CHAPTER 21

Planning for Profit and Cost Control

LEARNING OBJECTIVES

After you have mastered the material in this chapter you will be able to:

1. **Describe the budgeting process and the benefits it provides.**
2. **Explain the relationship between budgeting and human behavior.**
3. **Prepare a sales budget and related schedule of cash receipts.**
4. **Prepare an inventory purchases budget and related schedule of cash payments.**
5. **Prepare a selling and administrative expense budget and related schedule of cash payments.**
6. **Prepare a cash budget.**
7. **Prepare a pro forma income statement, balance sheet, and statement of cash flows.**

Chapter 21

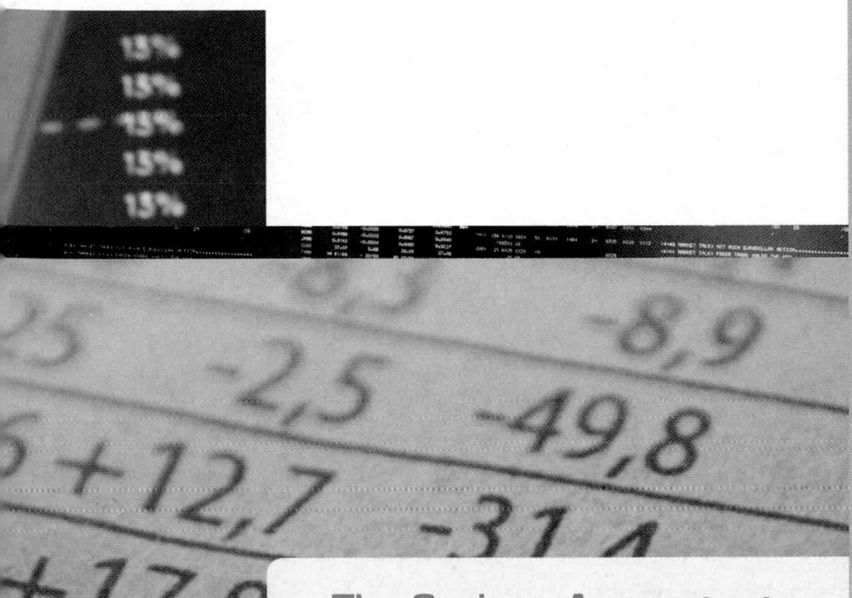

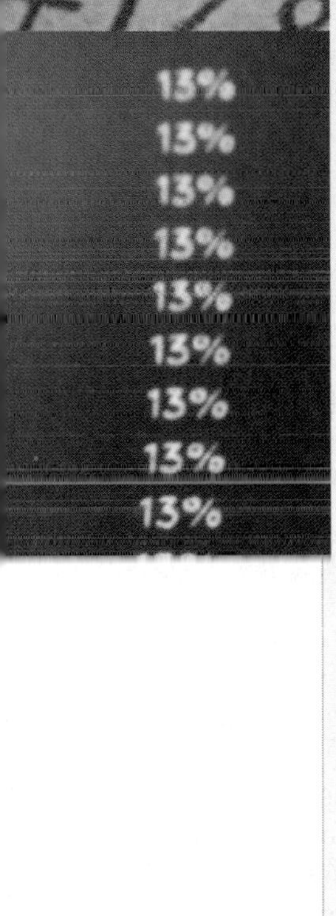

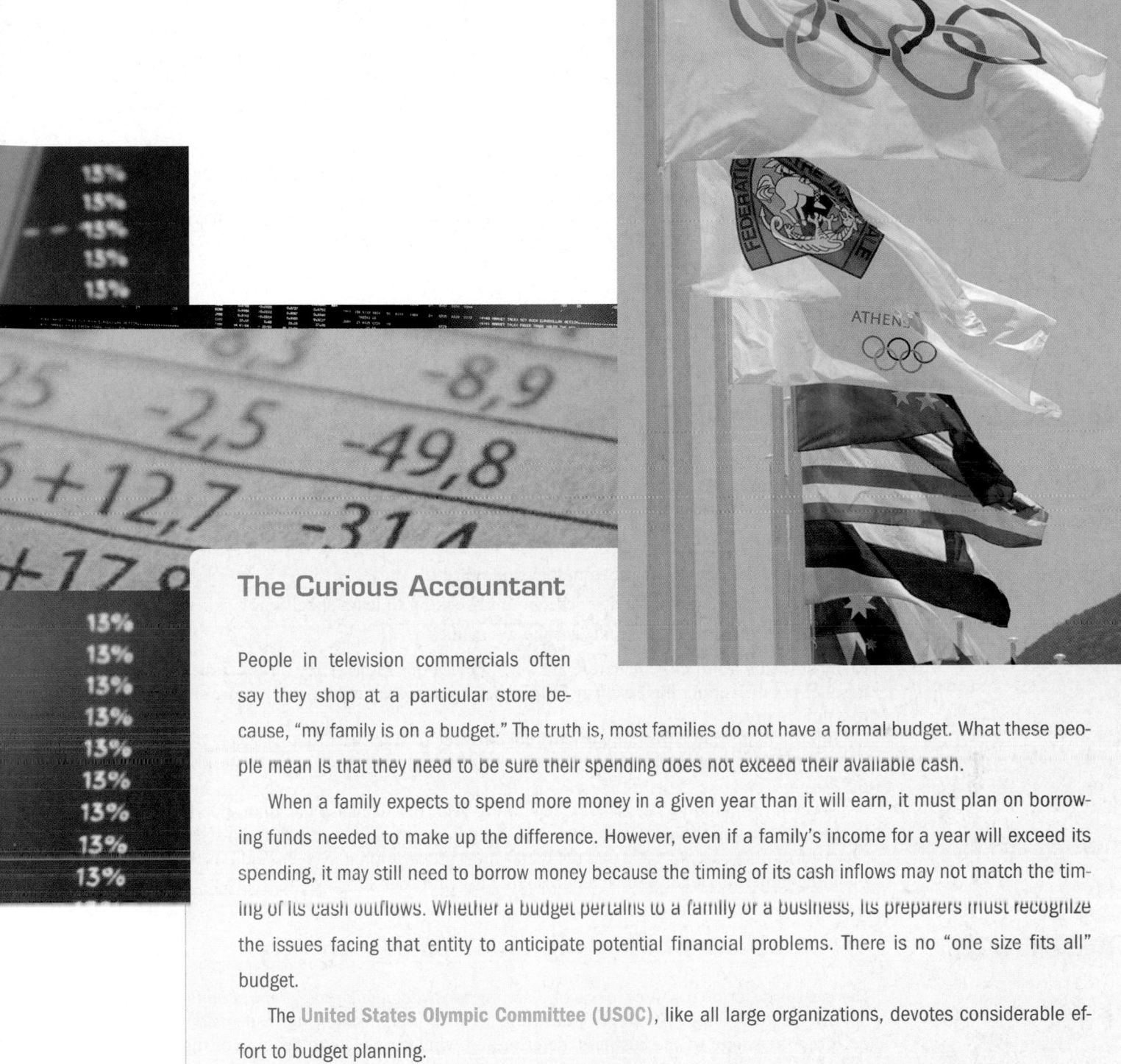

The Curious Accountant

People in television commercials often say they shop at a particular store because, "my family is on a budget." The truth is, most families do not have a formal budget. What these people mean is that they need to be sure their spending does not exceed their available cash.

When a family expects to spend more money in a given year than it will earn, it must plan on borrowing funds needed to make up the difference. However, even if a family's income for a year will exceed its spending, it may still need to borrow money because the timing of its cash inflows may not match the timing of its cash outflows. Whether a budget pertains to a family or a business, its preparers must recognize the issues facing that entity to anticipate potential financial problems. There is no "one size fits all" budget.

The **United States Olympic Committee (USOC)**, like all large organizations, devotes considerable effort to budget planning.

Think about the Olympic Games, and how the USOC generates revenues and incurs expenditures. Can you identify any unusual circumstances facing the USOC that complicate its budgeting efforts? (Answer on page 1033.)

CHAPTER OPENING

Planning is crucial to operating a profitable business. Expressing business plans in financial terms is commonly called **budgeting.** *The budgeting process involves coordinating the financial plans of all areas of the business. For example, the production department cannot prepare a manufacturing plan until it knows how many units of product to produce. The number of units to produce depends on the marketing department's sales projection.*

The marketing department cannot project sales volume until it knows what products the company will sell. Product information comes from the research and development department. The point should be clear: a company's master budget results from combining numerous specific plans prepared by different departments.

Master budget preparation is normally supervised by a committee. The budget committee is responsible for settling disputes among various departments over budget matters. The committee also monitors reports on how various segments are progressing toward achieving their budget goals. The budgeting committee is not an accounting committee. It is a high-level committee that normally includes the company president, vice presidents of marketing, purchasing, production, and finance, and the controller. ■

The Planning Process

LO 1

Describe the budgeting process and the benefits it provides.

Topic Tackler PLUS

21-1

Planning normally addresses short, intermediate, and long-range time horizons. Short-term plans are more specific than long-term plans. Consider, for example, your decision to attend college. Long-term planning requires considering general questions such as:

- Do I want to go to college?
- How do I expect to benefit from the experience?
- Do I want a broad knowledge base, or am I seeking to learn specific job skills?
- In what field do I want to concentrate my studies?

Many students go to college before answering these questions. They discover the disadvantages of poor planning the hard way. While their friends are graduating, they are starting over in a new major.

Intermediate-range planning usually covers three to five years. In this stage, you consider which college to attend, how to support yourself while in school, and whether to live on or off campus.

Short-term planning focuses on the coming year. In this phase you plan specific courses to take, decide which instructors to choose, schedule part-time work, and join a study group. Short-term plans are specific and detailed. Their preparation may seem tedious, but careful planning generally leads to efficient resource use and high levels of productivity.

Three Levels of Planning for Business Activity

Businesses describe the three levels of planning as *strategic planning, capital budgeting,* and *operations budgeting.* **Strategic planning** involves making long-term decisions such as defining the scope of the business, determining which products to develop or discontinue, and identifying the most profitable market niche. Upper-level management is responsible for these decisions. Strategic plans are descriptive rather than quantitative. Objectives such as "to have the largest share of the market" or "to be the best-quality producer" result from strategic planning. Although strategic planning is an integral component of managing a business, an in-depth discussion of it is beyond the scope of this text.

Capital budgeting focuses on intermediate range planning. It involves such decisions as whether to buy or lease equipment, whether to stimulate sales, or whether to increase the company's asset base. Capital budgeting is discussed in detail in a later chapter.

The central focus of this chapter is the *master budget* which describes short-term objectives in specific amounts of sales targets, production goals, and financing plans. The master budget describes how management intends to achieve its objectives and directs the company's short-term activities.

The master budget normally covers one year. It is frequently divided into quarterly projections and often subdivides quarterly data by month. Effective managers cannot wait until year-end to know whether operations conform to budget targets. Monthly data provide feedback to permit making necessary corrections promptly.

Many companies use **perpetual,** or **continuous, budgeting** covering a 12-month reporting period. As the current month draws to a close, an additional month is added at the end of the budget period, resulting in a continuous 12-month budget. A perpetual budget offers the advantage of keeping management constantly focused on thinking ahead to the next 12 months. The more traditional annual approach to budgeting invites a frenzied stop-and-go mentality, with managers preparing the budget in a year-end rush that is soon forgotten. Changing conditions may not be discussed until the next year-end budget is due. A perpetual budget overcomes these disadvantages.

Advantages of Budgeting

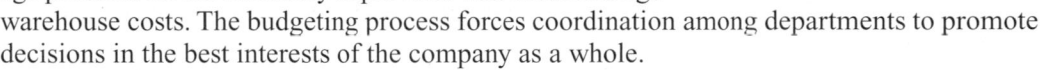

Budgeting is costly and time-consuming. The sacrifices, however, are more than offset by the benefits. Budgeting promotes planning and coordination; it enhances performance measurement and corrective action.

Planning

Almost everyone makes plans. Each morning, people think about what they will do during the day. Thinking ahead is planning. Most business managers think ahead about how they will direct operations. Unfortunately, planning is frequently as informal as making a few mental notes. Informal planning cannot be effectively communicated. The business manager might know what her objectives are, but neither her superiors nor her subordinates know. Because it serves as a communication tool, budgeting can solve these problems. The budget formalizes and documents managerial plans, clearly communicating objectives to both superiors and subordinates.

Coordination

Sometimes a choice benefits one department at the expense of another. For example, a purchasing agent may order large quantities of raw materials to obtain discounts from suppliers. But excessive quantities of materials pose a storage problem for the inventory supervisor who must manage warehouse costs. The budgeting process forces coordination among departments to promote decisions in the best interests of the company as a whole.

Performance Measurement

Budgets are specific, quantitative representations of management's objectives. Comparing actual results to budget expectations provides a way to evaluate performance. For example, if a company budgets sales of $10 million, it can judge the performance of the sales department against that level. If actual sales exceed $10 million, the company should reward the sales department; if actual sales fall below $10 million, the company should seek an explanation for the shortfall from the sales manager.

Corrective Action

Budgeting provides advance notice of potential shortages, bottlenecks, or other weaknesses in operating plans. For example, a cash budget alerts management to when the company can expect cash shortages during the coming year. The company can make borrowing arrangements before it needs the money. Without knowing ahead of time, management might be unable to secure necessary financing on short notice, or it may have to pay excessively high interest rates to obtain funds. Budgeting advises managers of potential problems in time for them to devise effective solutions.

Budgeting and Human Behavior

LO 2

Explain the relationship between budgeting and human behavior.

Effective budgeting requires sensitivity on the part of upper management to the effect on employees of budget expectations. People are often uncomfortable with budgets. Budgets are constraining. They limit individual freedom in favor of an established plan. Many people find evaluation based on budget expectations stressful. Most students experience a similar fear about testing. Like examinations, budgets represent standards by which performance is evaluated. Employees worry about whether their performance will meet expectations.

The attitudes of high-level managers significantly impact budget effectiveness. Subordinates are keenly aware of management's expectations. If upper-level managers degrade, make fun of, or ignore the budget, subordinates will follow suit. If management uses budgets to humiliate, embarrass, or punish subordinates, employees will resent the treatment and the budgeting process. Upper-level managers must demonstrate that they view the budget as a sincere effort to express realistic goals employees are expected to meet. An honest, open, respectful atmosphere is essential to budgeting success.

Participative budgeting has frequently proved successful in creating a healthy atmosphere. This technique invites participation in the budget process by personnel at all levels of the organization, not just upper-level managers. Information flows from the bottom up as well as from the top down during budget preparation. Because they are directly responsible for meeting budget goals, subordinates can offer more realistic targets. Including them in budget preparation fosters development of a team effort. Participation fosters more cooperation and motivation, and less fear. With participative budgeting, subordinates cannot complain that the budget is management's plan. The budget is instead a self-imposed constraint. Employees can hold no one responsible but themselves if they fail to accomplish the budget objectives they established.

Upper management participates in the process to ensure that employee-generated objectives are consistent with company objectives. Furthermore, if subordinates were granted complete freedom to establish budget standards, they might be tempted to adopt lax standards to ensure they will meet them. Both managers and subordinates must cooperate if the participatory process is to produce an effective budget. If developed carefully, budgets can motivate employees to achieve superior performance. Normal human fears must be overcome, and management must create an honest budget atmosphere.

The Master Budget

LO 1

Describe the budgeting process and the benefits it provides.

Topic Tackler PLUS

21-2

The **master budget** is a group of detailed budgets and schedules representing the company's operating and financial plans for a future accounting period. The master budget usually includes (1) *operating budgets,* (2) *capital budgets,* and (3) *pro forma financial statements.* The budgeting process normally begins with preparing the **operating budgets** which focus on detailed operating activities. This chapter illustrates operating budgets for Hampton Hams, a retail sales company that uses (1) a sales budget, (2) an inventory purchases budget, (3) a selling and administrative (S&A) expense budget, and (4) a cash budget.

The sales budget includes a schedule of cash receipts from customers. The inventory purchases and S&A expense budgets include schedules of cash payments for inventory and expenses. Preparing the master budget begins with the sales forecast. Based on the sales forecast, the detailed budgets for inventory purchases and operating expenses are developed. The schedules of cash receipts and cash payments provide the foundation for preparing the cash budget.

The **capital budget** describes the company's intermediate-range plans for investments in facilities, equipment, new products, store outlets, and lines of business. The capital budget affects several operating budgets. For example, equipment acquisitions result in additional depreciation expense on the S&A expense budget. The cash flow effects of capital investments influence the cash budget.

The operating budgets are used to prepare *pro forma statements.* **Pro forma financial statements** are based on projected (budgeted) rather than historical information. Hampton Hams prepares a pro forma income statement, balance sheet, and statement of cash flows.

EXHIBIT 21.1

Information Flows in the Master Budget

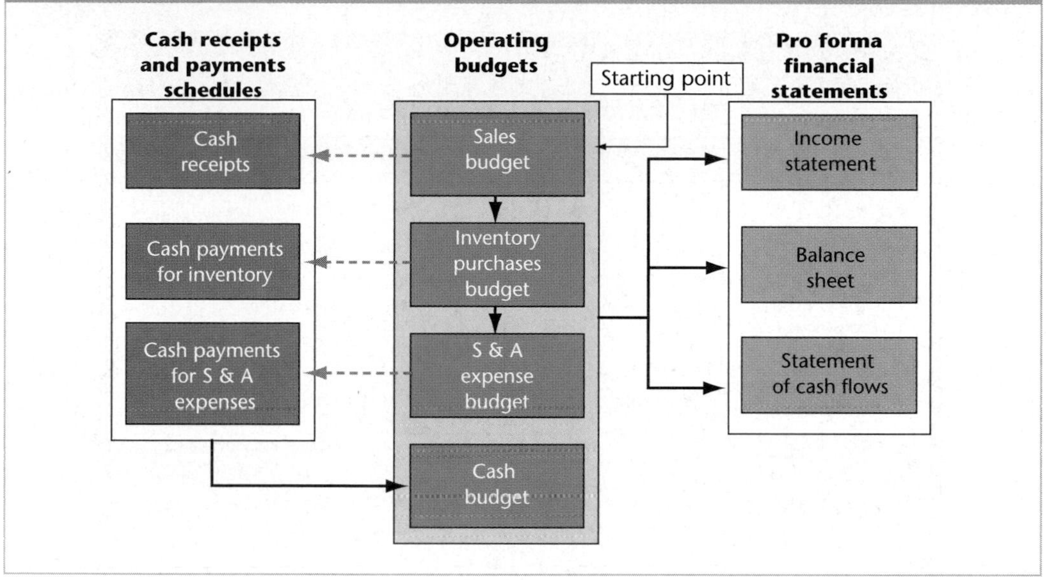

Exhibit 21.1 shows how information flows in a master budget.

Hampton Hams Budgeting Illustration

Hampton Hams (HH), a major corporation, sells cured hams nationwide through retail outlets in shopping malls. By focusing on a single product and standardized operations, the company controls costs stringently. As a result, it offers high-quality hams at competitive prices.

HAMPTON HAMS

Hampton Hams has experienced phenomenal growth during the past five years. It opened two new stores in Indianapolis, Indiana, last month and plans to open a third new store in October. Hampton Hams finances new stores by borrowing on a line of credit arranged with National Bank. National's loan officer has requested monthly budgets for each of the first three months of the new store's operations. The accounting department is preparing the new store's master budget for October, November, and December. The first step is developing a sales budget.

Sales Budget

LO 3

Prepare a sales budget and related schedule of cash receipts.

Preparing the master budget begins with the sales forecast. The accuracy of the sales forecast is critical because all the other budgets are derived from the sales budget. Normally, the marketing department coordinates the development of the sales forecast. Sales estimates frequently flow from the bottom up to the higher management levels. Sales personnel prepare sales projections for their products and territories and pass them up the line where they are combined with the estimates of other sales personnel to develop regional and national estimates. Using various information sources, upper-level sales managers adjust the estimates generated by sales personnel. Adjustment information comes from industry periodicals and trade journals, economic analysis, marketing surveys, historical sales figures, and changes in competition. Companies assimilate this data using sophisticated computer programs, statistical techniques, and quantitative methods, or, simply, professional judgment. Regardless of the technique, the senior vice president of sales ultimately develops a sales forecast for which she is held responsible.

To develop the sales forecast for HH's new store, the sales manager studied the sales history of existing stores operating in similar locations. He then adjusted for start-up conditions.

EXHIBIT 21.2

Sales Budget

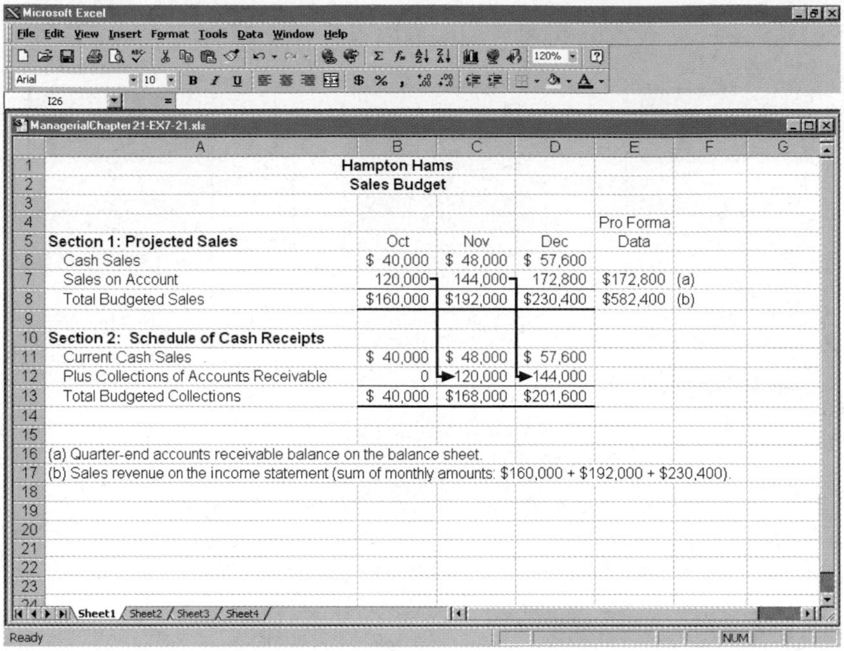

	Hampton Hams Sales Budget				
				Pro Forma	
Section 1: Projected Sales	Oct	Nov	Dec	Data	
Cash Sales	$ 40,000	$ 48,000	$ 57,600		
Sales on Account	120,000	144,000	172,800	$172,800	(a)
Total Budgeted Sales	$160,000	$192,000	$230,400	$582,400	(b)
Section 2: Schedule of Cash Receipts					
Current Cash Sales	$ 40,000	$ 48,000	$ 57,600		
Plus Collections of Accounts Receivable	0	120,000	144,000		
Total Budgeted Collections	$ 40,000	$168,000	$201,600		

(a) Quarter-end accounts receivable balance on the balance sheet.
(b) Sales revenue on the income statement (sum of monthly amounts: $160,000 + $192,000 + $230,400).

October is an opportune time to open a new store because customers will learn the store's location before the holiday season. The sales manager expects significant sales growth in November and December as customers choose the company's hams as the centerpiece for many Thanksgiving and winter holiday dinner tables.

The new store's sales are expected to be $160,000 in October ($40,000 in cash and $120,000 on account). Sales are expected to increase 20 percent per month during November and December. Based on these estimates, the sales manager prepared the sales budget in Exhibit 21.2.

Projected Sales

The sales budget has two sections. Section 1 shows the projected sales for each month. The November sales forecast reflects a 20 percent increase over October sales. For example, November *cash sales* are calculated as $48,000 [$40,000 + ($40,000 × 0.20)] and December *cash sales* as $57,600 [$48,000 + ($48,000 × 0.20)]. *Sales on account* are similarly computed.

Schedule of Cash Receipts

Section 2 is a schedule of the cash receipts for the projected sales. This schedule is used later to prepare the cash budget. The accountant has assumed in this schedule that Hampton Hams will collect accounts receivable from credit sales *in full* in the month following the sale. In practice, collections may be spread over several months, and some receivables may become uncollectible accounts. Regardless of additional complexities, the objective is to estimate the amount and timing of expected cash receipts.

In the HH case, *total cash receipts* are determined by adding the current month's *cash sales* to the cash collected from the previous month's *credit sales* (accounts receivable balance). Cash receipts for each month are determined as follows:

- October receipts are projected to be $40,000. Because the store opens in October, no accounts receivable from September exist to be collected in October. Cash receipts for October equal the amount of October's cash sales.
- November receipts are projected to be $168,000 ($48,000 November cash sales + $120,000 cash collected from October sales on account).

FOCUS ON INTERNATIONAL ISSUES

CASH FLOW PLANNING IN BORDEAUX

The year 2000 was considered the greatest year for wine in the Bordeaux region of France since at least 1982, and the winemakers could look forward to selling their wines for record prices, but there was one catch: these wines would not be released to consumers until late in 2003. The winemakers had incurred most of their costs in 2000 when the vines were being tended and the grapes were being processed into wine. In many industries this would mean the companies would have to finance their inventories for almost four years—not an insignificant cost. A company must finance its inventory by either borrowing the money, which results in out-of-pocket interest expense, or using its own funds. The second option generates an opportunity cost resulting from the interest revenue that could have been earned if these funds were not being used to finance the inventory.

To address this potential cash flow problem, many of the winemakers in Bordeaux offer some of their wines for sale as "futures." That means the wines are purchased and paid for while they are still aging in barrels in France. Selling wine as futures reduces the time inventory must be financed from four years to only one to two years. Of course there are other types of costs in such deals. For one, the wines must be offered at lower prices than they are expected to sell for upon release. The winemakers have obviously decided this cost is less than the cost of financing inventory through borrowed money, or they would not do it.

Companies in other industries use similar techniques to speed up cash flow, such as factoring of accounts receivable. A major reason entities prepare cash budgets is to be sure they will have enough cash on hand to pay bills as they come due. If the budget indicates a temporary cash flow deficit, action must be taken to avoid the problem, and revised budgets must be prepared. Budgeting is not a static process.

- December receipts are projected to be \$201,600 (\$57,600 December cash sales + \$144,000 cash collected from November sales on account).

Pro Forma Financial Statement Data

The Pro Forma Data column in the sales budget displays two figures HH will report on the quarter-end (December 31) budgeted financial statements. Since HH expects to collect December credit sales in January, the *accounts receivable balance* will be \$172,800 on the December 31, 2006, pro forma balance sheet (shown later in Exhibit 21.7).

The \$582,400 of *sales revenue* in the Pro Forma Data column will be reported on the budgeted income statement for the quarter (shown later in Exhibit 21.6). The sales revenue represents the sum of October, November, and December sales (\$160,000 + \$192,000 + \$230,400 = \$582,400).

Inventory Purchases Budget

LO 4

Prepare an inventory purchases budget and related schedule of cash payments.

The inventory purchases budget shows the amount of inventory HH must purchase each month to satisfy the demand projected in the sales budget. The *total inventory needed* each month equals the amount of inventory HH plans to sell that month plus the amount of inventory HH wants on hand at month-end. To the extent that total inventory needed exceeds the inventory on hand at the beginning of the month, HH will need to purchase additional inventory. The amount of inventory to purchase is computed as follows:

Cost of budgeted sales	XXX
Plus: Desired ending inventory	XXX
Total inventory needed	XXX
Less: Beginning inventory	(XXX)
Required purchases	XXX

It is HH's policy to maintain an ending inventory equal to 25 percent of the next month's *projected cost of goods sold.* HH's cost of goods sold normally equals 70 percent of *sales.* Using this information and the sales budget, the accounting department prepared the inventory purchases budget shown in Exhibit 21.3.

Projected Purchases

Section 1 of the inventory purchases budget shows required purchases for each month. HH determined *budgeted cost of goods sold* for October by multiplying October *budgeted sales* by 70 percent ($160,000 × 0.70 = $112,000). Budgeted cost of goods sold for November and December were similarly computed. The October *desired ending inventory* was computed by multiplying November *budgeted cost of goods sold* by 25 percent ($134,400 × 0.25 = $33,600). Desired ending inventory for November is $40,320 ($161,280 × .25). Desired ending inventory for December is based on January projected cost of goods sold (not shown in the exhibit). HH expects ham sales to decline after the winter holidays. Because January projected cost of goods sold is only $140,000, the December desired ending inventory falls to $35,000 ($140,000 × .25).

Schedule of Cash Payments for Inventory Purchases

Section 2 is the schedule of cash payments for inventory purchases. HH makes all inventory purchases on account. The supplier requires that HH pay for 60 percent of inventory purchases in the month goods are purchased. HH pays the remaining 40 percent the month after purchase.

Cash payments are projected as follows (amounts are rounded to the nearest whole dollar):

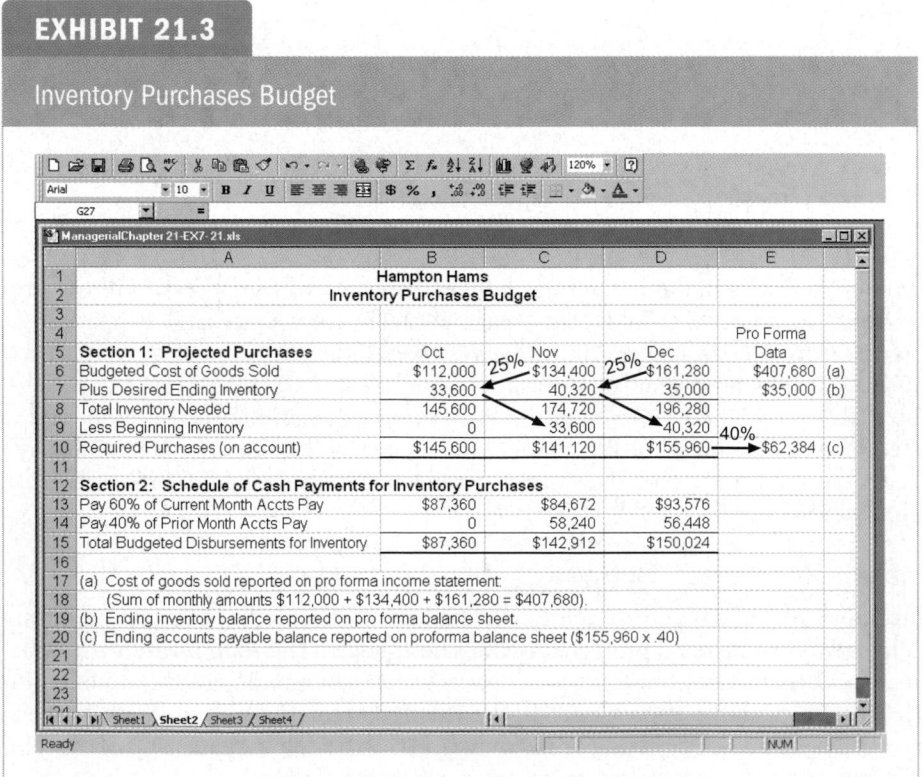

EXHIBIT 21.3

Inventory Purchases Budget

Hampton Hams
Inventory Purchases Budget

	Oct	Nov	Dec	Pro Forma Data	
Section 1: Projected Purchases					
Budgeted Cost of Goods Sold	$112,000	$134,400	$161,280	$407,680	(a)
Plus Desired Ending Inventory	33,600	40,320	35,000	$35,000	(b)
Total Inventory Needed	145,600	174,720	196,280		
Less Beginning Inventory	0	33,600	40,320		
Required Purchases (on account)	$145,600	$141,120	$155,960	$62,384	(c)
Section 2: Schedule of Cash Payments for Inventory Purchases					
Pay 60% of Current Month Accts Pay	$87,360	$84,672	$93,576		
Pay 40% of Prior Month Accts Pay	0	58,240	56,448		
Total Budgeted Disbursements for Inventory	$87,360	$142,912	$150,024		

(a) Cost of goods sold reported on pro forma income statement
(Sum of monthly amounts $112,000 + $134,400 + $161,280 = $407,680).
(b) Ending inventory balance reported on pro forma balance sheet.
(c) Ending accounts payable balance reported on proforma balance sheet ($155,960 x .40)

- October cash payments for inventory are $87,360. Because the new store opens in October, no accounts payable balance from September remains to be paid in October. Cash payments for October equal 60 percent of October inventory purchases.
- November cash payments for inventory are $142,912 (40 percent of October purchases + 60 percent of November purchases).
- December cash payments for inventory are $150,024 (40 percent of November purchases + 60 percent of December purchases).

Pro Forma Financial Statement Data

The Pro Forma Data column in the inventory purchases budget displays three figures HH will report on the quarter-end budgeted financial statements. The $407,680 *cost of goods sold* reported on the pro forma income statement (shown later in Exhibit 21.6) is the sum of the monthly cost of goods sold amounts ($112,000 + $134,400 + $161,280 = $407,680).

The $35,000 *ending inventory* as of December 31, 2006, is reported on the pro forma balance sheet (shown later in Exhibit 21.7). December 31 is the last day of both the month of December and the three-month quarter represented by October, November, and December.

The $62,384 of *accounts payable* reported on the pro forma balance sheet (shown later in Exhibit 21.7) represents the 40 percent of December inventory purchases HH will pay for in January ($155,960 × .40).

CHECK YOURSELF 21.1

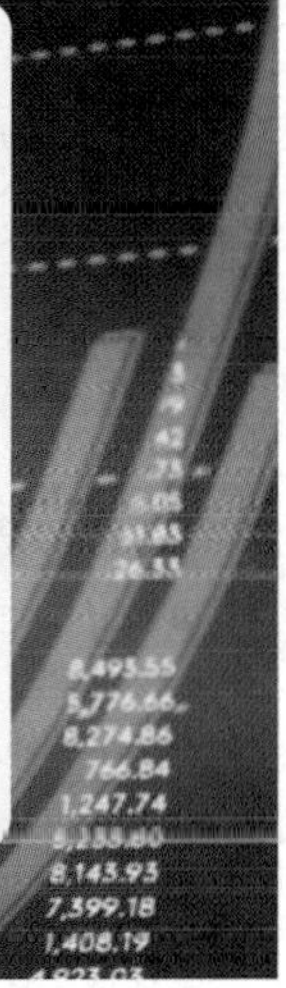

Main Street Sales Company purchased $80,000 of inventory during June. Purchases are expected to increase by 2 percent per month in each of the next three months. Main Street makes all purchases on account. It normally pays cash to settle 70 percent of its accounts payable during the month of purchase and settles the remaining 30 percent in the month following purchase. Based on this information, determine the accounts payable balance Main Street would report on its July 31 balance sheet.

Answer

Purchases for the month of July are expected to be $81,600 ($80,000 × 1.02). Main Street will pay 70 percent of the resulting accounts payable in cash during July. The remaining 30 percent represents the expected balance in accounts payable as of July 31. Therefore, the balance would be $24,480 ($81,600 × 0.3).

Selling and Administrative Expense Budget

Projected S&A Expenses

LO 5

Prepare a selling and administrative expense budget and related schedule of cash payments.

Section 1 of Exhibit 21.4 shows the selling and administrative (S&A) expense budget for Hampton Hams' new store. Most of the projected expenses are self-explanatory; depreciation and interest, however, merit comment. The depreciation expense is based on projections in the *capital expenditures budget.* Although not presented in this chapter, the capital budget calls for the cash purchase of $130,000 of store fixtures on October 1. The supplier allows a thirty-day inspection period. As a result, payment for the fixtures is budgeted for the end of October. The fixtures are expected to have a useful life of 10 years and a $10,000 salvage value. Using the straight-line method, HH estimates annual depreciation expense at $12,000 [($130,000 − $10,000) ÷ 10]. Monthly depreciation expense is $1,000 ($12,000 annual charge ÷ 12 months).

Interest expense is missing from the S&A expense budget. HH cannot estimate interest expense until it completes its borrowing projections. Expected borrowing (financing activities) and related interest expense are shown in the *cash budget.*

Schedule of Cash Payments for Selling and Administrative Expenses

Section 2 of the S&A expense budget shows the schedule of cash payments. There are several differences between the S&A expenses recognized on the pro forma income statement

EXHIBIT 21.4

Selling and Administrative Expense Budget

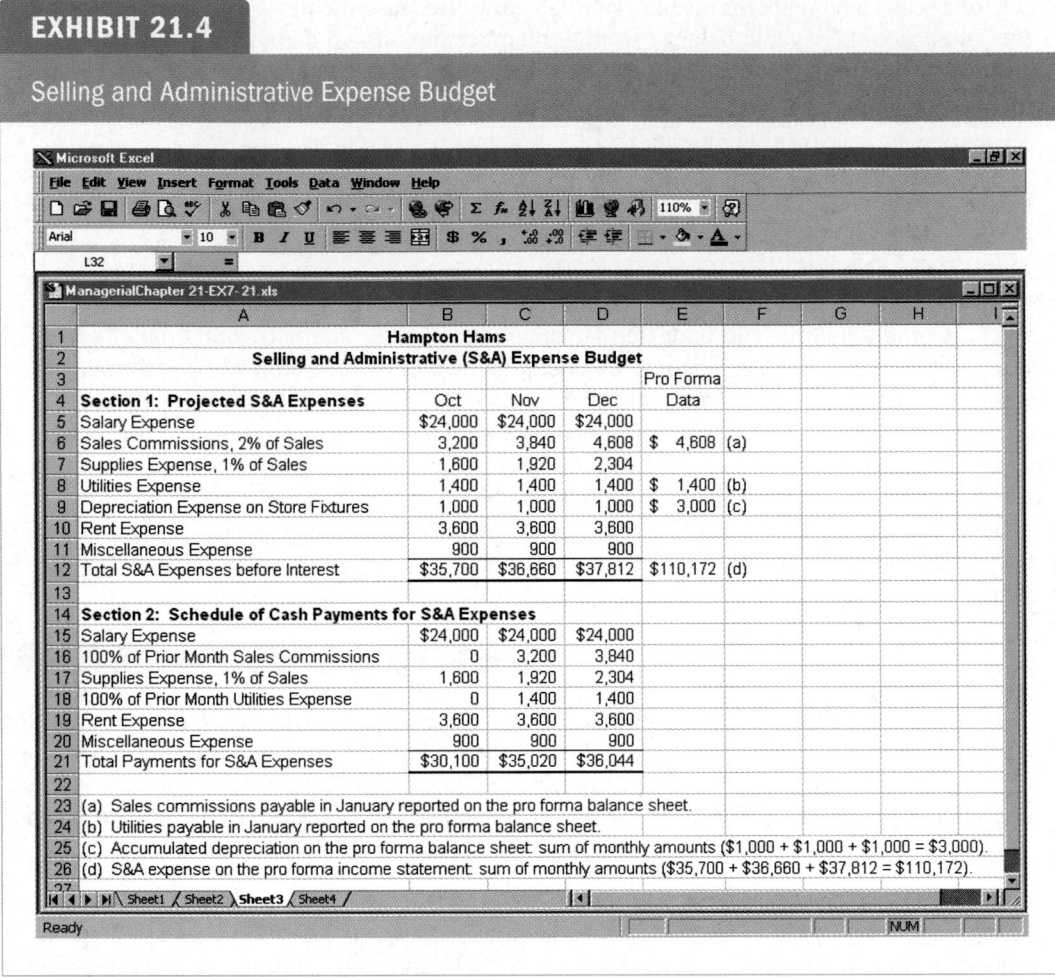

	A	B	C	D	E	
1	Hampton Hams					
2	Selling and Administrative (S&A) Expense Budget					
3					Pro Forma	
4	**Section 1: Projected S&A Expenses**	Oct	Nov	Dec	Data	
5	Salary Expense	$24,000	$24,000	$24,000		
6	Sales Commissions, 2% of Sales	3,200	3,840	4,608	$ 4,608	(a)
7	Supplies Expense, 1% of Sales	1,600	1,920	2,304		
8	Utilities Expense	1,400	1,400	1,400	$ 1,400	(b)
9	Depreciation Expense on Store Fixtures	1,000	1,000	1,000	$ 3,000	(c)
10	Rent Expense	3,600	3,600	3,600		
11	Miscellaneous Expense	900	900	900		
12	Total S&A Expenses before Interest	$35,700	$36,660	$37,812	$110,172	(d)
13						
14	**Section 2: Schedule of Cash Payments for S&A Expenses**					
15	Salary Expense	$24,000	$24,000	$24,000		
16	100% of Prior Month Sales Commissions	0	3,200	3,840		
17	Supplies Expense, 1% of Sales	1,600	1,920	2,304		
18	100% of Prior Month Utilities Expense	0	1,400	1,400		
19	Rent Expense	3,600	3,600	3,600		
20	Miscellaneous Expense	900	900	900		
21	Total Payments for S&A Expenses	$30,100	$35,020	$36,044		
22						
23	(a) Sales commissions payable in January reported on the pro forma balance sheet.					
24	(b) Utilities payable in January reported on the pro forma balance sheet.					
25	(c) Accumulated depreciation on the pro forma balance sheet: sum of monthly amounts ($1,000 + $1,000 + $1,000 = $3,000).					
26	(d) S&A expense on the pro forma income statement: sum of monthly amounts ($35,700 + $36,660 + $37,812 = $110,172).					

and the cash payments for S&A expenses. First, Hampton Hams pays sales commissions and utilities expense the month following their incurrence. Since the store opens in October there are no payments due from September. Cash payments for sales commissions and utilities in October are zero. In November, HH will pay the October expenses for these items and in December it will pay the November sales commissions and utility expenses. Depreciation expense does not affect the cash payments schedule. The cash outflow for the store fixtures occurs when the assets are purchased, not when they are depreciated. The cost of the investment in store fixtures is in the cash budget, not in the cash outflow for S&A expenses.

Pro Forma Financial Statement Data

The Pro Forma Data column of the S&A expense budget displays four figures HH will report on the quarter-end budgeted financial statements. The first and second figures are the sales commissions payable ($4,608) and utilities payable ($1,400) on the pro forma balance sheet in Exhibit 21.7. Because December sales commissions and utilities expense are not paid until January, these amounts represent liabilities as of December 31. The third figure in the column ($3,000) is the amount of accumulated depreciation on the pro forma balance sheet in Exhibit 21.7. Since depreciation accumulates, the $3,000 balance is the sum of the monthly depreciation amounts ($1,000 + $1,000 + $1,000 = $3,000). The final figure in the Pro Forma Data column ($110,172) is the total S&A expenses reported on the pro forma income statement in Exhibit 21.6. The total S&A expense is the sum of the monthly amounts ($35,700 + $36,660 + $37,812 = $110,172).

EXHIBIT 21.5

Cash Budget

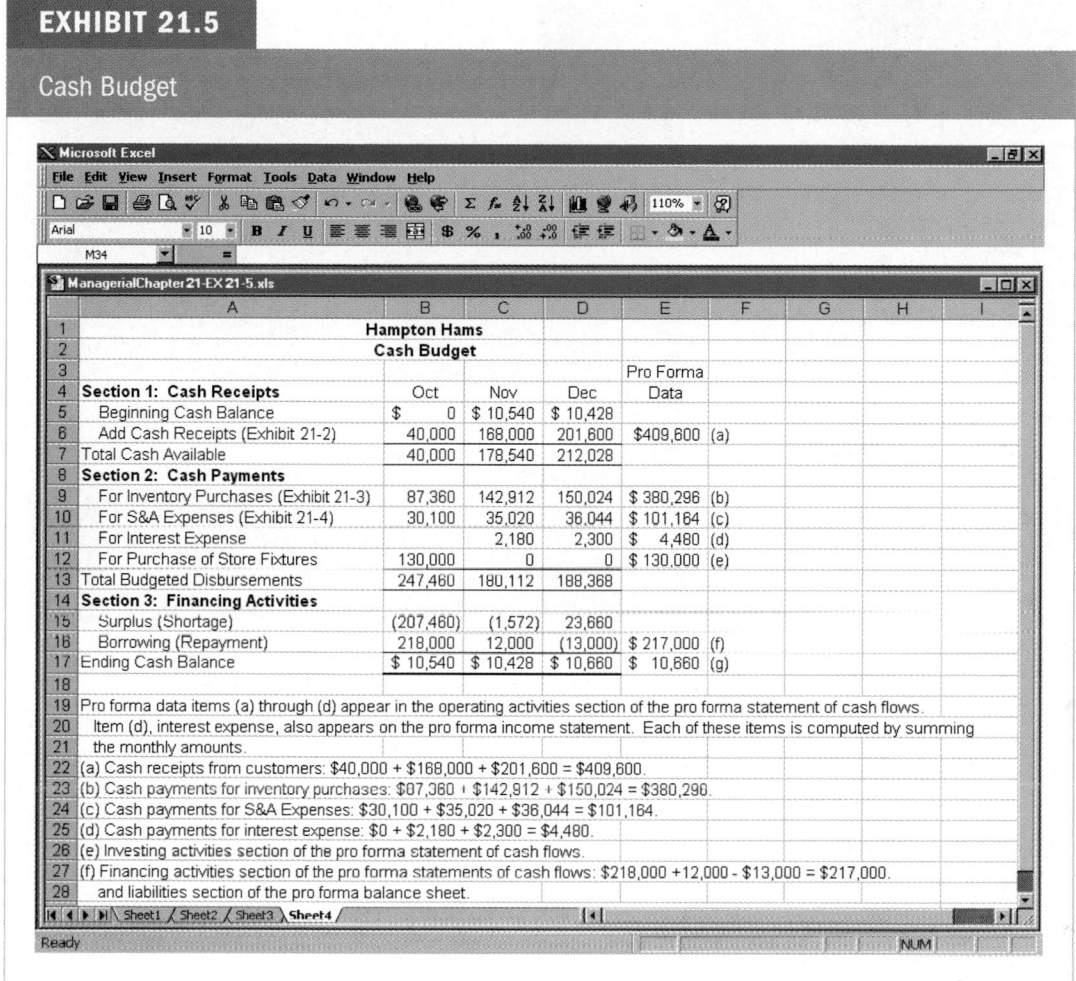

	A	B	C	D	E	F
1	**Hampton Hams**					
2	**Cash Budget**					
3					Pro Forma	
4	**Section 1: Cash Receipts**	Oct	Nov	Dec	Data	
5	Beginning Cash Balance	$ 0	$ 10,540	$ 10,428		
6	Add Cash Receipts (Exhibit 21-2)	40,000	168,000	201,600	$409,600	(a)
7	Total Cash Available	40,000	178,540	212,028		
8	**Section 2: Cash Payments**					
9	For Inventory Purchases (Exhibit 21-3)	87,360	142,912	150,024	$ 380,296	(b)
10	For S&A Expenses (Exhibit 21-4)	30,100	35,020	36,044	$ 101,164	(c)
11	For Interest Expense		2,180	2,300	$ 4,480	(d)
12	For Purchase of Store Fixtures	130,000	0	0	$ 130,000	(e)
13	Total Budgeted Disbursements	247,460	180,112	188,368		
14	**Section 3: Financing Activities**					
15	Surplus (Shortage)	(207,460)	(1,572)	23,660		
16	Borrowing (Repayment)	218,000	12,000	(13,000)	$ 217,000	(f)
17	Ending Cash Balance	$ 10,540	$ 10,428	$ 10,660	$ 10,660	(g)
18						
19	Pro forma data items (a) through (d) appear in the operating activities section of the pro forma statement of cash flows.					
20	Item (d), interest expense, also appears on the pro forma income statement. Each of these items is computed by summing					
21	the monthly amounts.					
22	(a) Cash receipts from customers: $40,000 + $168,000 + $201,600 = $409,600.					
23	(b) Cash payments for inventory purchases: $87,360 + $142,912 + $150,024 = $380,296.					
24	(c) Cash payments for S&A Expenses: $30,100 + $35,020 + $36,044 = $101,164.					
25	(d) Cash payments for interest expense: $0 + $2,180 + $2,300 = $4,480.					
26	(e) Investing activities section of the pro forma statement of cash flows.					
27	(f) Financing activities section of the pro forma statements of cash flows: $218,000 +12,000 - $13,000 = $217,000.					
28	and liabilities section of the pro forma balance sheet.					

Cash Budget

LO 6 Prepare a cash budget.

Little is more important to business success than effective cash management. If a company experiences cash shortages, it will be unable to pay its debts and may be forced into bankruptcy. If excess cash accumulates, a business loses the opportunity to earn investment income or reduce interest costs by repaying debt. Preparing a **cash budget** alerts management to anticipated cash shortages or excess cash balances. Management can plan financing activities, making advance arrangements to cover anticipated shortages by borrowing and planning to repay past borrowings and make appropriate investments when excess cash is expected.

The cash budget is divided into three major sections: (1) a cash receipts section, (2) a cash payments section, and (3) a financing section. Much of the data needed to prepare the cash budget are included in the cash receipts and payments schedules previously discussed; however, further refinements to project financing needs and interest costs are sometimes necessary. The completed cash budget is shown in Exhibit 21.5.

Cash Receipts Section

The total cash available (Exhibit 21.5, row 7) is determined by adding the beginning cash balance to the cash receipts from customers. There is no beginning cash balance in October because the new store is opening that month. The November beginning cash balance is the October ending cash balance. The December beginning cash balance is the November ending cash balance. Cash receipts from customers comes from the *schedule of cash receipts* in the sales budget (Exhibit 21.2, section 2, row 13).

REALITY BYTES

Budgeting in Governmental Entities

This chapter has presented several reasons organizations should prepare budgets, but for governmental entities, budgets are not simply good planning tools—law requires them. If a manager at a commercial enterprise does not accomplish the budget objectives established for his or her part of the business, the manager may receive a poor performance evaluation. At worst, they may be fired. If managers of governmental agencies spend more than their budgets allow, they may have broken the law. In some cases the manager could be required to personally repay the amount by which the budget was exceeded. Since governmental budgets are enacted by the relevant elected bodies, to violate the budget is to break the law.

Because budgets are so important for governments and are not to be exceeded, government accounting practices require that budgeted amounts be formally entered into the bookkeeping system. As you have learned, companies do not make formal accounting entries when they order goods; they only make an entry when the goods are received. Governmental accounting systems are different. Each time goods or services are ordered by a government, an "encumbrance" is recorded against the budgeted amount so that agencies do not commit to spend more money than their budgets allow.

Cash Payments Section

Cash payments include expected cash outflows for inventory purchases, S&A expenses, interest expense, and investments. The cash payments for inventory purchases comes from the *schedule of cash payments for inventory purchases* (Exhibit 21.3, section 2, row 15). The cash payments for S&A expenses comes from the *schedule of cash payments for S&A expenses* (Exhibit 21.4, section 2, row 21).

HH borrows or repays principal and pays interest on the last day of each month. The cash payments for interest are determined by multiplying the loan balance for the month by the monthly interest rate. Since there is no outstanding debt during October, there is no interest payment at the end of October. HH expects outstanding debt of $218,000 during the month of November. The bank charges interest at the rate of 12% per year, or 1% per month. The November interest expense and cash payment for interest is $2,180 ($218,000 × .01). The outstanding loan balance during December is $230,000. The December interest expense and cash payment for interest is $2,300 ($230,000 × .01). Determining the amount to borrow or repay at the end of each month is discussed in more detail in the next section of the text.

Finally, the cash payment for the store fixtures comes from the *capital expenditures budget* (not shown in this chapter).

Financing Section

HH has a line of credit under which it can borrow or repay principal in increments of $1,000 at the end of each month as needed. HH desires to maintain an ending cash balance of at least $10,000 each month. With the $207,460 projected cash shortage in row 15 of the cash budget ($40,000 cash balance in row 7 less $247,460 budgeted cash payments in row 13), HH must borrow $218,000 on October 31 to maintain an ending cash balance of at least $10,000. This $218,000 balance is outstanding during November. On November 30, HH must borrow an additional $12,000 to cover the November projected cash shortage of $1,572 plus the $10,000 desired ending cash balance. HH projects a surplus of $23,660 for the month of December. This surplus will allow HH to repay $13,000 of debt and still maintain the desired $10,000 cash balance.

Pro Forma Financial Statement Data

Figures in the Pro Forma Data column of the cash budget (Exhibit 21.5) are alphabetically referenced. The cash receipts from customers, item (a), and the cash payment items (b), (c), and (d) are reported in the operating activities section of the pro forma statement of cash flows (Exhibit 21.8). The interest expense, item (d), is also reported on the pro forma income statement (Exhibit 21.6). The figures are determined by summing the monthly amounts. The $130,000 purchase of store fixtures, item (e), is reported in the investing activities section of the pro forma statement of cash flows. The $217,000 net borrowings, item (f), is reported in the financing activities section of the pro forma statement of cash flows (Exhibit 21.8) and also as a liability on the pro forma balance sheet (Exhibit 21.7). The $10,660 ending cash balance, item (g), is reported as the ending balance on the pro forma statement of cash flows and as an asset on the pro forma balance sheet.

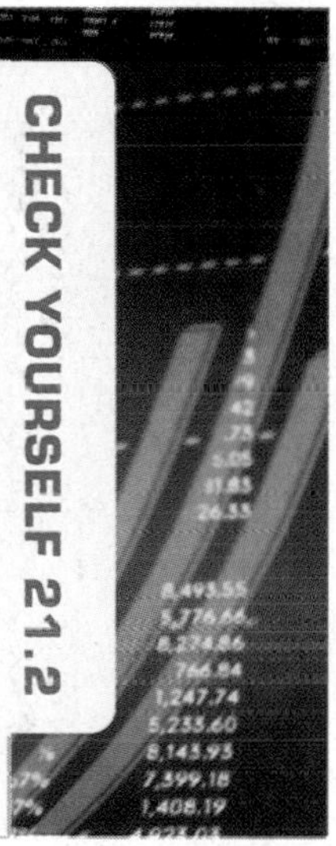

CHECK YOURSELF 21.2

Astor Company expects to incur the following operating expenses during September: salary expense, $25,000; utility expense, $1,200; depreciation expense, $5,400; and selling expense, $14,000. In general, it pays operating expenses in cash in the month in which it incurs them. Based on this information alone, determine the total amount of cash outflow Astor would report in the operating activities section of the pro forma statement of cash flows.

Answer

Depreciation is not included in cash outflows because companies do not pay cash when they recognize depreciation expense. The total cash outflow is $40,200 ($25,000 + $1,200 + $14,000).

Pro Forma Income Statement

LO 7

Prepare a pro forma income statement, balance sheet, and statement of cash flows.

Exhibit 21.6 shows the budgeted income statement for Hampton Hams' new store. The figures for this statement come from Exhibits 21.2, 21.3, 21.4, and 21.5. The budgeted income statement provides an advance estimate of the new store's expected profitability. If expected profitability is unsatisfactory, management could decide to abandon the project or modify planned activity. Perhaps HH could lease less costly store space, pay employees a lower rate, or reduce the number of employees hired. The pricing strategy could also be examined for possible changes.

Budgets are usually prepared using spreadsheets or computerized mathematical models that allow managers to easily undertake "what-if" analysis. What if the growth rate differs from expectations? What if interest rates increase or decrease? Exhibits 21.2 through 21.5 in this chapter were prepared using Microsoft Excel. When variables such as growth rate, collection assumptions, or interest rates are changed, the spreadsheet software instantly recalculates the budgets. Although managers remain responsible for data analysis and decision making, computer technology offers powerful tools to assist in those tasks.

EXHIBIT 21.6

HAMPTON HAMS
Pro Forma Income Statement
For the Quarter Ended December 31, 2006

		Data Source
Sales Revenue	$582,400	Exhibit 21.2
Cost of Goods Sold	(407,680)	Exhibit 21.3
Gross Margin	174,720	
Selling and Administrative Expenses	(110,172)	Exhibit 21.4
Operating Income	64,548	
Interest Expense	(4,480)	Exhibit 21.5
Net Income	$ 60,068	

Pro Forma Balance Sheet

Most of the figures on the pro forma balance sheet in Exhibit 21.7 have been explained. The new store has no contributed capital because its operations will be financed through debt and retained earnings. The amount of retained earnings equals the amount of net income because no earnings from prior periods exist and no distributions are planned.

EXHIBIT 21.7

HAMPTON HAMS
Pro Forma Balance Sheet
As of the Quarter Ended December 31, 2006

			Data Source
Assets			
Cash		$ 10,660	Exhibit 21.5
Accounts Receivable		172,800	Exhibit 21.2
Inventory		35,000	Exhibit 21.3
Store Fixtures	$130,000		Exhibit 21.4 Discussion
Accumulated Depreciation	(3,000)		Exhibit 21.4 Discussion
Book Value of Store Fixtures		127,000	
Total Assets		$345,460	
Liabilities			
Accounts Payable		$ 62,384	Exhibit 21.3
Sales Commissions Payable		4,608	Exhibit 21.4
Utilities Payable		1,400	Exhibit 21.4
Line of Credit Borrowings		217,000	Exhibit 21.5
Equity			
Retained Earnings		60,068	
Total Liabilities and Equity		$345,460	

Pro Forma Statement of Cash Flows

Exhibit 21.8 shows the pro forma statement of cash flows. All information for this statement comes from the cash budget in Exhibit 21.5.

EXHIBIT 21.8

HAMPTON HAMS
Pro Forma Statement of Cash Flows
For the Quarter Ended December 31, 2006

Cash Flow from Operating Activities		
Cash Receipts from Customers	$409,600	
Cash Payments for Inventory	(380,296)	
Cash Payments for S&A Expenses	(101,164)	
Cash Payments for Interest Expense	(4,480)	
Net Cash Flow for Operating Activities		$ (76,340)
Cash Flow from Investing Activities		
Cash Outflow to Purchase Fixtures		(130,000)
Cash Flow from Financing Activities		
Inflow from Borrowing on Line of Credit		217,000
Net Change in Cash		10,660
Plus Beginning Cash Balance		0
Ending Cash Balance		$ 10,660

Answers to The Curious Accountant

Budget preparation at the USOC is complicated by the fact that the timing of its revenues does not match the timing of its expenditures. The USOC spends a lot of money helping to train athletes for the United States Olympic team. Training takes place year-round, every year, for many athletes. The USOC's training facilities in Colorado must also be maintained continuously.

Conversely, much of the USOC's revenues are earned in big batches, received every two years. This money comes from fees the USOC receives for the rights to broadcast the Olympic games on television in the United States. Most companies have a one-year budget cycle during which they attempt to anticipate the coming year's revenues and expenses. This model would not work well for the USOC.

Every business, like every family, faces its own set of circumstances. Those individuals responsible for preparing an entity's budget must have a thorough understanding of the environment in which the entity operates. This is the reason the budget process must be participatory if it is to be successful. No one person, or small group, can anticipate all the issues that will face a large organization in the coming budget period; they need input from employees at all levels.

CHECK YOURSELF 21.3

How do pro forma financial statements differ from the financial statements presented in a company's annual report to stockholders?

Answer

Pro forma financial statements are based on estimates and projections about business events that a company expects to occur in the future. The financial statements presented in a company's annual report to stockholders are based on historical events that occurred prior to the preparation of the statements.

A Look Back <<

The planning of financial matters is called *budgeting.* The degree of detail in a company's budget depends on the budget period. Generally, the shorter the time period, the more specific the plans. *Strategic planning* involves long-term plans, such as the overall objectives of the business. Examples of strategic planning include which products to manufacture and sell and which market niches to pursue. Strategic plans are stated in broad, descriptive terms. Capital budgeting deals with intermediate investment planning. *Operations budgeting* focuses on short-term plans and is used to create the master budget.

A budgeting committee is responsible for consolidating numerous departmental budgets into a master budget for the whole company. The *master budget* has detailed objectives stated in specific amounts; it describes how management intends to achieve its objectives. The master budget usually covers one year. Budgeting supports planning, coordination, performance measurement, and corrective action.

Employees may be uncomfortable with budgets, which can be constraining. Budgets set standards by which performance is evaluated. To establish an effective budget system, management should recognize the effect on human behavior of budgeting. Upper-level management must set a positive atmosphere by taking budgets seriously and avoiding using them to humiliate subordinates. One way to create the proper atmosphere is to encourage subordinates' participation in the budgeting process; *participative budgeting* can lead to goals that are more realistic about what can be accomplished and to establish a team effort in trying to reach those goals.

The primary components of the master budget are the *operating budgets,* the *capital budget,* and the *pro forma financial statements.* The budgeting process begins with preparing the operating budgets, which consist of detailed schedules and budgets prepared by various company departments. The first operating budget to be prepared is the sales budget. The detailed operating budgets for inventory purchases and S&A expenses are based on the projected sales from the sales budget. The information in the schedules of cash receipts (prepared in conjunction with the sales budget) and cash payments (prepared in conjunction with the inventory purchases and S&A expense budgets) is used in preparing the cash budget. The cash budget subtracts cash payments from cash receipts; the resulting cash surplus or shortage determines the company's financing activities.

The capital budget describes the company's long-term plans regarding investments in facilities, equipment, new products, or other lines of business. The information from the capital budget is used as input to several of the operating budgets.

The pro forma financial statements are prepared from information in the operating budgets. The operating budgets for sales, inventory purchases, and S&A expenses contain information that is used to prepare the income statement and balance sheet. The cash budget includes the amount of interest expense reported on the income statement, the ending cash balance, the capital acquisitions reported on the balance sheet, and most of the information included in the statement of cash flows.

>> A Look Forward

Once a company has completed its budget, it has defined its plans. Then the plans must be followed. The next chapter investigates the techniques used to evaluate performance. You will learn to compare actual results to budgets, to calculate variances, and to identify the parties who are normally accountable for deviations from expectations. Finally, you will learn about the human impact management must consider in taking corrective action when employees fail to accomplish budget goals.

SELF-STUDY REVIEW PROBLEM

The Getaway Gift Company operates a chain of small gift shops that are located in prime vacation towns. Getaway is considering opening a new store on January 1, 2007. Getaway's president recently attended a business seminar that explained how formal budgets could be useful in judging the new store's likelihood of succeeding. Assume you are the company's accountant. The president has asked you to explain the budgeting process and to provide sample reports that show the new store's operating expectations for the first three months (January, February, and March). Respond to the following specific requirements:

Required

a. List the operating budgets and schedules included in a master budget.

b. Explain the difference between pro forma financial statements and the financial statements presented in a company's annual reports to shareholders.

c. Prepare a sample sales budget and a schedule of expected cash receipts using the following assumptions. Getaway estimates January sales will be $400,000 of which $100,000 will be cash and $300,000 will be credit. The ratio of cash sales to sales on account is expected to remain constant over the three-month period. The company expects sales to increase 10 percent per month. The company expects to collect 100 percent of the accounts receivable generated by credit sales in the month following the sale. Use this information to determine the amount of accounts receivable that Getaway would report on the March 31 pro forma balance sheet and the amount of sales it would report on the first quarter pro forma income statement.

d. Prepare a sample inventory purchases budget using the following assumptions. Cost of goods sold is 60 percent of sales. The company desires to maintain a minimum ending inventory equal to 25 percent of the following month's cost of goods sold. Getaway makes all inventory purchases on account. The company pays 70 percent of accounts payable in the month of purchase. It pays the remaining 30 percent in the following month. Prepare a schedule of expected cash payments for inventory purchases. Use this information to determine the amount of cost of goods sold Getaway would report on the first quarter pro forma income statement and the amounts of ending inventory and accounts payable it would report on the March 31 pro forma balance sheet.

Solution to Requirement *a*

A master budget would include (1) a sales budget and schedule of cash receipts, (2) an inventory purchases budget and schedule of cash payments for inventory, (3) a general, selling, and administrative expenses budget and a schedule of cash payments related to these expenses, and (4) a cash budget.

Solution to Requirement *b*

Pro forma statements result from the operating budgets listed in the response to Requirement *a.* Pro forma statements describe the results of expected future events. In contrast, the financial statements presented in a company's annual report reflect the results of events that have actually occurred in the past.

Solution to Requirement *c*

General Information				
Sales growth rate		**10%**		**Pro Forma Statement Data**
Sales Budget	**January**	**February**	**March**	
Sales				
Cash sales	$100,000	$110,000	$121,000	
Sales on account	300,000	330,000	363,000	$ 363,000*
Total sales	$400,000	$440,000	$484,000	$1,324,000†
Schedule of Cash Receipts				
Current cash sales	$100,000	$110,000	$121,000	
Plus 100% of previous month's credit sales	0	300,000	330,000	
Total budgeted collections	$100,000	$410,000	$451,000	

*Ending accounts receivable balance reported on March 31 pro forma balance sheet.

†Sales revenue reported on first quarter pro forma income statement (sum of monthly sales).

Solution to Requirement *d*

General information				
Cost of goods sold percentage		**60%**		**Pro Forma Statement Data**
Desired ending inventory percentage of CGS		**25%**		
Inventory Purchases Budget	**January**	**February**	**March**	
Budgeted cost of goods sold	$240,000	$264,000	$290,400	$794,400*
Plus: Desired ending inventory	66,000	72,600	79,860	79,860†
Inventory needed	306,000	336,600	370,260	
Less: Beginning inventory	0	(66,000)	(72,600)	
Required purchases	$306,000	$270,600	$297,660	89,298‡
Schedule of Cash Payments for Inventory Purchases				
70% of current purchases	$214,200	$189,420	$208,362	
30% of prior month's purchases	0	91,800	81,180	
Total budgeted payments for inventory	$214,200	$281,220	$289,542	

*Cost of goods sold reported on first quarter pro forma income statement (sum of monthly amounts).

†Ending inventory balance reported on March 31 pro forma balance sheet.

‡Ending accounts payable balance reported on pro forma balance sheet ($297,660 × 0.3).

KEY TERMS

budgeting 1019
capital budget 1022
capital budgeting 1020
cash budget 1029
master budget 1022
operating budgets 1022
participative budgeting 1022
perpetual (continuous) budgeting 1021
pro forma financial statements 1022
strategic planning 1020

QUESTIONS

1. Budgets are useful only for small companies that can estimate sales with accuracy. Do you agree with this statement?
2. Why does preparing the master budget require a committee?
3. What are the three levels of planning? Explain each briefly.
4. What is the primary factor that distinguishes the three different levels of planning from each other?
5. What is the advantage of using a perpetual budget instead of the traditional annual budget?
6. What are the advantages of budgeting?
7. How may budgets be used as a measure of performance?
8. Ken Shilov, manager of the marketing department, tells you that "budgeting simply does not work." He says that he made budgets for his employees and when he reprimanded them for failing to accomplish budget goals, he got unfounded excuses. Suggest how Mr. Shilov could encourage employee cooperation.
9. What is a master budget?
10. What is the normal starting point in developing the master budget?
11. How does the level of inventory affect the production budget? Why is it important to manage the level of inventory?
12. What are the components of the cash budget? Describe each.
13. The primary reason for preparing a cash budget is to determine the amount of cash to include on the budgeted balance sheet. Do you agree or disagree with this statement? Explain.
14. What information does the pro forma income statement provide? How does its preparation depend on the operating budgets?
15. How does the pro forma statement of cash flows differ from the cash budget?

EXERCISES—SERIES A

All Exercises in Series A are available with McGraw-Hill's Homework Manager.

L.O. 1, 2

Exercise 21-1A *Budget responsibility*

Janet Pace, the accountant, is a perfectionist. No one can do the job as well as she can. Indeed, she has found budget information provided by the various departments to be worthless. She must change everything they give her. She has to admit that her estimates have not always been accurate, but she shudders to think of what would happen if she used the information supplied by the marketing and operating departments. No one seems to care about accuracy. Indeed, some of the marketing staff have even become insulting. When Ms. Pace confronted one of the salesmen with the fact that he was behind in meeting his budgeted sales forecast, he responded by saying, "They're your numbers. Why don't you go out and make the sales? It's a heck of a lot easier to sit there in your office and make up numbers than it is to get out and get the real work done." Ms. Pace reported the incident, but, of course, nothing was done about it.

Required

Write a short report suggesting how the budgeting process could be improved.

Exercise 21-2A *Preparing the sales budget*

L.O. 3, 7

Digital Flash, which expects to start operations on January 1, 2007, will sell digital cameras in shopping malls. Digital Flash has budgeted sales as indicated in the following table. The company expects a 10 percent increase in sales per month for February and March. The ratio of cash sales to sales on account will remain stable from January through March.

Sales	January	February	March
Cash sales	$ 40,000	?	?
Sales on account	60,000	?	?
Total budgeted sales	$100,000	?	?

Required

a. Complete the sales budget by filling in the missing amounts.

b. Determine the amount of sales revenue Digital Flash will report on its second quarter pro forma income statement.

Exercise 21-3A *Preparing a schedule of cash receipts*

L.O. 3, 7

The budget director of Amy's Florist has prepared the following sales budget. The company had $200,000 in accounts receivable on July 1. Amy's Florist normally collects 100 percent of accounts receivable in the month following the month of sale.

Sales	July	August	September
Sales Budget			
Cash sales	$ 60,000	$ 66,000	$ 72,600
Sales on account	150,000	165,000	181,500
Total budgeted sales	$210,000	$231,000	$254,100
Schedule of Cash Receipts			
Current cash sales	?	?	?
Plus collections from accounts receivable	?	?	?
Total budgeted collections	$260,000	$216,000	$237,600

Required

a. Complete the schedule of cash receipts by filling in the missing amounts.

b. Determine the amount of accounts receivable the company will report on its third quarter pro forma balance sheet.

Exercise 21-4A *Preparing sales budgets with different assumptions*

L.O. 3

Stenton Corporation, which has three divisions, is preparing its sales budget. Each division expects a different growth rate because economic conditions vary in different regions of the country. The growth expectations per quarter are 2 percent for East Division, 3 percent for West Division, and 5 percent for South Division.

Division	First Quarter	Second Quarter	Third Quarter	Fourth Quarter
East Division	$300,000	?	?	?
West Division	400,000	?	?	?
South Division	100,000	?	?	?

Required

a. Complete the sales budget by filling in the missing amounts. (Round figures to the nearest dollar.)

b. Determine the amount of sales revenue that the company will report on its quarterly pro forma income statements.

L.O. 3

Exercise 21-5A *Determining cash receipts from accounts receivable*

Special Delivery operates a mail-order business that sells clothes designed for frequent travelers. It had sales of $400,000 in December. Because Special Delivery is in the mail-order business, all sales are made on account. The company expects a 25 percent drop in sales for January. The balance in the Accounts Receivable account on December 31 was $80,000 and is budgeted to be $60,000 as of January 31. Special Delivery normally collects accounts receivable in the month following the month of sale.

Required

a. Determine the amount of cash Special Delivery expects to collect from accounts receivable during January.

b. Is it reasonable to assume that sales will decline in January for this type of business? Why or why not?

L.O. 3

Exercise 21-6A *Using judgment in making a sales forecast*

Kandy Inc. is a candy store located in a large shopping mall.

Required

Write a brief memo describing the sales pattern that you would expect Kandy to experience during the year. In which months will sales likely be high? In which months will sales likely be low? Explain why.

L.O. 4

Exercise 21-7A *Preparing an inventory purchases budget*

Designer Lighting Company sells lamps and other lighting fixtures. The purchasing department manager prepared the following inventory purchases budget. Designer Lighting's policy is to maintain an ending inventory balance equal to 10 percent of the following month's cost of goods sold. April's budgeted cost of goods sold is $90,000.

	January	February	March
Budgeted cost of goods sold	$75,000	$80,000	$86,000
Plus: Desired ending inventory	8,000	?	?
Inventory needed	83,000	?	?
Less: Beginning inventory	16,000	?	?
Required purchases (on account)	$67,000	$80,600	$86,400

Required

a. Complete the inventory purchases budget by filling in the missing amounts.

b. Determine the amount of cost of goods sold the company will report on its first quarter pro forma income statement.

c. Determine the amount of ending inventory the company will report on its pro forma balance sheet at the end of the first quarter.

L.O. 4

Exercise 21-8A *Preparing a schedule of cash payments for inventory purchases*

Book Warehouse buys books and magazines directly from publishers and distributes them to grocery stores. The wholesaler expects to purchase the following inventory.

	April	May	June
Required purchases (on account)	$60,000	$80,000	$100,000

Book Warehouse's accountant prepared the following schedule of cash payments for inventory purchases. Book Warehouse's suppliers require that 90 percent of purchases on account be paid in the month of purchase; the remaining 10 percent are paid in the month following the month of purchase.

Schedule of Cash Payments for Inventory Purchases	April	May	June
Payment for current accounts payable	$54,000	?	?
Payment for previous accounts payable	4,000	?	?
Total budgeted payments for inventory	$58,000	$78,000	$98,000

Required

a. Complete the schedule of cash payments for inventory purchases by filling in the missing amounts.

b. Determine the amount of accounts payable the company will report on its pro forma balance sheet at the end of the second quarter.

Exercise 21-9A *Determining the amount of expected inventory purchases and cash payments* L.O. 4

Jakal Company, which sells electric razors, had $280,000 of cost of goods sold during the month of June. The company projects a 5 percent increase in cost of goods sold during July. The inventory balance as of June 30 is $30,000, and the desired ending inventory balance for July is $25,000. Jakal pays cash to settle 80 percent of its purchases on account during the month of purchase and pays the remaining 20 percent in the month following the purchase. The accounts payable balance as of June 30 was $32,000.

Required

a. Determine the amount of purchases budgeted for July.

b. Determine the amount of cash payments budgeted for inventory purchases in July.

Exercise 21-10A *Preparing a schedule of cash payments for selling and administrative expenses* L.O. 5

The budget director for Shining Window Cleaning Services prepared the following list of expected operating expenses. All expenses requiring cash payments are paid for in the month incurred except salary expense and insurance. Salary is paid in the month following the month in which it is incurred. The insurance premium for six months is paid on October 1. October is the first month of operations; accordingly, there are no beginning account balances.

	October	November	December
Budgeted Operating Expenses			
Equipment lease expense	$ 7,000	$ 7,000	$ 7,000
Salary expense	6,400	6,800	6,900
Cleaning supplies	2,600	2,860	3,146
Insurance expense	1,000	1,000	1,000
Depreciation on computer	1,600	1,600	1,600
Rent	1,800	1,800	1,800
Miscellaneous expenses	600	600	600
Total operating expenses	$21,000	$21,660	$22,046
Schedule of Cash Payments for Operating Expenses			
Equipment lease expense	?	?	?
Prior month's salary expense, 100%	?	?	?
Cleaning supplies	?	?	?
Insurance premium	?	?	?
Depreciation on computer	?	?	?
Rent	?	?	?
Miscellaneous expenses	?	?	?
Total disbursements for operating expenses	$18,000	$18,660	$19,346

Required

a. Complete the schedule of cash payments for operating expenses by filling in the missing amounts.

b. Determine the amount of salaries payable the company will report on its pro forma balance sheet at the end of the fourth quarter.

c. Determine the amount of prepaid insurance the company will report on its pro forma balance sheet at the end of the fourth quarter.

L.O. 4

Exercise 21-11A *Preparing inventory purchases budgets with different assumptions*

Executive officers of Cary Company are wrestling with their budget for the next year. The following are two different sales estimates provided by two difference sources.

Source of Estimate	First Quarter	Second Quarter	Third Quarter	Fourth Quarter
Sales manager	$400,000	$320,000	$300,000	$480,000
Marketing consultant	500,000	450,000	420,000	630,000

Cary's past experience indicates that cost of goods sold is about 70 percent of sales revenue. The company tries to maintain 10 percent of the next quarter's expected cost of goods sold as the current quarter's ending inventory. This year's ending inventory is $30,000. Next year's ending inventory is budgeted to be $32,000.

Required

a. Prepare an inventory purchases budget using the sales manager's estimate.

b. Prepare an inventory purchases budget using the marketing consultant's estimate.

L.O. 5, 7

Exercise 21-12A *Determining the amount of cash payments and pro forma statement data for selling and administrative expenses*

January budgeted selling and administrative expenses for the retail shoe store that Nell Walker plans to open on January 1, 2006, are as follows: sales commissions, $20,000; rent, $15,000; utilities, $5,000; depreciation, $4,000; and miscellaneous, $2,000. Utilities are paid in the month following their incursion. Other expenses are expected to be paid in cash in the month in which they are incurred.

Required

a. Determine the amount of budgeted cash payments for January selling and administrative expenses.

b. Determine the amount of utilities payable the store will report on the January 31st pro forma balance sheet.

c. Determine the amount of depreciation expense the store will report on the income statement for the year 2006, assuming that monthly depreciation remains the same for the entire year.

L.O. 6, 7

Exercise 21-13A *Preparing a cash budget*

The accountant for Tricia's Dress Shop prepared the following cash budget. Tricia's desires to maintain a cash cushion of $14,000 at the end of each month. Funds are assumed to be borrowed and repaid on the last day of each month. Interest is charged at the rate of 2 percent per month.

Cash Budget	July	August	September
Section 1: Cash Receipts			
Beginning cash balance	$ 42,500	$?	$?
Add cash receipts	180,000	200,000	240,600
Total cash available (a)	222,500	?	?
Section 2: Cash Payments			
For inventory purchases	165,526	140,230	174,152
For S&A expenses	54,500	60,560	61,432
For interest expense	0	?	?
Total budgeted disbursements (b)	220,026	?	?
Section 3: Financing Activities			
Surplus (shortage)	2,474	?	?
Borrowing (repayments) (c)	11,526	?	?
Ending Cash Balance (a − b + c)	$ 14,000	$ 14,000	$ 14,000

Required

a. Complete the cash budget by filling in the missing amounts. Round all computations to the nearest whole dollar.

b. Determine the amount of net cash flows from operating activities Tricia's will report on the third quarter pro forma statement of cash flows.

c. Determine the amount of net cash flows from financing activities Tricia's will report on the third quarter pro forma statement of cash flows.

Exercise 21-14A *Determining amount to borrow and pro forma statement balances*

L.O. 6, 7

Jane Hesline owns a small restaurant in New York City. Ms. Hesline provided her accountant with the following summary information regarding expectations for the month of June. The balance in accounts receivable as of May 31 is $50,000. Budgeted cash and credit sales for June are $100,000 and $500,000, respectively. Credit sales are made through Visa and MasterCard and are collected rapidly. Ninety percent of credit sales is collected in the month of sale, and the remainder is collected in the following month. Ms. Hesline's suppliers do not extend credit. Consequently, she pays suppliers on the last day of the month. Cash payments for June are expected to be $620,000. Ms. Hesline has a line of credit that enables the restaurant to borrow funds on demand; however, they must be borrowed on the last day of the month. Interest is paid in cash also on the last day of the month. Ms. Hesline desires to maintain a $20,000 cash balance before the interest payment. Her annual interest rate is 9 percent. Disregard any credit card fees.

Required

a. Compute the amount of funds Ms. Hesline needs to borrow for June, assuming that the beginning cash balance is zero.

b. Determine the amount of interest expense the restaurant will report on the June pro forma income statement.

c. What amount will the restaurant report as interest expense on the July pro forma income statement?

Exercise 21-15A *Preparing pro forma income statements with different assumptions*

L.O. 7

Andy Collum, the controller of Grime Corporation, is trying to prepare a sales budget for the coming year. The income statements for the last four quarters follow.

	First Quarter	Second Quarter	Third Quarter	Fourth Quarter	Total
Sales revenue	$160,000	$180,000	$200,000	$260,000	$800,000
Cost of goods sold	96,000	108,000	120,000	156,000	480,000
Gross profit	64,000	72,000	80,000	104,000	320,000
Selling & admin. expense	16,000	18,000	20,000	26,000	80,000
Net income	$ 48,000	$ 54,000	$ 60,000	$ 78,000	$240,000

Historically, cost of goods sold is about 60 percent of sales revenue. Selling and administrative expenses are about 10 percent of sales revenue.

Tim Grime, the chief executive officer, told Mr. Collum that he expected sales next year to be 10 percent above last year's level. However, Sara Lund, the vice president of sales, told Mr. Collum that she believed sales growth would be only 5 percent.

Required

a. Prepare a pro forma income statement including quarterly budgets for the coming year using Mr. Grime's estimate.

b. Prepare a pro forma income statement including quarterly budgets for the coming year using Ms. Lund's estimate.

c. Explain why two executive officers in the same company could have different estimates of future growth.

PROBLEMS—SERIES A

All Problems in Series A are available with McGraw-Hill's Homework Manager.

L.O. 3

excel

mhhe.com/edmonds2007

CHECK FIGURES
c. Feb: $96,000
March: $115,600

Problem 21-16A *Preparing a sales budget and schedule of cash receipts*

Bedimo Pointers Inc. expects to begin operations on January 1, 2007; it will operate as a specialty sales company that sells laser pointers over the Internet. Bedimo expects sales in January 2007 to total $100,000 and to increase 10 percent per month in February and March. All sales are on account. Bedimo expects to collect 60 percent of accounts receivable in the month of sale, 30 percent in the month following the sale, and 10 percent in the second month following the sale.

Required

a. Prepare a sales budget for the first quarter of 2007.
b. Determine the amount of sales revenue Bedimo will report on the first 2007 quarterly pro forma income statement.
c. Prepare a cash receipts schedule for the first quarter of 2007.
d. Determine the amount of accounts receivable as of March 31, 2007.

L.O. 4, 7

CHECK FIGURES
a. May: $71,000
c. June: $76,760

Problem 21-17A *Preparing the inventory purchases budget and schedule of cash payments*

Stine Inc. sells fireworks. The company's marketing director developed the following cost of goods sold budget for April, May, June, and July.

	April	May	June	July
Budgeted cost of goods sold	$60,000	$70,000	$80,000	$86,000

Stine had a beginning inventory balance of $3,600 on April 1 and a beginning balance in accounts payable of $14,800. The company desires to maintain an ending inventory balance equal to 10 percent of the next period's cost of goods sold. Stine makes all purchases on account. The company pays 60 percent of accounts payable in the month of purchase and the remaining 40 percent in the month following purchase.

Required

a. Prepare an inventory purchases budget for April, May, and June.
b. Determine the amount of ending inventory Stine will report on the end-of-quarter pro forma balance sheet.
c. Prepare a schedule of cash payments for inventory for April, May, and June.
d. Determine the balance in accounts payable Stine will report on the end-of-quarter pro forma balance sheet.

L.O. 7

CHECK FIGURE
a. 12.75%

Problem 21-18A *Preparing pro forma income statements with different assumptions*

Top executive officers of Chesnokov Company, a merchandising firm, are preparing the next year's budget. The controller has provided everyone with the current year's projected income statement.

	Current Year
Sales Revenue	$2,000,000
Cost of Goods Sold	1,400,000
Gross Profit	600,000
Selling & Admin. Expenses	260,000
Net Income	$ 340,000

Cost of goods sold is usually 70 percent of sales revenue, and selling and administrative expenses are usually 10 percent of sales plus a fixed cost of $60,000. The president has announced that the company's goal is to increase net income by 15 percent.

Required

The following items are independent of each other.

a. What percentage increase in sales would enable the company to reach its goal? Support your answer with a pro forma income statement.
b. The market may become stagnant next year, and the company does not expect an increase in sales revenue. The production manager believes that an improved production procedure can cut cost of goods sold by 2 percent. What else can the company do to reach its goal? Prepare a pro forma income statement illustrating your proposal.
c. The company decides to escalate its advertising campaign to boost consumer recognition, which will increase selling and administrative expenses to $340,000. With the increased advertising, the company expects sales revenue to increase by 15 percent. Assume that cost of goods sold remains a constant proportion of sales. Can the company reach its goal?

Problem 21-19A ***Preparing a schedule of cash payments for selling and administrative expenses***

L.O. 5, 6

CHECK FIGURE
a. Sept: $22,460

Shah is a retail company specializing in men's hats. Its budget director prepared the list of expected operating expenses that follows. All items are paid when the expenses are incurred except sales commissions and utilities, which are paid in the month after they are incurred. July is the first month of operations, so there are no beginning account balances.

	July	August	September
Salary expense	$12,000	$12,000	$12,000
Sales commissions (4 percent of sales)	1,600	1,500	1,800
Supplies expense	360	400	440
Utilities	1,200	1,200	1,200
Depreciation on store equipment	2,600	2,600	2,600
Rent	6,600	6,600	6,600
Miscellaneous	720	720	720
Total S&A expenses before interest	$25,080	$25,020	$25,360

Required

a. Prepare a schedule of cash payments for selling and administrative expenses.
b. Determine the amount of utilities payable as of September 30.
c. Determine the amount of sales commissions payable as of September 30.

Problem 21-20A ***Preparing a cash budget***

L.O. 6

CHECK FIGURE
Feb cash surplus before financing activities: $7,010

Hoyt Medical Clinic has budgeted the following cash flows.

	January	February	March
Cash receipts	$100,000	$106,000	$126,000
Cash payments			
For inventory purchases	90,000	72,000	85,000
For S&A expenses	31,000	32,000	27,000

Hoyt Medical had a cash balance of $8,000 on January 1. The company desires to maintain a cash cushion of $5,000. Funds are assumed to be borrowed, in increments of $1,000, and repaid on the last day of each month; the interest rate is 1 percent per month. Hoyt pays its vendor on the last day of the month also. The company had a $40,000 beginning balance in its line of credit liability account.

Required

Prepare a cash budget. (Round all computations to the nearest whole dollar.)

L.O. 3, 4, 5

excel

mhhe.com/edmonds2007

CHECK FIGURES

c. 1st QTR purchases for peaches: $141,120
2nd QTR purchases for oranges: $312,840

Problem 21-21A *Preparing budgets with multiple products*

Fresh Fruits Corporation wholesales peaches and oranges. Beth Fresh is working with the company's accountant to prepare next year's budget. Ms. Fresh estimates that sales will increase 5 percent annually for peaches and 10 percent for oranges. The current year's sales revenue data follow.

	First Quarter	Second Quarter	Third Quarter	Fourth Quarter	Total
Peaches	$220,000	$240,000	$300,000	$240,000	$1,000,000
Oranges	400,000	450,000	570,000	380,000	1,800,000
Total	$620,000	$690,000	$870,000	$620,000	$2,800,000

Based on the company's past experience, cost of goods sold is usually 60 percent of sales revenue. Company policy is to keep 20 percent of the next period's estimated cost of goods sold as the current period's ending inventory. (*Hint:* Use the cost of goods sold for the first quarter to determine the beginning inventory for the first quarter.)

Required

a. Prepare the company's sales budget for the next year for each quarter by individual product.

b. If the selling and administrative expenses are estimated to be $700,000, prepare the company's budgeted annual income statement.

c. Ms. Fresh estimates next year's ending inventory will be $34,000 for peaches and $56,000 for oranges. Prepare the company's inventory purchases budgets for the next year showing quarterly figures by product.

L.O. 3, 4, 5

excel

mhhe.com/edmonds2007

CHECK FIGURES

c. Dec. purchases: $113,250

g. Nov. surplus before financing activities: $19,505

Problem 21-22A *Preparing a master budget for a retail company with no beginning account balances*

Unici Company is a retail company that specializes in selling outdoor camping equipment. The company is considering opening a new store on October 1, 2006. The company president formed a planning committee to prepare a master budget for the first three months of operation. He assigned you, the budget coordinator, the following tasks.

Required

a. October sales are estimated to be $120,000 of which 40 percent will be cash and 60 percent will be credit. The company expects sales to increase at the rate of 25 percent per month. Prepare a sales budget.

b. The company expects to collect 100 percent of the accounts receivable generated by credit sales in the month following the sale. Prepare a schedule of cash receipts.

c. The cost of goods sold is 60 percent of sales. The company desires to maintain a minimum ending inventory equal to 10 percent of the next month's cost of goods sold. Ending inventory at December 31 is expected to be $12,000. Assume that all purchases are made on account. Prepare an inventory purchases budget.

d. The company pays 70 percent of accounts payable in the month of purchase and the remaining 30 percent in the following month. Prepare a cash payments budget for inventory purchases.

e. Budgeted selling and administrative expenses per month follow.

Salary expense (fixed)	$18,000
Sales commissions	5 percent of Sales
Supplies expense	2 percent of Sales
Utilities (fixed)	$1,400
Depreciation on store equipment (fixed)*	$4,000
Rent (fixed)	$4,800
Miscellaneous (fixed)	$1,200

*The capital expenditures budget indicates that Unici will spend $164,000 on October 1 for store fixtures, which are expected to have a $20,000 salvage value and a three-year (36-month) useful life.

Use this information to prepare a selling and administrative expenses budget.

f. Utilities and sales commissions are paid the month after they are incurred; all other expenses are paid in the month in which they are incurred. Prepare a cash payments budget for selling and administrative expenses.
g. Unici borrows funds, in increments of $1,000, and repays them on the last day of the month. The company also pays its vendors on the last day of the month. It pays interest of 1 percent per month in cash on the last day of the month. To be prudent, the company desires to maintain a $12,000 cash cushion. Prepare a cash budget.
h. Prepare a pro forma income statement for the quarter.
i. Prepare a pro forma balance sheet at the end of the quarter.
j. Prepare a pro forma statement of cash flows for the quarter.

Problem 21-23A *Behavioral impact of budgeting*

L.O. 2

CHECK FIGURE
a. NI: $945,000
c. NI: $1,035,000

Vanhorn Corporation has three divisions, each operating as a responsibility center. To provide an incentive for divisional executive officers, the company gives divisional management a bonus equal to 20 percent of the excess of actual net income over budgeted net income. The following is Dancy Division's current year's performance.

	Current Year
Sales revenue	$4,500,000
Cost of goods sold	2,700,000
Gross profit	1,800,000
Selling & admin. expenses	900,000
Net income	$ 900,000

The president has just received next year's budget proposal from the vice president in charge of Dancy Division. The proposal budgets a 5 percent increase in sales revenue with an extensive explanation about stiff market competition. The president is puzzled. Dancy has enjoyed revenue growth of around 10 percent for each of the past five years. The president had consistently approved the division's budget proposals based on 5 percent growth in the past. This time, the president wants to show that he is not a fool. "I will impose a 15 percent revenue increase to teach them a lesson!" the president says to himself smugly.

Assume that cost of goods sold and selling and administrative expenses remain stable in proportion to sales.

Required

a. Prepare the budgeted income statement based on Dancy Division's proposal of a 5 percent increase.
b. If growth is actually 10 percent as usual, how much bonus would Dancy Division's executive officers receive if the president had approved the division's proposal?
c. Prepare the budgeted income statement based on the 15 percent increase the president imposed.
d. If the actual results turn out to be a 10 percent increase as usual, how much bonus would Dancy Division's executive officers receive since the president imposed a 15 percent increase?
e. Propose a better budgeting procedure for Vanhorn.

EXERCISES—SERIES B

Exercise 21-1B *Budget responsibility*

L.O. 1, 2

Ken Chaney, the controller of Oxmoore Industries, Inc., is very popular. He is easygoing and does not offend anybody. To develop the company's most recent budget, Mr. Chaney first asked all department managers to prepare their own budgets. He then added together the totals from the department budgets to produce the company budget. When Sally Khatri, Oxmoore's president, reviewed the company budget, she sighed and asked, "Is our company a charitable organization?"

Required

Write a brief memo describing deficiencies in the budgeting process and suggesting improvements.

L.O. 3, 7

Exercise 21-2B *Preparing a sales budget*

Reese's Restaurant is opening for business in a new shopping center. Casey Mazur, the owner, is preparing a sales budget for the next three months. After consulting friends in the same business, Ms. Mazur estimated July revenues as shown in the following table. She expects revenues to increase 5 percent per month in August and September.

Revenues Budget	July	August	September
Food sales	$20,000	?	?
Beverage and liquor sales	12,000	?	?
Total budgeted revenues	$32,000	?	?

Required

a. Complete the sales budget by filling in the missing amounts.

b. Determine the total amount of revenue Reese's Restaurant will report on its quarterly pro forma income statement.

L.O. 3, 7

Exercise 21-3B *Preparing a schedule of cash receipts*

Tilden Imports Inc. sells goods imported from the Far East. Using the second quarter's sales budget, Sam Wu is trying to complete the schedule of cash receipts for the quarter. The company had accounts receivable of $430,000 on April 1. Tilden Imports normally collects 100 percent of accounts receivable in the month following the month of sale.

Sales	April	May	June
Sales Budget			
Cash sales	$160,000	$176,000	$168,000
Sales on account	480,000	568,000	500,000
Total budgeted sales	$640,000	$744,000	$668,000
Schedule of Cash Receipts			
Current cash sales	?	?	?
Plus: Collections from accounts receivable	?	?	?
Total budgeted collections	$590,000	$656,000	$736,000

Required

a. Help Mr. Wu complete the schedule of cash receipts by filling in the missing amounts.

b. Determine the amount of accounts receivable the company will report on the quarterly pro forma balance sheet.

L.O. 3

Exercise 21-4B *Preparing sales budgets with different assumptions*

Briggs International Inc. has three subsidiaries, Falcon Trading Company, Ammons Medical Supplies Company, and Ocean Shipping Company. Because the subsidiaries operate in different industries, Briggs's corporate budget for the coming year must reflect the different growth potentials of the individual industries. The growth expectations per quarter for the subsidiaries are 4 percent for Falcon, 1 percent for Ammons, and 3 percent for Ocean.

Subsidiary	Current Quarter Sales	First Quarter	Second Quarter	Third Quarter	Fourth Quarter
Falcon	$250,000	?	?	?	?
Ammons	350,000	?	?	?	?
Ocean	450,000	?	?	?	?

Required

a. Complete the sales budget by filling in the missing amounts. (Round the figures to the nearest dollar.)

b. Determine the amount of sales revenue Briggs will report on the quarterly pro forma income statements.

Exercise 21-5B *Determining cash receipts from accounts receivable*

L.O. 3

Otell Corporation is about to start a business as an agricultural products distributor. Because its customers will all be retailers, Otell will sell its products solely on account. The company expects to collect 60 percent of accounts receivable in the month of sale and the remaining 40 percent in the following month. Otell expects sales revenues of $200,000 in July, the first month of operation, and $250,000 in August.

Required

a. Determine the amount of cash Otell expects to collect in July.

b. Determine the amount of cash Otell expects to collect in August.

Exercise 21-6B *Using judgment in making a sales forecast*

L.O. 3

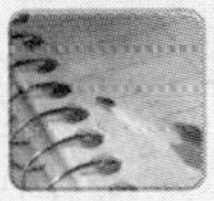

Merry Greetings Corporation sells greeting cards for various occasions.

Required

Write a brief memo describing the sales pattern that you would expect Merry Greetings to experience during the year. In which months will sales likely be high? Explain why.

Exercise 21-7B *Preparing an inventory purchases budget*

L.O. 4

Green Drugstores Inc. sells prescription drugs, over-the-counter drugs, and some groceries. The purchasing manager prepared the following inventory purchases budget. Green desires to maintain an ending inventory balance equal to 20 percent of the following month's cost of goods sold. April's budgeted cost of goods sold amounts to $50,000.

Inventory Purchases Budget	January	February	March
Budgeted cost of goods sold	$40,000	$35,000	$48,000
Plus: Desired ending inventory	7,000	?	?
Inventory needed	47,000	?	?
Less: Beginning inventory	8,000	?	?
Required purchases (on account)	$39,000	?	?

Required

a. Complete the inventory purchases budget by filling in the missing amounts.

b. Determine the amount of cost of goods sold the company will report on the first quarter pro forma income statement.

c. Determine the amount of ending inventory the company will report on the first quarter pro forma balance sheet.

Exercise 21-8B *Preparing a schedule of cash payments for inventory purchases*

L.O. 4

Hometown Grocery buys and sells groceries in a community far from any major city. Chuck Portelli, the owner, budgeted the store's purchases as follows:

	October	November	December
Required purchases (on account)	$25,000	$24,000	$32,000

Hometown's suppliers require that 80 percent of accounts payable be paid in the month of purchase. The remaining 20 percent is paid in the month following the month of purchase.

Schedule of Cash Payments for Inventory Purchases

	October	November	December
Payment for current accounts payable	$20,000	?	?
Payment for previous accounts payable	6,000	?	?
Total budgeted payments for inventory	$26,000	?	?

Required

a. Complete the schedule of cash payments for inventory purchases by filling in the missing amounts.

b. Determine the amount of accounts payable Hometown will report on the store's quarterly pro forma balance sheet.

L.O. 4

Exercise 21-9B ***Determining the amount of inventory purchases and cash payments***

Duval Oil Corporation, which distributes gasoline products to independent gasoline stations, had $480,000 of cost of goods sold in January. The company expects a 2.5 percent increase in cost of goods sold during February. The ending inventory balance for January is $25,000, and the desired ending inventory for February is $30,000. Duval pays cash to settle 70 percent of its purchases on account during the month of purchase and pays the remaining 30 percent in the month following the purchase. The accounts payable balance as of January 31 was $35,000.

Required

a. Determine the amount of purchases budgeted for February.

b. Determine the amount of cash payments budgeted for inventory purchases in February.

L.O. 5

Exercise 21-10B ***Preparing a schedule of cash payments for selling and administrative expenses***

The controller for Deluxe Laundry Services prepared the following list of expected operating expenses. All expenses requiring cash payments except salary expense and insurance are paid for in the month incurred. Salary is paid in the month following its incursion. The annual insurance premium is paid in advance on January 1. January is the first month of operations. Accordingly, there are no beginning account balances.

	January	February	March
Budgeted Selling and Administrative Expenses			
Equipment depreciation	$ 6,000	$ 6,000	$ 6,000
Salary expense	2,900	2,700	3,050
Cleaning supplies	1,000	940	1,100
Insurance expense	600	600	600
Equipment maintenance expense	500	500	500
Leases expense	1,600	1,600	1,600
Miscellaneous expenses	400	400	400
Total S&A expenses	$13,000	$12,740	$13,250
Schedule of Cash Payments for Selling and Administrative Expenses			
Equipment depreciation	?	?	?
Prior month's salary expense, 100%	?	?	?
Cleaning supplies	?	?	?
Insurance premium	?	?	?
Equipment maintenance expense	?	?	?
Leases expense	?	?	?
Miscellaneous expenses	?	?	?
Total payments for S&A expenses	$10,700	$ 6,340	$ 6,300

Required

a. Complete the schedule of cash payments for selling and administrative expenses by filling in the missing amounts.

b. Determine the amount of salaries payable the company will report on its quarterly pro forma balance sheet.

c. Determine the amount of prepaid insurance the company will report on its quarterly pro forma balance sheet.

Exercise 21-11B ***Preparing inventory purchases budgets with different assumptions*** L.O. 4

Alice Grant has been at odds with her brother and business partner, Larry, since childhood. The sibling rivalry is not all bad, however; their garden shop, Grant Gardens and Gifts, has been very successful. When the partners met to prepare the coming year's budget, their forecasts were different, naturally. Their sales revenue estimates follow.

Source of Estimate	First Quarter	Second Quarter	Third Quarter	Fourth Quarter
Alice	$360,000	$400,000	$300,000	$420,000
Larry	300,000	320,000	340,000	480,000

Past experience indicates that cost of goods sold is about 60 percent of sales revenue. The company tries to maintain 15 percent of the next quarter's expected cost of goods sold as the current quarter's ending inventory. The ending inventory this year is $25,000. Next year's ending inventory is budgeted to be $35,000.

Required

a. Prepare an inventory purchases budget using Alice's estimate.

b. Prepare an inventory purchases budget using Larry's estimate.

Exercise 21-12B ***Determining the amount of cash payments for selling and administrative expenses*** L.O. 5, 7

Doug Fleak, managing partner of Fleak Business Consulting, is preparing a budget for January 2007, the first month of business operations. Doug estimates the following monthly selling and administrative expenses: office lease, $5,000; utilities, $1,600; office supplies, $2,400; depreciation, $12,000; referral fees, $5,000; and miscellaneous, $1,000. Referral fees will be paid in the month following the month they are incurred.

Required

a. Determine the amount of budgeted cash payments for January selling and administrative expenses.

b. Determine the amount of referral fees payable the firm will report on the January 31 pro forma balance sheet.

c. Determine the amount of office lease expense the company will report on its 2007 pro forma income statement, assuming that the monthly lease expense remains the same throughout the whole year.

Exercise 21-13B ***Preparing a cash budget*** L.O. 6, 7

David Helmi, the accounting manager of Nile Antique Company, is preparing his company's cash budget for the next quarter. Nile desires to maintain a cash cushion of $4,000 at the end of each month. As cash flows fluctuate, the company either borrows or repays funds at the end of a month. It pays interest on borrowed funds at the rate of 1 percent per month.

Cash Budget	July	August	September
Section 1: Cash Receipts			
Beginning cash balance	$ 16,000	$?	$?
Add cash receipts	180,000	192,000	208,000
Total cash available (a)	196,000	?	?

continued

Cash Budget	July	August	September
Section 2: Cash Payments			
For inventory purchases	158,000	153,000	171,000
For S&A expenses	37,000	36,000	39,000
For interest expense	0	?	?
Total budgeted disbursements (b)	195,000	?	?
Section 3: Financing Activities			
Surplus (shortage)	1,000	?	?
Borrowing (repayments) (c)	3,000	?	?
Ending Cash Balance (a − b + c)	$ 4,000	$ 4,000	$ 4,000

Required

a. Complete the cash budget by filling in the missing amounts. Round all computations to the nearest whole dollar.

b. Determine the amount of net cash flows from operating activities Nile will report on its quarterly pro forma statement of cash flows.

c. Determine the amount of net cash flows from financing activities Nile will report on its quarterly pro forma statement of cash flows.

L.O. 6, 7

Exercise 21-14B *Determining amount to borrow and pro forma statement balances*

Ali Nassar, the president of Ali's Flowers, Inc., has been working with his controller to manage the company's cash position. The controller provided Ali the following data.

Balance of accounts receivable, June 30	$ 40,000
Balance of line of credit, June 30	0
Budgeted cash sales for July	74,000
Budgeted credit sales for July	320,000
Budgeted cash payments for July	400,000

The company typically collects 75 percent of credit sales in the month of sale and the remainder in the month following the sale. Ali's line of credit enables the company to borrow funds readily, with the stipulation that any borrowing must take place on the last day of the month. The company pays its vendors on the last day of the month also. Mr. Nassar likes to maintain a $15,000 cash balance before any interest payments. The annual interest rate is 12 percent.

Required

a. Compute the amount of funds Mr. Nassar needs to borrow on July 31, assuming that the cash balance on June 30 is zero.

b. Determine the amount of interest expense the company will report on the July pro forma income statement.

c. Determine the amount of interest expense the company will report on the August pro forma income statement.

L.O. 7

Exercise 21-15B *Preparing pro forma income statements with different assumptions*

Boylan Corporation's budget planning meeting is like a zoo. Todd Owens, the credit manager, is naturally conservative and Jenny Hoover, the marketing manager, is the opposite. They have argued back and forth about the effect of various factors that influence the sales growth rate, such as credit policies and market potential. Based on the following current year data provided by Peggy Sullivan, the controller, Todd expects Boylan's revenues to grow 5 percent each quarter above last year's level; Jenny insists the growth rate will be 8 percent per quarter.

Current Year	First Quarter	Second Quarter	Third Quarter	Fourth Quarter	Total
Sales revenue	$240,000	$200,000	$216,000	$314,000	$970,000
Cost of goods sold	122,000	101,000	106,000	156,000	485,000
Gross margin	118,000	99,000	110,000	158,000	485,000
Selling & admin. expenses	32,000	26,000	26,400	40,600	125,000
Net income	$ 86,000	$ 73,000	$ 83,600	$117,400	$360,000

Historically, cost of goods sold has been about 50 percent of sales revenue. Selling and administrative expenses have been about 12.5 percent of sales revenue.

Required

a. Prepare a pro forma income statement for the coming year using the credit manager's growth estimate.

b. Prepare a pro forma income statement for the coming year using the marketing manager's growth estimate.

c. Explain why two executives in the same company could have different estimates of future growth.

PROBLEMS—SERIES B

Problem 21-16B ***Preparing a sales budget and schedule of cash receipts*** L.O. 3

Isbell Corporation sells mail-order computers. In December 2005, it has generated $500,000 of sales revenue; the company expects a 20 percent increase in sales in January and 10 percent in February. All sales are on account. Isbell normally collects 80 percent of accounts receivable in the month of sale and 20 percent in the next month.

Required

a. Prepare a sales budget for January and February 2006.

b. Determine the amount of sales revenue Isbell would report on the bimonthly pro forma income statement for January and February 2006.

c. Prepare a cash receipts schedule for January and February 2006.

d. Determine the amount of accounts receivable as of February 28, 2006.

Problem 21-17B ***Preparing the inventory purchases budget and schedule of cash payments*** L.O. 4, 7

Rourke Company's purchasing manager, Milton Hayes, is preparing a purchases budget for the next quarter. At his request, Earl Vaiton, the manager of the sales department, forwarded him the following preliminary sales budget.

	October	November	December	January
Budgeted sales	$600,000	$750,000	$900,000	$800,000

For budgeting purposes, Rourke estimates that cost of goods sold is 75 percent of sales. The company desires to maintain an ending inventory balance equal to 20 percent of the next period's cost of goods sold. The September ending inventory is $90,000. Rourke makes all purchases on account and pays 70 percent of accounts payable in the month of purchase and the remaining 30 percent in the following month. The balance of accounts payable at the end of September is $90,000.

Required

a. Prepare an inventory purchases budget for October, November, and December.

b. Determine the amount of ending inventory Rourke will report on the end-of-quarter pro forma balance sheet.

c. Prepare a schedule of cash payments for inventory for October, November, and December.

d. Determine the balance in accounts payable Rourke will report on the end-of-quarter pro forma balance sheet.

L.O. 7

Problem 21-18B *Preparing pro forma income statements with different assumptions*

Arthur Winters, a successful entrepreneur, is reviewing the results of his first year in business. His accountant delivered the following income statement just five minutes ago.

	Current Year
Sales Revenue	$500,000
Cost of Goods Sold	350,000
Gross Profit	150,000
Selling & Admin. Expenses	90,000
Net Income	$ 60,000

Mr. Winters would like net income to increase 20 percent in the next year. This first year, selling and administrative expenses were 10 percent of sales revenue plus $40,000 of fixed expenses.

Required

The following questions are independent of each other.

a. Mr. Winters expects that cost of goods sold and variable selling and administrative expenses will remain stable in proportion to sales next year. The fixed selling and administrative expenses will increase to $68,000. What percentage increase in sales would enable the company to reach Mr. Winters' goal? Prepare a pro forma income statement to illustrate.

b. Market competition may become serious next year, and Mr. Winters does not expect an increase in sales revenue. However, he has developed a good relationship with his supplier, who is willing to give him a volume discount that will decrease cost of goods sold by 3 percent. What else can the company do to reach Mr. Winters' goal? Prepare a pro forma income statement illustrating your proposal.

c. If the company escalates its advertising campaign to boost consumer recognition, the selling and administrative expenses will increase to $150,000. With the increased advertising, the company expects sales revenue to increase by 25 percent. Assume that cost of goods sold remains constant in proportion to sales. Can the company reach Mr. Winters' goal?

L.O. 5

Problem 21-19B *Preparing a schedule of cash payments for selling and administrative expenses*

Perry Travel Services Inc. has prepared its selling and administrative expenses budget for the next quarter. It pays all expenses when they are incurred except sales commissions, advertising expense, and telephone expense. These three items are paid in the month following the one in which they are incurred. January is the first month of operations, so there are no beginning account balances.

	January	February	March
Salary expense	$10,000	$10,000	$10,000
Sales commissions	700	740	900
Advertising expense	500	500	600
Telephone expense	1,000	1,080	1,100
Depreciation on store equipment	4,000	4,000	4,000
Rent	10,000	10,000	10,000
Miscellaneous	800	800	800
Total S&A expenses before interest	$27,000	$27,120	$27,400

Required

a. Prepare a schedule of cash payments for selling and administrative expenses.

b. Determine the amount of telephone payable as of March 31.

c. Determine the amount of sales commissions payable as of February 28.

Problem 21-20B ***Preparing a cash budget*** L.O. 6

Mead Company has budgeted the following cash flows:

	April	May	June
Cash receipts	$320,000	$470,000	$624,000
Cash payments			
For inventory purchases	410,000	420,000	464,000
For S&A expenses	80,000	106,000	132,000

Mead had a $36,000 cash balance on April 1. The company desires to maintain a $60,000 cash cushion before paying interest. Funds are assumed to be borrowed, in increments of $1,000, and repaid on the last day of each month; the interest rate is 1.50 percent per month. Mead pays its vendors on the last day of the month also.

Required

Prepare a cash budget.

Problem 21-21B ***Preparing budgets with multiple products*** L.O. 3, 4, 5

Leath Enterprises Inc. has two products, palm-size computers and programmable calculators. Shirley Belvin, the chief executive officer, is working with her staff to prepare next year's budget. Ms. Belvin estimates that sales will increase at an annual rate of 10 percent for palm-size computers and 4 percent for programmable calculators. The current year sales revenue data follow.

	First Quarter	Second Quarter	Third Quarter	Fourth Quarter	Total
Palm-size computers	$500,000	$550,000	$620,000	$ 730,000	$2,400,000
Programmable calculators	250,000	275,000	290,000	325,000	1,140,000
Total	$750,000	$825,000	$910,000	$1,055,000	$3,540,000

Based on the company's past experience, cost of goods sold is usually 75 percent of sales revenue. Company policy is to keep 10 percent of the next period's estimated cost of goods sold as the current period ending inventory.

Required

a. Prepare the company's sales budget for the next year for each quarter by individual products.

b. If the selling and administrative expenses are estimated to be $500,000, prepare the company's budgeted annual income statement for the next year.

c. Ms. Belvin estimates the current year's ending inventory will be $78,000 for computers and $32,000 for calculators and the ending inventory next year will be $88,000 for computers and $42,000 for calculators. Prepare the company's inventory purchases budget for the next year showing quarterly figures by product.

Problem 21-22B ***Preparing a master budget for a retail company with no beginning account balances*** L.O. 3, 4, 5

Oversea Gifts Corporation begins business today, December 31, 2004. Sharon Ting, the president, is trying to prepare the company's master budget for the first three months (January, February, and March) of 2005. Since you are her good friend and an accounting student, Ms. Ting asks you to prepare the budget based on the following specifications.

Required

a. January sales are estimated to be $250,000 of which 30 percent will be cash and 70 percent will be credit. The company expects sales to increase at the rate of 10 percent per month. Prepare a sales budget.

b. The company expects to collect 100 percent of the accounts receivable generated by credit sales in the month following the sale. Prepare a schedule of cash receipts.

c. The cost of goods sold is 50 percent of sales. The company desires to maintain a minimum ending inventory equal to 20 percent of the next month's cost of goods sold. The ending inventory at March 31 is expected to be $33,000. Assume that all purchases are made on account. Prepare an inventory purchases budget.

d. The company pays 60 percent of accounts payable in the month of purchase and the remaining 40 percent in the following month. Prepare a cash payments budget for inventory purchases.

e. Budgeted selling and administrative expenses per month follow.

Salary expense (fixed)	$25,000
Sales commissions	8 percent of Sales
Supplies expense	4 percent of Sales
Utilities (fixed)	$1,800
Depreciation on store equipment (fixed)*	$5,000
Rent (fixed)	$7,200
Miscellaneous (fixed)	$2,000

*The capital expenditures budget indicates that Oversea will spend $350,000 on January 1 for store fixtures. The fixtures are expected to have a $50,000 salvage value and a five-year (60-month) useful life.

Use this information to prepare a selling and administrative expenses budget.

f. Utilities and sales commissions are paid the month after they are incurred; all other expenses are paid in the month in which they are incurred. Prepare a cash payments budget for selling and administrative expenses.

g. The company borrows funds, in increments of $1,000, and repays them on the last day of the month. It pays interest of 1.5 percent per month in cash on the last day of the month. For safety, the company desires to maintain a $50,000 cash cushion. The company pays its vendors on the last day of the month. Prepare a cash budget.

h. Prepare a pro forma income statement for the quarter.

i. Prepare a pro forma balance sheet at the end of the quarter.

j. Prepare a pro forma statement of cash flows for the quarter.

L.O. 2

Problem 21-23B *Behavioral impact of budgeting*

Anita Landy, the director of Mathis Corporation's Mail-Order Division, is preparing the division's budget proposal for next year. The company's president will review the proposal for approval. Ms. Landy estimates the current year final operating results will be as follows.

	Current Year
Sales revenue	$10,000,000
Cost of goods sold	5,680,000
Gross profit	4,320,000
Selling & admin. expenses	1,920,000
Net income	$ 2,400,000

Ms. Landy believes that the cost of goods sold as well as selling and administrative expenses will continue to be stable in proportion to sales revenue.

Mathis has an incentive policy to reward division managers whose performance exceeds their budget. Division directors receive a 10 percent bonus based on the excess of actual net income over the division's budget. For the last two years, Ms. Landy has proposed a 4 percent rate of increase, which proved accurate. However, her honesty and accuracy in forecasting caused her to receive no year-end bonus at all. She is pondering whether she should do something differently this time. If she continues to be honest, she should propose an 8 percent growth rate because of robust market demand. Alternatively, she can propose a 4 percent growth rate as usual and thereby expect to receive some bonus at year-end.

Required

a. Prepare a pro forma income statement, assuming a 4 percent estimated increase.
b. Prepare a pro forma income statement, assuming an 8 percent increase.
c. Assume the president eventually approves the division's proposal with the 4 percent growth rate. If growth actually is 8 percent, how much bonus would Ms. Landy receive?
d. Propose a better budgeting procedure for Mathis Corporation.

ANALYZE, THINK, COMMUNICATE

ATC 21-1 Business Applications Case *Preparing and using pro forma statements*

Nancy Chen and Tim Hoffer recently graduated from the same university. After graduation they decided not to seek jobs in established organizations but to start their own small business. They hoped this would provide more flexibility in their personal lives for a few years. Since both of them enjoyed cooking, they decided on a business selling vegetarian wraps and fruit juices from a street cart near their alma mater.

They bought a small enclosed cart for $3,500 that was set up for selling food. This cost, along with the cost for supplies to get started, a business license, and street vendor license, brought their initial expenditures to $4,500. They used $500 of their personal savings, and they borrowed $4,000 from Nancy's parents. They agreed to pay interest on the outstanding loan balance each month based on an annual rate of 6 percent. They will repay the principal over the next two years as cash becomes available.

After two months in business, September and October, they had average monthly revenues of $5,800 and out-of-pocket costs of $3,600 for ingredients, paper supplies, and so on, but not interest. Tim thinks they should repay some of the money they borrowed, but Nancy thinks they should prepare a set of forecasted financial statements for their first year in business before deciding whether or not to repay any principal on the loan. She remembers a bit about budgeting from a survey of accounting course she took and thinks the results from their first two months in business can be extended over the next 10 months to prepare the budget they need. They estimate the cart will last at least three years, after which they expect to sell it for $500 and move on to something else in their lives. Nancy agrees to prepare a forecasted (pro forma) income statement, balance sheet, and statement of cash flows for their first year in business, which includes the two months already passed.

Required

a. Prepare the annual pro forma financial statements that you would expect Nancy to prepare based on her comments about her expectations for the business. Assume no principal will be repaid on the loan.
b. Review the statements you prepared for the first requirement and prepare a list of reasons why Tim and Nancy's business results probably will not agree with their budgeted statements.

ATC 21-2 Group Assignment *Master budget and pro forma statements*

The following trial balance was drawn from the records of Havel Company as of October 1, 2005.

Cash	$ 16,000	
Accounts receivable	60,000	
Inventory	40,000	
Store equipment	200,000	
Accumulated depreciation		$ 76,800
Accounts payable		72,000
Line of credit loan		100,000
Common stock		50,000
Retained earnings		17,200
Totals	$316,000	$316,000

Required

a. Divide the class into groups, each with four or five students. Organize the groups into three sections. Assign Task 1 to the first section, Task 2 to the second section, and Task 3 to the third section.

Group Tasks

(1) Based on the following information, prepare a sales budget and a schedule of cash receipts for October, November, and December. Sales for October are expected to be $180,000, consisting of $40,000 in cash and $140,000 on credit. The company expects sales to increase at the rate of 10 percent per month. All of accounts receivable is collected in the month following the sale.

(2) Based on the following information, prepare a purchases budget and a schedule of cash payments for inventory purchases for October, November, and December. Cost of goods sold for October is expected to be $72,000. Cost of goods sold is expected to increase by 10 percent per month in November and December. Havel expects January cost of goods sold to be $89,000. The company desires to maintain a minimum ending inventory equal to 20 percent of the next month's cost of goods sold. Seventy-five percent of accounts payable is paid in the month that the purchase occurs; the remaining 25 percent is paid in the following month.

(3) Based on the following selling and administrative expenses budgeted for October, prepare a selling and administrative expenses budget for October, November, and December.

Cash payments for sales commissions and utilities are made in the month following the one in which the expense is incurred. Supplies and other operating expenses are paid in cash in the month in which they are incurred. As of October 1, no amounts were payable for either commissions or utilities from the previous month.

Sales commissions (10% increase per month)	$ 7,200
Supplies expense (10% increase per month)	1,800
Utilities (fixed)	2,200
Depreciation on store equipment (fixed)	1,600
Salary expense (fixed)	34,000
Rent (fixed)	6,000
Miscellaneous (fixed)	1,000

b. Select a representative from each section. Have the representatives supply the missing information in the following pro forma income statement and balance sheet for the fourth quarter of 2005. The statements are prepared as of December 31, 2005.

Income Statement		
Sales Revenue		$?
Cost of Goods Sold		?
Gross Margin		357,480
Operating Expenses		?
Operating Income		193,290
Interest Expense		(2,530)
Net Income		$190,760
Balance Sheet		
Assets		
Cash		$ 9,082
Accounts Receivable		?
Inventory		?
Store Equipment	$200,000	
Accumulated Depreciation Store Equipment	?	
Book Value of Equipment		118,400
Total Assets		$314,682
Liabilities		
Accounts Payable		?
Utilities Payable		?
Sales Commissions Payable		?
Line of Credit		23,936

continued

Equity	
Common Stock	50,000
Retained Earnings	?
Total Liabilities and Equity	$314,682

c. Indicate whether Havel will need to borrow money during October.

ATC 21-3 Research Assignment *Simplifying the budget process*

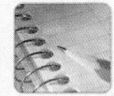

By their nature, large entities often generate big, complex budgets. There is a danger, however, that budgets can become so detailed and complex that they do not get used after being prepared. In the article, "Streamline Budgeting in the new Millennium: Concentrate on Simplicity and Usefulness, Not Unrealistic Numbers," *Strategic Finance,* December 2001, pp. 45–50, Bruce Neumann provides suggestions for improving the budgeting process. Read this article and complete the following requirements.

Required

a. What are the five steps of budgeting that the author identifies?

b. Briefly explain what the article means by "the Three C's" of motivation for those preparing a budget.

c. The article describes "activity budgeting" as one method for streamlining an entity's budget. Explain the basic concept of activity budgeting.

d. The article describes "global budgeting" as one method for streamlining an entity's budget. Explain the basic concept of global budgeting.

e. Does the author suggest that more budget categories be devoted to fixed-cost categories or variable-cost categories?

ATC 21-4 Writing Assignment *Continuous budgeting*

HON Company is the largest maker of mid-priced office furniture in the United States and Canada. Its management has expressed dissatisfaction with its *annual* budget system. Fierce competition requires businesses to be flexible and innovative. Building the effects of innovation into an annual budget is difficult because actions and outcomes often are evolutionary. Innovation unfolds as the year progresses. Consequently, HON's management team reached the conclusion that "when production processes undergo continuous change, standards developed annually for static conditions no longer offer meaningful targets for gauging their success."

Required

Assume that you are HON Company's budget director. Write a memo to the management team explaining how the practice of continuous budgeting could overcome the shortcomings of an annual budget process. (For insight, read the article "Continuous Budgeting at the HON Company," *Management Accounting,* January 1996. This article describes HON's real-world experience with a continuous budget system.)

ATC 21-5 Ethical Dilemma *Bad budget system or unethical behavior?*

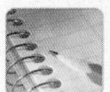

Clarence Cleaver is the budget director for the Harris County School District. Mr. Cleaver recently sent an urgent e-mail message to Sally Simmons, principal of West Harris County High. The message severely reprimanded Ms. Simmons for failing to spend the funds allocated to her to purchase computer equipment. Ms. Simmons responded that her school already has a sufficient supply of computers; the computer lab is never filled to capacity and usually is less than half filled. Ms. Simmons suggested that she would rather use the funds for teacher training. She argued that the reason the existing computers are not fully utilized is that the teachers lack sufficient computer literacy necessary to make assignments for their students.

Mr. Cleaver responded that it is not Ms. Simmons's job to decide how the money is to be spent; that is the school board's job. It is the principal's job to spend the money as the board directed. He informed Ms. Simmons that if the money is not spent by the fiscal closing date, the school board would likely reduce next year's budget allotment. To avoid a potential budget cut, Mr. Cleaver reallocated Ms. Simmons's computer funds to Jules Carrington, principal of East Harris County High. Mr. Carrington knows how to buy computers regardless of whether they are needed. Mr. Cleaver's final words were, "Don't blame me if parents of West High students complain that East High has more equipment. If anybody comes to me, I'm telling them that you turned down the money."

Required

a. Do Mr. Cleaver's actions violate the standards of ethical conduct shown in Exhibit 14.13 of Chapter 14?

b. Explain how participative budgeting could improve the allocation of resources for the Harris County School District.

COMPREHENSIVE PROBLEM

The management team of Magnificent Modems Inc. (MMI) wants to investigate the effect of several different growth rates on sales and cash receipts. Cash sales for the month of January are expected to be $10,000. Credit sales for January are expected to be $50,000. MMI collects 100 percent of credit sales in the month following the month of sale. Assume a beginning balance in accounts receivable of $48,000.

Required

Calculate the amount of sales and cash receipts for the months of February and March assuming a growth rate of 1 percent, 2 percent, and 4 percent.

The results at a growth rate of 1 percent are shown as an example.

Sales Budget

Sales	Jan	Feb	Mar
Cash sales	$10,000	$10,100	$10,201
Sales on account	50,000	50,500	51,005
Total budgeted sales	$60,000	$60,600	$61,206

Schedule of Cash Receipts

	Jan	Feb	Mar
Current cash sales	$10,000	$10,100	$10,201
Plus collections from accts. rec.	48,000	50,000	50,500
Total budgeted collections	$58,000	$60,100	$60,701

Use the following forms, assuming a growth rate of 2 percent.

Sales Budget

Sales	Jan	Feb	Mar
Cash sales	$10,000		
Sales on account	50,000		
Total budgeted sales	$60,000		

Schedule of Cash Receipts

	Jan	Feb	Mar
Current cash sales	$10,000		
Plus collections from accts. rec.	48,000		
Total budgeted collections	$58,000		

Use the following forms, assuming a growth rate of 4 percent.

Sales Budget

Sales	Jan	Feb	Mar
Cash sales	$10,000		
Sales on account	50,000		
Total budgeted sales	$60,000		

Schedule of Cash Receipts

	Jan	Feb	Mar
Current cash sales	$10,000		
Plus collections from accts. rec.	48,000		
Total budgeted collections	$58,000		

CHAPTER 22

Performance Evaluation

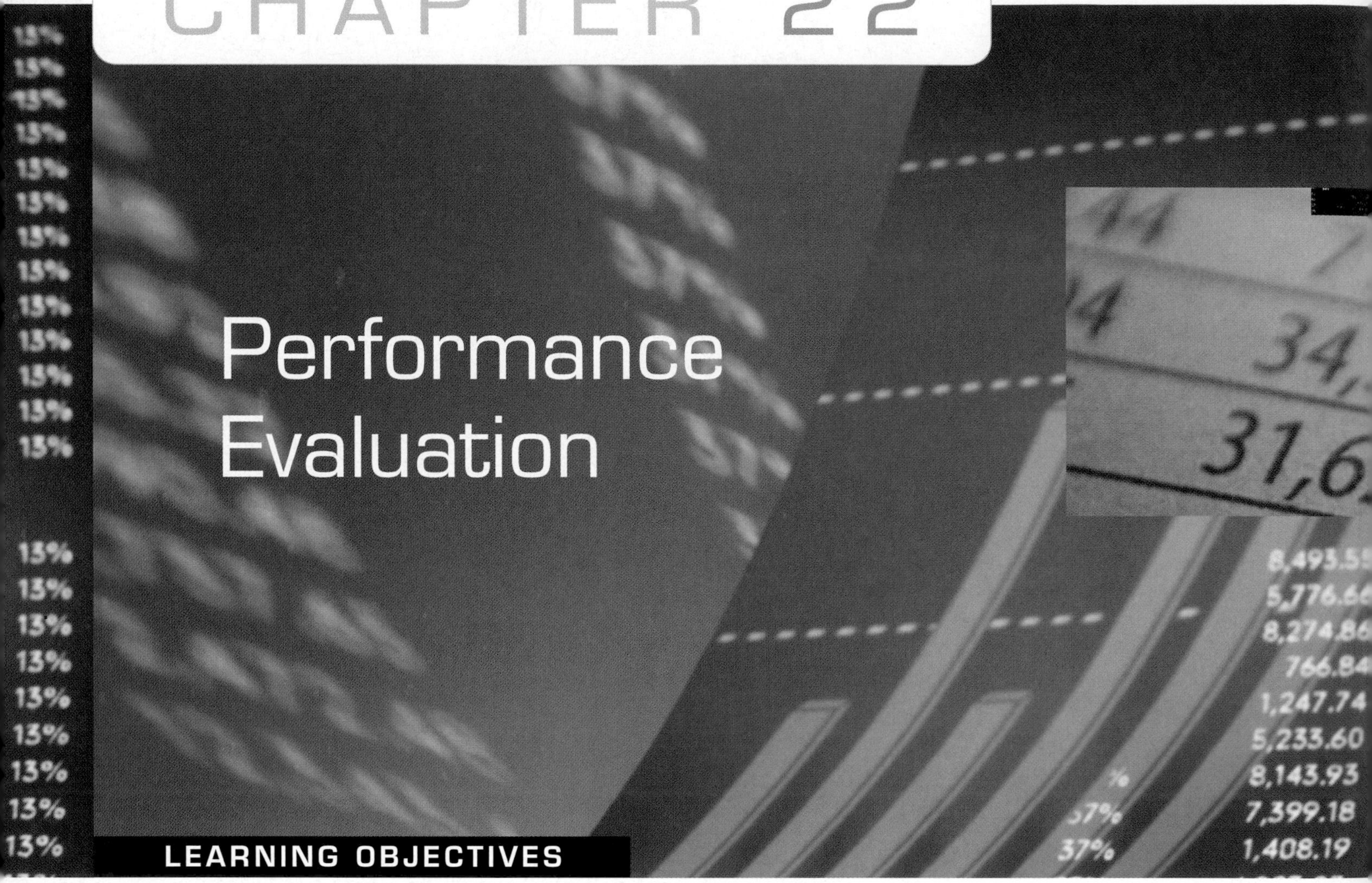

LEARNING OBJECTIVES

After you have mastered the material in this chapter you will be able to:

1. Distinguish between flexible and static budgets.
2. Use spreadsheet software to prepare flexible budgets.
3. Compute revenue and cost variances and interpret whether the variances signal favorable or unfavorable performance.
4. Compute sales volume variances (differences between static and flexible budgets) and explain how volume variances affect fixed and variable costs.
5. Compute and interpret flexible budget variances (differences between flexible budget and actual results).
6. Explain how practical standards can motivate employee performance without negative consequences such as lowballing (the human element).
7. Identify which variances are the most appropriate to investigate.
8. Calculate price and usage variances and identify the parties most likely responsible for them.

Chapter 22

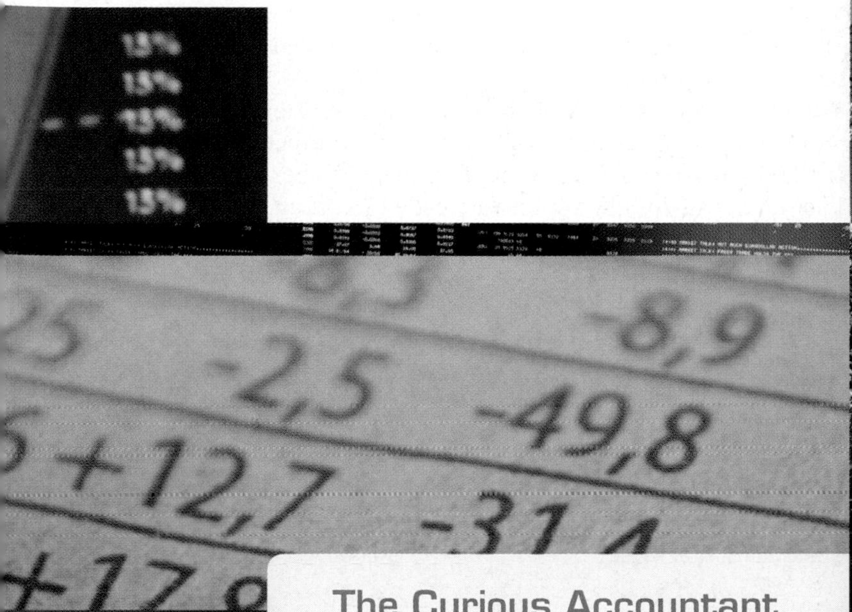

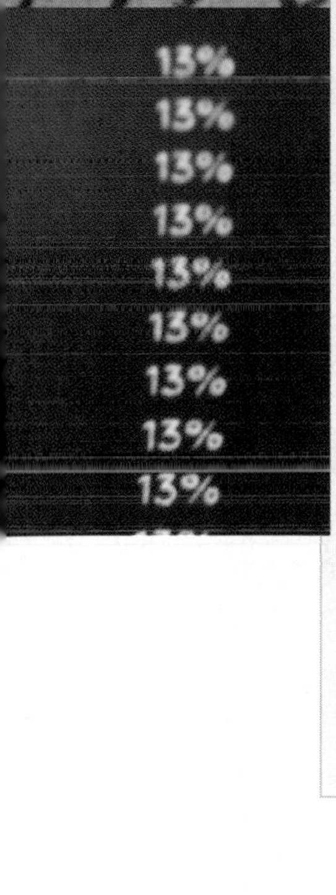

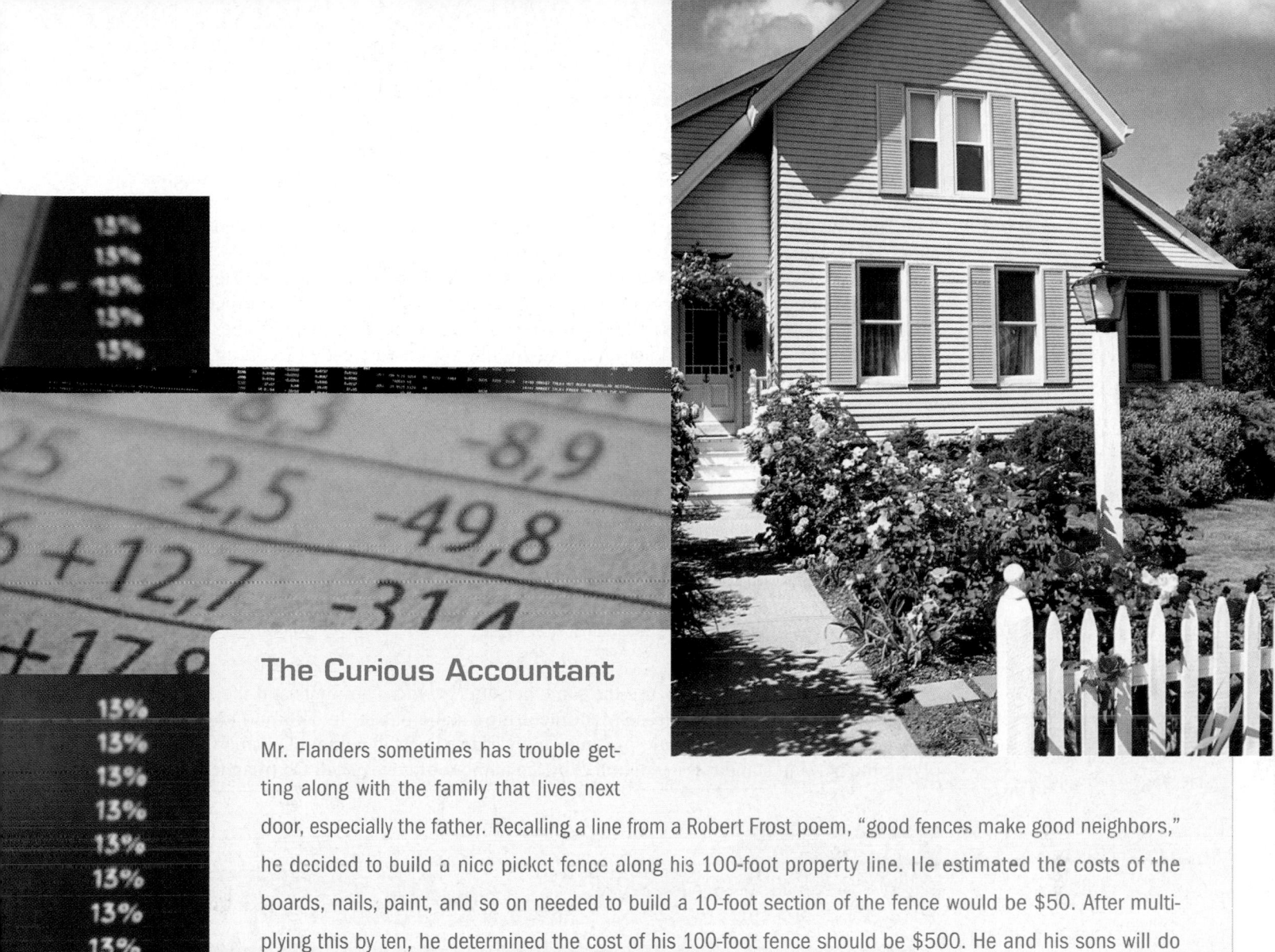

The Curious Accountant

Mr. Flanders sometimes has trouble getting along with the family that lives next door, especially the father. Recalling a line from a Robert Frost poem, "good fences make good neighbors," he decided to build a nice picket fence along his 100-foot property line. He estimated the costs of the boards, nails, paint, and so on needed to build a 10-foot section of the fence would be $50. After multiplying this by ten, he determined the cost of his 100-foot fence should be $500. He and his sons will do the work themselves, so his only cost will be for materials.

Being compulsive by nature, Flanders kept meticulous records of the amount he spent on materials. Upon completion of the fence, he discovered the actual cost of the fence was $578.

What are two general reasons that may explain why the fence cost more to construct than Mr. Flanders estimated? (Answer on page 1071.)

CHAPTER OPENING

Suppose you are a carpenter who builds picnic tables. You normally build 200 tables each year (the planned volume of activity), but because of unexpected customer demand, you are asked to build 225 tables (the actual volume of activity). You work hard and build the tables. Should management chastise you for using more materials, labor, or overhead than you normally use? Should management criticize the sales staff for selling more tables than expected? Of course not. Management must evaluate performance based on the actual volume of activity, not the planned volume of activity. To help management plan and evaluate performance, managerial accountants frequently prepare flexible budgets based on different levels of volume. Flexible budgets flex, or change, when the volume of activity changes.

Preparing Flexible Budgets

LO 1 Distinguish between flexible and static budgets.

Topic Tackler PLUS 22-1

A **flexible budget** is an extension of the *master budget* discussed in Chapter 21. The master budget is based solely on the planned volume of activity. The master budget is frequently called a **static budget** because it remains unchanged even if the actual volume of activity differs from the planned volume. Flexible budgets differ from static budgets in that they show expected revenues and costs at a *variety* of volume levels.

To illustrate the differences between static and flexible budgets, consider Melrose Manufacturing Company, a producer of small, high-quality trophies used in award ceremonies. Melrose plans to make and sell 18,000 trophies during 2006. Management's best estimates of the expected sales price and per unit costs for the trophies are called *standard* prices and costs. The standard price and costs for the 18,000 trophies follow.

Per unit sales price and variable costs	
Expected sales price	$80.00
Standard materials cost	12.00
Standard labor cost	16.80
Standard overhead cost	5.60
Standard general, selling, and administrative cost	15.00
Fixed costs	
Manufacturing cost	$201,600
General, selling, and administrative cost	90,000

LO 2 Use spreadsheet software to prepare flexible budgets.

Static and flexible budgets use the same per unit *standard* amounts and the same fixed costs. Exhibit 22.1 shows Melrose Manufacturing's static budget in column D of the Excel spreadsheet. The amounts of sales revenue and variable costs in column D come from multiplying the per unit standards in column C by the number of units in cell D4 (planned volume).

EXHIBIT 22.1

Static and Flexible Budgets in Excel Spreadsheet

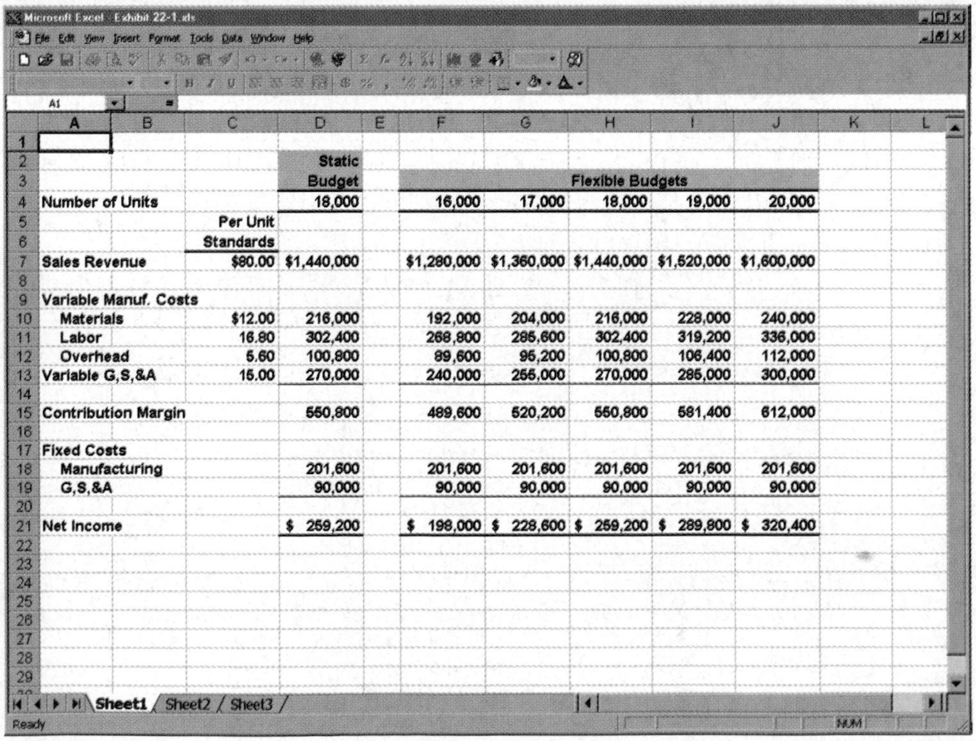

	Per Unit Standards	Static Budget	Flexible Budgets				
Number of Units		18,000	16,000	17,000	18,000	19,000	20,000
Sales Revenue	$80.00	$1,440,000	$1,280,000	$1,360,000	$1,440,000	$1,520,000	$1,600,000
Variable Manuf. Costs							
Materials	$12.00	216,000	192,000	204,000	216,000	228,000	240,000
Labor	16.80	302,400	268,800	285,600	302,400	319,200	336,000
Overhead	5.60	100,800	89,600	95,200	100,800	106,400	112,000
Variable G,S,&A	15.00	270,000	240,000	255,000	270,000	285,000	300,000
Contribution Margin		550,800	489,600	520,200	550,800	581,400	612,000
Fixed Costs							
Manufacturing		201,600	201,600	201,600	201,600	201,600	201,600
G,S,&A		90,000	90,000	90,000	90,000	90,000	90,000
Net Income		$ 259,200	$ 198,000	$ 228,600	$ 259,200	$ 289,800	$ 320,400

For example, the sales revenue in cell D7 comes from multiplying the per unit sales price in cell C7 by the number of units in cell D4 ($80 × 18,000 units = $1,440,000). The variable costs are similarly computed; the cost per unit amount in column C is multiplied by the planned volume in cell D4.

What if management wants to know the amount net income would be if volume were 16,000, 17,000, 18,000, 19,000, or 20,000 units? Management needs a series of *flexible budgets*. With little effort, an accountant can provide *what-if* information on the Excel spreadsheet. By copying to columns F through J the formulas used to determine the static budget amounts in column D, then changing the volume variables in row 4 to the desired levels, the spreadsheet instantly calculates the alternative flexible budgets in columns F through J.

Management can use the flexible budgets for both planning and performance evaluation. For example, managers may assess whether the company's cash position is adequate by assuming different levels of volume. They may judge if the number of employees, amounts of materials, and equipment and storage facilities are appropriate for a variety of different potential levels of volume. In addition to helping plan, flexible budgets are critical to implementing an effective performance evaluation system.

CHECK YOURSELF 22.1

The static (master) budget of Parcel Inc. called for a production and sales volume of 25,000 units. At that volume, total budgeted fixed costs were $150,000 and total budgeted variable costs were $200,000. Prepare a flexible budget for an expected volume of 26,000 units.

Answer

Budgeted fixed costs would remain unchanged at $150,000 because changes in the volume of activity do not affect budgeted fixed costs. Budgeted variable costs would increase to $208,000, computed as follows: calculate the budgeted variable cost per unit ($200,000 ÷ 25,000 units = $8) and then multiply that variable cost per unit by the expected volume ($8 × 26,000 units = $208,000).

Determining Variances for Performance Evaluation

LO 3

Compute revenue and cost variances and interpret whether the variances signal favorable or unfavorable performance.

One means of evaluating managerial performance is to compare *standard* amounts with *actual* results. The differences between the standard and actual amounts are called **variances;** variances can be either **favorable** or **unfavorable.** When actual sales revenue is greater than expected (planned) revenue, a company has a favorable sales variance because maximizing revenue is desirable. When actual sales are less than expected, an unfavorable sales variance exists. Because managers try to minimize costs, favorable cost variances exist when actual costs are *less* than standard costs. Unfavorable cost variances exist when actual costs are *more* than standard costs. These relationships are summarized below.

- When actual sales exceed expected sales, variances are favorable.
- When actual sales are less than expected sales, variances are unfavorable.
- When actual costs exceed standard costs, variances are unfavorable.
- When actual costs are less than standard costs, variances are favorable.

Sales Volume Variances

LO 4

Compute sales volume variances (differences between static and flexible budgets) and explain how volume variances affect fixed and variable costs.

The amount of a **sales volume variance** is the difference between the static budget (which is based on planned volume) and a flexible budget based on actual volume. This variance measures management effectiveness in attaining the planned volume of activity. To illustrate, assume Melrose Manufacturing Company actually makes and sells 19,000 trophies during 2006. The planned volume of activity was 18,000 trophies. Exhibit 22.2 shows Melrose's static budget, flexible budget, and volume variances.

EXHIBIT 22.2

Melrose Manufacturing Company's Volume Variances

	Static Budget	Flexible Budget	Volume Variances	
Number of units	18,000	19,000	1,000	Favorable
Sales revenue	$1,440,000	$1,520,000	$80,000	Favorable
Variable manufacturing costs				
Materials	216,000	228,000	12,000	Unfavorable
Labor	302,400	319,200	16,800	Unfavorable
Overhead	100,800	106,400	5,600	Unfavorable
Variable G, S, & A	270,000	285,000	15,000	Unfavorable
Contribution margin	550,800	581,400	30,600	Favorable
Fixed costs				
Manufacturing	201,600	201,600	0	
G, S, & A	90,000	90,000	0	
Net income	$ 259,200	$ 289,800	$30,600	Favorable

Interpreting the Sales and Variable Cost Volume Variances

Because the static and flexible budgets are based on the same standard sales price and per unit variable costs, the variances are solely attributable to the difference between the planned and actual volume of activity. Marketing managers are usually responsible for the volume variance. Because the sales volume drives production levels, production managers have little control over volume. Exceptions occur; for example, if poor production quality control leads to inferior goods that are difficult to sell, the production manager is responsible. The production manager is responsible for production delays that affect product availability, which may restrict sales volume. Under normal circumstances, however, the marketing campaign determines the volume of sales. Upper-level marketing managers develop the promotional program and create the sales plan; they are in the best position to explain why sales goals are or are not met. When marketing managers refer to **making the numbers,** they usually mean reaching the sales volume in the static (master) budget.

In the case of Melrose Manufacturing Company, the marketing manager not only achieved but also exceeded by 1,000 units the planned volume of sales. Exhibit 22.2 shows the activity variances resulting from the extra volume. At the standard price, the additional volume produces a favorable revenue variance of $80,000 (1,000 units × $80 per unit). The increase in volume also produces unfavorable variable cost variances. The net effect of producing and selling the additional 1,000 units is an increase of $30,600 in the contribution margin, a positive result. These preliminary results suggest that the marketing manager is to be commended. The analysis, however, is incomplete. For example, examining market share could reveal whether the manager won customers from competitors or whether the manager simply reaped the benefit of an unexpected industrywide increase in demand. The increase in sales volume could have been attained by reducing the sales price; the success of that strategy will be analyzed further in a later section of this chapter.

The unfavorable variable cost variances in Exhibit 22.2 are somewhat misleading because variable costs are, by definition, expected to increase as volume increases. In this case the unfavorable cost variances are more than offset by the favorable revenue variance, resulting in a higher contribution margin. The variable cost volume variances could be more appropriately labeled "expected" rather than unfavorable. However, the cost volume variances are described as unfavorable because actual cost is greater than planned cost.

Fixed Cost Considerations

The fixed costs are the same in both the static and flexible budgets. By definition, the budgeted amount of fixed costs remains unchanged regardless of the volume of activity. What insights can management gain by analyzing costs that don't change? Consider the *operating leverage* fixed costs provide. A small increase in sales volume can have a dramatic impact on profitability. Although the 1,000 unit volume variance represents only a 5.6 percent increase in revenue ($80,000 variance ÷ $1,440,000 static budget sales base), it produces an 11.8 percent increase in profitability ($30,600 variance ÷ $259,200 static budget net income base). To understand why profitability increased so dramatically, management should analyze the effect of fixed costs on the higher than expected sales volume.

Companies using a cost-plus pricing strategy must be concerned with differences between the planned and actual volume of activity. Because actual volume is unknown until the end of the year, selling prices must be based on planned volume. At the *planned volume* of activity of 18,000 units, Melrose's fixed cost per unit is expected to be as follows:

Fixed manufacturing cost	$201,600
Fixed G, S, & A cost	90,000
Total fixed cost	$291,600 ÷ 18,000 units = $16.20 per trophy

Based on the *actual volume* of 19,000 units, the fixed cost per unit is actually $15.35 per trophy ($291,600 ÷ 19,000 units). Because Melrose's prices were established using the $16.20 budgeted cost rather than the $15.35 actual cost, the trophies were overpriced, giving competitors a price advantage. Although Melrose sold more trophies than expected, sales volume might have been even greater if the trophies had been competitively priced.

Underpricing (not encountered by Melrose in this example) can also be detrimental. If planned volume is overstated, the estimated fixed cost per unit will be understated and prices will be set too low. When the higher amount of actual costs is subtracted from revenues, actual profits will be lower than expected. To avoid these negative consequences, companies that consider unit cost in pricing decisions must monitor volume variances closely.

The volume variance is *unfavorable* if actual volume is less than planned because cost per unit is higher than expected. Conversely, if actual volume is greater than planned, cost per unit is less than expected, resulting in a *favorable* variance. Both favorable and unfavorable variances can have negative consequences. Managers should strive for the greatest possible degree of accuracy.

Flexible Budget Variances

LO 5

Compute and interpret flexible budget variances (differences between flexible budget and actual results).

For performance evaluation, management compares actual results to a flexible budget based on the *actual* volume of activity. Because the actual results and the flexible budget reflect the same volume of activity, any variances result from differences between standard and actual per unit amounts. To illustrate computing and analyzing flexible budget variances, we assume that Melrose's *actual* per unit amounts during 2006 were those shown in the following table. The 2006 per unit *standard* amounts are repeated here for your convenience.

	Standard	Actual
Sales price	$80.00	$78.00
Variable materials cost	12.00	11.78
Variable labor cost	16.80	17.25
Variable overhead cost	5.60	5.75

Actual and budgeted fixed costs are shown in Exhibit 22.3.

Exhibit 22.3 shows Melrose's 2006 flexible budget, actual results, and flexible budget variances. The flexible budget is the same one compared to the static budget in Exhibit 22.2.

EXHIBIT 22.3

Flexible Budget Variances for Melrose Manufacturing Company

	Flexible Budget	Actual Results	Flexible Budget Variances	
Number of units	19,000	19,000	0	
Sales revenue	$1,520,000	$1,482,000	$38,000	Unfavorable
Variable manufacturing costs				
Materials	228,000	223,820	4,180	Favorable
Labor	319,200	327,750	8,550	Unfavorable
Overhead	106,400	109,250	2,850	Unfavorable
Variable G, S, & A	285,000	283,100	1,900	Favorable
Contribution margin	581,400	538,080	43,320	Unfavorable
Fixed costs				
Manufacturing	201,600	210,000	8,400	Unfavorable
G, S, & A	90,000	85,000	5,000	Favorable
Net income	$ 289,800	$ 243,080	$46,720	Unfavorable

Recall the flexible budget amounts come from multiplying the standard per unit amounts by the actual volume of production. For example, the sales revenue in the flexible budget comes from multiplying the standard sales price by the actual volume ($80 × 19,000). The variable costs are similarly computed. The *actual results* are calculated by multiplying the actual per unit sales price and cost figures from the preceding table by the actual volume of activity. For example, the sales revenue in the Actual Results column comes from multiplying the actual sales price by the actual volume ($78 × 19,000 = $1,482,000). The actual cost figures are similarly computed. The differences between the flexible budget figures and the actual results are the **flexible budget variances.**

Calculating the Sales Price Variance

Because both the flexible budget and actual results are based on the actual volume of activity, the flexible budget variance is attributable to sales price, not sales volume. In this case, the actual sales price of $78 per unit is less than the standard price of $80 per unit. Because Melrose sold its product for less than the standard sales price, the **sales price variance** is *unfavorable.* Even though the price variance is unfavorable, however, sales volume was 1,000 units more than expected. It is possible the marketing manager generated the additional volume by reducing the sales price. Whether the combination of lower sales price and higher sales volume is favorable or unfavorable depends on the amount of the unfavorable sales price variance versus the amount of the favorable sales volume variance. The *total* sales variance (price and volume) follows:

Actual sales (19,000 units × $78 per unit)	$1,482,000	
Expected sales (18,000 units × $80 per unit)	1,440,000	
Total sales variance	$ 42,000	Favorable

Alternatively,

Activity variance (i.e., sales volume)	$ 80,000	Favorable
Sales price variance	(38,000)	Unfavorable
Total sales variance	$ 42,000	Favorable

This analysis indicates that reducing the sales price had a favorable impact on *total* revenue. Use caution when interpreting variances as good or bad; in this instance, the unfavorable sales price variance was more than offset by the favorable volume variance. All unfavorable variances are not bad; all favorable variances are not good. Variances signal the need to investigate.

CHECK YOURSELF 22.2

Scott Company's master budget called for a planned sales volume of 30,000 units. Budgeted direct materials cost was $4 per unit. Scott actually produced and sold 32,000 units with an actual materials cost of $131,000. Determine the materials volume variance and identify the organizational unit most likely responsible for this variance. Determine the flexible budget variance and identify the organizational unit most likely responsible for this variance.

Answer

The volume (activity) variance is the difference between the expected materials usage at the planned volume of activity and the expected materials usage at the actual volume of activity [($4 × 30,000 units) − ($4 × 32,000) = $8,000]. The variance is unfavorable because expected direct materials cost at actual volume was higher than budgeted direct materials cost at planned volume. The unfavorable variance might not be a bad thing. The variance is due to increased volume, which could be a good thing. The organizational unit most likely responsible for the activity variance is the marketing department.

The flexible budget variance is the difference between the expected materials cost at the actual volume ($4 × 32,000 units = $128,000) and the actual materials cost of $131,000. The $3,000 ($128,000 − $131,000) variance is unfavorable because it cost more than expected to make the 32,000 units. Either the production department or the purchasing department is most likely responsible for this variance.

The Human Element Associated with Flexible Budget Variances

LO 6

Explain how practical standards can motivate employee performance without negative consequences such as lowballing (the human element).

The flexible budget cost variances offer insight into management efficiency. For example, Melrose Manufacturing Company's favorable materials variance could mean purchasing agents were shrewd in negotiating price concessions, discounts, or delivery terms and therefore reduced the price the company paid for materials. Similarly, production employees may have used materials efficiently, using less than expected. The unfavorable labor variance could mean managers failed to control employee wages or motivate employees to work hard. As with sales variances, cost variances require careful analysis. A favorable variance may, in fact, mask unfavorable conditions. For example, the favorable materials variance might have been caused by paying low prices for inferior goods. Using substandard materials could have required additional labor in the production process, which would explain the unfavorable labor variance. Again, we caution that variances, whether favorable or unfavorable, alert management to investigate further.

In general, variances should not be used to praise or punish managers. The purpose of identifying variances is to help management improve efficiency and productivity. If variances are used to assign rewards and blame, managers are likely to respond by withholding or manipulating information. For example, a manager might manipulate the cost standard for a job by deliberately overstating the amount of materials or labor needed to complete it. The manager's performance will later appear positive when the actual cost of materials or labor is less than the inflated standard. This practice is so common it has a name: **budget slack** is the difference between inflated and realistic standards. Sales staff may play a game called *lowballing* in which they deliberately underestimate the amount of expected sales, anticipating a reward when actual sales subsequently exceed the budget.

Gamesmanship can be reduced if superiors and subordinates participate sincerely in setting mutually agreeable, attainable standards. Once standards are established, the evaluation system that uses them must promote long-term respect among superiors and their subordinates. If standards are used solely for punitive purposes, gamesmanship will rapidly degrade the standard costing system.

Establishing Standards

LO 6

Explain how practical standards can motivate employee performance without negative consequences such as lowballing (the human element).

Establishing standards is probably the most difficult part of using a standard cost system. A **standard** represents the amount a price, cost, or quantity *should be* based on certain anticipated circumstances. Consider the complexity of establishing the standard cost to produce a pair of blue jeans. Among other things, managers need to know where they can get the best price for materials, who will pay transportation costs, if cash or volume discounts are available, whether the suppliers with the lowest price can reliably supply the quantities needed on a timely basis, how the material should be cut to conserve time and labor, in what order to sew pieces of material together, the wage rates of the relevant production employees, whether overtime will be needed, and how many pairs of jeans will be produced. Obtaining this information requires the combined experience, judgment, and forecasting ability of all personnel who have responsibility for price and usage decisions. Even when a multitalented group of experienced persons is involved in standard setting, the process involves much trial and error. Revising standards is common even with established systems.

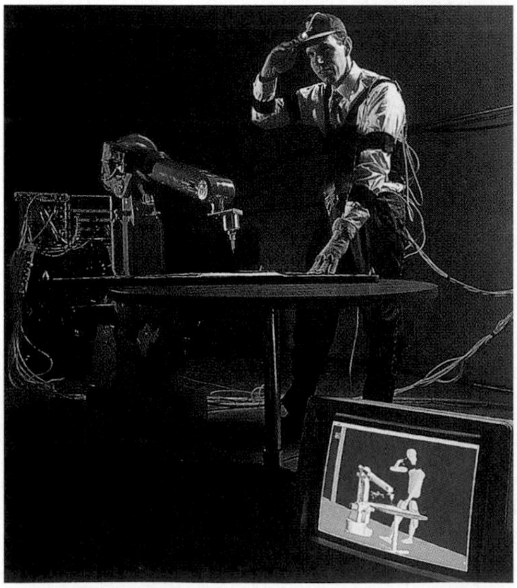

Historical data provide a good starting point for establishing standards. These data must be updated for changes in technology, plant layout, new methods of production, and worker productivity. Frequently, changes of this nature result from initiating a standard cost system. Remember that a *standard* represents what *should be* rather than what *is* or *was.* Engineers often help establish standards, recommending the most efficient way to perform required tasks. The engineers undertake time and motion studies and review material utilization in the process of developing standards. Established practices and policies are frequently changed in response to engineers' reports.

Management must consider behavioral implications when developing standards. Managers, supervisors, purchasing agents, and other affected employees should be consulted for two reasons: (1) their experience and expertise provide invaluable input to standard development and (2) persons who are involved in standard setting are more likely to accept and be motivated to reach the resulting standards. Management should also consider how difficult it should be to achieve standard performance. Difficulty levels can be described as follows: (1) ideal standards, (2) practical standards, and (3) lax standards.

Ideal standards represent flawless performance; they represent what costs should be under the best possible circumstances. They do not allow for normal materials waste and spoilage or ordinary labor inefficiencies caused by machine down time, cleanups, breaks, or personal needs. Meeting ideal standards is beyond the capabilities of most, if not all, employees. Ideal standards may motivate some individuals to constantly strive for improvement, but unattainable standards discourage most people. When people consistently fail, they become demotivated and stop trying to succeed. In addition, variances associated with ideal standards lose significance. They reflect deviations that are largely beyond employees' control, and they mask true measures of superior or inferior performance, considerably reducing their usefulness.

Practical standards represent reasonable effort; they are attainable for most employees. Practical standards allow for normal levels of inefficiency in materials and labor usage. An average worker performing diligently would be able to achieve standard performance. Practical standards motivate most employees; the feeling of accomplishment attained through earnest effort encourages employees to do their best. Practical standards also produce meaningful variances. Deviations from practical standards usually result from factors employees control. Positive variances normally represent superior performance, and negative variances indicate inferior performance.

Lax standards represent easily attainable goals. Employees can achieve standard performance with minimal effort. Lax standards do not motivate most people; continual success with minimal effort leads to boredom and lackluster performance. In addition, variances lose meaning. Deviations caused by superior or inferior performance are obscured by the built-in slack.

Management must consider employee ability levels when establishing standards. Standards that seasoned workers can attain may represent ideal standards to inexperienced workers. Management should routinely monitor standards and adjust them when it is appropriate to do so.

Need for Standard Costs

As the previous discussion suggests, standard costs are the building blocks for preparing the static and flexible budgets. Standard costs help managers plan and also establish benchmarks against which actual performance can be judged. By highlighting differences between standard (expected) and actual performance, standard costing focuses management attention on the areas of greatest need. Because management talent is a valuable and expensive resource, businesses cannot afford to have managers spend large amounts of time on operations that are functioning normally. Instead, managers should concentrate on areas not performing as expected. In other words, management should attend to the exceptions; this management philosophy is known as **management by exception.**

Standard costing fosters using the management by exception principle. By reviewing performance reports that show differences between actual and standard costs, management can focus its attention on the items that show significant variances. Areas with only minor variances need little or no review.

Selecting Variances to Investigate

LO 7

Identify which variances are the most appropriate to investigate.

Managerial judgment, developed through experience, plays a significant role in deciding which variances to investigate. Managers consider the *materiality* of a variance, the *frequency* with which it occurs, their *capacity to control* the variance, and the *characteristics* of the items behind the variance.

Standard costs are estimates. They cannot perfectly predict actual costs. Most businesses experience minor variances as part of normal operations. Investigating minor variances is not likely to produce useful information. Many companies therefore establish *materiality* guidelines for selecting variances to analyze. They set dollar or percentage thresholds and ignore variances that fall below these limits, investigating material variances only. A **material variance** is one that could influence management decisions. Material variances should be investigated whether they are favorable or unfavorable. As mentioned earlier, a favorable price variance can result from purchasing substandard materials; the quality of the company's products, however, will suffer from the inferior materials and sales will fall.

How *frequently* a variance occurs impacts materiality. A variance of $20,000 may be immaterial in a single month, but if the same variance occurs repeatedly throughout the year, it can become a material $240,000 variance. Variance reports should highlight frequent as well as large variations.

Capacity to control refers to whether management action can influence the variance. If utility rates cause differences between actual and standard overhead costs, management has little control over the resulting variances. Conversely, if actual labor costs exceed standard costs because a supervisor fails to motivate employees, management can take some action. To maximize their value to the firm, managers should concentrate on controllable variances.

The *characteristics* of the items behind the variance may invite management abuse. For example, managers can reduce actual costs in the short term by delaying expenditures for maintenance, research and development, and advertising. Although cost reductions in these areas may produce favorable variances in the current period, they will have a long-term detrimental impact on profitability. Managers under stress may be tempted to focus on short-term benefits. Variances associated with these critical items should be closely analyzed.

The primary advantage of a standard cost system is efficient use of management talent to control costs. Secondary benefits include the following.

1. Standard cost systems quickly alert management to trouble spots. For example, a standard amount of materials may be issued for a particular job. If requisitions of additional materials require supervisory approval, each time a supervisor must grant such approval, she is immediately aware that excess materials are being used and can act before excessive material usage becomes unmanageable.
2. If established and maintained properly, standard cost systems can boost morale and motivate employees. Reward systems can be linked to accomplishments that exceed the established performance standards. Under such circumstances, employees become extremely conscious of the time and materials they use, minimizing waste and reducing costs.
3. Standard cost systems encourage good planning. The failure to plan well leads to overbuying, excessive inventory, wasted time, and so on. A standard cost system forces managers to plan, resulting in more effective operations with less waste.

Flexible Budget Manufacturing Cost Variances

The *manufacturing costs* incurred by Melrose Manufacturing Company in 2006 are summarized here:

	Standard	Actual
Variable materials cost per unit of product	$ 12.00	$ 11.78
Variable labor cost per unit of product	16.80	17.25
Variable overhead cost per unit of product	5.60	5.75
Total per unit variable manufacturing cost (a)	$ 34.40	$ 34.78
Total units produced (b)	19,000	19,000
Total variable manufacturing cost (a × b)	$653,600	$660,820
Fixed manufacturing cost	201,600	210,000
Total manufacturing cost	$855,200	$870,820

The total flexible budget manufacturing cost variance is $15,620 ($870,820 − $855,200). Because Melrose actually incurred more cost than expected, this variance is unfavorable. The

Answers to The Curious Accountant

As this chapter demonstrates, there are two primary reasons a company spends more or less to produce a product than it estimated it would. First, the company may have paid more or less to purchase the inputs needed to produce the product than it estimated. Second, the company used a greater or lesser quantity of these inputs than expected. In the case of Mr. Flanders's fence, he may have had to pay more for boards, paint, nails, and so on than he thought he would. Or, he may have used more boards, paint, and nails than he expected. Of course, it could have been a combination of these factors.

If Mr. Flanders were a company in the business of building fences, it would be important for him to determine if the difference between his expected costs and his actual costs was because his estimates were faulty, or because his production process was inefficient. If his estimates were to blame, he would need to revise them so he can charge the proper price to his customers. If his production process is inefficient, he needs to correct it if he is to earn an acceptable level of profit. If his competitors are more efficient than he is, he will eventually be priced out of the market. Standard costs are not only used for preparing budgets, they are also used for evaluating performance.

sum of the individual flexible budget variances for manufacturing costs shown in Exhibit 22.3 equals this variance:

Variable manufacturing cost variances:		
Materials	$ 4,180	Favorable
Labor	8,550	Unfavorable
Overhead	2,850	Unfavorable
Total variable manufacturing cost variances	7,220	Unfavorable
Fixed manufacturing cost variance	8,400	Unfavorable
Total	$15,620	Unfavorable

Exhibit 22.4 shows how to algebraically compute the flexible budget variable manufacturing cost variances.

Note that the difference between the actual and standard cost is expressed as an absolute value. This mathematical notation suggests that the mathematical sign is not useful in interpreting the condition of the variance. To assess the condition of a variance, you must consider the type of variance being analyzed. With respect to cost variances, managers seek to attain actual costs that are lower than standard costs. In this case, the actual cost of materials is less than the standard cost, so the materials variance is favorable. Since the actual costs for labor and overhead are higher than the standard costs, those variances are unfavorable.

EXHIBIT 22.4

Flexible Budget Variances Calculated Algebraically

Variable Mfg. Costs	| Actual Cost Per Unit of Product	−	Standard Cost Per Unit of Product |	×	Actual Units	=	Flexible Budget Variance
Materials	| $11.78	−	$12.00 |	×	19,000	=	$4,180 Favorable
Labor	| 17.25	−	16.80 |	×	19,000	=	8,550 Unfavorable
Overhead	| 5.75	−	5.60 |	×	19,000	=	2,850 Unfavorable

Price and Usage Variances[1]

LO 8

Calculate price and usage variances and identify the parties most likely responsible for them.

Topic Tackler PLUS

22-2

For insight into what caused the flexible budget variances, management can analyze them in more detail. Consider the $4,180 favorable flexible budget materials cost variance. This variance indicates that Melrose spent less than expected on materials to make 19,000 trophies. Why? The price per unit of material may have been less than expected (price variance), or the company may have used less material than expected (usage variance). To determine what caused the total favorable variance, Melrose must separate the cost per unit of product into two parts, price per unit of material and quantity of material used.

Calculating Materials Price and Usage Variances

Melrose's accounting records indicate the materials cost per unit of product (trophy) is as follows:

	Actual Data	Standard Data
Price ***per pound*** of material	$ 1.90	$ 2.00
Quantity of materials per unit of product	× 6.2 pounds	× 6.0 pounds
Cost ***per unit*** of product	$11.78	$12.00

Based on this detail, the total quantity of materials is:

	Actual Data	Standard Data
Actual production volume	19,000 units	19,000 units
Quantity of materials per unit of product	× 6.2 pounds	× 6.0 pounds
Total quantity of materials	117,800 pounds	114,000 pounds

Confirm the price and usage components that make up the total flexible budget materials variance, as follows:

Actual Cost		Standard Cost	
Actual quantity used	117,800	Standard quantity	114,000
×	×	×	×
Actual price per pound	$1.90	Standard price per pound	$2.00
	$223,820		$228,000
	Total variance: $4,180 favorable		

To isolate the price and usage variances, insert a Variance Dividing column between the Actual Cost and Standard Cost columns. The Variance Dividing column combines standard and actual data, showing the *standard cost* multiplied by the *actual quantity* of materials purchased and used.[2] Exhibit 22.5 shows the result.

[1] Businesses use various names for price and usage variances. For example, materials price and usage variances are frequently called **materials price** and **quantity variances;** labor price and usage variances are frequently called **labor rate** and **efficiency variances.** Regardless of the names, the underlying concepts and computations are the same for all variable price and usage variances.

[2] In practice, raw materials are frequently stored in inventory prior to use. Differences may exist between the amount of materials purchased and the amount of materials used. In such cases, the price variance is based on the quantity of materials *purchased,* and the usage variance is based on the quantity of materials *used.* This text makes the simplifying assumption that the amount of materials purchased equals the amount of materials used during the period.

EXHIBIT 22.5

Materials Price and Usage Variances

Actual Cost		Variance Dividing Data		Standard Cost	
Actual quantity used	117,800	Actual quantity used	117,800	Standard quantity	114,000
×	×	×	×	×	×
Actual price per pound	$1.90	Standard price per pound	$2.00	Standard price per pound	$2.00
	$223,820		$235,600		$228,000

Materials price variance $11,780 favorable

Materials usage variance $7,600 unfavorable

Total variance: $4,180 favorable

Algebraic Solution. The materials price variance (difference between the Actual Cost column and the Variance Dividing column) can be computed algebraically as follows:

$$\begin{aligned}\text{Price variance} &= |\text{Actual price} - \text{Standard price}| \times \text{Actual quantity}\\ &= |\$1.90 - \$2.00| \times 117{,}800\\ &= \$0.10 \times 117{,}800\\ &= \$11{,}780 \text{ Favorable}\end{aligned}$$

Since the actual price ($1.90) is less than the standard price ($2.00), the materials price variance is favorable.

The materials usage variance (difference between the Variance Dividing column and the Standard Cost column) also can be determined algebraically, as follows:

$$\begin{aligned}\text{Usage variance} &= |\text{Actual quantity} - \text{Standard quantity}| \times \text{Standard price}\\ &= |117{,}800 - 114{,}000| \times \$2.00\\ &= 3{,}800 \times \$2.00\\ &= \$7{,}600 \text{ Unfavorable}\end{aligned}$$

Responsibility for Materials Variances. A purchasing agent is normally responsible for the *favorable price variance.* Management establishes the standard materials cost based on a particular grade of material and assumptions about purchasing terms including volume discounts, cash discounts, transportation costs, and supplier services. A diligent purchasing agent places orders that take advantage of positive trading terms. In such circumstances, the company pays less than standard costs, resulting in a favorable price variance. Investigating the favorable price variance could result in identifying purchasing strategies to share with other purchasing agents. Analyzing favorable as well as unfavorable variances can result in efficiencies that benefit the entire production process.

In spite of a purchasing agent's diligence, unfavorable price variances may still occur. Suppliers may raise prices, poor scheduling by the production department may require more costly rush orders, or a truckers' strike may force the company to use a more expensive delivery system. These conditions are beyond a purchasing agent's control. Management must be careful to identify the real causes of unfavorable variances. False accusations and overreactions lead to resentment that will undermine the productive potential of the standard costing system.

The nature of the *materials usage variance* is readily apparent from the quantity data. Because the actual quantity used was more than the standard quantity, the variance is unfavorable. If management seeks to minimize cost, using more materials than expected is unfavorable. The materials usage variance is largely controlled by the production department. Materials waste caused by inexperienced workers, faulty machinery, negligent processing, or poor planning results in unfavorable usage variances. Unfavorable variances may also be

REALITY BYTES

Do purchasing agents really make a difference? They certainly do—at least that is the opinion of Inspector General Eleanor Hill, who is in charge of policing waste and fraud at the **Department of Defense.** Explaining preposterous costs such as a $76 screw, Ms. Hill told a Senate Armed Services subcommittee that Pentagon buyers failed to obtain volume discounts, neglected to compare prices with competitors, or otherwise failed to pursue aggressive purchasing strategies. Specifically, Ms. Hill said, "Department of Defense procurement approaches were poorly conceived, badly coordinated, and did not result in the government getting good value for the prices paid both for commercial and noncommercial items. We found considerable evidence that the Department of Defense had not yet learned how to be an astute buyer in the commercial marketplace."

Source: John Diamond, "Audits Say Pentagon Continues to Overpay," *USA Today,* March 19, 1998, p. 2A.

caused by factors beyond the control of the production department. If the purchasing agent buys substandard materials, the inferior materials may lead to more scrap (waste) during production which would be reflected in unfavorable usage variances.

Calculating Labor Variances

Labor variances are calculated using the same general formulas as those used to compute materials price and usage variances. To illustrate, assume the labor cost per unit of product (trophy) for Melrose Manufacturing is as follows:

	Actual Data	Standard Data
Price ***per hour***	$11.50	$12.00
Quantity of labor per unit of product	× 1.5 hours	× 1.4 hours
Cost ***per unit*** of product	$17.25	$16.80

Based on this detail, the total quantity of labor is:

	Actual Data	Standard Data
Actual production volume	19,000 units	19,000 units
Quantity of labor per unit of product	×1.5 hours	×1.4 hours
Total quantity of labor	28,500 hours	26,600 hours

Using this cost and quantity information, the labor price and usage variances are computed in Exhibit 22.6.

Responsibility for Labor Variances. The *labor price variance* is favorable because the actual rate paid for labor is less than the standard rate. The production supervisor is usually responsible for the labor price variance because price variances normally result from labor use rather than underpayment or overpayment of the hourly rate. Because labor costs are usually fixed by contracts, paying more or less than established rates is not likely. However, us-

EXHIBIT 22.6

Labor Price and Usage Variances

Actual Cost		Variance Dividing Data		Standard Cost	
Actual hours used	28,500	Actual hours used (AHrs)	28,500	Standard hours (SHrs)	26,600
×	×	×	×	×	×
Actual price per labor hour (AP)	$11.50	Standard price per labor hour (SP)	$12.00	Standard price per labor hour	$12.00
	$327,750		$342,000		$319,200

Labor price variance $14,250 favorable

Labor usage variance $22,800 unfavorable

Algebraic solution: |AP − SP| × AHrs
|$11.50 − $12.00| × 28,500 = $14,250

Algebraic solution: |AHrs − SHrs| × SP
|28,500 − 26,600| × $12.00 = $22,800

Total variance: $8,550 unfavorable

ing semiskilled labor to perform highly skilled tasks or vice versa will produce price variances. Similarly, using unanticipated overtime will cause unfavorable variances. Production department supervisors control which workers are assigned to which tasks and are therefore accountable for the resulting labor price variances.

Labor usage variances measure the productivity of the labor force. Because Melrose used more labor than expected, the labor usage variance is unfavorable. Unsatisfactory labor performance has many causes; low morale or poor supervision are possibilities. Furthermore, machine breakdowns, inferior materials, and poor planning can waste workers' time and reduce productivity. Production department supervisors generally control and are responsible for labor usage variances.

Price and usage variances may be interrelated. Using less skilled employees who earned less but took longer to do the work could have caused both the favorable labor price variance and the unfavorable labor usage variance. As mentioned earlier, management must exercise diligence in determining causes of variances before concluding who should be held responsible for them.

CHECK YOURSELF 22.3

DogHouse Inc. expected to build 200 dog houses during July. Each dog house was expected to require 2 hours of direct labor. Labor cost was expected to be $10 per hour. The company actually built 220 dog houses using an average of 2.1 labor hours per dog house at an actual labor rate averaging $9.80 per hour. Determine the labor rate and usage variances.

Answer

Labor rate variance = |Actual rate − Standard rate| × Actual quantity

Labor rate variance = |$9.80 − $10.00| × (220 units × 2.1 hours) = $92.40 Favorable

Labor usage variance = |Actual quantity − Standard quantity| × Standard rate

Labor usage variance = |[220 × 2.1] − [220 × 2.0]| × $10 = $220.00 Unfavorable

Variable Overhead Variances

Variable overhead variances are based on the same general formulas used to compute the materials and labor price and usage variances. Unique characteristics of variable overhead costs, however, require special attention. First, variable overhead represents many inputs such as supplies, utilities, and indirect labor. The variable overhead cost pool is normally assigned to products based on a predetermined variable overhead allocation rate. Using a single rate to assign a mixture of different costs complicates variance interpretation. Suppose the actual variable overhead rate is higher than the predetermined rate. Did the company pay more than expected for supplies, utilities, maintenance, or some other input variable? The cost of some variable overhead items may have been higher than expected while others were lower than expected. Similarly, a variable overhead usage variance provides no clue about which overhead inputs were over- or underused. Because meaningful interpretation of the results is difficult, many companies do not calculate price and usage variances for variable overhead costs. We therefore limit coverage of this subject to the total flexible budget variances shown in Exhibit 22.3.

Fixed Overhead Variances

Variable costs can have both price and usage variances. *Fixed overhead costs* can also have price variances. Remember that a *fixed* cost remains the same relative to changes in production *volume;* it does not necessarily remain the same as *expected.* Companies may certainly pay more or less than expected for a fixed cost. For example, a supervisor may receive an unplanned raise, causing actual salary costs to be more than expected. Similarly, a manager may negotiate a reduced rental cost for manufacturing equipment, causing actual rental costs to be less than expected. The difference between the *actual fixed overhead costs* and the *budgeted fixed overhead costs* is the **spending variance.** The spending variance is favorable if the company spent less than expected (actual cost is less than budgeted cost). The variance is unfavorable if the company spent more than expected (actual is more than budget).

Analyzing fixed overhead costs differs from analyzing variable costs because there is no potential usage variance. If Melrose pays $25,000 to rent its manufacturing facility, the company cannot use more or less of this rent no matter how many units of product it makes. Because the rent cost is fixed, however, the *cost per unit* will differ depending on the number of units of product made. The more units Melrose produces, the lower the fixed overhead cost per unit and vice versa. Because the volume of activity affects the cost per unit, companies commonly calculate a volume variance for fixed overhead costs. The **volume variance** is the difference between the *budgeted fixed cost* and the *amount of fixed costs allocated to production.* The amount of fixed costs allocated to production is frequently called *applied fixed cost.*

To illustrate the fixed overhead variances, return to the overhead spending variance for Melrose Manufacturing Company shown in Exhibit 22.3. The spending variance is the difference between the budgeted fixed overhead and the actual fixed overhead (|$201,600 budgeted − $210,000 actual| = $8,400 spending variance). The variance is unfavorable because Melrose actually spent more than expected for fixed overhead costs. Recall there is no fixed overhead usage variance.

To calculate the overhead volume variance, first calculate the predetermined fixed cost overhead rate: divide budgeted fixed costs of $201,600 by planned volume of 18,000 trophies. The predetermined fixed overhead rate is $11.20 per trophy ($201,600 ÷ 18,000 trophies). Since Melrose actually produced 19,000 trophies, it applied (allocated) $212,800 ($11.20 × 19,000 units) of fixed overhead costs to production. The difference between the budgeted fixed overhead and the applied fixed overhead produces a volume variance of $11,200 (|$201,600 budgeted − $212,800 applied| = $11,200 variance). Exhibit 22.7 shows a summary of the fixed overhead variances.

Responsibility for Fixed Overhead Price Variances

There is no way to know who is responsible for the unfavorable fixed overhead spending variance because all of the fixed overhead costs have been pooled together. To improve accountability, significant controllable fixed overhead costs such as supervisory salaries should be tagged for individual analysis. Fixed overhead costs that are not controllable may nevertheless be reported for management oversight. Even if not controllable in the short term, management should stay abreast of fixed costs because they may be controllable in the long term.

EXHIBIT 22.7

Fixed Overhead Spending and Volume Variances for Melrose Manufacturing Company

Actual Fixed Overhead Cost		Variance Dividing Data		Standard Fixed Overhead Cost	
Actual fixed cost	$210,000	Budgeted fixed cost	$201,600	Applied fixed cost	$212,800
		Overhead spending variance $8,400 unfavorable		Overhead volume variance $11,200 favorable	

The fixed overhead volume variance is favorable because the actual volume of production was greater than the planned volume, resulting in a decreased cost per unit of product. The lower cost per unit does *not* result from reduced spending. Melrose actually spent more than expected on fixed overhead costs. The volume variance is caused by greater utilization of the company's manufacturing facilities. Melrose has benefited from *economies of scale.* As a rule, a company with high fixed costs should produce as high a volume as possible, thereby lowering its cost per unit of production. Of course, this rule assumes products produced can be sold at prevailing prices. An *unfavorable* volume variance alerts management to the underutilization of manufacturing facilities. In summary, a volume variance indicates over- or underutilization of facilities, not over- or underspending.

As previously discussed, production managers are not usually responsible for volume variances. The level of production is normally based on sales volume which is under the control of upper-level marketing managers. Although the volume variance measures the effectiveness of facilities use, the marketing department should be held accountable for volume variances because it is primarily responsible for establishing the volume of activity.

Summary of Manufacturing Cost Variances

To summarize, the total flexible budget variable manufacturing cost variance can be subdivided into materials, labor, and variable overhead variances. These variances can be further subdivided into price and usage variances. Manufacturing fixed cost can be subdivided into spending and volume variances. The *volume variance* is not a cost variance; it shows how volume affects fixed cost *per unit,* but it does not reflect a difference between the *total* amount of actual and expected costs. Exhibit 22.8 summarizes the relationships among the cost variances for Melrose Manufacturing Company. Exhibit 22.9 summarizes the algebraic formulas for the variable and fixed manufacturing cost variances discussed.

General, Selling, and Administrative Cost Variances

Variable general, selling, and administrative (G, S, & A) costs can have *price and usage* variances. For example, suppose Melrose decides to attach a promotional advertising brochure to each trophy it sells. Melrose may pay more or less than expected for each brochure (a price variance). Melrose also could use more or fewer of the brochures than expected (a usage variance). Businesses frequently compute variances for G, S, & A costs such as sales commissions, food and entertainment, postage, and supplies. The same algebraic formulas used to compute variances for variable manufacturing costs apply to computing variable G, S, & A cost variances.

Fixed G, S, & A costs are also subject to variance analysis. As shown in Exhibit 22.3, Melrose Manufacturing incurred a favorable $5,000 G, S, & A fixed cost *spending variance.* This means Melrose actually incurred less fixed G, S, & A cost than expected. A fixed cost *volume variance* could also be computed. Changes in sales volume affect the per unit amounts of fixed G, S, & A costs.

EXHIBIT 22.8

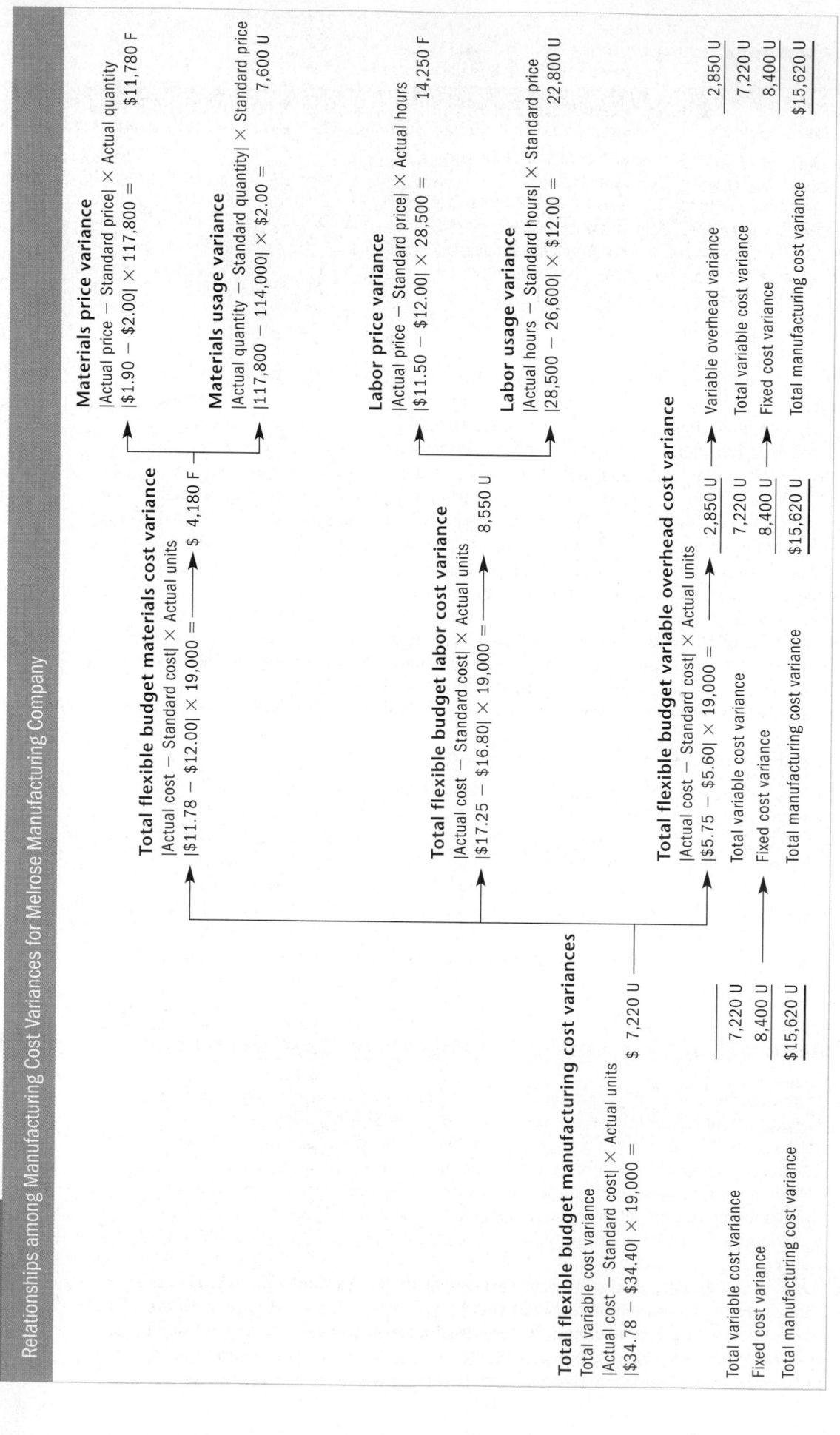

Relationships among Manufacturing Cost Variances for Melrose Manufacturing Company

Total flexible budget manufacturing cost variances

Total variable cost variance

|Actual cost − Standard cost| × Actual units

|$34.78 − $34.40| × 19,000 = $ 7,220 U

Total variable cost variance	7,220 U
Fixed cost variance	8,400 U
Total manufacturing cost variance	$15,620 U

Total flexible budget materials cost variance

|Actual cost − Standard cost| × Actual units

|$11.78 − $12.00| × 19,000 = $ 4,180 F

Materials price variance

|Actual price − Standard price| × Actual quantity

|$1.90 − $2.00| × 117,800 = $11,780 F

Materials usage variance

|Actual quantity − Standard quantity| × Standard price

|117,800 − 114,000| × $2.00 = 7,600 U

Total flexible budget labor cost variance

|Actual cost − Standard cost| × Actual units

|$17.25 − $16.80| × 19,000 = 8,550 U

Labor price variance

|Actual price − Standard price| × Actual hours

|$11.50 − $12.00| × 28,500 = 14,250 F

Labor usage variance

|Actual hours − Standard hours| × Standard price

|28,500 − 26,600| × $12.00 = 22,800 U

Total flexible budget variable overhead cost variance

|Actual cost − Standard cost| × Actual units

|$5.75 − $5.60| × 19,000 = 2,850 U

Total variable cost variance	7,220 U
Fixed cost variance	8,400 U
Total manufacturing cost variance	$15,620 U

Variable overhead variance	2,850 U
Total variable cost variance	7,220 U
Fixed cost variance	8,400 U
Total manufacturing cost variance	$15,620 U

REALITY BYTES

Does variance analysis apply to service companies as well as manufacturers? The answer is a definite yes! **Express Oil Change** could establish standard rates and times for the labor required to perform specific auto maintenance functions. Similarly, it could establish standards for materials such as oil, filters, and transmission fluid. Also, fixed overhead costs and measures of volume (i.e., number of vehicles serviced) exist. A full range of variances could be computed for the services provided.

EXHIBIT 22.9

Algebraic Formulas for Variances

1. Variable cost variances (materials, labor, and overhead)
   a. Price variance
      |Actual price − Standard price| × Actual quantity
   b. Usage variance
      |Actual quantity − Standard quantity| × Standard price
2. Fixed overhead variances
   a. Fixed overhead spending variance
      |Actual fixed overhead costs − Budgeted fixed overhead costs|
   b. Fixed overhead volume variance
      |Applied fixed overhead costs − Budgeted fixed overhead costs|

Many different individuals are responsible for G, S, & A cost variances. For example, lower level sales personnel are responsible for controlling the price and usage of promotional items. In contrast, upper-level administrative officers are responsible for fixed salary expenses. A full discussion of G, S, & A cost variances is beyond the scope of this text.

A Look Back <<

The essential topics of this chapter are the master budget, flexible budgets, and variance analysis. The *master budget* is determined by multiplying the standard sales price and per unit variable costs by the planned volume of activity. The master budget is prepared at the beginning of the accounting period for planning purposes. It is not adjusted to reflect differences between the planned and actual volume of activity. Since this budget remains unchanged regardless of actual volume, it is also called a *static budget*. *Flexible budgets* differ from static budgets in that they show the estimated amount of revenue and costs expected at different levels of volume. Both static and flexible budgets are based on the same per unit standard amounts and the same fixed costs. The total amounts of revenue and costs in a static budget differ from those in a flexible budget because they are based on different levels of volume. Flexible budgets are used for planning, cost control, and performance evaluation.

The differences between standard (sometimes called *expected* or *estimated*) and actual amounts are called *variances*. Variances are used to evaluate managerial performance and can be either favorable or unfavorable. *Favorable sales variances* occur when actual sales are greater than expected sales. *Unfavorable sales variances* occur when actual sales are less than expected sales. *Favorable cost variances* occur when actual costs are less than expected costs. *Unfavorable cost variances* occur when actual costs are more than expected costs.

Volume variances are caused by the difference between the static and flexible budgets. Since both static and flexible budgets are based on the same standard sales price and costs per unit, the volume variances are attributable solely to differences between the planned and the actual volume of activity. Favorable sales volume variances suggest that the marketing manager has performed well by selling more than was expected. Unfavorable sales volume variances suggest the inverse. Favorable or unfavorable variable cost volume variances are not meaningful for performance evaluation because variable costs are expected to change in proportion to changes in the volume of activity.

Flexible budget variances are computed by taking the difference between the amounts of revenue and variable costs that are expected at the actual volume of activity and the actual amounts of revenue and variable costs incurred at the actual volume of activity. Since the volume of activity is the same for the flexible budget and the actual results, variances are caused by the differences between the standard and actual sales price and per unit costs. Flexible budget variances are used for cost control and performance evaluation.

Flexible budget variances can be subdivided into *price and usage variances*. Price and usage variances for materials and labor can be computed with the following formulas. Variable overhead variances are calculated with the same general formulas; interpreting the results is difficult, however, because of the variety of inputs combined in variable overhead.

$$\text{Price variance} = |\text{Actual price} - \text{Standard price}| \times \text{Actual quantity}$$

$$\text{Usage variance} = |\text{Actual quantity} - \text{Standard quantity}| \times \text{Standard price}$$

The purchasing agent is normally accountable for the material price variance. The production department supervisor is usually responsible for the materials usage variance and the labor price and usage variances.

The fixed overhead cost variance consists of a spending variance and a volume variance computed as follows:

$$\text{Spending OH variance} = \text{Actual fixed OH costs} - \text{Budgeted fixed OH costs}$$

$$\text{OH volume variance} = \text{Budgeted fixed cost} - \text{Applied (allocated) fixed costs}$$

The overhead spending variance is similar to a price variance. Although fixed costs do not change relative to changes in production volume, they may be more or less than expected. For example, a production supervisor's salary will remain unchanged regardless of the volume of activity, but the supervisor may receive a raise resulting in higher than expected fixed costs. The fixed overhead volume variance is favorable if the actual volume of production is greater than the expected volume. A higher volume of production results in a lower fixed cost per unit. The volume variance measures how effectively production facilities are being used.

Management must interpret variances with care. For example, a purchasing agent may produce a favorable price variance by buying inferior materials at a low cost. However, an unfavorable labor usage variance may result because employees have difficulty using the substandard materials. The production supervisor is faced with an unfavorable usage variance for which she is not responsible. In addition, the purchasing agent's undesirable choice produced a favorable price variance. Favorable variances do not necessarily reflect good performance and unfavorable variances do not always suggest poor performance. The underlying causes of variances must be investigated before assigning responsibility for them.

A Look Forward >>

Chapter 23 introduces other techniques for evaluating managerial performance. The concept of decentralization and its relationship to responsibility accounting will be explained. You will learn how to calculate and interpret return on investment and residual income. Finally, you will study approaches used to establish the price of products that are transferred between divisions of the same company.

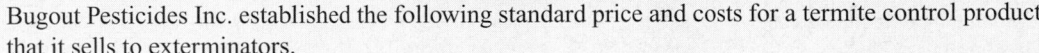

SELF-STUDY REVIEW PROBLEM

Bugout Pesticides Inc. established the following standard price and costs for a termite control product that it sells to exterminators.

Variable price and cost data (per unit)	Standard	Actual
Sales price	$52.00	$49.00
Materials cost	10.00	10.66
Labor cost	12.00	11.90
Overhead cost	7.00	7.05
General, selling, and administrative (G, S, & A) cost	8.00	7.92
Expected fixed costs (in total)		
Manufacturing	$150,000	$140,000
General, selling, and administrative	60,000	64,000

The 2006 master budget was established at an expected volume of 25,000 units. Actual production and sales volume for the year was 26,000 units.

Required

a. Prepare the pro forma income statement for Bugout's 2006 master budget.
b. Prepare a flexible budget income statement at the actual volume.
c. Determine the sales activity (volume) variances and indicate whether they are favorable or unfavorable. Comment on how Bugout would use the variances to evaluate performance.
d. Determine the flexible budget variances and indicate whether they are favorable or unfavorable.
e. Identify the two variances Bugout is most likely to analyze further. Explain why you chose these two variances. Who is normally responsible for the variances you chose to investigate?
f. Each unit of product was expected to require 4 pounds of material, which has a standard price of $2.50 per pound. Actual materials usage was 4.1 pounds per unit at an actual price of $2.60 per pound. Determine the materials price and usage variances.

Solution to Requirements *a, b,* and *c*

Number of units		25,000	26,000	
	Per Unit Standards	Master Budget	Flexible Budget	Volume Variances
Sales revenue	$52	$1,300,000	$1,352,000	$52,000 F
Variable manufacturing costs				
Materials	10	(250,000)	(260,000)	10,000 U
Labor	12	(300,000)	(312,000)	12,000 U
Overhead	7	(175,000)	(182,000)	7,000 U
Variable G, S, & A	8	(200,000)	(208,000)	8,000 U
Contribution margin		375,000	390,000	15,000 F
Fixed costs				
Manufacturing		(150,000)	(150,000)	0
G, S, & A		(60,000)	(60,000)	0
Net income		$ 165,000	$ 180,000	$15,000 F

The sales activity variances are useful in determining how changes in sales volume affect revenues and costs. Since the flexible budget is based on standard prices and costs, the variances do not provide insight into differences between standard prices and costs versus actual prices and costs.

Solution to Requirement *d*

Number of units		26,000	26,000	
	Actual Unit Price/Cost	**Flexible Budget***	**Actual Results**	**Flexible Budget Variances**
Sales revenue	$49.00	$1,352,000	$1,274,000	$78,000 U
Variable manufacturing costs				
Materials	10.66	(260,000)	(277,160)	17,160 U
Labor	11.90	(312,000)	(309,400)	2,600 F
Overhead	7.05	(182,000)	(183,300)	1,300 U
Variable G, S, & A	7.92	(208,000)	(205,920)	2,080 F
Contribution margin		390,000	298,220	91,780 U
Fixed costs				
Manufacturing		(150,000)	(140,000)	10,000 F
G, S, & A		(60,000)	(64,000)	4,000 U
Net income		$ 180,000	$ 94,220	$85,780 U

*The price and cost data for the flexible budget come from the previous table.

Solution to Requirement e

The management by exception doctrine focuses attention on the sales price variance and the materials variance. The two variances are material in size and are generally under the control of management. Upper-level marketing managers are responsible for the sales price variance. These managers are normally responsible for establishing the sales price. In this case, the actual sales price is less than the planned sales price, resulting in an unfavorable flexible budget variance. Mid-level production supervisors and purchasing agents are normally responsible for the materials cost variance. This variance could have been caused by waste or by paying more for materials than the standard price. Further analysis of the materials cost variance follows in Requirement *f*.

Solution to Requirement *f*

$$|\text{Actual price} - \text{Standard price}| \times \text{Actual quantity} = \text{Price variance}$$
$$|\$2.60 - \$2.50| \times |4.1 \text{ pounds} \times 26{,}000 \text{ units}| = \$10{,}660\ \text{U}$$

$$|\text{Actual quantity} - \text{Standard quantity}| \times \text{Standard price} = \text{Usage variance}$$
$$|(4.1 \times 26{,}000) - (4.0 \times 26{,}000)| \times \$2.50 = \$6{,}500\ \text{U}$$

The total of the price and usage variances [($10,660 + $6,500) = $17,160] equals the total materials flexible budget variance computed in Requirement *d*.

KEY TERMS

budget slack 1067
favorable variance 1063
flexible budget 1062
flexible budget variance 1066
ideal standard 1069
labor efficiency variance 1072
labor rate variance 1072
lax standard 1069
making the numbers 1064
management by exception 1069
material variance 1070
materials price variance 1076
materials quantity variance 1072
practical standard 1069
sales price variance 1066
sales volume variance 1063
spending variance 1076
standard 1068
static budget 1062
unfavorable variance 1063
variances 1063
volume variance 1076

QUESTIONS

1. What is the difference between a static budget and a flexible budget? When is each used?
2. When the operating costs for Bill Smith's production department were released, he was sure that he would be getting a raise. His costs were $20,000 less than the planned cost in the master budget. His supervisor informed him that the results look good but that a more in-depth analysis is necessary before raises can be assigned. What other considerations could Mr. Smith's supervisor be interested in before she rates his performance?
3. When are sales and cost variances favorable and unfavorable?
4. Joan Mason, the marketing manager for a large manufacturing company, believes her unfavorable sales volume variance is the responsibility of the production department. What production circumstances that she does not control could have been responsible for her poor performance?
5. When would variable cost volume variances be expected to be unfavorable? How should unfavorable variable cost volume variances be interpreted?
6. What factors could lead to an increase in sales revenues that would not merit congratulations to the marketing manager?
7. With respect to fixed costs, what are the consequences of the actual volume of activity exceeding the planned volume?
8. How are flexible budget variances determined? What causes these variances?
9. Minnie Divers, the manager of the marketing department for one of the industry's leading retail businesses, has been notified by the accounting department that her department experienced an unfavorable sales volume variance in the preceding period but a favorable sales price variance. Based on these contradictory results, how would you interpret her overall performance as suggested by her variances?
10. What three attributes are necessary for establishing the best standards? What information and considerations should be taken into account when establishing standards?
11. What are the three ranges of difficulty in standard setting? What level of difficulty normally results in superior employee motivation?
12. "So many variances," exclaimed Carl, a production manager with Bonnyville Manufacturing. "How do I determine the variances that need investigation? I can't possibly investigate all of them." Which variances will lead to useful information?
13. What is the primary benefit of using a standard cost system?
14. A processing department of Carmine Corporation experienced a high unfavorable materials usage variance. The plant manager initially commented, "The best way to solve this problem is to fire the supervisor of the processing department." Do you agree? Explain.
15. Sara Anderson says that she is a busy woman with no time to look at favorable variances. Instead, she concentrates solely on the unfavorable ones. She says that favorable variances imply that employees are doing better than expected and need only quick congratulations. In contrast, unfavorable variances indicate that change is needed to get the substandard performance up to par. Do you agree? Explain.
16. What two factors affect the total materials and labor variances?
17. Who is normally responsible for a materials price variance? Identify two factors that may be beyond this individual's control that could cause an unfavorable price variance.
18. John Jamail says that he doesn't understand why companies have labor price variances because most union contracts or other binding agreements set wage rates that do not normally change in the short term. How could rate variances occur even when binding commitments hold the dollar per hour rate constant?
19. Which individuals are normally held responsible for labor usage variances?
20. What is the primary cause of an unfavorable overhead volume variance?
21. What is the primary cause of a favorable overhead spending variance?

EXERCISES—SERIES A

All Exercises in Series A are available with McGraw-Hill's Homework Manager.

L.O. 3

Exercise 22-1A *Classifying variances as favorable or unfavorable*

Required

Indicate whether each of the following variances is favorable or unfavorable. The first one has been done as an example.

Item to Classify	Standard	Actual	Type of Variance
Sales volume	40,000 units	42,000 units	Favorable
Sales price	$3.60 per unit	$3.63 per unit	
Materials cost	$2.90 per pound	$3.00 per pound	
Materials usage	91,000 pounds	90,000 pounds	
Labor cost	$10.00 per hour	$9.60 per hour	
Labor usage	61,000 hours	61,800 hours	
Fixed cost spending	$400,000	$390,000	
Fixed cost per unit (volume)	$3.20 per unit	$3.16 per unit	

L.O. 3

Exercise 22-2A *Determining amount and type (favorable vs. unfavorable) of variance*

Required

Compute variances for the following items and indicate whether each variance is favorable (F) or unfavorable (U).

Item	Budget	Actual	Variance	F or U
Sales revenue	$490,000	$506,000		
Cost of goods sold	$385,000	$360,000		
Material purchases at 5,000 pounds	$275,000	$280,000		
Materials usage	$180,000	$178,000		
Sales price	$500	$489		
Production volume	950 units	900 units		
Wages at 4,000 hours	$60,000	$58,700		
Labor usage at $16 per hour	$96,000	$97,000		
Research and development expense	$22,000	$25,000		
Selling and administrative expenses	$49,000	$40,000		

L.O. 1

Exercise 22-3A *Preparing master and flexible budgets*

Burrel Manufacturing Company established the following standard price and cost data.

Sales price	$7.50 per unit
Variable manufacturing cost	3.00 per unit
Fixed manufacturing cost	3,000 total
Fixed selling and administrative cost	1,200 total

Burrel planned to produce and sell 1,100 units. Actual production and sales amounted to 1,200 units.

Required

a. Prepare the pro forma income statement in contribution format that would appear in a master budget.

b. Prepare the pro forma income statement in contribution format that would appear in a flexible budget.

Exercise 22-4A ***Determining sales volume variances*** **L.O. 4**

Required

Use the information provided in Exercise 22-3A.

a. Determine the sales volume variances.

b. Classify the variances as favorable (F) or unfavorable (U).

c. Comment on the usefulness of the variances with respect to performance evaluation and identify the member of the management team most likely to be responsible for these variances.

d. Explain why the fixed cost variances are zero.

e. Determine the fixed cost per unit based on planned activity and the fixed cost per unit based on actual activity. Assuming Burrel uses information in the master budget to price the company's product, comment on how the volume variance could affect the company's profitability.

Exercise 22-5A ***Determining flexible budget variances*** **L.O. 5**

Use the standard price and cost data provided in Exercise 22-3A. Assume that the actual sales price is $7.20 per unit and that the actual variable cost is $3.10 per unit. The actual fixed manufacturing cost is $2,850, and the actual selling and administrative expenses are $1,275.

Required

a. Determine the flexible budget variances.

b. Classify the variances as favorable (F) or unfavorable (U).

c. Comment on the usefulness of the variances with respect to performance evaluation and identify the member(s) of the management team who is (are) most likely to be responsible for these variances.

Exercise 22-6A ***Using a flexible budget to accommodate market uncertainty*** **L.O. 5**

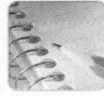

According to its original plan, Katta Consulting Services Company would charge its customers for service at $200 per hour in 2006. The company president expects consulting services provided to customers to reach 40,000 hours at that rate. The marketing manager, however, argues that actual results may range from 35,000 hours to 45,000 hours because of market uncertainty. Katta's standard variable cost is $90 per hour, and its standard fixed cost is $3,000,000.

Required

Develop flexible budgets based on the assumptions of service levels at 35,000 hours, 40,000 hours, and 45,000 hours.

Exercise 22-7A ***Evaluating a decision to increase sales volume by lowering sales price*** **L.O. 4, 5**

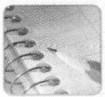

Rauch Educational Services had budgeted its training service charge at $80 per hour. The company planned to provide 40,000 hours of training services during 2007. By reducing the service charge to $70 per hour, the company was able to increase the actual number of hours to 42,000.

Required

a. Determine the sales volume variance, and indicate whether it is favorable (F) or unfavorable (U).

b. Determine the flexible budget variance, and indicate whether it is favorable (F) or unfavorable (U).

c. Did reducing the price of training services increase profitability? Explain.

Exercise 22-8A ***Responsibility for sales volume variance*** **L.O. 4**

Holbrook Company expected to sell 400,000 of its pagers during 2006. It set the standard sales price for the pager at $30 each. During June, it became obvious that the company would be unable to attain the expected volume of sales. Holbrook's chief competitor, Coker, Inc., had lowered prices and was pulling market share from Holbrook. To be competitive, Holbrook matched Coker's price, lowering its sales price to $28 per pager. Coker responded by lowering its price even further to $24 per pager. In an emergency meeting of key personnel, Holbrook's accountant, Vickie Dees, stated, "Our cost structure simply won't support a sales price in the $24 range." The production manager, Jean Volker, said, "I don't understand why I'm here. The only unfavorable variance on my report is a fixed cost volume variance and that one is not my fault. We can't be making the product if the marketing department isn't selling it."

Required

a. Describe a scenario in which the production manager is responsible for the fixed cost volume variance.

b. Describe a scenario in which the marketing manager is responsible for the fixed cost volume variance.

c. Explain how a decline in sales volume would affect Holbrook's ability to lower its sales price.

L.O. 5

Exercise 22-9A *Responsibility for variable manufacturing cost variance*

Slater Manufacturing Company set its standard variable manufacturing cost at $15 per unit of product. The company planned to make and sell 5,000 units of product during 2005. More specifically, the master budget called for total variable manufacturing cost to be $75,000. Actual production during 2005 was 5,200 units, and actual variable manufacturing costs amounted to $79,040. The production supervisor was asked to explain the variance between budgeted and actual cost ($79,040 − $75,000 = $4,040). The supervisor responded that she was not responsible for the variance that was caused solely by the increase in sales volume controlled by the marketing department.

Required

Do you agree with the production supervisor? Explain.

L.O. 8

Exercise 22-10A *Calculating the materials usage variance*

Evelyn Hill is the manager of the Southside Bagel Shop. The corporate office had budgeted her store to sell 4,000 ham sandwiches during the week beginning July 17. Each sandwich was expected to contain 6 ounces of ham. During the week of July 17, the store actually sold 4,500 sandwiches and used 27,450 ounces of ham. The standard cost of ham is $0.25 per ounce. The variance report from company headquarters showed an unfavorable materials usage variance of $650. Ms. Hill thought the variance was too high, but she had no accounting background and did not know how to register a proper objection.

Required

a. Is the variance calculated properly? If not, recalculate it.

b. Provide three independent explanations as to what could have caused the materials price variance that you determined in Requirement *a*.

L.O. 8

Exercise 22-11A *Determining materials price and usage variances*

Cathy's Florals produced a special Mother's Day arrangement that included six roses. The standard and actual costs of the roses used in each arrangement follow.

	Standard	Actual
Average number of roses per arrangement	6.0	6.5
Price per rose	× $0.40	× $0.36
Cost of roses per arrangement	$2.40	$2.34

Cathy's Florals planned to make 760 arrangements but actually made 800.

Required

a. Determine the total flexible budget materials variance and indicate whether it is favorable (F) or unfavorable (U).

b. Determine the materials price variance and indicate whether it is favorable (F) or unfavorable (U).

c. Determine the materials usage variance and indicate whether it is favorable (F) or unfavorable (U).

d. Confirm the accuracy of Requirements *a*, *b*, and *c* by showing that the sum of the price and usage variances equals the total variance.

L.O. 8

Exercise 22-12A *Responsibility for materials usage variance*

Ivy Fruit Basket Company assembles baskets of assorted fruit. The standard and actual costs of oranges used in each basket of fruit follow.

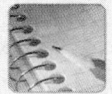

	Standard	Actual
Average number of oranges per basket	4.00	4.80
Price per orange	× $0.30	× $0.25
Cost of oranges per basket	$1.20	$1.20

Ivy actually produced 25,000 baskets.

Required

a. Determine the materials price variance and indicate whether it is favorable (F) or unfavorable (U).

b. Determine the materials usage variance and indicate whether it is favorable (F) or unfavorable. (U)

c. Explain why the purchasing agent may have been responsible for the usage variance.

Exercise 22-13A *Responsibility for labor price and usage variances*

L.O. 8

Jolly Manufacturing Company incurred a favorable labor price variance and an unfavorable labor usage variance.

Required

a. Describe a scenario in which the personnel manager is responsible for the unfavorable usage variance.

b. Describe a scenario in which the production manager is responsible for the unfavorable usage variance.

Exercise 22-14A *Calculating and explaining labor price and usage variances*

L.O. 8

Raman and Sons, a CPA firm, established the following standard labor cost data for completing what the firm referred to as a Class 2 tax return. Raman expected each Class 2 return to require 4.0 hours of labor at a cost of $50 per hour. The firm actually completed 600 returns. Actual labor hours averaged 4.4 hours per return and actual labor cost amounted to $46 per hour.

Required

a. Determine the total labor variance and indicate whether it is favorable (F) or unfavorable (U).

b. Determine the labor price variance and indicate whether it is favorable (F) or unfavorable (U).

c. Determine the labor usage variance and indicate whether it is favorable (F) or unfavorable (U).

d. Explain what could have caused these variances.

Exercise 22-15A *Determining the standard labor price*

L.O. 8

Wyman Car Wash Inc. expected to wash 1,000 cars during the month of August. Washing each car was expected to require 0.20 hours of labor. The company actually used 230 hours of labor to wash 920 cars. The labor usage variance was $368 unfavorable.

Required

a. Determine the standard labor price.

b. If the actual labor rate is $7.50, indicate whether the labor price variance would be favorable (F) or unfavorable (U).

Exercise 22-16A *Calculating the variable overhead variance*

L.O. 7, 8

Regan Company established a predetermined variable overhead cost rate at $10.00 per direct labor hour. The actual variable overhead cost rate was $9.60 per hour. The planned level of labor activity was 75,000 hours of labor. The company actually used 77,000 hours of labor.

Required

a. Determine the total flexible budget variable overhead cost variance.

b. Like many companies, Regan has decided not to separate the total variable overhead cost variance into price and usage components. Explain why Regan made this choice.

L.O. 8

Exercise 22-17A *Determining and interpreting fixed overhead variances*

Craig Company established a predetermined fixed overhead cost rate of $30 per unit of product. The company planned to make 9,000 units of product but actually produced only 8,000 units. Actual fixed overhead costs were $280,000.

Required

a. Determine the fixed overhead cost spending variance and indicate whether it is favorable or unfavorable. Explain what this variance means. Identify the manager(s) who is (are) responsible for the variance.

b. Determine the fixed overhead cost volume variance and indicate whether it is favorable or unfavorable. Explain why this variance is important. Identify the manager(s) who is (are) responsible for the variance.

PROBLEMS—SERIES A

All Problems in Series A are available with McGraw-Hill's Homework Manager.

L.O. 1, 4

CHECK FIGURES
a. NI = $81,000
b. NI at 29,000 units: $72,000

Problem 22-18A *Determining sales volume variances*

Tolbert Publications established the following standard price and costs for a hardcover picture book that the company produces.

Standard price and variable costs	
Sales price	$36.00
Materials cost	9.00
Labor cost	4.50
Overhead cost	6.30
General, selling, and administrative costs	7.20
Planned fixed costs	
Manufacturing	$135,000
General, selling, and administrative	54,000

Tolbert planned to make and sell 30,000 copies of the book.

Required

a. Prepare the pro forma income statement that would appear in the master budget.

b. Prepare flexible budget income statements, assuming production volumes of 29,000 and 31,000 units.

c. Determine the sales volume variances, assuming production and sales volume are actually 31,000 units.

d. Indicate whether the variances are favorable (F) or unfavorable (U).

e. Comment on how Tolbert could use the variances to evaluate performance.

L.O. 5

CHECK FIGURE
Flexible budget variance of NI: $20,450 U

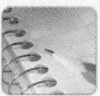

Problem 22-19A *Determining and interpreting flexible budget variances*

Use the standard price and cost data supplied in Problem 22-18A. Assume that Tolbert actually produced and sold 31,000 books. The actual sales price and costs incurred follow.

Actual price and variable costs	
Sales price	$35.00
Materials cost	9.20
Labor cost	4.40
Overhead cost	6.35
General, selling, and administrative costs	7.00
Actual fixed costs	
Manufacturing	$120,000
General, selling, and administrative	60,000

Required

a. Determine the flexible budget variances.

b. Indicate whether each variance is favorable (F) or unfavorable (U).

c. Identify the management position responsible for each variance. Explain what could have caused the variance.

Problem 22-20A *Flexible budget planning*

L.O. 1

eXcel

mhhe.com/edmonds2007

CHECK FIGURES

a. NI = $180,000

c. NI = $162,500

Tommie Okes, the president of Star Computer Services, needs your help. He wonders about the potential effects on the firm's net income if he changes the service rate that the firm charges its customers. The following basic data pertain to fiscal year 2007.

Standard rate and variable costs	
Service rate per hour	$80.00
Labor cost	40.00
Overhead cost	7.20
General, selling, and administrative cost	4.30
Expected fixed costs	
Facility repair	$525,000.00
General, selling, and administrative	150,000.00

Required

a. Prepare the pro forma income statement that would appear in the master budget if the firm expects to provide 30,000 hours of services in 2007.

b. A marketing consultant suggests to Mr. Okes that the service rate may affect the number of service hours that the firm can achieve. According to the consultant's analysis, if Star charges customers $75 per hour, the firm can achieve 38,000 hours of services. Prepare a flexible budget using the consultant's assumption.

c. The same consultant also suggests that if the firm raises its rate to $85 per hour, the number of service hours will decline to 25,000. Prepare a flexible budget using the new assumption.

d. Evaluate the three possible outcomes you determined in Requirements *a, b,* and *c* and recommend a pricing strategy.

Problem 22-21A *Determining materials price and usage variances*

L.O. 8

CHECK FIGURES

b. $0.27/cup

d. $8,160.60 U

Gibson Fruit Drink Company planned to make 200,000 containers of apple juice. It expected to use two cups of frozen apple concentrate to make each container of juice, thus using 400,000 cups (200,000 containers × 2 cups) of frozen concentrate. The standard price of one cup of apple concentrate is $0.25. Gibson actually paid $110,168.10 to purchase 408,030 cups of concentrate, which was used to make 201,000 containers of apple juice.

Required

a. Are flexible budget materials variances based on the planned volume of activity (200,000 containers) or actual volume of activity (201,000 containers)?

b. Compute the actual price per cup of concentrate.

c. Compute the standard quantity (number of cups of concentrate) required to produce the containers.

d. Compute the materials price variance and indicate whether it is favorable (F) or unfavorable (U).

e. Compute the materials usage variance and indicate whether it is favorable (F) or unfavorable (U).

Problem 22-22A *Determining labor price and usage variances*

L.O. 8

CHECK FIGURES

c. $616 U

d. $8,800 F

Amy's Doll Company produces handmade dolls. The standard amount of time spent on each doll is 1.5 hours. The standard cost of labor is $8 per hour. The company planned to make 10,000 dolls during the year but actually used 15,400 hours of labor to make 11,000 dolls. The payroll amounted to $123,816.

Required

a. Should labor variances be based on the planned volume of 10,000 dolls or the actual volume of 11,000 dolls?

b. Prepare a table that shows the standard labor price, the actual labor price, the standard labor hours, and the actual labor hours.
c. Compute the labor price variance and indicate whether it is favorable (F) or unfavorable (U).
d. Compute the labor usage variance and indicate whether it is favorable (F) or unfavorable (U).

L.O. 8

CHECK FIGURE
c. $5,000 F

Problem 22-23A *Computing fixed overhead variances*

In addition to other costs, Molton Phone Company planned to incur $212,500 of fixed manufacturing overhead in making 170,000 telephones. Molton actually produced 174,000 telephones, incurring actual overhead costs of $213,500. Molton establishes its predetermined overhead rate based on the planned volume of production (expected number of telephones).

Required

a. Calculate the predetermined overhead rate.
b. Determine the overhead spending variance and indicate whether it is favorable (F) or unfavorable (U).
c. Determine the overhead volume variance and indicate whether it is favorable (F) or unfavorable (U).

L.O. 8

excel
mhhe.com/edmonds2007

CHECK FIGURES
d. Price variance: $1,848 F
g. $900 F

Problem 22-24A *Computing materials, labor, and overhead variances*

The following data were drawn from the records of Walcott Corporation.

Planned volume for year (static budget)	4,000 units
Standard direct materials cost per unit	3 lbs. @ $2.00 per pound
Standard direct labor cost per unit	2 hours @ $4.00 per hour
Total expected fixed overhead costs	$18,000
Actual volume for the year (flexible budget)	4,200 units
Actual direct materials cost per unit	2.9 lbs. @ $2.10 per pound
Actual direct labor cost per unit	2.2 hrs. @ $3.80 per hour
Total actual fixed overhead costs	$17,600

Required

a. Prepare a materials variance information table showing the standard price, the actual price, the standard quantity, and the actual quantity.
b. Calculate the materials price and usage variances. Indicate whether the variances are favorable (F) or unfavorable (U).
c. Prepare a labor variance information table showing the standard rate, the actual rate, the standard hours, and the actual hours.
d. Calculate the labor price and usage variances. Indicate whether the variances are favorable (F) or unfavorable (U).
e. Calculate the predetermined overhead rate, assuming that Walcott uses the number of units as the allocation base.
f. Calculate the overhead spending variance. Indicate whether the variance is favorable (F) or unfavorable (U).
g. Calculate the overhead volume variance. Indicate whether the variance is favorable (F) or unfavorable (U).

L.O. 8

CHECK FIGURES
b. Usage variance: $2,781 U
d. Price variance: $8,916 U

Problem 22-25A *Computing materials, labor, and overhead variances*

Kingston Manufacturing Company produces a component part of a top secret military communication device. Standard production and cost data for the part, Product X, follow.

Planned production	30,000 units
Per unit direct materials	2 lbs. @ $1.80 per lb.
Per unit direct labor	3 hrs. @ $8.00 per hr.
Total estimated fixed overhead costs	$702,000

Kingston purchased and used 63,345 pounds of material at an average cost of $1.85 per pound. Labor usage amounted to 89,160 hours at an average of $8.10 per hour. Actual production amounted to 30,900 units. Actual fixed overhead costs amounted to $738,000. The company completed and sold all inventory for $1,800,000.

Required

a. Prepare a materials variance information table showing the standard price, the actual price, the standard quantity, and the actual quantity.

b. Calculate the materials price and usage variances. Indicate whether the variances are favorable (F) or unfavorable (U).

c. Prepare a labor variance information table showing the standard price, the actual price, the standard hours, and the actual hours.

d. Calculate the labor price and usage variances. Indicate whether the variances are favorable (F) or unfavorable (U).

e. Calculate the predetermined overhead rate, assuming that Kingston uses the number of units as the allocation base.

f. Calculate the overhead spending and volume variances and indicate whether they are favorable (F) or unfavorable (U).

g. Determine the amount of gross margin Kingston would report on the income statement.

Problem 22-26A *Computing variances*

L.O. 8

CHECK FIGURES
a. 1,760 lbs
d. $8.60

Kawa Manufacturing Company produces a single product. The following data apply to the standard cost of materials and labor associated with making the product.

Materials usage per unit	1 pound
Materials price	$5.00 per pound
Labor quantity per unit	2 hours
Labor price	$9.00 per hour

During the year, the company made 1,800 units of product. At the end of the year, the variance accounts had the following balances.

Materials Usage Variance account	$200 Favorable
Materials Price Variance account	$176 Unfavorable
Labor Usage Variance account	$900 Unfavorable
Labor Price Variance account	$1,480 Favorable

Required

a. Determine the actual amount of materials used.

b. Determine the actual price paid per pound for materials.

c. Determine the actual labor hours used.

d. Determine the actual labor price per hour.

Problem 22-27A *Computing standard cost and analyzing variances*

L.O. 8

excel
mhhe.com/edmonds2007

Ordeck Company manufactures molded candles that are finished by hand. The company developed the following standards for a new line of dipped candles.

Amount of direct materials per candle	1.6 pounds
Price of direct materials per pound	$0.75
Quantity of labor per unit	2 hours
Price of direct labor per hour	$6.00/hour
Total budgeted fixed overhead	$168,000

CHECK FIGURES
e. Usage variance for direct materials: $1,350 F
f. Volume variance: $33,600 U

During 2006, Ordeck planned to produce 40,000 dipped candles. Production lagged behind expectations, and it actually produced only 32,000 dipped candles. By year-end, direct materials purchased and used amounted to 49,400 pounds at a unit price of $0.60 per pound. Direct labor costs were actually $5.75 per hour and 61,400 actual hours were worked to produce the dipped candles. Overhead for the year actually amounted to $173,500. Overhead is applied to products using a predetermined overhead rate based on estimated units.

Required

(Round all computations to two decimal places.)

a. Compute the standard cost per candle for direct materials, direct labor, and overhead.
b. Determine the total standard cost for one dipped candle.
c. Compute the actual cost per candle for direct materials, direct labor, and overhead.
d. Compute the total actual cost per candle.
e. Compute the price and usage variances for direct materials and direct labor. Identify any variances that Ordeck should investigate. Offer possible cause(s) for the variances.
f. Compute the fixed overhead spending and volume variances. Explain your findings.
g. Although the individual variances (price, usage, and overhead) were large, the standard cost per unit and the actual cost per unit differed by only a few cents. Explain why.

L.O. 1, 3

Problem 22-28A *Analyzing not-for-profit entity variances*

CHECK FIGURE
b. Variance of surplus: $1,134 U

The Central Accounting Association held its annual public relations luncheon in April 2008. Based on the previous year's results, the organization allocated $21,150 of its operating budget to cover the cost of the luncheon. To ensure that costs would be appropriately controlled, Leigh Dilworth, the treasurer, prepared the following budget for the 2008 luncheon.

The budget for the luncheon was based on the following expectations.

1. The meal cost per person was expected to be $11.80. The cost driver for meals was attendance, which was expected to be 1,400 individuals.
2. Postage was based on $0.37 per invitation and 3,000 invitations were expected to be mailed. The cost driver for postage was number of invitations mailed.
3. The facility charge is $1,000 for a room that will accommodate up to 1,600 people; the charge for one to hold more than 1,600 people is $1,500.
4. A fixed amount was designated for printing, decorations, the speaker's gift, and publicity.

CENTRAL ACCOUNTING ASSOCIATION
Public Relations Luncheon Budget
April 2008

Operating funds allocated	$21,150
Expenses	
Variable costs	
Meals (1,400 × $11.80)	16,520
Postage (3,000 × $0.37)	1,110
Fixed costs	
Facility	1,000
Printing	950
Decorations	840
Speaker's gift	130
Publicity	600
Total expenses	21,150
Budget surplus (deficit)	$ 0

Actual results for the luncheon follow.

CENTRAL ACCOUNTING ASSOCIATION Actual Results for Public Relations Luncheon April 2008	
Operating funds allocated	$21,150
Expenses	
Variable costs	
Meals (1,620 × $12.50)	20,250
Postage (4,000 × $0.37)	1,480
Fixed costs	
Facility	1,500
Printing	950
Decorations	840
Speaker's gift	130
Publicity	600
Total expenses	25,750
Budget deficit	$ (4,600)

Reasons for the differences between the budgeted and actual data follow.

1. The president of the organization, Margaret Church, increased the invitation list to include 1,000 former members. As a result, 4,000 invitations were mailed.
2. Attendance was 1,620 individuals. Because of higher than expected attendance, the luncheon was moved to a larger room, thereby increasing the facility charge to $1,500.
3. At the last minute, Ms. Dilworth decided to add a dessert to the menu, which increased the meal cost to $12.50 per person.
4. Printing, decorations, the speaker's gift, and publicity costs were as budgeted.

Required

a. Prepare a flexible budget and compute the volume variances based on a comparison between the master budget and the flexible budget.

b. Compute flexible budget variances by comparing the flexible budget with the actual results.

c. Ms. Church was extremely upset with the budget deficit. She immediately called Ms. Dilworth to complain about the budget variance for the meal cost. She told Ms. Dilworth that the added dessert caused the meal cost to be $3,730 ($20,250 − $16,520) over budget. She added, "I could expect a couple hundred dollars one way or the other, but a couple thousand is totally unacceptable. At the next meeting of the budget committee, I want you to explain what happened." Assume that you are Ms. Dilworth. What would you tell the members of the budget committee?

d. Since this is a not-for-profit organization, why should anyone be concerned with meeting the budget?

EXERCISES—SERIES B

Exercise 22-1B *Classifying variances as favorable or unfavorable* **L.O. 3**

Required

Indicate whether each of the following variances is favorable (F) or unfavorable (U). The first one has been done as an example.

Item to Classify	Standard	Actual	Type of Variance
Sales volume	38,000 units	36,750 units	Unfavorable
Sales price	$6.90 per unit	$6.78 per unit	
Materials cost	$2.10 per pound	$2.30 per pound	
Materials usage	102,400 pounds	103,700 pounds	
Labor cost	$8.25 per hour	$8.80 per hour	
Labor usage	56,980 hours	55,790 hours	
Fixed cost spending	$249,000	$244,000	
Fixed cost per unit (volume)	$2.51 per unit	$3.22 per unit	

L.O. 3

Exercise 22-2B *Recognizing favorable vs. unfavorable variances*

Compute variances for the following items and indicate whether each variance is favorable (F) or unfavorable (U).

Item	Budget	Actual	Variance	F or U
Sales revenue	$620,000	$650,000		
Cost of goods sold	$450,000	$400,000		
Materials purchases at 10,000 pounds	$260,000	$290,000		
Materials usage	$270,000	$260,000		
Sales price	$550	$560		
Production volume	890 units	900 units		
Wages at 7,600 hours	$91,200	$90,800		
Labor usage	7,600 hours	8,000 hours		
Research and development expense	$81,000	$90,000		
Selling and administrative expenses	$75,000	$71,000		

L.O. 1

Exercise 22-3B *Preparing master and flexible budgets*

Lamar Manufacturing Company established the following standard price and cost data.

Sales price	$12 per unit
Variable manufacturing cost	8 per unit
Fixed manufacturing cost	40,000 total
Fixed selling and administrative cost	36,000 total

Lamar planned to produce and sell 36,000 units. It actually produced and sold 38,000 units.

Required

a. Prepare the pro forma income statement that would appear in a master budget. Use the contribution margin format.

b. Prepare the pro forma income statement that would appear in a flexible budget. Use the contribution margin format.

L.O. 4

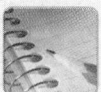

Exercise 22-4B *Determining sales activity (volume) variances*

Required

Use the information provided in Exercise 22-3B.

a. Determine the sales volume variances.

b. Classify the variances as favorable or unfavorable.

c. Comment on the usefulness of the variances with respect to performance evaluation and identify the member of the management team most likely to be responsible for these variances.

d. Explain why the fixed cost variances are zero.

e. Determine the fixed cost per unit based on planned activity and the fixed cost per unit based on actual activity. Assuming Lamar uses information in the master budget to price its product, explain how the volume variance could affect the company's profitability.

Exercise 22-5B *Determining flexible budget variances*

L.O. 5

Use the standard price and cost data provided in Exercise 22-3B. Assume the actual sales price was $11.90 per unit and the actual variable cost was $7.95 per unit. The actual fixed manufacturing cost was $42,000, and the actual selling and administrative expenses were $34,600.

Required

a. Determine the flexible budget variances.

b. Classify the variances as favorable or unfavorable.

c. Comment on the usefulness of the variances with respect to performance evaluation and identify the member(s) of the management team that is (are) most likely to be responsible for these variances.

Exercise 22-6B *Using a flexible budget to accommodate market uncertainty*

L.O. 5

Ritter Cable Installation Services Inc. is planning to open a new regional office. Based on a market survey Ritter commissioned, the company expects services demand for the new office to be between 30,000 and 40,000 hours annually. The firm normally charges customers $40 per hour for its installation services. Ritter's expects the new office to have a standard variable cost of $25 per hour and standard fixed cost of $550,000 per year.

Required

a. Develop flexible budgets based on 30,000 hours, 35,000 hours, and 40,000 hours of services.

b. Based on the results for Requirement *a*, comment on the likely success of Ritter's new office.

Exercise 22-7B *Evaluating a decision to increase sales volume by reducing sales price*

L.O. 4, 5

At the beginning of its most recent accounting period, Sturdy Roof had planned to clean 800 house roofs at an average price of $420 per roof. By reducing the service charge to $390 per roof, the company was able to increase the actual number of roofs cleaned to 900.

Required

a. Determine the sales volume variance and indicate whether it is favorable (F) or unfavorable (U).

b. Determine the flexible budget variance and indicate whether it is favorable (F) or unfavorable (U).

c. Did reducing the price charged for cleaning roofs increase profitability? Explain.

Exercise 22-8B *Responsibility for sales volume (activity) variance*

L.O. 4

Dion Manufacturing Company had an excellent year. The company had hired a new marketing director in January. The new director's great motivational appeal had inspired the sales staff, and, as a result, sales were 20 percent higher than expected. In a recent management meeting, the company president, Ken Steele, congratulated the marketing director and then criticized Mr. Cobb, the company's production manager, because of an unfavorable fixed cost spending variance. Mr. Cobb countered that the favorable fixed cost volume variance more than offset the unfavorable fixed cost spending variance. He argued that Mr. Steele should evaluate the two variances in total and that he should be rewarded rather than criticized.

Required

Do you agree with Mr. Cobb's defense of the unfavorable fixed cost spending variance? Explain.

Exercise 22-9B *Assessing responsibility for a labor cost variance*

L.O. 5

Gilliam Technologies Company's 2006 master budget called for using 30,000 hours of labor to produce 180,000 units of software. The standard labor rate for the company's employees is $19 per direct labor hour. Demand exceeded expectations, resulting in production and sales of 210,000 software units. Actual direct labor costs were $661,500. The year-end variance report showed a total unfavorable labor variance of $91,500.

Required

Assume you are the vice president of manufacturing. Should you criticize or praise the production supervisor's performance? Explain

L.O. 8

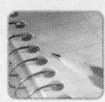

Exercise 22-10B *Calculating the materials usage variance*

Debbie Willis manages the Willis Candy Shop, which was expected to sell 4,000 servings of its trademark candy during July. Each serving was expected to contain 6 ounces of candy. The standard cost of the candy was $0.20 per ounce. The shop actually sold 3,800 servings and actually used 22,100 ounces of candy.

Required

a. Compute the materials usage variance.

b. Explain what could have caused the variance that you computed in Requirement *a*.

L.O. 8

Exercise 22-11B *Determining materials price and usage variances*

Rainbow Company makes paint that it sells in 1-gallon containers to retail home improvement stores. During 2007, the company planned to make 190,000 gallons of paint. It actually produced 198,000 gallons. The standard and actual quantity and cost of the color pigment for 1 gallon of paint follow.

	Standard	Actual
Quantity of materials per gallon	4.0 ounces	4.5 ounces
Price per ounce	× $0.25	× $0.26
Cost per gallon	$1.00	$1.17

Required

a. Determine the total flexible budget materials variance for pigment. Indicate whether the variance is favorable or unfavorable.

b. Determine the materials price variance and indicate whether the variance is favorable (F) or unfavorable (U).

c. Determine the materials usage variance and indicate whether the variance is favorable (F) or unfavorable (U).

d. Confirm your answers to Requirements *a*, *b*, and *c* by showing that the sum of the price and usage variances equals the total variance.

L.O. 8

Exercise 22-12B *Responsibility for materials price variance*

Chilly Delight Inc. makes ice cream that it sells in 5-gallon containers to retail ice cream parlors. During 2008, the company planned to make 100,000 containers of ice cream. It actually produced 97,000 containers. The actual and standard quantity and cost of sugar per container follow.

	Standard	Actual
Quantity of materials per container	2 pounds	2.1 pounds
Price per pound	×$0.39	×$0.40
Cost per container	$0.78	$0.84

Required

a. Determine the materials price variance and indicate whether the variance is favorable (F) or unfavorable (U).

b. Determine the materials usage variance and indicate whether the variance is favorable (F) or unfavorable (U).

c. Explain how the production manager could have been responsible for the price variance.

L.O. 8

Exercise 22-13B *Responsibility for labor rate and usage variance*

Quincy Manufacturing Company incurred an unfavorable labor rate variance.

Required

a. Describe a scenario in which the personnel manager is responsible for the unfavorable rate variance.

b. Describe a scenario in which the production manager is responsible for the unfavorable rate variance.

Exercise 22-14B *Calculating and explaining labor price and usage variances* L.O. 8

Lowder Landscaping Company established the following standard labor cost data to provide complete lawn care service (cutting, edging, trimming, and blowing) for a small lawn. Lowder planned each lawn to require 2 hours of labor at a cost of $12 per hour. The company actually serviced 500 lawns using an average of 1.75 labor hours per lawn. Actual labor costs were $14 per hour.

Required

a. Determine the total labor variance and indicate whether the variance is favorable (F) or unfavorable (U).

b. Determine the labor price variance and indicate whether the variance is favorable (F) or unfavorable (U).

c. Determine the labor usage variance and indicate whether the variance is favorable (F) or unfavorable (U).

d. Explain what could have caused the variances computed in Requirements *b* and *c*.

Exercise 22-15B *Determining standard labor hours* L.O. 8

Hair Styles, Inc., a hair salon, planned to provide 120 hair color treatments during December. Each treatment was planned to require 0.5 hours of labor at the standard labor price of $20 per hour. The salon actually provided 125 treatments. The actual labor price averaged $18. The labor price variance was $150 favorable.

Required

a. Determine the actual number of labor hours used per treatment.

b. Indicate whether the labor usage variance would be favorable (F) or unfavorable (U).

Exercise 22-16B *Calculating a variable overhead variance* L.O. 8

Winters Manufacturing Company established a predetermined variable overhead cost rate of $10 per direct labor hour. The actual variable overhead cost rate was $9.50 per direct labor hour. Winters planned to use 150,000 hours of direct labor. It actually used 152,000 hours of direct labor.

Required

a. Determine the total flexible budget variable overhead cost variance.

b. Many companies do not subdivide the total variable overhead cost variance into price and usage components. Under what circumstances would it be appropriate to distinguish between the price and usage components of a variable overhead cost variance? What would be required to accomplish this type of analysis?

Exercise 22-17B *Determining and interpreting fixed overhead variances* L.O. 8

Pino Manufacturing Company established a predetermined fixed overhead cost rate of $200 per unit of product. The company planned to make 19,000 units of product but actually produced 20,000 units. Actual fixed overhead costs were $4,000,000.

Required

a. Determine the fixed overhead cost spending variance. Indicate whether the variance is favorable (F) or unfavorable (U). Explain what this variance means. Identify the manager(s) who is (are) responsible for the variance.

b. Determine the fixed overhead cost volume variance. Indicate whether the variance is favorable (F) or unfavorable (U). Explain what the designations *favorable* and *unfavorable* mean with respect to the fixed overhead volume variance.

PROBLEMS—SERIES B

Problem 22-18B *Determining sales volume variances* L.O. 1, 4

Drake Food Corporation developed the following standard price and costs for a refrigerated TV dinner that the company produces.

Standard price and variable costs	
Sales price	$25.96
Materials cost	9.00
Labor cost	2.60
Overhead cost	0.56
General, selling, and administrative costs	4.20
Planned fixed costs	
Manufacturing cost	$500,000
General, selling, and administrative costs	360,000

Drake plans to make and sell 200,000 TV dinners.

Required

a. Prepare the pro forma income statement that would appear in the master budget.

b. Prepare flexible budget income statements, assuming production and sales volumes of 180,000 and 220,000 units.

c. Determine the sales volume variances, assuming production and sales volume are actually 190,000 units.

d. Indicate whether the variances are favorable (F) or unfavorable (U).

e. Comment on how Drake could use the variances to evaluate performance.

L.O. 5

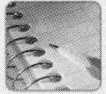

Problem 22-19B *Determining and interpreting flexible budget variances*

Use the standard price and cost data supplied in Problem 22-18B. Assume that Drake actually produced and sold 216,000 units. The actual sales price and costs incurred follow.

Actual price and variable costs	
Sales price	$25.80
Materials cost	8.80
Labor cost	2.68
Overhead cost	0.56
General, selling, and administrative costs	4.40
Actual fixed costs	
Manufacturing cost	$512,000.00
General, selling, and administrative costs	356,000.00

Required

a. Determine the flexible budget variances.

b. Indicate whether each variance is favorable (F) or unfavorable (U).

c. Identify the management position responsible for each variance. Explain what could have caused the variance.

L.O. 1

Problem 22-20B *Flexible budget planning*

Executive officers of Meikung Seafood Processing Company are holding a planning session for fiscal year 2008. They have already established the following standard price and costs for their canned seafood product.

Standard price and variable costs	
Price per can	$3.00
Materials cost	1.05
Labor cost	0.64
Overhead cost	0.10
General, selling, and administrative costs	0.25
Expected fixed costs	
Production facility costs	$215,000.00
General, selling, and administrative costs	180,000.00

Required

a. Prepare the pro forma income statement that would appear in the master budget if the company expects to produce 600,000 cans of seafood in 2008.

b. A marketing consultant suggests to Meikung's president that the product's price may affect the number of cans the company can sell. According to the consultant's analysis, if the firm sets its price at $2.70, it could sell 810,000 cans of seafood. Prepare a flexible budget based on the consultant's suggestion.

c. The same consultant also suggests that if the company raises its price to $3.25 per can, the volume of sales would decline to 400,000. Prepare a flexible budget based on this suggestion.

d. Evaluate the three possible outcomes developed in Requirements *a, b,* and *c* and recommend a pricing strategy.

Problem 22-21B *Determining materials price and usage variances* L.O. 8

Hearn Swimsuit Specialties Inc. makes fashionable women's swimsuits. Its most popular swimsuit, with the Sarong trade name, uses a standard fabric amount of 6 yards of raw material with a standard price of $5.00 per yard. The company planned to produce 100,000 Sarong swimsuits in 2007. At the end of 2007, the company's cost accountant reported that Hearn had used 636,000 square yards of fabric to make 102,000 swimsuits. Actual cost for the raw material was $3,307,200.

Required

a. Are flexible budget material variances based on the planned volume of 100,000 swimsuits or actual volume of 102,000 swimsuits?

b. Compute the actual price per square yard of fabric.

c. Compute the standard quantity (square yards of fabric) required to produce the swimsuits.

d. Compute the materials price variance and indicate whether it is favorable (F) or unfavorable (U).

e. Compute the materials usage variance and indicate whether it is favorable (F) or unfavorable (U).

Problem 22-22B *Determining labor price and usage variances* L.O. 8

As noted in Problem 22-21B, Hearn Swimsuit makes swimsuits. In 2007, Hearn produced its most popular swimsuit, the Sarong, for a standard labor price of $30 per hour. The standard amount of labor was 1.0 hour per swimsuit. The company had planned to produce 100,000 Sarong swimsuits. At the end of 2007, the company's cost accountant reported that Hearn had used 107,000 hours of labor to make 102,000 swimsuits. The total labor cost was $3,295,600.

Required

a. Should the labor variances be based on the planned volume of 100,000 swimsuits or on the actual volume of 102,000 swimsuits?

b. Prepare a table that shows the standard labor price, the actual labor price, the standard labor hours, and the actual labor hours.

c. Compute the labor price variance and indicate whether it is favorable (F) or unfavorable (U).

d. Compute the labor usage variance and indicate whether it is favorable (F) or unfavorable (U).

Problem 22-23B *Computing fixed overhead variances* L.O. 8

Sartin Sporting Goods Co. manufactures baseballs. According to Sartin's 2006 budget, the company planned to incur $300,000 of fixed manufacturing overhead costs to make 200,000 baseballs. Sartin actually produced 187,000 balls, incurring $296,000 of actual fixed manufacturing overhead costs. Sartin establishes its predetermined overhead rate on the basis of the planned volume of production (expected number of baseballs).

Required

a. Calculate the predetermined overhead rate.

b. Determine the overhead spending variance and indicate whether it is favorable (F) or unfavorable (U).

c. Determine the overhead volume variance and indicate whether it is favorable (F) or unfavorable (U).

Problem 22-24B *Computing materials, labor, and overhead Variances* L.O. 8

Victor Kemp was a new cost accountant at Beck Plastics Inc. He was assigned to analyze the following data that his predecessor left him.

Planned volume for year (static budget)	10,000 units
Standard direct materials cost per unit	2 lbs. @ $1.50 per pound
Standard direct labor cost per unit	0.5 hours @ $10.00 per hour
Total planned fixed overhead costs	$12,000
Actual volume for the year (flexible budget)	10,800 units
Actual direct materials cost per unit	1.9 lbs. @ $1.60 per pound
Actual direct labor cost per unit	0.6 hrs. @ $8.00 per hour
Total actual fixed overhead costs	$12,400

Required

a. Prepare a materials variance information table showing the standard price, the actual price, the standard usage, and the actual usage.

b. Calculate the materials price and usage variances and indicate whether they are favorable (F) or unfavorable (U).

c. Prepare a labor variance information table showing the standard price, the actual price, the standard hours, and the actual hours.

d. Calculate the labor price and usage variances and indicate whether they are favorable (F) or unfavorable (U).

e. Calculate the predetermined overhead rate, assuming that Beck Plastics uses the number of units as the allocation base.

f. Calculate the overhead spending variance and indicate whether it is favorable (F) or unfavorable (U).

g. Calculate the overhead volume variance and indicate whether it is favorable (F) or unfavorable (U).

L.O. 8

Problem 22-25B ***Computing materials, labor, and overhead variances***

Evans Corporation makes mouse pads for computer users. After the first year of operation, Shirley Evans, the president and chief executive officer, was eager to determine the efficiency of the company's operation. In her analysis, she used the following standards provided by her assistant.

Units of planned production	400,000
Per unit direct materials	1 square foot @ $0.25 per square foot
Per unit direct labor	0.2 hrs. @ $7.00 per hr.
Total estimated fixed overhead costs	$200,000

Evans purchased and used 460,000 square feet of material at an average cost of $0.24 per square foot. Labor usage amounted to 79,200 hours at an average of $6.90 per hour. Actual production amounted to 416,000 units. Actual fixed overhead costs amounted to $204,000. The company completed and sold all inventory for $1,414,400.

Required

a. Prepare a materials variance information table showing the standard price, the actual price, the standard quantity, and the actual quantity.

b. Calculate the materials price and usage variances and indicate whether they are favorable (F) or unfavorable (U).

c. Prepare a labor variance information table showing the standard price, the actual price, the standard hours, and the actual hours.

d. Calculate the labor price and usage variances and indicate whether they are favorable (F) or unfavorable (U).

e. Calculate the predetermined overhead rate, assuming that Evans uses the number of units as the allocation base.

f. Calculate the overhead spending and volume variances and indicate whether they are favorable (F) or unfavorable (U).

g. Determine the amount of gross margin Evans would report on the income statement.

Problem 22-26B *Computing variances*

L.O, 8

A fire destroyed most of Omar Products Corporation's records. Sherry Hill, the company's accountant, is trying to piece together the company's operating results from salvaged documents. She discovered the following data.

Standard materials usage per unit	2.5 pounds
Standard materials price	\$2 per pound
Standard labor usage per unit	0.6 hour
Standard labor price	\$12 per hour
Actual number of products produced	8,000 units
Materials price variance	\$792 favorable
Materials usage variance	\$400 favorable
Labor price variance	\$1,952 unfavorable
Labor usage variance	\$960 unfavorable

Required

a. Determine the actual amount of materials used.

b. Determine the actual price per pound paid for materials.

c. Determine the actual labor hours used.

d. Determine the actual labor price per hour.

Problem 22-27B *Computing standard cost and analyzing variances*

L.O. 8

Nash Manufacturing Company, which makes aluminum alloy wheels for automobiles, recently introduced a new luxury wheel that fits small sports cars. The company developed the following standards for its new product.

Amount of direct materials per wheel	4 pounds
Price of direct materials per pound	\$5.50
Quantity of labor per wheel	5.0 hours
Price of direct labor per hour	\$8.00/hour
Total budgeted fixed overhead	\$336,000

In its first year of operation, Nash planned to produce 3,000 sets of wheels (four wheels per set). Because of unexpected demand, it actually produced 3,600 sets of wheels. By year-end direct materials purchased and used amounted to 60,000 pounds of aluminum at a cost of \$351,000. Direct labor costs were actually \$8.40 per hour. Actual hours worked were 4.4 hours per wheel. Overhead for the year actually amounted to \$360,000. Overhead is applied to products using a predetermined overhead rate based on the total estimated number of wheels to be produced.

Required

(Round all computations to two decimal places.)

a. Compute the standard cost per wheel for direct materials, direct labor, and overhead.

b. Determine the total standard cost per wheel.

c. Compute the actual cost per wheel for direct materials, direct labor, and overhead.

d. Compute the actual cost per wheel.

e. Compute the price and usage variances for direct materials and direct labor. Identify any variances that Nash should investigate. Based on your results, offer a possible explanation for the labor usage variance.

f. Compute the fixed overhead spending and volume variances. Explain your findings.

Problem 22-28B *Analyzing not-for-profit organization variances*

L.O. 3, 4, 5

The Finance Department of Dothan State University planned to hold its annual distinguished visiting lecturer (DVL) presentation in October 2008. The secretary of the department prepared the following budget based on costs that had been incurred in the past for the DVL presentation.

FINANCE DEPARTMENT Distinguished Visiting Lecturer Budget October 2008	
Variable costs	
Beverages at break	$ 375
Postage	296
Step costs*	
Printing	500
Facility	250
Fixed costs	
Dinner	200
Speaker's gift	100
Publicity	50
Total costs	$1,771

*Step costs are costs that change abruptly after a defined range of volume (attendance). They do not change proportionately with unit volume increases (i.e., the cost is fixed within a range of activity but changes to a different fixed cost when the volume changes to a new range). For instance, the facility charge is $250 for from 1 to 400 attendees. From 401 to 500 attendees, the next larger room is needed, and the charge is $350. If more than 500 attended, the room size and cost would increase again.

The budget for the presentation was based on the following expectations:

1. Attendance was estimated at 50 faculty from Dothan State and neighboring schools, 125 invited guests from the business community, and 200 students. Beverage charge per attendee would be $1.00. The cost driver for beverages is the number of attendees.
2. Postage was based on $0.37 per invitation; 800 invitations were expected to be mailed to faculty and finance business executives. The cost driver for postage is the number of invitations mailed.
3. Printing cost was expected to be $500 for 800 invitations and envelopes. Additional invitations and envelopes could be purchased in batches of 100 units with each batch costing $50.
4. The DVL presentation was scheduled at a downtown convention center. The facility charge was $250 for a room that has a capacity of 400 persons; the charge for one to hold more than 400 people was $350. The convention center provided refreshments at break except beverages.
5. After the presentation, three Dothan State faculty members planned to take the speaker to dinner. The dinner had been prearranged at a local restaurant for $200 for a three-course dinner.
6. A gift for the speaker was budgeted at $100.
7. Publicity would consist of flyers and posters placed at strategic locations around campus and business offices, articles in the business section of the local newspapers, and announcements made in business classes and school newspapers. Printing for the posters and flyers had been prearranged for $50.
8. The speaker lives in the adjoining state and had agreed to drive to the presentation at his own expense.

The actual results of the presentation follow.

1. Attendance consisted of 450 faculty, business executives, and students.
2. An additional 100 invitations were printed and mailed when the Finance Department decided that selected alumni should also be invited.
3. Based on RSVP responses, the department rented the next size larger room at a cost of $350 for the presentation.
4. The speaker's gift cost was as budgeted.
5. The department chairperson decided to have a four-course dinner, which cost $230.
6. Because of poor planning, the posters and flyers were not distributed as widely as expected. It was decided at the last minute to hire a temporary assistant to make phone calls to alumni. The actual publicity cost was $75.

Required

a. Prepare a flexible budget and compute activity variances based on a comparison between the master budget and the flexible budget. Briefly explain the meaning of the activity variances.

b. Compute flexible budget variances by comparing the flexible budget with the actual results. Briefly explain the meaning of the variable cost flexible budget variances. Discuss the fixed cost variances.

c. Calculate the expected and actual fixed cost per attendee. Discuss the significance of the difference in these amounts.

d. Since the department is a not-for-profit entity, why is it important for it to control the cost of sponsoring the distinguished visiting lecturer presentation?

ANALYZE, THINK, COMMUNICATE

ATC 22-1 Business Applications Case *Static versus flexible budget variances*

Vince Jacobs is the manufacturing production supervisor for High-Five Inline Skates Company. Trying to explain why he did not get the year-end bonus he had expected, he told his wife, "This is the dumbest place I ever worked. Last year the company set up this budget assuming it would sell 200,000 skates. Well, it sold only 190,000. The company lost money and gave me a bonus for not using as much materials and labor as was called for in the budget. This year, the company has the same 200,000 goal and it sells 210,000. The company's making all kinds of money. You'd think I'd get this big fat bonus. Instead, management tells me I used more materials and labor than was budgeted. They say the company would have made a lot more money if I'd stayed within my budget. I guess I gotta wait for another bad year before I get a bonus. Like I said, this is the dumbest place I ever worked."

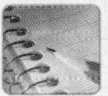

High-Five Company's master budget and the actual results for the most recent year of operating activity follow.

	Master Budget	Actual Results	Variances	F or U
Number of units	200,000	210,000	10,000	
Sales revenue	$40,000,000	$42,630,000	$2,630,000	F
Variable manufacturing costs				
Materials	(6,000,000)	(6,115,200)	115,200	U
Labor	(5,600,000)	(5,974,500)	374,500	U
Overhead	(2,400,000)	(2,471,700)	71,700	U
Variable general, selling, and admin. costs	(7,600,000)	(8,110,200)	510,200	U
Contribution margin	18,400,000	19,958,400	1,558,400	F
Fixed costs				
Manufacturing overhead	(8,150,000)	(8,205,000)	55,000	U
General, selling, and admin. costs	(7,200,000)	(7,176,000)	24,000	F
Net income	$ 3,050,000	$ 4,577,400	$1,527,400	F

Required

a. Did High-Five increase unit sales by cutting prices or by using some other strategy?

b. Is Mr. Jacobs correct in his conclusion that something is wrong with the company's performance evaluation process? If so, what do you suggest be done to improve the system?

c. Prepare a flexible budget and recompute the budget variances.

d. Explain what might have caused the fixed costs to be different from the amount budgeted.

e. Assume that the company's material price variance was favorable and its material usage variance was unfavorable. Explain why Mr. Jacobs may not be responsible for these variances. Now, explain why he may have been responsible for the material usage variance.

f. Assume the labor price variance is favorable. Was the labor usage variance favorable or unfavorable?

g. Is the fixed overhead volume variance favorable or unfavorable? Explain the effect of this variance on the cost of each set of inline skates.

ATC 22-2 Group Assignment *Variable price and usage variances and fixed cost variances*

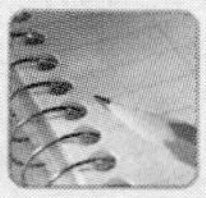

Kemp Tables Inc. (KTI) makes picnic tables of 2 × 4 planks of treated pine. It sells the tables to large retail discount stores such as Wal-Mart. After reviewing the following data generated by KTI's chief accountant, Arianne Darwin, the company president, expressed concern that the total manufacturing cost was more than $0.5 million above budget ($7,084,800 − $6,520,000 = $564,800).

	Actual Results	Master Budget
Cost of planks per table	$ 44.10	$ 40.00
Cost of labor per table	26.10	25.50
Total variable manufacturing cost per table (a)	$ 70.20	$ 65.50
Total number of tables produced (b)	82,000	80,000
Total variable manufacturing cost (a × b)	$5,756,400	$5,240,000
Total fixed manufacturing cost	1,328,400	1,280,000
Total manufacturing cost	$7,084,800	$6,520,000

Ms. Darwin asked Conrad Pearson, KTI's chief accountant, to explain what caused the increase in cost. Mr. Pearson responded that things were not as bad as they seemed. He noted that part of the cost variance resulted from making and selling more tables than had been expected. Making more tables naturally causes the cost of materials and labor to be higher. He explained that the flexible budget cost variance was less than $0.5 million. Specifically, he provided the following comparison.

	Actual Results	Flexible Budget
Cost of planks per table	$ 44.10	$ 40.00
Cost of labor per table	26.10	25.50
Total variable manufacturing cost per table (a)	$ 70.20	$ 65.50
Total number of tables produced (b)	82,000	82,000
Total variable manufacturing cost (a × b)	$5,756,400	$5,371,000
Total fixed manufacturing cost	1,328,400	1,280,000
Total manufacturing cost	$7,084,800	$6,651,000

Based on this information, he argued that the relevant variance for performance evaluation was only $433,800 ($7,084,800 − $6,651,000). Ms. Darwin responded, "*Only* $433,800! I consider that a very significant number. By the end of the day, I want a full explanation as to what is causing our costs to increase."

Required

a. Divide the class into groups of four or five students and divide the groups into three sections. Assign Task 1 to the first section, Task 2 to the second section, and Task 3 to the third section.

Group Tasks

(1) Based on the following information, determine the total materials cost variance and the price and usage variances. Assuming that the variances are an appropriate indicator of cause, explain what could have caused the variances. Identify the management position responsible.

	Actual Data	Standard Data
Number of planks per table	21	20
Price per plank	× $2.10	× $2.00
Materials cost per table	$44.10	$40.00

(2) Based on the following information, determine the total labor cost variance and the price and usage variances. Assuming that the variances are an appropriate indicator of cause, explain what could have caused each variance. Identify the management position responsible.

	Actual Data	Standard Data
Number of hours per table	2.9	3.0
Price per hour	×$9.00	×$8.50
Labor cost per table	$26.10	$25.50

(3) Determine the amount of the fixed cost spending and volume variances. Explain what could have caused these variances. Based on the volume variance, indicate whether the actual fixed cost per unit would be higher or lower than the budgeted fixed cost per unit.

b. Select a spokesperson from each section to report the amount of the variances computed by the group. Reconcile any differences in the variances reported by the sections. Reconcile the individual variances with the total variance. Specifically, show that the total of the materials, labor, and overhead variances equals the total flexible budget variance ($433,800).

c. Discuss how Ms. Darwin should react to the variance information.

ATC 22-3 Research Assignment *Nonfinancial performance measures*

The article "How Nonfinancial Performance Measures Are Used" (*Management Accounting,* February 1998) describes several emerging performance measures that do not rely on financial data. Read this article and complete the following requirements.

Required

a. What are nonfinancial performance measures? Provide several examples.

b. The article describes five categories of nonfinancial performance measures. Identify these categories. Which category do executives consider most important?

c. Can you compute variances for nonfinancial performance measures? Explain.

d. Comment on the extent to which executives use nonfinancial measures.

e. The authors indicate that their study identified three red flags that executives need to address to use nonfinancial performance measures more effectively. Identify and briefly discuss these three red flags.

ATC 22-4 Writing Assignment *Standard costing—the human factor*

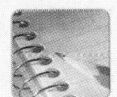

Kemp Corporation makes a protein supplement called Power Punch™. Its principal competitor for Power Punch is the protein supplement Superior Strength™, made by Jim Adams Company (JAC). Mr. Adams, a world-renowned weight-lifting champion, founded JAC. The primary market for both products is athletes. Kemp sells Power Punch to wellness stores, which sell it, other supplements, and health foods to the public. In contrast, Superior Strength is advertised in sports magazines and sold through orders generated by the ads.

Mr. Adams's fame is an essential factor in his company's advertising program. He is a dynamic character whose personality motivates people to strive for superior achievement. His demeanor not only stimulates sales but also provides a strong inspirational force for company employees. He is a kind, understanding individual with high expectations who is fond of saying that "mistakes are just opportunities for improvement." Mr. Adams is a strong believer in total quality management.

Mr. Quayle, president of Kemp Corporation, is a stern disciplinarian who believes in teamwork. He takes pride in his company's standard costing system. Managers work as a team to establish standards and then are held accountable for meeting them. Managers who fail to meet expectations are severely chastised, and continued failure leads to dismissal. After several years of rigorous enforcement, managers have fallen in line. Indeed, during the last two years, all managers have met their budget goals.

Even so, costs have risen steadily. These cost increases have been passed on to customers through higher prices. As a result, Power Punch is now priced significantly higher than Superior Strength. In fact, Superior Strength is selling directly to the public at a price that is below the wholesale price that Kemp is charging the wellness stores. The situation has reached a critical juncture. Sales of Power

Punch are falling while Superior Strength is experiencing significant growth. Given that industry sales have remained relatively stable, it is obvious that customers are shifting from Power Punch to Superior Strength. Mr. Quayle is perplexed. He wonders how a company with direct market expenses can price its products so low.

Required

a. Explain why JAC has been able to gain a pricing advantage over Kemp.

b. Assume that you are a consultant whom Kemp's board of directors has asked to recommend how to halt the decline in sales of Power Punch. Provide appropriate recommendations.

ATC 22-5 Ethical Dilemma *Budget games*

Melody Lovelady is the most highly rewarded sales representative at Swift Corporation. Her secret to success is always to understate your abilities. Ms. Lovelady is assigned to a territory in which her customer base is increasing at approximately 25 percent per year. Each year she estimates that her budgeted sales will be 10 percent higher than her previous year's sales. With little effort, she is able to double her budgeted sales growth. At Swift's annual sales meeting, she receives an award and a large bonus. Of course, Ms. Lovelady does not disclose her secret to her colleagues. Indeed, she always talks about how hard it is to continue to top her previous performance. She tells herself if they are dumb enough to fall for this rubbish, I'll milk it for all it's worth.

Required

a. What is the name commonly given to the budget game Ms. Lovelady is playing?

b. Does Ms. Lovelady's behavior violate any of the standards of ethical conduct shown in Exhibit 14.13 of Chapter 14?

c. Recommend how Ms. Lovelady's budget game could be stopped.

COMPREHENSIVE PROBLEM

The management of Magnificent Modems Inc. (MMI) is uncertain as to the volume of sales that will exist in 2007. The president of the company asked the chief accountant to prepare flexible budget income statements assuming that sales activity amounts to 3,000 and 6,000 units. The static budget is shown in the following form.

Required

a. Complete the following worksheet to prepare the appropriate flexible budgets.

b. Calculate and show the flexible budget variances for the static budget versus the flexible budget at 6,000 units.

c. Indicate whether each variance is favorable or unfavorable.

Flexible Budget Income Statements				
		Static Budget	**Flexible Budget**	**Flexible Budget**
Number of Units		5,000	3,000	6,000
	Cost per Unit			
Sales Revenue	$120.00	$600,000		
Variable Manuf. Costs				
Materials	40.00	200,000		
Labor	25.00	125,000		
Overhead	4.00	20,000		
Variable G, S, & A	6.00	30,000		
Contribution Margin		225,000		
Fixed Costs				
Manufacturing Rent		50,000		
Dep. on Manu. Equip.		60,000		
G, S, & A Expenses		71,950		
Dep. On Admin. Equip.		12,000		
Net Income (Loss)		$ 31,050	$(58,950)	$76,050

CHAPTER 23

Responsibility Accounting

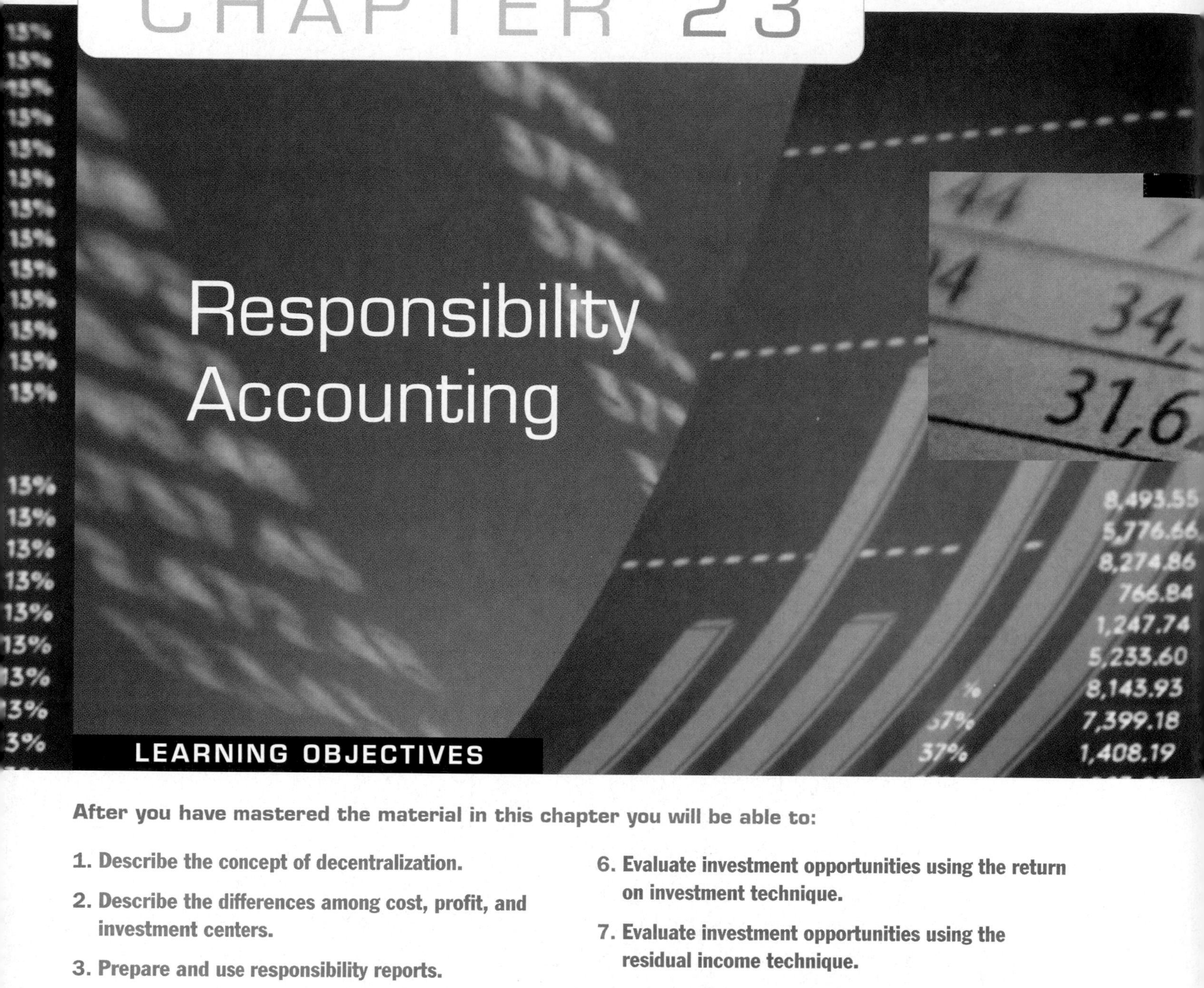

LEARNING OBJECTIVES

After you have mastered the material in this chapter you will be able to:

1. **Describe the concept of decentralization.**
2. **Describe the differences among cost, profit, and investment centers.**
3. **Prepare and use responsibility reports.**
4. **Explain how the management by exception doctrine relates to responsibility reports.**
5. **Explain the controllability concept.**
6. **Evaluate investment opportunities using the return on investment technique.**
7. **Evaluate investment opportunities using the residual income technique.**
8. **Describe the three common approaches used to establish transfer prices. (Appendix)**

Chapter 23

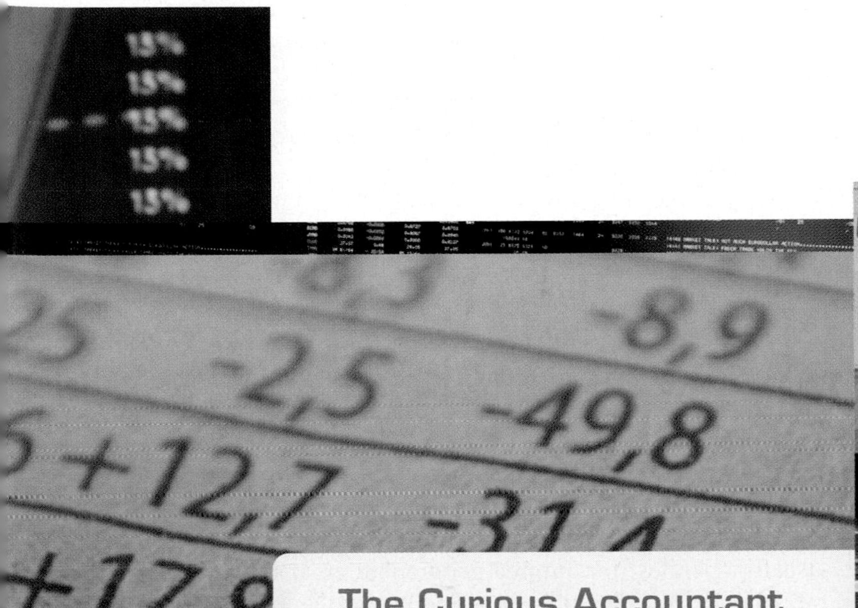

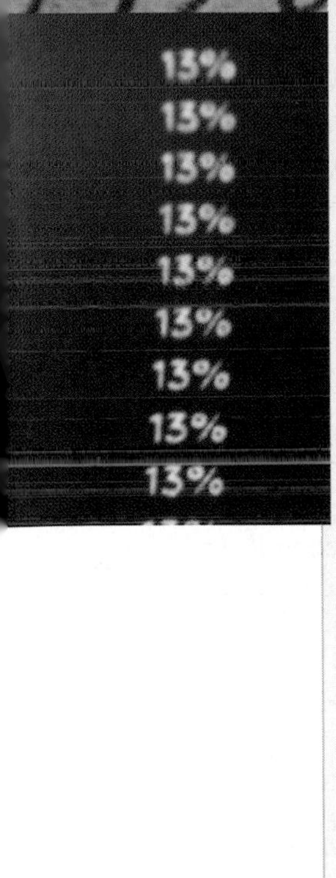

The Curious Accountant

In 1978 Bernie Marcus and Arthur Blank founded **The Home Depot, Inc.**, and their first store opened in 1979. One year later they had four stores, 300 employees, and sales of $22 million. By 2000 there were 1,123 Home Depot stores with 226,000 employees and annual sales of $45.7 billion. Mr. Marcus was the company's CEO during these 20 years of tremendous growth, and he ran the company with a decentralized management style. He wanted store managers to operate individual stores as if they were their owners. Using this strategy, he saw the company's stock price rise from less than $1 per share to over $45 per share (when adjusted for stock splits). In December 2000, Mr. Marcus stepped down as Home Depot's CEO and an outsider, Bob Nardelli, was appointed as his replacement.

Two significant things happened during the first two years of Mr. Nardelli's tenure. First, he began implementing a much more centralized management system, and second, the stock price fell by 51 percent. A few examples of his management changes are: he required stores to hire more part-time employees and fewer full-time employees whether the local manager wanted to or not; he implemented a centralized purchasing system; he required local stores to carry new product lines, such as small appliances, even if the store manager objected. As a result of the change in management style, several long-time store managers left the company, and others complained. Despite these problems, Mr. Marcus, who still yielded considerable influence as a major stockholder and member of the board of directors, stood behind Mr. Nardelli and the changes he was implementing.

What could explain why a company that had enjoyed so much success under a decentralized management system would switch to a more centralized system? Why would the architect of the decentralized system that had been so successful support the man who replaced his system? (Answers on page 1114.)

CHAPTER OPENING

Walter Keller, a production manager, complained to the accountant, Kelly Oberson, that the budget system failed to control his department's labor cost. Ms. Oberson responded, "people, not budgets, control costs." Budgeting is one of many tools management uses to control business operations. Managers are responsible for using control tools effectively. ***Responsibility accounting*** *focuses on evaluating the performance of individual managers. For example, expenses controlled by a production department manager are presented in one report and expenses controlled by a marketing department manager are presented in a different report. This chapter discusses the development and use of a responsibility accounting system.* ■

Decentralization Concept

LO 1

Describe the concept of decentralization.

Effective responsibility accounting requires clear lines of authority and responsibility. Divisions of authority and responsibility normally occur as a natural consequence of managing business operations. In a small business, one person can control everything: marketing, production, management, accounting. In contrast, large companies are so complex that authority and control must be divided among many people.

Consider the hiring of employees. A small business usually operates in a limited geographic area. The owner works directly with employees. She knows the job requirements, local wage rates, and the available labor pool. She is in a position to make informed hiring decisions. In contrast, a major corporation may employ thousands of employees throughout the world. The employees may speak different languages and have different social customs. Their jobs may require many different skills and pay a vast array of wage rates. The president of the corporation cannot make informed hiring decisions for the entire company. Instead, he delegates *authority* to a professional personnel manager and holds that manager *responsible* for hiring practices.

Decision-making authority is similarly delegated to individuals responsible for managing specific organization functions such as production, marketing, and accounting. Delegating authority and responsibility is referred to as **decentralization.** Decentralization offers advantages like the following.

1. *Encourages upper-level management to concentrate on strategic decisions.* Because local management makes routine decisions, upper-level management can concentrate on long-term planning, goal setting, and performance evaluation.
2. *Improves the quality of decisions by delegating authority down a chain of command.* Local managers are better informed about local concerns. Furthermore, their proximity to local events allows them to react quickly to changes in local conditions. As a result, local managers can generally make better decisions.
3. *Motivates managers to improve productivity.* The freedom to act coupled with responsibility for the results creates an environment that encourages most individuals to perform at high levels.
4. *Trains lower-level managers for increased responsibilities.* Decision making is a skill. Managers accustomed to making decisions about local issues are generally able to apply their decision-making skills to broader issues when they are promoted to upper management positions.
5. *Improves performance evaluation.* When lines of authority and responsibility are clear, credit or blame can be more accurately assigned.

Organization Chart

Exhibit 23.1 displays a partial organization chart for Panther Holding Company, a decentralized business. The chart shows five levels of authority and responsibility arranged in a hierarchical order from the top down. Other companies may have more or less complex organizational charts, depending on their decentralization needs and philosophy.

Responsibility Centers

Decentralized businesses are usually subdivided into distinct reporting units called responsibility centers. A **responsibility center** is an organizational unit that controls identifiable revenue or expense items. The unit may be a division, a department, a subdepartment, or even a single machine. For example, a transportation company may identify a semitrailer truck as a responsibility center. The company holds the truck driver responsible for the revenues and expenses associated with operating the truck. Responsibility centers may be divided into three categories: cost, profit, and investment.

A **cost center** is an organizational unit that incurs expenses but does not generate revenue. In the Panther organization chart (Exhibit 23.1), the finishing department and the production department are cost centers. Cost centers normally fall on the lower levels of an organization chart. The manager of a cost center is judged on his ability to keep costs within budget parameters.

A **profit center** differs from a cost center in that it not only incurs costs but also generates revenue. In the Panther organization chart, the companies at the third level (Wilson Carpet Company, Selma Sopha Corporation, and Tables Incorporated) are considered profit centers. The manager of a profit center is judged on his ability to produce revenue in excess of expenses.

Investment center managers are responsible for revenues, expenses, and the investment of capital. Investment centers normally appear at the upper levels of an organization chart. The second-level division managers (managers of the lumber, home, and furniture divisions) in the Panther organization are responsible for investment centers. Managers of investment centers are accountable for assets and liabilities as well as earnings.

EXHIBIT 23.1

Organization Chart

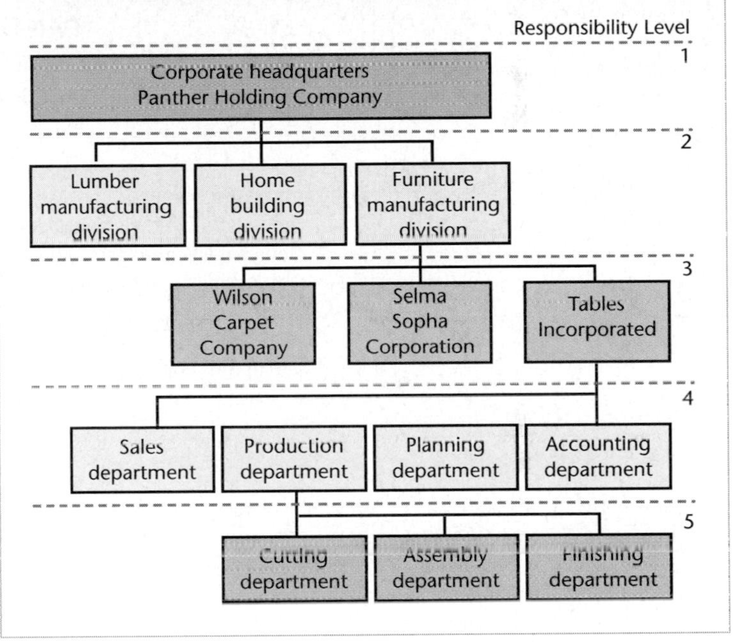

LO 2 Describe the differences among cost, profit, and investment centers.

Responsibility Reports

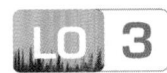

LO 3 Prepare and use responsibility reports.

A **responsibility report** is prepared for each manager who controls a responsibility center. The report compares the expectations for the manager's responsibility center with the center's actual performance. A typical report lists the items under the manager's control, both the budgeted amount and the actual amount spent for each item, and the differences between budgeted and actual amounts (variances).

Management by Exception and Degree of Summarization

LO 4 Explain how the management by exception doctrine relates to responsibility reports.

Responsibility reports are arranged to support using the **management by exception** doctrine. Exhibit 23.2 illustrates a partial set of responsibility reports for Panther Holding Company. From the lower level upward, each successive report includes summary data from the preceding report. For example, the detailed information about the finishing

EXHIBIT 23.2

Responsibility Reports

PANTHER HOLDING COMPANY
Second Level: Furniture Manufacturing Division
For the Month Ended January 31, 2004

	Budget	Actual	Variance
Controllable expenses			
Administrative division expense	$ 20,400	$ 31,100	$10,700 U
Company president's salary	9,600	9,200	400 F
Wilson Carpet Company	82,100	78,400	3,700 F
Selma Sopha Corporation	87,200	116,700	29,500 U
Tables Incorporated	48,600	51,250	2,650 U
Total	$247,900	$286,650	$38,750 U

PANTHER HOLDING COMPANY
Third Level: Tables Incorporated
For the Month Ended January 31, 2004

	Budget	Actual	Variance
Controllable expenses			
Administrative division expense	$ 3,000	$ 2,800	$ 200 F
Department managers' salaries	10,000	11,200	1,200 U
Sales department costs	9,100	8,600	500 F
Production department costs	13,500	13,750	250 U
Planning department costs	4,800	7,000	2,200 U
Accounting department costs	8,200	7,900	300 F
Total	$ 48,600	$ 51,250	$ 2,650 U

PANTHER HOLDING COMPANY
Fourth Level: Production Department
For the Month Ended January 31, 2004

	Budget	Actual	Variance
Controllable expenses			
Administrative staff expense	$ 900	$ 1,100	$ 200 U
Supervisory salaries	2,800	2,800	0
Cutting department costs	1,400	1,200	200 F
Assembly department costs	2,800	2,900	100 U
Finishing department costs	5,600	5,750	150 U
Total	$ 13,500	$ 13,750	$ 250 U

PANTHER HOLDING COMPANY
Fifth Level: Finishing Department
For the Month Ended January 31, 2004

	Budget	Actual	Variance
Controllable expenses			
Wages expense	$ 3,200	$ 3,000	$ 200 F
Direct materials	1,100	1,400	300 U
Supplies	400	500	100 U
Small tools	600	650	50 U
Other expenses	300	200	100 F
Total	$ 5,600	$ 5,750	$ 150 U

department (a level five responsibility center) is summarized as a single line item ($150 unfavorable variance) in the report for the production department (a level four responsibility center).

The lack of detailed information may appear to hinder the production manager's ability to control costs. In fact, it has the opposite effect. The supervisor of the finishing department should use her responsibility report to identify and correct problems without bothering the production manager. The production manager should become concerned only when one of his supervisors loses control. The summary data in the production manager's report will adequately advise him of such situations. With this format, managers will concentrate only on significant deviations from expectations (management by exception) because the deviations are highlighted in their responsibility reports.

Applying the management by exception doctrine to the variances in her responsibility report, the division manager of the Furniture Manufacturing Division (second level responsibility center) should concentrate her efforts on two areas. First, the $29,500 unfavorable variance for Selma Sopha Corporation indicates Selma's expenditures are out of line. Second, the $10,700 unfavorable variance for the division manager's own administrative expenses indicates those costs are significantly above budget expectations. The division manager should request detailed reports for these two areas. Other responsibility centers seem to be operating within reason and can be left to their respective managers. This reporting format focuses management's attention on the areas where it is most needed.

The complete responsibility accounting report would also include the first responsibility level, corporate headquarters. At the corporate level, responsibility reports normally include year-to-date income statements to inform management of the company's overall performance. To facilitate decision making, these income statements are normally prepared using the contribution margin format. Exhibit 23.3 shows the January 2004 income statement for Panther Holding Company.

Controllability Concept

LO 5

Explain the controllability concept.

The **controllability concept** is crucial to an effective responsibility accounting system. Managers should only be evaluated based on revenues or costs they control. Holding individuals

EXHIBIT 23.3

Panther Income Statement (Contribution Margin Format)

PANTHER HOLDING COMPANY
Income Statement for Internal Use
For the Month Ended January 31, 2004

	Budget	Actual	Variance
Sales	$984,300	$962,300	$22,000 U
Variable expenses			
Variable product costs	343,100	352,250	9,150 U
Variable selling expenses	105,000	98,000	7,000 F
Other variable expenses	42,200	51,100	8,900 U
Total variable expenses	490,300	501,350	11,050 U
Contribution margin	494,000	460,950	33,050 U
Fixed expenses			
Fixed product cost	54,100	62,050	7,950 U
Fixed selling expense	148,000	146,100	1,900 F
Other fixed expenses	23,000	25,250	2,250 U
Total fixed expenses	225,100	233,400	8,300 U
Net income	$268,900	$227,550	$41,350 U

Answers to The Curious Accountant

The management at **The Home Depot**, along with former CEO Bernie Marcus, understands that the environment in which a business operates changes and successful companies are willing to alter the way they do business to keep up with those changes. For example, in 2000, Home Depot had nine regional purchasing offices that operated independently. Mr. Nardelli consolidated these into one central office. This reduced the cost of ordering inventory—one purchase order is cheaper to process than nine—and it gave the company more power to negotiate lower prices from its suppliers.

One of Mr. Nardelli's changes was to implement a more detailed performance measurement system for each store. Among other things, this system allowed the company to reduce the amount of inventory it carries, thus saving the company the cost of financing that inventory.

The new CEO was willing to admit if a change did not work and to quickly make another change. His requirement to use more part-time employees led to some customer dissatisfaction, so it was revised.

To be fair, the drop in Home Depot's stock price had many causes. The stock price had grown rapidly over the years because the company had grown rapidly. However, the larger a company becomes, the harder it is to maintain a given growth rate. For example, if a company has only ten stores, it can open one new one and realize a ten percent growth rate. If the company has 1,000 stores, it must open 100 new stores to realize a ten percent growth rate. Furthermore, the economy in general was much weaker during 2001 and 2002 than it had been during the 1990s.

Even though Home Depot's stock price fell during Mr. Nardelli's first two years as CEO, its profit margins were up and its cash balance was up. Also, its sales increased by 27 percent from 2000 to 2002, and its earnings were up 42 percent.

Sources: Company disclosures, stock-market data, and Dan Morse, "A Hardware Chain Struggles to Adjust to a New Blueprint," *The Wall Street Journal*, January 17, 2003, pp. A-1 and A-6.

responsible for things they cannot control is demotivating. Isolating control, however, may be difficult, as illustrated in the following case.

Dorothy Pasewark, a buyer for a large department store chain, was criticized when stores could not resell the merchandise she bought at the expected price. Ms. Pasewark countered that the sales staff caused the sluggish sales by not displaying the merchandise properly. The sales staff charged that the merchandise had too little sales potential to justify setting up more enticing displays. The division of influence between the buyer and the sales staff clouds the assignment of responsibility.

Since the exercise of control may be clouded, managers are usually held responsible for items over which they have *predominant* rather than *absolute* control. At times responsibility accounting may be imperfect. Management must strive to ensure that praise or criticism is administered as fairly as possible.

Qualitative Reporting Features

Responsibility reports should be expressed in simple terms. If they are too complex, managers will ignore them. The reports should include only the budgeted and actual amounts of *controllable* revenues and expenses, with variances highlighted to promote management by exception. Report preparers and report users should communicate regularly to ensure the reports provide relevant information. Furthermore, reports must be timely. A report that presents yesterday's problem is not nearly as useful as one that presents today's problem.

Managerial Performance Measurement

A primary reason for a responsibility accounting system is to evaluate managerial performance. Managers are assigned responsibility for certain cost, profit, or investment centers. They are then evaluated based on how their centers perform relative to specific goals and objectives. The measurement techniques (standard costs and contribution margin format income reporting) used for cost and profit centers have been discussed in previous chapters. The remainder of this chapter discusses performance measures for investment centers.

Return on Investment

LO 6

Evaluate investment opportunities using the return on investment technique.

Topic Tackler PLUS

23-1

Society confers wealth, prestige, and power upon those who have control of assets. Unsurprisingly, managers are motivated to increase the amount of assets employed by the investment centers they control. When companies have additional assets available to invest, how do upper-level managers decide which centers should get them? The additional assets are frequently allotted to the managers who demonstrate the greatest potential for increasing the company's wealth. Companies often assess managerial potential by comparing the return on investment ratios of various investment centers. The **return on investment (ROI)** is the ratio of wealth generated (operating income) to the amount invested (operating assets) to generate the wealth. ROI is commonly expressed with the following equation.

$$\text{ROI} = \frac{\text{Operating income}}{\text{Operating assets}}$$

To illustrate using ROI for comparative evaluations, assume Panther Holding Company's corporate (first level) chief financial officer (CFO) determined the ROIs for the company's three divisions (second level investment centers). The CFO used the following accounting data from the records of each division:

	Lumber Manufacturing Division	Home Building Division	Furniture Manufacturing Division
Operating income	$ 60,000	$ 46,080	$ 81,940
Operating assets	300,000	256,000	482,000

The ROI for each division is:

Lumber manufacturing: $\frac{\text{Operating income}}{\text{Operating assets}} = \$60{,}000 \div \$300{,}000 = 20\%$

Home building: $\frac{\text{Operating income}}{\text{Operating assets}} = \$46{,}080 \div \$256{,}000 = 18\%$

Furniture manufacturing: $\frac{\text{Operating income}}{\text{Operating assets}} = \$81{,}940 \div \$482{,}000 = 17\%$

All other things being equal, higher ROIs indicate better performance. In this case the Lumber Manufacturing Division manager is the best performer. Assume Panther obtains additional funding for expanding the company's operations. Which investment center is most likely to receive the additional funds?

If the manager of the Lumber Manufacturing Division convinces the upper level management team that his division would continue to outperform the other two divisions, the Lumber Manufacturing Division would most likely get the additional funding. The manager of the lumber division would then invest the funds in additional operating assets which would in turn increase the division's operating income. As the division prospers, Panther would reward the manager for exceptional performance. Rewarding the manager of the lumber division would likely motivate the other managers to improve their divisional ROIs. Internal competition would improve the performance of the company as a whole.

CHECK YOURSELF 23.1

Green View is a lawn services company whose operations are divided into two districts. The District 1 manager controls $12,600,000 of operating assets. District 1 produced $1,512,000 of operating income during the year. The District 2 manager controls $14,200,000 of operating assets. District 2 reported $1,988,000 of operating income for the same period. Use return on investment to determine which manager is performing better.

Answer

District 1

ROI = Operating income ÷ Operating assets = $1,512,000 ÷ $12,600,000 = 12%

District 2

ROI = Operating income ÷ Operating assets = $1,988,000 ÷ $14,200,000 = 14%

Because the higher ROI indicates the better performance, the District 2 manager is the superior performer. This conclusion is based solely on quantitative results. In real-world practice, companies also consider qualitative factors.

Qualitative Considerations

Why do companies compute ROI using operating income and operating assets instead of using net income and total assets? Suppose Panther's corporate headquarters closes a furniture manufacturing plant because an economic downturn temporarily reduces the demand for furniture. It would be inappropriate to include these nonoperating plant assets in the denominator of the ROI computation. Similarly, if Panther sells the furniture plant and realizes a large gain on the sale, including the gain in the numerator of the ROI formula would distort the result. Since the manager of the Furniture Manufacturing Division does not control closing the plant or selling it, it is unreasonable to include the effects of these decisions in computing the ROI. These items would, however, be included in computing net income and total assets. Most companies use operating income and operating assets to compute ROI because those variables measure performance more accurately.

Measuring Operating Assets

The meaning of ROI results is further complicated by the question of how to *value* operating assets. Suppose Echoles Rental Company's two divisions, Northern and Southern, each rent to customers a vending machine that originally cost $5,000. The vending machines have five-year useful lives and no salvage value. The Northern Division purchased its machine one year ago; the Southern Division purchased its machine three years ago. At the end of the current year, the book values of the two machines are as follows:

	Northern Division's Vending Machine	Southern Division's Vending Machine
Original cost	$5,000	$5,000
Less accumulated depreciation	(1,000)	(3,000)
Book value	$4,000	$2,000

Each machine generates operating income averaging $800 per year. The ROI for each machine this year is as follows:

$$\text{Northern Division: } \frac{\text{Operating income}}{\text{Operating assets}} = \$800 \div \$4{,}000 = 20\%$$

$$\text{Southern Division: } \frac{\text{Operating income}}{\text{Operating assets}} = \$800 \div \$2{,}000 = 40\%$$

Is the manager of the Southern Division outperforming the manager of the Northern Division? No. The only difference between the two divisions is that Southern is using an older asset than Northern. Using book value as the valuation base can distort the ROI and cause severe motivational problems. Managers will consider comparisons between different investment centers unfair because the ROIs do not accurately reflect performance. Furthermore, managers may avoid replacing obsolete equipment because purchasing new equipment would increase the dollar amount of operating assets, reducing the ROI.

Companies may minimize these problems by using original cost instead of book value in the denominator of the ROI formula. In the vending machine example, using original cost produces an ROI of 16 percent ($800 ÷ $5,000). Using original cost, however, may not entirely solve the valuation problem. As a result of inflation and technological advances, comparable equipment purchased at different times will have different costs. Some accountants advocate using *replacement cost* rather than *historical cost* as the valuation base. This solution is seldom used because determining the amount it would cost to replace particular assets is difficult. For example, imagine trying to determine the replacement cost of all the assets in a steel mill that has been operating for years.

Selecting the asset valuation base is a complex matter. In spite of its shortcomings, most companies use book value as the valuation base. Management must consider those shortcomings when using ROI to evaluate performance.

Factors Affecting Return on Investment

Management can gain insight into performance by dividing the ROI formula into two separate ratios as follows:

$$\text{ROI} = \frac{\text{Operating income}}{\text{Sales}} \times \frac{\text{Sales}}{\text{Operating assets}}$$

The first ratio on the right side of the equation is called the margin. The **margin** is a measure of management's ability to control operating expenses relative to the level of sales. In general, high margins indicate superior performance. Management can increase the margin by reducing the level of operating expenses necessary to generate sales. Decreasing operating expenses increases profitability.

The second ratio in the expanded ROI formula is called turnover. **Turnover** is a measure of the amount of operating assets employed to support the achieved level of sales. Operating assets are scarce resources. To maximize profitability, they must be used wisely. Just as excessive expenses decrease profitability, excessive investments in operating assets also limit profitability.

Both the short and expanded versions of the ROI formula produce the same end result. To illustrate, we will use the ROI for the Lumber Manufacturing Division of Panther Holding Company. Recall that the division employed $300,000 of operating assets to produce $60,000 of operating income, resulting in the following ROI:

$$\text{ROI} = \frac{\text{Operating income}}{\text{Operating assets}} = \frac{\$60{,}000}{\$300{,}000} = 20\%$$

Further analysis of the accounting records indicates the Lumber Manufacturing Division had sales of $600,000. The following computation demonstrates that the expanded ROI formula produces the same result as the short formula:

$$\begin{aligned}\text{ROI} &= \text{Margin} \times \text{Turnover}\\ &= \frac{\text{Operating income}}{\text{Sales}} \times \frac{\text{Sales}}{\text{Operating assets}}\\ &= \frac{\$60{,}000}{\$600{,}000} \times \frac{\$600{,}000}{\$300{,}000}\\ &= .10 \times 2\\ &= 20\%\end{aligned}$$

The expanded formula may seem more complicated. It is generally more useful, however, because it helps managers see a variety of strategies to improve ROI. The expanded formula shows that profitability and ROI can be improved in three ways: *by increasing sales, by reducing expenses,* or *by reducing the investment base.* Each of these possibilities is demonstrated using the Lumber Manufacturing Division (LMD) of Panther Holding Company.

1. *Increase ROI by increasing sales.* Because some expenses are fixed, sales can be increased while those expenses are constant. Managers may even be able to reduce variable expenses by increasing productivity as sales increase. As a result, managers can increase their ROIs by increasing sales while limiting growth in expenses. To illustrate, assume the manager of LMD is able to increase sales from \$600,000 to \$660,000 while controlling expense growth so that net income increases from \$60,000 to \$72,600. Assuming investment in operating assets remains constant at \$300,000, ROI becomes:

$$\begin{aligned} \text{ROI} &= \text{Margin} \times \text{Turnover} \\ &= \frac{\text{Operating income}}{\text{Sales}} \times \frac{\text{Sales}}{\text{Operating assets}} \\ &= \frac{\$72{,}600}{\$660{,}000} \times \frac{\$660{,}000}{\$300{,}000} \\ &= .11 \times 2.2 \\ &= 24.2\% \end{aligned}$$

2. *Increase ROI by reducing expenses.* Suppose the manager of LMD takes a different approach. He decides to eliminate waste. By analyzing spending, he is able to cut expenses without affecting sales or the investment in operating assets. As a result of controlling expenses, operating income increases from \$60,000 to \$72,000. Assume the other variables remain the same as in the original example. ROI becomes:

$$\begin{aligned} \text{ROI} &= \text{Margin} \times \text{Turnover} \\ &= \frac{\text{Operating income}}{\text{Sales}} \times \frac{\text{Sales}}{\text{Operating assets}} \\ &= \frac{\$72{,}000}{\$600{,}000} \times \frac{\$600{,}000}{\$300{,}000} \\ &= .12 \times 2 \\ &= 24\% \end{aligned}$$

3. *Increase ROI by reducing the investment base.* Managers who focus too narrowly on income frequently overlook this possibility. Reducing the amount of funds invested in operating assets such as inventory or accounts receivable can increase profitability because the funds released can be invested in other, more productive assets. This effect is reflected in the ROI computation. For example, assume the manager of LMD launches a *just-in-time* inventory system that allows the division to reduce the amount of inventory it carries. The manager also initiates an aggressive campaign to collect receivables which significantly reduces the outstanding receivables balance. As a result of these two initiatives, the assets employed to operate LMD fall from \$300,000 to \$240,000. All other variables remain the same as in the original example. ROI becomes:

$$\begin{aligned} \text{ROI} &= \text{Margin} \times \text{Turnover} \\ &= \frac{\text{Operating income}}{\text{Sales}} \times \frac{\text{Sales}}{\text{Operating assets}} \\ &= \frac{\$60{,}000}{\$600{,}000} \times \frac{\$600{,}000}{\$240{,}000} \\ &= .10 \times 2.5 \\ &= 25\% \end{aligned}$$

The $60,000 of funds released by reducing the operating assets can be returned to headquarters or be reinvested by LMD depending on the opportunities available.

The benefits of increasing the *margin* by increasing sales or reducing expenses are intuitive. They are so obvious that, in their zeal to increase margins, managers for many years overlooked the effect of *turnover*. Growing use of the ROI ratio has alerted managers to the benefits of controlling operating assets as well as expenses. Because ROI blends many aspects of managerial performance into a single ratio that enables comparisons between companies, comparisons between investment centers within companies, and comparisons between different investment opportunities within an investment center, ROI has gained widespread acceptance as a performance measure.

CHECK YOURSELF 23.2

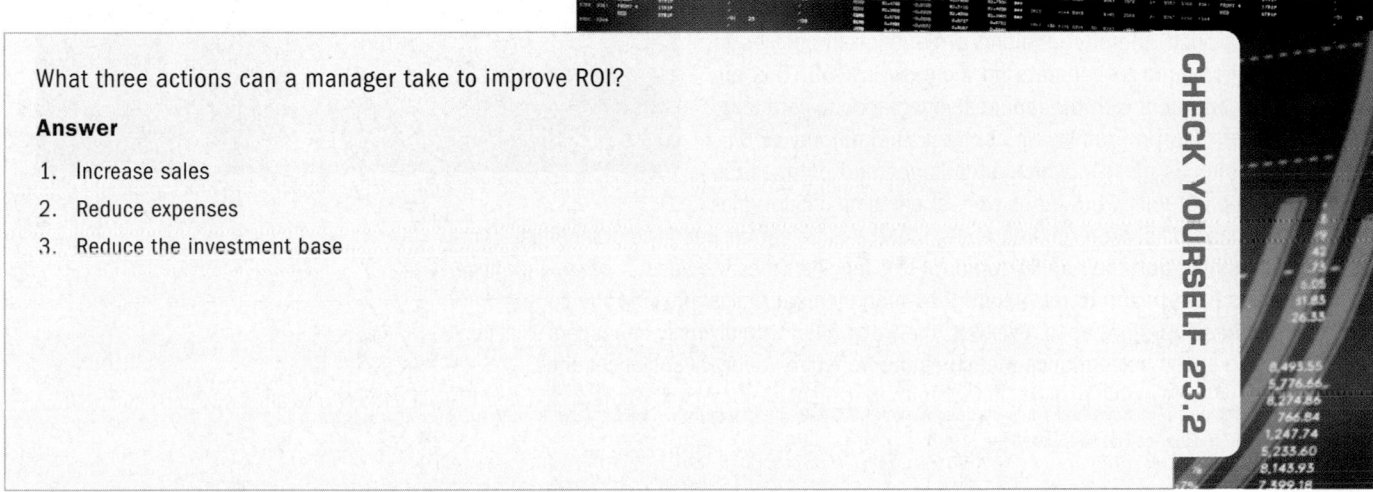

What three actions can a manager take to improve ROI?

Answer

1. Increase sales
2. Reduce expenses
3. Reduce the investment base

Residual Income

LO 7 Evaluate investment opportunities using the residual income technique.

Topic Tackler PLUS 23-2

Suppose Panther Holding Company evaluates the manager of the Lumber Manufacturing Division (LMD) based on his ability to maximize ROI. The corporation's overall ROI is approximately 18 percent. LMD, however, has consistently outperformed the other investment centers. Its ROI is currently 20 percent. Now suppose the manager has an opportunity to invest additional funds in a project likely to earn a 19 percent ROI. Would the manager accept the investment opportunity?

These circumstances place the manager in an awkward position. The corporation would benefit from the project because the expected ROI of 19 percent is higher than the corporate average ROI of 18 percent. Personally, however, the manager would suffer from accepting the project because it would reduce the division ROI to less than the current 20 percent. The manager is forced to choose between his personal best interests and the best interests of the corporation. When faced with decisions such as these, many managers choose to benefit themselves at the expense of their corporations, a condition described as **suboptimization.**

To avoid *suboptimization*, many businesses base managerial evaluation on **residual income.** This approach measures a manager's ability to maximize earnings above some targeted level. The targeted level of earnings is based on a minimum desired ROI. Residual income is calculated as follows:

$$\text{Residual income} = \text{Operating income} - (\text{Operating assets} \times \text{Desired ROI})$$

To illustrate, recall that LMD currently earns $60,000 of operating income with the $300,000 of operating assets it controls. ROI is 20 percent ($60,000 ÷ $300,000). Assume Panther's desired ROI is 18 percent. LMD's residual income is therefore:

$$\begin{aligned}\text{Residual income} &= \text{Operating income} - (\text{Operating assets} \times \text{Desired ROI})\\ &= \$60{,}000 - (\$300{,}000 \times .18)\\ &= \$60{,}000 - \$54{,}000\\ &= \$6{,}000\end{aligned}$$

FOCUS ON INTERNATIONAL ISSUES

DO MANAGERS IN DIFFERENT COUNTRIES STRESS THE SAME PERFORMANCE MEASURES?

Companies operating in different countries frequently choose different performance measures to evaluate their managers. For example, although U.S. companies tend to favor some form of return on investment (ROI), Japanese companies tend to emphasize return on sales (ROS) as a primary measure of financial performance.* In general, the Japanese assume a constant sales price, thereby requiring a reduction in cost or an increase in volume to generate an increase in ROS. This approach is consistent with the Japanese orientation toward long-term growth and profitability. In contrast, the majority of U.S. companies focus on ROI, which encourages and emphasizes short-term profitability. U.S. firms were at one time criticized for their emphasis on short-term profitability, but the more entrenched style of Japanese companies has hindered their ability to adapt to changing times. As a result, many Japanese companies have begun to reevaluate their management philosophy and the corresponding measures of performance. Even so, in a world filled with diversity, managers will likely continue to stress performance measures that reflect a variety of social customs.

*Robert S. Kaplan, "Measures for Manufacturing Excellence," *Emerging Practices in Cost Management* in WG&L Corporate Finance Network Database, 1998.

Now assume that Panther Holding Company has \$50,000 of additional funds available to invest. Because LMD consistently performs at a high level, Panther's corporate management team offers the funds to the LMD manager. The manager believes he could invest the additional \$50,000 at a 19 percent rate of return.

If the LMD manager's evaluation is based solely on ROI, he is likely to reject the additional funding because investing the funds at 19 percent would lower his overall ROI. If the LMD manager's evaluation is based on residual income, however, he is likely to accept the funds because an additional investment at 19 percent would increase his residual income as follows:

$$\text{Operating income} = \$50{,}000 \times .19 = \$9{,}500$$

$$\begin{aligned}\text{Residual income} &= \text{Operating income} - (\text{Operating assets} \times \text{Desired ROI})\\ &= \$9{,}500 - (\$50{,}000 \times .18)\\ &= \$9{,}500 - \$9{,}000\\ &= \$500\end{aligned}$$

Accepting the new project would add \$500 to LMD's residual income. If the manager of LMD is evaluated based on his ability to maximize residual income, he would benefit by investing in any project that returns an ROI in excess of the desired 18 percent. The reduction in LMD's overall ROI does not enter into the decision. The residual income approach solves the problem of suboptomization.

The primary disadvantage of the residual income approach is that it measures performance in absolute dollars. As a result, a manager's residual income may be larger simply because her investment base is larger rather than because her performance is superior.

To illustrate, return to the example where Panther Holding Company has \$50,000 of additional funds to invest. Assume the manager of the Lumber Manufacturing Division (LMD) and the manager of the Furniture Manufacturing Division (FMD) each have investment

REALITY BYTES

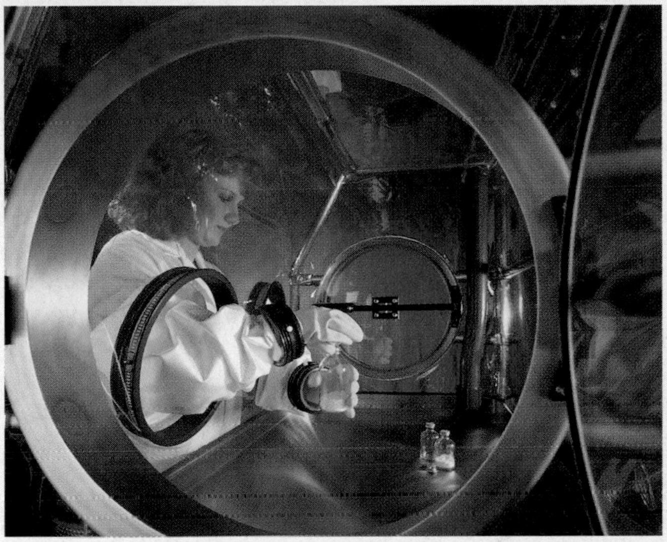

In recent years the residual income approach has been refined to produce a new technique called economic value added (EVA). EVA was developed and trademarked by the consulting firm Stern Stewart & Co. EVA uses the basic formula behind residual income [Operating income 2 (Operating assets 3 Desired ROI)]. EVA, however, uses different definitions of operating income and operating assets. For example, research and development (R&D) costs are classified as operating assets under EVA. In contrast, R&D costs are classified as expenses under traditional accounting. As a result, operating assets and operating income are higher under EVA than they are under the residual income approach. There are more than 100 such differences between EVA and residual income. However, most companies make only a few adjustments when converting from the residual income approach to EVA. Even so, these refinements seem to have had significant benefits. In a recent article in Fortune magazine, Shawn Tully concluded "Managers who run their businesses according to the precepts of EVA have hugely increased the value of their companies. Investors who know about EVA, and know which companies are employing it, have grown rich."

opportunities expected to earn a 19 percent return. Recall that Panther's desired ROI is 18 percent. If corporate headquarters allots $40,000 of the funds to the manager of LMD and $10,000 to the manager of FMD, the increase in residual income earned by each division is as follows:

$$\text{LMD's Residual income} = (\$40{,}000 \times .19) - (\$40{,}000 \times .18) = \$400$$

$$\text{FMD's Residual income} = (\$10{,}000 \times .19) - (\$10{,}000 \times .18) = \$100$$

Does LMD's higher residual income mean LMD's manager is outperforming FMD's manager? No. It means LMD's manager received more operating assets than FMD's manager received.

CHECK YOURSELF 23.3

Young Company's desired rate of return is 14 percent. Christina Fallin, manager of Young's northeastern investment center, controls $12,600,000 of operating assets. During the most recent year, Fallin's district produced operating income of $1,839,600. Determine the amount of the northeastern investment center's residual income.

Answer

$$\text{Residual income} = \text{Operating income} - (\text{Operating assets} \times \text{Desired ROI})$$

$$\text{Residual income} = \$1{,}839{,}600 - (\$12{,}600{,}000 \times 0.14) = \$75{,}600$$

Responsibility Accounting and the Balanced Scorecard

Throughout the text we have discussed many financial measures companies use to evaluate managerial performance. Examples include standard cost systems to evaluate cost center managers; the contribution margin income statement to evaluate profit center managers; and ROI / residual income to evaluate the performance of investment center managers. Many companies may have goals and objectives such as "satisfaction guaranteed" or "we try harder" that are more suitably evaluated using nonfinancial measures. To assess how well they accomplish the full range of their missions, many companies use a *balanced scorecard.*

A **balanced scorecard** includes financial and nonfinancial performance measures. Standard costs, income measures, ROI, and residual income are common financial measures used in a balanced score card. Nonfinancial measures include defect rates, cycle time, on time deliveries, number of new products or innovations, safety measures, and customer satisfaction surveys. Many companies compose their scorecards to highlight leading versus lagging measures. For example, customer satisfaction survey data is a leading indicator of the sales growth which is a lagging measure. The balanced scorecard is a holistic approach to evaluating managerial performance. It is gaining widespread acceptance among world-class companies.

<< A Look Back

The practice of delegating authority and responsibility is referred to as *decentralization.* Clear lines of authority and responsibility are essential in establishing a responsibility accounting system. In a responsibility accounting system, segment managers are held accountable for profits based on the amount of control they have over the profits in their segment.

Responsibility reports are used to compare actual results with budgets. The reports should be simple with variances highlighted to promote the *management by exception* doctrine. Individual managers should be held responsible only for those revenues or costs they control. Each manager should receive only summary information about the performance of the responsibility centers under her supervision.

A *responsibility center* is the point in an organization where control over revenue or expense is located. *Cost centers* are segments that incur costs but do not generate revenues. *Profit centers* incur costs and also generate revenues, producing a measurable profit. *Investment centers* incur costs, generate revenues, and use identifiable capital investments.

One of the primary purposes of responsibility accounting is to evaluate managerial performance. Comparing actual results with standards and budgets and calculating *return on investment* are used for this purpose. Because return on investment uses revenues, expenses, and investment, problems with measuring these parameters must be considered. The return on investment can be analyzed in terms of the margin earned on sales as well as the turnover (asset utilization) during the period. The *residual income approach* is sometimes used to avoid *suboptimization,* which occurs when managers choose to reject investment projects that would benefit their company's ROI but would reduce their investment center's ROI. The residual income approach evaluates managers based on their ability to generate earnings above some targeted level of earnings.

>> A Look Forward

The next chapter expands on the concepts in this chapter. You will see how managers select investment opportunities that will affect their future ROIs. You will learn to apply present value techniques to compute the net present value and the internal rate of return for potential investment opportunities. You will also learn to use less sophisticated analytical techniques such as payback and the unadjusted rate of return.

REALITY BYTES

If a company does business in only one country, the issue of transfer pricing is mostly relevant to performance evaluation of investment centers and their managers. Transfer prices do not affect the overall profit of the company, because the cost that will be recorded as an expense for the company as a whole is the actual cost incurred, not the transfer price. However, the situation can be different if the producing division is in one country and the acquiring division is in another. This difference occurs because income tax rates are not the same in all countries.

Assume the Global Tool Company manufactures a product in South Korea for the equivalent of $10. The product is transferred to another segment that operates in the United States where it is ultimately sold for $18. Now, assume the income tax rate is 40 percent in South Korea and 30 percent in the United States. Ignoring all other costs, what amount of taxes will the company pay if the transfer price is $10? What amount of taxes will the company pay if the transfer price is $18?

If a $10 transfer price is used, then all of the company's $8 per unit profit ($18 − $10) will be recognized in the Unites States. Since the item is assumed to have been "sold" in Korea at an amount equal to its production cost, there will be no profit for the Korean division of the company ($10 − $10 = $0). The United States division will pay $2.40 in taxes ($8 × .30 = $2.40). Conversely, if the transfer price is $18, then all of the profit will be reported in Korea, and $3.20 per unit of taxes will be paid ($8 × .40 = $3.20).

The Internal Revenue Service has rules to prevent companies from setting transfer prices simply for the purpose of reducing taxes, but various companies have been accused of such practices over the years. It is often impossible to prove exactly what the best transfer price should be. Even though the company in our hypothetical example could not get away with such extreme transfer prices as $10 or $18, it might try to set the price a bit lower than it should be in order to shift more profit to the segment in the United States where the assumed tax rate was lower. Regarding the use of transfer prices to reduce taxes, an article in *BusinessWeek* noted, "Last year, a General Accounting Office study reported that, from 1989 to 1995, an outright majority of corporations, both U.S. and foreign-controlled, paid zero U.S. income taxes."*

*"The Creative Economy," *BusinessWeek,* August 28, 2000, p. 76.

APPENDIX

Transfer Pricing

LO 8

Describe the three common approaches used to establish transfer prices. (Appendix)

In vertically integrated companies, one division commonly sells goods or services to another division. For example, in the case of Panther Holding Company (Exhibit 23.1), the Lumber Manufacturing Division may sell lumber to the Home Building and Furniture Manufacturing Divisions. When such intercompany sales occur, the price to charge is likely to become a heated issue.

In a decentralized organization, each division is likely to be defined as an investment center. Division managers are held responsible for profitability. When goods are transferred internally, the sales price charged by the selling division becomes a cost to the buying division. The amount of profit included in the **transfer price** will increase the selling division's earnings and decrease the purchasing division's earnings (via increased expenses). The selling division benefits from getting the highest possible price; the purchasing division seeks the lowest possible price. When managers are competitively

EXHIBIT 23.4

What Companies Actually Use As Transfer Prices

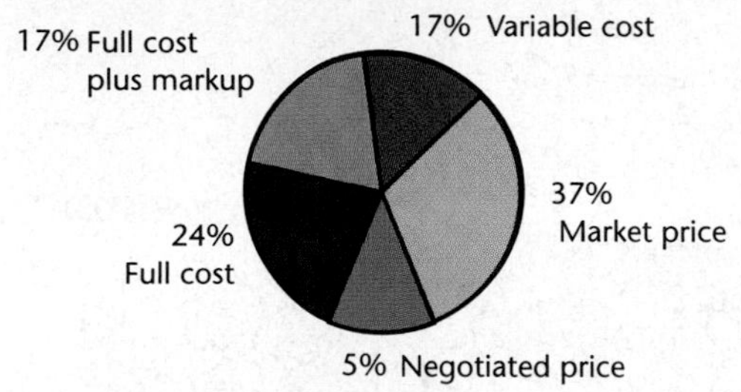

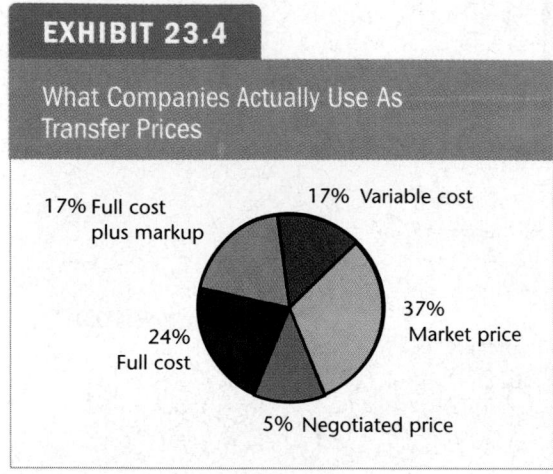

Source: R. Tang, "Transfer Pricing in the 1990s," *Management Accounting*, February 1992, pp. 22–26.

evaluated based on profitability measures, the transfer price is the subject of considerable controversy.

Companies use three common approaches to establish transfer prices: (1) price based on market forces; (2) price based on negotiation; and (3) price based on cost. Exhibit 23.4 shows some specific measures and the frequency of their use.

Market-Based Transfer Prices

The preferred method for establishing transfer prices is to base them on some form of competitive market price. Ideally, selling divisions should be authorized to sell merchandise to outsiders as well as, or in preference to, other divisions. Similarly, purchasing divisions should have the option to buy goods from outsiders if they are able to obtain favorable prices. However, both selling and purchasing divisions would be motivated to deal with each other because of savings in selling, administrative, and transportation costs that arise as a natural result of internal transactions.

Market-based transfer prices are preferable because they promote efficiency and fairness. Market forces coupled with the responsibility for profitability motivate managers to use their resources effectively. For example, Jerry Lowe, the manager of the lumber division, may stop producing the high-quality boards the furniture division uses if he finds it is more profitable to produce low-quality lumber. The furniture division can buy its needed material from outside companies that have chosen to operate in the less-profitable, high-quality market sector. The company as a whole benefits from Mr. Lowe's insight. An additional advantage of using market prices is the sense of fairness associated with them. It is difficult for a manager to complain that the price she is being charged is too high when she has the opportunity to seek a lower price elsewhere. The natural justice of the competitive marketplace is firmly implanted in the psyche of most modern managers.

Negotiated Transfer Prices

In many instances, a necessary product is not available from outside companies or the market price may not be in the best interest of the company as a whole. Sometimes a division makes a unique product that only one of its company's other divisions uses; no external market price is available to use as a base for determining the transfer price. Other times, market-based transfer prices may lead to suboptimization, discussed earlier.

Consider the case of Garms Industries. It operates several relatively autonomous divisions. One division, TrueTrust Motors, Inc., makes small electric motors for use in appliances such as refrigerators, washing machines, and fans. Another Garms division, CleanCo, makes and sells approximately 30,000 vacuum cleaners per year. CleanCo currently purchases the motors used in its vacuums from a company that is not part of Garms Industries. The president of Garms asked the TrueTrust division manager to establish a price at which it could make and sell motors to CleanCo. The manager submitted the following cost and price data.

Variable (unit-level) costs	$45
Per unit fixed cost at a volume of 30,000 units	15
Allocated corporate-level facility-sustaining costs	20
Total cost	$80

TrueTrust has enough excess capacity that its existing business will not be affected by a decision to make motors for CleanCo. However, TrueTrust would be required to buy additional equipment and hire a supervisor to make the motors that CleanCo requires.

The TrueTrust manager added a profit margin of $10 per unit and offered to provide motors to CleanCo at a price of $90 per unit. When the offer was presented to the CleanCo division manager, she rejected it. Her division was currently buying motors in the open market for $70 each. Competitive pressures in the vacuum cleaner market would not permit an increase in the sales price of her product. Accepting TrueTrust's offer would significantly increase CleanCo's costs and reduce the division's profitability.

After studying the cost data, Garms' president concluded the company as a whole would suffer from suboptimization if CleanCo were to continue purchasing motors from a third-party vendor. He noted that the allocated corporate-level facility-sustaining costs were not relevant to the transfer pricing decision because they would be incurred regardless of whether TrueTrust made the motors for CleanCo. He recognized that both the variable and fixed costs were relevant because they could be avoided if TrueTrust did not make the motors. Since TrueTrust's avoidable cost of $60 ($45 variable cost + $15 fixed cost) per unit was below the $70 price per unit that CleanCo was currently paying, Garms would save $10 per motor, thereby increasing overall company profitability by $300,000 ($10 cost savings per unit × 30,000 units). The president established a reasonable range for a negotiated transfer price.

If the market price were less than the avoidable cost of production, the supplying division (TrueTrust) and the company as a whole (Garms) would be better off to buy the product than to make it. It would therefore be unreasonable to expect TrueTrust to sell a product for less than its avoidable cost of production, thereby establishing the avoidable cost as the bottom point of the reasonable range for the transfer price. On the other hand, it would be unreasonable to expect an acquiring division (CleanCo) to pay more than the price it is currently paying for motors. As a result, the market price becomes the top point of the reasonable range for the transfer price. The reasonable transfer price range can be expressed as follows:

$$\text{Market price} \geqslant \text{Reasonable transfer price} \geqslant \text{Avoidable product cost}$$

In the case of Garms Industries, the reasonable range of the transfer price for vacuum cleaner motors is between the market price of $70 per unit and the avoidable production cost of $60.[1] Any transfer price within this range would benefit both divisions and the company as a whole. Garms' president encouraged the two division managers to negotiate a transfer price within the reasonable range that would satisfy both parties.

Under the right set of circumstances, a **negotiated transfer price** can be more beneficial than a market-based transfer price. Allowing the managers involved to agree to a negotiated price preserves the notion of fairness. The element of profit remains intact and the evaluation concepts discussed in this chapter can be applied. Negotiated prices may offer many of the same advantages as market prices. They should be the first alternative when a company is unable to use market-based transfer prices.

Suppose the two division managers cannot agree on a negotiated transfer price. Should the president of Garms Industries establish a reasonable price and force the managers to accept it? There is no definitive answer to this question. However, most senior-level executives recognize the motivational importance of maintaining autonomy in a decentralized organization. So long as the negative consequences are not disastrous, division managers are usually permitted to exercise their own judgment. In other words, the long-term benefits derived from autonomous management outweigh the short-term disadvantages of suboptimization.

Cost-Based Transfer Prices

The least desirable transfer price option is a **cost-based transfer price.** To use cost, it must first be determined. Some companies base the transfer price on *variable cost* (a proxy for avoidable cost). Other companies use *full cost* (variable cost plus an allocated portion of fixed cost) as the transfer price. In either case, basing transfer prices on cost removes the profit motive. Without profitability as a goal, the incentive to control cost is diminished. One department's inefficiency is simply passed on to the next department. The result is low companywide profitability. Despite this potential detrimental effect, many companies base transfer prices on cost because cost represents an objective number that is available. When a company uses cost-based transfer prices, *it should use standard rather than actual costs.* Departments will therefore at least be responsible for the variances they generate which will encourage some degree of cost control.

[1] This discussion assumes the supplying division (TrueTrust) has excess capacity. When the supplying division is operating at full capacity and has external buyers, the minimum price for the reasonable transfer price range would include not only the avoidable cost but also an opportunity cost. An opportunity cost exists when the supplying division must forgo the opportunity to profit from sales it could otherwise make to external buyers. On the other hand, if the supplying division has enough capacity to fill both existing orders and the additional orders on which the transfer price is negotiated, the opportunity cost is zero. In other words, the supplying division does not have to give up anything to accept an order from another division. A full discussion of opportunity cost is complex. It is covered in more advanced courses.

SELF-STUDY REVIEW PROBLEM

The following financial statements apply to Hola Division, one of three investment centers operated by Costa Corporation. Costa Corporation has a desired rate of return of 15 percent. Costa Corporation Headquarters has $80,000 of additional operating assets to assign to the investment centers.

HOLA DIVISION
Income Statement
For the Year Ended December 31, 2006

Sales Revenue	$78,695
Cost of Goods Sold	(50,810)
Gross Margin	27,885
Operating Expenses	
Selling Expenses	(1,200)
Depreciation Expense	(1,125)
Operating Income	25,560
Nonoperating Expense	
Loss on Sale of Land	(3,200)
Net Income	$22,360

[redacted]

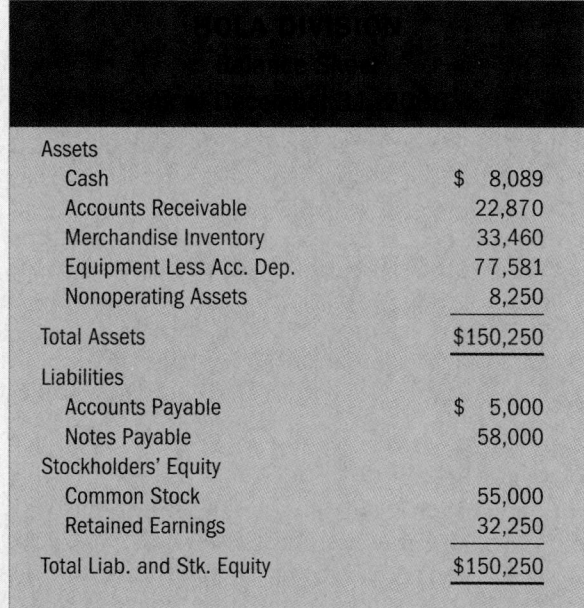

Assets	
Cash	$ 8,089
Accounts Receivable	22,870
Merchandise Inventory	33,460
Equipment Less Acc. Dep.	77,581
Nonoperating Assets	8,250
Total Assets	$150,250
Liabilities	
Accounts Payable	$ 5,000
Notes Payable	58,000
Stockholders' Equity	
Common Stock	55,000
Retained Earnings	32,250
Total Liab. and Stk. Equity	$150,250

Required:

a. Should Costa use operating income or net income to determine the rate of return (ROI) for the Hola investment center? Explain.

b. Should Costa use operating assets or total assets to determine the ROI for the Hola investment center? Explain.

c. Calculate the ROI for Hola.

d. The manager of the Hola division has an opportunity to invest the funds at an ROI of 17 percent. The other two divisions have investment opportunities that yield only 16 percent. The manager of Hola rejects the additional funding. Why would the manager of Hola reject the funds under these circumstances?

e. Calculate the residual income from the investment opportunity available to Hola and explain how residual income could be used to encourage the manager to accept the additional funds.

Solution to Requirement *a*

Costa should use operating income because net income frequently includes items over which management has no control, such as the loss on sale of land.

Solution to Requirement *b*

Costa should use operating assets because total assets frequently includes items over which management has no control, such as assets not currently in use.

Solution to Requirement *c*

ROI = Operating Income/Operating Assets = $25,560/$142,000 = 18%

Solution to Requirement d

Since the rate of return on the investment opportunity (17 percent) is below the Hola's current ROI (18 percent), accepting the opportunity would decrease Hola's average ROI, which would have a negative effect on the manager's performance evaluation. While it is to the advantage of the company as a whole for Hola to accept the investment opportunity, it will reflect negatively on the manager to do so. This phenomenon is called *suboptimization.*

Solution to Requirement *e*

Operating income from the investment opportunity is $13,600 ($80,000 × .17)

Residual income = Operating income − (Operating assets × Desired ROI)

Residual income = $13,600 − ($80,000 × .15)

Residual income = $13,600 − $12,000

Residual income = $1,600

Since the investment opportunity would increase Hola's residual income, the acceptance of the opportunity would improve the manager's performance evaluation, thereby motivating the manager to accept it.

KEY TERMS

balanced scorecard 1122
controllability concept 1113
cost-based transfer price 1125
cost center 1111
decentralization 1110
investment center 1111
management by exception 1111
margin 1117
market-based transfer price 1124
negotiated transfer price 1125
profit center 1111
residual income 1119
responsibility accounting 1110
responsibility center 1111
responsibility reports 1111
return on investment 1115
suboptimization 1119
transfer price 1123
turnover 1117

QUESTIONS

1. Pam Kelly says she has no faith in budgets. Her company, Kelly Manufacturing Corporation, spent thousands of dollars to install a sophisticated budget system. One year later the company's expenses are still out of control. She believes budgets simply do not work. How would you respond to Ms. Kelly's beliefs?
2. All travel expenses incurred by Pure Water Pump Corporation are reported only to John Daniels, the company president. Pure Water is a multinational company with five divisions. Are travel expenses reported following the responsibility accounting concept? Explain.
3. What are five potential advantages of decentralization?
4. Who receives responsibility reports? What do the reports include?
5. How does the concept of predominant as opposed to that of absolute control apply to responsibility accounting?
6. How do responsibility reports promote the management by exception doctrine?
7. What is a responsibility center?
8. What are the three types of responsibility centers? Explain how each differs from the others.
9. Carmen Douglas claims that her company's performance evaluation system is unfair. Her company uses return on investment (ROI) to evaluate performance. Ms. Douglas says that even though her

ROI is lower than another manager's, her performance is far superior. Is it possible that Ms. Douglas is correct? Explain your position.

10. What two factors affect the computation of return on investment?

11. What three ways can a manager increase the return on investment?

12. How can a residual income approach to performance evaluation reduce the likelihood of suboptimization?

13. Is it true that the manager with the highest residual income is always the best performer?

14. Why are transfer prices important to managers who are evaluated based on profitability criteria?

15. What are three approaches to establishing transfer prices? List the most desirable approach first and the least desirable last.

16. If cost is the basis for transfer pricing, should actual or standard cost be used? Why?

EXERCISES—SERIES A

All Exercises in Series A are available with McGraw-Hill's Homework Manager.

L.O. 1

Exercise 23-1A *Organization chart and responsibilities*

The production manager is responsible for the assembly, cleaning, and finishing departments. The executive vice president reports directly to the president but is responsible for the activities of the production department, the finance department, and the sales department. The sales manager is responsible for the advertising department.

Required

Arrange this information into an organization chart and indicate the responsibility levels involved.

L.O. 5

Exercise 23-2A *Responsibility report*

Grover Department Store is divided into three major departments: Men's Clothing, Women's Clothing, and Home Furnishings. Each of these three departments is supervised by a manager who reports to the general manager. The departments are subdivided into different sections managed by floor supervisors. The Home Furnishings Department has three floor supervisors, one for furniture, one for lamps, and one for housewares. The following items were included in the company's most recent responsibility report.

Travel expenses for the housewares buyer
Seasonal decorations for the furniture section
Revenues for the Home Furnishings Department
Administrative expenses for the Men's Clothing Department
Utility cost allocated to the Home Furnishings Department
Cost of part-time holiday season help for the Women's Department
Delivery expenses for furniture purchases
Salaries for the sales staff in the lamp section
Storewide revenues
Salary of the general manager
Salary of the Men's Clothing Department manager
Allocated companywide advertising expense
Depreciation on the facility

Required

Which items are likely to be the responsibility of the Home Furnishings Department manager?

L.O. 1, 5

Exercise 23-3A *Organization chart and controllable costs*

Jewel Company has employees with the following job titles.

President of the company	Controller
Vice president of marketing	Vice president of manufacturing
Product manager	Treasurer

Regional sales manager
Personnel manager
Cashier
Vice president of finance
Fringe benefits manager
Board of directors
Production supervisors
Vice president of administration
Sales office manager

Required

a. Design an organization chart using these job titles.

b. Identify some possible controllable costs for the person holding each job title.

Exercise 23-4A *Income statement for internal use*

L.O. 1, 3

Geis Company has provided the following 2005 data.

Budget	
Sales	$408,000
Variable product costs	164,000
Variable selling expense	48,000
Other variable expenses	4,000
Fixed product costs	16,800
Fixed selling expense	25,200
Other fixed expenses	2,400
Interest expense	900
Variances	
Sales	8,800 U
Variable product costs	4,000 F
Variable selling expense	2,400 U
Other variable expenses	1,200 U
Fixed product costs	240 F
Fixed selling expense	400 F
Other fixed expenses	160 U
Interest expense	100 F

Required

Prepare in good form a budgeted and actual income statement for internal use. Separate operating income from net income in the statements.

Exercise 23-5A *Evaluating a cost center including flexible budgeting concepts*

L.O. 1, 3

Herrera Medical Equipment Company makes a blood pressure measuring kit. Cedric Major is the production manager. The production department's static budget and actual results for 2005 follow.

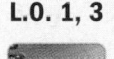

	Static Budget	Actual Results
	20,000 kits	21,000 kits
Direct materials	$150,000	$161,700
Direct labor	135,000	138,600
Variable manufacturing overhead	35,000	44,600
Total variable costs	320,000	344,900
Fixed manufacturing cost	180,000	178,000
Total manufacturing cost	$500,000	$522,900

Required

a. Convert the static budget into a flexible budget.

b. Use the flexible budget to evaluate Mr. Major's performance.

c. Explain why Mr. Major's performance evaluation does not include sales revenue and net income.

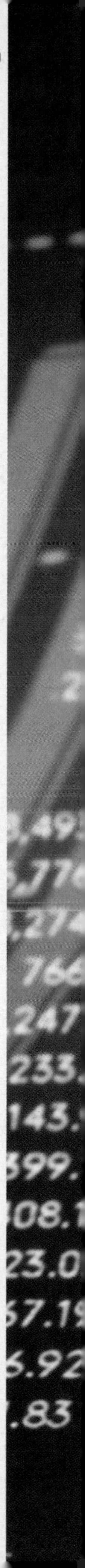

L.O. 2, 3

Exercise 23-6A *Evaluating a profit center*

Shelia Parham, the president of Best Toys Corporation, is trying to determine this year's pay raises for the store managers. Best Toys has seven stores in the southwestern United States. Corporate headquarters purchases all toys from different manufacturers globally and distributes them to individual stores. Additionally, headquarters makes decisions regarding location and size of stores. These practices allow Best Toys to receive volume discounts from vendors and to implement coherent marketing strategies. Within a set of general guidelines, store managers have the flexibility to adjust product prices and hire local employees. Ms. Parham is considering three possible performance measures for evaluating the individual stores: cost of goods sold, return on sales (net income divided by sales), and return on investment.

Required

a. Using the concept of controllability, advise Ms. Parham about the best performance measure.

b. Explain how a balanced scorecard can be used to help Ms. Parham.

L.O. 6

Exercise 23-7A *Return on investment*

An investment center of Milton Corporation shows an operating income of $7,200 on total operating assets of $30,000.

Required

Compute the return on investment.

L.O. 6

Exercise 23-8A *Return on investment*

Giddens Company calculated its return on investment as 15 percent. Sales are now $180,000, and the amount of total operating assets is $300,000.

Required

a. If expenses are reduced by $18,000 and sales remain unchanged, what return on investment will result?

b. If both sales and expenses cannot be changed, what change in the amount of operating assets is required to achieve the same result?

L.O. 7

Exercise 23-9A *Residual income*

Tyler Corporation has a desired rate of return of 10 percent. Andy Tan is in charge of one of Tyler's three investment centers. His center controlled operating assets of $3,000,000 that were used to earn $390,000 of operating income.

Required

Compute Mr. Tan's residual income.

L.O. 7

Exercise 23-10A *Residual income*

Brannon Cough Drops operates two divisions. The following information pertains to each division for 2005.

	Division A	Division B
Sales	$180,000	$60,000
Operating income	$ 18,000	$ 9,600
Average operating assets	$ 72,000	$48,000
Company's desired rate of return	20%	20%

Required

a. Compute each division's residual income.

b. Which division increased the company's profitability more?

L.O. 6, 7

Exercise 23-11A *Return on investment and residual income*

Required

Supply the missing information in the following table for Haley Company.

Sales	$300,000
ROI	?
Operating assets	?
Operating income	?
Turnover	2
Residual income	?
Margin	0.10
Desired rate of return	18%

Exercise 23-12A *Comparing return on investment with residual income* — L.O. 6, 7

The Spokane Division of Cascade Inc. has a current ROI of 20 percent. The company target ROI is 15 percent. The Spokane Division has an opportunity to invest $4,000,000 at 18 percent but is reluctant to do so because its ROI will fall to 19.2 percent. The present investment base for the division is $6,000,000.

Required

Demonstrate how Cascade can motivate the Spokane Division to make the investment by using the residual income method.

Appendix

Exercise 23-13A *Transfer pricing* — L.O. 8

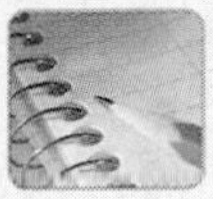

Kader Company has two divisions, A and B. Division A manufactures 8,000 units of product per month. The cost per unit is calculated as follows.

Variable costs	$ 8
Fixed costs	24
Total cost	$32

Division B uses the product created by Division A. No outside market for Division A's product exists. The fixed costs incurred by Division A are allocated headquarters-level facility-sustaining costs. The manager of Division A suggests that the product be transferred to Division B at a price of at least $32 per unit. The manager of Division B argues that the same product can be purchased from another company for $19 per unit and requests permission to do so.

Required

a. Should Kader allow the manager of Division B to purchase the product from the outside company for $19 per unit? Explain.

b. Assume you are the president of the company. Write a brief paragraph recommending a resolution of the conflict between the two divisional managers.

Exercise 23-14A *Transfer pricing and avoidable cost* — L.O. 8

The Tire Division of Durable Tires Company (DTC) produces a radial all-purpose tire for trucks that it sells wholesale to automotive manufacturers. Per unit sales and cost data for this tire follow.

Selling price	$54
Unit-level variable cost	$36
Corporate-level fixed cost	$15
Manufacturing capacity	30,000 units
Average sales	25,000 units

DTC also has a Trucking Division that provides delivery service for outside independent businesses as well as divisions of DTC. The Trucking Division, which uses approximately 4,000 tires a year, presently buys tires for its trucks from an outside supplier for $51 per tire.

Required

Recommend a transfer price range for the truck tires that would be profitable for both divisions if the Trucking Division purchased the tires internally. Assume that both divisions operate as investment centers.

L.O. 8

Exercise 23-15A *Transfer pricing and fixed cost per unit*

The Saginaw Parts Division of Sims Company plans to set up a facility with the capacity to make 10,000 units annually of an electronic computer part. The avoidable cost of making the part is as follows.

Costs	Total	Cost per Unit
Variable cost	$300,000	$30
Fixed cost	80,000	8 (at capacity)

Required

a. Assume that Sims' Borden Division is currently purchasing 6,000 of the electronic parts each year from an outside supplier at a market price of $50. What would be the financial consequence to Sims if the Saginaw Parts Division makes the part and sells it to the Borden Division? What range of transfer prices would increase the financial performance of both divisions?

b. Suppose that the Borden Division increases production so that it could use 10,000 units of the part made by the Saginaw Parts Division. How would the change in volume affect the range of transfer prices that would financially benefit both divisions?

PROBLEMS—SERIES A

All Problems in Series A are available with McGraw-Hill's Homework Manager.

L.O. 5

Problem 23-16A *Determining controllable costs*

John Crew is the manager of the production department of Strong Corporation. Strong incurred the following costs during 2005.

Production department supplies	$ 8,000
Administrative salaries	300,000
Production wages	652,000
Materials used	529,200
Depreciation on manufacturing equipment	361,600
Corporate-level rental expense	240,000
Property taxes	68,600
Sales salaries	286,800

Required

Prepare a list of expenditures that Mr. Crew controls.

L.O. 3, 5

Problem 23-17A *Controllability, responsibility, and balanced scorecard*

Sally Voigt manages the production division of Yates Corporation. Ms. Voigt's responsibility report for the month of August follows.

	Budget	Actual	Variance	
Controllable costs				
Raw materials	$ 60,000	$ 75,000	$15,000	U
Labor	30,000	41,400	11,400	U
Maintenance	6,000	7,200	1,200	U
Supplies	5,100	3,600	1,500	F
Total	$101,100	$127,200	$26,100	U

The budget had called for 7,500 pounds of raw materials at $8 per pound, and 7,500 pounds were used during August; however, the purchasing department paid $10 per pound for the materials. The wage rate used to establish the budget was $30 per hour. On August 1, however, it increased to $36 as the result of an inflation index provision in the union contract. Furthermore, the purchasing department did not provide the materials needed in accordance with the production schedule, which forced Ms. Voigt to use 100 hours of overtime at a $54 rate. The projected 1,000 hours of labor in the budget would have been sufficient had it not been for the 100 hours of overtime. In other words, 1,100 hours of labor were used in August.

Required

a. When confronted with the unfavorable variances in her responsibility report, Ms. Voigt argued that the report was unfair because it held her accountable for materials and labor variances that she did *not* control. Is she correct? Comment specifically on the materials and labor variances.

b. Prepare a responsibility report that reflects the cost items that Ms. Voigt controlled during August.

c. Will the changes in the revised responsibility report require corresponding changes in the financial statements? Explain.

d. Explain how a balanced scorecard may be used to improve the performance evaluation.

Problem 23-18A *Performance reports and evaluation*

L.O. 3, 4, 5

eXcel

mhhe.com/edmonds2007

CHECK FIGURE

a. Total actual controllable costs: $407,160

Hester Corporation has four divisions: the assembly division, the processing division, the machining division, and the packing division. All four divisions are under the control of the vice president of manufacturing. Each division has a manager and several departments that are directed by supervisors. The chain of command runs downward from vice president to division manager to supervisor. The processing division is composed of the paint and finishing departments. The May responsibility reports for the supervisors of these departments follow.

	Budgeted*	Actual	Variance	
Paint Department				
Controllable costs				
Raw materials	$28,800	$ 30,000	$1,200	U
Labor	60,000	66,000	6,000	U
Repairs	4,800	3,840	960	F
Maintenance	2,400	2,280	120	F
Total	$96,000	$102,120	$6,120	U
Finishing Department				
Controllable costs				
Raw materials	$22,800	$ 22,560	$ 240	F
Labor	43,200	39,600	3,600	F
Repairs	2,880	3,240	360	U
Maintenance	1,680	2,040	360	U
Total	$70,560	$ 67,440	$3,120	F

*Hester uses flexible budgets for performance evaluation.

Other pertinent cost data for May follow.

	Budgeted*	Actual
Cost data of other divisions		
Assembly	$324,000	$318,240
Machining	282,000	288,480
Packing	421,440	412,920
Other costs associated with		
Processing division manager	240,000	237,600
Vice president of manufacturing	132,000	137,040

*Hester uses flexible budgets for performance evaluation.

Required

a. Prepare a responsibility report for the manager of the processing division.

b. Prepare a responsibility report for the vice president of manufacturing.
c. Explain where the $6,000 unfavorable labor variance in the paint department supervisor's report is included in the vice president's report.
d. Based on the responsibility report prepared in Requirement *a*, explain where the processing division manager should concentrate his attention.

Problem 23-19A ***Different types of responsibility centers***

L.O. 2

First National Bank is a large municipal bank with several branch offices. The bank's computer department handles all data processing for bank operations. In addition, the bank sells the computer department's expertise in systems development and excess machine time to several small business firms, serving them as a service bureau.

The bank currently treats the computer department as a cost center. The manager of the computer department prepares a cost budget annually for senior bank officials to approve. Monthly operating reports compare actual and budgeted expenses. Revenues from the department's service bureau activities are treated as other income by the bank and are not reflected on the computer department's operating reports. The costs of serving these clients are included in the computer department reports, however.

The manager of the computer department has proposed that bank management convert the computer department to a profit or investment center.

Required

a. Describe the characteristics that differentiate a cost center, a profit center, and an investment center from each other.
b. Would the manager of the computer department be likely to conduct the operations of the department differently if the department were classified as a profit center or an investment center rather than as a cost center? Explain.

Problem 23-20A ***Comparing return on investment and residual income***

L.O. 6, 7

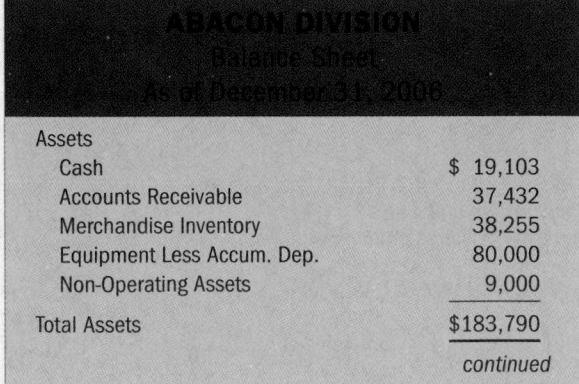

CHECK FIGURE
c. 16.60%

Hannant Corporation operates three investment centers. The following financial statements apply to the investment center named Abacon Division.

ABACON DIVISION
Income Statement
For the Year Ended December 31, 2006

Sales Revenue	$91,285
Cost of Goods Sold	(59,620)
Gross Margin	31,665
Operating Expenses	
Selling Expenses	(1,445)
Depreciation Expense	(1,200)
Operating Income	29,020
Nonoperating Expense	
Gain on Sale of Land	4,180
Net Income	$33,200

ABACON DIVISION
Balance Sheet
As of December 31, 2006

Assets	
Cash	$ 19,103
Accounts Receivable	37,432
Merchandise Inventory	38,255
Equipment Less Accum. Dep.	80,000
Non-Operating Assets	9,000
Total Assets	$183,790

continued

Liabilities	
Accounts Payable	$ 7,000
Notes Payable	65,700
Stockholders' Equity	
Common Stock	70,000
Retained Earnings	41,090
Total Liab. and Stk. Equity	$183,790

Required

a. Should operating income or net income be used to determine the rate of return (ROI) for the Abacon investment center? Explain your answer.
b. Should operating assets or total assets be used to determine the ROI for the Abacon investment center? Explain your answer.
c. Calculate the ROI for Abacon.
d. Hannant has a desired ROI of 12 percent. Headquarters has $100,000 of funds to assign its investment centers. The manager of the Abacon division has an opportunity to invest the funds at an ROI of 15 percent. The other two divisions have investment opportunities that yield only 14 percent. Even so, the manager of Abacon rejects the additional funding. Explain why the manager of Abacon would reject the funds under these circumstances.
e. Explain how residual income could be used to encourage the manager to accept the additional funds.

Problem 23-21A *Return on investment*

L.O. 6

excel

mhhe.com/edmonds2007

Tipton Corporation's balance sheet indicates that the company has $300,000 invested in operating assets. During 2006, Tipton earned operating income of $45,000 on $600,000 of sales.

CHECK FIGURES

c. 15%

d. (3) 18.75%

Required

a. Compute Tipton's margin for 2006.
b. Compute Tipton's turnover for 2006.
c. Compute Tipton's return on investment for 2006.
d. Recompute Tipton's ROI under each of the following independent assumptions.
   (1) Sales increase from $600,000 to $750,000, thereby resulting in an increase in operating income from $45,000 to $60,000.
   (2) Sales remain constant, but Tipton reduces expenses resulting in an increase in operating income from $45,000 to $48,000.
   (3) Tipton is able to reduce its invested capital from $300,000 to $240,000 without affecting operating income.

Problem 23-22A *Comparing return on investment and residual income*

L.O. 6, 7

The manager of the Cranston Division of Wynn Manufacturing Corporation is currently producing a 20 percent return on invested capital. Wynn's desired rate of return is 16 percent. The Cranston Division has $6,000,000 of capital invested in operating assets and access to additional funds as needed. The manager is considering a new investment in operating assets that will require a $1,500,000 capital commitment and promises an 18 percent return.

CHECK FIGURES

b. The ROI would decline to 19.60%.

c. RI would increase by $30,000.

Required

a. Would it be advantageous for Wynn Manufacturing Corporation if the Cranston Division makes the investment under consideration?
b. What effect would the proposed investment have on the Cranston Division's return on investment? Show computations.
c. What effect would the proposed investment have on the Cranston Division's residual income? Show computations.
d. Would return on investment or residual income be the better performance measure for the Cranston Division's manager? Explain.

Appendix

Problem 23-23A *Transfer pricing*

L.O. 8

Rankin Radio Corporation is a subsidiary of Gibon Companies. Rankin makes car radios that it sells to retail outlets. It purchases speakers for the radios from outside suppliers for $30 each. Recently,

CHECK FIGURE
The price should range between $18 and $30.

Gibon acquired the Levine Speaker Corporation, which makes car radio speakers that it sells to manufacturers. Levine produces and sells approximately 200,000 speakers per year which represents 70 percent of its operating capacity. At the present volume of activity, each speaker costs $26 to produce. This cost consists of a $18 variable cost component and an $8 fixed cost component. Levine sells the speakers for $32 each. The managers of Rankin and Levine have been asked to consider using Levine's excess capacity to supply Rankin with some of the speakers that it currently purchases from unrelated companies. Both managers are evaluated based on return on investment. Levine's manager suggests that the speakers be supplied at a transfer price of $32 each (the current selling price). On the other hand, Rankin's manager suggests a $26 transfer price, noting that this amount covers total cost and provides Levine a healthy contribution margin.

Required

a. What transfer price would you recommend?

b. Discuss the effect of the intercompany sales on each manager's return on investment.

c. Should Levine be required to use more than excess capacity to provide speakers to Rankin? In other words, should it sell to Rankin some of the 200,000 units that it is currently selling to unrelated companies? Why or why not?

EXERCISES—SERIES B

L.O. 1

Exercise 23-1B *Organizational chart and responsibilities*

Yesterday Wesson Corporation's board of directors appointed Cheryl Buford as the new president and chief executive officer. This morning, Ms. Buford presented to the board a list of her management team members. The vice presidents are Bill Riggins, regional operations; Dan Nelson, research and development; and Carol Mercer, chief financial officer. Reporting to Mr. Riggins are the directors of American, European, and Asian operations. Reporting to Mr. Nelson are the directors of the Houston, Seattle, and Charlotte laboratories. Reporting to Ms. Mercer are the controller and the treasurer.

Required

Arrange the preceding information into an organization chart and indicate the responsibility levels involved.

L.O. 5

Exercise 23-2B *Responsibility report*

Wesson Corporation divides its operations into three regions: American, European, and Asian. The following items appear in the company's responsibility report.

European director's salary
Revenues of the French branch
Office expenses of the Japanese branch
Corporation president's salary
Asian director's salary
Revenues of the Taiwanese branch
Revenues of the British branch
Office expenses of the French branch
Revenues of the U.S. branch
Administrative expenses of the corporate headquarters
Office expenses of the Taiwanese branch
Office expenses of the Canadian branch
Revenues of the Japanese branch
Revenues of the Canadian branch
Office expenses of the British branch
Office expenses of the U.S. branch
American director's salary

Required

Which items should Wesson include in the responsibility report for the director of Asian operations?

Exercise 23-3B *Organizational chart and controllable cost*

L.O. 1, 5

Dan Nelson, Wesson Corporation vice president of research and development, has overall responsibility for employees with the following positions:

Directors of the Houston, Seattle, and Charlotte laboratories
Senior researchers reporting to laboratory directors
A personnel manager in each laboratory
An accounting manager in each laboratory
Research assistants working for senior researchers
Recruiters reporting to a personnel manager
Bookkeepers reporting to an accounting manager

Required

a. Design an organization chart using these job positions.

b. Identify some possible controllable costs for persons holding each of the job positions.

Exercise 23-4B *Income statement for internal use*

L.O. 1, 3

Saunders Company has provided the following data for 2006:

Budget	
Sales	$400,000
Variable product costs	120,000
Variable selling expense	39,000
Other variable expenses	8,000
Fixed product costs	56,000
Fixed selling expense	21,000
Other fixed expenses	2,000
Interest expense	1,000
Actual results	
Sales	$414,000
Variable product costs	122,000
Variable selling expense	42,000
Other variable expenses	7,000
Fixed product costs	60,000
Fixed selling expense	19,200
Other fixed expenses	10,000
Interest expense	1,050

Required

a. Prepare in good form a budgeted and actual income statement for internal use. Separate operating income from net income in the statements.

b. Calculate variances and identify them as favorable (F) or unfavorable (U).

Exercise 23-5B *Evaluating a cost center (including flexible budgeting concepts)*

L.O. 1

Edwin Wingo, president of Wingo Door Products Company, is evaluating the performance of Tim Shirley, the plant manager, for 2005, the last fiscal year. Mr. Wingo is concerned that production costs exceeded budget by over $17,000. He has available the 2005 static budget for the production plant, as well as the actual results, both of which follow:

	Static Budget	Actual Results
	5,000 Doors	5,250 Doors
Direct materials	$200,000	$204,750
Direct labor	85,000	99,750
Variable manufacturing overhead	35,000	34,650
Total variable costs	320,000	339,150
Fixed manufacturing overhead	180,000	178,000
Total manufacturing cost	$500,000	$517,150

Required

a. Convert the static budget into a flexible budget.

b. Use the flexible budget to evaluate Mr. Shirley's performance.

c. Explain why Mr. Shirley's performance evaluation doesn't include sales revenue and net income.

L.O. 2, 5

Exercise 23-6B *Evaluating a profit center*

Jean Reeder, president of World Travel Company, a travel agency, is seeking a method of evaluating her seven branches. Each branch vice president is authorized to hire employees and devise competitive strategies for the branch territory. Ms. Reeder wonders which of the following three different measures would be most suitable: return on investment, operating income, or return on sales (operating income divided by sales).

Required

a. Using the concept of controllability, advise Ms. Reeder about the best performance measure.

b. Explain how a balanced scorecard can be used for Ms. Reeder.

L.O. 7

Exercise 23-7B *Computing return on investment*

An Imhof Corporation investment center shows an operating income of $80,000 and an investment in operating assets of $640,000.

Required

Compute the return on investment.

L.O. 6

Exercise 23-8B *Return on investment*

With annual sales of $5,000,000 and operating assets of $2,500,000, Gibbon Company achieved a 10 percent ROI.

Required

a. If Gibbon reduces expenses by $50,000 and sales remain unchanged, what ROI will result?

b. If Gibbon cannot change either sales or expenses, what change in the investment base is required to achieve the same result you calculated for Requirement *a*?

L.O. 7

Exercise 23-9B *Computing residual income*

Niblett Corporation's desired rate of return is 15 percent. North Division, one of Niblett's five investment centers, earned an operating income of $4,800,000 last year. The division controlled $30,000,000 of operational assets.

Required

Compute North Division's residual income.

L.O. 7

Exercise 23-10B *Computing residual income*

Quick Oil Change operates two divisions. The following pertains to each division for 2006:

	Houston Division	Dallas Division
Sales	$800,000	$600,000
Operating income	$ 60,000	$ 40,000
Average operating assets	$250,000	$200,000
Company's desired rate of return	15%	15%

Required

a. Compute each division's residual income.

b. Which division increased the company's profitability more?

Exercise 23-11B *Supply missing information regarding return on investment and residual income*

L.O. 6, 7

Required

Supply the missing information in the following table for Tapley Company.

Sales	?
ROI	12%
Investment in operating assets	$500,000
Operating income	?
Turnover	?
Residual income	?
Margin	0.08
Desired rate of return	11%

Exercise 23-12B *Contrasting return on investment with residual income*

L.O. 6, 7

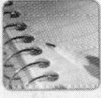

The Boston Division of Massachusetts Garage Doors Inc. is currently achieving a 16 percent ROI. The company's target ROI is 10 percent. The division has an opportunity to invest in operating assets an additional $600,000 at 13 percent but is reluctant to do so because its ROI will fall to 15.5 percent. The division's present investment in operating assets is $3,000,000.

Required

Explain how management can use the residual income method to motivate the Boston Division to make the investment.

Appendix

Exercise 23-13B *Transfer pricing*

L.O. 6, 7

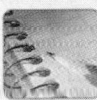

Welch Company makes household water filtration equipment. The Aquafresh Division manufactures filters. The Sweet Water Division then uses the filters as a component of the final product Welch sells to consumers. The Aquafresh Division has the capacity to produce 8,000 filters per month at the following cost per unit:

Variable costs	$14
Division fixed costs	10
Allocated corporate-level facility-sustaining costs	8
Total cost per filter	$32

Sweet Water currently uses 6,000 Aquafresh filters per month. Jim Sanders, Sweet Water's manager, is not happy with the $32 transfer price charged by Aquafresh. He points out that Sweet Water could purchase the same filters from outside vendors for a market price of only $26. Amy Mead, Aquafresh's manager, refuses to sell the filters to Sweet Water below cost. Mr. Sanders counters that he would be happy to purchase the filters elsewhere. Because Aquafresh does not have other customers for its filters, Ms. Mead appeals to Frank Pell, the president of Welch, for arbitration.

Required

a. Should the president of Welch allow Mr. Sanders to purchase filters from outside vendors for $26 per unit? Explain.

b. Write a brief paragraph describing what Mr. Pell should do to resolve the conflict between the two division managers.

Exercise 23-14B *Transfer pricing and avoidable cost*

L.O. 8

Gonzalez Household Equipment Corporation recently acquired two new divisions. The Purdy Division manufactures vacuum cleaner motors. The Oak Mountain Division makes household vacuum cleaners. Each division was formerly an independent company and continues to maintain its own customer base. Purdy Division data pertaining to vacuum cleaner motors follow:

Selling price per motor	$40
Unit-level variable costs per motor	$24
Division-level fixed costs per motor	$6
Corporate-level fixed costs per motor	$4
Manufacturing capacity	54,000 units per year
Average sales	32,000 units per year

The Oak Mountain Division currently buys motors for its vacuum cleaners from an outside supplier at a price of $33 per unit. Oak Mountain uses approximately 20,000 motors per year.

Required

Recommend a transfer price range for the motors that would be profitable for both divisions if the Oak Mountain Division purchased the motors internally. Assume both divisions operate as investment centers.

L.O. 8

Exercise 23-15B *Transfer pricing and fixed cost per unit*

The Murdock Division of Yesso Company currently produces electric fans that desktop computer manufacturers use as cooling components. The Hart Division, which makes laptop computers, has asked the Murdock Division to design and supply 20,000 fans per year for its laptop computers. Hart currently purchases laptop fans from an outside vendor at the price of $28 each. However, Hart is not happy with the vendor's unstable delivery pattern. To accept Hart's order, Murdock would have to purchase additional equipment and modify its plant layout. The additional equipment would enable the company to add 35,000 laptop fans to its annual production. Murdock's avoidable cost of making 20,000 laptop fans follows:

Costs	Total	Per Unit
Variable costs	$200,000	$10
Fixed cost	240,000	12

Required

a. What would be the financial consequence to Yesso Company if the Murdock Division makes the laptop fans and sells them to the Hart Division? What range of transfer prices would increase the financial performance of both divisions?

b. Suppose the Hart Division increases production so that it could use 35,000 Murdock Division laptop fans. How would the change in volume affect the range of transfer prices that would financially benefit both divisions?

PROBLEMS—SERIES B

L.O. 5

Problem 23-16B *Determining controllable costs*

At a professional conference just a few days ago, Dick Garrison, the president of Browning Corporation, learned how the concept of controllability relates to performance evaluation. In preparing to put this new knowledge into practice, he reviewed the financial data of the company's sales department.

Salaries of salespeople	$ 560,000
Cost of goods sold	45,000,000
Facility-level corporate costs	820,000
Travel expenses	64,000
Depreciation on equipment	200,000
Salary of the sales manager	120,000
Property taxes	8,000
Telephone expenses	78,000

Required

Help Mr. Garrison prepare a list of expenditures that the sales manager controls.

Problem 23-17B ***Controllability, responsibility, and balanced scorecard***

L.O. 3

Patrick Laird, president of Ebitz Corporation, evaluated the performance report of the company's production department. Mr. Laird was confused by some arguments presented by Darlene Rait, the production manager. Some relevant data follow.

Variances	Amount
Materials usage variance	$200,000 U
Materials price variance	120,000 F
Labor price variance	38,000 F
Labor usage variance	138,000 U
Volume variance	300,000 U

Ms. Rait argues that she had done a great job, noting the favorable materials price variance and labor price variance. She argued that she had had no control over factors causing the unfavorable variances. For example, she argued that the unfavorable materials usage variance was caused by the purchasing department's decision to buy substandard materials that resulted in a substantial amount of spoilage. Moreover, she argued that the unfavorable labor usage variance resulted from the substantial materials spoilage which in turn wasted many labor hours, as did the hiring of underqualified workers by the manager of the personnel department. Finally, she said that the sales department's failure to obtain a sufficient number of customer orders really caused the unfavorable volume variance.

Required

a. What would you do first if you were Patrick Laird?

b. Did Ms. Rait deserve the credit she claimed for the favorable variances? Explain.

c. Was Ms. Rait responsible for the unfavorable variances? Explain.

d. Explain how a balanced scorecard can be used to improve performance evaluation.

Problem 23-18B ***Performance reports and evaluation***

L.O. 3, 4, 5

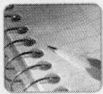

The mortgage division of Kemp Financial Services Inc. is managed by a vice president who supervises three regional operations. Each regional operation has a general manager and several branches directed by branch managers.

The Coleman region has two branches, Cahaba and Garner. The March responsibility reports for the managers of these branches follow.

	Budgeted*	Actual	Variance
Cahaba Branch			
Controllable costs			
Employee compensation	$288,000	$300,800	$12,800 U
Office supplies	72,000	70,000	2,000 F
Promotions	152,000	128,000	24,000 F
Maintenance	16,000	21,200	5,200 U
Total	$528,000	$520,000	$ 8,000 F
Garner Branch			
Controllable costs			
Employee compensation	$260,000	$250,000	$10,000 F
Office supplies	76,000	84,000	8,000 U
Promotions	144,000	150,000	6,000 U
Maintenance	20,000	19,200	800 F
Total	$500,000	$503,200	$ 3,200 U

*Kemp uses flexible budgets for performance evaluation.

Other pertinent cost data for March follow.

	Budgeted*	Actual
Cost data of other regions		
Helena	$1,400,000	$1,452,000
Alabaster	1,720,000	1,688,000
Other costs controllable by		
Coleman region general manager	280,000	292,000
Vice president of mortgage	384,000	392,000

*Kemp uses flexible budgets for performance evaluation.

Required

a. Prepare a responsibility report for the general manager of the Coleman region.

b. Prepare a responsibility report for the vice president of the mortgage division.

c. Explain where the $24,000 favorable promotions variance in the Cahaba branch manager's report is included in the vice president's report.

d. Based on the responsibility report prepared in Requirement *a*, explain where the Coleman region's general manager should concentrate her attention.

L.O. 2

Problem 23-19B *Different types of responsibility center*

Rosser Industries Inc. has five different divisions; each is responsible for producing and marketing a particular product line. The electronic division makes cellular telephones, pagers, and modems. The division also buys and sells other electronic products made by outside companies. Each division maintains sufficient working capital for its own operations. The corporate headquarters, however, makes decisions about long-term capital investments.

Required

a. For purposes of performance evaluation, should Rosser classify its electronic division as a cost center, a profit center, or an investment center? Why?

b. Would the manager of the electronic division be likely to conduct the operations of the division differently if the division were classified as a different type of responsibility center than the one you designated in Requirement *a*? Explain.

L.O. 6, 7

Problem 23-20B *Comparing return on investment and residual income*

Kenton Corporation operates three investment centers. The following financial statements apply to the investment center named Sumter Division.

SUMTER DIVISION
Income Statement
For the Year Ended December 31, 2006

Sales Revenue	$250,975
Cost of Goods Sold	(128,635)
Gross Margin	122,340
Operating Expenses	
Selling Expenses	(13,200)
Administrative Expense	(2,400)
Operating Income	106,740
Nonoperating Expense	
Interest Expense	(6,800)
Net Income	$ 99,940

[redacted]

Assets	
Cash	$ 68,360
Accounts Receivable	380,290
Merchandise Inventory	53,750
Equipment Less Accum. Dep.	428,600
Nonoperating Assets	48,000
Total Assets	$979,000
Liabilities	
Accounts Payable	$115,000
Notes Payable	100,000
Stockholders' Equity	
Common Stock	520,000
Retained Earnings	244,000
Total Liab. and Stk. Equity	$979,000

Required

a. Should operating income or net income be used to determine the rate of return (ROI) for the Sumter investment center? Explain your answer.

b. Should operating assets or total assets be used to determine the ROI for the Sumter investment center? Explain your answer.

c. Calculate the ROI for Sumter.

d. Kenton has a desired ROI of 8 percent. Headquarters has $300,000 of funds to assign its investment centers. The manager of the Sumter division has an opportunity to invest the funds at an ROI of 10 percent. The other two divisions have investment opportunities that yield only 9 percent. Even so, the manager of Sumter rejects the additional funding. Explain why the manager of Sumter would reject the funds under these circumstances.

e. Explain how residual income could be used to encourage the manager to accept the additional funds.

Problem 23-21B *Return on investment*

L.O. 6

Gentry Corporation's balance sheet indicates that the company has $750,000 invested in operating assets. During 2006, Gentry earned $120,000 of operating income on $2,400,000 of sales.

Required

a. Compute Gentry's margin for 2006.

b. Compute Gentry's turnover for 2006.

c. Compute Gentry's return on investment for 2006.

d. Recompute Gentry's ROI under each of the following independent assumptions.

(1) Sales increase from $2,400,000 to $2,700,000, thereby resulting in an increase in operating income from $120,000 to $141,750.

(2) Sales remain constant, but Gentry reduces expenses, thereby resulting in an increase in income from $120,000 to $126,000.

(3) Gentry is able to reduce its operating assets from $750,000 to $720,000 without affecting income.

Problem 23-22B *Comparing return on investment and residual income*

L.O. 6, 7

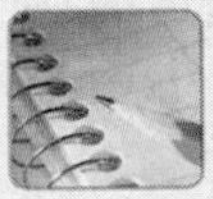

Christie House, the manager of Cunny Division, Lockard Corporation, has enjoyed success. Her division's return on investment (ROI) has consistently been 16 percent on a total investment in operating assets of $5,000,000. Lockard evaluates its division managers based on ROI. The company's desired ROI is 12 percent. Ms. House is evaluating an opportunity that will require a $1,000,000 investment in additional operating assets and is expected to result in a 13 percent return.

Required

a. Would it be advantageous for Lockard Corporation if Ms. House makes the investment under consideration?

b. What effect will making the proposed investment have on Cunny Division's ROI? Show computations.

c. What effect will making the proposed investment have on Cunny Division's residual income (RI)? Show computations.

d. Would ROI or RI be the better performance measure for Ms. House? Explain.

Appendix

L.O. 8

Problem 23-23B *Transfer pricing*

Yousuf Electronics Corporation makes a modem that it sells to retail stores for $75 each. The variable cost to produce a modem is $35 each; the total fixed cost is $5,000,000. Yousuf is operating at 80 percent of capacity and is producing 200,000 modems annually. Yousuf's parent company, Marsh Corporation, notified Yousuf's president that another subsidiary company, Kent Technologies, Inc., has begun making computers and can use Yousuf's modem as a part. Kent needs 40,000 modems annually and is able to acquire similar modems in the market for $72 each.

Under instruction from the parent company, the presidents of Yousuf and Kent meet to negotiate a price for the modem. Yousuf insists that its market price is $75 each and will stand firm on that price. Kent, on the other hand, wonders why it should even talk to Yousuf when Kent can get modems at a lower price.

Required

a. What transfer price would you recommend?

b. Discuss the effect of the intercompany sales on each president's return on investment.

c. Should Yousuf be required to use more than excess capacity to provide modems to Kent if Kent's demand increases to 60,000 modems? In other words, should it sell some of the 200,000 modems that it currently sells to unrelated companies to Kent instead? Why or why not?

ANALYZE, THINK, COMMUNICATE

ATC 23-1 Business Applications Case *Analyzing segments at Coca-Cola*

The following excerpt is from **Coca-Cola Company's** 2002 annual report filed with the SEC.

Management evaluates the performance of its operating segments separately to individually monitor the different factors affecting financial performance. Segment profit or loss includes substantially all the segment's costs of production, distribution and administration. Our Company typically manages and evaluates equity investments and related income on a segment level. However, we manage certain significant investments, such as our equity interests in Coca-Cola Enterprises, at the Corporate segment. Our Company manages income taxes on a global basis. We manage financial costs, such as exchange gains and losses and interest income and expense, on a global basis at the Corporate segment. Thus, we evaluate segment performance based on profit or loss before income taxes and cumulative effect of accounting change.

Below are selected segment data for Coca-Cola Company for the 2002 and 2001 fiscal years.

	North America	Africa	Europe, Eurasia & Middle East	Latin America	Asia
2002 Fiscal Year					
Net operating revenues	$6,264	$684	$5,262	$2,089	$5,054
Segment income before taxes and effect of accounting change	1,515	187	1,540	1,081	1,848
Identifiable operating assets	4,999	565	4,576	1,205	2,370

continued

	North America	Africa	Europe, Eurasia & Middle East	Latin America	Asia
2001 Fiscal Year					
Net operating revenues	$5,729	$633	$3,961	$2,181	$4,861
Segment income before taxes and effect of accounting change	1,472	262	1,413	1,279	1,808
Identifiable operating assets	4,738	517	2,292	1,681	2,121

Required

a. Compute the ROI for each of Coke's geographical segments for each fiscal year. Which segment appears to have the best performance during 2002 based on their ROI's? Which segment showed the most improvement from 2001 to 2002?

b. Assuming Coke's management expects a minimum return of 20 percent, calculate the residual income for each segment for each fiscal year. Which segment appears to have the best performance based on their residual incomes? Which segment showed the most improvement from 2001 to 2002?

c. Explain why the segment with the highest ROI is not the segment with the highest residual income.

d. Assume the management of Coke is considering a major expansion effort for the next five years. On which geographic segment would you recommend Coke focus its expansion efforts? Explain the rationale for your answer.

ATC 23-2 Group Assignment *Return on investment versus residual income*

Bellco, a division of Becker International Corporation, is operated under the direction of Antoin Sedatt. Bellco is an independent investment center with approximately $72,000,000 of assets that generate approximately $8,640,000 in annual net income. Becker International has additional investment capital of $12,000,000 that is available for the division managers to invest. Mr. Sedatt is aware of an investment opportunity that will provide an 11 percent annual net return. Becker International's desired rate of return is 10 percent.

Required

Divide the class into groups of four or five students and then organize the groups into two sections. Assign Task 1 to the first section and Task 2 to the second section.

Group Tasks

1. Assume that Mr. Sedatt's performance is evaluated based on his ability to maximize return on investment (ROI). Compute ROI using the following two assumptions: Bellco retains its current asset size and Bellco accepts and invests the additional $12,000,000 of assets. Determine whether Mr. Sedatt should accept the opportunity to invest additional funds. Select a spokesperson to present the decision made by the group.
2. Assume that Mr. Sedatt's performance is evaluated based on his ability to maximize residual income. Compute residual income using the following two assumptions: Bellco retains its current asset base and Bellco accepts and invests the additional $12,000,000 of assets. Determine whether Mr. Sedatt should accept the opportunity to invest additional funds. Select a spokesperson to present the decision made by the group.
3. Have a spokesperson from one of the groups in the first section report the two ROIs and the group's recommendation for Mr. Sedatt. Have the groups in this section reach consensus on the ROI and the recommendation.
4. Have a spokesperson from the second section report the two amounts of residual income and disclose the group's recommendation for Mr. Sedatt. Have this section reach consensus on amounts of residual income.
5. Which technique (ROI or residual income) is more likely to result in suboptimization?

ATC 23-3 Research Assignment *Centralized or decentralized management*

The Curious Accountant story in this chapter related how one company, The Home Depot, grew from a small business into a large business in about 20 years. Another company that has experienced explosive growth since its founding in 1971 is **Bed Bath & Beyond, Inc.** Read the article "What's Beyond for Bed Bath & Beyond?" by Nanette Byrnes that appears on pages 46 and 50 of the January 19, 2004, issue of *BusinessWeek* and answer the following questions.

Required

a. Does the management at Bed Bath & Beyond operate using a centralized or decentralized organizational style?

b. Give specific examples from the article to support your conclusion in Requirement *a*.

c. Some analysts think Bed Bath & Beyond may not be able to maintain its historic growth rate into the future. What are some of their concerns, and how might a centralized or decentralized management style affect these issues?

d. Based on the related article, "Like Father Like Son," that appears next to the Bed Bath & Beyond story, what role do the children of the founders of Bed Bath & Beyond play at the company, and what are the reasons for this?

ATC 23-4 Writing Assignment *Transfer pricing*

Green Lawn Mower Inc. recently acquired Hallit Engines, a small engine manufacturing company. Green's president believes in decentralization and intends to permit Hallit to continue to operate as an independent entity. However, she has instructed the manager of Green's lawn mower assembly division to investigate the possibility of purchasing engines from Hallit instead of using the current third-party supplier. Hallit has excess capacity. The current full cost to produce each engine is $96. The avoidable cost of making engines is $78 per unit. The assembly division, which currently pays the third-party supplier $90 per engine, offers to purchase engines from Hallit at the $90 price. Hallit's president refuses the offer, stating that his company's engines are superior to those the third-party supplier provides. Hallit's president believes that the transfer price should be based on the market price for independent customers, which is $132 per engine. The manager of the assembly division agrees that Hallit's engines are higher quality than those currently being used but notes that Green's customer base is in the low-end, discount market. Putting more expensive engines on Green mowers would raise the price above the competition and would hurt sales. Green's president tries to negotiate a settlement between the assembly manager and Hallit's president, but the parties are unable to agree on a transfer price.

Required

a. Assuming that Green makes and sells 40,000 lawn mowers per year, what is the cost of suboptimization resulting from the failure to establish a transfer price?

b. Assume that you are a consultant asked by the president of Green to recommend whether a transfer price should be arbitrarily imposed. Write a brief memo that includes your recommendation and your justification for making it.

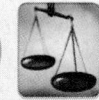

ATC 23-5 Ethical Dilemma *Manipulating return on investment and residual income*

The October 5, 1998, issue of *BusinessWeek* includes the article "Who Can You Trust?" authored by Sarah Bartlett. Among other dubious accounting practices, the article describes a trick known as the "big bath," which occurs when a company makes huge unwarranted asset write-offs that drastically overstate expenses. Outside auditors (CPAs) permit companies to engage in the practice because the assets being written off are of questionable value. Because the true value of the assets cannot be validated, auditors have little recourse but to accept the valuations suggested by management. Recent examples of questionable write-offs include **Motorola's** $1.8 billion restructuring charge and the multibillion-dollar write-offs for "in-process" research taken by high-tech companies such as **Compaq Computer Corp.** and **WorldCom, Inc.**

Required

a. Why would managers want their companies to take a big bath? (*Hint:* Consider how a big bath affects return on investment and residual income in the years following the write-off.)

b. Annual reports are financial reports issued to the public. The reports are the responsibility of auditors who are CPAs who operate under the ethical standards promulgated by the American Institute of Certified Public Accountants. As a result, attempts to manipulate annual report data are not restricted by the Institute of Management Accountants Standards of Ethical Conduct shown in Exhibit 14.13 of Chapter 14. Do you agree or disagree with this conclusion? Explain your position.

COMPREHENSIVE PROBLEM

Assume Magnificent Modems (MM) is a division of Gilmore Business Products (GBP). GBP used ROI as the primary measure of managerial performance. GBP has a desired return on investment (ROI) of 3 percent. The company has $100,000 of investment funds to be assigned to its divisions. The president of MM is aware of an investment opportunity for these funds that is expected to yield an ROI of 3.5 percent.

Required

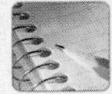

a. Explain why you believe the president of MM will accept or reject the $100,000 investment opportunity. Support your answer by calculating MM's existing ROI. Base your computation on the information contained in the income statement and balance sheet that you prepared in Chapter 14 (page 742).

b. Name the term used to describe the condition that exists in Requirement *a*. Provide a brief definition of this term.

c. If GBP changes its performance measurement criteria from ROI to residual income (RI), will the new evaluation approach affect the president's decision to accept or reject the $100,000 investment opportunity? Support your answer by calculating MM's residual income for the investment opportunity.

CHAPTER 24

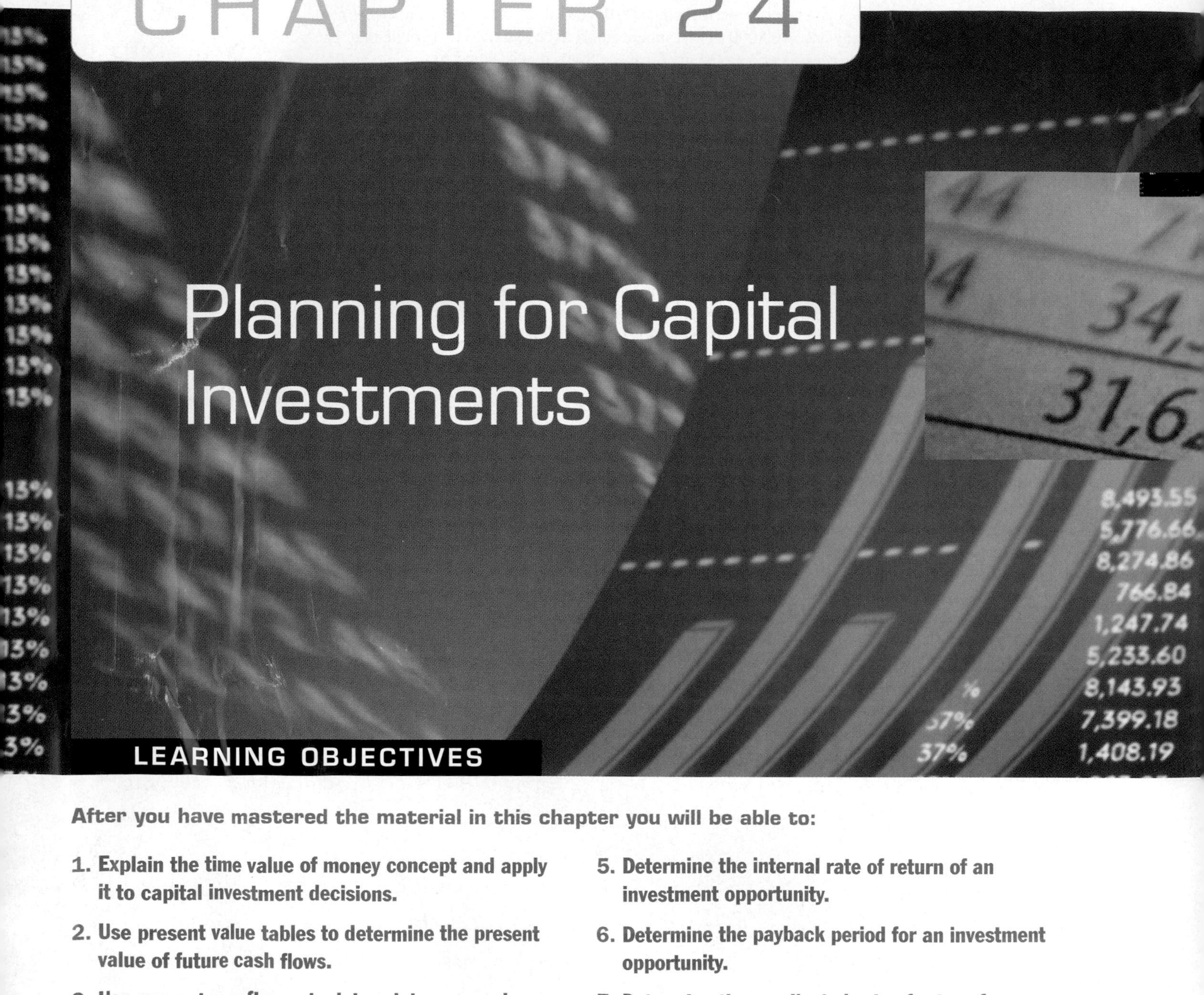

Planning for Capital Investments

LEARNING OBJECTIVES

After you have mastered the material in this chapter you will be able to:

1. **Explain the time value of money concept and apply it to capital investment decisions.**
2. **Use present value tables to determine the present value of future cash flows.**
3. **Use computer software in determining present values.**
4. **Determine and interpret the net present value of an investment opportunity.**
5. **Determine the internal rate of return of an investment opportunity.**
6. **Determine the payback period for an investment opportunity.**
7. **Determine the unadjusted rate of return for an investment opportunity.**
8. **Conduct a postaudit of a completed investment.**

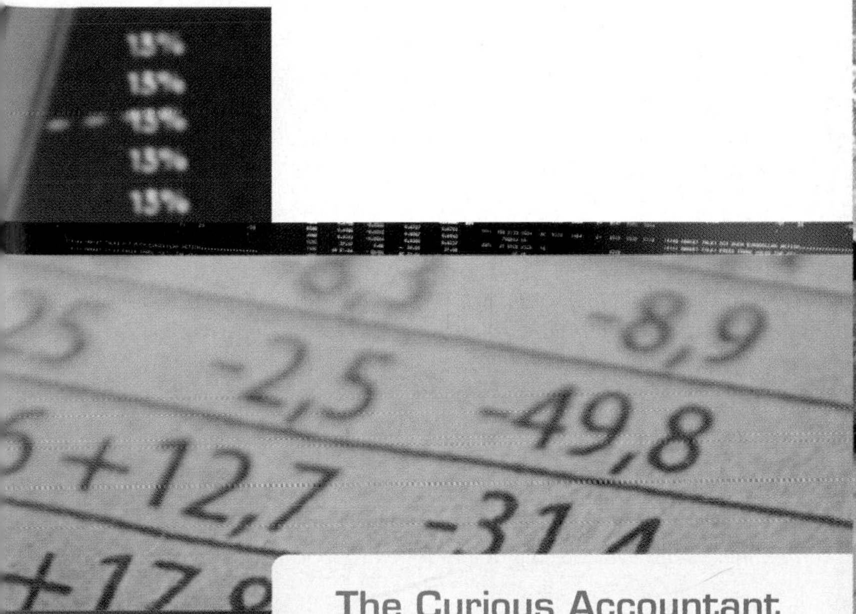

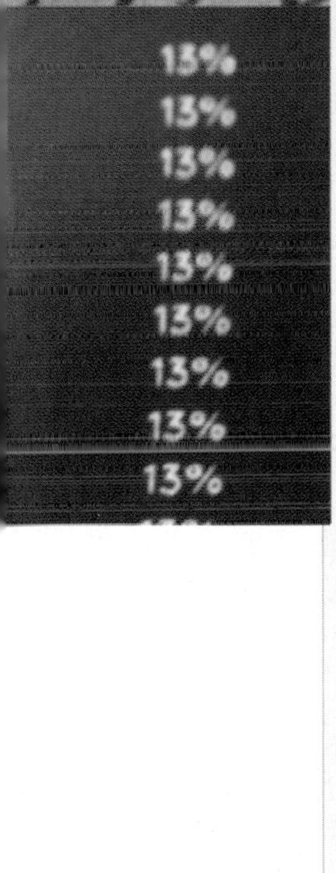

Chapter 24

The Curious Accountant

Ginger and Fred want to replace the windows in the older house they purchased recently. The company they have talked to about doing the work, RWC, claims that its new windows will reduce Ginger and Fred's heating and cooling costs by around 33 percent. RWC also estimates that they will get back 70 percent of the cost of the new windows when they sell their house, and their real estate agent verifies that this is a good estimate. The new windows will cost \$10,000.

The couple gathered the following information to help them make their decision. The heating and cooling costs for Fred and Ginger's house average around \$1,800 per year, so they expect to save \$600 on these costs per year if they get the new windows. The new windows should also increase the resale value by \$7,000 (.70 × \$10,000) when they decide to move. They expect to stay in this house for 10 years, so the total savings in energy costs are estimated at \$6,000 (10 × \$600). These savings, along with the higher resale value, bring the total return on their investment to \$13,000 (\$6,000 + \$7,000).

To pay for the windows they would have to withdraw the money from a mutual fund that has earned an average annual return of only 4 percent over the past few years. They are hesitant about liquidating the mutual fund, but think that spending \$10,000 today in order to receive future savings and income of \$13,000 seems like a good deal.

Can Fred and Ginger simply compare the \$13,000 future cash inflows to the \$10,000 cost of the windows in order to decide if replacing them is a good idea? If not, what analysis should they perform in order to make their decision? (Answer on page 1163.)

CHAPTER OPENING

The president of EZ Rentals (EZ) is considering expanding the company's rental service business to include LCD projectors that can be used with notebook computers. A marketing study forecasts that renting projectors could generate revenue of $200,000 per year. The possibility of increasing revenue is alluring, but EZ's president has a number of unanswered questions. How much do the projectors cost? What is their expected useful life? Will they have a salvage value? Does EZ have the money to buy them? Does EZ have the technical expertise to support the product? How much will training cost? How long will customer demand last? What if EZ buys the projectors and they become technologically obsolete? How quickly will EZ be able to recover the investment? Are there more profitable ways to invest EZ's funds?

Spending large sums of money that will have long-term effects on company profits makes most managers anxious. What if a cell phone manufacturer spends millions of dollars to build a factory in the United States and its competitors locate their manufacturing facilities in countries that provide cheap labor? The manufacturer's cell phones will be overpriced, but it cannot move overseas because it cannot find a buyer for the factory. What if a pharmaceutical company spends millions of dollars to develop a drug which then fails to receive FDA approval? What if a communications company installs underground cable but satellite transmission steals its market? What if a company buys computer equipment that rapidly becomes technologically obsolete? Although these possibilities may be remote, they can be expensive when they do occur. For example, Wachovia Bank's 1997 annual report discloses a $70 million dollar write-off of computer equipment. This chapter discusses some of the analytical techniques companies use to evaluate major investment opportunities.

Capital Investment Decisions

LO 1

Explain the time value of money concept and apply it to capital investment decisions.

Purchases of long-term operational assets are **capital investments.** Capital investments differ from stock and bond investments in an important respect. Investments in stocks and bonds can be sold in organized markets such as the New York Stock Exchange. In contrast, investments in capital assets normally can be recovered only by using those assets. Once a company purchases a capital asset, it is committed to that investment for an extended period of time. If the market turns sour, the company is stuck with the consequences. It may also be unable to seize new opportunities because its capital is committed. Business profitability ultimately hinges, to a large extent, on the quality of a few key capital investment decisions.

A capital investment decision is essentially a decision to exchange current cash outflows for the expectation of receiving future cash inflows. For EZ Rentals, purchasing LCD projectors, cash outflows today, provides the opportunity to collect $200,000 per year in rental revenue, cash inflows in the future. Assuming the projectors have useful lives of four years and no salvage value, how much should EZ be willing to pay for the future cash inflows? If you were EZ's president, would you spend $700,000 today to receive $200,000 each year for the next four years? You would give up $700,000 today for the opportunity to receive $800,000 (4 × $200,000) in the future. What if you collect less than $200,000 per year? If revenue is only $160,000 per year, you would lose $60,000 [$700,000 − (4 × $160,000)]. Is $700,000 too much to pay for the opportunity to receive $200,000 per year for four years? If $700,000 is too much, would you spend $600,000? If not, how about $500,000? There is no one right answer to these questions. However, understanding the *time value of money* concept can help you develop a rational response.

Time Value of Money

The **time value of money** concept recognizes that *the present value of a dollar received in the future is less than a dollar.* For example, you may be willing to pay only $0.90 today for a promise to receive $1.00 one year from today. The further into the future the receipt is expected to occur, the smaller is its present value. In other words, one dollar to be received two years from today is worth less than one dollar to be received one year from today. Likewise,

one dollar to be received three years from today is less valuable than one dollar to be received two years from today, and so on.

The present value of cash inflows decreases as the time until expected receipt increases for several reasons. First, you could deposit today's dollar in a savings account to earn *interest* that increases its total value. If you wait for your money, you lose the opportunity to earn interest. Second, the expectation of receiving a future dollar carries an element of risk. Changed conditions may result in the failure to collect. Finally, *inflation* diminishes the buying power of the dollar. In other words, the longer you must wait to receive a dollar, the less you will be able to buy with it.

When a company invests in capital assets, it sacrifices present dollars in exchange for the opportunity to receive future dollars. Since trading current dollars for future dollars is risky, companies expect compensation before they invest in capital assets. The compensation a company expects is called *return on investment (ROI)*. As discussed in Chapter 23, ROI is expressed as a percentage of the investment. For example, the ROI for a $1,000 investment that earns annual income of $100 is 10 percent ($100 ÷ $1,000 = 10%).

Determining the Minimum Rate of Return

To establish the minimum expected *return on investment* before accepting an investment opportunity, most companies consider their cost of capital. To attract capital, companies must provide benefits to their creditors and owners. Creditors expect interest payments; owners expect dividends and increased stock value. Companies that earn lower returns than their cost of capital eventually go bankrupt; they cannot continually pay out more than they collect. *The* **cost of capital** *represents the* **minimum rate of return** *on investments.* Calculating the cost of capital is a complex exercise which is beyond the scope of this text. It is addressed in finance courses. We discuss how management accountants *use* the cost of capital to evaluate investment opportunities. Companies describe the cost of capital in a variety of ways: the *minimum rate of return*, the *desired rate of return*, the *required rate of return*, the *hurdle rate*, the *cutoff rate,* or the *discount rate*. These terms are used interchangeably throughout this chapter.

CHECK YOURSELF 24.1

Study the following cash inflow streams expected from two different potential investments.

	Year 1	Year 2	Year 3	Total
Alternative 1	$2,000	$3,000	$4,000	$9,000
Alternative 2	4,000	3,000	2,000	9,000

Based on visual observation alone, which alternative has the higher present value? Why?

Answer

Alternative 2 has the higher present value. The size of the discount increases as the length of the time period increases. In other words, a dollar received in year 3 has a lower present value than a dollar received in year 1. Since most of the expected cash inflows from Alternative 2 are received earlier than those from Alternative 1, Alternative 2 has a higher present value even though the total expected cash inflows are the same.

Converting Future Cash Inflows to Their Equivalent Present Values

Given a desired rate of return and the amount of a future cash flow, present value can be determined using algebra. To illustrate, refer to the $200,000 EZ expects to earn the first year it leases LCD projectors.[1] Assuming EZ desires a 12 percent rate of return, what amount of cash would EZ be willing to invest today (present value outflow) to obtain a $200,000 cash inflow at the end of the year (future value)? The answer follows:[2]

$$\text{Investment} + (0.12 \times \text{Investment}) = \text{Future cash inflow}$$
$$1.12\ \text{Investment} = \$200{,}000$$
$$\text{Investment} = \$200{,}000 \div 1.12$$
$$\text{Investment} = \$178{,}571$$

If EZ invests $178,571 cash on January 1 and earns a 12 percent return on the investment, EZ will have $200,000 on December 31. An investor who is able to earn a 12 percent return on investment is indifferent between having $178,571 now or receiving $200,000 one year from now. The two options are equal, as shown in the following mathematical proof:

$$\text{Investment} + (0.12 \times \text{Investment}) = \$200{,}000$$
$$\$178{,}571 + (0.12 \times \$178{,}571) = \$200{,}000$$
$$\$178{,}571 + \$21{,}429 = \$200{,}000$$
$$\$200{,}000 = \$200{,}000$$

LO 2

Use present value tables to determine the present value of future cash flows.

Present Value Table for Single-Amount Cash Inflows. The algebra illustrated above is used to convert a one-time future receipt of cash to its present value. One-time receipts of cash are frequently called **single-payment,** or **lump sum,** cash flows. Because EZ desires a 12 percent rate of return, the present value of the first cash inflow is $178,571. We can also determine the present value of a $200,000 single amount (lump sum) at the end of the second, third, and fourth years. Instead of using cumbersome algebraic computations to convert these future values to their present value equivalents, financial analysts frequently use a table of conversion factors to convert future values to their present value equivalents. The table of conversion factors used to convert future values into present values is commonly called a **present value table.**[3] A typical present value table presents columns with different return rates and rows with different periods of time, like Table 1 in the Appendix.

To illustrate using the present value table, locate the conversion factor in Table 1 at the intersection of the 12% column and the one period row. The conversion factor is 0.892857. Multiplying this factor by the $200,000 expected cash inflow yields $178,571 ($200,000 × 0.892857). This is the same value determined algebraically in the previous section of this chapter. The conversion factors in the present value tables simplify converting future values to present values.

The conversion factors for the second, third, and fourth periods are 0.797194, 0.711780, and 0.635518, respectively. These factors are in the 12% column at rows 2, 3, and 4, respectively. Locate these factors in Table 1 of the Appendix. Multiplying the conversion factors by the future cash inflow for each period produces their present value equivalents, shown in Exhibit 24.1. Exhibit 24.1 indicates that investing $607,470 today at a 12 percent rate of return is equivalent to receiving $200,000 per year for four years. Because EZ Rentals desires to earn (at least) a 12 percent rate of return, the company should be willing to pay up to $607,470 to purchase the LCD projectors.

Present Value Table for Annuities. The algebra described previously for converting equal lump-sum cash inflows to present value equivalents can be further simplified by adding the present value table factors together before multiplying them by the cash inflows. The total of the present value table factors in Exhibit 24.1 is 3.037349 (0.892857 + 0.797194 + 0.711780 + 0.635518). Multiplying this **accumulated conversion factor** by the expected annual cash inflow results in the same present value equivalent of $607,470 ($200,000 ×

[1] The following computations assume the $200,000 cash inflow is received on the last day of each year. In actual practice the timing of cash inflows is less precise and present value computations are recognized to be approximate, not exact.

[2] All computations in this chapter are rounded to the nearest whole dollar.

[3] The present value table is based on the formula $[1 \div (1 + r)^n]$ where r equals the rate of return and n equals the number of periods.

EXHIBIT 24.1

Present Value of a $200,000 Cash Inflow to be Received for Four Years

PV	=	FV	×	Present Value Table Factor	=	Present Value Equivalent
Period 1 PV	=	$200,000	×	0.892857	=	$178,571
Period 2 PV	=	200,000	×	0.797194	=	159,439
Period 3 PV	=	200,000	×	0.711780	=	142,356
Period 4 PV	=	200,000	×	0.635518	=	127,104
Total						$607,470

3.037349). As with lump-sum conversion factors, accumulated conversion factors can be calculated and organized in a table with *columns* for different rates of return and *rows* for different periods of time. Table 2 in the Appendix is a present value table of accumulated conversion factors. Locate the conversion factor at the intersection of the 12% column and the fourth time period row. The factor at this intersection is 3.037349, confirming that the accumulated conversion factors represent the sum of the single-payment conversion factors.

The conversion factors in Table 2 apply to annuities. An **annuity** is a series of cash flows that meets three criteria: (1) equal payment amounts; (2) equal time intervals between payments; and (3) a constant rate of return. For EZ Rentals, the expected cash inflows from renting LCD projectors are all for equivalent amounts ($200,000); the expected intervals between cash inflows are equal lengths of time (one year); and the rate of return for each inflow is constant at 12 percent. The series of expected cash inflows from renting the projectors is therefore an annuity. The present value of an annuity table can be used only if all of these conditions are satisfied.

The present value of an annuity table (Table 2) simplifies converting future cash inflows to their present value equivalents. EZ Rentals can convert the cash inflows as shown in Exhibit 24.1, using four conversion factors, multiplying each conversion factor by the annual cash inflow (four multiplications), and adding the resulting products. In contrast, EZ can recognize that the series of payments is an annuity, which requires multiplying a single conversion factor from Table 2 by the amount of the annuity payment. Regardless of the conversion method, the result is the same (a present value of $607,470). Recall that EZ can also make the conversion using algebra. The table values are derived from algebraic formulas. The present value tables reduce the computations needed to convert future values to present values.

LO 3

Use computer software in determining present values.

Software Programs that Calculate Present Values. Software programs offer an even more efficient means of converting future values into present value equivalents. These programs are frequently built into handheld financial calculators and computer spreadsheet programs. As an example, we demonstrate the procedures used in a Microsoft Excel spreadsheet.

An Excel spreadsheet offers a variety of financial functions, one of which converts a future value annuity into its present value equivalent. This present value function uses the syntax PV(*rate,nper,pmt*) in which *rate* is the desired rate of return, *nper* is the number of periods, and *pmt* is the amount of the payment (periodic cash inflow). To convert a future value annuity into its present value equivalent, provide the function with the appropriate amounts for the rate, number of periods, and amount of the annuity (cash inflows) into a spreadsheet cell. Press the Enter key and the present value equivalent appears in the spreadsheet cell.

The power of the spreadsheet to perform computations instantly is extremely useful for answering what-if questions. Exhibit 24.2 demonstrates this power by providing spreadsheet conversions for three different scenarios. The first scenario demonstrates the annuity assumptions for EZ Rentals, providing the present value equivalent ($607,470) of a four-year cash inflow of $200,000 per year at a 12 percent rate of interest. The present value is a *negative* number. This format indicates that an initial $607,470 *cash outflow* is required to

EXHIBIT 24.2

Microsoft Excel Spreadsheet Present Value Function

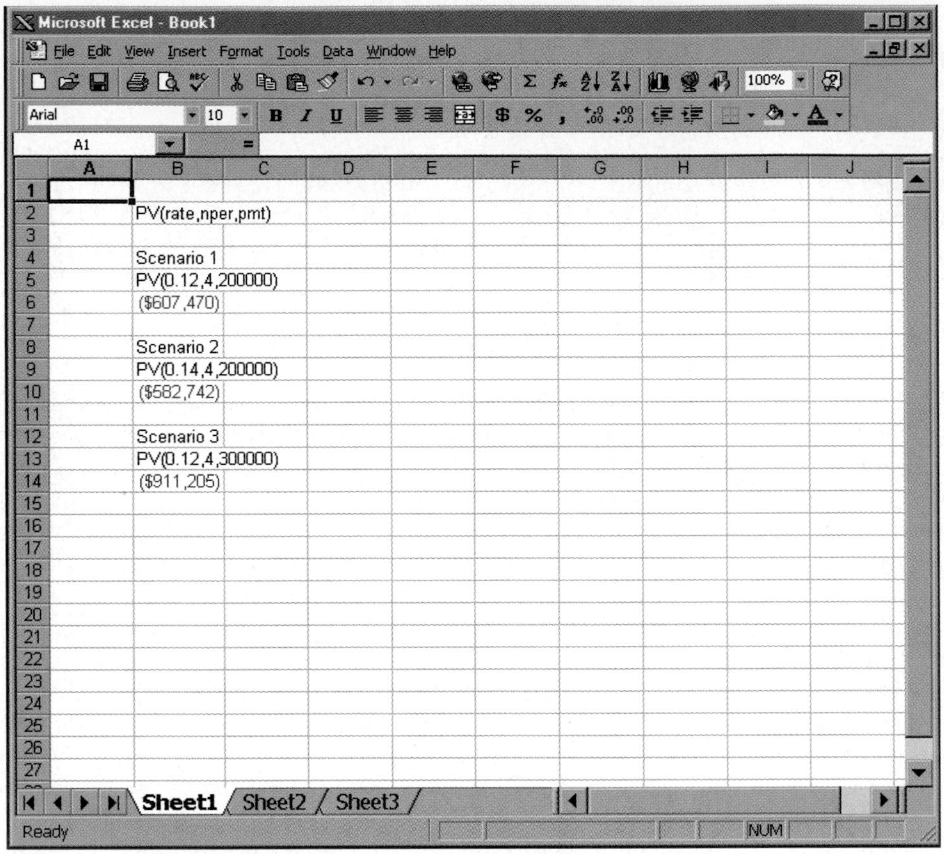

obtain the four-year series of cash inflows. The present value equivalent in Scenario 2 shows the present value if the annuity assumptions reflect a 14 percent, rather than 12 percent, desired rate of return. The present value equivalent in Scenario 3 shows the present value if the annuity assumptions under Scenario 1 are changed to reflect annual cash inflows of $300,000, rather than $200,000. A wide range of scenarios could be readily considered by changing any or all the variables in the spreadsheet function. In each case, the computer does the calculations, giving the manager more time to analyze the data rather than compute it.

Although software is widely used in business practice, the diversity of interfaces used by different calculators and spreadsheet programs makes it unsuitable for textbook presentations. This text uses the present value tables in the Appendix in the text illustrations and the end-of-chapter exercises and problems. If you use software to solve these problems, your answers will be the same. All these tools—formulas, conversion tables, software—are based on the same mathematical principles and will produce the same results.

Ordinary Annuity Assumption. All the conversion methods described above assume the cash inflows occur at the *end* of each accounting period. This distribution pattern is called an **ordinary annuity.**[4] In practice, cash inflows are likely to be received throughout the period, not just at the end. For example, EZ Rentals is likely to collect cash revenue from renting projectors each month rather than in a single lump-sum receipt at the end of each of the four

[4] When equal cash inflows occur at the beginning of each accounting period, the distribution is called an *annuity due.* Although some business transactions are structured as annuities due, they are less common than ordinary annuities. This text uses the ordinary annuity assumption.

years. Companies frequently use the ordinary annuity assumption in practice because it simplifies time value of money computations. Because capital investment decisions are necessarily based on uncertain projections about future cash inflows, the lives of investment opportunities, and the appropriate rates of return, achieving pinpoint accuracy is impossible. Sacrificing precision for simplicity by using the ordinary annuity assumption is a reasonable trade-off in the decision-making process.

Reinvestment Assumption. The present value computations in the previous sections show that investing $607,470 today at a 12 percent rate of return is equivalent to receiving four individual $200,000 payments at the end of four successive years. Exhibit 24.3 illustrates that a cash inflow of $200,000 per year is equivalent to earning a 12 percent rate of return on a $607,470 investment.[5]

EXHIBIT 24.3

Cash Flow Classifications for EZ's Investment in Projectors

Time Period	(a) Investment Balance During the Year	(b) Annual Cash Inflow	(c) Return on Investment (a × 0.12)	(d) Recovered Investment (b − c)	(e) Year-End Investment Balance (a − d)
1	$607,470	$200,000	$ 72,896	$127,104	$480,366
2	480,366	200,000	57,644	142,356	338,010
3	338,010	200,000	40,561	159,439	178,571
4	178,571	200,000	21,429	178,571	0
Totals		$800,000	$192,530	$607,470	

It is customary to assume that the desired rate of return includes the effects of *compounding*.[6] Saying an investment is "earning the desired rate of return," assumes the cash inflows generated by the investment are reinvested at the desired rate of return. In this case, we are assuming that EZ will reinvest the $200,000 annual cash inflows in other investments that will earn a 12 percent return.

Techniques for Analyzing Capital Investment Proposals

Managers can choose from among numerous analytical techniques to help them make capital investment decisions. Each technique has advantages and disadvantages. A manager may apply more than one technique to a particular proposal to take advantage of more information. Since most companies have computer capabilities that include a variety of standard capital budgeting programs, applying different techniques to the same proposal normally requires little extra effort. Limiting analysis to only one tool could produce biased results. Obtaining more than one perspective offers substantial benefit.

Topic Tackler PLUS 24-1

LO 4 Determine and interpret the net present value of an investment opportunity.

Net Present Value

By using the present value conversion techniques described earlier, EZ Rentals' management determined it would be willing to invest $607,470 today (present value) to obtain a four-year,

[5] Exhibit 24.3 is analogous to an amortization table for a long-term note with equal payments of principal and interest.

[6] *Compounding* refers to reinvesting investment proceeds so the total amount of invested capital increases, resulting in even higher returns. For example, assume $100 is invested at a 10 percent compounded annual rate of return. At the end of the first year, the investment yields a $10 return ($100 × 0.10). The $10 return plus any recovered investment is reinvested so that the total amount of invested capital at the beginning of the second year is $110. The return for the second year is $11 ($110 × 0.10). All funds are reinvested so that the return for the third year is $12.10 [($110 + $11) × 0.10].

$200,000 future value annuity cash inflow. The $607,470 investment is *not* the cost of the LCD projectors, it is the amount EZ is willing to pay for them. The projectors may cost EZ Rentals more or less than their present value. To determine whether EZ should invest in the projectors, management must compare the present value of the future cash inflows ($607,470) to the cost of the projectors (the current cash outflow required to purchase them). Subtracting the cost of the investment from the present value of the future cash inflows determines the **net present value** of the investment opportunity. A positive net present value indicates the investment will yield a rate of return higher than 12 percent. A negative net present value means the return is less than 12 percent.

To illustrate, assume EZ can purchase the projectors for $582,742. Assuming the desired rate of return is 12 percent, EZ should buy them. The net present value of the investment opportunity is computed as follows.

Present value of future cash inflows	$607,470
Cost of investment (required cash outflow)	(582,742)
Net present value	$ 24,728

The positive net present value suggests the investment will earn a rate of return in excess of 12 percent (if cash flows are indeed $200,000 each year). Because the projected rate of return is higher than the desired rate of return, this analysis suggests EZ should accept the investment opportunity.

CHECK YOURSELF 24.2

To increase productivity, Wald Corporation is considering the purchase of a new machine that costs $50,000. Wald expects using the machine to increase annual net cash inflows by $12,500 for each of the next five years. Wald desires a minimum annual rate of return of 10 percent on the investment. Determine the net present value of the investment opportunity and recommend whether Wald should acquire the machine.

Answer

Present value of future cash flows = Future cash flow × Table 2 factor (n = 5, r = 10%)

Present value of future cash flows = $12,500 × 3.790787 = $47,385

Net present value = PV of future cash flows − Cost of machine

Net present value = $47,385 − $50,000 = ($2,615)

The negative net present value indicates the investment will yield a rate of return below the desired rate of return. Wald should not acquire the new machine.

Internal Rate of Return

LO 5

Determine the internal rate of return of an investment opportunity.

The net present value method indicates EZ's investment in the projectors will provide a return in excess of the desired rate, but it does not provide the actual rate of return to expect from the investment. If EZ's management team wants to know the rate of return to expect from investing in the projectors, it must use the *internal rate of return method.* The **internal rate of return** is the rate at which the present value of cash inflows equals the cash outflows. It is the rate that will produce a zero net present value. For EZ Rentals, the internal rate of return can be determined as follows. First, compute the *present value table factor* for a $200,000 annuity that would yield a $582,742 present value cash outflow (cost of investment).

Present value table factor × $200,000 = $582,742

Present value table factor = $582,742 ÷ $200,000

Present value table factor = 2.91371

Second, since the expected annual cash inflows represent a four-year annuity, scan Table 2 in the Appendix at period n = 4. Try to locate the table factor 2.91371. The rate listed at the top of the column in which the factor is located is the internal rate of return. Turn to Table 2 and determine the internal rate of return for EZ Rentals before you read further. The above factor is in the 14 percent column. The difference in the table value (2.913712) and the value computed here (2.91371) is due to truncation. If EZ invests $582,742 in the projectors and they produce a $200,000 annual cash flow for four years, EZ will earn a 14 percent rate of return on the investment.

The *internal rate of return* may be compared with a *desired rate of return* to determine whether to accept or reject a particular investment project. Assuming EZ desires to earn a minimum rate of return of 12 percent, the preceding analysis suggests it should accept the investment opportunity because the internal rate of return (14 percent) is higher than the desired rate of return (12 percent). An internal rate of return below the desired rate suggests management should reject a particular proposal. The desired rate of return is sometimes called the *cutoff rate* or the *hurdle rate.* To be accepted, an investment proposal must provide an internal rate of return higher than the hurdle rate, cutoff rate, or desired rate of return. These terms are merely alternatives for the *cost of capital*. Ultimately, to be accepted, an investment must provide an internal rate of return higher than a company's cost of capital.

Techniques for Measuring Investment Cash Flows

The EZ Rentals example represents a simple capital investment analysis. The investment option involved only one cash outflow and a single annuity inflow. Investment opportunities often involve a greater variety of cash outflows and inflows. The following section of this chapter discusses different types of cash flows encountered in business practice.

Cash Inflows

Cash inflows generated from capital investments come from *four basic sources*. As in the case of EZ Rentals, the most common source of cash inflows is incremental revenue. **Incremental revenue** refers to the *additional* cash inflows from operating activities generated by using additional capital assets. For example, a taxi company expects revenues from taxi fares to increase if it purchases additional taxicabs. Similarly, investing in new apartments should increase rent revenue; opening a new store should result in additional sales revenue.

A second type of cash inflow results from *cost savings*. Decreases in cash outflows have the same beneficial effect as increases in cash inflows. Either way, a firm's cash position improves. For example, purchasing an automated computer system may enable a company to reduce cash outflows for salaries. Similarly, relocating a manufacturing facility closer to its raw materials source can reduce cash outflows for transportation costs.

An investment's *salvage value* provides a third source of cash inflows. Even when one company has finished using an asset, the asset may still be useful to another company. Many assets are sold after a company no longer wishes to use them. The salvage value represents a one-time cash inflow obtained when a company terminates an investment.

Companies can also experience a cash inflow through a *reduction in the amount* of **working capital** needed to support an investment. A certain level of working capital is required to support most business investments. For example, a new retail store outlet requires cash, receivables, and inventory to operate. When an investment is terminated, the decrease in the working capital commitment associated with the investment normally results in a cash inflow.

Cash Outflows

Cash outflows fall into *three primary categories*. One category consists of outflows for the *initial investment*. Managers must be alert to all the cash outflows connected with purchasing a capital asset. The purchase price, transportation costs, installation costs, and training costs are examples of typical cash outflows related to an initial investment.

A second category of cash outflows may result from *increases in operating expenses*. If a company increases output capacity by investing in additional equipment, it may experience higher utility bills, labor costs, and maintenance expenses when it places the equipment into service. These expenditures increase cash outflows.

Third, *increases in working capital* commitments result in cash outflows. Frequently, investments in new assets must be supported by a certain level of working capital. For example, investing in a copy machine requires spending cash to maintain a supply of paper and toner. Managers should treat an increased working capital commitment as a cash outflow in the period the commitment occurs.

Exhibit 24.4 lists the cash inflows and outflows discussed. The list is not exhaustive but does summarize the most common cash flows businesses experience.

EXHIBIT 24.4

Typical Cash Flows Associated With Capital Investments

Inflows	Outflows
1. Incremental revenue	1. Initial investment
2. Cost savings	2. Incremental expenses
3. Salvage values	3. Working capital commitments
4. Recovery of working capital	

Techniques for Comparing Alternative Capital Investment Opportunities

The management of Torres Transfer Company is considering two investment opportunities. One alternative, involving the purchase of new equipment for $80,000, would enable Torres to modernize its maintenance facility. The equipment has an expected useful life of five years and a $4,000 salvage value. It would replace existing equipment that had originally cost $45,000. The existing equipment has a current book value of $15,000 and a trade-in value of $5,000. The old equipment is technologically obsolete but can operate for an additional five years. On the day Torres purchases the new equipment, it would also pay the equipment manufacturer $3,000 for training costs to teach employees to operate the new equipment. The modernization has two primary advantages. One, it will improve management of the small parts inventory. The company's accountant believes that by the end of the first year, the carrying value of the small parts inventory could be reduced by $12,000. Second, the modernization is expected to increase efficiency, resulting in a $21,500 reduction in annual operating expenses.

The other investment alternative available to Torres is purchasing a truck. Adding another truck would enable Torres to expand its delivery area and increase revenue. The truck costs $115,000. It has a useful life of five years and a $30,000 salvage value. Operating the truck will require the company to increase its inventory of supplies, its petty cash account, and its accounts receivable and payable balances. These changes would add $5,000 to the company's working capital base immediately upon buying the truck. The working capital cash outflow is expected to be recovered at the end of the truck's useful life. The truck is expected to produce $69,000 per year in additional revenues. The driver's salary and other operating expenses are expected to be $32,000 per year. A major overhaul costing $20,000 is expected to be required at the end of the third year of operation. Assuming Torres desires to earn a rate of return of 14 percent, which of the two investment alternatives should it choose?

Net Present Value

LO 4

Determine and interpret the net present value of an investment opportunity.

Begin the analysis by calculating the net present value of the two investment alternatives. Exhibit 24.5 shows the computations. Study this exhibit. Each alternative is analyzed using three steps. Step 1 requires identifying all cash inflows; some may be annuities, and others may be lump-sum receipts. In the case of Alternative 1, the cost saving is an annuity, and the inflow from the salvage value is a lump-sum receipt. Once the cash inflows have been identified, the appropriate conversion factors are identified and the cash inflows are converted to their equivalent present values. Step 2 follows the same process to determine the present value of the cash outflows. Step 3 subtracts the present value of the outflows from the present value of the inflows to determine the net present value. The same three-step approach is used to determine the net present value of Alternative 2.

EXHIBIT 24.5

Net Present Value Analysis

	Amount	×	Conversion Factor	=	Present Value
Alternative 1: Modernize Maintenance Facility					
Step 1: Cash inflows					
1. Cost savings	$21,500	×	3.433081*	=	$73,811
2. Salvage value	4,000	×	0.519369†	=	2,077
3. Working capital recovery	12,000	×	0.877193‡	=	10,526
Total					$86,414
Step 2: Cash outflows					
1. Cost of equipment					
($80,000 cost–$5,000 trade-in)	$75,000	×	1.000000§	=	$75,000
2. Training costs	3,000	×	1.000000§	=	3,000
Total					$78,000
Step 3: Net present value					
Total present value of cash inflows					$86,414
Total present value of cash outflows					(78,000)
Net present value					$ 8,414
Alternative 2: Purchase Delivery Truck					
Step 1: Cash inflows					
1. Incremental revenue	$69,000	×	3.433081*	=	$236,883
2. Salvage value	30,000	×	0.519369†	=	15,581
3. Working capital recovery	5,000	×	0.519369†	=	2,597
Total					$255,061
Step 2: Cash outflows					
1. Cost of truck	$115,000	×	1.000000§	=	$115,000
2. Working capital increase	5,000	×	1.000000§	=	5,000
3. Increased operating expense	32,000	×	3.433081*	=	109,859
4. Major overhaul	20,000	×	0.674972⁺	=	13,499
Total					$243,358
Step 3: Net present value					
Total present value of cash inflows					$255,061
Total present value of cash outflows					(243,358)
Net present value					$ 11,703

*Present value of annuity table 2, $n = 5$, $r = 14\%$.

†Present value of single payment table 1, $n = 5$, $r = 14\%$.

‡Present value of single payment table 1, $n = 1$, $r = 14\%$.

§Present value at beginning of period 1.

⁺Present value of single payment table 1, $n = 3$, $r = 14\%$.

With respect to Alternative 1, the original cost and the book value of the existing equipment are ignored. As indicated in a previous chapter, these measures represent *sunk costs*; they are not relevant to the decision. The concept of relevance applies to long-term capital investment decisions just as it applies to the short-term special decisions that were discussed in Chapter 20. To be relevant to a capital investment decision, costs or revenues must involve different present and future cash flows for each alternative. Since the historical cost of the old equipment does not differ between the alternatives, it is not relevant.

Since the *net present value* of each investment alternative is *positive*, either investment will generate a return in excess of 14 percent. Which investment is the more favorable? The data could mislead a careless manager. Alternative 2 might seem the better choice because it

REALITY BYTES

Developing proficiency with present value mathematics is usually the most difficult aspect of capital budgeting for students taking their first managerial accounting course. In real-world companies, the most difficult aspect of capital budgeting is forecasting cash flows for several years into the future. Consider the following capital budgeting project.

In 1965 representatives from the **Georgia Power Company** visited Ms. Taylor's fifth grade class to tell her students about the Edwin I. Hatch Nuclear Plant that was going to be built nearby. One of the authors of this text was a student in that class.

In 1966 construction began on the first unit of the plant, and the plant started producing electricity in 1975. The next year, 10 years after hearing the presentation in his fifth grade class, the author worked on construction of the second unit of the plant during the summer before his senior year of college. This second unit began operations in 1978.

In its 2002 annual report, the **Southern Company,** which is now the major owner of the plant, stated that the Hatch plant is expected to operate until 2038, and that decommissioning of the plant will continue until 2042. The cost to construct both units of the plant was \$934 million. The estimated cost to dismantle and decommission the plant is over \$1 billion.

It seems safe to assume that the students in Ms. Taylor's fifth grade class were not among the first to hear about the power company's plans for the Hatch plant. Thus, we can reasonably conclude that the life of this capital project will be at least 85 years, from around 1960 until 2042.

Try to imagine that you were assigned the task of predicting the cash inflows and outflows for a project that was expected to last 85 years. Clearly, mastering present value mathematics would not be your biggest worry.

has a greater present value than Alternative 1 (\$11,703 vs. \$8,414). Net present value, however, is expressed in *absolute dollars*. The net present value of a more costly capital investment can be greater than the net present value of a smaller investment even though the smaller investment earns a higher rate of return.

To compare different size investment alternatives, management can compute a **present value index** by dividing the present value of cash inflows by the present value of cash outflows. *The higher the ratio, the higher the rate of return per dollar invested in the proposed project.* The present value indices for the two alternatives Torres Transfer Company is considering are as follows.

$$\text{Present value index for Alternative 1} = \frac{\text{Present value of cash inflows}}{\text{Present value of cash outflows}} = \frac{\$86{,}414}{\$78{,}000} = 1.108$$

$$\text{Present value index for Alternative 2} = \frac{\text{Present value of cash inflows}}{\text{Present value of cash outflows}} = \frac{\$255{,}061}{\$243{,}358} = 1.048$$

Management can use the present value indices to rank the investment alternatives. In this case, Alternative 1 yields a higher return than Alternative 2.

LO 5

Determine the internal rate of return of an investment opportunity.

Internal Rate of Return

Management can also rank investment alternatives using the internal rate of return for each investment. Generally, *the higher the internal rate of return, the more profitable the invest-*

ment. We previously demonstrated how to calculate the internal rate of return for an investment that generates a simple cash inflow annuity. The computations are significantly more complex for investments with uneven cash flows. Recall that the internal rate of return is the rate that produces a zero net present value. Manually computing the rate that produces a zero net present value is a tedious trial-and-error process. You must first estimate the rate of return for a particular investment, then calculate the net present value. If the calculation produces a negative net present value, you try a lower estimated rate of return and recalculate. If this calculation produces a positive net present value, the actual internal rate of return lies between the first and second estimates. Make a third estimate and once again recalculate the net present value, and so on. Eventually you will determine the rate of return that produces a net present value of zero.

Many calculators and spreadsheet programs are designed to make these computations. We illustrate the process with a Microsoft Excel spreadsheet. Excel uses the syntax *IRR* (*values, guess*) in which *values* refers to cells that specify the cash flows for which you want to calculate the internal rate of return and *guess* is a number you estimate is close to the actual internal rate of return (IRR). The IRRs for the two investment alternatives available to Torres Transfer Company are shown in Exhibit 24.6. Study this exhibit. Excel requires netting cash outflows against cash inflows for each period in which both outflows and inflows are expected. For your convenience, we have labeled the net cash flows in the spreadsheet. Labeling is not necessary to execute the IRR function. The entire function, including values and guess, can be entered into a single cell of the spreadsheet. Persons familiar with spreadsheet programs learn to significantly simplify the input required.

The IRR results in Exhibit 24.6 confirm the ranking determined using the present value index. Alternative 1 (modernize maintenance facility), with an internal rate of return of 18.69 percent, ranks above Alternative 2 (purchase a truck) with an internal rate of return of 17.61 percent, even though Alternative 2 has a higher net present value (see Exhibit 24.5). Alternative 2, however, still may be the better investment option, depending on the amount available

EXHIBIT 24.6

Microsoft Excel Spreadsheet Internal Rate of Return Function

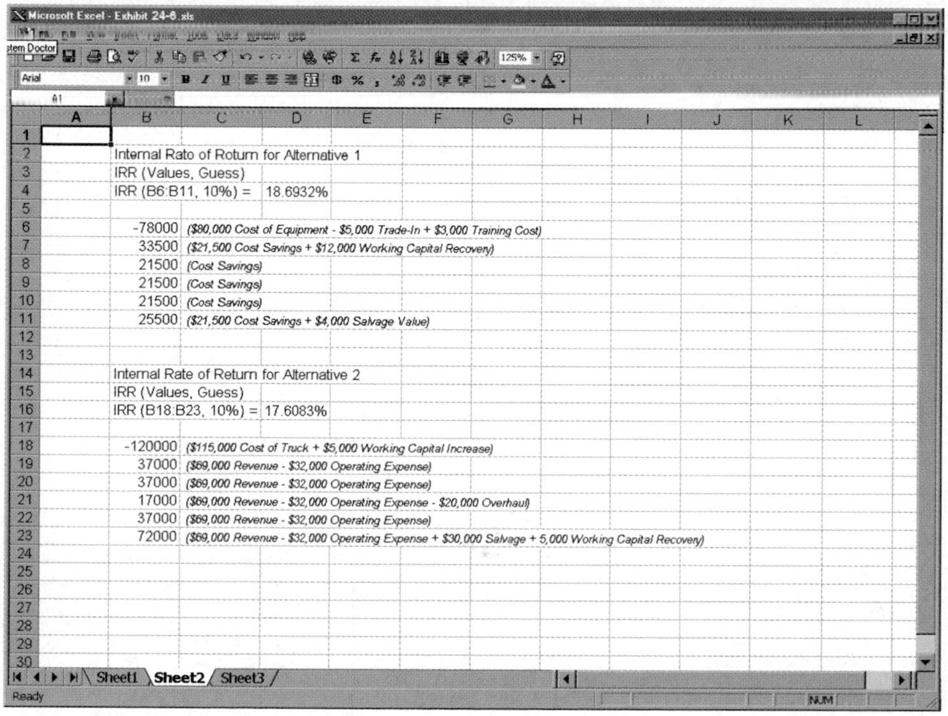

to invest. Suppose Torres has $120,000 of available funds to invest. Because Alternative 1 requires an initial investment of only $78,000, $42,000 ($120,000 − $78,000) of capital will not be invested. If Torres has no other investment opportunities for this $42,000, the company would be better off investing the entire $120,000 in Alternative 2 ($115,000 cost of truck + $5,000 working capital increase). Earning 17.61 percent on a $120,000 investment is better than earning 18.69 percent on a $78,000 investment with no return on the remaining $42,000. Management accounting requires exercising judgment when making decisions.

Relevance and the Time Value of Money

Suppose you have the opportunity to invest in one of two capital projects. Both projects require an immediate cash outflow of $6,000 and will produce future cash inflows of $8,000. The only difference between the two projects is the timing of the inflows. The receipt schedule for both projects follows.

	Project 1	Project 2
2007	$3,500	$2,000
2008	3,000	2,000
2009	1,000	2,000
2010	500	2,000
Total	$8,000	$8,000

Because both projects cost the same and produce the same total cash inflows, they may appear to be equal. Whether you select Project 1 or Project 2, you pay $6,000 and receive $8,000. Because of the time value of money, however, Project 1 is preferable to Project 2. To see why, determine the net present value of both projects, assuming a 10 percent desired rate of return.

Computation of Net Present Value for Project 1 and Project 2

Net Present Value for Project 1

Period	Cash Inflow	×	Conversion Factor Table 1, $r = 10\%$	=	Present Value
1	$3,500	×	0.909091	=	$3,182
2	3,000	×	0.826446	=	2,479
3	1,000	×	0.751315	=	751
4	500	×	0.683013	=	342
Present value of future cash inflows					6,754
Present value of cash outflow					(6,000)
Net present value Project 1					$ 754

Net Present Value for Project 2

	Cash Inflow Annuity	×	Conversion Factor Table 2, $r = 10\%$, $n = 4$	
Present value of cash inflow	$2,000	×	3.169865	$6,340
Present value of cash outflow				(6,000)
Net present value Project 2				$ 340

The net present value of Project 1 ($754) exceeds the net present value of Project 2 ($340). The timing as well as the amount of cash flows has a significant impact on capital investment returns. Recall that to be relevant, costs or revenues must differ between alterna-

Answers to The Curious Accountant

Ginger and Fred should not simply compare $10,000 spent today with $13,000 in energy savings and higher resale value that are to be received in the future. A dollar received in the future is worth less than a dollar spent today because of the time value of money. In order to decide if the replacement windows are worth their cost, today's $10,000 must be compared in common values with the $13,000 that they estimate will be received in the future.

This problem can be solved using the net present value approach that is explained in this chapter. This method calculates the present value of all dollars spent and received, and chooses the option with the highest present value. These computations are shown below. Note that a discount rate of 4 percent is used, because this is the rate that will be lost if the mutual fund is liquidated. This 4 percent is an opportunity cost.

The windows cost more than the present value of their future benefits, so this opportunity has a negative net present value of $404.51 ($10,000.00 − $9,595.49). Therefore, from a strictly financial point of view, Fred and Ginger should not buy the windows. Of course there may be nonquantitative factors in favor of buying the windows that the analysis above did not consider. Perhaps Ginger and Fred believe their new neighbors will like them more if they improve the looks of their house. If Fred and Ginger believe that being liked by their neighbors is worth $404.51, they should go ahead and purchase the windows.

Annual savings in heating and cooling costs	$ 600	
× Present value factor of a 10-year annuity, at 4%	8.110896	
Present value of the annual energy savings		$ 4,866.54
Increase in resale value of the house	$ 7,000	
× Present value factor of $1 in 10 years, at 4%	0.675564	
Present value of the increase in resale value		4,728.95
Total present value of buying the windows		$ 9,595.49
Cost of the new windows, today		$10,000.00

tives. Differences in the timing of cash flow payments or receipts are also relevant for decision-making purposes.

Tax Considerations

The previous examples have ignored the effect of income taxes on capital investment decisions. Taxes affect the amount of cash flows generated by investments. To illustrate, assume Wu Company purchases an asset that costs $240,000. The asset has a four-year useful life, no salvage value, and is depreciated on a straight-line basis. The asset generates cash revenue of $90,000 per year. Assume Wu's income tax rate is 40 percent. What is the net present value of the asset, assuming Wu's management desires to earn a 10 percent rate of return after taxes? The first step in answering this question is to calculate the annual cash flow generated by the asset, as shown in Exhibit 24.7.

Because recognizing depreciation expense does not require a cash payment (cash is paid when assets are purchased, not when depreciation is recognized), depreciation expense must be added back to after-tax income to determine the annual cash inflow. Once the cash flow is determined, the net present value is computed as shown here.

Cash flow annuity	×	Conversion factor Table 2, $r = 10\%$, $n = 4$	=	Present value cash inflows	−	Present value cash outflows	=	Net present value
$78,000	×	3.169865	=	$247,249	−	$240,000	=	$7,249

The depreciation sheltered some of the income from taxation. Income taxes apply to income after deducting depreciation expense. Without depreciation expense, income taxes each year would have been $36,000 ($90,000 × 0.40) instead of $12,000 ($30,000 × 0.40).

EXHIBIT 24.7

Determining Cash Flow from Investment

	Period 1	Period 2	Period 3	Period 4
Cash revenue	$90,000	$90,000	$90,000	$90,000
Depreciation expense (noncash)	(60,000)	(60,000)	(60,000)	(60,000)
Income before taxes	30,000	30,000	30,000	30,000
Income tax at 40%	(12,000)	(12,000)	(12,000)	(12,000)
Income after tax	18,000	18,000	18,000	18,000
Depreciation add back	60,000	60,000	60,000	60,000
Annual cash inflow	$78,000	$78,000	$78,000	$78,000

The $24,000 difference ($36,000 − $12,000) is known as a *depreciation tax shield.* The amount of the depreciation tax shield can also be computed by multiplying the depreciation expense by the tax rate ($60,000 × 0.40 = $24,000).

Because of the time value of money, companies benefit by maximizing the depreciation tax shield early in the life of an asset. For this reason, most companies calculate depreciation expense for tax purposes using the *modified accelerated cost recovery system (MACRS)* permitted by tax law rather than using straight-line depreciation. MACRS recognizes depreciation on an accelerated basis, assigning larger amounts of depreciation in the early years of an asset's useful life. The higher depreciation charges result in lower amounts of taxable income and lower income taxes. In the later years of an asset's useful life, the reverse is true, and lower depreciation charges result in higher taxes. Accelerated depreciation does not allow companies to avoid paying taxes but to delay them. The longer companies can delay paying taxes, the more cash they have available to invest.

Techniques that Ignore the Time Value of Money

Topic Tackler PLUS

24-2

Several techniques for evaluating capital investment proposals ignore the time value of money. Although these techniques are less accurate, they are quick and simple. When investments are small or the returns are expected within a short time, these techniques are likely to result in the same decisions that more sophisticated techniques produce.

Payback Method

LO 6

Determine the payback period for an investment opportunity.

The **payback method** is simple to apply and easy to understand. It shows how long it will take to recover the initial cash outflow (the cost) of an investment. The formula for computing the payback period, measured in years, is as follows.

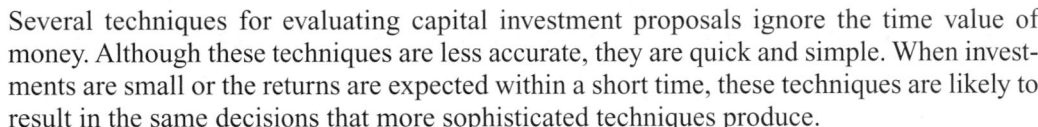

Payback period = Net cost of investment ÷ Annual net cash inflow

To illustrate, assume Winston Cleaners can purchase a new ironing machine that will press shirts in half the time of the one currently used. The new machine costs $100,000 and will reduce labor cost by $40,000 per year over a four-year useful life. The payback period is computed as follows.

Payback period = $100,000 ÷ $40,000 = 2.5 years

Interpreting Payback. Generally, investments with shorter payback periods are considered better. Because the payback method measures only investment recovery, not profitability, however, this conclusion can be invalid when considering investment alternatives. To illustrate, assume Winston Cleaners also has the opportunity to purchase a different machine that costs $100,000 and provides an annual labor savings of $40,000. However, the second machine will last for five instead of four years. The payback period is still 2.5 years ($100,000 ÷ $40,000), but the second machine is a better investment because it improves profitability by providing an additional year of cost savings. The payback analysis does not measure this difference between the alternatives.

Unequal Cash Flows. The preceding illustration assumed Winston's labor cost reduction saved the same amount of cash each year for the life of the new machine. The payback method requires adjustment when cash flow benefits are unequal. Suppose a company purchases a machine for $6,000. The machine will be used erratically and is expected to provide incremental revenue over the next five years as follows.

2007	2008	2009	2010	2011
$3,000	$1,000	$2,000	$1,000	$500

Based on this cash inflow pattern, what is the payback period? There are two acceptable solutions. One accumulates the incremental revenue until the sum equals the amount of the original investment.

Year	Annual Amount	Cumulative Total
2007	$3,000	$3,000
2008	1,000	4,000
2009	2,000	6,000

This approach indicates the payback period is three years.

A second solution uses an averaging concept. The average annual cash inflow is determined. This figure is then used in the denominator of the payback equation. Using the preceding data, the payback period is computed as follows.

1. Compute the average annual cash inflow.

$$\begin{array}{l}2007 + 2008 + 2009 + 2010 + 2011 = \text{Total} \div 5 = \text{Average}\\ \$3{,}000 + \$1{,}000 + \$2{,}000 + \$1{,}000 + \$500 = \$7{,}500 \div 5 = \$1{,}500\end{array}$$

2. Compute the payback period.

$$\frac{\text{Net cost of}}{\text{investment}} \div \frac{\text{Average annual}}{\text{net cash inflow}} = \$6{,}000 \div \$1{,}500 = 4 \text{ years}$$

The average method is useful when a company purchases a number of similar assets with differing cash return patterns.

Unadjusted Rate of Return

LO 7

Determine the unadjusted rate of return for an investment opportunity.

The **unadjusted rate of return** method is another common evaluation technique. Investment cash flows are not adjusted to reflect the time value of money. The unadjusted rate of return is sometimes called the *simple rate of return.* It is computed as follows.

$$\text{Unadjusted rate of return} = \frac{\text{Average incremental increase in annual net income}}{\text{Net cost of original investment}}$$

To illustrate computing the unadjusted rate of return, assume The Dining Table Inc. is considering establishing a new restaurant that will require a $2,000,000 original investment. Management anticipates operating the restaurant for 10 years before significant renovations will be required. The restaurant is expected to provide an average after-tax return of $280,000 per year. The unadjusted rate of return is computed as follows.

$$\text{Unadjusted rate of return} = \$280{,}000 \div \$2{,}000{,}000 = 14\% \text{ per year}$$

The accuracy of the unadjusted rate of return suffers from the failure to recognize the recovery of invested capital. With respect to a depreciable asset, the capital investment is normally recovered through revenue over the life of the asset. To illustrate, assume we purchase a \$1,000 asset with a two-year life and a zero salvage value. For simplicity, ignore income taxes. Assume the asset produces \$600 of cash revenue per year. The income statement for the first year of operation appears as follows.

Revenue	\$600
Depreciation Expense	(500)
Net Income	\$100

What is the amount of invested capital during the first year? First, a \$1,000 cash outflow was used to purchase the asset (the original investment). Next, we collected \$600 of cash revenue of which \$100 was a *return on investment* (net income) and \$500 was a **recovery of investment.** As a result, \$1,000 was invested in the asset at the beginning of the year and \$500 was invested at the end of the year. Similarly, we will recover an additional \$500 of capital during the second year of operation, leaving zero invested capital at the end of the second year. Given that the cash inflows from revenue are collected somewhat evenly over the life of the investment, the amount of invested capital will range from a beginning balance of \$1,000 to an ending balance of zero. On average, we will have \$500 invested in the asset (the midpoint between \$1,000 and zero). The average investment can be determined by dividing the total original investment by 2 (\$1,000 ÷ 2 = \$500). The unadjusted rate of return based on average invested capital can be calculated as follows.

$$\begin{aligned}\text{Unadjusted rate of return (Based on average investment)} &= \frac{\text{Average incremental increase in annual net income}}{\text{Net cost of original investment} \div 2} \\ &= \frac{\$100}{\$1{,}000 \div 2} = 20\%\end{aligned}$$

To avoid distortions caused by the failure to recognize the recovery of invested capital, the unadjusted rate of return should be based on the *average investment* when working with investments in depreciable assets.

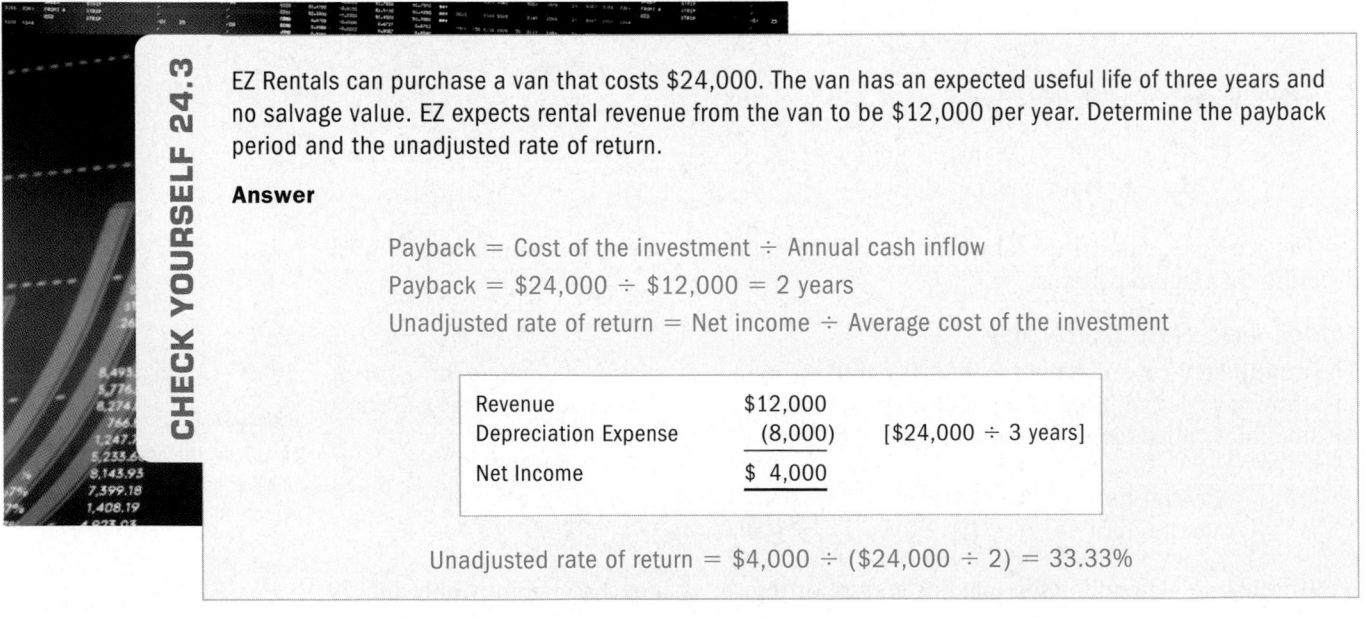

CHECK YOURSELF 24.3

EZ Rentals can purchase a van that costs \$24,000. The van has an expected useful life of three years and no salvage value. EZ expects rental revenue from the van to be \$12,000 per year. Determine the payback period and the unadjusted rate of return.

Answer

Payback = Cost of the investment ÷ Annual cash inflow
Payback = \$24,000 ÷ \$12,000 = 2 years
Unadjusted rate of return = Net income ÷ Average cost of the investment

Revenue	\$12,000	
Depreciation Expense	(8,000)	[\$24,000 ÷ 3 years]
Net Income	\$ 4,000	

Unadjusted rate of return = \$4,000 ÷ (\$24,000 ÷ 2) = 33.33%

Real-World Reporting Practices

In a recent study, researchers found that companies in the forest products industry use discounted cash flow techniques more frequently when the capital project being considered is a long-term timber investment. The use of techniques that ignore the time value of money increased when other shorter-term capital investment projects were being considered. Exhibit 24.8 shows the researchers' findings.

EXHIBIT 24.8

Forestry Industry Investments

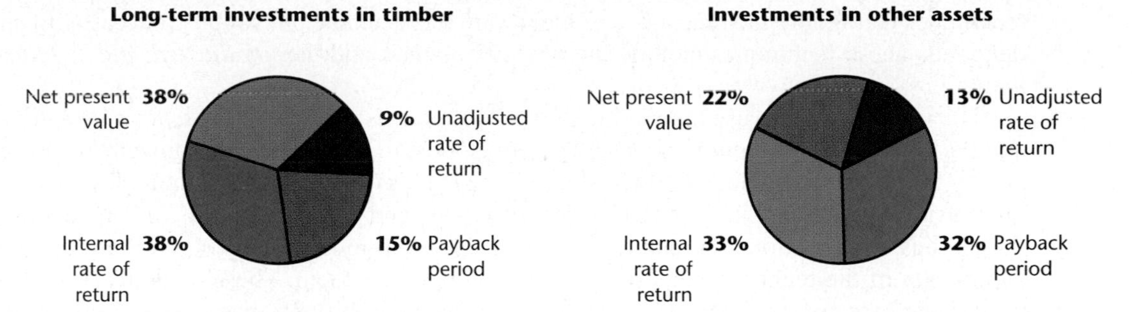

Data Source: J. Bailes, J. Nielsen, and S. Lawton, "How Forest Product Companies Analyze Capital Budgets," *Management Accounting,* October 1998, pp. 24–30.

Postaudits

LO 8

Conduct a postaudit of a completed investment.

The analytical techniques for evaluating capital investment proposals depend highly on estimates of future cash flows. Although predictions cannot be perfectly accurate, gross miscalculations can threaten the existence of an organization. For example, optimistic projections of future cash inflows that do not materialize will lead to investments that do not return the cost of capital. Managers must take their projections seriously. A postaudit policy can encourage managers to carefully consider their capital investment decisions. A **postaudit** is conducted at the completion of a capital investment project, using the same analytical technique that was used to justify the original investment. For example, if an internal rate of return was used to justify approving an investment project, the internal rate of return should be computed in the postaudit. In the postaudit computation, *actual* rather than estimated cash flows are used. Postaudits determine whether the expected results were achieved.

Postaudits should focus on continuous improvement rather than punishment. Managers who are chastised for failing to achieve expected results might become overly cautious when asked to provide estimates for future projects. Being too conservative can create problems as serious as those caused by being too optimistic. Managers can err two ways with respect to capital investment decisions. First, a manager might accept a project that should have been rejected. This mistake usually stems from excessively optimistic future cash flow projections. Second, a manager might reject a project that should have been accepted. These missed opportunities are usually the result of underestimating future cash flows. A too cautious manager can become unable to locate enough projects to fully invest the firm's funds.

Idle cash earns no return. If projects continue to outperform expectations, managers are probably estimating future cash flows too conservatively. If projects consistently fail to live up to expectations, managers are probably being too optimistic in their projections of future cash flows. Either way, the company suffers. The goal of a postaudit is to provide feedback that will help managers improve the accuracy of future cash flow projections, maximizing the quality of the firm's capital investments.

A Look Back <<

Capital expenditures have a significant, long-term effect on profitability. They usually involve major cash outflows that are recovered through future cash inflows. The most common cash inflows include incremental revenue, operating cost savings, salvage value, and working capital releases. The most common outflows are the initial investment, increases in operating expenses, and working capital commitments.

Several techniques for analyzing the cash flows associated with capital investments are available. The techniques can be divided into two categories: (1) techniques that use time value of money concepts and (2) techniques that ignore the time value of money. Generally, techniques that ignore the time value of money are less accurate but simpler and easier to understand. These techniques include the *payback method* and the *unadjusted rate of return method.*

The techniques that use time value of money concepts are the *net present value method* and the *internal rate of return method.* These methods offer significant improvements in accuracy but are more difficult to understand. They may involve tedious computations and require using experienced judgment. Computer software and programmed calculators that ease the tedious computational burden are readily available to most managers. Furthermore, the superiority of the techniques justifies learning how to use them. These methods should be used when investment expenditures are larger or when cash flows extend over a prolonged time period.

>> A Look Forward

This chapter probably completes your introduction to accounting. We sincerely hope that this text has provided you a meaningful learning experience that will serve you well as you progress through your academic training and ultimately, your career. Good luck and best wishes!

APPENDIX

TABLE 1 Present Value of $1

n	4%	5%	6%	7%	8%	9%	10%	12%	14%	16%	20%
1	0.961538	0.952381	0.943396	0.934579	0.925926	0.917431	0.909091	0.892857	0.877193	0.862069	0.833333
2	0.924556	0.907029	0.889996	0.873439	0.857339	0.841680	0.826446	0.797194	0.769468	0.743163	0.694444
3	0.888996	0.863838	0.839619	0.816298	0.793832	0.772183	0.751315	0.711780	0.674972	0.640658	0.578704
4	0.854804	0.822702	0.792094	0.762895	0.735030	0.708425	0.683013	0.635518	0.592080	0.552291	0.482253
5	0.821927	0.783526	0.747258	0.712986	0.680583	0.649931	0.620921	0.567427	0.519369	0.476113	0.401878
6	0.790315	0.746215	0.704961	0.666342	0.630170	0.596267	0.564474	0.506631	0.455587	0.410442	0.334898
7	0.759918	0.710681	0.665057	0.622750	0.583490	0.547034	0.513158	0.452349	0.399637	0.353830	0.279082
8	0.730690	0.676839	0.627412	0.582009	0.540269	0.501866	0.466507	0.403883	0.350559	0.305025	0.232568
9	0.702587	0.644609	0.591898	0.543934	0.500249	0.460428	0.424098	0.360610	0.307508	0.262953	0.193807
10	0.675564	0.613913	0.558395	0.508349	0.463193	0.422411	0.385543	0.321973	0.269744	0.226684	0.161506
11	0.649581	0.584679	0.526788	0.475093	0.428883	0.387533	0.350494	0.287476	0.236617	0.195417	0.134588
12	0.624597	0.556837	0.496969	0.444012	0.397114	0.355535	0.318631	0.256675	0.207559	0.168463	0.112157
13	0.600574	0.530321	0.468839	0.414964	0.367698	0.326179	0.289664	0.229174	0.182069	0.145227	0.093464
14	0.577475	0.505068	0.442301	0.387817	0.340461	0.299246	0.263331	0.204620	0.159710	0.125195	0.077887
15	0.555265	0.481017	0.417265	0.362446	0.315242	0.274538	0.239392	0.182696	0.140096	0.107927	0.064905
16	0.533908	0.458112	0.393646	0.338735	0.291890	0.251870	0.217629	0.163122	0.122892	0.093041	0.054088
17	0.513373	0.436297	0.371364	0.316574	0.270269	0.231073	0.197845	0.145644	0.107800	0.080207	0.045073
18	0.493628	0.415521	0.350344	0.295864	0.250249	0.211994	0.179859	0.130040	0.094561	0.069144	0.037561
19	0.474642	0.395734	0.330513	0.276508	0.231712	0.194490	0.163508	0.116107	0.082948	0.059607	0.031301
20	0.456387	0.376889	0.311805	0.258419	0.214548	0.178431	0.148644	0.103667	0.072762	0.051385	0.026084

TABLE 2 Present Value of an Annuity of $1

n	4%	5%	6%	7%	8%	9%	10%	12%	14%	16%	20%
1	0.961538	0.952381	0.943396	0.934579	0.925926	0.917431	0.909091	0.892857	0.877193	0.862069	0.833333
2	1.886095	1.859410	1.83393	1.808018	1.783265	1.759111	1.735537	1.690051	1.646661	1.605232	1.527778
3	2.775091	2.723248	2.673012	2.624316	2.577097	2.531295	2.486852	2.401831	2.321632	2.245890	2.106481
4	3.629895	3.545951	3.465106	3.387211	3.312127	3.239720	3.169865	3.037349	2.913712	2.798181	2.588735
5	4.451822	4.329477	4.212364	4.100197	3.992710	3.889651	3.790787	3.604776	3.433081	3.274294	2.990612
6	5.242137	5.075692	4.917324	4.766540	4.622880	4.485919	4.355261	4.111407	3.888668	3.684736	3.325510
7	6.002055	5.786373	5.582381	5.389289	5.206370	5.032953	4.868419	4.563757	4.288305	4.038565	3.604592
8	6.732745	6.463213	6.209794	5.971299	5.746639	5.534819	5.334926	4.967640	4.638864	4.343591	3.837160
9	7.435332	7.107822	6.801692	6.515232	6.246888	5.995247	5.759024	5.328250	4.946372	4.606544	4.030967
10	8.110896	7.721735	7.360087	7.023582	6.710081	6.417658	6.144567	5.650223	5.216116	4.833227	4.192472
11	8.760477	8.306414	7.886875	7.498674	7.138964	6.805191	6.495061	5.937699	5.452733	5.028644	4.327060
12	9.385074	8.863252	8.383844	7.942686	7.536078	7.160725	6.813692	6.194374	5.660292	5.197107	4.439217
13	9.985648	9.393573	8.852683	8.357651	7.903776	7.486904	7.103356	6.423548	5.842362	5.342334	4.532681
14	10.563123	9.898641	9.294984	8.745468	8.244237	7.786150	7.366687	6.628168	6.002072	5.467529	4.610567
15	11.118387	10.379658	9.712249	9.107914	8.559479	8.060688	7.606080	6.810864	6.142168	5.575456	4.675473
16	11.652296	10.837770	10.105895	9.446649	8.851369	8.312558	7.823709	6.973986	6.265060	5.668497	4.729561
17	12.165669	11.274066	10.477260	9.763223	9.121638	8.543631	8.021553	7.119630	6.372859	5.748704	4.774634
18	12.659297	11.689587	10.827603	10.059087	9.371887	8.755625	8.201412	7.249670	6.467420	5.817848	4.812195
19	13.133939	12.085321	11.158116	10.335595	9.603599	8.905115	8.364920	7.365777	6.550369	5.877455	4.843496
20	13.590326	12.462210	11.469921	10.594014	9.818147	9.128546	8.513564	7.469444	6.623131	5.928841	4.869580

SELF-STUDY REVIEW PROBLEM

The CFO of Advo Corporation is considering two investment opportunities. The expected future cash inflows for each opportunity follow:

	Year 1	Year 2	Year 3	Year 4
Project 1	$144,000	$147,000	$160,000	$178,000
Project 2	204,000	199,000	114,000	112,000

Both investments require an initial payment of $400,000. Advo's desired rate of return is 16 percent.

Required

a. Compute the net present value of each project. Which project should Advo adopt based on the net present value approach?

b. Use the summation method to compute the payback period for each project. Which project should Advo adopt based on the payback approach?

Solution to Requirement *a*

Project 1	Cash Inflows		Table Factor*		Present Value
Year 1	$144,000	×	0.862069	=	$124,138
Year 2	147,000	×	0.743163	=	109,245
Year 3	160,000	×	0.640658	=	102,505
Year 4	178,000	×	0.552291	=	98,308
PV of cash inflows					434,196
Cost of investment					(400,000)
Net present value					$ 34,196

*Table 1, n = 1 through 4, r = 16%

Project 2						
	Cash Inflows		Table Factor*		Present Value
Year 1	$204,000	×	0.862069	=	$175,862
Year 2	199,000	×	0.743163	=	147,889
Year 3	114,000	×	0.640658	=	73,035
Year 4	112,000	×	0.552291	=	61,857
PV of cash inflows					458,643
Cost of investment					(400,000)
Net present value					$ 58,643

*Table 1, n = 1 through 4, r = 16%

Advo should adopt Project 2 since it has a greater net present value.

Solution to Requirement *b*

Cash Inflows	Project 1	Project 2
Year 1	$144,000	$204,000
Year 2	147,000	199,000
Total	$291,000	$403,000

By the end of the second year, Project 2's cash inflows have more than paid for the cost of the investment. In contrast, Project 1 still falls short of investment recovery by $109,000 ($400,000 − $291,000). Advo should adopt Project 2 since it has a shorter payback period.

KEY TERMS

accumulated conversion factors 1152
annuity 1153
capital investments 1150
cost of capital 1151
incremental revenue 1157
internal rate of return 1156
minimum rate of return 1151
net present value 1156
ordinary annuity 1154
payback method 1164
postaudit 1167
present value index 1160
present value table 1152
recovery of investment 1166
single-payment (lump-sum) 1152
time value of money 1150
unadjusted rate of return 1165
working capital 1157

QUESTIONS

1. What is a capital investment? How does it differ from an investment in stocks or bonds?
2. What are three reasons that cash is worth more today than cash to be received in the future?
3. "A dollar today is worth more than a dollar in the future." "The present value of a future dollar is worth less than one dollar." Are these two statements synonymous? Explain.
4. Define the term *return on investment.* How is the return normally expressed? Give an example of a capital investment return.
5. How does a company establish its minimum acceptable rate of return on investments?
6. If you wanted to have $500,000 one year from today and desired to earn a 10 percent return, what amount would you need to invest today? Which amount has more value, the amount today or the $500,000 a year from today?
7. Why are present value tables frequently used to convert future values to present values?
8. Define the term *annuity.* What is one example of an annuity receipt?

9. How can present value "what-if" analysis be enhanced by using software programs?

10. Receiving $100,000 per year for five years is equivalent to investing what amount today at 14 percent? Provide a mathematical formula to solve this problem, assuming use of a present value annuity table to convert the future cash flows to their present value equivalents. Provide the expression for the Excel spreadsheet function that would perform the present value conversion.

11. Maria Espinosa borrowed $15,000 from the bank and agreed to repay the loan at 8 percent annual interest over four years, making payments of $4,529 per year. Because part of the bank's payment from Ms. Espinosa is a recovery of the original investment, what assumption must the bank make to earn its desired 8 percent compounded annual return?

12. Two investment opportunities have positive net present values. Investment A's net present value amounts to $40,000 while B's is only $30,000. Does this mean that A is the better investment opportunity? Explain.

13. What criteria determine whether a project is acceptable under the net present value method?

14. Does the net present value method provide a measure of the rate of return on capital investments?

15. Which is the best capital investment evaluation technique for ranking investment opportunities?

16. Paul Henderson is a manager for Spark Company. He tells you that his company always maximizes profitability by accepting the investment opportunity with the highest internal rate of return. Explain to Mr. Henderson how his company may improve profitability by sometimes selecting investment opportunities with lower internal rates of return.

17. What is the relationship between desired rate of return and internal rate of return?

18. What typical cash inflow and outflow items are associated with capital investments?

19. "I always go for the investment with the shortest payback period." Is this a sound strategy? Why or why not?

20. "The payback method cannot be used if the cash inflows occur in unequal patterns." Do you agree or disagree? Explain.

21. What are the advantages and disadvantages associated with the unadjusted rate of return method for evaluating capital investments?

22. How do capital investments affect profitability?

23. What is a postaudit? How is it useful in capital budgeting?

EXERCISES—SERIES A

All Exercises in Series A are available with McGraw-Hill's Homework Manager.

Exercise 24-1A *Identifying cash inflows and outflows*

L.O. 1

Required

Indicate which of the following items will result in cash inflows and which will result in cash outflows. The first one is shown as an example.

Item	Type of Cash Flow
a. Incremental revenue	Inflow
b. Initial investment	
c. Salvage values	
d. Recovery of working capital	
e. Incremental expenses	
f. Working capital commitments	
g. Cost savings	

Exercise 24-2A *Determining the present value of a lump-sum future cash receipt*

L.O. 1, 2

Mark Nelson turned 20 years old today. His grandfather established a trust fund that will pay Mr. Nelson $50,000 on his next birthday. However, Mr. Nelson needs money today to start his college

education. His father is willing to help and has agreed to give Mr. Nelson the present value of the future cash inflow, assuming a 10 percent rate of return.

Required

a. Use a present value table to determine the amount of cash that Mr. Nelson's father should give him.

b. Use an algebraic formula to prove that the present value of the trust fund (the amount of cash computed in Requirement *a*) is equal to its $50,000 future value.

L.O. 1, 2

Exercise 24-3A *Determining the present value of a lump-sum future cash receipt*

Ginger Smalley expects to receive a $300,000 cash benefit when she retires five years from today. Ms. Smalley's employer has offered an early retirement incentive by agreeing to pay her $180,000 today if she agrees to retire immediately. Ms. Smalley desires to earn a rate of return of 12 percent.

Required

a. Assuming that the retirement benefit is the only consideration in making the retirement decision, should Ms. Smalley accept her employer's offer?

b. Identify the factors that cause the present value of the retirement benefit to be less than $300,000.

L.O. 1, 2

Exercise 24-4A *Determining the present value of an annuity*

The dean of the School of Social Science is trying to decide whether to purchase a copy machine to place in the lobby of the building. The machine would add to student convenience, but the dean feels compelled to earn an 8 percent return on the investment of funds. Estimates of cash inflows from copy machines that have been placed in other university buildings indicate that the copy machine would probably produce incremental cash inflows of approximately $8,000 per year. The machine is expected to have a three-year useful life with a zero salvage value.

Required

a. Use Present Value Table 1 in Appendix A to determine the maximum amount of cash the dean should be willing to pay for a copy machine.

b. Use Present Value Table 2 in Appendix A to determine the maximum amount of cash the dean should be willing to pay for a copy machine.

c. Explain the consistency or lack of consistency in the answers to Requirements *a* and *b*.

L.O. 4

Exercise 24-5A *Determining net present value*

Transit Shuttle Inc. is considering investing in two new vans that are expected to generate combined cash inflows of $20,000 per year. The vans' combined purchase price is $65,000. The expected life and salvage value of each are four years and $15,000, respectively. Transit Shuttle has an average cost of capital of 14 percent.

Required

a. Calculate the net present value of the investment opportunity.

b. Indicate whether the investment opportunity is expected to earn a return that is above or below the cost of capital and whether it should be accepted.

L.O. 4

Exercise 24-6A *Determining net present value*

Travis Vintor is seeking part-time employment while he attends school. He is considering purchasing technical equipment that will enable him to start a small training services company that will offer tutorial services over the Internet. Travis expects demand for the service to grow rapidly in the first two years of operation as customers learn about the availability of the Internet assistance. Thereafter, he expects demand to stabilize. The following table presents the expected cash flows.

Year of Operation	Cash Inflow	Cash Outflow
2006	$5,400	$3,600
2007	7,800	4,800
2008	8,400	5,040
2009	8,400	5,040

In addition to these cash flows, Mr. Vintor expects to pay $8,400 for the equipment. He also expects to pay $1,440 for a major overhaul and updating of the equipment at the end of the second year of operation. The equipment is expected to have a $600 salvage value and a four-year useful life. Mr. Vintor desires to earn a rate of return of 8 percent.

Required

(Round computations to the nearest whole penny.)

a. Calculate the net present value of the investment opportunity.

b. Indicate whether the investment opportunity is expected to earn a return that is above or below the desired rate of return and whether it should be accepted.

Exercise 24-7A *Using present value index*

L.O. 4

Wrencher Company has a choice of two investment alternatives. The present value of cash inflows and outflows for the first alternative is $60,000 and $56,000, respectively. The present value of cash inflows and outflows for the second alternative is $146,000 and $142,000, respectively.

Required

a. Calculate the net present value of each investment opportunity.

b. Calculate the present value index for each investment opportunity.

c. Indicate which investment will produce the higher rate of return.

Exercise 24-8A *Determining the internal rate of return*

L.O. 5

Medina Manufacturing Company has an opportunity to purchase some technologically advanced equipment that will reduce the company's cash outflow for operating expenses by $1,280,000 per year. The cost of the equipment is $6,186,530.56. Medina expects it to have a 10-year useful life and a zero salvage value. The company has established an investment opportunity hurdle rate of 15 percent and uses the straight-line method for depreciation.

Required

a. Calculate the internal rate of return of the investment opportunity.

b. Indicate whether the investment opportunity should be accepted.

Exercise 24-9A *Using the internal rate of return to compare investment opportunities*

L.O. 5

Smith and Hough (S&H) is a partnership that owns a small company. It is considering two alternative investment opportunities. The first investment opportunity will have a five-year useful life, will cost $9,335.16, and will generate expected cash inflows of $2,400 per year. The second investment is expected to have a useful life of three years, will cost $6,217.13, and will generate expected cash inflows of $2,500 per year. Assume that S&H has the funds available to accept only one of the opportunities.

Required

a. Calculate the internal rate of return of each investment opportunity.

b. Based on the internal rates of return, which opportunity should S&H select?

c. Discuss other factors that S&H should consider in the investment decision.

Exercise 24-10A *Determining the cash flow annuity with income tax considerations*

L.O. 1, 2

To open a new store, Ross Tire Company plans to invest $640,000 in equipment expected to have a four-year useful life and no salvage value. Ross expects the new store to generate annual cash revenues of $840,000 and to incur annual cash operating expenses of $520,000. Ross's average income tax rate is 30 percent. The company uses straight-line depreciation.

Required

Determine the expected annual net cash inflow from operations for each of the first four years after Ross opens the new store.

Exercise 24-11A *Evaluating discounted cash flow techniques*

L.O. 8

Kay Vickery is angry with Gene Libby. He is behind schedule developing supporting material for tomorrow's capital budget committee meeting. When she approached him about his apparent

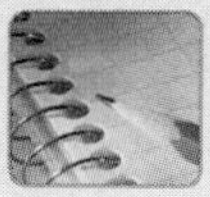

lackadaisical attitude in general and his tardiness in particular, he responded, "I don't see why we do this stuff in the first place. It's all a bunch of estimates. Who knows what future cash flows will really be? I certainly don't. I've been doing this job for five years, and no one has ever checked to see if I even came close at these guesses. I've been waiting for marketing to provide the estimated cash inflows on the projects being considered tomorrow. But, if you want my report now, I'll have it in a couple of hours. I can make up the marketing data as well as they can."

Required

Does Mr. Libby have a point? Is there something wrong with the company's capital budgeting system? Write a brief response explaining how to improve the investment evaluation system.

L.O. 6

Exercise 24-12A *Determining the payback period*

Cascade Airline Company is considering expanding its territory. The company has the opportunity to purchase one of two different used airplanes. The first airplane is expected to cost $1,800,000; it will enable the company to increase its annual cash inflow by $600,000 per year. The plane is expected to have a useful life of five years and no salvage value. The second plane costs $3,600,000; it will enable the company to increase annual cash flow by $900,000 per year. This plane has an eight-year useful life and a zero salvage value.

Required

a. Determine the payback period for each investment alternative and identify the alternative Cascade should accept if the decision is based on the payback approach.

b. Discuss the shortcomings of using the payback method to evaluate investment opportunities.

L.O. 6

Exercise 24-13A *Determining the payback period with uneven cash flows*

Shaw Company has an opportunity to purchase a forklift to use in its heavy equipment rental business. The forklift would be leased on an annual basis during its first two years of operation. Thereafter, it would be leased to the general public on demand. Shaw would sell it at the end of the fifth year of its useful life. The expected cash inflows and outflows follow.

Year	Nature of Item	Cash Inflow	Cash Outflow
2008	Purchase price		$48,000
2008	Revenue	$20,000	
2009	Revenue	20,000	
2010	Revenue	14,000	
2010	Major overhaul		6,000
2011	Revenue	12,000	
2012	Revenue	9,600	
2012	Salvage value	6,400	

Required

a. Determine the payback period using the accumulated cash flows approach.

b. Determine the payback period using the average cash flows approach.

L.O. 7

Exercise 24-14A *Determining the unadjusted rate of return*

Tharpe Painting Company is considering whether to purchase a new spray paint machine that costs $3,000. The machine is expected to save labor, increasing net income by $450 per year. The effective life of the machine is 15 years according to the manufacturer's estimate.

Required

a. Determine the unadjusted rate of return based on the average cost of the investment.

b. Discuss the shortcomings of using the unadjusted rate of return to evaluate investment opportunities.

L.O. 6, 7

Exercise 24-15A *Computing the payback period and unadjusted rate of return for one investment opportunity*

Padgett Rentals can purchase a van that costs $48,000; it has an expected useful life of three years and no salvage value. Padgett uses straight-line depreciation. Expected revenue is $24,000 per year.

Required

a. Determine the payback period.
b. Determine the unadjusted rate of return based on the average cost of the investment.

PROBLEMS—SERIES A

All Problems in Series A are available with McGraw-Hill's Homework Manager.

Problem 24-16A ***Using present value techniques to evaluate alternative investment opportunities***

L.O. 4

excel

mhhe.com/edmonds2007

CHECK FIGURES

a. NPV of the vans investment: $100,811.42
b. NPV index of the trucks investment: 1.126

Parcel Delivery is a small company that transports business packages between Boston and Philadelphia. It operates a fleet of small vans that moves packages to and from a central depot within each city and uses a common carrier to deliver the packages between the depots in the two cities. Parcel recently acquired approximately $4 million of cash capital from its owners, and its president, Roger Makris, is trying to identify the most profitable way to invest these funds.

Nick Wells, the company's operations manager, believes that the money should be used to expand the fleet of city vans at a cost of $720,000. He argues that more vans would enable the company to expand its services into new markets, thereby increasing the revenue base. More specifically, he expects cash inflows to increase by $280,000 per year. The additional vans are expected to have an average useful life of four years and a combined salvage value of $100,000. Operating the vans will require additional working capital of $40,000, which will be recovered at the end of the fourth year.

In contrast, Leigh Young, the company's chief accountant, believes that the funds should be used to purchase large trucks to deliver the packages between the depots in the two cities. The conversion process would produce continuing improvement in operating savings with reductions in cash outflows as the following:

Year 1	Year 2	Year 3	Year 4
$160,000	$320,000	$400,000	$440,000

The large trucks are expected to cost $800,000 and to have a four-year useful life and a $80,000 salvage value. In addition to the purchase price of the trucks, up-front training costs are expected to amount to $16,000. Parcel Delivery's management has established a 16 percent desired rate of return.

Required

a. Determine the net present value of the two investment alternatives.
b. Calculate the present value index for each alternative.
c. Indicate which investment alternative you would recommend. Explain your choice.

Problem 24-17A ***Using the payback period and unadjusted rate of return to evaluate alternative investment opportunities***

L.O. 6, 7

CHECK FIGURES

a. Payback period of the yogurt investment: 1.77 years
Unadjusted rate of return of the cappuccino investment: 52.86%

Brice Looney owns a small retail ice cream parlor. He is considering expanding the business and has identified two attractive alternatives. One involves purchasing a machine that would enable Mr. Looney to offer frozen yogurt to customers. The machine would cost $2,700 and has an expected useful life of three years with no salvage value. Additional annual cash revenues and cash operating expenses associated with selling yogurt are expected to be $1,980 and $300, respectively.

Alternatively, Mr. Looney could purchase for $3,360 the equipment necessary to serve cappuccino. That equipment has an expected useful life of four years and no salvage value. Additional annual cash revenues and cash operating expenses associated with selling cappuccino are expected to be $2,760 and $810, respectively.

Income before taxes earned by the ice cream parlor is taxed at an effective rate of 20 percent.

Required

a. Determine the payback period and unadjusted rate of return (use average investment) for each alternative.
b. Indicate which investment alternative you would recommend. Explain your choice.

L.O. 4, 5

CHECK FIGURES

a. NPV of A: $17,950.68

b. Rate of return of B: 12%

Problem 24-18A ***Using net present value and internal rate of return to evaluate investment opportunities***

Jane Crawford, the president of Crawford Enterprises, is considering two investment opportunities. Because of limited resources, she will be able to invest in only one of them. Project A is to purchase a machine that will enable factory automation; the machine is expected to have a useful life of four years and no salvage value. Project B supports a training program that will improve the skills of employees operating the current equipment. Initial cash expenditures for Project A are $400,000 and for Project B are $160,000. The annual expected cash inflows are $126,188 for Project A and $52,676 for Project B. Both investments are expected to provide cash flow benefits for the next four years. Crawford Enterprise's cost of capital is 8 percent.

Required

a. Compute the net present value of each project. Which project should be adopted based on the net present value approach?

b. Compute the approximate internal rate of return of each project. Which one should be adopted based on the internal rate of return approach?

c. Compare the net present value approach with the internal rate of return approach. Which method is better in the given circumstances? Why?

L.O. 4, 6

CHECK FIGURES

a. NPV of #1: $164,189.94

b. Payback period of #2: less than 2 years.

Problem 24-19A ***Using net present value and payback period to evaluate investment opportunities***

Lowell Cox saved $800,000 during the 25 years that he worked for a major corporation. Now he has retired at the age of 50 and has begun to draw a comfortable pension check every month. He wants to ensure the financial security of his retirement by investing his savings wisely and is currently considering two investment opportunities. Both investments require an initial payment of $600,000. The following table presents the estimated cash inflows for the two alternatives.

	Year 1	Year 2	Year 3	Year 4
Opportunity #1	$178,000	$188,000	$252,000	$324,000
Opportunity #2	328,000	348,000	56,000	48,000

Mr. Cox decides to use his past average return on mutual fund investments as the discount rate; it is 8 percent.

Required

a. Compute the net present value of each opportunity. Which should Mr. Cox adopt based on the net present value approach?

b. Compute the payback period for each project. Which should Mr. Cox adopt based on the payback approach?

c. Compare the net present value approach with the payback approach. Which method is better in the given circumstances?

L.O. 4, 6, 7

eXcel

mhhe.com/edmonds2007

CHECK FIGURES

a. NPV = $71,810

d. Payback period: 2.32 years

Problem 24-20A ***Effects of straight-line versus accelerated depreciation on an investment decision***

Hilyer Electronics is considering investing in manufacturing equipment expected to cost $184,000. The equipment has an estimated useful life of four years and a salvage value of $24,000. It is expected to produce incremental cash revenues of $96,000 per year. Hilyer has an effective income tax rate of 30 percent and a desired rate of return of 12 percent.

Required

a. Determine the net present value and the present value index of the investment, assuming that Hilyer uses straight-line depreciation for financial and income tax reporting.

b. Determine the net present value and the present value index of the investment, assuming that Hilyer uses double-declining-balance depreciation for financial and income tax reporting.

c. Why do the net present values computed in Requirements *a* and *b* differ?

d. Determine the payback period and unadjusted rate of return (use average investment), assuming that Hilyer uses straight-line depreciation.
e. Determine the payback period and unadjusted rate of return (use average investment), assuming that Hilyer uses double-declining-balance depreciation. (Note: Use average annual cash flow when computing the payback period and average annual income when determining the unadjusted rate of return.)
f. Why are there no differences in the payback periods or unadjusted rates of return computed in Re-quirements *d* and *e*?

Problem 24-21A ***Applying the net present value approach with and without tax considerations***

L.O. 4

excel

mhhe.com/edmonds2007

CHECK FIGURE

a. $(46,120.48)

Buck Novak, the chief executive officer of Novak Corporation, has assembled his top advisers to evaluate an investment opportunity. The advisers expect the company to pay $400,000 cash at the beginning of the investment and the cash inflow for each of the following four years to be the following.

Year 1	Year 2	Year 3	Year 4
$84,000	$96,000	$120,000	$184,000

Mr. Novak agrees with his advisers that the company should use the discount rate (required rate of return) of 12 percent to compute net present value to evaluate the viability of the proposed project.

Required

a. Compute the net present value of the proposed project. Should Mr. Novak approve the project?
b. Lydia Hollman, one of the advisers, is wary of the cash flow forecast and she points out that the advisers failed to consider that the depreciation on equipment used in this project will be tax deductible. The depreciation is expected to be $80,000 per year for the four-year period. The company's income tax rate is 30 percent per year. Use this information to revise the company's expected cash flow from this project.
c. Compute the net present value of the project based on the revised cash flow forecast. Should Mr. Novak approve the project?

Problem 24-22A ***Comparing internal rate of return with unadjusted rate of return***

L.O. 5, 7

CHECK FIGURE

b. Internal rate of return: 12%

Masters Auto Repair Inc. is evaluating a project to purchase equipment that will not only expand the company's capacity but also improve the quality of its repair services. The board of directors requires all capital investments to meet or exceed the minimum requirement of a 10 percent rate of return. However, the board has not clearly defined the rate of return. The president and controller are pondering two different rates of return: unadjusted rate of return and internal rate of return. The equipment, which costs $400,000, has a life expectancy of five years. The increased net profit per year will be approximately $28,000, and the increased cash inflow per year will be approximately $110,800.

Required

a. If it uses the unadjusted rate of return (use average investment) to evaluate this project, should the company invest in the equipment?
b. If it uses the internal rate of return to evaluate this project, should the company invest in the equipment?
c. Which method is better for this capital investment decision?

Problem 24-23A ***Postaudit evaluation***

L.O. 8

CHECK FIGURE

b. NPV: $(654,174)

Sean Roberts is reviewing his company's investment in a cement plant. The company paid $15,000,000 five years ago to acquire the plant. Now top management is considering an opportunity to sell it. The president wants to know whether the plant has met original expectations before he decides its fate. The company's discount rate for present value computations is 8 percent. Expected and actual cash flows follow.

	Year 1	Year 2	Year 3	Year 4	Year 5
Expected	$3,300,000	$4,920,000	$4,560,000	$4,980,000	$4,200,000
Actual	2,700,000	3,060,000	4,920,000	3,900,000	3,600,000

Required

a. Compute the net present value of the expected cash flows as of the beginning of the investment.

b. Compute the net present value of the actual cash flows as of the beginning of the investment.

c. What do you conclude from this postaudit?

EXERCISES—SERIES B

L.O. 1

Exercise 24-1B *Identifying cash inflows and outflows*

Required

Seth Gunn is considering whether to invest in a dump truck. Mr. Gunn would hire a driver and use the truck to haul trash for customers. He wants to use present value techniques to evaluate the investment opportunity. List sources of potential cash inflows and cash outflows Mr. Gunn could expect if he invests in the truck.

L.O. 1, 2

Exercise 24-2B *Determining the present value of a lump-sum future cash receipt*

One year from today Mary Bray is scheduled to receive a $100,000 payment from a trust fund her father established. She wants to buy a car today but does not have the money. A friend has agreed to give Mary the present value of the $100,000 today if she agrees to give him the full $100,000 when she collects it one year from now. They agree that 8 percent reflects a fair discount rate.

Required

a. You have been asked to determine the present value of the future cash flow. Use a present value table to determine the amount of cash that Mary's friend should give her.

b. Use an algebraic formula to verify the result you determined in Requirement *a*.

L.O. 1, 2

Exercise 24-3B *Determining the present value of a lump-sum future cash receipt*

Kyle Matthews has a terminal illness. His doctors have estimated his remaining life expectancy as three years. Kyle has a $1,500,000 life insurance policy but no close relative to list as the beneficiary. He is considering canceling the policy because he needs the money he is currently paying for the premiums to buy medical supplies. A wealthy close friend has advised Kyle not to cancel the policy. The friend has proposed instead giving Kyle $750,000 to use for his medical needs while keeping the policy in force. In exchange, Kyle would designate the friend as the policy beneficiary. Kyle is reluctant to take the $750,000 because he believes that his friend is offering charity. His friend has tried to convince Kyle that the offer is a legitimate business deal.

Required

a. Determine the present value of the $1,500,000 life insurance benefit. Assume a 10 percent discount rate.

b. Assuming 10 percent represents a fair rate of return, is Kyle's friend offering charity or is he seeking to profit financially from Kyle's misfortune?

L.O. 1, 2

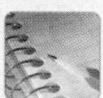

Exercise 24-4B *Determining the present value of an annuity*

Andrea James is considering whether to install a drink machine at the gas station she owns. Andrea is convinced that providing a drink machine at the station would increase customer convenience. However, she is not convinced that buying the machine would be a profitable investment. Friends who have installed drink machines at their stations have estimated that she could expect to receive net cash inflows of approximately $4,000 per year from the machine. Andrea believes that she should earn 10 percent on her investments. The drink machine is expected to have a two-year life and zero salvage value.

Required

a. Use Present Value Table 1 to determine the maximum amount of cash Andrea should be willing to pay for a drink machine.

b. Use Present Value Table 2 to determine the maximum amount of cash Andrea should be willing to pay for a drink machine.

c. Explain the consistency or lack of consistency in the answers to Requirement *a* versus Requirement *b*.

Exercise 24-5B ***Determining the net present value*** **L.O. 4**

Heidi Kahn, manager of the Grand Music Hall, is considering the opportunity to expand the company's concession revenues. Specifically, she is considering whether to install a popcorn machine. Based on market research, she believes that the machine could produce incremental cash inflows of $1,600 per year. The purchase price of the machine is $5,000. It is expected to have a useful life of three years and a $1,000 salvage value. Ms. Kahn has established a desired rate of return of 16 percent.

Required

a. Calculate the net present value of the investment opportunity.

b. Should the company buy the popcorn machine?

Exercise 24-6B ***Determining the net present value*** **L.O. 4**

Marcus Carroll has decided to start a small delivery business to help support himself while attending school. Mr. Carroll expects demand for delivery services to grow steadily as customers discover their availability. Annual cash outflows are expected to increase only slightly because many of the business operating costs are fixed. Cash inflows and outflows expected from operating the delivery business follow:

Year of Operation	Cash Inflow	Cash Outflow
2006	$6,800	$3,200
2007	7,600	3,600
2008	8,400	3,840
2009	9,200	4,000

The used delivery van Mr. Carroll plans to buy is expected to cost $13,200. It has an expected useful life of four years and a salvage value of $2,400. At the end of 2007, Mr. Carroll expects to pay additional costs of approximately $640 for maintenance and new tires. Mr. Carroll's desired rate of return is 12 percent.

Required

(Round computations to the nearest whole penny.)

a. Calculate the net present value of the investment opportunity.

b. Indicate whether the investment opportunity is expected to earn a return above or below the desired rate of return. Should Mr. Carroll start the delivery business?

Exercise 24-7B ***Using the present value index*** **L.O. 4**

Two alternative investment opportunities are available to Byron Osborne, president of Osborne Enterprises. For the first alternative, the present value of cash inflows is $266,000, and the present value of cash outflows is $254,000. For the second alternative, the present value of cash inflows is $460,000, and the present value of cash outflows is $446,000.

Required

a. Calculate the net present value of each investment opportunity.

b. Calculate the present value index for each investment opportunity.

c. Indicate which investment will produce the higher rate of return.

Exercise 24-8B ***Determining the internal rate of return*** **L.O. 5**

Joel Hodge, CFO of Kleiser Enterprises, is evaluating an opportunity to invest in additional manufacturing equipment that will enable the company to increase its net cash inflows by $600,000 per year. The equipment costs $1,794,367.20. It is expected to have a five-year useful life and a zero salvage value. Kleiser's cost of capital is 18 percent.

Required

a. Calculate the internal rate of return of the investment opportunity.

b. Indicate whether Kleiser should purchase the equipment.

L.O. 5

Exercise 24-9B ***Using the internal rate of return to compare investment opportunities***

Rachel Allen has two alternative investment opportunities to evaluate. The first opportunity would cost $149,512.23 and generate expected cash inflows of $21,000 per year for 17 years. The second opportunity would cost $136,909.44 and generate expected cash inflows of $18,000 per year for 15 years. Ms. Allen has sufficient funds available to accept only one opportunity.

Required

a. Calculate the internal rate of return of each investment opportunity.

b. Based on the internal rate of return criteria, which opportunity should Ms. Allen select?

c. Identify two other evaluation techniques Ms. Allen could use to compare the investment opportunities.

L.O. 1, 2

Exercise 24-10B ***Determining a cash flow annuity with income tax considerations***

Rick Howell is considering whether to invest in a computer game machine that he would place in a hotel his brother owns. The machine would cost $14,000 and has an expected useful life of three years and a salvage value of $2,000. Mr. Howell estimates the machine would generate revenue of $7,000 per year and cost $1,200 per year to operate. He uses the straight-line method for depreciation. His income tax rate is 30 percent.

Required

What amount of net cash inflow from operations would Mr. Howell expect for the first year if he invests in the machine?

L.O. 8

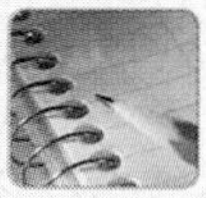

Exercise 24-11B ***Evaluating discounted cash flow techniques***

Four years ago Valerie Bowen decided to invest in a project. At that time she had projected annual net cash inflows would be $72,000. Over its expected four-year useful life, the project had produced significantly higher cash inflows than anticipated. The actual average annual cash inflow from the project was $84,000. Bowen breathed a sigh of relief. She always worried that projects would not live up to expectations. To avoid this potential disappointment she tried always to underestimate the projected cash inflows of potential investments. She commented, "I prefer pleasant rather than unpleasant surprises." Indeed, no investment approved by Ms. Bowen had ever failed a postaudit review. Her investments consistently exceeded expectations.

Required

Explain the purpose of a postaudit and comment on Ms. Bowen's investment record.

L.O. 6

Exercise 24-12B ***Determining the payback period***

The management team at Nisbett Manufacturing Company has decided to modernize the manufacturing facility. The company can replace an existing, outdated machine with one of two technologically advanced machines. One replacement machine would cost $200,000. Management estimates that it would reduce cash outflows for manufacturing expenses by $80,000 per year. This machine is expected to have an eight-year useful life and a $5,000 salvage value. The other replacement machine would cost $252,000 and would reduce annual cash outflows by an estimated $90,000. This machine has an expected 10-year useful life and a $25,000 salvage value.

Required

a. Determine the payback period for each investment alternative and identify which replacement machine Nisbett should buy if it bases the decision on the payback approach.

b. Discuss the shortcomings of the payback method of evaluating investment opportunities.

L.O. 6

Exercise 24-13B ***Determining the payback period with uneven cash flows***

Mountain Snowmobile Company is considering whether to invest in a particular new snowmobile model. The model is top-of-the-line equipment for which Mountain expects high demand during the first year it is available for rent. However, as the snowmobile ages, it will become less desirable and its rental revenues are expected to decline. The expected cash inflows and outflows follow.

Year	Nature of Item	Cash Inflow	Cash Outflow
2006	Purchase price	–	$14,000
2006	Revenue	$8,000	–
2007	Revenue	6,000	–
2008	Revenue	5,500	–
2008	Major overhaul	–	2,000
2009	Revenue	3,000	–
2010	Revenue	2,000	–
2010	Salvage value	1,600	–

Required

a. Determine the payback period using the accumulated cash flows approach.

b. Determine the payback period using the average cash flows approach.

Exercise 24-14B *Determining the unadjusted rate of return* L.O. 7

Airport Shuttle Service Inc. is considering whether to purchase an additional shuttle van. The van would cost $20,000 and have a zero salvage value. It would enable the company to increase net income by $3,350 per year. The manufacturer estimates the van's effective life as five years.

Required

a. Determine the unadjusted rate of return based on the average cost of the investment.

b. What is the shortcoming of using the unadjusted rate of return to evaluate investment opportunities?

Exercise 24-15B *Computing the payback period and unadjusted rate of return for the same investment opportunity* L.O. 6, 7

Star Lake Marina (SLM) rents pontoon boats to customers. It has the opportunity to purchase an additional pontoon boat for $36,000; the boat has an expected useful life of four years and no salvage value. SLM uses straight-line depreciation. Expected rental revenue for the boat is $12,000 per year.

Required

a. Determine the payback period.

b. Determine the unadjusted rate of return based on the average cost of the investment.

c. Assume that the company's desired rate of return is 30 percent. Should SLM purchase the additional boat?

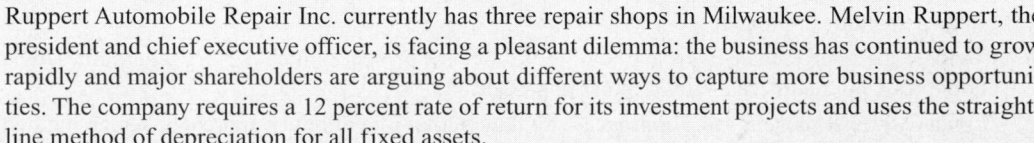

PROBLEMS—SERIES B

Problem 24-16B *Using present value techniques to evaluate alternative investment opportunities* L.O. 4

Ruppert Automobile Repair Inc. currently has three repair shops in Milwaukee. Melvin Ruppert, the president and chief executive officer, is facing a pleasant dilemma: the business has continued to grow rapidly and major shareholders are arguing about different ways to capture more business opportunities. The company requires a 12 percent rate of return for its investment projects and uses the straight-line method of depreciation for all fixed assets.

One group of shareholders wants to open another shop in a newly developed suburban community. This project would require an initial investment of $480,000 to acquire all the necessary equipment, which has a useful life of five years with a salvage value of $160,000. Once the shop begins to operate, another $120,000 of working capital would be required; it would be recovered at the end of the fifth year. The expected net cash inflow from the new shop follows.

Year 1	Year 2	Year 3	Year 4	Year 5
$48,000	$96,000	$152,000	$192,000	$240,000

A second group of shareholders prefers to invest $400,000 to acquire new computerized diagnostic equipment for the existing shops. The equipment is expected to have a useful life of five years with a salvage value of $80,000. Using this state-of-the-art equipment, mechanics would be able to pinpoint automobile problems more quickly and accurately. Consequently, it would allow the existing shops to increase their service capacity and revenue by $120,000 per year. The company would need to train mechanics to use the equipment, which would cost $40,000 at the beginning of the first year.

Required

a. Determine the net present value of the two investment alternatives.

b. Calculate the present value index for each alternative.

c. Indicate which investment alternative you would recommend. Explain your choice.

L.O. 6, 7

Problem 24-17B *Using the payback period and unadjusted rate of return to evaluate alternative investment opportunities*

Alberta and Tony Services is planning a new business venture. With $100,000 of available funds to invest, it is investigating two options. One is to acquire an exclusive contract to operate vending machines in civic and recreation centers in a small suburban city for four years. The contract requires the firm to pay the city $40,000 cash at the beginning. The firm expects the cash revenue from the operation to be $50,000 per year and the cash expenses to be $28,000 per year.

The second option is to operate a printing shop in an office complex. This option would require the company to spend $72,000 for printing equipment that has a useful life of four years with a zero salvage value. The cash revenue is expected to be $85,000 per year and cash expenses are expected to be $47,000 per year. The firm uses the straight-line method of depreciation. Its effective income tax rate is expected to be 20 percent.

Required

a. Determine the payback period and unadjusted rate of return (use average investment) for each alternative.

b. Indicate which investment alternative you would recommend. Explain your choice.

L.O. 4, 5

Problem 24-18B *Using net present value and internal rate of return to evaluate investment opportunities*

Alex Doyle's rich uncle gave him $100,000 cash as a birthday gift for his 40th birthday. Unlike his spoiled cousins who spend money carelessly, Mr. Doyle wants to invest the money for his future retirement. After an extensive search, he is considering one of two investment opportunities. Project 1 would require an immediate cash payment of $88,000; Project 2 needs only a $40,000 cash payment at the beginning. The expected cash inflows are $28,800 per year for Project 1 and $14,000 per year for Project 2. Both projects are expected to provide cash flow benefits for the next four years. Mr. Doyle found that the interest rate for a four-year certificate of deposit is about 7 percent. He decided that this is his required rate of return.

Required

a. Compute the net present value of each project. Which project should Mr. Doyle adopt based on the net present value approach?

b. Compute the approximate internal rate of return of each project. Which project should Mr. Doyle adopt based on the internal rate of return approach?

c. Compare the net present value approach with the internal rate of return approach. Which method is better in the given circumstances?

L.O. 4, 6

Problem 24-19B *Using net present value and payback period to evaluate investment opportunities*

Vivian Ogard just won a lottery and received a cash award of $800,000 net of tax. She is 61 years old and would like to retire in four years. Weighing this important fact, she has found two possible investments, both of which require an immediate cash payment of $640,000. The expected cash inflows from the two investment opportunities are as follows.

	Year 1	Year 2	Year 3	Year 4
Opportunity A	$364,800	$208,000	$118,400	$134,400
Opportunity B	91,200	107,200	236,800	540,800

Ms. Ogard decided that her required rate of return should be 10 percent.

Required

a. Compute the net present value of each opportunity. Which should Ms. Ogard choose based on the net present value approach?

b. Compute the payback period for each opportunity. Which should Ms. Ogard choose based on the payback approach?

c. Compare the net present value approach with the payback approach. Which method is better in the given circumstances?

Problem 24-20B ***Effects of straight-line versus accelerated depreciation on an investment decision*** **L.O. 4, 6, 7**

Gulf Pipe Inc. spent $80,000 to purchase new state-of-the-art equipment for its manufacturing plant. The equipment has a five-year useful life and a salvage value of $20,000. The company expects the equipment to generate additional cash revenue of $32,000 per year. Gulf Pipe's required rate of return is 10 percent; its effective income tax rate is 25 percent.

Required

a. Determine the net present value and the present value index of the investment, assuming that Gulf Pipe uses straight-line depreciation for financial and income tax reporting.

b. Determine the net present value and the present value index of the investment, assuming that Gulf Pipe uses double-declining-balance depreciation for financial and income tax reporting.

c. Why are there differences in the net present values computed in Requirements *a* and *b*?

d. Determine the payback period and unadjusted rate of return (use average investment), assuming that Gulf Pipe uses straight-line depreciation.

e. Determine the payback period and unadjusted rate of return (use average investment), assuming that Gulf Pipe uses double-declining-balance depreciation. (Note: Use average annual cash flow when computing the payback period and average annual income when computing the unadjusted rate of return.)

f. Why are there no differences in the payback period or unadjusted rate of return computed in Requirements *d* and *e*?

Problem 24-21B ***Applying the net present value approach with and without tax considerations*** **L.O. 4**

Jerry Ray, the president of Jerry's Moving Services, Inc., is planning to spend $500,000 for new trucks. He expects the trucks to increase the company's cash inflow as follows.

Year 1	Year 2	Year 3	Year 4
$130,800	$142,572	$155,404	$169,388

The company's policy stipulates that all investments must earn a minimum rate of return of 10 percent.

Required

a. Compute the net present value of the proposed purchase. Should Mr. Ray purchase the trucks?

b. Kim Wells, the controller, is wary of the cash flow forecast and points out that Mr. Ray failed to consider that the depreciation on trucks used in this project will be tax deductible. The depreciation

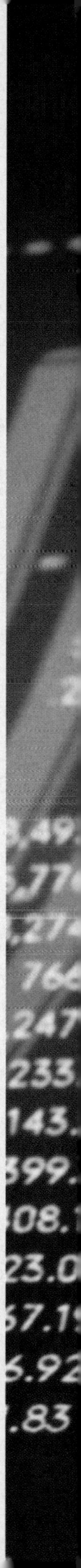

is expected to be $120,000 per year for the four-year period. The company's income tax rate is 30 percent per year. Use this information to revise the company's expected cash flow from this purchase.

c. Compute the net present value of the purchase based on the revised cash flow forecast. Should Mr. Ray purchase the trucks?

L.O. 5, 7

Problem 24-22B ***Comparing internal rate of return with unadjusted rate of return***

Elliott Computers Inc. faces stiff market competition. Top management is considering the replacement of its current production facility. The board of directors requires all capital investments to meet or exceed a 9 percent rate of return. However, the board has not clearly defined the rate of return. The president and controller are pondering two different rates of return: unadjusted rate of return and internal rate of return. To purchase a new facility with a life expectancy of four years, the company must pay $360,000. The increased net profit per year resulting from improved conditions would be approximately $40,000; the increased cash inflow per year would be approximately $110,000.

Required

a. If it uses the unadjusted rate of return (use average investment) to evaluate this project, should the company invest in the new facility?

b. If it uses the internal rate of return to evaluate this project, should the company invest in the new facility?

c. Which method is better for this capital investment decision?

L.O. 8

Problem 24-23B ***Postaudit evaluation***

Derric Pawlik is wondering whether he made the right decision four years ago. As the president of Pawlik Health Care Services, he acquired a hospital specializing in elder care with an initial cash investment of $2,800,000. Mr. Pawlik would like to know whether the hospital's financial performance has met the original investment objective. The company's discount rate (required rate of return) for present value computations is 14 percent. Expected and actual cash flows follow.

	Year 1	Year 2	Year 3	Year 4
Expected	$920,000	$960,000	$1,000,000	$1,200,000
Actual	800,000	760,000	1,280,000	1,400,000

Required

a. Compute the net present value of the expected cash flows as of the beginning of the investment.

b. Compute the net present value of the actual cash flows as of the beginning of the investment.

c. What do you conclude from this postaudit?

ANALYZE, THINK, COMMUNICATE

ATC 24-1 Business Applications Case ***Lottery winnings consulting job***

The February 20, 2004, drawing for the Mergmillions multistate lottery produced one winning ticket. More than a month after the drawing no one had come forward to claim the $239 million prize. Perhaps the winner was simply confused about whether to take the winnings as a lump-sum, immediate payment, or annual payments over the next 26 years.

Assume that you work as a personal financial planner, and that one of your clients held the winning lottery ticket. He faces the choice of (1) taking annual payments of $9,192,308 over the next 26 years ($239 million ÷ 26), or (2) taking an immediate one-time payment of $136 million.

Required

a. Assume you believe you can invest your client's winnings and safely earn an average annual return of 7 percent. Should he take the immediate cash payment or should he take the 26 annual payments? Ignore tax considerations and show the supporting computations used to reach your answer.

b. Assume your client is not convinced you can safely earn an annual rate of 7 percent on his money. What is the minimum annual rate of return you would need to earn for him before he would be better off taking the immediate cash payout of $136 million rather than the 26 annual payments of $9,192,308? Ignore tax considerations and show the supporting computations used to reach your answer.

(The tables in the Appendix for Chapter 24 end at 24 periods, so the factors for 26 periods are provided below.)

Present Value of $1

n	4%	5%	6%	7%	8%	9%	10%	12%	14%
26	0.3607	0.2812	0.2198	0.1722	0.1352	0.1064	0.0839	0.0525	0.0331

Present Value of an Annuity of $1

n	4%	5%	6%	7%	8%	9%	10%	12%	14%
26	15.9828	14.3752	13.0032	11.8258	10.8100	9.9290	9.1609	7.8957	6.9061

ATC 24-2 Group Assignment *Net present value*

Espada Real Estate Investment Company (EREIC) purchases new apartment complexes, establishes a stable group of residents, and then sells the complexes to apartment management companies. The average holding time is three years. EREIC is currently investigating two alternatives.

1. EREIC can purchase Harding Properties for $4,500,000. The complex is expected to produce net cash inflows of $360,000, $502,500, and $865,000 for the first, second, and third years of operation, respectively. The market value of the complex at the end of the third year is expected to be $5,175,000.
2. EREIC can purchase Summit Apartments for $3,450,000. The complex is expected to produce net cash inflows of $290,000, $435,000, and $600,000 for the first, second, and third years of operation, respectively. The market value of the complex at the end of the third year is expected to be $4,050,000.

   EREIC has a desired rate of return of 12 percent.

Required

a. Divide the class into groups of four or five students per group and then divide the groups into two sections. Assign Task 1 to the first section and Task 2 to the second section.

Group Tasks

(1) Calculate the net present value and the present value index for Harding Properties.

(2) Calculate the net present value and the present value index for Summit Apartments.

b. Have a spokesperson from one group in the first section report the amounts calculated by the group. Make sure that all groups in the section have the same result. Repeat the process for the second section. Have the class as a whole select the investment opportunity that EREIC should accept given that the objective is to produce the higher rate of return.

c. Assume that EREIC has $4,500,000 to invest and that any funds not invested in real estate properties must be invested in a certificate of deposit earning a 5 percent return. Would this information alter the decision made in Requirement *b*?

d. This requirement is independent of Requirement *c*. Assume there is a 10 percent chance that the Harding project will be annexed by the city of Hoover, which has an outstanding school district. The annexation would likely increase net cash flows by $37,500 per year and would increase the market value at the end of year 3 by $300,000. Would this information change the decision reached in Requirement *b*?

ATC 24-3 Research Assignment *Real world capital budgeting issues*

In recent years companies have devoted considerable time trying to decide if new software systems should be purchased. Vendors trying to sell the systems in question are happy to provide their own analysis to the prospective buyer showing how profitable their system will be. Not surprisingly, buyers are often skeptical of the objectivity of such analysis, and prefer to do their own. "Sizing up Your Payoff," *BusinessWeek,* October 29, 2001, presents anecdotal evidence about problems companies have encountered when evaluating the profitability of proposed software systems. Read this article and complete the following requirements.

Required

a. The focus of the article is on "return on investment" (ROI) analysis. Of the four techniques presented in this chapter for analyzing capital projects, which of them do you think is most closely related to the ROI analysis discussed by the article?

b. Give an example from the article of a company that appears to be using the payback method, at least in part, for capital budgeting decisions.

c. Give an example from the article of a company that appears to be using the internal rate of return method, at least in part, for capital budgeting decisions.

d. Give an example from the article of a company that used a postaudit to evaluate a capital budgeting decision it had made. What were the results of this postaudit?

e. The article discusses a capital project study that **Metreo, Inc.,** undertook before buying a software system. How long did this study take? How many employees were asked to provide input into the analysis?

ATC 24-4 Writing Assignment *Limitations of capital investment techniques*

Webb Publishing Company is evaluating two investment opportunities. One is to purchase an Internet company with the capacity to open new marketing channels through which Webb can sell its books. This opportunity offers a high potential for growth but involves significant risk. Indeed, losses are projected for the first three years of operation. The second opportunity is to purchase a printing company that would enable Webb to better control costs by printing its own books. The potential savings are clearly predictable but would make a significant change in the company's long-term profitability.

Required

Write a response discussing the usefulness of capital investment techniques (net present value, internal rate of return, payback, and unadjusted rate of return) in making a choice between these two alternative investment opportunities. Your response should discuss the strengths and weaknesses of capital budgeting techniques in general. Furthermore, it should include a comparison between techniques based on the time value of money versus those that are not.

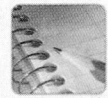

ATC 24-5 Ethical Dilemma *Postaudit*

Gaines Company recently initiated a postaudit program. To motivate employees to take the program seriously, Gaines established a bonus program. Managers receive a bonus equal to 10 percent of the amount by which actual net present value exceeds the projected net present value. Victor Holt, manager of the North Western Division, had an investment proposal on his desk when the new system was implemented. The investment opportunity required a $250,000 initial cash outflow and was expected to return cash inflows of $90,000 per year for the next five years. Gaines' desired rate of return is 10 percent. Mr. Holt immediately reduced the estimated cash inflows to $70,000 per year and recommended accepting the project.

Required

a. Assume that actual cash inflows turn out to be $91,000 per year. Determine the amount of Mr. Holt's bonus if the original computation of net present value were based on $90,000 versus $70,000.

b. Is Mr. Holt's behavior in violation of any of the standards of ethical conduct in Exhibit 14.13 of Chapter 14?

c. Speculate about the long-term effect the bonus plan is likely to have on the company.

d. Recommend how to compensate managers in a way that discourages gamesmanship.

COMPREHENSIVE PROBLEM

Magnificent Modems Inc. (MMI) has several capital investment opportunities. The term, expected cash inflows, and the cost of each opportunity are outlined in the following table. MMI has established a desired rate of return of 16 percent for these investment opportunities.

Opportunity	A	B	C	D
Investment term	4 years	5 years	3 years	5 years
Expected cash inflow	$ 6,000	$ 5,000	$ 8,000	$ 4,800
Cost of investment	$16,000	$15,000	$18,000	$16,000

Required

a. Compute the net present value of each investment opportunity manually using the present value tables. Record your answers in the following table. The results for investment opportunity A have been recorded in the table as an example.

Opportunity	A	B	C	D
Cash inflow	$ 6,000.00	$ 5,000.00	$ 8,000.00	$ 4,800.00
Times present value factor	2.798181			
Present value of cash flows	16,789.09			
Minus cost of investment	(16,000.00)	(15,000.00)	(18,000.00)	(16,000.00)
Net present value	$ 789.09			

b. Use Excel spreadsheet software or a financial calculator to determine the net present value and the internal rate of return for each investment opportunity. Record the results in the following table. The results for investment opportunity A have been recorded in the following table as an example. Note that the manual computation yields the same net present value amounts as the financial function routines of Excel or a financial calculator.

Opportunity	A	B	C	D
Net present value	$789.09			
Internal rate of return	18.45%			

Accessing the EDGAR Database Through the Internet

Successful business managers need many different skills, including communication, interpersonal, computer, and analytical. Most business students become very aware of the data analysis skills used in accounting, but they may not be as aware of the importance of "data-finding" skills. There are many sources of accounting and financial data. The more sources you are able to use, the better.

One very important source of accounting information is the EDGAR database. Others are probably available at your school through the library or business school network. Your accounting instructor will be able to identify these for you and make suggestions regarding their use. By making the effort to learn to use electronic databases, you will enhance your abilities as a future manager and your marketability as a business graduate.

These instructions assume that you know how to access and use an Internet navigator, such as Netscape. After you activate the Navigator program on your computer, follow the instructions to retrieve data from the Securities and Exchange Commission's EDGAR database. Be aware that the SEC may have changed its interface since this appendix was written. Accordingly, be prepared for slight differences between the following instructions and what appears on your computer screen. Take comfort in the fact that changes are normally designed to simplify user access. If you encounter a conflict between the following instructions and the instructions provided in the SEC interface, remember that the SEC interface is more current and should take precedence over the following instructions.

1. To connect to EDGAR, type in the following address: **http://www.sec.gov/**.
2. After the SEC home page appears, under the heading **Filings & Forms (EDGAR),** click on **Search for Company Filings.**
3. From the screen that appears, click on **Companies & Other Filers.**
4. On the screen that appears, enter the name of the company whose file you wish to retrieve and click on the **Find Companies** button.
5. The following screen will present a list of companies that have the same, or similar, names to the one you entered. Identify the company you want and click on the CIK number beside it.
6. Enter the SEC form number that you want to retrieve in the window titled **Form Type** that appears in the upper right portion of the screen that appears. For example, if you want Form 10-K, which will usually be the case, enter **10-K,** and click on the **Retrieve Filings** button.
7. A list of the forms you requested will be presented, along with the date they were filed with the SEC. You may be given a choice of **[text]** or **[html]** file format. The **[text]** format will present one large file for the form you requested. The **[html]** format will probably present several separate files from which you must choose. These will be named Document 1 . . ., Document 2 . . ., etc. Usually, you should choose the file whose name ends in **10k.txt.** Form 10-K/A is an amended Form 10-K and it sometimes contains more timely information, but usually, the most recent Form 10-K will contain the information you need.
8. Once the 10-K has been retrieved, you can search it online or save it on your hard drive or diskette. If you want to save it, do so by using the **Save As** command from the pull-down menu at the top of the screen named **File.**
9. The financial statements are seldom located near the beginning of a company's 10-K, so it is necessary to scroll down the file until you find them. Typically, they are located about one-half to three-fourths of the way through the report.

Topps Annual Report 2003

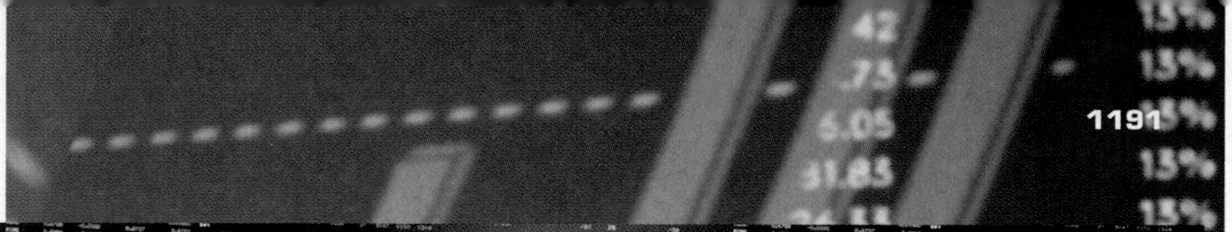

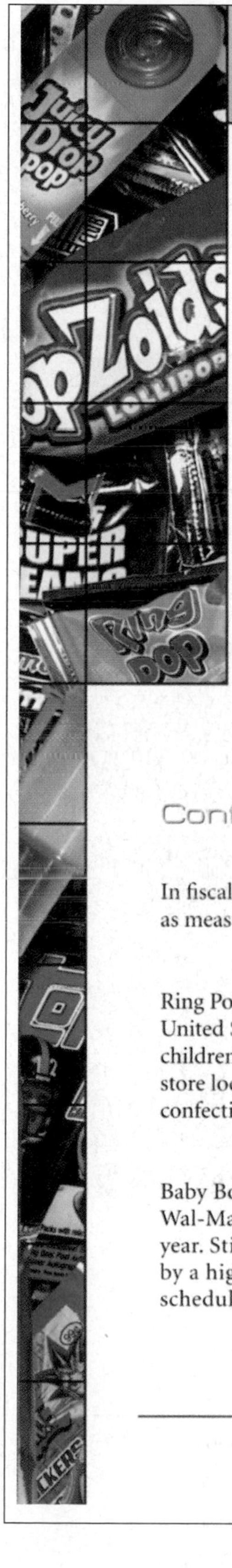

Stockholders' Letter

Dear Stockholders:

Fiscal 2003, ended March 1, 2003, marked the beginning of a Company-wide program devoted to building for future growth. In last year's Annual Report, we characterized the upcoming year as one of strategic investment. It was all of that and more as the Company made meaningful progress against targeted initiatives, in a difficult business environment.

Overall, we aimed to strengthen Topps position as a global marketer of branded confectionery and entertainment products. In fact, we recently announced that we will be reporting the sports and entertainment segments as one business—Entertainment —due to their similarities and the way we are now organized to manage them.

Here is a sampling of Topps strategies that guided our activities last year along with some specific achievements against them to date. For financial details see Management's Discussion beginning on page 7.

Confectionery

In fiscal 2003, we set out to grow the core brand franchises of Ring Pop, Push Pop and Baby Bottle Pop, as measured by heightened consumer awareness, greater retail distribution, and increased sales.

Ring Pop and Push Pop brands both delivered strong performances with impressive sales gains in the United States. The impetus for progress was execution against our three-pronged strategy—providing children with compelling high quality products, expanding product availability (distribution and in-store location) and advertising on kids' television programs. Overseas, we also aimed to secure confectionery listings in several key retailers and were on the mark in virtually every instance.

Baby Bottle Pop presented a particular challenge, coming off a year-long special retail promotion at Wal-Mart, as well as our expectation of lower sales in Japan after the product's rollout there last year. Still, we had reason to envision that much, if not all, of that lost ground could be made up by a highly anticipated brand extension. "Baby Bottle Pop with Candy Juice," was originally scheduled to reach market early enough in the fiscal year to impact financial results. Technical difficulties, however, delayed its introduction until this past January when first shipments were made, at last.

Fast-forwarding to today, we are very encouraged by early reports of consumer response to the new entry as well as solid trade acceptance. "Candy Juice" may well turn out to have been worth the wait. Further, a new brand, "Juicy Drop Pop," is making its initial appearance overseas as we speak.

Another goal for us in fiscal 2003 was to begin branching out into other kids' confectionery segments by creating one or more brands outside the lollipop category, for marketing in fiscal 2004. We analyzed the candy universe to identify areas of opportunity based on a variety of factors such as segment size and growth, price points, trade channel development and competitive framework. Qualitative and quantitative research was conducted to gain consumer insights about targeted segments. That data was used to guide internal and external new product development activities.

At present, there are several candidates in development, at least one of which is expected to see light of day this fiscal year. Work on these and other new confectionery products continues apace.

Entertainment

In fiscal 2003, the principal focus was on leveraging our strengths (brands and know-how) against current products and new formats. As mentioned earlier, this segment is now comprised of sports and non-sports products, including trading cards, stickers, albums, internet, and other entertainment offerings.

Our traditional sports card products performed relatively well during the period, winning an enviable number of industry awards and, as best one can tell, gaining market share.

Nonetheless, the consumer base for traditional cards declined yet again and there is little protection for sales and margins in such a lengthy down cycle. Simply too many competitors vie for bits of too small a pie. Accordingly, in the fourth quarter, we significantly modified our expectations regarding next year's traditional card sales and took the steps necessary to bring staffing, costs and marketing plans more in line with reality.

That said, we are as resolved as ever to advance the market leadership position Topps has held for decades, by continuing to create innovative products with purpose and appeal. After all, the Topps brand itself is and can continue to be a powerful sponsor for traditional and non-traditional offerings alike. Take "etopps" for instance, a relatively new brand of cards we sell exclusively on the internet via Initial Player Offerings (IPOs). Last year the number of registered etopps users and buyers expanded and we will continue to invest in its future. If you haven't already done so, we invite you to go to the site (www.etopps.com) and see for yourself what etopps is all about.

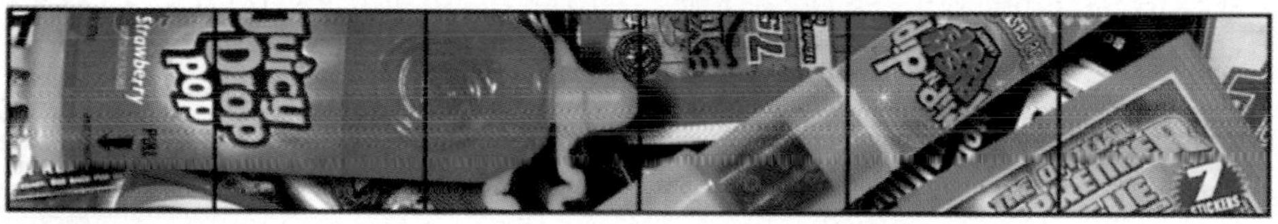

Another major strategy in fiscal 2003 was to improve the performance of our European football sticker album products. Results were outstanding, even excluding World Cup sales which occur only once every four years. We offered consumers compelling product innovations, utilized considerably more in-store merchandising than before and increased album sampling which appears to have brought more sticker buyers into the fold.

By way of example, Topps Italy successfully introduced a brand new concept marketed through our confectionery distribution system – Bubble Gum with Mini Stickers – featuring Calcio football players. This product was a significant success, making the case that combining creativity with brand equity is more than a good idea. It is an imperative going forward. Additional efforts along this line can be anticipated.

Last but not least, other Entertainment opportunities continue to dot our radar screen such as Simpsons Sticker Gum, released late last year. Presently scheduled for marketing this year are Yu-Gi-Oh! Stickers and Albums, The Incredible Hulk cards and punch-out cards featuring Beyblade, a popular Japanese animation property. We remain highly selective as to which licenses are pursued.

Conclusion

We hope the foregoing is helpful in providing perspective on last year's performance. No doubt, attention to strategic goals will continue to play a key role in shaping the Company's future.

We would like to express our appreciation to the entire Topps family of employees, both here and abroad, for their tireless efforts. These are the people in every discipline of the business that make the trains go on time, so to speak, and not bump into one another. And Happy Anniversary Bazooka Joe—50 years young is worth celebrating!

On behalf of the Organization, we also thank our fans, collectors, customers, licensors, stockholders and suppliers for their valued support.

Chairman, Chief Executive Officer and President

OFFICERS OF THE TOPPS COMPANY, INC.

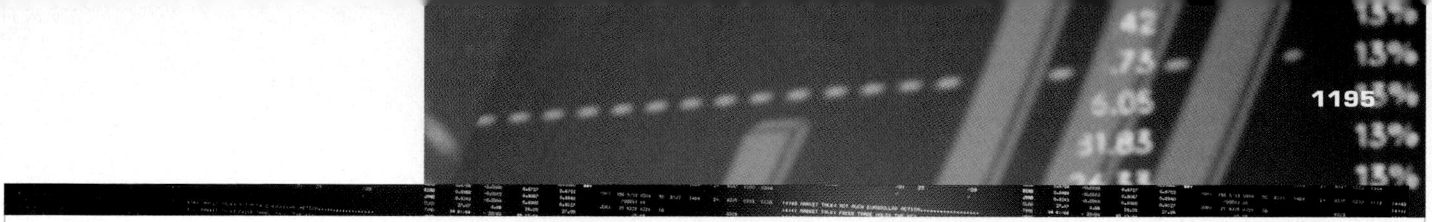

PAGE

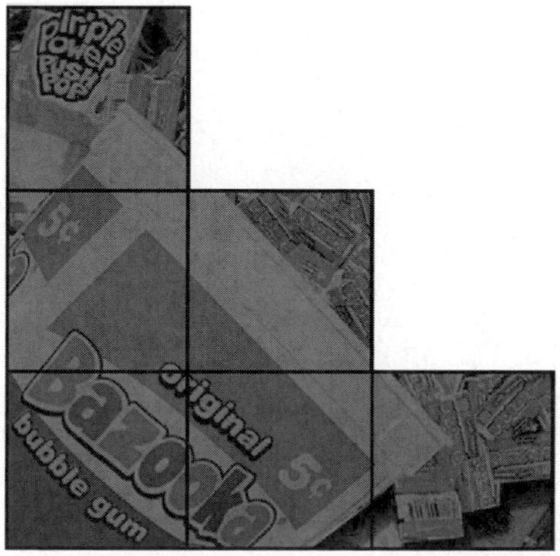

financial highlights

	Year Ended		
	March 1, 2003	March 2, 2002	March 3, 2001
	(In thousands of dollars, except share data)		
Net sales	**$ 290,079**	$ 300,180	$ 437,440
Income from operations	**20,782**	36,564	121,917
Net income	**16,936**	28,462	88,489
Cash provided by operations	**6,200**	1,619	104,120
Working capital	**141,484**	136,389	140,487
Stockholders' equity	**196,768**	194,054	196,542
Net income per share - basic	**$ 0.41**	$ 0.66	$ 1.97
- diluted	**$ 0.40**	$ 0.64	$ 1.91
Weighted average shares outstanding - basic	**41,353,000**	43,073,000	45,011,000
- diluted	**42,065,000**	44,276,000	46,366,000

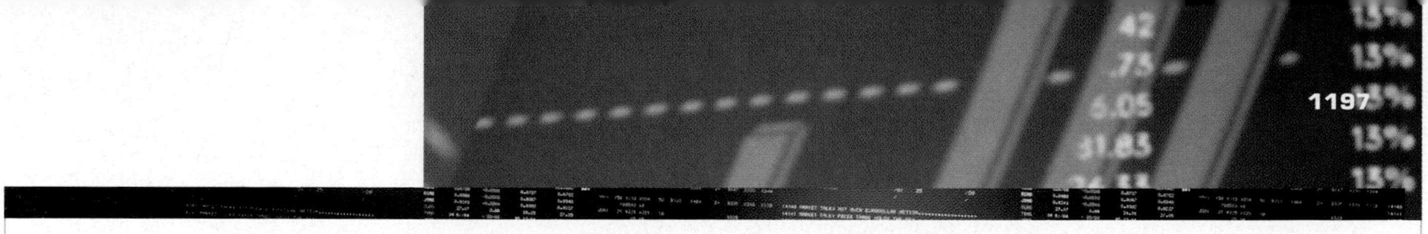

The Company has two reportable business segments: Confectionery and Entertainment. Consistent with Topps organizational structure and product line similarities, Entertainment now combines the former Sports and Entertainment segments into one.

The following table sets forth, for the periods indicated, net sales by key business segment:

	Year Ended		
	March 1, 2003	March 2, 2002	March 3, 2001
	(In thousands of dollars)		
Confectionery	**$146,865**	$152,127	$170,700
Entertainment	**143,214**	148,053	266,740
Total	**$290,079**	$300,180	$437,440

Fiscal 2003 Versus 2002*

In fiscal 2003, the Company's consolidated net sales decreased 3.4% to $290.1 million from $300.2 million in fiscal 2002. This decrease was primarily a function of a reduction in the popularity of products featuring Pokémon, which generated $6.0 million in sales in fiscal 2003 versus $24.1 million in fiscal 2002. Stronger European currencies served to increase fiscal 2003 sales by $3.9 million.

Net sales of the Confectionery segment, which includes Ring Pop, Push Pop, Baby Bottle Pop and Bazooka brand bubble gum, decreased 3.5% in 2003 to $146.9 million from $152.1 million in 2002. Excluding sales of Pokémon products, confectionery sales decreased 0.7%. Sales results reflect growth in the U.S. of Ring Pop and Push Pop, the successful roll out of Pro Flip Pop in Japan and the introduction of Yu-Gi-Oh! sticker pops in the U.S. and Canada. These gains were offset by lower sales of Baby Bottle Pop. Confectionery products accounted for 51% of the Company's consolidated net sales in both 2003 and 2002.

Net sales of the Entertainment segment, which includes cards, sticker albums and Internet activities, decreased 3.3% in fiscal 2003 to $143.2 million. Excluding sales of Pokémon products which decreased to $4.5 million in fiscal 2003 from $18.2 million, Entertainment sales increased 6.9%. Sales of European sports sticker albums increased significantly, driven by the World Cup soccer tour which occurs once every four years, substantial increases in sales of U.K. Premier League soccer products and the successful introduction of a new concept — bubble gum with mini stickers — in Italy. Internet activities, which include etopps (cards sold online via an IPO format) and thePit.com (an online sports card exchange), generated $11.9 million in sales and $0.7 million in contributed margin losses (before overhead) in 2003 versus $5.8 million in sales and $1.4 million in contributed margin losses in the prior year. Sales of traditional U.S. sports cards were lower in fiscal 2003, reflecting continued industry declines. In February 2003, the Company restructured its U.S. sports operations, reducing headcount and the number of products it expects to release going forward. In fiscal 2003, the Company also marketed products featuring the Star Wars, Spider-Man, Yu-Gi-Oh! and Hamtaro properties, among others. Entertainment products represented 49% of the Company's consolidated net sales in both 2003 and 2002.

Consolidated gross profit as a percentage of net sales decreased to 35.1% in 2003 from 37.9% in 2002. Margins this year were negatively impacted by the reduction in sales of high-margin Pokémon products, an increase in sales of lower margin products and the absence of rebates received last year from a foreign distributor.

Other income (expense) was $184,000 this year versus an expense of $215,000 last year, in part the result of government cash incentives to maintain our New York office location received in 2003, versus non-cash foreign exchange losses in 2002 on dollar-denominated cash balances held in Europe.

Selling, general & administrative expenses ("SG&A") increased as a percentage of net sales to 28.0% in 2003 from 25.7% a year ago. SG&A dollar spending increased to $81.1 million from $77.1 million due to the absence of a $2.4 million favorable Internet-related legal settlement received in 2002, a $1.6 million unfavorable legal settlement recorded in 2003 and an increase in marketing costs primarily related to etopps. Partially offsetting these increases was the elimination of goodwill amortization in 2003 in accordance with FAS 142, which totaled $1.6 million, and lower costs associated with the employee incentive compensation program.

Net interest income decreased to $2.5 million in fiscal 2003 from $4.9 million in fiscal 2002

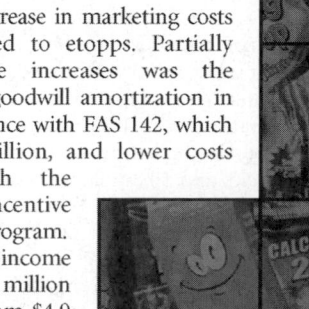

* *Unless otherwise indicated, all date references to 2003, 2002 and 2001 refer to the fiscal years ended March 1, 2003, March 2, 2002 and March 3, 2001, respectively.*

reflecting less favorable interest rates and a lower average cash balance.

The effective tax rate in 2003 of 27.3% reflects provisions for federal, state and local income taxes in accordance with statutory income tax rates. The decrease versus the 2002 rate of 31.3% was a function of certain one-time R&D and foreign tax benefits received this year.

Net income in fiscal 2003 was $16.9 million, or $0.40 per diluted share, versus $28.5 million, or $0.64 per diluted share in 2002.

Fiscal 2002 Versus 2001

In fiscal 2002, the Company's consolidated net sales decreased $137.2 million or 31.4% to $300.2 million from $437.4 million in fiscal 2001. This decrease was primarily a function of a $155.5 million decline in Pokémon sales to $24.1 million in fiscal 2002 from $179.6 million in fiscal 2001.

Net sales of the Confectionery segment decreased $18.6 million or 10.9% in 2002 to $152.1 million from $170.7 million in 2001. Sales of Pokémon confectionery products decreased $33.0 million to $5.9 million in 2002 from $38.9 million in 2001. Topps branded (non-Pokémon) confectionery sales increased 10.9%, reflecting strong domestic growth of Ring Pop and Push Pop, worldwide growth of Baby Bottle Pop and the introduction of seasonal candy products. Confectionery products accounted for 51% of the Company's consolidated net sales in 2002, compared with 39% in 2001.

Net sales of the Entertainment segment decreased $118.7 million or 44.5% in fiscal 2002 to $148.1 million, reflecting a $122.4 million decrease in sales of Pokémon products to $18.2 million. Sales of traditional sports products decreased 8.4% due to lower sales of football and basketball products, partially offset by higher sales of baseball and European soccer products. Internet activities, which include etopps and thePit.com, generated $5.8 million in sales and $1.4 million in contributed margin losses (before overhead) in the year versus $0.1 million in sales and $0.5 million in contributed margin losses in the prior year. Non-sports card and sticker album releases in 2002 included Lord of the Rings, Monsters, Inc., Planet of the Apes and Enduring Freedom. Entertainment products represented 49% of the Company's consolidated net sales in 2002, compared with 61% in 2001.

Consolidated gross profit as a percentage of net sales decreased to 37.9% in 2002 from 45.7% in 2001. Margins in 2002 were impacted by the reduction in sales of high-margin Pokémon products as well as an increase in sports autograph and relic costs and lower gross profit margins at thePit.com.

Other income (expense) was an expense of $215,000 in 2002 versus income of $3.0 million in 2001 primarily as a result of non-cash foreign exchange losses in 2002 on dollar-denominated cash balances held in Europe, as well as lower levels of prompt payment discounts on European inventory purchases.

Selling, general & administrative expenses increased as a percentage of net sales to 25.7% in 2002 from 18.5% in 2001 as a result of lower sales. SG&A dollar spending decreased to $77.1 million from $81.0 million due to a $2.4 million favorable Internet-related legal settlement, a reduction in etopps overhead expenses and lower marketing expenditures overseas.

Net interest income decreased to $4.9 million in fiscal 2002 from $5.7 million in fiscal 2001 reflecting lower interest rates and a lower average cash balance than in 2001.

The effective tax rate in 2002 of 31.3% reflects provisions for federal, state and local income taxes in accordance with statutory income tax rates. The increase versus the 2001 rate of 30.7% was a function of the lower mix of international earnings and the lower effective rates on those earnings as well as the absence of certain one-time tax benefits present in 2001.

Net income in fiscal 2002 was $28.5 million, or $0.64 per diluted share, versus $88.5 million, or $1.91 per diluted share in 2001.

Quarterly Comparisons

Management believes that quarter-to-quarter comparisons of sales and operating results are affected by a number of factors, including but not limited to new product introductions, the scheduling of product releases, seasonal products and the timing of various expenses such as advertising. Thus, quarterly results vary. See Note 17 of Notes to Consolidated Financial Statements.

Inflation

In the opinion of management, inflation has not had a material effect on the operations of the Company.

Liquidity and Capital Resources

Management believes that the Company has adequate means to meet its liquidity and capital resource needs over the foreseeable future as a result of the combination of cash on hand, anticipated cash from operations and credit line availability.

As of March 1, 2003, the Company had $114.3 million in cash and cash equivalents.

On June 26, 2000, the Company entered into a credit agreement with Chase Manhattan Bank and LaSalle Bank National Association. The agreement provides for a $35.0 million unsecured facility to cover revolver and letter of credit needs and expires on June 26, 2004. Interest rates are variable and a function of the Company's EBITDA. The credit agreement contains restrictions and prohibitions of a nature generally found in loan agreements of this type and requires the Company, among other things, to comply with certain financial covenants, limits the Company's ability to repurchase its shares, sell or acquire assets or borrow additional money and prohibits the payment of dividends. The credit agreement may be terminated by the Company at any point over the four-year term (provided the Company repays all outstanding amounts thereunder) without penalty. The full $35.0 million credit line was available as of March 1, 2003.

In October 1999, the Board of Directors authorized the Company to purchase up to 5 million shares of the Company's common stock. In October 2001, purchases against this authorization were completed, and the Board of Directors authorized the purchase of up to an additional 5 million shares of stock. As of March 2003, the Company had purchased 2.6 million shares against this new authorization. During fiscal 2003, the Company purchased a total of 1.6 million shares at an average price per share of $9.01.

During 2003, the Company's net decrease in cash and cash equivalents was $6.8 million versus a decrease of $37.7 million in 2002. Cash flow from operating activities in 2003 was $6.2 million versus $1.6 million last year, primarily as a result of European tax payments in 2002 on the prior year's Pokémon product sales, partially offset by lower net income in 2003. Cash flow from investing activities this year reflects $3.8 million in capital expenditures, principally on computer software and systems and Ring Pop production equipment, versus the $5.7 million acquisition of thePit.com and $5.1 million in capital expenditures last year. Cash flow from financing activities was driven by treasury stock purchases net of cash received from options exercised of $12.9 million this year versus $24.3 million last year.

Stockholders' equity of $196.8 million in fiscal 2003 was $2.7 million above fiscal 2002 levels, as net income of $16.9 million was partially offset by $12.9 million in net treasury stock purchases.

Future minimum payments under non-cancelable leases which extend into the year 2014 are $1,531,000 (2004), $1,531,000 (2005), $1,531,000 (2006), $1,454,000 (2007), $1,400,000 (2008) and $2,980,000 thereafter.

Future minimum payments required under the Company's existing sports and entertainment contracts, with various expiration dates extending into the year 2004, are estimated to be $12,162,000.

Critical Accounting Policies

The preparation of financial statements in conformity with accounting principles generally accepted in the United States of America requires Topps management to make estimates and assumptions that affect the reported amounts of revenue, expenses, assets, liabilities and the disclosure of contingent assets and liabilities.

On an on-going basis, Topps management evaluates its estimates and judgments, including those related to revenue recognition, intangible assets and reserves, based on historical experience and on various other factors that are believed to be reasonable under the circumstances. Actual results may differ from these estimates. Note 1 to the Company's consolidated financial statements, "Summary of Significant Accounting Policies," summarizes each of its significant accounting policies. Additionally, Topps management believes the following critical accounting policies, among others, affect its more significant judgments and estimates used in the preparation of its consolidated financial statements.

Revenue Recognition: Revenue related to sales of the Company's products is generally recognized when products are shipped, the title and risk of loss has passed to the customer, the sales price is fixed or determinable and collectibility is reasonably assured. Sales made on a returnable basis are recorded net of a provision for estimated returns. These estimates are revised, as necessary, to reflect actual experience and market conditions.

Intangible Assets: Intangible assets include trademarks and the value of sports, entertainment and proprietary product rights. Amortization is by the straight-line method over estimated lives of up to twenty years. Management evaluates the recoverability of intangible assets under the provisions of SFAS 144, based on undiscounted projections of future cash flows attributable to the individual assets.

Estimates: The preparation of financial statements in conformity with generally accepted accounting principles requires management to make estimates and assumptions which affect the reporting of assets and liabilities as of the dates of the financial statements and revenues and expenses during the reporting period. These estimates primarily relate to the provision for sales returns, allowance for doubtful accounts, inventory obsolescence and asset valuations. Actual results could differ from these estimates.

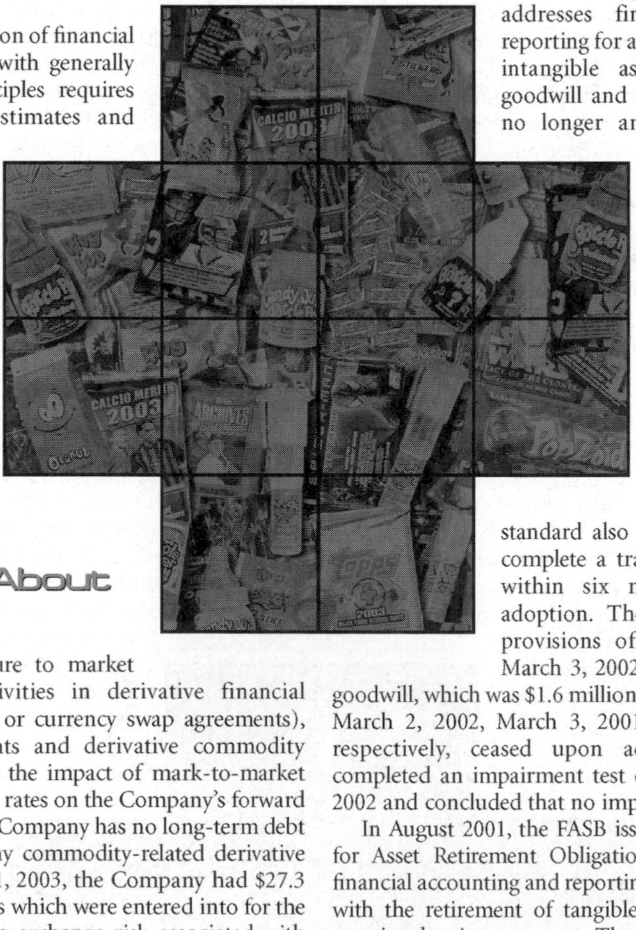

Disclosures About Market Risk

The Company's exposure to market risk associated with activities in derivative financial instruments (e.g., hedging or currency swap agreements), other financial instruments and derivative commodity instruments is confined to the impact of mark-to-market changes in foreign currency rates on the Company's forward contracts and options. The Company has no long-term debt and does not engage in any commodity-related derivative transactions. As of March 1, 2003, the Company had $27.3 million in forward contracts which were entered into for the purpose of hedging foreign exchange risk associated with forecasted receipts and disbursements.

New Accounting Pronouncements

In June 2001, the FASB issued SFAS 141 "Business Combinations." SFAS 141 applies prospectively to all business combinations initiated after June 30, 2001 and to all business combinations accounted for using the purchase method for which the date of acquisition is July 1, 2001, or later. The Company adopted SFAS 141 during fiscal 2002. The adoption of this standard did not have a material impact on the Company's financial condition or results of operations.

In June 2001, the FASB issued SFAS 142 "Goodwill and Other Intangible Assets." SFAS 142 addresses financial accounting and reporting for acquired goodwill and other intangible assets. Under SFAS 142, goodwill and some intangible assets are no longer amortized, but rather are reviewed for impairment on a periodic basis. In addition, the standard includes provisions for the reclassification of certain intangibles as goodwill, reassessment of the useful lives of intangibles and the identification of reporting units for purposes of assessing potential future impairment of goodwill. The standard also required the Company to complete a transitional impairment test within six months of the date of adoption. The Company adopted the provisions of this Statement effective March 3, 2002. Amortization of existing goodwill, which was $1.6 million for each of the years ended March 2, 2002, March 3, 2001 and February 26, 2000, respectively, ceased upon adoption. The Company completed an impairment test of goodwill on August 31, 2002 and concluded that no impairment exists.

In August 2001, the FASB issued SFAS 143 "Accounting for Asset Retirement Obligations." SFAS 143 addresses financial accounting and reporting for obligations associated with the retirement of tangible long-lived assets and the associated retirement costs. The adoption of SFAS 143 was effective March 3, 2002. The adoption of this standard did

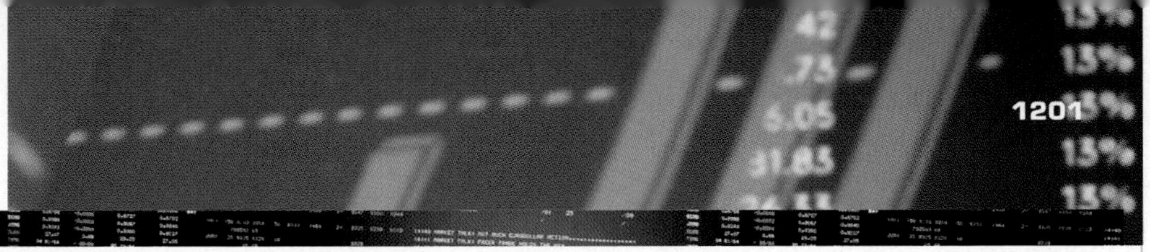

not have a material impact on the Company's financial condition or results of operations.

In October 2001, the FASB issued SFAS 144 "Accounting for the Impairment or Disposal of Long-Lived Assets." SFAS 144 superseded previous guidance for financial accounting and reporting for the impairment or disposal of long-lived assets and for segments of a business to be disposed of. The Company adopted SFAS 144 during fiscal 2002. The adoption of this standard did not have a material impact on the Company's financial condition or results of operations.

In April 2002, the FASB issued SFAS 145 "Rescission of FASB Statements No. 4, 44, and 64, Amendment of FASB Statement No. 13, and Technical Corrections." Among other changes, SFAS 145 rescinded SFAS 4 "Reporting Gains and Losses from Extinguishment of Debt," which required all gains and losses from the extinguishment of debt to be aggregated and, if material, to be classified as an extraordinary item, net of related income tax effects. The rescission of SFAS 4 is effective for fiscal years beginning after May 15, 2002. The primary impact of SFAS 145 on the Company is that future gains and losses from the extinguishment of debt will be subject to the criteria of APB Opinion 30 "Reporting the Results of Operations – Reporting the Effects of Disposal of a Segment of a Business, and Extraordinary Unusual and Infrequently Occurring Events and Transactions." Therefore, debt extinguishments in future periods may not be classified as an extraordinary item, net of related income tax effects, but instead as a component of income from continuing operations. The adoption of this standard did not have a material impact on the Company's financial condition or results of operations.

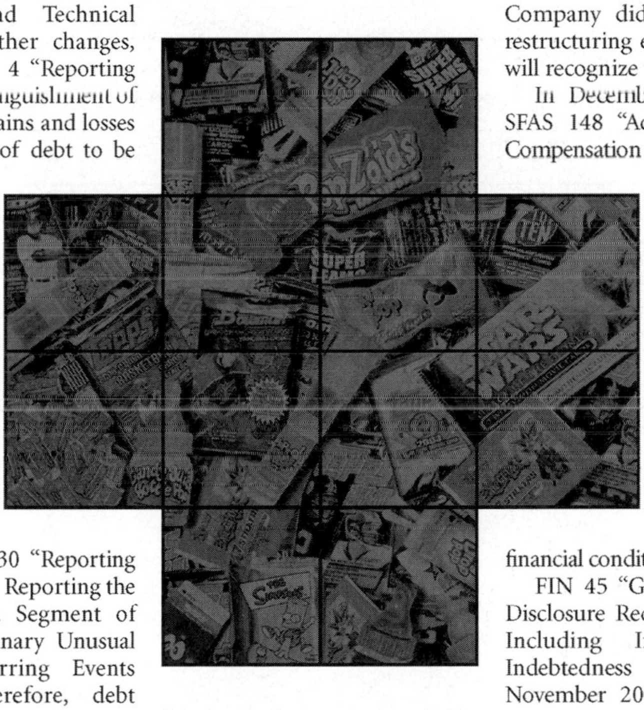

In June 2002, the FASB issued SFAS 146 "Accounting for Costs Associated with Exit or Disposal Activities" which is effective for exit or disposal activities initiated after December 31, 2002. SFAS 146 addresses financial accounting and reporting for costs incurred in connection with exit or disposal activities, including restructurings, and supersedes Emerging Issues Task Force (EITF) Issue No. 94-3 "Liability Recognition for Certain Employee Termination Benefits and Other Costs to Exit an Activity (including Certain Costs Incurred in a Restructuring)." Under SFAS 146, a liability related to an exit or disposal activity is not recognized until such liability has actually been incurred, as opposed to a liability being recognized at the time of a commitment to an exit plan, which was the standard for liability recognition under EITF Issue 94-3. As a result of adopting SFAS 146, the Company did not record $570,000 in restructuring expenses in fiscal 2003 and will recognize them in fiscal 2004.

In December 2002, the FASB issued SFAS 148 "Accounting for Stock-Based Compensation - Transition and Disclosure" which is effective for fiscal years ending after December 15, 2002. SFAS 148 provides alternative methods of transition for any entity that voluntarily changes to the fair value based method of accounting for stock-based employee compensation. The Company does not expect the adoption of SFAS 148 to have a material effect on its financial condition or results of operations.

FIN 45 "Guarantor's Accounting and Disclosure Requirements for Guarantees, Including Indirect Guarantees of Indebtedness of Others" was issued in November 2002. FIN 45 elaborates on certain disclosure requirements and clarifies certain recognition criteria related to guarantees. The disclosure requirements of FIN 45 are effective for periods ending after December 15, 2002, and the recognition criteria of FIN 45 are effective on a prospective basis for guarantees issued or modified after December 31, 2002. The impact of FIN 45 on the Company's financial condition or results of operations is not determinable since FIN 45 primarily impacts guarantees issued or modified in future periods.

consolidated statements of operations

The Topps Company, Inc. and Subsidiaries
(In thousands of dollars, except share data)

	Year Ended March 1, 2003	March 2, 2002	March 3, 2001
Net sales	**$ 290,079**	$ 300,180	$ 437,440
Cost of sales	**188,345**	186,339	237,529
Gross profit on sales	**101,734**	113,841	199,911
Other income (expense)	**184**	(215)	2,964
Selling, general and administrative expenses	**81,136**	77,062	80,958
Income from operations	**20,782**	36,564	121,917
Interest income, net	**2,516**	4,894	5,717
Income before provision for income taxes	**23,298**	41,458	127,634
Provision for income taxes	**6,362**	12,996	39,145
Net income	**$ 16,936**	$ 28,462	$ 88,489
Net income per share - basic	**$ 0.41**	$ 0.66	$ 1.97
- diluted	**$ 0.40**	$ 0.64	$ 1.91
Weighted average shares outstanding - basic	**41,353,000**	43,073,000	45,011,000
- diluted	**42,065,000**	44,276,000	46,366,000

See Notes to Consolidated Financial Statements.

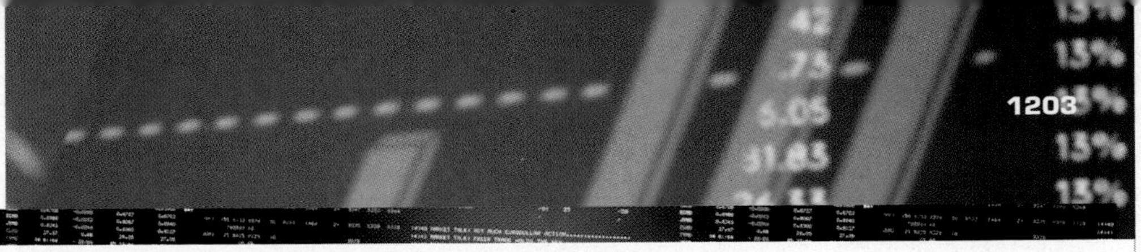

consolidated balance sheets

The Topps Company, Inc. and Subsidiaries
(In thousands of dollars, except share data)

	March 1, 2003	March 2, 2002
ASSETS		
Current assets:		
Cash and cash equivalents	**$ 114,259**	$ 121,057
Accounts receivable, net	**25,205**	20,039
Inventories	**28,681**	23,096
Income tax receivable	**2,029**	3,230
Deferred tax assets	**3,267**	4,343
Prepaid expenses and other current assets	**10,302**	11,807
Total current assets	**183,743**	183,572
Property, plant and equipment, net	**14,606**	14,606
Goodwill	**48,839**	46,773
Intangible assets, net	**6,041**	7,251
Other assets	**8,399**	5,748
Total assets	**$ 261,628**	$ 257,950
LIABILITIES AND STOCKHOLDERS' EQUITY		
Current liabilities:		
Accounts payable	**$ 9,074**	$ 10,966
Accrued expenses and other liabilities	**29,243**	30,274
Income taxes payable	**3,942**	5,943
Total current liabilities	**42,259**	47,183
Deferred income taxes	**-**	-
Other liabilities	**22,601**	16,713
Total liabilities	**64,860**	63,896
Commitments and contingencies	**-**	-
Stockholders' equity:		
Preferred stock, *par value $.01 per share, authorized 10,000,000 shares, none issued*	**-**	-
Common stock, *par value $.01 per share, authorized 100,000,000 shares, issued 49,244,000 in 2003 and 49,189,000 in 2002*	**492**	492
Additional paid-in capital	**27,344**	26,824
Treasury stock, *8,564,000 shares in 2003 and 7,143,000 shares in 2002*	**(80,791)**	(67,415)
Retained earnings	**262,877**	245,941
Accumulated other comprehensive loss	**(13,154)**	(11,788)
Total stockholders' equity	**196,768**	194,054
Total liabilities and stockholders' equity	**$ 261,628**	$ 257,950

See Notes to Consolidated Financial Statements.

consolidated statements of cash flows

The Topps Company, Inc. and Subsidiaries
(In thousands of dollars, except share data)

	Year Ended March 1, 2003	Year Ended March 2, 2002	Year Ended March 3, 2001
Operating Activities			
Net income	**$ 16,936**	$ 28,462	$ 88,489
Add (subtract) non-cash items included in net income:			
Depreciation and amortization	**5,038**	5,525	4,345
Deferred taxes on income	**1,076**	(3,242)	2,007
Net effect of changes in:			
Receivables	**(5,166)**	(9,176)	14,960
Inventories	**(5,585)**	789	(2,188)
Income tax receivable	**1,201**	8,339	(11,317)
Prepaid expenses and other current assets	**1,505**	(7,446)	1,029
Payables and other current liabilities	**(4,924)**	(26,439)	7,752
Other	**(3,881)**	4,807	(957)
Cash provided by operating activities	**6,200**	1,619	104,120
Investing Activities			
Purchase of subsidiary	**-**	(5,680)	-
Net additions to property, plant and equipment	**(3,807)**	(5,108)	(3,360)
Cash used in investing activities	**(3,807)**	(10,788)	(3,360)
Financing Activities			
Exercise of employee stock options	**1,449**	5,074	3,266
Purchase of treasury stock	**(14,305)**	(29,364)	(21,374)
Cash used in financing activities	**(12,856)**	(24,290)	(18,108)
Effect of exchange rate changes on cash and cash equivalents	**3,665**	(4,225)	236
Net (decrease) increase in cash and cash equivalents	**(6,798)**	(37,684)	82,888
Cash and cash equivalents at beginning of year	**121,057**	158,741	75,853
Cash and cash equivalents at end of year	**$ 114,259**	$ 121,057	$ 158,741
Supplemental disclosure of cash flow information:			
Interest paid	**$ 91**	$ 83	$ 119
Income taxes paid	**$ 12,578**	$ 24,024	$ 30,854

See Notes to Consolidated Financial Statements.

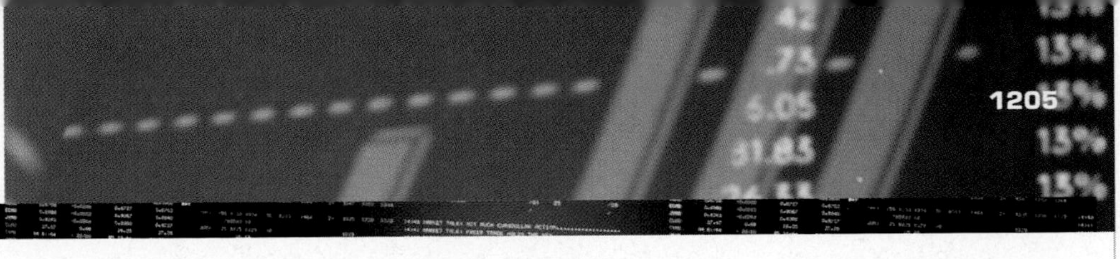

consolidated statements of stockholders' equity and comprehensive income

The Topps Company, Inc. and Subsidiaries
(In thousands of dollars)

	Total	Common Stock	Additional Paid-in Capital	Treasury Stock	Retained Earnings	Other Comprehensive Income (Loss)
Stockholders' equity as of 2/26/2000	$ 129,175	$ 478	$ 18,498	$ (16,677)	$ 128,990	$ (2,114)
Net income	88,489	-	-	-	88,489	-
Translation adjustment	(1,430)	-	-	-	-	(1,430)
Minimum pension liability	(1,584)	-	-	-	-	(1,584)
Total comprehensive income	85,475	-	-	-	88,489	(3,014)
Purchase of treasury stock	(21,374)	-	-	(21,374)	-	-
Exercise of employee stock options	3,266	6	3,260	-	-	-
Stockholders' equity as of 3/3/2001	$ 196,542	$ 484	$ 21,758	$ (38,051)	$ 217,479	$ (5,128)
Net income	28,462	-	-	-	28,462	-
Translation adjustment	(3,304)	-	-	-	-	(3,304)
Minimum pension liability	(3,356)	-	-	-	-	(3,356)
Total comprehensive income	21,802	-	-	-	28,462	(6,660)
Purchase of treasury stock	(29,364)	-	-	(29,364)	-	-
Exercise of employee stock options	5,074	8	5,066	-	-	-
Stockholders' equity as of 3/2/2002	$ 194,054	$ 492	$ 26,824	$ (67,415)	$ 245,941	$ (11,788)
Net income	16,936	-	-	-	16,936	-
Translation adjustment	3,399	-	-	-	-	3,399
Minimum pension liability	(4,765)	-	-	-	-	(4,765)
Total comprehensive income	15,570	-	-	-	16,936	(1,366)
Purchase of treasury stock	(14,305)	-	-	(14,305)	-	-
Exercise of employee stock options	1,449	-	520	929	-	-
Stockholders' equity as of 3/1/2003	**$ 196,768**	**$ 492**	**$ 27,344**	**$ (80,791)**	**$ 262,877**	**$ (13,154)**

See Notes to Consolidated Financial Statements.

notes to consolidated financial statements

NOTE 1

Summary of Significant Accounting Policies

Principles of Consolidation: The consolidated financial statements include the accounts of The Topps Company, Inc. and its subsidiaries ("the Company"). All intercompany items and transactions have been eliminated in consolidation.

The Company and its subsidiaries operate and report financial results on a fiscal year of 52 or 53 weeks which ends on the Saturday closest to the end of February. Fiscal 2001 was comprised of 53 weeks versus 52 weeks in both fiscal 2002 and fiscal 2003.

Foreign Currency Translation: The financial statements of subsidiaries outside the United States, except those subsidiaries located in highly inflationary economies or where costs are primarily U.S. dollar-based, are generally measured using the local currency as the functional currency. Assets and liabilities of these subsidiaries are translated at the rates of exchange as of the balance sheet date. The resultant translation adjustments are included in accumulated other comprehensive income. Income and expense items are translated at the average exchange rate for the month. Gains and losses from foreign currency transactions of these subsidiaries are included in net income. For subsidiaries operating in highly inflationary economies or where inventory costs are U.S. dollar-based, the financial statements are measured using the U.S. dollar as the functional currency. Gains and losses from balance sheet translation adjustments are also included in net income.

Derivative Financial Instruments: Derivative financial instruments are used for hedging purposes by the Company in the management of its foreign currency exposures. The Company does not hold or issue derivative financial instruments for trading purposes.

Gains or losses arising from the derivative financial instruments are recorded in earnings. On March 4, 2001, the Company adopted the provisions of SFAS 133 "Accounting for Derivative Instruments and Hedging Activities" and related standards, as amended. SFAS 133 provides a comprehensive standard for the recognition and measurement of derivatives and hedging activities.

Cash Equivalents: The Company considers investments in highly liquid debt instruments with a maturity of three months or less to be cash equivalents.

Inventories: Inventories are stated at lower of cost or market. Cost is determined on the first-in, first-out basis.

Property, Plant and Equipment ("PP&E"): PP&E is stated at cost. Depreciation is computed using the straight-line method. Estimated useful lives used in computing depreciation are twenty-five years for buildings, three to twelve years for machinery, equipment and software and the remaining lease period for leasehold improvements. In accordance with SFAS 144, the Company periodically evaluates the carrying value of its PP&E for circumstances which may indicate impairment.

Intangible Assets: Intangible assets include trademarks and the value of sports, entertainment and proprietary product rights. Amortization is by the straight-line method over estimated lives of up to twenty years. Management evaluates the recoverability of intangible assets under the provisions of SFAS 144, based on undiscounted projections of future cash flows attributable to the individual assets.

Revenue Recognition: Revenue related to sales of the Company's products is generally recognized when products are shipped, the title and risk of loss has passed to the customer, the sales price is fixed or determinable and collectibility is reasonably assured. Sales made on a returnable basis are recorded net of a provision for estimated returns. These estimates are revised, as necessary, to reflect actual experience and market conditions.

Estimates: The preparation of financial statements in conformity with generally accepted accounting principles requires management to make estimates and assumptions which affect the reporting of assets and liabilities as of the dates of the financial statements and revenues and expenses during the reporting period. These estimates primarily relate to the provision for sales returns, allowance for doubtful accounts, inventory obsolescence and asset valuations. Actual results could differ from these estimates.

Reclassifications: Certain items in the prior years' financial statements have been reclassified to conform with the current year's presentation. Beginning in the first quarter of fiscal 2002, prepress, autograph and relic costs related to future period releases, which previously had been included in prepaid expenses and other current assets, were reclassified to inventory. Autograph, relic and freight costs related to merchandise sold in the period, which previously were included in selling, general and administrative expenses, were reclassified to cost of goods sold.

The Company has adopted the EITF Issue 01-9 accounting standards that require certain trade promotion expenses, such as slotting fees, to be reported as a reduction of net sales rather than as marketing expense. This presentation has been reflected on the Consolidated Statements of Operations for the fiscal years ended March 1, 2003, March 2, 2002 and March 3, 2001.

Income Taxes: The Company provides for deferred income

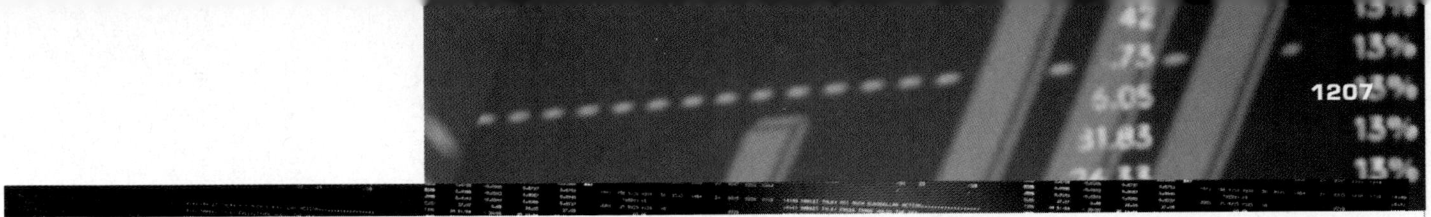

taxes resulting from temporary differences between the valuation of assets and liabilities in the financial statements and the carrying amounts for tax purposes. Such differences are measured using the enacted tax rates and laws that will be in effect when the differences are expected to reverse.

Employee Stock Options: The Company accounts for stock-based employee compensation based on the intrinsic value of stock options granted in accordance with the provisions of APB 25 "Accounting for Stock Issued to Employees." Information relating to stock-based employee compensation, including the pro forma effects had the Company accounted for stock-based employee compensation based on the fair value of stock options granted in accordance with SFAS 123 "Accounting for Stock-Based Compensation," is as follows:

	2003		2002		2001	
	(In thousands of dollars, except share data)					
	As reported	**Pro forma**	As reported	Pro forma	As reported	Pro forma
Net income	**$ 16,936**	**$ 15,586**	$ 28,462	$ 26,721	$ 88,489	$ 87,279
Earnings per share	**$ 0.40**	**$ 0.37**	$ 0.64	$ 0.60	$ 1.91	$ 1.88

In determining the preceding pro forma amounts under SFAS 123, the fair value of each option grant is estimated as of the date of grant using the Black-Scholes option-pricing model with the following assumptions: no dividend yield in any year; risk free interest rate, estimated volatility and expected life, as follows: fiscal 2003 - 4.5%, 35% and 6.5 years respectively; fiscal 2002 - 5.7%, 59% and 6.7 years respectively; and fiscal 2001 - 6.5%, 56% and 6.6 years respectively

NOTE 2

Earnings Per Share

Earnings per share is computed in accordance with SFAS 128. Basic EPS is computed using weighted average shares outstanding, while diluted EPS is computed using weighted average shares outstanding plus shares representing stock distributable under stock-based plans computed using the treasury stock method.

The following table represents the computation of weighted average shares outstanding - diluted:

	Year Ended		
	March 1, 2003	March 2, 2002	March 3, 2001
Weighted average shares outstanding:			
Basic	**41,353,000**	43,073,000	45,011,000
Effect of dilutive stock options	**712,000**	1,203,000	1,355,000
Diluted	**42,065,000**	44,276,000	46,366,000

In the above calculation, the following shares were not included in the effect of dilutive stock options because they had an anti-dilutive effect: 1,532,000 (2003), 469,000 (2002) and 918,000 (2001).

NOTE 3

Accounts Receivable

	March 1, 2003	March 2, 2002
	(In thousands of dollars)	
Gross receivables	**$ 43,250**	$ 37,565
Reserve for returns	**(16,443)**	(15,877)
Allowance for discounts and doubtful accounts	**(1,602)**	(1,649)
Net	**$ 25,205**	$ 20,039

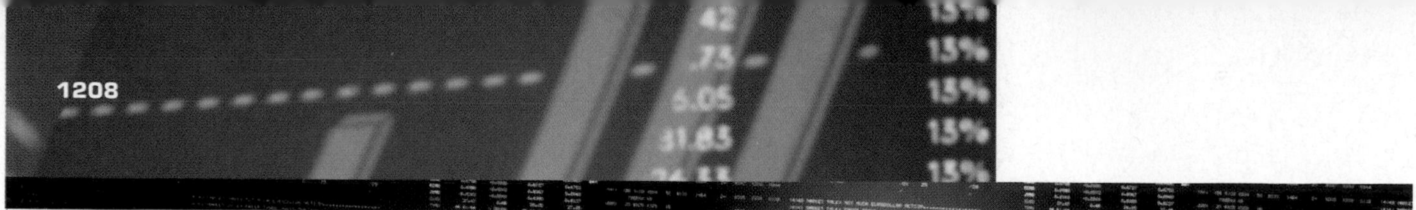

NOTE 4

Inventories

	March 1, 2003	March 2, 2002
	(In thousands of dollars)	
Raw materials	**$ 6,162**	$ 6,395
Work in process	**2,229**	1,274
Finished products	**20,290**	15,427
Total	**$ 28,681**	$ 23,096

NOTE 5

Property, Plant and Equipment, Net

	March 1, 2003	March 2, 2002
	(In thousands of dollars)	
Land	**$ 42**	$ 42
Buildings and improvements	**2,278**	2,291
Machinery, equipment and software	**26,621**	22,801
Total PP&E	**$ 28,941**	$ 25,134
Accumulated depreciation and amortization	**(14,335)**	(10,528)
Net	**$ 14,606**	$ 14,606

NOTE 6

Intangible Assets

On March 3, 2002, the Company adopted SFAS 141 "Business Combinations" and SFAS 142 "Goodwill and Other Intangible Assets" which require the Company to prospectively cease amortization of goodwill and instead conduct periodic tests of goodwill for impairment. The table below compares reported earnings and earnings per share for the year ended March 1, 2003, with earnings and earnings per share assuming pro forma application of the new accounting standards for the year ended March 2, 2002.

	March 1, 2003	March 2, 2002
	(In thousands of dollars)	
Net income	**$ 16,936**	$ 28,462
Add back:		
Goodwill amortization	-	1,568
Adjusted net income	**$ 16,936**	$ 30,030
Adjusted basic net income per share	**$ 0.41**	$ 0.70
Adjusted diluted net income per share	**$ 0.40**	$ 0.68

The Company has evaluated its goodwill and intangible assets acquired prior to June 30, 2002 using the criteria of SFAS 141, and has determined that no intangible assets should be reclassified to goodwill. The Company has also evaluated its intangible assets and determined that all such assets have determinable lives. Furthermore, the Company has reassessed the useful lives and residual values of all intangible assets to review for any necessary amortization period adjustments. Based on that assessment, no adjustments were made to the amortization period or residual values of the intangible assets. In order to conform with the definitions contained in SFAS 142, the Company reclassified $1.5 million in deferred financing fees from intangible assets to other assets and $0.8 million in software development costs from intangible assets to property, plant and equipment. Additionally, $1.9 million of deferred tax assets related to thePit.com acquisition were reclassified to goodwill.

SFAS 142 prescribes a two-phase process for impairment testing of goodwill. The first phase, completed on August 31, 2002, screens for impairment; while the second phase (if

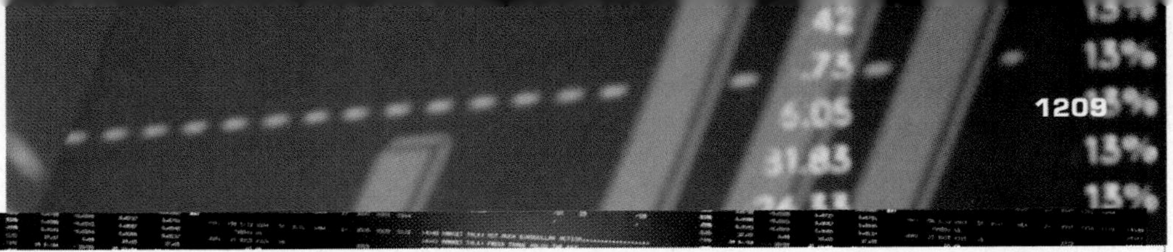

necessary), required to be completed by March 1, 2003, measures the impairment. The Company has completed the first phase and has concluded that no impairment of goodwill exists. Therefore, completion of phase two of the transitional impairment test was not necessary.

For the year ended March 1, 2003, no goodwill or other intangibles were acquired, impaired or disposed. Intangible assets consisted of the following as of March 1, 2003 and March 2, 2002:

March 1, 2003

	Gross Carrying Value	Accumulated Amortization	Net
	(In thousands of dollars)		
Licenses & contracts	$ 21,879	$ (16,594)	$ 5,285
Intellectual property	12,584	(12,473)	111
Software & other	2,953	(2,602)	351
FAS 132 pension	294	-	294
Total intangibles	$ 37,710	$ (31,669)	$ 6,041

March 2, 2002

	Gross Carrying Value	Accumulated Amortization	Net
	(In thousands of dollars)		
Licenses & contracts	$ 21,879	$ (15,717)	$ 6,162
Intellectual property	12,584	(12,315)	269
Software & other	2,953	(2,477)	476
FAS 132 pension	344	-	344
Total intangibles	$ 37,760	$ (30,509)	$ 7,251

Over the next five years the Company expects the annual amortization of the intangible assets detailed above to be as follows:

Fiscal Year	Amount (in thousands)
2004	$ 1,060
2005	$ 826
2006	$ 826
2007	$ 748
2008	$ 670

NOTE 7

Accrued Expenses and Other Liabilities

	March 1, 2003	March 2, 2002
	(In thousands of dollars)	
Royalties	**$ 6,407**	$ 9,009
Employee compensation	**5,563**	7,136
Payments received in advance	**3,700**	1,391
Advertising and marketing expenses	**2,271**	2,908
Legal settlement	**1,612**	-
Other	**9,690**	9,830
Total	**$ 29,243**	$ 30,274

NOTE 8

Depreciation and Amortization

	Year Ended		
	March 1, 2003	March 2, 2002	March 3, 2001
	(In thousands of dollars)		
Depreciation expense	**$ 3,756**	$ 2,601	$ 1,685
Amortization of intangible assets	**1,160**	1,237	1,004
Amortization of goodwill	**-**	1,568	1,568
Amortization of deferred financing fees	**122**	119	88
Total	**$ 5,038**	$ 5,525	$ 4,345

NOTE 9

Long-Term Debt

On June 26, 2000, the Company entered into a credit agreement with Chase Manhattan Bank and LaSalle Bank National Association. The agreement provides for a $35.0 million unsecured facility to cover revolver and letter of credit needs and expires on June 26, 2004. Interest rates are variable and a function of the Company's EBITDA. The credit agreement contains restrictions and prohibitions of a nature generally found in loan agreements of this type and requires the Company, among other things, to comply with certain financial covenants, limits the Company's ability to repurchase its shares, sell or acquire assets or borrow additional money and prohibits the payment of dividends. The credit agreement may be terminated by the Company at any point over the four-year term (provided the Company repays all outstanding amounts thereunder) without penalty. The full $35.0 million credit line was available as of March 1, 2003.

NOTE 10

Income Taxes

The Company provides for deferred income taxes resulting from temporary differences between the valuation of assets and liabilities in the financial statements and the carrying amounts for tax purposes. Such differences are measured using the enacted tax rates and laws that will be in effect when the differences are expected to reverse.

U.S. and foreign operations contributed to income before provision for income taxes as follows:

	Year Ended		
	March 1, 2003	March 2, 2002	March 3, 2001
	(In thousands of dollars)		
United States	**$ 14,157**	$ 25,275	$ 36,359
Europe	**7,861**	15,744	89,201
Canada	**992**	739	1,762
Latin America	**288**	(300)	312
Total income before provision for income taxes	**$ 23,298**	$ 41,458	$ 127,634

Provision for income taxes consists of:

	Year Ended		
	March 1, 2003	March 2, 2002	March 3, 2001
	(In thousands of dollars)		
Current income taxes:			
Federal	**$ 3,899**	$ 8,609	$ 6,467
Foreign	**3,301**	3,889	27,323
State and local	**146**	614	2,459
Total current	**$ 7,346**	$ 13,112	$ 36,249
Deferred income taxes (benefit):			
Federal	**$ (434)**	$ (719)	$ 1,554
Foreign	**(330)**	262	1,020
State and local	**(220)**	341	322
Total deferred	**$ (984)**	$ (116)	$ 2,896
Total provision for income taxes	**$ 6,362**	$ 12,996	$ 39,145

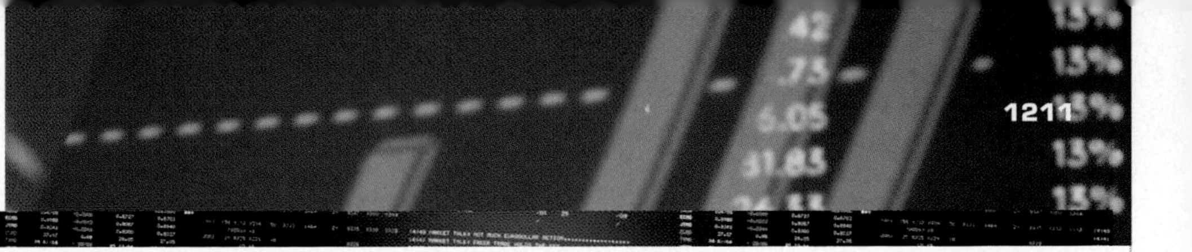

The reasons for the difference between the provision for income taxes and the amount computed by applying the statutory federal income tax rate to income before provision for income taxes are as follows:

	Year Ended		
	March 1, 2003	March 2, 2002	March 3, 2001
	(In thousands of dollars)		
Computed expected tax provision	**$ 8,154**	$ 14,510	$ 44,672
Increase (decrease) in taxes resulting from:			
State and local taxes, net of federal tax benefit	**617**	900	2,327
Foreign and U.S. tax effects attributable to foreign operations	**(1,387)**	(2,274)	(7,080)
Amortization of intangibles	**-**	549	549
R&D	**(502)**	-	-
Other permanent differences	**(520)**	(689)	(1,323)
Provision for income taxes	**$ 6,362**	$ 12,996	$ 39,145

Deferred U.S. income taxes have not been provided on undistributed earnings of foreign subsidiaries as the Company considers such earnings to be permanently reinvested in the businesses as of March 1, 2003. These undistributed foreign earnings could become subject to U.S. income tax if remitted, or deemed remitted, as a dividend. Determination of the deferred U.S. income tax liability on these unremitted earnings is not practical, since such liability, if any, is dependent on circumstances existing at the time of the remittance. The cumulative amount of unremitted earnings from foreign subsidiaries that is expected to be permanently reinvested was approximately $27.8 million on March 1, 2003.

During the year the Company received a refund in the amount of $1.3 million from a foreign tax credit carryback claim that was filed with the Internal Revenue Service and reduced the provision for income taxes. The successful claim resulted from a favorable ruling in a prior tax year.

Taxing authorities periodically challenge positions taken by the Company on its tax returns. On the basis of present information, it is the opinion of the Company's management that any assessments resulting from current tax audits will not have a material adverse effect on the Company's consolidated results of operations or its consolidated financial position.

The components of deferred income tax assets and liabilities are as follows:

	Year Ended	
	March 1, 2003	March 2, 2002
	(In thousands of dollars)	
Deferred income tax assets:		
Provision for estimated losses on sales returns	**$ 1,290**	$ 929
Provision for inventory obsolescence	**852**	1,075
Tax assets of thePit.com	**581**	1,937
Total deferred income tax assets*	**$ 2,723**	$ 3,941
Deferred income tax liabilities:		
Amortization	**$ 1,224**	$ 2,786
Depreciation	**625**	383
Post-retirement benefits	**(1,889)**	(1,593)
Other	**(504)**	(1,978)
Total deferred income tax liabilities*	**$ (544)**	$ (402)

** Net deferred tax assets of $3,267 and $4,343 are presented on the Consolidated Balance Sheet in fiscal 2003 and 2002 respectively.*

NOTE 11

Employee Benefit Plans

The Company maintains qualified and non-qualified defined benefit pensions in the U.S. and Ireland as well as a postretirement healthcare plan in the U.S. for all eligible non-bargaining unit personnel. The Company has previously not included information on the Irish pension in this footnote. The Company is also a participant in a multi-employer defined contribution pension plan covering domestic bargaining unit employees.

In addition, the Company sponsors a defined contribution plan, which qualifies under Sections 401(a) and 401(k) of the Internal Revenue Code (the "401(k) Plan"). While all non-bargaining unit employees are eligible to participate in the 401(k) Plan, participation is optional. The Company does not contribute to the 401(k) Plan.

The following tables summarize benefit costs, as well as the benefit obligations, plan assets and funded status associated with the Company's U.S. and Irish pension and U.S. postretirement healthcare benefit plans.

	Pension Benefits		**Postretirement Healthcare Benefits**	
	March 1, 2003	March 2, 2002	**March 1, 2003**	March 2, 2002
	(In thousands of dollars)			
Reconciliation of change in benefit obligation				
Benefit obligation at beginning of year	**$ 31,662**	$ 27,691	**$ 6,981**	$ 6,836
Service cost	**1,184**	1,003	**225**	217
Interest cost	**2,316**	1,984	**514**	479
Benefits paid	**(1,120)**	(1,200)	**(546)**	(546)
Actuarial (gains) losses	**3,376**	1,467	**2,390**	(5)
Plan amendments/Effect of foreign currency	**440**	717	**(46)**	-
Benefit obligation at end of year	**$ 37,858**	$ 31,662	**$ 9,518**	$ 6,981
Reconciliation of change in the fair value of plan assets				
Fair value of plan assets at beginning of year	**$ 20,329**	$ 17,101	**$ -**	$ -
Actual return on plan assets	**(2,445)**	20	**-**	-
Employer contributions	**689**	4,639	**546**	546
Benefits paid	**(1,120)**	(1,200)	**(546)**	(546)
Participant's contributions/Effect of foreign currency	**738**	(231)	**-**	-
Fair value of plan assets at end of year	**$ 18,191**	$ 20,329	**$ -**	$ -

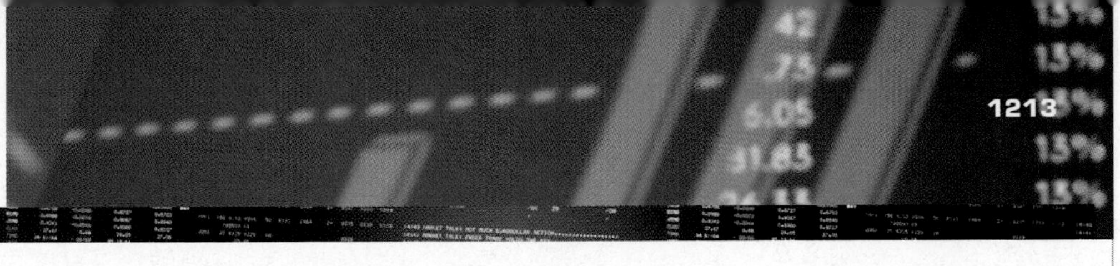

	Pension Benefits		Postretirement Healthcare Benefits	
	March 1, 2003	March 2, 2002	**March 1, 2003**	March 2, 2002
	(In thousands of dollars)			
Funded status				
Funded status	**$ (19,667)**	$ (11,332)	**$ (9,518)**	$ (6,981)
Unrecognized actuarial (gains) losses	**15,995**	9,486	**1,347**	(915)
Unrecognized prior service cost	**539**	697	**-**	-
Unrecognized initial transition obligation	**(707)**	(608)	**2,298**	2,774
Net amount recognized in the consolidated balance sheets	**$ (3,840)**	$ (1,757)	**$ (5,873)**	$ (5,122)
Components of amounts recognized in the consolidated balance sheets				
Prepaid benefit cost	**$ 1,890**	$ 3,474	**$ -**	$ -
Accrued benefit liability	**(16,879)**	(11,686)	**(5,873)**	(5,122)
Intangible asset	**539**	691	**-**	-
Accumulated other comprehensive expense	**10,610**	5,764	**-**	-
Net amount recognized in the consolidated balance sheets	**$ (3,840)**	$ (1,757)	**$ (5,873)**	$ (5,122)

	Pension Benefits			Postretirement Healthcare Benefits		
	March 1, 2003	March 2, 2002	March 3, 2001	**March 1, 2003**	March 2, 2002	March 3, 2001
	(In thousands of dollars)					
Components of net periodic benefit cost						
Service cost	**$ 1,184**	$ 1,003	$ 817	**$ 225**	$ 217	$ 175
Interest cost	**2,316**	1,984	1,896	**514**	479	474
Expected return on plan assets	**(1,643)**	(1,457)	(1,451)	**-**	-	-
Amortization of initial transition obligation	**(51)**	180	152	**221**	221	221
Prior service cost	**133**	66	(15)	**-**	-	-
Actuarial (gains) losses/Special charges	**875**	491	192	**337**	(22)	(82)
Net periodic benefit cost	**$ 2,814**	$ 2,267	$ 1,591	**$ 1,297**	$ 895	$ 788

As of March 1, 2003 and March 2, 2002, both the qualified and non-qualified pension plans had accumulated benefit obligations in excess of plan assets. Information is as follows:

	Pension Benefits	
	March 1, 2003	March 2, 2002
	(In thousands of dollars)	
Projected benefit obligation	**$ 33,990**	$ 29,150
Accumulated benefit obligation	**$ 30,495**	$ 25,802
Fair value of plan assets	**$ 15,280**	$ 17,420

The weighted-average actuarial assumptions used for the U.S. pension and postretirement healthcare plans are as follows:

	Pension and Postretirement Healthcare Benefits	
	March 1, 2003	March 2, 2002
Discount rate	**6.3%**	7.0%
Expected return on plan assets	**8.0%**	8.5%
Rate of compensation increase	**4.5%**	5.0%

Assumptions for healthcare cost increases are as follows: 10% in fiscal 2003, trending down to a 5.0% increase in fiscal 2008. Increases in healthcare costs could significantly affect the reported postretirement benefits cost and benefit obligations. A one percentage point change in assumed healthcare benefit cost trends would have the following effect:

	1-Percentage Point (In thousands of dollars)	
	Increase	Decrease
On total service and interest cost component	$ 118	$ (97)
On postretirement benefit obligation (APBO)	$ 1,066	$ (914)

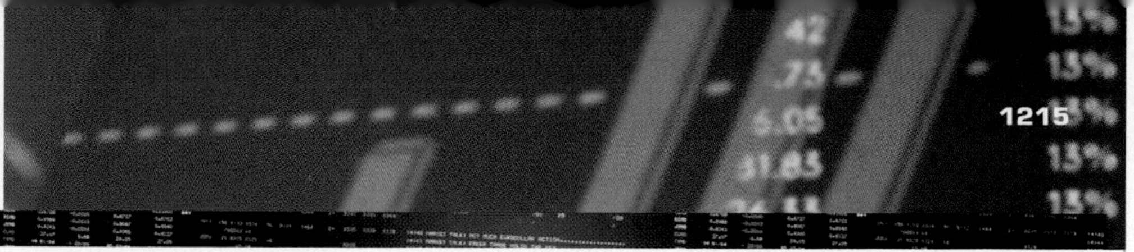

NOTE 12

Stock Option Plans

The Company has Stock Option Plans that provide for the granting of non-qualified stock options, incentive stock options and stock appreciation rights (SARs) to employees, non-employee directors and consultants within the meaning of Section 422A of the Internal Revenue Code. Options granted generally vest over two or three years and expire ten years after the grant date. The following table summarizes information about the Plans.

	March 1, 2003		March 2, 2002		March 3, 2001	
Stock Options	**Shares**	**Weighted Average Exercise Price**	Shares	Weighted Average Exercise Price	Shares	Weighted Average Exercise Price
Outstanding at beginning of year	**3,956,127**	**$ 6.88**	4,309,369	$ 6.34	4,684,052	$ 5.81
Granted	**166,000**	**$ 10.12**	599,306	$ 10.55	569,550	$ 9.35
Exercised	**(220,750)**	**$ 6.21**	(768,335)	$ 4.93	(587,058)	$ 3.57
Forfeited	**(143,400)**	**$ 15.68**	(184,213)	$ 14.24	(357,175)	$ 11.25
Outstanding at end of year	**3,757,977**	**$ 6.73**	3,956,127	$ 6.88	4,309,369	$ 6.34
Options exercisable at end of year	**3,383,854**	**$ 6.32**	3,181,109	$ 6.08	3,491,735	$ 5.97
Weighted average fair value of options granted during the year	**$4.12**		$6.86		$5.84	

Summarized information about stock options outstanding and exercisable at March 1, 2003 is as follows:

	Options Outstanding			Options Exercisable	
Exercise Price Ranges	Outstanding as of 3/1/03	Weighted Average Remaining Contractual Life	Weighted Average Exercise Price	Exercisable as of 3/1/03	Weighted Average Exercise Price
$1.76 - $3.53	939,984	4.9	$ 2.60	939,984	$ 2.60
$3.54 - $5.29	612,250	5.5	$ 4.55	612,250	$ 4.55
$5.30 - $7.05	246,500	3.6	$ 6.20	246,500	$ 6.20
$7.06 - $8.81	603,500	3.2	$ 7.81	603,500	$ 7.81
$8.82 - $10.57	1,020,493	7.2	$ 9.90	704,495	$ 9.76
$10.58 - $12.34	335,250	5.6	$ 11.10	277,125	$ 11.00
	3,757,977	5.3	$ 6.73	3,383,854	$ 6.32

NOTE 13

Capital Stock

In October 1999, the Board of Directors authorized the Company to purchase up to 5 million shares of stock. In October 2001, purchases against this authorization were completed, and the Board of Directors authorized the purchase of up to an additional 5 million shares of stock. As of March 1, 2003, the Company had purchased 2.6 million shares against this new authorization. During fiscal 2003, the Company purchased a total of 1.6 million shares at an average price per share of $9.01.

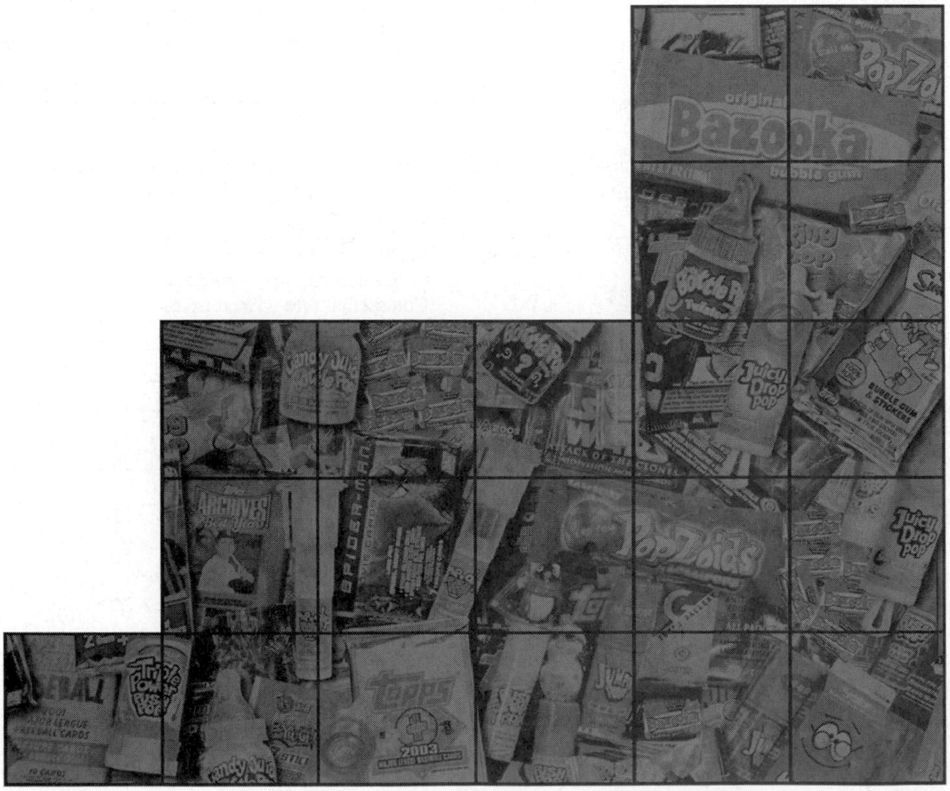

NOTE 14

Segment and Geographic Information

Following is the breakdown of industry segments as required by SFAS 131. The Company has two reportable business segments: Confectionery and Entertainment. Consistent with Topps organizational structure and product line similarities, Entertainment now combines the former Sports and Entertainment segments into one.

The Confectionery segment consists of a variety of lollipop products including Ring Pop, Push Pop and Baby Bottle Pop, the Bazooka bubble gum line and other novelty confectioneries including Pokémon products.

The Entertainment segment primarily consists of cards and sticker album products featuring sports and non-sports licenses, including Pokémon.

The Company's management regularly evaluates the performance of each segment based upon its contributed margin, which is profit after cost of goods, product development, advertising and promotional costs and obsolescence, but before unallocated general and administrative expenses and manufacturing overhead, depreciation and amortization, other income, net interest income and income taxes.

The Company does not allocate assets among its business segments and therefore does not include a breakdown of assets or depreciation and amortization by segment.

Business Segments

	Year Ended		
	March 1, 2003	March 2, 2002	March 3, 2001
	(In thousands of dollars)		
Net Sales			
Confectionery	**$ 146,865**	$ 152,127	$ 170,700
Entertainment	**143,214**	148,053	266,740
Total Net Sales	**$ 290,079**	$ 300,180	$ 437,440
Contributed Margin			
Confectionery	**$ 52,101**	$ 54,880	$ 64,390
Entertainment	**39,313**	47,464	119,653
Total Contributed Margin	**$ 91,414**	$ 102,344	$ 184,043
Reconciliation of contributed margin to income before provision for income taxes			
Total contributed margin	**$ 91,414**	$ 102,344	$ 184,043
Unallocated general and administrative expenses and manufacturing overhead	**(65,778)**	(60,040)	(58,917)
Depreciation & amortization	**(5,038)**	(5,525)	(4,345)
Other income	**184**	(215)	2,964
Income from operations	**20,782**	36,564	121,917
Interest income, net	**2,516**	4,894	5,717
Income before provision for income taxes	**$ 23,298**	$ 41,458	$ 127,634

Net sales to unaffiliated customers and income from operations, as presented below, are based on the location of the ultimate customer. Income from operations is defined as contributed margin less unallocated general and administrative expenses and manufacturing overhead, depreciation and amortization, and other income. Identifiable assets, as presented below, are those assets located in each geographic area.

Geographic Areas

	Year Ended		
	March 1, 2003	March 2, 2002	March 3, 2001
	(In thousands of dollars)		
Net Sales			
United States	**$ 212,464**	$ 220,368	$ 216,780
Europe	**48,555**	48,387	180,419
Other	**29,060**	31,425	40,241
Total Net Sales	**$ 290,079**	$ 300,180	$ 437,440
Income from Operations			
United States	**$ 12,306**	$ 22,579	$ 32,591
Europe	**5,406**	11,216	80,132
Other	**3,070**	2,769	9,194
Total Income from Operations	**$ 20,782**	$ 36,564	$ 121,917
Identifiable Assets			
United States	**$ 213,840**	$ 216,170	$ 171,385
Europe	**41,020**	35,271	101,819
Other	**6,768**	6,509	7,068
Total Identifiable Assets	**$ 261,628**	$ 257,950	$ 280,272

NOTE 15

Acquisition of thePit.com, Inc.

On August 26, 2001, the Company acquired all of the outstanding common stock of thePit.com, Inc., which operates a sports card exchange, for a net $5.7 million in cash. The acquisition was accounted for using the purchase method of accounting. The financial statements of thePit.com, Inc. have been consolidated into the financial statements of the Company. As part of the purchase price allocation, $780,000 ($470,000 for technology and $310,000 for marketing agreements) was reclassified from goodwill to intangibles and is being amortized over 5 years. The amount of goodwill remaining after the reclassification was $4.1 million.

NOTE 16

Fair Value of Financial Instruments

The carrying value of cash, accounts receivable, accounts payable and accrued liabilities approximates fair value due to their short-term nature.

The Company enters into foreign currency forward contracts to hedge its foreign currency exposure. As of March 1, 2003, the Company had outstanding foreign currency forward contracts, which will mature at various dates, in the amount of $27,286,000, with over 60% of the contracts maturing within six months, as compared to $12,504,000 as of March 2, 2002. The fair value of these forward contracts is the amount the Company would receive or pay to terminate the contracts. The approximate pre-tax impact on earnings to the Company to terminate these agreements as of March 1, 2003 and March 2, 2002 was $(400,000) and $519,000, respectively. The Company believes there is no significant credit risk of non-performance by counter parties of the foreign currency forward contracts.

NOTE 17

Quarterly Results of Operations (Unaudited)

	2003				2002			
	1st	**2nd**	**3rd**	**4th**	1st	2nd	3rd	4th
	(In thousands of dollars, except share data)							
Net sales	**$ 87,739**	**$ 69,999**	**$ 66,656**	**$ 65,685**	$ 86,892	$ 81,214	$ 72,052	$ 60,022
Gross profit on sales	**32,635**	**25,296**	**21,649**	**22,154**	37,702	36,207	22,259	17,673
Income from operations	**10,665**	**6,311**	**813**	**2,993**	16,993	12,295	5,917	1,359
Net income	**7,341**	**4,692**	**2,910**	**1,993**	11,629	8,852	6,532	1,449
Net income per share								
- basic	**$ 0.17**	**$ 0.11**	**$ 0.07**	**$ 0.05**	$ 0.27	$ 0.20	$ 0.15	$ 0.03
- diluted	**$ 0.17**	**$ 0.11**	**$ 0.07**	**$ 0.05**	$ 0.26	$ 0.20	$ 0.15	$ 0.03

NOTE 18

Commitments and Contingencies

Future minimum payments under non-cancelable leases which extend into the year 2014 are $1,531,000 (2004), $1,531,000 (2005), $1,531,000 (2006), $1,454,000 (2007), $1,400,000 (2008) and $2,980,000 thereafter.

Future minimum payments required under the Company's existing sports and entertainment contracts, with various expiration dates extending into the year 2004, are estimated to be $12,162,000.

Total royalty expense under the Company's sports and entertainment licensing contracts was $25,344,000 (2003), $25,669,000 (2002) and $46,727,000 (2001).

Advertising and marketing expenses (which encompass media spending and consumer promotions costs) included in selling, general and administrative expenses amounted to $20,145,000 (2003), $18,790,000 (2002) and $21,514,000 (2001).

The Company transacts business in many countries, utilizing many different currencies. It is thus exposed to the effect of exchange rate fluctuations on sales and purchase transactions. The Company enters into both foreign currency forward contracts and options on currency forward contracts to manage these exposures and to minimize the effects of foreign currency transactions on cash flow. Such contracts are entered into primarily to hedge against future commitments. The Company does not engage in foreign currency speculation. The Company may be exposed to credit losses in the event of non-performance by counterparties to these instruments. Management believes, however, the risk of incurring such losses is remote as the contracts are entered into with major financial institutions.

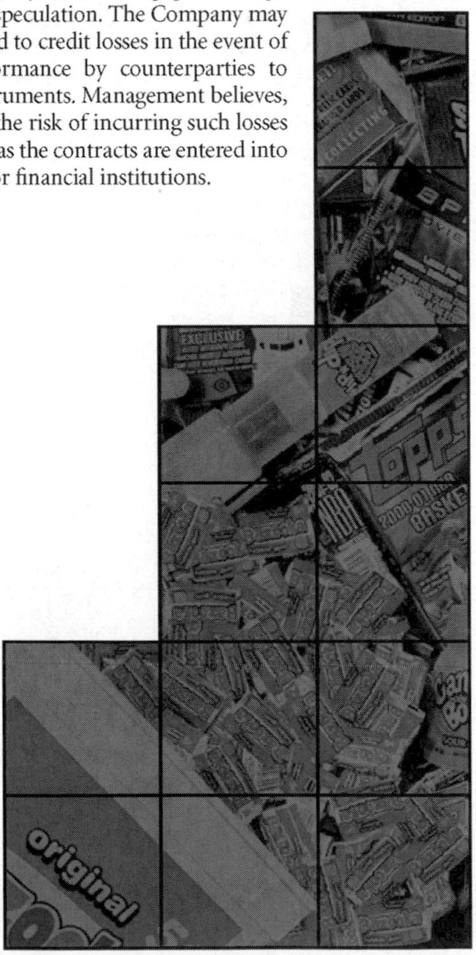

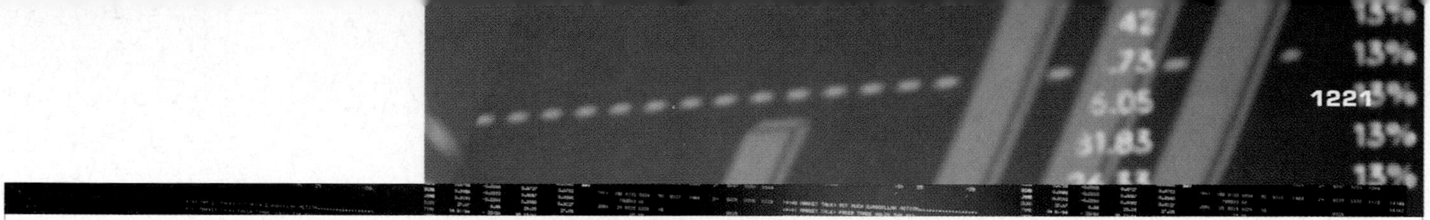

Report of Independent Public Accountants

Board of Directors and Stockholders
The Topps Company, Inc.:

We have audited the accompanying consolidated balance sheets of The Topps Company, Inc. and Subsidiaries as of March 1, 2003 and March 2, 2002, and the related consolidated statements of operations, stockholders' equity and cash flows for each of the three years in the period ended March 1, 2003. These financial statements are the responsibility of the Company's management. Our responsibility is to express an opinion on these financial statements based on our audits.

We conducted our audits in accordance with auditing standards generally accepted in the United States of America. Those standards require that we plan and perform the audit to obtain reasonable assurance about whether the financial statements are free of material misstatement. An audit includes examining, on a test basis, evidence supporting the amounts and disclosures in the financial statements. An audit also includes assessing the accounting principles used and significant estimates made by management, as well as evaluating the overall financial statement presentation. We believe that our audits provide a reasonable basis for our opinion.

In our opinion, such financial statements present fairly, in all material respects, the financial position of The Topps Company, Inc. and Subsidiaries as of March 1, 2003 and March 2, 2002 and the results of their operations and cash flows for each of the three years in the period ended March 1, 2003 in conformity with accounting principles generally accepted in the United States of America.

As discussed in Note 6 of the notes to the consolidated financial statements, in 2003 the Company changed its method of accounting for goodwill and other intangible assets to conform to Statement of Financial Accounting Standards ("SFAS") No. 142.

Deloitte & Touche LLP

DELOITTE & TOUCHE LLP
New York, New York
April 4, 2003

Market and Dividend Information

The Company's common stock is traded on the Nasdaq National Market under the symbol TOPP. The following table sets forth, for the periods indicated, the high and low sales price for the common stock during the last two fiscal years as reported on the Nasdaq National Market. As of March 1, 2003, there were approximately 4,500 holders of record.

	Fiscal year ended March 1, 2003		Fiscal year ended March 2, 2002	
	High Price	**Low Price**	High Price	Low Price
First quarter	**$ 11.06**	**$ 9.35**	$ 10.40	$ 8.78
Second quarter	**$ 10.57**	**$ 8.20**	$ 12.29	$ 9.60
Third quarter	**$ 9.93**	**$ 7.36**	$ 12.16	$ 9.05
Fourth quarter	**$ 9.97**	**$ 7.79**	$ 12.49	$ 9.06

The Company did not pay a dividend in fiscal 2003, and any future dividend payments, should they occur, would require an amendment of the Company's Credit Agreement. See "Management's Discussion and Analysis of Financial Condition and Results of Operations - Liquidity and Capital Resources" and "Notes to Consolidated Financial Statements - Note 9."

selected consolidated financial data

	2003	2002	2001	2000	1999
		(In thousands of dollars, except share data, unaudited)			
OPERATING DATA:					
Net sales	**$ 290,079**	$ 300,180	$ 437,440	$ 374,193	$ 229,414
Gross profit on sales	**101,734**	113,841	199,911	166,895	93,037
Selling, general and administrative expenses	**81,136**	77,062	80,958	72,798	70,534
Income from operations	**20,782**	36,564	121,917	94,852	26,658
Interest income (expense), net	**2,516**	4,894	5,717	1,712	(454)
Net income	**16,936**	28,462	88,489	59,215	15,571
Income from operations per share					
- basic	**$ 0.50**	$ 0.85	$ 2.71	$ 2.04	$ 0.57
- diluted	**$ 0.49**	$ 0.83	$ 2.63	$ 2.00	$ 0.57
Net income per share					
- basic	**$ 0.41**	$ 0.66	$ 1.97	$ 1.28	$ 0.34
- diluted	**$ 0.40**	$ 0.64	$ 1.91	$ 1.25	$ 0.33
Cash dividends	**-**	-	-	-	-
Wtd. avg. shares outstanding					
- basic	**41,353,000**	43,073,000	45,011,000	46,398,000	46,415,000
- diluted	**42,065,000**	44,276,000	46,366,000	47,463,000	46,678,000
BALANCE SHEET DATA:					
Cash and equivalents	**$ 114,259**	$ 121,057	$ 158,741	$ 75,853	$ 41,728
Working capital	**141,484**	136,389	140,487	71,952	24,919
Net property, plant and equipment	**14,606**	14,606	11,181	9,181	7,429
Long-term debt, less current portion	**-**	-	-	-	5,158
Total assets	**261,628**	257,950	280,272	203,313	151,453
Stockholders' equity	**$ 196,768**	**$ 194,054**	$ 196,542	$ 129,175	$ 77,224

Certain items in the prior years' financial statements have been reclassified to conform with the current year's presentation.

Fiscal 2000 and 1999 Net sales and SG&A do not reflect the reclassification of slotting expenses included in the figures for fiscal 2001, 2002 and 2003.

Fiscal 1999 Income from operations includes non-recurring income of $3.5 million related to the sale of the Company's manufacturing facility in Cork, Ireland and of equipment in Cork, Ireland and Duryea, Pennsylvania.

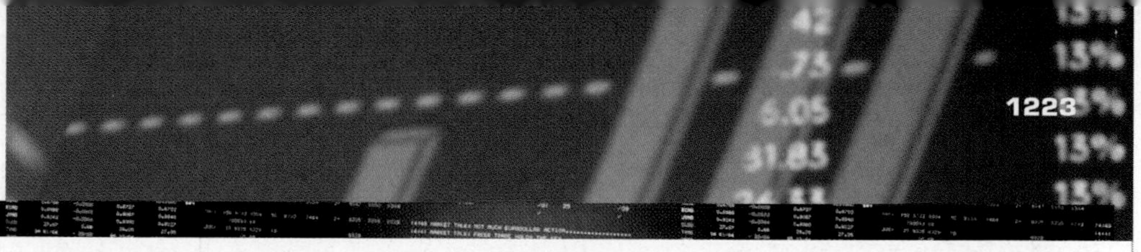

Board of Directors

Arthur T. Shorin*
Chairman, Chief Executive Officer and President

Allan A. Feder
Independent Business Consultant

Stephen D. Greenberg
Managing Director
Allen & Company, LLC

Ann Kirschner
President, Comma International

David Mauer
Chief Executive Officer
E & B Giftware, LLC

Edward D. Miller*
Senior Advisor
Former President and CEO
AXA Financial, Inc.

Jack H. Nusbaum
Senior Partner and Chairman
Willkie Farr & Gallagher

Richard Tarlow
Chairman
Carlson & Partners

Stanley Tulchin*
Chairman
Stanley Tulchin Associates, Inc.

*Nominated to stand for re-election to the Company's Board of Directors at the 2003 Annual Meeting of Stockholders.

Officers

Arthur T. Shorin
Chairman, Chief Executive Officer and President

Scott Silverstein
Executive Vice President

Ronald L. Boyum
Vice President - Marketing and Sales and General Manager Confectionery

Edward P. Camp
Vice President and President -Hobby Division

Michael P. Clancy
Vice President - International and Managing Director, Topps International Limited

Michael J. Drewniak
Vice President - Manufacturing

Ira Friedman
Vice President - Publishing and New Product Development

Warren Friss
Vice President - Internet Business and General Counsel

Leon J. Gutmann
Assistant Treasurer and Assistant Secretary

Catherine K. Jessup
Vice President - Chief Financial Officer

William G. O'Connor
Vice President Administration

John Perillo
Vice President - Operations

Subsidiaries

Topps Argentina, SRL
Managing Director -
Juan P. Georgalos

Topps UK Limited
Managing Director -
Jeremy Charter

Topps Italia, SRL
Managing Director -
Furio Cicogna

Topps Canada, Inc.
General Manager -
Michael Pearl

Topps International Limited
Managing Director -
Michael P. Clancy

Topps Europe Limited
Managing Director -
Christopher Rodman

Topps Enterprises, Inc.

Topps Finance, Inc.

Corporate Information

Annual Meeting
Thursday, June 26, 2003
10:30 A.M.
J.P. Morgan Chase & Co.
270 Park Avenue
New York, NY 10017

Investor Relations
Brod Group LLC
445 Park Avenue
New York, NY 10036

Corporate Counsel
Willkie Farr & Gallagher
787 Seventh Avenue
New York, NY 10019

Independent Auditors
Deloitte & Touche LLP
Two World Financial Center
New York, NY 10281

Registrar and Transfer Agent
American Stock Transfer & Trust Company
59 Maiden Lane
New York, NY 10038
877-777-0800 ext 6820

Form 10-K — A copy of the Company's Annual Report on Form 10-K as filed with the Securities and Exchange Commission will be available at the Topps website www.topps.com or upon written request to the Assistant Treasurer.

GLOSSARY

absolute amounts Dollar totals reported in accounts on financial reports that can be misleading because they make no reference to the relative size of the company being analyzed. *p. 651*

absorption (full) costing Practice of capitalizing all product costs, including fixed manufacturing costs, in inventory and expensing costs when goods are sold. *p. 848*

accelerated depreciation methods Depreciation methods that recognize depreciation expense more rapidly in the early stages of an asset's life than in the later stages of its life. *p. 393*

account balance Difference between total debits and total credits in an account. *p. 118*

account receivable Expected future cash receipt(s) arising from permitting a customer to *buy now and pay later;* characterized by relatively small balance with a short term to maturity. *pp. 60, 331*

accounting Service-based profession that provides reliable and relevant financial information useful in making decisions. *p. 3*

accounting controls Procedures designed to safeguard assets and to ensure accuracy and reliability of the accounting records and reports. *p. 288*

accounting cycle A cycle consisting of these stages: recording accounting data, adjusting the accounts, preparing the financial statements, and closing the nominal accounts; when one accounting cycle ends, a new one begins. *p. 66*

accounting equation Expression of the relationship between the assets and the claims on those assets. *p. 9*

accounting event Economic occurrence that causes changes in an enterprise's assets, liabilities, or equity. *p. 11*

accounting period Span of time covered by the financial statements, normally one year, but may be a quarter, a month or some other time span. *p. 17*

accounts receivable turnover Financial ratio that measures how fast accounts receivable are turned into cash; computed by dividing sales by accounts receivable. *pp. 350, 657*

accounts Records used for the classification and summary of transaction data. *p. 9*

accrual Recognition of events before exchanging cash. *p. 60*

accrual accounting Accounting system that recognizes expenses or revenues when they occur regardless of when cash is exchanged. *p. 59*

accrual transactions Transactions involving the recognition of revenue or expense before the corresponding cash receipt or payment. *p. 605*

accrued expenses Expenses that are recognized before cash is paid. An example is accrued salaries expense. *p. 62*

accrued interest Interest revenue or expense that is recognized before cash has been exchanged. *p. 345*

accumulated conversion factors Factors used to convert a series of future cash inflows into their present value equivalent and that are applicable to cash inflows of equal amounts spread over equal interval time periods and that can be determined by computing the sum of the individual single factors used for each period. *p. 1152*

accumulated depreciation Contra asset account that indicates the sum of all depreciation expense recognized for an asset since the date of acquisition. *p. 390*

acid-test ratio (quick ratio) Measure of immediate debt-paying ability; calculated by dividing very liquid assets (cash, receivables, and marketable securities) by current liabilities. *p. 656*

activities The actions taken by an organization to accomplish its mission. *p. 714*

activity base Factor that causes changes in variable cost; usually some measure of volume when used to define cost behavior. *p. 756*

activity-based management (ABM) Management of the activities of an organization to add the greatest value by developing products that satisfy the needs of that organization's customers. *p. 714*

adjusting entry Entry that updates account balances prior to preparing financial statements. *pp. 62, 345*

administrative controls Procedures designed to evaluate performance and the degree of compliance with a firm's policies and public laws. *p. 288*

adverse opinion Audit opinion for a set of financial statements issued by a certified public accountant that means that part of or all of the financial statements are not in compliance with GAAP and the auditors believe this noncompliance would be material to the average prudent investor. *p. 303*

aging of accounts receivable Classifying each account receivable by the number of days it has been outstanding. The purpose of the aging schedule is to develop a more accurate estimate of the amount of uncollectible accounts. *p. 340*

allocation Process of dividing a total cost into parts and apportioning the parts among the relevant cost objects. *p. 796*

allocation base Cost driver that constitutes the basis for the allocation process. *p. 796*

allocation rate Factor used to allocate or assign costs to a cost object; determined by taking the total cost to be allocated and dividing it by the appropriate cost driver. *p. 796*

Allowance for Doubtful Accounts Contra asset account that contains an amount equal to the accounts receivable that are expected to be uncollectible. *p. 332*

allowance method of accountiing for uncollectible accounts Method of accounting for bad debts in which bad debts are estimated and expensed in the same period in which the corresponding sales are recognized. The receivables are reported in the financial statements at net realizable value (the amount expected to be collected in cash). *p. 332*

allowances Reduction in the selling price of goods extended to the buyer because the goods are defective or of lower quality than the buyer ordered to encourage a buyer to keep merchandise that would otherwise be returned. *p. 189*

amortization Method of systematically allocating the costs of intangible assets to expense over their useful lives; also a term for converting the discount on a note or a bond to interest expense over a designated period. *pp. 386, 497*

amortizing See amortization. *p. 463*

annual report Document in which an organization provides information to stockholders, usually on an annual basis. *p. 25*

annuity Series of equal payments made over a specified number of periods. *pp. 520, 1153*

applied overhead Amount of overhead costs assigned during the period to work in process using the predetermined overhead rate. *p. 838*

appropriated retained earnings Retained earnings restricted by the board of directors for a specific purpose (e.g., to repay debt or for future expansion); although a part of total retained earnings, not available for distribution as dividends. *p. 570*

articles of incorporation Items on an application filed with a state agency for the formation of a corporation; contains such information as the corporation's name, its purpose, its location, its expected life, provisions for its capital stock, and a list of the members of its board of directors. *p. 556*

articulation A term used to describe interrelationships among the financial statements. For example, the amount of net income reported on the income statement is added to beginning retained earnings as a component in the calculation of the ending retained earnings balance reported on the statement of stockholders' equity. *p. 15*

asset exchange transaction A transaction that decreases one asset while increasing another asset so that total assets do not change; for example, the purchase of land with cash. *p. 61*

asset source transaction Transaction that increases an asset and a claim on assets; three types of asset source transactions are acquisitions from owners (equity), borrowings from creditors (liabilities), or earnings from operations (revenues). *pp. 11, 60*

asset turnover ratio The amount of net income divided by average total assets. *p. 661*

asset use transaction Transaction that decreases an asset and a claim on assets; the three types are distributions (transfers to owners), liability payments (to creditors), or expenses (used to operate the business). *p. 61*

assets Economic resources used by a business to produce revenue. *p. 9*

audits Detailed examinations of financial statements and the documents that support the information presented in those statements. *p. 301*

authority manual A document that outlines the chain of command for authority and responsibility. The authority manual provides guidelines for specific positions such as personnel officer as well a general authority such as all vice presidents are authorized to spend up to a designated limit. *p. 289*

authorized stock Number of shares that the corporation is approved by the state to issue. *p. 562*

available-for-sale securities Marketable securities that are not properly classified as held-to-maturity or trading securities. *p. 254*

average cost The total cost of making products divided by the total number of products made. *p. 703*

average number of days to collect accounts receivable Length of the average collection period for accounts receivable; computed by dividing 365 by the accounts receivable turnover ratio. *pp. 350, 657*

average number of days to sell inventory (average days in inventory) Financial ratio that measures the average number of days that inventory stays in stock before being sold. *pp. 252, 658*

avoidable costs Future costs that can be avoided by taking a specified course of action. To be avoidable in a decision-making context, costs must differ among the alternatives. For example, if the cost of material used to make two different products is the same for both products, that cost could not be avoided by choosing to produce one product over the other. Therefore, the material's cost would not be an avoidable cost. *p. 971*

balance sheet Statement that lists the assets of a business and the corresponding claims (liabilities and equity) on those assets. *p. 18*

balanced scorecard A management evaluation tool that includes financial and nonfinancial measures. *p. 1122*

bank reconciliation Schedule that identifies and explains differences between the cash balance reported by the bank and the cash balance in the firm's accounting records. *p. 293*

bank statement Statement issued by a bank (usually monthly) that denotes all activity in the bank account for that period. *p. 293*

bank statement credit memo Memo that describes an increase in the account balance. *p. 293*

bank statement debit memo Memo that describes a decrease in the account balance. *p. 293*

basket purchase Acquisition of several assets in a single transaction with no specific cost attributed to each asset. *p. 387*

batch-level costs The costs associated with producing a batch of products. For example, the cost of setting up machinery to produce 1,000 products is a batch-level cost. The classification of batch-level costs is context sensitive. Postage for one product would be classified as a unit-level cost. In contrast, postage for a large number of products delivered in a single shipment would be classified as a batch level cost. *p. 972*

benchmarking Identifying the best practices used by world-class competitors. *p. 714*

best practices Practices used by world-class companies. *p. 714*

board of directors Group of individuals elected by the stockholders of a corporation to oversee its operations. *p. 559*

bond certificates Debt securities used to obtain long-term financing in which a company borrows funds from a number of lenders, called *bondholders;* usually issued in denominations of $1,000. *p. 501*

bond discount Difference between the selling price and the face amount of a bond sold for less than the face amount. *p. 508*

bondholder The party buying a bond (the lender or creditor). *p. 501*

bond premium Difference between the selling price and the face amount of a bond that is sold for more than the face amount. *p. 512*

book value Historical (original) cost of an asset minus the accumulated depreciation; alternatively, undepreciated amount to date. *p. 391*

book value per share Value of stock determined by dividing the total stockholders' equity by the number of shares of stock. *pp. 562, 664*

books of original entry Journals in which transactions are first recorded. *p. 129*

bottleneck A constraint limiting the capacity of a company to produce or sell its products. An example is a piece of equipment that cannot produce enough component parts to keep employees in the assembly department busy. *p. 987*

break-even point Point where total revenue equals total cost; can be expressed in units or sales dollars. *p. 932*

budgeting Form of planning that formalizes a company's goals and objectives in financial terms. *p. 1019*

budget slack Difference between inflated and realistic standards. *p. 1067*

by-products Products that share common inputs with other joint products but have relatively insignificant market values relative to the other joint products. *p. 808*

callable bonds Bonds that include a feature allowing the issuer to pay them off prior to maturity. *p. 503*

call premium Difference between the call price (the price that must be paid for a called bond) and the face amount of the bond. *p. 504*

call price Specified price that must be paid for bonds that are called; usually higher than the face amount of the bonds. *p. 504*

capital budget Budget that describes the company's plans regarding investments, new products, or lines of business for the coming year; used as input to prepare many of the operating budgets and becomes a formal part of the master budget. *p. 1022*

capital budgeting Financial planning activities that cover the intermediate range of time such as whether to buy or lease equipment, whether to purchase a particular investment, or whether to increase operating expenses to stimulate sales. *p. 1020*

capital expenditures (on an existing asset) Substantial amounts of funds spent to improve an asset's quality or to extend its life. *p. 400*

capital investments Expenditures for the purchase of operational assets that involve a long-term commitment of funds that can be critically important to the company's ultimate success; normally recovered through the use of the assets. *p. 1150*

carrying value Face amount of a bond liability less any unamortized bond discount or plus any unamortized bond premium. *p. 509*

cash Coins, currency, checks, balances in checking and certain savings accounts, money orders, bank drafts, certificates of deposit, and other items that are payable on demand. *p. 290*

cash budget A budget that focuses on cash receipts and payments that are expected to occur in the future. *p. 1029*

cash discount Discount offered on merchandise sold to encourage prompt payment; offered by sellers of merchandise and represent sales discounts to the seller when they are used and purchase discounts to the purchaser of the merchandise. *p. 188*

cash inflows Sources of cash. *p. 603*

cash outflows Uses of cash. *p. 603*

Cash Short and Over Account used to record the amount of cash shortages or overages; shortages are considered expenses and overages are considered revenues. *p. 298*

certified check Check guaranteed by a bank to be drawn on an account having funds sufficient to pay the check. *p. 295*

certified public accountant (CPA) Accountant who has met certain educational and experiential requirements and is licensed by the state government to provide audit services to the public. *p. 301*

certified suppliers Suppliers who have gained the confidence of the buyer by providing quality goods and services at desirable prices and usually in accordance with strict delivery specifications; frequently provide the buyer with preferred customer status in exchange for guaranteed purchase quantities and prompt payment schedules. *p. 979*

chart of accounts List of all ledger accounts and their corresponding account numbers. *p. 128*

checks Prenumbered forms, sometimes multicopy, with the name of the business issuing them preprinted on the face, indicating to whom they are paid, the amount of the payment, and the transaction date. *p. 293*

claims Owners' and creditors' interests in a business's assets. *p. 9*

claims exchange transaction Transaction that decreases one claim and increases another so that total claims do not change. For example, the accrual of interest expense is a claims exchange transaction; liabilities increase, and the recognition of the expense causes retained earnings to decrease. *p. 62*

classified balance sheet Balance sheet that distinguishes between current and noncurrent items. *p. 458*

closely held corporation Corporation whose stock is exchanged between a limited number of individuals. *p. 556*

closing see closing the books. *p. 66*

closing entries Entries used to transfer the balances in the Revenue, Expense, and Dividends accounts to the Retained Earnings account at the end of the accounting period. *p. 132*

closing the books Process of transferring balances from nominal accounts (Revenue, Expense, and Dividends) to the permanent account (Retained Earnings). *p. 66*

Code of Professional Conduct A set of guidelines established by the American Institute of Certified Public Accountants (AICPA) to promote high ethical conduct among its membership. *p. 21*

collateral Assets pledged as security for a loan. *pp. 344, 514*

common size financial statements Financial statements in which amounts are converted to percentages to allow a better comparison of period-to-period and company-to-company financial data since all information is placed on a common basis. *p. 201*

common stock Basic class of corporate stock that carries no preferences as to claims on assets or dividends; certificates that evidence ownership in a company. *pp. 10, 563*

compounding Earning interest on interest. *p. 518*

compound interest Practice of reinvesting interest so that interest is earned on interest as well as on the initial principal. *p. 518*

comprehensive annual financial report (CAFR) An annual report that provides information regarding all funds and account groups under the jurisdiction of a government reporting entity. *p. 578*

confidentiality Code of ethics requirement that prohibits CPAs from voluntarily disclosing information they acquire as a result of accountant-client relationships. *p. 304*

conservatism A principle that guides accountants in uncertain circumstances to select the alternative that produces the lowest amount of net income. *p. 67*

consistency A principle that encourages the continuing use of the same accounting method(s) so that financial statements are comparable across time. *p. 243*

consolidated financial statements Financial statements that represent the combined operations of a parent company and its subsidiaries. *p. 258*

constraints Factors that limit a business's ability to satisfy the demand for its products. *p. 987*

contingent liability Obligations with amounts due that depend on events that will be resolved in the future. *p. 445*

continuity Concept that describes the fact that a corporation's life may extend well beyond the time at which any particular shareholder decides to retire or to sell his or her stock. *p. 558*

continuous improvement Total quality management (TQM) feature that refers to an ongoing process through which employees learn to eliminate waste, reduce response time, minimize defects, and simplify the design and delivery of products and services to customers. *p. 714*

contra asset account Account subtracted from another account with which it is associated; has the effect of reducing the asset account with which it is associated. *pp. 333, 390*

contra liability account Account reported in the liability section of the balance sheet that has a debit balance; reduces total liabilities. A discount on a note payable is an example of a contra liability account. *p. 462*

contribution margin Difference between a company's sales revenue and total variable cost; represents the amount available to cover fixed cost and thereafter to provide a profit. *p. 751*

contribution margin per unit The contribution margin per unit is equal to the sales price per unit minus the variable cost per unit. *p. 932*

contribution margin ratio Result of dividing the contribution margin per unit by the sales price; can be used in cost-volume-profit analysis to determine the amount of the break-even sales volume expressed in dollars or to determine the dollar level of sales required to attain a desired profit. *p. 943*

controllability concept The practice that evaluates a manager only on the revenue and costs under his or her direct control. *p. 1113*

convertible bonds Bonds that can be converted (exchanged) to an ownership interest (stock) in the corporation. *p. 503*

copyright Legal protection of writings, musical compositions, and other intellectual property for the exclusive use of the creator or persons assigned the right by the creator. *p. 403*

corporation Legal entity separate from its owners; formed when a group of individuals with a common purpose join together in an organization according to state laws. *p. 556*

cost A resource such as cash that has been exchanged for another resource (asset) or that has been consumed in the process of earning revenue. Incurring a cost results in an asset exchange or expense recognition. *p. 68*

cost accumulation Process of determining the cost of a particular object by accumulating many individual costs into a single total cost. *p. 808*

cost allocation Process of dividing a total cost into parts and assigning the parts to relevant objects. *pp. 708, 794*

cost averaging Method to determine the average cost per unit of a product or service by dividing the total cost by the activity base used in defining the cost; often is more relevant to decision making than actual costs. Pricing, performance evaluation, and control depend most often on average costs. *p. 756*

cost-based transfer price Transfer price based on the historical or standard cost incurred by the supplying segment. *p. 1125*

cost behavior How a cost reacts (goes up, down, or remains the same) relative to changes in some measure of activity (e.g., the behavior pattern of the cost of raw materials is to increase as the number of units of product made increases). *p. 745*

cost center Type of responsibility center which incurs costs but does not generate revenue. *p. 1111*

cost driver Any factor, usually some measure of activity, that causes cost to be incurred, sometimes referred to as *activity base* or *allocation base*. Examples are labor hours, machine hours, or some other measure of activity whose change causes corresponding changes in the cost object. *p. 794*

cost method of accounting for treasury stock Method of accounting for treasury stock in which the purchase of treasury stock is recorded at its cost to the firm but does not consider the original issue price or par value. *p. 567*

cost objects Objects for which managers need to know the cost; can be products, processes, departments, services, activities, and so on. *p. 793*

cost of capital Return paid to investors and creditors for the use of their assets (capital); usually represents a company's minimum rate of return. *p. 1151*

cost of goods available for sale Total costs paid to obtain goods and to make them ready for sale, including the cost of beginning inventory plus purchases and transportation-in costs, less purchase returns and allowances and purchase discounts. *p. 182*

cost of goods sold Total cost incurred for the goods sold during a specific accounting period. *p. 182*

cost per equivalent unit Unit cost of product determined by dividing total production costs by the number of equivalent whole units. It is used to allocate product costs between processing departments (compute ending inventory and the amount of costs transferred to the subsequent department). *p. 896*

cost-plus pricing Pricing strategy that sets the price at cost plus a markup equal to a percentage of the cost. *pp. 702, 932*

cost pool Many individual costs that have been accumulated into a single total for the purposes of allocation. *p. 806*

cost structure Company's cost mix (relative proportion of variable and fixed costs to total cost). When sales change, the size of the corresponding change in net income is directly related to the company's cost structure. Companies with a large percentage of fixed cost to variable costs have more fluctuation in net income with changes in sales. *p. 749*

cost tracing Relating specific costs to the objects that cause their incurrence. *p. 795*

cost-volume-profit (CVP) analysis Analysis that shows the interrelationships among sales prices, volume, fixed, and variable costs; an important tool in determining the break-even point or the most profitable combination of these variables. *p. 931*

credit Entry that increases liability and equity accounts or decreases asset accounts. *p. 118*

creditors Individuals or institutions that have loaned goods or services to a business. *p. 4*

cumulative dividends Preferred dividends that accumulate from year to year until paid. *p. 563*

current (short-term) assets Assets that will be converted to cash or consumed within one year or an operating cycle, whichever is longer. *pp. 385, 457*

current (short-term) liability Obligation due within one year or an operating cycle, whichever is longer. *p. 457*

current ratio Measure of liquidity; calculated by dividing current assets by current liabilities. *pp. 459, 656*

date of record Date that establishes who will receive the dividend payment: shareholders who actually own the stock on the record date will be paid the dividend even if the stock is sold before the dividend is paid. *p. 568*

debentures Unsecured bonds backed by the general credit of the organization. *p. 503*

debit Entry that increases asset accounts or decreases liability and equity accounts. *p. 118*

debt security Type of security acquired by loaning assets to the investee company. *p. 253*

debt to assets ratio Financial ratio that measures a company's level of risk. *pp. 138, 659*

debt to equity ratio Financial ratio that compares creditor financing to owner financing, expressed as the dollar amount of liabilities for each dollar of stockholder's equity. *p. 659*

decentralization Practice of delegating authority and responsibility for the operation of business segments. *p. 1110*

declaration date Date on which the board of directors actually declares a dividend. *p. 568*

deferral Recognition of revenue or expense in a period after cash is exchanged. *p. 60*

deferral transactions Accounting transactions in which cash payments or receipts occur before the associated expense or revenue is recognized. *p. 608*

deferred tax liability Taxes not paid until future years because of the difference in accounting methods selected for financial statements and methods required for tax purposes (e.g., a company may select straight-line depreciation for financial statement reporting but will be required to use MACRS for tax reporting). *p. 399*

depletion Method of systematically allocating the costs of natural resources to expense as the resources are removed from the land. *p. 386*

deposits in transit Deposits recorded in a depositor's books but not received and recorded by the bank. *p. 294*

deposit ticket Bank form that accompanies checks and cash deposited into a bank account; normally specifies the account number, name of the account, and a record of the checks and cash being deposited. *p. 293*

depreciable cost Original cost minus salvage value *p. 388*

depreciation Method of systematically allocating the costs of long-term tangible assets to expense over their useful lives. *p. 386*

depreciation expense Portion of the original cost of a long-term tangible asset allocated to an expense account in a given period. *p. 388*

differential revenues Future-oriented revenues that differ among the alternatives under consideration. *p. 971*

direct cost Cost that is easily traceable to a cost object and for which the sacrifice to trace is small in relation to the information benefits attained. *p. 795*

direct labor Wages paid to production workers whose efforts can be easily and conveniently traced to products. *p. 706*

direct method Method of preparing the statement of cash flows that reports the total cash receipts and cash payments from each of the major categories of activities (collections from customers, payments to suppliers, etc.). *p. 617*

direct raw materials Costs of raw materials used to make products that can be easily and conveniently traced to those products. *p. 705*

direct write-off method Method of recognizing bad debts expense only when accounts are determined to be uncollectible. *p. 342*

disclaimer of opinion Position that an auditor can take with respect to financial statements when there is not enough information to confirm compliance or noncompliance with GAAP; is neither positive nor negative. *p. 303*

discount Amount of interest included in the face of a note; the discount (interest) is subtracted from the face amount of the note to determine the principal amount of cash borrowed. *p. 461*

discount note a note that has the interest included in its face value. *p. 461*

Discount on Bonds Payable Contra liability account used to record the amount of discount on a bond issue. *p. 509*

Discount on Notes Payable Contra liability account subtracted from the Notes Payable account to determine the carrying value of the liability. *p. 462*

dividend Transfer of wealth from a business to its owners. *pp. 13, 255*

dividends in arrears Cumulative dividends on preferred stock that have not been paid; must be paid prior to paying dividends to common stockholders. *p. 563*

dividend yield Ratio for comparing stock dividends paid in relation to the market price; calculated as dividends per share divided by market price per share. *p. 665*

double-declining-balance depreciation Depreciation method that recognizes larger amounts of depreciation in the early stages of an asset's life and progressively smaller amounts as the asset ages. *p. 393*

double-entry accounting (bookkeeping) Method of keeping records that provides a system of checks and balances by recording transactions in a dual format. *pp. 12, 119*

double taxation Policy to tax corporate profits distributed to owners twice, once when the income is reported on the corporation's income tax return and again when the dividends are reported on the individual's return. *p. 557*

downstream costs Costs, such as delivery costs and sales commissions, incurred after the manufacturing process is complete. *p. 712*

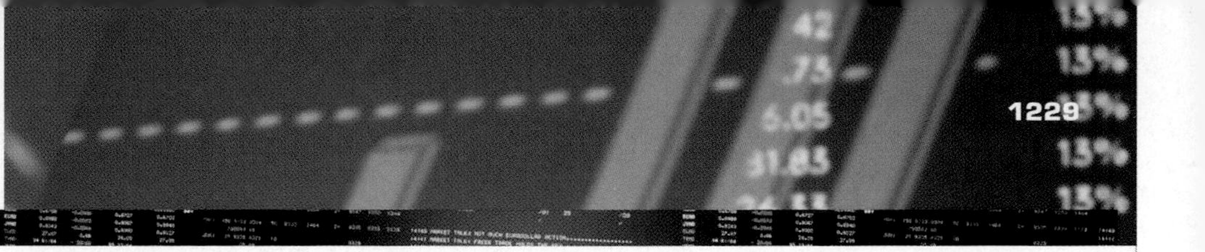

earnings The difference between revenues and expenses. Same as net income or profit. *p. 4*

earnings per share Measure of the value of a share of common stock in terms of company earnings; calculated as net income available to common stockholders divided by the average number of outstanding common shares. *p. 663*

effective interest rate Yield rate of bonds, which is usually equal to the market rate of interest on the day the bonds are sold. *p. 508*

effective interest rate method Method of amortizing bond discounts and premiums that computes interest based on the carrying value of liability. As the liability increases or decreases, the amount of interest expense also increases or decreases. *p. 522*

elements Primary components of financial statements including assets, liabilities, equity, contributions, revenue, expenses, distributions, and net income. *p. 8*

employee An individual whose labor is supervise, directed, and controlled by a business. *p. 449*

Employee's Withholding Allowance Certificate, Form W4 A form used by an employee to report the number of withholding allowances claimed by the employee. Each withholding allowance reduces the amount of income tax withheld from the employee's pay. *p. 451*

Employer's Quarterly Federal Tax Return, Form 941 The form used to show the amounts due and paid to the government for federal tax withholdings. *p. 452*

entity See reporting entities. *p. 8*

entrenched management Management that may have become ineffective but because of political implications may be difficult to remove. *p. 559*

equation method Cost-volume-profit analysis technique that uses a basic mathematical relationship among sales, variable costs, fixed costs, and desired net income before taxes and provides a solution in terms of units. *p. 944*

equipment replacement decisions Decisions regarding whether existing equipment should be replaced with newer equipment based on identification and comparison of the avoidable costs of the old and new equipment to determine which equipment is more profitable to operate. *p. 983*

equity Portion of assets remaining after the creditors' claims have been satisfied (i.e., Assets Liabilities Equity); also called residual interest or net assets. *p. 10*

equity method Method of accounting for investments in marketable equity securities; is required when the investor owns more than 20 percent of the investee company. The amount of investments carried under the equity method represents a measure of the book value of the investee rather than the cost or market value of the investment security. *p. 258*

equity security An equity security is certificate that evidences an ownership interest in a company. An example is a common stock certificate. *p. 254*

equivalent whole units Result of expressing partially completed goods in an equivalent number of fully completed goods. *p. 895*

estimated useful life Time for which an asset is expected to be used by a business. *p. 388*

ex-dividend Stock traded after the date of record but before the payment date; does not receive the benefit of the upcoming dividend. *p. 569*

expense transactions Transactions completed in the process of operating a business that decrease assets or increase liabilities. *p. 606*

expenses Economic sacrifices (decreases in assets or increase in liabilities) that are incurred in the process of generating revenue. *pp. 13, 65*

face value Amount of the bond to be paid back (to the bondholders) at maturity. *p. 501*

facility-level costs Costs incurred on behalf of the whole company or a segment of the company; not related to any specific product, batch, or unit of production or service and unavoidable unless the entire company or segment is eliminated. *p. 972*

fair value The price at which securities or other assets sell in free markets. Also called *market value*. *p. 254*

favorable variance Variance that occurs when actual costs are less than standard costs or when actual sales are higher than standard sales. *p. 1063*

Federal Unemployment Tax Act (FUTA) The Act that requires employers to pay unemployment tax for the establishment of a fund that is used to provide temporary relief to qualified unemployed persons. *p. 455*

fidelity bond Insurance policy that a company buys to insure itself against loss due to employee dishonesty. *p. 288*

financial accounting Field of accounting designed to meet the information needs of external users of business information (creditors, investors, governmental agencies, financial analysts, etc.); its objective is to classify and record business events and transactions to facilitate the production of external financial reports (income statement, balance sheet, statement of cash flows, and statement of changes in equity). *pp. 6, 700*

Financial Accounting Standards Board (FASB) Privately funded organization with the primary authority for the establishment of accounting standards in the United States. *pp. 7, 701*

financial audit Detailed examination of a company's financial statements and the documents that support the information presented in those statements; includes a verification process that tests the reliability of the underlying accounting system used to produce the financial reports. *p. 302*

financial leverage Concept of increasing earnings through debt financing; investment of money at a higher rate than that paid to borrow the money. *p. 138, 515*

financial resources Money or credit arrangements supplied to a business by investors (owners) and creditors. *p. 4*

financial statements Primary means of communicating the financial information of an organization to the external users. The four general-purpose financial statements are the income statement, statement of changes in equity, balance sheet, and statement of cash flows. *p. 8*

financing activities Cash inflows and outflows from transactions with investors and creditors (except interest). These cash flows include cash receipts from the issue of stock, borrowing activities, and cash disbursements associated with dividends. *pp. 18, 604*

finished goods End result of the manufacturing process measured by the accumulated cost of raw materials, labor, and overhead.

Finished Goods Inventory Asset account used to accumulate the product costs (direct materials, direct labor, and overhead) associated with completed products that have not yet been sold. *pp. 702, 834*

first-in, first-out (FIFO) cost flow method (1) Inventory cost flow method that treats the first items purchased as the first items sold for the purpose of computing cost of goods sold. (2) Method used to determine equivalent units when accuracy is deemed to be important; accounts for the degree of completion of both beginning and ending inventories but is more complicated than the weighted-average method. *pp. 238, 896*

fiscal year Year for which a company's accounting records are kept. *p. 117*

fixed cost Cost that in total remains constant when activity volume changes; varies per unit inversely with changes in the volume of activity. *p. 745*

fixed interest rate Interest rate (charge for the use of money) that does not change over the life of the loan. *p. 497*

flexible budgets Budgets that show expected revenues and costs at a variety of different activity levels. *p. 1062*

flexible budget variances Differences between budgets based on standard amounts at the actual level of activity and actual results; caused by differences in standard and actual unit cost since the volume of activity is the same. *p. 1066*

FOB (free on board) destination Term that designates the seller as the responsible party for freight costs (transportation-in costs). *p. 189*

FOB (free on board) shipping point Term that designates the buyer as the responsible party for freight costs (transportation-in costs). *p. 189*

franchise Exclusive right to sell products or perform services in certain geographic areas. *p. 403*

full disclosure A principle that requires financial statements to include all relevant information about an entity's operations and financial condition. Full disclosure is frequently accomplished by adding footnotes to the financial statements. *p. 243*

fund Independent accounting entity with a self-balancing set of accounts segregated for the purposes of carrying on specific activities. *p. 576*

fund accounting Type of accounting used by governmental entities. *p. 576*

future value Amount an investment will be worth at some point in the future, assuming a specified interest rate and the reinvestment of interest each period that it is earned. *p. 519*

gains Increases in assets or decreases in liabilities that result from peripheral or incidental transactions. *p. 199*

general authority Policies and procedures that apply across different levels of a company's management, such as everyone flies coach class. *p. 289*

general journal Journal in which all types of accounting transactions can be entered but which is commonly used to record adjusting and closing entries and unusual types of transactions. *p. 129*

general ledger Complete set of accounts used in accounting systems. *pp. 14, 128*

general uncertainties Uncertainties such as competition and damage from storms. These uncertainties are distinguished from contingent liabilities because they arise from future rather than past events. *p. 445*

general, selling, and administrative costs All costs not associated with obtaining or manufacturing a product; in practice are sometimes referred to as *period costs* because they are normally expensed in the period in which the economic sacrifice is incurred. *p. 707*

generally accepted accounting principles (GAAP) Rules and regulations that accountants agree to follow when preparing financial reports for public distribution. *pp. 7, 701*

going concern assumption Assumption that a company will continue to operate indefinitely, will pay its obligations, and should therefore report those obligations at their full face value in the financial statements. *p. 441*

goodwill Added value of a successful business that is attributable to factors—reputation, location, and superior products—that enable the business to earn above-average profits; stated differently, the excess paid for an existing business over the appraised value of the net assets. *p. 403*

gross earnings The total amount of employee wages or salaries before any deductions or withholdings. Gross earnings include the total of regular pay plus any bonuses, overtime, or other additions. *p. 450*

gross margin (gross profit) Difference between sales revenue and cost of goods sold; the amount a company makes from selling goods before subtracting operating expenses. *p. 182*

gross margin method Method of estimating ending inventory that assumes that the percentage of gross margin to sales remains relatively stable from one accounting period to the next. *p. 249*

gross margin percentage Expression of gross margin as a percentage of sales computed by dividing gross margin by net sales; the amount of each dollar of sales that is profit before deducting any operating expenses. *p. 201*

gross profit See *gross margin. p. 182*

half-year convention Tax rule that requires six months of depreciation expense to be taken in the year of purchase of the asset and the year of disposal regardless of the purchase date. *p. 398*

held-to-maturity securities Debt securities intended to be held until maturity. *p. 254*

high-low method Method of estimating the fixed and variable components of a mixed cost; determines the variable cost per unit by dividing the difference between the total cost of the high and low points by the difference in the corresponding high and low volumes. The fixed cost component is determined by subtracting the variable cost from the total cost at either the high or low volume. *p. 759*

historical cost concept Recording an asset at the actual price paid for it when purchased. *pp. 14, 387*

horizontal analysis Analysis technique that compares amounts of the same item over several time periods. *p. 651*

horizontal statements model Arrangement of a set of financial statements horizontally across a sheet of paper. *p. 19*

hybrid cost systems Cost system that blends some of the features of a job-order costing system with some of the features of a process cost system. *p. 884*

ideal standard Highest level of efficiency attainable, based on all input factors interacting perfectly under ideal or optimum conditions. *p. 1069*

imprest basis Description of the periodic replenishment of a fund to maintain it at its specified original amount. *p. 299*

income Added value created in transforming resources into more desirable states. *p. 4*

income statement Statement that reports the difference between the revenues and the expenses associated with running a business. *p. 17*

incremental revenue Additional cash inflows from operations generated by using an additional capital asset. *p. 1157*

independent auditor Certified public accountant licensed to perform audits who is independent of the company being audited. *p. 302*

independent contractor An individual who is paid by a business but retains individual control and supervisory authority over the work performed. *p. 449*

indirect cost Cost that cannot be easily traced to a cost object and for which the economic sacrifice to trace is not worth the informational benefits. *pp. 707, 795*

indirect method Method of preparing the statement of cash flows that uses the net income from the income statement as a starting point for reporting cash flow from operating activities; adjustments necessary to convert accrual-based net income to a cash-equivalent basis are shown in the operating activities section of the statement of cash flows. *p. 617*

information overload Situation in which presentation of too much information confuses the user of the information. *p. 650*

installment notes Obligations requiring principal repayments at regular intervals over the life of the loan. *p. 498*

intangible assets Assets that may be represented by pieces of paper or contracts that appear tangible; however, the true value of an intangible asset lies in the rights and privileges extended to its owners. *p. 386*

interest Fee paid for the use of borrowed funds; also refers to revenue from debt securities. *pp. 5, 255, 344*

interest-bearing notes Notes that require the payment of the face value plus accrued interest at maturity. *p. 461*

internal controls A company's policies and procedures designed to reduce the opportunity for fraud and to provide reasonable assurance that its objectives will be accomplished. *pp. 23, 288*

internal rate of return Rate that will produce a present value of an investment's future cash inflows that equals cash outflows required to acquire the investment; alternatively, the rate that produces a net present value of zero. *p. 1156*

inventory cost flow methods Methods used to allocate the cost of goods available for sale between cost of goods sold and inventory. *p. 240*

inventory holding costs Costs associated with acquiring and retaining inventory including cost of storage space; lost, stolen, or damaged merchandise; insurance; personnel and management costs; and interest. *p. 715*

inventory turnover Ratio of cost of goods sold to inventory that indicates how many times a year the average inventory is sold (turned over). *pp. 251, 658*

investee Company that receives assets or services in exchange for a debt or equity security. *p. 253*

investing activities One of the three categories of cash inflows and outflows shown on the statement of cash flows; includes cash received and spent by the business on productive assets and investments in the debt and equity of other companies. *pp. 18, 604*

investment center Type of responsibility center for which revenue, expense and capital investments can be measured. *p. 1111*

investment securities Certificates that describe the rights and privileges that investors receive when they loan or give assets or services to investees. *p. 254*

investors Companies or individuals who give assets or services and receive security certificates in exchange. *pp. 4, 253*

issued stock Stock sold to the public. *p. 362*

issuer Individual or business that issues a note payable, bonds payable, or stock (the party receiving cash). See also *maker. pp. 442, 501.*

job cost sheet Document used in a job-order cost system to accumulate the materials, labor, and overhead costs of a job through the various stages of production; at job completion, contains a summary of all costs that were incurred to complete that job; also known as *job-order cost sheet* or *job record. p. 884*

job-order cost system System used to determine the costs of distinct, one-of-a-kind products. Costs are traced to products that are produced individually (e.g., custom designed building) or produced in batches (e.g., an order for 100 wedding invitations). *p. 882*

joint costs Common costs incurred in the process of making two or more products. *p. 806*

joint products Products derived from joint cost. *p. 806*

journal Book of original entry in which accounting data are entered chronologically before posting to the ledger accounts. *p. 128*

just in time (JIT) Inventory flow system that minimizes the amount of inventory on hand by making inventory available for customer consumption on demand, therefore eliminating the need to store inventory. The system reduces explicit holding costs including financing, warehouse storage, supervision, theft, damage, and obsolescence. It also eliminates hidden opportunity costs such as lost revenue due to the lack of availability of inventory. *p. 716*

labor efficiency variance Variance occurring in a standard cost accounting system when the actual amount or quantity of direct labor used differs from the standard amount required. *p. 1072*

labor rate variance Variance that occurs when the actual pay rate differs from the standard pay rate for direct labor. *p. 1072*

labor resources Both intellectual and physical labor used in the process of converting goods and services to products of greater value. *p. 5*

last-in, first-out (LIFO) cost flow method Inventory cost flow method that treats the last items purchased as the first items sold for the purpose of computing cost of goods sold. *p. 238*

lax standards Easily attainable goals that can be accomplished with minimal effort. *p. 1069*

legal capital Amount of assets that should be maintained as protection for creditors; the number of shares multiplied by the par value. *p. 561*

liabilities Obligations of a business to relinquish assets, provide services, or accept other obligations. *p. 10*

limited liability Concept that investors in a corporation may not be held personally liable for the actions of the corporation (the creditors cannot lay claim to the owners' personal assets as payment for the corporation's debts). *p. 558*

limited liability companies (LLC) Organizations offering many of the best features of corporations and partnerships and with many legal benefits of corporations (e.g., limited liability and centralized management) but permitted by the Internal Revenue Service to be taxed as a partnership, thereby avoiding double taxation of profits. *p. 558*

line of credit Preapproved credit arrangement with a lending institution in which a business can borrow money by simply writing a check up to the approved limit. *p. 501*

liquidation Process of dividing up the assets and returning them to the resource providers. Creditors normally receive first priority in business liquidations; in other words, assets are distributed to creditors first. After creditor claims have been satisfied, the remaining assets are distributed to the investors (owners) of the business. *p. 4*

liquidity Ability to convert assets to cash quickly and meet short-term obligations. *pp. 18, 347, 458*

liquidity ratios Measures of short-term debt-paying ability. *p. 655*

long-term liabilities Liabilities with maturity dates beyond one year or the company's operating cycle, whichever is longer; noncurrent liabilities. *p. 497*

long-term operational assets Assets used by a business to generate revenue; condition of being used distinguishes them from assets that are sold (inventory) and assets that are held (investments). *p. 385*

losses Decreases in assets or increases in liabilities that result from peripheral or incidental transactions. *p. 199*

low-ball pricing Pricing a product below competitors' price to lure customers away and then raising the price once customers depend on the supplier for the product. *p. 979*

lower-of-cost-or-market rule Accounting principle of reporting inventories at market value if their value declined below their cost, regardless of the cause. *p. 246*

maker The party issuing a note (the borrower). *p. 344*

making the numbers Expression that indicates that marketing managers attained the sales volume indicated in the master budget. *p. 1064*

management by exception Use of management resources on areas that are not performing in accordance with expectations; a philosophy that directs management to concentrate on areas with significant variances. *pp. 1069, 1111*

managerial accounting Branch of accounting that provides information useful to internal decision makers and managers in operating an organization. *pp. 6, 700*

manufacturing businesses Makers of goods sold to customers. *p. 24*

manufacturing overhead Production costs that cannot be traced directly to products. *p. 707*

Manufacturing Overhead account Temporary account used during an accounting period to accumulate the actual overhead costs incurred and the total amount of overhead applied to the Work in Process account. At the end of the period, a debit balance in the account implies that overhead has been underapplied and a credit balance implies that overhead has been overapplied. The account is closed at year end in an adjusting entry to the inventory and Cost of Goods Sold accounts. If the balance is insignificant, it is closed only to Cost of Goods Sold. *p. 838*

margin Component in the determination of the return on investment. Computed by dividing operating income by sales. *p. 1117*

margin of safety Difference between break-even sales and budgeted sales expressed in units, dollars, or as a percentage; the amount by which actual sales can fall below budgeted sales before a loss is incurred. *p. 938*

market Gathering of people or organizations for the purpose of buying and selling resources. *p. 4*

marketable securities Securities that are readily traded in the secondary securities market. *p. 254*

market-based transfer price Transfer price based on the external market price less any savings in cost; the closest approximation to an arm's-length transaction that segments can achieve. *p. 1124*

market interest rate Current interest rate available on a wide range of alternative investments. *p. 513*

market value Value at which securities sell in the secondary market; also called *fair value. pp. 254, 562*

master budget Composition of the numerous separate but interdependent departmental budgets that cover a wide range of operating and financial factors such as sales, production, manufacturing expenses, and administrative expenses. *p. 1022*

matching concept Process of matching expenses with the revenues they produce; three ways to match expenses with revenues include matching expenses directly to revenues, matching expenses to the period in which they are incurred, and matching expenses systematically with revenues. *pp. 67, 345*

material amounts or matters that would influence a user's judgment, see *materiality. p. 302*

materiality Concept that recognizes practical limits in financial reporting by allowing flexible handling of matters not considered material; information is considered material if the decisions of a reasonable person would be influenced by its omission or misstatement; can be measured in absolute, percentage, quantitative, or qualitative terms. *p. 651*

materials price variance Variance that occurs when actual prices paid for raw materials differ from the standard prices. *p. 1072*

materials quantity variance Variance that occurs when the actual amounts of raw materials used to produce a good differ from the standard amounts required to produce that good. *p. 1072*

materials requisition form A form used to request or order the materials needed to begin a designated job; can be a paper document or an electronic impulse delivered through a computer. Materials requisitioned for a job are summarized by the accounting department on a job cost sheet. *p. 884*

material variance Variance that would affect decision making. *p. 1070*

maturity date The date that a liability is due to be settled (the date the borrower is expected to repay a debt). *p. 344*

Medicare Health insurance provided by the government primarily for retired workers. *p. 452*

merchandise inventory Supply of finished goods held for resale to customers. *p. 181*

merchandising businesses Companies that buy and sell merchandise inventory. *pp. 24, 181*

minimum rate of return Minimum amount of profitability required to persuade a company to accept an investment opportunity; also known as *desired rate of return, required rate of return, hurdle rate, cutoff rate,* and *discount rate. p. 1151*

mixed costs (semivariable costs) Costs composed of a mixture of fixed and variable components. *p. 758*

Modified Accelerated Cost Recovery System (MACRS) Prescribed method of depreciation for tax purposes that provides the maximum depreciation expense deduction permitted under tax law. *p. 397*

mortgage bond Type of secured bond that conditionally transfers title of a designated piece of property to the bondholder until the bond is paid. *p. 503*

most-favored customer status Arrangement by which a supplier and customer achieve mutual benefit by providing each other with favorable treatment that is not extended to other associates. *p. 716*

multistep income statement Income statement format that matches particular revenue items with related expense items and distinguishes between recurring operating activities and nonoperating items such as gains and losses. *p. 195*

natural resources Mineral deposits, oil and gas reserves, and reserves of timber, mines, and quarries are examples; sometimes called *wasting assets* because their value wastes away as the resources are removed. *p. 386*

negotiated transfer price Transfer price established by agreement of both the selling and buying segments of the firm. *p. 1125*

net income Increase in net assets resulting from operating the business. *p. 17*

net income percentage Another term for *return on sales.* Refer to *return on sales* for the definition. *p. 202*

net loss Decrease in net assets resulting from operating the business. *p. 17*

net margin Profitability measurement that indicates the percentage of each sales dollar resulting in profit; calculated as net income divided by net sales. *p. 661*

net method A method of accounting for cash discounts that records inventory purchases at the net price (the list price minus the purchase discount). *p. 188*

net pay Employee's gross pay less all deductions (withholdings). *p. 454*

net present value Evaluation technique that uses a desired rate of return to discount future cash flows back to their present value equivalents and then subtracts the cost of the investment from the present value equivalents to determine the net present value. A zero or positive net present value (present value of cash inflows equals or exceeds the present value of cash outflows) implies that the investment opportunity provides an acceptable rate of return. *p. 1156*

net realizable value Face amount of receivables less an allowance for accounts whose collection is doubtful (amount actually expected to be collected). *p. 332*

net sales Sales less returns from customers and allowances or cash discounts given to customers. *p. 201*

noncash investing and financing activities Business transactions that do not directly affect cash, such as exchanging stock for land or purchasing property by using a mortgage; reported as both an inflow and outflow in a separate section of the statement of cash flows. *p. 604*

non-sufficient-funds (NSF) check Customer's check deposited but returned by the bank on which it was drawn because the customer did not have enough funds in its account to pay the check. *p. 295*

nonvalue-added activities Tasks undertaken that do not contribute to a product's ability to satisfy customer needs. *p. 714*

note payable Liability that results from the execution of a legal document called a *promissory note* that describes interest charges, maturity date, collateral, and so on. *p. 442*

notes receivable Notes that evidence rights to receive cash in the future; usually specify the maturity date, rate of interest, and other credit terms. *p. 331*

not-for-profit entities Organizations (also called *nonprofit* or *nonbusiness entities*) whose primary motive is something other than making a profit, such as providing goods and services for the social good. Examples include state-supported universities and colleges, hospitals, public libraries, and public charities. *p. 6*

operating activities Cash inflows and outflows associated with operating the business. These cash flows normally result from revenue and expense transactions including interest. *pp. 18, 604*

operating budgets Budgets prepared by different departments within a company that will become a part of the company's master budget; typically include a sales budget, an inventory purchases budget, a selling and administrative budget, and a cash budget. *p. 1022*

operating cycle Time required to turn cash into inventory, inventory into receivables, and receivables back to cash. *pp. 351, 457*

operating income Income statement subtotal determined by subtracting operating expenses from operating revenues. Gains and losses and other peripheral activities are added to or subtracted from operating income to determine net income or loss. *p. 195*

operating leverage Operating condition in which a percentage change in revenue produces a proportionately larger percentage change in net income; measured by dividing the contribution margin by net income. The higher the proportion of fixed cost to total costs, the greater the operating leverage. *p. 746*

opportunity cost Cost of lost opportunities such as the failure to make sales due to an insufficient supply of inventory or the wage a working student forgoes to attend class. *pp. 203, 717, 973*

ordinary annuity Annuity whose cash inflows occur at the end of each accounting period. *p. 1154*

outsourcing The practice of buying goods and services from another company rather than producing them internally. *p. 977*

outstanding checks Checks deducted from the depositor's cash account balance but not yet presented to the bank for payment. *p. 294*

outstanding stock Stock owned by outside parties; normally the amount of stock issued less the amount of treasury stock. *p. 562*

overapplied overhead Result of allocating more overhead costs to the Work in Process account than the amount of the actual overhead costs incurred. *p. 839*

overhead Costs associated with producing products that cannot be cost effectively traced to products including indirect costs such as indirect materials, indirect labor, utilities, rent, and depreciation. *p. 702*

overhead costs Indirect costs of doing business that cannot be directly traced to a product, department, or process, such as depreciation. *p. 795*

paid-in capital in excess of par (stated) value Any amount received above the par or stated value of stock when stock is issued. *p. 564*

parent company Company that holds a controlling interest (more than 50 percent ownership) in another company. *p. 258*

participative budgeting Budget technique that allows subordinates to participate with upper-level managers in setting budget objectives, thereby encouraging cooperation and support in the attainment of the company's goals. *p. 1022*

partnership agreement Legal document that defines the responsibilities of each partner and describes the division of income and losses. *p. 556*

partnerships Business entities owned by at least two people who share talents, capital, and the risks of the business. *p. 556*

par value Arbitrary value assigned to stock by the board of directors. *p. 561*

patent Legal right granted by the U.S. Patent Office ensuring a company or an individual the exclusive right to a product or process. *p. 403*

payback method Technique that evaluates investment opportunities by determining the length of time necessary to recover the initial net investment through incremental revenue or cost savings; the shorter the period, the better the investment opportunity. *p. 1164*

payee The party collecting cash. *p. 344*

payment date Date on which a dividend is actually paid. *p. 569*

percentage analysis Analysis of relationships between two different items to draw conclusions or make decisions. *p. 652*

percent of receivables method A method of estimating the amount of uncollectible accounts by taking a percent of the outstanding receivables balance. The percentage is frequently based on a combination of factors such as historical experience, condition of the economy, and the company's credit policies. *p. 340*

percent of revenue method A method of estimating the amount of uncollectible accounts by taking a percent of revenue that was earned on account during the accounting period. The percentage is frequently based on a combination of factors such as historical experience, condition of the economy, and the company's credit policies. *p. 338*

period costs General, selling, and administrative costs that are expensed in the period in which the economic sacrifice is made. *pp. 67, 182, 707*

periodic inventory system Method of accounting for changes in the Inventory account only at the end of the accounting period. *p. 205*

permanent accounts Accounts that contain information transferred from one accounting period to the next. *p. 66*

perpetual (continuous) budgeting Continuous budgeting activity normally covering a 12-month time span by replacing the current month's budget at the end of each month with a new budget; keeps management constantly involved in the budget process so that changing conditions are incorporated on a timely bases. *p. 1021*

perpetual inventory system Method of accounting for inventories that increases the Inventory account each time merchandise is purchased and decreases it each time merchandise is sold. *p. 184*

petty cash fund Small amount of cash set aside in a fund to pay for small outflows for which writing checks is not practical. *p. 299*

petty cash voucher A document prepared by the petty cash custodian that evidences a petty cash disbursement. The person who receives the cash signs the voucher as evidence of receiving the money. Supporting documents, such as an invoice, restaurant bill, or parking fee receipt, should be attached to the petty cash voucher. *p. 299*

physical flow of goods Physical movement of goods through the business; normally a FIFO flow so that the first goods purchased are the first goods delivered to customers, thereby reducing the likelihood of obsolete inventory. *p. 238*

physical resources Natural resources used in the transformation process to create resources of more value. *p. 5*

plant assets to long-term liabilities Financial ratio that suggests how well a company manages its long-term debt. *p. 660*

postaudit Repeat calculation using the techniques originally employed to analyze an investment project; accomplished with the use of actual data available at the completion of the investment project so that the actual results can be compared with expected results based on estimated data at the beginning of the project. Its purpose is to provide feedback as to whether the expected results were actually accomplished in improving the accuracy of future analysis. *p. 1167*

posting Process of copying information from journals to ledgers. *p. 130*

practical standard Level of efficiency in which the ideal standard has been modified to allow for normal tolerable inefficiencies. *p. 1069*

predetermined overhead rate Rate determined by dividing the estimated overhead costs for the period by some measure of estimated total production activity for the period, such as the number of labor hours or machine hours. The base chosen should provide some logical measure of overhead use. The rate is determined before actual costs or activity are known. Throughout the accounting period, the rate is used to allocate overhead costs to the Work in Process Inventory account based on actual production activity. *pp. 806, 838*

preferred stock Stock that receives some form of preferential treatment (usually as to dividends) over common stock; normally has no voting rights. *p. 563*

prepaid items Deferred expenses. An example is prepaid insurance. *p. 68*

present value The value today of a future cash payment or payments, assuming a given interest rate. *p. 519*

present value index Present value of cash inflows divided by the present value of cash outflows. Higher index numbers indicate higher rates of return. *p. 1160*

present value table Table that consists of a list of factors to use in converting future values into their present value equivalents; composed of columns that represent different return rates and rows that depict different periods of time. *p. 1152*

prestige pricing Pricing strategy that sets the price at a premium (above average markup above cost) under the assumption that people will pay more for the product because of its prestigious brand name, media attention, or some other reason that has piqued the interest of the public. *p. 942*

price-earnings (P/E) ratio Measurement used to compare the values of different stocks in terms of earnings; calculated as market price per share divided by earnings per share. *pp. 77, 664*

primary securities market Market made up of transactions between the investor and investee. *p. 254*

principal Amount of cash actually borrowed. *pp. 344, 461*

procedures manual Manual that sets forth the accounting procedures to be followed. *p. 289*

proceeds The amount of cash received. An example is the principal amount borrowed on a discount note payable. *p. 461*

process cost system System used to determine the costs of homogeneous products, such as chemicals, foods or paints, that distributes costs evenly across total production; determines an average by dividing the total product costs of each production department by the number of units of product made in that department during some designated period of time. The total costs in the last production department include all costs incurred in preceding departments so that the unit cost determined for the last department reflects the final unit cost of the product. *p. 882*

product costing Classification and accumulation of individual inputs (materials, labor, and overhead) for determining the cost of making a good or providing a service. *p. 702*

product costs All costs related to obtaining or manufacturing a product intended for sale to customers; accumulated in inventory accounts and expensed as cost of goods sold at the point of sale. For a manufacturing company, product costs include direct materials, direct labor, and manufacturing overhead. *pp. 182, 702*

productive assets Assets used to operate the business; frequently called *long-term assets*. *p. 18*

product-level costs Costs incurred to support different kinds of products or services; can be avoided by the elimination of a product line or a type of service. *p. 972*

profit Value created by transforming goods and services to more desirable states. *p. 4*

profitability ratios Measurements of a firm's ability to generate earnings. *p. 665*

profit center Type of responsibility center for which both revenues and costs can be indentified. *p. 1111*

pro forma financial statements Budgeted financial statements prepared from the information in the master budget. *p. 1022*

promissory note A legal document representing a credit agreement between a lender and a borrower. The note specifies technical details such as the maker, payee, interest rate, maturity date, payment terms, and any collateral. *p. 344*

property, plant, and equipment Category of assets, sometimes called *plant assets*, used to produce products or to carry on the administrative and selling functions of a business; includes machinery and equipment, buildings, and land. *p. 386*

purchase discount Reduction in the gross price of merchandise extended under the condition that the purchaser pay cash for the merchandise within a stated time (usually within 10 days of the date of the sale). *p. 188*

qualified opinion Opinion issued by a CPA that falls between an unqualified opinion (see later definition) and an adverse opinion; means that for the most part, the company's financial statements are in compliance with GAAP, but the auditors have reservations about something in the statements or have other reasons not to give a fully unqualified opinion; reasons that a qualified opinion is being issued are explained in the auditor's report. *p. 303*

qualitative characteristics Nonquantifiable features such as company reputation, welfare of employees, and customer satisfaction that can be affected by certain decisions. *p. 975*

quantitative characteristics Numbers in decision making subject to mathematical manipulation, such as the dollar amounts of revenues and expenses. *p. 975*

quick ratio See *acid-test ratio. p. 656*

ratio analysis See *percentage analysis. p. 655*

raw materials Physical commodities (e.g., wood, metal, paint) used in the manufacturing process. *p. 705*

Raw Materials Inventory Asset account used to accumulate the costs of materials such as lumber, metals, paints, and chemicals that will be used to make the company's products. *p. 834*

realization A term that usually refers to transactions that involve the collection or payment of cash. *p. 59*

recognition Reporting an accounting event in the financial statements. *p. 59*

recovery of investment Recovery of the funds used to acquire the original investment. *p. 1166*

reengineering Business practices designed by companies to make production and delivery systems more competitive in world markets by eliminating or minimizing waste, errors, and costs. *p. 714*

reinstate Recording an account receivable previously written off back into the accounting records, generally when cash is collected long after the original due date. *p. 337*

relative fair market value method Method of assigning value to individual assets acquired in a basket purchase in which each asset is assigned a percentage of the total price paid for all assets. The percentage assigned equals the market value of a particular asset divided by the total of the market values of all assets acquired in the basket purchase. *p. 387*

relaxing the constraints The process of opening bottlenecks that constrain the profitable operations of a business. *p. 987*

relevant costs Future-oriented costs that differ between business alternatives; also known as *avoidable costs. p. 971*

relevant information Decision-making information about costs, costs savings, or revenues that have these features: (1) future-oriented information and (2) the information differs between the alternatives; decision specific (information that is relevant in one decision may not be relevant in another decision). *p. 970*

relevant range Range of activity over which the definitions of fixed and variable costs apply. *p. 755*

reliability concept Information is reliable if it can be independently verified. Reliable information is factual rather than subjective. *p. 14*

reporting entities Particular businesses or other organizations for which financial statements are prepared. *p. 8*

residual income Approach that evaluates managers on their ability to maximize the dollar value of earnings above some targeted level of earnings. *p. 1119*

responsibility accounting Accounting system in which the accountability for results is assigned to a segment manager of the firm based on the amount of control or influence the manager possesses over those results. *p. 1110*

responsibility center Point in an organization where the control over revenue or expense items is located. *p. 1111*

responsibility reports Reports of the performance of various responsibility centers of the firm with respect to controllable items; show the variances that result from comparing budgeted and actual controllable items. *p. 1111*

restrictive covenants Special provisions specified in the loan contract that are designed to prohibit management from taking certain actions that place creditors at risk. *p. 514*

retail companies Companies that sell goods to consumers. *p. 181*

retained earnings Equity account that includes all earnings retained in the business since inception (revenues minus expenses and distributions for all accounting periods). *p. 10*

return on assets ratio Ratio that measures the relationship between the level of net income and the size of the investment in assets. *p. 137*

return on equity Measure of the profitability of a firm based on earnings generated in relation to stockholders' equity; calculated as net income divided by stockholders' equity. *p. 662*

return on equity ratio Ratio that measures the relationship between the amount of net income and the stockholders' equity of a company. *p. 138*

return on investment Measure of profitability based on the asset base of the firm. It is calculated as net income divided by average total assets. ROI is a product of net margin and asset turnover. *pp. 662, 1115*

return on sales Percent of net income generated by each $1 of sales; computed by dividing net income by net sales. *p. 202*

revenue An economic benefit (an increase in assets or a decrease in liabilities) that is gained by providing goods and services to customers. *pp. 12, 73*

revenue expenditures Costs incurred for repair or maintenance of long-term operational assets; recorded as expenses and subtracted from revenue in the accounting period in which incurred. *p. 400*

revenue transactions Transactions completed in the process of operating a business that increase assets or decrease liabilities by providing services or products. *p. 606*

salaries The term used to describe amounts due employees who are paid a set amount per week, month, or other earnings period regardless of how many hours they work during that period. *p. 450*

salaries payable Amounts of future cash payments owed to employees for services that have already been performed. *p. 62*

sales discount Cash discount extended by the seller of goods to encourage prompt payment. When the buyer of the goods takes advantage of the discount and pays less than the original selling price, the difference between the selling price and the cash collected is the sales discount. *p. 196*

sales price variance Difference between actual sales and expected sales based on the standard sales price per unit times the actual level of activity. *p. 1066*

sales volume variance Difference between sales based on a static budget (standard sales price times standard level of activity) and sales based on a flexible budget (standard sales price times actual level of activity). *p. 1063*

salvage value Expected selling price of an asset at the end of its useful life. *p. 388*

Sarbanes-Oxley Act of 2002 An act of Congress that was established to promote ethical behavior in corporate governance and fairness in financial reporting. Key provisions of the act include a requirement that a company's chief executive officer (CEO) and chief financial officer (CFO) must certify in writing that they have reviewed the financial reports being issued, and that the reports present fairly the company's financial status. An executive who falsely certifies the company's financial reports is subject to significant fines and imprisonment. The act also establishes the Public Company Accounting Oversight Board (PCAOB). This board assumes the primary responsibility for developing and enforcing auditing standards for CPAs who audit SEC companies. The Sarbanes-Oxley Act also prohibits auditors from providing most types of nonaudit services to companies they audit. *pp. 557, 701*

scattergraph method Method of estimating the variable and fixed components by which cost data are plotted on a graph and a regression line is visually drawn through the points so that the total distance between the data points and the line is minimized. *p. 760*

schedule of cost of goods manufactured and sold Schedule that summarizes the flow of manufacturing product costs; its result, cost of goods sold, is shown as a single line item on the company's income statement. *p. 846*

schedule of cost of goods sold Schedule that reflects the computation of the amount of the cost of goods sold under the periodic inventory system; an internal report not shown in the formal financial statements. *p. 205*

secondary securities market Market in which securities are exchanged between investors. *p. 254*

secured bonds Bonds secured by specific identifiable assets. *p. 503*

Securities Act of 1933 and Securities Exchange Act of 1934 Acts passed after the stock market crash of 1929 designed to regulate the issuance of stock and govern the stock exchanges; created the Securities and Exchange Commission (SEC), which has the authority to establish accounting policies for companies registered on the stock exchanges. *p. 557*

Securities and Exchange Commission (SEC) Government organization responsible for overseeing the accounting rules to be followed by companies required to be registered with it. *p. 700*

segment Component part of an organization that is designated as a reporting entity. *p. 980*

selling and administrative costs Costs that cannot be directly traced to products that are recognized as expenses in the period in which they are incurred. Examples include advertising expense and rent expense. *p. 182*

sensitivity analysis Spreadsheet analysis that executes "what-if " questions to assess the sensitivity of profits to simultaneous changes in fixed cost, variable cost, and sales volume. *p. 941*

separation of duties Internal control feature of, whenever possible, assigning the functions of authorization, recording, and custody to different individuals. *p. 288*

serial bonds Bonds that mature at specified intervals throughout the life of the total issue. *p. 503*

service businesses Organizations—accountants, lawyers, and dry cleaners—that provide services to consumers. *p. 24*

service charges Fees charged by a bank for services performed or a penalty for the depositor's failing to maintain a specified minimum cash balance throughout the period. *p. 295*

shrinkage A term that reflects decreases in inventory for reasons other than sales to customers. *p. 108*

signature card Bank form that records the bank account number and the signatures of the people authorized to write checks on an account. *p. 292*

simple interest Interest computed by multiplying the principal by the interest rate by the number of periods. Interest earned in a period is not added to the principal, so that no interest is earned on the interest of previous periods. *p. 518*

single-payment (lump-sum) A one-time receipt of cash which can be converted to its present value using a conversion factor. *p. 1152*

single-step income statement Single comparison between total revenues and total expenses. *p. 195*

sinking fund Fund to which the bond issuer annually contributes to ensure the availability of cash for the payment of the face amount on the maturity date. *p. 503*

Social Security Insurance provided by the federal government to qualified individuals. Also called old age, survivors, and disability insurance (OASDI). *p. 452*

sole proprietorships Businesses (usually small) owned by one person. *p. 556*

solvency Ability of a business to pay liabilities in the long run. *p. 458*

solvency ratios Measures of a firm's long-term debt-paying ability. *p. 658*

source documents Documents such as a cash register tape, invoice, time card, or check stub that provide accounting information to be recorded in the accounting journals and ledgers. *p. 128*

special journals Journals designed to improve the efficiency of recording specific types of repetitive transactions. *p. 129*

special order decisions Decisions of whether to accept orders from nonregular customers who want to buy goods or services significantly below the normal selling price. If the order's relevant revenues exceed its avoidable costs, the order should be accepted. Qualitative features such as the order's effect on the existing customer base if accepted must also be considered. *p. 975*

specific authorizations Policies and procedures that apply to designated levels of management, such as the policy that the right to approve overtime pay may apply only to the plant manager. *p. 289*

specific identification Inventory method that allocates costs between cost of goods sold and ending inventory using the cost of the specific goods sold or retained in the business. *p. 238*

spending variance Difference between actual fixed overhead costs and budgeted fixed overhead costs. *p. 1076*

split-off point Point in the production process where products become separate and identifiable. *p. 806*

spread Difference between the rate a bank pays to obtain money (e.g., interest paid on savings accounts) and the rate that the bank earns on money it lends to borrowers. *p. 515*

stakeholders Parties interested in the operations of a business, including owners, lenders, employees, suppliers, customers, and government agencies. *p. 6*

standard The expected unit price or cost based on a certain set of anticipated circumstances. *p. 1068*

stated interest rate Rate of interest specified in the bond contract that will be paid at specified intervals over the life of the bond. *p. 502*

stated value Arbitrary value assigned to stock by the board of directors. *p. 561*

statement of activities Statement that reports the revenues, expenses, gains, and losses that increase or decrease the net assets of a not-for-profit organization. *p. 575*

statement of cash flows Statement that explains how a business obtained and used cash during an accounting period. *pp. 18, 575*

statement of changes in stockholders' equity Statement that summarizes the transactions occurring during the accounting period that affected the owners' equity. *p. 17*

statement of financial position Statement that reports the assets, liabilities, and net assets of a not-for-profit organization. *p. 575*

static budgets Budgets such as the master budget based solely on the level of planned activity; remain constant even when volume of activity changes. *p. 1062*

stock certificate Evidence of ownership interest issued when an investor contributes assets to a corporation; describes the rights and privileges that accompany ownership. *p. 556*

stock dividend Proportionate distribution of additional shares of the declaring corporation's stock. *p. 569*

stockholders Owners of a corporation. *pp. 10, 559*

stockholders' equity Stockholders' equity represents the portion of the assets that is owned by the stockholders. *p. 10*

stock split Proportionate increase in the number of outstanding shares; designed to reduce the market value of the stock and its par value. *p. 570*

straight-line amortization Method of amortization that allocates bond discount or premium in equal amounts to each period over the life of the bond. *p. 510*

straight-line depreciation Method of computing depreciation that allocates the cost of an asset to expense in equal amounts over its life. The formula for calculating straight-line depreciation is [(Cost - Salvage)/ Useful Life] *p. 389*

strategic planning Planning activities associated with long-range decisions such as defining the scope of the business, determining which products to develop, deciding whether to discontinue a business segment, and determining which market niche would be most profitable. *p. 1020*

suboptimization Situation in which managers act in their own self-interests even though the organization as a whole suffers. *p. 1119*

subordinated debentures Unsecured bonds that have a lower priority than general creditors, that is, are paid off after the general creditors are paid in the case of liquidation. *p. 503*

subsidiary company Company controlled (more than 50 percent owned) by another company. *p. 258*

sunk costs Costs that have been incurred in past transactions and therefore are not relevant for decision making. *p. 970*

T-account Simplified account form, named for its shape, with the account title placed at the top of a horizontal bar, debit entries listed on the left side of the vertical bar, and credit entries shown on the right side. *p. 118*

T-account method Method of determining net cash flows by analyzing beginning and ending balances on the balance sheet and inferring the period's transactions from the income statement. *p. 606*

tangible assets Assets that can be touched, such as equipment, machinery, natural resources, and land. *p. 386*

target pricing (target costing) Pricing strategy that begins with the determination of a price at which a product will sell and then focuses on the development of that product with a cost structure that will satisfy market demands. *p. 935*

temporary accounts Accounts used to collect information for a single accounting period (usually revenue, expense, and distribution accounts). *p. 66*

term bonds Bonds in an issue that mature on a specified date in the future. *p. 503*

theory of constraints (TOC) Practice used by many businesses to increase profitability by managing bottlenecks or constrained resources by identifying the bottlenecks restricting the operations of the business and then opening them by relaxing the constraints. *p. 987*

times interest earned Ratio that computes how many times a company would be able to pay its interest by using the amount of earnings available to make interest payments; amount of earnings is net income before interest and income taxes. *pp. 516, 659*

time value of money Recognition that the present value of a promise to receive a dollar some time in the future is worth less than a dollar because of interest, risk, and inflation factors. For example, a person may be willing to pay $0.90 today for the right to receive $1.00 one year from today. *pp. 518, 1150*

total quality management (TQM) Management philosophy that includes (1) a continuous systematic problem-solving philosophy that engages personnel at all levels of the organization to eliminate waste, defects, and nonvalue-added activities; and (2) to manage quality costs in a manner that leads to the highest level of customer satisfaction. *p. 714*

trademark Name or symbol that identifies a company or an individual product. *p. 403*

trading securities Securities bought and sold to generate profit from short-term appreciation in stock and bond prices. *p. 254*

transaction Particular event that involves the transfer of something of value between two entities. *p. 11*

transferability Concept referring to the practice of dividing the ownership of corporations into small units that are represented by shares of stock, which permits the easy exchange of ownership interests. *p. 558*

transfer price Price at which products or services are transferred between divisions or other subunits of an organization. *p. 1123*

transferred-in costs Costs transferred from one department to the next; combined with the materials, labor, and overhead costs incurred in the department so that when goods are complete, the total product cost of all departments is transferred to the Finished Goods Inventory account. *p. 883*

transportation-in (freight-in) Cost of freight on goods purchased under terms FOB shipping point that is usually added to the cost of inventory and is a product cost. *p. 189*

transportation-out (freight-out) Freight cost for goods delivered to customers under terms FOB destination; a period cost expensed when it is incurred. *p. 189*

treasury stock Stock first issued to the public and then bought back by the corporation. *p. 562*

trend analysis Study of the performance of a business over a period of time. *p. 651*

trial balance List of ledger accounts and their balances that provides a check on the mathematical accuracy of the recording process. *p. 131*

true cash balance Actual balance of cash owned by a company at the close of business on the date of the bank statement. *p. 293*

turnover Component in the determination of the return on investment. Computed by dividing sales by operating assets. *p. 1117*

2/10, n/30 Term indicating that the seller will give the purchaser a 2 percent discount on the gross invoice price if the purchaser pays cash for the merchandise within 10 days from the date of purchase. *p. 188*

unadjusted bank balance Ending cash balance reported by the bank as of the date of the bank statement. *p. 293*

unadjusted book balance Balance of the Cash account as of the date of the reconciliation before making any adjustments. *p. 293*

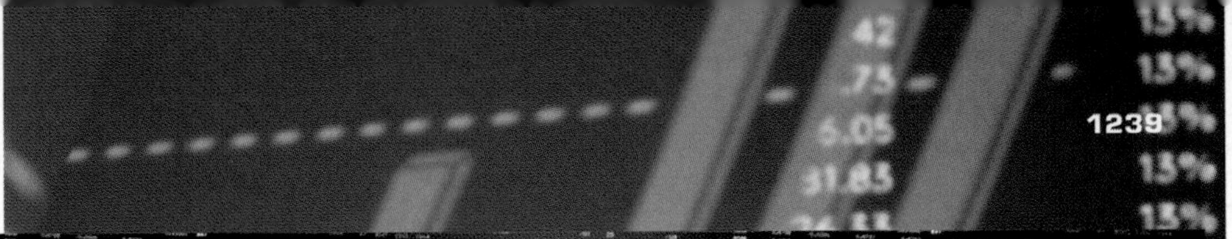

unadjusted rate of return Measure of profitability computed by dividing the average incremental increase in annual net income by the average cost of the original investment (original cost ÷ 2). *p. 1165*

uncollectibe accounts expense Expense associated with uncollectible accounts receivable; amount recognized may be estimated using the allowance method, or actual losses may be recorded using the direct write-off method. *p. 333*

underapplied overhead Result of allocating less overhead costs to the Work in Process account than the amount of the actual overhead costs incurred. *p. 839*

unearned revenue Revenue for which cash has been collected but the service has not yet been performed. *p. 69*

unfavorable variance Variance that occurs when actual costs exceed standard costs or when actual sales are less than standard sales. *p. 1063*

unit-level costs Costs incurred each time a company makes a single product or performs a single service and that can be avoided by eliminating a unit of product or service. Likewise, unit-level costs increase with each additional product produced or service provided. *p. 971*

units-of-production depreciation Depreciation method based on a measure of production rather than a measure of time; for example, an automobile may be depreciated based on the expected miles to be driven rather than on a specific number of years. *p. 395*

unqualified opinion Opinion on financial statements audited by a CPA that means the auditor believes the financial statements are in compliance with GAAP. *p. 303*

unrealized gain or loss Paper gain or loss on investment securities that has not yet been realized and is not realized until the securities are sold or otherwise disposed of. *p. 256*

unsecured bonds Also known as *debentures*, bonds backed by the general credit of the organization. *p. 503*

unsubordinated debentures Unsecured bonds that have equal claims with the general creditors. *p. 503*

upstream costs Costs incurred before the manufacturing process begins, for example, research and development costs. *p. 712*

users Individuals or organizations that use financial information for decision making. *p. 6*

value-added activity Any unit of work that contributes to a product's ability to satisfy customer needs. *p. 714*

value-added principle The benefits attained (value added) from the process should exceed the cost of the process. *p. 701*

value chain Linked sequence of activities that create value for the customer. *p. 714*

variable cost Cost that in total changes in direct proportion to changes in volume of activity; remains constant per unit when volume of activity changes. *p. 745*

variable costing Product costing system that capitalizes only variable cost in inventory; its income statement subtracts variable costs from revenue to determine contribution margin. Fixed costs, including product cost, are subtracted from the contribution margin to determine net income. In this format the amount of net income is not affected by the volume of production. *p. 849*

variable interest rate Interest rate that fluctuates (may change) from period to period over the life of the loan. *p. 497*

variances Differences between standard and actual amounts. *p. 1063*

vertical analysis Analysis technique that compares items on financial statements to significant totals. *p. 653*

vertical integration Attainment of control over the entire spectrum of business activity from production to sales; for example, a grocery store that owns farms. *p. 979*

vertical statements model Arrangement of a full set of financial statements on a single page with account titles arranged from the top to the bottom of the page. *p. 75*

visual fit line Line drawn by visual inspection to minimize the total distance between the data points and the line; used to estimate fixed and variable cost. *p. 760*

volume variance Difference between the budgeted fixed cost and the amount of fixed costs allocated to production. *p. 1076*

Wage and Tax Statement, Form W2 Form used by employers to notify each employee of the amount of his or her gross earnings for the year and the amounts withheld by the employer. *p. 451*

wages The term used to describe amounts due employees who are paid according to the number of hours they actually work. *p. 450*

warranties Promises to correct deficiencies or dissatisfactions in quality, quantity, or performance of products or services sold. *p. 446*

weighted average method Method often used in a process cost system for determining equivalent units; ignores the state of completion of items in beginning inventory and assumes that items in beginning inventory are complete. *p. 896*

weighted average cost flow method Inventory cost flow method in which the cost allocated between inventory and cost of goods sold is based on the average cost per unit, which is determined by dividing total costs of goods available for sale during the accounting period by total units available for sale during the period. If the average is recomputed each time a purchase is made, the result is called a *moving average*. *p. 238*

wholesale companies Companies that sell goods to other businesses. *p. 181*

withdrawals Distributions to the owners of proprietorships and partnerships. *p. 560*

working capital Current assets minus current liabilities. *pp. 655, 1157*

working capital ratio Another term for the current ratio; calculated by dividing current assets by current liabilities. *p. 656*

Work in Process Inventory Asset account used to accumulate all product costs (direct materials, direct labor, and overhead) associated with incomplete products in production. *p. 834*

work ticket Mechanism (paper or electronic) used to accumulate the time spent on a job by each employee; sent to the accounting department where wage rates are recorded and labor costs are determined. The amount of labor costs for each ticket is summarized on the appropriate job-order cost sheet; sometimes called a *time card*. *p. 884*

PHOTO CREDITS

Chapter 1
p. 3 Corbis, p. 4 Don Farrall/Getty Images, p. 7 Corbis, p. 10 Don Farrall/ Getty Images, p. 23 Reuters/Corbis, p. 24 PhotoLink/Getty Images, p. 24 Steele/Getty Images

Chapter 2
p. 59 Reader's Digest, p. 67 Photodisc/Getty Images, p. 79 Corbis, p. 81 AP/Wide World Photos

Chapter 3
p. 117 Daniel Acker/Bloomberg News/Landov, p. 131 Courtesy Intuit, Inc, p. 139 © Royalty-Free/CORBIS, p. 140 J. Luke/PhotoLink/Getty Images

Chapter 4
p. 181 Spencer Grant/PhotoEdit, Inc., p. 182 StockTrek/Getty Images, p. 203 Royalty-Free/CORBIS, p. 205 Ovark Arsian

Chapter 5
p. 237 Royalty Free/Corbis, p. 238 The McGraw-Hill Companies, Inc./Ken Karp photographer, p. 242 Royalty-Free/CORBIS, p. 246 Spencer Grant PhotoEdit, Inc., p. 247 Royalty-Free/CORBIS, p. 249 Ryan McVay/Corbis, p. 252 H. Wiesenhofer/PhotoLink/Getty Images

Chapter 6
p. 287 AP/Wide World Photos, p. 288 PhotoLink/Getty Images, p. 289 Courtesy of Nordstrom, p. 292 Keith Brofsky/Getty Images, p. 295 Keith Brofsky/Getty Images, p. 303 Bradley C. Bower/Bloomberg News/Landov, p. 304 PhotoLink/Getty Images

Chapter 7
p. 331 France Freeman/Costco Wholesale, p. 337 Jack Star/PhotoLink/ Getty Images, p. 348 Janis Christie/Getty Images, p. 352 Jack Star/ PhotoLink/Getty Images, p. 353 Don Farrall/Getty Images

Chapter 8
p. 385 Photodisc/Getty Images, p. 386 © Royalty-Free/CORBIS, p. 393 Ryan McVay/Getty Images, p. 404 Photodisc/Getty Images, p. 405 AP/ Wide World Photos, p. 409 Ryan McVay/Getty Images

Chapter 9
p. 441 Dave Thompson/Life File/Getty Images p. 445 PhotoDisc/Getty Images, p. 450 Ryan McVay/Getty Images p. 452 C. Sherburne/PhotoLink/ Getty Images, p. 459 Royalty-Free/CORBIS

Chapter 10
p. 497 Mario Tama/Getty Images, p. 504 AP/Wide World Photos, p. 514 Keith Brofsky/Getty Images, p. 516 Royalty Free/Corbis

Chapter 11
p. 555 Amy Etra/PhotoEdit, Inc., p. 556 Royalty Free/Corbis, p. 557 Royalty-Free/CORBIS, p. 559 Courtesy of AT&T, p. 562 Jeff Smith/Getty Images, p. 572 Royalty-Free/CORBIS

Chapter 12
p. 603 Nick Koudis/Getty Images, p. 609 Royalty Free/Corbis, p. 620 IBM Corporate Archives

Chapter 13
p. 649 Brian Marcus/Bloomberg News/Landov, p. 650 Don Farrall/Getty Images, p. 658 PhotoLink/Getty Images, p. 661 John Rizzo/ Bloomberg News/Landov, p. 667 AP/Wide World Photos

Chapter 14
p. 699 PhotoLink/Getty Images, p. 700 Image reprinted by arrangement with Sears Roebuck and Co., p. 714 Win McNamee/Reuters/Landov, p. 715 Ryan McVay/Getty Images, p. 716 Courtesy of Ford Motor Company

Chapter 15
p. 745 Courtesy of Southwest Airlines, p. 747 Cer/Corbis Sygma, p. 757 Costco Wholesale, p. 762 Corbis

Chapter 16
p. 793 Royalty-Free/Corbis, p. 794 Cele Seldon, p. 797 Courtesy of Southwest Airlines, p. 804 Royalty Free/Corbis, p. 809 Keith Brofsky/ Getty Images

Chapter 17
p. 833 Stickley Furniture, L & L.G. Stickley, Inc., p. 835 Royalty Free/ Corbis, p. 839 Allan H./ShoemakerTaxi/Getty Images, p. 844 Spike Mafford/Getty Images

Chapter 18
p. 881 F. Schussler/PhotoLink/Getty Images, p. 882 Courtesy Everett Collection, p. 885 Russell Illig/Getty Images, p. 895 Royalty Free/Corbis, p. 904 Jules Frazier/Getty Images

Chapter 19
p. 931 Royalty Free/Corbis, p. 935 Royalty Free/Corbis, p. 940 SAP AG Headquarters, p. 942 Royalty Free/Corbis

Chapter 20
p. 969 Photodisc/Getty Images, p. 970 Royalty Free/Corbis, p. 972 Stephen Mallon/Getty Images, p. 974 Janice Christie/Getty Images, p. 979 Ryan McVay/Getty Images

Chapter 21
p. 1019 Karl Mathis/EPA/Landov, p. 1021 Kim Steele/Getty Images, p. 1025 PhotoLink/Getty Images, p. 1030 R. Morley/ PhotoLink/Getty Images

Chapter 22
p. 1061 Peter Gridley/Photographers Choice/Getty Images, p. 1064 Royalty Free/Corbis, p. 1068 PhotoLink/Getty Images, p. 1074 Rob Crandall/Stock Boston, p. 1079 Royalty Free/Corbis

Chapter 23
p. 1109 Photo Courtesy of Home Depot, p. 1110 Royalty Free/Corbis, p. 1120 PhotoLink/Getty Images, p. 1121 PhotoLink/Getty Images, p. 1123 PhotoLink/Getty Images

Chapter 24
p. 1149 Beateworks Inc/Brand X Pictures/Getty Images, p. 1151 Photodisc/Getty Images, p. 1157 Royalty Free/Corbis, p. 1160 PhotoLink/ Getty Images

INDEX

A

D

G

H

I

J

K

N

O

P

Q

R

T

U

V

W

X

Z

eInstruction
Partnering with teachers to inspire the next generation

CPS
Classroom Performance System

What is CPS?

The Classroom Performance System is a revolutionary system that brings ultimate interactivity to the lecture hall or classroom. CPS is a wireless response system that gives you immediate feedback from every student in the class. CPS units include easy-to-use software for creating and delivering questions and assessments to your class. With CPS you can ask subjective and objective questions. Then every student simply responds with their individual, wireless response pad, providing instant results. CPS is the perfect tool for engaging students while gathering important assessment data.

Features and Benefits:

- Better interactivity – Receive instant feedback on what students have learned
- Increased class discussion – Anonymous opinion polls can be used to generate debate
- Improved attendance by "alert" students
- Automatically graded testing
- Simple to install, set up and use
- Low cost
- Reliable technical support available

For more information on CPS go to www.mhhe.com/cps or contact your McGraw-Hill textbook representative.

The McGraw-Hill Companies

McGraw-Hill Higher Education

Come visit us at **www.mhhe.com/edmonds/concepts**

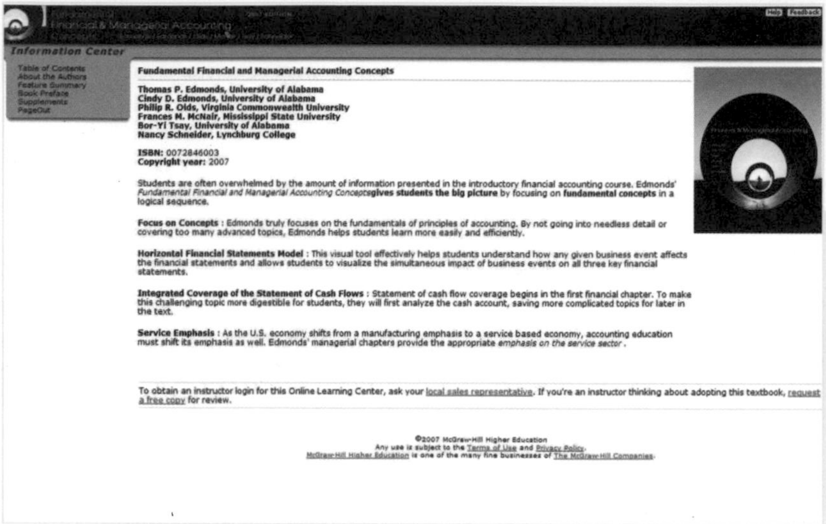

More and more students are studying online. That's why we offer an **Online Learning Center (OLC)** that supports *Fundamental Financial and Managerial Accounting Concepts.*

As students study and learn from this book, they can access the OLC Website and work with a multitude of helpful tools including:

- Chapter Learning Objectives
- Excel Spreadsheets
- Key Term Flashcards
- Interactive Quizzes
- Topic Tackler Plus
- E Lectures (audio-narrated Slide Presentations)
- Check Figures
- Excel Spreadsheet Tips
- Text Updates
- Text Glossary
- Mobile Resources

Instructors rely on the Internet to present and manage course material. That's why the **Online Learning Center** provides the most complete and up-to-date collection of web resources.

Whether you're an instructor building a lesson plan or a student preparing for an exam, the *Fundamental Financial and Managerial Accounting Concepts* **Online Learning Center** is the perfect resource.